THE NEW SOTHEBY'S WINE ENCYCLOPEDIA

THE NEW SOTHEBY'S WINE ENCYCLOPEDIA

TOM STEVENSON

A Dorling Kindersley Book

DK

LONDON, NEW YORK, SYDNEY, DELHI, PARIS,
MUNICH, AND JOHANNESBURG

Third edition (2001)

Senior Editor • Edward Bunting
Senior Art Editor • Anna Benjamin
Editors • Maggie Crowley, Cathy Rubinstein, Mary Scott
DTP Designer • Sonia Charbonnier
Managing Editor • Sharon Lucas
Senior Managing Art Editor • Derek Coombes
Production Controller • Louise Daly
Maps produced by Lovell Johns Limited, Oxford

Second edition (1997)

Senior Editors • Heather Jones, Paul Docherty
Art Editors • Nicola Powling, Mark Johnson Davies
Assistant Project Editor • Colette Connolly
Editors • Jane Sarluis, Samantha Gray, Nichola Thomasson
Designer • Carla De Abreu
Design Assistant • Michelle Fiedler
DTP Designers • Zirrinia Austin, Mark Bracey
Managing Editor • Gwen Edmonds
Managing Art Editor • Claire Legemah
Production Manager • Meryl Silbert
Picture Researcher • Victoria Walker

Third American Edition, 2001
03 04 05 10 9 8 7 6 5

Published in the United States by DK Publishing, Inc.
375, Hudson Street, New York, New York, 10014
Second American edition published 1997
First edition published in 1988 (as *Sotheby's World Wine Encyclopedia*)

Copyright © 1997, 2001 Dorling Kindersley Limited, London
Text copyright © 1997, 2001 Tom Stevenson
Serena Sutcliffe's Foreword and Introduction
copyright © 1997 Serena Sutcliffe

Library of Congress Cataloging-in-Publication Data
Stevenson, Tom.
  The new Sotheby's wine encyclopedia / by Tom Stevenson. -- 3rd
    American ed.
      p. cm
  Includes index
  ISBN 0–7894–8039–5
  1. Wine and wine making. I Title.
TP548.S724   2001
641.2'2'03--DC21 97–16170

Color reproduction by Colourscan, Singapore
Printed and bound in Spain by Artes Gráficas Toledo S.A.U.
D.L.TO:1235-2003

See our complete catalog at
www.dk.com

✦ CONTENTS ✦

Sotheby's Introduction 7

AUTHOR'S INTRODUCTION 16–51

The WINES *of* FRANCE 52–259

Château Gruaud-Larose, St.-Julien, France

Louis Roederer Champagne Label

The WINES *of*
GERMANY 258–303

Rieschen Vineyard, Meersburg, Germany

The WINES *of*
ITALY 304–345

Conca d'Oro estate, Vulture, Basilicata, Italy

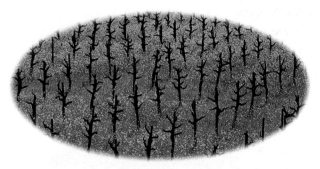

Spring Mustard Flowers and Vines, Napa Valley, California, US

Cabernet sauvignon grapes, Chile

✦SOTHEBY'S INTRODUCTION✦

Foreword and introduction by Serena Sutcliffe, MW
Head of Sotheby's International Wine Department

THIRST FOR KNOWLEDGE has a special meaning for wine lovers. They acquire that knowledge most directly by tasting, and drinking, wine, but they also deepen and broaden their experience through reading. Background information on growing vines and making wine can enhance appreciation of how a wine smells and tastes. Even something as "dry" as learning about wine laws (as opposed to wine lores, which are picturesque but unreliable) becomes interesting when applied to the flavour in the bottle. Tom Stevenson's *New Sotheby's Wine Encyclopedia* circles the vinous world in all its immense variety. It is a labour of love, full of fact and opinion based on those facts, which is what makes a book come alive. And this Encyclopedia is very much alive – it breathes its subject and each page resonates with directly acquired experience blended with unquenchable enthusiasm.

So much has happened in the wine world over the last decade. Wine producers and wine lovers have never travelled and exchanged knowledge as much as now. There has been a veritable cross-fertilization of ideas that has been extremely positive, benefiting consumers worldwide and at all price levels. Wine is now produced, and drunk, from China to Uruguay, and this Encyclopedia reflects the rich diversity of the global wine trade on the threshold of the new millennium.

Tom's text is incisive and clear, delivering hard-packed, fascinating material. Even esoteric grape varieties and obscure soil types become entrancing nuggets of information on which to muse. A good Encyclopedia should lead the reader up myriad paths of discovery. This one takes you into the vineyards and cellars, and ultimately leads you to the glass, which is where all wine lovers should meet.

I shall find this book indispensable.

ENJOYING WINE

A T WINE LECTURES and tastings as well as at Sotheby's wine courses and seminars many people ask me – how do I describe this wine? They are looking for words that will accurately reflect their olfactory sensations. The best way to gain a useful (but not ludicrously esoteric) vocabulary is to listen to someone who combines a perceptive nose and palate, a respectable amount of experience, and the ability to communicate clearly and with flair. Often a shared word or phrase suddenly makes sense of all the myriad smells and tastes emanating from a fine wine. A graphic description of a bouquet or flavour can reveal distinct new dimensions to a wine, marking the memory and increasing the wine's significance. It is comparable to being guided round a gallery of paintings by someone who has spent years studying the artist – you perceive nuances that previously you could not.

THE SHAPE OF THE GLASS

Whether tasting or drinking, the shape of the glass is important. Any decent-sized tulip-shaped glass is the perfect vessel for any wine. Its bulbous base and inwardly-sloping sides concentrate the aromas in the top of the glass, allowing the drinker the full benefit of the wine's bouquet. The glass must be large enough to ensure that a "good glassful" takes up barely more than half the glass, thus allowing the aromas to circulate. The worst possible glasses are those that are too small, have straight sides or sides that lean outwards, and the so-called Champagne *coupe* – its wide brim allows both the bubbles and the bouquet to escape. In the past, traditional glass shapes and even colours (*see* p.265) have evolved in the most famous winemaking regions, whereas the trend today is to develop a certain shape and size of glass to match a particular style of wine rather than the wines of one region. The Austrian fine glassware manufacturer Georg Riedel even claims that the same wine tastes different in each style of glass he produces.

Clean long-stemmed glasses that taper towards the top are best for winetasting.

T.S.

WINE TASTINGS

One marvellous aspect of wine tasting is that you do not need a mass of paraphernalia to enjoy your "sport". Just turn up with nose and palate intact and then all you need is clean, well-shaped glasses, a few bottles of wine, and a corkscrew. Fine glass is the most suitable, as it does not get between you and the wine, and if the glasses have long stems, they are easier to hold. A glass that narrows at the top holds the wine's bouquet better and prevents spillage from too vigorous "swirling", which is done merely to aerate the wine and encourage its bouquet to emerge. It helps if you also have good light, white tablecloths and chlorine-free water for light relief. There are many different types of wine tastings, from trade marathons to judge a new vintage to gatherings of friends who each bring a bottle. The latter is more fun if you also include a meal, for most wines are made to accompany, and complement, food. However, you can always play it seriously and have your first taste of each wine before starting eating, so that you can compare the "before" and "after" result.

Just as a pianist will develop a series of exercises that allows the highest standard of play to be achieved, so each taster has a routine when tasting, and my own is simple: I look at the colour, swirl the wine around in the glass, sniff, and finally, I taste. I then spit out the wine into a spittoon, or some such recipient, as swallowing a number of wines tends to impair judgement. However, no-one, thank goodness, spits at dinner parties. By spitting, you do not lose any of the wine's after-taste – only its mellowing effect.

That, in a nutshell, is wine-tasting, and you could spend the rest of your life embroidering on this theme. Anyone who possesses the basic biological equipment, in the form of a nose and palate, can taste wine. In more years of wine-tasting than I would like to remember, I have rarely met a person with a genuine physical "block" to tasting, although now and again one can encounter the tasting equivalent of someone who is tone deaf! The vast majority of people have all the necessary tools of the trade, but they may need to learn how to use them. It is one of the joys of tasting that practice makes perfect. Taste with like-minded friends and, by all means, drink with them – the rewards are great.

COLLECTING WINE

FORMING A WINE COLLECTION is fun. The catalyst that decides someone to begin collecting might be finding some extra space at home, enjoying a friend's collection, or a financial bonus just waiting to be transformed into liquid form. The only other prerequisite is a love of wine – a passion shared by an increasing amount of people around the world.

A wine collection can range from a few dozen bottles gathered from wine merchants, mail-order companies, and visits to wineries, to strategically planned cellars of thousands of bottles acquired at auction and through fine-wine specialists. The only criterion for the type of collection you start is whether it suits your needs. There is the small matter of depth of pocket, but one joy of this hobby is that a collection can start out small and grow larger.

WINES FOR PLEASURE AND INVESTMENT

The first question to ask when starting a collection is what will it be used for? Is it for early drinking, long-term keeping, or a mixture of the two, with wines of varying type and age to ensure gradual consumption of bottles as they mature? With a clear idea of what is wanted, better advice can be given by experts in auction houses, reputable wine merchants, and stores.

My first advice would be don't buy modest everyday wines. These can be bought hand to mouth and will be better and fresher as a result. Wines for storage, however short or long-term, should be more interesting, better quality, and, of course, suitable for ageing.

I also ask any prospective collector if the aim of acquiring a cellar is pleasure, investment, or a combination, which is both feasible and sensible. The more the collector favours the investment element, the

more blue-chip, and the less adventurous, should be the wines bought. Most people who acquire modest wine collections do it purely for pleasure, their own and that of their friends, which is an added joy and very much part of wine culture – sharing bottles and opinions with like-minded wine lovers is convivial and life enhancing. With a reasonable disposable income, an enthusiast can build up a collection that is large enough for investment wines to be sold from time to time in order to finance personal drinking, a solution that has a wisdom all of its own.

PRACTICAL ASPECTS

Unless collecting for investment purposes only, everyone wishes to buy wines that they actually like. So do taste as often as possible at restaurants, in-store tastings, pre-sale tastings given by auction houses for catalogue subscribers, with friends, or at wine courses. It is only by tasting that you discover favourite wine-producing areas and grape varieties. Then, concentrate on collecting those types of wine. There are several practical aspects to consider before arriving at the store or saleroom. How much money is there to spend, how much storage space is available, and, if it is at home, is it suitably cold?

The more information you can give an adviser on your vinous needs and tastes, the more pleasure you will derive from your collection. The most gifted of Masters of Wine cannot guide you to the wines of your dreams without being advised of your tastes: young or old, dry or sweet, gutsy and tannic, or light and floral. Of course, it is permitted to like them all. Read, discuss, and above all, taste as much as possible as you build up your wine collection, and keep all your options open – new and exciting experiences lie around the corner.

1985 Domaine de la Romanée-Conti Methuselah collection sold at Sotheby's London in May 1996 for £148,500.

LAYING DOWN A CELLAR

THE CELLAR SPACE IS FOUND, the credit card is willing, so... what to buy for the cellar? If you are the sort of person who loves variety and choice, and perhaps equally enjoys travel and holidays in winemaking areas, there is a good chance that your ideal wine collection should be international.

This might mean bottles, perhaps cases, of wine from Europe, the US, South America, Australia, New Zealand, and South Africa. However, you might be more of a classicist, with a penchant for Bordeaux, Burgundy, and the Rhone, as well as top-of-the-line Californian wines. If you sometimes like to sip port with Stilton cheese, add some vintage port to the collection. Should you appreciate sweet wine, do not forget Sauternes and late-picked, very ripe German Rieslings. If you appreciate vintage champagne with some bottle age, buy the new vintages from the great champagne houses when they appear on the market.

Good wine merchants, specialists, qualified professionals, and, indeed, books such as this one will pinpoint actual producers and wineries. They will also give guidance on vintages, which further determine the character of most wines (*see* Guide to Good Vintages, pp.569–570). Hot weather can produce big, full, long-lasting wines, while a rainy year may produce lighter wines. If you are laying down a cellar that will last for decades, the choice will have to be great wines from great vintages, as they have the best potential longevity. However, if you need only a small cellar for pleasurable drinking over the next few years, you should look for lighter, fruity vintages that age faster, or more mature wines (here auctions, especially, are a good source of supply) that are virtually ready for drinking.

Andrew Lloyd Webber's cellar at Sydmonton Court in southern England.

Finding out whether your personal preference is for young, lively wines, or older, mature, perhaps more complex wines is one of the many delights of wine tasting, and this will dictate the type of cellar you should develop. Higher quality wines do age better than most moderately priced wines, which are designed for relatively early drinking. Another consideration is that not all wines grow more beautiful with the years – some simply grow older.

INVESTMENT WINES

A cellar that is laid down with the prime aim of providing an investment should be chosen with great care and with the advice of those who really know the fine-wine market. The field of wine investment is dominated by top clarets, the great red wines from Bordeaux's classed growths. Those Médoc châteaux that were classified as First Growths in the 1855 classification are the blue-chips of the wine investment world, along with the First Growth from the Graves, Château Haut Brion. Other châteaux that fall into this category are La Mission Haut Brion in Graves, and the most renowned of the Médoc Second Growths, such as Pichon Longueville Comtesse de Lalande, Cos d'Estournel, and Leoville Lascases. Then there are châteaux from elsewhere in the "*classement*" that are also sure to increase in value – the Fifth Growth Lynch Bages is a classic example. However, precise advice is vital because the fortunes of châteaux can fluctuate – Pichon Longueville Baron, for example, became highly desirable from the vintages of the late 1980s onwards. There are also certain châteaux in Pomerol and

St.-Émilion that fall into the investment category, such as Pétrus, Cheval Blanc, Latour à Pomerol, Lafleur, and, recently, Le Pin.

Investment cellars might also include Sauternes, such as Château d'Yquem and Rieussec, and Vintage Port from houses such as Taylor, Fonseca, Graham, Warre, and Noval. The investment wines of Burgundy are fewer in number, as the estates are far smaller and the market fragmented and complex. This area is dominated by the seven wines of the Domaine de la Romanée-Conti, followed by estates such as Comtes de Vogüé, Armand Rousseau, Henri Jayer (for past vintages), and Leflaive for white wine. California's red wines may be part of an investment cellar, and the wines of Caymus, Mondavi, Ridge, Grace Family, Heitz Martha's Vineyard, Stag's Leap, and Opus One would be most likely to feature, especially their top reserve wines. The one Australian wine with international investment value is Grange, while in Italy Sassicaia leads the field.

The Thurn und Taxis cellar at Regensburg, which was sold by Sotheby's in October 1993.

enjoyment is more fun if it is easily accessible at home. In those countries where the climate is cold or moderate this is often possible, but collectors who live where the summers are hot, or where a tropical climate prevails all year round, will have to provide air-conditioned cellarage. Some wine lovers convert a spare room, others establish cellars outside or underground, while some opt for a "cold cupboard" small cellar, such as Eurocave. Just as good wine merchants and auction houses are able to advise you on the choice of wine, they can also recommend suppliers and constructors of cellars, many of whom also advertise in wine magazines.

EN PRIMEUR WINES

Some cellar owners are interested in buying wines that require ageing when they are very young, and these are known either as *en primeur* wines or as "futures". As this practice involves buying and paying for top Bordeaux châteaux wines long before they are in bottle, you should always choose a supplier with an impeccable reputation in order to be assured of eventual safe delivery. The most important aspects of a personal wine cellar, however, are that it should be easy to use and should be formed with the owner's palate in mind.

WHAT TYPE OF CELLAR IS BEST?

A serious investment cellar might be better stored in professional cellars, but a cellar built up for personal

CELLAR CONDITIONS

STORAGE TEMPERATURES
While 11°C (52°F) is the ideal storage temperature for wine, anything between 5 and 18°C (40–65°F) is fine, provided there is no great temperature variation. Higher temperatures do, however, increase the rate of oxidation of a wine, so a bottle stored at 18°C (65°F) will age more quickly than the same wine stored at 11°C (52°F). A constant 18°C (65 F) is kinder to a wine than erratic temperatures that often hit 11°C (52°F), but jump 3°C (5°F) up one day and 3°C (5°F) below the next.

THE EFFECT OF LIGHT
Ultraviolet light is most harmful to wine, but sunlight and artificial lighting should also be avoided. Darkness is of equal importance to temperature in the storage of wine.

PHYSICALLY STORING BOTTLES
Bottles and cases should be stored or stacked on their sides to keep the corks moist, thus fully swollen and airtight, avoiding oxidation. Humidity is harmless to wine and may accompany cellars with low temperatures.

WINE AUCTIONS

WINE AUCTIONS are a wine lover's paradise, a forum for buying and selling wine, and a vital part of the international wine market. The finest wines of the world are sold at auction and the saleroom sets the market price. The saleroom is, in fact, the wine lover and buyer, as the successful bid price is settled on the floor by consumers who are bidding against each other in the room, over the telephone, or by fax before the sale. The buyer is the barometer.

Auctions of fine wine are open to all – it is not a closed world of rarefied treasures accessible to only a few *cognoscenti*. All you need is a catalogue in order to follow the sale and enable you to bid. Both young and old wines are sold at auction, with prices varying from the astronomical for historic wines of great repute, to much more modest sums for highly drinkable wines designed to be enjoyed more often.

While media coverage of esoteric great wines fetching record prices makes for exciting reading, such reports can give the misleading impression that wine auctions are beyond the reach of ordinary mortals. Nothing could be further from the truth, as a quick survey of people who buy wine at auction would prove. Clients' tastes and ages are as diverse as the wines that parade through the saleroom, and the only real common denominator that links wine-auction participants from all continents is a love of the subject.

People sell and buy wine for many different reasons. Some acquire cellars purely for pleasure while others also look at this happy pursuit from an investment angle. Fine-wine lovers from all walks of life use the auction room and this has become particularly apparent during the last decade. The most marked recent change has been the internationalization of the wine-auction market. Whereas in the past auctions were virtually the sole domain of the British, wine lovers from every continent in the world now use wine auctions to stock their cellars and sometimes to dispose of them. The most recent recruits to the joys of wine auctions are from Asia, especially Hong Kong, Singapore, and Taiwan, and Latin America is making an increasing appearance as a buying force.

One of the most commonly asked questions about wine auctions is where does the wine come from? Traditionally, in the auction world, there is a saying that auctions result from the three Ds – death, divorce, and debt. Apart from sounding rather morbid, this is most certainly not the whole picture. Some wine collectors simply buy too much – they run out of space, or years in which to drink their wine. Many sales on behalf of vendors are partial disposals of cellars, a thinning out because of a surplus to requirements, or a change of emphasis in a cellar. A wine collector might wish to sell some older wines and replenish stocks with younger vintages, or enthusiasms for untried wine regions might result in a reshuffle in the cellar. For many, wine variety is the spice of life. It can happen that an auction client will even buy and sell in the same sale, astutely creating diversity in his collection. Others build up a cellar, watch it mature, and then sell part of it to subsidize their continuing consumption. Buyers at auction profit from this fluidity in the market, which ensures a tempting array of wine sales throughout the year and across the globe.

On the whole, European collections of wine are sold at auction in Europe, while American cellars are sold at auction in the United States. Sales in Asia are mostly of wines coming from Europe. The majority of wine auctions are made up of many different individual cellars, each separately identified in the catalogue. However, now and again the major auction houses hold single-owner wine sales, which always generate extra

The £3.7 million sale of the Andrew Lloyd Webber Wine Collection on 20-21 May, 1997 at Sotheby's London broke the previous world record for a wine auction.

excitement. In these instances, the name of the owner features and the sale of the wine collection in its entirety, or a substantial part of it, is of great quality and interest. Sotheby's has sold many such remarkable collections at auction, from the classic wines of Lord McAlpine in England, to the massive cellar of Prince Thurn und Taxis of Bavaria, to the record-breaking greatest cellar of all, the Andrew Lloyd Webber Wine Collection, sold in May 1997 in London.

When Sotheby's is approached to sell a quantity of wine, the auction house first provides low and high estimates for the collection, whether it consists of an entire cellar or a few cases of fine wine. If the vendor then wishes to sell, the wines are inspected, lotted up, and catalogued by Sotheby's expert wine-department staff. The auction house will check the condition of the wines and will describe any significant features such as the level of the wine in the bottle, the condition of the labels, and whether the wine is packed in original wooden cases or Sotheby's cartons.

"Damp-soiled" labels denote a damp cellar, which pleases knowledgeable wine lovers as it indicates the wine has been kept under ideal conditions – people do not drink pretty labels, they drink the bottle's contents! Where old, or very precious and expensive, wines are concerned, particular care must be taken to check authenticity and provenance. Just as great pictures have a story attached to them, great old wines do not appear mysteriously from nowhere – they should have ancestry that can be traced. It is increasingly important for wine lovers to be cautious in this respect. Accurate cataloguing and the availability of experts to give more information is reassuring and part of auction-house service. Wines for sale are moved to Sotheby's own cellarage before the auction, or may remain in professional storage, especially in countries where the stocks are "bonded", or lying tax free.

Auction catalogues are available about three weeks before the sale. This gives clients ample time to plan their purchases and, if they cannot attend the sale in person, to fax their bids in advance. Absentee, or commission, bids form a very important part of wine auctions, as people feel confident about buying wines they know, or have had recommended to them, in this easy-to-understand way. Live telephone bidding is accepted for important lots, or from clients who wish to buy significant quantities of wine.

For those who attend a wine auction, it is sensible to remain alert, as the bidding is very fast. With so many cases in a sale, a good auctioneer might sell over 200 lots an hour (a lot can be a case of wine, or even

a bottle if it is very old and precious). Every buyer registers for a paddle on arrival at the sale, which is used to attract the attention of the auctioneer when bidding. If successful in your bid, the auctioneer will call out your paddle number after bringing down the gavel and say the price at which the lot was sold. All lots are sold at one increment, or bidding step, above the previous bid.

One feature of wine sales are "parcels" of the same wine, maybe six separate lots of one case each of Château X 1982. The buyer of the first lot in the parcel may be asked by the auctioneer if he wishes to "go on", i.e. to buy the further five lots of similar wine at the same price. This is entirely at the auctioneer's discretion, but it does mean that if you really want some of the wine in the parcel, it might be as well to start bidding at the outset. Increments are always printed in the catalogue, so you will not be surprised by unexpected quantum leaps in price.

As with most things, when you pay for the wine you have bought at auction, it can be collected or delivered to you. If, for any reason, the wine is not as catalogued, the auction house should be contacted immediately and will take responsibility. However, do not buy mature red Burgundy if you actually like young red Californian Cabernets!

Auctions can be addictive and wine auctions have a special charm, as your purchase can soon be in your glass. Wine sales have existed for centuries and have been a great source of satisfaction to wine lovers everywhere. As Sotheby's puts its first wine catalogue on the Internet, the future looks exciting.

Serena Sutcliffe MW

One double magnum of Château Mouton Rothschild 1975, the label illustrated and signed by Andy Warhol, sold at Sotheby's New York in February 1997 for $3,738

❖AUTHOR'S INTRODUCTION❖

This is my kind of book – quite literally. Nothing else I have written, or am ever likely to write, presents the same challenge. I planned to write the first edition in two years, but it took three, so I thought it would be a doddle to update the Encyclopedia in the same amount of time, yet it took me five years. The reason was that so much had changed in the previous ten years that merely tweaking the text was unthinkable. So much had to be totally rewritten or added that the book has expanded from 480 pages to 600, and that was achieved only after ruthless cuts. Italy alone has swollen from 25 pages to almost 40. I had looked forward to introducing

a section of producer profiles for Italy, but the expansion of that section is due solely to the explosion of its appellations. If you have the original edition of the Encyclopedia, just compare the maps for an instant idea of the magnitude of growth that has taken place.

The aim is still the same, to provide a beautifully illustrated book that is evocative of each winemaking region, to cram it with information, and to do this in a user-friendly format that does not interrupt the flow of text and thus appeal to the novice and expert alike.

Tom Stevenson, April 2001

USING THIS BOOK

Each chapter of the Encyclopedia is arranged on a country-by-country basis, within which each wine region is dealt with; any districts within regions are examined, as are any smaller winemaking areas in each district. Within each chapter, there are two basic types of page: general Introductory text and Taste Guides. Introductory text has two regular features, "How to Read Wine Labels" and "Factors Affecting Taste and Quality", which may be given at either the national or regional level (*see* below). Taste Guides are variously titled "The Appellations of...", "The Wine Styles of...", and "The Wine Producers of...". Where appropriate – in

Bordeaux for example –, a listing of generic appellations provides an overview before the more specific appellations are dealt with. Various levels of information may be included in the Taste Guides, depending on the importance of a wine and/or its producer. Look for red, white, rosé, and sparkling tasting notes, with symbols denoting other information as detailed on the facing page.
Quick reference When consulting the Encyclopedia for a comment on a particular wine, look up the wine producer in the index. If you find that the producer is not listed, then look up the wine's appellation or style (by country or region).

COUNTRY AND REGION INTRODUCTION PAGES

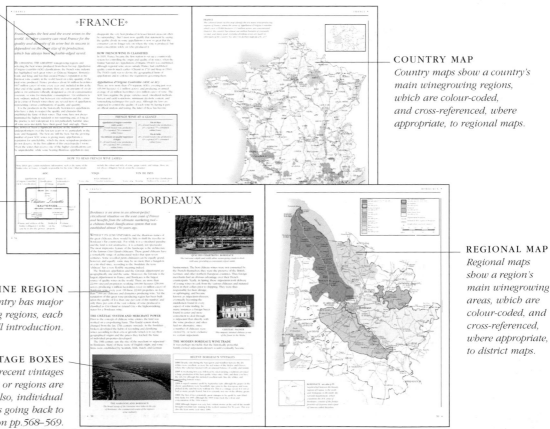

CHAPTER INTRODUCTION
This gives a broad-brush picture of a country or region. Much of the statistical and technical data is compartmentalized in boxes to avoid interrupting the flow of text while enabling readers seeking such information to zero-in on it quickly.

TABLES, CHARTS, AND BOXES
A wealth of statistical information is given in various charts, tables, and information boxes.

HOW TO READ THE WINE LABELS OF...
Often illustrated with a sample label, these features aim to supply all the information needed to understand the labels of a country or a region.

MAIN WINE REGION
If a country has major winemaking regions, each is given a full introduction.

VINTAGE BOXES
In each chapter, recent vintages of countries or regions are reviewed. Also, individual vintage scores going back to 1963 are given on pp.568–569.

COUNTRY MAP
Country maps show a country's main winegrowing regions, which are colour-coded, and cross-referenced, where appropriate, to regional maps.

REGIONAL MAP
Regional maps show a region's main winegrowing areas, which are colour-coded, and cross-referenced, where appropriate, to district maps.

DISTRICTS AND TASTE GUIDES

WINE DISTRICTS
In France and California, each individual winegrowing district within a region is examined separately.

DISTRICT MAP
These maps show colour-coded winegrowing areas, and, like some regional maps, also show intensive wine-growing zones and indicate the location of the best wine producers.

APPELLATIONS TEXT
Each winemaking area or appellation of a country, region, or district, whether legally defined or not, is listed and reviewed. The best producers in each appellation are listed. Symbols (see below) form part of the text.

WINE STYLES
If a country or region has a purely geographical system of appellations, then its wines may be described under the heading "The Wine Styles of…". The best producers of each style are listed.

ILLUSTRATIONS
Colour photographs capture the flavour of each region.

FACTORS AFFECTING TASTE AND QUALITY
In the introductory text for countries or regions and districts, a tinted panel gives a quick-reference guide to the fundamental conditions that determine the quality and style of the wines produced in each area. Symbols (see below) form part of the text.

WINE PRODUCERS
The best and most famous wine producers in countries, regions, and districts are reviewed on Wine Producer pages. Star ratings are given where applicable, and particular wines are recommended.

AUTHOR'S CHOICE
In each chapter, Tom Stevenson takes the reader on an armchair tasting tour of wines that highlights the present state of the various winemaking areas.

SYMBOLS

Factors Affecting Taste and Quality Boxes appear on the introduction pages of countries or regions and districts. The Taste Guides (Appellations, Producers, and Wine Styles) follow the introductions.

FACTORS AFFECTING TASTE AND QUALITY

- Aspect
- Climate
- Location
- Soil
- Viticulture
- Primary grape variety

TASTE GUIDE SYMBOLS

When to drink for optimum enjoyment. This is usually given as a range (e.g. 3–7 years) from date of vintage. "Upon purchase" is for wines that should be both bought and drunk while young. "Upon opening" is for fortified wines that can keep for many years but, contrary to popular belief, do not keep well once opened.

Grape varieties in the wine.

The very best producers, vineyards, and wines in the author's experience.

STAR RATING SYSTEM

Stars are given for a producer's general quality and do not necessarily apply to each wine. No stars or cross indicates an acceptable but not outstanding standard.

Half-stars indicate intermediate ratings

★ Wines that excel within their class or style.

★★ Very exceptional wines. The local equivalent of a Bordeaux super-second. *See Glossary, p.579.*

★★★ The best wines that money can buy, without any allowances

made for limitations of local style and quality.

V Wines of exceptional value for money, whether inexpensive or not.

? Wines that are inconsistent, or too rustic, or judgement has been reserved for stated reason.

✗ Underperformers for their category or style.

THE TASTE OF WINE

The difference between tasting and drinking is similar to test-driving a car you may buy and the relish of driving it afterwards. One is a matter of concentration, as you seek out distinguishing merits and faults, while the other is a far more relaxed and enjoyable experience. Tasting is a matter of concentration, and almost anyone can acquire the technique.

WHEN TASTING A WINE IT IS IMPORTANT to eliminate all distractions, especially comments made by others; it is all too easy to be swayed. The wine should be tasted and an opinion registered before any ensuing discussions. Even at professionally led tastings, the expert's job is not to dictate but to educate, to lead from behind, putting into perspective other people's natural responses to smells or tastes through clear and concise explanation. The three "basics" of wine-tasting are sight, smell, and taste, known as "eye", "nose", and "palate".

THE SIGHT OR "EYE" OF A WINE

The first step is to assess the wine's limpidity, which should be perfectly clear. Many wines throw a deposit, but this is harmless if it settles to yield a bright and clear wine. If it is cloudy or hazy, the wine should be discarded. Tiny bubbles that appear on the bowl or cling persistently to the edge of the glass are perfectly acceptable in a few wines, such as Muscadet sur lie and Vinho Verde, but probably indicate a flaw in most other still wines, particularly if red and from classic Old World regions.

The next step is to swirl the wine gently around the glass. So-called "legs" or "tears", thin sinewy threads of wine that run down the side of the glass, may appear. Contrary to popular belief, they are not indicative of high glycerol content, but are simply the effect of alcohol on wine's viscosity, or the way the wine flows. The greater the alcohol content the less free-flowing, or more viscous, the wine actually becomes.

The colour of wine

Natural light is best for observing a wine's colour, the first clue to its identity once its condition has been assessed. Look at the wine against a white background, holding the glass at the bottom of the stem and tilting it away from you slightly. Red wines vary in colour from *clairet*, which is almost rosé, to tones so dark and opaque that they seem black. White wines range from a colourless water-white to deep gold, although the majority are a light straw-yellow colour. For some reason there are very few rosé wines that are truly pink in colour, the tonal range extending from blue-pink, through purple-pink to orange-pink. Disregard any impression about a wine's colour under artificial lighting because it will never be true – fluorescent light, for example, makes a red wine appear brown.

Factors affecting colour

The colour and tonal variation of any wine, whether red, white, or rosé, is determined by the grape variety. It is also influenced by the ripeness of the actual grapes, the area of production, the method of vinification and the age of the wine. Dry, light-bodied wines from cooler climates are the lightest in colour, while fuller-bodied or sweeter-styled wines from hotter regions are the deepest. Youthful red wines usually have a purple tone, whereas young white wines may hint of green, particularly if they are from a cooler climate. The ageing process involves a slow oxidation that has a browning effect similar to the discolouration of a peeled apple that has been exposed to the air.

THE SMELL OR "NOSE" OF A WINE

Whenever an experienced taster claims to be able to recognize in excess of 1,000 different smells, many wine-lovers give up all hope of acquiring even the most basic tasting skills. Yet they should not be discouraged. Almost everybody can detect and distinguish over 1,000 different smells, the majority of which are ordinary everyday odours. Ask anyone to write down all the

VISUAL EXAMINATION
Unless it has an extreme colour or hue, the appearance of a wine is the least interesting aspect of a tasting note for most readers, which is why most authors use colour descriptions sparingly. The eye is, however, one of the most important sensory organs for professional tasters, as even the most subtle shade or nuance can provide numerous clues to the wine's identity.

NOSING A WINE
As we smell most flavours, rather than taste them, a good sniff tells us a lot about a wine. But refrain from continuously sniffing as this will dull your sense of smell. Take one good sniff, then pause for thought. Do not rush on to tasting the wine. Remember that no smells are specific to wine – they can all be compared to something familiar, but you need time to work out what they are.

smells they can recognize and most will be able to list several hundred without really trying. Yet a far greater number of smells are locked away in our brains waiting to be triggered.

The wine-smelling procedure is quite simple: give the glass a good swirl, put your nose into the glass, and take a deep sniff. While it is essential to take a substantial sniff, it is not practicable to sniff the same wine again for at least two minutes. This is because each wine activates a unique pattern of nerve ends in the olfactory bulb; these nerve ends are like small candles that are snuffed out when activated and take a little time to reactivate. As a result, subsequent sniffs of the same smell can reveal less and less, yet it is perfectly feasible to smell different smells, therefore different wines, one after the other.

THE TASTE OR "PALATE" OF A WINE

As soon as one sniffs a wine the natural reaction is to taste it, but do this only after all questions concerning the nose have been addressed. The procedure is simple, although it may look and sound rather strange to the uninitiated. Take a good mouthful and draw air into the mouth through the wine; this makes a gurgling sound, but it is essential to do it in order to magnify the wine's volatile characteristics in the back of the throat.

The tongue itself reveals very little; sweetness is detected on its tip, sourness or acidity on the sides, bitterness at the back and top, and saltiness on the front and sides. Apart from these four basic taste perceptions, we smell tastes rather than taste them. Any food or drink emits odorous vapours in the mouth that are automatically conveyed to the roof of the nasal passages. Here the olfactory bulb examines, discerns, and catalogues them – as they originate from the palate the natural inclination is to perceive them as tastes. For many of us it is difficult to believe that we taste with an organ located behind the eyes at the top of the nose, but when we eat ice-cream too quickly, we painfully experience precisely where the olfactory bulb is, as the chilly ice-cream aromas literally freeze this acutely delicate sensory organ. The texture of a wine also influences its taste; the prickly tactile sensation of CO_2, for example, heightens our perception of acidity while increased viscosity softens it.

SPITTING OUT
When tasting a large number of wines, each mouthful should be ejected after due assessment to avoid alcohol affecting the ability to taste. Yet some wine will remain, even after spitting out, coating the inner surface of the mouth, where it is absorbed directly into the bloodstream. Contrary to popular belief, the more you taste the better you taste, but it is a race between the wine sharpening the palate and the alcohol dulling the brain!

QUALITY AND TASTE: WHY OPINIONS DIFFER

Whether you are a novice or a Master of Wine, it is always personal preference that is the final arbiter when you are judging wine. The most experienced tasters can often argue endlessly over the relative merits and demerits of certain wines.

We all know that quality exists, and more often than not agree which wines have it, and yet we are not able to define it. Lacking a solid definition, most experienced tasters would happily accept that a fine wine must have natural balance and finesse and show a definite, distinctive, and individual character within its own type or style. If we occasionally differ on the question of the quality of wine, should we disagree on what it tastes like? We may love or hate a wine, but surely the taste we perceive is the same?

Conveying specific taste characteristics from the mind of one person to that of another is difficult enough, whether one is writing a book or simply discussing a wine at a tasting. Much of this difficulty lies in the words we choose, but the problem is not confined to semantics. In a world of perfect communication, conveying impressions of taste would still be an inexact art because of the different threshold levels at which we pick up elementary tastes and smells, and because of the various tolerance levels at which we enjoy them. If individuals require different quantities of acidity, tannin, alcohol, sugar, esters, and aldehydes in a wine before actually detecting them, then the same wine has, literally, a different taste for each of us. In the unlikely event of people having the same threshold for every constituent and combination of constituents, disagreement would probably ensue because we also have different tolerance levels; therefore, some of us would enjoy what others dislike because we actually like the tastes and smells they dislike. Thresholds and tolerance levels vary enormously; the threshold for detecting sweetness, for example, varies by a factor of five, which explains the "sweet tooth" phenomenon, and there are an infinite number of tolerance levels. Apply this to every basic aroma and flavour and it is surprising that we agree on the description of any wine.

MAGNIFYING THE TASTE OF A WINE
The tongue discerns only sweetness, sourness, bitterness, and saltiness. Every other "taste" we smell. By drawing air through a mouthful of wine, the volatalized aromas are taken into the back of the throat where they are picked up by the olfactory bulb, which automatically analyses them and transmits the information to the brain as various so-called flavours.

HOW TO ASSESS A WINE

It would be impossible to answer many of the following questions without some experience, however limited. Likewise, it would be difficult to identify a particular wine, or type of wine, having never tasted it. Do not panic – your knowledge will increase with every tasting.

SIGHT

Look at the colour: is it deep or pale, is there a positive quality to it, a specific hue that reminds you of a particular grape variety, the growing climate, or the area of production? Is the colour vivid and youthful, or is there browning that might suggest its age?

What does the rim, or meniscus, indicate? Does it retain the intensity of colour to the rim of the glass, which suggests a quality product, or does it fade to an unimpressive, watery finish?

SMELL

If the first impression is very heady, is the wine fortified? (Classic fortified wines, such as Port, Sherry, and Madeira, do have easily recognizable characteristics, but it can still be difficult to distinguish between a robust wine with a naturally high alcohol level produced in a hot country and a fortified wine.) Does the wine have any distinctive aromas, or are they obscure or bland or simply reticent? Does the wine smell as youthful or as mature as it

A SAMPLE TASTING

This chart provides a few examples from a whole range of the possible options that are open in the complex business of tasting. It also demonstrates that it is possible to approach the task systematically and rationally. When tasting it is important to keep your options open until

you have assessed the sight, smell, and taste of the wine. At each stage you should be seeking to confirm at least one of the possibilities that has arisen during the previous stage. Be confident and do not be afraid to back your own judgement – it is the only way to learn.

SIGHT
The clear, well-defined garnet colour of medium intensity suggests only moderately hot climatic origins. The tinge of purple on the meniscus could indicate youth.

SMELL
This is dominated by the distinctive pear-drop aroma of *macération carbonique*, hallmark of all but the best *cru* Beaujolais. Often mistaken for the varietal aroma of Gamay (from which Beaujolais is made), the aroma is characteristic of all wines fermented in this way. If this is a Beaujolais, the colour suggests something more serious than a lighter basic Beaujolais or Nouveau.

TASTE
The balance between fruit, acidity, and alcohol confirms that this is Beaujolais. The good depth of spicy-grapey fruit beneath the pervasive pear-drop character indicates that it is better-than-average.

CONCLUSION
Grape variety Gamay
Region Beaujolais
Age 2–3 years old
Comment Beaujolais Villages

SIGHT
Water-white, this wine has obvious cool climatic origins, although the tiny bubbles collecting on the glass suggest it could be a *Vinho Verde*. But the palest usually have a tell-tale hint of straw colour. Probably a modest *Qualitätswein* from the Mosel-Saar-Ruwer.

SMELL
This is not Vinho Verde. Its crisp, youthful, sherbet aroma is typical Mosel Riesling. Considering its colour, the nose would confirm that this is probably a *Qualitätswein*, or a *Kabinett* at most, of a modest vintage, but from a very good grower who is possibly as high up as the Saar tributary.

TASTE
Youthful, tangy fruit with the flower of the Riesling still evident. More flavour than expected, and a nice dry, piquant finish with a hint of peach on the aftertaste.

CONCLUSION
Grape variety Riesling
Region Mosel-Saar-Ruwer
Age about 18–24 months
Comment *Kabinett*, top grower

SIGHT
Intense, almost black colour that is virtually opaque. Obviously from a thick-skinned grape variety like the Syrah, which has ripened under a very hot sun. Australia's Swan Valley or France's Rhône Valley? California?

SMELL
As intense on the nose as on the eye. Definitely Syrah, and judging by its spicy aroma with hints of herbal scrub, almost certainly from the Northern Rhône. Australia and California can now be ruled out. More massive than complex, it must be from an exceptional vintage.

TASTE
Powerful and tannic, the spicy-fruit flavour is rich with blackberries, blackcurrants, plums, and cinnamon. Beginning to develop, but has a long way to go. This is a high-quality Rhône Syrah, but without quite the class of Hermitage, or the finesse of Côte Rôtie.

CONCLUSION
Grape variety Syrah
Region Cornas, Rhône Valley
Age about 5 years old
Comment top grower, great year

SIGHT
The brick-red colour and watery meniscus immediately suggest a young Bordeaux of petit-château quality. But first impressions can deceive – more evidence is needed.

SMELL
An attractive violet aroma with a restrained hint of soft, spicy fruit. Nothing contradicts my impressions, although the lack of blackcurrant suggests that the wine is a Bordeaux with a high proportion of Merlot rather than Cabernet sauvignon.

TASTE
The palate perfectly reflects the nose. This is a medium-bodied, modest claret of no great age. However, the fruit is well-rounded and the soft-tannin structure indicates that in little more than another two, possibly three, years it will be at its peak.

CONCLUSION
Grape variety Merlot-dominated blend
Region Bordeaux
Age 2 years old
Comment *petit château* or good generic

appears to the eye? Is it smooth and harmonious, suggesting the wine is ready to drink? If so, should it be drunk? If it is not ready, can you estimate when it will be? Is there a recognizable grape variety aroma? Are there any creamy or vanilla hints to suggest that it has been fermented or aged in new oak? If so, which region ages such wine in oak? Is it a simple wine or is there a degree of complexity? Are there any hints as to the area of production? Is its quality obvious or do you need confirmation on the palate?

TASTE

This should reflect the wine's smell and therefore confirm any judgements that you have already made. Should. But human organs are fallible, not least so the brain, therefore keep an open mind. Be prepared to accept contradiction as well as confirmation. Ask yourself all the questions you asked on the nose, but before you do, ask what your palate tells you about the acidity, sweetness, and alcoholic strength.

If you are tasting a red wine, its tannin content can be revealing. Tannin is derived from the grape's skin, and the darker and thicker it is, and the longer the juice macerates with the

skins, the more tannin there will be in the wine. A great red wine will contain so much tannin that it will literally pucker the mouth, while early-drinking wines will contain little.

If you are tasting a sparkling wine, on the other hand, its mousse, or effervescence, will give extra clues. The strength of the mousse will determine the style – whether it is fully sparkling, semi-sparkling, or merely *pétillant* – and the size of bubbles will indicate the quality; the smaller they are, the better.

CONCLUSION

Just try to name the grape variety and area of origin, and give some indication of the age and quality of the wine. Wise tasters will not risk their credibility by having a stab at anything more specific, such as the producer or vineyard, unless he or she is 100 per cent sure. In the Master of Wine examination, marks are given for correct rationale, even if the conclusion that is drawn is wrong, while it has been known for a candidate to name the wine in precise detail but, because of defective reasoning, to receive no score at all. Wine tasting is not a matter of guessing, it is about deduction, and getting it wrong should be encouraged as that is the only way to learn.

SIGHT
This distinctive yellow-gold colour retains its intensity to the rim. Various possibilities: a sweet wine, a full-bodied dry wine, a mature wine, or something obscure like Retsina. If none of these, it could be a Gewürztraminer.

SMELL
Gewürztraminer! Full, rich, and spicy, the aroma hits you between the eyes and the first instinct is to think of Alsace. Usually you will be right, but bear in mind the possibility of a top grower in the Rheinpfalz or Austria. If the aroma were muted, it might be Italian; if exotic, Californian or Australian. This, however, seems to be a classic example of a ripe Alsace vintage of maybe four years of age.

TASTE
A rich-flavoured wine; full, fat, and fruity with well-developed spice and a soft, succulent finish. Evidently made from very ripe grapes.

CONCLUSION
Grape variety Gewürztraminer
Region Alsace
Age about 4–5 years old
Comment very good quality

SIGHT
Stunning colour, more distinctive even than the Gewürztraminer, the old gold immediately suggests a full, rich, and probably very sweet wine. Sauternes springs to mind, but Austria, or even an oddity from Australia are also possible.

SMELL
This has the amazingly full, rich, and opulent nose of a botrytized wine. Anyone who dislikes sweet wine should smell a wine like this before giving up on it altogether. A touch of creamy-spicy oak rules out Austria and its maturity, probably between 10 and 15 years, probably disposes of Australia.

TASTE
Everything is here from peaches, pineapple, and cream to the honeyed aromatics of a fairly mature wine. Only a classic Sauternes can have such intense flavours, yet possess such great finesse.

CONCLUSION
Grape variety mostly Sémillon
Region Sauternes
Age about 15 years old
Comment *Premier Cru*, great vintage

SIGHT
The orange-pink of this wine almost certainly pins it to Provence or Tavel, although, if the orange hue is not indicative of the style and vinification of the wine, it could be almost any over-the-hill rosé.

SMELL
Put the dunce's hat on and stand in the corner! The high-toned Pinot noir aroma dismisses the firm conviction of a Tavel or Provence rosé. But what is it? It is not oxidized, so it cannot be an otherwise obvious wine that has gone over. Is the orange hue a clue to its origin? More data is needed; must taste the wine.

TASTE
Definitely Burgundian, but with a very distinctive piquant Pinot noir taste. At its peak now, but certainly not on the way down. By eliminating what it cannot be, only Rosé de Marsannay fits the bill.

CONCLUSION
Grape variety Pinot noir
Region Burgundy
Age 4–5 years old
Comment medium quality

SIGHT
This sparkling wine has an attractive, lively, lemon-yellow colour. Not young, but not old, its mousse is evident, but its power and size of bubble cannot be assessed without tasting it. Its star-bright limpidity just makes it look like a fine wine.

SMELL
Its quality is immediately evident, with the autolytic characteristics of a wine with several years on its first cork (in contact with its lees prior to disgorgement), which eliminates every possibility other than a fine Champagne. It has the zippy tang of ripe Chardonnay grapes. This must be a Champagne *blanc de blancs* with a high proportion of wine from the Côte des Blancs.

TASTE
A gently persistent mousse of ultra-fine bubbles. The fresh, lively flavour has a long finish but needs five years more to reach perfection.

CONCLUSION
Grape variety Chardonnay
Region Champagne
Age about 5 years old
Comment top quality

FACTORS AFFECTING TASTE AND QUALITY

The same grape grown in the same area can make two totally different wines, owing to seemingly inconsequential factors such as a change of soil or aspect. And yet different grapes grown continents apart may produce two wines that are very similar.

THERE ARE CERTAIN, CONSTANT FACTORS that affect the taste and quality of wine. These include grape variety, always the most important factor; location; climate, determining the ability to grow grapes; aspect, responsible for enhancing or negating local conditions; soil (*see* pp.28–29); viticulture, because the cultivation techniques used can stretch or concentrate varietal character; vinification, which, like cooking methods, can produce a range of options from the same basic ingredient (*see* pp.32–35, How Wine is Made); vintage, the vagaries of which can make or break a harvest; and the winemaker, the idiosyncratic joker in the pack.

GRAPE VARIETY

The grape variety used for a wine is the most influential factor in determining its taste. The factors that determine the inherent flavour of any grape variety are the same as those that determine the varietal taste of any fruit. How they affect the taste of wine is outlined below (*see also* pp.42–49, Glossary of Grape Varieties).

SIZE

The smaller the fruit, the more concentrated the flavour will be. Thus most classic grape varieties, such as Cabernet sauvignon and Riesling, have small berries, although some varieties that rely more

on elegance than power of concentration, such as the Pinot noir, may yield large berries. Many varieties are known as *petit-* or *gros-*something, and it is usually the *petit* that is the better variety – Petit vidure is Cabernet sauvignon, for example, and Gros vidure is Cabernet franc; Petit rhin is Riesling and Gros rhin is Sylvaner.

SKIN STRUCTURE

The skin contains most of the aromatic characteristics with which we associate the varietal identity of any fruit. Its construction and thickness is, therefore, of paramount importance. For example, the thick-skinned Sauvignon blanc produces an aromatic wine that, when ripe, varies in pungency from "peach" in a warm climate to "gooseberry" in a cool climate, and when underripe through various degrees of herbaceousness, ranging from "grassy" to "elderflower" and even "cat's pee". Meanwhile the thin-skinned Sémillon produces a rather neutral wine, although its thin skin makes it susceptible to "noble rot" and is thus capable of producing one of the world's greatest botrytized sweet wines, with mind-blowing aromatics.

SKIN COLOUR AND THICKNESS

A dark-coloured, thick-skinned grape, such as Cabernet sauvignon, produces very deep-coloured wines, while the lighter-coloured, thin-skinned grapes, such as Merlot, produce a less intense colour.

ACID/SUGAR RATIO AND PRESENCE OF OTHER CONSTITUENTS

The grape's sugar content dictates the alcohol level and whether any natural sweetness is possible; this, together with the acidity level, determines the balance. The proportion of the grape's other

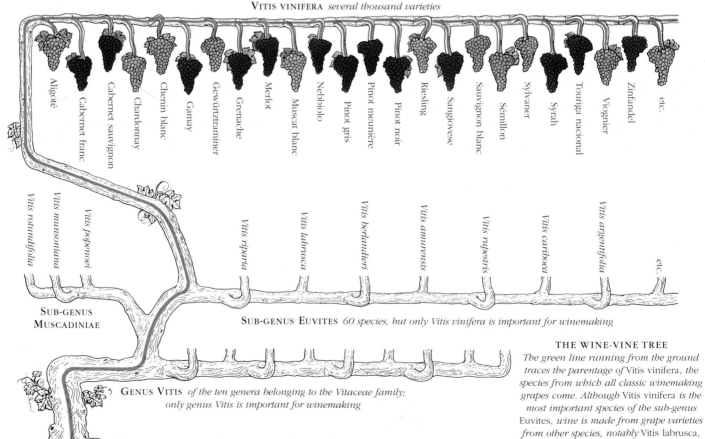

VITIS VINIFERA *several thousand varieties*

Aligoté · Cabernet franc · Cabernet sauvignon · Chardonnay · Chenin blanc · Gamay · Gewürztraminer · Grenache · Merlot · Muscat blanc · Nebbiolo · Pinot gris · Pinot meunière · Pinot noir · Riesling · Sangiovese · Sauvignon blanc · Sémillon · Sylvaner · Syrah · Touriga nacional · Viognier · Zinfandel · etc.

Vitis rotundifolia · Vitis munsoniana · Vitis popenoei · Vitis riparia · Vitis labrusca · Vitis berlandieri · Vitis amurensis · Vitis rupestris · Vitis cariboea · Vitis argentifolia · etc.

SUB-GENUS MUSCADINIAE

SUB-GENUS EUVITES *60 species, but only Vitis vinifera is important for winemaking*

THE WINE-VINE TREE
The green line running from the ground traces the parentage of Vitis vinifera, the species from which all classic winemaking grapes come. Although Vitis vinifera is the most important species of the sub-genus Euvites, wine is made from grape varieties from other species, notably Vitis labrusca, which is native to North America.

GENUS VITIS *of the ten genera belonging to the Vitaceae family; only genus Vitis is important for winemaking*

BOTANICAL FAMILY *Vitaceae (also called Ampelidaceae)*

constituents, or their products after fermentation, form
the subtle nuances that differentiate the various varietal
characters. Although soil, rootstock, and climate have their
effect on the ultimate flavour of the grape, the basic recipe
for these ingredients is dictated by the genetics of the vine.

THE VITIS FAMILY
The vine family is a large and diverse family of plants ranging
from the tiny pot-plant Kangaroo Vine to Virginia Creeper.
The Wine Vine Tree, (*see* opposite), shows how the *Vitis
vinifera*, the classic winemaking species, relates to the rest
of the vine family. The species *Vitis vinifera*, called *vinifera*
for short, is one of many belonging to the sub-genus *Euvites*.
Other species in this sub-genus are used for rootstock.

PHYLLOXERA VASTATERIX – PEST OR BLESSING?
The vine louse – *phylloxera vastaterix* – that devastated the
vineyards of Europe in the late 19th century still infests the
soils of nearly all the world's wine-growing regions. At the
time, it was considered the greatest disaster in the history of
wine, but with hindsight, it was a blessing in disguise.

Before phylloxera arrived, many of Europe's greatest wine
regions had gradually been devalued because of an increase
in the demand for their wines. This led to bulk-producing,
inferior varieties being planted, and vineyards being extended
into unsuitable lands. As phylloxera spread, it became apparent
that every vine had to be grafted on to phylloxera-resistant
American rootstock. This forced a much-needed rationalization,
in which only the best sites in the classic regions were
replanted and only noble vines were cultivated, a costly and
time-consuming operation that owners of vineyards in lesser
areas could not afford. The grafting took France 50 years, and
enabled the the *Appellation d'Origine Contrôlée* system to be
established. It is hard to imagine what regional or varietal
identities might now exist, if phylloxera had not occurred.

ROOTSTOCK
Hundreds of rootstock varieties have been developed from
various vine species, usually *berlandieri*, *riparia*, or *rupestris*,
because they are the most phylloxera-resistant. The choice of
rootstock depends on its suitability to the vinestock on which
it is to be grafted. It is also dependent on the rootstock's
adaptability to the geographical location and soil type. But
the choice can increase or decrease a vine's productivity,
and thus has a strong effect upon the quality of the wine.
Generally, the lower the quantity, the higher the quality.

LOCATION
The location of a vineyard is fundamental in determining whether
its climate is suitable for viticulture. Virtually all the world's wine-
producing areas, in both hemispheres, are located in the temperate
zones between 30° and 50° latitude, where the annual mean
temperature is between 10°C (50°F) and 20°C (68°F). The most
northerly vineyards of Germany are at the outermost limit,
between 50° and 51° latitude (almost 53° if we include the
scattered vineyards of former East Germany), but survive because
of the continental climatic influence, which assures the hotter
summers. The shorter days also retard the cane growth in favour
of fruit maturity, allowing the grapes to ripen before the harsh
continental winter. Interestingly, most of the world's finest wines
are produced in west-coast locations, which tend to be cooler
and less humid than east-coast areas. Forests and mountain ranges
protect the vines from wind and rain. A relatively close proximity
to forests and large masses of water can influence the climate
through transpiration and evaporation, providing welcome
humidity in times of drought, although they can encourage rot.
Thus some factors can have both positive and negative effects.

APPLE TREE IN CALVADOS, NORMANDY
*Methods of vine-training are applicable to other cultivated fruits,
as this spur-trained apple tree in Calvados illustrates.*

THE WORLD OF WINE
*The most important areas of
cultivation in both the northern
and southern hemispheres lie
mainly between latitudes 30° and
50°. However, there are a number
of smaller winemaking areas closer
to the equator. Indeed, equatorial*
vinifera *wines are produced in tiny
quantities in Kenya and Peru.*

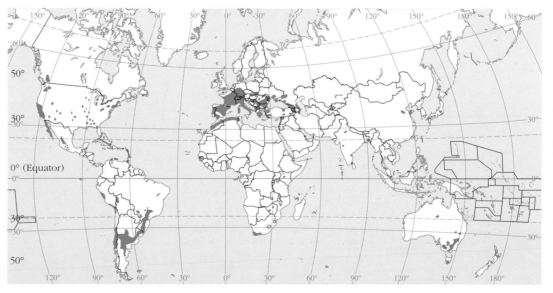

CLIMATE AND WEATHER

Climate and weather are the most important factors that influence the growth of grapes for quality wines. Climate is determined by geographical location, whereas weather is the result of how nature decides to affect that climate on a daily basis. In other words, climate is what it should be, weather is what it is. A grower must select a region with an amenable climate and hope that nature does not inflict too many anomalies.

Although some vines survive under extreme conditions, most, and all classic, winemaking vines are confined to two relatively narrow climatic bands between 30º and 50º latitude and require a combination of heat, sunshine, rain, and frost.

HEAT

Vines will not provide grapes suitable for winemaking if the annual mean temperature is less than 10°C (50°F). The ideal mean temperature is 14º to 15°C (57º to 59°F), with an average of no less than 19°C (66°F) in summer and –1°C (30°F) in the winter. In order for the vines to produce a good crop of ripe grapes, the minimum heat-summation, measured in "degree-days" with an average of above 10°C (50°F) over the growing season, is 1,000º (using °C to calculate) or 1,800º (using °F to calculate). Below are the degree-day totals over the growing season for a variety of vineyards from around the world.

AREA/REGION	DEGREE-DAYS CELSIUS (FAHRENHEIT)
Trier, Mosel, Germany	945 (1,700)
Bordeaux, France	1,320 (2,375)
McLaren Vale, South Australia	1,350 (2,425)
Russian River, California, USA	2,000 (3,600)

SUNSHINE

While light is required for photosynthesis, which is the most important biological process of green plants, there is sufficient light for this even in cloudy conditions. For winegrowing, sunshine is needed more for its heat than its light. Approximately 1,300 hours is the minimum amount of sunshine required per growing season, but 1,500 hours is preferable.

RAINFALL

A vine requires 68 centimetres (27 inches) of rain per year. Ideally, most of the rain should fall in the spring and the winter, but some is needed in the summer too. Vines can survive with less water if the temperature is higher, although rain in warm conditions is more harmful than rain in cool conditions. A little rain a few days before the harvest will wash the grapes of any sprays, and is therefore ideal if followed by sun and a gentle, drying breeze. Torrential rain, however, can split berries and cause fungus.

Below are annual rainfall figures for a variety of vineyards from around the world.

AREA/REGION	RAINFALL
McLaren Vale, South Australia	60 cm (24 in)
Trier, Mosel, Germany	65 cm (26 in)
Bordeaux, France	90 cm (36 in)
Russian River, California, USA	135 cm (53 in)

FROST

Surprising as it may seem, some frost is desirable, providing it is in the winter, as it hardens the wood and kills spores and pests that the bark may be harbouring. However, frost can literally kill a vine, particularly at bud-break and flowering (*see* p.30).

PREPARING FOR RAIN
In southern Spain furrows are dug horizontally between rows of vines to provide channels for any rain.

CLIMATIC CONDITIONS

Favourable

• Fine, long summers with warm, rather than hot, sunshine. This weather ensures that the grapes ripen slowly, resulting in a good acid-sugar balance.
• A dry, sunny autumn is essential for ripening grapes and avoiding rot, but, again, it must not be too hot.
• The winter months from November to February (May to August in the southern hemisphere) are climatically flexible, with the vine able to withstand temperatures as low as –20°C and anything other than absolute flood or drought.
• Within the above parameters, the climate must suit the viticultural needs of specific grape varieties; for example a cooler climate for Riesling, hotter for Syrah, etc.

Unfavourable

• Major dangers are frost, hail, and strong winds, all of which can denude a vine and are particularly perilous when the vine is flowering or the grapes are ripening and at their most susceptible.
• Rain and/or cold temperatures during the flowering may cause imperfect fertilization, which results in a physiological disorder called *millerandage*. The affected grapes contain no seeds and will be small and only partially developed when the rest of the cluster is fully matured.
• Persistent rain at, or immediately before, the harvest can lead to rot or can dilute the wine, both of which can cause vinification problems.
• Sun is not often thought of as a climatic danger, but, just as frost can be beneficial to the vine, so sun can be harmful. Too much sun encourages the sap to go straight past the embryo grape clusters to the leaves and shoots. This causes a physiological disorder called *coulure*, which, is often confused with *millerandage*. However, it is totally different, although both disorders can appear together due to the vagaries of climate. Most seeds suffering from *coulure* drop to the ground, and those that remain do not develop.
• Excessive heat during the harvest rapidly drops the acid level of grape juice and makes the grapes too hot, creating problems during fermentation. It is especially difficult to harvest grapes at an acceptable temperature in very hot areas, such as South Africa. As a result, some wine estates harvest the grapes at night when the grapes are at their coolest.

ASPECT

The aspect of a vineyard refers to its general topography – which direction the vines face, the angle and height of slope, and so on – and how it interrelates with the climate.

There are few places in the world where winemaking grapes – as opposed to table grapes – are successfully growing under the full effect of a prevailing climate. The basic climatic requirements of the vine are usually achieved by manipulating local conditions, keeping sunshine, sunstrength, drainage, and temperature in mind.

SUNSHINE

South-facing slopes (north-facing in the southern hemisphere) attract more hours of sunshine. In hotter areas, however, the opposite facing slopes tend to be cultivated.

SUN STRENGTH AND DRAINAGE

Because of the angle, vines on a slope absorb the greater strength of the sun's rays. In temperate regions the sun is not directly overhead, even at noon, and therefore its rays fall more or less perpendicular to a slope. Conversely, the sun's rays are dissipated on flat ground across a wider area, so their strength is diluted on the plains (which are also susceptible to flooding and have soils that are usually too fertile, yielding larger crops of correspondingly inferior fruit). Lake- and river-valley slopes are particularly well suited for vines because they receive rays reflected from the water.

A sloping vineyard also affords natural drainage. However, vines grown on hilltops are too exposed to wind and rain and deprive vines below of their protective forested tops. Forested hilltops not only supply humidity in times of drought, but also absorb the worst of any torrential rain that could wash away the topsoil below.

TEMPERATURE

While slopes are very desirable sites, it must be remembered that for every 100 metres (330 feet) above sea level, the temperature falls 1°C (1.8°F). This can result in 10 to 15 days extra being needed for the grapes to ripen and, because of the extra time, the acidity will be relatively higher. Thus a vineyard's altitude can be a very effective way of manipulating the quality and character of its crop. Riverside and lakeside slopes also have the advantages of reflected sunlight and the water acting as a heat reservoir, releasing at night heat that has been stored during the day. This not only reduces sudden drops in temperature that can be harmful, but reduces the risk of frost. However, depressions in the slopes and the very bottom of valleys collect cold air, are frost-prone, and retard growth.

SOIL

Topsoil is of primary importance to the vine because it supports most of its root system, including most of the feeding network. Subsoil always remains geologically true. Main roots penetrate several layers of subsoil, whose structure influences drainage, the root system's depth, and its ability to collect minerals.

The metabolism of the vine is well known, and the interaction between it and the soil is generally understood. The ideal medium in which to grow vines for wine production is one that has a relatively thin topsoil and an easily penetrable (therefore well-drained) subsoil with good water-retaining characteristics. The vine does not like "wet feet", so drainage is vital, yet it needs access to moisture, so access to a soil with good water-retention is also important. The temperature potential of a soil, its heat-retaining capacity, and heat-reflective characteristics affect the ripening period of grapes: warm soils (gravel, sand, loam) advance ripening, while cold soils (clay) retard it. Chalk comes in between these two extremes, and dark, dry soils are obviously warmer than light, wet soils. High pH (alkaline) soils (such as chalk) encourage the vine's metabolism to produce sap and grape juice with a relatively high acid content. The continual use of fertilizers has lowered the pH level of some viticultural areas in France, and these are now producing wines of higher pH (less acidity).

THE MINERAL REQUIREMENTS OF THE VINE

Just as various garden flowers, shrubs, and vegetables perform better in one soil type as opposed to another, so too do different grape varieties. Certain minerals essential to plant growth are found in various soils. Apart from hydrogen and oxygen (which is supplied as water) the most important soil nutrients are nitrogen, which is used in the production of a plant's green matter; phosphate, which directly encourages root development and indirectly promotes an earlier ripening of the grapes (an excess inhibits the uptake of magnesium); potassium, which improves the vine's metabolism, enriches the sap, and is essential for the development of the following year's crop; iron, which is indispensable for photosynthesis (a lack of iron will cause chlorosis); magnesium, which is the only mineral constituent of the chlorophyll molecule (lack of magnesium also causes chlorosis); and calcium, which feeds the root system, neutralizes acidity and helps create a friable soil structure (although an excess of calcium restricts the vine's ability to extract iron from the soil and thus causes chlorosis). For information on specific soil types *see* pp.28–29.

TERRACED VINEYARDS OVERLOOKING THE RHINE
Vines beside water masses benefit from the sun's rays reflecting off the water, an advantage in areas where the climate is cooler.

HILLS NEAR SANCERRE
In the spring, vineyards give the rolling countryside in France's Loire Valley a speckled appearance. Most soils in the area are dominated by clay or limestone.

VINTAGE

The anomalies of a vintage can bring disaster to reliable vineyards and produce miracles in unreliable ones. A vintage is made by weather, which is not at all the same as climate. While the climate may be generally good, uncommon weather conditions can sometimes occur. In addition to this, the vintage's annual climatic adjustment can be very selective; on the edge of a summer hail-storm, for example, some vineyards may be destroyed and produce no wine at all, while others are virtually unharmed and may produce good wine. Vines situated between the two might be left with a partial crop of fruit that could result in wines of an exceptional quality, if given a further two to three months of warm sunshine before the harvest, as reduced yields per vine produce grapes with a greater concentration of flavour.

THE WINEMAKER

The winemaker, and that includes the winegrower, can maximize or minimize the fruits of nature by his or her skill. Time and again I have seen that neighbouring winemakers can make totally different quality wine using virtually the same raw product and the same technology. Chemical analyses of the wines in question may be virtually indistinguishable, yet one wine will have all the definition, vitality, and expression of character that the other lacks. Why does this occur? No doubt there are valid reasons that science may one day establish, but in our current state of ignorance I can only say that it is always the winemakers with passion who are able to produce the finer, more characterful wines. Of course many inferior wines are made by the misuse of up-to-date technology, but I have seen dedicated winemakers produce absolutely spell-binding wines using what I would consider to be totally inadequate or inferior equipment. Some winemakers have even been known to sleep by their vats during a particularly difficult fermentation, so that they are on hand to make any adjustments immediately if anything goes wrong. From the grower who never hesitates to prune the vine for low yields, yet always agonizes over the optimum time to harvest, to the winemaker who literally nurses the wines through each and every stage of fermentation and maturation, who bottles at precisely the right time and at exactly the correct temperature, the human element is most seriously the joker in the pack when it comes to factors affecting the taste and quality of the wines produced.

INSPECTING MATURING WINE
Auguste Clape, one of the finest winemakers in France's Northern Rhône area, checks the progress of his oak-matured wine.

VITICULTURE

While it is the variety of grape that determines the basic flavour of a wine, it is the way in which the variety is grown that has the most profound effect on the quality of the wine.

VINE TRAINING

In vine training, it is absolutely crucial to ensure that no cane ever touches the ground. Should a cane find its way to the ground, its natural inclination is to send out suckers that will put down roots. Within two or three years the majority of the grafted vine's above-ground network would be dependent not upon grafted roots, but upon the regenerated root system of the producing vine. Not only would this have the effect of putting the vine at the mercy of phylloxera, but, ironically, that part of the vine still receiving its principal nourishment from the grafted rootstock would send out its own shoots and, unchecked by any sort of pruning, these

BASIC SYSTEMS OF VINE TRAINING

There are two basic systems of vine training: cane training and spur training, on which there are many local variations. Cane-trained vines have no permanent branch because all but one of the strongest canes (which will be kept for next season's main branch) are pruned back each year to provide a vine consisting of almost entirely new growth. Apart from the trunk, the oldest wood on a cane-trained vine is the main branch and that is only one year old.

This system gives a good spread of fruit over a large area, and allows easier regulation of annual production, because the number of fruiting buds can be increased or decreased. With spur training there is no annual replacement of the main branch, thus a solid framework is formed. It is easy, therefore, to know which basic training system has been applied to a vine simply by looking at the main branch. Even if you cannot recognize the specific style of training, if the main branch is thin and smooth, you will know that it has been cane trained, whereas if it is thick, dark, and gnarled, it has been spur trained.

Will be next year's main cane (A)		Will be next year's main cane (A)
A		
Beginning of season	Height of season	End of season

GUYOT – AN EXAMPLE OF CANE-TRAINING
In the winter, the main horizontal cane is cut off and the spare cane (A) bent horizontally to be tied to the bottom wire, where it will become next season's main cane, while another shoot close to the trunk will be allowed to grow as the next season's spare cane.

Beginning of season	Height of season	End of season

GOBELET – AN EXAMPLE OF SPUR-TRAINING
The main canes on a spur-trained vine are all permanent, and will only be replaced if they are damaged. Only the year-old shoots are pruned back.

would produce hybrid fruit. Therefore, the fundamental reason for training and pruning a vine is to avoid phylloxera and to ensure that the purity of the fruiting stock is maintained.

The manner in which a vine is trained will guide the size, shape, and height of the plant towards reaping maximum benefits from the local conditions of aspect and climate. Vines can be trained high to avoid ground frost, or low to hug any heat that may be reflected by stony soils at night. There may be a generous amount of space between rows to attract the sun and avoid humidity. On the other hand, vines may be intensively cultivated to form a canopy of foliage to avoid too much sun.

STYLES OF VINE TRAINING
Within the two basic systems of cane training and spur training, hundreds of different styles are employed, each developed for a reason, and all having their own advantages and disadvantages. In order to discern the style used in a particular vineyard, it is always best to look at the vines between late autumn and early spring when the branches are not camouflaged with leaves. In the illustrations below, which are not drawn to scale, vines are shown as they appear during their winter dormancy, with the following season's fruiting canes shown in green. For cane-trained systems, a green-brown tint has been used to pick out the one-year-old wood used as next season's main branch.

Bush vine - *Spur-training system*
An unsupported version of the Gobelet system (*see* opposite), the term "bush vine" originated in Australia, where a few old vineyards, usually planted with Grenache, are still trained in this fashion. Bush vines are traditional in Beaujolais (where both supported and unsupported methods are referred to as Gobelet) and are common throughout the most arid areas of the Mediterranean. Being unsupported, the canes often flop downwards when laden with fruit, giving the vine a  sprawling, straggly look. In the Beaujolais *crus*, the number of canes is restricted to between three and five, but in other, less controlled wine areas a Bush Vine may have up ten canes. It is only suitable for low-vigour vines.

Chablis - *Spur-training system*
As the name implies, this style of vine training was originally developed in the Chablis district, although the method employed there now is, in fact, the Guyot Double. Champagne is the most important winemaking region to use the Chablis system for training vines, where it accounts for more than 90 per cent of all the Chardonnay grown. Either three, four, or five permanent branches may be cultivated, each one being grown at yearly intervals. This results in a three-year-old vine (the minimum age for AOC Champagne) having three branches, a four-year-old having four branches, and so forth. The distance between each vine in the same row determines the eventual life of the oldest branch because, when it encroaches upon the next vine, it is removed and a new one cultivated from a bud on the main trunk. The Chablis spur-training system is, in effect, little more than a slanting bush vine unsupported by a central post.

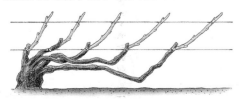

Cordon de Royat - *Spur-training system*
This is to Champagne's Pinot noir what Chablis is to its Chardonnay and is nothing more complicated than a spur-trained version of Guyot Simple (*see below*). There is even a double variant, although this is 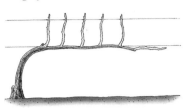 rarely cultivated purely for its own ends, its primary reason for existence being to replace a missing vine on its blind side. When, after their winter pruning, they are silhouetted against the sky, Cordon de Royat vines look very much like columns of gnarled old men in perfect formation; they all face forward, bent almost double, as if with one arm dug into the pit of the back and the other seeking the support of a stick.

Geneva Double Curtain - *Spur-training system*
This downward-growing, split-canopy system was developed by Professor Nelson Shaulis of the Geneva Experimental Station in New York state in the early 1960s to increase the volume and ripening of locally-grown Concord grapes. Since then, GDC, as it is often referred to, has been adopted all over the world (particularly in Italy). However, unlike Concord varieties, classic *vinifera* vines have an upward-growing tendency, which makes the system more difficult to apply. Successful results are obtained by shoot positioning, which can either be accomplished via a movable wire (as in Scott Henry, *see* p.26), by hand, or even by machine. Yields from GDC are 50 per cent higher than those from the standard VSP trellis (*see* p.27), and the system offers increased protection from frosts (due to height above ground).
It is ideal for full mechanization of medium- to high-vigour vineyards on deep fertile soils (low-vigour vines do not benefit).

Guyot - *Cane-training system*
Developed by Jules Guyot in 1860, both the double and simple forms shown here represent the most conservative style of cane training possible. It is the least complicated concept for growers to learn and, providing the number of fruiting canes and the number of buds on them are restricted, Guyot is the easiest means of restraining yields. Even when growers abuse the system, it is still the most difficult vine-training method with which to pump up 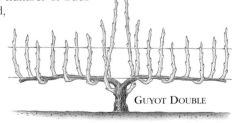 production. Commonly used in Bordeaux, where the number of canes and buds are restricted by AOC rules (although, like most French bureaucratic systems, much depends on self-regulation – as I have never seen an INAO inspector in the middle of a vineyard checking the variety of vines or counting them, let alone counting the number of canes or buds on canes!). Guyot is also used for some of the finest wines throughout the winemaking world, Old and New.

GUYOT DOUBLE

GUYOT SIMPLE

Lyre – *Spur-training system*

Also called the "U" system, the canopy is divided, allowing a better penetration of light (improving ripeness levels) and air (reducing the incidence of cryptogamic disorders). Although developed in Bordeaux, the Lyre system is more common in the New World where vine vigour is a problem, although not a major one. As with all split-canopy systems, Lyre is of no use whatsoever for low-vigour vineyards. Some growers have successfully adapted Lyre to cane training.

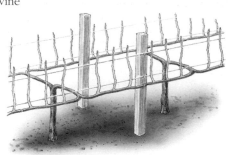

Minimal Pruning – *Spur-training system*

A wild, unruly mass that contains a central thicket of unpruned dead wood, which by definition has no disciplined form and is thus impossible to illustrate. Some of the central thicket may be mechanically removed in the winter, but will still be a tangled mass. Initially, several canes are wrapped loosely around a wire, either side of the trunk, about 1.5 to 2 metres (5 to 6 feet) off the ground. The vine is then left to its own devices, although if necessary some of the summer shoots will be trimmed to keep the fruit off the ground. Some growers give up quite quickly because yields can initially be alarmingly high and as the volume increases, so the quality noticeably deteriorates. However, if they are patient, the vine eventually achieves a natural balance, reducing the length of its shoots and, consequently, the number of fruiting nodes on them. Although mature minimally pruned vines continue to give fairly high yields, the quality begins to improve after two or three years. By the sixth or seventh year the quality is usually significantly superior to the quality achieved before minimal pruning was introduced – only the quantity is substantially greater. The ripening time also increases, which can be an advantage in a hot climate, but disastrous in a cool one, particularly if it is also wet. Furthermore, after a number of years, the mass of old wood in the central thicket and the split-ends of machine-pruned cane ends surrounding it can make the vine vulnerable to various pests and diseases, especially rot and mildew, which is why minimally pruned vines in wet areas like New Zealand are more heavily pruned than they are in the hotter areas of Australia – such as Coonawarra and Padthaway – where minimal pruning first emerged and is still used to great effect.

Pendelbogen – *Cane-training system*

Also known as the "European Loop", or "Arc-Cane Training", this vine-training system, which is a variant of the Guyot Double (*see* p.25), is most popular in Switzerland and the flatter Rhine Valley areas of Germany and Alsace, although it can also be found in

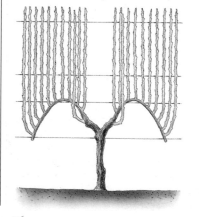

Mâcon, British Columbia, and Oregon. By bending the canes in an arch, Pendelbogen has more fruit-bearing shoots than the Guyot Double system thereby providing higher yields. The arching does promote better sap distribution, which helps the production of more fruit, but it can also reduce ripeness levels, making the prime motive for adopting Pendelbogen one of economy, not of quality.

Scott Henry – *Cane-training system*

Developed by Scott Henry at the Scott Henry Vineyard in Oregon, this system effectively doubles the fruiting area provided by Guyot Double. It also offers a 60 per cent increase in fruiting area over the standard VSP Trellis system (*see* opposite). Scott Henry not only provides larger crops, but riper, better quality fruit and because the canopy is split and, therefore, less dense, the wines are less herbaceous, with smoother tannins.

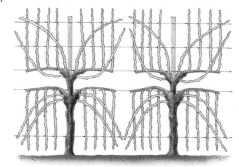

Increased yields and increased quality may seem unlikely, but Kim Goldwater of Waiheke Island has records to prove it and as *Goldwater Estate* is consistently one of New Zealand's best red wines, that is good enough for me. When I have asked growers who have tried the Scott Henry why they have given it up, they invariably reply "Have you ever tried to grow vine shoots downwards? It doesn't work!", but the downward-growing shoots actually grow upwards for most of the season. They are separated from the other upward-growing shoots by a moveable wire that levers half the canopy into a downwards position. The secret of this system's success is to move the wire no earlier than two or three weeks before the harvest, which gives the canes no time to revert and, with the increasing weight of the fruit, no inclination. In areas where grazing animals coexist with vines (as sheep do in New Zealand, for instance), the fact that both halves of the canopy are a metre (two feet) or so above the ground most of the time allows under-vine weeds and water-shoots to be controlled without herbicides or manual labour, without fear of the crop being eaten in the process. Scott Henry is found mainly in the New World and is becoming increasingly popular.

Scott Henry – *Spur-training system*

When adapted to spur training, each vine has two permanent spurs, instead of four annual canes, and produces either top canopies or bottom, but not both. The vines are pruned at alternating heights to replicate the effect of cane training, and all canopies grow upwards until those on the lower vines are levered

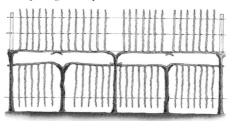

downwards (as shown here). The detailed structure of the Scott Henry system is almost impossible to identify when the vines are shrouded in foliage.

Sylvos – *Spur-training system*

This is like Guyot Double, only the trunk is much longer – up to two metres (four feet) – the main branches permanent, and the fruiting canes tied downwards, not upwards. Sylvos requires minimal pruning and is simple to maintain, lending itself to mechanization, but yields are low, unless pruned very lightly. *Vinifera* varieties do not like being forced downwards, but shoot positioning has been introduced by growers in

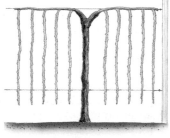

Australia (where it is called "Hanging Cane") and New Zealand. The system was originally conceived by Carlo Sylvos in Italy, where it is still very popular and is sometimes operated without a bottom wire, the canes falling downwards under their own weight. The main disadvantage is the dense canopy, which makes the vines prone to bunch-rot.

Sylvos (Hawke's Bay variant) – *Spur-training system*
This version of the Sylvos system was developed by Gary Wood of Montana Wines in the early 1980s on a Hawke's Bay vineyard belonging to Mark Read. The difference between this and the similar Scott Henry system is that it has two main spurs instead of four. With alternate fruiting canes on the same spur trained

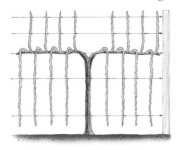

upwards then downwards, the canopy is more open, and grape clusters are further apart. This reduces bunch-rot significantly and facilitates better spray penetration. Yields are increased by as much as 100 per cent. The only disadvantage is the longer ripening time needed, which is a risk in areas where late harvests have their dangers.

VSP Trellis – *Cane-training system*
The VSP or Vertical Shoot Positioned trellis is widely used, particularly in New Zealand, where it is commonly referred to as the "standard" trellising system. With

the fruiting area contained within one compact zone on wires of a narrow span, it is ideally suited to mechanized forms of pruning, leaf removal, harvesting, and spraying, but it is prone to high vigour and shading. It is, therefore, a very economic method and when properly maintained is capable of producing good, but not top, quality wines. VSP is suitable for low-vigour vines only. A spur-trained version with just two main spurs is commonly encountered in France and Germany.

VITICULTURAL SPRAYS
The use of sprays was once confined to protecting the vine against pests and diseases and for controlling weeds, but they now have additional uses. Foliar feeds supply nutrients direct to the vine, while other sprays halt the growth of foliage, rendering summer pruning unnecessary; some sprays deliberately induce two disorders called *millerandage* and *coulure* to reduce the yield and, hopefully, increase the quality.

PRUNING
Important for controlling quantity, pruning is equally important for producing quality fruit. As with any crop, be it grapes or prize roses, if the quantity is reduced, the quality is increased. Reducing the number of fruiting buds lowers the quantity of fruit.

FLOWERING
The most critical period of a vine's life is when it flowers – at this stage frost, hail, rain, wind, and excessively high or low temperatures could wipe out a crop before the growing season begins in earnest. Even quality-conscious growers usually leave a couple of extra buds on each vine in case of poor weather during

flowering. It follows that if the weather permits a perfect flowering, even the best growers' vines end up with too many grape bunches. The weather is not often so kind in classic areas, but when it is, the perfect solution is to remove some of the embryo bunches. Most growers wait until the beginning of *veraison*, when the grapes start to take on colour and begin to ripen, before cutting off unwanted bunches. By now the vine has already wasted much of its energy on developing the clusters about to be discarded, but their removal will help the remaining bunches of grapes to ripen.

THE TIMING OF THE GRAPE HARVEST
When to pick is one of the most crucial decisions a grower has to make each year. As grapes ripen, there is a reduction in their acidity (which is also converted from mostly malic acid to primarily tartaric acid) and an increase in sugar, colour, various minerals, and essential aromatic compounds. The decision when to pick will vary according to the grape variety, the location of the vineyard, and the style of wine that is to be made. White wine generally benefits from the extra acidity of early-harvested grapes, but they also need the varietal aroma and richness that can only be found in ripe grapes. It is essential to get the balance right. Red wine requires relatively low acidity and profits from the increased colour, sugar, and tannin content of later-harvested grapes. The grower must also take the vagaries of the weather into account. Those who have the nerve to wait for perfectly ripe grapes every year can produce exceptional wines in even the poorest vintages, but run the risk of frost, rot, or hail damage. This can totally destroy not only an entire crop, but also an entire year's income. Those who never take a chance may always harvest healthy grapes, but in poor years the disadvantage of this approach is that the crop will be unripe and the wine mediocre.

TRANSPORTING THE GRAPES
In the race against time to get the grapes from the vineyard to the winery, everything possible should be done to cosset the fruit. Ideally, the winery and the vineyards should be as close as possible and the grapes transported in plastic crates small enough to prevent damage from their own weight. The crates should be designed so that stacking one on top of the other does not crush the fruit. The fact that some of the best-value wines of Eastern Europe are dumped into huge skips and take hours to reach their destination is fine for red wine, but currently less useful for white, as it splits the grapes, thereby encouraging oxidation and a loss of aromatics.

MECHANICAL HARVESTING
Mechanical harvesting is a contentious subject. The advantages of mechanization are dramatically reduced labour costs and a quick harvest of the entire crop at optimum ripeness, but the vineyard has to be adapted to the machine chosen and the reception and fermentation facilities must be enlarged to cope with the larger amounts and quicker throughput, which is costly. Disadvantages relate to the efficiency of the machinery and the quality of the wine.

As the machines beat the vine trunks with rubber sticks, the grapes drop on to a conveyor along with leaves and other matter, most of which is ejected as the fruit is sorted on its way to the hold. Apart from the rubbish that remains with the harvested grapes – which is becoming less as machines become more sophisticated – the main disadvantage is the inability to distinguish between the ripe and unripe, and the healthy and the diseased or plain rotten (the first thing to drop from any plant when shaken.)

Despite these inadequacies many excellent red wines have been made from mechanically harvested grapes. From a practical point of view it would seem that this method of harvesting is better for red wine than it is for white, particularly sparkling, as it splits the grapes, which encourages oxidation, loss of aromatics and, when harvesting black grapes for white sparkling wine, this creates an undesirable colouration of the juice.

GUIDE TO VINEYARD SOILS

The geological origin of rocks is vital, of course, to geologists, but not to the wine amateur. Does it matter whether two clay soils were laid down in different eras if, as far as it affects the growth of vines, the soil is similar in both cases? I think not. If one clay soil is heavier, or more silty, sandy, or calcareous, then that is relevant, but there is enough jargon used when discussing wine, to think of mixing it with rock-speak.

Aeolian soil Sediments deposited by wind (eg. loess).

Albariza White-surfaced soil formed by diatomaceous deposits, found in southern Spain.

Alluvial deposits (noun – alluvium) Material that has been transported by river and deposited. Most alluvial soils contain silt, sand, and gravel, and are highly fertile.

Aqueous rocks This is one of the three basic rock forms (*see* Rock). Also called sedimentary or stratified.

Arenaceous rocks Formed by the deposits of coarse-grained particles, usually siliceous and often decomposed from older rocks (eg. sandstone).

Argillaceous soils This term covers a group of sedimentary soils, commonly clays, shales, mudstones, siltstones, and marls.

Basalt Material that accounts for as much as 90 per cent of all lava-based volcanic rocks. It contains various minerals, is rich in lime and soda, but not quartz, the most abundant of all minerals, and it is poor in potash.

Bastard soil A *bordelais* name for medium-heavy, sandy-clay soil of variable fertility.

Boulbènes A *bordelais* name for a very fine siliceous soil that is easily compressed and hard to work. This "beaten" earth covers part of the Entre-Deux-Mers plateau.

Boulder *See* Particle size

Calcareous clay Argillaceous soil with carbonate of lime content that neutralizes the clay's intrinsic acidity. Its low temperature also delays ripening, so wines produced on this type of soil tend to be more acidic.

Calcareous soil Any soil, or mixture of soils, with an accumulation of calcium and magnesium carbonates. Essentially alkaline, it promotes the production of acidity in grapes, although the pH of each soil will vary according to its level of "active" lime. Calcareous soils are cool, with good water-retention. With the exception of calcareous clays (*see* above), they allow the vine's root system to penetrate deeply and provide excellent drainage.

Carbonaceous soil Soil that is derived from rotting vegetation under anaerobic conditions. The most common carbonaceous soils are peat, lignite, coal, and anthracite.

CHALK
Pristine white chalk on the Côtes des Blancs.

Chalk A type of limestone, chalk is a soft, cool, porous, brilliant-white, sedimentary, alkaline rock that encourages grapes with a relatively high acidity level. It also allows the vine's roots to penetrate and provides excellent drainage, while at the same time retaining sufficient moisture for nourishment. One of the few finer geological points that should be adhered to is that which distinguishes chalk from the numerous hard limestone rocks that do not possess the same physical properties.

Clay A fine-grained argillaceous compound with malleable, plastic characteristics and excellent water-retention properties. It is, however, cold, acid, offers poor drainage and, because of its cohesive quality, is hard to work. An excess of clay can stifle the vine's root system, but a proportion of small clay particles mixed with other soils can be advantageous.

Clayey-loam A very fertile version of loam, but heavy to work under wet conditions with a tendency to become waterlogged.

Cobble *See* Particle size.

Colluvial deposits (noun – colluvium) Weathered material transported by gravity or hill-wash.

Crasse de fer Iron-rich hard-pan found in the Libournais area of France. Also called machefer.

Crystalline May either be igneous (eg. granite) or metamorphic.

Dolomite A calcium-magnesium carbonate rock. Many limestones contain dolomite.

Feldspar or **Felspar** One of the most common minerals, feldspar is a white- or rose-coloured silicate of either potassium-aluminium or sodium-calcium-aluminium and is present in a number of rocks, including granite and basalt.

Ferruginous clay Iron-rich clay.

Flint A siliceous stone that stores and reflects heat, and is often associated with a certain "gun-flint" smell that sometimes occurs in wines, although this is not actually proven and may simply be the taster's auto-suggestion, unless it is picked up in a blind tasting.

Galestro A Tuscan name for the rocky, schistous soil that is commonly found in most of the region's best vineyards.

Glacial moraine A gritty scree that has been deposited by glacial action.

Gneiss A coarse-grained form of granite.

Granite A hard, mineral-rich rock that warms quickly and retains its heat. Granite contains 40 to 60 per cent quartz and 30 to 40 per cent potassium feldspar, plus mica or hornblende, and various other minerals. It has a high pH that reduces wine acidity. Thus, in Beaujolais, it is the best soil for the acidic Gamay grape. It is important to note that a soil formed from granite is a mixture of sand (partly derived from a disintegration of quartz and partly from the decomposition of feldspar with either mica or hornblende), clay, and various carbonates or silicates derived from the weathering of feldspar, mica or hornblende.

Gravel A wide-ranging term that covers siliceous pebble of various sizes. This soil is loose,

GRAVEL
Château de France, Leognan, Gironde.

granular, airy, and affords excellent drainage. It is also acid, infertile, and encourages the vine to send its roots down deep in search of nutrients. Therefore, gravel beds that are located above limestone subsoils produce wines with markedly more acidity than those located above clay subsoils.

Gypsum Highly absorbent, hydrated calcium-sulphate that was formed during the evaporation of sea-water.

Gypsiferous marl A marly soil permeated with Keuper or Muschelkalk gypsum fragments, which improve the soil's heat-retention and water-circulation properties.

Hard-pan A dense layer of clay that forms if the subsoil is more clayey than the topsoil at certain depths. As hard-pans are impermeable to both water and roots, they are not desirable too close to the surface, but may provide an easily reachable water-table if located deep down. A sandy, iron-rich hard-pan known as iron-pan is commonly found in parts of Bordeaux.

Hornblende A silicate of iron, aluminium, calcium, and magnesium, it constitutes the main mineral found in many crystalline rocks, such as basalt, and is a major component of some granite, gneiss etc.

Humus Organic material that contains bacteria and other micro-organisms that are capable of converting complex chemicals into simple plant foods. Humus makes soil fertile; without it soil is nothing more than finely-ground rock.

Igneous rock One of the three basic rock forms (*see* Rock), igneous rocks are formed from molten or partially molten material. Most igneous rocks are crystalline.

Iron-pan A sandy, iron-rich hard-pan.

Keuper Often used when discussing wines in Alsace, Keuper is a stratigraphic name for the Upper Triassic period, and can mean marl (varicoloured, saliferous grey or gypsiferous grey) or limestone (ammonoid).

Kimmeridgian soil A greyish-coloured limestone originally identified in, and so named after, the village of Kimmeridge in Dorset, England. A sticky, calcareous clay containing this limestone is often called Kimmeridgian clay.

Lignite The "brown coal" of Germany and the "black gold" of Champagne, this is a brown carbonaceous material intermediate between coal and peat. Warm and very fertile, it is mined and used as a natural fertilizer in Champagne.

Limestone Any sedimentary rock consisting essentially of carbonates. With the exception of chalk, few limestones are white, with grey- and buff-coloured probably the most commonly found limestone in wine areas. The hardness and water-retention of this rock varies, but being alkaline it generally encourages the production of grapes with a relatively high acidity level.

Loam A warm, soft, crumbly soil with roughly equal proportions of clay, sand, and silt. It is perfect for large-cropping mediocre-quality wines, but too fertile for fine wines.

Loess An accumulation of wind-borne, mainly silty material, that is sometimes calcareous, but usually weathered and decalcified. It warms up relatively quickly and also has good water-retention properties.

Machefer *See* **Crasse de fer**.

Marl A cold, calcareous clay that delays ripening and adds acidity to wine.

Marlstone Clayey limestone that has a similar effect to marl.

Metamorphic rocks One of the three basic categories of rock (*see* **Rock**), it is caused by great heat or pressure, often both.

Mica A generic name encompassing various silicate minerals, usually in a fine, decomposed-rock format.

Millstone Siliceous, iron-rich, sedimentary rock.

Moraine *See* **Glacial moraine**.

Mudstone A sedimentary soil similar to clay but without its plastic characteristics.

Muschelkalk Often used when discussing wines in Alsace, Muschelkalk is a stratigraphic name for the Middle Triassic period, and can mean anything from sandstone (shelly, dolomitic, calcareous, clayey, pink, yellow, or millstone) to marl (varicoloured or fissile), dolomite, limestone (crinoidal or grey), and shingle.

Oolite A type of limestone.

Oolith A term used for small, round, calcareous pebbles that have grown through fusion of very tiny particles.

Palus A *bordelais* name for a very fertile soil of modern alluvial origin that produces medium-quality, well-coloured, robust wines.

Particle size The size of a rock determines its descriptive name. No handful of soil will contain particles of a uniform size, unless it has been commercially graded, of course, so all such descriptions can only be guestimates, but it is worth noting what they should be,

otherwise you will have nothing to base your guestimates on. According to the Wentworth-Udden scale, they are: boulder (greater than 256mm), cobble (64mm–256mm), pebble (4mm–64mm), gravel (2mm–4mm), sand ($^1/_{16}$mm–2mm), silt ($^1/_{256}$mm–$^1/_{16}$mm) and clay (smaller than $^1/_{256}$mm). Notice that even by this precise scale, Wentworth and Udden have allowed overlaps, thus a $^1/_{16}$mm particle might either be sand or silt and, of course, sub-divisions are possible within each group, as there is such a thing as fine, medium, or coarse sand and even gritty silt.

Pebble *See* **Particle size**

Perlite A fine, powdery, light, and lustrous substance of volcanic origin with similar properties to diatomaceous earth.

Porphyry A coloured igneous rock with high pH.

Precipitated salts A sedimentary deposit. Water charged with acid or alkaline material, under pressure of great depth, dissolves various mineral substances from rocks on the sea-bed, which are then held in solution. When the water flows to a place of no great depth or is drained away or evaporates, the pressure is reduced, the minerals are no longer held in solution and precipitate in deposits that may be just a few centimetres or several thousand metres deep. There are five groups: oxides, carbonates, sulphates, phosphates, and chlorides.

Pudding stones A term used for a large, heat-retaining conglomerate of pebbles.

Quartz The most common and abundant mineral found in various sizes and in almost all soils, although sand and coarse silt contain the largest amount. Quartz has a high pH, which reduces wine acidity, but quartz that is pebble-sized or larger, stores and reflects heat, which increases alcohol potential.

Red earth *See* **Terra rossa**.

Rock A rock may be loosely described as a mass of mineral matter. There are three basic types of rock: igneous, metamorphic, and sedimentary (or aqueous or stratified).

Sand Tiny particles of weathered rocks and minerals that retain little water, but constitute a warm, airy soil that drains well and is supposedly phylloxera-free

Sandstone Sedimentary rock composed of sand-sized particles that have either been formed by pressure or bound by various iron minerals.

Sandy-loam Warm, well-drained, sand-dominated loam that is easy to work and suitable for early-cropping grape varieties.

Schist Heat-retaining, coarse-grain, laminated, crystalline rock that is rich in potassium and magnesium, but poor in nitrogen and organic substances.

Scree Synonymous with colluvium deposits.

Sedimentary rock One of the three basic rock forms (*see* **Rock**), it includes arenaceous (eg. sandstone), argillaceous (eg. clay), calcareous (eg. limestone), carbonaceous (eg. peat, lignite, or coal), siliceous (eg. quartz), and the five groups of precipitated salts, (oxides, carbonates, sulphates, phosphates, and chlorides). Sedimentary rocks are also called aqueous or stratified.

Shale Heat-retaining, fine-grain, laminated, moderately fertile sedimentary rock. Shale can turn into slate under pressure.

Shingle Pebble or gravel sized rounded by water-action.

Siliceous soil A generic term for acid rock of a crystalline nature. It may be organic (flint and kieselguhr) or inorganic (quartz) and have good heat retention, but no water retention unless

SLATE
Slate soil of the Mosel valley.

found in a finely-ground form in silt, clay, and other sedimentary soils. Half of the Bordeaux region is covered with siliceous soils.

Silt A very fine deposit, with good water retention. Silt is more fertile than sand, but is cold and offers poor drainage.

Slate Hard, dark grey, fine-grain, plate-like rock formed under pressure from clay, siltstone, shale, and other sediments. It warms up quickly, retains its heat well, and is responsible for many fine wines, most notably from the Mosel.

Steige A type of schist found on the north side of Andlau in Alsace, it has metamorphosed with the Andlau granite and is particularly hard and slaty. It has mixed with the granitic sand from the top of the Grand Cru Kastelberg and makes a dark, stony soil.

Stone This word should be used with rock types, such as limestone and sandstone, but is often used synonymously with pebble.

Stratified rock One of the three basic rock forms (*see* **Rock**), also called sedimentary or aqueous.

Terra rossa A red, clay-like, sometimes flinty sedimentary soil that is deposited after carbonate has been leached out of limestone. It is often known as "Red earth".

Tufa Various vent-based volcanic rocks, the chalk tufa of the Loire being the most important viticulturally speaking.

Volcanic soils Derived from two sources, volcanic soils are lava-based (the products of volcanic flow) and vent-based (material blown into the atmosphere). Some 90 per cent of lava-based rocks and soils are comprised of basalt, while others include andesite, pitchstone, rhyolite, and trachyte. Vent-based matter has either been ejected as molten globules, cooled in the air, and dropped to earth as solid particles (pumice), or as solid material and fractured through the explosive force with which it was flung (tufa).

PUDDING STONE
Large stones (galettes), Château de Beaucastel, in Châteauneuf-du-Pape.

TERRA ROSSA
The red soil of Wynns, Coonawarra, South Australia.

ANNUAL LIFE-CYCLE OF THE VINE

The calendar of events by which any well-established vine seeks to reproduce, through the production of grapes, is outlined below, along with a commentary on how the vine is cultivated to encourage the best possible grapes for wine-making. The vine's year starts and finishes with the end and approach of winter, although a winegrower is active almost all year, with vineyard maintenance continuing into winter.

FEBRUARY Northern hemisphere
AUGUST Southern hemisphere

Weeping

Weeping is the first sign of the vine awakening after a winter of relative dormancy. When the soil at a depth of 25 centimetres (10 inches) reaches 10.2°C (50°F), the roots start collecting water and the sap in the vine rises, oozing out of the cane-ends which were pruned in winter, in a manifestation called "weeping". This occurs suddenly, rapidly increases in intensity, and then decreases gradually. Each vine loses between half and five-and-a-half litres (ten pints) of sap. Weeping is the signal to prune for the spring growth. However, this poses a problem for the grower

As the soil warms up the vine awakes, pushing sap out of its cane ends.

because the vine, once pruned, is at its most vulnerable to frost. But waiting for the danger of frost to pass wastes the vine's preciously finite energy and retards its growth, delaying the ripening of the fruit by as much as ten days, and thus risking exposure of the fruit to autumn frosts later on.

APRIL – MAY Northern hemisphere
OCTOBER – NOVEMBER Southern hemisphere

Emergence of shoots, foliage, and embryo bunches

Embryo bunches, the vine's flowers, form.

Following bud-break, foliage develops and shoots are sent out. In mid-April (mid-October in the southern hemisphere), after the fourth or fifth leaf has emerged, tiny green clusters form. These are the flowers which, when they bloom, will develop into grapes. Commonly called embryo bunches, they are the first indication of the potential size of a crop. In the vineyard, spraying to ward off various vine pests, or cure diseases and other disorders starts in May (November), and continues until the harvest. Many of these sprays are combined with systemic fertilizers to feed the vine directly through its foliage. These spraying operations are normally done by hand or tractor, but may sometimes be carried out by helicopter if the slopes are very steep or the vineyards too muddy to enter. At this time of year the vine can be affected by *coulure* or *millerandage* (*see* p.22).

MARCH – APRIL Northern hemisphere
SEPTEMBER – OCTOBER Southern hemisphere

Bud-break

In the spring, some 20 to 30 days after the vine starts to weep, the buds open. Different varieties bud-break at different times; there are early bud-breakers and the same variety can bud-break at different times in different years due to climatic changes. The type of soil can also affect the timing; clay, which is cold, will retard the process, while sand, which is warm, will promote it. Early bud-break varieties are susceptible to frost in northerly vineyards (southerly in the southern hemisphere), just as late-ripeners are prone to

Buds begin to open at a time determined by variety and climate.

autumn frosts. In the vineyard, pruning continues into March (September in the southern hemisphere). The vines are secured to their training frames, and the earth that was ploughed over the grafting wound to protect it in the winter is ploughed back, aerating the soil and levelling off the ground between the rows.

MAY – JUNE Northern hemisphere
NOVEMBER – DECEMBER Southern hemisphere

Flowering of the vine

For about ten days the vine flowers – a vulnerable period.

The embryo bunches break into flower after the 15th or 16th leaf has emerged on the vine. This is normally about eight weeks after the bud-break and involves pollination and fertilization, and lasts for about ten days. The weather must be dry and frost-free, but temperature is the most critical requirement. A daily average of at least 15°C (59°F) is needed to enable a vine to flower and between 20º and 25°C (68º–77°F) is considered ideal. Heat summation, however, is more important than temperature levels, so the length of day has a great influence on the number of days the flowering will last. Soil temperature is more significant than air temperature, so the soil's heat-retaining capacity is a contributory factor. Frost is the greatest hazard, and many vineyards are protected by stoves or sprinkling systems.

JUNE – JULY Northern hemisphere
DECEMBER – JANUARY Southern hemisphere

Fruit set

After the flowering, the embryo bunches rapidly evolve into true clusters. Each fertilized berry expands into a grape, the first visible sign of the actual fruit that will produce the wine. This is called fruit-set. The number of grapes per embryo bunch varies from variety to variety, as does the percentage that actually set into grapes. The panel below illustrates this. In the vineyard, spraying continues and summer pruning (cutting away some bunches) will concentrate the vine's energy on making fruit. In

Clearly recognizable grapes begin to form.

some vineyards this is the time for weeding, but in others the weeds are allowed to grow as high as 50 centimetres (20 inches) before they are mown and ploughed into the soil to break up the soil and provide the vines with excellent green manure.

VARIETY	BERRIES PER EMBRYO BUNCH	GRAPES IN A RIPE CLUSTER	PERCENTAGE OF FRUIT-SET
Chasselas	164	48	29%
Gewürztraminer	100	40	40%
Pinot gris	149	41	28%
Riesling	189	61	32%
Sylvaner	95	50	53%

AUGUST Northern hemisphere
JANUARY Southern hemisphere

Ripening of the grapes

As the grape develops its fleshy fruit, very little chemical change takes place inside the berry until its skin begins to turn a different colour – the process known as *veraison*. Throughout the grape's green stage, the sugar and acid content remains the same, but during August (January in the southern hemisphere), the ripening process begins in earnest – the skin changes colour, the sugar content dramatically increases, and the hard malic acid diminishes as the riper tartaric acid builds up. Although the tartaric acid content begins to

The grapes begin to change colour, the sign of true ripening.

decline after about two weeks, it always remains the primary acid. It is at this stage that the grape's tannins are gradually hydrolyzed. This is a crucial moment because only hydrolyzed tannins are capable of softening as a wine matures. In the vineyard, spraying and weeding continue, and the vine's foliage is thinned to facilitate the circulation of air and thus reduce the risk of rot. Care has to be taken not to remove too much foliage as it is the effect of sunlight upon the leaves, not the grapes, that causes the grapes to ripen.

AUGUST – OCTOBER Northern hemisphere
FEBRUARY – MARCH Southern hemisphere

Grape harvest

Grapes are picked at a time determined by the winemaker.

The harvest usually begins mid- to late-September (mid-to-late-February in the southern hemisphere) and may last for a month or more, but, as is the case with all vineyard operations, the timing is earlier nearer to the equator and is dependent on the weather. Picking may, therefore, start as early as August (February) and finish as late as November (April). White grapes ripen before black grapes and must, in any case, be harvested that little bit more early to achieve a higher acidity balance.

NOVEMBER – DECEMBER Northern hemisphere
APRIL – MAY Southern hemisphere

Grapes affected by botrytis cinerea

Rotting grapes, soon to be harvested for sweet botrytized wine.

In November the sap retreats to the protection of the vine's root system. As a result, the year-old canes begin to harden and any remaining grapes, cut off from the vine's metabolic system, start to dehydrate. The concentrated pulp that they become is subject to severe cold. This induces complex chemical changes in a process known as *passerillage*. In specialist sweet-wine areas the grapes are deliberately left on the vine to undergo this quality-enhancing experience and, in certain vineyards with suitable climatic conditions, growers pray for the appearance of *botrytis cinerea* or "noble rot".

DECEMBER – JANUARY Northern hemisphere
MAY – JUNE Southern hemisphere

Eiswein

Grapes still on the vine may yet become wine.

In Germany, it is possible to see grapes on the vine in December and even January. This is usually because the grower has hoped for *botrytis cinerea*, or *Edelfäule* as it is called in Germany, but it has failed to occur on some grapes. Should frost or snow freeze the grapes, they can be harvested to produce Eiswein, one of the world's most spectacular wines. As it is only the water that freezes, this can be skimmed off once the grapes are pressed in order to leave a super-concentrated unfrozen pulp that produces Eiswein.

HOW WINE IS MADE

Although the internationalization of winemaking techniques is a topic that is always much discussed, methods of production can still vary greatly not just from country to country, but from region to region, and quite commonly even from grower to grower within the same village.

IN WINEMAKING, much depends upon whether traditional values are upheld or innovations are sought, and for the latter, whether the technology is available. Whatever the winemaker decides, certain principles will, essentially, remain the same. These are described below, followed by sections on styles of wine and the processes common or unique to each one.

THE DIMINISHING QUALITY FACTOR

The quality of the grapes when they are harvested represents the maximum potential of any wine that can be made from them.

However, a winemaker will never be able to transfer 100 per cent of this inherent quality to the wine, because deterioration sets in from the moment a grape is disconnected from the vine's metabolism. Furthermore, the very process of turning grapes into wine is necessarily a destructive one, so every action that the winemaker takes, however quality-conscious, will inevitably erode some of the wine's potential. Winemakers, therefore, can only attempt to minimize the loss of potential quality.

It is relatively easy to retain approximately 80 per cent of the potential quality of a wine, but very difficult to claw-back every percentile point after that. It is also relatively easy to double or even treble the basic grape quality by a better selection of vineyard sites, improved training methods, the use of superior clones, correct rootstock, and a reduction in yields. As a result, research has now swung from the winery back to the vineyard.

That said, oenological practices are still important and how they are employed will have a profound effect not only on quality, but also on the style of the wine produced.

PRINCIPLES OF VINIFICATION

With modern technology, good everyday-drinking wines can be made anywhere that grapes are grown. When such wines are not made, the reason is invariably a lack of equipment and expertise. Finer quality wines require vineyards that have a certain potential and winemakers with a particular talent. When not even good everyday-drinking wines are made from fine wine vineyards, it is usually due to a combination of excessive yields and poor winemaking, and there is no excuse for either.

FERMENTATION

The biochemical process that transforms fresh grape juice into wine is called fermentation. Yeast cells excrete enzymes that convert natural fruit sugars into almost equal quantities of alcohol and carbonic gas. This process ceases when the supply of sugar is exhausted or when the alcoholic level reaches a point that is toxic for the yeast enzymes (usually 15 to 16 per cent, although certain strains can survive at 20 to 22 per cent). Traditionally, winemakers racked their wine from cask to cask (*see* p.34) until he was sure that fermentation had stopped, but there are now many other methods that halt fermentation artificially. They can involve the use of heat, sulphur dioxide, centrifugal filtration, alcohol, pressure, or carbonic gas.

• **Heat** There are various forms of pasteurization (for table wines), flash-pasteurization (for finer wines), and chilling operations that are used to stabilize wine. These operate on the basis that yeast cells are incapacitated at temperatures above 36°C (97°F), or below –3°C (26°F), and that yeast enzymes are destroyed above 65°C (149°F). Flash-pasteurization subjects wines to a temperature of about 80°C (176°F) for between 30 seconds and one minute, whereas fully fledged pasteurization involves lower temperatures of 50 to 60°C (122 to 140°F) for a longer period.

• **Addition of sulphur dioxide or sorbic acid** Dosing with one or more aseptic substances will kill off the yeasts.

• **Centrifugal filtration or filtration** Modern equipment is now capable of physically removing all the yeasts from a wine, either by filtration, which is simply pouring the wine through a medium that prevents certain substances passing through, or by centrifugal filtration, which is a process that separates unwanted matter from wine (or grape juice, if used at an earlier stage) by so-called "centrifugal force".

• **Addition of alcohol** Fortification raises the alcohol content to a level toxic to yeast.

• **Pressure** Yeast cells are destroyed by pressure in excess of eight atmospheres (the pressure inside a Champagne bottle is around six atmospheres).

• **Addition of carbonic gas (CO_2)** Yeast cells are destroyed in the presence of 15 grams per litre or more of carbonic gas.

THE USE OF SULPHUR

Sulphur is used in winemaking from the time the grapes arrive at the winery until just before the wine is bottled. It has several qualities, including anti-oxidant and aseptic qualities, that make it essential for commercial winemaking. To some extent, all wines are oxidized from the moment the grapes are pressed and the juice is exposed to the air, but the rate of oxidation must be controlled. This is where sulphur is useful, because it has a chemical attraction for the tiny amounts of oxygen that are present in wine. One molecule of sulphur will combine with two molecules of oxygen, to form sulphur dioxide (SO_2), or fixed sulphur. Once it is combined with the sulphur, the oxygen is neutralized and can no longer oxidize the wine. More oxygen will be absorbed by wine during the vinification process, of course, and there will also be a small head of air between the wine and the cork after bottling.

YEAST THE FERMENTER

The yeasts used for fermentation may be divided into two categories: cultured yeasts and natural yeasts.

Cultured yeasts are nothing more than thoroughbred strains of natural wine yeasts that have been raised in a laboratory. They may be used because the juice has been cleansed prior to fermentation of all organisms, including its yeasts, or because the winemaker prefers their reliability, or for a specific purpose, such as withstanding higher alcohol levels or the increased osmotic pressure that affects bottle-fermented sparkling wines.

Natural yeasts are to be found adhering to the *pruina*, a waxy substance that covers the skin of ripe grapes and other fruits. By the time a grape has fully ripened, the coating of yeasts and other micro-organisms, commonly referred to as the "bloom", contains an average of ten million yeast cells, although only one per cent or just 100,000 cells are so-called "wine-yeasts". A yeast cell is only a tiny fraction of an inch, yet under favourable conditions it has the ability to split 10,000 sugar molecules every second during fermentation.

It is for this reason that wines are bottled with a set amount of free sulphur (the amount of the total sulphur content that is not fixed). Occasionally a winemaker claims that sulphur is completely superfluous to the winemaking process, but whereas low-sulphur regimes are actually to be encouraged, wines produced without it are usually dire or have a very short shelf-life.

One famous wine that claimed not to use any sulphur was so long-lived I had a bottle independently analysed, only to find that it did contain sulphur. The quantity was small, but far too significant to have been created during fermentation (which is possible in tiny amounts). It was, therefore, an example of how effective a low-sulphur regime can be. Methods of reducing the level of SO_2 are well known, the most important being a very judicious initial dosage because a resistance to sulphur builds up and, as a result, later doses have to be increased.

Some wines can be over-sulphured and, although they are less common than they used to be, they are by no means rare. Over-sulphured wines are easily recognizable by their smell, which ranges from the slight whiff of a recently ignited match (which is the clean smell of free sulphur) to the pong of bad eggs (which is H_2S, where the sulphur has combined with hydrogen – literally the stuff of stink-bombs). When H_2S reacts with ethyl alcohol or one of the higher alcohols, foul-smelling compounds called mercaptans are formed. They can smell of garlic, onion, burnt rubber, or stale cabbage, depending on the exact nature of the compound. Mercaptans are extremely difficult for the winemaker to remove and can ruin a wine, which illustrates just how important it is to maintain a low-sulphur regime.

MALOLACTIC FERMENTATION

Malolactic fermentation is positively encouraged for red wines and fuller, fatter, more complex whites, but may sometimes be avoided for lighter, crisper whites and certain styles of sparkling wine.

Malolactic fermentation is sometimes known as the secondary fermentation, but this is an inappropriate description. The malolactic, or "malo" as it is sometimes called, is a biochemical process that converts the "hard" malic acid of unripe grapes into two-parts "soft" lactic, or "milk", acid (so-called because it is the acid that makes milk sour) and one-part carbonic gas. Malic acid is a very strong-tasting acid, which reduces during the fruit's ripening process. However, a significant quantity persists in ripe grapes, and, although reduced by fermentation, also in wine. The quantity of malic acid present in a wine may be considered too much and the smoothing effect of replacing it with just two-thirds the quantity of the much weaker lactic acid is often desirable. The smoothing effect is considered vital for red wine, but optional for white, rosé, and sparkling wine. To ensure that the malo can take place, it is essential that specific bacteria are present. These are found naturally on grape skins among the yeasts and other micro-organisms. To undertake their task, they require a medium of a certain warmth, a low level of sulphur, a pH between 3 and 4, and a supply of various nutrients found naturally in the grapes.

STAINLESS STEEL OR OAK?

The use of stainless steel and oak containers for fermentation and maturation is not simply dependent on the cost (*see right*). The two materials produce opposing effects upon wine, so the choice is heavily dependent upon whether the winemaker wants to add character to a wine or to keep its purity.

A stainless-steel vat is a long-lasting, easy-to-clean vessel made from an impervious and inert material that is ideally suited to all forms of temperature control, and has the capacity to produce the freshest wines with the purest varietal character. An oak cask has a comparatively limited life, is not easy to clean (it can never be sterilized), makes temperature control very difficult, and is neither impervious nor inert. It allows access to the air, which encourages a faster rate of oxidation, but also causes evaporation, which

STAINLESS-STEEL VATS
Stainless-steel is the cornerstone of modern winemaking technology. The bands around each tank contain a coolant to regulate fermentation temperatures.

concentrates the flavour. Vanillin, the essential aromatic constituent of vanilla pods, is extracted from the oak by oxidation, and, with various wood lactones and unfermentable sugars, imparts a distinctive, sweet and creamy vanilla nuance to wine. This oaky character takes on a smoky complexity if the wine is allowed to go through its malolactic fermentation in contact with the wood, and becomes even more complex, and certainly better integrated, if the wine has undergone all or most of its alcoholic fermentation in cask. Oak also imparts wood tannins to low tannin wine, absorbs tannins from tannic wine, and can exchange tannins with some wines. Oak tannins also act as catalysts, provoking desirable changes in grape tannins through a complex interplay of oxidations.

NEW OAK BARRELS
A meticulous display of brand-new, French oak barriques in the first year chai of Château Mouton-Rothschild.

THE COST OF NEW OAK

Two hundred 225-litre (49-gallon) oak casks with a total capacity of 450 hectolitres (9,900 gallons) cost between four and ten times the cost of a single 450 hectolitre (9,900 gallon) stainless-steel vat. After two years of much higher labour costs to operate and maintain the large number of small units, the volume of wine produced in the oak casks is 10 per cent less because of evaporation, and the winemaker faces the prospect of purchasing another two hundred casks.

POST-FERMENTATION PROCEDURES

Numerous procedures can take place in the winery after fermentation and, where applicable, malolactic fermentation has ceased. However, the five most basic procedures are racking, fining, cold stabilisation, filtration, and bottling.

Racking

Draining the clear wine off its lees, or sediment, into another vat or cask is known as "racking" because of the different levels, or racks, on which the wine is run from one container into another. In modern vinification, this operation is usually conducted several times throughout the maturation period in vat or cask. The wine gradually throws off less and less of a deposit. Some wines, such as Muscadet sur lie are never racked.

Fining

After fermentation, wine may, or may not, look hazy to the eye, and yet still contain suspended matter that threatens cloudiness in the bottle. Fining usually assists the clarification of wine at this stage, in addition to which, special fining agents may be employed to remove unwanted characteristics. When a fining agent is added to wine, it adheres to cloudy matter by physical or electrolytic attraction, creating tiny clusters, known as colloidal groups, which drop to the bottom of the vat as sediment. The most commonly encountered fining agents are egg white, tannin, gelatine, bentonite, isinglass, and casein. Winemakers have their preferences and individual fining agents also have their specific uses. Thus positively charged egg white fines out negatively charged matter, such as unwanted tannins or anthocyanins, while negatively charged bentonite fines out positively charged matter, such as protein haze and other organic matter.

Cold stabilization

When wines are subjected to low temperatures, a crystalline deposit of tartrates can form a deposit in the bottle. Should the wine be dropped to a very low temperature for a few days before bottling, this process can be precipitated, rendering the wine safe from the threat of a tartrate deposit in the bottle. For the past 20 years, cold stabilization has been almost obligatory for cheap commercial wines, and it is now increasingly used for those of better quality as well. This recent trend is a pity because the crystals are, in fact, entirely harmless and their presence is a completely welcome indication of a considerably more natural, rather than heavily processed, wine.

Filtration

Various methods of filtration exist, and they all entail running wine through a medium that prevents particles of a certain size from passing. Filtration has become a controversial subject in recent times, with some critics claiming that anything that removes something from wine must be bad. Depending on who you listen to, this "something" is responsible for a wine's complexity, body, or flavour. However, although it is undeniable that filtration strips something from a wine, if it is unfiltered, it will throw a much heavier deposit and do so relatively quickly. The mysterious "something" is, therefore, purged from all wines at some time or other, whether they are filtered or not, and whether the critics like it or not. Filtration, like so many things, is perfectly acceptable if it is applied in moderation. The fact that many of the world's greatest wines are filtered is a testament to this.

I prefer less filtration or no filtration, as do most quality-conscious winemakers. This is not because of any romantic, unquantifiable ideal, it is simply because I prefer wine to be as unprocessed and as natural as possible. This is a state that can only be achieved through as much of a hands-off approach as the wine will allow. Generally the finer the wine, the less filtration required, as consumers of expensive wines expect sedimentation

ROTARY DRUM VACUUM FILTER
One of the most efficient forms of filtration available, Rotary Drum Vacuum Filters are often used to extract the last drop of wine from the lees.

and are prepared to decant. Delicate reds, such as Pinot noir, should be least filtered of all, as I swear they lose fruit just by looking at them, and they certainly lose colour – that, at least, is quantifiable. No wine with extended barrel-ageing should ever require filtration, just a light, natural fining.

Each filtration is expensive and time-consuming, thus even producers of the most commercial, everyday wines (which even filtration critics accept must be filtered) should keep these operations to a minimum. The principle means of achieving this is by ensuring the best possible clarification by settling and racking. Fining should always take precedence, as it is both kinder on the wine and much cheaper than filtering. There are four basic types of filtration: Earth, Pad, Membrane, and Crossflow.

• **Earth Filtration** This system is primarily used after racking for filtering the wine-rich lees that collect at the bottom of the fermentation tank. A medium, usually kieselguhr, a form of diatomaceous earth, is continuously fed into the wine and used with either a Plate and Frame Filter or a Rotary Drum Vacuum Filter. Both types of filter are precoated with the medium, but in a Plate and Frame Filter, the wine and medium mix is forced, under pressure, through plates, or screens, of the medium, in a manner similar to that of any other filter. For the Rotary Drum Vacuum Filter, however, the precoat adheres to the outside of a large perforated drum by virtue of the vacuum that is maintained inside. The drum revolves through a shallow bath into which the wine is pumped and literally sucks the wine through the precoat into the centre, where it is piped away. The advantage of this system is that on one side of the shallow bath there is a scraper that constantly shaves the coating on the drum to the desired thickness. The medium thus falls into the wine, with which it mixes, and is then sucked back on to, and through, the drum. It is a continuous process and a very economical one, as the amount of medium used is limited. In a Plate and Frame Filter, the medium is enclosed and eventually clogs up, requiring the operation to be stopped, and the equipment to be dismantled and cleaned before the process can resume.

• **Pad Filtration** Also called Sheet Filtration, this requires the use of a Plate and Frame Filter with a variable number of frames into which filter pads or sheets can slide. Before it was outlawed, these used to be made of asbestos. They now contain numerous filtration mediums, ranging from diatomaceous earth to regular cellulose pads, which are the most commonly used medium. Special filter formats include active carbon (to remove unwanted colour, which is frowned upon for all but the most commercial, high-volume wines) and electrostatically charged pads. These are designed to attract any matter that is suspended in the wine, most of which will possess a negative or positive charge. It is claimed that these electrostatically charged pads are more effective in filtering out matter than the same pads without a charge.

• **Membrane Filtration** This is also called Millipore, because the membranes contain microscopic holes capable of removing yeasts and other micro-organisms. As these holes account for 80 per cent of the sheet's surface, the throughput of wine can be extremely fast provided it has undergone a light pre-filtration. Both filtration and pre-filtration can now, however, be done at the same time with new Millipore cartridge filters. These contain two or more membranes of varying porosity, thus the coarser ones act as a screen for those with the most minuscule holes.

• **Crossflow Filtration** Originally designed to purify water, crossflow filtration varies from the others (with the exception of Rotary Drum Vacuum Filter) because it is self-cleaning and never clogs-up. The wine flows across the membrane, not into it, so only some of it penetrates. Most of it returns to the chamber from which it came and, because it flows very fast, takes with it any matter filtered out by the membrane.

BOTTLING

When visiting larger producers, automated bottling lines are the wine journalist's *bête noire*. They get faster and more complex each year and, having invested vast sums in the very latest bottling line, it is understandable that proprietors are keen to show off their new high-tech toy. However, as John Arlott once told me, as he resolutely refused to set foot in the bottling hall of Piper-Heidsieck, "I have not written a single word about bottling lines in my life and I'm not going to start now". They make a very dull experience and inevitably break down just as one's host boasts that it is the fastest bottling line in the world, but their smooth operation most days of the week is essential if the wine is to remain as fresh as possible in the bottle. All that readers need to know is that the bottles should be sterile, that fully-automated lines cork, capsule, label, and box the wines, and that there is a device to detect any impurities before the bottles are boxed. All European systems either print on the label, or laser-print directly on to the bottle a lot number, which identifies the date each batch was bottled. This means that in an emergency, a specific batch can be recalled, rather than the entire production having to be cleared from every wholesaler and retailer stocking a particular line.

FROM GRAPE TO GLASS

Virtually every ingredient of a fresh grape can be found in the wine it makes, although additional compounds are produced when wine is made and any sedimented matter is disposed of before it is bottled. The most significant difference in the two lists below is the disappearance of fermentable sugar and the appearance of alcohol, although the constituents will vary according to the variety and ripeness of the grape and the style of wine produced.

THE "INGREDIENTS" OF FRESH GRAPE JUICE

Percentage by volume

73.5	Water	
25	Carbohydrates, of which:	
	5%	Cellulose
	20%	Sugar (plus pentoses, pectin, inositol)
0.8	Organic acids, of which:	
	0.54%	Tartaric acid
	0.25%	Malic acid
	0.01%	Citric acid (plus possible traces of succinic acid and lactic acid)
0.5	Minerals, of which:	
	0.025%	Calcium
	0.01%	Chloride
	0.025%	Magnesium
	0.25%	Potassium
	0.05%	Phosphate
	0.005%	Silicic acid
	0.035%	Sulphate
	0.1%	Others (aluminium, boron, copper, iron, molybdenum, rubidium, sodium, zinc)
0.13	Tannin and colour pigments	
0.07	Nitrogenous matter, of which:	
	0.05%	Amino acids (arginine, glutamic acid, proline, serine, threonine, and others)
	0.005%	Protein
	0.015%	Other nitrogenous matter (humin, amide, ammonia, and others)
Traces	Mainly vitamins (thiamine, riboflavin, pyridoxine, pantothenic acid, nicotinic acid, and ascorbic acid)	

WATER INTO WINE

The individual flavouring elements in any wine represent barely two per cent of its content, but although we can determine with great accuracy the amount and identity of 99 per cent of these constituents, the mystery is that if we assembled them and added the requisite volume of water and alcohol, the result would taste nothing like wine, let alone like the specific wine we would be trying to imitate.

THE "CONTENTS" OF WINE

Percentage by volume

86	Water	
12	Alcohol (ethyl alcohol)	
1	Glycerol	
0.4	Organic acids, of which:	
	0.20%	Tartaric acid
	0.15%	Lactic acid
	0.05%	Succinic acid (plus traces of malic acid citric acid)
0.2	Carbohydrates (unfermentable sugar)	
0.2	Minerals, of which:	
	0.02%	Calcium
	0.01%	Chloride
	0.02%	Magnesium
	0.075%	Potassium
	0.05%	Phosphate
	0.005%	Silicic acid
	0.02%	Sulphate
	Traces	Aluminium, boron, copper, iron, molybdenum, rubidium, sodium, zinc
0.1	Tannin and colour pigments	
0.045	Volatile acids (mostly acetic acid)	
0.025	Nitrogenous matter, of which:	
	0.01%	Amino acids (arginine, glutamic acid, proline, serine, threonine, and others)
	0.015%	Protein and other nitrogenous matter (humin, amide, ammonia, and others)
0.025	Esters (mostly ethyl acetate, but traces of numerous others)	
0.004	Aldehydes (mostly acetaldehyde, some vanillin, and traces of others)	
0.001	Higher alcohols (minute quantities of amyl plus traces of isoamyl, butyl, isobutyl, hexyl, propyl, and methyl may be present)	
Traces	Vitamins (thiamine, riboflavin, pyridoxine, pantothenic acid, nicotinic acid, and ascorbic acid)	

HOW RED WINE IS MADE

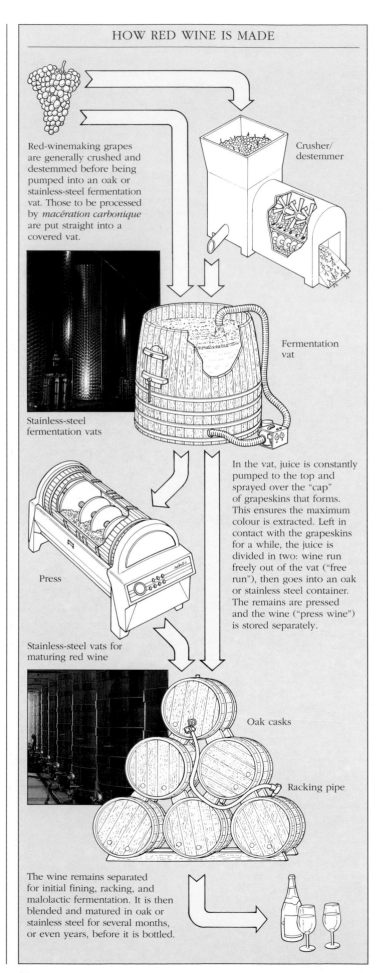

Red-winemaking grapes are generally crushed and destemmed before being pumped into an oak or stainless-steel fermentation vat. Those to be processed by *macération carbonique* are put straight into a covered vat.

Crusher/destemmer

Stainless-steel fermentation vats

Fermentation vat

Press

In the vat, juice is constantly pumped to the top and sprayed over the "cap" of grapeskins that forms. This ensures the maximum colour is extracted. Left in contact with the grapeskins for a while, the juice is divided in two: wine run freely out of the vat ("free run"), then goes into an oak or stainless steel container. The remains are pressed and the wine ("press wine") is stored separately.

Stainless-steel vats for maturing red wine

Oak casks

Racking pipe

The wine remains separated for initial fining, racking, and malolactic fermentation. It is then blended and matured in oak or stainless steel for several months, or even years, before it is bottled.

RED WINES

On arrival at the winery the grapes are usually crushed and destemmed, although in the past it was the accepted practice to leave the stems in order to promote a more tannic wine. However, the tannins in the stems are too harsh and fail to soften as the wine matures. Knowing this, the modern winemaker can include a small percentage of stems if the grape variety he uses requires extra structure or if the vintage in question needs firming up.

FERMENTATION

After the grapes are destemmed and lightly crushed, they are pumped into a vat where fermentation may begin as early as 12 hours, or as late as several days later. Even wines that will be cask-fermented must start off in vats, whether they are old-fashioned oak *foudres* or modern stainless-steel tanks. This is because they must be fermented along with a *manta*, or cap, of grapeskins. To encourage fermentation, the juice may be heated and selected yeast cultures or partially fermented wine from another vat added. During fermentation the juice is pumped from the bottom of the vat to the top and sprayed over the *manta* to keep the juice in contact with the grapeskins. This ensures that the maximum colour is extracted. Other methods involve the *manta* being pushed under the fermenting juice with poles. Some vats are equipped with crude but effective grids that prevent the *manta* from rising, others rely on the carbonic gas that is given off during fermentation to build up pressure, releasing periodically and pushing the *manta* under the surface; another system keeps the *manta* submerged in a "vinimatic", a sealed, rotating stainless-steel tank, based on the cement-mixer principle.

The higher the temperature during fermentation, the more colour and tannin will be extracted; the lower the temperature, the better the bouquet, freshness, and fruit will be. The optimum temperature for the fermentation of red wine is 29.4°C (85°F). If it is too hot, the yeasts produce certain substances (decanoic acid, octanoic acids, and corresponding esters), which inhibit their own ability to feed on nutrients, and cause the yeasts to die. It is, however, far better to ferment hot fresh juice than to wait two weeks (which is normal in many cases) to ferment cool but stale juice. The fuller, darker, more tannic and potentially longer-lived wines remain in contact with the skins for anything between ten and 30 days. Lighter wines, on the other hand, are separated from the skins after only a few days.

VIN DE GOUTTE AND VIN DE PRESSE

The moment the skins are separated from the juice, every wine is divided into two – free-run, or *vin de goutte*, and press wine, or *vin de presse*. The free-run juice runs out of the vat when the tap is opened. The remains, the *manta* of grapeskins, pips, and other solids, is put into a press to extract the very dark, extremely tannic "press wine". The free-run wine and the press wine are then pumped into separate vats or casks depending on the style of the wine being made. These wines then undergo their malolactic conversion separately, are racked several times, fined, racked again, blended, then fined and racked once more before bottling.

MACÉRATION CARBONIQUE

There are several variations of *macération carbonique*, a technique used almost exclusively for making red wine, involving an initial fermentation under pressure of carbonic gas. The traditional method, dating back at least 200 years, was to put the uncrushed grapes in a closed container, where, after a while a natural fermentation inside the grapes would take place. When the grapes eventually exploded, filling the container with carbonic gas, a normal fermentation continued and the grapes macerated in their own skins. Today the grapes are often placed in vats filled with carbonic gas from a bottle. *Macération carbonique* produces light wines with good colour, soft fruit, and a "pear-drop" aroma.

WHITE WINES

Until fairly recently it could be said that two initial operations distinguished the white-winemaking process from the red one: first, an immediate pressing to extract the juice and separate the skins, and, second, the purging, or cleansing, of this juice. But for white wines of expressive varietal character the grapes are now often crushed and then macerated in a vinimatic (*see* Glossary) for 12 to 48 hours to extract the aromatics that are stored in the skins. The juice that is run out of the vinimatic, and the juice that is pressed out of the macerated pulp left inside it, then undergoes cleansing and fermentation like any other white wine.

However, with the exception of wines macerated in a vinimatic, the grapes are either pressed immediately on arrival at the winery or lightly crushed and then pressed. The juice from the last pressing is murky, bitter, and low in acidity and sugar, so only the first pressing, which is roughly equivalent to the free-run juice in red wine, together with the richest elements of the second pressing, should be used for white-wine production. Once pressed, the juice is pumped into a vat where it is purged, or cleansed, which in its simplest form means simply leaving the juice to settle so that particles of grapeskin and any other impurities fall to the bottom. This purging may be helped by chilling, adding sulphur dioxide and, possibly, a fining agent. Light filtration and centrifugation may also be applied during this process.

After cleansing, the juice is pumped into the fermenting vat or directly into barrels if the wine is to be cask-fermented. The opportunity to add selected yeast cultures occurs more often in the production of white wine because of the wine's limited contact with the yeast-bearing skins and the additional cleansing that reduces the potential amount of wine yeasts available. The optimum temperature for fermenting white wine is 18°C (64°F), although many winemakers opt for between 10°C and 17°C (50°F and 63°F), and it is possible to ferment wine at temperatures as low as 4°C (39°F). At lower temperatures, more esters and other aromatics are created, less volatile acidity is produced, and a lower dose of sulphur dioxide is required, but the wines are lighter in body and contain less glycerol.

With acidity an essential factor in the balance of fruit and, where appropriate, sweetness in white wines, many products are not permitted to undergo malolactic conversion and are not bottled until some 12 months after the harvest. Oak-matured wines which, incidentally, always undergo malolactic conversion, may be bottled between 9 and 18 months, but wines that are made especially for early drinking are nearly always racked, fined, filtered, and bottled as quickly as the process will allow in order to retain as much freshness and fruitiness as possible.

ROSÉ WINES

With the exception of pink Champagne, most of which is made by blending white wine with red, all quality rosés are produced either by bleeding, pressing, or limited maceration. A true-bled rosé is made from the juice that issues from black grapes pressed under their own weight. This is a sort of *tête du cuvée*, which, after fermentation, is a very pale *vin gris* colour, but has a rich, fruity, and exquisitely fresh flavour. Pressed rosé is made by pressing black grapes until the juice takes on enough colour. It, too, has a pale *vin gris* colour, but lacks the true richness of a *tête de cuvée* rosé. Limited maceration is the most common method used in the production of rosé. During this process, rosé is made in exactly the same way as red wine, except that skin-contact is limited to what is sufficient to give the desired pink tint. (All shades of rosé exist, ranging from barely perceptible to *clairet*, or almost red.) Some superior rosé wines made by this last method are virtually by-products of red-wine production. In certain areas that lack the appropriate climate for deep red wines, some free-run juice might be run off in order to produce rosé, thus leaving a greater ratio of colouring pigment in the juice that remains.

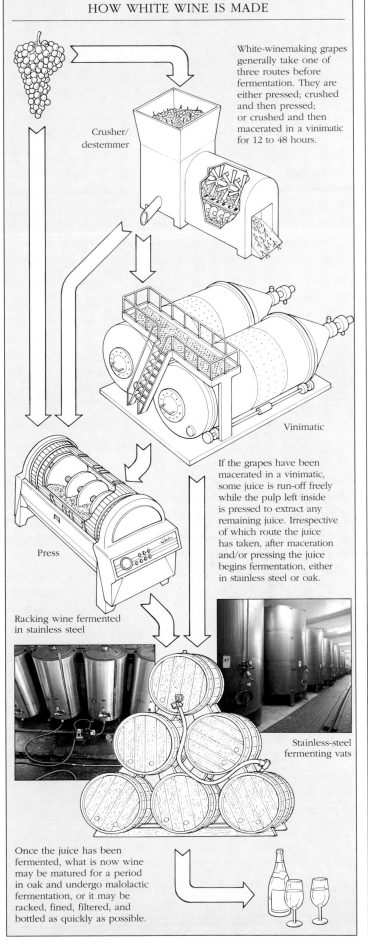

HOW WHITE WINE IS MADE

Crusher/destemmer

White-winemaking grapes generally take one of three routes before fermentation. They are either pressed; crushed and then pressed; or crushed and then macerated in a vinimatic for 12 to 48 hours.

Vinimatic

If the grapes have been macerated in a vinimatic, some juice is run-off freely while the pulp left inside is pressed to extract any remaining juice. Irrespective of which route the juice has taken, after maceration and/or pressing the juice begins fermentation, either in stainless steel or oak.

Press

Racking wine fermented in stainless steel

Stainless-steel fermenting vats

Once the juice has been fermented, what is now wine may be matured for a period in oak and undergo malolactic fermentation, or it may be racked, fined, filtered, and bottled as quickly as possible.

SPARKLING WINES

When grape juice is fermented, sugar is converted into alcohol and carbonic gas. For still wines the gas is allowed to escape, but if it is prevented from doing so, by putting a lid on a vat or a cork in a bottle, it will remain dissolved in the wine until the lid or cork is removed. When the gas is released it rushes out of the wine in the form of bubbles. The production of all natural sparkling wines is based on this essential principle, using one of four different methods – *méthode champenoise*, bottle-fermented, *methode rurale*, and *cuve close*.

MÉTHODE CHAMPENOISE

Also referred to as *méthode traditionnelle* or *méthode classique* (France), *metodo classico* (Italy), and *Cap Classique* (South Africa), this term indicates a sparkling wine that has undergone a second fermentation in the bottle in which it is sold. A label may refer to a wine being "Individually fermented in this bottle", which is the beautifully simple American equivalent of *méthode champenoise*.

BOTTLE-FERMENTED

This refers to a wine produced through a second fermentation in a bottle, but (and this is the catch) not necessarily in the bottle in which it is sold. It may have been fermented in one bottle, transferred to a vat and, under pressure at –3°C (26°F), filtered into another bottle. This is also known as the "transfer method".

MÉTHODE RURALE

This refers to the precursor of *méthode champenoise*, which is still used today, albeit only for a few obscure wines. It involves no second fermentation, the wine being bottled before the first alcoholic fermentation is finished.

CUVE CLOSE, CHARMAT, OR TANK METHOD

This is used for the bulk production of inexpensive sparkling wines that have undergone a second fermentation in large tanks before being filtered and bottled under pressure at –3°C (26°F). Contrary to popular belief, there is no evidence to suggest that this is an intrinsically inferior method of making sparkling-wine. It is only because it is a bulk production method that it tends to attract mediocre base wines and encourage a quick throughput. I genuinely suspect that a *cuve close* produced from the finest base wines of Champagne and given the autolytic benefit of at least three years on its lees before bottling might well be indistinguishable from the "real thing".

CARBONATION

This is the cheapest method of putting bubbles into wine and simply involves injecting it with carbon dioxide. Because this is the method used to make lemonade, it is incorrectly assumed that the bubbles achieved through carbonation are large and short-lived. They can be, and fully sparkling wines made by this method will indeed be cheapskates, but modern carbonation plants have the ability to induce the tiniest of bubbles, even to the point of imitating the "prickle" of wine bottled *sur lie*.

FORTIFIED WINES

Any wine, dry or sweet, red or white, to which alcohol has been added is classified as a fortified wine, whatever the inherent differences of vinification may be. Still wines usually have a strength of 8.5 to 15 per cent alcohol; fortified wines a strength of 17 to 24 per cent. The spirit added is usually, but not always, brandy made from local wines. It is totally neutral, with no hint of a brandy flavour. The amount of alcohol added, and exactly when and how it is added, is as critical to the particular character of a fortified wine as is its grape variety or area of production. Mutage, early fortification, and late fortification are all methods that may be used to fortify wines.

MUTAGE

This is the addition of alcohol to fresh grape juice. This prevents fermentation and produces fortified wines, known as *vins de liqueurs* in France, such as Pineau des Charentes in the Cognac region, Floc de Gascogne in Armagnac, and Ratafia in Champagne.

EARLY FORTIFICATION

This is the addition of alcohol after fermentation has begun. This is often done in several small, carefully measured, timed doses spread over several hours or even days. The style of fortified wine being made will dictate exactly when the alcohol is added, and the style itself will be affected by the variable strength of the grapes from year to year. On average, however, alcohol is added to Port after the alcohol level has reached six to eight per cent, and added to the *vins doux naturels* of France, such as Muscat de Beaumes de Venise, at any stage after five and before ten per cent.

LATE FORTIFICATION

This is the addition of alcohol after fermentation has ceased. The classic drink produced by this method is Sherry, which is always vinified dry, with any sweetness added afterwards.

AROMATIZED WINES

With the exception of Retsina, the resinated Greek wine, aromatized wines are all fortified. They also all have aromatic ingredients added to them. The most important aromatized wine is Vermouth, which is made from neutral white wines aged two to three years old, which are blended with an extract of wormwood (Vermouth is a corruption of the German *wermut* meaning "wormwood"), vanilla, and various other herbs and spices. Italian Vermouths are produced in Apulia and Sicily, and French Vermouths in Languedoc and Roussillon. Chambéry is a delicate generic Vermouth from the Savoie and Chambéryzette, a red-pink version flavoured with alpine strawberries, but such precise geographical aromatized wines are rare. Most, in fact, are made and sold under internationally recognized brands such as Cinzano and Martini. Other well-known aromatized wines include Amer Picon, Byrrh, Dubonnet (both red and white), Punt e Mes, St.-Raphael, and Suze.

MANUFACTURING ALCOHOL
At a government distillery in the Douro, Portugal, alcohol used to fortify Port is made with mechanized efficiency.

THE CHOICE OF OAK

I have seen the question only once in print, yet it is the most fundamental question that could possibly be asked: why oak? Why out of all the woods around the world is oak, and to any significant degree, only oak, used for barrel-making?

THE ANSWER IS THAT OTHER WOODS are either too porous or contain overpowering aromatic substances that unpleasantly taint the wine. It is not entirely true to say that only oak is used in winemaking; chestnut, for example, is occasionally found in the Rhône and elsewhere, but it is so porous and so tannic that it is usually lined with a neutral substance, rendering the wood no different from any other lined construction material (such as concrete). A beech variety called *rauli* used to be popular in Chile until its winemakers, suddenly exposed to international markets, soon discovered they had become so used to the wood that they had not realized that it gave their wines a musty joss-stick character. Large, redwood tanks are still used in California and Oregon, but they are not greatly appreciated and, as the wood cannot be bent very easily, it is not practical for small barrels. Pine has a strong resinous character that the Greeks seem to enjoy, although they have had 3,000 years to acquire the taste. Most tourists try Retsina, but very few continue to drink it by choice when they return home. Moreover it is made by adding resin, with no direct contact with the wood and, apart from an oddity called "Tea Wine", produced on La Palma in the Canary Islands, no wine to my knowledge is produced in barrels made of pine. Eucalyptus also has a resinous affect, acacia turns wine yellow, and hardwoods are impossible to bend and contain aromatic oils that are undesirable.

White oak, on the other hand, is easily bent, has a low porosity, acceptable tannin content, and mild, creamy aromatic substances that either have an intrinsic harmony with wine or, like the Greeks, we have grown accustomed to the effect.

LARGE OR SMALL?
The size of the cask is critical to its influence because the smaller it is, the larger the oak-to-wine ratio, and a greater oaky flavour it imparts. A 200-litre *barrique* has, for example, one-and-a-half times the internal surface area of oak for every litre of wine as a 500-litre cask. Traditional sizes for *barriques* range from 205 litres in Champagne, to 225 litres in Bordeaux and Spain, 228 litres in Burgundy, and 300 to 315 litres in Australia and New Zealand.

AN OAK BARREL
The staves of a barrel are held together by metal hoops, which are sometimes positioned at slightly different distances, depending on the traditions of the cooper, or *tonnelier*, in question. There may be a red colour between the two innermost hoops, but this is merely where some winemakers wish to conceal their own dribble marks around the bung by dyeing the entire middle area with wine, which can look very impressive. When fermenting white

wines, the bung is always uppermost and, even with a good ullage, or space, the hole may be left open during the most tumultuous period, but will be sealed with an air-lock valve when the fermentation process settles down and will remain closed during the malolactic fermentation. After racking, when all wines undergo several months of maturation, the barrels are filled to the very top, and positioned so that the tightly sealed bung is to one side, visually reminding cellar-workers that the casks are full.

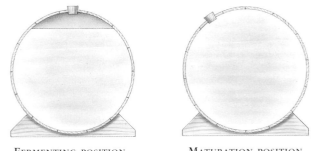

FERMENTING POSITION   MATURATION POSITION

Square barrels were even developed to increase the ratio of oak-to-wine and, although treated as a novelty, were actually more practical and economical than normal casks. More practical because they make more efficient use of storage space, and more economical because their straight sides could be reversed to create a new oak barrel from an old one. An Australian firm even built a square stainless-steel tank with two oak panels made from oak staves that could be replaced, reversed, and adjusted in size to give different oak-to-wine ratios. However, all such barrels became superfluous, with the advent and widespread use of oak chips.

CHIPS OFF THE OLD BLOCK
Using old oak barrels for the finest *barrique*-fermented or *barrique*-matured wines is a question of style rather than a consideration of cost. But for less expensive wines, it is almost entirely a question of economics, as barrels can double, for example, the cost of a *vin de pays*.

The use of new oak *barriques* for just a small percentage of a wine blend can add a certain subliminal complexity to it, although not the overt oakiness that so many people find attractive, yet so few are willing to pay very much for. Oak chips or shavings are the answer. Although generally believed to be a recent phenomenon, the use of oak chips was sufficiently widespread by 1961 to warrant statutory controls in the US. In fact, as a by-product of barrel-making, today's ubiquitous chip probably has an equally long, if somewhat more covert, history. Oak chips have been one of the most potent weapons in the New World's armoury, producing relatively inexpensive, but distinctly premium-quality wines to conquer international markets. This has been particularly evident in Australia, where flying wine-makers have not only perfected oak chip wines, but by the early

Bung — Stave — Hoop — Head — Middle stave — Chimb

AMERICAN OAK DUST
Light-toast

FRENCH OAK CHIPS
Medium-toast

AMERICAN OAK CHIPS
High-toast

1990s had exported the techniques to virtually every winemaking country in the world. Some experiments have demonstrated that wine matured with oak chips used in old barrels is "virtually indistinguishable" from the same wine stored in new oak. The range of oak chip products is now very comprehensive, covering the entire range of oak varieties and different toast levels. Some are even impregnated with malolactic bacteria. If a wine label mentions oak, but not *barriques*, barrels, or casks, it is probably a clue that oak chips have been employed in the winemaking and, if the wine is cheap, you can bet on it.

ANYONE FOR TOAST?

Toasting is one operation in the barrel-making process that has a very direct effect on the taste of the wine. In order to bend the staves, heat is applied in three stages: warming-up (*pre-chauffrage*), shaping (*cintrage*), and toasting (*bousinage*), each of which browns, or chars, the internal surface of the barrel. However, it is only the last stage – *bousinage* – that determines the degree of toasting. During toasting, furanic aldehydes (responsible for "roasted" aromas) reach their maximum concentration, the vanilla aroma of vanillin is heightened, and various phenols, such as eugenol (the chief aromatic constituent of oil of cloves),

BOUSINAGE
The final barrel-firing operation puts a light, medium, or heavy toast on the inner surface.

add a smoky, spicy touch to the complexity of oak aromas in wine.

There are three degrees of toasting: light, medium, and heavy. A light toasting is used by winemakers who seek the most natural oak character (although it is not as neutral as using staves that have been bent with steam); medium varies between a true

medium, which suits most red wine demands, and the so-called medium-plus, which is the favourite for fermenting white wines; the third, a heavy toast, dramatically reduces the coconutty-lactones and leaves a distinctly charred-smoke character that can be overpowering unless used only as a small component in a blend. Furthermore, with time, the high carbon content of heavily toasted barrels can leach the colour out of some wines, so it tends to be used for white wines (often big, brash Chardonnays), although it is best-suited to maturing Bourbon whiskey.

THE DIFFERENT OAKS

Both American and European oaks are used for winemaking. The aromatics of fast-growing, wide-grained American white oak, *Quercus alba*, are more pungent, while there are more tannins, finer in texture, in slow-growing, tight-grained European brown oaks, *Quercus robur* (*syn.* pedunculate oak), and *Quercus sessilis* (syn. *Quercus petraea* and *Quercus rouvre*). Much of the appealing, if obvious, coconut character in American oak is also due to the very different barrel-making techniques used in the US.

Unlike European oak, American is sawn, not split. This ruptures the wood cells, releasing aromatic substances, especially vanillin and up to seven different lactones, which together explain the coconut aroma. American oak is also kiln-dried, which concentrates the lactones, while European oak is seasoned outside for several years, a process that leeches out some of the most aromatic substances, and reduces the more aggressive tannins. The whole process tends to accentuate the character of American oak, while subduing that of European oak.

Many French winemakers consider American oak vulgar. Even so, a little-known fact is that in ultra-conservative Bordeaux, at least 60 châteaux are experimenting with it. Coconut-flavoured claret is by no means a forgone conclusion, but oak is expensive, a little sawn *Quercus alba* goes a long way, and a small percentage of American oak, either as barrels or mixed staves, could, in fact, significantly reduce the percentage of new oak needed each year.

LIGHT TOAST   **MEDIUM TOAST**   **HEAVY TOAST**

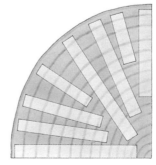
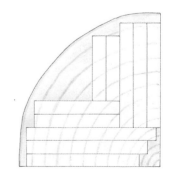

EUROPEAN SPLIT VERSUS AMERICAN SAWN
After the bark has been stripped from a log destined for barrel-making, it will be split (in Europe) or sawn (in the US), into quarters. The examples above clearly show that it is more economical to saw staves from a quarter, as opposed to splitting them. This is the major reason why American oak barrels cost half the price of European ones.

REGIONAL OAK VARIETIES

For winemaking, the tighter the size of the oak grain, the better. The slower the tree grows, the tighter the grain – thus, cooler-climate European oak is older and tighter-grained than warmer-climate American oak. Of the European oaks, forest oak (*Quercus sessilis*) is preferred to solitary oak trees (*Quercus robur*) because its branches start higher and the trunk is longer and straighter. Solitary oaks grow faster and have a larger grain because they tend to grow in fertile soil where there is more water. *Quercus sessilis* is also preferred to *Quercus robur* because it is four times richer in aromatic components.

AMERICAN *Quercus alba*

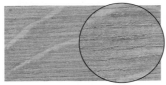

This oak covers most of the eastern US. Some winemakers think that Minnesota and Wisconsin are the best, while others find them too tannic and consider Appalachian oak, particularly from Pennsylvania, to be superior. Other popular oaks are Ohio, Kentucky, Mississippi, and Missouri. All are white oaks, fast-growing, wide-grained, with lower tannin (except for Oregon) than any European brown oaks, but with higher, sweeter, more coconutty aromatics. *Quercus alba* is favoured for traditional Rioja, Australian Shiraz, and California Zinfandel.

OREGON *Quercus gariana*

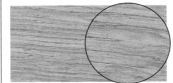

Although a white oak, *Quercus gariana* has a significantly tighter grain than *Quercus alba*. Relatively few barrels have been made from Oregon oak, and it has always been sawn, making it hard to evaluate the claim that it is similar to European oak. In 1996, however, barrels were made from split, open-air seasoned Oregon oak, so watch this space.

ALLIER *Quercus sessilis*

Tight-grained with well-balanced, medium tannin and aromatics, Allier is highly regarded.

ARGONNE *Quercus sessilis*

Tight-grained with low aromatics and tannin, this oak was used for Champagne before the advent of stainless-steel. Now seldom used.

AMERICAN OAK FORESTS

EUROPEAN OAK FORESTS

BOURGOGNE *Quercus sessilis*

Tight-grained with high tannin and low aromatics, most of this oak goes to Burgundian cellars.

LIMOUSIN *Quercus robur*

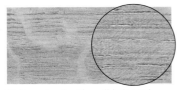

Wider-grained with high tannin and low aromatics, this oak used to be favoured for Chardonnay, but is most widely used for brandy.

NEVERS *Quercus sessilis*

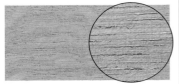

Tight-grained with well-balanced, medium tannin and aromatics, Nevers is highly regarded.

TRONÇAIS *Quercus sessilis*

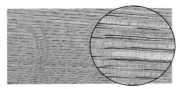

The tightest-grained and, with Vosges, the highest tannin content, Tronçais grows in the Allier forest. It is highly suitable for long-term maturation, owing to its understated aromatics, and has been long sought after.

VOSGES *Quercus sessilis*

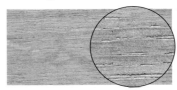

The tight grain, very high tannin content, and understated but slightly spicy aromatics make Vosges an especially well-balanced oak for winemaking. It is underrated, particularly in its home-region of Alsace, where even though few winemakers use *barriques*, those who do ironically seem to experiment with virtually every French forest except the one that is actually on their own doorstep. Vosges is especially popular in California and New Zealand, where some winemakers think it is similar to Allier and Nevers. Vosges deserves to receive greater recognition.

BALKAN *Quercus robur*

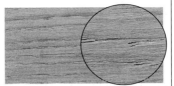

Often called Slavonian or Yugoslav oak, the grain is tight, with medium tannin and low aromatics. Balkan oak is popular for large oval casks, particularly in Italy. Diminishing use due to recent troubles.

PORTUGUESE *Quercus gariana*

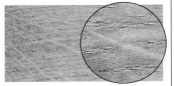

Cooperage oak (*Quercus gariana*) is far less of a commercial concern in Portugal than stunted cork-industry oak (*Quercus suber*), but the former's medium-grain wood has good aromatic properties, making it preferable in Portugal itself, where it is much cheaper than French oak.

RUSSIAN *Quercus sessilis*

Tight-grained with low aromatics and easy to confuse with French oak under blind conditions, this was the major oak in Bordeaux during the 19th century and up until the 1930s. Thus all the great old vintages owe something to it. Thanks to investment from Seguin Moreau, which set up a cooperage in the Adygey region near the Black Sea, French producers have begun to use Russian oak again, although it is mysteriously just ten per cent cheaper than French.

GLOSSARY OF GRAPE VARIETIES

There are thousands of winemaking grape varieties grown throughout the world. The varieties that are the most significant to one degree or another in the areas where they are cultivated, are profiled over the following pages.

CROSSES AND HYBRIDS

A cross between grape varieties within one species is called a cross, whereas a cross between varieties from different species is called a hybrid. Cross the same grape varieties more than once and the odds are that the new strains produced will not be the same. Thus *Sylvaner* x *Riesling* is not only the parentage of the Rieslaner, but also the Scheurebe, two totally different grapes. It is also possible to cross a variety with itself and produce a different grape. In this glossary, and throughout the book, the parentage of crosses and hybrids are always in italic.

CLONES AND CLONING

Within varietal limitations, intensive selection can produce a vine to suit specific conditions, such as to increase yield, resist certain diseases or to thrive in a particular climate. Identical clones of this vine can then be replicated an infinite number of times by micro-biogenetic techniques. Clones are named by number and initial. For instance, "Riesling clone 88Gm" is the 88th clone of the Riesling variety produced at Geisenheim (Gm), the German viticultural research station.

A "localized" clone is a vine that has evolved naturally under specific conditions within a particular environment. These may be named first by grape variety and then by locality and referred to as sub-varieties. However, the name of the original variety is often entirely forgotten with the passing of time, so that the variety acquires a new name altogether.

GRAPE COLOUR

Most white wines are made from "white" grapes, which actually range from green to amber-yellow. On the other hand, most red or rosé wines are made from "black" grapes, which vary from red to blue-black. White wine can also be made from most black grapes because, with only a few exceptions (categorized as *teinturier* grapes, literally "dyer" grapes) only the skin is coloured, not the juice. But red wine can only be made from black grapes, because it is pigments in the skin, called anthocyanins, that give the wine its colour. The acidity in the skin's sap also affects the colour of its wine: high acid levels gives a ruddy colour, while the lower the acidity the more purple, and eventually violet, the wine becomes.

WHITE GRAPE VARIETIES

Note Some pink-coloured varieties, such as Gewürztraminer and Pinot Gris, are included in this section because the wine they make is essentially white.

ALBALONGA
A *Rieslaner* x *Sylvaner* cross developed and grown in Germany for its naturally high sugar level and early-ripening qualities.

ALIGOTÉ
See box, below.

ALTESSE
The finest of Savoie's traditional varieties, this grape makes delightfully rich and fragrant wines.

ALIGOTÉ
A thin-skinned grape of unexceptional quality grown in Burgundy and Bulgaria. It makes tart wines of moderate alcoholic content, but in exceptionally hot years they can have good weight and richness. The variety's best wines come from certain Burgundian villages, especially Bouzeron, where the quality may be improved by the addition of a little Chardonnay.

ALVARINHO
The classic Vinho Verde grape, although it might not rank as a classic grape variety *per se.*

ARBOIS
An interesting but very localized variety cultivated in the Loire Valley, where it is sometimes blended with another obscure grape called the Romorantin.

ARINTO
One of Portugal's potentially excellent white grapes. Its use in Bucelas is to make a crisp, lemony wine that ages well.

ASSYRTIKO
One of the better-quality indigenous varieties of Greece.

AUXERROIS
Often confused with the Pinot blanc, but in fact a totally separate variety, this grape is grown most successfully in Alsace and is up-and-coming in England. Its wine is fatter than that of the Pinot blanc and so suits cooler situations. Its musky richness has immediate appeal, but it is inclined to low acidity and can become too fat and blowzy in hotter climates.

BACCHUS
A (*Riesling* x *Sylvaner*) x *Müller-Thurgau* cross that is one of Germany's more superior crosses. In recent years a considerable acreage has been grown in Germany's Rheinhessen region. It is also grown in England because of its inherently high sugar level and can produce vivacious, fruity wines in both countries.

BLANQUETTE
A synonym for the Colombard in the department of Tarn-et-Garonne in France, the Clairette in the department of Aude, and the Ondenc in the Bordeaux region.

BORRADO DES MOSCAS
A Dão grape, literally called "fly droppings", Borrado des Moscas retains high natural acidity at high alcohol levels, making it well suited to white winemaking in hot areas.

BOUVIER
A modest-quality grape variety significantly cultivated in Austria and one which, under its Ranina synonym, produces the "Tiger's Milk" wine of Slovenia.

BUAL
The richest and fattest of Madeira's four classic grape varieties. The Bual may also be grown in many parts of southern Portugal.

CHARDONNAY
See box, opposite.

CHASSELAS
A modest-quality variety producing the best-forgotten Pouilly-sur-Loire wines (not to be confused with Pouilly-Blanc Fumé from the same area). It is probably at its modest best in the Valais, Switzerland (where it is known as the Fendant). The Chasselas is the most popular table grape in France, but, strange as it may seem, good eating grapes rarely make good wine grapes.

CHENIN BLANC
See box, opposite.

CLAIRETTE
A sugar-rich, intrinsically flabby grape best known for its many wines of southern France. It is the Muscat though, not the Clairette, which is chiefly responsible for the "Clairette de Die" in the Rhône.

COLOMBARD
This produces thin, acidic wine ideal for the distillation of Armagnac and Cognac. It has also adapted well to the hotter winelands of California and South Africa, where its high acidity is a positive attribute.

CRUCHEN BLANC
Widely-cultivated, this variety usually, but incorrectly, has the tag of Riesling attached to it.

CHARDONNAY
The greatest dry white wine grape in the world, despite its proliferation in virtually every commercial wine-making area. Once erroneously thought to be a member of the Pinot family, this classic variety is responsible for producing the greatest white Burgundies and is one of the three major grape types used in the production of Champagne.

CHENIN BLANC
A variety that acquired its name from Mont-Chenin in the Touraine district in about the 15th century, but can be traced back to Anjou, around AD 845. The grape has a good acidity level, thin skin, and a high natural sugar content, making it very suitable for either sparkling or sweet wines, although some dry wines, notably Savennières, are made from it.

DELAWARE
This American hybrid of uncertain parentage was developed in Frenchtown, New Jersey, and propagated in Delaware, Ohio, in the mid 19th century. Although grown in New York State and Brazil, it is far more popular in Japan.

EHRENFELSER
A *Riesling* x *Sylvaner* cross, this is one of the best of Germany's new breed of crosses.

ELBLING
This variety was once held in high esteem in both Germany and France. The major Mosel grape in the 19th century, it is now mostly confined to the Ober-mosel where its very acid, neutral flavour makes it particularly useful for the German *Sekt* industry. In Alsace it was known as the *Knipperlé* and its former position was such that one of the *Grand Cru* Guebwiller slopes was named after it.

EMERALD RIESLING
A *Muscadelle* x *Riesling* cross, this grape was developed for cultivation in California by a Professor Olmo of UC-Davis fame as the sister to his Ruby cabernet cross, which is a combination of Cabernet sauvignon and Carignan.

FABER
A *Weissburgunder* x *Müller-Thurgau* cross grown in Germany, where it produces a fruity wine with a distinctive light Muscat aroma.

FOLLE BLANCHE
Traditionally used for the distillation of Armagnac and Cognac, the Folle Blanche grape also produces the Gros plant wine of the Nantais district of the Loire Valley.

FORTA
A little of this *Madeleine Angevine* x *Sylvaner* cross is grown in Germany, where it produces good-quality grapes that are rich in sugar.

FREISAMER
A *Sylvaner* x *Pinot gris* cross that is grown in Germany and produces a full, neutral, Sylvaner-like wine.

FURMINT
This strong, distinctively flavoured grape is the most important variety used to make Tokij in Hungary.

GARGANEGA BIANCO
An Italian variety that is the principal grape used in the production of Soave.

GEWÜRZTRAMINER
See box, below.

GLORIA
A *Sylvaner* x *Müller-Thurgau* cross grown in Germany, where it produces grapes that are rich in sugar, but make wines of a rather neutral character.

GRENACHE BLANC
This is the white Grenache variant that is widely planted in France and Spain. It is an ancient Spanish variety with the potential to produce a good-quality, full-bodied wine.

GRÜNER VELTLINER
This is the most important wine grape in Austria, where it produces fresh, well-balanced wines, with a light, fruity, sometimes slightly spicy, flavour. Top-quality Grüner Veltliner from the Wachau can have a penetrating pepperiness.

GUTENBORNER
This *Müller-Thurgau* x *Chasselas* cross is grown in Germany and England. It produces grapes with intrinsically high sugar levels, but makes rather neutral wines.

HARSLEVELÜ
A Hungarian grape that is the second most important Tokay variety. It produces a full, rich, and powerfully perfumed wine.

HUXELREBE
A *Chasselas* x *Muscat courtillier* cross that is grown in Germany and England, and is capable of producing good-quality wine.

JACQUÈRE
The work-horse grape of the Savoie, the Jaquère is subject to rot, has a neutral flavour and high acidity.

JOHANNISBERG RIESLING
This is a synonym often used to distinguish a wine that is made from the true Riesling grape. Many people believe that the Riesling is at its classic best when grown in the Rheingau vineyards of Johannisberg, thus the synonym most probably evolved as a way of indicating that a wine contained Riesling grapes "as grown in Johannisberg".

KANZLER
A *Müller-Thurgau* x *Sylvaner* cross that produces a good Sylvaner substitute in the Rheinhessen.

KERNER
A *Trollinger* x *Riesling* cross grown in Germany, South Africa, and England. It produces Riesling-like wines with a high natural sugar content and good acidity, but a very light aroma.

LEN DE L'ELH
This is a flavoursome, naturally sugar-rich grape that is used in Gaillac, France.

MACABÉO
This is a Spanish variety used to "lift" a sparkling Cava blend and give it freshness. Bearing the name of Viura, it is also responsible for the "new wave" of fresh, unoaked white Rioja.

MADELEINE ANGEVINE
This is a *Précoce de Malingre* x *Madeleine royale* cross that is grown quite successfully in England, where it produces a characteristically light-bodied, aromatic wine.

GEWÜRZTRAMINER
At its most clear-cut and varietally distinctive in Alsace, this variety produces very aromatic wines, which are often described as spicy, although its complex bouquet can range from grapey-muskiness to pungent pepperyness. Originally from the Pfalz region in Germany, the Gewürztraminer was introduced into Alsace after 1871, since when it has been successfully transplanted as far afield as South Africa and California, where its characteristics are softer.

MUSCAT À PETITS GRAINS

There are two versions of this variety – the Muscat blanc à petits grains and the Muscat rosé à petits grains – and some vines that seem to produce a motley crop somewhere between the two. Where one is cultivated, the other is often intermingled or growing close by. The two greatest products produced by petits grains are the dry wines of Alsace and the sweet and lightly fortified Muscat de Beaumes de Venise, although in the production of the former the variety is giving way to the Muscat ottonel.

MANSENG

The Gros manseng and Petit manseng are grown in southwest France, and are well known mainly for producing the legendary Jurançon Moelleux.

MARIENSTEINER

A *Sylvaner* x *Rieslaner* cross that is grown in Germany and is generally considered superior to the Sylvaner.

MARSANNE

This grape makes fat, rich, full wines and is one of the two major varieties used to produce the rare white wines of Hermitage and Châteauneuf-du-Pape.

MAUZAC

A late-ripening grape with good natural acidity, grown in southwest France, Mauzac is flexible in the wines it produces, but is particularly suitable for sparkling wine.

MELON DE BOURGOGNE

This variety was transplanted from Burgundy to the Nantais district to replace its less hardy vines after the terrible winter of 1709. Most famous for its production of Muscadet. When fully ripe, it produces very flabby wines, lacking in acidity.

MERLOT BLANC

This variety is cultivated on a surprisingly large scale on the right-bank of the Gironde. Yet, according to ampelographer Pierre Galet, it is not related to the more famous black Merlot variety.

MORIO-MUSKAT

This *Sylvaner* x *Pinot blanc* cross is widely grown in the Rheinpfalz and Rheinhessen of Germany. Intriguingly, it has a powerfully aromatic character, the inverse of the neutral character of its parents.

MÜLLER-THURGAU

This variety was bred at Geisenheim in 1882 by Professor Hermann Müller, who hailed from the canton of Thurgau in Switzerland, and was named after him by August Dern in 1891. It was originally believed to be a *Riesling* x *Sylvaner* cross, but not one single plant has ever reverted to Sylvaner, and the closest resemblance to it is the Rabaner, a *Riesling (clone 88Gm)* x *Riesling (clone 64Gm)*. This seems to confirm the theory that the Müller-Thurgau is, in fact, a self-pollinated Riesling seed. It is more prolific than the Riesling, has a typically flowery bouquet and good fruit, but lacks the Riesling's characteristic sharpness of definition. Although this variety has a justifiably important position in the production of German *Tafelwein*, its cultivation in the classic Riesling vineyards of the Mosel devalues that great wine region. It is widely planted in English and New Zealand vineyards, although in both cases the acreage has shrunk markedly in the 1990s.

MULTANER

A *Riesling* x *Sylvaner* cross, a small amount of this variety is grown in Germany. However, the area planted is declining because the grapes need to be very ripe to produce good-quality wine.

MUSCADELLE

A singular variety that has nothing to do with the Muscat family, although it does, in fact, have a distinctive musky aroma and there is, confusingly, a South African synonym for the Muscat – the Muskadel. It is not related to the Muscadet or Melon de Bourgogne grape, despite the inference of one of its synonyms being Muscadet. In Bordeaux, small quantities add a certain lingering "after-smell" to some of the sweet wines, but the Muscadelle is at its sublime best in Australia where it is called the Tokay and produces a fabulously rich and sweet "liqueur wine".

MUSCAT

A family name for numerous related varieties, sub-varieties, and localized clones of the same variety, all of which have a distinctive musky aroma and a pronounced grapey flavour. The wines that are produced range from dry to sweet, still to sparkling, and fortified.

MUSCAT À PETITS GRAINS

See box, left.

MUSCAT D'ALEXANDRIE

An extremely important grape in South Africa, where it makes mostly sweet, but some dry, wines. In France it is responsible for the fortified wine Muscat de Rivesaltes (a very tiny production of unfortified dry Muscat is also made in Rivesaltes), and the grape is also used for both wine and raisin production in California.

MUSCAT OTTONEL

An east-European variety which, because of its relative hardiness, is now in the process of replacing the Muscat à petits grains in Alsace.

NOBLESSA

This is a low-yielding *Madeleine Angevine* x *Sylvaner* cross grown in Germany, which produces grapes with a high sugar level.

NOBLING

A *Sylvaner* x *Chasselas* cross grown in Baden, Germany, its grapes have high sugar and acidity levels.

ONDENC

A grape once widely planted in southwest France and particularly popular in Bergerac, it is now grown more in Australia than in France. Its intrinsically high acidity makes it useful for sparkling wines.

OPTIMA

Developed in 1970, this (*Riesling* x *Sylvaner*) x *Müller-Thurgau* cross is already widely grown in Germany because it ripens even earlier than the early-ripening Müller-Thurgau.

PINOT GRIS

A variety undoubtedly at its best in Alsace, where it can produce succulent, rich, and complex wines of great quality, and a spiciness seldom encountered elsewhere. It is also responsible for many sweet fortified wines throughout the world.

RIESLING

A classic German grape variety. Although other German grapes and crosses can make good commercial wines, the Riesling, if properly handled, produces a wine of such tremendous fruit-acidity ratio that it is in a different class. It is light in body and low in alcohol, yet intensely flavoured and very long-lived. With some bottle age, the finest Rieslings develop a vivid and zesty bouquet that may be referred to as "petrolly". The grape's susceptibility to botrytis also makes it one of the most scintillating producers of intensely sweet wines.

ORTEGA

A *Müller-Thurgau* x *Siegerrebe* cross that is grown in both Germany and England, its aromatic grapes have a naturally high sugar content and make a pleasantly fragrant and spicy wine.

PALOMINO

The classic Sherry grape variety.

PARELLADA

This is the major white grape variety of Catalonia, used for still and sparkling Cava wines. In a Cava blend it imparts a distinctive aroma and is used to soften the firm Xarello grape.

PERLE

A *Gewürztraminer* x *Müller-Thurgau* cross grown in Franken, Germany, this grape can survive winter temperatures as low as –30°C (–22°F), and produces a light, fragrant, and fruity wine, but in low yields.

PINOT BLANC

A variety that is perhaps at its best in Alsace where it is most successful, producing fruity, well-balanced wines with good grip and alcohol content. Plantings of the true Pinot blanc are gradually diminishing worldwide.

PINOT GRIS

See box, opposite.

PINOT LIÉBAULT

A black grape authorized for the production of various Burgundian appellations, it is very similar to the Pinot noir. It could be closely related and is probably a localized variant.

POULSARD

The Jura's famous grape with pink skin and pink juice can produce a fine and aromatic *vin gris*.

PROSECCO

This grape is responsible for producing a great deal of very ordinary Italian sparkling wine.

RABANER

This *Riesling (clone 88Gm)* x *Riesling (clone 64Gm)* cross has the dubious honour of being the variety that most resembles the Müller-Thurgau. It is grown in Germany on an experimental basis.

RABIGATO

This is the main white Port grape variety. It is also known as Rabo di ovelha or "ewe's tail".

REGNER

The parents of this *Luglienca bianca* x *Gamay* cross are a curious combination. Why anyone would consider crossing a table grape with the red wine grape of Beaujolais to create a German white wine variety is a mystery. It produces sugar-rich grapes and mild, Müller-Thurgau-like wines.

REICHENSTEINER

This *Müller-Thurgau* x *Madeleine angevine* x *Calabreser-fröhlich* cross is grown in Germany and England. Its sugar-rich grapes produce a mild, delicate, somewhat neutral, Sylvaner-like wine.

RHODITIS

This grape is used as a supporting variety in the making of Retsina, a use only eclipsed by its suitability for the distilling pot!

RIESLANER

A *Riesling* x *Sylvaner* cross mainly grown in Franken, Germany, where it produces sugar-rich grapes and full-bodied, rather neutral wines.

RIESLING

See box, opposite.

RKATSITELI

A grape variety that is grown extensively in Russia, on a scale that would cover the vineyards of Champagne at least ten times over. The Soviets consider it to be a high-quality wine grape; it is also grown in Bulgaria, China, California, and New York State.

SÉMILLON

In Sauternes and Barsac, this is the grape particularly susceptible to botrytis, or "noble rot". Some experts say its aroma is reminiscent of lanolin, but as pure lanolin is virtually odourless, the comparison hardly conveys the Sémillon's distinctive bouquet. Melon or fig are more helpful comparisons but quite often one is trying to describe the odour and character of botrytized grapes, rather than of the Sémillon itself.

ROBOLA

Confined to the island of Cephalonia, this is a good-quality Greek grape.

ROMORANTIN

An obscure variety that is confined to the Loire Valley, Romorantin, and which can produce a delicate, attractive, and flowery wine if it is not overcropped.

ROUSSANNE

One of two major varieties used to produce the rare white wines of Hermitage and Châteauneuf-du-Pape in France's Rhône Valley, this grape makes the finer, more delicate wines, while those made from the Marsanne are fatter and richer.

SACY

A minor grape variety that produces bland "stretching" wine and is grown in small quantities in the Chablis district. Its high acidity could make it very useful in the production of sparkling wines.

SAINT-ÉMILION

This is a synonym for the Ugni blanc in France and for the Sémillon in Romania.

SAUVIGNON BLANC

See box, left.

SAVAGNIN

This is the grape responsible for the Sherry-like *Vin Jaune* of the Jura, of which the best known is Château Chalon. The wine, in fact, takes the name of a commune, rather than a specific château. A Savagnin rosé grows in the village of Heiligenstein, Alsace, where it is known as the Klevener, as opposed to the Klevner, which is a synonym for the Pinot blanc. The Savagnin noir is, in fact, merely a synonym for the Pinot noir.

SAVATIANO

This grape was used by the Greeks to make Retsina. A pure, unresinated Savatiano called Kanza is made in Attica, the heartland of Retsina.

SCHEUREBE

A *Riesling* x *Sylvaner* cross, this is one of the best of Germany's new varieties. When ripe, it makes very good varietal wines, but, if it is harvested too early, the bouquet can be quite unpleasant.

SCHÖNBURGER

A *Spatburgunder* x (*Chasselas rosé* x *Muscat Hamburg*) cross, this grape is grown in Germany and England. It produces sugar-rich grapes that make wine with good aromatic qualities but low acidity.

SÉMILLON

See box, above.

SEPTIMER

A *Gewürztraminer* x *Müller-Thurgau* cross grown in Germany, where it is early-ripening and produces sugar-rich grapes that are made into aromatic wines.

SERCIAL

This classic grape of Madeira is reputed to be a distant relative of the Riesling. However, judging by its totally different leaf shape, this seems rather unlikely.

SEYVAL BLANC

This *Seibel 5656* x *Seibel 4986* hybrid is the most successful of the many Seyve-Villard crosses. It is grown in France, New York State, and England, where it produces attractive wines.

SIEGERREBE

This is a *Madeleine-Angevine* x *Gewürztraminer* cross, a grape that is widely grown in Germany.

SAUVIGNON BLANC

Sauvignon blanc is at its best-defined in the central vineyards of the Loire, where it produces characteristically aromatic dry wines. In Bordeaux, the dry wines it makes have a dusty quality, although with earlier picking and improved vinification techniques this is now changing. It is also used in Sauternes and Barsac blends.

SYLVANER
Originally from Austria, this variety is widely planted throughout Central Europe. It is prolific, early maturing, and yields the dry wines of Franken and Alsace. It is also widely believed to be the Zierfandler of Austria. Sylvaner has a tart, earthy, yet neutral flavour, which takes on a tomato-like richness in the bottle.

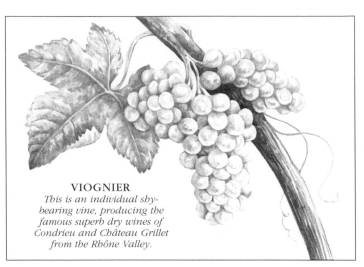

VIOGNIER
This is an individual shy-bearing vine, producing the famous superb dry wines of Condrieu and Château Grillet from the Rhône Valley.

STEEN
This is a South African synonym for the Chenin blanc. The term "Stein" is also used in South Africa, but refers to a semi-sweet white wine that usually, but not necessarily, contains a percentage of Steen wine.

SYLVANER
See box, above.

TROUSSEAU GRIS
This grape is now more widely grown in California and New Zealand than in its traditional home

of the northern Jura, France. It is yet another grape that has been erroneously tagged with the Riesling name in the New World but does not resemble that grape in the slightest.

UGNI BLANC
A variety that usually makes light, even thin wines that have to be distilled, the Ugni blanc is ideal for making Armagnac and Cognac. There are a few exceptions, but most are light, fresh, quaffing wines at their very best.

VERDELHO
Successful in Australia and possibly connected to the Verdello of Italy, Verdelho is best known, however, as a classic Madeira grape (a Verdelho *tinto* also exists on the island).

VERDICCHIO
As well as being used to make Verdicchio wine, this grape is also employed for blending.

VILLARD BLANC
This *Seibel 6468* x *Seibel 6905* hybrid is the widest-cultivated of the Seyve-Villard crosses in France. Its slightly bitter, iron-rich wine cannot be compared with the attractive wine of the Seyve-Villard 5276 or Seyval blanc grown in England.

VIOGNIER
See box, above.

WELSCHRIESLING
No relation whatsoever to the true Riesling, this variety is grown throughout Europe, producing ordinary medium-dry to medium-sweet white wines.

WÜRZER
This grape is a German variety with the same *Gewürztraminer* x *Müller-Thurgau* origins as the Perle.

XARELLO
Very important to the sparkling Cava industry, this Spanish grape makes firm, alcoholic wines, softened by Parellada and Macabéo grapes.

BLACK GRAPE VARIETIES

AGIORGITIKO
An excellent indigenous Greek variety responsible for the rich and often oak-aged wines of Nemea.

ALICANTE BOUSCHET
A *Petit bouschet* x *Grenache* cross, this is a *teinturier* grape, with vivid, red juice. It is surprisingly widely planted in France and Corsica, is an authorized variety for the production of Port, and is cultivated in Italy, Lebanon, North Africa, South Africa, and California. In California, this variety is usually planted in the Central Valley and blended into cheap wine.

ARAMON
The fact that this is the Ugni noir of the wine world says it all. Its wines are usually thin and harsh, but its importance in terms of quantity has to be recognized.

BAGA
Based on the potential of the Bairrada region of Portugal, where this grape accounts for 80 per cent of all grapes grown, it must surely be a dependable variety. However, it has yet to establish truly fine varietal characteristics.

BARBERA
A prolific Italian variety grown in Piedmont, the Barbera makes light, fresh, fruity wines that are sometimes very good.

BASTARDO
This is the classic Port grape and is identified as the Trousseau, an ancient variety once widely cultivated in the Jura, France.

BLAUFRÄNKISCH
Some believe this Austrian variety to be the Gamay, and, judging from its light and poor-quality wine, they could be close to the truth.

CABERNET
This is an ambiguous name that refers to the Cabernet sauvignon or Cabernet franc.

CABERNET FRANC
See box, right.

CABERNET SAUVIGNON
See box, opposite.

CAMINA
This German *Portugieser* x *Pinot noir* cross yields grapes with more sugar and acidity than either parent.

CAMPBELL'S EARLY
This is an American hybrid that is particularly popular in Japan.

CANAIOLO NERO
A secondary grape, the Canaiolo nero adds softness to Chianti's principal variety, the Sangiovese.

CARIGNAN
A Spanish grape grown extensively in southern France and California. One of its synonyms – Mataro – is a common name for the Mouvèdre, which also provides a well-coloured, but not quite as harsh wine. A Carignan blanc and a gris also exist.

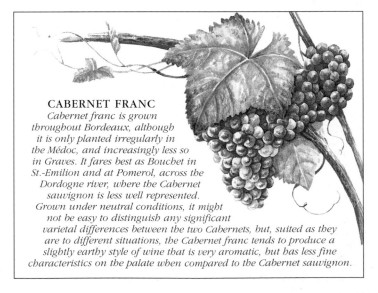

CABERNET FRANC
Cabernet franc is grown throughout Bordeaux, although it is only planted irregularly in the Médoc, and increasingly less so in Graves. It fares best as Bouchet in St.-Emilion and at Pomerol, across the Dordogne river, where the Cabernet sauvignon is less well represented. Grown under neutral conditions, it might not be easy to distinguish any significant varietal differences between the two Cabernets, but, suited as they are to different situations, the Cabernet franc tends to produce a slightly earthy style of wine that is very aromatic, but has less fine characteristics on the palate when compared to the Cabernet sauvignon.

CABERNET SAUVIGNON

The noblest variety of Bordeaux, the Cabernet sauvignon, rich in colour, aroma, and depth, is vitally important to the classic Médoc wines. Many of its classical traits have been transplanted as far afield as California, Chile, and Australia. The complexities that this grape can achieve transcend simplistic comparisons to cedar, blackcurrants, or violets.

CARMENÈRE
A Bordeaux grape, not very widely cultivated, that produces deliciously rich, soft-textured wines with an excellent colour.

CÉSAR
A minor grape variety of moderate quality that is still used in some areas of Burgundy, most notably for Bourgogne Irancy.

CINSAULT
A prolific grape found mainly in southern Rhône and Languedoc-Roussillon vineyards, where it makes robust, well-coloured wines. Best results are obtained when it is blended, as happens at Châteauneuf-du-Pape, for example.

CONCORD
The widest-cultivated variety in North America outside of California, this variety has an extremely pronounced "foxy" flavour.

CORVINA
A prolific Italian variety, this is found mainly in the Veneto, where it is blended into the wines of Bardolino and Valpolicella. The grape's thick skin contributes colour and tannin.

DECKROT
A *Pinot gris* x *Teinturier färbertraube* cross, the Deckrot produces a coloured juice that is welcomed by growers in the cool climate of Germany's vineyards. This is because they are unable to grow black grapes with a dark skin in order to produce red wines in the normal way.

DOMINA
A *Portugieser* x *Pinot noir* cross, this is more suited to Germany's vineyards than either of its parents.

GAMAY
See box, above.

GRACIANO
An important variety used in the production of Rioja, where a small amount lends richness and fruit to a blend, Graciano could be the next pure varietal to grab the headlines.

GRENACHE
See box, below.

GROLLEAU
A prolific grape with a high natural sugar content, it is important for the bulk production of Anjou rosé, but rarely interesting in terms of quality.

HEROLDREBE
A *Portugieser* x *Limberger* cross, this grape produces light-coloured, neutral-flavoured wines in Germany.

KADARKA
Hungary's most widely-cultivated grape variety is grown throughout the Balkans. It was once thought to be the same as the Zinfandel but this theory no longer persists. It makes pleasant, light, and fruity wine.

KOLOR
One of Gemany's *teinturier* varieties, this *Pinot noir* x *Teinturier Färbertraube* cross was developed to put colour into the blends of the country's northern red wines.

LAMBRUSCO
An Italian variety, this is famous for its production of the medium-sweet, red, frothy wine of the same name in the Emilia-Romagna area.

MALBEC
This grape is traditionally used in Bordeaux blends in order to provide colour and tannin. It is also grown in the Loire, Cahors, and Mediterranean regions, among many others, and was the grape responsible for the "black wine of Cahors" – a legendary name, if not wine, in the 19th century. However, Cahors is now made from a blend of grapes and is an infinitely superior wine to its predecessor.

MAVROUD
This Bulgarian variety produces dark, rich, and plummy wines.

MAZUELO
A variety grown in Rioja, it is believed to be the Carignan, although it bears little resemblance to it, and produces wines of light, yet rich, fruit and low alcohol.

GAMAY

The mass-produced basic product of this famous grape from Beaujolais, has a tell-tale "pear-drop" aroma, indicative of its macération carbonique *style of vinification. These wines should be drunk very young and fresh, although traditionally vinified wines from Beaujolais' nine classic* crus *can be aged like other red wines and, after 10 or 15 years, will develop Pinot noir varietal traits. This may be just a phenomenon or it may be because the grape is an ancient, natural clone of the Pinot noir. In France, Gamay Beaujolais is the synonym for the true Gamay, but in California it refers to the Pinot noir. As Leon Adams notes in* The Wines of America, *this erroneous American synonym arose out of genuine confusion when Paul Masson brought back several Burgundian grapes to his winery, one of which he believed was the Gamay of Beaujolais. It was identified as the Pinot noir in the mid 1960s, but by then several Californian wineries were selling their own brand of Gamay Beaujolais. Before its true identity was revealed, another grape – the Napa gamay – that had been grown in California for some time, was identified as the true Gamay.*

Gamay teinturiers Gamay fréaux, Gamay de bouze, Gamay Castille, Gamay teinturier mouro, Fréaux hatif

GRENACHE

The Grenache is grown in southern France where it is partly responsible for the wines of Châteauneuf-du-Pape, Tavel, and many others. It is the mainstay of Rioja, makes port-style and light rosé wines in California, and is also grown in South Africa. Its wines are rich, warm, and alcoholic, sometimes too much so, and require blending with other varieties. The true Grenache has nothing to do with the Grenache de Logroña of Spain, which is, in fact, the Tempranillo or Tinto de Rioja. Some sources say the Alicante (a synonym of the Grenache) is the Alicante bouschet (or plain Bouschet in California), but this too is misleading. The Alicante/Grenache has colourless juice, whereas the Alicante bouschet has bright-red juice derived from the teinturier half of its parentage. The Petit bouschet (in its true form, and not as the synonym of the Cabernet sauvignon) is itself a cross of teinturier du cher x Aramon.

MERLOT
Merlot produces nicely-coloured wines, soft in fruit but capable of great richness. It is invaluable in Bordeaux, bringing fruity lusciousness and a velvet quality to wines that might otherwise be rather hard and austere. It is the chief grape in Château Pétrus, the top name in Pomerol.

PINOT MEUNIER
An important variety in Champagne, where vinified white gives more up-front appeal of fruit than the Pinot noir when young, and is therefore essential for early-drinking Champagnes. Its characteristics are more immediate, but less fine and somewhat earthier than those of the Pinot noir. The Pinot meunier is extensively cultivated in the Marne Valley area of Champagne, where its resistance to frost makes it the most suitable vine.

MERLOT
See box, above.

MONTEPULCIANO
A late-ripening variety that performs best in the Abruzzi region of Italy, where its wines are very deep in colour, and can either be full, soft, fat, luscious fruit, or made in a much firmer, more tannic, style.

MONASTRELL
An underrated Spanish variety that is usually hidden in blends. However, it does have a full and distinctive flavour and could make individual wines of some appeal.

MONDEUSE
This variety may have originally hailed from Friuli in northeastern Italy, where it is known as the Refosco. It is now planted as far afield as the Savoie in France, parts of the US, including California, Switzerland, Italy, the Argentine, and Australia, where it is often an important constituent of the fortified port-type wines.

MOURVÈDRE
This excellent-quality grape variety has been used more than other lesser varieties in Châteauneuf-du-Pape blends in recent years. It is grown extensively throughout the Rhône and the French Midi, and, under the name of the Mataro, also in Spain. The Mataro is Australia's fifth widest-cultivated black grape, but is a declining force in southern California.

NEBBIOLO
See box, below.

PAMID
This is the most widely cultivated of Bulgaria's indigenous black grape varieties. It makes light and fruity quaffing wine.

PETIT VERDOT
A grape that has been used to good effect in Bordeaux because it is a late-ripener, bringing acidity to the overall balance of a wine. Certain modern techniques of viticulture and vinification have rendered it less valuable, which might prove to be a pity because it also produces a characterful, long-lived, and tannic wine when ripe.

PINEAU D'AUNIS
This grape is best known for its supporting role in the production of Rosé d'Anjou.

PINOTAGE
A *Pinot noir* x *Cinsault* cross developed in 1925, it occupies an important position in South African viticulture where its rustic and high-toned wine is greatly appreciated.

PINOT MEUNIER
See box, above.

PINOT NOIR
See box, below.

PORTUGIESER
The most widely planted black grape variety in Germany, it originates in the Danube district of Austria, not in Portugal as its name suggests. As it makes very ordinary and extremely light red wine, it is often used in bad years to blend with the too acidic white wine.

PRIMITIVO
An Italian variety grown in Apulia where it produces rich wines, sometimes sweet or fortified. Some think it is the same variety as Zinfandel.

RONDINELLA
An Italian variety, secondary to the Corvina grape in terms of area planted, it is used in the production of Bardolino and Valpolicella.

ROTBERGER
A *Trollinger* x *Riesling* cross, the parents seem an odd couple, but the offspring is surprisingly successful, producing some excellent rosé wines.

RUBY CABERNET
An American *Carignan* x *Cabernet sauvignon* cross that originated in 1936, first fruited in 1940, and made its first wine in 1946.

SANGIOVESE
This is the principal variety used in Chianti. In a pure varietal form it can lack fruit and have a metallic finish.

SYRAH
See box, opposite.

TANNAT
This grape originated from the Basque region, and has the potential to produce deeply-coloured, tannic wines of great longevity (although there are certain modern methods of vinification that often change the traditional character of Tannat wines). The variety's best known wines are the attractive red Madiran and Irouléguy. A little Tannat wine is used for blending purposes in and around the town of Cahors.

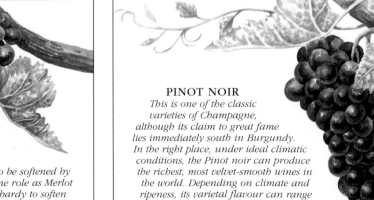

NEBBIOLO
Famous for its production of Barolo, this grape is also responsible, totally or in part, for the other splendid wines of Piedmont in Italy, such as Gattinara, Barbaresco, Carema, and Donnaz. It often needs to be softened by the addition of Bonarda grapes, which have the same role as Merlot grapes in Bordeaux. In fact, Merlot is used in Lombardy to soften Nebbiolo grapes for the production of Valtelina and Valtelina Superiore wines, of which Sassella can be the most velvety of all.

PINOT NOIR
This is one of the classic varieties of Champagne, although its claim to great fame lies immediately south in Burgundy. In the right place, under ideal climatic conditions, the Pinot noir can produce the richest, most velvet-smooth wines in the world. Depending on climate and ripeness, its varietal flavour can range from cherries to strawberries.

SYRAH
A variety whose name, derived from Shiraz, the capital of Fars, a province of Iran, causes most people to believe that the vine must have originated in Persia, possibly as far back as 600 BC. In Hermitage, in the northern Rhône, the grape makes big, rich, tannic wines, with a good deal of fruit.

ZINFANDEL
The Zinfandel is probably the Primitivo of southern Italy. However, in California it makes singularly unique wine and is regarded as a native grape. The style can vary from being light and elegant, as in the white or rosé wines, to massive and tannic in the red wines, but the grape's intrinsic berry-like character always comes through.

TEMPRANILLO
This is the most important variety in Rioja, where it is traditional to blend the grapes, although many pure Tempranillo wines of excellent quality are made. It is capable of producing long-lived wines of some finesse and complexity. It is also an important variety in Argentina.

TINTA AMARELA
This is an important Port grape due to high yield and great colour.

TINTA BARROCA
One of the Douro's up-and-coming varieties, this grape makes very full, well-coloured wines that can be somewhat rustic compared with the two Touriga varieties (*see* below).

TINTA CÃO
This is one of the best Port grapes.

TOURIGA FRANCESA
This classic Port grape is no relation of the Touriga nacional. Its wine is less concentrated, but of fine quality.

TOURIGA NACIONAL
The finest Port grape in the entire Douro, it produces fantastically rich and tannic wine, with masses of fruit, which is capable of great longevity and complexity.

TROLLINGER
This variety is mainly restricted to around Württemberg in Germany. It produces fresh and fruity red wine.

VERDELHO TINTO
A classic Madeira grape.

VRANAC
A grape indigenous to Croatia, Montenegro, and Macedonia, it makes dark-coloured, full-bodied, characterful wines.

XYNOMAVRO
Xyno means "acid" and "mavro" black, an indication of how dark and longlived the wines of this excellent Greek variety can be.

ZINFANDEL
See box, above.

GRAPE VARIETY SYNONYMS

Many grape varieties are known by several different synonyms. The Malbec, for example, has at least 34 names, including Pressac, Auxerrois, Balouzet, Cot, Estrangey, and Grifforin. This would not be too confusing if the synonyms applied, uniquely, to the same grape variety, but this is not the case. The Malbec is a good example: a black grape, it is known as the Auxerrois in Cahors, but in Alsace and Chablis, the Auxerrois is a white grape, while in other parts of France the Malbec is known as the Cahors!

SYNONYMS RELATING TO LOCALIZED clones or sub-varieties are often regarded as singularly separate varieties in their own right. The Italian Trebbiano, itself a synonym for the French Ugni blanc, has many sub-varieties recognized by the Italian vine regulations. Also, many synonyms revolve around the name of another grape variety, although they are not necessarily related. Ampelographers distinguish between "erroneous" and "misleading" synonyms. The former refers to varieties that have mistakenly been given the name of another, totally different variety, whereas the latter refers to varieties whose names suggest, incorrectly, that they are related to another variety – for example, the Pinot chardonnay, which is Chardonnay, and not remotely related to any pinot variety whatsoever.

Alben – Elbling
Albig – Elbling
Alcaing – Macabéo
Alcabéo – Macabéo
Alicante – Grenache
Alicante grenache – Grenache
Alva (in Portugal) – Elbling
Alzeyer perle – Perle
Angélicant – Muscadelle
Angélico – Muscadelle
Aragad – Grenache
Aragonez – Tempranillo
Arnaison – Chardonnay
Aubaine – Chardonnay
Auvernat – Pinot noir
Auvernat blanc – Muscadelle
Auvernat gris – Pinot gris
Auvernat gris – Pinot meunier
Auxerrois – Malbec
Auxerrois gris – Pinot gris
Auxois – Pinot gris
Balkan kadarka – Kadarka
Balouzet – Malbec
Balzac – Mourvèdre
Banatski rizling – Welschriesling
Beaunois – Chardonnay
Beaunois – Pinot blanc
Beli muscat – Muscat blanc à petits grains
Beni carlo – Mourvèdre
Béquin (in Bordeaux) – Ondenc
Bergeron – Roussanne
Biela sladka grasica – Welschriesling
Bigney – Merlot

Black Hamburg – Trollinger
Black malvoisie – Cinsault
Blanc de Troyes – Aligoté
Blanc doux – Sémillon
Blanc d'Anjou – Chenin blanc
Blanc fumé – Sauvignon blanc
Blanc select – Ondenc
Blanc vert – Sacy
Blanche feuille – Pinot meunier
Blanc-lafitte – Mauzac
Blanquette – Clairette
Blanquette – Colombard
Blanquette – Ondenc
Blauburgunder – Pinot noir
Blauer limberger – Blaufränkisch
Blauer malvasier – Trollinger
Blauer spätburgunder – Pinot noir
Blaufränkisch – Gamay
Bobal – Monastrell
Bois dur – Carignan
Bordeleza belcha – Tannat
Borgogna crna – Gamay
Bötzinger – Sylvaner
Bouchet – Cabernet franc
Bouchet – Cabernet sauvignon
Bourdalès – Cinsault
Bourgvignon noir – Gamay
Bouschet sauvignon – Cabernet franc
Bouschet sauvignon – Cabernet sauvignon
Bouviertraube – Bouvier
Bovale – Monastrell
Breton – Cabernet franc

Briesgaver riesling – Elbling
Briesgaver – Elbling
Brown muscat – Muscat blanc à petits grains
Brunello (in Montalcino) – Sangiovese
Buisserate – Jacquère
Burger elbling – Elbling
Cabarnelle – Carmenère
Cabernet gris – Cabernet franc
Cabernet – Cabernet franc
Cahors – Malbec
Calabrese – Sangiovese
Camobraque – Folle blanche
Cape riesling (in South Africa) – Cruchen blanc
Carignan noir – Carignan
Carignane – Carignan
Carinena – Carignan
Carmelin – Petit verdot
Carmenelle – Carmenère
Carmenet – Cabernet franc
Catalan – Carignan
Catalan – Mourvèdre
Catape – Muscadelle
Cavalier – Len de l'Elh
Cencibel – Tempranillo
Chalosse – Folle blanche
Chardonnay – Chasselas
Chardonnay – Pinot blanc
Chasselas blanc – Chasselas
Chasselas doré – Chasselas
Chasselas – Chardonnay
Chaudenet gras – Aligoté
Chenin noir – Pineau d'aunis
Chevier – Sémillon
Chevrier – Sémillon
Chiavennasca – Nebbiolo
Chira – Syrah
Christkindltraube – Gewürztraminer
Cinq-saou – Cinsault
Cinsaut – Cinsault
Clairette à grains ronds – Ugni blanc
Clairette blanc – Clairette
Clairette blanche – Clairette
Clairette de Vence – Ugni blanc
Clairette ronde – Ugni blanc
Clare riesling (in Australia) – Cruchen blanc
Clevner – Gewürztraminer
Clevner – Pinot blanc
Codarka – Kadarka
Collemusquette – Muscadelle
Colombar – Colombard
Colombier – Colombard
Colombier – Sémillon
Cortaillod – Pinot noir
Corvina veronese – Corvina
Cot à queue rouge – Pineau d'aunis
Cot – Malbec
Crabutet noir – Merlot
Crna moravka – Blaufränkisch
Crucillant – Sémillon
Cruina – Corvina
Crujillon – Carignan
Cugnette – Jacquère
Cuviller – Cinsault
Dannery – Romorantin
Dorin – Chasselas
Douzanelle – Muscadelle
Dreimanner – Gewürztraminer
Drumin – Gewürztraminer
Dusty miller – Pinot meunier
Edeltraube – Gewürztraminer
Elben – Elbling
Enragé – Folle blanche
Enrageade – Folle blanche
Entournerien – Syrah
Epinette blanche – Chardonnay
Ermitage blanc – Marsanne
Espagna – Cinsault
Espar – Mourvèdre
Esparte – Mourvèdre
Estrangey – Malbec
Estreito – Rabigato
Etaulier – Malbec

Etranger – Malbec
Farine – Sacy
Fauvet – Pinot gris
Fehérburgundi – Pinot blanc
Feiner weisser burgunder – Chardonnay
Fendant blanc – Chasselas
Fendant – Chasselas
Fermin rouge – Gewürztraminer
Fié dans le Neuvillois – Sauvignon blanc
Flaischweiner – Gewürztraminer
Folle enrageat – Folle blanche
Formentin (in Hungary) – Savagnin
Franken riesling – Sylvaner
Franken – Sylvaner
Frankenriesling – Sylvaner
Frankenthaler – Trollinger
Frankinja crna – Gamay
Frankinja modra – Gamay
Frankisch – Gewürztraminer
Frauentraube – Chasselas
Fréaux hatif – a Gamay *teinturier*
French colombard – Colombard
Frenscher – Gewürztraminer
Fromenté – Savagnin
Fromenteau rouge – Gewürztraminer
Fromentot – Pinot gris
Frontignac – Muscat blanc à petits grains
Fumé blanc – Sauvignon blanc
Fuszeres – Gewürztraminer
Gaamez – Gamay
Gamay Beaujolais – Gamay
Gamay blanc à feuille ronds – Melon de bourgogne
Gamay blanc – Melon de bourgogne
Gamay Castille – a Gamay *teinturier*
Gamay de Bouze – a Gamay *teinturier*
Gamay de Chaudenay – a Gamay *teinturier*
Gamay fréaux – a Gamay *teinturier*
Gamay noir à just blanc – Gamay
Gamay noir – Gamay
Gamay rond – Gamay
Gamay teinturier mouro – a Gamay *teinturier*
Gamé – Blaufränkisch
Gamza – Kadarka
Garnacha blanca – Grenache blanc
Garnacha – Grenache
Garnache – Grenache
Garnacho blanco – Grenache blanc
Garnacho – Grenache
Garnaxta – Grenache blanc
Gelber muscatel – Muscat blanc à petits grains
Gelber muscateller – Muscat blanc à petits grains
Gelber muskatel – Muscat blanc à petits grains
Gelber muskateller – Muscat blanc à petits grains
Gelder ortlieber – Elbling
Gentilduret rouge – Gewürztraminer
Gentin à romorantin – Sauvignon blanc
Giboudot – Aligoté
Glera – Prosecco
Golden chasselas – Chasselas
Gordo blanco – Muscat d'Alexandrie
Goujan – Pinot meunier
Gourdoux – Malbec
Graisse blanc – Ugni blanc
Graisse – Ugni blanc
Granaccia – Grenache
Grand picot – Mondeuse
Grande vidure – Carmenère
Grasica – Welschriesling
Grassevina – Welschriesling
Grau clevner – Pinot blanc
Grauer mönch – Pinot gris
Grauerburgunder – Pinot gris
Grauklevner – Pinot gris
Gray riesling – Trousseau gris
Greffou – Roussanne
Grenache de Logrono – Tempranillo
Grenache nera – Grenache

Grey friar – Pinot gris
Grey pinot – Pinot gris
Grey riesling – Trousseau gris
Grifforin – Malbec
Gris cordelier – Pinot gris
Gris meunier – Pinot meunier
Gris rouge – Gewürztraminer
Gros auxerrois – Melon de bourgogne
Gros blanc – Sacy
Gros bouchet – Cabernet franc
Gros bouchet – Cabernet franc
Gros cabernet – Cabernet franc
Gros lot – Grolleau
Gros monsieur – César
Gros noir Guillan rouge – Malbec
Gros noir – César
Gros plant du Nantais – Folle blanche
Gros plant – Folle blanche
Gros Rhin – Sylvaner
Gros rouge du pays – Mondeuse
Gros vidure – Cabernet franc
Groslot – Grolleau
Grosse roussette – Marsanne
Grosse syrah – Mondeuse
Grossriesling – Elbling
Gross-vernatsch – Trollinger
Grünedel – Sylvaner
Grüner Silvaner – Sylvaner
Grüner – Grüner veltliner
Grünfrankisch – Sylvaner
Grünling – Sylvaner
Grünmuskateller – Grüner veltliner
Guenille – Colombard
Guépie – Muscadelle
Guépie-catape – Muscadelle
Guillan – Muscadelle
Guillan-musqué – Muscadelle
Gutedel – Chasselas
Haiden – Gewürztraminer
Hanepoot – Muscat d'Alexandrie
Harriague – Tannat
Heida – Gewürztraminer
Hermitage blanc – Marsanne
Hermitage – Cinsault
Hignin noir – Syrah
Hignin – Syrah
Hocheimer – Riesling
Hunter riesling (in Australia) – Sémillon
Hunter River riesling (in Australia) – Sémillon
Ilegó – Macabéo
Iskendiriye misketi – Muscat d'Alexandrie
Island belle – Campbell's early
Italianski rizling – Welschriesling
Italiansky rizling – Welschriesling
Jacobain – Malbec
Johannisberg riesling – Riesling
Johannisberger – Riesling
Kadarska – Kadarka
Kékfrankos – Blaufränkisch
Kékfrankos – Gamay
Klavner – Gewürztraminer
Klein reuschling – Elbling
Kleinberger – Elbling
Kleiner räuschling – Elbling
Kleinergelber – Elbling
Kleinweiner – Gewürztraminer
Klevner – Pinot blanc
Klevner – Pinot noir
Knipperlé – Elbling
Kurztingel (in Austria) – Elbling
Lardot – Macabéo
Laski rizling – Welschriesling
Laskiriesling – Welschriesling
Lemberger – Blaufränkisch
Lexia – Muscat d'Alexandrie
Limberger – Gamay
Liwora – Gewürztraminer
Luckens – Malbec
Lyonnaise blanche – Melon de bourgogne
Macabéo – Macabéo
Maccabeu – Macabéo
Mâconnais – Altesse
Madiran – Tannat
Magret – Malbec

Mala dinka – Gewürztraminer
Malaga Morterille noire – Cinsault
Malbeck – Malbec
Malmsey – Pinot gris
Malvagia – Pinot gris
Malvasia – Pinot gris
Malvoisie – Pinot gris
Manseng blanc – Manseng
Marchigiano – Verdicchio
Mataro – Carignan
Mataro – Mourvèdre
Mausat – Malbec
Maussac – Mauzac
Mauzac blanc – Mauzac
Mauzac – Malbec
Mavrud – Mavroud
Mazuelo – Carignan
Médoc noir – Merlot
Melon blanc – Chardonnay
Melon d'Arbois – Chardonnay
Melon – Melon de bourgogne
Menu pineau – Arbois
Moisac – Mauzac
Molette noir – Mondeuse
Monemrasia – Pinot gris
Monterey riesling (in California) – Sylvaner
Montonec – Parellada
Montonech – Parellada
Moravka silvanske (in Czechoslovakia) – Sylvaner
Morellino – Sangiovese
Morillon taconé – Pinot meunier
Morillon – Pinot noir
Morrastel – Graciano
Moscata bianca – Muscat blanc à petits grains
Moscata – Muscat blanc à petits grains
Moscatel bravo – Rabigato
Moscatel de Alejandria – Muscat d'Alexandrie
Moscatel de grano menudo – Muscat blanc à petits grains
Moscatel de Málaga – Muscat d'Alexandrie
Moscatel de Setúbal – Muscat d'Alexandrie
Moscatel dorado – Muscat blanc à petits grains
Moscatel gordo blanco – Muscat d'Alexandrie
Moscatel gordo – Muscat d'Alexandrie
Moscatel menudo bianco – Muscat blanc à petits grains
Moscatel romano – Muscat d'Alexandrie
Moscatel rosé – Muscat rosé à petits grains
Moscatel samsó – Muscat d'Alexandrie
Moscatel – Muscat blanc à petits grains
Moscatel – Muscat d'Alexandrie
Moscatel – Muscat d'Alexandrie
Moscatello bianco – Muscat blanc à petits grains
Moscatello – Muscat blanc à petits grains
Moscato di Canelli – Muscat blanc à petits grains
Moscato d'Asti – Muscat blanc à petits grains
Moscato – Muscat blanc à petits grains
Mosel riesling – Riesling
Moselriesling – Riesling
Mosttraube – Chasselas
Mourane – Malbec
Moustère – Malbec
Moustrou – Tannat
Moustroun – Tannat
Mueller-Thurgau – Müller-thurgau
Müller rebe – Pinot meunier
Müller schwarzriesling – Pinot meunier
Müllerrebe – Pinot meunier
Muscade – Muscadelle
Muscadel ottonel – Muscat ottonel
Muscadet doux – Muscadelle
Muscadet – Chardonnay
Muscadet – Melon de bourgogne

Muscadet – Muscadelle
Muscat aigre – Ugni blanc
Muscat Canelli – Muscat blanc à petits grains
Muscat Cknelli – Muscat blanc à petits grains
Muscat de Frontignan – Muscat blanc à petits grains
Muscat doré de Frontignan – Muscat blanc à petits grains
Muscat doré – Muscat blanc à petits grains
Muscat d'Alsace – Muscat blanc à petits grains
Muscat d'Alsace – Muscat rosé à petits grains
Muscat fou – Muscadelle
Muscat gordo blanco – Muscat d'Alexandrie
Muscat rosé à petits grains d'Alsace – Muscat rosé à petits grains
Muscat roumain – Muscat d'Alexandrie
Muscat – Muscat blanc à petits grains
Muscatel branco – Muscat blanc à petits grains
Muscatel – Muscat blanc à petits grains
Muscateller – Muscat blanc à petits grains
Muskadel – Muscadelle
Muskat – Muscat blanc à petits grains
Muskateller – Muscat blanc à petits grains
Muskat-silvaner – Sauvignon blanc
Muskotaly – Muscat blanc à petits grains
Muskotály – Muscat ottonel
Muskuti – Muscat blanc à petits grains
Musquette – Muscadelle
Nagi-burgundi – Pinot noir
Nagyburgundi – Pinot noir
Napa gamay – Gamay
Naturé – Savagnin
Nebbiolo Lampia – Nebbiolo
Nebbiolo michet – Nebbiolo
Nebbiolo rosé – Nebbiolo
Nebbiolo spanna – Nebbiolo
Negri – Malbec
Negron – Mourvèdre
Nerino – Sangiovese
Noir de Pressac – Malbec
Noir doux – Malbec
Noiren – Pinot noir
Oesterreicher – Sylvaner
Ojo de liebre – Tempranillo
Olasz rizling – Welschriesling
Olaszriesling – Welschriesling
Oporto – Portugieser
Ormeasco – Dolcetto
Ortlieber – Elbling
Paarl riesling (in South Africa) – Cruchen blanc
Pansa blanca – Xarello
Panse musquée – Muscat d'Alexandrie
Parde – Malbec
Perpignanou – Graciano
Petit bouschet – Cabernet sauvignon
Petit cabernet – Cabernet sauvignon
Petit Dannezy – Romorantin
Petit gamai – Gamay
Petit mansenc – Manseng
Petit merle – Merlot
Petit pineau – Arbois
Petit rhin – Riesling
Petit riesling – Riesling
Petit verdau – Petit verdot
Petite sainte-marie – Chardonnay
Petite syrah (France) – Syrah
Petite-vidure – Cabernet sauvignon
Petit-fer – Cabernet franc
Picardin noir – Cinsault
Picotin blanc – Roussanne
Picoutener – Nebbiolo
Picpoul – Folle blanche
Picpoule – Folle blanche
Picutener – Nebbiolo

Pied de perdrix – Malbec
Pied noir – Malbec
Pied rouge – Malbec
Pied-tendre – Colombard
Pinat cervena – Gewürztraminer
Pineau blanche de Loire – Chenin blanc
Pineau de la Loire – Chenin blanc
Pineau de Saumur – Grolleau
Pineau rouge – Pineau d'aunis
Pineau – Pinot noir
Pinot beurot – Pinot gris
Pinot blanc (in California) – Melon de bourgogne
Pinot blanc chardonnay – Chardonnay
Pinot blanc vrai auxerrois – Pinot blanc
Pinot blanc – Chardonnay
Pinot chardonnay – Chardonnay
Pinot de la Loire – Chenin blanc
Pinot grigio – Pinot gris
Pinot vérot – Pinot noir
Piperdy – Malbec
Pisse vin – Aramon
Plant Boisnard – Grolleau
Plant de brie – Pinot meunier
Plant dore – Pinot noir
Plant d'arles – Cinsault
Plant d'Aunis – Pineau d'aunis
Plousard – Poulsard
Portugais bleu – Portugieser
Portugalka – Portugieser
Prèchat – Malbec
Pressac – Malbec
Primativo – Primitivo
Primitivo – Zinfandel
Prolongeau – Malbec
Prugnolo (in Montepulciano) – Sangiovese
Ptinc cerveny – Gewürztraminer
Pugnet – Nebbiolo
Puiechou – Sauvignon blanc
Punechon – Sauvignon blanc
Quercy – Malbec
Queue-tendre – Colombard
Queue-verte – Colombard
Rabo de ovelha – Rabigato
Raisinotte – Muscadelle
Rajinski rizling – Riesling
Rajnai rizling – Riesling
Ranfoliza – Gewürztraminer
Ranina – Bouvier
Räuschling – Elbling
Rcatziteli – Rkatsiteli
Rdeci traminac – Gewürztraminer
Red trollinger – Trollinger
Refosco – Mondeuse
Reno – Riesling
Resinotte – Muscadelle
Rezlink rynsky – Riesling
Rezlink – Riesling
Rhein riesling – Riesling
Rheingau riesling – Riesling
Rheingauer – Riesling
Rheinriesling – Riesling
Rhine riesling – Riesling
Riesler – Riesling
Riesling (in Australia) – Sémillon
Riesling du rhin – Riesling
Riesling italianski – Welschriesling
Riesling italico – Welschriesling
Riesling italien – Welschriesling
Riesling renano – Riesling
Rieslinger – Riesling
Riesling-sylvaner – Müller-thurgau
Rislig rejnski – Riesling
Rismi – Welschriesling
Rivaner – Müller-thurgau
Rizling rajinski bijeli – Riesling
Rizling vlassky – Welschriesling
Romain – César
Ronçain – César
Rössling – Riesling
Rossola – Ugni blanc
Rotclevner – Gewürztraminer
Rotclevner – Pinot noir
Rotedel – Gewürztraminer

Roter nurnberger – Gewürztraminer
Roter traminer – Gewürztraminer
Rotfranke – Gewürztraminer
Rotter muscateller – Muscat rosé à petits grains
Rotter muskateller – Muscat rosé à petits grains
Roussan – Ugni blanc
Roussanne – Ugni blanc
Rousselet – Gewürztraminer
Roussette – Altesse
Roussillon tinto – Grenache
Roussillonen – Carignan
Royal muscadine – Chasselas
Ruländer – Pinot gris
Rulonski Szürkebarát – Pinot gris
Rusa – Gewürztraminer
Rynski rizling – Riesling
Saint-Emilion (in Romania) – Sémillon
Saint-Emilion – Ugni blanc
Salvagnin – Savagnin
Sangiovese di lamole – Sangiovese
Sangiovese dolce – Sangiovese
Sangiovese gentile – Sangiovese
Sangiovese Toscano – Sangiovese
Sanvicetro – Sangiovese
Sargamuskotaly – Muscat blanc à petits grains
Sauvagnin – Savagnin
Sauvignon jaune – Sauvignon blanc
Sauvignon vert (in California) – Muscadelle
Savagnin blanc – Savagnin
Savagnin musqué – Sauvignon blanc
Savagnin noir – Pinot noir
Savagnin rosé – Gewürztraminer
Savignin – Pinot noir
Savoyanche – Mondeuse
Scharvaner – Sylvaner
Schiava-grossa – Trollinger
Schiras – Syrah
Schwartz klevner – Pinot noir
Schwarze frankishe – Blaufränkisch
Schwarzriesling – Pinot meunier
Séme – Malbec
Semijon – Sémillon
Sémillon muscat – Sémillon
Sémillon roux – Sémillon
Sercial (in Australia) – Ondenc
Serenne – Syrah
Seretonina (in Yugoslavia) – Elbling
Serine – Syrah
Serprina – Prosecco
Seyve-Villard 5276 – Seyval blanc
Seyve-Villard – Seyval blanc
Shiraz – Syrah
Shyraz – Syrah
Silvain vert – Sylvaner
Silván (in Czechoslovakia) – Sylvaner
Silvaner bianco – Sylvaner
Silvaner – Sylvaner
Sipon – Furmint
Sirac – Syrah
Sirah – Syrah
Sirrah – Syrah
Sirras – Syrah
Sonoma riesling (in California) – Sylvaner
Spanna – Nebbiolo
Spätburgunder – Pinot noir
Spauna – Nebbiolo
Steen – Chenin blanc
Surin – Sauvignon blanc
Süssling – Chasselas
Syra – Syrah
Syrac – Syrah
Syras – Syrah
Szilváni (in Hungary) – Sylvaner
Talia – Sylvaner
Talijanski rizling – Welschriesling
Tamyanka – Muscat blanc à petits grains
Tanat – Tannat
Teinturier – Malbec
Tempranilla – Tempranillo
Tempranillo de la Rioja – Tempranillo

Termeno aromatico – Gewürztraminer
Terranis – Malbec
Terrano – Mondeuse
Tinta roriz – Tempranillo
Tinto aragonés – Grenache
Tinto de la Rioja – Tempranillo
Tinto de Toro – Tempranillo
Tinto fino – Tempranillo
Tinto Madrid – Tempranillo
Tinto mazuela – Carignan
Tinto – Mourvèdre
Tokaier – Pinot gris
Tokay (in Australia) – Muscadelle
Tokay d'Alsace – Pinot gris
Tokay – Pinot gris
Tokayer – Pinot gris
Tokay-Pinot gris – Pinot gris
Touriga – Touriga nacional
Traminac creveni – Gewürztraminer
Traminac – Gewürztraminer
Traminer aromatico – Gewürztraminer
Traminer aromatique – Gewürztraminer
Traminer musqué – Gewürztraminer
Traminer parfumé – Gewürztraminer
Traminer rosé – Gewürztraminer
Traminer rosso – Gewürztraminer
Traminer roz – Gewürztraminer
Traminer rozovy – Gewürztraminer
Traminer – Gewürztraminer
Tramini piros – Gewürztraminer
Tramini – Gewürztraminer
Trebbiano (often with local place name appendaged) – Ugni blanc
Tresallier – Sacy
Ugni noir – Aramon
Ull de llebre – Tempranillo
Uva di spagno – Grenache
Uva marana – Verdicchio
Veltliner – Grüner veltliner
Veltlini (in Hungary) – Grüner veltliner
Verdet – Arbois
Verdone – Verdicchio
Verdot rouge – Petit verdot
Verdot – Petit verdot
Verneuil – Romorantin
Véron – Cabernet franc
Vert doré – Pinot noir
Vidure – Cabernet sauvignon
Vionnier – Viognier
Vitraille – Merlot
Viura – Macabéo
Wälschriesling – Welschriesling
Weiss clevner – Pinot blanc
Weiss musketraube – Muscat blanc à petits grains
Weissburgunder – Pinot blanc
Weisse muskateller – Muscat blanc à petits grains
Weissemuskateller – Muscat blanc à petits grains
Weisser clevner – Chardonnay
Weisser elbling – Elbling
Weisser riesling – Riesling
Weisserburgunder (in Germany) – Melon de bourgogne
Weissgipfler – Grüner veltliner
White Frontignan – Muscat blanc à petits grains
White hermitage – Ugni blanc
White pinot – Chenin blanc
White riesling – Riesling
Wrotham pinot – Pinot meunier
Xarel-lo – Xarello
Zibibbo – Muscat d'Alexandrie
Zinfandel – Primitivo
Zingarello – Primitivo
Zingarello – Zinfandel
Zuti muscat – Muscat blanc à petits grains

The WINES of

FRANCE

FRENCH WINES ARE REGARDED AS THE BEST in the world, and a thread of this belief is even shared by France's fiercest New-World competitors. Although the winemakers of Australia and California, for instance, no longer try to copy famous French wine styles they still consider them benchmarks. The great French wine regions are an accident of geography, climate, and *terroir*. No other winemaking country in the world has such a wide range of cool climates, and this has enabled France to produce the entire spectrum of classic wine styles – from the crisp sparkling wines of Champagne through the smooth reds of Burgundy to the rich sweet wines of Sauternes. Over many centuries of trial and error, the French have discovered that specific grapes are suited to certain soils and, through this, distinctive regional wine styles have evolved, so that every wine drinker knows what to expect from a bottle of Bordeaux, Burgundy, Champagne, or Rhône, and this has been the key to success for French wines.

THE MOON RISING OVER CHÂTEAU LATOUR
The magnificent tower of Château Latour is bathed in moonlight, evoking the majesty of one of the world's greatest wines.

✦FRANCE✦

France makes the best and the worst wines in the world. No other country can rival France for the quality and diversity of its wine but its success is dependent on the sheer size of its production, which has always been a double-edged sword.

BY CHOOSING THE GREATEST winegrowing regions and selecting the best wines produced from them for top *Appellation d'Origine Contrôlée* (AOC) classifications, the French wine industry has highlighted such great wines as Château Margaux, Romanée-Conti, and Krug, and has thus created France's reputation as the foremost wine country in the world based on a tiny quantity of the total wine produced. France produces over 67 million hectolitres (745 million cases) of wine every year and, included in this at the other end of the quality spectrum, there are vast amounts of *vin de table* or *vin ordinaire* (officially designated as *vin de consommation courante*, or wine for immediate consumption). *Vin ordinaire* is very ordinary indeed, but between *vin ordinaire* and the *crème de la crème* of French wines there are several tiers of appellation, representing various combinations of quality and quantity.

It is the producers in the historically best-known appellations who have a duty to respect the quality and character that established the fame of their wines. That some have not always maintained the highest standards is not surprising and, as long as the practice is not widespread, it is not particularly harmful, since all wine areas inevitably have their good, bad, and ugly. There has, however, been a significant increase in the number of underperformers over the last ten years or so, particularly in the Loire and Burgundy. The best are still the best, but the growing number of poor AOC wines is giving many appellations a reputation for unreliability, which the more scrupulous producers do not deserve. In the first edition of this encyclopedia I wrote: "Even the wines that receive one of the higher classifications can be unpredictable: while some bearing illustrious appellations may

disappoint, the very best produced in lesser known areas can often be outstanding". But I must now qualify that statement by saying the quality divide in some appellations is now so great that the consumer can no longer rely on where the wine is produced, but must concentrate solely on who produced it.

HOW FRENCH WINE IS CLASSIFIED
In 1935, France became the first nation to set up a countrywide system for controlling the origin and quality of its wines, when the Institut National des Appellations d'Origine (INAO) was established, although regional wine areas outside France had established quality controls much earlier (Chianti in 1716 and Rioja in 1560). The INAO's task was to devise the geographical limits of appellations and to enforce the regulations governing them.

Appellation d'Origine Contrôlée (AOC or AC)
There are now more than 470 separate AOCs, covering almost 490,000 hectares (1.2 million acres), and producing an annual average of 29 million hectolitres (322 million cases) of wine. The AOC laws regulate the grape varieties used, viticultural methods, harvest and yield restrictions, minimum alcoholic content, and winemaking techniques for each area. Although the laws are supposed to control the quality of each wine by having it pass an official analysis and tasting, the latter of these has become

---

FRENCH WINE AT A GLANCE

Appellation d'Origine Contrôlée (AOC or AC)	*Vin de Pays*
Over 52% of total French wine production – 27% exported, 73% consumed within France	29% of total French wine production – 23% exported, 77% consumed within France
	Vin de Table
Vin Délimité de Qualité Supérieure (VDQS)	18% of total French wine production – 13% exported, 87% consumed within France
Less than 1% of total French wine production – 20% exported, 80% consumed within France	

HOW TO READ FRENCH WINE LABELS

Wine labels give certain mandatory information, such as the name of the bottler who, in France, is legally responsible for the wine. Other details include the colour and style of wine, grape variety, and vintage; these are not always obligatory but do assist the consumer.

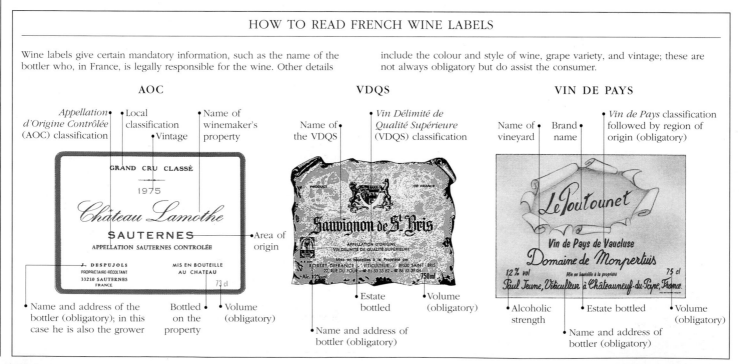

AOC
- Appellation d'Origine Contrôlée (AOC) classification
- Local classification
- Vintage
- Name of winemaker's property
- Area of origin
- Name and address of the bottler (obligatory); in this case he is also the grower
- Bottled on the property
- Volume (obligatory)

GRAND CRU CLASSÉ
1975
Château Lamothe
SAUTERNES
APPELLATION SAUTERNES CONTRÔLÉE
J. DESPUJOLS
PROPRIÉTAIRE-RÉCOLTANT
33210 SAUTERNES
FRANCE
MIS EN BOUTEILLE
AU CHATEAU
73 cl

VDQS
- Name of the VDQS
- *Vin Délimité de Qualité Supérieure* (VDQS) classification
- Estate bottled
- Volume (obligatory)
- Name and address of bottler (obligatory)

Sauvignon de St Bris
APPELLATION D'ORIGINE
VIN DÉLIMITÉ DE QUALITÉ SUPÉRIEURE
ROBERT DEFRANCE · VITICULTEUR · 89530 SAINT-BRIS
22, RUE DU FOUR · ☎ 86 53 33 82 · ☎ 86 53 39 04
Alc. 12% vol
750ml

VIN DE PAYS
- Name of vineyard
- Brand name
- *Vin de Pays* classification followed by region of origin (obligatory)
- Alcoholic strength
- Estate bottled
- Name and address of bottler (obligatory)
- Volume (obligatory)

Le Poutounet
Vin de Pays de Vaucluse
Domaine de Monpertuis
12% vol
Paul Jeune, Viticulteur à Châteauneuf-du-Pape, France
75 cl

FRANCE

*The coloured areas on this map identify the ten main wine-producing
regions of France, where the areas of* Appellation d'Origine Contrôlée,
*which cover 490,000 hectares (1.2 million acres), are concentrated.
However, the country has almost one million hectares of vineyards
in total, and many good, everyday-drinking wines are made in
other parts of the country. See also* Vin de Pays *maps pp.246, 247.*

Bordeaux
See also p.59

Burgundy
See also p.131

Champagne
See also pp.165, 169

Alsace
See also p.182

The Loire Valley
See also p.192

The Rhône Valley
See also p.211

Jura and Savoie
See also p.222

Southwest France
See also p.226

Languedoc-Roussillon
See also p.233

Provence and Corsica
See also p.242

---------- *Département* boundary

▲ Height above sea level (metres)

something of a farce, since panels of tasting judges are today composed almost entirely of the very people who actually make the wine. Virtually all the producers I spoke to admitted that only those wines with faults – and obvious ones at that – are likely to be rejected, with no account taken of either quality or whether a wine reflects the character of the grapes used or expresses any regional style. Some were honest enough to explain that most people are too afraid to start the ball rolling on the issue of quality or style for fear that someone whose wine has already been rejected might seek revenge by rejecting other wines indiscriminately. It is little surprise, therefore, that only around two or three per cent of wines fail to pass these tastings.

In 1995, Michel Bettane, one of France's top wine writers, was quoted as saying "Today, *appellation contrôlée* guarantees neither quality nor authenticity"; and even Alain Berger, who at the time was the director of the Institut National des Appellations d'Origine or INAO (i.e. he was the man in charge of running the entire French appellation system), confessed that "One can find on the market scandalously poor products with the *appellation contrôlée* halo". The AOC tasting system is obviously deficient as, presumably, are the VDQS and *vin de pays* tastings, although with no famous names or grand history, the expectations for such wines are relatively low and not prone to the same degree of scandal that expensive AOCs of very poor quality will inevitably attract. The French accept there is a problem and, even as I write, the INAO has set up a commission to study how improvements can be made. Until such improvements are agreed and implemented, however, the onus is very much on the knowledge of the consumer.

Vin Délimité de Qualité Supérieure (VDQS)
There are just over 40 VDQS wines, covering less than 8,000 hectares (under 20,000 acres), and producing an annual average of 515,000 hectolitres (just over 5.7 million cases) under similar controls to those applied to AOC wines, but with yields that may be higher and alcoholic strengths that are often lower. The overall quality standard is not as high, although it may be argued in certain cases that the quality is easily comparable.

Since the emergence of *vins de pays* in the 1970s, there have been persistent rumours of the imminent demise of VDQS, but the INAO, which is the regulatory body for both AOC and VDQS wines, has found this category to be such a convenient staging post for potential AOCs that it would be madness to remove it. VDQS wines promoted to AOC status include Coteaux du Tricastin (promoted in 1973), St.-Chinian (1982), Coteaux du Lyonnais (1984), and Côtes du Marmandais (1990).

It would be a mistake, however, to think of all VDQS wines as purely transitory. It is not a guaranteed halfway house to full AOC status, as can be demonstrated by those wines that still retain VDQS classification 40 years after this category came into fruition, and the fact that the majority of surviving VDQS wines actually date from the 1960s and 1970s. It is not beyond imagination that the French might elevate these crusty old VDQS wines at some date in the future, but most potential new AOC wines will be selected from those VDQS wines that have come up through the now mature *vin de pays* ranks.

Vin de Pays
There are just over 140 *vin de pays* or "country wine" appellations, covering 200,000 hectares (494,200 acres), producing an annual average of 16 million hectolitres (178 million cases). Officially established in 1968, the *vins de pays* did not become a marketable reality until 1973, when the rules for production were fixed. They were created, quite simply, by authorizing some *vins de table* to indicate their specific geographic origin and, if desired, the grape varieties used, but the effect was more profound than that. For a long while, it was even obligatory for these wines to carry the term "Vin de Table" in addition to their *vin de pays* appellation,

but this regulation was discontinued in 1989. Allowing producers of potentially superior table wine areas to market, for the first time, the origin and content of their wines gave them back a long-lost pride. The best producers started to care more about how they tended their vines and made their wines, and began to uproot low-quality varieties, replant with better ones, and restrict yields.

There are three categories of *vin de pays*, each with its own controls, but all regulated by the Office National Interprofessionnel des Vins or ONIVINS. Although every *vin de pays* must have a specified origin on the label, a wide range of grape varieties can be used and high yields are allowed – with the result that the quality of the wine varies greatly. This is, nevertheless, a most interesting category of wines, often infiltrated by foreign winemakers – usually Australian – producing some of the most exciting, inexpensive, and upfront-fruity wines. Many *vins de pays* are, of course, bland and will never improve, but some will make it up the hierarchical ladder to VDQS and, possibly, full AOC status. Certain individual producers, such as Aimé Guibert of Mas de Daumas Gassac, could not care less about AOC status, as they

---

VINS DE PRIMEUR

We tend to think of Beaujolais Nouveau as the only *vin de primeur* or "new wine", but there are no less than 55 different wines that are allowed by AOC regulations to be sold in the year they are harvested, and 25 of these must be labelled *primeur* or *nouveau*. They are made in a style that is at its peak in the first year of its life. So, for those who like drinking wine when it has only just stopped fermenting, why not look out for the following?

Wines that must be clearly labelled *primeur* or *nouveau* and which may be sold as from the third Thursday of November following the harvest:

1 Anjou Gamay
2 Beaujolais (red or rosé)
3 Beaujolais Supérieur (red or rosé)
4 Beaujolais-Villages (red or rosé)
5 Beaujolais with village name but not *cru* (red or rosé)
6 Bourgogne (white only)
7 Bourgogne Aligoté (white only)
8 Bourgogne Grand Ordinaire (white only)
9 Cabernet d'Anjou (rosé)
10 Cabernet de Saumur (rosé)
11 Coteaux du Languedoc (red or rosé)
12 Coteaux du Lyonnais (red, white, or rosé)
13 Coteaux du Tricastin (red, white, or rosé)
14 Côtes-du-Rhône (red sold

only as a *vin de café* or rosé)
15 Côtes du Roussillon (red, white, or rosé)
16 Côtes du Ventoux (red, white, or rosé)
17 Gaillac (red Gamay or white)
18 Mâcon (white or rosé)
19 Mâcon Supérieur (white only)
20 Macon-Villages (white only)
21 Macon with village name (white only)
22 Muscadet
23 Muscadet de Sèvre et Maine
24 Muscadet des Coteaux de la Loire
25 Muscadet Côtes de Grand-Lieu
26 Rosé d'Anjou
27 Tavel (rosé only)
28 Touraine Gamay (red only)
29 Touraine (rosé only)

The following wines may be sold from 1 December after the harvest without any mention of *primeur* or *nouveau*:

1 Anjou (white only)
2 Bergerac (white or rosé, but not red)
3 Blayais (white only)
4 Bordeaux (*sec*, rosé, or *clairet*)
5 Buzet (white or rosé)
6 Cabernet d'Anjou (rosé)
7 Cabernet de Saumur (rosé)
8 Corbières (white or rosé)
9 Costières de Nîmes (white or rosé)
10 Coteaux d'Aix-en-Provence (white or rosé)
11 Coteaux du Languedoc (white or rosé)
12 Coteaux Varois (white or rosé)
13 Côtes de Bourg (white only)
14 Côtes de Duras (white or rosé)
15 Côtes du Marmandais (white or rosé)
16 Côtes de Provence (white or rosé)
17 Côtes-du-Rhône (white or rosé)
18 Côtes du Ventoux (white or rosé)
19 Entre-Deux-Mers (white only)
20 Faugères (rosé only)
21 Graves (white only)
22 Graves des Vayres (white only)
23 Jurançon Sec
24 Minervois (white or rosé)
25 Montravel (white or rosé)
26 Muscadet
27 Muscadet de Sèvre et Maine
28 Muscadet des Coteaux de la Loire
29 Muscadet Côtes de Grand-Lieu
30 Premières Côtes de Blaye (white only)
31 Rosé d'Anjou
32 Rosé de Loire
33 St.-Chinian (rosé only)
34 Ste.-Foy-Bordeaux (white only)
35 Saumur (white only)
36 Touraine (white only)

BREAKDOWN OF FRENCH WINE PRODUCTION MEASURED IN HECTOLITRES

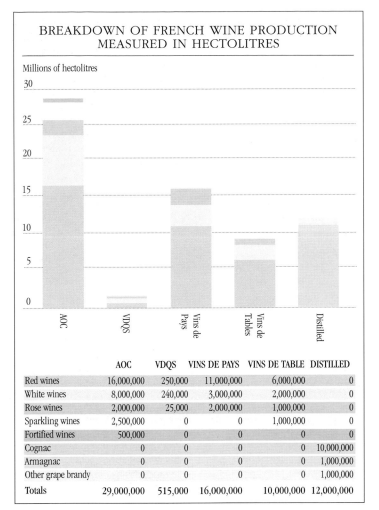

Millions of hectolitres

	AOC	VDQS	VINS DE PAYS	VINS DE TABLE	DISTILLED
Red wines	16,000,000	250,000	11,000,000	6,000,000	0
White wines	8,000,000	240,000	3,000,000	2,000,000	0
Rose wines	2,000,000	25,000	2,000,000	1,000,000	0
Sparkling wines	2,500,000	0	0	1,000,000	0
Fortified wines	500,000	0	0	0	0
Cognac	0	0	0	0	10,000,000
Armagnac	0	0	0	0	1,000,000
Other grape brandy	0	0	0	0	1,000,000
Totals	29,000,000	515,000	16,000,000	10,000,000	12,000,000

FRENCH WINE PRODUCTION BY TYPE

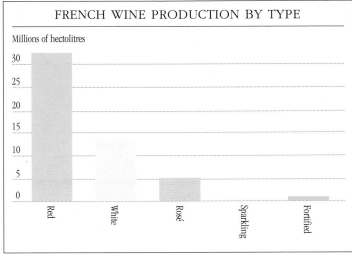

Millions of hectolitres

FRENCH WINE PRODUCTION BY TYPE

Some 55 million hectolitres of wine are currently produced in France, plus 12 million hectolitres that are distilled primarily for cognac. Since the mid-1980s, French wine production has dropped by 27 per cent in response to a move away from *vins de table* (now 10 million hectolitres, compared to 34 million ten years ago) to higher quality wines, such as *vin de pays* and AOC wines.

WHO DRINKS FRENCH WINE?

Although production of French wine fell by 27 per cent in the 1990s, exports rose by more than 3 million hectolitres to a record 16.1 million hectolitres. This level was achieved in 1999 as part of the millennium celebrations, thus exports dropped back to 14.9 million hectolitres in 2000, but even this was almost 2 million more than in the 1980s, a period that is still perceived as the hey-day of French wine exports. Germany remains the largest importer of French wines, although much of this volume is focused on the cheaper end of the market, which is why it is only the third largest importing country in terms of value and the UK is number one. With less than half the volume that the UK purchased for almost the same price, the USA continues to pay top dollar.

happen to be making wines under the less draconian *vin de pays* system that already have reputations as good as those of the finest French appellations and demand even higher prices than expensive AOC wines. For a description of the various *vin de pays* categories, a map showing the areas producing *vins de pays*, and profiles of every *vin de pays* and their finest producers, *see* pp.246–57.

Vin de Table

There are more than 170,000 hectares (420,000 acres) of unclassified vineyards in France, producing an annual average of 10 million hectolitres (more than 150 million cases) of *vins de table*, although this includes some two million hectolitres (22 million cases) of grape juice, grape concentrate, and wine vinegar.

Also known as *vins ordinaires*, these wines are cheap in every sense of the word. They are not intended for keeping and some cynics might argue that they are not fit for drinking, since much of this wine has to be diluted with water before even the French can bring themselves to drink it.

Vins de table come under the auspices of ONIVINS, but there are no controls apart from negative ones, such as not being allowed to mention any grape names or indicate an origin more specific than France. The address of the producer seldom has any bearing on the origin of the wine, although some producers do try to fabricate a style in accordance with their local image, thus a *négociant* based in Nuits-St.-Georges might attempt to make a *vin de table* with some sort of Burgundian character, but the consumer cannot be sure that any of the wines used will be from Burgundy, and the likelihood is that they won't. Some winemerchants pride themselves on the quality of their basic *vin de table* brand, but it's a dead-end category as far as being able to discover useful information, let alone rely on it.

FRENCH WINE EXPORTS 2000

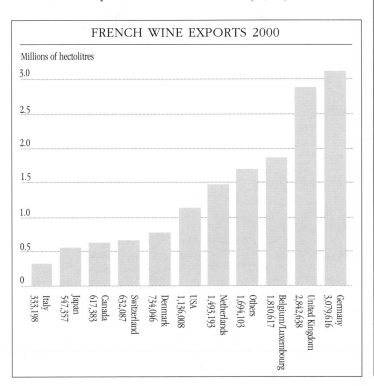

Millions of hectolitres

Italy 333,198 / Japan 547,357 / Canada 617,383 / Switzerland 632,087 / Denmark 734,046 / USA 1,136,008 / Netherlands 1,493,193 / Others 1,694,103 / Belgium/Luxembourg 1,810,617 / United Kingdom 2,842,638 / Germany 3,079,616

BORDEAUX

Bordeaux is an area in an almost-perfect viticultural situation on the west coast of France and benefits from the ultimate marketing tool – a château-based classification system that was established almost 150 years ago.

THE LAST DECADE OF THE 21ST CENTURY severely tested Bordeaux's reputation. With rain-drenched harvests, its claim to be the ultimate viticultural paradise has been put into question, whilst the depressingly poor quality of its generic wines attracted almost as much bad publicity as the grossly inflated prices of the top châteaux from the relatively modest 1997 vintage. However, this will be no more than *déjà vu* for most of those who have been following Bordeaux for the last 20 years or so. The only difference now is that faced with competition at all price points from the New World and the effect of virtually instantaneous communication, the Bordelais are more likely to do something about it this time around.

The Bordeaux appellation and the Gironde *département* are geographically one and the same. Moreover, the Gironde is the largest *département* in France and Bordeaux is the largest source of quality wines in the world. There are more than 22,000 vineyard proprietors working in excess of 113,000 hectares (280,000 acres), producing 6 million hectolitres (over 66 million cases) of Bordeaux wine every year. Of these 22,000 properties, no less than 7,000 are châteaux and domaines producing wine. Yet the reputation of this great wine-producing region has been built upon the quality of less than one per cent of this number,

and only three per cent of the vast volume of wine produced is classified as *Cru Classé* or *Grand Cru* – the highest-ranking status for a Bordeaux wine.

THE CHÂTEAU SYSTEM AND MERCHANT POWER
Prior to the concept of château wine estates, the land was worked on a crop-sharing basis. This feudal system slowly changed from the late 17th century onwards. As the *bordelais* brokers developed the habit of recording and classifying wines according to their *cru* or growth (which is to say their geographical origin) and the prices they fetched, the fame of individual properties developed.

The 19th century saw the rise of the merchant or *négociant* in Bordeaux. Many of these were of English origin, and some firms were established by Scottish, Irish, Dutch, and German businessmen. The best château wines were not consumed by the French themselves; they were the preserve of the British, German, and other northern European countries. Thus foreign merchants had an obvious advantage over their French counterparts. Yearly, in Spring, these *négociants* took delivery of young wines in cask from the various châteaux and matured them in their cellars prior to shipping. They were thus responsible for their *élevage*, or upbringing, and became known as *négociants-éleveurs*, eventually becoming the middlemen found in every aspect of wine trading. In many instances a foreign buyer found it more convenient to deal through a *négociant* than directly with the wine producer and often had no alternative, since a number of châteaux were owned by, or were exclusive to, certain *négociants*.

CHÂTEAU PALMER
This majestic turreted château is one of the finest in the Médoc.

THE MODERN BORDEAUX WINE TRADE
It was perhaps inevitable that the historically powerful, family-owned *négociants-éleveurs* would eventually become a spent force. They lacked the resources required to finance adequately the huge increase in demand for Bordeaux in the 1960s, and if they did not founder during the oil crisis of the early- to mid-1970s, they fell prey to the economic depressions of the next two decades.

As proud old firms were either taken over or went bankrupt, so the power shifted from the *négoce* to the châteaux, and in order to cope with a boom in world markets, many Bordeaux properties expanded their vineyards or added large shiny new fermentation facilities. Many of these projects were financed with bank loans when interest rates were low. When sales slumped and interest rates shot up the repayments became unbearable. Consequently, apart from a few entrepreneurial owners, power has shifted relatively recently from châteaux to investors – not only banks but insurance groups, pension funds, and the like.

In today's market, therefore, the *négoce* has much less influence than before, with its *élevage* role primarily restricted to branded wines. The *élevage* of fine *Cru Classé* wine is either handled by the individual château itself or dispensed with by selling wines ridiculously young through French supermarkets or through the worldwide *en primeur* trade (*see* p.62). A number of château owners have carved out their own little empires, collecting estates or developing their own *négociant* businesses.

BORDEAUX & CHIPS

In 1999, when genuine quality issues needed to be addressed, the Bordeaux Appeal Tribunal found four châteaux guilty of adulteration and fined them approximately £8,000 ($13,000) each. Adulteration might sound very serious, but all the châteaux concerned (Giscours, Cap de Haut, Greysac and Lacroix-Merlin) had done was to use oak chips, a practice that has long been widespread outside France, particularly throughout the New World. Whether a second growth such as Giscours should contemplate such an economy is debatable, but it is reasonable to expect less expensive châteaux to experiment with oak chips and their use cannot reasonably be described as adulteration. In fact, until this case oak chips were not specifically illegal in Bordeaux, but as Jacques Fanet of INAO stated at the time 'We are against this because in the original decree for the AOCs dating back to 1935 it stipulates that "All oenological practices must conform to the local practices, which are faithful and constant". In Bordeaux this means putting wine into wood, not wood into wine.'

That may be a clever thing to say, amusing even, but it is utter nonsense. To apply such a generalised rule rigidly would entail banning everything from stainless-steel vats to the latest technological advances, throwing Bordeaux back to the primitive practices prior to Peynaud, Ribéreau-Gayon, Dubourdieu et al. As far as wood is concerned, Monsieur Fanet will find that Bordeaux was primarily using Russian oak in the 1930s. Very few châteaux used French oak and absolutely none used American, yet as I reported in the previous edition, more than 60 Bordeaux châteaux, including crus classés, have been using American oak. If INAO does not pursue these cases, then to be even-handed it should petition the Bordeaux Appeal Tribunal to annul its verdict on Giscours, Cap de Haut, Greysac and Lacroix-Merlin.

It does make outsiders wonder why the French continue to shoot themselves in the foot whenever it comes to defending their appellations in general, and their most famous wines in particular.

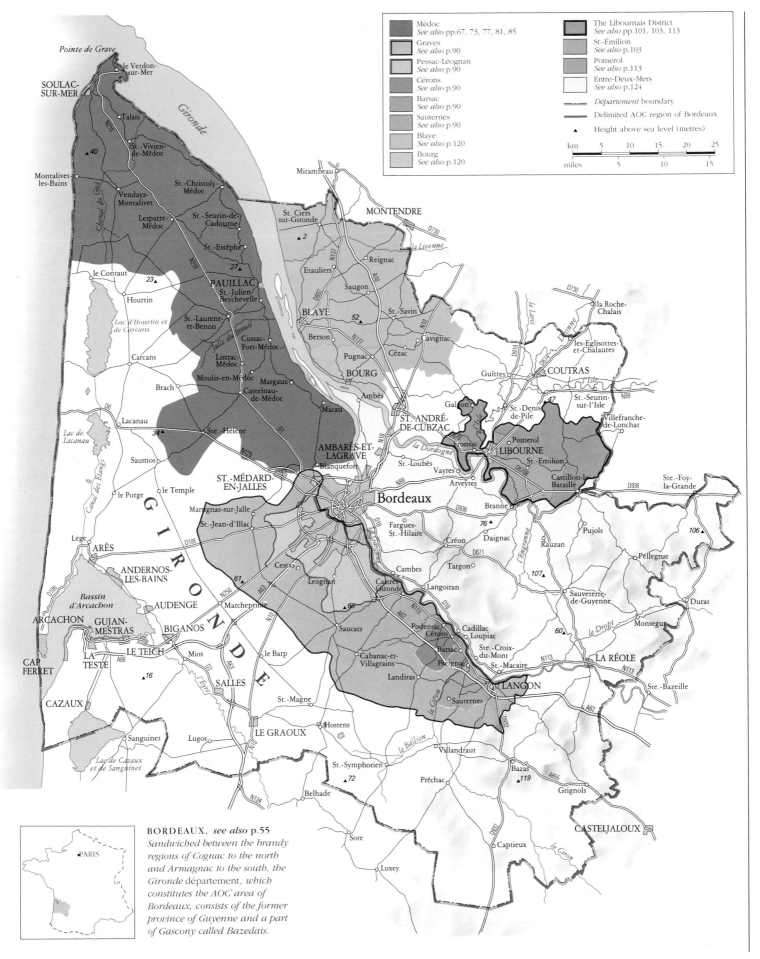

Médoc
See also pp.67, 73, 77, 81, 85

Graves
See also p.90

Pessac-Léognan
See also p.90

Cérons
See also p.90

Barsac
See also p.90

Sauternes
See also p.90

Blaye
See also p.120

Bourg
See also p.120

The Libournais District
See also pp.101, 103, 113

St.-Émilion
See also p.103

Pomerol
See also p.113

Entre-Deux-Mers
See also p.124

Département boundary

Delimited AOC region of Bordeaux

Height above sea level (metres)

km   5   10   15   20   25
miles   5   10   15

BORDEAUX, *see also p.55*
Sandwiched between the brandy regions of Cognac to the north and Armagnac to the south, the Gironde département, which constitutes the AOC area of Bordeaux, consists of the former province of Guyenne and a part of Gascony called Bazedais.

PARIS

Some of the new elite in Bordeaux are named below:

• Jean-Michel Cazes, owner of Château Lynch-Bages and former head of AXA (an insurance group with wine investments that stretch from Bordeaux to Tokay in Hungary) still commands great respect and it will be interesting to see if his successor at AXA, Christian Sealey, has the same influence.

• Eric Dulong, the dynamic vice-president of the CIVB and instigator of a 25-point quality control programme for producers who deal through his family-owned négociant firm.

• Frédéric Engerer, who became the youngest president of Château Latour, shaking Bordeaux to its roots when he sacked both the winemaker and maître de chais in the same year.

• André Lurton, of La Louvière and Cluzeau, which are the quality leaders in a growing number of Graves properties.

• Jacques and François Lurton, the sons of André, who are merchants in their own right and have taken on the Australian winemakers at their own game in France, making French-inspired wine all over the globe, including, ironically, Australia itself.

• Jean-François Mau of Yvon Mau, a busy Bordeaux négociant who floods Europe with wines from petits châteaux.

• The Merlaut family, who control Groupe Taillan, which recently purchased Cos d'Estournel and Gruaud-Larose. Groupe Taillan also owns Citran, Ferrière, La Gurgue, Haut-Bages-Libéral, Chasse-Spleen, and Bordeaux wine merchant Ginestet.

• Christian and Jean-Jacques Moueix of Pétrus fame and other holdings concentrated in the Libournais district.

• Stephan Von Neipperg for his charismatic contribution to the Côtes de Castillon.

THE CLASSIFICATION OF BORDEAUX WINES

Of all the Bordeaux classifications that exist, it is the 1855 Classification which is meant whenever anyone refers to "The Classification". It was commissioned by the Bordeaux Chamber of Commerce, which was required by the government of the Second Empire to present a selection of its wines at the 1855 Exposition Universelle in Paris. For their own ends, the brokers of the Bordeaux Stock Exchange traditionally categorized the most famous Bordeaux properties on the basis of the prices they fetched, so they were charged by the Chamber of Commerce to submit a "complete list of classified red Bordeaux wines, as well as our great

HOW TO READ BORDEAUX LABELS

Since 2000 all wines from this region must state "Vin de Bordeaux" or "Grand Vin de Bordeaux". This is a welcome clarification for many consumers who until now might not have realised that certain AOC (e.g., Fronsac) are in fact Bordeaux appellations.

VINTAGE
Local variations in vintage quality must always be considered. The excellent 1970 vintage was not quite as good in St.-Émilion, yet the 1971 was far more successful there than in the Médoc. Do not be disillusioned by the complexity of it all: the experts are still arguing about the 1961 and 1945 vintages. Master of Wine Michael Broadbent freely admits it took him 40 years to opt for 1945; however, he would not turn down a 1961!

APPELLATION
The first thing to do is to search out the appellation. All the famous châteaux have small, specific appellations. If the wine is from one of the generic Bordeaux appellations or from a lesser area such as Bourg, Blaye, or Entre-Deux-Mers, it might be good, but it will not be great.

PRODUCE OF FRANCE
OR *PRODUIT DE FRANCE*
It is a legal requirement that the country of production should be shown on the label of any wine due for export. There is one reason why this might not, in fact, appear: Bordeaux wines tend to pass through many owners in various countries before being consumed and can end up almost anywhere.

NAME
Is it a brand name or does it purport to be a château? Branded wines will normally be from generic appellations and should be moderately priced. If it is a château, does it have a reputation you are prepared to pay for?

GRAND CRU CLASSÉ
In the Médoc and Graves, this term is used synonymously with *Cru Classé* (see below).

PROPRIETOR
The name and address of the proprietor of the château.

IS IT CHÂTEAU BOTTLED?
All great Bordeaux wines now clearly show the term "*Mis en bouteille au château*" on both the cork and the label, but earlier vintages might have been bottled by a *négociant* in Bordeaux, or shipped in cask and bottled abroad, and should be significantly cheaper. If the bottler is (or was) a reputable merchant, the wine could be a bargain way of enjoying an old vintage – this Château Batailley 1966, bottled by Peter Dominic was, in fact, quite superb. Buying old vintages is risky anyway, but buying an English-, Scottish-, Belgian-, or Bordeaux-bottled old vintage is supposed to increase that risk, hence the lower price.

(Label reads:)
CHÂTEAU BATAILLEY
LE GRAND BATAILLEY
GRAND CRU CLASSÉ
APPELLATION PAUILLAC CONTROLÉE
1966
HÉRITIERS BORIE MANOUX, PROPRIÉTAIRES A PAUILLAC
PRODUCE OF FRANCE
Shipped & Bottled by
Peter DOMINIC Ltd
LONDON, S. W. I.

The following classifications may be found on Bordeaux labels. Some apply only to St.-Émilion (*see* p.104):

CRU ARTISAN
A traditional title in the Médoc, but not recognized by the EU, although an association of 250 estates, representing 11 per cent of the total Médoc production, is petitioning for its official acceptance.

CRU BOURGEOIS
This is a category of good-quality, non-classified wines representing one-third of the production of the various appellations of the Médoc. These wines fall between the categories of *petits châteaux* and *Crus Classés*, and come from more than 300 estates that represent 49 per cent of the total Médoc production. With so many wines in this category, standards do vary, but some *Cru Bourgeois* can be outstanding.

CRU CLASSÉ
This phrase means "Classed Growth", and in Bordeaux this can only be used if the property and vineyard are an officially classified growth.

PREMIER CRU OR PREMIER GRAND CRU CLASSÉ
The First Growths of Bordeaux may boast their classification; the Second to Fifth rarely do.

GRAND CRU
An annually awarded classification for certain St.-Émilion wines, up to and including the 1985 vintage.

GRAND CRU CLASSÉ
This permanent classification of St.-Émilion is a higher category than wines bearing "*Grand Cru*" without any indication of the word *classé*.

The term "Grand Cru Classé" is also synonymous with *Cru Classé* in the Médoc and Graves regions.

PREMIER GRAND CRU
Ranked above *Grand Cru Classé*, this is the highest-quality category of permanently classified St.-Émilion.

GRAND VIN
Although this term has no legal significance, it should refer to the "Great Wine" or principal label of a château. The so-called "Second Wines" are sold under other labels.

THE 1855 CLASSIFICATION OF THE WHITE WINES OF THE GIRONDE

PREMIER CRU SUPÉRIEUR
(Superior First Growth)
Yquem, Sauternes

PREMIER CRUS
(First Growths)
Latour Blanche, Bommes
(now *Château La Tour Blanche*)
Peyraguey, Bommes (now two
properties: *Château Lafaurie-
Peyraguey* and *Château Clos
Haut-Peyraguey*)
Vigneau, Bommes (now *Château
Rayne-Vigneau*)
Suduiraut, Preignac
Coutet, Barsac
Climens, Barsac
Bayle, Sauternes (now *Château
Guiraud*)
Rieusec, Sauternes (now *Château
Rieussec*, Fargues)
Rabeaud, Bomme (now two
properties: *Château Rabaud-Promis*
and *Château Sigalas-Rabaud*)

DEUXIÈME CRUS
(Second Growths)
Mirat, Barsac (now *Château Myrat*)
Doisy, Barsac (now three
properties: *Château Doisy-Daëne,
Château Doisy-Dubroca,* and
Château Doisy-Védrines)
Pexoto, Bommes (now part of
Château Rabaud-Promis)
D'arche, Sauternes (now *Château
d'Arche*)
Filhot, Sauternes
Broustet Nérac, Barsac (now two
properties: *Château Broustet* and
Château Nairac)
Caillou, Barsac
Suau, Barsac
Malle, Preignac (now *Château de
Malle*)
Romer, Preignac (now two
properties: *Château Romer* and
Château Romer-du-Hayot, Fargues)
Lamothe, Sauternes (now two
properties: *Château Lamothe* and
Château Lamothe-Guignard)

white wines". The classifications listed above and right give the 19th-century names in the original form as listed by the brokers on 18 April, 1855. The frequent absence of the word château has been followed, as has the circumflex in *Crûs*, and the use of *Seconds Crûs* for red wines and *Deuxièmes Crûs* for whites.

THE CLASSIC GRAPE VARIETIES OF BORDEAUX

Contrary to what one might expect, it is Merlot, not Cabernet sauvignon, that is the most important grape variety in Bordeaux. Cabernet sauvignon represents only 18 per cent of the vines cultivated in Bordeaux, whereas Merlot accounts for more than 32 per cent. It is nearer the truth, therefore, to say that Cabernet sauvignon gives backbone to Merlot, rather than to suggest that Merlot softens Cabernet sauvignon. Although Château Mouton-Rothschild contains no less than 90 per cent Cabernet sauvignon, it is an exception, as even on the Médoc's hallowed ground, where it is blasphemy to mention the name of Merlot, 40 per cent of the vines grown are of that variety. Château Pétrus

THE MERLOT GRAPE VARIETY
Almost twice as much Merlot as Cabernet sauvignon grows in Bordeaux.

(*see* p.114), one of the most expensive wines in the world, contains 95 per cent Merlot, without any Cabernet sauvignon at all. Cabernet sauvignon is a classic grape, quite possibly the greatest red-wine grape in the world, but its importance for Bordeaux is often overstated.

Sémillon is the most important white grape variety grown in Bordeaux. It is important both in terms of its extent of cultivation and quality. This grape variety is susceptible to botrytis, the "noble rot" that results in classic Sauternes and Barsac. It is therefore considered to be the world's greatest sweet-wine grape.

THE 1855 CLASSIFICATION OF THE RED WINES OF THE GIRONDE

PREMIER CRUS *(First Growths)*
Château Lafite, Pauillac
(now *Château Lafite-Rothschild*)
Château Margaux, Margaux
Château Latour, Pauillac
Haut-Brion, Pessac (Graves)

SECONDS CRUS
(Second Growths)
Mouton, Pauillac (now *Château
Mouton-Rothschild* and a First
Growth since 1973)
Rauzan-Ségla, Margaux
Rauzan-Gassies, Margaux
Léoville, St.-Julien (now three
properties: *Châteaux Léoville-Las-
Cases, Léoville-Poyferré,* and
Léoville-Barton)
Vivens Durfort, Margaux
(now *Château Durfort-Vivens*)
Gruau-Laroze, St.-Julien
(now *Château Gruaud-Larose*)
Lascombe, Margaux
(now *Château Lascombes*)
Brane, Cantenac (now *Château
Brane-Cantenac*)
Pichon Longueville, Pauillac
(now two properties: *Château
Pichon-Longueville-Baron* and
*Château Pichon-Longueville-
Comtesse-de-Lalande*)
Ducru Beau Caillou, St.-Julien
(now *Château Ducru-Beaucaillou*)
Cos Destournel, St.-Estèphe
(now *Château Cos d'Estournel*)
Montrose, St.-Estèphe

TROISIÈME CRUS
(Third Growths)
Kirwan, Cantenac
Château d'Issan, Cantenac
Lagrange, St.-Julien
Langoa, St.-Julien (now *Château
Langoa-Barton*)
Giscours, Labarde
St.-Exupéry, Margaux (now *Château
Malescot-St.-Exupéry*)
Boyd, Cantenac (now two
properties: *Châteaux Boyd-
Cantenac* and *Château Cantenac
Brown*)
Palmer, Cantenac
Lalagune, Ludon (now *Château
La Lagune*)
Desmirail, Margaux
Dubignon, Margaux (no longer in
existence, but some of these
original vineyards now belong to
*Châteaux Malescot-St.-Exupéry,
Château Palmer,* and *Château
Margaux*)
Calon, St.-Estèphe (now *Château
Calon-Ségur*)

Ferrière, Margaux
Becker, Margaux (now *Château
Marquis d'Alesme-Becker*)

QUATRIÈMES CRUS
(Fourth Growths)
St.-Pierre, St.-Julien (now *Château
St.-Pierre-Sevaistre*)
Talbot, St.-Julien
Du-Luc, St.-Julien (now *Château
Branaire-Ducru*)
Duhart, Pauillac (at one time
Château Duhart-Milon Rothschild,
but now *Château Duhart-Milon,*
although still Rothschild-owned)
Pouget-Lassale, Cantenac
(now *Château Pouget*)
Pouget, Cantenac (now *Château
Pouget*)
Carnet, St.-Laurent (now *Château
La Tour-Carnet*)
Rochet, St.-Estèphe (now *Château
Lafon-Rochet*)
Château de Beychevele, St.-Julien
(now *Château Beychevelle*)
Le Prieuré, Cantenac
(now *Château Prieuré-Lichine*)
Marquis de Thermes, Margaux
(now *Château Marquis-de-Terme*)

CINQUIÈMES CRUS
(Fifth Growths)
Canet, Pauillac (now *Château
Pontet-Conet*)
Batailley, Pauillac (now two
properties: *Château Batailley* and
Château Haut-Batailley)
Grand Puy, Pauillac (now *Château
Grand-Puy-Lacoste*)
Artigues Arnaud, Pauillac
(now *Château Grand-Puy-
Ducasse*)
Lynch, Pauillac (now *Château
Lynch-Bages*)
Lynch Moussas, Pauillac
Dauzac, Labarde
Darmailhac, Pauillac (now *Château
d'Armailhac*)
Le Tertre, Arsac (now *Château
du Tertre*)
Haut Bages, Pauillac (now *Château
Haut-Bages-Libéral*)
Pédesclaux, Pauillac (now *Château
Pédesclaux*)
Coutenceau, St.-Laurent
(now *Château Belgrave*)
Camensac, St.-Laurent
Cos Labory, St.-Estèphe
Clerc Milon, Pauillac
Croizet-Bages, Pauillac
Cantemerle, Macau

Sémillon also accounts for most of the finest dry white wines of Bordeaux, but these are relatively few and lack prestige. Sauvignon blanc plays the supporting role in the production of sweet wines, and is used to a greater or lesser degree for dry wines. Many of the less expensive dry white wines are pure Sauvignon blanc varietals.

VARIETAL CONTRIBUTIONS TO A CUVÉE

There are several varieties of red and white grape that are grown in Bordeaux and each variety is used to make its own contribution to a particular wine.

The Cabernet sauvignon is the most complex and distinctive of all black Bordeaux grapes. It has a firm tannic structure, yet with time reveals a powerful, rich, and long-lasting flavour. Wines from this grape can have great finesse; their bouquets often possess a "blackcurrant" or "violets" character. Cabernet franc has similar characteristics to Cabernet sauvignon, but may also have a leafy, sappy, or earthy taste depending on where it is cultivated. It does, however, shine through as the superior variety when grown in St.-Émilion and Pomerol, and can compete on even terms with its more famous cousin in parts of Graves. Merlot is soft, silky, and sometimes opulent. It is a grape that charms, and can make wines with lots of juicy-rich and spicy fruit. Petit verdot is a late ripener with a naturally high acidity, while Malbec has a thick skin that is rich in colour pigments. Small amounts of Petit verdot and Malbec were traditionally used to correct the colour and acidity of a blended wine. The cultivation and use of these two varieties for this purpose has been on the decrease for the last 20 years owing to the various modern techniques of viticulture and vinification.

The white Sémillon grape provides a wine naturally rich in flavour and high in alcohol. It makes succulent sweet white wines that are capable of great longevity, but its intrinsically low acidity is unsuitable for producing dry wines. In exceptional circumstances the highest quality Sémillon does make a fine dry white wine – if matured in new oak. This enhances the aromatic character of the wine and gives it a firm structure without which it would be too "fat" and "flabby".

The Sauvignon blanc in Bordeaux is soft, delicate, and easy to drink. It does not have the same bite as it does in the Loire vineyards of Sancerre or Pouilly-Fumé, but the varietal character is more pronounced today than it was a few years ago. Early harvesting, pre-fermentation maceration on the grape skins to draw out the aromatics, and longer, cooler fermentation in stainless steel, have all combined to produce a far more interesting, medium-quality, dry white wine.

FERMENTATION AND MATURATION

Although some properties producing *Crus Classés* retain their wooden vats for the fermentation process (more because they lack the funds to re-equip than for any idealistic reasons), hardly any of them actually invest in new oak vats, preferring those made of stainless steel. The one startling exception is Château Margaux. This great property has spent more money, following the advice of the legendary oenologist Professor Peynaud, than any other château in Bordeaux. This is puzzling because it was principally at his recommendation that virtually everyone else in Bordeaux invested in stainless steel.

THE VINIFICATION PROCESS
The proportion of grape varieties grown and the intrinsic potential of a château's terroir determine the basic quality and character of Bordeaux's finest wines. Manipulating the vinification process has, however, always been the method of honing the style of this region's best châteaux. Processes include adding up to 15 per cent vin de presse; grape-skin contact, (which can be for up to a month); maturation, which used to take 3 to 5 years, but now takes 15 to 18 months, and a percentage of new oak, always the hallmark of Bordeaux's First Growths.

ADDING VIN DE PRESSE

One technique that is more characteristic of red winemaking in Bordeaux than in any other region is the addition of a certain amount of *vin de presse*. This is produced after the wine has completed its alcoholic fermentation and has undergone malolactic conversion. The wine is drawn off its lees into casks and the residue of skin and pips at the bottom of the vat is pressed. Normally this requires two pressings: the first *vin de presse* is the best and represents about ten per cent of the total wine produced, the second provides a further five per cent. *Vin de presse* is relatively low in alcohol, very dark, and extremely tannic. In a wine made for early drinking, *vin de presse* would be harsh and unpleasant, but with the structure of a classic oak-matured Bordeaux, it gives extra body and increases longevity.

OAK CASK MATURATION

After fermentation and prior to bottling, all the best red Bordeaux are matured in 225-litre (59-gallon) Bordeaux oak casks called *barriques*. The duration of this operation and the percentage of new oak casks used should depend entirely on the quality and

BARRELS IN A BORDEAUX CHAIS
These new oak barriques *at Château Langoa-Barton contain the wines of Château Léoville-Barton. Both properties belong to the Barton family (who are of British descent) but Léoville-Barton has no* chais *of its own.*

structure of the wine, and this will vary according to the vintage. The bigger the wine, the more new oak it can take and the longer maturation it will need. The greatest wines – all the First Growths – require at least 18 to 24 months in 100 per cent new oak to reach maturity. Other fine-quality Bordeaux wines do not need so much time, maybe only 12 to 18 months, and do not benefit from 100 per cent new oak; between 30 and 50 per cent may be enough. If you get the chance, put your nose into a new oak cask before it has been used. The wonderful creamy-smoky, vanilla-and-charcoal aroma is the very essence of what should come through when a fine wine has been properly matured in oak.

THE PRESENT AND THE FUTURE

During the early 1980s, the idea of "second wines"– always a factor in the production of the finest Bordeaux growths – began to catch on among the properties producing *Crus Bourgeois*, enabling modest properties to make much better wines through stricter selection of their *grands vins*. Towards the end of the 1980s, "green harvesting" or crop-thinning became *de rigueur* for all quality-conscious châteaux (even though the Romans considered such practices essential 2,000 years ago!). The most significant advance in Bordeaux over the last 20 years was in 1994, when a decision was taken to harvest grapes according to tannin ripeness, rather than sugar-acidity ripeness. Unripe tannins are not hydrolyzed; they are hard and will never soften, whereas ripe tannins are hydrolyzed, have a certain suppleness from day one, and will always soften. This phenomenon has long been known, but precisely when it occurs can vary from region to region. In Bordeaux tannin ripeness has been under study since 1986 by Vincent Dupuch, who discovered that grapes deemed physiologically ripe in Bordeaux by their sugar-acidity ratio actually possessed a high proportion of unripe tannins. In 1994 many *bordelais* harvested according to Dupuch's tannin ripeness parameters and were surprised to discover the optimum moment to pick was in fact much later than they had previously thought. This means not only that many Bordeaux wines will be riper, but also that by determining ripeness in this way, the winemaker is aware of the precise phenolic content, and this allows the fine-tuning of maceration and fermentation for each batch of grapes. The 21st century will see a continuation in the rise of super-premium boutique wines, particularly from St.-Émilion. However, the increase in the density of vines to raise general standards in several Bordeaux appellations has been delayed. According to decrees issued in 1994 these new standards were to be fast-tracked, but new decrees in 1998 mean that some of these higher densities will not now be legally enforceable until 2025.

RECENT BORDEAUX VINTAGES

2000 God forgave the Bordelais its transgressions and excesses of the recent past, and smiled on the world's foremost red wine region for the last vintage of the millennium. He held back the rains until almost everyone had brought their harvest in. The reds on both banks are beautifully coloured, high in alcohol, with the weight and plumpness of a truly great vintage. Some excellent, full-bodied wines have been produced and even though the late-picking Sauternes and Barsac districts were hit by rain during the harvest, the results are not that bad, with quality equalling that of 1999.

1999 This is the year when almost everything that could go wrong did go wrong in Bordeaux. It was as if the last vintage of the 1990s was a testament to the climatic difficulties that masked this decade, with disease in the vineyards, rain at harvest and a huge crop of unripe grapes. Very patchy, but most of the best wines were made in St.-Émilion, some excellent Margaux and St.-Julien, with some Sauternes that can vie with the 1998s, though not the 1997s. It is in vintages such as 1999 that the difference in quality between Bordeaux as a whole and that found when tasting at the top 100 or so Bordeaux estates becomes so marked.

1998 A very good vintage that could have been great but for rain at the end of September, but this did not cause dilution as such because the wines are

marked by exceptional colour. Merlot promised well from the start, but the Cabernets have developed much better than expected, particularly from the top châteaux. Great Pomerol, excellent St.-Émilion, and very good Sauternes.

1997 Although only 1990 was harvested under better conditions, the weather throughout the growing season was patchy, resulting in irregular ripeness and uneven quality. At their best the reds are soft and elegant, but they lack the concentration of the previous two vintages. Furthermore this year provided the largest crop in Bordeaux's history, yet prices were 30% above the 1996s and those were the highest on record at the time. This underlines just how greedy the Bordelais can be, although they must be a different breed in Fronsac, one of the few Bordeaux appellations where value could be found. The dry whites lacked acidity, but Sauternes and Barsac yielded superb quality.

1996 Despite rain during the Sauvignon and Sémillon harvest, the dry whites were excellent, as were the red wines of the Médoc and Graves, where the Cabernet ripened with an unusual balance of acidity and tannin. Some St.-Émilion, Pomerol, and Sauternes were patchy, but some were exceptional.

THE APPELLATIONS OF GENERIC
BORDEAUX

There are more than 50 appellations in Bordeaux and every one has its generic wines, produced by a *négociant* or local *coopérative*. The appellations below bear the region's name and are therefore as widely generic as can be found, yet many individual wines are forced to utilize these AOCs due to their location.

BORDEAUX AOC

As with any large, and thus variable, appellation, the generic Bordeaux AOC is responsible for the good, bad, and ugly wines of the region. Its overall quality is of a decent standard even though the best wines are hardly likely to fit the classic descriptions that have made this region famous. Wines carrying the generic appellation may come from any AOC vineyard in the entire Gironde. Some of the most interesting wines are from classic areas where the more specific appellation is confined to a precise style of wine: for example, a red Bordeaux produced by a château in Sauternes. If the wine is a brand, it should be ready to drink. If it is a château wine, the address should reveal its probable area of origin, and the price will be an indication of its quality and a guide to when it should be drunk.

RED Most are simply dry luncheon claret styles, that are made for early drinking and usually softened by a high Merlot content.

🍇 Cabernet sauvignon, Cabernet franc, Carmenère, Merlot, Malbec, Petit verdot

🍷 1–5 years

WHITE All of these medium-dry basic white Bordeaux contain at least four grams of residual sugar per litre, so they have a certain sweetness. However, this is by far the most variable category of the appellation, with many dull and boring wines. If the wine contains less than four grams of residual sugar per litre, the Bordeaux appellation must be qualified by "Sec". These dry whites are almost as variable, but most of the best wines of the appellation are found among them. They may be sold from 1 December without any mention of *primeur* or *nouveau*.

🍇 Sémillon, Sauvignon, Muscadelle plus up to 30% in total of Merlot blanc, Colombard, Mauzac, Ondenc, Ugni blanc

🍷 1–2 years

ROSÉ When made by individual properties, this medium-dry, medium-bodied wine can be attractive. These wines may be sold from 1 December following the harvest without any mention of *primeur* or *nouveau*.

🍇 Cabernet sauvignon, Cabernet franc, Carmenère, Merlot, Malbec, Petit verdot

🍷 Immediately

BORDEAUX CLAIRET AOC

"Clairet" is a term that refers to a red wine that is light in body and colour. *Vin claret* in Old French was a term of respect; this suggests that Bordeaux achieved a reputation for limpidity before other wines.

ROSÉ Rich, dark rosé or failed, feeble red? The best examples of this medium-dry, medium-bodied wine come from the village of Quinsac in the Premières Côtes de Bordeaux.

🍇 Cabernet sauvignon, Cabernet franc, Carmenère, Merlot, Malbec, Petit verdot

🍷 1–2 years

BORDEAUX ROSÉ AOC

The theory is that this appellation is reserved for wine deliberately produced as rosé, while "Bordeaux Clairet" is for a light-coloured red wine. Both may simply be labelled "Bordeaux AOC". For technical details see Bordeaux AOC.

BORDEAUX SEC AOC

White Bordeaux with less than four grams of residual sugar per litre. For more details *see* Bordeaux AOC.

BORDEAUX SUPÉRIEUR AOC

Technically superior to Bordeaux AOC by only half a degree of alcohol, yet most of these wines do seem to have a greater consistency of quality, and therefore value. All generics are variable, but this one is less so than most.

RED These dry, light-bodied or medium- to full-bodied wines vary a lot but are generally fuller and richer than most red wines using the basic Bordeaux appellation.

🍇 Cabernet sauvignon, Cabernet franc, Carmenère, Merlot, Malbec, Petit verdot

🍷 2–6 years

WHITE Dry and sometimes sweet, light- to medium-bodied white wines that are little seen.

🍇 Sémillon, Sauvignon, Muscadelle plus up to 30% in total of Merlot blanc, Colombard, Mauzac, Ondenc, Ugni blanc; the proportion of Merlot blanc must not exceed 15%

🍷 1–2 years

BORDEAUX SUPÉRIEUR CLAIRET AOC

This is a little-seen appellation: the wines are either sold as "Bordeaux Supérieur" or "Bordeaux Clairet".

ROSÉ Medium-dry and medium-bodied as Bordeaux Clairet, but with an extra half-degree of alcohol.

🍇 Cabernet sauvignon, Cabernet franc, Carmenère, Merlot, Malbec, Petit verdot

🍷 1–2 years

BORDEAUX SUPÉRIEUR ROSÉ AOC

This appellation has a small cast – and Château Lascombe's Rosé de Lascombes still tops the bill.

ROSÉ As few examples of these medium-dry, medium-bodied wines exist, it is possible to generalize and describe them as fuller, richer, and having more class than any Bordeaux Rosé AOC wines.

🍇 Cabernet sauvignon, Cabernet franc, Carmenère, Merlot, Malbec, Petit verdot

🍷 1–2 years

CRÉMANT DE BORDEAUX AOC

This was introduced in 1990 to replace the old Bordeaux Mousseux AOC, which was phased out on 31 December 1995. Although preferable to a lot of poorly produced Loire sparkling wines, there is nothing special about Bordeaux bubbly. Changing the appellation has done nothing to change the product because, like its predecessor, Crémant de Bordeaux is merely a modest and inoffensive fizz. It lacks the spirit and expressiveness to stand out from the sea of far cheaper, but equally boring, sparkling wines that exist almost everywhere. I have tasted much better from areas far less suited to sparkling wine than Bordeaux.

SPARKLING WHITE Varies from dry to sweet and light- to medium-bodied, but is almost always bland.

🍇 Sémillon, Sauvignon, Muscadelle, Ugni blanc, Colombard, Cabernet sauvignon, Cabernet franc, Carmenère, Merlot, Malbec, Petit verdot

🍷 1–2 years

SPARKLING ROSÉ The authorities should have taken advantage of the introduction of a new appellation to allow the inclusion of white grapes for this style, as this would have improved the potential quality.

🍇 Cabernet sauvignon, Cabernet franc, Carmenère, Merlot, Malbec, Petit verdot

🍷 2–3 years

BORDEAUX'S BEST GENERIC BRANDS

Bordeaux has the greatest reputation for red wine in the world, but as in all regions, ordinary wines do exist. In Bordeaux, such products can boast the same illustrious appellations as the greatest wines. Remember, however, that more than money separates a generic Margaux from Château Margaux. The former is the blended product of relatively inferior wines grown anywhere within the appellation, the latter a selection of only the finest wines grown on one estate – the *premier* growth of Margaux. As a branded generic Bordeaux wine can be a disappointing introduction to the world's greatest wine region, the following brands are suggested:

DOURTHE NUMÉRO 1
Probably the best largest-selling branded Bordeaux available.

LA COUR PAVILLON
One of the most reliable and underrated generics on the market. Made at IDVs Château Loudenne, this wine always has good fruit, but with enough structure to keep a while.

MAÎTRE D'ESTOURNEL
This has the same connection to Château Cos d'Estournel as "Mouton Cadet" has to Château Mouton-Rothschild, which is absolutely non-existent as far as the wine is concerned, but hopes to sell on the back the château's name.

There is a difference, of course: "Maître d'Estournel" happens to be an expressive, early-drinking wine that can also take a few years in bottle, whereas "Mouton Cadet" is mutton dressed up as lamb.

MICHEL LYNCH
Produced by Michel Cazes of Château Lynch-Bages in an unashamedly upfront, fruity style. Red, white, and rosé are all thoroughly recommended.

SICHEL SIRIUS
This is as serious as it sounds. Excellent oak-aged generic Bordeaux that will improve for a further year or two in bottle.

THE WINE PRODUCERS OF
BORDEAUX AND BORDEAUX SUPÉRIEUR

BORDEAUX

CHÂTEAU BALLUE-MONDON
Gensac

Soft and fruity "organic" claret.

CHÂTEAU DE BERTIN
Targon

Powerful Cabernet sauvignon-dominated wines that age gracefully.

CHÂTEAU BERTINERIE
Cavignac

A serious rosé, pleasantly romantic, with delicately rich, floral fruit on the palate and a smooth finish.

CHÂTEAU BONHOSTE
St.-Jean-de-Blaignac
★✪

Classic white Bordeaux at its best.

DOMAINE DU BRU
St.-Avit–St.-Nazaire

Refreshing clairet: light in colour and body and easy to drink.

CHÂTEAU CARSIN
Rions

Popular in the UK, New World influenced.

CHÂTEAU COURTEY
St.-Macaire
★✪

These are intensely flavoured old-style wines, possessing quite a remarkable bouquet.

CHÂTEAU FAUGAS
Cadillac

Well-balanced reds with attractive berry-fruit flavours.

CHÂTEAU DU GRAND MOUEYS
Capian

Consistently elegant red wines.

CHÂTEAU GRAND VILLAGE
Mouillac

Rich and easy Merlot-dominated, oak-aged red, and a good second wine under the "Beau Village" label.

CHÂTEAU DE HAUX
Haux

Gorgeously ripe and dry white wine, with very fresh and elegant fruit.

CHÂTEAU LAGROSSE
Tabanac
★✪

Elegant, ripe, and long, with lemony-rich, oaky fruit.

CHÂTEAU LAPÉYÈRE
Cadillac

Well-structured red, dominated by Cabernet sauvignon.

CHÂTEAU DE LUGUGNAC
Pellegrue

Romantic 15th-century château making attractive, firm, and fleshy red that can show some finesse.

CHÂTEAU MARJOSSE
Branne
★✪

This is Pierre Lurton's home, where he makes lush and upfront reds with creamy-silky fruit and a beautiful dry white.

CHÂTEAU MORILLON
Monségur
★✪

Rich, fat, and juicy wines.

CLOS DE PELIGON
St.-Loubès

Fine, full-bodied red with a hint of oak.

CHÂTEAU PLAISANCE
Capian

This château makes excellent, lightly rich Bordeaux Blanc Sec, made from 50-year-old vines and fermented in oak.

CHÂTEAU DE PLASSAN
Tabanac
★✪

The basic Bordeaux Blanc Sec has fresh, swingeing Sauvignon fruit, while the more expensive Bordeaux Blanc Sec, which is fermented and aged in oak, has lovely creamy fruit and a fine, lemony-vanilla finish.

CHÂTEAU POUCHAUD-LARQUEY
La Réole

Full and rich red with lots of fruit.

CAVE DE QUINSAC
La Tresne

Delicately-coloured, light-bodied, rosé-styled wines sold as clairet.

CHÂTEAU RENON
Langoiran
★✪

This is a pleasantly fresh and floral Sauvignon-style wine.

CHÂTEAU REYNON
Cadillac
★✪

This is a star-performing château that produces *Cru Classé* dry white wine under the auspices of Denis Dubourdieu. The elite Vieilles Vignes *cuvée* is quite extraordinary, but everything produced here can be relied upon, right down to the aptly named "Le Second de Reynon". Also very good red.

CHÂTEAU ROC-DE-CAYLA
Targon

Easy-drinking, well-balanced reds with good fruit and some finesse.

LE ROSÉ DE CLARKE
Castelnau-de-Médoc

From Château Clarke, this has all the fragrance expected from a classic dry rosé.

CHÂTEAU THIEULEY
Créon
★✪

These are medium-bodied, elegant reds that possess more than just a hint of cask-ageing. Also fine, fresh, floral, and fruity white wines.

CHÂTEAU TIMBERLAY
St.-André-de-Cubzac
★✪

Deep-coloured, full of flavour, but not without a certain elegance.

BORDEAUX SUPÉRIEUR

CHÂTEAU DES ARRAS
St.-André-de-Cubzac
★✪

Deep-coloured wines with good structure and lots of chunky fruit.

MARQUIS DE BOIRAC
Castillon-la-Batille
★✪

Super value *coopérative* wine with a big, oaky aroma and fruit to match.

CHÂTEAU FONCHEREAU
St.-Loubès
★✪

Well-structured, finely-balanced *vins de garde* of extremely good quality.

CHÂTEAU FOUCHÉ
Bourg-sur-Gironde

This wine is firm yet has fat, juicy fruit and a smooth finish.

CHÂTEAU GROSSOMBRE
Branne
★✪

Nicely concentrated, very good red wine which will improve for 12 to 18 months, and represents exceptional value.

CHÂTEAU LACOMBE-CADIOT
Blanquefort

These well-coloured wines have a big bouquet, and are oaky with delicious fruit.

CHÂTEAU LAGRANGE-LES-TOURS
St.-André-de-Cubzac

Well-made, full, flavoursome wines.

CHÂTEAU LATOUR
Sauveterre-de-Guyenne

These medium-bodied wines have consistently good fruit, smooth flavour, and make a cheap punt to get the "latour" name on the table!

CHÂTEAU LAVILLE
St.-Loubès

Rich, tannic, and powerfully structured wines with spicy fruit.

CHÂTEAU MÉAUME
Coutras

Alan Johnson-Hill used to be a UK wine merchant before settling north of Pomerol. Since then he has gained a reputation for cleverly tailoring this red Bordeaux to young British palates.

CHÂTEAU LA MICHELERIE
St.-André-de-Cubzac

Another property producing a big, tannic style of wine.

CHÂTEAU LES MOINES-MARTIN
Galgon

This is well-made wine for reasonably early drinking, with an attractive bouquet, round fruit, and fine balance.

CHÂTEAU DE PIERREDON
Sauveterre-de-Guyenne
★✪

Serious Cabernet Sauvignon-dominated Bordeaux from the Haut-Benauge.

CHÂTEAU PUYFROMAGE
Lussac

Attractive, well-balanced, medium-bodied, and easy to drink.

ROSÉ DE LASCOMBES
Margaux

Refreshing, fruity rosé of excellent character, quality, and finesse.

CHÂTEAU SARRAIL-LA-GUILLAMERIE
St.-Loubès

Rich and fleshy wine that softens nicely with age.

CHÂTEAU DE SEGUIN
La Tresne

Look out for the Cuvée Prestige, which is rich and smoother than the basic Château Seguin.

CHÂTEAU TOUR-DE-L'ESPÉRANCE
Galgon
★✪

This is soft and smooth wine, full of fat, ripe, and juicy fruit, yet not without finesse.

CHÂTEAU TOUR PETIT PUCH
St.-Germain-du-Puch
★✪

Attractively coloured, well-made, well-balanced wines, with a touch of spice.

CHÂTEAU DE LA VIEILLE TOUR
St.-Michel-Lapujade
★✪

Consistently rich and smooth, even in notoriously harsh vintages.

CHÂTEAU VIEUX MOULIN
Villegouge

These are well-rounded, long, and supple wines, which are of consistently fine quality.

THE MÉDOC

The style of wine alters more radically over short distances in the Médoc than in any other French red wine district. The wines are mild and unexceptional immediately northwest of Bordeaux, but from Ludon onwards, they become progressively more characterful, acquire finesse, and – after Margaux – gain considerable body. Beyond St.-Estèphe, the firmness of body of the wines eventually turns to coarseness, and their finesse fades.

THE MÉDOC TAKES its name from the Latin phrase *medio aquae* – "between the waters" – referring to the Gironde estuary and the Atlantic ocean. It is a long, thin strip of prized vines, extending northwest from the city limits of Bordeaux to the Pointe de Grave. At its centre is the classic area of Bordeaux, where the vast majority of the most famous châteaux are located, and yet this was the last major district of Bordeaux to be cultivated. While winemaking in the Libournais district of St.-Émilion began as early as the Roman occupation, it was another thousand years before scattered plots of vines spread along the Médoc. Across the large, brown expanse of water called the Gironde, the Romans viewed Bourg and considered its hilly area far more suitable for growing vines. At that time the marshland of the Médoc was difficult to cross and impossible to cultivate. Today, the Médoc is the envy of winemakers the world over and Bourg is merely a source of inexpensive, if good-value, basic Bordeaux.

THE MÉDOC STYLE: VARIATIONS ON A THEME

The four famous communes of Margaux, St.-Julien, Pauillac, and St.-Estèphe, plus the two lesser-known but developing communes of Listrac and Moulis, are to be found in a region within the Médoc known as the Haut-Médoc, where the wines are fine, firm, and fleshy. The Haut-Médoc begins at the southern outskirts of the city of Blanquefort, along the northern reaches of the Graves

FACTORS AFFECTING TASTE AND QUALITY

LOCATION
The Médoc lies on the left bank of the Gironde estuary, stretching northwest from Bordeaux in the south to Soulac in the north.

CLIMATE
Two large masses of water either side of the Médoc – the Atlantic and the Gironde – act as a heat-regulator and help provide a microclimate ideal for viticulture. The Gulf Stream generally gives the Médoc mild winters, warm summers, and long, sunny autumns. The district is protected from westerly and north-westerly winds by the continuous coastal strip of pine forest which runs roughly parallel to the Médoc.

ASPECT
Undulating hillsides with knolls and gentle slopes are characteristic of the Médoc. The best vineyards can "see the river" and virtually all areas of the Haut-Médoc gradually slope from the watershed to the Gironde. Marshy areas, where vines cannot be grown, punctuate most communes.

SOIL
Similar topsoils lie over different subsoils in the Médoc. Its topsoils are typically outcrops of gravel, consisting of sand mixed with siliceous gravel of varying particle size. Subsoils may contain gravel and reach a depth of several metres, or may consist of sand, often rich in humus, and some limestone and clay.

VITICULTURE AND VINIFICATION
Only red wines can use the Médoc appellation. Mechanical harvesting is commonplace and all grapes are destalked prior to fermentation in tanks, or in vats increasingly made of stainless steel. Skin-contact lasts for one to two weeks, although some châteaux have reverted to the once standard four weeks.

PRIMARY GRAPE VARIETIES
Cabernet sauvignon, Cabernet franc, Merlot

SECONDARY GRAPE VARIETIES
Carmenère, Petit verdot, Malbec

PROPORTION OF AOC AREA UNDER VINE REPRESENTED BY CRUS CLASSÉS

APPELLATION	TOTAL HA (ACRES)		CRUS CLASSÉS IN HA (ACRES)		REPRESENTS
Médoc	4,700	(11,614)	–	–	No *Crus Classés*
Haut-Médoc	4,160	(10,279)	255	(630)	6% of AOC, 9% of *Crus Classés*
Listrac	660	(1,630)	–	–	No *Crus Classés*
Moulis	600	(1,483)	–	–	No *Crus Classés*
St.-Estèphe	1,380	(3,410)	226	(558)	16% of AOC, 8% of *Crus Classés*
Pauillac	1,170	(2,891)	842	(2,081)	72% of AOC, 30% of *Crus Classés*
St.-Julien	910	(2,249)	628	(1,552)	69% of AOC, 22% of *Crus Classés*
Margaux	1,340	(3,311)	854	(2,100)	64% of AOC, 31% of *Crus Classés*
TOTAL	14,920	(36,867)	2,805	(6,921)	19% of Médoc AOCs, 100% of *Crus Classés*

DISTRIBUTION OF MÉDOC CRUS CLASSÉS THROUGHOUT THE APPELLATIONS

APPELLATION	GROWTHS					
	1ST	2ND	3RD	4TH	5TH	TOTAL
Haut-Médoc	0	0	1	1	3	5
St.-Estèphe	0	2	1	1	1	5
Pauillac	3	2	0	1	12	18
St.-Julien	0	5	2	4	0	11
Margaux	1	5	10	3	2	21
TOTAL	4	14	14	10	18	60

district where the wines are fairly neutral. The greatest wines of the Haut-Médoc are found in the area beginning at Ludon with Château la Lagune – the first *Cru Classé* encountered moving north from Blanquefort. Fine *Crus Bourgeois*, such as Château d'Agassac, are to be found in this same area as well.

The wines at Margaux are soft and velvety and full of charm, although they are very much *vins de garde* and will improve well with age. The wines of St.-Julien are elegant with a very pure flavour. They have the delicate touch of Margaux, yet lean closer to Pauillac in body. The wines of Pauillac are powerful, often having a rich blackcurrant flavour with hints of cedar and tobacco. These are wines of great finesse, and Pauillac can be considered the greatest appellation of the Médoc. St.-Estèphe includes many minor growths of rustic charm and a few classic wines, and technology is changing the robustness of its spicy wines to richness.

Beyond St.-Estèphe lies the commune of St.-Seurin-de-Cadourne, whose wines are entitled to use the Haut-Médoc appellation, after which the appellation becomes simply AOC

Médoc. This area, formerly known as the Bas-Médoc, has a lesser reputation than the Haut-Médoc. However, many exceptional wines are made here: the triangle formed by St.-Yzans, Lesparre, and Valeyrac contains such outstanding minor growths as Loudenne, Potensac, la Cardonne, Blaignan, les Ormes-Sorbet, la Tour-St.-Bonnet, la Tour-de-By, and Patache d'Aux. In general the style is more simplistic than in the Haut-Médoc.

THE FIGHT FOR GRAVEL

The best soils for vine-growing also happen to be the most suitable for gravel quarrying. After the war, in the absence of any legislation, gravel quarrying started in abandoned vineyards. Once the gravel was gone, the opportunity to reclaim the area as a vineyard was lost. There is plenty of gravel in the Gironde estuary, but it is more profitable to take it from an open pit. Quarrying companies will continue to plunder the Médoc's finite resources until the government agrees to protect them.

THE MÉDOC, *see also p.59*
The Médoc, a narrow strip of land between the Gironde estuary and the Atlantic ocean, stretches northwards from the city of Bordeaux to the Pointe de Grave. The climate is Bordeaux's mildest, moderated by both the estuary and the ocean. The region's many forests protect the vineyards from strong ocean winds.

BARREL-MAKING AT LAFITE ROTHSCHILD
Wines are aged in new oak at Château Lafite-Rothschild, although for a shorter length of time than in the past. The barrels are made with great care in a time-honoured, traditional manner.

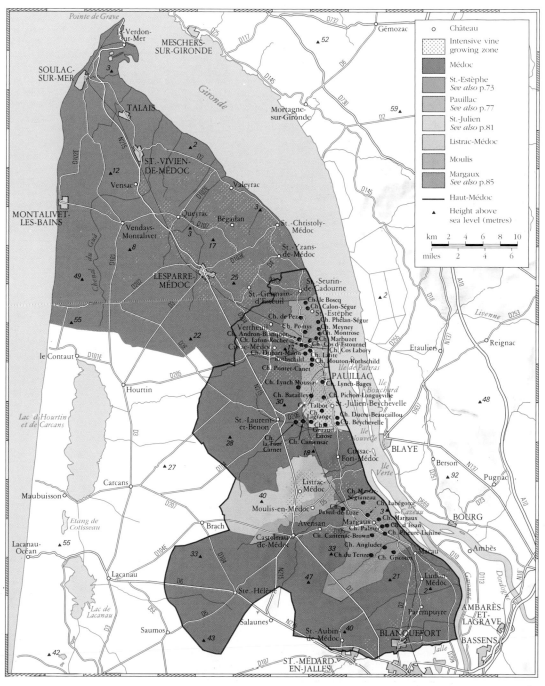

THE APPELLATIONS OF
THE MÉDOC

HAUT-MÉDOC AOC

This AOC encompasses the Médoc's four finest communes – Margaux, St.-Julien, Pauillac, and St.-Estèphe – as well as the less well-known Listrac and Moulis communes. Wines produced outside these six appellations but within the Haut-Médoc, are not generally as thrilling, although infinitely superior to those of Médoc. Among these very reliable wines are a few great-value *Crus Classés* and many high-quality *Crus Bourgeois*, but although Haut-Médoc is a name to look out for on the label of Château-bottled wines, it counts for little on a generic.

RED These dry wines have a generosity of fruit tempered by a firm structure, and are medium- to full-bodied.

🍇 Cabernet sauvignon, Cabernet franc, Merlot, Malbec, Petit verdot, Carmenère

🍷 6–15 years (*Crus Classés*)
5–8 years (others)

LISTRAC-MÉDOC AOC

Significant funds have been invested in a number of high-performance châteaux in this commune, although its heavy clay soil does not have anything like as much potential as the gravel ridges found in the most famous Médoc appellations.

RED These dry, medium- to full-bodied wines have the fruit and finesse of St.-Julien combined with the firmness of St.-Estèphe. The most successful wines tend to have a large proportion of Merlot, which enjoys the Haut-Médoc's clay soil.

🍇 Cabernet sauvignon, Cabernet franc, Carmenère, Merlot, Malbec, Petit verdot

🍷 5–10 years

MARGAUX AOC

The best Margaux are potentially the greatest wines in the whole of Bordeaux, but this is an appellation that covers five communes encompassing a great diversity of soil and some of its wines not unnaturally have a tendency to disappoint. Margaux benefits enormously from having a namesake château, which is unique in Bordeaux, and the fact that this property sets the most extraordinary high standards has done no harm to the reputation and price of these wines generally. The phenomenal success of Château Margaux has, however, unfairly raised expectations of many lesser quality châteaux in the area, but those critics who widely accuse proprietors of sacrificing quality for quantity could not be further from the truth. There are individual châteaux that overproduce and therefore fail to achieve their full potential, but excessive volume is not typically the problem

with this appellation, since it has the lowest yield per hectare of the four famous Médoc AOCs.

RED Exquisite, dry, medium-bodied, and sometimes full-bodied, wines that can be deep-coloured and fabulously rich, yet they have great finesse and a silky finish.

🍇 Cabernet sauvignon, Cabernet franc, Carmenère, Merlot, Malbec, Petit verdot

🍷 5–20 years (*Crus Classés*)
5–10 years (others)

MÉDOC AOC

Technically this appellation covers the entire Médoc, but most wines actually come from north of the Haut-Médoc in the area which was formerly called the Bas-Médoc. Its vineyards have undergone a rapid and extensive expansion since the mid-1970s.

RED The best of these dry, medium-bodied wines are similar in style to good Haut-Médocs, although the style is less sophisticated.

🍇 Cabernet sauvignon, Cabernet franc, Carmenère, Merlot, Malbec, Petit verdot

🍷 4–8 years

MOULIS AOC *OR*
MOULIS-EN-MÉDOC AOC

One of the two communal appellations located on the Atlantic side of the Médoc, Moulis-en-Médoc is smaller and potentially more interesting than its neighbour Listrac. Like Listrac, it has no *Cru Classé* châteaux, despite adjoining Margaux, the appellation that has the highest number of such properties in the Médoc.

RED These dry, medium-bodied, sometimes full-bodied, wines have more power than those of Margaux, but far less finesse.

🍇 Cabernet sauvignon, Cabernet franc, Carmenère, Merlot, Malbec, Petit verdot

🍷 5–12 years

PAUILLAC AOC

This commune vies with Margaux as the most famous appellation, but is without doubt the most rock solid and consistent of Bordeaux AOCs, while its First Growths of Latour, Lafite, and Mouton make it the most important.

RED Dark and virtually opaque, great Pauillac is a dry, powerfully constructed wine, typically redolent of blackcurrants and new oak. It might be unapproachable when young, but is always rich with fruit when mature. Although it does not have the grace of great Margaux, Pauillac brings power and style together to produce wines of incomparable finesse for their size.

🍇 Cabernet sauvignon, Cabernet franc, Carmenère, Merlot, Malbec, Petit verdot

🍷 9–25 years (*Crus Classés*)
5–12 years (others)

ST.-ESTÈPHE AOC

The potential of St.-Estèphe is exemplified by Cos d'Estournel, which is one of the best Second Growths in the Médoc, but the strength of this appellation lies in its range of *Crus Bourgeois*. The area under vine is slightly less than that of Margaux, which has the largest area, but St.-Estèphe has far more unclassified châteaux, and even the best wines are wonderfully cheap.

RED If Pauillac is the stallion of the four famous appellations, St.-Estèphe must be the shire-horse. These dry, full-bodied wines are big and strong, yet not without dignity. St.-Estèphe demands affection and, with the rich fruit of a sunny year, deserves it. These most enjoyable, sweet-spice, and cedary wines can have lots of honest, chunky fruit. Cos d'Estournel is the thoroughbred of the commune.

🍇 Cabernet sauvignon, Cabernet franc, Carmenère, Merlot, Malbec, Petit verdot

🍷 8–25 years (*Crus Classés*)
5–12 years (others)

ST.-JULIEN AOC

St.-Julien is the smallest of the four famous appellations and the most intensively cultivated, with almost 50 per cent of the commune under vine. There are no First Growths, but there are as many as five Seconds, and the standard and consistency of style is very high. This AOC overlaps part of the commune of Pauillac and, historically, châteaux Latour and Pichon-Longueville-Comtesse-de-Lalande could as easily have become St.-Julien AOC as Pauillac AOC.

RED These are dry, medium-bodied, sometimes full-bodied, wines that have purity of style, varietal flavour, and can be long-lived. Well balanced and elegant, these wines fall somewhere between the lushness that is typical of Margaux and the firmer structure of Pauillac.

🍇 Cabernet sauvignon, Cabernet franc, Carmenère, Merlot, Malbec, Petit verdot

🍷 6–20 years (*Crus Classés*); 5–12 years (others)

THE WINE PRODUCERS OF
THE MÉDOC

CHÂTEAU D'AGASSAC

AOC Haut-Médoc *Cru Bourgeois*

★✩Ⓥ

This is one of the best unclassified wines in the Haut-Médoc.

RED Dark-coloured, plummy wine, with a lot of soft, ripe fruit.

🍇 Cabernet sauvignon 60%, Merlot 40%

🍷 4–10 years

CHÂTEAU D'AURILHAC

AOC Haut-Médoc, *Cru Bourgeois*

★

A relative newcomer that has quickly developed a cult following.

RED Huge, dark and dense with masses of fruit to balance the ripe tannins and extrovert oak.

🍇 Cabernet sauvignon 67%, Cabernet franc 3%, Merlot 27%, Petit verdot 3%

🍷 5–15 years

Second Wine: *Château la Fagotte*

CHÂTEAU BEAUMONT

AOC Haut-Médoc *Cru Bourgeois*
This large property consistently produces wines of good quality.

RED These are aromatically attractive wines with elegant fruit and supple tannin.

🍇 Cabernet sauvignon 56%, Merlot 36%, Cabernet franc 7%, Petit verdot 1%

🍷 4–8 years

Second Wine: *Château Moulin d'Arvigny*

CHÂTEAU BÉCADE

AOC Haut-Médoc *Cru Bourgeois*

★✩Ⓥ

The well-situated vineyard of Château Bécade makes wines that regularly win medals on the international circuit.

RED These well-coloured wines of good bouquet are medium- to full-bodied with generous fruit and supple tannins.

🍇 Cabernet sauvignon 75%, Merlot 25%

🍷 4–8 years

Second Wine: *La Fleur Bécade*

CHÂTEAU BEL-AIR LAGRAVE

AOC Moulis

★✩Ⓥ

This growth was classified *Cru Bourgeois* in 1932, but not included in the *Syndicat's* 1978 list, although it is superior to some that were.

RED These vividly coloured wines have a fine bouquet and firm tannic structure.

🍇 Cabernet sauvignon 60%, Merlot 35%, Petit verdot 5%

🍷 8–20 years

CHÂTEAU BELGRAVE

AOC Haut-Médoc *5ème Cru Classé*

★✩Ⓥ

Situated on a good gravel bank behind Château Lagrange, the wine, which is matured in wood for 24 months with up to 50 per cent new oak, has improved consistently throughout the 1990s.

RED A good balance of blackcurrant fruit and ripe acidity, with firm tannin structure and vanilla overtones of new oak.

🍇 Cabernet sauvignon 60%, Merlot 35%, Petit verdot 5 %

🍷 8–16 years

Second Wine: *Diane de Belgrave*

CHÂTEAU BEL-ORME-
TRONQUOY-DE-LALANDE

AOC Haut-Médoc *Cru Bourgeois*

✩

This property has a confusingly similar name to Château Tronquoy-Lalande, St.-Estèphe.

RED These are firm, fruity, four-square wines.

🍇 Cabernet franc 30%, Cabernet sauvignon 30%, Merlot 30%, Malbec and Petit verdot 10%

🍷 7–15 years

CHÂTEAU BERNADOTTE

AOC Haut-Médoc

★✩Ⓥ

Consistently performing above its class, this château is situated on fine, gravelly ground that once had the right to the Pauillac appellation and formed part of a *Cru Classé*. Sold to the redoubtable Mme. Lencquesaing in 1997.

RED These wines are very stylish, with lush Cabernet fruit backed up by the creamy richness of new oak.

🍇 Cabernet sauvignon 60%, Merlot 30%, Cabernet franc 10%

🍷 6–12 years

CHÂTEAU
BISTON-BRILLETTE

AOC Moulis *Cru Bourgeois*

★✩Ⓥ

This top-quality Moulis property ages its wines in wood for 15 to 20 months, with 20 per cent new oak.

RED Wines that are very rich in colour and fruit with a full, spicy-cassis character and a supple tannin structure.

🍇 Cabernet sauvignon 55%, Merlot 40%, Petit verdot and Malbec 5%

🍷 5–15 years

CHÂTEAU LE BOURDIEU

AOC Haut-Médoc
Situated between Vertheuil and St.-Estèphe, this château was classified *Cru Bourgeois* in 1932, but not included in the *Syndicat's* 1978 list; it is superior to a few that were.

RED Well-coloured, full-bodied wines of robust character, which are not lacking in charm.

🍇 Cabernet sauvignon 50%, Merlot 30%, Cabernet franc 20%

🍷 7–15 years

Second Wine: *Château Les Sablons*
Other wines: *Château La Croix des Sablons*

CHÂTEAU
BRANAS-GRAND-POUJEAUX

AOC Moulis

★✩Ⓥ

These excellent and rapidly improving wines are aged in wood for 18 to 22 months, with one-third new oak.

RED This is a well-structured wine with plenty of accessible fruit, charming aromatic properties, and increasing finesse.

🍇 Cabernet sauvignon 60%, Merlot 35%, Petit verdot 5%

🍷 5–12 years

CHÂTEAU BRILLETTE

AOC Moulis *Cru Bourgeois*

★✩Ⓥ

This Château's name reputedly derives from its glinting, pebbly soil. The wine is matured in wood for 15 to 18 months, with a third new oak.

RED These are attractively coloured wines of full but supple body, with delightful summer-fruit and vanilla aromas. Easily equivalent to *Cru Classé* quality.

🍇 Cabernet sauvignon 55%, Merlot 40%, Petit verdot 5%

🍷 5–12 years

CHÂTEAU
CAMBON-LA-PELOUSE

AOC Haut-Médoc
Under the same ownership as Château Grand Barrail-Lamarzelle-Figeac, this estate was classified *Cru Bourgeois* in 1932, but not included in the *Syndicat's* 1978 list.

RED Soft, medium- to full-bodied wines with fresh and juicy flavours.

🍇 Merlot 50%, Cabernet sauvignon 30%, Cabernet franc 20%

🍷 3–8 years

CHÂTEAU CAMENSAC

AOC Haut-Médoc *5ème Cru Classé*

★Ⓥ

Situated behind Château Belgrave, this property was renovated in the mid-1960s. It began making wine equivalent to its classification in the late 1970s and since 1995 has been performing beyond its class. It is matured in wood for 14 to 18 months, with 40 per cent new oak.

RED Well-structured wine, with a medium weight of fruit and a certain amount of finesse.

🍇 Cabernet sauvignon 60%, Cabernet franc 20%, Merlot 20%

🍷 8–20 years

CHÂTEAU CANTEMERLE

AOC Haut-Médoc *5ème Cru Classé*

★✩Ⓥ

In 1980, new stainless-steel fermentation vats replaced the old wooden ones that had been responsible for some stingy vintages. Also discarded were all the old casks, so the 1980 vintage was uniquely matured in 100 per cent new oak. The wine is normally matured in wood for 18 to 20 months, with one-third new oak. It is currently performing above its classification.

RED Deliciously rich wines of fine colour, creamy-oaky fruit, beautiful balance, and increasing finesse.

🍇 Cabernet sauvignon 45%, Merlot 45%, Cabernet franc 10%

🍷 8–20 years

Second Wine: *Baron Villeneuve de Cantemerle*

CHÂTEAU LA CARDONNE
AOC Médoc *Cru Bourgeois*
★ ❶

This property was purchased by the Rothschilds of Lafite in 1973 and has since been expanded and renovated.

RED These are attractive, medium-bodied wines with a good, grapey perfume and a silky texture, made in an elegant style.

🍇 Merlot 58%, Cabernet sauvignon 34%, Cabernet franc 8%

⏳ 6–10 years

CHÂTEAU CARONNE-STE.-GEMME
AOC Haut-Médoc *Cru Bourgeois*
★ ★ ❶

This property is situated south of Château Lagrange – a superb island of vines on a gravel plateau.

RED Full-bodied wines rich in flavour with undertones of creamy-oak, and a supple tannin structure.

🍇 Cabernet sauvignon 65%, Merlot 35%

⏳ 8–20 years

CHÂTEAU CASTÉRA
AOC Médoc *Cru Bourgeois*
★ ❶

The original château was reduced to ruins by the Black Prince in the 14th century.

RED Soft-textured, medium-bodied wines best drunk relatively young.

🍇 Cabernet sauvignon and Cabernet franc 60%, Merlot 40%

⏳ 4–8 years

Second Wine: *Château Bourbon La Chapelle*

CHATEAU CHARMAIL
AOC Haut-Médoc *Cru Bourgeois*
★

The wines from this château have improved dramatically since the 1996 vintage and are performing well in recent blind tastings.

RED Rich, spicy, and long, with well-rounded, ripe tannins.

🍇 Cabernet sauvignon 30%, Cabernet franc 20%, Merlot 48%, Petit Verdot 2%

⏳ 3–7 years

CHÂTEAU CHASSE-SPLEEN
AOC Moulis *Cru Bourgeois*
★ ★ ❶

The proprietor of this quality-conscious property also owns the *Cru Classé* Château Haut-Bages-Libéral and the excellent unclassified growth of Château la Gurgue in Margaux. The wine is matured in wood for 18 to 24 months with 50 per cent new oak, and is usually of *Cru Classé* quality.

RED Full-bodied wines of great finesse, vivid colour, with a luxuriant, creamy-rich flavour of *cassis* and chocolate with warm, spicy-vanilla undertones. Easily equivalent to *Cru Classé* quality.

🍇 Cabernet sauvignon 50%, Merlot 45%,

Petit verdot 3%, Cabernet franc 2%

⏳ 8–20 years

Second Wine: *L'Ermitage de Chasse-Spleen*

CHÂTEAU CISSAC
AOC Haut-Médoc *Cru Bourgeois*
★ ❶

Château Cissac is always good value, especially in hot years. It is fermented in wood and matured in cask with no *vin de presse*.

RED These are well-coloured, full-bodied wines.

🍇 Cabernet sauvignon 75%, Merlot 20%, Petit verdot 5%

⏳ 8–20 years

Second Wine: *Les Reflets*

CHÂTEAU CITRAN
AOC Haut-Médoc *Cru Bourgeois*

A substantial-sized property once run by Château Coufran, until it passed to Jean Casseline. It is now owned by Groupe Bernard Taillan.

RED A solid, if plodding, Médoc of robust character.

🍇 Cabernet sauvignon 50%, Merlot 40%, Cabernet franc 10%

⏳ 8–15 years

CHÂTEAU CLARKE
AOC Listrac *Cru Bourgeois*
★ ❶

This estate's vines were dug up and its château pulled down in 1950. All was abandoned until 1973, when it was purchased by Baron Edmund de Rothschild. He completely restored the vineyard and installed an ultra-modern winery. Since the 1981 vintage, it has become one of the Médoc's fastest-rising stars. The wine is fermented in stainless steel and matured in wood for 12 months, with up to 60 per cent new oak. This is a wine to watch.

RED These well-coloured, medium- to full-bodied wines have a good measure of creamy-smoky oak and soft fruit.

🍇 Cabernet sauvignon 48%, Merlot 35%, Cabernet franc 14%, Petit verdot 3%

⏳ 7–25 years

CHÂTEAU COUFRAN
AOC Haut-Médoc *Cru Bourgeois*

These wines are matured in wood

for 13 to 18 months, with 25 per cent new oak.

RED Frank and fruity, this medium- to full-bodied wine has a chunky, chocolaty flavour, which is dominated by Merlot.

🍇 Merlot 85%, Cabernet sauvignon 10%, Petit verdot 5%

⏳ 4–12 years

Second Wine: *Domaine de la Rose-Maréchale*

CHÂTEAU DUTRUCH-GRAND-POUJEAUX
AOC Moulis *Cru Bourgeois*
★ ❶

Dutruch is one of the best Grand-Poujeaux satellite properties. It also makes two other wines from the specific-named plots "La Bernède" and "La Gravière".

RED These are fine, full-bodied wines of excellent colour, fruit, and finesse.

🍇 Cabernet sauvignon and Cabernet franc 60%, Merlot 35%, Petit verdot 5%

⏳ 7–15 years

Other wines: *La Bernède-Grand-Poujeaux, La Gravière-Grand-Poujeaux*

CHÂTEAU FONRÉAUD
AOC Listrac *Cru Bourgeois*

This splendid château has south-facing vineyards situated on and around a knoll, Puy-de-Menjon.

RED Attractive medium- to full-bodied wines of good fruit and some style.

🍇 Cabernet sauvignon 66%, Merlot 31%, Petit verdot 3%

⏳ 6–12 years

Second Wine: *Château Chemin-Royal-Moulis-en-Médoc*

Other wines: *Fontaine-Royale*

CHÂTEAU FOURCAS-DUPRÉ
AOC Listrac *Cru Bourgeois*
★ ❶

A charming house, with vineyards situated on gravel over iron-pan soil, which can excel in hot years.

RED The good colour, bouquet, and tannic structure of these wines is rewarded with rich fruit in good years.

🍇 Cabernet sauvignon 50%, Merlot 30%, Cabernet franc 10%, Petit verdot 2%,

⏳ 6–12 years

Second Wine: *Château Bellevue-Laffont*

CHÂTEAU FOURCAS-HOSTEN
AOC Listrac *Cru Bourgeois*
★ ❶

Under multi-national ownership (French, Danish, and American) since 1972, the wine making facilities here have been renovated.

RED Deeply coloured and full-bodied wines, rich in fruit and supported by a firm tannic structure, although the style is becoming more supple, and can even be quite fat in ripe years like 1982.

🍇 Cabernet sauvignon 50%, Merlot 40%, Cabernet franc 10%

⏳ 8–20 years

CHÂTEAU GRESSIER-GRAND-POUJEAUX
AOC Moulis
★ ❶

This château was classified *Cru Bourgeois* in 1932, but not in 1978, although it always has been superior to some that were. It has in recent years produced successful wines that compare well with good *Crus Classés*.

RED Full-bodied wines with plenty of fruit and flavour. Well worth laying down.

🍇 Cabernet sauvignon 50%, Merlot 40%, Cabernet franc 10%,

⏳ 6–12 years

CHÂTEAU GREYSAC
AOC Médoc *Cru Bourgeois*
★ ❶

Since it was purchased by Baron de Gunzbourg in 1973, the facilities of this château have undergone extensive modernization. The quality of the wine is excellent and its future promising.

RED Stylish, medium-bodied wines with silky-textured, ripe-fruit flavours.

🍇 Cabernet sauvignon 50%, Merlot 38%, Cabernet franc 10%, Petit verdot 2%

⏳ 6–10 years

CHÂTEAU HANTEILLAN
AOC Haut-Médoc *Cru Bourgeois*
★ ❶

This large property produces a consistently good standard of wine.

RED The wine has a fine colour, spicy bouquet with underlying vanilla-oak tones, ripe fruit, and supple tannins.

🍇 Cabernet sauvignon 48%, Merlot 42%, Cabernet franc 6%, Malbec and Petit verdot 4%

ﬁ— 6–12 years

Second Wine: *Château Larrivaux Hanteillan*

CHÂTEAU DU JUNCA
AOC Haut-Médoc *Cru Bourgeois*
★ ✔

This is a small 8-hectare (20-acre) property producing good-quality Haut-Médoc capable of medium-term ageing even in lesser years.

RED This is a classic, well-structured wine that is dominated by a Cabernet finish.

🍇 Cabernet sauvignon 60%, Merlot 30%, Cabernet franc 10%

ﬁ— 7–10 years

CHÂTEAU LA LAGUNE
AOC Haut-Médoc *3ème Cru Classé*
★ ✦ ✔

Owned by the Ducellier family of Champagne Ayala, the immaculate vineyard of this fine château is situated on sand and gravel soil. It is the first *Cru Classé* encountered after leaving Bordeaux.

RED These wines are deep-coloured with complex *cassis* and stone-fruit flavours intermingled with rich, creamy-vanilla oak nuances. They are are full-bodied but supple.

🍇 Cabernet sauvignon 55%, Cabernet franc 20%, Merlot 20%, Petit verdot 5%

ﬁ— 10–30 years

Second Wine: *Ludon-Pomies-Agassac*

CHÂTEAU LAMARQUE
AOC Haut-Médoc *Cru Bourgeois*
✔

This is a large and steadily-improving property.

RED This wine has the supple style of Médoc with plenty of real fruit flavour, and an enticingly perfumed bouquet.

🍇 Cabernet sauvignon 50%, Merlot 25%, Cabernet franc 20%, Petit verdot 5%

ﬁ— 5–12 years

Second Wine: *Réserve du Marquis d'Evry*

CHATEAU LAMOTHE-CISSAC
AOC Haut-Médoc *Cru Bourgeois*
★

An up and coming wine from one of Bordeaux's oldest properties,

Lamothe-Cissac is matured in 20% new oak and recently started to outperform Cissac.

RED Classically proportioned, Cabernet-dominated wines of excellent potential longevity.

🍇 Cabernet sauvignon 70%, Merlot 26%, Petit verdot 4%

ﬁ— 4–16 years

CHÂTEAU LANESSAN
AOC Haut-Médoc
★ ✔

This château was classified *Cru Bourgeois* in 1932, but not included in the *syndicat's* 1978 list.

RED Big, intensely flavoured wines of deep, often opaque, colour and a quality that closely approaches that of a *Cru Classé*.

🍇 Cabernet sauvignon 75%, Merlot 20%, Cabernet franc and Petit verdot 5%

ﬁ— 7–20 years

Second Wine: *Domaine de Ste.-Gemme*

CHÂTEAU LAROSE-TRINTAUDON
AOC Haut-Médoc *Cru Bourgeois*
★ ✦ ✔

This is the largest estate in the Médoc and was under the same ownership as Château Camensac until 1986, during which time vast sums were spent on renovation. The standard of these wines, which are matured in wood for 24 months with up to one-third new oak, is consistently high.

RED Medium-bodied, and sometimes full-bodied, wines with an elegantly rich flavour of juicy summer fruits, vanilla, and truffles, backed up by supple tannins. Larose-Perganson is more of a *tête de cuvée* than a second wine. Representing just 15 per cent of the total production, this wine is exclusively from the oldest vines and the grapes are all hand-picked in contrast to Larose-Trintaudon, which is machine-picked.

🍇 Cabernet sauvignon 60%, Cabernet franc 20%, Merlot 20%

ﬁ— 6–15 years

Second Wine: *Larose-Perganson*

CHÂTEAU LESTAGE-DARQUIER-GRAND-POUJEAUX
AOC Moulis *Cru Bourgeois*
★ ✔

This is the least encountered of the plethora of Poujeaux châteaux,

but well worth digging out.

RED Densely coloured wines, rich in bouquet and fruit, with a powerful structure.

🍇 Cabernet sauvignon 50%, Merlot 40%, Cabernet franc 10%

ﬁ— 8–20 years

CHÂTEAU LIVERSAN
AOC Haut-Médoc *Cru Bourgeois*
★ ✔

The estate of Château Liversan was purchased in 1984 by Prince Guy de Polignac, when it was inexorably linked with Champagne Pommery, but now leased to the owners of Patache d'Aux. The vineyard is on fine, sandy gravel over a limestone subsoil, and the wine is fermented in stainless steel and matured in wood for 18 to 20 months, with up to 50 per cent new oak.

RED Rich and flavourful wines, of full body and some style. They are gaining in class with each vintage.

🍇 Cabernet sauvignon 49%, Merlot 38%, Cabernet franc 10%, Petit verdot 3%

ﬁ— 7–20 years

CHÂTEAU LOUDENNE
AOC Médoc *Cru Bourgeois*
★ ✔

This pink-washed, Chartreuse-style château, with its lawns running down to the Gironde, once belonged to W. & A. Gilbey, who ran it in a style that harked back to the last days of the British Empire. Gilbeys ran residential courses at this château, in what was the best school of wine opened to the public. Sold to Jean-Paul Lagragette in 1999. The wine is matured in wood for 15 to 18 months, with 25 per cent new oak. Loudenne also produces a dry white wine that is attractive when drunk one to two years after the harvest.

RED Full-bodied wines with a spicy-blackcurrant bouquet, sometimes silky and hinting of violets, with underlying vanilla oak, a big mouthful of rich and ripe fruit, excellent extract, and considerable length.

🍇 Cabernet sauvignon 55%, Merlot 38%, Cabernet franc 7%

ﬁ— 5–15 years

CHÂTEAU DE MALLERET
AOC Haut-Médoc *Cru Bourgeois*

Château de Mallert is a vast estate, which incorporates a stud farm with two training race-tracks and stables for both hunting and racing. The vineyard boasts 60 hectares (148 acres).

RED Delightful wines of good bouquet, medium body, and juicy-rich fruit.

🍇 Cabernet sauvignon 70%, Merlot 15%, Cabernet franc 10%, Petit verdot 5%

ﬁ— 5–12 years

Second Wine: *Château Barthez*
Other wines: *Château Nexon, Domaine de l'Ermitage Lamourous*

CHÂTEAU MAUCAILLOU
★ ✦ ✔
AOC Moulis *Cru Bourgeois*

Château Maucaillou is consistently one of the greatest-value wines produced in Bordeaux.

RED Deep-coloured, full-bodied wine with masses of velvety-textured fruit, beautiful *cassis* and vanilla flavours, and supple tannins.

🍇 Cabernet sauvignon 45%, Merlot 35%, Cabernet franc 15%, Petit verdot 5%

ﬁ— 6–15 years

Second Wine: *Château Franc-Caillou*

CHÂTEAU MAUCAMP
AOC Haut-Médoc *Cru Bourgeois*
★ ✔

Situated between Macau itself and the *Cru Classé* Cantemerle to the south, this château makes superb use of its 15 hectares (37 acres) of fine, gravelly vineyards.

RED Always a deep-coloured, full-bodied wine with plenty of fruit flavour supported by supple tannins.

🍇 Cabernet sauvignon 50%, Merlot 40%, Petit verdot 10%

ﬁ— 5–12 years

CHÂTEAU LE MEYNIEU
AOC Haut-Médoc *Cru Bourgeois*
★ ✔

This property is under the same ownership as Château Lavillotte, which is situated in St.-Estèphe. The deep-coloured wine is not filtered before it is bottled.

RED This is a deep, dark, brooding wine of dense bouquet and solid fruit which promises very well for the future.

🍇 Cabernet sauvignon 70%, Merlot 30%

ﬁ— 7–15 years

CHÂTEAU MOULIN-À-VENT
AOC Moulis *Cru Bourgeois*

One-third of the property of Château Moulin-à-Vent overlaps the commune of Listrac, but its appellation is still Moulis.

RED Medium-bodied wines with an elegant bouquet and a full flavour.

🍇 Cabernet sauvignon 65%, Merlot 30%, Petit verdot 5%

🍷 7–15 years

Second Wine: *Moulin-de-St.-Vincent*

CHÂTEAU PATACHE-D'AUX
AOC Médoc *Cru Bourgeois*

This old property once belonged to the Aux family, descendants of the counts of Armagnac. Although Patache-d'Aux is always reliable, it has performed particularly well since its stunning 1990 vintage.

RED Stylish, highly perfumed, medium-bodied wine with very accessible fruit.

🍇 Cabernet sauvignon 70%, Merlot 20%, Cabernet franc 10%

🍷 4–8 years

Second Wine: *Le Relais de Patache d'Aux*

CHÂTEAU PLAGNAC
AOC Médoc

Since this château's acquisition by Cordier in 1972 it has deserved more recognition. The wine is matured in wood for 18 to 20 months, with a little new oak. Since the late 1970s, this property has produced consistently good-value red Bordeaux.

RED Full-bodied and full-flavoured, with some breed; lots of upfront Merlot fruit, and a smooth finish.

🍇 Cabernet sauvignon 60%, Merlot 40%,

🍷 4–10 years

CHATEAU PONTEY
AOC Médoc, *Cru Bourgeois*
★☆

Owned by Bordeaux *négociant*, this château occupies an excellent location on a gravel plateau, and its wines benefit from one-third new oak.

RED Cleverly constructed wines brimming with lush, oaky fruit.

🍇 Cabernet sauvignon 60%, Merlot 40%

🍷 3–12 years

Second Wine: *Château Vieux Prezat*

CHÂTEAU POTENSAC
AOC Médoc *Cru Bourgeois*
★Ⓥ

This property is under the same ownership as Château Léoville-Las-Cases in St.-Julien. The wines often aspire to *Cru Classé* quality.

RED Full-bodied wines of a lovely brick-red colour, with lots of fruit and underlying chocolate and spice flavours.

🍇 Cabernet sauvignon 60%, Merlot 25%, Cabernet franc 15%

🍷 6–15 years

Second Wine: *Château Lassalle*

Other wines: *Château Gallais-Bellevue, Goudy la Cardonne*

CHÂTEAUX POUJEAUX
AOC Moulis *Cru Bourgeois*
★★Ⓥ

After Chasse-Spleen, this Château produces the best wine in Moulis and easily the equivalent of a good *Cru Classé*.

RED Full-bodied and deep-coloured wine with a very expansive bouquet and creamy-rich, spicy fruit.

🍇 Cabernet sauvignon 40%, Merlot 36%, Petit verdot 12%, Cabernet franc 12%

🍷 10–25 years

Second Wine: *Château La Salle-de-Poujeaux*

CHÂTEAU RAMAGE-LA-BATISSE
AOC Haut-Médoc *Cru Bourgeois*
★Ⓥ

This property has excelled itself in recent years and is making wines of remarkable quality-price ratio.

RED Rich, well-flavoured, oaky wines that are immediately attractive in light years and ridiculously inexpensive *vins de garde* in the best vintages.

🍇 Cabernet sauvignon 60%, Merlot 30%, Cabernet franc 10%

🍷 7–15 years

Second Wine: *Le Terrey*

Other wines: *Château Dutellier*

CHATEAU ROLLAN DE BY
AOC Haut-Médoc, *Cru Bourgeois*
★☆

A new cult wine on the Bordeaux scene, with 100 per cent new oak and a string of blind tasting victories.

RED Lots of upfront fruit, but long and classy, with plenty of finesse. Not big and, surprising, not over-oaked.

🍇 Cabernet sauvignon 25%, Merlot 70%, Petit verdot 5%

🍷 4–12 years

Second Wine: *Château Haut-Condessas*

CHÂTEAU ST.-BONNET
AOC Médoc *Cru Bourgeois*
★

Some 35 of this important estate's 55 hectares (86 of its 134 acres) are planted with vines.

RED Full-flavoured wines of promising quality and immediate aromatic appeal.

🍇 Merlot 50%, Cabernet sauvignon 28%, Cabernet franc 22%

🍷 5–10 years

CHÂTEAU SOCIANDO-MALLET
AOC Haut-Médoc *Cru Bourgeois*
★★Ⓥ

This property has been making a name for itself since 1970, when Jean Gautreau, raised standards to near *Cru Classé* quality. The quality has continued to increase throughout the 1990s, when between 80 and 100 per cent new oak became the norm.

RED These are powerfully built wines that are rich in colour and extract. Often totally dominated by vanilla oak in their youth, they are backed up with plenty of concentrated *cassis* fruit.

🍇 Cabernet sauvignon 60%, Merlot 30%, Cabernet franc 10%

🍷 10–25 years

Second Wine: *Château Lartigue-de-Brochon*

CHATEAU LA TOUR DE-BY
AOC Médoc *Cru Bourgeois*
★Ⓥ

The tower of Tour-de-By was once a lighthouse. The wine is of very good *Cru Bourgeois* quality.

RED These deeply coloured, full-bodied, richly flavoured wines have good spicy fruit, backed up by a firm tannic structure.

🍇 Cabernet sauvignon 70%, Merlot 25%, Cabernet franc 5%

🍷 6–12 years

Second Wine: *La Roque-de-By*

Other wines: *Moulin de Roque*

CHÂTEAU LA TOUR-CARNET
AOC Haut-Médoc *4ème Cru Classé*
★

This charming, 13th-century, miniature moated castle has a well-kept vineyard. Unfortunately, the reputation of its wines is very lacklustre, although some critics believe it is improving.

RED Medium-bodied and sometimes full-bodied wines of good colour, but light in fruit and lacking any real richness of flavour.

🍇 Cabernet sauvignon 53%, Merlot 33%, Cabernet franc 10%, Petit verdot 4%

🍷 6–12 years

Second Wine: *Le Sire de Camin*

CHATEAU TOUR HAUT-CAUSSAN
AOC Médoc, *Cru Bourgeois*
★★☆

An up and coming property owned by Philippe Courrian, who also makes wine in Corbières.

RED A great concentration of fruit with nicely integrated oak.

🍇 Cabernet sauvignon 50%, Merlot 50%

🍷 4-10 years

Second Wine: *Château Landotte*

CHATEAU LA TOUR SAINT-BONNET
AOC Médoc *Cru Bourgeois*
★Ⓥ

Situated on fine, gravelly ridges, this property was known as Château la Tour Saint-Bonnet-Cazenave in the 19th century.

RED Firm, full-flavoured, well-coloured wines of consistent quality.

🍇 Merlot 50%, Cabernet sauvignon 28%, Cabernet franc 22%

🍷 7–15 years

Second Wine: *Château La Fuie-Saint-Bonnet*

CHÂTEAU VERDIGNAN
AOC Haut-Médoc *Cru Bourgeois*
★☆Ⓥ

The property of the Miailhe family since 1972. The wine is fermented in stainless steel and matured in wood for 18 to 20 months.

RED Medium-bodied, fruity wines, made in a soft and silky style.

🍇 Cabernet sauvignon 60%, Merlot 35%, Cabernet franc 5%

🍷 5–10 years

Other wines: *Château Plantey-de-la-Croix*

CHÂTEAU VILLEGORGE
AOC Haut-Médoc

This château was classified *Cru Bourgeois* in 1932. It was purchased by Lucien Lurton in 1973, but he then resigned from the *Syndicat* and, therefore, the château was not included in its 1978 list, although it is superior to a few that were.

RED Well-coloured, full-bodied wines, which have a spicy flavour.

🍇 Merlot 60%, Cabernet sauvignon 30%, Cabernet franc 10%

🍷 6–12 years

SAINT-ESTÈPHE

Although St.-Estèphe can be considered the least sexy of the Médoc's famous four appellations, it has an abundance of high-quality bourgeois growths, which make it indubitably the "bargain basement" of Bordeaux wines.

WITH ONLY FIVE CRUS CLASSÉS covering a mere six per cent of the commune, St.-Estèphe is a rich source of undervalued clarets, where the prices paid by wine-drinkers are unlikely to be "gazumped" by wine-investors.

CHÂTEAU COS D'ESTOURNEL

St.-Estèphe might lack classed growths, but it is not lacking in class. If it had only one *Cru Classé* – the stunning, stylish Château Cos d'Estournel – St.-Estèphe would still be famous. The reputation of this château soared after Bruno Prats took over control in 1971. Essentially, this success can be put down to his maximizing the true potential of Cos d'Estournel's exceptional *terroir*, a superb, south-facing ridge of gravel with perfect drainage. Those vineyards on heavier soil with less gravel and more clay tend to produce more rustic wines.

HARVEST, CHÂTEAU COS D'ESTOURNEL
The bizarre eastern façade of this purpose-built winery overlooks the vineyards. The château was owned by perfectionist Bruno Prats before it was sold to the Bernard Taillan group in October 1998.

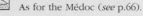

FACTORS AFFECTING TASTE AND QUALITY

LOCATION
St.-Estèphe, is the most northerly of the four classic communes of the Médoc. It is situated 18 km (11 miles) south of Lesparre, bordering the Gironde.

CLIMATE
As for the Médoc (*see* p.66).

ASPECT
St.-Estèphe has well-drained, well-sited, softly sloping vineyards. The southeast-facing crest of gravel overlooks Château Lafite-Rothschild in Pauillac and is relatively steep for the Médoc.

SOIL
The topsoil is gravelly and more fertile than in communes further south, with clay subsoil exposed in parts, consisting of clay beds, stony-clay, and limestone over iron-pan.

VITICULTURE AND VINIFICATION
Only the red wines have the right to the appellation in this commune. With increasing emphasis placed on the Merlot grape, which can now account for up to 50 per cent of the vines cultivated in some châteaux, less use of *vin de presse*, and improved vinification techniques, these wines are becoming far more accessible in less sunny years. During the vinification, all grapes must be destalked, and duration of skin contact averages three weeks. Maturation in cask currently varies between 15 and 24 months.

PRIMARY GRAPE VARIETIES
Cabernet sauvignon, Cabernet franc, Merlot
SECONDARY GRAPE VARIETIES
Carmenère, Malbec, Petit verdot

MODERN ST.-ESTÈPHE

Most wines from St.-Estèphe have always been well structured, with natural longevity, but they now have more lushness of fruit, which allows the wines to be accessible when relatively young. It was once essential to buy only the greatest vintages and wait twenty years or more before drinking them. The increasing use of the Merlot grape as well as Cabernet sauvignon and Cabernet franc, and a tendency to favour vinification techniques that extract colour and fruit in preference to the harsher tannins, provide richer, fruitier, and eminently drinkable wines in most vintages.

ST.-ESTÈPHE, *see also* p.68
Of the Haut-Médoc's four best-known communes, St.-Estèphe is the most northerly, although the actual AOC area covers only part of the commune.

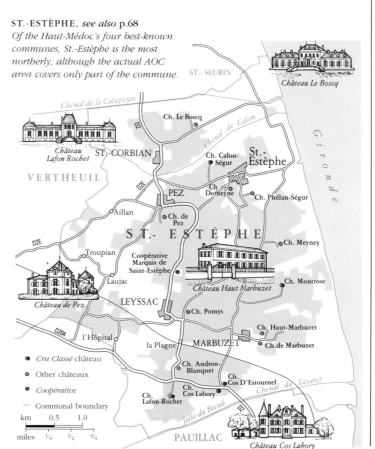

ST.-ESTÈPHE PROFILE

Appellation area Covers parts of the commune of St.-Estèphe only	**Surface area of *Crus Classés*** 226 ha (558 acres) 6% of commune, 16% of AOC
Size of commune 3,757 ha (9,284 acres)	**Special comments** Approximately 5 ha (12.3 acres) of vineyards within
AOC area under vine 1,380 ha (3,410 acres) 37% of commune	St.-Estèphe are classified as AOC Pauillac

ST.-ESTÈPHE CRU CLASSÉ STATISTICS

***Crus Classés* in AOC St.-Estèphe** 5 châteaux (by number: 8% of *Crus Classés* in the Médoc) with 226 ha (558 acres) of vineyards (by area: 8% of *Crus Classés* in the Médoc and 16% of this AOC)	**3rd Growths** 1 château (by number: 7% of 3rd Growths in the Médoc) with 48 ha (119 acres) of vineyards (by area: 11% of 3rd Growths in the Médoc)
1st Growths None	**4th Growths** 1 château (by number: 10% of 4th Growths in the Médoc) with 45 ha (111 acres) of vineyards (by area: 10% of 4th Growths in the Médoc)
2nd Growths 2 châteaux (by number: 14% of 2nd Growths in the Médoc) with 121 ha (299 acres) of vineyards (by area: 15% of 2nd Growths in the Médoc)	**5th Growths** 1 château (by number: 6% of 5th Growths in the Médoc) with 12 ha (30 acres) of vineyards (by area: 2% of 5th Growths in the Médoc)

THE WINE PRODUCERS OF
SAINT-ESTÈPHE

CHÂTEAU ANDRON-BLANQUET
Cru Bourgeois
★Ⓥ

Under the same ownership as Château Cos Labory, the vineyards of this property are situated above the gravel crest of *Cru Classé* châteaux that overlook Château Lafite-Rothschild in Pauillac.

RED An exceptionally well-made wine that consistently rises above its *petit château* status. Fermented and matured in cask, it has good fruit and a distinctive style.

🍇 Merlot 35%, Cabernet franc 30%, Cabernet sauvignon 30%, Petit verdot 5%

🍷 4–10 years

Second Wine: *St.-Roch*

CHÂTEAU BEAU-SITE
Cru Bourgeois
★Ⓥ

This property should not be confused with Château Beau-Site Haut-Vignoble, a lesser St.-Estèphe.

RED A stylish, medium-bodied, sometimes full-bodied, wine that often has an elegant finish reminiscent of violets.

🍇 Cabernet sauvignon and Cabernet franc 65%, Merlot 35%

🍷 3–10 years

CHÂTEAU LE BOSCQ
★✩Ⓥ

This property has always produced good wine, but quality increased dramatically in the 1980s; taken over by Dourthe-Kressman in 1995.

RED Superbly aromatic, almost exotic, full-bodied wine that is elegant and rich with the flavour of summer fruits, and is nicely backed up with new oak.

🍇 Cabernet sauvignon 60%, Merlot 40%

🍷 5–12 years

CHÂTEAU CALON-SÉGUR
3ème Cru Classé
★✩Ⓥ

From the Gallo-Roman origins of this château grew the community of St.-Estèphe. The first wine estate in the commune, it used to boast "*Premier Cru* de St.-Estèphe" on its label until other producers objected.

RED Full, fruity, well-structured wine that has a creamy, rich flavour. It is of consistently good quality and improves well in bottle.

🍇 Cabernet sauvignon 60%, Cabernet franc 20%, Merlot 20%

🍷 3–20 years

Second Wine: *Marquis de Ségur*

CHÂTEAU CAPBERN GASQUETON
Cru Bourgeois
★Ⓥ

This property is under the same ownership as Château Calon-Ségur. The vineyards are found north and south of the village of St.-Estèphe.

RED Medium-weight, ripe, and fruity wine of consistent quality; it is mellowed by 24 months in wood.

🍇 Cabernet sauvignon 60%, Merlot 25%, Cabernet franc 15%

🍷 4–12 years

CHÂTEAU CHAMBERT-MARBUZET
Cru Bourgeois
★✩Ⓥ

Technically faultless wine produced in limited quantities from the sister château of Haut-Marbuzet. Many would rate it easily equivalent to a *Cru Classé*.

RED Aromatically attractive, medium-bodied, sometimes full-bodied, wine. It is rich, ripe, and fruity, with plenty of caramel-oak and sufficient tannin to age well.

🍇 Cabernet sauvignon 70%, Merlot 30%

🍷 3–10 years

Second Wine: *MacCarthy*

CHÂTEAU COS D'ESTOURNEL
★★★Ⓥ
2ème Cru Classé

This was one of the very first super-seconds to emerge and this was the achievement of one man, Bruno Prats, although he would claim it to be teamwork. In 1998 Prats was forced by French tax laws to sell out to Groupe Taillan, who in 2001 sold it on to Michel Reybier, a Geneva-based food manufacturer. Cos d'Estournel has no château as such, merely a bizarre facade to the winery with huge, elaborately carved oak doors that once adorned the palace of the Sultan of Zanzibar. Bruno Prats's son Jean-Guillaume manages the property for Reybier and the wine is made in the same careful way that his father introduced. This involves some of the wine being fermented in stainless steel, but all of it is matured in cask for 18–24 months, with 100 per cent new oak for big years, and up to 70 per cent for lighter vintages.

RED A rich, flavoursome, and attractive wine of full body, great class, and distinction; without doubt the finest wine in St.-Estèphe. It is uniquely generous for the appellation and capable of amazing longevity, even in the poorest years. This is a complex wine with silky fruit and great finesse.

🍇 Cabernet sauvignon 60%, Merlot 38%, Cabernet franc 2%

🍷 8–20 years

Second Wine: *Les Pagodes de Cos*

CHÂTEAU COS LABORY
5ème Cru Classé
★

Until the late 19th century, this property formed part of Château Cos d'Estournel. During the 1920s, it was purchased by distant cousins of Madame Audoy, the current owner. The wine is matured in wood for 15 to 18 months; one-third of the casks are new oak.

RED These wines used to be merely light and elegant with a certain degree of finesse, even when at their best. However, recent vintages have displayed a very welcome change to a distinctly fuller, fruitier, and fatter style.

🍇 Cabernet sauvignon 60%, Merlot 38%, Petit verdot 5%, Cabernet franc 2%

🍷 5–15 years

CHÂTEAU LE CROCK
Cru Bourgeois
★

This property is under the same ownership as Château Léoville-Poyferré of St.-Julien.

RED These dark-coloured, substantial wines have surged in quality since 1995 under the personal guidance of Michel Rolland.

🍇 Cabernet sauvignon 58%, Merlot 24%, Cabernet franc 12%, Petit verdot 6%

🍷 6–15 years

CHÂTEAU DOMEYNE

This property was not classified *Cru Bourgeois* in 1932, nor was it listed by the *Syndicat* in 1978, but it certainly should have been.

RED These are typically deep-coloured, rich-flavoured wines that have an excellent marriage of fruit and oak. They are smooth and well-rounded wines that can be drunk while fairly young.

🍇 Cabernet sauvignon 75%, Merlot 25%

🍷 3–8 years

CHÂTEAU FAGET

Château Faget was classified *Cru Bourgeois* in 1932, but was not included in the *Syndicat's* 1978 list. However, this *coopérative*-produced wine is now superior to some that were included.

RED This is a well-made wine that gives a solid mouthful of flavour, and ages well.

🍇 Cabernet sauvignon 60%, Merlot 30%, Cabernet franc 10%

🍷 6–10 years

CHÂTEAU LA HAYE
★Ⓥ

New equipment, 25 per cent new oak casks every year, and a fair proportion of old vines, combine to produce some exciting vintages at this property.

RED Always limpid, this medium-bodied, sometimes full-bodied, wine is rich in colour and flavour, well balanced, and lengthy with vanilla-oak evident on the finish.

🍇 Cabernet sauvignon 65%, Merlot 30%, Petit verdot 5%

🍷 5–8 years

CHÂTEAU HAUT-MARBUZET
Cru Bourgeois
★✩Ⓥ

This is one of several properties belonging to Henri Duboscq. These wines receive 18 months in 100 per cent new oak, which is extremely rare for *Cru Classé* châteaux.

RED These full-bodied, deep-coloured wines are packed with juicy fruit, backed up by supple tannin. They are marked by a generous buttered-toast and creamy-vanilla character.

🍇 Merlot 50%, Cabernet sauvignon 40%, Cabernet franc 10%

🍷 4–12 years

Second Wine: *Tour de Marbuzet*

CHÂTEAU HOUISSANT

This property was classified *Cru Bourgeois* in 1932, but was not included in the *Syndicat's* 1978 list.

It is, however, superior to a few that were included.

RED These are well-produced, full-flavoured wines that are medium-bodied and sometimes full-bodied.

🍇 Cabernet sauvignon 70%, Merlot 30%

🍷 3–8 years

CHÂTEAU LAFON-ROCHET
4ème Cru Classé

When Guy Tesseron purchased this vineyard which is situated on the borders of Pauillac, in 1959, he embarked on a project to increase the proportion of Cabernet sauvignon grapes used in the wine. However, this proved to be a mistake for Lafon Rochet's *terroir* and has been rectified in recent years. The wine produced here is matured in wood for 18 to 24 months and one-third of the casks are new oak.

RED This wine is not typical St.-Estèphe, either of the traditional school or of the fruitier new wave. The Cabernet sauvignon has been reduced and the Merlot has been doubled in a bid to eradicate the astringent character that used to blight these wines. They are much better, but there is still room for improvement.

🍇 Cabernet sauvignon 55%, Merlot 40%, Cabernet franc 5%

🍷 5–12 years

Second Wine: ✓ *Numero 2*

CHÂTEAU LAVILOTTE
Cru Bourgeois
★☆ Ⓥ

This is a star-performing château that gives good value.

RED These are dark-coloured wines with a deep and distinctive bouquet. Smoky, full-bodied, intense, and complex.

🍇 Cabernet sauvignon 75%, Merlot 25%

🍷 5–12 years

CHÂTEAU DE MARBUZET
Cru Bourgeois
★

Under the same ownership as Cos d'Estournel, Marbuzet used to include the wines rejected from the *grand vin* of that "super-second". However, all the wine from this château has been produced exclusively from its own vineyards since 1994.

RED These elegant, medium-bodied and sometimes full-bodied wines are well-balanced and have good fruit and a supple finish.

🍇 Merlot 56%, Cabernet sauvignon 44%

🍷 4–10 years

LE MARQUIS DE SAINT-ESTÈPHE
Ⓥ

These wines are produced by the conscientious Cave Coopérative Marquis de Saint-Estèphe.

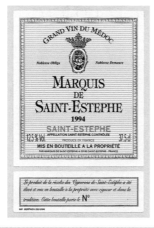

RED These are consistently well-made, good-value, medium-bodied, although sometimes full-bodied, wines.

🍇 Cabernet franc and Cabernet sauvignon 60%, Merlot 35%, Malbec and Petit verdot 5%

🍷 3–6 years

CHÂTEAU MEYNEY
Cru Bourgeois
★ Ⓥ

This château is consistent in managing to produce fine wines in virtually every vintage.

RED These wines used to be big, beefy, chunky, and chewy and required at least ten years in bottle. They have changed, and for the better. They have acquired a silky-textured finesse and no longer require many years in bottle, but age gracefully.

🍇 Cabernet sauvignon 70%, Merlot 24%, Cabernet franc 4%, Petit verdot 2%

🍷 5–25 years

Second Wine: *Prieuré de Meyney*

CHÂTEAU MONTROSE
2ème Cru Classé
★☆ Ⓥ

This youngest of the *Cru Classé* vineyards produces wines that are matured in wood for 24 months, with up to one-third new oak.

RED The inhibiting factor of Montrose has always been its "stemmy" tannins, and it requires a vintage of exceptional richness and

fatness to overcome the aggressive character produced by these tannins. The excellent 1994 gives me hope that this château has started to harvest the grapes when they are tannin-ripe (*see* p.63) and is now applying more specific maceration techniques. If so, the next millennium may see Montrose rise to the rank of a super-Second.

🍇 Cabernet sauvignon 65%, Merlot 25%, Cabernet franc 10%

🍷 8–25 years

Second Wine: *La Dame de Montrose*

CHÂTEAU LES ORMES DE PEZ
Cru Bourgeois
★☆ Ⓥ

Owner Jean-Michel Cazes of Château Lynch-Bages in Pauillac installed new stainless-steel vats in 1981 and has raised the quality of these wines from good to sensational. Matured in wood for at least 12 to 15 months, this relatively cheap wine is easily equivalent to a good *Cru Classé*.

RED Dark and fruity, yet capable of ageing with a herbal complexity.

🍇 Cabernet sauvignon 55%, Merlot 35%, Cabernet franc 10%

🍷 3–15 years

CHÂTEAU DE PEZ
★☆ Ⓥ

This property was purchased by Champagne Louis Roederer in 1995. The wines are fermented in wooden vats then aged for 20 to 22 months in casks, a quarter of which are new. These wines are easily the equivalent of *Cru Classé* quality.

RED Consistently one of the best *bourgeois* growths in the entire Médoc. A medium-bodied wine, it has a rich fruit flavour, and good tannic structure, and can mature into a sublime, cedary wine.

🍇 Cabernet sauvignon 70%, Cabernet franc 15%, Merlot 15%

🍷 6–20 years

CHÂTEAU PHÉLAN-SÉGUR
Cru Bourgeois
Ⓥ

This has greatly improved since the 1988 vintage and is now one of the best-value wines in the Médoc.

RED Still very firm wines, but no longer lacking charm or elegance.

🍇 Cabernet sauvignon 50%, Merlot 40%, Cabernet franc 10%

🍷 5–10 years

Second Wine: *Franck Phélan*

CHÂTEAU POMYS
Ⓥ

This property was classified *Cru Bourgeois* in 1932, but was not included in the 1978 list, although it is superior to a few that were. The wines are aged in wood for 24 months with 25 per cent new oak.

RED Substantial wines with good fruit and tannin balance.

🍇 Cabernet sauvignon 50%, Merlot 25%, Cabernet franc 20%, Petit verdot 5%

🍷 3–10 years

CHÂTEAU LES PRADINES
Ⓥ

This *coopérative*-produced, château-bottled wine was not classified as a *Cru Bourgeois* in 1932, nor included in the 1978 list, but it certainly should have been.

RED This is a positive wine, full of fruit and character, with a very satisfying finish.

🍇 Cabernet sauvignon 60%, Merlot 35%, Cabernet franc 5%

🍷 2–7 years

CHÂTEAU TOUR DE PEZ
★ Ⓥ

Huge investment has paid off in the 1990s.

RED An elegant, medium-bodied, wine with good, fleshy fruit. The 1996 is a stunner!

🍇 Cabernet sauvignon 45%, Cabernet franc 10%, Merlot 40%, Petit verdot 5%

🍷 3–7 years

CHÂTEAU TRONQUOY-LALANDE
Cru Bourgeois

Owned by Arlette Castéja-Texier with active input from the Dourthe-Kressman winemaking team.

RED These wines range from being pleasantly fruity to dark and tannic, with improvement noted as from 1996.

🍇 Cabernet sauvignon 45%, Merlot 45%, Petit verdot 10%

🍷 3–7 years

PAUILLAC

If any Bordeaux appellation can be described as "big, black, and beautiful", it is Pauillac – the commune most famous for the three First Growths of Latour, Lafite, and Mouton, which allows the wine to evolve very slowly, achieving an astonishing degree of finesse.

PAUILLAC IS, HOWEVER, an appellation of quite surprising contrasts. Although it boasts three-quarters of the Médoc's First Growths, it also contains two-thirds of the region's Fifth Growths. Very little lies between these two extremes, and *Crus Bourgeois* are, therefore, the exception rather than the rule. Cabernet sauvignon is at its most majestic in Pauillac and while the much-vaunted blackcurrant character of this grape may be elusive in many clarets, it is certainly very much in evidence in Pauillacs, which allows the wine to evolve very slowly, achieving an astonishing degree of finesse for its weight. In this wine, the *cassis* character is always beautifully balanced by a tannic structure.

PAUILLAC CRU CLASSÉ STATISTICS

Crus Classés in AOC Pauillac
18 châteaux (by number: 30% of *Crus Classés* in the Médoc) with 842 ha (2,080 acres) of vineyards (by area: 30% of *Crus Classés* in the Médoc and 72% of this AOC)

1st Growths
3 châteaux (by number: 75% of 1st Growths in the Médoc) with 230 ha (568 acres) of vineyards (by area: 75% of 1st Growths in the Médoc)

2nd Growths
2 châteaux (by number: 14% of 2nd Growths in the Médoc) with 90 ha (222 acres) of vineyards (by area: 11% of 2nd Growths in the Médoc)

3rd Growths
None

4th Growths
1 château (by number: 10% of 4th Growths in the Médoc) with 45 ha (111 acres) of vineyards (by area: 10% of 4th Growths in the Médoc)

5th Growths
12 châteaux (by number: 67% of 5th Growths in the Médoc) with 477 ha (1,179 acres) of vineyards (by area: 63% of 5th Growths in the Médoc)

Note Only Margaux has more *Cru Classé* châteaux than Pauillac, and no communal AOC has a greater concentration of *Cru Classé* vines (79%)

CHÂTEAU LATOUR
Due to radical changes in vinification techniques introduced in the 1960s, Château Latour became the most consistent of Bordeaux's great First Growths. It produces the archetypal Pauillac wine, which is full of finesse.

FACTORS AFFECTING TASTE AND QUALITY

LOCATION
Pauillac is sandwiched between St.-Estèphe to the north and St.-Julien to the south.

CLIMATE
As for the Médoc (*see* p.66)

ASPECT
Pauillac consists of two large, low-lying plateaux, one to the northwest of the town of Pauillac, the other to the southwest. Exposure is excellent, and both drain down gentle slopes, eastwards to the Gironde, westwards to the forest, or north and south to canals and streams.

SOIL
Pauillac's two plateaux are massive gravel beds, reaching a greater depth than any found elsewhere in the Médoc. The water

drains away before the iron-pan subsoil is reached. St.-Sauveur consists of shallow sand over a stony subsoil to the west, and gravel over iron-pan (or more gravel) in the centre and south.

VITICULTURE AND VINIFICATION
Only red wines have the right to the Pauillac appellation. Some *vin de presse* is traditionally used by most châteaux. Skin-contact duration averages between 3 and 4 weeks and maturation in cask currently varies between 18 and 24 months.

PRIMARY GRAPE VARIETIES
Cabernet sauvignon, Cabernet franc, Merlot
SECONDARY GRAPE VARIETIES
Carmenère, Petit verdot, Malbec

PAUILLAC PROFILE

Appellation Area	AOC area under vine
Covers parts of the commune of Pauillac, plus 34 ha (84 acres) in St.-Sauveur, 16 ha (40 acres) in St.-Julien, 5 ha (12.4 acres) in St.-Estèphe, and 1 ha (2.5 acres) in Cissac	1,170 ha (2,891 acres) 46% of commune
	Surface area of *Crus Classés* 842 ha (2,080 acres) 3% of commune 72% of AOC
Size of Commune 2,539 ha (6,274 acres)	

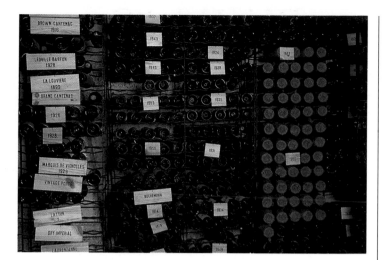

CAVEAU PRIVÉ, CHÂTEAU PICHON-LONGUEVILLE-COMTESSE-DE-LALANDE
One wall of the château's private cellars encapsulates a wine-making history, particularly of Bordeaux, stretching back nearly 200 years.

PAUILLAC, *see also p.68*
Blessed with three First Growths, Lafite-Rothschild and Mouton-Rothschild in the north, and Latour to the south, Pauillac is sandwiched between St.-Estèphe and St.-Julien.

PAUILLAC
The town of Pauillac, the largest of the Médoc, sits on the west bank of the Gironde. Despite its size and position, it still retains a quiet, rural character.

LABELS DESIGNED FOR CHÂTEAU MOUTON-ROTHSCHILD (*see* p.80)

In 1922, at the age of 20, Baron Philippe Rothschild took over the management of Château Mouton-Rothschild. One of his first actions was to commission Jean Carlu, a young artist to design a new label for the 1924 vintage – the famous sheep's head and five arrows. The label was used for several vintages, including some produced (but not bottled) before 1922. The label was changed for the 1928 and 1929 vintages and then again in 1933. Each vintage since 1945 has had a new label designed by a famous artist.

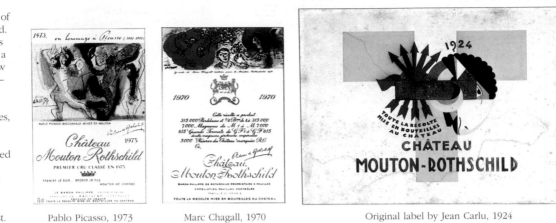

Pablo Picasso, 1973

Marc Chagall, 1970

Original label by Jean Carlu, 1924

THE WINE PRODUCERS OF
PAUILLAC

CHÂTEAU D'ARMAILHAC
5ème Cru Classé
⭐

Baron Philippe de Rothschild purchased Château Mouton d'Armailhac in 1933. In 1956 he renamed it Château Mouton Baron-Philippe. In 1975 it was changed to Mouton-Baronne-Philippe in honour of the baron's late wife. In 1991 it reverted to d'Armailhac, but without the Mouton tag because the Baron believed the wine to be in danger of assuming Second-Wine status due to the overwhelming prestige of Mouton-Rothschild. This property borders that of Mouton and one of Baron Philippe's reasons for acquiring it was to provide an easier, more impressive access to the famous First Growth. The wines, which are matured in wood for 22 to 24 months, with 20 per cent new oak, are produced with the same care and consideration.

RED Austere in youth, the light and attenuated style of this wine proves that even money cannot buy *terroir*.

🍇 Cabernet sauvignon 65%, Merlot 30%, Cabernet franc 5%

🍷 10–20 years

CHÂTEAU BATAILLEY
5ème Cru Classé
⭐⭐

This is a château that responds well to sunny years and produces underrated and undervalued wine. The 1985 was possibly the best bargain in Bordeaux, and the 1986 is probably even better. The wine is matured in wood with at least one-third new oak for 16 to 18 months.

RED This wine has sometimes been rustic and too assertive in the past, but now shows its class with fine, succulent fruit supported by a ripe tannic structure and a complex creamy-oak aftertaste.

🍇 Cabernet sauvignon 74%, Merlot 20%, Cabernet franc 5%, Petit verdot 1%

🍷 10–25 years

CHÂTEAU BECASSE

This château is a rapidly rising star that was not classified as a *Cru Bourgeois* in either 1932 or 1978, but certainly deserves the status now.

RED A consistently deep-coloured, well-structured wine that is rich in fruit, hinting of blackcurrants, and obviously matured in a certain percentage of new oak.

🍇 Cabernet sauvignon 70%, Merlot 20%, Cabernet franc 10%

🍷 5–12 years

CHÂTEAU CLERC MILON
5ème Cru Classé
⭐

This property was purchased by Baron Philippe de Rothschild in 1970. After more than a decade of investment and quite a few disappointing vintages along the way, it came good in 1981, achieved sensational quality in 1982, and now consistently performs well above its classification. This wine, which is matured in wood for 22 to 24 months with 20 to 30 per cent new oak, is one worth watching.

RED A deep-coloured, medium-bodied, sometimes full-bodied, wine with *cassis*-cum-spicy-oak aromas and rich berry flavours well balanced by ripe acidity.

🍇 Cabernet sauvignon 70%, Merlot 20%, Cabernet franc 10%

🍷 10–20 years

CHÂTEAU COLOMBIER-MONPELOU
Cru Bourgeois
⭐ V

In the third edition of *Bordeaux and its Wines*, published in 1874, this property was described as a Fourth Growth. Of course it was never classified as such, but its use of 30 per cent new oak gives this château a touch of *Cru Classé* luxury.

RED Rich, spicy, fruit with fine Cabernet characteristics, backed up by good, ripe tannic structure and vanilla-oaky undertones.

🍇 Cabernet sauvignon 70%, Merlot 20%, Cabernet franc 5%, Petit verdot 5%

🍷 5–12 years

Second Wine: *Grand Canyon*

CHÂTEAU DE CORDEILLAN-BAGES
AOC Pauillac
⭐

Jean-Michel Cazes of Château Lynch-Bages was the driving force behind the group of Médoc growers who renovated Château de Cordeillan, turning it into an hotel, restaurant and wine school complex. A tiny production from just two hectares made by the Lynch-Bages winemaking team.

RED As dark and as dense as could be expect with the Lynch-Bages influence, with smoky-oak, tobacco plant and violet aromas weaving their way through the chocolatey Cabernet fruit.

🍇 Cabernet sauvignon 60%, Merlot 30%, Malbec 5%, Petit Verdot 5%

🍷 3-8 years

CHÂTEAU CROIZET-BAGES
5ème Cru Classé
❷

Under the same ownership as Château Rauzan-Gassies of Margaux, and situated on the Bages plateau, Croizet-Bages is a classic example of a "château with no château". Its wine is matured in wood for 18 months and although not unattractive, it lacks class and rarely excites. Improvements are slowly taking place, however.

RED Not one of the most deeply coloured Pauillacs, this medium-bodied, easy-drinking wine has a clean, fruity flavour.

🍇 Cabernet sauvignon 37%, Cabernet franc 30%, Merlot 30%, Malbec and Petit verdot 3%

🍷 6–12 years

Second Wine: *Enclos de Moncabon*

CHÂTEAU DUHART-MILON-ROTHSCHILD
4ème Cru Classé
⭐⭐

Another "château with no château", Duhart-Milon was purchased by the Lafite branch of the Rothschild family in 1962. Its wines prior to this date were almost entirely Petit Verdot and so only in abnormally hot years did it excel with this late-ripening grape, which is traditionally cultivated for its acidity. Interestingly, in the near-tropical heat of 1947, Duhart-Milon managed to produce a wine that many considered to be the best of the vintage. The Rothschilds expanded these vineyards bordering those of Lafite, and replanted them with the correct combination of varieties to suit the *terroir*. In 1994 Charles Chevalier arrived and since 1996 he has moved these wines up a gear. The wine is matured for at least 18 to 24 months in wood with one-third new oak.

RED These wines are elegantly perfumed, deliciously rich in creamy-oaky fruit, and have exceptional balance and finesse.

Cabernet sauvignon 65%, Merlot 30%, Cabernet franc 5%

8–16 years

Second Wine: *Moulin de Duhart*

CHÂTEAU LA FLEUR-MILON
Cru Bourgeois

A "château with no château", La Fleur-Milon produces a wine accumulated from various parcels of vines bordering such prestigious properties as Lafite, Mouton, and Duhart-Milon.

RED A consistently firm, solid, and decent sort of wine, which somehow fails to live up to the favoured origins of its vines.

Cabernet sauvignon 45%, Cabernet franc 20%, Merlot 35%

4–10 years

CHÂTEAU FONBADET
★✫

This growth was classified *Cru Bourgeois* in 1932, but was not included in the *Syndicat's* 1978 list, although it is superior to a few that were. Many of the vines are up to 80 years old and the wine is matured in 15 per cent new oak. Great-value Pauillac.

RED This typical Pauillac has a deep, almost opaque colour, an intense *cassis*, cigar-box, and cedarwood bouquet, a concentrated spicy, fruit flavour with creamy-oak undertones, and a long finish.

Cabernet sauvignon 60%, Cabernet franc 15%, Merlot 19%, Malbec 4%, Petit verdot 2%

6–15 years

Second Wine: *Haut-Pauillac*
Other Wines: *Château Tour du Roc Milon*

CHÂTEAU GRAND-PUY-DUCASSE
5ème Cru Classé
★✫

Under the same owners as Château Rayne-Vigneau in Sauternes, this property produces an undervalued wine that comes from various plots scattered across half the commune and is matured in wood for 15 to 18 months. This is one of the best value *Cru Classé* wines available.

RED Well-balanced, relatively early-drinking, medium-bodied, sometimes full-bodied, wine of classic Pauillac *cassis* character and more suppleness than is usual for this commune.

Cabernet sauvignon 70%, Merlot 25%, Petit verdot 5%

5–10 years

Second Wine: *Château Artigues-Arnaud*

CHÂTEAU GRAND-PUY-LACOSTE
5ème Cru Classé
★✫✫

Under the same ownership as Château Ducru-Beaucaillou, Grand-Puy-Lacoste is going from strength to strength under the skilful guidance of François-Xavier Borie. The wine is matured in wood for 18 to 20 months, with one-third new oak.

RED Deep-coloured with complex *cassis*, spice, and vanilla bouquet, lots of fruit, length, and finesse.

Cabernet sauvignon 62%, Merlot 37%, Petit verdot 1%

10–20 years

Second Wine: *Lacoste-Borie*

CHÂTEAU HAUT-BAGES-AVEROUS
★✫

This growth was classified *Cru Bourgeois* in 1932, but not included in the *Syndicat's* 1978 list, although this property, owned by Jean-Michel Cazes of Château Lynch-Bages, is superior to a few that were. The Second Wines of Château Lynch-Bages are blended with this wine.

RED Spice, balance, and fine acidity are the hallmarks of this wine. This is a medium- to full-bodied wine of very good quality. In some rich years, such as 1983, there is an additional, attractive, minty-herbal touch.

Cabernet sauvignon 75%, Merlot 15%, Cabernet franc 10%

5–12 years

CHÂTEAU HAUT-BAGES-LIBERAL
5ème Cru Classé
★

Under the same ownership as the *bourgeois* growth of Château Chasse-Spleen in Moulis and the excellent unclassified Château la Gurgue in Margaux, this dynamic property is currently producing sensational wines. They are matured for 18 to 20 months in wood, with up to 40 per cent new oak. The 1986 has to be tasted to be believed.

RED Dark, full-bodied wines with masses of concentrated spicy-*cassis* fruit, great tannic structure, and ripe, vanilla oak. In a word – complete.

Cabernet sauvignon 75%, Merlot 20%, Petit verdot 5%

10–20 years

Second Wine: *Chapelle de Bages*

CHÂTEAU HAUT-BATAILLEY
5ème Cru Classé
★

This property is under the same ownership as châteaux Grand-Puy-Lacoste and, in St.-Julien, Ducru-Beaucaillou. When the Borie family purchased Château Batailley in 1942, this part of the vineyard was given to one son, while the bulk of the property, including the château itself, was given to the other. The wine is matured in wood for 20 months, with one-third new oak.

RED Haut-Batailley is well-coloured and medium-bodied and shows more elegance and finesse than Batailley, although it can lack the latter's fullness of fruit.

Cabernet sauvignon 65%, Merlot 25%, Cabernet franc 10%

7–15 years

Second Wine: *Château La Tour l'Aspic*

CHÂTEAU LAFITE-ROTHSCHILD
1er Cru Classé
★★★

Since 1994 this famous château, the vineyard of which includes a small plot in St.-Estèphe, has been run along traditional lines and with fastidious care by Charles Chevalier for Baron Eric of the French branch of the Rothschilds. The St.-Estèphe portion of the Lafite vineyard is allowed to bear the Pauillac appellation, having been part of the Lafite-Rothschild estate for several hundred years. A change of style occurred in the mid-1970s, when the decision was taken to give the wines less time in cask, but under Chevalier they have gone into hyperdrive and are often the very best of the First Growths.

RED Not the biggest of the First Growths, but Lafite is nevertheless textbook stuff: a rich delicacy of spicy fruit flavours, continuously unfolding, supported by an array of creamy-oak and ripe tannins; a wine with incomparable finesse.

Cabernet sauvignon 70%, Merlot 20%, Cabernet franc 10%

25–50 years

Second Wine: *Carraudes de Lafite*
Other wines: *Moulin des Carruades*

CHÂTEAU LATOUR
1er Cru Classé
★★★

The Pearson Group of London was accused by the French of turning this First Growth into a dairy when temperature-controlled, stainless-steel vats were installed in 1964 (conveniently ignoring the fact that Château Haut-Brion had done the same three years earlier). Pearson actually owned just over half of Latour at the time and Harveys of Bristol owned a quarter. Together they paid less than one million pounds for almost 80 per cent of this First Growth. It was a bargain, for although they invested heavily in renovating the vineyards and winery, Allied-Lyons (owners of Harvey's) paid almost £60 million in 1989 for Pearson's share, valuing the entire property at £110 million. Allied-Lyons lost out, however, when in 1993 they needed to liquidate various shareholdings to finance takeovers and sold Latour to François Pinault, the French industrialist, for £86 million. Pinsault appointed Frédéric Engerer, a graduate of one of France's top business schools, as the young new president of Latour. He has revolutionized working practices in both the vineyard and winery and with Frédéric Ardouin, his new, even younger winemaker at his side, the change in gear at Latour promised to be as dramatic as it was at Margaux. Since Latour is already a top performer, this could well bring Korbut-like problems to the classification of Latour in future editions of this encyclopedia, but I suppose there are worse problems in life. The wine is matured in wood for 20 to 24 months, with 100 per cent new oak.

RED Despite its close proximity to the neighbouring commune of St.-Julien, Latour is the archetypal Pauillac. Its ink-black colour accurately reflects the immense structure and hugely concentrated flavour of this wine. If Lafite is the ultimate example of finesse, then Latour is the ideal illustration of how massive a wine can be while still retaining great finesse.

🍇 Cabernet sauvignon 80%, Merlot 4%, Cabernet franc 15%, Petit verdot 1%

🍷— 30–60 years

Second Wine: *Les Forts de Latour*
Other wines: *Pauillac de Latour*

CHÂTEAU LYNCH BAGES
5ème Cru Classé
★★✓

This château is sited on the edge of the Bages plateau, a little way out of Pauillac. It is on the southern fringe of the small town of Bages. Jean-Michel Cazes produces wines that some people describe as "poor man's Latour (or Mouton)". Well, that cannot be such a bad thing, but if I were rich, I would drink as much Fifth Growths from this château as First Growths from elsewhere. No expense was spared in building the new vinification and storage facilities at this château, and since 1980 the successes in off-vintages have been extraordinary, making it more consistent than some Second Growths. The wine is matured in wood for 12 to 15 months, with 50 per cent new oak.

RED An intensely deep purple-coloured wine of seductive character that is packed with fruit and has obvious class. It has a degree of complexity on the nose, a rich, plummy flavour, supple tannin structure, and a spicy, blackcurrant and vanilla aftertaste.

🍇 Cabernet sauvignon 75%, Merlot 15%, Cabernet franc 10%

🍷— 8–30 years

Second Wine: ✓ *Château Haut-Bages-Avérous* (a little white wine is also produced).

CHÂTEAU LYNCH MOUSSAS
5ème Cru Classé
❓

Owned by Emile Castéja of Borie-Manoux, this property has been renovated and the wines could well improve. The wine is matured in wood for 18 to 20 months, with 25 per cent new oak.

RED Not unpleasant; merely light, rather insubstantial wines of no specific character or quality, although the 1985 was exceptionally stylish.

🍇 Cabernet sauvignon 70%, Merlot 30%

🍷— 4–8 years

CHÂTEAU MOUTON-ROTHSCHILD
1er Cru Classé
★★★

The famous case of the only wine ever to be officially reclassified since 1855, Baron Philippe de Rothschild's plight ending with Mouton's status being justly raised to First Growth in 1973. Through promotion of Mouton's unique character, he was probably responsible for elevating the Cabernet sauvignon grape to its present high profile. Part of his campaign to keep this château in the headlines was the introduction of a specially commissioned painting for the label of each new vintage. The wine is matured in wood for 22 to 24 months, with 100 per cent new oak.

RED It is difficult to describe this wine without using the same descriptive terms as those used for Latour, but perhaps the colour of Mouton reminds one more of damsons and the underlying character is more herbal, sometimes even minty. And although it ages just as well as Latour, it becomes accessible slightly earlier.

🍇 Cabernet sauvignon 85%, Cabernet franc 10%, Merlot 5%

🍷— 20–60 years

Second Wine: *La Petite Mouton*
Other wines: *Aile d'Argent* (white)

CHÂTEAU PEDESCLAUX
5ème Cru Classé

Little-seen *Cru Classé* produced from two very well-situated plots of vines, one bordering Lynch Bages, the other between Mouton-Rothschild and Pontet-Canet. Most of its exported production goes to Belgium. It is matured in wood for 20 to 22 months, with 50 per cent new oak. Wine rejected for the *Grand Vin* is blended into the wine of Château Belle Rose, a *Cru Bourgeois* under the same ownership.

RED Full, firm, traditional style of Pauillac that is slow-maturing and long-lasting.

🍇 Cabernet sauvignon 70%, Merlot 20%, Cabernet franc 5%, Petit verdot 5%

🍷— 15–40 years

CHÂTEAU AU BARON DE PICHON-LONGUEVILLE
2ème Cru Classé
★★★☆

The smaller of the two Pichon vineyards and until very recently the least inspiring, although many experts reckoned the *terroir* of Pichon-Baron to be intrinsically superior to that of its neighbour, the star-performing Pichon-Comtesse. Indeed, ten years ago, I even suggested that Mme de Lencquesaing should buy this château and cast her seemingly irresistible spell on what would inevitably be the still greater *terroir* of the two properties combined. Whether she had such an ambition or even the cash to consider it, the AXA insurance company got there first and has been embarrassingly successful at conjuring the most incredible quality from Pichon-Baron. Embarrassing because as consistently sensational as Cazes's Lynch-Bages is, Pichon-Baron is even better. Which just goes to prove how accurate the 1855 Classification still is and fulfils musing in the first edition that Pichon-Baron might one day live up to its potential. The wine is matured in wood for 24 months, with one third new oak.

RED Intensely coloured, full-bodied wine with concentrated spicy-*cassis* fruit backed up by supple tannins, which are rich and heady with smoky-creamy oak and complexity.

🍇 Cabernet sauvignon 75%, Merlot 24%, Malbec 1%

🍷— 8–25 years

Second Wine: ✓ *Les Tourelles de Longueville*

CHÂTEAU PICHON-LONGUEVILLE-COMTESSE-DE-LALANDE
2ème Cru Classé
★★★☆

There is a limit to the quality of any wine and this is determined by the potential quality of its grapes. But at Pichon-Comtesse (as it is known), the formidable Madame de Lencquesaing demands the maximum from her *terroir* – and consistently gets it. The wine is matured in wood for 18 to 20 months, with 50 per cent new oak.

RED This temptress is the Château Margaux of Pauillac. It is silky-textured, beautifully balanced, and seductive. A wine of great finesse, even in humble vintages.

🍇 Cabernet sauvignon 46%, Merlot 34%, Cabernet franc 12%, Petit verdot 8%

🍷— 10–30 years

Second Wine: ✓ *Réserve de la Comtesse*

CHÂTEAU PONTET-CANET
5ème Cru Classé
★

The reputation of this Château has suffered in recent decades, but many thought the situation would be reversed when Guy Tesseron purchased the property in 1975. The 1985 vintage gave a glimmer of hope, but it was not until 1995 that the breakthrough occurred, and the 1998 is nothing less than outstanding. A wine to watch? It is matured in wood for 18 to 24 months, with one-third new oak.

RED Since the mid-1990s these wines have been fruity and graceful with a rich, oaky touch.

🍇 Cabernet sauvignon 68%, Merlot 20%, Cabernet franc 10%, Malbec 2%

🍷— 6–12 years

Second Wine: *Les Hauts de Pontet*

LA ROSE PAUILLAC

This is the local *coopérative*'s wine – and pretty good it is, too.

RED This medium-bodied wine has good fruit and is a typical, if lesser, version of true Pauillac without seeming attenuated or disappointing.

🍇 Cabernet sauvignon and Cabernet franc 45%, Merlot 40%, Petit verdot 15%

🍷— 5–10 years

CHÂTEAU LA TOUR-PIBRAN
★✓

This growth was classified *Cru Bourgeois* in 1932, but was not in the *Syndicat*'s 1978 list, although it is superior to a few that were.

RED This wine has bags of blackcurranty fruit, yet retains the characteristic Pauillac structure and firm finish. The superb 1985 is not unlike a "mini-Mouton".

🍇 Cabernet sauvignon 75%, Merlot 15%, Cabernet franc 10%

🍷— 6–16 years

SAINT-JULIEN

The commune's fame is disproportionate to its size, since it is smaller than any of the other three classic Médoc appellations – St.-Estèphe, Pauillac, and Margaux. It has, however, a higher concentration of AOC vineyards than its neighbours, and its châteaux have discernibly larger estates and are better known.

ST.-JULIEN HAS NO FIRST GROWTHS, nor Fifth Growths, although some châteaux sometimes produce wines that are undeniably of First-Growth quality. The concentration of its 11 *Crus Classés* in the middle of the Classification is St.-Julien's real strength, enabling this commune justly to claim that it is the most consistent of the Médoc appellations; these quintessential clarets have a vivid colour, elegant fruit, superb balance, and great finesse.

It is perhaps surprising that wines from as far as 16 hectares (40 acres) inside St.-Julien's borders may be classified as AOC Pauillac, particularly in view of the perceived difference in style between these appellations. This illustrates the "grey area" that exists when communal boundaries overlap the historical borders

of great wine estates, and highlights the existence and importance of blending, even in a region reputed for its single-vineyard wines. Although time has allowed us to discern the communal differences of style, we should not be too pedantic about them: if the communal borders of the Médoc followed local history, Château Latour, the most famous château of Pauillac, would today be in St.-Julien – and that makes me wonder how the wines of this commune might be described under such circumstances?

ST.-JULIEN PROFILE

Appellation area Covers part of the commune of St.-Julien only	**Surface area of Crus Classés** 628ha (1,552 acres) 40% of commune, 69% of AOC
Size of commune 1,554 ha (3,840 acres)	**Special comments** Some 16 hectares (40 acres) of St.-Julien are classified as AOC Pauillac
AOC Area under vine 910 ha (2,249 acres) 59% of commune	

FACTORS AFFECTING TASTE AND QUALITY

LOCATION
St.-Julien lies in the centre of the Haut-Médoc, 4 km (2½ miles) south of Pauillac.

CLIMATE
As for the Médoc (*see* p.66).

ASPECT
The gravel crest of St.-Julien slopes almost imperceptibly eastwards towards the village and drains into the Gironde.

SOIL
Fine, gravel topsoil of good-sized pebbles in vineyards within sight of the Gironde. Further inland, the particle size decreases and the soil begins to mix with sandy loess. The subsoil consists of iron-pan, marl, and gravel.

VITICULTURE & VINIFICATION
Only red wines have the right to the appellation. All grapes must be destalked. Some *vin de presse* may be used according to the needs of the vintage. Skin-contact duration averages two to three weeks and most châteaux allow 18–22 months maturation in cask.

PRIMARY GRAPE VARIETIES
Cabernet sauvignon, Cabernet franc, Merlot
SECONDARY GRAPE VARIETIES
Carmenère, Malbec, Petit verdot

ST.-JULIEN CRU CLASSÉ STATISTICS

***Crus Classés* in AOC St.-Julien** 11 châteaux (by number: 18% of *Crus Classés* in the Médoc) with 628 ha (1,552 acres) of vineyards (by area: 22% of *Crus Classés* in the Médoc and 64% of this AOC)	**3rd Growths** 2 châteaux (by number: 14% of 3rd Growths in the Médoc) with 69 ha (170 acres) of vineyards (by area: 16% of 3rd Growths in the Médoc)
1st Growths None	**4th Growths** 4 châteaux (by number: 40% of 4th Growths in the Médoc) with 241 ha (596 acres) of vineyards (by area: 51% of 4th Growths in the Médoc)
2nd Growths 5 châteaux (by number: 36% of 2nd Growths in the Médoc) with 318 ha (786 acres) of vineyards (by area: 40% of 2nd Growths in the Médoc)	**5th Growths** None

ST.-JULIEN-BEYCHEVELLE
The Médoc's most consistent appellation has two small villages as its major centres, St.-Julien-Beychevelle itself and, to the south, Beychevelle.

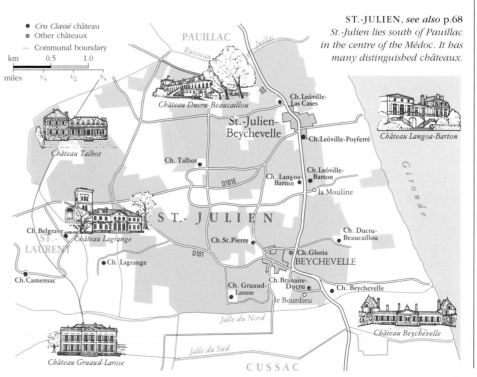

● *Cru Classé* château
● Other châteaux
— Communal boundary

ST.-JULIEN, *see also* p.68
St.-Julien lies south of Pauillac in the centre of the Médoc. It has many distinguished châteaux.

THE IMPORTANCE OF TERROIR

Bordeaux's château- or *cru*-system is based on the importance of *terroir*. The word "terroir" literally means "soil", but in a viticultural sense the term refers to the complete growing environment of a specific area, comprising only natural components such as soil, aspect, and climate. In the commune of St.-Julien, Château Talbot and Château Gruaud-Larose (*described below*)

demonstrate the dramatic effect that *terroir* can have on wines, since these neighbouring properties produce very different wines in peculiarly similar situations. The human factor used not to account for the difference in the wines because they used to be made by same Cordier winemaking team, and indeed this remains the case for the vast majority of vintages in distribution.

CHÂTEAU TALBOT

CLASSIFICATION
Fourth Growth

AREA UNDER VINE
102 ha (252 acres)

LOCATION
Plateau, west of St.-Julien

ASPECT
Southwest-facing

SOIL
Sand and medium-sized siliceous gravel over chalky-marl, and some iron-pan. The geological nature of these layers is different from that of Gruaud-Larose.

VIN DE PRESSE
6–8%

NEW OAK
One-third

CASK MATURATION
15–18 months

FINING AGENT
Egg white

FILTERING
Light plate

OENOLOGIST
Thierry Rustmann

GRAPE VARIETIES CULTIVATED
Cabernet sauvignon 66%, Merlot 24%, Cabernet franc 3%, Petit verdot 5%, Malbec 2%

DENSITY OF VINES
7,500–10,000 per ha (3,000–4,000 per acre)

AGE OF VINES
40 years

AVERAGE YIELD
42–45 hl/ha (189–202 cases per acre)

AVERAGE PRODUCTION AFTER REJECTION OF ANY UNSUITABLE WINES
40,000 cases

SECOND WINES
Connétable Talbot
(15–20% of production)

FERMENTATION
In stainless steel and wooden vats, maximum of 30°C (86°F), natural yeasts.

CHÂTEAU GRUAUD-LAROSE

CLASSIFICATION
Second Growth

AREA UNDER VINE
82 ha (203 acres)

LOCATION
Plateau, west of Beychevelle. Slightly higher than Talbot and nearer the river.

ASPECT
South-facing, undulating.

SOIL
Deep bed of large siliceous gravel over chalky-marl. This soil has a higher clay and iron-pan content than the Talbot soil, and so needs pipes to improve drainage.

VIN DE PRESSE
8–10%

NEW OAK
One-third

CASK MATURATION
16–18 months

FINING AGENT
Egg white

FILTERING
Light plate

OENOLOGIST
Georges Pauli

GRAPE VARIETIES CULTIVATED
Cabernet sauvignon 57%, Merlot 30%, Cabernet franc 7%, Petit verdot 4%, Malbec 2%

DENSITY OF VINES
7,500–10,000 per ha (3,000–4,000 per acre)

AGE OF VINES
40 years

AVERAGE YIELD
40–42 hl/ha (180–189 cases per acre)

AVERAGE PRODUCTION AFTER REJECTION OF ANY UNSUITABLE WINES
35,000 cases

SECOND WINE
Sarget de Gruaud-Larose
(15–20% of production)

FERMENTATION
In wooden vats (installed 1995), maximum of 30°C (86°F), natural yeasts.

DIFFERENCE BETWEEN THE WINES

The small difference in the proportion of grape varieties grown is unlikely to produce a discernible variation. Any difference should, in theory, be a greater fullness in the Talbot due to its higher ratio of Cabernet sauvignon, yet it is consistently lighter, while Gruaud-Larose has a fullness that can be almost fat. Despite both properties using the same plant density and methods of training and pruning, the average yield of Talbot is slightly higher than that of Gruaud-Larose. It is only in rare comparisons like this,

that we can discern just how significant the most minuscule changes in *terroir* can be. Variations in soil, location, elevation, and aspect affect the vine's metabolism, producing grapes of contrasting skin thickness with juice bearing different permutations of trace elements. The only human factor that magnifies the difference in these wines is the amount of *vin de presse* added. The lighter the wine, the less *vin de presse* it can support, thus even in this respect the winemakers' hands are tied by *terroir*.

THE WINE PRODUCERS OF
SAINT-JULIEN

CHÂTEAU BEYCHEVELLE
4ème Cru Classé
★★

The immaculate and colourful gardens of this château never fail to catch the breath of passers-by. Beychevelle also boasts one of the most famous legends of Bordeaux: its name is said to be a corruption of "*basse-voile*", the command to "lower sail". This arose because the Duc d'Épernon, a former owner who was also an admiral of France, apparently required the ships that passed through the Gironde to lower their sails in respect. His wife would then wave her kerchief in reply. This story, however, is not true. Épernon actually held the title of Baron de Beychevelle prior to being made the Amiral de Valette, and did not actually live at Beychevelle. I prefer the story of the sailors who lowered their trousers and revealed their sterns, which shocked the duchess, but made her children laugh. The wines are matured in wood for 20 months with 40 per cent new oak.

RED Medium- to full-bodied wines of good colour, ripe fruit, and an elegant oak and tannin structure. They can be quite fat in big years.

🍇 Cabernet sauvignon 59%, Merlot 30%, Cabernet franc 8%, Petit verdot 3%

🍷 12–20 years

Second Wine: ✓ *Réserve de l'Amiral*

Other wines: *Les Brulières de Beychevelle*

CHÂTEAU BRANAIRE-DUCRU
4ème Cru Classé
★ ❎

The vineyards of this château are situated further inland than those of Beychevelle and Ducru-Beaucaillou and its soil contains more clay and iron-pan than theirs, so the wine here is fuller and can be assertive, although never austere. It is matured in wood for 18 months, with up to 50 per cent new oak, and is remarkably consistent.

RED This is a quite full-bodied wine, which is richly flavoured, and can show a certain chocolate character in big years. It has a distinctive bouquet that sets it apart from other St.-Juliens.

🍇 Cabernet sauvignon 75%, Merlot 20%, Cabernet franc 5%

🍷 12–25 years

Second Wine: *Duluc*

CHÂTEAU LA BRIDANE
Cru Bourgeois
The owners of this property have maintained a vineyard here since the 14th century.

RED Attractive, fruity, medium-bodied wine that is easy to drink.

🍇 Cabernet sauvignon 55%, Merlot 45%

🍷 3–6 years

CHÂTEAU DUCRU-BEAUCAILLOU
2ème Cru Classé
★★★⯨

One of the super-Seconds, the quality of this classic St.-Julien château, the flagship property of the Borie empire, is both legendary and inimitable. In both good years and bad it remains remarkably consistent and, although relatively expensive, the price fetched falls short of those demanded by First Growths, making it a relative bargain. The wine is matured in wood for 20 months, with 50 per cent new oak.

RED This wine has a fine, deep colour that can belie its deft elegance of style. There is richness of fruit, complex spiciness of oak, great finesse, and exquisite balance.

🍇 Cabernet sauvignon 65%, Merlot 25%, Cabernet franc 10%

🍷 15–30 years

Second Wine: *La Croix*

CHÂTEAU DU GLANA
Cru Bourgeois
This property is under the same ownership as Château Plantey in Pauillac and Château la Commanderie in St.-Estèphe.

RED Du Glana is normally an unpretentious and medium-weight wine, but it excels in really hot years, when it can be deliciously ripe and juicy.

🍇 Cabernet sauvignon 68%, Merlot 25%, Petit verdot 5%, Cabernet franc 2%

🍷 3–6 years

CHÂTEAU GLORIA
★

Gloria excites opposite passions in wine drinkers: some consider it the equal of several *Cru Classé* wines – even superior in some cases – while others believe it earns an exaggerated price based on the reputation of merely a handful of vintages. Certainly the exceptional 1970 would not appear out of place in a blind tasting with some of the best *Crus Classés* of that vintage and there are lesser *Cru Classé* wines that most vintages of Gloria would match or beat. The wine is matured in wood for 16 months, with 40 per cent new oak.

RED A deep plum-coloured, full-bodied wine with masses of fruit and a rich, exuberant character.

🍇 Cabernet sauvignon 65%, Merlot 25%, Cabernet franc 5%, Petit verdot 5%

🍷 12–30 years

Second Wine: *Peymartin*

Other wines: *Haut-Beychevelle-Gloria*

CHÂTEAU GRUAUD-LAROSE
2ème Cru Classé
★★ ❎

This large property produces consistently great wines of a far more solid structure than most St.-Julien wines. Anyone who has tasted the supposedly mediocre 1980 Sarget de Gruaud-Larose (made from the wines rejected from the *grand vin*), will realize the true potential of Château Gruaud-Larose in any year.

RED Full-bodied, rich, and plummy wine with masses of fruit. Its spicy blackcurrant flavour is supported by a structure of ripe tannins.

🍇 Cabernet sauvignon 57%, Merlot 30%, Cabernet franc 7%, Petit verdot 4%, Malbec 2%

🍷 10–40 years

Second Wine: ✓ *Sarget de Gruaud-Larose*

Other Wines: *La Roseraie de Gruaud-Larose, Chevalier de Gruaud-Larose*

CHÂTEAU HORTEVIE
★⯨ ❎

There is no château as such on this property. This tiny vineyard's wine is made at Château Terrey-Gros-Caillou by Henri Pradère, the owner of both properties.

RED This is a silky-soft, rich, and succulent wine of excellent quality. This great-value wine is easily equivalent to *Cru Classé* quality.

🍇 Cabernet franc and Cabernet sauvignon 70%, Merlot 25%, Petit verdot 5%

🍷 7–15 years

CHÂTEAU DE LACOUFOURQUE

This tiny 1.25-hectare (three-acre) vineyard is mentioned not because of its past performance, but because it is unique in Bordeaux in being a 100 per cent Cabernet franc varietal, and it should be preserved.

RED This wine is sold in bulk as generic St.-Julien, which makes it impossible to make generalizations about its character.

🍇 Cabernet franc 100%

CHÂTEAU LAGRANGE
3ème Cru Classé
★★⯨ ❎

When the *Ban de Vendanges* was held at this Japanese-owned château in 1986, everyone realized that the Japanese were not simply content to apply state-of-the-art technology; they seriously intended to make Lagrange the best-quality wine in St.-Julien. They could well succeed in this ambition. The formidable Bordeaux oenologist Professor Peynaud has dubbed Lagrange a "dream estate", and describes its vinification centre as "unlike any other in the whole of Bordeaux". Each vat is, according to Peynaud, a "wine-making laboratory". The wine spends 20 months in wood with from 30 per cent new oak in light years to 50 per cent in big years.

RED A deeply-coloured wine with intense spicy-fruit aromas. It is full-bodied, silky-textured, and rich, with an exquisite balance and finish.

🍇 Cabernet sauvignon 66%, Merlot 27%, Cabernet franc and Petit verdot 7%

🍷 8–25 years

Second Wine: ✓ *Fiefs de Lagrange*

CHÂTEAU LALANDE-BORIE
★ ● ❤

Under the same ownership as the illustrious Château Ducru-Beaucaillou, Lalande-Borie is an inexpensive introduction to the wines of St.-Julien.

RED These are well-coloured wines, dominated by rich, blackcurranty Cabernet sauvignon flavours. Some vintages are fat and juicy, while others are more ethereal and tannic.

🍇 Cabernet sauvignon 65%, Merlot 25%, Cabernet franc 10%

⏱ 5–10 years

CHÂTEAU LANGOA-BARTON
3ème Cru Classé
★ ● ❤

This beautiful château was known as Pontet-Langlois until 1821, when it was purchased by Hugh Barton, grandson of "French Tom" Barton, the founder of Bordeaux *négociant* Barton & Guestier, and is now run by Anthony Barton. Both Langoa-Barton and Léoville-Barton are made here using very traditional techniques. The wine is matured in wood for 24 months, with a minimum of one-third new oak.

RED Attractive, easy-drinking wine with good fruit and acidity. It is lighter than the Léoville and can sometimes taste a little rustic in comparison, but has gained a degree of extra elegance and finesse in recent years.

🍇 Cabernet sauvignon 70%, Merlot 20%, Cabernet franc 8%, Petit verdot 2%

⏱ 10–25 years

Second Wine: ✓ *Lady Langoa* (a blend of Langoa-Barton and Léoville-Barton formerly sold simply as "*St.-Julien*")

CHÂTEAU LÉOVILLE-BARTON
2ème Cru Classé
★★☆ ❤

A quarter of the original Léoville estate was sold to Hugh Barton in 1826, but the château remained in the hands of the Léoville estate and is now called Château Léoville-Las Cases (*see below*). This wine is made by Anthony Barton at Langoa-Barton (*see above*). It is matured in wood for 24 months, with a minimum of one-third new oak. Although it is the better of the two Barton estates, it has been considered significantly beneath the standard set by Léoville-Las Cases – since the late 1980s, however, it has performed equally as well. A great château in ascendency.

RED Excellent wines of great finesse and breeding; they are darker, deeper, and richer than the Langoa-Barton, which is itself of very good quality. With maturity, a certain cedarwood complexity develops in this wine and gradually overwhelms its youthful *cassis* and vanilla character.

🍇 Cabernet sauvignon 70%, Merlot 20%, Cabernet franc 8%, Petit verdot 2%

⏱ 15–30 years

Second Wine: ✓ *Lady Langoa* (a blend of Langoa-Barton and Léoville-Barton formerly sold simply as "*St.-Julien*")

CHÂTEAU LÉOVILLE-LAS CASES
2ème Cru Classé
★★★

The label reads "*Grand Vin* de Léoville du Marquis de Las Cases", although this wine is commonly referred to as "Château Léoville-Las Cases". This estate represents the largest portion of the original Léoville estate. This is a great wine, and it certainly qualifies as one of the super-Seconds, while "Clos du Marquis" is one of the finest Second Wines available and probably the best value St.-Julien. The *Grand Vin* spends 18 months in wood, with 50 per cent new oak.

RED This dark, damson-coloured, full-bodied, and intensely flavoured wine is complex, classy, and aromatically stunning. A skilful amalgam of power and finesse.

🍇 Cabernet sauvignon 65%, Merlot 19%, Cabernet franc 13%, Petit verdot 3%

⏱ 15–35 years

Second Wine: ✓ *Clos du Marquis*
Other Wines: *Domaine de Bigarnon*

CHÂTEAU LÉOVILLE POYFERRÉ
2ème Cru Classé
★☆

This property once formed a quarter of the original Léoville estate, and probably suffers from being compared to the other two châteaux whose properties were also part of Léoville – Léoville-Barton and Léoville-Las Cases. Yet in the context of St.-Julien as a whole, it fares very well, and since 1982 it has had some extraordinary successes. Since the involvement of Michel Rolland from the mid-1990s, quality has gone up another gear. Wine is matured in wood for 18 months, with one-third new oak.

RED This wine has always been tannic, but is now much fuller in fruit, richer in flavour, and darker in colour, with oaky nuances.

🍇 Cabernet sauvignon 65%, Merlot 30%, Cabernet franc 5%

⏱ 12–25 years

Second Wine: *Moulin-Riche*

CHÂTEAU MOULIN-DE-LA-ROSE

This vineyard is well situated, being surrounded by *Crus Classés* on virtually all sides. Its wine is fermented in stainless steel and aged in cask for 18 months, with 25 per cent new oak.

RED This attractively aromatic wine is unusually concentrated and firm for a minor St.-Julien, but rounds out well after a few years in bottle.

🍇 Cabernet sauvignon 65%, Merlot 25%, Petit verdot 8%, Cabernet franc 2%

⏱ 6–12 years

CHÂTEAU ST.-PIERRE
4ème Cru Classé
★☆❤

This property was bought in 1982 by Henri Martin, who owns the *bourgeois* growth, Château Gloria. The wine is matured in wood for between 18 and 20 months with 50 per cent new oak.

RED Once an astringent, coarse wine that is now ripe, fat, and full of cedarwood, spice, and fruit.

🍇 Cabernet sauvignon 70%, Merlot 20%, Cabernet franc 10%,

⏱ 8–25 years

Second Wine: *Saint-Louis-le-Bosq*
Other wines: *Clos d'Uza*

CHÂTEAU TALBOT
4ème Cru Classé
★☆❤

Named after the English Commander who fell at the Battle of Castillon in 1453, this property remains under Cordier family ownership, while its sister château Gruaud-Larose now belongs to Groupe Taillan. To contrast the style of these two St.-Juliens is justifiable, but to compare their quality is not: Château Talbot is a great wine and the closer to the style of a classic St.-Julien, but intrinsically it does not have the quality nor the consistency of Château Gruaud-Larose (*see also* p.82). Talbot is matured in wood for between 15 and 18 months, with one-third new oak.

RED A graceful wine, medium-bodied, with elegant fruit, gently structured by ripe oak tannins and capable of considerable finesse.

🍇 Cabernet sauvignon 66%, Merlot 24%, Cabernet franc 3%, Petit verdot 5%, Malbec 2%

⏱ 8–30 years

Second Wine: ✓ *Connétable Talbot*
Other Wines: *Caillou Blanc*

CHÂTEAU TERREY-GROS-CAILLOU
Cru Bourgeois
★☆❤

This establishment is under the same ownership as Château Hortevie (whose wine it also makes), and is itself a top-performing property.

RED This beautifully coloured, medium- to full-bodied wine always has rich fruit and is often equivalent to a good *Cru Classé*.

🍇 Cabernet sauvignon 65%, Merlot 30%, Petit verdot 5%

⏱ 5–12 years

CHÂTEAU TEYNAC
❤

This fine gravel vineyard once formed part of *Cru Classé* Château Saint-Pierre.

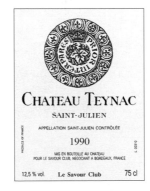

RED Well-balanced, medium- to full-bodied wine with good spice and a firm tannin structure.

🍇 Cabernet sauvignon 65%, Merlot 35%

⏱ 6–10 years

MARGAUX

Situated in the south of the Médoc district, Margaux is the most famous of all Bordeaux appellations. While it bathes in the reflected glory of its namesake First Growth, it is also the largest and most inconsistent of the four classic Médoc appellations.

WHILE THE OTHER THREE great Médoc AOCs – St.-Estèphe, Pauillac, and St.-Julien – are connected in one unbroken chain of vineyards, Margaux stands alone to the south, with its vines spread across five communes – Labarde, Arsac, and Cantenac to the south, Margaux in the centre, and Soussans to the north.

Margaux and Cantenac are the most important communes and, of course, Margaux contains the First Growth of Château Margaux itself. Cantenac has a slightly larger area under vine and no less than eight classified growths, including the star-performing Château Palmer, which was partly owned by the late Peter Sichel.

Margaux and Pauillac are the only appellations in the Médoc with First Growth vineyards, but only Margaux can boast vineyards in all five categories of the Classification. It also has more *Cru Classé* châteaux than any other Médoc appellation, including an impressive total of ten Third Growths.

FACTORS AFFECTING TASTE AND QUALITY

LOCATION
In the centre of the Haut-Médoc, some 28 km (17 miles) northwest of Bordeaux, encompassing the communes of Cantenac, Soussans, Arsac, and Labarde in addition to Margaux itself.

CLIMATE
As for the Médoc (*see* p.66).

ASPECT
One large, low-lying plateau centring on Margaux plus several modest outcrops that slope west towards the forest.

SOIL
Shallow, pebbly, siliceous gravel over a gravel subsoil interbedded with limestone.

VITICULTURE AND VINIFICATION
Only red wines have the right to the appellation. All grapes must be destalked. On average, between five and ten per cent *vin de presse* may be used in the wine, according to the needs of the vintage. Skin-contact duration averages 15–25 days, with the period of maturation in cask currently varying between 18 and 24 months.

PRIMARY GRAPE VARIETIES
Cabernet sauvignon, Cabernet franc, Merlot

SECONDARY GRAPE VARIETIES
Carmenère, Malbec, Petit verdot

MARGAUX CRU CLASSÉ STATISTICS

***Crus Classés* in AOC Margaux**
21 châteaux (by number: 35% of *Crus Classés* in the Médoc) with 854 ha (2,110 acres) of vineyards (by area: 35% of *Crus Classés* in the Médoc and 64% of this AOC)

1st Growths
1 château (by number: 25% of 1st Growths in the Médoc) with 75 ha (185 acres) of vineyards (by area: 25% of 1st Growths in the Médoc)

2nd Growths
5 châteaux (by number: 36% of 2nd Growths in the Médoc) with 271 ha (670 acres) of vineyards (by area: 34% of 2nd Growths in the Médoc)

3rd Growths
10 châteaux (by number: 72% of 3rd Growths in the Médoc) with 305 ha (754 acres) of vineyards (by area: 72% of 3rd Growths in the Médoc)

4th Growths
3 châteaux (by number: 30% of 4th Growths in the Médoc) with 105 ha (259 acres) of vineyards (by area: 22% of 4th Growths in the Médoc)

5th Growths
2 châteaux (by number: 11% of 5th Growths in the Médoc) with 98 ha (242 acres) of vineyards (by area: 13% of 5th Growths in the Médoc)

CHÂTEAU MARGAUX
Margaux's celebrated First Growth vineyards are matched by the grandeur of the building itself. Both the building and the wine are justifiably famous.

MARGAUX, *see also* p.68
Of the classic Médoc appellations, Margaux – the most famous – stands alone to the south, and can boast more Cru Classé *châteaux than any of the others.*

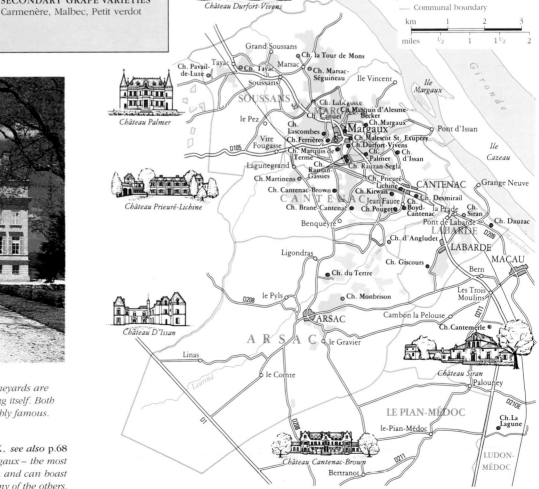

MARGAUX PROFILE

Appellation covers: parts of the communes of Arsac, Cantenac, Labarde, Margaux, and Soussans as follows.

REGION	SIZE OF COMMUNE	AOC AREA UNDER VINE	VINE AREA AS PROPORTION OF	
			COMMUNE	APPELLATION
Arsac	3,219 ha (7,954 acres)	203 ha (502 acres)	6%	15%
Cantenac	1,417 ha (3,502 acres)	370 ha (914 acres)	26%	28%
Labarde	475 ha (1,174 acres)	106 ha (262 acres)	22%	8%
Margaux	843 ha (2,083 acres)	390 ha (964 acres)	46%	29%
Soussans	1,558 ha (3,850 acres)	271 ha (670 acres)	17%	20%
TOTAL	7,512 ha (18,562 acres)	1,340 ha (3,311 acres)	18%	100%

Total size of all five communes: 7,512 ha (18,562 acres)
Total AOC area under vine: 1,340 ha (3,311 acres) (18% of communes)
Surface area of *Crus Classés*: 854 ha (2,110 acres)
(11% of communes, 64% of AOC)

NEW CELLAR AT CHÂTEAU MARGAUX
Evidence of the investment made in Château Margaux since the late 1970s is the refurbished wine store and its full complement of new oak barrels.

SOUTIRAGE, CHÂTEAU MARGAUX
As the wine matures in the barrel, its clarity is checked regularly. It spends between 18 and 24 months in new oak.

AN OUTSTANDING WINE

If the massive Pauillac wines of Château Latour and Château Mouton are an object lesson in how it is possible to bombard the senses with power and flavour, and yet retain quite remarkable finesse, then the exquisite wines of Margaux at their very best are perfect proof that complexity does not necessarily issue from an intense concentration of flavour.

However, this is not to suggest that Margaux wines do not actually possess some concentration; indeed Château Margaux has a particularly remarkable concentration of flavour, and it remains the quintessential wine of this appellation.

CHÂTEAU CANTENAC BROWN
This Third Growth was originally part of Château Boyd, but after the Boyds and Browns – who were joined by marriage in the late 18th century – had a family crisis, the property was divided into Château Boyd-Cantenac and Château Cantenac Brown.

CHÂTEAU D'ANGLUDET
Angludet, home of the Sichel family, dates back to Bertrand d'Angludet, who in 1313 swore allegiance to Edward II of England. Owned by Sichel from 1960 till 1999, this property exudes its English heritage, with swans gliding on the brook at the bottom of the garden.

THE WINE PRODUCERS OF
MARGAUX

CHÂTEAU ANGLUDET
Cru Bourgeois
★✩

This château is owned by the Sichel family, who are also part-owners of the star-performing Château Palmer. Since the late 1980s this château has established itself as *Cru Classé* quality. It will be interesting to see what the next decade brings. The wine is matured in wood for 12 months, with up to a third new oak.

RED Vividly coloured, medium- to full-bodied wines with excellent fruit, finesse, and finish – classic Margaux.

🍇 Cabernet sauvignon 55%, Merlot 35%, Petit verdot 10%

🍷 10–20 years

Second Wine: *La Ferme d'Angludet*

Other Wines: *Clairet d'Angludet*

CHÂTEAU D'ARSAC
AOC Margaux *Cru Bourgeois*

Until recently this was the only property in Arsac not to benefit from the Margaux appellation. Since a change in ownership this estate has expanded its vineyards from just over 11 hectares to 102, of which 40 are now classified as Margaux. The wines are matured in wood for 12 to 18 months, with 20 per cent new oak.

RED These are deep-coloured, full-bodied wines.

🍇 Cabernet sauvignon 80%, Merlot 15%, Cabernet franc 5%

🍷 7–15 years

Second Wine: *Château Ségur-d'Arsac*

Other wines: *Château Le Monteil-d'Arsac*

CHÂTEAU BEL-AIR MARQUIS D'ALIGRE
❽

Château Bel-Air Marquis d'Aligre was classified *Cru Bourgeois* in 1932, but was not included in the *Syndicat's* 1978 list, although it is superior to a few that were. The vineyard has limestone subsoil and only organic fertilizers are used.

RED Well-made wines of fine colour, elegant fruit, with a distinctive style are produced by Château Bel-Air Marquis d'Aligre.

🍇 Merlot 35%, Cabernet sauvignon 30%, Cabernet franc 20%, Petit verdot 15%

🍷 6–12 years

Second Wine: *Château Bel-Air-Marquis-de-Pomereu*

CHÂTEAU BOYD-CANTENAC
3ème Cru Classé

Château Boyd-Cantenac is a property producing traditional-style wines from old vines. The wine is made at owner Monsieur Guillemet's other property, Château Pouget, under the supervision of Professor Peynaud. It is matured in wood for 24 months, with 30 per cent new oak and, in my opinion, would benefit from more Merlot and no Petit verdot.

RED Full-bodied, firm wine of good colour that needs a long time in bottle to soften. The mediocre 1980 was particularly successful.

🍇 Cabernet sauvignon 70%, Merlot 20%, Cabernet franc 5%, Petit verdot 5%

🍷 12–20 years

CHÂTEAU BRANE-CANTENAC
2ème Cru Classé
★✩★

This property is a superb plateau of immaculately kept vines situated on gravel over limestone and is owned and run by Henri Lurton. The wine is matured in wood for 18 months, with 25 to 30 per cent new oak.

RED These stylish wines have a smoky-cream and new-oak bouquet, deliciously rich fruit, and finesse on the palate. They are top-quality wines, velvety and beautifully balanced.

🍇 Cabernet sauvignon 70%, Cabernet franc 15%, Merlot 13%, Petit verdot 2%

🍷 8–25 years

Second Wines: *Le Baron de Brane*

Other wines: *Domaine de Fontarney, Château Notton*

CHÂTEAU CANTENAC BROWN
3ème Cru Classé

Ever since I drank a 50-year-old half-bottle of 1926 Cantenac Brown in splendid condition, I have had a soft spot for this château, which has, frankly, been disproportionate to the quality of its wines. Despite heavy investment after being purchased by AXA these wines have not noticeably improved, although in the late 1980s, early 1990s there was hope and some evidence that they might. The wines are matured in wood for 18 months, with one-third new oak.

RED This wine has always had a similar weight to Brane-Cantenac, but with a less velvety and generally more rustic style. The vintages of the 1980s have more finesse than those of the 1970s, but the quality and concentration took a sharp upward turn in 1989 and 1990.

🍇 Cabernet sauvignon 65%, Merlot 25%, Cabernet franc 10%

🍷 10–25 years

Second Wine: *Canuet*

Other Wines: *Lamartine*

CHÂTEAU CHARMANT

This property was not classified as a *Cru Bourgeois* in 1932, nor listed by the *Syndicat* in 1978, but it certainly deserves recognition today.

RED An elegant wine with plenty of fruit and a soft finish. It makes delightful drinking when young.

🍇 Cabernet sauvignon 60%, Merlot 35%, Cabernet franc 5%

🍷 3–8 years

CHÂTEAU DAUZAC
5ème Cru Classé
★

Now owned by MAIF and managed by Vignobles André Lurton, the quality of the wines from this château has steadily increased since the mid-1990s. The wine, which is matured in wood for 16 to 18 months with one-third new oak, is steadily improving.

RED Ruby-coloured, medium-bodied, round, and attractively fruity wines that are easy to drink.

🍇 Cabernet sauvignon 65%, Merlot 25%, Cabernet franc 5%, Petit verdot 5%

🍷 6–12 years

Second Wine: *Labarde*

Other wine: *La Bastide*

CHÂTEAU DESMIRAIL
3ème Cru Classé
✩

A "château with no château" (because the building that was its château was purchased by Château Marquis d'Alesme-Becker), Desmirail has been on the ascent since its purchase by the Lurton family, but it still has a way to go before it becomes a true third growth. Owned and run by Denis Lurton. The wine is matured in wood for 20 months, with 25 to 50 per cent new oak; Professor Peynaud advises.

RED A medium-bodied wine that is nicely balanced with gentle fruit flavours and supple tannins. It is well made and gradually gaining in finesse.

🍇 Cabernet sauvignon 80%, Merlot 10%, Cabernet franc 9%, Petit verdot 1%

🍷 7–15 years

Second Wine: *Château Baudry*

Other wines: *Domaine de Fontarney*

CHÂTEAU DEYREM-VALENTIN

This château was classified *Cru Bourgeois* in 1932, but was not included in the *Syndicat's* 1978 list, although it is superior to a few that were. Its vineyards adjoin those of Château Lascombes.

RED Honest, medium-bodied, fruity wine of some elegance.

🍇 Cabernet sauvignon 45%, Merlot 45%, Cabernet franc 5%, Petit verdot 5%

🍷 4–10 years

CHÂTEAU DURFORT-VIVENS
2ème Cru Classé
★❽

Owned by Gonzague Lurton, who is married to Claire Villars, the Administrator of châteaux Chasse-Spleen and Haut-Bages-Libéral. Dufort-Vivans has become one of the best value cru classé wines of Margaux since the mid-1990s. This property matures its wine in wood for 18 to 20 months, with up to one-third new oak.

RED Higher tannic structure than Brane-Cantenac, but without the luxurious new-oak character, and with less fruit and charm. The 1985 was particularly rich and impressive.

🍇 Cabernet sauvignon 82%, Cabernet franc 10%, Merlot 8%

🍷 10–25 years

Second Wine: *Second de Durfort*

Other Wines: *Domaine de Curé-Bourse*

CHÂTEAU FERRIÈRE
3ème Cru Classé
★❽

When managed by Château Lascombes this was little more than second-label status, but it has gained in both exposure and quality since this property was purchased by the Villars family.

RED Quick-maturing wine of medium weight and accessible fruit.

🍇 Cabernet sauvignon 75%, Merlot 20%, Petit verdot 5%

🍷 4–8 years

Second Wine: *Les Remparts de Ferrière*

CHÂTEAU GISCOURS
3ème Cru Classé
★✩

This property is situated in the commune of Labarde. It was purchased in 1952 by the Tari family who have restored the château, the vineyard and the quality of its wine to their former glory. In 1995 the château was sold to Eric Albada Jelgerms, a Dutch businessman who has at least maintained the quality and arguably improved it. The wine is matured in wood for 20 to 34 months, with 50 per cent new oak.

RED Vividly coloured wine, rich in fruit and finesse. Its vibrant style keeps it remarkably fresh for many years.

🍇 Cabernet sauvignon 75%, Merlot 22%, Cabernet franc 2%, Petit verdot 1%

🍷⊶ 8–30 years

Second Wine: *La Sirène de Giscours*
Other Wines: *Cantelaude*

CHÂTEAU LA GURGUE

This property was classified *Cru Bourgeois* in 1932, but not included in the *Syndicat's* 1978 list, although it is superior to a few that were. Its proprietor also owns the *Cru Classé* Haut-Bages-Libéral, and the *Cru Bourgeois* Chasse-Spleen.

RED Soft, elegant, medium-bodied wine of attractive flavour and some finesse.

🍇 Cabernet sauvignon 70%, Merlot 25%, Petit verdot 5%

🍷⊶ 4–12 years

CHÂTEAU D'ISSAN
3ème Cru Classé
★★

This beautiful 17th-century château is frequently cited as the most impressive in the entire Médoc, and its remarkable wines, matured in wood for 18 months, with up to one-third new oak, are consistently just as spectacular.

RED This wine really is glorious! Its luxuriant bouquet is immediately seductive, its fruit is unbelievably rich and sumptuous. A great wine of great finesse.

🍇 Cabernet sauvignon 85%, Merlot 15%

🍷⊶ 10–40 years

Second Wine: *Blason d'Issan*
Other Wines: *De Candel*

CHÂTEAU KIRWAN
3ème Cru Classé
★✫Ⓥ

Château Kirwan is a well-run and improving property owned by the Bordeaux *négociant* Schröder & Schÿler with Michel Rolland consulting. The wine is matured in wood for 18 to 24 months, with up to 50 per cent new oak.

RED Deep-coloured, full-bodied, rich and concentrated wines that are well made and gaining in generosity, riper tannins, and new oak influence with each passing vintage.

🍇 Cabernet sauvignon 40%, Merlot 30%, Cabernet franc 20%, Petit verdot 10%

🍷⊶ 10–35 years

Second Wine: *Les Charmes de Kirwan*

CHÂTEAU LABÉGORCE
★Ⓥ

This château was classified *Cru Bourgeois* in 1932, but not included in the *Syndicat's* 1978 list. Since Hubert Perrodo, a wine-loving oil tycoon, purchased Labégorce in 1989, the quality and price of its wines have increased steadily. The wine is matured in wood for 18 months, with up to one-third new oak.

RED Well-coloured wine with good balance of concentration and finesse.

🍇 Cabernet sauvignon 55%, Merlot 40%, Cabernet franc 5%

🍷⊶ 5–15 years

CHÂTEAU LABÉGORCE-ZÉDÉ
★✫Ⓥ

Classified *Cru Bourgeois* in 1932, but not included in the 1978 list, although it is one of the best non-*Cru Classé* wines of the commune.

RED Fine flavour and great length, combined with a certain complexity, give the wines of this château a slight edge over those of Château Labégorce.

🍇 Cabernet sauvignon 50%, Merlot 35%, Cabernet franc 10%, Petit verdot 5%

🍷⊶ 5–15 years

Second Wine: *Château de l'Amiral*

CHÂTEAU LASCOMBES
2ème Cru Classé
★★

Owned by Bass Group, the wines of this large property have always been good, yet they have improved dramatically, under René Vanatelle.

It was Vantaelle who recognized that only 50 of Lascombe's 83 hectares (125 of 208 acres) were of authentic second growth potential. He therefore segregated the vineyard and sold the lesser wines as Château Segonnes. This accounted for the noticeable step up in quality in the 1980s. Then in 1997, the year before he retired, Vanatelle introduced a true second wine, Chevalier des Lascombes, which has pushed standards up yet another gear, before handing over to Bruno Lemoine, formerly of Montrose. The wine is matured in wood for 14 to 20 months, with one-third new oak.

RED Full-bodied, rich, and concentrated wine with ripe fruit, a lovely cedarwood complexity, and supple tannin.

🍇 Cabernet sauvignon 55%, Merlot 40%, Petit verdot 5%

🍷⊶ 8–30 years

Second Wine: *Chevalier Lascombes,*
Other wines: *Château Segonnes, Gombaud, Rosé de Lascombes, Vin Sec Chevalier Lascombes*

CHÂTEAU MALESCOT ST.-EXUPÉRY
3ème Cru Classé
★

English-owned until 1955 when it was purchased by Roger Zuger, whose brother owns Château Marquis-d'Alesme-Becker. The wine is matured in wood for 18 months, with 20 per cent new oak.

RED Richer, more complex wines have been produced since 1996.

🍇 Cabernet sauvignon 50%, Merlot 35%, Cabernet franc 10%, Petit verdot 5%

🍷⊶ 8–25 years

Second Wine: *Château De Loyac, La Dame de Malescot*
Other wines: *Balardin*

CHÂTEAU MARGAUX
1er Cru Classé
★★★

This is the most famous wine in the world and, since its glorious rebirth in 1978, the greatest. Its quality may occasionally be matched, but it is never surpassed. Purchased in 1977 for 72 million francs by the late André Mentzelopoulos, who spent an equal sum renovating it, this fabulous jewel in the crown of the Médoc is now run by his daughter, Corinne Mentzelopoulos. Both Château Margaux and its Second Wine, "Pavillon Rouge", are vinified in oak vats and matured for 18 to 24 months in 100 per cent new oak.

RED If finesse can be picked up on the nose, then the stunning and complex bouquet of Château Margaux is the yardstick. The softness, finesse, and velvety texture of this wine belies its depth. Amazingly rich and concentrated, with an elegant, long, and complex

finish supported by ripe tannins and wonderful smoky-creamy oak aromas. This is as near perfection as we will ever get.

🍇 Cabernet sauvignon 75%, Merlot 20%, Cabernet franc and Petit verdot 5%

🍷⊶ 15–50 years

Second Wine: ✓ *Pavillon Rouge du Château Margaux*
Other wines: *Pavillon Blanc du Château Margaux*

CHÂTEAU MARQUIS D'ALESME-BECKER
3ème Cru Classé

Like Château Malescot St.-Exupéry, this was English-owned until purchased by Jean-Claude Zuger, who also purchased the maison of neighbouring Desmirail to act as its château. The wine is matured in wood for 12 months, with one-sixth new oak.

RED Austere and charmless wines from my point of view, although they have their admirers. They are well made, but lack sufficient selection, although the *terroir* has potential.

🍇 Cabernet sauvignon 40%, Merlot 30%, Cabernet franc 20%, Petit verdot 10%

🍷⊶ 8–20 years

Second Wine: *Marquise d'Alesme*

CHÂTEAU MARQUIS-DE-TERME
4ème Cru Classé

Situated next to Château Margaux, this once majestic estate developed the reputation for producing tight, tannic, one-dimensional wines, but its quality has picked up since the late 1970s and has been performing extremely well since 1983. The wine is matured in wood for 24 months, with one-third new oak.

RED Appears to be developing a style that is ripe and rich, with definite and delightful signs of new oak. The 1984 was quite a revelation.

🍇 Cabernet sauvignon 60%, Merlot 30%, Petit verdot 7%, Cabernet franc 3%

🍷⊶ 10–25 years

Second Wine: *Terme des Goudat*

CHÂTEAU MARSAC-SÉGUINEAU

This property was classified *Cru Bourgeois* in 1932, but not included in the *Syndicat's* 1978 list, although it is superior to a few that were. The vineyards of this château include some plots that originally belonged to a *Cru Classé*.

RED Medium- to full-bodied wines of good bouquet and a soft style.

🍇 Cabernet sauvignon 65%, Merlot 35%

🍷⊶ 5–12 years

Second Wine: *Château Gravières-de-Marsac*

CHÂTEAU MONBRISON
Cru Bourgeois
★ ✪

These vineyards used to be part of *Cru Classé* Château Desmirail; the wines were excellent ten years ago, and now vie with those of true *Cru Classé* standard.

RED This Château's second label offers a brilliant selection of beautifully deep-coloured wines with spicy-oak, super-rich juicy fruit, and a fine structure of supple tannin.

🍇 Merlot 35%, Cabernet franc 30%, Cabernet sauvignon 30%, Petit verdot 5%

⌛ 8–15 years

Second Wine: ☑️ *Château Cordat*

CHÂTEAU MONTBRUN

Château Montbrun was classified *Cru Bourgeois* in 1932, but not included in the *Syndicat's* 1978 list, although it is superior to a few that were. This used to be part of *Cru Classé* Château Palmer.

RED Beautifully made, ripe, and juicy, medium- to full-bodied, Merlot-dominated wines.

🍇 Merlot 75%, Cabernet franc and Cabernet sauvignon 25%

⌛ 5–12 years

CHÂTEAU PALMER
3ème Cru Classé
★★☆

Only Château Margaux outshines this property, jointly owned by Belgian, French, and British (the Sichel family) interests. Château Palmer 1961 and 1966 regularly fetch prices at auction that equal those fetched by the First Growths. Judged at the very highest level, it could be more consistent. It is usually excellent, but not always astonishing – although when it is, it can stand shoulder to shoulder with First Growths in a blind tasting. A true super-second that promises to achieve even greater heights since the introduction of Alto Ego, a sort of super-premium of second wines, in 1998. The wine is matured in wood for 18 to 24 months, with one-third new oak.

RED Deep-, almost opaque-coloured wine and masses of *cassis* fruit and an exceedingly rich, intense, and complex construction of creamy, spicy, cedarwood, and vanilla flavours, supported by a fine tannic structure.

🍇 Cabernet sauvignon 50%, Merlot 40%, Cabernet franc 7%, Petit verdot 3%

⌛ 12–35 years

Second Wine: ☑️ *Alto Ego*, ☑️ *Réserve du Général*

CHÂTEAU PONTAC-LYNCH
★ ✪

This property was classified *Cru Bourgeois* in 1932, but not included in the *Syndicat's* 1978 list, although it is superior to a few that were. The vineyards are well-situated, and surrounded by *Crus Classés*.

RED Richly perfumed, deeply coloured, full-bodied wines of good structure.

🍇 Cabernet sauvignon and Merlot 47%, Cabernet franc 45%, Petit verdot 8%

⌛ 6–15 years

Second Wine: *Château Pontac-Phénix*

CHÂTEAU POUGET
4ème Cru Classé
❓

Under the same ownership as Boyd-Cantenac, this property houses the winemaking and storage facilities for both châteaux. The wine is matured in wood for 22 to 24 months, with 30 per cent new oak.

RED Well-coloured, full-bodied wine with good depth of flavour. Good, but not great, and could be more consistent.

🍇 Cabernet sauvignon 70%, Merlot 17%, Cabernet franc 8%, Petit verdot 5%

⌛ 10–25 years

CHÂTEAU PRIEURÉ-LICHINE
4ème Cru Classé
★

The late Alexis Lichine purchased Château Prieuré in 1951 and added his name to it. To develop the small run-down vineyard he bought various prized plots of vines from Palmer, Kirwan, Giscours, Boyd-Cantenac, Brane-Cantenac, and Durfort-Vivens – some 60 hectares (148 acres). The composite Classification must be higher than its official status – the wines certainly are. Lichine's son Sacha ran the property until 1999, when he sold it to its current owners, the Ballande family. The wines are matured in wood for 19 months, with one-third new oak.

RED Well-coloured, full-bodied wines, plummy and rich, with good blackcurrant fruit supported by supple tannins and a touch of vanilla-oak.

🍇 Cabernet sauvignon 54%, Merlot 39%, Cabernet franc 2%, Petit verdot 5%

⌛ 7–20 years

Second Wine: *Château De Clairefont*

CHÂTEAU RAUZAN-GASSIES
2ème Cru Classé
★

Until the French Revolution of 1789, this property and Château Rauzan-Ségla were one large estate. The globe-trotting Professor Peynaud was brought in to steer this wine back on course in the early 1980s but he failed miserably. Jean-Louis Camp, formerly of Loudenne, seems to be having more success. The wine is matured in wood for 17 to 20 months, with 20 per cent new oak, although there is little evidence of it on the palate.

RED The last vintage I really enjoyed was 1961; 1996 and particularly 1998 could herald an upturn in quality.

🍇 Cabernet sauvignon 40%, Merlot 39%, Cabernet franc 20%, Petit verdot 1%

⌛ 7–15 years

Second Wine: *Enclos de Moncabon*

CHÂTEAU RAUZAN-SÉGLA
2ème Cru Classé
★★☆

The quality of this once-disappointing château began improving in the 1980s due to significant investment in the property from its owner, the Bordeaux *négociant* house of Eschenauer, which also instigated a far stricter selection of the *Grand Vin*. In 1994 Rauzan-Ségla was sold to Chanel, the under-bidder for Latour (which was sold by Allied-Lyons to the French industrialist François Pinault), since when key personnel from the First Growth have been brought in to keep the improvements at this château in full swing. The wine is matured in wood for 20 months, with 50 per cent new oak, and is currently one of Bordeaux's top-performing Second Growths.

RED In classic years, this wine is deep and dark, with a powerful tannic construction, and more than enough intensely flavoured fruit to match. Lesser vintages are dark for the year, but much more lush, with softer tannins.

🍇 Cabernet sauvignon 65%, Merlot 30%, Cabernet franc 5%

⌛ 15–30 years

Second Wine: *Ségla*

Other Wines: *Lamouroux*

CHÂTEAU SIRAN
★★☆ ✪

Château Siran was classified *Cru Bourgeois* in 1932, but not included in the *Syndicat's* 1978 list, although it is superior to a few that were. The vineyard is well situated, with immaculately manicured vines that border those of châteaux Giscours and Dauzac. The wine is matured in wood for 24 months, with one-third new oak, in air-conditioned cellars. Monsieur Miailhe, the owner, also likes to provide his guests with every facility.

RED Stylish, aromatic wines of good body, creamy-spicy fruit, length, and obvious class. Easily equivalent to *Cru Classé* quality.

🍇 Cabernet sauvignon 50%, Merlot 25%, Petit verdot 15%, Cabernet franc 10%

⌛ 8–20 years

Second Wine: *Château Bellegarde*

Other wines: *Château St.-Jacques*

CHÂTEAU TAYAC
Cru Bourgeois

As Bernard Ginestet, whose family owned Château Margaux for 40 years, once wrote, "this is one of the largest of the smaller properties, and one of the smallest of the larger".

RED Firm, medium- to full-bodied wines of good character, although somewhat rustic; they tend to be coarse in lesser years.

🍇 Cabernet sauvignon 65%, Merlot 25%, Cabernet franc 5%, Petit verdot 5%

⌛ 6–12 years

CHÂTEAU DU TERTRE
5ème Cru Classé
★★☆

An underrated *Cru Classé,* this château has well-situated vineyards. Under the same ownership as Giscours since 1998. The wine is matured in wood for 24 months, with 25 per cent new oak.

RED Although the scent of violets is supposed to be a common characteristic in the wines of Margaux, this is one of the few in which I pick it up. The wine is medium- to full-bodied, rich in fragrant fruit, and has excellent balance, with obvious class.

🍇 Cabernet sauvignon 85%, Cabernet franc 5%, Merlot 10%

⌛ 8–25 years

CHÂTEAU LA TOUR DE MONS
Cru Bourgeois

These wines are aged in wood for 22 months, with 20 per cent new oak and have improved enormously since the late 1980s. Easily equivalent to *Cru Classé* quality.

RED As richly flavoured as ever, but without the tannins or acidity that used to be this wine's pitfall.

🍇 Cabernet sauvignon 45%, Merlot 40%, Cabernet franc 10%, Petit verdot 5%

⌛ 10–30 years

Second Wine: *Château Rucheterre*

CHÂTEAU DES TROIS-CHARDONS
★☆ ✪

A tiny production of very high-quality wine from a château named after the current owner, a Monsieur Chardon, and his two sons.

RED Ultra-clean, soft, fruity but serious wines of some finesse and well defined Margaux character.

🍇 Cabernet sauvignon 50%, Merlot 40%, Cabernet franc 10%

⌛ 6–15 years

GRAVES, CÉRONS, SAUTERNES, AND BARSAC

The finest red Graves wines are produced in Pessac-Léognan, good red and improving dry white wines in the centre of Graves, and the great sweet wines of Sauternes and Barsac in the South. The emphasis in production is on classic red wines.

THE SILKY-SMOOTH RED WINES of the Graves district have been famous since the Middle Ages, when they were protected by local laws that punished those who dared to blend them with other Bordeaux wines. Château Haut-Brion was the only red wine outside the Médoc to be classified in 1855, and such was its reputation that it was placed alongside the First Growths of Latour, Lafite, Mouton, and Margaux. Beneath Haut-Brion, there are a few great wines equivalent in quality to Second or Third Growth but only a few.

The relative lack of superstars in Graves is offset by a higher base quality of wine and greater consistency of performance in the red wines at least. There are 43 communes in this appellation. Much the best are Léognan, Talence, and Pessac, after which Martillac and Portets are the most outstanding, followed by Illats and Podensac. All the greatest wines are therefore in the north of the Graves district, amid the urban sprawl of Bordeaux, and this presents something of a problem. The once-peaceful left bank of the Garonne is slowly and inexorably disappearing. As the city bursts outwards, more rural vineyards are encircled by the concrete jungle, and many quite simply vanish. How many Bordeaux aficionados who fly directly to the airport in Mérignac stop to consider the cost of such progress? In 1908 there were 30 winemaking properties in the commune of Mérignac; today there is just one – Château Picque-Caillou. The conurbated communes of Cadaujac, Gradignan, Léognan, Martillac, Mérignac, Pessac, Talence, and Villenave d'Ornon have lost 214 wine châteaux over the same period.

THE PROBLEM OF WHITE GRAVES SOLVED

Well almost! While the quality and reputation of the red wines have always been well established, white Graves had a serious identity problem that came to a crisis point in the mid-1980s. Although fine white Graves were being produced, most of it was in the northern communes, but they were tarred with the same brush as the worst white wines from further south. It was not simply a north-south divide; there was also an identity problem – should they be making rich, oak-aged blends or light and fluffy Sauvignon blanc? Paradoxically, the worst wines came from some of the best properties in the north, produced by winemakers who

FERMENTATION VATS AT CHÂTEAU HAUT-BRION
This illustrious château was one of the first to install stainless-steel vats.

GRAVES, CÉRONS, SAUTERNES, AND BARSAC, *see also* p.59
The winemaking area that includes Graves, Cérons, Sauternes, and Barsac forms a swathe that sweeps down from Bordeaux, parallel with the Garonne.

VINES AT HAUT-BRION
Rose bushes at the end of each row act as a pest early-warning system.

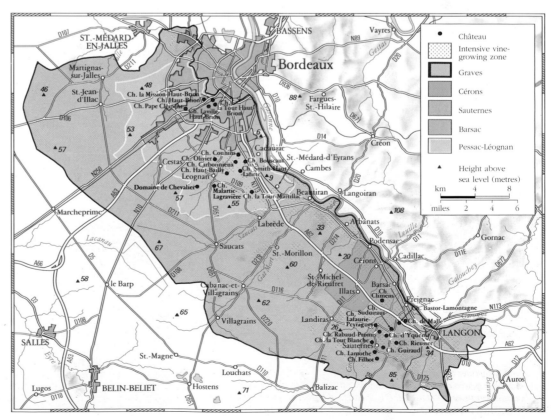

THE CLASSIFICATION OF GRAVES

The only Graves property to be classified in 1855 was Château Haut-Brion. The *Syndicat* for the defence of the Graves appellation wanted to create its own classification, but was prevented from doing so until the 1921 law was changed in 1949. The first classification was not made until 1953, and this itself was later modified in 1959.

Distinction is made between red wines and white wines, but no attempt at ranking between the various growths is made – they all have the right to use the term *Cru Classé*. It can be seen from the current size of the classified properties listed below that less than 19 per cent of the 1,900 hectares (4,695 acres) growing black grapes and less than five per cent of the 1,430 hectares (3,534 acres) growing white grapes qualify for *Cru Classé* status.

RED WINES	COMMUNE	AREA CURRENTLY UNDER VINE	
Château Bouscaut	Cadaujac	50 ha	(124 acres)
Château Carbonnieux	Léognan	45 ha	(111 acres)
Domaine de Chevalier	Léognan	31 ha	(77 acres)
Château de Fieuzal	Léognan	35 ha	(86 acres)
Château Haut-Bailly	Léognan	28 ha	(69 acres)
Château Haut-Brion	Pessac	40 ha	(99 acres)
Château La Mission-Haut-Brion	Pessac	21 ha	(52 acres)
Château Latour-Haut-Brion	Talence	5 ha	(12 acres)
Château La Tour-Martillac	Martillac	32 ha	(79 acres)
Château Malartic-Lagravière	Léognan	15 ha	(37 acres)
Château Olivier	Léognan	30 ha	(74 acres)
Château Pape-Clément	Pessac	30 ha	(74 acres)
Château Smith-Haut-Lafite	Martillac	45 ha	(111 acres)
TOTAL AREA UNDER VINE		**407 HA**	**(1,005 ACRES)**

WHITE WINES	COMMUNE	AREA CURRENTLY UNDER VINE	
Château Bouscaut	Cadaujac	20 ha	(49 acres)
Château Carbonnieux	Léognan	45 ha	(111 acres)
Domaine de Chevalier	Léognan	4 ha	(10 acres)
Château Couhins-Lurton	Villenave	6 ha	(15 acres)
Château Haut-Brion	Pessac	4 ha	(10 acres)
Château La Tour-Martillac	Martillac	5 ha	(12 acres)
Château Laville-Haut-Brion	Talence	4 ha	(10 acres)
Château Malartic-Lagravière	Léognan	4 ha	(10 acres)
Château Olivier	Léognan	14 ha	(35 acres)
TOTAL AREA UNDER VINE		**106 HA**	**(262 ACRES)**

either did not know how to, or did not care to, clean up their act, as they continued to sell tired, over-sulphured, oxidized, and flabby wines on the back of their decaying reputations.

An official north-south divide, however, proved to be the solution for, since 1987, when the Pessac-Léognan AOC was introduced, things have never looked better for Graves. The Pessac-Léognan appellation is a single appellation for both red and white wines from the communes Cadaujac, Canéjan, Gradignan, Léognan, Martillac, Mérignac, Pessac, St.-Médard-d'Eyrans, Talence, and Villenave d'Ornon. This has had the effect of giving the northern châteaux the official quality recognition they both wanted and deserved. It was a bit slow to start off – after all, Pessac-Léognan hardly trips off the tongue and there were worries about its marketability. There is still a tendency to put Graves on labels, and use Pessac-Léognan to qualify the wine as if it were a higher classification of Graves, which for all practical purposes it is.

Once the châteaux realized that foreign markets were picking up on the superior connotation of Pessac-Léognan, use of the appellation soon became widespread. Whether by their own volition or due to peer pressure, many of the underperformers have become the most quality-conscious châteaux in the appellation, and it has spurred producers in the south to improve their wines. They do not like being considered inferior, and as they intend to prove they are not, the consumer can only gain.

CÉRONS

This is an area situated within the boundaries of Graves. It is the stepping stone between dry white Graves, and sweet white Sauternes and Barsac. The châteaux of Cérons have been given the official right to make both red and white Graves, Graves Supérieur (which may be dry but is usually sweet) and, of course,

THE GLOWING TINTS OF CHÂTEAU D'YQUEM
Château d'Yquem vintages, stretching back from a bottle of the 1980. The younger wines are a rich gold with a greenish tinge, deepening to old gold and amber with the older vintages.

CHÂTEAU D'YQUEM: THE INNER COURTYARD
A huge stone well dominates the square central courtyard of this beautiful château, which comprises disparate elements dating from the 15th, 16th, and 17th centuries.

VINEYARDS AT CHÂTEAU D'YQUEM
Here, the winter vineyard shows the characteristic sandy-pebbly clay topsoil and the system of wires and stakes that supports the vines. Yquem's clay subsoil contains 100 kilometres (62 miles) of terracotta pipes, which were laid down at the end of the 19th century to provide perfect drainage.

the sweet wine of Cérons – a wine that has enjoyed a modest reputation for nearly 200 years. In fact, only 20 per cent of the production in this area is sold as Cérons since the appellation covers three communes, those of Illats, Podensac, and Cérons itself. Many of the vineyards comprise scattered plots, some of which are partially planted with acacias.

SAUTERNES AND BARSAC

The gap between ordinary sweet white wines and the great wines of Sauternes and Barsac is as wide as that between sweet and dry wines. What creates this gap is something called "complexity" – to find out what that is, sample the aroma of a glass of mature Sauternes. The wines produced in Sauternes are not only the world's most luscious, but also the most complex wines. I have seen hardened men who resolutely refuse to drink anything sweeter than lemon juice go weak at the knees

TRADITIONAL HORSE-DRAWN PLOUGH
At Château d'Yquem work-horses are used to help plough the topsoil between the rows, both after the harvest and again in March.

CHÂTEAU DE FARGUES
The original family home of the Lur-Saluces family is now a ghostly ruin. The family moved to Yquem in 1785 upon its union with the De Sauvage family.

FACTORS AFFECTING TASTE AND QUALITY

LOCATION
The left bank of the Garonne river, stretching southeast from just north of Bordeaux to 10 km (6 miles) east of Langon. Cérons, Sauternes, and Barsac are tucked into the southern section of the Graves district.

CLIMATE
Very similar to the Médoc, but fractionally hotter and with slightly more rainfall. In Sauternes and Barsac it is mild and humid, with an all-important autumnal alternation of misty mornings and later sunshine, the ideal conditions for "noble rot".

ASPECT
The suburbs of Bordeaux sprawl across the northern section of this district, becoming more rural beyond Cadaujac. Graves has a much hillier terrain than the Médoc, with little valleys cut out by myriad streams that drain into the Garonne. Some of the vineyards here are quite steep. The communes of Sauternes, Bommes, and Fargues are hilly, but Preignac and Barsac, on either side of the Ciron – a small tributary of the Garonne – have gentler slopes.

SOIL
Travelling south through the district, the gravelly topsoil of Graves gradually becomes mixed with sand, then with weathered limestone and eventually with clay. The subsoil also varies, but basically it is iron-pan, limestone, and clay, either pure or mixed. Cérons has a stony soil, mostly flint and gravel, over marl; there is reddish clay-gravel over clay, or gravelly iron-pan in Sauternes, and clay-limestone over clay-gravel in Fargues. The gravel slopes of Bommes are sometimes mixed with heavy clay soils, while the plain is sandy clay with a reddish clay or limestone subsoil. Preignac is sand, gravel, and clay over clay-gravel in the south, becoming more alluvial over sand, clay, and limestone closer to Barsac. Where the classified growths of Barsac are situated, the soil is clay-limestone over limestone, elsewhere the topsoil mingles with sandy gravel.

VITICULTURE AND VINIFICATION
Some châteaux add a certain amount of *vin de presse* to the red wine. The *cuvaison* varies between eight and 15 days, although some Graves châteaux permit 15–25 days. Maturation in cask is generally between 15 and 18 months. The sweet white wines of Sauternes and Barsac are made from several *tries* of late-harvested, overripe grapes which, ideally, have "noble rot". Destalking is usually unnecessary. The fermentation of grape juice so high in sugar content is difficult to start and awkward to control, but it is usually over within two to eight weeks. The exact period of fermentation depends upon the style desired. Many of the best wines are matured in cask for 1½– 3½ years.

PRIMARY GRAPE VARIETIES
Cabernet sauvignon, Cabernet franc, Merlot, Sémillon, Sauvignon blanc
SECONDARY GRAPE VARIETIES
Malbec, Petit verdot, Muscadelle

after one sniff of Château Suduiraut, and I defy the most stubborn and bigoted anti-sweet wine drinker not to drool over a glass of Château d'Yquem 1967. Astonishingly, there are dissenters, but for me Yquem is by far the best wine of these two appellations, Sauternes and Barsac. The battle for second place is always between the soft, luscious style of Suduiraut, and the rich, powerful character of Rieussec, with Climens, Nairac, and the non-classified growths of Gilette and de Fargues in close pursuit. Guiraud has the potential to go right to the top, and with so many châteaux seriously improving, they could all end up chasing each other for the number two spot.

The "noble rot"

Yquem might be the ultimate sweet white wine, but many other great wines are made in these two small areas tucked away in the Bordeaux backwaters. What gives all these wines their hallmark of complexity is, literally, a lot of rot – namely "noble rot", or the fungal growth *Botrytis cinerea*. The low-lying hills of Sauternes and, to a lesser extent, of Barsac, together with a naturally warm but humid climate, provide a natural breeding ground for botrytis, the spores of which are indigenous to the area. They remain dormant in the vineyard soil and on vine bark until they are activated by suitable conditions – alternate moisture and heat (the early-morning mist being followed by hot, mid-morning sunshine). The spores latch on to the skin of each grape, replacing its structure with a fungal growth and feeding on moisture from within the grape. They also devour five-sixths of the grape's acidity and one-third of its sugar, but as the amount of water consumed is between one-half and two-thirds, the effect is to concentrate the juice into a sticky, sugar-rich pulp. A healthy, ripe grape with a potential of 13 per cent alcohol is thus converted into a mangy-looking mess with a potential of between 17.5 per cent and 26 per cent. The spread of botrytis through a vineyard is neither orderly nor regular, and the harvest may take as long as ten weeks to complete, with the pickers making various sorties, or *tries*, through the vineyard. On each *trie*, only the affected grapes should be picked, but care must be taken to leave some rot on each bunch to facilitate its spread. The longer the growers await the miraculous "noble rot", the more the vines are prone to the ravages of frost, snow, hail, and rain, any of which could destroy an entire crop.

The viticulture of Sauternes and Barsac is the most labour-intensive of any region. The yield is very low, officially a maximum of 25 hectolitres per hectare (112 cases per acre), about half that in the Médoc, and the levels achieved in the best châteaux are much lower, around 15 to 20 hectolitres per hectare (67–90 cases per acre). At Yquem it is even less, the equivalent of one glass per vine. On top of all this, the vinification is, at the very least, difficult to handle, and maturation of a fine sweet wine demands a good proportion of very expensive new oak.

Variations in character

Not all the sugar is used up during fermentation, even when a wine of perhaps 14 to 15 per cent alcohol is made. The remaining unfermented sugar, often between 50 and 120 grams per litre, gives the wine its natural sweetness. However, unlike Sauternes'

German counterparts, its alcohol level is crucial to its character. Its strength, in harmony with the wine's sweetness, acidity, and fruit give it a lusciousness of concentration that simply cannot be matched. Its complexity is not, however, the effect of concentration, although an increased mineral level is no doubt an influence. Complexity is created by certain new elements that are introduced into the grape's juice during the metabolic activities of its botrytis – glycerol, gluconic acid, saccharic acid, dextrin, various oxidizing enzymes, and an elusive antibiotic substance called "botrycine". It is easy to explain how these components of a botrytized wine that form its inimitably complex character can vary. When tasting wine from different *tries* at the same château, the intensity of botrytized character varies according to the "age" of the fungus when the grapes are harvested. Wines made from the same percentage of botrytized grapes collected at the beginning and end of the harvest are noticeably mute compared to those in the middle when the rot is at its most rampant. If it is not surprising that youthful *Botrytis cinerea* has an undeveloped character, the same cannot be said of late-harvested. Many people believe that the longer botrytis establishes itself, the more potent its effect, but this is not true.

The rewards, the reality, and the future

A good Sauternes is the most arduous, expensive, and frustrating wine in the world to produce – and what is the winemaker's reward? Very little, I'm afraid. Apart from Château d'Yquem – not only the greatest Sauternes but the greatest wine *per se* – the wines of this region fail to realize their true worth. This is predictable in a world where the trend is towards lighter and drier styles of wine, and may have a positive effect for Sauternes aficionados, for it means a cheaper supply of their favourite wine. In the long term this is not a positive way to operate, and some proprietors simply cannot afford to go on. The Comte de Pontac uprooted all the vines at his Second Growth Château de Myrat in Barsac, and even optimistic Tom Heeter, former owner of Château Nairac, said "You have to be at least half-crazy to make a living out of these wines". I feel we certainly do not deserve the luscious wines of Sauternes and Barsac if we continue to ignore them, but if the authorities had more sense, and the owners more business acumen, these wines could literally be "liquid gold".

The only way ahead

The vineyards of Sauternes and Barsac should also be allowed to sell red and dry white wines under the Graves appellation. If this is a right accorded to modest Cérons, why not to its illustrious neighbours? Many châteaux already make red and dry white wines, but they are sold under the cheaper "Bordeaux" appellation. Tom Heeter was right, the proprietors must be half-crazy, because their motivation for producing these alternative products is to subsidize the cost of making their botrytized wine, when they should be trying to supplement their income. Given the incentive of a superior appellation, the châteaux should concentrate on making the finest red and dry white wines every year. Only when conditions appear favourable should some of the white grape crop be left on the vine, with fingers crossed for an abundance of *Botrytis cinerea*. Instead of these châteaux investing in new oak for modest vintages, they should utilize the casks for the red and the dry white. The result would be a tiny amount of the world's most luscious wine, maybe three or four years in ten. It would no longer be necessary to attempt the impossible task of selling an old-fashioned image to young wine drinkers; the limited supply would outstrip the current demand. After 30 years of watching this area's vain attempts to win over popular support for its wines, I have come to accept the view of Comte Alexandre de Lur-Saluces, proprietor of Château d'Yquem. When asked to justify the price of Yquem, he simply said his wines are not made for everyone; they are made for those who can afford them.

THE "POURRITURE NOBLE", OR NOBLE ROT

A bunch of Sémillon grapes ready for the first trie. *Some of the grapes are still unaffected by the fungus, some are affected and discoloured but not shrivelled, others are dried, withered, and covered with the fungus bloom.*

GRAVES, CÉRONS, SAUTERNES, AND BARSAC

BARSAC AOC

The commune of Barsac is one of five that have the right to the Sauternes appellation. (The others are Preignac, Fargues, Bommes, and Sauternes itself.) Some generic wines sold in bulk may take advantage of this, but all individual properties are sold as Barsac. The wine must include overripe botrytized grapes harvested in *tries*.

WHITE Luscious, intensely sweet wines similar in style to Sauternes, but perhaps lighter in weight, slightly drier, and less rich. As in Sauternes, 1983 is one of the best vintages of the 20th century.

🍇 Sémillon, Sauvignon blanc, Muscadelle

🍷 6–25 years for most wines; between 15–60 years for the greatest

CÉRONS AOC

These inexpensive wines from an area adjacent to Barsac are the best value-for-money sweet wines in Bordeaux. They must include overripe botrytized grapes harvested in *tries*.

WHITE Lighter than Barsac, but often just as luscious, the best of these wines can show true botrytis complexity.

🍇 Sémillon, Sauvignon blanc, Muscadelle

🍷 6–15 years for most wines

GRAVES AOC

This appellation begins at the Jalle de Blanquefort, where the Médoc finishes and runs for 60 kilometres (37 miles) along the left bank of the Garonne. Almost two-thirds of the wine is red, and is consistently high in quality and value.

RED I was brought up on the notion that with full maturity a Graves reveals itself through a certain earthiness of character. Experience has taught me the opposite. The biggest Graves from hot years can have a denseness that may combine with the smoky character of new oak to give the wine a roasted or tobacco-like complexity, but Graves is intrinsically clean. Its hallmark is its vivid fruit, clarity of style, silky texture, and hints of violets.

🍇 Cabernet sauvignon, Cabernet franc, Merlot Secondary grape varieties: Malbec, Petit verdot

🍷 6–15 years

WHITE This is the disappointing half of the appellation: light- to full-bodied, from pure Sauvignon to pure Sémillon (with all proportions of blends in between, flabby to zingy, and unoaked to heavily-oaked). Pay strict attention to the château profiles on the following pages. These wines may be sold from 1 December following the harvest without any mention of *primeur* or *nouveau*.

🍇 Sémillon, Sauvignon blanc, Muscadelle

🍷 1–2 years for modest wines; 8–20 years for the best

GRAVES SUPÉRIEUR AOC

Some surprisingly good would-be Barsacs lurk beneath this appellation that is rarely seen, yet accounts for more than one-fifth of all white Graves produced.

WHITE This wine can be dry, but most is a sweet style, similar to Barsac.

🍇 Sémillon, Sauvignon blanc, Muscadelle

🍷 6–15 years

PESSAC-LÉOGNAN AOC

Introduced in September 1987, this appellation covers the ten best communes that have the right to the Graves AOC and it is not by chance that it also encompasses 55 of the best estates, including all the *Crus Classés*. The technical requirements are similar to Graves except that the Carmenère may be used for red wines; white wines must contain at least 25 per cent Sauvignon blanc and a slightly stricter yield. If you are not sure which château to buy in the Graves, it is worth remembering this appellation and paying a premium for it.

RED Soft, silky reds of great violety elegance, and not lacking either concentration or length. Most have been aged in a percentage of new oak, which adds a smoky or tobacco-like complexity.

🍇 Cabernet sauvignon, Cabernet franc, Merlot, Malbec, Petit verdot, Carmenère

🍷 6–20 years

WHITE The serious styles are invariably oaked these days, with oodles of flavour, often tropical and fruity, with a firm acid structure. These wines may be sold from 1 December following the harvest without any mention of *primeur* or *nouveau*.

🍇 A minimum of 25% Sauvignon blanc, plus Sémillon, Muscadelle

🍷 Usually 3–8 years, but up to 20 years for the best

SAUTERNES AOC

The much hillier communes of Bommes, Fargues, and Sauternes produce the richest of all Bordeaux's dessert wines, while the châteaux in the lower-lying, flatter Preignac make wines very close in style to Barsac. The wine must include overripe botrytized grapes harvested in *tries*.

WHITE Golden, intense, powerful, and complex wines that defy the senses and boggle the mind. They are rich in texture, with masses of rich, ripe, and fat fruit. Pineapple, peach, apricot, and strawberry are some of the lush flavours that can be found, and the creamy-vanilla character of fruit and new oak matures into a splendid honeyed sumptuousness that is spicy and complex. Above all, these wines are marked by the distinctive botrytis character.

🍇 Sémillon, Sauvignon blanc, Muscadelle

🍷 10–30 years for most wines; between 20 and 70 years for the greatest

GRAVES AND CÉRONS

CHÂTEAU D'ARCHAMBEAU
Illats
★★☆ⓥ

Sited in Podensac, one of the communes of Cérons, this fine

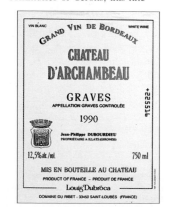

property is owned by Dr Jean Dubourdieu, nephew of Pierre Dubourdieu of Doisy-Daëne, a Second Growth in Barsac. He produces a fine-quality, fragrant, and attractively aromatic red wine, which has the typical silky Graves texture. The deliciously fresh, crisp, and fruity dry white Graves is better than some efforts by certain *Cru Classé* châteaux. His soft, fruity Cérons is *moelleux* with the emphasis more on perfume than richness.

Second Wine: *Château Mourlet, Château La Citadelle*

CHÂTEAU LA BLANCHERIE
La Brède

This fresh and lively dry white Graves is cool fermented, and has plenty of juicy fruit flavour balanced with ripe acidity.

CHÂTEAU LA BLANCHERIE-PEYRAT
La Brède
★ⓥ

The red wine of La Blancherie is sold under this label. It is a medium- to full-bodied wine that is matured in casks and has an engaging, spicy bouquet and a rich, fruity flavour.

CHÂTEAU BOUSCAUT
Cadaujac
Cru Classé (red and white)
★★☆ (white only)

Belongs to Sophie and Louis Lurton. The red wine is matured in wood for 18 months, with 25 per cent new oak. The white wine is fermented and matured for up to six months in 100 per cent new oak.

RED Until the 1980s this wine was big, tough, and tannic with little charm. Recent vintages have shown increasing suppleness, but the wine still struggles to find form. The second wine, Château Valoux, is a really excellent wine for its class.

🍇 Merlot 55%, Cabernet sauvignon 35%, Cabernet franc 5%, Malbec 5%

🍷 8–20 years

Second Wine: *Château Valoux*

WHITE This dry, medium-bodied white wine has exotic fruit flavours supported by gentle oak.

🍇 Sémillon 70%, Sauvignon 30%

🍷 5–10 years

CHÂTEAU DE CALVIMONT
Cérons

This red wine of Château de Cérons is an interesting pure Cabernet sauvignon Graves. The châteaux's proprietor, Jean Perromat, also owns châteaux Mayne-Binet, De Bessanes, Ferbos, and Ferbos-Lalanette in Cérons, and Prost in Barsac.

CHÂTEAU CARBONNIEUX
Léognan
Cru Classé (red and white)
★ ☆ ❤ (white only)

This is the largest wine estate in Graves. The white wine, the better known of the two styles, is cool-fermented in stainless steel and matured in 100 per cent new oak for three months.

RED I frankly did not care for this wine until the splendid 1985 vintage, which seduced me with its creamy-oak nose, silky-textured fruit, and supple tannin.

🍇 Cabernet sauvignon 55%, Merlot 30%, Cabernet franc 10%, Malbec, and Petit verdot 5%

🍷 6–18 years

WHITE Once solid and uninspiring, this wine has really come into its own since the early 1990s. From this time Château Carbonnieux has been lush and creamy with well-integrated new oak and not a little finesse.

🍇 Sauvignon 60%, Sémillon 40%

🍷 2–5 years

Second Wine: *Château La Tour Léognan*

CHÂTEAU DE CARDAILLAN
Toulenne
★ ☆ ❤

Under the same ownership as Château de Malle, this is a Second Growth Sauternes in the commune of Preignac. This excellent property produces a technically brilliant red Graves with a voluptuous blackcurrant flavour, which develops quickly, yet ages well.

🍇 Cabernet sauvignon 80%, Merlot 20%

CHÂTEAU LES CARMES-HAUT-BRION
Pessac

From 1584 until the French Revolution in 1789, this property belonged to the white friars Carmes, hence the name. Its wine is a reliable, soft, Merlot-dominated shadow of its more famous neighbour, Haut-Brion, although it is always capable of ageing. Vintages since 1995 have revealed a possible shift upwards in quality.

CHÂTEAU DE CÉRONS
Cérons

This 17th-century château, which makes an attractively light, sweet white Cérons, is owned by Jean Perromat, owner of Mayne-Binet, de Bessanes, Ferbos, Ferbos-Lalanette in Cérons, and Prost in Barsac.

CHÂTEAU DE CHANTEGRIVE
Podensac
★ ❤

This château produces a substantial quantity of an excellent, soft, and fruity red Graves (Cabernet

sauvignon 50 per cent, Merlot 40 per cent, Cabernet franc 10 per cent) that is matured in wooden vats for six months and then transferred to casks for a further 12 months with 20 per cent new oak. It also produces an elegant, aromatic, cool-fermented dry white Graves that is produced entirely from the first pressing (Sémillon 60 per cent, Sauvignon 30 per cent, Muscadelle 10 per cent). The proprietor also owns Château d'Anice.

Second Wine: *Château Mayne-Lévêque*

Other wines: *Château Bon-Dieu-des-Vignes*

DOMAINE DE CHEVALIER
Léognan
Cru Classé (red and white)
★★★ ❤

One of the top three Graves after Haut-Brion, this extraordinary property gives me more pleasure than any other in this AOC. It utilizes the most traditional methods to produce outstanding red and dry white wine. Fermenting red wine at a temperature as high as 32°C (89°F) might encourage some problems elsewhere, but under the meticulous care of those at the Domaine de Chevalier, this practice, designed to extract the maximum tannins and colouring material, is a positive advantage. The red wine is matured in wood for up to 24 months, with 50 per cent new oak. The white wine is fermented and matured in wood for 18 months, with up to 25 per cent new oak.

RED Deep-coloured, medium-to-full or full-bodied wines, stunningly rich in fruit and oak, with intense cedarwood and tobacco overtones, yet subtle, seductive, and full of finesse. These are wines of great quality, longevity, and complexity.

🍇 Cabernet sauvignon 65%, Merlot 30%, Cabernet franc 5%

🍷 15–40 years

WHITE Even better than the red, but produced in frustratingly small quantities, this star-bright, intensely flavoured dry wine is almost fat with exotic fruit and epitomizes finesse.

🍇 Sauvignon 70%, Sémillon 30%

🍷 8–20 years

CHÂTEAU CHICANE
Toulenne

Château Chicane is one of the chateaux that produce only red wine. It is typical of the large number of properties in the area that consistently produce an excellent basic Graves. Here is an elegant, medium-bodied red wine, with a bouquet of violets, and heaps of clean, silky-smooth fruit.

CHÂTEAU COUHINS
Villenave-d'Ornon
Cru Classé (white only)

The Institut National de La Récherche Agronomique (INRA) and Lucien Lurton share this estate.

INRA produces a separate wine, which is cool fermented with no maturation in wood.

WHITE Clean, crisp, and fruity dry white wines that are well made.

🍇 Sauvignon 50%, Sémillon 50%

🍷 2–4 years

Note Château also produces a red Graves, but it is not a *Cru Classé*.

CHÂTEAU COUHINS-LURTON
Villenave-d'Ornon
Cru Classé (white only)
★★ ☆ ❤

The highest-performing half of the Couhins estate owned by André Lurton. The wine is fermented and matured in 100 per cent new oak.

WHITE Delicious dry wines that have all the advantages of freshness and fruitiness, plus the complexity of oak. Surprisingly fat for pure Sauvignon.

🍇 Sauvignon 100%

🍷 3–8 years

Second Wine: *Château Cantebau*

CHÂTEAU DE CRUZEAU
St-Médard-d'Eyrans
★ ❤

Situated on a high, south-facing crest of deep, gravel soil, this property belongs to André Lurton, owner of Château Couhins-Lurton, the high-performance white Graves *Cru Classé*. De Cruzeau makes 18,000 cases of full-bodied red Graves (Cabernet sauvignon 60 per cent, Merlot 40 per cent) that is ripe and velvety with a spicy-cedarwood complexity.

This château also produces around 5,000 cases of a fine-quality white Graves (Sauvignon 90 per cent, Sémillon 10 per cent) that after some five years of maturation, develops an intense citrous bouquet and flavour.

CHÂTEAU FERRANDE
Castres

A large property that, like so many in Graves, makes better red wine than white. The red wine (Cabernet sauvignon 35 per cent, Merlot 35 per cent, Cabernet franc 30 per cent) is a consistently good-quality, chocolaty Graves that is matured in wood for 15 to 18 months, with 10 to 15 per cent new oak. The dry white Graves

(Sémillon 60 per cent, Sauvignon 35 per cent, Muscadelle 5 per cent) is somewhat less inspiring.

CHÂTEAU DE FIEUZAL
Léognan
Cru Classé (red only)
★★

This property occupies the highest and best exposed gravel crest in the commune. The vineyard and the château are immaculate, which is reflected in the style of its wines.

RED A deeply coloured, full-bodied, rich, stylish wine with typical Graves silky texture and ample finesse.

🍇 Cabernet sauvignon 60%, Merlot 30%, Malbec 5%, Petit verdot 5%

🍷 12–30 years

Second Wine: *L'Abeille de Fieuzal*

Note De Fieuzal also produces a rich, exotic, and oaky dry white wine that is not *Cru Classé*, yet is one of the finest white Graves produced.

CLOS FLORIDÈNE
Pujols-sur-Ciron
★★ ❤

Owned by Bordeaux's white wine revolutionary, Denis Dubourdieu, who is producing a sensational dry white Graves (Sémillon 70 per cent, Sauvignon 30 per cent) from this small estate. The red Clos Floridène (Cabernet sauvignon 80%, Merlot 20%) possesses an extraordinary combination of rich fruit and elegant new oak, and is the equivalent of a top *Cru Classé*.

Second Wine: *Second de Floridène*

GRAND ENCLOS DU CHÂTEAU DE CÉRONS
Cérons
★ ☆ ❤

This property, entirely enclosed by a wall, once formed the largest part of the estate of Château de Cérons. The wines produced here – far superior to those of Château de Cérons, and possibly the best of the appellation – are fat and rich, with good ageing potential and some complexity. The proprietor also makes dry white wines at nearby Château Lamouroux.

DOMAINE DE LA GRAVE
Portets
★ ❤

Formerly owned by maestro Peter Vinding-Diers, the Danish-born, Australian-trained winemaker who isolated the famous "RZ" yeast strain. Vinding-Diers sold this property along with Landiras to Van Quikelberg in 1998. The wines are for medium-term consumption, with a very soft, vibrantly fruity, easy-to-drink red and a lovely oak-aged white.

CHÂTEAU HAURA
Illats

Château Haura produces wines under the Cérons appellation. Although not as consistent as it should be, it can sometimes produce a fine, honey-sweet wine with some distinction and concentration. The residence on this property is known as Château Hillot and red and dry white Graves are sold under this name that come from vines contiguous with those of Haura. The proprietor also owns Château Tucau in Barsac.

CHÂTEAU HAUT-BAILLY
Léognan
Cru Classé (red only)
★★☆❶

This château's well-kept vineyard is located on an excellent gravel crest bordering the eastern suburbs of Léognan. This red Graves is matured for up to 20 months, with 50 per cent new oak.

RED The class of fruit and quality of new oak is immediately noticeable on the creamy-ripe nose of this medium-bodied wine. Never block-busting stuff, but always elegant and stylish.

Cabernet sauvignon 60%, Merlot 30%, Cabernet franc 10%

12–25 years

Second Wine: *Le Pardre de Haut-Bailly*

CHÂTEAU HAUT-BRION
Pessac
Cru Classé (red and white)
★★★

In 1663 this famous château was mentioned in Pepys's Diary as "Ho Bryan". It has been under American ownership since 1935, when it was purchased by Clarence Dillon, the banker. The parent company is called Domaine Clarence Dillon, and Dillon's granddaughter, the Duchesse de Mouchy, is the president. Jean Delmas is the technical director. The red wine is fermented in stainless steel and matured in wood for 24 to 27 months, with 100 per cent new oak. The white wine is fermented and matured in 100 per cent new oak.

RED This supple, stylish, medium- to full-bodied wine has a surprisingly dense flavour for the weight, and a chocolaty-violet character. The ideal commercial product, it develops quickly and ages gracefully.

Cabernet sauvignon 55%, Merlot 25%, Cabernet franc 20%

10–40 years

Second Wine: *Bahans-Haut-Brion*

WHITE This is not one of the biggest white Graves, but it is built to last. It is sumptuous, oaky, and teeming with citrous and more exotic fruit flavours.

Sauvignon 50%, Sémillon 50%

5–20 years

CHÂTEAU LANDIRAS
Landiras
M. and Mme. van Quikelberg purchased this property in 1998. Production is four-fifths white and potentially of *Cru Classé* quality.

CHÂTEAU LARRIVET-HAUT-BRION
Léognan
Originally called Château Canolle, the name was at one point changed to Château Haut-Brion-Larrivet. Larrivet is a small stream that flows through the property, and Haut-Brion means "high gravel", referring to the gravel plateau west of Léognan on which the vineyard is situated.

Château Haut-Brion took legal action over the re-naming, and since 1941 the property and its wines have been known as Château Larrivet-Haut-Brion. The red wine (Cabernet sauvignon 55 per cent, Merlot 45 per cent), which is matured in wood for 18 months with 25 per cent new oak, is certainly *Cru Classé* standard, being a well-coloured and full-bodied Graves with good flavour, spicy-cedarwood undertones, and a firm tannic structure. The white wine (Sauvignon blanc 85 per cent, Sémillon 15 per cent) has leapt in quality since 1996.

CHÂTEAU LAVILLE-HAUT-BRION
Talence
Cru Classé (white only)
★★

Since 1983, this small vineyard has been owned by Clarence Dillon, American proprietor of Château Haut-Brion. This "château with no château" is thought of as the white wine of La Mission. The wine is fermented and matured in cask.

WHITE Until 1982, the style was full, rich, oaky, and exuberant, tending to be more honeyed and spicy with a floral finesse since 1983. Both styles are stunning and complex.

Sauvignon 60%, Sémillon 40%

6–20 years

CHÂTEAU LA LOUVIÈRE
Léognan
★★❶

Part of André Lurton's Graves empire, this château has made a smart about-turn since 1985 as far as the quality of its red wine goes. A string of dull, lifeless vintages has come to an end with the beautiful, deep, and vividly coloured wines of the years 1985 and 1986. These are truly splendid, full-bodied red Graves that are rich in spicy-blackcurrant fruit and new oak (Cabernet sauvignon 70 per cent, Merlot 20 per cent, Cabernet franc 10 per cent). The white wines of Château La Louvière have always

been excellent, but even here there has been a gigantic leap in quality. These are exciting and complex wines that deserve to be among the very best *Crus Classés*.

Second Wine: *Château Coucheroy*

Other wines: *"L" de Louvière* (dry white), *Château Les Agunelles, Château Cantebau, Château Clos-du-Roy, Château Le Vieux-Moulin*

CHÂTEAU MAGENCE
St.-Pierre-de-Mons
A good property making 5,000 cases of a supple, well-perfumed, red wine (Cabernet sauvignon 40 per cent, Cabernet franc 30 per cent, Merlot 30 per cent) and 10,000 cases of attractive, aromatic, cool-fermented dry white Graves (Sauvignon 64 per cent, Sémillon 36 per cent).

CHÂTEAU MALARTIC-LAGRAVIÈRE
Léognan
Cru Classé (red and white)
★★

This 20-hectare (50-acre) vineyard forms a single block around the château. An underrated property, which has consistently produced much higher quality wines since the 1980s. The red wine is fermented in stainless steel at a low temperature (16°C/61°F), and matured in wood for 20 to 22 months, with one-third new oak. The white wine is now matured in 100 per cent new oak for seven to eight months.

RED Rich, garnet-coloured with an opulent sweet-oak nose, penetrating flavour, and supple tannin structure.

Cabernet sauvignon 50%, Cabernet franc 25%, Merlot 25%

7–25 years

WHITE Recent vintages of this once lacklustre white Graves prove the worth of new oak. It is not difficult to mistake this honey-rich, ripe, and succulent wine for pure Sémillon.

Sauvignon 100%

5–12 years

CHÂTEAU MAYNE-BINET
Cérons
Proprietor Jean Perromat also owns several other châteaux, namely De Cérons, De Bessanes, Ferbos, and Ferbos-Lalanette in Cérons and

Château Prost in Barsac. At Mayne-Binet he produces a fine sweet white Cérons.

CHÂTEAU MILLET
Portets
★ ❶ (red only)
The red is a deep, dark-coloured wine made in a traditional style with a dense flavour of concentrated spicy fruit. Although it has a firm tannin structure, this quickly rounds out with a few years in bottle. There is a dry white Graves, but it lacks the boldness and character of the red.

Other wines: *Château Du Clos Renon*

CHÂTEAU LA MISSION-HAUT-BRION
Pessac
Cru Classé (red only)
★★★☆

Under the ownership of Henri Woltner, this was the pretender to the throne of Graves. Little wonder, then, that Clarence Dillon of Haut-Brion snapped it up when the opportunity arose in 1983. The red wine is matured in wood for 24 months, with 50 per cent new oak.

RED Despite different winemaking techniques, Dillon's La Mission is no less stunning than Woltner's. Both styles are deeper, darker, and denser than any other wine Graves can manage. They are essentially powerful wines that require great bottle-age, but they do lack finesse.

Cabernet sauvignon 60%, Merlot 30%, Cabernet franc 10%

15–45 years

Second Wine: *La Chapelle de la Mission-Haut-Brion*

CHÂTEAU OLIVIER
Léognan
Cru Classé (red and white)
❓

There has never been any doubt about this château's *terroir*, which has as much potential as any Graves *Cru Classé*, but it was one of the appellation's most disappointing producers until 1990. Since then progress has been agonizingly slow and patchy, but this is still, I hope, a château to watch. The red wine is matured in wood for 18 months; the white wine up to three months, with 100 per cent new oak.

RED The fruit is now easier-drinking and the oak, which used to be aggressive, more supple and creamy.

Cabernet sauvignon 70%, Merlot 30%

WHITE This wine actually began to sparkle as early as 1985, with 1992 and 1994 being quite outstanding and the 1995 even more so. There seems to be added freshness, real fruit flavour, and some character developing.

Sémillon 65%, Sauvignon 30%, Muscadelle 5%

3–7 years

CHÂTEAU PAPE-CLÉMENT
Pessac
Cru Classé (red only)
★★

After a disastrous period in the 1970s and early 1980s, Pape-Clément began to improve in 1985 and 1986, due to stricter selection of the *Grand Vin* and the introduction of a Second Wine. Some critics rate these two vintages highly, and they were very good wines, but when examined in the context of the enormous potential of this vineyard, my brain tells me they were not at all special, even if my heart wants them to be.

The trio of 1988, 1989, and 1990 wines turned out to be the best this château has produced since 1953, although they are nowhere near as great and still not special at the very highest level of Graves wine. However, even in the string of lesser vintages Bordeaux experienced in the early 1990s, Pape-Clément managed to produce good wines, and with 1995, 1996, 1998, and 1999, it has truly regained the reputation of its former glory years. The red wine from this chateau is matured in wood for 24 months, with a minimum of 50 per cent new oak.

RED Medium-bodied wines of excellent deep colour, a distinctive style, and capable of much finesse.

🍇 Cabernet sauvignon 67%, Merlot 33%

Second Wine: *Le Clémentin*

Note This château also produces a little non-*Cru Classé* white Graves, made from equal proportions of Sémillon, Sauvignon, and Muscadelle.

CHÂTEAU RAHOUL
Portets

The wine produced by Château Rahoul is not quite as exciting as it was in the 1980s, when the property was home to – although never owned by – the maestro, Peter Vinding-Diers (*see* Domaine de la Graves and Château Landiras). However, both red and white wines are still reliable sources of very good value oak-aged Graves.

Second Wine: *Château Constantin*
Other Wines: *Petit Rahoul*

CHÂTEAU RESPIDE-MÉDEVILLE
Toulenne
★ ⓥ

Christian Médeville, the man responsible for Château Gilette, the rising star of Sauternes, produces excellent wines here using a totally

different wine philosophy. Both the red and the white are fine examples of the best of modern vinification combined with new oak. The red is a well-coloured wine with rich, ripe fruit, some spice, and a creamy, new-oak aftertaste, good for early drinking. The white is a rich, creamy-vanilla concoction with soft, succulent fruit and a fat finish.

CHÂTEAU DU ROCHEMORIN
Martillac
★ ⓥ

Originally called "La Roche Morine", (the moorish rock) this estate has a history that extends at least as far back as the eighth century when Bordeaux was defended by the Moors from attacking Saracens. Another château belonging to André

Lurton, Rochemorin produces a fine, elegant, fruity red Graves that is well balanced and has a good spicy finish (Cabernet sauvignon 60 per cent, Merlot 40 per cent). Rochemorin also produces a very clean and correct dry white Graves.

CHÂTEAU DE ROQUETAILLADE-LA-GRANGE
Mazères
★ ★ ⓥ (red only)

This is a very old property, that produces some 12,000 cases of an attractive, well-coloured red Graves that has an aromatic bouquet and a delicious spicy-*cassis* flavour. This wine is made from Merlot 40 per cent, Cabernet sauvignon 25 per cent, Cabernet franc 25 per cent, Malbec 5 per cent, and Petit verdot 5 per cent. Its firm, tannic structure means it matures gracefully over 15 or more years. The white wine, which is made from Sémillon 80 per cent, Sauvignon 20 per cent, is less successful.

Second wine: *Château de Carolle*
Other wines: *Château de Roquetaillade-le-Bernet*

CLOS SAINT-GEORGES
Illats
★ ⓥ

This property produces a small amount of red Graves, but is most famous for its scintillating sweet Graves Supérieur. A stunningly rich and flavoursome wine, full of botrytis complexity.

CHÂTEAU DU SEUIL
Cérons
★ ⓥ

Up-and-coming Graves property producing fine, elegant reds and fruity, oak-aged whites, both proving to be of increasingly excellent value.

CHÂTEAU SMITH-HAUT-LAFITTE
Martillac
Cru Classé (red only)
★ ★ ⓥ

This château has 50 hectares (124 acres) of fine vineyards and with Michel Rolland consulting on the red wines and Christophe Ollivier on the whites, its reputation and quality are soaring. The red wine is matured in wood for 18 months, with 50 per cent new oak.

RED These wines are now in a richer style with creamy-oak undertones, up-front fruit, and a soft finish.

🍇 Cabernet sauvignon 69%, Merlot 20% Cabernet franc 11%,

Second Wine: *Les Hauts-de-Smith-Haut-Lafitte*

Note A white Graves is also made, but it is not a *Cru Classé*, yet ironically now considered one of the finest white wines in Pessac-Léognan.

CHÂTEAU LA TOUR-HAUT-BRION
Talence
Cru Classé (red only)
★★

This château is situated close to Château La Mission-Haut-Brion. By 1980 sold under the label of this château was merely regarded as the Second Wine of Château La Mission-Haut-Brion. All the grapes from both vineyards were vinified together, and the two wines made by selection. However, after its acquisition by Domaine Clarence Dillon in 1983, some 4.5 hectares (11 acres) of vines were delimited as Château La Tour-Haut-Brion, and from 1984 all its wines can be said to be from one specific site. The wine is matured in wood for 24 months, with 50 per cent new oak.

RED This is an extremely dark, tannic, and full-bodied wine bulging with chocolaty, tannic fruit, and an underlying earthy-smoky bitterness of undeveloped extract. Despite its awesome attack of flavour it is not at all heavy and always shows great balance and finesse.

🍇 Cabernet sauvignon 60%, Merlot 30%, Cabernet franc 10%

🍷 20–40 years

CHÂTEAU LA TOUR-MARTILLAC
Martillac
Cru Classé (red and white)
★ ★

This property has its own herd of cattle to supply manure for the château's strictly "organic" wine. Its

red wine is not as consistent as the very best Graves and tends to lack charm in cask. These factors make it an underrated wine. It is matured in wood for 18 to 22 months with one-third new oak. The white is fermented in stainless steel, and matured in 100 per cent new oak.

RED Not big or bold wines that appeal immediately; the reds are elegant wines of some finesse. The fruit in recent vintages has tended to be a bit more plump, but it is in bottle that these wines take on their richness, developing a creamy-oak flavour.

🍇 Cabernet sauvignon 60%, Merlot 25%, Cabernet franc 6%, Malbec 5%, Petit verdot 4%

🍷 8–20 years

Second Wine: *Château La Grave-Martillac*

WHITE The stunning 1986 vintage heralds a new era of exciting dry white wines. It has very fresh, elegant, and stylish fruit, and this is gently balanced by complex nuances of oak.

🍇 Sémillon 55%, Sauvignon 35%, Muscadelle 3%, old diverse varieties 7%

🍷 4–8 years

THE WINE PRODUCERS OF
SAUTERNES and BARSAC

CHÂTEAU D'ARCHE
Sauternes
2ème Cru Classé
★ ♥

This property, which dates from 1530, was known as Cru de Bran-Eyre until it was bought by the Comte d'Arche in the 18th century. It has suffered from inconsistency. The wine is matured in up to 50 per cent new oak.

WHITE The successful Château d'Arche is an elegantly balanced wine that is more in the style of Barsac than Sauternes. It is sweet, rich, and has complex botrytis flavours, which often puts it on par with a First Growth, although its lusciousness is less plump than most Sauternes. Easily equivalent to a classed growth in quality and the Crème de Tête is even better.

🍇 Sémillon 80%, Sauvignon 15%, Muscadelle 5%

⌛ 8–25 years

Second Wine: Cru de Braneyre
Other Wines: d'Arche-Lafaurie

CHÂTEAU BASTOR-LAMONTAGNE
Preignac
★ ♥

A large property that deserves Second-Growth status. The wine is matured in wood for up to 36 months, with 10 to 15 per cent new oak. Lighter years such as 1980, 1982, and 1985 lack botrytis but are successful in an attractive mellow, citrus style. Big years such as 1983 lack nothing: the wines are full, rich, and stylish with concentrated botrytis flavour and ample class. 1989, 1990, 1996, 1997, 1998, and 1999 all very successful.

Second Wine: Les Remparts du Bastor

CHÂTEAU BOUYOT
Barsac
★ ☆ ♥

Jammy Fonbeney, the winemaker at this little-known property, is producing some stunning wines that deserve recognition. They have classic Barsac elegance, light in body, but not in flavour, with rich pineapple and creamy botrytis fruit, some spice, and fine length.

CHÂTEAU BROUSTET
Barsac
2ème Cru Classé
★ ♥

The wine produced at Château Broustet is matured in wood for 20 months with what was until recently just ten per cent new oak, but this increased to 40 per cent after the 1986 vintage.

WHITE Château Broustet can be a delightful wine, with a fruit-salad-and-cream taste, a very elegant balance, and some spicy-botrytis complexity.

🍇 Sémillon 63%, Sauvignon 25%, Muscadelle 12%

⌛ 8–25 years

Second Wine: Château de Ségur

CHÂTEAU CAILLOU
Barsac
2ème Cru Classé
★ ☆ ♥

This château gets its name from the cailloux, the stones that are brought to the surface during ploughing. These have been used to enclose the entire 15-hectare (37-acre) vineyard and to provide hardcore for the tennis courts. M. Bravo, the owner, has run out of uses but he is still churning them up. This is not one of the better-known Second Growths, but it consistently produces wines of a very high standard, and so deserves to be.

WHITE A rich, ripe, and spicy-sweet Barsac with concentrated botrytis flavours underscored by refined oak. Not the fattest of Barsacs, but made in the richer rather than lighter style.

🍇 Sémillon 90%, Sauvignon 10%

⌛ 8–30 years

Second Wine: Petit-Mayne
Other wines: Cru du Clocher (red), Château Caillou Sec (dry white), Rosé St.-Vincent (dry rosé)

CHÂTEAU DE LA CHARTREUSE
Preignac
★ ♥

This is the same stunning wine as Château Saint-Amande, but under a different exclusive label. See also Château Saint-Amande

CHÂTEAU CLIMENS
Barsac
1er Cru Classé
★ ★ ☆

Under the ownership of Bérénice Lurton, this property has long been considered one of the top wines of both appellations. The wine is matured in wood for 24 months with up to one-third new oak.

WHITE The fattest of Barsacs, yet its superb acidity and characteristic citrus style give it an amazingly fresh and zippy balance. This wine has masses of creamy-ripe botrytis fruit supported by good cinnamon and vanilla-oak flavours.

🍇 Sémillon 98%, Sauvignon 2%

⌛ 10–40 years

Second Wine: Les Cyprès de Climens

CHÂTEAU CLOS HAUT-PEYRAGUEY
Bommes
1er Cru Classé
★ ★

Originally part of Château Lafaurie-Peyraguey, this property has been owned by the Pauly family since 1934. A good dose of sulphur dioxide used to be the method of stopping fermentation at Clos Haut-Peyragey and the bouquet was often marred by an excess of sulphur. Thankfully this has not been evident since the 1985 vintage, when coincidentally, the wines began to benefit from some new oak. The wine is now matured in wood for 18 months, with up to 25 per cent new oak.

WHITE This wine now flaunts a positively eloquent bouquet, and has a rich flavour with complex botrytis creamy-oak nuances – very stylish.

🍇 Sémillon 83%, Sauvignon 15%, Muscadelle 2%

⌛ 8–25 years

Second Wine: Château Haut-Bommes

CHÂTEAU COUTET
Barsac
1er Cru Classé
★ ★

This château is usually rated a close second to Climens, but in fact it is capable of matching it in some vintages and its occasional production of tiny quantities of tête de cuvée called "Cuvée Madame" often surpasses it. It is fermented and matured for 24 months in cask with 30 to 50 per cent new oak. The dry white "Vin Sec" is an AOC Graves and very disappointing.

WHITE This wine has a creamy vanilla-and-spice bouquet, an initially delicate richness that builds on the palate, good botrytis character, and oaky fruit.

🍇 Sémillon 75%, Sauvignon 23%, Muscadelle 2%

⌛ 8–25 years (15–40 years for Cuvée Madame)

Other wines: ✓ Cuvée Madame, Vin Sec du Château Coutet

CHÂTEAU DOISY-DAËNE
Barsac
2ème Cru Classé
★ ★ ♥

Owner Pierre Dubourdieu cool ferments this wine in stainless steel until the desired balance of alcohol and sweetness is achieved, and then matures it in 100 per cent new oak for a short while. The wine also undergoes various low-sulphur techniques. The result is a wine equal to a Barsac First Growth.

WHITE This is a wine of great floral freshness and elegance, with a delightful honeyed fragrance of deliciously sweet fruit, delicate botrytis character, hints of creamy oak, and perfect balance.

🍇 Sémillon 100%

⌛ 8–20 years

Second Wine: Château Cantegril
Other wines: Vin Sec de Doisy-Daëne

CHÂTEAU DOISY-DUBROCA
Barsac
2ème Cru Classé

This property is run in conjunction with Climens, and is the smallest part of the original Doisy estate. But the wine, although consistent, is not in the same class as Doisy-Daëne, let alone Climens. It is matured in cask for 24 to 30 months with 25 per cent new oak.

🍇 Sémillon 90%, Sauvignon 10%

⌛ 6–15 years

Second Wine: La Demoiselle de Doisy

CHÂTEAU DOISY-VEDRINES
Barsac
2ème Cru Classé
★ ☆ ♥

This is the original and largest of the three Doisy châteaux. It is owned by Pierre Castéja, the head of Bordeaux négociant Roger Joanne. The wine is matured in wood for 18 months with one-third new oak.

WHITE This wine was somewhat lacklustre until 1983, since when it has exploded with character. Rich, ripe, and oaky, with a concentrated botrytis complexity.

🍇 Sémillon 80%, Sauvignon 20%

⌛ 8–25 years

Other wines: Château La Tour-Védrines

CHÂTEAU DE FARGUES
Fargues
★ ★

The eerie ruin of Château de Fargues is the ancestral home of the Lur-Saluces family. The small production of ultra-high-quality wine is made by essentially the same fastidious methods as Yquem, including fermentation and maturation in 100 per cent new oak. It is powerful and viscous, very rich, succulent, and complex, with a fat, toasty character (Sémillon 80 per cent, Sauvignon 20 per cent). Easily equivalent to a classed growth.

CHÂTEAU FILHOT
Sauternes
2ème Cru Classé
★

The beautiful Château Filhot was built between 1780 and 1850. This splendid château has a potentially great vineyard that consistently produces boring wine. Investment is required on a large scale in nearly every department: the proportion of Sémillon should be increased, the number of tries should be increased, the wine should contain more botrytized grapes and should be matured in cask, with some new oak.

WHITE At best these are well-made, simply fruity, and sweet.

🍇 Sémillon 60%, Sauvignon 37%, Muscadelle 3%

CHÂTEAU GILETTE
Preignac
★

Christian Médeville rejects modern marketing methods, preferring instead to keep his precious nectar (made from Sémillon 94 per cent, Sauvignon 4 per cent, Muscadelle 2 per cent) in vats under anaerobic conditions for an amazing 20 years before bottling and selling it. The Crème de Tête is First Growth quality with a powerful bouquet and intense flavour of liquorice and peaches and cream, followed by a long barley-sugar aftertaste. The Crème de Tête deserves ★★, but I am less impressed with Château Gilette's regular bottlings (if, indeed, any bottling at this property can be so described!).

CHÂTEAU GUIRAUD
Sauternes
1er Cru Classé
★★

This property has been on the up since 1981, when the Narby family of Canada purchased it. The château and vineyards were in a very run-down state. Narby dug up much of the Sauvignon and planted Sémillon, then totally re-equipped the winery and renovated the château. Only Yquem is on as high ground as Guiraud and as drainage is a key factor affecting the quality of the greatest Sauternes, where heavy clay soils dominate, the potential for this wine is very exciting and one that has been skilfully exploited with the help of Xavier Plantey, ex-manager of Château la Gaffelière. The wine is matured in wood for 30 months with at least 50 per cent new oak. The first vintages of the dry white Vin Blanc Sec "G" were dull, but subsequent efforts have improved.

WHITE After two dismal decades, great Sauternes arrived at this château with the classic 1983 vintage, the first true botrytis wine under Narby's ownership. Guiraud is now plump with Sémillon fruit and fat with botrytis character. A deliciously sweet wine with luxuriant new oak, complexity, and considerable finesse.

🍇 Sémillon 70%, Sauvignon 30%

⌛ 12–35 years

Second Wine: *Le Dauphin*

Other wines: *Vin Blanc Sec "G"* (dry white)

CHÂTEAU HAUT-BOMMES
Bommes

The owner, Jacques Pauly, prefers to live here rather than at his First Growth Château Clos Haut-Peyraguey. Occasionally the wine used to excel for an unclassified growth; the recent improvements at Château Clos Haut-Peyraguey augur well for the future.

CHÂTEAU LES JUSTICES
Preignac
★ Ⓥ

Under the same ownership as the star-performing Château Gilette, but here Christian Médeville gives his wines only four years ageing in vats. Les Justices is a consistent wine of excellent quality that is riper and fruitier than Gilette and the equivalent of a Second Growth.

CHATEAU LAFAURIE-PEYRAGUEY
Bommes
1er Cru Classé
★★⯪ Ⓥ

As with Cordier properties, this wine shows remarkable consistency. It is matured in wood for between 18 and 20 months with up to 50 per cent new oak.

WHITE The combination of botrytis and oak is like pineapples and peaches and cream in this elegant wine that keeps fresh and retains an incredibly light colour in old age.

🍇 Sémillon 98%, Sauvignon 2%

⌛ 8–30 years

CHÂTEAU LAMOTHE-DESPUJOLS
Sauternes
2ème Cru Classé

In 1961 the Lamothe vineyard was split in two. The section belonging to Jean Despujols has been the most disappointing half up until the 1985 vintage, but it has really come into its own since 1990.

WHITE Fuller, richer, and sweeter than previously expected, and in an oily, fuller bodied style, with overtly attractive tropical fruit character.

🍇 Sémillon 70%, Sauvignon 20%, Muscadelle 10%

CHÂTEAU LAMOTHE-GUIGNARD
Sauternes
2ème Cru Classé
★⯪ Ⓥ

The Guignards are really trying to achieve something with their section of the Lamothe vineyard. It was called Lamothe-Bergey until the name was changed in 1981. The wine is matured in wood for 24 months with 20 per cent new oak.

WHITE Rich, spicy, and concentrated wines of full body and good botrytis character.

🍇 Sémillon 85%, Muscadelle 10%, Sauvignon 5%

⌛ 7–20 years

CHÂTEAU LIOT
Barsac
★⯪ Ⓥ

This wine is elegant, with light but fine botrytis character and creamy vanilla of new oak – probably the equivalent of a Second Growth in quality and is excellent value. Owner Jean-Nicol David also produces Château Saint-Jean, a dry white Graves, and Château Pinsas, a fruity red Graves.

CHÂTEAU DE MALLE
Preignac
2ème Cru Classé

Dry white wine is produced under the "Chevalier de Malle" label, and red Graves from contiguous vineyards under the Château du Cardaillan label. While this vineyard does not shine every year (1989 and 1990 are its best-ever vintages), when it does, it can be superb value.

WHITE These are firm, well-concentrated wines often influenced more by *passerillage* than botrytis. Delicious, rich, and luscious.

🍇 Sémillon 75%, Sauvignon 22%, Muscadelle 3%

⌛ 7–20 years

Second Wine: *Château St.-Hélène*

Other Wines: *Chevalier de Malle*

CHÂTEAU DU MAYNE
Barsac
Ⓥ

There is a good proportion of old vines at this property which adds concentration and weight to these wines, which are fatter than the norm for Barsac. Owned by the Sanders family of the splendid Château Haut-Bailly of Graves.

CHÂTEAU MÉNOTA
Barsac
Ⓥ

This quaint old property – with its historic towers and ramparts – has exported its wines to England since the 16th century. Château de Ménota produces very good Barsac, despite the unusually high proportion of Sauvignon blanc (Sauvignon 60 per cent, Sémillon 40 per cent).

CHÂTEAU NAIRAC
Barsac
2ème Cru Classé
★⯪

Tom Heeter established the practice of fermenting and maturing his wine in up to 100 per cent new oak – Nevers for vanilla and Limousin for backbone – and his perfectionist ex-wife, Nicole Tari, has continued this format with great success.

WHITE These are rich and oaky wines that require ample ageing to show true finesse. With enough bottle maturity the tannin and vanilla harmonize with the fruit, and the rich botrytis complexity emerges.

🍇 Sémillon 90%, Sauvignon 6%, Muscadelle 4%

⌛ 8–25 years

CHÂTEAU PERNAUD
Barsac
★ Ⓥ

This property was once part of the Sauvage d'Yquem estate. It was then owned by the Lur-Saluces family, but was abandoned after the oidium fungus devastated Bordeaux in the late 18th century. It has been completely replanted and renovated, and is now building up something of a reputation. This slightly richer style of Barsac (Sémillon 70 per cent, Sauvignon 25 per cent, Muscadelle 5 per cent) has a typically elegant balance and is certainly a wine to watch.

CHÂTEAU RABAUD-PROMIS
Bommes
1er Cru Classé
★⯪

The wines of this once-grand property used to be awful. It was sad to see the vineyard, château, and wine so neglected. What a joy to witness such a dramatic change. It began with the 1983; and the vintages are now something special.

WHITE A lovely gold-coloured wine with full, fat, and ripe botrytis character on the bouquet and palate.

🍇 Sémillon 80%, Sauvignon 18%, Muscadelle 2%

⌛ 8–25 years

CHÂTEAU RAYMOND-LAFON
Sauternes

As I wrote in the last edition, it is easy to understand how people can get carried away by the idea of a vineyard so close to Yquem as Raymond-Lafon, especially when its owner, Pierre Meslier, was *régisseur* at Yquem. This was, however, an overrated and overpriced wine in the mid-1980s, and although things have improved since the 1989 and 1990 vintages, it is performing at only Second Growth level and is consequently overrated and overpriced. Now that the style has been cleaned up and plumped out, Raymond-Lafon (Sémillon 80 per cent, Sauvignon 20 per cent) is a nice Sauternes, but not worth three times the price of Rieussec or two-and-a-half times as much as Climens.

CHÂTEAU RAYNE-VIGNEAU
Bommes
1er Cru Classé
★

The quality of Rayne-Vigneau had plummeted to dismal depths until as recently as 1985. The wine is now matured in wood for 24 months with 50 per cent new oak. It has a higher Sémillon content than the statistics would suggest, due to the 5,000 cases of dry Sauvignon blanc that are sold as "Rayne Sec".

WHITE Chateau Rayne Vigneau is now a very high-quality wine that has an elegant peachy ripeness to its botrytis character.

🍇 Sémillon 65%, Sauvignon 35%

⌛ 8–25 years

Second Wine: *Clos l'Abeilley*

Other wines: *Rayne Sec*

CHÂTEAU RIEUSSEC
Fargues
1er Cru Classé
★★☆

This fine property promises to make even better wine since its acquisition by Domaines Rothschild in 1984. None of the Sauvignon produced here is used for Château Rieussec (it goes in the "R"), effectively making the wine 96 per cent Sémillon. It is barrel-fermented and cask matured for 18 to 30 months with 50 per cent new oak.

WHITE This wine is one of the richest and most opulent of Sauternes, with intense pineapple fruit and a heavily botrytized character.

Sémillon 75%, Sauvignon 22%, Muscadelle 3%

⌀— 12–35 years

Second Wine: ✓ *Clos Labère, Mayne des Carmes*

Other wines: *"R" de Château Rieussec* (dry white)

CHÂTEAU DE ROLLAND
Barsac

The château of this estate has been turned into a hotel with a good restaurant, and is under separate ownership. The vineyard of Château de Rolland belongs to Jean and Pierre Guignard, who also own the excellent Château de Roquetaillade-la-Grange at Mazères in Graves. The wines (Sémillon 60 per cent, Sauvignon 20 per cent, Muscadelle 20 per cent) are fresh and elegant with a particular emphasis on fruit.

CHÂTEAU ROMER
Fargues
2ème Cru Classé
❷

The original Romer estate was divided in 1881, and at just five hectares (13 acres) this is the smallest part. I have never come across the wine.

Sémillon 50%, Sauvignon 40%, Muscadelle 10%

CHÂTEAU ROMER-DU-HAYOT
Fargues
2ème Cru Classé
❶

Monsieur André du Hayot owns these ten hectares (25 acres) of vines on a fine clayey-gravel crest that was once part of the original Romer estate. The wines are little seen, but represent very good value.

WHITE The 1980 and 1983 are in the fresh, not oversweet, fruit-salad and cream style, with light botrytis character and an elegant balance. More recent vintages have not been tasted.

Sémillon 70%, Sauvignon 25%, Muscadelle 5%

⌀— 5–12 years

CHÂTEAU ROUMIEU
Barsac
★ ❶

This property, which borders the classified growths of Climens and Doisy-Vedrines, has produced luscious sweet wines of a richer than normal style in some vintages (Sémillon 90 per cent, Sauvignon 10 per cent).

CHÂTEAU ROUMIEU-LACOSTE
Barsac
★ ❶

A Dubourdieu property producing consistently fine Barsac (Sémillon 80 per cent, Sauvignon 20 per cent) with good botrytis concentration.

CHÂTEAU SAINT-AMANDE
Preignac
❶

An elegant and stylish wine (Sémillon 67 per cent, Sauvignon 33 per cent) that is very attractive when young, yet some vintages have potentially excellent longevity and are often equivalent to a classed growth in quality. Part of the production of this property is sold under the Château de la Chartreuse label.

Second Wine: *Château la Chartreuse*

CHÂTEAU SIGALAS-RABAUD
Bommes
1er Cru Classé
★★☆

This is the largest part of the original Rabaud estate. The proprietor contracted Cordier to manage this property as from 1995 and the wines have already shown a marked improvement.

WHITE A stylish early-drinking wine with an elegant botrytis bouquet and deliciously fresh fruit on the palate.

Sémillon 85%, Sauvignon 15%

⌀— 6–15 years

CHÂTEAU SIMON
Barsac

A combination of modern and traditional methods produces a mildly sweet wine from Sémillon 70 per cent, Sauvignon 30 per cent. Most Sauternes and Barsacs are aged in Nevers or Limousin oak. Sometimes Allier is used, but at Simon they mature the wine in Merrain oak for two years.

CHÂTEAU SUAU
Barsac
2ème Cru Classé

The vineyard belongs to Roger Biarnès, who makes the wine at his Château Navarro in Cérons because the château is under different ownership. These wines do not have a particularly high reputation, but if the attractive wine produced in the very modest 1980 vintage is anything to go by it is worth the benefit of the doubt.

WHITE The 1980 is an attractive, fresh, and fragrantly fruity wine

with a gentle citrus-and-spice botrytis complexity.

Sémillon 80%, Sauvignon 10%, Muscadelle 10%

⌀— 6–12 years

CHÂTEAU SUDUIRAUT
Preignac
1er Cru Classé
★★★☆

This splendid 17th-century château, with its picturesque parkland, effectively evokes the graceful beauty found in its luscious wines. Suduiraut's superb 100-hectare (245-acre) vineyard enjoys a good susceptibility to "noble rot", and adjoins that of Yquem. The wines went through an inconsistent patch in the 1980s, but have improved dramatically under the watchful eye of Jean-Michel Cazes's AXA insurance group. The wines are fermented and matured in cask for 24 months, with at least one-third new oak.

WHITE Soft, succulent, and sublime, this is an intensely sweet wine of classic stature. It is rich, ripe, and viscous, with great botrytis complexity that benefits from good bottle-age.

Sémillon 80%, Sauvignon 20%

⌀— 8–35 years

Second Wine: *Castelnau de Suduiraut*

CHÂTEAU LA TOUR BLANCHE
Sauternes
1er Cru Classé
★★☆

This property was placed at the head of the premiers crus in 1855, when only Yquem was deemed to be superior, but until relatively recently it failed to live up to this reputation. Even at its lowest ebb, few critics would have denied that these vineyards truly possessed great potential, but the wines were ordinary. This was made all the more embarrassing by the fact that the state-owned La Tour Blanche was a school of agriculture and oenology that was supposed to teach others how to make Sauternes. This depressing situation began to change, however, in the mid-1980s when Château la Tour Blanche started increasing the proportion of Sémillon, picking much riper grapes, and implementing stricter selection in both vineyard and chais. Fermentation is in wood (with up to 90 per cent new oak but averaging 25 per cent in most years), and the results have been exciting with excellent wines produced in 1988, 1989, 1990, (its greatest ever), 1994, 1995, 1996, 1997, and 1998.

WHITE These are now so rich they are almost fat and bursting with plump, ripe, juicy fruit and oodles of complex botrytis character.

Sémillon 78%, Sauvignon 19%, Muscadelle 3%

⌀— 8–20 years

Second Wine: *Mademoiselle de Saint-Marc*

CHÂTEAU D'YQUEM
Sauternes
1er Cru Supérieur
★★★

This most famous of all châteaux belonged to the English crown from 1152 to 1453. It then passed into the hands of Charles VII, King of France. In 1593 Jacques de Sauvage acquired tenant's rights to the royal property and in 1711 his descendants purchased the fiefdom of Yquem. In 1785 it passed into the hands of the Lur-Saluces family.

The property has been run with passionate care by succeeding generations, although LVMH (which owns Moët & Chandon in Champagne) purchased a majority shareholding in 1999 (after three years of acrimony between members of the Lur-Saluces family). Alexandre Lur-Saluces lost his independence, but won a handsome contract to remain in his former home. He is still very much in charge.

The *tries* tradition was kept alive at Yquem when it was long forgotten by other noble châteaux. Like Pétrus, one of Yquem's "secrets" is its pickers. They are all skilled; they know what to pick and, just as important, what to leave. The gap between *tries* can vary from three days to several weeks. Housing and feeding 120 pickers for several weeks of inactivity is not cheap.

In 1972 the harvest consisted of 11 *tries* spread over 71 days. In that year no wine was sold as Château d'Yquem. This is not to say that Yquem's fastidious attention to selection and quality does not pay off in some poor vintages. But in good years, because of the strict selection in the vineyard, the amount of wine that is finally used is as high as 80 to 90 per cent. The wines are matured for up to 42 months with 100 per cent new oak. Other *terroirs* in Sauternes and Barsac are potentially comparable, but, no matter how conscientious their owners, none makes the same sacrifices as Yquem.

WHITE This wine represents the ultimate in richness, complexity, and class. No other botrytis wine of equal body and concentration has a comparable finesse, breeding, and balance. Some of the characteristic aromas and flavours include peach, pineapple, coconut, nutmeg, and cinnamon, with toasty-creamy vanilla and caramel flavours of new oak.

Sémillon 80%, Sauvignon 20%

⌀— 20–60 years

Other wines: *"Y" de Château d'Yquem* (dry white)

THE LIBOURNAIS & FRONSADAIS

The right bank of the Dordogne river, known as the Libournais district, is red-wine country. Dominated by the Merlot grape, this district produces deep-coloured, silky- or velvety-rich wines of classic quality in the St.-Émilion and Pomerol regions, and wines of modest quality but excellent value and character in the "satellite" appellations that surround them.

IN THE MID-1950s, many Libournais wines were harsh, and even the best AOCs did not enjoy the reputation they do today. Most growers believed that they were cultivating too much Cabernet sauvignon and Malbec for their particular *terroir* and decided that they should plant more Cabernet franc. A few argued for the introduction of Merlot, which was allowed by the regulations, because it would give their wines the suppleness they desired. Even if they could have agreed on united action, changing the *encépagement* of an entire district would have been very long-term, as well as being hugely expensive. However, in 1956, frost devastated the vineyards, forcing the Libournais growers into action. With short crops inevitable for some years to come, prices soared, enabling them to carry out the massive replanting which, ironically, they could not have afforded prior to the crisis. This devastation led to the wholesale cultivation of Merlot and Cabernet franc, which established a totally different style of wines, providing the catalyst for the spectacular post-war success of St.-Émilion and Pomerol.

THE SATELLITE APPELLATIONS OF ST.-ÉMILION AND POMEROL

The wines of Lussac, Montagne, Parsac, Puisseguin, Sables, and St.-Georges were once sold as St.-Émilion, but in 1936 these outer areas were given their own AOCs. This was done to protect the image of the greatest St.-Émilion châteaux, but through the historical use of this famous name these areas won the right to attach the name of St.-Émilion to theirs. The tiny Sables area was later reclaimed by the St.-Émilion AOC, and in 1972 a new appellation, Montagne–St.-Émilion, was created. This appellation, which covered a large region, could be adopted by growers who had previously used either Parsac–St.-Émilion AOC or St.-Georges–St.-Émilion AOC, but the executive order that created Montagne–St.-Émilion AOC in 1972 did not disband either of these smaller appellations. So, a situation arose where growers could choose between two very similar AOCs. In 1993, however, Parsac–St.-Émilion was finally disbanded, since it was noticed that virtually all the producers of Parsac–St.-Émilion were not using the original AOC but opting for Montagne–St.-Émilion AOC. Many growers in St.-Georges–St.-Émilion, however, were still using the original appellation and so disbanding this would not have been so simple. All five combined St.-Émilion AOCs would in fact benefit from merging, since they all produce wines of essentially similar nature, under identical regulations.

WINDMILLS IN MONTAGNE
It would make commercial sense if all the St.-Émilion satellites (Lussac–St.-Émilion, Puisseguin–St.-Émilion, and St.-Georges–St.-Émilion) were combined under the Montagne–St.-Émilion appellation.

THE LIBOURNAIS DISTRICT
See also p.59
This great red-wine area includes St.-Émilion, Pomerol, and their satellites. In the Libournais district, the Merlot grape reigns supreme, its succulent fruit essential to the local style.

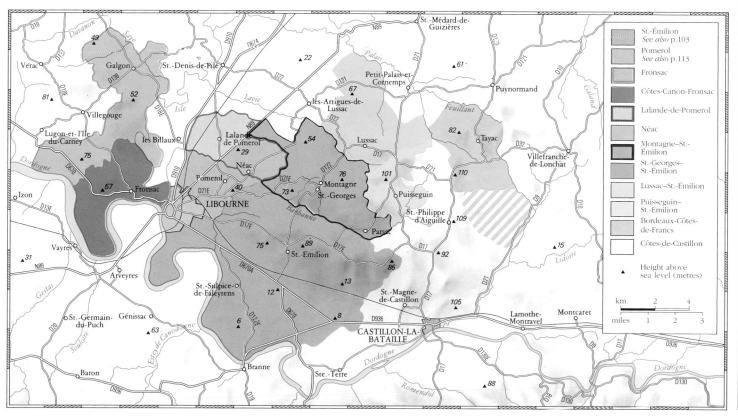

Legend:
- St.-Émilion *See also p.103*
- Pomerol *See also p.113*
- Fronsac
- Côtes-Canon-Fronsac
- Lalande-de-Pomerol
- Néac
- Montagne–St.-Émilion
- St.-Georges–St.-Émilion
- Lussac–St.-Émilion
- Puisseguin–St.-Émilion
- Bordeaux-Côtes-de-Francs
- Côtes-de-Castillon
- ▲ Height above sea level (metres)

THE APPELLATIONS OF
THE LIBOURNAIS & FRONSADAIS

BORDEAUX-CÔTES-DE-FRANCS AOC

This forgotten area's vineyards are contiguous with those of Puisseguin–St.-Émilion and Lussac–St.-Émilion, and have a very similar clay-limestone over limestone and iron-pan soil. The Bordeaux Supérieur version of these wines differs only in its higher alcohol level.

RED These are essentially robust, rustic, full-bodied wines that are softened by their high Merlot content.

🍇 Cabernet franc, Cabernet sauvignon, Malbec, Merlot

🍷 5–10 years

WHITE Little-seen dry, semi-sweet, and sweet wines of clean, fruity character.

🍇 Sauvignon blanc, Sémillon, Muscadelle

🍷 5–10 years

BORDEAUX-CÔTES-DE-FRANCS LIQUOREUX AOC

This style of Bordeaux-Côtes-de-Francs wine must by law be naturally sweet and made from overripe grapes that possess at least 223 grams of sugar per litre. The wines must have a minimum level of 11.5 per cent alcohol and 27 grams of residual sugar per litre.

WHITE Rich, genuinely *liquoreux* wines; only tiny amounts are made.

🍇 Sauvignon blanc, Sémillon, Muscadelle

🍷 5-15 years

BORDEAUX SUPÉRIEUR CÔTES-DE-FRANCS AOC

See Bordeaux-Côtes-de-Francs AOC

CANON-FRONSAC AOC

See Côtes-Canon-Fronsac AOC

CÔTES-CANON-FRONSAC AOC

Fronsac AOC and Côtes-Canon-Fronsac AOC will no doubt be the next wines to be "discovered" by budget-minded Bordeaux drinkers. The best of these wines are Côtes-Canon-Fronsac AOC, sometimes called Canon-Fronsac AOC. With lower yields and stricter selection, these wines could equal all but the best of St.-Émilion and Pomerol.

RED Full-bodied, deep-coloured, rich, and vigorous wines with dense fruit, fine spicy character, plenty of finesse, and good length.

🍇 Cabernet franc, Cabernet sauvignon, Malbec, Merlot

🍷 7–20 years

CÔTES-DE-CASTILLON AOC

This is an attractive hilly area squeezed between St.-Émilion, the Dordogne river, and the Dordogne *département*. Its wine has long been appreciated for quality, consistency, and value. These wines used to be sold as Bordeaux and Bordeaux Supérieur wine until the 1989 vintage, when Côtes-de-Castillon received its own AOC status.

RED Firm, full-bodied, fine-coloured wines with dense fruit and finesse.

🍇 Cabernet franc, Cabernet sauvignon, Carmenère, Malbec, Merlot, Petit verdot

🍷 5–15 years

FRONSAC AOC

This generic appellation covers the communes of La Rivière, St.-Germain-la-Rivière, St.-Aignan, Saillans, St.-Michel-de-Fronsac, Galgon, and Fronsac.

RED These full-bodied, well-coloured wines have good chunky fruit and a fulsome, chocolaty character. Not quite the spice or finesse of Côtes-Canon-Fronsac, but splendid value.

🍇 Cabernet franc, Cabernet sauvignon, Malbec, Merlot

🍷 6–15 years

LALANDE-DE-POMEROL AOC

This good-value appellation covers the communes of Lalande-de-Pomerol and Néac. No matter how good they are, even the best are but pale reflections of classic Pomerol.

RED Firm, meaty Merlots with lots of character but without Pomerol's texture and richness.

🍇 Cabernet franc, Cabernet sauvignon, Malbec, Merlot

🍷 7–20 years

LUSSAC–ST.-ÉMILION AOC

A single-commune appellation nine kilometres (five-and-a-half miles) northeast of St.-Émilion.

RED The wines produced on the small gravelly plateau to the west of this commune are the lightest, but have the most finesse. Those produced on the cold, clayey lands to the north are robust and earthy, while those from the clay-limestone in the southeast have the best balance of colour, richness, and finesse.

🍇 Cabernet franc, Cabernet sauvignon, Carmenère, Malbec, Merlot

🍷 5–12 years

MONTAGNE–ST.-ÉMILION AOC

This appellation includes St.-Georges–St.-Émilion, a former commune that is today part of Montagne–St.-Émilion. St.-Georges–St.-Émilion AOC and Montagne–St.-Émilion AOC are the best of all the appellations that append "St.-Émilion" to their names.

RED Full, rich, and intensely flavoured wines that mature well.

🍇 Cabernet franc, Cabernet sauvignon, Malbec, Merlot

🍷 5–15 years

NÉAC AOC

This appellation has not been employed since the proprietors have been allowed to use the Lalande-de-Pomerol appellation. *See* Lalande-de-Pomerol AOC.

POMEROL AOC

The basic wines of Pomerol fetch higher prices than those of any other Bordeaux appellation. The average Merlot content of a typical Pomerol is around 80 per cent.

RED It is often said that these are the most velvety-rich of the world's classic wines, but they also have the firm tannin structure that is necessary for successful long-term maturation and development. The finest also have surprisingly deep colour, masses of spicy-oak complexity, and great finesse.

🍇 Cabernet franc, Cabernet sauvignon, Malbec, Merlot

🍷 5–10 years (modest growths)
    10–30 years (great growths)

PUISSEGUIN–ST.-ÉMILION AOC

This commune has a clay-limestone topsoil over a stony subsoil and the wines it produces tend to be more rustic than those of the Montagne–St.-Émilion AOC.

RED These are rich and robust wines with a deep flavour and lots of fruit and colour, but they are usually lacking in finesse.

🍇 Cabernet franc, Cabernet sauvignon, Carmenère, Malbec, Merlot

🍷 5–10 years

ST.-ÉMILION AOC

These wines must have a minimum of 10.5 per cent alcohol, but in years when chaptalization (the addition of sugar to grape juice to increase alcohol content) is allowed there is also a maximum level of 13 per cent.

RED Even in the most basic St.-Émilions the ripe, spicy-juiciness of the Merlot grape should be supported by the firmness and finesse of the Cabernet franc. The great châteaux achieve this superbly: they are full, rich and concentrated, chocolaty, and fruit-cakey.

🍇 Cabernet franc, Cabernet sauvignon, Carmenère, Malbec, Merlot

🍷 6–12 years (modest growths)
    12–35 years (great growths)

ST.-GEORGES–ST.-ÉMILION AOC

Along with the Montagne region of Montagne–St.-Émilion, this is the best parish of the outer areas.

RED These are deep-coloured, plummy wines with juicy, spicy fruit, and good supporting tannic structure.

🍇 Cabernet franc, Cabernet sauvignon, Malbec, Merlot

🍷 5–15 years

SAINT-ÉMILION

The Romans were the first to cultivate the vine in St.-Émilion, a small area that has exported its wines to various parts of the world for over eight hundred years. In the first half of this century it lapsed into obscurity, but in the last forty years it has risen like a phoenix.

ST.-ÉMILION AS WE KNOW it is a phenomenon of the post-war era, but there are many reminders of this wine's ancient past – from the famous Château Ausone, named after the Roman poet Ausonius, to the walled hilltop village of St.-Émilion itself, which has survived almost unchanged since the Middle Ages. In contrast, the Union de Producteurs, the largest single-appellation *coopérative* in France, is a graphic illustration of the best in modern, technologically sophisticated wine production. Today, there are over a thousand *crus* within ten kilometres (six miles) of the village of St.-Émilion that may use this appellation.

THE APPEAL OF ST.-ÉMILION WINES

For those who find red wines too harsh or too bitter, St.-Émilion, with its elegance and finesse, is one of the easiest with which to make the transition from white to red. The difference between the wines of St.-Émilion and those of its satellites is comparable to the difference between silk and satin, whereas the difference between St.-Émilion and Pomerol is like the difference between silk and

velvet: the quality is similar, but the texture is not – although, of course, we must be humble about categorizing such complex entities as wine areas. It could justifiably be argued that the *graves* (gravelly terrain) that produces two of the very best St.-Émilions – Châteaux Cheval-Blanc and Figeac – has more in common with Pomerol than with the rest of the appellation.

CHÂTEAU FIGEAC
Without doubt in a class of its own within Class B of Premiers Grands Crus Classés, Château Figeac has long fought to be classified with Ausone and Cheval Blanc.

A LARGE PRODUCTION

If you look at the map of the entire Bordeaux region (*see* p.59) you will be amazed by how small this appellation of a thousand châteaux really is. It is a surprising but regular occurrence that an appellation as small as St.-Émilion produces more wine than all the famous appellations of the Médoc combined – St.-Estèphe, Pauillac, St.-Julien, and Margaux.

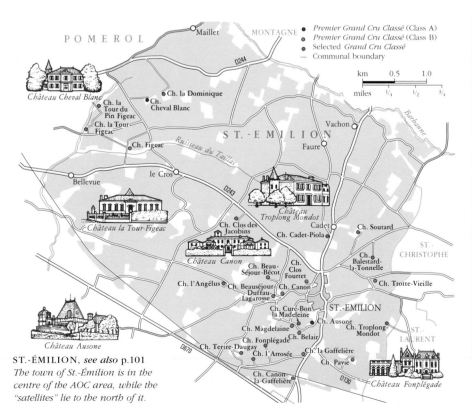

ST.-ÉMILION, *see also* p.101
The town of St.-Émilion is in the centre of the AOC area, while the "satellites" lie to the north of it.

CHÂTEAU AUSONE
From its hilltop perch, this ancient château commands a spectacular view of the sweeping vineyards below.

THE CLASSIFICATION OF ST.-ÉMILION

St.-Émilion wines were first classified in 1958, with the intention that the classification be revised every ten years according to the performance of properties during the previous decade. Three basic categories were established: *Premier Grand Cru Classé*, *Grand Cru Classé*, and *Grand Cru*. Of the 12 châteaux that were classified *Premiers Grands Crus Classés*, Ausone and Cheval-Blanc were placed in a superior subsection. The rest were listed alphabetically, not qualitatively, as were the 64 *Grands Crus Classés*. The classification was revised in 1969, 1985 (some six years late), and again in 1996 – which brought the reclassification period back to that anticipated.

Beware the distinction between *Grand Cru* (unclassified growths) and *Grand Cru Classé* (classified growths) because the difference is considerable. In St.-Émilion, *Grand Cru* merely indicates a minimum alcoholic strength 0.5% higher than that required by the basic St.-Émilion appellation, and a slightly lower yield. Any producer may apply for a *Grand Cru*, and hundreds do so. It is not a classification, but merely an adjunct to the appellation, and would be more accurately conveyed as a new appellation called St.-Émilion Supérieur, since the difference between *Grand Cru* and *Grand Cru Classé* is akin to that between basic Bordeaux and Bordeaux Supérieur.

ST.-ÉMILION CLASSIFICATION OF 1958, 1969, 1985, AND 1996
Incorporating vineyard soil classification

PREMIER GRAND CRU CLASSÉ Class A

1 Château Ausone
Soil: *Côte and St.-Émilion plateau*
2 Château Cheval Blanc
Soil: *Graves and ancient sand*

PREMIER GRAND CRU CLASSÉ Class B

3 Château l'Angélus [7]
Soil: *Pied de côte and ancient sand*
4 Château Beau-Séjour Bécot [1, 7]
Soil: *St.-Émilion plateau and côte*
5 Château Beauséjour (Duffau Lagarosse)
Soil: *Côte*
6 Château Belair
Soil: *St.-Émilion plateau and côte*
7 Château Canon
Soil: *St.-Émilion plateau and côte*
8 Château-Figeac
Soil: *Graves and ancient sand*
9 Clos Fourtet
Soil: *St.-Émilion plateau and ancient sand*
10 Château la Gaffelière
Soil: *Côte, pied de côte*
11 Château Magdelaine
Soil: *St.-Émilion plateau, côte, and pied de côte*
12 Château Pavie
Soil: *Côte and St.-Émilion plateau*
13 Château Trottevieille
Soil: *St.-Émilion plateau*

GRAND CRU CLASSÉ

14 Château l'Arrosée
Soil: *Côte*
15 Château Baleau (now Château Côte de Baleau) [1, 3]
Soil: *Côte and ancient sand*
16 Château Balestard la Tonnelle
Soil: *St.-Émilion plateau*
17 Château Bellevue
Soil: *Côte and St.-Émilion plateau*
18 Château Bergat
Soil: *Côte and St.-Émilion plateau*
19 Château Berliquet [2]
Soil: *Côte and pied de côte*
20 Château Cadet-Bon [1, 8]
Soil: *St.-Émilion plateau and côte*
21 Château Cadet-Piola
Soil: *St.-Émilion plateau and côte*
22 Château Canon-la-Gaffelière
Soil: *Pied de côte and sandy-gravel*
23 Château Cap de Mourlin
Soil: *Côte and ancient sand*

- Château la Carte [4]
Soil: *St.-Émilion plateau and ancient sand*
- Château Chapelle-Madeleine [5]
Soil: *Côte and St.-Émilion plateau*
24 Château le Châtelet [9]
Soil: *Côte and ancient sand*
25 Château Chauvin
Soil: *Ancient sand*
26 Château Clos des Jacobins
Soil: *Côte and ancient sand*
27 Château la Clotte
Soil: *Côte*
28 Château la Clusière
Soil: *Côte*
29 Château Corbin
Soil: *Ancient sand*
30 Château Corbin Michotte
Soil: *Ancient sand*
31 Château la Couspaude [1, 8]
Soil: *St.-Émilion plateau*
32 Château Coutet [1]
Soil: *Côte*
- Château le Couvent [6]
Soil: *St.-Émilion plateau*
33 Couvent des Jacobins [3]
Soil: *Ancient sand and pied de côte*
34 Château Croque Michotte [9]
Soil: *Ancient sand and graves*
35 Château Curé Bon la Madeleine
Soil: *St.-Émilion plateau and côte*
36 Château Dassault [3]
Soil: *Ancient sand*
37 Château la Dominique
Soil: *Ancient sand and graves*
38 Château Faurie de Souchard
Soil: *Pied de côte*
39 Château Fonplégade
Soil: *Côte*
40 Château Fonroque
Soil: *Côte and ancient sand*
41 Château Franc-Mayne
Soil: *Côte*
42 Château Grand Barrail Lamarzelle Figeac [9]
Soil: *Ancient sand*
43 Château Grand Corbin [9]
Soil: *Ancient sand*
44 Château Grand-Corbin-Despagne [9]
Soil: *Ancient sand*
45 Château Grand Mayne
Soil: *Côte and ancient sand*
46 Château Grandes Murailles [1, 8]
Soil: *Côte and ancient sand*
47 Château Grand-Pontet
Soil: *Côte and ancient sand*
48 Château Guadet St.-Julien
Soil: *St.-Émilion plateau*
49 Château Haut-Corbin
Soil: *Ancient sand*

50 Château Haut-Sarpe [3]
Soil: *St.-Émilion and St.-Christophe plateaux and côtes*
51 Château Jean Faure [1]
Soil: *Ancient sand*
52 Château Laniote [3]
Soil: *Ancient sand and pied de côte*
53 Château Larcis Ducasse
Soil: *Côte and pied de côte*
54 Château Larmande
Soil: *Ancient sand*
55 Château Laroque [8]
Soil: *St.-Émilion plateau and côte*
56 Château Laroze
Soil: *Ancient sand*
57 Clos la Madeleine [9]
Soil: *St.-Émilion plateau and côte*
58 Château la Marzelle (now Château Lamarzelle)
Soil: *Ancient sand and graves*
59 Château Matras [3]
Soil: *Pied de côte*
60 Château Mauvezin
Soil: *St.-Émilion plateau and côte*
61 Château Moulin du Cadet
Soil: *Côte and ancient sand*
62 Clos de l'Oratoire [3]
Soil: *Pied de côte*
63 Château Pavie Décesse
Soil: *St.-Émilion plateau and côte*
64 Château Pavie Macquin
Soil: *St.-Émilion plateau, côte, and sandy gravel*
65 Château Pavillon-Cadet [9]
Soil: *Côte and ancient sand*
66 Château Petit-Faurie-de-Soutard
Soil: *Ancient sand and côte*
67 Château le Prieuré
Soil: *St.-Émilion plateau and côte*
68 Château Ripeau
Soil: *Ancient sand*
69 Château St.-Georges (Côte Pavie)
Soil: *Côte and pied de côte*
70 Clos St.-Martin
Soil: *Côte and ancient sand*
71 Château Sansonnet [9]
Soil: *St.-Émilion plateau*
72 Château la Serre
Soil: *St.-Émilion plateau*
73 Château Soutard
Soil: *St.-Émilion plateau and côte*
74 Château Tertre Daugay [3]
Soil: *St.-Émilion plateau and côte*
75 Château la Tour Figeac
Soil: *Ancient sand and graves*
76 Château la Tour du Pin Figeac (Owner: Giraud-Belivier)
Soil: *Ancient sand and graves*
77 Château la Tour du Pin Figeac (Owner: Moueix)
Soil: *Ancient sand and graves*

78 Château Trimoulet
Soil: *Ancient sand and graves*
- Château Trois-Moulins [4]
Soil: *St.-Émilion plateau and côte*
79 Château Troplong Mondot
Soil: *St.-Émilion plateau*
80 Château Villemaurine
Soil: *St.-Émilion plateau*
81 Château Yon-Figeac
Soil: *Ancient sand*

See opposite for an explanation of soil types.

Notes
[1] One *Premier Grand Cru Classé* and six *Grands Crus Classés* demoted in the 1985 revision.
[2] This property was not in the original 1958 classification, nor was it included in the 1969 revision, but was awarded *Grand Cru Classé* status in 1985.
[3] These properties were not in the original 1958 classification, but were awarded *Grand Cru Classé* status in the 1969 revision.
[4] These two properties were merged with *Premier Grand Cru Classé* Château Beau-Séjour-Bécot in 1979. Wines bearing both labels can be found up to the 1978 vintage, and it is possible that they might reappear sometime in the future, particularly as the expansion of Château Beau-Séjour-Bécot vineyard was primarily responsible for its demotion in the 1985 classification.
[5] This property was merged with *Premier Grand Cru Classé* Château Ausone in 1970. Wines with this label can be found up to the 1969 vintage.
[6] This property changed hands prior to the 1985 revision and did not apply to be considered; it was not demoted, but simply ignored.
[7] Two properties were promoted to *Premier Grand Cru Classé* (B) in 1996.
[8] Four properties were promoted to *Grand Cru Classé* in 1996.
[9] Eight properties were demoted to *Grand Cru* in 1996.

THE QUESTION OF QUALITY

The diverse nature of St.-Émilion's soil has led to many generalizations that attempt to relate the quantity and character of the wines produced to the soils from which they come. Initially the wines were lumped into two crude categories, *côtes* (literally "hillside" or "slope") and *graves* (literally "gravelly terrain"). The term *côtes* was supposed to describe fairly full-bodied wines that develop quickly; the term *graves*, fuller, firmer, and richer wines that take longer to mature.

The simplicity was appealing, but it ignored the many wines produced on the stretch of deep sand between St.-Émilion and Pomerol, and those of the plateau, which has a heavier topsoil than the *côtes*. It also failed to distinguish between the eroded *côtes* and the deep-soiled bottom slopes. But most importantly, it ignored the fact that many châteaux are spread across more than one soil type (*see* the list of classified growths opposite) and that they have various other factors of *terroir*, such as aspect and drainage, which affect the character and quality of a wine (*see* Soil Survey of St.-Émilion, below).

The map below shows the positions of the 81 classified châteaux of St.-Émilion, listed with their soil types (*see* opposite). Châteaux la Carte, Chapelle-Madeleine, le Couvent, and Trois-Moulins are listed but do not appear on the map (*see* notes opposite).

SOIL SURVEY OF ST.-ÉMILION

The map below shows the area covered by *Premier Grand Cru Classé* and *Grand Cru Classé* châteaux. Each soil type is described (*right*) and colour keyed on the map. The numbers of the châteaux are listed opposite.

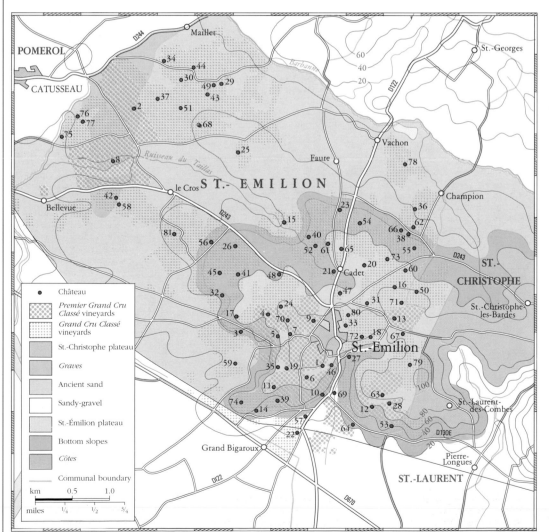

ST-CHRISTOPHE PLATEAU
Clay-limestone and clay-sand topsoil over limestone and *terra rossa* subsoil. *Terra rossa* is a red, clay-like soil.

GRAVES
Deep gravel topsoil with a subsoil of large-grain sand over a very deep, hard, and impermeable sedimentary rock called *molasse*. The gravel is similar to that found in the Médoc.

ANCIENT SAND
Thick blanket of large-grain sand over a subsoil of *molasse*. The bulk of this sand extends northeast from the village of St.-Émilion towards Pomerol. Although this area seems to have a gentle slope all round it, and the sand is very permeable, the *molasse* below is flat and impermeable. The water collects, saturating root systems and increasing soil acidity. Some châteaux benefit greatly from underground drainage pipes.

SANDY-GRAVEL
Sandy and sandy-gravel topsoil over sandy-gravel, ferruginous gravel, and iron-pan.

ST-ÉMILION PLATEAU
Shallow clay-limestone and clay sand, shell debris, and silt topsoil over eroded limestone subsoil.

BOTTOM SLOPES
The gentler bottom slopes of the *côtes* have a deep, reddish-brown, sandy-loam topsoil over yellow sand subsoil.

CÔTES
The lower-middle to upper slopes of the *côtes* have a shallow, calcareous, clay-silty-loam topsoil with a high active lime content. Quite sandy on the middle slopes, the topsoil thins out higher up. The subsoil is mostly *molasse*, not the impermeable type found under the ancient sand and *graves*, but a weathered, absorbent *molasse* of limestone or sandstone.

THE WINE PRODUCERS OF
SAINT-ÉMILION

CHÂTEAU ANGÉLUS
Premier Grand Cru Classé (B)
★★

This is a large property with a single plot of vines on the south-facing *côtes*. At one time the château produced wines in the old "farmyard" style, but that ended with the 1980 vintage. Two-thirds of the wine is matured for 14 to 16 months in wood with 100 per cent new oak. This château is a rising star, and was promoted to *Premier Grand Cru Classé* (B) in 1996.

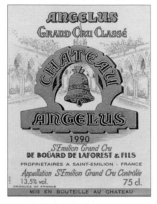

RED This is a soft, silky, and seductive wine. The luxury of new oak is having a positive effect on the quality, character, and ageing potential of this wine.

🍇 Cabernet franc 50%, Merlot 45%, Cabernet sauvignon 5%

🍷 7–20 years

Second Wine: *Carillon de l'Angélus*

CHÂTEAU L'ARROSÉE
Grand Cru Classé
★☆Ⓥ

This property sits on the *côtes* above the local *coopérative*. Through excellent selection of only its finest grapes, it has consistently produced wines that are a class above those of many of its peers.

RED This medium- to full-bodied wine has a lovely ruby colour, a voluptuous bouquet, and soft, creamy-rich fruit backed up by supple oak tannin.

🍇 Merlot 50%, Cabernet sauvignon 35%, Cabernet franc 15%

🍷 5–15 years

Second Wine: *Les Coteaux du Château l'Arrosée*

CHÂTEAU AUSONE
Premier Grand Cru Classé (A)
★★★

Since gifted winemaker Pascal Delbeck took control of Château Ausone in 1975, this prestigious property has produced wines of stunning quality, and it now deserves its superstar status. In 1997, after a power struggle between the two owners, Alain Vauthier took control and sacked

Delbeck and hired Michel Rolland as consultant. The vineyard of Château Ausone has a privileged southeast exposure and its vines are fairly established at between 40 and 45 years of age. They are capable of yielding very concentrated wines, which are then matured in wood for between 16 and 22 months, with 100 per cent new oak. The only question-mark hanging over Ausone has been its cellar, and one of Vauthier's first decisions was to store the wine in a drier cellar during the winter. If and when Ausone's cellar is thoroughly overhauled, this First Growth could well do an Olga Korbut, as Margaux has done and Latour is doing. Then I'll have to reassess all the wines in this encyclopedia by a new yardstick!

RED These rich, well-coloured wines have opulent aromas and scintillating flavours. They are full in body, compact in structure, and refined in character, with masses of spicy-*cassis* fruit and creamy-oak undertones. These wines are the quintessence of class, complexity, and finesse.

🍇 Cabernet franc 50%, Merlot 50%

🍷 15–45 years

CHÂTEAU BALESTARD LA TONNELLE
Grand Cru Classé
★

The label of this wine bears a 15th-century poem by François Villon that cites the name of the château. One-third of the wine is matured in 100 per cent new oak for up to 24 months, one-third is aged in two-year-old barrels, and the remainder rests in stainless-steel vats until bottling, when it is all blended together.

RED The gentle, ripe aromas of this wine belie its staunchly traditional style. It is a full-bodied wine of great extract, tannin, and acidity that requires time to soften, but it has masses of fruit, and so matures gracefully.

🍇 Merlot 65%, Cabernet franc 20%, Cabernet sauvignon 10%, Malbec 5%

🍷 10–30 years

Second Wine: *Les Tourelles de Balestard*

CHÂTEAU BEAU-SÉJOUR BÉCOT
Premier Grand Cru Classé (B)
★☆

Since 1979, this property has almost doubled in size by merging with two *Grands Crus Classés*, Château la Carte and Château Trois Moulins. In 1985, Beau-Séjour Bécot was the only *Premier Grand Cru Classé* to be demoted in the revision of the St.-Émilion classification. The demotion was not due to its quality or performance, but because of its expansion. However, the general application of such criteria would mean demoting nearly all the Bordeaux châteaux classified in 1855! The problem was that expansion within reasonable limits is allowed in the Médoc, but not in St.-Émilion. This has since been rectified and in 1996 this château was promoted and is once again a *Premier Cru Classé* (B). The wine is fermented in stainless steel and matured in wood for 18 months, with 90 per cent new oak.

RED Once lightweight and high-tone, this wine is now full, rich, and truly characterful. The silky Merlot fruit develops quickly, but is backed up with creamy new oak.

🍇 Merlot 70%, Cabernet franc 15%, Cabernet sauvignon 15%

🍷 7–25 years

Second Wine: *La Tournelle des Moines*

CHÂTEAU BEAUSÉJOUR
(Owner: Duffau-Lagarosse)
Premier Grand Cru Classé (B)
★

These little-seen wines consistently underwhelmed critics until the 1980s, since when Château Beauséjour began to produce darker, fuller wines with more class.

RED Not huge, but these wines are now quite rich, full-flavoured, and deeply coloured wine with plummy fruit.

🍇 Merlot 50%, Cabernet franc 25%, Cabernet sauvignon 25%

🍷 7–15 years

Second Wine: *La Croix de Mazerat*

CHÂTEAU BELAIR
Premier Grand Cru Classé (B)
★★

Pascal Delbeck, the gifted winemaker of Château Ausone, lives here and makes the wine with the same care and attention as he used to apply at Ausone. The wine is matured in wood for 16 to 20 months. Up to half is aged in new oak, the rest in casks that have been used for one wine at Ausone. This is one of the very best *Premiers Grands Crus*.

RED This is a deep-coloured, full-bodied wine with a rich flavour of plums, chocolate, black cherries, and *cassis*. It has great finesse, an alluring style, and a scintillating, spicy-cedarwood complexity.

🍇 Merlot 60%, Cabernet franc 40%

🍷 10–35 years

Second Wine: *Roc Blanquet*

CHÂTEAU BELLEVUE
Grand Cru Classé
✪

This small property was originally called "Fief-de-Bellevue" and belonged to the Lacaze family from 1642 to 1938. It is situated on the *côtes* and produces a wine that is seldom seen outside France.

RED I have tasted only the 1982 vintage – it is an attractive and fruity wine of medium body and elegant bouquet, but is no better than many unclassified St.-Émilions.

🍇 Merlot 67%, Cabernet franc 16.5%, Cabernet sauvignon 16.5%

🍷 5–10 years

CHÂTEAU BERGAT
Grand Cru Classé

This small vineyard is managed by Philippe Castéja of Château Trottevieille. Its wine is rarely seen and I have never tasted it.

🍇 Merlot 50%, Cabernet franc 40%, Cabernet sauvignon 10%

CHÂTEAU BERLIQUET
Grand Cru Classé
★☆

This was the only property to be upgraded to *Grand Cru Classé* in the 1985 reclassification. With Patrick Valette consulting since 1997 there has been an upward trend in quality, and if this continues it would be difficult to deny Berliquet *Premier Grand Cru Classé* status during a future revision. The wine is made under the supervision of the local *coopérative*. It is fermented in stainless steel vats and matured in wood for 18 months, with 30 per cent new oak.

RED These are deep, dark, and dense wines with spicy-*cassis* fruit and good vanilla oak.

Merlot 70%,
Cabernet franc and
Cabernet sauvignon 30%

10–30 years

CHÂTEAU CADET-BON
Grand Cru Classé

This property was demoted from *Grand Cru Classé* status in the 1985 reclassification, but after a period of improvement was reinstated in the 1996 reclassification.

Merlot 60%,
Cabernet franc 40%

CHÂTEAU CADET-PIOLA
Grand Cru Classé
★

With the exception of the vintages of 1980 and 1981, which were very light, this property usually shows great consistency and exquisite style. Up to 50 per cent of the wine is matured in new oak.

RED These are full-bodied, intensely flavoured wines with powerful, new-oak character and great tannic strength.

Merlot 51%,
Cabernet sauvignon 28%,
Cabernet franc 18%, Malbec 3%

12–25 years

Second Wine: *Chevalier de Malte*

CHÂTEAU CANON
Premier Grand Cru Classé (B)
★★ 🅥

Many years ago this château used to produce a second wine called "St.-Martin-de-Mazerat", which was the old Parish name before Château Canon was absorbed by St.-Émilion. Excellent wines were made under Eric Forner and although he sold out in 1996 the quality has been maintained. In summer 2000 the new owners, Chanel Inc., bought the nearby property Curé Bon la Madelaine with INAO agreement to incorporate it into Canon from the 2000 vintage. So goodbye Curé Bon! The *Grand Vin*, fermented in oak vats and matured in wood for 20 months with 50 per cent new oak, is one of the best of St.-Émilion's *Premiers Grands Crus Classés*.

RED These wines have a deep purple colour, an opulent *cassis* bouquet, and are very rich and voluptuous on the palate with masses of juicy Merlot fruit and spicy-complexity.

Merlot 55%, Cabernet franc 40%,
Cabernet sauvignon 3%,
Malbec 2%

8–30 years

Second Wine: *Clos J. Kanon*

CHÂTEAU CANON-LA-GAFFELIÈRE
Grand Cru Classé
★★☆

This is one of the oldest properties in St.-Émilion. Its wine was fermented in stainless steel vats until wooden vats were installed in 1997. Malolactic is in Barrel and the wines matured for 18 months, with up to 50 per cent new oak.

RED In the best years when this château excels itself, and invests in 50 per cent new oak, the wine can be really plump, full of vivid fruit and creamy oak.

Merlot 65%,
Cabernet franc 30%,
Cabernet sauvignon 5%

8–20 years

Other wines: *Côte Mignon-la-Gaffelière*

CHÂTEAU CAP DE MOURLIN
Grand Cru Classé

Until 1982 there were two versions of this wine, one bearing the name of Jacques Capdemourlin and one that of Jean Capdemourlin. This property is run by Jacques. The wine is matured in wood for up to 24 months, with one-third new oak.

RED Attractive, well-made, medium-bodied wines, with exquisitely fresh fruit, and a smooth finish.

Merlot 60%,
Cabernet franc 25%,
Cabernet sauvignon 12%,
Malbec 3%

6–15 years

Second Wine: *Mayne d'Artagnan*

CHÂTEAU LA CARTE
Grand Cru Classé

Since 1980, the vineyards of this property have been merged with those of *Premier Grand Cru Classé* Château Beau-Séjour-Bécot.

CHÂTEAU CHAPELLE-MADELEINE
Grand Cru Classé until 1996

Since 1971, these vineyards have been merged with those of *Premier Grand Cru Classé* Château Ausone.

CHÂTEAU CHAUVIN
Grand Cru Classé

This property's wine is matured in wood for 18 months, with one-third new oak. It is difficult to find, but its quality makes it deserving of better distribution.

RED When on form, Château Chauvin can have excellent colour, an aromatic bouquet, full body, and chunky, plummy fruit.

Merlot 60%,
Cabernet franc 30%,
Cabernet sauvignon 10%

4–10 years

Second Wine: *Chauvin Variation*

CHÂTEAU CHEVAL BLANC
Premier Grand Cru Classé (A)
★★★

The unusual aspect of this great wine is its high proportion of Cabernet franc, which harks back to the pre-1956 era. Switching to a majority of Merlot vines was advantageous for most Libournais properties but keeping a proportion of 60 per cent Cabernet franc was even better for Château Cheval Blanc. In 1998 this château was bought by two businessmen, Albert Frère from Belgium and Barnard Arnault, the head of LVMH. The wine is matured in wood for 20 months, with 100 per cent new oak.

RED These wines have all the sweet, spicy richness one expects from a classic St.-Émilion property situated on *graves*.

Cabernet franc 60%,
Merlot 37%, Malbec 2%,
Cabernet sauvignon 1%

12–40 years

Second Wine: *Le Petit Cheval*

CHÂTEAU CLOS DES JACOBINS
Grand Cru Classé
★

Clos des Jacobins, which is kept in the impeccable style to which all the Cordier properties are accustomed, is impressive even during "off-vintages".

RED These are rich, fat wines, bursting with chocolate and black-cherry flavours.

Merlot 85%, Cabernet franc 10%,
Cabernet sauvignon 5%

8–25 years

CHÂTEAU LA CLOTTE
Grand Cru Classé
🅥

This property is under the same ownership as the Logis de la Cadène restaurant in St.-Émilion, where much of its wine is sold. The Libournais *négociant* Jean-Pierre Moueix takes three-quarters of the crop.

RED Although not as consistent as some *Grands Crus Classés*, when successful this estate can make attractive and elegant wines with lots of soft, silky fruit that are a match for its peers.

Merlot 70%, Cabernet franc 30%

5–12 years

CHÂTEAU LA CLUSIÈRE
Grand Cru Classé

This is a small enclave within the property of Château Pavie and is under the same ownership as Pavie and Château Pavie Décesse. This wine is fermented in stainless steel vats and matured in wood (two-year-old barrels from Château Pavie) for up to 24 months.

RED This wine has a certain elegance, but lacks finesse and has a high-tone style that does not appeal to me. To be fair, I must point out that those who appreciate this style often find la Clusière solid and characterful.

Merlot 70%,
Cabernet franc 20%,
Cabernet sauvignon 10%

5–10 years

CHÂTEAU CORBIN
Grand Cru Classé
🅥

This property has the same owners as Château Grand Corbin – the Corbin estate, which is now divided into five separate properties bordering the Pomerol district. The wine is fermented in stainless steel and one-third of the production is matured in 100 per cent new oak.

RED Deep-coloured, full-bodied, and deliciously rich, but rather rustic for a classified growth.

Merlot 67%, Cabernet franc and Cabernet sauvignon 33%

6–12 years

Other wines: *Latour Corbin, Château Corbin-Vieille-Tour*

CHÂTEAU CORBIN MICHOTTE
Grand Cru Classé
★

This is one of five Corbin and two Michotte estates! This wine is fermented in stainless steel and some is matured in wood, with one-third new oak.

RED A dark, deeply flavoured, full-bodied wine that has rich, juicy Merlot fruit and some finesse.

Merlot 65%, Cabernet franc 30%,
Cabernet sauvignon 5%

6–15 years

Second Wine: *Les Abeilles*

CHÂTEAU CÔTE DE BALEAU
Grand Cru Classé until 1985
★

This property was unjustly demoted from its *Grand Cru Classé* status in the 1985 revision. Côte de Baleau deserves its former classification and is under the same ownership as Château Grandes Murailles and Clos St.-Martin, the former of which was also unfairly demoted. This wine is aged in wood and 25 per cent of the barrels are renewed every four years.

RED Full, rich, and well-balanced wines that have good fruit, some fat, and an attractive underlying vanilla character.

🍇 Merlot 70%,
 Cabernet sauvignon 20%,
 Cabernet franc 10%

⌐ 4–12 years

Second Wine: *Des Roches Blanches*

CHÂTEAU LA COUSPAUDE
Grand Cru Classé
★

This property was demoted from its *Grand Cru Classé* status in 1985 but, following a string of good vintages, promoted in 1996 back to its original classification. The wine is matured in wood, with up to 80 per cent new oak.

RED This wine now has lots of upfront, juicy-Merlot fruit with an increasing amount of finesse.

🍇 Merlot 60%, Cabernet franc and Cabernet sauvignon 40%

⌐ 3–7 years

Second Wine: *Hubert*

CHÂTEAU COUTET
Grand Cru Classé until 1985
❷

This property was demoted from its *Grand Cru Classé* status in 1985. It has a record of producing finer wines than la Couspaude (*see* previous entry), but unfortunately has the same lack of consistency.

RED Most vintages have a light but elegant style, with a firm tannin structure.

🍇 Cabernet franc 45%,
 Merlot 45%,
 Cabernet sauvignon 5%,
 Malbec 5%

⌐ 4–8 years

CHÂTEAU LE COUVENT
Grand Cru Classé until 1985
❷

This property was purchased by Marne & Champagne in 1982. They did not apply for reclassification in 1985 and were consequently ignored, rather than demoted. The wine is matured in wood for 24 months with 100 per cent new oak.

RED I have not tasted this wine as often as I would like, but the best of those I have tasted were very successful, well-coloured, medium- to full-bodied wines with rich Merlot fruit and some creamy-spicy oak complexity.

🍇 Merlot 55%, Cabernet franc 25%, Cabernet sauvignon 20%

⌐ 6–15 years

COUVENT DES JACOBINS
Grand Cru Classé
★

The wine from the young vines of this property is not included in its *Grand Vin*, but is used to make a Second Wine called "Château Beau Mayne". One-third of the production is matured in wood, with 100 per cent new oak.

RED The delicious, silky-seductive fruit in this consistently well-made wine is very stylish and harmonious.

🍇 Merlot 66%, Cabernet franc and Cabernet sauvignon 33%, Malbec 1%

⌐ 5–15 years

Second Wine: *Château Beau Mayne*

CHÂTEAU CROQUE MICHOTTE
Grand Cru Classé until 1996
★

This property certainly deserves its *Grand Cru Classé* status. The wine is fermented in stainless steel and matured in wood for between 18 and 24 months, with up to one-third new oak. I have not tasted the most recent vintages, but I have heard no suggestion of any downward trend in quality. It was demoted in the official 1996 St.-Émilion Classification.

RED A delightful and elegant style of wine, brimming with juicy, soft, and silky Merlot fruit.

🍇 Merlot 80%, Cabernet franc and Cabernet sauvignon 20%

⌐ 5–12 years

CHÂTEAU CURÉ BON LA MADELEINE
Grand Cru Classé
★

Surrounded by *Premiers Grands Crus Classés* such as Ausone, Belair, and Canon, this property has had an excellent record, but was absorbed by Château Canon in the summer of 2000. This entry is retained for the time being because the wines are still in the market-place and could well become collectors' items. They were matured in wood for 18 to 24 months, with a small proportion of new oak.

RED Elegant, well-defined wine with fine fruit, supple structure, and some finesse.

🍇 Merlot 90%, Cabernet franc 5%, Malbec 5%

⌐ 7–20 years

CHÂTEAU DASSAULT
Grand Cru Classé
★★❂

This property was promoted to *Grand Cru Classé* in the 1969 revision of the 1954 St.-Émilion classification. It has an excellent record and more than deserves its classification. The wine is fermented in stainless steel and matured in wood for 12 months, with one-third of the casks being new oak, and undergoes as many as six rackings. With its beautifully understated Lafite-like label, Dassault's presentation is perfect.

RED Supremely elegant wines that always display a delicate marriage of fruit and oak in perfect balance, with fine acidity and supple tannin.

🍇 Merlot 65%,
 Cabernet franc 20%,
 Cabernet sauvignon 15%

⌐ 8–25 years

Second Wine: *Merissac*

CHÂTEAU LA DOMINIQUE
Grand Cru Classé
★★❂❂

This property, one of the best of the *Grands Crus Classés*, is situated close to Château Cheval Blanc on the *graves* in the extreme west of St.-Émilion. The wine is fermented in stainless-steel vats that are equipped with grilles to keep the *marc* (residue of pips, stalks, and skin) submerged during the *cuvaison* (skin-contact fermentation). It is matured in wood for 24 months, with 50 per cent new oak.

RED Very open and expressive wines that are plump and attractive, full of ripe, creamy fruit with elegant underlying oak.

🍇 Merlot 60%, Cabernet franc 15%, Cabernet sauvignon 15%, Malbec 10%

⌐ 8–25 years

Second Wine: *St.-Paul de la Dominique*

CHÂTEAU FAURIE DE SOUCHARD
Grand Cru Classé
❷

The most positive thing I was able to say in 1988 was that at least this château did not turn out a last-minute string of good vintages in order to influence the 1985

reclassification, but the modestly attractive 1986 did herald the start of an improvement in quality.

RED This is still a medium-bodied wine, but since 1986 the vintages have increased in colour and concentration. Not yet a complex wine, but certainly accessible.

🍇 Merlot 65%,
 Cabernet franc 26%,
 Cabernet sauvignon 9%

⌐ 4–7 years

Other wines: *Cadet-Peychez*

CHÂTEAU-FIGEAC
Premier Grand Cru Classé (B)
★★★

Some critics suggest that the unusually high proportion of Cabernet sauvignon in the *encépagement* (varietal blend) of this great château is wrong, but owner Thierry de Manoncourt refutes this. He has bottles of pure varietal wines produced at Figeac going back 30 years. As far as I am concerned, his blended *Grand Vin* says it all every year. This château belongs with the elite of Ausone and its *graves* neighbour, Cheval Blanc. The wine is matured in wood for 18 to 20 months, with z100 per cent new oak.

RED Impressively ripe, rich, and concentrated wines with fine colour, a beautiful bouquet, stunning creamy-ripe fruit, great finesse, and a wonderful spicy complexity.

🍇 Merlot 30%,
 Cabernet franc 35%,
 Cabernet sauvignon 35%

⌐ 12–30 years

Second Wine: *La Grange Neuve*

CHÂTEAU FONPLÉGADE
Grand Cru Classé

Under the same ownership as Château la Tour du Pin Figeac, this property belongs to Armand Moueix, cousin of Jean-Pierre Moueix of Château Pétrus *et al*. The wine is matured in wood for 12 to 15 months, using one-third new oak.

RED Until quite recently I found these wines astringent and vegetal, but this impression has changed – they are now delightfully clean and attractive, literally bursting with the soft, ripe, juicy fruit flavours of raspberries and strawberries.

🍇 Merlot 60%, Cabernet franc 35%, Cabernet sauvignon 5%

⌐ 5–12 years

Second Wine: *Clos Goudichaud*

CHÂTEAU FONROQUE
Grand Cru Classé

Located just northwest of St.-Émilion itself, this secluded property has belonged to the *négociant* J.-P. Moueix since 1931. The wine is matured in wood for 24 months.

RED This is a deep-coloured, well-made wine with a fine plummy character that shows better on the bouquet and the initial and middle palate than on the finish.

🍇 Merlot 70%, Cabernet franc 30%

🍷 6–15 years

FRANC-MAYNE
Grand Cru Classé
❓

This property was bought in 1996 by a Belgian consortium headed by Georgy Fourcroy, who brought in Michel Rolland as consultant.

RED A deep colour, rich and concentrated.

🍇 Merlot 72%,
Cabernet franc 14%
Cabernet sauvignon 14%

🍷 6–12 years

CLOS FOURTET
Premier Grand Cru Classé (B)
★ ⓥ

This property had an inconsistent record, but has steadily improved throughout the 1990s. The wines are matured in wood for 12 to 18 months, using 70 per cent new oak.

RED Opulent and medium-bodied with silky Merlot fruit, gaining in complexity and finesse.

🍇 Merlot 60%,
Cabernet franc 20%,
Cabernet sauvignon 20%

🍷 6–12 years

Second Wine: *Domaine de Martialis*

CHÂTEAU LA GAFFELIÈRE
Premier Grand Cru Classé (B)
★

This property belongs to Comte Léo de Malet-Roquefort, who also owns the very old estate of Château Tertre Daugay, a *Grand Cru Classé*. After a string of aggressive, ungenerous vintages, Gaffelière has produced increasingly excellent wines since the mid-1980s. The wine is matured in wood for 18 months, with 100 per cent new oak.

RED These wines are concentrated and tannic, but they now have much more finesse, fat, and mouth-tingling richness than previously.

🍇 Merlot 65%,
Cabernet franc 20%,
Cabernet sauvignon 15%

🍷 12–35 years

Second Wine: *Clos la Gaffelière*
Other wines: *Roquefort*

CHÂTEAU LA GOMERIE
Grand Cru
★★

Owned by Gérard and Dominique Bécot of Beau-Séjour-Bécot fame, I rather get the impression that the tiny production of this 100 per cent Merlot vinified in 100 per cent new oak is the vinous equivalent of sticking one finger up to the authorities. The unfair demotion of Beau-Séjour-Bécot in 1985 (rectified in 1996) was a cruel and unjustified blow to the Bécots, who had improved the quality of their wine. By producing an unclassified super-premium St.-Émilion that demands and receives a higher price than its own Premier Grand Cru Classé, the Bécots have demonstrated that the classification is meaningless.

RED Masses of rich, ripe Merlot fruit dominate this wine, despite its 100 per cent new oak. A stunning wine that deserves its cult following.

🍇 Merlot 100%

🍷 4–18 years

CHÂTEAU GRAND CORBIN
Grand Cru Classé until 1996
❓

This property shares the same history and ownership as Château Corbin – it once belonged to the Black Prince, but is now owned by Alain Giraud. Production techniques differ between these properties, however, as the wine at Grand Corbin is fermented not in stainless steel, but in concrete, and matured in wood, using 25 per cent new oak. It was demoted in the official 1996 St.-Émilion Classification.

RED These wines are somewhat lighter in colour than Château Corbin wines and have less richness and body, but they are well made and not without their own appeal.

🍇 Merlot 60%,
Cabernet franc 20%,
Cabernet sauvignon 20%

🍷 4–10 years

CHÂTEAU GRAND-CORBIN-DESPAGNE
Grand Cru Classé until 1996
★

This part of the Corbin estate was bought by the Despagne family – hence the name. It was demoted in the 1996 St.-Émilion Classification. The wine is fermented in stainless steel and matured in wood for up to 18 months, with some new oak.

RED A well-coloured wine of full and rich body with plenty of creamy fruit and oak, supported by supple tannin.

🍇 Merlot 90%,
Cabernet franc 10%

🍷 7–25 years

Second Wine: *Reine-Blanche*

CHÂTEAU GRAND MAYNE
Grand Cru Classé
★ ⓥ

This château ferments its wine in stainless-steel vats and ages it in wood with 80 per cent new oak.

RED This is a firm, fresh, and fruity style of wine that had a rather inconsistent reputation until the 1990s when the wines have had much more richness than in previous years.

🍇 Merlot 50%,
Cabernet franc 40%,
Cabernet sauvignon 10%

🍷 4–10 years

Second Wine: *Les Plantes du Mayne*
Other wines: *Cassevert, Château Beau Mazerat*

CHÂTEAU GRANDES MURAILLES
Grand Cru Classé
★

This property was demoted from its *Grand Cru Classé* status in 1985, unjustly I think. The wines produced here are better and more consistent than those of many châteaux that were not demoted at that time. Château Grandes Murailles was, however, promoted back to its previous status in the 1996 St.-Émilion Classification. It is under the same ownership as Château Côte de Baleau and Clos St.-Martin, the former of which was also unfairly demoted. The wine is fermented in stainless steel vats and matured in wood for 20 months, using up to 25 per cent new oak.

RED These elegant, harmonious wines have good extract and a supple tannin structure that quickly softens. They are a delight to drink when relatively young, although they also age gracefully.

🍇 Merlot 60%,
Cabernet franc 20%,
Cabernet sauvignon 20%

🍷 5–20 years

CHÂTEAU GRAND-PONTET
Grand Cru Classé
★★ ⓥ

Since 1980 this property has been under the same ownership as Château Beau-Séjour Bécot. The wine is matured in wood for 12–18 months with 50 per cent new oak.

RED After a string of very dull vintages, this property is now producing full-bodied wines of fine quality and character. They are fat and ripe, rich in fruit and tannin, with delightful underlying creamy-oak flavours.

🍇 Merlot 60%,
Cabernet franc and
Cabernet sauvignon 40%

🍷 6–15 years

CHÂTEAU GUADET ST.-JULIEN
Grand Cru Classé
★

This property consistently produces wines that well deserve their status. They are matured in wood for 18 to 20 months, using up to one-third new oak.

RED These are wines that show the silky charms of Merlot very early, and then tighten up for a few years before blossoming into finer and fuller wines.

🍇 Merlot 75%,
Cabernet franc and
Cabernet sauvignon 25%

🍷 7–20 years

CHÂTEAU HAUT-CORBIN
Grand Cru Classé
★

This wine is matured in wood for 24 months, with up to 20 per cent new oak. Same ownership as Canteneste, with a string of good vintages in the 1990s.

🍇 Merlot 70%,
Cabernet franc and
Cabernet sauvignon 30%

Second Wine: *Vin d'Edouard*

CHÂTEAU HAUT-SARPE
Grand Cru Classé
★

Although not one of the top performers, this château certainly deserves its status. The wine is matured in wood for 20 to 22 months, using 25 per cent new oak.

RED Elegant, silky, and stylish medium-bodied wines that are best appreciated when young.

🍇 Merlot 70%,
Cabernet franc 30%

🍷 4–8 years

CHÂTEAU JEAN FAURE
Grand Cru Classé until 1985

This property was demoted from its *Grand Cru Classé* status in 1985. I have not tasted vintages beyond 1983. The wine is matured in wood for 24 months, with 25 per cent new oak.

RED These wines have good colour and easy, attractive, supple fruit.

Cabernet franc 60%, Merlot 30%, Malbec 10%

3–8 years

CHATEAU LA MARZELLE
Grand Cru Classé
✩

Under the same ownership as Grand Barrail Lamarzelle Figeac, this property preserved its classification in 1996, while the other château was demoted. Distributed by Dourthe Kressmann.

RED Forward, fruity wines that have improved throughout the 1990s.

Cabernet franc 80%, Merlot 20%

3–7 years

CHÂTEAU LANIOTE
Grand Cru Classé
❷

An old property that incorporates the "Holy Grotto" where St.-Émilion lived in the 8th century. The wine is fermented and matured in wood with 25 per cent new oak.

RED Infrequently tasted, but those I have tasted are light- to medium-bodied wines of some elegance.

Merlot 70%, Cabernet franc 20%, Cabernet sauvignon 10%

6–12 years

CHÂTEAU LARCIS DUCASSE
Grand Cru Classé

This property, whose vineyard is situated on the Côte de Pavie, matures its wine in vat and wood for 24 months.

RED Fuller, richer wines in the 1990s, particularly in the best years.

Merlot 65%, Cabernet franc and Cabernet sauvignon 35%

4–8 years

CHÂTEAU LARMANDE
Grand Cru Classé
★✩

Consistently one of the best *Grands Crus Classés* in St.-Émilion, fermented in stainless steel vats and matured

in wood for 12 to 18 months, with 35 to 50 per cent new oak.

RED These superb wines are typified by their great concentration of colour and fruit. They are rich and ripe with an abundancy of creamy *cassis* and vanilla flavours that develop into a cedarwood complexity.

Merlot 65%, Cabernet franc 30%, Cabernet sauvignon 5%

8–25 years

Second Wine: *Le Cadet de Larmande*

Other Wines: *Des Templiers*

CHÂTEAU LAROQUE
Grand Cru Classé
Made a *Grand Cru Classé* in 1996, this is one of three *Grands Crus Classés* châteaux that are not situated in the commune of St.-Émilion itself.

RED As smooth and fruity as might be expected, with good tannic edge and increasing oak influence.

Merlot 80%, Cabernet franc 15%, Cabernet sauvignon 5%

4–16 years

Second Wine: *Les Tours de Laroque*

CHÂTEAU LAROZE
Grand Cru Classé
★ⓥ

This 19th-century château was named Laroze after a "characteristic scent of roses" was found in its wines. The wine is matured in wood for one to three years.

RED The wine does have a soft and seductive bouquet, although I have yet to find "roses" in it. It is an immediately appealing wine of some finesse that is always a delight to drink early.

Merlot 50%, Cabernet franc 45%, Cabernet sauvignon 5%

4–10 years

CLOS LA MADELEINE
Grand Cru Classé until 1996
This tiny three-hectare (7½-acre) vineyard is in an excellent situation. So far, it has not lived up to its potential and was demoted in the 1996 St.-Émilion Classification.

RED This honest, well-made wine is attractive, supple, and fruity.

Cabernet franc 50%, Merlot 50%

5–10 years

Other wines: *Magnan la Gaffelière.*

CHÂTEAU MAGDELAINE
Premier Grand Cru Classé (B)
★★ⓥ

This could be considered the Pétrus of St.-Émilion. It is the grandest St.-Émilion estate in the Jean-Pierre Moueix Libournais empire, but as fine as the *terroir* is, and as much as Moueix does to extract the maximum quality from it, the wine inevitably falls short of Pétrus. The wine is matured in wood for 18 months, with one-third new oak.

RED These well-coloured wines have excellent concentration, yet

great finesse and a certain delicacy of style. They have a multi-layered flavour and a long, elegant, and complex finish.

Merlot 80%, Cabernet franc 20%

10–35 years

CHÂTEAU MATRAS
Grand Cru Classé
❷

This wine is matured in tank for 12 months, followed by 12 months in one-third new oak. A fine 1990.

Cabernet franc 60%, Merlot 30%, Malbec 10%

CHÂTEAU MAUVEZIN
Grand Cru Classé
❷

This property deserves its *Grand Cru Classé* status. The wine is fermented and matured in new oak.

RED The style usually has been aromatic and supple with some oaky finesse.

Cabernet franc 50%, Merlot 40%, Cabernet sauvignon 10%

7–15 years

CHATEAU MONBOUSQUET
Grand Cru
★✩

This was hypermarket owner Gérard Perse's first venture into wine and he openly admits that he bought the property because of its beauty, rather than out of any detailed analysis of its viticultural potential. That said, he has, with the help of consultant Michel Rolland, taken this château to unbelievable heights and, having done so, set about analysing what could and should be purchased in St.-Émilion from a purely viticultural perspective. He set his sights on Pavie and Pavie-Décesse, which he purchased in 1998 and 1997. Monbousquet remains his home.

RED Voluptuous, velvety and hedonistic, these wines lack neither complexity nor finesse, but they are so delicious to drink that their more profound qualities easily slip by. Or should that be slip down?

Cabernet sauvignon 10%, Cabernet franc 40%, Merlot 50%

4–15 years

CHATEAU MONDOTTE
Grand Cru
★★

Since the 1996 vintage, Stephan Von Neipperg's unclassified vin de garage has surpassed the quality and price of his excellent Grand Cru Classé Château Canon-la-Gafelière. Low yield, 100 per cent oak and ludicrous prices.

RED Extraordinary colour, density, and complexity for a wine that is not in the slightest bit heavy and makes such charming and easy drinking.

Cabernet franc 10%, Merlot 90%

5–20 years

CHÂTEAU MOULIN DU CADET
Grand Cru Classé
★

This château, which is farmed by the Libournais *négociant* J.-P. Moueix, is consistently one of the best *Grands Crus Classés*. The wine is matured in wood for 18 months, with a small proportion of new oak.

RED These wines have good colour, a fine bouquet, delightfully perfumed Merlot fruit, excellent finesse, and some complexity. They are not full or powerful, but what they lack in size, they more than make up for in style.

Merlot 85%, Cabernet franc 15%

6–15 years

CLOS DE L'ORATOIRE
Grand Cru Classé
★★

This property belongs to Stephan Von Neipperg, who should develop a cult-following for this wine. The wine is matured in wood for 18 months, with one-third new oak.

RED These fine, full-flavoured wines tend to have great concentration and style.

Merlot 75%, Cabernet franc 25%

7–15 years

CHÂTEAU PAVIE
Premier Grand Cru Classé (B)
★★ⓥ

This top-performing château was purchased in 1998 along with Pavie-Décesse and La Clusière by Gérard Perse. Perse used to own a group of hypermarkets, but his love of fine wine began to take over his working life in 1993, when he purchased Monbousquet. The link between Pavie under its previous owners, the Valette family, and now is Michel Rolland, who has been retained as consultant. Although Pavie has produced some of the greatest wines of St.-Émilions in recent decades, the obvious advantage for Rolland is that Perse has poured a small fortune into new installations. Could Pavie one day equal the likes of Latour or Margaux? I certainly hope so, otherwise the 1998 and 1999, which both sold for First Growth prices, would be grossly overpriced.

RED Great, stylish wines packed with creamy fruit and lifted by exquisite new oak. Fabulous concentration in the 1998 and 1999 without losing any finesse.

🍇 Merlot 55%,
Cabernet franc 25%,
Cabernet sauvignon 20%

🍷 8–30 years

CHÂTEAU PAVIE DÉCESSE
Grand Cru Classé

★★

This property was under the same ownership as Château Pavie when the Valette family were the owners, and still is under Perse. Although it is not one of the top *Grands Crus Classés*, it is consistent and certainly worthy of its status.

RED Huge seachange in colour, quality, and concentration in the 1998 and 1999 vintage.

🍇 Merlot 60%,
Cabernet franc 25%,
Cabernet sauvignon 15%

🍷 6–12 years

CHÂTEAU PAVIE MACQUIN
Grand Cru Classé

★

This property was named after Albert Macquin, a local grower who pioneered work to graft European vines on to American rootstock. These wines have noticeably improved throughout the 1990s, when Nicolas Thienpont of Vieux Château Certan has overseen the production.

RED Much richer, with more fruit and new oak in recent years.

🍇 Merlot 75%, Cabernet franc
and Cabernet sauvignon 25%

🍷 4–8 years

CHÂTEAU PAVILLON-CADET
Grand Cru Classé (until 1996)
❷

This small vineyard's wine is rarely seen on export markets. It is matured in wood for up to 24 months. The proprietors did not submit Pavillon-Cadet for reclassification in the official 1996 St.-Émilion Classification, thus the château has lost its status.

RED A well-coloured wine with a generous bouquet and chunky, chocolaty fruit – an enjoyable wine, but not really *Grand Cru Classé* quality.

🍇 Cabernet franc 50%, Merlot 50%

🍷 4–8 years

CHÂTEAU PETIT-FAURIE-DE-SOUTARD
Grand Cru Classé

★★

This excellent property used to be part of the neighbouring Château Soutard, but is now run by Jacques Capdemourlin, who also runs Château Cap de Mourlin and

---

Château Balestard la Tonnelle. Half of its production is matured in wood for up to a year.

RED This wine has soft, creamy aromas on the bouquet, some concentration of smooth Merlot fruit on the palate, a silky texture, and a dry, tannic finish. It is absolutely delicious when young but gains a lot from a little bottle-age.

🍇 Merlot 60%,
Cabernet franc 30%,
Cabernet sauvignon 10%

🍷 3–8 years

CHÂTEAU LE PRIEURÉ
Grand Cru Classé

★

This property is under the same ownership as Château Vray Croix de Gay in Pomerol and Château Siaurac in Lalande-de-Pomerol. The wine produced here is matured in wood for 18 to 24 months, with 25 per cent new oak.

RED Light but lengthy wines of some elegance that are best enjoyed when young and fresh.

🍇 Merlot 60%,
Cabernet franc 30%,
Cabernet sauvignon 10%

🍷 4–8 years

Second Wine: *L'Olivier*

CHÂTEAU RIPEAU
Grand Cru Classé
❷

Situated close to Château Cheval Blanc and the Pomerol district but on sandy, not gravelly, soil, this property changed hands in 1976, since when it has undergone considerable expansion and renovation. Although this is an inconsistent performer, one gets the feeling that it will all come together in the not too distant future. Part of the production is matured in wood, with an increasing proportion of new oak.

RED When successful, this wine has fine aromatic character, easy-drinking fruit, and plenty of oak.

🍇 Merlot 60%,
Cabernet franc 20%,
Cabernet sauvignon 20%

🍷 4–10 years

CHÂTEAU ST.-GEORGES (CÔTE PAVIE)
Grand Cru Classé

★

Owned by Jacques Masson, this small property's vineyard is well situated, lying close to those of châteaux Pavie and la Gaffelière. The wine is fermented in stainless steel and matured in wooden casks for 24 months.

RED This is a delicious medium-bodied wine with plump, spicy-juicy Merlot fruit, made in an attractive early-drinking style that does not lack finesse.

🍇 Merlot 50%,
Cabernet franc 25%,
Cabernet sauvignon 25%

🍷 4–8 years

CLOS ST.-MARTIN
Grand Cru Classé

★

These wines are made at Château Côte Baleau alongside those of that property and those of Château Grandes Murailles. Of these three wines, only Clos St.-Martin retained *Grand Cru Classé* status after the reclassification of 1985. It is aged in wood with 25 per cent new barrels every four years.

RED Vivid colour with ripe Merlot fruit, silky texture, and elegant style.

🍇 Merlot 75%,
Cabernet franc 25%

🍷 6–15 years

CHÂTEAU SANSONNET
Grand Cru Classé until 1996
❷

Supposedly purchased in 1999 by François d'Aulan, the former owner of Piper-Heidsieck and the master puppeteer behind numerous wine-related deals ever since. One of my spies reports that the previous owner is still there. If d'Aulan is serious about taking this château on, then we can expect some investment and improvement. However, if it's just part of one of his deals, don't hold your breath.

RED This wine is inconsistent and many vintages lack concentration, but the 1982, which is very light for the year, is supple and attractive.

🍇 Merlot 60%,
Cabernet franc 20%,
Cabernet sauvignon 20%

🍷 3–7 years

CHÂTEAU LA SERRE
Grand Cru Classé

★★ V

This is another property that is improving tremendously in quality. It occupies two terraces on St.-Émilion's limestone plateau, one in front of the château and one behind. The wine is fermented in lined concrete tanks and matured in wood for 16 months with a small proportion of new oak.

RED This wine initially charms, then goes through a tight and sullen period, making it reminiscent of Château Guadet St.-Julien. Their styles, however, are very different. When young, this is quite a ripe and plump wine, totally dominated by new oak. In time, the fruit emerges to form a luscious, stylish wine of some finesse and complexity.

🍇 Merlot 80%,
Cabernet franc 20%

🍷 8–25 years

Second Wine: *Menuts de la Serre*

CHÂTEAU SOUTARD
Grand Cru Classé

★★ V

The large and very fine château on this estate was built in 1740 for the use of the Soutard family in summer. Vines have grown here since Roman times. The wine of Soutard is matured in wood for 18 months, with up to one-third new oak casks.

RED This dark, muscular, and full-bodied wine is made in true *vin de garde* style, which means it improves greatly while ageing. It has great concentrations of colour, fruit, tannin, and extract. With time it can also achieve great finesse and complexity.

🍇 Merlot 65%, Cabernet franc 30%,
Cabernet sauvignon 5%

🍷 12–35 years

Second Wine: *Clos de la Tonnelle*

CHÂTEAU TERTRE DAUGAY
Grand Cru Classé

★

This property was purchased in 1978 by Comte Léo de Malet-Roquefort, the owner of *Premier Grand Cru Classé* Château la Gaffelière. The wine of Château Tertre Daugay, which is matured in wood with one-third new oak, is excellent and is getting better by the vintage.

RED These wines are rich, plump, and fruity with a fine bouquet, ripe underlying oak, great finesse, and surprising longevity.

🍇 Merlot 60%, Cabernet franc 30%,
Cabernet sauvignon 10%

🍷 7–20 years

Second Wine: *De Roquefort*
Other Wines: *Moulin du Biguey*

CHÂTEAU TERTRE-RÔTEBOEUF
★★

François Mitjavile's cult wine is yet more proof that the only important classification is made by the consumer. This was considered to be outrageously expensive before Mondotte. The price has not gone down, but in France you can get four or five bottles of Tertre-Rôteboeuf for the cost of one bottle of Mondotte.

RED Huge, oaky, complex, and cultish: the Leonetti of St.-Émilion!

🍇 Cabernet franc 20%, Merlot 80%

🍷 5–20 years

CHÂTEAU LA TOUR FIGEAC
Grand Cru Classé
★☆

This property was attached to Château Figeac in 1879 and today it is one of the best of the *Grands Crus Classés*. The wine is matured in wood for 18 months, with one-third new oak.

RED These are fat and supple wines with a very alluring bouquet and masses of rich, ripe *cassis* fruit gently supported by smoky-creamy oak.

🍇 Merlot 60%, Cabernet franc 40%

🍷 4–8 years

CHÂTEAU LA TOUR DU PIN FIGEAC
(Owner: Giraud-Bélivier)
Grand Cru Classé
❷

This property is run by André Giraud, who also owns Château le Caillou in Pomerol. Unfortunately, these wines have never impressed me and so I am unable to recommend them.

🍇 Merlot 75%, Cabernet franc 25%

CHÂTEAU LA TOUR DU PIN FIGEAC
(Owner: Moueix)
Grand Cru Classé
★☆

This property is one of the best of the *Grands Crus Classés*. It is now part of the Armand Moueix stable of châteaux. The wine is matured in wood for 12 to 15 months, with one-third new oak.

RED These consistently well-made wines always show a beautiful balance of spicy-juicy Merlot fruit, creamy oak, and supple tannin.

🍇 Merlot 60%, Cabernet franc 30%, Cabernet sauvignon and Malbec 10%

🍷 6–15 years

CHÂTEAU TRIMOULET
Grand Cru Classé
★

This is an old property overlooking St.-Georges–St.-Émilion. The wine is matured in wood for 12 months, with 100 per cent new oak.

RED This well-coloured wine has an overtly ripe and fruity aroma, lots of creamy-oaky character, a fruit flavour, and supple tannin.

🍇 Merlot 60%, Cabernet franc 20%, Cabernet sauvignon 20%

🍷 7–20 years

CHÂTEAU TROIS-MOULINS
Grand Cru Classé

These vineyards have been incorporated with those of Château Beau-Séjour Bécot since 1979.

CHÂTEAU TROPLONG MONDOT
Grand Cru Classé
★★

This property is owned by Claude Valette and is run by his daughter Christine. Half the production is matured in wood for 18 months with 80 per cent new oak.

RED Since the introduction of temperature-controlled fermentation and a second wine in 1985, some critics have believed the quality of this wine to be on a par with that of a *Premier Grand Cru Classé*, but for me, Troplong Mondot came on stream with the sensational 1988, 1989, 1990, 1992, and 1996 (those between being merely excellent!).

🍇 Merlot 65%, Cabernet franc and Malbec 20%, Cabernet sauvignon 15%

🍷 4–8 years

Second Wine: *Mondot*

CHÂTEAU TROTTEVIEILLE
Premier Grand Cru Classé (B)
★☆

This property has the reputation of producing a star wine every five years or so, interspersed by very mediocre wines indeed, but has been made very consistent since 1985, and now makes true *Premier Grand Cru Classé* quality wine every year. The wine is matured in wood for 18 months, with up to 100 per cent new oak.

RED The quality has dramatically improved since the mid-1980s. It has fabulous Merlot-fruit richness with new oak and the power of a true *Premier Grand Cru Classé*.

🍇 Merlot 50%, Cabernet franc 40%, Cabernet sauvignon 10%

🍷 8–25 years (successful years only)

CHÂTEAU VALANDRAUD
Grand Cru
❷★★

Château Valandraud is yet another St.-Émilion super-premium cult wine. A sign of the time perhaps, but this district is so wide open to the phenomenon once known as the boutique winery. At just 500FF or £50 at the time of writing, this wine is a veritable bargain, costing one-sixth that of Mondotte, yet the latter is merely the product of 100 per cent new oak, whereas Valandraud received 200 per cent! How come, you may well ask. Well, the wine goes into new oak, but when it is racked, it is not racked back into the same barrels:

it is racked into new oak barrels! This after such extraction that more colour could not be obtained at gunpoint. You might consider this to be a case of dual-ranking, depending on how many splinters you prefer in your wines. The Malbec content is unusual for St.-Émilion these days.

RED Wines that even Gary Figgins at Leonetti (Washington) might complain were too oaky! I suspect that I might reverse an opinion or two about some of the vintages in 20 years' time.

🍇 Cabernet franc 20%, Merlot 75%, Malbec 5%

🍷 6–25 years

CHÂTEAU VILLEMAURINE
Grand Cru Classé

Château Villemaurine belongs to Robert Giraud, which is a *négociant* concern owning not only this property, but also some 20 other *petits châteaux* in various Bordeaux districts. The wine is matured in wood for 18 to 24 months, with 50 per cent new oak.

RED These are full-bodied wines of excellent, spicy Merlot fruit, good underlying oak, and firm structure.

🍇 Merlot 70%, Cabernet sauvignon 30%

🍷 8–25 years

Other wines: *Maurinus, Beausoleil*

CHÂTEAU YON-FIGEAC
Grand Cru Classé

This is an important property situated near Pomerol. The wine is matured for 18 months with 100 per cent new oak.

RED This wine is attractive and easy-to-drink but not special, although the 1997, 1998, and 1999 are the best vintages ever.

🍇 Cabernet franc and Cabernet sauvignon 70%, Merlot 30%

🍷 5–15 years

THE BEST OF THE REST

With more than a thousand châteaux in this one district, it is not practical to feature every recommendable wine, therefore I list here the "best of the rest", being those châteaux not mentioned above which consistently make wines that stand out for either quality or value, or sometimes both. Those châteaux marked with a star sometimes produce wines that are better than many *Grands Crus Classés*.

Château du Barry
Château Cheval Noir
★ Château la Commanderie
★ Château Destieux
Château de Ferrand
★ Château la Fleur
★ Château Fleur Cardinale
Château la Fleur Pourret
★ Château Fombrauge
Château Franc Bigoroux
Château Grand Champs
★ Château la Grave Figeac

★ Château Haut Brisson
★ Château Haut Plantey
Château Haut-Pontet
★ Haut-Quercus
Clos Labarde
Château Lapelletrie
★ Château Laroque
Château Magnan la Gaffelière
Château Martinet
Clos des Menuts
Château Patris
★ Château Pavillon Figeac

★ Château Petit-Figeac
Château Petit-Gravet
★ Château Petit Val
Château Peyreau
★ Château Pindefleurs
Château Puy Razac
Château Roc Blanquant
★ Château Rolland-Maillet
Château Tour St.-Christophe

POMEROL

The most velvety and sensuous clarets are produced in Pomerol, yet the traveller passing through this small and rural area, with its dilapidated farmhouses at every turn, few true châteaux and no really splendid ones, must wonder how this uninspiring area can produce such magnificently expensive wines.

THE PROSPERITY OF RECENT YEARS has enabled Pomerol's properties to indulge in more than just an extra lick of paint, but renovation can only restore, not create, and Pomerol essentially remains an area with an air of obscurity. Even Château Pétrus, which is the greatest growth of Pomerol and produces what for the last twenty years has been consistently the world's most expensive wine, is nothing more than a simple farmhouse. It is interesting to reflect that, if this revered wine had achieved its current reputation and price under the *nouveau* aristocracy of the First Empire, the finest architect in France would have been summoned to the backwoods of Libourne to construct a magnificent château as a monument to its glorious success.

There has been no attempt to publish an official classification of Pomerol wines, but Château Pétrus is universally accepted as the leading growth and, since it commands prices that dwarf those of wines such as Mouton and Margaux, it could not be denied a status equivalent to that of a First Growth. Indeed, Le Pin has very recently become considerably more expensive than Pétrus and Lafleur; L'Evangile, La Fleur Pétrus, La Conseillante, Trotanoy, and a few others can all cost as much as Médoc First Growths, and many are more expensive. It is difficult to imagine, but Pomerol was once considered to be an inferior sub-appellation of St.-Emilion. Pomerol obtained its independent status in 1900, but even Château Pétrus did not become sought after until the mid-1960s.

FACTORS AFFECTING TASTE AND QUALITY

LOCATION
Pomerol is a small rural area on the western extremity of the St.-Émilion district, just northeast of Libourne.

CLIMATE
The same as for St.-Émilion (*see* p.105).

ASPECT
This modest mound, with Château Pétrus and Château Vieux Certan, situated at its centre, is the eastern extension of the Pomerol-Figeac *graves* (gravelly terrain). The vines grow on slightly undulating slopes that, over a distance of 2 km (1.2 miles), descend from between 35 and 40 m above sea level (115–130 ft) to 10 m (33 ft).

SOIL
Pomerol's soil is sandy to the west of the national highway and to the east, where the best properties are situated on the sandy-gravel soil of the Pomerol-Figeac *graves*. The subsoil consists of an iron-pan known as *crasse de fer* or *machefer*, with gravel in the east and clay in the north and centre. The château of Pétrus lies in the very centre of the Pomerol-Figeac *graves*, on a unique geological formation of sandy-clay over *molasse* (sandstone).

VITICULTURE AND VINIFICATION
Some of Pomerol's châteaux use a proportion of *vin de presse* according to the requirement of the vintage. At Pétrus, the *vin de presse* is added earlier than is normal practice, in order to allow it to mature with the rest of the wine – this is believed to reduce harshness. The duration of skin-contact is usually between 15 and 21 days, but is sometimes as brief as ten days or as long as four weeks. The wines stay in cask for between 18 and 20 months.

PRIMARY GRAPE VARIETIES
Cabernet franc, Cabernet sauvignon, Merlot
SECONDARY GRAPE VARIETIES
Malbec

POMEROL, *see also* p.101
The sleepy area of Pomerol and Lalande-de-Pomerol fans out above the riverside town of Libourne. None of the so-called "châteaux" is particularly imposing: among the most attractive are Château Nénin and Vieux Château Certan.

THE VINEYARDS OF VIEUX CHÂTEAU CERTAN
After Château Pétrus, this is one of the best wine-producing properties in Pomerol. A quaint signpost marks the boundary of the vineyard.

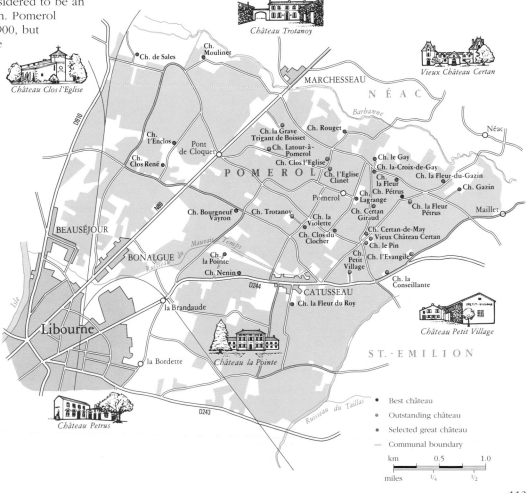

- Best château
- Outstanding château
- Selected great château
- Communal boundary

km   0.5   1.0
miles 1/4   1/2

WHAT MAKES PÉTRUS THE WORLD'S MOST EXPENSIVE WINE? (*See p.116*)

Pétrus is the most expensive wine in the world, and over the last decade, blue-chip First Growths in general have proved their investment value: the auction price of a case of 1961 Margaux, Mouton, Latour, or Lafite has risen by between 125 and 170 per cent to £3,800–£6,200; the legendary 1967 Yquem has risen by 125 per cent to £3,600; and the 1961 Romanée Conti has leapt by 400 per cent to £4,500. Pétrus 1961 has also performed well, having risen in price in the last decade from around £8,100 per case to up to £26,800 – an increase of around 140 per cent. Why is Pétrus so special? The answer is nothing to do with the weather – the neighbouring vineyards enjoy precisely the same climatic conditions. The most important factor is the soil of Pétrus.

THE MERLOT GRAPE
Of the 11.5 hectares (28 acres), barely four per cent is Cabernet franc; most of this is not used in the *Grand Vin* unless it is exceptionally ripe. Most Pétrus is virtually 100 per cent Merlot.

FROST
Pomerol is susceptible to frost and this quite often cuts the potential yield of its vineyards, producing wines of greater concentration.

PRUNING
The famous firm that runs Château Pétrus, J.-P. Moueix, never relies on the frost for pruning and always restricts the number of buds to eight per vine. Ten buds would increase the yield by 25 per cent, but the wine would lose its essential Pétrus character.

CROP THINNING
Cutting healthy bunches of grapes in July would be lunacy for most growers, but they are not making as expensive or concentrated a wine as Pétrus.

HARVESTING
Moueix has a highly-skilled force of 180 pickers for its empire of Libournais châteaux and they are all kept on alert for Château Pétrus. The day the grapes reach perfect maturation and there is no threat of rain, the entire force

CHATEAU PÉTRUS
The greatest growth of Pomerol.

descends on Pétrus. They pick only in the afternoon, by which time the sun has evaporated all the dew that would otherwise dilute the wine. This also yields grapes at a temperature favourable to fermentation.

VIN DE PRESSE
This is not added during the *assemblage* of the *Grand Vin*, but is immediately mixed with the free-run juice. Christian Moueix believes that it can take on a bitter taste if kept separately, but softens if allowed to age and develop with the *Grand Vin*.

MALOLACTIC CONVERSION
This process is encouraged to coincide with the alcoholic fermentation by adding lactic bacteria.

NEW OAK
The wine is matured in 100 per cent new oak for 18 to 22 months.

THE UNIQUE SOIL
All the above factors that affect quality could be replicated by any of the neighbouring châteaux, but the soil – the so-called "buttonhole" – of Pétrus is unique. The "buttonhole" is situated in the centre of the gravelly area that overlaps St.-Émilion, the "Pomerol-Figeac" *graves* that is responsible for the quality of Pomerol's best wines. Extraordinarily, it is the sandy-clay anomaly within it that is responsible for the even greater quality of Pétrus (*see also* Soil description, p.113.). The "buttonhole" is no ordinary soil and its clay is unlike the riverside clay, which produces rather coarse wine. Pétrus is positioned on a rise of *molasse* bedrock that was left bare when the bank of ancient gravel was laid down. Exposed to wind and water, the *molasse* was eroded and chemically altered, creating a sandy-clay. Subsequent decomposition and various climatic changes eventually formed three basic soil types: sandy-loam, sandy-clay-loam, and clay. One aspect of these soils is that they are essentially acid and so produce wines that are inversely lower in acidity.

TEAM OF PICKERS IN A POMEROL VINEYARD
Christian Moueix, whose family owns Château Pétrus, says of the decision of when to harvest: "Things have to be done the day they have to be done".

POMEROL COUNTRY
Pomerol is flat and unprepossessing, divided into smallholdings and dotted with unpromising-looking properties, but they actually produce some of Bordeaux's finest wines.

THE WINE PRODUCERS OF
POMEROL

CHÂTEAU BEAUREGARD
★ ☆

An American architect who visited Pomerol after World War I built a replica of Beauregard called "Mille Fleurs" on Long Island, New York. Quality changed dramatically at Beauregard in 1985, two years before the arrival of Michel Rolland, who followed 1985's superb wine with others and was generally responsible for turning this château around. The wine is matured in wood for 24 months with 60 per cent new oak.

RED Firm, elegant, and lightly rich wine with floral-cedarwood fruit.

🍇 Merlot 48%, Cabernet franc 44%, Cabernet sauvignon 6%, Malbec 2%

🍷 5–10 years

Second Wine: *Le Benjamin de Beauregard*

CHÂTEAU BONALGUE

This small property lies on gravel and sand northwest of Libourne. The wine is matured in wood.

RED This medium- to full-bodied wine has always been of respectable quality with a frank attack of refreshing fruit flavours, a supple tannin structure, and a crisp finish.

🍇 Merlot 65%, Cabernet franc and Cabernet sauvignon 30%, Malbec 5%

🍷 5–10 years

Second Wine: *Burgrave*

CHÂTEAU LE BON PASTEUR
★

This good and steadily improving wine is matured in wood for 24 months, with 35 per cent new oak.

RED These intensely coloured, full-bodied, complex wines are packed with *cassis*, plum, and black-cherry flavours.

🍇 Merlot 75%, Cabernet franc 25%

🍷 8–25 years

CHÂTEAU BOURGNEUF-VAYRON

This property is situated close to Château Trotanoy. It has an honourable, if not exciting, record and a 25-hectare (ten-acre) vineyard.

RED These wines are fresh and light, made in a quick-maturing style with soft fruit and a light herbal finish.

🍇 Merlot 85%, Cabernet franc 15%

🍷 4–8 years

CHÂTEAU LA CABANNE
★

This is a fine estate producing increasingly better wine. The wine is matured in wood for 18 months, with one-third new oak.

RED These medium-bodied, sometimes full-bodied, wines have fine, rich, chocolaty fruit.

🍇 Merlot 60%, Cabernet franc 30%, Malbec 10%

🍷 7–20 years

Second Wine: *Domaine de Compostelle*

CHÂTEAU CERTAN DE MAY DE CERTAN
★ ★

This can be a confusing wine to identify because the "De May de Certan" part of its name is in very small type on the label and it is usually referred to as "Château Certan de May". It is matured in wood for 24 months, with 50 per cent new oak.

RED This is a firm and tannic wine that has a powerful bouquet bursting with fruit, spice, and vanilla.

🍇 Merlot 65%, Cabernet franc 25%, Cabernet sauvignon and Malbec 10%

🍷 15–35 years

CHÂTEAU CLINET
★ ★

This wine, which is matured in wood with one-third new oak, has undergone a revolution in recent years. It used to disappoint those looking for the typically fat, gushy-juicy style of Pomerol, and critics often blamed this on the wine's high proportion of Cabernet sauvignon. The 1985 vintage was more promising (a touch plumper than previous vintages, with more juicy character), so Clinet's previous lack of typical Pomerol character was evidently not entirely due to the blend of grape varieties, although the vineyard has since undergone a radical change in varietal proportions. There was talk of a turnaround in quality beginning with the 1986 vintage, but it was not until the stunning 1989 and 1990 vintages that we really saw this wine take off.

RED Château Clinet is now producing exceedingly fine, rich, ripe wine with ample, yet supple tannin structure mixed with oaky tannins to produce a creamy-herbal-menthol complexity.

🍇 Merlot 75%, Cabernet sauvignon 15%, Cabernet franc 10%

🍷 7–20 years

CLOS DU CLOCHER
★ ☆ ⓥ

This belongs to the Libournais *négociant* Audy. The wine is rotated in thirds between new oak, one-year-old casks, and vat, and is one of the most undervalued Pomerols.

RED These are deliciously deep-coloured, attractive, medium-bodied, sometimes full-bodied, wines that have plenty of plump, ripe fruit, a supple structure, intriguing vanilla undertones, and plenty of finesse.

🍇 Merlot 80%, Cabernet 20%

🍷 8–20 years

Second Wine: *Esprit de Clocher*

Other Wines: *Château Monregard-Lacroix*

CHÂTEAU LA CONSEILLANTE
★ ★ ☆

If Pétrus is rated a "megastar", this property must be rated at least a "superstar" in the interests of fairness. The wine is matured in wood for 20 to 24 months, with 50 per cent new oak.

RED This wine has all the power and concentration of the greatest wines of Pomerol, but its priorities are its mindblowing finesse and complexity.

🍇 Cabernet franc 45%, Merlot 45%, Malbec 10%

🍷 10–30 years

CHÂTEAU LA CROIX

This property's wine is matured in wood for 20 to 24 months.

RED These attractive wines are quite full-bodied, yet elegant and quick-maturing, with fine, spicy Merlot fruit.

🍇 Merlot 60%, Cabernet sauvignon 20%, Cabernet franc 20%

🍷 5–10 years

Second Wine: *Le Gabachot*

CHÂTEAU LA CROIX DE GAY

This property is situated in the north of Pomerol on sandy-gravel soil, and the wine is matured in wood for 18 months, with up to 30 per cent new oak.

RED This red wine is somewhat lightweight, but attractive, with easy-drinking qualities.

🍇 Merlot 80%, Cabernet sauvignon 10%, Cabernet franc 10%

🍷 4–8 years

Other wines: *Château le Commandeur, Vieux-Château-Groupey*

CHÂTEAU DU DOMAINE DE L'ÉGLISE

This is the oldest estate in Pomerol. The wine is matured in wood for 18 to 24 months, with one-third new oak.

RED This is another attractive, essentially elegant wine that is light in weight and fruit.

🍇 Merlot 90%, Cabernet franc 10%

🍷 4–8 years

CLOS L'ÉGLISE
★ ☆

There are several "Église" properties in Pomerol. The wine from this one is matured in wood for 24 months, with some new oak.

RED A consistently attractive wine with elegant, spicy Merlot fruit and firm structure; it is eventually dominated by violet Cabernet perfumes.

🍇 Merlot 55%, Cabernet sauvignon 25%, Cabernet franc 20%

🍷 6–15 years

Second Wine: *La Petite Église*

CHÂTEAU L'ÉGLISE-CLINET
★ ★

The wine produced by Château L'Église-Clinet, which is matured in wood for up to 24 months with as much as 50 per cent new oak, is fast becoming one of the most exciting Pomerols. Quality in overdrive since the 1990s.

RED These are deeply coloured wines with a rich, seductive bouquet and a big, fat flavour bursting with spicy blackcurrant fruit and filled with creamy-vanilla oak complexity.

🍇 Merlot 80%, Cabernet franc 20%

🍷 8–30 years

Second Wine: *La Petite l'Église*

CHÂTEAU L'ENCLOS
★ ⓥ

The vineyard is situated on an extension of the sandy-gravel soil from the better side of the N89. The wine is matured in wood for 20 months, with a little new oak.

RED These are deliciously soft, rich, and voluptuous wines, full of plump, juicy Merlot fruit and spice.

Merlot 80%,
Cabernet franc 19%,
Malbec 1%

7–15 years

CHÂTEAU L'EVANGILE
★★☆

Situated close to two superstars of Pomerol, Vieux Château Certan and Château la Conseillante, this château produces stunning wines that are matured in wood for 15 months with 20 per cent new oak.

RED Dark but not brooding, these fruity wines are rich, and packed with summer fruits and cedarwood.

Merlot 65%, Cabernet franc and Cabernet sauvignon 35%

8–20 years

CHÂTEAU FEYTIT-CLINET
★

J.-P. Moueix, who is not this château's owner, does produce the wine and sells it on an exclusivity basis. Some vines are over 70 years old. The wine is matured in wood for 18 to 22 months.

RED Consistently well-coloured and stylish wines that are full of juicy plum and black-cherry flavours.

Merlot 80%, Cabernet franc 20%

7–15 years

CHÂTEAU LA FLEUR-PÉTRUS
★★

Château La Fleur-Pétrus, producer of one of the best Pomerols, is situated close to Château Pétrus, but on soil that is more gravelly. Four hectares (ten acres) of Château le Gay were purchased in 1994 and incorporated in this property, fattening out the style. The wine is matured in wood for 18 to 22 months.

RED Although recent vintages are relatively big and fat, these essentially elegant wines rely more on exquisiteness than richness. They are silky, soft, and supple.

Merlot 80%, Cabernet franc 20%

6–20 years

CHÂTEAU LE GAY
★Ⓥ

This is another château exclusive to the Libournais négociant J.-P. Moueix. The wine is matured in wood for 18 to 22 months.

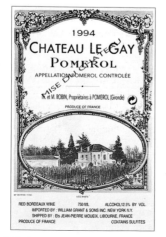

RED Firm and ripe, this big wine is packed with dense fruit and coffee-toffee oak.

Merlot 70%, Cabernet franc 30%

10–25 years

CHÂTEAU GAZIN
★★☆Ⓥ

This château's record was disappointing until the stunning 1985 vintage, and it has been on a roll ever since, having abandoned harvesting by machine, introduced new, thermostatically controlled vats, and employed various quality-enhancing practices, not the least being a Second Wine, which enables stricter selection of grapes. The wine is matured in wood for 18 months with up to one-third new oak.

RED Marvellously ripe and rich wine with plump fruit. It should have a great future.

Merlot 80%, Cabernet franc 15%, Cabernet sauvignon 5%

8–20 years

Second Wine: Hospitalet de Gazin

CHÂTEAU LA GRAVE

The gravelly vineyard of this property has an excellent location. The Trignant de Boisset element of this château's name has been dropped. It is owned by Christian Moueix and farmed by J.-P. Moueix. The wine is matured in wood with 25 per cent new oak.

RED Supple, rich and fruity, medium-bodied wines of increasing finesse.

Merlot 95%, Cabernet franc 5%

7–15 years

CHÂTEAU HOSANNA
★★Ⓥ

This property was called Château Certan-Marzelle until 1956 and was purchased in 1999 by Jean-Paul Moueix, with Christian Moueix in control. Almost immediately four hectares (ten acres) of less well-positioned vineyards were sold to Nénin and strict selection imposed on the 1999 vintage. Watch this space! The wine is matured in wood for 24 months, with 15 per cent new oak.

RED These ripe, voluptuous wines become darker and denser since 1999.

Merlot 67%, Cabernet franc and Cabernet sauvignon 33%

8–20 years

Second Wine: Clos du Roy

Other wines: Château Certan-Marzelle

CHÂTEAU LAFLEUR
★★★

This property has a potential for quality second only to Château Pétrus itself, but it has a very inconsistent record. The quality and concentration of the wines have soared since 1985.

RED This is a well-coloured wine with a rich, plummy-porty bouquet, cassis fruit, a toasty-coffee oak complexity and great finesse.

Cabernet franc 50%, Merlot 50%

10–25 years

Second Wine: Les Pensées de Lafleur

CHÂTEAU LAFLEUR-GAZIN
★

This property has been run by the J.-P. Moueix team on behalf of its owners since 1976. It produces a wine that is matured in wood for 18 to 22 months.

RED Well-made wines of good colour and bouquet, supple structure, and some richness and concentration.

Merlot 70%, Cabernet franc 30%

6–15 years

CHÂTEAU LAGRANGE
★

Not to be confused with its namesake in St.-Julien, this property belongs to the firm J.-P. Moueix. The wine is aged in wood for 18 to 22 months, with some new oak.

RED The recent vintages of this full-bodied wine have been very impressive, with an attractive and accessible style.

Merlot 90%, Cabernet franc 10%

8–20 years

CHÂTEAU LATOUR À POMEROL
★★

Château Latour à Pomerol now belongs to the last surviving sister of Madame Loubat, Madame Lily Lacoste (owner of one-third of Château Pétrus). The wine is matured in wood with 25 per cent new oak.

RED These deep, dark wines are luscious, voluptuous, and velvety. They have a great concentration of fruit and a sensational complexity of flavours.

Merlot 90%, Cabernet franc 10%

12–35 years

CHÂTEAU MAZEYRES
★☆

Two-thirds of this wine is matured in wood with 30 per cent new oak, and one-third is aged in vat.

RED These elegant wines are rich, ripe, and juicy, and have silky Merlot fruit and some oaky finesse.

Merlot 70%, Cabernet franc 30%

5–12 years

CHÂTEAU MOULINET
★☆Ⓥ

This large estate belongs to Armand Moueix. The wine is matured in wood for 18 months, with one-third new oak.

RED These red wines are attractively supple with a light, creamy-ripe fruit and oak flavour.

Merlot 60%, Cabernet sauvignon 30%, Cabernet franc 10%

5–10 years

CHÂTEAU NÉNIN
✪

A large and well-known property between Catussau and the outskirts of Libourne. The wine has had a disappointing record, but since this property was purchased by Jean-Hubert Delon in 1997 there have been signs of improvement, albeit slow and incremental.

RED The 1997 and 1998 are the best wines yet, and with the addition of four hectares (ten acres) from Certan-Giraud, future vintages should be even better.

Merlot 70%, Cabernet franc 20%, Cabernet sauvignon 10%

4–8 years

Second Wine: Château St.-Roche

CHÂTEAU PETIT-VILLAGE
★★

This property borders Vieux Château Certan and Château La Conseillante, and it therefore has the advantage of a superb terroir and a meticulous owner. The result is a wine of superstar quality, even in poor years. Petit-Village is matured in wood for 18 months with at least 50 per cent of the casks made from new oak.

RED These wines seem to have everything. Full and rich with lots of colour and unctuous fruit, they have a firm structure of ripe and supple tannins and a luscious, velvety texture. Classic, complex, and complete.

Merlot 80%, Cabernet franc 10%, Cabernet sauvignon 10%

8–30 years

CHÂTEAU PÉTRUS
★★★

The Libournais négociant J.-P. Moueix has been in technical control of this estate since 1947. Before the previous owner, Madame Loubat, died in 1961, she gave one-third of Pétrus to Monsieur Moueix. She had no children, just two sisters who were not on the best of terms, so Madame Loubat wisely gave Moueix the means of ensuring that family disagreements would not be able to harm the day-to-day running of Château Pétrus. In 1964 Moueix purchased one of the other two shares and has controlled the destiny of this world-famous château ever since.

RED The low acidity of Château Pétrus makes it an intrinsically soft wine which, when combined with the inherent lusciousness of the Merlot grape, enables Pétrus to produce intensely coloured, super-concentrated wines that would otherwise be too harsh to drink.

Merlot 95%, Cabernet franc 5%

20–50 years

CHÂTEAU LE PIN
★★

This tiny one-hectare (2½-acre) property was purchased in 1979 by the Thienpont family, who also own the neighbouring Vieux Château Certan. Since the 1981 vintage, there has been a deliberate attempt to outclass Pétrus in quality and also, as you may have guessed, in price. The yield is very low and the wine is fermented in stainless steel and matured in wood for 18 months with 100 per cent new oak. Those who are not convinced by le Pin keep asking whether there is enough concentration in these wines to match the oak; my guess is that there is, and that their wonderfully voluptuous style belies their true size and structure, but it will be a long time before we really know the answer.

RED These oaky wines are very full-bodied, and powerfully aromatic with a sensational spicy-*cassis* flavour dominated by decadently rich, creamy-toffee, toasty-coffee oak.

Merlot 100%

15–40 years

CHÂTEAU PLINCE
★ V

This property is owned by the Moreau family, but its wines are sold by the Libournais *négociant* J.-P. Moueix. It is matured in vats for six months and in wood for 18 months, with 15 per cent new oak.

RED These wines are fat, ripe, and simply ooze with juicy Merlot flavour. Although they could not be described as aristocratic, they are simply delicious.

Merlot 75%, Cabernet franc 20%, Cabernet sauvignon 5%

4–8 years

CHÂTEAU LA POINTE
✕

Until 1985, these light, lacklustre wines have given me the impression of an overcropped vineyard. I had hoped the 1985 would prove to be a turning point in the reputation of this important château but it was a one-off. The wine is matured in wood for 18 to 20 months with 35 per cent new oak.

RED Apart from the elegant, stylish, and reasonably priced 1985 vintage, the wines produced by Château La Pointe are lacking in every quality that makes Pomerol so lush.

Merlot 80%, Cabernet franc 15%, Malbec 5%

5–12 years

Second Wine: *La Pointe Riffat*

CLOS RENÉ
★ V

This property is situated just south of l'Enclos on the western side of the N89. The wine is matured in wood for 24 months with up to 15 per cent new oak. An underrated wine, it represents good value.

RED These wines have a splendid spicy-blackcurrant bouquet, plenty of fine plummy fruit on the palate, and a great deal of finesse. They are sometimes complex in structure, and are always of excellent quality.

Merlot 60%, Cabernet franc 30%, Malbec 10%

6–12 years

Other wines: *Moulinet-Lasserre*

CHÂTEAU ROUGET
★ V

One of the oldest properties in Pomerol. The proprietor also owns the neighbouring estate of Vieux Château des Templiers. The wine is matured in wood for 24 months.

RED Château Rouget produces excellent red wines with a fine bouquet and elegant flavour. Fat and rich, with good structure and lots of ripe fruit, they are at their most impressive when mature.

Merlot 90%, Cabernet franc 10%

10–25 years

CHÂTEAU DE SALES
★ V

At 48 hectares (119 acres), this is easily the largest property in the Pomerol appellation. It is situated in the very northwest of the district. Despite an uneven record, it has demonstrated its potential and inherent qualities on many occasions and the wine, which is matured in wood for 18 months with 35 per cent new oak, is one to watch for the future.

RED When successful, these wines have a penetrating bouquet and a palate jam-packed with deliciously juicy flavours of succulent stone-fruits such as plums, black cherries, and apricots.

Merlot 70%, Cabernet franc 15%, Cabernet sauvignon 15%

7–20 years

Second Wine: *Château Chantalouette*
Other wines: *Château de Délias*

CHÂTEAU DU TAILHAS

The wines of this château are matured in wood for 18 months with 50 per cent new oak.

RED Consistently attractive, with silky Merlot fruit and creamy oak.

Merlot 80%, Cabernet franc 10%, Cabernet sauvignon 10%

5–12 years

CHÂTEAU TAILLEFER
❓

This potentially excellent property belongs to Bernard Moueix. The wines are matured in wood for between 18 and 22 months, with the addition of some new oak.

RED At best these wines are attractively light and fruity, revealing their potential, but more often than not they are simply light and dilute.

Merlot 55%, Cabernet franc 30%, Cabernet sauvignon 15%

4–8 years

Second Wine: *Clos Toulifaut*

CHÂTEAU TROTANOY
★★½

Some consider this to be second only to Château Pétrus, although in terms of price l'Évangile and Lafleur have overtaken it. The wine is matured in wood for up to 24 months, with 50 per cent new oak.

RED This inky-black, brooding wine has a powerful bouquet and a rich flavour, which is supported by a firm tannin structure and a complex, creamy-toffee, spicy-coffee oak character.

Merlot 90%, Cabernet franc 10%

15–35 years

VIEUX CHÂTEAU CERTAN
★★½

This was once regarded as the finest-quality growth in Pomerol. It has not so much dropped its standards as witnessed the rapid rise of a new star – Pétrus – and all its pretenders. Vieux Château Certan remains one of Bordeaux's great wines. This wine is matured in wood for 18 to 24 months with up to 60 per cent new oak.

RED This is an attractive, garnet-coloured, full-bodied wine that has a smouldering, smooth, and mellow flavour. It displays great finesse and complexity of structure.

Merlot 50%, Cabernet franc 25%, Cabernet sauvignon 20%, Malbec 5%

12–35 years

Second Wine: *La Gravette de Certan*

CHÂTEAU LA VIOLETTE
★ ❓

In the same way as Château Laroze in St.-Émilion is said to be named after its aroma of roses, so this château is named after its aroma of violets – or so the story goes. It is located in Catussau and its vineyards are scattered about the commune. The wine, matured in wood for up to 24 months, can be inconsistent, but I think it has great potential.

RED I have not tasted this wine as frequently as I would like, but I can enthusiastically recommend the best vintages, when they have a rich and jubilant flavour of Merlot fruit, which is ripe and fat.

Merlot 95%, Cabernet franc 5%

5–15 years

CHÂTEAU VRAY CROIX DE GAY

A small property on good gravelly soil next to Château le Gay and under the same ownership as Château le Prieuré. The wine is matured in wood in 18 months.

RED The wine can be full, rich, chocolate- and black-cherry-flavoured, with the best vintages showing more fat and oak.

Merlot 80%, Cabernet franc 15%, Cabernet sauvignon 5%

5–10 years

THE WINE PRODUCERS OF THE FRONSADAIS AND THE
SAINT-ÉMILION AND POMEROL SATELLITES

CHÂTEAU D'AIGUILHE
AOC Bordeaux-Côtes-de-Castillon
★✫ Ⓥ

Purchased in 1998 by Stephan Von Neipperg, who has restored the property. One to watch.

Second wine: *Seigneurs d'Aiguilhe*

CHÂTEAU DES ANNEREAUX
AOC Lalande-de-Pomerol

Attractive, fruity, medium-bodied wines of some elegance.

CHÂTEAU BARRABAQUE
AOC Côtes Canon-Fronsac
★✫ Ⓥ

Situated on the mid-côte, this 70 per cent Merlot has really shone since the late 1990s.

CHÂTEAU BEL-AIR
AOC Puisseguin-St.-Émilion

This property makes generous, fruity, early-drinking wines.

CHÂTEAU DE BEL-AIR
AOC Lalande-de-Pomerol
★ Ⓥ

One of the best of the appellation, this property has fine, sandy gravel.

CHÂTEAU BELAIR-MONTAIGUILLON
AOC St.-Georges–St.-Émilion
★ Ⓥ

Consistently rich, deliciously fruity. The best wine selected from old vines and matured in cask, including some new oak, is sold as Château Belair-St.-Georges.

CHÂTEAU DE BELCIER
AOC Bordeaux-Côtes-de-Francs and Bordeaux Supérieur Côtes-de-Francs
This property produces fruity wines that can claim the Côtes de Castillon or Côtes de Francs appellations.

CHÂTEAU CALON
AOC Montagne-St.-Émilion and AOC St.-George-St.-Émilion

This château is under the same ownership as the *Grand Cru Classé* Château Corbin-Michotte. The wine is good quality, with a juicy style, and very Merlot in character. Part of this vineyard falls within the St.-George-St.-Émilion area and this produces the best wine.

CHÂTEAU CANON
AOC Côtes Canon-Fronsac
★✫ Ⓥ

This is one of several Fronsadais properties formerly owned, and still managed by, J.-P. Moueix. It was sold to a member of the Carrefour family in September 2000. It produces the best wine in this appellation from 100 per cent Merlot.

CHÂTEAU CANON DE BREM
AOC Côtes Canon-Fronsac
★ Ⓥ

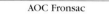

No longer owned by J.-P. Moueix, Château Canon de Brem was sold to a member of the Carrefour family in September 2000. It produces fine, firm, and flavoursome *vins de garde* that are deep coloured and powerful, yet complex and spicy.

Second Wine: *Château Pichelèbre*

CHÂTEAU CANON MOUEIX
AOC Côtes Canon-Fronsac
★ Ⓥ

Sold to a member of the Carrefour family in September 2000, this property was known as Château Pichelèbre until 1985, when it was purchased by J.-P. Moueix. Although under new ownership, it is still managed by J.-P. Moueix; whether the name remains is uncertain.

CHÂTEAU CAP DE MERLE
AOC Lussac–St.-Émilion
Château Cap de Merle is wine guru Robert Parker's best Lussac performer for the 1981–83 vintages.

CHÂTEAU CARLES
AOC Fronsac
★ Ⓥ

The primary wine is attractive and juicy, but it is the ★✫ blockbusting

95 per cent Merlot selection sold as Château Haut Carles that really stands out here.

Other wine: ✓ *Château Haut Carles*

CHÂTEAU CASSAGNE-HAUT-CANON
AOC Côtes Canon-Fronsac
★ Ⓥ

This château produces rich, full, fat, fruit-cake-flavoured wines that are especially attractive when they are still young.

CHÂTEAU DE CLOTTE
AOC Bordeaux-Côtes-de-Castillon and AOC Bordeaux Supérieur Côtes-de-Castillon

This property has the right to both the Côtes-de-Castillon and Côtes-de-Francs appellations, but uses only the former.

CHÂTEAU DU COURLAT
AOC Lussac–St.-Émilion

These are spicy-tannic wines with good fruit flavours.

CHÂTEAU COUSTOLLE VINCENT
AOC Côtes Canon-Fronsac

Château Coustolle Vincent's wines are well-flavoured, and matured in up to 20 per cent new oak.

CHÂTEAU LA CROIX CANON
AOC Côtes Canon-Fronsac
★✫ Ⓥ

Another former Moueix property that has sold to a member of the Carrefour family and yet remains managed by established team. Attractive Merlot-dominated wines are full of juicy fruit.

CHÂTEAU DALEM
AOC Fronsac
★✫ Ⓥ

These soft and velvety wines develop quickly but have finesse and are amongst the very best of their appellation.

CHÂTEAU DE LA DAUPHINE
AOC Fronsac

This property has been sold to a member of the Carrefour family, but is still run by the Moueix team,

who produce fresh and fruity wines that mature in oak, 20 per cent of which is new.

CHÂTEAU DURAND LAPLAIGNE
AOC Puisseguin–St.-Émilion
★ Ⓥ

The excellent-quality wine produced by Château Durand Laplaigne is grown using clay-and-limestone soil, with a strict selection of grapes, and modern vinification techniques.

CHÂTEAU LA FLEUR DE BOÜARD
AOC Lalande de Pomerol
★ Ⓥ

Very good wines getting much better since this property was purchased by the owner of Angelus in 1998.

Second wine: *Château La Fleur St-Georges*

CHÂTEAU FONTENIL
AOC Fronsac
★✫ Ⓥ

This rich, velvety 90 per cent Merlot high-flyer has lashings of new oak and is from Michel Rolland's own property.

CHÂTEAU GRAND-BARIL
AOC Montagne–St.-Émilion
Attractive, fruity wine made by the agricultural school in Libourne.

CHÂTEAU GRAND ORMEAU
AOC Lalande de Pomerol
★ Ⓥ

A rich and lusciously fruity wine that is matured in 50 per cent new oak, Grand Ormeau is very classy for its appellation.

Second wine: *Château d'Haurange*

CHÂTEAU GUIBEAU-LA FOURVIEILLE
AOC Puisseguin-St-Emilion
★✫ Ⓥ

Much investment has gone into this property, the wines of which are now considered to be the best in Puisseguin.

Second wines: *Le Vieux Château Guibeau, Château La Fourvieille*

CHÂTEAU HAUT-CHAIGNEAU
AOC Lalande-de-Pomerol
★ Ⓥ

Look out for Château Le Sergue ★★✫, which is selected from this property's best wines and matured in 80 per cent new oak. A poor man's Mondotte?

Other wines: ✓ *Château Le Sergue*

CHÂTEAU HAUT-CHATAIN
AOC Lalande-de-Pomerol
★✫ Ⓥ

Fat, rich, and juicy wines with definite hints of new-oak vanilla are made by Château Haut-Chatain.

CHÂTEAU LES HAUTS-CONSEILLANTS
AOC Lalande-de-Pomerol

Château les Hauts-Conseillants is another fine Néac property.

Other wines: *Château les Hauts-Tuileries* (export label)

CHÂTEAU HAUT-TUQUET
AOC Bordeaux-Côtes-de-Castillon and AOC Bordeaux Supérieur Côtes-de-Castillon

This wine is consistently good.

CHÂTEAU JEANDEMAN
AOC Fronsac

This château produces fresh, fruity wine with good aroma.

CHÂTEAU JUNAYME
AOC Côtes Canon-Fronsac
★ ✪

Well-known wines of finesse.

CHÂTEAU LA ROCHE-GABY
AOC Côtes Canon-Fronsac
★ ✪

Château La Roche-Gaby produces intensely flavoured, attractive, and well-structured wines, which are designed to have a long life.

CHÂTEAU DES LAURETS
AOC Puisseguin-St.-Émilion

The appellation's largest property.

Other wines: *Château la Rochette, Château Maison Rose*

CHÂTEAU DE LUSSAC
AOC Lussac-St.-Émilion

Château de Lussac produces well-balanced, early-drinking wine.

CHÂTEAU DU LYONNAT
AOC Lussac-St.-Émilion

The appellation's largest property.

Other wines: *La Rose Peruchon*

CHÂTEAU MAISON BLANCHE
AOC Montagne–St.-Émilion

Château Maison Blanche produces attractive wine that is easy to drink.

CHÂTEAU MAQUIN-ST.-GEORGES
AOC St.-Georges–St.-Émilion

This wine is 70 per cent Merlot.

Other wines: *Château Bellonne-St.-Georges*

CHÂTEAU MAUSSE
AOC Côtes Canon-Fronsac

Wines with good aroma and flavour.

CHÂTEAU MAYNE-VIEIL
AOC Fronsac

Easy-drinking wines with good Merlot spice and fruit.

CHÂTEAU MAZERIS
AOC Côtes Canon-Fronsac

There is an unusually high proportion of Cabernet sauvignon in these wines.

CHÂTEAU MILON
AOC Lussac–St.-Émilion
★ ✪

A château that produces a fine-quality, full, yet fragrant, wine.

CHÂTEAU MONCETS
AOC Lalande-de-Pomerol
★ ✪

This Néac property makes a fine, rich, and elegant Pomerol look-alike.

CHÂTEAU MOULIN HAUT-LAROQUE
AOC Fronsac

Well-perfumed, quite fat wines with lots of fruit and good tannin.

CHÂTEAU MOULIN NEUF
AOC Bordeaux-Côtes-de-Castillon and AOC Bordeaux Supérieur Côtes-de-Castillon
★ ✪

These wines regularly win medals.

CHÂTEAU LA PAPETERIE
AOC Montagne–St.-Émilion

Wines with a rich nose and a big fruit-filled palate.

CHÂTEAU DU PONT DE GUESTRES
AOC Lalande-de-Pomerol
★ ✪

This château produces full, ripe, fat wines of good quality.

CHÂTEAU DU PUY
AOC Bordeaux-Côtes-de-Francs and AOC Bordeaux Supérieur Côtes-de-Francs

Red wines from this property are rustic and overtly fruity.

CHÂTEAU PUYCARPIN
AOC Bordeaux-Côtes-de-Castillon and AOC Bordeaux Supérieur Côtes-de-Castillon

This property produces a well-made red, and a little dry white.

CHÂTEAU PUYGUERAUD
AOC Bordeaux-Côtes-de-Francs and AOC Bordeaux Supérieur Côtes-de-Francs

Aromatically attractive wines with good colour and supple fruit.

CHÂTEAU DE LA RIVIÈRE
AOC Fronsac
★ ✪

Magnificent wines that are built to last: they are rich, tannic, and fruity, and matured in up to 40 per cent new oak.

CHÂTEAU ROBIN
AOC Bordeaux-Côtes-de-Castillon and AOC Bordeaux Supérieur Côtes-de-Castillon
★ ✪

Château Robin produces award-winning red wines.

CHÂTEAU ROCHER-BELLEVUE
AOC Bordeaux-Côtes-de-Castillon and AOC Bordeaux Supérieur Côtes-de-Castillon
★ ✪

A good St.-Émilion look-alike that regularly wins medals.

Other wines: *La Palène, Coutet-St.-Magne*

CHÂTEAU ROUDIER
AOC Montagne–St.-Émilion
★ ★ ✪

Quality wines that are well-coloured, richly flavoured, finely balanced, and long and supple.

CHÂTEAU SIAURAC
AOC Lalande-de-Pomerol

Fine, firm, and fruity wines.

CHÂTEAU STE-COLOMBE
AOC Bordeaux-Côtes-de-Castillon
★ ✪

This château was purchased in 1999 by Gérard Perse of Pavie et al and Alain Reynaud of La Croix-de-Gay. These wines look very promising indeed.

CHÂTEAU ST.-GEORGES
AOC St.-Georges–St.-Émilion
★ ★ ✪

Super quality wine of great finesse.

CHÂTEAU TARREYO
AOC Bordeaux-Côtes-de-Castillon and AOC Bordeaux Supérieur Côtes-de-Castillon

Château Tarreyo (Gascon for "knoll

of stones") is sited on a limestone mound, as its name suggests.

CHÂTEAU THIBAUD-BELLEVUE
AOC Bordeaux-Côtes-de-Castillon and AOC Bordeaux Supérieur Côtes-de-Castillon

Medium-bodied, fruity red wine.

CHÂTEAU TOUMALIN
AOC Côtes Canon-Fronsac

Fresh, fruity wine from a property under the same ownership as Château La Pointe in Pomerol.

CHÂTEAU TOUR-DU-PAS-ST.-GEORGES
AOC St.-Georges–St.-Émilion
★ ✪

An excellent and inexpensive *entrée* into the world of *Premier Cru* claret.

CHÂTEAU DES TOURELLES
AOC Lalande-de-Pomerol
★ ✪

Fine wines with vanilla undertones.

CHÂTEAU TOURNEFEUILLE
AOC Lalande-de-Pomerol
★ ★ ✪

This rich, long-lived wine is the best of the appellation.

CHÂTEAU DES TOURS
AOC Montagne–St.-Émilion
★ ✪

The largest property in the appellation. The wine is big, full, and fleshy, yet soft and easy to drink.

CHÂTEAU LA VALADE
AOC Fronsac
★ ✪

Elegant, aromatic, and silky-textured wines, which are made exclusively from Merlot grapes.

CHÂTEAU LA VIEILLE CURE
AOC Fronsac
★ ★

Very fresh and velvety with delightful floral, summer fruit aromas, these wines are at the very top of their appellation. The 1998 is stunning.

CHÂTEAU LA VILLARS
AOC Fronsac
★ ✪

Soft, fat, and juicy wines of excellent quality, one-third of which are matured in new oak.

VIEUX-CHÂTEAU-ST.-ANDRÉ
AOC Montagne–St.-Émilion
★ ★ ✪

A soft, exciting wine, full of cherry, vanilla, and spice flavours.

CHÂTEAU VRAY-CANON-BOYER
AOC Côtes Canon-Fronsac

This château produces a fruity, medium-bodied wine that is attractive for early drinking from 90 per cent Merlot grapes.

BOURG AND BLAYE

Ninety-five per cent of the wine produced in Bourg and Blaye is good-value red. Tiny Bourg makes more wine than its five-times-larger neighbour, Blaye, and most of the vines grown in Blaye come from a cluster of châteaux close to the borders of Bourg.

AS ONE WOULD EXPECT of an area that has supported a settlement for 400,000 years, Bourg has a close-knit community. Comparatively recently, the Romans used neighbouring Blaye as a *castrum*, a fortified area in the defence system that shielded Bordeaux. According to some sources, the vine was cultivated in Bourg and Blaye as soon as the Romans arrived. Vineyards were certainly flourishing here long before those of the Médoc, just the other side of the Gironde.

Bourg is a compact, heavily cultivated area with pretty hillside vineyards at every turn. The vine is less important in Blaye, which has other interests, including a caviare industry based at its ancient fishing port where sturgeon is still a major catch. The south-facing vineyards of Blaye are mostly clustered in the countryside immediately bordering Bourg and, despite the similarity of the countryside, traditionally produce slightly inferior wines to those of Bourg. The D18 motorway appears to be a barrier beyond which the less intensely cultivated hinterland takes on a totally different topography, where the more expansive scenery is dotted with isolated forests.

FACTORS AFFECTING TASTE AND QUALITY

LOCATION
The vineyards fan out behind the town of Bourg, which is situated on the right bank of the confluence of the Dordogne and the Garonne, some 20 km (12½ miles) north of Bordeaux. Blaye is a larger district that unfolds beyond Bourg.

CLIMATE
These two areas are less protected than the Médoc from westerly and northwesterly winds, and have a higher rainfall.

ASPECT
Bourg is very hilly with vines cultivated on steep limestone hills and knolls up to a height of 80 m (260 ft). In the southern section of Blaye the country is rich and hilly, with steep slopes overlooking the Gironde that are really just a continuation of those in Bourg. The northern areas are gentle and the hills lower, with marshes bordering the viticultural areas.

SOIL
In Bourg the topsoil is clay-limestone or clay-gravel over a hard limestone subsoil, although in the east the subsoil sometimes gives way to gravel and clay. The soil in Blaye is clay or clay-limestone over hard limestone on the hills overlooking the Gironde, getting progressively sandier going east.

VITICULTURE AND VINIFICATION
There are many grape varieties here, some of which are far too inferior or unreliable to contribute to the quality of these wines, particularly the whites. Bourg produces the best reds, Blaye the best whites, but there is relatively little white wine made in both appellations – even Blaye is 90 per cent red and Bourg is in excess of 99 per cent red. Very few *petits châteaux* in both areas can afford the use of casks, let alone new ones, and much of the wine in Bourg is made by one of its five *coopératives*.

PRIMARY GRAPE VARIETIES
Cabernet franc, Cabernet sauvignon, Merlot, Sauvignon blanc, Sémillon
SECONDARY GRAPE VARIETIES
Malbec, Prolongeau, Cahors, Béguignol (Fer), Petit verdot, Merlot blanc, Folle blanche, Colombard, Chenin blanc, Muscadelle, Ugni blanc

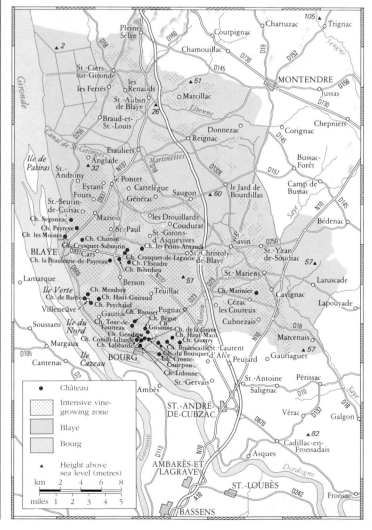

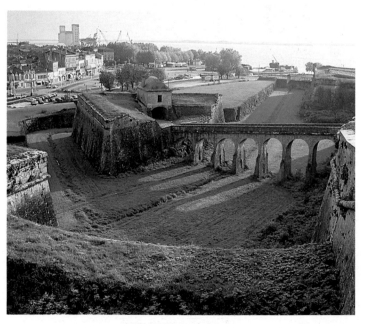

THE TOWN OF BLAYE
The attractive fishing port of Blaye with, in the foreground, the ruins of its ancient citadel guarding against the approach of marauders from the sea.

BOURG AND BLAYE, *see also* p.59
Most of the best growths of Bourg and Blaye are clustered behind the respective ports that give this wine-producing area its name. Bourg, the smaller area, has a higher concentration of vineyards and generally produces the better wines.

THE POTENTIAL OF BOURG AND BLAYE

To the Romans, these south-facing vineyards overlooking the Gironde seemed the ideal place to plant vines. Indeed, the quality achieved today in these vineyards would have surpassed the most optimistic hopes of those past masters of the vine. Since Roman times, however, new and different ideas of what a classic wine should be have relegated Bourg and Blaye to a viticultural backwater. I am sure the potential of these wines will one day be realized but probably not for some ten or twenty years and only after the world has woken up to such wines as Canon-Fronsac in the Libournais and has elevated Canon-Fronsac to the level of St.-Émilion. When wine lovers are prepared to pay higher prices for these wines, proprietors will be able to restrict yields, improve vinification techniques, and indulge in a percentage of new oak.

CHENIN BLANC IN BORDEAUX

The Chenin blanc of Loire fame (or infamy, as the case may be) is allowed in the white wines of Bourg, albeit restricted to a maximum of ten per cent. However, in the AOCs of Blayais and Côtes de Blaye (but not Premières Côtes de Blaye), this interloper from the north has a free run, or could have, if a producer wanted to market a pure Chenin blanc varietal wine.

I have never been a fan of Chenin blanc in the Loire, except in those idyllic vintages when the sublime *moelleux* style can be produced in quantity, and it is very hard not to produce liquid magic. The problem with Chenin in the Loire is that it grows like weed, but rarely has the degree of sunshine this grape likes to luxuriate in. Combine that with the inclination of far too many growers to over-yield and season it with those who have less than clinically clean vinification habits, and it is clear why Loire Chenin, particularly dry Loire Chenin, has such a poor reputation. On the other hand even cheap, mass-produced Chenin blanc wines in the New World have lovely ripe, tropical fruit flavours. Not all of them, of course, the New World has its good, bad, and ugly too, but I believe that the longer hours of warmer sunshine in Bordeaux could produce some excellent dry Chenin wines. A pure Chenin blanc Bordeaux would be a novelty.

VINEYARDS ALONG THE DORDOGNE AT BOURG
The Romans planted these south-facing vineyards, believing this to be a far more ideal place to grow vines than on the other side of the confluence of the Dordogne and Garonne estuaries where, understandably, they failed to realize the possibilities of the Médoc concealed beyond its virtually impenetrable marshes.

CHÂTEAU SEGONZAC, ST.-GENÈS-DE-BLAYE
A short distance from the fortress of Blaye, these sweeping vineyards belong to Château Segonzac, a wine estate created in 1887 by Jean Dupuy, the owner of the "Petit Parisiane", the largest-circulation newspaper in the world at the time.

THE APPELLATIONS OF
BOURG AND BLAYE

The number of appellations in this area, and their various differences, are very confusing for the consumer. The system should be tidied up and there is no reason why just two AOCs – Côtes de Blaye and Côtes de Bourg – could not be used for all the wines produced here.

BLAYE AOC

Blaye or Blayais is a large and diverse appellation of variable quality.

RED Few properties cultivate obscure varieties such as Pronlongeau and Béguignol, thus many utilize the prestigious sounding Premières Côtes de Blaye AOC, hence hardly anyone bothers to sell the wine under this plain appellation.

🍇 Cabernet sauvignon, Cabernet franc, Merlot, Malbec, Prolongeau, Béguignol, Petit verdot

🍷— 3–7 years

WHITE Since 1997 Ugni blanc has dominated, with Merlot blanc and Folle blanche banned. The ripeness level has been lowered from 170 to 153 grams of sugar, with no more than four grams residual allowed in the finished wine, and a maximum of 12.5 per cent alcohol imposed, thus ensuring fresher, crisper wines. These wines may be sold from 1 December following the harvest without any mention of *primeur* or *nouveau*.

🍇 Ugni blanc plus up to 10% in total of Folle blanche, Colombard, Chenin blanc, Sémillon, Sauvignon blanc, Muscadelle

🍷— 1–2 years

BLAYAIS AOC
See Blaye AOC

BOURG AOC

Also called Bourgeais, this appellation, which covers both red and white wines, has fallen into disuse because the growers prefer to use the Côtes de Bourg AOC, which is easier to market but conforms to the same regulations. *See also* Côtes de Bourg AOC.

BOURGEAIS AOC
See Bourg AOC

CÔTES DE BLAYE AOC

Unlike the Bourg and Côtes de Bourg appellations, which cover red and white wines, Côtes de Blaye is white only. Blaye, however, may be red or white.

WHITE As much white Côtes de Blaye is produced as basic Blaye. The wines are similar in style and quality.

🍇 Merlot blanc, Folle blanche, Colombard, Chenin blanc, Sémillon, Sauvignon blanc, Muscadelle

🍷— 1–2 years

CÔTES DE BOURG AOC

Bourg is one-fifth the size of Blaye yet it traditionally produces a greater quantity and, more importantly, a much finer quality of wine than that produced at Blaye.

RED Excellent value wines of good colour, which are full of solid, fruity flavour. Many are very stylish indeed.

🍇 Cabernet sauvignon, Cabernet franc, Merlot, Malbec

🍷— 3–10 years

WHITE A very small quantity of this light, dry wine is produced and sold each year. It may be sold from 1 December following the harvest without any mention of *primeur* or *nouveau*.

🍇 Sémillon, Sauvignon blanc, Muscadelle, Merlot blanc, Colombard, plus a maximum of 10% Chenin blanc

🍷— 1–2 years

PREMIÈRES CÔTES DE BLAYE AOC

This covers the same area as Blaye and Côtes de Blaye, but only classic grapes are used and the minimum alcoholic strength is higher. The area has very good potential for producing quality wines.

RED There are one or two excellent properties that use a little new oak.

🍇 Cabernet sauvignon, Cabernet franc, Merlot, Malbec

🍷— 4–10 years

WHITE Dry, light-bodied wines that may have a fresh, lively, grapey flavour.

🍇 Sémillon, Sauvignon blanc, Muscadelle

🍷— 1–2 years

THE WINE PRODUCERS OF
BOURG

CHÂTEAU DE BARBE
Villeneuve
Château de Barbe is a property that makes substantial quantities of light-styled, Merlot-dominated, gently fruity red wines, which are easy to drink.

CHÂTEAU BÉGOT
Lansac
This property produces some 5,000 cases of agreeably fruity red wine, which is best drunk young.

CHÂTEAU BRULESCAILLE
Tauriac

Château Brulescaille's vineyards are very well-sited and produce agreeable wines for early drinking.

CHÂTEAU DU BOUSQUET
Bourg-sur-Gironde
★ 🅥
This large, well-known château produces some 40,000 cases of red wine of excellent value for money. The wine is fermented in stainless steel and aged in oak, has a big bouquet, and a smooth feel.

CHÂTEAU CONILH-LIBARDE
Bourg-sur-Gironde
Soft, fruity red wines are made at this small vineyard overlooking Bourg-sur-Gironde and the river.

CHÂTEAU CROUTE-COURPON
Bourg-sur-Gironde
A small but recently enlarged estate, it produces honest, fruity red wines.

CHÂTEAU EYQUEM
Bayon-sur-Gironde
Owned by the serious winemaking Bayle-Carreau family which also owns several other properties, this wine is not normally, however, purchased for its quality. It is enjoyable as a light luncheon

claret, but the real joy is in the spoof of serving a red Eyquem.

CHÂTEAU GÉNIBON
Bourg-sur-Gironde
This small vineyard produces attractive wines that have all the enjoyment upfront and are easy to drink.

CHÂTEAU GRAND-LAUNAY
Teuillac
★ 🅥
This property has been developed from the vineyards of three estates: Domaine Haut-Launay, Château

Launay, and Domaine les Hermats. Mainly red wine is produced, although a very tiny amount of white is also made. The star-performing wine at this château is a superb, special reserve *cuvée* of red that is sold under the Château Lion Noir label.

CHÂTEAU DE LA GRAVE
Bourg-sur-Gironde
An important property situated on one of the highest points of Bourg-sur-Gironde, it produces a large quantity of light, fruity Malbec-influenced red wine and a very tiny amount of white.

CHÂTEAU GUERRY
Tauriac
★ 🅥
Some 10,000 cases of really fine wood-aged red wines are produced at this château. The wines have good structure, bags of fruit, and a smooth, elegant flavour.

CHÂTEAU GUIONNE
Lansac
These are easy-drinking wines, full of attractive Merlot fruit, good juicy flavour, and some finesse. A little white wine of some interest and depth is also made.

CHÂTEAU HAUT-GUIRAUD

St.-Ciers-de-Canesse

★ **V**

This red-only château produces medium- to full-bodied, well-structured red wine teeming with ripe fruit flavours. This property is under the same ownership as Châteaux Castaing and Guiraud-Grimard in the same commune.

CHÂTEAU HAUT-MACÔ

Tauriac

This rustic red wine is full of rich, fruity flavours, and good acidity. The proprietors also own a property called Domaine de Lilotte in Bourg-sur-Gironde producing attractive, early-drinking red wines under the Bordeaux Supérieur appellation.

Other wines: *Les Bascauds*

CHÂTEAU HAUT-ROUSSET

Bourg-sur-Gironde

Some 12,000 cases of decent, everyday-drinking red wine and 1,000 cases of white are produced at this fairly large property. The red wines from a small vineyard close by are sold under the Château la Renardière label.

CHÂTEAU DE LIDONNE

Bourg-sur-Gironde

★

This very old property produces an excellent-quality red wine, powerfully aromatic and full of Cabernet character. Its name comes from the 15th-century monks who looked after the estate and offered lodgings to passing pilgrims: "Lit-Donne" or "Give Bed".

CHÂTEAU MENDOCE

Villeneuve

★ **V**

The reputation of this turreted château is well deserved; it produces a rich red wine, which is full, smooth, and lingers on the palate.

CHÂTEAU PEYCHAUD

Teuillac

These fruity red wines are easy to drink when young. A little white is also made. Its is under the same ownership as Château Peyredoulle and Château le Peuy-Saincrit.

CHÂTEAU ROC DE CAMBES

Bourg-sur-Gironde

★★☆

You can expect to pay five times the price of any other Côtes de Bourg for this blockbuster, which is made by François Mitjavile, the owner of Tertre-Rôteboeuf. However, the 1995 and 1996 were worth it.

CHÂTEAU ROUSSET

Samonac

★☆ **V**

A fine estate of gravel vineyards producing lightly rich, juicy, Merlot-dominated wines of some finesse; they are perfect to drink when two or three years old.

CHÂTEAU SAUMAN

Villeneuve

These immaculate vineyards produce a good-quality red wine for medium-term maturity. The proprietor also owns the red-wine producing Domaine du Moulin de Mendoce in the same commune.

CHÂTEAU TOUR-DE-TOURTEAU

Samonac

★ **V**

This property was once part of Château Rousset. However, the wines are definitely bigger and richer than those of Rousset.

THE WINE PRODUCERS OF
BLAYE

CHÂTEAU BARBÉ

Cars

★☆ **V**

This château produces well-made, and overtly fruity red and white wines. Château Barbé is one of several properties owned by the Bayle-Carreau family (*see also* La Carelle and Pordaillan).

CHÂTEAU BOURDIEU

Berson

This is an old and well-known property producing Cabernet-dominated red wines of a very firm structure that receive time in oak. Seven hundred years ago this estate was accorded the privilege of selling "clairet", a tradition it maintains today by ageing the blended production of various vineyards in oak. It is also producing white wines of improving quality.

CHÂTEAU LA CARELLE

St.-Paul

More than 11,000 cases of agreeable red wines and just 1,500 cases of white are made at this property. The owner also runs châteaux Barbé and Pardaillan in Cars.

CHÂTEAU DE CASTETS

Plassac

A promising property, it produces attractive red and white wines for early drinking.

CHÂTEAU CHARRON

St.-Martin-Lacaussade

★☆ **V**

These very attractive, well-made, juicy-rich, Merlot-dominated red wines are matured in oak, some of which is new. A small amount of white wine is also made.

CHÂTEAU CRUSQUET-DE-LAGARCIE

Cars

★☆ **V**

A tremendously exciting, richly styled red wine, which is deep coloured, bright, big, full of fruit, vanilla, and spice. A small amount of dry white wine is sold under the name "Clos-des-Rudel" and an even smaller quantity of sweet white wine as "Clos-Blanc de Lagarcie". The châteaux Les-Princesses-de-Lagarcie and Touzignan, also in Cars, are under the same ownership.

CHÂTEAU L'ESCADRE

Cars

★☆

These elegant red wines are well-coloured, full, and fruity. They can be enjoyed young, but also improve with age. A small amount of fruity white wine is produced.

Second Wine: *Château la Croix St.-Pierre*

DOMAINE DU GRAND BARRAIL

Plassac

★☆ **V**

This Château makes a fine-quality red wine that attracts by its purity of fruit. A little white wine is produced. The proprietor also owns Château Gardut-Haut-Cluzeau and Domaine du Cavalier in Cars.

CHÂTEAU DU GRAND PIERRE

Berson

★ **V**

This property can produce tremendous value medium- to full-bodied red wine with sweet, ripe fruit. Fresh, zesty, dry white wine of agreeable quality is also made.

CHÂTEAU HAUT BERTINERIE

Cubnezais

★★☆ **V**

The consistent class of this wine, with its silky fruit and beautifully integrated oak, makes it stand out above the rest as the best-value dry white currently made in Bordeaux.

CHÂTEAU DE HAUT SOCIONDO

Agreeably light and fruity red and white wines are made here.

CHÂTEAU LES JONQUEYRES

St.-Paul-de-Blaye

★★☆ **V**

This château produces lush Merlot-dominated reds with lots of well-integrated creamy oak. The wines are impeccably produced.

CHÂTEAU LAMANCEAU

St.-Androny

★ **V**

Production at this property is entirely red and of an excellent standard: richly coloured wine full of the juicy spice of Merlot.

CHÂTEAU MARINIER

Cézac

★☆ **V**

Twice as much red wine as white is produced. The red is agreeably fruity, but the white is much the better wine: smooth, well balanced, lightly rich, and elegant. Red and rosé wines are also produced under the Bordeaux appellation.

CHÂTEAU MENAUDAT

St.-Androny

★ **V**

These are extremely attractive, full, and fruity red wines.

CHÂTEAU LES MOINES

Blaye

A red-only château, producing a light- to medium-bodied, fresh and fruity wine for easy drinking.

CHÂTEAU PARDAILLAN

Cars

Well made, enjoyable, fruity red wines that are best drunk young.

CHÂTEAU LES PETITS ARNAUDS

Cars

★☆ **V**

Attractively aromatic red wines, pleasingly round and fruity. Dry white Blaye and a *moelleux* white Bordeaux are also produced.

CHÂTEAU PEYREDOULLE

Berson

This 15th-century property produces mainly good-quality red wine, although some white is made. The proprietors also own Château Peychaud in the Bourgais commune of Teuillac and the Bordeaux AOC of Château le Peuy-Saincrit.

CHÂTEAU PEYREYRE

St.-Martin-Lacaussade

★ **V**

This château produces well-structured, rich-flavoured red wines of some finesse. Bordeaux Rosé is also made.

CHÂTEAU SEGONZAC

St.-Genès-de-Blaye

★ **V**

Château Segonzac's easy-drinking red wines are light, well made, fresh, firm, and agreeably fruity.

ENTRE-DEUX-MERS

Entre-Deux-Mers, which literally means "between two seas" is situated between the Dordogne and Garonne rivers. It is Bordeaux's largest district, and produces inexpensive dry white wines and an increasing volume of excellent value-for-money red wines that are entitled to the Bordeaux or Bordeaux Supérieur appellations or, most prestigious of all, to the Premières-Côtes-de-Bordeaux appellation.

TECHNOLOGICAL PROGRESS in winemaking occurred earlier and more quickly in Entre-Deux-Mers than in any other district of Bordeaux. As early as the 1950s and 1960s, there was a grass-roots viticultural movement to drop the traditional low vine-training systems and adopt the revolutionary "high-culture" system which can be either the cordon or Guyot method (*see* p.25) and contrasted with the low vine training methods common throughout Bordeaux. These new vineyard techniques were followed in the 1970s by a widespread adoption of cool-fermentation techniques. With fresh, light, and attractively dry white wines being made at many châteaux, the major export markets suddenly realized it would be easier to sell the name Entre-Deux-Mers rather than continue to sell what had become boring Bordeaux Blanc. This was even better if the wine could boast some sort of individual *petit château* personality.

THE "HIGH-CULTURE" SYSTEM OF VINE TRAINING

Entre-Deux-Mers in the late 1940s and early 1950s was a sorry place. The wines were sold in bulk, ending up as anonymous Bordeaux Blanc, and much of the decline in the Bordeaux region was centred on this district. But the new post-war generation of winegrowers were not content with this state of affairs. Although

CHÂTEAU BONNET
In 1898 this vineyard was acquired by Léonce Recapet, one of the first to carry out replanting after the devastation of the Gironde vineyard by phylloxera at the turn of the century. His son-in-law, François Lurton, succeeded him, and in 1956 his grandson, André Lurton, became the owner.

times were difficult and the economy was deteriorating, the young, technically minded *vignerons* realized that the district's compressed *boulbènes* soil, which was choking the vines, could not be worked by their ancestors' outdated methods, and they therefore took a considerable financial risk to rectify the situation. They grubbed up every other row of vines, thus increasing the spacing between the rows, and trained the plants on a "high-culture" system similar to that practised further south in Madiran and Jurançon (also in Austria where it was originally conceived and was called the Lenz Moser system). This system allowed

LOUPIAC CHURCH
The local church neighbours the vineyards of Château Loupiac, which are situated on the right bank of the Garonne.

ENTRE-DEUX-MERS
See also p.59
The varied countryside of this district spreads out between the rivers Dordogne and Garonne as their paths diverge. The Premières Côtes form a narrow strip along the south side.

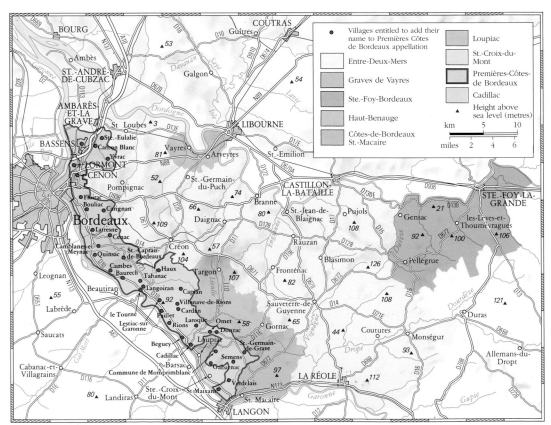

FACTORS AFFECTING TASTE AND QUALITY

LOCATION
A large area east of Bordeaux between the Garonne and Dordogne rivers.

CLIMATE
More blustery and wetter than the Médoc; areas near the rivers are liable to flood.

ASPECT
Quiet and very attractive countryside of vine-covered hillsides, orchards, and meadows.

SOIL
Very varied topsoils, ranging from alluvium by the river to gravel on some hillsides and crests, and clay-gravel or clay-limestone on various plateaus. At the western end of the district a soil called *boulbènes* dominates. This is extremely fine and sandy and has a tendency to compress into an impermeable barrier. Vines must be grafted on to special root-stock in order to be productive in such soil. Much of the subsoil is limestone or limestone-based, but sandy-clay, clay-and-limestone rubble, a quarry stone called *aslar*, and *ribot* – a sandstone containing gravel and iron deposits – are also found.

VITICULTURE AND VINIFICATION
This area is famed for its "high and wide" method of vine training, which was developed in the early 1950s and is similar to the Lenz Moser system used in Austria. Greater emphasis is now placed on the Sauvignon grape and cool fermentation in stainless-steel vats.

PRIMARY GRAPE VARIETIES
Sémillon, Sauvignon blanc, Muscadelle
SECONDARY GRAPE VARIETIES
Merlot blanc, Colombard, Mauzac, Ugni blanc

machinery to work the land and break up the soil. It also increased the canopy of foliage, which intensified chlorophyll assimilation and improved ripening.

COOL FERMENTATION

In the 1970s, university-trained personnel at the well-funded Entre-Deux-Mers *coopératives* invested in temperature-controlled stainless-steel vats and led the way in cool-fermentation techniques. Prior to this, fermentation temperatures were often in excess of 28°C (83°F), but it was soon discovered that the lower the temperature, the more aromatic compounds were released. They discovered that fermentation could take place at temperatures as low as 4°C (39°F), although the risk of stuck-fermentation (when the fermentation process stops) was greater at such low temperatures. It soon became clear that the ideal fermentation temperature was thought to be somewhere between 10°C (50°F) and 18°C (64°F). This increased the yield of alcohol and important aromatic and flavour compounds. It also reduced both the loss of carbonic gas and the presence of volatile acidity and required less sulphur dioxide. In the mid-1980s it was confirmed that 18°C (64°F) is the optimum temperature for fermentation. Lower temperatures also produce amylic aromas, which in small quantities are fine, but the lower the temperature, the more the wine is dominated by these nail-varnish aromas.

THE APPELLATIONS OF
ENTRE-DEUX-MERS

BORDEAUX HAUT-BENAUGE AOC

Situated above the Premières Côtes, opposite Cérons, this area corresponds to the ancient and tiny county of Benauge. To claim this appellation, as opposed to Entre-Deux-Mers–Haut-Benauge, the grapes are restricted to the three classic varieties and must be riper, with a minimum sugar level of 195 grams per litre instead of 170 grams per litre. The yield is 10 per cent lower and the minimum alcoholic level 1.5 per cent higher.

WHITE Dry, medium-sweet, and sweet versions of this light-bodied, fruity wine may be made.

Sémillon, Sauvignon blanc, Muscadelle

1–3 years for dry and medium-sweet wines; 3–6 years for sweet wines

CADILLAC AOC

Of the trio of sweet-wine areas on the right bank of the Garonne, Cadillac is the least known. It encompasses 21 communes, 16 of which form the canton of Cadillac, yet very little wine is produced under this appellation – just one-fifth of that made in Loupiac, or one-tenth of that made in St.-Croix-du-Mont. The regulations state that the wines must be made from botrytized grapes harvested in successive *tries*, but there is little evidence of this in the wines, which at best have the character of *passerillage*. The *terroir* could produce wines of a much superior quality, but it would be costly to do so, and sadly, this appellation does not fetch a high enough price to justify the substantial investment needed.

WHITE Attractive honey-gold wines with fresh, floral aromas and a semi-sweet, or sweet, fruity flavour.

Sémillon, Sauvignon blanc, Muscadelle

3–8 years

CÔTES-DE-BORDEAUX-ST.-MACAIRE AOC

These little-seen wines come from an area at the eastern extremity of the Premières-Côtes-de-Bordeaux. Of the 2,300 hectares (6,000 acres) of vineyards that may use this appellation, barely 30 hectares (75 acres) bother to do so.

WHITE Medium-bodied, medium-sweet, or sweet wines that are attractive in a fruity way, but unpretentious.

Sémillon, Sauvignon blanc, Muscadelle

1–3 years

ENTRE-DEUX-MERS AOC

This is the largest district in the region, and after the generic Bordeaux Blanc, it is its greatest-volume white-wine appellation. Entre-Deux-Mers has a growing reputation for exceptional-value wines of a high technical standard.

WHITE Crisp, dry, light-bodied wines that are fragrant, aromatic, and usually predominantly Sauvignon Blanc. These are clean, cool-fermented wines. They may be sold from 1 December following the harvest without any mention of *primeur* or *nouveau*.

At least 70 per cent Sémillon, Sauvignon blanc, and Muscadelle, plus a maximum of 30 per cent Merlot blanc and up to 10 per cent in total of Colombard, Mauzac, and Ugni blanc

1–2 years

ENTRE-DEUX-MERS-HAUT-BENAUGE AOC

These wines are drier than those of the Bordeaux-Haut-Benauge appellation, and their blends may include a greater number of grape varieties, although the same nine communes comprise both appellations. The wines comply with the less rigorous regulations of Entre-Deux-Mers and, consequently, this AOC produces four times the volume of wine than does Bordeaux-Haut-Benauge. Entre-Deux-Mers-Haut-Benauge has so far produced only dry wines, with the exception of 1983, when a luscious vintage arrived that was easy to make into sweet wines.

WHITE These dry wines are very similar to those of Entre-Deux-Mers.

At least 70 per cent Sémillon, Sauvignon blanc, and Muscadelle, plus a maximum of 30 per cent Merlot blanc and up to 10 per cent in total of Colombard, Mauzac, and Ugni blanc

1–3 years

GRAVES DE VAYRES AOC

An enclave of gravelly soil on the left bank of the Dordogne, this appellation produces a substantial quantity of excellent-value red and white wines.

RED These are well-coloured, aromatic, medium-bodied wines with fragrant, juicy-spicy, predominantly Merlot fruit. They are richer than those found elsewhere in Entre-Deux-Mers.

Cabernet sauvignon, Cabernet franc, Carmenère, Merlot, Malbec, Petit verdot

4–10 years

WHITE Mostly dry and off-dry styles of fresh, fragrant, and fruity wines made for early drinking. Occasionally, sweeter styles are made. These wines may be sold from 1 December following the harvest without any mention of *primeur* or *nouveau*.

Sémillon, Sauvignon blanc, and Muscadelle plus a maximum of 30 per cent Merlot blanc

1–3 years

LOUPIAC AOC

This appellation is located on the right bank of the Garonne, opposite Barsac. It is by far the best sweet-wine appellation in Entre-Deux-Mers and its wines are always excellent value. According to the regulations, Loupiac must be made with the "assistance" of overripe botrytized grapes and, unlike Cadillac, these wines often have the honeyed complexity of "noble rot". The best Loupiac wines come from vineyards with clay-and-limestone soil.

WHITE Luscious medium- to full-bodied wines that are sweet or intensely sweet, honey-rich, and full of flavour. They can be quite complex, and in suitable years have evident botrytis character.

Sémillon, Sauvignon blanc, Muscadelle

5–15 years (25 in exceptional cases)

PREMIÈRES-CÔTES-DE-BORDEAUX AOC

A 60-kilometre (37-mile) strip of southwest-facing slopes covering 170 hectares (63 acres) of vines scattered through 37 communes, each of which has the right to add its name to this appellation. They are: Bassens, Baurech, Béguey, Bouliac, Cadillac, Cambes, Camblanes, Capian, Carbon Blanc, Cardan, Carignan, Cenac, Cenon, Donzac, Floirac, Gabarnac, Haux, Langoiran, Laroque, Lestiac, Lormont, Monprimblanc, Omet, Paillet, Quinsac, Rions, Sémens, St.-Caprais-de-Bordeaux, St.-Germain-de-Graves, St.-Maixant, Ste.-Eulalie, Tabanac, Le Tourne, La Tresne, Verdelais, Ville-nave de Rions, and Yvrac.

RED The best red wines come from the northern communes. These well-coloured, soft, and fruity wines are a cut above basic Bordeaux AOC.

Cabernet sauvignon, Cabernet franc, Carmenère, Merlot, Malbec, Petit verdot

4–8 years

WHITE Since the 1981 harvest, no dry wines have been allowed under this generally unexciting appellation. They must have at least some sweetness, and most are in fact semi-sweet. Simple, fruity wines, well made for the most part, but lacking character.

Sémillon, Sauvignon blanc, Muscadelle

3–7 years

STE.-CROIX-DU-MONT AOC

This is the second-best sweet-white appellation on the right bank of the Garonne, and it regularly produces more wine than Barsac. Like Loupiac wines, these wines must be made with the "assistance" of overripe botrytized grapes. They have less honeyed complexity of "noble rot" than Loupiac wines, but often have more finesse.

WHITE Fine, viscous, honey-sweet wines that are lighter in body and colour than Loupiac wines. Excellent value when they have rich botrytis character.

Sémillon, Sauvignon blanc, Muscadelle

5–15 years (25 in exceptional cases)

STE.-FOY-BORDEAUX AOC

Until relatively recently, Ste.-Foy-Bordeaux was known primarily for its white wines, but it now produces as much red as white. There is a high proportion of "organic" winemakers in this area.

RED Ruby-coloured, medium-bodied wines made in a soft, easy drinking style.

Cabernet sauvignon, Cabernet franc, Merlot, Malbec, Petit verdot

3–7 years

WHITE Mellow, semi-sweet wines of uninspiring quality, and fresh, crisp dry white wines that have good aroma and make attractive early drinking. These wines may be sold from 1 December following the harvest without any mention of *primeur* or *nouveau*.

Sémillon, Sauvignon blanc, and Muscadelle, and up 10 per cent in total of Merlot blanc, Colombard, Mauzac, and Ugni blanc

1–3 years

THE WINE PRODUCERS OF
ENTRE-DEUX-MERS

CHÂTEAU ARNAUD-JOUAN
Cadillac
★ V
AOC Premières-Côtes-de-Bordeaux and AOC Cadillac
This large, well-situated vineyard makes interesting, attractive wines.

DOMAINE DU BARRAIL
Monprimblanc
★ V
AOC Premières-Côtes-de-Bordeaux and AOC Cadillac
Both the red Premières Côtes and sweet white Cadillac produced at this property are worth watching.

CHÂTEAU DE BEAUREGARD
AOC Entre-Deux-Mers and AOC Bordeaux-Haut-Benauge
The red and white wines are well-made. The red has good structure, but is softened by the spice of the Merlot.

CHÂTEAU BEL-AIR
Vayres
AOC Graves de Vayres
Most of the wines made here are red and well-coloured. They are aromatic wines of a Cabernet character.

CHÂTEAU BIROT
Béguey
★ V
AOC Premières-Côtes-de-Bordeaux and AOC Cadillac
Popular for its easy-drinking whites, this property also produces well-balanced red wines of some finesse.

CHÂTEAU LA BLANQUERIE
Mérignas
AOC Entre-Deux-Mers
Dry white wine with a Sauvignon character and a fine finish.

CHÂTEAU BONNET
Grézillac
AOC Entre-Deux-Mers
★ ★ ☆

This top-performing Entre-Deux-Mers château is owned by André Lurton. It produces crisp, fresh, and characterful white wines, and soft, fruity, extremely successful (Bordeaux Supérieur) red.

Second Wine: *Le Colombey*
Other Wines: *Tour-de-Bonnet, Château Gourmin, Château Peyraud*

CLOS BOURGELAT
Cérons
AOC Cérons
★ ★ ☆ V
These botrytized wines have great aroma, finesse, and complexity.

CHÂTEAU BRÉTHOUS
Camblanes-et-Meynac
AOC Premières-Côtes-de-Bordeaux and AOC Cadillac
★ V
The red wines are forward and attractive, yet well-structured while the whites are succulent and sweet.

CHÂTEAU CANET
Guillac
AOC Entre-Deux-Mers
★ V
These excellent white wines are clean and crisp, with good fruit and an elegant balance.

CHÂTEAU CAYLA
Rions
★ V
AOC Premières-Côtes-de-Bordeaux
The reds are elegant and accessible with just a touch of new oak.

CHÂTEAU DE CÉRONS
Cérons
AOC Cérons
★ V
Jean Perromat also owns Château d'Arche, and consistently produces superb, white botrytized wines.

Other wines: *De Calvimont* (dry white)

DOMAINE DE CHASTELET
Quinsac
AOC Premières-Côtes-de-Bordeaux and AOC Cadillac
★ V
Domaine de Chastelet produces red wine that is delicious, yet firm and complex, with very well-balanced blackcurrant fruit flavours and a hint of vanilla-oak.

CHÂTEAU LA CLYDE
Tabanac
AOC Premières-Côtes-de-Bordeaux and AOC Cadillac
★ V
These aromatic, deep-coloured, ruby-red wines show good spice and fruit. The white has finesse and balance.

CHÂTEAU DU CROS
Loupiac
AOC Loupiac
★ V
These fine, fat, succulent sweet wines of this château are among the best of the appellation.

CHÂTEAU DINTRANS
Ste.-Eulalie
AOC Premières-Côtes-de-Bordeaux and AOC Cadillac
This château produces attractive, nicely coloured, fruity red wines.

CHÂTEAU DE L'ESPLANADE
Capian
AOC Premières-Côtes-de-Bordeaux
Produced by Patrick & Sabine Bayle of Château Plaisance, these

primarily Merlot wines are cheaper and simpler than those of Château Plaisance, but are easy-drinking nevertheless. They are also sold under the Château Florestan label.

CHÂTEAU FAYAU
Cadillac
AOC Premières-Côtes-de-Bordeaux and AOC Cadillac
This château produces succulent sweet wines in addition to red, clairet, and dry white wines.

Other wines: *Clos des Capucins*

CHÂTEAU FLORESTAN
See Château de l'Esplanade

CHÂTEAU FONGRAVE
Gornac
AOC Entre-Deux-Mers
These dry white wines have a fresh and tangy taste.

Second Wine: *Château de la Sablière Fongrave* (red wines)

CHÂTEAU DE GORCE
Haux
AOC Premières-Côtes-de-Bordeaux and AOC Cadillac
This château produces fruity reds and fresh, floral whites.

CHÂTEAU GOUDICHAUD
Vayres
AOC Graves de Vayres
This property also extends into St.-Germain-du-Puch in Entre-Deux-Mers, where it produces some very respectable wines.

CHÂTEAU GOUMIN
Dardenac
AOC Entre-Deux-Mers
Goumin is another successful André Lurton château. It produces up to 10,000 cases of pleasant, soft, fruity red wine and 5,000 cases of white wine that is slightly fuller than other similar Lurton products.

GRAND ENCLOS DU CHÂTEAU DE CÉRONS
Cérons
AOC Cérons
Although historically part of Château de Cérons, this is not under the same ownership. The original estate belonged to the Marquis de Calvimont, but was split in two by the route from Bordeaux to Spain, which was constructed in 1875. The marquis then sold the property in three separate lots, one of which was called Grand Enclos and was purchased by the Lataste family, who are still the owners today. The white wines of Grand Enclos are equally as rich and potentially complex as those of Château de Cérons itself (which is so-called because it retains the marquis' château).

CHÂTEAU GRAND MONEIL
Salleboeuf
AOC Entre-Deux-Mers
★ⓥ
Barely more than a thousand cases of white, but 35,000 cases of excellent-quality, soft, quaffing red.

CHÂTEAU DU GRAND-MOÜEYS
Capian
★ⓥ
AOC Premières-Côtes-de-Bordeaux
Excellent-value reds for medium-term ageing are currently made at this château.

CHÂTEAU GRAVELINES
Sémens
AOC Premières-Côtes-de-Bordeaux and AOC Cadillac
★ⓥ
This large property produces equal quantities of excellent red and white wines.

CHÂTEAU GROSSOMBRE
Branne
AOC Entre-Deux-Mers
★ⓥ

The daughter of André Lurton runs this property which produces lush yet elegant white wines, and a beautifully concentrated red, the latter of which is sold under the Bordeaux Supérieur AOC and must be one of Bordeaux's greatest bargains.

CHÂTEAU DU GUA
Ambarès-et-Lagrave
AOC Premières-Côtes-de-Bordeaux and AOC Cadillac
An attractive, well-structured red wine is produced from this eight-hectare (20-acre) vineyard of fine gravel.

CHÂTEAU HAUT-BRIGNON
Cénac
AOC Premières-Côtes-de-Bordeaux and AOC Cadillac
★
This property has been steadily improving since the late-1980s, producing a soft, velvety red and crisp dry white, plus one of Cadillac's better wines.

CHÂTEAU DE HAUX
Haux
AOC Premières-Côtes-de-Bordeaux
★ⓥ
These red and white wines are gorgeously ripe and ready to drink, absolutely fresh and very elegant and, under the Château Frère label, a fabulous oak-fermented white is also produced. Probably the top-performing château in the Premières Côtes for both red and white.

CLOS JEAN
Loupiac
AOC Loupiac

The wines produced by Clos Jean are similar quality to those of Château du Cros, but more refined and ethereal in character.

CHÂTEAU DU JUGE
Cadillac
AOC Premières-Côtes-de-Bordeaux and AOC Cadillac
Respectable red and dry white wines are produced at Château du Juge, and in some years, a little sweet white wine of high quality is also made. Both red and white wines are extraordinarily good value.

CHÂTEAU DU JUGE
Haux
AOC Premières-Côtes-de-Bordeaux and AOC Cadillac
These promising red wines are easy drinking, and full of juicy fruit flavours. Decent, if unexciting whites are also made.

CHÂTEAU LABATUT
St.-Maixant
AOC Premières-Côtes-de-Bordeaux and AOC Cadillac
The red wines are aromatic, and full of flavour while the sweet white wines are exceptional quality. Decent dry white is also produced.

CHÂTEAU LAFITTE
Camblanes-et-Meynac
AOC Premières-Côtes-de-Bordeaux and AOC Cadillac

Nothing like the real thing (the famous First Growth), of course, but the wine is decent, well structured, and capable of improving with age – a cheap way to get a Château Lafitte on the table, even if it is not *the* Château Lafite.

CHÂTEAU LAFUE
Cadillac
AOC Ste.-Croix-du-Mont
★
Attractive, sweet white wines with more of a fruity than a botrytis character. Nearly a quarter of the production is red wine.

CHÂTEAU LAGAROSSE
Tabanac
AOC Premières-Côtes-de-Bordeaux
The red is easy-drinking with soft fruit and an easy finish.

CHÂTEAU LAGRANGE-HAMILTON
Rions
AOC Premières-Côtes-de-Bordeaux
This property is run by Hamilton Narby, formerly of Château Guiraud in Sauternes. I have not yet tracked down this wine, but if Hamilton Narby devotes a mere fraction of the effort he put into reviving Guiraud, then this château should be worth keeping an eye on.

CHÂTEAU LAMOTHE
Haux
AOC Premières-Côtes-de-Bordeaux and AOC Cadillac
Some exceptionally good wines have been produced in recent years at this château, which derives its name from "La Motte", a rocky spur that protects the vineyard.

CHÂTEAU LAROCHE BEL AIR
Baurech
AOC Premières-Côtes-de-Bordeaux
Absolutely delicious-drinking reds under the basic Château Laroche label, and an even better selection of oak-aged reds under Laroche Bel Air.

CHÂTEAU LATOUR
Camblanes-et-Meynac
AOC Premières-Côtes-de-Bordeaux and AOC Cadillac
This is another everyday-drinking claret with this prestigious name.

CHÂTEAU LATOUR
St.-Martin-du-Puy
AOC Entre-Deux-Mers
From this ancient château, parts of which date back to the 14th century, 10,000 cases of attractive, well-balanced, smooth, red Bordeaux Supérieur are produced every year. This château's technically sound wines often win prizes and enable its devotees to claim that they can afford to drink Château Latour every day, at minimum expense.

CHÂTEAU LAUNAY
Soussac
AOC Entre-Deux-Mers

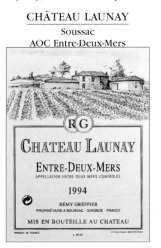

This large property produces 40,000 cases of a fresh dry white wine and 15,000 cases of a red wine sold under the "Haut-Castanet" label.

Other wines: *Bradoire, Château Dubory, Château Haut-Courgeaux, Château La Vaillante*

CHÂTEAU LAURETTE
Cadillac
AOC Ste.-Croix-du-Mont
☆

This property is under the same ownership as Château Lafue, and run along similar lines.

CHÂTEAU LOUBENS
Cadillac
AOC Ste.-Croix-du-Mont
★

This château produces rich, liquorous, superbly balanced sweet white wines. Dry white wines are sold as "Fleur Blanc" and a little red wine is also made.

Other wines: *Fleur Blanc de Château Loubens*

CHÂTEAU LOUPIAC-GAUDIET
Loupiac
AOC Loupiac
Fine, honey-rich sweet wines hinting of crystallized fruit are produced here.

CHÂTEAU LOUSTEAU-VIEIL
Cadillac
AOC Ste.-Croix-du-Mont
★

This property produces richly flavoured, high-quality sweet wines.

CHÂTEAU MACHORRE
St.-Martin-de-Sescas
AOC Côtes-de-Bordeaux-St.-Macaire

The sweet white wine of this château has an attractive, fresh, fruit-salad flavour and is one of the best examples of the appellation. Very respectable red and dry Sauvignon wines are also produced, which are sold under the Bordeaux appellations.

CHÂTEAU DES MAILLES
Cadillac
AOC Ste.-Croix-du-Mont
Some outstanding sweet wines are produced at Château des Mailles, but the wines can occasionally be disappointing.

CHÂTEAU LA MAUBASTIT
AOC Ste.-Foy-de-Bordeaux
Some 5,000 cases of white and 2,000 of red, both "organic" wines, are sold under the Bordeaux appellation.

CHÂTEAU MORLAN-TUILIÈRE
St.-Pierre-de-Bat
AOC Entre-Deux-Mers-Haut-Benauge and Bordeaux Haut-Benauge
One of the best properties of the area, producing a vibrant, crystal-clear Entre-Deux-Mers-Haut-Benauge, a Bordeaux Supérieur in the *moelleux* style, and a fairly full-bodied red AOC Bordeaux.

CHÂTEAU MOULIN DE LAUNAY
Soussac
AOC Entre-Deux-Mers
Despite the vast quantity produced, the dry white wine is crisp, and fruity, and of a very fine standard. A little red is also produced.

Other wines: *Plessis, Château Tertre-de-Launay, Château de Tuilerie, Château la Vigerie*

CHÂTEAU MOULIN DE ROMAGE
AOC Ste.-Foy-de-Bordeaux

BICENTENAIRE DE LA RÉVOLUTION FRANÇAISE
1789 1989
CHÂTEAU MOULIN de ROMAGE
SAINTE-FOY BORDEAUX
APPELLATION STE.-FOY BORDEAUX CONTRÔLÉE
12,5% vol. — 1988 — 75 cl
A. PROUX, PROPRIÉTAIRE À ROMAGE
LES LÈVES ET THOUMEYRAGUES (GIRONDE) FRANCE

This château produces equal quantities of "organic" red and white.

DOMAINE DU NOBLE
Loupiac
AOC Loupiac
This property consistently produces fine botrytized wines that combine sweetness and strength with elegance and a fresh, long finish.

CHÂTEAU PETIT-PEY
St.-André-du-Bois
AOC Côtes-de-Bordeaux-St.-Macaire
Good, sweet white St.-Macaire and agreeably soft red AOC Bordeaux are made at this property.

CHÂTEAU PEYREBON
Grézillac
AOC Entre-Deux-Mers

GRAND VIN DE BORDEAUX
CHÂTEAU PEYREBON
Entre-Deux-Mers
APPELLATION ENTRE-DEUX-MERS CONTRÔLÉE
J. ROBINEAU
PROPRIÉTAIRE À GRÉZILLAC 33420
MIS EN BOUTEILLE AU CHÂTEAU

Produces red and white wine in almost equal quantities. The dry white is fine and flavoursome.

CHÂTEAU PEYRINES
Mourens
AOC Entre-Deux-Mers-Haut-Benauge and Bordeaux Haut-Benauge
★☆

The vineyard of this château has an excellent southern exposure and produces fruity red and white wines.

CHÂTEAU DE PIC
Le Tourne
AOC Premières-Côtes-de-Bordeaux
The basic red is a lovely, creamy-sweet, easy-drinking fruity wine. A superb oak-aged red under the *Cuvée* Tradition label is also made.

CHÂTEAU PICHON-BELLEVUE
Vayres
AOC Graves de Vayres
The red wines are variable but the dry whites are delicate and refined.

CHÂTEAU PLAISANCE
Capian
AOC Premières-Côtes-de-Bordeaux
The *Cuvée* Tradition, in which the wine is aged in oak and is unfiltered, gives rich, ripe fruit with supple tannin structure and smoky-oak.

Other wines: *De l'Esplanade, Château Florestin*

CHÂTEAU DE PLASSAN
Tabanac
AOC Premières-Côtes-de-Bordeaux

The basic red has a lot of character, with cherry-minty undertones in riper years. However, the fuller, more complex *Cuvée Spéciale* is worth paying for, particularly if you want a wine to accompany food.

CHÂTEAU PONTETTE-BELLEGRAVE
Vayres
AOC Graves de Vayres
This property has a reputation for subtly flavoured, dry white wines.

CHÂTEAU PUY BARDENS
Cambes
AOC Premières-Côtes-de-Bordeaux
This top-performing château produces reds with sweet, ripe, fat fruit and a soft, velvety finish.

CHÂTEAU LA RAME
Cadillac
AOC Ste.-Croix-du-Mont
One of the top wines of the appellation, La Rame can have fruit, with cream and honey flavours.

CHÂTEAU REYNON-PEYRAT
Béguey
AOC Premières-Côtes-de-Bordeaux
This property produces a superb, oak-aged Premières Côtes red wine, and two dry white wines under the Château Reynon label.

CHÂTEAU RICAUD
Loupiac
AOC Loupiac

APPELLATION 1ère CÔTES DE BORDEAUX CONTRÔLÉE
CHÂTEAU DE RICAUD
1ère CÔTES DE BORDEAUX
ALAIN THIÉNOT, PROPRIÉTAIRE, CADILLAC (GIRONDE)
MIS EN BOUTEILLES AU CHÂTEAU

The wines of Château Ricaud are once again the best in the Loupiac appellation. They suffered a significant decline under the previous proprietor, but have at last recovered, and now display great class under new ownership.

CHÂTEAU DE LA SABLIÈRE-FONGRAVE
Gornac
AOC Entre-Deux-Mers-Haut-Benauge and Bordeaux Haut-Benauge
Sold as a Bordeaux Supérieur, the red wine of Château de la Sablière-Fongrave is fairly robust and requires time in bottle to soften. A much better-quality dry white is produced and sold under the Entre-Deux-Mers appellation.

CHÂTEAU TANESSE
Langoiran
AOC Premières-Côtes-de-Bordeaux and AOC Cadillac
A Cordier property, Château Tanesse produces a decent Cabernet-dominated red, and fine-quality, Sauvignon-styled dry white.

CHÂTEAU DES TASTES
Cadillac
AOC Ste.-Croix-du-Mont
★☆

The sweet white wine is truly exciting; luxurious in texture, with creamy-rich flavours showing the classic complex character of botrytis.

CHÂTEAU TERFORT
Cadillac
AOC Ste.-Croix-du-Mont
☆

A small amount of excellent sweet white wine is produced by Château Terfort.

CHÂTEAU THIEULEY
La Sauve
AOC Entre-Deux-Mers
☆

SEC SEC
1988
Château Thieuley
BORDEAUX
APPELLATION BORDEAUX CONTRÔLÉE
CÉPAGE SAUVIGNON
COURSELLE, PROPRIÉTAIRE À LA SAUVE (GIRONDE)
12% Vol. MISE EN BOUTEILLES AU CHÂTEAU 750ml

Château Thieuley is owned by Professor Courselle, a former Médoc professor of viticulture and oenology. His dry white combines good fruit flavour with a fine Sauvignon style, while the red is good and silky.

CHÂTEAU DE TOUTIGEAC
Targon
AOC Entre-Deux-Mers–Haut-Benauge and Bordeaux Haut-Benauge
★☆ ✔

Château de Toutigeac is a well-known property that produces full, rich red wine. It is made for early drinking, and is the best the château produces.

AUTHOR'S CHOICE

*Because virtually all the greatest Bordeaux wines are described within their own château profiles,
it seemed only logical to confine my choice to the most outstanding second wines and to
other top-performing styles of wine not described in the main entry text.*

PRODUCER	WINE	STYLE	DESCRIPTION	⌐
Château de Fieuzal (*see* p.95)	Château de Fieuzal Blanc	WHITE	Although not a *Cru Classé*, this wonderfully exotic dry white wine is jam-packed with rich, oaky, tropical fruit flavours, making it the greatest unclassified white wine produced in Bordeaux.	3–7 years
Château Gruaud-Larose (*see* p.83) V	Sarget de Gruaud-Larose	RED	This second wine was aggressively marketed in the early 1980s by Cordier. Unbelievably deep and dark at times, Sarget de Gruaud-Larose has masses of sweet, ripe mulberry fruit and fine spicy-oak, with an excellent tannin structure.	4–15 years
Château Haut-Bailly (*see* p.96) V	Le Pardre de Haut-Bailly	RED	The fruit in this *cuvée* is extraordinarily ripe and voluptuous for a second wine, although understandably it does not quite have the finesse or as much creamy-oak as the *grand vin*.	4–10 years
Château Haut-Brion (*see* p.96)	Bahans-Haut-Brion	RED	This classic claret vies with Château Léoville-Las Cases's Clos du Marquis for runner-up to Les Forts de Latour, the greatest second wine produced in Bordeaux. Bahans-Haut-Brion has beautifully structured fruit supported by complex, toasty-cedarwood oak.	5–15 years
Château Lafite-Rothschild (*see* p.79)	Carraudes de Lafite	RED	Formerly known as Moulin des Carraudes, this wine is one of the most consistent second wines available, full of creamy, refined fruit and a great bargain considering its First Growth origins.	4–12 years
Château Lafleur (*see* p.116)	Les Pensées de Lafleur	RED	This wine can be quite opaque and serious looking, yet it is the most sensuous, seductive, and beguiling of all second wines, as befits its illustrious origins.	5–10 years
Château Langoa-Barton and Château Léoville-Barton (*see* p.84)	Lady Langoa	RED	Made from a blend of wines de-selected from the *grands vins* of both Langoa-Barton and Léoville-Barton, this is a very classy wine. It has a delicious, well-focused flavour of ripe summer fruits, violety-vanilla oak, and plenty of fine tannin on the finish.	6–15 years
Château Latour (*see* p.79)	Les Forts de Latour	RED	A deep-flavoured archetypal Pauillac, Les Forts de Latour is full of the scents of soft forest fruits, rich and powerful on the palate, yet totally accessible, and laced with creamy-spicy oak. Easily the equivalent of a Second Growth, the 1978 and 1990 can even battle it out with the "super seconds", while the 1982, the greatest vintage of Les Forts de Latour made so far, has never come last in a blind tasting of First Growths from that great year. One of the reasons why this is such a great second wine is that it, too, is the result of selection, there being a third wine, which is sold simply as Pauillac.	10–25 years
Château Léoville-Las Cases (*see* p.84) V	Clos du Marquis	RED	Second only to Les Forts de Latour, as far as the second wines of Bordeaux are concerned, Clos du Marquis is on a par with Bahans-Haut-Brion, not quite achieving the finesse and complexity of that wine in the greatest vintages, but bettering it in merely good vintages and trouncing it in off-years. Very consistent, dark, plummy-spicy fruit, supported by fine vanilla-oak.	5–15 years
Château Margaux (*see* p.88) V	Pavillon Rouge du Château Margaux	RED	Some prefer Pavillon Blanc to Pavillon Rouge, but the former does not have the finesse of even a middle-rung Graves *blanc*, while the soft and seductively oaky Pavillon Rouge has more than a touch of the fine, flowery finesse and sweet perfume of Margaux's *grand vin*, although the texture is more silk than velvet.	5–15 years
Château Montrose (*see* p.75)	La Dame de Montrose	RED	Strangely, I sometimes prefer this wine to the *grand vin*, although it does not have its class or quality in great years such as 1990.	5–12 years
Château Palmer (*see* p.89)	Réserve du Général	RED	Not as deep as Palmer itself, and more floral than *cassis*, Réserve du Général does, however, have much of the fine tannic structure and creamy-spicy cedarwood complexity of the *grand vin*.	5–15 years
Château Pichon-Longueville-Comtesse-de-Lalande (*see* p.80)	Réserve de la Comtesse	RED	With its rich, almost exotic, aroma, exquisitely ripe fruit, and silky tannins, Réserve de la Comtesse shows extraordinary finesse for a second wine, and is at least Third Growth quality.	5–12 years
Château Talbot (*see* p.84) V	Connétable Talbot	RED	Talbot's second wine can be fuller than Gruaud-Larose's (reversing the *grand vin* situation). Indeed, Connétable can be dark and brooding, and both second wines age extremely well.	4–15 years

BURGUNDY

Villages with double-barrelled names are the key to Burgundy's greatest wines because they hijacked the names of their most famous vineyards, so that humble village wines could sell on the back of the finest Grand Crus. The village of Gevrey was the first to do this when in 1848 it took the name of its Chambertin vineyard to become Gevrey-Chambertin. You cannot become a Burgundy expert overnight, but if you remember the second part of every double-barrelled Burgundian village is one of its best vineyards, you will instantly know some of Burgundy's best wines.

SAY "BURGUNDY" and most people think of the famous wines of the Côtes de Nuits and Côtes de Beaune, but Burgundy in fact stretches from Chablis in the north, which is close to the Aube vineyards of Champagne, down to Beaujolais in the south, in the Rhône *département*.

Burgundy still produces the world's greatest Chardonnay and Pinot noir wines, and the only Gamay wines ever to achieve classic status, but it is increasingly debased by a growing number of lack-lustre, sometimes quite disgusting, supermarket wines that rely solely upon the reputation of the famous Burgundian names, which their producers abuse to sell low-quality wines at high prices.

Burgundy, or Bourgogne as it is known in French, is an area rich in history, gastronomy, and wine, but unlike the great estates of Bordeaux, the finest Burgundian vineyards are owned by a proliferation of smallholders. Prior to 1789, the church owned most of the vineyards in Burgundy, but these were seized and broken up as a direct result of the Revolution, which was as much anti-church as anti-aristocracy. While in Bordeaux, although some of the large wine estates were owned by the aristocracy,

VIRÉ, MÂCONNAIS
Viré is the most ubiquitous of Mâcon's village appellations, but makes consistently fine wines. There are moves to upgrade this village and Clessé to superior appellations.

many were owned by the *bourgeoisie*, who, because of their long association with the English, were anti-papist, and so escaped the full wrath of the Revolution. In Burgundy the great vineyards were further fragmented by inheritance laws, which divided the plots into smaller and smaller parcels. Consequently, many *crus* or growths are now owned by as many as 85 individual growers.

HOW TO READ BURGUNDY LABELS

GRAND VIN DE BOURGOGNE
This literally means "Grand" or "Great" wine of Burgundy, but has no official significance whatsoever.

SÉLECTIONNÉ, ÉLEVÉ, MIS EN BOUTEILLE PAR
This means "Selected, raised, and bottled by" the name of the *négociant* that follows, but not therefore produced from his own vines. When the wine was bottled on the property where the grapes were grown, you will see the term *Mis en bouteille au domaine*.

THE PRODUCER
If it is a merchant's wine, the label will not mention either Propriétaire or Domaine, unless of course the wine is produced entirely from that firm's own domaine (always a plus). This particular wine is from Olivier Leflaive Frères, who is generally considered one of the best producers in Burgundy.

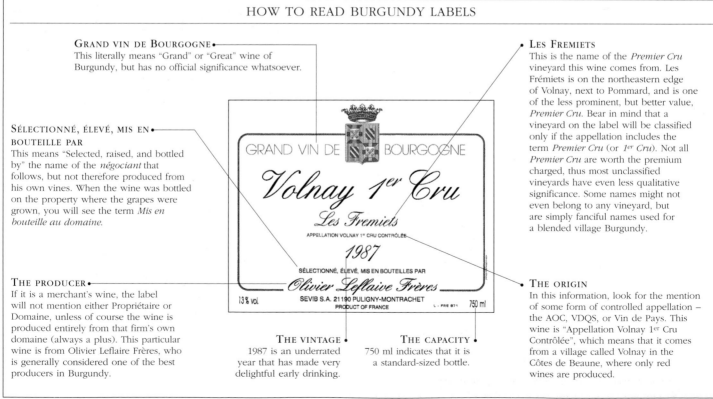

GRAND VIN DE BOURGOGNE
Volnay 1er Cru
Les Fremiets
APPELLATION VOLNAY 1er CRU CONTRÔLÉE
1987
SÉLECTIONNÉ, ÉLEVÉ, MIS EN BOUTEILLES PAR
Olivier Leflaive Frères
13 % vol.   SEVIB S.A. 21190 PULIGNY-MONTRACHET
PRODUCT OF FRANCE   L - FRE 871   750 ml

THE VINTAGE
1987 is an underrated year that has made very delightful early drinking.

THE CAPACITY
750 ml indicates that it is a standard-sized bottle.

LES FREMIETS
This is the name of the *Premier Cru* vineyard this wine comes from. Les Frémiets is on the northeastern edge of Volnay, next to Pommard, and is one of the less prominent, but better value, *Premier Cru*. Bear in mind that a vineyard on the label will be classified only if the appellation includes the term *Premier Cru* (or *1er Cru*). Not all *Premier Cru* are worth the premium charged, thus most unclassified vineyards have even less qualitative significance. Some names might not even belong to any vineyard, but are simply fanciful names used for a blended village Burgundy.

THE ORIGIN
In this information, look for the mention of some form of controlled appellation – the AOC, VDQS, or Vin de Pays. This wine is "Appellation Volnay 1er Cru Contrôlée", which means that it comes from a village called Volnay in the Côtes de Beaune, where only red wines are produced.

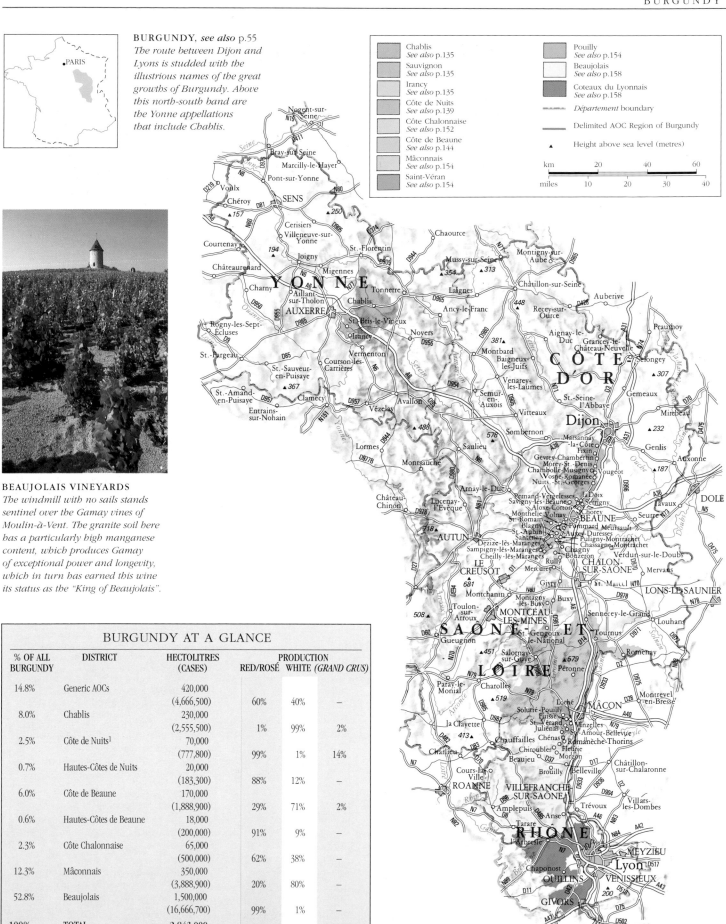

BURGUNDY, *see also* p.55
The route between Dijon and Lyons is studded with the illustrious names of the great growths of Burgundy. Above this north-south band are the Yonne appellations that include Chablis.

PARIS

Legend:

Chablis
See also p.135

Sauvignon
See also p.135

Irancy
See also p.135

Côte de Nuits
See also p.139

Côte Chalonnaise
See also p.152

Côte de Beaune
See also p.144

Mâconnais
See also p.154

Saint-Véran
See also p.154

Pouilly
See also p.154

Beaujolais
See also p.158

Coteaux du Lyonnais
See also p.158

- - - - - *Département* boundary

———— Delimited AOC Region of Burgundy

▲ Height above sea level (metres)

km   20   40   60
miles   10   20   30   40

BEAUJOLAIS VINEYARDS
The windmill with no sails stands sentinel over the Gamay vines of Moulin-à-Vent. The granite soil here has a particularly high manganese content, which produces Gamay of exceptional power and longevity, which in turn has earned this wine its status as the "King of Beaujolais".

BURGUNDY AT A GLANCE

% OF ALL BURGUNDY	DISTRICT	HECTOLITRES (CASES)	PRODUCTION		
			RED/ROSÉ	WHITE	(GRAND CRUS)
14.8%	Generic AOCs	420,000 (4,666,500)	60%	40%	–
8.0%	Chablis	230,000 (2,555,500)	1%	99%	2%
2.5%	Côte de Nuits[1]	70,000 (777,800)	99%	1%	14%
0.7%	Hautes-Côtes de Nuits	20,000 (183,300)	88%	12%	–
6.0%	Côte de Beaune	170,000 (1,888,900)	29%	71%	2%
0.6%	Hautes-Côtes de Beaune	18,000 (200,000)	91%	9%	–
2.3%	Côte Chalonnaise	65,000 (500,000)	62%	38%	–
12.3%	Mâconnais	350,000 (3,888,900)	20%	80%	–
52.8%	Beaujolais	1,500,000 (16,666,700)	99%	1%	
100%	TOTAL	2,843,000 (28,177,800)	74%[2]	26%[2]	7%[2]

[1]Including other wines of the Yonne   [2]Average percentage for region

The initial effect of this proprietorial carve-up was to encourage the supremacy of *le négoce*. Few commercial houses had been established prior to the mid-18th century because of the difficulty of exporting from a land-locked area, but with better transport and no opposition from land-owning aristocracy, merchant power grew rapidly. A network of brokers evolved in which dealers became experts on very small, localized areas.

As ownership diversified even further, it became a very specialized, and therefore rewarding, job to keep an up-to-date and comprehensive knowledge of a complex situation. The brokers were vital to the success of a *négociant*, and the *négoce* itself was essential to the success of international trade and therefore responsible for establishing the reputation of Burgundy.

THE ROLE OF THE NÉGOCIANT

Until as recently as the early 1980s, virtually all Burgundy would be sold through *négociants* and, although many of them had their own vineyards, these wines were seldom domaine-bottled. Faced with the rise of domaine-bottled Burgundies from small growers, most of the old-fashioned merchants were devoured by

CORTON, CÔTE DE BEAUNE
Capped by the Bois de Corton, this magnificent slope produces the Côte de Beaune's most famous red wines and minuscule amounts of Corton Charlemagne, possibly the greatest of all white Burgundies.

Boisset, which has become the largest merchant of its kind. Boisset might survive by marketing a mass of different labels, particularly in the supermarket sector or at the bottom end of the restaurant market, but the recent hiring of Pascal Marchand indicates that it has changed its strategy. Marchand is the French-Canadian whose wine-wizardry enabled the quality at Domaine Comte Armand to soar in the second half of the 1990s and by enticing him away Boisset has shown a determination to join the ranks of the few traditional *négociants* who can be said to be top-performing. These currently include Bouchard Père, Drouhin, Louis Jadot, and Leroy, who have not only enlarged their own domaines but have also taken an increasingly proactive role in the vineyards of their suppliers, tending now to buy in grapes or must, rather than wines. Until this new strategy evolved, the purchase of wine rather than grapes was the major difference between the old-style *négociant* and the new-wave growers-cum-merchants. The best of the latter include the likes of Jean-Marc

Boillot, Michel Colin, Bernard Morey and Sauzet, who tend to buy grapes to expand their range of single-vineyard wines, in contrast to the old-style merchant, who still churns out nearly every village wine under the Burgundian sun.

The decline of the old-style merchant is clearly highlighted by domaine-bottling statistics. Today as much as 90 per cent of all *Grand Cru* wines (and 50 per cent of all *Premiers Crus*) are domaine bottled, although only 24 per cent of the entire production of Burgundy is domaine bottled.

BURGUNDY'S RICH DIVERSITY

Chablis in the north of Burgundy produces the crispest white Chardonnay wines in the world and is geographically closer to Champagne, of which it was once a part, than to the rest of Burgundy. After travelling more than 100 kilometres (60 miles) southwest from Champagne, we reach the great Burgundy districts of the Côte d'Or: the Côte de Nuits is encountered first and followed by the Côte de Beaune. If you associate Nuits with "night" or "darkness" and Beaune with "bone-white", then you will easily remember which area is most famous for what: for although both *côtes* make excellent red and white wines, most of the greatest red burgundies come from the Côte de Nuits, whereas most of the greatest white burgundies come from the Côte de Beaune.

The Côte Chalonnaise or Mercurey region – probably the least well-known, but certainly the best-value, wine district of Burgundy – produces similar, if somewhat less classic, styles of red and white wines as those in the Côte de Beaune. Softer still are the primarily white wines of Mâcon, where Pouilly Fuissé AOC rules supreme and should never be confused with Pouilly Fumé AOC in the Loire.

Still in Burgundy, but further south, is the Beaujolais region, which is in the Rhône *département*, although its soft, light, fluffy, fruity red wines are far removed from the archetypal full-bodied red wines that we immediately perceive as coming from the Rhône Valley. Beaujolais can be delicious, but most is not. Whereas Beaujolais Nouveau was never meant to be considered as a serious wine, it is now a joke and far too many of even the best *Crus* Beaujolais are simply overpriced, but that is part of Burgundy's rich tapestry.

Great Pinot and Chardonnay

I was pleased to read in the second edition of Anthony Hanson's book "Burgundy" that he had revised his opinion that "Great burgundy smells of shit". Although semi-subliminal faults can add to the complexity, interest, and enjoyment of a wine, they should never dominate, particularly in a Pinot noir wine, where purity of fruit and varietal character play such an important role. Just as the once celebrated "sweaty saddle" smell of Hunter Valley Shiraz turned out to be a fault, so has *"ça sent la merde"*. Hanson now admits: "I certainly oversimplified the case when I wrote in 1982 that great burgundy smells of shit… if I perceive decaying vegetable and animal smells, I now mostly find them unacceptable".

While the Californian wineries of Santa Barbara, Carneros, and Russian River lead the way in the search for the winemaker's Holy Grail – successful Pinot noir – and individual wineries in other parts of California, and in Oregon and New Zealand, are not far behind, rarely can anyone outside Burgundy manage to produce a deep-coloured, full-bodied example of Pinot noir and still retain its varietal purity, finesse, and elegance. Even in Burgundy it does not come easy and cannot be attempted on grapes coming from anywhere but the best growths. It is, however, a relatively common occurrence.

Chardonnay is so ubiquitous it is probably cultivated in every wine-producing country in the world. Australian versions of this varietal are consistent and quaffable, even at the lowest level, but more expensive Chardonnays exist in Australia, just as they do in New Zealand, South Africa, Chile, California, Oregon, and lots of other places. This is why it is easy to forget just how different great white burgundy is. When it is right, good white burgundy is in a class of its own, and the incomparable richness, complexity, and longevity of the very greatest *Grands Crus* must be experienced to be believed.

GRAND CRU VALMUR, CHABLIS
At the very heart of Chablis' Grands Crus lies Valmur. Bordered by Grenouilles and Vaudesir on one side and Les Clos on the other, this vineyard is renowned for the fine bouquet and rich flavour of its wines.

THE GENERIC APPELLATIONS OF
BURGUNDY

BOURGOGNE AOC

Many writers consider Bourgogne AOC to be too basic and boring to warrant serious attention, but for me it is the most instructive of all Burgundy's appellations. If a producer cares about the quality of the Bourgogne, how much more effort does that producer put into making higher-quality wines? I delight in finding a delicious, easy-to-drink Bourgogne, and I often get more of a kick discovering one that will improve for several years than I do from a superior appellation that should age well, considering its famous name and high price. Light-red/dark-rosé wines may be sold as Bourgogne Clairet AOC, but the style is outmoded and the appellation rarely seen.

RED Despite the grape varieties that may be used to make this wine, the only Bourgogne worth seeking out is that with the flavour and aroma of pure Pinot noir. Many producers indicate the grape variety on the label.

🍇 Pinot noir, Pinot gris, Pinot liébault plus, in the Yonne district, César, Tressot, and Gamay (if declassified from one of the ten Beaujolais *Crus*)

🍷 2–5 years

✓ **Bourgogne Rouge** *Pascal Bouley • Château de Chamilly • J.-F. Coche-Dury • Domaine Joseph Drouhin • Louis Jadot • Domaine Henri Jayer • Domaine Michel Juillot • Labouré-Roi • Domaine Michel Lafarge • Louis Latour • Dominique Laurent • Olivier Leflaive • Domaine Hubert Lignier • Moillard • Domaine Denis Mortet • Domaine Parent • Domaine de la Pousse d'Or • Domaine Daniel Rion & Fils • Domaine Tollot-Beaut • Vallet Frères • A. & P. de Villaine • Cave Coopérative de Viré*

WHITE There are a lot of boring white wines made under this appellation, and unless you have access to something more interesting

like J.-F. Coche-Dury or Clos du Château du Meursault, it is probably safer to buy an inexpensive Mâcon AOC. These wines may be sold as *primeur* or *nouveau* as from the third Thursday of November following the harvest.

🍇 Chardonnay, Pinot blanc

🍷 1–4 years

✓ **Bourgogne Blanc** *Simon Bize & Fils • Jean-Marc Boillot • J.-F. Coche-Dury • Louis Jadot • Patrick Javillier • Domaine François Jobard • Labouré-Roi • Domaine Michel Lafarge • Domaine Leflaive • Olivier Leflaive • Domaine Lorenzon • Clos du Château du Meursault • Pierre Morey • Antonin Rodet • Domaine Tollot-Beaut • A. & P. de Villaine*

ROSÉ The wines produced under this appellation are acceptable, but they are never special – it is the least exciting category of Bourgogne.

🍇 Pinot noir, Pinot gris, Pinot liébault, plus, in the Yonne district, César and Tressot

🍷 1–4 years

Note For other more local generic wines, *see* **Chablis** Bourgogne Chitry AOC, Bourgogne Coulange-la-Vineuse AOC, Bourgogne Epineuil AOC, Bourgogne Irancy AOC, Bourgogne Saint-Bris AOC, Bourgogne Saint-Jacques AOC, Bourgogne Côtes d'Auxerre AOC (p.137) • **Côte de Nuits** and **Hautes-Côtes de Nuits** Bourgogne Hautes-Côtes de Nuits AOC, Bourgogne La Chapelle Notre-Dame AOC,

Bourgogne Le Chapitre AOC, Bourgogne Montrecul AOC (p.140) • Côte de Beaune and Hautes-Côtes de Beaune Bourgogne Hautes-Côtes de Beaune AOC (p.140) • Côte Chalonnaise Bourgogne Côte Chalonnaise AOC (p.153)

BOURGOGNE-ALIGOTÉ AOC

The finest Bourgogne-Aligoté wines come from the village of Bouzeron in the Mercurey region, which has its own appellation (*see also* Bourgogne Aligoté Bouzeron AOC, p.153). With the exception of the wines below, the remaining Aligoté can be improved by adding *Crème de Cassis*, a local blackcurrant liqueur, to create an aperitif known as a "Kir".

WHITE Dry wines that are usually thin, acid, and not very pleasant: bad examples are even worse and are becoming widespread. When good, however, Aligoté can make a refreshing change from Burgundy's ubiquitous Chardonnay wines. Bourgogne-Aligoté may be sold as *primeur* or *nouveau* from the third Thursday of November following the harvest.

🍇 Aligoté and a maximum of 15% Chardonnay

🍷— 1–4 years

✓ *Domaine Boyer-Martenot • Marc Brocot • Domaine Chevrot • J.-F. Coche-Dury • Domaine du Corps de Garde • Domaine Naudin-Ferrand • Domaine François Jobard • Jacky Renard • Thévenot-le-Brun & Fils • A. & P. de Villaine*

BOURGOGNE GRAND-ORDINAIRE AOC

In English-speaking markets the "*Grand*" sounds very grand indeed, and the fact that it qualifies "*Ordinaire*", not "Bourgogne", seems to get lost in the translation. Light-red/dark-rosé wines may be sold as Bourgogne Clairet Grand-Ordinaire AOC, but the style is outmoded and the appellation is rarely encountered.

RED These are mostly inferior wines made from the Gamay grape, but there are some interesting Pinot noir-dominated versions.

🍇 Pinot noir, Gamay, plus, in the Yonne district, César and Tressot

🍷— 2–6 years

WHITE These dry wines are even more dismal than standard-issue Bourgogne blanc. Buy Mâcon blanc instead! These wines may be sold as *primeur* or *nouveau* as from the third Thursday of November following the harvest.

🍇 Chardonnay, Pinot blanc, Aligoté, Melon de Bourgogne, plus, in the Yonne district, Sacy

🍷— 1–4 years

ROSÉ The Hautes-Côtes *coopérative* produces a dry, light but elegant wine under this appellation, "Rosé d'Orches".

🍇 Pinot noir, Gamay, plus, in the Yonne district, César and Tressot

🍷— 1–3 years

✓ *J.-C. Boisset • Edmond Cornu & Fils*

BOURGOGNE MOUSSEUX AOC

Since December 1985 this appellation has been limited to, and remains the only outlet for, sparkling red Burgundy.

SPARKLING RED A favourite fizzy tipple in the pubs of pre-war Britain. This wine's sweet flavour is very much out of step with today's sophisticated consumers.

🍇 Pinot noir, Gamay, plus, in the Yonne district, César and Tressot

🍷— Upon purchase

BOURGOGNE ORDINAIRE AOC

See Bourgogne Grand-Ordinaire AOC

BOURGOGNE PASSETOUTGRAINS AOC

Made from a *mélange* of Pinot noir and Gamay grapes, *passetoutgrains* is the descendant of an authentic peasant wine. A grower would fill his vat with anything growing in his vineyard and ferment it all together. Thus *passetoutgrains* once contained numerous grape varieties. The Pinot noir and Gamay varieties were, however, the widest planted, and the wine naturally evolved as a two-grape product. Up until 1943 a minimum of one-fifth Pinot noir was enforced by law; now the minimum is one-third.

RED Many *passetoutgrains* used to be drunk too early, as the better-quality examples require a few years of bottle-ageing to show the aristocratic influence of their Pinot noir content. With an increase in Pinot Noir production and more modern vinification techniques, more producers have begun making softer, less rustic *passetoutgrains*, which are easier to drink when young. They remain relatively modest wines.

🍇 Pinot noir plus a maximum of one-third Gamay and a combined maximum of 15% Chardonnay, Pinot blanc, and Pinot gris

🍷— 2–6 years

ROSÉ This dry, pink version is worth trying.

🍇 A maximum of one-third Gamay plus Pinot noir and Pinot liébault

🍷— 1–3 years

✓ *Edmond Cornu & Fils • Domaine Michel Lafarge • Domaine Lejeune • Daniel Rion & Fils*

CRÉMANT DE BOURGOGNE AOC

This appellation was created in 1975 to supersede the Bourgogne Mousseux AOC, which failed to inspire a quality image because the term "*mousseux*" also applied to cheap sparkling wines. Bourgogne Mousseux is now for red wines only. The major production centres for Crémant de Bourgogne are the Yonne, Region de Mercurey, and the Mâconnais. There are already many exciting wines, and the quality is certain to improve as more producers specialize in cultivating grapes specifically for sparkling wines, rather than relying on excess or inferior grapes, as was traditional in Burgundy.

SPARKLING WHITE Dry but round, the styles range from fresh and light to rich and toasty.

🍇 Pinot noir, Pinot gris, Pinot blanc, Chardonnay, Sacy, Aligoté, Melon de Bourgogne, and a maximum of 20% Gamay

🍷— 3–7 years

SPARKLING ROSÉ Until now the best pink Crémant produced outside of Champagne has come from Alsace. Good examples are made in Burgundy, but have not realized their potential.

🍇 Pinot noir, Pinot gris, Pinot blanc, Chardonnay, Sacy, Aligoté, Melon de Bourgogne, and a maximum of 20% Gamay

🍷— 2–5 years

✓ *Caves de Bailly • André Bonhomme • Paul Chollet • André Delorme • Roux Père • Caves de Viré*

THE CHABLIS DISTRICT

An island of vines that is closer to Champagne than the rest of Burgundy, Chablis is one of Burgundy's two classic white-wine areas, yet its Chardonnay grape is grown on soils and under climatic conditions that are more champenois *than Burgundian.*

LIKE CHAMPAGNE, Chablis owes much of its success to a cool and uncertain northern climate that puts viticulture on a knife-edge. This is a source of constant worry and not a little diabolical wine, but when everything comes together just right, Chablis can produce the most electrifying Chardonnay in the world.

Known as the "Golden Gate", this area has the advantage of being the inevitable first stop for anyone visiting the region by car, whether directly from Paris or via Champagne. Situated in the Yonne *département*, much of which once formed part of the ancient province of Champagne, Chablis gives the traveller the distinct impression of an area cut off not simply from the rest of Burgundy but from the rest of France. Indeed, the great *négociants* of the Côte d'Or rarely visit Chablis and have never made any significant penetration into what appears to be a closed-shop trade.

THE VARYING STYLES OF CHABLIS

The traditional description of Chablis is of a wine of clear, pale colour with a green hue around the rim. It is very straight and

THE TOWN OF CHABLIS
Above the town of Chablis, the vines face southeast and southwest, clinging to hills along the banks of the Serein, a small tributary of the Yonne. These are the Grand Cru *vineyards that make this district's finest wines.*

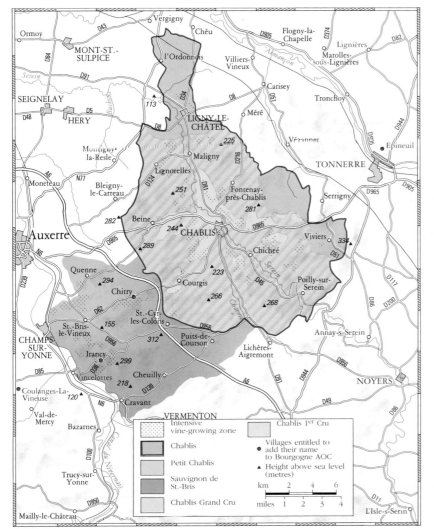

FOURCHAUME
Just north of Chablis itself, Fourchaume is one of only two Premier Cru *slopes that face southwest. The other is Montée de Tonnerre. It is probably no coincidence that, out of a total of seventeen Chablis* Premiers Crus, *these vineyards are always among the top three.*

CHABLIS DISTRICT
Overlooked by its Grands Crus *and surrounded by* Premiers Crus, *Chablis lies at the centre of its eponymous wine-producing area, which is geographically and climatically closer to Champagne than to the rest of Burgundy.*

FACTORS AFFECTING TASTE AND QUALITY

LOCATION
Chablis is isolated halfway between Beaune and Paris, 30 km (19 miles) from the southernmost vineyards of Champagne, but 100 km (60 miles) from the rest of Burgundy.

CLIMATE
This area has a semi-continental climate with minimal Atlantic influence, which results in a long, cold winter, a humid spring, and a fairly hot, very sunny summer. Hail storms and spring frosts are the greatest hazards.

ASPECT
All the *Grands Crus* are located on one stretch of southwest-facing slopes just north of Chablis itself, where the vineyards are at a height of between 150 and 200 m (490–660 ft). Apart from the southwest-facing slopes of "Fourchaume" and "Montée de Tonnerre", the *Premier Cru* slopes face southeast.

SOIL
This area is predominantly covered with calcareous clay, and the traditional view is that of the two major types, Kimmeridgian and Portlandian, only the former is suitable for classic Chablis; but this is neither proven nor likely.

Geologically they have the same Upper Jurassic origin. Any intrinsic geographical differences should be put down to aspect, microclimate, and the varied nature of the sedimentary beds that underlie and interbed with the Kimmeridgian and Portlandian soils.

VITICULTURE AND VINIFICATION
The vineyards in Chablis have undergone rapid expansion, most particularly in the generic appellation and the *Premiers Crus*, both of which have doubled in size since the early 1970s. Mechanical harvesting has now found its way to the *Grands Crus* slopes of Chablis, but smaller producers still pick by hand. Most Chablis is fermented in stainless steel, but oak barrels are making a comeback, although too much new oak fights against the lean, austere intensity of the Chardonnay grown in this district.

PRIMARY GRAPE VARIETIES
Chardonnay
SECONDARY GRAPE VARIETIES
Pinot noir, Pinot blanc, Pinot gris (*syn.* Pinot beurot), Pinot liébault, Sauvignon blanc, Gamay, César, Tressot, Sacy, Aligoté, Melon de Bourgogne

---

positive, with an aggressive, steely character, very direct attack, and a high level of acidity that needs a few years to round out. This description, however, rarely applies, as much has changed in the way these wines are made at both ends of the quality spectrum.

Thirty years ago most Chablis did not undergo malolactic fermentation. The wines that resulted had a naturally high acidity, and were hard, green, and ungenerous in their youth, although they often matured into wines of incomparable finesse. Now, most Chablis undergo malolactic fermentation and cold stabilization, which is used to precipitate tartrates (although some wines fermented or matured in small oak casks do not), which makes the wines fuller, softer, and rounder.

At the top end of the market there are two distinctly different schools. Some wines are fermented in stainless steel and bottled early to produce the most direct and attacking style, while others are fermented in wood and matured in casks with an increasing amount of new oak. Writers often describe the unoaked, stainless-steel-fermented Chablis as traditional, but these vats were introduced in the 1960s, so it cannot be a well-established tradition. The oak barrel is much older, of course, and thus far more traditional, but what the critics really mean is that new oak has never been a feature of Chablis winemaking, therefore the crisp, clean style of Chablis fermented in stainless steel is closer to the original style: traditional by default. Obviously the most authentic style of Chablis is the "unoaked wine" made in old or, more accurately, well-used casks or wooden vats.

What makes the divide between oaked and unoaked Chablis even wider is the fact that the leaner, more mineral style of wine produced in this district can fight against the effects of new oak, whereas the fatter, softer, more seductive wines of the Côte d'Or embrace it with open arms. Recognizing that some people enjoy more new oak characteristics than others, the recommendations in this book include producers of the best oaky Chablis.

There has always been a certain inconsistency about Chablis, which is only to be expected given its uncertain climate and has never deterred its devotees. However, things have gone from bad to worse over the last decade and it is not the weather that has always been to blame – it is the increasing yields by greedy producers and sloppy winemaking. There are still great joys to be had with the best and most passionately produced of Chablis, from the lowliest appellation to the greatest *Grands Crus*, but wine buyers must be increasingly vigilant.

OTHER WINES OF YONNE

Other than Chablis, the two best-known wines of the Yonne are the red wines of Irancy and the white of Sauvignon de Saint-Bris. The former is an AOC and sells under the Bourgogne Irancy appellation, the latter a VDQS made from the Sauvignon grape, a trespasser from the Loire. Other grapes peculiar to Yonne are the César and Tressot, which are black, and the Sacy, which is white. None is permitted in any Burgundian appellation other than AOC Bourgogne from Yonne, and they are not even widely cultivated here. César is the most interesting of these varieties, albeit rather rustic. It is a low-yielding vine that produces a thick, dark, tannic wine and does not have the balance to be a pure varietal wine, although Simonnet-Febvre makes one of the better examples. César grows best at Irancy and can make a positive contribution to a wine when it is carefully blended with Pinot noir. Just five or ten per cent of César is required, but a few growers use as much as 20 per cent and this tends to knock all the elegance out of the intrinsically light-bodied local Pinot noir. The Tressot is thin, weak, and without merit whatsoever, but this blank canvas together with the advantage of its typically high yield made it the obvious partner to the César in bygone times. Occasionally encountered, it usually tastes like a thin, coarse Beaujolais. This district's other viticultural oddity is the steadily declining Sacy, a high-yielding white grape that produces acidic, neutrally flavoured wines best utilized for the production of Crémant de Bourgogne, although most of it has traditionally been sold to Germany for the production of *Sekt*.

MACHINE-HARVESTING IN DOMAINE STE.-CLAIRE AT PRÉHY
Machine-harvesting, which can lower the quality of white wines in particular, is widespread in Chablis, even on the Grands Crus. *The technique is most appropriate at Préhy, where the vineyards are of lesser quality.*

THE APPELLATIONS OF

THE CHABLIS DISTRICT

BOURGOGNE CHITRY AOC
•
BOURGOGNE COULANGES-LA-VINEUSE AOC
•
BOURGOGNE EPINEUIL AOC
•
BOURGOGNE IRANCY AOC
•
BOURGOGNE SAINT-BRIS AOC*

The villages listed above do not have their own separate appellations. However, all except Saint-Bris may add their name to the Bourgogne AOC. Only Chitry and Epineuil are true single-village appellations, as the wines of Irancy also include those of Cravant and Vincelottes, and the far-flung borders of Coulanges-la-Vineuse encompass no fewer than six communes in addition to its own: Charentenay, Escolives-Sainte-Camille, Migé, Mouffy, Jussy, and Val-de-Mercy. Irancy is supposed to be the "famous" red wine of Chablis, but is not really that well known, although it is the only one of these Bourgogne appellations that is restricted to red wine production. With the exception of Saint-Bris and Irancy, the others can be made in red, white, rosé, or "clairet" style, although Chitry is best known for white, mostly Chardonnay but also some pretty decent Aligoté (officially Bourgogne Aligoté, not that they bother with such technicalities), while Epineuil and Coulanges-la-Vineuse are essentially red-wine appellations. *Bourgogne Saint-Bris is the real exception here, as it does not officially exist! (*See also* Sauvignon de St.-Bris.) I make no apologies for including it, however, because in practical terms it does. In fact it is a ubiquitous anomaly. Only Sauvignon has the right to the Saint-Bris appellation and it is merely VDQS. I have seen many AOC Bourgogne displaying the name of Saint-Bris in exactly the same way and just as prominently as the four other villages listed above, including those of Robert Defrance, Domaine Félix, Domaine Patrice Fort, Ghislaine & Jean-Hugues Goisot, Serge & Arnaud Goisot, Domaine Jacky Renard, Domaine Sainte-Claire, and Jean-Paul Tabit. As the AOC system was developed to acknowledge local usage, the authorities will no doubt one day realize that Bourgogne Saint-Bris is a fact and officially recognize the wine.

RED Most of these wines are primarily Pinot noir with a small dash of César. Most are simply frank and fruity, but the best can be quite rich, with truly expressive fruit.

🍇 Pinot noir, Pinot liébault, Pinot gris, César, Tressot

🍷 2–5 years

WHITE At its most basic level, not worth buying, but top-performing white wines from these appellations are superior to the cheapest, but much more expensive, Chablis. They are invariably pure Chardonnay, yet rarely taste like Chablis, being softer and smoother.

🍇 Chardonnay, Pinot blanc

🍷 1–3 years

ROSÉ Typically light, dry, and refreshing, the best examples often come from Epineuil, although Saint-Bris also does well.

🍇 Pinot noir, Pinot gris, Pinot liébault, César, Tressot

🍷 1–2 years

✓ Bourgogne Chitry *Joël & David Griffe* • Bourgogne Coulanges-la-Vineuse *Le Clos du Roi* • Bourgogne Epineuil *Dominique Gruhier* • Bourgogne Irancy *Léon Bienvenu, Anita & Jean-Pierre Colinot* (Palotte, Les Mazelots, Les Bessys, Côte de Moutier), *Roger Delalogue, Domaine Félix* • Bourgogne Saint-Bris *Domaine Félix, Jacky Renard*

BOURGOGNE CÔTES D'AUXERRE AOC

The Côtes d'Auxerre cover various parcels of vines scattered throughout the hillsides overlooking Augy, Auxerre-Vaux, Quenne, St.-Bris-le-Vineux, and in that part of Vincelottes which does not qualify for Irancy. Exactly the same grape varieties are used as for the Bourgogne appellations detailed above and, not surprisingly, the wines are very similar in style.

✓ *Patrice Fort* • *Ghislaine & Jean-Hugues Goisot Domaine du Corps de Garde*

BOURGOGNE CÔTE ST.-JACQUES AOC

This appellation was expected to be authorized in 1997, along the same lines as the three Bourgogne *lieux-dits* created in 1993 (*see* Bourgogne La Chapelle Notre Dame, p.147, Bourgogne Le Chapitre, p.140, and Bourgogne Montrecul, p.140). Côte St.-Jacques overlooks Joigny, which has the most northerly vineyards in Burgundy. Vines were first permitted to grow here for basic Bourgogne AOC in 1975, but just a few hectares were planted. Currently the largest vineyard owner is Alain Vignot, whose father pioneered winemaking in the area, but the local *coopérative*, which also has vineyards in the area, is planting a large proportion of the 90 hectares (220 acres) that were officially classified as Côte St.-Jacques. Currently the area barely manages to produce a light-bodied white wine, although Vignot makes a *vin gris* from Pinot noir and Pinot gris, which Joigny was famous for in pre-phylloxera times. What they need here is the true Auxerrois of Alsace, which would be a good idea as Auxerre is close by, although it has no connection whatsoever with this variety. The reasoning would be exactly the same as for Alsace, where more Auxerrois is used to make so-called Pinot Blanc wine the further north the vineyards are. In the Côte de Nuits it would be too fat and spicy, but in Joigny it would simply bring some generosity to the wines.

CHABLIS AOC

With careful selection, basic Chablis can be a source of tremendous value, classic 100 per cent Chardonnay wine, particularly in the best vintages, but the appellation covers a relatively large area with many vineyards that do not perform well and there are far too many mediocre winemakers. Basic Chablis needs to come from the most favourable locations, where the grower restricts the yield and the winemaker selects only the best wines, but it is not an appellation in which such cuts can be taken. Cheap Chablis can be dire, even in superior appellations: better therefore to pay for a top *cuvée* of basic Chablis, such as La Chablisienne Vieilles Vignes, than to be seduced by a cut-price *Premier Cru. See also* Chablis Premier Cru AOC and Petit Chablis AOC.

WHITE When successful, these wines have the quintessential character of true Chablis – dry, clean, green, and expressive, with just enough fruit to balance the "steel".

🍇 Chardonnay

🍷 2–6 years

✓ *Christian Adine* • *Domaine Baillard* • *Billaud-Simon* • *Jean-Marc Brocard* • *La Chablisienne* (especially Vieilles Vignes) • *Domaine de Chantemerle* • *Jean Collet* • *Jean Defaix* • *René & Vincent Dauvissat* • *Jean-Paul Droin* (especially Vieilles Vignes) • *Gérard Duplessis* • *William Fèvre Domaine de la Maladière* • *Domaine des Malandes* (especially Tour de Roi) • *Jean-Pierre Grossot* • *Domaine Michel Laroche* • *Louis & Anne Moreau* (especially Domaines de Biéville and Cèdre Doré) *Sylvain Mosnier* (Vieilles Vignes) • *Gilbert Picq* (especially Vieilles Vignes) • *François Raveneau*

CHABLIS GRAND CRU AOC

The seven *Grands Crus* of Chablis are all located on one hill that overlooks the town of Chablis itself. They are Blanchot, Bougros, Les Clos, Grenouilles, Les Preuses, Valmur, and Vaudésir. One vineyard called "La Moutonne" is not classified in the appellation as a *Grand Cru*, but the authorities permit the use of the coveted status on the label because it is physically part of other *Grands Crus*. In the 18th century "La Moutonne" was in fact a one-hectare (two-and-a-half-acre) *climat* of Vaudésir, but under the ownership of Louis Long-Depaquit its wines were blended with those of three other *Grands Crus* (namely, Les Preuses, Les Clos, and Valmur). This practice came to a halt in 1950 when, in a bid to get "La Moutonne" classified as a separate *Grand Cru*, Long-Depaquit agreed to limit its production to its current location, which cuts across parts of Vaudésir and Les Preuses. Its classification never actually took place, but the two *Grands Crus* that it overlaps are probably the finest of all Chablis's *Grands Crus*.

WHITE Always totally dry, the *Grands Crus* are the biggest, richest, and most complex of all Chablis, many showing new oak characteristics that unfortunately dominate the wine. Their individual styles depend very much on how the winemaker vinifies and matures his wine, but when well made they are essentially as follows: "Blanchot" has a floral aroma and is the most delicate of the *Grands Crus*; "Bougros" has the least frills of all the *Grands Crus*, but is vibrant with a penetrating flavour; "Les Clos" is rich, luscious, and complex with great mineral finesse and beautiful balance; "Grenouilles" should be long and satisfying, yet elegant, racy, and aromatic; "Les Preuses" gets the most sun and is vivid, sometimes exotic, quite fat for Chablis, yet still expressive and definitely complex, with great finesse; "Valmur" has a fine bouquet, rich flavour, and smooth texture; "Vaudésir" has complex, intense flavours that display great finesse and spicy-complexity; and "La Moutonne" is fine, long-flavoured, and wonderfully expressive.

🍇 Chardonnay

🍷— 6–20 years

✓ Blanchot *Domaine Michel Laroche, Jean-Marie Raveneau, Domaine Vocret* • Bougros *William Fèvre Domaine de la Maladière, Domaine Michel Laroche* • Les Clos *Billaud-Simon, Domaine Pascal Bouchard, René & Vincent Dauvissat, Jean-Paul Droin, Domaine Joseph Drouhin, Caves Duplessis, William Fèvre, Domaine de la Maladière, Domaines des Malandes, Louis Michel, J. Moreau (lieu-dit Clos des Hospices), Domaine Pinson, Jean-Marie Raveneau* • Grenouilles *La Chablisienne* (Château Grenouilles), *Louis Michel* • La Moutonne *Domaine Long-Depaquit* • Les Preuses *Billaud-Simon, René & Vincent Dauvissat, William Fèvre* • Valmur *Jean Collet, Jean-Paul Droin, Jean-Marie Raveneau* • Vaudésir *Domaine Billaud-Simon, Jean-Paul Droin, Domaine des Malandes, Domaine Pascal Bouchard, William Fèvre, Louis Michel*

CHABLIS PREMIER CRU

Premiers Crus: Les Beauregards, Beauroy, Berdiot, Chaume de Talvat, Côte de Jouan, Côte de Léchet, Côte de Vaubarousse, Fourchaume, Les Fourneaux, Montée de Tonnerre, Montmains, Mont de Milieu, Vaillons, Vaucoupin, Vau-de-Vey (or Vaudevey), Vau Ligneau, and Vosgros.

Unlike the *Grands Crus*, the 17 *Premiers Crus* of Chablis are scattered among the vineyards of 15 surrounding communes, and the quality and style is patchy. Montée de Tonnerre is the best *Premier Cru* throughout the different producers and across the many vintages. One of its *lieux-dits*, Chapelot, is considered by many to be the equivalent of a *Grand Cru*. After Montée de Tonnerre, Côte de Léchet, Les Forêts (which is a *climat* within Montmains), Fourchaume, Mont de Milieu and Vaillons form a tight bunch for second place among Chablis's *Premiers Crus*.

WHITE Dry wines that can vary from light- to fairly full-bodied, but should always be finer and longer-lasting than wines of the basic Chablis appellation, although without the concentration of flavour expected from a *Grand Cru*.

🍇 Chardonnay

🍷— 4–15 years

✓ Les Beauregards *None* • Beauroy *Sylvain Mosnier* • Berdiot *None* • Chaume de Talvat *None* • Côte de Jouan *Michel Cobois* • Côte de Léchet *Jean-Paul Droin, Jean Defaix, Sylvain Mosnier* • Côte de Vaubarousse *None* • Fourchaume *Billaud-Simon, La Chablisienne, Domaine de Chantemerle, Jean-Paul Droin, Gérard Duplessis, Jean Durup, William Fèvre, Lamblin & Fils, Domaine Michel Laroche, Domaine des Malandes, Louis Michel, Francine & Olivier Savary* • Les Forêts *Domaine Pinson* • Les Fourneaux *Jean-Pierre Grossot, Louis & Anne Moreau* • Montée de Tonnerre *Domaine Billaud-Simon, Jean-Paul Droin (Vieilles Vignes), Caves Duplessis, William Fèvre, Louis Michel, Jean-Marie Raveneau (including Chapelot and Pied d'Aloue lieux-dits), Guy Robin* • Montmains *La Chablisienne, René & Vincent Dauvissat (La Forest [sic] lieu-dit), Jean-Paul Droin, Caves Duplessis, Domaine des Malandes, Domaine des Marronniers, Louis Michel, Georges Pico, Domaine Pinson, Jean-Marie Raveneau (Butteaux lieu-dit), Guy Robin (Butteaux lieu-dit), Domaine Robert Vocoret (La Fôret lieu-dit)* • Mont de Milieu *Domaine Barat, Billaud-Simon (especially Vieilles Vignes), Jean Collet, Jean-Pierre Grossot, Domaine de Meulière, Domaine Pinson* • Vaillons *Domaine Barat, Jean Defaix, René & Vincent Dauvissat, Billaud-Simon, R & V Dauvissat (Séchet lieu-dit), Jean-Paul Droin, Gérard Duplessis, Domaine Michel Laroche, François Raveneau* • Vaucoupin *Jean-Pierre Grossot, Château de Viviers* • Vau-de-Vey *Jean Durup, Domaine Michel Laroche* • Vau Ligneau *Thierry Hamelin, Louis & Anne Moreau* • Vosgros *Gilbert Picq, Jean-Paul Droin*

PETIT CHABLIS AOC

A depreciatory appellation that covers inferior soils and expositions within the same area as generic Chablis, with the exception of Ligny-le-Châtel, Viviers, and Collan. Although I have found four more reliable producers than last time, this appellation should downgraded to VDQS or uprooted. The rumour is that it will be phased out, but do not misunderstand: this does not mean that they will uproot the vines, simply that the inferior land will continue to produce Chablis, albeit of a *petit vin* quality.

WHITE Apart from the occasional pleasant surprise, most are mean and meagre dry wines of light- to medium-body. The producers below provide most of the best surprises.

🍇 Chardonnay

🍷— 2–3 years

✓ Jean-Marc Brocard • Jean Durup • Vincent Gallois • Thierry Hamelin • Francine & Olivier Savary

SAUVIGNON DE ST.-BRIS VDQS

This single-village wine is as good as most Sauvignon blancs that have full AOC status, and considerably better than many other white AOCs made from lesser grape varieties. Ten years ago I did not believe it possible that Sauvignon de St.-Bris would ever rise to the ranks of *Appellation Contrôlée*, since the chauvinistic Burgundians, I thought, would never allow this upstart grape to rival their noble Chardonnay. Ghislaine et Jean-Hugues Goisot Domaine du Corps de Garde is the undisputed monarch of this appellation in its present format, but who knows under its wider scope?

WHITE Fine wet-grass or herbaceous aromas, full smoky-Sauvignon flavours, and a correct, crisp, dry finish. Jean-Hugues Goisot's Cuvée du Corps de Garde is probably the best and most consistent wine in this appellation.

🍇 Sauvignon blanc

🍷— 2–5 years

✓ Jean-Marc Brocard • Robert Defrance • Jean-Hugues Goisot

VÉZELAY

Although not yet an official appellation, it is rumoured to become one and I have come across good quaffing Bourgogne Vézelay in both red (Pinot noir) and white (a Chardonnay and a Melon de Bourgogne) from Marc Meneau. Apparently the new appellation will extend some 300 hectares (740 acres), although barely more than a third of this is currently planted. The vines are all situated on the steep, upper slopes, above the frost-line, which is dreaded in these parts, and they overlook the village of Vézelay itself.

✓ Marc Meneau

THE GRANDS CRUS OF CHABLIS
The slopes of the district's greatest vineyards rise quietly and majestically on the other side of the Serein river beyond the northern outskirts of Chablis itself.

CÔTE DE NUITS AND HAUTES-CÔTES DE NUITS

The Côte de Nuits is essentially a red-wine-producing area, and although capable of extraordinary white wine in Musigny and Nuits-St.-George Clos de l'Arlot, with 22 of Burgundy's 23 red Grands Crus, it is the place par excellence for Pinot noir.

THE CÔTE D'OR or "golden slope" is the departmental name for both the Côte de Nuits and the Côte de Beaune. Firmness and weight are the key words to describe the wines produced here, and these characteristics intensify as the vineyards progress north. A string of villages with some of the richest names in Burgundy – Gevrey-Chambertin, Chambolle-Musigny, Vosne-Romanée, and Nuits-St.-Georges – these slopes ring up dollar signs in the minds of merchants throughout the world. Ironically, the most famous appellations also produce some of Burgundy's worst wines.

CLOS ARLOT OF DOMAINE DE L'ARLOT
Purchased in 1987 by the dynamic AXA group, Domaine de l'Arlot is one of the most consistent, high-quality producers in Nuits-St.-Georges, making text-book Pinot noir and, from its monopole Clos Arlot, minuscule amounts of sublime white wine.

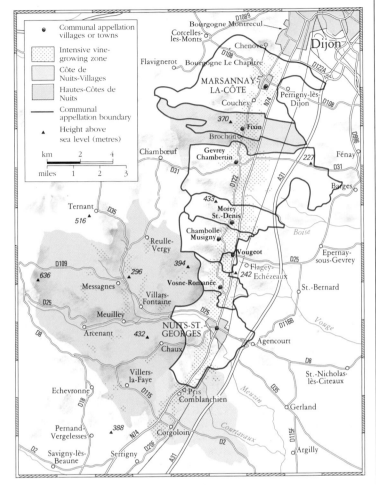

CÔTES DE NUITS AND HAUTES-CÔTES DE NUITS, *see also* p.131
The best vineyards of the Côte de Nuits form a tighter, more compact strip than those of the Côte de Beaune, (see also p.144), and the wines produced are, coincidentally, tighter, with more compact fruit.

FACTORS AFFECTING TASTE AND QUALITY

LOCATION
The Côte de Nuits is a narrow, continuous strip of vines stretching from Dijon to just north of Beaune, with the Hautes-Côtes de Nuits in the southwestern hinterland.

CLIMATE
Semi-continental climate with minimal Atlantic influence, which results in a long, cold winter, a humid spring, and a fairly hot, very sunny summer. Hail is its greatest natural hazard and heavy rain is often responsible for diluting the wines and causing rampant rot.

ASPECT
A series of east-facing slopes which curve in and out to give some vineyards northeastern, some southeastern aspects. The vines grow at an altitude of between 225 and 350 m (740–1,150 ft) and, apart from Gevrey-Chambertin and Prémeaux-Prissey, those vineyards that have the right to the village and higher appellations rarely extend eastwards beyond the RN 74.

SOIL
A subsoil of sandy-limestone, which is exposed in places, but usually covered by a chalky scree mixed with marl and clay particles on higher slopes and richer alluvial deposits on lower slopes. Higher slopes sometimes have red clay.

VITICULTURE AND VINIFICATION
The vines are trained low to benefit from heat reflected from the soil at night. For red wines, the grapes are almost always destemmed and the juice is kept in contact with the skins for between eight and ten days. Less than three per cent of the wine produced is white, but this is mostly high quality and traditionally cask fermented. The best wines are matured in oak.

PRIMARY GRAPE VARIETIES
Pinot noir, Chardonnay
SECONDARY GRAPE VARIETIES
Pinot gris (known locally as Pinot beurot), Pinot liébault, Pinot blanc, Aligoté, Melon de Bourgogne, Gamay

CONFRÉRIE DES CHEVALIERS DU TASTEVIN

After the three terrible vintages of 1930, 1931, and 1932, and four years of world slump following the Wall Street Crash of 1929, Camille Rodier and Georges Faiveley formed the Confrérie des Chevaliers du Tastevin to revive Burgundy's fortunes.

They fashioned their initiative on the Ordre de la Boisson, a fraternity that had flourished, and died, during the reign of Louis XIV. Adopting colourful medieval robes and dramatic rituals, they created four ranks: Chevalier, Commandeur, Commandeur-Major, and Grand Officer and named the brotherhood after the traditional Burgundian *tastevin*, a shallow, dimpled, silver tasting-cup with a fluted edge. This object dates from the 16th century and is worn around the neck, supported by a scarlet and gold ribbon.

The first investitures took place on 16 November 1934 in a cellar in Nuits-St.-Georges; the Confrérie now boasts thousands of members in numerous foreign chapters and averages 20 banquets a year at Château du Clos de Vougeot.

THE CÔTE DE NUITS AND HAUTES-CÔTES DE NUITS

Note Each *Grand Cru* of Côte de Nuits has its own appellation and is listed individually below. However, the *Premiers Crus* do not, and are therefore listed under the appellation of the village in which the vineyards are situated. *Premiers Crus* that are virtually contiguous with *Grand Cru* vineyards are in italics; they are possibly superior to those that do not share a boundary with one or more *Grand Crus*, and generally superior to those that share boundaries with village AOC vineyards.

BONNES MARES AOC
Grand Cru

Bonnes Mares is the largest of the two *Grands Crus* of Chambolle-Musigny. It covers 13.5 hectares (33½ acres) in the north of the village, on the opposite side to Musigny, the village's other *Grand Cru*, and extends a further one-and-a-half hectares (3½ acres) into Morey-St.-Denis.

RED This wine combines a fabulous femininity of style with sheer depth of flavour to give something rich and luscious, yet complex and complete.

🍇 Pinot noir, Pinot gris, Pinot liébault

⌛ 12–25 years

✓ *Bouchard Père & Fils • Joseph Drouhin • Domaine Dujac • R. Groffier • Louis Jadot • J. F. Mugnier • Domaine Georges Roumier • Domaine Comte Georges de Vogüé*

BOURGOGNE LA CHAPITRE AOC
•
BOURGOGNE MONTRECUL *or* MONTRE-CUL *or* EN MONTRE-CUL AOC

Two of three Bourgogne *lieux-dits* created in 1993, La Chapitre is located in Chenove, which is between Marsannay and Dijon, whereas Montrecul is in Dijon. According to Anthony Hanson (*Burgundy*), the wines of Chenove once fetched higher prices than those of Gevrey. Chenove's most famous vineyard is Clos du Roi, which Labouré-Roi took management of in 1994. Clos de Chapitre is solely owned by Michel Pont of Savigny, but the appellation is obviously much wider than that one *monopole*. Hanson also points out that a Bourgogne Montrecul is sold by Charles Quillardet, which is now part of Patriarche, but it is equally unlikely that an AOC was invented for just one owner, thus it can be taken for granted that others will produce the wine in due course. Both these appellations may produce red, white, and rosé wines, and the grapes allowed are the same as for Bourgogne AOC (*see* p.133).

BOURGOGNE HAUTES-CÔTES DE NUITS AOC

A source of good-value wines, these vineyards have expanded since the 1970s, and the quality is improving noticeably. Half-red/half-rosé wines may be sold as Bourgogne Clairet Hautes-Côtes de Nuits AOC, but the style is outmoded and the appellation rarely encountered.

RED Medium-bodied and medium- to full-bodied wines with good fruit and some true Côte de Nuits character. The wines from some growers have fine oak nuances.

🍇 Pinot noir, Pinot liébault, Pinot gris

⌛ 4–10 years

WHITE Just five per cent of the production is dry white. Most have a good weight of fruit, but little finesse.

🍇 Chardonnay, Pinot blanc

⌛ 1–4 years

ROSÉ Little-seen, but those that have cropped up have been dry, fruity, and delicious wines of some richness.

🍇 Pinot noir, Pinot liébault, Pinot gris

⌛ 1–3 years

✓ *Domaine Bertagna • J.-C. Boisset • Domaine Yves Chaley • Guy Dufouleur • Michel Gros • Robert Jayer-Gilles • Domaine de Montmain • Domaine Naudin-Ferrand • Thévenot-le-Brun & Fils • Alain Verdet • Thierry Vigot-Battault*

CHAMBERTIN AOC
Grand Cru

This is one of the nine *Grands Crus* of Gevrey-Chambertin. All of them (quite legally) add the name Gevery-Chambertin to their own and one, Clos de Bèze, actually has the right to sell its wines as Chambertin.

RED Always full in body and rich in extract, Chambertin is not, however, powerful like Corton, but graceful and feminine with a vivid colour, stunning flavour, impeccable balance, and lush, velvety texture.

🍇 Pinot noir, Pinot gris, Pinot liébault

⌛ 12–30 years

✓ *Joseph Drouhin • Domaine Leroy • Bouchard Père & Fils • Domaine Henri Rebourseau • Domaine Armand Rousseau • Jean & Jean-Louis Trapet*

CHAMBERTIN-CLOS DE BÈZE AOC
Grand Cru

Another Gevrey-Chambertin *Grand Cru*. The wine may be sold simply as Chambertin, the name of a neighbouring *Grand Cru*, but Chambertin may not call itself Clos de Bèze.

RED This wine is reputed to have a greater finesse than Chambertin but slightly less body. It is just as sublime.

🍇 Pinot noir, Pinot gris, Pinot liébault

⌛ 12–30 years

✓ *Bruno Clair • Joseph Drouhin • Domaine Faiveley • R. Groffier • Louis Jadot • Domaine Armand Rousseau*

CHAMBOLLE-MUSIGNY AOC

This village is very favourably positioned, with a solid block of vines nestled in the shelter of a geological fold.

RED Many of these medium- to fairly full-bodied wines have surprising finesse and fragrance for mere village wines.

🍇 Pinot noir, Pinot gris, Pinot liébault

⌛ 8–15 years

✓ *Ghislaine Barthod • J. F. Mugnier • Geantet Pansiot • Domaine Perrot-Minot • Daniel Rion • Domaine Georges Roumier • De Vogüé*

CHAMBOLLE-MUSIGNY PREMIER CRU AOC

Premiers Crus: Les Amoureuses, Les Baudes, Aux Beaux Bruns, *Les Borniques,* Les Carrières, Les Chabiots, Les Charmes, Les Châtelots, *La Combe d'Orveau,* Aux Combottes, Les Combottes, Les Cras, Derrière la Grange, Aux Echanges, Les Feusselottes, *Les Fuées,* Les Grands Murs, Les Groseilles, Les Gruenchers, Les Hauts Doix, *Les Lavrottes,* Les Noirots, Les Plantes, Les Sentiers. The outstanding *Premier Cru* is Les Amoureuses, with Les Charmes a very respectable second.

RED The best have a seductive bouquet and deliciously fragrant flavour.

🍇 Pinot noir, Pinot gris, Pinot liébault

⌛ 10–20 years

✓ *Domaine Amiot-Servelle • Domaine Ghislaine Barthod • Domaine J. Confuron-Cotetidot • R. Groffier • Domaine Joseph Drouhin • Domaine Moine Hudelot • Denis Mortet • Domaine Mugnier • Perrot-Minot • Domaine Georges Roumier • De Vogüé*

CHAPELLE-CHAMBERTIN AOC
Grand Cru

This is one of the nine *Grands Crus* of Gevrey-Chambertin, comprised of two *climats* called "En la Chapelle" and "Les Gémeaux".

RED The lightest of all the *Grands Crus*, with a delightful bouquet and flavour.

🍇 Pinot noir, Pinot gris, Pinot liébault

⌛ 8–20 years

✓ *Louis Jadot • Domaine Jean & Jean-Louis Trapet*

CHARMES-CHAMBERTIN AOC
Grand Cru

The largest Gevrey-Chambertin *Grand Cru*, part of the vineyard is known as "Mazoyères", from which Mazoyères-Chambertin has evolved.

RED Soft, sumptuous wines with ripe-fruit flavours and pure Pinot character, although some slightly lack finesse.

🍇 Pinot noir, Pinot gris, Pinot liébault

⌛ 10–20 years

✓ *Denis Bachelet • Confuron-Cotétidot • Domaine Joseph Drouhin • Domaine Claude Dugat • Bernard Dugat-Py • Géantet-Pansiot • Domaine Perrot-Minot • Sérafin Père & Fils • Domaine Joseph Roty • Christophe Roumier • Rousseau*

CLOS DE BÈZE AOC

An alternative appellation for Chambertin-Clos de Bèze. See Chambertin-Clos de Bèze AOC.

CLOS DES LAMBRAYS AOC
Grand Cru

This vineyard was classified as one of the four *Grands Crus* of Morey-St.-Denis only as recently as 1981, although the previous owner used to put "*Grand Cru Classé*" (illegally) on the label.

RED The vineyard was replanted under new ownership and now produces fine, elegant wines with silky fruit of a good, easily recommendable quality.

🍇 Pinot noir, Pinot gris, Pinot liébault

⌛ 10–20 years

✓ *Domaine des Lambrays*

CLOS DE LA ROCHE AOC
Grand Cru

Covering an area of almost 17 hectares (42 acres), Clos de La Roche is twice the size of the other *Grands Crus* of Morey-St.-Denis.

RED A deep-coloured, rich, and powerfully flavoured *vin de garde* with a silky texture. Many consider it the greatest *Grand Cru* of Morey-St.-Denis.

🍇 Pinot noir, Pinot gris, Pinot liébault

⌛ 10–20 years

✓ *Domaine Dujac • Domaine Leroy • Domaine Hubert Lignier • Domaine Ponsot • Armand Rousseau*

CLOS ST.-DENIS AOC
Grand Cru

This is the *Grand Cru* that the village of Morey attached to its name when it was the best growth in the village, a position now contested by Clos de la Roche and Clos de Tart.

RED Strong, fine, and firm wines with rich liquorice and berry flavours that require time to come together.

🍇 Pinot noir, Pinot gris, Pinot liébault

⌛ 10–25 years

✓ *Philippe Charlopin • Domaine Dujac • Louis Jadot • Domaine Ponsot*

CLOS DE TART AOC
Grand Cru

This is one of the four *Grands Crus* of Morey-St.-Denis. It is entirely owned by the *négociant* Mommessin. In addition to Clos de Tart itself, a tiny part of the Bonnes Mares *Grand Cru* also has the right to this appellation.

RED This monopoly yields wines with a penetrating Pinot flavour, to which *Mommessin* add such a spicy-vanilla character from 100 per cent new oak that great bottle-maturity is required for a completely harmonious flavour.

🍇 Pinot noir, Pinot gris, Pinot liébault

⌛ 15–30 years

✓ *Mommessin*

CLOS DE VOUGEOT AOC
Grand Cru

The only *Grand Cru* of Vougeot, it is a massive 50-hectare (123½-acre) block of vines with no less than 85 registered owners. It has been described as "an impressive sight, but a not very impressive site". This mass ownership situation has often been used to illustrate the classic difference between Burgundy and Bordeaux, where an entire vineyard belongs to one château and so the wine can be blended to a standard quality and style every year.

RED With individual plots ranging in quality from truly great to very ordinary, operated by growers of varying skills, it is virtually impossible to unravel the intrinsic characteristics of this *Cru*. Its best wines, however, have lots of silky Pinot fruit, an elegant balance, and a tendency towards finesse rather than fullness.

🍇 Pinot noir, Pinot gris, Pinot liébault

⌛ 10–25 years

✓ *Domaine Amiot-Servelle • Robert Arnoux • Bouchard Père & Fils • J.J. Confuron • Domaine J. Confuron-Cotetidot • Joseph Drouhin • Drouhin-Laroze • Domaine René Engel • Faiveley • Domaine Jean Grivot • Domaine Anne & François Gros • Michel Gros • Alfred Haegelyn • Alain Hudelot-Noëllat • Louis Jadot • Dominique Laurent • Domaine Leroy • Méo-Camuzet • Dr. Georges Mugneret • Domaine Prieuré Roch • Daniel Rion & Fils • Jean Tardy • Domaine de Château la Tour*

CLOS VOUGEOT AOC
See Clos de Vougeot AOC

CÔTE NUITS-VILLAGES AOC

This appellation covers the wines produced in one or more of five communes: Fixin and Brochon situated in the north of the district and Comblanchien, Corgoloin, and Prissy in the south.

RED Firm, fruity, and distinctive wines made in true, well-structured, Côte de Nuits style.

🍇 Pinot noir, Pinot gris, Pinot liébault

⌛ 6–10 years

WHITE Very little is made – just four hectolitres (44 cases) in 1985 – and I have never encountered it.

🍇 Chardonnay, Pinot blanc

✓ *Domaine de l'Arlot • Michel Esmonin • Domaine Naudin-Ferrand*

ECHÉZEAUX AOC
Grand Cru

This 30-hectare (74-acre) vineyard is the larger of the two *Grands Crus* of Flagey-Echézeaux and is comprised of 11 *climats* owned by no less than 84 smallholders.

RED The best have a fine and fragrant flavour that relies more on delicacy than power, but too many deserve no more than a village appellation.

🍇 Pinot noir, Pinot gris, Pinot liébault

⌛ 10–20 years

✓ *Domaine J. Confuron-Cotetidot • Joseph Drouhin • Domaine Dujac • Engel • Faiveley • Forey Père & Fils • Grivot • Louis Jadot • Robert Jayer-Gilles • Mongeard-Mugneret • Mugneret-Gibourg • Domaine de la Romanée-Conti • Emmanuel Rouget • Domaine Fabrice Vigot*

FIXIN AOC

Fixin was at one time the summer residence of the Dukes of Burgundy.

RED Well-coloured wines that can be firm, tannic *vins de garde* of excellent quality and even better value.

🍇 Pinot noir, Pinot gris, Pinot liébault

⌛ 6–12 years

WHITE Rich, dry, and concentrated wines that are rare, but exciting and well worth seeking out. Bruno Clair shows what Pinot blanc can produce when it is not over-cropped.

🍇 Chardonnay, Pinot blanc

⌛ 3–8 years

✓ *Domaine Bart • Domaine Berthaut • Bruno Clair • Pierre Gelin • Philippe Joliet • Mongeard-Mugneret*

FIXIN PREMIER CRU AOC

Premiers Crus: Les Arvelets, Clos du Chapitre, Aux Cheusots, Les Hervelets, Le Meix Bas, La Perrière, Queue de Hareng (located in neighbouring Brochon), En Suchot, Le Village.

The best *Premiers Crus* are La Perrière and Clos du Chapitre. Clos de la Perrière is a monopoly owned by Philippe Joliet that encompasses En Souchot and Queue de Hareng as well as La Perrière itself.

RED Splendidly deep in colour and full in body with masses of blackcurrant and redcurrant fruit, supported by a good tannic structure.

🍇 Pinot noir, Pinot gris, Pinot liébault

⌛ 10–20 years

WHITE I have not encountered any but it would not be unreasonable to assume that it might be at least as good as a basic Fixin *blanc*.

✓ *Domaine Berthaut • Pierre Gelin • Philippe Joliet • Mongeard-Mugneret*

GEVREY-CHAMBERTIN AOC

Famous for its *Grand Cru* of Chambertin, the best growers also produce superb wines under this appellation. Some vineyards overlap the village of Brochon.

RED These well-coloured wines are full, rich, and elegant, with a silky texture and a perfumed aftertaste reminiscent of the pure fruit of Pinot noir.

🍇 Pinot noir, Pinot gris, Pinot liébault

⌛ 7–15 years

✓ *Denis Bachelet • Alain Burguet • Philippe Charlopin • Domaine Drouhin-Laroze • Bernard Dugat-Py • Domaine Dujac • Labouré-Roi Denis Mortet • Geantet Pansiot*

GEVREY-CHAMBERTIN PREMIER CRU AOC

Premiers Crus: Bel Air, La Bossière, Les Cazetiers, Champeaux, *Champitennois*, Champonnet, Clos du Chapitre, *Cherbaudes*, *Au Closeau*, Combe au Moine, *Aux Combottes*, Les Corbeaux, Craipillot, En Ergot, Etournelles (or Estournelles), Fonteny, Les Goulots, Lavaut (or Lavout St.-Jacques), *La Perrière, Petite Chapelle*, Petits Cazetiers, *Plantigone* (or *Issarts*), Poissenot, *Clos Prieur-Haut* (or *Clos Prieure*), La Romanée, Le Clos St.-Jacques, Les Varoilles.

RED These wines generally have more colour, concentration, and finesse than the village wines, but, with the possible exception of Clos St.-Jacques, do not quite match the *Grands Crus*.

🍇 Pinot noir, Pinot gris, Pinot liébault

⌛ 10–20 years

✓ *Alain Burguet • Domaine Bruno Clair • Drouhin-Laroze • Domaine Claude Dugat • Bernard Dugat-Py • Domaine Dujac • Frédéric Esmonin • Michel Esmonin • Faiveley • Herezstyn • Louis Jadot • Denis Mortet • Geantet Pansiot • Domaine Joseph Roty • Domaine Armand Rousseau • Sérafin • Domaine Jean & Jean-Louis Trapet*

GRAND ECHÉZEAUX AOC
Grand Cru

The smaller and superior of the two *Grands Crus* of Flagey-Echézeaux, this area is separated from the upper slopes of the Clos de Vougeot by a village boundary.

RED Fine and complex wines that should have a silky bouquet, often reminiscent of violets.

The flavour can be very round and rich, but is balanced by a certain delicacy of fruit.

🍇 Pinot noir, Pinot gris, Pinot liébault

🍷 10–20 years

✓ *Joseph Drouhin • Engel • Domaine François Lamarche • Mongeard-Mugneret • Domaine de la Romanée-Conti*

LA GRANDE RUE AOC
Grand Cru

The newest *Grand Cru* of Vosne-Romanée, La Grande Rue was generally considered to have the best potential of all the *Premiers Crus* in this village. Officially upgraded in 1992, although the quality of wine produced by its sole owner, François Lamarche, was erratic to say the least. The *terroir* is, however, undeniably superior for a *Premier Cru* and as Domaine Lamarche has been on form since its promotion, perhaps the cart should come before the horse sometimes.

RED When Lamarche gets this right, the wine is well coloured with deep, spicy-floral, black cherry fruit.

🍇 Pinot noir, Pinot gris, Pinot liébault

🍷 7–15 years

✓ *Domaine Lamarche*

GRIOTTES-CHAMBERTIN AOC
Grand Cru

The smallest of the nine *Grands Crus* of Gevrey-Chambertin.

RED The best growers produce deep-coloured, delicious wines with masses of soft-fruit flavours and all the velvety texture that could be expected of Chambertin itself.

🍇 Pinot noir, Pinot gris, Pinot liébault

🍷 10–20 years

✓ *Domaine Joseph Drouhin • Domaine Claude Dugat • Frédéric Esmonin • Louis Jadot • Domaine Ponsot • Joseph Roty*

LATRICÈRES-CHAMBERTIN AOC
Grand Cru

One of the nine *Grands Crus* of Gevrey-Chambertin, situated above the Mazoyères *climat* of Charmes-Chambertin. A tiny part of the adjoining *Premier Cru*, Aux Combottes, also has the right to use this AOC.

RED Solid structure and a certain austerity connect the two different styles of this wine (early-drinking and long-maturing). They sometimes lack fruit and generosity, but wines from the top growers recommended below are always the finest to be found.

🍇 Pinot noir, Pinot gris, Pinot liébault

🍷 10–20 years

✓ *Drouhin-Laroze • Faiveley • Domaine Leroy • Domaine Ponsot • Domaine Jean & Jean-Louis Trapet*

MAZIS-CHAMBERTIN AOC
Grand Cru

Sometimes known as Mazy-Chambertin. One of the nine *Grands Crus* of Gevrey-Chambertin.

RED These complex wines have a stature second only to Chambertin and Clos de Bèze. They have a fine, bright colour, super-silky finesse, and a delicate flavour that lasts.

🍇 Pinot noir, Pinot gris, Pinot liébault

🍷 10–20 years

✓ *Auvenay • Frédéric Esmonin • Faiveley • Domaine Leroy • Domaine Bernard Maume • Joseph Roty • Armand Rousseau*

MAZOYÈRES-CHAMBERTIN AOC

An alternative appellation for Charmes-Chambertin. *See* Charmes-Chambertin AOC.

MOREY-ST.-DENIS AOC

This excellent little wine village tends to be overlooked. The fact that it is situated between two world-famous places, Gevrey-Chambertin and Chambolle-Musigny, coupled with the fact that Clos St.-Denis is no longer considered to be Gevrey-Chambertin's top *Grand Cru*, does little to promote the name of this village.

RED The best of these village wines have a vivid colour, a very expressive bouquet, and a smooth flavour with lots of finesse. A Morey-St.-Denis from a domaine such as Dujac can have the quality of a top *Premier Cru*.

🍇 Pinot noir, Pinot gris, Pinot liébault

🍷 8–15 years

WHITE Domaine Dujac produces an excellent Morey-St.-Denis *blanc*, but more interesting, although less consistent, is Domaine Ponsot Monts Luissants *blanc*. Although Monts Luissants is a *Premier Cru*, the upper section from which this wine comes is part of the village appellation (the southeastern corner is classified *Grand Cru* and sold as Clos de la Roche!). When Ponsot gets the Monts Luissants *blanc* right, it can be a superbly fresh, dry, buttery-rich wine and some writers have compared it to a Meursault.

🍇 Chardonnay, Pinot blanc

🍷 3–8 years

✓ *Domaine Pierre Amiot • Philippe Charlopin • Domaine Dujac • Hubert Lignier • Michel Magnien • Domaine Perrot-Minot • Domaine Ponsot • Domaine Georges Roumier*

MOREY-ST.-DENIS PREMIER CRU AOC

Premiers Crus: Clos Baulet, Les Blanchards, La Bussière, *Les Chaffots,* Aux Charmes, *Les Charrières,* Les Chénevery, Aux Cheseaux, *Les Faconnières, Les Genevrières,* Les Gruenchers, *Les Millandes, Monts Luissants, Clos des Ormes,* Clos Sorbè, Les Sorbès, Côte Rôtie, La Riotte, *Les Ruchots,* Le Village.

RED These wines should have all the colour, bouquet, flavour, and finesse of the excellent village wines plus an added expression of *terroir*. The best *Premiers Crus* are: Clos des Ormes, Clos Sorbè, and Les Sorbès.

🍇 Pinot noir, Pinot gris, Pinot liébault

🍷 10–20 years

WHITE The only white Morey-St.-Denis I know is from the upper section of "Monts Louisants" belonging to Domaine Ponsot (*see* Morey-St.-Denis AOC above). To my knowledge, no other white Morey-St.-Denis Premier Cru is made.

🍇 Chardonnay

✓ *Pierre Amiot • Domaine Dujac • Herezstyn • Hubert Lignier • Perrot-Minot • Georges Roumier*

MUSIGNY AOC
Grand Cru

Musigny is the smaller of Chambolle-Musigny's two *Grands Crus*. It covers some ten hectares (25 acres) on the opposite side of the village to Bonnes Mares.

RED These most stylish of wines have a fabulous colour and a smooth, seductive, and spicy bouquet. The velvet-rich fruit flavour

constantly unfolds to reveal a succession of taste experiences.

🍇 Pinot noir, Pinot gris, Pinot liébault

🍷 10–30 years

WHITE Musigny *blanc* is a rare and expensive dry wine produced solely at Domaine Comte Georges de Vogüé. It combines the steel of a Chablis with the richness of a Montrachet, although it never quite achieves the quality of either.

🍇 Chardonnay

🍷 8–20 years

✓ *Joseph Drouhin • Louis Jadot • Domaine Leroy • Domaine Mugnier (Château de Chambolle-Musigny) • Georges Roumier & Fils • Domaine Comte Georges de Vogüé*

NUITS AOC
See Nuits-St.-Georges AOC

NUITS PREMIER CRU AOC
See Nuits-St.-Georges Premier Cru AOC

NUITS-ST.-GEORGES AOC

More than any other, the name of this town graphically projects the image of full flavour and sturdy structure for which the wines of the Côte de Nuits are justly famous.

RED These are deep-coloured, full, and firm wines, but they can sometimes lack the style and character of wines such as Gevrey, Chambolle, and Morey.

🍇 Pinot noir, Pinot gris, Pinot liébault

🍷 7–15 years

WHITE I have not tasted this wine. (*See* white Nuits-St.-Georges Premier Cru).

✓ *Domaine de l'Arlot • R. Chevillon • J. Chauvenet • J.J. Confuron • Domaine J. Confuron-Cotetidot • Bertrand Marchard de Gramont • A. Michelot • Domaine Daniel Rion & Fils*

NUITS-ST.-GEORGES PREMIER CRU AOC

Premiers Crus: Les Argillats, Les Argillières*, Clos Arlot*, Aux Boudots, Aux Bousselots, Les Cailles, Les Chaboeufs, Aux Chaignots, Chaine-Carteau (or Chaines-Carteaux), Aux Champs Perdrix, Clos des Corvées*, Clos des Corvées Pagets*, Aux Cras, Les Crots, Les Damodes, Les Didiers*, Les Forêts* (or Clos des Forêts St.-Georges*), Les Grandes Vignes*, Château Gris, Les Hauts Pruliers, Clos de la Maréchale*, Aux Murgers, Aux Perdrix*, En la Perrière Noblet (or En la Perrière Noblot), Les Perrières, Les Porets, Les Poulettes, Les Procès, Les Pruliers, La Richemone, La Roncière, Rue de Chaux, Les St.-Georges, Clos St.-Marc (or Aux Corvées), Les Terres Blanches, Aux Thorey, Les Vallerots, Les Vaucrains, Aux Vignerondes.
*In the village of Prémeaux-Prissey.

RED These wines have a splendid colour, a spicy-rich bouquet, and a vibrant fruit flavour which can be nicely underpinned with vanilla.

🍇 Pinot noir, Pinot gris, Pinot liébault

🍷 10–20 years

WHITE Henri Gouges's "La Perrière" is dry, powerful, almost fat, with a spicy-rich aftertaste. The vines used for this wine were propagated from a mutant Pinot noir that produced bunches of both black and white grapes. Gouges cut a shoot from a white-grape-producing branch of the mutant vine in the mid-1930s, and there is now just less than half a hectare (just over one acre) of the vines planted by Gouges, none of which have ever reverted to producing black grapes.

🍇 Chardonnay, Pinot blanc

🍷— 5–10 years

✓ *Bertrand Ambroise • Domaine de l'Arlot Bouchard Père & Fils • Jean Chauvenet Robert Chevillon • J.J. Confuron • Jacky Confuron-Cotétidot • Dubois & Fils • Joseph Faiveley • Forey Père & Fils • Henri Gouges • Jean Grivot • Alain Hudelot-Noëllat Louis Jadot • Robert Jayer-Gilles • Léchenaut Philippe & Vincent • Alain Michelot • Dr. Georges Mugneret • Gérard Mugneret • Gilles Remoriquet • Domaine Daniel Rion & Fils • Jean Tardy • Thomas-Moillard*

RICHEBOURG AOC
Grand Cru

One of the six *Grands Crus* at the heart of Vosne-Romanée's vineyards.

RED This is a gloriously rich wine that has a heavenly bouquet and is full of velvety and voluptuous fruit flavours.

🍇 Pinot noir, Pinot gris, Pinot liébault

🍷— 12–30 years

✓ *Domaine Jean Grivot • Domaine Anne Gros • Alain Hudelot-Noëllat • Domaine Leroy • Domaine Méo-Camuzet • Domaine de la Romanée-Conti*

LA ROMANÉE AOC
Grand Cru

This vineyard is owned by the Domaine du Chateau de Vosne-Romanée, which is owned by the Liger-Belair family, but the wine is matured, bottled, and sold by Bouchard Père & Fils. Less than one hectare (two-and-a-half acres), it is the smallest *Grand Cru* of Vosne-Romanée.

RED This is a full, fine, and complex wine that might not have the voluptuous appeal of a Richebourg, but that certainly has the class to age gracefully.

🍇 Pinot noir, Pinot gris, Pinot liébault

🍷— 12–30 years

✓ *Domaine du Château de Vosne-Romanée*

ROMANÉE-CONTI AOC
Grand Cru

This Vosne-Romanée *Grand Cru* is under two hectares (five acres) in size and belongs solely to the famous Domaine de la Romanée-Conti.

RED As the most expensive Burgundy in the world, this wine must always be judged by higher standards than all the rest. Yet I must admit that I never fail to be amazed by the stunning array of flavours that continuously unfold in this fabulously concentrated and utterly complex wine.

🍇 Pinot noir, Pinot gris, Pinot liébault

🍷— 15–35 years

✓ *Domaine de la Romanée-Conti*

ROMANÉE-ST.-VIVANT AOC
Grand Cru

The largest of the six *Grands Crus* on the lowest slopes and closest to the village.

RED This is the lightest of the fabulous *Grands Crus* of Vosne-Romanée, but what it lacks in power and weight it makes up for in finesse.

🍇 Pinot noir, Pinot gris, Pinot liébault

🍷— 10–25 years

✓ *Robert Arnoux • Sylvain Cathiard • Domaine J.J. Confuron • Joseph Drouhin • Alain Hudelot-Noëllat • Leroy • Moillard • Domaine de la Romanée-Conti • Thomas-Moillard*

RUCHOTTES-CHAMBERTIN AOC
Grand Cru

This is the second-smallest of the nine *Grands Crus* of Gevrey-Chambertin. It is situated above Mazis-Chambertin and is the last *Grand Cru* before the slope turns to face north.

RED Normally one of the lighter Chambertin lookalikes, but top growers like Roumier and Rousseau seem to achieve a bag-full of added ingredients in their splendidly rich wines.

🍇 Pinot noir, Pinot gris, Pinot liébault

🍷— 8–20 years

✓ *Mugneret-Gibourg • Frédéric Esmonin Christophe Roumier • Domaine Armand Rousseau*

LA TÂCHE AOC
Grand Cru

One of Vosne-Romanée's six *Grands Crus*, this fabulous vineyard belongs to the world-famous Domaine de la Romanée-Conti (DRC), which also owns the *Grand Cru* Romanée-Conti.

RED While this wine is indeed extremely rich and very complex, it does not in comparative terms quite have the richness of Richebourg, nor the complexity of Romanée-Conti. It does, however, have all the silky texture anyone could expect from the finest of Burgundies, and no other wine surpasses La Tâche for finesse.

🍇 Pinot noir, Pinot gris, Pinot liébault

🍷— 12–30 years

✓ *Domaine de la Romanée-Conti*

VOSNE-ROMANÉE AOC

This is the most southerly of the great villages of the Côte de Nuits. Some Vosne-Romanée vineyards are in neighbouring Flagey-Echézeaux. This village includes the Romanée-Conti vineyard.

RED Sleek, stylish, medium-bodied wines of the purest Pinot noir character and with the silky texture so typical of the wines of this village.

🍇 Pinot noir, Pinot gris, Pinot liébault

🍷— 10–15 years

✓ *Robert Arnoux • Sylvain Cathiard • Bruno Clavelier • Engel • Jacky Confuron-Contédidot • Forey Père & Fils • Domaine Jean Grivot • Anne Gros • Michel Gros • Méo-Camuzet • Domaine Mugneret Gibourg • Dr Georges Mugneret • Emmanuel Rouget • Domaine Fabrice Vigot*

VOSNE-ROMANÉE PREMIER CRU AOC

Premiers Crus: Les Beaux Monts, Les Beaux Monts Bas*, Les Beaux Monts Hauts*, *Les Brûlées*, Les Chaumes, La Combe Brûlées, *La Croix Rameau, Cros-Parantoux, Les Gaudichots, Les Hauts Beaux Monts, Aux Malconsorts, En Orveaux*, Les Petits Monts,* Clos des Réas, *Aux Reignots, Les Rouges du Dessus*, Les Suchots.*
*These *Premier Cru* vineyards of Vosne-Romanée are in Flagey-Echézeaux.

RED These are well-coloured wines with fine aromatic qualities that are often reminiscent of violets and blackberries. They have a silky texture and a stylish flavour that is pure Pinot noir. The best *Premiers Crus* to look out for are: Les Brûlées, Cros-Parantoux, Les Petits-Monts, Les Suchots, and Les Beaumonts (an umbrella name for the various "Beaux Monts", high and low).

🍇 Pinot noir, Pinot gris, Pinot liébault

🍷— 10–20 years

✓ *Domaine de l'Arlot • Robert Arnoux • Sylvain Cathiard • Engel • Domaine Jean Grivot • Alain Hudelot-Noëllat • Henri Jayer • Domaine Lamarche • Leroy • Domaine Leroy • Domaine Méo-Camuzet • Gérard Mugneret • Daniel Rion & Fils • Domaine Emmanuel Rouget*

VOUGEOT AOC

The modest village wines of Vougeot are a relative rarity, this appellation covering less than five hectares (12½ acres), which is less than a tenth of the area encompassed by the *Grand Cru* of Clos de Vougeot itself.

RED Little-seen, fine-flavoured, well-balanced wines that are overpriced due to their scarcity. It is better to buy a *Premier Cru* or a well-selected Clos de Vougeot.

🍇 Pinot noir, Pinot gris, Pinot liébault

🍷— 8–20 years

WHITE I used to think this was just a theoretical possibility until I came across Vougeot *blanc* from Domaine Bertagna.

✓ *Domaine Bertagna • Mongeard-Mugneret*

VOUGEOT PREMIER CRU AOC

Premiers Crus: Les Crâs, Clos de la Perrière, Les Petits Vougeots, La Vigne Blanche.

The *Premiers Crus* are located between Clos de Vougeot and Musigny and, from a *terroir* point of view, should produce much better wines than they do.

RED The wines recommended below are nicely coloured, medium bodied, and have an attractive flavour with a good balance and a certain finesse.

🍇 Pinot noir, Pinot gris, Pinot liébault

🍷— 10–20 years

WHITE A clean, rich, and crisp wine of variable quality, called Clos Blanc de Vougeot, is produced by L'Héritier Guyot from the *Premier Cru* of La Vigne Blanche.

🍇 Chardonnay, Pinot blanc

🍷— 4–10 years

✓ *Domaine Bertagna • Domaine Lamarche*

CÔTE DE BEAUNE AND HAUTES-CÔTES DE BEAUNE

Pinot noir in the Côte de Beaune is renowned for its softness and finesse, characteristics that become more evident as one progresses south across the region, but with seven of Burgundy's eight white Grands Crus this is really Chardonnay country, and the wines produced are the richest, longest-lived, most complex, and stylish white wines in the world.

ENTERING THE CÔTE DE BEAUNE from the Nuits-St.-Georges end, the most immediate viticultural differences are its more expansive look and the much greater contrast between the deep, dark, and so obviously rich soil found on the inferior eastern side of the RN 74 and the scanty patches of pebble-strewn thick drift that cover the classic slopes west of the road.

It is often said that the slopes of the Côte de Beaune are gentler than those of the Côte de Nuits, but there are many parts that are just as sheer, although the best vineyards of the Côte de

CÔTE DE BEAUNE VINEYARDS
The slopes of the Côte de Beaune vineyards are generally a little gentler than those of the Côte de Nuits. In both areas, Pinot noir and Chardonnay vines are planted but it is here that Chardonnay is king.

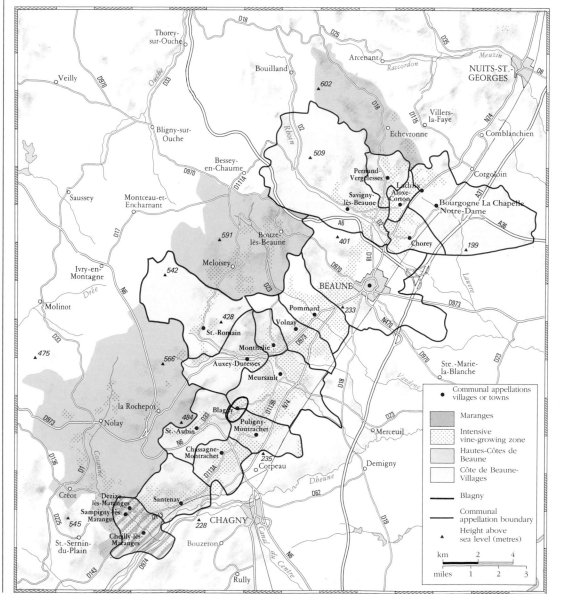

LADOIX-SERRIGNY
Situated to the west of Aloxe-Corton, parts of Ladoix-Serrigny are encompassed by that village's appellations, including the Grands Crus of Corton and Corton-Charlemagne.

CÔTE DE BEAUNE AND HAUTES-CÔTES DE BEAUNE
See also p.131
The Côte d'Or is a hilly ridge that follows the trajectory of the Autoroute du Soleil. Most of the village and Hautes-Côtes appellations are clustered between Nuits-St.-Georges in the north and Chagny in the south.

Beaune are located on the middle slopes, which have a gentler incline. The steeper, upper slopes produce good but generally lesser wines in all cases, except the vineyards of Aloxe-Corton – which are, anyway, more logically part of the Côte de Nuits than the Côte de Beaune.

FACTORS AFFECTING TASTE AND QUALITY

LOCATION
The Côte de Beaune abuts the Côte de Nuits on its southern tip and stretches almost 30 km (18½ miles) past the town of Beaune to Cheilly-lès-Maranges. Its vines are unbroken, although those of the Hautes-Côtes de Beaune in the western hinterland are divided into two by the Côte de Beaune vineyards of St.-Romain.

CLIMATE
This area has a slightly wetter, more temperate, climate than the Côte de Nuits and the grapes tend to ripen a little earlier. Hail is still a potential hazard, but less so, with wet winds and heavy rain being a greater nuisance.

ASPECT
Comprised of a series of east-facing slopes, up to 2 km (1¼ miles) wide, which curve in and out to give some of the vineyards northeastern and others southeastern aspects. Here the vines grow at an altitude of between 225 and 380 m (740–1,250 ft) on slightly less steep slopes than those of the Côte de Nuits. South of Beaune, no vines with the right to the village (and higher) appellations extend past the RN 74 on to the flat and fertile ground beyond.

SOIL
A limestone subsoil with sporadic beds of oolitic ironstones with flinty clay and calcareous topsoils. Light-coloured marl topsoil is found in the vineyards of Chassagne and Puligny.

VITICULTURE AND VINIFICATION
The vines are trained low to benefit from heat reflected from the soil at night. In the south of the district, the system employed is similar to that used in parts of Champagne and slightly different from elsewhere on the Côte de Beaune. For red wines, the grapes are almost always destemmed and the juice kept in contact with the skins for between eight and ten days. Classic white wines are cask fermented and the best wines, both red and white, matured in oak. The flavour of the Pinot noir grape can easily be overwhelmed by oak so it always receives less new-oak maturation than Chardonnay does.

PRIMARY GRAPE VARIETIES
Pinot noir, Chardonnay
SECONDARY GRAPE VARIETIES
Pinot gris (*syn.* Pinot beurot), Pinot liébault, Pinot blanc, Aligoté, Melon de Bourgogne, Gamay

THE HOSPICES DE BEAUNE LABEL

This distinctive label indicates that the wine comes from vineyards belonging to the Hospices de Beaune, a charitable institution that has cared for the sick and poor·of Beaune since 1443. Half a millennium of gifts and legacies has seen the accumulation of vineyards that now total some 62 hectares (153 acres) of *Premiers* and *Grands Crus.* Since 1859 these wines have been sold by auction and, because of the publicity gained by this annual event, the prices fetched are now generally much higher than the going rate. We must be prepared to pay a relatively higher price for these wines and help the cause.

After some criticism of the unreliability of certain wines, a new *cuverie* was built at the rear of the famous Hôtel-Dieu, known for its magnificent Flemish-crafted roof. All the wines are now matured in new oak casks. There remain, however, the variations that result from the different *élevages* of the various casks of the same *cuvée*, for after they have been auctioned they become the responsibility of the purchaser. At the most innocent level, these may result from one *négociant* giving his wine more or less cask-maturation than another, and temperature and humidity levels can radically change the wine's alcohol and extract content. The cellar management of less scrupulous firms is also a consideration.

THE HOSPICES DE BEAUNE CUVÉES

RED WINES

CUVÉE CLOS DES AVAUX
AOC Beaune
Unblended Les Avaux

CUVÉE BILLARDET
AOC Pommard
A blend of Petits-Epenots,
Les Noizons, Les Arvelets, Les Rugiens

CUVÉE BLONDEAU
AOC Volnay
A blend of Champans, Taille Pieds
Roceret, En l'Ormeau

CUVÉE BOILLOT
AOC Auxey-Duresses
Unblended Les Duresses

CUVÉE BRUNET
AOC Beaune
A blend of Les Teurons, La Mignotte
Les Bressandes, Les Cents Vignes

CUVÉE SUZANNE CHAUDRON
AOC Pommard
Unblended Pommard

CUVÉE MADELEINE COLLIGNON
AOC Mazis-Chambertin
Unblended Mazis-Chambertin

CUVÉE RAYMOND CYROT
AOC Pommard
A blend of Pommard and Pommard
Premier Cru

CUVÉE CYROT-CHAUDRON
AOC Beaune
Unblended Beaune Les Montrevots

CUVÉE CYROT-CHAUDRON ET GEORGES KRITTER
AOC Pommard
Unblended Clos de la Roche

CUVÉE DAMES DE LA CHARITÉ
AOC Pommard
A blend of Les Épenots,
Les Rugiens Les Noizons,
La Refène, Les Combes Dessus

CUVÉE DAMES HOSPITALIÈRES
AOC Beaune
A blend of Les Bressandes,
LaMignotte, Les Teurons,
Les Grèves

CUVÉE MAURICE DROUHIN
AOC Beaune
A blend of Les Avaux,
Les Grèves, Les Bourcherottes,
Champs Pimont

CUVÉE CHARLOTTE DUMMAY
AOC Corton
A blend of Renardes, Les Bressandes,
Clos du Roi

CUVÉE FORNERET
AOC Savigny-lès-Beaune
A blend of Les Vergelesses,
Aux Gravains

CUVÉE FOUQUERAND
AOC Savigny-lès-Beaune
A blend of Basses Vergelesses,
Les Talmettes, Aux Gravains,
Aux Serpentières

CUVÉE GAUVAIN
AOC Volnay
A blend of Les Santenots,
Les Pitures

CUVÉE ARTHUR GIRARD
AOC Savigny-lès-Beaune
A blend of Les Peuillets,
Les Marconnets

CUVÉE GUIGONE DE SALINS
AOC Beaune
A blend of Les Bressandes,
En Sebrey, Champs Pimont

CUVÉE HUGUES ET LOUIS BÉTAULT
AOC Beaune
A blend of Les Grèves, La Mignotte
Les Aigrots, Les Sizies,
Les Vignes Franches

CUVÉE LEBELIN
AOC Monthélie
Unblended Les Duresses

CUVÉE JEHAN DE MASSOL
AOC Volnay-Santenots
Unblended Les Santenots

CUVÉE GÉNÉRAL MUTEAU
AOC Volnay
A blend of Volnay-le-Village, Carelle
sous la Chapelle, Cailleret Dessus
Fremiet, Taille-Pieds

CUVÉE DOCTEUR PESTE
AOC Corton
A blend of Bressandes, Chaumes
Voirosses, Clos du Roi, Fiètre,
Les Grèves

CUVÉE RAMEAU-LAMAROSSE
AOC Pernand-Vergelesses
Unblended Les Basses Vergelesses

CUVÉE NICOLAS ROLIN
AOC Beaune
A blend of Les Cents Vignes,
Les Grèves, En Genêt

CUVÉE ROUSSEAU-DESLANDES
AOC Beaune
A blend of Les Cent Vignes,
Les Montrevenots, La Mignotte,
Les Avaux

WHITE WINES

CUVÉE DE BAHÈZRE DE LANLAY
AOC Meursault-Charmes
A blend of Les Charmes Dessus,
Les Charmes Dessous

CUVÉE BAUDOT
AOC Meursault-Genevrières
A blend of Genevrières Dessus,
Les Genevrières Dessous

CUVÉE PHILIPPE LE BON
AOC Meursault-Genevrières
A blend of Genevrières Dessus
Les Genevrières Dessous

CUVÉE PAUL CHANSON
AOC Corton-Vergennes
Unblended Corton-Vergennes

CUVÉE DAMES DE FLANDRES
AOC Bâtard-Montrachet
Unblended Bâtard-Montrachet

CUVÉE GOUREAU
AOC Meursault
A blend of Le Poruzot, Les Pitures, Les Cras

CUVÉE ALBERT-GRIVAULT
AOC Meursault-Charmes
Unblended Les Charmes Dessus

CUVÉE JEHAN HUMBLOT
AOC Meursault
A blend of Le Poruzot,
Grands Charrons

CUVÉE LOPPIN
AOC Meursault
Unblended Les Criots

CUVÉE FRANÇOIS POISARD
AOC Pouilly-Fuissé
Unblended Pouilly-Fuissé

CUVÉE FRANÇOISE-DE-SALINS
AOC Corton-Charlemagne
Unblended Corton-Charlemagne

THE APPELLATIONS OF
THE CÔTE DE BEAUNE
AND HAUTES-CÔTES DE BEAUNE

Note All the *Grands Crus* of Côte de Beaune have their own separate appellations and are therefore listed individually below. However, the *Premiers Crus* do not, and are therefore listed under the appellation of the village in which the vineyards are situated. *Premiers Crus* that are virtually contiguous with *Grand Cru* vineyards are italicized; they are possibly superior to those that do not share a boundary with one or more *Grands Crus*, and generally superior to those that share boundaries with village AOC vineyards.

ALOXE-CORTON AOC

This village is more Côte de Nuits than Côte de Beaune, as its 99 per cent red-wine production suggests.

RED These deeply coloured, firm-structured wines with compact fruit are reminiscent of reds from northern Côte de Nuits. They are excellent value for money.

🍇 Pinot noir, Pinot gris, Pinot liébault

🍷 10–20 years

WHITE Very little Aloxe-Corton *blanc* is made, but Daniel Senard makes a lovely buttery-rich, concentrated pure Pinot gris wine (which although it is definitely a white wine makes it red according to the regulations!).

🍇 Chardonnay

🍷 4–8 years

✓ *Edmond Cornu & Fils*
• *Domaine P. Dubreuil-Fontaine*
• *Follin-Arbelet* • *Domaine Maurice Martray*
• *Daniel Senard* • *Domaine Tollot-Beaut*

ALOXE-CORTON PREMIER CRU AOC

Premiers Crus: Les Chaillots, *La Coutière**, Les Fournières, Les Guérets, *La Maréchaude**, *Clos des Maréchaudes, Les Maréchaudes,* Les Meix (or Clos du Chapitre), *Les Moutottes**, *Les Paulands, Les Petites Lolières**, *La Toppe au Vert**, *Les Valozières,* Les Vercots.
*Premier Cru vineyards of Aloxe-Corton in Ladoix-Serrigny.

RED These wines can have an intense bouquet and a firm, spicy fruit flavour. The best *Premiers Crus* are Les Fournières, Les Valozières, Les Paulands, and Les Maréchaudes.

🍇 Pinot noir, Pinot gris, Pinot liébault

🍷 10–20 years

WHITE I have never encountered any.

✓ *Capitain-Gagnerot*
• *Domaine Antonin Guyon* • *André Masson*
• *Prince Florent de Mérode*

AUXEY-DURESSES AOC

A beautiful village, set in an idyllic valley behind Monthélie and Meursault.

RED Attractive wines not very deep in colour, but with a softness of fruit and a little finesse.

🍇 Pinot noir, Pinot gris, Pinot liébault

🍷 6–12 years

WHITE Medium-bodied wines with a full, spicy-nutty flavour, like that of a modest Meursault.

🍇 Chardonnay, Pinot blanc

🍷 3–7 years

✓ *Robert Ampeau* • *Jean-Pierre Diconne*
• *Alain Gras* • *Louis Jadot* • *Henri Latour*
• *Domaine Leroy* • various *Prunier* (all and sundry) • *Dominique & Vincent Roy*

AUXEY-DURESSES-CÔTES DE BEAUNE AOC

Alternative appellation for red wines only. *See* Auxey-Duresses AOC.

AUXEY-DURESSES PREMIER CRU AOC

Premiers Crus: Bas des Duresses, Les Bretterins, La Chapelle, Climat du Val, Les Duresses, Les Écusseaux, Les Grands-Champs, Reugne.

RED The *Premiers Crus* provide nicely coloured soft wines with good finesse. The best have fine redcurrant Pinot character with the creamy-oak of cask maturity.

🍇 Pinot noir, Pinot gris, Pinot liébault

🍷 7–15 years

WHITE Excellent value, smooth, and stylish wines in the Meursault mould.

🍇 Chardonnay, Pinot blanc

🍷 4–10 years

✓ *Jean-Pierre Diconne* • *Michel Prunier*
• *Domaine Vincent Prunier*

BÂTARD-MONTRACHET AOC
Grand Cru

This *Grand Cru* is situated on the slope beneath Le Montrachet and overlaps both Chassagne-Montrachet and Puligny-Montrachet.

WHITE Full-bodied, intensely rich wine with masses of nutty, honey-and-toast flavours. It is one of the best dry white wines in the world.

🍇 Pinot chardonnay (*sic*)

🍷 8–20 years

✓ *Jean-Marc Boillot* • *Michel Morey-Coffinet*
• *Jean-Noël Gagnard* • *Louis Latour*
• *Domaine Leflaive* • *Pierre Morey*
• *Michel Niellon* • *Domaine Paul Pernot*
• *Domaine Ramonet* • *Antonin Rodet*
• *Domaine Étienne Sauzet*

BEAUNE AOC

Beaune gives its name to village wines and *Premiers Crus*, but not to any *Grands Crus*.

RED These soft-scented, gently fruity wines are consistent and good value.

🍇 Pinot noir, Pinot gris, Pinot liébault

🍷 6–14 years

WHITE An uncomplicated dry Chardonnay wine with a characteristic soft finish.

🍇 Chardonnay, Pinot blanc

🍷 3–7 years

✓ *Bouchard Père & Fils* • *Bertrand Darviot*
• *François Germain (Château de Chorey-lès-Beaune)* • *Machard de Gramont*
• *Louis Jadot* • *Tollot-Beaut*

BEAUNE PREMIER CRU AOC

Premiers Crus: Les Aigrots, Aux Coucherias (or Clos de la Féguine), Aux Cras, Clos des Avaux, Les Avaux, Le Bas des Teurons, Les Beaux Fougets, Belissand, Les Blanches Fleurs, Les Boucherottes, Les Bressandes, Les Cents Vignes, Champs Pimont, Les Chouacheux, l'Écu (or Clos de l'Écu), Les Epenottes (or Les Epenotes), Les Fèves, En Genêt, Les Grèves, Clos Landry (Clos Ste.-Landry), Les Longes, Le Clos des Mouches, Le Clos de la Mousse, Les Marconnets, La Mignotte, Montée Rouge, Les Montrevenots, En l'Orme, Les Perrières, Pertuisots, Les Reversées, Clos du Roi, Les Seurey, Les Sizies, Clos Ste.-Anne (or Sur les Grèves), Les Teurons, Les Toussaints, Les Tuvilains, La Vigne de l'Enfant Jésus, Les Vignes Franches (or Clos des Ursules).

RED The best *Crus* are medium-bodied with a delightfully soft rendition of Pinot fruit and lots of finesse.

🍇 Pinot noir, Pinot gris, Pinot liébault

🍷 10–20 years

WHITE These wines have lovely finesse and can display a toasty flavour more common to richer growths.

🍇 Chardonnay, Pinot blanc

🍷 5–12 years

✓ *Arnoux Père & Fils* • *Bouchard Père & Fils*
• *Domaine Joseph Drouhin* • *François Germain (Château de Chorey)* • *Camille Giroud* • *Louis Jadot* • *Domaine Michel Lafarge* • *Bernard Morey* • *Albert Morot*
• *Domaine Jacques Prieur* • *Domaine Tollot-Beaut*

BIENVENUES-BÂTARD-MONTRACHET AOC
Grand Cru

This is one of Puligny-Montrachet's four *Grands Crus*.

WHITE Not the fattest dry wines from this village, but they have great finesse, immaculate balance, and some of the nuttiness, and honey-and-toast flavours expected in all Montrachets.

🍇 Chardonnay

🍷 8–20 years

✓ *Domaine Louis Carillon & Fils*
 • *Domaine Leflaive* • *Domaine Paul Pernot*
 • *Domaine Ramonet* • *Étienne Sauzet*

BLAGNY AOC

A red-only appellation from Blagny, a tiny hamlet shared by the communes of Meursault and Puligny-Montrachet.

RED These rich, full-flavoured, Meursault-like red wines are underrated.

🍇 Pinot noir, Pinot gris, Pinot liébault

🍷— 8–15 years

✓ *Robert Ampeau* • *Domaine Matrot*

BLAGNY-CÔTE DE BEAUNE AOC

Alternative appellation for Blagny.
See Blagny AOC.

BLAGNY PREMIER CRU AOC

Premiers Crus: La Garenne (or Sur la Garenne), Hameau de Blagny (in Puligny-Montrachet), La Jeunelotte, La Pièce sous le Bois, Sous Blagny (in Meursault), Sous le Dos d'Ane, Sous le Puits.

RED These rich wines have even more grip and attack than basic Blagny.

🍇 Pinot noir, Pinot gris, Pinot liébault

🍷— 10–20 years

✓ *Robert Ampeau* • *François Jobard*
 • *Domaine Leflaive* • *Domaine Matrot*

BOURGOGNE LA CHAPELLE NOTRE-DAME AOC

One of three Bourgogne *lieux-dits* created in 1993. La Chapelle Notre Dame is located in Serrigny, which is just east of Ladoix. Red, white, and rosé may be produced according to the same grapes and rules as for Bourgogne AOC (*see* p.133). Domaine P. Dubreuil-Fontaine has produced a wine from this *lieu-dit* for many years. It has always been decent, not special, but capable of improving in bottle. André et Jean-René Nudant also makes a light, fresh red from this appellation.

BOURGOGNE HAUTE-CÔTES DE BEAUNE AOC

This appellation is larger and more varied than Hautes-Côtes de Nuits. Half-red/half-rosé wines may be sold as Bourgogne Clairet Hautes-Côtes de Beaune AOC, but the style is outmoded and the appellation rarely encountered.

RED Ruby-coloured, medium-bodied wines with a Pinot perfume and a creamy-fruit finish.

🍇 Pinot noir, Pinot gris, Pinot liébault

🍷— 4–10 years

WHITE Not very frequently encountered, but Guillemard-Dupont's pure Pinot buerot (Pinot gris) is rich, dry, and expressive. Its grape variety makes it a very pale white, red, or rosé according to the regulations!

🍇 Chardonnay, Pinot blanc

🍷— 1–4 years

ROSÉ Pleasantly dry and fruity wines with some richness and a soft finish.

🍇 Pinot noir, Pinot gris, Pinot liébault

🍷— 1–3 years

✓ *Domaine Jean Joliot & Fils* • *Didier Montchovet* • *Domaine Claude Nouveau* • *Domaine Naudin-Ferrand*

CHARLEMAGNE AOC
Grand Cru

This white-only *Grand Cru* of Aloxe-Corton overlaps Pernand-Vergelesses and is almost, but not quite, identical to the *Grand Cru* of Corton-Charlemagne.

CHASSAGNE-MONTRACHET AOC

These village wines have a lesser reputation than those of Puligny-Montrachet.

RED Firm, dry wines with more colour and less softness than most Côte de Beaune reds.

🍇 Pinot noir, Pinot gris, Pinot liébault

🍷— 10–20 years

WHITE An affordable introduction to the great wines of Montrachet.

🍇 Chardonnay, Pinot blanc

🍷— 5–10 years

✓ *Fontaine-Gagnard* • *Jean-Noël Gagnard* • *Marquis de Laguiche* • *Bernard Morey* • *Jean-Marc Morey* • *Domaine Ramonet*

CHASSAGNE-MONTRACHET-CÔTE DE BEAUNE AOC

Alternative appellation for red wines only.
See Chassagne Montrachet AOC.

CHASSAGNE-MONTRACHET PREMIER CRU AOC

Premiers Crus: Abbaye de Morgeot, Les Baudines, *Blanchot Dessus*, Les Boirettes, Bois de Chassagne, Les Bondues, La Boudriotte, Les Brussonnes, En Cailleret, La Cardeuse, Champ Jendreau, Les Champs Gain, La Chapelle, Clos Chareau, Les Chaumées, Les Chaumes, Les Chenevottes, Les Combards, Les Commes, Ez Crets, Ez Crottes, *Dent de Chien*, Les Embrazées, Les Fairendes, Francemont, La Grande Borne, La Grande Montagne, Les Grandes Ruchottes, Les Grands Clos, Guerchère, Les Macherelles, *La Maltroie*, Les Morgeots, Les Murées, Les Pasquelles, Petingeret, Les Petites Fairendes, Les Petits Clos, Clos Pitois, Les Places, Les Rebichets, En Remilly, La Romanée, La Roquemaure, Clos St.-Jean, Tête du Clos, Tonton Marcel, Les Vergers, *Vide Bourse*, Vigne Blanche, Vigne Derrière, En Virondot.

RED The wines of Chassagne-Montrachet have the weight of a Côte de Nuits and the softness of a Côte de Beaune.

🍇 Pinot noir, Pinot gris, Pinot liébault

🍷— 10–25 years

WHITE Flavoursome dry wines, but lacking the finesse of those in the neighbouring appellation of Puligny.

🍇 Chardonnay, Pinot blanc

🍷— 6–15 years

✓ *Marc Colin* • *Michel Colin-Deléger* • *Fontaine-Gagnard* • *Jean-Noël Gagnard* • *Henri Germain* • *Château de la Maltroye* • *Michel Niellon* • *Domaine Ramonet* • *Domaine Roux* • *Verget*

CHEVALIER-MONTRACHET AOC
Grand Cru

This is one of Puligny-Montrachet's four *Grands Crus*.

WHITE Fatter and richer than Bienvenues-Bâtard-Montrachet, this wine has more explosive flavour than Bâtard-Montrachet.

🍇 Chardonnay

🍷— 10–20 years

✓ *Auvenay* • *Bouchard Père et Fils* • *Georges Déléger* • *Louis Jadot* • *Louis Latour* • *Domaine Leflaive* • *Michel Niellon*

CHOREY-LÈS-BEAUNE AOC

This satellite appellation of Beaune produces exciting, underrated wines.

RED Although next to Aloxe-Corton, Chorey has all the soft and sensuous charms that are quintessentially Beaune.

🍇 Pinot noir, Pinot gris, Pinot liébault

🍷— 7–15 years

WHITE Less than one per cent of the wines produced in this village are white.

✓ *Arnoux Père & Fils* • *Domaine Germain (Château de Chorey)* • *Domaine Maillard Père & Fils* • *Domaine Maurice Martray* • *Domaine Tollot-Beaut*

CHOREY-LÈS-BEAUNE CÔTE DE BEAUNE AOC

Alternative appellation for red wines only.
See Chorey-lès-Beaune AOC.

CORTON AOC
Grand Cru

This is one of the *Grands Crus* of Aloxe-Corton (it extends into Ladoix-Serrigny and Pernand-Vergelesses). Corton is the only *Grand Cru* in the Côte de Beaune that includes red and white wines and thus parallels the Côte de Nuits *Grand Cru* Musigny. The following 20 *climats* may hyphenate their names (with or without the prefix) to the Corton appellation: Les Bressandes, Le Charlemagne, Les Chaumes, Les Chaumes et la Voierosse, Les Combes, Le Corton, Les Fiétres, Les Grèves, Les Languettes, Les Maréchaudes, Les Miex, Les Meix Lallemand, Les Paulands, Les Perrières, Les Pougets, Les Renardes, Le Rognet-Corton, Le Clos de Roi, Les Vergennes, La Vigne au Saint. So it is possible to get a red Corton-Charlemagne!

RED These wines may sometimes appear intense and broody in their youth, but, when fully mature, a great Corton has such finesse and complexity that it can stun the senses.

🍇 Pinot noir, Pinot gris, Pinot liébault

🍷— 12–30 years

WHITE A medium- to full-bodied wine with a fine, rich flavour.

🍇 Chardonnay

⌛ 10–25 years

✓ *Arnoux Père & Fils • Bouchard Père & Fils • Domaine Delarche • Louis Jadot • Bonneau du Martray • Domaine Chandon de Briailles • Faiveley • Domaine Michel Juillot • Domaine Leroy • Prince Florent de Mérode • Domaine Jacques Prieur • Domaine Rapet Père & Fils • Domaine Comte Daniel Senard • Domaine Tollot-Beaut*

CORTON-CHARLEMAGNE AOC

Grand Cru

This famous *Grand Cru* of Aloxe-Corton extends into Ladoix-Serrigny and Pernand-Vergelesses.

WHITE This is the most sumptuous of all white Burgundies. It has a fabulous concentration of rich, buttery fruit flavours, a dazzling balance of acidity, and delicious overtones of vanilla, honey, and cinnamon.

🍇 Chardonnay

⌛ 5–25 years

✓ *Bonneau du Martray • J.-F. Coche-Dury • Joseph Drouhin • Domaine Antonin Guyon • Louis Jadot • Patrick Javillier • Michel Juillot • Maison Louis Latour • Olivier Leflaive • Domaine Rapet Père & Fils • Remoissenet Père & Fils • Christophe Roumier*

CÔTE DE BEAUNE AOC

Wines that are entitled to the actual Côte de Beaune appellation are restricted to a few plots on the Montagne de Beaune above Beaune itself.

RED These are fine, stylish wines that reveal the purest of Pinot noir fruit. They are produced in the soft Beaune style.

🍇 Pinot noir, Pinot gris, Pinot liébault

⌛ 10–20 years

WHITE Little-seen, dry basic Beaune.

🍇 Chardonnay, Pinot blanc

⌛ 3–8 years

✓ *Lycée Agricole & Viticole de Beaune • Joseph Drouhin*

CÔTE DE BEAUNE-VILLAGES AOC

While AOC Côte de Nuits-Villages covers red and white wines in a predominantly red-wine district, AOC Côte de Beaune-Villages applies only to red wines in a district that produces the greatest white Burgundies!

RED Excellent value fruity wines, made in true soft Beaune style.

🍇 Pinot noir, Pinot gris, Pinot liébault

⌛ 7–15 years

✓ *Bernard Bachelet & Fils • Coron Père & Fils • Lequin Roussot*

CRIOTS-BÂTARD-MONTRACHET AOC

Grand Cru

The smallest of Chassagne-Montrachet's three *Grands Crus*.

WHITE This wine has some of the weight of its great neighbours and a lovely hint of honey-and-toast richness, but it is essentially the palest and most fragrant of all the Montrachets.

🍇 Pinot chardonnay (*sic*)

⌛ 8–20 years

✓ *Joseph Belland • Blain-Gagnard*

LADOIX AOC

Parts of Ladoix-Serrigny have the right to use the Aloxe-Corton Premier Cru appellation or the *Grands Crus* of Corton and Corton-Charlemagne. Ladoix AOC covers the rest of the wine produced in the area.

RED Many wines are rustic versions of Aloxe-Corton, but there are some fine grower wines that combine the compact fruit and structure of a Nuits with the softness of a Beaune.

🍇 Pinot noir, Pinot gris, Pinot liébault

⌛ 7–20 years

WHITE Just five per cent of the production is white and it is not very well distributed.

🍇 Chardonnay, Pinot blanc

⌛ 4–8 years

✓ *Capitain-Gagnerot • Edmond Cornu & Fils • Domaine Maurice Martray • Prince Florent de Mérode*

LADOIX-CÔTE DE BEAUNE AOC

See Ladoix AOC

Alternative appellation for red wines only.

LADOIX PREMIER CRU AOC

Premiers Crus: Basses Mourottes, Bois Roussot, Les Buis, Le Clou d'Orge, La Corvée, Les Gréchons, *Hautes Mourottes*, Les Joyeuses, La Micaude, En Naget, *Rognet et Corton*.

These *premiers cru* vineyards were expanded from 14 to 24 hectares in 2000.

RED These wines are decidedly finer in quality and deeper in colour than those with the basic village appellation.

🍇 Pinot noir, Pinot gris, Pinot liébault

⌛ 7–20 years

WHITE Prince Florent de Mérode of Domaine de Serrigny makes the only white Ladoix Premier Cru I know: Ladoix Hautes Mourottes blanc.

✓ *Capitain-Gagnerot • Edmond Cornu & Fils • Prince Florent de Mérode • Domaine Naudin-Ferrand • Domaine André Nudant & Fils • Domaine G. & P. Ravaut*

MARANGES AOC

In 1989 Maranges AOC replaced three separate appellations: Cheilly-lès-Maranges AOC, Dézize-lès-Maranges AOC, and Sampigny-lès-Maranges AOC, a trio of villages sharing the once moderately famous *Cru* of Marange, which is on a well-exposed hillside immediately southwest of Santenay. The red wines may also be sold as Côte de Beaune AOC or Côte de Beaune-Villages AOC. Production used to be erratic, with most of the wine (including much of that qualifying for *Premier Cru*) sold to *négociants* for blending into Côte de Beaune-Villages, but two or three dedicated growers are beginning to get the name around.

RED Wines with a very pure Pinot perfume, which are developing good colour and body.

🍇 Pinot noir, Pinot gris, Pinot liébault

⌛ 2–7 years

WHITE Rarely produced in any of the three villages and never in Dézize-lès-Maranges, as far as I am aware, although it is allowed.

✓ *Domaine Fernand Chevrot • Jaffelin • René Martin • Edward Monnot • Claude Nouveau*

MARANGES CÔTE DE BEAUNE AOC

Alternative appellation for red wines only. *See* Maranges AOC.

MARANGES PREMIER CRU AOC

Premiers Crus: Clos de la Boutière, Le Croix Moines, La Fussière, Le Clos des Loyères, Le Clos des Rois, Les Clos Roussots.

Some of these *climats* officially designated as *Premiers Crus* are a bit of a puzzle. Clos de la Boutière, for example, was originally just plain old La Boutière, and Les Clos Roussots once adjoined a *Premier Cru* called Les Plantes de Marange, but was never classified as one itself. According to maps prior to the merging of the three appellations, Les Plantes de Marange, Maranges, and En Maranges were the authentic names of the most important vineyards in the area classified as *Premier Cru*, but they have since adopted less repetitive *lieux-dits*, and such revisionism is probably justified from a marketing aspect.

RED The best examples are well coloured, with a good balance of fruit, often red fruits, and a richer, longer finish than those wines bearing the basic Maranges appellation.

🍇 Pinot noir, Pinot gris, Pinot liébault

WHITE Rarely encountered.

🍇 Chardonnay, Pinot blanc

✓ *Bernard Bachelet & Fils • Domaine Fernand Chevrot • Yvon & Chantal Contat-Grangé • Edward Monnot • Claude Nouveau*

MEURSAULT AOC

While the greatest white Côte de Beaune is either Montrachet or Corton-Charlemagne, Meursault is probably better known and is certainly more popular.

RED This is often treated as a novelty, but it is a fine wine in its own right, with a firm edge.

🍇 Pinot noir, Pinot gris, Pinot liébault

⌛ 8–20 years

WHITE Even the most basic Meursault should be deliciously dry with a nutty-buttery-spice quality added to its typically rich flavour.

🍇 Chardonnay, Pinot blanc

🍷 5–12 years

✓ *Robert Ampeau* • *Bouchard Père & Fils* • *Boyer-Martenot* • *Alain Coche-Bizouard* • *J.-F. Coche-Dury* • *Drouhin* • *Jean-Philippe Fichet* • *Henri Germain* • *Domaine Albert Grivault* • *Patrick Javillier* • *François Jobard* • *Rémy Jobard* • *Domaine des Comtes Lafon* • *Domaine Michelot* (any Michelot, hyphenated or otherwise, with a Meursault address) • *François Mikulski* • *Pierre Morey* • *Domaine Guy Roulot*

MEURSAULT-BLAGNY PREMIER CRU AOC

Premiers Crus: La Jeunelotte, La Pièce sous le Bois, Sous Blagny, Sous le Dos d'Âne.

An alternative appellation for Meursault wines from vineyards in the neighbouring village of Blagny. The wines must be white, otherwise they claim the Blagny *Premier Cru* appellation. *See* Meursault Premier Cru AOC.

MEURSAULT-CÔTE DE BEAUNE AOC

Alternative red-wine-only appellation for Meursault. *See* Meursault AOC.

MEURSAULT PREMIER CRU AOC

Premiers Crus: Aux Perrières, Les Bouchères, Les Caillerets, Les Charmes-Dessous (or Les Charmes-Dessus), Les Chaumes de Narvaux, Les Chaumes des Perrières, Les Cras, Les Genevrières-Dessous (or Les Genevrières-Dessus), Les Gouttes d'Or, La Jeunelotte, Clos des Perrières, Les Perrières-Dessous (or Les Perrières-Dessus), La Pièce sous le Bois, Les Plures, Le Porusot, Les Porusot-Dessous (or Le Porusot-Dessus), Clos des Richemont (or Cras), Les Santenots Blancs, Les Santenots du Milieu, Sous Blagny, Sous le Dos d'Âne.

RED Finer and firmer than the basic village wines, these reds need plenty of time to soften.

🍇 Pinot noir, Pinot gris, Pinot liébault

🍷 10–20 years

WHITE Great Meursault should always be rich. Their various permutations of nutty, buttery, and spicy Chardonnay flavours may often be submerged by the honey, cinnamon, and vanilla of new oak until considerably mature.

🍇 Chardonnay, Pinot blanc

🍷 6–15 years

✓ *Michel Bouzereau & Fils* • *J.-F. Coche-Dury* • *François Jobard* • *Domaine Leroy* • *Domaine des Comtes Lafon* • *Domaine Matrot* • *Domaine Michelot* (any Michelot, hyphenated or otherwise, with a Meursault address) • *Pierre Morey* • *Domaine Jacques Prieur* • *Remoissenet Père & Fils* • *Domaine Guy Roulot*

MEURSAULT-SANTENOTS AOC

This is an alternative appellation for Meursault *Premier Cru* that comes from a part of the Volnay-Santenots appellation. *See* Volnay-Santenots AOC.

MONTHELIE AOC

Monthelie's wines, especially the *Premiers Crus*, are probably the most underrated in Burgundy.

RED These excellent wines have a vivid colour, expressive fruit, a firm structure, and a lingering, silky finish.

🍇 Pinot noir, Pinot gris, Pinot liébault

🍷 7–15 years

WHITE Relatively little white wine is produced.

🍇 Chardonnay, Pinot blanc

🍷 3–7 years

✓ *Eric Boigelot* • *Domaine Denis Boussey* • *Eric Boussey* • *J.-F. Coche-Dury* • *Paul Garaudet* • *Domaine des Comtes Lafon* • *Domaine Monthelie-Douhairet* • *Annick Parent*

MONTHELIE-CÔTE DE BEAUNE AOC

Alternative appellation for red wines only. *See* Monthelie AOC.

MONTHELIE PREMIER CRU AOC

Premiers Crus: Le Cas Rougeot, Les Champs Fulliot, Les Duresses, La Château Gaillard, Le Clos Gauthey, Le Meix Bataille, Les Riottes, Sur la Velle, La Taupine, Les Vignes Rondes, Le Village de Monthelie.

RED Monthelie's *Premiers Crus* are hard to find, but worth the effort.

🍇 Pinot noir, Pinot gris, Pinot liébault

🍷 8–20 years

WHITE Paul Garaudet's delicately perfumed Champs-Fulliot blanc is the only white *Premier Cru* I have come across.

✓ *Eric Boigelot* • *Denis Boussey* • *Domaine Jehan Changarnier* • *Gérard Doreau* • *Paul Garaudet* • *Château de Monthelie* • *Annick Parent*

MONTRACHET AOC

Grand Cru

Many consider Montrachet to be the greatest dry white wine in the world. On the other hand, I do remember reading somewhere that its flavours can be so intense that it is difficult to know whether it is a joy to drink or whether you are giving your palate an end-of-term exam. It definitely is a joy to drink, but I know what the writer means.

WHITE When it is fully mature, Montrachet has the most glorious and expressive character of all dry white wines. Its honeyed, toasty, floral, nutty, creamy, and spicy aromas are simply stunning.

🍇 Pinot chardonnay (*sic*)

🍷 10–30 years

✓ *Domaine Amiot-Bonfils* • *Bouchard Père & Fils* • *Marc Colin* • *Louis Jadot* • *Domaine Leflaive* • *Marquis de Laguiche* (made and sold by Joseph Drouhin) • *Pierre Morey* • *Domaine Jacques Prieur* • *Domaine Ramonet* • *Domaine de la Romanée-Conti*

LE MONTRACHET AOC

See Montrachet AOC

PERNAND-VERGELESSES AOC

This village, near Aloxe-Corton, is the most northerly appellation of the Côte de Beaune.

RED With the exception of the silky wines recommended below, too many of these are rustic and overrated and would be better off in a *négociant* Côte de Beaune-Villages blend.

🍇 Pinot noir, Pinot gris, Pinot liébault

🍷 7–15 years

WHITE Although this village is famous for its Aligoté, growers such as François Germain of Domaine Jacques Germain produce smooth, deliciously balanced wines that deserve more recognition.

🍇 Chardonnay, Pinot blanc

🍷 4–8 years

✓ *Denis Père & Fils* • *Domaine P. Dubreuil-Fontaine* • *Domaine Jacques Germain* • *Olivier Leflaive*

PERNAND-VERGELESSES-CÔTE DE BEAUNE AOC

Alternative appellation for red wines only. *See* Pernand-Vergelesses AOC.

PERNAND-VERGELESSES PREMIER CRU AOC

Premiers Crus: En Caradeux, Creux de la Net, Les Fichots, Île des Hautes Vergelesses, Les Basses Vergelesses.

RED These wines repay keeping until the fruit develops a silkiness that hangs gracefully on the wine's structure and gives Pernand's *Premiers Crus* the class its village wines lack.

🍇 Pinot noir, Pinot gris, Pinot liébault

🍷 10–20 years

WHITE The Beaune firm of Chanson Père & Fils produces a consistent wine of medium body, which is dry but mellow.

🍇 Chardonnay, Pinot blanc

🍷 4–8 years

✓ *Domaine Delarche* • *Domaine P. Dubreuil-Fontaine* • *Roger Jaffelin* • *Maison Louis Latour* • *Domaine Rapet Père & Fils* • *Rollin Père & Fils*

POMMARD AOC

A very famous village with a "reborn" image built up by a group of dedicated and skilful winemakers.

RED The "famous" dark, alcoholic, and soupy wines of Pommard are now mostly a thing of the past, having been replaced by exciting fine wines.

🍇 Pinot noir, Pinot gris, Pinot liébault

🍷 8–16 years

✓ *Robert Ampeau* • *Domaine Comte Armand* • *Billard-Gonnet* • *Jean-Marc Boillot* • *Bernard & Louis Glantenay* • *Domaine Leroy* • *Aleth Leroyer-Girardin* • *Hubert de Montille* • *Domaine Parent* • *Château Pommard*

POMMARD PREMIER CRU AOC

Premiers Crus: Les Arvelets, Les Bertins, Clos Blanc, Les Boucherottes, La Chanière, Les Chanlins-Bas, Les Chaponnières, Les Charmots, Les Combes-Dessus, Clos de la Commaraine, Les Croix Noires, Derrière St.-Jean, Clos des Epeneaux, Les Fremiers, Les Grands Epenots, Les Jarolières, En Largillière (or Les Argillières), Clos Micot, Les Petits Epenots, Les Pézerolles, La Platière, Les Poutures, La Refène, Les Rugiens-Bas, Les Rugiens-Hauts, Les Saussilles, Clos de Verger, Village.

RED The best *Crus* are the various *climats* of Les Rugiens (deep and voluptuous) and Les Epenots (soft, fragrant, and rich).

🍇 Pinot noir, Pinot gris, Pinot liébault

🍷 10–20 years

✓ *Domaine Comte Armand* • *Billard-Gonnet*
• *Jean-Marc Boillot* • *Domaine de Courcel*
• *Domaine Lejeune* • *Domaine Leroy*
• *Aleth Leroyer-Girardin* • *Hubert de Montille* • *Pierre Morey* • *Domaine Parent*
• *Domaine Pothier-Rieusset*
• *Domaine de la Pousse d'Or*

PULIGNY-MONTRACHET AOC

One of two Montrachet villages producing some of the greatest dry whites in the world.

RED Although some fine wines are made, Puligny-Montrachet *rouge* demands a premium for its scarcity.

🍇 Pinot noir, Pinot gris, Pinot liébault

🍷 10–20 years

WHITE Basic Puligny-Montrachet from a top grower is a very high-quality wine: full bodied, fine, and steely, requiring a few years to develop a nutty honey-and-toast flavour.

🍇 Chardonnay, Pinot blanc

🍷 5–12 years

✓ *Robert Ampeau* • *Jean-Marc Boillot*
• *Domaine Louis Carillon & Fils* • *Domaine Leflaive* • *Olivier Leflaive* • *Étienne Sauzet*

PULIGNY-MONTRACHET-CÔTE DE BEAUNE AOC

Alternative appellation for red wines only. *See* Puligny-Montrachet AOC.

PULIGNY-MONTRACHET PREMIER CRU AOC

Premiers Crus: Le Cailleret (or *Demoiselles*), Les Chalumeaux, Champ Canet, Champ Gain, Au Chaniot, Clavaillon, Les Combettes, Ez Folatières, Les Folatières, La Garenne (or Sur la Garenne), Clos de la Garenne, Hameau de Blagny, La Jaquelotte, Clos des Meix, Clos de la Mouchère (or Les Perrières), Peux Bois, *Les Pucelles*, Les Referts, En la Richarde, Sous le Courthil, Sous le Puits, La Truffière.

RED I have never encountered any.

🍇 Pinot noir, Pinot gris, Pinot liébault

WHITE A *Premier Cru* Puligny made by a top grower such as Étienne Sauzet is one of the most flavour-packed taste experiences you are likely to encounter.

🍇 Chardonnay, Pinot blanc

🍷 7–15 years

✓ *Robert Ampeau* • *Jean Boillot*
• *Jean-Marc Boillot*
• *Michel Bouzereau & Fils*
• *Domaine Louis Carillon & Fils*
• *Domaine Leflaive* • *Domaine de Montille*
• *Domaine Jacques Prieur*
• *Étienne Sauzet*

ST.-AUBIN AOC

This underrated village has many talented winemakers and is an excellent source for good-value wines.

RED Delicious, ripe but light, fragrant, and fruity red wines that quickly develop a taste of wild strawberries.

🍇 Pinot noir, Pinot gris, Pinot liébault

🍷 4–8 years

WHITE Super-value white wines – a sort of "Hautes-Côtes Montrachet"!

🍇 Chardonnay, Pinot blanc

🍷 3–8 years

✓ *Jean-Claude Bachelet*
• *Denis & Françoise Clair*
• *Domaine Clerget* • *Domaine Marc Colin*
• *Hubert Lamy & Fils*

ST.-AUBIN-CÔTE DE BEAUNE AOC

Alternative appellation for red wines only. *See* St.-Aubin AOC.

ST.-AUBIN PREMIER CRU AOC

Premiers Crus: Le Bas de Gamay à l'Est, Bas de Vermarain à l'Est, Les Castets, Les Champlots, Es Champs, Le Charmois, La Chatenière, Les Combes au Sud, Les Cortons, En Créot, Derrière chez Edouard, Derrière la Tour, Echaille, Les Frionnes, Sur Gamay, Marinot, En Montceau, Les Murgers des Dents de Chien, Les Perrières, Pitangeret, Le Puits, En la Ranché, En Remilly, Sous Roche Dumay, Sur le Sentier du Clou, Les Travers de Marinot, Vignes Moingeon, Le Village, En Vollon à l'Est.

The best of these *Premiers Crus* are Les Frionnes and Les Murgers des Dents de Chien, followed by La Chatenière, Les Castets, En Remilly, and Le Charmois.

RED Very appealing strawberry, and oaky-vanilla wines that are delicious young, yet improve further with age.

🍇 Pinot noir, Pinot gris, Pinot liébault

🍷 5–15 years

WHITE These dry wines are often superior to the village wines of Puligny-Montrachet and always much cheaper.

🍇 Chardonnay, Pinot blanc

🍷 4–10 years

✓ *Jean-Claude Bachelet*
• *Domaine Clerget* • *Domaine Marc Colin*
• *Bernard Morey Henri Prudhon et Fils*
• *Gérard Thomas*

ST.-ROMAIN AOC

A little village amid picturesque surroundings in the hills above Auxey-Duresses.

RED Good-value, medium-bodied, rustic reds that have a good, characterful flavour.

🍇 Pinot noir, Pinot gris, Pinot liébault

🍷 4–8 years

WHITE Fresh and lively, light- to medium-bodied dry white wines of an honest Chardonnay style.

🍇 Chardonnay, Pinot blanc

🍷 3–7 years

✓ *Joseph Drouhin* • *Alain Gras*
• *Thévenin-Monthelie*

ST.-ROMAIN-CÔTE DE BEAUNE AOC

Alternative appellation for red wines only. *See* St.-Romain AOC.

SANTENAY AOC

This most southerly village appellation of the Côte d'Or (but not of the Côte de Beaune) is a source of good-value Burgundy.

RED These wines are fresh and frank, with a clean rendition of Pinot noir fruit supported by a firm structure.

🍇 Pinot noir, Pinot gris, Pinot liébault

🍷 7–15 years

WHITE Only two per cent of Santenay is white, but some good buys can be found among the top growers.

🍇 Chardonnay, Pinot blanc

🍷 4–8 years

✓ *Bernard Bachelet & Fils* • *Roger Belland*
• *Denis & Françoise Clair*
• *Vincent Girardin* • *Alain Gras*
• *Domaine Prieur-Brunet*

SANTENAY-CÔTE DE BEAUNE AOC

Alternative appellation for red wines only. *See* Santenay AOC.

SANTENAY PREMIER CRU AOC

Premiers Crus: Beauregard, Le Chainey, La Comme, Comme Dessus, Clos Faubard, Les Fourneaux, Grand Clos Rousseau, Les Gravières, La Maladière, Clos des Mouches, Passetemps, Petit Clos Rousseau, Clos de Tavannes.

The best are Clos de Tavannes, Les Gravières, La Maladière, and La Comme Dessus.

RED In the pure and frank mould of Pinot noir wines, but with an added expression of *terroir*.

🍇 Pinot noir, Pinot gris, Pinot liébault

🍷 6–15 years

WHITE Rarely encountered.

🍇 Chardonnay, Pinot blanc

🍷 5–10 years

✓ *Roger Belland · Denis & Françoise Clair · Vincent Girardin · Alain Gras* (also sold as René Gras-Boisson) *· Bernard Morey · Lucien Muzard & Fils · Domaine de la Pousse d'Or*

SAVIGNY AOC

See Savigny-lès- Beaune AOC

SAVIGNY-CÔTE DE BEAUNE AOC

Alternative appellation for red wine only. *See* Savigny-lès-Beaune AOC.

SAVIGNY-LÈS-BEAUNE AOC

This village has gifted winemakers producing very underrated and undervalued wines.

RED Delicious, easy-to-drink, medium-bodied wines that are very soft and Beaune-like in style.

🍇 Pinot noir, Pinot gris, Pinot liébault

🍷 7–15 years

WHITE Some excellent dry wines with good concentration of flavour, a smooth texture and some finesse, but they are difficult to find.

🍇 Chardonnay, Pinot blanc

🍷 4–10 years

✓ *Robert Ampeau · Simon Bize & Fils · Bouchard Père & Fils · Camus-Brochon · Maurice Giboulot · Girard-Vollot · Pierre Guillemot · Lucien Jacob · Louis Jadot · Domaine Parent · Jean-Marc Pavelot · Domaine du Prieuré · Rollin Père & Fils · Domaine Tollot-Beaut*

SAVIGNY-LÈS-BEAUNE-CÔTE DE BEAUNE AOC

Alternative appellation for red wines only. *See* Savigny-lès-Beaune AOC.

SAVIGNY PREMIER CRU AOC

See Savigny-lès-Beaune Premier Cru AOC

SAVIGNY-LÈS-BEAUNE PREMIER CRU AOC

Premiers Crus: Aux Clous, Aux Fournaux, Aux Gravains, Aux Guettes, Aux Serpentières, Bas Marconnets, Basses Vergelesses, Clos la Bataillères (*or* Aux *or* Les Vergelesses), Champ Chevrey (*or* Aux Fournaux), Les Charnières, Hauts Jarrons, Les Hauts Marconnets, Les Jarrons (*or* La Dominodes), Les Lavières, Les Narbantons, Petits Godeaux, Les Peuillets, Redrescut, Les Rouvrettes, Les Talmettes

RED These wines have a very elegant, soft, and stylish Pinot flavour that hints of strawberries, cherries, and violets. The best are: Les Lavières, La Dominodes, Aux Vergelesses, Les Marconnets, and Aux Guettes.

🍇 Pinot noir, Pinot gris, Pinot liébault

🍷 7–20 years

WHITE Domaine des Terregelesses produces a splendidly rich, dry wine.

🍇 Chardonnay, Pinot blanc

🍷 5–15 years

✓ *Simon Bize & Fils · Bouchard Père & Fils · Camus-Brochon · Domaine Chandon de Briailles · Chanson Père & Fils · Domaine Bruno Clair · Domaine Maurice Ecard · Machard de Gramont · Louis Jadot · Domaine Leroy · Pavelot · Domaine Tollot-Beaut*

VOLNAY AOC

Volnay ranks in performance with such great growths as Gevrey-Chambertin and Chambolle-Musigny. It is the most southerly red-wine-only appellation in the Côte d'Or, and the only great wine village located above its vineyards.

RED These wines are not cheap, but they are firm and well coloured with more silky finesse than should be expected from a village appellation.

🍇 Pinot noir, Pinot gris, Pinot liébault

🍷 6–15 years

✓ *Marquis d'Angerville · Domaine Michel Lafarge · Domaine Régis Rossignol*

VOLNAY PREMIER CRU AOC

Premiers Crus: Les Angles, Les Aussy, La Barre, Bousse d'Or (or Clos de la Bousse d'Or), Les Brouillards, En Cailleret, Les Cailleret, Cailleret Dessus (part of which may be called Clos des 60 Ouvrées), Carelles Dessous, Carelle sous la Chapelle, Clos de la Caves de Ducs, En Champans, Chanlin, En Chevret, Clos de la Chapelle, Clos des Chênes (or Clos des Chânes), Clos de Ducs, Clos du Château des Ducs, Frémiets (or Clos de la Rougeotte), La Gigotte, Les Grands Champs, Lassolle, Les Lurets, Les Mitans, En l'Ormeau, Pitures Dessus, Pointes d'Angles, Robardelle, Le Ronceret, Taille Pieds, En Verseuil (or Clos du Verseuil), Le Village.

RED No *Grands Crus*, but its silky-smooth and fragrant *Premiers Crus* are great wines, showing tremendous finesse.
The best are: Clos des Chêne, Taille Pieds, Bousse d'Or, Clos de Ducs, the various *climats* of Cailleret, Clos des 60 Ouvrées, and En Champans.

🍇 Pinot noir, Pinot gris, Pinot liébault

🍷 8–20 years

✓ *Marquis d'Angerville · Jean Boillot · Jean-Marc Boillot · Domaine Antonin Guyon · Louis Jadot · Domaine Michel Lafarge · Domaine des Comtes Lafon · Domaine de Montille · Domaine de la Pousse d'Or · Domaine Régis Rossignol*

VOLNAY-SANTENOTS PREMIER CRU AOC

This confusing appellation is in Meursault, not Volnay, although it does run up to the boundary of that village. It dates back to the 19th century, when the Meursault *lieu-dit* of Les Santenots du Milieu became famous for its red wines. White wines cannot be called Volnay-Santenots and must be sold as Meursault or, if produced from the two-thirds of this vineyard furthest from the Volnay border, they may be sold as Meursault Premier Cru AOC or Meursault-Santenots. The right to the Volnay-Santenots appellation was accorded by Tribunal at Beaune in 1924.

RED These wines, which are not often found, are similar to Volnay with good colour and weight, but can lack its silky elegance.

🍇 Pinot noir, Pinot gris, Pinot liébault

🍷 8–20 years

✓ *Robert Ampeau · Domaine des Comtes Lafon · Leroy · Matrot · François Mikulski · Jacques Prieur · Prieur-Brunet*

GRAND CRU VINEYARD CORTON CLOS DES VERGENNES
The tiny vineyard of Corton Clos des Vergennes is under single ownership and the wines are distributed by Moillard-Grivot.

THE CÔTE CHALONNAISE

This is a simple district in winemaking terms, with just five appellations, two exclusively white and three red or white. Despite the fact that many of the wines are little known, their quality in all appellations is very good, and the value for money is even better.

THE CÔTE CHALONNAISE, or Région de Mercurey, as it is sometimes called, was once the forgotten area of Burgundy, perceived as too serious for its own good. Because its flavoursome reds and buttery whites have more in common with the wines of the Côte de Beaune than elsewhere, merchants categorized them as inferior or pretentious. Perhaps the Côte Chalonnaise need not have been forgotten had merchants thought of it more as a superior Mâconnais than as an inferior Côte de Beaune. However, over the last ten years, as merchants across the world have become more willing to seek out lesser-known wines, it has built up a reputation as one of Burgundy's best sources of quality wines.

EXCELLENT NÉGOCIANTS
The Burgundy drinker is blessed with a fine choice of *négociants* in the Côte Chalonnaise, including Chandesais, Delorme, and Faiveley. There is a good *coopérative* at Buxy, and an increasing number of talented growers. This area produces fine Crémant de Bourgogne and has the only single-village appellation of Aligoté wine.

FACTORS AFFECTING TASTE AND QUALITY

LOCATION
These three islands of vines are situated to the west of Châlon-sur-Saône, 350 km (217 miles) southeast of Paris, between the Côte de Beaune in the north and the Mâconnais in the south.

CLIMATE
Slightly dryer than that of the Côte d'Or, with many of the best slopes protected from the worst ravages of frost and hail.

ASPECT
This is a disjointed district in which the great plateau of the Côte d'Or peters out into a complex chain of small hills with vines clinging to the most favourable slopes, at an altitude of between 230 and 320 m (750–1,050 ft), in a far more sporadic fashion than those in the Côte d'Or.

SOIL
Limestone subsoil with clay-sand topsoils that are sometimes enriched with iron deposits. At Mercurey there are limestone ooliths mixed with iron-enriched marl.

VITICULTURE AND VINIFICATION
The wines are produced in an identical way to those of the Côte de Beaune, with no exceptional viticultural or vinification techniques involved, *see pp.32–35*.

PRIMARY GRAPE VARIETIES
Pinot noir, Chardonnay
SECONDARY GRAPE VARIETIES
Pinot gris (*syn.* Pinot beurot), Pinot liébault, Pinot blanc, Aligoté, Melon de Bourgogne, Gamay

THE CHANTE FLÛTÉ LABEL OF MERCUREY
Since 1972, the Confrérie St.-Vincent et des Disciples de la Chante Flûté de Mercurey has held annual tastings as the *Tastevinage* have done in the Côte de Nuits. Although the Mercurey AOC has a reputation for fine wines, these Chante Flûté wines are among the very best from the Côte Chalonnaise.

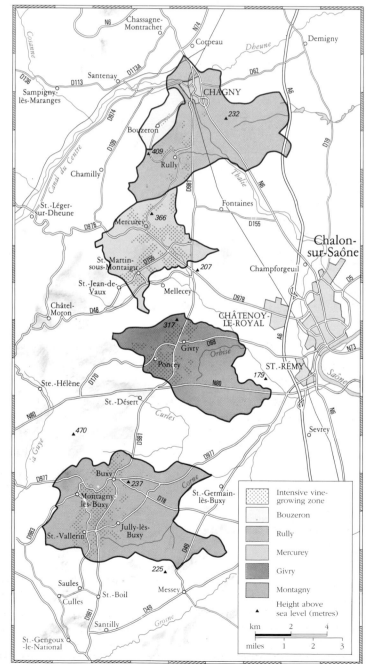

VINEYARD AND CHÂTEAU OF RULLY
With the most northerly AOC vineyards of the Côte Chalonnaise, Rully produces excellent dry Chardonnay wines and some pleasant red wines as well.

THE CÔTE CHALONNAISE, *see also* p.131
The vine-growing zones form three separate "islands" west of Chalon, between the Côte de Beaune to the north and the Mâconnais to the south.

THE APPELLATIONS OF
THE CÔTE CHALONNAISE

BOURGOGNE ALIGOTÉ BOUZERON AOC

In 1979 Bouzeron became the only *Cru* to have its own appellation specifically for the Aligoté grape and is shortly to be renamed Bouzeron AOC, with no mention of Aligoté, although the wines will still have to be 100 per cent Aligoté.

WHITE This excellent and interesting dry wine is much the fullest version of Aligoté available. In weight, fruit, and spice its style is nearer to Pinot gris than to Chardonnay.

🍇 Aligoté with up to 15% Chardonnay

🍷 2–6 years

✓ *Ancien Domaine Carnot (sold by Bouchard Père & Fils) • Domaine Chanzy Frères • André Delorme • A. & P. de Villaine*

BOURGOGNE CÔTE CHALONNAISE AOC

As from the 1990 vintage, basic Bourgogne made exclusively from grapes harvested in the region may be sold under this specific appellation.

✓ *René Bourgeon • Caves de Buxy • Émile Chandesais • André Delorme • Michel Derain • Michel Goubard • Guy Narjoux*

GIVRY AOC

Underrated wines from just south of Mercurey.

RED Light- to medium-bodied, soft, and fruity wine with delightful nuances of cherry and redcurrant.

🍇 Pinot noir, Pinot gris, Pinot liébault

🍷 5–12 years

WHITE Just ten per cent of Givry is white – a deliciously clean, dry Chardonnay that can have an attractive spicy-buttery hint on the aftertaste.

🍇 Chardonnay, Pinot blanc

🍷 3–8 years

✓ *René Bourgeon • Chofflet-Vaudenaire • Michel Derain • Mme du Jardin • Domaine Joblot • Maison Louis Latour • François Lumpp • Parize & Fils • Jean-Paul Ragot • R. Remoissenet & Fils • Baron Thénard*

GIVRY PREMIER CRU AOC

Premiers Crus: Clos de la Barraude, Les Berges, Bois Chevaux, Bois Gauthier, Clos de Cellier aux Moines, Clos Charlé, Clos du Cras Long, Les Grandes Vignes, Grand Prétants, Clos Jus, Clos Marceaux, Marole, Petit Marole, Petit Prétants, Clos St.-Paul, Clos St.-Pierre, Clos Salomon, Clos de la Servoisine, Vaux, Clos du Vernoy, En Vignes Rouge, Le Vigron.

RED Best examples are medium bodied, soft, rich, and fruity with delightful nuances of cherry and redcurrant.

🍇 Pinot noir, Pinot gris, Pinot liébault

🍷 5–12 years

WHITE Similar in character to Givry AOC, the deliciously clean, dry Chardonnay can have an attractive spicy-buttery hint on the aftertaste.

🍇 Chardonnay, Pinot blanc

🍷 3–8 years

✓ *René Bourgeon • Chofflet-Vaudenaire • Michel Derain • Mme du Jardin • Domaine Joblot • Maison Louis Latour • François Lumpp Parize & Fils • Jean-Paul Ragot • R. Remoissenet & Fils • Baron Thénard*

MERCUREY AOC

The wines of Mercurey, including the *Premiers Crus*, account for two-thirds of the production of the entire Côte Chalonnaise.

RED Medium-bodied wines with excellent colour and fine varietal character that have an exceptional quality-for-price ratio.

🍇 Pinot noir, Pinot gris, Pinot liébault

🍷 5–12 years

WHITE Dry wines that combine the lightness and freshness of the Mâconnais with some of the fat and butteriness of the Côte de Beaune.

🍇 Pinot chardonnay (*sic*)

🍷 3–8 years

✓ *Château de Chamilly • Château de Chamirey Émile Chandesais • Louis Desfontaine • Domaine Lorenzon • Antonin Rodet*

MERCUREY PREMIER CRU AOC

Premiers Crus: La Bondue, Les Byots, La Cailloute, Champs Martins, La Chassière, Le Clos, Clos des Barraults, Clos Château de Montaigu, Clos l'Evêque, Clos des Myglands, Clos du Roi, Clos Tonnerre, Clos Voyens (or Les Voyens), Les Combins, Les Crêts, Les Croichots, Les Fourneaux (or Clos des Fourneaux), Grand Clos Fortoul, Les Grands Voyens, Griffères, Le Levrière, Le Marcilly (or Clos Marcilly), La Mission, Les Montaigus (or Clos des Montaigus), Les Naugues, Les Petits Voyens, Les Ruelles, Sazenay, Les Vasées, Les Velley

During the last decade the *Premiers Crus* have increased in number from 5 to 27 and in area from 15 to over 100 hectares (37–250 acres).

RED These wines should have all the pure Pinot characteristics of basic Mercurey, but with added depth and more finesse.

🍇 Pinot noir, Pinot gris, Pinot liébault

🍷 5–15 years

WHITE I have encountered white Mercurey only at the basic village level.

✓ *Brintet • Émile Chandesais • Chartron et Trebuchet • Domaine Faiveley • Jeannin-Nastet • Domaine Émile Juillot • Michel Juillot • Domaine Lorenzon • Guy Narjoux • François Raquillet*

MONTAGNY AOC

As all the vineyards in this AOC are *Premiers Crus*, the only wines that appear under the basic village appellation are those that fail to meet the technical requirement of 11.5 per cent alcohol before chaptalization.

WHITE These dry white wines are good-value, fuller versions of the white Mâcon type.

🍇 Chardonnay

🍷 3–10 years

✓ *Domaine Maurice Bertrand & François Juillot • Caves de Buxy • Domaine Faiveley • Maison Louis Latour • Moillard • Antonin Rodet*

MONTAGNY PREMIER CRU AOC

Premiers Crus: Les Bassets, Les Beaux Champs, Les Bonnevaux, Les Bordes, Les Bouchots, Le Breuil, Les Burnins, Les Carlins, Les Champs-Toiseau, Les Charmelottes, Les Chandits, Les Chazelles, Clos Chaudron, Le Choux, Les Clouzeaux, Les Coères, Les Combes, La Condemine, Cornevent, La Corvée,

Les Coudrettes, Les Craboulettes, Les Crets, Creux des Beaux Champs, L'Epaule, Les Garchères, Les Gouresses, La Grand Pièce, Les Jardins, Les Las, Les Males, Les Marais, Les Marocs, Les Monts Cuchots, Le Mont Laurent, La Mouillère, Moulin l'Echenaud, Les Pandars, Les Pasquiers, Les Pidans, Les Platières, Les Resses, Les St.-Mortille, Les St.-Ytages, Sous les Roches, Les Thilles, La Tillonne, Les Treufferes, Les Varignys, Le Vieux Château, Vignes Blanches, Vignes sur le Clou, Les Vignes Couland, Les Vignes Derrière, Les Vignes Dessous, La Vigne Devant, Vignes Longues, Vignes du Puits, Les Vignes St-Pierre, Les Vignes du Soleil.

With every one of its 60 vineyards classified as *Premier Cru*, Montagny is unique among the villages of Burgundy.

WHITE These delicious dry wines have a Chardonnay flavour that is more akin to that of the Côte de Beaune than it is to Mâconnais.

🍇 Chardonnay

🍷 4–12 years

✓ *Stéphane Aladame • Arnoux Père & Fils • Caves de Buxy • Château de Davenay (blanc) • Domaine Maurice Bertrand & François Juillot • Château de la Saule • Jean Vachet*

RULLY AOC

The Côte Chalonnaise's northernmost appellation produces wines that are closest in character to those from the southern Côte de Beaune.

RED Delightfully fresh and fruity wines of light to medium body and some finesse, which are uncomplicated when young but develop well.

🍇 Pinot noir, Pinot gris, Pinot liébault

🍷 5–12 years

WHITE Serious dry wines that tend to have a crisper balance than wines made further south in Montagny, although a few can be quite fat.

🍇 Chardonnay

🍷 3–8 years

✓ *Émile Chandesais • Domaine Chanzy Frères • André Delorme • Joseph Drouhin • Raymond Dureuil-Janthial • Domaine de Folie • Henri-Paul Jacqueson • Domaine de la Renard • Antonin Rodet (Château de Rully)*

RULLY PREMIER CRU AOC

Premiers Crus: Agneux, Bas de Vauvry, La Bressaude, Champ-Clou, Chapitre, Clos du Chaigne, Clos St.-Jacques, Les Cloux (or Cloux), Ecloseaux, La Fosse, Grésigny, Margotey (or Margoté), Marissou, Meix-Caillet, Mont-Palais, Moulesne (or Molesme), Phillot, Les Pieres, Pillot, Préau, La Pucelle, Raboursay (or Rabourcé), Raclot, La Renarde, Vauvry.

RED Fine-quality, medium-bodied wines with a silky texture added to the summer-fruit flavour.

🍇 Pinot noir, Pinot gris, Pinot liébault

🍷 5–15 years

WHITE Generally finer, fuller, and richer dry wines, many with excellent finesse.

🍇 Chardonnay

🍷 4–12 years

✓ *Domaine Belleville • Jean-Claude Brelière • Michel Briday • Émile Chandesais • Chartron et Trebuchet • André Delorme • Domaine de Folie • Henri-Paul Jacqueson • Laborde-Juillot*

THE MÂCONNAIS

The Mâconnais produces three times more white wine than the rest of Burgundy put together and, although it never quite matches the heights of quality achieved in the Côte d'Or, it is easily the best-value pure Chardonnay wine in the world.

THE MÂCONNAIS IS AN ANCIENT viticultural area that was renowned as long as 1,600 years ago when Ausonius, the Roman poet of St.-Émilion, mentioned its wines. Today, it makes sense to couple it with the Beaujolais because, while Chardonnay is the dominant white grape in both districts (as it is in the rest of Burgundy), the Gamay is the dominant black grape, which it is not elsewhere; this forms a link between the two. The Mâconnais can be seen as essentially a white-wine producing area while the Beaujolais is almost entirely red.

MÂCON ROUGE – A RELIC OF THE PAST?

Although the Mâconnais is a white-wine district in essence, some 25 per cent of the vines planted here are in fact Gamay; and a further seven-and-a-half per cent are Pinot noir. The Gamay does not, however, perform very well in the limestone soils of the Mâconnais, and despite the smoothing effect of modern

FACTORS AFFECTING TASTE AND QUALITY

LOCATION
Situated halfway between Lyon and Beaune, the vineyards of the Mâconnais adjoin those of the Côte Chalonnaise to the north and overlap with those of Beaujolais to the south.

CLIMATE
The climate is similar to that of the Côte Chalonnaise, but with a Mediterranean influence gradually creeping in towards the south, so occasional storms are more likely.

ASPECT
The soft, rolling hills in the north of the Mâconnais, which are a continuation of those in the Côte Chalonnaise, give way to a more closely knit topography with steeper slopes and sharper contours becoming increasingly prominent as one travels further south into the area that overlaps the Beaujolais.

SOIL
The topsoil consists of scree and alluvium, or clay and clay-sand, and covers a limestone subsoil.

VITICULTURE AND VINIFICATION
Some exceptional wines (such as the "Vieilles Vignes" Château de Fuissé made in Pouilly Fuissé) can stand a very heavy oak influence, but most of the white wines are fermented in stainless steel and bottled very early to retain as much freshness as possible. The red wines are vinified by *macération carbonique*, either fully or in part.

PRIMARY GRAPE VARIETIES
Chardonnay, Gamay
SECONDARY GRAPE VARIETIES
Pinot noir, Pinot gris (*syn.* Pinot beurot), Pinot liébault, Pinot blanc, Aligoté, Melon de Bourgogne

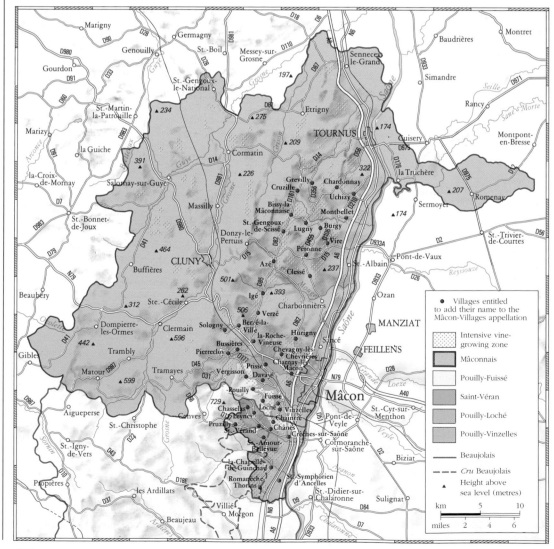

Villages entitled to add their name to the Mâcon-Villages appellation

Intensive vine-growing zone

Mâconnais

Pouilly-Fuissé

Saint-Véran

Pouilly-Loché

Pouilly-Vinzelles

Beaujolais

Cru Beaujolais

▲ Height above sea level (metres)

THE ROCK OF SOLUTRÉ
The dramatic shape of the Rock of Solutré towers over the village's vineyard. Solutré is one of the 42 villages of the Macon-Villages appelation, and a commune of Pouilly-Fuissé.

THE MÂCONNAIS
See also p.131
Concentrated to the west of the river Saône, the famous appellations of the Mâconnais interlace with those of Beaujolais to the south and spread out over the area northwest of Mâcon itself.

vinification techniques, these wines will always be of rustic quality with a characteristic hard edge. I well remember a particular blind tasting I once organized as editor of *The Sunday Telegraph Good Wine Guide*. All that the tasters knew about the wines was that they were produced from the Gamay grape and were thus most probably Beaujolais. British Master of Wine Christopher Tatham simply wrote "Limestone's the trouble!" against one wine. It turned out to be the only non-Beaujolais wine; it was Mâcon Rouge, which meant that limestone was indeed the problem. Such an accurate observation under blind conditions highlights how inappropriate the Gamay is in the Mâconnais.

It is possible to make a pure Pinot noir Mâcon *rouge*, but because the market assumes that this appellation is pure Gamay, there is little incentive for producers to plant the more noble grape. It is, however, far more suitable and capable of producing wines of some finesse in the limestone vineyards of the Mâconnais. Perhaps it is time to introduce a Mâcon Rouge Pinot Noir appellation, or maybe producers should print the grape variety boldly on the label of the existing appellation.

BERZÉ-LE-CHÂTEL, SAÔNE-ET-LOIRE, MÂCONNAIS
The massive fortifications of Berzé-le-Châtel, the seat of the first feudal barony of Mâcon, boasts 13 medieval towers.

THE APPELLATIONS OF
THE MÂCONNAIS

MÂCON AOC

Most wines from this district-wide appellation are produced in the area north of the Mâcon-Villages area.

RED Better vinification techniques have improved these essentially Gamay wines, but Gamay is still a grape that does not like limestone.

🍇 Gamay, Pinot noir, Pinot gris

🍷 2–6 years

WHITE These are basic-quality Chardonnay wines that are also fresh, frank, tasty, and dry; easy to quaff and superb value. They may be sold as *primeur* or *nouveau* from the third Thursday of November following the harvest.

🍇 Chardonnay, Pinot blanc

🍷 1–4 years

ROSÉ These lightweight wines have an attractive, pale raspberry colour and light fruit flavour, and are more successful than their counterparts. They may be sold as *primeur* or *nouveau* from the third Thursday of November after the harvest.

🍇 Gamay, Pinot noir, Pinot gris

🍷 1–3 years

✓ *Bénas Frères* • *E. Brocard* (rouge) • *Maison Desvignes* • *Domaine des Deux Roches* (Pierreclos rouge & Chavigne rouge) • *Maurice Gonon* (rouge) • *Jean Thévenet* (Clessé rouge Cuvée Botrytis) • *Henri Lafarge* (Braye rouge) • *Domaine Saumaize-Michelin* (Les Bruyères rouge)

MÂCON SUPÉRIEUR AOC

All of France's so-called "*Supérieur*" appellations merely demand extra alcohol (usually one degree more than the basic appellation), which does not necessarily make a superior wine.

RED Apart from those listed, these well-coloured, medium-bodied wines are nothing special.

🍇 Gamay, Pinot noir, Pinot gris

🍷 3–8 years

WHITE It is curious that almost a quarter of Mâcon Supérieur is white. The wines could just as easily sell as Mâcon AOC plain and simple. These wines may be sold as *primeur* or

nouveau from the third Thursday of November following the harvest.

🍇 Chardonnay, Pinot blanc

🍷 1–4 years

ROSÉ These are attractively coloured wines with a fresh and tasty fruit flavour.

🍇 Gamay, Pinot noir, Pinot gris

🍷 1–2 years

✓ *Collin & Bourisset* • *Henri Lafarge* • *Eugène Lebreton* • *Pierre Santé* • *Jean Signoret* • *Jean-Claude Thévenet*

MÂCON-SUPÉRIEUR (VILLAGE NAME) AOC

See Mâcon (village name) AOC

MÂCON-VILLAGES AOC

This white-only appellation covers 42 villages, eight of which also fall within the Beaujolais-Villages appellation (*see* p.160); four of these have the additional right to the St.-Véran AOC (*see* p.157). If the wine comes from a single village, it may replace the "Villages" part of this appellation with the name of that specific village (*see* the list below for details of all 42 villages).

WHITE These are some of the world's most delicious, thirst-quenching, easy-drinking, dry Chardonnay wines. They also represent tremendous value. These wines may be sold as *primeur* or *nouveau* commencing from the third Thursday of November following the harvest.

🍇 Chardonnay, Pinot blanc

🍷 1–4 years

✓ *André Bonhomme* • *Carpi-Gobet* (Château London) • *Domaine des Chazelles* • *Domaine Cordier* • *Domaine Corsin* • *Domaine des Deux Roches* • *Domaine des Granges* • *Domaine Guffens-Heynen* • *Domaine Jean Manciat* • *René Michel & Fils* • *Mommessin* • *Groupement de Producteurs de Prissé* • *Claudius Rongier* • *Cellier des Samsons*

THE 42 VILLAGES OF MÂCON-VILLAGES

The single-village version of Mâcon-Villages AOC covers the white wines from 42 villages:

MÂCON-AZÉ AOC

This village has a good *coopérative*, and its wines a reputation for fatness and consistency.

✓ *Georges Blanc* (Domaine d'Azenay) • *Domaine des Grand Bruyères* • *Duvergey-Taboureau* (Domaine de la Garonne)

MÂCON-BERZÉ-LE-VILLE AOC

I have not encountered these wines.

MÂCON-BISSY-LA-MÂCONNAISE AOC

I have not encountered these wines.

MÂCON-BURGY AOC

I have very rarely encountered these wines, but elegant examples from Domaine de Chervin demonstrate its potential.

✓ *Domaine de Chervin*

MÂCON-BUSIÈRES AOC

Rarely encountered.

✓ *Domaine du Terroir de Jocelyn*

MÂCON-CHAINTRE AOC

Chaintre is home to Georges Duboeuf's older brother, Roger. Since this village is one of five that form the appellation of Pouilly-Fuissé, its wines are entitled to two appellations.

✓ *Cave Coopérative de Chaintre* • *Roger Duboeuf* • *Domaine des Granges* • *Domaine Valette*

MÂCON-CHÂNES AOC

This village is also part of the Beaujolais-Villages and St.-Véran areas, so its wines have a choice of three appellations.

MÂCON-LA CHAPELLE-DE-GUINCHAY AOC

This village is also part of the Beaujolais-Villages area and its wines therefore have the right to both appellations.

MÂCON-CHARDONNAY AOC

These wines have a certain following due in part, no doubt, to the novelty of their name. The *coopérative*, however, produces fine wines.

✓ *Cave Coopérative de Chardonnay* (only Cuvée du Millénaire, which is from old vines and may be sold as Château du Chardonnay)

MÂCON-CHARNAY-LÈS-MÂCON AOC

Excellent wines produced east of Pouilly-Fuissé.

✓ *E. Chevalier & Fils • Domaine Jean Manciat • Domaine Manciat-Poncet*

MÂCON-CHASSELAS AOC

Unfortunately, Chasselas is also the name of a table grape known for producing inferior wines. The growers here usually sell their wines as basic Mâcon or as St.-Véran.

MÂCON-CHEVAGNY-LÈS-CHEVRIÈRES AOC

Reasonable wines, but not easy to find.

✓ *Groupement de Producteurs de Prissé*

MÂCON-CLESSÉ AOC

This appellation is due to lapse as of 2002. See Viré-Clessé AOC.

✓ *Domaine Guillemot-Michel • René Michel • Gilbert Mornand • Claudius Rongier • Jean Signoret • Jean Thévenet* (Domaine de la Bongran and Domaine Émélian Gillet)

MÂCON-CRÈCHES-SUR-SAÔNE AOC

I have not encountered these wines.

MÂCON-CRUZILLE AOC

These are rare wines from a tiny hamlet in the extreme north of the *villages* appellation area.

✓ *Demessy* (Château de Messy) *• Guillot-Broux*

MÂCON-DAVAYÉ AOC

Some excellent wines are made here, although they are usually sold as St.-Véran AOC.

✓ *Domaine des Deux Roches • Lycée Viticole de Davayé*

MÂCON-FUISSÉ AOC

This village is one of five communes that form Pouilly-Fuissé AOC. You might think it foolish to sell a wine as Mâcon-Fuissé AOC rather than Pouilly-Fuissé AOC, but I have found four very worthwhile cases that do just that.

✓ *Domaine Cordier • Domaine Defussiacus • Le Moulin du Pont • Domaine la Soufrandise • Jean-Paul Thibert*

MÂCON-GRÉVILLY AOC

A village with a good reputation, Mâcon-Grévilly is located in the extreme north of the *villages* appellation area.

✓ *Guillot-Broux*

MÂCON-HURIGNY AOC

I have not encountered these wines.

MÂCON-IGÉ AOC

The wines from this village are not very often seen, but have a good reputation.

✓ *Les Vignerons d'Igé*

MÂCON-LEYNES AOC

This village is also part of the Beaujolais-Villages and St.-Véran AOCs and its wines therefore have a choice of all three appellations.

✓ *André Depardon*

MÂCON-LOCHÉ AOC

This village also has the right to the Pouilly-Loché and Pouilly-Vinzelles AOCs and its wines therefore have a choice of all three appellations.

✓ *Caves des Crus Blancs • Château de Loché*

MÂCON-LUGNY AOC

Louis Latour has done much to promote the wines of this village.

✓ *Louis Latour • Cave de Lugny • Domaine du Prieuré*

MÂCON-MILLY-LAMARTINE AOC

I have not encountered these wines.

MÂCON-MONTBELLET AOC

Rarely encountered wines that develop well after a couple of years in bottle.

✓ *Henri Goyard* (Domaine de Roally)

MÂCON-PÉRONNE AOC

These wines seem to be fuller on the nose and stronger on the palate than those of most villages, but with less charm, although their producers say this is because they take longer than most Mâcon to "come around".

✓ *Maurice Josserand • Domaine des Légères • Cave de Lugny • Domaine du Mortier • Daniel Rousset*

MÂCON-PIERRECLOS AOC

Domaine Guffens-Heynen is by far the best producer here.

✓ *Domaine Guffens-Heynen • Henri de Villamont*

MÂCON-PRISSÉ AOC

This village is also part of the St.-Véran area and its wines therefore have a choice of two appellations.

✓ *Groupement de Producteurs de Prissé • Domaine de Thibert Père & Fils*

MÂCON-PRUZILLY AOC

This village is situated in the Beaujolais-Villages area and its wines therefore have a choice of two appellations.

MÂCON-LA ROCHE VINEUSE AOC

These underrated wines of Mâcon-La Roche Vineuse are produced on west- and south-facing slopes north of Pouilly-Fuissé, the potential of which is pushed to the very limits by Oliver Merlin, one of Mâcon's greatest winemakers.

✓ *Olivier Merlin • Groupement de Producteurs de Prissé*

MÂCON-ROMANÈCHE-THORINS AOC

The village of Mâcon-Romanèche-Thorins is also part of the Beaujolais-Villages area, so its wines have a choice of two appellations. Most of its production is red.

MÂCON-ST.-AMOUR-BELLEVUE AOC

Mâcon-St.-Amour Bellevue is a village famous for its *Cru* Beaujolais St.-Amour and also forms part of the Beaujolais-Villages and St.-Véran areas. Some of its vineyards therefore have a choice of four appellations and this one is the least appealing.

MÂCON-ST.-GENGOUX-DE-SCISSÉ AOC

I have not encountered these wines.

MÂCON-ST.-SYMPHORIEN-D'ANCELLES AOC

As Mâcon-St.-Symphorien-d'Ancelles is also part of the Beaujolais-Villages area, its wines therefore have the advantage of a choice between two appellations.

MÂCON-ST.-VÉRAND AOC

This village is in an area that is also part of the Beaujolais-Villages and the similarly spelled St.-Véran areas and its wines therefore have a choice of all three appellations.

MÂCON-SOLOGNY AOC

The village of Mâcon-Sologny lies just north of Pouilly-Fuissé AOC and produces a fresh, crisp, herbaceous wine.

✓ *Ets Bertrand • Cave de Sologny*

MÂCON-SOLUTRÉ AOC

This village is one of the five communes of Pouilly-Fuissé and also forms part of the St.-Véran area. Its wines therefore have a choice of three appellations.

✓ *André Depardon • Jean-Michel & Béatrice Drouhin • Chantal & Dominique Vaupré*

MÂCON-UCHIZY AOC

More commonly seen than a few years ago, the wines from this village, which is adjacent to Chardonnay, are usually of a good, thirst-quenching quality.

✓ *Domaine Raphaël Sallet* (also sold as R. & G. Sallet) *• Paul & Philebert Talmard*

MÂCON-VERGISSON AOC

This village of Mâcon-Vergisson is one of five communes that form the Pouilly-Fuissé AOC. Its wines are richer than most, and can be aged a few years in bottle.

✓ *Daniel Barraut • Michel Forest*

MÂCON-VERZÉ AOC

Rarely encountered.

✓ *Domaine du Clos Gandin*

MÂCON-VINZELLES AOC

This village also has the right to Pouilly-Vinzelles AOC and its wines therefore have a choice of two appellations.

✓ *Caves des Crus Blancs*

MÂCON-VIRÉ AOC

This appellation is due to lapse as of 2002. See Viré-Clessé AOC.

✓ *André Bonhomme • Jean-Noël Chaland • Domaine des Chazelles • Domaine Guillemot-Michel Henri Goyard* (Domaine de Roally) *• Jean Thévenet* (Domaine de

la Bongran and Domaine Émélian Gillet)
• *Cave Coopérative de Viré*

MÂCON (VILLAGE NAME) AOC

This appellation differs from the Mâcon-Villages AOC above (which may attach a village name and has to be white) in that it covers a slightly different range of villages, the names of which must (rather than may) be indicated on the label, and it applies only to red and rosé wines. Fewer villages use this appellation, but Mâcon-Bissy, Mâcon-Braye, Mâcon-Davayé, and Mâcon-Pierreclos are the most common of those villages that do.

RED There is some indication that a few villages (or more accurately, individual growers with isolated plots of vines growing in favourable soils within a few villages) can make better-balanced wines than the Gamay has hitherto been expected to produce in Mâcon.

🍇 Gamay, Pinot noir, Pinot gris

WHITE These wines may be sold as *primeur* or *nouveau* from the third Thursday of November following the harvest.

🍇 Chardonnay

🍷 1–4 years

ROSÉ I have not encountered these wines.

🍇 Gamay, Pinot noir, Pinot gris

✓ *Pierre Mahuet* • *Domaine du Prieuré*
  • *Jean-Claude Thevenet*

PINOT CHARDONNAY-MÂCON AOC

This is an alternative appellation for white Mâcon. *See* Mâcon AOC.

POUILLY-FUISSÉ AOC

This pure Chardonnay wine should not be confused with Pouilly-Fumé, the Sauvignon Blanc wine from the Loire. This appellation covers a wide area of prime vineyards, but there is considerable variation.

WHITE These dry wines range from typical Mâcon *blanc* style, through slightly firmer versions, to the power-packed, rich oaky flavours of Michel Forrest and Vincent's Château Fuissé "Vieilles Vignes". Although these last two are widely regarded as the finest in Pouilly-Fuissé, they are by no means typical of Mâcon, leaning more towards the Côte Chalonnaise, sometimes even the Côte de Beaune, and ardent admirers of the more traditional, light, and fluffy Mâcon will not even touch them. On the other hand wines from producers such as Guffens-Heynen can be just as rich and intense as either Forest or Château Fuissé, but without any oak whatsoever.

🍇 Chardonnay

🍷 3–8 years

✓ *Auvigne* (also sold as Burrier Revel & Cie)
  • *Daniel Barraud* • *Domaine Cordier*
  • *Domaine Corsin* • *Jean-Michel & Béatrice Drouhin* • *Georges Duboeuf* (Fût de Chêne)
  • *Domaine J. A. Ferret* • *Michel Forest*
  • *Michel Galley-Golliard* • *Domaine Guffens-Heynen* • *Roger Lassarat*
  • *Domaine Manciat-Poncet* • *Olivier Merlin*
  • *Domaine René Perraton* • *Groupement de Producteurs de Prissé* • *Domaine Pascal Renaud* • *Domaine Robert-Denogent*
  • *Château des Rontets* • *Jacques & Nathalie Saumaize* • *Domaine Saumaize-Michelin*
  • *Domaine de la Soufrandise* • *Domaine Valette* • *Verget* • *Vincent & Fils* (Château de Fuissé Vieilles Vignes)

POUILLY-LOCHÉ AOC

One of Pouilly-Fuissé's two satellite appellations.

WHITE This village may produce Mâcon-Loché AOC, Pouilly-Loché AOC, or Pouilly-Vinzelles AOC. The dry wines of this village are more of the Mâcon style, whatever the AOC.

🍇 Chardonnay

🍷 1–4 years

✓ *Caves des Crus Blancs* • *Domaine des Duc*
  • *Gilles Noblet* • *Domaine René Perraton*
  • *Domaine Saumaize-Michelin*
  • *Domaine St.-Philbert*

POUILLY-VINZELLES AOC

One of Pouilly-Fuissé's two satellite appellations.

WHITE More the Mâcon-type of Pouilly-Fuissé, for similar reasons to those of Pouilly-Loché.

🍇 Chardonnay

🍷 1–4 years

✓ *Caves des Crus Blancs* • *Domaine René Perraton* • *Jean-Jacques Martin*
  • *Jean-Paul Thibert* • *Château de Vinzelles*

ST.-VÉRAN AOC

This appellation overlaps the Mâconnais and Beaujolais districts, and is itself bisected by the Pouilly-Fuissé AOC, with two villages to the north (Davayé and Prissé) and five to the south (Chânes, Chasselas, Leynes, St.-Amour, and St.-Vérand). St.-Véran was named after St.-Vérand, but the "d" was dropped in deference to the growers in certain other villages, who it was feared would not support the new appellation if they felt their wines were being sold under the name of another village. This appellation was introduced in 1971 to provide a more suitable outlet for white wines produced in Beaujolais than the Beaujolais *blanc* appellation.

WHITE Excellent value, fresh, dry, and fruity Chardonnay wines that are very much in the Mâcon-Villages style. Vincent, the proprietor of Château Fuissé, produces an amazingly rich

wine that is far closer to Pouilly-Fuissé than to Macon-Villages, with hints of oak and honey.

🍇 Chardonnay

🍷 1–4 years

✓ *Auvigne* (also sold as Burrier Revel & Cie)
  Domaine Corsin • *Domaine des Deux Roches* • *Antoine Depagneux* • *Jean-Michel & Béatrice Drouhin* • *Duboeuf*
  • *Roger Lassarat* • *Domaine Jean Manciat*
  • *Jean-Jacques Martin* • *Olivier Merlin*
  • *Groupement de Producteurs de Prissé*
  • *Jacques & Nathalie Saumaize* (Vieilles Vignes) • *Domaine Saumaize-Michelin*
  • *Verget* • *Vincent & Fils*

VIRÉ-CLESSÉ AOC

This new appellation was created in November 1998, but effectively backdated to include the vintage of that year. It was formed by combining the Mâcon-Viré and Mâcon-Clessé sub-appellations, and recognising the wines from Viré-Clessé in their own right, above and beyond Mâcon-Villages. Viré was always the most ubiquitous of the Mâcon-Villages wines, but it was also the most consistent and one of the best, while Clessé showed the most finesse, thus it will be interesting to see how the reputation of this new appellation develops. However, if it is to stand alone, the wines should be subject to stricter yields, as the wines produced in the various Pouilly appellations do. It should be noted that some growers (notably Jean Thévenet) have vowed not to use this umbrella appellation.

🍇 Chardonnay

🍷 1–4 years

✓ All those recommended under Mâcon-Viré and Mâcon-Clessé are potential recommendations here, but those that have actually excelled are: *André Bonhomme*
  • *Domaine Philippe* • *Maison Rickaert*
  • *Cave Coopérative de Viré*

VILLAGE OF FUISSÉ SURROUNDED BY ITS VINEYARDS
*Fuissé, which dates back to Neanderthal settlements, sits
at the centre of an amphitheatre of vineyards.*

THE BEAUJOLAIS

This huge district is famous for producing the only Gamay wine to gain classic status – a purple-coloured, fresh, light, and quaffing wine that accounts for no less than six out of every ten bottles of Burgundy produced each year.

THE BEST PRODUCERS in the ten *Crus* Beaujolais make a Gamay wine that truly deserves its classic status. Basic Beaujolais, however, should be simply fresh, purple-coloured, juicy-fruity wine. The problem is that most Beaujolais falls short of even these basic standards: the majority of it, including bad *Cru* Beaujolais, smells of bubble-gum or bananas and tastes of pear-drops. The trade calls it "lollipop" wine and it is ideal for anyone who does not actually enjoy the characteristics of real wine. The factors that make most Beaujolais the lollipop wine it is are the method of vinification and the sheer volume of production – the grape variety has nothing to do with it. A massive amount

HARVESTING IN FLEURIE
To encourage semi-carbonic maceration, the Gamay grapes must arrive at the cuverie in whole bunches, on their stalks, and as uncrushed as possible.

of Beaujolais is produced each year: two-and-a-half times the entire red- and white-wine production of the rest of Burgundy put together! More than half is sold only a few weeks after the harvest as Beaujolais Nouveau or Primeur and all of this, plus a great chunk of Beaujolais, Beaujolais Supérieur, and Beaujolais-Villages, not to mention rip-off *Cru* Beaujolais, is made by semi-carbonic maceration (a variant of *macération carbonique, see* p.36), which creates a preponderance of the same chemical compounds (amyl-acetate and ethyl-acetate) that give bubble-gum, banana, and pear-drops their trademark aroma. This process also creates the pungent aroma of nail-varnish, of which some of the worst Beaujolais Nouveau can smell, although I hasten to add that it is not harmful. The amount of antipathy, even in Burgundy,

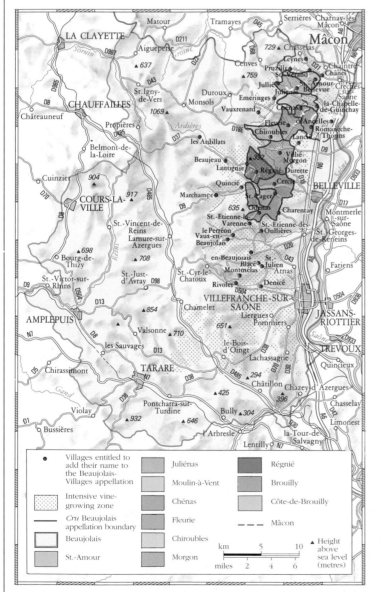

THE BEAUJOLAIS, *see also* p.131
Forming the southernmost part of the Burgundy region, the Beaujolais area is planted almost entirely with Gamay vines, the best vineyards being on granite soil.

Map legend:
- Villages entitled to add their name to the Beaujolais-Villages appellation
- Intensive vine-growing zone
- *Cru* Beaujolais appellation boundary
- Beaujolais
- St.-Amour
- Juliénas
- Moulin-à-Vent
- Chénas
- Fleurie
- Chiroubles
- Morgon
- Régnié
- Brouilly
- Côte-de-Brouilly
- Mâcon
- ▲ Height above sea level (metres)

FACTORS AFFECTING TASTE AND QUALITY

LOCATION
Beaujolais, the most southerly of Burgundy's districts, is located in the Rhône *département*, 400 km (250 miles) southeast of Paris.

CLIMATE
Beaujolais has an essentially sunny climate tempered by the Atlantic and Mediterranean, as well as by continental influences. Although the annual rainfall and temperature averages are ideal for winegrowing, they are subject to sudden stormy changes due to the influence of the Mediterranean.

ASPECT
A hilly district where vines grow at between 150 and 550 m (500–2,000 ft) on slopes facing all points of the compass.

SOIL
The northern Beaujolais, which encompasses the famous *crus* and those communes entitled to the Beaujolais-Villages AOC, is an area renowned for its granite-based soil, the only type on which the Gamay has so far excelled. The topsoils are often schistous or comprised of decomposed granite mixed with sand and clay.

The southern section is essentially limestone-based and this is a problem for the Gamay grape, which accordingly produces much lighter wines, which lack the class of those in the north.

VITICULTURE AND VINIFICATION
The vines are trained and pruned to the Gobelet system (*see* p.24), which gives them a totally different appearance from those in the rest of Burgundy. Grapes are hand-harvested and undergo whole-bunch fermentation by carbonic semi-maceration, which encourages the accumulation of carbon dioxide in the top half of the vat, although *Crus* Beaujolais wines are more traditionally produced, have greater skin contact (averaging seven days as opposed to just two days for Beaujolais Nouveau), and may even be matured with some new oak.

PRIMARY GRAPE VARIETIES
Gamay
SECONDARY GRAPE VARIETIES
Chardonnay, Pinot noir, Pinot gris (*syn.* Pinot beurot), Pinot liébault, Pinot blanc, Aligoté, Melon de Bourgogne

BARRELS AND FLOWERS AT ST.-AMOUR, BEAUJOLAIS
Just five Crus *Beaujolais were originally classified in 1936 (Chénas,
Chiroubles, Fleurie, Morgon, and Moulin-à-Vent), a further three (Brouilly,
Côte de Brouilly, and Juliénas) in 1938, while St.-Amour became
the ninth* Cru *in 1946 and Régnié the tenth in 1988.*

to this style of Gamay is revealed by Anthony Hanson, who,
in his book *Burgundy*, quotes Jean-Marie Guffens describing
the fermentation method used in much Beaujolais as "carbonic
masturbation". The profit generated by Beaujolais Nouveau is
considerable, but the wine itself should not be taken too seriously.
No producer of Beaujolais Nouveau claims it is a fine wine.
Such a claim would destroy the carefully marketed image of a
young, unpretentious wine intended to be consumed in copious
quantities. Beaujolais Nouveau should be fun and used to promote
a greater awareness of wine *per se*, just as Liebfraumilch can
attract new wine drinkers, but readers should be aware that these
"lollipop" wines are not good-quality Gamay, whereas the best
Cru Beaujolais are the world's greatest Gamay wines.

THE LEGEND OF "PISSE VIEILLE"

The vineyard of "Pisse Vieille" in Brouilly amuses English-speaking
consumers, who are dismayed by those writers who dare only to
print the vineyard's story in French. It goes like this:

One day, an old woman called Mariette went to confession.
The priest was new to the village and unaware of its dialect. He also
did not know that Mariette was hard of hearing. When he heard her
confession, he merely said *"Allez! Et ne péchez plus!"* ("Go! And do
not sin again!"). Mariette misheard this as *"Allez! Et ne piché plus"*,
which in the dialect meant "Go! And do not piss again", *piché* being
the local form of *pisser*. Being a devout Catholic, Mariette did
exactly as she was told. When her husband asked what terrible sin
she had committed she refused to tell and, after several days, he
went to ask the new priest. When he found out the truth he hurried
home, and as soon as he was within shouting distance, began
yelling *"Pisse, vieille!"* ("Piss, old woman!").

THE APPELLATIONS OF
THE BEAUJOLAIS

BEAUJOLAIS AOC

This generic Beaujolais appellation accounts
for half the wine produced in the district and
more than half of this is sold as Beaujolais
"Primeur". The basic quality of these wines
means that they cannot be bought from the
great *négociants* of the Côte d'Or, although
Crus Beaujolais can be.

RED Due to their method of vinification, most
of these wines have a "pear-drop" character to
their fruitiness. The best also have a delightful
freshness and frankness that beg for the wine
to be consumed in large draughts.

🍇 Gamay, Pinot noir, Pinot gris
🍷 1–3 years

WHITE Less than half of one per cent of the
production of this basic appellation consists
of dry white wine, and the specialist producers
of this usually make very fine wines. Pierre
Charmet's Beaujolais *blanc* is aromatic
and peachy.

🍇 Chardonnay, Aligoté
🍷 1–3 years

ROSÉ Fresh, "pretty", and fruity.

🍇 Gamay, Pinot noir, Pinot gris
🍷 1–3 years

✓ *Charles & Christine Brechard*
• *Cave Beaujolais du Bois-d'Oingt* (rosé)
• *Cave Coopérative Beaujolaise de Saint-
Vérand* • *Blaise Carron* • *Pierre Carron*
(blanc) • *Vignoble Charmet* • *Domaine
Pierre-Marie Chermette* • *Jean Garlon*
• *Domaine des Granges* (blanc) • *Pierre
Jomard* • *Domaine du Plateau de Bel-Air*
• *Domaine des Terres Dorées*

BEAUJOLAIS NOUVEAU AOC
See Beaujolais Primeur AOC

BEAUJOLAIS PRIMEUR AOC

More than half of all the Beaujolais produced
is sold as *vin de primeur*, a wine made by
intensive semi-carbonic maceration methods
that enable it to be consumed in export markets
from the third Thursday of each November.
"Beaujolais Nouveau" is synonymous with
"Beaujolais Primeur" and the former is the
name more often seen on export market labels,
while the latter is more popular on the French
market itself. Beaujolais Nouveau is supposed
to be a fun wine, but the merrymaking wears
a bit thin when it smells like nail-varnish and
tastes of bubble-gum. What else can you
expect from something that was swinging from
the vine just a few weeks before? "Lollipop"
wine is how it's known in the trade. If you
want real Beaujolais and great Gamay, then
try any of the wines recommended under
any of the other appellations.

BEAUJOLAIS SUPÉRIEUR AOC

Only one per cent of all Beaujolais wines
carry this appellation. It is very rare to find a
Beaujolais Supérieur that is superior in anything
other than strength to basic Beaujolais AOC,
since this appellation merely indicates that the
wines contain an extra one per cent alcohol.
Red and rosé Beaujolais Supérieur may be
sold as *primeur* or *nouveau* from the third
Thursday of November following the harvest.

RED By no means superior to Beaujolais AOC
– buy basic Beaujolais for fun or *Cru* Beaujolais
for more serious drinking.

🍇 Gamay, Pinot noir, Pinot gris

🍷 3–8 years

WHITE Barely five per cent of this tiny
appellation produces white wine. Fine as it
may be, it has no intrinsic superiority over the
quaffing quality of basic Beaujolais *blanc.*

🍇 Chardonnay, Aligoté

🍷 1–3 years

ROSÉ I have not encountered any pink versions
of this appellation.

✓ *Cave Beaujolais du Bois-d'Oingt • Cave
Coopérative Beaujolaise de Saint-Vérand
• Thierry Doat*

BEAUJOLAIS (VILLAGE NAME) AOC

Of the 38 villages that may add their names
to this appellation, very few do. One reason is
that all or part of 15 of these villages (asterisked
below) qualify for one of the superior *Cru*
Beaujolais appellations and it makes no sense
to use a less famous name to market the wines.
Another is that eight of the villages are entitled
to the Mâcon-Villages AOC (marked "M") and
four of these are also within the St.-Véran AOC
(*see also* p.157), marked "S-V", which overlaps
with Mâconnais and Beaujolais; some of these
villages, of course, produce more white wine
than red. These village names are also under-
exploited because, apart from a few that are
famous (the best wines of which will claim *Cru*
Beaujolais status), the rest are either unknown
or more suggestive of Mâcon than Beaujolais,
thus it is easier to sell them as nothing more
specific than Beaujolais-Villages. The wines may
be sold as *primeur* or *nouveau* from the third
Thursday of November following the harvest.

The following is a complete list of villages
that may use the appellation: Arbuisonnas;
Les Ardillats; Beaujeu; Blacé; Cercié (*);
Chânes (M, S-V); La Chapelle-de-Guinchay
(M, *); Charentay; Chénas; Chiroubles (*);
Denicé; Durette; Emeringes (*); Fleurie (*);
Jullié (*); Juliénas (*); Lancié; Lantignié; Leynes
(M, S-V); Marchampt; Montmelas; Odenas; Le
Perréon; Pruzilly (M, *); Quincié (*); Régnié (*);
Rivolet; Romanèche-Thorins (M, *); St.-Amour-
Bellevue (M, S-V, *); St.-Étienne-des-Ouillères;
St.-Étienne-la Varenne (*); St.-Julien; St.-Lager;
St.-Symphorien-d'Ancelles (M); St.-Vérand (M,
S-V); Salles; Vaux; Vauxrenard; Villié-Morgon (*)

RED When you find good examples, they should
be richly flavoured Gamay wines that are similar
in quality to non-specific Beaujolais-Villages, but
with more personality.

🍇 Gamay, Pinot noir, Pinot gris

🍷 3–8 years

WHITE I have rarely encountered these wines.

🍇 Chardonnay, Aligoté

🍷 1–3 years

ROSÉ I have rarely encountered these wines.

🍇 Gamay, Pinot noir, Pinot gris

🍷 1–3 years

✓ *Jean Bererd* (Le Perréon) • *Jean Berthelot*
(Quincié) • *Domaine de Granite Bleu*
(Perréon) • *Bruno Jambon* (Laitigne)
• *Claude & Michelle Joubert*
• *Bernard Nesmé* (Laitigne)

BEAUJOLAIS-VILLAGES AOC

The 38 villages that may add their names to the
Beaujolais AOC (*see* Beaujolais [village name]
AOC) also have the right to this appellation
and must use it if the wine is a blend of wines
from two or more villages.

RED If you find a good example, these wines
are well coloured with a rich Gamay flavour
and should have all the superiority that
Beaujolais Supérieur wines mysteriously lack.

🍇 Gamay, Pinot noir, Pinot gris

🍷 3–8 years

WHITE Very little encountered, but more
Villages *blanc* is produced than Beaujolais
blanc. These wines may be sold as *primeur*
or *nouveau* from the third Thursday of
November following the harvest.

🍇 Chardonnay, Aligoté

🍷 1–3 years

ROSÉ Seldom encountered, but the Cave
Beaujolais du Bois-d'Oingt makes an attractive
wine. These wines may be sold as *primeur*
or *nouveau* from the third Thursday of
November following the harvest.

🍇 Gamay, Pinot noir, Pinot gris

🍷 1–3 years

✓ *Domaine Auccoeur Noël • Domaine Berrod*
• *Cave Beaujolais du Bois-d'Oingt • Geny
de Flammerécourt • Evelyne & Claude
Geoffray • Château de Grand Vernay*
• *Château des Jacques • Jacky Janodet*
• *Méziat Père & Fils • Alain Passot*
• *Jean-Charles Pivot • Gilles Roux*
• *Château Thivin • Frédéric Trichard*
• *La Maison des Vignerons*

BROUILLY AOC
Cru Beaujolais

The largest and most southerly of the ten *Crus*
villages, this is the only one, with Côte de
Brouilly, to permit grapes other than Gamay.

RED Most Brouilly are serious wines, even if
they do not rank among the best *Crus* Beaujolais.
They are not quite as intense as Côte de

Brouilly wines, but they are full, fruity, and
supple, if a little earthy. They should be rich
and can be quite tannic.

🍇 Gamay, Chardonnay, Aligoté,
Melon de Bourgogne

🍷 2–7 years (4–12 years for *vin de garde*
styles produced in the very best vintages)

✓ *Domaine des Coteaux de Vuril • Domaine
H. & P. Dubost* (Vieilles Vignes) • *Henry
Fessy* (Cuvée Pur Sang de Bel Air)
• *Domaine Lafond • André Large • Jean
Lathuilière • Alain Marchaud • Château de
Nervers • Domaine du Plateau de Bel-Air*
• *Château Thivin*

CHÉNAS AOC
Cru Beaujolais

The smallest of the *Crus* Beaujolais, situated on
the slopes above Moulin-à-Vent. These slopes
used to be occupied by oak trees, and so its
name derives from *chêne*, the French for oak.

RED Although most Chénas cannot match the
power of the wines from neighbouring Moulin-
à-Vent, they are nevertheless in the full and
generous mould, and wines made by gifted
growers such as Jean Benon and Domaine
Champagnon are seductively rich and powerful,
the former oaked, the latter not.

🍇 Gamay

🍷 3–8 years (5–15 years for *vin de garde*
styles produced in the very best vintages)

✓ *Jean Benon • Château de Chénas*
• *Domaine des Duc • Bernard Santé*
• *Domaine Champagnon • Hubert Lapierre*
• *Henri Lespinasse • Georges Trichard*
• *Jacques Trichard*

CHIROUBLES AOC
Cru Beaujolais

Situated high in the hills above the Beaujolais
plain, the terrace of Chiroubles produces the
most fragrant of all the *Crus* Beaujolais.

RED These light-bodied wines have a
perfumed bouquet and a deliciously delicate,
crushed-grape flavour. They are charming to
drink when young, but exceptional examples
can improve with age.

🍇 Gamay

🍷 1–8 years (5–15 years for *vin de garde*
styles produced in the very best vintages)

✓ *Domaine Émile Cheysson • Domaine André
Métrat • Alain Passot • Domaine de la
Source • La Maison des Vignerons*

CÔTE DE BROUILLY AOC
Cru Beaujolais

If there were such things as *Grands Crus* in Beaujolais, Côte de Brouilly would undoubtedly be classified as the *Grand Cru* of Brouilly (the vineyards of which practically surround those of this appellation).

RED A fine Côte de Brouilly is full, rich, and flavoursome. Its fruit should be vivid and intense, with none of the earthiness that may be found in a Brouilly.

🍇 Gamay, Pinot noir, Pinot gris

🍷 3–8 years (5–15 years for *vin de garde* styles produced in the very best vintages)

☑ *Château du Grand Vernay • André Large • Château Thivin* (La Chapelle) *• Domaine de la Voûte des Crozes*

COTEAUX DU LYONNAIS AOC

This is not part of the true Beaujolais district, but it falls within its sphere of influence and certainly utilizes classic Beaujolais grapes. In May 1984, this wine was upgraded from VDQS to full AOC status.

RED Light-bodied wines with fresh Gamay fruit and a soft balance. These wines may be sold as *primeur* or *nouveau* from the third Thursday of November following the harvest.

🍇 Gamay

🍷 2–5 years

WHITE Fresh and dry Chardonnay wine that is softer than a Mâcon and lacks the definition of a Beaujolais *blanc*. These wines may be sold as *primeur* or *nouveau* from the third Thursday of November following the harvest.

🍇 Chardonnay, Aligoté

🍷 1–3 years

ROSÉ I have not encountered these wines.

☑ *Pierre Jomard • Domaine de Petit Fromentin • Cave de Sain-Bel*

FLEURIE AOC
Cru Beaujolais

The evocatively-named Fleurie is the most expensive of the *Crus* and its finest wines are the quintessence of classic Beaujolais.

RED The wines of Fleurie quickly develop a fresh, floral, and fragrant style. Not as light and delicate as some writers suggest, their initial charm belies a positive structure and a depth of fruit that can sustain the wines for many years.

🍇 Gamay

🍷 2–8 years (4–16 years for *vin de garde* styles produced in the very best vintages)

☑ *Hospice de Belleville • Domaine Berrod • Château de Chénas • Domaine Pierre-Marie Chermette* (Les Garants) *• Jean-Paul Champagnon • Michel Chignard • L. J. Denojean-Burton • Guy Depardon* (Domaine du Point du Jour) *• Jean-Marc Despris • Georges Duboeuf* (Château des Déduits) *• Cave Coopérative de Fleurie*

• *Château de Labourons • André Métrat* (La Roilette Vieilles Vignes) *• Méziat Père & Fils • Alain Passot • Clos de la Roilette*

JULIÉNAS AOC
Cru Beaujolais

Situated in the hills above St.-Amour, Juliénas is named after Julius Caesar and, according to local legend, was the first Beaujolais village to be planted. It is probably the most underrated of the ten *Crus* Beaujolais.

RED The spicy-rich, chunky-textured fruit of a youthful Juliénas will develop a classy, satin-smooth appeal if given sufficient time to develop in bottle.

🍇 Gamay

🍷 3–8 years (5–15 years for *vin de garde* styles produced in the very best vintages)

☑ *Mme Ernest Aujas • Jean Benon • François Condemine • J. M. Coquenlorge • Château de Juliénas • Henri Lespinasse*

MORGON AOC
Cru Beaujolais

Just as the Côte de Brouilly is a finer and more concentrated form of Brouilly, so the wines of Mont du Py in the centre of Morgon are far more powerful than those of the surrounding vineyards in this commune.

RED Although these wines are variable in character and quality, the best of them rank with those of Moulin-à-Vent as the most sturdy of all Beaujolais. They have a singularly penetrating bouquet and very compact fruit.

🍇 Gamay

🍷 4–9 years (6–20 years for *vin de garde* styles produced in the very best vintages)

☑ *Domaine Aucoeur Noël • Domaine Jean-Marc Burgaud • Louis-Claude Desvignes • Georges Duboeuf* (Domaine Jean Descombes) *• Jean Foillard • Jacky Janodet • M. Lapierre • Méziat Père & Fils • Jacky Passot • Domaine Passot les Rampaux • Dominique Piron • Pierre Savoye • La Maison des Vignerons • Vincent & Fils*

MOULIN-À-VENT AOC
Cru Beaujolais

Because of its sheer size, power, and reputation for longevity, Moulin-à-Vent is known as the "King of Beaujolais". The exceptionally powerful character of Moulin-à-Vent has been attributed to the high manganese content of its soil. Does this make sense? The availability of manganese to the vine's metabolic system depends on the pH of the soil, and in the acid, granite soil of Beaujolais, manganese is all too readily available. For a healthy metabolism, however, the vine requires only the tiniest trace of manganese, so its abundance at Moulin-à-Vent could be toxic (to the vine that is, not the consumer!), may well cause chlorosis, and would certainly affect the vine's metabolism. This naturally restricts yields and could alter the composition of the grapes produced.

RED These well-coloured wines have intense fruit, excellent tannic structure, and, in many cases, a spicy-rich oak flavour.

🍇 Gamay

🍷 4–9 years (6–20 years for *vin de garde* styles produced in the very best vintages)

☑ *Domaine Berrod • Domaine Bourrisset • Domaine de Champ de Cour • Domaine Champagnon • Château de Chénas • Domaine Pierre-Marie Chermette* (Rochegrès) *• Domaine Desperrier Père & Fils • Georges Duboeuf • Domaine Gay-Coperet • Château des Jacques* (Clos de la Roche, Clos du Grand Carquelin) *• Domaine Paul Janin • Jacky Janodet • Clos des Maréchaux • Le Clos du Moulin-à-Vent • Château du Moulin-à-Vent • Thorin* (Esprit)

RÉGNIÉ AOC
Cru Beaujolais

The growers claim this village was the first to be planted with vines in Beaujolais, but so do the growers of Juliénas. Régnié was upgraded to full *Cru* Beaujolais status in December 1988. Too many half-hearted efforts nearly sunk the ship while it was being launched, but the best growers are gradually carving a reputation for this fledgling *Cru*.

RED There are two distinct styles of red wine here: one is light and fragrant, the other much fuller and more meaty, but all the best examples are fruity and supple, showing a fresh, invigorating aroma.

🍇 Gamay

🍷 2–7 years (4–12 years for *vin de garde* styles produced in the very best vintages)

☑ *René Desplace • Georges Duboeuf • Méziat Père & Fils • Domaine Passot les Rampaux • Domaine de Ponchon • Joël Rochette • La Maison des Vignerons • Georges & Gilles Roux*

ST.-AMOUR AOC
Cru Beaujolais

This is the most northerly of the ten *Crus*, and is more famous for its Mâcon produce than for its *Cru* Beaujolais. Despite its modern-day connotations, St.-Amour has nothing to do with love, but derives from St.-Amateur, a Roman soldier who was converted to Christianity and founded a monastery in the locality.

RED Charming wines of fine colour, seductive bouquet, and fragrant flavour. They reveal a soft, fruity flavour, but they will also repay a little ageing.

🍇 Gamay

🍷 2–8 years (4–12 years for *vin de garde* styles produced in the very best vintages)

☑ *Domaine des Duc • Jean-Paul Ducoté • André Poitevin • Michel Tête • Georges Trichard*

AUTHOR'S CHOICE

I could have chosen two or three times as many wines as this, and still many famous wines would be missing. After a lot of agonizing, I whittled the list down to the following and have picked those wines that achieve a balance between value and money.

PRODUCER	WINE	STYLE	DESCRIPTION	⌇
Bonneau du Martray	Corton-Charlemagne AOC, *Grand Cru* (*see* p.148)	WHITE	This is always one of Burgundy's great white wines, even in off-years such as 1972, 1984, and 1987. The 1972 was still fresh and thrilling in the early 1990s. This proves the special quality of the Corton-Charlemagne *terroir*, which is just under 50 hectares (125 acres), of which Bonneau du Martray owns nine. A typical vintage is luxuriously rich with lots of lush, creamy fruit.	5–20 years
La Chablisienne ⓥ	Vieilles Vignes, Chablis AOC (*see* p.137)	WHITE	This textbook Chablis has real depth and a singular intensity that makes it better than many *Premiers Crus*. It is, without doubt, the best-value Chablis year in, year out.	3–8 years
Domaine Champagnon	Chénas AOC, *Cru Beaujolais* (*see* p.160)	RED	This wine has an immaculate, fresh-floral Gamay aroma, heaps of refreshing, juicy fruit, and a wonderfully deep purple colour for lovers of serious unoaked Beaujolais.	3–8 years
Clos du Château du Meursault ⓥ	Bourgogne AOC, Blanc (*see* p.133)	WHITE	This is the only wine from *négociant* Patriarche I have consistently liked and it is one I happen to adore. It would be Meursault AOC today but for the fact that vines occupy a patch of Château de Meursault's garden that was wooded at the time the appellation was delimited. It is a single vineyard wine, whereas Château de Meursault is a blend. At its best, Château de Meursault is superior, but Clos de Château is more consistent.	4–12 years
J.-F. Coche-Dury ⓥ	Bourgogne AOC, Blanc (*see* p.133)	WHITE	Robert Parker reckons that Jean-François Coche-Dury is not only the greatest maker of white wine in Burgundy, but is also "one of the greatest winemakers on planet Earth", and I cannot argue.	2–7 years
J.-F. Coche-Dury	Corton-Charlemagne AOC *Grand Cru* (*see* p.148)	WHITE	This is probably the most concentrated, sumptuous white wine it is possible to make in a dry style. Without its balance of refreshing acidity, the richness of this wine would overwhelm. Alas, with its tiny vineyard, Coche-Dury is rare and expensive.	5–25 years
J.-F. Coche-Dury	Les Perrières, Meursault AOC (*see* p.149)	WHITE	This wine is certainly worth the expense. It too is a huge wine, with masses of rich, creamy fruit, and a restrained use of new wood, which gives the wine its fine, lemony-oak finesse.	3–15 years
Jean Collet	Valmur, Chablis Grand Cru AOC (*see* p.138) & Mont de Milieu, Chablis Premier Cru AOC (*see* p.138)	WHITE	If your preference is for Chablis fermented in new oak, these two *Crus* should make your most hedonistic dreams come true. There is no mistaking their smoky-creamy vanilla of well-toasted new oak, but they lack none of the cold-steel structure or fine mineral intensity that is the hallmark of true Chablis.	5–20 years
René & Vincent Dauvissat	Les Preuses, Chablis Grand Cru AOC (*see* p.138)	WHITE	It is hard to choose between Vincent Dauvissat and Jean-Marie Raveneau, but the former will be the preference for those who prefer just a whisper of smoky-oak. His Les Clos is of equal quality, and Vaillons and La Forest (*sic*) are close behind.	5–15 years
Domaine Guffens-Heynen	Vieilles Vignes, Mâcon-Pierreclos AOC (*see* p.156)	WHITE	This wine has extraordinary, stylish fruit for a Mâcon village. You must choose between waiting for its concentrated flavours to blossom out but losing its youthful freshness, or drinking it young, vital, and zesty but missing its potential complexity.	2–7 years
Domaine Guffens-Heynen ⓥ	La Roche, Pouilly-Fuissé AOC (*see* p.157)	WHITE	Intensely rich fruit with great mineral finesse consistently make this the finest unoaked Pouilly-Fuissé available.	2–7 years
Patrick Javillier	Cuvée Oligocène, Bourgogne AOC, Blanc	WHITE	As Clive Coates once wrote, "Best Bourgogne Blanc on Earth?"	2–5 years
Domaine Michel Juillot	Clos des Barraults, Mercurey Premier Cru AOC (*see* p.153)	RED	The succulent black cherry fruit in Juillot's Clos des Barraults demonstrates the outstanding value for money that Côte Chalonnaise red wine can offer. It has exceptional finesse.	3–8 years
Jacky Janodet	Moulin-à-Vent AOC, *Cru Beaujolais* (*see* p.161)	RED	This wine is the essence of Gamay produced from old vines and is the stuff of legends.	4–12 years
Domaine Joblot	Clos de la Servoisine, Givry Premier Cru (*see* p.153)	RED	Often exceptionally dense purple in colour for Côte Chalonnaise Pinot Noir, with opulent fruit, and creamy-vanilla spicy-oak.	3–8 years

PRODUCER	WINE	STYLE	DESCRIPTION	⌇
Domaine des Comtes Lafon	Les Charmes, Les Genevrières, and Les Perrières, Meursault Premiers Crus AOC (see p.149)	WHITE	These are three of the greatest Meursault made; it is impossible to pick between them on a pure quality basis, as only style separates them. Les Charmes is the most buttery, and develops relatively quickly in bottle; Les Genevrières has the greatest potential longevity; and Les Perrières the most finesse.	6–20 years
Maison Louis Latour V	Montagny AOC (see p.153)	WHITE	I suspect they knock it out by the bucket-load, but that just makes it all the more admirable because this wine is always super, and it is not even *Premier Cru.*	3–7 years
Dominique Laurent V	Bourgogne AOC, Premier (see p.133)	RED	This is the best-value Burgundy and is made by an up-and-coming small *négociant* who uses up to "200 per cent" new oak (which means it is racked from new oak to new oak!).	4–7 years
Dominique Laurent	Ruchottes-Chambertin AOC, *Grand Cru* (see p.143)	RED	Laurent's most expensive wine is richly coloured, with red fruits, cherries, vanilla, and cinnamon on the palate, and must be sheer luxury for those who love an oak-beam or two in their wine.	5–15 years
Domaine Leflaive	Les Pucelles, Puligny-Montrachet Premier Cru AOC (see p.150)	WHITE	If money is no object, then buy Bâtard-Montrachet or Chevalier-Montrachet, but of all other Leflaive *Premiers Crus*, Les Pucelles is almost as good as these most years, and has undeniable finesse.	5–8 years
Domaine Leroy V	Auxey-Duresses AOC (see p.146)	RED	Owned by Madame Bize-Leroy, former co-director of Domaine Romanée-Conti, Domaine Leroy is the greatest red-wine estate in the Côte d'Or, and this is her best-value red. The Auxey-Duresses is a truly classy Burgundy, and gives an affordable glimpse of the extraordinary quality found in Bize-Leroy's top wines.	5–10 years
Domaine Leroy	Chambertin AOC, *Grand Cru* (see p.140)	RED	Chambertin is the greatest wine in the Domaine Leroy range. In the best vintages, it remains dense, dark, and impenetrable for 10 to 15 years before blossoming into a potpourri of red and black fruits with finesse and complexity.	12–35 years
Domaine Leroy	Richebourg AOC, *Grand Cru* (see p.143)	RED	I find it impossible to choose between this wine and Domaine de la Romanée-Conti Richebourg, but it would be an academic exercise because I cannot afford either.	10–30 years
Louis Michel	Vaudésir, Chablis Grand Cru AOC (see p.138)	WHITE	Louis Michel's Chablis are absolutely straight, unwooded, and intensely focused, but for true devotees of this style his Vaudésir must rank as the finest, most naturally aromatic example available.	4–15 years
Jean-Marie Raveneau	Les Clos, Chablis Grand Cru AOC (see p.138)	WHITE	A perfect example of classic Chablis, this wine comes from the greatest *Grand Cru,* and arguably the greatest winemaker, in the district. Made according to the most traditional of methods, with no oaky vanilla to blur the wine's vivid style, it has an intensity of flavour and razor-sharp acidity. It remains on a knife-edge inside the bottle for many years, but will be breathtaking when ready. Many rate Raveneau's *Grand Cru* Valmur and *Premier Cru lieux-dits* Chapelot and Butteaux on par with his Chablis Les Clos.	6–20 years
Domaine de la Romanée-Conti	Richebourg AOC, *Grand Cru* (see p.143)	RED	This was indisputably Burgundy's greatest red-wine estate prior to an inconsistent phase in the 1970s and early 1980s. Since the late 1980s, however, all the wines produced here have been great. The Richebourg is my favourite, for no matter how dark and complex the wine is, it always has the most silky texture.	8–25 years
Domaine de la Romanée-Conti	Romanée-Conti AOC, *Grand Cru* (see p.143)	RED	This is one of the greatest red wines in the world. So good they named it twice: Romanée-Conti Romanée-Conti. Quite how the Pinot noir grape can produce such an opaque, complex wine with pure varietal character is a mystery.	10–30 years
Château de la Saule V	Montagny Premier Cru *AOC* (see p.153)	WHITE	This wine has a concentrated flavour and rich buttery fruit, firmly underpinned by vanilla-oak.	4–8 years
Jean Thévenet V	Domaine de la Bongran, Mâcon-Clessé AOC (see p.156)	WHITE	When it comes to the quintessential unoaked style of Mâcon, it is difficult to choose between Jean-Marie Guffens and Jean Thévenet. Thévenet makes several different *cuvées* of Mâcon-Clessé, from the "basic" *Cuvée* Tradition to various botrytized *vins moelleux.*	2–7 years
Domaine Tollot-Beaut V	Bourgogne AOC, Rouge (see p.133)	RED	One of the best-value red Burgundies. Tollot-Beaut does not know how to make a bad wine and its Bourgogne Rouge has more fruit and body than anyone would dare to expect.	3–8 years
Domaine Tollot-Beaut V	Chorey-lès-Beaune AOC (see p.147)	RED	This is the best-value red Burgundy that money can buy.	3–8 years
Vincent & Fils	Château de Fuissé Vieilles Vignes, Pouilly-Fuissé (see p.157)	WHITE	This is a rich, firm, classic Chardonnay, whose structure and underlying lemony fruit belie its Mâconnais origin. It is in a different class from almost every other Mâcon wine, although some may not appreciate this style of wine.	2–5 years

CHAMPAGNE

If you can afford good Champagne and have become accustomed to its quality and character, then there is really no other sparkling wine that makes a worthy substitute – and the very best of Champagne's competitors are almost as expensive as the real thing.

NO OTHER VINE-GROWING REGION can challenge Champagne's claim to produce the world's greatest sparkling wine because no other area resembles this viticultural twilight zone where the vine struggles to ripen grapes each year. In order to produce a truly great sparkling wine in the classic *brut* sense, the grapes must be harvested with a certain balance of richness, extract, and acidity, which can be achieved only through the long-drawn-out ripening process that occurs when the vine is grown on a knife-edge between success and failure. The Champagne *terroir*, which includes a cold, sometimes mean, northern climate and lime-rich chalk soil, is the key to the wine's intrinsic superiority, yet if such an area were to be discovered today, modern wine experts would quickly dismiss it as unsuitable for viticulture, thus economically unsound for winemaking.

ASPERSION
Aspersion (water-sprinkling) is performed by a system that operates automatically whenever the vineyard temperature drops below freezing.

COMBATTING FROST
Vines are protected from frost, the most harmful of Champagne's natural hazards, by aspersion (see above). The frost expends its energy in freezing the water, leaving the delicate shoots and buds safely cocooned in ice.

THE FIVE MAJOR DISTRICTS

There are five major districts in Champagne, and each produces numerous base wines that differ distinctly within a region as well as between regions. When these wines are blended in various proportions, many contrasting styles are produced. The best way to appreciate regional influences is to seek out grower-producer Champagnes.

MONTAGNE DE REIMS
The vineyards of the northern *montagne* face north and would not ripen grapes but for the fact that the *montagne* itself is a free-standing formation, which allows the chilled night air to slip down the slopes on to the plain, to be replaced by warmer air from a thermal zone that builds up above the *montagne* during the day. The vines here generally produce darker-coloured, bigger-bodied wines than those from the southern *montagne*, which often have a deeper flavour, more aromatic character, and greater finesse.
Primary grape variety Pinot noir
Best villages Ambonnay, Aÿ-Champagne, Bouzy, Verzenay, Verzy

CÔTE DES BLANCS
The name of this area is derived from its almost exclusive cultivation of white Chardonnay grapes. The wines produced from these grapes have become the most sought after in all Champagne. They contribute finesse and delicacy yet mature to an unequalled intensity of flavour.
Primary grape variety Chardonnay
Best villages Cramant, Avize, le Mesnil-sur-Oger

VALLÉE DE LA MARNE
Essentially easy-drinking, fruity, and forward wines produced from an extremely high proportion of Pinot meunier, which is cultivated in the frost-prone valley vineyards due to its late bud-break and early ripening.
Primary grape variety Pinot meunier
Best villages Mareuil-sur-Aÿ (for Pinot noir), Dizy & Hautvillers (for both Pinot noir and Pinot meunier), Cumières, Leuvrigny, and Ste.-Gemme (for Pinot meunier)

THE AUBE
Ripe, fruity wines are produced in this southern part of Champagne, which is closer to Chablis than to the classic vineyards of the Marne. The wines are cleaner in style and better in quality than those of the outer areas of the Vallée de la Marne around Château-Thierry.
Primary grape variety Pinot noir
Best village les Riceys

CÔTE DE SÉZANNE
The Sézannais is a rapidly developing area 16 km (10 miles) southwest of the Côte des Blancs. Like its neighbour, the Sézannais favours Chardonnay, but its wines are fruitier, with less finesse, than those of the Côte des Blancs, and can be quite exotic and musky. These wines are ideal for people who enjoy New World sparkling wines but may have difficulty coming to terms with the more classic style of Champagne.
Primary grape variety Chardonnay
Best villages Bethon, Villenauxe-la-Grande

A SPECIFIC WINE, NOT A STYLE

Contrary to beliefs in some parts of the world, Champagne is not a generic term for any sparkling wine but the protected name of a sparkling wine produced from grapes grown within a specific, legally defined area of northern France.

In Europe and various countries throughout the world, strict laws ensure that only true Champagne may be sold under the name "Champagne", but this principle is not respected in a number of places. The most blatant misuse in the developed world is in the US, although the Americans are not entirely to blame since the *champenois* have stubbornly refused even to consider a compromise, such as "Champagne Style". Considering this intransigence and the fact that for many years some of the most powerful Champagne houses have sold the sparkling wines they produce in South America under the name "*Champaña*", which is Spanish for Champagne, the *champenois* deserve the treatment they get in the US.

In 1985, the term *Méthode Champenoise* was banned for all wines produced or sold in the EEC (now the EU). The term, while not a guarantee, had proved useful for sorting the wheat from the chaff, since the quality of the product must warrant the cost of fermenting in bottle. Now consumers have to look for linguistic variations along the *Méthode Traditionelle* or *Classique* theme. In addition, there are Crémant AOCs in France, Cava DO in Spain, as well as new terms (e.g. Talento in Italy), which crop up all the time.

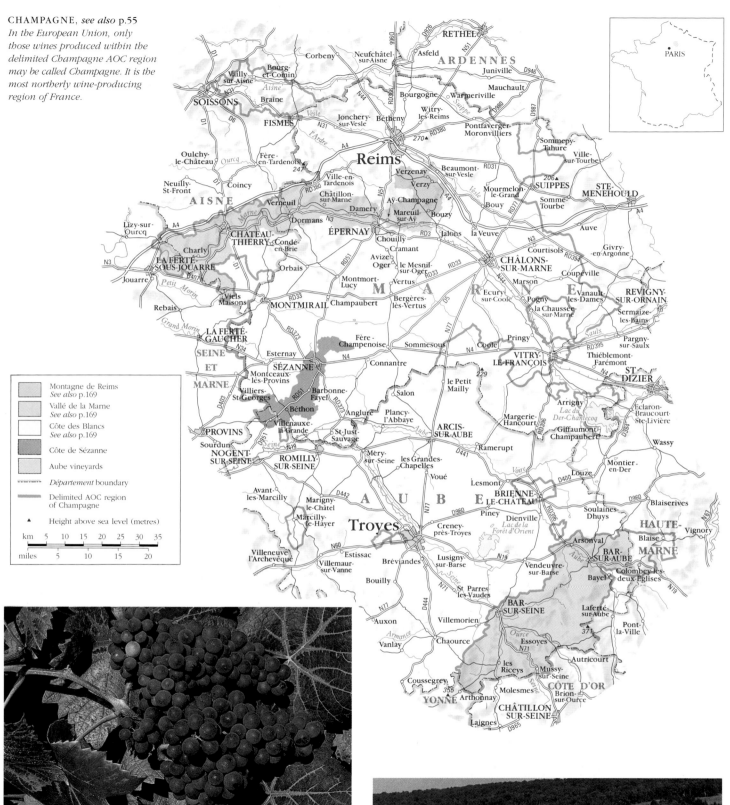

CHAMPAGNE, *see also p.55*
In the European Union, only those wines produced within the delimited Champagne AOC region may be called Champagne. It is the most northerly wine-producing region of France.

Montagne de Reims
See also p.169

Vallé de la Marne
See also p.169

Côte des Blancs
See also p.169

Côte de Sézanne

Aube vineyards

------- *Département* boundary

Delimited AOC region of Champagne

▲ Height above sea level (metres)

km 5 10 15 20 25 30 35
miles 5 10 15 20

PARIS

RIPE PINOT NOIR GRAPES IN VERZENAY
Although Champagne is primarily a white wine, the majority of grapes used to make it are black – either classic Pinot noir (above), or Pinot meunier – and special care is taken when pressing to ensure minimum coloration.

CHAMPAGNE'S CHALK SUBSOIL
This subsoil is part of a seabed that dried up 65 million years ago and is geologically part of the same bed of chalk as the white cliffs of Dover. It was formed by the slow accumulation of coccoliths, a calcareous matter secreted by sea-organisms. It took 1,000 billion coccoliths to produce each cubic inch of this pure-white chalk.

HOW CHAMPAGNE IS MADE

Champagne may be made from one or more of three grape varieties – Chardonnay, Pinot noir, and Pinot meunier. Wines made from these grape varieties are subjected to the so-called *méthode champenoise*, the complexities of which are explained below, but essentially involve a second fermentation inside the bottle in which they are sold.

THE HARVEST

Because of its northerly situation (145 kilometres [90 miles] northeast of Paris), Champagne's harvest usually takes place around mid-October, although in exceptional years it has commenced as early as August and as late as November. Due to the uncertain, Atlantic-influenced climate, rain invariably interrupts the flowering, resulting in at least two crops, although the second, known as the *bouvreux*, rarely ripens and is traditionally left for the birds. More often than not a potentially great vintage will be diluted or ruined by rain during the picking. These common setbacks are, however, the price that the *champenois* must pay for the *terroir* that enables them to produce the world's greatest sparkling wine

SORTING GRAPES

Harvesting is still done by hand in Champagne, but the once-traditional sorting into shallow trays called *osiers* is rarely carried out today. Roederer and Bollinger both sort their grapes on occasions, but not so thoroughly, yet most houses do not use any form of selection. With rot being a regular problem, intensive sorting should be a legal requirement. If a minimum percentage of grapes must be discarded for Châteauneuf-du-Pape in the sunny south of France, why not have the same law in rainy Reims?

PRESSING

Since more than 70 per cent of Champagne's vines grow black grapes, the grapes are never destemmed because their fibrous stem material creates a network of canals through which the juice rapidly drains, and this avoids coloration of the juice. Although modern horizontal presses, both hydraulic and pneumatic, are used, trials have recently proved that the best press is still the

CHAMPAGNE PRESS
The design of the pressoir coquard is basically the same as it was in the 17th century, when Dom Pérignon devised several winemaking methods still practised in Champagne today.

TRADITIONAL FERMENTATION
Some producers still favour fermentation in wooden casks or vats, through which oxygen can pass, because of the potential oxidative complexity achieved by this method.

MODERN FERMENTATION METHODS
The use of stainless steel is now widespread, and has resulted in cleaner styles of Champagne, although this does not necessarily mean lighter, less complex wines, as the rich, biscuity, stainless-steel-fermented Veuve Clicquot demonstrates.

traditional vertical *pressoir coquard,* and modern, computer-controlled versions of it are now available. The first pressing is called the *cuvée*, the second the *taille*, but "first" and "second" are misnomers because several pressings are necessary to extract this juice. In a traditional *coquard*, which has a capacity of 4,000 kilograms (8,818 lbs) of grapes, only 2,550 litres (561 gallons) of juice may be extracted – the first 2,050 being the *cuvée*, the last 500 the *taille*. Prior to 1992 an additional 116 litres (26 gallons) of *taille* could be pressed.

THE FIRST FERMENTATION

There is nothing mysterious about the initial fermentation, which results in a dry, still wine, very acid to taste and seemingly quite unremarkable in character. It must be neutral in character for the subtle influence of the second fermentation (and the process of autolysis that follows it) to work their effect on the flavour.

MALOLACTIC CONVERSION

Champagne normally undergoes what is called malolactic "fermentation". This is not strictly speaking a fermentation, but another biochemical process that converts hard malic acid to soft lactic acid. Those who cask-ferment their wines usually bottle without this conversion having taken place, since it is difficult to achieve in wood and is generally believed not to occur in bottle during or after the second fermentation. A Champagne that has not undergone malolactic conversion is quite often austere in character and hard to appreciate until properly matured, but will remain at its peak far longer than other Champagnes.

TRADITIONAL SORTING
Although harvesting is still carried out by hand in Champagne, the methodical sorting of grapes is rarely practised today.

FROM VINEYARD TO PRESS
The grapes are taken to the press-house in panniers de mannequin – *baskets or plastic trays that are small enough to prevent squashing.*

ASSEMBLAGE – THE BLENDER'S ART

In other wine regions blending is frowned upon, and the best wines made on one estate come from a single vintage. The traditional view in Champagne could not be a greater contrast, since a non-vintage blend of different grapes, from many different areas and several harvests, is the most classic of Champagnes. The critical operation of *assemblage*, or blending, is highly skilled and painstaking. To blend from as many as 70 different base wines – each of which changes in character from year to year – a consistent non-vintage *cuvée* of a specific house style is a remarkable feat and one that is more successful in some years than in others.

BLENDING
The highly skilful art of blending a fine Champagne can be compared to a game of chess: the winemaker, like the chessplayer, must think several moves ahead – this is necessary in order to predict how the wine will react to each addition to the blend.

The *assemblage* takes place in the first few months of the year following the harvest. At its most basic, and without taking into consideration any particular house style, it is a matter of balancing the characteristics of two or more of the three available grape varieties. The Chardonnay is often steely in its youth, but has the greatest finesse and potential longevity, although it is arguably less complex than great Pinot noir, which itself is no ephemeral beast. What the Pinot noir provides in abundance, however, is much of the backbone and body of a Champagne and real depth and richness of fruit. The Pinot meunier is a grape of immediate fruity-flowery appeal and in a blend of all three varieties in equal parts it is the first to dominate the wine, particularly on the nose.

RESERVE WINE

Reserve wines are quite literally wines kept in reserve from previous years and they are essential for, indeed restricted to, the production of non-vintage Champagne. The idea that reserve wines are primarily used to make *cuvées* conform to a particular house style no matter what the quality or character of the base-wine year is a misconception. That task, if at all possible, is achieved when blending the different *crus*. The job of reserves is, if anything, closer to that of the *dosage* in that they both make Champagne easier to drink at a younger age. Reserve wines also provide a certain richness, fullness, and mellowed complexity, which is why it is generally considered that the more reserve wines added the better. However, unless kept on their yeast, reserve wines can dilute the autolysis process, thus there may come a point when potential finesse is traded for instant complexity. The amount of reserves added can vary according to the producer or year (a blend from a great year will require less "help" than even the most fastidiously blended poor year). Reserves are kept in several ways: in tank under inert conditions, in cask of various sizes, and, in the case of Bollinger, bottled in magnums with a tiny amount of sugar and yeast to promote a slight *pétillance* for added freshness.

THE SECOND FERMENTATION

The second fermentation is actually the essence of the *méthode champenoise*, and is the only way to produce a fully sparkling wine. After the blended wine has undergone its final racking, the *liqueur de tirage*, or bottling liquor, is added. This is a mixture of still Champagne, sugar, selected yeasts, yeast nutrients, and a

CHAMPAGNE LYING SUR LATTES
Throughout the second fermentation and until required for disgorgement, bottles of Champagne are traditionally stacked on thin, wooden lathes in the coolest part of the cellar.

clarifying agent. The amount of sugar added depends on the degree of effervescence required and the amount of natural sugar in the wine. The wines are bottled (usually in May or thereabouts) and capped with a temporary closure, which used to be a cork secured by a metal clip called an *agrafe*, but a crown-cap (which is like a beer-bottle cap) is almost universally utilized these days and, if used, holds in place a small plastic pot to catch the sediment produced during this fermentation.

REMUAGE

The second fermentation can take between ten days and three months, after which the bottles can be transferred to *pupitres* to undergo *remuage*. A *pupitre* consists of a pair of heavy, hinged, rectangular boards, each containing 60 holes, which have been cut at an angle to enable the bottle to be held by the neck in any position in the 90° between horizontal and vertical (neck pointing downwards). *Remuage* is a method of riddling the bottles to loosen sediment, encouraging it to move to the neck of the bottle, where it collects. By hand this takes about eight weeks, although many companies now have computerized 504-bottle pallets that perform the task in just eight days. A technique involving the use of porous yeast capsules, which trap the sediment inside them, reduces *remuage* to a mere eight seconds.

SEDIMENT
The Champagne's second fermentation creates a sediment that falls in separate sticky layers; it must be worked down the bottle by an operation called remuage

HOW REMUAGE WORKS

After second fermentation and the desired yeast-ageing period, which can be anything from nine months to several years, the wines are taken from *sur lattes* and placed horizontally in the pupitre (1). Each time the *remueur* swiftly rotates the bottles backwards and forwards to dislodge the settlement without disturbing it, he tilts the bottle (2 and 3) to encourage it to slide down towards the neck until it rests just above the crown cap (4) and is ready for disgorgement.

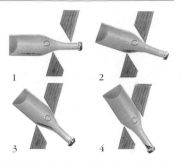

AGEING THE WINE

After *remuage*, the wine undergoes a period of ageing *sur point* (in a fully inverted position) before the sediment is removed. The minimum age for non-vintage Champagne is 15 months from 1 January following the harvest (prior to 1997, this used to be just 12 months) but most receive 18 to 30 months ageing. Vintage Champagne cannot be sold until three years after the harvest, but most are aged for much longer. Ageing Champagne improves its quality because the sediment contains dead yeast cells that break down by a process known as autolysis, which contributes to the wine's inimitable "champagny" character. The optimum duration of yeast-ageing depends on the quality of the wine and how it has been processed. Some do not improve beyond one or two years, while others can benefit for up to a decade, after which they merely remain fresher than earlier disgorged wine, since further toasty and biscuity aromas are suppressed.

DISGORGEMENT

Disgorgement is the removal of the sediment from the wine, which is usually collected in a plastic pot. The method usually used today is known as *dégorgement à la glace*, which involves the immersion of the bottle neck in a shallow bath of freezing brine. This causes the sediment to adhere to the base of the plastic pot, enabling the bottle to be turned upright without disturbing the sediment. When the crown-cap is removed, the semi-frozen sediment is ejected by the internal pressure of the bottle. Only a little wine is lost, as the wine's pressure is reduced by its lowered temperature.

DÉGORGEMENT À LA VOLÉE
The removal of sediment is still carried out by hand at a few houses with low production, in a process known as dégorgement à la volée *(which literally means "with a bang") because an experienced* dégorgeur *can detect any off aromas in the process, thereby eliminating the odd faulty bottle. Although* dégorgement à la glace, *which freezes the sediment, is the more common technique, even the most modern houses must disgorge large-sized bottles by hand.*

ADDING THE LIQUEUR D'EXPÉDITION

Before corking, bottles are topped up to their previous level and *liqueur d'expédition* is added. In all cases except for *Extra Brut*, this *liqueur* includes a small amount of sugar: the younger the wine, the greater the *dosage* of sugar required to balance its youthful acidity. High acidity is crucial to a fine Champagne, since it keeps the wine fresh during its lengthy bottle-ageing method of production and also during any additional cellaring by the consumer. High acidity is also necessary to carry the flavour to the palate through the tactile effect caused by thousands of minuscule bursting bubbles. This acidity rounds out with age, thus the older the Champagne, the smaller the *dosage* required.

SWEETNESS CHART

The sweetness of a Champagne can be accurately indicated by its residual sugar level, which is measured in grams per litre. The percentage *dosage* applied, which some books refer to, is not an accurate indicator because the *liqueur* added in the *dosage* itself varies in sweetness. The legal levels are as follows:

Brut Nature
0–3 grams per litre
Absolutely bone dry!

Extra Brut
0–6 grams per litre
Bone dry

Brut
0–15 grams per litre
Dry to very dry, but never austere

Extra Sec or Extra Dry
12–20 grams per litre
A misnomer – dry to medium-dry

Sec or Dry
17–35 grams per litre
A bigger misnomer –
medium to medium-sweet

Demi-Sec or Rich
35–50 grams per litre
Definitely sweet, but not
true dessert sweetness

Doux
50+ grams per litre
Very sweet; this style was favoured
by the tsars, but is no longer
commercially produced

CORKING

Although a used Champagne cork has a distinctive mushroom-like shape, it is the same cylindrical shape as any other cork prior to bottling, albeit in a significantly fatter format. It is inserted just halfway, after which a protective metal cap is placed over it with a pulverizing blow that gives the cork its special shape. A wire muzzle is then used to secure the cork to the bottle, which will be automatically shaken to homogenize the wine and *liqueur*. The very best *cuvées* are kept for at least three months prior to shipment, as this helps to marry the *liqueur*, but it is always worth giving any good Champagne a year or two of extra ageing.

CHAMPAGNE CORKS

1 A crown-cap to seal the wine during second fermentation.
2 The plastic pot in which the deposit is collected after a successful *remuage*.
3 A cork before insertion, which is cylindrical.
4 A cork from a youthful Champagne, which shows the mushroom head achieved when ramming it into the bottle.
5 The cork of a more mature Champagne, which has shrunk and straightened through age.

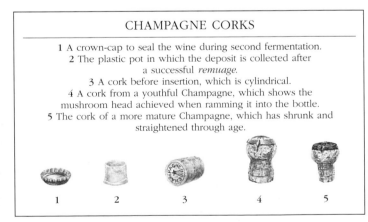

POST-DISGORGEMENT AGEING

The period that a producer keeps Champagne prior to shipment is seldom sufficient to build up the toasty, biscuity complexity that so many Champagne drinkers enjoy, which is given by the mellow bottle aromas that develop after disgorgement. This is, however, not to say that these aromas cannot be found in recently disgorged Champagnes, but they would have to be very mature.

THE CLASSIFICATION OF CHAMPAGNE VINEYARDS

Champagne's vineyards are quality-rated on a village-by-village basis using a percentile system known as the *Échelle des Crus*, which constitutes a pro-rata basis for grape prices. Villages with the maximum *échelle* of 100 per cent are *Grands Crus*, while those rated between 90 and 99 per cent are *Premiers Crus* and receive a correspondingly lower price for their grapes. The lowest-rated villages are currently classified at 80 per cent, but the *Échelle des Crus* was originally a true percentile system, starting at just 22.5 per cent. It would be unrealistic for any such system to commence at one per cent, since no village with merely one-hundredth the potential of a *Grand Cru* should even be part of the Champagne appellation, but when first conceived, the *Échelle des Crus* had a comprehensive structure of *Crus* covering the middle ground, which is something that it lacks today. Due to various *ad hoc* reclassifications and political posturing, the minimum *échelle* has gradually increased from 22.5 per cent to 80 per cent, and in truth the present system is nothing more than a 20-point scale.

There are 17 villages possessing official *Grand Cru* status. Until 1985 there were only 12. The five villages elevated to *Grand Cru* in 1985 were Chouilly, le Mesnil-sur-Oger, Oger, Oiry, and Verzy.

AUTUMNAL VIEW OF VILLEDOMMANGE
The Premier Cru *vineyards of Villedommange completely surround the village, which is located in the Petite Montagne, a few kilometres southwest of Reims. Pinot meunier reigns supreme, although the Pinot noir, shown above, accounts for 30 per cent of the vines grown.*

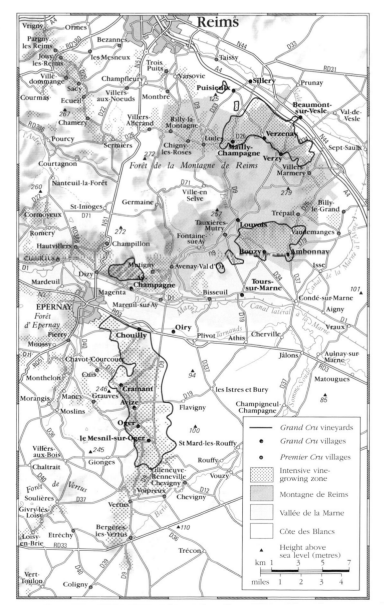

THE GRAND CRU AND PREMIER CRU VILLAGES
Within the three important districts surrounding Épernay, 17 villages have Grand Cru *status and 40 the status of* Premier Cru.

FACTORS AFFECTING TASTE AND QUALITY

LOCATION
This most northerly of the AOC wine regions of France lies some 145 km (90 miles) northeast of Paris, and is separated from Belgium by the forested hills of the Ardennes. Four-fifths of the region is in the Marne, and the balance is spread over the Aube, Aisne, Seine-et-Marne, and the Haute-Marne.

CLIMATE
This cold and wet northern climate is greatly influenced by the Atlantic, which has a cooling effect on its summer and makes the seasons generally more variable. Its position at the northern edge of the winemaking belt stretches the duration of the vine's growth cycle to the limit, making frost a major problem during spring and autumn.

ASPECT
Vineyards are planted on the gently rolling east- and southeast-facing slopes of the Côte des Blancs at altitudes of of 120–200 m (380–640 ft). On the slopes of the Montagne de Reims (a plateau) the vines grow at altitudes similar to those on the Côte. The best valley vineyards lie in sheltered situations on the right bank of the Marne.

SOIL
The vineyards of the Côte des Blancs, Montagne de Reims, Marne valley, and Côte de Sézanne are all situated on a porous chalk subsoil up to 300 m (960 ft) thick, which is covered by a thin layer of drift derived in various proportions from sand, lignite, marl, loam, clay, and chalk rubble. The pure white chalk in Champagne's soil drains well, yet retains enough water for the vines to survive a drought. The chalk's high active lime content encourages the vines to produce grapes that have a relatively high acid content when they become ripe.

VITICULTURE AND VINIFICATION
No mechanical harvesting is allowed and most grapes are still pressed using the traditional, vertical Champagne press or *pressoir coquard*. Increasing use is being made of stainless-steel vats with temperature-controlled conditions for the first fermentation, but a few houses and many growers still ferment part or all of their wines in cask. The second fermentation gives the wine its sparkle and this always takes place in the bottle in which it is sold.

PRIMARY GRAPE VARIETIES
Chardonnay, Pinot noir, and Pinot meunier
SECONDARY GRAPE VARIETIES
Arbanne, Petit meslier, and Pinot blanc vrai

WHAT HAPPENED TO THE GRANDES MARQUES?

In 1991 a poll of the Syndicat de Grandes Marques revealed that although every member believed that membership was a declaration of superior quality, almost all of them dismissed the notion that membership should be subject to any sort of quality criteria. Furthermore, they rejected the idea that the Syndicat should be opened up to any producer that meets such criteria, whether it be a grower or indeed a cooperative. Christian Bizot, then head of Bollinger, was so outraged with his *Grande Marque* colleagues that he launched the now famous "Charter of Ethics & Quality".

A year or so after the poll, the Syndicat elected a new chairman, Jean-Claude Rouzaud of Roederer, who promised he would achieve a rebirth of the *Grandes Marques* with "quality criteria and more open membership" or he would resign. Along the way he achieved some major victories, such as banning the purchase of *vins sur lattes*, but in the end it was impossible to get agreement on other quality criteria or on a more open *syndicat*. However, it was not just Rouzaud who resigned, he took the whole *syndicat* with him. And so in 1997 the *Grandes Marques* were disbanded. Regrettably this also revoked the ban on *sur lattes*.

KRUG'S CLOS DU MESNIL, LE MESNIL-SUR-OGER
One of the few true clos *in the region, the* blancs de blancs *it produces vies with Bollinger's Vieille Vignes Françaises as the world's most expensive Champagne.*

RECENT CHAMPAGNE VINTAGES

2000 A non-vintage year rather than a true vintage. However, good Champagne can be made in almost any year through selection, and some producers still believe that 2000 is a magical number, so expect this year to be more widely declared than it should be.

1999 The last vintage of the 1900s brought vintage-quality ripeness, but the worst acidity and pH readings for a couple of decades. Good Champagne will only be made through severe selection.

1998 On paper the 1998s are not quite as good as the 1997s. They are, if you like, the 1993s in comparison to the 1997s' similarity to the 1992s (see below). To continue the analogy, despite the 1997s having a slight edge, some of the 1998s have been more impressive, thus like 1992/1993 the best wines of 1997/1998 will vary from producer to producer. In other words another vintage by selection.

1997 Not a top Champagne vintage and certainly nothing like as special as 1996, but the base wines of this year were similar and slightly superior to the those of 1992, which produced a large number of very good vintage Champagnes. Like 1992, the best of this vintage will be the product of selection.

1996 In typical *champenois* fashion, they wait five years for a vintage, then two come along in successive years. The 1996 vintage is certainly better than the 1995, but whether it is as good as 1990 or, as some have suggested, as 1928, only time will tell.

1995 After four consecutive years of sporadic vintage declarations, most houses will declare 1995, the first truly universal vintage since 1990, particularly for Chardonnay. The best Champagnes will be close in quality to those of 1988.

HOW TO READ CHAMPAGNE LABELS

R.D.
This is a trademark belonging to Bollinger. It stands for *Récemment Dégorgé*, indicating the wine, usually a mature vintage, has just been disgorged, and thus will be fresher than normally disgorged bottles of the same vintage. Other producers also do this, but must use other terms such as Late Disgorged.

VINTAGE
In a vintage Champagne, 100% of the grapes used are from the year indicated.

THE VILLAGE
Village names in large type denote the sole origin of the Champagne, otherwise, as here, place names merely indicate the location of the producer.

THE MARQUE
The *marque* is usually the name of the producer, but it may be a brand name such as René Florancy, used by Union Champagne in Avize.

THE STYLE
An indication of style here is optional, and if none is found then you may take it that the Champagne will be a non-vintage *brut* and almost certainly blended from the three primary grape varieties, unless from a Marne valley village, when it will be predominantly Pinot meunier.

MATRICULATION NUMBER
The initials in front of this little code are the key to whether the Champagne has been produced by a house (NM), grower (RM), or *coopérative* (CM). If the initials are SR, this is a Société de Récoltants – the *récoltants* share premises to make and market more than one brand; ND is a *Négociant-Distributeur*, which means that the company selling the Champagne did not make it; and MA stands for *marque d'acheteur*, a brand name that is owned by the purchaser, such as a restaurant or supermarket.

THE WINE STYLES OF
CHAMPAGNE

NON-VINTAGE BRUT

No wine depends upon the winemaker's blending skills more than non-vintage Champagne, which accounts for more than 75 per cent of all Champagne sold. Although non-vintage Champagnes are not usually the finest Champagnes, they are capable of being so. Their base wine, to which reserve wines may be added, will always be from the last harvest. Most producers make up between 10 and 15 per cent of their blends from reserves from the previous two or three years, but some utilize as much as 40 per cent, while a few will add much less reserve wine in volume, but from a greater number of much older vintages. Many growers have no reserve wines, thus their non-vintage will in fact be from one year, but of a lesser quality than the *cuvée* selected for their vintage Champagne. All but the most dynamic *coopératives* typically make up just five per cent of their blends from reserves from the year immediately preceding that of the base wine – they seldom excel.

✓ *Michel Arnould • Paul Bara • Beaumont des Crayères • Bertin & Fils* (Carte Or) *• Billecart-Salmon • H. Billiot • Bollinger* (magnums) *• Th. Blondel • Raymond Boulard • Château de Boursault • Charles de Cazanove* (Brut Azure) *• Guy de Chassey • Chauvet • Gaston Chiquet • André Clouet • Hubert Dauvergne • Debas-Comin • Deutz* (Classic) *• Vve A. Devaux • Drappier • Gatinois • Michel Genet • Paul Gobillard • Philippe Gonet • Gosset* (Grande Réserve) *• Gosset-Brabant • Henri Goutorbe • Alfred Gratien • Jean Hanotin* (Grand Brut) *• Charles Heidsieck • Henriot • A. Jacquart* (Cuvée Spéciale) *• Jacquesson • Pierre Jamain • Lanson • Léon Launois • Launois Père • Laurent-Perrier • Etienne Lefevre • Lilbert Fils • Henri Mandois • Serge Mathieu • Jean Milan • Moët & Chandon* (but must be cellared for 12 months) *• Jean Moutardier* (Sélection) *• Napoleon* (Carte Or) *• De Nauroy • Bruno Paillard • Palmer • Joseph Perrier • Perrier-Jouët* (Blason de France) *• Pertois-Moriset • Philipponnat* (Brut and Le Reflet) *• Pierron-Lèglise • Michel Pithois • Ployez-Jacquemart • Renaudin • Louis Roederer • Ruinart • François Secondé • Jacques Sélosse • Taittinger • Veuve Clicquot • Vilmart & Cie* (Cuvée Cellier)

VINTAGE BRUT

Not more than 80 per cent of any year's harvest may be sold as vintage Champagne, so at least 20 per cent of the best years' harvests are conserved for the future blending of non-vintage wines. Some houses stick rigidly to declaring a vintage in only the greatest years, but many, sadly, do not, which is why we have seen vintage Champagnes from less than ideal years such as 1980, 1987, and even 1984. Most *coopératives* and a large number of grower-producers produce a vintage virtually every year, which is possible, of course, but rather defeats the object and debases the value of the product. However, even in great years, a vintage Champagne is more the result of tightly controlled selection of base wines than a reflection of the year in question and this makes these wines exceptionally good value.

The character of a vintage Champagne is more autolytic, giving it an acacia-like floweriness, than that of a non-vintage of the same age because it has no reserve-wine mellowness. If you like those biscuity or toasty bottle-aromas, you should keep vintage for a few years.

✓ *Paul Bara • Herbert Beaufort* (Corte d'Or) *• Billecart-Salmon • Bollinger • Pierre Callot • Cattier • Claude Cazals • Chauvet • André Clouet • Paul Déthune • Deutz • Drappier • Egly-Ouriet • Gardet • Michel Genet • Paul Gobillard • Henri Goutorbe • Alfred Gratien • J. M. Gremillet • Charles Heidsieck* (from 1989 onwards) *• Henriot • Krug • Lanson • Laurent-Perrier • Henri Mandois • Ph. Mouzon-Leroux • Lilbert Fils • Mailly Grand Cru • Serge Mathieu • Moët & Chandon • Napoleon • De Nauroy • Bruno Paillard • Palmer • Joseph Perrier • Perrier-Jouët • Michel Pithois • Ployez-Jacquemart • Pol Roger • Pommery • Louis Roederer • Taittinger • Ruinart • Patrick Soutiran • Sugot Feneuil* (Special Club) *• F. Vauversin • Veuve Clicquot • Vilmart & Cie* (Grand Cellier & Grand Cellier d'Or)

BLANC DE BLANCS
Non-vintage, vintage, and prestige

Literally meaning "white of whites", this wine is produced entirely from white Chardonnay grapes and possesses the greatest ageing potential of all Champagnes. *Blanc de blancs* may be made in any district of Champagne, but the best examples come from a small part of the Côte des Blancs between Cramant and Le Mesnil-sur-Oger. If consumed too early, a classic *blanc de blancs* can be austere and seem to lack fruit and generosity, yet with proper maturity this style of Champagne can be very succulent. Given a few years bottle-ageing after purchase, most *blanc de blancs* develop a toasty-lemony bouquet together with intense, beautifully focused fruit.

✓ *Non-vintage Boizel, De Castellane, Chauvet* (Carte Vert), *Delamotte, Pierre Gimonnet, Paul Goerg, Henriot, Larmandier-Bernier, R. & L. Legras, De Meric, Pierre Moncuit, Mumm* (Mumm de Cramant), *Bruno Paillard* (Réserve Privée), *Joseph Perrier, Pierre Peters* (Perlé de Mesnil), *Vilmart & Cie* • **Vintage** *Billecart-Salmon, Le Brun*

de Neuville, De Castellane (Cuvée Royal), *Delamotte, Deutz, Robert Doyard, Drappier, Duval-Leroy, Pierre Gimonnet, Paul Goerg, J. M. Gremillet, Gruet & Fils, Jacquart* (Cuvée Mosaïque), *Jacquesson, Guy Larmandier, Pierre Moncuit, Philipponnat, Pol Roger, Alain Robert, Louis Roederer, Vazart-Coquart* (Grand Bouquet), *De Venoge* • **Prestige cuvée** *Charles Heidsieck* (Cuvée de Millénaires), *Krug* (Clos du Mesnil), *Larmandier-Bernier* (Spécial Club), *Pierre Moncuit* (Vieilles Vignes Nicole Moncuit), *Ruinart* (Dom Ruinart), *Salon "S", Taittinger* (Comtes de Champagne)

BLANC DE NOIRS
Non-vintage, vintage, and prestige

Literally translated as "white of blacks", these Champagnes are made entirely from black grapes, either Pinot noir or Pinot meunier, or from a blend of the two. The most famous and most expensive is Bollinger's Vielles Vignes Françaises, which is a unique example of pure Pinot noir Champagne made from two tiny plots of ungrafted vines, which between them cannot produce more than 3,000 bottles, hence the hefty price tag. Apart from Bollinger, few producers have traditionally used the term *blanc de noirs*, but the "Vieilles Vignes Françaises" has given it a certain cachet and a few commercially minded houses have begun to cash in on the term (Beaumet, Jeanmaire, Mailly Grand Cru, Oudinot, and De Venoge, for example). Many supermarkets now sell their own-label brand of *blanc de noirs*.

Bollinger inadvertently created the myth that a *blanc de noirs* is intrinsically a big, full, and muscular Champagne, but it is generally little different in style from the other *cuvées* a house may produce. If you try Serge Mathieu's black label, you will discover a Champagne so elegant that you would never guess it is made only from Pinot noir, let alone that it is grown in the Aube.

✓ *Bollinger* (Vieilles Vignes Françaises)

EXTRA SEC, SEC, AND DEMI-SEC (RICH)
Non-vintage and vintage

In theory, *doux* is the sweetest Champagne style available, with a residual-sugar level in excess of 50 grams per litre. However, this style is no longer used. The last *doux* sold was a 1983-based Roederer Carte Blanche. That *cuvée* is now a *demi-sec*, although 100 years ago it contained a fabulous 180 grams of sugar per litre.

The extinction of *doux* has meant that *demi-sec* has, for all practical purposes, become the sweetest of the Champagne categories. A *demi-sec* may contain between 33 and 50 grams of residual sugar per litre, although most of them contain only 35 grams. Only a few contain as much as 45 grams.

While these wines are not dry, they certainly are not sweet and are nothing like a top Sauternes, which in great years will average between 90 and 108 grams per litre. A *demi-sec* thus falls between two stools and because it is primarily sold to an unsophisticated market, the *champenois* have been able to get away with using wines of decreasing quality. There are exceptions, of course, but Champagne *demi-sec* is now so adulterated that few *champenois* take the style seriously.

The exceptions that do exist are not sweet enough to accompany desserts and are best served with the main course or even with starters.

✓ **Non-vintage** *Billecart-Salmon* (Demi-Sec Réserve), *Gatinois* (Demi-Sec), *Jacquart* (Onctueuse Cuvée Rosé Extra Dry), *Lanson* (Ivory Label), *Moët & Chandon* (Nectar), *Philipponnat* (Sublime), *Pol Roger* (Demi-Sec*), *Jacques Sélosse* (Cuvée Exquise Sec), *Veuve Clicquot* (Demi-Sec) • **Vintage** *Veuve Clicquot* (Rich)

ROSÉ
Non-vintage, vintage, and prestige
The first record of a commercially produced rosé Champagne is by Clicquot in 1777 and this style has enjoyed ephemeral bursts of popularity ever since. It is the only European rosé that may be made by blending white wine with a little red; all other rosé, whether still or sparkling, must be produced by macerating the skins and juice to extract pigments. More pink Champagne is produced by blending than through skin contact and in blind tasting it has been impossible to tell the difference. Both methods produce good and bad wine that can be light or dark in colour and rich or delicate in flavour. A good pink Champagne will have an attractive colour, perfect limpidity, and a snow-white *mousse*.

✓ **Non-vintage** *Beaumont des Crayères* (Privilège), *Billecart-Salmon, Th. Blondel, André Clouet, Hubert Dauvergne, Gatinois, René Geoffroy, Etienne Lefevre, Serge Mathieu, Moët & Chandon, De Nauroy, Joseph Perrier, Perrier-Jouët* (Blason de France), *Eric Rodez* • **Vintage** *Bollinger, Boizel, Vve A. Devaux* (Cuvée Distinction), *Jacquart* (Cuvée Mosaïque), *Moët & Chandon* • **Prestige cuvée** *Billecart-Salmon* (Cuvée Elisabeth), *Gosset* (Grand Rosé), *Jacquesson* (Signature), *Krug, Laurent-Perrier* (Cuvée Grand Siècle Alexandra), *Moët & Chandon* (Dom Pérignon), *Perrier-Jouët* (Belle Epoque), *Pommery* (Cuvée Louise Pommery), *Pol Roger, Louis Roederer* (Cristal & straight vintage), *Ruinart* (Dom Ruinart), *Taittinger* (Comtes de Champagne), *Veuve Clicquot*

NON-DOSAGE
Non-vintage and vintage
The first non-*dosage* Champagne to be sold was Laurent-Perrier's Grand Vin Sans Sucre in 1889. Officially *Brut Extra*, but commercially labelled variously as *Brut Zéro, Brut Sauvage, Ultra Brut*, or *Sans Sucre*, these wines became fashionable in the early 1980s, when consumers began seeking lighter, drier wines. This trend was driven by critics who had been privileged to taste wonderful old vintages straight off their

lees, which led them to believe that a Champagne without any *dosage* was somehow intrinsically superior to a Champagne with a *dosage*. It is, of course, if it is of superior quality and at least ten years old before *disgorgement*, particularly if given a further 12–18 months ageing to develop toasty post-*disgorgement* bottle-aromas. It is not superior, however, when the Champagne is of normal commercial age, when it can only be austere, tart, and unpleasant to drink, which is why the fashion was so short-lived.

✓ **Non-vintage** *De Bruyne, Mailly Cassiopee* • **Vintage** *Pommery* (Flacon d'Excellence Nature)

CUVÉES DE PRESTIGE
Non-vintage and vintage
Also known as *special* or *deluxe cuvées*, Cuvées de Prestige should be the best that Champagne has to offer, regardless of the price. "Dom Pérignon" was the first commercial example of these Champagnes, launched in 1936, although Roederer's "Cristal" has a far longer history, having first been produced in 1876, but that was made exclusively for Tsar Alexander II. The first commercially available Cristal *cuvée* was not produced until 1945.

A typical *prestige cuvée* may be made entirely of wines from a firm's own vineyards, and the blend is often restricted to the *Grands Crus*. Most of these are vintage Champagnes, and many are produced by the most traditional methods (fermented in wood, sealed with a cork and *agrafe* rather than a crown-cap, then hand-disgorged), aged for longer than normal, and sold in special bottles at very high prices. Some are clearly overpriced, others are over-refined, having so much mellowness that all the excitement has been oozed out of them, but a good number are truly exceptional Champagnes and worth every penny.

✓ **Non-vintage** *Hubert Dauvergne* (Fine Fleur de Bouzy), *Paul Déthune* (Princesse des Thunes), *Krug* (Grande Cuvée), *Laurent-Perrier* (Grand Siècle "La Cuvée"), *De Meric* (Cathérine de Medici) • **Vintage** *Ayala* (Grande Cuvée), *Paul Bara* (Comtesse Marie de France), *Billecart-Salmon* (Cuvée N. F. Billecart), *De Castellane* (Cuvée Commodore & Cuvée Florens de Castellane), *Guy Charlemagne* (Mesnillésime), *Delamotte* (Nicolas Louis Delamotte), *Deutz* (Cuvée William Deutz), *Lanson* (Cuvée Noble), *Laurent-Perrier* (Grand Siècle Exceptionellement Millésimé), *Moët & Chandon* (Dom Pérignon), *Perrier-Jouët* (Belle Epoque), *Piper-Heidsieck* (Rare), *Pol Roger* (Cuvée Sir Winston Churchill & Cuvée Réserve Speciale PR), *Pommery* (Cuvée Louise Pommery), *De Venoge* (Cuvée des Princes), *Veuve Clicquot* (Grande Dame), *Vilmart* (Coeur de Cuvée)

Note Top-performing *prestige cuvées* that are *blanc de blancs, blanc de noirs*, rosé, or single-vineyard Champagnes are not recommended above, but under their respective headings.

SINGLE VINEYARD
Non-vintage and vintage
Although the winemakers of Champagne are gradually becoming aware of the concept of single-vineyard sparkling wines, it is only a handful of houses that are doing this and not the growers, who are those best-equipped to take advantage of and promote the concept of wines that are expressive of *terroir*.

✓ **Non-vintage** *Cattier* (Clos du Moulin) • **Vintage** *Drappier* (Grande Sendrée), *Krug* (Clos du Mesnil), *Philipponnat* (Clos des Goisses)

COTEAUX CHAMPENOIS AOC
Non-vintage and vintage
The still wines (red, white, and rosé) that are produced in Champagne are low in quality and high in price. The white and rosé are the least interesting, although with modern technology they could be made more successful and easier to drink. It is Coteaux Champenois *rouge* that can be the most fascinating of them, although Champagne's notoriously inclement climate is very punishing on those who try to make red wine every year. Black grapes rarely ripen sufficiently to obtain a good colour without over-extraction, which merely brings out the harsh, unripe tannins. Most reds are, therefore, light- to medium-bodied wines that barely hint at the flush of fruit found in a good burgundy at the most basic level.

However, the all-too-rare exceptions can be singly impressive in their deep colour and rich fruit. Such wines often have a slightly smoky style reminiscent of Pinot noir. Bouzy is the most famous of these wines, but a good vintage rarely occurs in the same village more than once in ten years and various other growths can be just as good. The best reds from a successful vintage in Ambonnay, Aÿ, or any other winegrowing village in Champagne can certainly be compared to Bouzy.

Because of this intrinsic unreliability, it is impossible to recommend any Coteaux Champenois on a regular basis. However, virtually all the famous houses have a bottle or two of an amazing *rouge* – usually Bouzy from venerable vintages such as 1929, 1947, or 1959 – but their current commercial bottlings are usually pretty mediocre. Bollinger is the exception, with a *barrique*-matured Aÿ rouge from the *lieu-dit* La Côte aux Enfants, which consistently tries hard, even if it is more successful in some years than others. Joseph Perrier's Cumières Rouge is also worth keeping an eye on. To give readers a starting point, I have had most joy from the following:

✓ *Paul Bara* (Bouzy) • *Edmond Barnault* (Bouzy) • *André Clouet* (Bouzy) • *Denois* (Cumières) • *Paul Déthune* (Ambonnay) • *Egly-Ouriet* (Bouzy) • *Gatinois* (Aÿ) • *René Geoffroy* (Cumières) • *Gosset-Brabant* (Aÿ) • *Patrick Soutiran* (Ambonnay)

ROSÉ DES RICEYS AOC
This is not part of the Coteaux Champenois AOC, but is a totally separate appellation. This pure Pinot noir, still, pink wine is made in the commune of Les Riceys in the Aube *département* and is something of a legend locally, its fame dating back to the 17th century and Louis XIV, who is said to have served it as often as he could. It should be dark pink, medium-bodied, and aromatic. The best are often reminiscent of chocolate, herbs, and even mint, and can possess a penetrating, fruity flavour with a long, smooth finish. Production has greatly increased in recent years, with even Vranken, the most commercial of commercial houses, producing one, but quality is erratic and I have never tasted an example anywhere near Horiot's 1971. Try Vve A. Devaux, Gallimard, and Morel – but be prepared for more disappointments than successes.

THE PRODUCERS OF
CHAMPAGNE

Notes

GM Former *Grande Marque* (*see* p.170)

NV Non-vintage

V Vintage

PC *Prestige Cuvée* (*see* p.172)

SV Single vineyard

Where "Entire range" is recommended, this applies to Champagne only, not to Coteaux Champenois.

MICHEL ARNOULD
28 rue de Mailly
51360 Verzenay
★

Arnould is a traditional grower specializing in pure Verzenay Champagne, including a very rich but exquisitely balanced *blanc de noirs* Grand Cru Brut Réserve.

✓ *Grand Cru Brut*
• *Grand Cru Brut Réserve* (NV)

AYALA & CO *GM*
Château d'Aÿ
51160 Aÿ-Champagne
★❶V

This house is back on form after a disappointing period between the late 1980s and early 1990s, and is again making good-value, easy-to-drink *Grande Marque* Champagnes.

✓ *Brut* (NV) • *Brut* (V)
• *Grande Cuvée* (V)

BEAUMONT DES CRAYÈRES
64 rue de la Liberté
Mardeuil 51318 Epernay
★❶V

This cooperative's 210 members own just 80 hectares (200 acres) of vineyards and they are mostly of modest origin, but they are tended like gardens, without resort to machines or chemical treatments. Winemaker Jean-Paul Bertus regularly produces richly flavoured Champagne with a light dosage.

✓ *Fleur de Rosé* (V)
• *Fleur de Prestige* (V)

BILLECART-SALMON *GM*
40 rue Carnot
Mareuil-sur-Aÿ
★★★

Billecart-Salmon is a family-owned *Grande Marque* of exceptionally high quality. This house has a reputation for the delicate style of its rosé Champagnes, which it has been producing since 1830 and which account for almost one in every five bottles it produces. The Cuvée Elisabeth Salmon Rosé really is a Champagne to die for!

✓ *Entire range*

TH. BLONDEL
Domaine des Monts Fournois
51500 Ludes
★

This is a small house producing an elegant style of Champagne with fragrant aromas and biscuity fruit.

✓ *Brut* (NV) • *Rosé* (NV)

BOIZEL
14 rue de Bernon
51200 Epernay
★❶V

Boizel is now part of BCC (Boizel-Chanoine Champagne), one of the industry's youngest and most dynamic companies. Bruno Paillard is the chairman and the largest shareholder, although the Roques-Boizel family and Philippe Baijot of Chanoine are almost equal partners. Although the non-vintage Boizel has occasionally been prone to the ubiquitous pear-drop style, quality has been more consistent since 1995 and the *blanc de blancs*, rosé, and *prestige cuvée* have always stood out.

✓ *Brut* (NV) • *Rosé* (V)
• *Joyau de France* (PC)

BOLLINGER *GM*
Rue Jules Lobet
Aÿ-Champagne
★★★

The non-vintage Special Cuvée can seem austere, but it is merely an extreme example of the classic, lean style and, although it contains considerably aged reserves, this wine is always freshly disgorged to order and benefits from further ageing. It mellows beautifully if laid down for two or three years. Magnums are fruitier and easier to drink when sold. Bollinger is, however, a house par excellence for vintage Champagne.

✓ *Entire range*

CHÂTEAU DE BOURSAULT
Boursault
51480 prés Epernay
★❶V

Château de Boursault NV has started to develop a real finesse since 1995, and the rosé has always been a joy. Made by owner Harald Fringhian, these Champagnes are now outperforming the château's modest 84 per cent *échelle*, which is probably helped by the fact that the vineyards are a genuine *clos* (an enclosed plot of land).

✓ *Brut* (NV) • *Rosé* (NV)

CANARD DUCHÊNE *GM*
1 rue Edmond Canard
51500 Ludes
Rilly-la-Montagne
★❶V

Owned by Veuve Clicquot since 1978, the value-for-money quality of these easy-drinking Champagnes has improved since the mid-1990s.

✓ *Brut* (NV) • *Rosé* (NV)
• *Charles VII Blanc de Noirs* (NV)

DE CASTELLANE
57 rue Verdun
51200 Epernay
★❶V

Part of the Laurent-Perrier group, this is an excellent source of under-valued, ripe, exotic *blanc de blancs*, as are the more expensive Cuvée Commodore and Cuvée Florens de Castellane, despite their presentation – the former looks *circa* 1950s while the latter is decidedly kitsch.

✓ *Chardonnay* (NV)
• *Cuvée Royale Chardonnay* (V)
• *Cuvée Commodore* (PC)
• *Cuvée Florens de Castellane* (PC)

CATTIER
6 et 11 rue Dom Pérignon
51500 Chigny-les-Roses
★❶❶V

I have always respected Clos du Moulin, Cattier's great single-vineyard Champagne, but have not been impressed – or depressed for that matter – by any of the other *cuvées*, until I first tasted its trio of particularly stunning vintages: 1988, 1989, and 1990.

✓ *Brut* (V) • Clos du Moulin (SV)

CHARLES DE CAZANOVE
1 rue des Cotelles
51204 Epernay
★❶V

This house has worked very hard to improve its wines during the 1990s and the quality can only get better now that Thierry Lombard, whose family owns the business, has divested himself of "Marie Stuart", a Champagne that could have been much better, but that merely

drained his resources. Since the early to mid-1990s, these wines have had an elegant style, often showing particularly fine autolytic floweriness.

✓ *Brut Azure* (NV)

CHANOINE
avenue de Champagne
51100 Reims
★

This *marque* was established in 1730 (just one year after Ruinart, the oldest house in Champagne) but was relaunched by Philippe Baijot in 1991. I was greatly impressed with the first *cuvées* following the relaunch, but their brilliant quality has never been recaptured. Well, not in the basic vintage and non-vintage, but the more recent Tsarine *cuvées* promise to grab attention (and I don't only mean because of the convoluted bottle shape, which comes out of the same mould as a certain brand of Asti!).

✓ *Tsarine* (NV) • *Tsarine* (V)

CHAUVET
41 avenue de Champagne
51150 Tours-sur-Marne
★❶V

A small, quality-conscious house situated opposite Laurent Perrier, Champagne Chauvet is owned by the Paillard-Chauvet family, who are wonderfully eccentric. They are related to Pierre Paillard in Bouzy, Bruno Paillard in Reims, and the Gossets of Aÿ. I have always enjoyed Chauvet's Carte Vert *blanc de blancs*, which is an excellent non-vintage blend of exclusively *Grand Cru* wines, and I have also greatly admired the consistency and quality of their entire range since the early 1990s.

✓ *Entire range*

GASTON CHIQUET
890-912 avenue du Général-Leclerc
Dizy 51310 Epernay
★❶V

Antoine and Nicolas Chiquet are grower cousins of *négociants* Jean-Hervé and Laurent Chiquet of Jacquesson, which is also in Dizy. The style here is succulent and creamy, with moreish juicy fruit.

✓ *Entire range*

ANDRÉ CLOUET
8 rue Gambetta
Bouzy 51150
Tours-sur-Marne
★

André Clouet, a small, quality-conscious grower, produces a very large range of attractive, rich, and beautifully made Champagnes.

✓ *Entire range*

DELAMOTTE PÈRE & FILS
5 rue de la Brèche
51190 Le Mesnil-sur-Oger
★❶V

Part of the Laurent-Perrier group and situated next door to Champagne Salon, which also belongs to Laurent-Perrier, Delamotte is a small, underrated, high-quality, good-value house that has been privately owned by the Nonancourt family (the owners of Laurent-Perrier) since the end of World War I, when it was purchased by Marie Louise de Nonancourt, the sister of Victor and Henri Lanson.

✓ *Brut* (**NV**)
- *Blanc de Blancs* (**NV**)
- *Blanc de Blancs* (**V**)
- *Nicolas Louis Delamotte* (**PC**)

DELBECK
**39 rue du Général Sarrail
51100 Reims**
❓

Delbeck is a lavishly packaged Champagne that was launched by François d'Aulan after he had sold Piper-Heidsieck. D'Aulan sold Delbeck to Bruno Paillard in 1994, who sold all but ten per cent to Pierre Martin, the mayor of Bouzy. Since its inception, Delbeck has been sourced from at least three different producers, but with Martin's 18 hectares (seven acres) of prime Bouzy vineyards, it should soon establish its own high-quality house style, and with Olivier de la Giraudière (who came from Laurent-Perrier) being a minor shareholder and in charge of sales, we should see more of this brand.

PAUL DÉTHUNE
**2 rue du Moulin
51150 Ambonnay**
★ⓥ

As one of the more consistent growers, Paul Déthune always makes good vintage and rosé, but is best known for his *prestige cuvée*, the luxuriously rich, big, deliciously creamy Princesse des Thunes, which is made from an *assemblage* of mature vintages.

✓ *Grand Cru Rosé* (**NV**)
- *Millésimé* (**V**)
- *Princesse des Thunes* (**PC**)

DEUTZ *GM*
**16 rue Jeanson
51160 Aÿ-Champagne**
★★

The profitability and quality of Deutz suffered from underfunding until Roederer acquired it in 1983. Its resurgence began a little shakily with the 1985 vintage but was firmly established by 1988, when it returned to making very stylish Champagnes. Now on stunning form. Deutz also own Délas Frères in the Rhône and Château Vernous in the Médoc, and have a partnership with Montana to produce Deutz Marlborough in New Zealand.

✓ *Entire range*

VVE A. DEVAUX
**Domaine de Villeneuve
10110 Bar-sur-Seine**
★ⓥ

There are two men, Laurent Gillet and Claude Thibaut, responsible for this being the most dynamic *coopérative* in Champagne. Gillet is the man in charge and he was the one who had the vision to raise standards throughout the Aube, while Thibaut is the talented winemaker whose experience at Yellowglen in Australia and Iron Horse in California has obviously rubbed off in the clean, well-focused fruit found in these Champagnes.

✓ *Grande Réserve Brut* (**NV**)
- *Cuvée Rosée (sic)* (**NV**)
- *Blanc de Noirs* (**NV**)
- *Cuvée Distinction Rosé* (**V**)

ROBERT DOYARD
**61 avenue de Bammental
51130 Vertus**
★

It was Robert Doyard's father, Maurice Doyard who, with Robert-Jean de Vogüé, persuaded the Germans to establish the CIVC (Comité Interprofessionnel du Vin de Champagne) by suggesting that the Third Reich had more important things to do than to get bogged down in the day-to-day operations of the Champagne industry. This not only enabled the *champenois* to run their own industry under the noses of their invaders, but the organization they set up became the most efficient and powerful in the entire French wine industry. Yannick Doyard, the grandson, is now the winemaker.

✓ *Blanc de Blancs* (**V**)
- *Oeil de Perdrix Rosé* (**V**)

DRAPPIER
**Grande rue
10200 Urville
Cellars in Reims:
11 rue Godot
51100 Reims**
★★☆ⓥ

Drappier's Champagnes are brilliantly consistent, ultra-fruity, and rapidly acquire mellow biscuity complexity.

✓ *Entire range*

DUVAL-LEROY
**65 avenue de Bammental
51130 Vertus**
★★☆ⓥ

Duval-Leroy's light, elegant house-style offers a very high quality-to-price ratio, not least because up to 70 per cent of its annual turnover of 5.5 million bottles is sold under other labels. The own-label wines are superior examples of their type, but Duval-Leroy is eager to see its own brand sales grow, so it makes sure every bottle bearing its own name attracts repeat buyers.

✓ *Entire range*

GARDET & CIE
**13 rue Georges Legros
51500 Chigny-les-Roses**
★★ⓥ

This Champagne used to be sold as Georges Gardet in the UK and Charles Gardet in France, but the emphasis is now on Gardet plain and simple. Gardet has always prided itself on the longevity of its wines, but I prefer the vintage almost before it is even released, although the greatest Gardet I have ever tasted was the 1964 in 1995. A very welcome addition to the range is the succulent new *blanc de blancs*, the first vintage of which was 1990.

✓ *Brut Spécial* (**NV**) • *Brut* (**V**)
- *Blanc de Blancs* (**V**)

RENÉ GEOFFROY
**150 rue du Bois-des-Jots
Cumières 51480 Damery**

The Geoffroy family have been growers in Cumières since 1600 and conscientiously harvest their grapes in *tries*. The Champagne, which does not go through malolactic "fermentation" and may be matured in oak *foudres*, is classic in style, longlived, and capable of great complexity.

✓ *Cuvée Sélectionnée Brut* (**NV**)
- *Brut Rosé* (**NV**)

PIERRE GIMONNET
**1 rue de la République
51530 Cuis**
★★☆

This excellent grower's vineyards are all planted with Chardonnay, hence every wine is a *blanc de blancs*, which is a very rare phenomenon, even among growers on the Côte des Blancs. Quality is exceptionally high and prices very reasonable.

✓ *Entire range*

PAUL GOBILLARD
**Château de Pierry
Pierry 51200 Epernay**
★

Bruno Gobillard runs a munificent venture in Château de Pierry called La Maison du Millésime, providing visitors with the rare opportunity to taste older vintages of Champagne in perfect condition from the cellars of famous houses. Gobillard's own Champagne is usually excellent in a weighty, yet crisp and elegant, style.

✓ *Brut* (**NV**) • *Brut* (**V**)
- *Cuvée Régence* (**PV**)

PAUL GOERG
**4 Place du Mont Chenil
51130 Vertus**

This small but superior *coopérative* produces very fine and elegant yet rich, concentrated Champagnes.

✓ *Blanc de Blancs* (**NV**)
- *Brut* (**V**)

GOSSET *GM*
**69 rue Jules Blondeau
51160 Aÿ-Champagne**
★★★

Established in 1584, Gosset is the oldest house in the region, but for still wines, not sparkling. In 1992, Gosset became the first new *Grande Marque* for more than 30 years, then in 1994, after 400 years of family ownership, the house was

sold. This was profoundly sad but not such a bad thing as Gosset was not taken over by one of the large groups but by the Cointreau family, and is under the direct control of Béatrice Cointreau, a fiery young lady who has breathed some fresh air into the Champagne trade. The *chef de caves* and oenologist remain the same, as do the winemaking techniques. I have always rated the Grande Réserve, the Grand Millésimé, and the Grand Millésimé Rosé as three of the consistently greatest Champagnes available.

HENRI GOUTORBE
**11 rue Jeanson
51160 Aÿ-Champagne**
★★☆ⓥ

With 15 hectares (six acres) of vineyards and half a million bottles in stock, this is one of the larger wine growers. Henri Goutorbe produces some rich, classic, and well-structured Champagnes that become very satisfying with age.

✓ *Entire range*

ALFRED GRATIEN
**30 rue Maurice-Cerveaux
51201 Epernay**
★★☆ⓥ

This house is part of Gratien, Meyer, Seydoux & Cie, who also sell a range of Loire *méthode champenoise* wines under the Gratien and Meyer brand. Alfred Gratien is one of the most traditionally produced Champagnes available. The old vintages never fail to amaze, as they are brilliant in quality and retain a remarkable freshness for decades. The non-vintage wine is beautifully fresh with mature reserves coming through on the palate, making it a wine to drink now, yet one that will improve with age.

✓ *Entire range*

CHARLES HEIDSIECK *GM*
**12 allée du Vignoble
Murigny 51061 Reims**
★★ⓥ

Charles Heidsieck is part of Rémy-Cointreau's Champagne group, which also includes Piper-Heidsieck. The superb quality of the house of Charles Heidsieck is guided by the masterly hand of Daniel Thibault, who is one of Champagne's greatest winemakers.

✓ *Entire range*

HEIDSIECK & CO MONOPOLE *GM*
**83 rue Coquebert
51100 Reims**
❓

Not to be confused with either Charles Heidsieck or Piper-Heidsieck, this brand was owned by Mumm until 1996, when it was eventually sold to Vranken.

HENRIOT
**3 place des Droits-de-l'Homme
51100 Reims**
★

Now back under family ownership with Joseph Henriot at the helm, this Champagne house is trying to re-establish itself on export markets, where I prefer the wines, as they usually have good landed-age, which brings a certain desirable biscuity complexity to their elegant richness.

✓ *Entire range*

JACQUART
5 rue Gosset
51066 Reims
★★⊙

This CRVC (Coopérative Régionale des Vins de Champagne) *coopérative* cleverly converted its primary brand into a *négociant-manipulant* Champagne by making its members shareholders. The quality of Jacquart is always acceptable at the very least, and some vintages, such as the 1985, can be outstanding.

✓ *Cuvée Mosaïque Blanc de Blancs* (V) • *Cuvée Mosaïque Rosé* (V) • *Cuvée Onctueuse Rosé* (NV)

JACQUESSON & FILS
68 rue du Colonel Fabien
Dizy 51310 Epernay
★★★⊬

This small, family-owned house is run by the Chiquet brothers, two of the most charming people you are likely to meet. They make utterly sublime Champagnes, which are beautifully presented.

✓ *Entire range*

PIERRE JAMAIN
Route de Chantemerle
51260 La Celle-sous-Chantemerle
★⊙

Elisabeth Jamain produces delicious Champagnes from one of the first vineyards to be planted in the Sézannais. The pure Chardonnay non-vintage *brut* is particularly successful, with exotic fruit flavours and lively acidity.

✓ *Brut* (NV)

ANDRÉ JARRY
Rue Principale
51260 Bethon
★⊙

Excellent Champagne in a style that is midway between the classic character of Champagnes from the Marne *département* and the exotic character of Sézannais Champagnes, full of biscuity richness yet with an aftertaste of vanilla and peaches.

✓ *Cuvée Special* (NV)

KRUG & CO *GM*
5 rue Coquebert
51051 Reims
★★★

Krug puts quality first and makes Champagne in its own individual style, regardless of popular taste or production costs. With the possible exception of Salon, this sort of quality is not equalled by any other Champagne house, although it could be if they were willing to sell tiny quantities at very high prices. If everyone did this, it would be a disaster – Champagne has to be affordable – but that at least one house does is not just laudable, it is very important for Champagne.

✓ *Entire range*

LANSON PÈRE & FILS *GM*
12 boulevard Lundy
51056 Reims
★★⊬⊙

This house was purchased in 1991 by Marne et Champagne, a house specializing in *sous marque* and own-label Champagnes (they have over 360 different brands!). Lanson has always excelled at making classic, slow-maturing, biscuity vintage Champagne. The Black Label non-vintage has improved tremendously over the last two or three years.

✓ *Brut* (NV) • *Brut* (V) • *Noble Cuvée* (PC) • *Demi Sec* (NV)

GUY LARMANDIER
30 rue du Général Koenig
51130 Vertus
★

Guy and François Larmandier have a well-earned reputation for finely balanced wines of surprising depth and obvious finesse.

✓ *Blanc de Blancs Cramant* (NV)

LARMANDIER-BERNIER
43 rue du 28 août
51130 Vertus
★

These high quality *blanc de blancs* Champagnes are made by Pierre Larmandier, the president of the Young Winegrowers of Champagne.

✓ *Entire range*

LAURENT-PERRIER *GM*
Avenue de Champagne
51150 Tours-sur-Marne
★★⊙

This house used to head a sprawling vinous empire until its outposts in Burgundy and Bordeaux were sold off to concentrate Laurent-Perrier's efforts and finances on its Champagne holdings, including De Castellane, Delamotte, Lemoine, and Salon. Although owner Bernard de Nonancourt has retired from day-to-day running of the company,

this great *champenois* is still firmly in control of the Laurent-Perrier group. Winemaker Alain Terrier has a passion for elegantly rich Champagnes of great finesse.

✓ *Entire range*

LECLERC BRIANT
67 rue de la Chaude-Ruelle
51204 Epernay
⊙

Pascal Leclerc can come up with the odd Champagne to dumbfound people, such as his blood-red Rubis 1989 Rosé des Noirs and, when he does, they represent excellent value for money, but there could be slightly more consistency here. Furthermore, I am not sure about his Les Authentiques range of single-vineyard Champagnes. This was a brilliant marketing concept, but the wines, while enjoyable enough when launched, have failed to display any consistent and distinctive *terroir* character. A *cuvée* called Divine is the best of the range, despite its gaudy label.

✓ *Divine* (PC)

LILBERT FILS
223 rue du Moutier
51200 Cramant
★

This house is a consistent producer of firm *blanc de blancs* that show finesse and age gracefully.

✓ *Entire range*

MAILLY GRAND CRU
28 rue de la Liberation
51500 Mailly-Champagne
★⊙

This mono-cru cooperative has great potential, but its lower order Champagnes lack consistency.

✓ *Cassiopee* (NV) • *Cuvée des Echansons* (V) • *L'Intomporolle* (V) • *Cuvée du 60e Anniversaire* (V)

HENRI MANDOIS
66 rue du Gal-de-Gaulle
51200 Pierry
★⊬⊙

The house style of Henri Mandois is for elegant Champagnes that have a very satisfying length of attractive, creamy-fruit, and a fine balance. Most *cuvées* peak at between five and six years of age and do not attain great complexity. However, they do represent great value and give much satisfaction.

✓ *Entire range*

MARNE & CHAMPAGNE
22 rue Maurice-Cerveaux
Epernay
★⊙

This is the second-largest producer in Champagne but is relatively unknown. Until recently "Alfred Rothschild" was its best-known brand, and most of its output had been under some 200 obscure labels. Its presence has been more noticeable, however, since its acquisition of Bessarat de Bellefon and the *Grande Marque* house of Lanson. Quality, even under the most obscure label, can be very good.

SERGE MATHIEU
Les Riceys
10340 Avirey-Lingey
★⊬

Mathieu, a small grower in the Aube, consistently produces excellent Champagnes that are beautifully focused, have much finesse, and a real richness of fruit for such light and elegantly balanced wines.

✓ *Entire range*

MERCIER *GM*
75 avenue de Champagne
51200 Epernay
⊙

Mercier, established by Eugène Mercier in 1858, was the original owner of the Dom Pérignon brand, although it never utilized it and, in a strange twist of fate, sold it to Moët & Chandon in 1930. Moët liked the product so much that it bought Mercier, albeit some 40 years later. Mercier is still the best-selling brand in France, no matter how hard the parent company tries to make Moët number one, although Moët is way ahead in global sales.

✓ *Brut* (V)

DE MERIC
17 rue Gambetta
51160 Aÿ-Champagne
★

De Meric, whose wines are made by Christian Besserat, ranges from the simple but elegant and fruity non-vintage *Brut* to the sublime and very special Cuvée Catherine de Medicis, with various fine and fragrant *cuvées* in between.

✓ *Blanc de Blancs* (NV) • *Rosé* (NV) • *Cuvée Catherine de Medicis* (PC)

MOËT & CHANDON *GM*
20 avenue de Champagne
54120 Epernay
★★⊬

The largest Champagne house by a mile, Moët is also the leading company in the LVMH group, which also includes Mercier, Krug, Ruinart, Pommery, Veuve Clicquot, and Canard-Duchêne. In 1994, after the most exhaustive testing any non-vintage Champagne has ever been put through, I became convinced that – contrary to general belief – Moët's Brut Impérial is remarkably consistent in quality and character. When first released, the soft style of Brut Impérial makes it amenable to everyone and offensive to no one, but being relatively neutral it rarely does well in competitive tastings. After a further 12 months bottle-age, however, it mellows into a much fuller, toasty-rich Champagne that can win any competitive tasting. Between the unfairly criticized non-vintage and the universally praised Dom Pérignon, the vintage Brut Impérial and Brut Impérial Rosé have both been ignored and underrated. These two *cuvées* tend to offer the best value for money, whilst the fairly recent addition of an excellent non-vintage rosé, an innovative Premier Cru blend and a quality *demi-sec* called Nectar, Moët has demonstrated that it is not content to rest on its laurels. What next? A barrel-fermented super-Meunier *cuvée*?

✓ *Brut Impérial* (NV) • *Brut Impérial* (V) • *Brut Impérial Rosé* (V) • *Dom Pérignon* (PC) • *Dom Pérignon Rosé* (PC)

G. H. MUMM & CO *GM*
29 & 34 rue du Champ-de-Mars
51053 Reims
✰

Mumm has successfully pulled its act together, weeded out the dross, and shipped much better wines since early 1995. Before this time, the wines had lost their authentic house style, but they are now once again light, fragrant, and never too *brut*, and they have become cleaner, fresher, and more elegant with each successive shipment.

✓ *Cordon Rouge* (NV)
• *Mumm de Cramant* (NV)
• *Cordon Rouge* (V)

GRAND CHAMPAGNE NAPOLEON
2 rue de Villiers-aux-Bois
Vertus
★

This small, quality-conscious house is run by Etienne Prieur, whose brother Vincent makes the wines in one of the tiniest Champagne cellars I've seen. The Carte Or is richer and more mature than the Carte Vert, with some biscuity complexity. The Prieurs traditionally sell vintages of greater maturity than those of most houses and their vintage is often two or three years behind the rest of Champagne.

✓ *Carte Or* (NV)

BRUNO PAILLARD
avenue du Champagne
51100 Reims
★✰Ⓥ

Bruno Paillard is Champagne's fastest-rising star. He opts for elegance rather than body or character and his Premier Cuvée is not just elegant, it is one of the most consistent non-vintage Champagnes on the market. This house belongs personally to Bruno Paillard and is not part of the BCC group, which he heads.

✓ *Entire range*

PALMER & CO
67 rue Jacquart
51100 Reims
★Ⓥ

Palmer is generally acknowledged to be one of the highest-quality and most reliable *coopératives* in Champagne, on top of which it has a growing reputation for the excellent Champagnes sold under its own label and is particularly well known for its mature vintages. The chief oenologist is Liliane Vignon, one of a small but growing number of talented female winemakers in Champagne.

✓ *Entire range*

PANNIER
23 rue Roger Catillon
02400 Château-Thierry
★Ⓥ

For some time now this *coopérative* has been able to produce some very good vintage Champagne, especially its *prestige cuvée* Egérie de Pannier, but the basic "Brut Tradition" was always foursquare. This changed with the 1990-based Brut Tradition. Although this was and still is Pannier's best *cuvée*, due no doubt to the year in question, it also marked a general increase in finesse and this promises better quality ahead.

✓ *Brut Tradition* (NV)
• *Brut Vintage* (V)

JOSEPH PERRIER *GM*
69 avenue de Paris
51005 Châlons-sur-Marne
★Ⓥ

This house is still run by Jean-Claude Fourmon, even though he has sold a 51 per cent share in the business to his cousin Alain Thienot via an ephemeral interest by Laurent-Perrier. The style of these Champagnes is rich and mellow, although the difference when switching from one *cuvée* or vintage to the next can be quite severe, and the wines need to be laid down for 12 months or so.

✓ *Cuvée Royale* (NV) • *Cuvée Royale Rosé* (NV) • *Cuvée Royale Blanc de Blancs* (NV) • *Cuvée Royale* (V) • *Cuvée Joséphine* (PC)

PERRIER-JOUET *GM*
26/28 avenue de Champagne
51200 Epernay
★★✰

The basic non-vintage *brut* of Seagram's top-quality *Grande Marque* went through the same sour-cream and pickled cabbage malolactic aromas that blighted its sister brand Mumm. Although now sorted out, it is still well worth the premium asked to take a step up in quality to the non-vintage Blason de France *brut* and rosé, although this house is best known for its superb Belle-Époque Champagne.

✓ • *Blason de France Rosé* (NV)
• *Grand Brut* (NV & V)
• *Belle Époque Brut* (PC)
• *Belle Époque Rosé* (PC)
• *Belle Époque Blanc de Blancs* (V)

PHILIPPONNAT
13 rue du Pont
Mareuil-sur-Aÿ
★★✰
51160 Aÿ-Champagne

This house was purchased from an ailing Marie-Brizard by the BCC group in 1997. BCC's chairman finally persuaded Charles Philipponnat, a direct descendent and a sharp player in the grape-buying business, to leave his high-powered job at Moët. If the fabulously rich, mellow, Pinot-dominated non-vintage disgorged in March 2000 and on sale when this edition was put to bed is anything to go by, Philipponnat is going to be a name to watch in the future. The new Sublime *demi-sec* is truly sublime, but Clos des Goisses remains Philipponnat's jewel in the crown. One of the greatest Champagnes available, Clos des Goisses is a fully south-facing vineyard of very steep incline overlooking the Marne canal.

✓ *Entire range*

PIPER-HEIDSIECK *GM*
51 boulevard Henri Vasnier
51100 Reims
★Ⓥ

After working his miracles on Charles Heidsieck, Daniel Thibault upgraded the quality of Piper-Heidsieck without upsetting the supremacy of its sister brand. He achieved this by pouring more fruit into the blend and sourcing much of it from the warm Aube

vineyards, giving the wine a soft but simple, fruity aroma, and very moreish fruit on the palate.

✓ *Brut Rosé* (NV)
• *Brut Millésimé* (V)

PLOYEZ-JACQUEMART
Ludes
51500 Rilly-la-Montagne
★Ⓥ

The fragrant, creamy-lemony non-vintage *brut* of this small, family-run, quality-conscious house has never been better. Although the *prestige cuvée* L. d'Harbonville has always been excellent, it has jumped up a class since the 1989 vintage, when it was fermented in small oak barrels and not put through its malolactic fermentation. This made it even more succulent and mouthwatering than usual, with ample *dosage* to balance its electrifying acidity.

✓ *Entire range*

POL ROGER & CO *GM*
1 rue Henri Lelarge
51206 Epernay
★★★✰Ⓥ

If I were to choose just one house from which to source a vintage Champagne to lay down, there is no question that I would choose Pol Roger. There are always exceptions, of course, but, generally speaking, these Champagnes last longer and remain fresher than those of any other house, however justified their great reputations may be, and I base this opinion on tasting a good number of vintages spanning back a century or more at many houses.

✓ *Entire range*

POMMERY *GM*
5 place Général-Gouraud
51053 Reims
★★

Pommery has been on a roll since 1995, which is no mean feat for such a light and elegant Champagne with a production of almost seven million bottles, because the lighter the wine's style, the more difficult it is to maintain the quality as production increases. Currently on a roll!

✓ *Entire range*

R. RENAUDIN
Domaine des Conardins
51530 Moussy

Renaudin is a grower Champagne of consistently high quality. Its style is very expressive and elegant, from the Brut Réserve, which has classic structure and ages gracefully into a fine biscuity richness with minuscule bubbles, through the elegant, well-perfumed rosé, to the Cuvée Réserve CD, which is a splendidly rich blend produced from four vintages.

✓ *Brut Réserve* (**NV**) • *Cuvée Réserve CD* (**NV**) • *Rosé* (**NV**)

ALAIN ROBERT
25 avenue de la République
51190 le Mesnil-sur-Oger
★★☆

This grower owns vineyards in several villages throughout the Côte des Blancs and all his Champagnes are of excellent quality, but he is best known for lavishly packaged, beautifully produced, pure Le Mesnil Chardonnay, which shows exquisite finesse with age.

✓ *Mesnil Séduction* (**V**)
• *Mesnil Tradition* (**V**)
• *Mesnil Réserve* (**V**)

LOUIS ROEDERER *GM*
21 boulevard Lundy
51100 Reims
★★★☆ **V**

Louis Roederer is the most profitable house in Champagne, and should be an object lesson for those houses that count success in terms of the number of bottles they sell. The keys to real success in Champagne are an impeccable reputation, which guarantees a premium price, enough vineyards to guarantee consistent quality for a production large enough to rake in the money, and the self-discipline required not to go beyond that level. Jean-Claude Rouzaud knows that if he goes too far beyond Roederer's current production of 2.5 million bottles, he will be unable to guarantee the quality he demands and his brand would soon lose the cachet of relative exclusiveness. He does not, however, like to see his capital lie idle, which is why he would rather take over Deutz than increase his own production.

✓ *Entire range*

RUINART *GM*
4 rue de Crayère
51053 Reims
★★

Established in 1729 by Nicolas Ruinart, this is the oldest commercial producer of sparkling Champagne. This house was taken over in 1963 by Moët & Chandon, but has managed to maintain the image of an independent, premium-quality Champagne in spite of it being part of LVMH, the largest Champagne group, and trebling its production in the meantime.

✓ *Entire range*

SALON *GM*
le Mesnil-sur-Oger
51190 Avize
★★★

Now owned by Laurent-Perrier, Salon is assured of remaining one of the greatest Champagnes available. Only one *cuvée* is produced and it is exclusively vintage, making it the only winery in the world not to produce a wine every year. The wine does not usually undergo malolactic fermentation, is often kept on its sediment for ten years or more, and continues to benefit from at least an equal amount of ageing after disgorgement. To illustrate this, in 1995 when the trio of vintages 1988, 1989, and 1990 were dominating Champagne sales, the 1982 Salon was gradually being phased out and the 1983 phased in, a process that should take a few years, after which the 1985 will be gradually filtered on to the market.

✓ *Salon Cuvée "S"* (**V**)

JACQUES SÉLOSSE
22 rue Ernest Vallée
51190 Avize
★★☆

Anselme Sélosse has found a niche in the market for classic, wood-fermented, non-malolactic wines that receive minimal *dosage* and usually require several years extra post-disgorgement cellarage to show their full potential. Generally far too much raw oak for my liking, but there is no denying the quality of the wine underneath.

✓ *Entire range* (but with care)

TAITTINGER *GM*
9 place Saint-Niçaise
51061 Reims
★★

This house uses a high proportion of Chardonnay in its non-vintage Brut Réserve, making it one of the most elegant and delicate of *Grande Marque* Champagnes. Comtes de Champagne *blanc de blancs* and rosé are two of the greatest Champagnes produced, but I cannot understand why people rave about Taittinger's Art Collection Champagnes in their kitsch plastic casings. Except for the first two vintages (1978 and 1981), the wines have been identical to Taittinger's straight vintage *cuvées*, so you are paying a lot for a casing. Plastic cladding on a Champagne bottle is about as tasteful as stone cladding on a brick house, and spraying it with a replica of the Mona Lisa will not enhance the image one jot.

✓ *Entire range*

MARCEL & THIERRY TRIOLET
22 rue des Pressoirs
51260 Bethon

The Triolets own vineyards in Bethon, Villenauxe-la-Grande, and Montgenost, and make some of the best Champagnes in the Sézanne area, although they are more mature and traditional than is usual, with less intensity of the typical Sézanne exotic fruits.

✓ *Brut* (**NV**)

UNION CHAMPAGNE
7 rue Pasteur
51190 Avize
★ **V**

Champagne de St.-Gall is this *coopérative's* primary brand, and its biggest fault until now has been the confusing similarity of the blue label found on most of its very different *cuvées*. Recently, however, there has been an additional problem in that almost all the wines have had insufficient ageing following disgorgement. The one exception is the *prestige cuvée* Cuvée Orpale, which has consistently been well aged and shows surprising finesse.

✓ *Cuvée Orpale* (**PC**)

DE VENOGE
30 avenue de Champagne
51200 Epernay
★☆ **V**

This house has greatly improved over the last ten years, but could do itself a great favour by getting rid of the ridiculous, tear-shaped bottle used for the often excellent Cuvée des Princes. Champagne's lengthy ageing process means that it would take five years to get a new bottle on the shelf and a significant investment to achieve, but one only has to consider how the image of Grande Dame changed overnight to know that it would be well worth the expense.

✓ *Blanc de Noirs* (**V**)
• *Brut* (**V**)
• *Cuvée des Princes* (**PC**)

GEORGES VESSELLE
20 rue des Postes
51150 Bouzy
★☆

Better known than Jean Vesselle, but not quite as good or as consistent, although if the releases as from 2000 are anything to go by, we might be witnessing a distinctive step up in quality.

✓ *Brut* (**NV**)
• *Brut Rosé* (**NV**)
• *Brut Millésimé* (**V**)
• *Brut Juline* (**V**)

JEAN VESSELLE
4 rue Victor-Hugo
51150 Bouzy
★

Produced by Delphine Vesselle, who is a quality-conscious grower with Champagnes that are always rich, mature, and distinctive.

✓ *Entire range*

VEUVE CLICQUOT-PONSARDIN *GM*
12 rue du Temple
51054 Reims
★★★☆

The quality and image of this producer is surprisingly luxurious for such a large house. Admittedly, this is simpler to achieve for a house such as Clicquot that makes a full-bodied and characterful Champagne than it is for a maker of lighter-styled Champagne. The more delicately constructed a wine is, the easier it is to see the slightest flaw. That said, producing a big style of Champagne does not automatically guarantee its quality. Indeed, while it is easier to hide faults behind a fuller style, it is harder to achieve finesse and the one thing that comes across about the Clicquot style is that it is not just big, but it is also beautiful. This is not achieved merely through the selection of grapes, which is emphatically driven by Montagne Pinot and often Bouzy, but also by the natural, hands-off approach to winemaking at this house. The fermentation temperature is not excessively low at Veuve Clicquot-Ponsardin, there is no filtering before blending, and only a light filtration prior to bottling, with reserves stored on their lees.

✓ *Entire range*

VILMART
4 rue de la République
51500 Rilly-la-Montagne
★★★☆

In 1991 I wrote that "Vilmart is the greatest Champagne-grower I know", which could have been an albatross around my neck. However, while many growers have made, and still make, individual Champagnes that please me as much or almost as much as Vilmart, none has achieved quite such stunning consistency throughout its entire range, year in, year out. The top *cuvées* have become too oaky, but Vilmart has gone through this heavy-handy phase and emerged all the better for it, although it will be some time before we see the results in wines that are ready for drinking.

✓ *Entire range*

VRANKEN
42 avenue de Champagne
Epernay
❓

The house of Vranken is owned by the Belgian Paul Vranken, whose ideas on quality I do not share but who undoubtedly has one of the cleverest commercial brains in the region. His brands include Charles Lafitte, René Lallement, Demoiselle, Vranken, Barancourt, and Heidsieck & Co Monopole. He also owns subsidiaries in Portugal (Port: Quinta do Convento, Quinta do Paco & Sao Pedro) and Spain (Cava: Senora & Vranken).

AUTHOR'S CHOICE

Many good-value wines have already been recommended in the preceding pages. As Champagne is my first specialist subject – the second being Alsace – I decided to grasp the nettle and select 25 all-time-great Champagnes. However, no matter how hard I tried, I could not whittle it down to less than 27 and even then I had to cheat by lumping different styles of some cuvées *together.*

PRODUCER	WINE	STYLE	DESCRIPTION	🍾
Billecart-Salmon (*see p.173*)	Blanc de Blancs	SPARKLING WHITE	This is the *cuvée* that seems to slip by the critics, but it is a rich and luscious style of *blanc de blancs* that evolves very slowly.	5–20 years
Billecart-Salmon (*see p.173*)	Brut	SPARKLING WHITE	My ultimate choice for the best elegant-but-succulent style of non-vintage. It is ripe and generous, yet light, and delicate in balance, with just a touch of vanilla-finesse on the finish.	Up to 2 years
Bollinger (*see p.173*)	Vieilles Vignes Françaises, Blanc de Noirs	SPARKLING WHITE	This is not a classic *cuvée*, it is an idiosyncratic Champagne of sensational quality, made exclusively from Pinot noir grapes, and sells for an outrageous price.	10–30 years
Cattier (*see p.173*) ⓥ	Clos du Moulin	SPARKLING WHITE	An old favourite of mine, this vineyard on the northern Montagne yields just 15–20,000 bottles, less than 40 per cent of its potential production. It is a blend of three vintage years, and needs post-disgorgement ageing to show its true class.	8–20 years from the youngest of three vintages
Pierre Gimonnet (*see p.174*) ⓥ	Premier Cru Chardonnay	SPARKLING WHITE	The purity of fruit, sheer concentration and great elegance add up to Chardonnay of amazing finesse, yet it is just *premier cru*, not *grand cru*. This is only possible through restricted yields and great passion, both in the vineyard and in the winery.	5–20 years
Charles Heidsieck (*see p.174*) ⓥ	Brut Réserve Mis en Cave	SPARKLING WHITE	Since relaunched in 1989 with 40 per cent reserves, many critics have wondered whether the standard of this *cuvée* could be maintained. Its full-bodied, biscuity-rich, vanilla-hued, mellow character has remained uncannily consistent. It is the best-value serious-quality non-vintage Champagne available.	Up to 4 years
Jacquesson & Fils (*see p.175*) ⓥ	Signature	SPARKLING WHITE and SPARKLING ROSÉ	With a tremendous run of vintages since 1975, the Signature Brut has shown its reliability for a balanced, succulently fruity Champagne. Exceptionally seductive on release, it repays cellaring with wonderfully complex aromas.	6–15 years
Jacquesson & Fils (*see p.175*) ⓥ	Blanc de Blancs	SPARKLING WHITE	Until 1995, this was a non-vintage blend acknowledged as one of Jacquesson's most successful Champagnes. That year, the Chiquet brothers launched the first vintage with the 1990 *cuvée*, and its rich, creamy Chardonnay flavour was a great success.	6–10 years
Krug & Co. (*see p.175*)	Clos du Mesnil, Blanc de Blancs	SPARKLING WHITE	What can I say about this wine, other than can you afford it? Clos du Mesnil less than half the size of Clos du Moulin, yet it produces a similar quantity of more concentrated wine, due to the sun-trap of its high walls. This wine can change its character many times over the years.	10–100 years
Krug & Co. (*see p.175*)	Grande Cuvée	SPARKLING WHITE	Grande Cuvée contains on average 35–50 per cent of reserve wines from 6–10 different vintages, spends 5–7 years on its yeast, and is the same price as the most expensive prestige Champagnes. Huge, lemony-oak aromas, and rich, exotic fruit.	Up to 15 years
Krug & Co. (*see p.175*)	Vintage	SPARKLING WHITE	These are great wines without exception. The massively flavoured yet beautifully balanced house style is legendary, while its character varies with the year.	12–30 years
Laurent-Perrier (*see p.175*) ⓥ	Grand Siècle	SPARKLING WHITE and SPARKLING ROSÉ	The original Grand Siècle "La Cuvée" is still my favourite of the two *brut* styles and at just over half the price of the Exceptionellement Millésimé, it is an amazing bargain *prestige cuvée*. With classic biscuity aromas, crisp fruit, and a hint of violets, it ages as gracefully as the very best vintage Champagnes.	Up to 40 years
Moët & Chandon (*see p.175*)	Dom Pérignon	SPARKLING WHITE and SPARKLING ROSÉ	The quality and fame of Cuvée Dom Pérignon are such that many people think it is a separate house. The *brut* is capable of tremendous finesse, and is surprisingly longlived, but most bottles are consumed too young, and far too cold. The rosé, produced in tiny amounts, has an exquisite richness of red fruits.	10–30 years
Bruno Paillard (*see p.176*) ⓥ	Premier Cuvée	SPARKLING WHITE	I thought long and hard about whether to include this relatively new Champagne, but whenever I have been in a restaurant with a companion who has preferred a light, elegant style of non-vintage, it has proved to be the most consistent choice.	Up to 3 years

PRODUCER	WINE	STYLE	DESCRIPTION	⌐~~
Perrier-Jouët (see p.176)	Belle Époque	SPARKLING WHITE and SPARKLING ROSÉ	This is sold in the famous "flower bottle" created by Émile Gallé at the turn of the century to evoke the Belle Époque of the 1890s. Perrier-Jouët has always ensured that the very finest ingredients are used. The *brut* is always quite firm when released, but after about ten years the Chardonnay element of the blend blossoms into rich, toasty aromas.	8–25 years
Philipponnat (see p.176)	Clos des Goisses	SPARKLING WHITE	Another favourite of mine, Clos des Goisses is a very special wine that requires at least 10 to 15 years to show its full potential. Six hectares of vineyards varying from steep incline to gentle slopes enable Philipponnat to employ a flexibility for the blending of this single-vineyard Champagne.	10–40 years
Pol Roger & Co. (see p.176) ⓥ	Brut Vintage	SPARKLING WHITE	No other house makes classic Champagnes that evolve slower or more gracefully than Pol Roger. Here you can find the 1928, 1921, 1919, and 1914 all in brilliant condition. I bet you a case of Pol Roger 1990 the next hundred years of vintages will be as great as the last.	7–50 years (up to 105 years for exceptional vintages!)
Pol Roger & Co. (see p.176) ⓥ	Cuvée Sir Winston Churchill	SPARKLING WHITE	This is the greatest *prestige cuvée* of recent times. The first vintage was 1975, available in magnums only, and launched in 1984. It was nectar then, and will age gracefully for another 30 years or more. All vintages reveal luscious fruit and fine floweriness upon release and this slowly acquires complex toasty aromas of great finesse.	10–40 years
Louis Roederer (see p.177) ⓥ	Brut Premier	SPARKLING WHITE	Although Roederer's most famous Champagne is Cristal, its small production means the non-vintage Brut Premier must act as its flagship, perfectly expressing the style of this house. It contains just 10 to 20 per cent of reserve wines, but it is the style and quality of these which are important. They are kept in old casks, infusing Brut Premier with its creamy-biscuit potential.	Up to 4 years
Louis Roederer (see p.177) ⓥ	Cristal	SPARKLING WHITE and SPARKLING ROSÉ	These extraordinary *cuvées* show hardly any special quality when released, but undergo a most profound change in the three years following disgorgement. Cristal Rosé is made in tiny quantities from the ripest Pinot noir. All vintages of the rosé and *brut* with the exception of 1986 are enthusiastically recommended.	8–20 years
Ruinart (see p.177)	Dom Ruinart	SPARKLING WHITE and SPARKLING ROSÉ	The *blanc de blancs* is best known and has succulent fruit that develops full, smoky aromas after eight years in bottle. Equally good, the rosé has a bouquet of red summer fruits. To know what pure Pinot noir smells like, open any 10-year-old bottle of Dom Ruinart Rosé, although it is 80 per cent Chardonnay!	8–12 years
Salon (see p.177)	Cuvée "S" Blanc de Blancs	SPARKLING WHITE	Light in flavour when young, Salon develops an intense, creamy-richness with age. A mature vintage has a complex range of aromas and flavours, including toasted macaroons, creamy brazil nuts, and coffee.	Within 10–50 years
Taittinger (see p.177)	Comtes de Champagne	SPARKLING WHITE and SPARKLING ROSÉ	Comtes de Champagne Blanc de Blancs is an elegant wine, but given ten years or more, it demonstrates just how full and rich top-notch Chardonnay Champagnes can be. Conversely, Comtes de Champagne Rosé can seem a bit top-heavy when young, but this *cuvée* will always achieve perfect balance in the end.	10–20 years
Veuve Clicquot-Ponsardin (see p.177)	La Grande Dame	SPARKLING WHITE	The difference between La Grand Dame and Veuve Clicquot's equally classic Vintage Reserve is often, but not always, that La Grande Dame is lighter, riper, more elegant, with particularly pure fruit and greater finesse. There will soon be a rosé version of La Grande Dame, which should be worth looking out for, coming from the house that invented the style.	8–40 years
Veuve Clicquot-Ponsardin (see p.177)	Vintage Reserve	SPARKLING WHITE and SPARKLING ROSÉ	Fuller than La Grande Dame and distinctly toasty, rather than biscuity, the straight vintage from this house appeals particularly to those who enjoy the classic, Pinot-dominated style of Champagne. The *Rich* version of vintage has raised the quality perception of sweeter Champagne styles and the rosé is about as classic as rosé gets.	8–40 years (6–15 years for rosé)
Vilmart (see p.177)	Coeur de Cuvée	SPARKLING WHITE	Vilmart did not rest on the laurels garnered by its superb Grand Cellier and Grand Cellier d'Or. The latter was the top of its range, but it has been surpassed by a super-deluxe *prestige cuvée* called Coeur de Cuvée, which, as its name implies, is made from the heart of the *cuvée*. Only a tiny quantity of such a refined product is possible, of course, and the authenticity of each numbered bottle is verified by a local magistrate.	5–30 years (presumably)
Vilmart (see p.177)	Grand Cellier d'Or	SPARKLING WHITE	Extremely rich, biscuity Champagne of great length and persistence. A sort of poor man's Krug!	5–20 years

ALSACE

Alsace is the only classic French wine region that has built a reputation on the concept of varietal wines. The region produces rich dry white wines with beautifully focused fruit. The wines are equally well suited to food as they are to drinking on their own.

A FASCINATING MIXTURE of French and German characteristics pervade this northeastern fragment of France, cut off from the rest of the country by the barrier of the Vosges mountains, and separated from neighbouring Germany by the mighty Rhine. The colourful combination of cultures is the result of wars and border squabbles that have plagued the ancient province since the Treaty of Westphalia put an end to the Thirty Years' War in 1648. This gave the French sovereignty over Alsace, and royal edicts issued in 1662, 1682, and 1687 proffered free land to anyone willing to

restore it to full productivity. As a result of this, Swiss, Germans, Tyroleans, and Lorrainers poured into the region. In 1871, at the end of the Franco-Prussian war, the region once again came under German control, and remained so until the end of World War I, when it once again became French. At this juncture, Alsace began to reorganize the administration of its vineyards in line with the new French AOC system, but in 1940 Germany reclaimed the province from France before this process was complete. Only after World War II, when Alsace reverted to France, was the quest for AOC status resumed, finally being realized in 1962.

The vineyards of Alsace are dotted with medieval towns of cobbled streets and timbered buildings, reflecting – as do the wines – the region's myriad Gallic and Prussian influences. The grapes are a mixture of German, French, and the exotic, with the German Riesling and Gewurztraminer (written without umlaut in Alsace), the French Pinot gris, and the decidedly exotic Muscat

HEADQUARTERS OF HUGEL & FILS
The small wine shop, cellars, and offices of the merchants Hugel & Fils in Riquewihr are marked by a typically Alsatian sign.

RECENT ALSACE VINTAGES

2000 Everyday drinking varieties such as Sylvaner, Pinot Blanc, and Auxerrois are extremely fruity. Excellent *Vendanges Tardives*, particularly in Riesling and Gewurztraminer.

1999 A large crop of easy-drinking wines, with good *vins de garde* from lower-yielding domaines.

1998 Good quality from early-picked aromatic varieties and excellent *Sélection de Grains Nobles*. Riesling excelled, Pinot Gris the least consistent.

1997 Better than 1996 and 1995, particularly for Gewurztraminer, this super-ripe vintage has produced

classic *Vendanges Tardives* in such volume that most of the standard bottlings are easily of this level. Beware the residual sweetness in many standard wines. Wines labelled as *Vendanges Tardives* are comparable to *Sélection de Grains Nobles* in a normal vintage and those labelled as *Sélection de Grains Nobles* are simply stunning!

1996 A potentially great vintage that should have been at least as good as 1995, although for both years you need to be very selective when it comes to Gewurztraminer, and the worst wines of 1996 have an unpleasantly distinctive aroma and unyielding acidity.

HOW TO READ ALSACE LABELS

GRAPE VARIETY •
This is the first thing to look for – in this case Riesling. Another name, in addition to the grape variety, will most probably be a brand name, but could refer to a village or vineyard, as is the case here. The Mambourg vineyard is a limestone *coteaux* overlooking the town of Sigolsheim. If there is no grape variety specified, the wine will either be Crémant d'Alsace, which is a good quality *méthode champenoise* sparkling wine, or a blend of different grape varieties, which may or may not refer to itself as an Edelzwicker.

GRAND CRU •
This applies to 50 classified vineyards whose wines reflect their individual *terroir*, but there is a significant premium over most other Alsace wines, which is not a guarantee of quality, so it is wise to follow recommended producers.

ALSACE GRAND CRU
APPELLATION ALSACE GRAND CRU CONTRÔLÉE

Ringenbach Moser

GEWURZTRAMINER 1985
14,5% vol   GRAND CRU MAMBOURG   750 ml

MIS EN BOUTEILLE PAR
RINGENBACH-MOSER A SIGOLSHEIM (HT-RHIN) FRANCE
PRODUCE OF FRANCE

• **APPELLATION**
All Alsace wines are made within the appellation of Alsace, and are so labelled. If the vineyard is classified as *Grand Cru*, this information is incorporated with the appellation.

• **PRODUCER AND VINTAGE**
The label may reveal both. In this case, 1985 is a great vintage, and Ringenbach Moser a very good grower whose vineyards are scattered over five different villages in, around, and including Sigolsheim. The small print at the bottom of the label clearly states that the wine was bottled on the domaine by the proprietor, and gives the address of the proprietor. This is obligatory, as is mentioning the country of origin if the wine is for export, and the bottle capacity.

Other information regarding style or quality may also be present:

MÉDAILLE D'OR
The medals of Colmar, Mâcon, and Paris have been devalued by the growing number of "winners". Many excellent wines are to be found

bearing the gold-medal stickers, but they are now so common that their presence has become practically meaningless. However, one medal that is definitely well worth looking out for is the "Sigillé de Qualité", issued by the Confrérie St.-Étienne.

VENDANGE TARDIVE
A late-harvested wine that is rich and powerful, and may be sweet.

SÉLECTION DE GRAINS NOBLES
A relatively rare, intensely sweet, yet remarkably elegant wine made from botrytized grapes.

ELEVÉ EN FÛTS
This indicates wine aged in cask and should taste and smell oaky.

SÉLECTION, RÉSERVE, AND SPÉCIALE CUVÉE
These terms suggest, and quite often mean, superior wine.

LA PETITE VENISE, COLMAR
This charming town, closely associated with the wine trade, boasts many architectural delights as well as a picturesque canal district.

comprising the four principal varieties. Sylvaner, another German grape, also features to some extent, while other French varieties include Pinot noir, Pinot blanc, Auxerrois, and Chasselas. While Gewurztraminer is definitely German (and fine examples are still to be found in the Pfalz, its area of origin), only in Alsace is it quite so spicy. And only in Alsace do you find spicy Pinot gris, a grape that is neutral elsewhere. Even the Pinot blanc may produce spicy wines in Alsace, although this is normally due to the inclusion of the fat-spicy Auxerrois grape.

Very little red wine is made in Alsace. What is produced is intended principally for local restaurants and *Weinstuben*. Ninety per cent of the wine in Alsace is white. Traditionally, the style of these very fruity wines is dry, although some varieties, such as the Gewurztraminer, have always been made less dry than others. With the introduction of Vendange Tardive and Sélection de Grains Nobles wines, growers have deliberately reduced yields to chase high sugar levels. This practice has resulted in even the most basic *cuvées* being too rich for a truly dry style, so the tendency to produce less dry wine has now spread to other varieties.

PINOT GRIS, ROTENBERG
A view of Turckheim from the steep slopes of Rotenberg vineyard in Wintzenheim, where Domaine Humbrecht produces fabulously fat Pinot Gris wines with powerful aromatic qualities.

FACTORS AFFECTING TASTE AND QUALITY

LOCATION
The northeast corner of France, flanked by the Vosges mountains and bordered by the Rhine and Germany's Black Forest. Six rivers rise in the fir-capped Vosges, flowing through the 97–km (60–mile) strip of vineyards to feed the river Ill.

CLIMATE
Protected from the full effect of Atlantic influences by the Vosges mountains, these vineyards are endowed with an exceptional amount of warm sunshine and a very low rainfall. The rain clouds tend to shed their load on the western side of the Vosges as they climb over the mountain range.

ASPECT
The vineyards nestle on the lower east-facing slopes of the Vosges at a relatively high altitude of about 180–360 m (600–1,200 ft), and at an angle ranging between 25° on the lower slopes and 65° on the higher ones. The best vineyards have a south or southeast aspect, but many good growths are also found on north- and northeast-facing slopes. In many cases the vines are cultivated on the top as well as the sides of a spur, but the best sites are always protected by forested tops. Too much cultivation of the fertile plains in the 1970s has led to recent over-production problems. However, some vineyards on the plains do yield very good-quality wines due to favourable soil types.

SOIL
Alsace has the most complex geological and solumological situation of all the great wine areas of France. The three basic morphological and structural areas are: the siliceous edge of the Vosges; limestone hills; and the hydrous alluvial plain. The soils of the first include: colluvium and fertile sand over granite, stony-clay soil over schist, various fertile soils over volcanic sedimentary rock, and poor, light, sandy soil over sandstone; of the second, dry, stony, and brown alkaline soil over limestone, brown sandy calcareous soils over sandstone and limestone, heavy fertile soils over clay-and-limestone, and brown alkaline soil over chalky marl; and of the third, sandy-clay and gravel overalluvium, brown decalcified loess, and dark calcareous soils over loess.

VITICULTURE AND VINIFICATION
The vines are trained high on wires to avoid spring ground frost. Traditionally, the wines are fermented as dry as possible, although many are no longer as dry as they used to be, due to growers lowering their yields in the last ten years in order to produce the higher sugar levels required for the new Vendange Tardive and Sélection de Grains Nobles wines (*see* below).

PRIMARY GRAPE VARIETIES
Gewurztraminer, Muscat blanc à petits grains, Muscat rosé à petits grains, Muscat ottonel, Riesling
SECONDARY GRAPE VARIETIES
Auxerrois, Chardonnay, Chasselas, Pinot gris, Sylvaner

VENDANGE TARDIVE AND SELECTION DE GRAINS NOBLES

"Vendange Tardive" or late-harvested wines have occasionally been made by a handful of quality-conscious producers throughout the history of Alsace, among them Hugel & Fils, who had long sold such wines under the German descriptions: "Auslese" and "Beerenauslese". Wanting to introduce Francophile terms, the firm pioneered the decree authorizing and controlling the commercial designations of Vendange Tardive and Sélection de Grains Nobles. The decree was passed in March 1984, and these styles have been universally produced since the botrytis-rich vintage of 1989.

THE WINES OF LORRAINE

Viticulture in these parts dates back to Roman times, and when the *départements* of Meurthe-et-Moselle and Moselle formed part of the old Province of Lorraine, their vineyards covered some 30,000 hectares (74,000 acres). This area was more than twice that of neighbouring Alsace today. They currently cover a mere 70 hectares (173 acres), virtually all of which are in the Meurthe-et-Moselle *département*. The viticultural outcrops of the Moselle are particularly sparse and make a sorry sight compared to their former glory; nowadays it is the *Route de la Mirabelle* (damson road), not the *Route du Vin* (wine road), that is flourishing. Growing damsons, it would seem, is far less risky than growing vines, although most people find that working in the industrialized town of Metz is more profitable

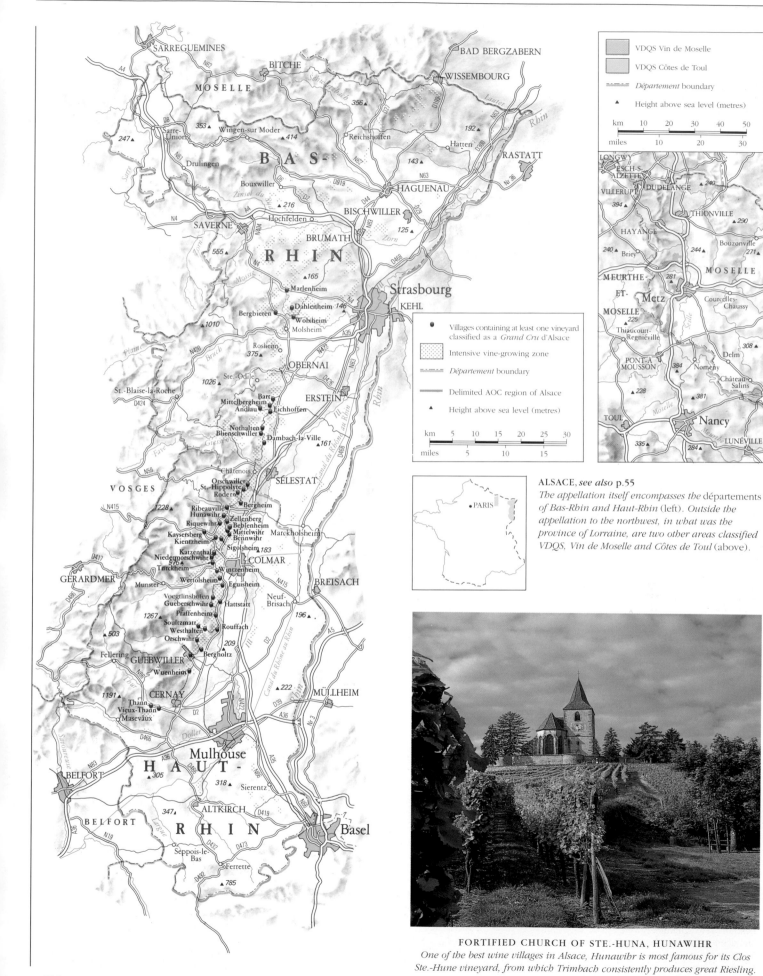

SARREGUEMINES
BITCHE
BAD BERGZABERN
WISSEMBOURG
MOSELLE
356▲
353▲ Wingen-sur Moder
247▲ 414▲
Sarre-Union
Reichshoffen
192▲
143▲
RASTATT
Drulingen
Hatten
B A S -
Bouxwiller
216▲
HAGUENAU
Hochfelden
BISCHWILLER
125▲
R H I N
SAVERNE
BRUMATH
555▲
165▲
Marlenheim
Strasbourg
Dahlenheim 146▲
KEHL
Bergbieten
Wolxheim
Molsheim
1010▲
Rosheim
OBERNAI
375▲
Ste.-Odile
St.-Blaise-la-Roche
1026▲
Barr
ERSTEIN
Mittelbergheim
Andlau Eichhoffen
Nothalten
Blienschwiller
Dambach-la-Ville
161▲
Châtenois
Orschwiller
SÉLESTAT
St.-Hippolyte
Rodern
VOSGES
1228▲
Bergheim
Ribeauvillé
Hunawihr
Zellenberg
Riquewihr
Beblenheim
Mittelwihr
Marckholsheim
Kaysersberg
Bennwihr
Kientzheim
Sigolsheim 183▲
Katzenthal
976▲
Niedermorschwihr
COLMAR
Turckheim
Wintzenheim
GERARDMER
Wettolsheim
Munster
Eguisheim
BREISACH
Voegtlinshofen
Neuf-Brisach
Gueberschwihr Hattstatt
196▲
1267▲
Pfaffenheim
Soultzmatt
Rouffach
Westhalten
503▲
Orschwihr
209▲
Bergholtz
GUEBWILLER
Wuenheim
MÜLLHEIM
222▲
1191▲
Thann
CERNAY
Vieux-Thann
Masevâux
D466
Mulhouse
305▲
H A U T -
318▲
Sierentz
BELFORT
347▲
ALTKIRCH
BELFORT
R H I N
Basel
Seppois-le-Bas
Ferrette
785▲

VDQS Vin de Moselle
VDQS Côtes de Toul
Département boundary
▲ Height above sea level (metres)
km 10 20 30 40 50
miles 10 20 30

LONGWY
ESCH-S.-
ALZETTE
VILLERUPT DUDELANGE
240▲
394▲
THIONVILLE
290▲
HAYANGE
240▲ Briey
244▲
Bouzonville
271▲
MEURTHE-
281▲
M O S E L L E
ET-
Metz
Courcelles-
MOSELLE
225▲
Chaussy
Thiaucourt-
Regniéville
PONT-A-
MOUSSON
384▲
Delm
308▲
Nomeny
228▲
Château-
Salins
TOUL
381▲
Nancy
335▲
284▲
LUNÉVILLE

• Villages containing at least one vineyard classified as a *Grand Cru* d'Alsace
Intensive vine-growing zone
Département boundary
Delimited AOC region of Alsace
▲ Height above sea level (metres)
km 5 10 15 20 25 30
miles 5 10 15

•PARIS

ALSACE, *see also* p.55
The appellation itself encompasses the départements *of Bas-Rhin and Haut-Rhin* (left). *Outside the appellation to the northwest, in what was the province of Lorraine, are two other areas classified VDQS, Vin de Moselle and Côtes de Toul* (above).

FORTIFIED CHURCH OF STE.-HUNA, HUNAWIHR
One of the best wine villages in Alsace, Hunawihr is most famous for its Clos Ste.-Hune vineyard, from which Trimbach consistently produces great Riesling.

THE GRANDS CRUS OF
ALSACE

The original *Grand Cru* legislation was introduced in 1975, but it was not until 1983 that the first list of 25 *Grand Cru* sites apeared. Three years later a further 23 were added, and there are now 50, although this number is the subject of much controversy, not least because it excludes what is acknowledged as one of the most famous, truly great *crus* of Alsace – Kaefferkopf in Ammerschwihr. While the *Grands Crus* will be of long-term benefit to both Alsace and the consumer, the limitation of *Grand Cru* to pure varietal wines of just four grapes – Muscat, Riesling, Pinot gris, and Gewurztraminer – robs us of the chance to drink the finest quality of Pinot Noir, Pinot Blanc, Sylvaner, and Chasselas.

Even if these wines might not be in the same league as the big four, it seems wholly unreasonable to prevent their cultivation for AOC Alsace Grand Cru when market forces dictate that most growers will, in any case, plant the four classic varieties in their most prized *Grand Cru* sites because they fetch the highest prices. If, however, a grower on a *Grand Cru* is determined to make the best possible wine from any of the less lucrative varieties or, indeed, to produce a classic blend, why should we, the buyers, be prevented from knowing where the grapes came from because the law prevents the grower from mentioning *Grand Cru* on the label of such wines?

I have been aware of these shortcomings since the publication of *The Wines of Alsace* (Faber & Faber, 1993), so it was particularly heartening when in 2000 various impeccable sources informed me that the *Grand Cru* appellation will shortly be opened up to include varieties other than the so-called noble grapes. Apparently Zotzenberg will be the first (for Sylvaner), followed by Steinklotz (for Pinot Noir) and Altenberg de Bergheim (for a blend of grapes). It won't stop there because if Steinklotz is classified for Pinot Noir, then Vorbourg cannot be far behind, and Altenberg de Bergheim will certainly open the door for Kaefferkopf. The ball will just keep rolling because if Sylvaner from Zotzenberg why not Chasselas from Hengst? There will be fears that these wines will dilute the status of *Grand Cru* wines, and that may indeed happen, but it does not matter. In the long term it is the market that dictates status, not a decree. Reputations have to be earned, not bestowed. That's why the cheapest wine from Zind-Humbrecht is more expensive than some producers' *Grands Crus*. The classification Alsace Grand Cru was late in coming, but happened in a rush, leapfrogging any thought of an intermediate *Premier Cru* appellation, and the delimitation of many sites was a joke. However, the market is already starting to sort the chaff from the wheat and the same will happen to classified wines made from less classic varieties and grape blends.

ALTENBERG DE BERGBIETEN
Bergbieten
An exceptional growth, but not a truly great one. Its gypsum-permeated, clayey-marl soil is best for Gewurztraminer, which has a very floral character with immediate appeal, yet can improve for several years in bottle.

✓ *Frédéric Mochel*

ALTENBERG DE BERGHEIM
Bergheim
This Altenberg has been a true *Grand Cru* since the 12th century, and its calcareous clay soil is best suited to Gewurztraminer, which is tight and austere in youth, but gains in depth and bouquet with ageing. This *cru* will apply for classification of wines made from a blend of grapes.

✓ *Marcel Deiss • Domaine Spielmann*

ALTENBERG DE WOLXHEIM
Wolxheim
Even though appreciated by Napoleon, this calcareous clay *cru* cannot honestly be described as one of the greatest growths of Alsace, although it has a certain reputation for its Riesling.

✓ *Charles Dischler • Muhlberger*

BRAND
Turckheim
This *cru* might legitimately be called Brand New, the original Brand being a tiny *cru* of little more than three hectares. In 1924 it was expanded to include surrounding sites: Steinglitz, Kirchthal, Schneckenberg, Weingarten, and Jebsal, each with its own fine reputation. By 1980 it had grown to 30 hectares (74 acres) and it is now almost double. This confederation of *lieux-dits* is one of the most magnificent sights in the entire region, and the quality of the wines consistently excites me – great Riesling, Pinot Gris, and Gewurztraminer.

✓ *Albert Boxler • Domaines Dopff Au Moulin • JosMeyer • Pierre Sparr and the CV Turckheim • Domaine Zind Humbrecht*

BRUDERTHAL
Molsheim
Riesling and Gewurztraminer – reputedly the best varieties – occupy most of this calcareous clay *cru*. I have tasted good, fruity Riesling from Bernard Weber, which was elegant but not really top stuff, and the Riesling, Pinot Gris, and Gewurztraminer of Domaine Neumeyer have not impressed me at all.

EICHBERG
Eguisheim
This calcareous clay *cru* has the lowest rainfall in Colmar and produces very aromatic wines of exceptional delicacy, yet great longevity. Famous for Gewurztraminer, which is potentially the finest in Alsace, Eichberg is also capable of making superb long-lived Riesling and Pinot Gris.

✓ *Charles Baur • Léon Beyer* (contrary to the *Grand Cru* concept, Beyer's Cuvée des Comtes d'Eguisheim is 100% pure Eichberg) *• Paul Ginglinger • Albert Hertz • Kuentz-Bas • André Scherer • Gérard Schueller • Wolfberger*

ENGELBERG
Dahlenheim and Scharrachbergheim
One of the least-encountered *Grands Crus*, this vineyard gets long hours of sunshine and is supposed to favour Gewurztraminer and Riesling; but few of the wines I have tasted suggest anything special.

✓ *Jean-Pierre Bechtold*

FLORIMONT
Ingersheim and Katzenthal
Mediterranean flora abounds on the sun-blessed, calcareous clay slopes of this *cru* – hence its name, meaning "hill of flowers" – the excellent microclimate producing some stunning Riesling and Gewurztraminer.

✓ *CV Ingersheim • Bruno Sorg*

FRANKSTEIN
Dambach-la-Ville
Not so much one vineyard as four separate spurs, the warm, well-drained, granite soil of this *cru* is best suited to delicate, racy Riesling, and elegant Gewurztraminer. Hauller is by far and away the best producer of Frankstein, for both the Riesling and Gewurztraminer, and is generally underrated for his entire range of wines.

✓ *J. Hauller & Fils*

FROEHN
Zellenberg

This *cru* sweeps up and around the southern half of the hill upon which Zellenberg is situated. The marly-clay soil suits Muscat, Gewurztraminer, and Pinot gris, in that order, and the wines are typically rich and long lived.

✓ *Jean Becker*

FÜRSTENTUM
Kientzheim and Sigolsheim
This estate is best for Riesling, although the vines have to be well established to take full advantage of the calcareous soil. Gewurztraminer can also be fabulous – in an elegant, more floral, less spicy style – and Pinot gris excels even when the vines are very young.

✓ *Paul Blanck • Bott-Geyl • Albert Mann • Marc Tempé • Domaine Weinbach*

GEISBERG
Ribeauvillé
Geisberg has been well documented since as long ago as 1308 as Riesling country par excellence. The calcareous, stony-and-clayey sandstone soil produces fragrant, powerful, and long-lived wines of great finesse. Trimbach owns vines here and the wine produced forms a large part of its superb Cuvée Frédéric Émile.

✓ *Robert Faller • André Kientzler*

GLOECKELBERG
Rodern and St.-Hippolyte
This clay-granite *cru* is known for its light, elegant, and yet persistent style of wine, with Gewurztraminer and Pinot Gris most successful.

✓ *Charles Koehly • CV Ribeauvillé*

GOLDERT
Gueberschwihr

Dating back to the year 750, and recognized on export markets as long ago as 1728, Goldert derives its name from the colour of its wines, the most famous of which is the golden Gewurztraminer. The Muscat grape variety also excels on the calcareous clay soil, and whatever the varietal the style of wine is rich and spicy with a luscious creaminess.

☑ Ernest Burn (Clos St.-Imer) • Marcel Hertzog • Fernand Lichtlé • CV Pfaffenheim • Louis Scher • Clément Week • Domaine Zind Humbrecht

HATSCHBOURG
Hattstatt and Voegtlinshoffen

Gewurztraminer from this south-facing, calcareous marl soil slope excels, but Pinot Gris and Riesling are also excellent.

☑ Joseph Cattin • André Hartmann • Wolfberger

HENGST
Wintzenheim

Hengst Gewurztraminer is a very special, complex wine, seeming to combine the classic qualities of this variety with the orange zest and rose-petal aromas more characteristic of the Muscat grape variety. But Hengst is a very flexible cru. Besides Gewurztraminer, its calcareous marl soil also produces top-quality Muscat, Riesling, and Pinot Gris.

☑ Henri Ehrhart • JosMeyer • Albert Mann • Wunsch & Mann • Domaine Zind Humbrecht

KAEFFERKOPF
Ammerschwihr

Although not technically a Grand Cru, this is one of the greatest Alsace crus, superior to many of the officially nominated sites. Kaefferkopf was legally delimited in 1932, but the bureaucrats refuse to recognize all of it because it is not geologically uniform; yet some Grands Crus are less uniform and have swollen to 20 times their designated size. Contrary to the ethos of the AOC system, which is supposed to respect local usage

and custom, the authorities refuse to recognize the traditional Kaefferkopf practice of blending varieties – usually Riesling and Gewurztraminer.

☑ J.B. Adam • Kuehn • Meyer-Fonné • Martin Schaetzel • Pierre Sparr • François Wackenthaler

KANZLERBERG
Bergheim

Although this tiny cru adjoins the western edge of Altenberg de Bergheim, the wines of its gypsum-permeated, clayey-marl terroir are so different from those of the Altenberg growth that the vinification of the two sites has always been kept separate. The wines have the same potential longevity, but the Kanzlerbergs are fuller and fatter. Kanzlerberg has a reputation for both Riesling and Gewurztraminer, but their ample weight can be at odds with their varietal aromas when young, and both wines require plenty of bottle age to achieve their true finesse.

☑ Gustave Lorentz • Domaine Spielmann

KASTELBERG
Andlau

One of the oldest vineyards in Alsace, Kastelberg has been planted with vines since the Roman occupation. Situated on a small hill next to Wiebelsberg, Andlau's other Grand Cru, the very steep, schistous terroir has long proved to be an excellent site for racy and delicate Riesling, although the wines can be very closed when young and require a few years to develop their lovely bottle aromas. Kastelberg wines remain youthful for 20 years or more, and even show true Grand Cru quality in so-called "off" years.

☑ André Durrmann • Domaine Klipfel • Marc Kreydenweiss • Charles Moritz • Guy Wach

KESSLER
Guebwiller

Though a cru more premier than grand (the truly famous sites of Guebwiller being Kitterlé and Wanne, the latter not classified), the central part of Kessler is certainly deserving of Grand Cru status. Here, the vines grow in a well-protected, valley-like depression, one side of which has a very steep, south-southeast facing slope. Kessler is renowned for its full, spicy, and mellow Gewurztraminer, but Riesling can be much the greater wine.

☑ Domaine Dirler-Cadé • Domaines Schlumberger

KIRCHBERG DE BARR
Barr

The true Grands Crus of Barr are Gaensbroennel and Zisser, but these have been incorporated into the calcareous marl terroir of Kirchberg, which is known for its full-bodied yet delicate wines that exhibit exotic spicy fruit, a characteristic that applies not only to Pinot gris and Gewurztraminer but also to Riesling.

☑ Klipfel • Domaine Stoeffler • Willm

KIRCHBERG DE RIBEAUVILLÉ
Ribeauvillé

One of the few lieux-dits that has regularly been used to commercialize Alsace wine over the centuries. It is famous for Riesling, which typically is firm, totally dry, and long lived, developing intense petrolly characteristics with age. Kirchberg de Ribeauvillé also produces great Muscat with a discreet, yet very specific, orange-and-musk aroma, excellent acidity, and lots of finesse.

☑ Robert Faller • André Kientzler • Jean Sipp • Louis Sipp

KITTERLÉ
Guebwiller

Of all the grape varieties that are grown on this volcanic sandstone terroir, it is the crisp, petrolly Riesling that shows greatest finesse. Gewurztraminer and Pinot gris are also very good in a gently rich, supple, and smoky-mellow style.

☑ Domaines Schlumberger

MAMBOURG
Sigolsheim

The reputation of this cru has been documented since 783, when it was known as the "Sigolttesberg". A limestone coteau, with calcareous clay topsoil, Mambourg stretches for well over a kilometre (⅝ mile), penetrating further into the plain than any other spur of the Vosges foothills. Its vineyards, supposed to be the warmest in Alsace, produce wines that tend to be rich and warm, mellow and liquorous. Both the Gewurztraminer and the Pinot Gris have plenty of smoky-rich spice in them.

☑ Ringenbach-Moser • Pierre Schillé & Fils • Pierre Sparr • André Thomas

MANDELBERG
Mittelwihr and Beblenheim

Mandelberg – "almond tree hill" – has been planted with vines since Gallo-Roman times, and commercialized as an appellation since 1925. Its reputation has been built on Riesling, although today more Gewurztraminer is planted; high-quality Pinot gris and Muscat is also produced.

☑ Frédéric Mallo • Jean-Paul Mauler • CV Ribeauvillé • Edgard Schaller

MOENCHBERG
Andlau and Eichhoffen

Moenchberg – "monk's hill"– was owned by a Benedictine order until 1097, when it was taken over by inhabitants of Eichhoffen. With its clayey-marl soil, excellent exposure to the sun, and very hot, dry microclimate, this *cru* has built up a reputation for firm, intensely fruity, and very racy Riesling. Excellent though it is, however, the finest Moenchberg wines I have tasted have been Pinot Gris. Not to be confused with the equally excellent *Grand Cru* Muenchberg of Nothalten.

☑ *Armand Gilg • Domaine André & Rémy Gresser • Marc Kreydenweiss • Charles Moritz • Marcel Schlosser • Guy Wach*

MUENCHBERG
Nothalten

This sunny vineyard belonging to the abbey of Baumgarten, whose monks tended vines in the 12th century, nestles under the protection of the Undersberg, a 900-metre (2,950-feet) peak in the Vosges mountains. The striking style of Muenchberg's wines is due in part to the special microclimate it enjoys, and also to the ancient, unique, and pebbly volcanic sandstone soil.

☑ *Willy Gisselbrecht • Gérard Landmann • André Ostertag*

OLLWILLER
Wuenheim

Ollwiller's annual rainfall is one of the lowest in France, with Riesling and Gewurztraminer faring best on its clayey-sand soil – although it is not one of the greatest *Grands Crus*.

☑ *Château Ollwiller • CV Vieil Armand*

OSTERBERG
Ribeauvillé

This stony-clay growth abuts Geisberg, another Ribeauvillé *Grand Cru*, and makes equally superb Riesling country. The wines age very well, developing the petrolly nose of a fine Riesling. Gewurztraminer and Pinot gris also fare well.

☑ *André Kientzler • CV Ribeauvillé • Louis Sipp*

PFERSIGBERG *OR* PFERSICHBERG, *OR* PFIRSIGBERG
Eguisheim and Wettolsheim

A calcareous sandstone soil well known for its full, aromatic, and long-lived Gewurztraminer – although Pinot gris, Riesling, and Muscat also fare well here. The wines all share a common succulence of fruit acidity, and possess exceptional aromas.

☑ *Charles Baur • Léon Beyer* (contrary to the *Grand Cru* concept, Beyer's Cuvée Particulière is 100% pure Pfersigberg) *• Pierre Freudenreich • Alphonse Kuentz • Kuentz-Bas • André Scherer • Gérard Schueller • Bruno Sorg • Wolfberger*

PFINGSTBERG
Orschwihr

All four *Grand Cru* varieties grow well on the calcareous-marl and clayey-sandstone of this *cru*, producing wines of typically floral aroma, combined with rich, honeyed fruit.

☑ *Lucien Albrecht • François Braun*

PRAELATENBERG
Kintzheim and Orschwiller

Although Praelatenberg dominates the north side of the village of Orschwiller, virtually all the *cru* actually falls within the boundary of Kintzheim, 1.5 kilometres (1 mile) away. The locals say that all four varieties grow to perfection here, but Pinot gris has been best in my experience, followed by Riesling, and then Gewurztraminer.

☑ *Jean Becker • Raymond Engel* (Domaine des Prelats) *• Domaine Siffert*

RANGEN
Thann and Vieux-Thann

The 15th-century satirist Sebastian Brant, writing about the little-known travels of Hercules through Alsace, reveals that the mythical strongman once drank so much Rangen that he fell asleep. So ashamed was he on waking that he ran away, leaving behind his bludgeon – the club which today appears on Colmar's coat of arms.

So steep that it can be cultivated only when terraced, Rangen's volcanic soil is very poor organically, but extremely fertile minerally. It also drains very quickly, and its dark colour makes it almost too efficient in retaining the immense heat that pours into this sweltering suntrap. However, this fierce heat and rapid drainage are essentially responsible for the regular stressing of the vine, which is what gives the wines their famed power and pungency. Rangen produces great wines even in the poorest years, making it a true *Grand Cru* in every sense.

☑ *Bruno Hertz • Martin Schaetzel • Domaine Schoffit • Domaine Zind Humbrecht*

ROSACKER
Hunawihr

First mentioned in the 15th century, this *cru* has built up a fine reputation for Riesling, but one wine – Trimbach's Clos Ste.-Hune – is almost every year far and away the finest Riesling in Alsace. Occasionally other producers make an exceptional vintage that may challenge it, but none has consistently matched Clos Ste.-Hune's excellence. Trimbach makes no mention of Rosacker on its label because the family believes, as do a small number of internationally known producers, who avoid using the term, that much of Rosacker should not be classified as *Grand Cru* (although Trimbach used to sell Clos Ste.-Hune *Grand Cru* in the 1940s). Rosacker's calcareous and marly-clay soil is rich in magnesium and makes fine Gewurztraminer as well as top Riesling.

☑ *Mader • Frédéric Mallo • Mittnacht-Klack • Sipp-Mack • Trimbach* (Clos Ste.-Hune)

SAERING
Guebwiller

This vineyard, first documented in 1250 and commercialized since 1830, is situated below Kessler and Kitterlé, Guebwiller's other two *Grands Crus*. Like Kessler, this *cru* is more *premier* than *grand* (yet still better than many of the *Grands Crus*). The floral, fruity, and

elegant Riesling is best, especially in hot years, when it becomes exotically peachy, but Muscat and Gewurztraminer can also be fine.

☑ *Domaine Dirler-Cadé • Eric Rominger • Domaines Schlumberger*

SCHLOSSBERG
Kientzheim and Kaysersberg

The production of Schlossberg was controlled by charter in 1928, and in 1975 it became the first Alsace *Grand Cru*. Although its granite *terroir* looks equally shared by the two sites, less than half a hectare (1¼ acres) belongs to Kaysersberg. Schlossberg is best for Riesling, but Gewurztraminer can be successful in so-called "off" vintages. The wine is full of elegance and finesse, whether produced in a classic, restrained style, as Blanck often is, or with the more exuberant fruit that typifies Domaine Weinbach.

☑ *Paul Blanck • Albert Mann • Salzmann-Thomann • Pierre Sparr • Domaine Weinbach*

SCHOENENBOURG
Riquewihr

This vineyard has always had a reputation for producing great Riesling and Muscat, although modern wines show Riesling to be supreme, with Pinot Gris vying with Muscat for the number two spot. Schoenenbourg's gypsum-permeated, marly-and-sandy soil produces very rich, aromatic wines in a *terroir* that has potential for Vendange Tardive and Sélection de Grains Nobles.

☑ *Baumann & Fils • Marcel Deiss • Domaines Dopff Au Moulin • Dopff & Irion • François Lehmann • Mittnacht-Klack • René Schmidt • Daniel Wiederhirn*

SOMMERBERG
Niedermorschwihr and Katzenthal

Known since 1214, the fame of this *cru* was such that a strict delimitation was in force by the 17th century. Situated in the foothills leading up to Trois-Épis, its granite soil is supposed to be equally excellent for all four classic varieties, although Riesling stands out in my experience. Sommerberg wines are typically aromatic, with an elegant succulence of fruit.

☑ *Albert Boxler • Domaine Aimé Stentz • CV Turckheim*

SONNENGLANZ
Beblenheim

In 1935, two years after Kaefferkopf was defined by tribunal at Colmar, Sonnenglanz received a similar certification. Unlike at Kaefferkopf, however, its producers failed to exploit the appellation until 1952, when the local cooperative was formed. But Sonnenglanz is a *Grand Cru* and Kaefferkopf technically is not. Once renowned for its Sylvaner, the calcareous clay soil of Sonnenglanz is best suited to Gewurztraminer and Pinot Gris, which can be very ripe and golden in colour.

☑ *Frédéric Berger • Bott-Geyl • Jean-Paul Hartweg • CV Ribeauvillé*

SPIEGEL
Bergholtz and Guebwiller

Known for only 50 years or so, this is not one of the great *Grands Crus* of Alsace. However, its sandstone and marl *terroir* can produce fine, racy Riesling with a delicate bouquet, and good, though not great, Gewurztraminer and Muscat.

☑ *Dirler • Domaine Loberger • Eugène Meyer • Wolfberger*

SPOREN
Riquewihr

Sporen is one of the truly great *Grands Crus*, its stony, clayey-marl soil producing wines of remarkable finesse. Historically, this *terroir* is famous for Gewurztraminer and Pinot gris, which occupy virtually all of its vineyard today, but it was also traditional to grow a mix of varieties and vinify them together to produce a classic non-varietal wine. One such is Hugel & Fils's "Sporen Gentil", capable of ageing 30 years or more (and in a totally different class to that firm's own Gentil, which does not come from Sporen and is a blend of separately vinified wines).

☑ *Domaine Dopff Au Moulin • Hugel & Fils • Roger Jung • Mittnacht-Klack • CV Ribeauvillé • Bernard Schwach*

STEINERT
Pfaffenheim and Westhalten

Pinot Gris is the king of this stony, calcareous *cru*, although historically Schneckenberg (now part of Steinert) was always renowned for producing a Pinot Blanc that tasted more like Pinot Gris. The Pfaffenheim cooperative still produces a Pinot Blanc Schneckenberg (although not a *Grand Cru*, of course), and its stunning Pinot Gris steals the show. Steinert's Pinot Blanc-cum-Gris reputation illustrates the exceptional concentration of these wines. Gewurztraminer fares best on the lower slopes, Riesling on the higher, more sandy slopes.

☑ *Pierre Frick • CV Pfaffenheim • Rieflé • François Runner*

STEINGRUBLER
Wettolsheim

Although this calcareous-marl and sandstone *cru* is not one of the great names of Alsace, I have enjoyed some excellent Steingrubler wines, particularly Pinot Gris. This can be very rich, yet show great finesse. Certainly Steingrubler is one of the better lesser-known *Grands Crus*, and it could well be a great growth of the future.

☑ *Barmès-Buecher • Robert Dietrich • Albert Mann • Wunsch & Mann (Collection Joseph Mann)*

STEINKLOTZ
Marlenheim

Steinklotz ("block of stone") was in 589 part of the estate of the Merovingian king Childebert II, from which Marlenheim derives its still-flourishing reputation for Pinot Noir wines of red and rosé style, but since it has flown the *Grand Cru* flag, Steinklotz is supposed to be good for Pinot Gris, Riesling, and Gewurztraminer. However, local growers are determined to have their Pinot Noir recognized and will be applying for *grand cru* status for these wines.

☑ *Romain Fritsch*

VORBOURG
Rouffach and Westhalten

All four varieties excel in this calcareous sandstone *terroir*, whose wines are said to develop a bouquet of peaches, apricots, mint, and hazelnut – but Riesling and Pinot gris fare best. Muscat favours warmer vintages, when its wines positively explode with flavour, and Gewurztraminer excels in some years but not in others. Vorbourg catches the full glare of the sun from dawn to dusk and so is also well suited to Pinot noir, which is consequently heavy with pigment.

☑ *Muré* (Clos St.-Landelin)

WIEBELSBERG
Andlau

This vineyard has very good sun exposure, and its siliceous soil retains heat and drains well. Riesling does well, producing wines that can be very fine and floral, slowly developing a delicate, ripe-peachy fruit on the palate.

☑ *Domaine André & Rémy Gresser • Jean-Pierre Klein • Marc Kreydenweiss • Marcel Schlosser*

WINECK-SCHLOSSBERG
Katzenthal and Ammerschwihr

Wineck-Schlossberg's granite vineyards enjoy a sheltered microclimate that primarily favours Riesling, followed by Gewurztraminer. The wines are light and delicate, with a fragrant aroma.

☑ *Jean-Paul Ecklé • Klur-Stoecklé • Meyer-Fonné*

WINZENBERG
Blienschwiller

Locals claim that this *cru* is cited in "old documents" and that Riesling and Gewurztraminer fare best in its granite vineyards. The Riesling I have encountered has been light and charming, but not special. Gewurztraminer has definitely been much the superior wine, showing fine, fresh aromas with a refined spiciness of some complexity.

☑ *Hubert Metz • François Meyer*

ZINNKOEPFLÉ
Soultzmatt and Westhalten

Zinnkoepflé's hot, dry microclimate gives rise to a rare concentration of Mediterranean and Caspian fauna and flora near its exposed summit. The heat and the arid, calcareous sandstone soil are what gives it its reputation for strong, spicy, and fiery styles of Pinot Gris and Gewurztraminer. The Riesling is a delicate and most discreet wine, but this is deceptive and it can, given good bottle-age, be just as powerful.

☑ *Léon Boesch • Seppi Landmann • Landmann-Ostholt • Schlegel-Boeglin*

ZOTZENBERG
Mittelbergheim

First mentioned in 1364, when it was known as Zoczenberg, this calcareous clay *terroir* has been commercialized under its own *lieu-dit* since the beginning of the 20th century. It is historically the finest site in Alsace for Sylvaner, and is destined to become the first *Grand Cru* to be officially recognized for this supposedly lowly grape variety. Gewurztraminer and Riesling show a creamy richness of fruit.

☑ *E. Boeckel • Bernard & Daniel Haegi • André Wittmann*

THE VILLAGE OF RIQUEWIHR
Alsace is full of beautiful villages, but Riquewihr is one of the most delightful, having avoided much of the commercial exploitation that has made nearby Ribeauvillé a more thriving yet less intimate place.

THE APPELLATIONS OF
ALSACE AND LORRAINE

ALSACE AOC

This appellation covers all the wines of Alsace (with the exception of Alsace Grand Cru and Crémant d'Alsace), but 95 per cent of the wines are often sold according to grape variety. These are: Pinot (which may also be labelled Pinot Blanc, Clevner, or Klevner), Pinot Gris, Pinot Noir, Riesling, Gewurztraminer, Muscat, Sylvaner, Chasselas (which may also be labelled Gutedel), and Auxerrois. This practice effectively creates nine "varietal" AOCs under the one umbrella appellation, and these are listed separately.

ALSACE GRAND CRU AOC

The current production of *Grand Cru* wine is approximately 2.5 per cent of the total volume of AOC Alsace. Because every *cru*, or growth, makes a wine of a specific character, it is impossible to give a generalized description.

WHITE *See* The Grands Crus of Alsace p.183.

🍇 Muscat, Riesling, Gewurztraminer, Pinot gris

ALSACE SÉLECTION DE GRAINS NOBLES AOC

This is not an AOC in itself, but a subordinate designation that may be appended either to the basic appellation or to Alsace Grand Cru AOC. Its production is strictly controlled, and the regulations are far tougher than for any AOC elsewhere. In theory, these wines are harvested after Vendange Tardive, but in practice they are picked in several *tries* prior to the best Vendange Tardive, which will be produced from what remains on the vine after a further period of ripening.

These rare and sought-after wines are made from botrytis-affected grapes; unlike Sauternes, however, Alsace is no haven for "noble rot", which occurs haphazardly and in much reduced concentrations. The wines are, therefore, produced in tiny quantities and sold at very high prices. The sauternais are often amazed not only by the high sugar levels (while chaptalization is not permitted in Alsace, it has become almost mandatory in Sauternes), but also by how little sulphur is used, highlighting why Sélection de Grains Nobles has become one of the world's greatest dessert wines.

WHITE Now made with less alcohol and higher sugar than when first introduced, these wines possess even more finesse than before. While Gewurztraminer is almost too easy to make, Pinot Gris offers the ideal balance between quality and price; just a couple of Muscat have been produced, and Riesling Sélection de Grains Nobles is in a class of its own. Check the appropriate varietal entry for the best producers.

🍇 Gewurztraminer, Pinot gris, Riesling, Muscat

🍷 5–30 years

ALSACE VENDANGE TARDIVE AOC

This is not an AOC in itself, but a subordinate designation that may be appended either to the basic appellation or to Alsace Grand Cru AOC. Its production is controlled, and the regulations are far stricter than for any AOC elsewhere in France. Vendange Tardive is far less consistent in quality and character than Sélection de Grains Nobles. This is because some producers make these wines from grapes that have the correct minimum sugar content, but that were picked with the rest of the crop, not late-harvested. Such Vendange Tardive lacks the true character of a late-harvested wine, which is only brought about by the complex changes that occur inside a grape that has remained on the vine until November or December. As the leaves begin to fall and the sap retreats to the protection of the root system, the grapes, cut off from the vine's metabolic system, start dehydrating. The chemical compounds that this process (known as *passerillage*) produces are in turn affected by the prevailing climatic conditions. Thus, *passerillé* grapes that have endured progressively colder temperatures (the norm) and those that have enjoyed a late burst of warmth of an Indian summer (not uncommon) will produce entirely different wines. Until the regulations are changed to ensure that Vendange Tardive is always harvested after a certain specified date, stick to those wines recommended and look for a date of harvest on the back label.

Another aspect that requires regulating is the relative sweetness of the wine, as Vendange Tardive can be anything from almost dry to sweeter than some Sélection de Grains Nobles. Refer to the appropriate varietal entry for the best producers.

WHITE Whether dry, medium-sweet, or sweet, this relatively full-bodied wine should always have the true character of *passerillage* although sometimes this will be overwhelmed by botrytis. Gewurztraminer is the most commonly encountered variety, but only the best have the right balance; Pinot Gris and Riesling both offer an ideal balance between quality, availability, and price. Muscat is almost as rare for Vendange Tardive as it is for Sélection de Grains Nobles, as it tends to go very flabby when overripe.

🍇 Gewurztraminer, Pinot gris, Riesling, Muscat

🍷 5–20 years

AUXERROIS AOC

Theoretically this designation does not exist, but Auxerrois is one of the varieties permitted for the production of Pinot wine and makes such a distinctly different product that it has often been labelled separately. This practice, currently on the increase, is "officially tolerated".

WHITE Fatter than Pinot Blanc, with a more buttery, honeyed, and spicy character to the fruit, the greatest asset of Auxerrois is its natural richness and immediate appeal. Inclined to low acidity, it can easily become flabby and so musky it tastes almost foxy, but the best Auxerrois can give Pinot Gris a run for its money.

🍇 Auxerrois

🍷 Up to 5 years

✓ *Pierre Frick* • *Rolly Gassmann* • *JosMeyer* • *André Kientzler* • *Mark Kreydenweiss* • *Julien Rieffel* (the Klevner Vieilles Vignes is pure Auxerrois despite the Pinot blanc synonym) • *Bruno Sorg*

CHASSELAS AOC

Rarely seen, but enjoying something of a revival amongst a few specialist growers.

WHITE The best Chasselas wines are not actually bottled, but sit in vats waiting to be blended into anonymous *cuvées* of Edelzwicker. They are neither profound nor complex, but teem with fresh, fragrant fruit and are an absolute joy to drink; they taste better, however, before they are bottled than after. The fruit is so delicate that it needs a lift to survive the shock of being bottled, and the wine would probably benefit from being left on lees and bottled very cold to retain a bit of tongue-tingling carbonic gas.

🍇 Chasselas

🍷 Upon purchase

✓ *Paul Blanck* • *JosMeyer* • *André Kientzler* • *Robert Schoffit*

CLASSIC ALSACE BLENDS

Despite the varietal wine hype, Alsace is more than capable of producing the finest-quality classic blends, but their number is small and dwindles every year because so few consumers realize their true quality. It is difficult for producers to make potential customers appreciate why their blends are more expensive than ordinary Edelzwicker, but classic Alsace blends should no more be categorized with Edelzwicker than *Crus Classés* compared to generic Bordeaux. This category focuses attention on the region's top-performing blends which, whether or not they fetch them, deserve *Grand Cru* prices. Unlike the blending of Edelzwicker, for which various wines are mixed together – and where there is always the temptation to get rid of unwanted wines – the different varieties in most classic Alsace blends always come from the same vineyard and are traditionally harvested and vinified together. *See also* Kaefferkopf (p.184) and the third paragraph on page 183.

WHITE Most of these wines improve with age, but go through phases when one or other grape variety dominates, which is interesting to observe and should help you to understand why you prefer to drink a particular blend. Depending on the amounts involved, Gewurztraminer typically dominates in the young wine, followed by Pinot gris then, many years later, Riesling, but other varieties may also be involved when overripe.

🍇 Chasselas, Sylvaner, Pinot blanc, Pinot gris, Pinot noir, Auxerrois, Gewurztraminer, Muscat blanc à petits grains, Muscat rosé à petits grains, Muscat Ottonel, Riesling

✓ *Marc Kreydenweiss* (Clos du Val d'Eléon 70% Riesling, 30% Pinot gris) • *CV Ribeauvillé* (Clos du Zahnacker equal parts Gewurztraminer, Pinot gris, and Riesling) • *Jean Sipp* (Clos du Schlossberg (50% Riesling, 20% Gewurztraminer, 20% Tokay-Pinot gris, 10% Muscat) • *Louis Sipp* (Côtes de Ribeauvillé 40% Pinot blanc plus 60% Sylvaner, Riesling, and Gewurztraminer)

CLEVNER AOC

Commonly used synonym under which Pinot is commercialized, sometimes spelled Klevner, but not to be confused with Klevener. *See* Pinot AOC.

CÔTES DE TOUL VDQS

Part of the once-flourishing vineyards of Lorraine, these *côtes* are located in eight communes west of Toul, in the *département* of Meurthe-et-Moselle.

RED The Pinot noir is the most successful, and the wine is usually sold as a pure varietal. It can have surprisingly good colour for wine from such a northerly region, and good cherry-Pinot character.

🍇 Pinot meunier, Pinot noir

🍷 1–4 years

WHITE These wines represent less than two per cent of the VDQS, just 76 hectolitres (844 cases). Nevertheless, the Auxerrois is the best grape, its fatness making it ideal for such a northerly area with a calcareous soil.

🍇 Aligoté, Aubin, Auxerrois

🍷 1–3 years

ROSÉ Most Côtes de Toul is made and sold as *vin gris*, a pale rosé that is delicious when young.

🍇 Gamay, Pinot meunier, Pinot noir, plus a maximum of 15% Aligoté, Aubin, and Auxerrois

🍷 Upon purchase

✓ *Vincent Gorny • Michel & Marcel Laroppe • Lelièvre Frères • Yves Masson • Fernand Poirson • Société Vinicole du Toulouis • Michel Vosgien*

CRÉMANT D'ALSACE AOC

Although small growers like Dirler had made Vin Mousseaux d'Alsace as early as 1880, it was not until 1900 that Dopff Au Moulin created a sparkling wine industry on a commercial scale, and 1976 before an AOC was established. The quality is good, and is improving.

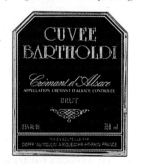

SPARKLING WHITE Although the Pinot blanc has perfect acidity for this sort of wine, it can lack sufficient richness, and after intensive tastings I have come to the conclusion that the Pinot gris has the right acidity and richness.

🍇 Pinot blanc, Pinot gris, Pinot noir, Auxerrois, Chardonnay, Riesling

🍷 5–8 years

SPARKING ROSÉ These delightful wines can have a finer purity of perfume and flavour than many pink Champagnes.

🍇 Pinot noir

🍷 3–5 years

✓ *Becker • Bestheim • Heimberger • Riéflé • Willm • Wolfberger*

EDELZWICKER AOC

This appellation – its name means "noble blend" – is reserved for wines blended from two or more of the authorized grape varieties, and it was indeed once noble. However, since the banning of AOC Zwicker, which was never meant to be noble, and due to the fact that there has never been a legal definition of which varieties are noble, producers simply renamed their Zwicker blends Edelzwicker. Consequently, this appellation has become so degraded that many producers prefer to sell their cheaper AOC Alsace wines under brand names rather than put the dreaded Edelzwicker on the label.

WHITE Essentially dry, light-bodied wines that have a clean flavour and are best drunk young. Most Edelzwickers are either Sylvaner or Pinot-blanc based, with better or slightly more expensive products having a generous touch of Gewurztraminer to fatten up the blend.

🍇 Chasselas, Sylvaner, Pinot blanc, Pinot gris, Pinot noir, Auxerrois, Gewurztraminer, Muscat blanc à petits grains, Muscat rosé à petits grains, Muscat ottonel, Riesling

🍷 Upon purchase

✓ *Rolly Gassmann • Domaines Schlumberger Cristal-Marée*

GEWURZTRAMINER AOC

No other wine region in the world has managed to produce Gewurztraminer with any real spice, which is probably why this is usually the first Alsace wine people taste. Its voluptuous, up-front style is always immediately appealing.

WHITE The fattest and most full-bodied of Alsace wines. Classic renditions of this grape have the aroma of banana when young and only develop a real pungency of spice in bottle, eventually achieving a rich gingerbread character when mature.

🍇 Gewurztraminer

🍷 3–10 years (20–30 years for great examples)

✓ *Barmès-Buecher • Charles Baur • Jean Becker • Léon Beyer • Paul Blanck • Bott-Geyl • Albert Boxler • Camille Braun • Marcel Deiss • Dirler • J. Hauller & Fils • Hugel & Fils • André Kientzler • Charles Koehly • Kuentz-Bas • Frédéric Mallo • Mittnacht-Klack • Muhlberger • Muré (Clos St.-Landelin) • Domaine Ostertag • Rolly Gassmann • Domaine Martin Schaetzel • Edgard Schaller • Gérard Schueller • Domaines Schlumberger • Jean Sipp • Bruno Sorg • Domaine Spielmann • F. E. Trimbach • Domaine Weinbach • Wolfberger • Domaine Zind Humbrecht*

Vendange Tardive *J. B. Adam • Léon Boesch • Joseph Cattin • René Fleith • Geschikt • Hugel & Fils • Roger Jung • André Kientzler • Kuentz-Bas • Domaine Ostertag • André Thomas • CV Turckheim • Domaine Weinbach • Domaine Zind Humbrecht*

Sélection de Grains Nobles *Paul Blanck • Léon Boesch • Albert Boxler • Dirler-Cadé • Hugel & Fils • Kuentz-Bas • Albert Mann • Muré (Clos St.-Landelin) • Rolly Gassmann • Seppi Landmann • Sick-Dreyer • Pierre Sparr • F. E. Trimbach • Domaine Weinbach • Domaine Zind Humbrecht*

GUTEDEL AOC

Synonym under which Chasselas may be commercialized. *See* Chasselas AOC.

KLEVENER DE HEILIGENSTEIN AOC

An oddity in Alsace for three reasons: firstly, the wine is made from a grape variety that is native to the Jura further south and not found anywhere else in Alsace; secondly, of all the famous village appellations (Rouge d'Ottrott, Rouge de Rodern, etc.), it is the only one specifically defined in the regulations; thirdly, it is the only grape confined by law to a fixed area within Alsace (the village of Heiligenstein). It is not to be confused with Klevner, a common synonym for the Pinot blanc.

WHITE Dry, light-bodied wines of a subdued, spicy aroma, and delicate, fruity flavour.

🍇 Savagnin rosé

🍷 2–4 years

✓ *CV Andlau • Jean Hewang • Ch. Wantz*

KLEVNER AOC

See Pinot Blanc AOC

MUSCAT AOC

The best Muscat wine, some growers believe, is made from the Muscat d'Alsace, a synonym for both the white and pink strains of the rich, full Muscat à petits grains. Others are convinced that the lighter, more floral, Muscat ottonel is best. A blend of the two is probably preferable. These wines are better in average years, or at least in fine years that have good acidity, rather than in truly great vintages.

WHITE Dry, aromatic wines with fine floral characteristics that often smell of orange-flower water and taste of peaches. A top-quality Muscat that is expressive of its *terroir* is a great wine.

🍇 Muscat blanc à petits grains, Muscat rosé à petits grains, Muscat ottonel

🍷 Upon purchase

✓ *Becker • Ernest Burn (Clos St.-Imer) • Dirler • Paul Ginglinger • Roger Jung • André Kientzler • Marc Kreydenweiss • Kuehn • Kuentz-Bas • Frédéric Mochel • Muré (Clos St.-Landelin) • Rolly Gassmann • Charles Schleret • Bruno Sorg • Domaine Spielmann • Domaine Weinbach • Daniel Wiederhirn • Domaine Zind Humbrecht*

Vendange Tardive *None*

Sélection de Grains Nobles *Jean Becker • Albert Mann* (Le Tri)

PINOT AOC

Not necessarily pure Pinot blanc, this white wine may be made from any of the Pinot grape varieties, including Auxerrois (often confused with Pinot blanc but in fact a totally separate variety). Most Pinot wines are a blend of Pinot blanc and Auxerrois; the further north the vines are cultivated, the more Àuxerrois is used to plump out the Pinot blanc.

WHITE Some Pinot wines are occasionally spineless, but lacklustre examples are not as common as they used to be, as it is the plump and juicy *cuvées* that have made this the fastest-growing category of Alsace wine.

🍇 Pinot blanc, Auxerrois, Pinot noir (vinified white), Pinot gris

🍷 2–4 years

✓ *J. B. Adam • Paul Blanck • Camille Braun • CV Cléebourg • Marcel Deiss • JosMeyer • Hugel & Fils • Koeberlé-Kreyer • Charles Koehly • Albert Mann • CV Pfaffenheim • Rolly Gassmann • Domaine Spielmann • Domaine Zind Humbrecht*

PINOT BLANC AOC

This designation should only be used if the wine is made from 100 per cent Pinot blanc. *See also* Pinot AOC.

PINOT GRIS AOC

This designation is now the most common way of commercializing wine from the rich Pinot gris grape. For me, this is the greatest of all Alsace wines; top Riesling can be much finer, but the variety is so sensitive that the quality is nowhere near as consistent across the board.

WHITE This full-bodied, off-dry wine is decadently rich, but has excellent acidity, and its fullness of flavour never tires the palate. A young Pinot Gris can taste or smell of banana, sometimes be smoky, with little or no spice, but as it matures it increasingly develops a smoky-spice, toasty-creamy richness, finally achieving a big, honeyed walnut-brazil complexity with good bottle age.

🍇 Pinot gris

🍽 5–10 years

✓ *Lucien Albrecht • Barmès-Buecher • Bott Frères • Albert Boxler • Maison Ernest Burn (Clos St.-Imer) • CV Cléebourg • Marcel Deiss • Robert Dietrich • Ehrhart • Pierre Frick • Hugel & Fils • André Kientzler • Charles Koehly • Marc Kreydenweiss • Kuentz-Bas • Seppi Landmann • Landmann-Ostholt • Frédéric Mallo • Albert Mann • Mittnacht-Klack • Muller-Koeberle • Muré (Clos St.-Landelin) • Domaine Ostertag • CV Pfaffenheim • Edgar Schaller • Schleret • Domaines Schlumberger • Domaine Schoffit • Jean Sipp • Bruno Sorg • F. E. Trimbach • CV Turckheim • Domaine Weinbach • Daniel Wiederhirn • Wolfberger • Bernard Wurtz • W. Wurtz • Domaine Zind Humbrecht • Zimmermann*

Vendange Tardive *Lucien Albrecht • Joseph Cattin • Marc Kreydenweiss • Kuentz-Bas • Hugel & Fils • Domaine Ostertag • Vignobles Reinhart • Domaine Zind Humbrecht*

Sélection de Grains Nobles *J. B. Adam • Albert Boxler • Marcel Deiss • Hugel & Fils • Marc Kreydenweiss • Kuentz-Bas • Domaine Ostertag • F. E. Trimbach • Domaine Weinbach • Domaine Zind Humbrecht*

PINOT NOIR AOC

Not so long ago, Pinot Noir d'Alsace was synonymous in style with rosé, but the trend has swung hard over towards a true red wine. After a steep learning curve, during which many wines were over-extracted, lacked elegance, were prone to rapid oxidation, and bore the most ungainly caramelized characteristics, Alsace winemakers have now managed to master the handling of oak and red-wine techniques.

RED When the first edition came out in 1988, the most consistent red wine was Wolfberger's Rouge d'Alsace (oak *cuvée*), it remains dependable, but many other producers make deep-coloured wines with real red-wine characteristics, elegance, and finesse. They will never compete with even medium-quality Burgundy Pinot Noir, but they have a purity of fruit and are truly expressive of Alsace.

🍇 Pinot noir

🍽 2–6 years (12 years for exceptional *cuvées*)

ROSÉ At its best, this dry, light-bodied wine has a deliciously fragrant aroma and flavour, which is reminiscent of strawberries, raspberries, or cherries.

🍇 Pinot noir

🍽 1–2 years

✓ *Barmes-Buecher (Vieilles Vignes) • Paul Blanck (Furstentum) • Marcel Deiss • Albert Hertz • Hugel & Fils • Muré (Clos St.-Landelin) • CV Pfaffenheim • CV Turckheim • Wolfberger*

RIESLING AOC

Riesling is the most susceptible to differences in soil: clay soils give fatness and richness; granite Riesling is also rich, but with more finesse; limestone adds obvious finesse but less richness; and volcanic soil makes for a powerfully flavoured, spicy style.

WHITE In youth, fine Rieslings can show hints of apple, fennel, citrus, and peach, but can be so firm and austere that they give no hint of the beautiful wines into which they can evolve.

🍇 Riesling

🍽 4–20 years

✓ *J. B. Adam • Barmès-Buecher • Léon Baur • Léon Beyer • Paul Blanck • Albert Boxler • François Braun • Marcel Deiss • Dirler • Pierre Freudenreich • Albert Hertz • Marc Kreydenweiss • Kuentz-Bas • Mader • Frédéric Mallo • Albert Mann • Frédéric Mochel • Muré (Clos St.-Landelin) • Rolly Gassmann • Martin Schaetzel • Edgard Schaller • Roland Schmitt • Domaines Schlumberger • Domaine Schoffit • Jean Sipp • Louis Sipp • Sipp-Mack • Bruno Sorg • Pierre Sparr • Domaine Spielmann • Bernard Schwach • F. E. Trimbach • Domaine Weinbach • Wunsch & Mann • Domaine Zind Humbrecht*

Vendange Tardive *Paul Blanck • Hugel & Fils • André Kientzler • Marc Kreydenweiss • Domaine Ostertag • Schlegel-Boeglin • Seppi Landmann • Domaine Weinbach*

• *Domaine Zind Humbrecht*

Sélection de Grains Nobles *J. B. Adam • Albert Boxler • Marcel Deiss • Hugel & Fils • André Kientzler • Domaine Ostertag • F.E. Trimbach • Domaine Weinbach • Domaine Zind Humbrecht*

SYLVANER AOC

Hugh Johnson once described the Sylvaner as "local tap-wine", and by the tap is exactly how it should be served – direct from the stainless-steel vat, with all the zip and zing of natural carbonic gas that is filtered out during the bottling process. Like the Muscat, it does not suit the heat of the greatest vintages, and is thus a wine to buy in poorer years. If Alsace producers want to guarantee a great Sylvaner wine every year, they should take a lesson from Angelo Publisi of Ballandean Winery (*see* p.543), who replicates the Vendange Tardive style by cutting the fruit-bearing canes just after *veraison*. This cuts the grape off from the vine's metabolism and the effect is much the same as when the leaves drop and sap returns to roots after the first snap of winter. The wine produced as a result is consistently fabulous.

WHITE Typically, an Alsace Sylvaner is not as fat as a Rheinpfalz Sylvaner, nor as spicy-earthy as a Franconian Silvaner (*sic*) or even as spicy, strange as it may seem for a region that can even put spice in the Pinot blanc. Sylvaner is an unpretentious, dry, light- to medium-bodied wine, with fragrance rather than fruitiness. It is generally best drunk young, but, like the Muscat, exceptionally long-living examples can always be found.

🍇 Sylvaner

🍽 Upon purchase

✓ *Paul Blanck • Christian Dolder • Dopff Au Moulin • J. Hauller • Rolly Gassmann • Domaine Martin Schaetzel • Domaine Schoffit • Domaine Weinbach • Domaine Zind Humbrecht*

VIN D'ALSACE AOC

Alternative designation for Alsace AOC.

VIN DE MOSELLE VDQS

Although many restaurants list German Mosel as "Moselle", the river and the wine it produces is called the Mosel in Germany, only becoming the Moselle when it crosses the border into France.

RED The few I have come across have been unimpressive.

🍇 A minimum of 30% Gamay plus Pinot meunier, and Pinot noir

🍽 Upon purchase

WHITE Light, dry, and insubstantial wines.

🍇 Auxerrois, Pinot blanc, Pinot gris, Riesling, Gewurztraminer, a maximum of 30% Sylvaner and, until it is replaced by other varieties, a maximum of 20% Ebling

🍽 Upon purchase

AUTHOR'S CHOICE

As most wine drinkers seldom encounter anything beyond inexpensive cooperative-produced wines from Alsace, possibly bought in good supermarkets and wine outlets, I have restricted my choice here to some of the very greatest wines this region can produce.

PRODUCER	WINE	STYLE	DESCRIPTION	
Jean Becker	1988 Froehn Grand Cru (*see* p.183), Muscat	WHITE	This wine is in a different class from anything ever made before in Alsace. As a result of picking fully botrytized grapes individually with an *escargot* fork, Philippe Becker achieved a fabulously concentrated botrytized flavour, which is boosted by a massive 204 grams of residual sugar per litre and balanced by exceptionally high acidity, which sounds more like an ultra-successful Alsace *vin de paille* than a Sélection de Grains Nobles. We can only hope he might be crazy enough to do it again someday.	5-15 years
Paul Blanck	Riesling, Furstentum Grand Cru (*see* p.183)	WHITE	The reputation of this *Grand Cru* rests almost solely on the wines of Paul Blanck. If I have tasted one Furstentum wine from Paul Blanck, I tave tasted fifty, such has been the producer's effort to understand this *cru* and exploit all its potential. Blanck's Furstentum Riesling is very fine indeed; elegant and floral when young, the fruit gaining great intensity with age, and as its flavour deepens, so its finesse increases.	4-12 years
Albert Boxler	Riesling Sélection de Grains Nobles, Sommerberg Grand Cru (*see* p.185)	WHITE	This is a sensationally rich wine, with stunning ripe-fruit intensity and great finesse. Its quality puts this wine up there with the big names such as Zind Humbrecht *et al.*	5-20 years
Maison Ernest Burn	Pinot Gris Clos St.-Imer, Goldert Grand Cru (*see* p.184), La Chapelle	WHITE	This wine has a stunning combination of exotic fruit, tremendous creamy richness, and great finesse.	5-12 years
Marcel Deiss	Pinot Gris Sélection de Grains Nobles Quintessence (*see* p.189)	WHITE	A fabulously rich wine with intensely sweet fruit so unctuous it would cloy but for the wine's scintillating acidity.	7-35 years
Marcel Deiss	Pinot Noir Bergheim Burlenberg Vieilles Vignes (*see* p.189)	RED	The frenetically expressive Jean-Michel Deiss produces a Pinot Noir of truly classic quality and proportion, as vividly rich as it is coloured. It is beautifully structured, with powerful varietal character and great toasty-smoky complexity.	5-12 years
Marcel Deiss	Riesling Sélection de Grains Nobles Quintessence (*see* p.189)	WHITE	Is this beautifully liquorous, super-concentrated nectar the greatest botrytized Riesling in the world? Certainly its electrifying balance of huge, honeyed sweetness and rip-roaring acidity can be compared only to the very greatest of Germany's legendary *Eiswein.*	7-35 years
Dopff Au Moulin	Crémant d'Alsace (*see* p.188), Cuvée Bartholdi	SPARKLING WHITE	Although dressed up to look like an upmarket Italian fizz, this is a very stylish wine that retains its youth for a considerable number of years, requiring about eight years from the date of harvest to show its full, classy potential. It was produced to commemorate Bartholdi, who was a native of Colmar and famous for sculpting the Statue of Liberty.	5-10 years
Hugel & Fils	Pinot Gris (*see* p.189), Vendange Tardive	WHITE	Made by the masters of late-harvest wines, this Pinot Gris is always plump and honeyed, with sweet, spicy-ripe fruit. It is a voluptuously complex wine of immense class and extraordinary longevity.	7-35 years
Hugel & Fils	Riesling (*see* p.189), Vendange Tardive	WHITE	No-one – not Trimbach, Weinbach, or Zind Humbrecht – makes Riesling Vendange Tardive quite like Hugel, who have, after all, been making it longer than anyone else and still have a number of 19th-century, late-harvest gems in their cellars. Made only in exceptional years, it ages gracefully over 60 years or more into a wonderfully honeyed wine.	10-60 years
Hugel & Fils	Riesling (*see* p.189), Sélection de Grains Nobles	WHITE	This famous old house has the greatest number of top-performing vintages of this style, which is ridiculously easy to drink as soon as it is bottled, yet a pity to disturb before its first flush of finesse at 15 to 20 years of age.	15-100 years
Kuentz-Bas	Gewurztraminer, Eichberg Grand Cru (*see* p.183)	WHITE	As delicious, voluptuous, and heady as any good Gewurztraminer should be, but with exceptional concentration and a degree of class and finesse seldom seen in this variety.	5-15 years

PRODUCER	WINE	STYLE	DESCRIPTION	🍷
Kuentz-Bas	Gewurztraminer Vendange Tardive, Eichberg Grand Cru (*see* p.183), Caroline	WHITE	This sublime wine brims with succulent, sweet-fruit intensity of great power and remarkable finesse. Always a great wine, in the ripest years this Vendange Tardive is better than many a Sélection de Grains Nobles and is worth paying a premium for.	5–25 years
Kuentz-Bas	Gewurztraminer Sélection de Grains Nobles, Pfersigberg Grand Cru (*see* p.183), Cuvée Jeremy	WHITE	A fabulously rich and voluptuous wine that is too stylish to be decadent, with intense yet elegantly focused spicy and floral fruit.	5–35 years
Rolly Gassmann	Muscat (*see* p.188), Moenchreben	WHITE	The luscious, exotic rose-and-orange-peel fruit in this wine is cleverly lifted and emphasized by a touch of residual sugar. It is not totally dry, but is completely satisfying.	1–4 years
Bruno Sorg	Muscat, Pfersigberg Grand Cru (*see* p.185)	WHITE	This is quite simply the best Muscat in Alsace.	2–5 years
F. E. Trimbach	Gewurztraminer (*see* p.188), Cuvée des Seigneurs de Ribeaupierre	WHITE	This style is in total contrast to the voluptuous Kuentz-Bas style, but has equal class and quality for those who expect their palates to be assaulted by the pungent, spice-shocking power Gewurztraminer has when given sufficient bottle age.	10–20 years
F. E. Trimbach	Gewurztraminer (*see* p.188), Sélection de Grains Nobles and Hors 1988	WHITE	Although less voluptuous than Kuentz-Bas Gewurztraminer Sélection de Grains Nobles, this has more structure and an equally fabulous honeyed botrytis concentration. The even more luscious Hors Choix is, however, a supercharged step up.	10–40 years
F. E. Trimbach	Riesling (*see* p.189), Clos Ste.-Hune	WHITE	What can I say about this quintessential Riesling? Distinctly lighter than Cuvée Frédéric Émile, it takes almost twice as long to develop in bottle, a factor that accounts for its far greater finesse and helps explain why it is probably the greatest dry Riesling in the world.	12–50 years
F. E. Trimbach	Riesling (*see* p.189), Cuvée Frédéric Émile	WHITE	Anyone tasting this and Clos Ste.-Hune together for the first time would be forgiven for thinking Cuvée Frédéric Émile the superior wine, since it is fatter, charms at a much younger age, and matures into a fabulously rich, classic, honeyed Riesling.	6–30 years
Domaine Weinbach	Gewurztraminer (*see* p.188), Cuvée Laurence and Cuvée Théo	WHITE	Both these wines are fat, stylish, and succulent, but the Cuvée Laurence is more exotic, with flowery spice and a smoky, honeyed complexity, while Cuvée Théo is bigger, bolder, and perhaps has a touch more class.	5–12 years
Domaine Weinbach	Pinot Gris (*see* p.189), Sélection de Grains Nobles Quintessence	WHITE	This is a decadently rich, fabulously complex wine that is always full of intense, raisiny botrytis flavour and has on occasions rivalled Yquem.	6–20 years
Domaine Weinbach	Riesling, Schlossberg Grand Cru (*see* p.185), Cuvée Ste.-Cathérine	WHITE	This wine has a beautifully floral aroma, utterly ravishing fruit, astonishing finesse, and, although a wine of pure joy, it has great potential complexity.	4–20 years
Domaine Weinbach	Riesling (*see* p.189), Sélection de Grains Nobles Quintessence	WHITE	Anyone who has tasted Mme. Faller's "basic" Sélection de Grains Nobles might well wonder how the immaculate quality of that wine could be improved upon, yet, since its inaugural 1989 vintage, Quintessence has deliciously demonstrated that it is a class apart.	5–30 years
Domaine Zind Humbrecht	Gewurztraminer, Rangen Grand Cru (*see* p.185), Clos St.-Urbain and Gewurztraminer Clos Windsbuhl	WHITE	All Zind Humbrecht Gewurztraminer show spectacular, smoky-buttery-spicy richness and complexity, but these two probably have the most finesse.	5–15 years
Domaine Zind Humbrecht	Gewurztraminer Sélection de Grains Nobles, Rangen Grand Cru (*see* p.185), Clos St.-Urbain	WHITE	This potentially super-spicy nectar must be the ultimate amalgam of heavily botrytized sweetness and firm structure.	8–40 years
Domaine Zind Humbrecht	Pinot Gris Clos St.-Urbain, Rangen Grand Cru (*see* p.185)	WHITE	Massively structured, this wine is so powerfully flavoured that it requires, even in lesser vintages, a good decade to obtain bottle mellowness, broaden the flavours, and provide any hint of the complexity and finesse that will develop from its succulently rich creamy-spiciness.	8–15 years
Domaine Zind Humbrecht	Pinot Gris (*see* p.189), Vendange Tardive Clos Windsbuhl	WHITE	A sensationally rich, intensely sweet, and tremendously concentrated wine, even for Vendange Tardive, and even for Zind Humbrecht. Due to the wine's firm structure and acidity, the huge, creamy-nutty, buttery-spicy complexity shows great finesse.	10–30 years

THE LOIRE VALLEY

In winemaking terms, the Loire valley is best imagined as a long ribbon with crisp white wines at either end and fuller wines of all types in the middle. It is the home of Sauvignon blanc, the only wine area in the world that specializes in Cabernet franc and, in truly great vintages, makes some of the most sublime and sumptuous botrytized wines.

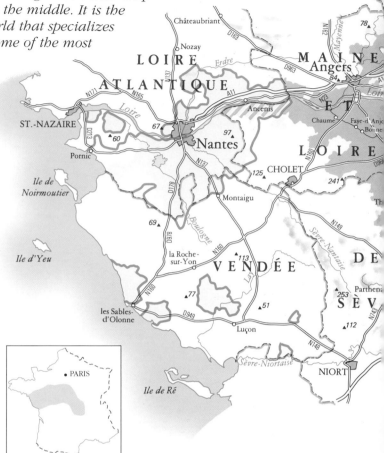

THE LOIRE IS THE LONGEST river in France. From its source in the Cévennes Mountains, it flows 1,000 kilometres (620 miles) through 12 *départements*. The variations in soil, climate, and grape varieties found along its banks and those of its tributaries are reflected in the wide range of wines grown in the four major wine-producing districts. Red, white, and rosé; still, *pétillant*, and fully sparkling wines are produced in some 60 different appellations ranging in style from bone dry to intensely sweet.

THE LOIRE'S MOST IMPORTANT GRAPE
The Chenin blanc grape produces four distinctly different styles of wine – dry, semi-sweet, sweet, and sparkling. This is due to traditional practices that have been forced on growers

RECENT LOIRE VINTAGES

2000 With heavy rain and cold temperatures in July and widespread mildew, this was a problematic year with extremely variable results. Contrary to expectations, the reds have good colour and represent one of the Loire's successes. They have an easy-drinking suppleness, but are not for keeping. However, it is the Sauvignon wines of the Central Loire that stand out most of all. Good Muscadet was made, with fruit as well as acidity for a change, but very few sweet wines of any note.

1999 Another difficult year that produced some surprisingly good, soft and supple reds (Alphonse Mellot in particular). The whites have good acidity. Tread carefully.

1998 The first of three arduous vintages in the Loire, with variable quality. This followed three excellent vintages, the vinous delights of which encouraged some critics to declare a resurgence of quality-minded producers in the Loire, but it was down to the exceptional weather. As 1998, 1999, and 2000 were to prove, you can only trust the best producers in average or poor years. Mind you, in 1998 the best producers have made lovely dry white wines (Didier Dagueneau, Henri Bourgeois) and a few stunning reds too (Vincent Pinard Sancerre Charlouise springs to mind).

1997 The last truly great Loire vintage, although the excellent ripeness levels made it difficult to produce crisp dry white. There was an abundance of great reds and sweet wines.

1996 While thunderstorms punctuated the very hot summer throughout most of France, the Loire escaped unscathed. The grapes ripened too quickly in Muscadet, so although hyped up, 1996 is not going to be one of the longest-lived vintages. This vintage has produced good Sauvignons, excellent sweet wines, and superb reds.

by the vagaries of climate. This grape has abundant natural acidity and, if it receives enough sun, a high sugar content. But the Loire is considered a northern area in viticultural terms, and the vine grower must contend with late frosts, cold winds, and variable summers. Given a sunny year, the grower's natural inclination is to make the richest wine possible with this sweet and tangy grape, but in many vintages, only a medium or a dry style can be achieved. This variation in style is the root of the Loire's problems because it is difficult to build a reputation on uncertainty. If you take into account overproduction, the all too often debilitating effect of rot, and the lack of almost any selection criteria for picking grapes for all styles of wine except those produced from late-harvested or botrytized grapes, then add an alarming spread of sloppy winemaking, you have all the reasons why, for me, the Loire has become the least exciting of all French wine regions.

With the exception of wines such as the best Savennières, dry Chenin blanc wines are all too often thin, harsh, and acidic. These wines do little to enhance the reputation of the Loire, but they do have similar characteristics to the wines of Champagne in that they are disappointing when still, yet appear glamorous when sparkling. It is little wonder, then, that as the Champagne trade rapidly evolved in the 19th century, so the seeds of a sparkling-wine industry were sown in Saumur, and today the Loire boasts the largest such market outside of Champagne itself.

THE LOIRE FROM CHAMPTOCEAUX
From well above the river this hillside town provides a panoramic view of the surrounding countryside.

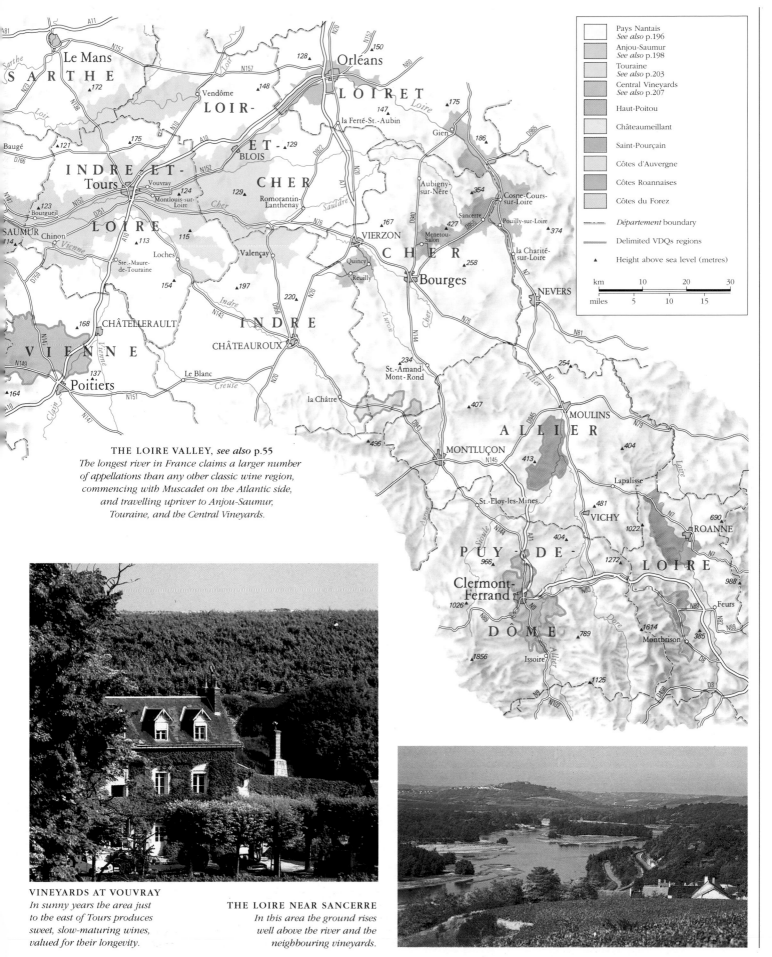

THE LOIRE VALLEY, *see also* p.55
*The longest river in France claims a larger number
of appellations than any other classic wine region,
commencing with Muscadet on the Atlantic side,
and travelling upriver to Anjou-Saumur,
Touraine, and the Central Vineyards.*

Legend:
- Pays Nantais *See also p.196*
- Anjou-Saumur *See also p.198*
- Touraine *See also p.203*
- Central Vineyards *See also p.207*
- Haut-Poitou
- Châteaumeillant
- Saint-Pourçain
- Côtes d'Auvergne
- Côtes Roannaises
- Côtes du Forez

— · — · *Département* boundary
——— Delimited VDQs regions
▲ Height above sea level (metres)

km | 10 | 20 | 30
miles | 5 | 10 | 15

VINEYARDS AT VOUVRAY
*In sunny years the area just
to the east of Tours produces
sweet, slow-maturing wines,
valued for their longevity.*

THE LOIRE NEAR SANCERRE
*In this area the ground rises
well above the river and the
neighbouring vineyards.*

193 •

To suggest that the Chenin blanc is fit only for fizzing up is to do the grape a great injustice. Firstly, it is not in fact suited to the classic *brut* style of sparkling wine, its aromatic qualities tending to fight rather than absorb the subtle effects of second fermentation. Secondly, it is this very character that makes Chenin blanc one of the world's greatest wine grapes when botrytized. However, it is not the grape that is intrinsically disappointing when it is vinified as a still wine, but merely the methods employed by the grower and winemaker.

Chenin blanc has been given pride of place in the Anjou-Saumur district, but unfortunately its cultivation has spread to unsuitable areas over the last 25 years. Producers more interested in making money than building a fine reputation have taken advantage of the Chenin blanc's natural inclination to over-crop. It is a grape that should be harshly pruned, but most growers lack the courage to do this, and when the weather is unsettled it is these same growers who are the first to harvest. The heavier the crop, the less ripe the grapes – especially when harvested early – and the less ripe the grapes, the more washed out the flavours. However, there are quality-conscious growers in the

THE SOURCE OF THE LOIRE
The river begins its journey high up in the Cévennes Mountains, embarking on a route north to Orléans, then west to Nantes and the Atlantic ocean.

Loire, who restrict their yield and allow the grapes to ripen, yet still agonize over whether to risk the weather for one more day's maturity.

It is from such top-performing growers as Domaine Baumard and Moulin Touchais in the Coteaux du Layon, Foreau and Huet in Vouvray, and Dominique Moyer in Montlouis that we get Chenin blanc wines that dazzle our palates.

FROM SOURCE TO SEA

For some inexplicable reason, most references restrict the Loire to its four major districts of Pays Nantais, Anjou-Saumur, Touraine, and Central Vineyards. Although some books incorporate the outlying areas of Fiefs Vendéens and Haut-Poitou, few mention the appellations of the Upper Loire, yet the wines of Côtes du Forez, Côte Roannaises, Côtes d'Auvergne, St.-Pourçain, and Châteaumeillant are equally legitimate members of the Loire's family of wines. And whereas the most famous appellations could and should rank among the most exciting wines of the world, there are so many underachievers that the major districts have become a minefield for wine-lovers, while growers in the lesser-known areas of the Upper Loire have everything to prove.

THE GENERIC AND OUTLYING APPELLATIONS OF
THE LOIRE

ANJOU-VILLAGES BRISSAC AOC

This village was singled out under the Anjou-Villages appellation in 1998 and backdated for wines as from 1996. Covers the Brissac-Quince area and nine surrounding communes.

√ *Château de Brissac • Château la Varière*

CHÂTEAUMEILLANT VDQS

Borders the Cher and Indre, around Bourges. Although only red-wine grapes are grown, white wine of some standing used to be made here, and its production is still permitted.

RED The Gamay grape usually dominates these. They should be drunk as young as possible.

⚜ Gamay, Pinot gris, Pinot noir

🍷 6–12 months

ROSÉ The best Châteaumeillant wines. They are fresh, grapey, and delicately balanced.

⚜ Gamay, Pinot gris, Pinot noir

🍷 6–12 months

√ *CV Châteaumeillant*
• *Maurice Lanoix • Raffinat & Fils*

CÔTES ROANNAISES AOC

Red and rosé wines made from a localized Gamay clone called Gamay Saint-Romain. Grown on south- and southwest-facing slopes

of volcanic soil on the left bank of the Loire some 40 kilometres (25 miles) west of the Mâconnais district of Burgundy. In the first edition of this book (1988), I stated that this appellation, although classified VDQS, deserved full AOC status; they duly achieved this promotion in 1994.

RED Some of these dry, medium- to full-bodied wines are produced using a form of *macération carbonique*, and a few are given a little maturation in cask. The result can vary between well-coloured wines that are firm and distinctive, and oaky and fruity Beaujolais-type versions for quaffing when young.

⚜ Gamay

🍷 1–5 years

ROSÉ Dry, medium-bodied, well-made wines that are crisp and fruity.

⚜ Gamay

🍷 2–3 years

√ *Robert Chaucesse • Michel Montroussier*
• *Domaine du Pavillon • Domaine de Perrier*
• *Robert Plasse • Marcel Vial*

CÔTES D'AUVERGNE VDQS

Côte d'Auvergne is located south of Saint-Pourçin and west of Côtes du Forez on the edge of the Massif Central. This is the most remotely situated of all the outer areas that fall officially within the Loire region. The wines from certain villages are superior and have therefore been given the right to use the following communal appellations: Côtes d'Auvergne-Boudes (villages of Boudes, Chalus, and St.-Hérant); Côtes d'Auvergne-Chanturgues (villages of Clermont-Ferrand and Cézabat [part]); Côtes d'Auvergne-Châteaugay (villages of Châteaugay and Cézabat [part]); Côtes d'Auvergne-Corent (villages of Corent, Les Martres-de-Veyre, La Sauvetat, and

Veyre-Monton); and Côtes d'Auvergne-Madargues (village of Riom).

RED The best of these dry, light-bodied, and fruity wines carry the Chanturgues appellation. Most are made from the Gamay, a grape that has traditionally been grown in the area, and are very much in the style of Beaujolais.

⚜ Gamay, Pinot noir

🍷 1–2 years

WHITE These dry, light-bodied wines made from Chardonnay have been overlooked but can be more accessible than the same variety grown in more classic areas of the Loire, thus they are surely a marketable commodity in view of the Chardonnay's upmarket status.

⚜ Chardonnay

🍷 1–2 years

ROSÉ These are dry, light-bodied wines with an attractive cherry flavour. They are made in the village of Clermont-Ferrand, and carry the Chanturgues appellation.

⚜ Gamay, Pinot noir

🍷 Within 1 year

√ *Henri Bourcheix • Pradier • Gilles Persilier*
• *Romeuf Raymond • Rougeyron*

CÔTES DU FOREZ VDQS

Similar to a VDQS Beaujolais, this wine is produced in the Loire *département* adjacent to Lyons. The wines are improving through the efforts of the *coopérative* and a few quality-conscious growers, but they could be better.

RED These are dry, light-bodied wines with some fruit. They are are best drunk young and at a cool temperature.

⚜ Gamay

🍷 Upon purchase

ROSÉ Simple, light-bodied, dry rosés that make attractive, unpretentious picnic wines.

🍇 Gamay

🍷 Upon purchase

✓ *Les Vignerons Foreziens*
• *Paul Gammon* • *Verdier-Logel*

CRÉMANT DE LOIRE AOC

Of all the Loire's sparkling wines, this is probably the most underrated, yet has the greatest potential because it can be blended from the wines of Anjou-Saumur and Touraine and from the widest range of grape varieties.

SPARKLING WHITE The better-balanced *cuvées* of these dry to semi-sweet, light- to medium-bodied wines are normally a blend of Chenin blanc in the main, with a good dash of Cabernet franc and Chardonnay. The best Chardonnay clones are yet to be established in the Loire, but at least it is widely utilized for sparkling wines, whereas Pinot noir is not and this is a mystery, as it is a proven variety in the region.

🍇 Chenin blanc, Cabernet franc, Cabernet sauvignon, Pineau d'Aunis, Pinot noir, Chardonnay, Arbois, Grolleau noir, and Grolleau gris

🍷 1–3 years

SPARKLING ROSÉ The best of these light- to medium-bodied wines are *brut*, and usually contain a high proportion of Cabernet franc and Grolleau noir grapes. Cabernet franc makes the most distinctive wine. A pure Pinot noir *crémant* rosé would be interesting to taste.

🍇 Chenin blanc, Cabernet franc, Cabernet sauvignon, Pineau d'Aunis, Pinot noir, Chardonnay, Arbois, Grolleau noir and gris

🍷 Most are best drunk upon purchase, although some benefit if kept 1–2 years

✓ *Alain Arnault* • *Baumard* • *Cray* • *Gratien & Meyer* • *Château Langlois* (Réserve Millésime) • *Michel Lateyron* (Perry de Malleyrand) • *Noël Pinot*

HAUT-POITOU VDQS

Situated 80 kilometres (50 miles) southwest of Tours, the Poitiers district produces wines that have achieved a remarkable reputation despite its hot, dry climate, and flat land that is more suited to arable farming than to viticulture. The local *cave coopérative* was responsible for this achievement, partly because of its high-tech establishment, which turned out clean wines during the late 1980s, when the rest of the Loire was going through its worst dirty wine period, and partly due to clever marketing. However, things went wrong on the financial side, Georges Duboeuf bought 40 per cent of the cooperative and it now operates as a *négociant*.

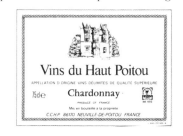

RED This is a wine to watch: although the really successful reds have until now been in short supply and confined mainly to Cabernet, there is a feeling that a general breakthrough is imminent. The quality of the entire appellation is likely to rise significantly, and there is promise of some exciting, pure varietal reds.

🍇 Pinot noir, Gamay, Merlot, Malbec, Cabernet franc, Cabernet sauvignon, and a maximum of 20% each of Gamay de Chaudenay and Grolleau

🍷 Within 3 years

WHITE Dry, light- to medium-bodied, varietal wines. Those made from pure Sauvignon are softer and more floral than most of their northern counterparts, yet retain the freshness and vitality that is so important to this grape variety.

🍇 Sauvignon blanc, Chardonnay, Pinot blanc, and up to a maximum of 20% Chenin blanc

🍷 Within 1 year

ROSÉ These dry, light- to medium-bodied wines are fresh and fruity. The *coopérative* produces a vivid raspberry-coloured Cabernet that is a bit too obvious, but other more subtle versions can be found.

🍇 Pinot noir, Gamay, Merlot, Malbec, Cabernet franc, Cabernet sauvignon, and a maximum of 20% each of Gamay de Chaudenay and Grolleau

🍷 Within 3 years

✓ *CV Haut-Poitou* • *Robert Champalou*
• *Gérard Descoux* • *Jacques Morgreau*
• *Domaine de Villemont*

ROSÉ DE LOIRE AOC

A dry rosé wine introduced in 1974 to exploit the international marketing success of Rosé d'Anjou and to take advantage of the trend for drier styles. However, the result has been very disappointing, although the few producers (recommended below) who have really tried demonstrate that very good-quality dry rosé can be made throughout the Loire.

ROSÉ Dry, light- to medium-bodied rosé from the Loire that could (and should) be the most attractive wine of its type – a few growers try, but most do not. These wines may be sold from 1 December following the harvest without any mention of *primeur* or *nouveau*.

🍇 Pineau d'Aunis, Pinot noir, Gamay, Grolleau, and at least 30% Cabernet franc and Cabernet sauvignon

🍷 Upon purchase

✓ *Clos de l'Abbaye* • *Domaine d'Ambinois*
• *Château de Breuil* • *Domaine Ogereau*

SAINT-POURÇAIN VDQS

The wines of Saint-Pourçain have a long and impressive history for what is, after all, an obscure VDQS, with vineyards first planted not by the Romans, as elsewhere in the Loire valley, but by the Phoenicians. The Saint-Pourçain area covers 19 communes southeast of the Bourges appellations of the Central Vineyards in the Allier *département*. The growers are quite ambitious, and many people think that these wines have a particularly promising future. There are 500 hectares (1,235 acres) of vineyards.

RED Dry, light- to medium-bodied wines, but they can vary from very light Beaujolais lookalikes to imitations of Bourgogne Passetoutgrains, depending on the grape varieties in the blend.

🍇 Gamay, Pinot noir, and up to a maximum of 10% Gamay teinturier

🍷 1–2 years

WHITE Dry, light- to medium-bodied wines. The Tresallier grape (which is known as the Sacy in Chablis), when blended with Chardonnay and Sauvignon, produces a crisp, toasty, full-flavoured wine that does have some merit. Very little is known about the Saint-Pierre-Doré, except that locals say it makes a "filthy wine" according to Master of Wine Rosemary George in *French Country Wines*.

🍇 A maximum of 50% Tresallier and 10% Saint-Pierre-Doré, plus Aligoté, Chardonnay, and Sauvignon blanc

🍷 1–2 years

ROSÉ Crisp, dry, light- to medium-bodied wines that have a fragrance that is reminiscent of soft summer fruits. The rosés are generally more successful than the red wines of the area but both styles are particularly refreshing and thirst-quenching.

🍇 Gamay, Pinot noir, and up to a maximum of 10% Gamay teinturier

🍷 1–2 years

✓ *Domaine de Bellevue* • *François Ray*
• *Union des Vignerons de Saint-Pourçain*

PAYS NANTAIS

Nantais is Muscadet country. The Sèvre-et-Maine produces the richest Muscadet, while the area immediately west has just been granted its own appellation (Côtes de Grandlieu) and the Coteaux de la Loire to the north produces wines with extra acidity.

SOUTHEAST OF NANTES are the vineyards of Muscadet. The best are those of the Sèvre-et-Maine district, named after two rivers, which is much hillier than the surrounding countryside and protected from northwesterly winds by Nantes itself. Sèvre-et-Maine accounts for one-quarter of the general appellation area, yet 85 per cent of all the Muscadet produced. Only in unusually hot or dry years, when they contain extra natural acidity, can the Muscadet grapes grown further north in the Coteaux de la Loire sometimes surpass those from Sèvre-et-Maine.

THE MUSCADET GRAPE AND ITS WINES

It is uncertain when the Muscadet grape, also known as the Melon de Bourgogne and the Gamay blanc, was first planted in the area. There is a plaque at Château de la Cassemichère that claims that the first Muscadet vine was transplanted there from Burgundy in 1740, but Pierre Galet, the famous ampelographer (vine botanist), tells us that "following the terrible winter of 1709, Louis XIV ordered that the replanting of the frozen vineyards of Loire-Atlantique be with Muscadet blanc".

The wine produced from the Muscadet grape is neutral in flavour and bears no hint of the muskiness its name implies. It must be harvested early to preserve acidity, and yet, in doing so, the grower risks making a wine that lacks fruit. But if the wine is left in contact with its sediment and bottled *sur lie*, this enhances the fruit, adds a yeasty-roundness, and, by retaining more of the carbonic gas created during fermentation, imparts a certain liveliness and freshness.

NANTES
The charm of the old quarter contrasts with the urban sprawl of the modern-day city, the gateway to the Loire valley.

MUSCADET VINES
In the heart of Muscadet country, to the southeast of Nantes, the village of St.-Fiacre-sur-Maine overlooks the surrounding vineyards.

FACTORS AFFECTING TASTE AND QUALITY

LOCATION
The Pays Nantais lies in the coastal area and the westernmost district of the Loire Valley, with vineyards occupying parts of the Loire-Atlantique and the Maine-et-Loire *départements*.

CLIMATE
Mild and damp, but winters can be harsh and spring frosts troublesome. Summers are generally warm and sunny, although they are also rainy.

ASPECT
Some of the vineyards are found on the flat land around the mouth of the Loire southwest of Nantes. There are rolling hills in the Sèvre-et-Maine and Coteaux de la Loire, with the best vineyards on gentle riverside slopes. Some of the smaller valleys are actually too steep for viticulture, and the vines in these areas occupy the hilltops.

SOIL
The best vineyards of the Sèvre-et-Maine are light and stony, with varying proportions of sand, clay, and gravel above a granitic, schistous, and volcanic subsoil that is rich in potassium and magnesium. The Coteau de la Loire is more schistous, while the Côtes de Grandlieu is schistous and granitic, and vineyards in the generic Muscadet appellation sand with silt. These soils provide good drainage, which is essential for such a damp growing district.

VITICULTURE AND VINIFICATION
The Muscadet is a frost-resistant, early-ripening grape that adapts well to the damp conditions of the Pays Nantais. It is harvested early (mid- to late September) to preserve its acidity. The best Muscadet is left in vat or barrel on its sediment – *sur lie* – until it is bottled. This imparts a greater depth and fruitiness, and a faint prickle of natural carbonic gas.

PRIMARY GRAPE VARIETIES
Muscadet, Folle blanche
SECONDARY GRAPE VARIETIES
Gamay, Gamay de Chaudenay, Gamay de Bouze, Négrette, Chardonnay, Cabernet franc, Cabernet sauvignon, Pinot noir, Chenin blanc, Groslot gris

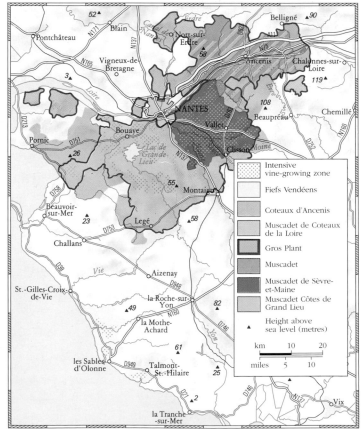

Intensive vine-growing zone
Fiefs Vendéens
Coteaux d'Ancenis
Muscadet de Coteaux de la Loire
Gros Plant
Muscadet
Muscadet de Sèvre-et-Maine
Muscadet Côtes de Grand Lieu
▲ Height above sea level (metres)

PAYS NANTAIS, *see also p.192*
The finest wines in the Pays Nantais are produced to the east of Nantes in Sèvre-et-Maine and Coteaux de la Loire.

THE APPELLATIONS OF
NANTAIS

COTEAUX D'ANCENIS VDQS

These varietal VDQS wines, which come from the same area as Muscadet Coteaux de la Loire, should be promoted to full AOC status.

RED Bone-dry to dry, and light- to medium-bodied wines that include Cabernets, made from both Cabernet franc and Cabernet sauvignon grapes. Surprisingly they are not as successful as the juicy Gamay wines which represent no less than 80 per cent of the total production of this appellation.

🍇 Cabernet sauvignon, Cabernet franc, Gamay, and up to a combined total of 5% Gamay de Chaudenay and Gamay de Bouze

🍷 2 years

WHITE Dry to medium-dry, light-bodied wines. The Pinot gris, also sold as "Malvoisie", is not as alcoholic as its Alsatian cousin, yet can possess a light richness that will linger in the mouth. The Chenin blanc, known locally as "Pineau de la Loire", rarely sparkles.

🍇 Chenin blanc, Pinot gris

🍷 12–18 months

ROSÉ Bone-dry to dry, light- to medium-bodied wines, some of which are fresh, firm, and lively. Gamay is the most popular grape variety.

🍇 Cabernet sauvignon, Cabernet franc, Gamay, and up to a combined total of 5% Gamay de Chaudenay and Gamay de Bouze

🍷 2 years

✓ *Jacques Guindon*

FIEFS VENDÉENS VDQS

A *vin de pays* until 1984, this appellation has been steadily improving and deserves its VDQS status. The regulations controlling the grape varieties permitted for this appellation are unique. They determine the proportion of each variety that must be cultivated in the vineyard, yet they do not limit the percentages of grapes contained in the final blend; thus blends and pure varietals are allowed.

RED The communes of Vix and Mareuil-sur-Lay-Disais produce the best wines. They are dry, medium-bodied, and firm, but not long-lived. They can have a grassy character, derived from the Cabernet franc, which is the predominant grape grown in both these two villages.

🍇 A minimum of 50% Gamay and Pinot noir plus Cabernet franc, Cabernet sauvignon, Négrette, and up to a maximum of 15% Gamay de Chaudenay

🍷 Within 18 months

WHITE Bone-dry to dry, light-bodied wines which, apart from those of Vix and Pissotte, are of limited quality. This could be because the Chenin blanc rarely ripens properly in a northerly coastal area. If some of the other permitted grape varieties were grown over a much wider area, quality might improve.

🍇 A minimum of 50% Chenin blanc, plus Sauvignon blanc and Chardonnay. A maximum of 20% Melon de Bourgogne in the communes of Vix and Pissotte and a maximum of 30% Groslot gris in the coastal vineyards around Les Sables d'Olonne

🍷 Upon purchase

ROSÉ Dry, light- to medium-bodied wines. The best wines of Vix and Mareuil-sur-Lay-Disais are soft, delicate, and underrated.

🍇 A minimum of 50% Gamay and Pinot noir plus Cabernet franc, Cabernet sauvignon, Négrette, and a maximum of 15% Gamay de Chaudenay. A maximum of 30% (was as high as 30% until 1994) Groslot gris in the coastal vineyards around Les Sables d'Olonne.

🍷 Within 18 months

✓ *Philippe Orion* (Domaine de la Barbinière) • *Philippe & Xavier Coirer*

GROS PLANT VDQS *OR* GROS PLANT NANTAIS VDQS

Gros plant is the local synonym for the Folle blanche – one of the grapes used to make Cognac.

WHITE Gros Plant is normally so dry, tart, and devoid of fruit and body that it seems tough and sinewy to taste. I would rather drink lemon juice than 99 per cent of the Gros Plant that I have had, but if yields are limited and the wine bottled *sur lie*, it can have sufficient depth to match its inherent bite.

🍇 Gros plant

🍷 Usually upon purchase

✓ *Domaine de Beauregard* • *Guy Bossard* • *Château de la Preuille* • *Clos Saint-Vincent des Rongères*

MUSCADET AOC

This basic appellation covers the whole Muscadet area, yet the wines produced under it account for only ten per cent of the total production.

WHITE Bone-dry, light-bodied wines which, with very few exceptions, are ordinary wines at best, and often lack balance. These wines may be sold as *primeur* or *nouveau* as from the third Thursday of November following the harvest.

🍇 Muscadet

🍷 Upon purchase

✓ *Domaine des Herbauges* • *Château de la Preuille*

MUSCADET DES COTEAUX DE LA LOIRE AOC

The Coteaux de la Loire is the most northerly wine area on the French coast, above which it is almost impossible to grow grapes of sufficient ripeness for winemaking.

WHITE Bone-dry, light-bodied wines of variable quality, usually lacking in fruit, but can be the best balanced of all Muscadets in very hot years.

🍇 Muscadet

🍷 Upon purchase

✓ *Château la Berrière "Clos Saint-Roch"* • *Domaine de la Garanderie* • *Jacques Guindon* • *Domaine des Herbauges* • *Château de la Roulière* • *Vignerons de la Noëlle*

MUSCADET CÔTES DE GRANDLIEU AOC *OR* MUSCADET CÔTES DE GRAND LIEU AOC

Delimited as recently as 1994, this area west of Sèvre-et-Maine once represented 73 per cent of the basic Muscadet appellation. The wines now fetch a nice premium above that received when they were merely perceived as generic Muscadets and while some deserve elevated price and status, many plainly do not.

WHITE Bone-dry, light-bodied variable wines.

🍇 Muscadet

🍷 Upon purchase

✓ *Domaine de la Chambaudière* • *Marquis de Goulaine* • *Domaine des Herbauges*

MUSCADET DE SÈVRE-ET-MAINE AOC

Classic Muscadet from a small area containing most of the best wines. Some 45 per cent of this appellation is bottled and sold as *sur lie*, having remained in contact with its sediment for at least one winter before bottling.

WHITE Bone-dry to dry, light-bodied wines. The best should have fruit, acidity, and elegance, but although they can be reminiscent of a modest white Burgundy and exceptional wines can survive considerable ageing, they seldom improve and always trade depth for finesse.

🍇 Muscadet

🍷 2 years, although some may last 3–4 years

✓ *Domaine de Beauregard* • *Guy Bossard* (Domaine de l'Ecu) • *Château de Briacé* • *Domaine de la Chambaudière* • *Domaines Chéreau Carré* • *Château du Coing de Saint-Fiacre* (Grande Cuvée Saint Hilaire) • *Domaine Gadais* • *Marquis de Goulaine* (La Cuvée du Millénaire) • *Manoir la Grange* • *Domaine de l'Hyvernière* • *Leroux Frères* (Clos de Beauregard) • *Pierre Luneau* (Le d'Or) • *Château de la Preuille* • *Château de la Ragotière* • *Domaine Dominique & Vincent Richard* • *Domaine de la Roche* • *Clos Saint-Vincent des Rongères* • *Serge Saupin* (Cuvée des Lions) • *Sauvion* (Château du Cléray, Cuvée Cardinal Richard and Découverte range) • *Domaine du Vieux Chai*

MUSCADET SUR LIE AOC

Until recently there were no controls and unscrupulous producers would simply describe an ordinary filtered wine as *sur lie* and thereby demand a higher price. Since 1994, however, this term may be applied to only one of the three sub-appellations (Coteaux du Loire, Côtes de Grandlieu, and Sèvre-et-Maine) and may not be used on any wines bearing the generic Muscadet AOC. Quite what the logic is to this is uncertain, since Gros Plant VDQS is permitted to use *sur lie* and it is even more inferior than the generic Muscadet appellation. The lesser the wine, the more need for a *sur lie* boost, thus rather than limiting its use, more emphasis should be placed on stricter controls.

At the moment Muscadet *sur lie* must remain in contact with its sediment for one winter, and may not be bottled before the third week of March following the harvest, with a second bottling period of mid-October to mid-November for fuller styles. The wine must also be bottled directly off its lees, and must not be racked or filtered, but there is still no regulation on the size and type of vessel in which the wine should be kept *sur lie*. Some growers would like the term applied only to wines kept in wooden barrels, arguing that the effect of keeping a wine in contact with its lees in huge vats is negligible, but at the very least vats over a certain size should be equipped with paddles to circulate the lees.

ANJOU-SAUMUR

Anjou-Saumur is a microcosm of the entire Loire Valley, producing virtually every style of wine imaginable, from almost every grape available in the Loire – from dry to sweet, red through rosé to white, and still wines to sparkling.

Saumur is the Loire's sparkling-wine centre, where tourists flock in the summer, visiting the numerous cellars hewn out of the solid tufa subsoil. The magnificent white tufa-stone castle that overlooks the town was built in the 14th century. It is regarded as one of the finest of the Loire châteaux, and is used by the Confrérie des Chevaliers du Sacavins (one of Anjou's several wine fraternities) for various inaugural ceremonies and celebrations.

VINEYARDS, COTEAUX DU LAYON
In favourable sites, the vines are sometimes attacked by "noble rot". The area is famous for its sweet white wines.

THE WINES OF ANJOU

Rosé still represents as much as 45 per cent of Anjou's total wine output, even though it is on the decline (the figure was 55 per cent in the late 1980s). However, although rosé remains this district's most popular wine, it has a down-market image and is essentially a blend of minor grapes; thus its commercial success has not propelled a specific variety to fame, and Anjou's most celebrated grape is the Chenin blanc used to make white wines. This vine has been cultivated in the area for well over a thousand years. It has many synonyms, from "Pineau de la Loire" to "Franc-blanc", but its principal name, Chenin blanc, stems from Mont-Chenin in 15th-century Touraine. Under other names it can be traced as far back as the year 845, to the abbey of Glanfeuil (south of the river in the Anjou district). The distinctive tang of

the Chenin blanc grape comes from its inherently high tartaric-acid content and this, combined with a naturally high extract, makes for unacceptably tart and often bitter styles of dry and medium-dry white. Exceptions to this rule are few and mostly confined to the four sun-blessed, southeast-facing slopes of Savennières. Anjou growers go by the rule rather than the exception, and the common practice has always been to leave the harvest of this variety until as late as possible. This invites the risk of rain, but by going over the vines several times in the time-

ANJOU-SAUMUR
See also p.192
Boasting sparkling wine, and more, from Saumur, and a range of wines from Angers's environs, Anjou-Saumur produces most types of wine found in the Loire as a whole.

BOTTLING AT SAUMUR-CHAMPIGNY
The appellation produces some of the Loire valley's finest red wines from the Cabernet franc.

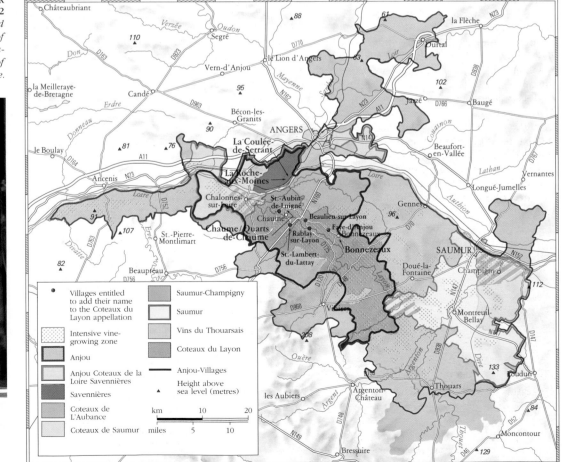

Villages entitled to add their name to the Coteaux du Layon appellation

Intensive vine-growing zone

Anjou

Anjou Coteaux de la Loire Savennières

Savennières

Coteaux de L'Aubance

Coteaux de Saumur

Saumur-Champigny

Saumur

Vins du Thouarsais

Coteaux du Layon

Anjou-Villages

Height above sea level (metres)

THE TOWN OF SAUMUR
*The 14th-century castle, one of the finest in the Loire, towers above
the bustling town of Saumur, the buildings distinguished by
the brilliant white tufa-stone typical of the area.*

honoured tradition of *tries*, picking only the ripest and healthiest
grapes on each and every sweep of the vineyard, a miraculous
wine may be made. Although this is a time-consuming, labour-
intensive operation, the unique quality of overripe grapes
produced can result in the most succulent and immaculately
balanced of sweet wines. Unlike poor and boring dry Chenin
blanc wines that only deteriorate with age, these treasures are
vinous investments that are capable of great maturity and can
achieve wonderfully complex honeyed characteristics.

THE SPARKLING SAUMUR INDUSTRY

With the rapid growth of the Champagne market in the 19th
century, producers in the Loire began to copy the effervescent
winemaking practices, believing that here, at last, was a potential
outlet for the surplus of thin, tart Chenin blanc wines with which
even the most quality-conscious growers were often lumbered.
Saumur eventually turned into the largest French sparkling-wine
industry outside Champagne. In many parts of the Loire the Chenin
blanc grape has the perfect acidity for a quality sparkling wine,
although devotees of the true yeasty character of Champagne can
find its bouquet sweet and aromatic, maintaining that its flavour
is too assertive to be properly transmuted by the *méthode
champenoise*. However, the wines are hugely popular, and the
admixture of Chardonnay and other neutral varieties can greatly
improve the overall blend. The most ardent admirer of Champagne
has been known to fall prey to the charms of a superior pure
Chenin-blanc bubbly from this region and even I have been
besotted by Bouvet's luxuriously ripe, oak-fermented Trésor.

TUFA SUBSOIL CELLARS
*The tufa-stone not only dominates the architecture;
the subsoil is ideal for the sparkling-wine cellars.*

THE REGION'S RED WINES

It is in Anjou, especially in the villages south of Saumur, that
the Cabernet franc emerges as the Loire's best red-wine grape.
However, beyond the neighbouring district of Touraine, its
cultivation rapidly diminishes. The Loire is the largest wine
region in France, yet surprisingly it boasts just three classic red
wines – Saumur-Champigny, Bourgueil, and Chinon – to which
we might now add Anjou-Villages. The fact that most of the
vineyards producing these wines are clustered together in
one tiny part of the region is less surprising, and is also no
coincidence. The reason is that they share a compact area
around the confluence of the Vienne and the Loire – two
rivers that long ago established the gravel terraces so prized
for growing the Cabernet franc today.

FACTORS AFFECTING TASTE AND QUALITY

LOCATION
West-central district with mostly left-bank vineyards situated between Angers and Saumur.

CLIMATE
A gentle Atlantic-influenced climate with light rainfall, warm summers, and mild autumns, but frost is a problem in Savennières.

ASPECT
Soft, rolling hills which hold back the westerly winds. The best sites are the south-facing rocky hillsides of Savennières and the steep-sided valley of the river Layon.

SOIL
In the west and around Layon, the soil is schist with a dark, shallow topsoil that stores heat well and helps ripen the grapes, but some colder clay-soil areas produce heavier wines. The chalk-tufa soil in the east of the district around Saumur produces lighter wines, while the shale and gravel in Saumur-Champigny favours Cabernet franc.

VITICULTURE AND VINIFICATION
The Chenin blanc is a particularly slow-ripening grape that is often left on the vine until November, especially in the Coteaux du Layon. The effect of the autumn sun on the dew-drenched, overripe grapes can encourage "noble rot", particularly in Bonnezeaux and Quarts-de-Chaume. In good years, pickers go through the vineyards several times, selecting only the ripest or most rotten grapes – a tradition known as *tries*. Most wines are bottled in the spring following the vintage, but wines produced from such richly sweet grapes take at least three months to ferment and, for this reason, might not be bottled until the following autumn.

PRIMARY GRAPE VARIETIES
Chenin blanc, Cabernet franc, Gamay, Grolleau
SECONDARY GRAPE VARIETIES
Chardonnay, Sauvignon blanc, Cabernet sauvignon, Pineau d'Aunis, Malbec

THE APPELLATIONS OF
ANJOU-SAUMUR

ANJOU AOC

The Anjou district encompasses the vineyards of Saumur; thus Saumur may be sold as Anjou, but not vice versa. The red wines are by far the best, the whites the worst, and the rosé wines, although waning in popularity, remain the most famous. Because "mousseux" has "cheap fizz" connotations, the wines officially designated as Anjou Mousseux appellation are often marketed simply as "Anjou".

RED Dry, medium- to full-bodied wines, made mostly from pure Cabernet franc or with a touch of Cabernet sauvignon. These delightful wines are best drunk young, although the odd oak-aged wine of surprising complexity can be found.

🍇 Cabernet franc, Cabernet sauvignon, Pineau d'Aunis

🍷— 1–3 years

✓ *Domaine d'Ambinois • Domaine de Bablut
Domaine des Baumard • Bouvet-Ladubay
• Godineau Père & Fils • Château d'Epiré
(Clos de la Cerisaie) • Château de
Montguéret • Château des Rochettes
• Domaine de Terrebrune*

WHITE Although these wines vary from dry to sweet and from light- to full-bodied types, there are too many aggressively acid-dry or simply mediocre medium-sweet Chenin blanc wines in the appellation. Some improvement has been made by growers maximizing the 20 per cent Chardonnay and Sauvignon allowance, while Jacques Beaujeu and a few others use oak to smooth out Chenin's jagged edges, and Domaine Ogereau even ferments *en barrique*. These wines may be sold as from 1 December following the harvest without any mention of *primeur* or *nouveau*.

🍇 A minimum of 80% Chenin blanc and a maximum of 20% Chardonnay and Sauvignon blanc

🍷— Upon purchase

✓ *Jacques Beaujeu* (Château la Varière)
• *Domaine Philippe Delesvaux*
• *Domaine Ogereau • Domaine Richou*

ROSÉ Once a marketing miracle, Anjou Rosé or Rosé d'Anjou sells less well in today's increasingly sophisticated markets. There is nothing intrinsically wrong with a wine that happens to be pink with some sweetness, although you would be forgiven for thinking this is why some critics turn up their noses at such wines. I prefer dry rosés, but I enjoy medium-sweet rosés when they are very fresh and fruity. The trouble with so many of these medium-sweet, light- to medium-bodied, coral-pink wines is that while they can be delicious in the early spring following the vintage, an alarming number quickly tire in the bottle. The moral is, therefore, that even when you have found an Anjou Rosé you like, never buy it by the case. These wines may be sold

as *primeur* or *nouveau* from the third Thursday of November following the harvest or from 1 December without any mention of *primeur* or *nouveau*.

🍇 Predominately Grolleau, with varying proportions of Cabernet franc, Cabernet sauvignon, Pineau d'Aunis, Gamay, Malbec

🍷— Upon purchase

ANJOU COTEAUX DE LA LOIRE AOC

This rare, white-only appellation is situated southwest of Angers. Production is small and will dwindle even further as vineyards are replanted with Cabernet for the increasingly popular Anjou Rouge appellation.

WHITE Although currently produced in dry through to medium styles, this was originally legally defined in 1946 as a traditionally sweet wine. Today, producers following the trend for drier styles are hampered by out-of-date regulations that set the alcoholic strength too high and the yield too low.

🍇 Chenin blanc

🍷— Within 1 year

✓ *Gilles Musset*

ANJOU GAMAY AOC

Gamay is only allowed in Anjou AOC wines if the name of the grape is added to the appellation on the label.

RED Dry to medium-dry, light-bodied wines that are rarely of great interest. These wines may be sold as *primeur* or *nouveau* as from the third Thursday of November following the harvest.

🍇 Gamay

🍷— Upon purchase

✓ *Domaine de Bablut*

ANJOU MOUSSEUX AOC

This *méthode champenoise* wine is softer, but less popular than its Saumur equivalent, although it may come from the communes within Saumur itself.

SPARKLING WHITE These dry to sweet, light- to medium-bodied wines desperately need a change of regulation to allow a little Chardonnay in the blend. The Chardonnay's fatter, more neutral character would enable producers to make a more classic, less frivolous style of sparkling wine.

🍇 A minimum of 60% Chenin blanc plus Cabernet sauvignon, Cabernet franc, Malbec, Gamay, Grolleau, Pineau d'Aunis

🍷— 1–2 years

SPARKLING ROSÉ If you want to know what Anjou Rosé tastes like with bubbles, try this light- to medium-bodied wine, which is mostly sold as *demi-sec*.

🍇 Cabernet sauvignon, Cabernet franc, Malbec, Gamay, Grolleau, Pineau d'Aunis

🍷— Upon purchase

ANJOU PÉTILLANT AOC

A little-used appellation for gently sparkling *méthode champenoise* wines with a minimum of nine months' bottle-age, which must be sold in ordinary still-wine bottles with regular corks.

SEMI-SPARKLING WHITE These are dry to *demi-sec*, light-bodied sparkling wines. Considering

the variable quality of Anjou Blanc, many producers might be better advised to fizz it up and sell it under this appellation.

🍇 A minimum of 80% Chenin blanc and a maximum of 20% Chardonnay and Sauvignon blanc

🍷— Upon purchase

SEMI-SPARKLING ROSÉ Dry to medium, light-bodied wines, which are rarely encountered outside the area and may be labelled "Anjou Pétillant", "Anjou Rosé Pétillant", or "Rosé d'Anjou Pétillant".

🍇 Grolleau, Cabernet franc, Cabernet sauvignon, Pineau d'Aunis, Gamay, Malbec

🍷— Upon purchase

ANJOU ROSÉ AOC
See Anjou AOC

ANJOU-VILLAGES AOC

This supposedly superior, red-wine only appellation was first delimited in 1986, but did not come into effect until 1991. It is supposed to encourage producers to make interesting red wines rather than nondescript whites and, with a considerably higher permitted yield, there was little doubt that it would succeed in this aim. After all, why produce Anjou AOC at 45 hectolitres per hectare for white or 40 hectolitres per hectare for red, when you can market the much grander-sounding Anjou-Villages AOC and increase yields to 50 hectolitres per hectare at the same time? It was such a good deal that growers outside the original delimitation wanted to be included and in 1994 the authorities duly obliged by expanding the appellation area. If you buy from the best growers, you will get some of the finest red wines that the Loire has to offer.

RED The very best wines can be deeply coloured with a creamy-raspberry aroma and flavour.

🍇 Cabernet franc, Cabernet sauvignon

🍷— 2–6 years

✓ *Domaine de Bablut • Château Pierre Bise
• Brault Père & Fils* (Domaine de Sainte Anne) *• Domaine Victor Lebreton
• Domaine Ogereau • Château la Varière*

ANJOU–VILLAGES BRISSAC AOC

This village was singled out under the Anjou-Villages appellation in 1998 and backdated for wines as from 1996 onwards. It covers the area of Brissac-Quince and nine surrounding communes.

✓ *Château de Brissac • Château la Varière*

BONNEZEAUX AOC

Grown on three south-facing river slopes of the commune of Thouarcé in the Coteaux du Layon, this is one of the undisputed great sweet wines of France. The grapes must be harvested in *tries* with the pickers collecting only the ripest, often botrytis-affected fruit, which can take up to two weeks. In fact, the minimum sugar ripeness for Bonnezeaux is higher than Sauternes or Barsac.

WHITE Intensely sweet, richer, and more full-bodied than Quarts-de-Chaume, the other great growth of the Layon valley, this wine has pineapple and liquorice fruit when young, achieving a beautiful honeyed-vanilla complexity with age.

🍇 Chenin blanc

🍷 Up to 20 years or more

✓ *Domaine de la Croix des Loges • Château de Fesles • Domaine Godineau* (Le Malabé) *• Domaine les Grandes Vignes • Domaine de Laffourcade* (Château Perray-Jouannet) *• Domaine de Terrebrune* (La Montagne) *• Château la Varière*

CABERNET D'ANJOU AOC

This appellation includes Saumur, and it was a *saumurois* named Taveau who, in 1905, was the first person to make an Anjou Rosé from Cabernet grapes. Despite its classic Cabernet content and an extra degree of natural alcohol, this is not as superior to Anjou Rosé as it should be because bulk sales at cheap prices have devalued its reputation.

ROSÉ Good examples of these medium to medium-sweet, medium-bodied wines produced by the best domaines have a clean and fruity character with aromas of raspberries. These wines may be sold as *primeur* or *nouveau* from the third Thursday of November following the harvest or from 1 December without any mention of *primeur* or *nouveau*.

🍇 Cabernet franc, Cabernet sauvignon

🍷 Upon purchase

✓ *Domaine de Bablut • Brault Père & Fils* (Domaine de Sainte Anne) *• Château de Breuil • Domaine Cady • Domaine des Maurières • Domaine du Petit Val*

CABERNET DE SAUMUR AOC

All Cabernet de Saumur wines have the right to claim the appellation Cabernet d'Anjou, but those sold as Saumur are usually finer in quality.

ROSÉ A delicate, medium-sweet, light- to medium-bodied wine with a hint of straw to its pink colour and a distinctive raspberry aroma. These wines may be sold as *primeur* or *nouveau* from the third Thursday of November following the harvest or from 1 December without any mention of *primeur* or *nouveau*.

🍇 Cabernet franc, Cabernet sauvignon

🍷 Upon purchase

✓ *Domaine du Val Brun*

COTEAUX DE L'AUBANCE AOC

These wines are made from old vines grown on the schistous banks of the river Aubance. To use this appellation growers must use grapes that are well ripened and harvested by *tries*, a labour-intensive system that is not cost-effective, so most growers produce Cabernet d'Anjou.

WHITE A few growers still make this rich and semi-sweet, medium- to full-bodied wine of excellent longevity and exceptional quality.

🍇 Chenin blanc

🍷 5–10 years

✓ *Domaine de Bablut • Domaine Victor Lebreton • Domaine Richou • Domaine des Rochelles • Château des Rochettes*

COTEAUX DU LAYON AOC

This appellation, which overlaps Anjou Coteaux de la Loire in the northwest and Saumur in the southeast, has been famous for its sweet white wines since the 4th century. In favourable sites the vines are sometimes attacked by "noble rot", but in all cases the grapes must be extremely ripe and harvested by *tries* to a minimum of 12° alcohol from a maximum 30 hectolitres per hectare. Due to the relatively low price this appellation commands, harvesting by *tries* is viable only for the top domaines.

WHITE Green-gold- to yellow-gold-coloured, soft-textured, sweet, medium- to full-bodied wines, rich in fruit, and potentially long lived.

🍇 Chenin blanc

🍷 5–15 years

✓ *Domaine Pierre Aguilas • Domaine Baumard* (Cuvée le Paon & Clos de Sainte Cathérine) *• Château Pierre Bise • J. L. Douet* (Château des Rochettes) *• Château de Fesles* (Château de la Roulerie) *• Jousset & Fils* (Carte d'Or and Logis de la Giraudière) *• Domaine des Landreau • Moulin Touchais • Domaine Ogereau* (Cuvée Prestige) *• Domaine de la Pierre Saint Maurille • Domaine de Touche Noir* (formerly Domaine de Millé)

COTEAUX DU LAYON-CHAUME AOC

In many ways, there is very little that separates this single-village appellation from Coteaux du Layon, although it does have a lower maximum yield of 25 hectolitres per hectare instead of 30 hectolitres per hectare, which itself is very low.

WHITE Sweet, medium- to full-bodied, fine, viscous wines that usually rank above most basic Coteaux du Layon.

🍇 Chenin blanc

🍷 5–15 years

✓ *Michel Blouin • Domaine Cady* (Cuvée Anatole) *• Château de Fesles* (Château de la Roulerie) *• Château de la Guimonière • Clos de la Herse • Château Montbenault • Domaine du Petit Metris • Domaine Rochais* (les Zariles) *• Domaine de la Soucherie*

COTEAUX DU LAYON VILLAGES AOC

Historically these six villages have consistently produced the cream of all the wines in the Coteaux du Layon, and thus have the right to add their names to the basic appellation.

WHITE Sweet wines that are medium- to full-bodied. According to the "Club des Layon Villages", Beaulieu has a soft, light aroma; Faye has a scent reminiscent of brushwood; Rablay is big, bold, and round; Rochefort is full-bodied, tannic, and matures well; St.-Aubin has a delicate aroma that develops; and St.-Lambert is robust yet round.

🍇 Chenin blanc

🍷 5–15 years

✓ **Beaulieu** *Domaine d'Ambinois* (Clos des Mulonières), *Château de Breuil, Château Pierre Bise* (L'Anciaie) *• Domaine Godineau* (Vieilles Vignes, Guy Tourtet) *•* **Rablay** *Domaine de la Bergerie, Domaine des Sablonettes •* **Rochefort** *Domaine des Haut Perras,*

Domaine de la Motte • **St.-Aubin** *Michel Blouin, Domaine Cady, Domaine Philippe Delesvaux, Domaine Jo Pithon •* **St.-Lambert** *Domaine Ogereau, Domaine Jo Pithon*

COTEAUX DE SAUMUR AOC

After the ban on the term *méthode champenoise* in 1985 for wines produced or sold in the EU (*see* p.164), there were moves to develop this little-used appellation as the principal still wine of the Saumur district in order to promote Saumur AOC as an exclusively sparkling wine. However, they seem to have ground to a halt.

WHITE Relatively rare, semi-sweet, medium- to full-bodied wines that are richly flavoured and worth seeking out.

🍇 Chenin blanc

🍷 5–10 years

✓ *Château de Brézé • Domaine des Hautes-Vignes • Château de Hureau • Clos Rougeard • Domaine de Saint-Just*

QUARTS-DE-CHAUME AOC

These wines are grown on the plateau behind the village of Chaume in the Coteaux-du-Layon commune of Rochefort-sur-Loire. The vineyards of Quarts-de-Chaume used to be run by the abbey of Ronceray, whose landlord drew a quarter of the vintage as rent.

WHITE These are semi-sweet to sweet, medium- to full-bodied wines. Although harvested by *tries* and produced in the same manner as Bonnezeaux, Quarts-de-Chaume comes from a more northerly area and as a result is slightly lighter in body. It also tends to have a touch less sweetness.

🍇 Chenin blanc

🍷 Up to 15 years or more

✓ *Domaine des Baumard • Château de Belle Rive • Domaine de Laffourcade* (Château de l'Echarderie, Château de Surronde, and Cuvée Novembre) *• Domaine du Petit Metris • Château Pierre Bise*

ROSÉ D'ANJOU AOC

See Anjou AOC

ROSÉ D'ANJOU PÉTILLANT AOC

See Anjou Pétillant AOC

SAUMUR AOC

Saumur, situated within the borders of the Anjou appellation, is regarded as the pearl of Anjou. Its wine may be sold as Anjou, but Anjou does not automatically qualify as Saumur. Unless made from Cabernet grapes, all rosé wines must adopt the Anjou Rosé appellation. Like Anjou, its white wines are variable, yet its red wines are excellent.

RED These fine, bone-dry to dry, medium- to full-bodied wines are often similar to the red wines of Anjou, although they can vary from light and fruity to deep-coloured and tannic.

🍇 Cabernet franc, Cabernet sauvignon, Pineau d'Aunis

🕰 1–10 years according to style

✓ *Clos de l'Abbaye • Bouvet-Ladubay • Domaine des Hautes Vignes • Langlois-Château • Château de Montreuil-Bellay • Cave des Vignerons* (Reserve) *• Domaine des Nerleux • Château de Passavent • Château de Targé*

WHITE Varying from bone-dry to sweet and from light- to full-bodied, these wines have a style more akin to Vouvray than Anjou, due to the limestone and the tufa soil. In poor-to-average years, however, a Saumur is easily distinguished by its lighter body, leaner fruit, and a tartness of flavour that can sometimes have a metallic edge on the aftertaste. These wines may be sold as from 1 December following the harvest without any mention of *primeur* or *nouveau*.

🍇 A minimum of 80% Chenin blanc and a maximum of 20% Chardonnay and Sauvignon blanc

🕰 Upon purchase

✓ *Cave de Vignerons • Château de Hureau • Langlois-Château* (Vieilles Vignes) *• Château de Villeneuve*

SPARKLING WHITE Although the production per hectare of this wine is one-third more than for its Anjou equivalent, Saumur is – or at least should be – better in quality and style due to its Chardonnay content and the tufa-limestone soil. Most wines are made in a true, bone-dry, *brut* style, although the full gamut is allowed and wines up to *demi-sec* sweetness are relatively common. The vast majority of these wines have a tart greengage character, lack finesse, and do not pick up toasty or biscuity bottle-aromas. The wines indicated below have an elegance sadly lacking in most Saumur, and possess gentler, more neutral fruit, which will benefit from a little extra time in bottle, although after a while all these wines tend to age rather than mature gracefully. The creamy-rich *barrique*-fermented Bouvet Trésor is the one big exception: not only is it just the best sparkling wine in the Loire, it can also be compared to very good-quality Champagne, although it is in a very different style.

🍇 Chenin blanc plus a maximum of 20% Chardonnay and Sauvignon blanc, and up to 60% Cabernet sauvignon, Cabernet franc, Malbec, Gamay, Grolleau, Pineau d'Aunis, and Pinot noir

🕰 3–5 years

✓ *Bouvet* (Vintage Crémant Saumur) *• Cave Coopérative des Vignerons de Saumur* (Saumur Cuvée Spéciale)

SPARKLING ROSÉ Pink Saumur can be made from several varieties, but many are pure Cabernet franc and an increasing number are showing very well these days. However, the aggressive potential of this grape can quickly turn a thrilling raspberry-flavoured fizz into something hideous. Pure Cabernet Sauvignon rosés can also be very good, although much

smoother, less overt, and not as intrinsically Saumur as a Cabernet franc *cuvée*.

🍇 Cabernet sauvignon, Cabernet franc, Malbec, Gamay, Grolleau, Pineau d'Aunis, Pinot noir

🕰 Upon purchase

✓ *Jean Douet • Domaine des Nerleux • De Neuville Saumur Brut • Noël Pinot*

SAUMUR-CHAMPIGNY AOC

Many people believe that the vineyards southeast of Saumur entitled to add the village name of Champigny to their appellation produce the best red wine in the Loire.

RED Bone-dry to dry, full-bodied wines with a distinctive deep colour and full and fragrant raspberry aromas, often tannic and long-lived.

🍇 Cabernet franc, Cabernet sauvignon, Pineau d'Aunis

🕰 5–10 years

✓ *Domaine Filliatreau • Château du Hureau* (Cuvée Lisagathe) *• René-Noël Legrand • Domaine des Roches Neuves • Clos Rougeard • Domaine de Saint-Just • Domaine du Val Brun • Château de Villeneuve*

SAUMUR D'ORIGINE AOC

When the EU banned the term *méthode champenoise*, this marketing term was developed by the producers of sparkling Saumur to promote and advertise their wines under. *See also* Saumur AOC.

SAUMUR MOUSSEUX AOC

This is the technically correct appellation for all fully sparkling white and rosé Saumur wines made by the *méthode champenoise*, but producers have shied away from the down-market term *mousseux*, selling the wines simply as Appellation Saumur Contrôlée. There is no allowance for this in the regulations, but it is so widespread that the authorities might as well integrate these wines in the basic Saumur AOC. Either that or officially embellish the Saumur d'Origine designation that producers created to market these wines under. A significant amount of red *méthode champenoise* is also produced, but this cannot claim AOC status. *See also* Saumur AOC.

SAUMUR PÉTILLANT AOC

Little-used appellation for gently sparkling *méthode champenoise* wines with a minimum of nine months' bottle-age, which must be sold in ordinary still-wine bottles with regular corks.

SEMI-SPARKLING WHITE These dry to *demi-sec*, light-bodied, and fruity wines are not dissimilar to the fine wines of the Montlouis Pétillant appellation and should be revived.

🍇 A minimum of 80% Chenin blanc and a maximum of 20% Chardonnay and Sauvignon blanc

🕰 Upon purchase

SAVENNIÈRES AOC

When this small portion of Anjou Coteaux de la Loire produced only sweet wines the AOC regulations set a correspondingly low maximum yield. This concentrates the wines on four southeast-facing slopes of volcanic debris that produce the world's greatest dry Chenin Blanc.

WHITE Bone-dry to dry wines of great mineral intensity, Savennières can be some of the longest-lived dry white wines in the world. Most critics believe that the single greatest

Savennières is Nicolas Joly's Clos de la Coulée de Serrant and, while I agree that it is one of the greatest wines of the Loire, I think that Baumard's Clos du Papillon (not to be confused with Clos du Papillon from other growers) consistently displays greater elegance and finesse. Over the last 15 years or so, a few producers have resurrected the semi-sweet style that used to be more popular in Savennières in the first half of the 20th century.

🍇 Chenin blanc

🕰 5–8 years (10–15 years for Clos de la Coulée de Serrant)

✓ *Domaine des Baumard* (Clos du Papillon, Clos de St.-Yves, and straight Savennières) *• Le Domaine du Closel* (Clos du Papillon) *• Château d'Epiré • Nicolas Joly* (Clos de la Bergerie, Clos de la Coulée de Serrant, Roche-aux-Moines) *• Domaine de Laffourcade* (Clos la Royauté) *• Domaine Soulez* (Château de Chamboureau, Chevalier Buliard, Clos du Papillon, Le Rigourd, Roche-aux-Moines)

SAVENNIÈRES COULÉE-DE-SERRANT AOC

One of just two single-vineyard designations authorized for Savennières, Coulée-de-Serrant is seven hectares and a mono-*cru*, solely-owned by Nicolas Joly of Château de la Roche-aux-Moines. Many consider this to be the single-greatest Loire dry white wine. *See also* Savennières AOC.

SAVENNIÈRES ROCHE-AUX-MOINES AOC

The second and largest of the two single-vineyard designations authorized for Savennières, Roche-aux-Moines is 17 hectares (42 acres) and owned by three producers: Nicolas Joly of Château de la Roche-aux-Moines, Pierre and Yves Soulez of Château de Chamboureau, and Mme Laroche of Domaine au Moines. *See also* Savennières AOC.

VINS DU THOUARSAIS VDQS

Michel Gigon is the sole producer of Vins du Thouarsais, a wine that could once boast over a hundred growers.

RED Dry, light- to medium-bodied, fruity reds, sometimes reminiscent of cherries and other stone fruit.

🍇 Cabernet franc, Cabernet sauvignon, Gamay

🕰 1–2 years

WHITE A lighter-bodied but far more fragrant version of dry and semi-sweet Anjou Blanc.

🍇 Chenin blanc plus up to 20% Chardonnay

🕰 Upon purchase

ROSÉ This is a splendid dry, light-bodied or light- to medium-bodied picnic wine.

🕰 Upon purchase

✓ *Michel Gigon*

TOURAINE

Wines bearing Touraine appellations are prolific and capable of giving good value, but they are not great. However, there are notable exceptions, such as the wines from Vouvray and the less well-known but equally elite wines of Montlouis, Bourgueil, and Chinon.

THE WINE-GROWING DISTRICT around Tours dates back to Roman times, as does the town itself. Tours was a place of pilgrimage as early as the 6th century and famous for its production of silk in the 15th and 16th centuries. The Cabernet franc, known locally as Breton, was flourishing in the vineyards of the abbey of Bourgueil 1,000 years ago and, as recently as 500 years ago, the Chenin blanc – today's predominant Touraine grape – acquired its name from Mont Chenin in the south of the district.

TOURAINE'S WINE REGIONS

With the possible exception of Saumur-Champigny, the best red wines in the Loire come from the appellations of Chinon and Bourgueil, which face each other across the river Loire, just west of Tours. Made predominantly from Cabernet franc, good vintages aged in oak may be complex and comparable to claret, while the more everyday wines have the fresh-picked aromas of strawberries and raspberries and can be drunk young and cool. To the east of Tours, Vouvray and Montlouis produce rich, sweet, long-lived *moelleux* wines from overripe Chenin blanc grapes in sunny years. North of Tours, the wines produced in Jasnières are from the same grape, but the dry style is distinctly different. Jasnières is a singular white sub-appellation within a wider red, white, and rosé AOC called the Coteaux du Loir. The "Loir" is not a typographical error for "Loire", but a confusingly spelt tributary of the great river. Also grown on the banks of the Loir, the larger VDQS area Coteaux du Vendômois produces the full spectrum of still-wine styles, as does Cheverny to the east, including a distinctive dry white wine from the obscure Romorantin grape. Touraine Sauvignon blanc makes an attractively priced, unassuming alternative to Sancerre, while the fruity Gamay makes easy-drinking reds and rosés. Other reds are made from the local Grolleau, or from the Pineau d'Aunis.

FACTORS AFFECTING TASTE AND QUALITY

LOCATION
East-central district with most of its vineyards in the *département* of Indre-et-Loire, but they also extend into those of Loir-et-Cher, Indre, and Sarthe.

CLIMATE
Touraine falls under some Atlantic influence, but the climate is less maritime than in the Nantes district and Anjou-Saumur. Protected from northerly winds by the Coteaux du Loir. Warm summer, low October rainfall.

ASPECT
Attractively rolling land, flatter around Tours itself, hillier in the hinterland. Vines are planted on gently undulating slopes, which are often south-facing, at between 40 and 100 m (130–330 ft) above sea level.

SOIL
Clay and limestone over tufa subsoil east of Tours around Vouvray and Montlouis. Tufa is chalk boiled by volcanic action.

It is full of minerals, retains water, and can be tunnelled out to make large, cool cellars for storing wine. Sandy-gravel soils in low-lying Bourgueil and Chinon vineyards produce fruity, supple wines; the slopes or coteaux of sandy-clay produce firmer wines.

VITICULTURE AND VINIFICATION
White-wine fermentation takes place at low temperatures and lasts for several weeks for dry wines, several months for sweet wines. The reds undergo malolactic fermentation. Some Bourgueil and Chinon is aged for up to 18 months in oak casks before bottling.

PRIMARY GRAPE VARIETIES
Chenin blanc, Cabernet franc, Sauvignon blanc, Grolleau
SECONDARY GRAPE VARIETIES
Cabernet sauvignon, Pinot noir, Meslier, Gamay, Gamay teinturier, Pineau d'Aunis, Romorantin, Arbois, Chardonnay, Malbec

The Chenin blanc is still the dominant variety here and, as in Anjou-Saumur, the tradition has been to produce naturally sweet wines in great years when these grapes are full of sugar, but lighter, not completely dry styles are more usual. The surplus of less-than-overripe grapes, like that in Anjou-Samur, is traditionally utilized for sparkling wines, although Touraine's sparkling-wine industry did not take off until the end of the 19th century.

TOURAINE, *see also* p.192
Surrounded by different appellations, the ancient city of Tours is the focal point of an area rich in the variety of its wines.

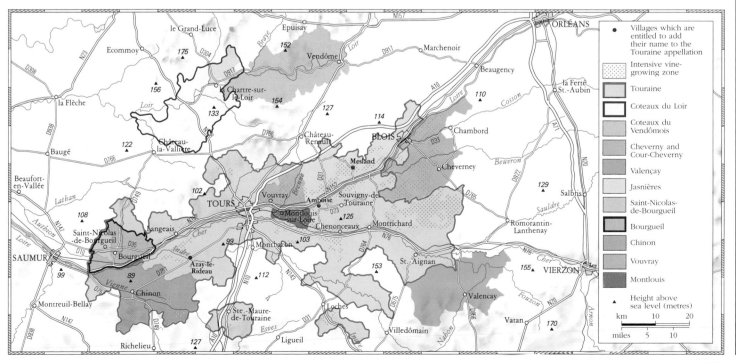

Legend:
- Villages which are entitled to add their name to the Touraine appellation
- Intensive vine-growing zone
- Touraine
- Coteaux du Loir
- Coteaux du Vendômois
- Cheverny and Cour-Cheverny
- Valençay
- Jasnières
- Saint-Nicolas-de-Bourgueil
- Bourgueil
- Chinon
- Vouvray
- Montlouis
- ▲ Height above sea level (metres)

km 10 20
miles 5 10

THE APPELLATIONS OF
TOURAINE

BOURGUEIL AOC

Most of the vines are grown on a sand-and-gravel plateau, or *terrasse,* by the river. The wines have a pronounced fruity character and are delicious to drink when less than six months old. Those grown on the south-facing clay and tufa slopes, or *coteaux,* ripen up to ten days earlier and produce more full-bodied, longer-lived wines.

RED Bone-dry to dry, medium-bodied, lively wines, full of soft-fruit flavours, which are often aged in cask. They are very easy to quaff when less than six months old; many close up when in bottle and need time to soften. Wines from the *terrasse* vineyards are best drunk young, while those from the *coteaux* repay keeping.

🍇 Cabernet franc with up to
   10% Cabernet sauvignon

🍷 Within 6 months or after 6 years

ROSÉ Bone-dry to dry, light- to medium-bodied wines that are very fruity with aromas of raspberries and blackberries and good depth of flavour. They deserve to be better known.

🍇 Cabernet franc with up to
   10% Cabernet sauvignon

🍷 2–3 years

✓ *Clos de l'Abbaye • Yannick Amirault • Domaine Breton • Domaine de la Chevalerie • Domaine Druet • Moïse Thierry Boucard • Max Cognard • Domaine Delaunay • Paul Gambier • Pierre Grégoire • Domaine des Mailloches*

CHEVERNY AOC

Upgraded from VDQS to full AOC status in 1993. These good-value, crisp, and fruity wines deserve their promotion and should be better known. Cheverny is usually made and marketed as a pure varietal wine, the most interesting of which, Romorantin, has been awarded its own AOC for the best vineyards around Cour-Cheverny itself. *See also* Cour-Cheverny AOC.

RED Dry, light- to medium-bodied wines. The smaller growers mostly produce pure Gamay wines of very acceptable quality, although the addition of ten per cent or more Pinot noir gives a smoother wine. Gamay teinturier de Chaudenay, which has coloured juice, is no longer permitted.

🍇 Between 40 and 65% Gamay, plus Pinot noir, Cabernet franc, Malbec, and until the year 2000, Cabernet sauvignon

🍷 1–2 years

WHITE Dry, light-bodied, modest wines with a fine, flowery nose, delicate flavour, and crisp balance. Now primarily a Sauvignon blanc wine, as Romorantin may not be used and the amount of Sauvignon in these wines has been regulated since 1993.

🍇 Between 65 and 80% Sauvignon blanc, plus Chardonnay, Chenin blanc, and Arbois

🍷 1–2 years

ROSÉ Only small quantities are produced but the wines are agreeably dry and light-bodied and very consistent in quality. Since acquiring full AOC status, Cabernet franc, Cabernet sauvignon, and Malbec have been allowed for the production of these wines, which has boosted the quantity even further.

🍇 At least 50% Gamay, plus Cabernet franc, Cabernet sauvignon, Malbec, Pineau d'Aunis, and Pinot gris

🍷 1–2 years

✓ *François Cazin • Jean-Michel Courtioux • Domaine de la Desoucherie • Domaine de la Gaudronnière • Domaine Sauger & Fils*

CHINON AOC

The appellations of Chinon and Bourgueil produce the best red wine in Touraine using the Cabernet franc grape, known locally as Breton. Chinon wines are generally lighter and more delicate than those of Bourgueil, but those from the tufa hill slopes have greater depth and flavour and age well.

RED Bone-dry to dry, light- to medium-bodied wines that are lively, soft, and delicate. Most growers use small oak casks for ageing and produce wines of very good quality.

🍇 Cabernet franc with up to
   10% Cabernet sauvignon

🍷 2–3 years

WHITE A tiny production of clean, dry, light- to medium-bodied wines that are strangely aromatic for Chenin blanc with an intriguing perfumed aftertaste.

🍇 Chenin blanc

🍷 1–2 years

ROSÉ These are dry, fairly light-bodied, smooth, and fruity wines which, like Bourgueil rosés, are very easy to drink and deserve to be better known.

🍇 Cabernet franc with up to
   10% Cabernet sauvignon

🍷 2–3 years

✓ *Philippe Alliet • Bernard Baudry • Logis de la Bouchardière • Domaine du Carroi Portier (Spelty) • Couly-Dutheil • Château de la Grille • Charles Joguet*

COTEAUX DU LOIR AOC

This is an area that had extensive vineyards in the 19th century. Production has since declined and these generally unexciting wines come from the Loir, which is a tributary of, and not to be confused with, the Loire.

RED These are dry, medium-bodied wines that can have a lively character and good extract in sunny years.

🍇 Minimum of 30% Pineau d'Aunis with Gamay, Pinot noir, Cabernet franc, and Cabernet sauvignon

🍷 1–2 years

WHITE Bone-dry to dry, light-bodied wines that are high in acidity that can be mean and astringent.

🍇 Chenin blanc

🍷 As early as possible

ROSÉ Dry, fairly light-bodied wines, a few of which are fruity and well balanced.

🍇 Pineau d'Aunis, Cabernet franc, Gamay, and Malbec with up to 25% Grolleau

🍷 Within 1 year

✓ *François Fresneau*

COTEAUX DU VENDÔMOIS VDQS

Situated on both banks of the Loir, upstream from Jasnières, this steadily improving district produces well-made, palatable, and very attractive wines.

RED Dry, fairly light-bodied wines that are full of soft-fruit flavours and very easy to drink.

🍇 Minimum of 30% Pineau d'Aunis with Gamay, Pinot noir, Cabernet franc, and Cabernet sauvignon

🍷 1–2 years

WHITE Dry, fairly light-bodied wines which, when made from pure Chenin blanc, have a tendency to be very astringent. Growers who blend Chardonnay with Chenin blanc produce better-balanced wines.

🍇 Primarily Chenin blanc with up to 20% Chardonnay

🍷 Within 1 year

ROSÉ Fresh and fragrant, Coteaux du Vendômois is one of the most appealing, yet little seen, of the Loire's dry rosés.

🍇 Pineau d'Aunis plus a maximum of 30% Gamay

🍷 1–2 years

✓ *Claude & Gisèle Minier • CV de Villiers-sur-Loir*

COUR-CHEVERNY AOC

Cheverny gained this special single-village appellation exclusively for Romorantin when it was upgraded in 1993 from a VDQS to an AOC, but it lost its right to produce sparkling wine. Romorantin is grown in the best sites around Cour-Cheverny. *See also* Cheverny AOC.

WHITE These are dry, light-bodied, modest wines, which have a fine, flowery nose, delicate flavour, and crisp balance.

🍇 Romorantin

🍷 1–2 years

✓ *François Cazin • Domaine de la Desoucherie*

JASNIÈRES AOC

This is the best area of the Coteaux du Loir – the wines produced here can, in hot years, achieve a richness that compares well to those of Savennières in Anjou (*see* p.202).

WHITE Medium-bodied wines that can be dry or sweet. They are elegant and age well in good years, but they can be unripe in poor years.

🍇 Chenin blanc

🍷 2–4 years

✓ *Domaine de la Charrière • Aubert de Rycke*

MONTLOUIS AOC

As in Vouvray, Montlouis produces wines that can be dry, medium-dry, or sweet depending on the vintage and, like those of its more famous neighbour, the greatest wines of Montlouis are the sweetest, most botrytis-rich wines often sold as *moelleux*. The wines are very similar in style to those of Vouvray, but Montlouis is terribly underrated whereas Vouvray is probably overrated. I would rank Moyer's 1959 and the 1947 Montlouis alongside even the greatest vintages of Château d'Yquem.

WHITE Light- to medium-bodied wines that can be dry or sweet. They are softer and more forward than the wines of Vouvray but can have the same honeyed flavour in fine years. Sweet Montlouis is aged in cask, but the best medium-dry styles are clean-fermented in stainless steel.

🍇 Chenin blanc

🍷 1–3 years for medium-dry, up to 10 years for sweeter wines

✓ *Berger Frères* (Domaine des Liards) • *Domaine de Bodet • Olivier Delétang • Domaine de la Milletière • Dominique Moyer • Jacky Petibon • Chaput Thierry*

MONTLOUIS MOUSSEUX AOC

In poor vintages the grapes are used to make sparkling *méthode champenoise* versions of Montlouis. The medium-dry (*demi-sec*) styles AOC are very popular in France.

SPARKLING WHITE These light- to medium-bodied wines can be *brut, sec, demi-sec*, or *moelleux*. The last two styles are only made in years that are particularly sunny.

🍇 Chenin blanc

🍷 Upon purchase

✓ *Alain Joulin • Daniel Mosny*

MONTLOUIS PÉTILLANT AOC

Gently effervescent, Montlouis Pétillant is one of the most successful yet least encountered, underrated, slightly sparkling French white wines.

SEMI-SPARKLING WHITE Light- to medium-bodied wines that can be dry or sweet. Very consistent in quality, with a rich, fruity flavour balanced by a delicate *mousse* of fine bubbles.

🍇 Chenin blanc

🍷 Upon purchase

✓ *Claude Levasseur • Dominique Moyer*

ST.-NICOLAS-DE-BOURGUEIL AOC

This is a commune with its own appellation in the northwest corner of Bourgueil. The soil is sandier than that of surrounding Bourgueil and the wines are lighter but certainly equal in terms of quality. These are some of the finest red wines in the Loire.

RED Bone-dry to dry, medium-bodied wines that age well and have greater finesse than the wines of Bourgueil.

🍇 Cabernet franc with up to 10% Cabernet sauvignon

🍷 After 5–6 years

ROSÉ A small amount of dry, medium-bodied rosé with firm, fruity flavour is produced.

🍇 Cabernet franc with up to 10% Cabernet sauvignon

🍷 Upon purchase

✓ *Yannick Amirault • Max Cognard • Pascal Lorieux • Jean-Paul Malibeau • Clos des Quarterons*

TOURAINE AOC

A prolific appellation with sparkling wines in dry and medium-dry styles, plus sweet white, red, and rosé still wines from all over Touraine. Most are pure varietal wines and the label should indicate which grape they have been made from. *See also* Touraine Mousseux AOC and Touraine Pétillant AOC.

RED Dry, light- to medium-bodied wines of little interest, which cannot be enhanced by the fact that the lacklustre Grolleau grape has been used in Touraine *rouge* since 1994. Those made from Gamay are fresh and fruity, and may be sold as *primeur* or *nouveau* from the third Thursday of November following the harvest.

🍇 Primarily Gamay and Cabernet franc but may also contain Cabernet sauvignon, Malbec, Pinot noir, Pinot meunier, Pinot gris, and Pineau d'Aunis

🍷 Within 3 years

WHITE These are bone-dry to dry, medium-bodied wines; when made from pure Sauvignon, they are fresh, aromatic, and fruity. Good Touraine Sauvignon is better than average Sancerre. Chardonnay has not been allowed in Touraine blanc since 1994. These wines may be sold from 1 December following the harvest without any mention of *primeur* or *nouveau*.

🍇 Primarily pure Sauvignon blanc, but may also contain Chenin blanc, Arbois, and a maximum of 20% Chardonnay

🍷 1–2 years

ROSÉ Dry, light- to medium-bodied wines, while those made from Pineau d'Aunis are drier and more subtle than Anjou rosé. They may be sold as *primeur* or *nouveau* from the third Thursday of November following the harvest.

🍇 Cabernet franc, Gamay, Grolleau, and Pineau d'Aunis with up to 10% Gamay teinturier de Chaudenay or Gamay de Bouze

🍷 1–2 years

✓ *Château de Chenonceau • GAEC Louet-Arcourt • Henri Marionnet • Domaine Michaud • Domaine Octavie • Oisly et Thésée • Domaine Jacky Preys*

TOURAINE-AMBOISE AOC

Modest white wines and light reds and rosés are produced by a cluster of eight villages surrounding, and including, Amboise. The vines are grown on both sides of the Loire adjacent to the Vouvray and Montlouis areas.

RED Dry, light-bodied wines that are mostly blended. Those containing a high proportion of Malbec are the best.

🍇 Cabernet franc, Cabernet sauvignon, Malbec, and Gamay

🍷 2–3 years

WHITE These bone-dry to dry, light-bodied Chenin Blancs are usually uninspiring; the rosés are superior.

🍇 Chenin blanc

🍷 Upon purchase

ROSÉ These dry, light-bodied, well-made wines are mouthwatering.

🍇 Cabernet franc, Cabernet sauvignon, Malbec, and Gamay

🍷 Within 1 year

✓ *Florent Catroux • Domaine Dutertre • Xavier Frissant • Michel Lateyron • Robert Mesliand • François Pequin*

TOURAINE AZAY-LE-RIDEAU AOC

Good-quality wines from eight villages on either side of the river Indre, a tributary of the Loire.

WHITE Delicate, light-bodied wines that are usually dry but may be *demi-sec*.

🍇 Chenin blanc

⌛ 1–2 years

ROSÉ Attractive, refreshing, dry wines that are coral-pink with the smell of strawberries.

🍇 Malbec and Gamay

⌛ 1–2 years

✓ *Gallais Père & Fils • Domaine du Haut-Baigneux, James Page • Pibaleau Père & Fils*

TOURAINE-MESLAND AOC

Wines from the vineyards of Mesland and five surrounding villages on the right bank of Loire. The reds and rosés of this appellation are definitely well worth looking out for.

RED These dry, medium- to full-bodied wines are the best of the AOC and, can be as good as those of Chinon or Bourgueil.

🍇 Cabernet franc, Cabernet sauvignon, Malbec, and Gamay

⌛ 1–3 years

WHITE Dry, light-bodied wines with a high acidity that is only tamed in the best and sunniest years.

🍇 Chenin blanc

⌛ 1–2 years

ROSÉ These dry, medium-bodied wines have more depth and character than those of Touraine-Amboise.

🍇 Cabernet franc, Cabernet sauvignon, Malbec, and Gamay

⌛ 1–3 years

✓ *Château Gaillard*

TOURAINE MOUSSEUX AOC

Very good-value *méthode champenoise* red, white, and rosé wines. While the grapes for the white and rosé can come from the entire AOC Touraine area, those for red Touraine Mousseux may come from only the following areas: Bourgueil, St.-Nicolas-de-Bourgueil, and Chinon.

SPARKLING RED Dry, light- to medium-bodied wines that are fruity and refreshing.

🍇 Cabernet franc

⌛ Upon purchase

SPARKLING WHITE These light- to medium-bodied wines are made in dry and sweet styles, and the quality is consistent due to the large production area, which allows for complex blending.

🍇 Primarily Chenin blanc but may also include Arbois and up to 20% Chardonnay

and a combined maximum of 30% Cabernet, Pinot noir, Pinot gris, Pinot meunier, Pineau d'Aunis, Malbec, and Grolleau

⌛ Upon purchase

SPARKLING ROSÉ Light- to medium-bodied wines that are attractive when *brut*, though a bit cloying if sweeter.

🍇 Cabernet franc, Malbec, Noble, Gamay, and Grolleau

⌛ 1–2 years

✓ *Serge Bonnigal • Prince Poniatowski*

TOURAINE PÉTILLANT AOC

Refreshing, slightly effervescent white and rosé wines made from the same grape varieties as Touraine Mousseux. None are exported.

SEMI-SPARKLING RED Medium-dry, light-bodied wines that are not very popular.

🍇 Cabernet franc

⌛ Upon purchase

SEMI-SPARKLING WHITE Well-made, refreshing, light-bodied wines, in dry and sweet styles.

🍇 Chenin blanc, Arbois, Sauvignon blanc, and up to 20% Chardonnay

⌛ Upon purchase

SEMI-SPARKLING ROSÉ Attractive, light, quaffing wines that are made in dry and sweet styles.

🍇 Cabernet franc, Malbec, Noble, Gamay, and Grolleau

⌛ Upon purchase

VALENÇAY VDQS

Situated in the southeast of Touraine around the river Cher, these vineyards produce well-made, attractive wines. They are rarely seen outside France.

RED Dry, light-bodied, fragrant wines that, when made from pure Malbec – labelled under the local synonym of Cot – are very smooth and full of character.

🍇 Cabernet franc, Cabernet sauvignon, Malbec, Gamay and up to 25% Gascon, Pineau d'Aunis, and a maximum of 10% Gamay de Chaudenay

⌛ 1–2 years

WHITE Simple, dry, light-bodied wines that are improved by the addition of Chardonnay or Romorantin to the blend.

🍇 Arbois, Chardonnay, Sauvignon blanc, and a maximum of 40% Chenin blanc and Romorantin

⌛ 1–2 years

ROSÉ Dry to medium-dry, light-bodied wines that can be full of ripe soft-fruit flavours. They are superior to many AOC Loire rosés.

🍇 Cabernet franc, Cabernet sauvignon, Malbec, Gamay, and up to 25% Gascon, Pineau d'Aunis, and a maximum of 15% Gamay teinturier de Chaudenay

⌛ Upon purchase

✓ *Marc Carré • Domaine Champieux • Gerard Toyer*

VOUVRAY AOC

These white wines may be dry, medium-dry, or sweet depending on the vintage. In sunny years, the classic Vouvray that is made from overripe grapes affected by the "noble rot" is still produced by some growers. In cooler years, the wines are correspondingly drier and more acidic, and greater quantities of sparkling wine are produced.

WHITE At its best, sweet Vouvray can be the richest of all the Loire sweet wines. In good years, the wines are very full bodied, rich in texture, and have the honeyed taste of ripe Chenin blanc grapes.

🍇 Chenin blanc but may also contain Arbois

⌛ Usually 2–3 years; the sweeter wines can last up to 50 years

✓ *Domaine des Aubuisières • Bourillon Dorleans • Gilles Champion • Clos Château Cherrie • Philippe Foreau (Clos Naudin) • Régis Fortineau • Château Gaudrelle • Benoît Gautier • Lionel Gautier-Homme • Huet-l'Echansonne • Daniel Jarry • Jean-Pierre Laisement • Prince Poniatowski (Clos Baudouin)*

VOUVRAY MOUSSEUX AOC

These sparkling wines are made from overripe grapes. In years when the grapes do not ripen properly they are converted into sparkling wines using the *méthode champenoise* and blended with reserve wines from better years.

SPARKLING WHITE Medium- to full-bodied wines made in both dry and sweet styles. They are richer and softer than sparkling Saumur but have more edge than sparkling Montlouis.

🍇 Chenin blanc and Arbois

⌛ Non-vintage 2–3 years, vintage *brut* and *sec* 3–5 years, vintage *demi-sec* 5–7 years

✓ *Marc Brédif • Jean-François Delaleu • Philippe Foreau • Huet-l'Echansonne • Jean-Pierre Laisement • Prince Poniatowski • Viticulteurs de Vouvray (Tête de Cuvée)*

VOUVRAY PÉTILLANT AOC

These are stylish and consistent semi-sparkling versions of Vouvray, but very little is produced.

SEMI-SPARKLING WHITE Medium- to full-bodied wines made in dry and sweet styles. They should be drunk young.

🍇 Chenin blanc and Arbois

⌛ Upon purchase

✓ *Gilles Champion • Régis Fortineau • Huet*

CENTRAL VINEYARDS

In this district of scattered vineyards, all the classic wines are dry variations of the Sauvignon Blanc, but there are some discernable differences between them – the concentrated flavour of Sancerre, the elegance of the best Pouilly-Fumé, the fresh-floral character of Menetou-Salon, the lighter but not lesser style of Reuilly, and the purity of Quincy, for example.

THE CENTRAL VINEYARDS are so called because they are in the centre of France, not the centre of the Loire Valley. This is a graphic indication of how far the Loire Valley is stretched out and, while it might not be such a surprise to discover the vineyards of Sancerre to be quite close to Chablis, it does take a leap of the imagination to accept that they are nearer to the Champagne region than to Tours. And who could discern by taste alone that Sancerre is equidistant between the production areas of such diverse wines as Hermitage and Muscadet?

Most well known of all the towns in this district is Orléans, famous for its liberation by Joan of Arc from the English in 1429. The other important town is Bourges, which is situated in the south between the wine villages of Reuilly, Quincy, and Menetou-Salon, and was once the capital of the Duchy of Berry. To the west is Romorantin, which gives its name to one of the Loire's more obscure grape varieties.

THE REGION'S SAUVIGNON BLANC WINES
The Sauvignon blanc is to the Central Vineyards what Muscadet is to the Pays Nantais. It produces the classic wine of the district, which, like Muscadet, also happens to be both white and dry.

But two dry white wines could not be more different in style and taste. In the best Muscadet *sur lie* there should be a yeasty fullness, which can sometimes be misread as the Chardonnay character of a modest Mâcon. In Central Vineyard Sauvignons, however, whether they come from Sancerre or Pouilly – or even from one of the lesser-known, but certainly not lesser-quality, villages around Bourges – the aroma is so striking it sometimes startles. The rasping dryness of the wine's flavour catches the breath and can come from only one grape variety.

A BURGUNDIAN INFLUENCE
Historically this district was part of the Duchy of Burgundy, which explains the presence of Pinot noir vines. After the scourge of *phylloxera*, the area under vine shrank and that which was brought back into production was mostly replanted with Sauvignon blanc, which began to dominate the vineyards, although isolated spots of Pinot noir were maintained. Some of the wines they produce today can be very good, although they are extremely delicate in style; and however fine the quality, they are but a shadow of the Burgundian Pinot.

CHÂTEAU DU NOZET, POUILLY-SUR-LOIRE
This 19th-century château at Pouilly-sur-Loire is the home of Patrick de Ladoucette, the baron of Pouilly.

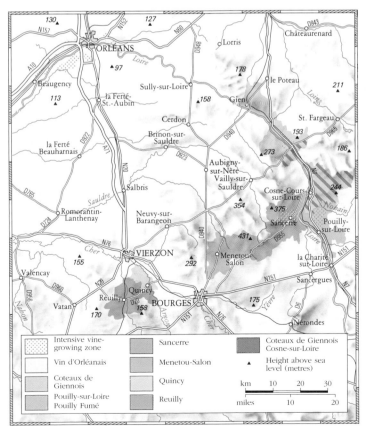

CENTRAL VINEYARDS, see also p.192
The most easterly of the Loire's vineyards, and the most central of France, the Central Vineyards are famous for wines made from the Sauvignon blanc grape.

Map legend
- Intensive vine-growing zone
- Vin d'Orléanais
- Coteaux de Giennois
- Pouilly-sur-Loire Pouilly Fumé
- Sancerre
- Menetou-Salon
- Quincy
- Reuilly
- Coteaux de Giennois Cosne-sur-Loire
- ▲ Height above sea level (metres)

km 10 20 30
miles 10 20

FACTORS AFFECTING TASTE AND QUALITY

LOCATION
The most easterly vineyards of the Loire are situated in the centre of France, chiefly in the *départements* of Cher, Nièvre, and Indre.

CLIMATE
More continental than areas closer to the sea; the summers are shorter and hotter and the winters longer and colder. Spring frosts and hail are particular hazards in Pouilly. Harvests are irregular.

SOIL
The soils are dominated by clay or limestone, topped with gravel and flinty pebbles. When mixed with chalk-tufa, gravelly soils produce lighter, finer styles of Sauvignon wines; when combined with Kimmeridgian clay, the result is firmer and more strongly flavoured.

ASPECT
Chalk hills in a quiet, green landscape. Vines occupy the best sites on hills and plateaux. At Sancerre they are planted on steep, sunny, sheltered slopes at an altitude of 200 m (660 ft).

VITICULTURE AND VINIFICATION
Some of the vineyard slopes in Sancerre are very steep so cultivation and picking are done by hand. Most properties are small and use the traditional wooden vats for fermentation, but some growers have stainless-steel tanks.

PRIMARY GRAPE VARIETIES
Sauvignon blanc, Pinot noir
SECONDARY GRAPE VARIETIES
Chasselas, Pinot blanc, Pinot gris, Cabernet franc, Chenin blanc, Gamay

THE APPELLATIONS OF THE
CENTRAL VINEYARDS

COTEAUX DU GIENNOIS VDQS

This once well-known appellation could boast nearly a thousand growers when it covered 40 times the size of today's vineyards at the turn of the 20th century. These wines may also use the appellation Côtes de Gien.

RED Dry, light-bodied red wines that often have less colour than many rosés.

🍇 Gamay, Pinot noir – since 1992, neither variety may exceed 80% of the total blend

⌛ 1–2 years

WHITE These very basic, dry, light-bodied wines lack interest. Chenin blanc can no longer be used to make this wine.

🍇 Sauvignon blanc

⌛ 1–2 years

ROSÉ Light-salmon-coloured, light-bodied wines that can have a fragrant citrous character.

🍇 Gamay, Pinot noir – since 1992, neither variety may exceed 80% of the total blend

⌛ 1 year

✓ *Domaine Balland-Chapuis • René Berthier • Paul Paulat & Fils • Poupat & Fils • Station Viticole INRA*

COTEAUX DU GIENNOIS COSNE-SUR-LOIRE VDQS

Of the 16 communes in the *départements* of Nièvre and Loiret that produce Coteaux du Giennois, only eight villages in the Nièvre are entitled to add Cosne-sur-Loire to the appellation. These wines may also use the appellation Côtes de Gien Cosne-sur-Loire.

RED Dry, bright ruby-coloured wines. Often full-tasting, but rarely with the body to match and sometimes quite tannic.

🍇 Gamay, Pinot noir – since 1992, neither variety may exceed 80% of the total blend

⌛ 1–2 years

WHITE These are dry, medium-bodied, curiously aromatic white wines that develop a full, toasty flavour with a little bottle-age.

🍇 Sauvignon blanc

⌛ 1–2 years

ROSÉ Light-salmon-coloured wines, slightly fuller bodied than the Coteaux du Giennois made a little further to the north, but equally capable of the same citrous fragrance.

🍇 Gamay, Pinot noir – since 1992, neither variety may exceed 80% of the total blend

⌛ 1–4 years

✓ *René Berthier • Paul Paulat & Fils • Station Viticole INRA*

MENETOU-SALON AOC

This underrated appellation covers the village of Menetou-Salon and the nine surrounding villages.

RED These are dry, light-bodied, crisp, and fruity wines with fine varietal aroma. They are best drunk young, although some oak-matured examples can age well.

🍇 Pinot noir

⌛ 2–5 years

WHITE Bone-dry to dry wines. They are definitely Sauvignon in character, but the flavour can have an unexpected fragrance.

🍇 Sauvignon blanc

⌛ 1–2 years

ROSÉ Extremely good-quality, dry, light-bodied aromatic wines, full of straightforward fruit.

🍇 Pinot noir

⌛ Within 1 year

✓ *Chasiot • Georges Chavet & Fils * • Henry Pellé **

*Particularly recommended for red or rosé

POUILLY BLANC FUMÉ AOC

See Pouilly Fumé AOC

POUILLY FUMÉ AOC

This used to be the world's most elegant Sauvignon blanc wine, but too many wines of ordinary and often quite dire quality have debased this once-great appellation. In Pouilly-sur-Loire and its six surrounding communes, only pure Sauvignon wines have the right to use "Fumé" in the appellation name, a term that evokes the grape's gunsmoke character.

WHITE Great Pouilly Fumé is rare but when found, its crisp, gooseberry flavour will retain its finesse and delicacy in even the hottest years.

🍇 Sauvignon blanc

⌛ 2–5 years

✓ *Jean-Claude Châtelain • Didier Dagueneau*

POUILLY-SUR-LOIRE AOC

This wine comes from the same area as Pouilly Fumé, but it is made from the Chasselas grape, although Sauvignon blanc is allowed for blending. Chasselas is a good dessert grape but makes very ordinary wine.

WHITE Dry, light-bodied wines. Most are neutral, tired, or downright poor.

🍇 Chasselas, Sauvignon blanc

⌛ Upon purchase

✓ *Landrat-Guyollot*

QUINCY AOC

These vineyards, on the left bank of the Cher, are situated on a gravelly plateau. Although located between two areas producing red, white, and rosé wines, Quincy only produces white wine from Sauvignon blanc.

WHITE Bone-dry to dry, quite full-bodied wines in which the varietal character of the Sauvignon blanc is evident. There is a purity that rounds out the flavour and seems to remove the rasping finish usually expected in this type of wine.

🍇 Sauvignon blanc

⌛ 1–2 years

✓ *Domaine Mardon • Domaine Meunier • Domaine de Maison Blanche*

REUILLY AOC

Due to the high lime content in the soil, Reuilly produces wines of higher acidity than those of neighbouring Quincy.

RED These are dry, medium-bodied wines. Some are surprisingly good, although often tasting more of strawberries or raspberries than the more characteristic redcurrant flavour associated with Pinot noir.

🍇 Pinot noir, Pinot gris

⌛ 2–5 years

WHITE These are bone-dry to dry, medium-bodied wines of good quality with more of

a grassy than a gooseberry flavour, yet possessing a typically austere dry finish.

🍇 Sauvignon blanc

⌛ 1–2 years

ROSÉ This bone-dry to dry, light-bodied wine is a pure Pinot gris wine, although simply labelled Pinot.

🍇 Pinot gris

⌛ 2–5 years

✓ *Jean-Michel Sorbe **

*Particularly recommended for red or rosé

SANCERRE AOC

This appellation is famous for its white wines, although originally its reds were better known. Recently the reds and rosés have developed greater style.

RED These wines have been more variable in quality than the whites, but the consistency is improving rapidly. They are dry, light- to medium-bodied wines, with a pretty floral aroma and a delicate flavour.

🍇 Pinot noir

⌛ 2–3 years

WHITE Classic Sancerre should be dry or bone dry, highly aromatic, and have an intense flavour, sometimes tasting of gooseberries or even peaches in a great year. However, too many growers overproduce, never get the correct ripeness, and make the most miserable little wines.

🍇 Sauvignon blanc

⌛ 1–3 years

ROSÉ Attractive, dry, light-bodied rosés with strawberry and raspberry flavours.

🍇 Pinot noir

⌛ Within 18 months

✓ *Henri Bourgeois • Cotat Frères • Lucien Crochet * • André Dezat * • Domaine Gitton • Alphonse Mellot • Henry Natter • Vincent Pinard • Christian Thirot (Domaine des Vieux Pruniers)*

*Particularly recommended for red or rosé

VINS DE L'ORLÉANAIS VDQS

These wines have been made for centuries, but only one-third of the appellation is worked now.

RED Dry, medium-bodied, fresh, and fruity wines that are given a short maceration, producing a surprisingly soft texture. They are usually sold as pure varietal wines: the Pinot can be delicate, the Cabernet franc is fuller.

🍇 Pinot noir, Pinot meunier, Cabernet franc

⌛ 1–2 years

WHITE Very small quantities of interesting wines are made from Chardonnay, known locally as Auvernat blanc. They are dry, medium-bodied, and surprisingly smooth and fruity.

🍇 Chardonnay (*syn.* Auvernat blanc), Pinot gris (*syn.* Auvernat gris)

⌛ 1–2 years

ROSÉ The local speciality is a dry, light- to medium-bodied rosé known as Meunier Gris – an aromatic *vin gris* with a crisp, dry finish.

🍇 Pinot noir, Pinot meunier, Cabernet franc

⌛ Within 1 year

✓ *Clos St.-Fiacre • Vignerons de la Grand'Maison*

AUTHOR'S CHOICE

Rather than choose classic examples of great moelleux *wines that anyone would perceive as world class,
I have concentrated on the finest wines of the Loire styles that seem to me the most problematical,
namely Muscadet, dry Chenin blanc, sparkling Saumur, Sancerre, and Pouilly Fumé – to show
that, despite a general lowering of quality, some consistently great wines are still produced.*

PRODUCER	WINE	STYLE	DESCRIPTION	
Bouvet	Trésor, Saumur AOC (*see* p.202)	SPARKLING WHITE	Made from very ripe grapes, part-fermented and aged in small, new oak barrels, then given three years on its lees, this wine demonstrates the fabulous quality that can be achieved when Saumur producers ignore volume and aim for quality. Very rich, ripe, and tending to become quite exotic, Bouvet Trésor might seem extremely expensive for a Loire sparkling wine, but it is better than many Champagnes that sell for much higher prices and in this respect it is tremendous value for money.	Up to 3 years from purchase
Domaine des Baumard	Clos du Papillon, Savennières AOC (*see* p.202)	WHITE	It is a matter of taste whether you opt for the almost unyielding steely intensity of Coulée de Serrant or the sheer elegance, purity, and finesse of Baumard's Clos du Papillon. For my taste, Baumard definitely comes first. Jean Baumard has always had a magic touch when it comes to the Chenin blanc, his wines never showing the slightest hint of the unclean or unripe character that blights so many other examples of this grape variety. I hope he has passed on the secret to his son Florent, who has assisted him since the late 1980s, so that we can look forward to a continuity of this soft, dry white wine with its ultra-fresh melon fruit.	3–7 years
Cotat Frères	La Grande Côte, Sancerre AOC (see p. 208)	WHITE	This *barrique*-fermented Sancerre is unfined, unfiltered, and produced in the tiniest of quantities to provide a rich, highly concentrated, beautifully balanced wine that, in defiance of the traditional concept of Sauvignon Blanc, demands to be aged. This is not the most expensive of Cotat's *lieu-dit* Sancerres, but invariably it stands out from its other truly wonderful wines.	1–3 years
Leroux Frères ⓥ	Clos de Beauregard, Muscadet de Sèvre-et-Maine AOC (*see* p.197)	WHITE	Fat, peachy fruit with hints of vanilla and botrytis make this an absolutely atypical wine that no regular Muscadet drinker would recognize. It must, however, be recognized for its pure, if idiosyncratic, quality and demonstrates that wines with the genuine richness of ripe grapes can be produced on a consistent basis in the cool climate of Nantes.	1–5 years
Château de Briacé ⓥ	Tiré sur lie, Muscadet de Sèvre-et-Maine AOC (*see* p.197)	WHITE	This is a beautifully made wine that has extremely fresh aromatic qualities and delicious, elegant, clean-as-a-whistle fruit, which retains the structure and crispness that make Château de Briacé consistently the finest Muscadet in terms of typicality.	1–2 years
Jean-Claude Châtelain	Châtelain Prestige and Les Charmes Châtelain, Pouilly Fumé AOC (*see* p.208)	WHITE	Jean-Claude Châtelain's wines are always beautifully made. The Châtelain Prestige typifies the house style: it has soft, delicately dry fruit and a light, elegant balance, yet is absolutely ripe and mellow, with amazing length for its weight; Les Charmes Châtelain, on the other hand, has a greater essence, and is jam-packed with unbelievably intense ripe-fruit flavour.	2–3 years
Didier Dagueneau	Silex, Pouilly Fumé AOC (*see* p.208)	WHITE	Pre-fermentation maceration gives this wine its great aromatic intensity, while part-fermentation in small new oak barrels adds a certain smoothness, fullness, and complexity.	2–3 years
Charles Joguet	Clos de la Dioterie, Chinon AOC (*see* p.204)	RED	I could not stop myself being sidetracked by this red wine. Charles Joguet is the greatest maker of red wine in the Loire and Clos de la Dioterie is, without question, his finest wine. Made from old vines on, strangely, a north-facing slope, this is extraordinarily dark and deep for what is not a massively built wine, and the fruit is richer and more complex than you will find in any other Loire red.	6–10 years
Christian Thirot	Domaine des Vieux Pruniers, Sancerre AOC (*see* p.208)		Christian Thirot always produces a delightful Sauvignon Blanc with elegant fruit. Any Sancerre that is this easy to drink deserves recognition, but this one is also made in a genuinely dry, classic Sancerre style.	2–3 years
Domaine du Vieux Chai ⓥ	Muscadet de Sèvre-et-Maine AOC (*see* p.197)	WHITE	This is another Muscadet de Sèvre-et-Maine that consistently has the peachy aroma and soft, ripe fruit that is so atypical for the appellation, but which makes a charming wine in its own right.	1–2 years

THE RHÔNE VALLEY

Famous for its full, fiery, and spicy-rich red wines, the Rhône Valley also produces a small quantity of rosé, a tiny amount of white throughout the region, and even some sparkling and fortified wines. Although essentially red-wine country, and great red-wine country at that, the Rhône has experienced a kind of revolution in white-wine production. There has been a growing number of exotic, world-class white wines in various appellations since the late 1980s, when just a few white wines began to emerge in Châteauneuf-du-Pape.

STRETCHING FROM VIENNE TO AVIGNON, the Côtes-du-Rhône appellation occupies a 200-kilometre (125-mile) length of the river Rhône. Beyond this great region other Rhône wines exist, and some are not even French. The banks of this mighty European river are clad with vines all the way from the Valais vineyards of Visp in Switzerland, just 50 kilometres (30 miles) from the Rhône's glacial origins in the Alps, to the *vin de pays* vineyards of the Bouches-du-Rhône, set amid the Rhône delta just west of Marseilles, where the river finally and sluggishly runs into the Mediterranean.

Only a tiny patch of vineyards in the very north of this region are in fact located within the Rhône *département* (which is a geographic misnomer as it actually accounts for 70 per cent of Burgundy's output). Comparing the contrasting character of Rhône and Burgundy wines produced within the one *département*

CÔTE BRUNE ON THE CÔTE RÔTIE, NORTHERN RHÔNE
The Côte Brune is an area of the Côte Rôtie where the rust colour of the earth is visible evidence of iron-rich elements in its granitic sandy soil.

BEAUMES-DE-VENISE, SOUTHERN RHÔNE
Home to one of the most elegant and consistent fortified Muscat wines in the world, Beaumes-de-Venise also produces a soft, peppery red wine under the Côtes-du-Rhône-Villages appellation.

LA LANDONNE VINEYARD, CÔTE RÔTIE
Syrah grapes are harvested on the steep slopes of Guigal's top-performing La Landonne vineyard in the Côte Brune area of Côte Rôtie, above Ampuis.

can have a humbling effect on all those who glibly talk about regional styles. For example, what could be further apart than a rich, classic Condrieu and a fresh, light Mâcon, or an intense, ink-black Côte Rôtie and a quaffing, cherry-coloured Beaujolais? Yet all of these wines are produced in the same *département* and could thus be described as coming from the same region.

A REGION DIVIDED

In terms of grape variety, the Rhône divides neatly into two – the Syrah-dominated north and the Grenache-influenced south – although there are those who confuse the issue by separating the southernmost section of the northern district and calling it the Middle Rhône. The north and south differ not only in terrain and climate, but also contrast socially, culturally, and gastronomically.

RECENT RHÔNE VINTAGES

2000 A brilliant year for reds in both the northern and southern Rhône, with the wines showing excellent colour, fruit, and tannin structure. The whites, however, are fat and blowsy.

1999 Soft, juicy, well-coloured reds in the northern Rhône have the edge over the southern reds, although those in the south who picked late have made wines to rival their northern cousins.

1998 One of the greatest Châteauneuf-du-Pape vintages in living memory overshadowed the good to very good red wines produced in the northern Rhône.

1997 A quaffing vintage; only the best Hermitage should be kept for very long.

1996 So many wine areas of France experienced a better year than 1995, which itself was the first decent vintage since 1990, but 1996 did not truly shine in the Rhône. In fact, 1996 is not even in the same league as 1995 when most wines are taken into consideration, although the whites are definitely finer.

1995 A good-quality vintage on a par with 1991 but not in the same league as 1990 and patchy due to the extreme heat, which caused the vine to shut down, leaving some vineyards with an unripe crop.

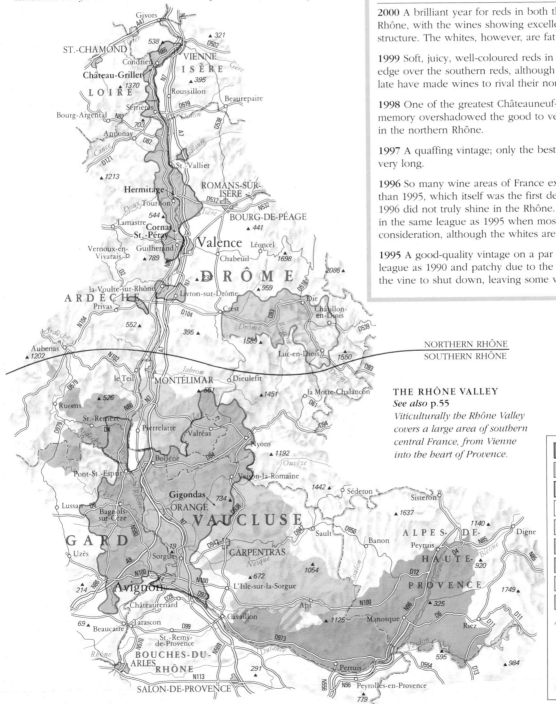

THE RHÔNE VALLEY
See also p.55
Viticulturally the Rhône Valley covers a large area of southern central France, from Vienne into the heart of Provence.

Côtes-du-Rhône
See also pp.212, 215

Côtes-du-Rhône-Villages
See also p.215

Clairette de Die
See also p.212

Châtillon-en-Diois
See also p.212

Coteaux du Tricastin
See also p.215

Coteaux de Pierrevert
See also p.215

Côtes du Lubéron
See also p.215

Côtes du Ventoux
See also p.215

Côtes du Vivarais
See also p.215

- - - *Département* boundary

▲ Height above sea level (metres)

km 10 20 30 40
miles 10 20

THE NORTHERN RHÔNE

The Northern Rhône is dominated by the ink-black wines of Syrah, the Rhône's only truly classic black grape. A small amount of white wine is also produced and, in the south of the district, at St.-Péray and Die, sparkling wines are produced.

THE NORTHERN RHÔNE might be the gateway to the south, but it has more in common with its northern neighbour, Burgundy, than it does with the rest of the Rhône, even though its wines cannot be compared to those from any other area. Indeed, it would be perfectly valid to isolate the north as a totally separate region called the Rhône, which would, therefore, allow the Southern Rhône to be more accurately defined as a high-quality extension of the Midi.

THE QUALITY OF THE NORTHERN RHÔNE

The ink-black classic wines of Hermitage and Côte Rôtie stand shoulder to shoulder with the *Crus Classés* of Bordeaux in terms of pure quality, and the elite wines such as the Hermitage produced by Chave and Jaboulet, or the Côte Rôtie of Guigal and Jasmin, for example, deserve the respect given to First Growths such as Latour, Mouton, or Lafite. Cornas is even bigger and blacker than Hermitage and Côte Rôtie, and a great vintage from Auguste Clape rivals the best of its better-known neighbours. While the fine, dry white wines of Condrieu and (potentially) Château Grillet are unique in character, the presence of such a style in this part of France is not as surprising as that of the sparkling white wines of St.-Péray and Die, particularly the latter, which Francophiles would describe as a superior sort of Asti!

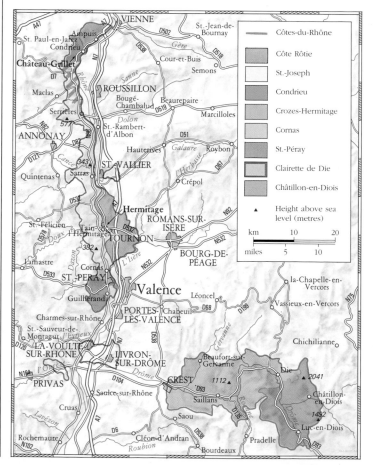

FACTORS AFFECTING TASTE AND QUALITY

LOCATION
The narrow strip of vineyards that belong to the Northern Rhône commences at Vienne, just south of Lyon, and extends southwards to Valence.

CLIMATE
The general effect of the Mediterranean is certainly felt in the Northern Rhône, but its climate has a distinctly continental influence. This results in the pattern of warmer summers and colder winters, which is closer to the climate of southern Burgundy, to the north, than to that of the Southern Rhône. The climatic factor that the area does have in common with the southern half of the Rhône is the mistral, a bitterly cold wind that can reach up to 145 km (90 miles) per hour and is capable of denuding a vine of its leaves, shoots, and fruit. As a result, many mistral-prone vineyards are protected by poplar and cypress trees. The wind can, however, have a welcome drying effect in humid harvest conditions.

ASPECT
The countryside is generally less harsh than that of the southern Rhône, with cherry, peach, chestnut, and other deciduous trees in evidence. The valley vineyards are cut far more steeply into the hillsides than they are in areas further south.

SOIL
The Northern Rhône's soil is generally light and dry, granitic and schistous. More specifically, it is made up of: granitic-sandy soil on the Côte-Rôtie (calcareous-sandy on the Côte Blonde and ruddy, iron-rich sand on the Côte Brune); granitic-sandy soil at Hermitage and Condrieu with a fine overlay of decomposed flint, chalk, and mica, known locally as *arzelle*; heavier soil in Crozes-Hermitage with patches of clay; granitic sand with some clay between St.-Joseph and St.-Péray, getting stonier towards the southern end of the region, with occasional outcrops of limestone; and limestone and clay over a solid rock base in the area that surrounds Die.

VITICULTURE AND VINIFICATION
Unlike the Southern Rhône, most Northern Rhône wines are produced entirely or predominantly from a single grape variety, the Syrah, despite the long list of grapes that are occasionally used (*see* Secondary grape varieties, below).

Viticultural operations are labour-intensive in the northern stretch of the district and, owing to the cost, the vineyards were once under the threat of total abandonment. Since that threat we pay much more for Côte Rôtie, but at least it has remained available. Vinification techniques are very traditional and, when wines are aged in wood, there is less emphasis on new oak than is given in Bordeaux or Burgundy, although chestnut casks are sometimes used.

PRIMARY GRAPE VARIETIES
Syrah, Viognier

SECONDARY GRAPE VARIETIES
Aligoté, Bourboulenc, Calitor, Camarèse, Carignan, Chardonnay, Cinsault, Clairette, Counoise, Gamay, Grenache, Marsanne, Mauzac, Mourvèdre, Muscardin, Muscat blanc à petits grains, Pascal blanc, Picardan, Picpoul, Pinot blanc, Pinot noir, Roussanne, Terret noir, Ugni blanc, Vaccarèse

Map legend

- Côtes-du-Rhône
- Côte Rôtie
- St.-Joseph
- Condrieu
- Crozes-Hermitage
- Cornas
- St.-Péray
- Clairette de Die
- Châtillon-en-Diois
- ▲ Height above sea level (metres)

km   10   20
miles 5   10

THE NORTHERN RHÔNE
See also p.211
At the heart of this region the towns of Tain and Tournon face each other across the river.

AMPUIS UNDER SNOW
These southeast-facing vineyards of Côte Rôtie form a dramatic stretch of scenery on the west bank of the Rhône, 9 km (5 miles) south of Vienne.

THE APPELLATIONS OF
THE NORTHERN RHÔNE

CHÂTEAU GRILLET AOC

Château Grillet is one of only two single-estate appellations in France, the other being Romanée-Conti (although you could also make an argument for Coulée-de-Serrant in the Loire's Savennières being a third). In the first edition of this book (1988), I commented that despite its fame as one of the world's great white wines, Grillet had yet to achieve its full potential – a belief based on some pretty good wines produced prior to the late 1970s, although they were not terribly exciting and were far from showing the potential of Château Grillet's *terroir*. Wines made in the early 1980s were not so good. Although the feeling was that they might develop, they hardly inspired confidence. In fact, these wines turned out to be even more feeble than feared, but there was a welcome resurgence in the late 1980s.

In view of the continual rise of Condrieu, which has spawned Viognier wines throughout southern France and spread them to all four corners of the wine world, the owners of this property have no option but to seek a dramatic increase in quality because there are going to be far too many truly exciting Condrieu wines on the market for the pretence of Château Grillet's *Grand Cru* status to survive.

WHITE In the most successful vintages, this is a pale-gold-coloured wine, with an entrancing floral-fruity bouquet, hinting of peaches and lime-blossom, a lingering, delicate flavour, and an elegant, peachy aftertaste. This is, potentially, a wine of great finesse and complex character, but not one to keep in bottle as long as some would have you believe.

🍇 Viognier

🍷 3–7 years

CHÂTILLON-EN-DIOIS AOC

This wine was raised to full AOC status in 1974, although it is hard to comprehend what merited such an elevation then or now.

RED Light in colour and body, thin in fruit, with little discernible character.

🍇 Gamay, plus up to 25% Syrah and Pinot noir

WHITE Sold as pure varietal wines, the light and fresh, gently aromatic Aligoté is as good as the richer, fuller, and rather angular Chardonnay.

🍇 Aligoté, Chardonnay

ROSÉ I have not encountered any.

🍇 Gamay, plus up to 25% Syrah and Pinot noir

✓ *UPVF du Diois*

CLAIRETTE DE DIE AOC

This dry sparkling wine is being phased out in favour of Crémant de Die from 1999 in what must be a classic example of Gallic logic – removing the name Clairette from an appellation of a wine that must be made from 100 per cent Clairette grapes, yet retaining it for one (*see below*) that does not have to contain any! See also Crémant de Die AOC.

CLAIRETTE DE DIE MÉTHODE DIOISE ANCESTRALE AOC

Formerly sold as Clairette de Die Tradition, this wine may contain Clairette, but it is not the primary grape. What makes it so different, however, is that it is produced from one fermentation only, as opposed to the two required by Crémant de Die, the old Clairette de Die Mousseux, and most other sparkling wines.

In the *Méthode Dioise Ancestrale*, the wine first undergoes a long, cold part-fermentation in bulk and when bottled must contain a minimum of 55 grams of residual sugar per litre and no *liqueur de tirage*. Fermentation continues inside the bottle, but when disgorged the wine must still retain at least 35 grams of residual sugar per litre. The wine undergoes *transvasage* (meaning it is filtered into a fresh bottle) and is corked without any addition of a *liqueur d'expédition*.

SPARKLING WHITE A very fresh, deliciously fruity, gently sparkling wine of at least *demi-sec* sweetness, with a ripe, peachy flavour.

🍇 At least 75% Muscat à petits grains (this went up in 1993 from a minimum of 50%), plus Clairette

🍷 Upon purchase

✓ *Archard-Vincent • Buffardel Frères • Clairdie • Caves Didier • Carod • Alain Poulet • UPVF du Diois • Domaine de Magord • Jean-Claude Raspail*

CONDRIEU AOC

This is the greatest white-wine appellation in the entire Rhône valley, with more up-and-coming young talent among its producers than anywhere else in the world. Initially the trend was to produce sweet and medium-sweet wines, but Condrieu has tended to be a distinctly dry wine for a couple of decades now. When the vintage permits, late-harvested sweeter wines are produced and these styles are very much part of Condrieu's recent revival as one of the undisputed great white wines of the world.

WHITE These pale-gold-coloured wines are essentially dry, but can have such an exotic perfume that you might easily think they are sweet when you first breathe in their heavenly aroma. The bouquet is fine, floral, and fruity, with heady, opulent aromas that can include may-blossom, honeysuckle, violets, roses, peaches, lime, and apricot, and in especially rich vintages there can also be some youthful honey wafting through. The fruit on the palate is always very perfumed and can give the impression of sweetness, even when completely dry. A great Condrieu has a beguiling balance of fatness, freshness, and finesse that produces an elegant, peachy-apricoty coolness of fruit on the finish. Do not be fooled into cellaring these wines – the dry ones in any case – as their greatest asset is the freshness and purity of fruit, which can only be lost over the years.

🍇 Viognier

🍷 4–8 years

✓ *Automnal du Condrieu • Clusel-Roch • Yves Cuilleron • Pierre Dumazet • Philippe Faury • Jean-Michel Gerin • E. Guigal • Antoine Montez • Didier Morion • André Perret • Philippe Pichon • Patrice Portet • Château du Rozay • Georges Vernay • François Villard*

CORNAS AOC

The sun-trap vineyards of Cornas produce the best value of all the Rhône's quality red wines, but you have to buy it as soon as it is released as it is always sold far too young, so there is none left when it starts to show its true potential.

RED Ink-black, full-bodied, strong-flavoured, pure Syrah wines with lots of blackcurrant and blackberry fruit, lacking only a little finesse if compared to a great Hermitage or Côte-Rôtie.

🍇 Syrah

🍷 7–20 years

✓ *Thierry Allemand • Guy de Barjac • René Bathazar • M. Chapoutier • Auguste Clape • Jean-Luc Colombo • Delas • Dumien-Serrette • Paul Jaboulet Aîné • Marcel Juge • Jacques Lémenicier • Jean Lionnet • Robert Michel • Tardieu-Laurent • Noël Verset • Alan Voge*

COTEAUX DE DIE AOC

This new appellation was created in 1993 to soak up wines from excess Clairette grape production that were formerly sold under previous sparkling-wine appellations.

WHITE Perhaps it is unfair to prejudge a wine that has had so little time to establish itself, but it is hard to imagine a quality wine made from this grape. In effect, Coteaux de Die is the still-wine version of Crémant de Die. It is easy to see why such a bland dry wine needs bubbles to lift it, but so few make the transition successfully.

🍇 Clairette

🍷 Upon purchase

✓ *Jean-Claude Raspail*

CÔTES-DU-RHÔNE AOC

Although generic to the entire region, relatively little Côtes-du-Rhône is made in this district.

CÔTE RÔTIE AOC

The terraces and low walls of the "burnt" or "roasted" slopes of Côte Rôtie must be tended by hand, but the reward is a wine of great class that vies with Hermitage as the world's finest example of Syrah.

RED A garnet-coloured wine of full body, fire, and power, made fragrant by the addition of Viognier grapes. The result is a long-living and complex wine with nuances of violets and spices, and great finesse.

🍇 Syrah, plus up to 20% Viognier

🍷 10–25 years

✓ *Pierre Barge • Vignoble de Boisseyt • Bernard Burgaud • Clusel-Roch • Yves Cuilleron • Delas* (Seigneur de Maugiron) *• Jean-Michel Gerin • E. Guigal • Paul Jaboulet Aîné • Joseph Jamet • Jasmin*

• *René Rostaing* • *Tardieu-Laurent*
• *Louis de Vallouit* • *Georges Vernay*
• *Vidal-Fleury* • *François Villard*

CRÉMANT DE DIE AOC

This dry sparkling wine was introduced in 1993 to replace Clairette de Die Mousseux, which was phased out by January 1999. Like the old Clairette de Die Mousseux appellation, Crémant de Die must be made by the *méthode champenoise*, but whereas the former could include up to 25 per cent Muscat à petit grains, the latter must be made entirely from Clairette.

SPARKLING WHITE It is too early to make a definitive pronouncement, but it looks as if Crémant de Die will be every bit as neutral and lacklustre as Clairette de Die.

🍇 Clairette

⌛ 1–3 years

CROZES-ERMITAGE AOC
See Crozes-Hermitage AOC

CROZES-HERMITAGE AOC

Crozes-Hermitage is produced from a relatively large area surrounding Tain, hence the quality is very variable, but a good Crozes-Hermitage will always be a great bargain.

RED These well-coloured, full-bodied wines are similar to Hermitage, but they are generally less intense and have a certain smoky-rustic-raspberry flavour that only deepens into blackcurrant in the hottest years. The finest wines do, however, have surprising finesse, and make fabulous bargains.

🍇 Syrah, plus up to 15% Roussanne and Marsanne

⌛ 6–12 years
8–20 years for top wines and great years

WHITE These dry white wines are improving and gradually acquiring more freshness, fruit, and acidity.

🍇 Roussanne, Marsanne

⌛ 1–3 years

✓ *Albert Belle* • *M. Chapoutier* (Les Meysonniers and Les Varonnières) • *Bernard Chave Domaine du Colombier* • *Domaine Combier* • *Château de Curson* • *Domaine des Entrefaux* • *Alain Graillot* • *Paul Jaboulet Aîné* (Thalabert) • *Etienne Pochon* • *CV Tain-Hermitage* • *Louis de Vallouit*

ERMITAGE AOC
See Hermitage AOC

HERMITAGE AOC

One of the great classic French red wines, produced entirely from Syrah grapes in virtually all cases, although a small amount of Marsanne and Roussanne may be added. The vines are grown on a magnificent south-facing slope overlooking Tain.

RED These wines have a deep and sustained colour, a very full body, and lovely, plummy,

---

lip-smacking, spicy, silky, violety, blackcurrant fruit. A truly great Hermitage has boundless finesse, despite the weighty flavour.

🍇 Syrah, plus up to 15% Roussanne and Marsanne

⌛ 12–30 years

WHITE These big, rich, dry white wines have a full, round, hazelnut and dried-apricot flavour. The wines have improved recently but are generally no more than curiosities.

🍇 Roussanne, Marsanne

⌛ 6–12 years

✓ *Albert Belle** • *M. Chapoutier** (Le Pavillon) • *Domaine Jean-Louis Chave** • *Domaine du Colombier* • *Delas* (Marquise de la Tourette and Les Bassards) • *Jean-Louis Grippat* • *E. Guigal* • *Paul Jaboulet Aîné* • *Marc Sorrel* • *Tardieu-Laurent*

*Particularly recommended for white as well as red.

HERMITAGE VIN DE PAILLE AOC

In the first edition of this book (1988), I wrote "In 1974 Gérard Chave made the last *vin de paille* of Hermitage, a wine that is now confined to the Jura vineyards of eastern France (*see* p.222). Monsieur Chave declares he made the wine for 'amusement'. Considering its success, it is extraordinary that some enterprising grower has not taken advantage of this appellation."

Chapoutier has since made several vintages of Hermitage *vin de paille* on a commercial basis – or as near commercial as you can get with this style of wine – and other producers include Michel Ferraton, Jean-Louis Grippat, and Guigal. Even the local *coopérative* has churned some out. At one time all Hermitage *blanc* was, in effect, *vin de paille*, a style that dates back in this locality to at least 1760 (Marc Chapoutier apparently drank the last wine of that vintage in 1964 when it was 204 years old!). The traditional *vin de paille* method in Hermitage is not as intensive as the one revived relatively recently in Alsace, where the grapes are dried out over straw beds until more than 90 per cent of the original juice has evaporated before they are pressed, as even Chave's legendary 1974 was made from grapes bearing as much as a third of their original juice, but some of the results have been equally as stunning. Despite decades between production, this wine still has its own AOC.

WHITE Some *vins de paille* are rich and raisiny whereas others – the best – have a crisp, vivid freshness about them, with intense floral-citrous aromas and a huge, long, honeyed aftertaste. After his famed 1974 vintage, Chave made a 1986 and at least a couple more vintages since. His *vin de paille* is reputed to be the greatest, but is practically unobtainable and certainly not available on the open market. Chapoutier's *vin de paille* is made in the most commercial quantity, yet this still amounts to hardly anything, since the wine is hard to find and very expensive. Jean-Louis Grippat made a *vin de paille* in 1985 and 1986, neither of which I have had the privilege to taste, but John Livingstone-Learmonth describes them as "not quite like late-harvest Gewürztraminer" in his seminal work *The Wines of the Rhône* (Faber & Faber).

🍇 Roussanne, Marsanne

⌛ Up to 30 years

✓ *Chapoutier* • *Domaine Jean-Louis Chave* • *Jean-Louis Grippat* • *E. Guigal* • *CV Tain-Hermitage*

L'ERMITAGE AOC
See Hermitage AOC

L'HERMITAGE AOC
See Hermitage AOC

ST.-JOSEPH AOC

At last, some truly exciting wines are being produced under this appellation. St.-Joseph has now replaced Cornas as the bargain-seeker's treasure trove.

RED The best wines are dark, medium- to full-bodied, with intense blackberry and blackcurrant fruit aromas and plenty of soft fruit, whereas mediocre St.-Joseph remains much lighter-bodied with a pepperiness more reminiscent of the Southern Rhône.

🍇 Syrah, plus up to 10% Marsanne and Roussanne

⌛ 3–8 years

WHITE At their best, clean, rich, and citrous-resinous dry wines.

🍇 Marsanne, Roussanne

⌛ 1–3 years

✓ *Domaine Chave* • *Pierre Coursodon* • *Yves Cuilleron* • *Pierre Gaillard* • *Domaine Gonan* • *Bernard Gripa* • *Domaine Jean-Louis Grippat* • *Paul Jaboulet Aîné* • *CV de St.-Désirat-Champagne* • *Trollat* • *Louis de Vallouit* • *Georges Vernay* • *François Villard*

ST.-PÉRAY AOC

This white-wine-only village appellation is curiously out of step with the rest of the area.

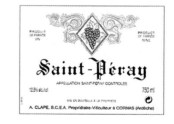

WHITE Firm and fruity, with good acidity for a wine from the south of the region, but unfortunately it usually lacks charm. Even the best growers within this region, recommended below, struggle to produce anything of interest.

🍇 Marsanne, Roussanne

⌛ 1–3 years

✓ *J.-F. Chaboud* • *Auguste Clape* • *Marcel Juge* • *Jean Lionnet* • *Alain Voge*

ST.-PÉRAY MOUSSEUX AOC

This is a *méthode champenoise* sparkling wine made from the wrong grapes grown on the wrong soil. The growers would be advised to rip the whole lot up and replant with black grapes for a red Côtes-du-Rhône.

SPARKLING WHITE An overrated, dry sparkling wine with a coarse *mousse*.

🍇 Marsanne, Roussanne

THE SOUTHERN RHÔNE

While the mellow warmth of the Grenache is found in most Southern Rhône wines, the wines do not revolve around one grape variety. It is a blender's paradise, with a choice of up to 23 different grape varieties, and wines of various styles and qualities are produced.

THE SOUTHERN RHÔNE is a district dominated by herbal scrubland, across which blows a sweet, spice-laden breeze. This is a far larger district than the slender northern *côtes*, and its production is, not unnaturally, much higher. Allowing the north a generous ten per cent of the generic Côtes-du-Rhône appellation, the southern Rhône still accounts for a staggering 95 per cent of all the wines produced in the region.

WINES OF THE MIDI OR PROVENCE?

At least half of the Southern Rhône is in what was once called the Midi, an area generally conceded to cover the *départements* of the Aude, Hérault, and Gard. This is never mentioned by those intent on marketing the Rhône's image of quality, because the Midi was infamous for its huge production of *vin ordinaire*. The Rhône river marks the eastern border of the Midi and the famous appellations of Châteauneuf-du-Pape, Muscat de Beaumes-de-Venise, and Gigondas further east are geographically part of Provence. But, viticulturally, these areas do not possess the quasi-Italian varieties that dominate the vineyards of Provence and may, therefore, be more rationally defined as a high-quality extension of the Midi.

THE SOUTHERN RHÔNE, *see also p.211*
The wider southern part of the Rhône valley area stretches its fingers down towards Provence and eastwards to the Alps.

FACTORS AFFECTING TASTE AND QUALITY

LOCATION
The Southern Rhône starts at Viviers, 50 km (31 miles) south of Valence, and runs south to Avignon.

CLIMATE
The Southern Rhône's climate is unmistakably Mediterranean and its vineyards are far more susceptible to sudden change and abrupt, violent storms than are those of the Northern Rhône.

ASPECT
The terrain in the south is noticeably Mediterranean, with olive groves, lavender fields, and herbal scrub amid rocky outcrops.

SOIL
The limestone outcrops that begin to appear in the southern area of the Northern Rhône become more prolific and are often peppered with clay deposits, while the topsoil is noticeably stonier. Châteauneuf-du-Pape is famous for its creamy-coloured drift boulders, which vary according to location. Stone-marl soils persist at Gigondas and weathered-grey sand in Lirac, Tavel, and Chusclan. The soils also incorporate limestone rubble, clay-sand, stone-clay, calcareous clay, and pebbles.

VITICULTURE AND VINIFICATION
The vines are traditionally planted at an angle leaning into the wind so that the mistral may blow them upright when they mature. The south is a district where blends reign supreme. Even Châteauneuf-du-Pape is a blend – usually of four or five varieties, although as many as 13 may sometimes be used. However, pure varietal wines are gaining ground. Traditional methods of vinification are used on some estates, but modern techniques are more common.

PRIMARY GRAPE VARIETIES
Carignan, Cinsault, Grenache, Mourvèdre, Muscat blanc à petits grains, Muscat rosé à petits grains
SECONDARY GRAPE VARIETIES
Aubun, Bourboulenc, Calitor, Camarèse, Clairette, Clairette rosé, Counoise, Gamay, Grenache blanc, Grenache gris, Macabéo, Marsanne, Mauzac, Muscardin, Oeillade, Pascal blanc, Picardan, Picpoul blanc, Picpoul noir, Pinot blanc, Pinot noir, Roussanne, Syrah, Terret noir, Ugni blanc, Vaccarèse, Vermentino (known locally as Rolle), Viognier

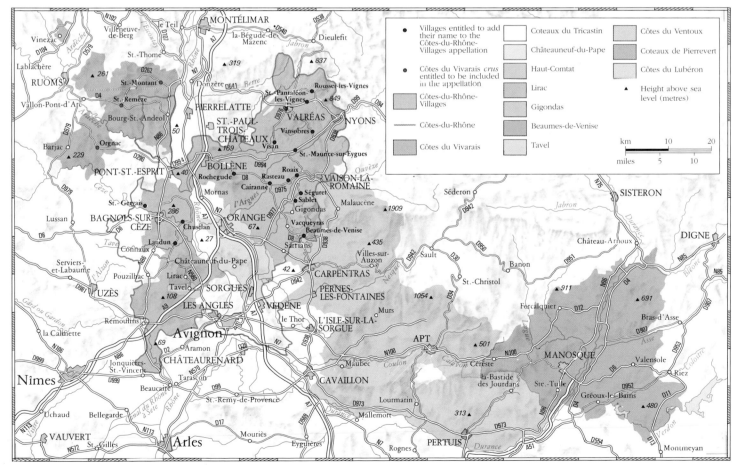

THE APPELLATIONS OF THE
SOUTHERN RHÔNE

BRÉZÈME-CÔTES-DU-RHÔNE AOC

A regulatory curiosity, Brézème is not one of the 16 Côtes-du-Rhône villages, which may attach their name only to the end of the appellation, but an anomalous village that through a peculiarity in the AOC laws is allowed to put its name before the basic Côtes-du-Rhône appellation.

RED This pure Syrah wine has been likened to a Crozes-Hermitage, but some *cuvées* (Grand Chêne and Eugène, for example) are aged in a percentage of new oak and are not at all like a northern Rhône wine.

🍇 The full spectrum of Côtes-du-Rhône grapes is allowed, but Syrah, Roussanne, and Marsanne are the only grapes cultivated

✓ *Jean-Marie Lombard*

CHÂTEAUNEUF-DU-PAPE AOC

The name Châteauneuf-du-Pape dates from the time of the dual Papacy in the 14th century. The appellation is well known for its amazingly stony soil, which at night reflects the heat stored during the day, but the size, type, depth, and distribution of the stones varies enormously, as does the aspect of the vineyards. These variations, plus the innumerable permutations of the 13 grape varieties that may be used, account for the diversity of its styles. In the early 1980s, some growers began to question the hitherto accepted concepts of *encépagement* and vinification; winemaking in Châteauneuf-du-Pape is still in an evolutionary state. The steady decline of the traditionally dominant Grenache has speeded up as more growers are convinced of the worth of the Syrah and Mourvèdre. The Cinsault and Terret noir are still well appreciated, and the Counoise is beginning to be appreciated for its useful combination of fruit and firmness. The use of new oak is under experimentation and it already seems clear that it is better suited to white wine than red.

The regulations for this appellation have a unique safeguard designed to ensure that only fully ripe grapes in the healthiest condition are utilized: between 5 and 20 per cent of the grapes harvested within the maximum yield for this AOC are rejected and may be used to make only *vin de table*. This process of exclusion is known as *le rapé*.

RED Due to the variations of *terroir* and almost limitless permutations of *encépagement*, it is impossible to describe a typical Châteauneuf-du-Pape, but there are two categories – the traditional, full, dark, spicy, long-lived style and the modern, easy-drinking Châteauneuf-du-Pape, the best of which are unashamedly upfront and brimming with lip-smacking, juicy-jammy fruit. Both are warmer and spicier than the greatest wines of Hermitage and Côte Rôtie.

🍇 Grenache, Syrah, Mourvèdre, Picpoul, Terret noir, Counoise, Muscardin, Vaccarèse, Picardan, Cinsault, Clairette, Roussanne, Bourboulenc

🍷 6–25 years

WHITE Early harvesting has reduced sugar levels and increased acidity, while modern vinification techniques have encouraged a drop in fermentation temperatures, so these wines are not as full as those produced previously. They can still be very rich, albeit in a more opulent, exotic fruit style, with a much fresher, crisper finish. The very best white Châteauneuf-du-Pape is generally agreed to be Château de Beaucastel Vieilles Vignes.

🍇 Grenache, Syrah, Mourvèdre, Picpoul, Terret noir, Counoise, Muscardin, Vaccarèse, Picardan, Cinsault, Clairette, Roussanne, Bourboulenc

🍷 1–3 years (4–6 years in exceptional cases)

✓ *Max Aubert • Lucien Barrot • Château de Beaucastel* • Domaine de Beaurenard • Bousquet des Papes • Château Cabrières • Domaine les Caillous • Réserve des Célestins • Gérard Charvin • Château Fortia • Château de la Gardine • Domaine de la Janasse • Domaine de Marcoux • Font de Michelle • Clos du Mont-Olivet • Château Mont-Redon* • Domaine de la Mordorée • Château la Nerthe • Clos des Papes* • Clos Pignan • Château Rayas* • Tardieu-Laurent • Pierre Usseglio • Vieux Donjon • Domaine du Vieux Télégraphe* • Domaine de Villeneuve*

*Particularly recommended for white as well as red

COTEAUX DE PIERREVERT AOC

This appellation consists of some 400 hectares (990 acres) and was upgraded from VDQS to full AOC status in 1998.

RED Dull, uninspiring wines with little original character to commend them.

🍇 Carignan, Cinsault, Grenache, Mourvèdre, Oeillade, Syrah, Terret noir

🍷 2–5 years

WHITE Unspectacular, light, dry white wines with more body than fruit.

🍇 Clairette, Marsanne, Picpoul, Roussanne, Ugni blanc

🍷 1–3 years

ROSÉ Well-made wines with a blue-pink colour and a crisp, light, fine flavour.

🍇 Carignan, Cinsault, Grenache, Mourvèdre, Oeillade, Syrah, Terret noir

🍷 1–3 years

✓ *Domaine de la Blaque • Château de Rousset*

COTEAUX DU TRICASTIN AOC

Established as a VDQS in 1964, Tricastin was upgraded to full AOC status in 1973.

RED Very good wines, especially the deeply coloured, peppery Syrah wines that are a delight after a few years in bottle. These wines may be sold as *primeur* or *nouveau* from the third Thursday of November following the harvest.

🍇 Grenache, Cinsault, Mourvèdre, Syrah, Picpoul noir, and a maximum of 20% Carignan; and 20% (in total) of Grenache blanc, Clairette, Bourboulenc, and Ugni blanc

🍷 2–7 years

WHITE Although I was unable to recommend Tricastin blanc in the first edition of this book (1988), the variety of grapes permitted has since been expanded to include Roussanne, Marsanne, and Viognier, which has enabled some producers to make richer, crisper, more interesting wines.

🍇 Grenache blanc, Clairette, Picpoul, Bourboulenc, and a maximum of 30% (in total) of Ugni blanc, Roussanne, Marsanne, and Viognier

ROSÉ A small production of fresh and fruity dry rosé that occasionally yields an outstandingly good wine. These wines may be sold as *primeur* or *nouveau* as from the third Thursday of November following the harvest.

🍇 Grenache, Cinsault, Mourvèdre, Syrah, Picpoul noir, and a maximum of 20% Carignan; and 20% (in total) of Grenache blanc, Clairette, Bourboulenc, and Ugni blanc

🍷 Upon purchase

✓ *CV Ardéchois • Le Cellier de Templiers • Domaine de Grangeneuve • Domaine Pierre Labeye • Domaine Saint-Luc • Domaine de la Tour d'Elyssas • Domaine du Vieux Micocoulier*

CÔTES DU LUBÉRON AOC

The wine of Côtes du Lubéron was promoted to full AOC status in February 1988. Much of the credit must go to Jean-Louis Chancel: his vineyards at Château Val-Joanis are still young, but the promise is such that this property has been described as the jewel in Lubéron's crown.

RED These are bright, well-coloured wines with plenty of fruit and character, improving with every vintage.

🍇 A blend of two or more varieties to include a minimum of 60% Grenache and Syrah (in total) – of which Syrah must represent at least 10%; a maximum of 40% Mourvèdre; 20% (each) of Cinsault and Carignan; and 10% (either singly or in total) of Counoise, Pinot noir, Gamay, and Picpoul

🍷 3–7 years

WHITE As white Lubéron has no established style or reputation, it seems bureaucratic nonsense to be so precise about the percentage of each grape variety that may or may not be included in its production. There was a feeling that some sort of quality and style was about to emerge in these wines in the late 1980s when Lubéron was merely a VDQS. Even then the regulation concerning grape varieties was unnecessarily complicated. Since its upgrade to full AOC status, the regulations have become even more confusing and I doubt if it is a coincidence that Lubéron blanc has completely lost its way over the same period.

🍇 A blend of two or more varieties, which can include Grenache blanc, Clairette, Bourboulenc, Vermentino, a maximum of 50% Ugni blanc, and up to 20% (of the blend) of Roussanne and/or Marsanne

🍷— 1–3 years

ROSÉ These attractively coloured, fresh, fruity wines are much better quality than most Provence rosé.

🍇 A blend of two or more varieties to include a minimum of 60% Grenache and Syrah (in total) – of which Syrah must represent at least 10%); a maximum of 40% Mourvèdre; 20% (each) of Cinsault and Carignan; 20% (in total) of Grenache blanc, Clairette, Bourboulenc, Vermentino, Ugni blanc, Roussanne, and Marsanne; plus 10% (either singly or in total) of Counoise, Pinot noir, Gamay, and Picpoul

🍷— Upon purchase

✓ *Château la Canorgue • Domaine de la Citadelle • Château de l'Isolette • Clos Mira-beau • Mas de Peyroulet • Tardieu-Laurent • Château Val-Joanis • La Vieille Ferme*

CÔTES-DU-RHÔNE AOC

A generic appellation that covers the entire Rhône region, although the vast majority of wines are actually produced in the Southern Rhône. There are some superb Côtes-du-Rhônes, but there are also some disgusting wines. The quality and character varies to such an extent that it would be unrealistic to attempt any generalized description. The red wines are the most successful, however, and many of the best rosés are superior in quality to those from more expensive Rhône appellations. The white wines have improved tremendously in the last few years (Vieux Manoir de Maransan being the best) and continue to do so in encouraging fashion.

RED, WHITE, and ROSÉ The red and rosé may be sold as *primeur* or *nouveau* from the third Thursday of November following the harvest, although the reds can be sold only unbottled as *vin de café*. Red, white, and rosé wines can be fully commercialized from 1st December without mention of *primeur* or *nouveau*.

🍇 The varieties and percentages of grapes permitted are the same for red, white, and rosé: Grenache, Clairette, Syrah, Mourvèdre, Picpoul, Terret noir, Picardan, Cinsault, Roussanne, Marsanne, Bourboulenc, Viognier; plus up to 30% Carignan; and a maximum of 30% (in total) of Counoise, Muscardin, Vaccarèse, Pinot blanc, Mauzac, Pascal blanc, Ugni blanc, Calitor, Gamay, and Camarèse

🍷— 2–8 years (red), 1–3 years (white and rosé)

✓ *Domaine de Bel-Air • Coudoulet de Beaucastel • Domaine Brusset • Domaine Delubac • CV d'Estezargues • Château de Fonsalette • Domaine Gramenon • Château du Grand Moulas • E. Guigal • Paul Jaboulet Aîné • Jean Lionnet • Domaine de l'Oratoire St.-Martin • Domaine Perrin • Domaine de la Réméjeanne • Domaine de Saint-Estève • Domaine la Soumade • Tardieu-Laurent*

CÔTES-DU-RHÔNE-VILLAGES AOC

Compared to the generic Côtes-du-Rhône, these wines generally have greater depth, character, and quality. The area covered by the appellation is entirely within the Southern Rhône. If the wine comes from one commune only, then it has the right to append that name to the appellation. Gigondas, Cairanne, Chusclan, and Laudun were the four villages that formed the original Côtes-du-Rhône-Villages appellation. Gigondas achieved its own AOC in 1971, but other villages have been added from time to time: there are now no less than 16 in the AOC.

RED These wines are mostly excellent.

🍇 A maximum of 65% Grenache; plus a minimum of 25% Syrah, Mourvèdre, and Cinsault; and up to 10% (in total) of Clairette, Picpoul, Terret noir, Picardan, Roussanne, Marsanne, Bourboulenc, Viognier, Carignan, Counoise, Muscardin, Vaccarèse, Pinot blanc, Mauzac, Pascal blanc, Ugni blanc, Calitor, Gamay, and Camarèse

🍷— 3–10 years

WHITE These wines are improving – Vieux Manoir du Frigoulas is the best.

🍇 A minimum of 80% Clairette, Roussanne, and Bourboulenc; plus up to 10% of Grenache blanc; and a maximum of 10% (in total) of Grenache, Syrah, Mourvèdre, Picpoul, Terret noir, Picardan, Cinsault, Bourboulenc, Viognier, Carignan, Counoise, Muscardin, Vaccarèse, Pinot blanc, Mauzac, Pascal blanc, Ugni blanc, Calitor, Gamay, and Camarèse

🍷— 1–3 years

ROSÉ These wines can be very good.

🍇 A maximum of 60% Grenache and 10% Carignan, plus a minimum of 10% Camarèse and Cinsault, and up to 10% (in total) of Clairette, Picpoul, Terret noir, Picardan, Roussanne, Marsanne, Bourboulenc, Vaccarèse, Pinot blanc, Mauzac, Pascal blanc, Ugni blanc, Calitor, Gamay, Syrah, and Mourvèdre

🍷— 1–3 years

✓ *Domaine de Cabasse • Domaine le Clos des Cazaux • Domaine Delubac • Château la Gardine • Domaine St.-Anne • CV St.-Hilaire d'Ozilhan • Château Signac • La Vieille Ferme* (La Réserve) *• Vieux Manoir du Frigoulas*

THE 16 VILLAGES OF THE CÔTES-DU-RHÔNE-VILLAGES

These single-villages versions of the above appellation wines can add their village name to the Côtes-du-Rhône Villages appellation.

CÔTES-DU-RHÔNE BEAUMES-DE-VENISE AOC

Famous for its delectable, sweet, Muscat wine, Beaumes-de-Venise also produces a pleasant red wine with a good peppery-raspberry fruit flavour. Dry white and rosé wines are produced under the generic AOC.

✓ *Domaine les Goubert • Château Redortier*

CÔTES-DU-RHÔNE CAIRANNE AOC

Since Vacqueyras was promoted to its own AOC, Cairanne is now the top village in the appellation. It is an excellent source of rich, warm, and spicy red wines that age very well.

✓ *Domaine Denis & Daniel Alary • Domaine des Amadieu • Domaine de l'Ameillaud • Max Aubert • Domaine Brusset • Domaine des Buisserons • CV des Coteaux de Cairanne • Domaine du Grand-Jas • Domaine de l'Oratoire St.-Martin • Domaine de la Présidente • Domaine Rabasse-Charavin • Domaine Marcel Richaud • Domaine des Travers*

CÔTES-DU-RHÔNE CHUSCLAN AOC

One of two single-village appellations whose wines actually come from more than one commune, Chusclan may also be made from vines growing in Bagnols-sur-Cèze, Cadolet, Orsan, and St.-Etienne-des-Sorts. These villages are situated just north of Lirac and Tavel, two famous rosé appellations, and make an excellent rosé. However, most of the wines are red, and produced in a good, quaffing style. The white is fresh, lively, and reliable.

✓ *Caves des Vignerons de Chusclan • Domaine du Lindas*

CÔTES-DU-RHÔNE LAUDUN AOC

Laudun, one of the appellation's four original villages, produces the other wine (*see* Côtes-du-Rhône Chusclan AOC) that can be made from vines grown outside the village indicated – in this case from St.-Victor-Lacoste and Tresques – and excels in making fine, fresh, and spicy red wines. It also makes the best white wines in the Côtes-du-Rhône-Villages appellation, and a small amount of quite delightful rosé wines.

✓ *Cave des Quatre Chemins • Domaine Rémy Estournel • Domaine Pélaquié • Louis Rousseau & Fils • Château St.-Maurice* (Cuvée Vicomte)

CÔTES-DU-RHÔNE RASTEAU AOC

This village is best known for its sweet Rasteau "Rancio" (*see below*) yet it produces nearly four times as much dry red, white, and rosé as it does Rasteau. Its red is the best: deep-coloured, full, and rich, with a spicy warmth, Rasteau *rouge* is a wine that can improve for up to ten years.

✓ *Caves des Vignerons de Rasteau • Didier Charavin • Domaine de la Grangeneuve • Domaine des Girasols • Domaine la Soumade • Domaine des Coteaux des Travers • Francis Vache*

CÔTES-DU-RHÔNE ROAIX AOC

Neighbouring the vineyards of Séguret, Roaix produces a similar dark-coloured red wine that requires two or three years in bottle to mellow. A little rosé is also produced.

✓ *Florimond Lambert • CV de Roaix-Séguret*

CÔTES-DU-RHÔNE ROCHEGUDE AOC

Only the red wine of Rochegude may claim the Côtes-du-Rhône-Villages appellation. I have encountered only the local *coopérative* wine, but it is good quality, well coloured, soft, and plummy. As at Beaumes-de-Venise, the white and rosé is sold as generic Côtes du Rhône.

✓ *Cave Coopérative Vinicole de Rochegude*

CÔTES-DU-RHÔNE
ROUSSET-LES-VIGNES AOC

The neighbouring villages of Rousset-les-Vignes and St.-Pantaléon-les-Vignes possess the most northerly vineyards of this appellation, close to the verdant Alpine foothills. With the coolest climate of all the Côtes-du-Rhône villages, the wines are light, but soft and quaffable. Production is monopolized by the local *coopérative*.

CÔTES-DU-RHÔNE SABLET AOC

This village's soft, fruity, and quick-maturing red and rosé wines are consistent in quality, and are always good value.

✓ *René Bernard • Domaine les Goubert • Domaine du Parandou • Domaine de Piaugier • Paul Roumanille • Château du Trignon • Domaine de Verquière*

CÔTES-DU-RHÔNE ST.-GERVAIS AOC

The valley vineyards of St.-Gervais are not those of the great river itself, but belong to the Cèze, one of its many tributaries. The red wines are deliciously deep and fruity, and the whites are fresh and aromatic with an excellent, crisp balance for wines from such a southerly location.

✓ *Domaine le Baine • Cave Coopérative de St.-Gervais • Domaine St.-Anne*

CÔTES-DU-RHÔNE ST.-MAURICE AOC
OR CÔTES-DU-RHÔNE
ST.-MAURICE-SUR-EYGUES AOC

Light, easy-drinking red and rosé wines. Production is dominated by the local *coopérative*.

✓ *CV des Coteaux St.-Maurice • Domaine de Deurre*

CÔTES-DU-RHÔNE
ST.-PANTALÉON-LES-VIGNES AOC

The neighbouring villages of St.-Pantaléon-les-Vignes and Rousset-les-Vignes possess the most northerly vineyards of this appellation. With the coolest climate of all the Côtes-du-Rhône villages, the wines are light, but soft and quaffable. Production is monopolized by the local *coopérative*, which has yet to make anything special.

CÔTES-DU-RHÔNE SÉGURET AOC

Séguret produces red wine that is firm and fruity with a good, bright, deep colour. A little white and rosé is also made but they seldom excel.

✓ *Jean-Pierre Brotte • Domaine de Cabasse • Domaine Garancière • Domaine du Sommier*

CÔTES-DU-RHÔNE VALREAS AOC

These are fine red wines with plenty of fruit flavour. A little rosé is also made.

✓ *Domaine de la Fuzière • Domaine des Grands Devers • Le Val des Rois*

CÔTES-DU-RHÔNE VINSOBRES AOC

This village consistently produces good-quality, firm red wines. It also produces a small amount of passable rosé.

✓ *Domaine des Ausellons • Domaine du Coriançon • Hubert Valayer* (Domaine de Deurre) • *Denis Vinson* (Domaine du Moulin)

CÔTES-DU-RHÔNE VISAN AOC

These red wines have good colour and true *vin de garde* character. Fresh, quaffing white wines are also made.

✓ *Cave Coopérative "les Coteaux de Visan" • Domaine de la Cantharide • Domaine de la Costechaude • Clos du Père Clément*

CÔTES DU VENTOUX AOC

The limestone subsoil of the Côtes du Ventoux appellation produces a lighter wine than is normal for the Rhône.

RED These fresh and fruity, easy-to-drink reds are the best wines in this AOC. The wines may be sold as *primeur* or *nouveau* from the third Thursday of November following the harvest.

🍇 Grenache, Syrah, Cinsault, and Mourvèdre, plus up to 30% Carignan, and a maximum of 20% (in total) of Picpoul noir, Counoise, Clairette, Bourboulenc, Grenache blanc, Roussanne, and – until the 2014 vintage – Ugni blanc, Picpoul blanc, and Pascal blanc

🍷— 2–5 years

WHITE A little white is produced, but it is seldom anything more than of minimal interest. These wines may be sold as *primeur or nouveau* from the third Thursday of November following the harvest.

🍇 Clairette, Bourboulenc, plus up to 30% (in total) of Grenache blanc, Roussanne, and – until the 2014 vintage – Ugni blanc, Picpoul blanc, and Pascal blanc

ROSÉ The fresh character and deliciously delicate fruit of these wines can be pure joy on a hot sunny day. They may be sold as *primeur or nouveau* from the third Thursday of November following the harvest.

🍇 Grenache, Syrah, Cinsault, and Mourvèdre, plus up to 30% Carignan, and a maximum of 20% (in total) Picpoul noir, Counoise, Clairette, Bourboulenc, Grenache blanc, Roussanne, and – until the 2014 vintage – Ugni blanc, Picpoul blanc, and Pascal blanc

🍷— Upon purchase

✓ *Domaine des Anges • Domaine de Fenouillet • CV des Coteaux du Mont Ventoux • Domaine St.-Croix • Château Pesquié • Domaine St.-Saveur • Domaine de Tenon • La Vieille Ferme • Château du Vieux-Lazaret*

CÔTES DU VIVARAIS VDQS

The *côtes* of Vivarais look across the Rhône river to the *coteaux* of Tricastin. Its best *cru* villages (Orgnac, St.-Montant, and St.-Remèze) may add their names to the Côtes du Vivarais appellation, and of these, the wines of the village of Orgnac stand out.

RED These light, quaffing reds are by far the best wines in the district.

🍇 Since 1995 Mourvèdre, Picpoul, Aubun, and Carignan have been banned and this wine must now contain a minimum of 90% (in total) of Syrah and Grenache; the Syrah must account for at least 40% and Grenache at least 30%, with Cinsault and Carignan optional

🍷— 1–3 years

WHITE These wines were always dull and disappointing, but with the recent improvement in the *encépagement*, standards have improved, and Vivarais *blanc* may very well prove to be interesting in the future.

🍇 Since 1995 Bourboulenc, Macabéo, Mauzac, Picpoul, and Ugni blanc have been banned and this wine must now be made from at least two varieties of the three recommended grapes – Clairette, Grenache, and Marsanne – with no single variety accounting for more than 75% of the total

🍷— 1–3 years

ROSÉ These pretty pink dry wines can have a ripe, fruity flavour and are generally better than the whites.

🍇 Since 1995 Mourvèdre, Carignan, Picpoul, and Aubun have been banned and this wine must now be made from at least two of three recommended grapes – Syrah, Grenache, and Cinsault – with no single variety accounting for more than 80% of the total

🍷— 1–3 years

✓ *Les Chais du Vivarais*

GIGONDAS AOC

Gigondas produces some of the most underrated red wines in the Rhône Valley.

RED The best have an intense black-red colour with a full plummy flavour.

🍇 A maximum of 80% Grenache, plus at least 15% Syrah and Mourvèdre, and a maximum of 10% (in total) of Clairette, Picpoul, Terret noir, Picardan, Cinsault, Roussanne, Marsanne, Bourboulenc, Viognier, Counoise, Muscardin, Vaccarèse, Pinot blanc, Mauzac, Pascal blanc, Ugni blanc, Calitor, Gamay, and Camarèse

🍷— 7–20 years

ROSÉ Good-quality, dry rosé wines.

🍇 A maximum of 80% Grenache and a maximum of 25% (in total) of Clairette, Picpoul, Terret noir, Picardan, Cinsault, Roussanne, Marsanne, Bourboulenc, Viognier, Counoise, Muscardin, Vaccarèse, Pinot blanc, Mauzac, Pascal blanc, Ugni blanc, Calitor, Gamay, and Camarèse

🍷— 2–5 years

✓ *Domaine Brusset • Domaine du Cayron • Domaine le Clos des Cazaux • Domaine de Font-Sane • Domaine les Goubert • Domaine de Longue-Toque • Château de Montmirail • l'Oustau Fauquet • Domaine les Pallières • Domaine du Pesquié • Domaine Raspail-Ay • Château Redortier • De Rocasère • Domaine de St.-Gayan • Domaine Santa-Duc • Domaine la Soumade • Château du Trignon*

LIRAC AOC

This appellation was once the preserve of rosé, but the production of red is now on the increase.

RED In really great years, the Syrah and Mourvèdre can dominate despite the quite small quantities used, which produces a more plummy wine with silky-spicy finesse.

A minimum of 40% Grenache and 25% (in total) of Syrah and Mourvèdre, plus up to 10% Carignan and no limit on the amount of Cinsault, although this used to be restricted to 20% and I suspect this relaxation is due to clerical error when the regulations were rewritten in 1992.

🍇 4–10 years

WHITE A fragrant dry white wine, the best of which has improved since 1992, when Marsanne, Roussanne, and Viognier were permitted for use in this appellation. The cheapest wines have dropped in quality because the amount of Clairette allowed has been doubled. Macabéo and Calitor are no longer permitted.

🍇 Up to 60% (each) of Bourboulenc, Clairette, and Grenache blanc; plus up to 25% (each) of Ugni blanc, Picpoul, Marsanne, Roussanne, and Viognier (but these secondary varieties must not represent more than 30% of the blend in total)

🍇 1–3 years

ROSÉ Production is declining in favour of red wine, but these dry rosés can have a delightful summer-fruit flavour that is fresher than either Tavel or Provence.

🍇 A minimum of 40% Grenache and 25% (in total) of Syrah and Mourvèdre, plus up to 10% Carignan, no limit on the amount of Cinsault (but see red wine grapes above), and up to 20% (in total) of Bourboulenc, Clairette, Grenache blanc, Ugni blanc, Picpoul, Marsanne, Roussanne, and Viognier

🍇 1–3 years

✓ *Château d'Aquéria • Château Boucarut • Château de Bouchassy • Domaine des Causses & St.-Eymes • Domaine de Devoy • Domaine la Fermade • Domaine les Garrigues • Domaine Maby • Domaine de la Mordorée • Domaine de la Pélaquié • Domaine du Château St.-Roche • Château de Ségriès • Domaine de la Tour de Lirac*

MUSCAT DE BEAUMES-DE-VENISE AOC

These wines from Muscat de Beaumes-de-Venise are the most elegant of the world's sweet fortified Muscat wines. Very little sweet Muscat was made before World War II. When the AOC was granted in 1945, the wine was classified as a *vin doux naturel*. The process by which this is made entails the addition of pure grape spirit, in an operation called *mutage*, after the spirit has achieved five per cent alcohol by natural fermentation. The final wine must contain at least 15 per cent alcohol, plus a minimum of 110 grams of residual sugar per litre. The Coopérative des Vins & Muscats, which was established in 1956, accounts for a formidable 90 per cent of the wine produced. It is often said that this wine is always non-vintage, but in fact ten per cent is sold with a vintage on the label.

WHITE/ROSÉ The colour varies between the rare pale gold and the common light apricot-gold, with an aromatic bouquet more akin to the perfume of dried flowers than fruit. You should expect Muscat de Beaumes-de-Venise to have hardly any acidity, which surprisingly does not make it cloying, despite its intense sweetness, but does enable it to be one of the very few wines to partner ice-cream successfully.

🍇 Muscat blanc à petits grains, Muscat rosé à petits grains

🍇 1–2 years

✓ *Domaine de Beaumalric • Domaine des Bernadins • CV Beaumes-de-Venise • Domaine de Coyeux • Domaine de Durban • Domaine de Fenouillet • Domaine de la Mordorée • Domaine de St.-Saveur*

RASTEAU AOC

This appellation was first created in the early 1930s, and was promoted to full AOC status on 1 January 1944. Rasteau was the first of the Rhône's two *vin doux naturel* appellations. In popularity and quality it is, however, second to Muscat de Beaumes-de-Venise.

RED A rich, sweet, coarse, grapey-flavoured concoction with plenty of grip, a rather awkward spirity aroma, and a pithy, apricot-skin aftertaste.

🍇 A minimum of 90% Grenache (gris or blanc), plus up to 10% (in total) of Clairette, Syrah, Mourvèdre, Picpoul, Terret noir, Picardan, Cinsault, Roussanne, Marsanne, Bourboulenc, Viognier, Carignan, Counoise, Muscardin, Vaccarèse, Pinot blanc, Mauzac, Pascal blanc, Ugni blanc, Calitor, Gamay, and Camarèse

🍇 1–5 years

WHITE/TAWNY/ROSÉ This wine can be white, tawny, or rosé depending on the technique used and on the degree of ageing. It does not have the grip of the red, but has a mellower sweetness.

🍇 A minimum of 90% Grenache (gris or blanc), plus up to 10% (in total) of Clairette, Syrah, Mourvèdre, Picpoul, Terret noir, Picardan, Cinsault, Clairette, Roussanne, Bourboulenc, Viognier, Carignan, Counoise, Muscardin, Vaccarèse, Pinot blanc, Mauzac, Pascal blanc, Ugni blanc, Calitor, Gamay, and Camarèse

🍇 1–5 years

✓ *Domaine de Char-à-Vin • Gourt de Mautens • Domaine de la Grangeneuve • Domaine la Soumade • Tardieu-Laurent • Francis Vache • Caves des Vignerons*

RASTEAU "RANCIO" AOC

These wines are similar to the wines of the Rasteau AOC (*see above*), except they must be stored in oak casks "according to local custom", which often means exposing the barrels to sunlight for a minimum of two years, which allows the wines to develop the maderized "rancio" character.

TAVEL AOC

Tavel is the most famous French dry rosé, but only the very best domaines live up to its reputation. In order to retain freshness, Tavel's alcoholic level is restricted to a maximum of 13 per cent alcohol.

ROSÉ Some properties still cling to the old-style vinification methods and, frankly, this means the wines are too old before they are sold. The top domaines in the appellation make clean-cut wines with freshly scented aromas and fine fruit flavours, which are invariably good food wines.

🍇 Grenache, Cinsault, Clairette, Clairette rosé, Picpoul, Calitor, Bourboulenc, Mourvèdre, and Syrah (none of which may account for more than 60% of the blend), plus a maximum of 10% Carignan

🍇 1–3 years

✓ *Château d'Aquéria • Domaine la Forcadière • Domaine de la Genestière • Prieuré de Montezargues • Domaine de la Mordorée • Château de Trinquevedel • Le Vieux Moulin de Tavel*

VACQUEYRAS AOC

Formerly one of the single-village wines under the AOC Côtes-du-Rhône-Villages, Vacqueyras was elevated to full AOC status in 1990, without any mention of Côtes-du-Rhône or Côtes-du-Rhône-Villages, and is now theoretically on a par with Gigondas.

RED The best are dark, rich, and robust, with a warm, black-pepper spiciness.

🍇 At least 50% Grenache plus up to 25% (in total – 20% as from the year 2000) of Syrah, Mourvèdre, and Cinsault; and no more than 10% (either singly or in total) of Terret noir, Counoise, Muscardin, Vaccarèse, Gamay, and Camarèse

🍇 4–12 years

WHITE This is the least successful style of the appellation; most tend to be either flabby or so dominated by modern, cool vinification methods that they are just fresh and could come from anywhere.

🍇 Grenache blanc, Clairette, and Bourboulenc, plus up to 50% in total of Marsanne, Roussanne, and Viognier

🍇 2–3 years

ROSÉ Can be lovely, fresh, and fruity.

🍇 Up to 60% Grenache plus no more than 15% in total of Mourvèdre or Cinsault, and up to 15% (either singly or in total) of Terret noir, Counoise, Muscardin, Vaccarèse, Gamay, and Camarèse

🍇 2–3 years

✓ *Domaine des Amouriers • Domaine les Clos des Cazaux • Domaine la Fourmone • Paul Jaboulet Aîné • Domaine de la Monardière • Domaine de Montuac • Château des Roques • Tardieu-Laurent • Château des Tours • Domaine de Verquière*

AUTHOR'S CHOICE

Because the Rhône is increasingly recognized as a classic red-wine area on a par with either Bordeaux or Burgundy, it is no longer the bargain basement it used to be. I have therefore split my choice between some of the truly great wines and the most stunning bargains that can still be found.

PRODUCER	WINE	STYLE	DESCRIPTION	⌇
Château de Beaucastel **Ⓥ**	Châteauneuf-du-Pape AOC (*see* p.216)	RED	It is the small yield of highly concentrated fruit from this vineyard's very old vines that is responsible for this wonderfully deep-coloured wine. Deliciously juicy with masses of black pepper and plummy-ripe, spicy-blackcurrant, and blackberry fruit, Château de Beaucastel is capable of great complexity.	10–30 years
Château de Beaucastel	Cuvée Jacques Perrin, Châteauneuf-du-Pape AOC (*see* p.216)	RED	At one time, many people solemnly swore that Château de Beaucastel was the greatest Châteauneuf-du-Pape and it has always been one of my two favourites (Vieux Télégraphe being the other). However, in 1989 the Perrin brothers brought out the first vintage of a new super-*cuvée* in honour of their father and it is, quite simply, in an entirely different league from any other Châteauneuf-du-Pape.	10–40 years
Château de Beaucastel	Roussanne Vieilles Vignes, Châteauneuf-du-Pape AOC (*see* p.216)	WHITE	A consistently minute yield from 70-year-old vines is the secret of this fabulously rich, exotic, oaky dry white wine with its multi-layered, honey-rich fruit, impeccable balance, and great finesse.	5–7 years
Jean-Luc Colombo	Les Ruchets, Cornas AOC (*see* p.213)	RED	It is astonishing how such deep, inky-black wine can be so smooth and supple, yet still possess huge depth, length, and concentration in its blackberry, raspberry, and *cassis* fruit.	6–15 years
Yves Cuilleron	Les Chaillets, Condrieu AOC (*see* p.213)	WHITE	Exquisitely made, crisp, bright, succulently fruity wine with exotic aromas of tropical fruits and flowers. Drink it on its own or with fresh asparagus, like a great Alsace Muscat.	2–4 years
M. Chapoutier	Cuvée de l'Orée, Hermitage AOC (*see* p.214)	WHITE	Made from 70-year-old vines and barrel-fermented, this extraordinarily rich wine has a botrytis-like richness, texture, and complexity of honeyed-peachy fruit.	5–15 years
Coudoulet de Beaucastel **Ⓥ**	Côtes-du-Rhône AOC (*see* p.217)	RED	Coudoulet is probably the most consistent, great-quality Côtes-du-Rhône. It has a gorgeous depth of flavour, rich, juicy fruit, and a black-pepper, spicy freshness that can achieve a degree of finesse and complexity way beyond its modest appellation.	4–10 years
Yves Cuilleron **Ⓥ**	Cuvée Prestige, St.-Joseph AOC (*see* p.214)	RED	Yves Cuilleron consistently makes one of the best wines from this great-value-for-money appellation, making it one of the Rhône's biggest bargains. Big, black, and sleek, with heaps of spicy brambly-blackcurranty fruit.	5–12 years
Delas	Seigneur de Maugiron, Côte-Rotie AOC (*see* p.213)	RED	If there is such a thing as bargain Côte-Rôtie (or Côte-Rotie as Delas insists on spelling it), then this super-fresh, super-delicious wine, which is loaded with elegant blackberry fruit, must be it.	5–12 years
Delas	Chante-Perdrix, Cornas AOC (*see* p.213)	RED	This costs slightly more than Delas Côte-Rotie Seigneur de Maugiron, although Cornas traditionally costs just one-fifth of the price of a Côte-Rôtie, but in terms of pure quality, this exquisitely perfumed Chante-Perdrix is indeed its equal.	5–12 years
Delas	Les Bassards, Hermitage AOC (*see* p.214)	RED	This wine is a huge, concentrated Hermitage that was first produced as recently as 1991, but quickly established itself as a class act, with its fine, black-pepper, spicy-black-fruit flavours, and long, smooth, elegant finish.	5–20 years
Domaine de Durban	Muscat de Beaumes-de-Venise AOC (*see* p.219)	FORTIFIED WHITE	Of all the fine Muscat de Beaumes-de-Venise, this probably displays the most complex array of Muscat aromas, ranging from the floral (rose petals, orange-blossom, and violets) through the creamy and nutty (vanilla and coconut) to the fruity (peach and orange).	Upon purchase
Domaine Gramenon **Ⓥ**	Cuvée de Laurentides, Côtes-du-Rhône AOC (*see* p.217)	RED	This fabulously rich and weighty wine has a lusty texture, oaky smoothness, and remarkable complexity for such an inexpensive Côtes-du-Rhône. This is possibly the Rhône's greatest bargain.	3–8 years
E. Guigal	La Doriane, Condrieu AOC (*see* p.213)	WHITE	The production of this single-vineyard Condrieu is tiny and the wine, which is fermented in *barriques*, has such vivid, luscious, and intense, floral-peachy fruit that there are no overtly oaky tones, just a soothing-smoothing effect on the long finish.	2–5 years

PRODUCER	WINE	STYLE	DESCRIPTION	⌐⊷
E. Guigal	La Landonne, Côte-Rôtie AOC (*see* p.213)	RED	La Landonne is made from only old Syrah vines on the Côte Brun, and is therefore potentially the biggest of Guigal's three single-vineyard Côte-Rôtie wines, although some vintages can be very opulent and smooth, as well as dense and powerful.	10–30 years
E. Guigal	La Mouline, Côte-Rôtie AOC (*see* p.213)	RED	La Mouline comes from relatively young vines on the Côte Blonde, and contains some ten per cent Viognier, making it the smoothest and most exotic of Guigal's three single-vineyard Côte-Rôtie, with an almost New World supple-tannin finish.	5–20 years
E. Guigal	La Turque, Côte-Rôtie AOC (*see* p.213)	RED	La Turque is the least seen and has the smallest production of Guigal's three superb, if outrageously expensive, single-vineyard wines. It has been produced only since 1985 compared to 1978 for La Landonne and 1976 for La Mouline. Like La Landonne, this wine comes from the Côte Brun, but is produced from relatively young vines, and on an even steeper slope. In some years it may receive a dash of Viognier. With these variations, it is not surprising that La Turque falls somewhere between the power and structure of La Landonne and the voluptuousness of La Mouline, some vintages being more exotic than others.	8–25 years
Paul Jaboulet Aîné ⓥ	Cornas AOC (*see* p.213)	RED	I regularly buy this wine as soon as it is offered, and by its eighth year, when its deep, dark, ripe, black-pepper, and spicy-blackberry fruit has deliciously mellowed, it is virtually unobtainable on the open market. If you are then lucky enough to find a bottle, it costs three times as much, making it one of the most consistent Rhône wine bargains still available.	8–20 years
André Perret	Coteau de Chéry, Condrieu AOC (*see* p.213)	WHITE	Very little of this single-vineyard, oak-fermented Condrieu is produced and even less finds its way on to the open market. This luscious, succulent dry white wine is *barrique*-fermented and kept *sur lie* for up to a year, which makes the fruit so fresh and breezy that it is like biting into the juicy-plump flesh of a perfectly ripe white peach.	2–5 years
Jean-Claude Raspail ⓥ	Clairette de Die Méthode Dioise Ancestrale AOC (*see* p.213)	SPARKLING WHITE	This is the freshest, most deliciously tangy and racy, sweet-ripe peachy Clairette de Die you can find.	2–5 years
Château Rayas	Châteauneuf-du-Pape AOC (*see* p.216)	RED	Many consider this to be the finest Châteauneuf-du-Pape. Its unique character can be attributed to its 100 per cent Grenache content, and to the extremely low-yielding very old vines that, in a great vintage, produce a concentrated but deliciously elegant wine. It has ripe, spicy, berry-fruit with a remarkable, sweet, herby-cedary complexity.	10–30 years
Marc Sorrel	Les Rocoules, Hermitage AOC (*see* p.214)	WHITE	This big, rich, Burgundian-like Hermitage *blanc* is one of the few white Rhône wines made in a truly *vin de garde* style, with beautifully pure honeyed-peach fruit that is capable of developing a spicy, citrous, honeyed-mineral complexity without losing its fresh, clean, crisp finish.	5–10 years
Domaine de la Soumade	Côtes-du-Rhône Rasteau AOC (*see* p.217)	RED	Owner-winemaker André Romero produces a stunning range of inexpensive Rasteau *cuvées*. They have rich, dark chocolate and cherry fruit, with fine toasted-roasted herbal complexity, demonstrating that the potential of this village is not far short of that of the Rhône's more famous appellations.	5–8 years
CV Tain-Hermitage ⓥ	Crozes-Hermitage AOC (*see* p.214)	RED	For the cheapest, most consistent Crozes-Hermitage, the lip-smacking black-pepper-dusted raspberries in the local *coopérative* are difficult to beat and in great vintages are a truly sensational bargain.	2–5 years (5–10 years in great vintages)
Domaine du Vieux Télégraphe	Châteauneuf-du-Pape AOC (*see* p.216)	RED	The new generation seems intent on pushing the quality of Vieux Télégraphe (one of my two favourite Châteauneuf-du-Pape, the other being Beaucastel) even higher. The warm, mellow, spicy glow of the Grenache is always beautifully balanced by the black-pepper and *cassis* of Syrah and the Mourvèdre, which gives this wine such finesse, but I think we can expect bigger, darker, more intense and openly powerful wines in future.	10–30 years
Vidal-Fleury	La Chatillonne, Côte Rôtie AOC (*see* p.213)	RED	This Côte Rôtie is produced from a single vineyard on the Côte Blonde. It is a wine of great elegance and poise, brimful of deliciously supple, creamy red fruits, yet is not at all big or heavy, and is nicely rounded off with creamy-smoky oak finish of great finesse.	8–12 years
François Villard	Les Terrasses de Pilat Condrieu, Condrieu AOC (*see* p.213)	WHITE	This is a fat, succulent, barrel-fermented dream of a wine from one of the fastest-rising young stars of Condrieu.	4–6 years

THE JURA AND SAVOIE

White wines dominate the production from these picturesque vineyards set amid the ski slopes of the French Alps. Sparkling wines are the speciality of Savoie, while Jura can boast the rare, sweet vins de paille and the amazingly long-lived vins jaunes.

THE JURA IS DOMINATED by the town of Arbois, a little alpine community reigned over by the winemaker Henri Maire. His infamous sparkling "Vin Fou", or "Mad Wine", has no appellation and comes in various different *cuvées*, of which some are better than others, but many taste the same. Despite the light-hearted approach to its consumption, "Vin Fou" has performed one admirable function: it has introduced wine drinkers to the district of Jura and Savoie and its many better wines. This could not have been achieved by the *vins de paille* and *vins jaunes*, due to their scarcity and high price. The very sweet *vin de paille* or "straw wine" is so called because the grapes were traditionally dried on straw mats to concentrate the juice into a syrup. The *vin jaune* or "yellow wine" derives its name from the colour that results from

its deliberate oxidation under a yeast *flor* when matured in casks that are not topped up for six years. This region also produces a number of more ordinary wines, often pure varietals, that are seldom exciting. The Jura's other claim to fame is, of course, as the birthplace of Louis Pasteur (1822–1895), who for all intents and purposes invented oenology, having been requested by Napoléon III to investigate the changes already observed during the maturation of wine. Born in the Arbois, where a small museum dedicated to him exists today, Pasteur's discoveries included the vital role of yeast during fermentation – totally unsuspected in his day, but without the knowledge of which the branch of chemistry called oenology would not exist. His vineyard, just outside Arbois, is now owned by the firm of Henri Maire.

The vineyards in the area between Lake Geneva and Grenoble, known as the Savoie, should be far more of a sparkling success than they are. I cannot imagine a better way to promote these wines than through the Savoie's built-in winter-sports trade. The only obstacle to their greater success is the failure of foreign wine merchants to import the wines in sufficient quantities.

RECENT JURA AND SAVOIE VINTAGES
Although 1995 stands out for all styles, variations in vintage are less significant for the Jura and Savoie than they are for most other French wine regions. You are best advised to buy the very latest vintage and, if you want, to keep the wine yourself rather than purchasing one that has been hanging around for a couple of years.

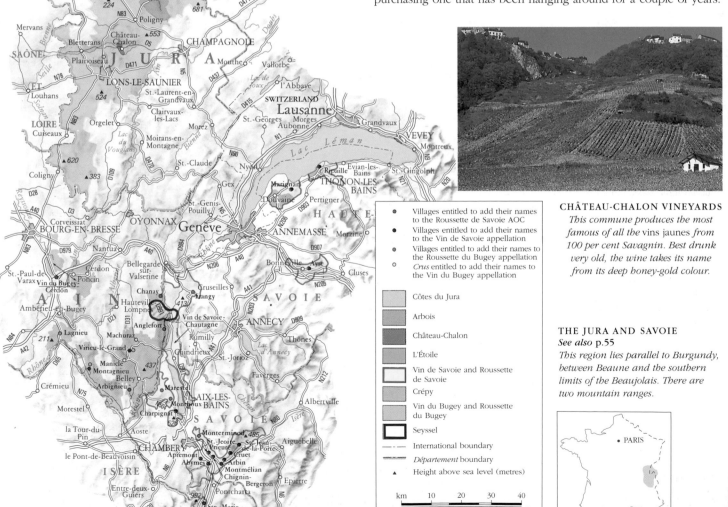

CHÂTEAU-CHALON VINEYARDS
This commune produces the most famous of all the vins jaunes *from 100 per cent Savagnin. Best drunk very old, the wine takes its name from its deep honey-gold colour.*

THE JURA AND SAVOIE
See also p.55
This region lies parallel to Burgundy, between Beaune and the southern limits of the Beaujolais. There are two mountain ranges.

Map legend:
- Villages entitled to add their names to the Roussette de Savoie AOC
- Villages entitled to add their names to the Vin de Savoie appellation
- Villages entitled to add their names to the Roussette du Bugey appellation
- *Crus* entitled to add their names to the Vin du Bugey appellation
- Côtes du Jura
- Arbois
- Château-Chalon
- L'Étoile
- Vin de Savoie and Roussette de Savoie
- Crépy
- Vin du Bugey and Roussette du Bugey
- Seyssel
- International boundary
- *Département* boundary
- Height above sea level (metres)

km 10 20 30 40
miles 10 20

FACTORS AFFECTING TASTE AND QUALITY

LOCATION
Running down the mountainous eastern border of France, the Jura and Savoie are parallel to the Burgundy region.

CLIMATE
The climate is continental, with hot summers and cold winters. The close proximity of the Jura and the Savoie mountain ranges can provoke sudden changes, although these may sometimes be mitigated by the calming effect of lakes Geneva and Bourget.

ASPECT
The vineyards of the Jura are situated on the lower slopes of the Jura mountains. The vines grow at an altitude of 250–500 m (820–1,640 ft). The Savoie vineyards lie lower than those of the Jura.

SOIL
The limestone of the Jura is generally mixed with clay over a subsoil of compacted marl. There are limestone and marl topsoils over a base of sandy and gravelly marls at Arbois and Château-Chalon and a limestone scree, calcareous sand, and clay-like sand with alluvial deposits at Bugey and Seyssel.

VITICULTURE AND VINIFICATION
The Jura is famous for two special techniques: the viticultural practice responsible for *vin de paille* and the vinification procedure required to make *vin jaune*. For *vin de paille*, wicker trays or wire mesh may be used, but in most cases bunches of grapes are hung from the rafters of heated huts, after which the shrivelled-up, super-concentrated, raisin-like grapes produce an amber-coloured sweet wine of great potential longevity. *Vin jaune* is produced entirely from the Savagnin grape which, after a normal fermentation, is left to age in wooden barrels for six years with no topping up. A yeast *flor* develops similar to that generated during the production of *fino* sherry and the results are not dissimilar.

GRAPE VARIETIES
Aligoté, Cabernet franc, Cabernet sauvignon, Chardonnay (*syn.* Melon d'Arbois or Gamay blanc), Chasselas, Chasselas roux, Chasselas vert, Etraire de la Dui, Frühroter Veltliner (*syn.* Malvoisie rosé or Veltliner rosé), Gamay, Gringet (close relation to Savagnin), Jacquère, Joubertin, Marsanne, Molette, Mondeuse, Mondeuse blanche, Persan, Pinot blanc, Pinot noir (*syn.* Gros noirien), Poulsard (*syn.* Poulsard), Roussette, Roussette d'Ayze, Savagnin (*syn.* Naturé), Serène, Trousseau, Verdesse

THE APPELLATIONS OF THE
JURA AND SAVOIE

ARBOIS AOC

This is the best-known appellation of the Jura, from in and around the town of Arbois.

RED Trousseau wines are rich, and sometimes coarse, and Pinot wines are light and rustic.

🍇 Trousseau, Poulsard, Pinot noir

🍷 2–8 years

WHITE Light, fresh Chardonnay wines are best, but Savagnin has a tendency to oxidize and is best suited to the famous local *vin jaune*.

🍇 Savagnin, Chardonnay, Pinot blanc

🍷 1–3 years

ROSÉ Famous for its firm and distinctive dry rosé wines made in the pale *vin gris* style.

🍇 Poulsard, Trousseau, Pinot noir

🍷 1–3 years

✓ *Lucien Aviet • Maurice Chassot • Fruitière Vinicole d'Arbois • Jean-Pierre & Marie-France Ligier • Henri Maire (Domaine de la Grange Grillard, Domaine du Sorbief) • Jean-François Nevers • Pierre Overnay • Jacques Puffeney • Domaine Rolet André & Mireille Tissot • Jacques Tissot*

ARBOIS MOUSSEUX AOC

This is a *méthode champenoise* sparkling wine seldom seen outside Arbois.

SPARKLING WHITE These fresh, dry sparkling wines show more potential than quality.

🍇 Savagnin, Chardonnay, Pinot blanc

🍷 1–3 years

✓ *Domaine Foret • Fruitière Vinicole d'Arbois* (Montboise)

ARBOIS VIN DE PAILLE AOC

This wine is made from grapes that are dried to concentrate the juice, followed by a long fermentation and up to four years in wood.

WHITE These are very sweet wines with an old-gold colour, complex bouquet, and a rich, nutty flavour.

🍇 Poulsard, Trousseau, Savagnin, Chardonnay

🍷 10–50 (or more) years

✓ *Fruitière Vinicole d'Arbois • Jacques Foret • Domaine Rolet • André & Mireille Tissot*

ARBOIS PUPILLIN AOC

This is a single-commune appellation for red, white, rosé, *vin jaune*, and *vin de paille* made to the same specification as Arbois AOC. *See* Arbois AOC, Arbois Vin de Paille AOC, and Arbois Vin Jaune AOC.

✓ *Désiré Petit & Fils • Fruitière Vinicole de Pupillin • Henri Maire (Domaine du Sorbief) • Domaine de la Pinte • Pierre Overnoy • Daniel Overnoy-Crinquand*

ARBOIS VIN JAUNE AOC

For details of production and style, *see* Château-Chalon AOC.

✓ *Lucien Aviet • Maurice Chassot • Fruitière Vinicole d'Arbois • Fruitière Vinicole de Pupillin • Domaine Michel Geneletti • Pierre Overnoy • Domaine de la Pinte • Jacques Puffeney • Domaine Rolet • André & Mireille Tissot • Jacques Tissot*

CHÂTEAU-CHALON AOC

The Jura's *vins jaunes* possess a unique style and Château-Chalon (which is the name of a commune) is its most legendary exponent. It is normally fermented, then left to age in sealed wooden barrels for six years with no topping up. During this time, a *flor* develops – a skin of yeast that floats on top of the wine. The changes induced by the *flor* give the acetaldehyde-dominated *vin jaune* a resemblance to a *fino* Sherry, but the fact that it is not fortified (whereas Sherry is) and is made from a different grape produces its unique character.

WHITE *Vin jaune* is something of an acquired taste and should be drunk when very old. The vast array of complex nuances of bouquet eventually subdue and transmute the Sherry-like smell of acetaldehyde. It has a dry flavour.

🍇 Savagnin

🍷 10–100 years

✓ *Domaine Berthet-Bondet • Jean Bourdy • Daniel Chalanard • Domaine Jean Macle*

CÔTES DU JURA AOC

This generic appellation contains some of the most widely encountered Jura wines. Its larger area of production gives it an edge over Arbois, the better known AOC within its boundaries.

RED Usually light in colour and body, with elegant fruit and a little finesse.

🍇 Poulsard, Trousseau, Pinot noir

🍷 2–8 years

WHITE Simple dry whites that make an ideal accompaniment to the local *raclette* cheese dish.

🍇 Savagnin, Chardonnay

🍷 1–3 years

ROSÉ These dry rosés have a fine and fragrant *vin gris* style, with solid fruit.

🍇 Poulsard, Trousseau, Pinot noir, Pinot gris, Savagnin, Chardonnay

🍷 1–3 years

✓ *Château d'Arlay • Daniel & Pascal Chalanard • Domaine Grand Frères • Domaine Labet • Domaine Jean Macle • Domaine Morel-Thibaut • Domaine Rolet • Domaine des Roussots • Hélène & Jean-Marie Salaün • André & Mireille Tissot*

CÔTES DU JURA MOUSSEUX AOC

Probably Jura's best sparkling-wine appellation.

SPARKLING WHITE These wines have a persistent *mousse* of tiny bubbles, excellent balance, surprising finesse, and great potential.

🍇 Savagnin, Chardonnay, Pinot blanc

🍷 1–3 years

✓ *Bernard Badoz • Hubert Clavelin • Gabriel Clerc • Château Gréa • Pierre Richard*

CÔTES DU JURA VIN DE PAILLE AOC

These wines are made from grapes that are dried to concentrate the juice, after which fermentation is long and the wine is given up to four years in wood.

WHITE These very sweet wines have old-gold, honey-gold, and amber-gold colours; a full, distinctive, and complex bouquet; a powerfully rich and nutty flavour; and a surprisingly crisp finish, with a raisiny, apricot-skin aftertaste.

🍇 Poulsard, Trousseau, Savagnin, Chardonnay

🍷 10–50 (or more) years

✓ *Château d'Arlay • Domaine Berthet-Bondet • Durand-Perron • Jacques Foret • Domaine Grand Frères • Désiré Petit & Fils • Pignier Père & Fils*

CÔTES DU JURA VIN JAUNE AOC

For details of production and style, *see* Château-Chalon AOC.

✓ *Château d'Arlay • Xavier Reverchon*

CRÉMANT DU JURA AOC

This appellation was introduced in 1995. It can be used for any wine conforming to *vin mousseux* AOCs of the Côtes du Jura, Arbois, and L'Étoile, and may be applied retrospectively to any of these wines from 1991 on. Part of the "*crémantization*" of French *méthode champenoise* appellations, when most sparkling wines in the region are marketed as Crémant du Jura, the unwieldy bunch of *mousseux* appellations (*see below*) will be quietly dropped.

✓ *Marcel Cabelier • Jacques Tissot*

CRÉPY AOC

These wines are well known to the skiing set, who enjoy them after a day on the *piste*.

WHITE Light, dry, and fruity wines, with a floral aroma and a slight spritz.

🍇 Chasselas roux, Chasselas vert

🍷 1–3 years

✓ *Goy Frères • Fichard • Mercier & Fils • Georges Roussiaude*

L'ÉTOILE AOC

These wines are named after the star-shaped fossils found in the local limestone.

WHITE Light, dry white wines whose aromas reveal the scents of alpine herbs and bracken.

🍇 Chardonnay, Poulsard, Savagnin

🍷 1–3 years

✓ *Domaine Michel Geneletti • Domaine de Montbourgeau*

L'ÉTOILE MOUSSEUX AOC

Not quite up to the standard of Côtes du Jura Mousseux, but this *méthode champenoise* has more potential than Arbois Mousseux.

SPARKLING WHITE Domaine de Montbourgeau makes a fine-quality, dry, sparkling wine.

🍇 Chardonnay, Poulsard, Savagnin

🍷 1–3 years

✓ *Château de l'Étoile • Domaine de Montbourgeau*

L'ÉTOILE VIN JAUNE AOC

See Château-Chalon AOC

🍇 Savagnin

🍷 10–100 years

✓ *Château de l'Étoile • Domaine Michel Geneletti • Jean Gros*

MACVIN AOC OR MACVIN DU JURA AOC

Macvin, a *vin de liqueur*, is made by adding *marc* (local brandy distilled from the residue of skins) to grape juice, preventing fermentation.

RED Typical dull *vin de liqueur* aroma, sweet and grapey.

🍇 Poulsard, Trousseau, Pinot Noir

🍷 Upon purchase or never

WHITE This has a typical dull *vin de liqueur* aroma, and is sweet and grapey. This is the most oxidative Macvin style.

🍇 Chardonnay, Poulsard, Savagnin

🍷 Never!

ROSÉ Typical dull *vin de liqueur* aroma, sweet and grapey.

🍇 Poulsard, Trousseau, Pinot Noir

🍷 Upon purchase or never

✓ *Désiré Petit & Fils • Château de l'Étoile • Henri Maire*

MOUSSEUX DU BUGEY AOC

See Vin du Bugey Mousseux VDQS

MOUSSEUX DE SAVOIE AOC

See Vin de Savoie Mousseux AOC

PÉTILLANT DU BUGEY VDQS

See Vin du Bugey Pétillant VDQS

PÉTILLANT DE SAVOIE AOC

See Vin de Savoie Pétillant AOC

ROUSSETTE DU BUGEY VDQS

The following villages may add their name to this appellation, if harvested within an extremely low yield: Anglefort, Arbignieu, Chanay, Lagnieu, Montagnieu, and Virieu-le-Grand.

WHITE Light, fresh, and agreeable off-dry wines with few pretensions.

🍇 Roussette, Chardonnay

🍷 1–3 years

✓ *Jean Peillot*

ROUSSETTE DE SAVOIE AOC

The following villages have the right to add their name to this appellation, if the wine is 100 per cent Roussette: Frangy, Marestel (or Marestel-Altesse), Monterminod, and Monthoux.

WHITE Drier than *Roussette de Bugey*, these wines have fine, tangy fruit.

🍇 Roussette, Mondeuse blanche, plus up to 50% Chardonnay

🍷 1–3 years

✓ *Domaine Dupasquier • Michel Gisard*

SEYSSEL AOC

This is a favourite après-ski wine.

WHITE These are fragrant, dry, refreshing wines.

🍇 Roussette

🍷 1–3 years

✓ *Maison Mollex • Clos de la Péclette • Varichon & Clerc*

SEYSSEL MOUSSEUX AOC

It was Varichon & Clerc that first carved a niche for Seyssel Mousseux in the export market.

SPARKLING WHITE With a full, yeasty nose, fine *mousse*, and elegant flavour, the Royal Seyssel Private Cuvée is a yardstick for other producers.

🍇 Molette, Chasselas, plus a minimum of 10% Roussette

🍷 1–3 years

✓ *Royal Seyssel*

VIN DU BUGEY VDQS

These are often pure varietals. The following villages may add their name: Virieu-le-Grand, Montagnieu, Manicle, Machuraz, and Cerdon.

RED Fresh wines that range from the fruity Pinot to the rich Mondeuse.

🍇 Gamay, Pinot noir, Poulsard, Mondeuse, plus up to 20% (in total) of Chardonnay, Roussette, Aligoté, Mondeuse blanche, Jacquère, Pinot gris, and Molette

🍷 2–8 years

WHITE Off-dry, fresh, light, and gently fruity.

🍇 Chardonnay, Roussette, Aligoté, Mondeuse blanche, Jacquère, Pinot gris, and Molette

🍷 1–3 years

ROSÉ Light and refreshing dry wines.

🍇 Gamay, Pinot noir, Poulsard, Mondeuse, plus up to 20% (in total) of Chardonnay, Roussette, Aligoté, Mondeuse blanche, Jacquère, Pinot gris, and Molette

🍷 1–3 years

✓ *Cellier de Bel-Air • Caveau Bugiste • Eugène Monin*

VIN DU BUGEY CERDON MOUSSEUX VDQS

Only Cerdon may add its name to the Vin du Bugey VDQS for *mousseux* wines. They must be white and made by the *méthode champenoise*.

VIN DU BUGEY CERDON PÉTILLANT VDQS

Only Cerdon may add its name to the Vin du Bugey VDQS for *pétillant* wines. They must be white and made by the *méthode rurale*.

VIN DU BUGEY MOUSSEUX VDQS

These white wines are presumably *méthode champenoise*.

VIN DU BUGEY PÉTILLANT VDQS

These are mostly drunk in local restaurants.

SEMI-SPARKLING WHITE These are off-dry wines with a lively fizz.

🍇 Chardonnay, Roussette, Aligoté, Mondeuse blanche, Jacquère, Pinot gris, Molette

🍷 1–3 years

✓ *Caveau Bugiste*

VIN JAUNE D'ARBOIS AOC

See Arbois Vin Jaune AOC

VIN JAUNE DE L'ÉTOILE AOC

See L'Étoile AOC

VIN DE PAILLE D'ARBOIS AOC

See Arbois Vin de Paille AOC

VIN DE PAILLE DE L'ÉTOILE AOC

See L'Étoile AOC

VIN DE SAVOIE AOC

The wines in this generic appellation are produced to a high standard. The following villages have the right to add their name to the appellation: Abymes, Apremont, Arbin, Ayze, Bergeron (white Roussanne only), Charpignat, Chautagne, Chignin, Chignin-Bergeron (white Roussanne only), Cruet, Marignan (Chasselas white only), Montmélian, Ripaille (Chasselas white), St.-Jean de la Porte, St.-Jeoire Prieuré, and Sainte-Marie d'Alloix.

RED Blends and single-variety wines; the blended wines are usually better.

🍇 Gamay, Mondeuse, Pinot noir, Persan and (in the Savoie *département*) Cabernet franc, Cabernet sauvignon, (in the Isère *département*) Etraire de la dui, Serène, and Joubertin, plus a maximum 20% (in total) of Aligoté, Roussette, Jacquère, Chardonnay, Mondeuse blanche, Chasselas, Gringet, Roussette, Marsanne, and Verdesse

🍷 2–8 years

WHITE These dry wines are the best of the AOC, with Abymes, Apremont, and Chignin the best villages. All are fine, rich, and complex.

🍇 Aligoté, Roussette, Jacquère, Chardonnay, Mondeuse blanche, plus (in the Ain and Haute-Savoie *départements*) Chasselas, (in the Haute-Savoie *département*) Gringet, Roussette d'Ayze, and (in the Isère *département*) Marsanne and Verdesse

🍷 1–3 years

ROSÉ Attractive, light, and fruity, dry to off-dry rosés made for early drinking.

🍇 Gamay, Mondeuse, Pinot noir, Persan and (in the Savoie *département*) Cabernet franc, Cabernet sauvignon, (in the Isère *département*) Etraire de la dui, Serène and Joubertin, plus a maximum 20% (in total) of Aligoté, Roussette, Jacquère, Chardonnay, Mondeuse blanche, Chasselas, Gringet, Roussette, Marsanne, and Verdesse

🍷 1–3 years

✓ *Domaine Dupasquier • Michel Gisard • Claude Marandon • André & Michel Quénard • Charles Trosset • Château de la Violette*

Best single-*cru* wines:

✓ **Abymes** *Vigneron Savoyard* • **Apremont** *Domaine Raymond Quénard* • **Arbin** *Louis Magnin, Charles Trosset* • **Chignin** *André & Michel Quénard, Domaine Raymond Quénard* • **Chignin-Bergeron** *Louis Magnin, André & Michel Quénard, Domaine Raymond Quénard* • **Montmélian** *Louis Magnin*

VIN DE SAVOIE AYZE PÉTILLANT *or* MOUSSEUX AOC

These are very promising, single-commune, *méthode champenoise* wines, but unfortunately are seldom encountered.

SEMI-SPARKLING WHITE Wispy-light wines with an Alpine-fresh, clean taste.

🍇 Gringet, Roussette, plus up to 30% Roussette d'Ayze

🍷 1–3 years

✓ *Bernard Cailler • Michel Menetrey*

VIN DE SAVOIE MOUSSEUX AOC

These wines are very consistent and undervalued generic *méthode champenoise*. The Savoie does not have a sparkling-wine industry as such, although it most certainly has the potential to build one. The tradition of making the effervescent wines in this part of eastern France dates back to 1910, when two growers, Messieurs Varichon and Clerc, joined together to make sparkling wine in Seyssel (*see also* p.224) from the sparkling Rousette grape, the wines of which were naturally *pétillant*, just as the Swiss wines made from the Chasselas, just across Lake Geneva, were, and still are, today.

SPARKLING WHITE These dry and delicately fruity wines have a fragrant aroma, fine acidity, and a good balance.

🍇 Aligoté, Roussette, Jacquère, Chardonnay, Pinot gris, Mondeuse blanche, plus (in the Ain and Haute-Savoie *départements*) Chasselas, (in the Haute-Savoie and Isère *départements*) Molette, (in the Haute-Savoie *département*) Gringet and Roussette d'Ayze, (in the Isère *département*) Marsanne and Verdesse

🍷 1–2 years

✓ *Cave Coopérative de Cruet*

VIN DE SAVOIE PÉTILLANT AOC

A very consistent and undervalued generic *méthode champenoise*.

SEMI-SPARKLING WHITE Attractive, early-drinking dry wines with a gentle, light *mousse* and a fragrant flavour.

🍇 Aligoté, Roussette, Jacquère, Chardonnay, Pinot gris, Mondeuse blanche, plus Chasselas (in the Ain and Haute-Savoie *départements*), Gringet, Rousset d'Ayze (in the Haute-Savoie *département*), Marsanne, and (in the Isère *département*) Verdesse

🍷 Within 1 year

✓ *Dominique Allion • Michel Menetrey • Perrier & Fils • Varichon & Clerc*

AUTHOR'S CHOICE

While some critics, particularly French ones, would no doubt include a number of vins jaunes *in their choice of wines from these two districts, I most definitely do not. It is the* vins de paille *that excite me.*

PRODUCER	WINE	STYLE	DESCRIPTION	🍷
Château d'Arlay	Côtes du Jura Vin de Paille AOC (*see* p.224)	White	The most consistent and classic of all the *vins de paille*, Château d'Arlay has a firm structure and luscious, raisiny richness with a distinctive, nutty complexity.	10–50 years
Jacques Foret	Arbois Vin de Paille AOC (*see* p.223)	White	The creamiest and fruitiest of Jura's *vins de paille*.	10–50 years
Pignier Père & Fils	Côtes du Jura Vin de Paille AOC (*see* p.224)	White	A sumptuously sweet and creamy Chardonnay-dominated *vin de paille* matured in new oak for up to 24 months.	10–50 years
André & Mireille Tissot	Arbois Vin de Paille AOC (*see* p.223)	White	Gloriously midway between classic, firm nuttiness, and luscious, creamy fruit.	10–50 years

SOUTHWEST FRANCE

This region encompasses numerous small, scattered areas that combine to produce an impressively wide range of excellent-value wines with diverse, but quite discernible, stylistic influences from Bordeaux, Spain, Languedoc-Roussillon, and the Rhône.

AT THE HEART OF THE REGION lies Gascony, the great brandy district of Armagnac. It was from here that d'Artagnan set out in around 1630 to seek fame and fortune in the King's Musketeers. The narrow tracks upon which his eventful journey began still wind their lonely way around wooded hills and across bubbling brooks. Apart from brightly coloured fields of cultivated sunflowers, surprisingly little has changed since Alexandre Dumas painted such a vivid and colourful picture of these parts, for they remain sparsely populated to this day. Time passes slowly even in the towns, where the main square is usually completely deserted all day long, except during the five o'clock rush hour, which can last for all of ten minutes.

RECENT SOUTHWEST FRANCE VINTAGES

2000 Good reds, particularly in Madiran, and an excellent year for sweeter Jurançon.

1999 Extremely variable for all styles.

1998 Low yields made for excellent reds, which rival the 1995s (which in turn were the best since 1989), while Jurançon *vendanges tardives* and *moelleux* can be compared to the 1997s and 1995s.

1997 The sweeter styles of Jurançon are very good, on a par with the 1995s, which were the best since 1990. The reds, however, are merely average.

1996 Better than those of either 1995 or 1994, the sweeter styles of Jurançon have a richness and complexity that has not been witnessed since 1989. Very good reds all over.

SOUTHWEST FRANCE, *see also* p.55
This diverse region bridges the southwest corner of France. While it is mostly subject to the climatic influence of the Atlantic, areas such as Gaillac are also affected by the Mediterranean.

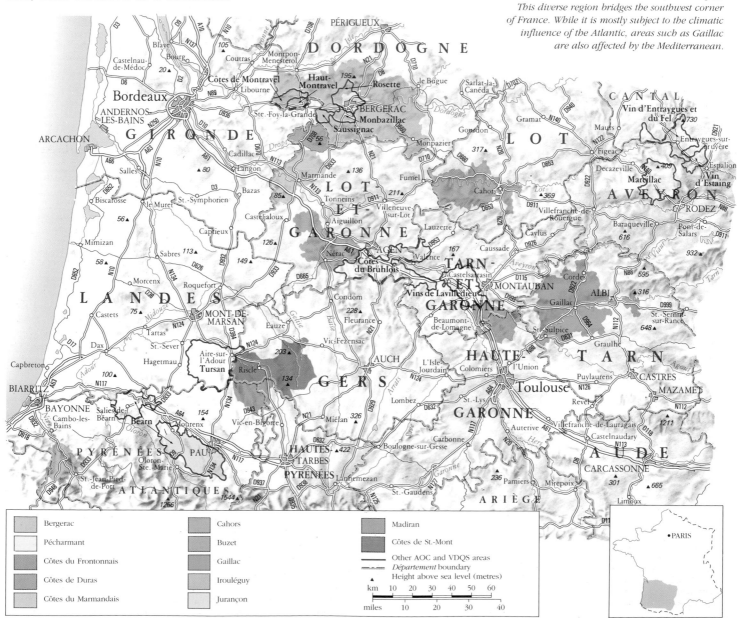

	Bergerac		Cahors		Madiran	
	Pécharmant		Buzet		Côtes de St.-Mont	
	Côtes du Frontonnais		Gaillac		Other AOC and VDQS areas	
	Côtes de Duras		Irouléguy		*Département* boundary	
	Côtes du Marmandais		Jurançon		▲ Height above sea level (metres)	

km 10 20 30 40 50 60
miles 10 20 30 40

• PARIS

CÔTES DE BUZET VINEYARDS
*This good-value Bordeaux satellite is barely 15 kilometres
(9 miles) from the Gironde département.*

FACTORS AFFECTING TASTE AND QUALITY

LOCATION
The southwest corner of France, bordered by Bordeaux, the Atlantic, the Pyrenees, and the Mediterranean vineyards of Languedoc-Roussillon.

CLIMATE
The climate of southwestern France is Atlantic-influenced, with wet winters and springs, warm summers, and long, sunny autumns. The vineyards of Cahors, Fronton, and Gaillac are subject to the greater heat but more changeable characteristics of the Mediterranean.

ASPECT
Mostly east- and east-through-to-south-facing slopes, affording protection from the Atlantic, in a varied countryside that can range from rolling and gently undulating to steep and heavily terraced.

SOIL
This collection of diverse areas has, not unexpectedly, a number of different soils: sandy-and-calcareous clay over gravel in the best vineyards of Bergerac; sandy soils on the Côte de Duras; calcareous and alluvial soils in the côtes of Buzet and Marmandais; gravel-clay and gravel crests over marly bedrock in the hilly hinterland of Cahors, and alluvial soils peppered with pebbly quartz, limestone, and gravel over a calcareous bedrock in the Lot valley; limestone, clay-and-limestone, and gravel at Gaillac; sandy soils in Madiran, Tursan, and Irouléguy; and stony and sandy soils in Jurançon.

VITICULTURE AND VINIFICATION
The viticultural traditions and vinification techniques of Bergerac, Buzet, Marmandais, and, to some extent, Cahors, are similar to those of Bordeaux. Other districts of this composite region have very much their own distinctive, individual practices: Béarn, Gaillac, and Jurançon produce almost every style of wine imaginable by many vinification techniques, among them the *méthode rurale* (known locally as the *méthode gaillaçoise*). Although the winemaking technique in these areas is generally very modern, the Basque district of Irouléguy remains stoutly traditional, allowing only the introduction of Cabernet sauvignon and Cabernet franc to intrude upon its set ways.

GRAPE VARIETIES
Abouriou, Arrufiac, Baroque, Cabernet franc, Cabernet sauvignon, Camaralet, Castet, Chardonnay, Chenin blanc, Cinsault, Clairette, Claret de Gers, Claverie, Colombard, Courbu blanc, Courbu noir, Cruchinet, Duras, Fer, Folle blanche, Fuella, Gamay, Gros manseng, Jurançon noir, Lauzet, Len de l'El, Malbec (*syn.* Cot), Manseng noir, Mauzac, Mauzac rosé, Mérille, Merlot, Milgranet, Mouyssaguès, Muscadelle, Négrette, Ondenc, Petit manseng, Picpoul, Pinot noir, Raffiat, Roussellou, Sauvignon blanc, Sémillon, Syrah, Tannat, Ugniblanc, Valdiguié

THE DIVERSITY OF THE SOUTHWEST'S APPELLATIONS

The Southwest does not have a single wine of truly classic status, yet it probably offers more value for money and is a greater source of hidden bargains than any other French region. From the succulent, sweet Jurançon *moelleux* and Monbazillac to the fine wines of Bergerac, Buzet, and Marmandais, the revitalized "black wines" of Cahors, the up-and-coming Frontonnais, the tannic Madiran, and the highly individual Irouléguy of the Basque country, this part of France represents tremendous potential for knowing wine drinkers.

Perhaps because it is a collection of diverse areas, rather than one natural region, the appellations of the Southwest seem at first numerous and confusing – even within one area there appear to be needless duplications. In Bergerac, for example, the dry white wines are reasonably easy to understand, since there are just two appellations (Bergerac Sec and Montravel). But there are three possibilities for red wines (Bergerac, Côtes de Bergerac, and Pécharmant), and a galaxy of sweet and semi-sweet appellations (Côtes de Bergerac Moelleux, Monbazillac, Côtes de Montravel, Haut-Montravel, Rosette, and Saussignac). When such a small and relatively minor area as Bergerac can develop so many different appellations, it is little wonder that a large and famous region such as Bordeaux has evolved into 50-odd appellations. It would surely be simpler to have a single Bergerac appellation to which certain villages might be allowed to add a communal name; if the same logic were applied throughout this region, more of its wines could achieve marketing success, rather than attracting only occasional attention as hidden bargains. With a more cohesive image and some enterprising wineries straddling the many different appellations, Southwest France should be at least as exciting as Languedoc-Roussillon has recently become. Flying winemakers have occasionally come to roost here in the last few years, but it will take a permanent New World winery for the exciting potential of Southwest France to be fully recognized.

THE APPELLATIONS OF
SOUTHWEST FRANCE

BÉARN AOC

This modest AOC shines in the local Basque area. Wines made in Bellocq, Lahontan, Orthez, and Saliès are allowed to add the communal designation Bellocq to the appellation.

RED Fresh, light, and fruity wines with a good balance, but lacking depth.

🍇 A maximum of 60% Tannat, plus Cabernet franc, Cabernet sauvignon, Fer, Manseng noir, Courbu noir

🍷 1–4 years

WHITE Light, dry, and aromatic wines.

🍇 Petit manseng, Gros manseng, Courbu blanc, Lauzet, Camaralet, Raffiat, Sauvignon blanc

🍷 1–2 years

ROSÉ Simple, fruity, dry rosés with a fresh floral aroma.

🍇 Tannat, Cabernet franc, Cabernet sauvignon, Fer, Manseng noir, Courbu noir

🍷 1–2 years

✓ *CV de Bellocq • Domaine Bouscassé (Château Montus) • Clos Guirouilh*

BÉARN-BELLOCQ AOC
See Béarn AOC

BERGERAC AOC

Ajoining Bordeaux, Bergerac produces wines that are sometimes mistaken for the modest appellations of its more famous neighbour. Its wines were shipped up to London as early as 1250. Supplies dried up after the Hundred Years War, which ended with the battle of Castillon, and Castillon-la-Bataille marks the ancient English–French boundary between Bergerac and Bordeaux.

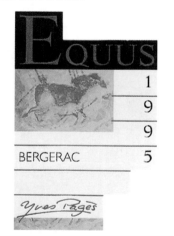

RED The best reds have a good garnet or ruby colour, fine fruit, and an elegant balance.

🍇 Cabernet sauvignon, Cabernet franc, Merlot, Malbec, Fer, Mérille

🍷 2–8 years

WHITE Mostly dry Bordeaux-style wines, but semi-sweet wines with up to 54 grams of residual sugar per litre are permitted. Until 1993, such wines had to be described as *moelleux*; however, as this is no longer compulsory, we will not know whether some of these wines are *moelleux* or not. Bergerac Blanc may be sold from 1 December following the harvest without any mention of *primeur* or *nouveau*.

🍇 Sémillon, Sauvignon blanc, Muscadelle, Ondenc, Chenin blanc, and up to 25% Ugni blanc (on the proviso that the quantity of Sauvignon blanc used is at least equal)

🍷 1–3 years

ROSE These are light, easy, and attractive dry wines. They may be sold from 1 December following the harvest without mention of *primeur* or *nouveau*.

🍇 Cabernet sauvignon, Cabernet franc, Merlot, Malbec, Fer, Mérille

🍷 1–3 years

✓ *Château Belingard • Château du Bloy • Château de la Colline • Domaine Constant • Domaine Grande-Maison • Château de la Mallevieille • Château le Mayne • Château la Plante • Château le Raz • Domaine de Richard • Château Tour des Gendres • Clos d'Yvigne*

BERGERAC SEC AOC

These white wines are distinguished from Bergerac *blanc* by having to be dry, with no more than four grams of residual sugar per litre.

WHITE Dry Bordeaux-style wines. They may be sold from 1 December following the harvest without any mention of *primeur* or *nouveau*.

🍇 Sémillon, Sauvignon blanc, Muscadelle, Ondenc, Chenin blanc, and up to 25% Ugni blanc (on the proviso that the quantity of Sauvignon blanc used is at least equal)

🍷 1–3 years

✓ *Château Belingrad • Clos la Croix Blanche • Château de la Colline • Domaine Constant • Château de la Mallevieille • Château le Raz • Château Richard (Cuvée Spéciale) • Château Tour des Gendres*

BUZET AOC

Formerly known as Côtes de Buzet, this super-value Bordeaux satellite is located on the northern edge of the Armagnac region.

RED The best are always very good, with considerable finesse and charm.

🍇 Merlot, Cabernet sauvignon, Cabernet franc, Malbec

🍷 3–10 years (15 in exceptional cases)

WHITE These dry whites are the least interesting wines in this appellation. They may be sold from 1 December following the harvest without any mention of *primeur* or *nouveau*.

🍇 Sémillon, Sauvignon blanc, Muscadelle

🍷 1–3 years

ROSÉ Ripe, fruity, dry rosés. They may be sold from 1 December following the harvest without any mention of *primeur* or *nouveau*.

🍇 Merlot, Cabernet sauvignon, Cabernet franc, Malbec

🍷 1–4 years

✓ *Vignerons de Buzet* (particularly Château Baleste, Château de Gueyze, Château de Pardère, and Baron d'Ardeuil) • *Château du Frandat • Le Lys • Château Pierron • Château Sauvagnères*

CAHORS AOC

The once-famous "black wine" of Cahors got its name from the Malbec grape, which, prior to phylloxera, produced dark, inky-coloured wines. The vines did not graft well to the earliest American rootstocks and Cahors fell into decline. Compatible rootstocks were developed, and with the introduction of the Merlot and Tannat, Cahors has started to claw back its reputation. The sheer number of good producers now makes Cahors one of the most reliable red wine appellations in France. Vieux Cahors must be aged in oak for at least three years.

RED Most Cahors wines have a deep colour with a blackcurrant tinge. They are full of fruit and have a good, plummy, Bordeaux-like taste, with a silky texture and a distinctive violet-perfumed aftertaste.

🍇 A minimum of 70% Malbec, plus up to 30% (in total) of Merlot and Tannat – Jurançon noir has not been permitted since 1996

🍷 3–12 years (20 in exceptional cases)

✓ *Château Bovila • Château la Caminade (La Commandery) • Château de Cèdre • Domaine de la Coustarelle • Clos la Coutale • Côtes d'Olt • Clos de Gamot • Domaine de Gaudou • Château Gautoul • Domaine des Grauzils • Château Lagrézette • Château Lamartine* (especially Cuvée Particulière) *• Domaine Pineraie • Château Quattre • Domaine des Savarines • Château du Souleillou* (Cuvée Diane) *• Clos Triguedina • Château Vincens*

CÔTES DE BERGERAC AOC

Geographically, there are no *côtes*; the only difference between this appellation and Bergerac is an extra degree of alcohol. The appellation Côtes de Bergerac Moelleux was withdrawn in 1993 (wines from this appellation must now be sold as Bergerac Moelleux), thus any wine bearing Côtes de Bergerac must now be red.

RED Should be richer than Bergerac AOC.

🍇 Cabernet sauvignon, Cabernet franc, Merlot, Malbec, Fer, Mérille

🍷 3–10 years

✓ *Château Belingard • Château du Bloy • Château de la Colline • Château Court-les-Muts • Château le Mayne • Château Panniseau • Château la Plante • Château le Raz • Domaine du Siorac • Château Tour des Gendres • Clos d'Yvigne*

CÔTES DE DURAS AOC

An appellation of increasing interest.

RED Light Bordeaux-style wines.

🍇 Cabernet sauvignon and franc, Merlot, Malbec

🍷 2–3 years

WHITE Clean, crisp, and dry wines, except for those designated *moelleux*, which must have a minimum of four grams of residual sugar per litre, although most good *moelleux*, such as Château Lafon, contain much more than this and are definitely sweet. With the exception of *moelleux*, these wines may be sold from 1 December following the harvest without any mention of *primeur* or *nouveau*.

🍇 Sauvignon blanc, Sémillon, Muscadelle, Mauzac, Chenin blanc, Ondenc, and up to 25% Ugni blanc (provided that the quantity of Sauvignon blanc used is at least equal)

🍷 1–3 years

ROSÉ These attractively coloured, dry, crisp, fruity rosés are firm and fresh. They may be sold from 1 December following the harvest without any mention of *primeur* or *nouveau*.

🍇 Cabernet sauvignon, Cabernet franc, Merlot, Malbec

🍷 1–3 years

✓ *Duc de Berticot • Clos du Cadaret • Domaine de Durand • Domaine de Ferrant • Château la Grave Bechade • Château Lafon • Domaine de Laulan • Château la Moulière • Château les Savignattes*

CÔTES DE MONTRAVEL AOC

This wine must have a minimum of eight grams and a maximum of 54 grams of sugar per litre in order to meet the requirements of the appellation. Any red wines produced here are sold as Bergerac AOC.

WHITE These fat, fruity wines are usually produced in a *moelleux* style.

🍇 Sémillon, Sauvignon blanc, Muscadelle

🍷 3–8 years

✓ *Château du Bloy • Domaine de la Roche Marot • Château le Raz*

CÔTES DE SAINT-MONT VDQS

Situated within the Armagnac region, the vineyards of this appellation extend northwards from Madiran. Wine production is dominated by the local *coopérative.*

RED Well-coloured wines of good flavour and medium body. They are not dissimilar to a lightweight Madiran, although they could become deeper, darker, and more expressive, if the *coopérative* were prepared to reduce yields and produce better-quality wine.

🍇 At least 70% Tannat, plus Cabernet sauvignon, Cabernet franc, Merlot, and Fer (which must constitute one-third of all the grapes other than the Tannat)

🍷 2–5 years

WHITE Fruity, dry wines with a tangy finish.

🍇 At least 50% Arrufiac, Clairette, and Courbu, plus Gros manseng, Petit manseng

🍷 1–2 years

ROSÉ Dry wines with a clean, fruity flavour.

🍇 At least 70% Tannat, plus Cabernet sauvignon, Cabernet franc, Merlot, and Fer (which must constitute one-third of all grapes other than the Tannat)

🍷 1–3 years

✓ *Producteurs Plaimont*

CÔTES DU BRULHOIS VDQS

Elevated from *vin de pays* in November 1984, this appellation encompasses vineyards along the Garonne immediately west of Buzet.

RED Decent, if unexciting, Bordeaux-like wine, though more rustic in style.

🍇 Cabernet franc, Cabernet sauvignon, Fer, Merlot, Malbec, Tannat

🍷 2–4 years

ROSÉ Fresh, easy-to-drink dry wine.

🍇 Cabernet franc, Cabernet sauvignon, Fer, Merlot, Malbec, Tannat

🍷 1–3 years

✓ *Château Bastide • CV de Goulens-en-Brulhois*

CÔTES DU FRONTONNAIS AOC

Situated just west of Gaillac. The wines of two villages, Fronton and Villaudric, are allowed to add their own name to the appellation.

RED These medium- to full-bodied wines have excellent colour and violetty perfumed fruit.

🍇 50–70% Négrette, up to 25% (in total) of Malbec, Mérille, Fer, Syrah, Cabernet franc, and Cabernet sauvignon, plus a maximum of 15% Gamay, Cinsault, and Mauzac

🍷 2–8 years

ROSÉ Overtly fruity wines.

🍇 50–70% Négrette, up to 25% (in total) of Malbec, Mérille, Fer, Syrah, Cabernet franc, and Cabernet sauvignon, plus a maximum of 15% Gamay, Cinsault, and Mauzac

🍷 1–3 years

✓ *Château Baudare • Château Bellevue la Forêt • Château Cahuzac • Château Flotis • Château le Roc*

CÔTES DU FRONTONNAIS FRONTON AOC
See Côtes du Frontonnais AOC

CÔTES DU FRONTONNAIS VILLAUDRIC AOC
See Côtes du Frontonnais AOC

CÔTES DU MARMANDAIS AOC

This successful Bordeaux imitation, upgraded from VDQS to AOC in 1990, is situated on the border of Bordeaux itself; its vines grow either side of the Garonne, on the left-bank Côtes de Cocumont and the right-bank Côtes de Beaupuy. Few French outside the region know anything about these wines, but the English have shipped them since the 14th century.

RED Fresh, clean, and impeccably made wines.

🍇 A maximum of 75% (in total) of Cabernet franc, Cabernet sauvignon, and Merlot, plus up to 50% (in total) of Abouriou, Malbec, Fer, Gamay, Syrah

🍷 2–5 years

WHITE These dry white wines are soft and delicious. They may be sold from 1 December following the harvest without any mention of *primeur* or *nouveau*.

🍇 At least 70% Sauvignon blanc, plus Ugni blanc, Sémillon

🍷 1–2 years

ROSÉ Ripe and dry wines. They may be sold from 1 December following the harvest without any mention of *primeur* or *nouveau*.

🍇 A maximum of 75% (in total) of Cabernet franc, Cabernet sauvignon, and Merlot, plus up to 50% (in total) of Abouriou, Malbec, Fer, Gamay, Syrah

🍷 1–2 years

✓ *Château de Beaulieu • CV de Beaupuy • CV de Cocumont*

GAILLAC AOC

These vineyards, among the oldest in France, have only recently begun to make their mark. In order to emphasize local styles, there has been a concerted move away from classic grapes towards different native varieties. Gaillac Liquoreux and Gaillac Moelleux are no longer permitted appellations, but such wines are still available under the Gaillac Doux appellation. The Gaillac Sec Perlé denomination for slightly *pétillant* dry white wines has been dropped (although Gaillac Perlé still seems to flourish), and the sparkling wines of Gaillac are now segregated by their method of production (*see* Gaillac Mousseux Méthode Deuxième Fermentation AOC and Gaillac Mousseux Méthode Gaillaçoise AOC).

RED Wines mostly made in the fresh, soft but light *macération carbonique* style. They may be sold as *primeur* or *nouveau* from the third Thursday of November following the harvest.

🍇 At least 60% Duras, Fer, and Syrah, plus Cabernet sauvignon, Cabernet franc, and Merlot – from the year 2000 Gamay has still been permitted but not mandatory, with a minimum of 20% each for Duras and Fer

🍷 1–3 years

WHITE Dry and fresh, these wines may be sold as *primeur* or *nouveau* as from the third Thursday of November following the harvest.

🍇 At least 15% of Len de l'El or Sauvignon blanc (or a blend of the two), plus Mauzac, Mauzac rosé, Muscadelle, Ondenc, and Sémillon

🍷 Upon purchase

ROSÉ Easy to drink, light, fresh, and dry rosés.

🍇 At least 60% Duras, Fer, and Syrah, plus Cabernet sauvignon, Cabernet franc, and Merlot – from the year 2000, Gamay has still been permitted but not mandatory, with a minimum of 20% each for Duras and Fer

🍷 1–2 years

✓ *Domaine des Bouscaillous • Domaine Jean Cros • Domaine de Labarthe • CV de Labastide-de-Levis • Manoir de l'Émeille • Château Montels • Mas Pignou • Robert Plageoles (Domaine de Très-Cantous) • Cave de Rabastens (particularly Château de Branes and Château d'Escabe) • René Rieux • Cave de Técou • Domaine des Terrisses*

GAILLAC DOUX AOC

These are naturally sweet wines that must contain a minimum of 70 grams of residual sugar per litre.

WHITE Sweet to very-sweet wines of ripe-peach, or richer, character.

🍇 At least 15% (each or in total) of Len de l'El and Sauvignon blanc, plus Mauzac, Mauzac rosé, Muscadelle, Ondenc, Sémillon

🍷 5–15 years

✓ *Domaine des Bouscaillous • Domaine de Labarthe • Manoir de l'Émeille • Robert Plageoles (Domaine de Très-Cantous) • René Rieux • Domaine des Terrisses • Domaine de Vayssette*

GAILLAC MOUSSEUX MÉTHODE DEUXIÈME FERMENTATION AOC

This is a sparkling wine made by the *méthode champenoise*. Expect to see a phasing out of the term *mousseux* on these and other Gaillac sparkling-wine appellations.

SPARKLING WHITE These wines are fresh and fragrant with a fine sparkle.

🍇 At least 15% (each or in total) of Len de l'El and Sauvignon blanc, plus Mauzac, Mauzac rosé, Muscadelle, Ondenc, Sémillon

🍷 1–3 years

SPARKLING ROSÉ Attractive, fresh, fruity wines.

🍇 At least 60% Duras, plus Fer, Gamay, Syrah, Cabernet sauvignon, Cabernet franc, Merlot

🍷 1–2 years

✓ *Manoir de l'Emeille • René Rieux*

GAILLAC MOUSSEUX MÉTHODE GAILLAÇOISE AOC

Sparkling wines made by the *méthode rurale*, involving just one fermentation, with no addition of a *liqueur de tirage*. The wine is bottled before the fermentation stops and no *liqueur d'expédition* is added prior to distribution, thus any residual sweetness is entirely from the original grape sugars. Styles include *brut* and *demi-sec*. A *doux* is also available, but is governed by stricter rules and is given its own appellation (*see below*).

SPARKLING WHITE These very fresh, fragrant, and grapey wines have a fine natural sparkle.

🍇 At least 15% (each or in total) of Len de l'El and Sauvignon blanc, plus Mauzac, Mauzac rosé, Muscadelle, Ondenc, Sémillon

🍷 1–3 years

SPARKLING ROSÉ These wines are attractive, fresh, and deliciously fruity.

🍇 At least 60% Duras, plus Fer, Gamay, Syrah, Cabernet sauvignon, Cabernet franc, Merlot

🍷 1–2 years

✓ *Château Clarès • Domaine Clement Termes • Jean Cros • Robert Plageoles (Domaine de Très-Cantous) • René Rieux • Domaine des Terrisses*

GAILLAC MOUSSEUX MÉTHODE GAILLAÇOISE DOUX AOC

This is a sparkling wine made by the *méthode rurale* (*see above*) from riper grapes (minimum of 11 per cent) than those of any other Gaillac sparkling-wine appellation, and with at least 45 grams of residual natural sugar per litre.

SPARKLING WHITE Not as exotic as, say, Clairette de Die Méthode Dioise Ancestrale, but delicious, grapey, and fragrant all the same.

🍇 At least 15% (each or in total) of Len de l'El and Sauvignon blanc, plus Mauzac, Mauzac rosé, Muscadelle, Ondenc, Sémillon

🍷 1–3 years

SPARKLING ROSÉ I have never come across a Gaillac Doux rosé, but if the white is anything to go by, it would be an interesting wine.

🍇 At least 60% Duras, plus Fer, Gamay, Syrah, Cabernet sauvignon, Cabernet franc, Merlot

🍷 1–2 years

✓ *Château Clarès • Domaine Clement Termes • Jean Cros • Robert Plageoles (Domaine de Très-Cantous) • René Rieux • Domaine des Terrisses*

GAILLAC PREMIÈRES CÔTES AOC

These are dry white wines, which come from 11 communes. The grapes must be riper than for ordinary Gaillac AOC and the wine must conform to the technical requirements of Gaillac Doux in all but sweetness.

✓ *Robert Plageoles (Domaine de Très-Cantous)*

HAUT-MONTRAVEL AOC

This wine must have a minimum of eight and a maximum of 54 grams of sugar per litre to meet the requirements of the appellation. Any red wines produced here are sold as Bergerac AOC.

WHITE Fat, fruity, and *moelleux* wines.

🍇 Sémillon, Sauvignon blanc, Muscadelle

🍷 3–8 years

✓ *Château Puy-Servain*

IROULÉGUY AOC

The local *coopérative* dominates this Basque appellation, which makes some of the most distinctive red wines in southwest France. Surprisingly, however, the production of rosé outweighs that of red.

RED These deep, dark, tannic wines have a rich and mellow flavour, with a distinctive earthy-and-spicy aftertaste.

🍇 Tannat, plus at least 50% (in total) of Cabernet sauvignon and Cabernet franc

🍷 4–10 years

WHITE These modest dry whites are the least interesting of this appellation.

🍇 Courbu, Manseng

ROSÉ This salmon-coloured, very fruity dry rosé is best drunk very young and fresh.

🍇 Tannat plus at least 50% (in total) of Cabernet sauvignon and Cabernet franc

🍷 Upon purchase

✓ *Domaine Brana • Domaine Etxegaraya • Domaine Ilarria (Cuvée Bixintxo) • CV d'Irouléguy (particularly Domaine de Mignaberry)*

JURANÇON AOC

The sweet version of this wine from the Pyrénées-Atlantiques was used at Henri de Navarre's christening in 1553 and is often sold today as *vendanges tardives* or *moelleux*. Most production is, however, tart, dry, and nervy, and sold as Jurançon Sec (*see below*).

WHITE The best wines have a fine, spicy, and tangy bouquet and flavour, and can hint of pineapples and peaches, candied peel, and cinnamon.

🍇 Petit manseng, Gros manseng, Courbu, plus up to 15% (in total) of Camaralet and Lauzet

🍷 5–20 years

✓ *Domaine Bellegarde • Domaine Brana • Domaine Bru-Baché • Domaine Cauhapé • Clos Guirouilh • Cru Lamouroux • Clos Lapeyre • Domaine Nigri • Clos Uroulat*

JURANÇON SEC AOC

This wine has to meet the same requirements as Jurançon AOC, but less residual sugar is allowed, and the grapes may be less ripe. It is best drunk young. These wines may be sold from 1 December following the harvest without any mention of *primeur* or *nouveau*.

WHITE If any wine in the world habitually has a certain nervousness, it has to be Jurançon Sec. Most lack any individual character that would make them stand out from other dry whites, and none has the complexity and richness of Jurançon's late-harvest wines, but the best can have an intensity that hints of grapefruit.

🍇 Petit manseng, Gros manseng, Courbu, plus up to 15% (in total) of Camaralet and Lauzet

🍷 2–5 years

✓ *Domaine Bellegarde • Domaine Bru-Baché • Domaine Cauhapé • Clos Guirouilh • Cru Lamouroux • Clos Lapeyre • Domaine Nigri • Clos Uroulat*

MADIRAN AOC

One of the most individually expressive appellations in southwest France, but there are as many disappointments as successes. Many domaines are trying new oak, and there is a trend towards more Cabernet franc.

RED You literally have to chew your way through the tannin in these dark, rich, and meaty wines when young.

🍇 At least 40% Tannat, plus Cabernet franc, Cabernet sauvignon, Fer

🍷 5–15 years

✓ *Château d'Aydie (including Domaine Frédéric Laplace) • Domaine Barréjat • Domaine Berthoumieu • Domaine de Bouscassé • Domaine Brana • Domaine Capmartin • Domaine Crampilh • Château Laffitte-Teston • Domaine de Lanestousse • La Chapelle Lenclos • Château Montus • Primo Palatum • Château de Peyros • Domaine Sergent*

MARCILLAC AOC

This rarely encountered wine from the northeastern borderlands was upgraded from Vin de Marcillac VDQS to Marcillac AOC in 1990, when greater focus was placed on the local Fer and Gamay – Jurançon noir, Mouyssaguès, and Valdiguié were disallowed.

RED Rough and rustic when young, these wines soften with age.

🍇 At least 90% Fer, plus Cabernet franc, Cabernet sauvignon, Merlot

🍷 3–6 years

ROSÉ Full, ripe, and attractive dry rosés that have expressed more individual style since the minimum Fer content has tripled.

🍇 At least 90% Fer, plus Cabernet franc, Cabernet sauvignon, Merlot

🍷 1–3 years

✓ *Domaine du Cros • Lacombe Père & Fils • CV du Vallon*

MONBAZILLAC AOC

An excellent value Sauternes-style appellation at the heart of Bergerac, these wines date back to 1080, when vines were planted by the abbey of St.-Martin on a hill called Mont Bazailhac.

WHITE These intensely sweet, rich wines are of a very high quality.

🍇 Sémillon, Sauvignon blanc, Muscadelle

🍷 7–20 years

✓ *Château Belingard • Château la Borderie • Domaine de Bosredon • Château Fonmorgues • Domaine Grande-Maison • Domaine de Pecoula • Château Treuil-de-Nailhac*

MONTRAVEL AOC

The largest of the three Montravel appellations and the only one that can (and must) be dry. Any red wines that are produced here are sold as Bergerac AOC.

WHITE Dry, crisp, and aromatic Sauvignon-dominated wines. These wines may be sold from 1 December following the harvest without any mention of *primeur* or *nouveau*.

🍇 Sémillon, Sauvignon blanc, Muscadelle, Ondenc, Chenin blanc, and up to 25% Ugni blanc (on the proviso that the quantity of Sauvignon blanc used is at least equal)

🍷 1–2 years

✓ *Château du Bloy • Château le Mayne • Château le Raz • Domaine de la Roche-Marot*

PACHERENC DU VIC-BILH AOC

New oak is being increasingly used in this white-only appellation, which covers the same area as Madiran.

WHITE Exotic floral aromas, a fruit salad of flavours, and a soft, flavour in off-dry (sold as *sec*), medium-sweet (*moelleux*), and sweet (*doux*) styles.

🍇 Arrufiac, Courbu, Gros manseng, Petit manseng, Sauvignon blanc, Sémillon

🍷 3–7 years

✓ *Château d'Aydie • Château Barrejat • Domaine Capmartin • La Chapelle Lenclos • Cave de Crouseilles • Domaine Frédéric Laplace • Château Laffitte-Teston • Domaine Sergent*

PÉCHARMANT AOC

These are the finest red wines of Bergerac; all but one (Saint-Saveur) of the communes in this appellation are also within the Rosette AOC.

RED All the characteristics of the Bergerac, but with a greater concentration of colour, flavour, and tannin.

🍇 Cabernet franc, Cabernet sauvignon, Merlot, Malbec

🍷 4–12 years

✓ *Château Champarel • Domaine des Costes • Cave du Fleix* (Domaine Brisseu-Belloc) *• Domaine du Grand-Jaure • Domaine du Haut-Pécharmant • Domaine de Puy Grave • Château de Tiregrand*

ROSETTE AOC

A white-wine appellation only. The wines must contain 8–54 grams of residual sugar per litre. Any red wines are sold as Bergerac AOC.

WHITE Château Puypezat has a soft and delicately sweet flavour.

🍇 Sémillon, Sauvignon blanc, Muscadelle

🍷 4–8 years

✓ *Château Puypezat*

SAUSSIGNAC AOC

A sweet-wine appellation; it must have a minimum of 18 grams of residual sugar per litre. Any red wines are sold as Bergerac AOC.

WHITE The best can be very rich, fat, and full.

🍇 Sémillon, Sauvignon blanc, Muscadelle, Chenin blanc

🍷 5–15 years

✓ *Château Court-les-Muts • Château les Miaudoux • Domaine de Richard • Clos d'Yvigne*

TURSAN VDQS

The reds rely on the Tannat, the same primary grape used in Madiran; the whites are essentially Baroque, a variety more at home in Tursan.

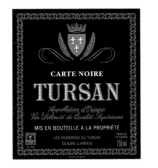

RED Rich, and chewy, or finer-flavoured and aromatic, depending on the dominant grape.

🍇 Tannat, plus at least 25% (in total) of Cabernet franc, Cabernet sauvignon, and Fer

WHITE The *coopérative* traditionally makes a full-bodied white with a solid, somewhat rustic, rich flavour, but it is gradually being influenced by the growing reputation of the wine made under the relatively new Château de Bachen label, which is far more aromatic and elegant.

🍇 Baroque, plus a maximum of 10% (in total) of Sauvignon blanc, Gros manseng, Petit manseng, Claverie, Cruchinet, Raffiat, Claret du Gers, Clairette

🍷 2–5 years

ROSÉ An unpretentious dry wine with good, juicy, fruit flavour.

🍇 Tannat, plus at least 25% (in total) of Cabernet franc, Cabernet sauvignon, and Fer

🍷 1–3 years

✓ *Château de Bachen • CV de Tursan*

VINS DE LAVILLEDIEU VDQS

Situated south of Cahors, this VDQS is a northern extension of the Frontonnais, with vines growing on a *boulbènes* soil that is similar to that of Bordeaux's Entre-Deux-Mers district. Production is dominated by the local *coopérative*, and the wines are seldom seen outside the locality.

RED Nicely coloured, medium-bodied wines with a fresh, fruity flavour.

🍇 A minimum of 80% (in total) of Mauzac, Mérille, Cinsault, Fuella, and Négrette (which must account for at least 35%), plus up to 20% (in total) of Syrah, Gamay, Jurançon noir, Picpoul, Milgranet, Fer

🍷 3–6 years

WHITE Dry, crisp, aromatic wines.

🍇 Mauzac, Sauvignon blanc, Sémillon, Muscadelle, Colombard, Ondenc, Folle blanche

🍷 1–3 years

✓ *Hugues de Verdalle*

VINS D'ENTRAYGUES AND DU FEL VDQS

This area overlaps the Aveyron and Cantal *départements* in the northeast of the region, but only a tiny amount is made and the wines are rarely encountered and never exported.

RED Light, rustic wines that are best consumed locally because they need all the local ambience they can get.

🍇 Cabernet franc, Cabernet sauvignon, Fer, Gamay, Jurançon noir, Merlot, Mouyssaguès, Négrette, Pinot noir

🍷 1–2 years

WHITE Light, dry, and crisp wines for unpretentious quaffing.

🍇 Chenin blanc, Mauzac

🍷 Upon purchase

ROSÉ Light, fresh, and dry rosés.

🍇 Cabernet franc, Cabernet sauvignon, Fer, Gamay, Jurançon noir, Merlot, Mouyssaguès, Négrette, Pinot noir

🍷 1–2 years

✓ *François Avallon*

VINS D'ESTAING VDQS

This area is contiguous with the southern tip of the above VDQS appellation and production is even more minuscule.

RED These wines are light bodied, attractive, and fruity.

🍇 Fer, Gamay, Abouriou, Jurançon noir, Merlot, Cabernet franc, Cabernet sauvignon, Mouyssaguès, Négrette, Pinot noir, Duras, Castet

🍷 1–3 years

WHITE These are unpretentious, dry white wines with a crisp flavour and a rustic, tangy style.

🍇 Chenin blanc, Roussellou, Mauzac

🍷 1–2 years

ROSÉ These pleasant dry wines are probably the most interesting in the appellation.

🍇 Fer, Gamay, Abouriou, Jurançon noir, Merlot, Cabernet franc, Cabernet sauvignon, Mouyssaguès, Négrette, Pinot noir, Duras, Castet

🍷 Upon purchase

✓ *Le Viala*

AUTHOR'S CHOICE

*There is such a diversity of styles in Southwest France that picking out my favourites
is a bit of a lucky dip, but I ended up favouring the dense, extracted reds
and the Southwest's relatively unknown late-harvest whites.*

PRODUCER	WINE	STYLE	DESCRIPTION	
Domaine Bouscassé **V**	Château Montus Cuvée Prestige, Madiran AOC *(see p.230)*	RED	This is a fabulously deep-coloured wine with an ample concentration of rich, firmly structured, oak-matured fruit. Château Montus is a separate property to Bouscassé, even though the label bears both names, and it is aged in new oak, whereas one-year-old barrels are used for the Madiran under the basic Domaine Bouscassé.	5–12 years
Domaine Bouscassé	Pacherenc du Vic-Bilh AOC *doux* *(see p.231)*	WHITE	A truly late-harvested wine, Domaine Bouscassé, which is the family home of owner-winemaker Alain Brumont, produces the most stunning, mellowed depth, and rich, honeyed complexity.	3–20 years
Domaine Brana **V**	Irouléguy AOC *(see p.230)*	RED	Although not as rough or as tough as the wines of this appellation usually are, this top-performing Irouléguy is just as dark and as deep, with more suppleness to the tannins, and marked by a distinctive, oak-driven complexity.	5–10 years
Domaine Cauhapé	Noblesse du Petit Manseng, Jurançon Sec AOC *(see p.230)*	WHITE	Whereas most producers use a blend of varieties for Jurançon, the best wines of Henri Ramonteu, the most innovative winemaker in the appellation, are often pure varietals. This is made from the Petit manseng, Jurançon's greatest grape, which is traditionally reserved for the sweetest and most expensive wines.	4–8 years
Domaine Cauhapé	Noblesse du Petit Manseng, Jurançon AOC *(see p.230)*	WHITE	The Petit manseng is the greatest Jurançon grape variety. The locals say "Petit manseng is the king, and the Gros manseng his page-boy", hence Henri Ramonteu's use of Noblesse for these varietals. This rich, unctuous dessert wine is fairly bursting with ripe peachy fruit and candied-peel complexity.	3–12 years
Domaine Cauhapé	Quintessence du Petit Manseng, Jurançon AOC *(see p.230)*	WHITE	Of all Jurançon late-harvest wines, Domaine Cauhapé is the richest, most luscious, and potentially most complex.	5–20 years
Château Gautoul **V**	Cuvée Prestige, Cahors AOC *(see p.228)*	RED	Since it was purchased in 1992 by well-known Parisian chef Alain Sendrens, this château has benefited from considerable investment and a quality-first philosophy, resulting in this brilliantly balanced, intensely flavoured Cahors of stunning finesse.	4–10 years
Château Laffitte-Teston **V**	Vieilles Vignes, Madiran AOC *(see p.230)*	RED	This is a big, rich, and deeply coloured red that gradually develops complex aromas to complement its slowly evolving, multilayered flavours with a long, very ripe, but heroically structured fruit finish.	5–10 years
Château Laffitte-Teston **V**	Erika, Pacherenc du Vic-Bilh *(see p.231)*	WHITE	Although this wine is a blend of Pacherenc's lesser grape varieties (Arrufiac, Courbu, and Gros manseng), through low yields and both fermentation and maturation in new oak, Jean-Marc Laffitte manages to produce a seductively rich, somewhat sweet white wine with oodles of creamy, exotic fruit.	5–10 years
Château Laffitte-Teston **V**	Pacherenc du Vic-Bilh *moelleux* *(see p.231)*	WHITE	This sumptuous blend of late-harvest Petit manseng and Petit courbu is aged in new oak. It is full of sweet, oaky fruit and has great length.	5–10 years
Château de Peyros	Le Couvent, Madiran AOC *(see p.230)*	RED	This top-flight Madiran is made under the auspices of the ubiquitous Professor Peynaud, who insists on manual harvest in *tries*, longer skin contact than normal, and maturation in small oak *barriques*, all of which virtually guarantees the impeccable quality of this blend of roughly half-and-half Tannat and Cabernet franc with a dash of Cabernet sauvignon.	5–12 years
Robert Plageoles	Domaine de Très-Cantous Vin de Voile Gaillac AOC *(see p.229)*	WHITE	As the Plageoles have been *vignerons* in Gaillac for half a millennium, it is not surprising that they know how to grow grapes or how to make make this luscious late-harvested wine, which remains remarkably pure and fruity for an extraordinary length of time in bottle.	10–20 years
Clos Uroulat **V**	Cuvée Marie, Jurançon Sec AOC *(see p.230)*	WHITE	Probably second only to Domaine Cauhapé in Jurançon, this particular *cuvée* has a long, satisfying, tangy fruitiness of tremendous finesse.	3–6 years

LANGUEDOC-ROUSSILLON

In recent years there has been an influx of Australian winemakers in this area of the South of France, who have bought up vineyards and built wineries, forcing up the quality and value of the wines that are produced. Their influence can only be for the good, but the French had started putting their own house in order long before the Australians began to arrive.

TEN YEARS AGO, Languedoc-Roussillon was already losing its image for cheap, but not-so-cheerful, plonk. A growing number of domaines began bottling their own wines and with the government *vins de pays* scheme that was already encouraging reduced yields and classic varieties, a new generation of winemakers had started to emerge as early as the late 1970s. By combining modern technology with the best traditional practices, including the use of some ageing with new oak, many exciting new wines had reached export markets by the early 1980s. As other growers realized the vastly increased prices that their pioneering neighbours were receiving, so more of them switched from selling in bulk to domaine-bottling, and it was this potential that attracted the Australians. It was the French who created the new-found pride that is so evident in Languedoc-Roussillon today, but perhaps the Australians have contributed to this by making the business of winemaking in this part of southern France so dynamic and forward looking.

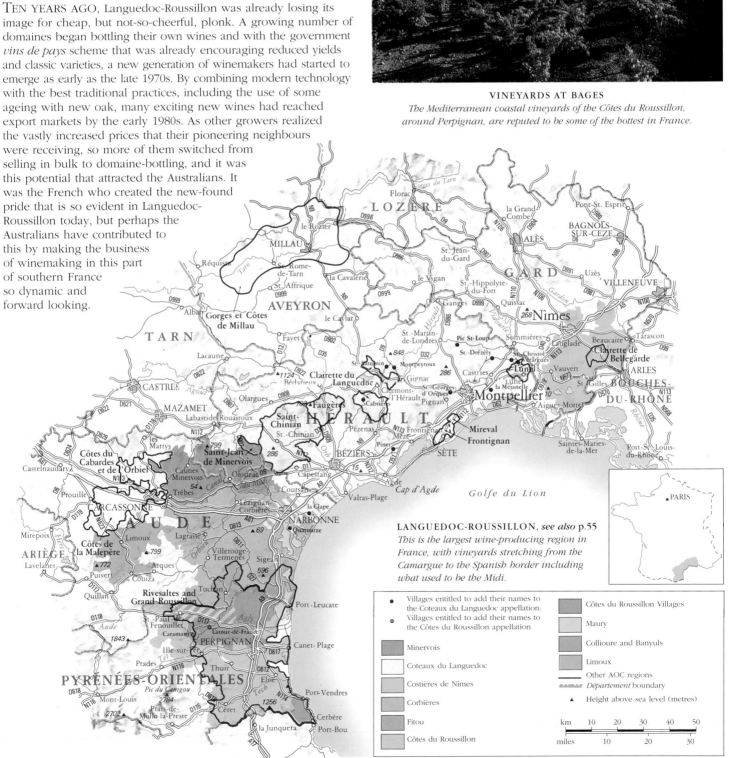

VINEYARDS AT BAGES
The Mediterranean coastal vineyards of the Côtes du Roussillon, around Perpignan, are reputed to be some of the hottest in France.

LANGUEDOC-ROUSSILLON, *see also* p.55
This is the largest wine-producing region in France, with vineyards stretching from the Camargue to the Spanish border including what used to be the Midi.

- Villages entitled to add their names to the Coteaux du Languedoc appellation.
- Villages entitled to add their names to the Côtes du Roussillon appellation

Minervois

Coteaux du Languedoc

Costières de Nîmes

Corbières

Fitou

Côtes du Roussillon

Côtes du Roussillon Villages

Maury

Collioure and Banyuls

Limoux

Other AOC regions

Département boundary

▲ Height above sea level (metres)

FACTORS AFFECTING TASTE AND QUALITY

LOCATION
A crescent of vineyards situated in southern France between the Rhône to the east and the Pyrenees to the southwest.

CLIMATE
The Mediterranean-influenced climate is generally well suited to the cultivation of the vine, although it is subject to occasional stormy weather. Two winds dominate: the cold and parching mistral, which blows down from the heights of the Alpine glaciers, and the wet and warm *marin,* which comes in from the sea and can cause rot at harvest time. There are many microclimates in this collection of isolated vine-growing areas.

ASPECT
Famous for its unending tracts of flat, *vin ordinaire* vineyards that stretch across the vast plains, the best sites of Languedoc-Roussillon, however, mostly occupy south-, southeast-, and east-facing *garrigues* and hillsides, or nestle beneath protective overhanging cliffs.

SOIL
In general terms, the plains and valleys have rich alluvial soils, while the hillsides are schist or limestone and the *garrigues,* or former moorlands, are comprised of stony, carbonaceous soils over fissured limestone. However, specific situations vary enormously.

VITICULTURE AND VINIFICATION
This remains the great *vin ordinaire* region of France, where everything is mechanized and the vines of the plain are farmed like wheat or corn. There is a trend towards developing single-domaine vineyards that have potentially expressive *terroirs,* growing classic varieties, combining various traditional methods with modern techniques. Limoux still practises the ancient *méthode rurale* – Blanquette Méthode Ancestrale AOC (*see below*), although the majority of the wines are pure *méthode champenoise* and sold under the new Crémant appellation.

GRAPE VARIETIES
Aspiran noir, Aspiran gris, Aubun (*syn.* Counoise), Bourboulenc (known in some areas as Malvoisie or Tourbat), Cabernet franc, Cabernet sauvignon, Carignan, Carignan blanc, Cinsault, Clairette, Duras, Fer, Grenache, Grenache blanc, Grenache gris, Lladoner pelut, Listan negra (the black version of Spain's Palomino), Malbec, Macabéo, Marsanne, Merlot, Mourvèdre, Muscat d'Alexandrie, Muscat blanc à petits grains, Muscat doré de Frontignan, Muscat rosé à petits grains, Négrette, Oeillade, Picpoul, Picpoul noir, Roussanne, Syrah, Terret, Terret noir, Ugni blanc, Vermentino (*syn. Rolle*).

THE APPELLATIONS OF
LANGUEDOC-ROUSSILLON

Note In the following entries, a wine described as a *vin doux naturel* (or VDN) is made from very ripe grapes and fortified with pure grape spirit after its fermentation has reached five or six per cent. It has the natural sweetness of the grape. To be labelled "Rancio" a VDN must be stored in oak casks "according to local custom", which often means exposing the barrels to direct sunlight for a minimum of two years. This imparts the distinctive *rancio* flavour that is so prized in Roussillon. Depending on the colour of the original wine, the wine technique used, and how long it has been aged, the style of the wine produced varies; it can be red/white/rosé or tawny.

BANYULS AOC

The most southerly appellation in France, the vineyards of this *vin doux naturel* are literally a stone's throw from those of Spain. The vines are grown on precipitous slopes of schist where man and mule have great difficulty in maintaining a foothold, mechanization is out of the question, yields are extremely low, and ripeness very high. You will often see "rimage" on labels; this word is derived from the Catalan "rime" or "grape" and refers to the vintage.

RED This is the deepest and darkest of all VDNs. A rich, sweet, red Banyuls (without too much barrel-age) has a chocolaty, bottled-fruitiness, which is the nearest France gets to the great wines of Portugal's Douro region. It lacks the fire of a great port, but has its own immense charm and after 15 to 20 years in bottle, a great Banyuls develops a curious but wonderful complexity that falls somewhere between the porty-plummy, dried-fruit spice of a mature vintage port and the coffee-caramel, nutty-raisiny smoothness of a fine old tawny.

⌛ 10–40 years

WHITE/ROSÉ/TAWNY Like all VDNs that may be made in red, white, and rosé style, they can all turn tawny with time, particularly "rancio" wines.

🍇 All wines: a minimum of 50% Grenache, plus Grenache gris, Grenache blanc, Macabéo, Tourbat, Muscat blanc à petits grains, Muscat d'Alexandrie, and a maximum 10% (in total) of Carignan, Cinsault, and Syrah

⌛ 10–20 years

✓ *Domaine de la Casa Blanca* • *CV l'Étoile* • *Château de Jau* • *Domaine du Mas Blanc* • *Clos de Paulilles* • *Domaine de la Rectorie* • *Cellier des Templiers* • *Domaine de la Tour Vieille* • *Domaine du Tragnier* • *Vial Magnières*

BANYULS GRAND CRU AOC

The requirements are the same as for Banyuls AOC, but a minimum of 75 per cent Grenache is required. The grapes must be destemmed and macerated for a minimum of five days and the wine matured in oak for at least 30 months. The wines are similar in character to those of the basic, although not at all ordinary, Banyuls appellation, but in terms of classic port styles, they veer more towards the tawny than vintage.

✓ *Cellier des Templiers* • *Domaine du Tragnier* • *Vial Magnières*

BANYULS GRAND CRU "RANCIO" AOC

See Banyuls Grand Cru AOC

BANYULS "RANCIO" AOC

See Banyuls AOC

BLANQUETTE DE LIMOUX AOC

Although this always has been a surprisingly good *méthode champenoise* wine for such sunny southern vineyards, the best Limoux have improved by leaps and bounds over the last decade, moving away from a somewhat rustic fizz to a much finer style, although not to the degree of finesse possible in a Crémant de Limoux. Some may regret its loss of individuality (more so for the Crémant appellation) and this is to a certain extent a true loss, but Limoux must adopt a more refined style if it is to compete in the international premium sparkling wine market. And let's not overstate the case, the best of these wines still retain a sufficiently distinctive style to stand out in any blind tasting. This has been assured by the Mauzac component, which rose from optional to a minimum of 90 per cent when the Crémant appellation was introduced.

SPARKLING WHITE These wines used to have the distinctive aroma of fresh-cut grass, but are now developing finer, more flowery, autolytic aromas.

🍇 A minimum of 90% Mauzac, plus Chardonnay, Chenin blanc

⌛ 1–3 years (up to 12 for vintages)

✓ *Antech* (Tête de Cuvée and Cuvée St.-Laurent) • *Domaine de Froin* (Au Temps de Pépé) • *Robert* • *Sieur d'Arques* (Diaphane Blanc de Blancs)

BLANQUETTE MÉTHODE ANCESTRALE AOC

Formerly called Vin de Blanquette, but still produced by the ancient *méthode rurale,* this wine was apparently invented by the monks at the Abbey of St.-Hilaire in 1531.

SPARKLING WHITE These succulently sweet sparkling wines are a hedonist's dream and should be far more commercially available. The ancient *méthode rurale* should be perfected so that prestige *cuvées* can be sold at a premium, allowing Limoux to capitalize on its historical value and individual wines' reputation.

🍇 Mauzac

✓ *Sieur d'Arques* (Dame d'Arques) • *Les Vignobles Vergnes de Martinolles*

CABARDÈS VDQS

An obscure appellation north of Carcassonne, these wines may also be sold as Côtes du Cabardès et de l'Orbiel, but as this hardly trips off the tongue, this shortened form is used.

RED The best wines have elegant fruit and a leaner, more Bordeaux-like balance than most of the warmer, spicy-ripe southern French reds.

🍇 At least 40% (in total) of Grenache, Syrah, and Cinsault (limited to a maximum of 20%), plus a 60% maximum (in total) of Cabernet sauvignon, Cabernet franc, Merlot, Malbec, and Fer, with up to 30% permitted until the year 2000 of Carignan and Aubun. Mourvèdre, Négrette, Picpoul noir, and Terret noir have not been permitted in these wines since 1992.

🍷 3–8 years

ROSÉ I have not encountered these wines.

🍷 Between 2–3 years

✓ *UC du Cabardès* • *Château de Pennautier* • *CV de Pézenas* • *Château Rivals*

CLAIRETTE DE BELLEGARDE AOC

When compared to all the best *vins de pays*, this appellation, which is dedicated to the lowly, intrinsically flabby Clairette grape, does not deserve to be a VDQS, let alone an AOC.

WHITE The two domaines below represent the soft, floral, modest height to which these unimpressive dry wines aspire.

🍇 Clairette

🍷 Before Christmas of the year of production

✓ *Domaine de l'Amarine* • *Domaine St.-Louis-la-Perdrix*

CLAIRETTE DU LANGUEDOC AOC

The appellation of Clairette du Languedoc covers three basic wine types. These are natural, fortified, and "Rancio". The "Rancio" must be aged in sealed casks for at least three years, and can be produced in both natural and fortified styles.

WHITE The natural wine is fuller and richer than Bellegarde, but has more alcohol and less sweetness in its "Rancio" form. The fortified version is off-dry to medium-sweet, with a resinous flavour that is stronger in "Rancio" character than the natural white.

🍇 Clairette

🍷 1–3 years for naturally fermented wines, 8–20 years for fortified wines and "Rancio" wines

✓ *Domaine d'Aubepierre* • *CV de Cabrières* • *Château de la Condamine-Bertrand*

CLAIRETTE DU LANGUEDOC "RANCIO" AOC

See **Clairette du Languedoc AOC**

COLLIOURE AOC

An obscure but exciting appellation for unfortified wines from normally harvested grapes grown in Banyuls, the eponymous wine of which is made from only the ripest, late-picked (but not botrytized) grapes.

RED These deep, dark, and powerful wines have a full and concentrated fruit flavour, with a soft, spicy aftertaste.

🍇 At least 60% (in total) of Grenache and Mourvèdre, plus a minimum of 25% (in total) of Carignan, Cinsault, and Syrah

ROSÉ I have not encountered these wines.

🍇 At least 60% (in total) of Grenache and Mourvèdre, plus a minimum of 25% (in total) of Carignan, Cinsault, Syrah, and a maximum of 30% Grenache Gris

🍷 3–15 years

✓ *Domaine de Baillaury* • *Château de Jau* • *Domaine du Mas Blanc* • *Clos de Paulilles* • *Domaine de la Rectorie* • *Celliers des Templiers* • *Domaine de la Tour Vieille*

CORBIÈRES AOC

When this appellation was elevated to full AOC status in December 1985, its area of production was practically halved to its current realm of 23,000 hectares (57,000 acres). The top estates often use *macération carbonique*, followed by 12 months or so in new oak and the results can be stunning. The only problem appears to be the difficulty of projecting any characteristic style, especially as there is such a great diversity of *terroirs* in the appellation.

This has led to the unofficial formation of 11 internal zones: Boutenac (central-north of Corbières, Mourvèdre apparently does well); Durban (wedged between the two hilly halves of Fitou, this zone is cut off from any Mediterranean influence); Fontfroide (extending from the northern tip of Durban to the eastern outskirts of Narbonne, this zone has a very low rainfall and is well-suited to Mourvèdre); Lagrasse (protected, limestone, valley vineyards immediately west of Boutenac); Lézignan (a low plateau of gravelly vineyards in the most northerly zone of Corbières); Montagne d'Alaric (northerly zone just west of Lézignan, with vines growing on well-drained slopes of gravel over limestone); Quéribus (most southerly zone, with vineyards on high, stony slopes); St.-Victor (the very heart of Corbières); Serviès (the northwestern perimeter, the wettest zone, with calcareous-clay soils particularly well-suited to Syrah); Sigean (the coastal strip of Corbières, where Syrah performs best); Termenès (the western perimeter, between Serviès and Quéribus, with the highest vineyards in the appellation).

RED These wines have an excellent colour, a full, spicy-fruity nose, and a creamy-clean, soft palate that often hints of cherries, raspberries, and vanilla.

🍇 A maximum of 40–60% (depending on location) of Carignan, a minimum of 25–35% (depending on location) of Grenache, Lladoner pelut, and Syrah, plus Mourvèdre, Picpoul, Terret, a maximum of 20% Cinsault, with Macabéo and Bourboulenc restricted to a proportion no greater than that of Carignan – Grenache gris has not been permitted since 1995

🍷 2–5 years (3–8 years in exceptional cases)

WHITE Soft, almost clinically clean, dry wines that have acquired a more aromatic character in recent vintages – Château Meunier St.-Louis is probably the best example – but many of the wines should be more expressive. There have been some successful experiments with oak-fermentation. These wines may be sold from 1 December following the harvest without any mention of *primeur* or *nouveau*.

🍇 A minimum of 50% Bourboulenc, Grenache blanc and Macabéo, plus Clairette, Muscat blanc à petit grains, Picpoul, Terret, Marsanne, Roussanne, and Vermentino

🍷 1–3 years

ROSÉ The best of these dry wines have an attractive colour and a pleasant, floral aroma, but are nothing special.

🍇 Same as for red wines

🍷 1–3 years

✓ *Château la Baronne* • *Château la Bastide* • *Château Caraguilhes* • *Château Cascadais* • *Château l'Étang des Colombes* • *Château Hélène* (particularly Cuvée Ulysse) • *Château des Lanes* • *Château de Lastours* • *Château Meunier St.-Louis* • *Val d'Orbieu* • *Château les Palais* • *Château St.-Auriol* • *Château la Voulte-Gasparets* (Romain Pauc)

COSTIÈRES DE NÎMES AOC

Formerly a VDQS called Costières du Gard, these wines have never been special, but most have been better than many a lacklustre wine from far more famous appellations, and in this respect Costières de Nîmes well deserved its promotion to AOC status in 1986, but since then the grape varieties permitted for all three styles – red, white, and rosé – have altered so radically that you have to wonder why they bother to have any controls whatsoever.

RED Simple, light, fruity wines are the norm, yet the best are round, aromatic, and spicy.

🍇 A maximum of 40% (each) of Carignan and Cinsault, a minimum of 25% Grenache, and at least 20% (in total or each) of Mourvèdre and Syrah

🍷 2–3 years (average wines), 3–8 years (better *cuvées*)

WHITE Fresh, soft, but uninspiring. These wines may be sold from 1 December following the harvest without any mention of *primeur* or *nouveau*.

🍇 Clairette, Grenache blanc, Bourboulenc, a maximum of 40% Ugni blanc and no more than 50% (in total) of Marsanne, Roussanne, Macabéo, and Rolle

🍷 1–2 years

ROSÉ Good-value dry wine with a delightful colour and ripe fruit. These wines may be sold from 1 December following the harvest without any mention of *primeur* or *nouveau*.

🍇 A maximum of 40% (each) of Carignan and Cinsault, a minimum of 25% Grenache, at least 20% (in total or each) of Mourvèdre and Syrah, plus up to 10% (in total) of Clairette, Grenache blanc, Bourboulenc, Ugni blanc, Marsanne, Roussanne, Macabéo, and Rolle

🍷 Within 1–2 years

✓ *Domaine de l'Amarine • Château Paul Blanc • Château de Campuget • Domaine le Grand Plaignol • Château Morgue du Grès • Tardieu-Laurent • Château Tuilerie*

COTEAUX DU LANGUEDOC AOC

This appellation consists of a collection of areas strung out across three *départements*, which gives rise to a variation in style, but the quality is remarkably consistent. After a decade of exciting red wine developments, it is now the time for white wines to buzz.

RED Full and honest red wines that make excellent everyday drinking. These wines may be sold as *primeur* or *nouveau* from the third Thursday of November following the harvest.

🍇 At least 40% (in total) of Grenache, Lladoner pelut, Mourvèdre, and Syrah, a maximum of 40% (in total) of Carignan and Cinsault plus up to 10% (in total) of Counoise, Grenache gris, Terret noir, and Picpoul noir

🍷 1–4 years

WHITE Getting better by the day, some wonderfully fresh, aromatic, dry white wines are being made by the appellation's younger *vignerons*, often with a little new oak and not infrequently from very old vines. These wines may be sold from 1 December of the vintage indicated without any mention of *primeur* or *nouveau*.

🍇 Grenache blanc, Clairette, Bourboulenc, Picpoul and up to 30% Marsanne, Roussanne, Rolle, Macabéo, Terret blanc, Carignan blanc, and Ugni blanc

ROSÉ These dry wines have good fruit and are far more enjoyable than many a pricey Provence rosé. These wines may be sold as *primeur* or *nouveau* from the third Thursday of November following the harvest.

🍇 Counoise, Grenache gris, Terret noir, Picpoul noir, Bourboulenc, Carignan blanc, Clairette, Macabéo, Picpoul, Terret blanc, and Ugni blanc

🍷 1–2 years

✓ *Domaine de l'Aiguelière • Henri Arnal • Mas Cal Demoura • Domaine Christin (Cuvée Tradition) • Domaine Guiraud-Boyer • Domaine de l'Hortus • Mas Jullien • Château de Lascaux • Château de la Négly • Val d'Orbieu • Domaine Peyre Rose • Prieuré St.-Jean de Bébian • Château Puech-Haut • Domaine St.-Martin de la Garrigue*

COTEAUX DU LANGUEDOC (VILLAGE NAME) AOC

Except where stated, the wines bearing the names of the following villages conform to the requirements of Coteaux du Languedoc AOC.

CABRIÈRES AOC

This is a single commune of steep schistous slopes in the centre of the Clairette du Languedoc sub-appellation. Cabrières' production is dominated by the local *coopérative*. This village produces mostly rosé; a fine, firm, and racy wine that contains more Cinsault than other Languedoc rosés. A little red is also produced, and its *vin vermeil*, so-called because of its vivid vermilion colour, is best known.

✓ *CV de Cabrières • Domaine du Temple (particularly Cuvée Jacques de Molay)*

COTEAUX DE LA MÉJANELLE AOC
See La Méjanelle AOC

COTEAUX DE ST.-CHRISTOL AOC
See St.-Christol AOC

COTEAUX DE VÉRARGUES AOC
See Vérargues AOC

LA CLAPE AOC

These red, white, and rosé wines come from vineyards on a limestone outcrop extending across five communes of the Aude *département* where the appellations of Coteaux du Languedoc and Corbières overlap. One of the only two whites allowed under the Coteaux du Languedoc appellation, it must be made from at least 60 per cent Bourboulenc and can be full, fine, and golden or firm, with an attractive Mediterranean spice. La Clape *blanc* is more expensive than the red, but the latter is easily best, with its full, rich favour and *vin de garde* style, while the rosé is refreshing, light and well worth seeking out.

✓ *Château de Complazens • Château Moujan • Château Pech-Céleyran • Château Pech Redon • Domaine de la Rivière-le-Haut • Château de Ricardelle de la Clape • Château Rouquette-sur-Mer • Domaine de Terre Megre • Domaine de Vires*

LA MÉJANELLE AOC

This appellation, which may also be sold as Coteaux de la Méjanelle, covers four communes in an area once part of the Rhône delta – river-smoothed boulders litter the vineyards.

ROSÉ Rosé is permitted, but La Méjanelle produces mostly red wines of a dark, rich, and well-structured *vin de garde* style and Château de Flaugergues consistently ranks as the best.

✓ *Château de Flaugergues • Château St.-Marcel d'Esvilliers*

MONTPEYROUX AOC

This village is located on shistous hills next to Saint-Saturnin, just north of the Clairette du Languedoc sub-appellation. The style of all but

the best of these red and rosé wines is firm and somewhat rustic, but they are honest and pleasing, and those recommended below rank among the finest in Languedoc.

✓ *Domaine de l'Aiguelière • Domaine d'Aupilhac*

PICPOUL-DE-PINET AOC

Covering six communes, this white-wine-only appellation, must be made, as the name suggests, from 100 per cent Picpoul, which in Pinet produces a lively young wine that quickly tires, and thus must be drunk as young as possible. Gaujal is undoubtedly the best.

✓ *Domaine d'Aupilhac • Domaine Gaujal (Cuvée Ludovic Gaujal) • Domaine de la Grangette*

PIC-ST.-LOUP AOC

Red and rosé wines from 12 communes in Hérault and one in Gard, all in the vicinity of the *pic* or peak of Mount Pic St.-Loup, including some high-altitude locations that must rank among the coolest vineyards in southern France. Permitted grape varieties for Pic-St.-Loup break from the norm – red wines must be made from a blend of at least two of the following: Grenache, Mourvèdre, and Syrah (no minimum or maximum restrictions), plus up to 10 per cent Carignan and Cinsault (Counoise, Grenache gris, Terret noir, Picpoul noir, and Lladoner pelut are not allowed). The grapes for rosé are the same, except that Carignan is excluded and as much as 30 per cent Cinsault may be used.

✓ *Mas Bruguière • Domaine de Cazeneuve • Clos Marie • Domaine de la Roque*

QUATOURZE AOC

These sandy soil vineyards just south of Narbonne overlap the Corbières appellation, but the wines, mostly red with some rosé, are rather stern and four-square, although the best can fill out and soften up with a few years in bottle.

✓ *Château Notre Dame*

ST.-CHRISTOL AOC

Just north of Lunel, the calcareous-clay soil of St.-Christol produces ripe, spicy, well-balanced red and rosé wines that may also be sold as Coteaux de St.-Christol AOC. The local *coopérative* dominates production.

✓ *Domaine de la Coste • Gabriel Martin • CV de St.-Christol*

ST.-DRÉZÉRY AOC

Both red and rosé wines are allowed under this village appellation north of Montpellier, but I have only encountered reds, and those have been of a very modest quality.

ST.-GEORGES-D'ORQUES AOC

Just west of Montpellier, the St.-Georges-d'Orques appellation extends over five communes and produces mostly red wines of very good colour, plenty of fruit, and no little finesse for this unpretentious Languedoc appellation. A small quantity of rosé is also made, the best having a bouquet of dried flowers and some summer fruits on the palate.

✓ *Château de l'Engarran • CV de St.-Georges-d'Orques*

ST.-SATURNIN AOC

Named after the first bishop of Toulouse, these red and rosé wines come from three communes in the foothills of the Cévennes Mountains, just

west of Montpeyroux, where deep-coloured, fine and full-flavoured red wines are possible, if not always evident. Production is dominated by the *coopératives* of St.-Félix-de-Lodez and St.-Saturnin, the former specializing in a pleasant, slightly *pétillant* rosé, while the latter makes a *vin d'une nuit*, a light-bodied red that has been macerated for only one night.

✓ *CV St.-Félix-de-Lodez • CV de St.-Saturnin*

VÉRARGUES AOC

Vérargues produces large quantities of quaffing, but otherwise unexceptional red and rosé wines from nine communes, four of which also constitute the Muscat de Lunel appellation. They are also sold as Coteaux de Vérargues AOC.

✓ *Château du Grès-St.-Paul*

CÔTES DU CABARDÈS ET DE L'ORBIEL VDQS

See Cabardès VDQS

CÔTES DE LA MALEPÈRE VDQS

Between the Razès *coopérative* and Domaines Virginie (Domaine des Bruyère), this is becoming one of the fastest-rising, value-for-money, superb-quality appellations in Languedoc-Roussillon. Why isn't this an AOC?

RED Well-coloured wines of medium- to full-body, with elegant, deliciously spicy fruit.

🍇 Up to 60% (each) of Merlot, Malbec, and Cinsault, plus a 30% maximum (in total) of Cabernet sauvignon, Cabernet franc, Grenache, Lladoner pelut, and Syrah

🍷 3–7 years

ROSÉ These attractive dry wines are totally different from the reds, due to the greater use and mellow effect of Grenache.

🍇 Cinsault, Grenache, Lladoner pelut, plus a 30% maximum (in total) of Merlot, Cabernet sauvignon, Cabernet franc, Syrah

🍷 1–3 years

✓ *Domaine des Bruyère • CV de Malepère* (Château de Festes, Domaine de Foucauld) • *Domaine de Matibat • CV de Razès* (Château Beauséjour, Domaine de Cazes, Domaine de Fournery, Château de Montclar) • *Château de Routier*

CÔTES DE MILLAU VDQS

Upgraded to VDQS in 1994 from *vin de pays* status (Gorges et Côtes de Millau), this appellation has yet to establish any characteristic style or reputation. There is no intrinsic reason why it should not, but with just 50 hectares (124 acres) under vine and one dominant *coopérative* (Aguessac), it will not be easy.

RED *Vin primeur* is a speciality.

🍇 A blend of at least two varieties, including a minimum of 30% Gamay and Syrah, plus Fer, Duras, and up to 20% Cabernet sauvignon

WHITE Very little is made and I have not encountered any.

🍇 Chenin blanc, Mauzac

ROSÉ Very little is made and I have not encountered any.

🍇 A blend of at least two varieties, including a minimum of 50% Gamay, plus Syrah, Cabernet sauvignon, Fer, and Duras

CÔTES DU ROUSSILLON AOC

Situated south of Corbières, this large appellation began to shrug off the sort of reputation that typified the wines of the Midi long before Languedoc. Although the latter region tends to grab most of the headlines these days, Roussillon still offers a tremendous choice of richly flavoured wines of exciting value and quality.

RED The best of these wines have a good colour and a generosity of southern fruit, with the tiniest hint of vanilla and spice. They may be sold as *primeur* or *nouveau* from the third Thursday of November following the harvest.

🍇 A blend of at least three varieties, no two of which may exceed 90% of the total, but since 1996 must include at least 20% Syrah and Mourvèdre, other permitted grapes being Carignan (60% maximum), Macabéo (10% maximum), Cinsault, Grenache, Lladoner pelut

🍷 3–8 years

WHITE The best of these floral wines are fat, but all too often lack acidity. They may be sold as *primeur* or *nouveau* from the third Thursday of November following the harvest.

🍇 Macabéo and Tourbat

🍷 1–2 years

ROSÉ Fresh and attractive dry wines, these rosés may be sold as *primeur* or *nouveau* from the third Thursday of November following the harvest.

🍇 A blend of at least three varieties, no two of which may exceed 90% of the total, but since 1996 it must include at least 20% Syrah and Mourvèdre, other permitted grapes being Carignan (60% maximum), Macabéo (30% maximum), Cinsault, Grenache, and Lladoner pelut

🍷 1–2 years

✓ *CV de Baïxas* (Dom Brial) • *Château de Canterrane • Domaine de la Casenove • CV Catalans* (particularly Château Cap de Fouste) • *Cazes Frères • Château Corneilla • Domaine Gauby • Château de Jau • Domaine Jaubert-Noury • Domaine du Mas Camo and Domaine du Mas Rous • Château Montner • Domaine Piquemal • Domaine de Rombeau • Domaine St.-François • Domaine St.-Luc • Domaine Sarda-Malet • Taïchat de Salvat*

CÔTES DU ROUSSILLON VILLAGES AOC

This appellation exclusively encompasses red wines from 25 villages along the river Agly and its hinterland, in the best area of the Côtes du Roussillon.

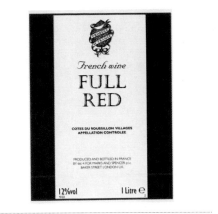

RED Just as good value as basic Côtes du Roussillon, the best can have even more character and finesse.

🍇 As for Côtes du Roussillon *rouge*, except with only 15% Syrah and Mourvèdre

🍷 3–10 years

✓ *SCA Aglya • CV de Baïxas* (Dom Brial) • *CV de Bélesta* (particularly Castel Riberbach Sélection Granite) • *Domaine de Casenove • CV Catalans • Domaine des Chênes • Mas Crémat • Clos des Fées • Domaine Força Real • Cazes Frères • Domaine Gardiés • Domaine Gauby • Domaine Piquemal • Domaine des Schistes • Maîtres Vignerons de Tautavel*

CÔTES DU ROUSSILLON VILLAGES CARAMANY AOC

This super-value red wine conforms to the requirements of Côtes du Roussillon Villages, except that at least 60 per cent of the wine (and all the Carignan) must be vinified by *macération carbonique* (this strange requirement stems from the fact that, in 1964, the local *coopérative* was the first in France to use this technique).

RED Simply the fullest, richest, and longest-living wines of Roussillon, despite the *macération carbonique*, which just goes to prove how useful that process can be when used to lift the natural fruit of a wine instead of dominating it with peardrop aromas.

🍷 3–15 years

✓ *CV Catalans*

CÔTES DU ROUSSILLON VILLAGES LATOUR-DE-FRANCE AOC

This is a fine-value red wine that conforms to the requirements of Côtes du Roussillon Villages. Virtually the entire production of Latour-de-France used to be sold to, and through, the national French wine-shop group Nicolas, which was a great advantage when this village obtained its own appellation, as its seemingly cheeky name was already known the length and breadth of the country.

RED Full in colour and body, these fine-value wines have a fruity flavour.

🍷 3–15 years

✓ *CV Latour-de-France*

CRÉMANT DE LIMOUX AOC

This provisional sparkling wine was introduced in 1989 to allow producers to decide the future name of their appellation: Blanquette de Limoux or Crémant de Limoux. The former relied primarily on the Mauzac grape and, on introducing the Crémant appellation, at least

90 per cent content of this local variety became compulsory. In contrast, the newly created Crémant de Limoux had a minimum content of Chardonnay and Chenin, albeit a more modest percentage. The choice was not merely about a name, but what direction and style the wine should follow. It was thought that Mauzac-based Blanquette de Limoux would take the slow lane while Chardonnay-influenced Crémant would be in the fast lane. By law, they should have made this decision by the end of 1994, but Crémant de Limoux did not take off as anticipated. Just a year before the deadline, only a 20th of Limoux's sparkling wine harvest had adopted the Crémant appellation. The lawmakers face a dilemma since two names are being used for one wine and there is much less support for the new appellation than expected. However, both styles deserve to exist.

SPARKLING WHITE Chardonnay tends to be the main base, with just enough Mauzac retained to assure a certain style, and Chenin blanc is used as a natural form of acid adjustment. The wines are generally more refined than Blanquette de Limoux and the best have a finesse that the more traditional products cannot match.

Mauzac plus a minimum of 30% Chardonnay and Chenin blanc (neither of which may exceed 20%).

✓ *Domaine de l'Aigle* • *Aimery* • *Antech* (Carte Or Prestige) • *Les Vignobles Vergnes de Martinolles* • *Robert* • *Sieur d'Arques* • *Héritiers Valent* (L'Evèche)

FAUGÈRES AOC

Although fair-sized, Faugères is an obscure and overlooked appellation, probably due to the fact that it was formerly known for *eau-de-vie* and fortified Muscat, with red wine a post-war development. Despite the similarity between the schistous, hillside vineyards and grape varieties here and in neighbouring St.-Chinian, the two appellations make distinctly different wines.

RED These rustic wines have a deep colour and are heavy with the spicy, warm flavours of Cinsault and Carignan.

3–10 years

ROSÉ Small production of attractively coloured, ripe, and fruity dry rosés. These wines may be sold as from 1 December following the harvest without any mention of *primeur* or *nouveau*.

All wines: up to 30% Carignan and Cinsault, plus at least 40% (in total) of Grenache, Lladoner pelut, Mourvèdre, and Syrah, of which the first two varieties must represent at least 20% (of the total blend) and the last two at least 15%, of which the Mourvèdre, must constitute at least 5%

3–10 years

✓ *Domaine Alquier* • *Château des Estanilles* • *Château de Grézan* • *CV de Laurens* (Château de Laurens, Cuvée Valentin Duc) • *Château la Liquière* • *Domaine Ollier-Taillefer*

FITOU AOC

When it was made an AOC in 1948, Fitou was fast asleep, but wine buyers beat a path to its desolate door in the early 1980s, making it the fastest-rising star in the Mediterranean firmament. It seems to have returned to its dozing state.

RED Even at the lowest level, these wines have a fine colour and a spicy warmth of Grenache that curbs and softens the concentrated fruit and tannin of low-yielding Carignan.

Carignan, Grenache, and Lladoner pelut must account for at least 90% of the wine (the Carignan being restricted to 75%), plus up to 10% Cinsault, Macabéo, Mourvèdre, and Syrah Terret noir

3–6 years (4–10 years in exceptional cases)

✓ *Bertrand Bergé* • *Caves du Mont-Tauch* • *Château de Nouvelles* • *Val d'Orbieu* • *Cave de Paziols* (Domaine de Cabrils) • *CV Pilote de Villeneuve-les-Corbières*

FRONTIGNAN AOC
See Muscat de Frontignan AOC

GRAND ROUSSILLON AOC

The largest appellation producing the least amount of wine, Grand Roussillon is a VDN that encompasses 100 communes, yet produces as little as 30 hectolitres (330 cases) of wine per year. This has nothing to do with low yields or a strict selection process – the appellation is apparently used as a sort of *sous-marque* or dumping ground for the inferior wines produced by the better VDNs within its boundaries.

Muscat (petit grains and Alexandria), Grenache (gris, blanc, and noir), Macabéo, Tourbat, plus up to 10% (in total) of Carignan, Cinsault, Syrah, and Listan

GRAND ROUSSILLON "RANCIO" AOC
See Grand Roussillon AOC

LIMOUX AOC

Until 1993, Mauzac was the only grape allowed for the still-wine version of Blanquette de Limoux, but new regulations reduced this to a minimum of 15 per cent and allowed the inclusion of Chardonnay and Chenin blanc. At the same time, Limoux became the first French AOC to insist upon barrel fermentation and some fabulous successes quickly established an enviable reputation for the Chardonnay-dominated wines of this appellation. The only question now is will Limoux have equal success with Chenin blanc?

WHITE Where the wines are merely still versions of Blanquette or Crémant de Limoux

blends, they are dull, although the best have a certain nervy appeal. Chardonnay varietals are sherbetty-fresh with a zesty style at minimum; the best are beautifully rich, with succulent, lemony-oaky fruit and mouthwatering acidity.

A minimum of 15% Mauzac, plus Chardonnay and Chenin blanc

✓ *Domaine de l'Aigle* • *Sieur d'Arques* (Toques et Clochers)

MAURY AOC

Despite the long list of possibilities, these fortified wines are mostly pure Grenache, a fact that is recognized by the gradual increase in the compulsory percentage of this grape – the minimum was just 50 per cent ten years ago.

RED/WHITE/ROSÉ/TAWNY Pale and intricate wines, they have a combination of tangy, toasty, berry flavours and nutty-raisiny richness.

At least 70% Grenache (a minimum of 75% from the year 2000), a maximum of 15% Macabéo (10% from 2000), plus Grenache gris, Grenache blanc, Muscat à petits grains, Muscat d'Alexandrie, Tourbat, and a combined maximum of 10% of Carignan, Cinsault, Syrah, and Listan Negra

10–30 years

✓ *Mas Amiel* • *Domaine de la Coume du Roy* • *Cave Jean-Louis Lafage* • *Cave de Maury* • *Maurydoré*

MAURY "RANCIO" AOC
See Maury AOC

MINERVOIS AOC

North of Corbières and adjoining the western extremity of the Coteaux du Languedoc, the rocky Minervois area has the typically hot and arid air of southern France. Elevated to full AOC status in February 1985, its vineyards are divided into zones and, as in Corbières, these are not official, but one day may become so: L'Argent Double (rough, rugged vineyards amid rocky outcrops in the arid heart of Minervois); La Clamoux (a cooler western area with a touch more rainfall than most Minervois zones, with Grenache and Syrah doing well, particularly on the higher altitude vineyards); La Clause (rugged, mountain climate and stony, *terra rosa* soil combine to produce rather rustic *vins de garde* in the north of Minervois); Les Côtes Noires (under a harsh mountain climate, these high-altitude vineyards situated in the northwestern corner of Minervois are better suited to the production of white wine rather than of red); Petit Causse (when it can get enough moisture, Mourvèdre does well on these baking hot, sheltered, limestone slopes in the arid heart of Minervois); Serres (very dry, stony vineyards over limestone subsoil, mostly planted with Carignan).

RED At worst, these wines are rough and ready for an AOC, but some of the best domaines also produce *vins de pays* that are better than the Minervois of other properties.

A maximum of 50% (40% as from 1999) Carignan, a minimum of 50% (60% as from 1999) in total of Grenache, Lladoner pelut, Syrah, and Mourvèdre (these last two must represent at least 10%), plus Cinsault, Picpoul noir, Terret noir, Aspiran noir

1–5 years

WHITE Less than one per cent of Minervois is white. A simple, dry, and fruity wine fermented at cooler temperatures than was once standard, it is now fresher and more aromatic.

Grenache blanc, Bourboulenc, Macabéo, Marsanne, Roussanne, Vermentino, plus up to 20% (in total) of Picpoul, Clairette, Terret blanc, and Muscat à petit grains, the last variety of which must not account for more than 10%

Within 1 year

ROSÉ These are good-value wines with a pretty pink colour, and a dry, fruity flavour.

As for red wines, plus up to 10% of white wine grapes

Within 1 year

✓ *Château Bassanel • Château Donjon • Domaine Domergue • Château de Gourgazaud • Château Maris • Domaine de Mayranne • Château les Ollieux • Château les Palais • Domaine Piccinini • Domaine Ste.-Eulalie • Domaine Tailhades Mayranne • Château Villerambert-Julien*

MUSCAT DE FRONTIGNAN AOC

It is claimed that the Marquis de Lur-Saluces visited Frontignan in 1700 and it inspired him to make sweet wines at Château d'Yquem, but Muscat de Frontignan is no longer botrytized – it is a fortified wine. Muscat de Frontignan may either be a *vin doux naturel* (VDN) or a *vin de liqueur* (VDL). In the latter, the spirit is added to the grape juice before any fermentation whatsoever can take place. If the label does not differentiate between the two, the small green tax mark on the cap should bear the letters VDN or VDL.

WHITE The VDNs are delightful, golden-coloured, raisiny-rich, sweet, and delicious wines that have a succulent, honeyed aftertaste with a somewhat fatter style than those of Beaumes, although many lack its finesse. The VDLs are much sweeter.

Muscat doré de Frontignan

1–3 years

✓ *Favier-Bel • CV du Muscat de Frontignan • Château de la Peyrade • Château de Stony*

MUSCAT DE LUNEL AOC

Situated on limestone terraces northeast of Montpellier, this under-valued VDN approaches Frontignan in terms of pure quality.

WHITE/ROSÉ Lighter than Frontignan, these wines nevertheless have fine, fragrant Muscat aromas of great delicacy and length.

Muscat blanc à petits grains, Muscat rosé à petits gains

1–3 years

✓ *Château du Grès St-Paul • Lacoste and CV du Muscat de Lunel*

MUSCAT DE MIREVAL AOC

This is a little-seen VDN appellation.

WHITE Light and sweet wines that can have a better balance and (relatively) more acidity than those from neighbouring Frontignan. Mireval wines can have more elegance although they may lack the raisiny-rich concentration.

Muscat blanc à petits grains

1–3 years

✓ *Domaine de la Capelle • Domaine du Mas Neuf • Domaine du Moulinas • Mas du Pigeonnier and CV Rabelais*

MUSCAT DE RIVESALTES AOC

This appellation should not be confused with the blended Rivesaltes VDNs that bear no mention of the Muscat grape.

WHITE/ROSÉ Rich, ripe, grapey-raisiny wines that are very consistent in quality.

Muscat blanc à petits grains, Muscat d'Alexandrie

1–3 years

✓ *CV de Baïxas* (Dom Brial) *• Bobé • Domaine Boudau • Cazes Frères • Château Corneilla • Domaine Força Real • Château de Jau • Domaine Mas Canclaux • Caves du Mont-Tauch • Château de Nouvelles • Vignerons de Rivesaltes* (Domaine Lacroix, Arnaud de Villeneuve) *• Domaine de Rozès • Domaine Sarda-Malet*

MUSCAT DE ST.-JEAN-DE-MINERVOIS AOC

This tiny sub-appellation of Minervois produces a little *vin doux naturel* that used to be grossly underrated but has gained excellent distribution on export markets over the last five years.

WHITE/ROSÉ These golden wines have a balanced sweetness and an apricoty flavour.

Muscat blanc à petits grains, Muscat rosé à petits grains

1–3 years

✓ *Domaine de Barroubio • CV de St.-Jean-de-Minervois • Domaine Simon*

RIVESALTES AOC

This appellation represents half of the *Vin Doux Naturel* produced in France.

RED The warm, brick-red glow of these wines belies their astringent-sweet, chocolate, and cherry-liqueur flavour and drying, tannic finish.

10–40 years

WHITE/ROSÉ/TAWNY Because much of the red version can be lightened after lengthy maturation in wood, all Rivesaltes eventually merge into one tawny style with time.

The whites do not, of course, have any tannic astringency and are more oxidative and raisiny, with a resinous, candied-peel character.

All wines: Muscat blanc à petits grains, Muscat d'Alexandrie, Grenache, Grenache gris, Grenache blanc, Macabéo, Tourbat, plus a combined maximum of 10% of Carignan, Cinsault, Syrah, and Palomino

10–20 years

✓ *CV de Baïxas* (Dom Brial) *• Domaine des Chênes • Domaine Força Real • Cazes Frères • Château Corneilla • Château de Jau • Domaine Piquemal • Domaine Sarda-Malet*

RIVESALTES "RANCIO" AOC

See Rivesaltes AOC

ST.-CHINIAN AOC

Upgraded from VDQS in May 1982, the excellent-value appellation of St.-Chinian is the nearest that native southern French grapes come to resembling Bordeaux. Similar grapes from comparable schistous hillsides in neighbouring Faugères make an entirely different, far more rustic wine that lacks the finesse of St.-Chinian, let alone Bordeaux.

RED Relatively light in colour and weight, these wines have an elegance that belies their Mediterranean origin.

2–6 years

ROSÉ These dry and delicately fruity rosés have an attractive, fragrant bouquet and flavour. They may be sold from 1 December following the harvest without any mention of *primeur* or *nouveau*.

All wines: at least 50% (in total) of Grenache, Lladoner pelut, Mourvèdre, and Syrah, plus a maximum of 40% Carignan and no more than 30% Cinsault

1–3 years

✓ *Clos Bagatelle • Mas Canet Valette • Château Cazal-Viel • Château Coujan • Domaine des Jougla • Château Milhau-Lacugue • CV du Rieu-Berlou • CV de Roquebrun • Val d'Orbieu* (Château St.-Celse)

VIN DE FRONTIGNAN AOC

See Muscat de Frontignan AOC

AUTHOR'S CHOICE

There is such a huge diversity of style, quality, and price in Languedoc-Roussillon today that any selection could be doubled. The pace of change is speeding up rather than slowing down, so while the wines recommended should remain top quality, there will continue to be plenty of competition.

PRODUCER	WINE	STYLE	DESCRIPTION	🍷
Domaine de l'Aigle Ⓥ	Limoux AOC (*see* p.238)	WHITE	Made from low-yield, hand-harvested grapes, which are whole-bunch pressed and 100 per cent barrel-fermented, this is the richest, creamiest Limoux Chardonnay on the market, with beautifully ripe acidity for everlasting freshness.	2–5 years
Domaine de l'Amarine Ⓥ	Cuvée des Bernis, Costières de Nîmes AOC (*see* p.236)	RED	This *cuvée*'s wickedly fat, ripe fruit, with an attractive hint of spice and oak, makes it dangerously easy to drink when young.	2–5 years
Domaine des Bruyère Ⓥ	Côtes de Malepère VDQS (*see* p.237)	RED	Rich, coconutty fruit wrapped up in supple tannins with a hint of mint on the finish make this one of France's best wine bargains.	2–4 years
L'Étoile	Grand Réserve, Banyuls AOC (*see* p.234)	RED	A luscious and long wine, with a rich Christmas-cake flavour, Demerara sweetness, and a smooth toffee-coffee finish.	15–30 years
Cazes Frères	Muscat de Rivesaltes AOC (*see* p.239)	WHITE	This is quite simply the freshest and most luscious of all Muscat de Rivesaltes. Drink it as young as possible.	Upon purchase
Château Hélène Ⓥ	Cuvée Ulysse, Corbières AOC (*see* p.235)	RED	If you like oak to hit you between the eyes, then this is for you. It has more than enough fruit to overcome the *woomph* of oak and has a fine tannin structure, which makes it very flexible with food.	5–8 years
Domaine de l'Hortus Ⓥ	Classique, Coteaux du Languedoc AOC (*see* p.236)	RED	This soft, rich and smooth wine has an elegant tannin balance with fat, ripe, sweet fruit, and a long finish of no little finesse.	2–5 years
Domaine du Mas Blanc	Vieilles Vignes, Banyuls AOC (*see* p.234)	RED	The wines of Dr André Parcé, the most famous producer in Banyuls, are by far the most expensive in that area, but they are worth the price for their sheer intensity and complexity of flavour.	15–30 years
Domaine du Mas Blanc	Collioure AOC (*see* p.235)	RED	Dr. André Parcé also produces the most expensive Collioure in Banyuls. This unfortified wine is massively coloured, structured, and flavoured and should ideally be aged for at least ten years.	5–20 years
Mas Jullien	Depierre and Cailloutis, Coteaux du Languedoc AOC (*see* p.236)	RED	Two of the finest Coteaux du Languedoc, both show a lovely depth of colour and intense, ripe, summer-fruit flavours, but the Depierre is for drinking, while the Cailloutis is for keeping.	3–5 years
Mas Jullien Ⓥ	Les Cépages Obiliées, Coteaux du Languedoc AOC (*see* p.236)	WHITE	This is a dry, aromatic, and exotic white wine made from Terret, Carignan blanc, and Grenache blanc grapes, grown on very old vines at very low yield and fermented in new oak.	1–3 years
Château Pech Redon Ⓥ	Coteaux du Languedoc, La Clape AOC (*see* p.236)	RED	This wine has an absolutely delightful fruit underpinned by bubble-gum oak to create a sort of raspberry-ripple effect. The result is an elegant, classy wine for its price and provenance.	3–6 years
Domaine de Rozès Ⓥ	Muscat de Rivesaltes AOC (*see* p.239)	WHITE	This wine has an amazingly fresh and billowy Muscat aroma followed by lusciously rich, intensely sweet fruit.	Upon purchase
Domaine St.-François Ⓥ	Côtes du Roussillon AOC (*see* p.237)	RED	This elegant, medium- to full-bodied red has lots of lovely, silky, blackcurrant fruit, making it ideal for both sipping and partnering food at a truly bargain price.	3–6 years
Sieur d'Arques Ⓥ	Toques et Clochers, Autan and Haute-Vallée, Limoux AOC (*see* p.238)	WHITE	Even the basic Chardonnay *cuvée* has lovely, rich fruit, but the single-*climat* wines show extraordinary finesse and intensity. In particular, the Haute-Vallée is superior to most *premier cru* Burgundies.	2–5 years
Domaine de Terre Megre Ⓥ	Les Dolomies, Coteaux du Languedoc, La Clape AOC (*see* p.236)	RED	In good vintages, this is a delicious, claret-style Coteaux du Languedoc with a quite extraordinary depth and finesse of blackcurranty fruit, the like of which you would have to pay at least twice the price for from Bordeaux itself.	3–6 years
Château de la Tuilerie Ⓥ	Costières de Nîmes AOC (*see* p.236)	ROSÉ	This dry rosé is full of fresh, mouthwatering, tropical-fruit flavours and can hold my interest sufficiently to plough through a bottle or two.	Upon purchase
Vignerons de Rivesaltes Ⓥ	Arnaud de Villeneuve, Muscat de Rivesaltes (*see* p.239)	WHITE	Beautifully made wine with elegant, musky aromas and deliciously rich, pure, succulent fruit showing the most enchanting balance.	Upon purchase

PROVENCE AND CORSICA

*If any wine does not travel, it has to be Provence rosé.
However, it is the romance surrounding the wine,
rather than the wine itself, that does not travel. If you
could take the blazing sun and care-free atmosphere
home in a bottle, the wine would taste much better.*

YOU CAN FORGET MOST PROVENCE ROSÉ. It may come in an
exotically-shaped bottle, but exotic is the last word that could be
used to describe its dull, flabby contents. They have been making
wine here for more than 2,600 years and by the time the Romans
arrived, in 125BC, it was already so good that they immediately
exported it back to Rome, but ask yourself this question: do you
think that wine was a rosé? Of course not; Provence Rosé is a
relatively recent phenomenon and, some would cynically say,
one that was deliberately designed to swindle the gold-draped
nouveau riche who flock here.

Rosé still represents more than half of all Provençal production,
although sales of rosé have declined in recent years, as the once-
exclusive resorts become more accessible to the sophisticated
middle classes, who recognize how dull these wines are. Quality
improved in the 1980s, but has reached a plateau and without
resorting to actually acidifying the wines, modern vinification
techniques will never be able to rid these wines of the dusty-
flabbiness that is their sunny southern heritage.

THE TRUE CLASSIC WINES OF PROVENCE
For most people Provence evokes the beaches of St.-Tropez or
the rich, *bouillabaisse*-laden aromas of back-street Marseilles, but
there are other experiences to be had in this sun-blessed corner
of southern France. For while the wines of Provence may not
have the classic status of Burgundy or Bordeaux, the reds, such as
the magnificent Bandol, the darkly promising Bellet, and the aptly
named Cassis, have an abundance of spice-charged flavours that
show more than a touch of class. Silly-shaped bottles are being

discarded by the more serious winemakers who find the classic,
understated lines of Bordeaux- and Burgundy-style bottles better
reflect the quality of their wines.

The top estates of the Riviera produce red wines of a far
more serious calibre than might be expected from an area better
known for its play than its work. Maximum yields are low,
however, and the potential for quality can be high. The smaller
AOCs of Bandol, Bellet, and Palette are restricted to a maximum
of 40 hectolitres per hectare (180 cases per acre), which is very
modest for a region that could easily average more than double
this amount. Even the all-embracing AOCs of Côtes de Provence
and Coteaux d'Aix-en-Provence are absolutely full of fine
vineyards capable of producing the exciting red wine that
must surely be Provence's future.

CORSICA – "THE ISLE OF BEAUTY"
In Corsica, the advent of France's *vin de pays* system meant
that one-third of its vineyards were uprooted and put to better
use. If the *vin de pays* system was intended to encourage the
production of superior-quality wines from the bottom of the

FACTORS AFFECTING TASTE AND QUALITY

LOCATION
Provence is situated in the
southeast of France, between the
Rhône delta and the Italian border.
A further 110 km (68 miles)
southeast lies Corsica.

CLIMATE
Winters are mild, as are
springs, which can also be humid.
Summers are hot and stretch into
long, sunny autumns. A vine
requires 1,300 hours of sunshine in
one growing season – 1,500 hours
is preferable, but in Provence, it
luxuriates in an average of 3,000
hours. The close proximity of the
Mediterranean, however, is also
capable of inducing sharp
fluctuations in the weather. Rain
is spread over a limited number
of days in autumn and winter.

ASPECT
The vineyards run down
hillsides and on to the plains.

SOIL
The geology of Provence is
complex. Many ancient soils have
undergone chemical changes and
numerous new soils have been
created. Sand, red sandstone, and
granite are, however, the most
regular common denominators,
with limestone outcrops that often
determine the extent of superior
terroirs: the Var *département* has
mica-schist, chalky scree, and
chalky tufa as well as granite
hillsides; there are excellent flinty-
limestone soils at Bandol; and
pudding stones (conglomerate
pebbles) that are rich in flint at
Bellet. The south of Corsica is
mostly granite, while the north
is schistous, with a few limestone
outcrops and deposits of sandy
and alluvial soils in between.

VITICULTURE AND
VINIFICATION
All the vines used to be planted in
gobelet fashion, but most are now
trained on wires. The recent trend
towards Cabernet sauvignon has
stopped; although many excellent
wines are still made from this
grape. The current vogue is to re-
establish a true Provençal identity
by relying exclusively (where
possible) on local varieties and
the laws have been changed to
encourage this particular evolution.
Much of the rosé has been
improved by modern cool-
vinification techniques, although
most remains tired and flabby.

GRAPE VARIETIES
Aragnan, Aramon, Aramon
gris, Barbarossa, Barbaroux,
Barbaroux rosé, Bourboulenc,
Braquet, Brun-Fourcat, Cabernet
sauvignon, Calitor (*syn.*
Pecoui-touar), Carignan, Castets,
Chardonnay, Cinsault (*syn.* Plant
d'Arles), Clairette, Clairette à gros
grains, Clairette à petits grains,
Clairette de Trans, Colombard,
Counoise, Doucillon, Durif, Fuella,
Grenache, Grenache blanc,
Marsanne, Mayorquin, Mourvèdre,
Muscat d'Aubagne, Muscat blanc
à petits grains, Muscat de Die,
Muscat de Frontignan, Muscat de
Hambourg, Muscat de Marseille,
Muscat noir de Provence, Muscat
rosé à petits grains, Nielluccio,
Panse muscade, Pascal blanc, Petit-
brun, Picardan, Picpoul, Pignerol,
Sauvignon blanc, Sémillon,
Sciacarello, Syrah, Téoulier (*syn.*
Manosquin), Terret blanc, Terret
gris (*syn.* Terret-bourret), Terret
noir, Terret ramenée, Tibouren
(*syn.* Tibourenc), Ugni blanc,
Ugni rosé, Vermentino (*syn.* Rolle)

CORSICAN VINEYARDS
*These vineyards of Domaine de Valrose at Borgo, near the east coast,
are typical of the Corsican landscape. The east coast plains are
backed by dramatic mountains and palm trees proliferate.*

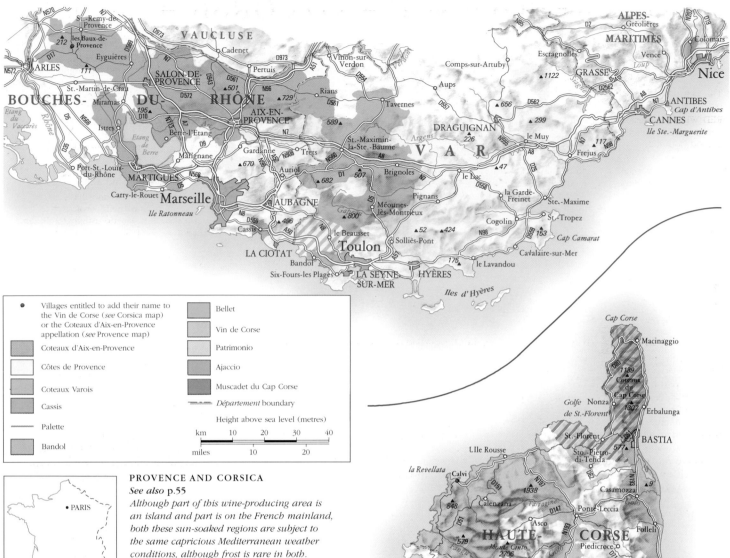

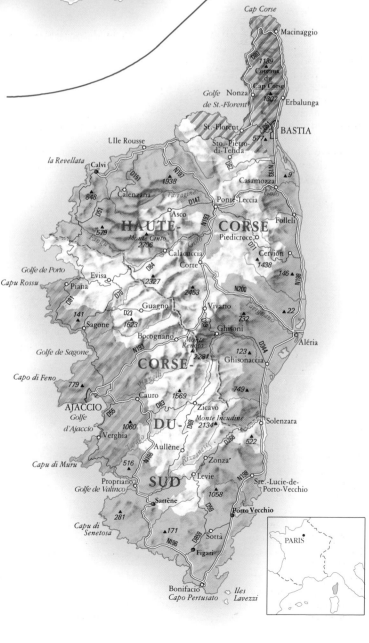

Legend:

- Villages entitled to add their name to the Vin de Corse (*see* Corsica map) or the Coteaux d'Aix-en-Provence appellation (*see* Provence map)
- Coteaux d'Aix-en-Provence
- Côtes de Provence
- Coteaux Varois
- Cassis
- Palette
- Bandol
- Bellet
- Vin de Corse
- Patrimonio
- Ajaccio
- Muscadet du Cap Corse
- *Département* boundary

Height above sea level (metres)

km 10 20 30 40
miles 10 20

PROVENCE AND CORSICA
See also p.55

Although part of this wine-producing area is an island and part is on the French mainland, both these sun-soaked regions are subject to the same capricious Mediterranean weather conditions, although frost is rare in both.

market upwards, then here at least it has been successful, for this island is no longer the generous contributor to Europe's "wine-lake" it used to be. The days when Corsica's wines were fit only for turning into industrial spirit are long gone, but this is not a potentially fine wine region either. Just 15 per cent of its vineyards are AOC and these yield barely more than five per cent of Corsica's total wine production. Although this is a fair and accurate reflection of its true potential, most critics agree that even within the modest limits of *vin de pays* production there should be many more individually expressive domaines. What has restricted their numbers is, however, something few are willing to talk about – intimidation and extortion by the local "Mafia", which has caused more than one brave new Corsican venture to flounder.

RECENT PROVENÇAL AND CORSICAN VINTAGES

Vintages in Provence and Corsica are very stable, even more so than those of the Southern Rhône, where the quality depends to a large extent on the success or otherwise of the Grenache grape. Even when Provence suffers an excess of good weather, as in 1985, when there was literally too much sun, the best growers manage to produce tremendously good wines.

THE APPELLATIONS OF
PROVENCE AND CORSICA

Note An asterisk denotes producers who are particularly recommended for Rosé.

AJACCIO AOC

This is a predominantly red-wine appellation on the west coast of Corsica.

RED When successful, this will inevitably be a medium-bodied Sciacarello wine with a good bouquet.

🍇 At least 60% (in total) of Barbarossa Nielluccio, Vermentino, and Sciacarello (the last of which must account for at least 40%), plus a maximum of 40% (in total) of Grenache, Cinsault, and Carignan (the last of which must not exceed 15%)

WHITE Decently dry and fruity, the best have a good edge of Ugni blanc acidity.

ROSÉ Average to good-quality dry rosé with a typical southern roundness.

🍇 As for the red

🍷 All wines: 1–3 years

✓ *Clos d'Alzeto • Domaine Comte Peraldi*

BANDOL AOC

The red wine of this Provence appellation is a true *vin de garde* and deserves greater recognition.

RED The best of these wines have a dark purple-black colour, a deep and dense bouquet, masses of spicy-plummy Mourvèdre fruit, and complex after-aromas that include vanilla, *cassis*, cinnamon, violets, and sweet herbs.

🍇 A blend of at least two of the following: Mourvèdre, Grenache, and Cinsault, of which a minimum of 50% Mourvèdre is obligatory, plus no more than 15% in total or 10% individually of Syrah and Carignan

🍷 3–12 years

WHITE These dry wines are now fresher and more fragrant than they were, but they are nothing special compared to the reds.

🍇 At least 60% (in total) of Bourboulenc, Clairette, and Ugni blanc plus a maximum of 40% Sauvignon blanc

🍷 Within 1 year

ROSÉ Well-made, attractive dry rosés, with body, structure, and a fine individual character.

🍇 As for red but no minimum Mourvèdre content

🍷 1–2 years

✓ *Domaine Bastide Blanche • Domaines Bunan* (Moulin des Costes, Château la Rouvière) *• Domaine du Cagueloup*

• *Domaine de Frégate • Domaine le Galantin • Château Jean-Pierre Gaussen • Domaine de l'Hermitage • Domaine de la Laidière • Domaine Lafran-Veyrolles* • *Domaine de la Noblesse • Domaines Ott* (Château Romassan) *• Château de Pibarnon • Château Pradeaux • Domaine Ray Jane • Château Roche Redonne • Château la Rouvière • Château Ste.-Anne* • *Domaine des Salettes • Domaine la Suffrene • Domaine Tempier* • *Domaine Terrebrune* • *Domaine de la Tour de Bon • Domaine Vannières**

LES BAUX DE PROVENCE AOC

Excellent red and rosé wines, sold under the sub-appellation of Coteaux d'Aix-en-Provence Les Baux until 1995, when they were given their own AOC and the requirements changed.

RED Deep, dark, and rich, with creamy-spicy cherry and plum flavours.

🍇 Grenache, Mourvèdre, Syrah plus a maximum of 40% Cinsault, Counoise, Carignan, and Cabernet Sauvignon

🍷 4–10 years

ROSÉ Domaine de la Vallongue is rich and ripe.

🍇 Cinsault, Grenache, Syrah plus a maximum of 40% Counoise, Carignon, Cabernet Sauvignon, and Mourvèdre

🍷 1–2 years

✓ *Mas de la Dame • Mas de Gourgonnier • Domaine Hauvette • Château Romanin • Mas Sainte-Berthe • Domaine de la Vallongue**

BELLET AOC

This tiny Provence appellation is cooled by Alpine winds and produces exceptionally fragrant wines for such a southerly location.

RED These wines have a good colour and structure, with a well-perfumed bouquet.

🍇 Braquet, Fuella, Cinsault, plus up to 40% (in total) of Grenache, Rolle, Ugni blanc, Mayorquin, Clairette, Bourboulenc, Chardonnay, Pignerol, and Muscat à petits grains

🍷 4–10 years

WHITE Fine, firm yet fragrant, and highly aromatic dry white wines of unbelievable class and finesse.

🍇 Rolle, Ugni blanc, Mayorquin, plus up to 40% Clairette, Bourboulenc, Chardonnay, Pignerol, and Muscat à petits grains

🍷 3–7 years

ROSÉ Fine, floral, dry rosés that are exceptionally fresh and easy to drink.

🍇 Braquet, Fuella, Cinsault, plus up to 40% (in total) of Grenache, Rolle, Ugni blanc, Mayorquin, Clairette, Bourboulenc, Chardonnay, Pignerol, and Muscat à petits grains

🍷 1–2 years

✓ *Château de Bellet • Château de Crémant*

CASSIS AOC

This is a decent but overpriced Provence appellation located around a beautiful rocky bay, a few kilometres east of Marseilles. In all but a few enterprising estates, these vineyards are on the decline.

RED These solid, well-coloured red wines can age, but most do not improve.

🍇 Grenache, Carignan, Mourvèdre, Cinsault, Barbaroux, plus up to 10% (in total) of Terret noir, Terret gris, Terret blanc, Terret ramenée, Aramon, and Aramon gris

WHITE These dry white wines have an interesting bouquet of herby aromas of gorse and bracken, but are usually flabby and unbalanced on the palate. However, Bagnol and St.-Magdeleine produce excellent, racy whites for such southerly vineyards and Ferme Blanche can be almost as good.

🍇 Ugni blanc, Sauvignon blanc, Doucillon, Clairette, Marsanne, Pascal blanc

ROSÉ Pleasantly fresh, dry rosés of moderately interesting quality.

🍇 Grenache, Carignan, Mourvèdre, Cinsault, Barbaroux, plus up to 10% (in total) of Terret noir, Terret gris, Terret blanc, Terret ramenée, Aramon, and Aramon gris

🍷 All wines: 1–3 years

✓ *Domaine du Bagnol • La Ferme Blanche • Clos St.-Magdeleine*

COTEAUX D'AIX-EN-PROVENCE AOC

This large appellation has many fine estates, several of which have been replanted and re-equipped.

RED The best are deeply coloured *vins de garde* with lots of creamy-*cassis*, spicy-vanilla, and cherry flavours, capable of some complexity.

🍇 Grenache, plus a maximum of 40% of Cinsault, Counoise, Mourvèdre, Syrah, Cabernet sauvignon, and Carignan (the last two of which must not exceed 30%)

🍷 3–12 years

WHITE Dry and fruity white wines that are of moderate quality, and are certainly improving. These wines may be sold from 1 December following the harvest without any mention of *primeur* or *nouveau*.

🍇 A maximum of 70% (each) of Bourboulenc, Clairette, Grenache blanc, Vermentino, up to 40% Ugni blanc and no more than 30% (each) of Sauvignon blanc and Sémillon

🍷 Upon purchase

ROSÉ Fine-quality dry rosés that are light in body, but bursting with deliciously fresh and ripe fruit. These wines may be sold from 1 December following the harvest without any mention of *primeur* or *nouveau*.

As for red, plus up to 10% (in total) of Bourboulenc, Clairette, Grenache blanc, Vermentino, Ugni blanc, Sauvignon blanc, and Sémillon

1–2 years

✓ *Château Barbelle* • *Commanderie de la Bargemone* • *Château Bas* • *Château des Béates (Béates)* • *Château de Beaupré* • *Château de Calissanne* • *Château de Fonscolombe* • *Château Revelette* • *Château de Rimauresq* • *Mas Sainte Berthe* • *Château St.-Jean* • *Domaine de St Julien les Vignes* (Cuvée du Château) • *Domaine de Trévallon*

COTEAUX VAROIS AOC

Upgraded from *vin de pays* to VDQS in 1985 and to AOC in 1993, this appellation covers an area of pleasant country wines in the centre of Provence.

RED The best have good colour, a deep fruity flavour, and some finesse.

A minimum in total of 70% (80% as from the year 2000) Mourvèdre, Syrah, and Grenache, plus a maximum of 20% (in total) of Cinsault, Carignan, and Cabernet sauvignon – the Tibouren is no longer admissible

WHITE Soft and fresh at best.

A minimum of 30% Vermentino, plus Clairette, Grenache blanc, a maximum of 30% Sémillon, and no more than 25% Ugni blanc

ROSÉ These attractive, easy-to-drink, dry rosés offer better value than some of the more famous pretentious wines of Provence.

A minimum of 70% (in total) of Mourvèdre, Syrah, and Grenache (the last of which must account for at least 40%), plus a maximum of 20% (in total) of Cinsault, Carignan, Cabernet sauvignon, and Tibouren – white grapes have not been allowed since 1993

All wines: 1–3 years

✓ *Domaine des Chaberts* (Cuvée Spéciale) • *Domaine du Deffends* • *Château la Galisse* • *Château Routas* • *Domaine de St.-Jean*

CÔTES DE PROVENCE AOC

While this AOC is famous for its rosés, it is the red wines of Côtes de Provence that have real potential, and they seem blessed with good vintages, fine estates, and talented winemakers. Inferior wines are made, but drink the best and you will rarely be disappointed. The major drawback of this all-embracing appellation is its very size. There are, however, several areas with peculiarities of soil and specific micro-climates that would make a Côtes de Provence Villages AOC a logical evolution and give the most expressive growers something to aim for.

RED There are too many exciting styles to generalize, but the best have a deep colour and many show an exuberance of silky Syrah fruit and plummy Mourvèdre. Some have great finesse, others are more tannic and chewy. The southern spicy-*cassis* of Cabernet sauvignon is often present and the Cinsault, Grenache, and Tibouren grapes also play important roles.

Up to 40% Carignan, plus Cinsault, Grenache, Mourvèdre, Tibouren, a maximum of 30% Syrah, and a 30% maximum (in total) of Barbaroux rosé, Cabernet sauvignon, Calitor, Clairette, Sémillon, Ugni blanc, and Vermentino

3–10 years

WHITE Moderate but improving soft, dry, fragrant, and aromatic wines. These wines may be sold from 1 December following the harvest without any mention of *primeur* or *nouveau*.

Clairette, Sémillon, Ugni blanc, Vermentino

1–2 years

ROSÉ Mediterranean sun is integral to the enjoyment of these wines, which are without doubt, wines made to accompany food, but even the best fail to perform against other rosés under blind conditions; their low acidity makes them seem flat and dull. These wines may be sold from 1st December following the harvest without any mention of *primeur* or *nouveau*.

Up to 40% Carignan, plus Cinsault, Grenache, Mourvèdre, Tibouren, a maximum of 30% Syrah, and a 30% maximum (in total) of Barbaroux rosé, Cabernet sauvignon, Calitor, Clairette, Sémillon, Ugni blanc, and Vermentino

1–2 years

✓ *Domaine de l'Abbaye* • *Château Barbey-rolles* • *Domaine la Bernarde* • *Château de Berne* • *Domaine de la Courtade* • *Château Coussin* • *Château d'Esclans* • *Domaines des Féraud* • *Château des Garcinières* • *Domaines Gavoty* • *Domaine de la Jeannette* • *Domaine de la Malherbe* • *Château Maravenne* • *Château Minuty* • *Commanderie de Peyrassol* • *Domaine des Planes* • *Domaine Rabiega* • *Château Réal Martin* • *Château Requier* (Tête de Cuvée*) • *Domaine Richeaume* • *Domaine de Rimauresq* • *Château Romassan* • *Domaine St.-André de Figuière* • *Domaine de St.-Baillon* • *Château de Selles* (also Clos Mireille) • *Château de la Tour l'Evéque* • *Vignerons Presqu'Ile St.-Tropez* (Château de Pampelonne, Carte Noire)

MUSCAT DU CAP CORSE AOC

When I first wrote this book in 1988, Corsica's only truly classic wine, the succulent sweet Muscat of Cap Corse, was not even recognized, let alone awarded the AOC status it deserved, and it took five more years to get it on the statute books. The Muscat du Cap Corse appellation overlaps Vin de Corse – Vin de Coteaux du Cap Corse and five of the seven communes that comprise the Patrimonio AOC.

WHITE The wines of Clos Nicrosi (in particular) demonstrate that Corsica has the ability to produce one of the most fabulous Muscats in the world. These wines are so pure and succulent with wonderful fresh aromas, that they have very little to gain through age.

Upon purchase

Muscat blanc à petit grains

✓ *Domaine de Catarelli* • *Clos Nicrosi*

PALETTE AOC

The ridiculously long list of permissible grapes here illustrates one of the worst excesses of the AOC system. What is the point of such a large number of diverse grape varieties? Ignoring the fact that it includes some low-quality ones that should, if anything, be

banned, it is obvious that no specific style could possibly result from the infinite permutation of varieties and percentages this AOC permits. Why not simply have an appellation that guarantees that Palette comes from Palette? Despite this farce, Palette is one of the best in Provence. It can be considered the equivalent of a *Grand Cru* of Coteaux d'Aix-en-Provence, standing out from surrounding vineyards by virtue of its calcareous soil. Three-quarters of this appellation is occupied by just one property – Château Simone.

RED Though not in the blockbusting style, this is a high-quality wine with good colour and firm structure, which can achieve finesse.

At least 50% (in total) of Mourvèdre, Grenache, and Cinsault, plus Téoulier, Durif, and Muscat (any variety planted), Carignan, Syrah, Castets, Brun-Fourcat, Terret gris, Petit-brun, Tibouren, Cabernet sauvignon and up to 15% (in total) of Clairette (any variety planted), Picardan, Ugni blanc, Ugni rosé, Grenache blanc, Muscat (any variety planted), Picpoul, Pascal, Aragnan, Colombard, and Terret-bourret

7–20 years

WHITE Firm but nervy dry wine with a pleasantly curious aromatic character.

At least 55% (in total) of Clairette (any variety planted), plus Picardan, Ugni blanc, Ugni rosé, Grenache blanc, Muscat (any variety planted), Picpoul, Pascal, Aragnan, Colombard, and a maximum of 20% Terret-bourret

Upon purchase

ROSÉ A well-made, but not exceptional wine, which is perhaps made too seriously for its level of quality.

At least 50% (in total) of Mourvèdre, Grenache, and Cinsault, plus Téoulier, Durif, and Muscat (any variety planted), Carignan, Syrah, Castets, Brun-Fourcat, Terret gris, Petit-brun, Tibouren, Cabernet sauvignon, and up to 15% (in total) of Clairette (any variety planted), Picardan, Ugni blanc, Ugni rosé, Grenache blanc, Muscat (any variety planted), Picpoul, Pascal, Aragnan, Colombard, and Terret-bourret

1–3 years

✓ *Château Crémade* • *Château Simone*

PATRIMONIO AOC

This is a small appellation situated west of Bastia in the north of Corsica.

RED Some fine-quality red wines of good colour, body, and fruit are made.

At least 75% Nielluccio, (90% by the year 2000), plus Grenache, Sciacarello, and Vermentino

WHITE Light and dry wines of a remarkably fragrant and floral character for Corsica.

At least 90% Vermentino (100% by the year 2000), but, in the meantime, a balance of Ugni blanc is allowed

ROSÉ Good-value dry rosés that have a coral-pink colour and an elegant flavour.

At least 75% Nielluccio (90% by the year 2000), plus Grenache, Sciacarello, and Vermentino

All wines: 1–3 years

✓ *Antoine Arena* • *Domaine de Catarelli* • *Domaine Gentile* • *Domaine Leccia* • *Clos Montemagni* • *Orenga de Gaffory* • *Domaine Aliso Rossi*

VIN DE BANDOL AOC

See Bandol AOC

VIN DE BELLET AOC

See Bellet AOC

VIN DE CORSE AOC

Vin de Corse is a generic appellation covering the entire island.

RED These honest wines are full of fruit, round and clean, with rustic charm.

🍇 At least 50% Nielluccio, Sciacarello, and Grenache noir, plus Cinsault, Mourvèdre, Barbarossa, Syrah, and a maximum of 20% (in total) of Carignan and Vermentino

WHITE The best are well made, clean, and fresh, but not of true AOC quality.

🍇 At least 75% Vermentino, plus up to 25% Ugni blanc

ROSÉ Attractive, dry, fruity, easy-to-drink wines.

🍇 At least 50% Nielluccio, Sciacarello, and Grenache noir, plus Cinsault, Mourvèdre, Barbarossa, Syrah, and a maximum of 20% (in total) of Carignan and Vermentino

🍷 All wines: 1–3 years

✓ *Domaine Colombu* • *Domaine Fiumicicoli* • *Domaine Gentile* • *Clos Landry* • *Domaine Maestracci*

VIN DE CORSE CALVI AOC

Lying north of Ajaccio, this sub-appellation of Vin de Corse AOC requires the same grape varieties and meets the same technical level.

✓ *Domaine Colombu* • *Domaine Maestracci* • *Clos Reginu*

VIN DE CORSE COTEAUX DU CAP CORSE AOC

A sub-appellation of Vin de Corse, this requires the same varieties, except that Codivarta may be used with Ugni blanc in support of Vermentino.

✓ *Clos Nicrosi*

VIN DE CORSE FIGARI AOC

Situated between Sartène and Porto Vecchio, Vin de Corse Figari is a sub-appellation of Vin de Corse AOC and requires the same grape varieties and technical level.

✓ *Poggio d'Oro* • *Domaine de Canella*

VIN DE CORSE PORTO VECCHIO AOC

The southeastern edge of Corsica, around Porto Vecchio, is a sub-appellation of Vin de Corse AOC and requires the same grape varieties and technical level.

✓ *Domaine de Torraccia*

VIN DE CORSE SARTENE AOC

South of Ajaccio, this sub-appellation of Vin de Corse AOC requires the same grape varieties and conforms to the same technical level.

✓ *Clos d'Alzeto*⁕ • *Domaine de San Michelle* • *Domaine de Tizzano*

AUTHOR'S CHOICE

With the exception of a stunning Muscat Cap Corse from Clos Nicrosi, Domaine de St.-Baillon's consistently mouthwatering rosé, and the powerful white wine of Château Simone, it is perhaps inevitable that my choice should be focused on this region's single-most successful style: its glorious reds.

PRODUCER	WINE	STYLE	DESCRIPTION	🍷
Domaine du Deffends ⓥ	Clos de la Truffière, Coteaux Varois AOC (*see* p.244)	RED	This single-vineyard wine has a beautifully sustained colour and much greater intensity than other Coteaux Varois reds.	3–6 years
Orenga de Gaffory ⓥ	Cuvée des Gouverneurs, Patrimonio AOC (*see* p.244)	RED	One of Corsica's few true *vins de garde*, spicy fruit is supported by creamy oak, illustrating the potential of the Nielluccio grape.	3–6 years
Château de Pibarnon	Bandol AOC (*see* p.243)	RED	Consistently one the most remarkable red Bandol wines, Pibarnon is full of lush, velvety fruit, nicely underpinned with supple tannins, with seductive, creamy oak on the finish.	4–12 years
Château Pradeaux	Bandol AOC (*see* p.243)	RED	A deep-coloured Bandol of heady bouquet and exceptional longevity, Pradeaux has been one of my favourite wines since Clive Coates MW imported it for the Malmaison Wine Club in the 1970s. Outstanding then and gets better with almost every vintage.	4–12 years
Domaine Rabiega ⓥ	Clos d'Tère Cuvée, Côtes de Provence AOC (*see* p.244)	RED	This beautifully coloured, well-structured wine is packed with soft, black fruit flavours that seems to smack far more of Syrah than the 30 per cent maximum allowed for that grape.	3–8 years
Domaine de St.-Baillon	Côtes de Provence AOC (*see* p.244)	ROSÉ	After all I have said, readers might be surprised to discover a rosé included here. No other Provence rosé can match St.-Baillon for consistency. It has lovely pure fruit, with good acidity and amazing freshness.	Upon purchase
Château Simone	Palette AOC (*see* p.244)	RED	Not for the faint-hearted, this is a burly-structured, tannic red, but has the fruit, flavour, and length to support it. Capable of great finesse and complexity.	5–10 years
Château Simone	Palette AOC (*see* p.244)	WHITE	This rich, oak-aged wine has a long and complex finish. The finest dry white in Provence, and *grand vin* by any standards.	2–5 years
Domaine Tempier	Cuvée Tourtine, Bandol AOC (*see* p.243)	RED	With a deep-colour, ripe berry and herbal aromas, and supple-tannin structure, this red wine is produced from one of Bandol's finest vineyards without the use of fertilizers or chemicals.	4–12 years
Domaine de Torraccia	Cuvée Oriu, Vin de Corse Porto Vecchio AOC (*see* p.245)	RED	Another rare *vin de garde* from Corsica, this well-coloured red comes from the south of the island. Lovely dense fruit flavours with a slightly smoky, sweet-tobacco complexity.	3–5 years
Domaine de Trévallon	Coteaux d'Aix-en-Provence AOC (*see* p.244)	RED	The most outstanding wine of the appellation, Domaine de Trévallon is a stunningly good, deep, dark Cabernet-Syrah blend that shows tremendous finesse and elegance for its size.	3–10 years

VINS DE PAYS

This category of wine includes some of the most innovative and exciting wines being produced in the world today, yet most of the 141 vin de pays *denominations are superfluous and confusing. The success of the* vin de pays *system lies not in creating more appellations, but in freeing producers from them, which allows the most talented individuals to carve out their own reputations.*

VINS DE PAYS OR "COUNTRY WINES" are supposed to be unpretentious, but many are better than average-quality AOC wines and the best rank as some of the finest wines that France can produce. This was never the intention; a *vin de pays* was merely meant to be a quaffing wine that should display, in a very rudimentary sense, the broadest characteristics of its region's greatest wines. It was to have a rustic charm and be a joy to drink, but nothing more. However, the *vin de pays* system, which had fewer restrictions than the AOC system, encouraged creative winemakers to produce wines in a way that they felt best expressed their *terroir* and, in so doing, they managed to equal and occasionally surpass the quality of the more famous local appellations.

As news of these exciting *vins de pays* hit the headlines of the international wine press, so the thought of shedding the shackles of AOC regulations attracted a new generation of winemakers, including a number of Australians. The idea of being allowed to produce, for example, a Cabernet Sauvignon in parts of Burgundy was simply too good to miss, and a combination of French and foreign winemakers opened up the *vin de pays* system, turning it into something its creators had never imagined.

This success, however, also attracted the attention of less quality-minded producers, who jumped on the bandwagon and now churn out megagallons of unbelievably bland *vins de pays*, but if this is the price of revolution at the bottom end of the French wine regime, I for one am pleased to pay it.

COUNTRY ORIGINS

The expression "Vin de Pays" first appeared in the statute books in a decree dated 8 February 1930. The law in question merely allowed wines to refer to their canton of origin provided they attained a certain alcoholic degree; for example "Vin de Pays de Canton X". These cantons were not controlled appellations as such: there was no way of enforcing a minimum standard of quality, and the relatively small amounts of these so-called *vins de pays* were often the product of inferior hybrid grapes. It was not until 1973 that the concept was officially born of *vins de pays* that were a superior breed of *vins de table*, originating from a defined area and subject to strict controls. By 1976, a total of 75 *vins de pays* had been established, but all the formalities were not worked out until 1979, and between 1981 and 1982 every single existing *vin de pays* was redefined and another 20 created. Currently there are 141, athough the number fluctuates as *vins de pays* are upgraded to VDQS, when new *vins de pays* are created or, as has happened recently, when some *départements* are denied the right to produce a *vin de pays* (*see* Vins de Pays at a Glance p.248).

Officially, a *vin de pays* is a *vin de table* from a specified area that conforms to quality-control laws that are very similar to those regulating AOC and VDQS wines, although obviously not quite as stiff. *Vin de pays* came of age in 1989, prior to which all such wines had to carry the additional descriptor *Vin de Table Français* or *Vin de Table de France*. From time to time *vins de pays* are upgraded to VDQS, which itself has become a staging post for

DOMAINE DE LA BAUME
This property is owned by Hardy, one of Australia's largest wine companies. Believing the French had not exploited varietal wines and seeing an opening in the market for Australian-made French wines, Hardy puchased Domaine de la Baume on the outskirts of Béziers just in time for the 1990 harvest.

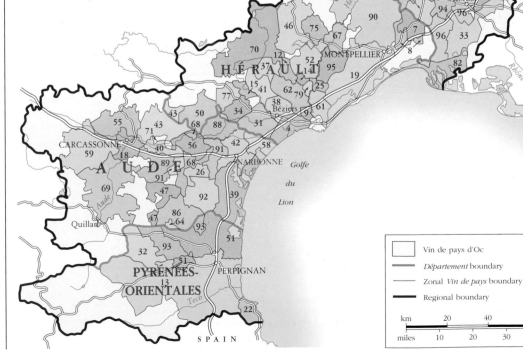

	Vin de pays d'Oc
	Département boundary
	Zonal *Vin de pays* boundary
	Regional boundary

VIN DE PAYS, MAP A
See also p.247
Languedoc-Roussillon encompasses the greatest concentration of zonal vins de pays *and is dominated by the regional* Vin de Pays d'Oc, *by far the most successful* vin de pays.

full AOC status. The last *vin de pays* to be promoted was Gorges et Côtes de Millau in 1994, which is now Côtes de Millau VDQS, and a number are expected to follow suit shortly.

IS VARIETAL THE SPICE OF LIFE FOR VIN DE PAYS?

Many *vins de pays* are made and marketed on a varietal basis. The number of Chardonnay and Cabernet Sauvignon *vins de pays* is truly mind-boggling. The French authorities agonize over the affect that this is having on their more famous appellations (the old story of customers saying "I don't want Chablis, I want Chardonnay"), but it is a fact of life and if some traditional, geographical-based

appellations fall by the wayside it will be due more to their not providing consumers with what they want than to any invasion of varietal names. After all, the New World is now using varietals grown in specific areas to establish geographical-based appellations. The argument cannot work both ways. However, as part of their plan to divert attention from single-varietal names, the French authorities introduced the twin-varietal concept (the Australian practice of naming wines Cabernet-Merlot, Chardonnay-Sémillon etc.) for *vins de pays* in 1996. Whether varietals are a problem, and whether twin-varietals will help to disperse it or double the confusion, remains to be seen.

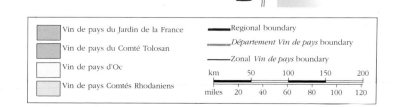

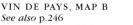

VIN DE PAYS, MAP B

See also p.246

This map shows all the regional and départemental vins de pays, *plus those zonal appellations that are situated beyond the boundaries of the Languedoc-Roussillon region.*

▨ Vin de pays du Jardin de la France	▬ Regional boundary
▨ Vin de pays du Comté Tolosan	▬ *Département Vin de pays* boundary
☐ Vin de pays d'Oc	▬ Zonal *Vin de pays* boundary
☐ Vin de pays Comtés Rhodaniens	

km 50 100 150 200
miles 20 40 60 80 100 120

VINS DE PAYS AT A GLANCE

141 VIN DE PAYS DENOMINATIONS IN TOTAL
From virtually zero production in 1973, to an annual average of 12 million hectolitres (133 million cases), *vin de pays* now represents 25 per cent of the total French wine production and this trend is continuing.

TYPES OF VINS DE PAYS
There are three basic categories of *vins de pays*: regional, *départemental*, and zonal. Although no official quality differences exist between these, it is not an unreasonable assumption that the zonal *vins de pays* may sometimes show more individual character than the much larger *vins de pays départementaux* or all-encompassing regional *vins de pays*, but this is not always so.

A grower within a specific zone may find it easier to sell wine under a more generic *vin de pays*, which explains why so many individual wines are to be found under the vast Vin de Pays d'Oc denomination. Also, the geographical size of a *vin de pays* can be deceptive, with many *départements* producing relatively little wine compared to some more prolific zonal *vins de pays*. In the Loire few producers bother with the *départemental* denominations.

REGIONAL VINS DE PAYS (23 per cent of total *vin de pays* output)
There are four of these wide-ranging appellations: Jardin de la France; Comté Tolosan; Comtés Rhodaniens; and Oc. Each encompasses two or more *départements*. They represented only 12 per cent of *vin de pays* production in 1990.

DÉPARTEMENTAL VINS DE PAYS (44 per cent of total *vin de pays* output)
These cover entire *départements*, and although 39 are officially in use, some will become redundant as producers opt for one of the more widely supported regional appellations, which are often easier to promote. In theory every *département* in France can claim a *vin de pays* under its own *départemental* denomination, but to avoid confusion with AOC wines the following were in 1995 expressly forbidden from exercising this right: the Marne and Aube (in Champagne), the Bas-Rhin

and Haut-Rhin (in Alsace), the Côte-d'Or (in Burgundy), and the Rhône (which encompasses Beaujolais but is likely to cause confusion with the Rhône AOC). Jura, Savoie, and Haut-Savoie were also disenfranchised.

ZONAL VINS DE PAYS (33 per cent of total *vin de pays* production)
No less than 95 denominations are included in this category, many of which are seldom encountered. It is limited to a local area, sometimes just one commune.

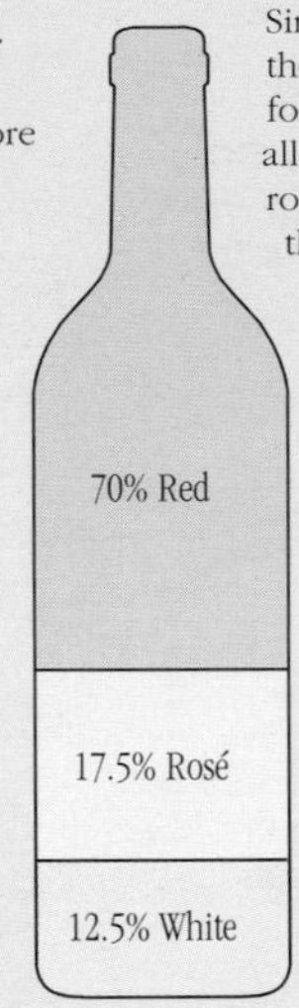

VINS DE PAYS PRIMEUR
Since 1990, all *vin de pays* denominations have been permitted to produce these wines, which may be marketed from the third Thursday of October following the harvest (much earlier than Beaujolais Nouveau). The regulations allow for red and white wines to be made as *vins primeurs*, but strangely not rosé, although by the very nature of their production many reds are lighter than some rosés, so it is a somewhat moot point. White wines are vinified by cool-fermentation techniques and red wines by one of three methods: *macération carbonique* (*see* Glossary), part-*macération carbonique* (some of the grapes are crushed and mixed with the whole bunches), and "short-classic" (traditional vinification with minimum skin-contact). Cool-fermented whites and *macération carbonique* reds are dominated by amylic aromas (peardrops, banana, nail-varnish etc), but "short-classic" rarely provides enough fruit, depth, or colour, whereas part-*macération carbonique* can be very successful in enhancing the fruitiness of a wine without drowning it in amylic aromas, but it has to be expertly applied.

Note Although *vins de pays* may use terms such as "Mas" and "Domaine" to designate the property producing the wine, for some obscure reason "château" is strictly forbidden. The vintage and up to two grape varieties may be specified on the front label. The minimum natural alcohol level is fixed at 9 per cent in northern denominations (which is higher than most AOCs in these regions) and 10 per cent in Mediterranean areas. A maximum alcoholic strength of 15 per cent applies to all *vins de pays*.

Bottle diagram:
70% Red
17.5% Rosé
12.5% White

THE VINS DE PAYS OF FRANCE

AGENAIS
Zonal *vin de pays* Map B, No.1
These red, white, and rosé wines are produced from a combination of classic *bordelais* grapes and some rustic regional varieties, including the Tannat and Fer. Although more than three-quarters of the output is red, it is the rosé made primarily from Abouriou that is best known.

AIGUES
Zonal *vin de pays* Map A, No.2
Created as recently as 1993, this *vin de pays* roughly corresponds to the Coteaux du Lubéron, and has a similar range of grape varieties.

ALLOBROGIE
Zonal *vin de pays* Map B, No.3
This is the *vin de pays* equivalent of the Vin de Savoie, although it extends beyond the borders of that AOC into cattle country where the existence of vines is very sporadic. The wines are similar to Vin de Savoie, if somewhat lighter and more rustic in style. Almost 90 per cent of production is white, made primarily from Jacquère, Chardonnay, and Chasselas, although Altesse, Mondeuse blanche, Roussanne, and Molette can also be used. The balance of the production is essentially red and may be made from Gamay, Mondeuse, and Pinot noir, with rosé accounting for less than one per cent.

ALPES DE HAUTE-PROVENCE
Départemental vin de pays Map B
Most of these wines come from the Durance valley in the east of the *département*. Production is mostly red, made from Carignan, Grenache, Cinsault, Cabernet sauvignon, Merlot, and Syrah.

Rosé accounts for 15 per cent and white made from Ugni blanc, Clairette, Chardonnay, and Muscat for just seven per cent.
☑ *Domaine de Réguesse*

ALPES-MARITIMES
Départemental vin de pays Map B
Some 70 per cent of production is red and 30 per cent rosé, made from Carignan, Cinsault, Grenache, Ugni blanc, and Rolle grapes, mostly from the communes of Carros, Mandelieu, and Mougins. White wines may also be produced.

ARDAILHOU
Zonal *vin de pays* Map A, No.4
This wine comes from an area on the Hérault coast west of Béziers. The modest production of this *vin de pays* is almost two-thirds red and one-third rosé, mostly from Cinsault (maximum of 50 per cent), Carignan (maximum of 40 per cent), and Grenache (minimum of ten per cent), although Syrah, Merlot, and Cabernet sauvignon may be used. A little white is produced from a range of up to 20 grape varieties, with Clairette, Terret, and Ugni blanc dominating.

ARDÈCHE
Départemental vin de pays Map B
Red and white wines, from a range of Rhône and *bordelais* grapes, are produced on a limited scale.

ARGENS
Zonal *vin de pays* Map A, No.5
This denomination covers part of the Côtes de Provence and almost half the wines are rosé of a similar style and quality to those of the

Vin de Pays du Var. Half the production is red, which is rich, tannic, and spicy, made from Carignan, Cinsault, Syrah, Roussanne du Var, Mourvèdre, and Cabernet sauvignon. A little white is also produced.

AUDE
Départemental vin de pays Map B

DORGAN
VIN DE PAYS DE L'AUDE
75cl e   12%Alc.Vol
Mis en bouteilles par les Producteurs du Mont Tauch à 11350 Tuchan - France

A vast production of fresh and fruity wine is made here, which is mostly red, with just five per cent each of rosé and white. Mediterranean grape varieties dominate.
☑ *Jacques Boyer • Producteurs du Mont Tauch* (Carignan/Syrah)

AVEYRON
Départemental vin de pays Map B
Since most of the wines produced in this *département*, which is situated between Cahors and Hérault, used to claim the Vin de Pays des

Gorges et Côtes de Millau (now Côtes de Millau VDQS) appellation, it will be interesting to see how many *vin de pays* producers utilize this denomination or prefer to use the wider Comté Tolosan appellation.

BALMES DAUPHINOISES
Zonal *vin de pays* Map B, No.6
In the denomination of Balmes Dauphinoises, dry white, made from Jacquère and Chardonnay, accounts for 60 per cent of production, and red, made from Gamay and Pinot noir, accounts for 40 per cent. Rosé may also be produced.

BÉNOVIE
Zonal *vin de pays* Map A, No.7
This denomination is located at the eastern extremity of the Coteaux du Languedoc and overlaps part of the Muscat-de-Lunel area. Almost 80 per cent of the production is a light, fruity red, made predominantly from Carignan, Grenache, Cinsault, and Syrah, although Merlot and Cabernet sauvignon may also be used. A fair amount of attractive rosé is made, mostly by the *saignée* method, plus a small quantity of Ugni-blanc based dry white.

BÉRANGE
Zonal *vin de pays* Map A, No.8
Production in Bérange is 75 per cent red, 20 per cent rosé, and five per cent white, made from a range of grape varieties very similar to those used in the Coteaux du Languedoc and neighbouring Bénvoie.

BESSAN
Zonal *vin de pays* Map A, No.9
This tiny, single-village denomination just east of Béziers is best known for its dry, aromatic rosé, which now accounts for 65 per cent of production. Just ten per cent red is made, with simple Ugni-blanc based white accounting for the balance.

BIGORRE
Zonal *vin de pays* Map B, No.10
Mostly full, rich, Madiran-type red wine is made here, plus a little good crisp, dry white. Rosé may also be produced.

BOUCHES-DU-RHÔNE
Départemental *vin de pays* Map B
This denomination has one of the largest *vin de pays* productions in the country, some 80 per cent of which is red and most of that comes from the Coteaux d'Aix-en-Provence area. These wines are warm, spicy, and often quite powerfully structured from Carignan, Grenache, Cinsault, Cabernet sauvignon, Merlot, and Syrah. The production of rosé is just 12 per cent, which is a reasonable proportion for the style, and also in view of the absence of the mystique of a name (it cannot have Provence on the label). The quality is invariably much better than most of the AOC rosé from this area. A little white is also made from Ugni blanc, Clairette, Bourboulenc, Vermentino, Chardonnay, and Chasan (a slightly aromatic Listan x Chardonnay cross).

✓ *Mas de Rey • Domaine de l'Île St.-Pierre • Château Revelette • Domaine de Trévallon*

BOURBONNAIS
Zonal *vin de pays* Map B, No.11
This is a rare wine from a white-only area in the Loire Valley.

CASSAN
Zonal *vin de pays* Map A, No.12
This area is in the Coteau-du-Languedoc north of Béziers and overlaps part of Faugères. Almost three-quarters of the wine is red and full-bodied, from Carignan, Cinsault, Grenache, Cabernet sauvignon, Merlot, Cabernet sauvignon, and Syrah. The balance is split between a well-flavoured rosé and a crisp, dry white made primarily from Ugni blanc, although Clairette and Terret may also be used.

CATALAN
Zonal *vin de pays* Map A, No.13
Very successful, well-coloured, uncomplicated, fruity reds account for almost 70 per cent of production, and are made mostly from Grenache and Carignan, although Mourvèdre, Merlot, Cabernet sauvignon, and Syrah are on the increase. Clean, easy-drinking, dry rosés account for 20 per cent of production, made from the same grape varieties, while the 10 per cent balance of dry white is made from Grenache blanc, Macabéo, Chardonnay, and a little Muscat. *Vins primeurs* are a speciality of this prolific *vin de pays*.

✓ *Mas Amiel • Domaine de Casenove • Domaine Cazes • Domaine Ferrer-Ribière • Château de Jau*

CAUX
Zonal *vin de pays* Map A, No.14
This *vin de pays* produces a good, typical, dry, and fruity rosé in a Languedoc style from vines growing north of Béziers. Some 40 per cent of the output is red and a little white is also made.

✓ *Domaine de Sallets*

CESSENON
Zonal *vin de pays* Map A, No.15
This appellation produces red wines of a rustic St.-Chinian style, plus a little rosé.

CÉVENNES
Zonal *vin de pays* Map A, No.16
This new appellation is an amalgamation of four former *vins de pays*: Coteaux Cévenols, Coteaux du Salavès, Côtes du Libac (originally Serre du Coiran), Mont Bouquet, and Uzège, each of which may add their name to the denomination Cévennes. Most of the wines are red, 15 per cent are rosé, with *saignée* rosé a speciality. Very small quantities of white *vin primeur* are also produced. Production is mostly of an honest, fruity Languedoc style.

✓ *Domaine de Gournier*

CHARENTAIS
Zonal *vin de pays* Map B, No.17
The dry white wines are really good, even though 50 per cent of the grapes used are Ugni blanc. It seems that this lowly variety and, indeed, the Colombard make light but very fresh, crisp, and tangy wine in the Charente, which is not only well suited to distilling Cognac, but makes a cheap, cheerful quaffable wine. Some red and rosé wines from Gamay and *bordelais* grapes are also made.

CHER
Départemental *vin de pays* Map B
Mostly Touraine-like, Gamay-based red wine, plus a small amount of dry rosé in a light *vin gris* style. A little dry white Sauvignon Blanc is also made, comparable to a rustic Sancerre or Menetou-Salon from the Loire.

CITÉ DE CARCASSONNE
Zonal *vin de pays* Map A, No.18
Red wines account for over 90 per cent of production, rosé five per cent, and white wine barely one per cent. The wines come from 11 communes around Carcassonne.

✓ *Domaine Auzias*

COLLINES DE LA MOURE
Zonal *vin de pays* Map A, No.19
More than 80 per cent of production is basic red, made from a choice of Carignan, Cinsault, Grenache, Syrah, Cabernet sauvignon, and Merlot, the last two of which are often vinified separately. A light, dry rosé accounts for about 15 per cent of production, but very little white is made and it is mostly from Ugni blanc. Although late-harvest rather than a *vin doux naturel*, it should still come as no surprise that this *vin de pays* denomination roughly corresponds to the AOCs Muscat de Mireval and Muscat de Frontignan.

✓ *Domaine de Terre Mégère • Domaine de Valmagne*

COLLINES RHODANIENNES
Zonal *vin de pays* Map B, No.20
A large denomination at the centre of Comtés Rhodaniens, this *vin de pays* straddles five *départements* (Rhône, Isère, Drôme, Ardèche, and Loire) and produces primarily red wines from Gamay, Syrah, Merlot, and Pinot noir. Some extremely small quantities are made of rosé and white, the latter coming from an interesting choice of Chardonnay, Marsanne, Roussanne, Viognier, Jacquère, Aligoté, and Clairette. With the range of body, fatness, aromatic complexity, and acidity that a successful blend of these varieties could bring, there is ample scope for Collines Rhodaniennes to develop a first-rate reputation for white wines.

✓ *Domaine Etienne Pochon*

COMTÉ DE GRIGNAN
Zonal *vin de pays* Map B, No.21
Virtually all the production of Comté de Grignan is red and most of that Grenache-dominated, although Syrah, Cinsault, Gamay, Carignan, Merlot, and Cabernet sauvignon are also allowed. Rosé accounts for just one per cent and white is virtually non-existent.

COMTÉ TOLOSAN
Regional *vin de pays* Map B
Modest quantities of mostly red wines are produced, with some rosé and a tiny amount of white, all of which are entitled to be made from a wide range of southwest grape varieties.

✓ *Domaine de Baudare • Plaimont*

COMTÉS RHODANIENS
Regional *vin de pays* Map B
Created in 1989, Comtés Rhodaniens encompasses eight *départements* and its name can be given only to wines that have already qualified as a zonal *vin de pays*.

CORRÈZE
Départemental *vin de pays* Map A
Mostly reds from Cabernet franc, Merlot, and Gamay – the limestone *coteaux* of Branceilles have historically produced the best.

✓ *Sauret Père* (Mille et Une Picrre)

CÔTE VERMEILLE
Zonal *vin de pays* Map A, No.22
Mostly red and rosé, these wines are the *vin de pays* equivalent of Collioure, which in turn is the table-wine equivalent of Banyuls.
✓ *Domaine Vial Magnères*

COTEAUX DE L'ARDÈCHE
Zonal *vin de pays* Map B, No.23

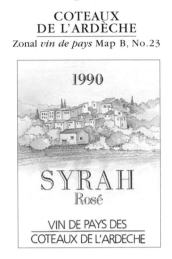

This large denomination has a very significant output and is particularly well known for its dark, spicy red wine, which accounts for 80 per cent of the total production. Often Syrah-dominated, this wine may also include Cabernet sauvignon, Carignan, Cinsault, Grenache, Gamay, and Merlot. Louis Latour's Chardonnay put this *vin de pays* on the map during the last ten years and over the next decade the same firm's stunning Pinot noir will make Coteaux de l'Ardèche a superstar. Just over ten per cent of this denomination's total output is rosé and just under ten per cent is white, the latter made from Bourboulenc, Marsanne, Viognier, Roussanne, Marsanne, Sauvignon blanc, and Ugni blanc. About 30 per cent of all wines produced are sold as pure varietal.
✓ *CV Ardèchois*
  • *Domaine du Colombier*
  • *La Cévenne Ardèchois*
  • *Louis Latour*
  • *Domaine de Vigier*

COTEAUX AUXOIS
New zonal *vin de pays*
This zonal *vin de pays* is due to replace the *départmental* denomination Côte d'Or and is awaiting delimitation at the time of writing.

COTEAUX DES BARONNIES
Zonal *vin de pays* Map B, No.24
Almost 90 per cent of Coteaux des Baronnies wines are red and ten per cent rosé, made from Cabernet sauvignon, Cinsault, Syrah, Grenache, Pinot noir, Gamay, and Merlot. Less than two per cent is white, with varietal wines generally increasing.
✓ *Domaine du Rieu Frais*

COTEAUX DE BESSILLES
Zonal *vin de pays* Map A, No.25
Fresh, light, rustic-style wines from the Coteaux du Languedoc immediately north of Pinet. Production is two-thirds red, one quarter rosé, and the balance white.
✓ *Domaine St.-Martin de la Garrigue*

COTEAUX DE LA CABRERISSE
Zonal *vin de pays* Map A, No.26
Mostly red wine, as might be expected from what is after all the heart of Corbières, with ten per cent rosé and just three per cent white, including some *vins primeurs*. There is a wide range of grape varieties permitted, particularly for the red, which may be made from Carignan, Grenache, Cinsault, Syrah, Mourvèdre, Terret noir, Cabernet sauvignon, Cabernet franc, Merlot, and the teinturier grape Alicante bouschet. White grapes include Terret, Grenache blanc, Clairette, Ugni blanc, and Macabéo.

COTEAUX DE CEZE
Zonal *vin de pays* Map A, No.27
This is a large denomination with a modest output of roughly 80 per cent red and 20 per cent rosé, with a minuscule amount of white.

COTEAUX CHARITOIS
Zonal *vin de pays* Map B, No.28
Basic white wines from the Loire Valley.
✓ *Cave des Hauts de Seyr* (Le Montaillant)

COTEAUX DU CHER ET DE L'ARNON
Zonal *vin de pays* Map B, No.29
The reds and *vin gris* are made from Gamay, and dry white from Sauvignon blanc.

COTEAUX DE COIFFY
Zonal *vin de pays* Map A, No.30
A relatively new and as yet untested *vin de pays* from way up north, between Champagne and Alsace, in the southeastern corner of the Haute-Marne *département*.

COTEAUX D'ENSÉRUNE
Zonal *vin de pays* Map A, No.31
This *vin de pays* west of Béziers used to produce two-thirds red and one-third rosé, but red wines now account for almost 90 per cent of the output, made from a typical range of Languedoc grapes. Just ten per cent rosé is produced, but hardly any white. However, Jeanjean makes a nice, soft, fruity dry white from Ugni blanc, Marsanne, and Chardonnay.
✓ *Jeanjean*

COTEAUX DES FENOUILLEDES
Zonal *vin de pays* Map A, No.32
Frank, and fruity wines that come from the hilly, northwestern corner of Roussillon. Production is 85 per cent red, 12 per cent rosé, and white wines account for just three per cent.

COTEAUX FLAVIENS
Zonal *vin de pays* Map A, No.33
From hills named after the Roman Emperor Flavius, this *vin de pays* just south of Nîmes in the Costières de Nîmes produces a full, warm-hearted red which accounts for 85 per cent of the output. Most of the rest is rosé, and just a small amount of white is made. Carignan, Grenache, Cinsault, Cabernet sauvignon, Merlot, and Syrah are the main grape varieties used.

COTEAUX DE FONTCAUDE
Zonal *vin de pays* Map A, No.34
This area overlaps much of Saint-Chinian in the eastern section of the Coteaux du Languedoc. Almost 80 per cent of the wines are red, and

these are made in a light, fresh but interesting style from Carignan, Cinsault, Grenache, Cabernet sauvignon, and Syrah. Rosé and a little white are also to be found.

COTEAUX DE GLANES
Zonal *vin de pays* Map B, No.35
This appellation produces mainly red wines, which are Gamay- or Merlot-dominated, plus a little rosé.

COTEAUX DU GRÉSIVAUDAN
Zonal *vin de pays* Map B, No.36
Red and rosé Savoie-style wines made from Gamay, Pinot, and Etraire de la dui (a local grape variety), and Jacquère-based dry whites.

COTEAUX DE LAURENS
Zonal *vin de pays* Map A, No.37
Some 85 per cent of these wines are a red *vin de pays* equivalent of Faugères, made mostly from Carignan, Cinsault, Syrah, and Grenache, but some of the better wines also include Cabernet sauvignon and Merlot. A small amount of rosé and even less white is made.
✓ *Domaine de la Commanderie de St.-Jean*

COTEAUX DU LIBRON
Zonal *vin de pays* Map A, No.38
Situated around Béziers itself, this *vin de pays* produces mainly red wines, made from Carignan, Grenache, Cinsault, Cabernet sauvignon, Merlot, and Syrah. Some 12 per cent of the output is rosé, and less than seven per cent white, the latter being made mainly from Ugni blanc, with a touch of Tarret and Clairette.

COTEAUX DU LITTORAL AUDOIS
Zonal *vin de pays* Map A, No.39
This area corresponds geographically to the unofficial Sigean zone of Corbières (*see also* p.235), where Syrah performs best and is used, not surprisingly, in many of these *vins de pays*, of which red wine accounts for no less than 98 per cent of the total output. Other black grape varieties permitted include Carignan, Grenache, Cinsault, Merlot, and Cabernet sauvignon. Minuscule amounts of rosé and white are produced; the latter is made mainly from Grenache blanc and Macabéo, but can also include Ugni blanc, Terret, and Clairette.

COTEAUX DE MIRAMONT
Zonal *vin de pays* Map A, No.40
Red wines from a typically Mediterranean range of *bordelais* and southern-Rhône grapes dominate this denomination, which bridges the Côtes de la Malepère and Corbières. Rosé and white together account for less than five per cent of output, including some *vins primeurs*.
✓ *Foncalieu* (Domaine des Pins
  • *Château Mansenoble*

COTEAUX DE MURVIEL
Zonal *vin de pays* Map A, No.41
Just next to the Saint-Chinian area, this *vin de pays* produces some very good reds, which account for 85 per cent of the output, made

from Carignan, Cinsault, Grenache, Cabernet sauvignon, Merlot, and Syrah. There are a number of rosés, but very few whites.

✓ *Domaine de Coujan* • *Domaine de Ravanès*

COTEAUX DE NARBONNE
Zonal *vin de pays* Map A, No.42

Mostly soft red wines, and just four per cent in total of white and rosé, come from this coastal edge of Corbières where the vines overlap with those of Coteaux du Languedoc.

✓ *Domaine Hospitalet*

COTEAUX DE PEYRIAC
Zonal *vin de pays* Map A, No.43

Full and rustic red wines, made from local grape varieties augmented by the Syrah, Cabernet, and Merlot, account for more than 80 per cent of the production of this *vin de pays* in the heart of Minervois. The remainder is mostly rosé, with less than one per cent white.

COTEAUX DU PONT DU GARD
Zonal *vin de pays* Map A, No.44

The Pont du Gard is a stunningly beautiful, three-tier Roman aqueduct from the first century BC. Its bottom tier is still strong enough to support modern traffic 2,000 years later, but the wines of Coteaux du Pont du Gard, though mostly rich and powerful reds, are built for a considerably shorter life-span. A small amount of white and rosé is also produced, with *vins primeurs* a local speciality.

COTEAUX DU QUERCY
Zonal *vin de pays* Map B, No.45

These are mainly richly coloured, full-bodied, but precocious Gamay- and Merlot-dominated red wines from just south of the Cahors area. Production includes just five per cent rosé in a soft, easy style, but no white wine.

COTEAUX DU SALAGOU
Zonal *vin de pays* Map A, No.46

Production is 80 per cent red and 20 per cent rosé, made from a range of typical Languedoc grape varieties.

COTEAUX DU TERMENÈS
Zonal *vin de pays* Map A, No.47

Red, white, rosé, and *vins primeurs* from vines in the centre of Hautes-Corbières, but production is irregular.

COTEAUX ET TERRASSES DE MONTAUBAN
Zonal *vin de pays* Map B, No.48

Red and rosé wines from the Pays de la Garonne.

COTEAUX DU VERDON
Zonal *vin de pays* Map B, No.49

This *vin de pays* in the northern hinterland of Côtes de Provence and Coteaux Varois was created as recently as 1992 and has no restriction on the grape varieties that may be used.

CÔTES DU BRIAN
Zonal *vin de pays* Map A, No.50

An area in Minervois, Côtes du Brian produces 90 per cent red, from Carignan for the most part, although Grenache, Cinsault, Cabernet sauvignon, Merlot, and Syrah may also be used. The balance of the production is principally rosé with very few white wines.

CÔTES CATALANES
Zonal *vin de pays* Map A, No.51

Lying east of the Coteaux des Fenouilledes in the *villages* area of the Côtes-du-Roussillon, this appellation produces mostly red wine, made from a typical southern combination of *bordelais* and Rhône grapes. Some 10 per cent rosé and 10 per cent white (Rhône grapes) is also made.

✓ *Domaine Cazes* (also sold as Le Canon de Maréchal)

CÔTES DU CÉRESSOU
Zonal *vin de pays* Map A, No.52

Typically light and fruity Languedoc wines are produced in fairly large amounts; 60 per cent is red, 15 per cent white, and 25 per cent rosé.

CÔTES DU CONDOMOIS
Zonal *vin de pays* Map B, No.53

Production includes 60 per cent red, dominated by the Tannat grape, and 40 per cent white, from the Colombard or Ugni blanc. A little rosé is also produced.

CÔTES DE GASCOGNE
Zonal *vin de pays* Map B, No.54

These deliciously tangy, dry white wines are the undistilled produce of Armagnac. Those made from the Colombard grape are the lightest, while those from the Ugni blanc are fatter and more interesting. Manseng and Sauvignon blanc are also used to good aromatic effect in some blends. Less than 20 per cent of production is red and barely one per cent rosé.

✓ *Patrick Azcué* • *La Coume de Peyre* • *Domaine de Papolle* (also Domaine de Barroque) • *Plaimont* (Colombelle) • *Domaine du Rey* • *Domaine de San de Guilhem*• *Domaine du Tariquet*

CÔTES DE LASTOURS
Zonal *vin de pays* Map A, No.55

This area roughly corresponds to the Cabardès VDQS and produces mostly red wines from a similar range of grapes. Just four per cent rosé and three per cent white (Mauzac, Chenin, Chardonnay, and Ugni Blanc) is made, with *vins primeurs* a local speciality.

✓ *Baron d'Ambres*

CÔTES DU LÉZIGNAN
Zonal *vin de pays* Map A, No.56

Formerly Coteaux du Léziznanais, this denomination corresponds to the unofficial Lézignan zone of Corbières (*see also* p.235)

and almost all its wines are red. They must not contain more than 50 per cent Carignan and half the Carignan content must be made by *macération carbonique* (which some of the best Corbières producers practise anyway). Other permitted grapes include Cinsault, Grenache, Syrah, Cabernet sauvignon, Cabernet franc, and Lladoner pelut. In other words it is Corbières in all but name. Equally tiny amounts of rosé and white are also made.

CÔTES DE MONTESTRUC
Zonal *vin de pays* Map B, No.57

Production includes reds, made from Alicanté bouschet, Cabernets, Malbec, Merlot, and Jurançon noir and white wines, made from the Colombard, Mauzac, and Ugni blanc.

CÔTES DE PÉRIGNAN
Zonal *vin de pays* Map A, No.58

This area is within the southern extremity of the Coteaux du Languedoc, just north of La Clape AOC and incorporates some of La Clape's northern slopes. Almost 90 per cent is red wine that is similar, if more rustic, in style to the wines of La Clape and made from a similar range of grape varieties, but with Grenache, Syrah, and Cinsault dominating. The fresh, dry rosé can be good quality and flavoursome too. Just one per cent of white wine is made, mainly from Clairette and Ugni blanc, but Terret and Macabéo are also permitted. *Vin primeur* is also made.

CÔTES DE PROUILLE
Zonal *vin de pays* Map A, No.59

These red, white, and rosé wines produced by the Côtes de Prouille appellation come from the Aude *département*.

CÔTES DU TARN
Zonal *vin de pays* Map B, No.60

Côtes du Tarn is the *vin de pays* equivalent of Gaillac: some 60 per cent is red, 30 per cent white, and the rest rosé. These wines are made from *bordelais* and southwestern grape varieties, plus, uniquely for France, the Portugais bleu. Gamay is often used for Côtes du Tarn Primeur, while together with Syrah it makes an appealing, delicate *saignée* rosé.

CÔTES DE THAU
Zonal *vin de pays* Map A, No.61

A small denomination west of Béziers, producing almost equal quantities of red, white, and rosé from all the usual Languedoc varieties. These wines used to be used for Vermouth until the upswing in *vin de pays*.

CÔTES DE THONGUE
Zonal *vin de pays* Map A, No.62
Just south of Faugères, this appellation produces mostly red wine, from grapes including
Grenache, Cinsault, Cabernet sauvignon, Merlot,
Syrah, and Carignan, with *vins primeurs* of the
last three varieties a speciality. Emphasis is placed
on pure varietal wines of all styles. Some 15 per
cent rosé and 10 per cent white is also made in
this up-and-coming *vin de pays*.

✓ *Clos de l'Arjolle • Domaine de la
Condamine l'Evêque* (Syrah) • *Domaine
Deshenrys • Domaine du Prieuré d'Amilhac
Prodis Boissons* (Domaine Coussergue)
• *Domaine de la Serre*

CÔTES DU VIDOURLE
Zonal *vin de pays* Map A, No.63
Wedged between the Coteaux du Languedoc
and Costières de Nîmes, more than 80 per cent
of the wines produced are red, from Carignan,
Grenache, Cinsault, Cabernet sauvignon, Merlot,
Cabernet franc, and Syrah. About 15 per cent
rosé is made, but white is seldom seen.

CUCUGNAN
Zonal *vin de pays* Map A, No.64
A tiny denomination of essentially red wines
in the midst of the Côtes du Roussillon Villages
district, produced from Rhône varieties boosted
by Cabernet sauvignon and Merlot. Rosé may
be made, but seldom is, although there is an
average of one per cent dry white from Mauzac,
Chenin blanc, Chardonnay, and Ugni blanc.

DEUX-SÈVRES
Départemental vin de pays Map B
These are simple wines of a frank nature,
from the vineyards with the richest soil (and
thus the poorest as far as wine production is
concerned) in the Nantais.

✓ *Bouvet-Ladubay*

DORDOGNE
Départemental vin de pays Map B
A rustic Bergerac-style of both red and white
wine is made here. Approximately 60 per cent
of the production is white. It is due to change
its denomination to Vin de Pays du Périgord.

DRÔME
Départemental vin de pays Map B
Red, white, and rosé wines, are produced from
typical Rhône varieties augmented by Gamay,
Cabernet sauvignon, and Merlot. More than
90 per cent of the output is red and similar
in style to Coteaux du Tricastin AOC. A small
amount of decent rosé is made, but white
wines represent barely one per cent.

✓ *Sud-Est Appellations* (Syrah)

DUCHÉ D'UZES
Zonal *vin de pays* Map A, No.65
In theory, this area is in the southern half of
Vin de Pays des Cévennes, but in practice the
two *vins de pays* are virtually identical and this
is recognized by the decree in 1995, in which
Duché d'Uzès overlaps all but ten of the
131 villages in Vin de Pays des Cévennes.

FRANCHE COMTÉ
Zonal *vin de pays* Map B, No.66
A vast area overlapping the Jura and Savoie,
Franche Comté produces fresh, clean, crisp but
otherwise unremarkable red and rosé wines.
Only the white, made from Chardonnay,
Pinot gris, and Pinot blanc, is of any note.

GARD
Départemental vin de pays Map B
A large production of mostly red wines made
from Carignan, Grenache, Cinsault, Cabernet
sauvignon, Merlot, and Syrah. Some 15 per
cent of the output is a clean, fruity rosé, and
the mainly Ugni-blanc-based white wines
account for less than three per cent.

✓ *Domaine Monpertuis • Domaine le Pian*

GERS
Départemental vin de pays Map B
Mostly white wines, similar in style to Côtes
de Gascogne.

✓ *Patrick Azcué*

GIRONDE
Départemental vin de pays Map B
Red and white wines made in isolated areas
not classified for the production of Bordeaux.

GORGES DE L'HÉRAULT
Zonal *vin de pays* Map A, No.67
This denomination is in Coteaux du Languedoc
and overlaps most of the Clairette du Languedoc
appellation, yet less than ten per cent of its
wines are white, with Ugni blanc and Terret
supporting Clairette. They are, however, better
known than the reds, which account for over 80
per cent of output. Some rosés are also made.

✓ *La Grange des Pères*

HAUTES-ALPES
Départemental vin de pays Map B
Very little wine is produced under this denom-
ination, which is just south of the Savoie.

HAUTE GARONNE
Départemental vin de pays Map B
Robust red and rosé wines made from Jurançon
noir, Négrette, and Tannat grapes grown in old
vineyards south of Toulouse, with a little Merlot,
Cabernet, and Syrah. A minuscule amount of dry
white is made, and total production of all styles
is very small, but Domaine de Ribonnet has put
this denomination on the viticultural map and is
in a class apart from all the other producers.

✓ *Domaine de Ribonnet*

HAUTE MARNE
Départemental vin de pays
Located adjacent to Champagne's Aube and
Burgundy's Côte d'Or, it is not surprising that
Le Muid Montsaugeonnais made some pretty
good Pinot Noir in 1998 and 1999.

✓ *Le Muid Montsaugeonnais*

HAUTERIVE
EN PAYS D'AUDE
Zonal *vin de pays* Map A, No.68
Production is primarily red, made from a range
of typical Languedoc and southwestern grapes
in the Corbières. A little *vin primeur* is made,
as well as small amounts of white and rosé.

HAUTE-VALLÉE DE L'AUDE
Zonal *vin de pays* Map A, No.69
Mostly dry whites, from Chardonnay, Chenin,
Mauzac, and Terret grapes grown in the Limoux
district. A quarter of the output is red, from
bordelais grapes, with just three per cent rosé.

✓ *Marc Ramires* (Prieuré d'Antugnac)

HAUTE-VALLÉE DE L'ORB
Zonal *vin de pays* Map A, No.70
A limited amount of mostly reds; some rosé.

HAUTS DE BADENS
Zonal *vin de pays* Map A, No.71
These red and rosé wines are produced in a
rustic Minervois style.

HÉRAULT
Départemental vin de pays Map B

Red wine accounts for 85 per cent of production
and is increasing. The choice of grapes is quite
wide, but most blends are based on Carignan,
Cinsault, Grenache, and Syrah, boosted by a
small proportion of bordelais varieties. About
ten per cent rosé and five per cent white wine
is produced, the latter made from Clairette,
Macabéo, Grenache blanc, and Ugni blanc.
Production is vast, over one million hectolitres
(11 million cases) and rising, as is quality,
thanks to the improved viticultural and
vinicultural techniques that have transformed
what was once the heart of Midi mediocrity.

The most famous wine bearing this most
modest of *vin de pays* denominations is, of
course, Mas de Daumas Gassac. Situated
northwest of Montpellier at Aninane, this
property has been dubbed "the Lafite of the
Languedoc", but when Aimé and Véronique
Guibert purchased it wine was the last thing on
their mind. That was, however, before the visit
of Professor Enjalbert, the Bordeaux geologist
and author, who discovered Daumas Gassac
had a rare and fine, powdery volcanic soil
that is an incredible 20 metres (65 feet) deep.
Enjalbert predicted that it would yield a world-
class wine if cultivated as a *Grand Cru* and that
is exactly what Aimé Guibert set out to do.

✓ *Domaine d'Aupilhac • Domaine du Bosc*
(also sold under Vin de Pays d'Oc)
• *Domaine Capion* (also sold under Vin de
Pays d'Oc) • *Domaine de la Fadèze • Mas
de Daumas Gassac* (other *vin de pays* sold
as Terrasses de Landoc) • *Domaine de la
Source* (Muscat) • *Domaine St.-Martin*
• *Domaine St.-Martin-de-la-Garrigue*

ÎLE DE BEAUTÉ
Zonal *vin de pays* Map B, No.72
With AOC wines accounting for just 15 per
cent of Corsica's wine output, its one all-
encompassing (though technically not
départemental) *vin de pays* has a huge impact
on the perceived quality of this island's wine.
Almost 60 per cent of this *vin de pays* is red
and 25 per cent rosé, both made from a wide
range of grapes including many indigenous
Corsican varieties. Some of these may be
related to certain Italian grapes: Aleatico
(red Muscat-like variety), Cabernet sauvignon,
Carignan, Cinsault, Grenache, Merlot, Syrah,
Barbarossa, Nielluccio (the widest planted

on the island and said to be related to Sangiovese), Sciacarello (echoes of Provence's Tibouren), and Pinot noir. A lot of effort is made to promote Corsican Pinot Noir, but at the time of writing this seems to be totally misguided. The best show decent varietal aroma, but lack an elegance of fruit and do not possess the essence of Pinot on the palate. Maybe someone will make good Corsican Pinot Noir, but it is a variety that requires a lot more care and attention in the vineyard and winery than is evident in any of the examples I have tasted so far. Niellucio has a certain reputation for making good rosé, but as Orenga de Gaffory of Patrimonio in Corsica has shown, it also has the ability to produce a very fine red wine. White wines from Chardonnay, Ugni blanc, Muscat, and Vermentino are usually more demonstrative of super-clean, anaerobic handling and very cool fermentation than they are of any expression of *terroir*.

✓ *Prodis Boissons* (Domaine Sette Piana Rosé)
• SICA UVAL (Domaine de Lischetto Chardonnay)

INDRE

Départemental vin de pays Map B

Red, white, and rosé wines, including a pale *vin gris* style, from traditional Loire grape varieties are produced under this appellation.

INDRE-ET-LOIRE

Départemental vin de pays Map B

From vineyards east of Tours, this *vin de pays* is 80 per cent red, made primarily from Gamay, although Cabernet franc and Grolleau are also used. A little white, but even less rosé is made.

JARDIN DE LA FRANCE

Regional *vin de pays* Map B

This *vin de pays* produces red, white, and rosé wines from 14 *départements* covering most of the Loire Valley. It would seem, from the wines most commonly encountered, that the majority of this vast output must be dry white, dominated by either Chenin blanc or Sauvignon blanc, but, according to the statistics, 60 per cent is red. Generally a disappointing appellation, with the thin, acid Chardonnays being the most depressing, but the Cabernet Sauvignon from Pierre & Paul Freuchet is surprisingly soft and perfumed for this northerly denomination.

✓ *Pierre & Paul Freuchet*
• *Château de la Ragotière*

LANDES

Départemental vin de pays Map B

Red, white, and rosé wines are produced under this appellation. Approximately 80 per cent is red, and the grapes used are traditional southwestern varieties.

✓ *Domaine du Comte*

LOIRE-ATLANTIQUE

Départemental vin de pays Map B

Red and rosé wines, including a pale *vin gris*, are made from Gamay and Grolleau, while Folle blanche and Melon de Bourgogne are used for white, with some interesting developments using Chardonnay.

LOIRET

Départemental vin de pays Map B

This appellation produces a small amount of red and rosé, including a pale *vin gris* style, made from Gamay. A Sauvignon Blanc white is also made.

LOIR-ET-CHER

Départemental vin de pays Map B

Red, white, and rosé wines, including a pale *vin gris*, are made from traditional Loire grape varieties, mostly from around Blois in the Cheverny area. Almost half the production is red and the rest white, but a touch more of the former is made, with very little rosé.

LOT

Départemental vin de pays Map B

Most wines in this *département* are red, and claim either the regional Comté Tolosan denomination or Vin de Pays des Coteaux de Glanes.

LOT-ET-GARONNE

Départemental vin de pays Map B

This *vin de pays* is seldom seen – the wines are mostly red and sold as Vin de Pays du Comté Tolosan.

MAINE-ET-LOIRE

Départemental vin de pays Map B

Production is 85 per cent red, and white and rosé account for the rest, made from traditional Loire grape varieties in the Anjou-Saumur district. Substantial quantities are produced, but most are sold from the back door.

MARCHES DE BRETAGNE

Zonal *vin de pays* Map B, No.73

Production includes red and rosé wines, made predominantly from Abouriou, Gamay, and Cabernet franc, plus a little white from Muscadet and Gros plant.

MAURES

Zonal *vin de pays* Map B, No.74

This denomination has a very large production and covers most of the southern part of the Côtes de Provence. Almost half the wines are rosé of a similar style and quality to those of the *Vin de Pays du Var*. The rest is red, which is rich, warm, and spicy, while white wine accounts for just five per cent of total output.

MEUSE

Départemental vin de pays Map B

This *vin de pays* produces red and rosé wines, including a pale *vin gris*, from Pinot noir and Gamay. Some white wine from Chardonnay, Aligoté, and Auxerrois is also made.

MONT BAUDILE

Zonal *vin de pays* Map A, No.75

Production is mostly red wine, from a typical Languedoc range of grapes grown in the foothills of the Causses de Larzac. Rosé and white account for less than 15 per cent of the total output, although crisp, dry whites are on the increase.

✓ *Domaine d'Aupilhac*

MONT CAUME

Zonal *vin de pays* Map B, No.76

Effectively the *vin de pays* of Bandol – it is indeed the red wines that are the best here, including some truly outstanding wines, such as Bunan's classic Cabernet Sauvignon. However, the main varieties for most red and rosé wines (which account for 45 per cent of the total production) are Carignan, Grenache, Cinsault, Syrah, and Mourvèdre. A little white is produced, but it is of little interest.

✓ *Bunan* (Cabernet Sauvignon)

MONTS DE LA GRAGE

Zonal *vin de pays* Map A, No.77

These red and rosé wines are produced in a basic Languedoc style, often beefed-up with Syrah grapes.

NIÈVRE

Départemental vin de pays Map B

Red, white, and rosé wines, production of which is mostly confined to the areas of Charité-sur-Loire, La Celle-sur-Nièvre, and Tannay.

OC

Regional *vin de pays* Map B

This vast appellation is the most successful of all *vins de pays*, commercially and qualitatively. It sells well because of the simplicity of its name, which even Anglo-Saxons have no difficulty pronouncing, and it encompasses most of the best *vins de pays* produced in France. The "Oc" of this regional *vin de pays* is southern dialect for "yes", it being "oui" elsewhere in France, thus Languedoc, the "tongue of Oc".

Some 70 per cent of production is red, with the balance split equally between white and rosé. Even though most of the finest *vins de pays* are produced here, the volume of output is so vast that the quality will inevitably be variable. What has enabled so many truly fine wines to emerge in this denomination is the role of the so-called *cépages améliorateurs*. These grapes, such as Cabernet sauvignon, Merlot, Syrah, Chardonnay, and Sauvignon blanc, are not traditional in the region, but add greatly to the quality and finesse of more rustic local varieties. They also make excellent varietal wines. Viognier is on the increase as a varietal wine and makes a super-value, juicy-fruity (sometimes creamy-oaky), more exotic alternative to Chardonnay. The quest for Pinot Noir du Vin de Pays d'Oc has been even less satisfactory. The best so far are the oaky renditions from Domaine Clovallon and Domaine Joseph de Bel Air, and the strawberry-milkshake-flavoured concoction from Domaine Virginie. They might succeed, but even these three are very far from doing so, and the efforts of others have been totally alien to any knowledgeable drinker's concept of this grape.

✓ *Domaine de l'Aigle* • *Domaine des Aspes* • *Domaine du Banes* (Chardonnay, Viognier)

• *Domaine Borie la Vitarèle* • *Domaine du Bosc* (also sold under Vin de Pays de l'Hérault) • *Domaine de Calvez* (Carignan) • *Domaine Capion* (also sold under Vin de Pays de l'Hérault) • *Domaine de Cazal-Viel* • *Chais Cuxac* (Viognier) • *Chantovent* (Domaine du Roc Viognier) • *Domaine Clovallon* • *Domaine de la Condamine l'Evêque* • *Cuckoo Hill* (Chardonnay, Viognier) • *Serge Dubois* • *Fair Martina Vermentino* • *Foncalieu* (Domaine de Massia Cabernet/Syrah) • *Fortant* (wines in the top price-tier are the best) • *Domaine de Gourgazaud* • *La Grange de Quatre Sous* • *BRL-Hardy* (Cuvée Australe, Philippe de Baudin, Domaine de la Baume, Domaine de Baumière) • *James Herrick* • *Château de Jau* • *Domaine Lalaurie* • *J. & F. Lurton* • *Domaine Mandeville* • *Domaine Maury* • *Gabriel Meffre* (Galet Vineyards) • *Montagne Noire* (Chardonnay) • *Domaine le Noble* • *Domaine Ormesson* • *Primo Palatum* • *Resplandy* • *Domaine Saint-François* (Sauvignon) • *Domaine St.-Hilaire* • *Skalli* (Robert Skalli Merlot, Robert Skalli Cabernet Sauvignon) • *Domaine de Terre Mégère* • *Château le Thou* • *Val d'Orbieu* (especially Cuvée Mythique) • *Le Vieux Mas* (Sauvignon) • *Domaine Virginie* (also sold as Domaine St.-Pierre and Pierre de Passendale) • *Les Vins du Littoral Mediterranéen* (Gris)

PÉRIGORD
New zonal *vin de pays* Map B
This name is due to replace the *départemental* Vin de Pays of Dordogne.

PETITE CRAU
Zonal *vin de pays* Map B, No.78
A small *vin de pays* just south of Avignon, production is almost 80 per cent red and 20 per cent rosé from mostly Carignan, Grenache, Cinsault, and Syrah. Most rosé wines are made from, or dominated by, the Cinsault using the *saignée* method. Insignificant amounts of white from Ugni blanc and Clairette are also produced.

PÉZENAS
Zonal *vin de pays* Map A, No.79
Just south of the Cabrières AOC, this single-village denomination produces mostly red wines. The grapes permitted are typical for Languedoc, with pure varietal wines on the increase, particularly Merlot, Cabernet Sauvignon, and Syrah. Rosé and white account for about ten per cent each, with crisp dry whites on the increase, including a tiny amount sold as *vins primeurs*.

PRINCIPAUTÉ D'ORANGE
Zonal *vin de pays* Map B, No.80
This is a full red wine, made predominantly from Rhône grape varieties grown around Orange, north of Avignon, in an area that bridges Châteauneuf-du-Pape and Côtes-du-Rhône Villages. Just four per cent rosé and barely one per cent white is made.

✓ *Domaine la Soumade*

PUY-DE-DÔME
Départemental *vin de pays* Map B
Red, white, and rosé wines of simple, rustic quality are made under this appellation. A *puy* is a volcano stack, a number of which are found in the Puy-de-Dôme *département*.

PYRÉNÉES-ATLANTIQUES
Départemental *vin de pays* Map B
Two-thirds red and one-third white wine from traditional southwestern grape varieties is produced under this appellation.

PYRÉNÉES-ORIENTALES
Départemental *vin de pays* Map B

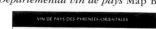

From the most southerly French *Département*, bordering Spain's Andorra region, much of the *vin de pays* in the Pyrénées-Orientales comes from the same area as the AOC Côtes-du-Roussillon and Vin de Pays Catalan. Most of the production consists of full, fruity reds, with just ten per cent rosé and five per cent white.

RETZ
Zonal *vin de pays* Map B, No.81
This denomination is best known for its rosé made from the Grolleau gris, although red wines from Grolleau, Gamay, and Cabernet franc account for as much as 70 per cent of production. A tiny amount of white from Grolleau gris can be found.

SABLES DU GOLFE DU LION
Zonal *vin de pays* Map A, No.82
A very go-ahead *vin de pays* situated along the Mediterranean coast of Gard, Hérault, and Bouches-des-Rhône, where the vines are mostly ungrafted and grown on an amazing sand-bar with seawater on both sides. Production is, unusually, two-thirds rosé, including a large proportion in pale *vin gris* style, plus 30 per cent red and a small amount of white wine.

✓ *Listel*

SAINT-SARDOS
Zonal *vin de pays* Map B, No.83
This *vin de pays* produces a small amount of mostly reds, with a little rosé, from a typically southwestern hotchpotch of grape varieties.

✓ *Domaine de Tucayne*

SARTHE
Départemental *vin de pays* Map B
Red, white, and rosé wines may be made, although production of this *vin de pays départemental* is minuscule and, as far as I am aware, limited to just one grower in Marçon.

TARN-ET-GARONNE
Départemental *vin de pays* Map B
Red wine accounts for 90 per cent of the tiny production of this appellation, although some rosé and a minuscule amount of white is also made. Most of these vines are west of Montauban, in an area that can also claim the

Vin de Pays Saint-Sardos, which overlaps part of a southwest VDQS called Vins de Lavilledieu. The grape varieties are similar to those for Lavilledieu, except for the fact that they can also include Merlot, Cabernet, and Tannat.

TERROIRS LANDAIS
Zonal *vin de pays* Map B, No.84
These are red, white, and rosé wines from four separate areas in Aquitaine, each of which may be appended to this *vin de pays* denomination: Les Sables de l'Océan (the romantic sounding "Sands of the Ocean" refers to vines growing in the sand dunes around Messanges); Les Coteaux de Chalosse (the largest area in the south of the Landes *département*, where vines grow in and around Dax and Murgon); Les Côtes de l'Adour (from vines around Aire-sur-Adour and Geaune), and Les Sables Fauves (the "Wild Sands" is a tiny enclave of vines west of Eauze). Reds and rosés are made from Tannat supported by *bordelais* varieties, while whites are primarily Ugni blanc plus Colombard, Gros mansenf, and Baroque.

✓ *Domaine de Lacquy*

THÉZAC-PERRICARD
Zonal *vin de pays* Map A, No.85
This is a small *vin de pays* adjoining the western extremity of Coteaux du Quercy.

TORGAN
Zonal *vin de pays* Map A, No.86
As this is geographically the *vin de pays* equivalent of Fitou AOC, it is no surprise to discover that 98 per cent of its wines are red. They are in fact made from a very similar range of grapes as that used to make Fitou, only certain other grapes are also permitted, including *bordelais* varieties and the teinturier Alicante Bouschet. Rosé may be made, but seldom is, and the minuscule amount of aromatic dry white may be made from Clairette, Macabéo, and Marsanne. This *vin de pays* used to be known as Coteaux Cathares.

✓ *Producteurs du Mont Tauch* (Domaine de Gardie)

URFÉ
Zonal *vin de pays* Map B, No.87
Red wine is mostly made in modest quantities. White and rosé may also be produced.

VAL-DE-CESSE
Zonal *vin de pays* Map A, No.88
These are mostly red wines, plus ten per cent rosé, and five per cent white from local grape varieties in the Minervois area.

VAL-DE-DAGNE
Zonal *vin de pays* Map A, No.89
This area overlaps part of the Côtes de Malepère and produces almost entirely red wines from a choice of Carignan, Grenache, Terret noir, Merlot, Cabernet sauvignon, Cabernet franc, and the teinturier Alicante bouschet. Very little rosé and white is made.

VAL DE MONTFERRAND
Zonal *vin de pays* Map A, No.90
Mostly red wines, but rosé accounts for 25 per cent of production and white for 15 per cent in this denomination, which encompasses the *garrigues* below the Cévennes. The usual Languedoc grapes are used. *Vin primeur* and *vin d'une nuit* are local specialities produced in relatively large quantities.

VAL D'ORBIEU
Zonal *vin de pays* Map A, No.91

This *vin de pays* can come from two areas of vines in the Corbières district, one between Narbonne and Lézignan, the other further west around Lagrasse. Production is mostly red from Carignan, Cinsault, Grenache, Terret noir, Cabernet sauvignon, Syrah, Mourvèdre, and the teinturier Alicante bouschet. Little rosé and white is made, but *vin primeur* is a local speciality.

✓ *Penfolds* (Laperouse)

VALLÉE DU PARADIS
Zonal *vin de pays* Map A, No.92
Mostly red wines from an area that overlaps Corbières and Fitou, made from Carignan, Syrah, Grenache, Cinsault, Cabernet sauvignon, and Merlot. Very little white wine is made (usually as *vin primeur*) and even less rosé. A heavenly name, even to Anglo-Saxon ears, which no doubt helps it on export markets, which account for almost half its sales.

✓ *Jeanjean*

VALS D'AGLY
Zonal *vin de pays* Map A, No.93
Located in the *villages* area of the Côtes du Roussillon, sandwiched between the Côtes Catalanes and Coteaux des Fenouilledes, three-quarters of these wines are red, made from a typically southern mix of *bordelais* and Rhône grape varieties, with white and rosé on the increase and *vin primeur* a local speciality.

✓ *Domaine des Chênes*

VAR
Départemental *vin de pays* Map B
This denomination is one of the largest producers of *vins de pays*. Covering the vast majority of the Côtes de Provence AOC, it not surprisingly produces a large quantity of rosé: no less than 45 per cent, in fact. The wines are usually made by the *saignée* method and range from very pale *vin gris* style, through orange to almost cherry-red. The quality is equally as variable. The big, rich, spicy reds are much better and of a more consistent quality, often utilizing Syrah, Mourvèdre, and Cabernet sauvignon to boost the Grenache, Cinsault, Carignan, and Roussane du Var, which the rosés mainly rely on. Some white wines are also made, but represent just five per cent of production. They are not usually very exciting, and are mostly made from Ugni blanc, Clairette, Bourboulenc, and Vermentino. The white from Domaine Rabiega is one of the exceptions, relying on Chardonnay for body and Viognier and Sauvignon blanc to lift the Ugni blanc base.

✓ *Domaine du Deffends • Domaine Rabiega • Château Vignelaure*

VAUCLUSE
Départemental *vin de pays* Map B
Three-quarters of output of this *vin de pays* is red, similar to basic Côtes-du-Rhone. Rosé can be fresh, and accounts for just ten per cent of output; white is generally the least interesting.

✓ *Domaine de la Citadelle • Domaine de la Monardière*

VAUNAGE
Zonal *vin de pays* Map A, No.94
Light red wines made in typical Languedoc style.

VENDÉE
Départemental *vin de pays* Map B
Red, white, and rosé wines are produced in small quantities, in a similar style to Fiefs Vendéens (which was a *vin de pays* until it was promoted to VDQS status in December 1984).

VICOMTÉ D'AUMELAS
Zonal *vin de pays* Map A, No.95
Overlapping part of Cabrières, this *vins de pays* produces mostly red wines of a simple, fresh, fruity style, from traditional southwestern grape varieties, such as the typical Languedoc grape. Just over ten per cent of wines are rosé, and a tiny amount of crisp, dry white is produced.

✓ *Domaine Puech*

VIENNE
Départemental *vin de pays* Map B
This appellation produces red, white, and rosé wines, which are produced in and around the Haut-Poitou district.

✓ *Domaine Ampelidae*

VISTRENQUE
Zonal *vin de pays* Map A, No.96
This appellation produces red and rosé wines, which are made in very small quantities. White wine may also be produced.

YONNE
Départemental *vin de pays* Map B
The Yonne is a white-only appellation, and its production of wines is quite small.

✓ *William Fèvre*

ARDÈCHE GORGE
This dramatic gorge is located at the heart of the Coteaux de l'Ardèche – an appellation that quickly established a reputation as one of the most progressive and quality-conscious vins de pays in the country, first for Syrah, then Chardonnay and, if Louis Latour's range of stunning new wines is anything to go by, Pinot Noir.

AUTHOR'S CHOICE

The only problem with choosing favourite vins de pays *is that it is such an exciting, fast-moving category that potential new favourites are cropping up all the time, but the following selections currently give me the most pleasure.*

PRODUCER	WINE	STYLE	DESCRIPTION	⏳
Domaine Cazes	Muscat, Vin de Pays de Catalan (*see* p.249)	WHITE	Deliciously dry and beautifully aromatic, this wine has elegant, floral (orange-water), peachy fruit.	6–18 months
Mas de Daumas Gassac	Vin de Pays de l'Hérault (*see* p.252)	RED	This is a world-class Cabernet-dominated blend made in true Médoc style, but with a touch of warm Mediterranean spice. A wine of great longevity, its initial vintages could be criticized for being too tough and tannic, but from 1985 onwards, they have become more supple in style and can now be compared to a top *Cru Classé* of Pauillac or St.-Estèphe.	8–20 years
Mas de Daumas Gassac	Vin de Pays de l'Hérault (*see* p.252)	ROSÉ	Not in the same class as the white (which is not in the same class as the red), this fresh, dry and very spritzy wine is not supposed to be anything more than an unpretentious quaffing wine. If I dared to suggest this might be considered the thinking person's Mateus, Aimé Guibert would not talk to me again, so never let it be said that I intimated anything of the sort!	Upon purchase
Mas de Daumas Gassac	Vin de Pays de l'Hérault (*see* p.252)	WHITE	Not in the same class as the red and far more exotic, this oak-aged dry white is very floral, aromatic, soft, and seductive, which in most years is a blend of Chardonnay, Viognier, and Petit Manseng with a good dollop of Muscat.	1–3 years
BRL-Hardy	La Baume Cuvée Australe, Vin de Pays d'Oc (*see* p.254)	RED	Its dry tannin structure belies the richness and depth of this classic French food wine made by Australian wizardry.	2–6 years
James Herrick	Chardonnay and Réserve Chardonnay, Vin de Pays d'Oc (*see* p.254)	WHITE	The pure, fresh, immaculate fruit in the basic wine stands out in the company of much more expensive Chardonnay, and the Réserve can stand up to famous Burgundy at twice the price.	1–2 years
James Herrick	Domaine la Motte Chardonnay, Vin de Pays d'Oc (*see* p.254)	WHITE	This is much richer and fatter than the basic Chardonnay and has even more finesse than the superb Réserve Chardonnay.	1–2 years
James Herrick	Cuvée Simone, Vin de Pays d'Oc (*see* p.254)	RED	Where can you buy such a lovely, rich mouthful of lip-smacking fruit and tannins bearing an AOC for such a reasonable price? Any red that is ready in one year yet improves for six is something special (it defies the Coates Law of Maturity, *see* Glossary).	1–6 years
Louis Latour	Pinot Noir, Vin de Pays de Coteaux de l'Ardèche (*see* p.250)	RED	This stunning wine is easily the greatest *vin de pays* Pinot Noir ever produced. It could be the greatest *vin de pays* that has ever been produced from any grape variety, but it is not possible or fair to compare wines of totally different grapes and styles and say which is best. I am certain, however, that it is the most exciting *vin de pays* I have ever tasted. It is so soft and silky, with such a purity of fruit and so much finesse that few Burgundians would believe this is not a Burgundy, and a fine one at that. It's not cheap for a *vin de pays*, but it is better than many Burgundies twice its price.	2–5 years
Louis Latour	Chardonnay, Vin de Pays de Coteaux de l'Ardèche (*see* p.250)	WHITE	Maison Louis Latour made waves in 1979 when it started selling pure *vin de pays* Chardonnay, one *cuvée* of which had been fermented in new oak *barriques* (unprecedented for such a lowly appellation at the time), and aggressively marketed the wine under the company's name in a not entirely un-Burgundian presentation. The first *cuvées* were hailed as ground-breaking by some, but in all honesty were too oaky. They soon got the balance right and the oak in the Grand Ardèche is now beautifully integrated. Although not cheap, this rich and classy Chardonnay puts many far more expensive oak-aged Burgundies to shame, whereas the lovely, unoaked Chardonnay fruit in the basic Ardèche shows up most Mâcons-Villages AOC wines.	18–30 months (Ardèche), 2–5 years (Grand Ardèche)

PRODUCER	WINE	STYLE	DESCRIPTION	🍴
Gabriel Meffre	Barrel Reserve Merlot, Vin de Pays d'Oc (*see* p.254)	RED	Unlike the Syrah (below), I cannot claim that the basic Merlot ever had any special reputation. There is nothing wrong with it (indeed, there is seldom anything wrong with any of this producer's wines), it is simply a bit "nervy" and it ranks with the Grenache Blanc as one of the two least interesting wines under the Galet Vineyards label. The Barrel Reserve, however, is a revelation – very smooth and rich with even the nervy quality in the basic *cuvée* seemingly transformed into an agreeable assertiveness, which makes it a much better wine to drink with food than the Barrel Reserve Syrah, although it is a matter of personal taste as to which is the better wine *per se*.	2–8 years
Gabriel Meffre	Barrel Reserve Syrah, Vin de Pays d'Oc (*see* p.254)	RED	The basic Syrah is one of the two wines (the other being Chardonnay) that created the Galet Vineyards' reputation for richly flavoured wines of great value, but this is so much fatter and richer that it is creamy and unctuous – an uncommon descriptor for red wines – with beautifully balanced classic fruit.	2–5 years
Gabriel Meffre	Fat Bastard Chardonnay, Vin de Pays d'Oc (*see* p.254)	WHITE	When British shipper Guy Anderson was visiting Meffre, the winemaker took him to a barrel and said "Taste this fat bastard", using a term picked up during a stint in Australia. Guy thought it sounded so funny in a French accent with that he persuaded him to put the barrel to one side and bottle the wine under the "Fat Bastard" label. It is big, and it is fat, but it is so delicious and seductive that this portly author uses it as his house white.	1–3 years
Domaine de Papolle	Vin de Pays des Côtes de Gascogne (*see* p.251)	WHITE	Made by an Englishman called Peter Hawkins, who married a French woman, has lived in France since 1970, and purchased Domaine de Papolle in the Bas-Armagnac region in 1981. He divides his time between engineering in the north of France and making and selling wine and Armagnac in the southwest. Both his Domaine Papolle and Domaine de Barroque have provided good, inexpensive dry white wines from modest grape varieties for more than a decade, but occasionally his wines transcend their intrinsic quality, producing the freshest, crispest, fruity style and titillating the palate with intense, flowery-grapey flavour that after a year in bottle develops a deliciously honeyed aftertaste.	6–18 months
Domaine du Rey	Vin de Pays des Côtes de Gascogne (*see* p.251)	WHITE	If there is one thing wrong with Côtes de Gascogne it is its predictability: it is always a refreshing, tangy-dry white wine. No one, however, could predict the gentle ripeness of fruit in this wine, which is a tip-top Côtes de Gascogne.	1–3 years
Terrasses de Landoc	Carignan, Vin de Pays de l'Hérault (*see* p.252)	RED	A wine that shows just how good the lowly and despised Carignan grape can be, this is a proper wine to drink with food. It has a rich and complex character that evolves as you drink, and fascinating aromas that unfold with every swirl of the glass.	2–4 years
Val d'Orbieu	Cuvée Mythique, Vin de Pays d'Oc (*see* p.254)	RED	This is the brainchild of Marc Dubernet, Val d'Orbieu's brilliant oenologist. I have to admit that between the excellence of his wine and the genius of his label, Val d'Orbieu has certainly created a myth and mystique about this wine. The oak aromas really intensify between its second and third year, when the wine billows with huge coconutty aromas that are more reminiscent of American oak than the French Allier oak claimed on the wine's back label. By the third year, the wine also attains a mellow richness, which is gently supported by supple tannins, giving it an ideal structure for food. Exactly when you will prefer to drink this wine will depend on how much complexity you like and how much freshness of fruit you're willing to trade for this, although fruit *per se* (rather than the freshness of fruit) remains ample for a good number of years.	3–7 years

The WINES *of*

GERMANY

CLASSIC GERMAN RIESLING IS INCOMPARABLE.
No other wine can offer in a single sip as much
finesse, purity of fruit, intensity of flavour, and
thrilling acidity as a fine Riesling. Almost every
wine writer agrees that German wines are
underrated, and the only course of action
is to rebuild their reputation on the back of
the Riesling grape variety. This would involve
the classification of the country's top wine
estates, but the owners are politically weak,
while the large, commercial bottlers are strong.
It is in the commercial interest of these large,
powerful firms and cooperatives to keep export
markets flooded with cheap, medium-sweet
wines made from almost every German white
grape variety except Riesling, and this is why,
in the fraternity of winemaking nations, Germany
is perceived as such a poor and unsophisticated
relation. However, great Riesling wines are still
made and the current situation, although
deplorable, does mean that at least fine
German wines can be purchased for a
reasonable price by the *cognoscente*.

THE RHEINGAU DISTRICT
*An autumnal view of the quaint Hallgarten chapel which
lies between the Schönhell and Würzgarten vineyards.*

✦ GERMANY ✦

When a German wine producer makes and bottles a wine, the aim is to capture the quintessential freshness of the grapes that went into it. From the most modest to the very finest German wines, the secret is the harmony between sweetness and acidity. The best German wines are better than ever, but the worst have never been as bad, and the new German Wine Law passed in 1994 to replace the flawed law of 1971 has unfortunately not improved matters.

EVERY GERMAN WINE IS GRADED by the natural sugar content of its grapes; the more sugar, the higher the quality, therefore the greatest German wines are inevitably the sweetest. Although the philosophy that equates ripeness with greatness is misguided and has proved harmful to Germany's reputation, it is not an unreasonable one, for ripe grapes are required to make fine wine, and in Germany's northerly climate it is usually only the best sites that can fully ripen grapes. Nonetheless, taken to its ultimate conclusion, the German ideal implies, nonsensically, that a drier wine is inherently inferior to a sweeter wine. In the quest for sweetness, the Riesling was gradually discarded in favour of German crosses such as Müller-Thurgau and Kerner, which easily ripened at much higher sugar levels and yielded far larger crops.

A GERMAN ESTATE-WINE REVIVAL?

In the 18th and 19th centuries, German wines from the Rhine were once as famous and as expensive as the wines of Bordeaux when Germany's system of aristocratic wine estates was on a par with the great wine châteaux of France. Today, almost every wine critic agrees that Germany's best wine estates must reassert the position they once had, if this country wants to regain its reputation for quality, but this is not currently possible because each estate makes far too many wines to project any sort of unified image, let alone reputation.

In Bordeaux one can speak of the style and quality of, say, Château Margaux *viz-à-viz* Château Latour, but what can be said about any top German estate, when the wines range from QbA, through *Kabinett, Spätlese, Auslese, Beerenauslese,* and *Trockenbeerenauslese* to *Eiswein* for each grape variety grown? At one time Germany's top wine estates were every bit as illustrious as the most famous French châteaux. They did not market a vast number of *Prädikat* wines. Instead, they built their reputations on a single, flagship *cuvée*, which was invariably pure Riesling

SCHLOSS JOHANNISBERG
This historic, mansion-style schloss, which dominates the Rheingau slope between Winkel and Geisenheim, was built in 1563.

THE WINE REGIONS OF GERMANY

Viticulturally, Germany is made up of four large *Deutscher Tafelwein* regions encompassing eight *Tafelwein* sub-regions, within which there are separate infrastructures for 13 *Qualitätswein* and 19 *Landwein* regions (the two *Qualitätswein* and two *Landwein* regions in former Eastern Germany fall outside the *Tafelwein* structure). The *Qualitätswein* regions called *Anbaugebiete* encompass 39 *Bereiche* (districts), containing 160 *Grosslagen* (collective sites), which in turn encapsulate 2,632 *Einzellagen* (single sites).

DEUTSCHER TAFELWEIN REGIONS	DEUTSCHER TAFELWEIN SUB-REGIONS	LANDWEIN REGIONS	QUALITÄTSWEIN REGIONS (ANBAUGEBIETEN)
Rhein-Mosel	Rhein	Ahrtaler *Landwein*	Ahr
		Starkenburger *Landwein*	Hessische Bergstrasse
		Rheinburgen *Landwein*	Mittelrhein
		Nahegauer *Landwein*	Nahe
		Altrheingauer *Landwein*	Rheingau
		Rheinischer *Landwein*	Rheinhessen
		Pfälzer *Landwein*	Pfalz
	Mosel	*Landwein* der Mosel	
	Saar	Saarländischer *Landwein*	Mosel-Saar-Ruwer
		Landwein der Ruwer	
Bayern	Main	Fränkischer *Landwein*	
	Donau	Regensburger *Landwein*	Franken
	Lindau	Bayerischer Bodensee *Landwein*	
Neckar	—	Schwäbischer *Landwein*	Württemberg
Oberrhein	Römertor	Südbadischer *Landwein*	Baden
	Burgengau	Unterbadischer *Landwein*	
		Taubertäler *Landwein*	
		Mitteldeutscher *Landwein*	Saale-Unstrut
		Sächsischer *Landwein*	Sachsen

QUALITY STRUCTURE OVERVIEW

This is a simplistic overview because each category varies according to the grape variety and its area of origin. More detailed analyses are given under each region (*see* Quality Requirements and Harvest Percentages box).

QUALITY CATEGORY	MINIMUM OECHSLE	MINIMUM POTENTIAL ALCOHOL
*Deutscher Tafelwein**	44–50°	5.0–5.9%
*Landwein**	47–55°	5.6–6.7%
Qualitätswein bestimmter Anbaugebiete (QbA)*	50–72°	5.9–9.4%
QUALITÄTSWEIN MIT PRÄDIKAT (QmP):		
Kabinett	67–85°	8.6–11.4%
Spätlese	76–95°	10.0–13.0%
Auslese	83–105°	11.1–14.5%
Beerenauslese	110–128°	15.3–18.1%
Eiswein	110–128°	15.3–18.1%
Trockenbeerenauslese (TBA)	150–154°	21.5–22.1%

*Chaptalization is allowed, and will be necessary if the wine has a potential alcoholic strength of less than 8.5 per cent.

and, no matter how many times the vineyards were combed for grapes, just one wine was produced. It would be like combining all the different *Prädikat* wines into one super-rich blend today. In the days of Germany's illustrious wine estates the wines were fermented more fully, rather than being arrested at artificially low alcohol levels in order to retain sweetness. Thus these flagship *cuvées* were not just richer than today's wines, but drier, fuller-bodied, and more alcoholic. It was this sort of wine that

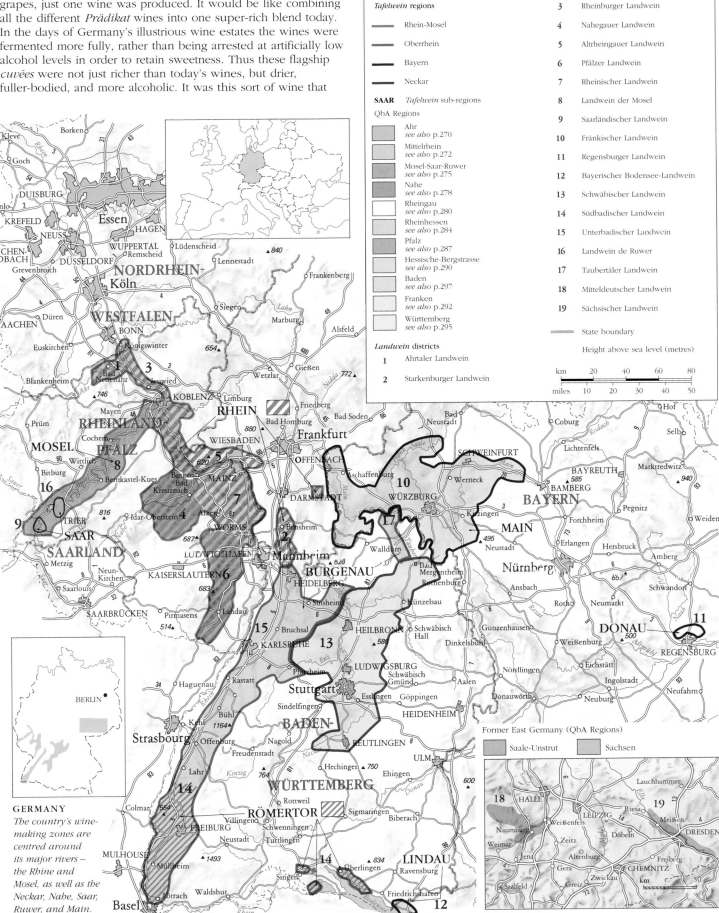

Tafelwein regions

— Rhein-Mosel
— Oberrhein
— Bayern
— Neckar

SAAR *Tafelwein* sub-regions

QbA Regions

- Ahr *see also p.270*
- Mittelrhein *see also p.272*
- Mosel-Saar-Ruwer *see also p.275*
- Nahe *see also p.278*
- Rheingau *see also p.280*
- Rheinhessen *see also p.284*
- Pfalz *see also p.287*
- Hessische-Bergstrasse *see also p.290*
- Baden *see also p.297*
- Franken *see also p.292*
- Württemberg *see also p.295*

Landwein districts

1 Ahrtaler Landwein
2 Starkenburger Landwein
3 Rheinburger Landwein
4 Nahegauer Landwein
5 Altrheingauer Landwein
6 Pfälzer Landwein
7 Rheinischer Landwein
8 Landwein der Mosel
9 Saarländischer Landwein
10 Fränkischer Landwein
11 Regensburger Landwein
12 Bayerischer Bodensee-Landwein
13 Schwäbischer Landwein
14 Südbadischer Landwein
15 Unterbadischer Landwein
16 Landwein de Ruwer
17 Taubertäler Landwein
18 Mitteldeutscher Landwein
19 Sächsischer Landwein

— State boundary

Height above sea level (metres)

km   20   40   60   80
miles 10   20   30   40   50

Former East Germany (QbA Regions)

Saale-Unstrut   Sachsen

GERMANY

The country's winemaking zones are centred around its major rivers – the Rhine and Mosel, as well as the Neckar, Nahe, Saar, Ruwer, and Main.

made Germany's finest wine estates famous throughout the world and only when they return to the same basic philosophy will they be able to rebuild their reputations.

THE 1971 GERMAN WINE LAW

In 1971 a wine law was established to take account of EEC legislation regulating wine production. The main aspect of the law was to reduce 30,000 *Einzellagen* (individually named vineyards) to 2,600. The law allowed the boundaries of each of the original *Einzellagen* to be extended in order to cover a minimum area of five hectares. The solution appeared efficient, but missed the point of why any plot of land evolves a name or reputation to distinguish it from neighbouring vineyards: *terroir* (*see* p.82). The enshrining of these amalgamated vineyards in law has duped the public into believing that highly priced wines come from specific, historical sites when in fact they may originate from the surrounding areas that, on average, are more than ten times the size.

This was nothing less than legalized fraud, but the bureaucratic bungling did not end there, as the lawmakers went on to create an entirely new geographical appellation called the "*Grosslage*", which has turned out to be an even greater deception. In fact, once this law's capacity to deceive was fully understood, it became known on English-speaking markets as the "Gross lie". A *Grosslage* or "collective site" is a very large area, not merely encompassing several *Einzellagen* (single sites as the term

DECODING THE AP NUMBER

All QbAs and QmPs, including *Deutscher Sekt*, must carry an AP number (*Amtliche Prüfnummer*). This proves that a wine has undergone and passed various tasting and analytical tests and its origin has been established to the board's satisfaction. Each time a producer applies for an AP number, specially sealed samples of the approved wine are kept by both the board and the producer. Should there be a fault or a fraud enquiry, these samples are analyzed and checked against a sample of the product on the market that has given rise to complaint or investigation. This sounds foolproof and it is indeed more stringent than the EU's Lot Number, which has been in operation since 1989, but like all systems it can be abused, which in this case would simply mean printing fictitious AP numbers on the label, although if noticed the penalty for this would be imprisonment, plus a ban from operating for the company, and a large fine. Understanding the AP number can be very useful. If the wine is a non-vintage QbA, it can give you some idea of how long it has been in bottle.

1991 "Weingut Grans-Fassian" Riesling Trocken Qualitätswein

3 = Examination Board number

529 = number of the commune where the wine was bottled

042 = the bottler's registered number

10 = the bottler's application number

92 = the year in which the bottler made the application

The communes' and bottlers' numbers run into thousands and are of the least significance to the consumer. It is the last two sets of numbers that provide the most useful information: the 10 and 92 reveal that this is the tenth application that Weingut Grans-Fassian has made in 1992 for the 1991 vintage of its Reisling Trocken. There must have been nine other shipments of the same wine earlier in 1992, thus this bottle would taste distinctly fresher than a bottle with, for example, an 01 application number. If the wine happens to be a non-vintage version of something that should be drunk as young as possible, the date of application could be a revelation.

literally means) but many villages, each of which comprises a large number of *Einzellagen*. On average, each *Grosslage* consists of 17 post-1971 *Einzellagen* or 197 pre-1971 *Einzellagen*. Such wines are widely blended and of modest quality, but this in itself would not have been a problem had it been obligatory for the term "*Grosslage*" to appear on the label before the name of the *Einzellage* itself, as "*Bereich*" (district) has to. Not only does the term *Grosslage* not have to appear anywhere on the label, but the name of the *Grosslage* appears after that of the village, in precisely the same way as the name of an *Einzellage* does, constantly leading consumers to believe that a *Grosslage* wine is from a single *Einzellage*. The criteria that originally established Germany as one of the great wine-producing countries of the world – the pre-eminence and defining quality of the Riesling grape, the famous villages or estates where it was grown, and the legendary quality of the individually named vineyards, or true *Einzellagen* – no longer applied after 1971.

THE 1994 WINE LAW

In 1994, when Germany was required to bring its wine law into line with other member states of the EU, it had a chance to remedy the flaws in the 1971 wine law and those who cared about quality bravely attempted reforms, but the large private and

COMPARISON OF GERMAN HARVESTS 1992–1995

Production varies enormously in Germany from as much as 15.4 million hectolitres (171 million cases) in 1982 to as little as 5.2 million hectolitres (58 million cases) in 1985, as does the spread of wines across the range of quality categories, shown by the table below:

	1992	1993	1994	1995
QUALITY CATEGORY				
Tafelwein to *Landwein*	2%	–	2%	1%
QbA	50%	34%	55%	79%
Kabinett	10%	11%	9%	–
Spätlese	8%	10%	9%	20%
Auslese to *TBA**	1%	2%	2%	–
SIZE OF HARVEST				
Millions of hectolitres	13.4	9.7	10.3	8.4
(Millions of cases)	148.8	107.7	114.4	93.3
Hectares under vine	102,995	103,450	103,727	103,727
(Acres)	254,500	255,625	256,309	256,309
Hectolitres per hectare	130.1	93.8	99.3	81.0
(Cases per acre)	585	421	446	364

*Includes Eiswein

HOW TO READ GERMAN WINE LABELS

MOSEL-SAAR-RUWER•
One of the 11 specified regions or *Anbaugebiete,* one of which must appear on the label of every QbA and QmP wine. In the case of a *Landwein,* one of its 15 regions must be indicated and the term *Deutscher Tafelwein* must also be mentioned.

ZELLER MARIENBURGER•
This reveals that the wine comes from the commune of Zell on the lower reaches of the Mosel river, between Reil and Bullay. In German, "-*er*" is an adjectival ending that is added to the name of the place where a wine comes from, in the same way that English-speaking people might add "-*er*" to describe a person from London or New York as a "Londoner" or "New Yorker". Marienburger is the name of an *Einzellage* (an individual site or vineyard) within Zell.

QUALITÄTSWEIN MIT PRÄDIKAT (QmP)•
The wine comes from the highest quality category of German wine and will carry one of the predicates that range from *Kabinett* up to *Trockenbeerenauslese.*

ERZEUGERABFÜLLUNG•
At one time this was considered to mean estate-bottled, but so many cooperatives used it that over the years it really came to mean producer-bottled.
   The term now supposedly meaning estate-bottled is *Gutsabfüllung.* It can only be used if the winemaker holds a diploma in oenology, so that any naturally-gifted winemaker who has not sat the examination, but owns an estate and makes brilliant wines, will not be able to print *Gutsabfüllung* on his label.

GRAPE VARIETY
This is often indicated on German labels. In this example the lable states "Riesling" and is in fact 100 per cent pure Riesling, although it need only be 85 per cent according to the regulations. If more than one grape variety is indicated on the label, then they must be listed in order of their importance in that wine; therefore a Riesling-Kerner contains more Riesling than Kerner.•

NAME AND ADDRESS•
The name and address of the owner of the estate and bottler of the wine must be shown on every German label. This example clearly shows that Kloster Machern is owned by Schneider'sche Weingüterverwaltung Kloster Machern, which is in fact part of Michel Schneider, a small, high-quality export house based in Zell.

•VINTAGE
A wine must be at least 85 per cent a product of the named year. It often carries the adjectival "-*er*" ending.

•KABINETT
The predicate at the end of this wine's name reveals that it is the lightest and driest predicate. The predicate can come either before or after the grape variety.

•AMTLICHE PRÜFNUMMER OR AMTLICHE PRÜFUNGSNUMMER
The AP number, as it is commonly called, is found on all QbA and QmP wines and literally means the "official proof number". The code is unique to each batch of wine presented to the official examination board and its presence is proof that the wine has passed the statutory origin, tasting, and laboratory analysis test. *See* Decoding the AP Number, p.262.

•PRODUCE (OR PRODUCT) OF GERMANY
This must be clearly shown on every bottle of exported German wine. If it is not, the wine is made from grapes grown in another country.

•KLOSTER MACHERN
The name of the estate. This property once belonged to an ancient Cistercian order that dates back to 1238.

•VOLUME
An indication of the liquid contents is mandatory at all levels of quality.

ALCOHOLIC STRENGTH
Mandatory for export wines only.

Other terms on wine labels:

BEREICH
If the wine carries the appellation of a *Bereich,* it will simply state this – "Bereich Zell", for example.

GROSSLAGE
This is one of the main problems with German wine labelling. A *Grosslage* ("collective site") is usually a large area, under which name modest wines are sold, but there is no way to distinguish it from a relatively rare *Einzellage* ("single site") wine.

INDICATION OF SWEETNESS (STILL WINE)
This is permitted, but not mandatory, not even for *Landwein,* which is rather strange as it is a wine that may be produced in only *Trocken* and *Halbtrocken* styles. The terms that might be found are: *Trocken* (dry) – must not contain more than four grams of residual sugar per litre, although up to nine grams per litre is permitted if the acidity is two grams per litre or less. *Halbtrocken* (half-dry) – must not contain more than 18 grams of residual sugar per litre and ten grams of acid per litre.

Lieblich (medium-sweet) – nearer to the French *moelleux* than medium-sweet, this wine may have up to 45 grams of residual sugar per litre. *Süss* (Sweet) – with in excess of 45 grams of residual sugar per litre, this is a truly sweet wine.
   Where applicable, *Rotwein* (red wine), *Weisswein* (white wine), or *Rotling* (rosé wine) must be indicated on the label of any category of *Tafelwein* up to and including *Landwein.* They must also be featured on the label of QbA and higher quality wines, but this is not mandatory, except in the case of *Rotling* or *Rosé,* which must be indicated on the label of QbA wines, although this is optional for QmP.

WEISSHERBST
This is a single-variety rosé produced from black grapes only. The grape variety must be indicated and the minimum quality of what was originally a botrytis wine is now QbA.

SCHILLERWEIN
A style of wine produced in Württemberg that is the same as a *Rotling,* which is to say it may be made from a blend of black and white grape varieties.

BADISCH ROTGOLD
A speciality rosé wine made from a blend of Ruländer and Spätburgunder. It must be of at least QbA level, and can be produced only in Baden.

PERLWEIN
Cheap, semi-sparkling wines made by carbonating a still wine. Mostly white, but may be red or rosé.

SCHAUMWEIN
With no further qualification, such as *Qualitätsschaumwein,* this indicates the cheapest form of sparkling wine, probably a carbonated blend of wines from various EU countries.

QUALITÄTSSCHAUMWEIN
A "quality sparkling wine" can be produced by any member state of the EU, but the term should be qualified by the country of origin (of the wine). Only *Deutscher Qualitätsschaumwein* will necessarily be from Germany.

DEUTSCHER SEKT OR DEUTSCHER QUALITÄTSSCHAUMWEIN
A sparkling wine made by any method (though probably *cuve close*), that is produced from 100 per cent German grapes. It may indicate a maximum of two grape names and should be at least ten months old when sold.

DEUTSCHER QUALITÄTS-SCHAUMWEIN OR DEUTSCHER SEKT BESTIMMTER ANBAUGEBIETE
A sparkling wine made by any method (probably *cuve close*), that is produced from 100 per cent German grapes from one specified region, although it may indicate an even smaller area of origin if 85 per cent of the grapes come from that named area.

FLASCHENGÄRUNG
Bottle-fermented *Sekt,* but not necessarily *méthode champenoise.*

FLASCHENGÄRUNG NACH DEM TRADITIONELLEN VERFAHREN
This indicates *Sekt* made by the *méthode champenoise,* although it is not usually a wine that shows much autolytic character.

FÜR DIABETIKER GEEIGNET
This phrase means "suitable for diabetics". The wines must be *Trocken* (dry), contain less than 1.5 grams per litre of sulphur dioxide (as opposed to 2.25 grams per litre) and no more than 12 per cent alcohol.

SÜSSRESERVE

Süssreserve is sterilized grape juice that may have just one or two degrees of alcohol, but has none if processed before fermentation can commence. It not only contributes the grapey freshness and sweetness for which German wines are famous, but also provides the winemaker with a convenient last-minute ingredient with which he can correct the balance of a wine. The origin of *Süssreserve* must, in essence, be the same as the wine to which it is added. Its quality, or degree of ripeness, should by law be at least the equivalent of the wine itself. The quantity added is not in itself restricted, but is indirectly controlled by the overall ratio of sugar to alcohol.

QUALITY	GRAMS OF ALCOHOL FOR EVERY GRAM OF RESIDUAL SUGAR PER LITRE	EXCEPTIONS	
Tafelwein	3g	Franconian red	5g
Qualitätswein	3g	Franconian red	5g
		Franconian white and rosé	3.5g
		Württemberg red	4g
		Rheingau white	2.5g
Kabinett	no controls	Franconian red	5g
		Franconian white and rosé	3g

WEINGUT MAX. FERD. RICHTER, MÜLHEIM
A producer of great Riesling, particularly from Juffer Sonnenuhr in Braunberg, Dr. Richter is justly famous for his superb Eiswein.

cooperative bottlers of inferior wine were too powerful, thus the bad law of 1971 was replaced by the even worse law of 1994. The *Grosslagen* and *Bereiche* could and should have been disposed of because they are unnecessary appellations that do not enhance the reputation of German wines. If such a simple but radical move was too difficult to accomplish, then a temporary yet perfectly adequate means of stopping the rot would have been to concentrate on reforming the *Grosslagen*, which are a deception as well as a distraction. This would have been easy to achieve simply by making it mandatory to print the term *Grosslage* on the label, in the same way that *Bereich* must appear. Until there is a consensus on the reform or eradication of the *Grosslagen*, there is no hope of reinstating the authentic names and boundaries of the *Einzellagen*, yet this is the only hope Germany has of reclaiming equal fine-wine status with France. Only a hierarchical classification of Germany's greatest vineyards will put this country back among

the elite winemaking nations of the world, but it would be meaningless to build one on the current tissue of lies. The number of *Einzellagen* was reduced to 2,600 in 1971 because, it was claimed, 30,000 was too confusing to contemplate, but this claim was without justification. It does not matter whether there are 30,000 or 300,000 – there are as many *Einzellagen* as there are; they all have the same right to exist, but only the outstanding ones will ever earn a reputation, so where is the potential for confusion? No one has suggested that all 30,000 *Einzellagen* should be classified. If the Germans ever conduct an official classification, it would probably consist of no more than the best 250 *Einzellagen* and only the top ten per cent of these would be required to create the sort of international reputation that Bordeaux's First Growths have so effectively achieved.

CHANGING IDEAS ABOUT GERMAN WINES

The modern idea of which German wines to drink, and how and when to drink them, is based on a tradition that is over a hundred years old. Outside Germany itself, the predilection for Rhine and Mosel is essentially a British one. Historically, this has always been so. Even two world wars failed to diminish the British fondness for these wines, and despite a 25 per cent drop in exports in the early 1990s, Britain remains Germany's biggest customer.

At one time, the British, whose tastes influenced the rest of the world, drank only Hock, a name that originally applied only to the wines of Hochheim in Rheingau, but soon became generic for all white Rhine wines. Unlike the light, grapey Rhine wines we know today, the passion in the 19th century was for mature, full-flavoured, amber-coloured wines. In fact, Hock glasses traditionally have brown stems

RECENT GERMAN VINTAGES

2000 Too much rain in July and October meant that 2000 was not as magical a year as some hoped it would be. Predominantly a Qualitätswein vintage with relatively small amounts of Prädikat wines produced. Definitely a year to stick to classic sites from top estates.

1999 With September rains, those who picked late rather than early turned out to be the winners, making the 1999 a high-quality vintage. Good ripeness levels in Riesling and Spätburgunder. Emphasis on Kabinett and Spätlese wines, although BA and TBA were produced.

1998 Summer temperatures were just too hot. Best areas were Pfalz and Baden, mixed reports from the Mosel-Saar-Ruwer.

1997 A great year in which rich and concentrated wines were made in most regions. Classic Rieslings. An Auslese year. The Ahr had one of its greatest vintages of the century, so grab those reds!

1996 After a bewildering display of climatic up and downs, the 1996 vintage turned out low in volume, but good in quality, especially for Riesling *Kabinett*, particularly in the middle Mosel where truly excellent wines have been produced. No major quantities of *Beerenauslese* or TBA, but a number of estates made *Eiswein*.

A LITTLE GERMAN

Those who don't speak German may find it helpful to know that the plural of German words ending in 'e' is achieved by adding an 'n', thus one *Grosslage*, two or more *Grosslagen*, while for plural of words ending with a consonant an 'e' is added, thus one *Bereich*, two or more *Bereiche*.

PICKING GRAPES IN THE MOSEL
Harvesting the Riesling in this region's steep vineyards is labour intensive, due to precipitous slopes and teacherous loose slate soil.

because they were deliberately made to reflect the desired amber hue of age into the wine (*see* box above). The Christie's auction of May 1777 listed "Excellent Genuine Old Hock" of the 1719 vintage, and another London sale offered "Hock Hocheim" 1726 in August of 1792. How a modern Hock might taste in 60 years or so is anyone's guess, but mine is that it would not be very pleasant by today's standards – unless it happened to be a *Trockenbeerenauslese*.

LIEBFRAUMILCH – NOT A WINE THE GERMANS DRINK OR EVEN KNOW!

More than one-third of all German wine exports are sold as Liebfraumilch, an inexpensive, bulk-blended product that few Germans have even heard of, let alone tasted. Less than 0.01 per cent of the 1.1 million hectolitres (12 million cases) produced each year is consumed in Germany itself and most of that is sold to foreign tourists and servicemen. Virtually 100 per cent of all Liebfraumilch is consumed by non-Germans and, although it is no longer fashionable among the new generation of drinkers in the UK, it nevertheless remains the number one best-selling wine in Britain's largest supermarket groups. While the two largest markets, the UK and US, continue to consume such vast quantities of Liebfraumilch, I am duty-bound to tell the full story.

Myriad theories surround the origin of the name Liebfraumilch (or Liebfrauenmilch), but many agree that it means "milk of Our Lady" and refers to the wine produced from one small and fairly indifferent vineyard in the suburbs of Worms that was once called Liebfrauenkirche or "Church of Our Lady". This is now part of Liebfrauenstift-Kirchenstück, which in turn is part of the 1,000-hectare (2,470-acre) *Grosslage* Liebfrauenmorgen. The single-vineyard wine that gave birth to the name of Liebfraumilch has no bearing whatsoever on the bulk-blended wine of today, nor, for that matter, any connection with the Liebfraumilch that was sold more than 100 years ago. What is interesting, however, is the nature of those early Liebfraumilch wines that gave the blended product of today its worldwide reputation and huge sales. The blurred and non-specific character of this wine was

officially classified by the Worms Chamber of Commerce in 1910, when it stated that Liebfraumilch was merely "a fancy name" that merchants "have made use of", applying it to "Rhine wines of good quality and character". The ill-defined use of this "fancy name" widened during the following 20 years. Even between 1945 and the advent of the new German wine laws in 1971, one-third of the wines blended into Liebfraumilch came from German regions other than the Rhine.

This should have ended when Liebfraumilch was granted *Qualitätswein* status under the 1971 German Wine Law because the law further stated that a *Qualitätswein* could come only from one specified region. However, the regulations also specified that Liebfraumilch could be made only from Rheinhessen, Pfalz, Rheingau, and Nahe grapes and, although few people doubted the spirit of the law, many producers interpreted this quite literally. They considered Liebfraumilch to be an umbrella designation that entitled the wine to come from any one or more of the four specified regions. Now, however, at least 85 per cent of every Liebfraumilch has to come from just one region, which must be indicated on the label.

There have been many moves to reclassify Liebfraumilch as a *Tafelwein*, which would permit it to be blended with grape varieties from the much wider *Tafelwein* regions and this would be more in keeping with its quality, which is not poor or bad *per se*, simply unpretentious and of non-specific character. However, Liebfraumilch producers disliked the idea of the *Tafelwein* classification – a misguided view in my opinion, not least because Liebfraumilch sells on its brand name. Although not intrinsically poor quality, far too many Liebfraumilch are bad wines, just as far too many cheap German wines in general are. Taken at its best, a decent Liebfraumilch should possess a fresh, flowery aroma and sweet, grapey taste. It has proved to be a

SEKT SWEETNESS CHART

SWEETNESS RATING	RESIDUAL SUGAR (GRAMS PER LITRE)
Extra Herb or *Extra Brut*	0–6
Herb or *Brut*	0–15
Extra Trocken or Extra Dry	12–20
Trocken * or Dry	17–35
Halbtrocken* or *Demi-Sec*	33–50
Süss, Drux, Doux, or Sweet	50+

*Not to be confused with still-wine limits, which are no more than 9 grams per litre for *Trocken* and 18 grams per litre for *Halbtrocken*.

BERNKASTEL-KUES, MOSEL-SAAR-RUWER
*Looking across the Mosel from Bernkastel-Kues, above which is the
famous Doctor vineyard, where some of Germany's greatest wines grow.*

good stepping-stone, with statistics showing that the vast majority
of seasoned wine-drinkers originally "cut their teeth" on this
accessible wine, but there will always be some Liebfraumilch
drinkers who never stray beyond it. Those drinkers, if honest,
dislike the taste of alcohol, but enjoy the effect it has and most
of them are not too keen on tannin, acidity, and the assertively
dry taste found in most "real" wines. There is no reason why
they should be – it is all a matter of taste.

WHAT IS LIEBFRAUMILCH?

Ironically, Germany's most criticized wine is the only one to
be defined by taste and sweetness in its wine laws. According to
the regulations, the minimum residual sugar allowed is 18 grams
per litre, equivalent to the maximum allowed for a *Halbtrocken*,
although few are actually this low, and some are twice as high.
Producers have their own idea of what level of sweetness is right
for the market and make their wines accordingly. Many buyers
insist on a certain ratio of sugar to acidity; most brands contain
between 22–35 grams of sugar per litre, with 27–28 grams of
sugar per litre as a good average. Liebfraumilch labels must now
show one of the four permitted regions; at least 85 per cent of
the wine must come from the region stated. On average, the
Rheinhessen and the Pfalz produce more than nine out of every
ten bottles of Liebfraumilch, while the Nahe makes very little and
the Rheingau virtually none. Any grape permitted for German
QbA wine may be used for the production of Liebfraumilch, the
only control being that at least 51 per cent of the blend must be
composed of one or more of the following varieties: Riesling,

Silvaner, Müller-Thurgau, and Kerner. According to the present
regulations, the wine should taste of these grapes, although I
have so far met no expert who can either describe or detect
a definitive blend of four such different varieties in the wine.
What I have discovered, however, is that some of the best blends
have actually been denied their AP numbers because they have
received a beneficial *süssreserve* of aromatic Morio-muskat. The
Liebfraumilch examining board apparently believes these eminently
more attractive wines to be untypical of the appellation.

SEKT – GERMANY'S SPARKLING WINE

Germany's *Sekt* or sparkling-wine industry is very important,
producing almost half a billion bottles a year, more than twice
the largest-ever Champagne crop. This is almost entirely made by
cuve close and over 85 per cent is not *Deutscher Sekt* at all, but
Sekt plain and simple, made from imported wines. Despite a fourfold
increase in exports over the last ten years, foreign markets
represent barely 8 per cent of sales. Thus Germans essentially
make *Sekt* for themselves and its bland, off-dry style with a very
young tartness to it has a peculiarly domestic appeal that sparkling
wine drinkers in most international markets cannot comprehend,
whether they are used to Champagne or New World fizz.
Deutscher Sekt is little better and the best *Deutscher Sekt* is seldom
encountered. On those rare occasions when bottle-fermented
wines are produced, *Sekt* will not appeal to most sparkling-wine
drinkers outside Germany itself because the grapes are too
aromatic for the expected mellow biscuity character to develop.

SCHLOSS VOLLRADS, RHEINGAU
*The vines of Schlossberg slope down towards Schloss Vollrads, a
famous old estate that has recently encountered troubled times.*

HOW TO USE THE "APPELLATIONS OF..." SECTIONS

The entries that follow for each of Germany's wine regions are set out in
a logical order. In each of these regions, or *Anbaugebiete*, every *Bereich* is
listed and the wine styles are described; this is followed by the *Grosslagen*
within that particular *Bereich*. Under each *Grosslage*, the best villages are
listed where applicable and, within each of these, the finest *Einzellagen*,
or vineyards are named.

In Germany, vineyards are rarely owned only by one estate, as they
are in Bordeaux for example (see "Germany's quality structure", p.260).
It is therefore important to be aware of not only which are the top vineyards,
but also who makes the best wines there, which is why I recommend growers
and estates within each of the finest vineyards. The term "village" covers both
Gemeinden – communes, which may be anything from a tiny village to a
large, bustling town – and *Ortsteile*, which are villages absorbed within the
suburbs of a larger *Gemeinde*. The term "*Grosslagenfrei*" refers to villages
and *Einzellagen* within one *Bereich* that are not part of any of its *Grosslagen*.

Where it is stated that there are no outstanding villages, vineyards, estates,
or growers in a particular *Grosslage*, excellent estates and growers might well

own vineyards there, but the wine produced in these vineyards may not
actually be of the highest standard.

All styles and descriptions of wines refer to Riesling, unless otherwise
stated. The following sample entry is given from the Franken region.

BEREICH	**BEREICH STEIGERWALD**
GROSSLAGE	**GROSSLAGE SCHLOSSBERG**
BEST VILLAGE	RÖDELSEE
BEST VINEYARD AND/OR BEST GROWERS	✓ Vineyard *Küchenmeister* **Grower** *Juliusspital Würzburg* • Vineyard *Schwanleite* **Grower** *Johann Ruck*

GENERIC WINES OF
GERMANY

Note The German wine categories below are listed in ascending order of quality, and not in alphabetical order. Only the broadest character can be given for each category, since so much depends upon the grape variety. The grape variety can even determine the colour of a wine, although some 90 per cent of the production is white. Most grape varieties likely to be encountered, including all the most important crosses, are included in the Glossary of Major Grape Varieties (*see* p. 42).

The area of origin also has a strong influence on the type of wine a particular grape variety will produce. A winemaker can either make the most of what nature brings, or fail. For full details on these two aspects, *see* the regional chapters in which styles are described and growers recommended.

WEIN

The existence of this term without the qualification "*Tafel-*", indicates a cheap, blended wine made from grapes grown outside the EU.

TAFELWEIN

Table wine may be a blend from different EU countries or the wine made in one member country from grapes harvested in another. Known as "Euroblends", these products are sometimes dressed up to look like German wines, but the wine beneath the Gothic writing and German language usually turns out to be an Italian or multi-state blend. This practice, once prolific, now less so, is tantamount to deception and contrary to Article 43 of EU Regulation 355/79. To be sure of drinking a genuine German product, check that "*Tafelwein*" is qualified by the all-important "*Deutscher*". The more successful of these wines are made in years when Germany is overburdened by such a huge yield of basic-quality wines that the wineries turn back the convoy of tankers from Italy and dump the excess production in their bulk-selling Euroblends. The best have a good dose of fresh and flowery Morio-Muskat *Süssreserve*.

🍷— Upon purchase

DEUTSCHER TAFELWEIN

This is the lowest grade of pure German wine, which about ten years ago represented between three and five per cent of the country's total production, but now, when added to *Landwein*, it accounts for between one and two per cent. The quality of production has not dramatically improved at the bottom end of the German wine market and the cheapest QbAs have actually deteriorated in quality – now you know why.

This wine must be 100 per cent German and, if at least 75 per cent comes from any one of the *Tafelwein* regions or sub-regions indicated earlier in the table, the label is allowed to show that name. These regional names are the most specific geographic location permitted, although, prior to the introduction of *Landwein* legislation, it was permissible sometimes to include the name of a *Bereich*.

A *Deutscher Tafelwein* should convey the basic characteristics of the region from which it comes, so a Rhein, for example, might be expected to have a more flowery aroma, but

less acidity than a Mosel. In practice, however, the wines are blended from such a hotchpotch of grape varieties, mostly crosses, that all one can hope for is something fresh and fruity in a medium-dry "Germanic" style!

🍷— Upon purchase

LANDWEIN

Landwein is a *Deutscher Tafelwein* from a specific region and the label must contain both terms. It was introduced in 1982 to parallel the French *vin de pays* system, although there are significant differences. The 130 or so *vins de pays* represent a group of wines that aspire to VDQS and, theoretically, AOC status and it has become one of the most exciting categories of wine in the world (*see* p.246). The German category is not a transitional one, it consists of 19 fixed areas that have no hope of achieving anything more illustrious than a "dressed-up" *Tafelwein* status.

Ten years ago I noted that the potential of *Landwein* could never be the same as that of a *vin de pays*, but it could and should have served a very useful, one might even say essential, purpose: to improve the quality of German wines in the QbA and QmP categories through selection. By syphoning off the lesser elements of these wines of superior status, it could have improved not only their quality, but the quality of *Landwein* itself. It would be great to think that the biggest producers had taken this category to heart and, through a genuine desire to raise standards all round, reduced yields and used *Landwein* to mop-up 15 or 20% of total German production. However, the authorities have opted to increase yields and so these wines, together with *Deutscher Tafelwein*, account for a measly one to two per cent, which is why Germany's reputation has never been lower, despite critics and importers doing their best to promote the fine quality of Riesling.

The major difference between *Landwein* and *Deutscher Tafelwein* is that the former must be made either as *Trocken*, with up to nine grams residual sugar per litre, or as *Halbtrocken*, with a maximum of 18 grams per litre.

🍷— Upon purchase

QUALITÄTSWEIN BESTIMMTER ANBAUGEBIETE *or* QBA

A QbA is literally a quality wine from one of the 13 specified regions. These wines may be (and invariably are) chaptalized to increase the alcohol content, and sweetened with *Süssreserve*.

The legal minimum potential alcoholic strength of a QbA is merely 5.9 per cent, so it can be understood why the alcohol level is not increased for its own sake, but to give the wine a reasonable shelf-life. The category includes Liebfraumilch and the vast majority of Niersteiner Gutes Domtal, Piesporter Michelsberg, and other generic wines. Most *Grosslage* and *Bereich* wines are sold as QbAs. There is no technical or legal reason why this is so, but it makes marketing sense if more specific wines, such as *Einzellagen* or estate-bottled wines, are sold as prestigious QmPs, as they can demand higher prices. Although a QbA has a lower Oechsle than a *Kabinett*, it is a more commercial product and therefore often distinctly sweeter.

🍷— 1–3 years (up to 10 years for exceptional wines)

QUALITÄTSWEIN MIT PRÄDIKAT *or* QMP

This means "a quality wine affirmed (predicated) by ripeness" and covers the categories *Kabinett*, *Spätlese*, *Auslese*, *Beerenauslese*, *Eiswein*, and *Trockenbeerenauslese*. The grower must give the authorities prior notice of his intention to harvest for any QmP wine and, whereas a QbA can be blended from grapes gathered from all four corners of an *Anbaugebiet*, providing it carries only the name of that region, the origin of a QmP must be a geographical unit of no greater size than a *Bereich*. A QbA can be chaptalized, but a QmP can not. A certain very highly respected estate owner who believes he could make much better QmP wines if he were allowed to chaptalize them, once made the interesting observation that the French chaptalize their best wines, while Germans chaptalize only their poorest! It is, however, permissible to add *Süssreserve*, although many growers maintain that it is not the traditional method and claim that sweetness is best achieved by stopping the fermentation before all the natural grape sugars have been converted to alcohol. (*See* the various QmP entries.)

KABINETT QMP

The term *Kabinett* once referred to wines that were stored for their rare and exceptional qualities, much as "Reserve" is commonly used today. In this context, it originated at Kloster Eberbach in the Rheingau in the early 18th century. The first documented existence of this word appeared as "Cabernedt" on an invoice from the Elville master cooper, Ferdinand Ritter, to the Abbot of Eberbach in 1730. Just six years later, another bill in Ritter's hand refers to the "Cabinet-Keller". (The meaning of "Cabinet" as a treasured store found its way into the French language as early as 1547, and is found in

German literature in 1677.) *Kabinett* is the first of the predicates in the Oechsle scale. Its grapes must reach an Oechsle level of 67-85°, the exact minimum varying according to the grape variety concerned and its geographical origin. With no chaptalization, this means that the wine has a minimum potential alcoholic strength of between 8.6 and 11.4 per cent by volume.

Although made from riper (thus sweeter) grapes than a QbA, a *Kabinett* is usually, though not necessarily, made in a slightly drier style. Some producers resolutely refuse to bolster the wine with *Süssreserve*. This makes *Kabinett* the lightest and, for some, the purest of German wine styles.

🍷 2–5 years (up to 10 years in exceptional cases)

SPÄTLESE QMP

Technically, "*Spätlese*" implies that a wine is made from late-harvested grapes, but it is important to remember that "late" is relative to the normal (early) occurrence of a harvest in Germany. As both QbA and *Kabinett* are produced from grapes that have not fully ripened, *Spätlese* can more accurately be seen as the first level of German wine to be produced from ripe grapes. The minimum Oechsle level of 76–95°, which would give a minimum potential strength of between 10 and 13 per cent by volume, is hardly an indication of overripe grapes. Although a *Spätlese* is made from grapes that merely have a modest degree of ripeness, the style of wine produced is traditionally sweet, with excellent balancing acidity.

🍷 3–8 years (up to 15 in exceptional cases)

AUSLESE QMP

This predicated wine is made from bunches left on the vines after the *Spätlese* harvest and as such is truly late-harvested. The regulations state that bunches of fully ripe to very ripe grapes free from disease or damage must be selected for this wine – how this can be achieved by machine-harvesting, which has been permitted for *Auslese* since the new German Wine Laws of 1994, is beyond the imagination of every quality-conscious German winemaker I have spoken to.

Auslese must also possess an Oechsle reading of 83–105°, the exact minimum varying according to the grape variety concerned and its geographical origin. With no chaptalization, this means that the wine has a minimum potential strength of between 11.1 and 14.5 per cent by volume.

Traditionally this rich and sweet wine is made in exceptional vintages only. There may be some hint of *Edelfäule* (botrytis), especially if the wine comes from a top estate that has a policy of under-declaring its wines, and thus

an *Auslese* might be borderline *Beerenauslese*, but even without *Edelfäule*, an *Auslese* is capable of considerable complexity. It is possible to find totally dry *Auslese* wine and this may or may not be labelled *Auslese/Trocken*, depending on the whim of the winemaker. *Auslese* is the ideal predicate for *Trocken* wines, because its natural ripeness provides a Burgundy-like degree of body, fullness of fruit, and alcohol.

🍷 5–20 years

BEERENAUSLESE QMP

A very rare wine made only in truly exceptional circumstances from overripe grapes that have been affected by *Edelfäule*. According to the regulations, each berry should be shrivelled, and be individually selected, on a grape-by-grape basis. They must achieve an Oechsle level of 110–128°, the exact minimum varying according to the grape variety concerned and its geographical origin. With no chaptalization, this means that the wine has a minimum potential strength of between 15.3 and 18.1 per cent by volume, but only 5.5 per cent need actually be alcohol, with residual sugar accounting for the rest.

These intensely sweet, full-bodied wines are remarkably complex and elegant. I actually prefer *Beerenauslese* to the technically superior *Trockenbeerenauslese* – it is easier to drink and be delighted by the former, whereas the latter requires concentration and appraisal.

🍷 10–35 years (up to 50 years in exceptional cases)

EISWEIN QMP

Until 1982 this was a qualification used in conjunction with one of the other predicates. It was previously possible to obtain *Spätlese Eiswein*, *Auslese Eiswein* and so on, but *Eiswein* is now a predicate in its own right, with a minimum Oechsle level for its grapes equivalent to *Beerenauslese*. An *Eiswein* occurs through extremely unusual circumstances whereby grapes left on the vine to be affected by *Edelfäule* are frozen by frost or snow. They are harvested, rushed to the winery and pressed in their frozen state. Only the water inside the grape actually freezes; this either remains caked inside the press or rises to the top of the vat in the form of ice, which is then skimmed off. What remains available for fermentation is a freeze-condensed juice that is rich, concentrated, and capable of producing wines that are the equivalent of, but totally different from, *Beerenauslese* or *Trockenbeerenauslese*.

This icy harvest can be very late. It seldom occurs before December and often takes place in January of the following year (although it must carry the previous year's vintage). The Oechsle level of an *Eiswein*, which must be at least the equivalent of a *Beerenauslese*, can be every bit as high as a *Trockenbeerenauslese*. Its quality is also comparable, although of an entirely different character, due essentially to

its far higher acidity balance. For me, it is the zippy, racy, tangy vitality of this acidity that makes it superior. The finest *Eiswein* has a finesse unequalled by other botrytis wine, but it remains to be seen what effect the 1994 German Wine Law will have on the reputation of these very special wines. The quality-minded wanted the new law to demand hand-picking for *Eiswein*, which would bring it in line with *Auslese*, *Beerenauslese,* and *Trockenbeerenauslese*, but the industrial bottlers not only fended this off, but made it legal for it to be machine-harvested, although anyone who has made *Eiswein* will tell you this method is impossible.

🍷 0–50 years

TROCKENBEERENAUSLESE QMP *or* TBA

Germany's legendary TBA is produced from heavily botrytized grapes, left on the vine to shrivel into raisin-like berries that must be individually picked. These grapes must reach an Oechsle level of 150–154°. With no chaptalization, the wine will have a minimum potential strength of between 21.5 and 22.1 per cent by volume, although only 5.5 per cent need be alcohol, the rest being residual sugar.

Consulting charts, however, does little to highlight the difference in style that exists between a *Beerenauslese* and a TBA, which is every bit as great as that between a *Kabinett* and a *Beerenauslese*. The first noticeable difference is often the colour. Going from *Auslese* to *Beerenauslese* is merely to progress from a light to a rich gold or buttercup yellow. The TBA colour range extends from a raisin khaki through various shades of brown, to dark iodine, with some distinctly odd orange-tawny hues in between. The texture is very viscous and its liqueur-like consistency is just one of many reasons why it is impossible to drink TBA. Taking a good mouthful of TBA is about as easy as swigging cough mixture – one can merely sip it. Its intensity and complexity, and the profundity of its aromas and flavours really must be experienced. It demands attention and provokes discussion, but is not really a wine to enjoy with, and is difficult to relax with.

🍷 12–50 years

TROCKEN WINES

These wines must not contain more than four grams of residual sugar per litre, although up to nine grams per litre is permitted if the acidity is a mere two grams per litre or less, although such a wine would be appallingly flabby. *Trocken* really started to take off in the early -1990s and now accounts for a staggering 20 per cent of all German wines produced, but most of these are thin, weak, and disappointing. There are some terrific *Trocken* wines, but to be any good, *Trocken* really has to be made from grapes of *Auslese* ripeness. Only then does it have the body, structure, and weight that most dry wine drinkers are used to. Many producers try to claim that a *Spätlese/Trocken* is ripe enough, but whereas odd examples are, nine out of ten are not. Some *Trocken* specialists utilize grapes of *Auslese* ripeness, but prefer to make and sell their wines as *Deutscher Tafelwein*, which releases them from unnecessarily restrictive rules, most of which have been developed with sweet and semi-sweet wine production in mind. Try Reichsgraf und Marquis zu Hoensbroech in Baden or Müller-Catoir in the Pfalz.

🍷⏴ 2–6 years

BARRIQUE WINE

Always classified as *Deutscher Tafelwein* (because the oak influence is not considered typical in official QbA and QmP tastings), this category is used for red and white *Trocken* wines fermented and/or aged in new oak casks, although there are no rules against *barrique*-aged *Rotling* or rosé. Riesling can be excellent if just fermented in barrel, with very little *barrique*-ageing as such, otherwise the main varieties aged in barrel are Weissburgunder, Grauburgunder and Spätburgunder (*see* Red Wine below). Although the first *barrique* wines were made in Baden as long ago as the late 1970s, it was still a very new wine style when the first edition of this book was published, but Schlossgut Diel in the Nahe was already establishing itself as one of Germany's foremost *barrique* specialists, a position it retains today. For other fine examples of this style, try Franz Keller-Schwarzer Adler.

🍷⏴ 2–6 years

RED WINE

The most commonly encountered German red wines are Dornfelder, Limberger, and Spätburgunder, and the best are sold as *Deutscher Tafelwein*, which allows producers the greatest freedom of expression. Dornfelder is grown mostly in the Pfalz (800 hectares), Rheinhessen (600 hectares), and Württemberg (200 hectares) and producers have developed three basic styles: *barrique*-aged for serious drinking (try Thomas Siegrist in the Pfalz), early-drinking Beaujolais-style (Lingenfelder, also in the Pfalz, or Wilhelm Laubenstein in Rheinhessen), and a sweet and grapey style (Gustav Adolf Schmitt, also in Rheinhessen). The Limberger, or Lemberger as it is sometimes

spelt, is grown almost entirely in Württemberg (800 hectares) and is invariably produced in a Beaujolais style, although a few growers maintain it will age (Graf Adelmann's Brüssele is best).

Spätburgunder is the German name for Pinot noir; it is the widest-planted black grape variety in the country and over the last ten years some talented winemakers have managed to produce some truly beautiful, silky-smooth, well-coloured red wines from this grape. At their best in southern Baden (try Dr Heger), good wines are also made in Pfalz (Friedrich Becker, Lingenfelder) and the Ahr (Mayer-Näkel).

🍷⏴ 2–6 years

SPARKLING WINE
SEKT

The common method of production for this anonymous sparkling wine is *cuve close*, although when the industry was born in the 1820s, all *Sekt* was bottle-fermented. Today, not only is it such an industrialized product, but most is made from grapes grown outside Germany, usually from Italy or the Loire Valley in France. Furthermore, until 1986, this Euro-fizz could be called *Deutscher Sekt*. This was because *Sekt* was considered to be a method of production and, so it was argued, if production took place in Germany, it must logically be German or *Deutscher Sekt*. As the vast majority of Germany's huge *Sekt* industry used imported grapes, juice, or wine (and still does), this was more a matter of lobbying by those with vested interests, than logic. However, much of the effort to dispose of this false logic came from

honourable sectors within the German wine industry itself. Common sense finally won through on 1 September, 1986, when an EU directive brought this appellation into line with the general philosophy of the EU's wine regime. There has been a noticeable upsurge in the number of what are now genuine German *Deutscher Sekt*, although *Sekt* plain and simple still dominates the market.

DEUTSCHER SEKT

Deutscher Sekt must be made from 100 per cent German grapes. The best are usually Riesling-based and do not allow autolysis (the enzymatic breakdown of yeast) to interfere with the pure varietal aroma and flavour of the wine, characteristics that are held in the greatest esteem by its producers and the vast majority of its German consumers. Try Max Ferdinand. The best *Sekt* I have ever tasted was Wegeler-Deinhard Bernkasteler Doctor, but it is rarely produced and very expensive. *See also Deutscher Qualitätsschaumwein bestimmter Anbaugebiete.*

🍷⏴ 3–8 years

DEUTSCHER SEKT BESTIMMTER ANBAUGEBIETE *OR* DEUTSCHER SEKT BA

See Deutscher Qualitätsschaumwein bestimmter Anbaugebiete

DEUTSCHER QUALITÄTSSCHAUMWEIN BESTIMMTER ANBAUGEBIETE *OR* DEUTSCHER QUALITÄTSSCHAUMWEIN BA

This *Deutscher Sekt* must be made entirely from grapes grown within one specified wine region and may come from a smaller geographical unit, such as a *Bereich*, *Grosslage*, or *Einzellage*, providing that at least 85 per cent of the grapes used come from the area indicated. An alternative appellation is *Deutscher Sekt bestimmter Anbaugebiete*.

🍷⏴ 3–8 years

IMMACULATE VINEYARDS, BADEN
Baden's greatest wines are produced around the extinct volcano of Kaiserstuhl, in neat vineyards that are perfect examples of Flurbereinigung.

THE AHR

It may seem surprising that black grapes can be cultivated here at all, considering the Ahr is one of Europe's most northerly wine regions, yet varieties such as Spätburgunder, Dornfelder, and Portugieser account for four-fifths of the Ahr's vines.

SPÄTBURGUNDER AND PORTUGIESER can grow here because the Ahr is a deep valley – protected by the Hohe Eifel hills – which captures sunlight in its rocky, slaty soil. The cumulative effect of the heat allows black grapes to ripen, but until recently few growers took advantage of these favourable conditions. Consequently the Ahr became known for mild, dilute red wines, popular with social clubs on weekend outings. A change in winemaking philosophy, however, has propelled a good number of the region's Spätburgunders into contention for Germany's red

QUALITY REQUIREMENTS AND HARVEST PERCENTAGES

MINIMUM OECHSLE	QUALITY CATEGORY	HARVEST BREAKDOWN			
		1992	1993	1994	1995
44°	Deutscher Tafelwein	6%	–	7%	5%
47°	Landwein				
50–60°	* QbA	92%	55%	86%	87%
67–73°	* Kabinett	2%	30%	6%	7%
76–85°	* Spätlese	–	15%	1%	1%
83–88°	* Auslese				
110°	Beerenauslese	–	–	–	–
110°	Eiswein				
150°	Trockenbeerenauslese				

*Minimum Oechsle levels vary according to grape variety; those that have a naturally lower sugar content may qualify at a correspondingly lower level.

OLD WINE-CASKS AT MAYSCHOSS
Beautiful carving depicts grapes and vines on old wooden casks at Mayschoss, up-river from Bad Neuenahr.

FACTORS AFFECTING TASTE AND QUALITY

LOCATION
The lower reaches of the Ahr river, 10 km (6 miles) south of Bonn.

CLIMATE
Despite its northerly position, the deep Ahr valley is sheltered by the surrounding Hohe Eifel hills and maintains temperatures that are favourable for viticulture.

ASPECT
The vineyards of the Ahr are sited mainly on inclines and the steeply terraced rocky valley sides.

SOIL
Deep, rich, loess soils in the lower Ahr valley and basalt and slaty stone soils with some tufa in the upper Ahr valley.

VITICULTURE AND VINIFICATION
Three-quarters of vineyards are worked by part-time farmers under labour-intensive conditions. Hence the wines are expensive to produce. More than half the crop is vinified by a small number of cooperatives. Red wines account for 70 per cent of the output. They used to be made into sweet and semi-sweet styles, but drier versions are more popular today. Pure varietal Weissherbst, usually Spätburgunder, is a speciality.

PRIMARY GRAPE VARIETIES
Dornfelder, Portugieser, Riesling, Spätburgunder

SECONDARY GRAPE VARIETIES
Domina, Kerner, Müller-Thurgau

THE AHR, *see also p.261*
Formerly the most northerly of Germany's wine-producing regions, the Ahr is made up of districts close to the River Ahr, a tributary of the Rhine.

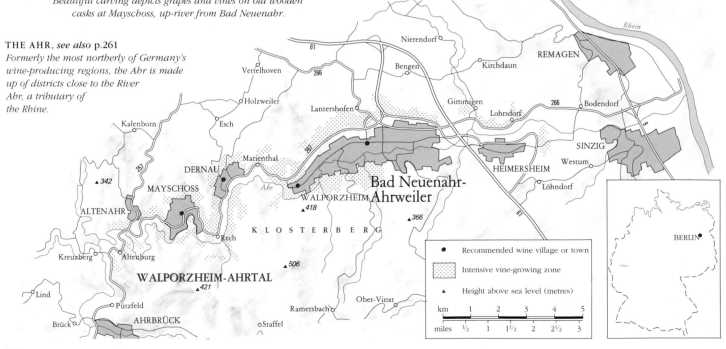

- Recommended wine village or town
- Intensive vine-growing zone
- ▲ Height above sea level (metres)

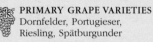

HARVESTING IN THE AHR
These steeply sloping vineyards at Marienthal are planted with the black grape varieties, Spätburgunder and a little Portugieser, and 80 per cent of the region's wines are in fact red.

THE REGION AT A GLANCE

Area under vine 632 ha (1,562 acres)	**Most important grape varieties** 52% Spätburgunder, 18% Portugieser, 30% Others
Average yield 74 hl/ha (333 cases/acre)	**Infrastructure** *Bereich* 1; *Grosslage* 1; *Einzellagen* 43
Red wine 80%	**Note:** The vineyards of the Ahr straddle 11 *Gemeinden* (communes), the names of which may appear on the label.
White wine 20%	

wine crown. Unfortunately quantities will always be too small to quench the international wine community's thirst, thus readers are unlikely to find the Ahr's best reds in their local wine shop. These remain the preserve of knowledgeable consumers willing to put on walking boots and take a trip to the Ahr to buy them direct. The region takes the name of the river that flows parallel to, and north of, the lower Mosel and joins the Rhine just south of Bonn. It is one of the world's most beautiful and serene viticultural landscapes, as anyone who has ever travelled along the *Rotweinwanderweg*, the Ahr's red-wine route, will verify.

RIESLING
Riesling grapes can produce fresh, racy, aromatic wines here, but over the years have given way to black grapes and now comprise under ten per cent of the region's vines. Given the healthy prices that Ahr reds command, Riesling is unlikely to regain its share.

THE APPELLATIONS OF
THE AHR

BEREICH WALPORZHEIM-AHRTAL

This is the only *Bereich* in the Ahr district. Walporzheim-Ahrtal produces many kinds of wines, from light, ruby-coloured Portugiesers to Spätburgunders of fair depth and Dornfelders with great intensity. Those areas in the *Bereich* with slaty soil give a vigorous wine, while those situated on rich loess soil produce a softer style. At one time, the wines used to be fairly sweet, but the trend nowadays is for drier wines. The Weissherbst is a soft and fruity wine, and the Riesling fresh and racy. Try the Rotwein with *Rauchfleisch* (smoked meats), the

Weissherbst with *Schinken* (ham), and the Riesling with trout or with the salmon that have recently been reintroduced into the river.

GROSSLAGE KLOSTERBERG
The only *Grosslage* in the *Bereich*, the area of Klosterberg is thus identical to that of Walporzheim-Ahrtal.

ALTENAHR
☑ Vineyard *Eck* Growers *Deutzerhof,*
Winzergenossenschaft Mayschoss-Altenahr

DERNAU
☑ Vineyard *Pfarrwingert*
Growers *H. J. Kreuzberg, Meyer-Näkel*
• Vineyard *Schieferlay*
Growers *H. J. Kreuzberg, Meyer-Näkel*

NEUENAHR
☑ Vineyard *Sonnenberg*
Growers *H.J. Kreuzberg, Burggarten*

RECH
Vineyard *Herrenberg*
Grower *Jean Stodden*

WALPORZHEIM
☑ Vineyard *Gärkammer*
Grower *J. J. Adeneuer*
• Premium Red Wine Blend: Growers
Deutzerhof (Caspar C., Grand Duc Select),
Meyer-Näkel (S), *Nelles* (B48, B52), *H.J.
Kreuzberg* (Devon), *Winzergenossenschaft
Mayschoss-Altenahr* (Ponsart),
J.J. Adeneuer (No.1)

THE MITTELRHEIN

Possessing precariously perched vineyards that have declined by almost 50 per cent since 1965, the Mittelrhein is a region that is all too often overlooked by serious wine drinkers. Yet it offers some of Germany's finest and most underrated wines.

IT WAS FROM THE MITTELRHEIN that the Celts spread out across Europe. With such ancient roots, it is not surprising that this region is so steeped in Germany's mythical history. It was at the Drachenfels in Königswinter, for instance, that Siegfried slew the dragon, and, in fact, the vineyards in this area produce a red Spätburgunder wine known as Drachenblut or "Dragon's blood". The river Rhine, associated with many myths and fables, flows past numerous medieval castles and towers, and rushes through the Rhine Gorge, past the famous "Loreley" rock on to which the siren lured many ships to their final and fatal destination.

SHRINKING VINEYARDS, GROWING TOURISM

The difficulty of working the steepest of the Mittelrhein's vineyard slopes has encouraged many of the workforce to forsake them and seek higher wages for easier work in Germany's industrial cities. This has led to a decline in the number of vineyards but the Mittelrhein is by no means deserted as its dramatic beauty makes it one of Germany's favourite tourist spots. In this region, where many tiny tributaries provide valley vineyards of a superior natural aspect for viticulture than most of those on the Rhine, there is much potential for producing high-quality Riesling on its slaty soil. There are a few excellent estates, making exciting wines that display a vigorous varietal character, intense flavour, and splendid acidity. The acidity, so prized that *Sekt* houses try to buy as much of the lesser quality and surplus wines as possible, makes the rare occurrence of *Auslese* and higher QmP wines something special.

THE MITTELRHEIN, *see also p.261*
North and south of Koblenz, the Mittelrhein's vineyards run up towards the steep, rocky escarpments that closely border this stretch of the Rhine.

THE REGION AT A GLANCE

Area under vine
662 ha (1,636 acres)

Average yield
78 hl/ha (351 cases/acre)

Red wine 6%

White wine 94%

Most important grape varieties
75% Riesling, 8% Müller-Thurgau, 5% Kerner, 12% Others

Infrastructure
Bereiche 2; *Grosslagen* 11; *Einzellagen* 111

Note The vineyards of the Mittelrhein straddle 59 *Gemeinden* (communes), the names of which may appear on the label.

FACTORS AFFECTING TASTE AND QUALITY

LOCATION
A 160-km (100-mile) stretch of the Rhine Valley between Bonn and Bingen.

CLIMATE
The benefits of the sun are maximized by the steep valley sides that afford protection from cold winds. The river acts as a heat-reservoir, tempering the low night and winter temperatures.

ASPECT
Vines on the steep valley sides benefit from any available sunshine. North of Koblenz the vineyards are on the east bank, while to the south most are on the west bank.

SOIL
Slaty soil lies on a clay base and a conglomerate rock of rounded pebbles and sand. There are also small, scattered deposits of loess and, towards the north, some vineyards are of volcanic origin.

VITICULTURE AND VINIFICATION
Virtually all remaining vineyards in this region have been *flurbereinigt* (modernized by abolishing terraces) and many of the steep slopes are a patchwork of precarious vineyards. With a high proportion of Riesling grapes giving an average yield that is very low by German standards, the quality is generally high. About 80 per cent of growers are part-time and one-quarter of the harvest is processed by the cooperatives using normal white-wine techniques.

PRIMARY GRAPE VARIETY
Riesling

SECONDARY GRAPE VARIETIES
Bacchus, Kerner, Müller-Thurgau, Optima, Scheurebe, Silvaner

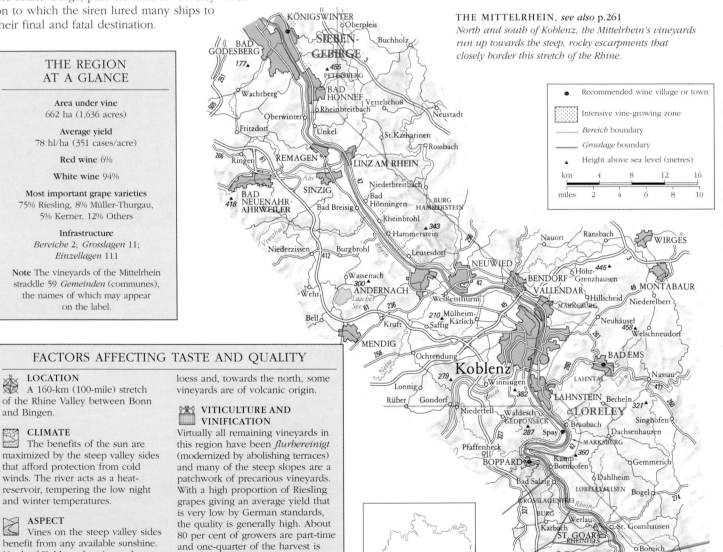

● Recommended wine village or town

▦ Intensive vine-growing zone

— *Bereich* boundary

— *Grosslage* boundary

▲ Height above sea level (metres)

QUALITY REQUIREMENTS AND HARVEST PERCENTAGES

MINIMUM OECHSLE	QUALITY CATEGORY	1992	1993	1994	1995
44°	*Deutscher Tafelwein*	29%	–	1%	7%
47°	*Landwein*				
50–60°	* *QbA*	70%	57%	70%	75%
67–73°	* *Kabinett*	1%	32%	22%	15%
76–85°	* *Spätlese*	–	11%	–	3%
83–88°	* *Auslese*				
110°	*Beerenauslese*	–	–	7%	–
110°	*Eiswein*				
150°	*Trockenbeerenauslese*				

*Minimum Oechsle levels vary according to grape variety;
those that have a naturally lower sugar content may
quality at a correspondingly lower level.

MITTELRHEIN VINEYARDS
*The region's weekend winegrowers have plenty to do to maintain these
slopes, which include some of the steepest vineyards in Germany.*

THE APPELLATIONS OF
THE MITTELRHEIN

BEREICH LORELEY

This new *Bereich* is formed from the two
former *Bereiche* of Bacharach (the very small
but heavily cultivated southern end of the
Mittelrhein, restricted to the west bank and
named after the beautiful old market town of
Bacharach) and Rheinburgengau (a very large,
successful town bordering the Rheingau).

GROSSLAGE SCHLOSS REICHENSTEIN

There are no outstanding villages, vineyards,
estates, or growers in this *Grosslage* that faces
the Rheingau across the river and neighbours
the Nahe to the south, but good wines are
made in the village of Niederheimbach,
especially the vineyard of Froher Weingarten.

GROSSLAGE SCHLOSS STAHLECK

There is perhaps more potential here, in the
south-facing vineyards that belong to tributaries
of the Rhine, than in the east-facing vineyards
on the great river itself. Yet it is wines from
Hahn and Posten at Bacharach, with both
easterly and southerly aspects, that excel.

BACHARACH
✓ Vineyard *Hahn* Grower *Toni Jost -
Hahnenhof* • Vineyard *Kloster Fürstental*
Growers *Dr. Rudolf Kauer* • Vineyard
Posten Grower *Fritz Bastian, Karl Heidrich*

GROSSLAGE BURG HAMMERSTEIN

Starting just south of Köningswinter and
stretching along the right bank, almost as far as
Koblenz, this long, scenic *Grosslage* comprises
scattered vineyards, with the only unbroken
stretch of fine Riesling vines at Hammerstein.

GROSSLAGE BURG RHEINFELS

A village-sized *Grosslage* on the west bank,
with its best vineyards situated on the
southeast-facing banks of a small tributary
at Werlau, an *Ortsteil* of Sankt Goar.

GROSSLAGE GEDEONSECK

A top-performing *Grosslage* where a bend in
the river allows for good east- and south-facing
vineyards, the best of which are situated within
an *Ortsteil* of Boppard.

BOPPARD HAMM
✓ Vineyard *Feuerlay* Growers *Bernhard
Didinger* (Oberspay), *Toni Lorenz, Müller,
Weingart* (Spay) • Vineyard *Mandelstein*
Growers *Heinrich Müller, August Perll,
Walter Perll* • Vineyard *Ohlenberg*
Growers *Weingart* (Spay), *Heinrich Müller*

GROSSLAGE HERRENBERG

The southeastern end of this *Grosslage* abuts
the western edge of the Rheingau, but all
of the *Einzellagen* are located in the north,
between Dörscheid and Kaub, just downstream
from Bacharach on the opposite bank.

KAUB
✓ Vineyard *Backofen*
Grower *Weingut Sonnenhang*

GROSSLAGE LAHNTAL

There are no outstanding villages, vineyards,
estates, or growers in this beautiful hinterland
Grosslage and its vineyards have been in a
state of decline for many years. However, the
Einzellage of Hasenberg at Bad Ems has a
certain reputation.

GROSSLAGE LORELEYFELSEN

Some fine Riesling vineyards set amid dramatic
scenery that includes the famous "Loreley" rock.

GROSSLAGE MARKSBURG

The vineyards on the Mittelrhein side of Koblenz
have mostly been overtaken by urban sprawl,
but one of the best remains in the *Ortsteil* of
Ehrenbreitstein. The others in this *Grosslage*
are located to the north and south of the city.
There is a natural similarity between these
wines and those of the lower Mosel.

GROSSLAGE SCHLOSS SCHÖNBURG

The reputation of the fine Riesling vineyards in
this *Grosslage* rests on two growers.

ENGELHÖLL
✓ Vineyard *Bernstein* Grower *Lanius-Knab*

OBERWESEL
✓ Vineyard *Römerkrug*
Growers *Goswin, Joseph Albert Lambrich*
• Vineyard *Sankt Martinsberg*
Growers *Goswin, Joseph Albert Lambrich*

SIEBENGEBIRGE

A single-*Grosslage Bereich* covering the
vineyards of Königswinter Siebengebirge.

GROSSLAGE PETERSBERG

The same area as *Bereich* Siebengebirge. There
are no outstanding villages, vineyards, estates,
or growers, although good wines are made in
the Drachenfels vineyard of Königswinter.

MOSEL-SAAR-RUWER

The greatest Rieslings grown along the Mosel river have an excruciating, but delightful, acidity, that can only be relieved through a knife-edge balance of sweetness. Unlike in the warmer Rhine regions, the Riesling grape is at its best here in hot vintages.

IF ANY GRAPE IS INTRINSICALLY RACY, it is the vigorous Riesling, and if any region can be singled out for emphasizing this raciness, it must be Mosel-Saar-Ruwer. Grown on the steepest, slaty slopes, Riesling combines a relatively high acidity with an irrefutable suggestion of lightness and elegance. But a fine Mosel-Saar-Ruwer is never thin, as these wines have surprisingly high extract levels that, together with the acidity, intensify the characteristics of flavour.

In even the hottest vintages, the best *Auslesen* and *Beerenauslesen* remain racy, while those from the other regions appear fat and overblown by contrast. Even the most modest wines retain a freshness and vitality in sunblessed years that will be lacking in those from the warmer regions.

THE GOOD DOCTOR

There are many great vineyards in this region, but none so famous as the legendary Bernkasteler Doctor, which produces Germany's most expensive wine. The story is that Boemund II, archbishop of Trier in the 14th century, was so ill that his doctors could do nothing for him. A wine-grower from Bernkastel recommended the restorative powers of the wine from his vineyard. Boemund drank some, made a miraculous recovery, and declared "The best doctor grows in this vineyard in Bernkastel". More recently, the Doctor vineyard has been the subject of a lengthy court case. The original vineyard comprised 1.35 hectares (3⅓ acres), but in 1971 the new German wine law proscribed a ban on all vineyards of less than 5 hectares (12⅓ acres), and the authorities planned to expand the Doctor almost equally to the west (into the *Einzellage* Graben) and to the east (into

an area classified merely as Grosslage Badstube). This enabled thirteen different producers to make and sell Bernkasteler Doctor, whereas only three owners of the true Doctor vineyards had existed before. It is not surprising that the owners of the original Doctor vineyard felt strong enough to take their objections to court.

The case continued until finally, in 1984, after an exhaustive study had been made of the vineyard's *terroir*, the court decided that the Doctor vineyard could legitimately be stretched to include all the Graben element and a small portion of the Badstube, making a total of 3.26 hectares (8 acres). The main reason why the Doctor vineyard was primarily expanded

---

FACTORS AFFECTING TASTE AND QUALITY

LOCATION
This region follows the Mosel river from Koblenz south to the border with France. It includes the vineyards of two major tributaries, the Saar and the Ruwer, which flow into the Mosel from the south.

CLIMATE
The moderate rainfall and rapid warming of the steep and protective valley sides provide ideal conditions for vines to flourish and produce grapes with high acidity, even when late harvested.

ASPECT
The Mosel has more loops and bends than any other German river, providing slopes of every aspect. The valleys have very steep sides where most of the vines grow at an altitude of between 100 and 350 m (330 and 1,150 ft).

SOIL
Soils in this region vary from sandstone, shell-limestone, and red marl in the upper Mosel, to Devon slate in the middle Mosel, Saar, and Ruwer, and clay slate and grey stony soil in the lower Mosel. Alluvial sand and gravel soils are also found in lower sites. Classic Riesling sites are slaty; the Elbling prefers limestone.

VITICULTURE AND VINIFICATION
Many of the greatest German wines come from the highest and steepest vineyards in this area, most of which are situated in the upper reaches of the valleys. Tending the vines is unavoidably labour-intensive and this, combined with a longer winter than experienced elsewhere in Germany, accounts for the higher prices asked for fine Mosel-Saar-Ruwer wines. The early onset of winter causes fermentation to take place at cool temperatures, and when the wines are bottled early they retain more carbonic gas, which emphasizes the crisp, steely character of the Riesling grape. There are about 13,750 growers owning very small plots of land and approximately 60 per cent of the total wine produced is distributed by merchants and shippers. Cooperatives sell 15 per cent of the total. The sales are increasing of growers and estates, who sell direct and account for 25 per cent.

PRIMARY GRAPE VARIETIES
Müller-Thurgau, Riesling
SECONDARY GRAPE VARIETIES
Auxerrois, Bacchus, Elbling, Kerner, Optima, Ortega

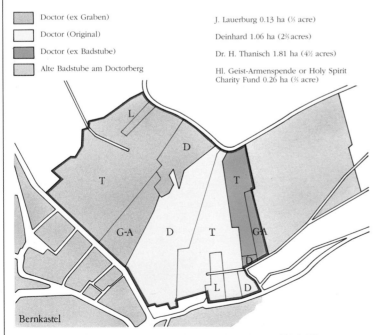

Doctor (ex Graben)
Doctor (Original)
Doctor (ex Badstube)
Alte Badstube am Doctorberg

J. Lauerburg 0.13 ha (⅓ acre)

Deinhard 1.06 ha (2⅔ acres)

Dr. H. Thanisch 1.81 ha (4½ acres)

Hl. Geist-Armenspende or Holy Spirit Charity Fund 0.26 ha (⅔ acre)

THE BERNKASTELER DOCTOR VINEYARD TODAY
The red outline encloses the area of the original vineyard (yellow) and those areas finally adopted in 1984 (light and mid-green). The area excluded in 1984 is pink.

BERNKASTEL FROM THE DOCTOR VINEYARD
Bernkasteler Doctor wines are some of Germany's most prestigious and expensive. Bernkastel lies in the Badstube Grosslage.

QUALITY REQUIREMENTS AND HARVEST PERCENTAGES

MINIMUM OECHSLE	QUALITY CATEGORY	HARVEST BREAKDOWN			
		1992	1993	1994	1995
44°	Deutscher Tafelwein	33%	–	4%	8%
47°	Landwein				
50–60°	* QbA	66%	63%	72%	86%
67–73°	* Kabinett	1%	27%	18%	5%
76–85°	* Spätlese	–	8%	6%	1%
83–88°	* Auslese				
110°	Beerenauslese	–	2%	–	–
110°	Eiswein				
150°	Trockenbeerenauslese				

*Minimum Oechsle levels vary according to grape variety; those that have a naturally lower sugar content may qualify at a correspondingly lower level.

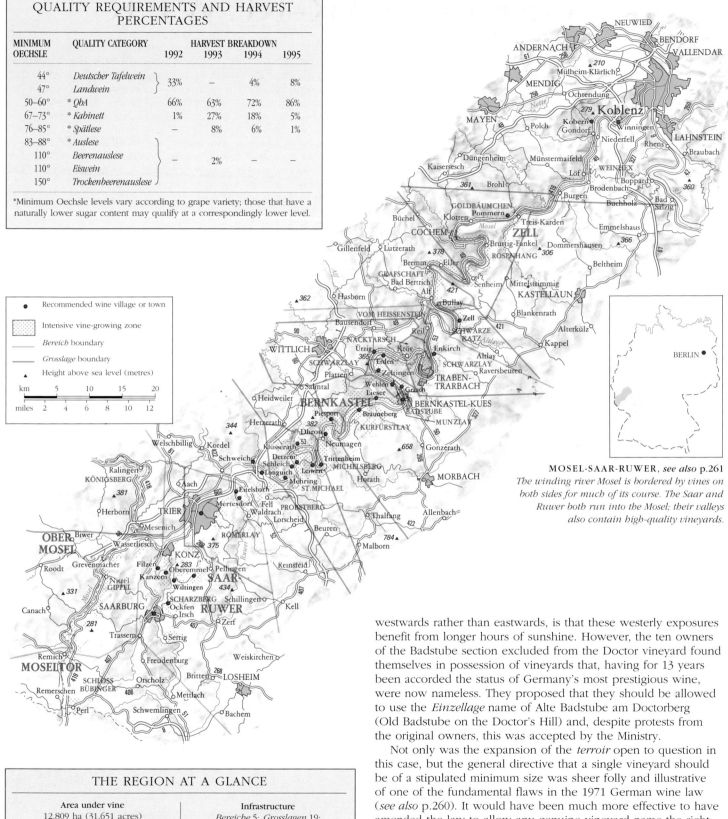

MOSEL-SAAR-RUWER, *see also p.261*
The winding river Mosel is bordered by vines on both sides for much of its course. The Saar and Ruwer both run into the Mosel; their valleys also contain high-quality vineyards.

THE REGION AT A GLANCE

Area under vine
12,809 ha (31,651 acres)

Average yield
100 hl/ha (450 cases/acre)

Red wine 1%

White wine 99%

Most important grape varieties
54% Riesling, 22% Müller-Thurgau,
9% Elbling, 8% Kerner, 7% Others

Infrastructure
Bereiche 5; *Grosslagen* 19;
Einzellagen 523

Note The vineyards of Mosel-Saar-Ruwer straddle 192 *Gemeinden* (communes), the names of which may appear on the label.

westwards rather than eastwards, is that these westerly exposures benefit from longer hours of sunshine. However, the ten owners of the Badstube section excluded from the Doctor vineyard found themselves in possession of vineyards that, having for 13 years been accorded the status of Germany's most prestigious wine, were now nameless. They proposed that they should be allowed to use the *Einzellage* name of Alte Badstube am Doctorberg (Old Badstube on the Doctor's Hill) and, despite protests from the original owners, this was accepted by the Ministry.

Not only was the expansion of the *terroir* open to question in this case, but the general directive that a single vineyard should be of a stipulated minimum size was sheer folly and illustrative of one of the fundamental flaws in the 1971 German wine law (*see also* p.260). It would have been much more effective to have amended the law to allow any genuine vineyard name the right to appear in small print on a label, and to establish a register of perhaps 100 or more (but certainly not 2,600) truly great vineyards that would have the right to appear on the label in a dominant size of print with an appropriate designation of elevated status. If the greatest German wines could trade on a reputation similar to that of the finest wines of France, the Mosel-Saar-Ruwer would probably have more *"Grands Crus"* than any other region, although the Rheingau would give it a good fight.

BEREICH ZELL

The lower Mosel is generally regarded as an area of unexciting wines, yet there are some good wines to be found.

GROSSLAGE GOLDBÄUMCHEN

There are few outstanding villages, vineyards, or growers in this *Grosslage*, although good wines are made in the village of Eller at Pommern.

GROSSLAGE GRAFSCHAFT

Good wines are made in the villages of Alf and Bullay, but the Riesling of Neef stands out from the rest.

GROSSLAGE ROSENHANG

This is a promising *Grosslage* which winds along the right bank of the Mosel downstream from *Grosslage* Schwarze Katz.

GROSSLAGE SCHWARZE KATZ

The village of Zell has some good *Einzellagen* with officially classified slopes that can make fine and aromatic Riesling, but it is best known for its *Grosslage* label that carries the famous Schwarze Katz "Black Cat" logo. In 1863, three merchants from Aachen were selecting wines in cellar in Zell, but could not decide which of three casks to buy. When the grower tried to take a second sample of one of the wines, his black cat leapt on to the barrel, arched its back, and hissed. The merchants thought that the cat was perhaps defending the best wine, thus purchased it, returning each year for what they dubbed the "Schwarze Katz" wine. As this story spread, so it became customary for other producers in Zell to label their best wines with the insignia of the black cat, but since Merl and Kaimt have been merged with Zell, it has become merely a blended *Grosslage* wine.

MERL
- Vineyard *Königslay Terrassen* Grower *Albert Kallfelz*
- Non-Einzellagen wines: Growers *Peter Thielen, Albert Kallfelz*

ZELL
- Non-Einzellagen wines: Growers *Peter Lehmen, Albert Kallfelz, Peter Thielen*

GROSSLAGE WEINHEX

This *Grosslage* extends over both banks of the Mosel and into the suburbs of Koblenz, encompassing some very steep slopes planted entirely with Riesling.

GONDORF
- Vineyard *Schlossberg* Grower *Andreas Barth*

WINNINGEN
- Vineyard *Uhlen* Grower *Heymann-Löwenstein* • Vineyard *Bruckstück* Growers *Knebel, Freiherr von Heddersdorf* • Vineyard *Röttgen* Growers *Knebel, Freiherr von Heddersdorf, Heymann-Löwenstein*

BEREICH BERNKASTEL

This covers the entire Mittelmosel, encompassing all of the river's most famous villages and towns, and most of its best vineyards. Much wine is sold under this *Bereich* appellation, but unfortunately most of it is disappointing.

GROSSLAGE BADSTUBE

Badstube must be the grandest *Grosslage* in Germany encompassing as it does the greatest, and certainly most famous, of all *Einzellagen*, the Doctor vineyard, as well as the almost equally well-known Lay, the superb Graben, and six other good sites. The quality of even the surplus wine from such great vineyards is so high that it is practically impossible to find poor Badstube, and the *Grosslage* wines are especially good in relatively poor years when grapes from the Doctor vineyard fail to achieve *Kabinett* level and are included in these blends.

BERNKASTEL
- Vineyard *Doctor* Growers *Wwe. Dr. H. Thanisch-Erben Thanisch, Reichsgraf von Kesselstatt, Geheimrat J. Wegeler* • Vineyard *Graben* Grower *Geheimrat J. Wegeler* • Vineyard *Lay* Growers *Franz Dahm, Dr. Loosen, Dr. Pauly-Bergweiler, Geheimrat J. Wegeler*

GROSSLAGE VOM HEISSEN STEIN

There is one grower that excels in this otherwise modest *Grosslage*.

PÜNDERICH
- Vineyard *Marienburg* Grower *Clemens Busch*

GROSSLAGE KURFÜRSTLAY

This includes the lesser wines of Bernkastel and the superior wines of Brauneberg, the best of which come from the fabulous vineyards on the south-southeast-facing Juffer hill that rises from the river opposite the village of Brauneberg. Its wines are remarkably racy considering their exceptional fullness of body and some prefer them to those of the Doctor, although I find it impossible to choose, and delight in their differences.

BERNKASTEL
- Vineyard *Johannisbrünnchen* Growers *J.J. Prüm, Dr. Weins-Prüm*

BRAUNEBERG
- Vineyard *Juffer* Growers *Fritz Haag, Karp-Schreiber, Max. Ferd. Richter, Reichsgraf von Kesselstatt* • Vineyard *Juffer Sonnenuhr* Growers *Fritz Haag, Willi Haag, Karp-Schreiber, Max Ferd. Richter, Paulinshof*

KESTEN
- Vineyard *Paulinshofberg* Growers *Bastgen-Vogel, Kees-Kieren, Paulinshof*

LIESER
- Vineyard *Niederberg Helden* Grower *Schloss Lieser*

GROSSLAGE MICHELSBERG

There are some great wines made in the village of Piesport in the Michelsberg *Grosslage*, but the thin, characterless Piesporter Michelsberg is not one of them. It is a *Grosslage* wine that comes not from steep, slaty slopes such as Goldtröpfchen or Domherr, but from very high-yielding, flat, alluvial land. No great grower would contemplate cultivating such fertile soil, the low-quality wines of which have unfairly debased the Peisporter village name to such a degree that its wine in the trade has become known as Piss-pot. The great wines of Trittenheim have not had to suffer from such great indignities, and the village of Dhron especially should not be forgotten for its produce.

MINHEIM
- Vineyard *Rosenberg* Grower *Molitor*

PIESPORT
- Vineyard *Domherr* Growers *Kurt Hain, Weller-Lehnert* • Vineyard *Goldtröpfchen* Growers *Reinhold Haart, Lehnert-Veit, Weller-Lehnert, Reuscher-Haart, St. Urbanshof*

TRITTENHEIM
- Vineyard *Apotheke* Growers *Ernst Clüsserath, Clüsserath-Eifel, Clüsserath-Weiler, Grans-Fassian, Josef Rosch, Laurentiushof Milz* • Vineyard *Felsenkopf* Grower *Laurentiushof Milz*

GROSSLAGE MÜNZLAY

The three villages in this *Grosslage* may lack the fame of Bernkastel and the popularity of Piesport, but they possess truly superb Mosel vineyards and boast an incomparable number of great growers and estates.

GRAACH
- Vineyard *Domprobst* Grower *Kees-Kieren, Max Ferd. Richter, Willi Schaefer, Selbach-Oster, Dr. Weins-Prüm* • Vineyard *Himmelreich* Growers *Kees-Kieren, Markus Molitor, J. J. Prüm, S. A. Prüm*

WEHLEN
- Vineyard *Sonnenuhr* Growers *Heribert Kerpen, Dr. Loosen, J. J. Prüm, S. A. Prüm, Dr. Weins-Prüm*

ZELTINGEN
- Vineyard *Sonnenuhr* Grower *Leo Kappes, Markus Molitor, Selbach-Oster*

GROSSLAGE NACKTARSCH

The labels of this *Grosslage* are collectors' items because of the naked bottoms featured on many of them – reflecting not only the name but also the quality of most of the wine. One grower is, however, trying harder than most.

KRÖV
✓ Vineyard *Letterlay*
Grower *Martin Müller* (Traben-Trarbach)

GROSSLAGE PROBSTBERG

There are no outstanding villages, vineyards, or growers except at Longuich and Schweich, which face each other across the Mosel, down river from its confluence with the Ruwer at Eitelsbach.

SCHWEICH
✓ Vineyard *Annaberg*
Growers *Bernhard Eifel, Werner & Sohn*

GROSSLAGE SCHWARZLAY

Erden and Uerzig are two of the Mittelmosel's most underrated villages. Their spectacular vineyards cling to cliff-like slopes in defiance of gravity and are capable of producing rich, racy wines of rapier-like acidity, stunning intensity, and immaculate style.

ENKIRCH
✓ Vineyard *Batterieberg*
Grower *Immich-Batterieberg*

ERDEN
✓ Vineyard *Treppchen*
Growers *J. J. Christoffel, Erben Stephan Ehlen, Dr. Loosen, Mönchhof-Robert Eymael, Dr. Weins-Prüm*

TRABEN
✓ Vineyard *Würzgarten* **Grower** *Rainer Knod*

ÜRZIG
✓ Vineyard *Goldwingert* **Grower** *Dr. Pauly-Bergweiler* • Vineyard *Prälat* **Grower** *Dr. Loosen* • Vineyard *Würzgarten* **Growers** *J. J. Christoffel, Dr. Loosen, Merkelbach*

GROSSLAGE ST. MICHAEL

Popular but generally overrated wines come from Klüsserath these days, although the wonderful wines of Kirsten and Franz-Josef Regnery are bringing back the glory days. Detzem, Mehring, and Schleich all have good potential, but it is Leiwen that truly excels, especially in its steepest and sunniest vineyards of Laurentiuslay and Klostergarten, which stretch up above the village, exposing their superb southwesterly aspect.

DETZEM
✓ Vineyard *Würzgarten* **Grower** *Walter Rauen*

KLÜSSERATH
✓ Vineyard *Bruderschaft*
Growers *Kirsten, Franz-Josef Regnery*

KÖWERICH
✓ Vineyard *Laurentiuslay*
Growers *Hoffmann-Simon* (Piesport), *Heinz Schmitt St. Nikolaushof, Schweicher*

LEIWEN
✓ Vineyard *Klostergarten*
Growers *Bernhard Werner, Heinz Schmitt, St. Urbanshof, Josef Rosch, Carl Loewen*
• Vineyard *Laurentiuslay*
Growers *Carl Loewen, St. Urbanshof, Stoffel, Grans-Fassian, Josef Rosch*

MEHRING
✓ Vineyard *Blattenberg*
Grower *Winfried Reh*

SCHLEICH
✓ Vineyard *Sonnenberg*
Grower *Winfried Reh*

BEREICH SAAR-RUWER

This contains two *Grosslagen* that cover the Mosel's two most famous tributaries, the Saar and the Ruwer. It is easy to remember which *Grosslage* belongs to which river as Scharzberg is on the Saar and Römerlay on the Ruwer.

GROSSLAGE RÖMERLAY

This covers the vineyards of the Ruwer and incorporates the ancient Roman city of Trier, as well as a few scattered plots on the Mosel, including one on the left bank facing Trier. The Ruwer is much the smaller of the two tributaries, yet it has its share of exceptional vineyards owned by gifted growers who make very aromatic, vital wines that are as racy as any on the Mosel, but not quite as biting as those of the Saar. The quality is high and few wines are seen under the *Grosslage* appellation.

EITELSBACH
✓ Vineyard *Karthäuserhofberg*
Grower *Karthäuserhof*

KASEL
✓ Vineyard *Kehrnagel*
Growers *Karlsmühle, Winzergenossenschaft Kasel*
• Vineyard *Nieschen*
Growers *Erben von Beulwitz, Reichsgraf von Kesselstatt, Karlsmühle*

LORENZHOF
✓ Vineyard *Felslay*
Grower *Karlsmühle*

MERTESDORF
✓ Vineyard *Herrenberg*
Grower *Morgen-Herres*

TRIER
✓ Vineyard *Deutschherrenberg*
Grower *Peter Terges*

GROSSLAGE SCHARZBERG

This covers the Saar and a small section of the Mosel between Konz and Trier to the north. These wines are so racy that they are positively biting and steely in their youth, but they age gracefully, harmonizing into exquisitely piquant flavours. Very modest Saar wines can be too thin and unripe to enjoy, but *Kabinett* and higher predicates from great growers are almost sure to please. Unlike the Ruwer's Römerlay, this *Grosslage* appellation is often used. Kanzem is also known for its red wine.

AYL
✓ Vineyard *Kupp*
Grower *Johann Peter Reinert*

FILZEN
✓ Vineyard *Herrenberg*
Growers *Edmund Reverchon, Peter Lauer*

KANZEM
✓ Vineyard *Altenberg*
Grower *Von Othegraven*

OBEREMMEL
✓ Vineyard *Karlsberg*
Grower *Reichsgraf von Kesselstatt*
• Vineyard *Hütte* **Grower** *Von Hövel*

OCKFEN
✓ Vineyard *Bockstein*
Growers *Jordan & Jordan, St. Urbanshof* (Leiwen)

SERRIG
✓ Vineyard *Schloss Saarstein*
Grower *Schloss Saarstein*
• Vineyard *Vogelsang*
Grower *Staatl. Weinbaudomäne*

SAARBURG
✓ Vineyard *Rausch*
Grower *Geltz Zilliken*

SCHARZHOFBERG
✓ Vineyard *Scharzhofberger*
Growers *Reichsgraf von Kesselstatt, von Hövel, Jordan & Jordan, Egon Müller*

SCHODEN
✓ Vineyard *Herrenberg*
Growers *Weinhof Herrenberg*

WILTINGEN
✓ Vineyard *Klosterberg*
Grower *Johann Peter Reinert*

BEREICH OBERMOSEL

The Obermosel, or Upper Mosel, runs parallel to the Luxembourg border and is planted mostly with Elbling. The wines are thin, acidic, and mostly made into *Sekt*.

GROSSLAGE KÖNIGSBERG

No outstanding villages, vineyards, or growers.

GROSSLAGE GIPFEL

No outstanding villages, vineyards, or growers, although respectable wines are made in the village of Nittel.

BEREICH MOSELTOR

This is the most southerly *Bereich* on the Mosel. It encompasses the upper reaches of the river that flows from its source in the Vosges mountains of France through Luxembourg and into Germany, hence the name Moseltor or "Mosel gate". Its wines are very light and acid, and of little significance except to the *Sekt* houses.

GROSSLAGE SCHLOSS BÜBINGER

Haven of the less than heavenly Elbling. While colleagues across the river in Luxembourg earn a good living out of wine and tourism, the acidic Elbling wines of this Grosslage do not make it easy for its growers to survive.

THE NAHE

In the Nahe region, a sunny microclimate and varied soils combine to produce wines that have the elegance of a Rheingau, the body of a light Rheinhessen, and the acidity of a Mosel. The perfumed aroma of a Nahe wine is unique to the region, as are its extremely fragrant flavour and soft, smooth style.

DESPITE AN ABUNDANCE of Roman roads and villas, viticulture came relatively late to the Nahe, the earliest documented record dating from the eighth century, at least 500 years after the Romans had established a flourishing wine industry in the Mosel valley. As with the rest of Germany, the vineyards underwent a great expansion in the 12th and 13th centuries, and by the 19th century the Nahe was universally considered to be on a par with the Rheingau. Strangely, by World War II it had become Germany's least-known region. This had nothing to do with a loss of either quantity or quality: excellent vineyards such as Kupfergrube at Schlossböckelheim, today widely acclaimed as the greatest of all Nahe vineyards, did not even exist before 1900. The decline was probably due instead to the fact that the region was a relatively small area of scattered vineyards, and as such it

was difficult to compete with larger, more compact ones. When those larger competitors also became industrialized, they prospered and developed sophisticated transport systems, edging the Nahe further into the cold. As a region with an essentially rural, non-industrialized, mixed-agricultural economy, it looked inwards. Yet its own population could consume most of its production with little trouble and so the Nahe's wines adopted an increasingly lower profile on national and international markets.

SMALL COULD BE SO BEAUTIFUL

If majority of the grape varieties cultivated in the Nahe were Riesling, the region would be able to capitalize on its limited size, and market the exclusive quality of its fine-wine production.

THE REGION AT A GLANCE

Area under vine
4,665 ha (11,527 acres)

Average yield
80 hl/ha (360 cases/acre)

Red wine 7%

White wine 93%

Most important grape varieties
27% Riesling, 23% Müller-Thurgau, 11% Silvaner, 8% Kerner, 31% Others

Infrastructure
Bereich 1; *Grosslagen* 7; *Einzellagen* 328

Note The vineyards straddle 80 *Gemeinden* (communes), the names of which may appear on the label.

QUALITY REQUIREMENTS AND HARVEST PERCENTAGES

MINIMUM OECHSLE	QUALITY CATEGORY	1992	1993	1994	1995
44°	*Deutscher Tafelwein*	20%	–	4%	4%
50°	*Landwein*				
57–60°	* QbA	76%	57%	80%	88%
70–73°	* Kabinett	3%	27%	14%	8%
78–82°	* Spätlese	1%	13%	2%	–
85–92°	* Auslese				
120°	Beerenauslese	–	3%	–	–
120°	Eiswein				
150°	Trockenbeerenauslese				

*Minimum Oechsle levels vary according to grape variety; those that have a naturally lower sugar content may qualify at a correspondingly lower level.

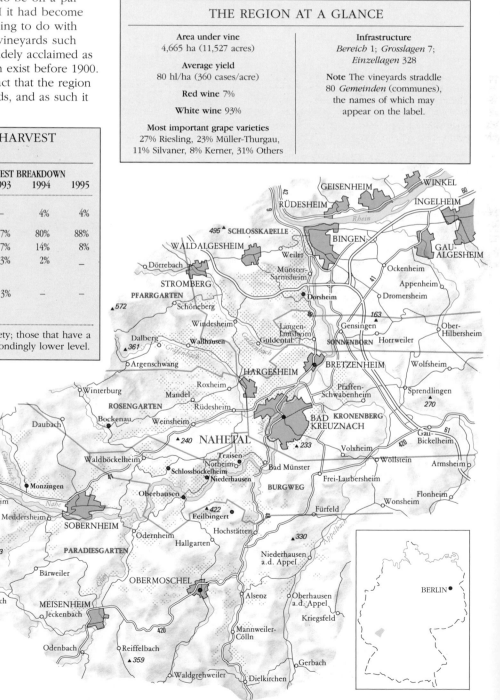

THE NAHE, *see also p.261*
Between Rheinhessen and the Mittelrhein nestles the self-contained wine-producing region of the Nahe. Its namesake river has many tributaries running between spectacular overhanging cliffs.

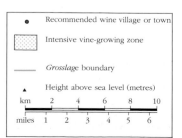

- Recommended wine village or town
- Intensive vine-growing zone
- *Grosslage* boundary
- ▲ Height above sea level (metres)

km 2 4 6 8 10
miles 1 2 3 4 5 6

FACTORS AFFECTING TASTE AND QUALITY

LOCATION
The region balloons out from between Rheinhessen and the Mittelrhein around the River Nahe, which runs parallel to, and 40 km (25 miles) southeast of, the Mosel.

CLIMATE
A temperate, sunny climate with adequate rainfall and no frosts. Local conditions are influenced by the Soonwald forest to the northeast and heat-retaining, rocky hills to the east. Protected south-facing vineyards enjoy microclimates that are almost Mediterranean.

ASPECT
Vineyards are found on both the gentle and steep slopes of the Nahe and its hinterland of many small tributary river valleys. Vines grow at altitudes of between 100 and 300 m (330–985 ft).

SOIL
Diverse soils ranging from quartzite and slate along the lower reaches to porphyry (hard rock poor in lime), melaphyry (hard rock rich in lime), and coloured sandstone in the middle and upper reaches. Near Bad Kreuznach, weathered clay, sandstone, loess, and loam soil may also be found. The greatest Riesling wines grow on sandstone.

VITICULTURE AND VINIFICATION
Since the mid-1960s, cultivation of Riesling and Silvaner has declined by 20 and 15 per cent respectively, yet Riesling is now the most widely planted variety, accounting for some 27 per cent of the Nahe's vineyards. This fluctuation in percentages is due to the increased cultivation of crosses such as Kerner, Scheurebe, and Bacchus. In the cellar, methods remain traditional and also very efficient, with technically up-to-date cooperatives processing just 20 per cent of the crop. As much as 40 per cent of all the wine made in this region is processed by small grower who sell direct to passing customers, with the remaining 40 per cent belonging to (or delivered by growers to) the traditional trade and export houses.

PRIMARY GRAPE VARIETIES
Müller-Thurgau, Riesling, Silvaner
SECONDARY GRAPE VARIETIES
Bacchus, Faberrebe, Kerner, Scheurebe, Ruländer, Weissburgunder

---

THE APPELLATIONS OF

THE NAHE

BEREICH NAHETAL

This region-wide Bereich replaces the former *Bereich* of Kreuznach, which covered the area once called Untere Nahe, or Lower Nahe, and Schlossböckelheim, which is the most famous.

GROSSLAGE BURGWEG

Not to be confused with the *Grosslagen* of the same name in the Rheingau and Franken, this Burgweg produces the Nahe's greatest range of fine Riesling wines; Schlossböckelheimer Kupfergrube is widely regarded as the best of all.

NIEDERHAUSEN
✓ Vineyard *Hermannshöhle*
Grower *Hermann Dönnhoff*
• Vineyard *Hermannsberg*
Growers *Staatsdomäne Niederhausen-Schlossböckelheim, Oskar Mathern*
• Vineyard *Rosenberg* Grower *Oskar Mathern*

NORHEIM
✓ Vineyard *Dellchen*
Growers *Lötzbeyer, Oskar Mathern*

OBERHAUSEN
✓ Vineyard *Brücke*
Grower *Hermann Dönnhof*

SCHLOSSBÖCKELHEIM
✓ Vineyard *Kupfergrube*
Grower *Staatsdomäne Niederhausen-Schlossböckelheim*
• Vineyard *Felsenberg* Grower *Hans Crusius*

NAHE
1988er
Schloßböckelheimer
Kupfergrube
Riesling
Beerenauslese
QUALITÄTSWEIN MIT PRÄDIKAT
A. P. Nr. 1 750 053 / 37 / 89
Erzeugerabfüllung
Verwaltung der Staatlichen Weinbaudomänen
Niederhausen-Schloßböckelheim
9,0 % vol   D-6551 Niederhausen   e 750 ml

TRAISEN
✓ Vineyard *Bastei* Grower *Staatsdomäne Niederhausen-Schlossböckelheim*
• Vineyard *Rotenfels* Grower *Hans Crusius*

GROSSLAGE KRONENBERG

This is not a branded beer, but one of the best *Grosslagen* in the Nahe, although all its finest wines, invariably Rieslings with a magical blend of perfumed fragrance and soft yet racy acidity, carry *Einzellage* names.

BAD KREUZNACH
✓ Vineyard *Krötenpfuhl* Grower *Paul Anheuser* • Vineyard *Narrenkappe* Grower *Paul Anheuser*

BRETZENHEIM
✓ Vineyard *Pastorei* Grower *K. Schmidt*

1554
Bretzenheimer Pastorei
Riesling Auslese

GROSSLAGE PFARRGARTEN

Although the *Grosslage* of Pfarrgarten is relatively small, it is intensively cultivated. Grosslage Pfarrgarten lies west and slightly north of Bad Kreuznach. The wines produced by Wallhausen are the best.

DALBERG
✓ Vineyard *Schlossberg* Grower *Prinz zu Salm*

WALLHAUSEN
✓ Vineyard *Johannisberg* Grower *Prinz zu Salm* • Vineyard *Schloss Wallhausen* Grower *Prinz zu Salm*

GROSSLAGE PARADIESGARTEN

This *Grosslage* consists of many scattered vineyards of extremely variable quality. With the exception of Oberndorf, all its finest wines come from the very eastern edge of the Nahe. It is worth noting that the relatively unknown wines usually offer excellent value for money.

FEILBINGERT
✓ Vineyard *Königsgarten* Grower *Adolf Lötzbeyer*

MONZINGEN
✓ Vineyard *Halenberg* Grower *Emrich-Schönleber*

OBERNDORF
✓ Non-Einzellagen wine *Alisencia* Grower *Hahnmühle*

GROSSLAGE ROSENGARTEN

The true, original, and famous Rüdesheimer Rosengarten is a great Rheingau Riesling from an Einzellage called Rosengarten. The Nahe version may be honest enough, but it is not particularly special, being merely a modest Grosslage wine and, in all probability, a blend of Müller-Thurgau and Silvaner.

BOCKENAU
✓ Vineyard *Stromberg* Grower *Schäfer-Fröhlich*

ROXHEIM
✓ Vineyard *Berg* Grower *Prinz zu Salm*

GROSSLAGE SCHLOSSKAPELLE

In this *Grosslage* there are a number of attractive, good-quality wines from Münster-Sarmsheim and Dorsheim, which are excellent value. In addition to some full and rich Riesling, the Weisser and Grauer Burgunder are also making a name for themselves.

DORSHEIM
✓ Vineyard *Goldloch* Grower *Schlossgut Diel*
• Vineyard *Pittermännchen* Grower *J.B. Schäfer*

MÜNSTER (-SARMSHEIM)
✓ Vineyard *Dautenpflänzer* Growers *Göttelmann, Kruger-Rumpf*
• Vineyard *Rheinberg* Grower *Göttelmann*
• Vineyard *Pittersberg* Grower *Kruger-Rumpf* Non-Einzellagen wine *Kruger-Rumpf*

GROSSLAGE SONNENBORN

Sonnenborn is a one-village *Grosslage*. A number of growers in Langenlonsheim produce some interesting and fulsome wines.

LANGENLONSHEIM
✓ Vineyard *Lauerweg* Grower *Wilhelm Sitzius*
• Vineyard *Löhrer Berg* Growers *Wilhelm Sitzius, Tesch*
• Vineyard *Steinchen* Grower *Bürgermeister Willi Schweinhardt*

THE RHEINGAU

There can be no doubt that Riesling, the King of Germany's grapes, is more at home in and around the village of Johannisberg in the Rheingau than anywhere else in the world. Nowhere else can it produce such lush, juicy-ripe wines with distinctive, silky-smooth peach fruit.

MANY COUNTRIES OF THE WORLD use the synonym "Johannisberg Riesling" to distinguish the true Riesling grape variety from the many false and inferior Rieslings that claim the name. There can be no doubt that the Riesling grape luxuriates on this single sun-blessed slope of the Johannisberg vineyard in a most unique way.

Even at QbA level, the relaxed and confident style of a good Rheingau wine will leave a soft, satisfying, and elegant taste of peaches in the mouth. This gradually merges into a youthful, honeyed character that is nothing to do with *Edelfäule*

VITICULTURE IN THE RHEINGAU
Over 80 per cent of the vines are Riesling, and it is here that it has historically ripened to such perfection that the wines have a juicy peachiness.

QUALITY REQUIREMENTS AND HARVEST PERCENTAGES

MINIMUM OECHSLE	QUALITY CATEGORY	HARVEST BREAKDOWN			
		1992	1993	1994	1995
44°	*Deutscher Tafelwein*	20%	–	3%	2%
53°	*Landwein*				
57–60°	* *QbA*	79%	40%	72%	89%
73–80°	* *Kabinett*	1%	53%	21%	8%
85–95°	* *Spätlese*	–	6%	4%	1%
55–105°	* *Auslese*				
125°	*Beerenauslese*	–	1%	–	–
125°	*Eiswein*				
150°	*Trockenbeerenauslese*				

*Minimum Oechsle levels vary according to grape variety; those that have a naturally lower sugar content may qualify at a correspondingly lower level.

THE REGION AT A GLANCE

Area under vine
3,288 ha (8,125 acres)

Average yield
64 hl/ha (288 cases/acre)

Red wine 10%

White wine 90%

Most important grape varieties
81% Riesling, 9% Spätburgunder,
4% Müller-Thurgau, 6% Others

Infrastructure
Bereich 1;
Grosslagen 10;
Einzellagen 118

Note The vineyards of Rheingau straddle 28 *Gemeinden* (communes), the names of which may appear on the label.

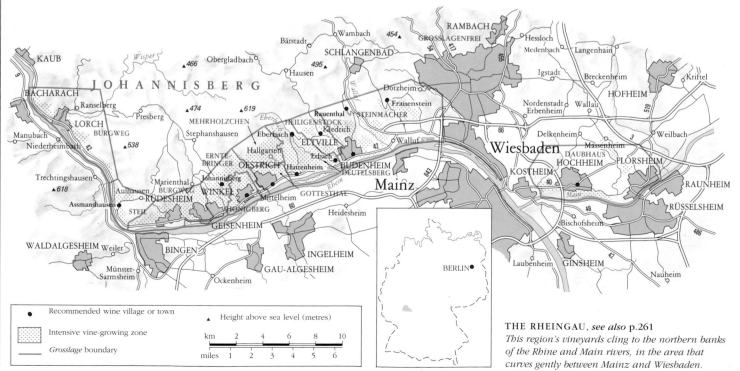

Recommended wine village or town

Intensive vine-growing zone

Grosslage boundary

Height above sea level (metres)

km 2 4 6 8 10
miles 1 2 3 4 5 6

THE RHEINGAU, *see also p.261*
This region's vineyards cling to the northern banks of the Rhine and Main rivers, in the area that curves gently between Mainz and Wiesbaden.

(botrytis or noble rot), overripeness, or bottle-ageing. One can prefer other stylistic renditions of the Riesling grape, but it is impossible to find finer, more graceful examples.

THE RHEINGAU'S INITIAL CHARTA FOR QUALITY
In the midst of the excitement generated by Germany's new *Trocken* wines, it became evident to various top Rheingau estates that most of the wines exported were bulk blended and of low commercial quality. Since these properties had traditionally produced naturally drier wines, they believed that a continuance of poor *Trocken* wines could damage their own image, so banded together to protect it. In 1983, the Association of Charta- (pronounced "CARTA") Estates was launched to "further the classic Rheingau Riesling style, to upgrade the quality of Rheingau wines, and to make them unique among wines from other growing areas". Although this could not have succeeded without the active support of almost all the best Rheingau producers, the engine that has relentlessly driven the Charta organisation has been the indefatigable Georg Breuer. Under his direction, Charta has become the antithesis of any official quality-control system, as it aspires to the highest possible quality, rather than succumbing to the lowest common denominator. When first drawn-up, the Charta's rules were uncommonly stiff, yet every few years, Breuer tightens the ratchet a bit more by issuing even tougher rules.

TROCKEN WINES
One in every five bottles of German wine is *Trocken* or dry, but many of these are thin and short. The intrinsically riper grapes grown by the Rheingau's Charta estates produce a fatter, fuller style of wine that adapts naturally to the *Tocken* style, particularly with food, but *Trocken* wines produced in other regions have come

on in leaps and bounds since the early 1990s. They are now well balanced, with an elegance that was missing from even the best of the best in the late 1980s. Due to the botrytis found in Spätlese and Auslese grapes used, they also possess a level of youthful complexity that is seldom encountered in other wines. They are very accessible when young, but rarely improve after their first flush of youth.

SCHLOSS VOLRADS
This famous wine Schloss *was built* circa *1300 by the Knights of Greiffenclau.*

THE CHARTA RULES

I have tasted many Charta wines and am convinced that they are indeed superior to other Rheingau wines. It must be emphasized, however, that it is only dry styles that are subject to the Charta Organisation's regulations – great QmP Rheingau wines of sweet styles from *Auslese* upwards are not affected. A Charta wine may be recognized by the traditional tall, slim, brown bottle typical of the Rheingau region and by the distinctive "Charta capsule" consisting of a Romanesque double-arch on a white ground. There is also a label on the back with the same insignia.

Charta wines are examined organoleptically (using only the senses of taste, smell, and sight) before and after bottling. There is a second examination to check the authenticity of the original sample.

Wines destined to receive the Charta imprimatur must be accompanied by official analysis documents and must also satisfy certain criteria laid down by the Association of Charta Estates, as follows:

The wines that are submitted for examination must be made in a "dry" style and conform to the following:

- 100 per cent own-estate production
- 100 per cent Riesling grapes
- Grapes hand-picked by *tries*
- Minimum of 12 per cent potential alcohol
- Maximum production of 50 hl/ha
- No *Prädikat* may be mentioned*

The wines must have the true characteristics of a Riesling, of the specific vintage, and of the vineyard where the grapes were grown.

Registration has to be made four weeks prior to the date of examination, indicating the vintage and category.

*Older vintages of *Prädikat* wines may be encountered. These will not have been produced according to the above rules if only for the simple reason that they have not been made in a dry style, but they will have undergone the same exhaustive tasting and, if selected, become "Charta Designated", rather than "Charta Approved".

As a control, normal wines of comparable location and category are tasted blind alongside wines submitted for examination. Charta wines have to surpass the quality of these standard wines in each of the required aspects. The wines provided for the second tasting, as well as being a control, have to be accompanied by the analysis of the AP number (*see* p.262). The results of these tests are lodged with the Association and can be used in the eventuality of any subsequent claim that a member is passing off an inferior wine as a Charta wine.

Charta bottle

Charta capsule · Back label

CAPSULE AND BACK LABEL
All wines that have passed the Charta examination are sealed with a capsule bearing the organization's logo consisting of a Romanesque double-arch that also appears on the back-label.

CHARTA BOTTLE
Originally all bottles were embossed with the Charta logo similar to the example here. However, the cost of embossing proved prohibitive for some of the smaller producers, and it is now optional.

BERG SCHLOSSBERG VINEYARDS, RÜDESHEIM
*These south-facing vineyards on the slopes of Berg Schlossberg
are blessed with perfect exposure to the sun's rays.*

FACTORS AFFECTING TASTE AND QUALITY

LOCATION
The Rheingau is a compact region only 36 km (22 miles) long, situated on the northern banks of the Rivers Rhine and Main between Bingen and Mainz.

CLIMATE
Vines are protected from cold by the tempering effect of the rivers and the shelter provided by the Taunus mountains. The region receives above-average hours of sunshine during the growth period of May to October.

ASPECT
The vines grow at an altitude of 100–300 m (330–985 ft) on a superb, fully south-facing slope.

SOIL
Quartzite and weathered slate-stone in the higher situated sites produce the greatest Riesling, while loam, loess, clay, and sandy gravel soils of the lower vineyards give a fuller, more robust style.

The blue phyllite-slate around Assmannshausen is traditionally thought to favour the Spätburgunder.

VITICULTURE AND VINIFICATION
There are some 500 independent wine estates and approximately 2,600 private growers. Many of these make and market their own wines while others supply the region's ten cooperatives. The Riesling grape variety represents 80 per cent of the vines cultivated and it is traditional in this region to vinify all but the sweetest wines in a drier style than would be used in other regions. Assmannshausen is famous for its red wine, one of Germany's best.

PRIMARY GRAPE VARIETY
Riesling
SECONDARY GRAPE VARIETIES
Ehrenfelser, Kerner, Müller-Thurgau, Silvaner, Spätburgunder

THE CHARTA'S NEW CLASSIFIED VINEYARD WINES

Look out for Charta *Einzellage* wines with a black bottom border bearing not one but three Romanesque double-arches on the front label. This is verification that the wine comes not from the grossly inflated official *Einzellagen*, but from the original, authentic site, which Charta has called *Erstes Gewächs* or First Growths. They must conform to the same rules as above (i.e. dry style with no mention of *Prädikat*), although new regulations to cover botrytis and even Spätburgunder *Erstes Gewächs* are under study.

The difference between official and authentic *Einzellage* size can be, as you can see, quite enormous. In fact, the 1971 German Wine Law is nothing less than the promotion of legalized fraud on a massive and widespread scale.

VILLAGE	EINZELLAGE	VINEYARD SIZE		1971 EXPANSION
		Official	Charta	
Lorch	Bodenthal-Steinberg	28.1	12.3	128%
Lorch	Kapellenberg	56.9	17.9	218%
Lorch	Krone	14.5	7.5	93%
Assmannshausen	Höllenberg	43.4	20.0	117%
Rüdesheim	Berg Schlossberg	25.5	23.2	10%
Rüdesheim	Berg Roseneck	26.7	16.2	65%
Rüdesheim	Berg Rottland	36.2	32.3	12%
Geisenheim	Fuchsberg	44.4	5.6	693%
Geisenheim	Rothenberg	26.8	9.0	198%
Geisenheim	Kläuserweg	57.6	14.3	303%
Geisenheim	Mäuerchen	32.6	3.6	806%
Johannisberg	Schloss Johannisberg	21.9	16.6	32%
Johannisberg	Klaus	2.0	2.0	0%
Johannisberg	Hölle	20.9	6.2	237%
Johannisberg	Mittelhölle	6.5	6.5	0%
Winkel	Jesuitengarten	31.2	26.0	20%
Winkel	Hasensprung	103.8	19.9	421%
Winkel	Schloss Vollrads	37.7	15.0	151%
Mittelheim	St. Nikolaus	44.8	6.7	569%
Oestrich	Lenchen	130.6	35.8	265%
Oestrich	Doosberg	137.9	38.4	259%
Hattenheim	Engelmannsberg	14.1	10.5	34%
Hattenheim	Mannberg	8.1	8.1	0%
Hattenheim	Pfaffenberg	6.6	6.6	0%
Hattenheim	Nussbrunnen	10.8	10.8	0%
Hattenheim	Wisselbrunnen	16.9	9.7	74%
Hattenheim	Steinberg	36.7	26.9	36%
Hallgarten	Schönhell	52.1	18.9	176%
Erbach	Marcobrunn	5.2	5.2	0%
Erbach	Steinmorgen	28.2	8.6	228%
Erbach	Siegelsberg	15.1	13.7	10%
Erbach	Hohenrain	17.1	5.8	195%

VILLAGE	EINZELLAGE	VINEYARD SIZE		1971 EXPANSION
		Official	Charta	
Erbach	Schlossberg	28.1	12.3	128%
Kiedrich	Gräfenberg	56.9	17.9	218%
Kiedrich	Wasseros	14.5	7.5	93%
Eltville	Sonnenberg	43.4	20.0	117%
Rauenthal	Baiken	25.5	23.2	10%
Rauenthal	Gehrn	26.7	16.2	65%
Rauenthal	Rothenberg	36.2	32.3	12%
Rauenthal	Nonnenberg	44.4	5.6	693%
Rauenthal	Wülfen	26.8	9.0	198%
Martinsthal	Wildsau	57.6	14.3	303%
Martinsthal	Langenberg	32.6	3.6	806%
Walluf	Walkenberg	21.9	16.6	32%
Wiesbaden	Neroberg	2.0	2.0	0%
Hochheim	Domdechaney	20.9	6.2	237%
Hochheim	Kirchenstück	6.5	6.5	0%
Hochheim	Hölle	31.2	26.0	20%
Hochheim	Königin Victoria Ber	103.8	19.9	421%

THE APPELLATIONS OF

THE RHEINGAU

BEREICH JOHANNISBERG

This *Bereich* covers the entire Rheingau. Trading off the famous village of Johannisberg, situated behind Schloss Johannisberg, lesser wines sell well under it. However, some producers have started using *Grosslage* names on labels and because they do not use the word "*Grosslage*", this implies the wine might be from one specific site, and perhaps of better quality.

GROSSLAGE BURGWEG

This is the westernmost *Grosslage*. If a wine bears its name on the label and clearly shows "Riesling", it may well be good, but it will not in any way compare with Burgweg's superb *Einzellage* wines that are produced by the great estates or small growers.

LORCH
✓ Vineyard *Bodental-Steinberg* Grower *Graf von Kanitz* • Vineyard *Kapellenberg* Grower *Graf von Kanitz*

GEISENHEIM
✓ Vineyard *Mäuerchen* Grower *Prinz von Hessen* • Vineyard *Rothenberg* Grower *Dr. Wegeler Erben*

RÜDESHEIM
✓ Vineyard *Berg Rottland* Growers *Georg Breuer, Johannishof Eser, Josef Leitz, Dr. Heinrich Nägeler* • Vineyard *Berg Schlossberg* Growers *Georg Breuer, August Kessler, Josef Leitz, Kloster Eberbach* • Vineyard *Bischofsberg* Growers *Georg Breuer, Schloss Schönborn* • Vineyard *Klosterberg* Grower *Josef Leitz*

GROSSLAGE DAUBHAUS

The best vines of Daubhaus, which is the most easterly *Grosslage* in *Bereich* Johannisberg, grow in just one tiny, isolated, but excellent strip at Hochheim. The wines are firm and full, but do not quite match the elegance of the Rheingau's very best.

HOCHHEIM
✓ Vineyard *Domdechaney* Grower *Domdechant Werner'sches Weingut* • Vineyard *Kirchenstück* Growers *Domdechant Werner'sches Weingut* • Vineyard *Hölle* Growers *Franz Künstler, W.J. Schäfer*

WICKER
✓ Vineyard *Mönchsgewann* Grower *Joachim Flick*

GROSSLAGE DEUTELSBERG

Grosslage Deutelsberg encompasses the great Erbach vineyards as well as the rather underrated wines of Hattenheim that have great strength and longevity. It also includes the famous Kloster Eberbach and Mariannenau Island vineyard, where there is a little Chardonnay grown.

HATTENHEIM
✓ Vineyard *Pfaffenberg* Grower *Domäne Schloss Schönborn* • Vineyard *Steinberg* Grower *Staatsweingüter Kloster Eberbach* • Vineyard *Wisselbrunnen* Growers *Freiherr zu Knyphausen, Hans Lang, Schloss Reinhartshausen, Hans Barth*
Non-Einzellagen wines: Grower *Hans Barth*

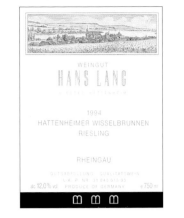

GROSSLAGE ERNTEBRINGER

The most often-seen of the Rheingau's *Grosslagen*, Erntebringer is also its best, although not comparable to the *Einzellagen*, particularly the legendary Schloss Johannisberg and the grossly underrated Klaus.

GEISENHEIM
✓ Vineyard *Kläuserweg* Grower *Prinz von Hessen*

JOHANNISBERG
✓ Vineyard *Goldatzel* Grower *Johannishof Eser* • Vineyard *Schloss Johannisberg* Grower *Domäne Schloss Johannisberg* • Vineyard *Klaus* Growers *Prinz von Hessen, Johannishof Eser*

GROSSLAGE GOTTESTHAL

It is strange that this *Grosslage*, sandwiched between the superb Deutelsberg and Honigberg, should be relatively disappointing in the wine it produces. However, some excellent, long-lived Riesling can be found.

OESTRICH
✓ Vineyard *Lenchen* Growers *J. Wegeler Erben, Peter Jakob Kühn* • Vineyard *Doosberg* Growers *Josef Spreitz, Peter Jakob Kühn*
Non-Einzellagen wines: Growers *Peter Jakob Kühn, Schloss Vollrads*

GROSSLAGE HEILIGENSTOCK

The best product of this small *Grosslage* is the fabulous, peach-and-honey Riesling of Kiedrich. The *Grosslage* wine can also be good.

KIEDRICH
✓ Vineyard *Gräfenberg* Grower *Robert Weil*

GROSSLAGE HONIGBERG

Wines of great vitality, finesse and all the elegant, mouthwatering, peachy fruit and youthful honey you could expect from top Rheingau wines.

ERBACH
✓ Vineyard *Hohenrain* Grower *Jakob Jung* • Vineyard *Marcobrunn* Growers *Schloss Schönborn, Staatsweingut Kloster Eberbach* • Vineyard *Michelmark* Grower *Jakob Jung* • Vineyard *Steinmorgen* Grower *Jakob Jung*

WINKEL
✓ Vineyard *Hasensprung* Growers *Fritz Allendorf, Prinz von Hessen* • Vineyard *Jesuitengarten* Growers *Fritz Allendorf, Breuer, Prinz von Hessen, J. Wegeler Erben*

GROSSLAGE MEHRHÖLZCHEN

The *Grosslage* of Mehrhölzchen, which is on higher, steeper slopes than the rest of the Rheingau, is tucked up beneath the Taunus hills. The area is planted almost entirely with Riesling, and the style of the wine is fat, almost heavy. It is sometimes full of fruit, displaying a unique spicy aroma.

HALLGARTEN
✓ Vineyard *Jungfer* Grower *Prinz*

GROSSLAGE STEIL

The tiny *Grosslage* of Steil divides the *Grosslage* of Burgweg. Steil is famous for its production of the red wines of Assmannshausen. These wines are very soft and delicate, and have a pure varietal style, but possess neither the body nor the tannin one is accustomed to finding to some degree in any red wine, whatever its grape variety or provenance. The majority of the vineyards in Grosslage Steil are situated on steep, southwest-facing slopes, but those of Höllenberg, which notably produce the best wine, are situated on a tiny, south-facing tributary.

ASSMANNSHAUSEN
✓ Vineyard *Höllenberg* Growers *August Kesseler, Staatsweingüter Assmannshausen, Robert König, Weingut Krone*

GROSSLAGE STEINMÄCHER

The vineyards of Grosslage Steinmächer are less intensively cultivated than those vineyards situated in the main body of the Rheingau's vine-growing area, but this does not necessarily mean that the wines they produce are in any way less impressive.

RAUENTHAL
✓ Vineyard *Baiken* Growers *Staatsweingüter Kloster Eberbach, Langwerth von Simmern*

WALLUF
✓ Vineyard *Walkenberg* Growers *J.B. Becker, Toni Jost - Hahnenhof (Bacharach)*

RHEINHESSEN

Rheinhessen is the most heavily cultivated of all Gemany's Qualitätswein *regions. The diversity of its soils and grape varieties makes it impossible to convey a uniform impression of its wines. Riesling is planted in just eight per cent of its vineyards. These vineyards produce cheap, unpretentious wines, ranging from mild Silvaner to aromatic Müller-Thurgau, but some truly fine wines are to be found.*

RHEINHESSEN IS INDISPUTABLY LINKED with the ubiquitous Liebfraumilch. This is partly because the area is responsible for producing one in every two bottles; partly because of the famous Liebfraumilch-Kirchenstück in Worms, where the Liebfraumilch story began, and partly because Sichel and Co. brews up perhaps the most famous Liebfraumilch ("Blue Nun") in sleepy Alzey. Nierstein carries a similar stigma to that of Liebfraumilch in the minds of many experienced drinkers, due to the huge quantities of the cheap Bereich Nierstein and Niersteiner Gutes Domtal that flood the market and which downgrade the reputation of the high-quality Niersteiner *Einzellagen*.

FACTORS AFFECTING TASTE AND QUALITY

LOCATION
This region is situated between the towns of Bingen, Mainz, and Worms, immediately south of the Rheingau.

CLIMATE
Rheinhessen enjoys a temperate climate and is protected from cold winds by the Taunus hills to the north and the Odenwald forest to the east. Vineyards that slope down to the river are protected by the Rhine terrace itself.

ASPECT
Vines grow on east- and southeast-facing slopes at an altitude of between 100 and 200 m (330–660 ft) on the river slopes of the Rhine Terrace, while those in Rheinhessen's hinterland are found at various heights and with every possible aspect.

SOIL
Mainly loess deposited during inter-glacial sandstorms, but also limestone, sandy-marl, quartzite, porphyry-sand, and silty-clay. Riesling growers favour heavier marl soil.

VITICULTURE AND VINIFICATION
Much of the wine is made from vast vineyard yields, bulk-blended into cheap generic wines such as Bereich Nierstein, and, of course, Liebfraumilch. At the other extreme, small quantities of some fine wines are produced on the best estates.

PRIMARY GRAPE VARIETIES
Müller-Thurgau, Silvaner
SECONDARY GRAPE VARIETIES
Bacchus, Faberrebe, Huxelrebe, Kerner, Morio-muskat, Portugieser, Riesling, Scheurebe

THE RHINE TERRACE
Despite the high volume of indifferent wines, there are many great growers and estates producing good wine in this region. If you are looking for an initial increase in quality for a modest price, look out for the "Rhein Terrasse" sticker on bottles of Rheinhessen wine.

The Rhine Terrace comprises nine villages on the slopes that descend from Rheinhessen's plateau to the river Rhine. These villages and their *Grosslagen* are as follows: Bodenheim in the St. Alban *Grosslage*; Nackenheim in the Gutes Domtal *Grosslage*; Nierstein,

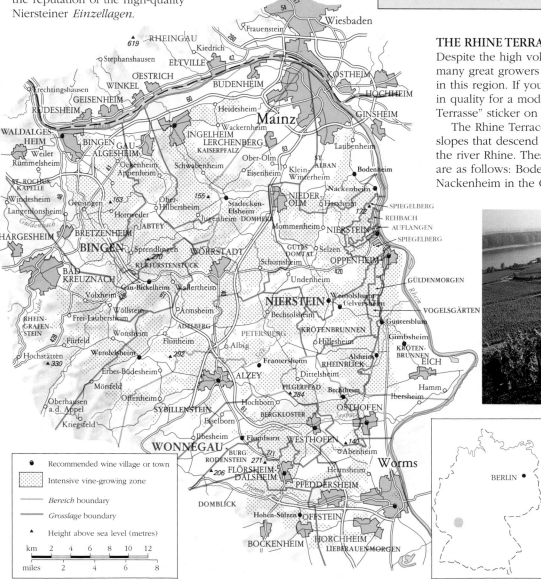

RHINE TERRACE VINEYARDS AT NIERSTEIN
Nierstein is one of the nine member villages of the "Rhein-Terrasse" group, which offers good-value, quality wines. New grape crosses are a feature of this area.

RHEINHESSEN, *see also p.261*
One of Germany's largest regions in terms of hectares under vine, this is an area of great variety where several different grapes are grown.

Map legend
- Recommended wine village or town
- Intensive vine-growing zone
- *Bereich* boundary
- *Grosslage* boundary
- ▲ Height above sea level (metres)

km 2 4 6 8 10 12
miles 2 4 6 8

which is shared by the *Grosslagen* of Gutes Domtal, Spiegelberg, Rehbach, and Auflangen; Oppenheim in the *Grosslagen* of Güldenmorgen and Krötenbrunnen; Dienheim, also in the Krötenbrunnen *Grosslage*; Guntersblum and Ludwigshöhe, both of which are in the Krötenbrunnen and Vogelsgarten *Grosslagen*; and Alsheim and Mattenheim, in the *Grosslage* of Rheinblick.

QUALITY REQUIREMENTS AND HARVEST PERCENTAGES

MINIMUM OECHSLE	QUALITY CATEGORY	HARVEST BREAKDOWN			
		1992	1993	1994	1995
44°	*Deutscher Tafelwein*	10%	–	1%	4%
53°	*Landwein*				
60–62°	* *QbA*	82%	38%	75%	80%
73–76°	* *Kabinett*	5%	28%	19%	15%
85–90°	* *Spätlese*	3%	29%	5%	1%
92–100°	* *Auslese*				
125°	*Beerenauslese*	–	5%	–	–
125°	*Eiswein*				
150°	*Trockenbeerenauslese*				

*Minimum Oechsle levels vary according to grape variety; those that have a naturally lower sugar content may qualify at a correspondingly lower level.

LIEBFRAUMILCH COUNTRY IN THE SPRING
The village of Grau-Heppenheim, near Alzey, the home of Blue Nun, in the large Petersberg Grosslage.

THE REGION AT A GLANCE

Area under vine
26,372 ha (65,165 acres)

Average yield
90 hl/ha (405 cases/acre)

Red wine 11%

White wine 89%

Most important grape varieties
23% Müller-Thurgau, 13% Silvaner, 9% Riesling, 9% Kerner, 8% Scheurebe, 7% Bacchus, 31% Others

Infrastructure
Bereiche 3; *Grosslagen* 24; *Einzellagen* 434

Note The vineyards of Rheinhessen straddle 167 *Gemeinden* (communes), the names of which may appear on the label.

THE APPELLATIONS OF
RHEINHESSEN

BEREICH BINGEN

Abutting the Nahe region to the west and separated by the Rhine from the Rheingau to the north, Bereich Bingen is the smallest of Rheinhessen's three *Bereiche* and the least important in terms of both the quantity and quality of the wine produced.

GROSSLAGE ABTEY

The *Grosslage* of Abtey does not have any outstanding villages, vineyards, or growers, although good-quality wines are produced in the village of St. Johann.

GROSSLAGE ADELBERG

Some good value wines can be found in the small town of Wörrstadt, but in terms of quality no vineyards or growers stand out.

GROSSLAGE KAISERPFALZ

Kaiserpfalz is a *Grosslage* consisting mainly of a small tributary valley located halfway between Bingen and Mainz, with vineyards facing to both the east and west. This *Grosslage* produces some of the region's most promising red wines from the Portugieser and Spätburgunder grapes. The village of Ingelheim is one of the places that claim to be the birthplace of the emperor Charlemagne.

INGELHEIM (-WINTERHEIM)
✓ Non-Einzellagen wines: **Grower** *Lunkenheimer-Lager*

JUGENHEIM
✓ **Vineyard** *St. Georgenberg* **Grower** *Rainer Schick*

GROSSLAGE KURFÜRSTENSTÜCK

Gau-Bickelheim is the home of Rheinhessen's huge central cooperative, but it has been the good growers or excellent *Staatsdomäne* from the *Einzellage* of Kapelle that have produced superior wines in the past.

GROSSLAGE RHEINGRAFENSTEIN

Not everything carrying the name Liebfrau is mediocre, as the wines from the Brühler Hof demonstrate.

VOLXHEIM
✓ **Vineyard** *Liebfrau* **Grower** *Brühler Hof*

GROSSLAGE SANKT ROCHUSKAPELLE

Bingen is often thought to belong more to the Nahe region than to Rheinhessen, but 14 of its 18 *Einzellagen* belong to this Rheinhessen *Grosslage*, which is the best in *Bereich* Bingen.

BINGEN-RÜDESHEIM
✓ **Vineyard** *Scharlachberg* **Grower** *Villa Sachsen*

BEREICH NIERSTEIN

Although this is a famous *Bereich* with many superb sites and great growers, most wines sold under its label include some of the most dull, characterless, and lacklustre in all Germany. Wine enthusiasts will find it best to choose the great *Einzellagen* and leave these *Grosslage* products alone.

GROSSLAGE AUFLANGEN

This is the best of the three *Grosslagen* that encompass some parts of Nierstein (the other two are Rehbach and Spiegelberg). Its vineyard area actually begins in the centre of the town, then stretches west to include the south and south-east facing vineyards of the tiny tributary of the Rhine that flows through Schwabsburg, and then north to the Kranzberg, which overlooks the Rhine itself.

NIERSTEIN
✓ **Vineyard** *Kranzberg* **Grower** *Reichert*
• **Vineyard** *Heiligenbaum* **Grower** *Seebrich*
• **Vineyard** *Ölberg* **Growers** *Heyl zu Herrnsheim, St. Antony, Seebrich, Senfter, Gunderloch, Staatliche Weinbaudomäne, J. Strub* • **Vineyard** *Orbel* **Growers** *Georg Albrecht Schneider, J. Strub*

GROSSLAGE DOMHERR

Once forming ecclesiastical vineyards (Domherr means "Canon of the Cathedral") this *Grosslage* has good vineyards on steep slopes, but there are few outstanding growers. Hedesheimer Hof/Beck, however, is building a serious reputation for Stadeckener Lenchen, but this is a very large and diverse vineyard, which few other growers have been able, or even inclined to attempt, to excel with.

STADECKEN
✓ Vineyard *Lenchen*
Grower *Hedesheimer Hof/Beck*

GROSSLAGE GÜLDENMORGEN

Güldenmorgen was once a fine-quality *Einzellage* belonging to Oppenheim, but now encompasses three villages and no longer has any connotation of quality, although some of its individual vineyards do. Please note that although the village of Uelversheim is clearly situated in the *Grosslage* of Krottenbrunnen, the eastern tail-end of its vineyards actually overlaps Güldenmorgen.

OPPENHEIM
✓ Vineyard *Sackträger* Grower *Kühling-Gillot*

GROSSLAGE GUTES DOMTAL

This district covers a vast area of Rhine hinterland behind the better *Grosslagen* of Nierstein. Although it encompasses 15 villages, most is sold under the ubiquitous Niersteiner Gutes Domtal (sometimes Domthal) name. Much is decidedly inferior and cheapens the reputation of Nierstein's truly great wines. The most famous village is Dexheim, because of its so-called Doktor, named after the old spelling of the great Bernkasteler Doctor vineyard. But neither Dexheim generally, nor Dexheimer Doktor specifically, warrant the attention.

WEINOLSHEIM
✓ Vineyard *Kehr* Grower *Erich Manz*

GROSSLAGE KRÖTENBRUNNEN

This district encompasses those parts of Oppenheim's vineyards that are not included in the *Grosslage* Güldenmorgen, and the wide-ranging vineyards of Guntersblum.

LUDWIGSHÖHE
✓ Non-Einzellagen wines: Grower *Dr. Becker*

GROSSLAGE PETERSBERG

This *Grosslage* lies behind Gutes Domtal and is wedged between the *Bereiche* of Bingen and Wonnegau. Although large, this *Grosslage* has few exciting sites or growers.

FRAMERSHEIM
✓ Vineyard *Kreuzweg* Grower *Dr. Hinkel*

GROSSLAGE REHBACH

Rehbach is one of the greatest *Grosslagen* in Rheinhessen, consisting of a long, thin strip of very steep terraced slopes overlooking the Rhine, just north of Nierstein. Riesling wines produced by these vineyards are aromatic, intense, and delightfully mellow, yet have a definite raciness on the finish.

NIERSTEIN
✓ Vineyard *Hipping* Growers *Georg Albrecht Schneider, St. Antony, Heinrich Braun, Franz-Karl Schmitt*
• Vineyard *Pettenthal* Growers *Heyl zu Herrnsheim, St. Antony, Gunderloch, Heinrich Braun, Julianenhof, Gehring*

GROSSLAGE RHEINBLICK

This district produces better-than-average *Grosslage* wines, in addition to one or two good grower wines.

ALSHEIM
✓ Vineyard *Frühmesse* Growers *H. L. Menger* (Eich), *Weingut Rappenhof*

GROSSLAGE ST. ALBAN

Named after the St. Alban monastery, which once owned most of the land in this underrated *Grosslage* situated between Mainz and Nierstein. The *Einzellage* wines have fine, positive character and usually represent excellent value for money.

BODENHEIM
✓ Vineyard *Burgweg*
Growers *Kühling-Gillot, Martinshof Acker*

GROSSLAGE SPIEGELBERG

The largest of Nierstein's riverside districts, its vineyards stretch to the north and south of both the famous town and the Grosslage Auflangen. Ignore the ubiquitous, mild, and neutral-flavoured *Grosslagen* wines and choose the wines of the finer *Einzellagen* that are situated between Nierstein and Oppenheim.

NACKENHEIM
✓ Vineyard *Rothenberg* Grower *Gunderloch*
NIERSTEIN
✓ Vineyard *Findling* Growers *Niersteiner Winzergenossenschaft, Winzergenossenschaft Rheinfront* • Vineyard *Hölle* Grower *J. und H. A. Strub* • Vineyard *Rosenberg* Grower *Gehring*

GROSSLAGE VOGELSGARTEN

This is not, in fact, one of the best Rheinhessen districts, although Weingut Ohnacker makes fine, rich, sometimes powerful wines that are well worth seeking out.

BEREICH WONNEGAU

The least-known of Rheinhessen's three *Bereiche*, Wonnegau contains the world-famous (although not world-class) Liebfrauenstift *Einzellage*, which had the rather dubious honour of giving birth to Liebfraumilch. Wonnegau means "province of great joy".

GROSSLAGE BERGKLOSTER

Some very good *non-Einzellage* wines are also made in Flomborn and Westhofen.

DINTESHEIM
✓ Non-Einzellagen wines: Grower *Rauh*
FLOMBORN
✓ Vineyard *Goldberg*
Grower *Michel-Pfannebecker*
WESTHOFEN
✓ Vineyard *Morstein* Grower *Wittmann*
• Vineyard *Steingrube* Grower *Wittmann*

GROSSLAGE BURG RODENSTEIN

A large proportion of the wines made in the Grosslage Burg Rodenstein district are sold under its *Grosslage* name. Most of it is well above average quality, although not in the same class as its best *Einzellage* wines.

DAHLSHEIM
(an *Ortsteil* of Flörsheim-Dalsheim)
✓ Vineyard *Hubacker*
Grower *Klaus und Hedwig Keller*
• Vineyard *Sauloch*
Growers *Göhring, Klaus und Hedwig Keller*
• Vineyard *Steig*
Grower *Klaus und Hedwig Keller*
Premium Red Wine Blend: Grower *Klaus und Hedwig Keller (Felix)*
FLÖRSHEIM-DALSHEIM
✓ Non-Einzellagen wines: Grower *Schales*
NIEDERFLÖRSHEIM
(an *Ortsteil* of Flörsheim-Dalsheim)
✓ Vineyard *Frauenberg*
Growers *Göhring, Scherner-Kleinhanns*

GROSSLAGE DOMBLICK

There are few outstanding growers here, although good wines are made in the village of Hohen-Sülzen and the *Grosslage* label usually offers sound value.

MONSHEIM
✓ Vineyard *Silberberg* Grower *Klaus und Hedwig Keller* (Flörsheim-Dalsheim)

GROSSLAGE GOTTESHILFE

A tiny district encompassing the excellent wine village of Bechtheim. Very little wine is seen on export markets under the *Grosslage* label.

BECHTHEIM
✓ Non-Einzellagen wines:
Growers *Göhring, Scherner-Kleinhans*

GROSSLAGE LIEBFRAUENMORGEN

This familiar sounding *Grosslage* includes the famous Liebfrauenstift-Kirchenstück vineyard in Worms, the birthplace of Liebfraumilch.

GROSSLAGE PILGERPFAD

This *Grosslage* stretches from the lesser vineyards of Bechtheim to the large Petersberg district in Bereich Nierstein.

BECHTHEIM
✓ Vineyard *Hasensprung* Grower *Meiser*
MONZERNHEIM
✓ Non-Einzellagen wines:
Grower *Weedenbornhof*

GROSSLAGE SYBILLENSTEIN

There are no outstanding villages, vineyards, or growers in this *Grosslage*, although good wines are made in the village of Alzey, and its Kappellenberg vineyard has a certain reputation for quality wines. Alzey is the location of Sichel & Co. master-blenders of "Blue Nun" Liebfraumilch.

ALZEY
✓ Non-Einzellagen wines:
Growers *Gysler, Schlossmühlenhof*

THE PFALZ

Germany's rising star, the Pfalz, or Rheinpfalz as it was called until recently, has always been capable of producing world-class wines, but has only just started doing so on any widespread scale. The best winemakers of the Pfalz now tend to make rich, powerful, spicy wines that are more reminiscent of Alsace than those of Alsace's mirror-image, Baden.

RARE PHYSICAL EVIDENCE of ancient German wines exists in the Pfalz at the Wine Museum at Speyer. Here a glass amphora contains genuine, golden 1,600-year-old wine, made by the Romans, beneath a thick layer of foul-looking resin and oil. By the 12th century, the Bishop of Speyer owned all the best vineyards in the Pfalz and they remained the property of the Church until they were acquired by Napoleon.

After the great Corsican emperor somewhat reluctantly left the region, the socio-economic composition of the Pfalz changed dramatically and irrevocably. With the restructuring came a considerably less monopolistic form of land ownership.

THE PFALZ TODAY

Sometimes referred to as the Palatinate, the Pfalz covers 80 kilometres (50 miles) of the sun-blessed vineyards on the crest of the Haardt mountain range and the Pfälzer Wald (Pfalz forest). It has some 25,000 smallholders, each of whom works less than one hectare (about two-and-a-half acres) on average. These smallholders generally tend their vines at the weekends, working in the cities and towns during the week. Many sell their grapes to cooperatives, who process about 25 per cent of the Pfalz's vast output. There is, however, still a large minority of estates that have considerably larger land-holdings than the average grower. The vast

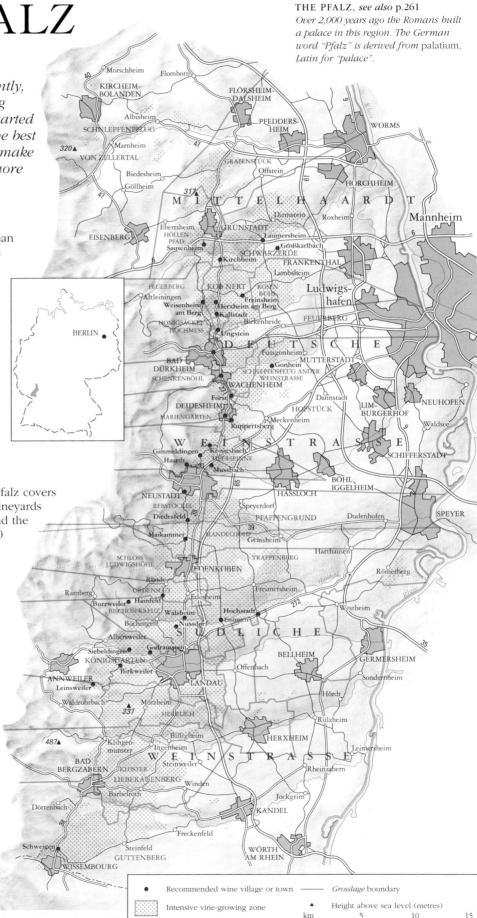

THE PFALZ, *see also p.261*
Over 2,000 years ago the Romans built a palace in this region. The German word "Pfalz" is derived from palatium, *Latin for "palace".*

BERLIN •

| Recommended wine village or town | — Grosslage boundary |

Intensive vine-growing zone

▲ Height above sea level (metres)

— Bereich boundary

km 5 10 15

miles 2 4 6 8

THE REGION AT A GLANCE

Area under vine
23,804 ha (58,820 acres)

Average yield
98 hl/ha (441 cases/acre)

Red wine 18%

White wine 82%

Most important grape varieties
21% Müller-Thurgau, 21% Riesling, 11% Kerner, 10% Portugieser, 7% Silvaner, 5% Scheurebe, 4% Dornfelder, 21% Others

Infrastructure
Bereiche 2; *Grosslagen* 26; *Einzellagen* 335

Note The vineyards of the Pfalz straddle 170 *Gemeinden* (communes), the names of which may appear on the label.

numbers of growers, grapes, soil types, and microclimates combine to create a diversity of wine styles, from close to half of all Liebfraumilch produced (Rheinhessen accounts for most of the other half) to an increasing wealth of expressive pure varietals. This region yields more wine than any other in Germany, and it is the smallest growers of the Pfalz that make this such a great region.

QUALITY REQUIREMENTS AND HARVEST PERCENTAGES

MINIMUM OECHSLE	QUALITY CATEGORY	HARVEST BREAKDOWN			
		1992	1993	1994	1995
44°	*Deutscher Tafelwein*	30%	–	12%	5%
50–53°	*Landwein*				
60–62°	** QbA*	60%	47%	78%	80%
73–76°	** Kabinett*	10%	32%	8%	14%
85–90°	** Spätlese*	–	17%	2%	1%
92–100°	** Auslese*				
120°	*Beerenauslese*				
120°	*Eiswein*		4%	–	–
150°	*Trockenbeerenauslese*				

*Minimum Oechsle levels vary according to grape variety; those that have a naturally lower sugar content may qualify at a correspondingly lower level.

FACTORS AFFECTING TASTE AND QUALITY

LOCATION
The second-largest German wine region, stretching 80 km (50 miles) from Rheinhessen to Alsace, bounded by the Rhine on the east and the Haardt Mountains on the west.

CLIMATE
The Pfalz is the sunniest and driest wine-producing region in Germany. Its climate is enhanced by the sheltering effect of the Haardt Mountains and Donnersberg hills.

ASPECT
Vineyards are sited mainly on flat land or gentle slopes, at an altitude of between 100 and 250 m (330–820 ft).

SOIL
A great variety of soils, ranging from loam and weathered sandstone to widely dispersed "islands" of limestone, granite, porphyry, and clayish slate.

VITICULTURE AND VINIFICATION
The Pfalz produces more wine than any other German wine region. The leading estates have a relatively high proportion of Riesling in their vineyards, and produce wines of the very highest quality, although speciality Gewürztraminers and Muskatellers can be extraordinarily good if vinified dry.

PRIMARY GRAPE VARIETIES
Kerner, Müller-Thurgau, Riesling
SECONDARY GRAPE VARIETIES
Bacchus, Gewürztraminer, Huxelrebe, Morio-muskat, Muskateller, Portugieser, Ruländer, Scheurebe, Silvaner

---

THE APPELLATIONS OF
THE PFALZ

Note In the Pfalz wine region, each *Grosslage* can be prefixed only by a specified village name. The village name has been listed under the name of the *Grosslage*.

BEREICH MITTELHAARDT-DEUTSCHE WEINSTRASSE

The quality of wines from this *Bereich* is so high, few are sold as anything less than *Einzellagen*.

GROSSLAGE FEUERBERG

Bad Dürkheim

A versatile *Grosslage*, producing a wide range of wines from full, spicy Gewürztraminers to soft, velvety Spätburgunders.

BAD DÜRKHEIM
√ Non-Einzellagen wines:
Growers *WG Vier Jahreszeiten, Egon Schmitt*
• Premium Wine Blends: Grower *Egon Schmitt* (Thur, Duca XI)

GROSSLAGE GRAFENSTÜCK

Bockenheim

One producer in this Grosslage now stands out with some excellent Spätburgunder.

KINDENHEIM
√ Non-Einzellagen wines: Grower *Ludi Neiss*

GROSSLAGE HOCHMESS

Bad Dürkheim

This is a small, but high-performance *Grosslage*. It includes the best vineyards of Bad Dürkheim, although some fine wines are also produced within the boundaries of the two neighbouring *Grosslagen* of Feuerberg and Schenkenböhl. The attractive wines of Grosslage Hochmess display a perfect harmony of full flavour and flowery fragrance.

BAD DÜRKHEIM
√ Vineyard **Hochbenn** Growers *Kurt Darting, WG Vier Jahreszeiten* • Vineyard *Spielberg* Growers *Kurt Darting, Fitz-Ritter, Karl Schaefer*
√ Non-Einzellagen wines: *WG Vier Jahreszeiten*

GROSSLAGE HOFSTÜCK

Deidesheim

Grosslage Hofstück produces homogeneous, noble, and elegant wines. The outstanding quality of these wines owes a great deal to the vineyard's favourable soil conditions.

DEIDESHEIM
√ Vineyard *Nonnenstück* Growers *Bürklin-Wolf, Reichsrat Buhl*
GÖNNHEIM
√ Vineyard *Sonnenberg* Grower *Eymann*
RUPPERTSBERG
√ Vineyard *Gaisböhl* Grower *Bürklin-Wolf* • Vineyard *Nussbien* Grower *A. Christmann* • Vineyard *Reiterpfad* Growers *Bassermann-Jordan, von Buhl, A. Christmann, Dr. Deinhard*

GROSSLAGE HÖLLENPFAD

Grünstadt

Produces a range of wines that are full and substantial in body but lack finesse.

GROSSLAGE HONIGSÄCKEL

Ungstein

This is a small *Grosslage* composed of varied soil and making full-bodied wines of intense flavour, especially Scheurebe.

UNGSTEIN
√ Vineyard *Herrenberg* Grower *Fuhrmann-Eymael*

GROSSLAGE KOBNERT

Kallstadt

A single vineyard prior to the 1971 wine law, this is now a *Grosslage*, but a very good one, particularly in the hands of somebody such as the talented Philippi from the Koehler-Ruprecht estate.

KALLSTADT
√ Vineyard *Saumagen* Grower *Koehler-Ruprecht*
√ Non-Einzellagen wines: *Philippi* Grower *Koehler-Ruprecht*

GROSSLAGE MARIENGARTEN

Forst an der Weinstrasse

Nowhere in the entire Pfalz can Riesling wines of such incomparable finesse and intensity be found. Virtually all the great Pfalz producers are here, and even the *Grosslage* wine can be outstanding in their hands.

GROSSLAGE MARIENGARTEN
√ Grosslage wine: Grower *J.F. Kimich*
DEIDESHEIM
√ Vineyard *Kieselberg* Grower *Deinhard* • Vineyard *Grainhübel* Growers *Josef Biffar, J.F. Kimich* • Vineyard *Herrgottsacker* Grower *Josef Biffar* • Vineyard *Hohenmorgen* Growers *Bassermann-Jordan, Bürklin-Wolf, A. Christmann* • Vineyard *Maushöhle* Grower *Josef Biffar*

FORST
✓ Vineyard *Freundstück*
Grower *Georg Mosbacher*
• Vineyard *Ungeheuer*
Growers *Bassermann-Jordan, von Buhl, Lucashof, Georg Mosbacher, Eugen Müller*
• Vineyard *Jesuitengarten*
Growers *Bassermann-Jordan, von Buhl, WG Vier Jahreszeiten*
• Vineyard *Kirchenstück*
Grower *Eugen Müller*
• Vineyard *Pechstein*
Growers *Bassermann-Jordan, von Buhl, Bürklin-Wolf, Lucashof, J.L. Wolf*

WACHENHEIM
✓ Vineyard *Gerümpel* **Growers** *Dr. Bürklin-Wolf, Karl Schaefer, J.L. Wolf* • Vineyard *Goldbächel* **Grower** *Josef Biffar* • Vineyard *Rechbächel* **Grower** *Dr. Bürklin-Wolf*

GROSSLAGE MEERSPINNE
Neustadt-Gimmeldingen
These climatically-pampered vineyards, on the sheltered slopes of the Haardt mountains, produce some of the very finest Pfalz wines.

GIMMELDINGEN
✓ Vineyard *Mandelgarten* **Growers** *von Buhl, A. Christmann, Müller-Catoir*
• Vineyard *Schlössel*
Grower *A. Christmann, Müller-Catoir*

HAARDT
✓ Vineyard *Bürgergarten* **Grower** *Müller-Catoir* • Vineyard *Herrenletten* **Growers** *Müller Catoir, Weegmüller* • Vineyard *Mandelring* **Growers** *Müller-Catoir, Weegmüller* • Vineyard *Herzog* **Grower** *Herbert Müller Erben*

KÖNIGSBACH
✓ Vineyard *Idig*
Growers *von Buhl, A. Christmann*

MUSSBACH
✓ Vineyard *Eselshaut* **Grower** *Müller-Catoir*

NEUSTADT
✓ Vineyard *Mönchgarten* **Grower** *Müller-Catoir*

GROSSLAGE PFAFFENGRUND
Neustadt-Diedesfeld
This is not an exceptional *Grosslage*, although there are some *Einzellagen* that can produce very good wines.

DUTTWEILER
✓ Vineyard *Kreuzberg* **Grower** *Bergdolt*

GROSSLAGE REBSTÖCKEL
Neustadt-Diedesfeld
There are no outstanding villages, vineyards, or growers in this *Grosslage*, although there are good wines produced in the village of Neustadt-Diedesfeld.

GROSSLAGE ROSENBÜHL
Freinsheim
These are light, attractive, easy-drinking wines that rarely rise into the fine-wine bracket. Reasonable red wines, made from the Portugieser grape, are also produced.

FREINSHEIM
✓ Vineyard *Goldberg*
Growers *Kassner-Simon, Lingenfelder*

GROSSLAGE SCHENKENBÖHL
Wachenheim
The third *Grosslage* to share the vineyards of Bad Dürkheim, this one ranks with Feuerberg – Hochmess being by far the best.

WACHENHEIM
✓ Vineyard *Fuchsmantel*
Grower *Karl Schaefer*

GROSSLAGE SCHNEPFENFLUG AN DER WEINSTRASSE
Forst an der Weinstrasse
Except for a small part of Forst's vineyards (the rest belong to Grosslage Mariengarten), few outstanding growers are to be found here.

FORST
✓ Vineyard *Stift* **Grower** *Heinrich Spindler*

GROSSLAGE SCHNEPFENFLUG VOM ZELLERTAL
Zell
There are no outstanding villages, vineyards, or growers, although good wines are made in the village of Zell.

GROSSLAGE SCHWARZERDE
Kirchheim
Mediocre Silvaner-based wines are standard here, but there are a couple of good growers in obscure villages that offer good value.

DIRMSTEIN
✓ Vineyard *Mandelpfad*
Grower *Knipser Johannishof*

GROSSKARLBACH
✓ Vineyards *Burgweg, Osterberg*
Grower *Knipser Johannishof*
✓ Non-Einzellagen wines *Lingenfelder*

LAUMERSHEIM
✓ Vineyards *Kapellenberg, Kirschgarten, Mandelberg* **Grower** *Knipser Johannishof*
• Premium Red Wine Blend:
Grower *Philipp Kuhn* (Luitmar)

BEREICH SÜDLICHE WEINSTRASSE
The lesser of the two Pfalz *Bereiche*, Südliche Weinstrasse's wines are dominated by rather dull and neutral Müller-Thurgau, but the younger winemakers are producing better Riesling and cooperative varietals from various grapes that are at worst clean and correct.

GROSSLAGE BISCHOFSKREUZ
Walsheim
Most wines are sound, if unexciting, though the three *Einzellagen* below are capable of producing exceptional wines in capable hands.

BÖCHINGEN
✓ Vineyard *Rosenkranz*
Grower *Theo Minges* (Flemlingen)

BURRWEILER
✓ Vineyard *Schlossgarten*
Grower *Herbert Messmer*

NUSSDORF
✓ Non-Einzellagen wines: **Grower** *Lorentz*

WALSHEIM
✓ Vineyard *Silberberg* **Grower** *Karl Pfaffmann*

GROSSLAGE GUTTENBERG
Schweigen
Beck produces excellent, expressive, if rarely encountered, Riesling.

SCHWEIGEN
✓ Vineyard *Sonnenberg* **Growers** *Friedrich Becker, Bernhart, Bruno Grimm, Scheu*
• Premium Red Wine Blend:
Grower *Friedrich Becker* (P.N.)

GROSSLAGE HERRLICH
Eschbach
An area easily capable of producing QmP wines. The *Auslese* are nothing special, but are exported and can be astonishingly cheap.

LEINSWEILER
✓ Non-Einzellagen wines:
Grower *Thomas Siegrist*

GROSSLAGE KLOSTER LIEBFRAUENBERG
Bad Bergzabern
No outstanding villages or vineyards, and no notable growers, although good wines are produced in the town of Bad Bergzabern.

GROSSLAGE KÖNIGSGARTEN
Godramstein
This *Grosslage* consists of some excellent wine villages and several talented winemakers.

ALBERSWEILER
✓ Vineyard *Latt*
Grower *Ökonomierat Rebholz*

BIRKWEILER
✓ Vineyard *Kastanienbusch*
Growers *Ökonomierat Rebholz, Dr. Wehrheim*
• Vineyard *Mandelberg*
Growers *Scholler, Dr. Wehrheim*

GODRAMSTEIN
✓ Vineyard *Münzberg*
Growers *Weingut Münzberg Lothar Kessler, Ökonomierat Rebholz*

SIEBELDINGEN
✓ Vineyard *Im Sonnenschein*
Growers *Ökonomierat Rebholz, Wilhelmshof*
• Premium Red Wine Blend:
Grower *Ökonomierat Rebholz* (R)

GROSSLAGE MANDELHÖHE
Maikammer
The best estates in this *Grosslage* produce some pleasant, attractive Rieslings.

MAIKAMMER
✓ Vineyard *Kapellenberg*
Grower *August Ziegler*
• Vineyard *Mandelberg* **Grower** *Bergdolt*

GROSSLAGE ORDENSGUT
Edesheim
Grosslage Ordensgut is currently improving in the quality of its produce, and a couple of growers have started to excel.

HAINFELD
✓ Vineyard *Letten* **Grower** *Gerhard Klein*
✓ Non-Einzellagen wines:
Growers *Koch, Möller*

GROSSLAGE SCHLOSS LUDWIGSHÖHE
Edenkoben
No outstanding villages, vineyards, or growers in this *Grosslage*, although good wines are produced in the village of St. Martin.

GROSSLAGE TRAPPENBERG
Hochstadt
Apart from Essingener Rossberg, there are few outstanding vineyards in this *Grosslage*, although there are some good wines made in the village of Hochstadt.

ESSINGEN
✓ Non-Einzellagen wines:
Grower *Weingut Frey*

THE HESSISCHE BERGSTRASSE

Situated between the Rheinhessen and Franken, the northern tip of Baden's vineyards is the Hessische Bergstrasse. This is the smallest and least-known of Germany's Qualitätswein regions, and its fruity wines are marked by a pronounced earthy acidity.

THIS REGION CORRESPONDS to the northern section of the old Roman *strata montana* or "mountain road", hence Bergstrasse. This ancient trade route ran from Darmstadt to Wiesloch, which is south of Heidelberg in what is now the Baden region. The Romans brought viticulture to this area, but without the monasteries, which developed, spread, and maintained the vineyards throughout the medieval period, the tradition of winemaking would have ceased long ago.

The vineyards of the Hessische Bergstrasse are dotted among orchards in a strip of foothills along the western edge of Odenwald. Protected by the Odenwald, the fragrance of fruit trees in full bloom noticeably hangs over these hills in springtime. Indeed, Odenwald's forested mountains offer such effective protection that the sun-trap vineyards of Bensheim boast the highest annual mean temperatures in Germany. This exceptional heat is, of course, relative to

UNTERHAMBACH
A vineyard above Unterhambach, where small scale winemaking is the norm. The cooperative at nearby Heppenheim receives over 70% of the region's grapes.

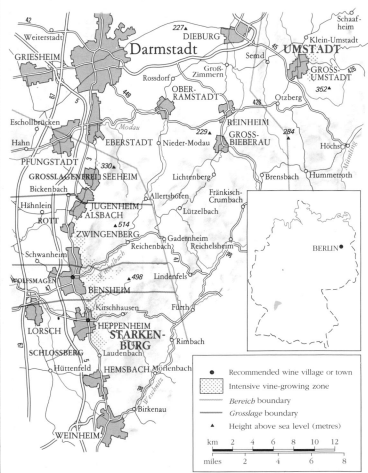

THE HESSISCHE BERGSTRASSE, *see also p.261*
This area is called the "spring garden", because of the early flowering of its fruit and almond orchards between which vineyards are planted.

QUALITY REQUIREMENTS AND HARVEST PERCENTAGES

MINIMUM OECHSLE	QUALITY CATEGORY	HARVEST BREAKDOWN			
		1992	1993	1994	1995
44°	*Deutscher Tafelwein*	15%	–	2%	3%
53°	*Landwein*				
57–66°	* *QbA*	83%	30%	71%	86%
73–80°	* *Kabinett*	2%	55%	25%	11%
85–95°	* *Spätlese*	–	15%	2%	–
95–105°	* *Auslese*				
125°	*Beerenauslese*	–	–	–	–
125°	*Eiswein*				
150°	*Trockenbeerenauslese*				

*Minimum Oechsle levels vary according to grape variety; those that have a naturally lower sugar content may qualify at a correspondingly lower level.

Germany's cool northern climate, and the wines produced here have an excellent level of acidity, but there is a definite peachiness to the finest Rieslings, which is an indication of their ripeness. The Hessische Bergstrasse is planted with a relatively high proportion of Riesling, particularly in the *Bereich* Starkenburg where the best wines are grown.

The vines, which grow on relatively rich soils, produce very fruity wines that have a typical and easily recognized, earthy acidity, with a style that is richer than most Rheinhessen wines and more reminiscent of a somewhat rustic Rheingau. The Müller-Thurgau is not Germany's best, but it can be fragrant; the Silvaner lacks the assertive character found in Franken to the east; but the Gewürztraminer can have a fine, subdued style.

The vineyards are farmed by more than 1,000 individual growers with the average-sized plot being barely more than one-third of a hectare (four-fifths of an acre). Most of these growers are part-timers who tend their plots at weekends. This helps to explain the anonymity of the area's wines, and this will remain until a number of large, quality-minded estates are established.

GRONAU HESSISCHE BERGSTRASSE
Looking down the south-facing slopes of the Hemsburg vineyard towards Gronau, an Ortsteil *of Bensheim.*

FACTORS AFFECTING TASTE AND QUALITY

LOCATION
Between Darmstadt and Heppenheim, beside the Odenwald mountains, with the Rhine to the west and the Main to the north.

CLIMATE
The vineyards on the southern slopes of the valleys flanking the Bergstrasse benefit from an average temperature of over 9°C (48°F). Combined with an annual rainfall of 75.5 cm (30 in), this produces ideal conditions. Bensheim is supposed to be the hottest place in Germany.

ASPECT
The best vineyards are on south- and west-facing slopes in Bereich Umstadt, and south- and east-facing slopes in Bereich Starkenburg. The terrain is more one of hilly hinterland than steep valleys.

SOIL
Most of the soil consists of varying amounts of light, finely-structured loess and basalt.

VITICULTURE AND VINIFICATION
The vineyards in this region are not of the modern *Flurbereinigung* type, but are planted rather haphazardly on old-established terraces among orchards. Although a great many individuals grow grapes, more than 80 per cent of the wines are processed in cooperatives.

PRIMARY GRAPE VARIETIES
Müller-Thurgau, Riesling
SECONDARY GRAPE VARIETIES
Ehrenfelser, Kerner, Ruländer, Scheurebe, Silvaner, Gewürztraminer

THE REGION AT A GLANCE

Area under vine
469 ha (1,159 acres)

Average yield
72 hl/ha (324 cases/acre)

Red wine 4%

White wine 96%

Most important grape varieties
56% Riesling, 15% Müller-Thurgau, 29% Others

Infrastructure
Bereiche 2
Grosslagen 3
Einzellagen 22

Note The vineyards of the Hessische Bergstrasse straddle 10 *Gemeinden* (communes), the names of which may appear on the label.

THE APPELLATIONS OF THE
HESSISCHE BERGSTRASSE

BEREICH STARKENBURG

This is the larger of this region's *Bereiche*, and the best in terms of quality. Riesling is planted in most of its vineyards.

GROSSLAGE ROTT

The largest of Starkenburg's three *Grosslagen*, this includes the northern section of Bensheim, one of the region's two best communes. The finest wine comes from its south-facing Herrnwingert vineyard.

GROSSLAGE SCHLOSSBERG

This Grosslage covers part of Bensheim and three villages to the south, with Heppenheim the most highly rated. A unique peachiness is associated with the sun-drenched Stemmler and Centgericht vineyards.

HEPPENHEIM
✓ **Vineyard** *Centgericht* **Growers** *Bergsträsser Winzer EG, Staatsweingut Bergstrasse*
• **Vineyard** *Stemmler*
Grower *Staatsweingut Bergstrasse*

GROSSLAGE WOLFSMAGEN

This includes the southern section of Bensheim with the two *Ortsteile* of Zell and Gronau.

BENSHEIM
✓ **Vineyard** *Kalkgasse* **Grower** *Staatsweingut Bergstrasse* • **Vineyard** *Kirchberg* **Grower** *Weingut der Stadt Bensheim*

BEREICH UMSTADT

There are no remarkable villages, vineyards, or *Grosslagen* in this *Bereich*, as its six *Einzellagen* are *Grosslagenfrei*. The grape varieties Müller-Thurgau, Ruländer, and Silvaner dominate.

ZELL VINEYARD
Vineyard in the Streichling Einzellage *at Zell, near Bensheim, Hessen.*

FRANKEN

Classic Franconian Silvaner wine is distinctly dry with an earthy or smoky aroma and is bottled in the traditional flask-shaped Bocksbeutel. *Unfortunately, in this region, the Silvaner grape variety is giving way to Müller-Thurgau among others.*

THERE IS ALMOST TWICE AS MUCH land under vine in Franken than in the Rheingau, for instance, but the vineyards are scattered over a far greater area and interspersed with meadows and forests. Franken is also a beer-producing region and many say that more pleasure can be had from a *Stein* of Würzburger beer than from a glass of Würzburger Stein, Franken's most famous wine. Exported wine invariably comes from the better estates and is relatively

THE CELLAR AT THE RESIDENZ, WÜRZBURG
The magnificent cellar under the baroque Residency at Würzburg has been state run since 1803.

QUALITY REQUIREMENTS AND HARVEST PERCENTAGES

MINIMUM OECHSLE	QUALITY CATEGORY	HARVEST BREAKDOWN			
		1992	1993	1994	1995
44°	Deutscher Tafelwein	13%	–	5%	–
50°	Landwein				
60°	* QbA	85%	27%	70%	94%
76–80°	* Kabinett	2%	59%	20%	5%
85–90°	* Spätlese	–	11%	5%	1%
100°	* Auslese				
125°	Beerenauslese	–	3%	–	–
125°	Eiswein				
150°	Trockenbeerenauslese				

*Minimum Oechsle levels vary according to grape variety; those that have a naturally lower sugar content may qualify at a correspondingly lower level.

THE REGION AT A GLANCE

Area under vine
6,078 ha (15,019 acres)

Average yield
85 hl/ha (382 cases/acre)

Red wine 5%

White wine 95%

Most important grape varieties
46% Müller-Thurgau, 20% Silvaner, 11% Bacchus, 23% Others

Infrastructure
Bereiche 3; *Grosslagen* 17; *Einzellagen* 171

Note The vineyards of Franken straddle 125 *Gemeinden* (communes), the names of which may appear on labels.

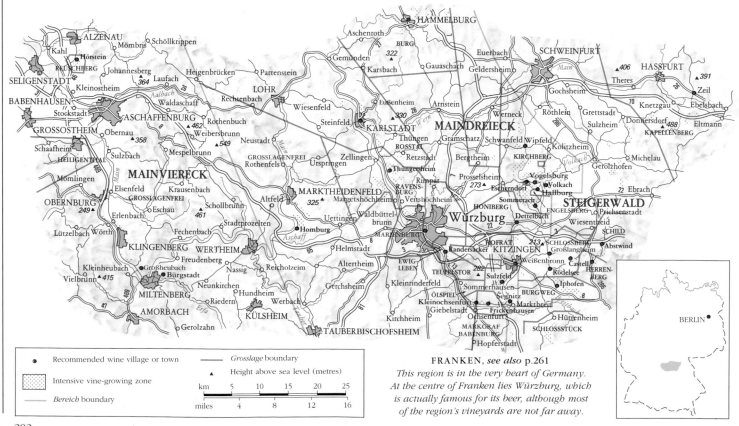

FRANKEN, *see also p.261*
This region is in the very heart of Germany. At the centre of Franken lies Würzburg, which is actually famous for its beer, although most of the region's vineyards are not far away.

Recommended wine village or town

Intensive vine-growing zone

Bereich boundary

Grosslage boundary

▲ Height above sea level (metres)

km 5 10 15 20 25
miles 4 8 12 16

FACTORS AFFECTING TASTE AND QUALITY

LOCATION
Situated in Bavaria, Franken is the most northeasterly of Germany's wine regions.

CLIMATE
The most continental climate of Germany's wine regions, with dry warm summers and cold winters. Severe frosts affect yields.

ASPECT
Many vineyards face south and are located on the slopes of the valleys of the Main and its tributaries, as well as on sheltered sites of the Steigerwald.

SOIL
Franken's three *Bereiche* have different soil structures: Mainviereck has predominantly weathered coloured sandstone; Maindreieck has predominantly weathered

limestone with clay and loess; and Steigerwald, weathered red marl.

VITICULTURE AND VINIFICATION
More than half the vineyards have been replanted since 1954. The classic Franconian vine, the Silvaner, has become less widely planted than the Müller-Thurgau. The wines are usually drier than most in Germany and accompany food well. There are 6,000 growers, allowing for a great range of styles, although half the wines are processed by cooperatives.

PRIMARY GRAPE VARIETIES
Müller-Thurgau, Silvaner
SECONDARY GRAPE VARIETIES
Bacchus, Kerner, Ortega, Perle, Riesling, Scheurebe, Traminer

INTERIOR OF THE RESIDENZ, WÜRZBURG
The Residency at Würzburg, with its Baroque grand staircase, is now part of the Bavarian State Domain.

expensive, particularly if bottled in the traditional *Bocksbeutel*. This region's Silvaner has a full taste and earthy bite, sometimes attaining smoky complexity, making it far more interesting than most examples of this variety. However, my favourite Franconian wine is Riesling, because although it accounts for less than three per cent of the vines grown and often fails to ripen here, it can be made into exceptional wines in sunny years. Rieslaner (*Riesling x Silvaner* cross), Bacchus, and Kerner are all successful, particularly as QmP, although it is rare to find a wine above *Auslese* level.

THE APPELLATIONS OF
FRANKEN

Note In Franken, certain *Grosslagen* can be prefixed only by a specified village name, which is listed immediately beneath the relevant *Grosslage* name.

BEREICH STEIGERWALD

Nowhere is the distinctive, earthy character of Franconian wine more evident than in *Bereich* Steigerwald, where heavier soil results in a range of fuller-bodied wines.

GROSSLAGE BURGWEG

This *Grosslage* (which shares its name with a *Grosslage* in the Nahe and another in the Rheingau) contains one of Franken's greatest wine villages, Iphofen.

IPHOFEN
☑ **Vineyard** *Julius-Echter Berg* **Growers** *Johann Ruck, Hans Wirsching, Juliusspital Würzburg* • **Vineyard** *Kalb* **Grower** *Hans Wirsching* • **Vineyard** *Kronsberg* **Grower** *Hans Wirsching*

GROSSLAGE HERRENBERG

There are a number of south-facing vineyards in Grosslage Herrenberg, but despite this, it is the northwest-facing vineyards of the village of Castell that produce the *Grosslage*'s most exceptional wines.

CASTELL
☑ **Vineyard** *Kugelspiel* **Grower** *Castell'sche Domäne* • **Vineyard** *Schlossberg* **Grower** *Castell'sche Domäne*

GROSSLAGE KAPELLENBERG

There are no outstanding villages, vineyards, or growers in Grosslage Kapellenberg, although a number of good wines are often produced in the village of Zeil.

GROSSLAGE SCHILD

This *Grosslage* has no outstanding villages, vineyards, or growers, although good wines are made in the village of Abtswind.

GROSSLAGE SCHLOSSBERG

Underrated, with excellent, sheltered vineyards.

RÖDELSEE
☑ **Vineyard** *Küchenmeister* **Growers** *Ernst Popp, Juliusspital Würzburg* • **Vineyard** *Schwanleite* **Grower** *Johann Ruck*

GROSSLAGE SCHLOSSTÜCK

No outstanding villages, vineyards, or growers, although good wines are made in Ippesheim.

BEREICH MAINDREIECK

Most of the vineyards are in the vicinity of Würzburg in this *Bereich*. Grapes grown on the limestone soils can produce exceptional wines.

GROSSLAGENFREI

Many vineyards in this *Bereich* are *Grosslagenfrei* (composed of individual *Einzellagen* that are not grouped under any *Grosslagen*).

GROSSLAGE BURG
Hammelburg
Robust, earthy Silvaners and the lighter, fragrant Müller-Thurgaus are the main attractions.

GROSSLAGE ENGELSBERG

A new *Grosslage*, God forbid, encompassing part of two *Einzellagen* formerly in the *Grosslage* Kirchberg, the Sommeracher vineyards of Katzenkopf and Rosenberg.

GROSSLAGE EWIG LEBEN

This *Grosslage* contains the greatest concentration of fine vineyards in Franken. It has the advantage of a particularly favourable microclimate, which helps create wines of a rare harmony. Rieslings from this area possess an original natural charm complemented by a bouquet often reminiscent of peaches.

RANDERSACKER

✓ Vineyard *Sonnenstuhl*
Grower *Schmitt's Kinder*
• Vineyard *Pfülben*
Growers *Josef Störrlein,*
Winzergenossenschaft Randersacker Hofrat

GROSSLAGE HOFRAT

Kintzingen

This is one of Franken's few relatively large *Grosslagen*, where the *Einzellagen* seldom excel, except for the vineyards on the lazy bend of the River Main north and south of Sulzfeld.

SEGNITZ

✓ Vineyard *Pfaffensteig*
Grower *Kreeglinger*

SULZFELD

✓ Vineyard *Cyriakusberg*
Grower *Zehnthof Theo Luckert*

GROSSLAGE HONIGBERG

In this *Grosslage* there are no particularly outstanding villages, vineyards, or growers, although a few good wines are made in the village of Dettelbach.

GROSSLAGE KIRCHBERG

Volkach

Grosslage Kirchberg contains some of the finest vineyards in all of Franken. The full potential offered by the land is perhaps not always exploited by the growers.

ESCHERNDORF

✓ Vineyard *Lump*
Growers *Weingut am Lump,*
Horst Sauer,
Egon Schäffer

NORDHEIM

✓ Vineyard *Vögelein*
Growers *Waldemar Braun,*
Helmut Christ,
Glaser-Himmelstoss

GROSSLAGE MARIENBERG

This has been created as a new *Grosslage* for the previously *Grosslagenfrei* vineyards north and west of Würzburg.

DORFPROZELTEN

✓ Vineyard *Predigtstuhl*
Grower *Staatlicher Hofkeller Würzburg*

WÜRZBURG

✓ Vineyard *Stein*
Growers *Staatlicher Hofkeller Würzburg,*
Bürgerspital Würzburg,
Juliusspital Würzburg
• Vineyard *Pfaffenberg*
Grower *Bürgerspital Würzburg*
• Vineyard *Abtsleite*
Growers *Juliusspital Würzburg,*
Bürgerspital Würzburg

GROSSLAGE MARKGRAF BABENBERG

There are no outstanding villages, vineyards, or growers in this *Grosslage* although some very good wines are made in the village of Frickenhausen.

GROSSLAGE OELSPIEL

This *Grosslage's* main feature is a fine strip of vineyards on the right bank of the Main, southeast of Würzburg. Schloss Sommerhausen has emerged as the district's leading producer.

SOMMERHAUSEN

✓ Vineyard *Steinbach*
Growers *Ernst Gebhardt,*
Schloss Sommerhausen
• Vineyard *Reifenstein*
Grower *Schloss Sommerhausen*

GROSSLAGE RAVENSBURG

Thüngersheim

Grosslage Ravensburg is situated rather downstream from Franken's best vineyards, but some of the wines from this area can still be quite attractive.

GROSSLAGE ROSSTAL

Karlstadt

One grower who has shown promise in this otherwise lacklustre *Grosslage* is the Weingut am Stein in Stetten.

STETTEN

✓ Vineyard *Stein* Grower *Weingut am Stein*

GROSSLAGE TEUFELSTOR

The *Grosslage* of Teufelstor is a continuation of Ewig Leben, but the quality of the wines it produces is not as good.

EIBELSTADT

✓ Vineyard *Kapellenberg*
Grower *Schloss Sommerhausen*

BEREICH MAINVIERECK

Mainviereck is the smallest of the *Bereiche*, as well as being the most westerly, and the wines it produces are modest.

GROSSLAGE HEILIGENTHAL

This *Grosslage* comprises one village, Grossostheim, with just two *Einzellagen*, most vineyards in the area being *Grosslagenfrei*.

GROSSLAGE REUSCHBERG

This *Grosslage* comprises one village, Hörstein, and just two *Einzellagen*, most vineyards in the area being *Grosslagenfrei*.

GROSSLAGENFREI

Most of Mainviereck's vineyards are *Grosslagenfrei* (individual *Einzellagen* not grouped under any *Grosslage*). Apart from those recommended below, there are few outstanding villages or vineyards, and few remarkable growers here, although decent red wine is produced in the villages of Klingenberg and Miltenberg.

BÜRGSTADT

✓ Vineyard *Centgrafnberg*
Grower *Rudolf Fürst*

KREUZWERTHEIM

✓ Vineyard *Kaffelstein*
Grower *Staatlicher Hofkeller Würzburg*

WÜRTTEMBERG

Württemberg is not well known as a wine region, principally because the wines produced in the region – a light red wine and a rosé called "Schillerwein" – are not styles that are much in demand outside the region itself.

WÜRTTEMBERG IS GERMANY'S red-wine-producing region. This is not red wine as most non-German wine drinkers would perceive it.

Black grape varieties grow in over half the vineyards in Württemberg, and half of these are planted with Trollinger, a grape that produces a light, fresh, and grapey wine that has none of the body, tannin, or other characteristics associated with a true red wine. The most concentrated Trollinger wines are made between Heilbronn and Winnenden, just northeast of Stuttgart. Even they do not compare with reds produced in the adjacent area of Baden.

Red Lemberger is enjoyed locally in **Württemberg, but until recently it produced** unimpressive, neutral-flavoured wines. A few growers have begun to get more out of this grape variety, but it is never going to shake things up in the red-wine world.

The rosé Schillerwein made here is a speciality and it usually has more character than the red wines made from other black varieties grown locally, such as the Schwarzriesling (Pinot meunier), which makes a better white wine than it does red or even rosé.

WHITE WINES

White Württemberg wines are usually of modest quality, although there are exceptions, such as robust, intensely flavoured Riesling, with pronounced acidity. The region's other white grape varieties make wines of a very ordinary quality, unless harvested at one of the higher QmP categories. One of these white grape varieties – Kerner – does, however, deserve a mention as this *Trollinger* x *Riesling* cross was created at the Württemberg's Weinsberg viticultural institute and named after the local 19th-century doctor and poet Justinus Kerner.

WÜRTTEMBERG, *see also p.261*
see also p.261
Most of the region's vineyards, in fertile districts near the river Neckar, are interspersed with farmland.

WÜRTTEMBERGISCHER UND BAYERISCHER BODENSEE

- ● Recommended wine village or town
- ⬚ Intensive vine-growing zone
- — *Bereich* boundary
- — *Grosslage* boundary
- ▲ Height above sea level (metres)

km	5	10	15	20	25
miles	4	8	12	16

THE REGION AT A GLANCE

Area under vine 11,204 ha (27,685 acres)	**Most important grape varieties** 24% Riesling, 22% Trollinger, 16% Schwarzriesling, 8% Kerner, 8% Lemberger, 22% Others
Average yield 96 hl/ha (432 cases/acre)	**Infrastructure** *Bereiche* 6; *Grosslagen* 17; *Einzellagen* 206
Red wine 56%	**Note** The vineyards of Württemberg straddle 230 *Gemeinden* (communes), the names of which may appear on the label.
White wine 44%	

QUALITY REQUIREMENTS AND HARVEST PERCENTAGES

MINIMUM OECHSLE	QUALITY CATEGORY	HARVEST BREAKDOWN			
		1992	1993	1994	1995
40°	*Deutscher Tafelwein*	8%	–	4%	1%
50°	*Landwein*				
57–63°	* *QbA*	90%	63%	92%	93%
72–78°	* *Kabinett*	2%	25%	3%	6%
85–88°	* *Spätlese*	–	11%	1%	–
95°	* *Auslese*				
124°	*Beerenauslese*	–	1%	–	–
124°	*Eiswein*				
150°	*Trockenbeerenauslese*				

*Minimum Oechsle levels vary according to grape variety; those that have a naturally lower sugar content may qualify at a correspondingly lower level.

FACTORS AFFECTING TASTE AND QUALITY

LOCATION
Situated on the eastern edge of Germany's vine-growing land, between Frankfurt to the north and Lake Constance to the south.

CLIMATE
Sheltered by the Black Forest to the west and the hilly Swabian Alb to the east, this area has an especially warm growing season.

ASPECT
The vineyards are fairly widely scattered either side of the River Neckar.

SOIL
Soils vary widely, but red marl, clay, loess, and loam dominate, with scatterings of shell-limestone in the main Neckar Valley area. The topsoils are deep and well drained,

producing full wines – in a German sense – with a firm acidity.

VITICULTURE AND VINIFICATION
There are 16,500 growers; most have tiny plots and tend them part-time, taking their grapes to the cooperatives that process the wines. Although more than half of the area is planted with black grapes, 70 per

cent of the wine is white (i.e. many black grapes are vinified white).

PRIMARY GRAPE VARIETIES
Müllerrebe, Müller-Thurgau, Riesling, Trollinger
SECONDARY GRAPE VARIETIES
Kerner, Lemberger, Pinot meunier, Portugieser, Ruländer, Silvaner, Spätburgunder

THE APPELLATIONS OF
WÜRTTEMBERG

BEREICH REMSTAL-STUTTGART

The second-largest *Bereich*, covering some 1,600 hectares (3,954 acres).

GROSSLAGE HOHENNEUFFEN

There are no outstanding villages, vineyards, or growers in this *Grosslage*, although good wines are made in Metzingen.

GROSSLAGE KOPF

Some improvements have been made in this once uninspiring *Grosslage*.

√ **Non-Einzellagen wines:**
Growers *Jürgen Ellwanger, Albrecht Schwegler*

GROSSLAGE SONNENBÜHL

No outstanding villages, vineyards, or growers.

GROSSLAGE WARTBÜHL

Squeezed between the unremarkable *Grosslagen* of Kopf and Sonnenbühl, these wines are superior. With very little to choose between the aspect, soil, and microclimate, Wartbühl is distinguished by its selection of grape varieties, all white and with a high percentage of Riesling.

STETTEN
√ **Vineyard** *Mönchberg*
Grower *Karl Haidle*
• **Vineyard** *Pulvermächer*
Grower *Karl Haidle*

GROSSLAGE WEINSTEIGE

Over the years the cooperative of Untertürkheim has produced consistently good wines in this *Grosslage*.

UNTERTÜRKHEIM
√ **Vineyard** *Herzogenberg*
Grower *Wöhrwag*
√ **Non-Einzellagen wines:**
Grower *Winzergenossenschaft Untertürkheim*

BEREICH WÜRTTEMBERGISCH UNTERLAND

This *Bereich* encompasses more than 70 per cent of Württemberg's vineyards throughout its nine *Grosslagen* near the town of Heilbronn.

GROSSLAGE HEUCHELBERG

Some of Württemberg's finest Rieslings come from the rich limestone soil west of Heilbronn.

DÜRRENZIMMERN
√ **Vineyard** *Mönchberg*
Grower *Winzergenossenschaft Dürrenzimmern*

SCHWAIGERN
√ **Vineyard** *Ruthe* **Grower** *Graf von Neipperg*

NEIPPERG
√ **Vineyard** *Schlossberg*
Grower *Graf von Neipperg*

GROSSLAGE KIRCHENWEINBERG

This area produces mostly black grapes; Pinot meunier dominates.

LAUFFEN
√ **Vineyard** *Katzenbeisser*
Grower *Winzergenossenschaft Lauffen*

GROSSLAGE LINDELBERG

A small, scattered area east of Heilbronn, where *barrique*-matured Lemberger red is making a name for itself in an area that is better suited to Riesling.
√ **Non-Einzellagen wines:**
Grower *Fürst zu Hohenlohe-Oehringen*

GROSSLAGE SALZBERG

Sandwiched between Heilbronn and Lindelberg; fine Rieslings could be produced on its steepest vineyards.

GROSSLAGE SCHALKSTEIN

Käsberg vineyard is the finest in this *Grosslage*. It specializes in full, dark red wines.

GROSSLAGE SCHOZACHTAL

Mostly white wines, including fine Riesling, but also some encouraging *barrique*-matured Lemberger and Spätburgunder.

GROSSLAGE STAUFENBERG

This covers the town of Heilbronn, its *Ortsteile*, and several outlying villages.

HEILBRONN
√ **Non-Einzellagen wines:**
Grower *Drautz-Able*

WEINSBERG
√ **Non-Einzellagen wines:**
Grower *Staatsweingut Weinsberg*

GROSSLAGE STROMBERG

A predominantly black-grape area.

BÖNNIGHEIM
√ **Vineyard** *Sonnenberg* **Grower** *Ernst Dautel*
Premium Red Wine Blend:
Grower *Ernst Dautel* (Kreation)

GROSSLAGE WUNNENSTEIN

For many years now Graf Adelmann has carried the torch for an area that could otherwise be regarded as vinous hinterland.

KLEINBOTTWAR
√ **Vineyard** *Süssmund* **Grower** *Graf Adelmann*

BEREICH KOCHER-JAGST-TAUBER

Although this small *Bereich* specializes in white wines, they rarely excel.

GROSSLAGE KOCHERBERG

No outstanding villages, vineyards, or growers, although good wines are made in Criesbach.

GROSSLAGE TAUBERBERG

This encompasses the river Tauber, and produces some good Rieslings, Traminers, and Muscats.

BEREICH OBERER NECKAR

A tiny *Bereich* with no outstanding vineyards.

BEREICH WÜRTTEMBERGISCH BODENSEE

A one-*Einzellage Bereich* on Lake Constance.

BEREICH BAYERISCHER BODENSEE

This has one *Grosslage* with four *Einzellagen*. Climatic conditions are not favourable enough for Reisling, and the small production consists mainly of Müller-Thurgau whites, Spätburgunder reds, and Spätburgunder Weissherbst.

GROSSLAGE LINDAUER SEEGARTEN

Although closest to the Baden *Grosslage* of Sonnenufer and politically part of Bavaria, which encompasses the QbA Franken, German wine law classifies this outpost of vines as part of Württemberg.

BADEN

Often described as Germany's southernmost wine-producing region, Baden is not so much one region as a hotchpotch of politically diverse districts that once produced wine in the now defunct Grand Duchy of Baden.

THE MOST NORTHERLY SECTION OF BADEN is parallel with the Mosel, bridging Franconia and Württemberg, while south from Baden-Baden, the vineyards are the mirror-image of Alsace across the border, and three pockets of vines on the shores of Bodensee are almost the most southerly in Germany; that dubious honour goes to Württemberg's nearby *Grosslage* of Lindauer Seegarten.

This variation of geographical, geological, and climatical conditions produces a wide range of wines, from mild Silvaner, through light, spicy Gutedel, to the full-bodied Ruländer, the attractive pink-coloured Weissherbst, a speciality of the region, and a good deal of Germany's best red wines. If, however, anything can be said to be the mark of a Baden wine it must be a certain warmth, roundness, and mellowness.

QUALITY REQUIREMENTS AND HARVEST PERCENTAGES

MINIMUM OECHSLE	QUALITY CATEGORY	HARVEST BREAKDOWN			
		1992	1993	1994	1995
50–55°	*Deutscher Tafelwein*	10%	–	6%	1%
55°	*Landwein*			90%	
60–72°	* *QbA*	85%	61%	3%	73%
76–85°	* *Kabinett*	4%	29%	1%	25%
86–92°	* *Spätlese*	1%	9%		1%
100–105°	* *Auslese*				
128°	*Beerenauslese*	–	1%	–	–
128°	*Eiswein*				
154°	*Trockenbeerenauslese*				

*Minimum Oechsle levels vary according to grape variety; those that have a naturally lower sugar content may qualify at a correspondingly lower level.

THE REGION AT A GLANCE

Area under vine
16,371 ha (40,453 acres)

Average yield
68 hl/ha (306 cases/acre)

Red wine 28%

White wine 72%

Most important grape varieties
33% Müller-Thurgau,
27% Spätburgunder,
9% Grauerburgunder, 8% Gutedel,
8% Riesling, 15% Others

Infrastructure
Bereiche 8; *Grosslagen* 16;
Einzellagen 306
Note The vineyards of Baden straddle
315 *Gemeinden* (communes). Their
names may appear on the label.

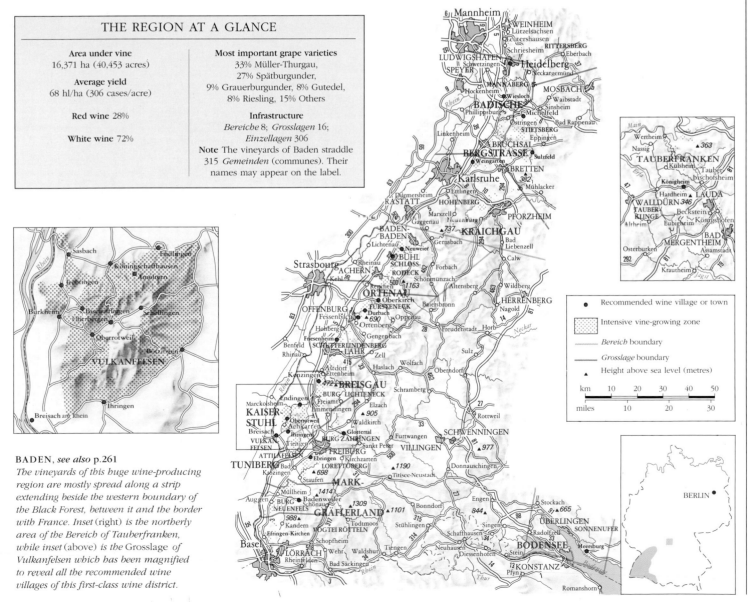

BADEN, *see also* p.261
The vineyards of this huge wine-producing region are mostly spread along a strip extending beside the western boundary of the Black Forest, between it and the border with France. Inset (right) *is the northerly area of the Bereich of Tauberfranken, while inset* (above) *is the Grosslage of Vulkanfelsen which has been magnified to reveal all the recommended wine villages of this first-class wine district.*

Recommended wine village or town

Intensive vine-growing zone

Bereich boundary

Grosslage boundary

Height above sea level (metres)

RIESCHEN VINEYARD
*The old and new castles above the Rieschen vineyard,
on the north shore of the Bodensee at Meersburg.*

Baden is considered to be one of Germany's newest wine regions, yet by 1800 it had become its largest, possessing more than 27,000 hectares (66,700 acres) of vines, almost twice the amount grown today. Ironically, it was when Germany acquired a wealthy and viticulturally prolific Alsace in 1871, as one of the spoils of the Franco-Prussian War, that Baden's vineyards began to decline. The downward trend continued, despite the formation of the Baden Wine Growers' Association founded by the priest and winemaker Heinrich Hansjakob at Hagnau in 1881. Even after the return of Alsace to French sovereignty in 1918, Baden's wine production continued to decline, primarily through lack of investment. In the 1920s wine production was adversely affected by inheritance laws that split Baden's vineyards into smaller and smaller units. By 1950, with barely 6,000 hectares (14,800 acres) of vines, Baden's wine industry was at its lowest ebb.

The eventual resurgence of Baden's wine industry began in 1952 with the formation of the Zentralkellerei Kaiserstuhler Winzergenossenschaften (Central Winery of Kaiserstuhl), which two years later expanded into the Zentralkellerei Badischer Winzergenossenschaften (Central Winery of Baden), or ZBW for short. ZBW built a £25 million vinification and storage plant at Breisach that helped to raise quality standards throughout the

region and adopted an aggressive marketing policy on the domestic scene. Baden established itself as Germany's third-largest wine producing region, yet its wines were virtually unknown outside the country until ZBW made a serious effort to export its products in the early 1980s. Sadly, Baden is now a victim of its own success, for ZBW, which accounts for some 90 per cent of the region's output, has established such a clear-cut identity for its wines that Baden is generally perceived to produce one style of well-made, but rather basic, characterless wine. The truth is that while this one style represents the bulk of ZBW's, and thus Baden's, production, both ZBW and the region's independent producers have a wealth of other wines that are seldom seen or spoken about outside their locality. It is now time for ZBW to turn its marketing expertise to the relatively small number of very high-quality wines within its region, and promote them as independent wine estates for the benefit of all.

BODENSEE (LAKE CONSTANCE)
*These vines are in the south of Baden, at Meersburg, the best village of the
Sonnenufer Grosslage, with some of the most southerly vineyards in Germany.*

FACTORS AFFECTING TASTE AND QUALITY

LOCATION
The longest *Anbaugebiete*, Baden stretches for approximately 400 km (250 miles), from Franken in the north, past Württemberg and the Badische Bergstrasse to Bodensee, or Lake Constance, some of Germany's most southerly vineyards.

CLIMATE
Compared to the rest of Germany, the bulk of Baden's vineyards have a sunny and warm climate, due in part to the shelter afforded by the Black Forest and the Odenwald Mountains.

ASPECT
Most vineyards are on level or gently sloping ground. Some, however, are to be found higher up the hillsides, and these avoid the frosts of the valley floors.

SOIL
Baden's soils are rich and fertile, varying from heat-retaining gravel near Lake Constance, through limestone, clay, marl, loam, granite, and loess deposits to limestone and Keuper, a sandy-marl, in the Kraichgau and

Taubergrund. Volcanic bedrock forms the main subsoil structure throughout most of the region.

VITICULTURE AND VINIFICATION
The relatively flat and fertile vineyards of this region are easily mechanized. Although the geographical spread and variety of soils has led to a large number of different, traditional styles of wine, they are over-shadowed by the mild and neutrally fruity, bulk-produced Baden QbA marketed by ZBW. More than 90 per cent of the winemaking in Baden is conducted by its 54 cooperatives, but there are several independent and top-quality estates among the region's 26,000 growers. A speciality that is unique to Baden is Badisch Rotgold, a soft, delicately-flavoured rosé made from pressing Ruländer and Spätburgunder grapes together.

PRIMARY GRAPE VARIETIES
Müller-Thurgau, Ruländer, Spätburgunder
SECONDARY GRAPE VARIETIES
Gutedel, Kerner, Nobling, Riesling, Silvaner, Traminer, Weissburgunder

THE APPELLATIONS OF
BADEN

BEREICH TAUBERFRANKEN

The most northerly of Baden's vineyards, Bereich Tauberfranken bridges Franken and Württemberg. The wines have a similar style to those produced in both regions. If anything, the crisp, dry, aromatic, and slightly earthy Müller-Thurgau and Silvaner wines bear more resemblance to Franken wines rather than to Württemberg wines. Only that part of the *Bereich* outside Franken itself is allowed to use Franken's famous *Bocksbeutel*.

GROSSLAGE TAUBERKLINGE

As well as at Königshofen, good wines are also made in the villages of Beckstein, Königheim, and Tauberbischofsheim.

KÖNIGSHOFEN
✓ Vineyard *Turmberg*
Grower *Winzergenossenschaft Beckstein*

REICHHOLZHEIM
✓ Vineyard *First*
Grower *Konrad Schlör*

BEREICH BADISCHE BERGSTRASSE-KRAICHGAU

This Bereich has four *Grosslagen*, two in the Badische Bergstrasse, north and south of Heidelberg, and two in the Kraichgau, a larger but sparsely cultivated area further south. Only one *Grosslage*, Stiftsberg, in the Kraichgau, has any reputation at all. Half the *Bereich* is planted with Müller-Thurgau grapes, but it makes mostly dull and lacklustre wine. When successful, the best wines are Ruländer and Riesling.

GROSSLAGE HOHENBERG

In this *Grosslage* there are no outstanding villages, vineyards, or growers, although good wines are made in the village of Weingarten.

GROSSLAGE MANNABERG

This *Grosslage* is situated just southeast of Mannheim and it encompasses the historic university town of Heidelberg, which has some fine steep vineyard slopes overlooking the river Neckar.

HEIDELBERG
✓ Vineyard *Herrenberg* Grower *Seeger/Leimen*
• Premium Red Wine Blend: Grower *Seeger*
(Leimen – "R")

GROSSLAGE RITTERSBERG

There are no outstanding villages, vineyards, or growers here although good wines are made in the villages of Leutershausen, Lützelsachen, Schriesheim, and Weinheim.

GROSSLAGE STIFTSBERG

Situated in the Kraichgau, this is the *Bereich's* most successful *Grosslage*. Nearly half of its vineyards are classified as "steep", which officially means sloping at more than 20 degrees, and this contributes to the extreme fruitiness of the Ruländer and the relatively racy character of the Riesling.

MICHELFELD
✓ Vineyard *Himmelberg* Grower *Reichsgraf und Marquis zu Hoensbroech*

SULZFELD
✓ Non-Einzellagen wines: Growers *Hagenbucher, Burg Ravensburg*

TIEFENBACH
✓ Premium Red Wine Blend:
Grower *Albert Heitlinger* (Master Etage)

BEREICH ORTENAU

Sheltered by the Black Forest, the two *Grosslagen* in this *Bereich* produce some of Baden's greatest wines. They are generally full, fruity, and often very spicy. The Riesling, known locally as Klingelberger, is extremely fine for such a powerful and spicy variation of this normally racy variety. Müller-Thurgau is particularly good and full, and a successful Ruländer-Spätburgunder blend called Badisch Rotgold is also produced. Confusingly, the Gewürztraminer is often called Clevner, which is usually a synonym for Pinot blanc.

GROSSLAGE FÜRSTENECK

This *Grosslage* sports some of Baden's finest estates. The range of grape varieties is greater here than anywhere else within Baden and the wines include Rieslings that range from firm and spicy to fine and delicate; powerful Gewürztraminer; some of Germany's best Müller-Thurgau; and some extraordinarily good Gutedel. Many of the wines are made in increasingly drier styles, although some estates are famous for their sweeter, late-harvested products.

BERGHAUPTEN
✓ Vineyard *Schützenberg*
Grower *Freiherr von und zu Frankenstein*

DURBACH
✓ Vineyard *Schloss Grohl* Grower *Gräflich Wolff Metternich'sches Weingut* • Vineyard *Schlossberg* Growers *Gräflich Wolff*

Metternich'sches Weingut • Vineyard *Plauelrain* Growers *Andreas Laible, Gräflich Wolff Metternich'sches Weingut* • Vineyard *Kochberg* Grower *Heinrich Männle*

ORTENBERG
✓ Non-Einzellagen wines:
Grower *Schloss Ortenberg*

GROSSLAGE SCHLOSS RODECK

Schloss Neuweier is the undisputed number one in this *Grosslage*, although there are also some respectable cooperatives. Once at the forefront of developments with Spätburgunder in barriques, the area has since had to concede its lead to producers from other regions.

NEUWEIER
✓ Vineyard *Mauerberg* Grower *Schloss Neuweier* • Vineyard *Schlossberg* Grower *Schloss Neuweier*

BEREICH BREISGAU

Strangely, the old city of Breisach is not part of the *Bereich* that takes its name; it is, in fact, situated in the *Bereich* of Kaiserstuhl-Tuniberg to the south. The wines of *Bereich* Breisgau do not compare with the better-known Kaiserstuhl-Tuniberg, although they can be attractive and easy to drink. There is a mild, fruity, off-dry Müller-Thurgau; a full and juicy Ruländer; and a popular Weissherbst made from Spätburgunder.

GROSSLAGE BURG LICHTENECK

Besides those of the villages recommended below, good wines are also made in Altdorf.

ETTENHEIM
✓ Vineyard *Kaiserberg*
Grower *Badischer Winzerkeller Breisach*

MALTERDINGEN
✓ Vineyard *Bienenberg*
Grower *Bernhard Huber*
• Premium Red Wine Blend:
Grower *Bernhard Huber* (R)

GROSSLAGE BURG ZÄHRINGEN

There are no outstanding villages, vineyards, or growers in this *Grosslage*, although good wines are made in the village of Glottertal.

GROSSLAGE SCHUTTER-LINDENBERG

There are no outstanding villages, vineyards, or growers in this *Grosslage*, although good wines are made in the village of Friesenheim.

BEREICH KAISERSTUHL

Formerly part of Kaiserstuhl-Tuniberg, this *Bereich* is dominated by the extinct volcano of Kaiserstuhl, whose immaculate slopes are copybook examples of *Flurbereinigung* (growing vines in rows up and down slopes).

In this, Germany's warmest and driest *Bereich*, there are microclimates that favour certain sites protected by the volcano. Some of Baden's best wines come from these *Einzellagen*, although most of the wine is sold under the *Bereich* name, usually with the grape name attached; Bereich Kaiserstuhl Müller-Thurgau dominates. But it is the very full white Ruländer and the assertive Weissherbst Ruländer that made the reputation of the *Bereich*. Some fine, rich Spätburgunder wines enhance this reputation.

GROSSLAGE VULKANFELSEN

Vulkanfelsen is the largest and most successful of the two *Grosslagen* that belonged to the now defunct Kaiserstuhl-Tuniberg. As its name implies (Vulkanfelsen means volcano rock), it covers the superior, high volcanic vineyards of the Kaiserstuhl mound itself. Above all else, it is the full, fiery intensity of Ruländer wines from the Kaiserstuhl that give this district its reputation.

ACHKARREN
✓ Vineyard *Schlossberg*
Growers *Winzergenossenschaft Achkarren, Dr. Heger, Reiner Probst*

BISCHOFFINGEN
✓ Vineyard *Steinbuck* Grower *Winzergenossenschaft Bischoffingen*
• Vineyard *Engelberg* Grower *Abril*
• Premium Red Wine Blend: Grower *Johner* (S. J.)

BREISACH
✓ Vineyard *Eckartsberg* Grower *Kageneck*

BURKHEIM
✓ Vineyard *Feuerberg* Grower *Bercher*
• Vineyard *Schlossgarten* Growers *Bercher, Winzergenossenschaft Burkheim*

ENDINGEN
✓ Vineyard *Engelsberg* Growers *L. Bastian, Reinhold und Cornelia Schneider, Knab*

JECHTINGEN
✓ Vineyard *Eichert* Grower *Bercher*
• Vineyard *Hochberg* Grower *Winzergenossenschaft Jechtingen*

IHRINGEN
✓ Vineyard *Winklerberg* Growers *Dr. Heger, Winzergenossenschaft Ihringen, Stigler, Gebr. Müller*

KÖNIGSSCHAFFHAUSEN
✓ Vineyard *Hasenberg* Grower *Bercher*
• Vineyard *Steingrüble* Grower *Winzergenossenschaft Königsschaffhausen*

OBERBERGEN
✓ Vineyard *Bassgeige* Grower *Winzergenossenschaft Oberbergen*
• Premium Red Wine Blends: Grower *Franz Keller-Schwarzer Adler* (A, S, Selection)

OBERROTTWEIL
✓ Vineyard *Eichberg* Growers *Freiherr von Gleichenstein, Winzergenossenschaft Oberrottweil, Salwey*

SASBACH
✓ Vineyard *Lützelberg* Grower *Winzergenossenschaft Saabach* • Vineyard *Scheibenbuck* Grower *Winzergenossenschaft Sasbach*
• Vineyard *Rote Halde* Grower *Winzergenossenschaft Sasbach*

SCHELINGEN
✓ Vineyard *Kirchberg* Grower *Th. Schätzle*

BEREICH TUNIBERG

Formerly part of Kaiserstuhl-Tuniberg, this *Bereich* is to the south of the mighty Kaiserstuhl and it is the far less awesome sight of the Tuniberg, another volcanic outcrop, that provides the only other topographical and viticultural relief. The Tuniberg's steeper, west-facing slopes are cultivated, but neither its reputation nor its bulk can match those of Kaiserstuhl's fabulous recommendations above.

GROSSLAGE ATTILAFELSEN
The potential for good wines at this small volcanic outcrop of the Tuniberg is fulfilled by the Gretzmeier estate in Merdingen.

MERDINGEN
✓ Non-Einzellagen wines: Grower *Gretzmeier*

BEREICH MARKGRÄFLERLAND

This is the second-most important Bereich in Baden. The principal grape variety is, unusually, Gutedel, which makes a light, dryish, and neutral wine that benefits from a slight spritz and can be most attractive when very youthful. Other prominent varieties include Nobling, an up-and-coming cross between Gutedel and Silvaner that makes a more characterful wine than the light Müller-Thurgau. The latter can be attractive nevertheless. Spätburgunder can be full and successful, and Gewürztraminer also fares well.

GROSSLAGE BURG NEUENFELS

The vast majority of vineyards in this *Grosslage* are on steep ground. These vineyards make some of Germany's most delicious Gutedel.

BRITZINGEN
✓ Vineyard *Rosenberg* Grower *Winzergenossenschaft Britzingen*

LAUFEN
✓ Non-Einzellagen wines: Grower *Schlumberger*

MAUCHEN
✓ Vineyard *Sonnenstück* Grower *Erste Markgräfler Winzergenossenschaft*
✓ Non-Einzellagen wines: Grower *Lämmlin-Schindler*

SCHLIENGEN
✓ Non-Einzellagen wines: Grower *Lämmlin-Schindler*

GROSSLAGE LORETTOBERG
There are no outstanding villages, vineyards, or growers in this *Grosslage*, although good wines are made in the village of Ebringen.

GROSSLAGE VOGTEI RÖTTELN
Although much wine is sold under this *Grosslage*, its exceptional vineyards are known for Gutedel and, to a lesser extent, Spätburgunder.

BEREICH BODENSEE

In the Hochrhein of Bodensee, or the Upper Rhine of Bodensee (known in English as Lake Constance), the wines are not great, but can be very acceptable. They range from the fruity and lively Müller-Thurgau to Rotwein and Weissherbst, both produced from Spätburgunder.

GROSSLAGE SONNENUFER
The steep sides of Lake Constance around Meersburg are the most spectacular vineyards here, but the gently sloping Fohrenberg *Einzellage* inside the town is the most successful. Winzerverein Meersburg, Germany's first state domain (since 1802), consistently performs well.

MEERSBURG
✓ Vineyard *Sängerhalde* Grower *Aufricht*

DURBACH, BADEN
A tractor carrying grape tubs passes through the main street of Durbach on its way to the winery, in the Bereich Ortenau. The hills of the Black Forest can be seen in the distance.

SAALE-UNSTRUT AND SACHSEN

These two eastern outposts of viticulture are the most northerly in Germany and even though their terraced vineyards are being renovated and replanted, and modern vinification facilities installed, their wines can never be more than a tourist curiosity.

PARADOXICALLY THIS LIMITATION may be the saving grace for the wines of Saale-Unstrut and Sachsen because they are far too small and rustically structured to stand any chance of competing with the large volumes of cheap dross churned out by cooperatives in Germany's more intensively cultivated wine regions. Furthermore, as Meissen and Dresden have already been designated as lucrative tourist areas, the wines must adhere to a certain standard if they are to satisfy tourists with far more sophisticated palates than those who consumed them under GDR mismanagement. I hope that, realizing this, local entrepreneurs and investors from the west will opt for efficient, but not excessive, production methods, which should at least concentrate the restricted potential into as attractive a wine as possible. With the exception of Köppelberg in Pforten (Saale-Unstrut) and Heinrichsburg in Diesbar-Seusslitz (Sachsen), few *Einzellagen* have shown any promise that makes them comparable to the finest wines found in Germany's classic QbA regions.

THE FUTURE – VARIETAL EVOLUTION
When Germany was reunified in 1989, the most commonly cultivated grape variety in the former GDR's rundown vineyards was Müller-Thurgau, and although it remains the most important grape, its days

FACTORS AFFECTING TASTE AND QUALITY

LOCATION
The most northerly wine regions in Germany, Saale-Unstrut is equidistant between Berlin and the Franken region, while Sachsen is approximately 128 km (80 miles) east, around Dresden, close to the border with the Czech republic.

CLIMATE
Despite their northerly position, the continental climate ensures high summer temperatures, but winters are long and very cold. The growing season is short and dry compared to other German regions, with spring and autumn frosts a particular danger, cutting yields by 20–70 per cent in Saale-Unstrut and by as much as 90 per cent in Sachsen.

ASPECT
Vineyards are on south and southeast facing valley slopes, but much of the terracing has deteriorated under Communist rule and the current reconstruction will take some time to complete.

SOIL
Limestone and a tiny amount of sandstone in Saale-Unstrut, with loam and loess over granite and volcanic subsoils in Sachsen.

VITICULTURE AND VINIFICATION
Yields were very low prior to reunification, but production has now increased. There are problems such as decimation of production by fierce attacks of frost, decaying terracing, dead vines, and rustic production methods, but it would be a pity if old vines were replaced and if the hardy but highest-yielding characterless crosses were introduced in place of classic varieties.

PRIMARY GRAPE VARIETIES
Müller-Thurgau, Silvaner
SECONDARY GRAPE VARIETIES
Bacchus, Dornfelder, Elbling, Gewürztraminer, Grauerburgunder, Gutedel, Kerner, Morio-Muscat, Portugieser, Weissburgunder

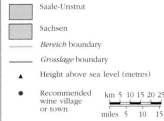

	Saale-Unstrut
	Sachsen
	Bereich boundary
	Grosslage boundary
▲	Height above sea level (metres)
●	Recommended wine village or town

km 5 10 15 20 25
miles 5 10 15

SAALE-UNSTRUT AND SACHSEN
See also p.261
Almost 700 hectares (1,700 acres) of vines grow in these areas, formerly part of East Germany. Production is centred at Bad Kösen, Freyburg, and near the confluence of the Saale and Unstrut rivers at Naumberg.

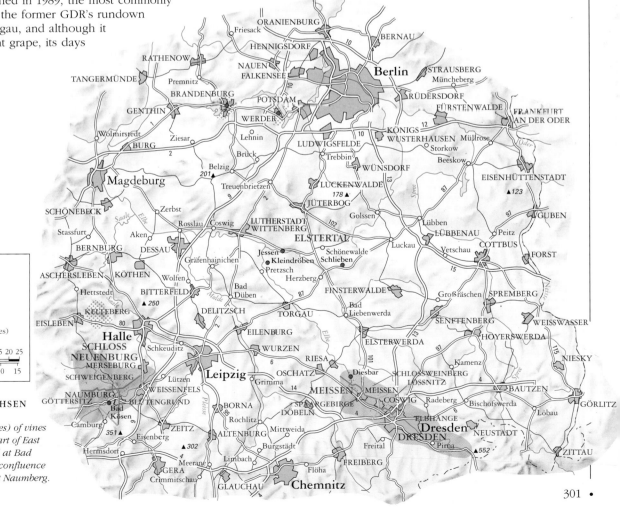

Area under vine	Most important grape varieties
690 ha (1,705 acres)	37% Müller-Thurgau, 16% Silvaner, 7% Weissburgunder, 40% Others
Average yield 50 hl/ha (225 cases/acre)	Infrastructure *Bereiche* 5; *Grosslagen* 8; *Einzellagen* 35
Red wine 6%	Note The vineyards of Saale-Unstrut and Sachsen straddle 63 *Gemeinden* (communes), the names of which may appear on the label.
White wine 94%	

VINEYARDS BY THE ELBE
*Most of Sachsen's vineyards are terraced and overlook
the Elbe river or one of its tributaries*

must be numbered. Riesling accounts for just five per cent of the vines grown, but it is Germany's greatest variety, thus more will be planted, if only for the sake of national pride. The area is, however, more suited to the full, rich, and distinctively earthy wine produced by Silvaner and, perhaps surprisingly for such a northerly, frost-prone region, also to red-wine grape varieties. The continental climate of Saale-Unstrut and, particularly, Sachsen makes for very hot summers, making red wines not

only possible, but preferable. The current choice is Portugieser, for its brash raspberryish fruit, and Dornfelder for colour. No doubt someone will try Trollinger, which dominates Württemberg, Germany's closest red-wine area, but hopefully Spätburgunder (Pinot noir) will prove to be suitable.

THE APPELLATIONS OF
SAALE-UNSTRUT AND SACHSEN

ANBAUGEBIET SAALE-UNSTRUT

Wines have been produced in this area for nearly 1,000 years, but it took the GDR less than 50 years to erase these once-well-known names from the memory of wine drinkers. This region comprises two *Bereiche*, and Müller-Thurgau is the most important grape variety. It accounts for some 35 per cent of the vines planted and black grapes account for some ten per cent.

BEREICH SCHLOSS NEUENBURG

By far the largest of Saale-Unstrut's two *Bereiche*, Schloss Neuenburg encompasses all but a tiny section in the very south of the Saale-Unstrut region, plus the island of vines just west of Halle.

GROSSLAGE BLÜTENGRUND

There are no outstanding villages, vineyards, or growers in this *Grosslage*.

GROSSLAGE GÖTTERSITZ

Whether there is anything intrinsically superior about the vineyards in this *Grosslage* it is far too early to say, but since reunification the wines of Pforten have been the only ones to stand out on any consistent basis.

PFORTEN
✓ Vineyard *Köppelberg*
Grower *Weingut Lützkendorf*

NAUMBURG
✓ Vineyard *Steinmeister* Grower *Gussek*

GROSSLAGE KELTERBERG

No outstanding villages, vineyards, or growers.

GROSSLAGE SCHWEIGENBERG

One grower has begun to shine in this previously lacklustre *Grosslage*.

KARSDORF
✓ Vineyard *Hohe Gräte*
Grower *Weingut Lützkendorf*

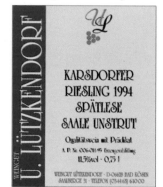

KARSDORFER
RIESLING 1994
SPÄTLESE
SAALE UNSTRUT

BEREICH THÜRINGEN

The southern tip of the Saale-Unstrut region does not contain any *Grosslagen*, just two *Einzellagen*, one in Grossheringen, the other in Bad Sulza.

BEREICHEFREI AND GROSSLAGENFREI MARK BRANDEBURG

Mark Brandenburg covers the vineyards around Werder, from which no outstanding wines have so far been made.

ANBAUGEBIET SACHSEN

Incorporating Dresden and Meissen, this *Aubaugebiet* produces wines that are grown along the River Elbe (Sachsen was formerly known as Elbethal). The area is even more prone to frost damage than Saale-Unstrut, with Riesling relatively more important (13 per cent as opposed to Saale-Unstrut's 5 per cent). The amount of black grapes is minuscule.

BEREICH MEISSEN

The northern end of the Sachsen region, Meissen itself will always be more well known for the porcelain it once produced than its wine. This area, however, did have something of a name for producing fine wine at the beginning of the 19th century. Wine drinkers can only wait and see if there is sufficient potential for that reputation to be recaptured sometime in the future.

GROSSLAGE SPAARGEBIRGE

There are no outstanding villages, vineyards, or growers in this *Grosslage*.

GROSSLAGE SCHLOSS-WEINBERG

North of Meissen, the best wines come from a bend in the Elbe at Diesbar-Seusslitz where the vineyards face south.

SEUSSLITZ
✓ Vineyard *Heinrichsburg*
Grower *Schloss Proschwitz*

BEREICH DRESDEN

This *Bereich* covers most of the southern half of Sachsen.

GROSSLAGE LÖSSNITZ

There are no outstanding villages or vineyards, and no remarkable growers to be recommended in this *Grosslage*.

GROSSLAGE ELBHÄNGE

There are no outstanding villages or vineyards, and no remarkable growers to be recommended in this *Grosslage*.

BEREICH ELSTERTAL

This is a *Bereich* consisting of three villages at the southern end of Sachsen. There are relatively few vines and, so far, no village has produced any outstanding wines.

AUTHOR'S CHOICE

The German categories Beerenauslesen, Trockenbeerenauslesen, *and* Eiswein *are by definition great wines but they are also anomalies, so I have not included these in my choice and have focused instead on the consistently best* Kabinett *styles for each QbA region in Germany. I have also included a few of the more successful* Trocken *wines.*

PRODUCER	WINE	STYLE	DESCRIPTION	⌛
Weingut Bercher	Burkheim Weisser Burgunder, Trocken Auslese (*see* p.300, Grosslage Vulkanfelsen)	WHITE	This wine and Weingut Keller's Dalsheimer Auslese Trocken are the world's best Pinot Blanc. Bercher has the edge for complexity, but their glorious tropical-fruit flavours are equally delicious.	2–5 years
Georg Breuer	Rüdesheim Berg Schlossberg, Riesling (*see* p.283, Grosslage Burgweg)	WHITE	Sold simply as *Qualitätswein*, Breuer's Rüdesheim Berg Schlossberg Riesling is invariably of *Spätlese* level and made, like all Charta wines, in a dry style. It has rich apricot fruit that quickly assumes a classic petrolly character, but ages gracefully.	3–10 years
Weingut Ernst Dautel	Lemberger -S- Deutscher, Tafelwein Neckar (*see* p.296, Grosslage Stromberg)	RED	A Lemberger *Tafelwein* might be modest in variety and appellation, but represents Württemberg well. While Graf Adelmann's Brüssele is the best Lemberger made to age, this unpretentious grape should produce easy, early-drinking wines, which is where Ernst Dautel shines through. Dautel has recently been making a name for itself with this variety, giving it a nicely understated *barrique*-ageing.	3–5 years
Weingut Göttelmann	Münsterer Rheinberg, Riesling Kabinett (*see* p.279, Grosslage Schlosskapelle)	WHITE	This wine comes from the lower part of the Rheinberg *Einzellage*. Göttelmann really excels with Riesling *Spätlese*, but also makes the best *Kabinett* in the Nahe. This wine has the Nahe's characteristic floweriness, but the fruit is so ripe and intense that an almost Rheingau-like peach-kernel nuance intrudes. In another part of Rheinberg, Göttelmann produces a rare Chardonnay *Auslese*.	2–8 years
Dr. Heger	Ihringer Winklerberg, Spätburgunder Spätlese Trocken (*see* p.300, Grosslage Vulkanfelsen)	RED	Spätburgunder (*syn.* Pinot Noir) is Germany's only great red-wine grape and, of the small but growing number of classy wines produced from it, this silky-smooth, deeply coloured red wine has repeatedly proved to be the finest, with lovely black cherry, strawberry, and raspberry fruit underpinned by beautifully blatant tannins and finishing with a wisp of smoky-vanilla oak.	3–6 years
Juliusspital-Weingut	Würzburger Stein, Silvaner Spätlese Trocken (*see* p.294, Grosslage Marienberg)	WHITE	Although Weinbau Egon Schäffer ran it close, I chose this stunning wine as the best representative of classic Franconian Silvaner. Its beautifully ripe pineapple flavours, refreshing acidity, and intense fruit set it apart from other typically earthy examples.	2–4 years
Weingut Keller	Dalsheimer Steig, Weisser Burgunder Auslese Trocken (*see* p.286, Grosslage Burg Rodenstein)	WHITE	A voluptuous wine that is bursting with liquorous fruit of wonderful botrytis richness, yet this does not make it at all heavy.	2–5 years
Staatsweingut Bergstrasse	Heppenheimer Centgericht, Grauer Burgunder Spätlese Trocken (*see* p.291, Grosslage Schlossberg)	WHITE	This lacks the spice of a great Alsace Pinot Gris, as do all German wines of that variety, but it is the best example of this grape produced in Germany, with a fluffier, more sherbetty fruit than the norm, and a slight spritz to enhance the crispness on the finish.	2–4 years
Staatsweingut Bergstrasse	Heppenheimer Centgericht, Riesling Spätlese Trocken (*see* p.291, Grosslage Schlossberg)	WHITE	Very intense, yet luscious, easily accessible, peachy fruit makes this wine easily the best Riesling from Hessische Bergstrasse.	2–7 years
Weingut Josef Albert Lambrich	Oberweseler Römerkrug Riesling Auslese Trocken (*see* p.273, Grosslage Schloss Schönburg)	WHITE	The hugely rich, pure botrytis fruit that Lambrich regularly piles into this wine invariably makes it infanticide to consume before its tenth year, yet it is utterly irresistible as soon as it's bottled.	5–15 years
Weingut Lanius-Knab	Engehöller Goldemund Riesling Kabinett (*see* p.273, Grosslage Schloss Schönburg)	WHITE	The sabre-edged acidity and exquisitely intense fruit in this wine make it stand out as the best Riesling *Kabinett* in the Mittelrhein most years, illustrating just how under-valued this region is.	2–10 years
Dr. Loosen	Erdener Treppchen Riesling Kabinett (*see* p.277, Grosslage Schwarzlay)	WHITE	I have chosen Loosen's Erdener Treppchen as the best Mosel Riesling *Kabinett* because of its extraordinary consistency in providing sharp, tangy, apple fruit when young, then developing into a classic racy Riesling after several years in bottle.	3–12 years
Weingut Schmitt's Kinder	Randersackerer Pfülben Riesling Kabinett (*see* p.294, Grosslage Ewig Leben)	WHITE	Schmitt's Kinder regularly produces the greatest Franconian Riesling *Kabinett* from its Pfülben vineyard, the intensity of extract being so great that it forms a bitterness in its youth, but after sufficient bottle-age this develops into a wonderfully rich, assertive flavour that is unlike that of any other German Riesling.	7–15 years

The WINES of

ITALY

THE WINES OF ITALY ARE RICH IN POTENTIAL
but lack focus, consequently the image is
muddled when it should really be diverse.
In Italy, vines are so easy to grow that one
even expects them to shoot up from cracks
in the pavement after a Mediterranean squall.
Furthermore, the number of interesting
indigenous grape varieties is greater than can
be found in any other winemaking country
of the world, including France. However, there
are no regions great or otherwise in Italy –
just provinces that abut each other. Consumers
cannot visualize Italian wines in the map of
their minds as they can with French wines.
Vine varieties and the types of wine they
make not only merge within provinces, but
overlap their boundaries, blurring the already
confused picture. Despite this, Italy, like
France, makes a quarter of the world's wines,
and Italian exports are healthy. If and when
Italy manages to project a coherent image
of distinct regional styles, France will
have a rival to worry about.

HILLSIDE VINES ABOVE FUMANE, VENETO
*The town of Fumane is in one of five valleys that
comprise the historic Valpolicella Classico area.*

✧ ITALY ✧

It is staggering to think that a quarter of the world's wine is Italian yet, despite 4,000 years of Italian winemaking history, the Italian wine industry remains in a state of flux. The dawning of a new millennium promises even more changes to come.

ITALY'S ENORMOUS WINE PRODUCTION has given many discerning wine drinkers a misleading impression of the country's true quality potential. Italy can, and does, make many fine wines, but they have always been surrounded by so much *vin ordinaire* that finding them is a hit-and-miss affair. Like Italy, France churns out a huge volume of wine and its production can include a fair amount of dross, but the names of great French wines roll off the tongue of even the uninitiated, and, rightly or wrongly, France has managed to get away with it, whereas Italy never has. What a pity this is, as Italy has at least as much potential in terms of

MONTALCINO
With its famous Brunello vines in the foreground, Montalcino basks in Tuscan sunshine. Viticulturally, the surrounding area is highly prestigious; its tannic red wines generally need at least ten years' maturation.

the diversity of its *terroir* and a plethora of native grape varieties. The fundamental problem is identity: in Italy vines grow in every corner of the country, whereas in France they are mostly confined to half a dozen major regions and each of these has its own recognizable style and reputation.

If the Italians want to enhance their winemaking image, they need only ask themselves what difficulty French wines would have if there were no regional names such as Bordeaux or Burgundy to unify the 50-odd appellations they encompass. If the entire winegrowing region of Tuscany were called Chianti, for example, a hierarchy of denominations could be established, which would then propel the very best Chianti (be it Brunello, Carmignano, Vino Nobile, or Chianti Classico itself) to the top of the Chianti tree. Under such a straightforward, easily discernible system, not only would consumers readily understand where each wine came from, but critics would also be as forgiving of generic Chianti as they are of basic Bordeaux. Had the French given the entire generic Bordeaux appellation the very highest ranking, as the Italians have done with Chianti DOCG (*Denominazione di Origine Controllata e Garantita*), the critics would condemn these wines for their ordinariness. If Chianti, however, was made the lowliest DOC (*Denominazione di Origine Controllata*) in the region, its very ordinariness would be expected and welcomed as a necessity of the selection process by which the very greatest wines of the region could attain and maintain the highest possible standards.

ITALY'S LAW OF MEDIOCRITY

Italy's DOC legislation was introduced in 1963, but this law was fundamentally flawed because it failed to establish a small number of easily identifiable regions, each bearing an umbrella name and style. It also actively encouraged increased volume by officially recognizing the most productive grape varieties and classifying the highest yielding areas on the edges of famous appellations. The late 1950s and early 1960s were crucial in the development of the modern wine industry in Europe and Italy's DOC system encouraged its largest bottlers to move out of the low-yielding, hilly, *classico* areas, which make better wines than the higher-yielding plains but are the more difficult and expensive to maintain. From this point, the Italian wine industry became increasingly dominated by mass production; most wineries became passionless factories and the quality of Italy's most famous wines sank as fast as the volume of production increased.

At first, out of respect for Senator Paolo Desana, who fathered the DOC concept, Italy ignored foreign criticism of its new wine regime. But by the early 1980s, its greatest wine names were so devalued that many of its best wines were being sold as *vini da tavola*, which made a mockery of the DOC system. In the end, even the most conservative Italians had to admit something must be done. Over the next ten years, successive agricultural ministers tried to overhaul Italy's wine laws, but failed owing to the political clout of the industrial bottlers, who gained a lot by flooding the market with cheap wines. When agricultural minister Giovanni

ITALY

As might be expected of a nation so geographically and culturally diverse, Italy produces a vast array of different types of wine. Away from the mainland, the islands of Sicily and Sardinia both have thriving wine industries.

Northwest Italy
See also pp.310, 311

Northeast Italy
See also p.319

West-Central Italy
See also pp.326, 327

East-Central Italy
See also p.333

Southern Italy and the Islands
See also pp.336, 337

Provincia boundary

▲ Height above sea level (metres)

2000 The grapes ripened quickly throughout Italy, but particularly in the Piedmont, which had a very early harvest; then, however, came the rain, thus a variable vintage, with only those who picked early enough making the best Barolo. Picking in Franciacorta was even earlier, with hopes for an excellent vintage. Tuscany had problems with overripeness, although some great full-bodied Chianti was produced.

1999 Except for individual cases, the wines this year were not quite up to the quality of the 1998s. Barolo was generally more successful than Chianti.

1998 Truly top-quality Barolo, particularly from the best producers. Very good Chianti too, although Tuscan reds were generally pipped by the heavyweight Barolo.

1997 Splendid year all round, but extraordinarily successful in Tuscany, with great Chianti and Brunello. Superb reds from all regions. Excellent whites from Veneto.

1996 After the great, but small, harvest of 1995, the Italian industry was praying for a bountiful vintage this year, as indeed were most Italian wine importers, who feared a sharp increase in prices. These prayers were almost answered, as the size of the 1996 was back to normal, but, of course, this left an overall shortage from the previous vintage, so prices went up. Overall the quality was good, especially in Piedmont and Lombardy, but Tuscany, Veneto, Latium, Sicily, and Sardinia fared less well.

Goria declared his intention of pressing for even more radical changes than any of his predecessors had, few took him seriously. No one would have bet a single lira on Goria's success, yet within ten weeks of his appointment a "New Disciplinary Code for Denomination of Wines of Origin" had been ratified by the Senate.

GORIA'S LAW
In February 1992 Law 164, now known simply as Goria's Law or the Goria Law, replaced Desana's wine regime. When the law first came into force, much attention was focused on the introduction of a brand new category called IGT or *Indicazioni Geografiche Tipiche*. The equivalent of French *vins de pays*, IGTs were supposed to form a buffer between the DOCs and *vini da tavola*, Goria having denied the latter the right to bear any geographical provenance other than Italy itself. Each IGT would come from an officially recognized zone of production, but could not claim to be anything more specific, such as the product of a village, microzone, estate, or single vineyard. Under Law 164 all such specific origins were restricted to DOC or DOCG wines.

In the euphoric first few months of this new law it was predicted that there would be 150 to 200 IGTs, accounting for some 12 million hectolitres (130 million cases) of wine, which should – according to Goria's own plans – rise to 40 per cent of the total Italian wine output, representing ten per cent of world production. For almost five years, no applications were received for IGT status. Without the right to mention the specific origins of these wines, yet being obliged to meet similar criteria to a DOC, why would producers bother, when they might as well opt for DOC or simply make *vino da tavola*? This is why the major thrust of Goria's ground-breaking law was considered, even in Italy, to have been stillborn. Then, with the 1996 harvest, the applications poured in, and there are now no less than 126 classified IGTs.

NEW RESPECT FOR THE DOCS?
Did the Goria Law successfully reconfigure the fundamentally flawed DOCs and DOCGs? The answer is yes and no. "No" because Italy's wines will never achieve their true potential until,

like those of France, they can be encapsulated within half-a-dozen major regions of recognizable style (*see* DOC's Lack of Specificity below) and reputation. Goria did not even attempt to tackle this problem. Furthermore, Italy's greatest wines will never receive the international acclaim they deserve until their delimited areas are reduced to the original hilly *classico* districts, about which Goria also did nothing. Although these unresolved issues are cardinal to the renaissance of fine Italian wines, what the Goria Law has done to enhance the reputation of Italy's DOCs and DOCGs is not insignificant: it has opened the door to official classification for all the very best *vini da tavola* that have, during the DOCs' darkest years, waved the flag for premium-quality Italian wine.

Until Goria's Law, many wines were denied the *vini da tavola* status because Italy's appellation system defined the characteristics of each DOC, and in so doing did not take into account the foreign grape varieties and non-traditional vinification methods that most premium *vini da tavola* came to employ. Giovanni Goria had the sense to realize that any system that did not recognize some of the country's finest wines is a discredited system. He thus made it easier for the "excesses" of such wines to be accepted within established DOCs and, should any local *consorzio* exercise the right to maintain more traditional standards, he also made it possible for new classics to create their own DOCs, even for appellations consisting of one wine only.

To qualify for DOC status, the wine or wines must have a history of at least five years' production. Any DOC with a further five years of recorded production can apply for a DOCG, providing it has acquired a "reputation and commercial impact both at home and at an international level".

DOC'S LACK OF SPECIFICITY
Part of the problem of Italian wines being unable to project a readily discernible image is the number of ways in which a single DOC wine may be interpreted. An appellation system should project and protect a recognizable style (and, one hopes, quality) through detailed regulations, or it should simply make sure the provenance of a wine is as stated – guaranteeing where it comes from, even if it is a blend of different areas. The very last thing that any wine regime should do is insist on an intricate recipe of grape-variety percentages and precise geographical limitation, then say it can be dry, off-dry, medium sweet, sweet, still, *passito*, *frizzantino* (slightly sparkling), *frizzante* (semi-sparkling), or *spumante* (fully sparkling). All this does is foster the uncertain image with which Italian wines have long been lumbered.

RIONERO, BASILICATA
A 17th-century farm building on the Conca d'Oro estate in Vulture, where Fratelli d'Angelo produces a great red wine called Aglianico del Vulture.

ALL THAT SPARKLES

No country has as many sparkling wine appellations as Italy, with its optional "may be *spumante*" clauses littering over 100 of its DOCs, including some of its truly greatest red wines. However, despite so many possibilities, Italy had no specific appellation for dry sparkling wine until 1995 when Franciacorta, the first and still the only appellation to insist on *méthode champenoise*, was given DOCG status. The rest of Italy's little-known, half-forgotten sparkling wine appellations are all *cuve close*, which is the ideal method for sweet sparkling wines such as Asti, but the worst method for a dry sparkling wine that may have aspirations to receiving international recognition or respect. This is not because *cuve close* is an intrinsically inferior method; in theory it could produce dry sparkling wines that are every bit as good as those made by *méthode champenoise* (*see* p.38), but in practice it does not. It is a bulk-production process, and consequently attracts the cheapest base wines. No one bothers to put top-quality base wines through *cuve close*, let alone keep them there for two or three years, and if they did, they would have to adapt the equipment to stir the lees. On the other hand, no one goes to the trouble and expense of using the *méthode champenoise* on the cheapest base wines. Bottle-fermentation does not guarantee quality, but it does encourage producers in the right direction, which is why it is a mistake for any dry sparkling DOC wine to be produced by any other process. Until all DOC *cuve close* is outlawed, no Italian dry sparkling wine will be taken seriously and Franciacorta's efforts to establish the country's first classic *brut* appellation will be frustrated.

HOW TO READ ITALIAN WINE LABELS

WINE NAME
Many Italian wines are named after a place alone, such as Barolo, Chianti, or Soave, but some carry the name of the grape variety first followed by the place where the grape was grown, such as Barbera d'Alba (which simply means Barbera grown in Alba). Some Italian wine names are anomalies. The wines of Montalcino, for example, have long been famous and considered fine or noble, hence Vino Nobile di Montalcino or noble wine of Montalcino.

VINTAGE
The words *annata*, meaning "year", or *vendemmia*, meaning "harvest", often precede or follow the vintage date. At least 85 per cent of the wine must be from the vintage indicated.

PRODUCER or BOTTLER
The producer on this example is Paola Silvestri Barioffi, whose Le Casalte estate regularly produces great Vino Nobile di Montepulciano.

VOLUME
All full bottles (i.e. not half bottles) must now contain 750 ml or 75 cl.

QUALITY DESIGNATION
Denominazione di Origine Controllata (DOC). There are currently more than 250 DOCs, but as some are multiple-varietal appellations covering as many as 12 different wines there are in excess of 600 DOC names. The classification claims an increasing number of the greatest Italian wines, but still includes a large proportion of the poorest.
Other quality categories are *Denominazione di Origine Controllata e Garantita* (DOCG), as used here, which is the highest quality category, and *Vino da Tavola* (VdT), a category that covers most of Italy's plonk as well as some of its greatest wines.

ESTATE BOTTLED
The words *Imbottigliato all'origine da*, *messo in bottiglia nell'origine*, or *del produttore all'origine* all mean estate-bottled.

PRODUCT OF ITALY
The country of origin need only be indicated on wines for export.

ALCOHOLIC STRENGTH
This is expressed in per cent by volume.

Other information regarding style or quality may also be present:

ABBOCCATO Slightly sweet

AMABILE Sweeter than *abboccato*

AMARO Bitter or very dry

ASCIUTTO Bone dry

AUSLESE
German term used in the Alto Adige for wines from selected grapes.

AZIENDA, AZIENDA AGRICOLA, AZIENDA AGRARIA, or AZIENDA VITIVINICOLA Estate winery

BIANCO White

CANTINA SOCIALE or COOPERATIVA Cooperative winery

CASCINA
North Italian term for a farm or estate.

CERASUOLO
Cherry red, used for vividly coloured rosés.

CHIARETTO
Wines falling between very light red and genuine rosé.

CLASSICO Best part of a DOC zone.

CONSORZIO
A group of producers who control and promote wine, usually insisting on higher standards than DOC regulations permit.

DOLCE Very sweet

FERMENTAZIONE NATURALE
Method of producing sparkling wine by natural refermentation in a tank or bottle.

FIORE
Term meaning "flower". Often part of a name, it indicates quality as it implies the first grape pressing has been used.

FRIZZANTE
Semi-sparkling, the equivalent of *pétillant*.

FRIZZANTINO Very lightly sparkling

LIQUOROSO
Usually fortified and sweet, but may also be dry wine that is simply high in alcohol.

LOCALITÀ, RONCO, or **VIGNETO**
Indicates a single-vineyard wine.

METODO CLASSICO The Italian for *méthode champenoise*.

PASSITO
Strong, often sweet wine made from semi-dried grapes.

PASTOSO Medium-sweet

RAMATO
Copper-coloured wine made from Pinot grigio grapes that are briefly macerated on their skins.

RECIOTO
Strong, sweet wine made from *passito* grapes.

RIPASSO
Wine refermented on the lees of a *recioto* wine.

RISERVA or **RISERVA SPECIALE**
DOC wines that have been matured for a statutory number of years (the *speciale* is older).

ROSATO Rosé

ROSSO Red

SECCO Dry

SEMI-SECCO Medium-sweet

SPUMANTE Fully sparkling

STRAVECCHIO Very old wines aged according to DOC rules.

SUPERIORE
DOC wines that usually have higher alcoholic strength, but may also be of higher quality. Although this term was dropped by the Goria Law, some producers still use it.

TALENTO
A registered trademark signifying a sparkling wine made by the *méthode champenoise*.

UVAGGIO
Wine blended from various grape varieties.

VECCHIO Old

VIN SANTO or **VINO SANTO**
Traditionally sweet, occasionally dry, white wine made from *passito* grapes stored in sealed casks, and not topped up for several years.

VINO NOVELLO Italian equivalent of Beaujolais *nouveau*.

VINO DA PASTO Ordinary wine

NORTHWEST ITALY

This area includes the great wine region of Piedmont as well as the regions of Liguria, Lombardy, and Valle d'Aosta. Generally the wines are fuller and richer than those of northeast Italy, which is generally a more mountainous region.

FEW AREAS ENCOMPASS such contrasting topographies as northwest Italy, from the alpine *pistes* of the Valle d'Aosta and the Apennines of Liguria to the alluvial plains of the river Po. Contrast is also evident in the character of its two most famous wines – the big, black, and tannic Barolo DOCG and the light, water-white, effervescent, and grapey-sweet Asti DOCG.

PIEDMONT (PIEMONTE)

Piedmont is dominated by two black grapes (Nebbiolo and Barbera) and one white (Moscato). Nebbiolo makes the magnificently rich and smoky Barolo and the elegant, more feminine, yet sometimes just as powerful, Barbaresco. The Barbera has a much greater yield than Nebbiolo but is potentially almost as fine. It is softer in tannin, at least as high in acidity, and excels around Alba and, to a slightly lesser extent, around Asti. White Asti, made from Moscato, is Italy's

most popular fine wine. Whether still, *frizzantino*, or *spumante*, Asti is light and succulently sweet, with a mesmerizing grapey character. Fully sparkling Asti is no longer called Asti Spumante because the term, like *mousseux*, has a cheap, low-quality connotation and Asti is undeniably the world's greatest dessert-style sparkling wine.

LOMBARDY (LOMBARDIA)

Northeast of Piedmont, Lombardy stretches from the flat plains of the Po Valley to snow-clad Alpine peaks. The region's finest wines

AVERAGE ANNUAL PRODUCTION		
REGION	**DOC PRODUCTION**	**TOTAL PRODUCTION**
Piedmont	1 million hl (11 million cases)	4 million hl (44 million cases)
Lombardy	400,000 hl (4 million cases)	2 million hl (22 million cases)
Liguria	7,000 hl (78,000 cases)	400,000 hl (4 million cases)
Valle d'Aosta	500 hl (5,550 cases)	30,000 hl (350,000 cases)

Percentage of total Italian production: Piedmont, 5.2%; Lombardy, 2.6%; Liguria, 0.52%; Valle d'Aosta, 0.04%.

NORTHWEST ITALY, *see also* p.307
The presence of the Alps gives this largely hilly region a hot growing season and a long autumn. The finest wines come from the foothills of Piedmont, which provide ideal growing conditions for the late-ripening Nebbiolo grape.

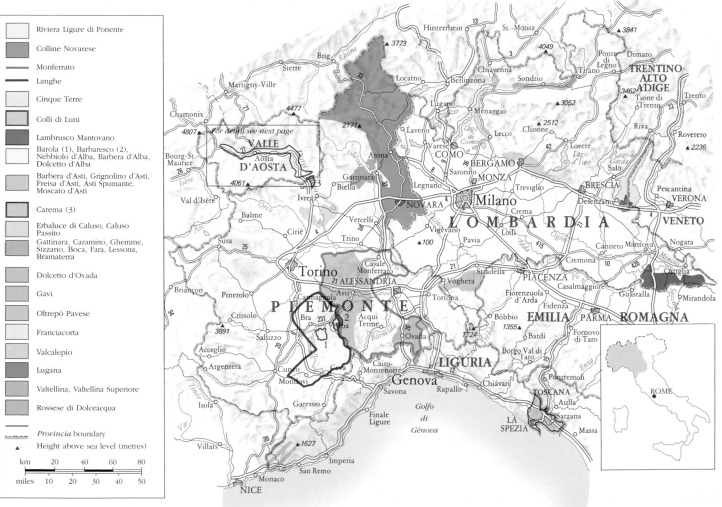

Legend:
- Riviera Ligure di Ponente
- Colline Novarese
- Monferrato
- Langhe
- Cinque Terre
- Colli di Luni
- Lambrusco Mantovano
- Barolo (1), Barbaresco (2), Nebbiolo d'Alba, Barbera d'Alba, Dolcetto d'Alba
- Barbera d'Asti, Grignolino d'Asti, Freisa d'Asti, Asti Spumante, Moscato d'Asti
- Carema (3)
- Erbaluce di Caluso, Caluso Passito
- Gattinara, Caramino, Ghemme, Sizzano, Boca, Fara, Lessona, Bramaterra
- Dolcetto d'Ovada
- Gavi
- Oltrepò Pavese
- Franciacorta
- Valcalepio
- Lugana
- Valtellina, Valtellina Superiore
- Rossese di Dolceacqua
- *Provincia* boundary
- ▲ Height above sea level (metres)

km 20 40 60 80
miles 10 20 30 40 50

FACTORS AFFECTING TASTE AND QUALITY

LOCATION
Flanked to the north and west by the Alps and by the Ligurian Sea to the south, northwest Italy contains the provinces of Piedmont, Lombardy, Liguria, and Valle d'Aosta.

CLIMATE
The winters are severe with frequent inversion fogs rising out of the valleys. Summers are hot, though not excessively so, but hail can damage the grapes at this time of year. Long autumns enable the late-ripening Nebbiolo grape to be grown very successfully.

ASPECT
This area covers mountains, foothills (*piedmont* means "foothills"), and the valley of Italy's longest river, the Po. Grapes are grown on hillsides that provide good drainage and exposure to the sun. In classic areas such as Barolo, every south-facing hillside is covered with vines, while in Lombardy many vineyards extend down to the rich, alluvial plains of the Po Valley.

SOIL
A wide range of soils with many local variations, the predominant type is calcareous marl (*see* p.28), which may be interlayered or intermingled with sand and clay.

VITICULTURE AND VINIFICATION
The great red wines of the region have suffered in the past from long ageing in large wooden vats, as many growers bottled their wine only when they sold it. This practice dried up the fruit and oxidized the wine. However, many wines are bottled at the optimum time although there is still no consensus about the best ageing vessels. The use of *cuve close* for sweet, grapey styles of wine from Asti has been very successful and these wines sell well internationally. Some of the same *spumante* houses have developed dry *spumante* from Pinot and Chardonnay grapes, using the *méthode champenoise*, to produce fine-quality sparkling wines.

PRIMARY GRAPE VARIETIES
Barbera, Muscat, (*syn.* Moscato), Nebbiolo (*syn.* Chiavennasca)

SECONDARY GRAPE VARIETIES
Arneis, Blanc de Morgex, Bonarda, Brachetto, Brugnola, Cabernet franc, Cabernet sauvignon, Casalese, Chardonnay, Cortese, Croatina (*syn.* Bonarda in Lombardy, but not the true Bonarda of Piedmont), Dolcetto (*syn.* Ormeasco in Liguria), Erbaluce, Favorita, Freisa, Fumin, Gamay, Grenache, Grignolino, Gropello, Incrocio terzi (Barbera x Cabernet franc), Lambrusco, Malvasia, Marzemino, Mayolet, Merlot, Neyret, Petit rouge (*syn.* Oriou), Petite arvine, Pigato, Pignola Valtellina, Pinot blanc (*syn.* Pinot bianco), Pinot gris (*syn.* Pinot grigio, Malvoisie, not Malvasia), Pinot noir (*syn.* Pinot nero), Premetta, Riesling (*syn.* Riesling Renano), Rossese, Rossola, Ruché, Schiava gentile, Syrah, Timorasso, Tocai Friulano (separate variety – neither Pinot grigio nor Malvasia), Trebbiano (*syn.* Buzzetto), Ughetta, Uva rara, Vermentino, Vespolina, Vien de Nus, Welschriesling (*syn.* Riesling Italico)

PERGOLA-TRAINED VINES
These Nebbiolo vines, grown near Carema in Piedmont, are trained on a Pergola Piemontese. *They are made into a fragrant, medium-bodied wine.*

include Franciacorta's full reds and its new DOCG for classic *brut* sparkling wines, plus the best of Valtellina's red Sassella. These wines are still relatively unknown compared with Piedmont's Barolo and Barbaresco and are good value.

LIGURIA
One of Italy's smallest regions, Liguria is more famous for its Riviera, which is set against the dramatic and beautiful backdrop of the Maritime Alps, than it is for its wines. Cinque Terre, which is the best-known Ligurian wine, is named after the *Cinque Terre*, or five villages, which are perched along the Ligurian coast above which the steep, intricately terraced vineyards tower like some great Aztec pyramid. Other than the Cinque Terre, interesting wines include the soft, spicy Rossese di Dolceacqua and the vividly coloured Albenga rosé of the Riviera Ligure di Ponente DOC. The Colli di Luni is almost Tuscan, and part of this DOC even overlaps that region, so it is not surprising that it is capable of producing a decent Sangiovese. However, most Ligurian wines belong to the category of pleasant holiday drinking, and some of the best potential vineyards have been grubbed up to accommodate the tourists who drink them.

VALLE D'AOSTA
If Liguria is a marginal wine region, then Valle d'Aosta is almost subliminal. High in the Alps, overlooked by Mont Blanc and the Matterhorn, the Valle d'Aosta looks at first as if it could as easily be a part of France or Switzerland, as of Italy, but the only easy, natural access is from Piedmont along the Dora Baltea river. Italy's smallest and most mountainous wine region, the Valle d'Aosta has picturesque, high-altitude vineyards that produce some enjoyable wines, particularly Chambave, Nus, and Torrette, which are just three of the 20 wines within the Valle d'Aosta DOC. However, most are tourist wines; the best are easy-drinking and unpretentious.

VALLE D'AOSTA, *see also* opposite
The winters here are cold and snowy, but summers in the valley can be very hot with contrastingly cold nights, which should make for some exciting wines.

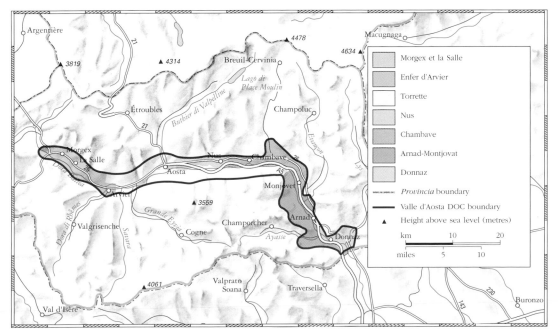

Morgex et la Salle

Enfer d'Arvier

Torrette

Nus

Chambave

Arnad-Montjovat

Donnaz

------ *Provincia* boundary

—— Valle d'Aosta DOC boundary

▲ Height above sea level (metres)

THE APPELLATIONS OF
NORTHWEST ITALY

CLASSIC BRUT SPARKLING WINES

All these wines are made by the *méthode champenoise*.

🍷 Upon purchase – for all regions

✓ **Lombardy** *Bellavista Cuvée Brut • Bellavista Gran Cuvée pas Operé • Berlucchi Brut Cuvée Impériale • Berlucchi Brut Cuvée Impériale Millesimato • Berlucchi Brut Cuvée Impériale Max Rosé • Ca' del Bosco Franciacorta Pinot Brut • Ca' del Bosco Franciacorta pas Dose • Ca' del Bosco Franciacorta Crémant Brut • Doria Pinot Brut • Mirabella Franciacorta Brut • Villa Mazzucchelli Brut • Villa Mazzucchelli pas Dose*

Piedmont *Stefano Barbero • Luigi Bosca Brut Nature • Contratto Brut*

ALBENGA DOC
Liguria

Vividly coloured, dry, and characterful, Liguria's best-known rosés are now classified as part of the Riviera Ligure di Ponente DOC. *See* Riviera Ligure di Ponente DOC.

ARENGO
Piedmont

A soft, light-bodied, fruity non-DOC Barbera red made by several Asti producers.

ARNAD-MONTJOVAT DOC
Valle d'Aosta

A red-only sub-appellation of the regional Valle d'Aosta DOC producing Nebbiolo-based red wines, with up to 30 per cent Dolcetto, Freisa, Neyret, Pinot noir, and Vien de Nus. *See* Valle d'Aosta DOC.

ARNEIS DI ROERO DOC
Piedmont

These wines are produced from the ancient Arneis grape grown in the hills north of Alba. Formerly a Vino da Tavola, the high price and reputation of these wines ensured they would eventually become part of the Roero DOC. The best are amazingly rich and full-flavoured white wines, yet soft and deftly balanced with a fine *frizzantino*. Essentially dry wines, some renditions are, however, less dry than others and Deltetto's Bric Tupin has started a trend for a lusciously sweet style. *See* Roero DOC.

🍷 3–5 years

✓ *Ceretto* (Blangé) • *Carlo Deltetto • Bruno Giacosa • Castello di Neive • Vietti*

ASTI DOCG
Piedmont

Formerly sold as Asti Spumante, the *spumante*, (which means "sparkling"), has been removed because it has become tarnished by cheap products that also use the term. It is now known simply as Asti and has been promoted to full DOCG status, which the best wines deserve, but an increasing number of under-performers do not. Italy's finest sparkling wine, and one of the most famous wines in the world, Asti is made by *cuve close*, which is far superior to *méthode champenoise* when producing an aromatic, sweet sparkling wine. The grapes used are grown in 52 communes throughout the provinces of Asti, Cuneo, and Alessandria.

The best Asti has a fine *mousse* of tiny bubbles, a fresh and grapey aroma, a luscious sweetness, and a light, delicately rich flowery-fruitiness that hints at peaches. Asti should be consumed as young as possible primarily because one of the most important compounds contributing to the Moscato aroma is geraniol, which is wonderful when fresh, but with bottle-age assumes a pungent geranium odour. Gancia's special selection *cuvée* called Camilo Gancia (no longer produced) was the best Asti I ever tasted. *See also* Moscato d'Asti DOCG.

🍷 Upon purchase

✓ *Barbero* (Conte di Cavour) • *Walter Barbero* (Acini Dolce) • *Batasiolo • Bersano • Capetta • Villa Carlotta • Cerutti* (Cesare) • *Conte di Cavour • Giuseppe Contratto • Romano Dogliotti* (La Selvatica) • *Fontanafredda* (Millesimato) • *Marenco • De Miranda • Mondoro • Perlino • Sperone • Tosti • Cantina Sociale Vallebelbo*

BARBACARLO
Lombardy

Dry, *frizzante*, red *vin de garde* that was originally classified as part of the Oltrepò Pavese DOC. However, Lino Maga has been legally recognized as its exclusive producer and it has returned to being a *vino da tavola*.

BARBARESCO DOCG
Piedmont

Generally more feminine and elegant than Barolo, Barbaresco has a greater suppleness, softer fruit, and a more obvious charm, although some producers overlap the weightier Barolo style. Produced from Italy's greatest indigenous grape variety, Nebbiolo, these wines must be aged for a minimum of two years, one of which must be in oak or chestnut casks.

🍷 5–20 years

✓ *Produttori di Barbaresco • Ceretto • Pio Cesare • Fratelli Cigliuti • Giuseppe Cortese • Angelo Gaja • Bruno Giacosa • Piero Busso • Cantina del Glicine • Marchese di Gresy • Moccagatta • Castello di Neive • Alfredo Prunotto • Bruno Rocca • Scarpa*

BARBERA
Piedmont

Although this grape can be a bit rustic, overly acidic, and may lack elegance if not grown in a suitable *terroir*, stunning *vini da tavola*, often aged in a *barrique*, are made in classic areas by producers who do not want to be restricted by the DOC and thus do not claim it.

✓ *Braida* (Bricco dell'Uccellone) • *Castello di Neive* (Rocca del Mattarello)

BARBERA D'ALBA DOC
Piedmont

Barbera is the most prolific Piedmont vine and, as such, has suffered unfairly from a somewhat lowly image. But in fact, it is one of Italy's great grapes and the best Barbera from Alba are magnificently rich and full of flavour, and quite capable of challenging

Barolo and Barbaresco very closely in terms of intrinsic quality. The production of Barbera d'Alba is very small, in fact often minute, in comparison with that of Barbera d'Asti.

🍷 5–12 years

✓ *Marziano Abbona • Pio Cesare • Fratelli Cigliuti • Clerico • Aldo Conterno • Giacomo Conterno • Conterno Fantino • Damonte • Franco Fiorina • Angelo Gaja • Gepin • Elio Grasso • Manzone • Giuseppe Mascarello • Prunotto • Renato Ratti • Bruno Rocca • Varja • Vietti • Roberto Voerzio*

BARBERA D'ALBA COLLINE NICESI DOC
Piedmont

The lower yield of this proposed sub-zone of Barbara d'Alba is intended to lead the way to full DOCG status for part or all of the current Barbera D'Alba DOC classified wines.

BARBERA D'ASTI DOC
Piedmont

Similar in character to Barbera d'Alba, but softer and more supple, with simpler generic wines, but equally profound single-vineyard wines.

🍷 3–8 years

✓ *Marchesi Alfieri* • *Cascina la Barbatella* • *Bava* (Stradivario) • *Alfiero Boffa* • *Braida* (Bricco della Figotta) • *Cascina Castelet* (Passum) • *Chiarlo* (Valle del Sole) • *Coppo* • *Cossetti* (Cascina Salomone) • *Neirano* (Le Croci) • *Antica Casa Vinicola Scarpa* • *Zonin* (Castello del Poggio)

BARBERA DEL MONFERRATO DOC
Piedmont

Most of the wines produced by Barbera Del Monferrato are lesser versions of Barbera d'Asti. Semi-sweet or *frizzante* styles may also be made.

✓ *CS di Castagnole Monferrato* (Barbera Vivace)

BAROLO DOCG
Piedmont

Barolo is unquestionably Italy's greatest wine appellation and its finest wines are the ultimate expression of the Nebbiolo grape. All the best vineyards of Barolo are located on a small, raised area of mostly gentle, but occasionally steep, slopes surrounded by the hills of the Langhe. The soil is essentially calcareous marl (*see* p.28), the northwestern half high in magnesium and manganese, the southeastern half more iron-rich. This small difference is deemed to be the reason why Barolo wines from the northwest have more elegance, while those from the southeast are fuller in body.

The biggest factor in the quality of Barolo has, however, been due more to man than to soil, especially with the trend over the last ten years to isolate the very best Barolo and market them under single-vineyard names. A vineyard name will not necessarily guarantee excellence, but hardly any of the very top Barolo are blended these days and quality should continue to rise under the Goria Law (*see* p.308), which requires significantly lower yields from any wine claiming single-vineyard status.

Great Barolo is incomparable, but there are still poor Barolo wines, although not as many as in the late 1980s. But even then the emergence of a new wave of fruit-driven Barolo was fairly evident. Initially, this split Barolo; the modern-style wines had more fruit, riper and more supple tannins, and were aged in small *barriques* of new oak, while the worst of the so-called traditionalists carried on producing thick, tannic, dried-out wines.

The popular belief that so many traditional Barolo are dried out because they are bottled late is only half right. The truth is that they are – or were – bottled to order. This meant that some of the shipments of the same vintage would be more dried-out than others. There is still a large number of producers who perceive themselves to be traditional, but this simply means that they eschew *barriques* and new oak. Most traditionalists now bottle their Barolo when the wines – not the orders – require it, which, in effect, is earlier than before. They also tend

to pick later and began to drop their yields even before the Goria Law of 1992. Today, both the modern and traditional schools of producers make stunning Barolo.

Modern styles are riper and more creamy than traditional ones, supported by the vanilla of new oak, whereas the traditional styles are arguably more complex, with tobacco, tar, and smoky aromas replacing the clean-cut vanilla. The best of both, however, are deep, sometimes inky-deep, in colour and share lashings of fruit. All Barolo should be powerfully built, even the more elegant, earlier-drinking styles, and they all have a surprising finesse for such weighty wines.

🍷 8–25 years

✓ *Marziano Abbona* • *Accomasso* • *Elio Altare* • *Abbazia dell'Annunzziata* • *Azelia* • *Fratelli Barale* • *Giacomo Borgogno* • *Bricco Roche* • *Fratelli Brovia* • *Giuseppe Cappellano* • *Cavalotto* • *Ceretto* • *Clerico* • *Aldo Conterno* • *Giacomo Conterno* • *Conterno-Fantino* • *Corino* • *Franco-Fiorina* • *Fratelli Oddero* • *Angelo Gaja* • *Bruno Giacosa* • *Manzone* • *Marcarini* • *Bartolo Mascarello* • *Giuseppe Mascarello* • *Alfredo Prunotto* • *Renato Ratti* • *Giuseppe Rinaldi* • *Luciano Sandrone* • *Antica Casa Vinicola Scarpa* • *Vietti* • *Roberto Voerzio*

BAROLO CHINATO DOCG
Piedmont

This Barolo, aromatized with quinine, is a DOCG, which is a bit like classifying Bordeaux's aperitif "Lillet" as a *cru classé*.

BLANC DE COSSAN
Valle d'Aosta

These are fresh, tart *blancs de noir* made by the Institut Agricol Régional from Grenache grapes grown at Cossan, just outside Aosta.

BOCA DOC
Piedmont

These are medium- to full-bodied, spicy red Nebbiolo wines. They are hard to find, but wines have been made here since Roman times and when found can be good value.

🍷 3–6 years

✓ *Antonio Vallana* • *Podere ai Valloni*

BOTTICINO DOC
Lombardy

Full-bodied, Barbera-based red wines with a good level of alcohol and a light tannic structure.

🍷 3–5 years

✓ *Miro Bonetti* • *Benedetto Tognazzi*

BRACHETTO
Piedmont

Sweet, red, non-DOC Brachetto is often made by Asti producers.

✓ *Batasiolo*

BRACHETTO D'ACQUI DOC
Piedmont

Sweet, *frizzante* (semi-sparkling) and sparkling red wines that are grapey and Muscat-like.

BRAMATERRA DOC
Piedmont

Good value, full-bodied red wines produced primarily from Nebbiolo, but which may include Bonarda, Croatina, and Vespolina grapes.

🍷 3–6 years

✓ *Luigi Perazzi* • *Fabrizio Sella*

BUTTAFUOCO DOC
Lombardy
See Oltrepò Pavese DOC

CABERNET FRANC
Lombardy

This grape is far more traditional in Lombardy than Cabernet sauvignon is, although the latter steals the limelight today. Mostly used in blends.

CABERNET-MERLOT
Lombardy

A relative newcomer to Lombardy, this classic Bordeaux mix has shown outstanding potential.

✓ *Bellavista* (Solesine) • *Ca' del Bosco* (Maurizio Zanella)

CABERNET SAUVIGNON
Piedmont

Thrives in Piedmont where *vini da tavola* can be excellent in quality as well as in value.

✓ *Angelo Gaja* (Darmagi)

CALUSO PASSITO DOC
Piedmont

Fragrant yet full-bodied, sweet white wines made from *passito* Erbaluce grapes.

🍷 3–5 years

✓ *Vittorio Boratto*

CAPRIANO DEL COLLE DOC
Lombardy

Rarely encountered red wines made from the Sangiovese, which are blended with Marzemino, Barbera, and Merlot, and tart white wines made from the Trebbiano.

CAREMA DOC
Piedmont

Soft, medium-bodied, Nebbiolo wines that are grown on the mountainous slopes close to the border with the Valle d'Aosta. They are good and reliable but rarely exciting.

🍷 2–5 years

✓ *Luigi Ferrando*

CASALESE
Piedmont

A local grape capable of light, delicately dry white wine with a characteristic bitter finish, both as DOC and *vino da tavola*.

CELLATICA DOC
Lombardy

This aromatic and flavoursome red wine has been made in the hills overlooking Bréscia for 400 years. Permitted grapes are Barbera, Marzemino, Schiava gentile, and Incrocio terzi.

🍷 2–6 years

✓ *Barbi*

CHAMBAVE DOC
Valle d'Aosta

A sub-appellation of the regional Valle d'Aosta DOC, Chambave produces attractively scented, crisp red wines primarily from Petit rouge grapes, plus up to 40 per cent Dolcetto, Gamay, and Pinot noir. Two white wines are also permitted; one sweet, long-lived, and *passito* in style, the other a highly perfumed, early-drinking, dry- to off-dry white – both from the Moscato grape. *See* Valle d'Aosta DOC.

🍷 2–3 years (red and *passito*), upon purchase (white)

✓ *La Crotta di Vegneron* • *Ezio Voyat*

CHARDONNAY
Lombardy, Piedmont, and the Valle d'Aosta

Most of the Chardonnay grown in Lombardy ends up in *méthode champenoise* wines, many of no specific origin, or in the Franciacorta and Oltrepò Pavese DOCs. However, there are a growing number of excellent, pure varietal *barrique*-aged *vini da tavola*, many of which are surprisingly full and lusty in style.

In contrast to Valle d'Aosta below, pure Chardonnay *vini da tavola* are quite common in Piedmont. Although the quality is variable, when Piedmont Chardonnay is good, it is rich and lush, yet classically structured and of a quality that few other Italian wine regions can touch. Many will no doubt receive official DOC status in years to come.

A few *barrique*-aged examples have proved the worth of this grape in Valle d'Aosta, but it is not a frequently encountered varietal, even though it is recognized in the regional DOC.

√ Lombardy *Bellavista* • *Ca' del Bosco* • *Cascina La Pertica* • *Tenuta Castello* • *Tronconero*

Piedmont *Angelo Gaja* • *Pio Cesare*

CINQUE TERRE or CINQUETERRE DOC
Liguria

These spectacular coastal vineyards produce good, though not exactly spectacular, delicately fruity dry white wines, and the somewhat more exciting Cinque Terre Sciacchetrà, which is a medium-sweet *passito* wine.

⌛ 1–3 years

√ *Forlini Cappellini*

COLLI DI LUNI DOC
Liguria

Sangiovese-based reds and Vermentino whites from the eastern extremity of Liguria, bordering and even overlapping part of Tuscany.

⌛ 2–5 years (red) and 1–2 years (white)

√ *La Colombiera*

COLLI MORENICI MANTOVANI DEL GARDA DOC
Lombardy

Although vines have been cultivated since ancient times in Lake Garda, today viticulture is one of the least important crops. The wines are dry, light-bodied, red, white, and rosé, produced from a mixture of grape varieties.

COLLINE NOVARESE DOC
Piedmont

A new DOC for red and white wines from the Novarese province northwest of Milan; the white is dry and made exclusively from the Erbaluce grape, whereas the red is a blend of at least 40 per cent Uva rara and 30 per cent Nebbiolo, plus up to 30 per cent Vespolina and Croatina.

COLLI TORTONESI DOC
Piedmont

Robust and rather rustic, full-bodied Barbera reds, and crisp, dry, rather lightweight, and sometimes *frizzante* Cortese whites.

CORTESE DELL'ALTO MONFERRATO DOC
Piedmont

Dry, crisp, still, *frizzante*, and fully sparkling white wines that often incline to a coarser style than expected for the Cortese grape.

CORTESE DI GAVI DOC
See Gavi DOC

DIANO D'ALBA DOC
See Dolcetto di Diano d'Alba DOC

DOLCETTO
Piedmont

Non-DOC Dolcetto can be excellent-value reds, gushing with soft, easy-drinking fruit.

√ *Clerico* • *Corino* • *Marchesi di Gresy* • *Marcarini* • *Luciano Sandrone*

DOLCETTO D'ACQUI DOC
Piedmont

Dolcetto is a plump grape with a low acid content that is traditionally used to make cheerful, Beaujolais-type wines that are deep purple in colour and best enjoyed young.

⌛ 1–3 years

√ *Viticoltori dell'Acquese* • *Villa Banficut*

DOLCETTO D'ALBA DOC
Piedmont

Dolcetto d'Alba DOC produces some soft, smooth, juicy wines that should be drunk while they are young, fresh, and fruity.

⌛ 1–3 years

√ *Elio Altare* • *Azelia* • *Batasiolo* • *Fratelli Brovia* • *Ceretto* • *Pio Cesare* • *Fratelli Cigliuti* • *Aldo Conterno* • *Cascina Drago* • *Franco Fiorina* • *Elio Grasso* • *Bartolo Mascarello* • *Pira* • *Roberto Voerzio*

DOLCETTO D'ASTI DOC
Piedmont

These wines are lighter than Dolcetto d'Alba.

DOLCETTO DELLE LANGHE MONREGALESI DOC
Piedmont

Rare wines produced in tiny quantities, reputed to have an exceptionally fine aroma.

DOLCETTO DI DIANO D'ALBA or DIANO D'ALBA DOC
Piedmont

Diano is a hilltop village just south of Alba, which produces wines that are slightly fuller and more grapey than most other Dolcetto wines.

⌛ 3–5 years

√ *Alario* • *Casavecchia* • *Colué* • *Fontanafredda* • *Giuseppe Mascarello* • *Cantina della Porta Rossa* • *Mario Savigliano* • *Veglio & Figlio*

DOLCETTO DI DOGLIANI DOC
Piedmont

Most Dolcetto from Dogliani used to be made to drink young, fresh, and fruity, but more is now being made in a *vin de garde* style. The best of such wines attain a lovely perfumed finesse with a few years in bottle.

√ *Chionetti* • *Luigi Einaudi* • *Angelo Gaja* • *Pira* • *Roberto Voerzio*

DOLCETTO DI OVADA DOC
Piedmont

These are the fullest and firmest of Dolcettos.

⌛ 3–6 years (up to 10 for the very best)

√ *Cascina Scarsi Olivi*

DOLCETTO-NEBBIOLO
Piedmont

When backed up by full, firm Nebbiolo, the soft, lush fruit of Dolcetto remains remarkably fresh for considerable time in bottle.

√ *Cascina Drago* (Bricco del Drago, especially Vigna le Mace)

DONNAZ or DONNAS DOC
Valle d'Aosta

Formerly its own DOC, but now a sub-appellation of the Valle d'Aosta DOC, Donnaz produces soft, well-balanced Nebbiolo-based red wines with a pleasant, slightly bitter aftertaste. *See also* Valle d'Aosta DOC.

ENFER D'ARVIER DOC
Valle d'Aosta

Formerly its own DOC, but now a sub-appellation of the regional Valle d'Aosta DOC, Enfer d'Arvier is a low-key, medium-bodied red wine made primarily from the Petit rouge grape, although Dolcetto, Gamay, Neyret, Pinot noir, and Vien de Nus may also be used. *See also* Valle d'Aosta DOC.

ERBALUCE DI CALUSO or CALUSO DOC
Piedmont

These are fresh, dry, light-bodied white wines made from the Erbaluce, which is a rather undistinguished grape. A far more interesting *passito* version exists and it is probably this that gave Erbaluce its overrated, albeit localized, reputation. *See also* Caluso Passito DOC.

⌛ 1–3 years

√ *Luigi Ferrando*

FARA DOC
Piedmont

In the hands of someone like Dessilani, Fara DOC proves to be an underrated, enjoyable, Nebbiolo-based wine with lots of fruit combined with a spicy-scented character.

√ *Luigi Dessilani* (Caramino)

FAVORITA
Piedmont

Descended from the Vermentino, this was once a popular table grape, but now makes dry, crisp white *vini da tavola* and, since 1995, DOC Langhe Favorita. The best varietal wines have a delicate floral aroma and refreshing acidity.

FLÉTRI
Valle d'Aosta

In this bilingual region, the French *flétri*, which means "shrivelled", may be used in preference to the Italian *passito*.

FRANCIACORTA DOCG
Lombardy

The sparkling white and rosé wines made by Franciacorta were promoted to DOC status in September 1995. Produced by the *méthode champenoise*, with 25 months ageing on the lees (or 37 if *riserva*), Franciacorta had already shown its potential for producing fine, biscuity, *brut*, and lightly rich style rosé sparkling wines when this book was first published. It not only deserves its prestigious classification, it is an object lesson for the rest of the Italian wine industry for two reasons. Firstly, the still wines have retained their former DOC status (*see* Terre di Franciacorta DOC), making it one of Italy's more prestigious appellations. Meanwhile the selection of only sparkling wines for DOCG enhances this new classification, whereas promoting an entire DOC devalues it. Not every region has a super-category to promote as Franciacorta has, but others could, for example, restrict production to the original *classico* area and a reduced yield. This would result in both a DOC and DOCG for the same region and, in the mind of the consumer, it would ensure that the "G" did guarantee an elevated quality equivalent to *Grand Cru*, for example. The second lesson is that as the first Italian wine to insist on bottle-fermentation, Franciacorta is currently the only Italian dry sparkling-wine appellation that can demand respect from the rest of the world. *See* Terre di Franciacorta DOC for still wines.

⌛— 2–5 years

✓ *Banfi • Bellavista • Fratelli Berlucchi • Bersi Serlini • Ca del'Bosco • Bredasole • Castelfaglia • Tenuta Castellino • Casteveder • Cavalleri • Cola • Ricci Curbastro • Faccoli • Lantieri de Paratico • Majolini • La Montina • Barone Pizzini • Lo Sparviere • Villa*

FREISA
Piedmont

The Freisa is a black grape of refreshing acidity, which makes ruby-red wines with characteristic raspberry and rose-petal aromas for early drinking. Non-DOC wines abound, particularly around Alba, where this variety excels in quality, despite the lack of official recognition.

✓ *Clerico • Aldo Conterno • Coppo*

FREISA D'ASTI DOC
Piedmont

Known for centuries, and a favourite of King Victor Emmanuel, this is the original and most famous Freisa. These fruity red wines may be made fully sparkling, *fizzante*, or still, and in both dry and sweet styles.

FREISA DI CHIERI DOC
Piedmont

Freisa di Chieri produces the same styles of wine as Freisa d'Asti from just outside Turin.

FUMIN
Valle d'Aosta

Very little is known about this grape, which is usually blended with others but occasionally makes a robust red on its own under the Valle d'Aosta DOC or as a *vino da tavola*.

GABIANO DOC
Piedmont

The full-bodied, red Barbera wines of Castello di Gabiano seemed to make this a promising DOC, but the appellation has not taken off and these wines are seldom encountered.

GAMAY
Valle d'Aosta

The non-DOC wines of Gamay are light-bodied with an attenuated earthy fruitiness.

GAMAY-PINOT NERO
Valle d'Aosta

A light and fruity *passetoutgrains* style.

GATTINARA DOCG
Piedmont

From Nebbiolo and up to ten per cent Bonarda grown on the right bank of the river Sesia in northern Piedmont, Gattinara can be a fine, though not a great, wine, especially now that overcropping problems have been reduced since Gattinara attained DOCG status. When young, the fruit can be chunky and rustic when compared with Barbaresco or Barolo, but the best Gattinara wines develop a fine, silky-textured flavour and a graceful, violet-perfumed finesse when mature. Gattinara earned its DOC and then full DOCG status through the almost single-handed efforts of Mario Antoniolo, whose wines have always been among the greatest produced in the area. Others have followed his example, but have been too few and too slow to give Gattinara the sort of reputation that a world-class wine appellation ought to have.

⌛— 6–15 years

✓ *Mario Antoniolo • Le Colline • Travaglini*

GAVI *or* CORTESE DI GAVI DOC
Piedmont

The quality and character of these highly fashionable wines is very uneven, although prices are uniformly high. At best, they are soft-textured, dry white wines with a slight *frizzantino* when young, and can develop a honey-rich flavour after a couple of years in bottle. Too many examples have all their character fermented out at low temperatures, which gives them an amylic peardrop aroma, and some are definitely *frizzante*.

⌛— 2–3 years

✓ *Nicola Bergaglio • Chiarlo* (Fior di Rovere) *• Carlo Deltetto • La Scolca*

GHEMME DOC
Piedmont

A Nebbiolo-based wine produced on the bank opposite Gattinara, Ghemme is usually seen as the inferior of the two appellations, but it has never been as persistently overcropped and is generally more consistent. Although not capable of reaching the heights of Antoniolo's Gattinara, for example, most Ghemme has just as much colour, body, and flavour as Gattinara in general, and starts off with a much finer bouquet and more elegant fruit. In addition to Nebbiolo, Vespolina and Bonarda may be used.

⌛— 4–15 years

✓ *Antichi Vignetti di Cantelupo • Le Colline • Luigi Dessilani*

GRIGNOLINO D'ASTI DOC
Piedmont

Grignolino d'Asti DOC produces lightly tannic red wines with a slightly bitter aftertaste.

GRIGNOLINO DEL MONFERRATO CASALESE DOC
Piedmont

These are light, crisp, fresh red wines made from Grignolino around the Casale Monferrato.

GRUMELLO DOC
Lombardy
See Valtellina Superiore DOC

INFERNO DOC
Lombardy
See Valtellina Superiore DOC

LAMBRUSCO MANTOVANO DOC
Lombardy

Not all Lambrusco comes from Emilia-Romagna. This one is produced just across the border on the plains of Mantua (Mantova). Formerly a *vino da tavola*, Mantovano is red and *frizzante* with a pink foam and may be dry or sweet.

⌛— Upon purchase

✓ *CS di Quistello*

LANGHE DOC
Piedmont

This area overlaps the DOCs Barbaresco, Barolo, Nebbiolo d'Alba, Dolcetto d'Alba, and Barbera d'Alba and, if used sensibly, through selection, could ensure the highest quality in those wines. White, red, and six varietal wines are permitted: Dolcetto, Freisa, and Nebbiolo for red; and Arneis, Favorita, and Chardonnay for white.

✓ *Chionetti • Aldo Conterno • Giuseppe Mascarello*

LESSONA DOC
Piedmont

These are red wines that can be delightfully scented, with rich fruit and some finesse.

LOAZZOLO DOC
Piedmont

From the village of Loazzolo, south of Canelli, this Moscato *passito* is aged for two years, including six months in *barriques*, to produce a golden-hued, richly-flavoured, lusciously-textured, exotically sweet wine. A wine that can age, but which is best drunk young.

⌛— 2–4 years

✓ *Borgo Maragliano • Borgo Sambui • Bricchi Mej • Giancarlo Scaglione*

LUGANA DOC
Lombardy

These are soft, smooth, dry white wines made from Trebbiano grown on the shores of Lake Garda, slightly overlapping Veneto in northeast Italy. There are many dullards, but the very best Lugana manage to transcend the lacklustre level normally expected from this grape variety.

⌛— 1–2 years

✓ *Cà dei Frati • Visconti*

MALVASIA
Lombardy
In many instances Malvasia, Malvoisie, and Pinot gris are the same variety of grape, but the Malvasia of Lombardy is the true Malvasia and a very different grape from the Malvoisie of Valle d'Aosta. A dark-skinned grape, Malvasia makes both red and white wines, still and sparkling, dry and sweet, and, most puzzling of all, full- and light-bodied, and neutral and aromatic.

✓ *La Muiraghina*

MALVASIA DI CASORZO D'ASTI DOC
Piedmont
These are lightly aromatic, sweet, red, and rosé wines that may also be sparkling.

🍷— 1–2 years

✓ *Bricco Mondalino*

MALVASIA DI CASTELNUOVO DON BOSCO DOC
Piedmont
The DOC of Malvasia di Castelnuovo Don Bosco produces attractive, lightly aromatic, sweet, red, still, and sparkling wines.

🍷— 1–2 years

✓ *Bava*

MALVOISIE
Valle d'Aosta
The Malvoisie of Valle d'Aosta is in fact Pinot gris, not Malvasia, and its dry, semi-sweet, and *passito* wines are, though not at all spicy, smooth and usually slightly bitter in both DOC and *vino da tavola* versions.

MONFERRATO DOC
Piedmont
This is a relatively new DOC, which was introduced in 1995 for red, white, and *ciaret* or *chiaretto* (rosé) Dolcetto, Casalese, and Freisa from a wide area overlapping the Asti region.

MORGEX ET LA SALLE DOC
Valle d'Aosta
A sub-appellation of the regional Valle d'Aosta DOC, the vineyards of these two communes reach as high as 1,300 metres (4,265 feet), which makes it one of the highest wine-growing areas in Europe. However, most vines in these two villages are grown between 900 and 1,000 metres (2,952–3,280 feet), although even this is remarkable as, in theory, grapes do not ripen above 800 metres (2,625 feet) in the Valle d'Aosta. However, in practice they ripen, and produce a fine, dry, *frizzantino* white. Brut, Extra Brut, and Demi Sec *spumante* versions are also made. *See also* Valle d'Aosta DOC.

🍷— 1–3 years

✓ *Alberto Vevey*

MOSCATO
Lombardy and Piedmont
Good non-DOC is made in Lombardy and the Moscato di Scanzo is undoubtedly the best. In the Piedmont, non-DOC Moscato is prolific in many styles and formats, and even a crisp, dry version to challenge Alsace is available from Alasia (an alliance between the flying winemaker Martin Shaw and the Araldica consortium of cooperatives).

✓ **Lombardy** *Celinate Ronchello* • *Il Cipresso* • *La Cornasella*
Piedmont *Alasia* (especially Muscaté Sec)

MOSCATO D'ASTI DOCG
Piedmont
Wines similar in flavour to Asti, but with a minimum pressure of three atmospheres, as opposed to five. Still, slightly *frizzantino*, and positively *frizzante* examples of Moscato d'Asti exist. Those with some degree of effervescence are bottled without any *dosage*, while the first fermentation is still underway, as opposed to Asti plain and simple, which is made by the *cuve close* method. Compared to Asti, Moscato d'Asti is generally, though not necessarily, less alcoholic (5.5 to 8 per cent instead of 7.5 to 9 per cent) and almost always much sweeter. If there is any criticism of this luscious, heavenly nectar, it is the unfortunate trend to make these wines fizzier, as there is often little difference between modern Moscato d'Asti and Asti itself. Rarely does one find a still Moscato d'Asti with the barest prickle, as in the past. That said, this is the Asti DOC to pick. As there are less than 3 million bottles as opposed to 85 million Asti, it is more expensive, and the best, such as Borgo Maragliano's La Caliera, which is in a completely different class from the rest, are definitely fine.

🍷— Upon purchase

✓ *Araldica* • *Castello Banfi* • *Alfiero Boffa* • *Borgo Maragliano* • *Redento Dogliotti* • *Gatti* • *Marchese di Gresy* • *Villa Lanata* • *Luciana Rivella* • *La Spinetta-Rivetti*

NEBBIOLO
Piedmont
Most *vini da tavola* from this grape are relatively simple red wines, as the best areas for Nebbiolo have long been known and have become famous DOCGs. Exceptionally fine examples have, however, been made in great years by the best Barolo and Barbaresco producers. It remains to be seen whether or not they will continue to do so now that they also have the choice of Nebbiolo d'Alba and Langhe Nebbiolo DOCs through which to sell such wines.

✓ *Elio Altare* • *Clerico* (Arté) • *Corino* • *Cascina Drago* • *I Paglieri* (Opera Prima)

NEBBIOLO-BARBERA
Piedmont
A strikingly successful *vino da tavola* blend that takes to *barrique*-ageing like a duck to water, producing delicious yet classy red wines with plump, juicy fruit, held together by supple tannins and a touch of smoky-oak. Some wines, such as Conterno Fantino's Monprà, contain more Barbera than Nebbiolo. *See also* Petit rouge.

✓ *Giacomo Ascheri* (Bric Milieu) • *Chiarlo* (Barilot) • *Valentino Migliorini* (Bricco Manzoni) • *Conterno Fantino* (Monprà) • *Vietti* (Fioretto) • *Roberto Voerzio* (Vignaserra) • *Oriou* (Valle d'Aosta)

NEBBIOLO D'ALBA DOC
Piedmont

Pure Nebbiolo wines come from between Barolo and Barbaresco. Most are fine, full, rich, and fruity. Sweet and sparkling versions are allowed.

🍷— 4–10 years

✓ *Ascheri* • *Tenuta Carretta* • *Ceretto* • *Pio Cesare* • *Aldo Conterno* • *Giacomo Conterno* • *Franco Fiorina* • *Angelo Gaja* • *Bruno Giacosa* • *Giuseppe Mascarello* • *Vietti*

NUS DOC
Valle d'Aosta
A sub-appellation of the Valle d'Aosta DOC, Nus makes an interesting red from Vien de Nus, Petit rouge, and Pinot noir grapes. Dry and *passito* styles of white wine are made from Pinot gris or Malvoisie de Nus. *See also* Valle d'Aosta DOC.

🍷— 2–4 years

✓ *La Crotta di Vegneron*

OLTREPÒ PAVESE DOC
Lombardy
The Oltrepò Pavese covers 42 communes south of the river Po, although much of the production is not marketed under this DOC, but sold to specialist wineries in Piedmont. These wineries turn it into non-DOC *spumante* by the *cuve close* process or the *méthode champenoise*. There

used to be three geographical sub-appellations, but Barbacarlo has since been recognized as the exclusive product of Lino Maga, reverting to *vino da tavola* status. The two remaining sub-appellations are **Oltrepò Pavese Buttafuoco** ("sparks of fire"), a deep-coloured, fruity, dry or semi-sweet *frizzante* red; and **Oltrepò Pavese Sangue di Giuda** (charmingly named "blood of Judas"), a soft, sweet, red *spumante*. Both wines are restricted to vineyards around the villages of Broni, Canetto Pavese, Castana, Cigognola, Montescano, Pietra de Giorgi, and Stradella. Apart from blended red, white, and rosé wines, Oltrepò Pavese permits eight varietal wines: Barbera, Bonarda (made from Croatina), and Pinot noir (still and *spumante*) for red; and Cortese, Moscato (still, *spumante* and *liquoroso*), Pinot gris, and Riesling (which may unfortunately contain anything up to 100 per cent Welschriesling) for white.

🍷— 1–3 years (white, rosé, and sparkling)
2–5 years (red)

✓ *Giacomo Agnes* • *Angelo Ballabio* • *Bianchina Alberici* • *Doria* (Pinot nero) • *Lino Maga* (*see also* Barbacarlo) • *Monsupello* • *Piccolo Bacco dei Quaroni* • *Tronconero* (Bonarda) • *Zonin* (Moscato *spumante*)

ORMEASCO
Liguria
Ormeasco is the local Ligurian variant of Dolcetto, which can produce some deliciously easy-to-drink, soft fruity red wines.

PETIT ROUGE
Valle d'Aosta

Deep, dark, and highly perfumed red wines from this low-yielding, local grape that can be met within both DOC and *vino da tavola* versions. There are many variants in the family of Petit rouge, but they can all be traced back to the Oriou, which may in future be used for its varietal wines. Moves have been underway since the early 1990s to change the name of the Petit rouge grape to Oriou owing to the belittling effect of *petit* in its name, even though this refers to the size of berry, not the quality of wine, and most classic varieties have smaller, rather than larger, grapes and this should thus be seen as a positive attribute.

PIEMONTE DOC
Piedmont

Introduced in 1995, this DOC embraces all the other DOC areas in the Piedmont and, with the exception of Piemonte Moscato and Piemonte Moscato Passito, which must be made from 100 per cent Moscato grapes, all wines claiming this appellation are required to contain at least 85 per cent of the variety indicated. Permitted red wine varietals are Barbera, Bonarda, Brachetto, Dolcetto, and Pinot noir, while in addition to the Moscato wines already mentioned above, white varietals include Cortese, Pinot blanc, and Pinot gris. The creation of this regional DOC probably explains why no IGT wines have been declared in the Piedmont, and it is doubtful whether any IGT will be in the future.

PINOT NERO
Lombardy

Most Pinot noir grown in northwest Italy goes into classic *brut spumante* wines. Still wines are made under the Oltrepò Pavese denomination (Doria being outstanding) and a small number of non-DOC examples are to be found. The two wines listed below are *barrique*-aged, and are exceptionally fine in quality.

√ *Ca' del Bosco* • *Tenuta Mazzolino*

PREMETTA
Valle d'Aosta

Lightly tannic, bright cherry-red wines from this local grape, Premetta, can be encountered in both DOC and *vino da tavola* versions.

RIVIERA DEL GARDA BRESCIANO *or* GARDA BRESCIANO DOC
Lombardy

This area makes light, fruity, slightly bitter red wines that are no more interesting than the bulk of Valpolicella, produced on the opposite bank of Lake Garda. Most are blended from Gropello, Sangiovese, Marzemino, and Barbera, but some are pure varietal wines from the Gropello grape and these tend to be superior. Although the whites may be pure Riesling, this is taken to mean either Riesling Renano, which is true Riesling, or Riesling Italico, which is not. Furthermore, as up to 20 per cent of other local grape varieties may be used, Garda Bresciano *bianco* has not been of much interest so far. The most successful wine here has been the rosé, or *chiaretto*, which, although it is made from exactly the same varieties as the *rosso*, can be much softer and easier to drink.

⌲ Upon purchase

√ *Costaripa*

RIVIERA LIGURE DI PONENTE DOC
Liguria

Four former *vini da tavola* are grouped together under this appellation, which covers the western riviera of Liguria. These are: *Ormeasco*, bright, cherry-red wines with juicy, raspberry, Dolcetto fruit; *Pigato*, full-flavoured yet somewhat precocious red wines; *Rossese*, well-scented, characterful reds; and *Vermentino*, rich, full, and characterful dry white wines.

ROERO DOC
Piedmont

This DOC covers light-bodied, easy-drinking, inexpensive Nebbiolo reds and the highly regarded, highly priced Arneis whites from the Roeri hills north of Alba. *See* Arneis di Roero.

⌲ 1–2 years

√ *Carlo Deltetto*

ROSSESE DI DOLCEACQUA *or* DOLCEACQUA DOC
Liguria

This DOC produces light, easy-drinking red wines that are capable of rich, lush fruit, a soft texture, and spicy-aromatic aftertaste.

⌲ 1–4 years

√ *Giobatta Cane* • *Lupi* • *Antonio Perrino*

RUBINO DI CANTAVENNA DOC
Piedmont

A full-bodied red wine blend of mostly Barbera, Grignolino, and sometimes Freisa. It is made by a *cooperativa* called Rubino, which was solely responsible for creating this appellation, but failed to interest other producers. As a result, the DOC has not taken off.

RUCHÉ
Piedmont

The Ruché is a rather mysterious grape of unknown origin that generally makes a light ruby-coloured wine with an aromatic twist, although through reduced yields much darker weightier, richer wines can be achieved

√ *Scarpa*

RUCHÉ DI CASTAGNOLE MONFERRATO DOC
Piedmont

When grown on the vineyards overlooking Castagnole Monferrato, the Ruché grape is supposed to produce an aromatic red wine that ages like Nebbiolo. Up to ten per cent Barbera and Brachetto may be used in production.

⌲ 3–5 years

√ *Piero Bruno* • *Ruché del Parrocco*

SAN COLOMBANO AL LAMBRO *or* SAN COLOMBANO DOC
Lombardy

Rich, robust, if somewhat rustic red wine made from Croatina, Barbera, and Uva rara are produced by this DOC. San Colombano is the only DOC in the Milan province.

⌲ 2–5 years

√ *Carlo Pietrasanta*

SAN MARTINO DELLA BATTAGLIA DOC
Lombardy

Dry, full-flavoured white wine with a flowery aroma and slightly bitter aftertaste, and a sweet, *liquoroso* wine, made from the Tocai Friulano.

SANGUE DI GIUDA DOC
See Oltrepò Pavese DOC

SASSELLA DOC
Lombardy
See Valtellina Superiore DOC

SAUVIGNON BLANC
Piedmont

These wines are virtually unknown in the region, although the soil and climate seem favourable. Angelo Gaja's *barrique*-aged pure Sauvignon Alteni di Brassica, in particular, shows potential.

√ *Angelo Gaga* (Alteni di Brassica)

SIZZANO DOC
Piedmont

These are good, full-bodied red wines that are produced from a Gattinara-like blend on a bank of the river Sesia, just south of Ghemme.

SPANNA
Piedmont

The local name for the Nebbiolo, Spanna merely represents the most basic wines from this grape variety, although in the hands of some specialists it can surpass many generic Barolo and Barbaresco.

√ *Luciano Brigatti* • *Villa Era*

SYRAH
Valle d'Aosta

The Institut Agricol Régional has produced very interesting *barrique* wine from this grape, the Syrah, since the late 1980s.

TERRE DI FRANCIACORTA DOC
Lombardy

Part of the original Franciacorta appellation since 1967, the still wines were renamed Terre di Franciacorta in 1995 when the name in its singular form, Terra di Franciacorta, was reserved for the newly created DOCG. Produced northeast of Milan, on hilly slopes near Lake Iseo, the red wines are typically well coloured, medium- to full-bodied, made from Cabernet franc and Cabernet sauvignon, with the possible addition of Barbera, Nebbiolo, and Merlot. Many are richly flavoured with good fruit and show some finesse. The dry white wines, primarily from Chardonnay with a little Pinot blanc permissible, have improved tremendously.

⌲ 3–8 years (red), 1–3 years (white)

√ *Enrico Gatti* • *Longhi-de Carli* • *Ragnoli*

TIMORASSO
Piedmont

Tipped by some to be the next trendy white grape variety, Timorasso has until now been confined to *vini da tavola* and *grappa*, with more emphasis definitely on the latter. Walter Massa in the upper Val Curone was the first to produce a varietal wine from Timorasso, almost by accident it would seem, when a *grappa* producer by the name of Antonella Bocchino became curious about this grape. She had seen it mentioned in 19th-century documents, but it was thought to be extinct until she tracked down a surviving plot on Massa's estate. As Bocchino was interested in making only *grappa* with the pressings, Massa was left with the wine on his hands and it turned out to be more than just a curiosity. Massa has supplied other estates with cuttings and several producers now make Timorasso, a varietal that could follow on the success of Gavi and Arneis.

TORRETTE DOC
Valle d'Aosta

A red-only sub-appellation of the regional Valle d'Aosta DOC, Torrette produces deep-coloured wines of good bouquet and body from the Petit rouge, plus up to 30 per cent Dolcetto, Fumin, Gamay, Mayolet, Pinot noir, Premetta, and Vien de Nus. *See also* Valle d'Aosta DOC.

✓ *Elio Cassol • Grosjean*

VALCALEPIO DOC
Lombardy

An up-and-coming appellation for well-coloured, deeply flavoured red wines made from a blend of Merlot and Cabernet sauvignon, and for light, delicately dry white wines made from Pinot blanc and Pinot gris.

🍷— 1–3 years (white), 3–7 years (red)

✓ *Tenuta Castello*

VALLE D'AOSTA *or* VALLÉE D'AOSTE DOC
Valle d'Aosta

A regional DOC encompassing 20 different styles of wine, Valle d'Aosta took under its wings the only two DOCs formerly recognized in the region: Donnaz and Enfer d'Arvier. These are now two of the seven sub-appellations within this DOC, the other five being Arnad-Montjovat, Chambave, Morgex et La Salle, Nus, and Torrette (*see* individual entries). The Valle d'Aosta DOC has revitalized this region's tiny production of somewhat low-key wines. Apart from blended red, white, and rosé, the following varietal wines are permitted: Fumin, Gamay, Nebbiolo, Petit rouge, Pinot noir, and Premetta for reds; and Chardonnay, Müller-Thurgau, Petit arvine, and Pinot gris for whites. There is also a Bianco de Pinot noir, which you might see labelled as a Blanc de Noir de Pinot Noir, as all Valle d'Aosta wines have official alternative French designations.

🍷— 1–3 years

✓ *Grosjean • La Crotta di Vegneron*

VALGELLA DOC
Lombardy
See Valtellina Superiore DOC

VALTELLINA DOC
Lombardy

Encompasses 19 communes of the province of Sondrio in Lombardy. Most products are light-scented, medium-bodied red wines of simple, although often pleasing, character. Many critics believe Valtellina to be grossly overrated, and the basic *appellatino* certainly is, but the truly fine wines are virtually all classified as Valtellina Superiore. *See also* Valtellina Superiore DOC.

VALTELLINA SUPERIORE DOC
Lombardy

The best wines of Valtellina are produced from a narrow strip of vineyards on the north bank of the river Adda near the Swiss border, and must contain a minimum of 12 per cent alcohol, as opposed to the 11 per cent required for Valtellina. Most of the wines come from four sub-districts: **Grumello** (the lightest), **Inferno** (supposedly the hottest, rockiest part of the valley), **Sassella** (the best), and **Valgella** (the most productive but least interesting). Essentially a Nebbiolo, but up to five per cent Pinot noir, Merlot, Rossola, Brugnola, and Pignola Valtellina may also be used. The richness of the best of these wines is belied by their elegance. They have good colour and are capable of developing exquisite finesse after several years in bottle. *Sfursat* or *Sforzato*, which literally means "strained" and is made from shrivelled grapes, is a dry, concentrated red wine that has a minimum of 14.5 per cent alcohol (try Nino Negri's), which makes it the equivalent of *amarone*.

🍷— 5–15 years

✓ *Enologica Valtellinese • Sandro Fay • Fondazione Fojanini • Nino Negri • Conti Sertoli-Salis • Fratelli Triacca*

VIEN DE NUS
Valle d'Aosta

A very similar grape to the Petit rouge, but whereas the Petit rouge is widely planted throughout the Valle d'Aosta, cultivation of the Vien de Nus is restricted to the vineyards around Nus itself.

VIN DE CONSEIL
Valle d'Aosta

Perfumed dry white made by the Institut Agricol Régional from Petite arvine.

NEW IGT WINES

The following Indicazioni Geografiche Tipiche wines were agreed at the end of 1996, but we have yet to see what style, quality, or consistency each one will establish:

Liguria *Colli Savonesi • Golfo del Tiguillio • Val Polcevera*

Lombardy *Alto Mincio • Benaco Bresciano • Bergamasca • Colina del Milanese • Quistello • Ronchi di Brescia • Sabbioneta • Sebino • Terrazze Retiche di Sondrio*

Piedmont *none*

Valle d'Aosta *none*

SPRINGTIME AT MORGEX, VALLE D'AOSTA
Grown at more than 900 metres (3,000 feet), these vines annually disprove the theory that grapes should not ripen above 800 metres (2,600 feet) in the Valle d'Aosta.

NORTHEAST ITALY

Freshness, crisp acidity, and purity of varietal character personify the wines of the northeastern regions of Trentino-Alto Adige, Friuli-Venezia Giulia, and the Veneto, but beware the mass-produced wines, which are so clean and pure that they lack any fruit.

THIS IS A MORE MOUNTAINOUS area than the Northwest (with the exception of that region's Valle d'Aosta), as just over half the land is occupied by the Dolomites and their precipitous foothills. Some of the finest wines are grown in the lush, verdant vineyards of the South Tyrol in the Alto Adige, just over the border from Austria. A great deal of wine is exported; the bulk of it is unexciting Soave and Valpolicella. Locally there is much greater variety and value to be had – a number of French and German grapes are grown in addition to fascinating local varieties, and dedicated producers continue to experiment. Austria to the north and Slovenia to the east have influenced the styles produced.

NORTHEAST ITALY, *see also p.307*
The variety of sites offered by the mountains and the hills of this area enables many grape varieties to be grown in addition to local ones. The most exciting wines come from the high vineyards of the South Tyrol, the hills of Friuli, and around Vicenza in the Veneto.

TERMENO VINEYARDS, ALTO ADIGE
The town of Termeno, or Tramin as it is also called, is situated between Bolzano and Trento, in the Alto Adige region. This is where the Traminer Aromatico, or Gewürztraminer, is supposed to have originated, but the local clone is far more restrained than the classic Alsace version, with hardly any spice to its character.

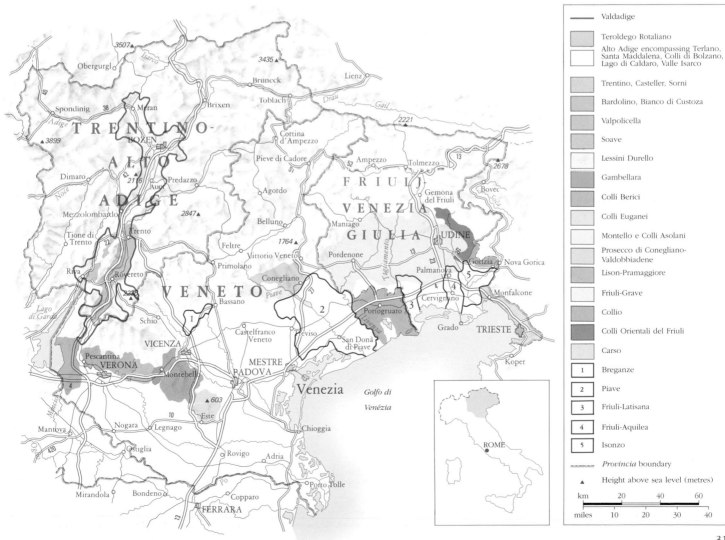

AVERAGE ANNUAL PRODUCTION

REGION	DOC PRODUCTION	TOTAL PRODUCTION
Veneto	1.5 million hl (17 million cases)	10 million hl (110 million cases)
Trentino-Alto Adige	700,000 hl (8 million cases)	1.5 million hl (17 million cases)
Friuli-Venezia Giulia	420,000 hl (5 million cases)	1.6 million hl (18 million cases)

Percentage of total Italian production: Veneto, 13%;
Trentino-Alto Adige, 2%; Friuli-Venezia Giulia, 1.5%.

TRENTINO-ALTO ADIGE

This is the most westerly and spectacular of the Northeast's three regions, and more than 90 per cent of its area is covered by mountainous countryside. It is made up of two autonomous provinces, the Italian-speaking Trento in the south and the German-speaking Bolzano, or South Tyrol, in the north. In the Bolzano the wines may possess alternative German names and can carry a QbA (*Qualitätswein Bestimmter Anbaugebiete*) designation. The generic Alto Adige DOC (Südtiroler QbA) is remarkably good and accounts for one-third of the region's total DOC output. There are also numerous fine wines produced in these cool, high vineyards.

THE VENETO

The Veneto stretches from the river Po to the Austrian border, between Trentino-Alto Adige to the west and Friuli-Venezia Giulia to the east, and most of the wines are grown on alluvial plains in the south. Once famous, but more recently infamous, for its Valpolicella and Soave, the Veneto is also one of the most exciting hunting grounds for some of Italy's best Bordeaux-type blends and there are signs that even the aforementioned abused wine names are beginning to regain a little of their former respectability.

FRIULI-VENEZIA GIULIA

Situated in the northeastern corner of Italy, this predominantly mountainous region has grown many non-Italian varieties since *phylloxera* wiped out its vineyards in the late 19th century. The naturally innovative Friulians (and South Tyrolians) used the opportunity to replant their vineyards with several better-quality foreign grape varieties, starting with the Merlot, which was brought to this region by Senator Pecile and Count Savorgnan in 1880. Over the last 100 years, the northeast has consistently demonstrated that the use of superior grape varieties and relatively lower yields can produce wines of dramatically improved quality.

BARDOLINO VINEYARDS
Ripening grapes adorn rows of vines in the Veneto's Bardolino area, which has a good reputation for light, dry-red, and rosé wines.

Friuli is the home of some of the country's finest wines, including many of its most complex Cabernet blends. Girolamo Dorigo's Montsclapade, which is the best of an exceptionally fine group of wines, is a typically Friulian blend of both Cabernets, Merlot, and Malbec. It is rare to find the Malbec variety on this side of the Alps, but it fares well in Friuli and might well be the key to the complexity of these wines. A few rather unconventional blends are found, the most unusual being Abbazia di Rosazzo's multi-national Ronco dei Roseti, which mixes the four Bordeaux varieties with the German Limberger, the Italian Refosco, and the obscure Tazzelenghe. Another Abbazia di Rosazzo wine, Ronco delle Acacie, is a rare masterpiece in the new Italian school of "super-deluxe" *vini da tavola* white wines – a category of dry white Italian wine that is expensive but mostly disappointing.

The largest volume of fine wines produced in the northeast comes from Colli Orientali del Friuli, one of Friuli's two *colli*, or "hilly" areas. This one is situated close to the former Yugoslav border and encompasses many varietal wines. These wines are well worth looking out for – with the exception of the Picolit, which is a grossly overrated and horrendously overpriced sweet wine wherever it comes from. The Picolit produced in Colli Orientali del Friuli is the only one in Italy to have DOC status, but, in fact, the wine is no better than other examples to be found throughout the country.

FACTORS AFFECTING TASTE AND QUALITY

LOCATION
The northeast of Italy is bounded by the Dolomites to the north and the Adriatic Sea to the south.

CLIMATE
Similar to the Northwest in that summers are hot and winters cold and harsh, but fog is less of a problem and hail more frequent. There are unpredictable variations in the weather from year to year so vintages are important, particularly for red wines.

ASPECT
Vineyards are found on a variety of sites ranging from the steep, mountainous slopes of Trentino-Alto Adige to the flat, alluvial plains of the Veneto and Friuli-Venezia Giulia. The best vineyards are always sited in hilly countryside.

SOIL
Most vineyards are on glacial moraine – a gritty mixture of sand, gravel, and sediment deposited during the Ice Age. Most are clayey or sandy clay and the best sites are often marly and rich in calcium. The light, stony soil in the South Tyrol is rapidly leached by weathering and fertilizers have to be added annually.

VITICULTURE AND VINIFICATION
The Northeast has led Italy's move towards more modern vinification techniques and experimentation with foreign grape varieties. It was the first area to use cold fermentation and, initially, the wines produced were so clean that they lacked natural character. There is now much experimentation into how to increase intensity of flavour through the use of new oak.

GRAPE VARIETIES
Blauer Portugieser (*syn.* Portoghese), Cabernet franc, Cabernet sauvignon, Chardonnay, Cortese (*syn.* Bianca fernanda), Corvina (*syn.* Corvinone or Cruina), Durello, Fraconia (*syn.* Limberger), Garganega, Gewürztraminer, Incrocio Manzoni 215 (*Prosecco* x *Cabernet sauvignon*), Incrocio Manzoni 6013 (*Riesling* x *Pinot blanc*), Kerner, Lagrein, Lambrusco a Foglia Frastagliata, Malbec, Malvasia, Marzemino, Merlot, Molinara (*syn.* Rossara or Rossanella), Mondeuse (*syn.* Refosco or Terrano), Muscat (*syn.* Moscato), Nosiola, Petit verdot, Picolit, Pinella, or Pinello, Pinot blanc (*syn.* Pinot bianco), Pinot gris (*syn.* Pinot grigio), Pinot noir (*syn.* Pinot nero), Prosecco (*syn.* Serprina or Serprino), Raboso (*syn.* Friularo), Ribolla, Riesling, Rossola (*syn.* Veltliner), Sauvignonasse (*syn.* Tocai Friulano), Sauvignon blanc, Schiava (*syn.* Vernatsch), Schioppettino, Tazzelenghe, Teroldego, Tocai, Ugni blanc (*syn.* Trebbiano), Verduzzo, Vespaiolo.

THE APPELLATIONS OF
NORTHEAST ITALY

THE BEST CLASSIC BRUT SPARKLING WINES

These wines all come from Trentino-Alto Adige and are made by the *méthode champenoise*.

- *Equipe 5 Brut Riserva* • *Equipe 5 Brut Rosé* • *Ferrari Brut* • *Ferrari Brut de Brut* • *Ferrari Brut Rosé* • *Ferrari Nature* • *Ferrari Riserva Giulio Ferrari* • *Methius Brut* • *Spagnolli Brut* • *Vivaldi Brut* • *Vivaldi Extra Brut*

ALTO ADIGE *or* SÜDTIROLER DOC

Trentino-Alto Adige

This generic appellation covers the entire Alto Adige, or South Tyrol, which is the northern half of the Valdadige DOC. It is remarkably consistent in terms of quality, considering that it represents more than a third of the region's total production. Where applicable, alternative German names are given in italics.

There are seven red-wine varietals: Cabernet covers either Cabernet Sauvignon or Cabernet Franc, or both, and ranges from simple, but delightful, everyday wines to deeper-coloured, fuller-bodied, richer wines that become warm, mellow, and spicy after five to ten years; Lagrein Scuro, or *Lagrein Dunkel*, is made from an underrated, indigenous grape and can have a fine, distinctive character and good colour; Malvasia, or *Malvasier*, is produced here as a red wine, although it would be better made into white or rosé; Merlot can be simply light and fruity or can attain greater heights, with a good spicy, sweet-pepper aroma and a fine, silky texture; Pinot Noir, or *Blauburgunder*, is a difficult varietal to perfect, but those from Mazzon are good and a speciality of this region (they will have Mazzoner on the label); Schiava, or *Vernatsch*, accounts for one in five bottles produced under this appellation and is the most popular tavern wine; Schiava Grigia, or *Grauervernatsch*, has recently been added to the list, as have two red-wine blends of Cabernet-Lagrein and Cabernet-Merlot.

There are no fewer than ten different white-wine varietals: Chardonnay can range from light and neutral to delicately fruity, and even *frizzantino* or verging upon *spumante* – the fuller versions can have recognizable varietal characteristics, but still lack the weight and intensity of flavour of even basic Burgundy; Moscato Giallo, or *Goldenmuskateller*, is made into delicious dessert wines; Pinot bianco, or *Weissburgunder*, is the most widely planted of all the white grape varieties and produces most of Alto Adige's finest white wines; Pinot grigio,

or *Ruländer*, is potentially as successful as Pinot blanc, but does not always occupy the best sites; Riesling Italico, or *Welschriesling*, is insignificant in both quantity and quality; Riesling Renano, or *Rheinriesling*, is fine, delicate, and attractive at the lowest level, but can be extraordinarily good in exceptional vintages; Riesling x Silvaner, or *Müller-Thurgau*, is relatively rare, which is a pity because it achieves a lively spiciness in this region; Sauvignon was very scarce in the early 1980s, but as the vogue for this grape spread so its cultivation increased and the crisp, dry, varietally pure Sauvignon is now one of the most successful wines of the Alto Adige; Silvaner is made mostly to be drunk young and fresh; Traminer Aromatico, or *Gewürztraminer*, is far more restrained than the classic Alsace version, even if, as some claim, the variety originated in the village of Tramin or Termeno, between Bolzano and Trento. If you can forget the full-blown spicy wine of Alsace, the delicate aroma and understated flavour of this wine can have a certain charm of its own.

Only three dry varietal *rosato*, or *Kretzer*, wines are allowed: Lagrein Rosato, or *Lagrein Kretzer*, is overtly fruity in a very round and smooth style; Merlot Rosato, or *Merlot Kretzer*, is a relatively recent addition and makes a curiously grassy or bell-pepper rosé; Pinot Nero Rosato, or *Blauburgunder Kretzer*, is more successful as a rosé than as a red.

Moscato Rosa, or *Rosenmuskateller*, are very flamboyant, deep-pink to scarlet-red, semi-sweet to sweet wines with an unusually high natural acidity, intense floral perfume, and an exaggerated Muscat flavour.

There is one sparkling-wine denomination for pure or blended Pinot blanc and/or Chardonnay with up to 30 per cent Pinot gris and Pinot noir, with both *cuve close* and *méthode champenoise* permissible.

In 1994 five former DOCs were incorporated into the Alto Adige, or Südtiroler, DOC as geographical sub-appellations. **Colli di Bolzano DOC**, or *Bozner Leiten*, for soft, fruity, early-drinking, Schiava-based red wines from the left bank of the Adige river, and both banks of the Isarco near Bolzano; **Meranese**, or **Meranese di Collina DOC**, or *Meraner Hügel*, from the hills around Merano, north of Bolzano, where the Schiava grape produces a light, delicately scented red wine, which may be labelled as Burgravito, or *Burggräfler*, if it comes from the part of the Meranese that was formerly part of the Contea di Tirol; **Santa Maddalena DOC**, or *Sankt Magdalener*, in the heart of the Colli di Bolzano (*see above*), where the Schiava-based red wines are just as soft and fruity, but fuller in body and smoother in texture – few Italian references today boast that Santa Maddalena was ranked by Mussolini (over-optimistically) as one of Italy's greatest wines; **Terlano DOC**, or *Terlaner*, which overlaps most of Caldaro DOC on the right bank of the Adige, running some 16 kilometres (10 miles) northwest of Bolzano to 24 kilometres (15 miles) south, and covers one blended, one *spumante*, and the following eight varietal white wines: Pinot Bianco (*Weissburgunder*), Chardonnay, Riesling Italico (*Welschriesling*), Riesling Renano (*Rheinriesling*), Silvaner, Müller-Thurgau, and Sauvignon; and, finally, **Valle Isarco DOC**, or *Eisacktaler*, which takes in both banks of the Isarco river from a few miles north of Bolzano

to just north of Bressanone, where the vineyards are high in altitude and the vines trained low to absorb ground heat. Six white-wine varietals are produced: Kerner, Müller-Thurgau, Pinot grigio, or *Ruländer*, Sylvaner, Traminer Aromatico, or *Gewürztraminer*, and Veltliner. Valle Isarco also includes a geographical blend called *Klausner Leitacher* for red wines from the villages of Chiusa (also known as *Klausen*), Barbiano, Velturno, and Villandro, which must be made from at least 60 per cent Schiava plus up to 40 per cent Portoghese and Lagrein. Furthermore, any Valle Isarco wine produced in Bressanone or Varna can be labelled "di Bressanone" or "*Brixner*".

🍷 2–10 years (red and rosé), 2–5 years (white), 1–3 years (sparkling)

✓ *Klosterkellerei Eisacktaler* • *Anton Gojer, Giorgio Grai* • *Klosterkellerei Muri Gries* • *Franz Haas* • *Josef Hofstätter* • *Kettmeir* • *Klosterkellerei Schreckbichl* • *Alois Lageder* • *Mazo Foradori* • *Stiftskellerei Neustift* • *Niedermayr* • *Heinrich Rottensteiner* • *San Michele* (Sanct Valentin) • *Santa Margherita* • *Schloss Rametz* • *Schloss Sallegg* • *Schloss Schwanburg* • *Tiefenbrunner* • *Wilhelm Walch* • *Baron Georg von Widmann*

AMARONE DELLA VALPOLICELLA *or* RECIOTO DELLA VALPOLICELLA AMARONE DOC

Veneto
See Valpolicella DOC

AQUILEA DOC

Friuli-Venezia Giulia
See Friuli-Aquilea DOC

BARDOLINO DOC

Veneto

Bardolino DOC produces dry, sometimes *frizzante*, red and rosé (*chiaretto*) wines from the southeastern shores of Lake Garda. The reds, made from Corvina, Molinara, and Negra, could be very interesting, but unfortunately most producers tend to make rather bland, lightweight wines.

🍷 1–3 years

✓ *Guerrieri-Rizzardi*

BIANCO DI CUSTOZA DOC
Veneto

Effectively the white wines of Bardolino, they can be scented with a smooth aftertaste and may sometimes be sparkling. Some critics compare Bianco di Custoza to Soave, which neatly sums up the quality. The grapes are Trebbiano, Garganega, Tocai Friulano, Cortese, and Malvasia.

BOZNER LEITEN or
COLLI DI BOLZANO DOC
Trentino-Alto Adige
See Alto Adige DOC

BREGANZE DOC
Veneto
This is one of Italy's unsung DOC heroes, largely due to the excellence of Maculan. As a generic red, Breganze is an excellent Merlot-based wine with the possible addition of Pinot noir, Freisa, Marzemino, Gropello gentile, Cabernet franc, and Cabernet sauvignon. As a white, it is fresh, zesty, and dry and made from Tocai Friulano with the possible addition of Pinot blanc, Pinot gris, Welschriesling, and Vespaiolo. But it is mostly sold as a varietal, of which there are two red (Cabernet and Pinot Nero) and three white (Pinot Bianco, Pinot Grigio, and Vespaiolo).

⌛ 2–5 years (red), 1–2 years (white)

√ *Bartolomeo da Breganze • Maculan*

CABERNET FRANC
Veneto
Most Cabernet wines are DOC, but a few non-DOC exist and are invariably well worth seeking out as they tend to be *barrique*-aged selections of ripe not too grassy fruit.

√ *Quintarelli* (Alerzo)

CABERNET-MERLOT
Trentino-Alto Adige and Veneto
There are so many Cabernet DOCs available in this region that few bother to produce a *vino da tavola*, but of those that do, the hellishly expensive San Leonardo is the very best. In Veneto, with one notable exception, Cabernet-based blends are not as common as one imagines they might be.

√ **Trentino-Alto Adige** *Tenuta San Leonardo* (Vallagrina)

Veneto *Conte Loredan-Gasparini* (Venegazzù della Casa, Venegazzù Capo di Stato)

CABERNET SAUVIGNON
Veneto
Less traditional in Veneto than Cabernet Franc, pure varietal wines of any real quality or concentration are rarely encountered, but Cabernet Sauvignon from Anselmi and Le Vigne de San Pietro can be superb.

⌛ 3–6 years

√ *Anselmi* (Realda)
• *Le Vigne de San Pietro* (Refolà)

CALDARO or
LAGO DI CALDARO or
KALTERER OR KALTERERSEE DOC
Trentino-Alto Adige
As this overlaps the heart of the Terlano area, Caldaro might as well be yet another sub-appellation of the Alto Adige DOC, along with Terlano and the other former DOCs that have now been absorbed. Schiava-based red wines with the possible addition of Lagrein and Pinot noir, they are usually soft and fruity, with a hint of almond, and easy to drink.

CARSO DOC
Friuli-Venezia Giulia
Carso Terrano must be at least 85 per cent Terrano (also known as Mondeuse or Refosco), which makes a deep, dark, and full red wine that can be fat and juicy. Carso Malvasia is a rich and gently spicy, dry white wine.

⌛ 1–3 years

√ *Edi Kante*

CASTELLER DOC
Trentino-Alto Adige
The thin strip of hilly vineyards that produces these wines is virtually identical to the Trentino DOC. Dry or semi-sweet, red and rosé wines for everyday drinking from Schiava, Merlot, and Lambrusco a Foglia Frastagliata grapes.

CHARDONNAY
Northeast Italy
A decade ago, only two pure Chardonnay DOCs existed in northeast Italy: Alto Adige and Grave del Friuli. Now it is one of the most ubiquitous varietals, but premium-priced non-DOC wines from this grape variety are still excellent quality.

√ *Azienda Agricola Inama* (Campo dei Tovi) • *Jermann* (Where The Dreams Have No End)

COLLI BERICI DOC
Veneto
In addition to a sparkling Garganega-based white wine, this DOC includes three red varietals (Merlot, Tocai Rosso, and Cabernet) and five white (Garganega, Tocai Bianco, Pinot Bianco, Sauvignon, and Chardonnay). The Cabernet can be rich and grassy with chocolaty fruit, and the Merlot, in the right hands, is plump and juicy; the red Tocai is unusual and interesting, and the Chardonnay suffices as usual. However, the other wines from this area immediately south of Vicenza are less exciting

⌛ 2–5 years (red), 1–2 years (white)

√ *Castello di Belvedere • Villa dal Ferro*

COLLI DI BOLZANO
OR BOZNER LEITEN DOC
Trentino-Alto Adige
See Alto Adige DOC

COLLI EUGANEI DOC
Veneto
Bordering Colli Berici to the southeast, this area produces soft, full-bodied, dry or semi-sweet red-wine blends (from Merlot plus Cabernet franc, Cabernet sauvignon, Barbera, and Raboso) and four red varietals: Cabernet, Cabernet Franc, Cabernet Sauvignon, and Merlot. There are dry or semi-sweet white-wine blends (from Prosecco, Garganega, and Tocai Friulano with the possible addition of Chardonnay, Pinot blanc, Pinella, and Welschriesling) and seven white varietals: Chardonnay, Fior d'arancio (from the Moscato giallo grape in sweet *frizzantino*, *spumante*, and *liquoroso* styles), Moscato (sweet *frizzantino* and *spumante* styles), Pinella or Pinello, Pinot bianco, Serprina or Serprino (dry or sweet in still, *frizzantino*, *frizzante*, or *spumante* styles), and Tocai Italico.

⌛ 2–5 years (red), 1–2 years (white)

√ *Villa Sceriman • Vignalta*

COLLI ORIENTALI
DEL FRIULI DOC
Friuli-Venezia Giulia

Larger than neighbouring Collio and initially more prestigious, both DOCs have now shown their excellent potential. In addition to a generic *rosato* blend, there are seven red varietals (Cabernet, Cabernet Franc, Cabernet Sauvignon, Merlot, Pinot Noir, Refosco, and Schioppettino); and 12 white (Chardonnay, Malvasia, Picolit, Pinot Bianco, Pinot Grigio, Ramandolo (dessert-style Verduzzo), Ribolla, Riesling Renano, Sauvignon, Tocai Friulano, and Verduzzo Friulano). The whites are especially outstanding, but the most famous, Picolit, is overrated and overpriced, even though this used to be the only Picolit in Italy to have its own DOC and should, therefore, have a reputation to maintain.

⌛ 3–8 years (red), 1–3 years (white)

√ *Abbazia di Rosazzo • Borgo del Tiglio*
• *Girolamo Dorigo • Livio Felluga*
• *Dorino Livon • Ronco del Gnemiz*
• *Torre Rosazza • Volpe Pasini*

COLLIO or
COLLIO GORIZIANO DOC
Friuli-Venezia Giulia
A large range of mostly white wines from a hilly area close to the Slovenian border, Collio now encompasses 19 different wines. With some top producers making very high-quality wines, this appellation is clearly in line for full DOCG status in the near future. As well as a blended dry white (primarily from Ribolla, Malvasia, and Tocai Friulano), which can be slightly *frizzantino*, and blended red (Merlot, Cabernet sauvignon, and Cabernet franc, plus Pinot noir and possibly one or two others), there are five red varietals (Cabernet, Cabernet Franc, Cabernet Sauvignon, Merlot, and Pinot Nero); and 12 white (Chardonnay, Malvasia, Müller-Thurgau, Picolit, Pinot Bianco, Pinot Grigio, Riesling Italico, Riesling Renano, Tocai Friulano, Ribolla, Sauvignon, and Traminer Aromatico).

⌛ 1–4 years (red), 1–3 years (white)

√ *Borgo Conventi* (Sauvignon)
• *Borgo del Tiglio • Livio Felluga*
• *Marco Felluga • Gradnik • Gravner*
• *Jermann • Dorino Livon • Ca' Ronesca*
• *Puiatti • Mario Schiopetto*

CORVINA

Veneto

Arguably the greatest grape in Veneto, Corvina is the key player in Bardolino and Valpolicella, particularly the *recioto* and *amarone* styles of the latter, but can also be found in a few premium *vini da tavola*.

✓ *Allegrini* (Pelara, La Poja)

EISACKTALER *OR* VALLE ISARCO DOC

Trentino-Alto Adige
See Alto Adige DOC

ETSCHTALER DOC

Trentino-Alto Adige
See Valdadige DOC

FRANCONIA *OR* BLAUFRANKISCH

Friuli-Venezia Giulia

Franconia is the synonym for the Limberger grape of Germany. The wine is made in a fuller, darker style than is possible in its homeland, yet it still possesses the same light, fruity flavour.

FRIULI-AQUILEA DOC

Friuli-Venezia Giulia

Formerly know simply as Aquileia, this is a wide-ranging appellation that covers five varietal red wines (Merlot, Cabernet, Cabernet Franc, Cabernet Sauvignon, and Refosco); eight white varietals (Chardonnay, Tocai Friulano, Pinot Bianco, Pinot Grigio, Riesling Renano, Sauvignon, Traminer, and Verduzzo Friulano); and a generic rosé of least 70 per cent Merlot plus Cabernet franc, Cabernet sauvignon, and Refosco. There is also a Chardonnay *spumante*. All are generally light, crisply-balanced wines, although some producers excel in better years.

⌑— 1–4 years (red),
1–3 years (white, rosé, and sparkling)

✓ *Zonin* (Tenuta Cà Bolani)

FRIULI-GRAVE DOC

Friuli-Venezia Giulia

Formerly called Grave del Friuli, this massive appellation spreads out on either side of the river Tagliamento between Sacile in the west and Cividale di Friuli in the east, and accounts for over half of the region's total production. It is a huge and complicated, but rapidly improving, multi-varietal DOC in which several winemakers regularly produce fine wines. In addition to generic red and white blends, there are six red varietals (Cabernet, Cabernet Franc, Cabernet Sauvignon, Merlot, Refosco, and Pinot Noir); and eight white varietals (Chardonnay, Pinot Bianco, Pinot Gris, Riesling Renano, Sauvignon, Tocai Friulano, Traminer Aromatico, and Verduzzo Friulano). There is a Chardonnay *frizzante*, Verduzzo *frizzante*, Chardonnay *spumante*, and a blended generic *spumante*.

⌑— 1–4 years (red),
1–3 years (white, rosé, and sparkling)

✓ *Borgo Magredo • Pighin
• Vignetti la Monde • Vignetti Pittaro*

FRIULI-LATISANA *or* LATISANA DOC

Friuli-Venezia Giulia

An area that stretches from the central section of the Friuli-Grave to the Adriatic coast at Lignano Sabbiadoro. In addition to a generic, blended rosé (Bordeaux varieties) and *spumante* (Chardonnay and Pinot varieties) there are five red varietal wines (Merlot,

Cabernet Sauvignon, Franconia [Limberger], Pinot Nero, and Refosco); and nine white varietals (Chardonnay, Malvasia, Pinot Bianco, Pinot Grigio, Riesling Renano, Sauvignon, Tocai Friulano, Traminer Aromatico, and Verduzzo Friulano). Chardonnay, Malvasia, and Pinot Nero may also be produced in a *frizzante* style.

GAMBELLARA DOC

Veneto

Produces scented, dry, or sometimes semi-sweet white wines and fruity, semi-sweet, still, *frizzante* or fully sparkling white *recioto*. A smooth, sweet *vin santo* is also produced here.

⌑— 2–5 years

✓ *La Biancara*

GARGANEGA

Veneto

The primary grape used for Soave – in skilled hands Garganega can produce a fabulously rich yet delicately balanced dry white, but has a tendency to overcrop, and most Garganega wines turn out bland.

GRAVE DEL FRIULI DOC

Friuli-Venezia Giulia
See Friuli-Grave DOC

ISONZO *or* INSONZO DEL FRIULI DOC

Friuli-Venezia Giulia

A small area south of Collio, producing a very good yet still improving quality wine. There are generic red- and white-wine blends, plus four red varietals (Cabernet, Merlot, Franconia [Limberger], and Refosco); and ten white varietals (Chardonnay, Malvasia, Pinot Bianco, Pinot Grigio, Riesling Italico, Riesling Renano, Sauvignon, Tocai Friulano, Traminer Aromatico, and Verduzzo Friulano); and a Pinot *spumante*.

⌑— 1–4 years (red), 1–3 years (white)

✓ *Borgo Conventi • Gallo* (Vie di Romans)

KALTERER *or* KALTERERSEE DOC

Trentino-Alto Adige
See Caldaro DOC

LAGREIN

Trentino-Alto Adige

An ancient Alto Adige variety, it was well known to Pliny, who called it Lageos. Although it is by no means the greatest grape grown in the region, Lagrein does, however, produce one of Alto Adige's most original and expressive wines, with rich, chunky, youthful fruit of relatively high acidity, but capable of developing a silky, violety finesse after a few years in bottle.

LATISANA DOC

Friuli-Venezia Giulia
See Friuli-Latisana DOC

LESSINI DURELLO DOC

Veneto

Dry white wine from just northeast of Soave, in still, *frizzantino*, and fully sparkling styles, from the Durello grape with the possible addition of Garganega, Trebbiano, Pinot blanc, Pinot noir, and Chardonnay.

✓ *Marcato*

LISON-PRAMAGGIORE DOC

Veneto and Friuli-Venezia Giulia

This DOC, which is in the very east of the Veneto, and overlaps a small part of Friuli, originally combined three former DOCs (Cabernet di Pramaggiore, Merlot di Pramaggiore, and Tocai di Lison) into one appellation. However, it has since been expanded to encompass a total of seven white varietal wines (Chardonnay, Pinot Bianco, Pinot Grigio, Riesling Italico, Sauvignon, Tocai Italico, and Verduzzo); and four reds (Cabernet, Cabernet Franc, Cabernet Sauvignon, and Refosco dal Peduncolo Rosso). Cabernet and Merlot are still the best in a rich, delicious, chocolaty style.

⌑— 3–8 years (red), 1–3 years (white)

✓ *Santa Margherita • Russola • Tenuta Sant'Anna • Villa Castalda* (Cabernet Franc)

LUGANA DOC

Veneto
See Lugana DOC (Lombardy)
under Northwest Italy

MARZEMINO

Trentino-Alto Adige

This grape variety was probably brought to Italy from Slovenia by the Romans. By the 18th century, it had achieved sufficient fame for Mozart to use it in his opera *Don Giovanni* as a preliminary to the seduction of Zerlina. A Marzemino cluster typically provides large, loosely bunched grapes, which make an aromatic, early-drinking red wine, either as DOC (Trentino) or *vino da tavola*.

MERANESE *or* MERANESE DI COLLINA *or* MERANER HÜGEL DOC

Trentino-Alto Adige
See Alto Adige DOC

MERLOT

Friuli-Venezia Giulia

A prolific grape in northeastern Italy, where it has been grown for almost 200 years. Far too many wishy-washy examples abound, but top producers achieve concentration and quality through low yields and strict selection. Although Merlot is a varietal wine in virtually all the DOCs of Friuli-Venezia Giulia, the only ones with any special reputation for it are of Colli Orientali, where the richest varietals are made, and Collio, which is less consistent, but the best are plump and juicy.

✓ *Borgo del Tiglio* (Rosso della Centa)

MONTELLO E COLLI ASOLANI DOC

Veneto

From vineyards at the foot of the aptly-named Mount Grappa, most of the production is varietal, comprising two reds (Merlot and Cabernet); four whites (Prosecco, Chardonnay, Pinot Bianco, and Pinot Grigio); and three *spumante* varietals (Chardonnay, Pinot

Bianco, and Prosecco). Any red wines that do not carry a varietal name will be primarily Cabernet-Merlot blends.

⌐ 1–3 years

✓ *Fernando Berta* • *Abazia di Nervesa*

NOSIOLA
Trentino-Alto Adige

Probably the least known of the Trentino's traditional grapes because it is mostly used for *vin santo*. However, dry white varietal wines are also made from this variety and, although it is best when blended with more aromatic varieties, as in Sorni DOC, it is even making a reputation as a premium *vino da tavola*.

✓ *Pravis* (Le Frate)

PIAVE *or* VINI DEL PIAVE DOC
Veneto

A large area to the west of Lison-Pramaggiore producing five red varietals (Merlot, Cabernet, Cabernet Sauvignon, Pinot Nero, and Raboso); and five white varietals (Chardonnay, Tocai Italico, Pinot Bianco, Pinot Grigio, and Verduzzo). The Cabernet and Raboso can be particularly good.

⌐ 1–3 years

✓ *Reichsteiner*

PICOLIT DOC
Friuli-Venezia Giulia
See Colli Orientali del Friuli DOC

PROSECCO
Veneto

Although it is one of the most traditional of Veneto's grape varieties, Prosecco originated in the village of that name in Friuli's Carso district. Latin-lovers adore the soft bubbly produced by this grape, but the vast majority is boring and it will take a revolution in quality to convince me that this grape is suitable for dry sparkling wines.

PROSECCO DI CONEGLIANO-VALDOBBIADENE DOC
Veneto

Dry and semi-sweet fizzy white wines of passable quality, although most of them have large bubbles and a coarse, dull flavour. A still version is also produced.

⌐ Upon purchase

✓ *Adami Adriano* (Vigneto Giardino)
• *Fratelli Bartolin Spumante*
• *Carpenè Malvolti*

RABOSO
Veneto

The indigenous Raboso grape has long produced excellent-value red wines that are full of sunny fruit and capable of improving after two to three years in bottle. There are two distinct, localized clones – Rabaso del Piave, which is most often used as a pure varietal, and the more productive Raboso Veronese, which does not have the richness or such a positive character, and is therefore merely a blending component. Most of the wines produced are *vini da tavola*, but DOC wines are available under the Piave appellation.

RECIOTO BIANCO DI CAMPOCIESA
Veneto

Soft, sweet, well-scented, golden-coloured, non-DOC white wines made from *passito* grapes.

RECIOTO DELLA VALPOLICELLA *or* RECIOTO DELLA VALPOLICELLA AMARONE DOC
Veneto
See Valpolicella DOC

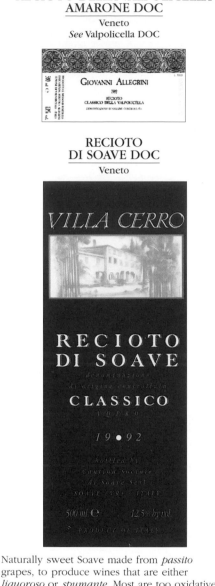

Naturally sweet Soave made from *passito* grapes, to produce wines that are either *liquoroso* or *spumante*. Most are too oxidative, but Pieropan is excellent and Anselmi is outstanding – both as pure as driven snow.

✓ *Anselmi* (I Capitelli) • *Pieropan* (Le Colombare Vendemia Tardiva)

REFOSCO
Friuli-Venezia Giulia

Otherwise known as Terrano in the Carso district, the Refosco is none other than the Mondeuse of France. It typically produces a deep-coloured red wine with soft, juicy, low-acid fruit, which can be somewhat one-dimensional, but is at its best in the Colli Orientali and Friuli-Grave.

SANTA MADDALENA *or* SANKT MAGDALENER DOC
Trentino-Alto Adige
See Alto Adige DOC

SCHIAVA
Trentino-Alto Adige

This is the most widely cultivated variety in the Alto Adige where it accounts for 60 per cent of the vines grown. In the Tyrol, where this grape is believed to have originated, it is known as Vernatsch, but most ampelographers refer to it as Schiava. There are four sub-varieties: Schiava grossa, Schiava gentile, Schiava grigia, and Schiava Meranese. Schiava wines are usually medium-bodied with an almond character to the fruit and a light bitterness on the finish.

SCHIOPPETTINO
Friuli-Venezia Giulia

An ancient Friulian variety, Schioppettino was nearly extinct until these wines suddenly became fashionable in the 1980s. It produces very ripe and round wines with a fine, spicy-scented bouquet and rich fruit flavour that attains great finesse only with maturity.

✓ *Ronchi di Cialla* • *Ronco del Gnemiz*
• *Giuseppe Toti*

SOAVE DOC
Veneto
See also Recioto di Soave DOC

Most Soave is still overcropped, thin, and acidic, but the top producers continue to make immensely enjoyable wines from Garganega and Trebbiano, when they are grown to restricted yields in the central, hilly, *classico* area. One or two growers, such as Stefano Inama of Azienda Agricola Inama, show promise for the future.

⌐ 1–4 years

✓ *Anselmi* (Capitel Foscarino, Capitel Croce)
• *Bolla* (Castellaro, Vignetti di Froscà)
• *Pieropan* (Vigneto Calvarino, Vigneto la Rocca) • *Fratelli Tedeschi* (Monte Tenda)

SORNI DOC
Trentino-Alto Adige

This tiny DOC is situated just south of Mezzolombardo at the confluence of the rivers Avisio and Adige. Soft Schiava-based reds are often improved by the addition of Teroldego and Lagrein. The light, fresh, delicate Nosiola-based white wines are usually charged with a good dollop of Müller-Thurgau, Silvaner, and Pinot blanc.

⌐ 2–3 years (red), up to 18 months (white)

✓ *Maso Poli*

SÜDTIROLER DOC
Trentino-Alto Adige
See Alto Adige DOC

TACELENGHE *or* TAZZELENGHE
Friuli-Venezia Giulia

This grape variety takes its name from the local dialect for *tazzalingua*, which means "a sharpness in the tongue", and is indicative of the wine's tannic nature. However, it does soften after five or six years in bottle.

TERLANO *or* TERLANER DOC
Trentino-Alto Adige
See Alto Adige DOC

TEROLDEGO
Trentino-Alto Adige

An indigenous black grape with a thick bluish skin, Teroldego is productive and makes a dark-coloured red wine with a distinctive aroma and a chewy, tannic raspberry richness that softens with age, attaining a silky-violety finesse. This has made it a very useful blending component in the past. However, more varietal wines are gradually being made and it has even started to be marketed as a premium *vino da tavola*.

✓ *Foradori* (Granato)

TEROLDEGO ROTALIANO DOC
Trentino-Alto Adige
Full-bodied red wines made from the Teroldego in the Rotaliano area, where the grape is said to have originated. There is also a fuller, more concentrated *Superiore* version and an attractive rosé.

⌐— 1–4 years

✓ *Foradori* (Vigneto Morei) • *Conti Martini*

TERRANO
Friuli-Venezia Giulia
See Refosco

TREBBIANO
Veneto
The Trebbiano of Soave and Lugana are supposedly superior to the Trebbiano of Tuscany, but there is much dross produced in both DOCs, and it is the producer who makes the real difference.

TRENTINO DOC
Trentino-Alto Adige

This appellation represents the southern half of the Valdadige DOC and its wines are generally softer and less racy than those from Alto Adige in the northern half, although there is an equally bewildering number of varietal wines. If no variety is indicated, white wines will be Chardonnay-Pinot blanc blends and reds Cabernet-Merlot. There are seven red-wine varietals (Cabernet, Cabernet Franc, Cabernet Sauvignon, Lagrein, Marzemino, Merlot, and Pinot Nero); and nine white (Chardonnay, Moscato Giallo, Müller-Thurgau, Nosiola, Pinot Bianco, Pinot Grigio, Riesling Italico, Riesling Renano, and Traminer Aromatico). Furthermore, the Nosiola can be made in *vin santo* style, while all Pinot (Blanc, Gris, and Noir) may be fully sparkling. There is also a bright scarlet, lusciously sweet Moscato Rosa, and both Moscato Rosa and Moscato Giallo may be made in *liquoroso* style.

✓ *Barone de Cles* • *Càvit* • *LaVis* • *Longariva* • *Madonna del Vittoria* • *Conti Martini* • *Pojer & Sandri* • *Giovanni Poli* • *Tenuta San Leonardo* • *Armando Simoncelli* • *de Tarczal* • *Vallarom* • *Roberto Zeni*

VALDADIGE *or* ETSCHTALER DOC
Trentino-Alto Adige and Veneto

This huge generic denomination encompasses both the Alto Adige and Trentino DOCs, a myriad of sub-appellations, and extends well into the Veneto. Few producers bother to use what is generally considered to be Trentino-Alto Adige's lowest quality DOC. If the IGTs proposed by the Goria Law actually existed and worked, the size and location of Valdadige would make it an ideal candidate, as producers could select their best wines to go out under Alto Adige, Trentino, or whatever, selling off the balance as an unpretentious Valdadige country wine. As it is already a DOC, nobody would dare suggest downgrading it to IGT, so the result is that hardly anyone uses it anyway. And, of the few who do, the dry and semi-sweet white and red wines that they sell inevitably attract a poor reputation as DOCs, whereas underselling the same products as IGTs would make them honest, good-value introductions to the finer wines of Trentino-Alto Adige.

VALLE ISARCO *or* EISACKTALER DOC
Trentino-Alto Adige
See Alto Adige DOC

VALPANTENA DOC
Veneto
See Valpolicella DOC
Sub-appellation for Valpolicella, in *recioto*, *amarone*, *spumante*, and regular *rosso* styles.

VALPOLICELLA DOC
Veneto
In the first edition I agreed with Robert Parker, the American wine writer, when he described most Valpolicella as "insipid industrial garbage", but technology has changed things over the last ten years. While most are still insipid and industrial, relatively few are as bad as garbage. Made from at least 80 per cent Corvina with the possible addition of Rossignola, Negrara, Trentina, Barbera, and Sangiovese, most Valpolicella are simply light-red and light-bodied, with lacklustre, attenuated fruit hinting of cherries, and a dry, slightly bitter finish. There are an increasing number of wines that are full of juicy cherry-fruit flavours, but they are still in a minority and for truly fine wines bearing the Valpolicella DOC you have to seek out exceptional wines from the tiny number of producers recommended below.

Valpolicella *recioto* is a bitter-sweet, yet very smooth, deep-coloured, Port-like wine made from *passito* grapes, although it may also be produced in a *spumante* style. *Amarone* is a derivative of *recioto*, with a similar deep colour, but in a dry or off-dry style, which seems to make the Port-like flavours more powerful and chocolaty-spicy with a distinctly bitter finish. There is also something very specific that marks the fruit in *amarone* wines, which wine writer Oz Clark once described – perfectly to my mind – as a "bruised sourness". This is an oxidative character that will not appeal to lovers of clean, precise, well-focused flavours, but its complexity is undeniable and such wines age wonderfully well. Quintarelli is the most outstanding producer, with Allegrini hard on his heels.

⌐— Upon purchase for most, 2–5 years for recommendations

✓ Valpolicella *Allegrini* (La Grola) • *Bolla* (Vigneti di Jago) • *Guerrieri-Rizzardi* (Villa Rizzardi Poiega) • *Quintarelli* • *La Ragose* • *Serègo Alighieri* • *Fratelli Tedeschi* (Capitel delle Lucchine, Capitel dei Nicalò) • *Tommasi* (Vigneto del Campo Rafael)
Recioto della Valpolicella *Allegrini* (Gardane) • *Masi* (Mazzanella) • *Quintarelli* • *Serègo Alighieri* (Casel dei Ronchi) • *Fratelli Tedeschi* (Capitel Monte Fontana)
Recioto della Valpolicella Amarone *Allegrini* (Fieramonte) • *Bertani* • *Tomasso Bussola*

• *Masi* (Mazzone) • *Fratelli Pasqua* (Vigneti Casterna) • *Quintarelli* • *Serègo Alighieri* (Vaio Armoron) • *Fratelli Tedeschi* (Fabriseria, Capitel Monte Olmi) • *Tommasi*

VALPOLICELLA "RIPASSO"
Veneto
Ripasso ("re-passed") wine has long been traditional in the Veneto. The best young Valpolicella is put into tanks or barrels that still contain the lees of the *recioto* for which they were previously used. When mixed with the young wine, active yeast cells in this sediment precipitate a second fermentation. This increases the alcohol content and gives it some *recioto* character. After this process, the wines usually cannot carry the Valpolicella appellation and are sold as *vino da tavola* under various brand names, although some Valpolicella are turbocharged by *ripasso* without any mention of this on the label.

⌐— 6–15 years

✓ *Allegrini* (Palazzo alla Torre) • *Boscaini* (Le Cane) • *Fratelli Tedeschi* (Capitel San Rocco) • *Masi* (Campo Fiorin)

VINI DEL PIAVE DOC
Veneto
See Piave DOC

WILDBACHER
Veneto
This black grape seems to be restricted to the Veneto and Western Styria in Austria, where it is called Blauer Wildbacher. Mostly used as a blending component, its distinctive, aromatic quality and high acidity are sometimes found in pure varietal form in non-DOC wines.

✓ *Le Case Bianche*

NEW IGT WINES

The following Indicazioni Geografiche Tipiche wines were agreed at the end of 1996, but we have yet to see what style, quality, or consistency each one will establish.

Friuli-Venezia Giulia Alto Livenza • *Delle Venezie* • *Venezia Giulia*

Trentino-Alto Adige Atesino • *Delle Venezie* • *Vallagarina*

Veneto Alto Livenza • *Colli Trevigiani* • *Conselvano* • *Delle Venezie* • *Marca Trevigiani* • *Provincia di Verona O Veronese* • *Vallagarina* • *Veneto* • *Veneto Orientale*

WEST-CENTRAL ITALY

The heart of Italy is also the centre of the country's most important quality-wine exports, which are dominated by famous red Sangiovese wines from the tiny Tuscan hills and valleys between Florence and the Umbria-Latium border.

TUSCANY (TOSCANA)

The home of traditional winemaking, Tuscany has also been the main focus of experimentation. Its powerful red Vino Nobile di Montepulciano was Italy's first DOCG, and has been followed by Brunello di Montalcino, Chianti, Carmignano, Vino Nobile di Montalcino, and Vernaccia di San Gimignano. But not all of its finest wines bear these famous appellations, a fact recognized by the Tuscan producers themselves, who, on one hand, sought the ideal DOCG solution for Chianti, while on the other began to invest in premium wines that were not restricted by the DOC. It was the uncompromising quality of their super-Tuscan wines that encouraged premium *vini da tavola* throughout the rest of Italy. Unfortunately, they were less successful with the DOCG of Chianti. The Tuscans had two sensible, forward-thinking approaches: one was to apply DOCG to the

Chianti Classico area and other isolated areas, such as parts of Rufina and the Colli Fiorentini, where most of the finest wines have traditionally been made, and to leave the rest as DOC Chianti; the other was to grant DOCG status to the best ten per cent, regardless of origin. Either would have made Chianti a success. But the biggest Chianti-producers had more political clout than the best producers and the new regulations gave DOCG status to the whole area and all Chianti wines, regardless of origin or quality.

It is true that the Trebbiano Toscano, a localized clone, is an intrinsically high-class Trebbiano and, indeed, it can make some charming wines, but it is not a fine-wine grape. Currently Tuscany has no white-wine sister for its red Sangiovese grape. Unfortunately, its best dry white-wine grape so far has been Chardonnay, a variety that excels in almost every half-decent wine area. Vermentino might be Tuscany's white-wine grape of the future, although it is really a Sardinian grape and currently mostly restricted to Tuscany's coastal areas. It is time someone managed to rekindle an ancient, all-but-extinct Tuscan white grape and rescue it with commercial success, much as the *piemontese* did with Arneis and, as I suspect, they will next try with Timorasso.

WEST-CENTRAL ITALY, *see also p.307*
The hills of this area provide the best sites for vineyards, tempering the summer's heat and providing a variety of microclimates suitable for classic French grape varieties as well as traditional ones.

FACTORS AFFECTING TASTE AND QUALITY

LOCATION
Located between the Apennines to the north and east and the Tyrrhenian Sea to the west.

CLIMATE
Summers are long and fairly dry and winters are less severe than in northern Italy. Heat and lack of rain can be a problem throughout the area during the growing season.

ASPECT
Vineyards are usually sited on hillsides for good drainage and exposure to the sun. Deliberate use is made of altitude to offset the heat, and red grapes grow at up to 550 m (1,800 ft) and white grapes at up to 700 m (2,275 ft). The higher the vines, the longer the ripening season and the greater the acidity of the grapes.

SOIL
These are very complex soils with gravel, limestone, and clay outcrops predominating. In Tuscany a rocky, schistose soil, known in some localities as *galestro*, covers most of the best vineyards.

VITICULTURE AND VINIFICATION
After much experimentation, particularly in Tuscany, with classic French grapes, the trend recently has been to develop the full potential of native varieties. Many stunning Cabernet-influenced, super-Tuscan wines still exist, and always will, but top-performing producers are seeking clones, *terroirs*, and techniques to maximize the fruit and accessibility of their own noble grapes. A traditional speciality is the sweet, white *vin santo*, which is made from *passito* grapes and dried on straw mats in attics. It is aged for up to six years, often in a type of *solera* system.

PRIMARY GRAPE VARIETIES
Sangiovese (*syn.* Brunello, Morellino, Prugnolo, Sangioveto, Tignolo, Uva Canina), Malvasia, Trebbiano (*syn.* Procanico)

SECONDARY GRAPE VARIETIES
Abbuoto, Aglianico, Albana (*syn.* Greco, but not Grechetto), Albarola, Aleatico, Barbera, Bellone, Bombino, Cabernet franc, Cabernet sauvignon, Canaiolo (*syn.* Drupeggio in Umbria), Carignan (*syn.* Uva di Spagna), Cesanese, Chardonnay, Cilíegiolo, Colorino, Gamay, Grechetto (*syn.* Greco, Pulciano), Inzolia (*syn.* Ansonica), Mammolo, Merlot, Montepulciano, Moscadelletto, Muscat (*syn.* Moscadello, Moscato), Nero Buono di Cori, Pinot blanc (*syn.* Pinot bianco), Pinot gris (*syn.* Pinot grigio), Roussanne, Sagrantino, Sauvignon blanc, Sémillon, Syrah, Verdello, Vermentino, Vernaccia, Welschriesling

TRADITION AND INNOVATION
This tranquil landscape appears to have remained unchanged for many centuries, but, while Tuscan winemaking is steeped in tradition, the area is now also experimenting with different grape varieties and barrique *ageing.*

BIRTH OF THE SUPER-TUSCANS
Ten years ago the largest number of exceptional Tuscan wines were the then relatively new *barrique*-aged super-Tuscans. Their story began in 1948 when the now famous Sassicaia wine was produced for the first time by Incisa della Rochetta using Cabernet sauvignon vines reputedly from Château Lafite-Rothschild. This was an unashamed attempt to produce a top-quality Italian wine from Bordeaux's greatest grape variety, decades before the idea became old hat in the wine world. It became so successful that in the wake of the 1971 vintage, a new red called Tignanello was introduced by Piero Antinori with a Sangiovese base and 20 per cent Cabernet sauvignon, as a compromise between Tuscany and Bordeaux. Although Frescobaldi had used Cabernet

ROME AND ITS ENVIRONS, *see also* **opposite**
The recent proliferation of appellations in the hills surrounding Italy's capital are evidence of a wine regime gone mad – this country's wines need cohesion, not more diversity.

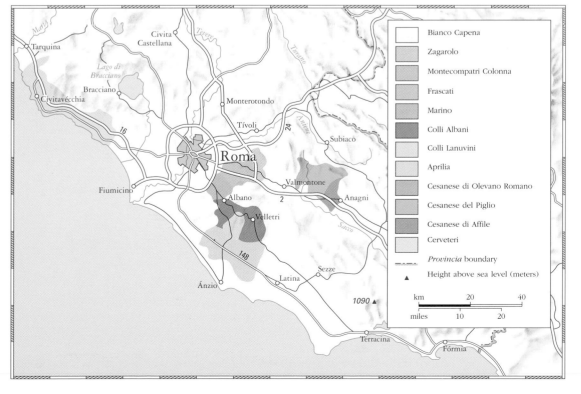

Bianco Capena
Zagarolo
Montecompatri Colonna
Frascati
Marino
Colli Albani
Colli Lanuvini
Aprilia
Cesanese di Olevano Romano
Cesanese del Piglio
Cesanese di Affile
Cerveteri

Provincia boundary
▲ Height above sea level (meters)

VERNACCIA VINES IN AUTUMN
These vines grow exclusively around the medieval Tuscan town of San Gimignano, whose impressive towers can be seen here in the distance. When it comes from good producers, the white Vernaccia can be a deliciously crisp, fruity dry wine.

AVERAGE ANNUAL PRODUCTION		
REGION	DOC PRODUCTION	TOTAL PRODUCTION
Tuscany	1 million hl (11 million cases)	4 million hl (44 million cases)
Latium	540,000 hl (6 million cases)	6 million hl (67 million cases)
Umbria	165,000 hl (2 million cases)	1.7 million hl (18 million cases)
Percentage of total Italian production: Latium, 7.8%; Tuscany, 5.2%; Umbria, 2.2%.		

sauvignon in its Nipozzano Chianti for over a century and it grew in the Carmignano area in the 18th century, nobody had truly appreciated the harmony that could be achieved between the two grapes until Tignanello appeared. The blend was akin to the natural balance of Cabernet and Merlot, only the Cabernet added weight to the Sangiovese and provided balance through a more satisfying flavour. Tignanello thus sparked off a new-wave of super-Tuscan *vini da tavola*. However, as the numbers grew, so they became an embarrassment, as observers realized that very few of the region's greatest wines actually qualified for DOC. But at the same time, many of the winemakers responsible for these French-influenced super-Tuscans were also working hard to make the Sangiovese stand alone. After extensive clonal and site selection, reduced yields, improved viticultural practices and vinification techniques, a new breed of super-Tuscan emerged; first as Sangiovese-dominated blends, such as Tignanello, then as pure Sangiovese wines. Now that the Goria Law has opened

the door for Italy's greatest *vini da tavola*, many who had resorted to making wines outside the DOC system are using their experience in remoulding the Sangiovese to re-establish the great old names of the past (Chianti, Brunello di Montalcino, Vino Nobile di Montepulciano) by making wines that are complete without the help of foreign varieties.

UMBRIA

Orvieto is Umbria's best-known and best-forgotten wine. Next to Frascati and Soave, it is the most used and abused name in the world's Italian restaurants. While there are a few good Orvieto wines, and tiny amounts of truly exciting *muffato* (a lusciously sweet botrytized version), they are in a lamentable minority. One of Umbria's few deservedly famous names is Lungarotti Rubesco Torgiano, whose reputation led to the Torgiano DOC and, more recently, to DOCG status for Torgiano Riserva. Lungarotti also leads in the production of Umbria's excellent new-wave wines. These use various grapes, both native and French, and are made in various styles, although nearly always aged in new-oak *barriques*.

LATIUM (LAZIO)

One of Italy's largest regions, Latium appropriately boasts one of its largest selling wines, Frascati, the Latin Liebfraumilch, and Est! Est!! Est!!!, probably the blandest tourist wine in existence. For a region responsible for Falernum, a classic wine of antiquity, it can now boast only two truly fine wines, Boncompagni Ludovisi's Fiorano Rosso and Cantina Colacicchi's Torre Ercolana, both innovative Cabernet-Merlot blends, which are very good.

THE APPELLATIONS OF
WEST-CENTRAL ITALY

CLASSIC BRUT SPARKLING WINES

The best sparkling Brut wines are made in Tuscany by the *méthode champenoise*.

✓ *Brut di Capezzana* • *Falchini Brut* • *Villa Banfi Brut*

ALEATICO
Tuscany

These are rare, rich, sweet red wines.

ALEATICO DI GRADOLI DOC
Latium

Sweet, sometimes fortified, red wines, without the reputation of the Aleatico di Puglia DOC.

APRILIA DOC
Latium

This DOC has two red varietals, Merlot and Sangiovese, and one white, Trebbiano, which is uninspiring. The washed-out flavours indicate that official yields are far too high.

ASSISI
Umbria

Assisi produces some soft, satisfying red, and fresh, easy-drinking white wines.

✓ *Sasso Rosso* • *Fratelli* • *Sportoletti* • *Tili*

BARCO REALE DI CARMIGNANO DOC
Tuscany

After Carmignano became a DOCG, this appellation was adopted for easy-drinking, Sangiovese-dominated (with a touch of

Cabernet) red wines in order to retain simple DOC status. This acted as a selection instrument to increase and maintain quality for the superior denomination. *See also* Carmignano DOC and Carmignano DOCG.

BIANCO CAPENA DOC
Latium

Bianco Capena is a large DOC northeast of Rome producing dry and semi-sweet Trebbiano-based white wines of modest quality.

BIANCO DELL'EMPOLESE DOC
Tuscany

This is an overrated, over-priced, and uninspiring dry white Trebbiano from the Empoli hills, west of Florence. A *passito* may be sold as *vin santo* under the same denomination.

BIANCO DELLA VAL DI NIEVOLE or BIANCO DELLA VALDINIEVOLE DOC
Tuscany

Dry, slightly *frizzante* white wines and soft, white *vin santo*, made primarily from Trebbiano grapes.

BIANCO DI PITIGLIANO DOC
Tuscany

This DOC produces delicate, refreshing, dry, and easy-drinking Trebbiano-based white wines, which are improved by the possible inclusion of Malvasia, Grechetto, Verdello, Chardonnay, Sauvignon, Pinot blanc, and Welschriesling. A *spumante* version is also allowed.

⌛ 1–2 years

✓ *La Stellata*

BIANCO PISANO DI SAN TORPÉ DOC
Tuscany

These dry white wines and dry or semi-sweet *vin santo* are made from Trebbiano grown in a large area southeast of Pisa.

BIANCO VERGINE DELLA VALDICHIANA DOC
Tuscany

This DOC produces off-dry, Trebbiano-based white wines with a bitter aftertaste. The best have a more delicate, floral fragrance.

⌛ 1–2 years

✓ *Poliziano*

BOLGHERI DOC
Tuscany

Until recently this was a relatively anonymous, pleasant, but hardly exciting DOC, producing delicate, dry whites and dry, slightly scented, Sangiovese *rosato*. Reds were ignored, even though it was home to Sassicaia, one of Italy's greatest wines. Now that reds are allowed,

Sassicaia even has its own sub-appellation, and two varietal whites (Sauvignon and Vermentino) and a pink *vin santo*, Occhio de Pernice, have also been added. It's a sure bet that Sassicaia will be upgraded to full DOCG status shortly, and it will probably leave behind a much healthier, better-known Bolgheri DOC with, hopefully, a number of aspiring new wines aiming to replicate its success. Look for Piero Antinori's new Vermentino, which promises to be Tuscany's first great white wine from a native variety, and for established super-Tuscan wines, such as Lodovico Antinori's Ornellaia.

🍷 1–3 years (white), 3–7 years (most reds), 8–25 years (Sassicaia and *vin santo*)

✓ *Antinori* (Guado al Tasso)
• *Le Macchiola* (Paleo)
• *Tenuta San Guido* (especially Sassicaia)

BRUNELLO DI MONTALCINO DOCG
Tuscany

One of Italy's most prestigious wines, made from Brunello, a localized clone of the Sangiovese. Many relatively unknown producers offer classic wines. The idea is that the wines should be so thick with harsh tannins that they must be left for at least 20 years. If they are ripe skin tannins and there is enough fruit, this can be a formula for a wine of classic stature. But too many Brunello wines are macerated for too long and are not destemmed, leaving the tannins in even the most expensive wines incapable of softening. The producers below all make wines requiring at least ten years' maturation, but they are packed with fruit that develops into layers of complex, smoky-spicy, plummy-fruit flavours. Look out especially for new Frescobaldi-Mondavi wines from the Solaria estate.

🍷 10–25 years

✓ *Altesino, Tenuta di Argiano* • *Villa Banfi* (especially Poggio all'Oro) • *Fattoria dei Barbi* (Vigna del Fiore) • *Campogiovanni, Tenuta Carpazo* • *Casanova* • *Case Basse* • *Castelgiocondo* • *Col d'Orca* • *Conti Costanti Frescobaldi* • *Lisini* • *Pertimali* • *Poggio Attico Tenuta Il Poggione* • *Talenti* • *Val di Suga*

CABERNET-MERLOT
West-central Italy

Cabernet-Merlot is a classic *bordelaise* blend that is best suited to Tuscany.

✓ **Tuscany** *Villa de Capezzana* (Ghiaie della Furbia) • *Tenuta dell'Ornellaia* (Ornellaia)
Latium *Cantina Colacicchi's* (Torre Ercolana) • *Fiorano Rosso* • *Colle Picchioni* (Vigna del Vassello)

CABERNET SAUVIGNON
Tuscany

Ideally suited to the Tuscan soil and climate.

✓ *Villa Banfi* (Tavernelle) • *Villa Cafaggio* (Cortaccio) • *Frescobaldi* (Mormoreto) • *Isole e Olena* • *Monsanto* (Nemo) • *Fattoria di Nozzole* (Il Pareto) • *Poliziano* (Le Stanze) • *Castello di Querceto* (Cignale)

CABERNET-SANGIOVESE BLENDS
Tuscany

Most contain at least 80 per cent Cabernet sauvignon, 20 per cent Sangiovese, and are the antithesis of the rising tide of Sangiovese blends.

✓ *Antinori* (Solaia) • *Tenuta di Bossi* (Mazzaferrata) • *Castellare di Castellina* (Coniale di Castellare) • *Castello di Gabbiano* (R e R) • *Lungarotti* (San Giorgio) • *Tenuta dell'Ornellaia* (Le Volte) • *Castello di Querceto* (Il Querciolaia) • *Castello dei Rampolla* (Sammarco) • *Rocca delle Macie* (Roccato)

CANAIOLO
Tuscany

This is a native Tuscan grape, which is capable of soft, seductively fruity red wines.

CANDIA DEI COLLI APUANI DOC
Tuscany

Delicate, slightly aromatic, dry or semi-sweet white wines from Vermentino and Albarola grapes grown in the hilly province of Massa Carrara.

CARMIGNANO DOC
Tuscany

Since Carmignano achieved DOCG status, the DOC has been used for *rosato*, *vin santo*, and *rosé vin santo*, called Occhio di Pernice (even though these styles were not allowed before the upgrading). The declassified Carmignano reds can now be sold as Barco Reale di Carmignano.

CARMIGNANO DOCG
Tuscany

Only traditional red Carmignano from this tiny appellation west of Florence may claim DOCG status. Other wines are classified as either Carmignano DOC or Barco Reale di Carmignano DOC. This DOCG is made from 45 to 65 per cent Sangiovese, 10 to 20 per cent Canaiolo nero, 6 to 10 per cent Cabernet sauvignon, 10 to 20 per cent Trebbiano, Canaiolo bianco or Malvasia, and up to 5 per cent Mammolo or Colorino. The result is similar to medium-bodied Chianti, but with less acidity, which, with its Cabernet content, gives a chocolaty-finesse to the fruit. *See also* Carmignano DOC and Barco Reale di Carmignano DOC.

🍷 4–10 years

✓ *Fattoria di Ambra* • *di Artimino* • *Fattoria di Bacchereto* • *Contini Bonacossi* (Villa di Capezzana, Villa di Trefiano) • *Fattoria Il Poggiolo*

CASTELLI ROMANI
Latium

Castelli Romani are rarely exciting, dry and semi-sweet white, red, and rosé wines.

CERVETERI DOC
Latium

Rustic Sangiovese-based reds, dry and semi-sweet Trebbiano-Malvasia white wines of decent, everyday quality, which are grown along the coast northwest of Rome.

CESANESE
Latium

This local black grape variety makes medium-bodied red wines of no special quality in all styles from dry to sweet, and still to sparkling.

CESANESE DEL PIGLIO *or* PIGLIO DOC
Latium

This DOC covers a complicated range of basically simple red wines, from Cesanese grapes grown in a hilly area southeast of Rome. The styles include bone-dry, off-dry, medium-dry, semi-sweet, and sweet, and may be still, *frizzantino*, *frizzante*, or *spumante*.

CESANESE DI AFFILE *OR* AFFILE DOC
Latium

This DOC produces the same styles as Cesanese del Piglio from a neighbouring area.

CESANESE DI OLEVANO ROMANO *or* OLEVANO ROMANO DOC
Latium

Much smaller than the previous two nearby Cesanese DOCs, but covering the same styles.

CHARDONNAY
Tuscany and Umbria

The great, if ubiquitous, Chardonnay first squeezed into the official wines of Tuscany when it was adopted by the Pomino DOC, but the best renditions are still *vini da tavola*. In Umbria, although there are only a few great Chardonnay wines, it has great potential in the region, whether in the pure form, as made by Lungarotti, or blended with a little Grechetto, as in the case of Antinori's Castello della Sala.

✓ **Tuscany** *Castello di Ama* (Colline di Ama) • *Caparzo* (Le Grance) • *Villa Banfi* (Fontanelle) • *Felsina Berardenga* (I Sistri) • *Isole e Olena* • *Ruffino* (Cabreo Vigneto la Pietra)
Umbria *Antinori Castello della Sala* (Cervaro della Sala) • *Lungarotti* (Vigna I Palazzi)

CHIANTI DOCG
Tuscany

When Chianti was granted DOCG status, its yields were reduced, the amount of white grapes allowed in Chianti Classico was cut, and up to ten per cent Cabernet sauvignon was permitted in the blend. However, the DOCG was applied to the entire Chianti production area and thus has failed to be a guarantee of quality. Most Chianti is still garbage, albeit in a cleaner, more sanitized form than it used to be. The best basic Chianti, however, is full of juicy cherry, raspberry, and plummy fruit flavours, which makes an enjoyable quaffer, although it is not what DOCG should be about. Only the finest wines of Chianti deserve DOCG status and they are usually sold as *classico* (the original, hilly Chianti area), although Rufina (from a small area northeast of Florence, which should not be confused with Ruffino, the brand name) and Colli Fiorentini (which bridges the Classico and Rufina areas), which are both outside the *classico* district, also produce *classico*-like quality. Both also have lower yields than the rest of Chianti, with the exception of Classico, which demands the lowest yield of all.

Whatever the industrial bottlers do to continue debasing Chianti's reputation, readers must not forget that the best wines from these three areas rank among the greatest in the world. Rufina and Colli Fiorentini are, however, just two of six sub-appellations collectively known as the Chianti Putto, which covers the peripheral areas surrounding Chianti Classico itself. The other four are Colli Senesi (the largest and most varied, and so inconsistent that few wines claim this provenance, two portions of which are better known for Brunello di Montalcino and Vino Nobile di Montepulciano); Colli Pisani (lightest of all Chianti); Colli Aretini (young, lively Chianti); and Montalbano (in effect the second wine of Carmignano, although there are two of those, so maybe it is the third wine?).

If they ever succeed in getting the regulations for this appellation right, Chianti will be as big a flagship for Italian quality as Bordeaux is for French. Look out for the neck seal of the Gallo Nero or "Black Rooster" used by the *consorzio*. Although not infallible, as some top estates are not members and occasionally those that are fail to deliver, it is a good rule-of-thumb and easy to remember.

All Chianti other than *classico* must contain between 75 and 90 per cent Sangiovese plus the possibility of 5 to 10 per cent Canaiolo nero, 5 to 10 per cent Trebbiano or Malvasia, and up to a maximum of 10 per cent Cabernet or any other specified black grape varieties. This recipe applied to Chianti Classico until 1995, when it was changed to allow up to 100 per cent Sangiovese, which should be a good move for those dedicated growers who are striving to get this difficult variety right. With the amount of Cabernet and other black grapes increased to 15 per cent, this DOC is wide open to many of the so-called "super-Tuscans" to be classified as Chianti Classico and thereby greatly enhance the reputation of this once great appellation.

🍷 3–5 years (inexpensive, everyday drinking), 4–8 years (more serious Chianti), 6–20 years (finest *classico*)

✓ *Antinori* (Pepole) • *Badia a Coltibuono* • *Castellare di Castellina* • *Castellini Villa* • *Castello di Ama* • *Castello di Brolio* • *Castello di Cacchiano* • *Castello Querceto* • *Castello di Rampolla* • *Castello di San Paolo in Rosso* • *Castello di Volpaia* • *Felsina Berardenga* • *Fontodi Isole e Olena* • *Monsanto* (Il Poggio) • *Podere Il Palazzino* • *Poggerino* • *Riecine* • *San Felice San Giusto* • *Terrabianca* • *Uggiano Vecchie Terre di Montefili*

COLLI ALBANI DOC
Latium
Soft and fruity, dry and semi-sweet white wines that can be *spumante*.

COLLI ALTOTIBERINI DOC
Umbria
An interesting DOC in the hilly upper Tiber valley area, which produces dry white wines from Trebbiano and Malvasia, and firm, fruity

reds from Sangiovese and Merlot. However, it is the crisp, fragrant rosés from the same red grape varieties that most people prefer.

COLLI AMERINI DOC
Umbria
Dry whites from Trebbiano with the possible addition of Grechetto, Verdello, Garganega, and Malvasia, with red and rosé from Sangiovese plus the possibility of Montepulciano, Ciliegiolo, Canaiolo, Merlot, and Barbera. A dry white pure Malvasia varietal may also be produced.

COLLI DELL'ETRURIA CENTRALE DOC
Tuscany
The idea was fine, to provide an alternative appellation for lesser red, white, and rosé wines produced in the Chianti area and thus improve the DOCG through selection. But the name hardly trips off the tongue and one might be forgiven for thinking it was agreed to by producers who wanted any excuse not to use it and so keep churning out as much Chianti as possible. Red wines may be referred to as *vermiglio*, which has historical connotations with Chianti, and *vin santo* may also be made.

COLLI DEL TRASIMENO DOC
Umbria
A very large DOC area on the Tuscan border. The dry and off-dry whites are ordinary, but the reds, in which the bitter edge of Sangiovese is softened with Gamay, Ciliegiolo, Malvasia, and Trebbiano are more interesting.

🍷 2–5 years

✓ *La Fiorita*

COLLI DI LUNI DOC
Tuscany
See Colli di Luni DOC (Liguria, Northwest Italy)

COLLI LANUVINI DOC
Latium
Smooth, white wines, either dry or semi-sweet.

COLLINE LUCCHESI DOC
Tuscany
This DOC produces light, soft, Chianti-like reds and bland, dry, Trebbiano-based whites.

COLLI MARTANI DOC
Umbria
This covers four varietal wines from a large but promising area encompassing the Montefalco DOC: Sangiovese, Trebbiano, Grechetto, and the single-commune Grechetto di Todi.

COLLI PERUGINI DOC
Umbria
Dry, slightly fruity, Trebbiano-based white wines, full-bodied red wines, and dry, fresh rosé wines, primarily from Sangiovese grapes. Produced in a large area between Colli del Trasimeno and the Tiber, covering six communes in the province of Perugia and one in the province of Terni.

CORI DOC
Latium
Little-seen and rarely exciting, dry, semi-sweet, or sweet white wines and smooth, vinous reds.

ELBA DOC
Tuscany
The range of wines from the holiday isle of Elba have been expanded to include ten types: Trebbiano-based dry white; Sangiovese-based

red, and *riserva* red; rosato; Ansonica dell'Elba (dry white from the Ansonica, better known as the Inzolia grape of Sicily); Ansonica Passito dell'Elba; Aleatico dell'Elba; Vin Santo dell'Elba; Vin Santo dell'Elba Occhio di Pernice; and a white *spumante*. However, these wines are mostly made for tourists.

🍷 *In situ* only

✓ *Acquabona*

EST! EST!! EST!!! DI MONTEFIASCONE DOC
Latium
The name is the most memorable thing about these dry or semi-sweet white wines made from Trebbiano and Malvasia grapes grown around Lake Bolsena, adjacent to the Soave district. Traditionally, the name dates to the 12th century, when a fat German bishop called Johann Fugger had to go to Rome for the coronation of Henry V. In order to drink well on his journey, he sent his *majordomo* ahead to visit the inns along the route and mark those with the best wine with the word "Est", short for "*Vinum est bonum*". When he arrived at Montefiascone, the *majordomo* so liked the local wine that he chalked "Est! Est!! Est!!!". Fugger must have agreed with him, because once he had tasted the wine he cancelled his trip and stayed in Montefiascone until his death. The truth of the story is uncertain, for, although a tomb in the village church bears Fugger's name, whether it contains his 800-year-old body or not is unknown. As for the wine, Hugh Johnson has accurately described it as an unextraordinary white wine that trades on its oddball name.

FALERNO *or* FALERNUM
Latium
Falernum was the famous wine of ancient Rome. Its modern equivalent is a typically dark and rustically rich Aglianico wine, the best of which is the Villa Matilde *riserva*, which has a full aroma and a better balance than most. A dry white wine is also produced.

FRASCATI DOC
Latium

Most Frascati used to be flabby or oxidized, but with recent improvements in vinification techniques they are now invariably fresh and clean, although many still have a bland, peardrop aroma and taste. The few exceptions come from virtually the same group of top-performing producers as they did a decade ago and these wines stand out for their noticeably full flavour, albeit in a fresh, zippy-zingy style. Frascati is made from Trebbiano and Malvasia grapes, primarily dry, but semi-sweet, sweet, and *spumante* styles are also made.

🍷 1–2 years

✓ *Colli di Catone* (especially Colle Gaio – other labels include Villa Catone and Villa Porziana) • *Fontana Candida* (Vigneti Santa Teresa) • *Villa Simone*

GALESTRO
Tuscany
This ultra-clean, light, fresh, and delicately fruity, dry white wine is made by a *consorzio* of Chianti producers to agreed standards. It is shortly due to receive DOC recognition.

GRECHETTO *or* GRECO
Umbria
Clean, fresh, dry and sweet white wines with a pleasant floral aroma that can make interesting drinking, but seldom excel, with the exception of Bigi's Marrano, which is aged in oak. The Maremma are well-made, light and fruity, dry red, white, and rosé wines, which come from the coastal Maremma hills.

✓ *Bigi* (Marrano) • *Maremma* (Tuscany)

MARINO DOC
Latium
A typically light and unexciting Trebbiano and Malvasia blend that may be dry, semi-sweet, or *spumante*. Paola di Mauro's deliciously rich and caramelized Colle Picchioni Oro stands out due to its relatively high proportion of Malvasia grapes, and the fact that it receives a prefermentation maceration on its skins and is matured in *barriques*.

⌐ 1–4 years

✓ *Colle Picchioni* (Oro)

MERLOT
Tuscany
There is only one classic Merlot produced in Tuscany, Masseto, and although it is one of the most expensive red wines in Italy, some vintages can stand shoulder to shoulder with Pétrus, which might make it look like a bargain, depending on your perspective.

✓ *Villa Banfi* (Mandrielle) • *Tenuta dell'Ornellaia* (Masseto)

MONTECARLO DOC
Tuscany
Some interesting dry white wines are starting to appear in this area situated between Carmignano and the coast. Although based on the bland Trebbiano, supplementary varieties (Roussanne, Sémillon, Pinot gris, Pinot blanc, Sauvignon blanc, and Vermentino) may account for 30 to 40 per cent of the blend, thus allowing growers to express individual styles, from light and delicate to full and rich, either with or without *barrique*-ageing. Red wines may be made from Sangiovese, Canaiolo, Cilíegiolo, Colorino, Syrah, Malvasia, Cabernet franc, Cabernet sauvignon, and Merlot. A white *vin santo* and a pink Occhio di Pernice *vin santo* are also allowed.

⌐ 4–10 years

✓ *Fattoria dell Buonamico* • *Carmignani* • *Fattoria Michi* • *Vigna del Greppo*

MONTECOMPATRI COLONNA *or* MONTECOMPATRI *or* COLONNA DOC
Latium
These dry or semi-sweet, Malvasia-based white wines may bear the name of one or both of the above towns on the label.

MONTEFALCO DOC
Umbria
There is a significant difference in quality between these basic red and white wines and the more interesting, characterful DOCG Sagrantino of Montefalco.

MONTEFALCO SAGRANTINO DOCG
Umbria
Upgraded to DOCG in 1992 and detached from the basic Montefalco denomination, these distinctive red wines in dry and sweet *passito* styles are made exclusively from the Sagrantino grape, which has the advantage of being grown on the best-exposed hillside vineyards southwest of Perugia. The *passito* wines are the most authentic in style, dating back to the 15th century, but the dry table-wine style, which hints of ripe, fresh-picked blackberries, is the best and most consistent.

⌐ 3–12 years

✓ *Fratelli Adanti* • *Antonelli* • *Villa Antico* • *Arnaldo Caprai*

MONTEREGIO DI MASSA MARITTIMA DOC
Tuscany
These are red, white, rosé, *novello*, and *vin santo* from the northern part of the province of Grosseto. A dry white Vermentino varietal wine and a pink *passito* called Occhio di Pernice are also included within Monteregio di Massa Marittima DOC.

MONTESCUDAIO DOC
Tuscany

A Trebbiano-based dry white wine, a soft, slightly fruity, Sangiovese-based red, and a *vin santo* from the Cecina valley.

⌐ 1–3 years

✓ *Poggio Gagliardo* • *Sorbaiano*

MORELLINO DI SCANSANO DOC
Tuscany
This DOC produces some good Brunello-like wines from 100 per cent pure Sangiovese, which are thick with tasty, ripe fruit and can age well.

⌐ 4–8 years

✓ *Erik Banti* • *Motta* • *Fattoria Le Pupille*

MOSCADELLO DI MONTALCINO DOC
Tuscany
An ancient style of aromatic, sweet Muscat that was famous long before Brunello. Fortified versions and sweet *frizzante* are also possible.

⌐ Upon purchase

✓ *Villa Banfi* (Vendemia Tardiva) • *Col d'Orca* • *Tenuta Il Poggione*

MOSCATO
Tuscany
There is just one Tuscan Moscato DOC, Moscadello di Montalcino, but a few delicately sweet rosé *vini da tavola* are made from the Moscato rosa grape. It is an exquisite wine well worth searching out.

⌐ Upon purchase

✓ *Castello di Farnatella* (Rosa Rosae)

ORVIETO DOC
Umbria and Latium
The vineyards for this popular, widely exported, dry or semi-sweet, Trebbiano-based white wine are primarily located in Umbria. In general, Orvieto is still disappointing, although Bigi's Vigneto Torricella remains outstanding and the number of wines aspiring to a similar quality is growing. The best semi-sweet, or *abboccato*, style will include a small proportion of botrytized grapes. Fully-botrytized, or *muffato*, Orvieto are extremely rare, but well worth tracking down as they offer a fabulous combination of elegance, concentration, and youthful succulence.

⌐ Upon purchase

✓ *Antinori* (Campogrande) • *Barberani* (Castagnolo) • *Bigi* (Torricella) • *Decugnano dei Barbi* • *Palazzone* (Terre Vineate)

PARRINA DOC
Tuscany

The dry whites of Parrina, the most southerly of Tuscany's DOCs, are the least interesting. The Sangiovese-based reds used to be merely soft, light, and attractive, but of late have become much darker, fuller, and richer, like an oaky Chianti, with just a touch of vanillin sweetness on the finish, and even an occasional wisp of mint on the aftertaste.

⌐ 3–7 years

✓ *Franca Spinola*

POMINO DOC
Tuscany
This wine dates back to 1716, and a Pomino was commercialized as a single-vineyard Chianti by Marchesi de' Frescobaldi long before it was resurrected as its own DOC in 1983. The white is a blend of Pinot blanc, Chardonnay, and Trebbiano, although Frescobaldi's Il Benefizio is pure Chardonnay. The red is a blend of Sangiovese, Canaiolo, Merlot, Cabernet franc, and Cabernet sauvignon. A semi-sweet *vin santo* is also produced in both red and white styles.

🍷 1–3 years (blended white)
3–7 years (red and Il Benefizio)

✓ *Frescobaldi* • *Fattoria Petrognano*

ROSATO DELLA LEGA
Tuscany

Rosato della Lega are dry, Tuscan, rosé wines, which are produced by members of the Chianti Classico *consorzio*.

ROSSO DELLA LEGA
Tuscany

These are reasonable, everyday red wines, which are produced by members of the Chianti Classico *consorzio*.

ROSSO DI MONTALCINO DOC
Tuscany

This appellation is for lesser or declassified wines of Brunello di Montalcino or for wines made from young vines. Although there has been a tendency in recent years to produce deeper, darker, more concentrated wines, as a rule the biggest Rosso di Montalcino wines are much more accessible in their youth than Brunello, which some readers may prefer.

🍷 5–15 years

✓ *Altesino* • *Castelgiocondo* • *Conti Costanti* • *Lisini* • *Tenuta Il Poggione* • *Val di Suga*

ROSSO DI MONTEPULCIANO DOC
Tuscany

This DOC is for the so-called lesser wines of Vino Nobile di Montepulciano and, like Rosso di Montalcino DOC, its wines are softer and more approachable when young.

🍷 5–15 years

✓ *Avignonesi* • *Bindella* • *Podere Boscarelli* • *Le Casalte* • *Contucci* • *Fattoria de Cerro* • *Poliziano* • *Tenuta Trerose*

SAGRANTINO
Umbria

Another local Italian variety that almost died out but has undergone a revival, Sagrantino traditionally makes both dry (normal harvest) and sweet, *passito* red wines. Some people believe its name is derived from *sagra*, which means "festival" and suggests that the wines it produced were originally reserved for feast days.

SANGIOVESE *or* SANGIOVESE-DOMINATED
Tuscany and Umbria

Although just ten years ago no-one believed that Sangiovese could stand alone, its success was merely a matter of reduced yields and a suitable *terroir*. With good, but not overstated, *barrique*-ageing, and bottling at the optimum moment for fruit retention, Sangiovese can be rich, lush, and satisfyingly complete, with a succulent, spicy-cedary oak complexity. It is commonly found in Umbria, but exceptional Sangiovese-based wines are relatively rare.

✓ **Tuscany** *Altesino* (Palazzo Altesi) • *Avignonesi* (I Grifi) • *Badia a Coltibuono* (Sangioveto) • *Castello di Cacchiano* (RF, Rocca di Montegrossi) • *Villa Cafaggio* (San Martino, Solataia Basilica) • *Podere Capaccia* (Querciagrande) • *Felsina Berardenga* (Fontalloro) • *Fontodi* (Flaccianello della Pieve) • *Isole e Olena* (Cepparello) • *Monsanto* (Bianchi Vigneti di Scanni) • *Podere Il Palazzino* (Grosso Senese) • *Poliziano* (Elegia) • *Castello di*

Querceto (La Corte) • *Ruffino* (Cabreo Il Borgo) • *Guicciardini Strozzi* (Sodole) • *Terrabianca* (Campaccio, Piano del Cipresso) • *Monte Vertine* (Le Pergole Torte)
Umbria *Lungarotti*

SANGIOVESE-CABERNET BLENDS
Tuscany

Cabernet sauvignon was originally blended with Sangiovese to supply fruit and accessibility within a classic fine-wine structure.

✓ *Altesino* (Alte d'Altesi) • *Antinori* (Tignanello) • *Caparzo* (Cà del Pazzo) • *Monsanto* (Tinscvil) • *Querciabella* (Camartina) • *Castello di Volpaia* (Balifico)

SANGIOVESE WITH OTHER ITALIAN GRAPES
Tuscany

✓ *Castellare di Castellina* (I Sodi de San Niccolò) • *Ricasoli-Firidolfi* (Geremia) • *Monte Vertine* (Il Sodaccio)

SAUVIGNON
Tuscany

The Sauvignon does not really seem at home in Tuscany, although judging by the remarkable success of Ornellaia's Poggio alle Gazze, you wouldn't think this was the case.

✓ *Tenuta dell'Ornellaia* (Poggio alle Gazze)

SYRAH
Tuscany

This classic Rhône grape shows tremendous potential, but at equally tremendous prices.

✓ *Fontodi* (Case Via) • *Isole e Olena* (L'Eremo)

TORGIANO DOC
Umbria

This DOC was built on the back of the reputation of one producer, Lungarotti (*see also* Torgiano Riserva DOCG). As before, Torgiano DOC covers generic blends for red and rosé (Sangiovese, Canaiolo, Trebbiano, Ciliégiolo, and Montepulciano) and white (Trebbiano, Grechetto, Malvasia, and Verdello), but also includes sparkling (Pinot noir and Chardonnay) as well as five varietal wines: Chardonnay, Pinot Grigio, Riesling Italico, Cabernet Sauvignon, and Pinot Noir.

🍷 3–8 years (red), 1–5 years (white and rosé)

✓ *Lungarotti*

TORGIANO RISERVA DOCG
Umbria

Lungarotti's best *rosso*, the *riserva* is a model example of how all DOCG denominations should work, and in respect of this it has deservedly been upgraded from DOC.

🍷 4–20 years

✓ *Lungarotti*

VAL D'ARBIA DOC
Tuscany

A large area south of the Chianti Classico district, producing a dry, fruity, Trebbiano-based white wine boosted by Malvasia and Chardonnay, which may be dried prior to fermentation for dry, semi-sweet, or sweet *vin santo*.

VAL DI CORNIA DOC
Tuscany

A large area of scattered vineyards in the hills east of Piombino and south of Bolgheri, Val di Cornia produces rarely seen Trebbiano-based dry

whites and Sangiovese-based reds and rosés, with the possible sub-appellations of Campiglia Marittima, Piombino, San Vincenzo, and Surveto.

VELLETRI DOC
Latium

Velletri DOC produces rather uninspiring, dry or semi-sweet white wines and vinous reds from the Castelli Romani area.

VERNACCIA DI SAN GIMIGNANO DOCG
Tuscany

This dry white wine was Italy's first-ever DOC, so DOCG status was inevitable, even if most are bland. The best have always been deliciously crisp and full of vibrant fruit, which makes them well worth seeking out, but not seriously worthy of DOCG status if this is supposed to signify one of the world's finest wines.

🍷 1–3 years

✓ *Falchini* • *Panizzi* • *Terruzi & Puthod*

VIGNANELLO DOC
Latium

This is a new and untested DOC for generic red, white, and rosé blends, plus pure Grechetto dry white wine in still and fully sparkling formats.

VIN SANTO
Tuscany and Umbria

A red or white *passito* wine that may be sweet, semi-sweet, or dry.

VINO NOBILE DI MONTEPULCIANO DOCG
Tuscany

Made largely from Prugnolo gentile, a clone of Sangiovese, plus Canaiolo and other local grapes, including white varieties, these wines come from Montepulciano. Most wines used to be overrated and overpriced, and a number still are, but a growing number of producers make wines that deserve DOCG status. The best wines resemble a fine *riserva* Chianti Classico, but have a more exuberant character, with generous ripe-fruit flavours hinting of cherry and plum.

🍷 6–25 years

✓ *Avignonesi* • *Bindella* • *Podere Boscarelli* • *Le Casalte* • *Contucci* • *Fattoria de Cerro* • *Poliziano* • *Tenuta Trerose*

ZAGAROLO DOC
Latium

This DOC has a tiny production of dry or semi-sweet white from Malvasia and Trebbiano grapes, which are grown east of Frascati in an area more famed for its wines half a millennium ago than it is now.

NEW IGT WINES

The following Indicazioni Geografiche Tipiche wines were agreed at the end of 1996, but we have yet to see what style, quality, or consistency each one will establish.

Latium *Castelli Romani* • *Circeo* • *Civitella d'Agliano* • *Colli Cimini* • *Colli delle Sabina* • *Colli Etruschi Viterbesi* • *Frusinate O del Frusinate* • *Lazio* • *Nettuno*

Tuscany *Alta Valle Della Greve* • *Colli della Topscana Central* • *Maremma Toscana* • *Orcia* • *Toscana O Toscano* • *Val di Magra*

Umbria *Allerona* • *Assisi* • *Bettona* • *Cannara* • *Lago di Corbara* • *Narni* • *Spello* • *Umbria*

EAST-CENTRAL ITALY

This area comprises the regions of Emilia-Romagna, the Marches, the Abruzzi, and Molise. The best-quality wines come from the Marches and the Abruzzi, but the best-known is Emilia-Romagna's lollipop wine, Lambrusco, which is exported in vast quantities.

IF THIS REGION, which extends across almost the entire width of northern Italy into Piedmont, appears geographically to wander off its central-east designation, it certainly does not do so topographically, for every hectare lies east of the Apennines on initially hilly ground that flattens out into alluvial plains stretching towards the Adriatic.

EMILIA-ROMAGNA

Emilia-Romagna is protected on its western flank by the Apennines, the source of seven major, and many minor, rivers. The rich soil results in abundant grape production, the most prolific varieties

FACTORS AFFECTING TASTE AND QUALITY

LOCATION
This area stretches along the Adriatic coast, from Molise in the south right up to Emilia-Romagna.

CLIMATE
The influence of the Mediterranean provides generally hot and dry summers, which get progressively hotter as one travels south, and cool winters. In hilly regions microclimates are created by the effects of altitude and aspect.

ASPECT
The best vineyards are invariably to be found on well-drained, foothill sites, but viticulture is spread across every imaginable type of terrain, with a heavy concentration on flat plains, particularly along the Po Valley in Emilia-Romagna, where grapes are produced in abundance.

SOIL
The soil is mostly alluvial, with some outcrops of granite and limestone.

VITICULTURE AND VINIFICATION
A wide variety of viticultural practices and vinification techniques are used here. Much bulk-blended

wine originates here, but some producers retain the most worthwhile traditions and augment them with modern methods.

GRAPE VARIETIES
Aglianico, Albana (*syn.* Biancame, Bianchello, Greco di Ancona, or Passerina), Ancellotta, Barbarossa, Barbera, Beverdino, Bombino bianco (*syn.* Pagadebit or Pagadebito), Cabernet franc, Cabernet sauvignon, Chardonnay, Ciliegiolo, Croatina (*syn.* Bonarda), Fortana (*syn.* Fruttana or Uva d'Oro), Incrocio Bruni 54 (Verdicchio x Sauvignon), Lacrima (*syn.* Gallioppa or Galloppo), Lambrusco, Maceratino, Malvasia, Merlot, Mondeuse (*syn.* Cagnina, Refosco or Terrano), Montepulciano, Montuni (*syn.* Montù or Bianchino), Muscat (*syn.* Moscato), Ortrugo (*syn.* Altra uva), Pecorino, Perricone (*syn.* Pignoletto), Pinot blanc (*syn.* Pinot bianco), Pinot gris (*syn.* Pinot grigio), Pinot noir (*syn.* Pinot nero), Sangiovese, Sauvignon (*syn.* Spergola), Toscano, Ugni blanc (*syn.* Campolese, Trebbiano or Albanella), Verdea, Verdicchio, Vernaccia Nera, Welschriesling (*syn.* Riesling Italico)

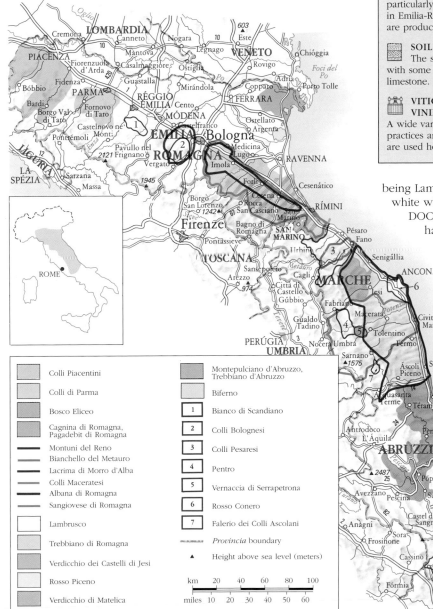

being Lambrusco, Trebbiano, and Albana, which produce rustic white wines that, unaccountably, have been given Italy's first DOCG for a white wine. Emilia-Romagna does, however, have some genuinely outstanding *vini da tavola*, such as Fattoria Paradiso's Vigna del Dosso, a red from the Barbarossa and, especially, a classy Sangiovese-Cabernet blend from Fattoria Zerbina, called Marzeno di Marzeno.

THE ABRUZZI (ABRUZZO)

Although its hills have a variety of soils and microclimates, and should be capable of producing many fine wines, the Abruzzi offers only one – Montepulciano d'Abruzzo. But winemakers are conservative here and only one producer, Santoro Corella, is experimenting with different varieties.

EAST-CENTRAL ITALY
See also p.307
With the Apennines forming the region's western border, the eastern part of central Italy is dominated by their foothills and the plains.

Map legend

- Colli Piacentini
- Colli di Parma
- Bosco Eliceo
- Cagnina di Romagna, Pagadebit di Romagna
- Montuni del Reno
- Bianchello del Metauro
- Lacrima di Morro d'Alba
- Colli Maceratesi
- Albana di Romagna
- Sangiovese di Romagna
- Lambrusco
- Trebbiano di Romagna
- Verdicchio dei Castelli di Jesi
- Rosso Piceno
- Verdicchio di Matelica
- Montepulciano d'Abruzzo, Trebbiano d'Abruzzo
- Biferno
- 1 Bianco di Scandiano
- 2 Colli Bolognesi
- 3 Colli Pesaresi
- 4 Pentro
- 5 Vernaccia di Serrapetrona
- 6 Rosso Conero
- 7 Falerio dei Colli Ascolani
- *Provincia* boundary
- ▲ Height above sea level (meters)

km 20 40 60 80 100
miles 10 20 30 40 50 60

THE MARCHES (MARCHE)

Tourism has been a factor in the success of the Marches's wines. This region has a beautiful coastline where holidaymakers quench their thirst with the local white – the dry Verdicchio. But there are more exciting wines to be found in the exceptionally fine DOCs of Rosso Cònero and Rosso Piceno and, in a few circumstances, Sangiovese dei Colli Pesaresi, together with excellent *vini da tavola*, such as Rosso di Corinaldo and Tristo di Montesecco.

MOLISE

This poor region with high unemployment has a badly equipped wine industry. Until 1963 it was combined with the Abruzzi and only gained its first DOC in 1983. Italian-wine expert Burton Anderson believes that it may one day provide wines of real class.

AVERAGE ANNUAL PRODUCTION

REGION	DOC PRODUCTION	TOTAL PRODUCTION
Emilia-Romagna	600,000 hl (6.6 million cases)	11 million hl (122 million cases)
Molise	450,000 hl (5 million cases)	550,000 hl (6 million cases)
Marches	275,000 hl (3 million cases)	2.5 million hl (28 million cases)
Abruzzi	250,000 hl (2.7 million cases)	4.5 million hl (50 million cases)

Percentage of total Italian production:
Emilia-Romagna 14%; Abruzzi 6%;
Marches 3%; Molise 0.7%.

THE APPELLATIONS OF
EAST-CENTRAL ITALY

ALBANA
Emilia-Romagna

In theory, this must be Italy's greatest white-wine grape, as Albana di Romagna was Italy's first DOCG. In practice, this high-yielding grape makes a rather rustic, almost common wine, improved to an extent by restricting production.

ALBANA DI ROMAGNA DOCG
Emilia-Romagna

These straightforward, fruity, sometimes dry, occasionally semi-sweet white wines are still or sparkling and may be in a very sweet style, either by regular vinification or from *passito* grapes. This is the very precise style, reputation, and quality that in 1987 became the first Italian white wine to receive DOCG status. From any angle, Albana di Romagna got its DOCG through a political fudge. This might not be surprising from the masters of political fudge, but it was monumentally stupid after the controversy surrounding the politically fudged Chianti DOCG. It's a bit like the French setting up a super-AOC and making Muscadet the first white to receive an elite status. On the bright side, the producers of Albana di Romagna have had so much stick that they have had to work hard at improving their product, and the wines are above average for an Italian white DOC.

⌛ In situ only
☑ *Fattoria Paradiso*

ANCELLOTTA
Emilia-Romagna

This is used to deepen the colour of Lambrusco.

BARBAROSSA
Emilia-Romagna

This variety is unique to Emilia-Romagna and produces one of the region's best red wines.

☑ *Fattoria Paradiso* (Vigna del Dosso)

BERTINORO DOC
Emilia-Romagna
See Pagadebit di Romagna DOC

BIANCHELLO DEL METAURO DOC
Marches

Dry, delicate white wines are made from the Bianchello grape (plus possibly Malvasia) grown in the lower Metauro valley.

BIANCO DI SCANDIANO DOC
Emilia-Romagna

Full-bodied, dry and semi-sweet white wines that may also be *spumante* and *frizzante*.

BIFERNO DOC
Molise

Smooth, slightly tannic, red and fruity rosé wines from Montepulciano, Trebbiano, and Aglianico grapes; and dry, lightly aromatic, white wines from Trebbiano, Bombino, and Malvasia.

BOSCO ELICEO DOC
Emilia-Romagna

A large coastal region, separated from the major Emilia-Romagna viticultural areas in the northeast of the region. There is a grapey, rustic red varietal from the mysterious Fortana grape, also known as the Uva d'Oro, although I know nothing of it and have not found it elsewhere. Bosco Eliceo Fortan can be dry or sweet, has a slightly bitter tannic bite, is *frizzante* and not dissimilar to Lambrusco. There is also a generic blended white (Trebbiano, Sauvignon, and Malvasia – may be *frizzante*); two pure varietal wines, a Merlot (sometimes *frizzantino*) and a Sauvignon (may also be *frizzantino*).

CAGNINA DI ROMAGNA DOC
Emilia-Romagna

Tannic but sweet and fruity red wines, with balancing high acidity.

COLLI BOLOGNESI DOC
Emilia-Romagna

Also known as Colli Bolognesi dei Castelli Medioevali or Colli Bolognesi di Monte San Pietro, this appellation covers an Albana-

and Trebbiano-based generic white; three red varietals, Barbera, Cabernet Sauvignon, and Merlot; and five whites, Riesling Italico, Sauvignon (the best, sometimes *frizzantino*), Pinot Bianco, Pignoletto, and Chardonnay. The last three are made still, *frizzante*, and fully *spumante*.

⌛ 1–3 years
☑ *Terre Rosse*

COLLI MACERATESI DOC
Marches

This huge area produces a dry, white-wine blend that used to be Trebbiano based, but now must contain at least 80 per cent Maceratino, and Verdicchio, Malvasia, and Chardonnay if possible.

COLLI DI PARMA DOC
Emilia-Romagna

Solid, slightly *frizzantino* red wines and two white varietals, Malvasia and Sauvignon, in dry, sweet, still, *frizzante,* or *spumante* styles.

COLLI PESARESI DOC
Marches

Originally a Sangiovese DOC, Colli Pesaresi now encompasses four different wines although the richly coloured, deeply flavoured Sangiovese-based red still stands out, with the best showing real class and finesse. Focara, another Colli Pesaresi red, may contain up to 15 per cent Pinot noir, but displays Sangiovese-like characteristics. There is also a Trebbiano-based, generic dry white and a very similar wine called Roncaglia.

⌛ 3–8 years
☑ *Constanini* (La Torraccia) • *Tattà* • *Umani Ronchi* • *Vallone* • *Villa Pigna*

COLLI PIACENTINI DOC
Emilia-Romagna

Fourteen wines produced in a vast district of the Piacenza hills where Julius Caesar's father-in-law made a wine that was traditionally drunk from a large vessel called a *gutturnium*. This story is the origin of *Guttornio*, the name of the DOC's most famous wine, a blend of Barbera and Bonarda. A red, it is usually dry and still, although a semi-sweet *frizzantino* or *frizzante* version is sometimes produced. There are two blended whites: an aromatic wine called Monterosso Val d'Arda (Malvasia, Moscato, Trebbiano, and Ortrugo plus the possibility of

Beverdino and Sauvignon) in dry, sweet, still, *frizzantino* or *frizzante* styles; and a slightly less aromatic wine called Val Nur (Malvasia, Moscato, Trebbiano, and Ortrugo), which may be dry or sweet, still, *frizzante*, or *spumante*. The following white varietals may be *frizzantino*, *frizzante*, or *spumante*: Chardonnay, Trebbiano Val Trebba, Malvasia, Ortrugo, Pinot Grigio, and Sauvignon. The Chardonnay, Pinot Grigio, and Sauvignon must be dry, but the others may be dry or sweet. There are three red varietals: Barbera, Cabernet Sauvignon, and Pinot Nero, which can be dry or sweet, still, *frizzantino*, *frizzante*, or *spumante*.

FALERIO DEI COLLI ASCOLANI DOC
Marches
Dry, lightly-scented white wines made from a blend of Trebbiano, Passerina, Verdicchio, Malvasia, Pinot blanc, and Pecorino.

🍷— 1–3 years

✓ *Cocci Grifoni* (Vigneti San Basso)

FOCARA DOC
Marches
See Colli Pesaresi DOC

GUTTURNIO *OR* GUTTURNIO DEI COLLI PIACENTINI DOC
Emilia-Romagna
See Colli Piacentini DOC

LACRIMA DI MORRO D'ALBA DOC
Marches
Nothing to do with the wine Lacryma Christi or the town of Alba in the Piedmont, this is a soft, medium-bodied red from the mysterious Lacrima grape grown in and around Morro d'Alba, in the province of Ancona. A seemingly single-village wine, this DOC has the largest appellation of the Marches region. Montepulciano and Verdicchio may also be used.

LACRYMA (*or* LACRIMA) CHRISTI DOC
Campania
See Vesuvio DOC (Southern Italy and the Islands)

LAMBRUSCO
Emilia-Romagna
Most Lambrusco is non-DOC, usually because screw-tops (illegal under DOC law) are used. Non-DOC Lambrusco is not interesting and the DOC only occasionally so. Lambrusco is an off-dry, cherry-red, frothy wine, which is low in alcohol (although the DOC is higher) and tastes of ripe cherries; export wines are mostly sweet. White and rosé styles are made and the sparkle varies from barely *frizzantino* to virtually *spumante*. Of the many sub-varieties, Grasparossa, Salamino, and Sorbara make the most interesting wines, but others include Foglia Frastagliata, Maestri, Marani, Monterrico, and Viadanese.

LAMBRUSCO DI SORBARA DOC
Emilia-Romagna
Mostly dry, although sometimes semi-sweet, these are medium-bodied, *frizzantino* reds or rosés with more body and depth of flavour than most.

LAMBRUSCO GRASPAROSSA DI CASTELVETRO DOC
Emilia-Romagna
Dry or semi-sweet, vinous, *frizzantino* reds and rosés, usually better than non-DOC versions, but not quite matching the Lambrusco di Sorbara.

LAMBRUSCO REGGIANO DOC
Emilia-Romagna
Dry or semi-sweet, *frizzante* red and rosé wines that are the lightest DOC Lambruscos.

LAMBRUSCO SALAMINO DI SANTA CROCE DOC
Emilia-Romagna
These dry or semi-sweet, vinous, semi-*spumante* red and rosé wines are the most aromatic of the Lambruscos and can come up to the standard of the Lambrusco di Sorbara.

MONTEPULCIANO D'ABRUZZO DOC
Abruzzi
This is the Abruzzi's only fine wine and there are two distinct styles. Made from Montepulciano with up to 15 per cent Sangiovese, both are very deep in colour, but one is full of soft, luscious fruit, the other firmer and more tannic. A lighter style called *cerasuolo* exists for cherry-pink wine with fresh fruit, but it is seldom as exciting.

🍷— 4–8 or 8–20 years (red), 1–3 years

✓ *Illuminati* • *Emidio Pepe* • *Tenuta del Priore* • *CS di Tollo* (Collo Secco) • *Valentini*

MONTEROSSO VAL D'ARDA DOC
Emilia-Romagna
See Colli Piacentini DOC

MONTUNI DEL RENO DOC
Emilia-Romagna
Light, dry or sweet, still or sparkling white wine with a slightly bitter finish.

PAGADEBIT DI ROMAGNA DOC
Emilia-Romagna
Dry and semi-sweet, still or *frizzante* white wines from the Bombino bianco grape, known locally as "Pagadebit". This DOC includes a single-village wine called Bertinoro, the characteristics of which are the same, although potentially finer.

PENTRO *or* PENTRO DI ISERNIA DOC
Molise
Smooth, slightly tannic reds and dry, fruity rosés from Montepulciano and Sangiovese; and dry, fresh whites from Trebbiano and Bombino.

PIGNOLETTO
Emilia-Romagna
Believed to be a distant relation of the Riesling.

RONCAGLIA DOC
Marches
See Colli Pesaresi DOC

ROSSO CÒNERO DOC
Marches
Fine Montepulciano-based wines that improve with *barrique*-ageing. Deep-coloured and rich.

🍷— 6–15 years

✓ *Garofoli* (Agontano) • *Umani Ronchi* (San Lorenzo) • *Marchetti* • *Mecvini*

ROSSO PICENO DOC
Marches
Small amounts of Trebbiano and Passerina may now be added to this excellent Sangiovese and Montepulciano wine. The best are firm and ruby-coloured with smooth fruit. Often *barrique*-aged.

🍷— 4–10 years

✓ *Cocci Grifoni* • *Villamagna* • *Villa Pigna*

SANGIOVESE-CABERNET
Emilia-Romagna
This blend is relatively rare in this region.

✓ *Fattoria Zerbina* (Marzeno di Marzeno)

SANGIOVESE DI ROMAGNA DOC
Emilia-Romagna
These solid red wines rarely excite, unless from exceptional vineyards.

🍷— 3–7 years

✓ *Fattoria Paradiso* (Vigneti delle Lepri)

TREBBIANO D'ABRUZZO DOC
Abruzzi
These are usually dry, neutral, and mediocre white wines, although they can be delicately scented and velvety in texture.

🍷— 1–3 years

✓ *Emidio Pepe* • *Tenuta del Priore* • *Valentini*

TREBBIANO DI ROMAGNA DOC
Emilia-Romagna
This producer makes dry, neutral white wines that are also made in dry, sweet, and semi-sweet *spumante* versions.

VAL NUR *or* VAL NUR DEI COLLI PIACENTINI DOC
Emilia-Romagna
See Colli Piacentini DOC

VERDICCHIO DEI CASTELLI DI JESI DOC
Marches
Popular, lean, fresh, and mostly uninteresting dry white wines. *Spumante*, *frizzante*, and *frizzantino* versions are also made.

🍷— 1–4 years

✓ *Brunori* • *Bucci* • *Fazi Battaglia* (Le Moie) • *Garofoli* • *Monte Schiavo* • *Umani Ronchi* • *Zaccagnini*

VERDICCHIO DI MATELICA DOC
Marches
Made in a hilly area in the centre of Verdicchio, these wines are slightly fatter than those of Castelli di Jesi, but most are just as uninteresting.

🍷— 1–4 years

✓ *Fratelli Bisci* • *La Monacesa*

VERNACCIA DI SERRAPETRONA DOC
Marches
Made from Vernaccia grapes, Sangiovese, Montepulciano, and Ciliegiolo may be added to these semi-sweet to sweet *spumante* reds.

NEW IGT WINES

The following IGT wines were agreed at the end of 1996, but we have yet to see what style, quality, or consistency each one will establish.

Abruzzi *Alto Tirino* • *Colli Aprutini* • *Colli del Sangro* • *Colline Frentane* • *Colline Pescaresi* • *Colline Teatime* • *Del Vastese O Histonium* • *Terre di Chieti* • *Valle Peligna*

Emilia-Romagna *Bianco del Sillaro* • *Bianco di Castelfranco Emilia* • *Colli Imolesi* • *Emilia O Dell'Emilia* • *Forlì* • *Fortana del Taro* • *Modena O Provincia di Modena* • *Ravenna* • *Rubicone* • *Val Tidone*

Marches *Marche*

Molise *Molise* • *Osco O Terre Íegli Osci* • *Rotac*

SOUTHERN ITALY AND THE ISLANDS

Hot and largely hilly, with volcanic soils, southern Italy is an ancient and prolific wine-growing area. Overproduction continues to be a problem, but well-made wines were starting to clean up Italy's southern-plonk image over a decade ago, since when a host of flying winemakers have made some remarkably expressive wines utilizing local varieties.

JUTTING OUT INTO THE BLUE WATERS of the Mediterranean, the vineyards of southern Italy receive very little natural moisture and bake rather than bask in unrelenting sunshine. This explains the deep-coloured wines with strong flavours and high alcoholic levels. Although these heavy wines do not suit modern tastes and southern Italy continues to produce a glut of these almost unsaleable wines, the region is subtly changing course. Its small but growing volume of cleaner, finer, more expressive wines may enable it to establish an identity capable of thriving in ever more sophisticated world-wine markets. In this respect it is being helped by foreign investment and flying winemakers, but the biggest obstacle to consolidating these isolated successes is the poverty that has for so long blighted southern Italy.

APULIA (PUGLIA)

Apulia's exceptionally fertile plains make it one of Italy's largest wine-producing regions, but until the 1970s most of its wines were seen as fit only for blending or for making Vermouth. Because of this, most Apulian producers chose to try to rid themselves of this lowly reputation, bringing about a radical transformation of their industry. A great number of very ordinary wines are still produced, but various changes have greatly improved the situation. Irrigation schemes, the introduction of lower-yielding, higher-quality grape varieties (including many classic French ones), and a move away from the single-bush cultivation, known as *alberello*, to modern wire-trained systems, have led to both new wines gaining favour and some traditional ones showing renewed promise. The two most important grape varieties are now the Primitivo, which has been identified as the Zinfandel of California and is the earliest-ripening grape grown in Italy, and the Uva di Troia, which has no connection with the

Legend

	Aleatico di Puglia		
	Solopaca	1	Falerno del Massico
	Taburno	2	Vesuvio
	Greco di Tufo	3	Ischia
	Fiano di Avellino	4	Capri
	Taurasi	5	San Severo
	Orta Nova	6	Cacc'e mmittee di Lucera
	Rosso di Cerignola	7	Aglianico del Vulture
	Rosso Barletta	8	Cilento
	Cirò	9	Gravina
	Moscato di Trani	10	Gioia del Colle
	Martina	11	Primitivo di Manduria
	Locorotondo	12	Rosso Canosa
	Ostuni	13	Melissa
	Brindisi	14	Sant'Anna di Isola Capo Rizzuto
	Squinzano	15	Lamezia
	Salice Salentino	16	Greco di Bianco
	Nardo		*Provincia* boundary
	Alezio	▲	Height above sea level (metres)
	Leverano		
	Matino		

km 40 80 120
miles 20 40 60 80

SOUTHERN ITALY, see also p.307
Southern Italy produces huge quantities of wine. Apulia makes distinguished wines, but apart from the Aglianico wines of Basilicata and Campania, the quality is

THE AMALFI COAST
These vines and citrus trees are terraced on cliffs typical to this area.

town of Troia in Apulia's northern province of Foggia, but refers to ancient Troy, from whence the grape originates. It was brought to the region by the first Greeks to settle in the Taranto area.

CAMPANIA

The best-known wine of Campania Felix, as the Romans called this area, is Lacryma Christi (Tears of Christ), but the best quality is the lesser-known Taurasi DOCG made from the underrated Aglianico grape. Falerno del Massico is an up-and-coming Aglianico-based DOC, but apart from wines made by individual producers such as Mastroberardino and Antica Masseria Venditti, there is little else of interest produced here.

BASILICATA

Basilicata is a dramatic and wild region dominated by the extinct volcano Mount Vulture. Manufacturing industry is scarce here, accounting for less than one per cent of the region's output, and the mountainous terrain makes mechanized agriculture extremely difficult. Lacking investment finance and with two in every three inhabitants unemployed, Basilicata has not had the means nor the

THE ISLANDS, *see also* p.307
Sicily and Sardinia are usually included with southern Italy because they are on the same latitude, but they had to be separated for mapping purposes in this edition because of the proliferation of new appellations, including the contentious DOCG status of Vermentino di Gallura in Sardinia.

AVERAGE ANNUAL PRODUCTION		
REGION	DOC PRODUCTION	TOTAL PRODUCTION
Sicily	270,000 hl (3 million cases)	10 million hl (110 million cases)
Sardinia	260,000 hl (2.8 million cases)	2.5 million hl (28 million cases)
Apulia	198,000 hl (2.2 million cases)	11 million hl (122 million cases)
Calabria	33,000 hl (367,000 cases)	1.2 million hl (13 million cases)
Campania	12,500 hl (139,000 cases)	2.5 million hl (28 million cases)
Basilicata	6,300 hl (70,000 cases)	0.42 million hl (4.7 million cases)

Percentage of total Italian production: Apulia, 14%; Sicily, 13%; Campania, 3.3%; Sardinia, 3.3%; Calabria, 1.6%; Basilicata, 0.6%

incentive to modernize its wine industry. Consequently, with the exception of the first-class, if idiosyncratic, Aglianico del Vulture, (Basilicata's solitary DOC), a wonderful non-DOC Aglianico called Canneto from Fratelli d'Angelo, and delicious Moscato and Malvasia from Fratelli d'Angelo and Paternosta, the fine-wine scene in Basilicata is as barren as the landscape although it should make fertile pastures for flying winemakers.

CALABRIA

The decline in Calabria's viticultural output since the 1960s has been for the better in terms of quality. Since then, the most unsuitable land has been abandoned, and the ten current DOCs, located in hilly and mountainous terrain, may eventually prove to be a source of quality wine. At the moment, however, improvement in wine technology is slow and, with the exception of Umberto Ceratti's succulent Greco di Bianco, a world-class dessert wine that is a relic of the past, and Odoardi's Vigna Vecchia, a fruity red from the obscure Gagloppo variety, and a luscious Moscato *vino da tavola* from Guido Lojelo, this region also has little in the way of interesting wine.

SICILY (SICILIA)

Sicily is the largest island in the Mediterranean and, in terms of quantity, it is one of Italy's most important wine regions, annually producing a quantity of wine roughly equal to Veneto or Emilia-Romagna. Many of the island's wines are consumed locally, although the branded wine "Corvo" has a fairly high export profile. The ancient port of Marsah-el-Allah, which was built under Arab rule, gives its name to Sicily's once popular classic wine, Marsala. Although products of a similar style can be traced back to the Romans, who boiled up wines to sweeten them, Marsala was invented in 1773 by John Woodhouse of Liverpool. He shipped Marsala back to England, where it quickly caught on, and Nelson even insisted on supplying his Mediterranean fleet with the wine. By the mid-19th century, Marsala had evolved into a style between that of Madeira and Sherry. This traditional fortified wine now finds itself unaligned with modern tastes, although there has been an effort to re-establish it by dropping the flavoured versions and concentrating on the lighter *vergine* style. Equally classic, but rarer, is the succulently sweet Moscato from the island of Pantelleria, which, in fact, is closer to Tunisia than Sicily.

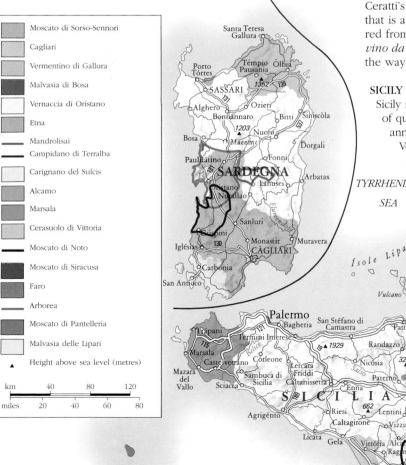

Moscato di Sorso-Sennori

Cagliari

Vermentino di Gallura

Malvasia di Bosa

Vernaccia di Oristano

Etna

Mandrolisai

Campidano di Terralba

Carignano del Sulcis

Alcamo

Marsala

Cerasuolo di Vittoria

Moscato di Noto

Moscato di Siracusa

Faro

Arborea

Moscato di Pantelleria

Malvasia delle Lipari

▲ Height above sea level (metres)

km 40 80 120
miles 20 40 60 80

THE POLLINO MOUNTAINS, CALABRIA
Spring flowers carpet the slopes above Frascineto, in the foothills of the Pollino Mountains. This small mountain range gives its name to the fruity chiaretto-style wine made from Gaglioppo, Greco nero, Malvasia, and Guarnaccia.

SARDINIA (SARDEGNA)

Sardinia is the second-largest island in the Mediterranean and while it produces virtually all styles of wine, the modernization its wine industry has undergone since the late 1970s has had a more radical effect on its white wines than on any other style. Although Sardinia produces no "fine" wines in the classic sense, the wines are generally well made and easy to enjoy, and a small number of top-performing wineries make interesting wines under the Carignano del Sulcis and Cagliari DOCs, while exceptional Malvasia *vini da tavola* are made by Gian Vittorio Naitana. Vermentino di Gallura was another enjoyable DOC, but

its controversial promotion was the most ludicrous abuse of DOCG status since Albana di Romagna. Gallura does offer the greatest potential for fine wines, but for reds, not whites. Its hilly terrain is naturally lower-yielding for black grape varieties, if they are to ripen fully, but it could produce intensely flavoured, age-worthy red wines from interesting local grape varieties like Cannonau, which is a local variant of Grenache.

FACTORS AFFECTING TASTE AND QUALITY

LOCATION
This area includes the southern mainland regions of Apulia, Campania, Basilicata, Calabria, the islands of Sicily further south, and Sardinia, across the Tyrrhenian Sea to the west.

CLIMATE
The south is by far the hottest and driest region of Italy, although the coastal areas and islands are tempered by maritime winds.

ASPECT
Most of the region is either mountainous or hilly, although vineyards are to be found on the flat land and gentle slopes of Apulia. The best sites are always found on the north-facing, higher slopes of hillsides where the vines receive less sun and benefit from the tempering effect of altitude, thus ensuring a longer growing season.

SOIL
Soil is predominantly volcanic and granitic, but there are some isolated outcrops of clay and chalk.

VITICULTURE AND VINIFICATION
This area, together with the Midi in France, is the principal source of Europe's infamous "wine lake". Nevertheless, producers using better-quality grape varieties grown on higher sites are making wines of a standard and style that deserve wider recognition. Flying winemakers have helped enormously by showing what can be done.

GRAPE VARIETIES
Aglianico, Albana (*syn.* Greco, but this Greco is not Grechetto), Aleatico, Alicante bouschet, Asprinio (*syn.* Asprino, Olivese, Ragusano, or Uva asprina), Barbera, Bianco d'Alessano, Biancolella (*syn.* Biancolelle, Ianculillo, Ianculella, Petit blanche, or Teneddu), Bombino, Bombino nero, Cabernet franc, Calabrese (*syn.* Nero d'Avola or Niura d'Avola), Carignan (*syn.* Carignano or Uva di Spagna), Carricante, Catarratti (*syn.* Cataratto), Chardonnay, Cinsault (*syn.* Ottavianello), Coda del Volpe (Caprettone, Coda di Pecora, or Pallagrello bianco), Damaschino, Falanghina, Fiano, Forastera, Francavidda (*syn.* Francavilla), Gaglioppo (*syn.* Arvino, Gaioppo, Lacrima nera, Magliocco, Mantonico nero, or Montonico nero), Garganega (*syn.* Grecanico), Girò, Grechetto, Greco nero, Grenache (*syn.* Cannonadu, Cannonatu, Cannonao, Cannonau, or Canonau), Grillo, Guarnaccia (*syn.* Cannamelu or Uarnaccia), Impigno, Incrocio Manzoni 6013 (Riesling x Pinot blanc), Inzolia (*syn.* Ansolia, Ansonica or Nzolia), Malbec, Malvasia, Malvasia nera, Mantonico, Marsigliana, Monastrell (*syn.* Bovale or Muristrellu), Monica (*syn.* Monaca, Munica, Niedda, Pacali, Passale, or Tintilla), Montepulciano, Muscat (*syn.* Moscato), Nasco (*syn.* Nascu or Nusco), Negroamaro, Nerello (*syn.* Frappato), Nocera, Notar domenico, Nuragus (*syn.* Abbondosa, Axina de Margiai, Axina de Poporus, Meragus, or Nuragus trebbiana), Pampanuto (*syn.* Pampanino), Perricone (*syn.* Pignatello), Piedirosso (*syn.* Palombina nera, Pedepalumbo, Per'e Palumme, Per'e Palummo, or Pied di Colombo), Pinot blanc (*syn.* Pinot bianco), Pinot gris (Pinot grigio), Pinot noir (*syn.* Pinot nero), Sangiovese, Sauvignon, Sciascinoso (*syn.* Olivella), Susumaniello, Torbato, Ugni blanc (*syn.* Trebbiano), Uva di Troia, Verdeca, Vermentino, Vernaccia, Zibibbo (Moscato variant), Zinfandel (*syn.* Primitivo or Zagarese)

THE APPELLATIONS OF
SOUTHERN ITALY AND THE ISLANDS

AGLIANICO
Basilicata

Many people think that this black grape is not dissimilar to the Barbera, and it has been respected since ancient Roman times, when it produced the famed wine of Falernum. One of Italy's two greatest Aglianico wines today is Basilicata's Aglianico del Vulture (the other is Campania's Taurasi). Its best producer, Fratelli d'Angelo, is also the greatest producer of a non-DOC Aglianico.

↦ 6–20 years

✓ *Fratelli d'Angelo* (Canneto)

AGLIANICO DEL TABURNO DOC
Campania
See Taburno DOC

AGLIANICO DEL VULTURE DOC
Basilicata

This is the only DOC in Basilicata to encompass the volcanic slopes of Mount Vulture and its surrounding hills, which make the best growing areas for the Aglianico grape. A big but balanced red wine of warm colour, rich, chocolate-cherry fruit, and firm tannin structure, Aglianico del Vulture can be slightly rustic in youth, yet develops a true silky finesse with age.

Some would argue that it is the greatest Aglianico and will doubtless achieve DOCG status. If described as *vecchio* (old), Aglianico del Vulture will have been aged for a minimum of three years, while *riserva* will have had five; both will have been aged for two years in wood. Aglianico del Vulture may also be sold as semi-sweet and *spumante*.

↦ 6–20 years

✓ *Fratelli d'Angelo* • *Paternosta*

ALCAMO *or* BIANCO ALCAMO DOC
Sicily

Dry, slightly fruity white wines from the Catarratto grape with the possible addition of Damaschino, Garganega, and Trebbiano. The soil is too fertile and yields far too high to produce wines of any real quality or character.

ALEATICO DI PUGLIA DOC
Apulia

Produced in tiny quantities throughout the region, this wine is rarely exported. Opulent and aromatic wines with a full, warming, smooth, and exotic flavour, ranging from very sweet and fortified (*liquoroso* or *liquoroso dolce naturel*) to medium-sweet and unfortified (*dolce naturel*). A *riserva* must be aged for at least three years from the date of harvest or, in the case of *liquoroso*, the date of fortification.

↦ Upon purchase

✓ *Francesco Candido*

ALEZIO DOC
Apulia

A DOC since 1983 for red and *rosato* wines made from Negroamaro, with the possible addition of Sangiovese, Montepulciano, and Malvasia nera. The red is alcoholic, slightly tannic, and not very interesting, but the dry rosé can be soft and flavourful with delicate fruit.

↦ Upon purchase (rosé)

✓ *Michele Calò* (Mjère)

ARBOREA DOC
Sardinia

Three varietal wines: Sangiovese red, Sangiovese *rosato*, and a dry or semi-sweet Trebbiano white.

ASPRINIO
Basilicata

This grape is always grown on its own rootstock and produces a green, often mean, dry white that is often *frizzante*.

ASPRINIO DI AVERSA DOC
Campania

Fresh, crisp, Vinho Verde lookalike dry white wine from Asprinio grapes grown on vines trained to trees. Usually still, *frizzantino*, or *frizzante*, but sometimes fully sparkling.

BIANCOLELLA
Campania

Almost exclusively grown on the island of Ischia where D'Ambra does a pure varietal bottling.

BRINDISI DOC
Apulia

Smooth, vinous red wines and dry, light, fruity rosés, both primarily from Negroamaro grapes, although Montepulciano, Malvasia nera, Sangiovese, and Susumaniello may also be used.

↦ 3–6 years (red)

✓ *Cosimo Taurino* (Patriglione)

CABERNET BLENDS
Calabria

Relatively few Cabernet-dominated wines stand out, but Gravello and Montevetrano are exceptionally fine.

✓ *Silvio Imparato* (Montevetrano) • *Librandi* (Gravello)

CACC'E MMITTEE DI LUCERA DOC
Apulia

The name of this full-bodied red *uvaggio*, which is made from seven grape varieties, loosely means "knock it back" (*cacc'e* means "drink" and *mmittee* means "pour"), which aptly applies to this simple, easy-drinking red wine.

CAGLIARI DOC
Sardinia

Four varietals: Malvasia (a smooth, delicately scented red wine in dry, sweet, and *liquoroso* styles); Moscato (rich, succulently sweet white wines that may be fortified; Nasco (finely scented, delicate, dry and sweet white wines that can also be *liquoroso*); and Nuragus (a large production of dry, semi-sweet, and *frizzante* white wines from the Nuragus grape).

↦ 1–2 years

✓ *Meloni*

CAMPIDANO DI TERRALBA *or* TERRALBA DOC
Sardinia

Soft yet full-bodied reds from the Monastrell, known locally as Bovale.

CAMPI FLEGEREI DOC
Campania

Two generic blends: red (Piedirosso, Aglianico, and Sciascinoso) and white (Falanghina, Biancolella, and Coda del Volpe); plus one red-wine varietal: Piedirosso (dry or *passito* dry-to-sweet); and one dry white varietal Falanghina (still or *spumante*).

CANNONAU DI SARDEGNA DOC
Sardinia

A DOC of variable quality that throws up the occasional gem, Cannonau, better known as the Grenache, encompasses dry, semi-sweet, or sweet red, rosé, and *liquoroso* styles.

CAPRI DOC
Campania

Easy-to-drink, dry white wines seldom seen beyond the Isle of Capri. The island's soil and climate suggests that these wines should be much finer, but the land for vines is scarce and expensive, encouraging growers to extract far too much from those vineyards that do exist.

CARIGNANO DEL SULCIS DOC
Sardinia

Promising red and rosé wines from the Carignan grape, to which may be added a little Monica, Pascale, and Alicante bouschet.

↦ 1–4 years

✓ *CS di Santadi* (Riserva Rocca Rubia, Terre Brune)

CASTEL DEL MONTE DOC
Apulia

The region's best-known wine is named after the 13th-century castle built by Emperor Frederick von Hohenstaufen. With the exception of a red *riserva* made by Rivera and called *Il Falcone* (The Falcon), the wines are less lofty than the name of this DOC suggests. In addition to the generic red and rosé, which are made from Uva di Troia and Aglianico grapes, and the basic dry white from Pampanuto and Chardonnay, there are two red varietals, Pinot Nero and Aglianico; four white varietals, Chardonnay, Pinot Bianco, Pinot Bianco da Pinot Nero, and Sauvignon; plus a rosé, Aglianico.

↦ 2–6 years
(red, but 8–20 years for Il Falcone)

✓ *Rivera* (especially Il Falcone and Terre al Monte)

CASTEL SAN LORENZO DOC
Campania
A relatively new DOC covering several communes in the province of Salerno, Castel San Lorenzo encompasses generic red and rosé (Barbera and Sangiovese), white (Trebbiano and Malvasia), one red wine varietal (Barbera) and one sweet white varietal (Moscato, still or *spumante*).

CERASUOLO DI VITTORIA DOC
Sicily
Cherry-coloured Nerello-Calabrese wines from the southeastern corner of Sicily.

CERDÈSER
Sicily
Red, white, and rosé wines produced in and around Cerda, close to Palermo.

CILENTO DOC
Campania
Vines struggle in the rocky vineyards of Cilento, where generic red and rosé are made from Aglianico, Piedirosso, and Barbera, and generic white from Fiano, Trebbiano, Greco, and Malvasia. An Aglianico varietal also exists, but has yet to prove itself.

CIRÒ DOC
Calabria
Strong, alcoholic Gaglioppo-based red and rosé, and Greco-based dry white wines that rely too heavily on the Cirò name, which was famous in ancient times.

CONTESSA ENTELLINA DOC
Sicily
This new DOC encompasses vineyards in the commune of Contessa Entellina in the province of Palermo for a delicate dry white blend of Inzolia, Catarratti, Garganega, Chardonnay, Sauvignon, and Müller-Thurgau; and three dry white-wine varietals, Chardonnay, Grecanico (Garganega), and Sauvignon.

COPERTINO DOC
Apulia

This appellation is named after the town of Copertino, although the wines that qualify for this DOC can also come from five other villages. These smooth, rich red wines and dry, finely scented rosés are made primarily from the Negroamaro grape with the possible addition of Malvasia nera, Montepulciano, and Sangiovese.

🍷— 2–5 years

☑ CS di Copertino (riserva)

CORVO
Sicily
The brand name for red, white, *spumante,* and fortified "Stravecchio di Sicilia" wines of Duca di Salaparuta, Corvo has no DOC but is probably the most famous wine in Sicily. The full, smooth, fruity red is by far the most successful and consistent of the range.

CREMOVO ZABAIONE VINO *or* CREMOVO ZABAIONE VINO AROMATIZZATO DOC
Sicily
See Marsala DOC

DONNICI DOC
Calabria
Fruity, cherry-coloured red and rosé wines (traditionally *chiaretto*) from Gaglioppo and Greco nero grapes grown in the province of Cosenza. They are best drunk young.

ELORO DOC
Sicily
This appellation straddles the provinces of Ragusa and Siracusa, where a generic red and rosé (Calabrese, Frappato, and Pignatello) are produced and, if the blend contains at least 80 per cent Calabrese, it may be called Pachino. These grapes are also vinified separately to produce three varietal wines, the Calabrese being sold under its local synonym Nero d'Avola.

ETNA DOC
Sicily
According to Homer, this is the wine that Ulysses used to intoxicate the Cyclops. There are three basic styles: a full red and fruity rosé from the Nerello grape, and a soft but bland dry white from Carricante and Catarratti with the possible addition of Trebbiano.

FALERNO DEL MASSICO DOC
Campania
This appellation celebrates Falernum, the wine so enjoyed in ancient Rome, which was made in the northwest of Campania and Latium. The deep-coloured, full-bodied, and rustically robust red generic is a blend of Aglianico and Piedirosso with the possible addition of Primitivo and Barbera. The round, fruity dry white generic is, in fact, pure Falanghina. A red varietal Primitivo is also produced.

🍷— 3–7 years (red)
      Upon purchase (white and rosé)

☑ Villa Matilde • Michele Moio (Primitivo)

FARO DOC
Sicily
Ruby-coloured, medium-bodied but firmly flavoured red wines from Nerello and Nocera grapes grown around Messina. Calabrese, Gaglioppo, and Sangiovese may also be used.

🍷— 2–5 years

☑ Bagni

FIANO DI AVELLINO DOC
Campania
Mastroberardino's Vignadora is the best wine in this unusual, but well above average, dry white wine DOC, made from Fiano grapes grown in the hilly hinterland of Avellino.

🍷— 1–3 years

☑ Mastroberardino

GIOIA DEL COLLE DOC
Apulia
For this large DOC in the province of Bari there are generic red and rosé blends (Primitivo, Montepulciano, Sangiovese, Negroamaro, and Malvasia nera); a dry white (Trebbiano and anything else that moves); and two varietals, a sweetish Primitivo and an intensely sweet Aleatico (which can be fortified).

GIRO DI CAGLIARI DOC
Sardinia
Smooth, alcoholic, dry and sweet red wines and dry and sweet fortified wines.

GRAGNANO DOC
Campania
See Penisola Sorrentina DOC

GRAVINA DOC
Apulia

Dry or semi-sweet, blended white wines that may be still or *spumante*, made from Malvasia, Greco, and Bianco d'Alessano, with the possible addition of Bombino, Trebbiano, and Verdeca.

GRECO DI BIANCO DOC
Calabria
Made on the very tip of Calabria, around Bianco, from the Grechetto grape, known locally as Greco Bianco. With the exception of Umberto Ceratti's exceptional rendition, Greco di Bianco is a simple *passito* wine. Ceratti harvests tiny, already shrivelled grapes and, apparently, plunges them into boiling water immediately after picking (to flash pasteurize the wine, which removes or reduces the need to use sulphur). His Greco di Bianco is deceptively strong, succulently sweet and smooth, with a vivacious bouquet, exuberant fruit, and a luscious, silk finish.

🍷— 3–5 years

☑ Umberto Ceratti

GRECO DI TUFO DOC
Campania
Delicate, dry, and soft white wines that may sometimes be *spumante*, from the true Greco grown north of Avellino.

🍷— Upon purchase

☑ Mastroberardino (Vignadangelo)

GUARDIA SANFRAMONDI *or* GUARDIOLO DOC
Campania
Located in the hilly terrain of the Benevento, this DOC consists of a generic dry white (Malvasia and Falanghina plus up to 30 per cent pick-and-mix), generic Sangiovese-based red and rosé, one dry white varietal (Falanghina), which may be *spumante*, and one red varietal (Aglianico).

ISCHIA DOC
Campania
Vinous, medium-bodied generic red (Guarnaccia and Piedirosso plus 20 per cent pick-and-mix); a lightly aromatic, generic dry white (Forastera and Biancolella), which may be *spumante*; two dry white varietal wines (Biancolella and Forastera); and one red varietal (Piedirosso), which can be either dry or *passito*.

⌇⏦ 2–4 years (red)
Upon purchase (white and rosé)

✓ *D'Ambra*

LAMEZIA DOC
Calabria
Originally a one-wine DOC for a light, delicately fruity, but otherwise unexceptional blended red wine (Nerello, Gaglioppo, Greco nero, and Marsigliana), Lamezia has now been expanded to include a generic, full dry white (Grechetto, Trebbiano, and Malvasia) and a white varietal called Greco, the local name for Grechetto. The light red has been split into red and rosé.

LETTERE DOC
Campania
See Penisola Sorrentina DOC

LEVERANO DOC
Apulia
Alcoholic red wines and fresh, fruity rosés (Negroamaro with the possible addition of Sangiovese, Montepulciano, and Malvasia nera), and soft, dry white wines (Malvasia plus Bombino and Trebbiano). Conti Zecca's elegant red Vigna del Sareceno stands out.

⌇⏦ 3–7 years (red)

✓ *Conti Zecca* (Vigna del Sareceno)

LIZZANO DOC
Apulia
Negroamaro-based red and rosé, still or *frizzante* style generic wines, which may be boosted by the addition of Montepulciano, Sangiovese, Bombino nero, Pinot noir, and Malvasia nera. The rosé can also be fully *spumante*, as can the generic white blend of Trebbiano and Chardonnay (with the possible addition of Malvasia, Sauvignon, and Bianco d'Alessano), which also comes in still or *frizzante* styles. There are two red varietal wines, Negroamaro and Malvasia Nera; and one rosé varietal, Negroamaro – all three in straightforward, dry still-wine styles.

LOCOROTONDO DOC
Apulia
Fresh, lightly fruity, dry white wines of improving quality from Verdeca and Bianco d'Alessano, with the possible addition of Fiano, Malvasia, and Bombino, made in still and *spumante* styles.

⌇⏦ Upon purchase

✓ *CS di Locorotondo*

MALVASIA
Basilicata and Sardinia
This grape plays a respectable second fiddle to Moscato in the *vini da tavola* stakes. Usually sweet, sometimes fizzy. In Sardinia, the wines are mostly fortified and DOC but Malvasia della Planargia is still *vino da tavola*, although many rank it as the finest in Sardinia.

✓ **Basilicata** *Fratelli d'Angelo* • *Paternosta*

Sardinia *Gian Vittorio Naitana* (Vigna Giagonìa, Vigna Murapiscados)

MALVASIA DELLE LIPARI DOC
Sicily
Sweet, aromatic, *passito* white wines.

⌇⏦ 2–5 years

✓ *Carlo Hauner*

MALVASIA DI BOSA DOC
Sardinia
Rich, sweet and dry white wines, and sweet and dry *liquoroso* wines. Generally fuller-bodied than Malvasia di Cagliari.

MALVASIA DI CAGLIARI DOC
Sardinia
Rich, sweet or dry, white wines, and dry or sweet, *liquoroso* wines. They are lighter but finer and more elegant wines than Malvasia di Bosa and traditionally are drier.

MALVASIA NERA
Apulia
Dark-skinned Malvasia is commonly found in the Salento district, and traditionally complements the local Negroamaro grape, although it is sometimes made into a pure varietal wine, both as DOC and *vini da tavola*. Alone, this grape produces a vivid red wine with slightly aromatic fruit and a dry but velvety-smooth finish.

MANDROLISAI DOC
Sardinia
Red and rosé wines with a bitter aftertaste blended from Bovale (Monastrell), Cannonau (Grenache), and Monica.

MARSALA DOC
Sicily
This wine was conceived by John Woodhouse, who began shipping it in 1773. Its name is Arabic, deriving from *Marsah-el-Allah*, the old name of the port of Marsala. The grapes used include Grillo (the original Marsala variety and still considered the best), Catarratto, Pignatello, Garganega, Calabrese, Damaschino, Nerello, and Inzolia. The wine is fortified by the adding of neutral spirit and, where appropriate, sweetened with grape concentrate made locally. Marsala can be dry (*secco*), semi-sweet (*semi-secco*), or sweet (*dolce*); is further defined by colour, gold (*oro*), amber (*ambra*), and red (*rubino*); and is made in four basic styles, *Fine, Superiore, Vergine*, and *Solera*. Marsala Fine, the lowest category, is aged for just a year (not necessarily in wood) with at least 17 per cent ABV. As Italian-wine expert David Gleave MW has put it, Marsala Fine is "usually anything but fine, being a cheap and rather nasty travesty of the name".

Marsala Superiore is aged for at least two years in wood (four years if *riserva*), with a minimum 18 per cent ABV. Marsala Vergine is aged for at least five years in wood, or ten if *stravecchio* or

riserva, is only *secco* (thus no grape concentrate allowed), and must have a minimum 18 per cent ABV. Marsala Solera is also aged for at least five years in wood, or ten years if *stravecchio* or *riserva*, is only *secco* (thus no grape concentrate allowed), and must have a minimum of 18 per cent ABV. Some historical abbreviations are still found on labels: IP (stands for Italy Particular – Marsala Fine), LP (London Particular – Marsala Superiore), SOM (Superior Old Marsala – Marsala Superiore), GD (Gariboldi Dolce – Marsala Superiore). Flavoured Marsala may be sold as Cremovo Zabaione Vino or Cremovo Zabaione Vino Aromatizzato (sickly sweet egg nog containing at least 80 per cent Marsala wine, eggs, and a minimum of 200 grams of residual sugar per litre), Preparato con l'impiego di Vino Marsala (for other Marsala-based products containing not less than 60 per cent Marsala wine), and you will find non-DOC Marsala-based concoctions with all sorts of flavourings (banana, chocolate, orange etc.). I must confess that, except for rare old bottlings of Vergine or Solera, most Marsala leaves me cold and the flavoured versions horrify me, but the best producers are well known.

⌇⏦ Upon purchase

✓ *Cantina de Bartoli* • *Florio* • *Carlo Pellegrino*

MARTINA *or* MARTINA FRANCA DOC
Apulia
These dry white wines in still or *spumante* styles are very similar to those of Locorotondo.

MATINO DOC
Apulia
Dry, robust red and slightly vinous rosé wines made from Negroamaro with the possible addition of Malvasia nera.

MELISSA DOC
Calabria
Full-bodied reds (Gaglioppo, Greco nero, Grechetto, Trebbiano, and Malvasia) and crisp, dry whites (Grechetto, Trebbiano, and Malvasia).

MENFI
Sicily
Decent red and white *vini da tavola* are made in and around Menfi at the western end of the south coast of the island.

METAPONTUM
Basilicata
Basic red and white *vini da tavola* are produced from the Ionian coastal plain either side of the Basento river around Metaponto in the eastern corner of Basilicata.

MONICA DI CAGLIARI DOC
Sardinia
See Sardegna DOC

MONICA DI SARDEGNA DOC
Sardinia
See Sardegna DOC

MOSCATO
Basilicata and Calabria

In Basilicata, the two best wine producers of these *vini da tavola* believe in the potential of Moscato, always sweet and usually fully *spumante*, from the Mount Vulture area. It is also grown all over Calabria, but is more often made into a *passito* wine than a *spumante* one.

✓ **Basilicata** *Fratelli d'Angelo* • *Paternosta*
Calabria *Guido Lojelo*

MOSCATO DI CAGLIARI DOC
Sardinia
See Cagliari DOC

MOSCATO DI NOTO DOC
Sicily

Still, *spumante*, or fortified semi-sweet and sweet Moscato wines.

MOSCATO DI PANTELLERIA DOC
Sicily

Sicily's best still, *spumante*, and fortified semi-sweet and sweet Moscato are made on the island of Pantelleria, closer to Tunisia than to Sicily.

✓ *De Bartoli* (Passito Bukkuram) • *Cantine Florio* (Morsi di Luce) • *Salvatore Murana*

MOSCATO DI SARDEGNA DOC
Sardinia
See Sardegna DOC

MOSCATO DI SIRACUSA DOC
Sicily

These sweet, smooth white wines are made from semi-*passito* grapes.

MOSCATO DI SORSO-SENNORI DOC
Sardinia

Sweet, rich, white Moscato and sweet, aromatic *liquoroso*. The wines are fuller than either Moscato di Cagliari or Moscato di Sardegna.

MOSCATO DI TRANI DOC
Apulia

Tiny production of luscious, ultra-smooth, sweet white Moscato wines, which may be fortified. These wines are high quality and distinctive.

🍷— Upon purchase

✓ *Fratelli Nugnes*

NARDO DOC
Apulia

Robust, alcoholic, red and delicate, cherry-red rosé wines from Negroamaro with the possible addition of Malvasia nera and Montepulciano.

NASCO DI CAGLIARI DOC
Sardinia
See Cagliari DOC

NEGROAMARO
Apulia

A very productive grape, the Negroamaro makes dark, potentially bitter red wines that used to be sold in bulk for blending purposes, but are starting to acquire their own reputation. It makes a delicious rosé under the Alezio DOC, but unless vinified with great care, the red wine it produces tends to be too strong, alcoholic, coarse, and bitter, although Calò's *barrique*-aged Vigna Spano and Vallone's *passito*-styled Graticcia are *vino da tavola* exceptions.

✓ *Michele Calò* (Vigna Spano) • *Vallone* (Graticcia)

NEGROAMARO-MALVASIA NERO
Apulia

The traditional red-wine blend of Salento.

✓ *Cosimo Taurino* (Notarpanaro)

NURAGUS DI CAGLIARI DOC
Sardinia
See Cagliari DOC

ORTA NOVA DOC
Apulia

These are full-bodied red and dry rosé Sangiovese-based wines from the villages of Orta Nova and Ordona in the province of Foggia.

OSTUNI DOC
Apulia

A delicate, dry white made from Impigno and Francavidda and a light-bodied red from the Cinsault grape, known locally as Ottavianello, with the possible addition of Negroamaro, Notar domenico, Malvasia nera, and Susumaniello.

OTTAVIANELLO DOC
Apulia
See Ostuni DOC

PELLARO
Campania

Ottavianello DOC produces powerful Alicante-based *chiaretto* wines from just south of Reggio di Calabria on the very toe of Italy.

PENISOLA SORRENTINA DOC
Campania

This is a relatively new DOC for former *vini da tavola* from the Sorrento peninsula, including a generic red (Piedirosso with the possible addition of Sciascinoso, Aglianico, and other unspecified non-aromatic varieties), which can also be made in a purple-coloured *frizzante* style, and a dry white generic (Falanghina with the possible addition of Biancolella, Greco, and other non-aromatic varieties). If the subzones Sorrento (for white and still red), Gragnano, or Lettere (red *frizzante*) appear on the label, the wines must conform to higher standards, including extra-ripe grapes.

PIEDIROSSO
Campania

An ancient variety identified by Pliny, Piedirosso is usually blended with more noble varieties, but has been produced as a varietal wine by D'Ambra on the island of Ischia, where the grape is commonly known as Per'e Palummo.

POLLINO DOC
Calabria

Full, fruity, *chiaretto* wines from Gaglioppo, Greco nero, Malvasia, and Guarnaccia.

PRIMITIVO
Apulia

Now proven to be the Zinfandel, although it generally makes a wine that has nowhere near Zinfandel's character, let alone its quality.

PRIMITIVO DI MANDURIA DOC
Apulia

Dry to semi-sweet, full-bodied red wines which may also be fortified and naturally sweet, and fortified and dry. Until I tasted Giordano's 1993 vintage in 1996, no Primitivo had shown any class.

🍷— 3–10 years (Giordano as from 1993)

✓ *Giordano* • *Vinicola Savese*

ROSSO BARLETTA DOC
Apulia

Medium-bodied, ruby-coloured, everyday-quality red wines made from Uva di Troia with the possible addition of Montepulciano, Sangiovese, and a small amount of Malbec. Most Rosso Barletta is consumed locally when very young.

ROSSO CANOSA DOC
Apulia

Vinous, slightly tannic red wines made from Uva di Troia with the possible addition of Montepulciano and Sangiovese.

ROSSO DI CERIGNOLA DOC
Apulia

Rare, rustic reds from Negroamaro and Uva di Troia with the possible addition of Sangiovese, Barbera, Montepulciano, Malbec, and Trebbiano.

SALICE SALENTINO DOC
Apulia

Full-bodied reds and smooth, alcoholic, rosés from Negroamaro with the possible addition of Malvasia nera, and, more recently, two dry white wines: a Chardonnay, which may be *frizzante*, and a Pinot Bianco, which may be *spumante*; plus a sweet red Aleatico, which can be fortified. The Negroamaro-based red wines are still, however, the best wines in this DOC.

🍷— 3–7 years

✓ *Francesco Candido* • *Leone de Castris* • *Cosimo Taurino* • *Vallone*

SAN SEVERO DOC
Apulia

Dry, vinous red and rosé wines made from Montepulciano and Sangiovese, and dry, fresh whites from Bombino and Trebbiano, with the possible addition of Malvasia and Verdeca.

SANT'AGATA DEI GOTI DOC
Campania

Relatively new DOC for generic red, dry white, and rosé from Aglianico and Piedirosso (thus the white is a blanc de noirs); two red wine varietals, Aglianico and Piedirosso; and two white varietals, Greco and Falanghina.

SANT'ANNA DI ISOLA CAPO RIZZUTO DOC
Calabria
Vinous red and rosé wines from Gaglioppo, Greco nero, and Guarnaccia grapes grown in the Ionian hills.

SAN VITO DI LUZZI DOC
Calabria
A new DOC covering generic red, rosé (Gaglioppo and Malvasia with the possible addition of Greco nero and Sangiovese), and dry white (Malvasia, Grechetto, and Trebbiano) wines produced in and near the village of Luzzi in the province of Conseza.

SARDEGNA DOC
Sardinia
This DOC is for wines made from grapes grown throughout the island, although in practice they are generally restricted to traditional areas. For Moscato, vines must not be grown above 450 metres (1,476 feet). Moscato di Sardegna is sweet and surprisingly delicate, usually in a natural still-wine style, although *spumante* is produced and the sub-appellations Tempio Pausania, Tempio, and Gallura are reserved for sparkling wines in the Gallura area. Monica di Sardegna is a fragrant red wine that may be dry or sweet, still or *frizzante*, but unlike Monica di Cagliari, is never fortified. Vermentino di Sardegna is a light-bodied, soft, clean, unexciting dry white wine that all too often has its flavours washed out by cool fermentation techniques.

SAVUTO DOC
Calabria
Fresh, fruity red or rosé wines from Gagloppo, Greco nero, Nerello, Sangiovese, Malvasia, and Pecorino grapes grown in Catanzaro province.

🍷— 1–3 years

✓ *Odoardi* (Vigna Vecchia)

SCAVIGNA DOC
Calabria
Generic red, rosé (Gaglioppo, Nerello, and Aglianico) and a fruity dry white (Trebbiano, Chardonnay, Grechetto, and Malvasia) from the communes of Nocera Terinese and Falerna.

Sicilia Rosso IGT

✓ *Abbazia Sant'Anastasia* (Passomaggio)

SOLOPACA DOC
Campania
Smooth generic red and rosé (Sangiovese and Aglianico with the possible addition of Piedirosso, Sciascinoso, and up to 30 per cent pick-and-mix), generic dry white (Trebbiano, Falanghina, Malvasia, and Coda di Volpe), one red wine varietal (Aglianico) and one white varietal (Falanghina – still or *spumante*). Solopaca comes from the Calore valley.

🍷— 1–4 years

✓ *Antica Masseria Venditti*

SORRENTO DOC
Campania
See Penisola Sorrentina DOC

SQUINZANO DOC
Apulia
Full-bodied red wines and lightly scented rosé wines from Negroamaro with the possible addition of Sangiovese and Malvasia nera, grown in Squinzano and the surrounding communes.

🍷— 2–4 years (red), upon purchase (rosé)

✓ *Villa Valletta*

TABURNO DOCG
Campania
This DOC started out life as Aglianico del Taburno in red and rosé, but it is one of those DOCs that just grows. It now includes a generic red (Sangiovese and Aglianico); white (Trebbiano and Falanghina, plus 30 per cent pick-and-mix); a *spumante* (Coda di Volpe and Falanghina, plus 40 per cent pick-and-mix); three white wine varietals (Falanghina, Greco, and Coda di Volpe); and one red (Piedirosso).

TAURASI DOCG
Campania
Red wines made primarily from Aglianico grapes (up to 15 per cent in total of Barbera, Piedirosso, and Sangiovese may be added) that are grown in Taurasi and 16 nearby villages. It was elevated to DOCG status in 1993. Along with Basilicata's thicker tasting Aglianico del Vulture, it is one of the country's greatest wines from this underrated grape variety, in an equally age-worthy style. Mastroberardino's *riserva* excels.

🍷— 5–10 years (some may last for as long as 20)

✓ *Mastroberardino* • *Giovanni Struzziero*

TERRALBA DOC
Sardinia
See Campidano di Terralba DOC

VERMENTINO DI GALLURA DOCG
Sardinia
Despite cool fermentation techniques this is the best Vermentino Sardinia offers, the hilly *terroir* of Gallura producing intense flavours that are hard to wash out. Although this wine was elevated to DOCG status in 1997, it could be much better quality and cheaper to produce if fermented at slightly higher temperatures.

🍷— 1–2 years

✓ *Tenuta di Capichera* • *CS di Gallura* • *CS del Vermentino*

VERMENTINO DI SARDEGNA DOC
Sardinia
See Sardegna DOC

VERNACCIA DI ORISTANO DOC
Sardinia
The DOC of Vernaccia di Oristano makes dry and lightly bitter white wines, which are Sherry-like in style. Also produced are *liquoroso* sweet and dry wines.

🍷— Upon purchase

✓ *Contini*

VESUVIO DOC
Campania
Restricted to vines on the volcanic slopes of Mount Vesuvius, a generic dry white (Coda di Volpe and Verdeca grapes, with the possible addition of Falanghina and Greco), and a generic rosé (Piedirosso and Sciascinoso with the possible addition of Aglianico) are produced by Vesuvio DOC. Those that are labelled Lacryma (or Lacrima) Christi del Vesuvio are usually dry white wines, but less commonly they may also be *spumante* or sweet and fortified.

NEW IGT WINES

The following IGT wines were agreed at the end of 1996, but we have yet to see what style, quality, or consistency each one will establish:

Apulia *Daunia* • *Murgia* • *Puglia* • *Salento* • *Tarantino* • *Valle d'Itria*

Basilicata *Basilicata*

Calabria *Arghilli* • *Bivongi* • *Calabria* • *Condoleo* • *Costa Viola* • *Esaro* • *Lipuda* • *Locride* • *Palizzi* • *Scilla* • *Val di Neto* • *Valdamato* • *Valle dell Crati*

Campania *Colli di Limvara* • *Isola dei Nuraghi* • *Marmilla* • *Nurra* • *Ogliastro* • *Parteolla* • *Planargia* • *Provincia di Nuoro* • *Romangia* • *Sibiola* • *Tharros* • *Trexenta* • *Valle del Tirso* • *Valle di Porto Pino*

Sicily *Camarro* • *Colli Ericini* • *Della Nivolelli* • *Fontanarossa di Cerda* • *Salemi* • *Salina* • *Sciacca* • *Sicilia* • *Valle Belice*

THE MARSALA PLAINS, SICILY
Vines on the hot, arid plains of western Sicily grow on a low-yielding soil called sciari, *producing the finest Marsala, while further east, but still within the DOC, the soil is more fertile and the wines are of lesser quality.*

AUTHOR'S CHOICE

I could easily fill this entire list with superb Barolo. Indeed, I could almost fill it with the wines of Aldo Conterno alone. In order therefore to include some of Italy's finest vini da tavola and a number of exciting but lesser-known DOCs, I have barely scraped the surface of the greatest wine appellations.

PRODUCER	WINE	STYLE	DESCRIPTION	🌡
Elio Altare	Barolo DOCG (see p.313)	RED	Altare's basic Barolo consistently out-paces many single-vineyard Barolo from top producers, with its creamy-rich fruit and fabulous toasty new-oak finish.	4–12 years
Elio Altare	Vigna Aborina VdT (Piedmont) (see p.316, Nebbiolo)	RED	Inky-black, massively fruity, pure Nebbiolo, *barrique*-aged red, this wine has great potential for complexity.	4–12 years
Altesino	Brunello di Montalcino DOCG (see p.329)	RED	Big in every sense of the word, from the intensity of its fruit to its firm tannin structure, this wine softens with age, achieving a lovely warm, cedary complexity.	8–20 years
Altesino	Palazzo Altesi VdT, Tuscany (see p.332, Sangiovese)	RED	This is sensational single-vineyard Sangiovese with toasty oak mellowing the rich, firm, and spicy varietal fruit.	6–15 years
Anselmi	I Capitelli, Recioto di Soave DOC (see p.324)	WHITE	This lusciously sweet botrytized wine has a gloriously golden colour, a luxuriant bouquet suggestive of honey, flowers, nuts, and molasses, a fabulously rich, sweet, and complex flavour of honeyed-spicy fruit, and a fine, smoky-creamy oak finish.	3–10 years
Anselmi	Capitel Foscarino, Soave Classico DOC (see p.324)	WHITE	If this wine is indicative of how classic Soave once tasted, then it is little wonder that the appellation achieved such widespread fame. One of Roberto Anselmi's secrets is his low-yielding, high-density vineyards and he cuts off whole bunches during the summer to further limit the potential harvest.	2–4 years
Anselmi	Capitel Croce, Soave Classico DOC (see p.324)	WHITE	This Soave is rich and ripe, with slightly exotic, yet always correctly crisp, fruit. It is full of the vanilla aroma of new oak. Although I would not like to see all Soave made in this style, such expressive and innovative winemaking is to be encouraged.	2–4 years
Antinori	Solaia VdT, Tuscany (see p.329, Cabernet-Sangiovese)	RED	Solaia is more Californian in style than Tignanello, using 80 per cent Cabernet sauvignon and 20 per cent Sangiovese. It is upfront and opulent, with gorgeously sweet, and sometimes quite jammy, fruit popping up through the smoky-vanilla oak.	7–20 years
Antinori	Tignanello VdT, Tuscany (see p.332, Sangiovese-Cabernet)	RED	The classic Sangiovese-Cabernet blend, rich and elegant, with opulent, smoky new oak and a distinctive Tuscan feel about it.	8–20 years
Avignonesi	Vino Nobile di Montepulciano DOCG (see p.332)	RED	The most consistent and elegant Vino Nobile, Avignonesi has a balance so deft that it belies the richness and typicity of its fruit, but only an intensity of flavour can produce such a long, lingering finish. Great finesse.	2–12 years
Braida	Bricco della Figotta, Barbera d'Asti DOC (see p.313)	RED	A huge concentration of Barbera fruit supported by a light, supple tannin structure and balanced by a luscious sweetness of new oak.	4–10 years
Ca' del Bosco	Maurizio Zanella VdT, Lombardy, (see p.313, Cabernet-Merlot)	RED	This is one of the finest Bordeaux-style blends produced in Italy so far. A full, rich, well-coloured wine with lots of new oak and obvious finesse, its delicious, juicy-fruitiness comes from the addition of a small proportion of *macération carbonique* wine.	3–10 years
Aldo Conterno	Single-vineyard Barolo DOCG (see p.313)	RED	Aldo Conterno is the greatest producer of single-vineyard Barolo. His Vigna Ciacala Busia is the most seductive, full of sumptuous, up-front fruit that is so accessible, yet capable of great longevity. Vigna Colonnello is a colossal wine, saturated and mega-concentrated, requiring many years bottle-ageing and repaying it with great finesse and mind-blowing, smoky-complexity. Granbussia is just as huge and potentially as complex as Vigna Colonnello, but shows finesse much earlier. All are produced in tiny quantities at extremely high prices.	8–25 years (10–30 years for Vigna Colonnello)
Cascina Drago	Bricco del Drago, Vigna le Mace VdT, Piedmont (see p.314, Dolcetto-Nebbiolo)	RED	The basic Bricco del Drago is a delicious *barrique*-aged Dolcetto and Nebbiolo blend, but this single-vineyard wine is even richer, teeming with summer fruits, juicy-plump black cherries, and sweet, ripe oak.	4–12 years
Felsina Berardenga	Fontalloro VdT, Tuscany (see p.332, Sangiovese)	RED	Few pure Sangiovese are as fat and accessible as this single-vineyard *vino da tavola*, which has oodles of sweet jammy fruit and ripe new oak.	4–10 years

PRODUCER	WINE	STYLE	DESCRIPTION	⌐—
Felsina Berardenga	Rancia Riserva, Chianti Classico DOCG (see p.330)	RED	This estate is known for big, rich, deeply coloured Chianti Classico, but the ripest grapes go into this single-vineyard wine, which is Berardenga's most intense, tight, and tannic. With good bottle-age, however, Rancia reveals very sweet, ripe, thick-tasting fruit. This is most definitely a food wine.	7–20 years
Angelo Gaja	Sori San Lorenzo, Barbaresco DOCG (see p.312)	RED	Angelo Gaja is without doubt the greatest producer of Barbaresco, and if anyone thinks that Barbaresco cannot compete with Barolo in size or quality, they should try Gaja's massively proportioned Barbaresco Sori Tilden. Also huge, if not quite as statuesque, Gaja's Barbaresco Sori San Lorenzo is, however, the greatest for finesse, showing deliciously rich and creamy fruit underpinned by supple tannins and a smoky, new-oak complexity.	10–25 years
Giordano	Primitivo di Manduria DOC (see p.342)	RED	The 1993 vintage of this wine was the first great Primitivo I ever tasted. The Primitivo is a synonym for the Zinfandel grape, but it has never produced a wine comparable, either in quality or character, to the best renditions from California. Giordano's Primitivo di Manduria is, however, a big, rich, oaky wine that ranks with the very best West Coast Zinfandel, although it has more of the weight, size, class, and complexity of a great Barolo.	3–8 years
Isole e Olena	L'Eremo VdT, Tuscany (see p.332, Syrah)	RED	By the mid-1990s, a number of Italian, pure Syrah wines were on the market. This wine from Isole e Olena was the first and, so far, none of the others has matched it for quality, finesse, and intensity of varietal character.	5–15 years
Jermann	Where The Dreams Have No End VdT, Friuli-Venezia Giulia (see p.322, Chardonnay)	WHITE	Silvio Jermann's first and only concession to the demand for barrique-ageing, this mysteriously named, expensive wine ranks with the greatest Chardonnay produced anywhere in Italy.	3–8 years
Maculan	Prato di Canzio, Breganze DOC (see p.322)	WHITE	This hedonistic blend of Tocai Friulano, Pinot blanc, and Riesling stands out as the best dry white wine in the Breganze DOC of Veneto. Its rich, gorgeously tangy flavour is the result of a knife-edge balance between ripe fruit and crisp acidity, with just the barest hint of spice and a kiss of sweet oak.	2–5 years
Tenuta dell'Ornellaia	Masseto VdT Bolgheri, Tuscany (see p.331, Merlot)	RED	Minute quantities of this single-vineyard Merlot are sold at three times the price of Ornellaia itself (below). These are deep purple, opaque, full-bodied wines with intense spicy-blackcurrant and new-oak flavour.	5–20 years
Tenuta dell'Ornellaia	Ornellaia VdT Bolgheri, Tuscany (see p.329, Cabernet-Merlot)	RED	Produced by Lodovico Antinori, there is definitely a family resemblance to brother Piero's Solaia, although Ornellaia is more focused and the opulence of its fruit shows earlier. Ornellaia is a Cabernet-Merlot blend, whereas Solaia is Cabernet-Sangiovese and they both represent the very greatest that Italian winemaking can aspire to.	5–20 years
Pertimali	Brunello di Montalcino DOCG (see p.329)	RED	Quintessential Brunello di Montalcino, deeply coloured, full in body, and rich in blackcurrant, blackberry, and black-cherry fruit; it is superconcentrated, multilayered, and has a supple tannin structure, a roasted-toasted oaky mellowness, and great potential complexity and finesse.	8–20 years
Poggerino	Chianti Classico DOCG (see p.330)	RED	Young Piero Lanza is the fastest-rising star in Chianti's firmament, producing the most fruit-driven wines in the district.	4–8 years
Rivera	Il Falcone, Castel del Monte Riserva DOC (see p.339)	RED	One of Apulia's greatest wines, Il Falcone is a deep-coloured, full-bodied, flavoursome red wine that, with good bottle-age, develops a very fine and deeply scented bouquet.	8–20 years
Tenuta San Guido	Sassicaia, Bolgheri DOC (see p.329)	RED	The granddaddy of the super-Tuscans and pioneer of Cabernet Sauvignon, Sassicaia received DOC status in 1994 and looks set to be the first former vino da tavola to become DOCG. A world-class Cabernet Sauvignon, it evolves away from its varietal identity towards great Tuscan typicity over many years in bottle.	8–25 years

The WINES of
SPAIN *and* PORTUGAL

SPAIN CONTINUES TO OVERPERFORM, providing more wines of real interest and quality than the most optimistic critic could reasonably hope for. As indigenous grape varieties go, Tempranillo is Spain's only class act and, except in parts of Rioja, Penedés, and the Ribera del Duero, there are no really world-class *terroirs* to be found, yet the number of truly fine Spanish wines continues to increase, with at least as much excitement at the lower end of the quality scale as at the higher. Most of the vineyards are not totally lacking potential, otherwise we would not have witnessed the revolution in Spanish wines that we have. Only 20 years ago, with the general exception of Rioja, most Spanish wines were either oxidized or over-sulphured. Never has an established, traditional winemaking nation got its act together so quickly and thoroughly as Spain has. Portugal seems set to repeat this Spanish phenomenon, adding breadth to its reputation for the great fortified wines of Port.

AUTUMNAL VINES AT LAROCO, BALDEORRAS
*Until Rías Baixas came on the scene, Laroco was
Galicia's up-and-coming white-wine district.*

◇SPAIN◇

In the early 1970s, Spanish wines had such a bad reputation that, by comparison, Italian wines seemed problem free. By the late 1980s, however, the wines of Spain were being taken seriously, whereas those of Italy generally were not.

THAT SPAIN COULD achieve such a swift turn around in the quality of its wines can be put down to its efforts to get out of the bulk-wine market. The Spanish did not stop selling bulk-wine altogether, but prevented this low-quality product from dominating exports. By its very volume, bulk-wine dilutes and downgrades a country's winemaking reputation, and in the 1970s Spanish bulk-wine was so bad that the country's worsening image threatened to undermine its share of global markets just as the culture of wine drinking was developing in the USA, UK, and other potentially lucrative markets.

CONSEJO REGULADOR STAMPS

Every current DO and DOCa possesses its own stamp, which usually appears somewhere on the label, offering a guarantee of authenticity.

HOW TO READ SPANISH WINE LABELS

APPELLATION
First establish where the wine comes from, as this should give you some indication of its quality and style. In this case it is Rioja, and the designation beneath the origin reveals that Rioja is a *Denominación de Origen Calificada*, which is the highest official classification. Rioja is the only wine so far to receive this status. More often than not, the label will simply state *Denominación de Origen* (controlled-quality wine region), *vino de la tierra* (literally "country wine", but similar to the French VDQS), or *vino comarcal* ("local wine" but the equivalent of *vin de pays*).

CONSEJO REGULADOR STAMP
The stamps of the various Consejo Reguladors, or regulating bodies, that guarantee the origin of a wine may be found on the label or capsule (*see above*).

WINE STYLE
There are various indications of style: *blanco* (white wine); *Cava* (a sparkling DO wine made by the *méthode champenoise*); *clarete* (mid-way between light-red and dark rosé, although this term is being superseded by *tintillo*); *rosado seco* (dry rosé); *cosechero* (a wine of the year or a synonym for *nuevo*, usually a *vino de mesa* made by grape-grower; *espumoso* (sparkling wine made by any method); *generoso* (fortified or dessert wine); *nuevo* (fresh, fruity "new" or *nouveau* style; *tintillo* (light-red wine similar to a *clarete*);

tinto (red wine); *viejo* (a term that should mean old, but its use is not controlled by law); *vino de aguja* (a semi-sparkling or *pétillant* wine); *vino de mesa* (literally "table wine" – this is likely to be found on the labels of ordinary, inexpensive wines); and *vino de pasto* (an ordinary, inexpensive, and often light style of wine).

NAME
This may be a brand name, or could relate to a specific vineyard, or might simply be the bodega that produced the wine. The following should help you to untangle who did what on the most complex of labels: *anejado por* ("aged by"); *bodega* (literally a "wine cellar", commonly used as part of the name of a wine firm, as in Bodega Carrion, for example); *criado por* ("blended by" and/or "matured by"); *criado y embotellado por* ("blended and bottled by"); *elaborado por* (as *criado por* but may also mean "made by"); *embotellado por* ("bottled by"); *viña* or *viñedo* (literally "vineyard", but often merely part of a brand name, and nothing to do with a specific vineyard).

VINTAGE
Since Spain joined the European Community, now the European Union, in 1986, every bottle bearing a vintage, or *cosecha*, must contain a minimum of 85 per cent of wine produced in the year indicated.

SWEETNESS
The sweetness of white wines is often indicated on Spanish labels, something many French producers might benefit from doing. The terms used are: *brut* (bone-dry to dry, a term usually used for sparkling wines); *seco* (dry); *semi-seco* (medium-dry); *semiduke* (medium-sweet); and *dulce* (sweet).

Other information regarding style or quality may also be present:

SIN CRIANZA
A wine without wood-ageing, including all cool-fermented, early-bottled wines and most rosé wines. *Sin crianza* is falling out of use in favour of *joven*.

VINO JOVEN
Wine made to be drunk within the year. There are moves to replace *sin crianza* with *vino joven*, but while wines in both categories must be

without any wood-ageing, some *sin crianza* wines are made to age well in bottle, unlike *vino joven*.

CRIANZE CORTA
Wines that have less than the legal minimum cask-age for any cask-age designation. Synonymous with *sin crianze*.

CON CRIANZA OR CRIANZA
A wine that has been aged in wood for a minimum of six months in cask, except in Rioja, Navarra, and Ribera del Duero, where it's twelve.

RESERVA
In good years, the best wines of a region are sold as *reserva*. These are matured for a minimum of three years for red wines and two years for white and rosé. The reds spend at least one year in oak, the whites and rosés six months. In Rioja only seven per cent of the wines sold are *reserva*.

GRAN RESERVA
Wines from the very best years that are considered capable of even further ageing. For red wines, the minimum is

two years in oak and three in bottle, or vice-versa. White and rosé *gran reservas* require four years' ageing, of which at least six months must be in oak.

DOBLE PASTA
This term refers to red wines that have been macerated with double the normal proportion of grape skins to juice during fermentation (*see p.36*). Such wines are opaque, with an intense colour, and may be sold in the bottle or for blending.

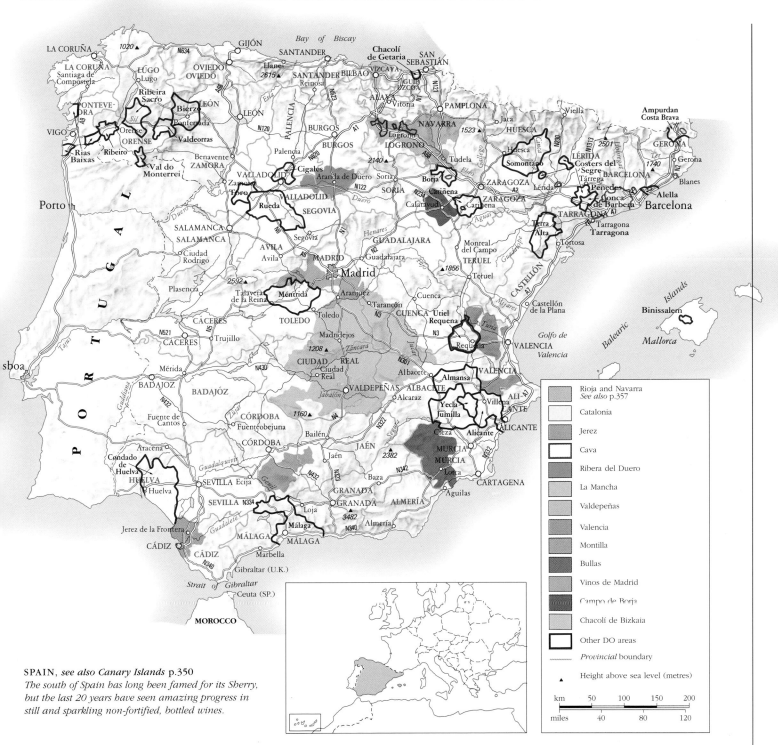

SPAIN, see also Canary Islands p.350
*The south of Spain has long been famed for its Sherry,
but the last 20 years have seen amazing progress in
still and sparkling non-fortified, bottled wines.*

It was not as if there was a meeting at which the entire Spanish
wine industry took a vote to change things, but there must have
been some sort of industry-wide determination to improve quality
because the situation was reversed so quickly. Spain's reputation
leapfrogged Italy's, despite having much less going for it in terms
of native grape varieties and *terroirs*, establishing the country as
one of the best-value sources in Europe.

ANCIENT ORIGINS
Vines were first planted in Spain *c.*1100 BC around Cádiz by, it is
believed, the Phoenicians. The earliest wines were by all accounts
rich, sweet, and heavy, the precursors of modern-day Sherry.
However, from the start of the 8th century until the end of the
15th, southern Spain was under the rule of the Moors, and being
Mohammedans, wine production was not a priority. This is not to
say that the Moors never drank wine; indeed, Al-Motamid, the last

Moorish king of Seville, enjoyed wine so much that he publicly
mocked anyone who drank water. The Moors also enjoyed the
grape as a fruit and for its fresh, unfermented juice, but under
a theoretically abstemious rule, winemaking stagnated. So,
while Spain can claim a 3,000-year history of wine, the diversity of its wine areas and styles did not commence until the
1490s, just 30 years before the Spanish planted the first vines in
the Americas. Some parts of the Old and New Worlds are much
closer in age, in terms of winemaking, than these terms imply.

SPAIN'S BEST WINES AND ITS APPELLATION SYSTEM
Vega Sicilia in the Ribera del Duero was once definitively Spain's
most expensive wine, leading many to believe that it must be
Spain's greatest. Others can now lay equal claim to be the most
expensive and greatest of Spanish wines (Clos l'Ermita, Dominio de
Pingus, and Cirsión are likely candidates), and many more are equal

in quality if not quite as ridiculously priced, including Pesquera, Rioja (Contino, Barón de Ley, Muga Prado Enea, Murrieta Castillo Ygay Gran Reserva), Penedés (Torres and Jean Léon), and even non-appellation wines such as Marqués de Griñón.

The *Denominación de Origen* (DO) system is Spain's equivalent of the French *Appellation d'Origine Contrôlée* (AOC) or Italian *Denominazione di Origine Controllata* (DOC) systems. The only higher Spanish classification is *Denominación de Origen Calificada* (DOCa) and Rioja remains the only recipient of this superior status since its inception in 1981, although other high-quality wines may be promoted in the future. Ribera del Duero, Navarra, Penedés, and Cava all spring to mind. If there is a lesson the Spanish could learn from Italy, it is not to overlook outstanding non-appellation wines such as Marqués de Griñón's Cabernet Sauvignon and Syrah from south of Madrid. Indisputably two of Spain's great wines, they should jump DO straight to DOCa status, if Spain's regime is to avoid the same fate as Italy's, whose best *vini da tavola* were forced to build up reputations at the expense of the official system.

RECENT SPANISH VINTAGES

2000 After a great flowering and excellent growing season the heavens opened up in perfect time for the harvest. Not likely to be a special vintage anywhere in Spain, but the price of grapes plummeted, so at least the wines won't be expensive!

1999 Good but not exceptional in Rioja, where growers suffered the worst frost for 60 years. Penedés also good.

1998 A very large crop of average quality in Rioja, where the reds lack concentration, but whites were fresh and fared better. Slightly better in Ribera del Duero.

1997 Very variable throughout Spain. Rioja not bad, but forget the Penedés except for wines from the most quality-conscious producers.

1996 This year marked the end of a five-year drought and, ironically, the authorization of irrigation, which will put Spain on an equal footing with the New World. Quality of this vintage generally good.

TRADITIONAL VERSUS MODERN STYLES

It used to be possible to speak of new-wave Spanish wines, as the tradition had been to leave wines in oak for longer than most modern winemakers consider wise and a younger generation of winemakers reacted by producing wines that were as fresh, clean, and unoaked as possible. However, although the old style for reds was dried-out and that for whites oxidized, the new style was so clean, it was clinical, and was no great improvement as such. The tendency now is to talk of modern style rather than new-wave, as the wines are much fruitier and the use of oak is not so much avoided, as restrained, with French casks more likely than American, and fermented rather than aged.

THE HILLTOP TOWN OF LAGUARDIA
Set against the majestic backdrop of the Sierra de Cantabria is the hilltop town of Laguardia, which boasts some of the finest vineyards of the Rioja Alava.

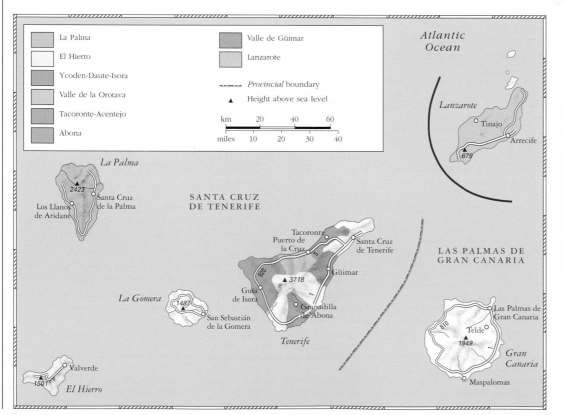

SAMPLING SHERRIES USING A VENENCIA
The development of a cask of Sherry is of crucial importance in determining its eventual style.

CANARY ISLANDS
The first of these appellations was established in 1992, but "Canary Sack" was famous in Shakespeare's time.

APPELLATIONS BELOW DENOMINACIÓN DE ORIGEN

The most baffling oddity in Spain's wine regime is the dual-level of its country-wine classification: *vino de la tierra* and *vino comarcal*. *Vino de la tierra* (VdlT) literally means "country wine", although it is closer to the French *Vin* *Délimité de Qualité Supérieure* (VDQS) than to *vin de pays*, as wines in this category aspire to *Denominación de Origen* (DO) status. *Vino comarcal* (VC) or "local wine" is a lesser appellation that is a closer equivalent of *vin de pays*.

ABANILLA VDLT
Murcia This flat, dry area has a scattering of vineyards whose wines have traditionally been blended with others in the Murcia region.

ALJARAFE VC
Andalucía These fortified wines are effectively an extension of the Condado de Huelva appellation.

ALTO JILOCA VC
Aragón Made mainly from Garnacha and Macabéo grapes, these wines were formerly sold with those of Daroca under the Alto Jiloca-Daroca appellation.

ANOIA VC
Catalonia Mostly soft, bland rosé wines from the Sumoll grape, as the whites are usually sold in bulk to Cava producers in Penedés.

BAGES VDLT
Catalonia Formerly the *vino comarcal* Artés, this area of Barcelona changed its appellation to Bages when it was upgraded to Catalonia's only *vino de la tierra*. Bages VdlT is now the DO Pla de Bages, although vintages of both are still available.

BAJO ARAGON VDLT
Aragón These wines are mostly *tinto* or *blanco* from red and white Garnacha grapes, although a fair amount of Macabéo, Mazuelo, and even Cabernet sauvignon grow in this very large area.

BAJO-EBROE-MONTSIA VC
Catalonia Meseguera, known locally as Exquitxagos, is the widest-planted grape variety in this area.

BENIARRÉS VC
Valencia This area produces robust, alcoholic reds and sweet Moscatel from Alicante.

BENAVENTE VC
Castilla-León This region was once quite famous for its *pétillant* rosé, but has yet to re-establish its historical reputation.

BETANZOS VC
Galicia A small amount of crisp, light-bodied, "Vinho Verde" style wines are produced here.

CADIZ VDLT
Andalucía These are light, white table wines of Jerez, pioneered and promoted by Barbadillo – they are fresh, but not special.

CAMPO DE CARTAGENA VDLT
Murcia Mostly oxidized whites, plus some rustic reds, although quality is apparently improving.

CAÑAMERO VDLT
Extremadura These rustic whites are produced in the foothills of the Sierra de Guadalupe. Now one of the six sub-regions of the DO Ribera del Guadiana although some producers refused to join the DO and are still labelling their wines as Cañamero VdlT.

CASTILLA VDLT
Castilla-La Mancha This VdlT was inaugurated in 1999 after lobbying by "maverick" winemakers in Castilla-La Mancha, headed by Carlos Falcó. It is a "Vin de Pays d'Oc" type classification allowing people to make the wines they want with minimal regulation throughout a vast region.

CEBREROS VDLT
Castilla-León A good source of cheap, fruity wines made from the Garnacha grape. Destined to achieve DO status.

CONCA DE TREMP VC
Catalonia A once-famous wine area at the foot of the Pyrenees, Conca de Tremp enjoys a warmer microclimate than surrounding areas and could produce some interesting wines.

CONTRAVIESA-ALPUJARA VDLT
Andalucía These rustic, fortified wines are from Granada and used to be called Costa-Albondón.

DAROCA VC
Aragón Made mainly from Garnacha and Macabéo grapes, these wines were formerly sold with those of Alto Jiloca.

FERMOSELLE-ARRIBES DEL DUERO VDLT
Castilla-León This is a large but shrinking viticultural area in which one of its secondary grape varieties, Juan García, could prove to be the most interesting. Destined to become the Arribes del Duero DO.

GALVEZ VDLT
Castilla-La Mancha Grape varieties in this large area southwest of Toledo are Tempranillo and Garnacha.

GRAN CANARIA-EL MONTE VDLT
Canary Islands These wines are made from the Negra común grape grown on Gran Canaria. Recently promoted to DO status under the appellation of Monte Lentiscal, although vintages of both are still available.

GRANDES PAGOS DE CASTILLA
Castilla-La Mancha & Castilla-León Literally meaning "Great Domains of Castile", this is a private designation utilized by an important group of producers throughout both parts of Castile. The wines they will make under this banner could be DO, VdlT or without regulations, but the corporate designation will take pride of place. The founder members include Mariano García, formerly of Vega Sicilia, plus various local-government dignitaries, the wine-writer Victor de la Serna and others. The president is – er – Carlos Falcó. One to watch.

LA GOMERA VDLT
Canary Islands Wines made from Forastera and Palomino grapes grown on the steep hillsides of La Gomera.

LA RIBERA DEL ARLANZA VC
Castilla-León This is a declining viticultural area, but high-altitude vineyards growing Tempranillo vines show potential.

LA SIERRA DE SALAMANCA VC
Castilla-León This area has potential, but some 70 per cent of its shallow granitic terraces overlooking the Alagón river are planted with Rufete, a high-yielding, low-quality Portuguese grape.

LAUJAR VC
Andalucía These are mostly rosé wines from an area better suited to the production of table grapes

LOPERA VC
Andalucía These are unfortified Pedro Ximénez wines, sold in bulk.

LOS PALACIOS VC
Andalucía These wines are mostly *mistela* (a combination of unfermented grape juice and alcohol) made from the Mollar grape or light, attenuated, white wines from Airén grapes.

MANCHUELA VDLT
Castilla-La Mancha These are effectively the lesser wines produced in the DO areas of Jumilla, La Mancha, and Utiel-Requena. This is now a DO, although vintages of both are still available.

MATANEGRA VDLT
Extremadura A very large area, Matanegra produces rather lacklustre whites, but interesting Tempranillo-based reds.

MONTANCHEZ VDLT
Extremadura This is a sizeable area in the province of Cáceres, producing rustic reds and whites from a mixture of varieties.

MUNIESA VC
Aragón This area is planted mostly with Garnacha, and the wines tend to be dark and tough.

PLA I LLEVANT DE MALLORCA VDLT
Balearic Islands Mallorca is seeking to replicate the fame of Majorca's Binissalem, which itself is but local. This is now a DO, although vintages of both are still available.

RIBEIRA DO ULLA VC
Galicia Albarella (*syn.* Albarello) is supposedly the best varietal to look for here.

RIBERA ALTA DEL GUADIANA VDLT
Extremadura There is promising potential here from both indigenous and foreign grape varieties.

RIBERA BAJA DEL GUADIANA VDLT
Extremadura This area has more in common – grapes, soil, and climate – with Tierra de Barros than with its neighbouring "Alta" VdlT.

POZOHONDO VDLT
Castilla-La Mancha The reds are made from Monastrell grapes, the whites from Airén. They have yet to achieve any reputation.

SACEDÓN-MONDÉJAR VDLT
Castilla-La Mancha An area southwest of Madrid producing mostly young, Tempranillo-based reds that are deep in colour and often sold in bulk. Also called Mondéjar-Sacedón. This is now the DO Mondéjar, although vintages of both are still available.

SAN MATEO VC
Valencia No reputation, not encountered, and no connection with the San Mateo festival in Rioja.

SIERRA DE ALCARAZ VDLT
Castilla-La Mancha: No reputation, not encountered, but I hear that this area is starting to show some serious form, mainly through Manuel Manzaneque, and could be a candidate for DO.

TIERRA BAJA DE ARAGON VDLT
Aragón These rough and ready Garnacha-dominated reds could well be improved over the next few years through increased cultivation of Tempranillo and Cabernet sauvignon.

TIERRA DE BARROS VDLT
Extremadura Bodegas Inviosa is demonstrating this area's potential for inexpensive fruity reds.

TIERRA DEL VINO DE ZAMORA VDLT
Castilla-León This traditional winegrowing area between Toro and Zamora is best known for its Tempranillo-based reds.

VALLE DEL MIÑO VDLT
Galicia These wines used to be sold as Ribeira del Sil prior to the best vineyards receiving DO status, while the remaining areas were relegated to this *vino de la tierra*.

VALDEVIMBRE-LOS OTEROS VDLT
Castilla-León Of all the VdlTs in Castilla-León, this area holds the most promise. Rocky-clay terraces either side of the Elsa river are planted with Prieto picudo, which produces wines that are similar to Tempranillo, but without the colour. They are traditionally blended to good effect with Garnacha and the underrated Mencía grape.

VALDEJALÓN VDLT
Aragón This has a similar history to that of Calatayud, but lags behind and has not quite the same potential. This VdlT is about to become a DO.

VILLAVICIOSA VC
Andalucía Wines from Córdoba of little reputation.

THE APPELLATIONS OF
SPAIN

Note Regions or provinces in which appellations are located are given in bold beneath each heading. "DO" is short for *Denominación de Origen*. A synonym for a grape variety is indicated by "*syn.*".

ABONA DO
Canary Islands

This new appellation was established in 1996 for white wines made in the south of Tenerife, where the vines are grown on terraces that are also planted with potatoes. Before they gained DO status, these wines were sold under the names of Granadilla, San Miguel, and Vilaflor.

🍇 Listán (*syn.* Palomino) and Malvasia

ALELLA DO
Catalonia

Tiny, predominantly white appellation just north of Barcelona, where grapes are traditionally grown on windy granite hills, but due to urban development the DO was extended in 1989 into the colder, limestone *vallès* of the Cordillera Catalana.

The red wines of Alella have good colour, medium body, and soft, fruity flavour. White and *rosado* are pale-coloured, fresh, and delicate, with good acidity when made with grapes from the best north-facing slopes.

🍇 Chardonnay, Chenin blanc, Garnacha, Grenache blanc (*syn.* Garnacha blanca), Garnacha peluda, Pansá rosada, Tempranillo (*syn.* Ull de Llebre), Xarel-lo (*syn.* Pansá blanca)

🍷 1–5 years (red), 1–2 years (white and rosé), 1–4 years (sweet)

✓ *Alta Alella Chardonnay* • *Alellasol* • *Marfil* • *Bodegas Parxet* (Marqués de Alella)

ALICANTE DO
Valencia

These mild-climate red, white, and rosé wines are grown on dark limey soil in the hills behind Alicante. The red wines are naturally deep in colour and, when made in a *doble pasta* style, they can be ink-black and astringent, but younger, fruitier styles are emerging, as indeed they are among *rosados* and whites. Fortified Moscatels are light and refreshing. A fortified wine of local repute called Fondillón is made from Monastrell grapes in a Tawny Port style.

🍇 Airén, Bobal, Garnacha, Garnacha tinta, Merseguera (*syn.* Merseguera), Moscatel Romano, Mourvèdre (*syn.* Monastrell), Planta fina, Tempranillo, Viura (*syn.* Macabéo)

🍷 6–12 years (reds)

✓ *Hijo de Luís García Poveda* (Costa Blanca)

ALMANSA DO
Castilla-La Mancha

This red and rosé appellation, which lies north of Jumilla and Yecla, bridges the heights of the central plains of La Mancha and the lowlands of Valencia.

These red wines are full-bodied and richly coloured, with the best being quite smooth and fruity. Good examples of *rosado* can be fruity and clean.

🍇 Airén, Garnacha, Meseguera (*syn.* Merseguera), Monastrell, Tempranillo (*syn.* Cencibel)

🍷 3–10 years (red), 1–3 years (rosé)

✓ *Alfonso Abellan* • *Bodegas Carrion* • *Bodegas Piqueras*

AMPURDAN-COSTA BRAVA DO
Catalonia

Lying at the foot of the narrowest section of the Pyrenees, this is the closest Spanish wine appellation to France. Most of the production is rosé and aimed at tourists, but the reds are much better, having a fairly deep, cherry-red colour, medium- to full-body, and a crisp, plummy flavour. Whites are fruity and may be off-dry or slightly sweet, with a pale, often greenish tinged colour, and are sometimes *pétillant* (lightly sparkling).

🍇 Carignan (*syn.* Cariñena), Grenache (*syn.* Garnacha), Grenache blanc (*syn.* Garnacha blanca), Viura (*syn.* Macabéo)

🍷 2–5 years (red), 9–18 months (white and rosé)

✓ *Cavas de Ampurdán* • *Convinosa* • *Oliveda*

BIERZO DO
Castilla-León

One of the more exciting of Spain's less traditional DOs, Bierzo includes red, white, and rosé wines. Young reds stand out, being made from a minimum of 70 per cent Mencía, an underrated variety capable of attractively aromatic wines.

🍇 Doña blanca, Garnacha, Godello, Malvasía, Mencía, Palomino

🍷 1–4 years (red), 9–18 months (white and rosé)

✓ *Bodegas CA del Bierzo* • *Bodegas Palacio de Arganza* (non-DO wines) • *Pérez Caramés* • *Casa Valdaiga*

BINISSALEM DO
Balearic Islands

This appellation owes its existence primarily to just one man, José Ferrer, but there are at least two other producers of Majorca's best-known

wine who are worth searching out. The white and rosé are simple, but the reds are slightly more serious and show some potential.

🍇 A minimum of 50% Manto negro (for reds) or 70% Moll (*syn.* Prensal blanco) for whites, plus Callet, Mourvèdre (*syn.* Monastrell), Parellada, Tempranillo, Viura (*syn.* Macabéo)

🍷 Upon purchase

✓ *José L. Ferrer* • *Jaume Mesquida* • *Bodegas Miguel Oliver*

BULLAS DO
Murcia

This is a large region just south of Jumilla where the soil is so poor that, apart from vines, only olives and almonds can survive. The young red wines here are made primarily from Monastrell grapes and seem to have the best potential, but white and rosé wines are also allowed. Bullas is, however, a new appellation that has yet to prove its quality.

🍇 Airén, Garnacha, Monastrell, Tempranillo (*syn.* Cencibel)

CAMPO DE BORJA DO
Aragón

This name derives from the notorious Borgia family, who used to run things here at the height of their power in the late 15th century. The whites are fresh, but somewhat neutral. The reds and rosés are full, robust, and can be alcoholic, but are they improving. Their character is sometimes compared to that which Navarra once had and Campo de Borja is now experimenting with Cabernet sauvignon in the same way as Navarra once did. This is a wine area to watch.

🍇 Garnacha, Garnacha blanca, Viura (*syn.* Macabéo)

🍷 3–8 years (red), 9–15 months (white and rosé)

✓ *Bodegas Bordeje* • *Agrícola de Borja* (Borsao) • *CA del Campo Union* • *Agraria del Santo Cristo* • *CA del Campo San Juan Bautista*

CARIÑENA DO
Aragón

Cariñena's low rainfall accounted for the traditionally high alcohol content of these wines, but modern vinification now makes a fresher, lighter, fruitier, more aromatic style. Reds are the best of this appellation. Some deliberately maderized *rancio* wines are still produced.

🍇 Cabernet Sauvignon, Carignan (*syn.* Cariñena), Garnacha, Grenache blanc (*syn.* Garnacha blanca), Juan Ibáñez, Moscatel Romano, Mourvèdre (*syn.* Monastrell), Parellada, Tempranillo, Viura

🍷 1–5 years (red), 9–18 months (white and rosé)

✓ *CA de Borja* • *CA de San Valero*

CALATAYUD DO
Aragón

A patchwork of vineyards, mostly planted with Garnacha vines, tussle with fruit trees for meagre sustenance from the poor, buff-coloured rocky soil. Increasing the amount of Tempranillo vines and temperature-controlled stainless-steel vats will eventually improve the potential here, but the best wines are still simple, fresh, fruity rosés.

🍇 Carignan (*syn.* Mazuelo),
  Grenache (*syn.* Garnacha),
  Grenache blanc (*syn.* Garnacha blanca),
  Juan Ibáñez (*syn.* Miguel de Arco),
  Malvasía, Moscatel Romano,
  Mourvèdre (*syn.* Monastrell),
  Tempranillo, Viura

🍾 Upon purchase

✓ *CA del Campo San Isidro* (Viña Alarba)
  • *CA de Maluenda* (Marqués de Aragón)

CAVA DO
See Cava and Penedés p.364

CHACOLÍ *or* TXAKOLINA DO
Cantabria
This appellation is split into two areas: Chacolí
de Guetaria (or Getariako Txakolina) and
Chacolí de Vizcaya (or Bizkaiko Txakolina).
The alternative names are Basque and, as this
is Basque country, these spellings will probably
take precedence. The wines are mostly white,
dry, and slightly *pétillant*, although a little red
is also produced. As typifies so many wines in
the northeastern corner of the Iberian peninsula,
the wines are high in acidity and low in alcohol.

🍇 Hondarribi beltza, Hondarribi zuri

✓ *Txomin Etxaniz*

CIGALES DO
Castilla-Léon
Since this appellation was established in
1991, it has been best known for fresh,
fruity, light reds and rosés.

🍇 Albillo, Garnacha, Palomino, Tempranillo,
  (*syn.* Tinto del País), Verdejo, Viura

✓ *CA de Cigales* (Escogido del Año,
  Viña Torondos) • *Frutos Villa*
  (Conde Ansurez, Viña Calderona,
  Viña Cansina, Viña Morejona)

CONCA DE BARBERA DO
Catalonia
This once little-known appellation for red,
white, and rosé wines from the hilly hinterland
of Penedés promises to be one of Spain's most
exciting areas. Chardonnay is outstanding here,
whether light and early-harvested as Ryman
makes, or rich, serious, and potentially complex,
as Torres demonstrates. Merlot is the most up-
and-coming variety in the red department, but
Trepat could mount a few surprises for fresh,
easy-drinking styles of both red and *rosado*.

🍇 Cabernet sauvignon, Grenache
  (*syn.* Garnacha), Merlot, Parellada,
  Tempranillo (*syn.* Ull de Llebre),
  Trepat, Viura (*syn.* Macabéo)

🍾 1–5 years

✓ *Torres* (Milmanda Chardonnay)

CONDADO DE HUELVA DO
Andalucía
The sweet dessert wines of this area, which
is sandwiched between the Sherry district of
southwest Spain and the Algarve of Portugal,
once had some fame for they were mentioned
by Chaucer in *The Canterbury Tales*. They
ended up, however, as blending fodder for
Sherry when that wine became more famous.
There are two basic types of fortified wine
here: *pálido* (young, pale-straw colour, dry,

austere wines, with 14–17% alcohol) and
viejo (solera-matured, mahogany hued, in
both dry and sweet styles that are deliberately
oxidized, with 15–23% alcohol). Light, dry
wines are a more recent phenomenon and
most are consumed locally.

🍇 Garrido fino, Palomino (*syn.* Listán), Zalema

🍾 Upon purchase

COSTERS DEL SEGRE DO
Catalonia
This is a top-performing appellation
encompassing four areas of different viticultural
character within the province of Lérida: Les
Garrigues and Valls de Riu Corb (primarily
white-grape districts); Artesa (planted almost
entirely with black grapes); and Raimat
(dominated by foreign grape varieties and
has quickly assumed classic status through
Codorníu's innovative Raimat Estate).

🍇 Cabernet sauvignon, Carignan
  (*syn.* Cariñena, Mazuelo), Chardonnay,
  Grenache (*syn.* Garnacha), Grenache blanc
  (*syn.* Garnacha blanca), Merlot, Mourvèdre
  (*syn.* Monastrell), Parellada, Trepat,
  Tempranillo (*syn.* Gotim Bru, Ull de
  Llebre), Viura (*syn.* Macabéo), Xarel-lo

🍾 2–6 years (red), 1–4 years (white)

✓ *Raïmat*
  • *Castell del Remei*

DO MONTERREI DO
Galicia
This area was awarded a provisional DO in
the early 1980s, but this was revoked when
too few of its growers showed any interest in
modernizing their estates. Some progress was
made in the late 1980s and this appellation has
now been granted full DO status, although it is
too early to make a rational assessment of any
improvement in its wines.

🍇 Alicante, Doña blanca, Gran negro,
  Mencía, Mouratón, Palomino (*syn.* Jerez),
  Verdello (*syn.* Godello)

EL HIERRO DO
Canary Islands
This new appellation was established in 1996
for El Hierro, the smallest and most westerly
island in the archipelago, yet the local
cooperative is one of the most advanced in
the Canary Islands. Before gaining DO status,
these wines were sold under the local names
of Frontera and Valverde. The best areas are
Valle de Golfo, El Pinar, and Echedo.

🍇 include: Listán (*syn.* Palomino), Malvasía,
  Moscatel, Negramoll (best for reds and
  rosés), Pedro Ximénez, Verdello,
  Verijadiego (best for whites)

JEREZ *or* JEREZ-XÉRÈS-SHERRY DO
See Sherry Country p.366

JUMILLA DO
Murcia
The high, hilly vineyards of Jumilla have
never been affected by phylloxera and most
of the vines are still ungrafted. Almost all the
wines produced here are red and until recently
were lacklustre, unless made in a *doble pasta*
style, which produces wines so thick and
intense that they are in great demand for
blending purposes throughout Spain and
abroad. The best reds carry the Jumilla
Monastrell varietal appellation and can be
very smooth, fruity, and aromatic, tending
to improve with age. With earlier picking and
temperature-controlled fermentation, lighter,
more accessible wines are now being made
that are best drunk when young and juicy,
including some soft, fruity whites and rosés.

🍇 Airén, Grenache (*syn.* Garnacha),
  Meseguera (*syn.* Merseguera), Mourvèdre
  (*syn.* Monastrell), Pedro Ximénez,
  Tempranillo (*syn.* Cencibel)

🍾 1–3 years (red, but up to 6 for *doble pasta*),
  9–15 months (white and rosé)

✓ *Bodegas Bleda* (Castillo Jumilla) • *Bodegas
  Señorío del Condestable* • *Jumilla Union
  Vitivinícola* (Cerrillares, Incunable)

LANZAROTE DO
Canary Islands
This new appellation was established in 1995
for the island of Lanzarote, where the lunar
landscape is dotted with vines in crater-like
depressions, protected by low stone walls.
The most spectacular example of this weirdly
beautiful form of viticulture can be viewed at
La Geria, an area west of Arrecife where no
less than 2,000 hectares (5,000 acres) of such
vineyards are to be found.

🍇 include: Caleta, Diego, Listán
  (*syn.* Palomino), Malvasia

LA PALMA DO
Canary Islands
This new appellation was established in 1995
for the island of La Palma. It was in Fuencaliente
in the south of the island that the famed "Canary
Sack" of Shakespeare's time was produced and
the grape responsible, Malvasia, still grows
here, amid four smoking volcanoes, in the
same sort of crater-like depressions that abound
on Lanzarote. An oddity aged in pine casks and
curiously called Vino del Tea ("Tea" being the

local name for a particular species of pine) is available in the north of the island, but only the most ardent admirers of Retsina should search it out.

🍇 include: Bujariego (best for whites), Gual, Listán (*syn.* Palomino), Malvasia, Negramoll (best for reds)

MÁLAGA DO
Andalucía

Just northeast of Jerez in southern Spain, the coastal vineyards of Málaga produce one of the most underrated classic dessert wines in the world. Most is matured by the *solera* system, involving some six scales (see Sherry Country, p.366) and may be blended in a Sherry-like manner using various grape-based colouring and sweetening agents, such as *arrope, vino de color, vino tierno,* and *vino maestro.* The colour of these fortified wines can range from gold through tawny to brown and red, depending on the style of Málaga, its age, and method of maturation, its degree of sweetness, and the grape variety used.

Málaga may be any one of the following: *Dulce color* is a dark, medium-bodied Málaga that has been sweetened with *arrope. Lágrima* is made from free-run juice only, and is the most luscious of all Málaga styles. *Moscatel* is a sweet, rich, raisiny, medium- to full-bodied wine that is similar to the Jerez version, only more luscious. *Old Solera* has the most finesse, depth, and length of all Málagas and is capable of complexity rather than lusciousness. It is medium- to full-bodied, still sweet yet with a dry finish. *Oscuro* is a dark, sweet Málaga that has been sweetened with *arrope* and coloured by *vino de color. Pajarette* or *Paxarete* is darkish in colour, and less sweet, but more alcoholic, than other Málagas. *Pedro Ximénez* is a smooth, sweet, deliciously rich varietal wine with an intense flavour, which is similar in character to the Jerez version. *Seco* is a pale, dry, tangy wine with a distinctive creamy hazelnut character.

🍇 Moscatel, Pedro Ximénez

🍷— Upon purchase (although it can last, but not improve, for several years)

✓ *Scholtz Hermanos • Pérez Texeira • Larios*

LA MANCHA DO
Castilla-La Mancha

VIÑA DEL CASTILLO
DE VINICOLA DE CASTILLA
1991

LA MANCHA
Denominación de Origen
DRY WHITE
PRODUCED SOLELY FROM AIREN GRAPES
PRODUCED AND BOTTLED BY
VINICOLA DE CASTILLA, S.A.
Manzanares - LA MANCHA - Spain
75 cl   PRODUCT OF SPAIN
11% vol.   R.E. M9-CR

Although its output remains enormous, accounting for some 40 per cent of all Spanish wines produced, the wine-land of Don Quixote has improved tremendously since the early 1980s. Many producers now harvest much earlier than previously and ferment at cooler temperatures (sometimes too cool), achieving fresher, lighter, more aromatic wines. The best wines of La Mancha are made in Valdepeñas, but there are an increasing number of very good, fruity wines made throughout this region.

🍇 Airén, Cabernet Sauvignon, Grenache (*syn.* Garnacha), Merlot, Moravia, Pardina (*syn.* Pardilla, Pardillo), Tempranillo (*syn.* Cencibel), Viura (*syn.* Macabéo)

🍷— 1–4 years (red), 9–15 months (white and rosé)

✓ *Bodegas Ayuso* (Estola Gran Reserva) • *Vinícola de Castilla* (Castillo de Alhambra, Señorío de Guadianeja) • *Jesús Díaz e Hijos* • *Bodegas C. Españolas* (Fuente del Ritmo) • *Bodegas Hermanos Morales* (Gran Créacion) • *CA del Campo Nuestra Señora de Manjavacas* (Zagarrón) • *CA del Campo Nuestra Padre Jesús de Perdon* (Casa la Teja, Lazarillo, Yuntero) • *Rama Corta* • *Rodriguez y Berger* (Viña Santa Elena) • *Julián Santos* • *Bodega Torres Filoso* (Arboles de Castollejo)

MANZANILLA DO
See Sherry Country p.369

MÉNTRIDA DO
Castilla-La Mancha

Cheap wine, consumed locally: deep-coloured, full-bodied, coarse reds and alcoholic rosé.

🍇 Garnacha, Tempranillo (*syn.* Cencibel, Tinto Madrid)

MONTILLA-MORILES DO
Andalucía

The Sherry-like wines of Montilla fall into three categories: *generosos* (fortified Finos, Amontillados, Olorosos, and magnificent PX); unfortified traditional wines (cream, medium, and dry at 14.5% abv); and *jóvenes afrutados* (ghastly).

🍇 Baladí, Lairén (*syn.* Airén), Moscatel, Pedro Ximénez, Torrontés

🍷— Can be kept, but consume upon opening

✓ *Marqués de la Sierra • Alvear • Bodegas Mora Chacon • Gracia Hermanos • Perez Barquero • Rodriguez Chiachio*

NAVARRA DO
See Rioja and Navarra p.359

PENEDÉS DO
See Cava and Penedés p.363

PRIORATO DO
Catalonia

This area has a dry climate and poor soil in which the vines' roots spread everywhere in search of moisture, the local saying being that Priorato vines can suck water out of stone. The best wines are currently being made around the hilltop town of Gratallops, by a group of young winemakers led by Bordeaux-trained Riojan oenologist Alvaro Palacios, who brought with him a wealth of experience from Château Pétrus to the Napa Valley. New-style reds are huge, serious, and stunningly rich, but old style are heavy, over-alcoholic and oxidized, although the best traditional wines fall somewhere between. One of the country's oldest appellations, Priorato is set to become a Spanish wine super-star.

🍇 Cabernet Sauvignon, Carignan (*syn.* Cariñena, Mazuelo), Grenache (*syn.* Garnacha), Grenache blanc (*syn.* Garnacha blanca), Merlot, Mourvèdre (*syn.* Monastrell), Pedro Ximénez, Syrah, Viura (*syn.* Macabéo)

🍷— 5–15 years (red)

✓ *Bodegas Alvaro Palacios* (Finca Dofi, Clos l'Ermita, Las Terrasses) • *René Barbier fill* (Clos Mogador) • *Clos Erasmus* • *Costers del Siurana* (Clos de l'Obac, Miserere) • *Masia Barril* • *De Muller* • *Scala Dei* (Cartoixa, El Cipres, Novell) • *Vinicola del Priorato* (Mas d'Alba, Onix)

RÍAS BAIXAS DO
Galicia

Spain's fastest-rising star in the DO firmament, the Rías Baixas appellation covers various red, white, and rosé wines, but the best-known and most enjoyable wines are the softly-perfumed, zippy whites made from low-yielding Albariño grapes, which can have real depth and fruit, and a fresh, lively acidity. Although I have always admired the best of these wines, I did wonder whether they are worth what appeared to be an increasingly high price. At the table, however, they accompany fine food beautifully, which in my book makes even the most expensive Rías Baixas well worth the price demanded.

🍇 Albariño, Brancellao, Caiño blanco, Caiño tinto, Espadeiro, Loureira blanca, Loureira tinta, Mencía, Sousón, Torrontés, Treixadura

🍷— 1–3 years

✓ *Albariño do Salnes • Pazo de Barrantes • Bodegas Cardalial • Lagar de Cevera • Bodegas del Palacio de Fefiñanes • Granxa Fillaboa • Morgadio-Agromiño • Bodegas de Vilariño Cambados* (Martín Códax, Organistrum) • *Santiago Ruíz*

RIBEIRA SACRA
Galicia

The most-planted grape variety here is Palomino, but on the steep, terraced vineyards of Ribeira Sacra, Albariño is far more exciting and Mencía shows promise for red wines.

🍇 Albariño, Brancellao, Caiño, Doña blanca, Espadeiro, Ferrón, Godello, Grenache (*syn.* Garnacha), Loureira, Loureira tinta, Mencía, Merenzao, Negrada, Palomino, Sousón, Torrontés

🍷— 1–3 years

✓ *Adegas Moure* (Albariño Abadia da Cova)

RIBEIRO DO
Galicia

Due to the Atlantic-influenced climate of northwest Spain, the styles of Ribeiro's red and white wines reflect that of Portugal's Vinhos Verdes, except that they are somewhat more fruity and aromatic.

🍇 Albariño, Albillo, Brancellao, Caiño, Ferrón, Garnacha (*syn.* Alicante), Godello, Jerez (*syn.* Palomino), Loureira, Mencía, Sousón, Tempranillo, Torrontés, Treixadura, Viura (*syn.* Macabéo)

🍷— 9–18 months

✓ *Bodegas Alanis • Bodegas Arsenio Paz • Bodegas Rivera • CA del Ribeiro*

RIBERA DEL DUERO DO
Castilla-León

From the upper reaches of the Duero river (which becomes the Douro, once it crosses the Portuguese border), the rosés are fresh, dry, fruity wines of a *clarete* or *claro* style, but are nowhere near the class of the best reds, which have a truly dense, black colour and are packed solid with rich, oaky-sweet, plummy-blackcurrant fruit flavours.

Ribera del Duero DO built its reputation on "Vega Sicilia", formerly Spain's most expensive wine. In the first edition of this book I categorically stated that contrary to the informed opinion of many other wine critics, this was not Spain's greatest red wine, although it was potentially the best. The problem was that ten or more years in wood took its toll on the fruit in a way that would destroy many of the greatest wines of Bordeaux.

There was also no logic to the duration of ageing at Vega Sicilia, which occurred in different sizes and ages of wooden cask, the various vintages being transferred from one vessel to another simply to fulfil the logistical necessity of moving the wines around in order to accommodate the incoming harvest. This explains why vertical tastings reveal such uneven results across many vintages. Sometimes, miraculously, this haphazard system yielded a phenomenal vintage (1982, 1976, 1975, 1962, and 1953 to name just a few), but quite often a critical taster would be left with the feeling that, although a particular vintage of Vega Sicilia was good, it could have been much better.

Since the first edition, however, Vega Sicilia has given its wines no more than six years in wood and now has a more disciplined approach to how long wines spend in various types and ages of cask, including new oak *barriques*. I claim no credit for these developments, for Vega Sicilia once aged its wines for 25 years in wood, thus the reduction in duration of ageing is merely part of the wine's natural evolution, but I welcome these long overdue changes, which will help ensure that Vega Sicilia remains one of Spain's very greatest wines.

🍇 Cabernet sauvignon, Grenache (*syn.* Garnacha), Malbec, Merlot, Pardina (*syn.* Albillo), Tempranillo (*syn.* Tinto fino, Tinto del País)

🍷 3–8 years (modern red), 5–25 years (traditional red), 1–2 years (rosé)

✓ *Ismael Arroyo* • *Balbás* • *Bodegas Alejandro Fernández* (Tinto Pesquera) • *Grandes Bodegas* (Marqués de Velilla) • *Hijos de Antonio Barceló* (Viña Mayor Reserva) • *Bodegas Mauro* • *Hermanos Pérez* (Viña Pedrosa) • *Pago de Carraovejas* • *Dominio de Pingus* • *Bodegas Reyes* • *Señorío de Nava* (Reserva) • *Bodegas Valduero* • *Vega Sicilia* (including Alión, which replaced the younger of the two Valbuena wines) • *Viñedos y Bodegas* (Matarromera)

RIOJA DOC
See **Rioja and Navarra** p.357

RUEDA DO
Castilla-León

This small district down-river from Ribeiro del Duero is known primarily for fresh, crisp, dry white wines made almost entirely from the Verdejo grape, but traditionally the wines were fortified in *fino* (Palido Rueda) and *rancio* (Dorado Rueda) styles, and these can still be found today. A *méthode champenoise* Rueda Espumoso is also allowed.

🍇 Palomino, Sauvignon blanc, Verdejo, Viura (*syn.* Macabéo)

🍷 1–2 years

✓ *Agricola Castellana* • *Marqués de Griñón* • *Marqués de Riscal*

SHERRY *or* JEREZ-XÉRÈS-SHERRY DO
See **Sherry Country** p.366

SITGES
Catalonia
This is a famous but rare non-DO fortified Malvasia and Moscatel wine made just south of the outskirts of Barcelona, from grapes that are allowed to shrivel on the vine.

✓ *Cellers Robert*

SOMONTANO DO
Aragón
Set at the foot of the Pyrenees, between Penedés and Navarra, Somontano is destined to become one of Spain's greatest wine regions. Chardonnay is by far the best for serious, barrel-fermented whites, but both Tempranillo and Cabernet sauvignon show superb potential for fragrant reds with a lively richness of fruit.

🍇 Alcanón, Cabernet sauvignon, Chardonnay, Grenache (*syn.* Garnacha), Grenache blanc (*syn.* Garnacha blanca), Moristel (*sic* – not Monastrell), Parreleta (*sic* – not Parellada), Tempranillo, Viura (*syn.* Macabéo)

🍷 2–5 years (red), 1–3 years (white)

✓ *Aragonesa* (Merlot/Cabernet Sauvignon Reserva) • *COVISA* (Viñas del Vero) • *Enate* • *Lalanne* • *Bodegas Pirineos* (Montesierra, Señorío de Lazán)

TACORONTE-ACENTEJO DO
Canary Islands
Established in 1992, this is the oldest

Canary Island appellation and, so far, the best, although it is too early to tell how the others will fare.

🍇 include: Castellano, Gual, Listán (*syn.* Palomino), Listán negro, Malvasía, Marmajuelo, Moscatel, Negra común, Negramoll, Pedro Ximénez, Tintillo, Torrontés, Verdello

✓ *Bodegas Monje* • *Viña Norte*

TARRAGONA DO
Catalonia
This is the largest appellation in Catalonia, but its potential quality is modest compared to that of neighbouring Penedés, although Australian winemakers Nick Butler and Mark Nairn have been quietly raising standards at Pedro Rovira, using hands-off methods to retain as much natural character as possible. The best red, white, and rosé can all be fresh, fruity, and rewarding. Even the local fortified wine, sold as Tarragona *classico*, can be worth looking out for.

🍇 Carignan (*syn.* Cariñena), Grenache (*syn.* Garnacha), Grenache blanc (*syn.* Garnacha blanca), Parellada, Tempranillo (*syn.* Ull de Llebre), Viura (*syn.* Macabéo), Xarel-lo

🍷 1–5 years (red), 1–2 years (white and rosé)

✓ *CA de Valls* • *José Lopez Beltrán* (Don Beltrán) • *Pedro Masana* (non-DO wines) • *De Müller* (Moscatel Seco, Parxete) • *Pedro Rovira*

TERRA ALTA DO
Catalonia
This slowly improving appellation lies in the highlands well away from the coast. It produces good, everyday-drinking reds and whites, but avoid the local sweet, fortified *mistela*.

🍇 Cabernet sauvignon, Carignan (*syn.* Cariñena, Mazuelo), Grenache (*syn.* Garnacha), Grenache blanc (*syn.* Garnacha blanca), Merlot, Moscatel, Parellada, Tempranillo, Viura (*syn.* Macabéo)

🍷 1–2 years

✓ *CA Gandesa* • *CA la Hermandad* • *Pedro Rovira* (Alta Mar, Viña d'Irto)

TORO DO
Castilla-León
I once told the manager of the local cooperative that although I had seen some grubby cooperatives in my time, his was the filthiest I had ever encountered. There were always a couple of producers who stood out from the rest, even then, but considerable improvements have occurred and the best wines – reds – are now less tannic and far more approachable in their youth, yet still quite meaty and ageing well.

🍇 Grenache (*syn.* Garnacha), Malvasía, Tempranillo (*syn.* Tinta de Toro), Verdejo blanco

🍷 2–8 years (red), 1–3 years (white)

✓ *Bodegas Frutos Villar* • *Bodegas Fariña* (especially Gran Colegiata)

TXAKOLINA DO
See **Chacoli DO**

UTIEL-REQUENA DO
Valencia
This large and important essentially red-wine district is situated in the extreme west of the province of Valencia. Although distilling wine

and *doble pasta* were once the area's forte, softer, more palatable reds are now being made and the best dry rosés are fresh and delicate for such sunny climes.

🍇 Bobal, Grenache (*syn.* Garnacha), Meseguera (*syn.* Merseguera), Planta nova (*syn.* Tardana), Tempranillo, Viura (*syn.* Macabéo)

🍷 2–5 years (red), 9–18 months (rosé)

✓ *Augusto Egli* (Casa Lo Alto)

VALDEORRAS DO
Galicia

Until Rías Baixas came on the scene, this was Galicia's most up-and-coming district. With vines planted on terraced, slaty hillsides flanking the river Sil and Valdeorras' northern, wet, Atlantic-influenced climate, these wines have never been overburdened with alcohol, as so much Spanish wine was once upon a time, and refreshing acidity is part of their charm. The best wineries have now been modernized and are even better than they used to be, particularly for white wines made from the Godello grape.

🍇 Garnacha, Godello, Gran negro, Lado, María Ardoña, Mencía, Merenzao, Palomino, Valenciana (*syn.* Doña blanca)

🍷 1–4 years (red), 1 year (white and rosé)

✓ *Bodegas Godeval* • *Bodega Jesus Nazareno* • *Joaquín Rebolledo*

VALDEPEÑAS DO
Castilla-La Mancha

This is Castilla-La Mancha's solitary fine-wine area. Despite the torrid heat (the climate has been described as nine months of winter, three months of hell) and an apathetic attitude held by far too many producers, some terrific wines are being made here by a minority of wineries and they are very good value. The rich, red, stony soil hides a water-retentive limestone base that helps offset the lack of rainfall.

The best reds are medium- to full-bodied, pure Tempranillo, with a wonderfully rich yet well-balanced flavour, and more and more new-oak influence. The rosé can be smooth and fruity, but it would take a complete

overhaul of the vineyards, replanting them with something decent, to make the white wines appealing, although there is no excuse for their not being fresh.

🍇 Airén, Tempranillo (*syn.* Cencibel)

🍷 2–6 years (red), 9–18 months (rosé)

✓ *Miguel Calatayud*
 • *Bodegas J.A. Megía*
 • *Bodegas Los Llanos*
 • *Bodegas Luis Megía* (Marqués de Gastañaga)
 • *Bodegas Felix Solis* (Viña Albali Reserva)
 • *Casa de la Viña* (Vega de Moriz)

VALENCIA DO
Valencia

This area was once renowned for its heavy, alcoholic, low-quality *vino de mesa* (table wine). However, most modern wineries nowadays produce much lighter wines than before, and they are are at least fresh and drinkable. There are some good reds from the Monastrell grape, which are smooth and medium-bodied and may sometimes be aged in oak. The deliciously sweet and raisiny Moscatel is consistently great value, often performing well under blind conditions against French Muscat de Beaumes de Venise that sells for twice the price.

🍇 Forcayat, Grenache (*syn.* Garnacha), Malvasía (*syn.* Riojana), Meseguera (*syn.* Merseguera), Mourvèdre (*syn.* Monastrell), Moscatel, Pedro Ximénez, Planta fina, Tempranillo, Tortosí, Viura (*syn.* Macabéo)

🍷 1–4 years (red), 9–18 months (white and rosé), upon opening (Moscatel)

✓ *CA de Villar* • *Vicente Gandía*
 • *Augusto Egli* (particularly good-value Moscatel)
 • *Bodegas Schenk* (Cavas Murviedro)
 • *Bodegas Tierra Hernández*

VALLE DE GÜIMAR DO
Canary Islands

This appellation was established in 1996 for wines from the eastern side of Tenerife, just south of down-town Santa Cruz. The vineyards here abut cultivated fields, which are irrigated and thus indirectly feed these vines. Before gaining DO status, these wines were not even sold locally, but consumed by the people who produced them.

🍇 mostly: Listán (*syn.* Palomino), Listán negro, Negramoll

VALLE DE LA OROTAVA DO
Canary Islands

Established in 1996, this appellation covers wines produced on the lush, northern side of Tenerife, between the appellations of Tacoronte-Acentejo and Ycoden-Daute-Isora. Before DO status, these wines were sold under the *vino de la tierra* (literally "country wine") of La Orotava-Los Realos.

🍇 mostly: Listán (*syn.* Palomino) and Listán negro

VINOS DE MADRID
Madrid

Much admired by Casanova, who sought refuge in Madrid at a time when the capital was rapidly expanding at the expense of its vineyards, these wines probably assumed a rarity value that outshone their intrinsic quality. By extending the appellation well beyond its

fast-disappearing 18th-century boundaries, Vinos de Madrid was resurrected in 1990, although you would have to be a greater lover of these wines than Casanova to declare your open admiration for them. There are, however, a couple of exceptions to the rule and one of these, Jesús Díaz e Hijos, is exceptional by any standards.

🍇 Airén, Albillo, Grenache (*syn.* Garnacha), Malvar, Tempranillo (*syn.* Tinto fino)

🍷 Upon purchase (2–3 years for recommended)

✓ *Bodega Francisco Figuero*
 • *Jesús Díaz e Hijos*

YCODEN-DAUTE-ISORA DO
Canary Islands

Established in 1995 for the wines produced on the northwestern corner of Tenerife, where the grapes are grown on terraces, which are often irrigated. Before they gained DO status, these wines were sold under the *vino de la tierra* of Icod de Los Vinos, a name that recalls their long-lost fame. After the Battle of Trafalgar, the Canaries were a favourite watering hole with the Royal Navy, and the orange-tinged white wines of this area were enjoyed by all ranks.

🍇 mostly: Listán (*syn.* Palomino) and Listán negro

YECLA DO
Murcia

You would think these stony-limestone vineyards between Alicante and Jumilla should do better, but although some decent wines can be found, nothing special stands out. The reds are either ink-black *doble pasta* or

cherry-coloured with good body and fruit. Wines from the Campo Arriba zone in the north of this appellation can add this name to the Yecla DO if they are red or rosé, and made from 100 per cent Monastrell grapes harvested at almost half the yield asked elsewhere in Yecla. Whites are at best fresh, clean, and fruity.

🍇 Grenache (*syn.* Garnacha), Meseguera (*syn.* Merseguera), Mourvèdre (*syn.* Monastrell), Verdil

🍷 2–5 years (red, 3–6 Yecla Campo Arriba), 1–2 years (white and rosé)

✓ *Bodegas Castaño* (Pozuelo, Las Gruesas)
 • *Ochoa Palao* (Cuvée Prestige)

YECLA CAMPO ARRIBA DO
See Yecla DO

XÉRÈS *or* JEREZ-XÉRÈS-SHERRY DO
See Sherry Country p.366

RIOJA AND NAVARRA

The first and, so far, the only wine to receive DOCa status, Spain's highest classification, Rioja is without doubt the country's greatest fine-wine region. Neighbouring Navarra, which was once regarded as the country's best source of rosado *but little else, is slowly developing a reputation for other styles, having upgraded its vineyards and wineries.*

ONLY A SHORT DRIVE from the shabby suburbs of the commercial city of Bilbao, and the dramatic beauty of an upland valley becomes apparent, rich with architectural treasures of the twelfth century, isolated hilltop *pueblos*, a philanthropic people, a generous tradition, and a hearty cuisine.

RIOJA
Rioja is oaky, and all attempts to rid the wine of oak are doomed to failure. Oak is the basis of its fame and the reason it became Spain's first and greatest red-wine success, and while critics who suggest that these wines are too oaky for today's more sophisticated consumers may have a point, there is precious little left in most Rioja once you take away the oak.

It was the French who originally blessed the wines of this region with their unmistakable sweet-vanilla oak identity. As early as the 18th century, a few enlightened *Riojanos* had looked to France, Bordeaux particularly, to improve their winemaking skills. The transformation that resulted was subtle compared to the radical changes that occurred in Rioja in the 1840s and 1860s, after phylloxera, a louse that attacks vine roots, had wreaked havoc on French vineyards. A number of *vignerons*, mostly *bordelais* but some Burgundian too, gave up hope of reviving their own vineyards and descended upon Rioja to set up new wineries. Their methods dramatically improved the quality and style of Rioja, while other Frenchmen, mostly merchants from Bordeaux, opened up an instantly lucrative trade for the wine, as they desperately sought to top-up the dwindling produce of their own devastated vineyards.

Origins
Wine has been made in Rioja since at least the second century BC, when the Romans conquered the area. Rioja was sufficiently well respected by 1560 that its producers forbade the use of grapes from outside the region, guaranteeing the authenticity of their wines with a brand on the *pellejos* (goat-skins) in which they were transported. Wooden barrels came into use in the 18th

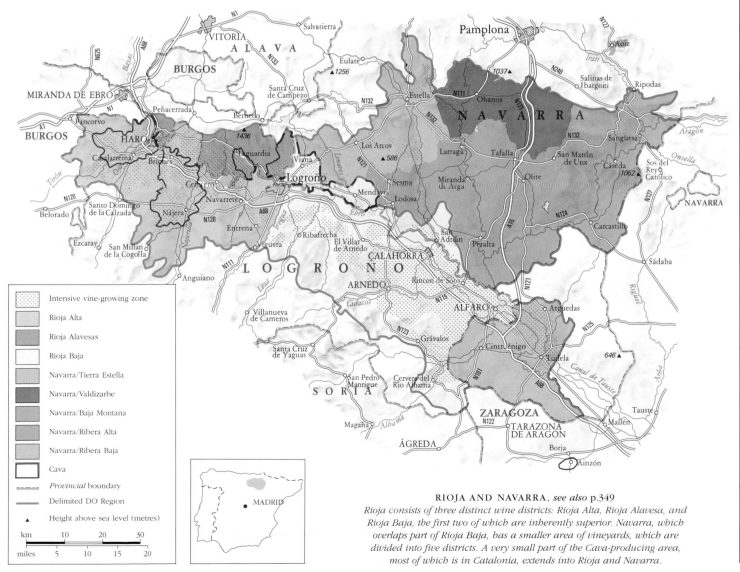

⸛	Intensive vine-growing zone
	Rioja Alta
	Rioja Alavesas
	Rioja Baja
	Navarra/Tierra Estella
	Navarra/Valdizarbe
	Navarra/Baja Montana
	Navarra/Ribera Alta
	Navarra/Ribera Baja
	Cava
— — —	*Provincial* boundary
——	Delimited DO Region
▲	Height above sea level (metres)

km   10   20   30
miles 5   10   15   20

RIOJA AND NAVARRA, *see also p.349*
Rioja consists of three distinct wine districts: Rioja Alta, Rioja Alavesa, and Rioja Baja, the first two of which are inherently superior. Navarra, which overlaps part of Rioja Baja, has a smaller area of vineyards, which are divided into five districts. A very small part of the Cava-producing area, most of which is in Catalonia, extends into Rioja and Navarra.

century, but were five times the size of casks today and it was not until 1860 at Marqués de Riscal that the first Bordeaux *barriques* were used (although there seems to be evidence that Manuel Quintano was the first, *c.*1800). One particularly influential Frenchman, Jean Pineau, was employed to teach French methods to local growers. In 1868, upon completion of his contract, Pineau was employed by Don Camilo Hurtado de Amezaga, the Marqués de Riscal, who was an admirer of Médoc wines and had lived in Bordeaux for 15 years. He had planted Cabernet sauvignon on his estate in 1863 and wanted Pineau to develop his new *bodega* in the manner of the most advanced wine châteaux in the Médoc.

RIOJA'S CLASSIC WINE DISTRICTS
Rioja's vineyards are located along the Ebro Valley, between Haro and Alfaro, and throughout its hinterland, with vines clustered around many of the Ebro's tributaries, one of which, the Oja River, has given its name to the region. Most Rioja is red and blended from wines or grapes (primarily Tempranillo and Garnacha) originating from the region's three districts (Rioja Alta, Rioja Alavesa, and Rioja Baja), although many of the best-quality are single-district wines and a handful of single-estate Rioja have also emerged in recent years.

Rioja Alta
Logroño and Haro, the principal towns of Rioja, are both in the Rioja Alta. Logroño is a very big town by Spanish standards, but Haro, at the western edge of the region, is an enclosed hilltop community and a much smaller, far more charming, older, and traditional place. The area's wine is Rioja's fullest in terms of fruit and concentration, and can be velvety smooth. Bodegas Muga makes fine examples of pure Rioja Alta, as do CVNE (Compañía Vinícola del Norte de España) – in the form of their Imperial range – in nine years out of every ten.

Rioja Alavesa
There are no large towns in the Alavesa, a district that is similar in climate to the Alta. Wines produced here are Rioja's fullest in body and reveal a much firmer character than those of the Alta and the Baja, with greater acidity. It was to the Alavesa that Pedro Domecq came, after years of intensive research, to plant a vast estate of 400 hectares (985 acres), cultivating his vines on wires as opposed to using the bush method traditional to the region. Apart from Bodegas Domecq, which produces mainly pure Alavesa wines, Remelluri and Contino, two single-estate Alavesas, are both typical of the district.

Rioja Baja
Baja is a semi-arid area influenced by the Mediterranean, and is hotter, sunnier, and drier than the Alta and the Alavesa, with rainfall averaging between 38 and 43 centimetres (15 and 17 inches) per year, but falling as low as 25 centimetres (10 inches) at Alfaro in the south. Some 20 per cent of the vines growing here come within, and can claim, the Navarra appellation. The wines are deep-coloured and very alcoholic, some as strong as 18 per cent, but lack acidity, aroma, and finesse, and are best used for blending.

NAVARRA
The wine-growing region of Navarra overlaps part of the Rioja Baja, but although not quite in the same league as Rioja in general, it is capable of producing some fine wines of exceptional value.

Recent marketing successes have halted the decline in Navarra's vineyards and encouraged various ambitious trials with foreign grapes such as Merlot, while previous experimental varieties such as Cabernet sauvignon are now fully recommended. According to the Estación de Viticultura y Enología de Navarra (EVENA), Spain's most advanced viticultural and oenological research station, these Bordeaux varieties are ideally suited to Navarra's soil and climate.

A rosy past
Navarra was once virtually synonymous with *rosado* and this style still accounts for almost half of total production, but what has really held back the reputation of this area has been the Garnacha (*syn.* Grenache) grape. This modest-quality grape variety can make good rosé, but except as part of a blend, rarely excels in red wines. Garnacha makes up more than 65 per cent of Navarra's vines, so the region is ill-equipped to develop beyond its *rosado* horizon. Furthermore, Tempranillo, the grape upon which Rioja's success has been built and indubitably Spain's finest red-wine variety, represents just 15 per cent of Navarra's vines. This proportion is, however, double what it was a decade ago and with Tempranillo and Cabernet sauvignon making up 60 per cent and 20 per cent respectively of all new vines currently being planted, Navarra is set to achieve a tremendous boost in quality over the next decade.

According to Javier Ochoa, former chief oenologist at EVENA, the perfect Navarra blend should be something in the order of 50 per cent Tempranillo, 30 per cent Garnacha, and 20 per cent Cabernet sauvignon, but I wonder if even this is tempered by the large amount of Garnacha that will still exist when the replanting programme has concluded. If there were, say, just two or three per cent in Navarra, would he actually advise increasing Garnacha to 30 per cent? Somehow I don't think so.

GRAPE VARIETIES IN RIOJA

Although there has been a recent trend towards pure varietal wines (particularly Tempranillo for *tinto* and Viura for *blanco*), most Rioja is blended, thus its character and quality depend to a large extent upon the producer's own house style. In addition to blending the strengths and weaknesses of different *terroirs*, there is usually an attempt to balance the various varietal characteristics of one or more of the seven grapes that are permitted in Rioja. These grape varieties are: Tempranillo, Garnacha, Graciano, Mazuelo, Viura, Malvasia, and the little-utilized Garnacha blanca.

A TYPICAL RED RIOJA BLEND
Tempranillo 70 per cent for its bouquet, acidity, and ageing qualities. It ripens some two weeks before the Garnacha (*temprano* means "early") and is also known in Spain as the Cencibel, Tinto fino, or Ull de Llebre. Tempranillo has a naturally low oxidizing enzyme content, giving its wines exceptional longevity.

Garnacha 15 per cent for body and alcohol – too much can make wine coarse. This is the Grenache of the Rhône, also known as the Lladoner and Aragonés. It is the major variety of the Rioja Baja, where it can produce wines of 16 per cent alcohol.

Graciano 7.5 per cent for freshness, flavour, and aroma. A singular variety with the unusual property of thin, yet tough black skin.

Mazuelo 7.5 per cent for colour, tannin, and good ageing characteristics. This is the Carignan of southern France and is also known in Spain as the Cariñena.

To the above a small proportion of white grapes, perhaps 5–10 per cent of Viura, may sometimes be added, but this tradition is fading. Cabernet sauvignon is not an authorized variety in Rioja, but is permitted by special dispensation for bodegas that have historically used the variety (such as Marqués de Riscal, which uses 15–60 per cent) and those who grow it on an trial basis. Although a number of bodegas have experimental plantations, Cabernet sauvignon is not of any great significance for the vast majority of Rioja wines.

A TYPICAL WHITE RIOJA BLEND
Viura 95 per cent for freshness and fragrance. This grape has reasonable acidity and a good resistance to oxidation. It is also known as the Macabéo and Alcañón in other parts of Spain, and is one of three major Cava varieties.

Malvasía 5 per cent for richness, fragrance, acidity, and complexity. Also known as the Rojal blanco and Subirat, this grape has a tendency to colour a patchy red when ripe, so pressing must be quick to avoid tainting the juice.

Most white wines are pure Viura, although some contain up to 50 per cent Malvasía. Some bodegas use a tiny amount of Garnacha blanca, particularly in lesser years, to increase alcohol levels, but they do so at the expense of a certain amount of freshness and aroma.

NAVARRA'S DISTRICTS

The region is divided into five districts:

Baja Montana

Situated in the Montana foothills, Baja Montana is the highest and wettest area of Navarra and the vintage is considerably later here than in the south of the region, hence the greater than normal importance placed on early-ripening Tempranillo. Extra rain causes the grape yield to be between 50 and 100 per cent higher than that of any of the other four areas. The district produces some of Navarra's best rosés, fresh and fruity in aroma and flavour.

Ribera Alta

With twice the amount of vineyards as Baja Montana and Tierra Estella, this is one of the two most important of Navarra's districts. Ribera Alta borders the Rioja Alta and produces some of the region's finest wines. The rosés are smooth and aromatic, and the reds soft and fruity, but with as much as 40 per cent Viura planted, this is a major white-wine player and the style is soft, dry, and fresh.

Ribera Baja

One of the two most important wine districts of Navarra, Ribera Baja is very hot and dry and includes approximately 20 per cent of what is effectively the Rioja Baja district. The wines produced

TIERRA ESTELLA, NAVARRA
The picturesque village of Maneru is situated near Estella, southwest of Pamplona. Tempranillo is the main variety grown in the area's vineyards.

are mostly red, made principally from the Garnacha (Grenache) grape, and typically deep-coloured, full, and robust. Muscat à petits grains accounts for ten per cent of the vines planted and produces a sweet Moscatel style wine.

Tierra Estella

Viticulturally as important as Baja Montana and climatically similar to Valdizarbe in the north, though gradually getting drier further south, the Tierra Estella makes pleasant, fruity reds and rosés from the Tempranillo, which is heavily planted here. The Garnacha variety is less important since its wines tend to oxidize. Some crisp white wines from the Viura grape are also produced.

Valdizarbe

The smallest of Navarra's five districts, Valdizarbe has a slightly drier climate than the Baja Montana and is an excellent source of good value red and rosé wines, although some of these have an unfortunate tendency to oxidize.

FACTORS AFFECTING TASTE AND QUALITY

LOCATION
Situated in northern Spain in the upper valley of the River Ebro, Rioja and Navarra are bounded to the northeast by the Pyrenees and to the southwest by the Sierra de la Demanda. Navarra has the second-most northerly vineyards in Spain.

CLIMATE
The Cantabrian Mountains, a range that is modest in elevation yet impressive in structure, provide a major key to the quality of Rioja, protecting the region from the devastating winds whipped up over the Bay of Biscay and holding in precarious check the influence of the Atlantic and Mediterranean. That of the former is at its strongest in Navarra, and of the latter in the Rioja Baja. Temperature rises and rainfall decreases as one moves eastwards towards the Mediterranean. The Pyrenees also provide shelter from the north, but winters can be cold and foggy, particularly in Navarra. Rioja can suffer from hailstorms and the hot, dry *solano* wind.

ASPECT
Vineyards are variously located, from the highest in the foothills of the Pyrenees in Navarra to those on the flatter lands of the Rioja Baja in the southeast. Generally, the best vineyards are in the central hill country of the Rioja Alta and the Alavesa.

SOIL
Although soils do vary, the common denominator is limestone. In Navarra, limestone contains between 25 and 45 per cent "active" lime, and is coated by a layer of silty-alluvium near the Ebro or by weathered limestone and sandstone

topsoil in drier areas. Limestone with either sandstone or calcareous clay and slaty deposits dominate the Rioja Alavesa and Alta, while a ferruginous-clay and a silty-loam of alluvial origin cover a limestone base in the Rioja Baja.

VITICULTURE AND VINIFICATION
Most wines are a blend of at least three grapes from different areas within a single appellation; very few are 100 per cent pure varietal or single-estate wines. The traditional vinification process, which is still used to produce the local *vino nuevo*, is a crude form of *macération carbonique* carried out in open vats; the grapes are trodden after the first few days of inter-cellular fermentation. This is much as Beaujolais wines used to be made, but the result here is much coarser, with a dark-damson colour and lots of youthful tannin.

Most wines are, however, vinified in the normal manner, but aged longer than other commercial wines. Although recent trends favour shorter oak-ageing and longer bottle-maturation, the character of Rioja still relies heavily on oak, and it is essential for its future that it should remain so.

PRIMARY GRAPE VARIETIES
Tempranillo, Viura (*syn.* Macabéo)
SECONDARY GRAPE VARIETIES
Cabernet sauvignon, Carignan (*syn.* Mazuelo), Chardonnay, Cinsault, Garnacha (*syn.* Grenache), Garnacha blanca (*syn.* Grenache blanc), Graciano, Malvasia, Mourvèdre (*syn.* Monastrell), Muscat (*syn.* Moscatel)

RIOJA'S DISTRICTS AT A GLANCE

GRAPE VARIETIES GROWN (IN HECTARES)

BLACK VARIETIES	RIOJA ALTA	RIOJA ALAVESA	RIOJA BAJA	REGIONAL TOTAL
Tempranillo	14,470	8,960	7,616	31,046
Garnacha	2,002	171	6,980	9,153
Mazuelo	500	89	1,224	1,813
Graciano	93	52	250	395
Others	4	-	170	174
Experimental	28	52	92	172
TOTAL	17,097	9,324	16,332	42,753

WHITE VARIETIES	RIOJA ALTA	RIOJA ALAVESA	RIOJA BAJA	REGIONAL TOTAL
Viura	4,471	1,442	1,675	7,588
Malvasia	79	30	18	127
Garnacho blanco	28	-	16	44
Others	147	12	43	202
Experimental	4	4	9	17
TOTAL	4,729	1,488	1,761	7,978
TOTAL (ALL VINES)	21,826	10,812	18,093	50,731

WINE PRODUCED (IN HECTOLITRES) AND BY ROUNDED PERCENTAGE

	RIOJA ALTA		RIOJA ALAVESA		RIOJA BAJA		TOTAL	
Red	836,000	74%	572,000	92%	339,000	80%	1,747,000	80%
White	150,000	13%	33,000	5%	18,000	5%	201,000	10%
Rosé	144,000	13%	19,000	3%	65,000	15%	228,000	10%
TOTAL	1,130,000	100%	624,000	100%	422,000	100%	2,176,000	100%

THE WINE PRODUCERS OF
RIOJA AND NAVARRA

Note Unless specifically stated otherwise, all recommendations (including "Entire range") are for red wine only. Reds from both regions are generally drinking well in their third year, but top *cuvées* often improve for up to ten years, and exceptional ones can age gracefully for decades, while most white and *rosado* wines are best fresh and should thus be consumed when purchased. *See* p.350 for details of the wine styles mentioned.

BODEGAS AGE
Rioja
See also Campo Viejo and Marques del Puerto

Part of Bebidas (formerly Savin), this *bodega* is now better known as Bodegas & Bebidas or ByB, and is under the same ownership as Campo Viejo and Marques del Puerto. The basic quality is rather uninspiring, but top of the range wines are usually very good value indeed. Labels include Agessimo, Azpilicueta Martínez, Credencial, Don Ernesto, Marqués del Romeral (traditional style and the best), and Siglo (modern style).

✓ *Reserva • Gran Reserva*

BODEGAS ALAVESAS
Rioja

This makes some long-lived *reserva* and *gran reserva* of surprising quality and elegance. Labels include Solar de Samaniego (primary) and Castillo de Bodala (secondary).

✓ *Reserva • Gran Reserva*

AMÉZOLA DE LA MORA
★
Rioja

I have encountered a couple of interesting wines from this Rioja Alta estate. One to watch.

✓ *Viña Amézola*
• *Señorío de Amézola*

ARAEX
Rioja

Formed in 1993, ARAEX is a group of nine bodegas selling Rioja under the following labels: Bodegas Don Balbino, Bodegas Luís Cañas (some excellent *reservas* that benefit from ageing ten years or more in bottle), Viña Diezmo, Bodegas Larchago (voluptuous fruit), Viña Lur, Bodegas Heredad de Baroja (heaps of fruit, firm tannin structure), Bodegas Muriel, Solagüen, and Valserano.

BARÓN DE LEY
★★★☆ Ⓥ
Rioja
See also El Coto

This is an exciting single-estate Rioja, which is produced by Barón de Ley using exclusively French, rather than American, oak. It is currently one of the two greatest Riojas in production (the other being Contino).

✓ *Entire range*

BARÓN DE OÑA
★★☆
Rioja
See also La Rioja Alta

This small bodega at Paganos was established in the late 1980s but sold to La Rioja Alta in 1995, long before its excellent wines had any chance of distribution in Spain, let alone abroad. With a high-tech, stainless-steel winery and use of 100 per cent new French oak, these wines make Barón de Oña a name to watch out for.

✓ *Entire range*

BODEGAS BERBERANA
★★ Ⓥ
Rioja

This producer can be disappointing at the lower end, but makes good to very good *reserva* and *gran reserva* wines that are full, fat, and sometimes even blowsy, with soft, oaky fruit. Berberana is also good value for older vintages. Labels include Preferido (*joven* style), Carta de Plata (younger style), Carta de Oro (bigger, richer), and Berberana *reserva* and *gran reserva* (best).

✓ *Reserva*
• *Gran Reserva*
• *Tempranillo*
• *Dragon Tempranillo*

BODEGAS BERCEO
Rioja

Berceo has few vineyards and makes ordinary basic wines, but good *reservas* and *gran reservas*. Bodegas Berceo, located at Haro in Rioja Alta, has the same owners as Bodegas Luís Gurpegui Muga at San Adrían, where Rioja Baja overlaps Navarra.

✓ *Gonzalo de Berceo Gran Reserva*

BODEGAS BERONIA
Rioja

These are firm, oaky reds and fresh whites from Gonzalez Byass.

✓ *Reserva • Gran Reserva*

BODEGAS BILBAÍNAS
☆
Rioja

Major vineyard owners, Bilbainas are producers of traditionally styled Rioja. Labels include Viña Pomal (deep, dark, and well-oaked with plummy fruit), Viña Zaco (even oakier), Vendimia Especial (excellent older vintages) and Royal Carlton (one of Rioja's Cava brands).

✓ *Reserva • Gran Reserva*

BODEGAS RAMÓN BILBAO
☆
Rioja

With few vineyards and a small production from mostly bought-in grapes, Ramón Bilbao's best wine is Viña Turzaballa. Its blend contains 90 per cent Tempranillo, and the wine is given plenty of time in oak, and also benefits from up to six years further ageing in bottle.

✓ *Viña Turzaballa Gran Reserva*

BODEGAS CAMPILLO
★☆ Ⓥ
Rioja
See also Faustino Martínez

Touted by many as a new Rioja, Campillo has been around for some years, starting out as a second label of Faustino Martínez. Even at the time of the first edition of this encyclopedia in 1988, Campillo was "often better than the principal label". This was because these wines were used to break in Faustino's new barrels, a strategy that caused Campillo to outshine Faustino's flagship wines. However, at least Faustino had the sense to capitalize on its own error and launch a new bodega under the Campillo brand.

✓ *Entire range*

BODEGAS CAMPO VIEJO
★ Ⓥ
Rioja
See also Bodegas AGE and Marqués del Puerto

A large producer with major vineyard holdings under the same ownership as Bodegas AGE and Marqués del Puerto, Campo Viejo has a well-earned reputation for good-quality wines of exceptional value. Its *tinto* wines are typically full-bodied and marked by a fatness of ripe fruit and rich vanilla-oak. Labels include Albor (*joven* style), Viña Alcorta (wood-aged pure varietals), San Asensio (exuberantly fruity) and Marqués de Villamagna (created for bottle-ageing, classic and fine rather than fat).

✓ *Reserva • Gran Reserva*
• *Marqués de Villamagna Gran Reserva*

BODEGAS CASTILLO DE MONJARDÍN
★
Navarra

This is an up-and-coming new bodega growing a high proportion of Tempranillo and French varieties. It also produces fresh, creamy-rich red and white wines, both with and without oak. It is a bodega that has exciting potential.

✓ *Chardonnay • Tinto Crianza*

BODEGAS JULIÁN CHIVITE
Navarra

Bodegas Julián Chivite typically produces soft, mellow, smooth, oaky wines with plenty of creamy-coconutty fruit flavour.

✓ *Chivite Reserva • Gran Feudo*
• *Viña Marcos*

CONTINO
★★★☆
Rioja

Owned by CVNE and a group of growers (whose combined holdings comprise the vineyards of this single-estate Rioja), Contino was not the first single-vineyard Rioja, but its great success encouraged other boutique wineries to follow. It also stimulated interest in French oak as opposed to American.

✓ *Contino Rioja Reserva*

BODEGAS CORRÁL
Rioja

This low-key but improving bodega has relatively few vineyards and is best-known for its Don Jácobo range, although the underrated Corral Gran Reserva is by far its best wine.

✓ *Corral Gran Reserva*

COSECHEROS ALAVESES
★☆ Ⓥ
Rioja

Perhaps one reason why this is one of Rioja's better cooperatives is that it is so small that it is hardly a cooperative in the commonly accepted definition of the term. The other reason is the excellent location of their vines around Laguardia in Rioja Alavesa. The style is always bright and fruity.

✓ *Artadi* (including blanco)
• *Orobio • Valdepomares*

BODEGAS EL COTO
★★☆
Rioja
See also Barón de Ley

These are wines of immaculate style, grace, and finesse, particularly the Coto de Imaz and, more recently, the single-vineyard Barón de Ley.

✓ *El Coto • Coto de Imaz Reserva*

CVNE
☆
Compañia Vinícola del Norte de España Rioja
See also Contino

Also known as Cune (pronounced "coonay"), Compañía Vinícola del Norte de España Rioja was once the most old-fashioned and traditional of Rioja producers and its vintages were legendary, easily lasting 30 years or more. Ironically these wines went through a dicey patch following the installation of a £12 million state-of-the-art winery, but CVNE seems to be coming to terms with this new technology. Recent vintages appear to be picking up, hence its half-star rating, and hopefully this bodega will return to its previous long-established quality, which should earn it two stars. Labels include Imperial (for finesse) and Viña Real (a plummier, fatter style) and Monopole (the best of the freshest, creamiest, oakiest style of *blanco*).

✓ *Gran Reserva* • *Monopole*

BODEGAS DOMECQ
Rioja

This famous sherry house has not only built up the largest vineyard holdings in Rioja, but has meticulously pieced together one consolidated block of vines, whereas other large holdings are scattered throughout the region. It is, if you like, a sort of super-sized Contino under single rather than multiple ownership. The original concept was thus to sell a single-vineyard Rioja under the Domecq Domaine label. This would create the desired prestige while the lesser-quality Marqués de Arienzo brand, produced from both own-vineyard and bought-in grapes, would attract a healthy cash-flow through high-volume sales. If the wines of Domecq Domaine had been significantly richer and better, it could have worked, but they were not, and marketing was further confused by these wines being called Privilegio Rey Sancho in Spain itself. Domecq could have been a super-single-vineyard Rioja, but Marqués de Arienzo has now assumed the mantle of this bodega's flagship wine, and a new cheaper brand is called Viña Eguia, and the house style continues to be light and refined, rather than either big or exciting. Stick to the *gran reserva*.

✓ *Gran Reserva*

BODEGAS FAUSTINO MARTÍNEZ
★
Rioja

If given sufficient bottle-age (keeping five years will do no harm) Faustino *reserva* and *gran reserva* can attain exceptional finesse, but are often outshone by Campillo, which started out as a second brand tasked with soaking up the unwanted oakiness from the bodega's new barrels.

✓ *Faustino V* (Reserva)
• *Faustino I* (Gran Reserva)

BODEGAS FRANCO ESPAÑOLAS
Rioja

Standard quality from an old-established house, labels of which include Viña Soledad (*blanco*), Bordón (young and fruity), and Royal (lightweight).

BODEGAS GUELBENZU
★
Navarra

Basic Guelbenzu Navarra is an exciting blend of Cabernet, Merlot, and Tempranillo, and the proportion of the Bordeaux varieties increases the further up the range the wines go. The top-of-the-line Evo is matured in 100 per cent French oak. Jardín is made from 30–40 year-old Garnacha vines. This is certainly a bodega to watch.

✓ *Jardín* • *Guelbenzu* • *Evo*

BODEGAS GURPEGUI
Rioja

Located at San Adrián in Rioja Baja, where it produces the Viñadrián and Dominio de la Plana ranges, Bodegas Gurpegui also owns Bodegas Berceo in Rioja Alta.

BODEGAS IRACHE
Navarra

This is a modern winery producing unpretentious, fruity wines.

✓ *Viña Irache*
• *Gran Irache*

BODEGAS LAGUNILLA
Rioja

Lagunilla is decent and dependable, but rarely exciting, even though the wines are usually pure Tempranillo and one of its labels, Viña Herminia, enjoys a good reputation in Spain itself. It is best to stick to older vintages and *gran reservas*.

BODEGAS LAN
Rioja

Lan was once good quality, but went through a patchy period in the early 1990s. In addition to Lan itself, labels include Lander (older vintages and more time in oak) and Viña Lanciano (more mature still and even oakier).

BODEGAS MAGAÑA
★
Navarra

Juan Magaña is best-known for varietal wines, particularly the excellent Merlot, but his Merlot-Tempranillo blend called Eventum has more finesse.

✓ *Eventum* • *Merlot*

MARQUÉS DE CÁCERES
★
Union Viti-vinícola

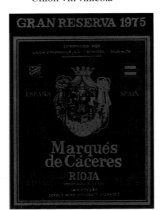

Marqués de Cáceres is often quoted as part of the modern school of Rioja winemaking, but is more accurately described as a traditional Bordeaux style. They are lighter, less rustic wines than those of modern Rioja style that benefit from bottle-ageing. Antea is an excellent barrel-fermented white.

✓ *Antea* • *Reserva* • *Gran Reserva*

MARQUÉS DE GRIÑÓN
★★☆ Ⓥ
Rioja

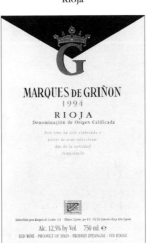

Marqués de Griñón is perhaps better known for its outstanding non-DO wines from south of Madrid, but it has also produced, in association with Berberana, an excellent run of modern-style Rioja since 1990.

✓ *Entire range*

MARQUÉS DEL PUERTO
Rioja
See also Bodegas AGE and Campo Vieja

Formerly known as Bodegas Lopez Agos, Marqués del Puerto is part of Bebidas (formerly Savin), along with Bodegas AGE and Campo Vieja, and produces an elegant style of Rioja, with ripe fruit and good acidity.

✓ *Reserva*

MARQUÉS DE MURRIETA
★★★
Rioja

Owned by Dominos de Creixell, along with Pazo de Barrantes (*see* Rías Baixas DO under "The Wine Appellations of Spain", p.354), Marqués de Murrieta is known for its pungently oxidative *blanco* Reserva, which is impossible to criticize, even if some vintages taste like a cup of lemon-tea brewed in new oak, as it is considered to be the epitome of its style. Marqués de Murrieta whites contain more freshness and fruit than they used to. A remarkable range of old vintages remain commercially available, especially the venerable Castillo Ygay.

✓ *Ygay Etiqueta Blanca* • *Ygay Reserva* • *Castillo Ygay*

MARQUÉS DE RISCAL
★★★☆
Rioja

When the first edition of this book came out, Riscal's Swiss importer faxed Francisco Hurtado de Amexaga a copy of this page claiming "the red wines from Rioja's most famous bodega have an unpleasant musty-mushroom character", upon receipt of which Hurtado de Amexaga recalled his top winemaker from Riscal's Rueda outpost to investigate. These wines had gradually acquired a musty character since the 1960s, prior to which they were always among the top three Riojas produced, but since they had the oldest and greatest reputation in Rioja, no one had dared mention this until this book was published in 1988. Hurtado de Amexaga was not sure whether this was true, but was honest enough to concede that if the mustiness had gradually crept into the wine over a long period, they might have developed a "cellar palate" at Riscal and failed to notice it. Every one of Riscal's 20,000 barrels was tasted and 2,000 were immediately destroyed, with the equivalent of 600,000 bottles of wine poured down the drain. Another 2,000 borderline barrels were earmarked for replacement the next year and a programme instigated to renew all 20,000 over ten years. With so much affected wine disposed of, the 1986 vintage was cleaned up and the 1988 had a purity of fruit not seen in a Riscal wine since the 1960s, but it is the 1989 and 1990 vintages in which the difference is really noticeable, due to the combination of superior wines and increasing new-oak content. In turning around the situation so quickly and with no expense spared, Hurtado de Amexaga showed the sort of determination and dedication that was absolutely vital for Riscal to regain its position amongst the world's finest wines.

✓ *Reserva* • *Gran Reserva*
• *Barón de Chirel*

BODEGAS MARTÍNEZ BUJANDA
★
Rioja

This high-tech winery consistently produces pure, fresh *blanco* and fine, firm, fruit-driven *tinto*.

✓ *Conde de Valdemar*

DOMINIO DE MONTALVO
★
Rioja

This is an innovative barrel-fermented, pure Viura *blanco*.

✓ *Dominio de Montalvo Viura*

BODEGAS MONTECILLO
★
Rioja

Owned by Osborne of Jerez, Montecillo covers the spread of styles, from fruity *crianza* reds, through zippy *blanco*, to great *gran reserva* reds.

✓ *Viña Cumbrero* (blanco)
• *Reserva* • *Gran Reserva*

BODEGAS MUGA
★★☆
Rioja
Lovely *rosado* here, but the reds are really top-class, especially Prado Enea. The basic Muga *crianza* is much younger and fresher, but can be bottle-aged to obtain a similar elegance and seductive, silky finish to those found in the Prado Enea.

✓ *Entire range*

BODEGAS MURUA
★
Rioja
This is a small winery dedicated to producing pure Rioja Alta Tempranillo of some finesse.

✓ *Reserva • Gran Reserva*

BODEGAS MUERZA
❷
Rioja
The cheapest reds made here are light, peppery wines that could come from anywhere, and that spoil the reputation of this bodega, which also produces relatively inexpensive *reservas* and *gran reservas* that are firm and oaky with good old-fashioned life-preserving acidity.

✓ *Rioja Vega*
(Reserva, Gran Reserva)

BODEGAS NEKEAS
★★
Navarra
The amazing discovery of the 1996 International Wine Challenge, Nekeas defeated some of the greatest Chardonnays from Burgundy and the New World to win the coveted Chardonnay Trophy. Made by Spain's former agricultural minister, Francisco San Martin, who certainly knows his vines, and probably his onions too.

✓ *Entire range*

BODEGAS OCHOA
❷
Navarra
The well-known Bodega Ochoa has been disappointing of late, but EVENA's (*see* p.358) former head oenologist certainly has the knowledge, equipment, and expertise to produce top-flight Navarra wines once again, so I will reserve my judgement.

BODEGAS OLARRA
★
Rioja
This ultra-modern, high-tech winery always used to produce a good Rioja across the range, but vintages became erratic in the mid-1980s, then decidedly poor, but improvements were first noticed with the 1990 vintage in the mid-1990s, so my fingers are crossed. Labels include La Catedral.

✓ *Añares and Cerro Añón ranges*

BODEGAS PALACIO
★★☆
Rioja
An old bodega that has truly excelled since the early 1990s, Palacio uses both French and American oak, with wines ranging from the pure Tempranillo Cosme Palacio y Hermanos, a very traditional Rioja that is consistently Palacio's best wine, and Milflores, which gushes with delicious, juicy fruit, making it one of the better *joven* wines produced.

✓ *Cosme Palacio y Hermanos*
• Glorioso • Milflores

PALACIO DE LA VEGA
★★☆
Navarra
José María Nieves produces beautifully packaged, stylish wines that are brimming with fruit and finesse made exclusively from vines grown on this excellent estate.

✓ *Cabernet Sauvignon* (Reserva)

FEDERICO PATERNINA
Rioja
These wines are generally light and lacking, especially Banda Azul, its best-known label. You must go up to *reserva* level to find real richness, although the *gran reserva* (Conde de Los Andes) is unpredictable, ranging from pure brilliance to absolute volatility.

✓ *Viña Vial* (Reserva)

BODEGAS PIEDEMONTE
★
Navarra
This is an up-and-coming bodega, which produces excellent Cabernet Sauvignon with a silky texture and a spicy finesse.

✓ *Oligitum Cabernet Sauvignon*

BODEGAS PRINCIPE DE VIANA
★☆❤
Navarra
Formerly known as Agronavarra Cenal and having devoured and dispensed with Bodegas Canalsa, Principe de Viana, the firm's premium product, has been adopted as the name of the high-tech *bodega*. The wines have become something of a bargain compared to those of other top Navarra *bodegas*, which have gained in price as they have achieved greater quality. Principe de Viana does not have the finesse of the best Navarra wines, but they are much cheaper and have oodles of rich, coconutty fruit, with which I associate American oak, although some of the wines claim to use French barrels. Labels include Agramont and Campo Nuevo.

✓ *Cabernet Sauvignon*
• Chardonnay

REMELLURI
★★
La Granja Nuestra Señora de Remelluri Rioja
These single-vineyard Riojas of consistently high quality from Labastida de Alava possess exquisite balance, elegance, and finesse, great richness of ripe fruit, and a long creamy-vanilla oak finish.

✓ *Labastida de Alava*

LA RIOJA ALTA
★★
Rioja
The Viña Alberdi *crianza* is an excellent introduction to these wines, but the serious business begins with the elegant Viña Arana and Viña Ardanza *reservas*, which are remarkably complex wines considering that they account for more than half of the firm's production. The Gran Reserva 904 is an exceptionally concentrated and classy wine, while the Gran Reserva 890 is a rare product indeed.

✓ *Barón de Oña*
• Viña Alberdi
• Viña Ardanza (Reserva)
• Gran Reserva 904
• Gran Reserva 890

BODEGAS RIOJANAS
★★☆
Rioja
A traditional *bodega* that has built its reputation on red wines, particularly the *reserva* and *gran reserva* versions of its rich-oaky Viña Albina and the dark, plummy Monte Real with its vanilla-spice aftertaste.

✓ *Canchales* (Vino Nuevo)
• Viña Albina (Reserva)
• Monte Real (Reserva)

BODEGAS RIOJA SANTIAGO
Rioja
Memories of excellent 1950s vintages from Rioja Santiago tasted in the 1970s are fading fast by today's acceptable, but hardly special, standards. Other labels nowadays include Vizconde de Ayala.

✓ *Gran Condal*
(Reserva, Gran Reserva)

BODEGA DE SARRÍA
★
Navarra
A large, well-established estate with a modern winery, which produces clean, fruity wines that are constantly improving despite the death of Francisco Morriones, the oenologist who was responsible for establishing this *bodega*'s current reputation. Labels include Viña del Portillo, Viña Ecoyen, and Viña del Perdón.

✓ *Gran Vino del Señorió de Sarría*
• Viña del Perdon
• Viña Ecoyen
• Blanco seco
• Rosado

BODEGAS CARLOS SERRES
Rioja
Carlos Serres was founded by Charles (who was later known as Carlos) Serres in 1869, one year after his fellow Frenchman Jean Pineau went to Bodegas Marqués de Riscal. The characteristic house style tends to be on the light side, but the *reserva* and *gran reserva* wines often have an elegant richness.

✓ *Carlomagno* (Reserva)
• Carlos Serres (Gran Reserva)

BODEGAS SIERRA CANTABRIA
★
Rioja
These are large vineyard owners producing an easy-drinking style of Rioja, with lush fruit, the fatness of which is often lifted by an intense tang of cherries. Other labels include Bodegas Eguran.

✓ *Codice • Reserva*

VIÑA IJALBA
★
Rioja
One of the smallest and potentially most exciting of Rioja *bodegas*, producing startling styles of wine in weird bottles, including a rare, pure Graciano. I'd be surprised if this producer does not warrant two stars by the next edition.

✓ *Ijalba* (Graciano)
• Solferino (Tempranillo)

VIÑA SALCEDA
★
Rioja
Fresh, gluggy reds at basic *crianza* level, but the *gran reservas* are huge, rich, and serious.

✓ *Gran Reserva*

VIÑA TONDONIA
★★☆
López de Heredia Viña Tondonia Rioja
Just up the hill from the very traditional Bodegas Muga is Tondonia, an old-fashioned firm that makes Muga look high-tech. It is impossible to find a more old-fashioned *bodega*, from the massive cobwebs in the tasting room to the religious dipping into wax of all bottle ends as if they contained Port. The style here is rich and oaky, and the wines are capable of great age. Tondonia is the finest wine, Bosconia the fattest, and Cubillo the youngest.

✓ *Viña Bosconia • Viña Cubillo*
• Viña Tondonia
(including blanco)

VINÍCOLA DE LABASTIDA
★☆
Rioja
This is probably the best cooperative in Rioja.

✓ *Gastrijo* (Reserva) • *Castillo Labastida* (Gran Reserva)

VINÍCOLA NAVARRA
❤
Navarra
Richly coloured and flavoured wines, sometimes a touch porty, but always cheap and good value, Vinicola Navarra is part of the sprawling ByB empire (Bodegas AGE, Campo Viejo etc.).

✓ *Las Campanas*
• Castillo de Tiebas (Reserva)

PENEDÉS: CAVA COUNTRY

The worldwide popularity of Cava – Spain's only méthode champenoise DO wine – together with the success of winemaking genius Miguel Torres, have made Penedés the most famous district in Catalonia, opening up the entire region's wine to export markets.

PRIOR TO PHYLLOXERA, which struck Penedés in 1876, more than 80 per cent of the vineyards here were planted with black grapes. When the vines were grafted on to American rootstock, white varieties were given priority due to the growing popularity of sparkling white wines. It is easy to recognize the classic imported varieties in the vineyards because they are trained along wires, whereas traditional Spanish vines grow in little bushes.

THE DISTRICTS OF PENEDÉS
Penedés can be divided into three wine districts: Bajo Penedés, Medio Penedés, and Alta Penedés (also called Penedés Superior).

Bajo (or Baix) Penedés
The following grape varieties are grown in the Bajo Penedés: Monastrell, Malvasía, Grenache (*syn.* Garnacha), Cariñena, and various other, mostly black, grape varieties.

This area occupies the coastal strip and is the warmest of all three areas. The land of the Bajo Penedés is low and flat, with vines growing on limestone, clay, and sandy soil. This area produces more and more full-bodied red wines such as Torres's Sangredetoro.

Medio (or Mitja) Penedés
The following grape varieties are grown: mostly Xarello and Macabéo; this is also the best area for Tempranillo, Cabernet sauvignon, Merlot, and Monastrell.

The middle section of the Penedés is slightly hilly, occasionally flat land at an altitude of some 200 metres (660 feet) in the foothills west of Barcelona, on a soil of mostly limestone and clay. It has a cooler climate than the Bajo, with most areas equivalent to Regions II and III of the California Heat Summation System (*see* p.448). This is essentially Cava country, but it also produces the best of the new-style reds, including Torres's various Coronas wines.

Alta (or Alt) Penedés
Grape varieties grown in this district are almost exclusively white, being mostly Parellada, plus Riesling, Gewürztraminer, and Muscat. A little Pinot noir is also grown.

This area is the furthest inland and the grapes are grown on chalky foothills at an altitude of between 500 and 800 metres (1,640–2,620 feet). Climatic conditions are the coolest in Penedés, equivalent to Regions I and II. It is so cool that Cabernet sauvignon will not ripen here and almost all wines produced are white, although Pinot noir for Torres's Mas Borras is grown at San Marti. Most pure Alta Penedés wines are fresh, of the cool-fermented type, and can show remarkably fine aroma and acidity.

CAVA: SPAIN'S SPARKLING WINE
The first Spanish sparkling wine was made by Antoni Gali Comas sometime prior to 1851, when he entered it in competition in

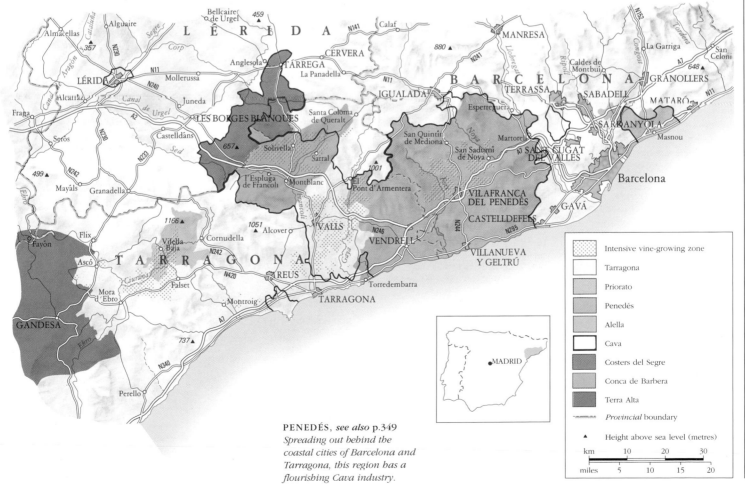

PENEDÉS, *see also* p.349
Spreading out behind the coastal cities of Barcelona and Tarragona, this region has a flourishing Cava industry.

Intensive vine-growing zone
Tarragona
Priorato
Penedés
Alella
Cava
Costers del Segre
Conca de Barbera
Terra Alta
Provincial boundary
▲ Height above sea level (metres)

FACTORS AFFECTING TASTE AND QUALITY

✦ LOCATION
Lying in the northeast corner of Spain, where Rioja's River Ebro enters the Mediterranean, Penedés is part of Catalonia, which also includes Alella, Tarragona, Priorato, and Terra Alta.

CLIMATE
A mild Mediterranean climate prevails in Penedés, becoming more continental (hotter summers and colder winters) moving westwards and inland towards Terra Alta. In the same way, problems with fog in the northeast are gradually replaced by the hazard of frost towards the southwestern inland areas. In the high vineyards of Alta Penedés, white and aromatic grape varieties are cultivated at greater altitudes than traditional ones; since they benefit from cooler temperatures.

ASPECT
Vines are grown on all types of land ranging from the flat plains of the Campo de Tarragona, through the 400-m (1,300-ft) high plateaux of Terra Alta, to the highest vineyards in the Alta Penedés, which reach an altitude of 800 m (2,620 ft). For every 100 m (330 ft) rise in altitude, the temperature drops 1°C (0.56°F).

SOIL
There is a wide variety of soils ranging from granite in Alella, through limestone-dominated clay, chalk, and sand in Penedés, to a mixture of mainly limestone and chalk with granite and alluvial deposits in Tarragona. The soil in Priorato is an unusual reddish slate with particles of reflective mica in the north, with schistose rock in the south.

VITICULTURE AND VINIFICATION
Catalonia is a hot-bed of experimentation. Ultra-modern winemaking techniques have been pioneered by Cava companies such as Codorníu and fine-wine specialists like Torres.

Viticultural and vinification practices are usually quite modern throughout Catalonia. This is especially so at the Raimat Estate in Lérida, where the technology ranges from the latest and most efficient "Sernagiotto" continuous press for bulk production to the "Potter gravity crusher". Described as the simplest press ever designed, this extracts no more than 50–60 per cent of the grape's potential juice.

🍇 PRIMARY GRAPE VARIETIES
Cabernet sauvignon, Carignan (*syn.* Cariñena, Mazuelo), Garnacha (*syn.* Lladoner, Aragonés), Mourvèdre (*syn.* Alcayata,Monastrell), Samsó, Tempranillo (*syn.* Ull de Llebre), Viura (*syn.* Macabéo); Xarel-lo (*syn.* Pansá blanca)
SECONDARY GRAPE VARIETIES
Cabernet franc, Chardonnay, Chenin blanc, Gewürztraminer, Merlot, Muscat d'Alsace, Parellada, Pinot noir, Riesling, Sauvignon, Subirat-Parent (*syn.* Malvasía Riojana)

Madrid. He did not persevere and the next milestone was Luis Justo i Villanueva, the Laboratory Director at the Agricultural Institute of Sant Isidre in Catalonia. It was under Villanueva that all the earliest commercial producers of Spanish sparkling wine learned the Champagne process. In 1872, three of his former students, Domenec Soberano, Francesc Gil, and Augusti Vilaret, entered their sparkling wines in a Barcelona competition. All used classic Champagne grapes grown in Catalonia; Soberano and Gil were awarded gold medals, while Vilaret, who used raspberry liqueur in the dosage, received a bronze. Vilaret firm, Caves Mont-Ferrant, is the only one of these pioneering firms to have survived.

The above facts are fully documented and thus contradict Codorníu's claim that it was first to produce Spanish sparkling wine in 1872. Codorníu did not in fact sell its first sparkling wines until 1879 and it would not be until 1893 that its production hit 10,000 bottles, a level that the three original firms achieved in the 1870s. What everyone seems agreed on, however, is that José Raventós i Fatjó of Codorníu was the first to make bottle-fermented sparkling wine out of Parellada, Macabéo, and Xarel.lo and that these grapes came to form the basis of the entire Cava industry.

CAVA'S SPANISH CHARACTER
The production of Cava is dominated by two firms: Codorníu and Freixenet. The latter has always been violently opposed to the invasion of Cava vineyards by foreign grape varieties. Freixenet's argument is certainly valid – that the introduction of foreign varieties could erode Cava's Spanish character. Cava is, after all,

the only dry sparkling-wine appellation of any repute outside France and, of course, Spain has its own indigenous varieties, thus internationally renowned grapes like Chardonnay can only dilute the wine's identity. However, as Codornuí has shown, blending with Chardonnay can fill out a Cava in a way that the traditional varieties (Macabéo, Parellada, and Xarello) cannot.

At a Cava shippers' dinner in 1991, when Manuel Duran, the chairman of Freixenet, admitted that they were still undecided as to whether Cava's varieties were ideally suited to sparkling wine, he was challenged not simply to find an indigenous substitute for Chardonnay, but to try to experiment with black Spanish varieties. Cava's traditionalists have, for some bizarre reason, always considered black grapes in a white Cava to be sacrilegious, yet Duran picked up the gauntlet, producing a Monastrell-Xarello *cuvée* (the first release was too flabby, but the second release in 1997 was much better – the Catalonians are not used to handling black grapes for white wines, and I expect this Cava to continue improving). Prior to Freixenet's project, Codorníu was the only house to try black grapes in white Cava and succeeded in producing one of the most sumptuous Spanish sparkling wines ever using Pinot noir.

Whether it is Monastrell, Grenache (*syn.* Garnacha), Trepat, Tempranillo, or some other Spanish grape, I believe that Cava will one day benefit from the use of indigenous black varieties and when that happens, Codorníu will, I am sure, use them, just as they will use any Spanish white variety that is discovered to be as useful in plumping up a *cuvée* as Chardonnay.

CAVA AND PENEDÉS
Although many Cava producers are either manual or computer-controlled girasols, which enable remuage to be performed by the pallet-load, some of the more traditional houses, such as the family-owned firm of Juvé y Camps, still use pupitres.

THE WINE PRODUCERS OF
CAVA AND PENEDÉS

Note For recommended wines of all other Catalonian appellations, see the relevant DO under "The Wine Appellations of Spain" on p.352. Included below are only those wines that come under Cava DO and Penedés DO. Reds from Penedés generally drink well in their third year, but top *cuvées* often improve for up to ten years, and exceptional ones can age gracefully for decades. Penedés white and *rosado* wines and sparkling Cava are best fresh and should thus be consumed when purchased.

ALBET I NOYA
★

Established as recently as 1981, Josep Albet i Noya soon became a respected producer of fresh, lively Cava and well-made white Penedés, but is now turning out some spectacular reds.

✓ *Cava* (Vintage) • *Blanc Novell*
  • *Cabernet Sauvignon*
  • *Tempranillo*

MASÍA BACH
★

Renowned more for its sweet, oak-aged white Extrísimo Bach, than for its reds, which have always been merely soft and acceptable, this Codorníu-owned firm began to take its red- winemaking seriously when it released a stunning 1985, simply labelled Masía Bach.

✓ *Masía Bach* (Reserva)
  • *Viña Extrísima* (Reserva)

RENÉ BARBIER FILL
★★

Not the old-established firm of René Barbier, which belongs to Freixenet, but René Barbier fill (or "son"), which is the relatively new company founded in Gratallops in Priorato.

✓ *Priorato* (Clos Mogador)

CAN RAFOLS DELS CAUS
★

This is an up-and-coming small estate producing excellent Cabernet (franc and sauvignon), and a Merlot blend called Gran Caus. Other labels include Petit Caus.

✓ *Gran Caus*

CASTELL DE VILARNAU
★

This producer is not as consistent as it should be, but has always been capable of richer, more complex Cava, even before the general improvement that lifted the industry in the mid-1990s.

✓ *Cava* (Vintage)

CASTELLBLANCH
★★ Ⓥ

Castellblanch is a firm, owned by Freixenet, and it produces a remarkably consistent Cava wine.

✓ *Cava* (Brut Zero)

CAVAS HILL
★

This old-established, family-owned estate produces elegant Cavas and some very good still wines.

✓ *Cava* (Reserva Oro Brut)
  • *Blanc Cru* • *Gran Civet*
  • *Gran Toc*

CODORNÍU
★

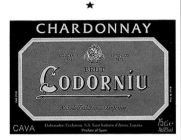

The largest and most innovative Cava firm, its production dwarfs even that of Moët & Chandon in Champagne. Codorníu started the foreign grape controversy by introducing Chardonnay, first through Raimat Cava in Conca de Barberà, then in its own range. When grown in the right area, Chardonnay does plump-up the quality, depth, and finesse of Cava, but there is opposition to non-traditional Spanish grape varieties from those who fear they will erode the intrinsically Spanish character of the wine.

✓ *Cava* (Anna de Codorníu Chardonnay, Jaume de Codorníu, Brut Rose)

CONDE DE CARALT
★

This is a reliable Cava from part of the Freixenet group.

✓ *Cava* (Brut)

COVIDES
★

This cooperative produces a surprisingly rich style of Cava.

✓ *Cava* (Duc de Foix Brut, Duc de Foix Vintage, Xenius)

FREIXENET
★

Freixenet is the second-largest Cava firm, and produces probably the best-known of all Cavas. Other labels include Castellblanch, Conde de Caralt, Paul Cheneau and Segura Viudas.

✓ *Cava* (Brut Nature, Carta Nevada)

GRAMONA
★

Of its tangy Cavas, Celler Battle shows rare vanilla-finesse on finish.

✓ *Celler Battle*
  • *Imperial III Lustros*

JUVÉ Y CAMPS

I have failed to discern any of the intrinsically superior qualities in this wine that some critics find, although I hasten to add that there is nothing wrong with the wines of this respected, traditional, family firm.

JEAN LÉON
★★

Following the death of Jean Léon, these wines are now made and marketed by Torres. These big, rich, oaky wines are stunning, but some vintages can disappoint.

✓ *Cabernet Sauvignon*
  • *Chardonnay*

MARQUÉS DE MONISTROL
★

This competent Cava firm, owned by Martini & Rossi, also makes a fine Reserva red Penedés wine and a fresh, youthful Merlot.

✓ *Cava* • *Penedés Reserva*
  • *Merlot*

CAVAS MASCARÓ
★

A small family-owned producer founded in the immediate post-war era, Mascaró is best known for its Don Narciso brandy, but also makes an underrated range of wines.

✓ *Cava* (Brut)
  • *Anima Cabernet Sauvignon*

MAS RABASSA
★

Mas Rabassa makes fresh and quite delicious, new-style wines.

✓ *Xarello* • *Macabéo*

MESTRES
★

Mestres is a small, traditional, family-owned Cava business, which produces numerous wines of fine autolytic character.

✓ *Cava* • *Clos Nostre Senyor*
  • *Mas-Via*

MONT MARÇAL
★

This is a well-made Cava produced by a private family firm.

✓ *Cava* (Nature, Chardonnay)

PARXET
★

Under the same ownership as Marqués de Alella, Parxet is capable of producing refined sparkling wines. Its pink-hued "Cuvée Dessert" is sweeter than a demi-sec and needs to be cellared for a couple of years. This firm is not afraid to go out on a limb.

✓ *Cava* (Brut Nature, Brut Reserva)

CELLARS PUIG I ROCA
★★

Cellars Puig and Roca are exciting, estate-bottled wines from ex-Torres trouble-shooter Josep Puig. The entrepreneurial Puig even produces a varietal vinegar from Cabernet sauvignon, which is aged in chestnut casks for flavour!

AUGUSTUS
✓ *Augustus* (Cabernet Sauvignon, Cabernet Sauvignon Rosado, Chardonnay, Merlot)

RAÏMAT
★★ Ⓥ

In the Conca de Barberà, the Raïmat estate is owned by Codorníu and utilizes innovative equipment to make an excellent range of fine wines using classic French grape varieties (Abadia, Tempranillo, Cabernet sauvignon, and Merlot) in addition to its Cava, which was Spain's first pure Chardonnay sparkling wine.

✓ *Cava* (Chardonnay) • *Gran Brut* (Abadia, Tempranillo, Cabernet Sauvignon, Merlot)

RAVENTOS I BLANC
★

Josep Maria, black sheep of the Raventós family, left Codorníu to set up his own Cava house, producing, fresh, lively *cuvées*, sometimes of excellent quality.

✓ *Cava* (Brut)

SEGURA VIUDAS
★★ Ⓥ

The best Cava house in the huge Freixenet group, Segura Viudas seems to have extra richness and relatively greater ageing potential.

✓ *Cava* (Aria, Heredad, Vintage Brut)

JAUME SERRA
★

Jaume Serra produces good Cava, but even better Penedés still wines, made in modern, fruit-driven style in collaboration with Chilean winemaker Ignacio Recabarren.

✓ *Cava* (Cristalino) • *Viña de Mar*

TORRES
★★

The Torres name conjures up French grape varieties and limited editions of world-class wines, but it is one of the largest family-owned wine producers in Spain, with 800 hectares (2,000 acres) of vineyard and annual sales of 1.4 million cases of wine. Considering that Sangre de Toro accounts for 300,000 cases, which is almost a quarter of Torres' total production, this modest hearty red is of a remarkable quality.

✓ *Entire range* (but especially Atrium Fransola, Viña Esmeralda, Mas la Plana Cabernet Sauvignon)

SHERRY COUNTRY

On 1 January 1996, Sherry regained exclusive use in Europe of its own name, which had suffered decades of abuse by producers of so-called "sherry" in other countries, especially Great Britain and Ireland. The governments of these countries had vetoed the protection of Sherry's name when Spain joined the Common Market in 1986.

SUCH ARE THE BLOCKS AND CHECKS of the EU (European Union) that it took ten years for this legislation allowing the abuse of Sherry's name to be reversed, ensuring that the name Sherry (also known as Jerez or Xérès) may now be used only for the famous fortified wines made around Cádiz and Jerez de la Frontera in the south of Spain. Due to the Sherry industry's own folly in trying to compete with these cheaper, fortified rip-offs, the vineyards of Jerez got into massive over-production problems, but this was recognized in the early 1990s when lesser-quality vineyards were uprooted, reducing the viticultural area from 17,500 hectares (43,000 acres) to the current 10,600 (26,000 acres).

SHERRY'S ANCIENT ORIGINS

The vinous roots of Sherry penetrate three millennia of history, back to the Phoenicians who founded Gadir (today called Cádiz), in 1100 BC. They quickly deserted Gadir because of the hot, howling *levante* wind that is said to drive men mad, and they established a town further inland called Xera, which some historians believe may be the Xérès or Jerez of today. It was probably the Phoenicians who introduced viticulture to the region. If they did not, then the Greeks certainly did, and it was the Greeks who brought with them their *hepsema*, the precursor of the *arropes* and *vinos de color* that add sweetness, substance, and colour to modern-day sweet or cream Sherries.

JEREZ DE LA FRONTERA
Palomino vines amid the brilliant white albariza *soil of Montigillilo, Emilio Lustau's superb 120-hectare (300-acre) vineyard, just north of Jerez.*

In the Middle Ages, the Moors introduced to Spain the *alembic*, a simple pot-still with which the people of Jerez were able to turn their excess wine production into grape spirit, which they added, along with *arrope* and *vino de color*, to their new wines each year to produce the first crude but true Sherry. The repute of these wines gradually spread throughout the western world, helped by the English merchants who had established wine-shipping businesses in Andalucía at the end of the 13th century. After Henry VIII broke with Rome, Englishmen in Spain were under constant threat from the Inquisition. The English merchants were rugged individualists and they survived, as they also did, remarkably, when Francis Drake set fire to the Spanish fleet in the Bay of Cádiz in 1587. Described as the day he singed the King of Spain's beard, it was the most outrageous of all Drake's raids, and when he returned home, he took with him a booty of 2,900 casks of Sherry. The exact size of these casks is not known, but the total volume is estimated to be in excess of 150,000 cases, which makes it a vast shipment of one wine for that period in history. It was, however, eagerly consumed by a relatively small population that had been denied its normal quota of Spanish wines during the war. England has been by far the largest market for Sherry ever since.

THE UNIQUENESS OF JEREZ SHERRY

It is the combination of Jerez de la Frontera's soil and climate that makes this region uniquely equipped to produce Sherry, a style of wine attempted in many countries around the world but never truly accomplished outside Spain. Sherry has much in common with Champagne, as both regions are inherently superior to all others in their potential to produce a specific style of wine. The parallel can be taken further: both Sherry and Champagne are made from neutral, unbalanced base wines that are uninspiring to drink before they undergo the elaborate process that turns them into high-quality, perfectly balanced, finished products.

The famous albariza soil

Jerez's *albariza* soil, which derives its name from its brilliant white surface, is not chalk but a soft marl of organic origin formed by the sedimentation of diatom algae during the Triassic period.

FACTORS AFFECTING TASTE AND QUALITY

LOCATION
This winemaking region is situated in the province of Cádiz, around Jerez de la Frontera in the southwest of Spain.

CLIMATE
This is the hottest wine region in Spain. Generally, the climate is Mediterranean, but towards the Portuguese border, the Atlantic influence comes into play and, further inland, around Montilla-Moriles, it becomes more continental. It is the Atlantic-driven *poniente* wind that produces the *flor* yeast of *fino* Sherry.

ASPECT
Vines are grown on all types of land, from the virtually flat coastal plains producing Manzanilla, through the slightly hillier Sherry vineyards rising to 100 m (330 ft), to the higher gentle inland slopes of Montilla-Moriles and the undulating Antequera plateau of Málaga at some 500 m (1,640 ft).

SOIL
The predominant soil in the Jerez is a deep lime-rich variety known as *albariza*, which soaks up and retains moisture. Its brilliant white colour also reflects sun on to the lower parts of the vines. Sand and clay soils also occur but, although suitable for vine-growing, they produce second-rate Sherries. The equally bright soil to the east of Jerez is not *albariza*, but a schisto-calcareous clay.

VITICULTURE AND VINIFICATION
Vinification is the key to the production of the great fortified wines for which this area is justly famous. Development of a *flor* yeast and oxidation by deliberately underfilling casks are vital components of the vinification, as, of course, is the *solera* system that ensures a consistent product over the years. The larger the *solera* the more efficient it is, because there are more butts. Montilla is vinified using the same methods as for Sherry, but is naturally strong in alcohol, and so less often fortified.

GRAPE VARIETIES
Palomino, Pedro Ximénez, Moscatel

The *albariza* begins to turn yellow at a depth of about one metre (three feet) and turns bluish after five metres (16 feet). It crumbles and is super-absorbent when wet, but extremely hard when dry. This is the key to the exceptional success of *albariza* as a vine-growing soil. Jerez is a region of baking heat and drought; there are about 70 days of rain each year, with a total precipitation of some 50 centimetres (20 inches). The *albariza* soaks up the rain like a sponge and, with the return of the drought, the soil surface is smoothed and hardened into a shell that is impermeable to evaporation. The winter and spring rains are imprisoned under this protective cap, and remain at the disposal of the vines, the roots of which penetrate some four metres (13 feet) beneath the surface. The *albariza* supplies just enough moisture to the vines, without making them too lazy or over-productive. Its high active-lime content encourages the ripening of grapes with a higher acidity level than would otherwise be the norm for such a hot climate. This acidity safeguards against unwanted oxidation prior to fortification.

HOW GREAT SHERRY IS MADE
The harvest

Twenty or more years ago, it was traditional to begin the grape harvest in the first week of September. After picking, Palomino grapes were left in the sun for 12–24 hours, Pedro Ximénez and Moscatel for 10–21 days. Older vines were picked before younger ones, and Pedro Ximénez and Moscatel were picked first of all because they required longer sunning than Palomino. At night, the grapes were covered with *esparto* grass mats as a protection against dew. This sunning is called the *soleo*, and its primary purpose is to increase sugar content, while reducing the malic acid and tannin content. Although some producers still carry out the *soleo*, most harvest in the second week of September and forgo the *soleo* for all grapes but Pedro Ximénez and Moscatel, used in the sweetest Sherry. The grapes are now left in the sun for far fewer than the traditional 10–21 days.

OSBORNE,
PUERTO DE SANTA MARÍA
The Bajamar solera of Osborne was established in 1772.

The levante and pontete winds

The hot, dry *levante* is one of Jerez de la Frontera's two alternating prevailing winds. This easterly wind blow-dries and vacuum-cooks the grapes on their stalks during the critical ripening stage. This results in a dramatically different metabolization of fruit sugars, acids, and aldehydes, which produces a wine with an unusual balance peculiar to Jerez. Alternating with the *levante* is the wet Atlantic *pontete* wind. This is of fundamental importance, as it allows the growth of several *Saccharomyces* strains in the microflora of the Palomino grape. This is the poetically named Sherry *flor* (*see* p.368), without which there would be no *fino* in Jerez.

SHERRY'S CLASSIC GRAPE VARIETIES

British Sherry expert Julian Jeffs believes that as many as 100 different grape varieties were once traditionally used to make Sherry and, in 1868, Diego Parada y Barreto listed 42 then in use. Today only three varieties are authorized: Palomino, Pedro Ximénez, and Moscatel fino. The Palomino is considered the classic Sherry grape and most Sherries are, in fact, 100 per cent Palomino, although they may be sweetened with Pedro Ximénez for export markets.

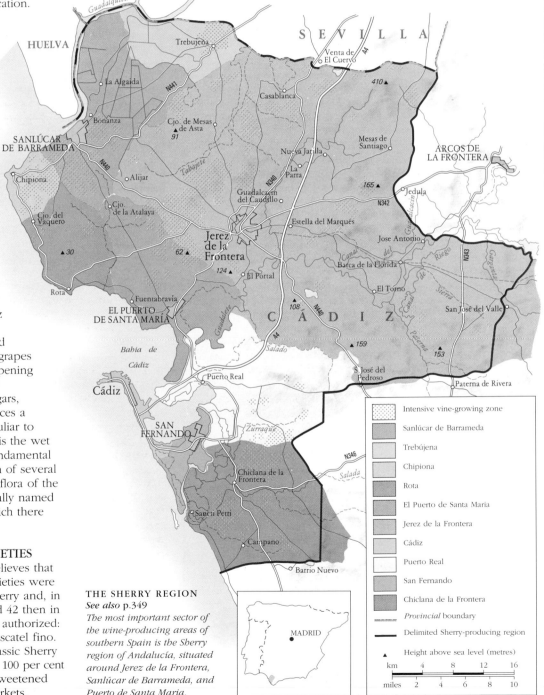

THE SHERRY REGION
See also p.349
The most important sector of the wine-producing areas of southern Spain is the Sherry region of Andalucía, situated around Jerez de la Frontera, Sanlúcar de Barrameda, and Puerto de Santa María.

Intensive vine-growing zone
Sanlúcar de Barrameda
Trebújena
Chipiona
Rota
El Puerto de Santa María
Jerez de la Frontera
Cádiz
Puerto Real
San Fernando
Chiclana de la Frontera
Provincial boundary
Delimited Sherry-producing region
Height above sea level (metres)

HOW THE FERMENTED SHERRY DEVELOPS

The larger bodegas like to make something of a mystery of the *flor*, declaring that they have no idea whether or not it will develop in a specific cask. There is some justification for this – one cask may have a fabulous froth of *flor* (looking like dirty soap-suds), while the cask next to it may have none. Any cask with good signs of dominant *flor* will invariably end up as *fino*, but others with either no *flor* or ranging degrees of it may develop into one of many different styles. There is no way of guaranteeing the evolution of the wines, but it is well known that certain zones can generally be relied on to produce particular styles.

ZONE	STYLE	ZONE	STYLE
Añina	*fino*	Madroñales	*Moscatel/sweet*
Balbaina	*fino*	Miraflores	*fino/Manzanilla*
Carrascal	*oloroso*	Rota	*Moscatel/sweet*
Chipiona	*Moscatel/sweet*	Sanlúcar	*fino/Manzanilla*
Los Tercios	*fino*	Tehigo	*colouring wines*
Macharnudo	*amontillado*	Torrebreba	*Manzanilla*

The yeso

Traditionally, prior to pressing the grapes, the stalks are removed and a small proportion of *yeso* (gypsum) is added to precipitate tartrate crystals. This practice, which is dying out, may have evolved when growers noticed that grapes covered by *albariza* dust produced better wine than clean ones. *Albariza* has a high calcium carbonate content that would crudely accomplish the task.

The pressing

Traditionally, four labourers called *pisadores* were placed in each *lagar* (open receptacle) to tread the grapes, not barefoot but wearing *zapatos de pisar*, heavily nailed cow-hide boots to trap the pips and stalks undamaged between the nails. Each man tramped 58 kilometres (36 miles) on the spot during a typical session lasting from midnight to noon. Automatic horizontal, usually pneumatic, presses are now in common use.

Fermentation

Some Sherry houses still ferment their wine in small oak casks purposely filled to only 90 per cent capacity. After 12 hours, the fermentation starts and continues for between 36 and 50 hours at 25–30°C (77–86°F), by which time as much as 99 per cent of available sugar is converted to alcohol; after a further 40 or 50 days, the process is complete. Current methods often use stainless-steel fermentation vats, and yield wines that are approximately one per cent higher in alcohol than those fermented in casks due to an absence of absorption and evaporation.

THE MAGICAL FLOR

For the majority of Sherry drinkers, *fino* is the quintessential Sherry style. It is a natural phenomenon called *flor* that determines whether or not a Sherry will become a *fino*. *Flor* is a strain of *Saccharomyces* yeast that appears as a grey-white film floating on a wine's surface, and it occurs naturally in the microflora of the Palomino grape grown in the Jerez district. It is found to one degree or another in every butt or vat of Sherry and Manzanilla, but whether or not it can dominate the wine and develop as a *flor* depends upon the strength of the *Saccharomyces* and the biochemical conditions. The effect of *flor* on Sherry is to absorb remaining traces of sugar, diminish glycerine and volatile acids, and greatly increase esters and aldehydes. To flourish, *flor* requires:

• An alcoholic strength of between 13.5 and 17.5%. The optimum is 15.3%, the level at which vinegar-producing acetobacter is killed.
• A temperature of between 15–30°C (59–86°F).
• A sulphur dioxide content of less than 0.018%.
• A tannin content of less than 0.01%.
• A virtual absence of fermentable sugars.

FIRST CASK-CLASSIFICATION AND FORTIFICATION

The cellarmaster's job is to sniff all the casks of Sherry and mark on each one in chalk how he believes it is developing, according to a recognized cask-classification system (*see* box, below). At this stage, lower-grade wines (those with little or no *flor*) are fortified to 18 per cent to kill any *flor*, thus determining their character once and for all and protecting the wine from the dangers of acetification. The *flor* itself is a protection against the acetobacter that threaten to turn wine into vinegar, but it is by no means invincible and will be at great risk until fortified to 15.3 per cent, or above, the norm for *fino*, and is not truly safe until it is bottled. A fifty-fifty mixture known as *mitad y mitad, miteado*, or *combinado* (half pure alcohol, half grape juice) is used for fortification. However, some producers prefer to use mature Sherry for fortification instead of grape juice.

Further cask-classification

The wines are often racked prior to fortification, and always after. A fortnight later, they undergo a second, more precise classification, but no further fortification, or other action, will take place until nine months have elapsed, after which they will be classified regularly over a period of two years to determine their final style.

CASK-CLASSIFICATION IN THE CELLAR

CHALK MARK	CHARACTER OF WINE	PROBABLE STYLE OF SHERRY	ACTION TO TAKE
FIRST CASK-CLASSIFICATION			
/ una raya	light and good	*fino/amontillado*	fortify up to 15.5%
/˙ raya y punto	slightly less promising	undecided	fortify up to 15.5%
// dos raya	less promising	*oloroso*	fortify up to 18%
/// tres rayas	coarse or acid	–	usually distil
Ve vinegar	–	–	immediately remove to avoid infection
SECOND CASK-CLASSIFICATION			
Y palma	a wine with breeding	has *flor*	–
/ raya	fuller	no *flor*	–
// dos rayas	tending to be coarse	no *flor*	–
# gridiron	no good at all	no *flor*	–
FURTHER CASK-CLASSIFICATION			
Y palma	Light and delicate	a *fino* sherry	–
¥ palma cortada	Fuller than a *fino*	*Fino-amontillado* or *amontillado*	–
+ palo cortado	No *flor*, but exceptional, full-bodied, and delicate	*Palo cortado*	–
/ raya	Darker, fuller, not breeding *flor*	Medium-quality *oloroso*	–
// dos rayas	Darker and fuller but coarser	Low-quality *oloroso*, for blending cheap Sherries that are usually sweetened	–
✓ pata de gallina	a *raya* that has developed the true fragrance of a fine *oloroso*	Top-quality *oloroso*, to be aged and kept dry	–

The solera blending system

Once the style of the Sherry has been established, the wines are fed into fractional-blending systems called *soleras*. A *solera* consists of a stock of wine in cask, split into units of equal volume but different maturation. The oldest stage is called the *Solera*; each of the younger stages that feed it is a *criadera*, or nursery. There are up to seven *criaderas* in a Sherry *solera*, and up to 14 in a Manzanilla *solera*. Up to one-third (the legal maximum) of the *Solera* may be drawn off for blending and bottling, although some bodegas may restrict their very high-quality old *Soleras* to one-fifth. The amount drawn off from the mature *Solera* is replaced by an equal volume from the first *criadera*, which is topped up by the second *criadera* and so on. When the last *criadera* is emptied of its one-third, it is refreshed by an identical quantity of *añada*, or new wine. This comprises like-classified Sherries from the current year's production, aged up to 36 months, depending on the style and exactly when they are finally classified.

THE EVOLUTION OF SHERRY STYLES

The tree shows the course taken by each Sherry to become one of the well-known styles by which it is sold.

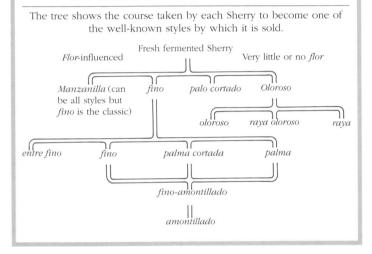

GRAPE-BASED SWEETENING AND COLOURING AGENTS

PX The most traditional most important sweetening agent in the production of Sherry, although gradually giving way to other less expensive ones, is that made from pure, overripe, sun-dried Pedro Ximénez grapes, also known as PX. After the *soleo* or sunning of the grapes (*see* p.367), the sugar content of the PX increases from around 23 per cent to between 43 and 54 per cent. The PX is pressed and run into casks containing pure grape spirit. This process, known as muting, produces a mixture with an alcohol level of about nine per cent and some 430 grams of sugar per litre. This mixture is tightly bunged and left for four months, during which it undergoes a slight fermentation, increasing the alcohol by about one degree and reducing the sugar by some 18 grams per litre. Finally the wine undergoes a second muting, raising the alcoholic strength to a final 13 per cent but reducing the sugar content to about 380 grams per litre. Other sweetening agents are:

MOSCATEL
This is prepared in exactly the same way as PX, but the result is not as rich and its use, which has always been less widespread than the use of PX, is technically not permitted under DO regulations.

DULCE PASA
Preparation is as for PX and Moscatel, but using Palomino, which achieves up to a 50 per cent sugar concentration prior to muting. Its use is on the increase. This must not be confused with *dulce racimo* or *dulce apagado*, sweetening agents that were once brought in from outside the region and are now illegal.

DULCE DE ALMIBAR *OR* **DULCE BLANCO**
A combination of glucose and laevulose blended with *fino* and matured, this agent is used to sweeten pale-coloured sherries.

SANCOCHO
A dark-coloured, sweet, and sticky non-alcoholic syrup made by reducing unfermented local grape juice to one-fifth of its original volume by simmering over a low heat. It is used in the production of *vino de color* – a "colouring wine".

ARROPE
This dark-coloured, sweet, and sticky non-alcoholic syrup, made by reducing unfermented local grape juice to one-fifth of its original volume, is also used in the production of *vino de color*.

COLOR DE MACETILLA
This is the finest *vino de color* and is produced by blending two-parts *arrope* or *sancocho* with one-part unfermented local grape juice. This results in a violent fermentation and, when the wine falls bright, it has an alcoholic strength of 9 per cent and a sugar content of 235 grams per litre. Prized stocks are often matured by *solera*.

COLOR REMENDADO
This is a cheap, commonly used *vino de color, which is* made by blending *arrope* or *sancocho* with local wine.

THE STYLES OF
SHERRY

The development of a Sherry can be natural, so that a *fino* can, without the help of increased fortification, turn into an *oloroso* (thus a natural *oloroso* may have developed with the aid of *flor*, whereas the increased fortification usually used to turn a *fino* into an *oloroso* would prevent the development of *flor*). A *palo cortado* can develop from either an *amontillado* or an *oloroso*. A genuine old *fino* sherry can surprise everyone and turn into an *oloroso*.

MANZANILLA

Sea winds in the Sanlúcar de Barrameda area create a more even temperature and higher humidity than those found in Jerez itself, which with the tradition of allowing more ullage (empty volume) in Manzanilla casks, encourages the thickest, whitest, and most vigorous growth of *flor* in the region. Fino is therefore the most classic style, but Manzanilla, too, has its *fino-amontillado* (called *pasada*) and *amontillado*. Oloroso and various intermediary styles are also produced, but these are invariably sold as Sherry, rather than Manzanilla, even when they are exclusively composed of the latter.

MANZANILLA FINA

Manzanilla (Sherry made in Sanlúcar de Barrameda) is a relatively modern, early-picked, *fino*. Its production differs from that of a traditional *fino* in that its fortification is lower and the *solera* system more complex. A true Manzanilla *fina* is pale, light-bodied, dry, and delicate with a definite *flor* nose, a touch of bitterness on the palate, and sometimes even a slightly saline tang. *See* general *fino* style below about freshness and when to consume. These wines are usually 100 per cent Palomino with an alcoholic strength of 15.5–17 per cent.

✓ *Barbadillo* (Eva) • *Diez-Mérito* (Don Zoilo)
• *Duff Gordon* (Cabrera)

MANZANILLA PASADA

When a Manzanilla begins to age, it loses its *flor*, gains alcoholic strength, and becomes the equivalent of a *fino-amontillado*, known in Sanlúcar de Barrameda as a *pasada*. These wines are invariably 100 per cent Palomino with an alcoholic strength of up to 20.5 per cent.

✓ *Barbadillo* (Solear) • *Delgado Zuleta* (Amontillado Fino, La Goya)
• *Hidalgo* (Pasada)

MANZANILLA AMONTILLADA

Fuller than a *pasada*, but lighter and more fragrant than Jerez *amontillado*, this is less common than the previous two, but can be excellent.

✓ *Barbadillo* (Principe)
• *Lustau* (Manuel Cuevas Jurado)

PUERTO FINO

This is a Manzanilla-type Sherry from El Puerto de Santa Maria, where the winds are almost as legendary as those of Sanlúcar de Barrameda.

✓ *Burdon* (Puerto Fino Superior Dry)
• *Osborne* (Coquinera Amontillado)

FINO

A *palma* is the highest quality of *fino* Sherry and may be graded in a rising scale of quality: *dos palmas*, *tres palmas*, *cuatro palmas*. A *palma cortada* is a *fino* that has developed more body, has a very dry, but smooth, almondy flavour, and is veering towards *amontillado*. An *entre fino* has little merit. Few *finos* remain *fino* with age in cask, which is why genuine Old Fino Sherry is rare. A *fino* is light, dry, and delicate; its *flor* nose should overpower any acetaldehyde.

This style is best appreciated straight from the cask, when it is crisp and vital, as it quickly tires once bottled and further declines rapidly as soon as it is opened. Until producers are required to declare the bottling date on the label (fat chance), the only sensible advice is not to buy *fino* until the day you want to drink it and, once opened, consume the entire contents: don't keep it. The wines are invariably 100 per cent Palomino with an alcoholic strength of between 15.5 and 17 per cent.

✓ *Tomás Abad* • *Domecq* (La Ina) • *Gonzalez Byass* (Tio Pepe) • *La Riva* (Tres Palmas) • *Williams & Humbert* (Pando)

PALE DRY

This style is synonymous with *fino*.

PALE CREAM

This is sweetened, usually lesser quality, *fino*.

AMONTILLADO

With age, a *fino* develops an amber colour in cask and becomes a *fino-amontillado* then, after at least eight years, a full *amontillado*, when it takes on a nutty character and acquires more body. A true *amontillado* is completely dry, with between 16 and 18 per cent alcohol, but will often be sweetened to a medium style for export markets.

The term *amontillado* means "Montilla style"; it was originally used to distinguish a Sherry with characteristics similar to those of Montilla (then part of the Jerez region – *see* p.366). Ironically, it was illegal for producers of Montilla to use the term *amontillado* under the Spanish republic, thus Sherry could be made in a montilla-style, but not Montilla! Under the EU, however, the law has changed and once again Montilla houses are shipping Montilla amontillado.

✓ *Domecq* (Botaina) • *Gonzalez Byass* (Duque) • *Sandeman* (Bone Dry Old Amontillado) • *Valdespino* (Coliseo, Don Tomás) • *Wisdom & Warter* (Very Rare Solera Muy Viejo)

MILK

Sweetened *amontillado*, usually of lesser quality.

OLOROSO

Oloroso means fragrant and, when genuinely dry, rich, and complex from age, I find it certainly has the greatest finesse and is the most rewarding wine in Jerez. Much of its character is due to the relatively high fortification it receives and the generous glycerine content that develops without the aid of *flor*. The alcoholic strength usually ranges between 18 and 20 per cent. Some high-quality, sweeter, dessert-style *oloroso* wines are also produced.

✓ **Dry** *Barbadillo* (Oloroso Seco) • *Diez-Mérito* (Victoria Regina) • *Domecq* (Río Viejo) • *Gonzalez Byass* (Alfonso, Apostles) • *Hidalgo* (Oloroso Seco) • *Lustau* (Don Nuno, Emperatríz Eugenia, Principe Rio, Tonel) • *Osborne* (Bailén, Alonso el Sabio) • *Diego Romero* (Jerezana) • *Sandeman* (Dry Old Oloroso) • *Valdespino* (Don Gonzalo)

Dessert style *Gonzalez Byass* (Mathúsalem) • *Sandeman* (Royal Corregedor) • *Valdespino* (Solera 1842)

BROWN

This sweetened *oloroso* is usually, but not always, of lesser quality than Oloroso. High-quality Brown Sherries used to be very popular in Scotland.

✓ *Williams & Humbert* (Walnut Brown)

CREAM *or* DARK CREAM

An *oloroso* style usually sweetened with Pedro Ximénez, the quality of which can range from commercial to top.

✓ *Diego Romero* (Jerezana) • *Lustau* (Premium Solera, Vendimia)

EAST INDIA

Some sources believe that this rich, sweet, Madeira-like style of Sherry dates back to as early as 1617, but the practice of shipping Sherry to the Orient and back gradually disappeared during the 19th century with the advent of steam-driven ships. It was revived in 1958 by the owners of the Ben Line and Alastair Campbell, an Edinburgh wine merchant, when they sent a hogshead of Valdespino Oloroso on a 32,000-kilometre (20,000-mile) round trip to the Far East, but although the style survives, the effects of the sea voyage, as with Madeira, are now replicated in the cellar.

✓ *Lustau* (Old East India) • *Osborne* (India Rare Solera Oloroso)

PALO CORTADO

This wine cannot be deliberately made, nor even encouraged (a *palo cortado solera* is very difficult to operate); only one butt in a thousand turns into a true *palo cortado*. A law unto itself, it is a naturally dry wine with a style somewhere between *amontillado* (on the nose) and *oloroso* (on the palate), but this does not by any means convey the stunning richness, nutty complexity, and fabulous finesse, which really must be experienced to be believed.

It should be totally dry, but some sweeter dessert-style *palo cortado* wines are produced and can be wonderful. Like *palma*, *palo cortado* may be graded; *dos cortados*, *tres cortados*, *cuatro cortados*.

✓ *Domecq* (Sibarita) • *Hidalgo* (Jerez) • *Lustau* (Peninsula) • *Rosario Fantante* (Dos Cortados) • *Sandeman* (Dry Old) • *Valdespino* (Cardenal) • *Williams & Humbert* (Dos Cortados)

Dessert style *Osborne* (Abocado Solera) • *Sandeman* (Royal Ambrosante) • *Wisdom & Warter* (Tizón)

MOSCATEL

Occasionally, releases of this wine can be rich, raisiny delights.

✓ *Lustau* (Las Cruzes, Solera Reserva Emelin)

PEDRO XIMÉNEZ

Although it is primarily produced as a sweetening agent, Pedro Ximénez is occasionally released in limited bottlings that are invariably very old and utterly stunning, huge, dark, deep, powerfully rich wines piled high with complex yet succulent, raisiny, Muscovado flavours.

These bottlings can be compared in quality, weight, and intensity – though not in character – with only some of the oldest and rarest Australian liqueur Muscats.

✓ *Gonzalez Byass* (Noe) • *Lustau* (Murillo, San Emilio) • *Sanchez Romate* (Superior) • *Valdespino* (Solera Superior) • *Wisdom & Warter* (Viale Viejisimo)

ALMACENISTA *or* BODEGAS DE ALMACENADO

This is not a style, but a category of increasing interest among Sherry enthusiasts. An *almacenista* is a private stockholder whose pure, unblended Sherries are held as an investment for 30 years or more, after which they are in great demand by large bodegas, who use them to improve their commercial blends. Lustau, itself an *almacenista* until the 1950s (and now part of the Caballero group), was the first firm to commercialize the concept, making these purest of Sherries available to consumers (and they registered "Almacenista" as a trademark in the process). All styles of Sherry and Manzanilla exist in *almacenista* form and are, almost by definition, guaranteed to be of extraordinary quality. Fractions on the label such as ⅛, ½, ⅟₄₀ etc. indicate the number of barrels in the *solera* from which it was drawn, therefore the lower the denominator (the number below the line), the greater the rarity of the wine and consequently the more expensive it will be.

✓ *Lustau*

✦PORTUGAL✦

*Once devoid of anything interesting beyond its
two classic fortified wines, Port and Madeira,
Portuguese winemakers have now woken up
to the tremendous potential of the* terroirs *and
native grape varieties that their country offers,
making it a hot-bed of innovation.*

THE JOINT VENTURE BETWEEN Bruno Prats, the former owner
and winemaker of Château Cos d'Estournel, and the Symington
family of Port fame to produce premium red wine in the Douro
will put the icing on the cake for Portugal's fine wine reputation.
This testament to the top-end potential of Portugal's wine industry
follows close on the heels of the red wine revolution that started
to materialize in its more inexpensive reds in the mid-1990s.

In the past, Dão had always typified the sort of wines we
had come to expect from Portugal, with its dried-out, fruitless
reds and dull, heavy, oxidized whites. But in 1995 deliciously
fruity, easily accessible reds and fresh, crisp whites came on
stream and, like a true revolution, the change started at the
lowest levels, with wines such as Alta Mesa and Ramada
from Estremadura. At the time these were, and still are,
some of the cheapest wines in the world. They had
already turned heads by being clean, easy-drinking
wines from what was formerly considered a lacklustre
wine country but, with the vintages of 1994 and
1995, they suddenly had twice the fruit, which
gave them instant gulpability and gained them
international recognition.

VINEYARDS, SETÚBAL
*The area's Moscatel vines
(Muscat d'Alexandrie) produce
a celebrated fortified wine that
has its own Denominacao de
Origem Controllada.*

PORTUGAL
*It is in the north of the country that the
most famous wines – Port and Vinho
Verde – are produced, along with the
most upwardly mobile, those from
Bairrada and Dão.*

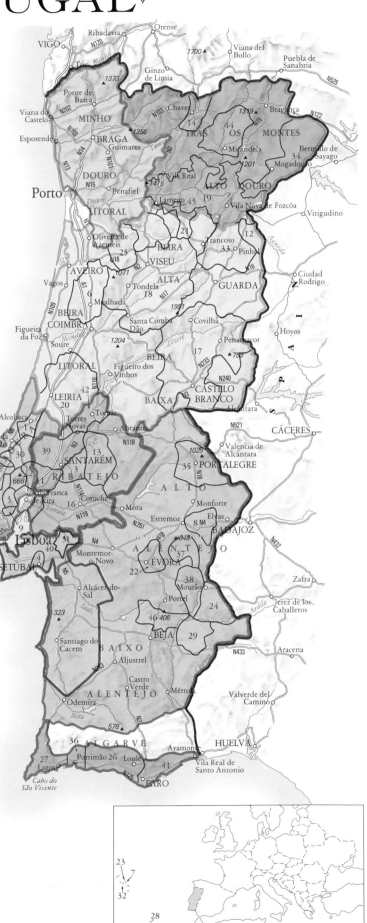

Major Wine Regions

Alentejo	
Algarve	
Beiras	
Estremadura	
Ribatejo	
Rios de Minho	

Tras-os-Montes	
Terras do Sado	
[1] Wine appellations	
—— International boundary	

Height above sea level (metres)

km 20 40 60 80 100
miles 20 40 60

CURRENT TRENDS

The rush of fruit has only just begun to filter its way upwards through the quality scale. This was in part due to the fact that more serious wines took longer to reach the market, thus while we were gulping 1994s and 1995s from Estremadura and other lesser-known Vinhos Regionals, such as Alentejo and Terras do Sado, the 1991s and 1992s from Dão and Bairrada were only just reaching the shelves. A few producers, such as Duque de Viseu in Dão, had got their act together by the early 1990s, but most had not and we still had to get through the dismal 1993 vintage before these more famous regions could show us what they were doing while the likes of Alta Mesa and Ramada were being knocked out.

Another reason for the delayed action in Portugal's fine-wine regions is that producers had until relatively recently been forced to buy wines. Quite extraordinarily, it was illegal for them to buy grapes. Most growers involved in the bulk market barely have a grasp of how to cultivate vines, let alone ferment wines, so being able to buy grapes has enabled firms like Sogrape (which makes Duque de Vieu) to have much greater control over the quality of the final product. When and if the same growers ever learn to grow grapes properly, the recent surge in quality will seem nothing and Portugal's finest wine areas should be catapulted to super-stardom.

HOW TO READ PORTUGUESE WINE LABELS

STYLE OF THE WINE •
Various terms found on Portuguese labels are descriptive of the wine's style. B*ranco* means "white" but on this example it has the term in English. Other possible terms include *adamado* (sweet); *aperitivo* (apéritif); *bruto* (Portuguese adaption of the French *brut*, used to describe a dry sparkling wine); *clarete* (Bordeaux-style); *claro* (new or "nouveau" wine); *doce* (sweet); *espumante* (sparkling wine that may be made by any method unless qualified by another term); *generoso* (an apéritif or dessert wine rich in alcohol and usually sweet); *licoroso* (a fortified wine); *maduro* (literally "matured" – it refers to a wine that has been kept in a vat). To many Portuguese consumers, a dried-out, oxidized wine is *maduro* and they prefer it that way; *quinado* (tonic wine); *rosado* (rosé); *séco* (dry); *tinto* (red).

NAME OF THE PROPERTY
The use of words such as *Casa, Palacio,* and *Solar* in the name of a wine may also indicate a single-vineyard wine. This wine is made at Quinta de Saes, and the presence of the term *Produzido e Engarrafado* or the more commonly encountered *Engarrafado na origem* confirms that it has been estate-bottled. The Portuguese have only just realized the importance that international markets place on estate-bottling and consequently many vineyards are not equipped to make and bottle wine, so that these functions may well be carried out elsewhere. *Vinha* means vineyard. *Adega,* literally "Cellar", is commonly used as part of the name of a company or cooperative, much in the way that the Spanish employ "Bodega", their equivalent term.

BOTTLED ON THE PROPERTY •
Engarrafado means "bottled at", or "by", and is followed by the name of the bottler. In this case, it is Qunita de Saes. *Produzido e Engarrafado* indicates that wine is estate-bottled and is one of the most useful, yet least encountered, terms on a Portuguese label. "Quinta", as part of a wine's name, should indicate that it is the product of a single farm or estate. Like the French term *château*, it has been somewhat abused in the past, but is now 95 per cent reliable (although by no means a guarantee of superior quality) and is to be the subject of continuous tightening up under the control of EU wine regulations.

DENOMINACAO DE ORIGEM CONTROLLADA (DOC)
This indicates that the wine comes from Portugal's top level of legally demarcated areas. In the example above, the wine is Vinho Verde from near Amares, in the Minho district. The next level down is *Indicaçao de Provência Regulamentada* (IPR), a number of which have been promoted to DOC status in recent years. The next level down is *Vinho Regional* (VR), which is similar to a large-sized *vin de pays*.

Other important and interesting terms on Portuguese wine labels:

CARVALHO Oak.
Oak casks were used in the maturation of the wine.

CASTA Grape variety.
Grape varieties are often indicated on Vinhos Verdes. The most common of these are: Alvarinho, Avesso, Azal, Loureiro, Pederña, and Trajadura. *Casta Predominante* refers to the major grape variety used in a wine.

COLHEITA
This means "Vintage" and is followed by the year of harvest.

ESCOLHA Choice or selection

GARRAFA Bottle

GARRAFEIRA
This term may be used only for a vintage-dated wine that possesses an extra 0.5 per cent of alcohol above the minimum requirement. Red wines must have a minimum of three years' maturation including one year in bottle;

white wines must have one year with six months in bottle. The wine may come from a demarcated region, or be blended from various areas.

RESERVA
A term that can be used only to qualify a vintage year of "outstanding quality", where the wine has an alcoholic strength of at least 0.5 per cent above the minimum requirement. Wine may come from a demarcated region, but does not have to; it could be blended from different areas.

VELHO
The meaning is literally "old". In the past, this term used not to have any legal definition. Now it can legally be applied only to wines with a strict minimum age: three years for red wines and two years for whites.

VINHO DE MESA
This is the table wine equivalent to the French *vin de table*. If the label does not state a specific DOC or Garrafeira (*see left*), the wine will simply be a cheap blend.

THE APPELLATIONS OF
PORTUGAL

Note DOC stands for *Denominacão de Origem Controllada*, Portugal's equivalent of France's AOC, Spain's DO etc.
IPR stands for *Indicação de Provência Regulamentada*, roughly equivalent to VDQS or a DOC in waiting, a number having been promoted to DOC status in recent years.
VR stands for *Vinho Regional*, a sort of large-sized *vin de pays*.

ALCOBAO IPR
Map (No.1)
These wines from the hills surrounding the old monastic town of Alcobaço are predominantly white. Yields arc unfavourably high, producing thin reds and light whites significantly lower in alcohol than wines from surrounding areas.

🍇 For all wines: Arinto, Baga, Fernão pires, Malvasia, Periquita, Tamarez, Trincadeira, Vital

ALENTEJO VR
Stretching up from the Algarve, the plains of Alto and Baixo Alentejo cover about one-third of Portugal. A sparsely populated area with large estates and a scattering of vines, Alentejo is better known for cork than vineyards, even though it has produced some of the country's most outstanding one-off wines and has achieved this with both indigenous and imported grape varieties.

🍇 Abundante, Alfrocheiro preto, Alicante bouschet, Antao vaz, Arinto, Cabernet sauvignon, Carignan, Chardonnay, Diagalves, Fernão pires, Grand noir, Manteudo, Moreto, Palomino (*syn.* Perrum), Periquita, Rabo de ovelha, Tempranillo (*syn.* Aragonez), Trincadeira

🍷 1–3 years (new-wave, fruity style)
2–5 years (others)

✓ *Apostolo* • *Cortes de Cima* • *Esporao* (other brands include Monte Velha) • *JP Vinhos* (Quinta da Anfora) • *Herdade do Mouchão* • *José de Sousa* • *Pêra Manca* • *AC de Reguengos* • *Quinta do Carmo* • *Sogrape* (Vinha do Monte)• *Tapada do Chaves*

ALENQUER IPR
Map (no.2)
The valley-side vineyards of Alenquer are well-suited to viticulture, ripening grapes easily and producing full, ripe-flavoured reds, with peppery-spicy aromas and soft, easy-going, creamy-dry whites.

🍇 Arinto, Camarate (possibly the same as Castelao nacional), Fernão pires, Graciano (*syn* Tinta miúda), Jampal, Mortágua, Periquita, Preto martinho, Vital

🍷 1–3 years (new-wave, fruity style)
2–5 years (others)

✓ *Quinta de Abrigada* • *Quinta de Plantos* • *Quinta do Carneiro*

ALGARVE VR
The quality is uninspiring, but the downgrading of Algarve to Vinho Regional was just a smoke-screen to gain acceptance for its four new internal DOCs: Lagos, Portimao, Lagoa, and Tavira. Lagoa used to have a reputation for fortified whites, which is not surprising considering its proximity to Jerez, but although wine is still produced, none of any interest, fortified or not, is made in the Algarve these days. It is wise to remember that the tourist economy, not quality, regulates wine appellations in the Algarve.

🍇 Arinto, Bastardo, Diagalves, Moreto, Negra mole, Periquita, Perrum, Rabo de Ovelha, Tamarez d'Algarve (possibly the same as Roupeiro)

ALMEIRIM IPR
Map (no.3)
An up-and-coming area in the Ribatejo region, rapidly becoming known as a source for cheap, fruity red and white wines, often from the plains, known locally as *lezíria* and simply sold as *vinho de mesa*. Terraced vines on the left bank of the Targus apparently have more potential.

🍇 Arinto, Baga (*syn* Poeirinha), Castelao nacional, Fernao pires, Periquita, Rabo de Ovelha, Tinta amarela (*syn.* Trincadeira preta), Trincadeira das Pratas (*syn.* Tamarez d'Azeitao), Ugni blanc (*syn.* Talia), Vital

🍷 6–18 months

✓ *AC de Almeirim* (including wines under Falcoaria and Quinta das Verandas labels)

ARRABIDA IPR
Map (no.4)
This area on the Setúbal peninsular has well-drained limestone soil and great quality potential, particularly for reds, but whether it takes off as an appellation, when the much wider, more flexible Terras do Sado VR is doing so well, remains to be seen.

🍇 Alfrocheiro, Arinto, Cabernet sauvignon, Periquita (Castelao francês), Fernão pires, Muscat d'Alexandrie (*syn.* Moscatel de Setúbal), Rabo de Ovelha, Roupeiro

ARRUDA IPR
Map (no.5)
From intensively cultivated hillsides surrounding the town of Arruda in the Estremadura region, come some of Portugal's cheapest, yet reliable, fruity reds.

🍇 Camarate (possibly the same as Castelao nacional), Fernão pires, Graciano (*syn.* Tinta miúda), Jampal, Trincadeira, Vital

🍷 1–3 years (new-wave, fruity style), 2–5 years (others)

✓ *AC de Arruda*

BAIRRADA DOC
Map (no.6)

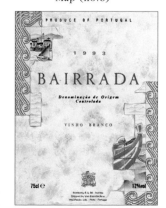

This area produces one of Portugal's two most important red wines and the best have a deep colour with good tannin and fine, capsicum-blackcurrany fruit. However, it is only just beginning to demonstrate its potential for white wines. Sogrape's Nobilis exemplifies Bairrada's fast-emerging rosé style, which really hits the spot with its freshness and depth of fruit.

🍇 Baga, Borrado das moscas (*syn.* Bical), Castelao francês, Fernao pires (*syn.* Maria gomes), Rabo de Ovelha, Tinta pinheira

🍷 3–12 years (reds)
1–3 years (rosés and whites)

✓ *José Maria da Fonseca* • *Gonçalves Faria* (Reserva) • *Luis Pato* (especially Quinta do Ribeirinho Vinhos Velhas) • *Quinta de Pedralvites* • *Casa de Saima* • *Caves Sao Joao* • *Sogrape* (Reserva, Nobilis Rosé) • *Terra Franca tinto*

BEIRAS VR
Located in the north of Portugal, encompassing the three Beira provinces of Alta, Baixa, and Litoral, containing the DOCs of Dão and Bairrada, plus the IPRs of Castelo Rodrigo, Cova de Beira, Lafoes, Lamego, Pinhel, Varosa, Encostas da Nave, and most of Encostas d'Aire, Beiras produces virtually every imaginable style of wine made, but standards vary enormously.

🍇 Arinto, Baga, Bastardo, Borrado das moscas (*syn.* Bical), Camarate (possibly the same as Castelao nacional), Cerceal, Esgana-cão, Fernão pires, Jaen, Malvasia, Marufo, Monvedro, Periquita, Rabo de Ovelha, Rufete, Tinta amarela (Trincadeira preta), Touriga nacional, Verdelho, Vital

🍷 1–3 years (new-wave, fruity style)
2–5 years (others)

✓ *Bright Brothers* (Baga) • *Buçaco* • *Conde de Santar* (Reserva) • *Entre Serras* • *Joao Pato* • *Quinta de Foz de Arouce*

BISCOITOS IPR
Map (no.7)
Rarely encountered fortified wines produced on the island of Terceira in the Azores.

🍇 Arinto, Terrantez, Verdelho

BORBA DOC
Map (no.8)
The first sub-appellation of the Alentejo region to gain recognition outside of Portugal itself, especially for its inexpensive, juicy red wines.

🍇 Aragonez, Periquita, Perrum, Rabo de Ovelha, Roupeiro, Tamarez, Trincadeira

🍷 1–3 years

✓ *AC de Borba* (Reserva)

BUCELAS DOC
Map (no.9)
The Arinto grape grows particularly well on the loam soil of this small district, but the antiquated winemaking methods are still holding back what is obviously a potentially fine white-wine appellation. Cool fermentation, early bottling, and a delicate touch of new oak would make this wine an international superstar, but so many wines are dried-out and over-acidic. Quinta da Romeira is the most consistent Bucelas, and is recommended in this context, but has failed to live up to its promise.

🍇 Arinto, Esgana-cão

🍷 Upon purchase

✓ *Quinta da Romeira* (Prova Régia)

CARCAVELOS DOC
Map (no.10)

Famous in Portugal itself since the late 18th century when the Marquis of Pombal owned a large vineyard and winery here. This area's oldest surviving vineyard, Quinta do Barao, stopped production in 1991, but a relatively new one, Quinta dos Pesos, is trying desperately to rekindle interest in Carcavelos. Rarely seen on export markets, it is a topaz-coloured, off-dry fortified wine with a nutty aroma, delicate almondy flavour, and a velvety texture.

🍇 Arinto, Boal, Galego dourado, Negra mole, Trincadeira Torneiro

🍷 5–20 years

✓ *Quinta dos Pesos*

CARTAXO IPR
Map (no.11)

This flat, fertile area overlaps the Estremadura and Ribatejo regions, producing good, fruity, value-for-money reds and whites.

🍇 Arinto, Castelao nacional, Fernão pires, Periquita, Preto martinho, Tinta amarela (Trincadeira preta), Trincadeira das Pratas (*syn.* Tamarez d'Azeitao), Ugni blanc (*syn.* Talia), Vital

🍷 1–3 years

✓ *Almeida*

CASTELO RODRIGO IPR
Map (no.12)

These full, spicy reds on the border with Spain, south of the Douro, in the Beiras region, show excellent potential, but have yet to establish an international reputation.

🍇 Arinto, Assario branco (*syn.* Arinto do Dao), Bastardo, Codo, Fonte-Cal, Marufo, Rufete, Touriga nacional

🍷 1–3 years (new-wave, fruity style)
  2–5 years (others)

✓ *Quinta do Cardo*

CHAMUSCA IPR
Map (no.13)

This sub-appellation of the Ribatejo region is adjacent to Almeirim and produces similar wines, but not quite of the same potential.

🍇 Arinto, Castelao nacional, Fernão pires, Periquita, Tinta amarela (Trincadeira preta), Trincadeira das Pratas (*syn.* Tamarez d'Azeitao), Ugni blanc (*syn.* Talia), Vital

CHAVES IPR
Map (no.14)

From the upper reaches of the river Tâmega in the Trás-os-Montes VR, this appellation tends to produce a similar but lighter style to that of the Douro DOC.

🍇 Bastardo, Boal, Codega (possibly the same as Roupeiro), Gouveio, Malvasia fina, Tinta carvalha, Tinta amarela

COLARES DOC
Map (no.15)

This small wine area is famous for its ungrafted Ramisco vines planted in trenches dug out of the sandy dunes of Sintra, which not only protects them from salt-blighting Atlantic winds, but also from the dreaded phylloxera louse. This is an historic wine, but should not be vinified in such an antiquated fashion if it is going to appeal to modern consumers. If the greatest Bordeaux châteaux have moved with the times, why not Colares? The reds are well-coloured and full-bodied, but have so much tannin that they are mouth-puckeringly astringent, smoothing out to a silky finish only with great age, when there is no fruit left. If the grapes could be picked according to tannin-ripeness, rather than fruit-ripeness, and more careful fermentation techniques employed, Colares could be world class. The dry whites are traditional *maduro*-style and not recommended.

🍇 Arinto, Jampal, Galego dourado, Malvasia, Ramisco

🍷 15–30 years (red)

✓ *Antonio Bernardino Paulo da Silva* (Chitas)

CORUCHE IPR
Map (no.16)

This appellation covers wines made from sandy, well-irrigated plains covering the southern half of the Ribatejo region, but Coruche is seldom encountered and has yet to make its mark.

🍇 Fernão pires, Periquita, Preto martinho, Tinta amarela (Trincadeira preta), Trincadeira das Pratas (*syn.* Tamarez d'Azeitao), Ugni blanc (*syn.* Talia), Vital

COVA DE BEIRA IPR
Map (no.17)

Located in the Beira Alta, between the Vinho Verde and Dão districts, Cova de Beira is the largest of Portugal's IPRs. As with the Beiras VR, every style of wine is produced in varying quality, but the area is best-known for its lightweight reds.

🍇 Arinto, Assario branco (*syn.* Arinto do Dão), Jaen, Marufo, Periquita, Pérola, Rabo de Ovelha, Rufete, Tinta amarela

DÃO DOC
Map (no.18)

For 20 years there have been rumours that Dão wines have more fruit and less tannin, but only over the last five have we seen this promise fulfilled in the glass, as fruit-filled Dão have begun to emerge. They have sufficient fruit to drink much earlier than the old-style Dão wines, but have a certain structure and dry, spicy-finesse that expresses their Portuguese origins. The best whites can be clean and fresh, but not yet truly special, although the Quinta de Saes *branco* is surprisingly good, especially when consumed with food.

🍇 Alfrocheiro preto, Assario branco (*syn.* Arinto do Dao), Barcelo, Bastardo, Borrado das moscas, Cercial, Encruzado, Jaen, Tempranillo (*syn.* Tinta roriz), Tinta pinheira, Touriga nacional, Verdelho

🍷 3–8 years (reds), 1–3 years (whites)

✓ *José Maria da Fonseca* (Garrafeira P)
  • *Campos da Silva Olivera*
  • *Casa da Insua* • *Duque de Viseu*

DOURO DOC
Map (no.19)

Known principally for its Port, the Douro Valley in fact makes as much table wine as fortified wine. Because the finest Port is produced on schist soils, most table wines are relegated to areas of the region's other dominant soil, granite. I remain surprised that the Syrah, which thrives in the Northern Rhône's hot, granite soil, has not been tried here, even though it has been experimented with in the Alentejo, where there is much less potential for this variety. The Douro's table wine quality potential is highlighted by Barca Velha, Portugal's most expensive table wine made by Ferreira at Quinta do Vale de Meao, although its second wine, Reserva Especial, is often just as good, if not better. Is it a coincidence that across the Spanish frontier, where the Douro becomes the Duero, Vega Sicilia, Spain's most expensive wine, grows on its banks? There is nothing Porty about these table wines, which range from the lighter, claret types to the fuller, richer Burgundian style. New oak is almost *de rigueur* for premium quality wines.

🍇 Bastardo, Donzelinho branco, Gouveio, Malvasia fina, Rabigato (probably not the same as Rabigato *syn.* Rabo de Ovelha), Mourisco tinto, Tempranillo (*syn.* Tinta roriz), Tinta amarela, Tinta barroca, Tinta cão, Touriga nacional, Touriga francesa, Viosinho

🍷 2–10 years (red, but up to 25 for Barca Velha), 1–4 years (white)

✓ *Bright Brothers* • *Ferreirinha* (Barca Velha, Reserva Especial) • *Niepoort* (Redoma and especially Quinta da Gaivosa) • *Quinta do Côtto* (Grande Escholha) • *Quinta do Crasto* • *Quinta de Passadouro* • *Quinta de la Rosa* • *Quinta do Vale da Raposa* • *Ramos-Pinto* (Duas Quintas) • *Sogrape* (Reserva) • *Vale do Bomfim* (Reserva)

ENCOSTAS DA AIRE IPR
Map (no.20)

Overlapping the Beiras and Estremadura region, the limestone hills of this appellation should produce some excellent wines, but most have so far been light and rather dried-out.

🍇 Arinto, Baga, Fernão pires, Periquita, Tamarez, Tinta amarela (Trincadeira preta), Vital

ENCOSTAS DA NAVE IPR
Map (no.21)

Not to be confused with Encostas da Aire, this is a much smaller appellation, located entirely within the Beiras region, adjacent to Varosa, and its wines are much fuller, resembling those of the Douro immediately north, but have yet to establish themselves.

🍇 Folgosao, Gouveio, Malvasia fina, Mourisco tinto, Tinta Barroca, Touriga francesa, Touriga nacional

ESTREMADURA VR

From Lisbon, Estremadura stretches north to the Bairrada region and encompasses the DOCs of Bucelas, Carcavelos, and Colares, plus the IPRs of Alenquer, Arruda, Obidos, Torres Vedras, and, in part, Encostas d'Aire (which overlaps Beiras) and Cartaxo (which overlaps Ribatejo).

This is Portugal's largest wine-producing region in terms of volume (although Beiras and Alentejo are much larger geographically) and, as such, Estremadura is often perceived as a source of cheap, uninteresting wine. While there are indeed cheap wines made here, they are good guzzlers and far from uninteresting, with a few *quintas* making much finer, more serious wines that are not remotely expensive.

ESPIGA
1995

VINHO TINTO
VINHO REGIONAL ESTREMADURA

Produzido e engarrafado na Quinta da Boavista por
COMPANHIA DAS VINHAS DE S. DOMINGOS, S.A.
2580 PORTUGAL
75 cl e   PRODUTO DE PORTUGAL   12% vol.

🍇 Alfrocheiro preto, Antao Vaz, Arinto, Baga, Bastardo, Borrado das moscas (*syn.* Bical), Cabernet Sauvignon, Camarate (possibly the same as Castelao nacional), Chardonnay, Esgana-cão, Fernão pires, Graciano (*syn.* Tinta miúda), Jampal, Malvasia, Moreto, Periquita, Rabo de Ovelha, Ramisco, Tamarez, Tinta amarella (Trincadeira preta), Trincadeira das Pratas (*syn.* Tamarez d'Azeitao), Ugni blanc (*syn.* Talia), Vital

🍷 2–4 years (reds, 4–8 years for better wines), 1–3 years (whites)

✓ *AC do Arruda* (selected cuvées) • *AC de Sao Mamede da Ventosa* • *AC do Torres Vedras* (selected cuvées) • *Espiga* • *Quinta da Folgorosa* • *Quinta de Pancas* • *Palha Canas*

EVORA IPR
Map (no.22)
This area of the Alentejo region is destined to be one of Portugal's most exciting appellations, especially for full-bodied, creamy-rich red.

🍇 Aragonez, Arinto, Periquita, Rabo de Ovelha, Roupeiro, Tamarez, Tinta Caida, Trincadeira

🍷 2–5 years

✓ *Heredad de Cartuxa* • *Pêra Manca* (branco)

GRACIOSA IPR
Map (no.23)
Rarely encountered light table wines produced on the island of Graciosa in the Azores.

🍇 Arinto, Fernão pires, Terrantez, Verdelho

GRANJA AMARELEJA IPR
Map (no.24)
The harsh climate and schistous soils of this sub-appellation of the Alentejo region can produce powerful, spicy reds, but it has yet to establish itself on export markets.

🍇 Manteudo, Moreto, Periquita, Rabo de Ovelha, Roupeiro, Trincadeira

LAFOES IPR
Map (no.25)
Light, acidic, red and white wines produced in a small area straddling the Vinho Verde and Dão regions.

🍇 Amaral, Arinto, Cerceal, Jaen

LAGOA DOC
Map (no.26)
Formerly known for fortified white wines, which are still made, but are not of interest, this sub-appellation of the Algarve does not deserve its DOC classification.

🍇 Crato branco, Negra mole, Periquita

LAGOS DOC
Map (no.27)
These Algarve wines do not deserve their DOC classification.

🍇 Boal branco, Negra mole, Periquita

MADEIRA DOC
Map (no.28)
See The styles of Madeira, p.384

MOURA IPR
Map (no.29)
Cool, red clay soil stretches out the grape's ripening period in this hot patch of the Alentejo, adding a certain finesse to the lush, plump fruit in these wines, which promise great things, but the appellation has not yet established itself.

🍇 Alfrocheiro, Antao vaz, Fernão pires, Moreto, Periquita, Rabo de Ovelha, Roupeiro, Trincadeira

OBIDOS IPR
Map (no.30)
The white wines from this area have traditionally been distilled, but the firm, cedary-oaky reds might have potential.

🍇 Arinto, Bastardo, Camarate (possibly the same as Castelao nacional), Fernão pires, Periquita, Rabo de Ovelha, Tinta miúda, Vital

PALMELA IPR
Map (no.31)
The Palmela area was first made famous by the Joao Pires off-dry white made from early-picked Muscat grapes, but it is equally good for full-bodied reds and the inspired, high-volume Joao Pires now claims the much larger Terras do Sado appellation, as have others, hence there are no recommendations, despite the excellent wines made here.

🍇 Alfrocheiro, Arinto, Fernão pires, Muscat d'Alexandrie (*syn.* Moscatel de Setúbal), Periquita, Rabo de Ovelha, Tamarez, Tinta amarela (*syn.* Espadeiro, but no connection with the Espadeiro of Vinho Verde)

PICO IPR
Map (no.32)
Rarely encountered fortified wines produced on the island of Pico in the Azores.

🍇 Arinto, Terrantez, Verdelho

PINHEL IPR
Map (no.33)
In the Beiras region, just south of the Douro, Pinhel makes dry, full, and earthy-tasting white wines, mostly sold to sparkling-wine producers.

🍇 Arinto, Assario branco (*syn.* Arinto do Dao), Bastardo, Codo, Fonte-cal, Marufo, Rufete, Touriga nacional

PLANALTO MIRANDES IPR
Map (no.34)
In the Trás-os-Montes region, in the very northeastern corner of Portugal, Planalto Mirandes borders Spain, producing full-bodied reds and heavy whites.

🍇 Bastardo, Gouveio, Malvasia fina, Mourisco tinto, Rabo de ovelha (*syn.* Rabigato), Tinta amarela, Touriga francesa, Touriga nacional, Viosinho

PORT DOC
See The Styles of Port, p.380

PORTALEGRE DOC
Map (no.35)
Powerful, yet elegant, spicy reds, and rather heavy, alcoholic whites produced in the Alentejo region, adjacent to the Spanish frontier.

🍇 Aragonez, Arinto, Assário, Fernão pires, Galego, Grand noir, Manteudo, Periquita, Roupeiro, Trincadeira

PORTIMAO DOC
Map (no.36)
These Algarve wines do not deserve their DOC classification.

🍇 Crato branco, Negra mole, Periquita

REDONDO DOC
Map (no.37)
A sub-appellation within the progressive Alentejo region, Redondo shows promise for the sort of gushy, upfront, fruity reds that are popping up all over Portugal at grassroots level.

🍇 Aragonez, Fernão pires, Manteudo, Moreto, Periquita, Rabo de Ovelha, Roupeiro, Tamarez, Trincadeira

🍷 1–3 years

✓ *AC de Redondo*

REGUENGOS DOC
Map (no.38)
An up-and-coming DOC in the Alentejo, Reguengos is already producing both gluggy and much finer reds, plus increasingly good whites, making it an appellation to watch.

🍇 Aragonez, Manteudo, Moreto, Periquita, Perrum, Rabo de Ovelha, Roupeiro, Trincadeira

🍷 1–3 years (new-wave, fruity style) 2–5 years (others)

✓ *AC de Reguengos* (tinto) • *JP Vinhos* (Quinta da Anfora)

RIBATEJO VR
This large province is sandwiched between Estremadura and Alentejo, and includes the following IPRs: Almeirim, Cartaxo (in part), Chamusca, Coruche, Santarém, Tomar, and Valada do Ribatejo. The temperate climate and rich alluvial plains of the River Tagus encourage high yields, making this the second most important wine region in Portugal. Some very good wines are made by those who restrict yields, particularly by Peter Bright in collaboration with the Fuiza family's vineyards.

🍇 Arinto, Cabernet sauvignon, Camarate (possibly the same as Castelao nacional), Carignan, Chardonnay, Esgana-cão, Fernão pires, Jampal, Malvasia fina, Malvasia rei (possibly the same as Palomino), Merlot, Periquita, Pinot noir, Rabo de Ovelha, Sauvignon, Syrah, Tamarez, Tinta amarela (Trincadeira preta), Tinta miúda, Touriga nacional, Trincadeira das Pratas (*syn.* Tamarez d'Azeitao), Ugni blanc (*syn.* Talia), Vital

🍷 1–5 years (reds), 1–3 years (whites)

✓ *Bright Brothers* • *Falua* • *Fuiza* • *Quinta do Lagoalva* • *Terra de Lobos*

RIOS DO MINHO VR

A sort of *vin de pays* Vinhos Verdes, except that this appellation also allows for still table wines from foreign varieties. Predictably lightweight.

🍇 Alvarinho, Arinto (*syn.* Paderna), Avesso, Azal branco, Azal tinto, Batoca, Borracal, Brancelho (*syn.* Alvarelho), Cabernet sauvignon, Chardonnay, Espadeiro, Loureiro, Merlot, Padreiro de Basto, Pedral, Rabo de Ovelha, Riesling, Trajadura, Vinhao (possibly the same as Sousao)

SANTARÉM IPR
Map (no.39)

A new appellation for the area around the capital of the Ribatejo region, Santarém should begin to establish itself over the next few years.

🍇 Arinto, Castelao nacional, Fernão pires, Periquita, Preto martinho, Rabo de Ovelha, Tinta amarela (Trincadeira preta), Trincadeira das Pratas (*syn.* Tamarez d'Azeitao), Ugni blanc (*syn.* Talia), Vital

SETÚBAL DOC
Moscatel de Setúbal
Map (no.40)

This style of fortified Muscat wine is believed to have been created by José-Maria da Fonseca, the old-established company that still has a quasi-monopoly over its production today. There are various wood-aged styles (5- or 6-Year-Old is best for freshness and the grapey-apricoty varietal character, while 20- or 25-Year-Old is darker and far more complex with a raisiny-nutty-caramel-apricoty intensity), but single-vintage Setúbal is top of the range.

🍇 Muscat d'Alexandrie (*syn.* Moscatel de Setúbal), Moscatel do Douro, Moscatel Roxo plus up to 30% Arinto, Boais, Diagalves, Fernão pires, Malvasia, Olho de lebre, Rabo de ovelha, Roupeiro, Tália, Tamarez, Vital

🍷— Upon purchase (but will last many years)

✓ *J. M. Fonseca*

TAVIRA DOC
Map (no.41)

These Algarve wines do not deserve their DOC classification.

🍇 Crato branco, Negra mole, Periquita

TERRAS DO SADO VR

Probably the cleverest appellation the Portuguese could conjure up, Terras do Sado covers a fairly large area fanning out from the Sado estuary far beyond the Setúbal Peninsular, where a good many innovative wines originated, but their development had been threatened by the urban sprawl south of Lisbon. If such wines take up the Terras do Sado appellation, they can be sourced from a much wider area. Joao Pires, Periquita, Quinta de Camarate, and Quinta da Bacalhôa have all claimed this humble VR status without it affecting the prices they command, which has made Terras do Sado an attractive appellation for future new wines.

🍇 **RED** At least 50% Aragonez, Cabernet sauvignon, Merlot, Moscatel roxo, Periquita (Castelao francês) and Touriga nacional, plus up to 50% Alfrocheiro preto, Alicante bouschet, Bastardo, Carignan, Grand noir, Monvedro, Moreto, Tinta miúda

🍇 **WHITE** At least 50% Arinto, Chardonnay, Fernão pires, Malvasia fina, Muscat

d'Alexandrie (*syn.* Moscatel de Setúbal) and Roupeiro, plus up to 50% Antao vaz, Esgana-cão, Sauvignon, Rabo de Ovelha, Trincadeira das Pratas (*syn.* Tamarez d'Azeitao), Ugni blanc (*syn.* Talia)

🍷— 1–3 years (new-wave style), 2–5 years (others)

✓ *J. M. Fonseca* (Joao Pires, Periquita, Quinta de Camarate tinto) • *JP Vinhos* (Quinta da Bacalhôa, Cova da Ursa)

TOMAR IPR
Map (no.42)

Red and white wines grown on limestone slopes of the right bank of the river Tagus in the Ribatejo region.

🍇 Arinto, Baga, Castelao nacional, Fernão pires, Malvasia, Periquita, Rabo de Ovelha, Ugni blanc (*syn.* Talia)

TORRES VEDRAS IPR
Map (no.43)

Originally called simply "Torres" until Miguel Torres objected, these high-yielding vineyards in the Estremadura region have traditionally supplied the largest producers with bulk wines for their high-volume branded *vinho de mesa.*

🍇 Arinto, Camarate (possibly the same as Castelao nacional), Fernão pires, Graciano (*syn.* Tinta miúda), Jampal, Mortágua, Periquita, Rabo de Ovelha, Seara nova, Vital

TRAS-OS-MONTES VR

The province of Trás-os-Montes is situated in northeastern Portugal, and encompasses the IPRs of Chaves, Valpaços and Planalto-Mirandês. The style of wine ranges from light-bodied in the higher altitude vineyards to full-bodied and alcoholic in the south. But the most important wine made in terms of volume is semi-sweet, semi-sparkling rosé.

🍇 Bastardo, Cabernet franc, Cabernet sauvignon, Chardonnay, Donzelinho, Gewürztraminer, Gouveio, Malvasia fina, Merlot, Mourisco tinto, Pinot noir, Rabo de ovelha (*syn.* Rabigato), Sauvignon blanc, Sémillon, Tempranillo (*syn.* Tinta roriz), Tinta amarela, Tinta barroca, Tinta cão, Touriga francesa, Touriga nacional, Viosinho

🍷— 1–3 years (new-wave style), 2–5 years (others)

✓ *Casal de Valle Pradinhos*
• *Quintas dos Bons Ares*

VALPAÇOS IPR
Map (no.44)

Firm reds and slightly *pétillant* rosés from the upper reaches of the Tua, a tributary of the Douro, in the Trás-os-Montes region.

🍇 Bastardo, Boal, Codega (possibly the same as Roupeiro), Cornifesto, Fernão pires, Gouveio, Malvasia fina, Mourisco tinto, Rabo de ovelha (*syn.* Rabigato), Tempranillo (*syn.* Tinta roriz), Tinta amarela, Tinta carvalha, Touriga francesa, Touriga nacional

VAROSA IPR
Map (no.45)

Like Pinhel, this Beiras sub-appellation has yet to establish a reputation above that of being a traditional source of base wines for the sparkling-wine industry.

🍇 Alvarelhao, Arinto, Borrado das moscas, Cercial, Chardonnay, Fernão pires, Folgosao, Gouveio, Malvasia fina, Pinot blanc, Pinot noir, Tempranillo (*syn.* Tinta roriz), Tinta barroca, Touriga francesa, Touriga nacional

VIDIGUEIRA DOC
Map (no.46)

This appellation takes its name from one of three towns around which vineyards flourish on volcanic soils, while the name of the town itself is derived from the word *videira*, meaning "wine", illustrating how long vines have been growing in this part of the Alentejo.

🍇 Alfrocheiro, Antao vaz, Manteudo, Moreto, Periquita, Perrum, Rabo de Ovelha, Roupeiro, Trincadeira

VINHO VERDE DOC

The vines literally grow on trees, up telegraph poles, and along fences – on anything that takes them above the ground. Training the vine in such a way enables the smallholders – and there are more than 60,000 of them in the Minho – to grow the cabbages, maize, and beans that the families survive on, and to produce grapes, which are either sold to large wineries or made into wine locally and sold to tourists. Genuine Vinho Verde is sharp, may be slightly fizzy, but should always be totally dry, either delicately or raspingly dry, depending primarily on the grape varieties used. The best two grape varieties are Alvarinho and Lourciro. The Alvarinho is a low-cropping variety that is more at home in the northern part of the Minho, between the Lima Valley and the Spanish border. It produces the most substantial Vinhos Verdes, with alcohol levels of 12.5 per cent ABV, compared to the norm of 9.5–10 per cent. Palacio da Brejoeira is the yardstick for this grape, and widely considered to be a class apart from any other Vinho Verde. The Loureiro is a heavier-cropping variety, producing aromatic wines. Vinhao is the most successful grape for red Vinho Verde, followed by Azal tinto and Espadeiro, and the best examples of these deep-purple wines have a peppery smack to them, even if it is quickly washed down the throat in a fizzy rush.

🍇 Alvarinho, Arinto (*syn.* Paderna), Avesso, Azal, Azal tinto, Brancelho (*syn.* Alvarelho), Borracal, Espadeiro, Loureiro, Perdal, Trajadura, Vinhao (possibly the same as Sousao)

🍷— Upon purchase (9–18 months maximum)

✓ **Red single-quintas** *Casa do Valle*
• *Ponte de Lima*

White single-quintas *Casa de Sezim*
• *Morgadio de Torre* • *Palacio da Brejoeira*
• *Ponte de Lima* • *Quinta de Azevedo*
• *Quinta de Franqueira* • *Quinta da Tamariz* • *Solar de Bouças*

White commercial blends *Cepa Velha* (Alvarinho) • *Chello* • *Gazela* • *Grinalda*

Trajadura da Aveleda

VINHO VERDE
REGIÃO DEMARCADA
DENOMINAÇÃO DE ORIGEM CONTROLADA
BRANCO SECO
ENGARRAFADO NA REGIÃO
BOTTLED AND SHIPPED BY:
AVELEDA - SOC. AGRICOLA E COMERCIAL DA QUINTA DA AVELEDA, S.A.
PENAFIEL

75 cl   *product of portugal*   10% vol.

PORT: THE DOURO VALLEY

No two neighbouring districts could produce wines of more contrasting styles than the deep-coloured, rich, sweet, warm, and spicy fortified Port of Portugal's Douro Valley, and the light, water-white, sharply dry, semi-sparkling Vinho Verde of the Minho region.

"IT SHOULD FEEL LIKE liquid fire in the stomach... it should burn like inflamed gunpowder... should have the tint of ink... it should be like the sugar of Brazil in sweetness and the spices of India in aromatic flavour." These words were written in 1754 by the agents for the Association of Port Wine Shippers, and such vivid accounts of Port remain a fair description of the great after-dinner wine we know today.

THE ORIGIN OF PORT

It is hard to imagine how such a wonderful winter-warming drink as Port could ever have been conceived in such a hot and sunny country as Portugal. Popular belief has it that that it was not the Portuguese but the British who were responsible for Port; however, this is not entirely accurate. We can thank the Portuguese for dreaming up this most classic of fortified wines; the British merely capitalized on their original idea.

In 1678, two Englishmen were sent by a Liverpool wine merchant to Viana do Castello, north of Oporto, to learn the wine trade. Holidaying up the Douro River, they were regally entertained by the Abbot of Lamego. Finding his wine "very agreeable, sweetish, and extremely smooth", they asked what made it exceptional among all others tasted on their journey. The Abbot confessed to doctoring the wine with brandy, but the Englishmen were so pleased with the result this had that they purchased the entire stock and shipped it home.

THE ORIGIN OF THE PORT TRADE

The ancient house of C.N. Kopke & Co. had been trading in Douro wines for nearly 40 years by the time the above encounter took place. Eight years before they stumbled upon the Abbot of Lamego, another Englishman named John Clark was busy building up a business that would become Warre & Co. In 1678, the same year as the encounter, Croft & Co was established, and this was followed by Quarles Harris in 1680 and Taylor's in 1692. By the time the Methuen Treaty of 1703 gave Portuguese wines preferential rates of duty in Britain, many British firms had set up trade in Oporto. Firms of other nationalities – Dutch, German, and French – followed, but it was the British shippers who virtually monopolized the trade, frequently abusing their power. In 1755, the Marquis of Pombal, who had assumed almost dictatorial powers over Portugal some five years before, put a curb on their activities through the Board of Trade. The privileges enjoyed by British merchants under two 100-year-old treaties were restricted. He also established the Oporto Wine Company, endowing it with the sort of powers to which the British had been accustomed.

GRAPE PICKERS NEAR AMARANTE, SOUTHERN MINHO
Grape pickers use ladders with buckets fixed to them to harvest the overhead bunches.

THE DOURO AND THE MINHO, *see also p.371*
These two northern areas produce the celebrated Port and Vinho Verde. The river Douro has long been crucial to the Port trade.

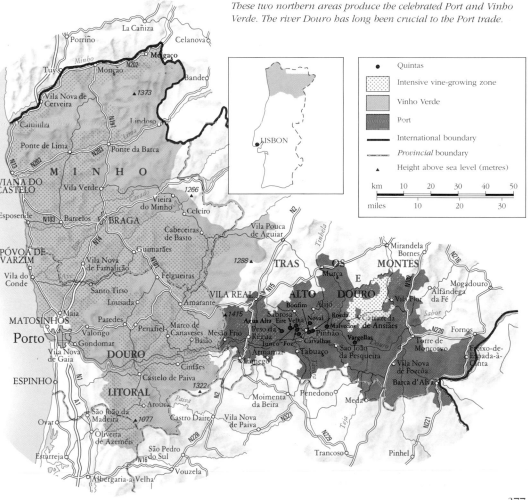

Even after several centuries, the Port trade is still dominated by the British. It is even possible to generalize about the stylistic difference between the wines of British- and Portuguese-owned Port houses. The British tend to go for bigger, darker, sweeter, fruit-driven wines and have made Vintage Port their particular niche, while the Portuguese opt for lighter, elegant, more mellow styles, the best of which are exquisitely aged Tawnies. At one time, some Portuguese houses rarely even declared a vintage, as they majored on Tawny. When they did, the wines were so much lighter in style that export countries often dismissed them as inferior. Although a few were indeed inferior, many were just different. Now, of course, world markets demand that if they are to survive, the Portuguese houses must declare as vintages often as British-owned houses.

When considering stylistic differences between Vintage Port and the lighter, tawny styles, it is probably more accurate to categorize the fuller, fatter Vintage Port as North European, not simply British, because this style is also preferred by Dutch, German, and French port houses.

HOW PORT IS MADE
If any wine is perceived as having been "trodden", then it is Port. This is perhaps because the pressing and winemaking traditionally takes place in the vineyards where, until relatively recently, affairs

This infuriated the British, but their protests were to no avail and Pombal went on to instigate many worthy, if unpopular, reforms, including limiting the Douro's production area to the finest vineyards, the banning of elderberries for colouring the wine, and the outlawing of manure, which reduced yields but greatly improved quality.

The production of Port had not been perfected at this time. Fifty years after the encounter with the Abbot of Lamego, the trade had widely accepted the practice of brandying, but the importance of when, and in what quantity, to administer the brandy had not been recognized. Ironically, the Abbot's wine was superior because he had added the brandy during, and not after, the fermentation, thus interrupting, or "muting", the process with the natural sweetness that had so attracted the two Englishmen.

THE HISTORIC BARCO RABELO
Based on the Viking warship, these flat-bottomed boats, loaded with pipes of Port, would sail for Oporto on the hazardous journey from the Upper Douro.

THE QUINTA CLASSIFICATION

A *quinta* is a wine-producing estate or vineyard. The Douro Valley covers 243,000 hectares (600,000 acres), of which 33,000 hectares (82,000 acres) are cultivated. Within this area, there are approximately 80,000 individual vineyards or *quintas* owned by 29,620 growers. Each vineyard is classified according to a points system allocated for the categories listed below. The better the classification, the higher official price a vineyard receives for its grapes and the greater its permitted production.

CATEGORY	MINIMUM	MAXIMUM
Location	-50	+600
Aspect	1,000	+250
Altitude; lowest is best	(-900)	(+150)
Gradient; steepest is best	(-100)	(+100)
Soil	-350	+100
Schist	(N/A)	(+100)
Granite	(-350)	(N/A)
Mixture	(-150)	(N/A)
Microclimate; sheltered best	0	+60
Vine varieties; official classification	-300	+150
Age of vines; oldest is best	0	+60
Vine density; lowest is best	-50	+50
Productivity; lowest is best	-900	+120
Vineyard maintenance	-500	+100
TOTAL	**-3,150**	**+1,490**

Vineyards are classified from **A**, for best, to **F**, for worst, as follows:
Class A (1,200 points or more); **Class B** (1,001–1,199 points);
Class C (801–1,000 points); **Class D** (601–800 points);
Class E (400–600 points); **Class F** (400 points or below).

CLASS A
Aciprestes (Royal Oporto), *Atayde* (Cockburn), *Bomfin* (Dow), *Bom-Retiro* (Ramos-Pinto), *Carvalhas* (Royal Oporto), *Carvalheira* (Calem & Filho), *Boa vista* (Offley Forrester), *Corte* (privately owned, managed by Delaforce), *Corval* (Royal Oporto), *Cruzeiro St. Antonio* (Guimaraens), Cavadinha (Warre), *Eira Velha* (privately owned, managed by Cockburn), *Ervamoira* (Ramos-Pinto), *Fontela* (Cockburn), *Fonte Santa* (Kopke), *Foz* (Calem & Filho), *La Rosa* (privately owned), *Lobata* (Barros, Almeida), *Madalena* (Warre), *Malvedos* (Graham), *Mesquita* (Barroa, Almeida), *Monte Bravo* (privately owned, managed by Dow), *Nova* (privately owned, managed by Warre), *Panascal* (Guimaraens), *Passa Douro* (Sandeman), *Sagrado* (Càlem & Filho), *Santo Antonio* (Càlem & Filho), *Sibio* (Royal Oporto), *St.Luiz* (Kopke), *Terra Feita* (Taylor's), *Tua* (Cockburn), *Vale de Mendiz* (Sandeman), *Vale Dona Maria* (Smith Woodhouse), *Vargellas* (Taylor's), *Vedial* (Càlem & Filho), *Zimbro* (privately owned, managed by Dow)

CLASS A–B
Aradas (Noval), *Avidagos* (Da Silva), *Casa Nova* (Borges & Irmao), *Ferra dosa* (Borges & Irmao), *Hortos* (Borges & Irmao), *Junco* (Borges & Irmao), *Leda* (Ferreira), *Marco* (Noval), *Meao* (Ferreira family), *Noval* (Noval),

Porto (Ferreira), *Roeda* (Croft), *Seixo* (Ferreira), *Silho* (Borges & Irmao), *Silval* (Noval), *Soalheira* (Borges & Irmao), *Urqueiras* (Noval), *Velho Roncao* (Pocas), *Vezuvio* (Symington family)

CLASS B
Carvoeira (Barros, Almeida), *Dona Matilde* (Barros, Almeida), *Laranjeira* (Sandeman), *San Domingos* (Ramos-Pinto), *Urtiga* (Ramos-Pinto)

CLASS B–C
Sta Barbara (Pocas)

CLASS C
Porrais (Ferreira family), *Quartas* (Pocas), *Valado* (Ferreira family)

CLASS C AND D
Sidro (Royal Oporto)

CLASS C,D AND E
Granja (Royal Oporto)

CLASS D
Casal (Sandeman), *Confradeiro* (Sandeman)

CLASS NOT DISCLOSED
Agua Alta (Churchill), *Alegria* (Santos), *Cachão* (Messias), *Côtto* (Champalimaud), *Crasto* (privately owned), *Fojo* (privately owned), *Forte* (Delaforce), *Infantado* (privately owned), *Rosa* (privately owned), *Val de Figueria* (Càlem & Filho), *Vau* (Sandeman)

were conducted on farms in a rather rustic style. Nowadays, few Ports are trodden, although several houses have showpiece *lagars* – troughs used for crushing grapes – for tourists. Many houses have "autovinificators" – rather antiquated devices that rely on the build-up of carbonic gas pressure given off during fermentation to force the juice up and over the *manta* of grape skins. The object is to extract the maximum amount of colouring matter from the skins, because so much is lost by fortification. It is possible also to achieve this using special vats and several have been installed throughout the Port industry.

Fermentation and fortification
The initial fermentation phase of Port differs little from that in the rest of the world, except that vinification temperatures are often as high as 32°C (90°F). This has no detrimental effect on Port and probably accounts for its chocolaty, high pH complexity. When a level of about six to eight per cent alcohol has been achieved, the wine is fortified, unlike Sherry, where the fermentation process is allowed to complete its natural course. Port derives its sweetness from unfermented sugars, whereas sweet Sherries are totally dry wines to which a syrupy concentrate is added. The timing of the addition of brandy is dependent on the sugar reading, not the alcohol level. When the sweetness of the fermenting juice has dropped to approximately 90 grams of sugar per litre, the alcoholic strength will normally be between six and eight per cent, but this varies according to the richness of the juice, which in turn is dependent on the grape variety, where it is grown, and the year.

The use of the word "brandy" is somewhat misleading. It is not, in fact, brandy, but a clear, flavourless, grape-distilled spirit of 77 per cent alcohol, known in Portugal as *aguardente*. It adds alcoholic strength to a Port, but not aroma or flavour. *Aguardente* is produced either from wines made in southern Portugal, or from excess production in the Douro itself. Its price and distribution to each shipper are strictly rationed. On average 110 litres (24 gallons) is added for every 440 litres (97 gallons) of wine, making a total of 550 litres (121 gallons) – the capacity of a Douro pipe, a specific size of cask used for shipping wine from the valley to the lodges at Vila Nova de Gaia. A drier Port has a slightly longer fermentation and requires less than 100 litres (22 gallons) of *aguardente*, while a particularly sweet (or *geropiga*) Port is muted with as much as 135 litres (30 gallons). If gauged correctly, the brandy which has been added to arrest the fermentation will eventually harmonize with the fruit and the natural sweetness of the wine. Our conception of balance between fruit, alcohol, and sweetness is, of course, greatly affected by what we are used to drinking. In deepest Douro a local farmer is likely to use a far higher proportion of alcohol for Port drunk by him than for the Port he makes for export. Generally, British shippers prefer more fruit and less brandy but all commercial shippers, British or Portuguese, would consider the domestic port of a Douro farmer to lack sufficient body to match the brandy.

Maturation and blending
Until 1986, all Port had by law to be matured and bottled at Vila Nova de Gaia on the left bank of the Douro estuary opposite Oporto. At some 75 kilometres (47 miles) from the region of production, this was like insisting that all Champagne be blended, bottled, and disgorged at Le Havre. The law bestowing Vila Nova de Gaia was made in 1756 and it was ostensibly created by and for the big shippers, as it effectively prevented small growers from exporting their wine, as they could not possibly afford the expense of a lodge at Vila Nova de Gaia. By the late 18th century, most of the famous Port names were already established, and this restrictive law enabled them to maintain the status quo, especially on the lucrative international markets. All this has changed, and though most Ports still come from the big shippers' lodges, many new Ports now find their way on to the market direct from privately owned Douro *quintas*.

THE STYLES OF
PORT

Note With the exception of White Port, there are just two basic styles from which all variants stem: Ruby and Tawny. What distinguishes these two styles is bottle-ageing for Rubies and cask-ageing for Tawnies.

RUBY STYLES

These are, in order of price and quality, Ruby (including Fine Old Ruby, Reserve, etc.), Vintage Character, Late-Bottled Vintage, Crusted, Single-*Quinta*, and Vintage. All but the cheapest Rubies improve in bottle, many shedding a deposit that requires decanting before serving.

BASIC RUBY PORT

The cheapest red Ports are Rubies with less than a year in cask and often no time at all. Sold soon after bottling, they do not improve if kept. Inexpensive Rubies have a basic, pepper-grapey flavour that can be quite fiery. Superior-quality wines are blended from various vintages with up to four years in cask, giving a more homogenous taste, though they should still have the fruity-spice and warmth of a young Ruby.

⌐— Upon purchase

✓ *Cockburn's* (Special Reserve) • *Fonseca* (Bin 27) • *Graham's* (Six Grapes) • *Quinta de la Rosa* (Finest Reserve) • *Warre's* (Warrior)

VINTAGE CHARACTER PORT

The suggestion that these wines, blended from various years and matured in cask for up to four years, have a "Vintage" character is misleading. They may be fine Ports, but the character is that of a genuine Fine Old Ruby, not a Vintage Port.

⌐— Upon purchase

✓ *Cálem* • *Churchill's* • *Ferreira* • *Royal Oporto* (The Navigator's) • *Sandeman's* (Signature)

CRUSTED PORT
or CRUSTING PORT

The greatest non-vintage Ruby Port, this is a blend of very high-quality wines from two or more years, given up to four years in cask and, ideally, at least three years in bottle. Like Vintage, it throws a deposit in bottle, hence the name. Ready to drink when purchased, providing it is carefully decanted, Crusting Port benefits from acclimatizing to new storage conditions, when it will shed further sedimentation before resuming the much slower process of maturation.

⌐— 1–10 years

✓ *Churchill's* • *Martinez* • *Smith Woodhouse*

LATE-BOTTLED
VINTAGE PORT (LBV)

A Late-Bottled Vintage is a pure Vintage Port from a good, but not necessarily great year. LBVs are usually made in lighter, generally undeclared years. Lighter, more precocious vintages are usually chosen for this less expensive category, and the wines are given between four and six years in cask to bring them on even quicker. LBVs are thus ready for drinking when sold, but will continue to improve in bottle for another five or six years.

⌐— 5–10 years

✓ *Burmester* • *Churchill's* • *Graham's* • *Quinta de la Rosa* • *Ramos-Pinto* • *Smith Woodhouse* • *Warre's*

SINGLE-*QUINTA* PORT

A wine from a single vineyard, this may be a classic Vintage Port from an established house or a special release from an undeclared vintage. Most Single-*Quinta* ports are as accessible as LBV because, after bottling, the wines are stored until more or less ready to drink. Many Single-*Quinta* and LBV Ports are the same age, although the former is aged longer *after* bottling, while the latter is aged longer *before*. With interest in these Ports increasing, the change in the law allowing Port to be matured at the *quintas*, and the fact that individual domaine wines are seen as more prestigious, this category could one day become more esteemed than Vintage Port itself.

⌐— 8–25 years

✓ *Cálem* (Quinta de Foz) • *Champalimaud* (Quinta do Cotto) • *Churchill's* (Quinta de Agua Alta) • *Ferreira* • (Quinta do Seixo) • *Fonseca* (Quinta do Panascal) • *Niepoort* (Quinta do Passadouro) • *Quinta de la Rosa* • *Quinta de Vesuvio* • *Quinta do Noval* • *Quinta do Sagrado* • *Ramos-Pinto* (Quinta da Urtiga) • *Taylor's* (Quinta de Vargellas) • *Warre's* (Quinta da Cavadinha)

VINTAGE PORT

By law, a Vintage Port must be bottled within two years. Maturation in bottle is more reductive than cask-ageing and the wine that results has a certain fruitiness that will not be found in any Fine Old Tawny. When mature, a fine Vintage Port is a unique taste experience with a heady bouquet and a sultry flavour. A warming feeling seems to follow the wine down the throat – more an "afterglow" than an aftertaste. The grape and spirit are totally integrated and the palate is near to bursting with warm, spicy-fruit flavours.

⌐— 12–30 years (but see individual producers)

✓ *Churchill's* • *Champalimaud* (Quinta do Cotto) • *Ferreira* • *Fonseca* • *Fonseca Guimaraens* • *Gould Campbell* • *Niepoort* • *Quinta do Noval* (especially Naçional) • *Taylor's*

TAWNY STYLES

These are, in ascending order of price and quality, Tawny Port (including Fine Old Tawny), Aged Tawny (10-, 20-, 30-, and Over 40 Years Old), Single-Quinta Tawny, and Vintage-Dated Tawny (Colheita) Ports. Ports in the last three categories can be equal in price and quality.

BASIC TAWNY PORT

These are often a blend of red and white Ports. Some skilful blends can be very good and have even the most experienced Port-tasters guessing whether they are Tawny by definition or blending. On the whole it is wise to pay more to ensure you are buying an authentically aged product. The best Tawnies are usually eight years old, although this is seldom indicated.

⌐— Upon purchase

✓ *Delaforce* (His Eminence's Choice) • *Dow's* (Boardroom) • *Warre's* (Nimrod)

AGED TAWNY PORT

These 10-, 20-, 30- Year-Old and Over 40 Years Old Ports are traditionally known as "Fine Old Tawnies" (FOT), but like Fine Old Rubies, there are no legal requirements. By constant racking over a period of 10, 20, or more years, Port fades to a tawny colour, falls bright, and will throw no further deposit. It assumes a smooth, silky texture, a voluptuous, mellow, nutty flavour, and complex after-aromas that can include freshly ground coffee, caramel, chocolate, raisins, nutmeg, and cinnamon. The years are merely an indication of age; in theory, a 20-Year-Old Tawny could be just a year old, if it could fool the Port Wine Institute. In practice, most blends probably have an age close to that indicated. Most Tawny Port experts find 20-Year-Old the ideal Tawny, but 30- and Over 40 Years Old Tawnies are not necessarily past it. The only relatively negative aspect of a good 30- or Over 40 Years Old is that it will be more like a liqueur than a Port.

⌐— Upon purchase

✓ **10-Year-Old** *Cálem* • *Churchill's* • *Cockburn's* • *Croft* • *Dow's* • *Ferreira* (Quinta do Porto) • *Fonseca* • *Graham's* • *Niepoort* • *Offley* (Baron Forrester) • *Ramos-Pinto* • *Robertson's* (Pyramid) • *Smith Woodhouse* • *Taylor's* • *Warre's* (Sir William)
20-Year-Old *Barros Almeida* • *Burmester* • *Cálem* • *Cockburn's* • *Croft* • (Director's Reserve) • *Dow's* • *Ferreira* (Duque de Bragança) • *Fonseca* • *Graham's* • *Niepoort* • *Noval* • *Offley* (Baron Forrester) • *Robertson's* (Privateer Reserve) • *Sandeman* (Imperial) • *Taylor's*
30-Year-Old *Cálem* • *Croft* • *Dow's* • *Fonseca* • *Niepoort* • *Ramos-Pinto*
Over 40 Years Old *Cálem* • *Fonseca* • *Graham's* • *Noval* • *Taylor's*

SINGLE-QUINTA TAWNY PORT

Although most single-vineyard Ports are Vintage and Ruby in style, some are made as Tawny, either with an indicated age or Vintage-dated.

⌐— Upon purchase

✓ **10-Year-Old**: *Quinta do Sagrado* • *Ramos-Pinto* (Quinta da Ervamoira) **20-Year-Old**: *Ramos-Pinto* (Quinta do Bom-Retiro) **Vintage-Dated**: *Borges' Quinta do Junco*

VINTAGE-DATES
TAWNY *or* COLHEITA PORT

These excellent-value, often sublime, cask-aged wines are from a single vintage, and may have 20 or 50 years in cask. They must not be confused with the plumper, fruitier Vintage Ports. There should be an indication of when the wine was bottled or a term such as "Matured in Wood". Some Vintage Ports are simply labelled "Vintage" and Tawnies "Colheita". Other clues are "Reserve", "Reserva", or "Bottled in" dates.

⌐— Upon purchase

✓ *Barros Almeida* • *Burmester* • *Cálem* • *Offley* (Baron Forrester) • *Niepoort* • *Noval*

WHITE PORT

Most dry White Ports taste like flabby Sherry, but there are some interesting sweet ones such as Ferreira's Superior White, which is creamy-soft and delicious. Truly sweet White Port is often labelled Lagrima. Niepoort pure Moscatel can make an nice alternative to Moscatel de Setúbal.

⌐— Upon purchase

✓ *Ferreira's Superior White*

THE WINE PRODUCERS OF THE
DOURO VALLEY

Note The age range for "when to drink" refers to the optimal enjoyment of Vintage Ports and appears only when this style is recommended. When the entire range is recommended, this includes all wines with the exception of the most basic Ruby and Tawny or any White Port, unless otherwise stated.

BARROS
Barros Almeida
★ ✿ ❤

Manuel de Barros started work as an office boy at Almeida & Co., ending up not only owning the company, but also building a Port empire, as he and his descendants took over Douro Wine Shippers and Growers, Feist, Feuerheerd, Hutcheson, Kopke, Santos Junior, and Viera de Sousa. Only Kopke and Barros Almeida itself retain any form of independence, and the others have become little more than brands.

✓ *20-Year-Old Tawny*
- *Vintage-Dated Tawny*
- *Colheitas*

BORGES & IRMAO
✗

Established in 1884, the Portuguese-owned house of Borges & Irmao is best known for its Soalheira 10-Year-Old and Roncão 20-Year-Old Tawnies, but the quality has suffered under a lack of direction from Portuguese government ownership.

BURMESTER
★ ❤

Of Anglo-German origin, Burmester is an underrated house that is best for mature Tawny styles, but also makes good Vintage.

✓ *Late-Bottled • Vintage*
- *20-Year-Old Tawny*
- *Colheitas • Vintage*

CÁLEM
★

Cálem was established in 1859 and is still owned by the Cálem family, who consistently produce elegant Tawny, single-*quinta*, and Vintage Port.

🍷 15–25 years

✓ *10-, 20-, 30-, and 40-Year-Old Tawny • Vintage Character*
- *Quinta de Foz • Vintage*

CHAMPALIMAUD
Quinta do Cotto
★ ☆

Although Miguel Montez Champalimaud can trace his family's viticultural roots in the Douro Valley back to the 13th century, he did not produce his first Port until 1982, when it became the world's first estate-bottled single-*quinta* Port, making him the fastest-rising star among the new wave of privately owned grower Ports.

🍷 12–25 years

✓ *Quinta do Cotto*

CHURCHILL'S
★ ☆

Established in 1981 by Johnny Graham, a member of the Graham's Port family who was married to Caroline (*née* Churchill), this was the first Port shipper to be established in recent times, and it has quickly risen to the top.

🍷 12–25 years

✓ *Entire range*

COCKBURN'S
★ ★

Founded in 1815 by Robert Cockburn, who married Mary Duff, a lady much admired by Lord Byron, this house is still British-owned (Allied-Domecq). Although Cockburn's best-selling Special Reserve and Fine Old Ruby are produced in vast quantities, they are exceptionally good and consistent in quality as are the Vintage Ports. *See also* Martinez.

🍷 15–30 years

✓ *Entire range*

CROFT
★

To many people, Croft is best known for its Sherries, yet it is one of the oldest Port houses, having started production in 1678. Its elegant style best suits Fine Old Tawnies, more characteristic of a Portuguese-owned house than a British-owned one. In all but a few years, its Vintage Ports are among the lightest. *See also* Morgan.

✓ *10-, 20-, and 30-Year-Old Tawny*

CRUZ
✗

The lacklustre quality of Cruz says a lot about the average Frenchman's appreciation of the world's greatest fortified wine. France takes nearly half of all the Port currently exported and this is the best-selling brand. The French could be forgiven if they cooked with it, but they actually drink the stuff.

DELAFORCE
★

Although owned by IDV (Grand Met) since 1968, and thus a sister company to both Croft and Morgan, this house still retains a certain amount of independence, with fifth-generation David Delaforce very much in day-to-day control. The style of Delaforce is very much on the lighter-bodied side, which particularly suits His Eminence's Choice, an exquisite old Tawny with a succulent balance as well as a lingering fragrance.

✓ *His Eminence's Choice Superb Old Tawny*

DOURO WINE SHIPPERS AND GROWERS
See Barros Almeida

DIEZ
Diez Hermanos
❓

Interesting recent vintages make this low-key producer one to watch.

DOW'S
Silva & Cosens
★ ★

Although the brand is Dow's, this firm is actually called Silva & Cosens. It was established in 1862 and James Ramsay Dow was made a partner in 1877, when his firm, Dow & Co., which had been shipping Port since 1798, was merged with Silva & Cosens. Dow's is now one of the many brands belonging to the Symington family, but consistently makes one of the very greatest Vintage Ports. *See also* Gould Campbell, Graham's, Quarles Harris, Smith Woodhouse, Warre's.

🍷 18–35 years

✓ *Entire range*

FEIST
See Barros Almeida

FERREIRA
★ ★

This house was established in 1761 and was family-owned until 1988, when it was taken over by Sogrape, the largest wine-shipper in Portugal. The brand leader in Portugal itself, Ferreira did not establish its present reputation until the mid-19th century, when it was under the control of Dona Antonia Adelaide Ferreira, who was so successful that when she died she left an estate of £3.4 million, valued at 1896 rates. Ever mindful of its Portuguese roots, it is not surprising that elegantly rich Tawny Port is Ferreira's forte. Equally consistent is the style of its Vintage Port. While this wine is typically light, smooth, and mellow, it does age beautifully.

🍷 12–30 years

✓ *Entire range*

FONSECA
Fonseca Guimaraens
★ ★ ☆

This house was originally called Fonseca, Monteiro & Co., but changed its name when it was purchased by Manuel Pedro Guimaraens in 1822. Although it has been part of Taylor, Fladgate & Yeatman since 1948, it operates in a totally independent fashion, utilizing its own *quintas* and contracted suppliers. Fonseca has always been the top-quality brand, but even its second wine, Fonseca Guimaraens, puts many Port houses to shame.

🍷 15–30 years

✓ *Entire range*

FEUERHEERD
See Barros Almeida

GOULD CAMPBELL

Although at the cheaper end of the Symington group, Gould Campbell, which was established in about 1797, produces fine, sometimes stunningly fine, Vintage Ports. *See also* Dow's, Graham's, Smith Woodhouse, Quarles Harris, Warre's.

🍷 12–25 years

✓ *Vintage*

GRAHAM'S
W & J Graham & Co
★ ★ ★ ☆

Graham's was founded as a textile business and only entered the Port trade when, in 1826, its Oporto office accepted wine in payment of a debt. Along the way, Graham's took over the firm of Smith Woodhouse and both of them became part of the Symington Port empire in 1970. Although it is the Vintage Port that earned Graham's its reputation, the entire range is of an equally high quality, category for category. *See also* Dow's, Gould Campbell, Quarles Harris, Smith Woodhouse, Warre's.

🍷 18–40 years

✓ *Entire range, including basic Six Grapes Ruby*

GUIMARAENS
See Fonseca

HUTCHESON
See Barros Almeida

KOPKE
See Barros Almeida

MARTINEZ
Martinez Gassiot
★ ☆ ❤

Martinez was founded in 1797 by Sebastian González Martinez, a Spaniard, but became affiliated to Cockburn in the early 1960s. Rather underrated, it produces small quantities of high-quality Vintage and great value Crusted, and is also a source of extraordinarily good own-label Port. *See also* Cockburn's.

🍷 12–20 years

✓ *Entire Range*

MORGAN
★ ☆ ❤

One of the oldest port houses, Morgan was purchased in 1952 by Croft (now part of IDV, thus Grand

Met), and now produces plummy Port, but is fast becoming known as an excellent source of good value, own-label Ports, particularly the 10-Year-Old Tawny. *See also* Croft.

✓ *Own-label Tawny*

NIEPOORT

★✩

This small Dutch-owned firm is best known for its elegantly rich Tawnies, especially the Colheitas, but also makes fine, underrated Vintage Port.

12–25 years

✓ *Entire range*

NOVAL

Quinta do Noval

★✩

(*Naçional* ★★★)

Originally a Portuguese house, having been founded in 1813 by Antonio José da Silva, Quinta do Noval was controlled by the Dutch van Zeller family for four generations until it was purchased by the French AXA group (*see* p.60). Although the firm is officially known as Quinta do Noval, it has been careful to market most products under the Noval brand, reserving the *quinta* name for those Ports made exclusively from the property itself.

15–35 years (25–70 years for Naçional)

✓ *Vintage • Naçional • 20- and 40-Year-Old Tawny*

OFFLEY

Offley Forrester

★✩

Established in 1737, this firm once belonged to the famous Baron Forrester, but is now owned by Sogrape. Offley makes excellent quality Colheitas, elegant Vintage Ports, and a deeper-coloured Single-Quinta Boa Vista.

12–25 years

✓ *Vintage • Boa Vista • Colheita • 10- and 20-Year-Old Tawny*

POÇAS

Poças Junior

Established in 1918, like many Portuguese-owned firms, Poças Junior started declaring Vintage Ports relatively recently (1960s) and is primarily known for its Tawnies and Colheitas. Second labels include Lopes, Pousada, and Seguro.

QUARLES HARRIS

Established in 1680 and the second-largest Port house in the 18th century, when it was taken over by Warre's, Quarles Harris is now one of the smallest Port brands under the control of the progressive Symington Group. *See also* Dow's, Gould Campbell, Graham's, Quarles Harris, Smith Woodhouse, Warre's.

QUINTA DE LA ROSA

★

Promising new estate-bottled, Single-Quinta Port. Look out for the new 10-Year-Old Tawny.

8–25 years

✓ *Finest Reserve • Late Bottled Vintage • Vintage*

QUINTA DO COTTO

See Champalimaud

QUINTA DO INFANTADO

❷

The Vintage Port from this estate-bottled single-*quinta* have been rather lightweight, but the 1991 Late-Bottled Vintage was a real gem, so it might be worth keeping an eye on future releases from this independent producer.

QUINTA DO NOVAL

See Noval

QUINTA DO VESUVIO

This massive, 400-hectare (990-acre), former Ferreira property was considered to be the greatest *quinta* in the Douro when planted in the 19th century. Owned since 1989 by the Symington group, which has already established its Vintage Port as exceptional, but how exceptional remains to be seen.

12–30 years

✓ *Vintage*

RAMOS-PINTO

★✩

Established in 1880 by Adriano Ramos-Pinto, when he was 20 years old, this firm remained in family ownership until 1990, when it was purchased by Champagne Louis Roederer. Ramos-Pinto always has produced excellent Tawnies, particularly the single-*quintas* 10- and 20-Year-Old and its Colheitas, but if the 1994 is anything to go by, Vintage Port could be its future forte.

12–25 years

✓ *Late-Bottled Vintage • Single-quinta* (Quinta da Ervamoira 10-Year-Old, Quinta do Bom-Retiro 20-Year-Old) • *Colheitas • Vintage* (from 1994)

REBELLO VALENTE

See Robertson Brothers and Co.

ROBERTSON BROTHERS AND CO.

✩

Established in 1881, this small port house is now a subsidiary of Sandeman and thus owned by Seagram. Best known for its Tawnies and, under the famous Rebello Valente label, very traditional Vintage Ports.

12–25 years

✓ *10- and 20-Year-Old Tawnies • Vintage*

ROYAL OPORTO

Real Companhia Velha

✩❷

Founded in 1756 by the Marquis de Pombal to regulate the Port trade, the future ownership of this firm looks uncertain at the time of writing, but its reputation as a good source of inexpensive Tawny and Vintage Character Ports should ensure its survival.

✓ *Vintage Character* (The Navigator's)

ROZES

❷

Part of the giant Moët-Hennessy group, Rozes has yet to establish a reputation beyond the French market, but with Moët & Chandon's globe-trotting "wine doctor" Richard Geoffroy getting involved, anything could happen.

SANDEMAN

✩

Also known for its Sherry and Madeira, Sandeman was established in 1790 and took over Robertson's and Rebello Valente in 1881, after which it acquired Diez and Offley (now part of Sogrape), and is itself owned by Seagram. The quality of Sandeman's Vintage Port is variable and seldom blockbusting, but its Tawnies are reliable, especially Imperial 20-Year-Old.

✓ *20-Year-Old Tawny* (Imperial) • *Vintage Character* (Signature)

SANTOS JUNIOR

See Barros Almeida

SILVA & COSENS

See Dow & Co.

SILVA, C DA

Small Dutch house producing inexpensive Ports; the Tawnies can sometimes be very good value.

SMITH WOODHOUSE

★✩❷

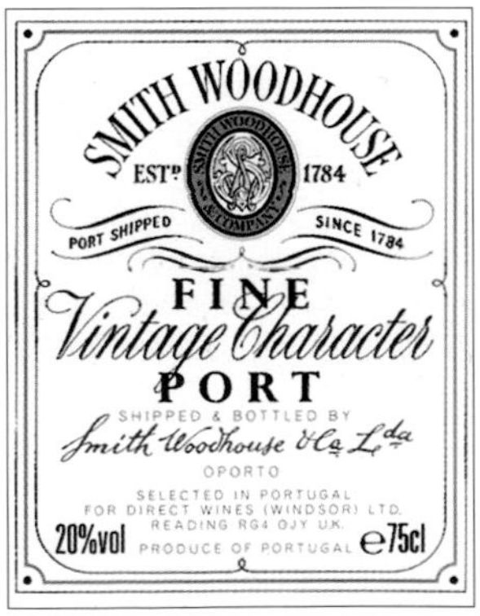

The products of this famous British Port house are not as well known in Portugal as they are on export markets, where they are much appreciated for tremendous value across the entire range, and also for some of the very greatest Vintage Ports ever made. *See also* Dow's, Gould Campbell, Graham's, Smith Woodhouse, Warre's.

12–25 years

✓ *Entire range*

SYMINGTON GROUP

The Symingtons are one of the most well-known and successful of all Port families, owning six brands, yet not one of these boasts the family name. *See also* Dow's, Gould Campbell, Graham's, Quarles Harris, Smith Woodhouse, Warre's.

TAYLOR'S

Taylor, Fladgate & Yeatman

★★★

Founded in 1692 by Job Bearsley, this house underwent no less than 21 changes of title before adopting its present one, which derives from the names of various partners: Joseph Taylor in 1816, John Fladgate in 1837, and Morgan Yeatman in 1844. At one time the firm was known as Webb, Campbell, Gray & Cano (Joseph Cano was, as it happens, the only American ever to be admitted into the partnership of a Port house). In 1744, Taylor's became the first shipper to buy a property in the Douro, but its most famous acquisition was Quinta de Vargellas in 1890, a prestigious property that provides the heart and soul of every Taylor's Vintage Port.

20–40 years

✓ *Entire range*

VIERA DE SOUSA

See Barros Almeida

WARRE'S

★★✩

Only the German-founded house of Kopke can claim to be older than Warre's, which was established in 1670, although it only assumed its present name in 1729 when William Warre entered the business. This house, which now belongs to the entrepreneurial Symington family, normally vies with Graham's, another Symington brand, as the darkest and most concentrated Vintage Port after that of Taylor's. *See also* Dow's, Gould Campbell, Graham's, Quarles Harris, Smith Woodhouse.

18–35 years

✓ *Entire range*

WEISE & KROHN

Weise & Krohn port house was originally founded in 1865 by two Norwegians of German extraction, Theodore Weise and Dankert Krohn. It has been owned by the Portuguese Carneiro family since the 1930s. It makes rather insubstantial Vintage Port, and is best known for its Tawnies.

✓ *Colheitas*

MADEIRA

The island of Madeira gives its name to the only wine in the world that must be baked in an oven! This fortified wine is deliberately heated to replicate the voyages of old during which the wine accidentally underwent maderization at equatorial temperatures.

PRINCE HENRY THE NAVIGATOR sent Captain Jào Gonçalves in search of new lands in the 15th century. The Captain's nickname was Zarco or "squinter", as he had been wounded in one eye while fighting the Moors. Although "squinter" seems an odd name for someone whose job it is to keep his eyes peeled for events on the horizon, particularly then when every sailor was worried about falling off the edge of the world, this nickname is fact not fiction. Indeed, he was so proud of being called the "squinter" that he adopted it as a surname, becoming Jào Gonçalves Zarco. Despite this impediment to his sight, Zarco not only navigated his ship safely, he actually managed to discover places. In 1418, for example, he found Madeira, although it must be admitted that he was searching for Guinea at the time. Zarco actually thought it was a cloud, but the more he squinted, the more suspicious he became:

it was always in the same position. One day he chased the cloud, sailed through it and bumped into an island. It was entirely covered in dense forest and the cloud was merely the mist of transpiration given off in the morning sun. The forest was impenetrable (Madeira means "island of woods"), so Zarco lit fires to denude areas of the island, sat back and waited. By all accounts he had a long wait, as the fires raged for seven years and consumed every bit of vegetation, infusing the permeable volcanic soil with potash, which by chance rendered it particularly suitable for vine-growing.

THE ORIGIN OF MADEIRA'S DISTINCTIVE WINE

As a source of fresh food and water, the island soon became a regular port of call for east-bound ships, which would often transport barrels of Madeira wine for sale in the Far East or Australia. As the ships journeyed through the tropics the wine was heated to a maximum of 45°C (113°F) and cooled again during the six-month voyage, giving it a very distinctive character. The winemakers of Madeira were totally unaware of this until one unsold shipment returned to the island. Since then, special ovens, called *estufas*, have evolved in order that this heating and cooling can be replicated in the *estufagem* process (cheaper wines do this in large concrete vats, while the casks of better-quality wines experience a much longer, gentler process in warm rooms). All Madeiras undergo a normal fermentation prior to the *estufagem* process. Drier wines are fortified prior to *estufagem*, the sweeter styles after.

The Future of Madeira

Although sales of Madeira are growing, they are doing so from a relatively low base. Madeira has fallen a long way from its height of fame in the 19th century, when Russia was its greatest market and one Grand Duke alone purchased the equivalent of 76,000 cases a year. Far too much Madeira today is cheap, made from the lowly Tinta negra mole grape, and sold in bulk to France, Germany, and Belgium, where the natural impulse is to cook with it. If Madeira is to survive, it must concentrate on quality by replanting with classic varieties, encouraging a new wave of independent producers, banning bulk wines, and updating the concept of Vintage Madeira. Pushing Madeira upmarket is not merely required to re-establish its reputation, it is simple logic – viticulture on this precipitous island is so labour-intensive that cheap wine makes no economic sense.

COASTAL VIEW, MADEIRA
Terraced vineyards cling to Madeira's rocky terrain, where irrigation is accomplished via a network of aqueducts.

MADEIRA, *see also p.371*
The island of Madeira, in the Atlantic Ocean west of Morocco, is famed for its fortified wine. Funchal is the capital, where many wine lodges are found.

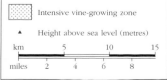

Intensive vine-growing zone

▲   Height above sea level (metres)

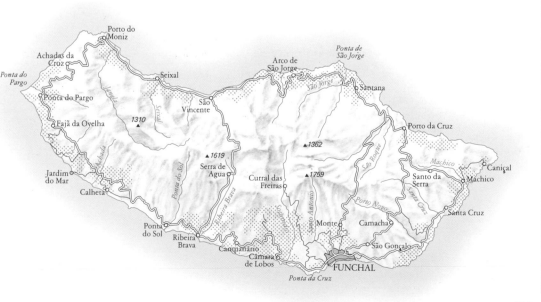

THE STYLES OF
MADEIRA

There have traditionally been four basic styles of Madeira, named after the following grape varieties: Sercial, Verdelho, Bual, and Malmsey. During the 20th century, however, the majority of Madeira produced has been blended with a high proportion of Tinta negra mole (or its variant Complexa) or of American hybrids. Since 1990, however, no hybrids have been allowed and since 1993, those wines made from Tinta negra mole may use only generic terms of sweetness (and not the stylistic terms listed below), such as *seco* (dry), *meio seco* (medium dry), *meio doce* (medium sweet), and *doce* (sweet), accompanied by descriptors such as pale, dark, full, or rich, while at least 85 per cent of a varietal wine must be made from the grape indicated.

Note Madeira should be ready to drink when sold and good Madeira will keep indefinitely, so no optimal drinking periods are given below.

FINEST *or* 3-YEAR-OLD MADEIRA

This, the lowest level of Madeira, will be the style of any Madeira whose age is not given. It consists primarily of Tinta negra mole, and some Moscatel. Three years is too short a time for any decent wine to evolve into a true Madeira and much is sold in bulk for cooking, and cannot be recommended.

RESERVE *or* 5-YEAR-OLD MADEIRA

This is the youngest age at which the noble varieties (Sercial, Verdelho, Bual, Malmsey, Bastardo, and Terrantez) may be used, so if no single variety is claimed, you can be sure that it is mostly, if not entirely, Tinta negra mole. Five years was once far too young for a classic Madeira from noble grapes, but they are much better than they used to be and some bargain five-year-old varietals can be found.

✓ *Barbeito* (Malmsey) • *Blandy's* (Sercial, Bual, Malmsey) • *Cossart* (Sercial)

SPECIAL RESERVE *or* 10-YEAR-OLD MADEIRA

This is where serious Madeira begins and even non-varietals are worth consideration because, although some wines in this style may be Tinta negra mole, producers will risk only superior wines from this grape for such extended ageing.

✓ *Blandy's* (Sercial, Malmsey) • *Cossart* (Verdelho, Malmsey) • *Henriques & Henriques* (Sercial, Malmsey) • *Power Drury* (Malmsey) • *Rutherford & Miles* (Bual, Malmsey)

EXTRA RESERVE *or* OVER 15-YEAR-OLD MADEIRA

This style is rarely encountered, but is always significantly richer and more complex than 10-Year-Old Madeira. The 15 years reference is excluded from some wines that are much older.

✓ *Barbeito* (25-Year-Old Bual) • *Cossart* (Malmsey 15-Year-Old Malmsey, Very Old Duo Centenary Celebration Bual, Very Old Duo Centenary Celebration Sercial)

SOLERA MADEIRA

Although an old *solera* will contain barely a few molecules from the year it was based on and boasts on the label, the best examples of authentic Madeira *soleras* (there have been several frauds) are soft, sensuous, and delicious.

✓ *Blandy's Solera 1863 Malmsey* • *Blandy's Solera 1880 Verdelho* • *Cossart Solera 1845 Bual*

VINTAGE MADEIRA

All Madeiras once bore a vintage, but this is unusual today, since most are blends or products of *solera* systems. Current regulations stipulate that Vintage Madeira must spend at least 20 years in cask, but if Madeira is to prosper, this outdated approach must be discarded and a system similar to that used for Vintage Port adopted. This is not to suggest that Vintage Madeira should not spend 20 years in cask, just that it ought not to be mandatory. Consumers worldwide perceive vintage wines to be superior to non-vintage ones and it does not matter that the opposite is sometimes true: if Madeira is to reclaim the world stage, producers must put the spotlight on Vintage Madeira, and the world will not wait 20 years for this to happen! Madeira must therefore release its vintages much younger and put the onus on consumers to age the wines. This would have the added advantage of feeding the auction circuit with a new investment and, as the different vintages are tasted and retasted, reported and discussed, this would raise consumer awareness, enhancing the reputation of Madeira in general.

SERCIAL

This grape is known on the Portuguese mainland as Esgana cao or "dog strangler" and is grown in the island's coolest vineyards. Sercial is the palest, lightest, and driest Madeira, but matures to a rich, yet crisp, savoury flavour with the sharp tang of acidic spices and citrus fruits. The legal limit for residual sugar is 18–65 grams per litre (the bottom end of this range tastes bone dry when balanced against an alcohol level of 17 per cent in such an intensely flavoured wine, and even 40 grams per litre can seem dry).

✓ *See* styles by age, earlier

VERDELHO

Some modern renditions of this style are almost as pale as Sercial, but Verdelho, both white and black varieties of which are grown on the island, traditionally produces a golden Madeira whose colour deepens with age. It is, however, always made in a medium-dry to medium-sweet style, which gives it somewhat more body than Sercial, and this can make it seem softer and riper than it actually is, although its true astringency is revealed on the finish. The legal limit for residual sugar is 49–78 grams per litre.

✓ *See* styles by age, earlier

BUAL

Definitely sweeter and darker than the styles above, Bual can often be recognized under blind conditions by its khaki-coloured meniscus. This style has soft, gentle fruit with noticeable fatness and ripeness, underscored by a baked, smoky complexity. The legal limit for residual sugar is 78–96 grams per litre.

✓ *See* styles by age, earlier

MALMSEY

Made from both white and black varieties of Malvasia grown on the island's lowest and warmest regions, Malmsey is the ultimate Madeira and my own favourite. It is the most luscious, the sweetest, and most honeyed of all Madeira styles. Potentially the most complex and long-lived Madeira, Malmsey matures to an ultra-smooth, coffee-caramel succulence, which lasts forever in the mouth. The legal limit for residual sugar is 96–135 grams per litre.

✓ *See* styles by age, earlier

TERRANTEZ

This white grape variety is virtually extinct, but the highly perfumed, rich, powerfully flavoured, tangy-sweet Madeira it produced is so highly regarded that old vintages still attract top prices at auction. If and when the Young Turks ever reach Madeira, this is one variety they will be replanting in earnest.

BASTARDO

Another rarity from Madeira's once glittering past, there is some question as to whether this black grape is related to the Douro variety of the same name, but there is no doubting its great potential quality, making it yet another golden oldie that is long overdue revival.

MOSCATEL

Madeira has made some interesting Moscatel, but only a few remain available for tasting today. With so many fortified Muscats of superb quality made throughout the world, Madeira's Moscatel should be reserved for blending purposes only.

RAINWATER

This is effectively a paler, softer version of a medium-dry Verdelho but, because varietal names are never used, making Rainwater with Verdelho would be a waste of this good-quality classic grape. Rainwater is more likely to be a paler, softer version of Tinta negra mole trying to emulate Verdelho. There are two theories about the origin of this curiously named Madeira style. One is that it came from the vines, which were grown on hillsides where it was impossible to irrigate, thus growers had to rely on rainwater. The other theory concerns a shipment that was bound for Boston: even though it was accidentally diluted by rain, the Madeira house in question had hoped to get away with it, and were shocked when the Americans loved it so much they wanted more!

AUTHOR'S CHOICE

It was my intention to include representative examples of both old and new wines from Spain, encompassing the best styles from the best appellations, but there were too many to make an easy choice. I therefore pulled twenty names out of a hat, which is why they make such an eclectic choice. Vintage Ports inevitably dominate my selection in Portugal.

PRODUCER	WINE	STYLE	DESCRIPTION	🍷
SPAIN				
Albet i Noya (*see* p.365) Ⓥ	Tempranillo, Penedés DO	RED	Fat, lush, and velvety-smooth, this Tempranillo is a weighty wine, but it is made to be enjoyed when young, soft, and fruity.	2–5 years
Barón de Ley (*see* p.360) Ⓥ	Reserva, Rioja DOC	RED	A smooth, classy wine of exceptional finesse and an elegantly rich flavour that builds and builds in the mouth, Barón de Ley comes from a single estate and a relatively new bodega that uses exclusively French oak, not American.	5–15 years
Bodegas Muga (*see* p.362)	Prado Enea Gran Reserva, Rioja DOC	RED	Lusciously rich red wine, this is made in a mellow Burgundian style, with a soft, succulent, mouthwatering mix of red and black cherries, spicy summer fruits, and a lovely smoky complexity.	7–20 years
Bodegas Palacio (*see* p.362)	Cosme Palacio y Hermanos, Rioja DOC	RED	Generously full and deliciously fruity, both elegant and expansive, this wine is one of the most beautifully balanced pure Tempranillo wines in the world.	5–10 years
Costers del Siurana	Clos de l'Obac, Priorato DO (*see* p.354)	RED	Rich and fruity, this new-wave Priorato has all the flavours of classic Bordeaux and Châteauneuf-du-Pape wrapped up in firm French oak with good tannins and a dusting of Spanish spice.	5–20 years
Contino (*see* p.360)	Reserva, Rioja DOC	RED	This single-vineyard, pure Alavesa Rioja has an excellent, deep black-purple colour, an aromatic bouquet, and a creamy-rich, blackcurrant-blackberry flavour, with a voluptuous vanilla finish.	5–15 years
Dominio de Pingus	Ribera del Duero DO (*see* p.355)	RED	Big and black with a great intensity of jammy fruit, and brilliant acidity for a red wine, Ribera del Duero DO has gorgeously supple tannins, and toasty-oak complexity.	2–8 years
Enate Ⓥ	Tempranillo-Cabernet Sauvignon, Somontano DO (*see* p.355)	RED	It is the Cabernet that dominates this elegant, firm-structured food wine, despite there being more Tempranillo in the blend.	3–8 years
Emilio Lustau Ⓥ	Premium Solera Cream Sherry (*see* p.370)	FORTIFIED	Except for the sweetness, which is relatively light, this has the nose, palate, and richness more reminiscent of an upmarket old *oloroso* than a commercial cream sherry.	Upon opening
Emilio Lustau Ⓥ	Old East India Sherry (*see* p.370)	FORTIFIED	A fabulously rich, rare, and succulently sweet style of Sherry, Old East India has been put through a similar process to that employed for Madeira. If you ever wondered what a Bual or Malmsey might taste like if made in Spain's Jerez district, try this extraordinary, voluptuous wine.	Upon opening
Marqués de Griñon (*see* p.361) Ⓥ	Domino de Valdepusa, Cabernet Sauvignon (non-DO)	RED	Deep coloured and full flavoured, this wine has heaps of succulent, juicy blackcurrant fruit underpinned by creamy-sweet vanilla oak. It was as recently as 1986 that Marqués de Griñon became an overnight success, not least because the grapes come from Malpica de Tajo, southwest of Madrid, which is the middle of nowhere as far as fine wines are concerned.	4–12 years
Marqués de Griñon (*see* p.361) Ⓥ	Domino de Valdepusa Syrah (non-DO)	RED	This deep, dark, and opaque wine is hugely seductive, rich, and savoury, with cleverly crafted smoky-fruit, full of blackcurrant and blueberry, and smoky-toasty vanilla oak complexity.	4–12 years
Marqués de Murrieta (*see* p.361)	Castillo Ygay, Gran Reserva, Rioja DOC	RED	At the time of writing, Murrieta was in danger of losing the mystique surrounding the venerable vintages of Castillo Ygay by releasing wines barely more than 20 years old! That might seem old enough in this day and age, but 1942 was the vintage available when the first edition was written. The 1942 is, for me, the yardstick for Castillo Ygay, having a succulence of ripe, mellow fruit, great length, and a silky smoothness that can be achieved only after 40 years in cask (albeit topped-up and refreshed by younger wine along the way, which is perfectly legal as long as the younger wine does not exceed 15 per cent of the total volume).	20–50 years

PRODUCER	WINE	STYLE	DESCRIPTION	
Pazo de Barrantes	Albariño, Rías Baixas DO (*see* p.354)	WHITE	A truly beautiful example of Albariño, Rías Baizas DO has elegant, peachy fruit and electrifying acidity.	1–3 years
Diego Romero ⓥ	Solera Jerezana, Rich Cream Sherry (*see* p.370)	FORTIFIED	Cream sherry is a British affectation and is responsible for over-sweetened styles, but this one is in a class of its own. Deep, rich, and lusciously sweet, with a beautiful sheen, this is flavour-packed, huge, and mellow.	Upon opening
Scholtz Hermanos	Solera 1885, Malaga DO (*see* p.354)	FORTIFIED	This wine has a full, luscious Moscatel nose with a rich toffee flavour and coffee-cream chocolate for an aftertaste.	Upon purchase
Torres (*see* p.365)	Gran Coronas Mas la Plana, Penedés DO	RED	Since 1978, Torres' famous Gran Coronas "Black Label" has been a single-vineyard, pure Cabernet Sauvignon wine and it is consistently one of Spain's greatest reds, with extremely rich fruit, beautifully integrated oak, and a succulently smooth finish.	5–20 years
Vega Sicilia	Reserva Especial, Ribera del Duero DO (*see* p.355)	RED	All Vega Sicilia wines are made primarily from Tempranillo and Cabernet sauvignon, with smaller amounts of Malbec, Merlot, and Albillo. This is a blend of old Unico vintages and always tastes remarkably youthful, like a super-smooth version of Unico itself. While they seem to promise a long life ahead, I have never cellared them for longer than two or three years for fear that each component vintage may evolve at a different rate, never quite achieving the same level of harmony these blends show when first released.	Within a few years of purchase
Vega Sicilia	Unico, Ribera del Duero DO (*see* p.355)	RED	A great Unico vintage is one of those experiences where the tremendous elegance seems miraculous in a wine of such dark, deep colour, huge body, and great complexity. At a youthful 12 years of age, it has rich, concentrated fruit, often tasting of blackcurrants and black cherries, and sweet, spicy oak. Over decades, these lively flavours slowly mellow, become toasted, even roasted, generating a complex array of aromas and aftertastes, commonly including tobacco, spices, and coffee.	12–45 years
Vega Sicilia	Valbuena, Ribera del Duero DO (*see* p.355)	RED	This is the so-called second wine of Vega Sicilia, which used to be released in two bottlings, one after just three years in wood, the other after five years, but since the introduction of Alion, another Vega Sicilia wine (from newly acquired vineyards), there is just one bottling. There are many vintages where I have preferred the vivacity of Valbuena to the uncertain potential of Unico and, as I write, the 1975 Valbuena is fetching the same price as the 1975 Unico. Now that the differential in cask-ageing has reduced from as much as 22 years to maybe one, the contrast in quality, rather than wood-ageing, should be more noticeable in future.	8–30 years

PORTUGAL

PRODUCER	WINE	STYLE	DESCRIPTION	
Churchill's (*see* p.381)	Vintage Port	FORTIFIED	Churchill's is a new producer that has quickly established a reputation for dark-coloured Vintage with intense fruit, spicy-sweetness, and classic tannin structure.	12–25 years
Cockburn's (*see* p.381)	Vintage Port	FORTIFIED	Cockburn's have produced some remarkable vintages recently. This wine has exceptionally good colour and depth, fine fruit, silky texture, and a chocolaty complexity.	15–30 years
Cossarts	Very Old Duo Centenary Celebration, (Over 15-years-old, *see* p.384) Madeira DOC	FORTIFIED	With wines aged in wood for between 15 and 60 years, the Sercial attains a stylish succulence rarely experienced at the dry end of the Madeira spectrum, and the Bual is so fabulously rich it tastes like a marvellously mature Vintage Malmsey.	Upon opening
Dow's (*see* p.381)	Vintage Port	FORTIFIED	Typically big, black, and backward, this is consistently one of the very best Vintage Ports. Dow's is a concentrated wine with a great depth of spicy-chocolaty fruit and a complex, tannic, somewhat drier character than most.	18–35 years
Duque de Viseu ⓥ	Dão DOC (*see* p.374.)	RED	Smooth and dark, full in body, with succulent fruit and a whisper of spice, this wine has the sort of quality we all knew Dão vineyards were capable of.	4–8 years
Espiga ⓥ	Estremadura VR (*see* p.375) Duque de Bragança 20-Years-	RED	Made by José Neiva, one of Portugal's most talented winemakers, Espiga has deliciously rich fruit that is beautifully underpinned by creamy oak, making it a classy wine on its own or with food, and ridiculously cheap.	2–5 years

PRODUCER	WINE	STYLE	DESCRIPTION	🍷
Ferreira (*see* p.381)	Old Port	FORTIFIED	One of the most elegantly rich Tawny Ports available, Ferreira's mellow Duque de Bragança has the classic smoothness and coffee-caramel complexity of authentically long cask-ageing.	Upon opening
Ferreirinha	Barca Velha, Douro DOC (*see* p.374)	RED	This is Portugal's answer to Vega Sicilia, except that Barca Velha undergoes optimum maturation in bottle, rather than over-ageing in cask, which gives the wine more silky finesse than its more famous Spanish counterpart. It is, however, just as ludicrously expensive.	6-20 years
Fonseca (*see* p.381) Ⓥ	Vintage Port	FORTIFIED	Although not quite as massive as Taylor's, Fonseca is very much in the same mould, only sweeter and more accessible. Classic Vintage Fonseca is deep coloured, with a deliciously rich and ripe flavour, and a sensual chocolaty-raisiny complexity that puts it among the best.	15-30 years
José Maria da Fonseca	20-Year-Old Setúbal DOC (*see* p.376)	FORTIFIED	This Moscatel, which has a deep mahogany colour, retains a certain grapiness, but is dominated by its intense creamy-caramel flavour and spicy-raisiny complexity.	Upon opening
Graham's (*see* p.381)	Vintage Port	FORTIFIED	Part of the Symington Port empire since 1970, Graham's reputation for big, black, beautifully sweet, and long-lived Vintage Port has never diminished.	18-40 years
Palacio da Brejoeira	Vinho Verde DOC (*see* p.376)	WHITE	Normally Vinhos Verdes should be consumed as early as possible, but this is the Premier Grand Cru of the Minho, and is fuller than most, with just the barest prickle, and actually benefits from a very modest time in bottle.	1-2 years
Palha Canas	Estremadura VR (*see* p.375)	RED	Also made by José Neiva, this is made in a more mellow style than his Espiga (*see* above), with the oak more dominant, but it is exquisitely smooth, with coffee-caramel complexity and finesse.	2-5 years
J. M. Fonseca Ⓥ	Joao Pires, Terras do Sado VR (*see* p.376)	WHITE	The early-picked Muscat grapes used for this succulently fruity dry white were previously sourced from Palmela, a sub-appellation of Terras do Sado. Joao Pires is more medium than dry, but that's the cleverest aspect of this wine, as its residual sugar makes the fruit seem juicy-ripe, exotic, and opulent.	Upon purchase
J. M. Fonseca Ⓥ	Quinta da Bacalhôa, Terras do Sado VR (*see* p.376)	RED	This *quinta* is owned by an American (Tom Scoville), and its truly international wine is made by an Australian (Peter Bright) and marketed by a Portuguese firm (J. P. Vinhos). Most credit should go to the American, who was obviously ahead of his time, having planted a north-facing limestone slope with Cabernet sauvignon and Merlot as early as the mid-1970s. The wine has a deep colour, rich blackcurrant fruit and supple tannins, supported by spicy-creamy new oak.	3-15 years
Quinta do Côtto Ⓥ	Douro DOC (*see* p.374)	RED	This creamy-rich wine with its voluptuous oaky fruit is made from the choicest selection of Champalimaud's grapes, the balance being fortified into Vintage Port. All other Douro *quintas* use their best grapes for the Vintage Port, and this might just explain why this is always so stunning.	12-25 years
Quinta do Noval (*see* p.382)	Nacional Vintage Port	FORTIFIED	Although this estate's Vintage Port is excellent, its most famous wine is not just a single-*quinta* Vintage Port, but a Vintage Port from a single plot of 5,000 ungrafted vines. They are so low-yielding that in great years they make the deepest and most densely coloured of all Vintage Ports. Naçional is a powerfully structured, super-concentrated wine that is reluctant to budge in terms of ageing, hugely rich and so overripe that it seems thick with liquorice and molasses, yet it is also on fire with spices, and retains the most remarkable grace and finesse.	25-70 years
Taylor's (*see* p.382)	Vintage Port	FORTIFIED	With the exception of Quinta do Noval Naçional, this is the darkest, deepest, and most massive of all Vintage Ports and the highest-valued on the auction market.	20-40 years
Warre's (*see* p.382)	Vintage Port	FORTIFIED	This big, black, massive Vintage Port is regularly one of the greatest produced and in stark contrast to Warre's tremendously elegant Tawny Ports.	18-35 years

The REST *of* EUROPE

and the LEVANT

READERS MIGHT BE AMAZED TO DISCOVER
no less than 500 vineyards in Great Britain,
but what about Dutch and even Danish
wines? The vineyards of the Netherlands and
Denmark are not exactly prolific, but they do
exist, and those referred to in this book are
fully exposed to the elements, not under glass.
They are, however, mere curiosities: the most
important part of this section is dedicated to
those countries I have included under the
heading Southeast Europe, particularly
Bulgaria, Hungary, and Romania. These
are already good sources of drinkable but
inexpensive wines, but have an even greater
potential, although this cannot be realized
until they recover economically from 50 years
of Communist rule. There is also Greece,
where viticulture originated. Yet Greek wines
have been disappointing for decades, even
centuries. It has, therefore, been heartening
to witness the widespread improvement in
this country's wines in recent years.

18,000-LITRE BARRELS IN SUHINDOL WINERY, BULGARIA
*The Suhindol Winery started the Bulgarian wine bandwagon rolling
in the mid-1970s with cheap but reliable Cabernet Sauvignon.*

❖ GREAT BRITAIN ❖

The future of English wine will be decided in the coming decades, when the Müller-Thurgau, Seyval blanc, and other French hybrids or German crosses that currently dominate these vineyards are grubbed up. It does not matter how good the wine from these grapes may occasionally be, their names on a bottle turn off most consumers.

ANY ENGLISH VINEYARD owner who does not have the courage to grow more popular grape varieties will eventually be doomed. Although English wine is destined to remain a cottage industry, this is not because it lacks serious or successful producers, it is due to two simple facts: English vineyards are a very recent phenomenon and Great Britain is a densely populated island. It will always be difficult to find suitable land for vineyards, therefore the potential growth of English wine is severely limited. Furthermore, if any *grand cru* sites ever existed they would be under concrete or asphalt today. It is a bit like starting up the French wine industry from scratch in a country half the size and twice as densely populated with a severely unfavourable climate.

DENBIES ESTATE, SURREY
In 1985 there were 430 hectares (1,060 acres) of vineyards in Great Britain of which 325 (800 acres) were in production. In 1995 the total production area under vine had risen to well over 1,000 hectares (2,470 acres) of vines, with 500 known vineyards in England and Wales.

FACTORS AFFECTING TASTE AND QUALITY

✦ LOCATION
Most of Great Britain's vineyards are located in England and Wales, south of a line drawn through Birmingham and the Wash.

❄ CLIMATE
Great Britain is at the northerly extreme of climates suitable for the vine, but the warm Gulf Stream tempers the weather sufficiently to make viticulture possible. Rainfall is relatively high and conditions vary greatly from year to year, making harvests somewhat unreliable. High winds can be a problem, but winter frosts are less troublesome than in many wine regions.

▨ ASPECT
Vines are planted on all types of land, but the best sites are usually sheltered, south-facing slopes with the consequent microclimate advantages that can be crucial for wine production in this marginal viticultural region.

▦ SOIL
Vines are grown on a wide variety of different soils ranging from granite through limestone, chalk, and gravel to clay.

⊞ VITICULTURE AND VINIFICATION
Vigour is a problem, as sap bypasses the fruit to produce an excessively luxuriant canopy of leaves, resulting in unnecessarily small grape clusters, delayed ripening, and overly herbaceous flavours. This problem is exacerbated by the use of rootstocks that actually promote vigour, but the New World influence that has already had its effect on English winemaking techniques will hopefully encourage the introduction of low-vigour rootstock. Although the British climate is least favourable for growing black grapes, an increasing amount of red and rosé has been produced since the early 1990s, but bottle-fermented sparkling wine is clearly the most up-and-coming of English wine styles, and two estates exclusively dedicated to it already exist.

🍇 GRAPE VARIETIES
Auxerrois, Bacchus, Blau-berger, Blauer Portugieser, Cabernet sauvignon, Cascade, Chardonnay, Chasselas, Dornfelder, Dunkelfelder, Ehrenfelser, Faberebe (*syn.* Faber), Findling, Gagarin blue, Gamay, Gewürztraminer, Gutenborner, Huxelrebe, Kanzler, Kerner, Kernling, Léon Millot, Madeleine Angevine, Müller-Thurgau, Optima, Ortega, Perle, Pinot blanc, Pinot gris, Pinot meunier, Pinot noir, Regner, Reichensteiner, Riesling, Sauvignon blanc, Scheurebe, Schönburger, Seibel, Seyval blanc, Siegerrebe, Triomphe d'Alsace, Wrotham pinot, Würzer, Zweigeltrebe

ANCIENT BRITONS
Winemaking in Britain is not new, but dates back to AD 43 when every important villa had a garden of vines. It was not until 1995, however, when a 20-acre Roman vineyard was excavated at Wollaston in Northamptonshire, that it was first realized how large the scale of this early viticulture was. The Domesday Book reveals the existence of some 40 vineyards of significance during the reign of William the Conqueror and by medieval times the number had risen to 300, most of which were run by monks. The Black Death took its toll in the mid-14th century and, almost 200 years later, the dissolution of the monasteries virtually brought an end to English winemaking. Apart from a couple of vineyards in the mid-18th century and two more in the late 19th century, winemaking on a commercial scale was almost non-existent until Hambledon was established in 1951. English vineyards began to boom in the late 1960s and peaked in the early 1970s, since when almost 500 have been planted, although fewer than 200 are in any sense commercial and fewer than half this number have created any semblance of a reputation.

Few vineyards in the UK can reasonably expect more than an average of 800 degree-days Celsius (1,440 degree-days Fahrenheit), which is well below the accepted minimum for winemaking of 1,000 degree-days Celsius (1,800 degree-days Fahrenheit), so even the best-situated vineyards risked failure when they were first established. Some vineyards were unsuccessful, but the 500 vineyards in existence today have proved the theoretical minimum conditions to be just that – theoretical.

FUTURE TRENDS

Although English wine will remain forever a cottage industry, this does not mean it cannot earn a reputation for quality. High-duty rates do mean, however, that it is difficult for the smallest vineyards, which have the highest overheads, to establish sales of a new product. Initially this problem was overcome by contract winemaking, with virtually all the oldest and largest vineyards providing a service for those where a winery was not a viable option. Since the early 1990s, however, cooperative groups have formed to produce large volumes of relatively inexpensive wines by blending wines from their members, all of whom also make and market their own single-vineyard products. The Harvest Group is the most famous example and the cleverly crafted Heritage Fumé its best-selling, bulk-blended brand. The next step to take in the development of English wine will be to rid the country of most of its crosses and hybrids. This has nothing to do with the European ban on hybrid grapes or the ill-informed view that they are somehow intrinsically inferior. For while it is true that there are far more interesting *vinifera* varieties, it is also easy to make bad wines from such grapes, whereas exceptionally fine wines can be made fairly easily from some hybrids. The most consistently high-quality hybrid wines are the Canadian Ice Wines, but they sell on the back of the Icewine term, not the Vidal hybrid name.

If English wine producers want success, they have to accept that hybrids have a negative impact on most consumers. Wine drinkers are attracted to classic varieties and even willing to dabble with more obscure *vinifera* grapes, particularly when indigenous to the wine-producing area of origin, but they either do not understand hybrids or find them a turn-off. As for German crosses, how can producers expect to establish an English or Welsh wine reputation with names like Reichensteiner or Siegerrebe?

Great Britain's more perceptive winemakers realized this some time ago, hence the move away from naming the varieties on wines such as Heritage Fumé, but this is a short-term solution, as consumers will eventually wonder what the grape varieties are and why they are no longer mentioned. The only long-term answer is to replace the unattractive grapes with more marketable ones, and if the vineyards cannot grow them to good enough standards, then English wine has no future.

The future of English and Welsh wine is not, however, merely a matter of upgrading vineyards. For the UK to have any impact above and beyond the minuscule size of its wine industry, it must be famous for something. With the climate-induced, low-alcohol, high-acidity wine produced in the UK, bottle-fermented sparkling wine represents its greatest potential, especially in the southeast, where even the chalk is exactly the same as that found in the Champagne region.

THE DELL ON DENBIES, DORKING, SURREY
Set amid Surrey countryside, Denbies Estate is the largest winery in Great Britain, surrounded by more than 100 hectares (250 acres) of vineyards.

THE WINE REGIONS OF
GREAT BRITAIN

Regional characteristics have not yet been established in the wine regions of Great Britain, and I am not sure that they ever will be, but it is very difficult to build up a proper spatial awareness of where English vineyards are located without first breaking them down into a small number of workable areas. The following regions are all officially recognized by UKVA or the United Kingdom Vineyard Association (which took over from EVA in 1996) and it would help English winemakers to help themselves if they were to utilize these regions on their labels as an appellation, in addition to a more specific location.

WEALD AND DOWNLAND

East and West Sussex, Kent, London South, Surrey
This region covers the "Garden of England", which probably says it all. It is not as wet as the west country, and milder than East Anglia, but not as warm as Thames and Chiltern. Soils range from clay to chalk. The latter forms the same basin that creates the chalk cliff at Dover and goes under the Channel to rise in Champagne.

WESSEX

Dorset, Hampshire, Isle of Wight, Wiltshire
The major factor linking these counties together is the interesting pattern of isotherms that form south of the Isle of Wight and provide a more temperate climate than the surrounding regions.

SOUTHWEST AND WALES

Avon, Cornwall, Devon, Gloucestershire, Herefordshire, Somerset, Wales, Worcestershire

Geographically the largest region, with vineyards as far apart as Cornwall, where the Gulf Stream has its greatest effect but which is also prone to wet weather, and North Wales, which takes the brunt of weather systems from the Atlantic. Although prevailing westerly winds make conditions difficult in the west of Cornwall and Wales, the region is generally milder than the east coast. The topography of the region ranges from mountainous to flat, with some areas below sea level. Soils vary tremendously from limestone through shale, clay, and peat to granite.

THAMES AND CHILTERN

Berkshire, Buckinghamshire, London West, Oxfordshire
This large area is the warmest of all the regions, and most vineyards are located on slopes of moisture-retaining soils. There are also many aquifers in the area, which prevent stress during drought conditions.

EAST ANGLIA

Bedfordshire, Cambridgeshire, Essex, Hertfordshire, London North, Norfolk, Suffolk
The flattest and most exposed of all the regions, East Anglia is subject to bitterly cold easterly and northeasterly winds, but has fertile soils, which can encourage significantly higher yields than some areas in England.

MERCIA

Cheshire, Derbyshire, Leicestershire, Northamptonshire, Nottinghamshire, Rutland, Shropshire, Staffordshire, Warwickshire, West Midlands, West Yorkshire
This is a very large and naturally diverse region, with vineyards planted both on flat ground and slopes, with soils ranging from light sand to heavy clay. About the only common factor is Madelaine Angevine, which seems to be the most reliable variety. At the time of writing, another ten vineyards have been planted, but are not yet in production.

THE WINE PRODUCERS OF
GREAT BRITAIN

1 ADGESTONE
Adgestone, Isle of Wight (Wessex)
A single, blended wine made dry or medium, according to the vintage, but which should be sparkling.

2 ASTLEY
Stourport on Severn (Southwest and Wales)
✓ *Huxelvaner • Kerner*
• *Madeleine Angevine*

3 BARDINGLEY
Hawkenbury, Kent (Weald and Downland)
✓ *Estate White*

4 BARKHAM MANOR VINEYARD
Uckfield, Sussex (Weald and Downland)
✓ *Bacchus • Kerner • Schöburger*

5 BARTON MANOR
East Cowes, Isle of Wight (Wessex)
Award-winning vineyard under new ownership since the early 1990s.

6 BATTLE WINE ESTATE
Whatlington, Sussex (Weald and Downland)
✓ *Saxon Valley Schönburger*

7 BEAULIEU
Nr Brockenhurst, Hampshire (Wessex)
This enthusiastic, aristocratic venture has been running since 1958.

8 BEENLEIGH MANOR
Harbertonford, Devon (Southwest and Wales)
✓ *Rosé*

9 BIDDENDEN
Biddenden, Kent (Weald and Downland)
✓ *Müller-Thurgau • Ortega*

10 BOOKERS
Bolney, Sussex (Weald and Downland)
Awaiting results of recently expanded vineyards.

11 BOSMERE
Nr Chippenham, Wiltshire (Wessex)
✓ *Huxelrebe*

12 BOTHY
Frilford Health, Oxfordshire (Thames and Chiltern)
✓ *Huxelrebe & Perle • Ortega & Optima*

13 BOZE DOWN
Whitchurch-on-Thames, Oxfordshire (Thames and Chiltern)
✓ *Dry Red • Dry White*

14 BOYTON VINEYARDS
Stoke-by-Clare, Suffolk (East Anglia)
✓ *Huxelrebe*

15 BREAKY BOTTOM
Northease, Sussex (Weald and Downland)
✓ *Müller-Thurgau • Seyval Blanc*

16 BRENCHLEY
Nr Tunbridge Wells, Kent (Weald and Downland)
✓ *Schönburger*

17 BRUISYARD
Bruisyard, Suffolk (East Anglia)
✓ *St. Peter*

18 CANE END
Cane End, Oxfordshire (Thames and Chiltern)
✓ *Late Harvest Bacchus • Medium White*

19 CARDEN
Tarpoley, Cheshire (Mercia)
This vineyard is part of Carden Park Leisure Centre. New owners turned the entire production over to sparkling wine in 1996.

20 CARR TAYLOR
Westfield, Sussex (Weald and Downland)
✓ *Pinot Blanc* (Kemsley Dry)
• *Reichensteiner*

21 CHAPEL DOWN
Tenterden, Kent (Weald and Downland)
✓ *Epoch 1*

22 CHÂTEAU LE CATILLON
Jersey, Channel Islands (Southwest and Wales)
✓ *Sec*

23 CHIDDINGSTONE
Chiddingstone, Kent (Weald and Downland)
✓ *Rosé*

24 CHILFORD HUNDRED
Linton, Cambridgeshire (East Anglia)
✓ *The Firmin Lifget Vat Rosé*

25 CHILTERN VALLEY
Hambleden, Oxfordshire (Thames and Chiltern)
✓ *Noble Bacchus*

26 CODDINGTON
Nr Ledbury, Herefordshire (Southwest and Wales)
✓ *Malvern Hills Bacchus*

27 CROFFTA
Pontyclun, Glamorgan (Southwest and Wales)
In the 19th century, the Marquis of Bute tried to revive English wine at nearby Castle Coch.

28 DEBEN VALLEY VINEYARD
Bromeswell, Suffolk (East Anglia)
✓ *Müller-Thurgau*

29 DENBIES
Dorking, Surrey (Weald and Downland)
✓ *Chardonnay • Late Harvest • Pinot Blanc • Pinot Gris • Pinot Rosé Brut • Special Reserve Noble*

30 DITCHLING
Ditchling, Sussex (Weald and Downland)
✓ *Müller-Thurgau*

31 EGLANTINE
Costock, Nottinghamshire (Mercia)
Over 80 grape varieties on trial.

32 ELHAM VALLEY
Barham, Kent (Weald and Downland)
✓ *Müller-Thurgau* (Medium Dry)

33 ELMHAM PARK
North Elmham, Norfolk (East Anglia)
✓ *Madelaine Angevine • Medium White*

34 GIFFORD'S HALL
Hartest, Suffolk (East Anglia)
✓ *Blush*

35 HALFPENNY GREEN
Bobbington, West Midlands (Mercia)
✓ *Madeleine Angevine*

36 HAMBLEDON VINEYARD
Hambledon, Hampshire (Wessex)
✓ *Hambledon*

37 HARVEST GROUP
Stanlake Park, Berks (Thames and Chiltern)
✓ *Heritage Fumé*

38 HEADCORN
Headcorn, Kent (Weald and Downland)
✓ *Seval Blanc*

39 HIDDEN SPRINGS
Horsham, Sussex (Weald and Downland)
✓ *Dark Fields Red • Dry White Reserve • Ortega • Rosé* (Sussex Sunset) • *Seyval Blanc • Vintage Brut*

40 HIGHFIELD
Tiverton, Devon (Southwest and Wales)
✓ *Madelaine Angevine • Siegerrebe*

41 KENTS GREEN
Taynton, Gloucestershire (Southwest and Wales)
✓ *Late Harvest*

42 LA MARE
Jersey, Channel Islands (Southwest and Wales)
The Channel Island's first vineyard and the only one open to visitors.

43 LAMBERHURST
Lamberhurst, Kent (Weald and Downland)
✓ *Bacchus • Blush • Müller-Thurgau*

44 LEVENTHORPE VINEYARD
Woodlesford, West Yorkshire (Mercia)
The country's most northerly vineyard is no curiosity, as it crops ripe grapes every year, and has its own winery.

45 LLANERCH VINEYARD
Hensol, Glamorgan (Southwest and Wales)
✓ *Cariad* (Dry White, Rosé Dry)

46 LODDISWELL
Lilwell, Devon (Southwest and Wales)
✓ *Reichensteiner*

47 MERSEA
Mersea Island, Essex (East Anglia)
✓ *Dry White*

48 MOORLYNCH
Bridgwater, Somerset (Southwest and Wales)
✓ *Somerset Moorlynch*

49 NEW HALL
Purleigh, Essex (East Anglia)
✓ *Bacchus • Chardonnay • Müller-Thurgau*

50 NORTHBROOK SPRINGS
Bishop Waltham, Hampshire (Wessex)
✓ *Noble Dessert*

51 NUTBOURNE MANOR
Nr Pulborough, Sussex (Weald and Downland)
✓ *Bacchus • Schönburger*

52 NYETIMBER
Pulborough, Sussex (Weald and Downland)
✓ *Blanc de Blanc Brut • Vintage Brut*

53 OATLEY VINEYARD
Cannington, Somerset (Southwest and Wales)
✓ *Kernling*

54 PARTRIDGE VINEYARD
Tarrant Keynston, Dorset (Southwest and Wales)
✓ *Bacchus*

55 PENBERTH VALLEY VINEYARD
St. Buryan, Cornwall (Southwest and Wales)
The most southwesterly vineyard in Britain.

56 PENGETHLEY MANOR
Nr Ross-on-Wye, Herefordshire (Southwest and Wales)
A country house hotel that began production of Reichensteiner wine in 1995.

57 PENSHURST
Penshurst, Kent (Weald and Downland)
✓ *Ehrenfelser • Seyval Blanc*

58 PILTON MANOR
Shepton Mallet, Somerset (Southwest and Wales)
✓ *Dry White • Westholme Late Harvest*

59 PULHAM
Pulham Market, Norfolk (East Anglia)
✓ *Müller-Thurgau*

60 QUEEN COURT
Ospringe, Kent (Weald and Downland)
✓ *Schönburger*

61 RIDGEVIEW ESTATE
Ditchling, Sussex (Weald and Downland)
Exclusively bottle-fermented sparkling-wine production, due to be released soon.

62 ROCK LODGE
Scayne's Hill, Sussex (Weald and Downland)
Sparkling-wine specialist.

63 ST. GEORGE'S
Nr Heathfield, Sussex (Weald and Downland)
✓ *Müller-Thurgau • Reichensteiner*

64 ST. NICHOLAS OF ASH
Ash, Kent (Weald and Downland)
✓ *Müller-Thurgau • Schönburger*

65 SANDHURST VINEYARDS
Sandhurst, Kent (Weald and Downland)
✓ *Bacchus* (Oak Aged) • *Seyval Blanc*

66 SCOTT'S HALL
Smeeth, Kent (Weald and Downland)
✓ *Rosé Brut*

67 SEDLESCOMBE
Robertsbridge, Sussex (Weald and Downland)
Organically grown wines.

68 SHARPHAM
Asprington, Devon (Southwest and Wales)
✓ *Bacchus*

69 SHAWSGATE
Framlingham, Suffolk (East Anglia)
✓ *Bacchus • Müller-Thurgau • Müller-Thurgau/Seyval-Blanc*

70 STAPLE ST. JAMES
Staple, Kent (Weald and Downland)
✓ *Müller-Thurgau • Huxelrebe • Reichensteiner*

71 STAPLECOMBE
Staplegrove, Somerset (Southwest and Wales)
✓ *Kerner*

72 STAVERTON
Woodbridge, Suffolk (East Anglia)
✓ *Bacchus*

[21] TENTERDEN
Tenterden, Kent (Weald and Downland)
✓ *Rosé • Seyval Reserve*

[37] THAMES VALLEY VINEYARD
Stanlake Park, Berkshire (Thames and Chiltern)
✓ *Clocktower Gamay Brut • Clocktower Selection Pinot Noir*

73 THORNCROFT
Leatherhead, Surrey (Weald and Downland)
✓ *Noble Harvest* • (and Elderflower "Champagne")

74 THREE CHOIRS
Newent, Gloucestershire (Southwest and Wales)
✓ *Bacchus • Huxelrebe • Rosé*

75 THROWLEY
Throwley, Kent (Weald and Downland)
✓ *Ortega*

76 TILTRIDGE
Upton-on-Severn, Worcestershire (Southwest and Wales)
✓ *Huxelrebe*

77 WELLOW
Romsey, Hampshire (Wessex)
Ambitiously sized project in a climatically exceptional situation. Wellow is making a comeback after non-business problems.

78 WOOLDINGS
Whitchurch, Hampshire (Wessex)
✓ *Vintage Brut* (but not 1993)
• *Dry Red • Schönburger*

79 WOOTTON
Shepton Mallet, Somerset (Southwest and Wales)
✓ *Auxerrois • Trinity*

80 WYKEN
Stanton, Suffolk (East Anglia)
✓ *Auxerrois • Bacchus • Kernling • Pinot Gris*

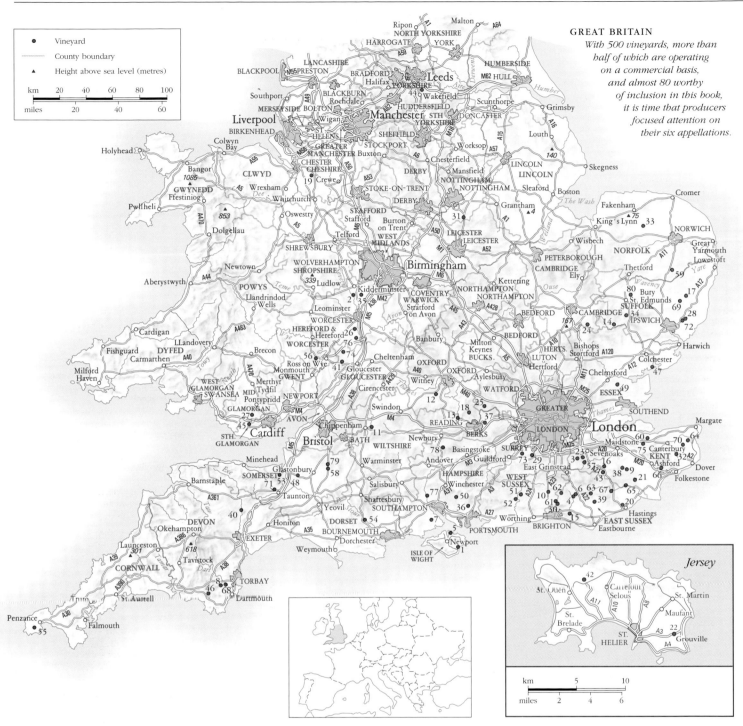

GREAT BRITAIN
With 500 vineyards, more than half of which are operating on a commercial basis, and almost 80 worthy of inclusion in this book, it is time that producers focused attention on their six appellations.

- • Vineyard
- — County boundary
- ▲ Height above sea level (metres)

Jersey

THE WINE STYLES OF
GREAT BRITAIN

Note Because of the variability of the climate in Great Britain, and the constantly evolving state of the English wine industry, some vineyards may not make all the styles of wine recommended below every year.

AUXERROIS

This grape variety is capable of producing fresh, creamy-rich wine that adapts well to oak and can also be a useful blending component for classic bottle-fermented sparkling wine.

✓ *Wootton • Wyken*

BACCHUS

Fat and grapey with rich, Muscat-like fruit when ripe, this grape provides high sugar levels even in cool climates, making it one of Great Britain's more successful German crosses. It does, however, develop an intensely herbaceous, elderflower style in cooler years and is downright catty when unripe.

✓ *Barkham • Coddington (Malvern Hills) • Lamberhurst • New Hall • Nutbourne Manor • Partridge • Sharpham • Shawsgate • Staverton • Three Choirs • Wyken*

CABERNET

Grown with Merlot in plastic tunnels at Beenleigh, this has promised deep, plummy fruit but has always been ruined during vinification.

CHARDONNAY

Mostly planted for sparkling wine, but Denbies uses it for both still and sparkling. Winemakers need to look to New Zealand for advice on how to handle this variety in a maritime-influenced growing environment.

✓ *Denbies • New Hall*

393 •

EHRENFELSER

Penshurst specializes in this grape, which is the darling of British Columbia in Canada, but to my mind it performs much better in Kent, where in warm years it is soft and ripe with a Riesling-like peach-stone intensity that develops well.

✓ *Penshurst*

GAMAY

The climate in Great Britain does not have the warmth to make good red wine from this grape, but if Thames Valley's first effort is not an anomaly, it could well be one of the most useful grapes for bottle-fermented sparkling wine.

✓ *Thames Valley* (Clocktower Gamay Brut)

HUXELREBE

Easy-going fruit that sometimes has a herbaceous-grapefruit bite and can become elderflower-tasting or catty in poor years.

✓ *Bosmere • Boyton Vineyards • Staple St. James • Three Choirs • Tiltridge*

KERNER

More aromatic in Great Britain than in Germany, where it was developed, Kerner is unsuitable for oak and is often grown for its late budding (thus frost avoidance) and high sugar level.

✓ *Astley • Barkham Manor • Staplecombe*

MADELEINE ANGEVINE

This grape has a light, floral aroma and after-perfume, and can have apricoty fruit, but often fights against an elderflower pungency.

✓ *Astley • Highfield • Elmham Park • Halfpenny Green*

MÜLLER-THURGAU

Müller-Thurgau is a typically German style that can become elderflower tasting or catty, although wines of real flavour are possible. Wines such as Bruisyard St. Peter, for example, can be extraordinarily fat and distinctive.

✓ *Biddenden • Breaky Bottom • Bruisyard* (St. Peter) *• Ditchling • Elham Valley* (Medium Dry) *• Lamberhurst • New Hall • Pulham • St. George's • Shawsgate • Staple St. James • Whitstone*

ORTEGA

Fat and jammy when ripe, becoming herbaceous in cooler years, with an elderflower, white currant character when unripe.

✓ *Biddenden • Hidden Springs • Throwley*

PINOT BLANC

Can be delicious, easy-drinking, and reminiscent of what Alsace does with this variety.

✓ *Carr Taylor* (Kemsley Dry) *• Denbies*

PINOT GRIS

England's Pinot gris is not the spiciest in the world, but it does offer richer fruit per gram of acidity than either Pinot blanc or Chardonnay. It can be successfully oaked, although the best-known example, Denbies 1995 Special Release, was over-oaked and would have been better if blended with another variety.

✓ *Denbies • Wyken*

PINOT NOIR

Some vineyard owners fear that English weather and this variety's susceptibility to rot will not mix, but those growers who have chosen the right clone have had less trouble than expected. In a good year, this grape is capable of making an elegant English red with a very attractive cherry and raspberry fruit flavour. In less ripe years, colour extraction can be a problem and a school of thought reckons that such grapes should then be utilized for sparkling wine, but Pinot noir that cannot produce a light red will not make good fizz, and would be better used making off-dry, New World-style blanc de noirs.

✓ *Thames Valley* (Clocktower Selection Pinot Noir)

REICHENSTEINER

Appreciated by growers for its resistance to rot and by winemakers for its high sugar levels, but its neutral character is seldom enjoyed by wine enthusiasts, although exceptions exist.

✓ *Carr Taylor • Loddiswell • St. George's • Staple St. James*

SCHÖNBURGER

Soft and peachy when ripe, good examples should have at least a light spiciness. There is nothing worse than a dry Schönburger from a cool year, when it smells like a tom-cat's spray.

✓ *Barkham Manor • Battle Wine Estate* (Saxon Valley) *• Brenchley • Nutbourne Manor • Queen Court • St. Nicholas of Ash • Wooldings*

SEYVAL BLANC

Relatively neutral and capable of oak-ageing, but classic English style is crisp and unoaked, with a grassy-elderflowery intensity that is very tangy and almost Sauvignon-like, although unlike Sauvignon, good Seyval ages well in bottle. However, it can be catty with less ripeness.

✓ *Breaky Bottom • Headcorn • Hidden Springs • Penshurst • Tenterden* (Reserve)

SIEGERREBE

A Madeleine-Angevine x Gewürztraminer cross that can produce fat wines with tangy fruit. Sometimes spritzy.

✓ *Highfield*

TRIOMPHE

This grape used to be called Triomphe d'Alsace because it was bred in Alsace. It has never been grown in Alsace vineyards, however, which led the EU, when it banned the grape along with all other hybrids, to insist on shortening its name as well. Triomphe is a red-wine hybrid with a cloying, foxy aftertaste, but this appalling characteristic can be hidden in a clever blend, such as Boze Down, which may contain up to 60 per cent Triomphe. Wooldings Red, which is pure Triomphe, has no foxiness, and some vintages taste like rustic Romanian Pinot Noir, sometimes with a pleasing touch of coffee, if winemaker Charles Cunningham uses more oak chips than he anticipated that year.

✓ *Wooldings • Boze Down*

OTHER STYLES

ROSÉ

Although the British climate makes it difficult (but by no means impossible) to produce a true red wine year in and year out, being on the viticultural fringe should be ideal for making crisp, ultra-fresh, off-dry rosés and a few vineyards are beginning to realize this potential.

✓ *Beenleigh • Chiddingstone • Chilford Hundred* (The Firmin Lifget Vat) *• Gifford's Hall* (Blush) *• Hidden Springs* (Sussex Sunset) *• Lamberhurst* (Blush) *• Llanerch* (Cariad Dry) *• Tenterden • Three Choirs*

UNOAKED WHITE BLENDS

Blending wines from different grape varieties and various vinification methods often produces more complete wines. With the tendency to avoid naming grape varieties, it is possible that some wines recommended here might well be pure varietals.

✓ *Astley* (Huxelvaner) *• Bardingly* (Estate White) *• Bothy Vineyard* (Huxelrebe & Perle, Ortega & Optima) *• Boze Down* (Dry) *• Cane End* (Medium) *• Château le Catillon* (Sec) *• Elmham Park* (Medium) *• Hambledon • Llanerch* (Cariad Dry) *• Mersea* (Dry) *• Pilton* (Dry) *• Shawsgate* (Müller-Thurgau/Seyval-Blanc)

OAKED WHITES

As in the US, English producers seem to have adopted the term *fumé* to indicate oak-ageing. Marginal climatic conditions produce wines of much leaner structure than those found on the continent of Europe or in the New World, thus oak can easily overwhelm, and winemakers tend to restrain its use. Normally only non-aromatic varieties such as Seyval blanc are oaked, but Bacchus is a surprising exception.

✓ *Harvest Group* (Heritage Fumé) *• Hidden Springs* (Dry Reserve) *• Sandhurst* (Bacchus Oak Aged) *• Tenterden* (Seyval Reserve) *• Wootton* (Auxerrois, Trinity)

RED BLENDS

Most English red wines are light and insubstantial, but New World influence has encouraged softer, more upfront fruity styles.

✓ *Boze Down • Chapel Down* (Epoch 1) *• Hidden Springs* (Dark Fields)

BOTRYTIS *OR* LATE-HARVEST

There's no doubt that the UK can guarantee sufficiently damp mornings to encourage rot, but it requires a strong burn-off from mid-morning sun for two weeks to encourage noble rot, which is not that common. When it occurs, however, these wines can have a stunning piquance of mouthwatering fruit and acidity.

✓ *Cane End* (Late Harvest Bacchus) *• Chiltern Valley* (Noble Bacchus) *• Denbies* (Late Harvest, Noble Harvest) *• Kents Green* (Late Harvest) *• Northbrook Springs* (Noble Dessert) *• Pilton* (Westholme Late Harvest) *• Thorncroft* (Noble Harvest)

BOTTLE-FERMENTED SPARKLING WINE

The best wines use non-aromatic varieties, preferably classic Champagne grapes. Stephen Skelton, one of the country's most respected winemakers, believes that Chardonnay will ripen only in exceptional years and that Pinot noir will succumb to rot, yet with the help of expert advice and the right clones, Stuart Moss at Nyetimber has shown that these varieties will ripen successfully every year.

✓ *Harvest Group* (Clock Tower Gamay Brut) *• Hidden Springs* (Vintage Brut) *• Nyetimber • Chapel Down* (Scott's Hall Brut Rosé) *• Wickham* (Premier Cuvée) *• Wooldings* (Vintage Brut – but not 1993)

✦SWITZERLAND✦

At their best, Swiss wines are as fresh and clean as the Alpine air. Although many grape varieties are cultivated, the most famous grape grown here is the Chasselas. In France this variety is perceived as a table grape, yet the Swiss make it into a light, dry, spritzy, and delicately delicious wine that is the perfect partner to the Swiss cheese fondue.

THE CHASSELAS CAN BE FOUND under the guise of the Dorin in the Vaud, the Perlan in Geneva and, most famous of all, the Fendant in the Valais, but although this country's most popular grape variety represents 40 per cent of the vines cultivated, nearly half of all Swiss wine produced is, most surprisingly, red.

There is, in fact, as much as 27 per cent Pinot noir, 14 per cent Gamay and, nowhere near as important, but very much on the increase, Merlot, which currently accounts for six per cent, leaving all the other varieties just 13 per cent of the vineyards.

Quality has certainly improved over the last decade, but yields have always been much too high in general (80 hectolitres per hectare on average, with some cantons producing as much as 120 hectolitres per hectare) for Switzerland to achieve a serious international reputation as a quality wine-producing country.

Producers who keep their yields low make some splendid wines, but they are too few to change the reputation of the country as a whole. The accepted wisdom is that the value of the Swiss franc and the high cost of living inevitably makes these

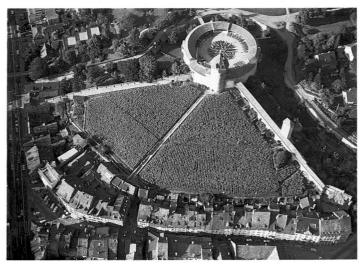

VINEYARDS AT SCHAFFHAUSEN
The Munot vineyard, situated in Schaffhausen itself, is one of the finest in this German-speaking Swiss canton. The orderly rows of vines reflect characteristic Swiss neatness.

wines expensive in international terms, especially the very best wines. As the Swiss drink twice as much wine as they can produce and are conditioned to high prices, there is no need to export and little incentive, therefore, to develop better-value wines. Price apart, the finest Swiss whites can be delightful, and the best reds are getting deeper and more velvety by the vintage.

SWITZERLAND
Switzerland is divided into three basic areas: French-speaking, German-speaking, and Italian-speaking. Some of the wine-producing cantons cross these "international" boundaries and possess alternative names, with most vineyards concentrated around the country's lakes and rivers.

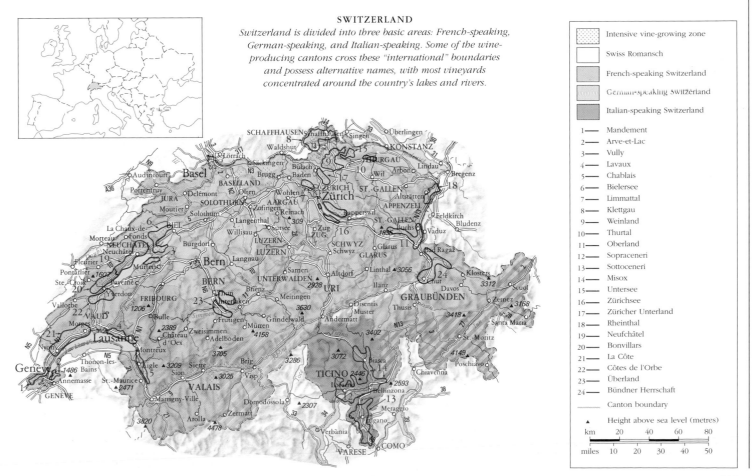

	Intensive vine-growing zone
	Swiss Romansch
	French-speaking Switzerland
	German-speaking Switzerland
	Italian-speaking Switzerland

1	Mandement
2	Arve-et-Lac
3	Vully
4	Lavaux
5	Chablais
6	Bielersee
7	Limmattal
8	Klettgau
9	Weinland
10	Thurtal
11	Oberland
12	Sopraceneri
13	Sottoceneri
14	Misox
15	Untersee
16	Zürichsee
17	Züricher Unterland
18	Rheinthal
19	Neufchâtel
20	Bonvillars
21	La Côte
22	Côtes de l'Orbe
23	Überland
24	Bündner Herrschaft
	Canton boundary
▲	Height above sea level (metres)

FACTORS AFFECTING TASTE AND QUALITY

LOCATION
Situated between the south of Germany, north of Italy, and the central-east French border.

CLIMATE
Continental Alpine conditions prevail, with local variations due to altitude, the tempering influence of lakes, and the sheltering effects of the various mountain ranges. An Alpine wind called the Foehn raises, rather than lowers, temperatures in some valleys. Rainfall is relatively low, and a number of areas, such as the Valais in the south, are very dry indeed. Spring frosts are a perennial threat in most areas.

ASPECT
Vines are grown in areas ranging from valley floors and lake shores to the steep Alpine foothill sites, which have an average altitude of 750 m (2,460 ft), although just south of Visp, they reach nearly 1,200 m (3,940 ft) and are reputedly the highest vineyards in Europe. The best sites are found on south-facing slopes, which maximize exposure to sun, and where the incline is too steep to encourage high yields.

SOIL
Mostly a glacial moraine (scree) of decomposed slate and schist, often with limestone over sedimented bedrock of limestone, clay, and sand. In the Vaud, Dézaley is famous for its "pudding stones", Chablais has limestone and marl, and Ollon and Bex both benefit from gypsum deposits.

VITICULTURE AND VINIFICATION
Terracing is required on the steeper sites, and so too is irrigation (with mountain water) in dry areas such as the Valais. Most vineyard work is labour-intensive, except in a few more gently sloping vineyards such as those around Lake Geneva (Lac Léman), where mechanical harvesting is practical. Careful vinification produces remarkably high yields. The last three decades have seen a growth in the production of red wine in what is generally a white-wine-dominated region.

GRAPE VARIETIES
Aligoté, Amigne, Ancellotta, Bacchus, Bonarda, Bondola, Cabernet franc, Cabernet sauvignon, Chardonnay, Charmont, Chasselas (*syn.* Dorin, Fendant, Gutedel, Perlan), Chenin blanc, Completer, Cornalin (*syn.* Landroter), Diolinoir, Doral, Elbling (*syn.* Räuschling), Freisa, Freishamer (*syn.* Frieburger), Gamaret, Gamay, Gewürztraminer (*syn.* Païen), Gouais (*syn.* Gwäss), Himbertscha, Humagne blanc, Humagne rouge, Kerner, Lafnetscha (possibly the same variety as Completer), Malbec, Marsanne (*syn.* Ermitage), Merlot, Müller-Thurgau (*syn.* Riesling x Sylvaner), Muscat à petits grains, Petite Arvine, Pinot blanc, Pinot gris (*syn.* Malvoisie, Ruländer), Pinot noir (*syn.* Blauburgunder, Clevner), Rèze, Riesling, Sauvignon blanc, Seibel (*syn.* Plantet), Sémillon, Seyval blanc, Sylvaner (*syn.* Silvaner), Syrah, Traminer (*syn.* Heida, Païn, Savagnin)

THE APPELLATIONS OF
SWITZERLAND

Note Under the federal appellation system all cantons have the right to their own appellation and each winemaking village within each canton can register its own appellation. Geneva was the first canton to comply in 1988, followed by Valais in 1991, Neuchâtel in 1993, and Vaud in 1995. Along with these village appellations, each canton may also designate generic district and stylistic appellations, the number of which is increasing all the time.

FRENCH-SPEAKING SWITZERLAND
Cantons *Fribourg, Geneva, Jura, Neuchâtel, Valais, Vaud*
District appellations *Vully* (part in Fribourg, part in Neuchâtel); *Arve-et-Lac, Arve-et-Rhône, Mandement* (Geneva); *Bonvillars, Chablais, La Côte, Côtes de l'Orbe, Lavaux* (Vaud)
Stylistic appellations *Oeil de Perdrix,* (Geneva, Neuchâtel, Valais, Vaud); *Perlan* (Geneva); *Amigne, Arvine, Cornalin, Dôle, Dôle Blanche, Ermitage, Fendant, Goron, Heidawein, Höllenwein, Pinot Noir, Vin de Païn, Vin du Glacier* (Valais); *Dorin, Salvagnin* (Vaud)
French-speaking Switzerland represents only 16 per cent of the country by area, yet manages to boast more than 80 per cent of its vineyards. Two-thirds of the wines are white, with Chasselas accounting for 90 per cent, while the Pinot noir and Gamay together represent 99 per cent of the black grapes planted. Valais is the longest-established, most famous, and by far the most intensively cultivated of Switzerland's cantons, with vineyards stretching along 50 kilometres (30 miles) of the Rhône, from Lac Léman (Lake Geneva) to Brig (in the German-speaking sector). The Valais canton accounts for more than one-third of the country's wines and even its lowliest wine villages are at least as good as the best villages of other Swiss cantons. The Vaud canton encompasses almost one-quarter of Switzerland's vineyards, which makes it the second most intensively cultivated canton in the country.

Villages *Auvernier · Cortaillod* (Neuchâtel); · *Salgesch · St.-Léonard · Vétroz* (Valais); *Calamin · Dézaley* (Vaud)
Growers *Château de Vaumarcus · André Ruedin* (Neuchâtel); *Charles Bonvin · Caves de Riondaz · Château Lichten · Domaine du Mont d'Or · Charles Favre · Maurice Gay · Alphonse Orsat, · Louis Vuignier* (Valais); *Henri Badoux · Château d'Allaman · Château Maison Blanche · Château de Vinzel · Clos de la George · Hammel · Domaine de la Lance · Domaine du Martheray · Domaine de Riencourt · Robert Isoz · Gérard Pinget · Rouvinez · J. & P. Testuz* (Vaud)

GERMAN-SPEAKING SWITZERLAND
Cantons *Aargau, Basel, Bern, Graubünden* (part), *St.-Gallen, Schwyz, Schaffhausen, Thurgau*
District appellations *Bielersee, Uberland* (Bern); *Bündner Herrschaft* (Graubünden); *Oberland, Rheinthal* (St.-Gallen); *Klettgau* (Schaffhausen); *Thurtal, Untersee* (Thurgau); *Flaachtal, Limmattal, Rafzerfelder, Züricher Unterland, Weinland* (Zürich)
Stylistic appellations *Clevner*
By far the largest of the three cultural divisions, German-speaking Switzerland (Eastern Switzerland) covers almost two-thirds of the country, yet encompasses only one-sixth of its total viticultural area. Aargau is best known for its red wines, but also produces off-dry, light, fragrant white wines of low alcohol content. Basel is a producer of white wine only. Although some rather thin and mean red wines are produced in Bern, the majority of grapes grown are white and produce wines that are fragrant and lively, with refreshing acidity. In Graubünden vineyards on the upper reaches of the Rhine, the Pinot noir ripens well and provides wines made from it with comparatively good colour and body. Saint-Gallen also encompasses the upper reaches of the Rhine and produces mostly red wine. The southern fringes of Graubünden fall within the Italian-speaking sector of Switzerland, where the canton is referred to locally as Grissons. The vines of Schaffhausen grow within sight of the famous falls of the Rhine. Thurgau is, of course, home of the famous Dr. Müller, who left his mark on world viticulture with his prolific Müller-Thurgau cross, and inevitably the grape grows there, although more than 50 per cent of the vines are Pinot noir and the fruity wine that grape produces is far superior. Zürich is the most important canton in German-speaking Switzerland, but it produces some of the most expensive, least impressive wines in the entire country, although Pinot noir grown on sheltered slopes with a good exposure to the sun can produce attractive fruity wines.

Villages *Brestenberger · Goldwand · Netteler* (Aargau) · *Schafis* (Bern) · *Fläsch · Jenins · Maenfeld · Malans* (Graubünden) · *Leutschen* (Schwyz) · *Hallau · Schaffhausen* (Schaffhausen)
Growers *Adelheid von Randenburg · Graaf von Spiegelberg · Hans Schlatter* (Schaffhausen)

ITALIAN-SPEAKING SWITZERLAND
Cantons *Ticino, Grissons* (part)
District appellations *Misox* (Grissons); *Sopraceneri, Sottoceneri* (Ticino)
Stylistic appellations
Bondola, Merlot del Ticino, Nostrano.
Italian-speaking Switzerland consists of the cantons of Ticino (also known as Tessin) and the southern fringes of Graubünden (also known as Grissons) and more than 80 per cent of the vineyards are planted with the Merlot grape variety. Merlot del Ticino is consistently one of the best wines produced in Switzerland. Labour costs are nowhere near as high as they are in the rest of the country, which also makes Merlot del Ticino the least expensive of Switzerland's finest wines.

Village *Misox* (Grissons)
Growers *Figli fu Alberto Daldini, Tamborini, Valsangiacomo* (Ticino)

THE WINE STYLES OF
SWITZERLAND

AMIGNE
Valais
WHITE Old Valais variety mostly grown at Vétroz, Amigne gives a full, rustic, smooth, dry white.

⌐⊸ 1–2 years

ARVINE
Valais
WHITE Another old Valais variety that makes an even richer, dry white, with a distinctive grapefruit character and good acidity. The Petite Arvine (to distinguish it from the lesser quality Grosse Arvine) adapts well to late-harvest styles and is highly regarded by Swiss wine lovers.

⌐⊸ 1–3 years

BLAUBURGUNDER
Eastern Switzerland

RED Synonym for Pinot noir used in German-speaking Switzerland; the best-coloured and velvety wines are made in Bündner Herrschaf.

⌐⊸ 2–7 years

BONDOLA
Ticino (Tessin)
RED An indigenous grape producing rustic reds on its own, Bondola is at its best in a wine called Nostrano, in which it is blended with Bonarda, Freisa, and other local varieties.

BONVILLARS
Vaud
WHITE Restricted to Chasselas grown around Lac de Neuchâtel in the villages of Côtes de l'Orbe and Vully, Bonvillars is lighter and more delicate and lively than Vaud wines of this variety grown further south.

⌐⊸ 1–2 years

CHABLAIS
Vaud
WHITE Restricted to Chasselas grown in the villages of Aigle, Bex, Ollon, Villeneuve, and Yvorne, Chablais is the most refined wine of this variety produced in Vaud, and should show some minerally complexity.

⌐⊸ 1–2 years

CHASSELAS
WHITE Called Fendant in the Valais, Dorin in the Vaud, and Perlan in Geneva, this is the most important Swiss grape variety and can be nicely flavoured, often having a charming *pétillance*. When grown on light, sandy soils it may have a lime-tree blossom aroma. The grape is sensitive to soil, with different characteristics depending on whether the soil is limestone, flint, gypsum, marl, schist, or whatever. Although it is possible to find relatively full, potentially long-lived wines from this variety, it is a wine best enjoyed young.

⌐⊸ 1–3 years

CLEVNER
Eastern Switzerland

RED Another official synonym for Pinot noir used in German-speaking Switzerland. *See* Blauburgunder.

COMPLETER
Graubünden
WHITE The Completer is rare grape variety of ancient origin that makes a fascinating, rich, *Auslese*-style of wine.

⌐⊸ 3–7 years

CORNALIN
Valais
RED Most vines of this indigenous Swiss variety are very old and make dark, powerful red wines that are rich and concentrated, with a full, spicy complexity.

⌐⊸ 3–10 years

LA CÔTE
Vaud
WHITE Restricted to Chasselas grown in the villages of Aubonne, Begnins, Bursinel, Coteau de Vincy, Féchy, Luins, Mont-sur-Rolle, Morges, Nyon, Perroy, and Vinzel, La Côte is the most floral and aromatic wine produced from Chasselas grapes in the Vaud.

⌐⊸ 1–2 years

CÔTES DE L'ORBE
Vaud
RED These are mostly light, fresh, fruity reds.

⌐⊸ 1–2 years

DÔLE
Valais
RED This wine is light red and consists of at least 50 per cent Pinot noir plus up to 50 per cent Gamay. It is the Swiss equivalent of Burgundy's Passetoutgrains.

⌐⊸ 3–7 years

DÔLE BLANCHE
Valais
WHITE The *blanc de noirs* version is popular, but does not carry its own appellation.

⌐⊸ 1–3 years

DORIN
Vaud
WHITE Chasselas made in a light, fresh, and easy-to-drink style.

⌐⊸ 9–18 months

ERMITAGE
Valais
WHITE A synonym for the old Rhône variety, Marsanne, used in the Valais. It makes delicately rich, sometimes quite refined, dry white wines that some enthusiasts like to age longer than I would advise.

⌐⊸ 1–4 years

FENDANT
Valais
WHITE This Chasselas is fleshy-styled and can have a flinty, lime-tree-blossom aroma.

⌐⊸ 1–3 years

GAMAY
Valais, Vaud

RED This Beaujolais grape in its pure varietal form makes red wines of little distinction, but blended with Pinot noir, it can be successful.

⌐⊸ 1–3 years

GAMAY DE GENÈVE
Geneva
RED These are light, fresh, easy-drinking red wines with gentle fruit and feeble colour.

⌐⊸ 1–2 years

GORON
Valais
RED This used to be an unclassified Dôle, made from grapes that failed to reach the minimum ripeness level, but it is now official.

⌐⊸ 1–2 years

HEIDAWEIN *OR* HEIDA
Valais
WHITE Fresh, lightly aromatic, dry and off-dry wine made from the Traminer grape.

⌐⊸ 1–2 years

HERMITAGE
See Ermitage AOC

HUMAGNE BLANC
WHITE The Humagne Blanc is a wine with a relatively high iron content, which could be the reason it used to be fed to babies, although it was probable that the dear little things cried when allowed to suck on Humagne blanc. It has a green bean or capsicum aroma, hints of

exotic fruit on the palate, and a touch of bitterness on the finish.

🍷— 1–3 years

HUMAGNE ROUGE
Valais

RED An old Valais variety, this dark-skinned grape hails from Italy's Valle d'Aosta and makes big, rich, rustic reds that traditionally go well with feathered game.

🍷— 4–8 years

JOHANNISBERG
Valais

WHITE This is not the Johannisberg Riesling, but is the official synonym for Sylvaner in the Valais. It is supposedly musky, but I have never noticed complexity in these wines, which are usually sappy and savoury with some sweetness.

🍷— 1–3 years

LAVAUX
Vaud

WHITE Restricted to Chasselas grown in the villages of Calamin, Chardonne, Dézaley, Epesses, Lutry, Saint-Saphorin, Vevey-Montreux, and Villette, Lavaux is the softest yet fullest wine of this variety produced in the Vaud.

🍷— 1–2 years

MALVOISIE
Valais

This synonym for the Pinot gris is used to identify sweet wines.

🍷— 2–5 years

MERLOT DEL TICINO
Ticini (Tessin)

RED The Merlot grape accounts for more than 80 per cent of the vines planted in Italian-speaking Switzerland, where it produces red wines that range from young and light-bodied to fuller, better-coloured wines that have a nice varietal perfume and are often aged in *barriques*. The VITI classification on a bottle of Merlot del Ticino used to be seen as a guarantee of superior quality, but now merely indicates the wine has had one year's ageing before being bottled.

🍷— 2–4 years (lighter styles),
3–10 years (*barrique* wines)

MÜLLER-THURGAU
Eastern Switzerland

WHITE This most prolific (supposedly) *Riesling* x *Sylvaner* cross was created in 1882 by Dr. Hermann Müller, who hailed from the canton of Thurgau, hence the name. It is rather ironic that the Swiss should call this grape *Riesling* x *Sylvaner* locally, rather than by the name that honours its Swiss origins, especially now that doubt over its parentage exists (many think it derived from a self-pollinated Riesling seed, *see* p.44), but the mild, grapey wine this variety produces even in its home canton is no more exciting than it is elsewhere, although relatively superior examples are produced in Aargau.

🍷— 1–2 years

MUSCAT
Valais

WHITE The Muscat à petits grains is traditionally grown in the Valais, in small quantities. It makes wines of very light body, with the grape's unmistakable varietal flowery aroma.

🍷— 1–2 years

NEUCHÂTEL
Neuchâtel

RED This Pinot noir wine is soft and smooth with elegant fruit, but does not have the weight, colour, or structure of those from the Valais.

WHITE This is a light, delicate, slightly spritzy pure Chasselas wine.

🍷— 2–4 years (red), 1–2 years (white)

NOSTRANO
Ticino

RED This used to be an inexpensive blend of *vin ordinaire* quality, produced from grapes that failed to reach appellation standard, but now it has its own official classification and the quality has certainly improved. Nostrano means "our" and literally refers to the local varieties used, as opposed to American hybrids.

🍷— 2–4 years

OEIL DE PERDRIX
Geneva, Neuchâtel, Valais, Vaud

ROSÉ Oeil de Perdrix, which literally means "partridge eye", is a French term for pale, dry rosé wines made from free-run Pinot noir. This version is mild and fruity.

🍷— 1–3 years

PERLAN
Geneva

WHITE These flowery, spritzy Chasselas wines must mention the canton of Geneva or one of the village names: L'Allondon, Bardonnex, Dardagny, Jussy, Lully, Peissy, Russin, or Satigny.

🍷— 9–18 months

PETITE ARVINE
See Arvine

PINOT NOIR
Valais

RED In a country like Switzerland that adores Burgundy, it is not surprising that top producers make some of Switzerland's most serious wines

with this grape variety – well coloured, velvety, with soft, cherry fruit and a touch of oak.

🍷— 3–6 years (up 10 years in exceptional cases)

PINOT NOIR

RED Non-appellation Pinot Noir wines are produced elsewhere in Switzerland, most notably the Vaud, but even the best wines cannot match the colour and intensity that is typical of the Valais appellation.

🍷— 2–4 years

RÄUSCHLING
Eastern Switzerland

WHITE This rarely seen variety is in decline and is now found only along the shore of Lake Zurich, where it is appreciated for its very fresh scents and fine acidity.

🍷— 9–18 months

RIESLING
Valais

WHITE Little is grown and apart from exceptional botrytized wines, Swiss Riesling does not have the quality or varietal intensity of Germany or Austria. This is a mystery, as the steepest and hottest slopes of the Rhône in the Valais should compare with the greatest wines of the Mosel and Wachau.

🍷— 2–4 years (up to 20 years for botrytis wines)

SALVAGNIN
Vaud

WHITE A light, supple red-wine blend of Pinot noir and Gamay, this is the Vaud's equivalent of the more famous Dôle.

🍷— 1–3 years

SÜSSDRUCK
Eastern Switzerland

ROSÉ A soft, fresh, dry rosé made exclusively from free-run Pinot noir.

🍷— 1–2 years

SYRAH
Valais

RED This grape is at home in the heat and exposure of the northern Côtes du Rhône, and in Valais the Rhône is as northerly as it gets. Peppery black fruits distinguish the wine.

🍷— 3–10 years

VIN DE PAIN
Valais

WHITE Fresh, gently aromatic, dry white wine made from the Traminer.

🍷— 1–3 years

VIN DU GLACIER
Valais

Although Switzerland's equivalent of Germany's Eiswein tends to be oxidative, this rare product does have its enthusiastic followers.

🍷— 2–5 years

❖AUSTRIA❖

Austria used to be seen as a winemaking clone of Germany, but over the last decade, Austria has slowly yet surely begun to establish its own unique wine identity, and it produces some exceptionally fine red wines.

IN THE LATE 1970s, Austrian wine production increased as domestic consumption declined, resulting in the largest wine lake outside the EC. Austria's wine industry was designed chiefly for exports to Germany, traditionally its only significant customer. After a succession of bumper harvests in both Germany and Austria, sales to Germany dried up, but overproduction in Austria continued. With hindsight, the so-called "anti-freeze" scandal which took place in 1985 can be seen as a godsend for Austrian wine. Call it a scam or a scandal, fraud, or deception, but it

AUSBRUCH – A RELIC OF THE AUSTRO-HUNGARIAN EMPIRE

Ausbruch is a still-popular style of wine that harks back to the days of the Austro-Hungarian Empire (and is also still produced in Hungary). At 138° Oechsle (*see* p.262), *Ausbruch* falls between the sweetness levels of *Beerenauslese* (127°) and *Trockenbeerenauslese* (150°). In terms of character, however, *Ausbruch* should be totally different from either a *Beerenauslese* or *Trockenbeerenauslese*. The name means "to break up"; the wine is made traditionally from the richest and sweetest botrytized grapes that are so shrivelled and dried-out that to press them is virtually impossible without first moistening the mass (breaking it up) with a more liquescent juice (the regulation stipulates *Spätlese* quality).

A true *Ausbruch* is overwhelmed by an intensely raisiny aroma and flavour that may be even more botrytized than a *Trockenbeerenauslese*, yet the wine itself need not necessarily be as rich.

Weinbauregion Niederösterreich
- Wachau
- Kamtal-Donauland
- Weinviertel
- Donauland-Carnuntum
- Thermenregion

Weinbauregion Wien
- Wien

Weinbauregion Burgenland
- Neusiedler See
- Neusiedler See-Hügelland
- Mittelburgenland
- Südburgenland

Weinbauregion Steiermark
- Weststeiermark
- Süd-Oststeiermark
- Südsteiermark
- Intensive vine-growing zone
- ● Best wine villages
- Provincial boundary
- ▲ Height above sea level (metres)

km 10 20 30 40 50
miles 5 10 15 20 25 30

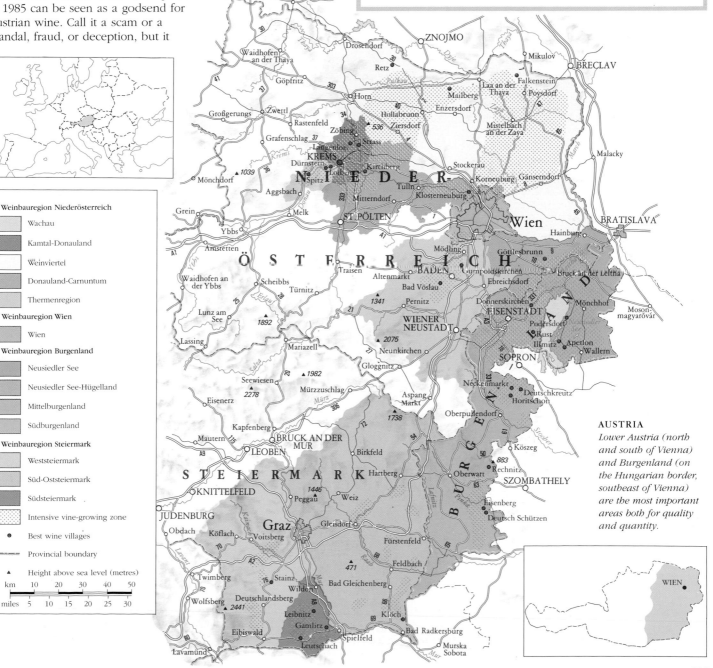

AUSTRIA
Lower Austria (north and south of Vienna) and Burgenland (on the Hungarian border, southeast of Vienna) are the most important areas both for quality and quantity.

was not the health scare it was made out to be. It did, however, have the effect of putting the Austrian government under enormous pressure to tighten up controls, with the result that Austria now has the most strictly controlled, safest wine industry in the world.

WHAT WAS THE ANTI-FREEZE SCANDAL?
In 1985, a handful of Austria's 40,000 wine producers used diethylene glycol to sweeten their wines artificially. The media throughout the world claimed that Austrian wines had been poisoned with anti-freeze, but it was not anti-freeze of course (ethylene glycol is). Diethylene glycol is in fact less toxic than alcohol, so adding it actually made the wines less poisonous.

THE MODERN WINE TRADE
Enthusiasts have always known that Austria produces some of the greatest botrytized wines in the world, yet just how electrifying these wines can be became clear when Willy Opitz, one of the smallest, but truly greatest, dessert wine producers, took the trouble to tour world markets and speak to people about his products. Over the last few years Austria has produced Cabernet sauvignon and Chardonnay to a very high standard and even St. Laurent, an obscure local variety, has proved to be quite stunning. What Austria must do now is promote its greatest Riesling, which can compare with the best from Germany, and export its top Grüner Veltliner, and keep pushing these wines.

STEINER HUND, WACHAU
An aerial view of some of Austria's most steeply terraced vineyards in the Steiner Hund, where some of the country's greatest Riesling wines are produced.

AUSTRIA VERSUS GERMANY

Both countries operate wine regimes that base levels of quality on degrees of ripeness by measuring the amount of sugar found in the grapes at the time of harvest. As in Germany, Austrian wines range from *Tafelwein*, through *Qualitätswein*, to *Trockenbeerenauslese*. The overview below shows that most Austrian wines conform to higher minimum standards than their German counterparts. More significant, however, is the fact that the minimum level for each category is rigid, so it has a distinctive style. This gives the consumer a clear idea of what to expect, whereas a German category varies according to the variety of grape and its area of origin. In Germany, only experience can reveal that a Mosel *Auslese*, for example, tastes no sweeter than a *Spätlese* from other regions. Also, *Süssreserve* is not allowed for any *Prädikat* wines, whereas in Germany this is permitted for *Kabinett*.

MINIMUM OECHSLE LEVELS

QUALITY CATEGORY	AUSTRIA	GERMANY
Tafelwein	63°	44–50°
Landwein	63°	47–55°
Qualitätswein	73°	50–72°
Kabinett	83.5°	67–85°
Spätlese	94°	76–95°
Auslese	105°	83–105°
Beerenauslese	127°	110–128°
Eiswein	127°	110–128°
Ausbruch	138°	N/A
Trockenbeerenauslese	156°	150–154°

FACTORS AFFECTING TASTE AND QUALITY

LOCATION
The vineyards are in the east of the country, north, and south of Vienna, bordering the Czech republic, Hungary, and Yugoslavia.

CLIMATE
The climate is a warm, dry continental type with annual rainfall varying between 57 and 77 cm (23–31 in). The hottest and driest area is Burgenland, where in the warm autumns, mists rising from the Neusiedler See help promote *Botrytis cinerea* (the "noble rot" beloved by winegrowers).

ASPECT
Vines are grown on all types of land, from the plains of the Danube to its valley sides – which are often very steep and terraced – and from the hilly Burgenland to the slopes of mountainous Styria.

SOIL
Soils vary from generally stony schist, limestone, and gravel (though occasionally loamy) in the north, through predominantly sandy soils on the shores of the Neusiedler See in Burgenland, to mainly clay with some volcanic soils in Styria.

VITICULTURE AND VINIFICATION
Not surprisingly, Austria's methods are similar to those of Germany but although modern techniques have been introduced here, far more Austrian wine is produced by traditional methods than is the case in Germany. More than 85 per cent of the country's vines are cultivated by the Lenz Moser system, which is a method of training vines to twice their normal height, thus achieving a comparatively higher ratio of quality to cost, by enabling the use of mechanized harvesting. This system brought fame to its Austrian inventor, Lenz Moser, and has been adopted by at least one grower in most winemaking countries. Harvesting is traditionally accomplished in *tries*, particularly on steeper slopes and for sweeter styles.

GRAPE VARIETIES
Blauberger, Blauer Portugieser, Blauer Wildbacher, Blaufränkisch, Bouviertraube, Cabernet franc, Cabernet sauvignon, Chardonnay, Frühroter Veltliner (*syn.* Malvasia), Furmint, Gewürztraminer, Goldburger, Grüner Veltliner, Pinot blanc, Pinot noir, Merlot, Müller-Thurgau, Muskateller, Muskatottonel, Neuburger, Pinot gris, Roter Veltliner, Rotgipfler, Sauvignon blanc, Scheurebe, St. Laurent, Silvaner, Trollinger, Riesling, Welschriesling, Zierfandler, Zweigelt

THE WACHAU
Much of Austria is very picturesque, making it a popular holiday destination; here the lush vineyards complement this typical Lower Austrian landscape.

THE WINE STYLES OF
AUSTRIA

BLAUBURGER

RED A *Blauer Portugieser* x *Blaufränkisch* cross that produces a well-coloured wine of little distinction, but tends to improve in bottle.

⌐⊷ 1–3 years

⊻ *Weingut Schützenhof Fam. Korpe*
• *Willi Opitz*

BLAUER PORTUGIESER

RED This used to be Austria's most widely planted black-grape variety and is still commonly found in Lower Austria, particularly Paulkautal, Retz, and the Thermenregion, where it makes a light-bodied but well-coloured red wine with a mild flavour, hinting of violets.

⌐⊷ 1–2 years

⊻ *Johann Gipsberg* • *H. V. Reinisch*

BLAUER WILDBACHER

RED/ROSÉ Otherwise known as Schilcher, this variety traditionally produces a light, dry, crisp, and fruity, pale rosé wine.

⌐⊷ 1–2 years

⊻ *E. & M. Müller*

BLAUFRÄNKISCH

RED Known as Lemberger in Germany and Kékfrankos in Hungary, this variety is popular in Neusiedler See-Hügelland Burgenland, where it produces tart, fruity wine with good tannin and an underlying hint of cherries and spice. The best examples of Blaufränkisch are fat and sometimes given time in oak.

⌐⊷ 2–4 years

⊻ *Weingut Gessellmann* (Creitzer)
• *Feiler-Artinger*
• *Weingut Fam. Igler*
• *Weingut H. und M. Krutzler*

BOUVIER

BOUVIER
Trockenbeerenauslese
Apetlon — Neusiedler See
1983

WHITE An early-ripening table grape that has a low natural acidity and is often used for high-quality *Prädikatswein*.

⌐⊷ 1–3 year (*Qualitätswein*)

⌐⊷ 2–8 years (*Prädikatswein*)

⊻ *Willi Opitz*

CABERNET SAUVIGNON

RED Very little of this variety used to be grown in Austria. Until 1982 the only commercial cultivation of Cabernet sauvignon was by Schlumberger at Bad Vöslau. Then Lenz Moser received special permission to cultivate 2.5 hectares (6 acres) at Mailberg, and the first Cabernet sauvignon was grown in 1986 in Lower Austria. Nowadays everyone seems to be growing Cabernet sauvignon.

⌐⊷ 5–6 years (*Qualitätswein*)

⌐⊷ 10–15 years (*Prädikatswein*)

⊻ *Lenz Moser* (Siegendorf Prestige)
• *Weingut Fam. Igler* • *Weingut Gessellmann*

CHARDONNAY

WHITE Also known in Austria as Feinburgunder, this grape variety has been grown for decades in Styria, where it is known as Morillon. Cultivation of this grape has risen rapidly since the early 1990s, producing some fat, rich wines.

⌐⊷ 2–5 years

⊻ *Weingut Bründlmayer* (Kabinett)
• *Juris-Stiegelmar* (Classic) • *H. V. Reinisch*
• *Andreas Schafler* • *Weingut Gottfried Schellmann* • *Weingut Tement*

FRÜHROTER VELTLINER

WHITE Sometimes labelled Malvasia, this dry Frühroter Veltliner has more alcohol and body than Austria's most widely grown white wine, Grüner Veltliner.

⌐⊷ 1–2 years

⊻ *Weingut Leth*

FURMINT

WHITE This is a rarely encountered Hungarian dry, medium- to full-bodied, rich, and fruity varietal that does well at Rust in Burgenland.

⌐⊷ 3–5 years

⊻ *Weinbau Ladislaus und Robert Wenzel*

GEWÜRZTRAMINER

WHITE Usually labelled Traminer or Roter Traminer, the wines from this variety range from light and floral to intensely aromatic. They may be dry or have one of various shades of sweetness. They are the fullest, richest, and most pungent of *Trockenbeerenauslesen*.

⌐⊷ 3–6 years

⊻ *Weingut Rheinhold Polz*
• *Andreas Schaefler* (Traminer)

GOLDBURGER

WHITE This is a *Welschriesling* x *Orangetraube* cross that produces white wines that are used for blending purposes.

⌐⊷ 1–3 years

GRÜNER VELTLINER

WHITE The Danube is the best area for great Grüner Veltliner, the finest examples of which have a fiery flavour that delivers a burning sensation reminiscent of freshly ground pepper. It certainly is not the bland *vin ordinaire* made by this grape in virtually every other area.

⌐⊷ 1–4 years (*Qualitätswein*)

⌐⊷ 3–10 years (*Prädikatswein*)

⊻ *Weingut Bründlmayer* (Langenloiser Berg Vogelsang Kabinett, Ried Lamm, Spätlese Trocken) • *Freie Weingärtner Wachau* (Weissenkirchner Achleiten "Smaragd") • *Graf Hardegg* (Dreikreuzen Kabinett, Maximilian Kabinett) • *Weingut Hirtzberger* (Rotes Tor "Smaragd", Spitzer Honifogl) • *Lenz Moser* (Knights of Malta) • *Weingut Mantlerhhof* (especially for older vintages) • *Metternich-Sandor* (Princess) • *Weingut Franz Prager* • *Weingut Wieninger* (Ried Herrenholz)

JUBLINÄUMSREBE

WHITE Another *Blauer Portugieser* x *Blaufränkisch* cross, this variety is allowed for *Prädikatswein* only, as its mild character is transformed by botrytis.

⌐⊷ 3–7 years

MERLOT

RED Small amounts are grown in Krems, Mailberg, and Furth in Lower Austria, plus in a few scattered plots in Burgenland. This variety has potential in Austria, as it can produce richly coloured red wines with soft, spicy-juicy fruit, but has been under-exploited until quite recently.

⌐⊷ 1–3 years (*Qualitätswein*)

⌐⊷ 3–5 years (*Prädikatswein*)

⊻ *Hofkellerei des Fürsten von Liechtenstein* (Herrenbaumgärtner Spätlese)

MÜLLER-THURGAU

WHITE Often labelled as *Riesling* x *Silvaner*, this is Austria's second most prolific grape variety. Austrian exporters should realize the value of Müller-Thurgau for adding fat to their Grüner Veltliners, most of which do not have the bite found in the best examples and lack a depth of fruit – outside Austria, the international taste is for a less peppery and more fruity style. The best of Austria's pure varietal Müller-Thurgaus have a fine, spicy character that is superior to the average German version.

⌐⊷ 1–2 years

⊻ *Weingut Hirtzberger*
• *Weingut Schützenhof Fam. Korper*

MUSKATELLER

WHITE The Muskateller is an under-exploited variety that makes some of Burgenland's finest *Prädikatswein* and excels in the sheltered sites of Styria.

⌐⊷ 1–3 years (*Qualitätswein*)

⌐⊷ 2–10 years (*Prädikatswein*)

⊻ *Weingut Leth* • *Weinhof Platzer*
• *Weinbau Ladislaus und Robert Wenzel*

MUSKAT-OTTONEL

WHITE Less weighty than the Muskateller, the Muskat-Ottonel variety has more immediate aromatic appeal and is best drunk when young.

⌐⊷ 2–4 years

⊻ *Willi Opitz*

NEUBURGER

WHITE An Austrian variety that excels on chalky soil, producing full-bodied wines with a typically nutty flavour in all categories of sweetness.

⌐⊷ 2–4 years (*Qualitätswein*)

⌐⊷ 3–8 years (*Prädikatswein*)

⊻ *Dip.-Ing. Kasl Alpart* • *H. V. Reinisch*

PINOT BLANC

WHITE Often called Klevner or Weisser Burgunder, this produces a fresh, light-bodied, easy-to-drink wine at lower quality levels. In exceptional years it can develop a fine spicy-richness in the upper *Prädikatswein* categories.

⌐⊷ 2–4 years (*Qualitätswein*)

⌐⊷ 3–8 years (*Prädikatswein*)

⊻ *Weingut Skoff* (Kabinett)

PINOT GRIS

WHITE More commonly sold in Austria as Ruländer or Grauer Burgunder, this is a fuller, spicier version of Pinot blanc but it has a typical nutty richness.

⌐— 2–4 years (*Qualitätswein*)

⌐— 3–8 years (*Prädikatswein*)

✓ *Weingut Tement*

PINOT NOIR

RED Labelled Blauer Burgunder, Blauer Spätburgunder, or Blauburgunder in different parts of Austria, the wines from this grape variety are often disappointing, although there are a few growers that excel.

⌐— 1–3 years

✓ *Weingut Bründlmayer • Johann Gipsberg • Juris-Stiegelmar • H. V. Reinisch*

RIESLING

WHITE In Austria the wines from this grape should be sold as Weisser Riesling or Rheinriesling, in order to distinguish it from Welschriesling. Wachau and Kremser Riesling can be compared with fine German examples.

⌐— 2–6 years (*Qualitätswein*)

⌐— 4–12 years (*Prädikatswein*)

✓ *Weingut Bründlmayer* (Spätlese) • *Freie Weingärtner Wachau* (Weissenkirchner Achleiten "Federspiel" & "Smaragd") • *Weingut Hirtzberger* (Spitzer Steinterrassen "Federspiel") • *Hofkellerei des Fürsten von Liechtenstein* (Spätlese) • *Weingut Thiery-Weber* (Kremser Sandgrube)

ROTER VELTLINER

WHITE The Roter Veltliner produces a rather neutral white wine that is usually blended into light, dry wines.

⌐— 1–3 years

ROTGIPFLER

WHITE This makes a robust, full-bodied, spicy wine of not dissimilar character to the Zierfandler, which is often made into a dry style, although the semi-sweet Rotgipfler of Gumpoldskirchen may be the most famous rendition of this grape.

⌐— 3–7 years

✓ *Weinbau Franz Kurz • Weingut Hoffer • Weingut Gottfried Schellmann*

ST. LAURENT

RED This is a variety that typically produces a light, mild-flavoured wine of quaffing character. St. Laurent is thought to be related to Pinot noir. Since 1990 it has to be said that producers such as Weingut Umathum in Neusiedler See-Hügelland and Weingut Gessellmann in Mittelburgenland can craft lovely, velvety wines of Pinot-like quality and style.

⌐— 1–3 years

✓ *Weingut Gessellmann • Johann Gipsberg • Weingut Umathum* (Vom Stein)

SAUVIGNON BLANC

WHITE Called Muskat-Silvaner (or occasionally Weisser sauvignon), this variety grown in Styria normally makes an austere, dry style, but can really excel at the higher levels of *Prädikatswein*.

⌐— 2–4 years (*Qualitätswein*)

⌐— 4–10 years (*Pradikätswein*)

✓ *Weingut Fam. Kollwentz* (Römerhof) • *Weingut Rheinhold Polz* • *Weingut Skoff* (Gamlitz Eckberg Edel Kabinett) • *Weingut Tement*

SCHEUREBE

WHITE This grape variety is not very pleasant at *Qualitätswein* level, but develops a beautiful aromatic character at higher levels of *Prädikatswein*.

⌐— 2–4 years

✓ *Weingut Gessellmann • Willi Opitz*

SILVANER

WHITE Seldom seen, tomato-tasting varietal.

⌐— 1–2 years

✓ *Weingut Sonnhof Josef Jurtschitsch*

WELSCHRIESLING

WHITE This is Austria's third most prolific variety, making very ordinary dry wines, but it can be rich and stylish at upper levels of *Prädikatswein*.

⌐— 1–3 years (*Qualitätswein*)

⌐— 2–8 years (*Pradikätswein*)

✓ *Weingut Bründlmayer • Willi Opitz • Weinhof Platzer • Weingut Tement*

ZIERFANDLER

WHITE Also known as Spätrot, this variety makes full-bodied and well-flavoured dry wine.

⌐— 2–6 years

✓ *Weinbau Franz Kurz • Weingut Hoffer • Weingut Gottfried Schellmann*

ZWEIGELT

RED Another mild red-wine variety, Zweigelt is sometimes given the name Blauer Zweigelt or Rotburger. The best examples have a structure that is suited to food, with big, peppery fruit, but the norm is rather light and lacklustre.

⌐— 1–3 years

✓ *Johann Gipsberg • Weingut Walter Glatzer* (Dornenvoge) • *Weingut Maria Magdalena Romer* (Schweizerreid)

OTHER STYLES

BLENDED RED

The finest of these blended red wines are usually oak-aged in new *barriques* and Cabernet-sauvignon-based for backbone, with Blaufrankish, St. Laurent, and sometimes Zweigelt added for fruit and softness.

⌐— 2–8 years

✓ *Weingut Gessellmann* (Opus Eximium) • *Weingut Igler* (Cuvée Vulcano) • *Weingut Josef Pöckl* (Admiral) • *H. V. Reinisch* (Cabernet-Merlot) • *Schlossweingut Malteser Ritterorden* (Cabernet Sauvignon-Merlot) • *Weingut Umathum* (Ried Hallebühl Cuvée Rot)

BLENDED WHITE

Cheap, commercial white wine blends are commonly found in Austria, whereas finer examples of the blender's art are thin on the ground. However, Franz Mayer produces an intriguing blend of Grüner Veltliner, Müller-Thurgau, Riesling, Silvaner, and Zierfandler.

✓ *Weingut Franz Mayer* (Grinzinger Reisenberg)

BOTTLE-FERMENTED SPARKLING

Austria's best-known sparkling wine is the bottle-fermented Schlumberge, produced in Vienna. Unfortunately, it seldom excels in quality. A small grower in Süd-Oststeiermark makes the best Austrian sparkling wine I have ever tasted.

✓ *Weinhof Platzer* (Pinot Cuvée)

THE APPELLATIONS OF
AUSTRIA

BURGENLAND

Austria's easternmost region is also its warmest. It consistently provides overripe grapes, almost guaranteeing a substantial production of *Prädikatswein* each year. The Mittelburgenland and Südburgenland are Austria's most important red-wine areas, with black varieties accounting for some 75 per cent of the vines cultivated.

NEUSIEDLER SEE

These vineyards and those of Neusiedler See-Hügelland are within the area of influence of Neusiedler See, a vast, shallow pan of water barely two metres (six and a half feet) deep. Its microclimate produces more botrytized grapes than any other wine area in the world.

✓ **Villages** *Apetlon • Illmitz • Podersdorf* **Growers** *Juris-Stiegelmar • Alois Kracher • Willi Opitz • Weingut Josef Pöckl • Weingut Umathum*

NEUSIEDLER SEE-HÜGELLAND

See Neusiedler See

✓ **Villages** *Donnerskirchen • Rust* **Growers** *Feiler-Artinger • Weingut Fam. Kollwentz* (Römerhof) • *Weinbau Ladislaus und Robert Wenzel*

MITTELBURGENLAND

Mittelburgenland was originally part of the old Rust-Neusiedler See but it is physically separated from the Neusiedler See by the Sopron wine area of Hungary. Mittelburgenland wines are more *passerillage* than botrytized in character. This is a red-wine district, with some 75 per cent of the production coming from varieties such as Blaufränkisch and Zweigelt.

The wines from this region do not have the body, tannin, and acidity balance that is associated with even the most modest red wines.

✓ **Villages** *Deutschkreuz*
• *Horitschon* • *Neckenmarkt*
Growers *Weingut Gessellmann*
• *Weingut Fam. Igler*

SÜDBURGENLAND

The red wines, mainly Blaufränkisch, are generally uninspiring. Some surprisingly fine *Prädikatswein* from the modest Welschriesling are also made.

✓ **Villages** *Deutsch Schützen*
• *Eisenberg* • *Rechnitz*
Growers *Weingut Schützenhof Fam. Korper*
• *Weingut H. und. M Krutzler*

KÄRNTEN

The wines of Kärnten are confined to a small area immediately to the west of Weststeiermark (Western Styria), comprising a few vineyards scattered between the towns of Klagenfurt and St. Andrä (not the St. Andrä in Südsteiermark). Red, white, Schilcher, and Bergwein wines are produced and sold by one or two small firms, but the quality of the wines is very modest.

LOWER AUSTRIA *or* NIEDERÖSTERREICH

This is Austria's premier dry-wine region. It is famous for its peppery Grüner Veltliners and the elegance of its Rieslings. Top Rieslings can be light and airy in their youth, but they attain a richness after a few years in bottle and can achieve a fine, racy balance comparable to some of the best German Rieslings. *Kabinett* is the style that dominates the classic wines of this region, although *Spätlese* and, occasionally, *Auslese* wines are made in the hottest years.

WACHAU

On a par with Kamtal-Donauland as Lower Austria's top-performing district, Wachau makes many fine varietals including Grüner Veltliner, the most important, and Riesling, the best.

✓ **Villages** *Durnstein* • *Loiben* • *Spitz*
Growers *Weingut Hirtzberger* • *Weingut Franz Prager* • *Freie Weingärtner Wachau*

KAMTAL-DONAULAND

As for the Wachau except that, if anything, it produces better Rieslings.

✓ **Villages** *Krems* • *Langenlois* • *Strass*
Growers *Weingut Bründlmayer*
• *Graf Hardegg* • *Weingut Sonnhof Josef Jurtschitsch* • *Weingut Mantlerhhof*
• *Metternich-Sandor* • *Weingut Thiery-Weber*

DONAULAND-CARNUNTUM

Donauland-Carnuntum is an area of historic, rather than intrinsic, viticultural importance, where the wines are good value, but not actually top class. Its winemaking fame extends back to Roman times. In addition, it boasts the world's oldest viticultural college, located at Klosterneuburg, and at Göttelsbrunn a

200-year-old Brauner veltliner vine is to be found. Believed to be the oldest in Europe, this vine produces an astonishing five hectolitres (55 cases) in a good vintage.

✓ **Villages** *Göttelsbrunn*
• *Kirchberg* • *Klosterneuburg*
Growers *Weingut Leth* • *Weingut Fam. Pitnauer* • *Weingut Neumayer*

WEINVIERTEL

This large area combines two former districts of Retz (the hinterland of Kamtal-Donauland) and Falkenstein, a totally separate area north of Vienna. Both extend northwards to the border with the Czech Republic. Some reds but mostly white wines are made. Although few could be said to have any class, they are well made, drinkable, and represent great value for money.

✓ **Villages** *Falkenstein* • *Mailberg* • *Retz*
Growers *Hofkellerei des Fürsten von Liechtenstein* • *Lenz Moser*
• *Schlossweingut Malteser Ritterorden*

THERMENREGION

One of Austria's warmest regions, producing red and white wines, with the Blauer Portugieser and Neuburger dominating. Zierfandler and Rotgipfler are specialities of Gumpoldskirchen.

✓ **Villages** *Bad Vöslau* • *Gumpoldskirchen*
Growers *Dip.-Ing. Kasl Alpart*
• *Johann Gipsberg* • *Weingut Hoffer*
• *H.V. Reinisch* • *Andreas Schafler*
• *Weingut Gottfried Schollmann*

OBERÖSTERREICH

This is a large region to the west of the Wachau, but with just 85 hectares (210 acres) of vineyards in the vicinity of Linz. To my knowledge, all the wines are sold under the "Weinbauer" brand in a *gasthof* at Hofkirchen.

STYRIA *or* STEIERMARK

Situated in the southeastern corner of Austria, this region has a high level of rainfall interspersed with exceptional levels of sunshine and warmth. The region makes red and very dry white wines and, although few particularly fine-quality wines are encountered, there are many interesting local specialities. The most famous is Schilcher. Made from the obscure Blauer wildbacher grape, it is a sort of blush-wine that results from the briefest maceration on the grape skins. There are three wine districts:

SÜDSTEIERMARK

The very best wines of this area have Stryia's naturally high acidity, but this is combined with delicate and pure fruit flavours, making for exceptional finesse, particularly in varieties such as Gewürztraminer, Chardonnay (known locally as Morillon), and Riesling.

✓ **Villages** *Gamlitz* • *Leibnitz* • *Leutschach*
Growers *Weingut Muster* • *Weingut Rheinhold Polz* • *Weingut Skoff*
• *Weingut Tement*

WESTSTEIERMARK

Made of some 70 per cent Schilcherwein, Zwiebelschilcher is an onion-skin-coloured Schilcher, which is grown on the slopes above Stainz. Another speciality is Sauvignon blanc, known locally as Muskat-Silvaner, a somewhat mystifying synonym since the searingly dry wines it produces in these vineyards (and elsewhere for that matter) have absolutely no hint of either Muskat or Silvaner, and the parentage of the Sauvignon blanc vine has, of course, no connection with either of these varieties.

✓ **Villages** *Stainz*
Grower *E. & M. Müller*

SÜD-OSTSTEIERMARK

The Müller-Thurgau and Welschriesling are surprisingly successful in the Süd-Oststeiermark, and the Gewürztraminer can be the most expressive in Austria. Weingut Gräflich Stügkh'sches is the oldest, best-known, and most traditional producer, but the wines of Manfred Platzer are more expressive.

✓ **Villages** *Kloch*
Grower *Weinhof Platzer*

VIENNA *or* WIEN

Until Madrid recently revived its ancient appellation, Vienna was the only capital city in Europe to have its own wine-growing region. Most of the wines are sold by the pitcher as *Wiener Heuriger*, in the city's many bars called *Heurigen* (also known as *Buschenschanken*). The wine is less than one year old when sold. As much as 28 per cent is blended, but pure varietals of classic grapes are on the increase. There are no inner districts, but there are several wine villages within the city limits, of which the most famous is Grinzing.

✓ **Growers** *Weingut Franz Mayer*
• *Weingut Wieninger*

TIROL

The Zirler Weinhof produces some 135 hectolitres (1,500 cases) of very ordinary wine from just 1.5 hectares (less than 4 acres) of Müller-Thurgau, Blauer Portugieser, and Zweigelt at Zirl. This might seem an unlikely place to plant a vineyard, if not for the fact that it is conveniently placed on the tourist route to the popular resort of Seefeld.

VORARLBERG

Vorarlberg is the westernmost region of Austria. It used to boast 100 hectares (247 acres) of vines, but only six hectares (15 acres) exist today, strung out between Bregenz, on Lake Constance (Bodensee), and Frastanz, close to Liechtenstein. The quality of the wine is unremarkably ordinary, and there are only about half-a-dozen growers who sell their wines commercially.

❖ SOUTHEAST EUROPE ❖

The vineyards of Southeast Europe stretch from Bohemia in the Czech Republic, close to the German border, to the shores of Kazakhstan on the Caspian sea. The area produces every conceivable style of wine, employing every conceivable viticultural and oenological practice – from the very crude to the latest high-tech.

SO MUCH HAS HAPPENED to reshape this part of the world since the first edition of this encyclopedia was published over a decade ago that it is easy to forget how Europe was then.

So much is in flux that it is very difficult to pin down international borders, let alone assess the current winemaking situation in many countries. The future is, I am afraid, not quite as bright or as certain as some observers make it out to be. Although there is a great deal of optimism about East European wines and there is certainly no denying that a huge potential exists, this will not be tapped for a very long time indeed. If it is going to take at least 20 years for former East Germany to come up to Western standards using the 110 billion dollars that the Federal Republic is pouring into its economy each year, how long will it take the rest of Eastern Europe, Russia, and other former USSR states to achieve the same?

Apart from an odd bit of equipment brought in here or there by flying winemakers and a number of showcase wineries (mostly in Bulgaria and Hungary), Eastern Europe's wineries are so primitive in many countries that the entire infrastructure of the wine industry will have to be discarded and rebuilt. The vineyards need replanting with the correct clones and rootstock. In these countries, transportation of grapes takes far too long and is commonly conducted in huge, rusting skips instead of small plastic crates, thus the vast bulk of every harvest fails to achieve its potential on the vine and much of the quality that does exist is thrown away as soon as it is picked. Re-equipping existing wineries is a waste of money. Eastern Europe and its wines must be put into perspective. There are many great-value wines and some of exceptional quality, too, but when you enjoy them do not be misled into concluding that Eastern Europe will be the next Australia. The level of investment required is enormous and wine is not high on the priority list.

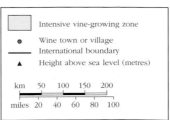

Intensive vine-growing zone
• Wine town or village
— International boundary
▲ Height above sea level (metres)

km 50 100 150 200
miles 20 40 60 80 100

SOUTHEAST EUROPE

Who would have guessed that within weeks of the Berlin wall coming down, the mood of freedom would touch every Eastern Bloc country? Few of us, I suspect, but it did and the effect was an unprecedented change to the face of Southeast Europe. As the precise borders and destiny of some nations will remain uncertain for many years to come, it seemed prudent for this edition to bring them together in one chapter with, for geographical and cartographical reasons, Greece.

LOW-TECH VINEYARDS IN ROMANIA

Rickety pergolas providing support for vines and old thatched-roof buildings reflect the conditions that most of Romania's agricultural industry has survived on since medieval times.

BULGARIA

Once the most reliable wine-producing country in Eastern Europe, Bulgaria was fashionable for cheap Cabernet Sauvignon as early as 1975, but it is no longer the most consistent source of cheap but good wine and its reputation is in danger of becoming passé. The privatization of the industry has, however, created vast new vineyards and, although wines are no longer blended into one dependable product, the best wines are more individual.

ALTHOUGH THE BULGARIANS have been cultivating vines for more than 3,000 years, winemaking came to a halt when the Turks imposed Muslim rule between 1396 and 1878. It was not until 1918 that winemaking began again in earnest, and it was only in the 1970s that the Bulgarians made any real effort to export their wines. During the mid-1970s Cabernet sauvignon was the most fashionable wine grape. At the same time, the economic depression that was affecting most western countries meant that established wine drinkers were on the lookout for cheaper alternatives to Bordeaux.

EXPORTING WINE

Cabernet Sauvignon from Bulgaria's Suhindol region was not simply cheap in the 1970s, it was extraordinarily well made, had a deep colour, full body, soft fruit, rich blackcurrant varietal flavour, and just a hint of wood-ageing on the finish.

Spurred on by the success of the Cabernet Sauvignon, Bulgaria soon became the world's fourth-largest exporter of wine, and state

THE SLIVEN WINERY
Huge stainless-steel tanks at the Sliven winery in the Sub-Balkan Region, where some of the world's cheapest Merlot is produced.

subsidies ensured that prices remained attractive. For many years Bulgarian wine was well known for its consistency and value for money, but Gorbachov's alcohol reforms in the mid-1980s resulted in the uprooting of many vineyards, which was the first factor to have a detrimental effect on its quality. Ironically, the second factor was democracy, as this was the precursor to privatization, which denied many of the largest former state-owned wineries some of their best sources of grapes. The result has been a rather mixed bag, as some wineries have gone completely private while most remain local cooperatives, and a large number of private growers have put their products (grapes now, but surely single-vineyard wines in the future) on the market for the very first time. In 1991, Domaine Boyar in Sofia became the first private wine company to be established in Bulgaria since 1947 and this has put it one step ahead of the rest in terms of sourcing by enabling it to forge links with ten of the best wineries in the country: Domaine Sakar Lubimetzm, LKV Targovischte, Lovico Suhindol, Menada Stara Zagora, Vinex Preslav, Vincom Burgas, Vinex Slaviantzi, Vinis Iambol, Vinprom Pomorie, and Vinzavod Assenovgrad.

There are other good producers in Bulgaria, of course, and, although a lot more dullard wines exist than before, and handling of oak by some wineries has been very clumsy indeed, there has also been much progress. The introduction of young, unvatted Cabernet and Merlot at the behest of a certain British supermarket group has shown what these wines can be like if bottled before the first flush of wonderfully fresh fruit is lost in vat. For all those who still like a lot of oak, some of the top Reserve wines are very good indeed. And huge strides have been made in white wine making, thanks to Australian flying winemakers. The future looks bright for Bulgaria and the days of it being a red-only country are over in more ways than one.

VIEW OVER MELNIK
Vineyards overlooking the town of Melnik, in the Southwestern Region, with the Pirin Mountains in the background.

THE APPELLATIONS OF
BULGARIA

Note Bulgaria's quality wines are divided into two categories: wines of Declared Geographical Origin or DGOs, which carry sub-regional, district, town, or village appellations, and *Controliran* wines, which are the highest-quality category, which have to be made from specified grape varieties grown in certain DGOs.

NORTHERN REGION
(DUNAVSKA RAUNINA)

DGO regions *Pleven, Vidin* (with sub-regions of Dunavski, Mizia, Novoseleski, Rabishki, Vidinski)
DGO districts *Aleksandrovo, Bjala, Bjala Cerkva, Bjala Slatina, Dimca, Dve Mogili, Dolni Dâbnik, Elena, Kamen, Komarevo, Krivodol, Levski, Lom, Magura, Mihajlovgrad, Nikopol, Orahovo, Polski Trâmbes, Resen, Rupci, Sevlievo, Strakika, Trojan, Varbovka, Vraca*
Controliran wines *Lyaskovetz, Lositza, Novo Selo, Pavlikeni, Russe, Suhindol, Svichtov*

This region accounts for 35 per cent of Bulgaria's vineyards, encompassing two sub-regional DGOs. Suhindol's reputation is based on Bulgaria's best-selling Cabernet Sauvignon, but two others from the district are worth trying: the grapey-oaky Gamza, which is a *Controliran* wine, and the interesting, soft-textured Merlot-Gamza blend, which is of equal quality but only a DGO. Cabernet Sauvignon from the Svichtov region is so rich it might be better used to pep-up lesser Cabernets. Russe (sometimes spelt Rousse or even Ruse) has produced gorgeously fruity, so-called "unvatted" reds and, under the guidance of winemaker Kym Milne, Lyaskovetz is now making easy-drinking, inexpensive blended whites. Russe makes an incredibly cheap, easy-to-drink Sauvignon Blanc called Début Fumé.

🐌 Cabernet sauvignon, Chardonnay, Gamza, Gamay, Muskat ottonel, Pinot noir, Red misket, Rkatsiteli, Sauvignon blanc, Traminer, Vrachanski misket

SOUTHERN REGION
(THRAKIISKA NIZINA)

DGO regions *Cirpan/Chirpan, Dolinata na Maritza, Haskovo, Iambol, Pazardzik, Plovdiv, Stara Zagora, Strandja*
DGO villages *Blatec, Brestovica, Brezovo, Dalboki, Elhovo, Gavrilovo, Granit, Kalugerovo, Korten, Liubimec, Nova Zagora, Perustica, Septemvri, Sivacevo, Svoboda, Vetren, Vinogradec, Zlatovrah*
Controliran wines *Assenovgrad, Brestnik, Oriachovitza, Sakar, Stambolovo*

This region accounts for 22 per cent of Bulgaria's vineyards and encompasses eight regional DGOs. Assenovgrad is justly famous for its dark, dry, plummy-spicy Mavrud wine,

which can age well for ten or more years. Plovdiv makes fine, firm, blackcurranty Cabernet Sauvignon, as does Stara Zagora, a district that boasts a superb Cabernet Sauvignon-Merlot *Controliran* wine from Oriachovitza. Oriachovitza also makes a Cabernet Sauvignon Reserve that has a lot of class. From the Strandja region comes Sakar Mountain Cabernet, which was one of the very first wines to establish a reputation on export markets, although it is the Merlot from the region that has *Controliran* status. East of Stara Zagora is Iambol (sometimes spelled Jambol), which produces a very rich Cabernet Sauvignon Reserve in which the oak can sometimes take on a spicy-caramel complexity, while in the very southeast of the region Elhovo is intent on churning out a much cheaper Cabernet with very obvious coconutty aromas that should suit budget-conscious oak-lovers. Another red in the coconutty-oak mould is Stambolovo Merlot.

🐌 Aligoté, Cabernet sauvignon, Dimiat, Gamay, Mavrud, Merlot, Pamid, Pinot noir, Red misket, Sauvignon blanc

EASTERN REGION
(TSCHERNOMORSKI RAION)

DGO regions *Burgas, Razgrad, Targovischte, Tolbuhin*
DGO villages *Ajtos, Bjala, Dragoevo, Euxinograd, Kabelskovo, Kavarna, Kamen Brjag, Kubrat, Medovetz, Pliska, Pomorie, Popovo, Preslav, Prosenik, Provadija, Sabla/Shabla, Silistra, Tutraken, Zarev Dol*
Controliran wines *Jujen Briag (South Coast), Khan Krum, Kralevo, Novi Pazar, Varna*

This region accounts for 30 per cent of Bulgaria's vineyards and encompasses four regional DGOs. The Schumen district has always been noted for white wines, particularly those from Khan Krum, but it was only recently that they came up to international standards, thanks to Australian expertise. Other well-known Schumen Chardonnays come from Novi Pazar and Preslav. Preslav now makes good, gluggy Chardonnay-Sauvignon blends. Khan Krum is also known for its Riesling & Dimiat, which has become very fresh and tangy. South Coast Rosé is an off-dry Cabernet Sauvignon blush wine from Burgas, an underrated district that produces many inexpensive yet very drinkable Country Wines.

🐌 Aligoté, Bolgar, Cabernet sauvignon, Chardonnay, Dimiat, Gewürztraminer (*syn.* Traminer), Pamid, Rkatsiteli, Red misket, Riesling (*syn.* Rheinriesling), Sauvignon blanc, Tamianka, Ugni blanc, Varneski misket, Welschriesling (*syn.* Italian riesling)

SOUTHWESTERN REGION
(JOLINAKA NA STRUMA)

DGO regions *Blagoevgrad, Kjustendil, Molina Dolina, Petric*
DGO villages *Bobosevo, Damjanica, Melnik, Sandanski*
Controliran wines *Harsovo*

This region accounts for just six per cent of Bulgaria's vineyards and encompasses four regional DGOs. The most famous wine is Melnik, which is made from the Shiroka Melnishka loza grape. The name means "broad vine of Melnik" and the grape is often simply called "Melnik". The wine itself is generally well coloured, rich, and warm, and may be tannic or soft, depending on how it is made. Damianitza Melnik is very smooth and rich.

🐌 Cabernet sauvignon, Chardonnay, Melnik (*syn.* Shiroka Melnishka loza), Tamianka

SUB-BALKAN REGION
(PODBALANSKI RAION)

DGO regions *Sliven*
DGO villages *Banja, Cernica, Hissar, Karnobat, Kasanlak, Pâderevo, Straldza*
Controliran wines *Karlovo, Rozova Dolina (Rose Valley), Slaviantzi, Sungurlare*

This region accounts for seven per cent of vineyards and encompasses one regional DGO. The Rozova Domina Misket is made in the Karlovo district and Sunguralre Misket in Slaviantzi. Both are light-golden, floral-scented, musky wines. Sliven makes one of the world's cheapest Merlot blends, using Pinot noir to add a touch of elegance to what is a very gluggy wine indeed.

🐌 Chardonnay, Red misket, Riesling, Ugni blanc

ROTARY FERMENTERS
Director of the Sliven winery discusses the performance of newly installed rotary fermenters.

HUNGARY

In the first edition of this book I wrote that Hungary offered little beyond Tokaji to excite the wine drinker. At the same time I also pointed out that the country had considerable potential. That was obvious from some of the experimental wines made by Hungary's research stations (despite the restrictions of micro-vinification) and, since 1993, we have seen some of this potential being realized.

WHEN DEMOCRACY ARRIVED in 1989, Hungary had the advantage over other Eastern Bloc countries because even under Communist rule it had long been dabbling with a mixed economy, and privatization was therefore less of an upheaval and foreign investment was easier to attract.

INVESTMENT IN TOKAJI
The first area that received investment was Tokaji. This is easy to understand, as this great sweet wine is the only classic wine of authentic historical reputation in all Eastern Europe. So great was the rush to invest in this region that the government restricted foreign ownership to a maximum of ten per cent of vineyards. Hugh Johnson and the Australian-trained, Anglo-Danish maestro winemaker Peter Vinding-Diers purchased the Royal Tokay Wine Company in Mád and 63 hectares (156 acres) of vineyards. Interestingly, these vineyards have never been state-owned (all other investors have been forced to buy vineyards from Borkombinat, the State Wine Farm), and almost 60 per cent are classified (dating back to 1700), including three First Growths (Nyulaszo, Szt Tamas, and Betsek) and one Second Growth (Birsalmas). After this dynamic duo came a number of others, mostly French, but including one Spanish venture. The most prominent French investor was AXA (*see* p.60) led by the redoubtable Jean-Michel Cazes, who purchased 130 hectares (320 acres) and built a brand new winery. The other French investors, also insurance companies, are GMF (75 per cent interest in the former royal estate of Hétszölö, which includes cellars and 36 hectares [89 acres] of vineyard, now replanted) and GAM Audy (controlling interest in two vineyards, totalling 140 hectares [346 acres] at Château Megyer and Pajzos), while the Spanish have invested in Oremus Kft, which has 37 hectares (91 acres) above Tolesva and several kilometres of cellars.

The one thing these investors have in common is a change in the methods whereby Tokaji is produced. It has been suggested that the French are intent on making Sauternes in Hungary; this has rankled local pride and some critics wonder "whether Tokaji should not legitimately remain an oxidative wine like Tawny Port". Tokaji is not, however, merely oxidative, it has been deliberately oxidized. The only possible comparison is Sherry and Vin Jaune because they are the only wines that are deliberately left in part-filled barrels to oxidize, whereas Tawny Port is kept topped up, undergoing a slow oxidation through the pores of the wood. But Sherry and Vin Jaune (*see* pp.367 and 223) are kept in part-filled barrels for a specific purpose, as the ullage allows for the growth of *flor*, which is responsible for the particular character and style of those wines. In the Tokaji process there is no such justification, the wine merely oxidizes under the influence of *flor*.

I adore the new-wave Tokaji, which have a stunning richness of fruit and pristine botrytis complexity, and I thank God for the revolution brought about by Johnson, Vinding-Diers, Cazes *et al*. Perhaps they can turn their attention to Egri Bikavér or "Bull's

SAMPLING TOKAJI
Gyula Borsos, deputy cellarmaster at Tolcsva, where I tasted pure Essencia with 640 grams per litre of residual sugar. It was still fermenting after 13 years, yet possessed an alcoholic strength of less than two per cent.

Blood", which is certainly no classic and not even a fine wine, but it does have a colourful reputation that dates back to 1552 and making it a joy to drink would do wonders for broadening the appeal of Hungarian wines.

IMPERIAL TOKAJI
The most famous wine is Imperial Tokaji, or Tokaji Aszú Essencia, an elixir so prized by the Tsars of Russia that they maintained a detachment of Cossacks solely for the purpose of escorting convoys of the precious liquid from Hungary to the royal cellars at St. Petersburg. Reputed to last at least three hundred years, it must surely have been considered an elixir of eternal youth. Until World War II, Fukier, the ancient wine merchants of Warsaw, had 328 bottles of Tokaji 1606 but, to my knowledge, none has emerged at auction since 1945. What is sold today as Tokaji Aszú and Tokaji Aszú Essencia does not have the same character, but can still be great wine.

How Tokaji is traditionally made
As with all great sweet wines, Tokaji owes its quality and character to semi-dried, extremely rich grapes (Furmint and Hárslevelü) that have been affected by *Botrytis cinerea*, or "noble rot". These shrivelled grapes, called Aszú (pronounced "ossu") are put into a wooden hod called a *putton* for six to eight days, during which time a highly concentrated juice collects at the

bottom of the container. This juice is pure Essencia. Each *putton* holds 25 kilograms (50 lbs) of Aszú grapes and yields only 0.2 litres (a quarter of a pint) of pure Essencia. After the Essencia has been removed, the *putton* of Aszú grapes is kneaded into a paste and added to a 140-litre (30-gallon) cask, called a *gönc*, of dry base wine. This base wine is made from a blend of non-botrytized Furmint and Hárslevelü grapes (wines labelled Muskotály Aszú will contain 100 per cent Muskotály grapes). The *gönc* is deliberately not filled up, an air-space being left to encourage the oxidized side of Tokaji's character. Naturally the sweetness of the wine depends on how many *puttonyos* (plural of *putton*) are added to the dry base wine: today's Tokaji Aszú Essencia contains about eight *puttonyos*.

The pure Essencia removed from the *putton* is the closest thing to the legendary drink of the past and is still made for sweetening. It is so rich in sugar that it requires a special strain of yeast to ferment it and even then it can take many decades to reach five or six per cent of alcohol. I was lucky enough to taste pure Essencia at the state cellars at Tolcsva. It had been fermenting for 13 years, yet had achieved less than two per cent of alcohol. With 640 grams of residual sugar per litre, it poured like oil, and had the most incredible bouquet, like the scent of a fresh rose in full morning bloom. But for the 38 grams per litre of acidity, it would have been like drinking syrup. It was intensely sweet, clean, and very grapey.

It is not just Aszú wines that are made in Tokaji. Szamorodni, which comes in two styles – dry (*száraz*) and sweet (*édes*) – is a product of the same blend of Furmint and Hárslevelü, but the grapes are seldom botrytized. Three pure varietal Tokaji wines – Tokaji Furmint, Tokaji Hárslevelü, and Tokaji Muskotályos – are made in *száraz* and *édes* styles.

BULL'S BLOOD AND OTHER WINES

Tokaji is not the only Hungarian wine to benefit from foreign winemaking expertise, as this country has attracted a veritable flock of flying winemakers – Nick Butler, Steve Donnelly, Lynette Hudson, Kym Milne, and Adrian Wing have made a contribution to raising standards and many of the local people they have worked with are fast becoming Hungary's new winemaking stars, namely Benjamin Bardos, Agi Dezsenyi, Marta Domokos, Akos Kamocksay, and Sandor Nemes.

Located halfway between Budapest and Tokaji is Eger, a region famous for the legend of Egri Bikavér or "Bull's Blood of Eger". The legend dates from 1552, when the fortress of Eger, fiercely defended by István Dobó and his Magyars, was besieged by the numerically superior force of the Turkish Army, led by Ali Pasha. It is said that, throughout the battle, the Magyars drank copious quantities of the local wine and that when the Turks saw the beards of their ferocious enemies stained red with wine, they ran in terror, thinking that all Magyars gained their strength by drinking the blood of bulls. Hence the name of this wine was born, Egri Bikavér or "Bull's Blood" of Eger. It was never a pretentious wine, but it was traditionally a robust, Kadarka-based red of firm structure and fiery flavour.

Since the early 1980s, however, Bull's Blood has been notoriously variable in both quality and character. Hungary will never earn a reputation for the depth and breadth of its wines until the consistency and modest quality of its second most famous wine is reinstated. Egri Leányka is a gold-coloured, medium-sweet wine from the same region.

Bordering Eger to the west is the Mátraalja, where at Gyöngyös the first truly excellent Hungarian white wine was produced, with Chardonnay. This wine steadily improved until 1995, when it jumped up another notch in quality and displayed lovely pineapple fruit. The fresh, flowery, medium-sweet Muscat from Kiskunhalas used to be the only wine to stand out in quality amid a sea of dull, dry Olaszrizlings from the Great Plain, but Kiskörös

now produces good, fresh, crisp, white-wine blends of unpretentious, easy-drinking, sherbety fruit. Azar-Neszmély is an up-and-coming region that is getting a reputation for excellent, dirt-cheap white wines. The Australian-influenced Neszmély winery produces a rich, tasty Pinot gris with a hint of real spice. Just south of Azar-Neszmély is the Mór region, which makes a Gewürztraminer that slowly builds up spicy bottle-aromas and a Chardonnay, with oodles of fruit and a spritz lift, that is very similar and just as cheap.

The winemaking potential of Lake Balaton was seldom fulfilled until the early 1990s, when Kym Milne started producing extremely rich, oak-aged Chardonnay at the Balatonboglár winery under the Chapel Hill label. At the same time, standard, semi-sweet Olaszrizling and full-flavoured, if rather heavy, Nagyburgundi are produced in Pécs. The best wines come from Villány and include dark, spicy Kadarka and greatly improving but variable-quality Cabernet Sauvignon. Some growers in Villány still train their vines to a single pole, instead of along wires, which is four times as labour-intensive and yields are reduced to as little as 15 or 20 hectolitres per hectare, rather than the normal 60. It will be interesting to see single-vineyard products from such grapes, when private growers start making and marketing their own wines.

Sopron is a potentially fine wine region in the west of Hungary, where too much emphasis used to be given to the light red wines of the Kékfrankos grape, until a few years ago when some attractive raspberry-like blends of Cabernet sauvignon and Cabernet franc were made.

MOUNT BADACSONY

A view of Lake Balaton from vineyards on the extinct volcano of Mount Badacsony, not far from the Balatonboglár winery where flying winemaker Kym Milne MW has produced some exceptional wines under the Chapell Hill label.

ROMANIA

Romania has at least as much potential as any other East European winemaking country, and recently gained a reputation for producing Pinot Noir wines. Other notable reds include Cabernet Sauvignon and Merlot. But among white-wine varieties, it is Gewürztraminer that has the most exciting potential.

THE BIGGEST PROBLEM is lack of consistency. The Pinot noir can be very elegant, although it is more often rather rustic and sometimes downright clumsy or dirty. The blockbusting 1993 vintage of a Gewürztraminer from the Transylvania region that appeared under the Posta Romana label could have stood alongside a number of Alsace wines, but while there was no vintage produced at all in 1994, the 1995 vintage turned into a medium-sweet, neutral wine of mere *vin de table* quality.

NEW VINEYARDS IN DEALUL MARE
A vineyard is staked out, waiting to support new vine growth in the Dealul Mare district of Mutenia.

THE APPELLATIONS OF
ROMANIA

BANAT
Wine districts *Minis, Recas-Tirol, Teremia*
The sandy plain of the Teremia district is best known for its large production of eminently drinkable white wines, while the hilly Minis area provides excellent, inexpensive reds from the Cardarca, Pinot noir, Cabernet, and Merlot grapes, grown on stony terraces. The mountain slopes of Recas-Tirol produce Valea Lunga, a pleasant, light-bodied red wine.

🍇 Cabernet sauvignon, Feteasca regala, Cadarca, Merlot, Mustoasa, Pinot noir, Riesling

DOBRUDJA
Wine districts *Murfatlar, Sarica-Niculitel*
Murfatlar is the most important and oldest winemaking district in Dobrudja, with well-organized vineyards on hills close to the Black Sea and an experimental state research station that has introduced many classic western varieties. Once reliant on its prestigious past, the wines used to be too old, oxidized, and heavy, but they are now clean and well balanced; the lovely, late-picked, softly sweet, and stylish Gewürztraminer is a good example of this style.

🍇 Cabernet sauvignon, Chardonnay, Gewürztraminer, Muscat ottonel, Pinot gris, Pinot noir, Riesling

MOLDAVIA
Wine districts *Cotnari, Dealurile-Moldovei, Odobesti* (sub-districts *Catchiest, Nicoresti), Tecuci-Galati*
The vineyards of Odobesti surrounding the industrial town of Focsani produce quantities of rather ordinary red and white wine. There are, however, exceptions: Cotesti, for example, has a good reputation for Pinot Noir and Merlot, while Nicoresti is known for its full-coloured, spicy red wine produced from the Babeaska grape. The vineyards of Cotnari are the most famous in Romania; their reputation dates back to the 15th century. The wine is a rich dessert wine, not unlike Tokaji but not as complex. The Bucium hills of Visan and Doi Peri overlook the city of Iasi and the cool conditions are reflected in Cabernet Sauvignon wines that have crisp, leafy characteristics.

🍇 Babeaska, Cabernet sauvignon, Feteasca alba, Feteasca neagra, Grasa, Merlot, Pinot noir, Welschriesling

MUTENIA
Wine district *Dealul Mare* (sub-district *Pietroasele*)
North of Bucharest is Dealul Mare, stretching across the lower, southeast facing slopes of the Carpathians. It is famous for Pinot noir, Cabernet sauvignon, and Merlot. There is a small area of chalky soil within this district that has a special microclimate best suited to the production of sweet white wines with fine balancing acidity. It is here that the vineyards of Pietroasele are situated. The area's Tamiîoasa or "Frankincense" grape is a Muscat-related variety that makes a lusciously sweet, gold-coloured wine of very expressive quality. One of the most remarkable Romanian wines I have tasted was a beautiful, botrytized Rosé *Edelbeerenlese* version of the normally lacklustre Feteasca neagra grape.

🍇 Babeasca neagra, Cabernet sauvignon, Feteasca neagra, Feteasca regala, Galbena, Merlot, Pinot gris, Pinot noir, Riesling, Tamiîoasa

OLTENIA
Wine districts *Arges-Stefanesti, Ragasani, Drobeta-Turnu, Severin, Segarcea*
Simburesti in the Dragasani district produces Oltenia's best reds. It is also known for a full, dry red wine from the Feteasca neagra grape, as well as Cabernet Sauvignon. Interesting sweet wines are found on the west side of the River Oltul. Arges-Stefánesti vineyards are planted close to the River Arges and produce mainly white wines. The Segarcea district produces red wines. The Pinot Noir produced here is good, although it is not as well known as the Cabernet Sauvignon.

🍇 Cabernet sauvignon, Feteasca neagra, Feteasca regala, Muscat ottonel, Pinot noir, Riesling, Sauvignon, Tamiîoasa

TRANSYLVANIA
Wine districts *Alba Iulia-Aiud, Bistrita-asaud, Tirnave (Trnave)*
Of all the wine-growing regions of Romania, Transylvania is perhaps the most exciting. The crisp fruit and good acidity of its white wines lies somewhere between the style of Alsace and South Tyrol. The steep Tirnave vineyards produce good-quality white wines with more than just a hint of Germanic style and delicacy. Not surprisingly, German settlers in Transylvania introduced many of their own grape varieties to the region. The native Feteasca grape is also successful.

🍇 Feteasca alba, Feteasca regala, Muscat ottonel, Pinot gris, Riesling, Sauvignon blanc, Traminer, Welschriesling

GREECE

At long last Greece has woken up to the fact that it had lost out to almost every other winemaking industry in the world and, now that poor winemaking is not so commonplace, new producers have appeared and clean, exciting, fine, and fruity wines of individual character are being made.

THIS IS GOOD NEWS, of course, but it used to be so easy when friends went to Greece for a holiday and asked what they should drink – "If it hasn't got Boutaris, Tsantalis, or Carras on the label", I would say "don't drink it. And if it's Retsina, pour it down the toilet as a pine disinfectant." These wines are still worth drinking, but there are now a lot of new boutique wineries to watch out for and even most of the cooperatives, once the scourge of the Greek wine industry, are making clean, drinkable wines these days. Mind you, Retsina is still more useful as a disinfectant.

ANCIENT GREEK WINES

Between the 13th and 11th centuries BC, long before a single vine existed in what are now the most famous wine regions of the world, Greek viticulture was at its peak and, together with wheat and olives, was of fundamental importance to the economy. The classic wines of ancient Greece were great wines indeed, relative to their era, and worthy of note in the writings of Hippocrates, Homer, Plato, Pliny, Virgil, and many others. Sources such as these show how sophisticated the viticulture at that time was. Vines were trained in parallel rows, just as they are today, with care taken to ensure proper spacing between each plant, and at least six different methods of pruning and training were employed, depending upon the variety of grape, type of soil, and strength of the wind.

It was the Greeks who taught the Romans all they knew about viticulture, and the Romans took this knowledge to France, Germany, and other parts of the Empire. Wine was the economic foundation of Greek civilization, but with the decline of this civilization went the famous wines of antiquity, and Greek wines now represent a mere two per cent of the gross national product.

GREEK WINE TODAY

Over ten years ago, in the first edition of this encyclopedia, I told a story about the time I asked Yannis Boutaris, then one of the country's few decent wine producers, why Greek wines were invariably oxidized, maderized, or sometimes just plain bad. Boutaris stretched, raised a gentle smile, and replied that most Greeks actually like oxidized wines and that if most Greek producers made fresh, clean wines, they would not be able to sell them on the domestic market, and would have to export them. He doubted this would work because most foreigners considered Greek wines to be either dross or Retsina, so no-one would buy them.

He was probably right: Greek wines have improved so much over the last decade, yet exports have made little progress. Consumption in Greece has declined sharply, along with other European countries, as younger consumers refuse the oxidized products their fathers still guzzle; instead they drink less, but better wine. In such circumstances, the only way the Greek wine industry has survived an influx of new producers has been by reducing production, which with the help of EU grants to uproot vineyards, is down a third in the last ten years.

It was the shipping magnate and multi-millionaire John Carras who established the first boutique winery, with the ambition of making the best wine in Greece. Not a great ambition in those days, but he believed that Greek viticulture could recapture its former glory. He built the winery quite close to his luxurious Porto Carras holiday complex on Sithonia, the middle prong of the three peninsulas that jut into the Aegean Sea from the Macedonian mainland. With advice from Professor Émile Peynaud, Carras surrounded the winery with 350 hectares (142 acres) of vineyards, including a large proportion of Bordeaux varieties, on the hilly terrain. When Peynaud said that some of the hills were in the wrong place or not the right shape, Carras ordered bulldozers to rectify the problem. The first vintage was 1972, but the Greek winemaker made mistakes and was sacked; Peynaud poured away most of the wine. The few barrels he retained were mixed with the next vintage, which was processed by Evangelos Gerovassiliou, who had trained in Bordeaux as one of Peynaud's oenology students.

Château Carras became a legend and Gerovassiliou is still making the wine, although he has also set up his own boutique winery, which is equally excellent, albeit on a far more modest scale. Other newcomers include Nicholas Cosmetatos of Cephalonia, who was one of the first Greeks to wonder why his fellow countrymen drank oxidized wines. Perhaps understandably, his first wine, Gentilini, started out so clean it was clinical, but it has moved on to become one of the country's finest, zippiest whites. Squeaky-cleanliness was a problem for Calligas too, but its top white, Château Calligas, has been fatter since the early 1990s and this has been lifted by a nifty touch of residual gas. In recent years, numerous small wineries of exceptional talent have cropped up. Some have been around for a while, others

HARVEST TIME
Harvesting the vineyards of Domaine Carras, which were bulldozed out of the slopes of Sithonia, the middle prong of Halkidiki's three peninsulas.

are very new, but the best of these include names such as Aidarinis, Antonopoulou, Castanioti, Chrisohoou, Emery, Hatzimichali, Château Lazaridi, Mercouri, Oenoforos, Papaioannou, Château Pegasus, Semeli, Sigalas, Skouras, and Strofiia, with many others, no doubt, waiting in the wings.

RETSINA – BOON OR BURDEN?

Retsina is wine (usually white) to which pine resin is added during fermentation. This practice dates back to antiquity, when wine was stored in jars and amphorae. As they were not airtight, the wines rapidly deteriorated. In the course of time, people learned to seal the jars with a mixture of plaster and resin and the wines lasted longer. This increased longevity was attributed to the antiseptic effect of resin, the aroma and flavour of which quickly tainted the stored wine. It was, of course, a false assumption, but in the absence of Pasteur's discoveries (then some twenty-five centuries in the future), it appeared to be supported by the fact that the more resinous the wine, the less it deteriorated. Within a short time, the resin was being added directly to the wine and the only difference between modern and ancient Retsina is that the resin is now added directly to the wine during fermentation, rather than after. The best Retsina is said to come from three areas, Attica, Evia, and Viota, and the best resin, which must be from the Alep or Aleppo pine, comes from Attica.

Strictly speaking, Retsina is not wine. It would be if its pine character were the result of maturation in pine casks, but having pine resin added makes it an aromatized wine, like Vermouth. In the first edition, I joked about the possibility of a matured wine in pine casks, but I have since discovered on La Palma "Tea Wine", which is exactly that. Insignificant in volume and oddity though it is, if it can be done in the Canary Islands, why not in Greece?

DOMAINE CARRAS
Looking out across the blue waters of the Aegean to the fishing village of Maramas, from the vineyards of Domaine Carras, which also consists of a luxurious leisure and sporting complex called Porto Carras.

THE APPELLATIONS OF
GREECE

AO = Appellation of Origin
TA = Traditional Appellation

AGIORITIKOS
Macedonia

These excellent wines come from 60 hectares (148 acres) of vineyards on Mount Athos (Agioritikos), the third peninsula of Halkidiki, immediately east of Sithonia. Leased from the Hourmistas monastery by the Tsantali winery, the vines are tended by Russian monks under the direction of the firm's vineyard manager. The best wine is the fine, dry, full-bodied red, which is made from Cabernet sauvignon and Limnio. There is also a dry and a medium-dry white wine, both fresh, clean, and fruity, and a delicious, dry rosé.

🕸 Cabernet sauvignon, Limnio, Sauvignon blanc

⊢⟶ 3–8 years (red), 1–2 years (white and rosé)

↯ *Tsantalis*

AMYNTEON AO
Macedonia

The most northerly of Greek appellations, where vines are grown at an altitude of 650 metres (2,130 feet) and the grapes are seldom overripe. The quality is sporadic, with a strangely blowzy brew from the local cooperative, but there are gems that clearly indicate its true potential.

🕸 Xynomavro

ANCHIALOS AO
Thessaly

This is a medium-bodied, dry white wine from the Nea Anchialos area on the Gulf of Pegassitikos near Volos. The local Demetra cooperative wine is clean, though unexciting.

🕸 Savatiano, Rhoditis, Sykiotis

ARCHANES AO
Crete

I have tasted the local cooperative's Armanti table wine, but I have not had the opportunity to taste this red appellation wine, which is apparently aged in old oak barrels.

🕸 Kotsifali, Mandilaria

COTES DE MELITON AO
Macedonia

This appellation covers the red, white, and rosé wines of Sithonia, the middle of Halkidiki's three peninsulas. They are made to a consistently high

standard because all the wines are from the excellent Domaine Porto Carras, the brainchild of the late John Carras. The project has been guided by Bordeaux's Professor Peynaud, with his ex-pupil Evanglos Gerovassiliou as winemaker. Made by modern vinification methods, the wines are generally light, and are best enjoyed young. The one exception is the top-of-the-range Château Carras, a rich-flavoured, full-bodied, deep-coloured, red wine of true *vin de garde* quality.

🕸 Assyrtico, Athiri, Cabernet franc, Cabernet sauvignon, Cinsault, Grenache, Limnio, Petite sirah, Rhoditis, Sauvignon blanc, Savatiano, Ugni blanc, Xynomavro

⊢⟶ 1–2 years (Château Carras: 5–8 years for lighter vintages; 10–20 years for bigger)

✓ *Domaine Carras* (Château Carras, Château Carras Cabernet Sauvignon, Limnio, Melisanthi)

DAPHNES AO
Crete
I have not tasted these dry red and sweet red, liqueur wines from Daphnes AO.

🍇 Liatiko

GOUMENISSA AO
Macedonia
A light-bodied red wine from the Goumenissa district, northeast of Naoussa. Usually a wine of good fruit and a certain elegance, the best undergo a light maturation in cask and can be relatively rich in flavour.

🍇 Xynomavro, Negoska

🍷 3–8 years

✓ *Aidarinis • Boutaris*

KANTZA AO
Central Greece

This dry white wine from the province of Attica is Retsina without the pine resin. The only one I have tasted is from Cambas and, although clean, I did not find it special.

🍇 Savatiano

LEMNOS *or* LIMNOS AO
The Aegean
A soft and flowery dry white wine with clean fruit and an attractive Muscat character from the island of Lemnos. The local cooperative version is consistently well made.

🍇 Limnio

🍷 Upon purchase

✓ *AC of Lemnos*

LESBOS
The Aegean
The wines of the island of Lesbos are consumed locally, and none is exported.

MANTINIA AO
Peloponnese
This is a dry white wine from mountain vineyards in the centre of the Peloponnese. The vines grow at an altitude of 650 metres (2,130 feet) and although there are some very fresh, young wines with nice lively fruit.

🍇 Moschophilero

🍷 Upon purchase

✓ *Antonopoulou • Tselepos*

MAVRODAPHNE OF CEPHALONIA AO
Ionian Islands
I have not tasted this sweet red liqueur wine; it should, however, be similar in character to the Mavrodaphne of Patras.

🍇 Mavrodaphne

MAVRODAPHNE OF PATRAS AO
Peloponnese
This is a rich, sweet, red liqueur wine from the Peloponnese, with a velvety smooth, sweet-oak finish. Often compared to a Recioto della Valpolicella, a good Mavrodaphne is in my opinion far better. One delightful aspect of this wine is that it can be drunk with equal pleasure when it is either young and fruity or smooth and mature, although it does have a similar raisiny-sherry oxidative aroma.

🍇 Mavrodaphne

🍷 1–20 years

✓ *Achaia Clauss* (Collector Series)

MUSCAT OF CEPHALONIA AO
Ionian Islands
This is one of the lesser-known, sweet liqueur wines from the Muscat grape. I tasted it once and found it acceptable, although I cannot comment on its consistency.

🍇 Muscat blanc à petits grains

MUSCAT OF LEMNOS AO
The Aegean
A superior liqueur Muscat wine that is richer and sweeter than Patras, though not in the class of Samos.

🍇 Muscat d'Alexandrie

🍷 Upon purchase

✓ *AC of Lemnos*

MUSCAT OF PATRAS AO
Peloponnese
An attractive, gold-coloured, sweet, liqueur Muscat wine that can be delicious in its typically raisiny way, Patras is the most widely available Greek Muscat on export markets.

🍇 Muscat blanc à petits grains

🍷 Upon purchase

✓ *AC of Patras Moschato*

MUSCAT OF RHODES AO
The Dodecanese
This is a good-quality, rich and sweet, golden, liqueur Muscat wine that I consider to be on a par with the Muscat of Patras.

🍇 Muscat blanc à petits grains, Traini muscat

🍷 Upon purchase

✓ *CAIR*

MUSCAT OF SAMOS AO
The Agean
One of the great sweet wines of the world, the local cooperative's Samos, Samos *Grand Cru*, Samos Nectar, and Samos Anthemis are, in increasing complexity, all superb, perfectly balanced, rich, and mellifluous wines. It also produces a deliciously dry and fresh, non-appellation version called Samena, which is as clean as a whistle, with a delightful orange flower-water aroma and delicate fruit.

🍇 Muscat blanc à petits grains

🍷 Upon purchase

✓ *Cambas • AC de Samos*

MUSCAT RION OF PATRAS AO
Peloponnese
This is similar to Muscat of Patras by all accounts, but I have not tasted or even seen it.

🍇 Muscat blanc à petits grains

NAOUSA AO
Macedonia
These generally reliable wines are grown west of Thessalonika, at a height of 350 metres (1,150 feet) on the southeastern slopes of Mount Velia. Although I can give only rock-solid recommendations, this is almost twice as many as in the first edition, with Castanioti and Chrisohoou the most exciting new arrivals, and I cautiously suggest that any Naousa could be worth the gamble; the growers take a pride in their wine that can be lacking elsewhere. Good Naousa is well-coloured, rich, and aromatic, with heaps of spicy fruit and a long finish.

🍇 Xynomavro

🍷 4–15 years

✓ *Boutaris • Castanioti • Chrisohoou • Château Pegasus • Tsantalis*

NEMEA AO
Peloponnese
This is a relatively reliable appellation and there is a local pride similar to that in Nauosa. Grown in the Corinth district at an altitude of between 250 and 800 metres (820–2,620 feet), the Agiorgitiko grape provides a deep-coloured, full, and spicy red wine that can be spoilt by dried-out fruit, or a lack of fruit. Known locally as the Blood of Hercules, because his blood was shed when he killed the Nemean lion, it has been produced for 2,500 years.

🍇 Agiorgitiko

⌛ 5–20 years

✓ *Boutaris* • *Kourtakis* • *Papaioannou* • *Semeli*

PAROS AO
The Cyclades
This is a deep-coloured, light-bodied red wine from the Mandilaria grape that I have tasted only once. My notes record a very strange, but difficult to describe, taste. A rich, dry, white wine from the Monemvassia grape (which some believe to be the original Malvasia), is also produced, but I have not tasted it.

🍇 Mandilaria, Monemvassia

PATRAS AO
Peloponnese
This is a light, dry white wine from the hilly hinterland of Patras in the Peloponnese. I have tasted only the local cooperative product and have found the wine both dull and flabby. However, the cooperative itself is capable of good quality, as evinced by its first-class Mavrodaphne and Muscat.

🍇 Rhoditis

PEZA AO
Crete
From my experience, which is based purely on the wines made by the local cooperative, I feel that great benefit could be gained if the malolactic process was prevented in the production of its Regalo dry white wine and if the Mantiko reds were bottled and sold when they were much younger, as both styles lack a certain freshness of fruit and vitality.

🍇 Kotsifali, Mandilaria, Vilana

RAPSANI AO
Thessaly
I have driven past these red wine regions in the vicinity of Mount Olympus, but have not had the opportunity to try the wine, and the vines I saw were on flat, uninspiring terrain.

🍇 Xynomavro, Krassato, Stavroto

RETSINA TA
Central Greece
Although rosé is not unknown, Retsina is almost invariably white, with 85 per cent of the blend coming from the Savatiano grape. It may be blended from various areas or can have a specific, usually superior, origin, but in every case Retsina carries the unique Traditional Appellation. This designation recognizes the ancient practice of resinating wine and the EU has confined its use to Greece.

There are degrees of resination, ranging from relatively light to heavy, and the quality of the pine resin itself can range from poor to fine; the better-quality pine resin makes better-quality Retsina. Despite its penetrating aroma and flavour, pine resin cannot hide a tired, flabby, oxidized, or simply bad wine. Personally, I do not like Retsina, but I have to admit that the aroma of fine pine resin is refreshing and I also agree that this aromatized wine has a useful cutting quality when drunk with oily Greek food.

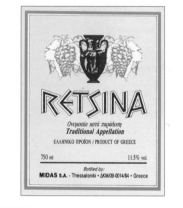

🍇 Rhoditis, Savatiano

⌛ As young and as fresh as possible.

✓ **Appellations** *Attica* • *Evia* • *Viota* • *Thebes*
Brands *Boutaris* • *Thives*

RHODES AO
The Dodecanese
Of the wines produced by the CAIR, the local cooperative, I have tasted a dull, oily, dry white wine called Ilios; a strong, but coarse, dry and sweet *méthode champenoise* sparkling wine; and a well-balanced, sweet, red Muscat wine called Amandia. Various other wines on this tourist island are also produced, but I have not tasted them.

🍇 Amorgiano, Athiri

⌛ Upon purchase

✓ CAIR

ROBOLA OF CEPHALONIA AO
Ionian Islands
A dry white wine that can be fresh and floral, with an almost racy nose and a tangy, lightly rich, delicate lemon-fruity flavour. However, it is all too often spoilt by sloppy winemaking.

🍇 Robola

⌛ 1–2 years

SANTA MAVRA
Ionian Islands
Deep-coloured, full-bodied red wine of local repute grown on terraces up to an altitude of 800 metres (2,620 feet) on the island of Lefkas.

🍇 Vertzami

SANTORINI AO
The Cyclades
This full-bodied, dry white wine can have as much as 17 per cent natural alcohol, plus a high acidity level. The wine is interesting and quite unusual, although, in my opinion, not particularly enjoyable. A sweet straw-wine called Santorini *liastos* (similar to *vin de paille*) is also produced.

🍇 Assyrtiko, Aidani

⌛ 2–5 years

✓ *Boutaris* • *Sigalas* (Oia Cask)

SITIA AO
Crete
These are deep-coloured, robust, dry red and sweet red liqueur wines.

🍇 Liatiko

VERDEA
Ionian Islands
An astringent, often oxidized, dry white wine made on the island of Zante, where it is famous for its delicate bouquet.

🍇 Pavlos, Skiadopoylo

ZITSA AO
Epirus
Dry and semi-sweet, slightly spritzy, clean and delicately fruity white wine from six villages around Zitsa, northwest of Ioánnina, where the vines grow at an altitude of 600 metres (1,970 feet). Most of the production is processed by the AC of Ioánnina and I recommend it.

🍇 Debina

⌛ Upon purchase

✓ AC of Ioánnina

OTHER NON-APPELLATION WINES
Some of the country's best wines have no appellation, simply because the system does not recognize a specific variety or blend grown in a particular place.

✓ **Red** *Achaia Clauss* (Château Clauss) • *Antonopoulou* (Kaberne Nea Dris) • *Boutaris* (Grande Reserve) • *Calligas* (Nostos) • *Gerovassiliou* (Ktima) • *Hatzimichali* (Cava, Merlot) • *Château Lazaridi* (Maghiko Vuono) • *Mercouri* • *Semeli* (non-vintage Vin de Table, Château Semeli) • *Skouras* (Mega Oenos) • *Strofiia* • *Thebes* (Saviatano – only a few vintages are good.) • *Tsantalis* (Rapsani)

White *Antonopoulou* (Adoli Ghis) • *Calligas* (Château Calligas) • *Chrisoboou* (Prekniariko) *Cosmetatos* (Fumé, Gentilini) • *Gerovassiliou* (Fumé, Ktima) • *Château Lazaridi* (Maghiko Vuono) • *Château Matsa* • *Oenoforos* (Asprolithi) • *Papaioannou* (Chardonnay) • *AC de Samos* (Samena – but must be very fresh) • *Vatis* (Château Vatis)

Dry rosé *Emery* (Grand Rosé) • *Oenoforos* (Espiritis)

Fortified *Cosmetatos* (Amano – sweet white) • *Montofli* (Vin de Liqueur – medium-sweet white)

THE APPELLATIONS OF
THE REST OF SOUTHEAST EUROPE

CZECH REPUBLIC

The Czech Republic is better known for its beer than its wine: its wine exports are negligible and Moravia is much more important than Bohemia in winemaking terms.

MORAVIA

Moravia accounts for the majority of Czech vineyards, with two major areas of production, Hustopece-Hodonin, on the River Morava, and Znojmo-Mikulov, on the River Dyje. The main grape varieties are Blauer Portugieser, Grüner-veltliner, Müller-Thurgau, Pinot blanc, Pinot gris, Pinot noir, St.-Laurent, Sauvignon blanc, and Traminer. There is a high level of winemaking expertise for aromatically fresh, light, and varietally elegant white wines. Good Cabernet Sauvignon has been produced at Pavlovice. Sparkling wines are produced in the towns of Mikulov and Bzenec by both *cuve close* and continuous methods.

BOHEMIA

This region northeast of Prague accounts for less than four per cent of the Czech Republic's vineyards and the grapes grown include Limberger, Neuberger, Pinot blanc, Pinot noir, Blauer Portugieser, Rynski Silván, and Welschrizling. Most vines are located around the towns of Melnik and Velke Zernoseky, on the banks of the rivers Ohre and Labe. The wines have a natural affinity with German wines, but are rarely encountered on export markets.

SLOVAKIA

Part of former Czechoslovakia until 1993, this country has twice as many vineyards as the Czech Republic, even though it is much smaller. Most wines are produced in the Little Carpathians and Nitra districts and the different grape varieties grown include Ezerjó, Grüner veltliner, Leányka, Müller-Thurgau, Muscat ottonel, Rulandské (Pinot gris), Rynski rizling (true Riesling), Sylvaner, Traminer, and Vlásskyrizling (Welschriesling). Sparkling wines have been made since 1825 at Sered and are still marketed under the "Hubert" brand, but quality is not high. Other wine districts are East Slovakia, Hlohovec-Trnava, Modry Kamen, Skalica-Záhorie, and, in the part of the Tokaji district that is Czechoslovakian, wines similar to the famous Hungarian version are reputed to be made.

SLOVENIA

By far the wealthiest part of former Yugoslavia, with *per capita* income close to that of Austria. With a sizeable chunk of the country under Italian rule until after World War II, Slovenia has always had ties with the West. Slovenia is divided into Inland and Coastal regions:

INLAND SLOVENIA (KONTINENTALNA SLOVENIJA)

Squeezed between Austria, Hungary, and Croatia are two winegrowing districts, each comprising several smaller areas: Podravina (Haloze, Lutomer-Ororske, Maribor, Prekmurje, Radgona-Kapela, Slovenske) and Posavina (Belakrajina, Bizeljsko-Sremic, Dolenjska, Smarje-Virstajn), and the grapes include Cabernet sauvignon, Sipon, Traminer, Pinot blanc, Riesling, Sauvignon blanc, and Welschriesling. This region always used to produce the best Yugoslavian white wines from its steep, hilly, vine-clad slopes, which are at the same latitude as central France. By far the most famous come from Lutomer. The best Lutomer wines are Gewürztraminer, a Sauvignon Blanc, and Lutomer Cabernet Sauvignon.

COASTAL SLOVENIA (PRIMORSKA SLOVENIJA)

This region is close to the Italian border and consists of four winegrowing districts: Brda, Karst, Koper, and Vipava. The climate is a mild Mediterranean type, except in Vipara and Briski Okolis, which come under the moderating influence of the Alps. The grapes include Barbera, Cabernet franc, Cabernet sauvignon, Chardonnay, Merlot, Picolit, Pinot blanc, Pinot gris, Rebula, Sauvignon blanc, Teran (Refosco), Tocai Friulano, and Zelen (Rotgipfler), and the wine of most local repute is a red, Kraski Teran.

CROATIA

Prior to hostilities Croatia was, with Slovenia, one of the two most prosperous states in Yugoslavia and it is today in a relatively stable condition, if stability is a word that can be used in the Balkans. Many vineyards were destroyed during the worst upheavals of the Croatian war, but the regions and districts still exist and replanting has even commenced in some places, as ordinary people try to resume a normal life. The vineyards of Croatia are divided into Inland and Coastal regions:

INLAND CROATIA

There are seven winegrowing districts: Bilogora-Drava, Kupa, Moslavina, Plesivica, Prigorje, Slavonski, and Zagorje-Medimurje. This region still boasts a fine amphitheatre of terraced vineyards set amid gently undulating landscape, growing mostly Traminer, Muscat ottonel, Pinot blanc, Pinot noir, Riesling, Sauvignon blanc, Sylvaner, and Grasevina (Welschriesling). The Kutjevacka Grasevina is a pale, straw-coloured wine with a fruity aroma from the Kutjevo. Interesting Traminer, Muscat Ottonel, and Pinot Blanc are also produced and the best come from the slopes of Baranja.

COASTAL CROATIA

This region has four winegrowing districts: Istria, Hrvatsko Primorje, Kvarner, and Dalmatia. Vineyards grow numerous varieties, including Babic, Bogdanusa, Debit-Grk, Dobricic, Malvazija, Merlot, Teran, Trebjac, Vranac, Vugava, and Zlahtina, but it is the Plavac mali, a black grape, that makes the region's finest wines. The best-known wine is Dingac, grown on the Peljesac peninsula; a deep-coloured, full-bodied red wine, this was the first appellation to be protected by law under the old Yugoslav system. Other wines made from Plavac mali include Postup, from Peljesac, Faros, from Hvar island, and Bolski Plavac from Brac island. The oldest and most common wine on the Istrian Peninsula is Motovunski Teran, a light-red wine.

BOSNIA-HERZEGOVINA

Before the conflict, there were vines in the south, where the climate and rocky soil favoured two indigenous varieties, Zilavka for white wine and Blatina for red, while Samotok was a free-run rosé. I hesitate to enquire about Bosnia's vineyards now, but I hope that one day lasting peace will allow them to flourish again.

SERBIA

Although the Federal Army made abortive attempts to put down independence in Slovenia and Croatia, and supported the Bosnian Serbs, it did not fight any battles on its home ground, and thus Serbian vineyards remain unaffected. There are three major viticultural regions: Kosovo, Vojvodina, and Serbia itself.

SERBIA

This covers five separate winegrowing districts: Sumadija-Velika Morava, Nisava-Juzna Morava, Pocerina-Podgora, Timok, and Zapadna Morava. The grapes include Cabernet sauvignon, Gamay, Pinot noir, Plemenka, Plovdina, Prokupac, Riesling, and Smederevka. It is by far the largest wine region in former Yugoslavia, and Sumadija-Velika Morava is easily its biggest district. The vineyards around Zupa have the best reputation in Serbia. Prokupac is the leading grape variety, and is used to make Zupska Ruzica, a light-bodied, dry rosé. Cabernet sauvignon is impressive, especially from Oplenac, and a Pinot noir and Gamay blend is also produced. The Smederevka is said to originate from Smederevo, where it accounts for 90 per cent of grapes and makes mild, fruity, medium-sweet white wines.

KOSOVO

Occupying just two wine districts, Severni and Juzni, where grapes grown include Cabernet franc, Gamay, Pinot noir, and Riesling, the vineyards of Kosovo are even less important than Herzegovina used to be before the civil war. Amselfelder Kosovsko Vino is the result

SOUTHERN ARMENIA
Widely spaced bush-vines on the foothills above the Ararat plains, in the south of the country.

of successful cooperation between Yugoslav producers and German marketeers. The wines are mostly red and come in dry and semi-sweet styles; dry white and rosé account for ten per cent each; small amounts of dry red Cabernet franc and Spätburgunder are made. The style is uninteresting and the quality disappointing.

VOJVODINA (VOIVODINA)

North of Serbia, bordering Croatia, Hungary, and Romania, Vojvodina has four winegrowing districts: Banat, Srem, Subotica, and Pescara. Grapes grown include Ezerjó, Traminer, Kadarka, Merlot, Rhine riesling, Sauvignon blanc, Sémillon, and Welschriesling (*syn.* Grasevina, Kreaca). Although the Welschriesling grape is called Grasevinahere or Kreaca, the wine is sold as Banatski Rizling. The Traminer is a more interesting alternative and the soft, fruity Merlot a good buy for red-wine drinkers.

MONTENEGRO

Viticulture is almost as unimportant here as it is in Kosovo. There are three winegrowing districts: Crnogorsko, Titogradski, Primorje, and the main grape varieties grown are Kratosija, Krstac, Merlot, and Vranac. The best-known vineyards of this region are those of Crnogorsko on the terraced southern slopes of Lake Skadar. In the 19th century, this wine was called Crmnicko Crno, was made from Vranac and Kratosija grapes, and was expensive. Today it is made entirely from Vranac grapes, is known as Crnogorski Vranac, and fetches a far more modest price. Merlot can be good. If you see 13 July on a bottle, it is not a sell-by date, just the name of the state-controlled cooperative.

MACEDONIA

Following the secession of Slovenia and Croatia in 1991, Macedonia received full international recognition in 1993. There are three wine districts: Povadarje, Plina-Osogovo, and Pelagonija-Polog, and the grapes grown include Grenache, Kadarka, Kratosija, Plovdina, Prokupac, Temjanika, and Vranac. Phylloxera, which devastated European vineyards in the late 19th century, did not reach Macedonia until 1912. The most popular wine is Kratosija, a deep-coloured red made from native Vranac and Kratosija varieties. It has a distinctive taste and aroma, full body, and a smooth flavour. It is bottled in its second year, when the bouquet is at its fullest, and is best drunk when very young. Prokupac and Kadarka make interesting reds, Belan is a neutral white Grenache wine, and Temjanika an aromatic white.

ALBANIA

Winemaking in Albania dates back to pre-Roman times, but although atheism was enforced for many years under the Communist regime, the majority in Albania are Muslim and therefore consumption of alcohol has been low and, with no exports, the potential for the country's wine industry was severely restricted over the last 40 years. Democracy has opened up international markets and the government has sought expert advice from the West, thus growth and development could result, but for the moment the Red Star cooperative at Durrës (Durazzo) is best known and Welschriesling, Mavrud, and Cabernet franc are its most important styles.

UKRAINE

As viticulture represents one-fifth of this recently re-established nation's agricultural economy, it will be instrumental in building up overseas trade. This is necessary to replace Ukraine's trade with Russia, upon which it is still dependent. The state's wine industry is mainly concerned with producing still white wines, although red and white sparkling wines are also produced in the Crimea and dessert wines are a local speciality. Crimea (Krym) is the peninsula that encloses the Sea of Azov. Sparkling "Krim" is a *méthode champenoise* wine made in five styles, from Brut through to Sweet, and in a semi-sweet red version. The grapes used include Chardonnay, Pinot noir, Rizling, Aligoté, and Cabernet. The wines are coarse and the traditional addition of brandy does not help, but the Brut and Demi-Sec Red are widely available in export markets and sell on novelty value. The Ruby of Crimea, which is a blend of Saperavi, Matrassa, Aleatika, Cabernet, and Malbec, is a robust, rustic, full-bodied red that is quite commonly encountered in various countries.

Nikolayev-Kherson, just northeast of Crimea, and Odessa, near the Moldova state border, produce various white, sparkling, and dessert wines. The best-known local wines are dry white wines such as Perlina Stepu, Tropjanda Zakarpatja, and Oksamit Ukrainy.

That this region is capable of not merely good but great wines of exceptional longevity is beyond doubt. In 1990 David Molyneux-Berry MW brought back some extraordinary wines for auction at Sotheby's in London. These came from the famous Massandra cellars, which were built on the outskirts of Yalta in the Crimea for the Russian imperial court at the end of the 19th century. This was not a winery, merely an ageing facility acting as the central hub to a complex of 25 satellite wineries. The wineries were in the surrounding hills of Krymskiye Gory, where the vineyards were situated, thus the grapes did not have to be transported, and almost every ounce of their potential quality was retained. This would be an ambitious project even by today's standards.

The wines Molyneux-Berry showed at a pre-auction tasting were nothing less than sensational. The Massandra Collection, as it has become known, consisted of fortified wines and I do not mean to be disparaging when I say that their maker deliberately mimicked classic styles such as Madeira, Port, and so on. How could you put down a 1932 White-Port-style wine that had more class, fragrance, and finesse at almost 60 years old than anything white and fortified that has ever been made in Oporto? The 1940 was let down by a spirity nose, but I would not keep a genuine White Port five years, let alone 50, and it blew away the 1932 on the palate anyway. The 1929 Muscat had as much toffee, caramel, and exotic fruit as the best Australian Muscats, but a balance that undeniably placed it in the northern hemisphere. The best Massandra wines I tasted that day were both Madeiras, a 1937 and a 1922 (No.31), but although I would like to see such wines made again (fortified wines are still made, but not of comparable quality), I do not for one moment suggest that the entire Crimea should be turned over to the production of classic-quality fortified wines. What I do mean, however, is that great wines can be made in the Ukraine, in certain parts, given the right vines, yield, and proper winemaking expertise.

MOLDOVA

A small country the size of Belgium, Moldova is, in fact, an extension of Romania's Moldavia and, historically, the two parts were one. Most vineyards need replanting, pruning should be more strict, grapes should not be dumped into huge skips for transporting, and an array of press-houses should be introduced throughout the vineyards to reduce oxidation. As for the wineries, the best and most modern are beyond repair and need pulling down. I have visited Moldova only once, in 1993, just months after civil war was averted, and they were cutting the corks in half to save money. Such is the scale of investment required, but that it should, somehow, be found and spent is not in question. Even under these crude conditions, some fine wines have been made and with a bit of patchwork improvement two flying winemakers, first Hugh Ryman and then Jacques Lurton, have made some surprisingly good wines with both foreign and indigenous grape varieties.

There are six important winemaking districts: Pucari, Balti, Ialoveni, Stauceni, Hincesti, Romanesti, and Cricova.

Pucari is 160 kilometres (100 miles) south of the capital in the heart of red wine country. Negru de Pucari is deep-coloured, firm-structured red wine blended from Cabernet sauvignon and Saperavi; Purpuruiu de Pucari is a softer Pinot-Merlot blend and Rosu de Pucari is a dark rosé made from Cabernet sauvignon, Merlot, and Malbec. There used to be many more vineyards in the north than there are today, but they were pulled up under Gorbachov and most are now located around Balti, where Aligoté, Rkatsiteli, and Sémillon predominate. The vineyards of Ialoveni are located near the capital, where Aligoté, Riesling, and Sauvignon blanc are grown for Moldovan sherry. Close by is Stauceni, which boasts one of the largest wineries in Moldova, where the surrounding vines are tended by pupils from the local wine school. To the south is Hincesti, which consumers in western countries are most likely to know, on account of the success of Kirkwood Chardonnay. Penfolds has also invested in the area. Romanesti's vineyards lie 50 kilometres (30 miles) farther north.

KRASNODAR, RUSSIA
Vines growing in the Black Sea vineyards of the Krasnodar district.

Romanesti was named after the Romanov Tzar Alexander I, who restarted the Moldovan wine industry by establishing his own winery here. Vines include Aligoté, Cabernet sauvignon, Malbec, Merlot, Pinot noir, and Rkatsiteli, but it is the Bordeaux varieties that do best. Halfway between Kishinev and Romanesti is Cricova, where unremarkable and often faulty sparkling wines are made in the most remarkable and elaborate underground city. Its entrance is a massive pair of steel doors in a rock face, through which the largest articulated lorries can drive, winding their way 80 metres (262 feet) below the surface where a city has been hewn out of solid rock. Its size corresponds to the area covered by 25 villages on the surface and it is serviced by 65 kilometres (40 miles) of underground roads, complete with traffic lights and road signs. In addition to these roads there are 120 kilometres (75 miles) of galleries, which almost equals the entire storage capacity of the Champagne region. Why, I asked myself, is this workplace equipped with opulent reception halls, a dining room the like of which I have not seen anywhere in Eastern Europe, and a cellar containing priceless old vintages of Mouton Rothschild, Latour, Romanée-Conti, and so on. I had absolutely no doubts that this was where the Politburo would head in a nuclear exchange.

RUSSIA

Climate is something of an obstacle to vinegrowing in Russia, as winters are generally very cold, often -30°C (-22°F), and the vines in many regions have to be buried in the earth to survive the bitterly cold months. Summers are very hot and dry and, but for the tempering effect of the Black and Caspian Seas, climatic conditions would probably be impossible for viticulture. There are five major winegrowing districts in Russia: Checheno-Ingush, Dagestan, Krasnodar, Rostov-na-Donu, and Stavropol, with grapes that include Aligoté, Caberne, Muscatel, Pinot gris, Pinot noir, Plechistik, Pukhljakovsky, Rizling, Rkatsiteli, Sylvaner, and Tsimlyansky. Russia concentrates on white and sparkling wines in the north and west, and red in the south and east.

In the mid-1950s, a system that has become known as the "Russian Continuous Flow Method" was developed for producing sparkling wine cheaply, easily, and quickly by a natural second fermentation. Krasnodar's most reputable vineyards are on southwest-facing coastal slopes overlooking the Black Sea. Abrau is known for its dry Riesling (Rizling), Cabernet, and Durso sparkling wine. Anapa, just along the coast to the north, also makes Rizling, while down the coast at Gelendzhik, Aligoté is the local speciality. To the east of Krasnodar and north of the Caucasus, Stavropol is known for its dry Rizling and Silvaner, as well as the Muscatel Praskoveiski dessert wines. Other dessert wines include the spicy Mountain Flower; and Rostov-na-Donu, located around the confluence of the rivers Don and Kan and the Taganrogskiy Zaliv estuary, is famous for its rich Ruby of the Don dessert wines. Plechistik is a grape used to give backbone to Tsimlyansky and, throughout the state, also makes decent, dry red wines.

On the east-facing slopes of the Caucasus Mountains, overlooking the Caspian Sea, are the vineyards of the republic of Dagestan. This is a black-grape area that is known for the full body and flavour of its dry red wines; the best come

THE VAIK REGION OF ARMENIA
Most of the wines produced from these trellised Muscadine vines in Armenia's mountainous Vaik region will go to produce sweet, fortified wines.

from Derbent in the south. Checheno-Ingush is another republic with vineyards on the Caucasus, but these are found inland, along its northern slopes, to the southeast of Stavropol. Most of the wines produced in this area are of the Port type.

GEORGIA

Political fractionalism still blights the peace in Georgia, which has one of the oldest winemaking traditions in the world. It has numerous valleys, each with its own favourable microclimate, which should propel this country to the forefront of the East European wine scene, but even without internal strife, Georgians seemed unable to recognize their own potential, let alone capitalize on it.

It is said that there are about 1,000 different grape varieties growing in Georgia, but the most important are Saperavi, Tsinandali, Gurdzhaani, Tsolikouri, Chinuri, Murkhranuli, and Tasitska.

ARMENIA

Although Armenia declared independence from the former Soviet Union in 1991, it was still reeling from the 1988 earthquake that destroyed one-tenth of its housing and one-tenth of its industrial base, including Yerevan nuclear power station, which supplied 40 per cent of the country's power. This disrupted all of Armenia's industries, including winegrowing, while the civil war in neighbouring Georgia and ethnic strife within its own borders have made its embryonic free-market trading with the outside world almost impossible.

The grapes grown in this mountainous republic include Chilar, Muscadine, Muscatel, Sersial, Verdelho, and Voskeat, from which high-strength red table wines and strong dessert wines are produced. In the Echmiadzin region, wineries produce fine, high-strength wines of Madeira, Port and Sherry types from such grape

varieties as Chilar, Sersial, Vardeljo, and Voskeat, while white and pink Muscadine grapes are used for dessert wines. Echmiadzin are reputed to be the best white table wines, with Norashen the best of the reds.

AZERBAIJAN

Azerbaijan is the least developed of the three independent Transcaucasian states, although it has been less affected by internal and external strife than either Armenia or Georgia, but its high Muslim population (87 per cent compared to just 11 per cent in Georgia and virtually none in Armenia) has restricted the development of its wine industry.

East of Armenia, Azerbaijan's largest wine-growing zone spreads over from Kirovabad to Akstafa. Wines are produced from local grape varieties such as Bayan shirei, Tavkveri, and others. The best-known table wines of Azerbaijan are dry white Sadilly and the soft and spicy red Matrassa. Akstafa and Alabashly are both high-strength fortified wines made in a Port style, and various dessert wines of local repute include Mil, Shamakhy, Kjurdamir, and Kara-Chanakh.

KAZAKHSTAN

The second-largest of the 15 former USSR states and the richest in natural resources, Kazakhstan has a bright future but for one thing: the fact that six million of its citizens, over a third of the population, are Russians, who were formerly favoured, but are now treated with contempt. If Kazakhstan can contain this problem, the country has the resources to develop a promising wine industry. The largest concentration of Kazakhstan's vineyards are in the extreme east, between Chimkent and Alma-Ata, in the foothills of the Tien Shan mountains, very close to the Chinese border, and thus part of Asia. Vines also grow on the west-facing shores of the Caspian Sea.

✦ THE LEVANT ✦

With the exception of one outstanding wine, Château Musar from Lebanon's Bekaa Valley, and to a somewhat lesser extent Château Kefraya (also in Lebanon), and the Golan Heights Winery in Israel, fine wine is non-existent in the Levant.

WINE WAS FIRST PRODUCED *circa* 4000 BC in Mesopotamia, an area roughly equivalent to modern-day Iraq. In recent times, most vineyards in the Levant have been used for the production of table grapes, sultanas, and currants. The success of Serge Hochar at Château Musar in the Lebanon has, however, confounded our perception of the wine potential in certain parts of the Levant.

TURKEY

Wine districts *Thrace-Marmara; Ankara; Mediterranean Coast; Black Sea Coast; Central Anatolia; Central-south Anatolia*
This country has the fifth-largest area under vine in the world, but because its population is predominantly Muslim, most vines produce either table grapes, sultanas, or currants. The wines that are produced in Turkey are generally flabby, too alcoholic, heavy, over-sulphured, and often oxidized. The best-known are Trakya (dry white Sémillon from Thrace), Trakya Kirmisi (a red blend of native grapes, also from Thrace), and the amusingly named duo Hosbag (red Gamay, from Thrace) and Buzbag (red wine made from native grapes grown in southeast Anatolia), but despite local fame these should all be avoided. The best Turkish wine is Villa Doluca, a clean, well-made, nicely balanced, pure red Gamay.

CYPRUS

Wine districts *Marathassa Afames; Pitsilia; Maheras Mountains; Troödos Mountains; Mesaoria*
Wines have been made on this beautiful island for at least 4,000 years and Cyprus's most famous wine, Commanderie St. John, is one of a handful that claim to be the world's oldest wine. It can be traced back to 1191, when Richard the Lionheart, King of England, acquired the island during the Crusades. He subsequently sold it to the Order of the Knights of the Temple, who established themselves as Commanderies and later became known as the

THE LEVANT

Among the disparate group of countries that forms the area known as the Levant, only Lebanon can boast a fine wine.

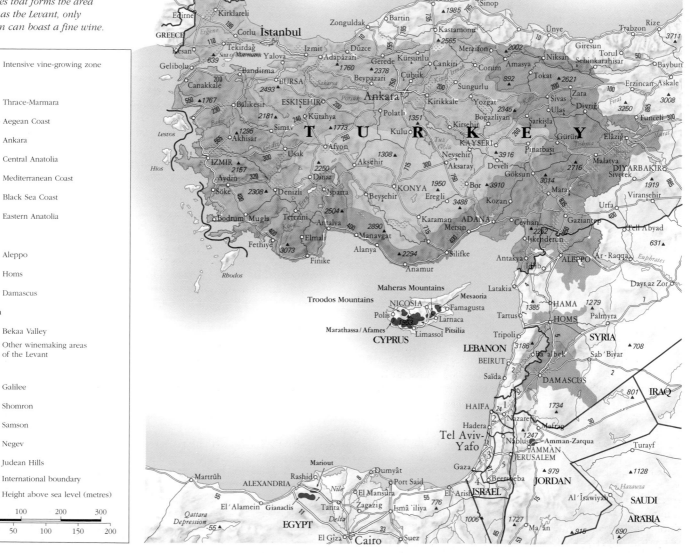

Intensive vine-growing zone

Turkey
- Thrace-Marmara
- Aegean Coast
- Ankara
- Central Anatolia
- Mediterranean Coast
- Black Sea Coast
- Eastern Anatolia

Syria
- Aleppo
- Homs
- Damascus

Lebanon
- Bekaa Valley
- Other winemaking areas of the Levant

Israel
- 1 Galilee
- 2 Shomron
- 3 Samson
- 4 Negev
- 5 Judean Hills

— International boundary
▲ Height above sea level (metres)

km 100 200 300
miles 50 100 150 200

CYPRIOT VINEYARDS
*One of the island's thriving winemaking areas is
situated in the foothills of the Troödos Mountains.*

Knights of the Order of St. John. Commanderie St. John is a *solera*-matured (*see* p.369), sweet dessert wine, which is made from a blend of black and white grapes that have been left in the sun for between 10 and 15 days after the harvest to shrivel and concentrate the grape sugars. It used to be rich and luscious with a fine toasty fullness, but there is nothing special about the wine produced today. Those privileged to taste rarities dating back to the turn of the 20th century can see just how great these wines once were.

In recent years, early harvesting, temperature-controlled stainless-steel vats, and various modern vinification techniques have revolutionized Cypriot winemaking techniques, producing much lighter, cleaner, and crisper wines. Few wines will excite, but KEO, the island's largest and most advanced winery, does produce some that can be safely consumed: Domaine d'Ahera (light, dry red); Bellapais (spritzy, semi-sweet, fruity white); Thisbe (mild, medium-sweet, fruity white); Heritage (oak-aged red); Othello (firm red); Rosella (fresh dry rosé).

SYRIA
Wine districts *Aleppo, Homs, Damascus*
There are approximately 90,000 hectares (220,000 acres) of vines in Syria, which produce mostly table grapes, sultanas, and currants. Since Muslims account for 90 per cent of the population, wine production rarely exceeds 8,000 hectolitres (90,000 cases) a year. It was, apparently, French troops stationed in the country during World War II who were the catalyst for what the wine industry that exists today because the French, being French, demanded wine. The above wine-growing districts are all situated on lower mountain slopes.

LEBANON
Wine district *Bekaa Valley*
The Lebanon's leading winemaker, Serge Hochar of Château Musar, performs a minor miracle in the Bekaa Valley. How he can be so cheerful, when his vineyards have had to contend with Syrian tanks, Israeli jets, and all sorts of militia is remarkable.

The wine is made from Cabernet sauvignon, Cinsault, and Syrah grapes grown at a cool climatic height of 1,000 metres (3,300 feet), on hillside slopes of gravelly soil over limestone bedrock. These vines receive no less than 300 days of sunshine per year and receive no rain during the harvest. Occasionally the wine tastes like Bordeaux, which pleases Hochar because he trained in Bordeaux, but more often than not there is a distinctly baked taste that is reminiscent of the best of good, old-fashioned Southern Rhône during the days when they were not averse to blending in a little wine from Algeria or Morocco. This is not to belittle the wine;

it is always a *vin de garde* and some vintages show remarkable finesse. Having so much success in such an unlikely location has made Hochar prone to detractors, who deprecate the wine, claiming that it is now no longer as stunning as it once was. Some critics even question whether he has any Cabernet sauvignon growing in his vineyards. To my mind the wine is of exactly the same quality, veering between Bordeaux and Rhône in style, although we might not be as excited by it as we once were.

The only other Lebanese wines of interest come from Château Kefraya, which used to be plain Domaine de Kefraya; there is no denying the rich quality of its Cabernet-dominated red. Both Musar and Kefrayer make whites, but despite having been livened up recently, they do not appeal to me. At Ksara there is a winery run by Jesuits, who produce clean, but so far uninteresting, whites. Most other producers still use very crude methods.

ISRAEL
Wine districts *Galilee/Galil, Shomron/Samaria, Samson/Shimshon, Judean Hills, Negev*
There are now five distinct growing districts in Israel, and at least 85 per cent of the wine in bottles bearing these names must come from the indicated appellation: Galilee (or Galil) is the country's premier wine region, especially in the Golan Heights; Shomron (or Samaria) is the largest region; Samson (or Shimshon) is the most ubiquitous appellation; the Judean Hills represent Israel's newest wine region; and Negev is still experimental.

It was not until 1987 that clean, expressive wines started to appear, notably Gamla Cabernet Sauvignon and Yarden Sauvignon Blanc. These were made with help from oenologists trained at UC Davis, using grapes from high-altitude vineyards planted in the Golan Heights where temperatures, even in the middle of summer, rarely rise above 25°C (77°F). Both wines are full of vibrant fruit flavours and getting better most years. The Golan Heights Winery also produces a bottle-fermented sparkling wine, Sauvignon blanc, and an excellent Merlot. Also look out for wines from Barkan, Israel's newest winery. Other wineries include Askalon (a family firm producing good reds, also called Segal or Carmel Zion), Baron (long-established family firm producing some fine white wines), Carmel (a large cooperative and Israel's oldest winery), Efrat (long-established producer, popular locally for low-cost wines), and Eliaz (also popular locally for low-cost wines).

JORDAN
Wine district *Amman-Zarqua*
A country where the vine once flourished, Jordan now has rapidly diminishing vineyards that cover just 3,000 hectares (7,400 acres), with only a small percentage of these responsible for its wine production, which averages just 6,000 hectolitres (67,000 cases) a year. Jordanians are not wine drinkers, preferring Arrack instead, the aniseed-flavoured spirit that is ubiquitous in the Levant.

EGYPT
Wine district *Abu Hummus*
Travelling to the Nile Delta, you are advised to refuse the ice, and the same advice should also apply to the foul-tasting Egyptian wine, which should be avoided at all costs. There are about 20,000 hectares (50,000 acres) of land under vine in Egypt, producing about 15,000 hectolitres (170,000 cases) of wine a year.

GRAPES OF THE LEVANT
Apart from the Mavro, which accounts for 75 per cent of all Cypriot vineyards, the most widely planted grape varieties that are common to the winegrowing areas of the Levant include Aramon, Cabernet franc, Cabernet sauvignon, Carignan, Chardonnay, Chasselas, Cinsault, Clairette, Gamay, Grenache, Muscat (various), Obaideh (possibly the same as Chardonnay), Palomino, Pinot noir, Riesling, Sémillon, Syrah, and Ugni blanc.

OTHER WINEMAKING COUNTRIES OF EUROPE

In the last edition of this book, I did not discuss Luxembourg or other small producers of Europe. I now include all those countries that produce even a tiny quantity of wine, and I must confess that, although I knew of Belgian, Dutch, and Liechtenstein wines, the wines of Denmark were a totally new discovery.

BELGIUM

In Belgium, winegrowing dates back to Roman times. Today, over 100 hectares (250 acres) of vineyards are cultivated by more than 100 growers, using mostly Müller-Thurgau, Auxerrois, Pinots blanc, gris, and noir, and a number of crosses, which are predominantly of German origin. Almost all of these vineyards are in southern Belgium; northeast of Charleroi in the province of Hainault, along the valleys of the Demer in Brabant, the Meuse in Liège, and the Semois in Luxembourg (the Belgian province, not the country). Belgian wines are light, particularly from the Pinot noir, which struggles at this latitude, but can be fresh, crisp, and, in good years, quite fruity. Apart from Hagelander of Aarschot in Brabant, most producers are unknown outside their own locality.

DENMARK

Although there are no commercial wineries in Denmark, I was surprised to discover that not only can grapes be grown so far north, but that there is even a "Danish Wine Growers Association" with 35 members. The vines grown are crosses and hybrids similar to those in English vineyards and the Danes are so keen to hone their skills that in 1995 they toured English vineyards and in 1996 applied to become Overseas Members of the United Kingdom Viticultural Association.

IRELAND

Better suited to stout and whiskey, Ireland had absolutely no winemaking history when, in 1972, Michael O'Callaghan planted vines at Mallow in County Cork. Whatever made him think that he could ripen grapes in a climate that was even less welcoming to viticulture than England? When I put this question to Mr. O'Callaghan, he told me, "I remember reading in a newspaper in the late 1960s or early 1970s something that Eamon De Valera said. He was in hospital abroad for treatment from an eye specialist, and seeing vines growing outside the window of his room, he mused, 'I wonder why we cannot grow grapes at home?'. Well, De Valera was my hero. Anything he said was like a command to me, so I planted vines and, do you know what? We can grow grapes at home!". Mr. O'Callaghan has just over one hectare (three acres) of Reichensteiner vines and his wine is sold exclusively in the restaurant of his country house hotel, Longueville House. Only one other Irish vineyard exists, just five kilometres (three miles) from Mallow, called Blackwater Valley. Knowing that viticulture was at least possible, the owner, Dr. Christopher, planted two hectares (five acres) between 1985 and 1988, since when he has extended it to the present size of five hectares (12 acres). Dr. Christopher also makes a Reichensteiner wine, in addition to which he produces a Madeleine Angevine wine. With four times the production of Longueville House, but no hotel of his own, Dr. Christopher sells his Blackwater Valley wines through restaurants and shops.

THE MOSELLE, LUXEMBOURG
Vineyards above the town of Ehnen, between Lenninger and Wormeldange, at the heart of Luxembourg's long, narrow viticultural region.

LIECHTENSTEIN

Situated between Germany and Switzerland, this is a tiny principality of 160 square kilometres (62 square miles), with just 15 hectares (37 acres) of vines. They are primarily Pinot noir and Chardonnay, and are mostly owned by the crown prince through his private winery the Hofkellerei Fürsten von Liechenstein. The wines are light, fresh, and well made.

LUXEMBOURG

Luxembourg's vineyards are to be found along the limestone banks of the Mosel river, which forms the border with Germany. There are 1,400 hectares (3,460 acres) of vine, which stretch across 42 kilometres (26 miles) of riverside slopes, from Schengen in the south to Wasserbilling in the north. There are over 700 growers in this area, but production is dominated by Vinsmoselle, the marketing organization of five cooperatives (Greiveldange, Remerschen, Stadtbredimus, Wellenstein, and Wormeldange), which processes over 70 per cent of Luxembourg's wines. The other 30 per cent is handled by 50 or so independent producers, including a dozen *négociants*.

Almost 50 per cent of the grapes that are grown within Luxembourg are Müller-Thurgau, which is a mild and fruity variety, and is sold as Rivaner. Elbling, cultivated here since Roman times, is the second most important variety, but the demand for its crisp, dry wine is gradually declining. Auxerrois is the third most important variety, and accounts for some ten per cent of the vines grown, and currently enjoys a growing reputation. Although it is not made in the same quantity or quality as Alsace Auxerrois, it is an extremely full, fat, and surprisingly rich wine that is well worth trying. Riesling is in decline, although the best wines from the warmest years are capable of showing fabulous finesse if they are given sufficient bottle-age. Pinot blanc is quite a rare variety, thankfully, as it tends to be rather one-dimensional; its producers would benefit from taking a leaf from the Alsatians' book and blending it with Auxerrois. Pinot gris from Luxembourg is quite mild and supple, with hardly a fleeting glimpse of the spice that makes this grape one of the kings of Alsace. A small amount of very light Pinot noir is also produced. Sparkling wine, both *cuve close* and bottle-fermented, is very popular, and Bernard Massard of Grevenmacher is the best-known brand on export markets.

On the whole, yields are too high (averaging 130 to 150 hectolitres per hectare) and controls are too lax. There is only one appellation, Moselle Luxembourgeois, which applies to all wines, regardless of village, grape variety, or style. Although there is an official classification system, which starts with *Marque National* and goes up supposedly in order of quality to *Vin Classé*, *Premier Cru*, and finally *Grand Premier Cru*, this is not in my opinion a reliable measure of quality. Furthermore, as there are no *Premier Cru* or *Grand Cru* vineyards as such, it goes against the entire ethos of the EU wine regime – a *cru* is a growth, not a score on a judge's notepad. Until this appellation system sorts itself out, I advise readers to look out for the *Domaines et Traditions* logo, which is awarded by a private organization that not only has tougher quality criteria than the appellation (albeit they could be tougher still), but also promotes the difference that *terroir* makes to wines from the same varieties grown in different villages.

MALTA
The tiny Mediterranean island of Malta has almost 1,000 hectares (2,500 acres) of vines and a winemaking history that dates back as far as to the Phoenicians. In order to meet tourist demand, most of the wines produced here are unfortunately blended with imported wines, but some authentic producers of Maltese wine do exist and Antinori is heading up a new venture.

NETHERLANDS
Although the Netherlands is north of Belgium, and therefore would seem an even more unlikely location for growing vines, almost all its vines grow east of Maastricht, so are actually situated further south than the Belgian vineyards of Brabant. In total, there are probably no more than 10 hectares (25 acres) of vines exsisting in the Netherlands, which is much less than even Liechtenstein has. Winegrowing dates back to the 14th century in the Netherlands, but it was an insignificant industry, and as a result died out completely in the early 19th century, not to be resurrected until as recently as the late 1960s. The grape varieties grown in the Netherlands include Riesling, Müller-Thurgau, Auxerrois, and the inevitable German crosses. Dutch wines rarely travel outside their own locality, but anyone wishing to track down the commercial products that do exist within the Netherlands should contact the Netherlands Wine Information Centre, or the equivalent organization in their own country.

AUTHOR'S CHOICE

Austria is represented by its top red and one of the world's greatest botrytized wine producers. My choice for Britain is its only world-class wine, Nyetimber. Although the selection for Hungary is all white, it should include some excellent reds in the near future. I have also included Lebanon in my round-up.

PRODUCER	WINE	STYLE	DESCRIPTION	
GREAT BRITAIN Nyetimber (*see* p.392)	Premiere Cuvée Chardonnay Brut	SPARKLING WHITE	This wine has the class to compete with some good-quality Champagnes and come out on top. It is a slow developer before and after disgorgement, which is a sign of a classic sparkling wine, building a lovely creamy-biscuity richness and complexity. This is based on the 1992, Nyetimber's first vintage, but I have tasted forward and was staggered to find the 1993 Chardonnay-Pinot blend even better, with great hopes for 1994 and 1995 (particularly Chardonnay 1995).	5–10 years
AUSTRIA Weingut Gesselmann (*see* p.402)	Opus Eximium (*see* p.402, Blended reds) and Cabernet Sauvignon	RED	Without doubt the best all-round red winemaker in Austria. The Opus Eximium is heaped full of flavour and the Cabernet Sauvignon is equally rich, yet extremely accessible.	5–8 years
Willi Opitz (*see* pp.400-402)	Entire range	RED & WHITE	Willi Opitz makes tiny quantities of fabulous wines in every single style he attempts, but he is the maestro when it comes to botrytized wines – not just in Austria, but on the world stage. He makes sumptuous *Beerenauslese* and *Trockenbeerenauslese* in a wide range of varietal styles, but even those who are accustomed to the power and glory of Willi Opitz's renderings should be tied to a chair before they taste his Weisser Schilfmandl, which is a sort of turbo-charged *vin de paille*.	2–20 years
BULGARIA Domaine Boyar (*see* p.406)	Vintage Blend Chardonnay-Sauvignon Blanc	WHITE	Lovely oaky Chardonnay, tweaked by a dash of crisp Sauvignon and definite hints of Australian wine wizardry.	1–2 years
HUNGARY Balaton Boglár Estate Winery, (*see* p.409) Ⓥ	Chapel Hill Barrique Aged Chardonnay	WHITE	Produced by flying winemaker Kym Milne MW, who selects the best wines for this oak-aged Chardonnay, which is so rich and satisfying on its own that food can only detract.	Upon purchase
Gyöngyös Estate Ⓥ (*see* p.409)	Chardonnay, Mátraalja	WHITE	Not as broad as Kym Milne's Chardonnay, this is more fruit driven, with delicious pineapple freshness.	Upon purchase
The Royal Tokay Company (*see* p.408)	Royal Tokaji Aszü 5 Puttonyos	WHITE	This pure, clean, beautifully focused botrytized wine is the best Tokaji currently available, but keep your eyes open for 6 *puttonyos* and *Essencia* in the future.	5–25 years
LEBANON Serge Hochar (*see* p.419)	Château Musar	RED	This full-bodied, rich Cabernet-based blend can sometimes be a bit too baked, but the best years mellow beautifully with age.	5–25 years

The WINES of

NORTH and SOUTH AFRICA

THE OLD WORLD MEETS THE NEW WORLD
on the same continent although they are
hundreds of kilometres apart. There is no
interest, let alone excitement, in the former
French colonies of Algeria, Morocco, or
Tunisia, but there is potential and it is only
a matter of time before a flock of flying
winemakers arrive to exploit it. When they
do, our perception of North African wine will
change rapidly and profoundly. The curiosities
are to be found in Kenya, where a one-off
vineyard and winery exists at Lake Naivasha
in the beautiful Rift Valley, and in Zimbabwe,
which has the potential to become a commercial
export proposition and its wines are likely to
trickle on to supermarket shelves over the
next year or two. The class act in Africa is,
of course, South African wine, the exports
of which have soared since the
demise of apartheid.

FRANSCHOEK VALLEY IN THE PAARL REGION, SOUTH AFRICA
*An aerial view of vineyards that are higher and steeper than
most of the Paarl region, and well suited to red wines.*

✦ NORTH AFRICA ✦

The wine industries of Algeria, Morocco, and Tunisia, and the appellation systems within which they work, are all based on the structure left behind by the colonial French. Today, the governments of each country play active roles in the further development of their wine industries, and although this has improved quality, no fine wines are produced. The quality of the wines can, however, be quite good, and the best are invariably Moroccan reds and Tunisian Muscats. If flying winemakers were ever to land here, they would have a field day.

ALGERIA

Wine districts of the *Département* of Oran *Coteaux de Mascara, Coteaux de Tlemcen, Monts du Tessalah, Mostaganem, Mostaganem-Kenenda, Oued-Imbert*

Wine districts of the *Département* of Alger *Aïn-Bessem-Bouïra, Coteaux du Zaccar, Haut-Dahra, Médéa*

In 1830, Algeria became the first North African country to be colonized by the French, which gave it a head start in viticulture over other North African countries. Algeria has always dominated North African viticulture in terms of quantity, if not quality. The demise of the country's wine industry after it gained independence in 1962 made it clear that cynical remarks about the use of its wine in bolstering Burgundies were true, but the ironic fact is that both the Moroccan and the Burgundian wines benefited from being blended together. It was not the best Burgundies that were enhanced with dark Algerian red, but the poorest, thinnest, and least attractive wines. After the blending, they were not Burgundian in character, but were superior to the original Burgundy.

BERBER WOMEN WORKING IN A TUNISIAN VINEYARD
The best and most reliable AOC wines in Tunisia are Muscats, although rosé enjoyed an ephemeral fashion just after World War II.

NORTH AFRICA
Morocco, Algeria, and Tunisia are all wine-producing countries. Most vineyards are concentrated along the coastal belts.

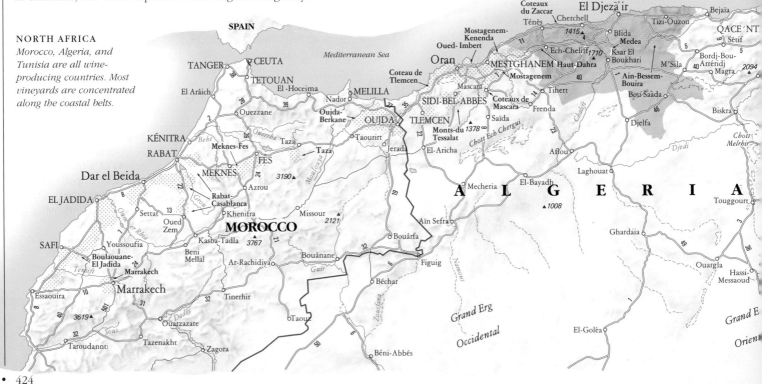

Since independence, Algeria's vineyards have shrunk by almost 50 per cent and the red wines produced that are unblended with French wines have not shown much improvement. The white and rosé wines, however, have improved enormously and are getting fresher with each new vintage. Of the few reds that can be honestly recommended, the best are from Coteaux de Mascara, where they are made in a solid, rustic, slightly coarse style.

MOROCCO

Wine districts *Meknès-Fez, Rabat-Casablanca, Oujda-Berkane, Marrakech*

Wines were made here during Roman times, but after more than 1,000 years of Muslim rule viticulture died out. In 1912, however, most of Morocco came under either French or Spanish control (with an international zone encompassing Tangiers) and it once

OLD MUSCAT VINES
Vineyards at Bizerte in the Bizerte-Mateur-Tébourba region at the northern tip of Tunisia.

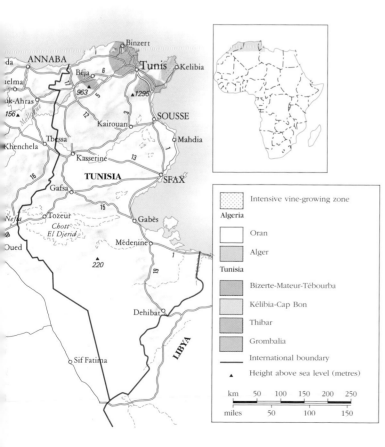

KHEMIS MILIANA, ALGERIA
Gently undulating vineyards south of Cherchell in the Alger region, just west of Haut-Dahra district.

more became an active winemaking country. When Morocco gained independence in 1956, the new government introduced a quality-control regime similar to the French AOC (*Appellation d'Origine Contrôlée*) system and, in 1973, it nationalized the wine industry. However, few wines carry the official *Appellation d'Origine Garantie* designation. Some pale rosés sold as *vin gris* can be pleasant when chilled but the best wines are red, the most successful being two Les Trois Domaines wines, which are called Tarik and Chante Bled on most export markets. These wines are made from Carignan, Cinsault, and Grenache grapes grown in the Meknès-Fez district. Of the two, the Tarik is bigger, the Chante Bled smoother. However, most Moroccan wines are sold on the home market, at undeserved high prices, to tourists who are not willing to pay the even more exorbitant prices demanded for heavily taxed imported wines, and poor storage conditions inevitably spoil both.

TUNISIA

Wine districts *Grombalia, Bizerte-Mateur-Tébourba, Kélibia-Cap Bon, Thibar*

Wines were first made around the Carthage area in Punic times, but production was forbidden for 1,000 years under Muslim rule. After French colonization in 1881, viticulture resumed and by Tunisian independence in 1955, the foundations of a thriving wine industry had been laid. At this time two basic appellations had been established – Vin Supérieur de Tunisie, for table wines, and Appellation Contrôlée Vin Muscat de Tunisie, for *liqueur* Muscat. These designations did not, however, incorporate any controls to safeguard origin, and in 1957 the government introduced a classification system that established four levels as follows: *Vins de Consommation Courante, Vins Supérieurs, Vins de Qualité Supérieure,* and *Appellation d'Origine Contrôlée.* The best Tunisian wines are those made from the Muscat grape – they range from the lusciously sweet, rich, and viscous Vin de Muscat grape de Tunisie, to fresh, delicate, dry Muscats such as the Muscat de Kelibia. There are also a small number of good red wines, such as Château Feriani, Domaine Karim, and Royal Tardi, with Carignan and Cinsault the most important grape varieties.

✦SOUTH AFRICA✦

The quality of South African wines has blossomed since this country became the rainbow state. By embracing a multiracial democracy, South Africa has opened up world markets that have been hungry for the next flavour of the month, and the revenue received was desperately needed to fund the production of better-quality wines.

AT FIRST, BETTER QUALITY simply meant stricter selection and, where appropriate, a massive investment in new oak, but an increasing amount of South Africa's growing export income has been ploughed into the industry's Vine Improvement Programme (VIP). Phase one of VIP concentrates on clonal selection and rootstock improvement, while phase two analyzes the suitability to specific *terroirs* of various combinations of the clones and rootstocks the scheme develops. It is so ambitious that the project will probably never end, but after such lengthy period of international isolation it was essential to revitalize the country's vineyards. However, VIP has already manifested itself in wines of richer varietal character and greater complexity than ever before, and South Africa, which was once ten years behind the rest of the world, is now at the forefront of viticultural research.

IN THE BEGINNING

Virtually all of South Africa's vineyards are located within a 160-kilometre (100-mile) sweep of Cape Town. The first vines were planted in 1655 and the wines were not, by all accounts, particularly successful. Simon van der Stel, who arrived in 1679, complained about the "revolting sourness" of the local wines. He proceeded to remedy the situation by founding Constantia, the most illustrious wine farm in the country's history (this has since been split into three properties: Groot Constantia, Klein Constantia, and Buitenverwachting).

HOW TO READ SOUTH AFRICAN WINE LABELS

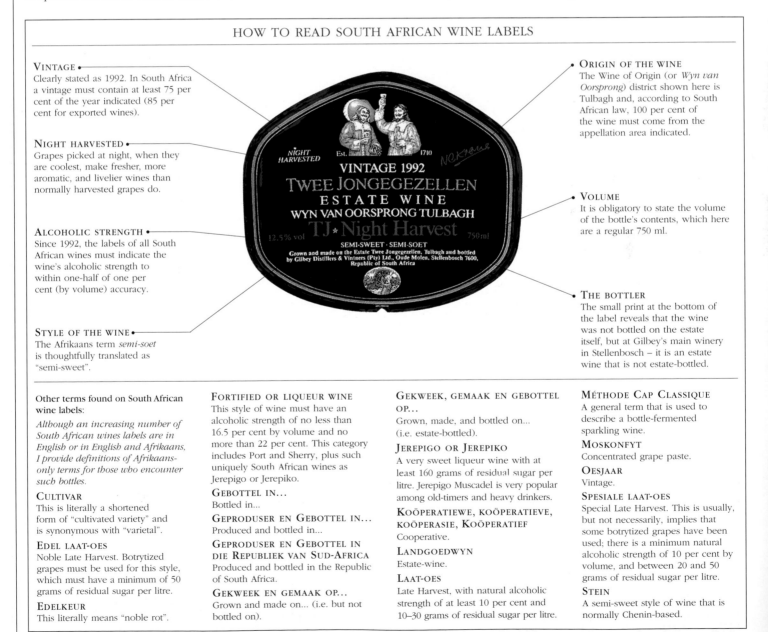

VINTAGE
Clearly stated as 1992. In South Africa a vintage must contain at least 75 per cent of the year indicated (85 per cent for exported wines).

NIGHT HARVESTED
Grapes picked at night, when they are coolest, make fresher, more aromatic, and livelier wines than normally harvested grapes do.

ALCOHOLIC STRENGTH
Since 1992, the labels of all South African wines must indicate the wine's alcoholic strength to within one-half of one per cent (by volume) accuracy.

STYLE OF THE WINE
The Afrikaans term *semi-soet* is thoughtfully translated as "semi-sweet".

ORIGIN OF THE WINE
The Wine of Origin (or *Wyn van Oorsprong*) district shown here is Tulbagh and, according to South African law, 100 per cent of the wine must come from the appellation area indicated.

VOLUME
It is obligatory to state the volume of the bottle's contents, which here are a regular 750 ml.

THE BOTTLER
The small print at the bottom of the label reveals that the wine was not bottled on the estate itself, but at Gilbey's main winery in Stellenbosch – it is an estate wine that is not estate-bottled.

Other terms found on South African wine labels:

Although an increasing number of South African wines labels are in English or in English and Afrikaans, I provide definitions of Afrikaans-only terms for those who encounter such bottles.

CULTIVAR
This is literally a shortened form of "cultivated variety" and is synonymous with "varietal".

EDEL LAAT-OES
Noble Late Harvest. Botrytized grapes must be used for this style, which must have a minimum of 50 grams of residual sugar per litre.

EDELKEUR
This literally means "noble rot".

FORTIFIED OR LIQUEUR WINE
This style of wine must have an alcoholic strength of no less than 16.5 per cent by volume and no more than 22 per cent. This category includes Port and Sherry, plus such uniquely South African wines as Jerepigo or Jerepiko.

GEBOTTEL IN...
Bottled in...

GEPRODUSER EN GEBOTTEL IN...
Produced and bottled in...

GEPRODUSER EN GEBOTTEL IN DIE REPUBLIEK VAN SUD-AFRICA
Produced and bottled in the Republic of South Africa.

GEKWEEK EN GEMAAK OP...
Grown and made on... (i.e. but not bottled on).

GEKWEEK, GEMAAK EN GEBOTTEL OP...
Grown, made, and bottled on... (i.e. estate-bottled).

JEREPIGO OR JEREPIKO
A very sweet liqueur wine with at least 160 grams of residual sugar per litre. Jerepigo Muscadel is very popular among old-timers and heavy drinkers.

KOÖPERATIEWE, KOÖPERATIEVE, KOÖPERASIE, KOÖPERATIEF
Cooperative.

LANDGOEDWYN
Estate-wine.

LAAT-OES
Late Harvest, with natural alcoholic strength of at least 10 per cent and 10–30 grams of residual sugar per litre.

MÉTHODE CAP CLASSIQUE
A general term that is used to describe a bottle-fermented sparkling wine.

MOSKONFYT
Concentrated grape paste.

OESJAAR
Vintage.

SPESIALE LAAT-OES
Special Late Harvest. This is usually, but not necessarily, implies that some botrytized grapes have been used; there is a minimum natural alcoholic strength of 10 per cent by volume, and between 20 and 50 grams of residual sugar per litre.

STEIN
A semi-sweet style of wine that is normally Chenin-based.

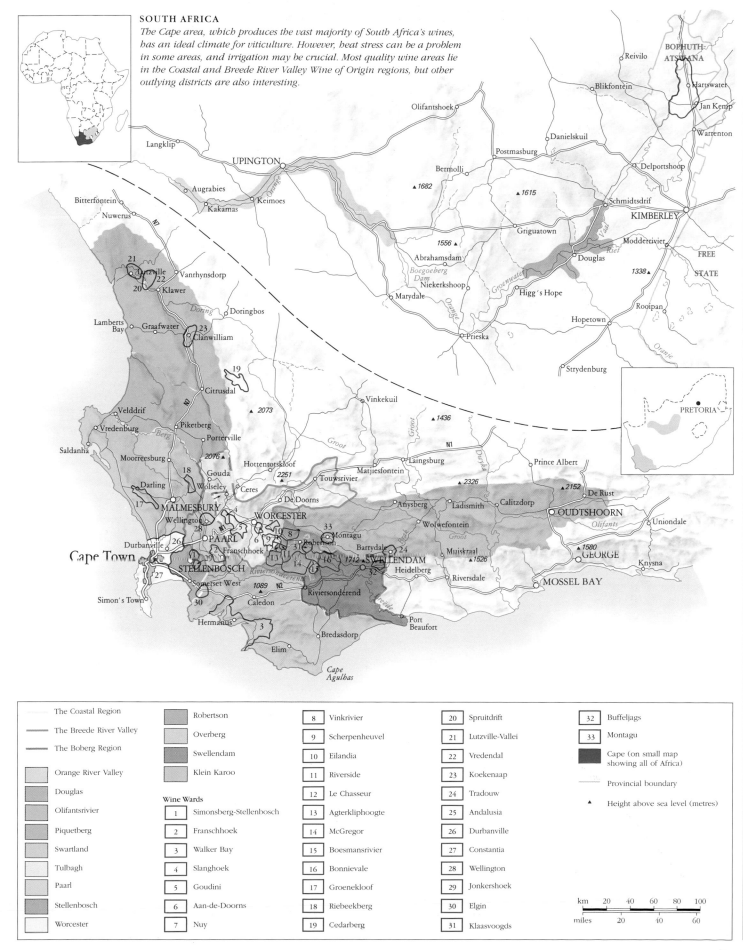

SOUTH AFRICA

The Cape area, which produces the vast majority of South Africa's wines, has an ideal climate for viticulture. However, heat stress can be a problem in some areas, and irrigation may be crucial. Most quality wine areas lie in the Coastal and Breede River Valley Wine of Origin regions, but other outlying districts are also interesting.

PRETORIA

Legend:

- .... The Coastal Region
- ——— The Breede River Valley
- ——— The Boberg Region

- Orange River Valley
- Douglas
- Olifantsrivier
- Piquetberg
- Swartland
- Tulbagh
- Paarl
- Stellenbosch
- Worcester

- Robertson
- Overberg
- Swellendam
- Klein Karoo

Wine Wards

1	Simonsberg-Stellenbosch
2	Franschhoek
3	Walker Bay
4	Slanghoek
5	Goudini
6	Aan-de-Doorns
7	Nuy

8	Vinkrivier
9	Scherpenheuvel
10	Eilandia
11	Riverside
12	Le Chasseur
13	Agterkliphoogte
14	McGregor
15	Boesmansrivier
16	Bonnievale
17	Groenekloof
18	Riebeekberg
19	Cedarberg

20	Spruitdrift
21	Lutzville-Vallei
22	Vredendal
23	Koekenaap
24	Tradouw
25	Andalusia
26	Durbanville
27	Constantia
28	Wellington
29	Jonkershoek
30	Elgin
31	Klaasvoogds

| 32 | Buffeljags |
| 33 | Montagu |

- Cape (on small map showing all of Africa)
- .... Provincial boundary
- ▲ Height above sea level (metres)

| km | 20 | 40 | 60 | 80 | 100 |
| miles | 20 | 40 | 60 | |

THELEMA MOUNTAIN VINEYARDS
These beautifully tended vineyards on the Simonsberg in Stellenbosch belong to Thelema Mountain, one of South Africa's youngest and most exciting wineries.

Three centuries of winemaking

The arrival of French Huguenots, with their viticultural and winemaking expertise, greatly improved the quality of Cape wines, and by the early 1700s they were beginning to be held in high esteem. When French Revolutionary forces entered Holland in 1806, the British occupied the Cape and, cut off from supplies of French wines, began exporting South African wines to the many corners of their Empire, enhancing the wines' growing reputation. By 1859, the export of Cape wines to Britain alone had reached 45,000 hectolitres (one million gallons). However, in Britain, Cobden (the "apostle of the free market") and Gladstone secretly negotiated a commercial treaty with the French that had a devastating effect on this trade. In 1860, Cape wine exports fell to 22,000 hectolitres; the next year this dropped to 5,700 hectolitres; and by 1865 it was as low as 4,200 hectolitres.

A time of struggle for South African wine

Despite this setback to the wine trade, production was not checked. In fact, the large influx of immigrants attracted by the discovery of gold and diamonds in the late 19th century prompted a rapid expansion of vineyards in anticipation of a vastly increased demand. This increase in demand was realised,

RECENT SOUTH AFRICAN VINTAGES

Differences in vintage are most significant in the Coastal Region and Overberg, but much less so in hot-climate areas. Quality has been steadily increasing since the 1994 vintage, whatever the vintage conditions, as vineyards are now replanted with new, better-ripening clones. Few whites improve with age, so best to rely on the producer and buy the most recent vintage.

2000 The third in a trio of fiercely hot and dry vintages in which those with water dams that did not run dry made good but alcoholic wines.

1999 Hot and dry, very good quality, but big and alcoholic.

1998 Hot and dry, very good quality, but big and alcoholic.

1997 A long, cool summer produced lovely fruit flavours and full yet elegant ripeness for those who picked late. Those who did not wait made lighter reds in which the fruit is less lush and the tannins quite green.

1996 An average year at best. The reds are light, lack complexity, and are marked with unripe tannins. Pinot Noir perhaps had the edge over other varieties, although Pinotage had greater highs and worst lows. A phenomenal Thelema Merlot bucked the trend.

FACTORS AFFECTING TASTE AND QUALITY

LOCATION
South Africa is on the southernmost tip of the African continent.

CLIMATE
The climate is generally mild Mediterranean, but coastal areas have a much higher rainfall and are cooler than inland parts in spring and autumn. All coastal areas are cooled by sea breezes chilled by the icy Benguela current from Antarctica. The coolest, Constantia, like Stellenbosch, rates as low Region III. Klein Karoo, Tulbagh, Olifants River, and parts of Paarl (Dal Josaphat) are the hottest, falling between high Region IV and low Region V (*see* p.448).

ASPECT
Most vines are cultivated flat on gently undulating valley floors. More recently, higher slopes have been increasingly cultivated and Klein Constantia, Thelema Mountain Vineyard, Bellingham, and Boschendal all have very steep vineyards.

SOIL
Soils range from gravel and heavy loams of sandstone, shale, and granitic origin on the coastal plain, to the deep alluvial, sandy, and lime-rich, red-shale soils of Klein Karoo and other river valleys.

VITICULTURE AND VINIFICATION
Contrary to popular belief, Cape vineyards sometimes fail even to ripen their grapes, although there are, of course, many hot areas where vines may suffer from heat-stress and grapes can quickly overripen. Irrigation is often necessary in Robertson, Worcester, and Vredendal, where successful cultivation depends on the availability of water. Where the heat factor is critical, some estates may conduct the harvest at night, under floodlight. South Africa has a history of overproduction (*see* KWV International p.435), due to having too much area under vine, too little emphasis on high-quality varieties, poor clones, and undesirably high yields, but is quickly upgrading its vineyards, and is now at the forefront of research on new clones and rootstock. Yields are also being lowered to appeal to export markets. Until the early 1990s, estates were slow to cultivate higher, cooler slopes, but this is changing fast.

PRIMARY GRAPE VARIETIES
Cabernet sauvignon, Chardonnay, Chenin blanc (*syn.* Steen), Cinsault, Colombard, Crouchen (*syn.* Cape riesling), Merlot, Muscat d'Alexandrie (*syn.* Hanepoot), Pinotage, Riesling (*syn.* Rhine riesling, Weisser riesling), Sauvignon blanc, Shiraz (*syn.* Syrah)
SECONDARY GRAPE VARIETIES
Alicante bouschet, Auxerrois, Barbarossa, Barbera, Bastardo, Bourboulenc, Bukettraube, Cabernet franc, Carignan, Chenel (*syn. Chenin blanc* x *Trebbiano*), Clairette blanche, Cornichon, Cornifesto, Emerald riesling, False Pedro, Ferdinand de Lesseps, Fernao Pires, Flame tokai (*syn.* Vlamkleur tokai), Folle blanche, Gamay, Gewürztraminer, Grenache (*syn.* Rooi grenache), Hárslevelü, Malbec, Morio muscat, Mouvedre, Muscadel, Muscat de Hambourg, Muscat ottonel, Palomino, Pedro Ximénez, Petit verdot, Pinot gris, Pinot noir, Sémillon (*syn.* Greengrape), Souzao, Tinta amarela (*syn.* Malvasia rey), Tinta barocca, Tinta Francisca, Tinta roriz, Ugni blanc, Viognier, Zinfandel

but the sudden wealth of these immigrants sparked off the Boer War, and sales of wine decreased at home and abroad. Yet unsaleable wine continued to be made.

In 1905, the Cape Government encouraged the formation of cooperatives, but nothing constructive was done either to reduce production or stimulate demand. Thus, when the Koöperatiewe Wijnbouwers Vereniging, or KWV as it is now known, was formed in 1918 with government-backed powers, its decision to distil half the country's annual wine production into brandy immediately and very effectively improved the quality of Cape wines. Its policy of blending the rest of the surplus into marketable export products did no less than save the South African wine industry.

NEW AREAS AND BETTER WINES

Stellenbosch and Paarl are traditionally viewed as the country's two greatest wine districts. With the establishment of Hamilton Russell's top-performing vineyard at Hermanus, however, the Walker Bay area of Overberg to the southeast is now seen by many as potentially as fine. Although there are just two wine estates in Hermanus at the moment, Elgin has developed into another startlingly good wine area. Elgin is the Cape's apple-growing capital, and, as Washington in the US quickly learned, wherever apple-growers choose to go, fine quality wine-grapes will follow. With Neil Ellis currently sourcing excellent Sauvignon

Blanc from Elgin, this area is certainly another feather in Overberg's cap. Most surprising of all is the even more recent establishment of Buitenverwachting and Klein Constantia, in 1985 and 1986 respectively, for these two estates have completed the cycle of exploration and development in South Africa's winelands. Constantia, once merely the site of an historic wine, is now one of the most exciting white-wine areas in all South Africa. Outside of the mainstream vineyard regions, Mossel Bay in the extreme east of the Cape district is a potentially fine wine-area, offering great hopes for aromatic white-wine varieties such as Riesling and Sauvignon blanc – some even think Pinot noir will do well there.

In 1995, South African wine estates were allowed for the first time to buy in grapes from other areas; these were not to blend with their own grapes, but to enable them to extend their range by offering single-vineyard wines from other locations. Thus, instead of struggling to produce, say, Sauvignon Blanc in red-wine territory (because customers demand the style), an estate may now source these grapes from a more ideal *terroir*, grub-up their own Sauvignon vines, and replant with more suitable varieties. This should lead to a certain polarizing of varieties in the areas where each performs best, which ties in with the second phase of the Vine Improvement Programme and the results can only be good for the future of South African wine.

THE APPELLATIONS OF
SOUTH AFRICA

Note Wine wards are the most specific type of WO (Wine of Origin) appellation. One or more WO wards may be contained in a larger WO dstrict, and one or more WO districts may be contained in a WO region.

ANDALUSIA WO

Although this ward is considered a wine district in its own right, its location some 80 kilometres (50 miles) north of Kimberley does in fact make it a part of the Orange River region for all practical purposes. Due to huge, irrigation-propelled yields, this area was once considered a source of bulk wines only, but the local cooperative, Vaalharts, markets some good value, easy-drinking bottled wines.

BENEDE ORANJE WO

Another single-ward appellation, Benede Oranje consists of a ten-kilometre (six-mile) stretch of the Orange River near Augrabies.

BOBERG WO

Wine districts *Paarl WO, Tulbagh WO*
This regional WO is restricted to fortified-wine made within the Paarl and Tulbagh districts.

BREEDE RIVER VALLEY WO

Wine districts *Robertson WO, Swellendam WO, Worcester WO*
The vineyards in this region, situated east of the Drakenstein Mountains, depend on irrigation, and mostly produce white or fortified wines. Dewetshot is perhaps the best-known winery.

CEDARBERG WO

This is an outlying area just east of the southern part of the Olifants River region, where the local cooperative, Cedarberg Kelders, offers a very good-value range, including an excellent Cabernet Sauvignon.

COASTAL REGION WO

Wine districts *Paarl WO, Stellenbosch WO, Swartland WO, Tulbagh WO*
The most frequently encountered appellation, the Coastal Region comprises two external wards (Constantia WO and Durbanville WO) in addition to the above four districts and their wards. The vineyards of Constantia are situated on the eastern, red-granitic slopes of Constantia Mountain, south of Cape Town. Bordered by sea on two sides, the climate is very moderate, of Mediterranean character, but it is quite wet with up to 120 centimetres (47 inches) annual rainfall. Durbanville is located in the lowlands of the Tygerberg hills and, although the rainfall is less than half that of Constantia,

the deep, well-weathered, red, granite-based soils have a particularly good water-retention, and the vines are cooled and dried by the sea-breezes coming in from Table Bay.

DOUGLAS WO

This district southwest of Kimberley was granted its own Wine of Origin status as recently as 1981, but it is in fact an extension of the Orange River appellation. The Douglas Cooperative is known for the excellence of its Muscat d'Alexandrie dessert wine.

KLEIN KAROO WO

Wine wards *Montagu WO, Tradouw WO*
This appellation is a long, narrow strip that stretches from Montagu in the west to De Rust in the east. The vineyards require irrigation to survive the hot and arid climate. The famous red, shale-based Karoo soil and the deep alluvium closer to the various rivers, are very fertile and well-suited to the Jerepigo, Muscadel, and other dessert wines for which this area is known. Klein Karoo's Boplass Estate makes South Africa's best "port" and Die Krans is another fortified-wine specialist, but most of the production is processed by cooperatives.

MOSSEL BAY

Although Mossel Bay is not a Wine of Origin area, it is highly thought of as a future source of very fine-quality Riesling, Sauvignon Blanc, and possibly Pinot Noir.

OLIFANTS RIVER *or* OLIFANTSRIVIER WO

Wine wards *Koekenaap WO, Lutzville-Vallei WO, Spruitdrift WO, Vredendal WO*
The vines in this long, narrow district grow on sandstone or lime-rich alluvial soil. The climate is hot and dry, with rainfall averaging just

26 centimetres (ten inches) and decreasing closer to the coast. There are no wine estates, the grapes grown being processed by some half-a-dozen cooperatives. Vredendal Winery is the largest and makes some very good wines indeed.

ORANGE RIVER *or* ORANJERIVIER REGION WO
Wine wards *none*
Also known as the Lower Orange River, this northernmost viticultural area is totally divorced from the rest of the country's vineyards. The climate is hot and dry, irrigation is essential, and the fertile soils are capable of high yields. No estate wines are produced here; all the grapes are processed by local cooperatives.

OVERBERG WO
Wine wards *Elgin WO, Walker Bay WO*
Overberg WO replaced Caledon WO, and consists of a huge, recently cultivated area southeast of Paarl and Stellenbosch. Fifteen years ago, there was only one estate here, Hamilton Russell Vineyards in Walker Bay, but this was obviously one of South Africa's most potentially exciting wine districts. Walker Bay and Elgin are now two of the hottest spots on South Africa's wine map. Hottest meaning coolest, of course. The wineries that have set up here since Hamilton Russell Vineyards include HRV, Bouchard Finlayson, Whalehaven, Cape Bay, Goedvertrouw, Newton Johnson, Bartho Eksteen and Beaumont, while Elgin now has Paul Cluver and Thandi. Many more about to begin production in both areas.

PAARL WO
Wine wards *Franschhoek WO, Wellington WO*
This district embraces the fertile Berg River valley and vineyards surrounding the towns of Franschhoek, Wellington, and Paarl itself. The vineyards are located on three main types of soil: granite in the Paarl district, Table Mountain sandstone along the Berg River, and Malmesbury slate to the north. The climate is Mediterranean with wet winters and hot, dry summers. Average annual rainfall is about 65 centimetres (26 inches), but this declines towards the northwest of the district. Although

this used to be a white-wine area, it is now more of a red wine area, with high-lying vineyards that are well-suited to the production of fine-quality reds.

PICKETBERG *or* PIQUETBERG WO
Wine wards *none*
This large district lies between Swartland and Tulbagh to the south and Olifants River district to the north. With very hot temperatures and rainfall as low as 17.5 centimetres (7 inches) in places, it is really not suited to viticulture, yet is starting to produce some interesting fruit.

ROBERTSON WO
Wine wards *Agterkliphoogte WO, Boesmansrivier WO, Bonnievale WO* (part overlaps the Swellendam district), *Le Chasseur WO, Eilandia WO, Klaasvoogds, McGregor WO, Riverside WO, Vinkrivier WO*
This district is bordered to the south by the Riversonderend Mountains and to the north by Langeberg Range. Soil, climate, and topography are, for the most part, similar to those of the Karoo, although somewhat more temperate.

STELLENBOSCH WO
Wine wards *Helderberg WO, Jonkershoek WO, Simonsberg-Stellenbosch WO*
This district is situated between False Bay to the south and Paarl to the north, where the greatest concentration of South Africa's finest wine estates are located. There are three types of soil: granite-based in the east (considered best for red wines), Table Mountain sandstone in the west (favoured for white wines), and alluvial soils around the Eerste River. With warm, dry summers, cool, moist winters and an average annual rainfall of 50 centimetres (20 inches), irrigation is usually unnecessary, except in some situations at the height of the summer season. Helderberg is the current hot-spot.

SWARTLAND WO
Wine wards *Groenekloof WO, Riebeekberg WO*
This replaced the Malmesbury WO district. Of the vast area covered by Swartland, most is arable land, with viticulture confined to the

southern section around Darling, Malmesbury, and Riebeek. The soils are Table Mountain sandstone and Malmesbury slate, and the rainfall is light, at around 24 centimetres (nine inches), which makes irrigation generally necessary, although some vineyards surprisingly manage without it.

SWELLENDAM WO
Wine wards *Bonnievale WO* (part overlaps Robertson district), *Buffeljags WO*
The vineyards here largely produce bulk-wine and are operated by the members of some half-a-dozen mostly average cooperatives, although the occasional excellent winery does exist.

TULBAGH WO
Wine wards *none*
This district is situated north of Paarl, on the eastern border of Swartland. Although Wolseley is geographically within this district, viticulturally it is part of the Breede River Region. The vineyards of the Tulbagh basin are surrounded by high mountains and located on sandy and shale-based soils. The climate is hot and relatively dry, with some 35 centimetres (14 inches) of annual rainfall, making irrigation necessary, although vines closer to the mountain slopes receive a higher rainfall.

WORCESTER WO
Wine wards *Nuy WO, Goudini WO, Slanghoek WO, Scherpenheuvel WO, Aan-de-Doorns WO*
On the western edge of Little Karoo, adjoining the eastern border of Paarl, the Worcester district is richly cultivated with vines in the Breede River catchment area. The soils are derived from Table Mountain sandstone and the fertile red shale of Little Karoo. The hot climate is tempered in the west by high rainfall, while in the east rainfall is very low. Although there are some good wine estates in Worcester, including the excellent Bergsig, the real stars of this district are the high-performing cooperatives that make exceptionally fine white and fortified wines.

THE WINE STYLES OF
SOUTH AFRICA

CABERNET FRANC
Like all maturing New World winemaking countries before it, South Africa has taken little notice of this grape, but elsewhere a growing number of wineries have discovered Cabernet franc can produce striking varietal wines and, if Warwick is anything to go by, this could be a growth area in the Cape too.

✓ *Avontuur* • Bellingham (Spitz) • *Cordoba* (Crescendo) • *KWV* (Cathedral Cellar) • *Warwick Estate*

CABERNET SAUVIGNON
PURE AND BLENDED Traditional, firm, assertive styles are made here, but the trend is towards more upfront wines driven by ripe, juicy *cassis* fruit with cedary, spicy-vanilla oak complexity. New-wave wines are often enjoyable when young, but some also develop in bottle. Cabernet

blends rank as one of South Africa's finest red-wine styles. Other constituents are usually Cabernet franc and Merlot, but may include Malbec, or, in the case of Boschendal Lanoy, even a dash of Shiraz (Shiraz-dominated blends are dealt with below).

🍷— 3–7 years (modern style), 5–10 years (traditional style, exceptional modern style)

✓ *Agusta* • Alto • *Ashwood* • Backsberg • *Graham Beck* (Coastal) • Bellingham • *Beyerskloof* • Boekenhoutskloof • *Le Bonheur* • Buitenverwachting • *Clos Malverne* • Cordoba • *Delheim* • Diemersdal • *Douglas Green* • Eikendal • *Neil Ellis Stellenbosch* • Fairview • *Genesis* • Grangehurst • *Hartenberg* • Kanonkop • *KWV* (Cathedral Cellar Stellenbosch, Cathedral Cellar Paarl) • *Laibach* • Meerlust • *Morgenhof*

• *Nederburg* (Auction) • Plaisir de Merle • *Le Riche* • Rustenberg (Stellenbosch, Peter Barlow) • *Saxenburg* (Private Collection) • *Simonsig* • Thelema • *De Trafford* • *Vergelegen* • Warwick

Cabernet Blends *Alto Rouge* • Backsberg (Klein Babylonstoren) • *Graham Beck* • Beyerskloof • *Le Bonheur* (Prima) • *Bouwland* • Buitenverwachting (Christine) • *Camberley* • Clos Malverne • *Diemersdal* (Private Collection) • *Eikendal* (Classique) • *Neil Ellis* (Inglewood) • Fairview • *Glen Carlou* (Grande Classique) • *Grangehurst* • *Groot Constantia* (Gouverneur's Reserve) • *Hazendal* • Jordan (Chameleon) • *Kanonkop* (Paul Sauer) • Klein Gustrouw • *KWV* (Cathedral Cellar Triptych) • *Laibach* • La Motte (Millennium) • *Meerlust* (Rubicon) • *Meinert*

• *Mulderbosch* (Faithful Hound)
• *Nederburg Edelrood* • *Overgaauw*
(Tria Corda) • *Le Riche* • *Rupert & De
Rothschild* (Baron Edmond de Rothschild)
• *Simonsig* (Tiara) • *Spice Route*
• *De Trafford* • *Veenwouden* (Classic)
• *Vergelegen* (Mill Race Red)
• *Vergelegen* (Reserve) • *Vergenoegd* (Reserve)
• *Villiera* (Cru Munro) • *Vriesenhof* (Kallista)
• *Warwick* (Trilogy) • *Welgemeend* (Douelle)
• *Weltevrede* • *Yonder Hill* (iNanda)

CHARDONNAY

Although this is South Africa's most improved
varietal, it was originally so bland that it could
only get better. The trouble was that as soon
as new oak became widely available for the
first time, many winemakers went over the top,
producing heavy, over-wooded Chardonnays.
These wines also suffered from poor raw material,
but this situation improved with clonal selection
and matching this variety to more suitable *terroirs*.
The best oaked Chardonnays are often barrel-
fermented, rather than just oak-aged, with just
a kiss of creamy new oak, although some less
refined if just as lip-smacking wines dominated
by yummy, coconutty-oak are also to be found.
The top unoaked versions, such as De Wetshof's
Grey Label, are very pure and exquisitely
balanced, and often belie their hot-climate origins.

🍷— 1–3 years (unoaked), 1–5 years (oaked)

☑ *L'Avenir* • *Avontuur* (Reserve) • *Backsberg*
• *Graham Beck Lonebill* • *Bellingham*
• *Boschendal* • *Bouchard Finlayson*
(Kaaimansgat, Missionvale) • *Brampton*
• *Buitenverwachting* • *Constantia Uitsig*
• *Dieu Donné* • *Durbanville Hills* • *Neil Ellis
Elgin* • *Fairview* • *Fort Simon* • *Glen Carlou*
• *Glen Carlou* (Reserve) • *Hamilton Russell*
• *Jordan* • *Kanu* • *Klein Constantia*
• *Longridge* • *Louisvale* • *Mont Rochelle*
(Oak matured) • *Rustenberg* (Five Soldiers)
• *Thelema* (Ed's Reserve) • *Vergelegen*
(Reserve) • *Warwick* • *De Wetshof*
(Bateleur, D'Honneur, Finesse, Sur Lie,
Limestone Hills)

CHENIN BLANC

Almost one-third of South Africa's vineyards are
covered with this variety, which is also known
locally as Steen. It generally produces cheap
and cheerful, off-dry whites, but some fine
bone-dry wines of greater intensity, sometimes
barrel-fermented, are also produced. As this
grape performs much better in the Cape than
it does at home in the Loire, why is there not
a botrytis style here? The nearest that South
Africa has got to a great Vouvray *moelleux* has
been the succulent, honeyed 1990 Noble Late
Harvest, made exclusively from Chenin Blanc
by the Perdeberg cooperative in Paarl.

🍷— Upon purchase

☑ *Beaumont* • *Boschendal* • *Fairview* • *Kanu*
• *Ken Forrester-Scholtzenhof* • *Kleine Zalze*
• *Morgenhof* • *Mulderbosch* • *Simonsvlei*
• *Spice Route* • *Swartland* • *De Trafford*
• *Verdun* • *Villiera* (Bush Vines)

CINSAULT

PURE AND BLENDED This undistinguished Rhône
varietal generally makes a light, ribby, washed-
out red wine in South Africa, but Vergenoegd
is the exception and Eikendal produces a fine-
quality Cinsault-dominated blend.

🍷— Upon purchase (except Eikendal Classique,
which give 3–7 years)

☑ *Landskroon* • *Swartland*

COLOMBARD

This variety is always inexpensive and usually
makes very fresh, floral, dry or, more often, off-
dry whites, the best of which are easy to drink,
have tropical fruit flavours, and a crisp finish.

🍷— Upon purchase

☑ *Bon Courage* • *Overhex*

GAMAY

This grape makes red wines that are similar to
light-bodied Cinsault, but with more exuberance
of fruit. They are not fine, by any means, but
they are cheap and, when fresh, more cheerful
than Beaujolais Nouveau.

🍷— Upon purchase

☑ *Fairview* • *Kleine Zalze* • *Verdun*

MALBEC

This grape is seldom seen as a pure varietal
and has a similar story to Cabernet franc
(*see* opposite), but Backsberg makes a stunner,
which hopefully might encourage other estates
to give Malbec – the original grape of Black
Wine of Cahors fame – a whirl.

🍷— 3–7 years

☑ *Backsberg* • *Fairview*

MERLOT

PURE AND BLENDED Cape winemakers are
following in California's footsteps, having
started with pure Cabernet Sauvignon, they then
moved on to Cabernet blends and then pure
Merlot wines. Cape Merlot is often spoiled by
green tannins, but the best have a persistence
of flavour that belies their softness. This softness
can be anything from the simple, fruit-driven
delight of, say, a Veenwouden Merlot to the
very classy, silky smoothness of Du Plessis
Havana Hills.

🍷— 2–5 years

☑ *Boschendal* • *Constantia Uitsig* • *Delheim*
• *Fairview* • *Fort Simon* • *Graceland* • *Jordan*
• *Jordan Cobbler's Hill* • *KWV* (Cathedral
Cellar) • *Laibach* • *Longridge* • *Meerlust*

• *Morgenhof* • *Plaisir de Merle* • *Du Plessis*
(Havana Hills) • *Rust en Vrede* • *Savanha
Sejana* • *Saxenburg* (Private Collection)
• *Spice Route* • *Steenberg* • *Thelema*
• *De Trafford* • *Veenwouden* • *Vergelegen*

MUSCAT

Unfortified Muscat is nowhere near as common
as the fortified stuff, but under the Cape sun its
super-concentrated, pristine fruit has a far more
lip-smacking quality to it.

🍷— Upon purchase

☑ *Nederburg* (Eminence)
• *Thelema* (Muscat de Frontignan)
• *Weltevrede* (Muscat de Hambourg)

PINOT NOIR

South Africa is not likely to challenge Burgundy
or, for that matter, California, Oregon, or New
Zealand when it comes to this fussy variety, but
a few highly-talented winemakers are crafting
some elegant exceptions.

🍷— 2–5 years

☑ *Bouchard Finlayson* (Galpin Peak,
Tête de Cuvée) • *Paul Cluver* • *Glen Carlou*
• *Hamilton Russell Vineyards* (Ashbourne)
• *Klein Constantia* • *Meerlust* • *Thandi*

PINOTAGE

This grape is to South Africa what Zinfandel is
to California and Shiraz to Australia. Or at least
it should be. The problem is that it does not
have half the potential of either of the other
two grapes and winemakers are in a bit of a
quandary about how it should be produced.
Pinotage is a *Cinsault* x *Pinot noir* cross that
traditionally made big, baked, earthy brews
with volatile aromas, until the first new-wave
attempts, which turned out like Beaujolais
Nouveau with bubble-gummy oak. The best
wines so far have fallen between tradition
and new wave, having a deep, inky colour
with just enough *macération carbonique* to
bring out the ultra-creamy-rich fruit without
going bubble-gummy, gently supported by
good grippy tannins. The strange thing is that
whatever their style, the wines seldom improve
for very long in bottle.

🍷— Upon purchase

☑ *L'Avenir* • *Avontuur* • *Beaumont*
• *Graham Beck* (Coastal) • *Bellingham Spitz*
• *Beyerskloof* • *Bouwland* • *Clos Malverne*
(Basket pressed) • *Darling Cellars*
• *Diemersdal* • *Neil Ellis Swansong* • *Fairview*
• *Grangehurst* • *Hidden Valley* • *Kaapzicht*
• *Kanonkop* • *Landskroon* • *Lanzerac*
• *Longridge* • *Mooiplaas* • *Simonsig Red Hill*
• *Spice Route* (Reserve) • *Southern Right*
• *Swartland* • *Thelema* • *Warwick*

RHINE RIESLING

Unless produced in a late-harvest or botrytized
style, Riesling in South Africa just does not seem
to have the fruit-acidity elegance I expect from
this variety, but I find that I am similarly picky
about Riesling throughout most of the New
World. Others find far more satisfaction in these
wines than I do, so perhaps I am being too
harsh in my judgement, but where we do agree,
I think, is on the exceptional style and quality
of the wines below.

☑ *Buitenverwachting* • *Paul Cluver* • *Groot
Constantia* • *Jordan* • *Klein Constantia*
• *Nederburg* • *Rhebokskloof* • *Simonsig*
• *Slanghoek* • *Thelema* • *Villiera*
• *Weltevrede* • *De Wetshof*

RUBY CABERNET

This underrated grape variety has at its best a delicious, juicy-ripe tomato, blood-orange fruitiness. Hopefully others will try to emulate Vredendal or even improve on its quality.

☑ *Long Mountain • Longridge • Capelands • McGregor*

SAUVIGNON BLANC

This is not this country's most successful varietal, despite the number of recommendations below. Their success is, however, disproportionate to the intrinsic quality Sauvignon has established in South Africa. The reason for this is that much of the industry seems committed to trying every which way in order to master this grape variety, and although the results show there are a lot of over-achievers out there, I had to drink my way through a sea of dross to find them. There are too many over-herbaceous wines from those who are trying too hard, and dull wines from those who are jumping on the bandwagon.

Most of these wines will never be a patch on your average New Zealand Sauvignon Blanc, although if there is such a thing as South Africa's answer to Marlborough, it could be Elgin. Note that "Fumé Blanc" or "Blanc Fumé" is used for barrel-fermented or oak-aged Sauvignon Blanc; Le Bonheur is the one exception to this, and honours the term's original French meaning, which is simply a synonym for the grape variety.

🍷— Upon purchase

☑ *L'Avenir • Graham Beck* (Coastal) *• Bellingham • Bloemendal • Bon Courage • Boschendal • Brampton • Buitenverwachting • Cape Point Vineyards • Paul Cluver • Constantia Uitsig • Darling Cellars • Durbanville Hills • Neil Ellis Groenekloof • Excelsior • Fairview • Fort Simon • Groote Post • Jordan • Ken Forrester-Scholtzenhof • Klein Constantia • McGregor • Mulderbosch • Robertson* (Wide River Retreat) *• Rustenberg • Simunye • Southern Right • Spice Route • Spier* (IV Spears) *• Springfield* (Life from Stone) *• Steenberg • Steenberg Reserve • Swartland • Vergelegen • Vergelegen* (Schaapenberg) *• Villiera* (Bush Vine) *• Welmoed*

SÉMILLON

Sémillon has great potential in South Africa, where it can produce rich yet refined wines on to which skilled winemakers can graft a lovely leesy complexity. The amount of recommendations is meagre because few producers take the potential of this grape seriously. If the industry applied half the effort to this variety that they have to Sauvignon Blanc, Sémillon would quickly become one of South Africa's most fashionable wines.

🍷— 18 months to 5 years

☑ *Boekenhoutskloof • Boschendal • Constantia Uitsig • Eikehof • Fairview • Stellenzicht*

SHIRAZ

PURE AND BLENDED Shiraz (as most Cape producers prefer to call the Syrah) in South Africa is planted far less widely than in Australia, but the top performers can give most Australian Shiraz a run for their money, albeit in a more restrained style that is closer to an opulent French Syrah. Now widely regarded as South Africa's most exciting red wine variety.

🍷— 2–8 years

☑ *Allesverloren • Graham Beck* (Coastal) *• Graham Beck* (The Ridge) *• Bellingham • Boekenhoutskloof • Boplaas • Boschendal*

• J.P. Bredell • Darling Cellars • Delheim • Diemersdal • Neil Ellis (Reserve) *• Fairview* (Cyril Back) *• Genesis • Gilga • Kaapzicht • Klein Constantia • Kleine Zalze • KWV* (Cathedral Cellar, Perold) *• Longridge • De Meye • Rust en Vrede • Saxenburg* (Private Collection) *• Simonsig* (Merindol) *• Slaley • Spice Route* (Reserve) *• Stellenzicht • De Trafford • Vera Cruz • Vergelegen • Zandvliet Kalkveld*

STEEN

This is a local synonym for Chenin Blanc.

STEIN

Not to be confused with Steen, this is a generic name for a commercial-quality, off-dry, soft-styled white wine blend. It may contain Chenin – indeed, it is likely to – but there is no guarantee that it will.

TINTA BARROCA

This Portuguese Port-wine variety is used mostly in blends, which it does make interesting.

🍷— 2–5 years

☑ *Allesverloren • Rust en Vrede*

ZINFANDEL

California's homespun grape is as variable here as it is there, although the secret is simply the right *terroir* (mountain slopes), training (bush), yield (very low) and, most importantly of all, meticulous harvesting (to avoid the underripe and overripe syndrome).

🍷— 2–7 years

☑ *Blaauwklippen • Fairview • Hartenberg*

OTHER WINE STYLES

CAP CLASSIQUE

This is South Africa's own term for *méthode champenoise*. Sparkling wine is generally less exciting here than in most other New World countries, which is probably due to the longer learning curve these wines demand. Most are merely in the fruity-fizz category, and only those recommended show promise of anything more serious, but we could well see a revolution for sparkling wines as we have for Chardonnay.

🍷— Upon purchase

☑ *Graham Beck* (Blanc de Blancs, Chardonnay-Pinot Noir, Pinotage) *• Boschendal* (Vintage Brut) *• Cabrière* (Pierre Jourdan) *• Morgenhof • Pongracz • J.C. Le Roux* (Chardonnay, Pinot Noir) *• Simonsig* (selected vintages of Kaapse Vonkel such as 1992) *• Villiera* (Munro, Tradition)

CLASSIC BLENDED WHITE

This category encompasses blends made from too many permutations of grapes to record here. Fairview, for example, comprises equal proportions of Sémillon and barrel-fermented Chardonnay, plus 20 per cent Pinot noir vinified white. Boschendal's Premier Cuvée, not at all sparkling despite the suggestion, is as much as 90 per cent Pinot noir vinified white, topped up with Chardonnay, with a hint of oak. Inglewood is basically a Sauvignon-Chenin blend that sometimes has a dash of Chardonnay, but never sees wood. Many, such as Bellingham's Sauvenay, are a blend of Sauvignon and Chardonnay.

☑ *Bellingham* (Sauvenay) *• Boschendal* (Premier Cuvée) *• Buitenverwachting*

(Buiten Blanc) *• Eersterivier* (Chardonnay-Sauvignon Blanc) *• Neil Ellis* (Inglewood Blanc de Blancs) *• Fairview • Hamilton Russell* (Chardonnay-Sauvignon Blanc) *• Nederburg* (Prelude) *• Stellenzicht* (Grand Vin Blanc/Collage) *• Trawal* (Classic Dry White) *• Weltevrede* (Privé du Bois)

LATE-HARVEST AND BOTRYTIS WINES

There are various categories of this style: Late Harvest must contain between 10 and 30 grams of residual sugar per litre; Special Late Harvest contains between 20 and 50 grams and usually, but not necessarily, implies that some botrytized grapes have been used; Noble Late Harvest contains a minimum of 50 grams of residual sugar, from botrytized grapes. Other naturally sweet, unfortified, non-botrytis dessert-style wines exist, including such marvellous oddities as Klein Constantia's Vin de Constance and Boschendal's Vin d'Or. All these styles will be seductive as soon as they are released, yet most will gain complexity over a great period of time.

🍷— Upon release and up to 20 years for Late Harvest; possibly 50 years or more for richer styles

☑ *Avontuur • Bon Courage • Klein Constantia Sauvignon Blanc • Lievland • Morgenhof • Nederburg* (Edelkeur) *• Neethlingshof • Stellenzicht • Vergelegen • De Wetshof* (Edeloes)

Other unfortified dessert wines *Boschendal* (Vin d'Or) *• Fairview* (Vin de Paille) *• Klein Constantia* (Vin de Constance) *• De Trafford* (Vin de Paille) *• De Wetshof* (Mine d'Or)

PORT STYLES

Authentic Port is made only in the Douro Valley of northern Portugal but Port-type fortified wines are made the world over, and South Africa has proved itself to be particularly adept at the style.

🍷— Usually fine upon release, but will improve for 25 years or more

☑ *Allesverloren • Axehill • Boplaas* (Cape Vintage) *• Bredell* (Cape Vintage) *• Glen Carlou • Die Krans* (Cape Vintage) *• KWV* (Tawny, Vintage) *• Landskroon • Morgenhof • Overgaauw • Rustenberg*

FORTIFIED DESSERT WINES

Other high-performance fortified wine styles include red and white Muscadel, which is often called Hanepoot when made from Muscat d'Alexandrie (also in red and white styles). Jerepigo (or Jerepiko) is the South African equivalent of *vin de liqueur*, in which grape spirit is added to grape juice before fermentation can begin (as opposed to *vin doux natural*, in which the grape spirit is added after fermentation has achieved an alcohol level of between 5 and 8 per cent). Red styles range in colour from cherry-bright to orange-gold and grow lighter with age, whereas white styles deepen with age (venerable vintages of both styles can become indistinguishable if they both assume an old-gold hue).

☑ **Red** *Nuy* (Red Muscadel) *• Rooiberg* (Rooi Jerepiko, Red Muscadel) *• Slanghoek* (Soet Hanepoot) *• Du Toitskloof* (Hanepoot Jerepigo) *• Weltevrede* (Oupa se Wyn)

White *Badsberg* (Hanepoot) *• Bon Courage* (Muscadel) *• Die Krans* (Jerepigo) *• Goudini* (Soet Hanepoot) *• Nuy* (White Muscadel) *• Robertson* (Muscadel) *• Simonsvlei* (White Muscadel) *• Weltevrede* (White Muscadel)

THE WINE PRODUCERS OF
SOUTH AFRICA

THE AFRICA COLLECTION
See Longridge Winery

AGUSTA
Franschhoek
★★✩

One of Franschhoek's newest and finest wineries.

✓ *Cabernet* • *Chardonnay*

ALLESVERLOREN ESTATE
Swartland

Traditionally one of the Cape's greatest Port producers, owner Fanie Malan also makes a great Shiraz, but I find his other varietals rather too hefty by modern standards.

✓ *Port* • *Shiraz*

ALTO ESTATE
Stellenbosch
★✩

Once the property of Fanie Malan, now of Hempies du Toit, Alto has a big and muscular style, with wines benefiting from as long as ten or 15 years in bottle.

✓ *Alto Rouge*
• *Cabernet Sauvignon*

ALTYDGEDACHT ESTATE
Durbanville
★✩

This property is owned by John and Oliver Parker, who learned their winemaking skills in California and New Zealand. Barbera and Tintoretto (a Barbera-Shiraz blend) are the most interesting wines here.

✓ *Barbera*

ASTONVALE
See Zandvliet

L'AVENIR
Stellenbosch
★

This property has shot to fame since François Naudé became the winemaker in 1992. The style is creamy, rich and accessible, yet not without considerable complexity in some of the wines.

AVONTUUR
Stellenbosch
Ⓥ

This is the winery that gave the world pink Chardonnay! Avontuur wines used to be very much in the quaffing style, but the style has much improved since the arrival of Lizelle Gerber.

✓ *Cabernet* (Reserve)
• *Chardonnay* (Le Chardon)
• *Merlot* (Reserve) • *Pinotage*

BACKSBERG ESTATE
Paarl
★★

This estate is owned by Michael Back and it produces some of South Africa's most consistent and classy wines, combining richness, finesse, and complexity with great success.

✓ *Cabernet Sauvignon* • *Klein Babylonstoren* (Cabernet blend)
• *Malbec* • *Merlot* • *Pinotage*

BAY VIEW
See Longridge Winery

GRAHAM BECK WINERY
Robertson
★★✩Ⓥ

Proprietor Graham Beck also owns Graham Beck Coastal and produces budget wines under the Madeba label. Winemaker Pieter Ferreira is one of South Africa's top sparkling winemakers and his sparkling Pinotage has caused quite a storm. Not quite the Cape's answer to Australia's sparkling Shiraz, it is nevertheless far more interesting than many still Pinotage.

✓ *Cap Classique* (Blanc de Blancs)
• *Chardonnay* (Lone Hill)

BELLINGHAM
Paarl
★★✩Ⓥ

Bellingham has changed from a good-value commercial brand sourced from wherever the price was right to a fine-quality range of own-vineyard wines, priced slightly more upmarket, but even better value for money.

✓ *Chardonnay* • *Sauvenay* (classic blended white)
• *Sauvignon Blanc* • *Shiraz*

BERGKELDER

This Stellenbosch-based organization is a subsidiary of the Distillers Corporation, and has seen much change in recent years, particularly through the departure of a number of estates from its fold. The Bergkelder is now responsible for the maturation, bottling, and marketing of wines from just seven member estates. Some are owned privately, others jointly. They consist of Allesverloren, Jacobsdal, Meerlust, La Motte, L'Ormarins, Rietvallei and Theuniskraal. The Bergkelder markets its own wines under the Fleur du Cap and Stellenryck labels.

BLAAUWKLIPPEN
Stellenbosch
★★✩

Pioneer of maturation in new oak, Blaauwklippen was one of the Cape's first great innovators. Its best wines are rich, warm, cedary reds, including what is widely considered to be South Africa's finest Zinfandel.

✓ *Cabernet Sauvignon* (Reserve)
• *Shiraz*
• *Zinfandel* (especially Reserve)

BLOEMENDAL
Durbanville
★

This up-and-coming winery already has a reputation for classic Cabernet Sauvignon and a promising pure-Chardonnay fizz.

✓ *Cabernet Sauvignon*
• *Cap Classique* (Brut)

BOEKENHOUTSKLOOF
Franschhoek
★★✩

Another new and rapidly rising star. Wines also sold under the Porcupine Ridge label.

✓ *Cabernet* • *Shiraz* • *Sémillon*

BOLAND WINE CELLAR
Paarl
★✩Ⓥ

This former cooperative is now a private company. Boland makes richly flavoured Cabernet and Chardonnay. Budget wines are sold in screw-top bottles under the Bon Vino label.

✓ *Cabernet Sauvignon*
• *Chardonnay*

BON COURAGE
Robertson
★✩

Although these wines were sold in bulk until the mid-1980s, owner Andre Bruwer was Champion Estate Winemaker in 1985 and 1986, and quality has if anything gone up since his son Jacques took over in 1995. The Cap Classique is promising.

✓ *Gewürztraminer Special Late Harvest* • *White Muscadel*

LE BONHEUR ESTATE
Stellenbosch

Uniquely, for South Africa, this estate's use of "Blanc Fumé" simply refers to grape variety, as the term is used in France. Le Bonheur's Blanc Fumé is widely considered to be one of the Cape's finest unoaked Sauvignon Blanc wines, but the Cabernet Sauvignon is just as classy and far more complex.

✓ *Cabernet Sauvignon*
• *Blanc Fumé*

BOPLAAS ESTATE
Klein Karoo
★

In this large range of commercially acceptable products, the Vintage Reserve Port not only stands out, but is head and shoulders above any other South African "port".

✓ *Vintage Reserve Port*

BOSCHENDAL ESTATE
Paarl
★

Although this large producer is best known as the Cape's pioneering *méthode champenoise* producer, Boschendal Estate also makes a vast range of still wines, many of which, particularly the reds, are much more exciting than the sparkling ones.

✓ *Cap Classique* (Boschendal Brut)
• *Chardonnay* • *Lanoy*
• *Vin d'Or* (dessert style)

BOUCHARD-FINLAYSON
Overberg
★★

This very young and small enterprise was started by Hamilton Russell's winemaker Peter Finlayson and a partner, who was joined by Paul Bouchard from Burgundy. In 2001, however, controlling interest in the winery was taken over by Bea and Stanley Tollman. Bouchard remains a partner and Finlayson continues as winemaker. Finlayson is a bit of a gentle giant and his wines reflect that, building quietly in the mouth to a remarkable elegance and depth of flavour. Total production is approximately 12,000 cases of which, 50 per cent of the grapes are grown at Bouchard Finlayson. The range is augmented by wines made from other "participating growers" (as they are described). These wines include the superb Kaaimansgat Chardonnay (Kaaimansgat literally means "Crocodile's Lair", although the Alpine-like source of these grapes at 700 metres (21 feet) above sea-level near Villiersdorp is the last place one would find a crocodile!), Sans Barrique Chardonnay (same source as Kaaimansgat, but without the French oak, the wine being kept on its lees for eight months prior to bottling) and Blanc de Mer

(originally Pinot Blanc, but since the 1999 vintage the wine also includes Pinot blanc giving way to Sauvignon blanc (10 per cent) for the first time. The other cultivars are Kerner, Riesling, Chardonnay and Gewürztraminer).

√ *Chardonnay* • *Pinot Noir*
• *Sauvignon Blanc*

BRAMPTON
See Rustenberg

JP BREDELL
Stellenbosch

This port specialist became quickly established.

√ *Port* (Vintage, Vintage Character, Vintage Reserve)

BUITENVERWACHTING
Constantia
★★

Part of the historical Constantia estate, Buitenverwachting was renovated and replanted in the 1970s. It produced its first vintage in 1985, and was already showing promise by 1988. Throughout the 1990s it has been outstanding in virtually every style produced.

√ *Buiten Blanc* (classic blended white) • *Buitenkeur* (Merlot blend) • *Cabernet Sauvignon* • *Chardonnay* • *Christine* (Cabernet blend) • *Rhine Riesling* • *Sauvignon Blanc*

CABRIERE ESTATE
Paarl
★★✩

This estate belongs to Achim von Arnim, formerly the winemaker at Boschendal, and not surprisingly, he carved out his initial reputation by specializing in fine *méthode champenoise* wines. Having done that, he seems intent on perfecting one of South Africa's truly great still red Pinot Noir wines.

√ *Cap Classique* (Pierre Jourdan Blanc de Blancs) • *Pinot Noir*

CAPE LANDS
See Longridge Winery

CATHEDRAL CELLAR
See KWV International

CHATEAU LIBERTAS

Not an individual-estate wine, but a Cabernet-based blend sourced from various locations. Its reputation suffered in the 1970s when Cabernet sauvignon came into vogue and supplies of this grape dried up, but the wine regained its rich flavour in the late 1980s and it remains one of the Cape's biggest-volume quality red wines.

CLARIDGE WINES
Paarl
★★ⓥ

This small, inexpensive boutique winery makes elegant, potentially complex Burgundian varietals and a fine blended red.

√ *Chardonnay* • *Pinot noir*
• *Wellington* (Cabernet blend)

CLOS MALVERNE
Stellenbosch
★

This is a relatively new venture noted for its deep-coloured, powerful, slow-developing wines.

√ *Cabernet Sauvignon*
• *Pinotage* (Reserve)
• *Cabernet Sauvignon/Pinotage*

PAUL CLUVER
Overberg
✩

These are pioneering wines from Elgin vineyards.

√ *Chardonnay* • *Weisser Riesling*

CONSTANTIA UITSIG
Constantia
★

Owned by Dave and Marlene McCay, Constantia Uitsig is one of South Africa's more lush Merlots.

√ *Chardonnay* • *Merlot*
• *Sauvignon Blanc* • *Semillon*

CORDOBA
Stellenbosch
★✩

These high mountain vineyards produce some of South Africa's finest reds, showing great length and finesse.

√ *Cabernet Franc* (Crescendo)
• *Cabernet Sauvignon*

CULEMBORG WINES
Paarl

These are clean, easy drinking wines for the budget-conscious.

DARLING CELLARS
Darling
★ⓥ

Abe Beukes produces accessible wines of extraordinarily good value at this former cooperative.

√ *Pinotage* • *Sauvignon Blanc*
• *Shiraz*

DELAIRE
Stellenbosch
★✩

Established by John Platter, South Africa's best-known wine writer; has since changed hands a couple of times. Delaire seems most consistent with Bordeaux-style blends and scintillating botrytized Riesling.

√ *Barrique* (Merlot blend)
• *Chardonnay* • *Noble Late Harvest* (Rhine Riesling)

DELHEIM WINES
Stellenbosch-Simonsberg
ⓥ

Always good value, but until recently the quality is more good than great, and more consistent than

outstanding. In recent years, however, Delheim has shown a dramatic improvement in quality.

√ *Grand Reserve* (Cabernet blend)
• *Noble Late Harvest* (Edelspatz)
• *Special Late Harvest*

DIEU DONNE VINEYARD
Paarl
★

This estate quickly made a reputation for fat, complex Chardonnay and rich, velvety Cabernet. Its Merlot also has potential.

√ *Cabernet Sauvignon*
• *Chardonnay*

DUC DE BERRY
See Eikendal

EIKEHOF
Paarl
★✩

This producer makes rich, fruity wines that can improve in bottle.

√ *Cabernet Sauvignon*
• *Chardonnay* • *Sémillon*

EIKENDAL VINEYARDS
Stellenbosch
✩

This Swiss-owned producer is perhaps best-known on export markets for its blockbuster Chardonnay, but it actually produces finer reds, and even manages to make a fine-quality Cinsault-dominated blend. Its second wines are made under the Duc de Berry label.

√ *Cabernet Sauvignon* • *Classique* (Cabernet blend) • *Chardonnay*
• *Eikendal Rouge* • *Merlot*

NEIL ELLIS VINEYARD SELECTION
Stellenbosch
★✩

The Cape's first and foremost winemaker-*négociant*, Ellis has displayed uncanny skill in sourcing grapes from leading-edge vineyard areas, and equal expertise in crafting some of South Africa's classiest wines from them. Neil Ellis is now very much a Cape front ranker. Inglewood is his budget label.

√ *Cabernet Sauvignon* • *Cabernet Sauvignon-Merlot* • *Chardonnay*
• *Elgin Sauvignon Blanc*
• *Groenkloof Sauvignon Blanc*
• *Inglewood Blanc de Blancs* (classic blended white)

FAIRVIEW ESTATE
Paarl
★★ⓥ

This estate is run by Charles Back, one of the most innovative wine producers in South Africa, offering a large and constantly expanding range of wine styles. The poorest wines here are good, and the best are sensational.

√ *Cabernet Sauvignon*
• *Chardonnay* • *Charles Gerard* (Sauvignon Blanc-Sémillon)
• *Fairview* (red and white flagship blends) • *Merlot* • *Pinotage*
• *Shiraz-Merlot* • *Shiraz Reserve*

FLEUR DU CAP
Stellenbosch
★ⓥ

Made and marketed by the Bergkelder at Stellenbosch, Fleur du Cap has established a high basic standard of quality for such a commercial range. Some vintages of the varietals recommended below can be quite spectacular.

√ *Cabernet Sauvignon*
• *Chardonnay* • *Merlot* • *Shiraz*

GLEN CARLOU
Paarl
★★

This young, successful venture is run by David Finlayson, who has had producer winemaking experience in Bordeaux and Australia. Donal Hess of The Hess Collection in Napa is a co-owner.

√ *Chardonnay* (especially Reserve) • *Grande Classique* (Cabernet blend) • *Les Trois* (Cabernet blend) • *Port*

GOEDE HOOP ESTATE
Stellenbosch
✩

This former Bergkelder estate is now expanding its range.

√ *Cabernet Sauvignon*
• *Vintage Rouge* (Shiraz blend)

GOUDINI
Worcester
✩ⓥ

This cooperative is swiftly improving.

√ *Soet Hanepoot*

GRANGEHURST
Stellenbosch
★★

One of the new breed of wine-makers who source grapes from various other growers. Grangehurst is still small, but nevertheless makes very good, well-crafted, elegant yet substantive wines.

√ *Cabernet-Merlot* • *Pinotage*

GROOT CONSTANTIA ESTATE
Constantia
★★

This government-run property is part of the original Constantia farm, the oldest and most famous of Cape estates, and is currently being run with passion and great skill.

√ *Chardonnay* • *Gouverneur's Reserve* (Cabernet blend)
• *Noble Late Harvest* • *Pinotage*
• *Shiraz* • *Weisser Riesling*

HAMILTON RUSSELL VINEYARDS
Overberg
★★

Established by Tim Hamilton Russell, this was once Africa's most southerly vineyard. Now there are many this far south and some further still. No expense was spared to ensure that this would become one of the finest wineries in the Cape, and winemaker Peter Finlayson helped make that dream come true. Finlayson left to establish his own

winery (just next door), which is now run by Hamilton Russell's son Anthony, whose new winemaker Kevin Grant has continued to make some of the Cape's most spell-binding Burgundian varietals.

✓ *Chardonnay*
  • *Chardonnay-Sauvignon Blanc*
  • *Pinot Noir* • *Sauvignon Blanc*

HARTENBERG ESTATE
Stellenbosch
★★☆

This winery was formerly known as Montagne but was renamed Hartenberg when it was purchased by Gilbeys. It is now once more under new ownership, has been completely renovated, and is turning out some stunning wines.

✓ *Cabernet Sauvignon-Shiraz*
  • *Chardonnay* • *Shiraz*
  • *Weisser Riesling* • *Zinfandel*

INGLEWOOD
See Neil Ellis

JORDAN VINEYARDS
Stellenbosch
★★☆

This property has been producing wines under its own label since 1993, very rapidly acquiring a reputation for rich and vibrant white wines. Now a Cape front ranker, especially for Merlot.

✓ *Chardonnay*
  • *Sauvignon Blanc* • *Merlot*

KAAPZICHT
Stellenbosch
★♥

Danie Steytler employs a low-sulphur regime to produce a brilliant combination of quality and value.

✓ *Pinotage* • *Shiraz*

KANONKOP ESTATE
Stellenbosch
★★

Winemaker Beyers Truter is generally considered to be one of the greatest Stellenbosch red-wine exponents.

✓ *Cabernet Sauvignon*
  • *Paul Sauer* (Cabernet blend)
  • *Pinotage* (especially Auction Reserve)

KEN FORRESTER-SCHOLTZENHOF
Stellenbosch
★

Scholtzenhof dates back to 1689, when the farm was called Zandberg, and by 1692 some 12,000 vines had been planted, but the first

wine in modern times was in 1994 when owners Ken and Teresa Forrester pressed a small quantity of our Sauvignon-Blanc grapes to produce a Blanc Fumé. They also own the wonderful restaurant opposite the vineyard called 96 Winery Road.

✓ *Chenin Blanc*
  • *Sauvignon Blanc*

KLEIN CONSTANTIA ESTATE
Constantia
★★

This property was part of Simon van der Stel's original Constantia estate, but after centuries of neglect it was replanted as recently as 1982. Note that Vin de Constance is not a botrytis wine, nor is it fortified; it is supposedly a faithful replication of the famous Constantia of old.

✓ *Chardonnay* • *Marlbrook* (Cabernet blend) • *Noble Late Harvest Sauvignon Blanc* • *Rhine Riesling* • *Sauvignon Blanc* • *Shiraz* • *Vin de Constance* (dessert style)

KLEINE ZALZE
Stellenbosch
★

This former Gilbeys property was purchased by Jan Malan in 1996, since when its wines have been put on the map and the reputation is rising fast.

✓ *Chenin Blanc*
  • *Gamay* • *Shiraz*

DIE KRANS ESTATE
Klein Karoo
★♥

This is a specialist in fortified wine.

✓ *Vintage Reserve Port*
  • *White Jerepigo*

KWV INTERNATIONAL
Paarl
★♥

Until 1995, this super-cooperative, which encompasses more than 70 local and regional cooperatives, officially controlled the entire South African wine industry. Now it has been privatized and has the same status as other Cape wine producers, albeit that no other cooperative or company is anything like the same size. This must make the industry more nervous than it was before, as until 1995 its official capacity prevented the KWV from selling any of its products, so well-known on export markets, in South Africa itself.

In 2001 the KWV was just about to sell on the domestic market. Apart from the KWV brand itself, wines of varying quality are also sold under a large number of brands, the most important being: Bon Esperance (cheap and clean), Cape Country (cheap, easy-drinking, fruit-driven), and Cathedral Cellar (a new top-flight range). *See also* Laborie Estate.

✓ *Cathedral Cellar* (Cabernet, Pinotage, Triptych-Cabernet blend) • *KWV* (Full Tawny Port, Limited Release Port,

Noble Late Harvest, Pinotage Shiraz, Vintage Port)

LABORIE ESTATE
★

KWV's flagship wine is now made, matured, and bottled on the estate, new facilities having been installed throughout 1995 and 1996. Granite Creek, the second label, is augmented with bought-in grapes.

✓ *Chardonnay*
  • *Sauvignon Blanc*

LAIBACH
Stellenbosch
★

This farm was called Good Success until it was purchased by Swiss-based German businessman Friedrich Laibach, who built a new cellar and bottled these wines for the first time in 1997.

✓ *Cabernet Sauvignon*
  • *Cabernet Blend* • *Merlot*

LANDSKROON ESTATE
Paarl
★☆♥

This is a very large estate of low-yielding, bush-trained vines that produce full, soft, smooth wines.

✓ *Cabernet Sauvignon*
  • *Port* • *Shiraz*

LANZERAC
Stellenbosch
★

This estate, owned by Christo Wiese, has no connection with the Lanzerac brand that has long been sold by Stellenbosch Wine Farmers/SFW other than the extraordinary agreement between the two in 1997 that allowed each party to share the name. This opened the way for Wiese to build a small winery and commence production that very year.

✓ *Pinotage*

LIEVLAND
Stellenbosch
❷

Named after one of its former owners, the Russian Baroness of Lievland, this is one of the Cape's most classic producers. There was a question over the ownership of this estate at the time of the last revise.

✓ *Cabernet Sauvignon*
  • *DBV* (Cabernet blend)
  • *Noble Late Harvest*
  • *Shiraz*
  • *Weisser Riesling*

JEAN DE LONG
See Boschendal Estate

LONG MOUNTAIN
Stellenbosch

This promising new range at Long Mountain was launched by the Pernod-Ricard venture under the guidance of Robin Day, the man who made Orlando's Jacob's Creek (Australia) a success.

✓ *Chenin Blanc*

LONGRIDGE WINERY
Stellenbosch

This winemaker-*négociant* shows promise for a decent fizz and various varietals. In addition to Longridge, labels include Bay View, Cape Lands, and The Africa Collection. Longridge is now part of the Australian wine giant Winecorp, which also owns Savanha, Cape-lands, Bayview and Spier. Longridge is one of the largest of the Cape's quality oriented producers.

✓ *Chardonnay* • *Merlot* • *Pinotage*
  • *Ruby Cabernet* • *Shiraz*

LOUISVALE
Stellenbosch
★

Louisvale offers a solid range of well-made wines, but is best-known for its big, leesy Chardonnay.

✓ *Chardonnay*
  • *Cabernet Blend* (Dominique)

MEERLUST ESTATE
Stellenbosch
★★

This is one of the Cape's most consistent estates, owned by Hannes Myburgh, who is served by the extremely gifted winemaker Giorgio Dalla Cia. Meerlust's Cabernet Sauvignon was one of the first stylish, fruit-driven wines to establish a classic reputation in South Africa (although good, it is now seen as this estate's least exciting wine). Then came Merlot and a Cabernet-Merlot called Rubicon, both of which were considered pioneering. Meerlust's Pinot Noir was also an original and, despite fears that the estate might be too hot, has produced some excellent vintages. The latest addition, Chardonnay, is not another South African first, of course, but it is Meerlust's first white wine and it's a mighty, rich, and ripe wine full of toasty-oak complexity.

✓ *Chardonnay*
  • *Merlot*
  • *Pinot Noir*
  • *Rubicon* (Cabernet blend)

MIDDELVLEI ESTATE
Stellenbosch
★

This estate made its reputation with Pinotage, but has been producing stunning Cabernet Sauvignon since 1981, has recently succeeded in perfecting a new-wave Pinotage, and now makes a beautifully rich and stylish Chardonnay.

✓ *Cabernet Sauvignon*
  • *Chardonnay*
  • *Pinotage*
  • *Shiraz*

MÔRESON-MATIN DU SOLEIL
Stellenbosch
★

Acquired by Richard Friedmann in 1985, this estate initially developed a reputation for its white wines, although it is its reds that have shone the most in recent vintages.

✓ *Cabernet Sauvignon*

MORGENHOF
Stellenbosch
★★✰

This historic wine estate is run by French immigrants with connections in Champagne and Cognac, who have rapidly revived its fortunes with some truly stylish wines.

✓ *Cabernet Blend* (Premiere Selection) • *Cabernet Sauvignon* • *Chardonnay* • *Merlot* • *Sauvignon Blanc*

LA MOTTE ESTATE
Paarl
★★

Owned by the daughter of Anton Rupert, the second-richest man in South Africa, its wines made by wine-wizard Jacques Borman, La Motte produces a small range compared to most estates, but every single wine is a winner. Part of a venture called Historic Wines Oude Meester.

✓ *Cabernet Sauvignon* • *Chardonnay* • *Merlot* • *Millennium* (Cabernet blend) • *Sauvignon Blanc* • *Shiraz*

MULDERBOSCH VINEYARDS
Stellenbosch
★★

These are top-flight wines from superbly sited mountain vineyards and crafted by skilful winemaking.

✓ *Chardonnay* • *Faithful Hound* (Cabernet blend) • *Sauvignon Blanc*

MURATIE ESTATE
Stellenbosch
❷

This historic wine estate was recently revived under new ownership.

✓ *Ansela* (Cabernet blend) • *Cabernet Sauvignon* • *Port*

NEDERBURG WINES
★★ⓥ

These wines are made and marketed by the Stellenbosch Farmers' Winery (SFW). As with Bergkelder's Fleur du Cap, the consistency is remarkable for such a commercial range, and some vintages of those recommended below can be outstanding. The annual Nederburg Auction is the largest fine wine sale in South Africa.

✓ *Cabernet Sauvignon* (especially Private Bin) • *Chardonnay* (especially Private Bin) • *Muscat de Frontignan* (Eminence) • *Noble Late Harvest* (especially Edelkeur, Sauvignon Blanc, and Private Bin Weisser Riesling) • *Prelude* (classic blended white) • *Shiraz* (Private Bin)

NEETHLINGSHOF ESTATE
Stellenbosch
★★✰

With vineyards and cellars both greatly expanded since new ownership in 1985, Neethlingshof has gradually improved on what was already a very good wine estate reputation.

✓ *Cabernet Sauvignon* • *Chardonnay* • *Lord Neethlingshof Reserve* (Cabernet blend) • *Noble Late Harvest* • *Weisser Riesling*

NUY COOPERATIVE
Worcester
★★ⓥ

Some say that Nuy is South Africa's best cooperative but, although others now vie for the title, which is currently the top performer, is a moot point. It certainly produces one of the country's finest Colombards, and its succulent Muscadel wines can compete with the best estate-produced products.

✓ *Colombard* • *Red Muscadel* • *White Muscadel*

L'ORMARINS ESTATE
Paarl
★★✰

Run by Toni Rupert, the son of Anton Rupert who, with virtually unlimited finance at his disposal, quickly established L'Ormarins at the very top of Cape winemaking. Toni Rupert had the pick of almost any wine estate he wanted and he chose L'Ormarins, which illustrates just how superbly sited it must be. This was not just another expensive toy to be tossed away when the novelty had worn thin, as more than 14 years on his boyish enthusiasm for viticulture remains undiminished. Part of a venture called Historic Wines Oude Meester.

✓ *Cabernet Sauvignon* • *Chardonnay* • *Optima* (Cabernet blend) • *Shiraz*

OVERGAAUW ESTATE
Stellenbosch
★

This is a technically superior operation that produces exciting wines with lots of class and very little sulphur dioxide. Overgaauw has been a pioneering wine estate for a quarter of a century.

✓ *Chardonnay* • *Merlot* • *Tria Corda* (Cabernet blend) • *Vintage Port*

PERDEBERG CO-OPERATIVE
Paarl
✰ⓥ

This cooperative has built up a serious reputation for its Chenin blanc in a country that is only just beginning to take this potentially fine quality grape seriously.

✓ *Chenin Blanc* • *Noble Late Harvest*

PLAISIR DE MERLE
Stellenbosch
★★

Grapes from Plaisir de Merle formed the heart of many Nederburg wines until 1993, when with the help of consultant Paul Pontallier of Château Margaux, owner-winemaker Niel Bester launched a range of estate-bottled wines that are worthy of SFW's flagship domaine.

✓ *Cabernet Sauvignon* • *Chardonnay* • *Merlot* • *Sauvignon Blanc*

PONGRÁCZ
Stellenbosch
★

Made by J.C. Le Roux, a subsidiary of the Distillers Corporation, this is one of South Africa's first successful bottle-fermented sparkling wines, and still one of its best.

✓ *Cap Classique* (Pongrácz)

RHEBOKSLOOF ESTATE
Paarl
❷

A relatively recent venture (its first vintage was produced in 1989) that has made good but unexciting wine, Rheboksloof has not yet achieved its full potential, although a new owner and a different winemaker in 1995 could make all the difference.

LE RICHE
Stellenbosch
★

Small up-and-coming winery making polished reds.

✓ *Cabernet* • *Caber*

RIETVALLEI ESTATE
Robertson
✰

Rietvallei Estate is a specialist producer of medal-winning, sweet, fortified, red Muscadel wine.

✓ *Rietvallei Rooi Muskadel*

ROBERTSON WINERY
Robertson
✰ⓥ

This cooperative produces a large range of good-value varietals and some truly excellent dessert wines.

✓ *Muscadel* • *Special Late Harvest* (Rheingold)

ROOIBERG CO-OPERATIVE
Robertson
✰ⓥ

Another medal-winning cooperative, Rooiberg enjoys a particularly high reputation for its fortified wines.

✓ *Jerepiko* (Rooi) • *Red Muscadel*

J.C. LE ROUX
★

This Bergkelder label was originally used exclusively for sparkling wines, but various still wines have since been added.

✓ *Cap Classique* (Pinot Noir)

RUSTENBERG ESTATE
Stellenbosch
★★

Once heralded as the very best of South Africa's top growths, the quality at Rustenberg Estate faltered in the early 1990s, but it picked up again as from the 1996 vintage and is, if anything, better than it has ever been. This winery is now under the direct control of Simon Barlow, who installed a brand new winery and has done everything necessary to ensure

that Rustenberg's reputation remains impeccable. Wines sold under the Brampton label sometimes rival Rustenberg at its best.

✓ *Cabernet Sauvignon* (Peter Barlow) • *Chardonnay* (Five Soldiers) • *Merlot-Cabernet* • *Port* • *Rustenberg Gold* • *Sauvignon Blanc*

RUST EN VREDE
Stellenbosch
★

Owned by Jannie Engelbrecht, a former Springbok, who produces only wines he likes to drink – rich, red, dense, well-balanced, and not sold until ready.

✓ *Cabernet Sauvignon* • *Estate Wine* (Cabernet-Shiraz blend) • *Merlot* • *Shiraz* • *Tinta Barocca*

SABLE VIEW
Stellenbosch

This is a standard export-quality commercial range produced by Stellenbosch Wine Farmers.

SAXENBURG
Stellenbosch
★

This Swiss-owned winery is a rising star for wines of complex style.

✓ *Cabernet Sauvignon* • *Chardonnay* • *Merlot* (Private Collection) • *Pinotage* (Private Collection) • *Shiraz* (Private Collection)

SEIDELBERG
Paarl
✰

Many interesting wines, but none more stunning than the Muscadel made from 80-year-old vines. Formerly trading as De Leuwen Jagt.

✓ *Muscadel*

SIMONSIG ESTATE
Stellenbosch
✰

This winery has a huge production, and its wines range from sensational down to pretty standard stuff.

✓ *Chardonnay* • *Pinotage* (especially Auction Reserve) • *Sauvignon Blanc* • *Shiraz*

SIMONSVLEI WINERY
Paarl
✰ⓥ

This former cooperative has a 40-year-old reputation for producing fine wines at remarkably low prices.

✓ *Cabernet Sauvignon* • *Shiraz* • *White Muscadel*

SPICE ROUTE
Malmesbury
★★✰

Originally owned by a consortium of Charles Back, Jabulani Ntshangase, John Platter and Gyles Webb, but now solely owned by Back. Spice Route excels at red wines and its signature style is typically deep, dark, rich and spicy with masses of black fruit. Its

Flagship Syrah is one of the best I've tasted from South Africa, whatever varietal name utilised. Second label Andrew's Hope is not to be sniffed at either.

✓ *Cabernet Blend* • *Merlot* • *Pinotage* • *Sauvignon Blanc* • *Shiraz* (Flagship Syrah)

STEENBERG
Constantia
★

Small quantities of gorgeously fresh Sauvignon Blanc made this winery the Constantia's newest rising star in 1995. Keep an eye open for other wine styles.

✓ *Sauvignon Blanc*

STELLENBOSCH VINEYARDS
Stellenbosch
★ ✪

The Eersterivier Vineyards and Helderberg cooperatives have now consolidated with Bottelary, Hoelenhof, and Welmoed.

✓ *Chardonnay-Sauvignon Blanc* • *Cabernet Sauvignon*

STELLENBOSCH FARMERS' WINERY *or* SFW

See Stellenbosch Wine Farmers

STELLENBOSCH WINE FARMERS

Otherwise known as Stellenbosch Farmers' Winery or SFW, this large group markets various brands which include Grand Mousseux, Lanzerac, Chateau Libertas, Lieberstein, Sable View and Zonnebloem, but is best known for its Nederburg range and, of course, Plaisir de Merle, its flagship estate.

STELLENRYCK COLLECTION
Durbanville
★ ✪

A high-quality range of individually crafted wines marketed by the Bergkelder as a sort of upmarket Fleur du Cap, the Stellenryck Collection has also been pioneering wines, its Blanc Fumé being the very first Sauvignon Blanc to show any real varietal style as early as the mid-1980s.

✓ *Blanc Fumé* • *Cabernet Sauvignon* • *Chardonnay*

STELLENZICHT
Stellenbosch
★ ★

Under the same ownership as Neethlingshof, Stellenzicht's mountain vineyards produce some of the finest new arrivals on the South African fine-wine scene.

✓ *Cabernet Sauvignon* • *Grand Vin Blanc* (classic blended white – called Collage on some markets) • *Noble Late Harvest* • *Sémillon* • *Shiraz* • *Stellenzicht* (Cabernet blend)

SWARTLAND WINE CELLAR
Swartland
★ ✪

This long-established, go-ahead cooperative now sells all its wines bottled, and a high proportion are exported. In addition to the technical excellence of its fruit handling and the vinification process, the prime reason the quality here is so exceptional for hot-climate vineyards is that much of the production comes from mostly non-irrigated bush vines.

✓ *Chenin Blanc* (especially Steen) • *Colombard* • *Sauvignon Blanc*

THELEMA MOUNTAIN
Stellenbosch
★ ★

One of the country's most exciting and fastest-rising young stars, Thelema Mountain produces stunningly rich and complex wines.

✓ *Cabernet Sauvignon* • *Cabernet Sauvignon-Merlot* • *Chardonnay* • *Merlot* • *Muscat de Frontignan* • *Reserve Cabernet* • *Rhine Riesling* • *Sauvignon Blanc*

THEUNISKRAAL ESTATE
Tulbagh
This is a white-wine specialist estate.

DU TOITSKLOOF COOPERATIVE
Worcester
✪

This cooperative has a long record of award-winning table wines and now produces top-flight dessert wines.

✓ *Hanepoot Jerepigo* • *Special Late Harvest*

DE TRAFFORD
Stellenbosch
★

This very new, ultra-small boutique winery is already establishing a reputation for beautifully crafted Cabernet, with whispers in the wind of things to come, including serious, *barrique*-fermented Chenin Blanc.

✓ *Cabernet Sauvignon*

TWEE JONGEGEZELLEN ESTATE
Tulbagh
❓

Nicky Krone was once the master-blender of South African sparkling wine, producing a classic vintaged fizz called Krone Borealis, which assumed excellent biscuity finesse after two or three years' further ageing. There have been times when Krone Borealis was the only worthwhile Cap Classique on the market. In 1999, however, Nicky harvested hardly any grapes

whatsoever, due to his over-zealous eco-friendly farming. This hiatus in production caused problems all round, not the least to Krone Borealis itself, which is now a non-vintage *cuvée* and a mere shadow of its former self. Anyone who remembers the 1990 and 1993 or indeed still has these wines will, like me, wish Nicky well in his quest to regain his reputation.

UITERWYK
Stellenbosch
An interesting Pinotage is made at Uiterwyk.

UITKYK ESTATE
Stellenbosch
★

Pronounced "ate-cake", Uitkyk has an established reputation for its burly Carlonet, which used to be a blend, but is now pure Cabernet Sauvignon.

✓ *Carlonet*

VAN LOVEREN
Robertson
★ ✪

The nearest you get to fine wines here are a blockbuster Chardonnay, a soft and smooth blended River Red, and an elegantly sweet and juicy Special Late Harvest Gewürztraminer. Van Loveren is more about innovative winemaking and unpretentious pricing, giving the masses a brash Blanc de Noirs Red Muscadel, with its wonderful, medium-sweet, grapy-Muscat aromas, and fruit full of honey, peaches, and roses on the palate. If Anjou Rosé were half as good, it would still be selling!

✓ *Blanc de Noirs* (Red Muscadel, Shiraz) • *Chardonnay* • *Special Late Harvest* (Gewürztraminer) • *River Red*

VEENWOUDEN
Paarl
★

This boutique winery was recently established by Deon van der Walt, South Africa's best-known tenor, with Giorgo Dalla Cia of Meerlust acting as consultant.

✓ *Merlot* • *Veenwouden* (Cabernet blend)

VERGELEGEN
Stellenbosch
★ ★

This immaculately restored, historic wine estate is now producing top-quality, complex wines. It is now very much a top ranked producer since the cellar has been taken over by Andre van Rensburg.

✓ *Merlot* • *Sauvignon Blanc*

VERGENOEGD ESTATE
Stellenbosch
★ ✪

Under sixth-generation ownership, this long-established wine estate's star performer is its Bordeaux-style Reserve, although Vergenoegd still makes eminently drinkable Cinsault.

✓ *Cabernet* (Reserve) • *Cinsault* • *Merlot* • *Port*

VILLIERA ESTATE
Paarl
★ ★

Villiera Estate was a rapidly rising star when the first edition of this encyclopedia was published ten years ago, and it is now a well-established producer by current Cape wine standards.

✓ *Blue Ridge Rouge* (Shiraz blend) • *Cap Classique* (Grande Cuvée, Tradition Reserve) • *Cru Monro* (Cabernet blend) • *Merlot* • *Sauvignon Blanc* (Traditional Bush Vine)

VLOTTENBURG CO-OPERATIVE
Stellenbosch
★ ✪

This medal-winning cooperative offers a large range of unpretentious, fruity super-value wines.

✓ *Cabernet Sauvignon* • *Chardonnay* • *Merlot* • *Reserve* (Shiraz blend) • *Riesling* • *Special Late Harvest*

VREDENDAL WINERY
Olifants River
★ ✪

Formerly known as Olifantsrivier Koöp Wynkelder, Vredendal is the country's largest cooperative, and processes the equivalent of more than the entire New Zealand harvest every year. Vredendal produces one of South Africa's best blood-orange-tasting Ruby Cabernets.

✓ *Ruby Cabernet*

VRIESENHOF
Stellenbosch
★

This estate is run by another ex-Springbok, Jan Boland Coetzee. Wines are also sold under the Paradyskloof and Talana Hill labels.

✓ *Chardonnay* • *Kallista* (Cabernet blend) • *Kestrel* (Merlot blend) • *Merlot*

WARWICK ESTATE
Stellenbosch
★ ★

Rich, complex wines make Warwick one of the youngest, smallest, and most exciting boutique wineries on the Cape winemaking scene.

✓ *Cabernet Franc* • *Merlot* • *Pinotage* (Traditional Bush Vine) • *Trilogy* (Cabernet blend)

WATERFORD
Stellenbosch
★

Promising new winery.

✓ *Shiraz*

WELGEMEEND ESTATE
Paarl
☆

Welgemeend Estate is a small, high-quality red-wine specialist. It was established in the 1970s, which was very early for a boutique winery in South Africa. So far the property has managed to maintain an enviable consistency.

✓ *Douelle*
  • *Estate Wine*

WELTEVREDE ESTATE
Robertson
★

Weltevrede means "well satisfied", which I am glad to say is still an apt description of anyone who has drunk the wines.

✓ *Chardonnay*
  • *Muscat de Hambourg*
  • *Privé du Bois* (classic blended white)
  • *Red Muscadel* (Oupa se Wyn)
  • *Special Late Harvest* (Therona)
  • *White Muscadel*

DE WET COOPERATIVE
Breede River

This cooperative is not to be confused with the private De Wetshof Estate, the wines of which are made by, even more confusingly, Danie de Wet. This wide and varied range includes such oddities as a wine made purely from Fernao Pires grapes.

DE WETSHOF ESTATE
Robertson
★★☆

Quite how Danie de Wet can make such exquisite wines as his Grey Label Chardonnay (particularly the 1993), when you can cook an egg on the rocks in his vineyard,

is a mystery, and such mysteries are part of the eternal fascination that wine holds for enthusiasts.

✓ *Rhine Riesling*
  • *Chardonnay*
  • *Sauvignon Blanc*
  • *Edeloes* (botrytis)

YONDER HILL
Stellenbosch
★

A recently established boutique winery, Yonder Hill makes beautifully crafted wine from mountain vineyards on the Helderberg. The name iNanda is Zulu for "Beautiful place".

✓ *iNanda* (Cabernet blend)
  • *Merlot*

ZANDVLIET ESTATE
Robertson
☆

Zandvliet is famous for its Shiraz. Astonvale is its second label.

✓ *Shiraz*

ZEVENWACHT
Stellenbosch

Zevenwacht grew rapidly in the 1980s, making wines that are fresh, frank, and aromatic, but not very exciting. The exception is Sauvignon Blanc and a one-off vintage (1994) of big, brash Pinot Noir.

✓ *Sauvignon Blanc*

ZONNEBLOEM WINES
★❖

Although this upmarket range produced by the Stellenbosch Wine Farmers has always been strong on reds, they have noticeably more oomph in recent vintages, and even the whites have become quite exciting. Zonnebloem's best wines represent extraordinary value for money.

✓ *Cabernet Sauvignon* • *Chardonnay*
  • *Chenin Blanc* (Blanc de Blancs) • *Laureat* (Cabernet blend) • *Merlot* • *Pinotage*
  • *Sauvignon Blanc* • *Shiraz*

OTHER WINES OF
AFRICA

KENYA

It was with utter amazement that I learned of the first Kenyan grape wines ever produced, just in time to scribble a few words for the first edition of this encyclopedia. Having now had the chance to visit these vineyards, I must say I'm impressed, not by any great quality or the beauty of the vineyards, merely by the fact that clean, drinkable wines can be produced in this equatorial area. The vineyards are located on volcanic soils beside Lake Naivasha, situated 1,900 metres (6,200 feet) above sea level in the Rift Valley, which is the Flower Garden of Africa, the blooms of which are flown to florists all over the world. You can grow anything here, and grow it twice a year too. You can certainly grow grapes here, as John and Elli D'Olier have done since 1982, when they first brought back cuttings from California.

John is a Kenyan of Huguenot stock, his father coming to East Africa from Ireland during World War I, and Elli is a Californian. The D'Oliers produced their first grape wines in 1986, having won a silver medal at Lisbon in 1985 for their papaya wine (a traditional Kenyan product that is very strong, thick, and oily – not the sort of thing that true wine enthusiasts are likely to enjoy). In an equatorial country the production of native wine is supposed to be something of a gamble, but the D'Oliers' Lake Naivasha wines have made me question this widely held belief. Not that these wines are in any way special, but they are clean and well-made, with no baked or otherwise off-putting hot-climate characteristics.

The idea that equatorial wine is impractical is essentially based on the vine's tendency to run rampant with foliage, to the detriment of fruit production, but Lake Naivasha proves that there are some equatorial locations that are suited to grape-growing, and its cool nights give surprisingly high acidity levels.

The biggest real disadvantage of winemaking in equatorial countries is that, without a wine industry as such, the ability of producers to acquire the right equipment and technology is hindered, and even when clean wines are produced, they often have to be transported long distances under horrendous conditions to be bottled in the nearest large city. Furthermore, the bottling-line staff may not have wine-bottling experience. Storage conditions are so bad that even imported wines suffer.

With all these disadvantages, it is surprising that Lake Naivasha is drinkable, but the Colombard Sur Lie is fresh, light, and friendly, with a touch of spritz, and the Sauvignon Blanc is fresh and correctly crisp, if lacking varietal character. The most disappointing wine was a coarse red wine from the Carnelian grape, but I found the Cabernet Sauvignon pleasant and was so impressed with a 1992 bottle-fermented fizz that I wanted to taste it back in the UK, on a cold, dank day, as far removed from the beauty of Lake Naivasha as possible, and side-by-side with other sparkling wines, but I had not managed to achieve this by the time of writing.

ZIMBABWE

Much has changed in Zimbabwe's wine industry over the last ten years, with low-quality grape varieties being dug-up, drip-irrigation installed, cool-fermentation technology introduced, and internationally trained winemakers employed.

The industry is very young, having been established as recently as the mid-1960s, and virtually all of its exports are still to neighbouring African states, although that could change in the short-term future. Familiar names such as Philips and Monis no longer exist, having been absorbed by the Mukuyu Winery, and brands such as Flame Lily, which made an ephemeral appearance on export markets such as the UK, have also fallen by the wayside.

The grape varieties grown in Zimbabwe include: Bukettraube, Cabernet sauvignon, Cinsault, Clairette blanche, Colombard, Chenin blanc (sometimes called Steen), Cruchen (also known as Cape riesling), Gewürztraminer, Merlot, Pinotage, Pinot noir, Riesling, Ruby cabernet, Sauvignon blanc, and Seneca.

There are now only two producers in Zimbabwe: African Distillers and Mukuyu. African Distillers, also known as Stapleford Wines, is situated north of Harare and owns 180 hectares (450 acres) of vineyards at Bulawayo, Odzi, and Gweru, the latter being the location of its winery. These grapes are supplemented with those from private growers, which account for some 40 per cent of the total product of 550,000 cases of wine per year.

Monis no longer exists, but the operation continues under the name of Mukuyu. Mukuyu is owned by Cairns Holdings, whose winery and 100 hectares (250 acres) of vineyards are situated south of a village called Marondera, 100 kilometres (62 miles) east of Harare. Production each year of around 165,000 cases is entirely from its own estate. Slightly up from the New Vineyard jug wines, under the Symphony label, are fruity, and drinkable wines, particularly the reds. The Meadows range includes an interesting dry white called L'Étoile, blended from several grapes including Gewürztaminer and Riesling. Single varietal wines (Sauvignon Blanc, Pinot Noir, and Merlot) are sold under the Select and Mukuyu ranges, the latter of which includes an interesting Brut de Brut sparkling wine made by the *Méthode Champenoise*.

This obscure winemaking country needs more producers before it will be taken seriously on international markets, but with its classic grape varieties and cool-fermentation technology, its wines may be on supermarket shelves very soon.

AUTHOR'S CHOICE

South Africa totally dominates this selection. This is itself a difficulty, since its producers are still getting to grips with the demands of a global market, and many wine styles are in a state of flux.

PRODUCER	WINE	STYLE	DESCRIPTION	🍷
Backsberg (*see p.433*)	Cabernet Sauvignon	RED	From my favourite South African red-wine producer, this Cabernet Sauvignon is top of the range. All Backsberg reds are great, but the Cabernet Sauvignon has the most class and finesse.	4–12 years
Graham Beck Winery (*see p.433*) Ⓥ	Chardonnay Blanc de Blancs Brut, Cap Classique	SPARKLING WHITE	The quality and style of classic sparkling wine is rapidly evolving all over the world, particularly in South Africa, where producers have a lot to catch up on after the period of exclusion severely restricted their development in this area. Graham Beck's Blanc de Blancs is currently South Africa's finest sparkling wine, with some creamy-malolactic complexity and nuances of toasty-biscuity bottle aromas adding a mellowing touch to the correctly crisp fruit.	1–2 years
Buitenverwachting (*see p.434*)	Cabernet Sauvignon	RED	Deep and dark with a powerful thrust of rich, spicy, blackcurrant fruit, this wine is supported by nicely structured, silky tannins.	5–10 years
Fairview Estate (*see p.434*) Ⓥ	Shiraz Reserve	RED	The step up from basic to Reserve Shiraz is about two staircases high, this wine having all the sumptuous, ripe-fruit fullness and complexity that is barely hinted at lower down the scale.	4–7 years
Glen Carlou (*see p.434*)	Chardonnay Reserve	WHITE	A big, rich, hit-you-between-the-eyes oaked Chardonnay, this wine is not at all blowzy or overblown, just huge flavoured and immensely enjoyable to drink.	1–4 years
Hamilton Russell Vineyards (*see p.435*)	Chardonnay	WHITE	Creamy Chardonnay fruit penetrates the varietal richness of this wine, despite the big, lemony-oaky and toasty complexity	2–5 years
Hamilton Russell Vineyards (*see p.435*)	Pinot Noir	RED	Brilliant varietal intensity, well-structured strawberry-redcurrant fruit, and grippy tannins keep Hamilton Russell Pinot Noir on top.	3–7 years
Kanonkop Estate (*see p.435*)	Paul Sauer	RED	A soft and sumptuously rich Cabernet-Merlot blend, this wine has a youthful complexity and mellow toasty-oak aromas.	3–8 years
Kanonkop Estate (*see p.435*)	Pinotage	RED	Anyone who has enjoyed Beyers Truter's supermarket Pinotage, which he labels under his own name, rather than under Kanonkop or the retailer's name, will adore this rich, riper, altogether far more succulent rendition.	4–8 years
Klein Constantia (*see p.435*)	Vin de Constance	WHITE	Although other Klein Constantia wines are arguably superior, Vin de Constance is one of South Africa's finest dessert-style wines and since it is a revival of the Cape's most historic wine, it would be inconceivable not to include it in my choice. Made famous by Jane Austen, Alexandre Dumas, and Henry Longfellow, Constantia was prized by Bismark and Napoleon. Like the original Constantia, Vin de Constance is a delicately rich, sweet, late-harvest wine that is neither fortified nor botrytized.	up to 20 years
Lievland (*see p.435*)	DVB	RED	A classy if decidedly oaky Cabernet-Merlot blend with heaps of vanilla-rich, spicy-*cassis* fruit, this is a wine that ages gracefully.	3–12 years
Meerlust (*see p.435*)	Merlot	RED	It was a toss-up between the Cabernet Sauvignon, since the 1975 was the first South African wine of classic quality I had tasted; Rubicon, the first vintage of which was, in 1980, literally like crossing the Rubicon as far as Cape winemaking was concerned; and Merlot, which is a relative newcomer, appearing on the scene in 1988. Merlot won on pure hedonism and current form.	3–6 years
Thelema Mountain (*see p.437*)	Reserve Cabernet	RED	This is blockbusting stuff! Although big is not necessarily best, in this case it definitely is.	5–15 years
De Wetshof Estate (*see p.438*)	Grey Label Chardonnay	WHITE	Quite how man-mountain Danie de Wet can produce such a delicate Chardonnay from vines growing in the baking hot plains of Robertson is hard to figure, but this wine is a pure delight.	1–3 years

The WINES of

NORTH
and SOUTH
AMERICA

THE MOST FAMOUS WINE REGIONS –
California, Washington, Oregon, and
Chile – are to be found inland from the
western coast. This is because eastern
seaboards are generally too humid and
prone to severely cold winters. California
is the major star, making large volumes of
wine, including some of the world's finest
Cabernet, Merlot, Zindfandel, and Chardonnay.
The best wines of Washington and Oregon
are at least as fascinating but, because
production is so much smaller, the quality
and diversity of these wines have less
impact. The expanding and rapidly improving
Canadian wine industry, both in Ontario and
British Columbia, should not be forgotten,
while Chile rules in South America, with a
tiny proportion of producers in Argentina
currently demonstrating that its wines could
rival those of Chile when the country
replaces quantity with quality.

MUSTARD FLOWERS IN CARNEROS, NAPA, CALIFORNIA
*Acting as a habitat for natural predators of wine pests,
Mustard also prevents evaporation of moisture.*

✦ NORTH AMERICA ✦

To talk of North American wine is not to discuss California alone. Although California would rank as the sixth-largest wine-producing nation in the world (if it were a nation), it is but one of 40 wine-producing states within the United States, and the vineyards of North America also encompass those of Ontario and British Columbia in Canada (see also p.494), and the Baja California and Sierra Madre in Mexico (see also p.502).

IN 1521, WITHIN ONE YEAR of invading Mexico, the Spanish planted vines and set about making the first North American wines. Fourteen years later, when French explorer Jacques Cartier sailed down the St. Lawrence to New France, he discovered a large island overrun by wild vines and decided to call it the Île de Bacchus. He had second thoughts, however, and later renamed it the Île d'Orléans, a calculated move in view of the fact that the then Duke of Orléans was the son of King Francis I of France. It is assumed that, *circa* 1564, the Jesuit settlers who followed in the wake of Cartier's explorations were the first winemakers in what was to become Canada. The earliest wines made in what is now the United States of America came from Florida. Between 1562 and 1564, French Huguenot settlers produced wines from native Scuppernong grapes on a site that would become Jacksonville.

NATIVE NORTH AMERICAN GRAPE VARIETIES
All classic grape varieties belong to one species, *Vitis vinifera*, but North America's native varieties belong to several different species, not one of which happens to be *Vitis vinifera* (*see* p.20). There were plenty of native vines growing wild wherever the early

MT. PLEASANT VINEYARDS
These vineyards in Augusta, Missouri were America's first Approved Viticultural Area.

settlers travelled, and so they came to rely on them for their initial wine production. Settlers in Australia, on the other hand, were forced to wait for precious shipments of classic European vines before they could plant vineyards. Although various European varieties were taken across the Atlantic in the 19th century, nearly all North American wines apart from Californian ones remained products of native varieties until relatively recently.

The most common native North American species, *Vitis labrusca*, has such a distinctive aroma and flavour that it seems truly amazing that those pioneers who were also winemakers did not pester their home countries for supplies of more acceptable vines. The *labrusca* character, commonly referred to as "foxy", is so exotic, it cloys at the back of the throat, and is generally not appreciated by European and antipodean palates.

PROHIBITION IN THE UNITED STATES
Although total Prohibition in the United States was confined to 1920–1933, the first "dry legislation" was passed as early as 1816, and the first state to go completely dry was Maine, in 1846. By the time the 18th Amendment to the Constitution was put into effect in 1920, forbidding "the manufacture, sale, or transport of intoxicating liquors", more than 30 states were already totally dry.

The result of Prohibition was chaos. It denied the government legitimate revenue and encouraged bootleggers to amass fortunes. The number of illicit stills multiplied quicker than the authorities could find and dismantle them, and the speakeasy became a way of life in the cities. Not only did the authorities often realize that it was much easier to turn a blind eye to what was going on, the federal government actually found it useful to open its own speakeasy in New York! Many vineyards were uprooted, but those grapes that were produced were often concentrated, pressed, and sold as "grape bricks". These came complete with a yeast capsule and instructions to dissolve the brick in one gallon of water, but warned against adding the yeast because it would start a fermentation. This would turn the grape juice into wine "and that would be illegal", the warning pointed out.

Prohibition and the wine industry
By the mid-to-late 19th century, the Californian wine industry had such a reputation that great French wine areas, such as Champagne, began to form *syndicats* to protect themselves, in part, from the potential of California's marketing threat. However, the 13 years of Prohibition coincided with a vital point in the evolution of wine, and set the Californian wine industry back a hundred years, as other wine regions had just recovered from the effects of phylloxera (*see* p.448), and were busily re-establishing their reputations and carving out future markets.

JEKEL VINEYARDS, CALIFORNIA
An irrigation pipe skirts rows of vines in one of the drier parts of Monterey County. Conditions are a far cry from those around the Finger Lakes, New York.

1707
6193 ALASKA Fairbanks
ANCHORAGE
YUKON
Skagway
Whitehorse *2966*
Prince Rupert
BRITISH
COLUMBIA
4042 Kamloops
Vancouver I. VANCOUVER
Victoria Penticton
SEATTLE
WASH. Spokane
PORTLAND
Eugene OREGON
4316
CALIFORNIA
San
Francisco
SAN JOSE
SACRAMENTO
Bakersfield
Los Angeles
SAN DIEGO
Northern Baja
California
3055
Caborca
Nogales
Hermosillo
3200
La Paz Culiacán
Mazatlan
ACAPULCO

Inuvik
472 Coppermine
NORTHWEST TERRITORIES
Yellowknife
Fort Nelson
Fort McMurray
ALBERTA
EDMONTON
CALGARY
Saskatoon
Regina
MONTANA
Great Falls
IDAHO
Boise *3857*
WYOMING
NEVADA Reno
SALT LAKE
CITY *4114*
Las
Vegas
3982 UTAH
Grand
Valley
ARIZONA COLORADO DENVER
PHOENIX
Middle
Rio Grande
Albuquerque
NEW
Mimbres MEXICO
Valley Mesilla
Valley
El Paso
Escondido
Valley
Fredericksburg *2389*
CHIHUAHUA
Delicias
2445
Laguna
Torreón Parras
Saltillo
MONTERREY
Zacatecas
Aguascalientes
GUADALAJARA
San Juan del Río
Mexico City
5452
Oaxaca

Victoria
Island
Great
Bear
L.
Mackenzie
240
Back
Great
Slave L. *610*
SASK.
747
N.
DAKOTA
Grand
Forks
52 *693*
Rapid S.
City DAKOTA
1036
NEBRASKA
OMAHA
Cheyenne
Colorado
Grand
Valley
Arkansas *2008*
OKLAHOMA
CITY
TEXAS
Bell
Mtn.
SAN
ANTONIO Austin
Rio Grande

Baffin
Island
Hudson Strait
Southampton
I.
Hudson
Bay
CANADA
Churchill
MANITOBA
Lake Winnipeg
WINNIPEG
Kapuskasing
ONTARIO
Albany *259*
Duluth
MINN.
MINNEAPOLIS
Des
Moines IOWA
Chicago
ILL.
KANSAS CITY
KANSAS
Wichita
Tulsa
ARK.
Little
Rock
MISSOURI
ST. LOUIS Augusta
Hermann
LOUISVILLE KY.
Memphis
Mississippi
Delta
Birmingham MISS.
ALA.
Dallas
Houston
NEW
ORLEANS
Gulf of Mexico
St. Petersburg
MIAMI

Labrador
Sea
NEWFOUNDLAND
Fort Chimo
Scheffervile
Goose
Bay
QUÉBEC
774
Sept-Iles
138
QUÉBEC
Montréal
MAINE *1916*
N.B. P.E.I.
NOVA
SCOTIA
Halifax
Portland
N.H.
Boston
MASS.
R.I.
Ottawa CONN.
Toronto
New York
N.J.
Detroit
MICH.
Cleveland PENN. Philadelphia
Pittsburgh Washington D.C.
OHIO W. MD.
IND. VA.
Virginia
Greensboro
N. CAROLINA
TENN.
ATLANTA S. CAROLINA
GEORGIA Savannah
Jacksonville *42*
FLORIDA
Cancún
Mérida
Veracruz
Villahermosa

Pacific Ocean

Kauai
Lihue
Niihau Oahu HONOLULU
Molokai
Lanai Maui
Tedeschi *3033*
Hawaiian Islands
4169 Hilo
Volcano
Winery
Hawaii

●	Winery
▲	Height above sea level (metres)

km 100 200 300 400 500
miles 100 200 300

NORTH AMERICA
Wine is produced across the entire continent of North America, in Canada,
the United States, and Mexico, whether from native grapes or vinifera *varieties.*
Winemakers work in enormously varied conditions according to climate.

	California *See also p.448*
	Pacific Northwest *See also p.479*
	Atlantic Northeast *See also p.487*
	Canada *See also pp.494, 495*
	Ozark Mountain
	Ozark Highlands
	Texas High Plains
	Texas Hill Country
	Other winemaking areas
●	Mexican winemaking areas
—	International boundary
—	State/Provincial boundary
▲	Height above sea level (metres)

km 200 400 600 800 1000
miles 200 400 600

VINEYARDS, UPSTATE NEW YORK
Rows of vines combine to form an emerald-green patchwork on the gently sloping countryside near Hammondsport. In the distance is Keuka Lake, one of the finger-shaped lakes that have a moderating influence on the area's climate.

In Europe, World War I had robbed every industry of its young, up-and-coming generation, but the rich tradition of the wine industry enabled it to survive until the arrival of a new generation. The early 1900s were also the era of the foundation of the French *Appellation Contrôlée* laws, a quality-control system that many other serious winemaking countries would eventually copy.

The United States also lost much of one generation in World War I, but it had less of a winemaking tradition to fall back on and, by 1920, there was virtually no wine industry whatsoever to preserve. After Prohibition came one of the worst economic depressions in history, followed by World War II that took yet another generation of bright young minds. It was, therefore, little wonder that by the late 1940s the wine industry of the United States was so out of date. It had lost touch with European progress and resorted to the production of awful *labrusca* wines that had been the wine drinker's staple diet in pre-Prohibition days. California produced relatively little *labrusca* compared to the eastern states, but its winemakers also resorted to old-fashioned styles, making heavy, sweet, fortified wines. The fact that Californian wine today is a match for the best of its European counterparts and that its industry is healthy, growing fast, and looking to compete on foreign markets, clearly proves that in the United States opportunity is boundless.

THE APPELLATION SYSTEM OF THE UNITED STATES

The older generation of appellations of the United States is based on political boundaries such as counties or states. During the mid-1970s, the Department of Treasury's Bureau of Alcohol, Tobacco, and Firearms (BATF) considered the concept of specific controlled appellations based on geography and climate, and in September 1978 BATF published its first laws and regulations designed to introduce a system of Approved Viticultural Areas (AVAs), to supplement the old system.

Every state, from Hawaii to Alaska, and the counties they contain, are recognized in law as their own individual appellations of origin, but other generic appellations are also recognized:

American or United States This appellation classifies blended and varietal wines from anywhere in the US, including the District of Columbia and the Commonwealth of Puerto Rico. These wines,

like *vins de tables* in France, are not allowed to carry a vintage, which is, in my opinion, irrational. It is the only appellation allowed for wines shipped in bulk to other countries.

Multi-state Appellation This appellation is used to classify a wine from any two or three contiguous states. The percentage of wine from each state must be clearly indicated on the label.

State Appellation A wine from any state may use this appellation; at least 75 per cent of grapes must come from grapes grown within the one state indicated. Thus wine claiming the appellation of California may contain up to 25 per cent produce of one other state, or a variety of several other states. The same principle applies to County Appellations.

Multi-county Appellation This appellation classifies a wine from any two or three contiguous counties. The percentage of wine from each state must be clearly indicated on the label.

County Appellation A wine from any county within any state may use this appellation: at least 75 per cent of the wine must come from grapes grown within the one county indicated.

Note For the purposes of the above appellations, the definition of "state" also includes the District of Columbia and the Commonwealth of Puerto Rico.

THE STATUS OF APPROVED VITICULTURAL AREAS

There are no AVA rules governing the varieties grown, the methods of vine-training employed, the yields allowed, or the style of wines produced, and AVAs are all the better for it. Although some have evolved to a point where they can be said to favour certain grape varieties and produce an identifiable style, many have not and never will – but is there any reason why they should? America's AVAs are much-maligned by various American critics, yet they are the healthy product of New World free enterprise. There are those who complain that the BATF knows nothing about wine and bemoan the fact that some AVAs are merely fabrications designed to allow larger producers to get away with putting "estate bottled" on wines blended from several different old-style appellations. What does this matter? All consumers are concerned about is that if a wine claims to be the product of a certain AVA, that the appellation exists and the wine actually comes from there. The draconian measures used to enforce European wine regimes have proved to be infinitely fallible and the wines produced highly susceptible to competition from better-value New World products. Perhaps French wines would benefit from a more *laissez-faire* system administered by people who know nothing about wine?

HEALTH WARNINGS ON AMERICAN WINE LABELS

The following "Government Warning" must appear on every bottle of wine sold in the United States: 1 According to the Surgeon General, "women should not drink alcoholic beverages during pregnancy because of the risk of birth defects"; 2 "Consumption of alcoholic beverages impairs your ability to drive a car or operate machinery and may cause health problems". In my opinion, however, the warning is grossly misleading, and contains half-truths and unsubstantiated claims.

As to the first part of the warning, which states that "women should not drink alcoholic beverages during pregnancy because of the risk of birth defects", women alcoholics can give birth to children deformed by "foetal alcohol syndrome", but a study of 2,000 Australian women concluded (in line with other reports) that "there is no significant relationship between light and moderate maternal alcohol intake and foetal growth effect". There can be no argument with the first part of the second warning because the "consumption of alcoholic beverages" does "impair" the ability to "drive a car or operate machinery" but, while the second part is true – that alcohol may cause health problems – it is grossly misleading because it does not put into context the word "may". The US government was forced to use this word because only excessive alcohol consumption is a potential health hazard, whereas drinking in moderation is actually beneficial to health. Tests and studies throughout the world, many of them by America's most respected institutes, have shown that compared to both non-drinkers and heavy drinkers, moderate drinkers:

• are sharper-minded when asked to perform cognitive skills (National Academy of Sciences, Journal of the American Geriatric Society, Journal of the American Medical Association *et al*);

• are less prone to stress, high blood pressure, heart-attack (55 per cent lower incidence at three glasses of wine a day), cerebral thrombosis (the risk of the most common form of stroke is halved for moderate drinkers), rheumatoid arthritis, late-onset (non-insulin dependent) diabetes, Leukoaraiosis (associated with mental dysfunction, vascular dementia, Alzheimer's type dementia, and cerebrovascular disease), post-menopausal osteoporosis (due to increased bone density), and gallstones (17 per cent lower incidence at two glasses of wine per day, 33 per cent at two to four glasses, and 42 per cent at more than four glasses);

• have greater protection against food-borne bacteria such as salmonella, E-coli, and shigella (more effective than bismuth salicylate, the active ingredient in proprietary medicines for traveller's diarrhoea), and an 85 per cent greater resistance against one of five strains of the common cold virus (this was a surprise to the scientist conducting the research, who had expected moderate drinkers to be among the most prone);

• are likely to live two to five years longer than non-drinkers. Excessive alcohol consumption is not good for you, but moderate drinking offers many health advantages and the US government should not give the opposite impression. From an objective assessment of all available information, the only advice the government should give is: "The contents of this bottle, drunk in moderation, are good for you – especially your heart – and may add up to five years to your life" (this wording was suggested by Kathryn McWhirter in the UK paper *The Independent on Sunday*).

What truly amazes me is that a country regarded by the rest of the world as litigation-mad has a wine industry that does not have the conviction to stand up for itself. Why not hire the largest firm of first-rate lawyers in the country and sue the Surgeon General, BATF and the US Government for $50 billion? I am informed that it would be impossible to prove the Surgeon General's unsubstantiated claim about birth defects in a Court of Law.

HOW TO READ AMERICAN WINE LABELS

WINERY •
By law, the producer's name and address must both be on the label. The latter is at the label's base. Bainbridge Island Winery is a few kilometres west of Seattle.

VINTAGE •
At least 95 per cent of the wine must be from the vintage indicated. Until the early 1970s, BATF regulations demanded that the figure was 100 per cent, but winemakers, particularly those producing higher-quality wines aged in small oak barrels, petitioned for a limited margin to enable topping-up, and this was granted.

GRAPE VARIETY •
The wine must contain at least 75 per cent of the grape variety indicated (90 per cent in Oregon). Although the potential of varietal labelling was recognized in Alsace in the 1920s, the international marketing phenomenon these wines represent today was brought about by the widespread application of the concept by Californian wineries.

HEALTH WARNING
Health warnings are required by federal law (*see* discussion above), yet none of the proven health advantages are permitted (*see* opposite).

APPELLATION
The appellation is always the first thing to look for on a label. Unfortunately, the law does not insist that any AVA indicated should be followed by the term "Approved Viticultural Area". As a result, who is to know if Puget Sound has any official connotation whatsoever? It would also surely be sensible for county appellations to be followed by the term "County Appellation" (plus the state in which the county is located) and, if only for the benefit of export markets, it would do no harm to add the term "State Appellation" where appropriate.

ALCOHOLIC STRENGTH
This must be stated by law.

Other information regarding style or quality may also be present:

TABLE WINE OR LIGHT WINE
A wine with an alcohol level not in excess of 14 per cent by volume.

NATURAL WINE
A wine may be called "natural" only if it has not been fortified with grape brandy or alcohol.

DESSERT WINE
A wine with an alcoholic content of at least 14 per cent by volume, but not in excess of 24 per cent. Wines designated as "sherry" must contain at least 17 per cent and those bearing the names of "angelica", "madeira", "muscatel", or "port"

musthave a minimum of 18 per cent. If any of the aforementioned types of wine have an alcoholic strength in excess of 14 per cent, but less than 18 per cent (or 17 per cent in the case of "sherry"), they must be prefixed with the term "light", for example "light sherry" or "light madeira".

VOLUME
This must be stated somewhere on the bottle by law.

SPARKLING WINE
This term may be used to describe "carbonated", *cuve close*, "bottle fermented", or *méthode champenoise* wine. If the label bears no other information, the consumer should fear the worst (carbonated or *cuve close*).

However, the label may refer to the wine by any of the following terms:

CHAMPAGNE
A sparkling wine derived through a second fermentation in "glass containers of not greater than one (US) gallon capacity".

BOTTLE FERMENTED
As above, this term could be used for *méthode champenoise*, but usually refers to a wine that, after second fermentation, is decanted and filtered under pressure before rebottling.

FERMENTED IN THIS BOTTLE
A simple and clever way of describing a wine that has been made by the *méthode champenoise*.

CRACKLING WINE
As for "champagne", although with a lesser degree of effervescence and may also be called *pétillant*, *frizzante*, or *crémant*.

CRACKLING WINE – BULK METHOD
As for "crackling wine" but made by *cuve close*.

CARBONATED WINE
Still-wine made bubbly through the addition of CO_2 from a bottle of gas, the method used to produce fizzy drinks such as lemonade or cola.

Note For information on Mexican labels, *see* p.503.

THE AVAs OF THE UNITED STATES

The number of AVAs is set to rise. The current total is 128.

Alexander Valley California
Established 23 November 1984

Altus Arkansas
Established 29 June 1984

Anderson Valley California
Established 19 September 1983

Arkansas Mountain Arkansas
Established 27 October 1986

Arroyo Grande Valley California
Established 5 February 1990

Arroyo Seco California
Established 16 May 1983

Atlas Peak California
Established 23 January 1992

Augusta Missouri
Established 20 June 1980

Bell Mountain Texas
Established 10 November 1986

Ben Lomond Mountain California
Established 8 January 1988

Benmore Valley California
Established 18 October 1991

California Shenandoah Valley California
Established 27 January 1983

Carmel Valley California
Established 15 January 1983

Catoctin Maryland
Established 14 November 1983

Cayuga Lake New York
Established 25 March 1988

Central Delaware Valley Pennsylvania and New Jersey
Established 18 April 1984

Chalk Hill California
Established 21 November 1983

Chalone California
Established 14 July 1982

Cienega Valley California
Established 20 September 1982

Clarksburg California
Established 22 February 1984

Clear Lake California
Established 7 June 1984

Cole Ranch California
Established 16 March 1983

Columbia Valley Oregon and Washington
Established 13 December 1984

Cucamonga Valley California
Established 31 March 1995

Cumberland Valley Maryland and Pennsylvania
Established 26 August 1985

Dry Creek Valley California
Established 6 September 1983

Dunnigan Hills California
Established 13 May 1993

Edna Valley California
Established 11 June 1982

El Dorado California
Established 14 November 1983

Escondido Valley Texas
Established 15 May 1992

Fennville Michigan
Established 19 October 1981

Fiddletown California
Established 3 November 1983

Finger Lakes New York
Established 1 October 1982

Fredericksburg Texas
Established 22 December 1988

Grand River Valley Ohio
Established 21 November 1983

Grand Valley Colorado
Established 25 November 1991

Guenoc Valley California
Established 21 December 1981

Hames Valley California
Established 27 March 1994

Herman Missouri
Established 10 September 1983

Howell Mountain California
Established 30 January 1984

Hudson River Region New York
Established 6 July 1982

Isle St. George Ohio
Established 20 September 1982

Kanawha River Valley West Virginia
Established 8 May 1986

Knights Valley California
Established 21 November 1983

Lake Eric New York, Pennsylvania, and Ohio
Established 21 November 1983

Lake Michigan Shore Michigan
Established 14 November 1983

Lake Wisconsin Wisconsin
Established 5 January 1994

Lancaster Valley Pennsylvania
Established 11 June 1982

Leelanau Peninsula Michigan
Established 29 April 1982

Lime Kiln Valley California
Established 6 July 1982

Linganore Maryland
Established 19 September 1983

Livermore Valley California
Established 1 October 1982

Lodi California
Established 7 March 1986

Loramie Creek Ohio
Established 27 December 1982

Los Carneros California
Established 19 September 1983

Madera California
Established 7 January 1985

Malibu-Newton Canyon California
Established 13 June 1996

Martha's Vineyard Massachusetts
Established 4 February 1985

McDowell Valley California
Established 4 January 1982

Mendocino California
Established 16 July 1984

Merritt Island California
Established 16 June 1983

Mesilla Valley New Mexico and Texas
Established 18 March 1985

Middle Rio Grande Valley New Mexico
Established 2 February 1988

Mimbres Valley New Mexico
Established 23 December 1985

Mississippi Delta Louisiana, Mississippi, and Tennessee
Established 1 October 1984

Monterey California
Established 16 July 1984

Monticello Virginia
Established 22 February 1984

Mt. Harlan California
Established 29 November 1990

Mt. Veeder California
Established 22 March 1990

Napa Valley California
Established 27 February 1981

Northern Neck – George Washington Birthplace Virginia
Established 21 May 1987

Northern Sonoma California
Established 17 June 1985

North Fork of Long Island New York
Established 10 November 1986

North Fork of Roanoke Virginia
Established 16 May 1983

North Yuba California
Established 30 August 1985

Oakville California
Established 2 July 1993

Ohio River Valley Indiana, Ohio, West Virginia, and Kentucky
Established 7 October 1983

Old Mission Peninsula Michigan
Established 8 July 1987

Ozark Highlands Missouri
Established 30 September 1987

Ozark Mountain Arkansas, Missouri, and Oklahoma
Established 1 August 1986

Pacheco Pass California
Established 11 April 1984

Paicines California
Established 15 September 1982

Paso Robles California
Established 3 November 1983

Potter Valley California
Established 14 November 1983

Puget Sound Washington
Established 4 October 1995

Redwood Valley California
Established 23 December 1996

Rocky Knob Virginia
Established 11 February 1983

Rogue Valley Oregon
Established 22 February 1992

Russian River Valley California
Established 21 November 1983

Rutherford California
Established 2 July 1993

San Benito California
Established 4 November 1983

San Lucas California
Established 2nd March 1987

San Pasqual Valley California
Established 16 September 1981

San Ysidro District California
Established 5 June 1990

Santa Clara Valley California
Established 28 March 1989

Santa Cruz Mountains California
Established 4 January 1982

Santa Maria Valley California
Established 4 September 1981

Santa Ynez Valley California
Established 16 May 1983

Shenandoah Valley Virginia and West Virginia
Established 27 January 1983

Sierra Foothills California
Established 18 December 1987

Solano Country Green Valley California
Established 28 January 1983

Sonoita Arizona
Established 26 November 1984

Sonoma Coast California
Established 13 July 1987

Sonoma County Green Valley California
Established 21 December 1983

Sonoma Mountain California
Established 22 February 1985

Sonoma Valley California
Established 4 January 1982

Southeastern New England Connecticut, Rhode Island, and Massachusetts
Established 27 April 1984

Spring Mountain District California
Established 13 May 1993

St. Helena California
Established 11 September 1995

Stag's Leap District California
Established 27 January 1989

Suisun Valley California
Established 27 December 1982

Temecula California
Established 23 November 1984

Texas High Plains Texas
Established 2 March 1992

Texas Hill Country Texas
Established 29 November 1991

The Hamptons Long Island, New York
Established 17 June 1985

Umpqua Valley Oregon
Established 30 April 1984

Virginia's Eastern Shore Virginia
Established 2 January 1991

Walla Walla Valley Washington and Oregon
Established 7 March 1984

Warren Hills New Jersey
Established 8 August 1988

Western Connecticut Highlands Connecticut
Established 9 February 1988

Wild Horse Valley California
Established 30 November 1988

Willamette Valley Oregon
Established 3 January 1984

Willow Creek California
Established 9 September 1983

Yakima Valley Washington
Established 4 May 1983

York Mountain California
Established 23 September 1983

CALIFORNIA

America's Golden State has always been a natural home for classic grape varieties and since the early 1980s, when many of its winemakers began to reject overblown styles in favour of a balance between natural power and finesse, California has produced an abundance of world-class wines.

CALIFORNIA WAS FIRST SETTLED by the Spanish in 1769 and formed part of Mexico until 1848, when it was ceded to the United States, becoming a State of the Union in 1850. The first Californian wine was made in 1782 at San Juan Capistrano, by Fathers Pablo de Mugártegui and Gregorio Amurrió. Mission grapes, from vines brought to California by Don José Camacho on the San Antonio, which docked at San Diego on 16 May 1778, were used to make the wine. However, it was not until 1833 that *bordelais* Jean-Louis Vignes established California's first commercial winery. He was the first Californian winemaker to import European vines and, in 1840, he became the first to export Californian wines.

THE AMAZING HARASZTHY

Eight years before California passed from Mexican to American sovereignty, a certain Hungarian political exile called Agoston Haraszthy de Mokesa settled in Wisconsin. Haraszthy was a colourful, flamboyant entrepreneur in the mould of Barnum or Champagne Charlie. Among other things, he founded a town in Wisconsin and modestly called it Haraszthy (it was later renamed Sauk City), ran a Mississippi steamboat, and cultivated the first vineyard in Wisconsin – all within two years of beginning a new life in a strange country.

In 1849, Haraszthy moved to San Diego, leaving his business interests in the hands of a partner who promptly took advantage of a rumour that he had perished during his transcontinental trek, sold all the business and properties, and vanished with the money. Haraszthy was broke, yet within six months he was farming his own 65-hectare (160-acre) fruit and vegetable ranch. Such rapid success followed by disaster then an even greater triumph was to become Haraszthy's trademark. Within a few months of acquiring his ranch he also became the owner of a butcher's shop and a livery stable in Middleton, a part of San Diego that still boasts an Haraszthy Street. In addition, he ran an omnibus company, started a construction business, was elected the first sheriff of San Diego, was made a judge, and became a Lieutenant in the volunteer militia. He also began importing cuttings of numerous European vine varieties.

RECENT CALIFORNIA VINTAGES

2000 Cold weather and rain in October held back late-ripening varieties such as Cabernet Sauvignon. The result was the longest harvest season in memory; whites and light reds fared best.

1999 A later harvest due to cool temperatures in spring and summer, but an excellent vintage throughout California and for all the different varieties, although Cabernet Sauvignon has the edge.

1998 Perhaps the most difficult harvest of the 1990s in California. The whites have high acidity and this crispness is welcome in those wines that also possess fruit. A very good year for Pinot Noir.

1997 The fourth outstanding California white vintage in a row. The reds, however, were even better. A great year for Zinfandel.

NAPA VALLEY VINEYARDS
Of all California's winemaking regions, Napa Valley is the best known and its wines are the most sought after. The first vines were planted here in 1838, and today the valley boasts a vast area under vine, with a bewildering array of grape varieties.

The Buena Vista Winery

Having imported no fewer than 165 different vine varieties from Europe, in 1857 Haraszthy purchased 230 hectares (560 acres) of land near the town of Sonoma, in an area called the Valley of the Moon. Here, he built a winery, which he named Buena Vista, and dug six cellars out of the sandstone hill. With North California's first significant wine estate, Haraszthy won several awards and attracted much publicity for both his vineyard and his wine. This venture drew so much attention that, in 1861, the governor of California commissioned Haraszthy to visit Europe and report on its winegrowing areas. Haraszthy's trip took him to every wine region in France, Germany, Italy, Spain, and Switzerland, where he interviewed thousands of winegrowers, took notes, consulted foreign literature and so accumulated a library of reference material. He returned to the United States with a staggering 100,000 cuttings of 300 different vine varieties, only to have the state Senate plead poverty when he presented them with a bill for 12,000 dollars for his trip, although the cuttings alone were worth three times that amount. He was never reimbursed for his trouble and many of the cuttings, which he had expected to be distributed among the state's other winegrowers, simply rotted away.

Haraszthy was not deterred: within seven years he managed to expand Buena Vista to 2,430 hectares (6,000 acres). In doing so, he totally changed the course of Californian viticulture, transferring

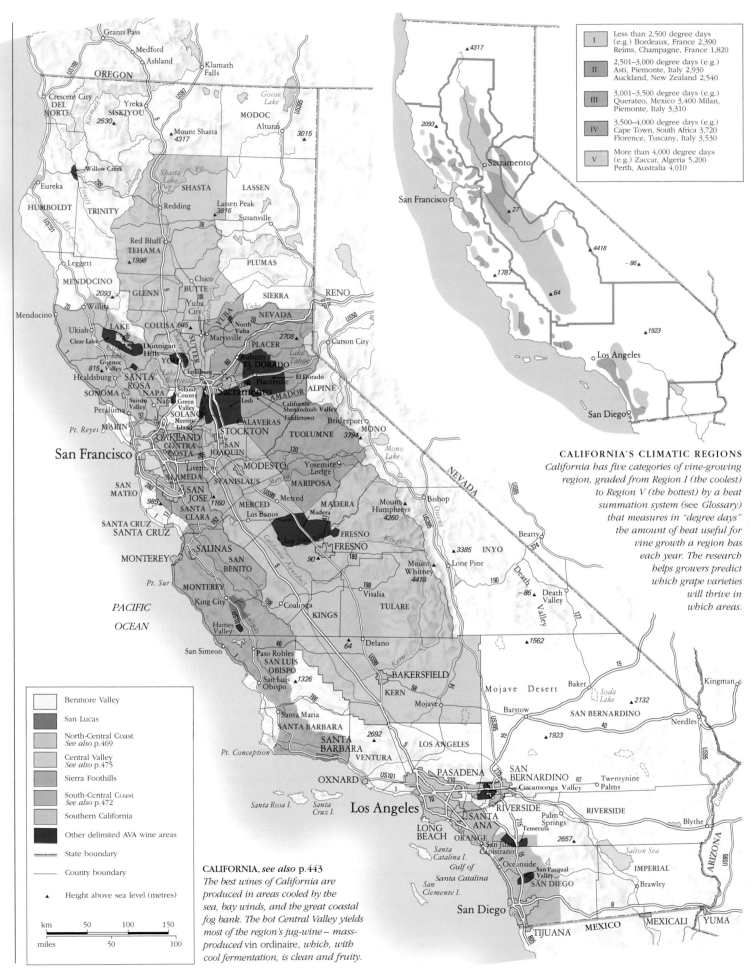

Grants Pass
Medford
Ashland
OREGON
Klamath Falls

Crescent City
DEL
NORTE
Yreka
SISKIYOU
2530 ▲
Mount Shasta
4317 ▲
MODOC
Alturas
3015 ▲

Willow Creek
Eureka
HUMBOLDT
TRINITY
SHASTA
Shasta Lake
Pit
LASSEN
Lassen Peak
3816 ▲
Susanville

Redding
Red Bluff
TEHAMA
1998 ▲
Chico
PLUMAS

Leggett
GLENN
BUTTE
Yuba City
SIERRA
RENO

MENDOCINO
2093 ▲
Willits
COLUSA
645 ▲
Marysville
North Yuba
YUBA
NEVADA
2708 ▲
PLACER
Carson City

Mendocino
LAKE
Clear Lake
Ukiah
Dunnigan Hills
YOLO
SUTTER
Auburn
Clarksburg
EL DORADO
Placerville
El Dorado
Lake Tahoe

815 ▲
Guenoc Valley
Healdsburg
SANTA ROSA
SONOMA
NAPA
Solano County Green Valley
Napa
Sacramento
Lodi
AMADOR
California Shenandoah Valley
Fiddletown
ALPINE

Petaluma
Suisun Valley
SOLANO
Merritt Island
CALAVERAS
Bridgeport
MONO

Pt. Reyes
MARIN
STOCKTON
TUOLUMNE
3794 ▲
Mono Lake

San Francisco
OAKLAND
CONTRA COSTA
SAN JOAQUIN
MODESTO
Yosemite Lodge
120

SAN MATEO
ALAMEDA
Livermore
STANISLAUS
MARIPOSA
Merced
Mount Humphreys
4260 ▲
Bishop

SAN JOSE
SANTA CLARA
1160 ▲
MERCED
Los Banos
MADERA
Madera
FRESNO
NEVADA

SANTA CRUZ
SANTA CRUZ
PACIFIC OCEAN

SALINAS
SAN BENITO
90 ▲
FRESNO
180
Mount Whitney
4418 ▲
INYO
3385 ▲
Lone Pine
Beatty

Pt. Sur
MONTEREY
MONTEREY
King City
Coalinga
KINGS
Visalia
198
TULARE
190
Death Valley
–86 ▲

Hames Valley
46
64
Delano
1562 ▲

San Simeon
Paso Robles
SAN LUIS OBISPO
San Luis Obispo
1326 ▲
BAKERSFIELD
KERN
Kern
59
Baker
Soda Lake
2132 ▲
Kingman

Santa Maria
SANTA BARBARA
2692 ▲
14
Mojave
Barstow
SAN BERNARDINO
40
Needles

Pt. Conception
SANTA BARBARA
VENTURA
LOS ANGELES
Mojave Desert
1923 ▲

OXNARD
PASADENA
SAN BERNARDINO
Twentynine Palms
Cucamonga Valley

Santa Rosa I.
Santa Cruz I.
Los Angeles
SANTA ANA
ORANGE
RIVERSIDE
RIVERSIDE
Palm Springs
Blythe

LONG BEACH
San Juan Capistrano
Temecula
2657 ▲
Salton Sea
ARIZONA

Santa Catalina I.
Gulf of Santa Catalina
San Clemente I.
Oceanside
San Pasqual Valley
SAN DIEGO
IMPERIAL
Brawley

San Diego
TIJUANA
MEXICO
MEXICALI
YUMA

Legend (climatic regions)

I	Less than 2,500 degree days (e.g.) Bordeaux, France 2,390 Reims, Champagne, France 1,820
II	2,501–3,000 degree days (e.g.) Asti, Piemonte, Italy 2,930 Auckland, New Zealand 2,540
III	3,001–3,500 degree days (e.g.) Quereteo, Mexico 3,400 Milan, Piemonte, Italy 3,310
IV	3,500–4,000 degree days (e.g.) Cape Town, South Africa 3,720 Florence, Tuscany, Italy 3,530
V	More than 4,000 degree days (e.g.) Zaccar, Algeria 5,200 Perth, Australia 4,010

4317 ▲
2093 ▲
Sacramento
San Francisco
27 ▲
4418 ▲
1787 ▲
–86 ▲
64 ▲
1923 ▲
Los Angeles
San Diego

CALIFORNIA'S CLIMATIC REGIONS

California has five categories of vine-growing region, graded from Region I (the coolest) to Region V (the hottest) by a heat summation system (see Glossary) that measures in "degree days" the amount of heat useful for vine growth a region has each year. The research helps growers predict which grape varieties will thrive in which areas.

Map legend

	Benmore Valley
	San Lucas
	North-Central Coast *See also p.469*
	Central Valley *See also p.475*
	Sierra Foothills
	South-Central Coast *See also p.472*
	Southern California
	Other delimited AVA wine areas
---	State boundary
—	County boundary
▲	Height above sea level (metres)

km   50   100   150
miles   50   100

CALIFORNIA, *see also p.443*

The best wines of California are produced in areas cooled by the sea, bay winds, and the great coastal fog bank. The hot Central Valley yields most of the region's jug-wine – mass-produced vin ordinaire, which, with cool fermentation, is clean and fruity.

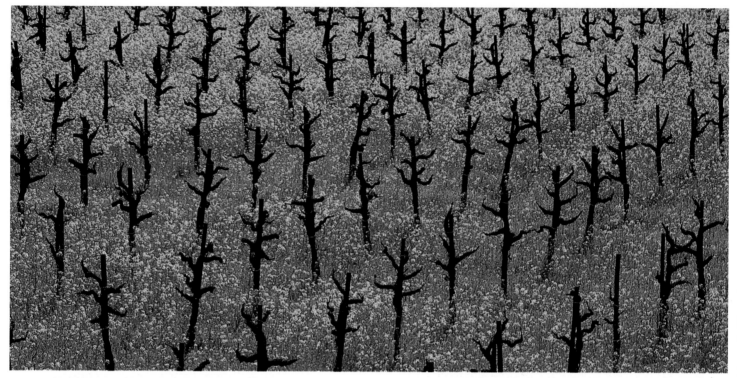

SPRING MUSTARD FLOWERS IN THE NAPA VALLEY
*This bright yellow carpet of mustard seed in full bloom will soon
be ploughed in as a "green manure" to feed the vines.*

the focus of attention from the south of the state to the north.
At the height of its fame Buena Vista had offices in San Francisco,
Philadelphia, Chicago, New York, and London. However, this
success was purely superficial, for the vineyard was described
in 1864 as "the largest wine-growing estate in the world and the
most unprofitable". Haraszthy also suffered a number of losses

on the stock exchange and was faced with a new tax on brandy,
which resulted in further loss of income. A fire at the winery then
destroyed much of his stock and the bank proceeded to cut off
his credit. Enough was enough, even for Agoston Haraszthy de
Mokesa. He left California for Nicaragua, where he was successful
in obtaining a government contract to distil rum from sugar. An
enigmatic character to the end, Haraszthy disappeared altogether
in 1869, presumed drowned while trying to cross an alligator-
infested stream on his plantation.

THE SECOND COMING

Because phylloxera, a root-feeding insect, came from the US to destroy
European vineyards, which were saved only when the vines were grafted
on to phylloxera-resistant native American varieties, there is a widespread
belief that California's vineyards have always been safe. Nothing could
be further from the truth. Phylloxera's home was east of the Rockies,
where over aeons native vines, such as *berlandieri* and *riparia*, developed
a natural resistance to phylloxera. When European *vinifera* vines were
introduced to California, phylloxera was bound to follow, via the waggon
trains across the Rockies or on the vines themselves, and *vinifera*
varieties proved to be as vulnerable in California as anywhere else.

THE ANTI-BEAST
Phylloxera was first identified at Sonoma in 1873, coincidentally at the
same time as another native American bug, *Tyroglyphus*, was being
shipped to France. The idea of using *Tyroglyphus*, which was harmless to
the vine but a deadly enemy of phylloxera, to infect phylloxera-infested
vineyards was an imaginative one. Unfortunately, unlike phylloxera,
Tyroglyphus did not care for the European climate and failed to settle.

In California, the effect of phylloxera was devastating. By 1891 Napa could
boast 7,200 hectares (18,000 acres) of vines, but by the turn of the century,
this had been reduced to a mere 1,200 hectares (3,000 acres). Under the
auspices of Professor Hilgard, Head of Agriculture at the Department
of Viticulture and Enology in the University of California at Davis,
California's growers eventually adopted the same method as the Europeans
to control the pest, grafting *vinifera* vines on to phylloxera-resistant
varieties. Ironically, it was some time before Californians realized these
wonder vines originated from eastern American states and initially they
imported them from France. Only half the vineyards had been grafted
when they were hit by another, even more lethal plague – Prohibition.

By the late 1940s, UC Davis had assembled one of the most formidable
teams of viticultural and oenological experts in the world. Headed by
such legendary figures as Amerine, Olmo, and Winkler, the university
was primarily responsible for making California the wine force it is
today. Along the way, however, they made some errors, such as placing
too much emphasis on volume and technical correctness. The biggest
mistake of all was recommending AxR#1 rootstock.

ROOT CAUSE
Despite warnings from various European sources about its susceptibility
to phylloxera (all acknowledged but brushed aside by numerous
University text books), UC-Davis recommended AxR's use on fertile
valley floors, such as Napa, because of its ability to increase yields. As
Winkler *et al* put it in *General Viticulture* (University of California Press)
"This is a case where the choice of (root)stock cannot be based entirely
on its resistance to phylloxera".

These words came back to haunt the faculty at Davis in the 1980s
when, slowly but inexorably, vineyards grafted on to AxR failed and
the culprit, phylloxera, was identified. Three out of every four vines
in California will have to be replaced, which will bring financial ruin
to many, although for the Californian wine industry as a whole, it will
ultimately be recognized as a blessing in disguise as undesirable grapes
will not only be replaced by selected clones of better-quality varieties,
but will also be grafted on to less productive rootstocks and planted
at higher densities. I wonder however, whether anyone has thought
of trying that bright 19th-century idea of deliberately infesting the
vineyards with phylloxera's arch-enemy *Tyroglyphus*. The only reason
it did not work in France was because of the climate, but perhaps
Tyroglyphus might prefer California sunshine?

Learning curve

With California's natural abundance of sun and what to most Europeans seems like America's preoccupation with size, it was perhaps inevitable that the 1950s and early 1960s saw a series of massive, ink-black, tannic Cabernet Sauvignon blockbusters hitting the shelves. The late 1960s witnessed the introduction of high-tech wineries and the use of 100 per cent new oak, and the precision of style and focus of fruit that resulted were welcomed at the time, as were the supple tannins that replaced harsh ones. The mid-1970s saw the irresistible rise of Chardonnay, but the wines were blatantly too rich and oaky. Sidetracked by the quest for finesse, the wines went too far in the wishy-washy vintages of 1982 and 1983, when over-acidified, tart, and downright stingy wines were made. Some winemakers wanted to sacrifice the voluptuousness that is inherent in this sunny state in a fruitless bid to fabricate some sort of European-styled, slower-developing, longer-lived wine (a number still pursue this misguided idea), but the truly magnificent 1985 vintage, the best year since 1974, was a turning point for California's wine industry. Virtually everyone got it right. Since then, the wines of all those who sought elegance without stripping away their natural expression have deliciously demonstrated that the original quest for finesse was no folly. This learning curve has established in California, as it has elsewhere, that the secret of fine wine is merely a matter of balance. The difficulty is in achieving it, for perfect balance is by definition a natural state that can be achieved only in the vineyard, not the winery.

Longevity

Now that most of California's makers of fine wines have found their direction, the only obstacle to prevent them from achieving their full potential (apart from the vagaries of vintage and occasional over-zealousness), is the problem of cellarage temperature. Air-conditioning is vital in California, but few people seem to realise that at 14°C, which seems to be the norm here, potentially fine white wines will fall over after two or three years and the longevity of even the best quality red wines will be halved. The additional cost of maintaining a temperature just a few degrees lower can be considerable, but once the bottle maturation process has set in, it can only be speeded-up, not slowed down, so it is a cost that cannot be cut. The *champenois* know this more than anyone else, as even their cheapest products must spend years in their cellars prior to distribution, which is why they are stored at between 10 and 11°C. Once most California cellars are kept at no more than 12°C, the notion that these wines rapidly mature will be shown to be a myth.

CALIFORNIA'S GRAPE VARIETIES

The area under vine in California has decreased by approximately 4,000 hectares (9,880 acres) over the last ten years, but this obscures the fact that, because of phylloxera (*see* p.449), this industry has undergone an exhaustive replanting programme and will continue to do so well into the next millennium. Wine grape varieties have, in fact, increased the area they cover by 4,598 hectares (11,361 acres), even though great swathes of vines have had to be uprooted, while raisin- and table-grape areas have decreased. Tellingly, the acreage of rootstock has swollen by more than 70 per cent. The breakdown of vines in 1995 was as follows:

VINE TYPE	ACRES	HECTARES
Wine grape varieties	354,417	143,431
Raisin grape varieties	277,190	112,177
Table grape varieties	85,539	34,617
Rootstock	1,597	646
TOTAL	718,743	290,871

From the breakdown below of wine grape varieties by colour, there has been a swing from a strong emphasis on red wine varieties in 1975 to almost half-and-half in 1995. In the 1980s, when the demand for Chardonnay was at its height and most people in the US believed that lighter meant healthier, white wine grapes accounted for as much as 57 per cent, but whether the pendulum has swung the other way because of the so-called "French Paradox" (*see* Glossary), which was much publicized on American CBS television's *60 Minutes* programme, or whether it is merely an anomaly caused by replanting phylloxera-ravaged vineyards, is impossible to tell at the moment.

GRAPE COLOUR	1975 HECTARES	1975 ACRES	%	1995 HECTARES	1995 ACRES	%
Black	52,886	130,681	62%	72,737	179,733	51%
White	31,880	78,775	38%	70,694	174,684	49%
TOTAL	84,766	209,456	100%	143,431	354,417	100%

CALIFORNIA'S TOP TEN BLACK GRAPE VARIETIES
Expressed as a percentage of total vineyard area

Over the ten year period 1985–1995, black grape varieties have polarized, with the three most widely cultivated varieties accounting for almost 60 per cent of the area under vine, as opposed to just over 40 per cent a decade earlier. Zinfandel and Cabernet sauvignon have tightened their grip on the number one and two spots respectively, while Merlot has come from nowhere to be the state's third most popular red wine grape.

VARIETY	1985		1995
1 Zinfandel	17%	(1)	24%
2 Cabernet sauvignon	15%	(2)	21%
3 Merlot	2%	(11)	14%
4 Grenache	10%	(4)	6%
5 Barbera	10%	(5)	6%
6 Rubired	5%	(6)	6%
7 Pinot noir	5%	(7)	5%
8 Carignan	11%	(3)	5%
9 Ruby cabernet	7%	(6)	4%
10 Petite Sirah	3%	(9)	1%
Others	15%	–	9%
TOTAL	100%		100%

CALIFORNIA'S TOP TEN WHITE GRAPE VARIETIES
Expressed as a percentage of total vineyard area

With over 70 per cent of the area under vine accounted for by the top three varieties in 1985, white grape varieties have always been more polarized than black, but they now account for 80 per cent, primarily due to the huge recent plantations of Chardonnay, which is now the number one grape.
[1] Includes Muscat d'Alexandrie, Muscat blanc and Orange Muscat.
[2] Authentic Johannisberg Riesling.

VARIETY	1985		1995
1 Chardonnay	14%	(3)	41%
2 Colombard	38%	(1)	26%
3 Chenin blanc	21%	(2)	13%
4 Sauvignon blanc	8%	(4)	7%
5 Muscat [1]	1%	(13)	4%
6 Riesling [2]	5%	(5)	2%
7 Malvasia	1%	(12)	2%
8 Burger	1%	(10)	1%
9 Gewürztraminer	2%	(6)	1%
10 Sémillon	2%	(7)	1%
Others	7%	–	2%
TOTAL	100%		100%

Note all percentages are rounded up or down, and the 1985 positions are given in brackets following that year's percentage (Alicante bouschet was in fact 10th in 1985. Emerald riesling, Palomino, and Pinot blanc, not in the 1995 list, were 8th, 9th, and 11th respectively.)

THE WINE STYLES OF
CALIFORNIA

ALICANTE BOUSCHET

The Alicante bouschet was a favourite during Prohibition, when the rich colour of its juice enabled bootleggers to stretch the wine with water and sugar. Cultivation of this *teinturier* grape has now dropped to less than two per cent of all California's black grapes. Many moons ago, Angelo Papagni's death-defying Alicante bouschet was not to be missed, but it is seldom seen as a varietal these days.

⌛ 5–8 years

☑ *Coturri* (Ubaldi Vineyard)
• *Il Podere dell' Olivos* • *Topolos*

BARBERA

This Italian grape is mostly cultivated in the Central Valley, where its high natural acidity makes it useful for blending purposes. This said, it is cultivated on a much smaller scale in fine-wine areas, particularly Sonoma and Mendocino, and more than 30 wineries produce a pure varietal Barbera in one form or another.

⌛ 3–6 years (up to 10 in exceptional cases)

☑ *Bonny Doon* • *Eberle* • *Robert Mondavi*
• *Pellegrini* • *Il Podere dell' Olivos* • *Preston*

BORDEAUX-STYLE BLENDED RED

On balance I would say that Bordeaux-style blends are more successful in California than pure Cabernet Sauvignon varietals. However, it has proved very difficult to persuade California-wine drinkers that they should pay the same price, let alone a premium, for such wines. For this reason the Meritage Association was formed (*see* Meritage), but not all wineries are members and some of the greatest Bordeaux-style blends do not actually use the *portmanteau*. Therefore all the best blends, whether Meritage or otherwise, are recommended here.

⌛ 3–5 years (inexpensive), 5–12 years (top wineries), 8–25 (or more) years (exceptional wines)

☑ *Beringer* (Alluvium) • *Buena Vista* (L'Année) • *Cain Cellars* (Cain Five) • *Carmenet* (Sonoma Estate Red) • *Clos Pegase* (Hommage) • *Cosentino* (The Poet Meritage) • *Dalla Vale* (Maya) • *Deblinger* • *Dominus* (1990 onwards) • *Ferrari-Carano* (Reserve Red) • *Flora Springs* (Trilogy) • *Franciscan Vineyards* (Oakville Estate Magnificent Meritage) • *Geyser Peak* (Reserve) • *Guenoc* (Langtree Meritage) • *Havens* (Bouriquot) • *Kendall-Jackson* (Cardinale Meritage) • *Laurel Glen* (Terra Rosa) • *Merryvale* (Profile) • *Peter Michael* (Les Pavots) • *Morago* (Bel Air) • *Newton* (Claret) • *Niebaum-Coppola* (Rubicon) • *Opus One* • *Pahlmeyer* (Caldwell Vineyard) • *Joseph Phelps* (Insignia) • *Rancho Sisquoc* (Cellar Select) • *Ravenswood* (Pickberry) • *Stag's Leap Wine Cellars* (Cask 23) • *Stonestreet* (Legacy) • *Viader* • *White Rock* (Claret)

BORDEAUX-STYLE BLENDED WHITE

The combination of Sauvignon and Sémillon is a good one, the traditional view being that the Sauvignon provides the aromatics, freshness, acidity, and crispness, while the Sémillon adds the necessary fat, weight, depth, and complexity. In some New World areas, however, including California, the Sauvignon is too soft and neutral for this philosophy to work successfully and is much better used to play the Sémillon's role, whereas a small quantity of that grape can provide, if harvested early enough, a grassy herbaceousness that is more like Sauvignon than Sauvignon. The effect is similar, but the cause somewhat back to front.

⌛ 2–4 years

☑ *Beringer* (Alluvium) • *Hidden Cellars* (Alchemy) • *Merryvale* (Vignette) • *Ojai* (Cuvée Spéciale Sainte Hélène) • *Rabbit Ridge* (Mystique) • *Simi* (Sendal)

BOTRYTIZED and LATE HARVEST STYLES

Some of the world's most succulent botrytized and late-harvest wines are made in California, where the sunshine state brings a wonderfully ripe peachiness to Riesling and mouthwatering tropical fruit freshness to Chenin and Muscat. Several excellent Icewines (*see* p.471) have been made, including one from Bonny Doon's irrepressible Randall Grahm, even though he openly admits to shoving the grapes into his freezer before pressing them!

⌛ Ready when released (but last well in bottle)

☑ *Arrowood* (Preston Ranch Late Harvest White Riesling) • *Bonny Doon* • *Far Niente* (Dolce) • *Château St. Jean* (Special Late Harvest Johannisberg Riesling) • *Freemark Abbey* (Edelwein Gold Late Harvest Johannisberg Riesling) • *Robert Pecota* (Moscato di Andrea) • *Joseph Phelps* (Muscat Vin du Mistral) • *Renaissance* (Riesling, Sauvignon Blanc) • *St. Francis* (Muscat Canelli Late Harvest) • *Swanson* (Late Harvest Sémillon)

BOTTLE-FERMENTED SPARKLING WINES

California used to be notorious for its cheap sparkling wine until Schramsberg and Domaine Chandon led the way in the early 1970s. Then in 1991, by dint of tasting back, it could be discerned that a number of houses had come of age with the wines that were made only four years earlier. Roederer Estate, in particular, was in a class of its own, and still is, but so many other producers dramatically improved the style and finesse of their wines that the quality of Californian sparkling wine in general had quadrupled by 1995.

⌛ 2–5 years (up to 10 in very exceptional cases)

☑ *S. Anderson* (Vintage Brut, Vintage Rosé) • *Codorníu Napa* (NV Brut, Vintage Carneros Cuvée) • *Domaine Carneros* • *Domaine Chandon* (Reserve, Rosé Brut) • *Gloria Ferrer* (NV Brut) • *Handley* (Vintage Blanc de Blancs, Vintage Brut, Vintage Rosé) • *Robert Hunter* (Vintage Brut de Noirs) • *Iron Horse* (Vintage Brut, Vintage Blanc de Blancs, Vintage Rosé) • *Jordan* ('J') • *Mumm* (NV Sparkling Pinot Noir, Vintage DVX, Vintage Blanc de Blancs, Vintage Blanc de Noirs – labelled Rosé on export markets – Vintage Winery Lake) • *Piper Sonoma* (Blanc de Noirs, NV Brut, Tête de Cuvée) • *Roederer Estate* (Quartet on export markets – NV Brut, NV Rosé, L'Ermitage)

• *Scharffenberger* (Blanc de Blancs, NV) • *Schramsberg* (Blanc de Blancs, Reserve, J. Schram) • *Thornton* (Vintage Blanc de Noirs Brut Reserve)

CABERNET FRANC

California's cultivation of this Bordeaux variety tripled between 1983 and 1988. At that time it was primarily used for effecting better-balanced Cabernet Sauvignon blends, and the only pure varietal versions readers were likely to encounter were rosés from the North Coast area. Since then, the area occupied by Cabernet franc vines has doubled and pure varietals will shortly become commonplace. Top California Cabernet Franc seems to have a fragrance and finesse not dissimilar to the way it performs in the bestSt.-Émilion vineyards.

⌛ 1–4 years

☑ *Deblinger* • *The Gainey Vineyard* (Limited Selection) • *Ironstone* • *Konocti* • *Longoria* • *Madrona* • *Niebaum-Coppola* • *Rancho Sisquoc* • *Sebastiani* • *Vita Nova*

CABERNET SAUVIGNON

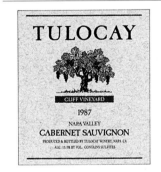

This grape accounts for 15 per cent of California's black grape varieties and, although Chardonnay inevitably stole the limelight when the trend was towards dry white wines, Cabernet sauvignon has always been California's finest grape variety. In areas that are too cool, Cabernet Sauvignon wines can have an herbaceous character of capsicum or green bean, but in most other areas they generally tend to combine the deliciously ripe, blackcurranty style, with a velvety texture and violet or mint after-aromas. Oak is now used intelligently and some of the most exciting Cabernet wines are blended with Merlot and Cabernet franc, as they are in Bordeaux. *See* Bordeaux-Style Blends, and Meritage.

⌛ 3–5 years (inexpensive), 5–12 years (top wineries), 8–25 (or more) years (exceptional wines)

☑ *Araujo* (Eisel Vineyards) • *Arrowood* (Reserve Speciale) • *Caymus* (especially Special Selection) • *Château Souverain* (Library Reserve, Winemaker's Reserve) • *Château Woltner* (particularly Titus Vineyard) • *B. R. Cohn* (Olive Hill) • *Clos du Val* (Reserve) • *Dalla Vale* • *Deblinger* • *Diamond Creek* (Red Rock Terrace, Lake Vineyard, Gravelly Meadow, Volcanic Hill) • *Duckhorn* • *Dunn* • *Eberle* • *Elyse* (Morisoli Vineyard) • *Etude* • *Gary Farrell* (Lad's Vineyard) • *Far Niente* • *Flora Springs* (Reserve) • *Forman* • *Foxen Vineyard* • *Freemark Abbey* (Bosché, Sycamore

Vineyards) • *Geyser Peak* (Reserve) • *Girard* (especially Reserve) • *Gundlach-Bundschu* (Rhinefarm Vineyard) • *The Hess Collection* (especially Reserve) • *Jordan* • *La Jota* • *Kenwood* (Jack London Vineyard) • *Kunde* (Reserve) • *Laurel Glen* • *Long Vineyards* • *Robert Mondavi* (Oakville, Reserve) • *Monticello* (Corley Reserve) • *Mount Eden* (Old Vine Reserve) • *Newton* • *Niebaum-Coppola* • *Joseph Phelps* (Backus, Eisele) • *Pine Ridge* (Andrus Reserve, Stags Leap District) • *Rochioli* (Reserve) • *St. Francis* (Reserve) • *Seavey* • *Sequoia Grove* • *Shafer* (Hillside Select) • *Signorello* (Founder's Reserve) • *Silverado Vineyards* (Limited Reserve) • *Silver Oak* (Alexander Valley) • *Simi* (Reserve) • *Spottswoode* • *Staglin* • *Stag's Leap Wine Cellars* (Fay Vineyard, S.L.V.) • *Stonestreet* • *Swanson* • *Philip Togni* • *Whitehall Lane* (Morisoli Vineyard) • *ZD*

CARIGNAN

Provides a high yield of well-coloured, strong-flavoured, coarse, and tannic wine; useful for blending both in California and in its native south of France, where it is one of the 13 grapes permitted in Châteauneuf-du-Pape. It has a less harsh character in California's coastal districts, where some wineries produce a pure varietal version. In California it is often spelt "Carignane".

⌛ 3–6 years
(up to 10 years in exceptional cases)

✓ *La Jota* (Little J) • *Pellegrini* • *Trentadue*

CHARBONO

This variety is the Corbeau, an almost extinct French variety that is also known as the Charbonneau. It produces a wine with vibrant cherry fruit, tingling ripe acidity, and of a similar style to Barbera. Indeed, Inglenook Vineyards, which was the first winery to make a pure varietal wine from this grape, labelled it Barbera until Dr. Winkler of the UC-Davis nursery identified it properly as Charbono.

⌛ 2–4 years

✓ *Duxoup*

CHARDONNAY

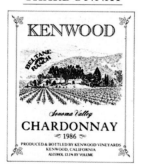

It's still as fashionable as ever, depite the efforts of the ABC (for which read either "Anything But Chardonnay" or "Anything But Cabernet") thugs to sidetrack consumers. I enjoy drinking all good wines, whatever the variety or blend, but I won't be told by self-appointed Thought Police what I should or should not drink, and no matter how prolific Chardonnay becomes, nothing can alter the fact that it is one of the world's greatest grapes and always will be. There have always been great Californian Chardonnays, even when the trend was for massive, blockbusting wines positively reeking

of oak, although too many were simply too fat and too blowzy. These days, "finesse" is very much the buzz-word. The biggest problem currently facing producers of fine Californian Chardonnay is how to convince the American public that "Chardonnay" and oak are not synonymous. It is not such a problem for more sophisticated, well-travelled wine drinkers, but give many Americans a great white Burgundy that has not seen a single stave of new oak and they won't believe it is Chardonnay.

⌛ 2–8 years
(15 or more years in very exceptional cases)

✓ *Arrowood* (Cuvée Michel Berthod) • *Au Bon Climat* • *Belvedere* (particularly Preferred Stock) • *Byron* (Reserve) • *Chalone* • *Clos du Bois* (particularly Calcaire and Flintwood) • *Château Souverain* (Allan Vineyard, Rochioli Vineyard, Sangiacomo Vineyard) • *Clos du Val* (Carneros) • *Conn Valley* • *Crichton Hall* • *Dehlinger* (Montrachet Cuvée) • *Durney* • *Flora Springs* (Barrel Fermented) • *Forman* • *Foxen Vineyard* • *Franciscan Vineyards* (Oakville Estate) • *Freemark Abbey* (Carpy Ranch) • *The Gainey Vineyard* (Limited Selection) • *Girard* (Reserve) • *Hanzell* • *Hartford Court* (Arrendell Vineyard) • *The Hess Collection* (Mount Veeder) • *Kendall-Jackson* (Camelot) • *Kistler* (especially all single-vineyard bottlings) • *Kunde* (Kinneybrook, Wildwood) • *Longoria* • *Long Vineyards* • *Marcassin* • *Martinelli* • *Merryvale* • *Peter Michael* • *Robert Mondavi* (Reserve) • *Mount Eden* (Santa Cruz) • *Newton* • *Niebaum-Coppola* • *Pahlmeyer* • *Joseph Phelps* (Ovation) • *Rabbit Ridge* • *Rochioli* (especially Reserve, Allen Vineyard, South River Vineyard) • *St. Francis* (Reserve) • *Salmon Creek* (Bad Dog Ranch) • *Sanford* (especially Barrel Select Sanford & Benedict) • *Santa Barbara Winery* (Lafond Vineyard) • *Shafer* (especially Red Shoulder Ranch) • *Signorello* (Founder's Reserve) • *Silverado Vineyards* (Limited Reserve) • *Sonoma-Cutrer* (Les Pierres) • *Sonoma-Loeb* (Private Reserve) • *Stag's Leap Wine Cellars* (especially Reserve) • *Steele* (particularly Lolonis Vineyard, Du Pratt Vineyard, Sangiacomo Vineyard) • *Stony Hill* • *Trefethen* (Library Selection) • *Swanson* • *Robert Talbott* (especially Diamond T) • *White Rock* • *Williams-Selyem* (Allen Vineyard) • *ZD*

CHENIN BLANC

This Loire-Valley grape is famous for wines such as the sweet, honey-rich Vouvray and the very dry, searingly flavoured, Savennières. In California it covers over one-fifth of the white-grape vineyards and, although the recent trend to improve the acidity balance has raised the standard of the wines made from this grape, it fares less well than in France. Since I am not a fan of any but the greatest Chenin Blancs, it is hard for me to work up any excitement for the Chenin blanc in California, so I do wonder at all the books that carry the same *spiel* – that Clarksburg is the only area to produce a regionally identifiable Chenin Blanc. Finding wines with any Central Valley AVA is something of a quest. The now defunct R. & J. Cook winery used to be the most prolific producer of wines bearing the Clarksburg appellation, but produced better Petite Sirah than Chenin, although it does not actually claim the appellation on the label, so we have to take

their word for it that they do indeed source some of their Chenin from Clarksburg. It is not exactly special, just fresh and quafable. Hacienda is another much-touted Chenin, but it too fails to mention the AVA. In my opinion the Napa Valley makes the best Chenin. The wines recommended are all dry or off-dry. *See* Botrytized and Late Harvest Wines for sweeter styles.

⌛ 1–4 years

✓ *Alexander Valley Vineyards* • *Chalone* • *Chappellet* • *Foxen Vineyard* (Barrel Fermented) • *Girard* • *Hacienda* • *Husch Vineyards* • *Robert Mondavi* • *Pine Ridge* • *Simi* • *Stearn's Wharf* (La Presta Vineyard)

CINSAULT

Until the Rhône-style wine revolution in California this variety was better known as the Black malvoisie. There is precious little in the state and what there is, is seldom put to good use, although Frick makes a statement with 30-year-old Cinsault vines in Sonoma's Dry Creek.

⌛ 2–5 years

✓ *Frick*

COLOMBARD

Accounting for almost 38 per cent of California's white-grape vineyards, Colombard, also known as French colombard, has always been more than adequate. But its true potential was only realized with the advent of cool fermentation (*see* p.37). A pure varietal Colombard is not a fine-quality wine, but it can be superb value in a totally unpretentious and absolutely delicious way, if it is consumed young and fresh.

⌛ Upon purchase

✓ *Carmenet* • *Parducci*

FORTIFIED STYLES

Forget the Sherry-style, but California produces excellent fortified Muscat and Port-style wines.

⌛ Ready when released (but last well in bottle)

✓ *Ficklin* (NV, Vintage) • *Il Podere dell' Olivos* (Pronto) • *Quady* (especially Electra and Essencia Muscat styles) • *Trentadue* (Merlot Port)

FUMÉ BLANC

A synonym for Sauvignon Blanc in France, much like *blanc de noirs*, Fumé Blanc has developed a New-World meaning of its own, as it is now perceived as a generic name for an oaked Sauvignon Blanc, ranging from a subtle, *barrique*-fermented influence to heavily oak-matured. *See also* Sauvignon Blanc

⌛ 1–3 years

✓ *Benzinger* • *Château St. Jean* (La Petite Étoile) • *Chimney Rock* • *Dry Creek* • *Ferrari-Carano* (especially Reserve) • *Grgich Hills Cellars* • *Kendall-Jackson* • *Robert Mondavi* (Reserve, Tokalon Estate) • *Murphy-Goode* (Reserve, Reserve Il la Deuce) • *Preston* (Cuvée de Fumé) • *Ivan Tamas*

GAMAY

Also called the Napa gamay, this grape is the true Gamay *à jus blanc* of Beaujolais fame (or infamy). It can make easy-drinking, fruity wines in many parts of California, sometimes quite brilliantly. Whereas California Gamay cannot match the best Cru Beaujolais, the average quality of this is considerably higher.

⌛ 1–3 years

✓ *Duxoup* • *J. Lohr* (Wildflower) • *Robert Pecota*

GAMAY BEAUJOLAIS

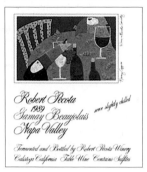

This was identified as a Pinot noir clone many years ago and categorically denounced as bearing no relation to the true Gamay. However, there could still be a connection, as many ampelographers seriously believe that the Gamay itself originated from an ancient clone of the Pinot noir. The name Gamay Beaujolais has been outlawed by BATF since 1993, but you still see it around, although quite why anyone would want to sell Pinot Noir as Gamay is beyond me.

⌐— 1–3 years

✓ *Beringer*

GEWÜRZTRAMINER

Although by no means one of California's commonly encountered varietal wines, Gewürztraminer must be one of its most overrated. The hype surrounding California's Gewürztraminers baffles me – most of them lack not only the varietal definition I expect of any classic grape, but their winemakers will insist on acidifying what is an intrinsically low-acid variety. The only way to extract the true pungency of spice that admirers of this varietal expect is through a pre-fermentation maceration. The spice will not be immediately apparent when bottled, but requires additional ageing for the spicy bottle-aromas to develop. The phenolics picked up from the skins during the pre-fermentation maceration are essential to the balance and length of such low-acid wines, providing a tactile impression that literally sears the spice on to the palate. It also gives such wines surprising longevity. The problem is that virtually every winemaker in California has been brainwashed into avoiding phenolics in white wine as if they were the plague. In case American readers should think I am taking an unreasonably European viewpoint, I quote Robert Parker: "Anyone who has tasted fine French Gewürztraminer must be appalled by what is sold under this name in California". About the only thing Californian Gewürztraminer has in common with its French counterparts is that classic dry renditions are equally rare.

⌐— 1–3 years

✓ *Bouchaine • Lazy Creek • Navarro*

GRENACHE

Although cultivation of this variety has been in decline in recent years, it still accounts for some ten per cent of California's black grapes and, despite being traditionally associated in this state with medium-dry rosé and tawny-port-type dessert wines, some truly delicious, high-quality pure varietals have surfaced.

⌐— 1–3 years

✓ *Bonny Doon* (Clos de Gilroy)
• *Forman* (La Grande Roche)

JOHANNISBERG RIESLING

Also known as White riesling, this grape covers more than five per cent of California's white-grape vineyards. Apart from the odd, sensational, tangy-dry exceptions, most wines are made in a slightly sweet, commercial style, which is invariably washed of any true varietal intensity. They range from being fine and restrained, through vivacious and juicy, to classically petrolly (Renaissance being a benchmark for the latter). *See* Botrytized and Late Harvest Wines for sweeter styles.

⌐— 1–3 years

✓ *Alexander Valley Vineyards*
• *Bonny Doon* (Pacific Rim)
• *Château Montelena* (Potter Valley)
• *Firestone • Greenwood Ridge • Navarro*
• *Fess Parker • Rancho Sisquoc • Renaissance*

MALBEC

Although a few wineries are now making good pure varietals from this grape, it has never really caught on in California, where, if it is not ignored entirely, Malbec is merely regarded as a blending component, much as it is in Bordeaux. Perhaps California's winemakers should look more to the 19th-century Black Wines of Cahors than to Bordeaux when considering this variety. When grown ungrafted or on low-yield rootstock, Malbec can produce excellent deep-coloured red wines with soft, chewy fruit and has demonstrated the capability of developing much individuality and complexity in most warm climes, particularly when grown on gravelly-clay and marly-clay soils.

⌐— 2–5 years

✓ *Arrowood • Benzinger*
• *Clos du Bois* (L'Étranger)

MERITAGE

Concocted from "merit" and "heritage", the term "Meritage" was devised and registered as a trademark for upmarket Bordeaux blends. There are no rules or regulations governing wines that use this trademark, other than that the wineries must be paid-up members of the Meritage Association. It is generally understood that such blends may consist of two or more of the following varieties: Cabernet sauvignon, Cabernet franc, Merlot, Malbec, and Petit verdot for reds; and Sauvignon blanc, Sémillon, and Muscadelle for whites. Certainly not the most inspired of American marketing terms, it has nevertheless been adopted by a wide range of wineries and restaurants, which often list these wines separately. The most outstanding of these wines, plus the many first-class blends that are not marketed as Meritage, are all recommended under Bordeaux-style Blends. *See also* Bordeaux-style Blends (Red), Bordeaux-style Blends (White), p.451.

MERLOT

It has always been obvious that Merlot possessed everything required to make it one of California's most fashionable and sought after varietals, and that is exactly what it became in the early 1990s. Its lush fruit and velvety texture are tailor-made for this sunshine state, although up to 15 per cent Cabernet sauvignon may be blended into supposedly pure varietal in order to give the wines added structure.

⌐— 3–8 years

✓ *Beaucanon • Bellerose • Beringer* (Bancroft Vineyard) • *Château St. Jean • Château Souverain • Cain Cellars • Clos du Val*
• *Clos Pegase • Duckhorn* (Three Palms)
• *Gary Farrell* (Lad's Vineyard)
• *Ferrari-Carano • Franciscan Vineyards* (Oakville Estate) • *Havens • Lewis Cellars* (Oakville Ranch) • *Matanzas Creek • Newton*
• *Pahlmeyer • Pine Ridge* (Carneros)
• *St. Francis* (Reserve) • *Seavey • Shafer*
• *Whitehall Lane* (Summer's Ranch)

MEUNIER

Occasionally used to bolster sparkling-wine *cuvées*, this makes unpretentious, soft, fruity reds, although it is seldom seen as a pure varietal. It is still referred to as Pinot meunier in the US.

⌐— 1–3 years

✓ *Bonny Doon • Domaine Chandon* (in winery restaurant only) • *Etude*

MOURVÈDRE

Sometimes known as Mataro, this is one of the most underrated Rhône varieties, and can produce dark, silky-soft, smooth wines that compare to the Syrah, but are not as rich or dense. In California, Mourvèdre can easily acquire a raspberry-jam flavour, which is fine for inexpensive wines and makes an ideal blending component, although exciting pure varietals are also beginning to emerge.

⌐— 2–5 years

✓ *Bonny Doon* (Old Telegram) • *Cline Cellars* (especially Reserve) • *Edmunds St. John*
• *Jade Mountain • Ridge* (Mataro) • *Sean Thackrey* (Taurus) • *Trentadue* (Old Patch)

MUSCAT BLANC
See Muscat Canelli

MUSCAT CANELLI

Also known as Muscat de Frontignan, Muscat blanc, and Moscato canelli, this grape is surprisingly successful in California, producing some delightfully perfumed, flowery-flavoured wines in off-dry through to very sweet and dessert styles. *See also* Botrytized and Late Harvest Wines for sweeter styles.

⌐— Upon purchase

✓ *Eberle*

ORANGE MUSCAT

Apart from Quady's fortified wine, I know of only one pure Orange Muscat produced in California, Mosby's Moscato di Fior, which is made in a compelling and distinctive dry style.

🍷— 1–3 years

✓ *Mosby* (Moscato di Fior)

PETITE SIRAH

In the first edition I suggested that ignorance was perhaps bliss in the case of Californian Petite sirah, an underrated grape, whose popularity, ever since it was identified as the lowly Durif of France, plummetted ridiculously, in spite of the fact that many wineries were regularly producing fine wines with it. There is now, however, a theory that it may not be the Durif, but the Syrah after all. As ironic as this may be, I am glad to say that even before this new theory started to circulate, the following for Petite Sirah had rapidly increased. It remains, however, California's most underrated varietal.

🍷— 4–8 years

✓ *Christopher Creek* • *Concannon*
• *Field Stone* • *Foppiano* (Reserve) • *Hop Kiln*
• *La Jota* (Howell Mountain) • *Marrietta Cellars* • *Ridge* (York Creek) • *Stag's Leap Wine Cellars* • *Stag's Leap Winery*
• *Sean Thackrey* (Sirius) • *Turley Cellars*

PINOT BLANC

When grown with care and barrel-fermented, it is virtually impossible to tell Pinot Blanc from a Chardonnay, particularly the examples from Napa, Monterey, and Sonoma. There are some excellent, very serious makers of pure varietal Pinot Blancs, but essentially this is one of California's most under-exploited varieties.

🍷— 1–3 years

✓ *Arrowood* (Saralee's Vineyard) • *Benzinger*
• *Byron* • *Chalone* • *Etude* • *Frick* • *Mirassou* (Harvest Reserve) • *Murphy-Goode* (Barrel Fermented) • *Steele* (Santa Barbara)
• *Wild Horse Winery*

PINOT GRIS

Even at its best, California Pinot Gris is not at all the spicy heavyweight of Alsace fame, but more like a superior Pinot Grigio, with riper, purer fruit – indeed, some of these wines are even sold as Pinot Grigio.

🍷— Upon purchase

✓ *Edmunds St. John* • *Elliston* • *Etude* • *Sterling*

PINOT NOIR

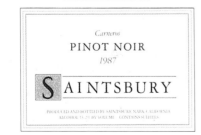

Carneros
PINOT NOIR
1987
SAINTSBURY
PRODUCED AND BOTTLED BY SAINTSBURY, NAPA, CALIFORNIA
ALCOHOL 13.5% BY VOLUME • CONTAINS SULFITES

Beyond all expectations, this Burgundian grape has found a natural home in parts of California, most notably in Sonoma's Russian River Valley, the Carneros area straddling Sonoma and Napa, and the Santa Ynez Valley in Santa Barbara. Santa Barbara does, I think, have the greatest potential of all; equally fine Pinot Noir will be made elsewhere, but the largest number of

Pinot Noir producers will eventually be seen to come from this southerly district. Other areas also show promise such as San Benito, Monterey, and the Arroyo Grande.

🍷— 2–5 years

✓ *Acacia* (Carneros) • *Au Bon Climat*
• *Babcock* • *Calera* • *Carneros Creek* (Signature) • *Chalone* • *Château St. Jean* (Durell Vineyard) • *Conn Valley* (Valhalla Vineyard) • *Dehlinger* (particularly Goldridge Vineyard and new Octagon Vineyard)
• *Etude* • *Gary Farrell* (particularly Howard Allen Vineyard) • *The Gainey Vineyard* (especially Sandford & Benedict) • *Hanzell*
• *Hartford Court* (Arrendell Vineyard)
• *Hartley & Ostini* (The Hitching Post)
• *Kent Rasmussen* (Carneros) • *Kistler* (especially all single-vineyard bottlings)
• *Longoria* • *Marcassin* • *Martinelli* • *Robert Mondavi* (particularly Reserve) • *Morgan* (especially Reserve) • *Rochioli* (especially East Block, Little Hill Block, Three Corner Vineyard, West Block) • *Sanford* (especially Barrel Select Sanford & Benedict)
• *Santa Barbara Winery* (Reserve) • *Steele* (Sangiacomo Vineyard) • *Marimar Torres*
• *Lane Tanner* (Sanford & Benedict Vineyard) • *Williams-Selyem* (particularly Allen Vineyard, Rochioli Vineyard)

RHÔNE-STYLE BLENDED RED

In the late 1980s, when Bonny Doon's Randall Grahm was virtually a Lone Rhône-Ranger, Rhône-style blends developed a cult following. While the whacky Grahm made, and continues to make, exceptionally fine wines, others make equally fine wines in a more earnest, often overly serious fashion. Most red Rhône-style blends will include two or more (usually three) of the following: Carignane, Mourvèdre, Grenache, Petite sirah, Syrah.

🍷— 3–7 years

✓ *Bonny Doon* (Cigare Volant) • *Cline Cellars* (Côtes d'Oakly) • *Edmunds St. John* (Les Côtes Sauvage) • *Jade Mountain* (Côtes du Soleil, Le Provençale) • *Joseph Phelps* (Le Mistral) • *R. H. Phillips* (Alliance) • *Preston* (Faux Castel, Sirah-Syrah) • *Quivira* (Dry Creek Cuvée) • *Qupé* (Los Olivos) • *Rabbit Ridge* (Allure) • *Zaca Mesa* (Cuvée Z)

RHÔNE-STYLE BLENDED WHITE

Not far behind red Rhône-style blends in popularity and catching up fast, these wines usually include two or more of the following: Marsanne, Roussanne, Viognier.

🍷— 1–4 years

✓ *Bonny Doon* (Le Sophiste)
• *Jade Mountain* (Marsanne et Viognier)

SANGIOVESE

Cultivation of this variety has increased over twenty-fold since the late 1980s, and much of this is due to the number of winemakers and grape-growers who have Italian ancestry. Its success will depend on the choice of site, where the vine should struggle, so there is no need to employ labour-intensive methods to reduce yields through green pruning.

🍷— 3–7 years
(15 years or more in exceptional cases)

✓ *Adelaida Cellars* • *Atlas Peak* • *Beringer* (Knights Valley) • *Coturri* (Jessandre Vineyard)
• *Flora Springs* • *Saddleback* • *Staglin* (Stagliano) • *Swanson* • *Trentadue* • *Viansa*

SAUVIGNON BLANC

Also known as the Fumé Blanc, a synonym now adopted for an oaked style that is dealt with separately. Many wines labelled Sauvignon Blanc rather than Fumé Blanc are also oaked, but it would be too confusing to list them in this category, so all recommended wines are listed according to their labels, whether they adhere to that style or not. A straight California Sauvignon Blanc should have a crisp style, with the vibrancy of its varietal fruit picked up by, and highlighted with, abundant ripe acidity. California Sauvignon Blanc has, however, an identity problem, as most are soft and neutral, and some are downright wishy-washy. Even the best Sauvignon Blanc, whether from California, New Zealand, France, or wherever, has upfront appeal that it tires easily in bottle. Some may last a few years, but they seldom improve, unless you are one of those who actually enjoy the bottle-aged aromas of asparagus and canned peas that develop.

JEPSON
1986
MENDOCINO
SAUVIGNON BLANC
GROWN, PRODUCED AND BOTTLED BY JEPSON VINEYARDS LTD.
ALC. 12.5% BY VOLUME • UKIAH, CA • CONTAINS SULFITES

🍷— Upon purchase

✓ *Adler Fels* • *Babcock* (especially 11 Oaks Ranch) • *Byron* (Reserve) • *Cain Cellars* (Musqué) • *Cakebread* • *Caymus* • *Clos du Bois* • *Cronin* • *Duckhorn* • *Flora Springs* (Soliloquy) • *The Gainey Vineyard* (Limited Selection) • *Hidden Cellars* • *Husch Vineyards*
• *Kendall-Jackson* (Grand Reserve) • *Kunde* (Magnolia Lane) • *Matanzas Creek* • *Peter Michael* (L'Après-Midi) • *Ojai* • *Parducci*
• *Robert Pecota* • *Robert Pepi* • *Quivira*
• *Rancho Sisquoc* • *Renaissance* • *Rochioli* (Reserve) • *Sanford* • *Santa Barbara Winery* (Reserve Musqué) • *Signorello* (Barrel Fermented) • *Spottswoode* • *Stonestreet* (Alexander Mountain) • *Strong* (Charlotte's Home Vineyard) • *Swanson* • *Trefethen* (White Riesling)

SÉMILLON

Also known as the Chevrier, this grape has long been favoured by California's winemakers, but not, it seems, by the consumer. Excellent oak-fermented dry wines can be made and are just starting to be acclaimed as they deserve. *See also* Botrytized and Late Harvest styles.

🍷— 1–5 years

✓ *Kalin* • *Kendall-Jackson* (Vintner's Reserve)
• *Signorello* (Barrel Fermented)
• *Vita Nova* (Reservatum)

SYLVANER

In California this classic Franconian and Alsace variety is also known as the Franken riesling, Monterey riesling, or the Sonoma riesling. The wines bear no resemblance to true Riesling, and tend to be off-dry and rather neutral in flavour, except from Rancho Sisquoc in Santa Barbara, where the vines are exceptionally old and the low-yield grapes deeply flavoured.

🍷— Upon purchase

✓ *Rancho Sisquoc*

SYMPHONY

Plantations of this *Muscat d'Alexandrie* x *Grenache gris* cross rapidly increased in the mid-1990s. The wine it makes is usually off-dry with a distinctly flowery-grapey Muscat aroma.

SYRAH

This classic Rhône grape illustrates how quickly things move in California. In the first edition I mentioned how surprised I was that the Syrah was not more widely planted. Since then it has increased from 45 hectares (110 acres) to 539 hectares (1,331 acres) and this is likely to double before the year 2000. There is a sumptuousness about Californian Syrah that makes it a totally different wine from either French Syrah or Australian Shiraz, although when full and ripe all three versions share the silky-*cassis* fruit and have the potential to develop a fine smoky-spicy complexity. From the top Syrahs listed below, it is obvious that this grape can be successfully grown in several California areas, but the warmer areas of Santa Barbara do seem to stand out.

⌁ 3–10 years

✓ *Araujo* (Eisel Vineyards) • *Arrowood* (Saralee's Vineyard) • *Beringer* • *Bonny Doon* • *Cambria* (Tepusquet Vineyard) • *Christopher Creek* • *Dehlinger* • *Duxoup* • *Edmunds St. John* (especially Durell Vineyard) • *Ferrari-Carano* • *Havens* • *Ironstone* (Shiraz) • *Jade Mountain* • *Kendall-Jackson* (Durell Vineyard) • *Kunde* • *Joseph Phelps* (Vin de Mistral) • *Ojai* • *Fess Parker* • *Qupé* • *Swanson* • *Sean Thackrey* (Orion) • *Zaca Mesa* (Zaca Vineyard)

TOCAI FRIULANO

This is none other than the Sauvignonasse, an insipid variety that virtually all Chilean wineries have at one time or other used in wines that are actually sold as Sauvignon Blanc.

✓ *Robert Mondavi* • *Wild Horse Winery*

VIOGNIER

This great Rhône white-wine grape was non-existent in California until 1985, when the first vines were planted by Joseph Phelps. Therefore, in 1988 when the first edition of this book was published, they were not even bearing fruit. At that time, just 4.5 hectares (11 acres) of vines existed and a further 5.7 hectares (14 acres) had been planted. Now there are almost 200 hectares (500 acres) and the number of vines are doubling every 15 months. While the vine seems to thrive in California, the wines seldom capture its elusive character. The same could be said about Château Grillet and Condrieu, of course, and as that has been overcome on one side of the Atlantic through the determination of the winemaker, there is no reason why more Californian winemakers cannot get it right. What does bother me, however, is that the notoriously difficult Viognier should thrive so well in the golden state: not only is there no problem with flowered vines failing to fruit, but the yield is exceptionally high even by the greediest French grower's standard. This leads me to suspect the authenticity of the vines being sold as Viognier in California or, if indeed they are genuine, to wonder what else might have been eradicated during the eight years it took UC-Davis to remove the virus from its Viognier bud stock before release. Perhaps the exquisiteness that makes the best Viognier wines great can be achieved only through debilitated vines?

⌁ Upon purchase

✓ *Arrowood* (Saralee's Vineyard) • *Beringer* (especially Hudson Ranch) • *Calera* • *Edmunds St. John* • *Kendall-Jackson* (Grand Reserve) • *Kunde* • *La Jota* • *Ojai* (Roll Ranch) • *Joseph Phelps*

ZINFANDEL

This was once thought to be America's only indigenous *Vitis vinifera* grape, but was later positively identified as the Primitivo grape of southern Italy by Isozyme "finger printing", a method of recording the unique pattern created by the molecular structure of enzymes found within specific varieties. There may yet be a twist to the story, for the earliest records of Primitivo in Italy date from the late 19th century and yet the Zinfandel is documented in the nursery catalogue of William Prince of Long Island, US, in 1830. Furthermore, Italian growers have often referred to their Primitivo as a foreign variety.

Depending on the way it is vinified, Zinfandel produces many different styles of wine, from rich and dark to light and fruity, or *nouveau* style, from dry to sweet, white to rosé, dessert wine or sparkling. The reason for such a variation in styles is that it is virtually impossible to harvest Zinfandel when all the grapes have an even ripeness. When most of the bunch achieves perfect ripeness, some grapes are green, but if the grower waits for these to ripen, the shoulder clusters quickly raisin. There are several ways to overcome this, but they are all labour-intensive, seemingly wasteful, and inevitably costly, which is why great Zinfandel is never cheap. Great Zinfandel is as rich and deep-coloured as only California could produce, with ripe, peppery-spicy fruit, liquorice intensity, and a chocolate-herb complexity. When young, such wines are chewy and have classic berry-fruit flavours, which can swing towards black-cherry or simply have a gluggy-jamminess. It is the only varietal that positively demands the coconutty aromas of American oak, and it is often improved when blended with Petite sirah for increased backbone. This is a wine that requires a certain amount of bottle-ageing to bring out the dried-fruit spiciness. Zinfandel is not one of California's longest-lived wines, but without sufficient time in bottle, the wine will merely have a richness of oak and berry fruits, and lack complexity.

⌁ 2–5 years (good but inexpensive wines), 5–15 years (expensive, more serious styles)

✓ *Adelaida Cellars* • *Cakebread* (Howell Mountain) • *Cline Cellars* (especially Big Break, Bridgehead Vineyard, and Reserve) • *Clos du Val* (Stags Leap District) • *De Loach* (particularly O.F.S.) • *Dry Creek*

Vineyard (Ol Vines) • *Eberle* • *Elyse* (Howell Mountain) • *Edmeades* (particularly Zeni Vineyard) • *Edmunds St. John* • *Gary Farrell* • *Franciscan Vineyards* (Oakville Estate) • *Ferrari-Carano* • *Fritz Cellars* (80 Year Old Vines) • *Green and Red* (Mill Vineyard) • *Gundlach-Bundschu* (Rhinefarm Vineyard) • *Hartford Court* (Hartford Vineyard) • *Hartley & Ostini* (The Hitching Post) • *Heitz* • *Hidden Cellars* (especially Pacini Vineyard) • *Hop Kiln* (Primitivo) • *Kendall-Jackson* (Ciapusci Vineyard, Dupratt Vineyard, Proprietor's Grand Reserve) • *Kunde* (Century Vines) • *Lava Cap* • *Martinelli* • *Robert Mondavi* • *Mosby* (Primitivo) • *Murphy-Goode* • *Quivira* • *Rafanelli* • *Ravenswood* (particularly Old Hill Vineyard) • *Nalle* • *Rabbit Ridge* • *Ridge* (Dusi Ranch, Lytton Springs, Pagain Ranch, Paso Robles) • *Rosenblum* • *St. Francis* (Old Vines) • *Steele* (Catfish Vineyard) • *Storybook Mountain* (Eastern Exposure) • *Joseph Swan* (Stellwagen Vineyard, Zeigler Vineyard) • *Whaler* (Flagship) • *Williams-Selyem* (Leo Martinelli Vineyard)

ROSÉ *or* BLANC DE NOIRS

One of the most overlooked wine styles in California, its well-made, unpretentious rosés can be delicious. All the wines recommended below are dry or off-dry.

⌁ Upon purchase

✓ *Bonny Doon* (Pinot Meunier, Vin Gris de Cigare) • *Heitz* (Grignolino) • *Joseph Phelps* (Vin du Mistral Grenache Rosé) • *Sanford* (Pinot Noir Vin Gris) • *Simi* (Rosé of Cabernet Sauvignon)

OTHER CLASSIC RED-WINE BLENDS

The term "classic" is used here to define a wine that has been blended up to a quality, rather than down to a price. Bordeaux- and Rhône-style blends are dealt with separately, thus the wines recommended here have all been blended from various other grape variety permutations, although they all share some distinction and personality, whether expensive or not. It could well be that a future edition will have to segregate Italian-style blends, particularly California versions of super-Tuscan blends, but they are not, for the moment, made in sufficient numbers to justify their own entry.

✓ *Atlas Peak Consenso* (Cabernet-Sangiovese) • *Elyse Nero Misto* (Petite Sirah-Zinfandel) • *Ferrari-Carano* (Siena) • *Jade Mountain* • *Les Jumeaux* (Cabernet-Mourvèdre) • *Marietta Cellars Old Vine Red Lot 18* (Petite Sirah-Cabernet-Zinfandel-Carignane) • *Robert Pepi Due Baci* (Cabernet-Sangiovese) • *R. H. Phillips* (Night Harvest Cuvée Rouge) • *Ridge Vineyards Geyserville* (Zinfandel-Carignane-Petite Sirah) • *Shafer Firebreak* (Sangiovese-Cabernet) • *Viansa Thalia* (Cabernet-Sangiovese)

OTHER CLASSIC WHITE-WINE BLENDS

As above, "classic" defines a wine blended up to a quality, rather than down to a price.

⌁ 1–3 years

✓ *Benzinger White Burgundy Imagery Series* (Chardonnay-Pinot Blanc-Meunier) • *Caymus Conundrum* (Chardonnay-Muscat-Sémillon-Sauvignon-Viognier) • *Geyser Peak Semchard* (Sémillon-Chardonnay)

MENDOCINO COUNTY

The best vineyards here are located on the fork of the Navarro and Russian rivers in the south of Mendocino, a district that has become a buzz-word for top-quality Californian sparkling wine since the emergence of Roederer Estate. Such is the climatic variation here that some excellent Zinfandel is made, and aromatic varieties may also do very well.

IN THE EARLY 1980S, Champagne Louis Roederer sunk some 15 million dollars into a 200-hectare (500-acre) vineyard and winery in the Anderson Valley, where the climate is considerably cooler than that of surrounding areas. A non-vintage wine in the *champenois* tradition, the first, 1986-based release was nothing special and has not improved over the years, yet the 1987-based release was the best sparkling wine produced anywhere in the world outside of Champagne itself, a quality that has been maintained ever since. The diversity of *terroir* within the sparkling-wine growing areas of Mendocino provides a fascinating contrast of styles, for Scharffenberger, just round the corner from Roederer, could hardly make a wine more different to Roederer. Whereas Roederer is rich, well-structured, and potentially complex in a style that leans decidedly towards Champagne, Scharffenberger is all lightness and elegance with a purity of fruit that gains in finesse every year. There are lots of reasons for this over and above that of *terroir*, including the good old joker in the pack – man – but it does suggest that we are witnessing the very earliest stages of development in California's sparkling-wine industry. In 20 years time there is every chance that the state's best sparkling-wine areas will be known, planted, and exploited to the extent that each will have many producers making contrasting styles from neighbouring vineyards.

THE GROWTH OF MENDOCINO'S WINE INDUSTRY

Because parts of Mendocino are too hot for classic wine production, there has been a tendency in the past to plant highly productive vines for jug-wine blends. However, the county has a complex climate, and there are some areas where coastal influences dominate and cooler Region I and II climates (*see* p.448) prevail. This has been recognized by the substantial amount of premium-quality varietals that were planted in the late 1970s, and by the rise in the number of wineries in the area, from 16 in 1981 to 29 in 1985 and 41 in 1995.

FACTORS AFFECTING TASTE AND QUALITY

LOCATION
160 km (100 miles) northwest of San Francisco, Mendocino is the most northerly of the major viticultural coastal counties.

CLIMATE
The mountain ridges surrounding the Upper Russian and Navarro rivers climb as high as 1,070 m (3,500 ft) and form a natural boundary that creates the reputed transitional climate of Mendocino. This climate is unusual in that either coastal or inland influences can dominate for long or short periods, although it generally has relatively warm winters and cool summers. This provides for a growing season with many warm, dry days and cool nights. The Ukiah Valley has the shortest, warmest growing season north of San Francisco.

ASPECT
Mainly flat ground at the bottom of valleys or gentle, lower slopes at a height of between 76 and 445 m (250–1,460 ft), with some rising to 490 m (1,600 ft). The vines generally face east, though just south of Ukiah they face west.

SOIL
Deep, diverse alluvial soils in the flat riverside vineyards, gravelly-loam in parts of the Russian River Valley, and a thin scree on the surrounding slopes.

VITICULTURE AND VINIFICATION
The average growing season is 268 days, compared to 308 in Sonoma (bud-break is 10 days earlier here), and 223 days in Lake County.

PRIMARY GRAPE VARIETIES
Cabernet sauvignon, Carignan, Chardonnay, Chenin blanc, Colombard, Sauvignon blanc, Zinfandel

SECONDARY GRAPE VARIETIES
Barbera, Burger, Cabernet franc, Charbono, Early Burgundy, Flora, Folle blanche, Gamay, Gamay Beaujolais, Gewürztraminer, Grenache, Grey riesling, Green Hungarian, Malvasia bianca, Merlot, Muscat blanc, Palomino, Petite sirah, Pinot blanc, Pinot noir, Ruby cabernet, Sauvignon vert, Sémillon, Sylvaner, Syrah, White riesling

VINEYARD LANDSCAPE
These typically flat Mendocino vineyards belong to Parducci Wine Cellars – a large firm producing a wide range of good-value wines.

MENDOCINO, see also p.448
This area's northerly location does not necessarily mean harsher microclimates. Inland regions are protected by the surrounding mountains, although the Anderson Valley is cooler.

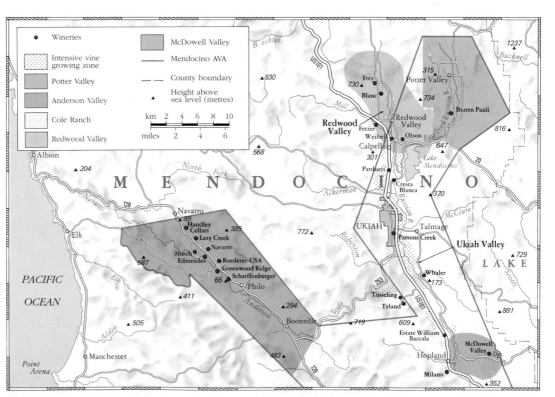

THE APPELLATIONS OF
MENDOCINO COUNTY

ANDERSON VALLEY AVA

This area consists of some 23,300 hectares (57,600 acres), a mere 240 hectares (600 acres) of which have been planted with vines. The valley's coastal-influenced microclimate is cooler than the "transitional" climate that prevails in the rest of Mendocino. The valley's soil is made up of more than 20 alluvial soils, which provides the diversity required for wineries such as Roederer Estate and Scharffenberger to produce a variety of base wines, the necessary building blocks of any fine-quality sparkling wine. The Anderson Valley should also be suitable for aromatic varieties such as Gewürztraminer and Pinot gris.

COLE RANCH AVA

Situated in a small, narrow valley, this appellation consists of a mere 25 hectares (62 acres) of Cabernet sauvignon, Chardonnay, and Johannisberg riesling vineyards, all owned by

the Cole family. The vines grow on soils ranging from deep, gravelly-clay-loam to shallow, gravelly-silty clay.

MCDOWELL VALLEY AVA

The McDowell Valley enjoys the natural protection of the mountains that encircle it. All the vineyards are restricted to the gravelly-loam soils found at approximately 300 metres (1,000 feet), the surrounding soils being unsuitable for vines. There is a microclimate here that warms up when other Mendocino areas are experiencing spring frosts. It is, however, slightly cooler during the growing season.

MENDOCINO AVA

This appellation may be used only for wines produced from grapes that are grown in the southernmost third of the county. It encompasses Mendocino's four other, smaller approved viticultural areas plus surrounding vineyards.

MENDOCINO COUNTY AO

This appellation, which is not an AVA, covers the wines from anywhere within the entire county of Mendocino.

POTTER VALLEY AVA

This appellation consists of 11,130 hectares (27,500 acres) situated northwest of Clear Lake, some 4,450 hectares (11,000 acres) of which are under vine. Vines grow on the valley floor and are protected by the surrounding hills.

REDWOOD VALLEY AVA

This area is where the first Mendocino vines were planted. It has been known as Redwood valley since it was settled in the mid-1850s and covers 90 square kilometres (35 square miles), with some 930 hectares (2,300 acres) of area under vine already in existence. The grapes ripen later than in the hotter and drier Ukiah area, providing higher acidity, colour, and tannin.

THE WINE PRODUCERS OF
MENDOCINO COUNTY

EDMEADES VINEYARDS
Philo
★

This small winery produces good-quality varietal wines. Zinfandel really stands out.

✓ *Zinfandel* (particularly Zeni Vineyard)

FETZER VINEYARDS
Redwood Valley
★ Ⓥ

Fetzer is owned by the Kentucky distilling group Brown-Forman (Jack Daniels, Southern Comfort *et al*) and has a reputation for exceptional value-for-money wines. Barrel-Select Pinot Noir can sometimes be delicious, with succulent strawberry fruit (as in the 1993, for example), but is not always consistent.

✓ *Chardonnay* (Sundial)
• *Petite Sirah* (Special Reserve)
• *Zinfandel*

GREENWOOD RIDGE VINEYARDS
Philo

Although these vineyards were planted in 1972, Greenwood Ridge did not begin to sell its own estate-bottled wines until 1980. Allan Green first made his name with Riesling, which is still his best wine, but now buys in grapes, offers a range of varietals, and is building a reputation for Sonoma Zinfandel in particular.

✓ *White Riesling*

HANDLEY
Philo
★

An excellent, underrated *méthode champenoise* specialist, Handley produces soft-lemony Vintage Blanc

de Blancs, a crisp Vintage Brut with creamy-vanilla richness, and a pale, exotic Vintage Rosé

✓ *Vintage Blanc de Blancs*
• *Vintage Brut* • *Vintage Rosé*

HIDDEN CELLARS
Ukiah
★

This is a cooperative venture on the oldest ranch in the Ukiah Valley between professional winemakers and a handful of partner-growers.

✓ *Alchemy* (white Bordeaux style) • *Sauvignon Blanc*
• *Zinfandel* (especially Pacini Vineyard)

HUSCH VINEYARDS
Philo
★ Ⓥ

Founded by Tony Husch, this winery was sold in 1979 to Hugo Oswald, the current owner and winemaker, who also has large vineyard holdings in the Anderson and Ukiah Valleys, from which his unpretentious white-wine varietals always stand out.

✓ *Chenin Blanc*
• *Sauvignon Blanc*

LAZY CREEK VINEYARD
Philo
★

The Gewürztraminer produced at this vineyard is considered to be one of California's finest and is a favourite wine of Michel Salgues at nearby Roederer Estate. It is good, and drier than most, but lacks phenolic spice and obviously has the potential to be much better.

✓ *Gewürztraminer* • *Pinot Noir*

NAVARRO VINEYARDS
Philo
★

These vineyards produce some of California's best Gewürztraminer, although it could be better. Navarro also makes a very good Pinot Noir for a white-wine specialist.

✓ *Gewürztraminer* • *Late Harvest Gewürztraminer* • *Pinot Noir*
• *Sauvignon Blanc*

PARDUCCI WINE CELLARS
Ukiah
★ Ⓥ

Parducci is a large winery, with over 142 hectares (351 acres), which was founded in Sonoma in 1918, and moved to Ukiah in 1931, where a new winery was built in preparation for the end of Prohibition. The wines are clean and fruity, and possess a good depth of flavour for their price.

✓ *French Colombard* • *Sauvignon Blanc* • *Petite Sirah* • *Zinfandel*

ROEDERER ESTATE
Philo
★★★

Owned by Louis Roederer, the second release (based on 1987) was the first sparkling wine made outside of Champagne that could be compared not simply to an average Champagne but to a good quality Champagne – and winemaker Michel Salgues has maintained this high standard ever since. The style is most definitely more Champagne than California, but if there is any criticism, it is that the wines are sometimes released without sufficient post-disgorgement ageing. This seems to have been overcome in the UK (where the same wine is sold as Quartet), although this could

simply be due to the importers giving it landed-age, but in the US Roederer Estate can be so young it tastes green. I can understand the problem, as the distribution network in America is notoriously complex and sluggish, but this is possibly the only Californian sparkling wine that positively needs ageing: one year after disgorgement to make it drinkable, two years to begin to see the class and quality, and three years to reveal its creamy-biscuity potential in full glory. By contrast, most Californian sparkling wines not only do not improve with extra bottle-age, but actually collapse a year or two after disgorgement.

✓ *NV Brut* • *NV Rosé* • *L'Ermitage*

SCHARFFENBERGER CELLARS
Ukiah
★★

Formerly owned by Pommery, but transferred to Veuve Clicquot since both Champagne houses became part of LVMH, this firm is thus technically a sister company of Domaine Chandon. The wines made by Scharffenberger Cellars have gained tremendously in elegance and finesse since the early 1990s, particularly the Blanc de Blancs. Scharffenberger NV improves dramatically if kept 9 to 12 months.

✓ *Blanc de Blancs* • *NV*

WHALER VINEYARDS
Ukiah
Ⓠ

Whaler Vineyards is a small, fine-quality winery, which specializes in dark, spicy Zinfandel.

✓ *Zinfandel* (Flagship)

SONOMA COUNTY

Six fertile valleys combine to make Sonoma county California's most prolific wine-producing area, with an output comprising equal quantities of red and white wine, and a reputation for quality now fast-approaching that of Napa County.

BECAUSE OF THE VOLUME of its production, Sonoma County was classed as little more than a source of blending wine until the late 1960s. It produced better-quality blending wine than the Central Valley, admittedly, but that wine was still nothing more than pep-up fodder for the bulk-produced anonymous generics. Then, in 1969, Russell Green, a former oil mogul and owner of a fast-growing vineyard in the Alexander Valley, purchased Simi, a once-famous winery founded in 1876, but at the time in decline. Green had ambitious plans for Simi, many of which he was successful in carrying out, but soaring costs forced him to sell up in 1973. During those four brief years, however, he managed to restore the pre-Prohibition reputation of the old winery by creating a new genre of high-quality varietal Sonoma wines. With this achievement, he made other winemakers in the district ambitious to improve the quality of their own wines.

Not only did the established Sonoma wineries re-evaluate what they were doing, resulting in a very pleasing plethora of interesting, vinous delights, but Green's activity also attracted new blood to the area. By 1985 there was a remarkable total of 93 wineries, and over the last ten years the number has increased to a staggering 160.

FACTORS AFFECTING TASTE AND QUALITY

LOCATION
North of San Francisco, between Napa and the Pacific.

CLIMATE
Extremes of climate range from warm (Region III, *see* p.448) in the north of the county to cool (Region I, *see* p.448) in the south, mainly due to ocean breezes. Fog is prevalent around Petaluma.

ASPECT
Sonoma Valley creek drains into the San Francisco Bay, and the Russian River flows directly into the Pacific. The vines grow at an altitude of approximately 120 m (400 ft) on flatland, or on the gentle lower slopes. Steeper slopes are being cultivated in the Sonoma Valley.

SOIL
The soil situation varies greatly, from low-fertile loams in the Sonoma Valley and Santa Rosa areas, to highly fertile alluvial soils in the Russian River Valley, with limestone at Cazadera, a gravelly soil in Dry Creek, and vent-based volcanic soils within the fall-out vicinity of Mount St. Helena.

VITICULTURE AND VINIFICATION
Bulk winemaking is still important in the Russian River Valley, but boutique wineries specializing in premium varietals are taking over.

PRIMARY GRAPE VARIETIES
Cabernet sauvignon, Chardonnay, Chenin blanc, Colombard, Gewürztraminer, Merlot, Petite sirah, Pinot noir, Pinot blanc, Sauvignon blanc, White riesling, Zinfandel

SECONDARY GRAPE VARIETIES
Aleatico, Alicante bouschet, Barbera, Cabernet franc, Carignan, Chasselas doré, Folle blanche, Gamay, Gamay Beaujolais, Grenache, Malbec, Malvasia, Muscat blanc, Palomino, Pinot St. George, Ruby cabernet, Sauvignon vert, Sémillon, Sylvaner, Syrah

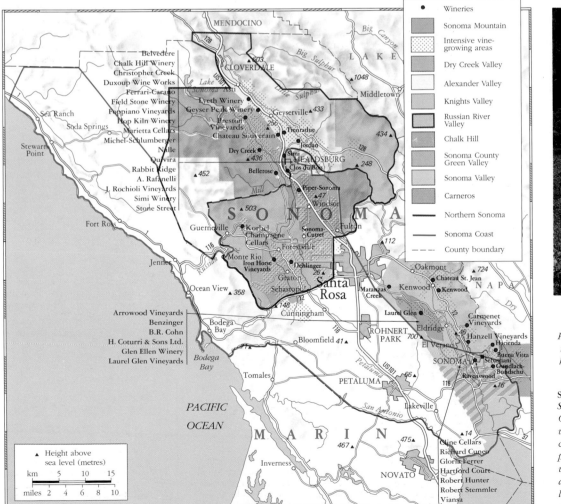

DRY CREEK VALLEY
Sonoma's Dry Creek lies close to the Russian River, of which Dry Creek is a tributary. Moist and fertile, the valley has a gravelly soil unique to the area, enabling it to claim AVA status.

SONOMA COUNTY
See also p. 448
One of California's most important wine regions, Sonoma has a varied climate with different soils, which produce a broad spectrum of wines. It is perhaps aptly named, as Sonoma is derived from the local Wintun Native American word for "nose".

THE APPELLATIONS OF
SONOMA COUNTY

ALEXANDER VALLEY AVA

Located in the northeast of the county, this appellation extends from the banks of the Russian River into the foothills of the Mayacamas Mountains. In 1986 its boundaries were extended so that it overlapped the Russian River AVA, and were further extended in 1990 to incorporate Sir Peter Michael's Gauer Ranch and Ellis Alden's Chestnut Springs vineyards in the foothills east of Geyserville. Cabernet sauvignon and Merlot are ideally suited to this area, where very fine Nebbiolo, Sangiovese, and Chardonnay can also be produced.

CHALK HILL AVA

This appellation covers 85 square kilometres (33 square miles) and encompasses 650 hectares (1,600 acres) of vineyards rising in altitude from 60 to 400 metres (200 to 1,300 feet). There is no chalk here; the soil's whiteness is in fact derived from volcanic ash with a high quartzite content. Emitted by Mount St. Helena over many centuries, the ash has mixed with local sandy and silty loams to provide a deep soil that is not particularly fertile. This area is protected by a thermal belt that promotes a September harvest, compared to October in surrounding areas.

DRY CREEK VALLEY AVA

This appellation faces that of the Alexander Valley across the Russian River. Its climate is generally wetter and warmer than surrounding areas, with a longer growing season than the Russian River appellation to the south, and varietal suitability is very flexible, stretching from Sauvignon blanc to Zinfandel.

KNIGHTS VALLEY AVA

Knight's valley covers an area of approximately 140 square kilometres (55 square miles) containing 400 hectares (1,000 acres) of vineyards. The vines grow on rocky and gravelly soil of low fertility at altitudes that are generally higher than those in the adjacent AVAs, making it ideal Cabernet country.

LOS CARNEROS AVA

The Los Carneros, or simply Carneros, appellation covers an area of low, rolling hills that straddle the counties of Sonoma and Napa. This was originally sheep country, but the cool sea breezes that come off San Pablo Bay to the south provide an excellent fine-wine growing climate, especially for Chardonnay, Pinot noir, and sparkling wine.

NORTHERN SONOMA AVA

The large appellation of Northern Sonoma completely encapsulates six other AVAs, those of Alexander Valley, Chalk Hill, Dry Creek Valley, Knights Valley, Russian River Valley, and Sonoma County Green Valley, and is separated from the Sonoma Valley appellation to the south by the city of Santa Rosa.

RUSSIAN RIVER VALLEY AVA

The name Russian River began appearing on wine labels as recently as 1970, although its vineyards date from the 19th century. The early morning coastal fog provides a cooler growing season than that of neighbouring areas, making the Russian River Valley well suited to Pinot noir – it produces some of California's finest.

SONOMA COAST AVA

An appellation covering 1,940 square kilometres (750 square miles), Sonoma Coast AVA is made up of the area directly inland from the length of Sonoma's Pacific coastline – the AVA's western boundary. It is significantly cooler than other areas owing to the persistent fog that envelops the Coast Ranges, the mountains that are within sight of the Pacific Ocean.

SONOMA COUNTY GREEN VALLEY AVA

Originally it was proposed that this area within the Russian River Valley AVA be called, simply, Green Valley, but to avoid confusion with Solano County's Green Valley appellation, it was decided to add "Sonoma County". The climate here is one of the coolest in the Russian River Valley and the soil is mostly fine sandy loam and well-suited to sparkling wine.

SONOMA MOUNTAIN AVA

This tiny appellation is within the Sonoma Valley AVA. Sonoma Mountain has a thermal belt phenomenon that drains cold air and fog from its steep terrain to the slopes below, creating a climate characterized by more moderate temperatures than the surrounding areas.

SONOMA VALLEY AVA

The first grapes were planted here in 1825 by the Mission San Francisco de Sonoma. Rainfall is lower than elsewhere in the county and fog rarely penetrates the Sonoma Mountains. It is red wine country; particularly for Cabernet sauvignon and Zinfandel.

THE WINE PRODUCERS OF
SONOMA COUNTY

ADLER FELS WINERY

Santa Rosa

Owner David Coleman was bitten by the wine bug when designing the labels for Château St. Jean. The vineyard overlooks the Valley of the Moon from a perch known locally as the Eagle's Nest.

✓ *Chardonnay* (Coleman Reserve) • *Sauvignon Blanc*

ARROWOOD VINEYARDS

Glen Ellen
★ ✓

Ex-Château St. Jean winemaker Richard Arrowood makes very stylish wines and the quality gets better each year, with the second label (Domaine de Grand Archer) representing exceptional value.

✓ *Cabernet Sauvignon* (Reserve Speciale) • *Chardonnay* (Cuvée Michel Berthod • *Malbec* • *Merlot* • *Pinot Blanc* (Saralee's Vineyard) • *Syrah* (Saralee's Vineyard) • *Viognier* (Saralee's Vineyard) • *White Riesling* (Preston Ranch Late Harvest)

BELLEROSE VINEYARD

Healdsburg

Rich, characterful wines from organic Dry Creek Valley vineyards.

✓ *Cuvée Bellerose* (red Bordeaux style) • *Merlot*

BELVEDERE

Healdsburg

Large vineyards enable owner Bill Hambrecht to make a wide range of wines, but his best and by far the most consistent is Chardonnay.

✓ *Chardonnay* (particularly Preferred Stock)

BENZINGER

Glen Ellen
★ ✓ ✓

Since selling its Glen Ellen and MG Vallejo brands to Heublein, Benzinger has managed to raise its image from penny-pinching to penny-saving, putting the focus on value for money.

✓ *Fumé Blanc* • *Imagery Series* (Malbec, Viognier, White Burgundy) • *Pinot Blanc*

BRYANT FAMILY VINEYARD

Napa
❷

This relatively new boutique winery is reputedly turning out masterly Cabernet Sauvignon.

BUENA VISTA WINERY

Sonoma
☆

Haraszthy's original winery (*see* p.447), but now German-owned, Buena Vista always made good wine, but never anything outstanding until the early 1990s.

✓ *Cabernet Sauvignon* (Private Reserve) • *Chardonnay* • *L'Année* (red Bordeaux style)

CARMENET VINEYARD

Sonoma
★

Owned by Chalone Vineyards of Monterey, Carmenet offers an excellent range of wines, although it is a pity that its Dynamite Cabernet-based wine is not as explosive on the palate as it sounds.

✓ *Chardonnay* (Sangiacomo Vineyard) • *Colombard* (Old Vines) • *Sonoma Estate Red* (Bordeaux style)

CHALK HILL WINERY

Healdsburg
★

This excellent operation was known as Donna Maria Vineyards when the owner only grew and sold grapes, but became Chalk Hill Winery when it first began to make and sell wines in 1981.

✓ *Cabernet Sauvignon* • *Chardonnay* (Reserve) • *Pinot Blanc* (especially Reserve)

CHATEAU ST. JEAN

Kenwood
★

Prior to former Japanese owners, Suntory, selling this prestigious winery to Beringer, the style of some of its wines swung from overt richness to elegance. The quality remains, but some American critics are less appreciative of the change.

✓ *Cabernet Sauvignon* (Alexander Valley Reserve, Belle Terre Vineyard) • *Chardonnay* (Robert Young Vineyard) • *Cinq Cépages* (red Bordeaux style) • *Fumé Blanc* (La Petite Étoile) • *Johannisberg Riesling* (Special Late-Harvest) • *Merlot* (Reserve) • *Pinot Noir* (Durell Vineyard)

CHÂTEAU SOUVERAIN
Geyserville
★☆ⓥ

This chateau has always produced a large amount of inexpensive, but good-value wines, although, until recently, they were rarely exciting. It is now firing on all cylinders, particularly with Chardonnay.

✓ *Cabernet Sauvignon* (Library Reserve, Winemakers Reserve) • *Chardonnay* (Allan Vineyard, Rochioli Vineyard, Sangiacomo Vineyard) • *Merlot*

CHÂTEAU WOLTNER
Angwin

What is it about the *bordelais* that when they come to California, they must make Chardonnay? The style is definitely Burgundian, looking more to structure than to weight of fruit, with a floral finesse on the nose and a certain mineral-like complexity.

✓ *Chardonnay* (particularly Titus Vineyard)

CHRISTOPHER CREEK
Healdsburg
★★☆

Formerly known as the Sotoyme Winery, Christopher Creek was snapped up by Englishman John Mitchell, who makes a wonderfully deep, rich, smoky Petite Sirah and, even better, a silky, stylish Syrah.

✓ *Petite Sirah* • *Syrah*

CLINE CELLARS
Sonoma
★★☆

These excellent Rhône-style wines range from the jammy Côtes d'Oakly to the serious, oaky Mourvèdre, but it is the superb range of full-throttle, all-American Zinfandel wines that Cline is truly famous for.

✓ *Côtes d'Oakly* (red Rhône style) • *Mourvèdre* • *Zinfandel* (especially Big Break, Bridgehead Vineyard, and Reserve)

CLOS DU BOIS
Healdsburg
★★☆

This winery has been under British ownership (Allied-Hiram Walker) since 1988 and, with a skilful new winemaker, Margaret Davenport, since 1990, Clos du Bois continues to make fleshy, well-textured, medal-winning wines from its massive 405 hectares (1,000 acres) of vineyards.

✓ *Cabernet Sauvignon* • *Chardonnay* (particularly Calcaire and Flintwood) • *Malbec* (L'Étranger) • *Marlstone* (red Bordeaux style) • *Sauvignon Blanc*

B. R. COHN
Glen Ellen
★☆ⓥ

Sometimes you have to spit the splinters out of these wines, but you cannot deny the quality and have to admire the enthusiasm.

✓ *Cabernet Sauvignon* (Olive Hill) • *Chardonnay* • *Merlot* (Silver Label)

H. COTURRI & SONS LTD
Glen Ellen
★★ⓥ

A wide range of sometimes excellent varietals, but as is often the case with organic winemaking, the quality ranges between rustic and brilliant. If they are drunk on release, the best examples of the following can be mind blowing.

✓ *Alicante Bouschet* (Ubaldi Vineyard) • *Cabernet Sauvignon* (Remick Ridge Vineyard) • *Sangiovese* (Jessandre Vineyard)

RICHARD CUNEO
Sonoma
★☆ⓥ

The Cuvée de Chardonnay under Sebastiani's sparkling-wine label is surprisingly well structured and capable of fine, biscuity complexity.

✓ *Cuvée de Chardonnay*

DEHLINGER WINERY
Sebastopol
★★

Tom Dehlinger is highly renowned for Pinot Noir of great finesse and style, but this should not distract readers from trying other varietals, particularly his cheekily labelled Chardonnay Montrachet Cuvée.

✓ *Cabernet Franc* • *Cabernet-Merlot* (red Bordeaux style) • *Cabernet Sauvignon* • *Chardonnay* (Montrachet Cuvée) • *Pinot Noir* (particularly Goldridge Vineyard and new Octagon Vineyard) • *Syrah*

DE LOACH VINEYARDS
Santa Rosa
★★☆

This winery is best known for its rich, buttery Chardonnays, but actually makes far more interesting Zinfandels, which are the smoothest you are ever likely to encounter; stylish wines oozing with deliciously spicy fruit and seamless oak.

✓ *Chardonnay* • *Zinfandel* (particularly O.F.S. and Papera Vineyard)

DRY CREEK VINEYARD
Healdsburg
★

Not all of David Stare's Dry Creek Vineyard wines actually come from the Dry Creek Valley AVA but he nevertheless maintains a high reputation for Fumé Blanc and Chardonnay, and since the early 1990s has started producing big, rich, and spicy Zinfandel.

✓ *Chardonnay* • *Fumé Blanc* • *Zinfandel* (Old Vines)

DUXOUP WINE WORKS
Healdsberg
★

The first time I visited Duxoup I got lost and asked to be excused for being two hours late, but Andy Cutter waved away my apology with "Don't worry, when your colleagues Robert Joseph and Charles Metcalfe paid a visit, they were two days late" and I am happy to say the wines are equally laid-back.

✓ *Charbono* • *Gamay* • *Syrah*

GARY FARRELL
Forestville
★★☆

The quality of these intense wines has soared since the early 1990s.

✓ *Cabernet Sauvignon* (Ladi's Vineyard) • *Chardonnay* (Howard Allen Vineyard) • *Merlot* (Ladi's Vineyard) • *Pinot Noir* (particularly Howard Allen Vineyard) • *Zinfandel*

FERRARI-CARANO
Healdsburg
★★☆

Don and Rhonda Carano sold up their Reno casino and hotel to buy 200 hectares (500 acres) of Sonoma vineyards in 1981, and Italian-styled wines have always been a feature.

✓ *Fumé Blanc* (especially Reserve) • *Merlot* • *Reserve Red* (red Bordeaux style) • *Siena* (classic red blend) • *Syrah* • *Zinfandel*

FIELD STONE WINERY
Healdsburg
★☆ⓥ

This underrated, underground winery produces fresh and fruity wines.

✓ *Cabernet Sauvignon* • *Petite Sirah*

FISHER VINEYARDS
Santa Rosa
★★☆

With two hillside vineyards in the Mayacamas Mountains and one on the Napa Valley floor, Fred Fisher has always crafted some high-quality wines, especially from Cabernet sauvignon.

✓ *Cabernet Sauvignon* (Coach Insignia, Lamb Vineyard, Wedding Vineyard) • *Chardonnay* (Whitney's Vineyard) • *Merlot* (RCF Vineyard)

FOPPIANO VINEYARDS
Healdsburg
★

After a period of inconsistency, this family-run winery is again making deep-flavoured varietal wines. Its second label is Riverside Vineyard.

✓ *Petite Sirah* (Reserve)

FRITZ CELLARS
Cloverdale
★

This is best known for Chardonnay and Sauvignon, but it is the intense, extraordinarily long-lived Zinfandel that excites most.

✓ *Zinfandel* (80 Year Old Vines)

GEYSER PEAK WINERY
Geyserville
★☆ⓥ

Penfolds owned fifty per cent of this winery from 1989 until 1992, when the Trione family, once again, became the sole owners. However, Australian winemaker Daryl Groom stayed on and the winery has not looked back since, consistently producing good-quality wines.

✓ *Cabernet Sauvignon* (Reserve) • *Reserve* (red Bordeaux style) • *Semchard* (classic white blend) • *Shiraz* • *Soft Johannisberg Riesling*

GLEN ELLEN WINERY
Glen Ellen
ⓥ

The Glen Ellen Winery used to be owned by Benzinger, but it was sold to Heublein (a diverse drinks group that also owns Beaulieu in Napa County), and now these wines are mostly penny-pinchers, but can sometimes offer good value.

GLORIA FERRER
Sonoma
★☆

Established by Cava-giant Freixenet in 1982 and named after the wife of José Ferrer, the Spanish firm's president, Gloria Ferrer quickly made an acceptable, if unexciting, NV Brut, but excelled with such vintage wines as the 1985 Carneros Cuvée. The NV Brut now ranks, with Codorniu, as equal second-best in California in the ready-to-drink stakes. (Piper Sonoma is ranked as number one.)

✓ *NV Brut*

GUNDLACH-BUNDSCHU WINERY
Sonoma
★

High-quality Cabernet and Zinfandel from the fifth generation of the family of the founder, Jacob Gundlach, this winery also shows promising signs for other varietals.

✓ *Cabernet Sauvignon* (Rhinefarm Vineyard) • *Zinfandel* (Rhinefarm Vineyard)

HACIENDA WINERY
Sonoma

This operation, which encompasses part of Haraszthy's original Buena Vista vineyard, was sold in 1993 to the Bronco Wine Company, which also owns Forest Glen, Grand Cru, Laurier, Napa Creek, and Rutherford Vintners. See also Laurier.

✓ *Chardonnay* (Claire de Lune) • *Dry Chenin Blanc*

HANZELL VINEYARDS
Sonoma

It was James Zellerbach, the founder of Hanzell Vineyards small winery, who in 1957 revolutionized the Californian wine industry. He achieved this by ageing a Chardonnay wine in imported Burgundian *barriques*.

✓ *Chardonnay* • *Pinot Noir*

HARTFORD COURT

Sonoma

★☆

Part of the Kendal-Jackson "Artisans & Estates" group of wineries, Hartford Court makes extremely classy Pinot Noir and Chardonnay, and a huge, oaky Zinfandel that is definitely out to grab attention.

✓ *Chardonnay* (Arrendell Vineyard) • *Pinot Noir* (Arrendell Vineyard) • *Zinfandel* (Hartford Vineyard)

HOP KILN WINERY

Healdsburg

★★☆

The hop-drying barn that houses Hop Kiln winery was built in 1905, and has already been declared a national historic landmark. The deep-coloured, luscious, fruity red wines are best.

✓ *Petite Sirah* • *Zinfandel* (Primitivo)

ROBERT HUNTER

Sonoma

☆

It was Robert Hunter's friend Dan Duckhorn who originally suggested that he should use his Pinot noir to make sparkling wine.

✓ *Vintage Brut de Noirs*

IRON HORSE VINEYARDS

Sebastopol

★☆

This was once the only railway stop in Sonoma Green Valley, hence the name, which also gave rise to its second label Tin Pony. I have always thought the fruit structure of Iron Horse superb for *méthode champenoise*, but the wines can be too austere when released, as with Roederer Estate. Coincidentally, 1987 was a turning point for Iron Horse too; its Vintage Blanc de Blancs that year had more finesse than any of this winery's previous *cuvées* and the vintages since then are the most complex *blanc de blancs* California has so far produced. All Iron Horse sparkling wines should have at least 18 months' additional ageing after purchase, with the exception of the deep-strawberry coloured, vivaciously fruity, brilliantly refreshing Vintage Rosé, which should be consumed as fast as you can drink it. Look out for a new *prestige cuvée* joint venture with the *grande marque* Champagne house Laurent-Perrier.

✓ *Cabernets* (red Bordeaux style) • *Chardonnay* (Cuvée Joy) • *Sparkling* (Vintage Brut, Vintage Blanc de Blancs, Vintage Rosé)

JORDAN

Healdsburg

★★☆

The rich, complex Cabernet Sauvignon has always been this winery's greatest wine, but it has been overshadowed by the launch of 'J' sparkling wine. The first releases had a bit of a terpene character, but although this was eradicated by the 1990 vintage, it was not until the tremendously elegant 1991 vintage that this brand was established as a world-class sparkling wine. Jordan now owns Piper Sonoma.

✓ *Cabernet Sauvignon* • *Sparkling* ('J')

KENWOOD VINEYARDS

Kenwood

★

Concentrated wines with good attack are consistently produced at these vineyards.

✓ *Cabernet Sauvignon* (Jack London Vineyard) • *Merlot* (Jack London Vineyard) • *Sauvignon Blanc* • *Zinfandel* (Jack London, Mazzoni)

KISTLER VINEYARDS

Trenton

★★

Mark Bixler and Steve Kistler are outstanding single-vineyard Chardonnay specialists who are now turning out masterly Pinot.

✓ *Chardonnay* (especially all single-vineyard bottlings) • *Pinot Noir* (especially all single-vineyard bottlings)

KORBEL CHAMPAGNE CELLARS

Guerneville

This is California's leading sparkling-wine specialist in the popular sector.

KUNDE ESTATE

Kenwood

★★☆

Kunde Estate winery was set up by a well-established group of Sonoma growers who started selling their own wines in 1990, and have rapidly made a huge impact with critics and consumers alike.

✓ *Cabernet Sauvignon* (Reserve) • *Chardonnay* (Kinneybrook, Wildwood) • *Sauvignon Blanc* (Magnolia Lane) • *Viognier* • *Zinfandel* (Century Vines)

LANDMARK VINEYARDS

Windsor

☆

These vineyards are best known for Chardonnay of a much fatter, richer, more complex style than they used to be, and are now developing a growing reputation for Pinot Noir.

✓ *Chardonnay* (especially Reserve) • *Pinot Noir*

LAUREL GLEN VINEYARD

Glen Ellen

★★

This vineyard has a well-established reputation for succulent Cabernet Sauvignon. Counterpoint and Terra Rosa are cheaper labels, the former used for more forward, lesser-quality estate wines, while the latter wines are bigger and more complex, but from grapes that are bought in.

✓ *Cabernet Sauvignon* • *Terra Rosa* (red Bordeaux-style blend)

LAURIER

Forestville

Formerly called Domaine Laurier, with production restricted to a 12-hectare (30-acre) vineyard, this is now a brand belonging to the Bronco Wine Company, which also owns Forest Glen, Grand Cru, Hacienda, Laurier, Napa Creek, and Rutherford Vintners. Apparently trying hard with Chardonnay and Pinot Noir, but I have not tasted them recently. *See also* Hacienda Winery.

LYETH WINERY

Geyserville

Pronounced "Leeth", this was an exciting new winery in the 1980s, but when the founder died in a plane crash in 1988, it was sold off and is now owned by Burgundian super-*négociant* Boisset. Their second label is Christophe.

✓ *Lyeth* (red and white Bordeaux style)

MARIETTA CELLARS

Healdsburg

★

Owner-winemaker Chris Bilbro started up this operation in 1980, after selling off his share in the Bandeira Winery, which he had established while still working as an administrator for Sonoma State Hospital. He built his reputation on lush Merlot and great-value wines.

✓ *Cabernet Sauvignon* • *Merlot* • *Old Vine Red Lot 18* (classic red blend) • *Petite Sirah* • *Zinfandel* (Cuvée Angeli)

MARTINELLI VINEYARDS

Fulton

★

Experienced grape growers, who turned winemakers in the early 1990s, the Martinelli family turns out lush, stylish wines under the skilful guidance of Helen Turley.

✓ *Chardonnay* • *Pinot Noir* • *Zinfandel*

MATANZAS CREEK WINERY

Santa Rosa

★

A small winery producing fine, rich, elegant wines with good fruit-acidity.

✓ *Chardonnay* • *Merlot* • *Sauvignon Blanc*

PETER MICHAEL WINERY

Calistoga

★★☆

Englishman Sir Peter Michael quickly carved out a name as a top producer of classy Californian wine. With no expense spared, Peter Michael has applied New World technology to the very best of traditional methods. Air-conditioning is vital in California, but this winery has computer controlled steam jets to maintain sufficient humidity to reduce evaporation through the staves of new oak to virtually zero. Peter Michael wines all have a certain balance, which enables them to enjoy the same quality that the best French wines possess, namely not to overwhelm when served with food, but to build in finesse and complexity in the glass.

✓ *Chardonnay* (Clos du Ciel and Monplaisir for elegance, Cuvée Indigènie and Cuvée Pointe Rouge for power) • *Les Pavots* (red Bordeaux style) • *L'Après-Midi* (Sauvignon Blanc)

MICHEL-SCHLUMBERGER

Healdsburg

Formerly known as Domaine Michel Winery, under the ownership of Swiss-born Jean-Jacques Michel, but it is now in collaboration with the Schlumberger family of Alsace.

NALLE

Healdsburg

★★☆

Doug Nalle was winemaker at Quivira when in 1984 he started making Zinfandel under his own label. He has no vineyards of his own, but buys only from low-yielding hill and mountain-side plots to produce this big, yet constantly refined, yardstick example.

✓ *Zinfandel*

PELLEGRINI FAMILY VINEYARDS

South San Francisco

★

These vineyards produce delicious, vividly flavoured Barbera and excellent Carignane with oodles of fresh, oaky fruit.

✓ *Barbera* • *Carignane*

PIPER SONOMA

Windsor

❷

Piper-Heidsieck, the Reims-based *grande marque* Champagne house, joined forces with Sonoma Vineyards to fund this venture and became the sole owner until 1997 when Jordan purchased the facility, but not the brand. The wines in the early 1980s were a bit curious, resinous even, but improved greatly towards the end of that decade and have taken on a lovely, zesty freshness since the early 1990s. Piper Sonoma is currently making the best ready-to-drink NV Brut in California, but whether it will remain so under the new arrangements will take a few years to discern, as the French-owned Piper-Sonoma brand will continue to be produced at these Jordan-owned premises.

✓ *Blanc de Noirs* • *NV Brut* • *Tête de Cuvée*

PRESTON VINEYARDS

Healdsburg

★

These Dry Creek vineyards are planted with an amazing and

successful mix of varieties and are capable of making high-quality wines.

✓ *Barbera* • *Cuvée de Fumé* • *Faux Castel* (red Rhône style) • *Sirah-Syrah* • *Zinfandel*

QUIVIRA
Healdsburg
★

Established in 1981 by Henry and Holly Wendt, Quivira was named after a legendary American kingdom that Europeans spent 200 years searching for. Not able to locate Quivira, the earliest settlers apparently used the name for this part of Northern California before it was called Sonoma. Doug Nalle first put this innovative winery on the wine map with, not surprisingly, Zinfandel, which remains Quivira's top wine, although Wendt makes other brightly flavoured varietals and, since 1992, has joined the ranks of California's Rhône rangers.

✓ *Dry Creek Cuvée* (red Rhône style) • *Sauvignon Blanc* • *Zinfandel*

RABBIT RIDGE
Healdsburg
★ Ⓥ

Part-owned by Erich Russell, who became chief winemaker at Belvedere in 1988, Rabbit Ridge offers a bewildering range of inexpensive, deliciously fruity wines. Second labels include Clairveaux and Meadow Glen.

✓ *Allure* (red Rhône style) • *Chardonnay* • *Mystique* (white Bordeaux style) • *Zinfandel*

A. RAFANELLI
Healdsburg
★

It was always said that Americo Rafanelli, who died in 1987, made wine "as they used to in the olden days". Well he would be proud of the blockbusters made by his son David from this small, unirrigated, hillside vineyard.

✓ *Zinfandel*

RAVENSWOOD
Sonoma
★★

Joel Peterson is the master when it comes to monstrous Zinfandel. Some growers of tiny mountain-side plots produce such low yields that their wines would be too intense to drink on their own, which is why even Ravenswood's Zinfandel blends can be quite sensational. Peterson's other first class varietals should not be overlooked.

✓ *Cabernet Sauvignon* (Gregory) • *Chardonnay* (Sangiacomo) • *Merlot* (Sangiacomo) • *Pickberry* (red Bordeaux style) • *Zinfandel* (particularly Old Hill)

J. ROCHIOLI VINEYARDS
Healdsburg
★★☆

The Rochioli family has been growing grapes at this long-established vineyard since the 1930s,

but did not build a winery until 1984, making their first wine the following year. They now offer a large range of all too drinkable estate-bottled wines.

✓ *Cabernet Sauvignon* (Reserve) • *Chardonnay* (especially Reserve, Allen Vineyard, South River Vineyard) • *Pinot Noir* (especially East Block, Little Hill Block, Three Corner Vineyard, West Block) • *Sauvignon Blanc* (Reserve)

ST. FRANCIS VINEYARD
Kenwood
★☆Ⓥ

Situated just across the road from Château St. Jean, the underrated winery of St. Francis is owned by Joseph Martin and Lloyd Canton, who produce some cracking good wines that are always intensely flavoured and seldom expensive.

✓ *Cabernet Sauvignon* (Reserve) • *Chardonnay* (Reserve) • *Merlot* (Reserve) • *Muscat Canelli* (Late Harvest) • *Zinfandel* (Old Vines)

SEBASTIANI
Sonoma
❷Ⓥ

The wines produced by Sebastiani are inexpensive, and although some bargains can be found, the quality is inconsistent and the wines below are recommended with this caution. Other labels include Pepperwood Grove, Talus, August Sebastiani, Vendange, and Richard Cuneo. *See also* Richard Cuneo.

✓ *Cabernet Franc* (Sebastiani label) • *Cabernet Sauvignon* • *Gewürztraminer* • *Muscat* • *Zinfandel*

SIMI WINERY
Healdsburg
★

Simi produces consistently improved wines every year, in a stunning, power-packed, ripe style that is 110 per cent California, yet amazingly never lacks elegance.

✓ *Cabernet Sauvignon* (Reserve) • *Chardonnay* • *Chenin Blanc* • *Rosé* (Cabernet Sauvignon) • *Sendal* (white Bordeaux style)

SONOMA-CUTRER VINEYARDS
Windsor
★

Sonoma-Cutrer Vineyards are a specialist winery, producing three good-quality but totally different styles of Chardonnays. Of these three, Les Pierres has proved to be consistently the finest.

✓ *Chardonnay* (Les Pierres)

SONOMA-LOEB
Geyserville
★

This producer is owned by John Loeb, a former American Ambassador to Denmark, who has grown grapes here since the early 1970s. However, he did not start making and selling wine under his own label until 1988.

✓ *Chardonnay* (Private Reserve)

ROBERT STEMMLER
Sonoma

Robert Stemmler formerly produced a full range of wines at his own winery in Healdsburg. Pinot Noir, which was the biggest seller, is the only wine remaining under this label today. The label has been sold to Buena Vista, where the wine is now produced and marketed.

✓ *Pinot Noir*

STONESTREET
Healdsburg
★★

One of the wineries in Kendal-Jackson's "Artisans & Estates" group, Stonestreet produces good Chardonnay, brilliant Sauvignon, and gorgeously sumptuous Cabernet and Merlot, but truly excels with its classy Legacy blend.

✓ *Cabernet Sauvignon* • *Legacy* (red Bordeaux style) • *Merlot* • *Sauvignon Blanc* (Alexander Mountain)

RODNEY STRONG VINEYARDS
Windsor
★❷

Although Rodney Strong Vineyards have produced some rich Cabernet Sauvignon and soft-styled Chardonnay, they lack consistency and fresh, easy-drinking Sauvignon is now emerging as his best wine.

✓ *Sauvignon Blanc* (Charlotte's Home Vineyard)

JOSEPH SWAN VINEYARDS
Forestville

These vineyards are run by the late Joe Swan's son-in-law, Rod Berglund, who continues the quest for the ultimate Zinfandel.

✓ *Zinfandel* (Stellwagen Vineyard, Zeigler Vineyard)

TOPOLOS RUSSIAN RIVER VINEYARDS
North Forestville
❷

From good vineyards around the winery and on Sonoma Mountain, Topolos sometimes comes up with

a gem in what can be an alarmingly wayward bunch of wines.

✓ *Alicante Bouschet* • *Petite Sirah* (Rossi Ranch)

MARIMAR TORRES VINEYARDS
Sebastopol
★

Miguel Torres planted his sister's vineyard with Chardonnay and Pinot noir, plus one experimental half hectare with Parellada (not one of my favourite grapes – hopefully Marimar will grub up the Parellada and replace it with a real quality Catalonian vine like Tempranillo). This vineyard is planted with four times as many vines per hectare than is the norm in California. This causes competition between the vines, yielding less fruit per vine, but the total volume per hectare is the same, and the quality higher. The Chardonnay is good, but the high-density vines work best for Pinot Noir, which has a combination of silky fruit, finesse, and age-worthiness that is uncommon in California.

✓ *Chardonnay* • *Pinot Noir*

TRENTADUE WINERY
Geyserville
★Ⓥ

The Trentadue Winery produces quite a characterful selection of good-value varietal wines that are rarely, if ever, filtered.

✓ *Carignane* • *Merlot Port* • *Old Patch* (red Rhône style) • *Petite Sirah* • *Sangiovese*

VIANSA
Sonoma
★

A contraction of "Vicky and Sam" Sebastiani, this beautiful Tuscan-styled winery was established in 1990 when Sam left Sebastiani.

✓ *Sangiovese* • *Thalia* (Classic red blend)

WILLIAMS-SELYEM
Fulton
★

This winery was established in 1981 by Burt Williams and Ed Selyem, who have since built up a reputation for small quantities of sought-after wines of beautiful balance and finesse.

✓ *Chardonnay* (Allen Vineyard) • *Pinot Noir* (particularly Allen Vineyard, Rochioli Vineyard) • *Zinfandel* (Leo Martinelli Vineyard)

NAPA COUNTY

Napa County is the heart and soul of the Californian wine industry. Its vineyards are the most concentrated in the state, it has more wineries than any other county, and they produce the greatest number and variety of fine wines in the entire North American continent.

IT IS HARD TO BELIEVE that Napa was planted after Sonoma, but it was, and by some 13 years; in 1838 a trapper from North Carolina by the name of George Yount acquired a few Mission vines from General Mariano Vallejo's Sonoma vineyard and planted them outside his log cabin, three kilometres (two miles) north of present-day Yountville. He merely wished to make a little wine for his own use. Little did he know that the entire Napa Valley would one day be carpeted with a lush green sea of vines. Within six years Yount himself was harvesting an annual average of 900 litres (200 gallons); by the turn of the decade various other

NAPA VINEYARDS
In this, the most famous of all California wine regions, vines grow mostly on the fertile valley floors, although more and more vineyards are being established in the wooded foothills, where the earliest settlers first planted vines.

vineyards had sprung up and, in 1859, Samuel Brannan, an ex-Mormon millionaire, purchased eight square kilometres (three square miles) of rich valley land and planted cuttings of various European vine varieties he had collected during his travels abroad. Within a further 20 years there were more than 7,300 hectares (18,000 acres) of vineyard in the county, more than half the amount currently cultivated and almost twice the area of vines now covering Mendocino.

Today, the Napa Valley's vinous reputation is well established throughout the world. Napa wines, particularly Chardonnay and Cabernet Sauvignon, are still the most sought-after and highly prized wines in the American continent, and will continue to be so for the foreseeable future at least.

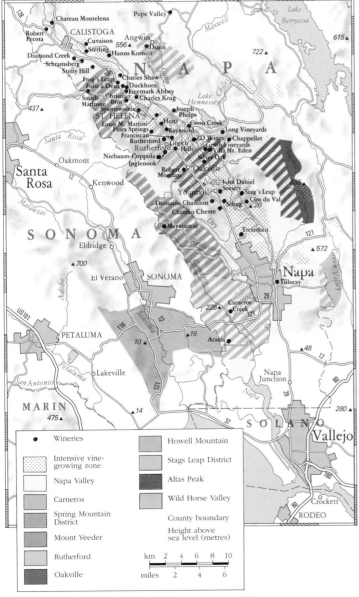

NAPA COUNTY, *see also p.448*
The intensive winegrowing areas of this illustrious Californian district occupy a long, narrow strip running roughly parallel to those of Sonoma County. Many famous names are crowded around Route 29.

FACTORS AFFECTING TASTE AND QUALITY

LOCATION
Starting alongside San Francisco Bay, Napa runs 54 km (34 miles) north and west to the foothills of Mount St. Helena. Flanking it are the Sonoma Valley to the west and Lake Berryessa to the east.

CLIMATE
This ranges from cool (Region I, *see* p.448) near the Bay, in the often foggy Carneros District, to warm (Region III, *see* p.448) in the northern section of the Napa Valley and in Pope Valley.

ASPECT
Vines are mostly planted on the valley floors but some are cultivated on slopes. Although flat, the altitude of the valley floors ranges from barely 5 m (17 ft) above sea level at Napa itself, to 70 m (230 ft) at St. Helena in the middle of the valley, and 122 m (400 ft) at Calistoga in the north. The wooded western slopes provide afternoon shade, which adds to the tempering effect of altitude and so favours white grapes, whereas the eastern slopes favour red varieties.

SOIL
Fertile clay and silt loams in the south of the region, and gravel loams of better drainage and lower fertility in the north.

VITICULTURE AND VINIFICATION
There is a vast range of wineries here, ranging from a small number of large firms employing the latest high-tech methods, to an increasing number of small boutique wineries. The latter have limited production based on traditional methods, although often with the help of judicious use of modern techniques. The great wines from this valley have established California's vinous reputation throughout the world.

PRIMARY GRAPE VARIETIES
Cabernet sauvignon, Chardonnay, Chenin blanc, Merlot, Pinot noir, Sauvignon blanc, White riesling, Zinfandel

SECONDARY GRAPE VARIETIES
Aleatico, Alicante bouschet, Barbera, Black malvoisie, Burger, Cabernet franc, Carignan, Early Burgundy, Colombard, Flora, Folle blanche, Gamay, Gamay Beaujolais, Gewürztraminer, Gray riesling, Green Hungarian, Grenache, Malbec, Malvasia bianca, Mataro, Mission, Muscat blanc, Palomino, Petite sirah, Pinot blanc, Pinot St. George, Ruby cabernet, Sauvignon vert, Sémillon, Sylvaner, Syrah

THE APPELLATIONS OF
NAPA COUNTY

ATLAS PEAK AVA

The Atlas Peak appellation consists of 4,600 hectares (11,400 acres) on and around Atlas Peak mountain, where more than a quarter of California's Sangiovese vines are planted.

CARNEROS AVA

Also known as Los Carneros, this AVA overlaps Napa and Sonoma counties. *See also* Los Carneros, Sonoma.

HOWELL MOUNTAIN AVA

The relatively flat table-top of Howell Mountain is a sub-appellation of the Napa Valley, covering 57 square kilometres (22 square miles) and encompassing some 81 hectares (200 acres) of vineyards at an altitude of between 420 and 890 metres (1,400–2,200 feet). Vines were first planted here in 1880. It is best for Cabernet Sauvignon but also capable of top-flight Zinfandel and Chardonnay.

MOUNT VEEDER AVA

Situated on the east-facing slopes of the Mayacamus Mountains and named after the volcanic peak that dominates this AVA, Mount Veeder is one of the hilly areas where winemakers went to escape the Napa Valley's fertile valley floor. Cool sea breezes from San Pablo Bay and occasional marine fogs temper the climate, while inversion prevents frost. Chardonnay and Cabernet sauvignon are the two dominant varieties, the latter being quite exceptional in its varietal intensity and completely different in structure from the lush valley-floor Cabernets.

NAPA COUNTY AO

This is an appellation that covers grapes grown anywhere in the entire county.

NAPA VALLEY AVA

This AVA includes all of the county with the exception of the area around Putah Creek and Lake Berryessa. The Napa Valley appellation is 40 kilometres (25 miles) long and between 12 and 16 kilometres (8–10 miles) wide, and is sheltered by two parallel mountain ranges. The majority of vineyards occupy the flat valley floor in a continuous strip from Napa to Calistoga, although the slopes are also beginning to be cultivated.

OAKVILLE AVA

If Rutherford has the greatest concentration of famous Cabernet sauvignon vineyards, then neighbouring Oakville, which is equally Napa's heartland, excels by its very diversity. Great Cabernet Sauvignon, Merlot, and Chardonnay are made here and even the Sauvignon Blanc from these vineyards can be extraordinary.

RUTHERFORD AVA

One of the most famous names in Napa, yet one of the last to gain AVA status because many growers feared that dividing the Napa Valley's heartland into smaller, possibly more prestigious sub-appellations would gradually have the effect of diluting the reputation of Napa itself. This AVA encompasses more than 30 wineries, including some of California's most famous, and contain's many of Napa's greatest Cabernet sauvignon vineyards.

ST. HELENA AVA

The latest AVA to be established in a bid to carve up the Napa Valley into communal districts in a similar manner to the Médoc, St. Helena is immediately north of Rutherford.

SPRING MOUNTAIN DISTRICT AVA

Originally proposed as Spring Mountain, but as this was already a brand name, the AVA was changed to Spring Mountain District to avoid confusion. This appellation is located within the Napa Valley AVA, just west of St. Helena, on the eastern flank of the Mayacamas Mountains, and comprises 3,480 hectares (8,600 acres), of which approximately 800 hectares (1,980 acres) are planted with vines.

STAGS LEAP DISTRICT AVA

Confusingly, Stags Leap is spelt in three slightly different ways: with an apostrophe before the "s" in the famous Stag's Leap Wine Cellars, with an apostrophe after the "s" in the lesser-known Stags' Leap Winery, and without an apostrophe in the AVA name. Stag's Leap Wine Cellar shot to fame in 1976 when its Cabernet Sauvignon trumped top Bordeaux wines at a blind tasting in Paris. Stags Leap District vies with Rutherford as the crème of Napa Valley Cabernet Sauvignon, but also makes good Petite Sirah, excellent Merlot, and stunning red Bordeaux-style blends.

WILD HORSE VALLEY AVA

Technically attached to Napa, Wild Horse Valley actually straddles the county line, occupying more of Solano than Napa.

THE WINE PRODUCERS OF
NAPA COUNTY

ABREU
Napa
?

I have no experience of these Cabernet Sauvignon wines, but wine writer Robert Parker has been waxing lyrical about recent vintages (1993, 1994, 1995), which he has provisionally scored at 94–96 percentile points. Such incredible praise from a respected source is better recycled than ignored, giving readers a chance to check it out.

ACACIA WINERY
Napa
★★☆

This Burgundian varietal specialist makes a fine Chardonnay with a touch of spice, and a lovely Pinot Noir that is all cherries and vanilla.

✓ *Chardonnay* (Marina Vineyard)
• *Pinot Noir* (Carneros)

S. ANDERSON VINEYARD
Napa

S. Anderson Vineyard is a small winery producing Chardonnay and

Cabernet from the Stags Leap District. Some impressive *méthode champenoise* wines are also made.

✓ *Cabernet Sauvignon* (Richard Chambers Vineyard)
• *Sparkling* (Vintage Brut, Vintage Rosé)

ARAUJO ESTATE
Calistoga
★

Bart and Daphne Araujo now own the highly regarded Eisele vineyard, which is north of Cuvaison, and the Cabernet is of outstanding quality.

✓ *Cabernet Sauvignon* (Eisele Vineyard)
• *Syrah* (Eisele Vineyard)

ATLAS PEAK
Atlas Peak
★

This exciting venture is backed with big bucks from Allied-Hiram Walker (which also owns Clos du Bois and William Hill) with expertise provided by Champagne Bollinger and the famous Chianti house of Antinori.

✓ *Consenso* • *Sangiovese*

BARNETT VINEYARDS
St. Helena
★★☆

These are delicious, very elegant Cabernet Sauvignons.

✓ *Cabernet Sauvignon*

BEAUCANON
St. Helena

Exceptionally well-structured Merlot is the best buy, but interesting oddities, such as the 1990 Late Harvest Chardonnay, are also made.

✓ *Merlot*

BEAULIEU VINEYARD
Rutherford

This was the centre of Californian innovation under the legendary winemaker, André Tchelistcheff.

✓ *Cabernet Sauvignon* (Georges de Latour)

BERINGER VINEYARDS
St. Helena
★★

Although all the products from Beringer Vineyards are among the finest in California, you do get

proportionately more for your money if you pay extra for the better *cuvées* or single-vineyard wines. They have soared in quality since the early 1990s.

Beringer.

✓ *Cabernet Sauvignon* (especially Chabot Vineyard and Private Reserve)
• *Chardonnay* (especially Private Reserve and Sbragia Select) • *Gamay Beaujolais*
• *Alluvium* (red and white)
• *Merlot* (Bancroft Vineyard)
• *Sangiovese* (Knights Valley)
• *Syrah* • *Viognier* (especially Hudson Ranch)

BIALÉ VINEYARDS

Napa
❷

A friend showed me this amazing wine (huge, rich, and gorgeously ripe), made from 60 year-old vines that survived Prohibition, on one of my trips through the Napa Valley. I must seek out the vineyard.

Zinfandel (Aldo's Vineyard)

BOUCHAINE VINEYARDS

Napa
★

Noticeable by its absence from most American critics' thoughts, Bouchaine's Pinot Noir and Chardonnay are probably too light and elegant to stir up much opinion in the US, but have a purity and finesse much appreciated by European palates.

Pinot Noir

BUEHLER VINEYARDS INC.

St. Helena
❷

This estate is again producing Cabernet Sauvignon reminiscent of the size and quality that once made it legendary.

Cabernet Sauvignon

BURGESS CELLARS

St. Helena
★

Owner Tom Burgess and winemaker Bill Sorenson often produce well-weighted, oaky wines of fine quality.

Chardonnay (Triere Vineyard)
• *Zinfandel*

CAIN CELLARS

St. Helena
★

These are interesting, innovative, and well-made wines.

Cain Five (red Bordeaux style)
• *Merlot* • *Sauvignon Musqué*

CAKEBREAD CELLARS

Rutherford

Bruce Cakebread has a reputation for fine, spicy Zinfandel, but also makes delicious Sauvignon Blanc.

Sauvignon Blanc
• *Zinfandel* (Howell Mountain)

CARNEROS CREEK WINERY

Napa
★

Although Carneros Creek went through a dull patch in the early 1980s, it was back on course by the end of that decade and produces some lovely wines today.

Pinot Noir (Signature)

CAYMUS VINEYARDS

Rutherford
★★

This high-quality winery produces a stunning range of Cabernet Sauvignon. Its second label is Liberty School.

Cabernet Sauvignon (especially Special Selection) • *Conundrum* (classic white wine blend)
• *Sauvignon Blanc*

CHAPPELLET VINEYARDS

St. Helena
★★

CHAPPELLET
·1986·
Napa Valley
JOHANNISBERG RIESLING

PRODUCED AND BOTTLED BY CHAPPELLET VINEYARD, B.W. 4537
PRITCHARD HILL, ST. HELENA, CA. U.S.A. ALCOHOL 11.5% BY VOLUME
RESIDUAL SUGAR 0.7% BY VOL.   CONTAINS GRAPES, YEAST, SULFITES

Chappellet is an excellent winery with a range of skilfully produced wines that show great finesse.

Cabernet Sauvignon
• *Chardonnay* • *Chenin Blanc*
• *Johannisberg Riesling* • *Merlot*

CHÂTEAU MONTELENA WINERY

Calistoga
★

The style of this small, prestigious winery has changed over the years, but the quality has always been high, especially for Cabernet.

Cabernet Sauvignon
• *Chardonnay* • *Johannisberg Riesling* (Potter Valley)
• *Zinfandel*

CHÂTEAU POTELLE

Mount Veeder

This winery was established in 1985 by a *bordelais* couple, who ironically are best known for their slow-evolving Chardonnay.

Cabernet Sauvignon
• *Chardonnay* • *Zinfandel*

CHIMNEY ROCK

Napa
★

In the early 1980s, Hack Wilson, an ex-Pepsi executive and former president of Rheingold Breweries, purchased the old Chimney Rock Golf Club, bulldozed nine holes, and planted a vineyard.

Elevage (red Bordeaux style)
• *Fumé Blanc*

CLOS DU VAL

Napa
★★

John Goelet is the owner, and Bernard Portet is the manager-winemaker. Goelet also owns Taltarni in Australia.

Cabernet Sauvignon (Reserve)
• *Chardonnay* (Carneros)
• *Merlot*
• *Zinfandel* (Stags Leap District)

CLOS PEGASE

Calistoga
★

A welcome, understated use of oak coupled with lush fruit produces wines of some elegance.

Cabernet Sauvignon
• *Chardonnay* • *Hommage* (red Bordeaux style) • *Merlot*

CODORNÍU NAPA

Napa
★

Buried in a Carneros hillside with a bunker-like protrusion, Spanish Cava giant Codorníu is now making sparkling wines of admirable quality, after a somewhat slow start.

NV Brut
• *Vintage Carneros Cuvée*

COLGIN-SCHRADER CELLARS

Napa
❷

I have not tasted this newcomer's wines, but understand that the Cabernet Sauvignon from Herb Lamb Vineyard on Howell Mountain might well rank among the greatest Napa wines produced.

CONN CREEK WINERY

St. Helena

This winery is owned by Stimson Lane, which also owns Château Ste. Michelle, Columbia Crest, and Villa Mount Eden. Conn Creek is best known for its supple, fruity Cabernet Sauvignon.

Cabernet Sauvignon
• *Triomphe* (red Bordeaux style)

CONN VALLEY

St. Helena
★★

Established in 1988, this impressive new winery has since produced a string of spectacular wines.

Cabernet Sauvignon
• *Chardonnay*
• *Pinot Noir* (Valhalla Vineyard)

CORISON

St. Helena
★★

After ten years as Chappellet's winemaker, Cathy Corison struck out on her own, and has not looked back since, purchasing small parcels of the finest Napa Valley grapes to produce lush, supple Cabernet wines of surprising longevity.

Cabernet Sauvignon

COSENTINO

Yountville
★

This former Central Valley winery moved from Modesto in 1989, since when Mitch Cosentino's hit-you-between-the-eyes wines have been made with alternating layers of exuberant fruit and oak. All the wines are worth trying at least once.

The Poet Meritage (red Bordeaux style) • *The Zin*

CRICHTON HALL

Rutherford
★

This British-owned winery is best known for a crisp, toasty-leesy Chardonnay, but also produces good Merlot and a serious, age-worthy Pinot Noir.

Chardonnay • *Merlot* • *Pinot Noir*

CUVAISON

Calistoga

This Swiss-owned winery is making better reds than whites.

Merlot

DALLA VALLE

Oakville
★★

Dalla Valle produces great Cabernet in addition to a truly heroic Cabernet-based blend.

Cabernet Sauvignon • *Maya*

DIAMOND CREEK VINEYARDS

Calistoga
★★

This small winery specializes in awesomely long-lived Cabernet Sauvignon.

Cabernet Sauvignon (Red Rock Terrace, Lake Vineyard, Gravelly Meadow, Volcanic Hill)

DOMAINE CARNEROS

Napa

This winery has the pristine façade of Taittinger's 17th-century Château de la Marquetterie in Champagne. The first harvest was in 1987, and the first couple of releases here were among the worst that any French-owned venture had produced. It is now one of the best.

Vintage Blanc de Blancs
• *Vintage Brut*

DOMAINE CHANDON

Yountville
★

The first French-financed sparkling-wine venture, Moët & Chandon's seal of approval kick-started the industry that, until then, had consisted of just one producer, Schramsberg. It is now exporting under the Shadow Creek label.

Reserve • *Rosé Brut*

DOMINUS

Yountville
★★

Christian Moueix of Château Pétrus joined forces with the daughters of John Daniel to produce Dominus, a massively structured Bordeaux-like blend from the historic Napanook vineyard. The best vintages are from 1990 onwards.

Dominus

DUCKHORN VINEYARDS

St. Helena
★★

These superb, dark, rich, and tannic wines have a cult following.

Cabernet Sauvignon • *Merlot* (Three Palms) • *Sauvignon Blanc*

DUNN VINEYARDS

Angwin
★★

Randy Dunn makes a very small quantity of top-quality Cabernet Sauvignon from his Howell Mountain vineyard.

Cabernet Sauvignon

DUNNEWOOD
St. Helena

This large-scale operation sells everyday varietal wines that are pitched a little further upmarket than those of its sister company Almadén (under the umbrella of Canandaigua, which also owns Inglenook and Cooks).

ELYSE
Napa
★⯪

I first tasted these wines when Bibendum showed them at the 1995 annual Californian tasting in London, and I was bowled over by their richness of fruit and expressive style.

✓ *Cabernet Sauvignon* (Morisoli Vineyard) • *Nero Misto* (classic red blend) • *Zinfandel* (Howell Mountain)

ETUDE
Oakville
★

This winery belongs to one of the top Napa wine consultants, Tony Soter (also consultant to Araujo, Dalla Valle, Moraga, Niebaum-Coppola, Spottswoode *et al*), who crafts beautifully proportioned, succulent, and stylish wines from bought-in grapes.

✓ *Cabernet Sauvignon* • *Pinot Blanc* • *Pinot Gris* • *Pinot Meunier* • *Pinot Noir*

FAR NIENTE

A revitalized pre-Prohibition winery that made its mark with fine Chardonnay in the 1980s, but that wine can sometimes be overblown, and Cabernet Sauvignon is the more consistent and classier bet.

✓ *Cabernet Sauvignon* • *Dolce*

FLORA SPRINGS
St. Helena
★

This winery produces an exciting Trilogy, a blend of Merlot with two Cabernets, and a Soliloquy, a barrel-fermented Sauvignon Blanc bottled *sur lie*.

✓ *Cabernet Sauvignon* (Reserve) • *Chardonnay* (Barrel Fermented) • *Sangiovese* • *Soliloquy* (Sauvignon Blanc) • *Trilogy* (red Bordeaux style)

FORMAN VINEYARDS
St. Helena
⯪

Rick Forman, formerly of Sterling Vineyard, set up this small winery in 1983. He has a following for classic yet opulent wines from his own vineyard, which sits on a gravel bed as deep as 17 metres.

✓ *Cabernet Sauvignon* • *Chardonnay* • *Grenache* (La Grande Roche)

FRANCISCAN VINEYARDS
Rutherford
★⯪

A consistent producer since the mid-1980s of smooth, stylish, premium-quality wines. Other labels include Estancia (fat, floral, good-value Chardonnay, easy-going Cabernet, and improving Meritage), Mount Veeder (intense, oaky-rich Chardonnay and Cabernet), and Pinnacles (light, easy-drinking Pinot Noir and fine, toasty Chardonnay).

✓ *Oakville Estate* (Chardonnay, Magnificent Meritage, Merlot, Zinfandel)

FREEMARK ABBEY
St. Helena
★

Although not as fashionable in the US as it used to be, Freemark Abbey continues to produce immaculately proportioned wines.

✓ *Cabernet Sauvignon* (Bosché, Sycamore Vineyards) • *Chardonnay* (Carpy Ranch) • *Edelwein Gold* (Late Harvest Johannisberg Riesling)

FROG'S LEAP WINERY
St. Helena
★

Winemaker Larry Turley established the reputation of these organic wines of great finesse for owners John and Julie Williams.

✓ *Cabernet Sauvignon* • *Chardonnay* • *Sauvignon Blanc* • *Zinfandel*

GIRARD WINERY
Oakville
★⯪

Top-quality, smooth, and stylish Chardonnay and Cabernet. The oak sometimes used to intrude, but is seamlessly integrated these days. Girard's Chenin Blanc is one of California's finest.

✓ *Cabernet Sauvignon* (especially Reserve) • *Chardonnay* (Reserve) • *Dry Chenin Blanc*

GRACE FAMILY VINEYARDS
St. Helena
★★

Produces minuscule amounts of huge, dark, hellishly expensive Cabernet Sauvignon wine, with wonderfully multilayered fruit, oak, and *terroir* flavours.

✓ *Cabernet Sauvignon*

GREEN AND RED VINEYARD
St. Helena

This hillside vineyard in the Chiles Valley southeast of Howell Mountain is making well-structured Zinfandel that requires time in bottle.

✓ *Zinfandel* (Mill Vineyard)

GRGICH HILLS CELLAR
Rutherford
★

Owned and run by Mike Grgich, once winemaker at Château Montalena, this winery produces intense, rich, and vibrant styles of high-quality wine.

✓ *Cabernet Sauvignon* • *Chardonnay* • *Fumé Blanc* • *Johannisberg Riesling*

GROTH VINEYARDS
Oakville
❓

Although these wines are not as consistent as they used to be, Groth can still produce some of the finest Cabernet in California.

✓ *Cabernet Sauvignon* (Reserve)

HARLAN ESTATE
Napa
❓

I have not tasted any, but I have heard that some vintages of this red Bordeaux-style blend rank among the very greatest Napa wines.

HAVENS WINE CELLARS
Napa
★⯪

Since Mike Havens set-up shop in 1984 he has attracted an enviable reputation for his supremely rich Merlot Reserve, but he also makes Syrah that is in a class of its own and a masterly Bordeaux-style red wine blend called Bouriquot.

✓ *Bouriquot* (red Bordeaux style) • *Merlot* (especially Reserve) • *Syrah*

HEITZ WINE CELLARS
St. Helena
★

I would love to know how much of the famed eucalyptus character of the wine from Heitz's Martha's Vineyard is oak-derived TCA. Perhaps none at all, but to me it does sometimes smell more like TCP than TCA!

✓ *Grignolino Rosé*

THE HESS COLLECTION
Napa
★

Swiss-born art collector David Hess makes wines to be consumed not collected, although they do last well. Readers should note that Hess Select is a second label, not a premium *cuvée*.

✓ *Cabernet Sauvignon* (especially Reserve) • *Chardonnay* (Mount Veeder)

WILLIAM HILL WINERY
Napa
★

Since 1994 this has been owned by the British company Allied-Hiram Walker (which also owns Atlas Peak and Clos du Bois). More importantly, it is now in the skilful hands of winemaker Jill Davies, who has already performed marvels here, after reviving Buena Vista in Sonoma.

✓ *Merlot* • *Sauvignon*

GRGICH HILLS CELLAR
INGLENOOK VINEYARDS
Rutherford

Founded by Gustave Niebaum in 1879, Inglenook became one of California's top wineries under Niebaum's grand-nephew, John Daniels, but the winery and vineyards are now part of the Niebaum-Coppola estate. Inglenook, which was purchased by Heublein and, more recently, Canandaigua, offers a large range of popularly priced wines.

JADE MOUNTAIN
Angwin
★

Oak can sometimes be too obtrusive in the wines of this high-quality Rhône-oriented winery.

✓ *Côtes du Soleil* (red Rhône Style) • *Les Jumeaux* (Cabernet-Mourvèdre) • *Marsanne et Viognier* • *Mourvèdre* • *Le Provençale* (red Rhône style) • *Syrah*

LA JOTA
Angwin
★⯪

La Jota is best known for luxuriously flavoured Cabernet Sauvignon, but is also developing an exciting reputation for Rhône varietals.

✓ *Cabernet Sauvignon* • *Carignane* (Little J) • *Petite Sirah* (Howell Mountain) • *Viognier*

ROBERT KEENAN WINERY
St. Helena
★

This Spring Mountain hillside winery produces admirably restrained Cabernet Sauvignon and Merlot.

✓ *Cabernet Sauvignon* • *Merlot*

KENT RASMUSSEN
Napa
★⯪

This vineyard is a great source for Carneros Pinot at its most luscious.

✓ *Pinot Noir* (Carneros)

CHARLES KRUG
St. Helena

Purchased by the Mondavi family in 1943 and run by Bob Mondavi's less prominent brother Peter, this winery used to be known for its Cabernet, but most of the production is jug wine and generics sold under a second label – C. K. Mondavi.

LEWIS CELLARS
Oakville
❓

A friend gave me a bottle of Merlot from this winery and it was stunning, like a Californian version of a really top-class Pomerol, but I know nothing about this operation other than what is on the label.

✓ *Merlot* (Oakville Ranch)

LONG VINEYARDS
St. Helena
★⯪

This was established in the 1970s by Robert and Zelma Long, who are now divorced, but still joint-owners, although Zelma is now better known for establishing Simi's reputation. Long Vineyards also has a high-quality reputation for its smooth and stylish estate-bottled wines.

✓ *Cabernet Sauvignon*
• *Chardonnay*

MARCASSIN

Calistoga
★☆

This small operation belongs to Helen Turley, who made her name at B. R. Cohn and the Peter Michael Winery, and is one of California's most sought-after consultants. It produces very stylish wines.

✓ *Chardonnay* • *Pinot Noir*

MARKHAM VINEYARDS

St. Helena
★Ⓥ

Japanese-owned since 1988, Markham has been making wines with greater fruit intensity since 1993. Markham is best known for Merlot and Cabernet from its Napa Valley vineyards situated at Calistoga, Yountville, and Oakville, but watch out for great-value whites.

✓ *Cabernet Sauvignon* • *Merlot*

LOUIS M. MARTINI

St. Helena
❷

The reputation of this winery is hanging on by the slim thread attached to its single-vineyard Cabernet Sauvignon Monte Rosso.

✓ *Cabernet Sauvignon*
(Monte Rosso)

MAYACAMAS VINEYARDS

Napa

This prestigious small winery is renowned for its tannic, long-lived Cabernet, but actually produces much better, more user-friendly Chardonnay as well.

✓ *Chardonnay*

MERRYVALE VINEYARDS

St. Helena
★

These are classy, stylish wines, particularly the Bordeaux-style blends.

✓ *Chardonnay* (Silhouette)
• *Profile* (red Bordeaux style)
• *Vignette* (white Bordeaux style)

ROBERT MONDAVI

Oakville
★★

Even Robert Mondavi's lowliest wines from the Napa surpass anything produced by the new Mondavi Woodbridge Winery label of the Central Valley, which in itself is a good, inexpensive introduction to Californian wine.

✓ *Barbera* • *Cabernet Sauvignon* (Napa Reserve, Oakville)
• *Chardonnay* (Napa Reserve)
• *Chenin Blanc* • *Fumé Blanc* (Reserve, Tokalon Estate)
• *Johannisberg Riesling*
• *Malvasia Bianco* • *Moscato d'Oro* • *Pinot Noir* (particularly Reserve) • *Tocai Friuliano*
• *Zinfandel*

MONTICELLO CELLARS

Napa
★

This producer used to be better for whites than reds, but Cabernet Sauvignon is now established as the most exciting of Monticello's wines.

✓ *Cabernet Sauvignon*
(Corley Reserve)

MUMM NAPA VALLEY

Rutherford
★★☆Ⓥ

This impeccably run sparkling-wine operation is under the helm of Greg Fowler, who was the winemaker at Schramsberg for seven years. Fowler really lets his winemaking skill fly with his Sparkling Pinot Noir, which has an outrageous deep cerise colour, an aroma of strawberries, and intensely perfumed Pinot fruit.

✓ *NV Sparkling Pinot Noir*
• *Vintage DVX* • *Vintage Blanc de Blancs* • *Vintage Blanc de Noirs* (Rosé on export markets)
• *Vintage Winery Lake*

MURPHY-GOODE

Geyserville

The top wines are all rich, oaky blockbusters, but I get just as much pleasure from Fumé Blanc and lesser varietals.

✓ *Chardonnay* (J. & K. Murphy Vineyard) • *Fumé Blanc* (Reserve, Reserve Il la Deuce)
• *Pinot Blanc* (Barrel Fermented) • *Zinfandel*

NEWTON VINEYARDS

St. Helena
★★☆

This top-notch estate has a track record for wines with impeccable oak integration, silky smooth fruit, and supple-tannin structure.

✓ *Cabernet Sauvignon*
• *Chardonnay* • *Claret* • *Merlot*

NIEBAUM-COPPOLA

Rutherford
★★☆

This winery is funded by Hollywood movie director Francis Ford Coppola, who purchased Gustave Niebaum's property, the vineyard responsible for the legendary Inglenook Cabernet Sauvignons. Since 1978, this vineyard has produced a Bordeaux-style red called Rubicon, which used to be the least-crafted of all Napa wines when made by Steve Beresini, who

just let the grapes do their own thing. This hands-off approach produced a wine that had a natural inclination to mimic Médoc. In the early 1990s, however, winemaker Scott McLeod and consultant Tony Soter (of Etude) were brought in, since when there has been a move to a more hands-on, new oak style that typifies Napa's luxury-priced Cabernet-based wines. It is still a great wine, and it will probably attract a higher price, but it is a pity that the last great natural wine of Napa has now disappeared.

✓ *Rubicon* • *Chardonnay*
• *Cabernet Franc*

OPUS ONE

Oakville
★★☆

The product of collaboration between Robert Mondavi and the late Baron Philippe de Rothschild, Opus One was the first Bordeaux–California joint venture and there is no denying the quality of this Cabernet–Merlot blend, just as there is no getting away from its outlandish price.

✓ *Opus One*

PAHLMEYER

Napa

Typical of the boutique wineries established by America's affluent professional class, this operation was founded in 1985 by lawyer Jason Pahlmeyer, who hired Randy Dunn of the tiny top-notch Dunn Vineyards to be his winemaker. The wines are now made under the guidance of Helen Turley.

✓ *Caldwell Vineyard* (red Bordeaux style) • *Chardonnay* • *Merlot*

PATZ AND HALL

Napa
★

This vineyard specializes in Chardonnay with an exotically rich, stirred-lees style.

✓ *Chardonnay*

ROBERT PECOTA WINERY

Calistoga
★Ⓥ

This underrated winery always made ravishing white wines, and now has an excellent Cabernet.

✓ *Cabernet Sauvignon* (Kara's Vineyard) • *Chardonnay*
• *Gamay* • *Muscato di Andrea* (late harvest) • *Sauvignon Blanc*

ROBERT PEPI WINERY

Oakville
★

This winery is still excellent for Sauvignon Blanc, but is developing a reputation for interesting Italian-based blends.

✓ *Colline di Sassi* (classic red blend) • *Du Baci* (classic red blend) • *Sauvignon Blanc*

JOSEPH PHELPS VINEYARDS

St. Helena
★★

This prestigious winery has always had a large range of top-quality

wines, but this has recently been expanded by the exciting Mistral range of Rhône-style wines, although Insignia remains its very greatest product.

✓ *Cabernet Sauvignon* (Backus, Eisele) • *Chardonnay* (Ovation)
• *Grenache Rosé* (Vin du Mistral) • *Insignia* (red Bordeaux style) • *Le Mistral* (red Rhône style) • *Muscat* (Vin du Mistral) • *Syrah* (Vin du Mistral) • *Viognier*

PINE RIDGE WINERY

Napa

These are interesting wines of exciting quality, which are in the mid-price range.

✓ *Cabernet Sauvignon* (Andrus Reserve, Stags Leap District)
• *Chenin Blanc*
• *Merlot* (Carneros)

PLUMPJACK

Napa

This new venture is owned by the Getty family. I have not tasted the wines as they are not due to be released until late 1997.

RAYMOND VINEYARD AND CELLAR

St. Helena

The Raymond family now have Japanese partners, but remain true to their reputation for vividly fruity Chardonnay and stylish Cabernet.

✓ *Cabernet Sauvignon*
• *Chardonnay*

RUTHERFORD HILL WINERY

Rutherford

Rutherford produces a range of good, flavoursome wines.

✓ *Cabernet Sauvignon* (XVS)
• *Chardonnay* (XVS)

SADDLEBACK

Oakville

Nils Venge, formerly at Groth, is a master par excellence of the massive, old-fashioned, port-like style of Zinfandel.

✓ *Sangiovese* • *Zinfandel*

ST. CLEMENT VINEYARDS

St. Helena
❷

This Japanese-owned winery has recently shown great signs of improvement. Cabernet Sauvignon is currently its best wine.

✓ *Cabernet Sauvignon*

SAINTSBURY

Napa
★★☆

David Graves and Dick Ward continue to make lovely, plump, juicy Pinot Noir at this increasingly impressive winery.

✓ *Pinot Noir* (especially Reserve)

SCHRAMSBERG VINEYARDS

Calistoga
★

This prestigious winery started the modern Californian sparkling-wine industry rolling in 1965 and, until Domaine Chandon was set up some eight years later, was the only producer of serious-quality bottle-fermented sparkling wine in the US. The head winemakers at Codornui, Franciscan, Kristone, Mumm Napa Valley, and Piper-Sonoma are all ex-Schramsberg – an indication of how owners Jack and Jamie Davies have influenced the development of other Californian producers.

✓ *Blanc de Blancs* (young, not L. D.) • *Reserve* • *J. Schram*

SCREAMING EAGLE
Oakville
❷

Although only minuscule quantities of Cabernet Sauvignon are made, they are causing a stir in Napa, so I thought I should pass on the tip.

SEAVEY
St. Helena
★

Small quantities of beautifully crafted, premium-quality wines are produced here.

✓ *Cabernet Sauvignon* • *Merlot*

SEQUOIA GROVE
Napa
★

Brothers Jim and Steve Allen have been producing great Cabernet Sauvignon since 1978, and are now sourcing fine Chardonnay from Carneros.

✓ *Cabernet Sauvignon* • *Chardonnay*

SHAFER VINEYARDS
Napa
★★☆

Although the Cabernet Sauvignon Hillside Select is definitely this winery's best wine, Shafer also makes very stylish Merlot and Chardonnay and the deliciously smooth Firebreak, which is a sort of Californian super-Tuscan.

✓ *Cabernet Sauvignon* (Hillside Select) • *Chardonnay* (especially Red Shoulder Ranch) • *Firebreak* (classic red blend) • *Merlot*

SIGNORELLO VINEYARDS
Napa
★★☆

Ray Signorello purchased a vineyard on the Silverado Trail as long ago as 1980, but has only recently come to the fore with a bewildering display of fruity yet complex wines.

✓ *Cabernet Sauvignon* (Founder's Reserve) • *Chardonnay* (Founder's Reserve) • *Sauvignon Blanc* (Barrel Fermented) • *Sémillon* (Barrel Fermented)

SILVERADO VINEYARDS
Napa
★

Siverado is owned by the widow of the late Walt Disney, but it has never produced Mickey Mouse wines.

✓ *Cabernet Sauvignon* (Limited Reserve) • *Chardonnay* (Limited Reserve)

SPRING MOUNTAIN VINEYARDS
St. Helena
☆

Known to millions as "Falcon Crest", this winery can produce wines that require ageing and develop finesse.

✓ *Cabernet Sauvignon*

STORYBOOK MOUNTAIN VINEYARDS
Calistoga
☆

This was established by Adam and Jacob Grimm in 1880. The present owner Jerry Seps, a former university professor, has devoted his 15-hectare (36-acre) vineyard to Zinfandel.

✓ *Zinfandel* (Eastern Exposure)

SUTTER HOME WINERY
St. Helena

Zinfandel of one style or another accounts for the majority of this winery's vast production.

✓ *Zinfandel* (Reserve)

SWANSON
Rutherford
★

Swanson Food heir Clarke Swanson caught the wine bug in the 1960s while studying at Stanford, and purchased his first vineyard in the early 1980s. The style is very silky and stylish, with noticeable Bordeaux and Tuscan traits from, no doubt, winemaker Marco Capelli, who gained experience in both regions before joining Swanson in 1986.

✓ *Cabernet Sauvignon* • *Chardonnay* • *Sangiovese* • *Sémillon* (Late Harvest) • *Syrah*

SILVER OAK CELLARS
Oakville
★

Concentrates solely on one variety, Cabernet Sauvignon, but there are three *cuvées* – Napa Valley, Bonny's Vineyard (also Napa Valley AVA), and Alexander Valley. I prefer the latter because it has the least oak and the most finesse, although those who enjoy big and oaky Cabernets will adore all three.

✓ *Cabernet Sauvignon* (Alexander Valley)

ROBERT SINSKEY VINEYARDS
Napa
★★☆

These vineyards produce vividly flavoured Pinot, classy Carneros Claret, luscious Merlot, and age-worthy Chardonnay.

✓ *Carneros Claret* (red Bordeaux style) • *Chardonnay* • *Merlot* (Los Carneros) • *Pinot Noir*

SMITH-MADRONE
St. Helena
★

This winery consists of some 16 hectares (40 acres) of high-altitude vines producing a small, high-quality range of wines.

✓ *Johannisberg Riesling*

SPOTTSWOODE
St. Helena
★★

On benchland in the Mayacamus Mountains, consultant Tony Soter produces tiny amounts of powerful but stylish wine.

✓ *Cabernet Sauvignon* • *Sauvignon Blanc*

STAGLIN
Napa
★★☆

This underrated winery produces lush, beautifully balanced Cabernet of great finesse, and stunningly rich yet silky-smooth Sangiovese.

✓ *Cabernet Sauvignon* • *Sangiovese* (Stagliano)

STAGS' LEAP WINE CELLARS
Napa
★★

A legendary Cabernet Sauvignon producer, but its Chardonnay should not be overlooked. Its second label is Hawk Crest.

✓ *Cabernet Sauvignon* (Fay Vineyard, S.L.V.) • *Cask 23* (red Bordeaux style) • *Chardonnay* (especially Reserve) • *Petite Sirah*

STAGS' LEAP WINERY
Napa
☆

This other Stags Leap winery is better known for one of California's finest Petite Sirah wines.

✓ *Petite Sirah*

STERLING VINEYARDS
Calistoga
★

Astonishingly high-quality in the mid-1970s, Sterling's standards dropped after Coca-Cola purchased it in 1978, but started a revival when Seagrams took over in 1983 and has continued to improve.

✓ *Cabernet Sauvignon* (Diamond Mountain Ranch) • *Malvasia* (Collection Series) • *Merlot* (Three Palms) • *Pinot Grigio* (Collection Series) • *Pinot Noir* (Winery Lake)

STONY HILL VINEYARD
St. Helena
★

The Chardonnays here are still world-class, but fatter than before.

✓ *Chardonnay*

PHILIP TOGNI VINEYARD
St. Helena
★

Philip Togni earned great respect at Chalone, Chappellet, Cuvaison, Mayacamus, and Chimney Rock, before establishing this vineyard.

✓ *Cabernet Sauvignon*

TREFETHEN VINEYARDS
Napa
☆

This winery combines high quality and consistency with good value.

✓ *Chardonnay* (Library Selection) • *White Riesling*

TURLEY CELLARS
Napa
★☆

The debut vintage from this exciting new venture by talented brother-and-sister winemakers Larry and Helen Turley was 1993, and the wines were an instant critical success.

✓ *Petite Syrah* (sic) • *Zinfandel*

VIADER
St. Helena
★

Tiny quantities of deeply coloured, concentrated red Bordeaux-style wine blended from vines grown on the steep slopes of Howell Mountain.

✓ *Viader*

VICHON WINERY
Oakville
★☆

The name Vichon was compiled from the names of the original restaurateur owners, Vierra, Brucher, and Watson, who sold the winery to nearby Mondavi in 1985.

✓ *Chevrignon* (white Bordeaux style)

VILLA MT. EDEN WINERY
Oakville
★ ❤

Owned by Stimson Lane (which owns Château Ste. Michelle, Columbia Crest, and Conn Creek), Villa Mt. Eden established a high reputation in the 1980s, but has become less exciting since branching into a wider range of wines.

✓ *Cabernet Sauvignon* (Signature) • *Chardonnay* (Grand Reserve) • *Pinot Blanc* (Grande Reserve)

WHITEHALL LANE WINERY
St. Helena
★

Established in 1979 by an architect and a plastic surgeon, sold in 1988 to a Japanese firm, and bought in 1993 by San Francisco wine-shop owner, Tom Leonardi. Despite various owners, Whitehall Lane consistently produces some inspired wines.

✓ *Cabernet Sauvignon* (Morisoli Vineyard) • *Merlot* (Summer's Ranch)

WHITE ROCK
Napa
★

This 100-year-old vineyard was restored in the late 1970s and is best known today for its Cabernet-based blend named Claret. Readers should not overlook the ripe Chardonnay.

✓ *Chardonnay* • *Claret* (red Bordeaux style)

ZD WINES
Napa
★☆❷

Pronounced "Zee Dee", this winery used to make variable Cabernet Sauvignons. It is now very consistent and challenges Chardonnay's position as ZD's best varietal.

✓ *Cabernet Sauvignon* • *Chardonnay*

THE NORTH-CENTRAL COAST

Originally a district where a small number of big companies produced a vast quantity of inexpensive wines, the North-Central Coast can now boast a large number of top-quality, highly individual wineries.

WINEMAKING IN THE NORTH-CENTRAL COAST district dates from the 1830s, when virtually all the vineyards were located in and around Santa Clara County, and this remained the situation until the late 1950s and early 1960s, when the growing urban sprawl of San Jose forced the wine industry to search out new areas for vine-growing. Happily, this search coincided with the publication of a climatic report based on heat-summation (*see* p.448) by the University of California. This report pinpointed cooler areas further south, particularly in Monterey, that should support fine-wine vineyards.

THE MOVE TO MONTEREY

In 1957, two companies, Mirassou and Paul Masson, were the first to make the move, purchasing some 530 hectares (1,300 acres) in the Salinas Valley. In the ensuing rush to plant the land, some areas were used that were too cool or exposed to excessive coastal winds. These failures were not the fault of the heat-summation maps, but were due to producers who could not conceive that grapes would not ripen in California.

In October 1966, the two authors of the heat-summation study, Professors Winkler and Amerine, were honoured at a special luncheon where a toast was made to "the world's first fine-wine district established as the direct result of scientific temperature research". Although this might have seemed premature, it has been substantiated by Monterey's viticultural growth. It was Bill Jekel who first brought the quality potential of this area to international fame, but this winery has been eclipsed by an eclectic bunch of wineries such as Bonny Doon, David Bruce, Calera, Chalone, Edmunds St. John, Frick, Morgan, Mount Eden, Ridge, Rosenblum, and Tamas.

JEKEL VINEYARDS
Oak barrels wait to be filled at one of the North-Central Coast's pioneering wineries. Vineyards stretch out across the flat plain of Salinas Valley, where intensive irrigation systems have made this hot and dry area more synonymous with crisp salad vegetables than with wines, and the new pioneering wineries have moved up into the hills.

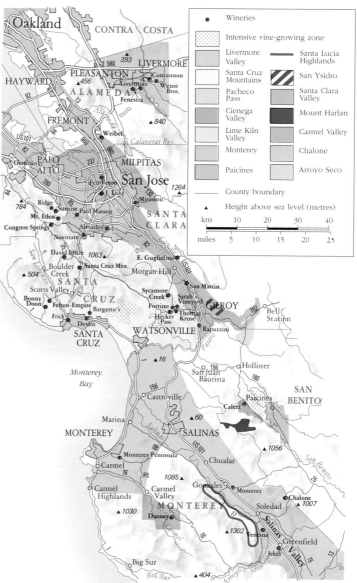

THE NORTH-CENTRAL COAST, *see also p.448*
Until the late 1950s, most wineries were in Santa Clara County, and although this is still the North-Central Coast's heartland, it has long been in a slow decline, while Monterey and Santa Cruz are the area's fastest-growing counties.

FACTORS AFFECTING TASTE AND QUALITY

LOCATION
The Central Coast's northern sector stretches from the San Francisco Bay area to Monterey.

CLIMATE
Generally warm (Region III, *see* p.448), but with variations such as the cooler (Region I, *see* p.448) areas of the Santa Cruz Mountains and the northern part of the Salinas Valley. Low rainfall in the south necessitates much irrigation, but there are microclimates with higher rainfall.

ASPECT
Vines are planted mainly on the flat and sloping lands of the various valleys. Variations are found: on the steep slopes of the Santa Cruz Mountains and the high benchland of the Pinnacles above Soledad, for example.

SOIL
A wide variety of gravel loams, often high in stone content and rich in limestone, in the Livermore Valley; clay and gravel loams in Santa Clara; sandy and gravelly loams over granite or limestone in San Benito; and gravelly, well-drained low-fertility soils in Monterey.

VITICULTURE AND VINIFICATION
A small number of big wine companies produce a vast quantity of inexpensive wines utilizing high-tech, production-line methods. The number of small wineries is growing. Many of these are quality-conscious and some are justifiably famous.

GRAPE VARIETIES
Barbera, Cabernet sauvignon, Carignan, Chardonnay, Chenin blanc, Colombard, Gamay, Gewürztraminer, Grenache, Grey riesling, Mourvèdre, Muscat, Pinot blanc, Pinot gris (*syn.* Pinot grigio), Pinot noir, Petite sirah, Riesling, Sauvignon blanc, Sémillon, Syrah, Trebbiano, Viognier, Zinfandel.

NORTH-CENTRAL COAST

ALAMEDA COUNTY AO

This appellation covers grapes grown anywhere within Alameda County.

ARROYO SECO AVA
Monterey County

This appellation covers 73 square kilometres (28 square miles) of triangular-shaped, sloping bench land adjacent to the Arroyo Seco Creek, a tributary of the Salinas River. Its vineyards are free from frost and adequately drained. The predominant soil is a coarse sandy loam, with a low lime content.

BEN LOMOND MOUNTAIN AVA
Santa Cruz County

This AVA covers 155 square kilometres (60 square miles) on Ben Lomond Mountain, northwest of Santa Cruz, and encompassing 28 hectares (70 acres) of vines.

CARMEL VALLEY AVA
Monterey County

This appellation covers 78 square kilometres (30 square miles) around the Carmel River and Cachagua Creek. A distinctive microclimate is created by the valley's higher elevation and its protective northeastern Tularcitos Ridge, which curbs the intrusion of marine fog and provides more sunny days than is usual in the county.

CHALONE AVA
Monterey County

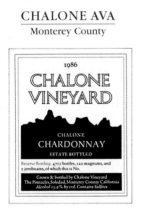

1986
CHALONE
VINEYARD

CHALONE
CHARDONNAY
ESTATE BOTTLED

This area covers 35 square kilometres (13½ square miles) of benchland between the North and South Chalone Peaks, 500 metres (1,650 feet) above sea level, with volcanic and granitic soils of high limestone content. Peak summertime temperatures in the Carmel Valley are hotter than the Salinas Valley, and it is not affected by maritime fog and so has more sunny days, but it is the altitude of this one-winery AVA (Chalone Vineyards) that makes its quality potential so superior for white wine varietals, particularly Chardonnay, Chenin blanc, and Pinot blanc.

CIENEGA VALLEY AVA
San Benito County

The Cienega valley is located at the base of the Gabilan (or Gavilan) Mountain Range where the Pescadero Creek is used artificially to augment the area's rainfall. The soil is loamy, well-drained, and often lies over weathered granite.

CONTRA COSTA COUNTY AO

The Contra Costa County AO is an appellation covering grape varieties grown anywhere within Contra Costa County.

HAMES VALLEY AVA
Monterey County

A new sub-appellation within the Monterey AVA, Hames is located in the south of the county, five kilometres (three miles) west of Bradley and 11 kilometres (seven miles) north of Lake Nacimiento, where more than 250 hectares (600 acres) of vineyards already exist.

LIME KILN VALLEY AVA
San Benito County

Although part of the Cienega Valley, Lime Kiln Valley is significantly different in its climate, with an annual rainfall ranging between 41 centimetres (16 inches) on the eastern valley floor and 102 centimetres (40 inches) in the mountainous western area, and in its soils, which are sandy and gravelly loams over a bedrock of limestone, with a high magnesium carbonate content.

LIVERMORE VALLEY AVA
Alameda County

The Livermore Valley is one of the coastal inter-mountain valleys surrounding San Francisco. The appellation has a moderate climate, cooled by sea breezes and morning fog, though with very little spring frost. Virtually all its annual 38 centimetres (15 inches) of rain falls in the winter and early spring. The South Bay Aqueduct, however, provides overhead sprinkler irrigation.

MONTEREY AVA
Monterey County

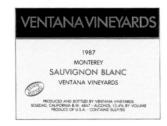

VENTANA VINEYARDS

1987
MONTEREY
SAUVIGNON BLANC
VENTANA VINEYARDS

This AVA is confined to the Monterey Bay area and the Salinas Valley, where the various sandy and gravelly loams are of an alluvial origin and differ from those of surrounding areas. It is also distinguished by a very dry climate that yields barely 25 centimetres (10 inches) of rain a year, although the watersheds of the Santa Lucia, Gabilan, and Diablo Mountain Ranges provide sufficient water, through the presence of underground aquifers, to irrigate the vineyards.

MONTEREY COUNTY AO

An appellation covering grapes that are grown anywhere within Monterey County.

MOUNT HARLAN AVA
San Benito County

Like Chalone, Mt. Harlan is, for all intents and purposes, a single-winery AVA (Calera in this instance), and is situated on rare limestone outcrops in the same range of hills (the San Benito Range), albeit at the other end and on the opposite facing flank. The Mount Harlan AVA is even higher – 670 metres (2,200 feet) – than Chalone, which also enabled Calera to seek a reputation based on Pinot Noir, although Chalone's vineyards were planted 30 years earlier, and thus have a good lead.

PACHECO PASS AVA
Santa Clara and San Benito Counties

The terrain sets this area apart from its neighbours. It is a small valley, with a flat or gently sloping topography that contrasts with the rugged hills of the Diablo Range to the east and west. The climate is moderate and wetter than that of the Hollister Basin to the south.

PAICINES AVA
San Benito County

Here the days are warm and the nights cool, and the annual rainfall ranges between 30 and 38 centimetres (12 and 15 inches). This AVA has fallen into disuse since Almadén, the winery that proposed it, moved to Santa Clara.

SAN BENITO AVA
San Benito County

Not to be confused with San Benito County, this AVA encapsulates the smaller AVAs of Paicines, Cienega Valley, and Lime Kiln Valley.

SAN BENITO COUNTY AO

This is an appellation covering grapes grown anywhere within San Benito County.

SAN LUCAS AVA
Monterey County

This AVA consists of a 16-kilometre (10-mile) segment of the Salinas Valley between King City and San Ardo, in the southern section of Monterey County. The soils in this area are mostly alluvial loams.

SAN MATEO COUNTY AO

This is an appellation covering grapes grown anywhere within San Mateo County.

SAN YSIDRO AVA
Santa Clara County

The appellation of San Ysidro covers a small enclave of vineyards at the southeastern end of the Santa Clara AVA. San Ysidro sits between two hills that channel the cool sea breezes coming up the Pajaro River, and is noted most particularly for Chardonnay.

SANTA CLARA COUNTY AO

This is an appellation covering grapes grown anywhere within Santa Clara County.

SANTA CLARA VALLEY AVA
Santa Clara County

Encompassing the entire municipality of San Jose to the north and better known as Silicon Valley in the south, this AVA must qualify as the most built-up wine appellation in the world. As it is the southern section where all the action is, why not just restrict the boundaries and call it Silicon Valley?

SANTA CRUZ MOUNTAINS AVA
Santa Clara County

The name "Santa Cruz Mountains" was first recorded in 1838. Its climate is influenced in the western section by ocean breezes and maritime fog movements, while the eastern area is moderated by the San Francisco Bay. Cool air coming down from the mountains forces warmer air up, lengthening the growing season to a full 300 days. The soils are forms of shale that are peculiar to the area.

THE WINE PRODUCERS OF THE
NORTH-CENTRAL COAST

ALMADÉN VINEYARDS
Santa Clara County
Almadén is now part of Canandaigua, which also owns Inglenook, Dunnewood, and Cooks. Founded in 1852, Almadén is the oldest continuously produced wine brand in the United States. A vast array of varietal and non-varietal wines are sold in various sizes and types of container with reuseable tops.

BONNY DOON VINEYARD
Santa Cruz County
★★
This is one of California's brightest, most bizarre, and most innovative stars, with wines that are electrifying in their brilliance, finesse, and style. I have got lost trying to find Bonny Doon on two occasions, but it was worth the effort just to meet the whacky winemaker, Randall Grahm. He specializes in Rhône varieties, is going over to Italian, makes sublime Pinot Noir, has produced an ice-wine with the help of a freezer, and once even made a *vin de paille*. This superb winery will soon be relocating to Livermore.

✓ *Barbera*
- *Cigare Volant* (red Rhône style)
- *Clos de Gilroy* (Grenache)
- *Muscat Canelli Vin de Glacier*
- *Old Telegram* (Mourvèdre)
- *Syrah* • *Vin Gris de Cigare Rosé*

DAVID BRUCE
Santa Cruz County
Some may long for the days when David Bruce produced a really concentrated Chardonnay, and I dare say it was as necessary for him to go through that phase as it was for California generally, but as he went through his own learning curve, so his wines have been tamed, and Pinot Noir has emerged as consistently his finest.

✓ *Pinot Noir*

CALERA WINE COMPANY
San Benito County
★★
This is one of California's premier pioneers in the continuing quest for perfect Pinot Noir. Potentially, it is probably the best, although its pursuit of elegance can produce a certain "prettiness" of style.

✓ *Pinot Noir* (especially Jensen and Selleck) • *Viognier*

CEDAR MOUNTAIN
Alameda County
This boutique winery was established in 1990 and early vintages are promising, if a little too correct and in need of a personal signature.

✓ *Cabernet Sauvignon*

CHALONE VINEYARD
Monterey County
★★
This winery's 63-hectare (155-acre) vineyard has its own AVA. Chalone Vineyard is dedicated to, and astonishingly successful at, producing a range of fine, complex wines of the most exquisite style.

✓ *Chardonnay* • *Chenin Blanc* • *Pinot Blanc* • *Pinot Noir*

CONCANNON VINEYARD
Alameda County
★

The Concannon family established this vineyard in 1883, but sold out in 1962. Deinhard became the new owner in 1988, but sold it to a partnership headed by the Wente family in 1992. Despite these changes of ownership, Concannon has continued to make one of California's finest Petite Sirah wines and the reason for this can be traced back to the early days of this vineyard, as the vines for this wine are nearly 80 years old.

✓ *Petite Sirah* (especially Reserve)

CRONIN VINEYARDS
San Mateo County
★
This winery is famous for full-throttle, toasty Chardonnay, but excellent Sauvignon Blanc is also produced here.

✓ *Chardonnay* • *Sauvignon Blanc*

DURNEY VINEYARD
Monterey County
★★
Although under new ownership since the death of Bill Durney, this winery continues to produce heroically dark, rich, densely-flavoured Cabernet Sauvignon, and is now also making splendidly long-lived Chardonnay.

✓ *Cabernet Sauvignon* • *Chardonnay*

EDMUNDS ST. JOHN
Alameda County
★★
Steven Edmunds and Cornelia St. John established this exciting winery in 1985 in what used to be the East Bay Wine Works, where they have honed some of California's most beautifully balanced wines.

✓ *Mourvèdre* • *Pinot Grigio* • *Syrah* • *Viognier*

FRICK WINERY
Santa Cruz County
★
This winery is an up-and-coming Rhône-style specialist with a hands-off approach to winemaking.

✓ *Cinsault* • *Petite Sirah*

ELLISTON VINEYARDS
Alameda County
★ ✔
Established in 1983 by Ramon and Amy Awtrey, two school teachers, who have always made a passable Pinot Gris, which has in recent years become deliciously fruity and unpretentious.

✓ *Pinot Gris* (Sunol Valley)

JEKEL VINEYARD
Monterey County
Once known for its fascinating range of Riesling, this winery is no longer the force it used to be.

J. LOHR
Santa Clara County
Best for fruity Gamay that is not just a good quaffer, but really quite elegant and well-perfumed with plenty of refreshing acidity.

✓ *Gamay* (Wildflower)

PAUL MASSON VINEYARDS
Monterey County
Founded by a Burgundian, this winery is one of the great jug-wine success stories of California. It is now part of Canandaigua (owners of Almadén, Inglenook, Dunnewood, and Cooks), with more emphasis on cheap varietals. Wines are also sold under the Taylor label.

MIRASSOU VINEYARDS
Santa Clara County
This company, known for its jug-wines, still makes one of California's best Pinot Blanc wines.

✓ *Pinot Blanc* (Harvest Reserve)

MONTEREY PENINSULA WINERY
Monterey County
This is under new ownership, but Zinfandel is still worth a look.

✓ *Zinfandel*

MORGAN WINERY
Monterey County
★
Possibly California's most underrated and age-worthy Pinot Noir is produced here. Good Chardonnay is also made but is not always in the same class. The fresh, zesty Sauvignon Blanc is improving.

✓ *Chardonnay* • *Pinot Noir* (especially Reserve) • *Sauvignon Blanc*

MOUNT EDEN VINEYARDS
Santa Clara County
★
This winery produces just three varietals, all of which are fine in quality. The Chardonnay excels, but the deep, dark, chocolaty Cabernet makes a close second.

✓ *Cabernet Sauvignon* (Old Vine Reserve) • *Chardonnay* (Santa Cruz)

MURRIETA'S WELL
Alameda County
Run by Phil Wente, whose wines are more understated but finer than those of his more prominent brother, Eric of Wente Bros.

✓ *Vendemia* (classic red blend) • *Zinfandel*

RIDGE VINEYARDS
Santa Clara County
★★
Those who wonder about the long-term maturation potential of Californian wines should taste these stunning ones, some of which need between 10 and 20 years in bottle before they are even approachable. Although I recommended all but the Paso Robles in the first edition of this book, I have to say that Paso Robles is today one of Ridge's finest examples of Zinfandel.

✓ *Cabernet Sauvignon* (Monte Bello) • *Chardonnay* (Howell Mountain, Santa Cruz Mountains) • *Geyserville* (blended red) • *Mataro* (Evangelo) • *Petite Sirah* (York Creek) • *Zinfandel* (Dusi Ranch, Lytton Springs, Pagain Ranch, Paso Robles)

ROSENBLUM CELLARS
Alameda County
With no less than five different *cuvées* of Zinfandel, Rosenblum has established himself as a worthy specialist, a reputation that is constantly enhanced by his various vineyard-designated bottlings today.

✓ *Zinfandel*

ROBERT TALBOTT VINEYARDS
Monterey County
Run by the son of the late-founder, the Talbott family is best known for the internationally renowned Monterey-based Talbott Tie Company.

✓ *Chardonnay* (especially Diamond T)

IVAN TAMAS
Alameda County
★ ✔
Quaffable, inexpensive wines of real interest are made by up-and-coming former *négociants* turned winemakers. Anyone who can make delicious wine from Trebbiano deserves success.

✓ *Fumé Blanc* • *Trebbiano*

WENTE BROS.
Alameda County
✔
Established for more than a century, Wente's wines can range from overtly fruity to distinctly dull. However, they are always inexpensive and some can be very good value. The company also owns Concannon Vineyard.

✓ *Sauvignon Blanc* (Livermore Valley)

THE SOUTH-CENTRAL COAST

An up-and-coming wine district in general, the South-Central Coast has very rapidly become one of the very best areas in the world, outside of Burgundy itself, for Pinot Noir. Chardonnay is equally exciting, and Italian varietals could well be the most prized wines of the next millennium.

PASO ROBLES WAS ORIGINALLY PLANTED with vines in the late 18th century; the Santa Ynez Valley, in Santa Barbara County, had a flourishing wine industry in pre-Prohibition times and the town of Santa Barbara itself was once dotted with vineyards. Yet both of the counties were virtually void of vines in the early 1960s, and it was not until Estrella, in Paso Robles, and Firestone, in the Santa Ynez Valley, had established very successful vineyards in 1972, that others began to follow.

Quite why Santa Barbara of all areas on the South-Central Coast has suddenly become the mecca for Pinot Noir specialists is difficult to unravel. In the late 1980s, California seemed the least likely place to be in a position to challenge Burgundy for the Holy Grail of winemaking. Oregon and New Zealand looked much more likely, but they have both since proved too small and prone to inconsistency. If it was going to be California, no one a decade ago would have put their money on Santa Barbara, way down south, just a stone's throw from Los Angeles; Carneros or Russian River seemed a more likely bet. The foundations for Santa Barbara's sudden surge of wonderful Pinot Noir wines were laid innocently in the 1970s, when the land was relatively cheap and planted with this variety in order to supply the sparkling-wine industry in the north of the state. It is impossible to pinpoint

exactly when local winemakers realized the potential of making their own still wine, but much of California's finest, purest, and most consistent Pinot Noir wines now come from this valley.

The Santa Ynez Valley makes the best Santa Barbara Pinot, yet the area where it excels is very restricted: 14 kilometres (nine miles) from the ocean and the valley is too cool to ripen grapes; 26 kilometres (16 miles) and it is ideal for Pinot noir; but for every 1.5 kilometres (one mile) further from the ocean the grapes gain an extra degree (ABV) of ripeness, and by 32 kilometres (20 miles) from the coast, this is Cabernet country. The best Pinot noir vineyard in the Santa Ynez Valley is Sanford & Benedict, much of which is used for the Sanford label, although Richard Sanford no longer owns all of the former property. In the Santa Maria Valley, which is also well-suited to Pinot noir, the best vineyard is Bien Nacido.

FACTORS AFFECTING TASTE AND QUALITY

LOCATION
This stretches southwards along the coast from Monterey, and includes the counties of San Luis, Obispo, and Santa Barbara.

CLIMATE
Generally warm (Region III, *see* p.448), except for areas near the sea, particularly around Santa Maria in the middle of the region where Regions I and II (*see* p.448) prevail because of the regular incursion of the tail of the great coastal fog bank. Annual rainfall ranges from 25 cm (10 in) to 114 cm (45 in).

ASPECT
Most vines grow on hillsides in San Luis Obispo and southern-facing bench land in Santa Barbara County, at altitudes that range from 37–180 m (120–600 ft) in the Edna Valley, to 180–305 m (600–1,000 ft) in Paso Robles, and 460 m (1,500 ft) on York Mountain.

SOIL
Mostly sandy, silty, or clay loams, but the soil can be more alkaline, as in the gravelly lime soils that are found on the foothills of the Santa Lucia Mountains.

VITICULTURE AND VINIFICATION
By the mid-1980s, the cooler areas had invited experimentation with the Burgundian varieties planted in the early 1970s to supply sparkling wine producers in the north of the state, and by the late 1980s a number of world class Pinot Noirs had been produced. This variety is the region's main claim to fame, although viticultural methods are still developing, as indeed are vinification processes. Open-top fermenters are commonly used, the cap being punched down frequently. Some producers have incorporated 15–30% whole-cluster, but most have shied away from this. A cold maceration is followed by natural yeast fermentation, the temperatures of which run nice and high. After a gentle pressing, the wines are matured in *barriques* with 25–50% new oak. The oak is all French, and nearly everyone prefers tight-grain, with many going for a heavy toast.

GRAPE VARIETIES
Barbera, Cabernet franc, Cabernet sauvignon, Chardonnay, Chenin blanc, Gewürztraminer, Malvasia, Muscat, Pinot blanc, Pinot noir, Riesling, Sangiovese, Sauvignon blanc, Sémillon, Sylvaner, Syrah, Tocai Friuliano, Zinfandel

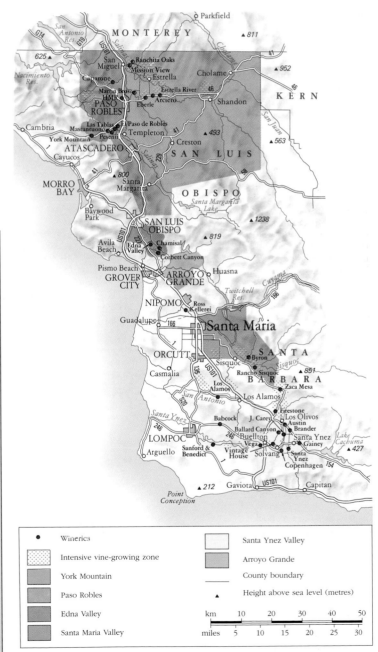

Wineries ·
Intensive vine-growing zone
York Mountain
Paso Robles
Edna Valley
Santa Maria Valley
Santa Ynez Valley
Arroyo Grande
County boundary
▲ **Height above sea level (metres)**

km 10 20 30 40 50
miles 5 10 15 20 25 30

THE SOUTH-CENTRAL COAST, *see also* p.448
Based on San Luis Obispo and Santa Barbara counties, this area has a fine reputation for top-quality Pinot Noir.

THE APPELLATIONS OF THE
SOUTH-CENTRAL COAST

ARROYO GRANDE VALLEY AVA
San Luis Obispo County

An area of 173 square kilometres (67 square miles) some 19 kilometres (12 miles) southeast of the town of San Louis Obispo, the Arroyo Grande Valley enjoys a Region I to II climate (*see* p.448), thanks primarily to its proximity to the ocean and the frequent fog produced by marine air in the mornings and evenings. Planted at an altitude of between 90 and 300 metres (300–1,000 feet), vines grow at much higher altitudes than those in the neighbouring Edna Valley AVA, and also receive slightly more rain. The hillsides cultivated range from moderate to very steep slopes, with deep, well-drained, sandy-clay and silty-clay loam soils. With a 17° C (30° F) drop in night-time temperatures, relatively high acidity levels are maintained throughout ripening. The potential for sparkling wine is considerable, so it is perhaps not surprising that Maison Deutz is the best-known winery here, with the largest vineyards in the appellation. Deutz has also produced some still Chardonnay and Pinot Noir, and although rather strange, disjointed, and hardly indicative of any potential for such wines, Au Bon Climat has had stunning success with these varieties.

EDNA VALLEY AVA
San Luis Obispo County

This elongated valley is located just south of Paso Robles, and is well-defined by the Santa Lucia Mountains to the northeast, the San Luis Range to the southwest, and a low hilly complex to the southeast. In the northwest, the Edna Valley merges with the Los Osos Valley, forming what is, in effect, a wide-mouthed funnel that sucks in ocean air from Morro Bay. This marine air flows unobstructed into the valley, where it is captured by the pocket of mountains and hills, providing a moderate summer climate that differentiates it from surrounding areas. The vines grow on the valley floor, rising to 120 metres (600 feet) in the Santa Lucia Mountains, on soils that are mostly sandy-clay loam, clay loam, and clay.

PASO ROBLES AVA
San Luis Obispo County

This area was given its name in the 18th century, when travellers passed through it on their way from the San Miguel to the San Luis Obispo missions. It is one of California's oldest winegrowing regions: grapes have been harvested in this area of rolling hills and valleys since *circa* 1797. There is no penetration by coastal winds or marine fog and, consequently, there is the equivalent of an additional 500 to 1,000 degree-days here compared to viticultural areas to the west and east. This obviously has a considerable effect on grape-ripening patterns making Paso Robles red-wine country, particularly for Zinfandel and Rhône varieties.

SAN LUIS OBISPO AO

An appellation covering grapes grown anywhere within the entire county of San Luis Obispo.

SANTA BARBARA AO

An appellation covering grapes grown anywhere within the entire county of Santa Barbara.

SANTA MARIA VALLEY AVA
Santa Barbara County

The Pacific winds blow along this funnel-shaped valley, causing cooler summers and winters and warmer autumns than in the surrounding areas. The terrain climbs from 60 to 240 metres (200–800 feet), with most of the vineyards concentrated at 90 metres (300 feet). The soil is sandy and clay loam, and is free from the adverse effects of salts. This is top-quality Pinot noir country and Bien Nacido (which many winemakers have access to) in the Tepesquet Bench area is far and away its best vineyard. Noises about Bien Nacido in the 1990s are reminiscent of the fuss made a decade earlier about the Sanford & Benedict vineyard in the Santa Ynez Valley. The Santa Maria Valley also grows top-quality Chardonnay and even one of California's best Syrahs.

SANTA YNEZ VALLEY AVA
Santa Barbara County

The Santa Ynez Valley is bounded by mountains to the north and south, by Lake Cachuma to the east, and by a series of low hills to the west. Close proximity to the ocean serves to moderate the weather with maritime fog, and this lowers the temperatures. The Santa Rita Hills block penetration of the coldest sea winds, however, so the middle and eastern end of the Valley do not have the coolest of coastal climates (2,680 degree-days), while Lompoc, just three kilometres (two miles) outside the appellation's western boundary, has just 1,970 degree days. The vineyards are located at an altitude of between 60 and 120 metres (200–400 feet) in the foothills of the San Rafael Mountains, on soils that are mostly well-drained, sandy, silty, clay, and shale loam. Santa Barbara's finest Pinot noir comes from the Sanford & Benedict vineyard (which a number of winemakers have access to) in the west, yet just a few miles further up the valley it is Cabernet and Zinfandel country. The Santa Ynez Valley also grows top-quality Chardonnay.

TEMPLETON
San Luis Obispo County

Templeton is situated within Paso Robles. It is not an AVA, but I have included it for the purposes of clarification, because various sources have stated that it is. Even official publications from California's Wine Institute have made the same error.

YORK MOUNTAIN AVA
San Luis Obispo County

This small appellation is just 11 kilometres (seven miles) from the sea, situated at an altitude of 450 metres (1,500 feet) in the Santa Lucia Mountains, close to the western border of Paso Robles. Its Region I (*see* p.448) climatic classification, and 114 centimetres (45 inches) of rain per year, set it apart from the warmer, and considerably drier, surrounding areas.

THE WINE PRODUCERS OF THE
SOUTH-CENTRAL COAST

ADELAIDA CELLARS

Established in 1983, this winery is headed by Bill Munch, whose best wines were initially Chardonnay, but they now seem to be the huge, rich, and deliciously fruity Sangiovese and Zinfandel.

✓ *Sangiovese* · *Zinfandel*

AU BON CLIMAT
Santa Barbara County
★★☆

I have never met anyone who talks quite as much as Jim Clendenen. He has no real need – his wines do all the talking necessary – but I listen because I love his wines and cannot get a word in anyway. The first time I came across one of his wines, it was thrust under my nose by UK wine merchant Jasper Morris MW,

who asked "What do you think that is?". A quick sniff, swirl, and spit and I said that it tasted like a mature village Burgundy of a good, but not great, year from the southern Côtes-de-Beaune. I told Jasper I knew it

was a trick, but why should I try to be clever: if he served it as a Santenay I would not have been suspicious. It was, in fact, 30 months-old Santa Barbara Pinot Noir from Au Bon Climat. I purchased a case.

✓ *Chardonnay* (especially Sanford & Benedict) · *Pinot Noir* (especially Sanford & Benedict for finesse and Rosemary's Vineyard from Arroyo Grande for a riper, fatter style)

BABCOCK VINEYARDS
Santa Barbara County
★★☆

Best for succulently sweet Pinot Noir and juicy, oaked Sauvignon Blanc. An exciting Santa Ynez Pinot Noir called Casa Cassara comes from Babcock's new hilltop vineyard.

✓ *Pinot Noir* · *Sauvignon Blanc* (especially 11 Oaks Ranch)

BYRON
Santa Barbara County
★★☆

Under Mondavi ownership since 1990, these wines are still made by founder Byron Ken Brown, whose white wines are even better than his Pinot Noir.

✓ *Chardonnay* · *Pinot Blanc* · *Pinot Noir* (Reserve) · *Sauvignon Blanc* (Reserve)

CAMBRIA
Santa Barbara County
★★☆

That Cambria, which is owned by Kendall-Jackson, can be so successful with both Pinot Noir and Syrah, two grape varieties that require diametrically opposed climates, illustrates the diversity of *terroirs* in the Santa Maria Valley.

✓ *Chardonnay* (particularly Katherine's Vineyard)
• *Pinot Noir*
• *Syrah* (Tepusquet Vineyard)

CHIMÈRE
Santa Barbara County
★✫❷

Chimère is a small producer of excellent Burgundian varietals, and I am told that owner–winemaker, Gary Mosby, also produces an interesting Nebbiolo.

✓ *Chardonnay* (Santa Barbara)
• *Pinot Noir* (Edna Valley)

EBERLE WINERY
San Luis Obispo County
★★✫

Look no further if you want massively-built Zinfandel, but the Cabernet is the better-balanced wine, and the Barbera is one of California's unsung heroes.

✓ *Barbera* • *Cabernet Sauvignon*
• *Muscat Canelli* • *Zinfandel*

EDNA VALLEY VINEYARD
San Luis Obispo County
★★✫

This vineyard produces superbly rich and toasty Chardonnay and very good Pinot Noir.

✓ *Chardonnay* • *Pinot Noir*

FESS PARKER WINERY
Santa Barbara County
★✫

Unless you enjoyed a 1950s childhood, the name Fess Parker is not likely to mean anything to you, but for me it will always be synonymous with Davy Crockett, so it was quite amusing to see a fat American lady at least twice my age swoon in front of this still imposing figure. Even more unfortunately she found all the wines too dry, even the excellent off-dry Riesling failed to please, but she did buy a poster of Mr. Crockett taking a bath wearing just his coonskin hat.

✓ *Johannisberg Riesling* • *Syrah*

FIRESTONE VINEYARD
Santa Barbara County
★✫

A very conscientious winery that makes fine wines. Although they can occasionally lapse, the wines

are usually rich and ripe, and can sometimes be magnificent.

✓ *Cabernet Sauvignon*
• *Johannisberg Riesling*

FOXEN VINEYARD
Santa Barbara County
✫

I am not as enamoured as some by this winery's Pinot Noir, but have great respect for virtually everything else produced here.

✓ *Cabernet Sauvignon*
• *Chardonnay* • *Chenin Blanc*
(Barrel Fermented)

THE GAINEY VINEYARD
Santa Barbara County
★★✫

A decade ago, winemaker Rick Longoria was knocking out stemmy Pinot Noir and sweet Riesling was his best offering. Now he makes one of Santa Barbara's best Pinots.

✓ *Cabernet Franc* (Limited Selection) • *Chardonnay* (Limited Selection) • *Pinot Noir* (especially Sanford & Benedict) • *Sauvignon Blanc* (Limited Selection)

HARTLEY OSTINI
Santa Barbara County
★★✫

Frank Ostini is the soft-spoken, friendly, fun-loving chef-owner of the Hitching Post restaurant in Santa Maria, which serves tasteful, unpretentious American barbecue food at its best. Hartley also enjoys making wines, in a corner of Jim Clendenen's Au Bon Climat vineyard.

✓ *The Hitching Post Pinot Noir* (especially Bien Nacido and Sanford & Benedict)
• *The Hitching Post Zinfandel*

KRISTONE
Santa Barbara County
★✫❷

Kendall-Jackson's prestige sparkling-wine project came to fruition in 1996 with the launch of a Blanc de Blancs and Blanc de Noirs, both from the 1991 vintage. Made by "Mad Harry" Harold Osborne (who was Schramsberg's first winemaker in the 1960s and consultant to Cloudy Bay for the development of their Pelorus sparkling wine), this first vintage of Kristone Blanc de Blancs was way too fat and blowzy, and dominated by huge toasty-oak aromas, but the Blanc de Noirs was beautifully crafted, with a succulent balance of fruit. Mad Harry believes in harvesting ripe fruit, rather than picking early when acid levels are correct. As he says, you can add acidity, but you cannot possibly put fruit and richness into a wine made from unripe grapes.

LONGORIA
Santa Barbara County
★★✫

Such is the modesty of Rick Longoria that he showed me just one wine from his own vineyard when I visited Gainey's, where he is the winemaker. It was not until later

that I discovered that he produced a range of different wines, albeit in very small quantities.

✓ *Cabernet Franc*
• *Chardonnay* • *Pinot Noir*

IL PODERE DELL' OLIVOS
Santa Barbara County
★★✫

Operating out of the Au Bon Climat winery, Il Podere dell Olivos makes one of California's finest Barbera wines – lovely acidity.

✓ *Barbera*
• *Pronto* (fortified Aleatico)

MAISON DEUTZ
San Luis Obispo County

A joint venture between Champagne Deutz and Beringer, Maison Deutz was established in 1985, and I have been waiting for it to come right ever since. Christian Rogunenant is highly knowledgeable and I am sure he will one day succeed.

MOSBY WINERY
Santa Barbara County

Bill and Jeri Mosby run this interesting, sometimes provocative, Italian-style specialist operation.

✓ *Moscato di Fior*
• *Primitivo*

QUPÉ
Santa Barbara County
★★✫❷

This Rhône-style specialist (owned by Bob Lindquist) also operates out of the Au Bon Climat winery. I am not so keen on the Marsanne.

✓ *Syrah* (Bien Nacido)
• *Los Olivos* (red Rhône style)

RANCHO SISQUOC
Santa Barbara County
★

These vividly fruity wines come from one of Santa Barbara's first vineyards. Rancho Sisquoc covers 80 hectares (200 acres) of the massive 14,500-hectare (36,000-acre) Flood Ranch.

✓ *Cabernet Franc* • *Cellar Select* (red Bordeaux style)
• *Chardonnay* • *Sylvaner*
• *Sauvignon Blanc*

SANFORD WINERY
Santa Barbara County
★★★✫

Richard Sanford's Barrel Select Sanford & Benedict is consistently one of California's finest Pinot Noirs, and the 1994 is probably the greatest example of this grape I have tasted outside of Burgundy.

✓ *Chardonnay* (especially Barrel Select Sanford & Benedict)
• *Pinot Noir* (especially Barrel Select Sanford & Benedict)
• *Sauvignon Blanc*

SANTA BARBARA WINERY
Santa Barbara County
★★✫♥

The oldest Santa Barbara winery dates back to the early 1960s, but did not get interested in premium-quality wines until a decade later. Now produces a number of great-value wines, particularly from Burgundian varieties.

✓ *Chardonnay* (Lafond Vineyard)
• *Pinot Noir* (Reserve)
• *Sauvignon Blanc* (Reserve Musqué) • *Zinfandel* (Beaujour)

LANE TANNER
Santa Barbara County
★★✫

The eponymous Lane Tanner established this small winery in 1989, since when he has honed a deliciously deep style of ripe, pure-flavoured Pinot Noir.

✓ *Pinot Noir* (Sanford & Benedict Vineyard)

VITA NOVA
Santa Barbara County
★♥

A joint venture between Jim Clendenen of Au Bon Climat and Qupé's Bob Lindquist, the emphasis is on elegance and the avoidance of overblown fruit.

✓ *Cabernet Franc* • *Chardonnay*
• *Sémillon* (Reservatum)

WILD HORSE
San Luis Obispo County
✫

Established in 1982 by Ken Volk, who has created a reputation for making beautiful wines from various lesser-known varieties, including Tocai Friuliano, which is none other than the Sauvignonasse of Chilean infamy, but this must be one of the greatest wines made from that otherwise despised grape.

✓ *Malvasia* (Barrel Fermented)
• *Pinot Blanc* • *Tocai Friulana*

ZACA MESA WINERY
Santa Barbara County

Good-value Chardonnay and Pinot Noir currently being eclipsed by more exciting, low-yield Rhône-style wines.

✓ *Cuvée Z* (red Rhône style)
• *Syrah* (Zaca Vineyard)

THE CENTRAL VALLEY

While California's coastal areas are its most famous wine districts and those most capable of producing fine wines, they are not as significant in terms of quantity as the baking-hot, flat, and dry Central Valley, which accounts for three-quarters of all Californian wine; one company, Gallo, produces half of that.

IF I HAD ANY PLANS AT ALL for the Californian section of this new edition, it was to shine a light on the Central Valley, which has always been brushed to one side by authors because of its jug-wine reputation. Looking through the first edition of this book, I was nagged by the same question – "Surely the source of three out of every four bottles of Californian wine is worthy of some attention?". To find an answer, I made two visits specifically to look for the wines of the Central Valley. I wanted to establish whether any areas or wines truly stood out and the reasons why.

Why do AVAs such as Clarksburg, Merritt Island, and Lodi exist, if they do not mean something? Clarksburg is supposed to be good for Chenin Blanc, and Lodi has an even greater, older reputation for Zinfandel, but if this is true, why aren't the UK and other price-conscious, value-minded markets flooded with such wines? Perhaps in this valley of giant producers there are a number of small wineries making some stunning wines for the price, but lacking the money or marketing muscle to get them noticed?

To get some answers I asked a local expert to set up a tasting of the best Central Valley AVA wines. I imagined there would be well over a hundred different wines, but he was able to assemble only 36 and a number of those were old vintages from wineries that no longer exist. After discounting those that were supposedly produced from pure or mostly Central Valley grapes, but did not make any such claims on the bottle and were not very interesting in any case, there were just eight wines currently available that proudly claimed their origins. Maybe more might be available by the time this book is published, but it was evident that there were not a lot of individually expressive wines waiting to be discovered in the Central Valley. I tasted some passable Chenin from Clarksburg, but nothing special and the best were only supposedly from Clarksburg, as they did not claim the AVA.

The wines from Bogle Vineyards on Merritt Island, at the heart of Clarksburg, were not particularly impressive at the tasting but, having had the opportunity to taste younger vintages at the

FRANZIA WINERY AT RIPON, NEAR MODESTO
Looking more like oil refineries than wineries, firms such as Franzia have perfected the art of industrialized winemaking.

winery itself, it was obviously one of the few independent Central Valley producers likely to succeed. I came away feeling that Bogle makes much better red than white wine, particularly Merlot, but it blends in up to 60 per cent bought-in grapes, using the generic Californian appellation. As for the Lodi Zinfandel, the few examples claiming the AVA were big, old-fashioned, tasted maderized, and sometimes stank quite foully.

Although I failed to find any outstanding wines, the experience taught me that the Central Valley AVAs are an irrelevance because the state's largest wineries (particularly Gallo, but also Mondavi at Woodbridge, in the heart of Lodi) have ignored them. When they select exceptional wines to bear and show off these AVAs, perhaps consumers will no longer be dismissive of the Central Valley?

FACTORS AFFECTING TASTE AND QUALITY

LOCATION
The viticultural area of this huge fertile valley stretches 640 km (400 miles) from Redding in the north to Bakersfield in the south, running between the Coastal Ranges to the west and the Sierra Nevada to the east.

CLIMATE
Generally homogenous from end to end, warming steadily from Region IV (*see* p.448) in the north to Region V (*see* p.448) in the south. The area around Lodi is the only exception, being cooled by sea air sweeping up the Sacramento River.

ASPECT
The vines are grown on the vast flat area of the valley floors, intersected and irrigated by a network of levees.

SOIL
Very fertile sandy loam dominates the length and breadth of the valley.

VITICULTURE AND VINIFICATION
Production of vast quantities of reliable-quality jug-wine, using the latest techniques of mechanization and irrigation, and a virtually continuous fermentation and bottling process. Somewhat higher-quality Zinfandel and sweet dessert wines are produced around Lodi.

GRAPE VARIETIES
Barbera, Cabernet sauvignon, Carnelian, Carignan, Chenin blanc, Colombard, Grenache, Merlot, Mourvèdre, Muscat, Petite sirah, Ruby cabernet, Sauvignon blanc, Sémillon, Zinfandel

HARVESTED CABERNET SAUVIGNON GRAPES
Despite its huge output, premium quality wines can be produced in Central Valley.

THE APPELLATIONS OF THE
CENTRAL VALLEY

CLARKSBURG AVA
Sacramento County

A large area south of Sacramento encompassing the AVA of Merritt Island, Clarksburg is cooled by the cool breezes that roll in off Suisun Bay. The average annual rainfall is 41 centimetres (16 inches), which is greater than the precipitation experienced in areas to the south and west, but less than that which occurs north and east. The area is crisscrossed by more than 1,600 kilometres (1,000 miles) of river and irrigation channels.

DUNNIGAN HILLS AVA
Yolo County

This is a new AVA located northwest of Sacramento in the rolling Dunnigan Hills. Much of the 445 hectares (1,100 acres) of vineyards cultivated in this area belongs to R. H. Phillips, a go-ahead winery that has led the Dunnigan Hills reputation for easy-drinking varietals.

LODI AVA
Sacramento and San Joaquin Counties

An inland area that comprises alluvial fan, plains that are prone to flood, and terrace lands both above and below the levees.

MADERA AVA
Madera and Fresno Counties

A viticultural area not to be confused with Madera County, Madera AVA is located in both the Madera and Fresno Counties and contains more than 14,500 hectares (36,000 acres) of wine grapes, plus substantial areas of raisin and table grapes.

MERRITT ISLAND AVA
San Joaquin County

An island bounded on the west and north by Elk Slough, by Sutter Slough on the south, and the Sacramento River on the east. Its climate is tempered by cooling southwesterly breezes from the Carquinez Straits, near San Francisco, which reduce the temperature substantially compared to that of the City of Sacramento, located just ten kilometres north. The soil is primarily sandy loam, while areas to the west have clay-type soil, and to the south, an organically structured, moderately fertile peat dirt.

NORTH YUBA AVA
Yuba County

North Yuba is located in the middle and upper foothills of Yuba County, immediately west of the Sierra Nevada and north of the Yuba River. This area escapes both the early frosts and the snow of higher elevations in the Sierra Nevadas and the heat, humidity, and fog common to the Sacramento Valley lowlands, and the climate is therefore relatively temperate compared to the rest of the AVA.

THE WINE PRODUCERS OF THE
CENTRAL VALLEY

BOGLE VINEYARDS
Sacramento County

Chris Smith, a former assistant winemaker at Kendall-Jackson in Lake County, is improving the quality at this winery, which has large vineyards on Merritt Island.

✓ *Merlot • Petite Sirah*

FICKLIN VINEYARDS
Madera County
☆

Ficklin is California's leading estate-bottled port-style specialist. The vineyards are planted with authentic Douro varieties such as Touriga nacional and Tinta cão, plus Souzao, which is used in Portugal for Dão.

✓ *NV Port • Vintage Port*

FRANZIA WINERY
San Joaquin County

Franzia produces a large amount of inexpensive, often overtly fruity wines. However, the better varietals, such as Cabernet Sauvignon, can be very sweet indeed. Other labels include Tribuno.

E. & J. GALLO WINERY
Stanislaus County

With production equivalent to one-and-a-half times the entire annual output of Australia, Gallo is not only California's largest winery, it is the largest wine producer in the world. On the basis of volume alone, Gallo should warrant at least 45 pages in a book of this size.

To say that Gallo is corporately nervous about wine journalists is an understatement. I did not manage to gain entry to the massive winery complex at Modesto until 1993, and that was only after I threatened to drive through the gates if they did not open them. There is no problem if a wine journalist wants to visit their upmarket estate in Sonoma, it is their pride and joy, but they cannot understand why anyone would want to tour their mass-production facilities. The answer is simple: it is an oenological miracle for any one firm to produce such mega-quantities and at the same time keep the wines drinkable.

From the air, the Modesto premises might look like an oil refinery, but from the ground as you enter the estate you see peacocks roaming freely over well-manicured lawns and inside the building there is a marble-bedecked reception, with waterfalls cascading into large pools surrounded by lush tropical vegetation, and containing carp the size of submarines. I cannot understand why Gallo are reluctant to show this off.

Gallo not only makes a lot of cheap plonk, it also produces inexpensive, yet drinkable varietal wines. The plonk comes under a variety of labels (Tott's André, Bartles & James, Carlo Rossi etc.), which encompass coolers, sweet wines from foxy-flavoured native grapes such as Concord, and most of the generics (i.e. Burgundy, Chablis, Rhine etc), while the varietals bear the Gallo name itself (the non-vintage Cabernet Sauvignon is a real penny-saver). Some generics such as Hearty Burgundy and Chablis Blanc can cross the divide into the reasonably drinkable (sometimes amazingly drinkable) category, and the better generics also carry the Gallo name; there is a big difference between Gallo Hearty Burgundy or Chablis Blanc and Carlo Rossi Burgundy or Chablis.

This is how the brothers Ernest and Julio Gallo, two struggling grape-growers who had to borrow money to buy a crusher when Prohibition ended, built up their business to become the most powerful wine producers in the world. This commercial success was not enough, however, as both brothers also wanted the critical acclaim of making some of California's finest wines, which is why they literally moved mountains to terraform their prized Sonoma estate.

But if Ernest Gallo is satisfied (Julio was tragically killed in an automobile accident in 1993), he should not be. To create Gallo Sonoma with the money he threw at it was no challenge at all. If he really does want respect and critical acclaim, then I have a real challenge for him: give the winemakers at Modesto a free rein to do two things: bottle-off small batches of anything exceptional, and allow them to develop pet projects.

I have never been one to condemn the huge wineries because of their size. The bigger they are, then the more likely they will come across an outstanding batch of grapes or wine. The choice of losing these little gems in some mega-blend or of giving them due recognition is what separates the best large wineries from the worst.

That Gallo has an army of highly qualified oenologists is beyond question, but it is obvious that those with any creativity will want to express that talent. If Gallo allowed its winemakers to propose and carry out their own pet projects (such as working with Lodi growers to make the best local Zinfandel possible), this would induce them to stay.

By following these two strategies, Gallo could very quickly attract rave reviews from the most hardened critics for limited bottlings of truly exciting wines. It would reveal the best that can be expected from California's Central Valley vineyards, verify whether the AVAs that exist deserve to be recognized, and pinpoint any other potential appellations that might exist. That would be a fitting achievement for a company that has benefited more than any other from the Central Valley, and an ideal legacy for which Gallo would always be remembered.

✓ *Cabernet Sauvignon* (Sonoma County, Northern Sonoma) • *Chardonnay* (Northern Sonoma, Stefani Vineyards) • *Merlot* (Frei Ranch Vineyard, Three Vineyard) • *Zinfandel* (Frei Ranch Vineyard)

R. H. PHILLIPS
Sacramento County
★☆❷

A spotless, hard to find winery on the Diamond G Ranch in the rolling Dunnigan Hills, R. H. Phillips is well worth searching out for supreme value wines that are wickedly easy to drink.

✓ *Alliance* (red Rhône style) • *Diamond G* (Sémillon–Sauvignon) • *Mourvèdre* (EXP) • *Night Harvest Cuvée Rouge*

QUADY WINERY
Madera County
★

Quady is an eclectic fortified wine specialist par excellence.

✓ *Fortified Muscat* (Electra, Elysium, Essensia) • *Port* (Starboard)

OTHER APPELLATIONS OF
CALIFORNIA

Note This section contains a round-up of the various California wine areas that are not dealt with in the preceding pages. Each of the AVAs listed below can be found on the regional California map (*see* p.448).

SIERRA FOOTHILLS

In the 1850s, this land of majestic vistas was California's gold-rush country, but since the 1970s scores of new wineries have opened up, mostly of the one-man "boutique" ilk. The Sierra Foothills is a quality-wine area that is definitely not part of the Central Valley. It attracts rugged specialists who, not content with the safe option of farming fertile valley floors, want the challenge of making expressive wine in limited quantities in one of the few areas of California where, owing to the altitude, cultivating grapes is not always possible. In the 19th century, Zinfandel was the king of these mountain vineyards, and quickly re-established itself as the big, blockbusting, spicy star of the 1980s. However, Sauvignon blanc and Riesling were quick to take up the challenge, with Barbera and, predictably, Cabernet sauvignon and Merlot not far behind.

CALIFORNIA SHENANDOAH VALLEY AVA

Amador County

The famous Shenandoah Valley is, of course, in Virginia and, like this AVA, received its status in 1983. The California Shenandoah Valley AVA, which is set amid the Sierra Foothills, was named by Virginian settlers who migrated to California during the gold rush. Vines were first grown here in 1881 when the diggers ran out of gold, and, as a result, turned to making wine instead. The soil is well-drained, moderately deep, and consists mostly of coarse sandy loams formed from weathered granitic rock over heavy, often clayey, loam.

EL DORADO AVA

El Dorado County

The soil is mostly decomposed granite, except on Apple Hill, east of Placerville, where an old lava flow exists (see Lava Cap winery). Apple Hill is one of two main winegrowing areas and, as the name suggests, the area is covered with orchards. Orchards invariably predate vineyards in the US and vines always do extremely well wherever apples have grown best. The other main vineyard is located in the southeast of the AVA, between Quitingdale and Fairplay. Go any further east and not only is it too cold for grapes, but grizzly bears become a real pest.

FIDDLETOWN AVA

Amador County

The Fiddletown viticultural area is located in the eastern Sierra Foothills of Amador County. It differs from the neighbouring Shenandoah Valley of California area because of its higher elevations, colder temperatures at night, and greater rainfall. Grapes are grown without any irrigation and the vineyards are located on deep, moderately well-drained, sandy loams.

NORTHERN CALIFORNIA

SEIAD VALLEY

Siskiyou County

Located just 21 kilometres (15 miles) south of the Oregon border, the Seiad Valley AVA is comprised of 877 hectares (2,165 acres) of which just over one (2.5 acres) is planted with vines.

WILLOW CREEK AVA

Humboldt County

This area is influenced primarily by two major climatic forces: the Pacific Ocean and the warmer climate of the Sacramento Valley 160 kilometres (100 miles) to the east. These create easterly winds that give Willow Creek fairly cool temperatures in the summer and infrequent freezes in the winter. The area to the east of Willow Creek experiences colder temperatures in winter and hotter temperatures in summer.

SOUTHERN CALIFORNIA

CUCAMONGA VALLEY AVA

Los Angeles and San Bernardino Counties

An area of more than 40,500 hectares (100,000 acres), some 72 kilometres (45 miles) from Los Angeles, the Cucamonga Valley was first planted with Mission grapes in about 1840. Despite Prohibition, the vineyards reached their peak in the 1950s, when more than 14,000 hectares (35,000 acres) were under vine. As the viticultural emphasis in California moved northwards, these vineyards declined, but there are still five operational wineries and some 800 hectares (2,000 acres) of vine.

MALIBU-NEWTON CANYON AVA

Los Angeles County

A one-vineyard appellation on the south-facing slopes of the Santa Monica Mountains.

SAN PASQUAL AVA

San Diego County

A natural valley located in the Santa Ysabel watershed, the San Pasqual Valley is fed by natural streams that feed the San Dieguito River, and is substantially affected by coastal influences. Temperatures are warm in the summer, but seldom very hot, and ocean breezes cool the area, especially during the night-time. The surrounding areas have a variety of very different climates ranging from tropical, through desert-like, to mountainous.

TEMECULA AVA

Riverside County

Temecula is located in Riverside County, Southern California, and includes Murrieta and Rancho California. Marine breezes entering the area through the Deluz and Rainbow Gaps cool the area to moderate temperatures. Sauvignon blanc and Chardonnay are the most widely planted varieties and Chenin blanc and Cabernet sauvignon the least successful.

LAKE, MARIN, *and* SOLANO COUNTIES

The only other counties of significance are Lake, Marin, and Solano, all of which are part of the North Coast AVA. Of these, Lake is the only area of real repute.

BENMORE VALLEY AVA

Lake County

Surrounded by the 1,000-metre (2,900-foot) peaks of the Mayacamus Mountains, this AVA encompasses 50 hectares (125 acres) of vines, but no wineries.

CLEAR LAKE AVA

Lake County

Located between the Mayacamas Mountains and the Mendocino National Forest, Clear Lake's large water-mass moderates the AVA's climate. Although this area is best for Chardonnay and Sauvignon Blanc, well-textured Cabernet Sauvignon is also produced.

GUENOC VALLEY AVA

Lake County

This appellation lies south of McCreary Lake and east of Detert Reservoir. Situated within the North Coast AVA, the valley has a more extreme climate, lower rainfall, and less severe fog than the nearby Middletown area.

SOLANO COUNTY GREEN VALLEY AVA

Solano County

Green Valley is sandwiched between the Napa Valley to the west and the Suisun Valley to the east. The soil here is a clay loam and the climate is influenced by the cool, moist winds that blow inland from the Pacific and San Francisco Bay almost continuously from spring through to autumn.

SUISUN VALLEY AVA

Solano County

Adjacent to Solano County Green Valley, and a stone's throw from the Central Valley, Suisun Valley AVA enjoys the same cool, moist winds that blow from spring until autumn in both of these areas. The soils consist of various forms of clay, and silty and sandy loams.

OTHER WINE PRODUCERS OF
CALIFORNIA

SIERRA FOOTHILLS

AMADOR FOOTHILL WINERY
Amador County

The wines from this winery, with its small Shenandoah Valley vineyards, are made by owner and ex-NASA chemist Ben Zeitman.

✓ *Zinfandel*

BOEGER WINERY
El Dorado County
☆

The first winery to re-open the pre-Prohibition Sierra Foothill vineyards, Boeger has established itself as a producer of understated fine wines that take time to flesh out in bottle, more appealing perhaps to European palates than to Californian ones.

✓ *Barbera • Cabernet Sauvignon • Merlot • Zinfandel*

IRONSTONE
Calaveras County
★

Opened in 1994, John Kautz's winery in gold-rush country has already shown a capability for smooth, lush Cabernet Franc and rich, oaky Syrah (labelled Shiraz, as in Australia).

✓ *Cabernet Franc • Shiraz*

KARLY WINES
Amador County
★

This underrated winery makes high-quality wines that are packed with flavour and show amazing finesse.

✓ *Sauvignon Blanc • Zinfandel*

LAVA CAP
Placerville
☆ⓥ

Underrated, inexpensive varietals grown on the volcanic soils, some 760 metres (2,500 feet) up Apple Hill in the El Dorado AVA.

✓ *Zinfandel*

MADRONA VINEYARDS
El Dorado County

These vineyards were established in 1980 high in the Sierra Foothills by engineering consultant Richard Bush.

✓ *Cabernet Franc • Quintet Reserve* (red Bordeaux-style)

MONTEVIÑA
Amador County

Best known for Zinfandel, Monteviña is hoping to start a Latino trend with Italian varieties planted in its Shenandoah Valley vineyards.

✓ *Zinfandel*

RENAISSANCE
Yuba County
★

Renaissance was founded by the Fellowship of Friends, a self-sufficient community of like-minded people dedicated to the fine arts. The range includes fine wines, which are made by Diana Werner in a clever, circular winery surrounded by an amphitheatre of vines in one of the most idyllic spots on earth.

✓ *Sauvignon Blanc* (Dry, Late Harvest) • *Riesling* (Dry, Late Harvest)

SHENANDOAH VINEYARDS
Amador County
❓

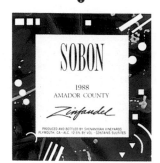

The Sobon family made some powerful wines here in the 1980s, but the produce of the following decade has been inconsistent.

✓ *Zinfandel* (Sobon Vineyard)

SOUTHERN CALIFORNIA

SOUTHERN CALIFORNIA

Southern California, site of the state's first vineyard, has even less land under vine than the Sierra Foothills. Since 1977 it has undergone a revival, particularly in Riverside and, to a lesser extent, San Diego counties.

CALLAWAY VINEYARD AND WINERY
Riverside County
☆

This was one of the first wineries to prove that parts of southern California have, in fact, excellent microclimates for producing fine-wine grapes.

✓ *Chardonnay* (Calla-Lees) • *Fumé Blanc • Chenin Blanc*

MORAGA
Los Angeles County
★

Six acres of Bel-Air real estate worth $3 million seems an odd place to grow vines when each bottle would have to retail at $50 for 22 years in order to gross – not cover – the original investment. Viticulturally, however, this tiny sandstone and limestone canyon is a good choice. It has a discernible microclimate with 61 centimetres (24 inches) of rain each year compared with 38 centimetres (15 inches) on nearby properties, and the wines are also truly fine by any standards. Most of owner Tom Jones' wine is a soft, deep-coloured red Bordeaux-style blend with seamless oak integration and beautifully layered fruit, the flavour building in the mouth.

He also makes a tiny amount of fresh, soft, delicately rich Sauvignon Blanc. My only suggestion might be that he should also try Viognier.

✓ *Moraga* (Bel Air) • *Sauvignon Blanc*

LEEWARD WINERY
Ventura County

The rich, toasty Chardonnay has been a favourite here for a long time.

✓ *Chardonnay*

THE OJAI VINEYARD
Ventura County
★☆

Adam Tolmach, a former partner in Au Bon Climat, teamed up with Helen Hardenbergh to create this boutique winery. Stylish, smoky-blackcurrant Syrah stands out, but Sauvignon Blanc and, particularly, Cuvée Spéciale Sainte Hélène Reserve should not be overlooked.

✓ *Cuvée Spéciale Sainte Hélène* (white Bordeaux style) • *Sauvignon Blanc • Syrah • Viognier*

THORNTON
San Diego County

John Culbertson has been making sparkling wine since the early 1980s. I have only recently been impressed, by the fruity yet elegant Vintage Blanc de Noirs Brut Reserve.

✓ *Vintage Blanc de Noirs Brut Reserve*

LAKE, MARIN, AND SOLANO COUNTIES

GUENOC WINERY
Lake County
☆ⓥ

This was once the property of Lillie Langtry (a mistress of Edward VII, when he was the Prince of Wales) whose picture is used to market one of these excellent-value wines.

✓ *Cabernet Sauvignon • Chardonnay • Langtree* (red Meritage) • *Zinfandel*

KONOCTI WINERY
Lake County
ⓥ

A cooperative of some 18 local growers backed by three investors, Konocti has built up a tremendous reputation for inexpensive, easy-drinking wines.

✓ *Cabernet Franc • Chardonnay • Fumé Blanc*

KALIN CELLARS
Marin County

Microbiologist Terry Leighton uses minimal handling techniques to craft ultra-high-quality wines that are deep, full, and rich, with great finesse and complexity.

✓ *Chardonnay* (especially Cuvée CH, Cuvée LD, Cuvée W) • *Pinot Noir • Sauvignon Blanc • Sémillon* (Livermore Valley)

KENDALL-JACKSON
Lake County
★★ⓥ

When the first edition was written, the Kendall-Jackson brand was barely four years old, yet had already gained a wide reputation. Since then, however, it has acquired and created an amazing range of wineries under its "Artisans & Estates" arm. These include Cambria, La Crema, Edmeades, Hartford Court, Kristone, Lakewood, Stonestreet, and also Vina Calina (all but the last profiled in this book). Kendall-Jackson's signature is its extraordinary quality-price ratio of wines.

✓ *Cabernet Sauvignon* (Grand Reserve) • *Cardinale Meritage* (red Bordeaux style) • *Chardonnay* (Camelot) • *Sauvignon Blanc* (Grand Reserve) • *Sémillon* (Vintner's Reserve) • *Syrah* (Durell Vineyard) • *Viognier* (Grand Reserve) • *Zinfandel* (Ciapusci Vineyard, Dupratt Vineyard, Proprietor's Grand Reserve)

STEELE
Lake County
★★

This is the personal label of Jed Steele, who is a former Kendall-Jackson winemaker and highly regarded wine consultant. His debut vintage was 1991, and his brightly-flavoured, brilliantly stylish wines made an instant impact. His second label is Shooting Star.

✓ *Chardonnay* (particularly Lolonis Vineyard, Du Pratt Vineyard, Sangiacomo Vineyard) • *Pinot Blanc* (Santa Barbara) • *Pinot Noir* (Sangiacomo Vineyard) • *Zinfandel* (Catfish Vineyard)

SEAN THACKREY AND COMPANY
Marin County
★

San Francisco art dealer Sean Thackrey loved Burgundy, which led him to establish this winery in 1980 and, naturally enough, try his hand at sculpting Pinot Noir. But it was not until the late 1980s that his wines began to appear and quickly attract attention, not for elegant Pinot, but for big, thick, richly-flavoured Rhône varietals.

✓ *Mourvèdre* (Taurus) • *Petite Sirah* (Sirius) • *Syrah* (Orion)

THE PACIFIC NORTHWEST

Although most wine enthusiasts will have heard of Oregon Pinot Noir, many would be surprised to find that vines are grown in Washington state at all, and even more surprised to learn that Washington has four times as many vineyards and produces twice as much wine as Oregon.

IN CONTRAST TO OREGON, the wines of Washington are not represented by any specific style, and this may well be the reason why this state has failed to register with wine drinkers. This will soon change, as Washington's wine producers, having dithered between sparkling wine and aromatic whites, realize that their state is really red-wine country and, in particular, a mecca for Merlot.

WASHINGTON STATE

In 1775 the Spanish laid claim to the land now known as Washington. Seventeen years later, Robert Gray, captain of the first US ship to circumnavigate the globe, claimed it for the Americans; and George Vancouver actually claimed it for the British a month before Gray even reached the area. In spite of this, it remained Spanish until 1819, although it was effectively controlled by America through the latter's domination of the fur trade. Washington became the 42nd state in the union in 1889.

The early wine trade

The first planting of vines in Washington was in about 1825 at Fort Vancouver on the Columbia River by traders working for the Hudson's Bay Company, though it is not known whether wine was actually produced. Washington's earliest winery was established at Walla Walla in the 1860s and the first *vinifera* vines were planted at Yakima in 1871, although the production of wine on a truly commercial scale was not effected until the post-Prohibition New Deal era allowed funding of the Columbia River irrigation project, which transformed an arid desert into an agricultural paradise.

Washington's wine industry grew rapidly, and no less than 42 wineries were in operation by 1937, but the vineyards, like those in the rest of North America, were essentially *labrusca-*

THE PACIFIC NORTHWEST
See also p.443

Encompassing thousands of square kilometres, the Pacific Northwest is a collection of well-dispersed winemaking areas. The ocean defines its western border from northern California in the south to the Canadian border in the north. The sea moderates the climate although it has little effect on inland Idaho.

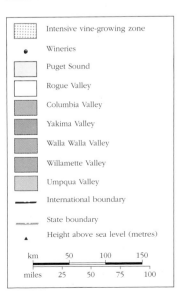

▦	Intensive vine-growing zone
•	Wineries
	Puget Sound
	Rogue Valley
	Columbia Valley
	Yakima Valley
	Walla Walla Valley
	Willamette Valley
	Umpqua Valley
▬	International boundary
—	State boundary
▲	Height above sea level (metres)

km   50   100   150
miles   25   50   75   100

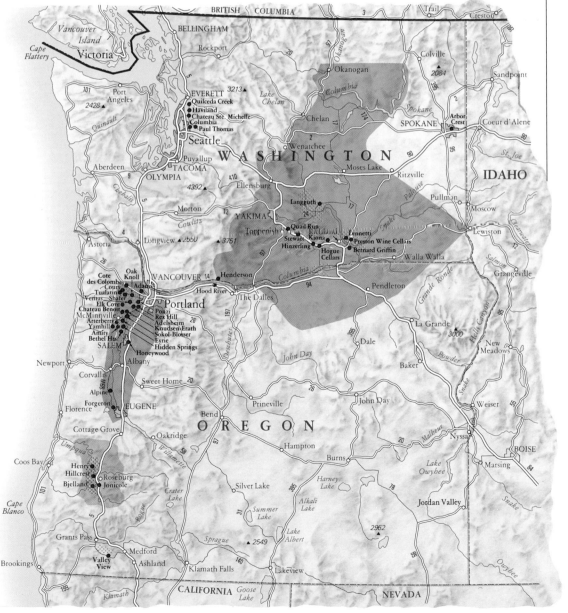

based. In addition to supplying California wineries with base wines for their abysmal "Cold Duck" blends (*see* p.498), the industry produced its own cheap, sweet, and often fortified wines from Concord, Island Belle, and other cloyingly foxy-tasting grapes.

Vitis vinifera did exist (*see* p.20): William Bridgman's Upland Winery in Yakima was making Muscat, Riesling, and Sémillon wines as early as 1934. It was not until 1951 that the first commercial

---

RECENT PACIFIC-NORTHWEST VINTAGES

2000 Both Washington and Oregon have high hopes of combining record level crops with excellent quality. This is the first year in which Washington's black grape vineyards have surpassed the state's white grape acreage.

1999 The best Washington reds ever. Very good Oregon Pinot Noir; on a par with the 1998s, but more accessible.

1998 The best Washington reds produced since 1994. Very good Oregon Pinot Noir, with better potential longevity, but in need of greater bottle-age.

1997 Excellent Washington reds, perhaps a tad better than the 1996s; however, this is the third in a trio of less than inspiring vintages for Oregon Pinot Noir.

1996 This year was the first in a row of four spectacularly successful vintages for Washington reds, but forgettable as far as Oregon Pinot Noir was concerned.

FACTORS AFFECTING TASTE AND QUALITY

LOCATION
An arbitrary grouping of three northwestern states: Washington, Oregon, and Idaho. The Yakima Valley, running through Washington, is at roughly the same latitude as northern Bordeaux and southern Burgundy.

CLIMATE
The temperatures generated by continental air masses are moderated in Washington and Oregon by westerly winds from the Pacific Ocean. Oregon is the coolest state, and Washington the wettest but, with the exception of Puget Sound, all the viticultural areas of Washington are not only hotter, but much drier than those of Oregon, with plentiful sunshine (averaging over 17 hours per day in June) and crisp, cool nights during the critical ripening period. Climatic conditions are generally more continental towards Idaho.

ASPECT
The vines are located in valleys, usually planted on low-lying slopes, but also on the valley floors and, in Oregon, in the hilly hinterland.

SOIL
The soils are deep, fertile, light-textured, silty, sandy, or clay loams over volcanic bedrock, and sometimes more clayey in Oregon.

 VITICULTURE AND VINIFICATION
Washington vines are ungrafted, irrigation is widely practised, with the oldest vines protected by

cutting off the water supply prior to winter, thus allowing them to become dormant before the cold sets in. According to various surveys, Washington's viticultural areas are almost phylloxera-free, but some growers say it is rife in the state's Concord vines, which are resistant to the pest, yet for some mysterious reason it has not attacked *vinifera* vines growing on the same soil in adjacent vineyards. There is a general belief that Washington will have to graft over its vines, but it is difficult from a survival point of view in areas where the winters are so cold.

Oregon is also looking at clonal and rootstock selection, but with much of Domaine Drouhin Oregon's success put down to the tight spacing of its vines, the big issue is whether to go for high-density vineyards. More than 50 per cent of Oregon's Pinot noir are planted at a density of less than 2,000 vines per hectare and 30 per cent are between 2,000 and 3,000. A small number have tried increasing the density to between 3,000 and 4,500 vines per hectare, but claim there is no discernible advantage. However, the benefits do not kick in until vine-density gets above 4,500 and Drouhin's vines are planted at 7,450 per hectare.

GRAPE VARIETIES
Cabernet sauvignon, Chardonnay, Chenin blanc, Gamay, Gewürztraminer, Merlot, Muscat ottonel, Pinot gris, Pinot noir, Riesling, Sauvignon blanc, Sémillon, Zinfandel

---

plantings of *vinifera* vines of the post-Prohibition period took place, but the example was not followed. Trial studies of *vinifera* varieties were conducted in the late 1950s at the Washington State University by Dr. Walter Clore. Clore's enthusiasm for these grapes earned him the nickname "Grandpa Grape" and encouraged the American Wine Growers (now called Château Ste.-Michelle) to start the *vinifera* ball rolling with the first of several considerable plantings in the early 1960s. By 1978 there were 1,000 hectares (2,500 acres) of *vinifera* vines being grown in Washington. Now there are 5,900 hectares (14,500 acres), from which some 85 wineries produce three million cases of wine, making Washington the second-largest producer of premium wines in the US.

Recent developments

When I visited Washington state to research the first edition of this book, Alex Golitzen's Quilceda Creek was the only red wine of consistently great quality that I could find, and it was produced in minuscule amounts with ricketty equipment that he kept stashed away in the back of his garage. Golitzen had an enviable reputation even then, although he has always had the unfair advantage of being the nephew of the legendary winemaker and wine-consultant André Tchelistcheff.

Things have certainly changed quite a lot since then, as Washington can now be described as quintessentially a red-wine region, even though almost 60 per cent of the varieties grown are white rather than black. A few years ago, 70 per cent of Washington's production was white. The quality of this region's rarely exciting white wine, however, compares unfavourably with that of its red, so much of which can be world class, and this has led to an increased production of Merlot, Cabernet Sauvignon, Cabernet Franc, and Syrah.

Alex Golizen at Quilceda Creek still makes classic wine, but knocks it out in such vast volumes that his son Paul has to help him and the Oldsmobile has been kicked out of the garage to make room for more sophisticated winemaking equipment. There are now many wineries making red wines of very high quality in Washington, including a number that can rival Quilceda Creek. After Merlot, the most important black grape variety is Cabernet sauvignon. On a much smaller scale, however, the plantings of Cabernet franc have recently doubled in number and there is a great deal of interest in other fashionable grapes from the New World such as Nebbiolo and Syrah.

IRRIGATION IN WASHINGTON
Although the state has a notoriously wet climate, some drier areas in eastern Washington, where most of the vineyards are located, rely on irrigation.

WASHINGTON VERSUS OREGON

The contrast of natural factors affecting viticulture in these two contiguous, coastal states offers a fascinating insight into why the wines they produce are so different:

	WASHINGTON	OREGON
Total vineyards	14,200 hectares	3,050 hectares
Vinifera vines	5,900 hectares	3,035 hectares
Black varieties	41%	49%
White varieties	59%	51%
Major varieties	24% Chardonnay	39% Pinot noir
	21% Merlot	20% Chardonnay
	16% Cabernet sauvignon	14% Pinot gris
	31% Others	27% Others

• All but one per cent of Washington vineyards are located on the hot, desert-dry, eastern side of the Cascades, whereas all of Oregon's vineyards are west of the Cascades where it is cooler, but where rain can be problematical.
• Washington irrigates, Oregon does not.
• Oregon's climate is marine-influenced, Washington's is more continental.
• Only the sturdiest varieties can withstand the cold of Washington's winter, which can kill grafted vines.
• It is Washington's extraordinary amount of sunshine (2,021 hours compared to Oregon's 1,660), rather than heat (1,240 degree days celsius compared to Oregon's 1,179) that gives Washington state vines the photosynthetic capability of ripening Cabernet and other thick-skin varieties, all of which struggle in Oregon.
• Washington has no cryptogamic diseases, whereas bunch-rot is a major problem in Oregon.

OREGON

The first *vinifera* vines were planted in Oregon's Rogue River Valley as early as 1854. These and other *vinifera* vineyards were still in existence at the time of Prohibition, but as in Washington, the wine industry in Oregon relied almost entirely on *labrusca* grapes of the Concord variety until the 1970s. Change began in a small way in the 60s and 70s when wineries were established by California drop-outs such as Richard Sommer (Hill Crest), David Lett (The Eyrie Vineyard), and Bill Fuller (Tualatin).

Oregon's overnight fame came in 1979 when Lett entered his 1975 Pinot Noir in a blind wine-tasting competition organized by Robert Drouhin. Drouhin's Chambolle-Musigny 1959 had won, but Lett's The Eyrie Vineyard 1975 Pinot Noir came second, trouncing Drouhin's fabulous 1961 Clos-de-Bèze and many other prestigious Burgundies in the process. Since that eventful day, most critics have believed that it would only be a matter of time before the Pinot Noirs of Oregon rival those of Burgundy.

By the mid-1980s such success seemed imminent, and the Oregon wine industry, with more than one eye on hyping up the publicity, declared McMinnville to be host of an annual World Pinot Noir Conference, thereby endorsing the perception that Oregon is Pinot country. More than a decade later, export markets are not exactly teeming with Oregon wines, so what went wrong? It is not so much a question of why Oregon has not fulfilled its early promise, as whether it will ever have enough vineyards and consistency of quality to be a commercial success.

Why Oregon is not yet at the end of its Pinot Noir Trail

Oregon has fewer than 1,200 hectares (2,960 acres) of Pinot noir, which has very little impact on a world market dominated by Burgundy's 26,000 hectares (64,240 acres). Furthermore, almost 70 per cent of all Oregon wines are sold on the home-state market, leaving the equivalent of 360 hectares (890 acres) of Pinot noir for the rest of the US and all the other wine-consuming countries of the world. This is not even commensurate with the vineyards of Fixin in the Côtes de Nuits, and Burgundy could not have established an international reputation based on the output of a solitary village. In the early 1980s, when the world first heard about David Lett's Pinot Noir, the situation was even more ludicrous, as there were less than 120 hectares (296 acres) in total, and all of that was consumed locally – with such a tiny

NEWBERG, OREGON
Young Pinot noir vines at Newberg in the Dundee Hills, where some of Oregon's finest wineries are located.

production, Oregon's market potential had been grossly overestimated from the start. Even now it has no chance of establishing a worldwide commercial reputation, but the Pinot noir area has increased ten-fold in 15 years and, if it can maintain this growth while tightening up on consistency, Oregon should just about be in a position to fulfil its destiny by the year 2010.

IDAHO

The smallest winemaking state in the northwest, Idahos's high-altitude vineyards are located on the Snake River, west of Boise, where it is sunny in the day, but extremely cold at night. This extreme diurnal difference produces wines with an unusually high acidity and alcohol balance. Although Ste. Chapelle is one of the largest wineries in the entire northwest, Idaho's wine industry remains embryonic, offering Ste. Chapelle very little competition.

OREGON'S OTHER VARIETIES

Whether Oregon Pinot Noir makes it to the big time or not, it is by no means a foregone conclusion that this is the state's best grape variety. Even in the Willamette Valley, where most of the best Oregon Pinot Noir wines are produced, Chardonnay has at least as much potential and there may well be some stunning Chardonnay wines from this area in future. Other white wines include early-picked Muscat, which is one of this state's most underrated wines, and Pinot Gris, which is probably the hottest tip for the future. The easiest way to taste the largest range of Oregon's many different varietals, wine areas, wineries, and vintages is to call at the Oregon Tasting Cellar, which is housed within The Lawrence Gallery at McMinnville.

THE APPELLATIONS OF THE
PACIFIC NORTHWEST

COLUMBIA VALLEY AVA
Oregon and Washington

Columbia Valley is Washington's largest appellation, encompassing two other AVAs, the Yakima Valley and Walla Walla Valley and no less than 99 per cent of the state's *vinifera* vines. At approximately 46,500 square kilometres (18,000 square miles), it is one-and-a-half times the size of Belgium, and consists of a large, treeless basin surrounding the Columbia, Yakima, and Snake rivers. There is a vast, undulating, semi-arid plateau of between 300 and 600 metres (1,000–2,000 feet) in altitude, through which these three rivers cut many dramatic gorges, particularly just south of their confluence, where the Columbia makes a 180 degree turn to follow the Oregon border, creating some of America's most vivid, striking, and contrasting scenery.

The Columbia Valley encompasses numerous microclimates, but they mostly fall between 1,240 and 1,440 degree-days celsius, which overlaps regions I and II on the Californian heat summation system (*see* p.448). Due to its northerly latitude and cloudless climate, the Columbia Valley averages two hours more sunlight during midsummer than the Napa Valley, a state and a half further south. Astonishingly, there are more than 300 cloud-free days every year, and although Washington as a whole is the wettest state in the nation, annual rainfall in the Columbia Valley is 38 centimetres (15 inches) or less.

Apart from the two sub-appellations of Yakima and Walla Walla, dealt with later, there are a number of other recognized areas within the Columbia Valley AVA. Without doubt, the most exciting of these is Canoe Ridge, which some people seem to think is in Walla Walla because that is where the Canoe Ridge winery is, but it is in fact 80 kilometres (50 miles) to the west, just beyond Paterson. The vines grow on the right bank of the Columbia, where there are great hopes for world-class Merlot, Cabernet, and Chardonnay, although some of its vineyards are prone to winds in excess of 40 kmh, the point at which viticulturists have recently discovered the vine temporarily shuts down its metabolism, hindering the ripening process. Other areas of note within the vast Columbia Valley AVA include Northern Columbia Valley (a convenient umbrella appellation for a collection of disparate wine regions, including Saddle Mountain, Wahluke Slope, Royal Slope, and Skookumchuck Creek, where the scenery is often breathtaking, but the wine seldom is) and Snake River (located between Red Mountain – *see* Yakima – and the Walla Walla, in the broad hills either side of the lower reaches of the Snake River, just a few kilometres east of Pasco, where it would seem that Cabernet and Merlot fare best).

IDAHO AO

This is not an AVA, although under US labelling regulations, Idaho has the right to its own appellation of origin, just as every state does. It is, however, quite surprising that after all this time not one AVA has been proposed for Idaho, especially as wines from this state have established a distinctive quality and style. Their characteristic intensity of fruit and vivid flavours are heightened by an intrinsically high acidity.

PUGET SOUND AVA
Washington

Seattle has a reputation as one of the world's wettest cities ("They don't tan in Seattle," Californians claim, "they rust!"), and rainfall initially put severe restrictions on what was grown. Bainbridge Island Winery boasts the nearest vines to downtown Seattle, with Müller-Thurgau and Siegerrebe growing just a couple of kilometres away by ferry, while further south on the mainland, Johnson Creek Winery grows Müller-Thurgau. Bainbridge Island was the first vineyard in Puget Sound to grow Pinot noir.

This AVA is a climatic contradiction since it is significantly drier than Burgundy and sunnier than Bordeaux, yet as cool as the Loire. And, in a state of such homogenous soil, the basin drained by rivers and streams that flow into the Sound is marked by a glacial moraine not seen anywhere else in the Pacific Northwest. However, these statistics are a bit like those used by Atlanta to secure the 100th Anniversary Olympics in 1996, as the annual rainfall within Puget Sound ranges between 43 and 114 centimetres (17–45 inches) so many areas are a lot wetter than Burgundy, even if the average is drier. Recognized areas within Puget Sound include Mount Baker and Lopez Island.

ROGUE VALLEY AVA
Oregon

Within a short distance of California, this is the most southerly and warmest of Oregon's wine regions. With a mixture of elevations and exposures, and soil types ranging from loam to clay and some decomposed granite, it has been difficult for growers to decide what grape to focus on, hence the mishmash of varieties planted. Not surprisingly, Chardonnay is the most consistent, after which Cabernet sauvignon and Pinot noir are the most widely cultivated, which illustrates how undecided everyone is. Even though the elevation of the Rogue Valley AVA is very high, it is the only area in Oregon where Bordeaux varieties ripen regularly.

UMPQUA VALLEY AVA
Oregon

A great variation in altitude, exposure, and other topographical factors has led to a much greater range of varieties than are grown elsewhere, with such diverse grapes as Riesling and Cabernet every bit as popular as both Pinot noir and Chardonnay.

WALLA WALLA VALLEY AVA
Washington and Oregon

This area has been called the Walla Walla Valley since it was settled in the 1850s, before the creation of either Oregon or Washington. With less than half of one per cent of the state's vineyards, Walla Walla would seem to lack the importance of warranting its own AVA, but it can receive up to 50 centimetres (20 inches)

of rain, which is more than twice as much as the rest of the Columbia Valley, and makes Walla Walla a truly distinctive viticultural area with the potential to produce outstanding non-irrigated wine. For every kilometre you travel west from Walla Walla towards the Blue Mountains, you get another 1.6 centimetres of rain.

From a viticultural point of view, the only problem with Walla Walla is that its wheat farmers have it so easy, vines seldom get a look in. When there is a shift from wheat, it is more often than not to alfalfa seed rather than vines, although one alfalfa farmer, Janet Rindal, has made a brave move to vines and her Waterbrook winery is extraordinarily successful. A few outsiders buy Walla Walla grapes: Mountain Dome, for example, which gets a third of its Chardonnay and almost all of its Pinot noir from Whisky Creek vineyard. The fact is, however, that Walla Walla has produced very few wines of its own despite its AVA (which also encompasses a small chunk of Oregon), although this is bound to change in the future. In the meantime the reputation of Walla Walla is firmly based on a small number of producers whose exceptionally fine wines rely heavily on fruit purchased from outside the area.

WILLAMETTE VALLEY AVA
Oregon

The Willamette Valley is well known for Pinot Noir, although this began as recently as 1970, when David Lett planted The Eyrie Vineyards in the Red Hills of Dundee. After Lett's 1975 Pinot Noir embarrassed Drouhin's 1961 Clos-de-Bèze, and Drouhin became serious about founding a winery in Oregon, it was no surprise that the Burgundian chose the Red Hills for the location. The Eola Hills, also in the Willamette Valley, which share the same volcanic soil as the hills of Dundee and straddle Yamhill and Polk counties, is an up-and-coming area within the Willamette Valley.

YAKIMA VALLEY AVA
Washington

One of the Columbia Valley's two sub-appellations, the Yakima Valley contains the greatest concentration of Washington's wineries and 40 per cent of the state's vineyards. It is in every sense the home and historical centre of the Washington wine industry. Most vineyards are on the southeast-facing slopes of the Rattlesnake Hills, especially in the mid-valley area from Sunnyside to Prosser, and intermingle with the apple, cherry, and peach orchards that are found between two old irrigation canals, the Roza and the Sunnyside. The Roza is higher up the slopes and sometimes an odd plot of vines, a windbreak of trees, or an orchard can be seen above this canal, where the deep, lush green of irrigated vegetation stands out in contrast to the yellow-ochre starkness of semi-arid desert. In this way, the Yakima is representative of the agricultural success brought to eastern Washington by irrigation projects dating back to the turn of the century, although real prosperity occurred under the great Columbia irrigation scheme funded by the New Deal. Everything grows here: apples, apricots, asparagus, cherries, hops, pears, lentils, mint, peas, plums, potatoes, and raspberries. The apple farmers arrived first and took all the best vineyard sites (apple trees and vines prefer a similar growing environment). In recent years vineyards have slowly encroached on prime apple orchards. Old cherry orchards have also proved quite favourable for the vine, but former apple sites have proven superior and those chosen for Red Delicious the best of all (because this variety needs a warm site and is susceptible to frost). Other recognized areas that are located within the Yakima Valley AVA are Red Mountain, Red Willow, and Cold Creek. Red Mountain is just northeast of Benton City, where the wild west is at its wildest and reminiscent of the Australian outback. Despite this, Red Mountain Cabernet Sauvignon has been an ingredient in such award-winning wines as Quilceda Creek and Woodward Canyon and is therefore an area for future viticultural development. Red

Willow is located 24 kilometres (15 miles) southwest of Yakima itself, on Ahtanum Ridge, which is on the opposite side of the valley to the Roza and Sunnyside canals. It has a steep slope, particularly on the west side where there is little topsoil, most of it having been dispersed by the winds that blow across the ridge. The west side produces small, thick-skinned berries, whereas the east side, which has less of a slope and a deep topsoil produces larger berries and softer, less tannic wines. Mike Sauer, who first planted Red Willow in 1973, reckons the complexity of the east-slope soils and the different air movements that occur over the various blocks of the vineyard create eight distinctly different microclimates. Red Willow is the source of Columbia Winery's best

Cabernet Sauvignon, its top class Syrah, and Milestone Merlot, and at least one winery is trying Nebbiolo there. Cold Creek is close to being the driest, warmest spot in the state and one of the first vineyards to start harvest, yet when the vineyards around Prosser are covered in an autumnal carpet of leaves, just over the low Rattlesnake Hills the vines of Cold Ridge are still verdant. The reason for this is that it has one of the longest growing seasons in Washington, so it is not only the first to start harvesting, but the last to finish, whereas the explanation for its name is that it is one of the most bitterly cold places in the state in winter. Originally noted for Chardonnay, Cold Creek Vineyard has matured into the consistent source for most of Château Ste. Michelle's premium varietal.

THE WINE PRODUCERS OF THE
PACIFIC NORTHWEST

IDAHO

INDIAN CREEK
Kuna
The owner of Indian Creek, Bill Stowe, is a Pinot Noir fanatic stuck in Riesling country, and not doing badly with either.

✓ *Pinot Noir* • *White Riesling*

PINTLER CELLAR
Nampa
In 1982, the Pintler family planted a south-facing vineyard on their large ranch in the Snake River Valley just west of Boise, but did not start selling wine until 1988.

✓ *Chardonnay*

ROSE CREEK VINEYARDS
Hagerman
Former Ste. Chapelle employee Jamie Martin makes some very creditable wine at Rose Creek Vineyards, from both Idaho and Washington fruit, pure and mixed.

✓ *Johannisberg Riesling* (Idaho)

STE. CHAPELLE
Caldwella
★
Established in 1976 and named after the Gothic Ste. Chapelle in Paris, Idaho's largest and oldest winery has set a particularly fine standard for others to follow. Ste. Chapelle is, in fact, the fourth-largest winery in the Northwest.

✓ *Blanc de Noirs Brut* • *Riesling* • *Chardonnay* • *Syrah* (Reserve)

OREGON

ADAMS VINEYARD
Portland
★✩
Carol and Peter Adams quickly established a reputation for these beautifully balanced Burgundian-like varietals.

✓ *Chardonnay* (especially Reserve) • *Pinot Noir*

ADELSHEIM VINEYARD
Newberg
★★
Fine wines across the range, and most successful for Pinot Noir, which are consistently among the best half-dozen in Oregon.

✓ *Chardonnay* • *Pinot Gris* • *Merlot* (Layne Vineyards Grant's Pass) • *Pinot Noir* (especially Elizabeth's Reserve, Seven Springs Vineyard) • *Sauvignon Blanc*

ARCHERY SUMMIT
Dundee
★✩
Newcomer Californian Gary Andrus has made a brilliant debut with gorgeously plump Pinot Noir.

✓ *Pinot Noir*

AMITY VINEYARDS
Amity
✩

1986 Willamette Valley
Oregon Pinot Noir
ALCOHOL 12.7% BY VOLUME

Most famous for Pinot Noir, which can be well structured and longer-lived than most of its neighbours, the Reserve can sometimes lack the fruit to support the tannin.

✓ *Gamay Noir* • *Pinot Gris* • *Pinot Noir*

ARGYLE WINERY
Dundee
★
This is a joint venture between Cal Knudson and Brian Croser (of Petaluma in Australia), with

Allen Holstein as vineyard manager, and is a great source for Riesling and Oregon's best sparkling wine. Occasionally the Chardonnay comes right, and Pinot Noir, once dire, has made dramatic progress.

✓ *Argyle Brut Vintage* (from 1989) • *Pinot Noir* (from 1994) • *Riesling* (Dry)

AUTUMN WIND VINEYARD
Newberg
★✩
This small vineyard in the Dundee Hills, run by Tom and Wendy Kreutner, makes beautifully balanced Pinot Noir, with ample fruit and great finesse.

✓ *Chardonnay* • *Pinot Noir*

BEAUX FRÈRES
Dundee
★✩
Wine critic Robert Parker owns a share of this vineyard and winery, which is run by his partner Mike Etzel. At approximately 6,000 vines per hectare, only Domaine Drouhin is planted at a higher density.

✓ *Pinot Noir*

BENTON-LANE
Sunnymount Ranch
✩♥
This is a joint venture between Stephen Girard of Girard Winery and Carl Doumani of Stag's Leap, both better known for Cabernet or Petite Sirah than Pinot Noir, but lovers of that grape and convinced that Oregon has great potential for Pinot. True to their beliefs, they purchased a 800-hectare (1,977-acre) ranch in the mid-1980s and planted 30 hectares (74 acres) of Pinot.

✓ *Pinot Noir*

BETHEL HEIGHTS VINEYARD
Salem
★★♥
One of the best half-dozen wineries in the state, Bethel Heights basic Pinot Noir (not the cheaper First Release) is often as good as the

individual block bottlings and sometimes can even be better balanced, so it not only ranks as one of Oregon's best-quality Pinot Noirs, it also ranks as one of the best value.

✓ *Chardonnay* • *Pinot Noir*

BRICK HOUSE VINEYARD
Newburg
✩
Wines made from organic grapes for those who like big, highly extracted, charred-oak Pinot Noir wines.

✓ *Pinot Noir*

BRIDGEVIEW
Cave Junction
✩♥

Bridgeview
OREGON
Willamette Valley
PINOT NOIR
Alcohol 12.5% By Volume

Located in the Illinois Valley in the Cascades, where the Chardonnay benefits from a fairly dense cultivation of just over 4,450 vines per hectare.

✓ *Chardonnay* • *Pinot Noir* (since 1994)

BROADLEY VINEYARDS
Monroe
★♥
Enjoying a very warm microclimate, this winery provides one of Oregon's more substantial Pinot Noirs.

✓ *Pinot Noir*

CALLAHAN RIDGE
Roseburg
☆

This vineyard in the Umpqua Valley is capable of producing world-class Riesling.

✓ *White Riesling*

CAMERON WINERY
Dundee
☆ ⓥ

An underrated winery with a good, easy-drinking, if sometimes bizarre, style.

✓ *Chardonnay* (Reserve)
• *Pinot Blanc* • *Pinot Noir*

CHÂTEAU BENOIT
Carlton
☆

An eclectic range, including a sparkling wine that tries hard to be fine, although it does not always succeed. It is worth a visit for the view alone.

✓ *Sauvignon Blanc*

CHÂTEAU LORANE
Lorane

Linde and Sharon Kester produce a wide range of varietals, including a refreshing white wine made from the Muscadet grape, which is sold under its synonym of Melon.

✓ *Melon*

CHEHALEM
Newburg
This is an up-and-coming venture.

✓ *Pinot Gris* (Ridgecrest Estate)
• *Pinot Noir*

COOPER MOUNTAIN
Beaverton
☆

This winery produces fine-quality, barrel-fermented Chardonnay from an extinct volcano overlooking the Tualatin Valley.

✓ *Chardonnay* • *Pinot Gris*

CRISTOM
Salem
☆

An up-and-coming new producer whose Pinot Noir has more fat and richness than most.

✓ *Chardonnay* (Barrel fermented)
• *Pinot Noir*

DAVIDSON
Tenmile
❷

Not always a conventionally balanced wine, Davidson's Pinot Noir can, however, be a joy to drink in some vintages.

DOMAINE DROUHIN
Dundee
☆☆

Joseph Drouhin has been intrigued by Oregon's potential since Oregon winemaker David Lett entered his 1975 Pinot Noir in a blind wine tasting Drouhin had organized. Although Drouhin's Chambolle-Musigny 1959 won, Lett's wine came second, trouncing Drouhin's Clos-de-Bèze 1961 and many other Burgundies. Ever since Domaine Drouhin's first vintage, 1988, was released, locals and critics alike have marvelled at how Drouhin's wine instantly possessed more colour, depth, and complexity than any other Oregon Pinot Noir, yet still maintained the grape's varietal purity and finesse. It appeared that Drouhin had planted his vines three-and-a-half-times closer than the average in Oregon. The notion that higher-density vines give better quality more quickly became established on the international grapevine as the reason for Drouhin's success. The locals knew, however, that the wine contained not a single grape from his own vineyard, which was too young. It was all down to the way that Drouhin had handled the grapes, which itself was ironic, because the only reason he started making wine in 1988 with bought grapes was because he wanted hands-on experience of Oregon fruit before committing himself with his own produce.

The 1989 vintage was a revelation and the 1990 was almost as good, but the stunning 1991 (the first made completely by Drouhin's daughter Véronique) was of such a significantly higher order that it led many to believe it was the first 100 per cent estate wine, but just one-third of the grapes were from Drouhin's own vineyards. This is hotly disputed by some critics, so I will identify where the balance, in roughly equal parts, came from: Bethel Heights, Canary Hill, Durant, Knudsen, Hyland, and Seven Springs. The 1991 has such structure, weight, and colour, yet nothing but the luscious fruit of pure Pinot Noir all the way to the bottom of the glass. I did not think that Oregon Pinot Noir could possibly get any better until, that is, I tasted it against the 1992 and was dumbfounded.

✓ *Pinot Noir*

DOMAINE SERENE
Carlton
☆

This winery made an excellent debut with the 1992 vintage but a shaky period followed. It is now finding its feet again.

✓ *Pinot Noir*

EDGEFIELD
Troutdale
This extraordinary property was at one time Multnomah County Poor Farm. It now makes some full, fruity wines.

✓ *Pinot Gris*

ELK COVE VINEYARDS
Gaston

Joe and Pat Campbell can produce easy-going, varietally pure Pinot Noir, but the quality is erratic.

✓ *Chardonnay* • *Pinot Gris* • *Pinot Noir* • *Riesling* (Late Harvest)

ERATH WINERY
Dundee
☆

Formerly Knudsen Erath, this is sometimes one of the best wineries in Oregon for Pinot Noir, but vintages can lurch between the firm-tannic and the soft, creamy, and voluptuous. Dick Erath started planting high-density Chardonnay vines in 1994, so watch out for a boost in this wine as from the late 1990s.

✓ *Chardonnay* • *Pinot Gris* • *Pinot Noir*

EVESHAM WOOD
Salem
☆☆

Evesham Wood is a small but expanding winery and is one of Oregon's rising stars.

✓ *Pinot Gris* • *Pinot Noir* (especially Cuvée J, *Seven Springs Vineyard*

THE EYRIE VINEYARDS
McMinnville
☆☆

Oregon's Pinot Noir pioneer, David Lett also makes a fine Pinot Gris, which is best drunk young.

✓ *Chardonnay*
• *Muscat Ottonel* • *Pinot Gris*
• *Pinot Noir* (Reserve)

FIRESTEED
Seattle
☆ ⓥ

This soft, delicious, easy-drinking wine offers brilliant value and is sourced from Oregon vineyards by Washington-based *négociant* Howard Rossbach. Originally devised to satisfy the demands of his mother, Eleanor, whose drinking prowess once featured in Vogue magazine, Firesteed is now a brand in its own right.

✓ *Pinot Noir*

FLYNN VINEYARDS
Rickreall
Wayne Flynn's bottle-fermented sparkling wines started improving with the 1988 vintage.

FORIS
Cave Junction
☆

Supposedly producing the best Gewürztraminer in Oregon, but is much better for other varieties.

✓ *Cabernet Sauvignon*
• *Chardonnay*
• *Merlot* • *Pinot Gris*

GIRARDET WINE CELLARS
Roseburg
Swiss-born Philippe Girardet loves his hybrids, but does not need to grow Seyval blanc and Maréchal Foch in the Umpqua Valley's climate because his Pinot Noir is, not surprisingly, much better.

✓ *Gewürztraminer* (Late Harvest)
• *Pinot Noir*

HENRY ESTATE
Umpqua
☆ ⓥ

The Henry Estate is not the most consistent of producers, but when on form can produce one of Oregon's best Pinot Noir wines.

✓ *Chardonnay* (Barrel Fermented)
• *Pinot Noir*
• *Riesling* (Select Clusters)

REX HILL VINEYARDS
Newberg
☆☆

Rex Hill is a producer of good Chardonnay and Riesling, but is best known for its range of fine, stylish Pinot Noir wines, which consistently rank in the top half-dozen in Oregon.

✓ *Chardonnay*
• *Pinot Noir* • *Riesling*

HILL CREST
Roseburg
☆

Richard Sommer, one of Oregon's pioneers, is generally supposed to produce one of the state's best Gewürztraminers, but his Pinot Noir is infinitely better and the best-quality wine here is in fact Riesling.

✓ *Riesling*

HINMAN VINEYARDS
Eugene
☆

This vineyard produces one of Oregon's better Gewürztraminers – also other delicious, fruity wines, and a Pinot Noir that balances richness and tannin. *See also* Silvan Ridge.

✓ *Early Muscat* • *Pinot Gris*
• *Pinot Noir* • *Riesling*

HOOD RIVER VINEYARDS
Hood River
Raisiny Zinfandel from the Oregon side of the Columbia Gorge.

KING ESTATE
Eugene
☆

This vast and still-expanding vineyard surrounds a high-tech, hilltop winery that promises to put Oregon on the commercial map with a 200,000-case capacity.

✓ *Chardonnay* • *Pinot Gris*

LANGE
Dundee
★
Californian Don Lange worked for various Santa Barbara wineries, then setup Lange in Oregon's Red Hills.

✓ *Pinot Gris • Pinot Noir*

LAUREL RIDGE
Forest Grove
Best-known for sparkling wine.

MARQUAM HILL VINEYARDS
Mollala
Smooth Willamette Valley Pinot Noir from vineyards situated around a lake at the foot of the Cascades.

✓ *Pinot Noir*

MONTINORE VINEYARDS
Forest Grove
❷
The quality of Montinore has been disappointing but it is such a large project by Oregon standards that someone will pull it round one day.

OAK KNOLL WINERY
Hillsboro
This winery used to produce one of Oregon's finest Pinot Noirs, but I much prefer its Riesling of late.

✓ *Riesling*

PANTHER CREEK
McMinnville
★★
This tiny winery specializes in opulent Pinot Noir wines that rank among the very finest in Oregon. It also makes a delicious white wine from the Muscadet grape, sold under its synonym of Melon.

✓ *Melon • Pinot Noir*

PONZI VINEYARDS
Beaverton
★★
One of Oregon's top-performing Pinot Noirs is made here, but Ponzi's other beautifully crafted wines should not be overlooked.

✓ *Chardonnay • Pinot Gris • Pinot Noir • Dry White Riesling*

RAINSONG
Cheshire
★❖
Formerly called Oregon Cellars, Rainsong consistently produces excellent, creamy-sweet Pinot Noir.

✓ *Pinot Noir*

REDHAWK VINEYARD
Salem
★
Proud winner of Decanter magazine's "Worst Wine Label Awards", Redhawk has an uncanny knack with Bordeaux varieties.

✓ *Cabernet Franc • Pinot Noir • Sauvignon Blanc (Safari Vineyard)*

ST. INNOCENT
Salem
★★
Vineyard-designated wines made from purchased grapes grown in the

---

Eola Hills that rank as some of Oregon's greatest Pinot Noirs.

✓ *Pinot Noir (especially Freedom Hill)*

SECRET HOUSE VINEYARDS
Veneta
Although some people value this winery for its Chardonnay, the leesy tasting wines I have come across have been fair, but not special. Pinot Noir sometimes seems better.

SEVEN HILLS
Milton-Freewater
☆
Disappointing Riesling, but well-structured reds from the Washington side of the Walla Walla AVA.

✓ *Cabernet Sauvignon • Merlot*

SILVAN RIDGE
Hinman Vineyards
Eugene
☆
Erratic Pinot Noir lurches between bizarre and brilliant, but Early Muscat is always gorgeously peachy, and occasionally there are some extraordinary late-harvest styles.

✓ *Chardonnay (Unfiltered) • Early Muscat (including the semi-sparkling version) • Early Muscat-Huxelrebe (Ultra Late Harvest) • Riesling (Botrytized Cluster Select)*

SOKOL BLOSSER WINERY
Dundee
★☆
This winery produces some lush, seductive, early-drinking Pinot Noirs that regularly rank among some of Oregon's finest.

✓ *Chardonnay • Pinot Noir*

SPRINGHILL CELLARS
Albany
☆
This is a reliable source of Riesling, and an outstanding Icewine.

✓ *Gewürztraminer Icewine • Riesling*

TORII MOR
Dundee
★
An up-and-coming producer of nicely oaked, fat, juicy Pinot Noir.

✓ *Pinot Noir (especially Reserve)*

TUALATIN VINEYARDS
Forest Grove
★
Blockbusting Chardonnay and elegant Pinot Noir are made here.

✓ *Chardonnay • Pinot Noir*

TYEE WINE CELLARS
Corvallis
Locals say that Tyee is good for Gewürztraminer, but the vintages I have tasted were not very good.

VALLEY VIEW VINEYARD
Jacksonville
★
This is one of the few consistent producers of Cabernet in Oregon.

Jacksonville in the Rogue Valley is one of those idyllic towns everyone should visit.

✓ *Chardonnay (Anna Maria) • Cabernet Sauvignon (Anna Maria) • Reserve (Anna Maria) • Sauvignon Blanc (Anna Maria)*

VERITAS VINEYARD
Newberg
☆
Veritas Vineyard produces wines of fine varietal character and structure.

✓ *Pinot Noir*

WEISINGER'S
Ashland
Most of the wines I have tasted from this winery have been light and unimpressive. These include the Pinot Noir and an Italian-style blend called Mescolare. The dark, dense 1989 Cabernet Sauvignon, however, shows the potential here.

WILLAMETTE VALLEY VINEYARDS
Turner
This newly established vineyard and winery was created through the pooled resources of more than 4,000 consumers who purchased public stock. Apart from producing an excellent Chardonnay, Willamette Valley Vineyards has yet to find its feet with other varieties.

✓ *Chardonnay (Shea Vineyard)*

KEN WRIGHT CELLARS
McMinnville
★★
This brilliant new winery was founded by the former Panther Creek owner Ken Wright, and has established a reputation for stylish Pinot Noir sold under single-vineyard names.

✓ *Chardonnay (Celio Vineyard) • Pinot Noir (especially Abbey Heights Whistling Ridge, Carter Vineyard)*

WASHINGTON

ANDREW WILL
Vachon
Andrew Will as a person does not actually exist, as Chris and Annie Camarda, owners of this winery, named it after their nephew Andrew and son Will.

✓ *Cabernet Sauvignon • Merlot (especially Ciel du Cheval, Pepper Bridge, "R")*

ARBOR CREST
Spokane
★
Arbor Crest was formerly a cherry winery. It is owned by the Mielke brothers, third generation farmers who specialize in producing white wines and, in fact, often make the best Sauvignon Blanc in the Northwest of the US.

✓ *Cabernet Sauvignon • Sauvignon Blanc (especially Bacchus Vineyard) • Riesling (Late Harvest)*

BAINBRIDGE ISLAND WINERY
Bainbridge Island
❷

Owners Gerard and JoAnn Bentryn once grew German crosses only, but planted Pinot noir in the early 1990s.

BARNARD GRIFFIN
Kennewick
★
Owners Deborah Barnard and Rob Griffin have a track record for Merlot and Chardonnay, but have made some splendid Cabernets since the early 1990s.

✓ *Cabernet-Merlot • Cabernet Sauvignon • Chardonnay (Reserve) • Fumé Blanc (Barrel Select) • Merlot (Reserve)*

BLUE MOUNTAIN CELLARS
Walla Walla
❷
This is a new venture whose part-owner is Gary Figgins' brother Rusty. He does not plan to upstage Leonetti Cellar, as all his wines will be Rhône varietals, starting with Grenache, then Syrah, and possibly even Viognier. The wines, due to be sold under the Glen Fiona label, should be worth watching out for.

BOOKWALTER
Pasco
☆
Jerry Bookwalter graduated from UC-Davis in 1962, but did not start up on his own until 1983, after 20 years' experience with Sagemoor Farms and various other vineyards in Washington and Oregon.

✓ *Cabernet Sauvignon (Columbia Valley)*

W. B. BRIDGMAN
Sunnyside
☆
I know little about this winery, but excellent reds have recently cropped up under this label.

✓ *Cabernet Franc • Merlot*

CANOE RIDGE
Walla Walla
★☆
A new venture owned by Chalone Vineyards of California, Canoe Ridge used Woodward Canyon and Hyatt Vineyards to make wines before setting up this winery to the east of its Canoe Ridge vineyards.

✓ *Chardonnay • Merlot*

CHÂTEAU STE. MICHELLE
Woodinville
★

This winery is owned by Stimson Lane. Château Ste. Michelle's sparkling wines showed great promise in the late 1970s, but they have been disappointing ever since. Efforts are being renewed to rediscover the original potential for this style of wine. In the meantime, however, varietal wines seem to be Château Ste. Michelle's strongest point and Cold Creek Vineyard its most consistent source.

✓ *Cabernet Franc* (Cold Creek)
• *Cabernet Sauvignon* (Cold Creek, Horse Heaven)
• *Chardonnay* (Cold Creek)
• *Chateau Reserve* (red Bordeaux style)
• *Merlot* (Cold Creek)

CHINOOK
Prosser
★

Californian viticulturist Clay Mackey met his winemaker wife Kay Simon when they both worked for Château Ste. Michelle prior to setting up this boutique winery together in 1993. Originally known for whites, Chinook now excels with reds.

✓ *Cabernet Sauvignon*
• *Sémillon* • *Merlot*

COLUMBIA CREST
Paterson
★ ✔

Owned by Stimson Lane, this is an impressive installation that was built to handle a high volume of tourists, but is in the middle of nowhere, and will never realize its potential in this respect. As tourism not only provides profit, but also increases the reputation of a wine area, it seems odd that Stimson Lane did not build its wine wonder-palace in the Yakima Valley, which has the greatest concentration of wineries and almost half the state's vineyards.

✓ *Merlot* • *Reserve*
• *Sémillon-Sauvignon*

COLUMBIA WINERY
Bellevue
★★

Formerly Associated Vintners, these wines are made by Master of Wine David Lake, who is unarguably one of Washington's best two or three producers of red wine.

✓ *Cabernet Sauvignon* (David Lake) • *Chardonnay*
• *Merlot* (Milestone, Red Willow Vineyard) • *Syrah* (Red Willow Vineyard)

COVEY RUN
Zillah
★

This winery started as a partnership between several Yakima farmers as an outlet for their grapes using the Quail Run label. They soon fell foul of Quail Ridge in California, and changed its name to Covey Run.

✓ *Cabernet Sauvignon* (Columbia Valley, Yakima Valley)
• *Chardonnay*

DE LILLE CELLARS
Woodinville
★

The D2 used to be pure Merlot until the early 1990s, when it became a blend of Cabernet sauvignon, Merlot, and Cabernet franc.

✓ *Cabernet Sauvignon* (Chaleur Estate, Harrison) • *D2* (red Bordeaux style) • *Sauvignon Blanc* (Chaleur Estate)

GORDON BROTHERS
Pasco
★

Jeff and Bill Gordon have made some very good wine in spite of early difficulties, and are now reaping the benefit.

✓ *Cabernet Sauvignon*
• *Chardonnay* (Reserve) • *Merlot*

HEDGES CELLARS
Benton City
★★ ✔

Tom Hedges has the amazing knack of being able to produce premium-quality Bordeaux-style reds that are lush, drinkable, and not lacking complexity and finesse within less than a year of the grapes being picked. I have never tasted Hedges wine that I would not want to drink.

✓ *Cabernet-Merlot*
• *Fumé Chardonnay*
• *Red Mountain Reserve*

THE HOGUE CELLARS
Prosser
★

After rearing cattle and growing spearmint for chewing-gum, Warren Hogue embarked upon running this ambitiously sized, yet family-run, vineyard and winery. The quality is high, particularly for white wines, and rapidly improving on the reds.

✓ *Cabernet Sauvignon* (Reserve, Yakima Valley)
• *Chardonnay* • *Fumé Blanc*
• *Merlot* (Reserve) • *Sémillon*

HYATT VINEYARDS
Zillah
★

Keyland Hyatt built his own winery in a bid to solve the problem of surplus grape production from his own vineyards, and has excelled.

✓ *Cabernet Sauvignon* (Reserve)
• *Merlot* (Reserve)

KIONA VINEYARDS
Benton City
★

The arid backdrop to this lush vineyard illustrates how irrigation can transform a desert. Kiona is the most important vineyard on Red Mountain and although it might not always hit the bull's eye in the Kiona wines themselves, the same fruit has consistently shown its potential in the wines of Woodward Canyon and has been one of three main ingredients of Quilceda Creek.

✓ *Cabernet Sauvignon*
• *Gewürztraminer* (Late Harvest) • *Lemberger*

LATAH CREEK
Spokane

Mostly white-wine production, but Latah Creek can produce excellent Cabernet Sauvignon (as in 1990).

✓ *Cabernet Sauvignon*

L'ÉCOLE
Lowden
★★

Marty Clubb has carved out quite a reputation from the wines made at this old school house. L'École No. 41, to give it its full title, is primarily known for its Sémillon, due in no small way to a string of rave reviews from wine writer Robert Parker, but although it is a very good wine, Marty's red wines are a class apart.

✓ *Sémillon* • *Merlot*
• *Cabernet Sauvignon*

LEONETTI CELLAR
Walla Walla
★★

Gary Figgins is a red-wine specialist with a cult-following that, judging by some of wine writer Robert Parker's reviews, includes the great man himself. The wines produced by Leonetti Cellar have led a charmed life since Leonetti's 1990 Cabernet Sauvignon became the only Washington wine to receive a perfect score of 100 from the Wine Spectator. The quality is almost always quite stunning, although the style might be too oaky for some.

✓ *Cabernet Sauvignon*
• *Merlot* • *Select*

MOUNTAIN DOME
Spokane
★

Mountain Dome has the potential to become one of the top half-dozen sparkling wines in the US. After an uncertain start, these wines became better focused with the 1990 and, particularly, the 1991 vintage, but need less oak and more acidity. In my opinion, it has merely been a matter of trying too hard to be too classic too early.

✓ *Brut Vintage*

PRESTON WINE CELLARS
Pasco
★

Bill Preston turned his retirement home into what was, in the 1970s, the largest privately owned winery in the Pacific Northwest. Although the quality can be very high, it is not always consistent.

✓ *Cabernet Sauvignon*
• *Platinum Red*

QUILCEDA CREEK
Seattle
★★

Washington's first truly great red wine and even now still one of the very elite, Quilceda Creek is produced in minute quantities by Alex Golitzen and his son.

✓ *Cabernet Sauvignon*

STATON HILLS
Wapato
★★ ✔

This winery started out with novelties such as a Riesling rosé (made by adding a little red wine), but now produces some of Washington's best-value and, in the case of Merlot, finest wines.

✓ *Fumé Blanc* • *Merlot*
• *Pinot Noir*

PAUL THOMAS
Bellevue
★★ ✔

This winery has so far been underrated because it began by making fruit wines only, which it still makes. As a result, many people have failed to take seriously the grape wines it now makes. However, winemaker Paul Thomas did master the art of making fruit wines, and it is probably because of, rather than despite, this ability that he now makes grape wines with such vivid fruit flavour.

✓ *Cabernet-Merlot* • *Chardonnay*
• *Sauvignon Blanc*

WALLA WALLA VINTNERS
Walla Walla
❾

A brand new venture with its own winery, the first releases were not due to be released until this edition is published, so no rating can be given, but should be worth watching for Cabernet Franc, Cabernet Sauvignon, and Merlot.

WASHINGTON HILLS
Sunnyside
★★

Washington Hills has produced a string of absolutely superb wines since 1990, particularly under the Apex label, which has put this winery among the very elite of Washington's producers.

✓ *Cabernet Sauvignon* (Apex)
• *Chardonnay* (Apex)
• *Merlot* (Apex) • *Riesling*

WOODWARD CANYON WINERY
Lowden

This Walla Walla winery has hardly put a foot wrong since it was established in 1981.

✓ *Cabernet Sauvignon* (especially Canoe Ridge)
• *Chardonnay* (Reserve, Roza Berg Vineyard) • *Merlot*

THE ATLANTIC NORTHEAST

All that holds back this region is its harsh winters. Although this does not prevent the cultivation of classic grape varieties, it does make grafting wounds highly vulnerable, and this dictates where such grafted vines are planted. If vineyards could be chosen for their ripening potential, rather than for winter survival, the eastern seaboard could rival California, as it has a much greater variation of soils and microclimates.

SINCE THE FIRST TRANSGENIC VINES were produced, only the identity of two genes has stood in the way of the Atlantic Northeast achieving its full potential – the gene that makes *Vitis amurensis* immune to Siberian winters, together with the one that enables native American vines to resist phylloxera. Within ten years of their discovery, Virginia could be more famous than the Napa Valley and, as it would also revolutionize the entire wine world, scientists from Baltimore to Bordeaux will be trying to isolate these genes.

AMERICA'S OLDEST WINE INDUSTRY

Wines have been made in America's Northeast since the middle of the 17th century, when vineyards were first established on Manhattan and Long Island. The emphasis, however, has always been on the notoriously "foxy" *labrusca* varieties. *Vinifera* vines were not cultivated until as recently as 1957, although the series of events that culminated in this most important development in the Atlantic Northeast's quest for quality wines began in 1934.

Immediately after Prohibition, Edwin Underhill, the President of Gold Seal Vineyards, went to Champagne and persuaded Charles Fournier, the *chef de cave* at Veuve Clicquot, to return with him to the United States. But Fournier found the *labrusca* grape varieties

LONG ISLAND, NEW YORK
These rows of vines are wide spaced to accommodate vineyard machinery, and are a far cry from the mid-17th century when Long Island was one of the first places in the Atlantic Northeast to be planted.

THE ATLANTIC NORTHEAST, see also p.443
The most prominent state in the Atlantic Northeast, New York is fast establishing this area's reputation for vinifera *wines, but Virginia and Maryland could rival this supremacy in the next century. The wine industries of the other states are dominated almost entirely by native* labrusca.

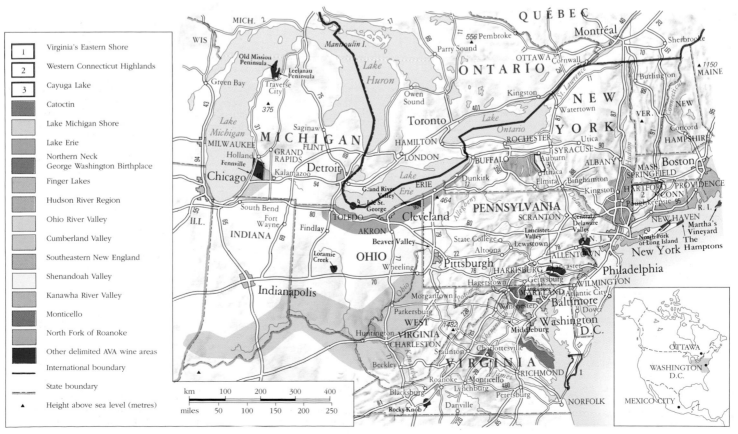

1	Virginia's Eastern Shore
2	Western Connecticut Highlands
3	Cayuga Lake
	Catoctin
	Lake Michigan Shore
	Lake Erie
	Northern Neck George Washington Birthplace
	Finger Lakes
	Hudson River Region
	Ohio River Valley
	Cumberland Valley
	Southeastern New England
	Shenandoah Valley
	Kanawha River Valley
	Monticello
	North Fork of Roanoke
	Other delimited AVA wine areas
	International boundary
	State boundary
▲	Height above sea level (metres)

MECHANICAL HARVESTING
Grapes are picked by machine at vineyards belonging to the Taylor Wine Company. Based at Hammondsport, the winery is one of New York State's most successful.

FACTORS AFFECTING TASTE AND QUALITY

LOCATION
An arbitrary group of states situated between the Great Lakes and the Atlantic Ocean.

CLIMATE
Despite severe winters, the tempering influence exerted by large masses of inland water, such as the Finger Lakes, creates microclimates that make cultivation of *vinifera* vines possible.

ASPECT
Many of the vineyards are planted on flat ground around the various lake shores, and on the nearby lower slopes of the various mountain ranges.

SOIL
New York: shale, slate, schist, and limestone in the Hudson River Region. Virginia: silty loam and gravel at Rocky Knob, limestone and sandstone at North Fork of Roanoke. Michigan: glacial scree in Fennville. Ohio: shallow drift soil over fissured limestone bedrock on Isle St. George. Pennsylvania: deep limestone-derived soils in the Lancaster Valley.

VITICULTURE AND VINIFICATION
In many areas, despite some advantageous microclimates, *vinifera* vines can survive the harsh winters only by being buried under several feet of earth before the winter arrives. Sparkling wines are a speciality of New York State and of the Finger Lakes area in particular. Through very careful vineyard practices, the use of the latest sprays, and the aid of new technology in vinification, the number of *vinifera* varietals produced is increasing and their reputation growing.

GRAPE VARIETIES
Native *labrusca* grapes such as Concord, Catawba, Delaware, and Ives predominate; French-American hybrids such as Vidal blanc, Seyval blanc, Chelois, Baco noir, Maréchal Foch, and Aurore are becoming increasingly important; and the quantity of *vinifera* varieties, such as Chardonnay, Riesling, Cabernet sauvignon, and Gewürztraminer, is small but increasing.

planted in New York State's Finger Lake vineyards far too aromatic. Persuaded by local wine-growers that *vinifera* vines could not survive the harsh winters, he began planting hybrid vines (crosses between French and native American varieties). These were initially shipped from France, and then acquired from a winemaker by the name of Philip Wagner, who had already established a considerable collection of hybrids at his Boordy Vineyard in Maryland.

In 1953 Fournier heard that one Konstantin Frank, a Ukrainian viticulturist who had arrived in the US in 1951, had been criticizing the industry for not planting European *vinifera* vines. On his arrival in the US, Frank, who spoke no English and had no money, had washed dishes to support his wife and three children. However, as soon as he had learnt enough English to get by, he applied for a job at the New York State viticultural research station at Geneva, informing his prospective employers of his studies in viticulture at Odessa, and his experience in organizing collective farms in the Ukraine, teaching viticulture and oenology at an agricultural institute, and managing farms in Austria and Bavaria. When told that the winters were too harsh for European vines, he dismissed the idea as absurd. Two years later, when Fournier heard Frank's claims, he employed him, taking the chance that his theory would prove correct. Frank's claims were justified, particularly after the great freeze of February 1957. Later that year, some of the hardiest *labrusca* vines failed to bear a single grape, yet less than ten per cent of the buds on Frank's Riesling and Chardonnay vines were damaged and they produced a bumper crop of fully ripe grapes.

In the 1980s Frank was still battling with the Geneva viticultural station. *Vinifera* had not taken off in New York State, despite Frank's success. He blamed this on the "Genevians", who maintained that *vinifera* was too risky to be cultivated by anyone other than an expert. Frank had, however, become articulate in his new language: "The poor Italian and Russian peasants with their shovels can do it, but the American farmer with his push-button tools cannot".

THE APPELLATIONS OF THE
ATLANTIC NORTHEAST

CATOCTIN AVA
Maryland
Situated west of the town of Frederick, this area's specific *terroir* was well known before the AVA was established, due to the fact that it roughly coincides with the Maryland Land Resource Area. This was determined by the US Soil Conservation Service on the basis of identifiable patterns of soil, climate, water availability, land use, and topography.

CAYUGA LAKE AVA
New York

PLANE'S
CAYUGA VINEYARD

1988
APPELLATION CAYUGA LAKE
CHARDONNAY

ESTATE GROWN AND BOTTLED BY
PLANE'S CAYUGA VINEYARD, INC.
OVID, NEW YORK
CONTAINS SULFITES
Alcohol 12.6% by Volume

This area encompasses vines along the shores of Lake Cayuga, making it part of the Finger Lakes AVA. The soil is predominantly shale and the growing season approximately one month longer than that of most of the Finger Lake area.

CENTRAL DELAWARE VALLEY AVA
Pennsylvania and New Jersey
This appellation covers 388 square kilometres (150 square miles), although very little of it is actually planted with vines. The Delaware river modifies the climate.

CUMBERLAND VALLEY AVA
Maryland and Pennsylvania
The Cumberland Valley is situated between the South Mountains and the Allegheny Mountains and is 120 kilometres (80 miles) long, bending in a northeasterly direction. Although this AVA covers approximately 3,100 square kilometres (1,200 square miles), its vines are confined to small areas where the soil, drainage, rainfall, and protection from lethal winter temperatures permit viticulture. Vineyards are found on high terraces along the north bank of the Potomac river, on the hills and ridges in the basin of the valley, and in the upland areas of the South Mountain.

FENNVILLE AVA
Michigan
Lake Michigan moderates this area's climate, providing slightly warmer winters and cooler summers than other areas within a 48-kilometre (30-mile) radius. Fennville covers 310 square kilometres (120 square miles) and has been cultivating various fruits for well over a century, including grapes for wine production. The soil is mostly scree of glacial origin.

FINGER LAKES AVA
New York
This name is derived from the 11 finger-shaped lakes in west-central New York State. These inland water masses temper the climate, and the topography of the surrounding land creates "air drainage", which moderates extremes of temperature in winter and summer.

GRAND RIVER VALLEY AVA
Ohio
Located within the Lake Erie AVA, the lake protects these vines from frost damage and forces a longer growing season than vineyards situated in inland areas. The river valley increases "air drainage", giving this AVA a sufficiently different microclimate to warrant its distinction from the Lake Erie AVA.

HUDSON RIVER REGION AVA
New York
This AVA encompasses all of Columbia, Dutchess, and Putnam Counties, the eastern parts of Ulster and Sullivan Counties, almost all of Orange County, and the northern parts of Rockland and Westchester Counties. This is the Taconic Province, one of the most complex geological divisions where the soil is made up of glacial deposits of shale, slate, schist, and limestone.

ISLE ST. GEORGE AVA
Ohio
The northernmost of the Bass Islands, vines have been grown here since 1853. Today they cover over half the island. Although tempered by Lake Erie, the climate is cooler in the spring and summer, and warmer in the winter than vineyards situated in mainland Ohio, and is frost-free for 206 days a year, which is longer than for any other area in Ohio. The shallow drift soil over fissured limestone bedrock is well suited to viticulture.

KANAWHA RIVER VALLEY AVA
West Virginia
This approved viticultural area covers 2,600 square kilometres (1,000 square miles), yet contains just six hectares of vines and one bonded winery.

LAKE ERIE AVA
New York, Pennsylvania, and Ohio
Overlapping three states, and encompassing the AVAs of Isle St. George and Grand River Valley, Lake Erie moderates the climate and is the fundamental factor that permits viticulture.

LAKE MICHIGAN SHORE AVA
Michigan
Located in the southwest corner of Michigan, this AVA is a geographically and climatically uniform region, although it does encapsulate smaller, very specific *terroirs* such as Fennville, which has its own AVA.

LANCASTER VALLEY AVA
Pennsylvania
Grapes have been grown in Lancaster County since the early 19th century but have only recently provoked outside interest. The vines are grown on a virtually level valley floor, at an average altitude of 120 metres (400 feet), where the deep, limestone-derived soils are well drained. Even so, they have good moisture retention, are highly productive, and differ sharply from those in the surrounding hills and uplands.

LEELANAU PENINSULA AVA
Michigan
Lake Michigan delays fruit development beyond the most serious frost period in the spring, and prevents sudden temperature drops in the Fall. It is situated on the western shore of Lake Michigan, northwest of Traverse City.

LINGANORE AVA
Maryland
Linganore, Maryland's first viticultural area, lies east of Frederick. It is generally warmer and wetter than the areas to the east, and slightly cooler and dryer than those to the west.

LORAMIE CREEK AVA
Ohio
This small AVA covers only 1,460 hectares (3,600 acres) in Shelby County, west-central Ohio. Moderate-to-poor drainage means vines must be grown on slopes and ridges to prevent "wet feet".

MARTHA'S VINEYARD AVA
Massachusetts
This AVA is an island in Massachusetts, and is surrounded to the north by Vineyard Sound, to the east by Nantucket Sound, and to the south and west by the Atlantic Ocean. The boundaries of the viticultural area include an area known as Chappaquiddick, which is connected to Martha's Vineyard by a sandbar. Ocean winds delay the coming of spring and make for a cooler autumn, extending the growing season to an average of 210 days, compared with 180 days on the mainland.

MONTICELLO AVA
Virginia

VIRGINIA

BARBOURSVILLE
VINEYARDS

1814
MONTICELLO
RIESLING

PRODUCED AND BOTTLED BY BARBOURSVILLE WINERY
BARBOURSVILLE, VA. • ALCOHOL 11.5% BY VOL. • 750 ML.

Monticello is well known as the home of Thomas Jefferson, who is recorded as having planted wine grapes here. Most of Virginia's best wineries are found in this AVA.

NORTHERN NECK GEORGE WASHINGTON BIRTHPLACE AVA
Virginia
This AVA lies on a peninsula 160 kilometres (100 miles) long, between the Potomac and Rappahannock rivers in the tidewater district of Virginia, which runs from Chesapeake Bay in the east to a few kilometres from the town of Fredericksburg to the west. The vines grow in sandy clay soils on the slopes and hills, and in alluvial soils on the river flats. The favourable climate, with excellent air-drainage, is moderated by the surrounding water.

NORTH FORK OF LONG ISLAND AVA
New York
Although the climate of this AVA is classified as "humid continental", the sea that surrounds it makes it more temperate than many other places of the same latitude in the interior of the US. The growing season is about one to three weeks longer than in the South Fork of the Island and, in general, the sandy soils contain less silt and loam, but are slightly higher in natural fertility.

NORTH FORK OF ROANOKE AVA

Virginia

A valley protected from excessive rainfall in the growing season by mountains to the west and east. The vines are on the limestone southeast-facing slopes and limestone-with-sandstone north-facing slopes. These soils are very different from those in the surrounding hills and ridges.

OHIO RIVER VALLEY AVA

Indiana, Ohio, West Virginia, and Kentucky

This is a vast AVA. Until 1859, Ohio was the leading wine-producing state. However, during the Civil War, black rot and powdery mildew took hold and destroyed nearly all its vineyards.

OLD MISSION PENINSULA AVA

Michigan

This AVA is surrounded on three sides by Grand Traverse Bay, and connected to the mainland at Traverse City. The waters, coupled with warm southwesterly winds, provide a unique climate that makes cultivation of *vinifera* vines possible.

ROCKY KNOB AVA

Virginia

This AVA is in the Blue Ridge Mountains, and in spring is colder than nearby areas. This means the vines flower later, enabling them to survive the erratic, very cold early spring temperatures. It also causes a late fruit-set, extending the growing season by about a week. The silty-loam and gravel soil provides good drainage.

SHENANDOAH VALLEY AVA

Virginia and West Virginia

The Shenandoah Valley lies between the Blue Ridge Mountains, and the Allegheny Mountains. This AVA extends south beyond the Shenandoah Valley almost as far as Roanoke.

SOUTHEASTERN NEW ENGLAND AVA

Connecticut, Rhode Island, and Massachusetts

An area distinguished in New England by the moderate climate, caused by its proximity to various coastal bodies of water.

THE HAMPTONS, LONG ISLAND AVA

New York

The Hamptons has been a productive agricultural area for 300 years. It lies within Suffolk County, next to North Fork of Long Island, with the Peconic River and Peconic Bay its northern boundary. This AVA includes Gardiners Island.

VIRGINIA'S EASTERN SHORE AVA

Virginia

This is located in Accomack and Northampton counties along the 120-kilometre (75-mile) narrow tip of the Delmarva Peninsula, with the Atlantic to the east and Chesapeake Bay to the west. The climatic influence of these two large bodies of water helps to alleviate the severest winter temperatures, but retards the ripening process and can be problematical at harvest time.

WARREN HILLS AVA

New Jersey

Wines made in the eastern half of the Central Delaware Valley AVA, which consists of five narrow valleys rather than one broad one, may use this sub-appellation. The narrow valleys provide more well-exposed hillsides and funnel the winds, reducing the risk of frost and rot.

WESTERN CONNECTICUT HIGHLANDS AVA

Connecticut

A vast 3,900-square kilometre (1,500-square-mile) area of rolling hills that rise to 150 metres (500 feet) above sea level, and the Western Connecticut Highlands, small mountains which reach to 460 metres (1,500 feet).

THE WINE PRODUCERS OF THE
ATLANTIC NORTHEAST

CONNECTICUT

CHAMARD
Clinton
⭐
This is a modern winery just three kilometres from Long Island Sound.

✓ *Chardonnay* (Estate Reserve)

STONINGTON VINEYARDS
Stonington
This small vineyard and winery was set up in 1986, and produces wines from both hybrid and *vinifera* grapes.

✓ *Chardonnay* (Estate)

Of the other nine Connecticut wineries, some interesting wines have been produced by **Crosswood Vineyard** (Johannisberg Riesling), **Haight Vineyards** (Chardonnay, Riesling), **Hamlet Hill Vineyards** (Seyval Blanc), and **Hopkins Vineyards** (Ravat Blanc).

INDIANA

CHÂTEAU THOMAS WINERY
Indianapolis
⭐
Dr. Charles Thomas is so passionate about the wine he drinks, and the cellar of fine European wines that he has built up, that he refuses to grow or buy grapes locally. If these wines seem special, it is because he buys grapes from only the best areas of the Napa Valley.

✓ *Chardonnay • Cabernet Sauvignon • Merlot*

OLIVER WINE COMPANY
Bloomington
⭐
In 1972, after lobbying for licenced winemaking in Indiana, Bill and Mary Oliver founded the state's first winery since Prohibition. Sadly, owing to climatic problems, the vineyard failed, but they still make wine from grapes from California, Washington, and New York.

✓ *Merlot • Sauvignon Blanc*

MARYLAND

BASIGNANI
Sparks
★
This small winery makes excellent Cabernet Sauvignon and its Merlot is good enough to attract attention.

✓ *Cabernet Sauvignon • Lorenzino* (red Bordeaux style) • *Merlot*

BOORDY VINEYARDS
Hydes

It was here that hybrids, a turning point in US viticultural history, were introduced to the Atlantic Northeast.

BYRD VINEYARDS
Myersville
❷
This pioneering *vinifera* winery has produced some medal-winning wines (especially Chardonnay, Cabernet Sauvignon, and Sauvignon Blanc).

CATOCTIN VINEYARDS
Brookeville
★ⓥ
These vineyards are owned by a partnership that includes Bob Lyon.

✓ *Cabernet Sauvignon* (Reserve)
• *Chardonnay* (Oak Fermented)
• *Johannisberg Riesling*

ELK RUN VINEYARD
Mount Airy
⭐
The owner-winemaker, Fred Wilson, trained with the legendary Dr. Konstantin Frank (*see* p.488).

✓ *Cabernet Sauvignon*
• *Chardonnay*

MONTBRAY WINE CELLARS
Westminster
Montbray produced America's first Riesling "Icewine" in 1974.

✓ *Chardonnay • Johannisberg Riesling • Seyval Blanc*

MASSACHUSETTS

CHICAMA VINEYARDS
West Tisbury
The first winery in Massachusetts, it was also the first to establish *vinifera* vines in Martha's Vineyard.

WESTPORT RIVERS
Westport
⭐
Bob and Carol Russell converted a 17th-century turnip farm into the largest vineyard in New England in 1986, establishing a winery in 1989.

✓ *Chardonnay*

MICHIGAN

BOSKYDEL VINEYARD
Lake Leelanau
The first vineyard to be established on the Leelanau Peninsula.

CHÂTEAU GRAND TRAVERS
Traverse City
Set up in 1974 by Edward O'Keefe, and the first Michigan vineyard to be planted with only *vinifera* vines.

✓ *Chardonnay* (Sur Lie)
• *Johannisberg Riesling*
(Botrytized Select Harvest, Dry Icewine, Late Harvest)

FENN VALLEY VINEYARDS
Fennville
Established in 1973, this was the first winery to produce wines under the Fennville AVA. Pinot Noir and Pinot Gris could be worth watching out for.

✓ *Johannisberg Riesling*

MADRON LAKE HILLS
Buchanan
Planted entirely with classic *vinifera* varieties, Madron Lake is best for Riesling. However, Pinot Noir is improving and there are interesting

things promised with varieties such as Pinot Gris and Barbera.

✓ *Pinot Noir* (Estate)
 • *White Riesling* (Estate Selected Late Harvest)

ST. JULIAN WINE COMPANY
Paw Paw

Founded in 1921 by an Italian, this was originally a Canadian winery called Meconi Wine Cellars. It became American when it moved to Detroit, and changed its name to the Italian Wine Company. Then, in 1938, the business moved to its current location and became the St. Julian Wine Company. Its sparkling wines are well regarded, but hybrids, such as Chambourcin, Chancellor, and Vignoles, have all been known to perform better.

TABOR HILL BRONTE WINES
Hartford

This winery was originally founded in Detroit as the Bronte Winery, which became the first firm to commercialize the infamous sparkling wine called "Cold Duck", a carbonated-Concord concoction that enjoyed an extraordinary vogue in the 1960s. With such an ignominious history, it is little wonder that the firm moved to a different neighbourhood and assumed another identity!

Of Michigan's 14 other wineries, **Mawby Vineyards** could be worth watching and the following have all produced worthwhile wines at some time in the past: **Leelanau Wine Cellars** (Chardonnay), **Lemon Creek Winery** (Riesling-Vidal blend), **Lakeside Vineyard** (Chardonnay, Johannisberg Riesling), and **Tabor Hill Vineyards** (Chardonnay – not to be confused with Tabor Hill Bronte Wines).

NEW JERSEY

ALBA VINEYARD
Milford

This vineyard has occasionally made good Cabernet, but is best for rich, sweet, plummy port-style wines.

✓ *Vintage Port*

TOMASELLO
Hammonton
☆

This winery, which opened up immediately after Prohibition was repealed, has had 50 years' decent sparkling-wine experience.

✓ *Sparkling Wine* (Blanc de Noirs)

UNIONVILLE VINEYARDS
Ringoes
☆

This is one of New Jersey's newest and fastest-rising wineries.

✓ *Riesling*

Of the 16 other New Jersey wineries, **Gross Highland Winery** has made some interesting Vidal Blanc.

NEW YORK

BEDELL
Cutchogue
★

The first harvest of this Long Island winery coincided with Hurricane Gloria in 1985, but subsequent vintages have stood the test of time.

✓ *Merlot* (Reserve)

BENMARL WINE COMPANY LTD
Marlboro

One of the state's most successful wineries. "Benmarl" is Gaelic for the vineyard's slate-marl soil, and although *vinifera* varieties are grown, Seyval Blanc has been the preferred wine here.

BIDWELL VINEYARDS
Cutchogue

Steadily fine Riesling.

✓ *White Riesling*

BRIDGEHAMPTON
Bridgehampton
★★

Long Island's fastest-rising star, Bridgehampton's wines have an intensity of fruit and a fine structure.

✓ *Chardonnay* • *Meritage* (red Bordeaux style) • *Merlot* • *Riesling* • *Sauvignon Blanc*

BROTHERHOOD WINERY
Washingtonville

The oldest winery in continuous operation in the US, Brotherhood Winery was established by a shoemaker called Jean Jacques, who initially sold wine to the First Presbyterian Church. The wines used to be very much of the old school, but are now fresher and crisper in character.

✓ *Marriage* (red Bordeaux style) • *Riesling*

CANANDAIGUA WINE COMPANY
Canandaigua

The Seneca Native American word *canandaigua* means "chosen place". Even in the late 1980s, this firm had a huge production, but it is now second only in size to Gallo and has diversified into premium varietals. Various Atlantic Northeast labels include Richards, J. Roget, and Virginia Dare, while in California Canandaigua owns Almadén Vineyards, Cooks, Dunnewood, Inglenook, Paul Masson, and Taylors. In Brazil, wines are sold under the Marcus James label.

CASA LARGA VINEYARDS
Fairport

Italian-born Andrew Coloruotolo grew mostly hybrid grapes until he met the late Dr. Konstantin Frank. Now the vineyards contain over 90 per cent *vinifera* vines.

✓ *Chardonnay* • *Johannisberg Riesling*

CHÂTEAU FRANK
Hammondsport

This winery is owned and run by Willy Frank, just down the road from where his father established Dr. Konstantin Frank's Vinifera Wine Cellars.

CLINTON VINEYARDS
Clinton Corners

This specialist winery makes one of the best Seyval Blancs in the state.

GLENORA WINE CELLARS
Dundee
★

Named after the nearby Glenora waterfall, this winery consistently produces crisp and stylish wines.

✓ *Chardonnay* • *Johann Blanc* • *Sparkling Wine* (Vintage Blanc de Blancs)

GOLD SEAL
Hammondsport

Originally called the Imperial Winery, this historic firm built its reputation on "New York Champagne". The quality of this sparkling wine was based on 100 years of Champagne expertise, in the form of Charles le Breton of Louis Roederer, Jules Crance of Moët & Chandon, Charles Fournier of Veuve Clicquot, and Guy Davaux of Marne & Champagne, who all worked at Gold Seal. Of these, it was Fournier who stood out, and his name lives on as the brand of this firm's quaffing fizz.

✓ *Charles Fournier Blanc de Noirs*

GREAT WESTERN WINERY
Hammondsport

Another historic winery, Great Western is now a subsidiary of The Taylor Wine Company. Its wines are less innovative, despite the occasional good *vinifera*.

GRISTINA
Cutchohue
☆

This North Fork vineyard was established in 1984 and started showing promise in the early 1990s.

✓ *Chardonnay* • *Merlot*

HARGRAVE VINEYARD
Cutchohue
★

After considering the potential of wine areas nationwide, including California, Alex and Louisa Hargrave established Long Island's first vineyard in 1973, on what used to be a potato farm.

✓ *Cabernet Sauvignon* • *Pinot Noir* (Le Noiren) • *Sauvignon Blanc*

HERON HILL VINEYARDS
Hammondsport

The name "Heron Hill" is a flight of fancy on the part of advertising copy writer Peter Johnstone, who so liked Finger Lake on a visit in 1968 that he stayed. He set up in business with major shareholder John Ingle, dreamt up Heron Hill in 1977, and has been the winemaker ever since.

✓ *Chardonnay* (Little Heron, Otter Spring) • *Johannisberg Riesling* (Ingle Vineyard) • *Seyval Blanc*

KNAPP VINEYARD
Romulus
☆

This producer has always made wines from *vinifera* as well as hybrid varieties, including one of the state's best Seyval Blancs.

✓ *Cabernet Sauvignon* • *Chardonnay*

LAMOREAUX LANDING
Lodi
★

Finger Lake's latest rising star was established as recently as 1991, and yet was showing off its products on export markets as early as 1994.

✓ *Chardonnay* • *Riesling* (Dry)

LENZ
Peconic
★

While running a restaurant, Patricia and Peter Lenz developed a passion for wine, which led them to establish this winery on a potato farm.

✓ *Chardonnay*

MILLBROOK
★★

This is the shooting star of the Hudson River Region.

✓ *Cabernet Franc* • *Chardonnay* (Proprietor's Special Reserve)

PALMER
Aquebogue
★★

The vineyard was converted from a potato-and-pumpkin farm in 1983, and the winery, built three years later, quickly started producing attention-grabbing wines. The reds, in particular, simply have more richness than other New York wineries can manage.

✓ *Cabernet Franc* • *Chardonnay* • *Merlot*

PAUMANOK VINEYARDS
Aquebogue

This is another of Long Island's up-and-coming stars.

✓ *Merlot* • *Riesling*

PELLEGRINI VINEYARDS
Cutchogue
★★

A recently established Long Island winery, Pellegrini is one of the most promising North Fork producers.

✓ *Cabernet Sauvignon* • *Chardonnay* • *Merlot*

PINDAR VINEYARDS
Peconic
★

With the intention of growing grapes, Dr. Herodotus Damianos converted a potato farm on Long Island into a vineyard. In 1982 he built a winery, named it after the Greek lyric poet, and it is now Long Island's largest producer, and also one of the best.

✓ *Sparkling Wine* (Premier Cuvée)
• *Chardonnay* • *Merlot*
• *Mythology* (red Bordeaux style)

DR. FRANK'S VINIFERA WINE CELLARS
Hammondsport
☆

A fascinating range of *vinifera* wines, especially Sereksia, which is made in a dessert wine style.

✓ *Johannisberg Riesling* (Dry, Semi-Dry) • *Sereksia*

WAGNER VINEYARDS
Route 414, Lodi
☆

Consistently high-quality wines.

✓ *Chardonnay* (Barrel Fermented)
• *Ravat* (Icewine)
• *Riesling* (Dry, Icewine)
• *Seyval Blanc* (Barrel Fermented)

HERMANN J. WEIMER VINEYARD
Dundee
☆

While working for a certain hybrid *aficionado*, Weimer produced some outstanding *vinifera* wines from his own vineyard. They received rave reviews, and he has not looked back.

✓ *Chardonnay*
• *Johannisberg Riesling*

Of the other 75 wineries in New York state, the following have at some time or other produced wines of interest: **Cascade Mountain** (Seyval Blanc, Vignoles Late Harvest), **Peconic Bay Vineyards** (Cabernet Sauvignon, Chardonnay, Merlot), **Plane's Cayuga Vineyard** (Chancellor, Chardonnay), **West Park Wine Cellars** (Chardonnay), **Windsor Vineyards** (Chardonnay), **Woodbury Vineyards** (Chardonnay, Johannisberg Riesling, Seyval Blanc).

OHIO

CHALET DEBONNÉ
Madison
This small winery was set up in 1971 by Tony Debevec, whose great grandfather, Anton Debevec, had in 1917 been the first person to grow grapes in the Grand River area along the south shore of Lake Erie. Vidal Blanc is the most consistent wine.

FIRELANDS WINERY
Sandusky
☆
This winery occupies the original Mantey Vineyard site, which was planted in 1880, and manages to attract 40,000 visitors a year.

✓ *Chardonnay* (Barrel Select)

MARKKO VINEYARD
Ridge Road, Conneaut
This vineyard is owned by Arnulf Esterer, the first of Konstantin Frank's followers to plant *vinifera* in Ohio.

✓ *Cabernet Sauvignon*
• *Chardonnay*

Of Ohio's other 46 wineries, these occasionally excel: **Grand River Wine** (Seyval Blanc), **Harpersfield Vineyard** (Geneva), **Klingshirn Winery** (Cabernet Sauvignon, Chardonnay), **Valley Vineyards** (Vidal Blanc).

PENNSYLVANIA

ALLEGRO VINEYARDS
Brogue
☆

John Crouch is a well-established producer of Cabernet, and is currently on form with Cadenza.

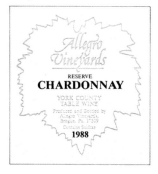

✓ *Cabernet Sauvignon*
• *Cadenza* (red Bordeaux-style)

CHADDSFORD WINERY
Chaddsford
★

It was too early to judge this winery ten years ago but now owners Eric and Lee Miller have turned Chaddsford into one of the rising stars of the Atlantic Northeast.

✓ *Chardonnay* (Philip Roth Vineyard) • *Pinot Grigio*

Of Pennsylvania's 60 other wineries, **Naylor Wine Cellars** has occasionally made some interesting wines (Chambourcin, Riesling).

RHODE ISLAND

SAKONNET VINEYARDS
Little Compton
☆

The first winery to open on Rhode Island after Prohibition.

✓ *Chardonnay*

VIRGINIA

BARBOURSVILLE VINEYARDS
Barboursville
☆

Once the property of James Barbour, a former governor of Virginia, this estate is now owned by Zonin of Piedmont in Italy. Keep an eye open for Barbera and Pinot Grigio.

✓ *Malvasia* (Reserve)

CHÂTEAU MORISETTE
Rocky Mount
A relatively well established (1982), but recently up-and-coming winery.

✓ *White Riesling*

HORTON
Charlottesville
★ • ☆

Dennis Horton is Virginia's lone Rhone Ranger, and he is performing brilliantly, but with vineyards planted between 1989 and 1990, the best is yet to come.

✓ *Côtes d'Orange*
• *Marsanne* • *Viognier*

INGLESIDE PLANTATION
Oak Grove
Ingleside produced Virginia's first sparkling wine in the early 1980s, but its Chardonnay and Cabernet Sauvignon are of more interest.

MEREDYTH VINEYARDS
Middleburg
When Archie Smith established this vineyard in 1972, he became the first grape-grower in Virginia's recent history. However, he was advised against classic *vinifera* varieties, so it was quite a few years before he made any premium-quality wine, and is now best regarded for Chardonnay.

MONTDOMAINE
Charlottesville
☆
Although it was established in 1977, Montdomaine has only just begun to realise its potential, as a result of changes in ownership.

✓ *Chardonnay* (Monticello Reserve)

NAKED MOUNTAIN
Markham
This is a small, improving winery best known for Chardonnay.

OASIS VINEYARD
Hume
★
When Dirgham Salahi planted this vineyard in 1975 he was warned, like everyone else, against *vinifera* varieties, and the locals thought he was mad when he not only ignored this advice, but decided to gamble exclusively on premium varieties. He was proved right and has since become one of the state's more consistent producers.

✓ *Chardonnay* • *Extra Dry Virginia Champagne*

PIEDMONT VINEYARDS AND WINERY INC
Middleburg
★ • ☆
When Elizabeth Furness planted *vinifera* grapes in 1973, no one advised her otherwise, presumably because she was born in 1898 and anyone who is crazy enough to start a new career at the age of 75 wouldn't listen anyway. Mrs. Furness proved to be one of Virginia's best winemakers and revelled in her new job until her death in 1986,

since when her daughter, Elizabeth Worrell, has carried on admirably.

✓ *Chardonnay*
• *Sémillon-Sauvignon*

PRINCE MICHAEL
Culpeper
Owned by French industrialist, Jean Leducq, Prince Michael is the largest vineyard in Virginia, and its production is supplemented with grapes from the company's own vineyards in Napa.

✓ *Cabernet Sauvignon*
• *Chardonnay*
• *Le Ducq* (red Bordeaux style)

RAPIDAN RIVER
Leon
This is also owned by Jean Leducq, but kept separate from his Prince Michael operation.

✓ *Riesling*

TARARA
Leesburg
☆
Established in 1989, this 16-hectare (40-acre) vineyard and winery started to shine almost immediately with its rich, buttery Chardonnay.

✓ *Chardonnay* (Barrel Fermented)

WILLIAMSBURG WINERY
Williamsburg
❷
Although established in 1984, this winery did not start to realize its potential until the 1990 vintage.

✓ *Chardonnay* (Act 12, John Adlum)

Of the 40-odd other wineries in Virginia, the following have showed some promise: **Autumn Hill** (Chardonnay, Riesling), **Burnley Vineyards** (Cabernet Sauvignon, Chardonnay, Riesling), **Linden Vineyards** (Cabernet, Chardonnay, Riesling-Vidal), **Misty Mountain Vineyards** (Chardonnay), **Oakencroft** (Seyval Blanc, Vidal Blanc), **Shenandoah Vineyards** (Chambourcin, Seyval Blanc), and **Simeon Vineyards** (Vin Gris de Pinot Noir).

WEST VIRGINIA
Of the nine wineries currently operating in West Virginia, **West-Whitehill** and **Pliska** have shown the most potential. Pliska provides employment for mentally handicapped adults, and its wines have been served at the American Embassy in Paris.

OTHER STATES
Other states in the Atlantic Northeast that have wineries include Maine (**Bartlett Maine Estate** at Gouldsboro and **Downeast Country** Wines at Trenton), New Hampshire (**The New Hampshire Winery** at Laconia) and Vermont (**Joseph Cerniglia Winery** at Proctorsville and **North River Winery** at Jacksonville).

OTHER WINEMAKING AREAS OF THE
UNITED STATES

ALABAMA

The first commercially cultivated vines were planted here in the 1830s, and the state had a flourishing wine industry prior to Prohibition. However, as many as half its counties remained "dry" until as recently as 1975, and legislation licensing farm wineries was not passed until 1978. Of the four Alabama wineries currently in production, only Braswell's has shown potential.

ARIZONA

Surprisingly, table grapes have long thrived in the irrigated Arizona deserts, but recently, classic wine-grape varieties have been cultivated in this state's solitary AVA of Sonoita, which is only made possible through its altitude of between 1,200 and 1,500 metres (4,000–5,000 feet).

SONOITA AVA

The Santa Rita, Huachuca, and Whetstone mountain ranges isolate this AVA. Geologically, this appellation is an upland basin rather than a valley, because it comprises the head-waters for three distinct drainages: Sonoita Creek to the south, Cienega Creek to the north, and the Babocamari River to the east. Local growers believe their *terra rosa* soil will determine the potential of this area.

ARKANSAS

More than 100 wineries sprang up in Arkansas after Prohibition, but lack of winemaking skills meant that barely half a dozen survived. The potential quality of these is, however, very high, although only one of the state's seven wineries is producing anything of interest.

ALTUS AVA

This plateau lies between the Arkansas River bottom lands and the climatically protective high peaks of the Boston Mountains.

ARKANSAS MOUNTAIN AVA

This AVA covers a huge area in the mountainous region of Arkansas. The Arkansas mountains moderate winter temperatures and provide shelter from violent northerly winds and sudden changes in temperature. Classic European grape varieties are grown in Arkansas Mountain, but cannot survive in the area immediately south because of Pierce's disease, a vine-destroying condition associated with warm climates that attacks *Vitis vinifera*.

OZARK MOUNTAIN AVA

Five major rivers make up this AVA's boundaries: the Mississippi, the Missouri, the Osage, the Neosho, and the Arkansas, and the area includes Mt. Magazine, the highest mountain in Arkansas. The Ozark Mountain appellation straddles parts of Missouri and Oklahoma, and is hilly-to-mountainous. The soils are stony, well drained, and contain clay from deeply weathered, well-consolidated sedimentary volcanic rocks.

COLORADO

The growing season in most of Colorado is too short to permit grape-growing, but the number of wineries have grown from just two a decade ago to 15 today, and there are more in the pipeline. Chardonnay and Merlot are the most popular *vinifera* varieties.

GRAND VALLEY AVA

Grand Valley is located just west of Grand Junction, and incorporates three localities known as Orchard Mesa, Redlands, and Vinelands.

FLORIDA

Not surprisingly, a lot of "orange wine" is made from the citrus fields of this semi-tropical state. A rather odd concoction it might be, yet it is superior to the wine made from the local Muscadine grapes, which are able to survive the humidity and Pierce's disease. Of the four wineries in Florida, Lafayette is most successful.

GEORGIA

Georgia has cultivated grapes since 1733 and by 1880 was the sixth-largest winegrowing state, but its wines, based on native Muscadine grapes, are an acquired taste by modern standards, which explains why there are currently only eight wineries in operation. Apart from an improving Chardonnay from Château Elan in Braselton, there is little of interest here.

HAWAII

Only Alaska seems a less likely wine-producing state, but vines were first planted here in 1814.

ILLINOIS

Until 1980, the winemaking importance of Illinois was vastly exaggerated because of the huge output of the David Morgan Corporation, which has now moved to New York.

IOWA

Most of Iowa's vineyards were destroyed in 1980 by "2, 4-D" pesticide used on neighbouring crops. Most of Iowa's 11 wineries make wines from bought-in grapes, although one producer, Private Stock Winery, has its own vineyard.

KANSAS

Kansas produced 110,000 cases of wine a year until they voted to go "dry" in 1880, and just three wineries exist today – Balkan Winery in Girard, Fields of Fair in Paxico, and Ludwigshof Winery in Eskridge.

KENTUCKY

Much of this state has remained dry since the Prohibition era. To my knowledge, only one winery, Premium Brand of Bardstown, exists.

LOUISIANA

Jesuit priests made altar wine here as early as 1750, and by Prohibition, there were many wineries. Louisana's climate is unsuitable for any vine other than Scuppernong, so grapes were imported from California, or other fruit was relied on for winemaking, particularly oranges. There are just two wineries in this state today – Church Point and Les Orangers Louisianais.

MINNESOTA

Vineyards have to be buried beneath several feet of earth in order to survive Minnesota's winters, which restricts cultivation to hybrids. Of the half-dozen wineries here, Alexis Bailly Vineyard has experimented with *vinifera* varieties.

MISSISSIPPI

The pattern here is very similar to that in Kentucky. However, heavy and restrictive taxes were reduced in 1984, when the Mississippi Delta was granted its own AVA.

MISSISSIPPI DELTA AVA

A fertile alluvial plain with loess bluffs that abruptly rise 30 metres (100 feet) along the entire eastern side of the delta that also covers parts of Louisiana and Tennessee.

MISSOURI

The first wines were produced in Missouri in the 1830s and the state had a flourishing wine industry in the mid-18th century. A small, wine industry exists once again; it relies primarily on hybrid vines, especially Cynthiana (*labrusca* x *aestivalis*) for reds.

AUGUSTA AVA

Grape-growing in Augusta, the country's first established AVA, dates from 1860. The bowl-like ridge of hills from west to east, and the Missouri River on the southern edge of the viticultural area, provide a microclimate that distinguishes Augusta from the surrounding areas.

HERMANN AVA

In 1904, this area furnished 97 per cent of the wine produced in Missouri. The soils are well drained, have a high water capacity, and provide good root development.

OZARK HIGHLANDS AVA

Located within the much larger Ozark Mountain AVA, this area's climate is frost-free and relatively cool during spring and autumn, compared to surrounding areas.

MONTANA

Although the growing season in Montana is too short for grape-growing, vines near Missoula cropped three successive harvests in the 1970s, but Mission Mountain in Drayton is the only surviving winery to my knowledge.

NEVADA

The growing season is theoretically too short for growing vines, but one winery does exist.

NEW MEXICO

Only Florida can claim an older winemaking industry than New Mexico's, which dates back to the early 1600s, but its future is modest, although there are now 20 wineries, including two owned by French Champagne producers.

MESILLA VALLEY AVA

An area that follows the Mesilla Valley along the Rio Grande River from an area just north of Las Cruces, New Mexico (where most of its vineyards are situated) to El Paso, Texas. Soils are alluvial, stratified, deep, and well drained.

MIDDLE RIO GRANDE VALLEY AVA

This narrow valley stretches along the Rio Grande River from Albuquerque to San Antonio. Franciscan missions grew vines here during the 17th century and winemaking existed until

Prohibition. At an altitude of between 1,465 and 1,585 metres (4,800–5,200 feet), the climate is characterized by low rainfall and hot summers.

MIMBRES VALLEY AVA

An area of the Mimbres River from north of Mimbres to south of Columbus.

NORTH CAROLINA

There are no AVAs established or planned for North Carolina as yet. The hot climate dictates that most wines are produced from the hardy, native Scuppernong vine, which produces unusual wine from large, cherry-like grapes. It was from North Carolina Scuppernong grapes that "Captain" Paul Garrett first made his notorious, best-selling Virginia Dare wine from a string of East Coast wineries at the turn of the century. After Prohibition, he created the first singing commercial for wine, and Virginia Dare once again became the country's biggest-selling wine. Scuppernong grapes were scarce, however, and despite successfully encouraging many growers in other southern states to grow this vine, he had to blend in more Californian wine, and in the process Virginia Dare lost its distinctive (and, by today's standards, not very attractive) character, so sales dropped. There are nine wineries in North Carolina, but it is still a hostile environment for anything other than Scuppernong.

OKLAHOMA

Prohibitive winery licence fees make this state unimportant in wine terms, although the Pete Schwarz Winery has been struggling against all the red tape with bought-in grapes since 1970, and Cimmaron Cellars has had its own Maréchal Foch vineyard since 1983. Oklahoma has nine wineries, but the quality is not special and, in the circumstances, this is understandable.

SOUTH CAROLINA

Winemaking began here as long ago as 1764, but it has never really recovered from Prohibition, and there is very little of interest from any of the five wineries that exist today.

TENNESSEE

Although Tennessee still has some "dry" counties, the state has recently passed legislation easing the establishment of farm wineries, of which there are now fourteen. *Vinifera* vines have been planted here, but they usually perish under severe winter conditions. Most producers purchase grapes (*vinifera*, hybrid, and native varieties such as Scuppernong) from both in-state and out-of-state sources (the generic American appellation is the give away). Some pure Tennessee wines are produced, but being authentic does not necessarily make them superior. Cordova Cellars, Highland Manor, and Laurel Hill are the most noted producers.

TEXAS

The Franciscan missions were making wines here at least 130 years before the first vines were grown in California and the first commercial Texan winery, Vel Verde, was established before the first Californian one. The revival of Texas wine began by accident in the mid-1950s, when Robert Reed, a professor of viticulture at Texas Tech University, took home some discarded vine cuttings. He planted them in his garden and was astonished at how well they grew. Reed and colleague Clinton McPherson planted an experimental vineyard of 75 grape varieties, which led to the founding of Llano Estacado winery in 1975. In 1987, Cordier, the famous Bordeaux *négociant*, invested in a massive 405-hectare (1,000-acre) vineyard called Ste. Geneviève, and with 26 Texan wineries now established, the potential that seemed evident ten years ago is just coming to fruition.

BELL MOUNTAIN AVA

Located in Gillespie County, north of Fredericksburg (another sub-appellation of the Texas Hill Country AVA), this is a single-winery denomination consisting of some 22 hectares (55 acres) of vines, growing on the southern and southwestern slopes of Bell Mountain. Over a third of the vines are Cabernet sauvignon, which has so far proved to be significantly better suited to this area than the Pinot noir, Sémillon, Riesling, and Chardonnay that also grow here. Bell Mountain is drier than the Pedernales Valley to the south and the Llano Valley to the north, and also cooler due to its elevation and its constant breezes. Its soils are sandy-loam, with light, sandy-clay subsoil.

ESCONDIDO VALLEY AVA

Proposed by Cordier, the Escondido Valley AVA in Pecos County encompasses the Ste. Geneviève winery. Escondido is an upland valley formed by ranges of mesas to the north and south, the vines growing at an elevation of between 795 and 825 metres (2,600–2,700 feet).

FREDERICKSBURG AVA

This AVA's full title is "Fredericksburg in the Texas Hill Country", but it is usually shortened to distinguish it from the massive Texas Hill Country appellation. Fredericksburg contained eight vineyards when established, but the area is primarily known for its peach orchards. As the peach tree has proved as sensitive to soil and climate as *vinifera* vines, many peach farmers have experimented with grapes, and a number of these are now in commercial production. The soil is sandy-loam over a mineral-rich reddish clay.

TEXAS HIGH PLAINS AVA

This massive appellation in the northwest of Texas covers 32,400 square kilometres (12,500 square miles), encompassing 24 counties and 800 hectares (2,000 acres) of vineyards. Soils are generally brown clay-loams to the north and fine sandy-loam to the south. Rainfall ranges from 14 inches (36 centimetres) in the west to 20 inches (51 centimetres) in the east.

TEXAS HILL COUNTRY AVA

A vast appellation, Texas Hill Country consists of the eastern two-thirds of the Edwards Plateau, encompassing two tiny AVA's (Bell Mountain and Fredericksburg) 40 commercial vineyards, and ten wineries. Most of the hillsides are on limestone, sandstone, or granite, while the valleys contain various sandy or clayey loams.

WISCONSIN

This state has a bigger reputation for its cherry, apple, and other "wines" (not serious in any true wine sense) than for those made from grapes.

LAKE WISCONSIN

Wisconsin Lake and River moderate the climate locally, providing winter temperatures that are several degrees higher than those to the north, south, and west, while the air circulation helps to prevent both frost and rot.

UTAH

Despite the enormous influence wielded by the powerful Mormon Church based in Salt Lake City, winemaking has a history in this state, ironically originating with the arrival of the seemingly abstemious Latter-Day Saints. Brigham Young, who led the Mormons to Utah in 1847, ordered vineyards to be planted and a winery to be built. He required one of his followers, an experienced German winemaker, to make as much wine as he could, and although he permitted Mormons to drink it for Communion (no longer allowed), he recommended that the bulk should be sold. His advice was not taken by the Dixie Mormons, who ran the winery and kept back their best wines for consumption. Winemaking peaked at the end of the 19th century, declining once the Church clamped down on drinking, and died out during Prohibition. Two wineries now exist.

OTHER WINE PRODUCERS OF THE
UNITED STATES

ARIZONA

CALLAGHAN VINEYARDS

Sonoita

Extraordinarily impressive wines are made here. Look out for future releases of Rhône and Italian varietals.

✓ *Cabernet Sauvignon*
(Caitlin's Selection) • *Dos Cabezas*
(Petite Sirah-Zinfandel blend)

ARKANSAS

WIEDERKEHR WINE CELLARS

Altus

This is not only the oldest of the state's seven wineries, its owner is the most successful winemaker in Arkansas, producing 70,000 cases.

✓ *Altus Spumante*
• *Johannisberg Riesling*

COLORADO

PLUM CREEK CELLARS

Palisada

★

That Colorado's wine industry is at an embryonic stage is underlined by the fact that this small winery, which produces only 2,000 cases, is actually the largest in the state.

✓ *Chardonnay* (Redstone)
• *Merlot* • *Riesling*

HAWAII

TEDESCHI VINEYARDS

Maui

Still and sparkling wines are made here from Carnelian grapes grown on the volcanic slopes of Maui

Island. Blanc de Noirs was the first *méthode champenoise* wine and although I have visited this winery just twice, the wines have been coarse and uninspiring on both occasions. The easy-going rosé-styled Rose Ranch Cuvée proved to be a less ambitious, more successful wine, but has not been made since 1990, as far as I am aware. Tedeschi also produces various still wines, including a Maui Nouveau, Maui Blush, and the two most recent additions, Plantation Red (pure Carnelian) and Ulupalakua Red (Carnelian-based blend), but the owners find it far less of a risk and much more profitable to make Maui Blanc from pineapples and, frankly, this tourist gimmick is their best product. There are, however, plans for growing other varieties, so quality may improve. With no winter as such, Tedeschi is also considering harvesting two crops a year.

✓ *Rose Ranch Cuvée*

VOLCANO WINERY
Hawaii

Veterinarian Doc McKinney planted this vineyard between two very active volcanos in 1987 in preparation for his retirement in 1992, when he "went from working six days a week to seven", as he puts it. Surrounded by continuous volcanic eruption, the winery is constantly prone to acid rain of such a strength that, in years such as 1993, production can be halved. McKinney has tried over 20 different varieties of vine, but just one is grown, Symphony, which he describes as "as close to Chardonnay as will grow on the Big Island". This might be correct, but there could hardly be a greater contrast to Chardonnay than the Muscat-like Symphony. However, its fresh, aromatic, slightly exotic character is probably as good a match to Hawaiian cuisine as any grape variety could offer. McKinney also produces fruit wines, and loves mixing the juice of different fruits, in much the same way as the pressings of different grape varieties can be mixed to produce wines of various styles. He also enjoys experimenting, and has just discovered that the cherry-pulp surrounding coffee beans (the vineyard is situated in the famous Kona coffee region) can be fermented, so we might soon have the world's first coffee wine!

ILLINOIS

ALTO VINEYARDS
Alto Pass

Retired university professor Guy Renzaglia planted Chardonnay and Riesling, as well as hybrids, but the *vinifera* vines did not survive.

✓ *Chambourcin • Vidal Blanc*

LYNFRED WINERY
Roselle

Fred Koehler makes a wide range of wines from bought-in grapes

(some from as far afield as California) as well as making a number of very successful fruit wines.

✓ *Fred's Red*

MISSISSIPPI

CLAIRBORNE VINEYARDS
Indianola

This tiny vineyard produces fresh, Seyval Blanc and Sauvignon Blanc.

There are at least three other wineries in Mississippi – **Almarla** in Matherville, **Old South Winery** in Natchez, and **Rushing Winery** in Merigold.

MISSOURI

MOUNT PLEASANT VINEYARDS
Augusta
★

A 19th-century winery resurrected in 1967 by Lucien Dressel, who in 1980 successfully proposed Augusta as the US's first AVA. Best known for its Vintage Port and clean-tasting Seyval Blanc and Vidal Blanc, but makes a surprisingly good Rayon d'Or and Cynthiana. It is trying with Chardonnay (Les Copain Vineyard) and a Bordeaux-style red blend (Private Reserve). It also produced an Icewine and, in 1993, stunned everyone with a wonderful individual Berry Select botrytis wine. However, there are no wines that I can highly recommend on a consistent basis.

STONE HILL WINERY
Hermann

Established in 1847, Stone Hill is the oldest winery in Missouri. Its cellars were used as a mushroom farm during Prohibition, but were revived in 1965 by Jim and Betty Held, who flirted briefly with *vinifera* varieties but gave up. Numerous Catawba and Concord wines are made, but this winery is best for Norton red and a barrel-fermented Seyval Blanc.

Other Missouri wineries worthy of consideration are **Hermannoff** (Norton, Vidal Blanc), and **Montelle** (Cynthiana Coyote Crossing Vineyard).

NEW MEXICO

ANDERSON VALLEY VINEYARDS
Albuquerque

Established in 1984 by mother-and-son team, Patty and Kris Anderson, who initially made Chardonnay and Chenin Blanc of a good quality for the day, but now produce a large range of wines and are more adept at Cabernet Sauvignon.

DOMAINE CHEURLIN
Truth or Consequences
★

This was established in 1981 by Jacques Cheurlin, whose family make Champagne in the Aube district. These wines have a fresh, crisp style.

✓ *New Mexico Brut*

GRUET
Albuquerque
★

The Gruet family established a cooperative in the Sézanne district of Champagne. Some of these wines have shown extraordinary acidity.

✓ *NV Brut*
  • *Vintage Blanc de Blancs*

There are 17 other wineries in New Mexico, but I have encountered very little of interest.

NORTH CAROLINA

BILTMORE ESTATE WINERY
Asheville
★

Classic French grape varieties were planted in 1979 by the grandson of George Washington Vanderbilt, who built the country's largest mansion (250 rooms) on this 3,200-hectare (8,000-acre) estate. At a height of 1,400 metres (4,500 feet) in the Blue Ridge Mountains, it is not only cool enough for classic *vinifera* varieties to grow, but can sometimes be too cold to ripen. The American appellation on these Biltmore Estate wines is worth noting, as it is a clue to the grapes that are trucked in from California, and the wines are, I am sure, all the better for it.

✓ *Chardonnay* (Barrel Fermented)

TEXAS

BELL MOUNTAIN
Fredericksberg

Although Bell Mountain's Cabernet Sauvignon is a medal-winner locally, owner Robert Oberhellman is still very much on a learning curve.

CAP*ROCK
Lubbock
★

Formerly known as Teysha Cellars, but under new ownership since 1992 when its name was changed to Cap*Rock. Tony Soter, the owner of Étude in the Napa Valley, now consults so this is a winery to watch.

✓ *Cabernet* (Reserve, Royale)
  • *Chenin Blanc*
  • *Sauvignon Blanc*

FALL CREEK VINEYARDS
Austin

Named after the waterfall that feeds Lake Buchanan from an upper ridge of Ed Auler's ranch, Fall Creek is planted on land where he once used to raise prize cattle, and has thus been well fertilized for many years. The wines are fruity and quaffable.

✓ *Cabernet Sauvignon*
  • *Chardonnay* (Grande Reserve)
  • *Sauvignon Blanc*

LLANO ESTACADO WINERY
Lubbock
★

Llano Estacado Winery is the first Texan winery to be established in

recent history. It is best for crisp, lively white wines, but the reds are improving.

✓ *Chardonnay • Chenin Blanc*
  • *Sauvignon Blanc*

MESSINA HOF WINE CELLARS
Bryan
★

Paul Bonnarrigo's family came from Messina in Italy, while his wife Merril has a German heritage, hence the name of this winery. Messina Hof Wine Cellars' white wines excel in quality.

✓ *Chenin Blanc • Johannisberg Riesling • Sauvignon Blanc*

PHEASANT RIDGE WINERY
Lubbock
★

Robert Cox of Pheasant Ridge Winery produces one of the state's few good red wines.

✓ *Cabernet Sauvignon* (Lubbock Reserve)

STE. GENEVIÈVE
Fort Stockton

The Ste. Geneviève winery was originally a Franco-Texan venture to cultivate 400 hectares (1,000 acres) of land leased from the University of Texas, but the partnership dissolved and the French partner, Cordier, took full ownership. Much of the huge production is sold in bulk.

✓ *Cabernet Sauvignon* (Grand Reserve) • *Sauvignon Blanc*

SLAUGHTER LEFTWICH
Austin

This 20-hectare (50-acre) vineyard is owned by the Slaughter-Leftwich family, who are sixth-generation Texans. Production includes some 11,000 cases of mostly white wine, but some Cabernet and bit of blush are also produced.

✓ *Chardonnay • Sauvignon Blanc*

UTAH

ARCHES VINEYARD
Spanish Fork

This is the most up-and-coming of Utah's wineries.

✓ *Riesling*

WISCONSIN

WOLLERSHEIM WINERY INC
Prairie du Sac

The Wollersheim Winery was built in 1858 by the Kehl family, from Nierstein in Germany, and then re-established in 1972 by Robert and Joann Wollersheim. Both hybrid and *vinifera* grapes are grown here, with interesting Domaine du Sac blended red and Dry Riesling also occasionally produced.

Of the 12 other wineries in Wisconsin, **Cedar Creek** has made some reasonable wines from bought-in grapes.

✦CANADA✦

When I wrote the first edition of this book I was of the opinion that Canada's wine industry was at a turning point, but in truth I was thinking only of Ontario, which had barely begun growing vinifera *vines at the time, and where red wine from premium varietals was almost non-existent. British Columbia hardly figured at all.*

WINE HAS BEEN COMMERCIALLY PRODUCED in Canada since at least 1860. For the first 100 years, Canadian palates preferred the sweet styles produced by the native *labrusca* grape varieties, although from 1913 the Horticultural Research Centre of Ontario at Vineland began its programme to develop hybrids.

ONTARIO

Ask most people, including many Canadians, if they were to trace a finger around a globe at the same latitude as Ontario, where it would point to in Europe, and they would say somewhere in Scandinavia. Some might think Holland or Belgium, but few would imagine Tuscany, which is in fact correct. It is only Canada's snowbound winter temperatures that stop Niagara Peninsula, the province's most important viticultural area, from being another California.

At the launch party of the first edition, I served Château des Charmes Cabernet Sauvignon and Inniskillin Pinot Noir because few knew that Canada even grew vines, let alone any of the classic varieties, and certainly no one imagined this country produced red wines. In fact, on my first visit to Niagara, I could find

THE VQA SEAL OF QUALITY

After 20 years of following appellation systems around the world, I am aware that none can guarantee quality, but whereas most legally imposed schemes indicate mediocrity, the self-regulated VQA seal has driven Canadian producers to higher and higher standards.
Look for the VQA seal, which guarantees:
• Provincial appellations, such as Ontario, use 100 per cent Canadian-grown grapes, a minimum of 85 per cent from the province indicated, and contain a minimum ripeness level.
• Specific appellations (*see* maps, below and opposite), such as Okanagan Valley, are 100 per cent from the province named, a minimum of 85 per cent from the area named, and contain only classic *vinifera* or preferred hybrid varieties of a minimum ripeness level.
• Estate Bottled wines are 100 per cent from grapes owned or controlled by the winery that is specified.
• Wines that are designated by vineyard names are 100 per cent from grapes grown in the particular vineyard indicated.

CANADA, ONTARIO, *see also p.443*
There are still some 2,800 hectares (7,000 acres) of labrusca *in Ontario and most of these vineyards are in the Lake Erie North Shore area, but they can be used only for fruit juice, fortified, and cheap sparkling-wine products. The premium* vinifera *area is the Niagara Peninsula.*

	Pelee Island
	Niagara District
	Lake Erie North Shore
•	Wineries
	Vine-growing zone
——	International boundary
----	State boundary
▲	Height above sea level (metres)

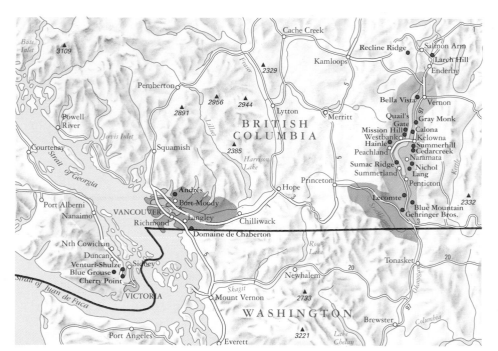

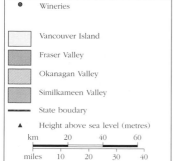

CANADA, BRITISH COLUMBIA, *see also p.443*
British Columbia is rapidly closing the gap with Ontario, Canada's premier wine region. When NAFTA gave cheap Californian wines free access to the Canadian market, both major regions had to upgrade their vineyards to survive. British Columbia's advantage was the relatively small size of its vineyards and the tiny amount of labrusca *planted, as this enabled the province rapidly to replace almost all of its hybrids with* vinifera *varieties, while Ontario still has 2,800 hectares of* labrusca *and close to 2,000 hectares of hybrids.*

FACTORS AFFECTING TASTE AND QUALITY

LOCATION
The chief areas are the Niagara Peninsula of Ontario in the east and the Okanagan Valley of British Columbia 3,200 kilometres (2,000 miles) away to the west. Vines also grow in Nova Scotia and Quebec.

CLIMATE
Eighty-five per cent of vines are grown in Ontario at the same latitude as the French vineyards of Provence and the hills of Tuscany. In Ontario, the temperature-moderating influence of Lakes Erie and Ontario, the windbreak effect of the Niagara Escarpment, and the circular airflow from the lakes, protect the vines from winter wind and frost damage.

The Okanagan Valley of British Columbia is on a more northerly latitude, some 49° to 50°N and approximately in line with Champagne and the Rheingau, but the area is technically a desert, with as little as 15 cm (6 in) of rain in the south. The summers have fierce daytime heat that rapidly builds up the grape sugars, followed by cold nights that allow the grapes to retain high acid levels. The glacial Okanagan lake provides a moderating effect, but winter quickly sets in and grapes do not develop beyond mid-October.

ASPECT
The vines in both Ontario and British Columbia are mostly grown on lakeside slopes. Those in Ontario are sheltered by the Niagara Escarpment, and the better grape varieties are grown on the steep north-facing slopes.

SOIL
Ontario soils cover a wide range from sandy loams to gravel, sand, and clay. Soil is sandy loam to clay on the west bank at the centre of British Columbia's Okanagan Valley, but stony-sandy clay on the east bank, more rocky and gravelly to the south, and much lighter and sandier to the north.

VITICULTURE AND VINIFICATION
The southern, red-wine producing end of the Okanagan valley is undergoing the most extensive planting in Canada, although Niagara Peninsula's vineyards are still growing rapidly. Ontario's wine industry is mature by Canadian terms, while the smaller British Columbia industry is growing at an even more ferocious rate. The level of technology is high, but as in any young wine industry, methods and practices are changing all the time, as winemakers gain experience. Apart from Icewine production, techniques are in a state of flux.

GRAPE VARIETIES
Agawam, Alden, Aligoté, Aurore, Auxerrois, Baco noir, Buffalo, Cabernet franc, Cabernet sauvignon, Canada muscat, Catawba, Chambourcin, Chancellor, Chardonnay, Chasselas, Chelois, Chenin blanc, Commandant, Concord, De Chaunac, Delaware, Dutchess, Elvira, Fredonia, Gamay, Gewürztraminer, Johannisberg riesling, Kerner, Léon Millot, Maréchal Foch, Merlot, New York muscat, Niagara, Okanagan riesling, Patricia, Petite sirah, Pinot blanc, Pinot gris, Pinot noir, President, Rosette, Rougeon, Seyval blanc, Siegfried rebe, Seyve villard, Van Buren, Vee blanc, Veeport, Ventura, Verdelet, Vidal blanc, Villard noir, Vincent, Zinfandel.

only three red wines made from *vinifera* grapes. On a recent visit, no less than 70 red wines were lined up for me to taste, such had been the progress since my initial visit.

Niagara's flagship wine is Icewine, because of the annual snowfall that guarantees that this area will always be the world's largest producer of this style of wine (Germany occasionally produces more, but the yield is erratic). Such wines are, however, hardly everyday drinking. If there is a more readily consumed style that excels on the Niagara Peninsula, it is Riesling, with Auxerrois and Gewürztraminer showing great promise. Although Pinot Noir is often seductive in barrel, it falls over too often in bottle and, while this may be part of the learning curve, Merlot and Cabernet franc have proved to be Ontario's most outstanding red wine grapes – two varieties that were unknown here a decade ago.

BRITISH COLUMBIA

The revolution in Ontario's wine industry over the last ten years has acted like an irresistible bait, luring British Columbia along the same premium-quality path. As in Ontario, winemaking here dates back to the 1860s, but the climate is more marginal and so the industry has always been smaller and – until recently – less adventurous. Large-scale plantings of *labrusca* varieties did not commence until the 1930s, whereas there were 2,000 hectares (5,000 acres) of these vines in Ontario by the end of the 19th century. Ontario started developing hybrids as early as 1913, whereas British Columbia did not plant such varieties until the 1950s and 1960s. The first *vinifera* varieties were planted in 1974, but they were not significant in terms of production until 1989, when two-thirds of the vineyards – all *labrusca* and the least fashionable hybrids – were grubbed up.

My first trip to British Columbia was in 1993, when the state of the industry was similar to that of Ontario in the mid- to late-1980s. There were only seven red wines made from premium varietals, although there were plenty made from hybrids. After seeing how rapidly Ontario changed from hybrid to *vinifera* wines, and how quickly this elevated the province's standing in the international wine community, British Columbia's winemakers are managing the same transition even quicker.

First impressions are that, with the exception of outstanding wines from three Ontario wineries – Inniskillin (Klose Vineyard), Reif Estate, and Stoney Ridge (Bebenek Vineyard and Puddicombe Vineyard) – British Columbia producers now make more consistent

Chardonnay than their western cousins, but the varieties that truly belong to this province are Pinot blanc and Auxerrois. Riesling shows almost as much promise as in Ontario, Gewürztraminer even more. Locals love their Ehrenfelser and, although I have tasted some nice examples, it usually makes a lacklustre wine and even the best will mean absolutely nothing to customers outside British Columbia. As for reds, I have tasted good Merlot from Sumac Ridge, but I have tasted even better red wines from hybrids such as Chelois and Chancellor. I have also had a Pinot Noir from Blue Mountain that was not Pinot Noir in any varietal sense, but an amazing wine – huge, dark, and fathomless – in its own right.

WINE PRODUCTION ONTARIO V BRITISH COLUMBIA

TYPE	ONTARIO	BRITISH COLUMBIA
Vinifera acres	3,500 (1.2m cases)	2,500 (0.9m cases)
Hybrid acres	4,800 (1.5m cases)	400 (0.2m cases)
Total wine	8,300 (2.7m cases)	2,900 (1.1m cases)
VQA areas	3	4
Red wines	40%	20%
White wines	60%	80%
Exports	2%	5%

THE APPELLATIONS OF
CANADA

FRASER VALLEY VQA
British Columbia
Six small farm wineries harvest hillside vineyards amid country lanes and historic towns, just one hour's drive from Victoria.

LAKE ERIE NORTH SHORE VQA
Ontario
In the southwest of Ontario, along the shoreline of Lake Erie, the shallowest and warmest of the five Great Lakes, this area has the most hours of sunshine in Canada and the grapes are picked weeks ahead of other areas. Its *vinifera* vineyards are just two per cent of the total vines.

NIAGARA PENINSULA VQA
Ontario
On the south shore of Lake Ontario, Niagara Peninsula is where the Lake-induced airflow is at its greatest, making viticulture most suitable, hence the area encompasses 97 per cent of Ontario's vineyards. Most vines grow at a height of 90 metres (300 feet) above sea level, as the land gently slopes from the foot of the Niagara

Escarpment to the lake. The escarpment rises to over 180 metres (600 feet) and contains a number of benches, about which there is increasing interest, especially in the Beamsville area.

OKANAGAN VALLEY VQA
British Columbia
The largest, oldest, and most important of BC's wine areas, this stretches 160 kilometres (100 miles), with some 970 hectares (2,400 acres) of vines: more than 96 per cent of BC's vineyards. French and German varieties are planted at the northern end, but much activity is focused on the fast-expanding vineyards in the south, which receive less than 152 millimetres (6 inches) of rain and where classic red-wine varieties thrive.

PELEE ISLAND VQA
Ontario
This is the site of Canada's first commercial winery, established in 1866. It is located in Lake Erie, 24 kilometres (15 miles) off the mainland, where its 200 hectares (500 acres) are marginally closer to the equator than Rome is. Picking

starts at the end of August and even late-harvested grapes are in by mid-October.

SIMILKAMEEN VALLEY VQA
British Columbia
To the southwest of the Okanagan Valley, through the mountains, in the high desert cattle country of the Similkameen Valley, Crowsnest Vineyards is leading a small band of pioneering wineries. The vines represents just over two per cent of BC's vineyards, yet make this the province's second-largest wine appellation.

VANCOUVER ISLAND VQA
British Columbia
The province's newest wine area, Vancouver Island's wet and windy climate might not seem ideal for viticulture, yet Divino moved here from what some considered to be the finest vineyards in the entire Okanagan Valley. In terms of wineries, Vancouver Island is the second most important wine area in BC and shortly promises to overtake the Similkameen Valley as second-largest for vineyards.

THE WINE PRODUCERS OF
CANADA

BRITISH COLUMBIA

ALDERLEA VINEYARD
Duncan
New venture on Vancouver Island where Roger Dosman grows Auxerrois, Pinot gris, and Pinot noir.

ANDRÉS WINES
This is the winery that introduced Canada to the delights of "Baby Duck", a popular and much-imitated sweet pink or red fizzy *labrusca* wine. The original version was known in Germany as "Kalte Ente" or "Cold Duck", and was made from the dregs of both red and white wines, to which some Sekt was added. For anyone not used to foxy-flavoured *labrusca* grapes, Andrés's commercial version was even more disgusting than the original concoction, but it took North America by storm. As *vinifera* wines gave Canada a wine industry

to be proud of, even Andrés was forced to sell premium varietals. However, it dawned on Andrés that the sort of discerning customer most likely to buy premium varietals would be the least likely to buy from a firm that was synonymous with "Baby Duck". The Peller Estates label (named after Andrew Peller, the founder of Andrés) was thus launched to market exclusively VQA *vinifera* wines. You can still buy "Baby Duck" – indeed, there are now other baby shams such as "Baby Duck White" and even "Baby Champagne".

BELLA VISTA
Vernon
This winery is best known for the hybrid Maréchal Foch, and *vinifera*-hybrid blends, such as Château Select, but has also produced Auxerrois, and is probably most famous for its Murder Mystery nights.

BLUE GROUSE
Duncan
This Vancouver Island winery in the Cowichan Valley is run by Hans Kiltz, who is known for his Pinot Blanc.

BLUE MOUNTAIN
Okanagan Falls
★
Ian Mavety's winery has come a long way since 1992, when it released its debut 1991 vintage, and the Pinot Gris – now one of BC's finest – was dull and toffee-like. Under the guidance of Raphael Brisbois (formerly at Omar Khayyam in India and Iron Horse in California), the sparkling wines from the Blue Mountain winery have proved to be particularly promising. This winery also makes an interesting Pinot Noir.

✓ *Pinot Blanc • Pinot Gris • Sparkling Wine* (Vintage Brut Vintage Reserve)

CALONA
Kelowna
★
Calona has been making wine since 1932. Its semi-sweet German-style Schloss Laderheim became Canada's bestseller in 1981, and has improved.

✓ *Merlot* (Cedar Creek) • *Sémillon* (Private Reserve)

CARRIAGE HOUSE

Oliver

Carriage House is known for Kerner, but has made Pinot Blanc and will be adding Chardonnay, Merlot, and Pinot Noir in 1997.

CEDAR CREEK

Kelowna

☆

I have tasted some interesting tank samples here, but with the exception of dessert wine styles (Late Harvest, Icewine etc.), most white wines tend to fall over fairly quickly once bottled, and could do with bottling at colder temperatures to preserve CO_2 content.

✓ *Chancellor* • *Ehrenfelser* (Late Harvest) • *Merlot Reserve* • *Optima* (Select Late Harvest) • *Riesling* (Icewine)

CHÂTEAU WOLFF

Nanaimo

Harry von Wolff's winery on Vancouver Island opened in 1996, when Chardonnay and Pinot noir were harvested.

CHERRY POINT

Cobble Hill

Wayne and Helena Ulrich heroically grow *vinifera* grapes on wet and windy Vancouver Island. A full and rich Pinot Noir is their ambition, but fresh and tasty Auxerrois and Pinot Blanc are more realistic, with Ortega and Müller-Thurgau planted for insurance.

CROWSNEST VINEYARDS

Keremeos

Since their first harvest in 1994, Andrea and Hugh McDonald have built up a steady reputation for Riesling and are just beginning to hone red-wine styles.

✓ *Riesling*

DIVINO WINERY

Cobble Hill

This former Okanagan winery is now on Vancouver Island, where Joe and Barbara Busnardo have planted eight hectares (20 acres).

DOMAINE DE CHABERTON

Langley

Owner Claude Violet has had winemaking experience in France and Switzerland and was the first to grow grapes in the Fraser Valley.

DOMAINE COMBRET

Osoyoos

With a reputation for Chardonnay and Cabernet Franc, Combret also produces Riesling and Gamay.

✓ *Chardonnay*

GEHRINGER BROTHERS

Oliver

Gordon and Walter Gehringer have produced many interesting wines, but none stranger than their red, raisiny Chancellor Icewine.

✓ *Ehrenfelser* • *Pinot Gris* • *Riesling* (Dry)

GRAY MONK CELLARS

Okanagan Centre

★ ⓥ

Gray Monk has a reputation for Gewürztraminer and the German clone growing in Broderson Vineyard is one of BC's more spicy.

✓ *Gewürztraminer* (Broderson Vineyard, Rotberger) • *Pinot Blanc* • *Pinot Auxerrois*

HAINLE

Peachland

I cannot fault Tilman Hainle's enthusiasm; he nearly always goes over the top, but can produce wonderfully exciting wines as a result, only to make a complete hash of the same *cuvée* in the following vintage. Serious, petrolly Riesling is his most outstanding wine at present, but keep taking chances Tilman.

✓ *Icewine* (Riesling) • *Kerner* (Fischer Vineyard) • *Pinot Gris* (Elizabeth's Vineyard) • *Riesling* (Dry Estate)

HAWTHORNE MOUNTAIN VINEYARDS

Okanagan Falls

☆

This winery is owned by Albert and Dixie LeComte, who wisely hired Eric von Krosig as winemaker. The winery was originally called LeComte and wines are still produced under that label, but since 1996, the emphasis has been on establishing the Hawthorne Mountain Vineyards name.

✓ *Pinot Noir* • *Riesling*

HESTER CREEK

Oliver

Located at the former Divino winery and vineyard (now re-established on Vancouver Island), the first harvest was 1996.

HILLSIDE

Penticton

☆

Vera Klokocka fled Czechoslovakia when the Soviets invaded in 1968. She has been growing grapes since the mid-1970s, and has been making some wonderfully gluggy wines since 1990.

✓ *Pinot Auxerrois* • *Riesling*

HOUSE OF ROSE

Kelowna

Vern Rose produces an eclectic range of wines, from Rose Rosé to Late Harvest Chardonnay.

INNISKILLIN OKANAGAN

Oliver

★

Ontario's premier publicist, Don Ziraldo, started making wines in 1994, when his winery became part of Vincor, but did not have his own premises until 1996, when Inniskillin acquired the former Okanagan Vineyards premises. Inniskillin's co-founder and winemaker, Karl Kaiser oversees

production while Christine Lerous, his former assistant in Ontario, is in day-to-day control.

✓ *Chenin Blanc* (Icewine) • *Merlot* (Inkameep Vineyard) • *Pinot Blanc*

JACKSON-TRIGGS

Oliver

☆

Vincor's new premium wine brand is building a reputation for elegance.

✓ *Riesling* (Dry Proprieter's Reserve, Icewine)

KETTLE VALLEY

Naramata

One of many up-and-coming small wineries established in the early 1990s. Owners Bob Fergusen and Tim Watts have produced Pinot Noir, Chardonnay, and Cabernet–Merlot. In 1995, they made novel Icewines from Chardonnay and Pinot Noir, while in 1996 the Pinot Noir was used for a Blanc de Noirs bottle-fermented sparkling wine.

LAKE BREEZE VINEYARDS

Naramata

Watch out for the 1996 Ehrenfelser Icewine from this winery.

LANG VINEYARDS

Naramata

Owner Guenther Lang left Germany in 1980 and set up Lang Vineyards, which became the first boutique farm winery in the province, in 1990.

✓ *Icewine* (Riesling)

LARCH HILL WINERY

Enderby

One of the most northerly vineyards in Okanagan Valley, the first vintage was 1995, released in 1997.

MISSION HILL VINEYARDS

Westbank

★

This operation has won more than its fair share of international medals since New Zealander John Simes took over as winemaker in 1992.

✓ *Chardonnay* (Barrel Select) • *Chardonnay-Semillon* • *Dune* (Port-style) • *Merlot-Cabernet* (Grand Reserve) • *Pinot Blanc*

NICHOL VINEYARD

Naramata

Alex and Kathleen Nichol have produced one of the Okanagan Valley's fastest-rising star wineries.

✓ *Ehrenfelser* (Select Late Harvest) • *Pinot Noir*

PARADISE RANCH

Naramata

Owned by Dr. Jeff Harries, this vineyard has been cropping for a few years now, but the winery was not due to be built until 1997.

PELLER ESTATES

Port Moody

★

This is Andrés premium-quality brand, exclusively dedicated to

VQA wines. The Trius Icewine is an innovation, made from three grape varieties and two regions.

✓ *Chardonnay* • *Ehrenfelser* (Late Harvest) • *Icewine* (Ehrenfelser, Trinity) • *Merlot* (Showcase) • *Pinot Blanc* (especially Showcase)

PINOT REACH CELLARS

Kelowna

Despite the name, this winery also produces Riesling, Bacchus, and Optima, while Pinot encompasses Pinot Blanc and Meunier (now thought to be a separate variety) as well as Pinot Noir.

POPULAR GROVE

Penticton

Ian and Gitta Sutherland had their first harvest of Cabernet and Merlot in 1995, and expect Chardonnay to come on stream in 1997.

PRPICH VINEYARDS

Okanagan Falls

This longtime grape-grower turned winemaker in the mid-1990s, but was not due to release any until his new winery was built in 1997.

QUAILS'S GATE

Kelowna

★

The Stewart family planted their vineyards in the 1960s, but there was an uncertain feel about these wines even until the early 1990s, but the arrival of Australian-born winemaker Jeff Martin has rapidly turned the quality around.

✓ *Cabernet Sauvignon* (Limited Release) • *Chardonnay* (Limited Release) • *Optima* (Late Harvest Botrytis Affected) • *Pinot Noir* (particularly Family Reserve) • *Riesling* (Icewine, Late Harvest)

ST. HUBERTUS

Kelowna

Erratic winemaking at this winery includes a strangely perfumed, almost foxy-tasting Pinot Blanc (1991) and Dry Rieslings that range from dull to fresh and invigorating.

✓ *Icewine* (Riesling)

SLAMKA CELLARS

Lakeview Heights

This is a small farm winery with a developing reputation.

SUMAC RIDGE

Summerland

★

Owned by Bob Wareham, but still very much run by one of his former partners, Harry McWatters, Harry's Private Reserve Gewürztraminer is one of the best examples of this variety found outside Alsace, and after a disappointing start, his bottle-fermented fizz is showing promise.

✓ *Cabernet Franc* • *Chardonnay* (Private Reserve) • *Chenin Blanc* • *Gewürztraminer* • *Merlot* • *Pinot Blanc* • *Red Meritage* • *Riesling*

SUMMERHILL ESTATE
Kelowna
★

Whether the pyramid of Cheops on this property actually focuses pyramid-power is open to question, but there is no doubt whatsoever that owner Stephen Cipes is eccentric. Without this special person, we would be denied the world's only Pyramid-Aged "Champagne". Locals also appreciate his Gewürztraminer, but he is most consistent for Pinot Blanc.

✓ *Chardonnay* • *Ehrenfelser* (Reserve) • *Icewine* (Pinot Noir, Riesling) • *Johannisberg Riesling* (Estate) • *Pinot Blanc* • *Riesling* (Late Harvest) • *Sparkling Wine* (Pinot Noir Brut, Icewine Dosage)

TINHORN CREEK
Oliver

Sandra Oldfield has quickly established a reputation, particularly for red wines, since her very recent debut vintage of 1994.

✓ *Icewine* (Kerner-Riesling) • *Pinot Noir*

VENTURI-SCHULZE
Cobble Hill

Giordano Venturi and Marilyn Schulze-Venturi on Vancouver Island are best known for Pinot Blanc wines and balsamic vinegar.

VIGNETTI ZANATTA
Duncan

Loretta Zanatta is known for her Pinot Blanc, which is made from the family vineyards in the Cowichan Valley of Vancouver Island.

VINCOR
Oliver

Formerly called Brights-Cartier, this vineyard is Canada's largest wine producer, owning the Inniskillin winery, and selling wines under the Jackson-Triggs and Sawmill Creek labels.

WILD GOOSE VINEYARDS
Okanagan Falls

Born in East Germany, Adolf Kruger and his family were one of the first producers to set up a farm winery here. He has built a reputation for red wines, primarily Maréchal Foch, but more recently for Merlot.

NOVA SCOTIA

The growing season here is short and cool, with very harsh winters, making vinegrowing more an act of faith than the result of hard work. There are almost 40 growers, but only three wineries. Most vineyards are located in the Annapolis Valley on the northwestern shore, where the grapes grown are mainly hybrids such as Seyval blanc, New York muscat, and Maréchal Foch, and a Russian *Amurensis* variety called Michurinetz. Grand Pré was the first commercial winery, established by the pioneering Roger

Dial, and now owned by Jim Landry and Karen Avery, who added Chardonnay to the varieties grown. The Jost Vineyard once held the record for Canada's most expensive Icewine, while Sainte Family has successfully grown Auxerrois, Chardonnay, and Riesling. Nova Scotia wines, like more generic Canadian wines, will probably be made from up to 100 per cent imported grapes, so it is difficult to identify pure province-grown wines.

ONTARIO

ANDRÉS WINES
Winona

Although this firm also produces Peller Estates wines under Ontario and Niagara Peninsula appellations, I have tasted only its BC products.

CAVE SPRING
Jordan
★★

A large, ambitious venture founded in 1986 by Leonard Penachetti, who has a great sense of humour, but is serious about establishing Cave Spring as one of Ontario's best wineries. The vineyards are located on the Beamsville Bench, west of St. Catharines, which is well suited to aromatic *vinifera* varieties.

✓ *Chardonnay* (Bench, Reserve) • *Chardonnay Musqué* • *Icewine* (Riesling) • *Riesling* (Botrytis Affected, Dry, Indian Summer)

CHÂTEAU DES CHARMES
St. Davids
★★

Established by Paul Bosc and run by his son who makes a decent fizz, Château des Charmes excels with red-wine styles.

✓ *Cabernet Sauvignon* • *Chardonnay* (Estate Bottled, St. David's Bench) • *Icewine* (Riesling) • *Merlot* (Paul Bosc Estate) • *Sparkling Wine* (Brut)

COLIO WINES
Harrow
★

Colio Wines was founded by a group of Italian businessmen who wanted to import Italian wines from their twin-town of Udine in Friuli-Venezia Giulia, but ultimately found that it was easier to build a winery and make their own.

✓ *Cabernet Franc* • *Pinot Gris* • *Riesling* (Lake Erie North Shore) • *Vidal*

CULOTTA WINES
Oakville

This winery has made both hybrid and *vinifera* varietals since 1979.

D'ANGELO ESTATE WINERY
Amherstburg

Sal D'Angelo has been growing hybrid vines since 1984, and making wines – including some from *vinifera* varieties – since 1990.

DE SOUSA
Beamsville

In 1987, John de Sousa became the first Portuguese-born winemaker to open a Canadian winery.

HENRY OF PELHAM
St. Catharines
★★

Established in 1988 by the Speck family, who have grown grapes in the area since 1974. After an initial period of inconsistency, this winery has settled to a high standard of quality. Hybrid enthusiasts should taste the Baco Noir, which is one of the best in the world.

✓ *Baco Noir* • *Cabernet-Merlot* • *Chardonnay* • *Icewine* (Riesling) • *Merlot* • *Riesling*

HERNDER ESTATE WINES
St. Catharines

The Hernder family have been Grape growers since 1967, and turned to producing wine in 1991. Ray Cornell is the winemaker here.

HILLEBRAND
Niagara-on-the-Lake
★

Initially called Newark (the original name of Niagara-on-the-Lake), the title of this winery changed when it was purchased by Scholl & Hillebrand of Rüdesheim in 1983.

✓ *Cabernet-Merlot* (Barrel Fermented Collector's Choice) • *Chardonnay* (Trius) • *Icewine* (no variety stated) • *Sparkling* (Mounier Brut) • *Trius* (Glenlake Vineyard – classic red blend)

INNISKILLIN
Niagara-on-the-Lake
★★

Founded by Don Ziraldo, an agronomist and one of Canada's greatest wine publicists, and the

winemaker, Karl Kaiser, a highly respected oenologist. You could not get two more contrasting characters, but the symbiotic relationship between extrovert Ziraldo and introvert Kaiser was essentially responsible for driving the Canadian wine industry from the backwaters to its present position on the international wine stage.

✓ *Auxerrois* • *Cabernet Franc* • *Cabernet Franc-Merlot* • *Cabernet Sauvignon* (Klose Vineyard) • *Chardonnay* (Reserve, Klose Vineyard, Seegar Vineyard) • *Gamay* • *Icewine* (Vidal) • *Maréchal Foch* • *Pinot Noir* • *Riesling* (Reserve) • *Vidal*

KITTLING RIDGE ESTATES
Grimsby

This is a relatively recent venture producing both wines and spirits.

KONZELMANN
Niagara-on-the Lake
★★

Established in 1984 by Herbert Konzelmann, who introduced the vertical trellising of vines to Canada. One of the most modest and gifted winemakers in Ontario, Herbert's vineyard has always displayed exceptional potential for Gewürztraminer. These wines sell out quickly every year. My only criticism is the label.

✓ *Chardonnay* (since 1992) • *Gewürztraminer* • *Icewine* (Gewürztraminer, Vidal) • *Pinot Blanc* • *Riesling* • *Riesling Traminer* (Select Late Harvest) • *Vidal* (Late Harvest)

LAKEVIEW CELLARS
Vineland

Award-winning amateur winemaker Eddy Gurinskas purchased a vineyard on the Beamsville bench in 1986 and went commercial in 1991.

LEBLANC ESTATE WINERY
Harrow

This family-owned vineyard was planted in 1984, but the winery is recent. 1993 was the debut vintage. Mostly aromatic whites are made.

LONDON WINERY
London

Founded in 1925 by the Knowles brothers from the Bahamas. They began making wine for medicinal purposes during Prohibition, and cleverly built up stocks of mature wine in readiness for the Repeal they knew would come.

MAGNOTTA WINERY
Mississauga

This winery, which has vineyards on the Beamsville Bench, has made some interesting Chardonnay and Icewine, but I am puzzled by Magnotta's sparkling wines, although I've tasted them only once. The Brut reminded me of Sherry, but with bubbles, while the Blanc de Blancs was like oak-aged Sherry with bubbles. Some great labels though.

√ *Chardonnay* (Lenko Vineyards)
• *Icewine* (Vidal)

MAPLE GROVE
Beamsville

Established as recently as 1994, the winemaker, Giovanni Follegot, who owns Vinoteca, has put a definite emphasis on red wines.

MARYNISSEN ESTATES
Niagara-on-the-Lake

This small farmgate winery (a farm-based vineyard with its own winery, which can sell from its own premises) was established in 1990 by John Marynissen, who has been growing *vinifera* grapes on the Niagara Peninsula longer than most winegrowers (he planted Cabernet vines in 1978). He has taken to winemaking like a duck to water.

√ *Cabernet Sauvignon*
• *Chardonnay*
• *Merlot* • *Pinot Noir*

PELEE ISLAND
Kingsville, Pelee Island
☆

It takes an hour on a ferry to reach this island in Lake Erie, one of Ontario's VQA areas and the location of Canada's most southerly vineyards. With the longest growing season in the country and the warmest climate, it comes as no surprise that Vin Villa, Canada's first commercial winery, was established here in the 1860s.

√ *Riesling* • *Cabernet Franc*
• *Chardonnay* (Premium Select)

PILLITTERI ESTATES WINERY
Niagara-on-the-Lake

The Pillitteri family has been growing grapes on the Niagara Peninsula for almost 50 years.

REIF ESTATE WINERY
Niagara-on-the-Lake
★☆

Firmly established as one of Niagara's top wineries, the wines

---

produced by Klaus Reif, just round the corner from Inniskillin, are 100 per cent estate bottled, often *barrique*-influenced, and they always show great elegance.

√ *Cabernet Sauvignon* (unfiltered)
• *Chardonnay* • *Riesling*

SOUTHBROOK FARMS
Vaughan

Established as recently as 1991, under the auspices of Brian Croser (of Petaluma in Australia), who also acted as consultant for the first vintage that year. The grapes came from Reif vineyard and Klaus Reif was the winemaker initially. Although various varietals have won awards internationally, I have been less impressed with them (so far) than with Southbrook's delectable Framboise, which has a heady, concentrated raspberry aroma.

√ *Cabernet Franc,*
Chardonnay, Framboise

STONECHURCH VINEYARDS
Niagara-on-the Lake
☆

Rick Hunse's family had been grape growers in the locality for more than 20 years when they opened Stonechurch vineyards and began making their own wine in 1990. After a dodgy start, some very nice wines are being produced.

√ *Cabernet Sauvignon*
• *Icewine* (Riesling)

STONEY RIDGE CELLARS
Winona
★★☆

Although founded as recently as 1990, Stoney Ridge has firmly established itself as one of the most outstanding wineries in Ontario.

√ *Cabernet Franc* • *Chardonnay*
(Bebenek Vineyard, Eastmann Vineyard, Puddicombe Vineyard) • *Icewine* (Vidal)
• *Merlot* (Lenko Vineyards)
• *Riesling* (Late Harvest)

THIRTY BENCH
Beamsville

I have heard good things about this small vineyard and winery. They also have nice, understated labels.

VINCOR
Niagara Falls

Formerly Brights-Cartier. Although Vincor makes Jackson-Triggs under the Niagara Peninsula appellation, I have tasted only its BC products.

VINELAND ESTATES
Vineland
☆

Formerly owned by Herman Weiss, whose family own a winery in the Mosel called St. Urban, Vineland Estates is now owned by John Howard, and BC-trained winemaker Allan Schmidt, whose father had been one of the original partners in Sumac Ridge.

√ *Icewine* (Vidal)
• *Riesling* (Late Harvest, Reserve, St. Urban Vineyards, Semi Dry)

VINOTECA
Woodbridge

Established in 1989 by Giovanni and Rosanne Follegot, Vinoteca was the first winery to be granted a licence in the greater metropolitan Toronto area, although the vineyards are located on the Niagara Peninsula.

WILLOW HEIGHTS
Beamsville

Owner–winemaker Speranzini is one of a new breed of Niagara vintners who believe that every wine produced must come from premium peninsular vineyards.

QUEBEC

If Nova Scotia wines seem improbable, then many readers may well wonder whether the vineyards of Quebec must surely be the figment of somebody's imagination or alternatively a scam to sell wines made from 100 per cent imported grapes. Surprisingly enough, these vineyards do exist. It was here, after all, that the Jesuits following in the wake of Jacques Cartier made Canada's first wines *circa* 1564. But even if Quebec were at the north pole, one gets the feeling that its French descendants would make an attempt to grow vines. It is in the blood. Making wine, however, is not so much a matter of honour to the French, it is a way of life, which explains why there are almost 20 wineries in existence. None is large, but the most important is L'Orpailleur, while others worth looking out for include Dietrich-Joos, Domaines des Côtes d'Ardoise, La Vitacée, and Vignoble Le Cep d'Argent. The vines are a mixture of hybrids and *vinifera*. Quebec is set to join the VQA scheme, which will raise standards of production.

INNISKILLIN VINEYARD UNDER SNOW
Inniskillin made its first Icewine in 1984, but it was not until 1986 that the technique was perfected and started to attract international interest, which was sealed by the gold medal won at Vinexpo in 1991 for the 1989 Vidal Icewine.

✦MEXICO✦

The biggest obstacle to Mexico's success as a winemaking region is not its hot climate, or the recent avalanche of cheap American imports but the absence of wine-drinking from the culture of its population.

IT WAS THE SPANISH who brought wine to Mexico, the oldest wine-producing country in the Americas. By 1521, just one year after invading Mexico, the conquistadors had planted vines and soon afterwards, they began making wine, the very first in the entire North American continent.

In 1524 Hernán Cortés, the governor of New Spain (Mexico), ordered that all Spanish residents who had been granted land and given Indians for forced labour, should annually plant "one thousand vines per hundred Indians" for a period of five years. By 1595 the country was almost self-sufficient in wine, and shipments of domestic Spanish wine had dwindled to such an extent that producers in the home country pressured Philip II into forbidding the planting of further vineyards in the New World.

THE ORIGINAL "TEQUILA SUNRISE"

When the Spanish encountered a strange, milky-white Aztec cactus wine called *pulque*, they were not very impressed. However, in a bid to utilize this popular local product, they tried distilling it – the crystal-clear, colourless spirit that resulted was far more to their taste, and was named *tequila*, after *Agave tequilana*, the variety of cactus used. Today tequila is one of Mexico's most important exports, and vast quantities of *pulque* are still produced and consumed by native Mexicans.

MODERN MEXICAN WINE

There are 50,000 hectares (125,000 acres) of vines in Mexico, but almost 40 per cent produce table grapes or raisins, and much of the wine produced is distilled into brandy. Of the average annual harvest of 650,000 tonnes of grapes, less than half ends up as wine, giving a typical production of approximately 2.4 million hectolitres (26.7 million cases).

It was not long ago that the best Mexican wines tasted little better than *pulque* but, by 1988, when the first edition of this encyclopedia was published, a combination of foreign investment and a tourist demand for more sophisticated products had already made significant improvements. At the time, many international oenologists were very optimistic about Mexico's future as a producer of good-quality wines, but unfortunately, although the potential remains the same, a lack of sales on the home market has seen more than half of Mexico's wineries close down. Most Mexicans drink beer or *pulque*, not wine. The consumption of wine *per capita* is less than one-thirtieth of that in the US, and that in turn is less than one-tenth of the European average. The wine industry in the States is only viable because of the sheer scale of its economy – the largest in the world – and the size and affluence of its middle classes. The truth is that Mexico's middle classes cannot support a fully-fledged domestic wine industry and

AREAS UNDER VINE IN MEXICO

STATE	HECTARES	ACRES
Sonora	18,200	45,000
Baja California Norte	7,500	18,500
Aguascalientes	6,500	16,050
Zacatecas	5,800	14,350
Coahuila	4,300	10,600
Chihuahua	3,500	8,650
Querétaro	2,500	6,200
Durango	1,700	4,200
TOTAL	50,000	123,550

FACTORS AFFECTING TASTE AND QUALITY

LOCATION
Eight of the country's states grow grapes, from Baja California in the north to San Juan del Rio, just north of Mexico City in the south.

CLIMATE
Half of Mexico lies south of the Tropic of Cancer, but altitude moderates the temperature of the vineyards. Most are situated on the high central plateau and some are cooled by the nearby ocean. Principal problems include extreme fluctuation of day and night temperatures, and the fact that most areas have either too little or too much moisture. The dry areas often lack adequate sources of water for irrigation, and the wet districts suffer from too much rain during the growing season.

ASPECT
In the states of Aguascalientes, Querétaro, and Zacatecas, vines are grown on flat plateau lands and the sides of small valleys, at altitudes of 1,600 m (5,300 ft), rising to nearly 2,100 m (7,000 ft) in Zacatecas State. In Baja California, vines are located in valley and desert areas at much lower altitudes of between 100 and 335 m (330–1,100 ft).

SOIL
The soils of Mexico can be divided into two wide-ranging categories: slope or valley soils are thin and low in fertility, while plains soils are of variable depth and fertility. In the Baja California, the soils range from a poor, alkaline sandy soil in Mexicali, to a thin spread of volcanic soil, which is intermixed with gravel, sand, and limestone to provide excellent drainage. In Sonora, the soils of Caborca are similar to those found in Mexicali, but those in Hermosillo are very silty and of alluvial origin. The high plains of Zacatecas have mostly volcanic and silty-clay soils. In the Aguascalientes, the soil in both the valley and the plains is of a scarce depth with a thin covering of calcium. The volcanic, calcareous sandy-clay soil in Querétaro has a good depth and drainage and is slightly alkaline, while in La Laguna the silty-sandy alluvium is very alkaline.

VITICULTURE AND VINIFICATION
Irrigation is widely practised in dry areas such as Baja California and Zacatecas. Most wineries are relatively new and staffed by highly trained oenologists.

GRAPE VARIETIES
Barbera, Bola dulce, Cabernet sauvignon, Cardinal, Carignan, Chenin blanc, French colombard, Grenache, Malaga, Malbec, Merlot, Mission, Muscat, Nebbiolo, Palomino, Perlette, Petite sirah, Rosa del Perú, Ruby cabernet, Sauvignon blanc, Trebbiano, Valdepeñas, Zinfandel

PEDRO DOMECQ WINERY

This firm produces a variety of red, white, and rosé wines at its modern winery where temperature-controlled, stainless-steel fermentation vats are used.

BAJA CALIFORNIA, MEXICO
*Petite sirah vines basking in the hot, midday Mexican sunshine,
with the foothills of the Sierra San Pedro Mártir in the background.*

since the North American Free Trade Agreement (NAFTA), their income has been diverted by the increasing flow of cheaper wines from north of the border. This may, however, be the silver lining because Mexico's wineries cannot compete in price with American jug wines, and will have to focus on quality to survive. This will lead to a whittling down of its vineyards, so that in a decade's time, with only the best areas cultivated with site-specific clones, the full potential of Mexico might finally be recognized.

HOW TO READ MEXICAN WINE LABELS

Many terms found on Mexican wine labels are the same as, or similar to, those seen on Spanish labels (*see* How to read Spanish wine labels, p.348). Some common terms are listed below:

Vino tinto	Red wine	*Viña*	Vineyard
Vino blanco	White wine	*Espumoso*	Sparkling
Variedad	Grape variety	*Seco, Extra Seco*	Dry, Extra Dry
Contenido neto	Contents	*Vino de Mesa*	Table wine
Cosechas Seleccionadas	Special blend	*Bodega*	Winery
		Hecho en Mexico	Made in Mexico

THE WINE PRODUCERS OF
MEXICO

BODEGAS DE SANTO TOMAS
Ensenada

This winery was founded next to the ruins of the Santo Tomás Mission by an Italian goldminer, who sold it to General Rodriguez in 1920. Rodriguez went on to become President of Mexico and the winery passed into the ownership of Esteban Ferro. He later sold it to Santo Thomas, who in turn sold it to Pedro Domecq. The winery now belongs to an importer in Mexico City, Elias Pando.

✓ *Cabernet Sauvignon*

CASA MADERO
Monterey
The second-oldest winery on the American continent, comprising 400 hectares (1,000 acres) of vineyards,

selling wines under the San Lorenzo and Varietales Madero labels. Flying winemaker John Worontschak has produced clean, easy-drinking wine here for Marks & Spencer, and hopefully Casa Madero has benefited from the experience.

✓ *Cabernet Sauvignon/Merlot*
• *San Lorenzo* (Red Table Wine)

CAVAS DE SAN JUAN
Cuauhtémoc
☆
The mile-high Cavas de San Juan owns some 250 hectares (625 acres) of vineyards, selling wines under the Hidalgo label.

L. A. CETTO
Tijuana
☆
I visited this winery's facility in Mexico City when most of its products were still branded as Domecq and the Cetto wines were unknown internationally. Even back then the quality here seemed more promising than at other producers. The wines come from the Baja, California's relatively cool Santo Tomas valley. Cetto's rich Petite Sirah is the most consistent wine, although not as good as some critics made out in the mid-1990s.

✓ *Cabernet Sauvignon* • *Nebbiolo*
• *Petite Sirah* • *Zinfandel*

CASA PEDRO DOMECQ
Mexico City
☆

This winery's top wine, Château Domecq, produced in Baja California, is still one of Mexico's best Cabernet Sauvignons.

✓ *Château Domecq*

CAVAS DE ALTIPLANO
Zacatecas
With vines growing at an altitude of 2,000 metres (7,000 feet), this winery operates in the highest wine region in Mexico.

MARQUÉS DE AGUAYO
Parras
Established in 1593, Marqués de Aguayo is the oldest winery in the entire American continent. However, it is now engaged solely in the production of brandy.

MONTE XANIC
Ensenada
★☆
Pronounced Sha-nic, Xanic is Cora Indian for "the first bloom after the rain" and it certainly is blossoming well as the finest winery in Mexico.

✓ *Cabernet Sauvignon*
• *Cabernet-Merlot* • *Chardonnay*

PRODUCTOS DE UVA
Tlanepantla
❷
I have, unfortunately, not tasted wine from here for quite a while, but I have enjoyed this winery's Riesling in Mexico itself, when it was the palest, freshest white wine in the country.

✓ *Riesling*

SALA VIVA
San Juan del Rio
★
Freixenet's sparkling-wine operation was making a fine, light, fresh sparkling wine that was better than some authentic Spanish Cava as early as 1988.

✓ *Brut*

Of the other Mexican wineries, those capable of producing interesting wines include: **Bodegas San Antonio**, **Cavas de Valmar**, **Casa Martell**, and **Vergel**.

✦SOUTH AMERICA✦

The Spanish introduced viticulture to the Americas: first to Mexico in 1521, and then further afield as the conquistadors opened up other areas of South America. Among its many wine regions, Chile stands out for quality, Argentina for quantity, while Brazil and Uruguay show some promise.

SOUTH AMERICA'S WINE INDUSTRIES are inextricably linked to Spain's expansionist policies of the 16th century, although the conquistadors were not primarily concerned with the spread of viticulture. They were in South America to plunder gold for Ferdinand of Spain, and when the Indians grew bored of the coloured glass beads traded for their treasures, the conquistadors took what they wanted by more direct and brutal methods. In response, the Indians poured molten gold down the throats of captured soldiers, which no doubt quenched the Spanish thirst for the precious metal, but also served as a sardonic retort to the Christian missionaries who had forced them to drink wine as part of the Sacrament. In more recent times it has been the traditional beer-drinking culture of the local populations that has held back the development of South American wines as a whole. This phenomenon has even affected the two major wine-producing countries here, Chile and Argentina. Brazil could be leading the way, however, as the switch from beer to wine among the younger generation makes this one of the few countries in the world where wine consumption is actually growing.

HARVEST IN THE RIO GRANDE, BRAZIL
Brazil's largest wine-producing region is Rio Grande do Sul. It borders the Atlantic and stretches down to Uruguay in the south.

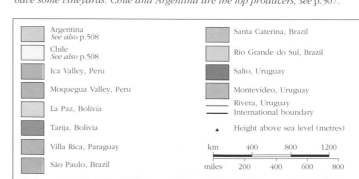

SOUTH AMERICA
Climatic conditions and inhospitable terrain preclude much of South America from producing wine, but such is the size of this continent that most countries have some vineyards. Chile and Argentina are the top producers, see p.507.

Argentina *See also p.508*	Santa Caterina, Brazil
Chile *See also p.508*	Rio Grande do Sul, Brazil
Ica Valley, Peru	Salto, Uruguay
Moquegua Valley, Peru	Montevideo, Uruguay
La Paz, Bolivia	—— Rivera, Uruguay
Tarija, Bolivia	—— International boundary
Villa Rica, Paraguay	▲ Height above sea level (metres)
São Paulo, Brazil	

km 400   800   1200
miles 200   400   600   800

VINEYARDS OF SAN PEDRO AT MOLINA, CHILE
*Part of the largest single vineyard in Chile, at Molina in the Curicó district,
200 kilometres (124 miles) south of Santiago, with the Andes in the distance.*

SOUTH AMERICAN COUNTRIES: AREA UNDER VINE AND YIELD

COUNTRY	HECTARES	(ACRES)	HECTOLITRES	(CASES)	YIELD
ARGENTINA	207,000	(511,497)	18,200,000	(202,000,000)	88 hl/ha
CHILE	114,000	(281,694)	3,600,000	(40,000,000)	32 hl/ha
BRAZIL	60,000	(148,260)	3,000,000	(33,000,000)	50 hl/ha
URUGUAY	11,000	(27,181)	710,000	(7,900,000)	65 hl/ha
PERU	10,000	(24,710)	80,000	(900,000)	8 hl/ha*
BOLIVIA	4,000	(9,884)	20,000	(220,000)	5 hl/ha*
COLOMBIA	1,500	(3,706)		N/A	N/A
VENEZUELA	1,000	(2,470)		N/A	N/A
ECUADOR	250	(618)		N/A	N/A
PARAGUAY	negligible			N/A	N/A

* These anomalies are because nearly all the wine is distilled into aromatic
grape-brandy. Discounting this production, yields can be as high as 160 hl/ha.

THE LAW THAT NEVER WAS

In 1993 I asked Yves Bénard, then the head of Moët & Chandon in Champagne, how the *champenois* could justify court actions to prevent the use of the name Champagne or Champaña on any sparkling wine produced outside the officially delimited Champagne region, when Moët had been selling South American sparkling wine as Champaña for more than 30 years.

Bénard told me that they had been trying to get the name Champaña banned, but were required by local laws to use the term, and this raised the question of why any Champagne house would set up business in countries that undermined their own appellation. What prompted my original question was that I had been told no such law existed by Trevor Bell, who was managing director of Piper-Heidsieck. I put it to Bénard that as Piper produced Argentinian sparkling wine, Bell should know what he was talking about, and they could not both be right.

Bénard maintained "It is the law. I know, because every time the CIVC (Comité Interprofessionnel du Vin de Champagne) takes a case to court, this very question is always raised by the other side and I am called to give evidence in defence of my company's actions."

I asked Bénard to supply the text of the law he was referring to. He offered a translation used as evidence in a Canadian court, but I insisted on a copy of the law itself in original Spanish for Argentina and Portuguese for Brazil, as they would have to be independently translated if there were to be no question about their interpretation.

This was duly promised, but did not turn up, and eventually I received a letter dated 25 June 1993 admitting that "The law in that country requires that sparkling wine should be specified as either champagne, champaña, vino espumoso or vino espumante. You should be aware that in Argentina to specify a wine as vino espumoso or vino espumante considerably depreciates the product in the mind of the consumer and nobody uses these terms." Yet this is precisely the argument used by producers of sparkling wines throughout the world, and the *champenois* take them to court to contest it.

No copy of the Brazil law turned up either, and Moët assured me "production is tiny, less than 200,000 cases, it is not really a problem". Yet when the *champenois* took Thorncroft to court over less than 3,000 cases of non-alcoholic Elderflower Champagne, they claimed it was "the thin-end of the wedge!".

The idea that sparkling wines in Argentina and Brazil must be labelled Champagne or Champaña by law has now been shattered. It is clear that the *champenois* involved were not legally obliged to use the term "Champaña" and the pity is that the court cases won by the *champenois* can now be challenged and, presumably, reversed.

THE MINOR WINE-PRODUCING COUNTRIES OF
SOUTH AMERICA

BOLIVIA

It is believed that vines were first cultivated in this country in the 1560s. Vineyards are found today at altitudes of between 1,600 and 2,400 metres (5,300–8,000 feet) on high plateau country around La Paz in the north and Tarija in the south. The soil is alluvial, the climate tropical, with rot-inducing humidity as great a problem as phylloxera, yet ironically most vines have to be irrigated. Muscat is by far the most important variety, and over half the wine produced is distilled into local Pisco brandy.

BRAZIL

According to some sources, Brazilian viticulture began under the Portuguese in São Paulo *circa* 1532, but winemaking was insignificant until 1815, when the Portuguese prince regent gave Brazil equal status to Portugal, and declared

Rio de Janeiro to be the seat of government for the co-kingdoms. Brazil could not be seen to be dependent on imported wine and thus allowed its vineyards to flourish. Domestic wine became a necessity following independence in 1822.

By far the largest wine region is in the southernmost state of Rio Grande do Sul, bordering Uruguay. Within its Palomas district is Santana do Livramento, Brazil's newest and most promising wine area, where vineyards on the Campanha Gaúcha – the vast Gaucho plainlands – are planted with more than 20 *vinifera* varieties, while eight out of every ten vines in the rest of the country are of the species *labrusca*. Quality has been elusive in Brazil, where the promise has always been evident but has seldom translated into actual quality. That Brazil will attain an international standard is not in question, only the timing is.

COLOMBIA

The Spanish conquest of Colombia commenced in 1525 with the founding of Santa Marta by Rodrigo de Bastidas, and vines were probably growing by 1559, when the *audienca* or Spanish Court of Santa Fé de Bogotá was established as part of the viceroyalty of Peru. Due to this country's accessibility by sea, however, it relied on imported wines from Spain to a greater extent than other west coast colonies, thus viticulture never flourished here. The first truly commercial vineyards were not established until the 1920s, but the industry was limited in size until wines imported from any country outside South America were banned in 1984, when the production of domestic wine rose rapidly. Most vines are concentrated in three zones: Cauce Valley, Sierra Nevada de Santa Marta, and Ocaña, where every conceivable variety of table grape is grown. Although many wineries utilize table grapes for winemaking, the most widely planted vine is Isabella, a *labrusca* variety, with *vinifera* varieties such as Barbera, Cabernet sauvignon, Chardonnay, Müller-Thurgau, Muscat, Pinot noir, Pedro Ximénez, Riesling, and Sylvaner accounting for a very small proportion of the vines grown. Many wines are made solely or in part from other fruits, plus grapes, juice, and concentrate imported from other countries.

ECUADOR

Viticulture in Ecuador probably commenced after 1534, when Villa de San Francisco de Quito was founded by Sebastian de Belalcázar, and the Spanish established a colony of large estates in Ecuador. Historically, most vineyards have been planted in coastal areas to take advantage of maritime breezes, but the largest area under vine today is found high up in the mountainous provinces. Wine production is, however, minuscule compared to coffee, which is this country's most famous drink.

PARAGUAY

Vines have been cultivated under Paraguay's sub-tropical climate since sometime after 1537, when the first colonial settlement at Asunción was established. Despite its long-lived history, the wine produced in Paraguay today is less important to the country's economy than palm cabbages or concentrated beef broth.

PERU

One of South America's oldest winegrowing countries, Peru has had vineyards since at least 1563, when Francesco de Carabantes planted vines in the Ica Valley, but many sources believe that Francisco Pizarro, the famous conquistador who built Lima, might have planted vines in 1531. Today, Peruvian vineyards are still mostly located in the province of Ica, in a fertile oasis, which is surrounded by desert, where it is hot and semi-arid, necessitating irrigation. With cool nights, the diurnal difference means that crisp, vividly flavoured wines should be possible, however, the achievements have yet to match the potential. The vineyards are composed of deep alluvial soil over a stony and sandy subsoil and, unlike its neighbour Chile, Peru has a problem with phylloxera.

URUGUAY

Since commercial production began in the 1870s, wine output has soared. If the idea of Uruguayan wine is difficult for Europeans to swallow, it is not for the locals, who have little left over for export. The vineyards are located on rolling hills of volcanic origin spread across Montevideo, Canalones, San José, Florida, Soriano, Paysandú, and along the River Plate in Maldonado. Summers are warm, and rainfall adequate. The most widespread vine is the Harriague, which is the Tannat of southwestern France and acquired its name from Pascual Harriagues, one of Uruguay's 19th-century winegrowing pioneers.

VENEZUELA

Spanish Jesuits at Cumana, the oldest colonial settlement in South America are thought to have started viticulture here. Most vines grown today are hybrids, but a few *vinifera* remain.

THE WINE PRODUCERS OF
SOUTH AMERICA

BRAZIL

AURORA
Bento Goncalves
This cooperative has more than 1,000 members who between them account for more than one third of Brazil's vineyards, and supply 95 per cent of the country's total wine exports. Various labels include Conde Foucolde, Clos de Nobles, and the Canandaigua-owned Marcus James brand (which has phenomenal sales in the US). Flying winemaker John Worontschak has made various wines here for British supermarkets. This is one of Brazil's most successful wineries, but, like most others, there is more promise than actual quality.

CASA MOËT & CHANDON
Rio Grande do Sul
★
The famous Champagne firm produces still and sparkling wines, which can be good but are sold shamelessly on the Brazilian market as Champaña.

✓ *M. Chandon* (syn. Diamantina)

CASTEL PUJOLS
Santana do Livramento
This well-known Uruguayan producer also makes wines in Brazil.

DREHER
Sao Paulo
Formerly called Heublein do Brasil, Dreher sells wine under various labels including Bratage, Castel Chatelet, Castelet, Lejon, and Marjolet.

FORESTIER
Rio Grande do Sul
★
Owned by Seagram, this is a boutique winery, unlike Seagram's Palomas winery, and currently makes the best wines in Brazil.

✓ *Cabernet Sauvignon*

DE-LANTIER
Garibaldi
This large, modern winery is owned by Martini & Rossi, who produce some of Brazil's better wines. Top-of-the-range varietals are marketed under the Baron De-Lantier brand, while lower-priced wines are sold under the Château Duvalier label, and bottle-fermented sparkling wines are sold as De-Greville.

PALOMAS
Santana do Livramento
Established in 1974, this modern winery with its lavish 1,200-hectare (3,000-acre) vineyard of exclusively classic *vinifera* vines, remains Brazil's most ambitious wine venture. It was supposed to help set the country's wine industry on a quality footing, but even when its wines were the best in Brazil, they were bland, and now other wineries are producing much better wines. When Seagram took over Palomas in 1989, no one held their breath for the new broom to sweep clean, but the potential remains, and Seagram (who own Forestier, one of the country's leading wineries) has the means to exploit it.

VINICOLA RIOGRANDENSE
Caxias do Sul
These specialists in *vinifera* wines since the 1930s sell most of their wines under the Granja Uniao label.

COLOMBIA
Of the 112 wineries in Colombia, the following are the most important:

Bodegas Andaluzas, Vinicola Andiña, Bodegas Añejas, Vinerias del Castillo, Cinzano, Viños de la Corte, Divinos, Pedro Domecq Colombia, Grajales, Inverca, Martini & Rossi, David & Eduardo Puyana, Viña Ramariz, Rojas, Bodegas Sevillanas, and Bodegas Venecians.

PERU

TACAMA
Ica
This is the only significant producer in the country and, although the wine is exported, only the Malbec is acceptable by international standards. Other reds are short or bitter, the whites are fresh but uninteresting, and the sparkling wines unpleasantly explosive. Bordeaux professors Peynaud and Ribereau-Gayon have consulted here and flying winemaker John Worontschak has made some quaffing wines (Malbec and Chenin) for British supermarkets.

✓ *Malbec*

Other Peruvian wineries include Ocucaje and Vista Alegre.

URUGUAY

CASTILLO VIEJO
San José
The winery of Castillo Viejo makes fresh, crisp whites and sharp, fruity reds from a private estate, which is 100 kilometres (60 miles) northwest of Montevideo. Flying winemaker John Worontschak has made wines here under the Pacific Peak label for British supermarket store Tesco.

✓ *Chardonnay-Sauvignon*
• *Tannat-Merlot*

ESTABLECIMENTO JUANICO
Canelones
★
These private cellars are producing wines to an international standard, both through the Don Pascual brand and with the help of flying winemaker Peter Bright.

✓ *Chardonnay*
• *Chardonnay-Viognier*
• *Merlot* • *Merlot-Tannat*

IRURTIA
Cerro Carmelo
This is the largest vineyard-owner in the country, with 300 hectares (740 acres) of *vinifera* varieties.

✓ *Pinot Blanc* (Novello) • *Tannat*

H. STAGNARI
Canelones
Surprisingly good Gewürztraminer and a decent, tasty Merlot.

✓ *Gewürztraminer*

VINOS FINOS JUAN CARRAU
Cerro Chapeau
This winery owns vineyards at Cerro Chapeau in northeastern Rivera, opposite Brazil's Santana do Livramento winegrowing area, where the climate and soil are particularly well-suited to *vinifera* varieties. However, most of the wines produced here are merely drinkable. The Castel Pujol label might be worth watching.

✓ *Museo 1752*

VENEZUELA
Of the dozen or so wineries in Venezuela, Bodegas Pomar is that most likely to be of interest.

✦CHILE AND ARGENTINA✦

If Chile is the showcase of South America's wine-producing countries, Argentina is its bottomless vat, yet wineries such as Catena and Weinert have shown that Argentina can compete with Chile for quality, if its producers will only reduce yields.

CHILE

The only problem with Chile is that most of its vineyards are in the wrong place. In such a long country it was natural for the population to live in or near the capital of Santiago, and to plant their vineyards thereabouts, especially as the melting snows of the nearby Andes provided an inexhaustible supply of irrigation.

As Chile became South America's best wine region, there was little incentive to search out better viticultural areas in uninhabited, less accessible parts of the country. New areas, such as the Casablanca Valley, are merely the fringe of the country's best wine area, the Secano region, which is a strip of coastal hills. Here, the cool maritime breezes temper the midday sun and sufficient rainfall permits viticulture without irrigation – if, that is, producers are content with lower yields. Casablanca nudges into the northern end of this future wine area, the greatest potential of which extends as far south as Concepcion. Ironically, the only people with vines here are peasants who cannot afford irrigation (hence its name Secano, which means "unirrigated") and grow País for their own use, but a chain-saw and chip-budding could convert these vineyards overnight, while properly planted ones are laid and, most importantly, roads are built to connect these forgotten areas to the pan-American highway.

CABERNET SAUVIGNON, CHILE
This Cabernet Sauvignon vine is more than 100 years old, and grows on ungrafted roots in the Maipo Valley.

FACTORS AFFECTING TASTE AND QUALITY

🧭 LOCATION
In Chile, vines are grown along 1,300 km (800 miles) of Pacific coast, and are most concentrated south of Santiago. In Argentina, vines grow mainly in the provinces of Mendoza and St. Juan, east of the Andes foothills and west of Buenos Aires.

CLIMATE
Extremely variable conditions prevail in Chile, ranging from arid and extremely hot in the north to very wet in the south. The main wine area around Santiago is dry, with 38 cm (15 in) of rain per year, no spring frosts, and clear, sunny skies. The temperature drops substantially at night due to the proximity of the snow-covered peaks of the Andes, enabling the grapes' acidity levels to remain high. Relatively new areas, such as the Casablanca Valley, are proving far more suitable for winegrowing, particularly for white wines, but inevitably the coastal range of hills will be Chile's fine-wine future, since they receive enough rainfall to allow viticulture at modest yields without the need for irrigation. This is the area most affected by the ice-cold Humbolt Current, which supposedly brings a tempering arctic chill to all Chilean vineyards, but is effectively blocked from flowing elsewhere in Chile by the coastal hills.

In Argentina's intensively cultivated Mendoza district, the climate is officially described as continental-semi-desertic, and has even less rainfall than Chile, a mere 20–25 cm (8–10 in) per year, although this is mercifully spread over the summer growing months, and temperatures range from 10°C (50°F) at night to 40°C (104°F) during the day.

ASPECT
In both countries, most vines are grown on the flat coastal and valley plains extending into the foothills of the Andes. In Chile, the unirrigated hillside vineyards are found in the Central Zone, although irrigation is widely utilized in other parts of this country. In Argentina, by contrast, the hillside vineyards are usually levelled to a minimal slope in order to allow for more efficient use of water.

SOIL
Vines are grown on a vast variety of soils in these countries. The deeper limestone soils of some parts of Chile are one reason for the generally better quality of wines from this country, but its most famous attribute is a total absence of phylloxera. In Argentina, the soils range from sandy to clay, with a predominance of deep, loose soils of alluvial and aeolian origin.

VITICULTURE AND VINIFICATION
While Chile uses traditional methods for most of its wines and often uses Bordeaux techniques, Argentina relies more on bulk-production methods. But traditional methods are also harnessed in Argentina for its increasing production of higher-grade premium varietals. Since Chile's economic policy of 1974, modern equipment, stainless-steel vats, and improved technology have been introduced into many of its wineries. Thanks to Miguel Torres Jnr., many of Chile's quality-wine producers are using cold-fermentation and other techniques, and producing much fresher, fruitier white wines as a result.

🍇 GRAPE VARIETIES
Barbera, Bonarda, Cabernet franc, Cabernet sauvignon, Cereza, Chardonnay, Chenin blanc, Criolla, Ferral, Grenache, Grignolino, Johannisberg riesling, Lambrusco, Malbec, Malvasia, Merlot, Muscat, Nebbiolo, País, Palomino, Pedro Ximénez, Petit verdot, Pinot blanc, Pinot gris, Pinot noir, Refosco, Renano, Sangiovettoe, Sauvignon blanc, Sémillon, Sylvaner, Syrah, Tempranillo, Torrontes, Ugni blanc

---

From red wines to white

As Chile exported more wine during the 1980s, it became evident that, while it made some really good-value reds, its white wines left much to be desired. In the late 1970s, the quality of Chilean wines greatly improved with the introduction of temperature-controlled, stainless-steel vats. The early- to mid-1980s saw the removal from the winemaking process of *raule* wood, a native variety of beech, which left a taint in the wines that the Chileans had got used to but that international markets found unpleasant.

With the introduction of new oak *barriques*, mostly of French origin, the 1989 vintage saw a transformation in the quality of Chardonnay, and with this it was widely imagined that Chile had at long last cracked the secret to successful white-wine production, but it soon became evident that even the best producers could not improve their dismal Sauvignon Blanc. Why was this so?

Non-existent Sauvignon

When I confronted producers, most confessed that virtually all the wine sold as Chilean Sauvignon Blanc was, in fact, Sauvignonasse. Sauvignonasse literally means "Sauvignon-like", but this variety is not related to Sauvignon and has no Sauvignon character whatsoever. Whenever I tried to get acreage figures for Sauvignon, the Chileans would lump it together with Sauvignonasse and Sémillon, because they seemed to think it was difficult to distinguish these varieties. When I tried to get the three varieties broken down, the nearest to a firm figure I could squeeze out of any member of the Chilean wine trade was at least 12,500 hectares (31,000 acres) of Sauvignonasse, no more than 2,000 hectares (5,000 acres) of Sauvignon blanc, and between 2,500 and 4,000 hectares (6,000–10,000 acres) of Sémillon. Therefore, if these statistics were correct, there was on average less than 12 per cent Sauvignon blanc in virtually every supposed Chilean Sauvignon Blanc wine up until at least the early 1990s. I was later to discover that even these statistics were greatly exaggerated. Little wonder, then, that Chilean Sauvignon Blancs possessed little varietal character – they contained very little Sauvignon blanc!

Unhappy with the statistics I had been given, I returned to Chile with the express purpose of trying to locate and identify Sauvignon blanc in its vineyards. I got my first clue to the true state of affairs while visiting Miguel Torres' vineyard at Curicó. He cocked his head and with a little grin asked, "So, Tom, tell me how you identify Sauvignon blanc in the field?". I could see in his pocket exactly the same page from Pierre Galet's *Practical Ampelography* that I had been studying on the plane going over, so I launched into the distinct differences between the inferior and superior sinuses of the Sauvignon's leaf when compared to those of Sauvignonasse and Sémillon. He must have been utterly amazed by my technical expertise! Here was a world-famous viticulturist who had actually trained under Galet at Montpellier, and he found it necessary to carry around a copy of his former teacher's text book in the vineyard while I seemingly rattled it off verbatim.

Having agreed with the ampelographic points I had churned out, Miguel Torres then set about pointing these out on the vines in front of us – only they were not there. He did not, in fact, have a pure strain of Sauvignon blanc. We concluded that he had a mutated form of Sauvignon blanc that was probably crossed with Sémillon but this was impossible to determine for sure in a single vineyard inspection. On that trip I saw Sauvignonasse – lots of it – and what appeared to be mutations or crosses such as *Sémillon* x *Sauvignon*, *Sauvignonasse* x *Sauvignon*, and *Sauvignonasse* x *Sémillon*, but the only place I actually saw

CHILE AND ARGENTINA, see also p.504

South America's southernmost countries are its best wine producers. Both come under the climatic influence of the Andes mountains – one of the factors that has prevented the entry of phylloxera to Chile.

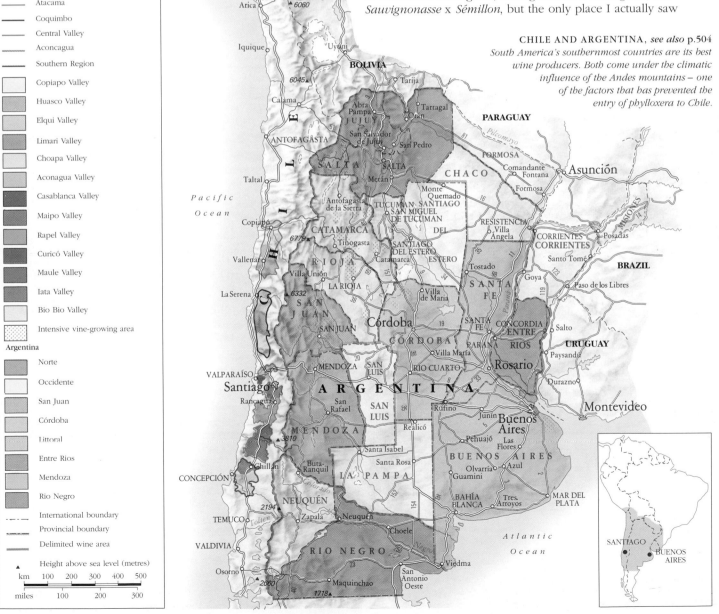

Chile

	Atacama
	Coquimbo
	Central Valley
	Aconcagua
	Southern Region
	Copiapo Valley
	Huasco Valley
	Elqui Valley
	Limari Valley
	Choapa Valley
	Aconagua Valley
	Casablanca Valley
	Maipo Valley
	Rapel Valley
	Curicó Valley
	Maule Valley
	Iata Valley
	Bio Bio Valley
	Intensive vine-growing area

Argentina

	Norte
	Occidente
	San Juan
	Córdoba
	Littoral
	Entre Rios
	Mendoza
	Rio Negro

- - - International boundary
Provincial boundary
Delimited wine area

▲ Height above sea level (metres)

km 100 200 300 400 500
miles 100 200 300

authentic Sauvignon blanc was at Viña Canepa, and this was about the only producer engaged in making wine that actually tasted of the variety at that particular time.

After I exposed Chile's non-existent Sauvignon blanc in an article called "Chile's Mutant Hero" (*Wine & Spirit International*, July 1991), a number of Chilean wineries commissioned French experts to go through their vineyards with a fine toothcomb. They came to the same conclusion that I had, since when great swathes of vines have been zapped and chip-budded over to true Sauvignon blanc. In the meantime, however, most wineries tried to make their Sauvignonasse more Sauvignon'ish by harvesting early, only they picked the grapes when too unripe (instead of staggering the crop as they do in New Zealand, for example), which resulted in wines that were terribly green and mean. Many such wines still exist, but as the chip-budded vineyards mature, so Chile has begun to produce much better Sauvignon Blanc wines.

ARGENTINA

This is the fifth-largest wine country in the world, and could be a major force in the premium-quality sector, if only its excessive yields could be curbed. While Chile has strengthened its position as South America's premier-quality wine-producing country by significantly reducing yields over the last ten years in order to concentrate on quality, Argentina has done the opposite. On the face of it, Argentina appears to have reduced production by some ten per cent over the same period, but the fact is it has ripped up a third of its vineyards, thus its yield has actually increased from 66 to 88 hectolitres per hectare (297 to 396 cases per hectare).

Scarce rainfall dictates that Argentina's vineyards must depend on irrigation, but it is so cheap and plentiful that growers simply have to turn the tap to increase the water supply in order to grow more grapes with which to make more wine, and this has killed the passion for quality among almost all the producers.

A few wineries, such as Catena and Weinert, have resolutely refused to go along this route, and have given us a glimpse of the quality that Argentina can produce. It is their example that the entire industry will have to follow if it wants to sell wines internationally, as the world is awash with *vin ordinaire*, and what really excites modern consumers is premium-quality wine at bargain (but not necessarily cheap) prices. Argentina is perfectly placed to supply this demand, when its producers wake up to the fact. If and when they do, the producers of Chile might have something to worry about. At the moment, however, Chile has nothing to fear from Argentina.

THE APPELLATIONS OF
CHILE AND ARGENTINA

CHILE

ACONCAGUA VITICULTURAL REGION

Wine districts *Aconagua Valley, Casablanca Valley*
The Aconagua Valley is known primarily for Errazuriz, the only major winery in the region, and grows mostly Cabernet sauvignon, Cabernet franc, and Merlot, with recent trials of Shiraz (note the Australian terminology). The cooler Casablanca Valley is the country's newest internationally recognized district, and has become famous for the freshness and fruitiness of its wines, particularly Chardonnay and Sauvignon Blanc, but Pinot noir and other black grape varieties are also showing exciting potential.

ATACAMA VITICULTURAL REGION

Wine districts *Copiapo Valley, Huasco Valley*
The coastal hills are mountainous and join the Andes, with no central valley. Rainfall is virtually non-existent and viticulture is possible only with irrigation. In certain years, when there is rain, plants and insects awaken and what is one of the most arid deserts in the world suddenly bursts into multi-coloured bloom. No quality wines are currently made from these vineyards, which produce mostly table grapes.

CENTRAL VALLEY VITICULTURAL REGION

Wine districts *Curicó Valley, Maipo Valley, Maule Valley, Rapel Valley*
Wine areas *Lontue Valley, Tenue Valley* (Curicó Valley); *Del Claro Valley, Locomilla Valley, Tutaven Valley* (Maule Valley); *Cachapoal Valley, Colchagua Valley* (Rapel Valley)
The oldest, most central, and most traditional wine region, the Central Valley Viticultural Region contains four wine districts encompassing seven wine areas. The Curicó Valley is situated 200 kilometres (120 miles) south of Santiago, and is home to such brand leaders as Caliterra,

Montes, Torres, and Valdivieso. Curicó is known principally for Chardonnay, but also produces fine Cabernet Sauvignon, Merlot, and Pinot Noir. The Maipo Valley around Santiago itself is still the country's most intensively cultivated district and therefore its most famous wine appellation. It is one of the warmest growing districts in the country and, although by no means the best, it is still capable of regularly producing very good wines, particularly reds. Furthest south of all is the Maule Valley, which contains three wine areas and is generally better suited to red wines than whites, but is really quite variable overall, and consequently vast amounts of the local País grapes are grown solely for local consumption.

COQUIMBO VITICULTURAL REGION

Wine districts *Elqui Valley, Limari Valley, Choapa Valley*
Like those in the Atacama Viticultural Region, the coastal hills in the Coquimbo Viticultural Region are a mountainous adjunct to the Andes, and viticulture is possible only with irrigation. The Elqui Valley is also known as the Magical Valley, because it lies at the southern end of the spectacular "flowering desert". The vines in all three valleys are found in discrete blocks, rather than in one contiguous section as is the case further south, and the wines, which are high in alcohol and low in acidity, are mostly used for local Pisco brandy. Viña Francisco de Aguire is the only exporting wine producer I am aware of (under the Palo Alto, Piedras Atlas, Tierra Arena, and Tierras Atlas labels).

SOUTHERN VITICULTURAL REGION

Wine districts *Iata Valley, Bio Bio Valley*
The País is the most commonly cultivated vine here and, apart from oddities such as a Gewürztraminer from Concha-y-Toro, this region is not known for the quality of its wines.

ARGENTINA

CATAMARCA

This has a very small area under vine, the grapes of which are mostly used for local brandy.

LA RIOJA

Unlike its original Spanish counterpart, this is a ferociously hot region producing wines high in alcohol, low in acidity, and, as often as not, oxidized in the bottle.

MENDOZA

This is the largest viticultural region in Argentina and accounts for more than two-thirds of its total wine production. There are more than 30,000 individual growers in this predominantly red-wine region, where Malbec is the most important variety, Cabernet sauvignon the best; others include Tempranillo, Pinot noir, and Syrah. White grapes include Chardonnay, Chenin blanc, Johannisberg riesling, and Muscat.

RIO NEGRO

This region is the most suitable for grape-growing, yet possesses less than five per cent of Argentina's vineyards. Now that this country has a more stable political climate, the Rio Negro could well attract much-needed foreign expertise, whether European, Antipodean, or Californian, and prove to be the hub of Argentina's future fine-wine production.

SALTA

This region covers less than half of one per cent of all the vines in the country. The quality is, however, reasonable in Argentinian terms, and, with an injection of foreign expertise, could prove to be a surprise fine-wine area.

SAN JUAN

Much of this dry, hot region's high-alcohol, low-acidity grapes are exported as grape concentrate.

THE WINE PRODUCERS OF
CHILE AND ARGENTINA

CHILE

AGRICOLA DOÑA JAVIERA
El Monte

This small producer makes clean, fresh, easy-drinking wines from the coastal end of the Maipo Valley. The wines were recently launched under the Arlequin label, and the Merlot is the best wine so far. Emilio de Solminihac of Santa Monica and Domaine Paul Bruno consults.

DOMAINE PAUL BRUNO
Quebrada de Macul

After a disappointing start, this expensively-priced Cabernet wine from a recently planted vineyard in the Maipo Valley has just started to produce the sort of quality its founders, Bruno Prats of Château Cos d'Estournel, Paul Pontallier of Château Margaux, and Emilio de Solminihac of Santa Monica, had originally envisaged.

CALITERRA
Curicó
★

This was originally a joint venture between Errazuriz and Franciscan Vineyards of California, but when the latter dropped out, the wines became inconsistent (the Sauvignon Blanc was particularly dire) and Caliterra almost assumed the mantle of an Errazuriz second label. Robert Mondavi has now become an equal partner and plans are afoot to establish Caliterra as a Chilean equivalent of Mondavi's "Opus One".

✓ *Cabernet Sauvignon* (Reserve)
• *Chardonnay*

CANEPA
Santiago
★✫ **V**

This is a high-tech winery producing elegant wines with a perfectly clean line, great clarity of fruit, and excellent finesse. Terrific value wines also sold under Montenuevo, Petroa, and Rowan Brook labels.

✓ *Cabernet Sauvignon* (especially Magnificum) • *Chardonnay* (Rancagua) • *Merlot*
• *Sauvignon Blanc* • *Zinfandel*

CARMEN
Alto Jahuel
★✫

Established in 1850, this is the oldest brand in Chile. Now part of the same group as Santa Rita, Carmen has a spanking new winery overseen by Alvaro Espinoza, one of Chile's best winemakers.

✓ *Cabernet Sauvignon*
• *Grand Vidure* • *Merlot* (especially Reserve) • *Petite Sirah* • *Sémillon* (Oak Aged)

CARTA VIEJA
Villa Allegre
V

This small, family winery is run by the Del Pedregal family, who have owned these vineyards since 1825, and are becoming ever more capable of producing good-value wines.

✓ *Cabernet Sauvignon*
(Antigua Selection)

CASA LAPOSTOLLE
Las Condes
★★

This is a Franco-Chilean venture between the Marnier-Lapostolle family of Grand Marnier renown (they also own Château de Sancerre) and the Rabats, an old Chilean family whose connections in the wine trade extend back to the 1920s, with Michel Rolland of Château Le Bon Pasteur acting as consulting winemaker.

✓ *Merlot* (especially Selection, Cuvée Alexandre)
• *Sauvignon Blanc*

CHÂTEAU LOS BOLDOS
Requinoa
★✫ **V**

This long-established vineyard has been revitalized by its owners, the Massenez family of Alsace (*Eaux-de-Vie* distillers), who make very good-value wines of richness, finesse, and complexity.

✓ *Cabernet Sauvignon*
• *Chardonnay* • *Merlot*

CONCHA Y TORO
Santiago
★★

Now one of the very best producers in the country, this firm's seriously talented winemaker, Pablo Morandé, was the first to realize the potential of Casablanca. There are some stunningly rich wines, ranging from vibrantly fruity to the complex and age-worthy. Look out particularly for Syrah. Excellent-value wines are produced through Concha y Toro's Santa Emiliana winery under the Andes Peak, Palmeras Estate, and Walnut Crest labels. Concha y Toro is one of the partners in Villard and also owns Cono Sur.

✓ *Cabernet Sauvignon* (especially Don Melchor, Marques de Casa Concha, Palmeras Estate)
• *Chardonnay* (especially Amelia, Casillero del Diablo, Cordillera Estate) • *Merlot* (especially Casillero del Diablo, Marques de Casa Concha, Trio)
• *Sauvignon Blanc* (Casablanca)

CONO SUR
Chimbarongo
★✫ **V**

These wines are produced by Viña Tocornal, which is owned by Concha y Toro, and was put on the map by Californian Ed Flaharty, who made his name with the stunning El Liso Tempranillo in Spain's La Mancha of all places. Flaharty has since moved on to Errazuriz. Under his guidance, Cono Sur gradually achieved great quality and, through its Isla Negra label, has released some really excellent-value wines. Under the Tocornal name for supermarket own-labels, this winery has produced cheap but smooth and fruity reds with silky-oak. Cono Sur remains top quality.

✓ *Cabernet Sauvignon*
• *Chardonnay* (Reserve)
• *Isla Negra* (Chardonnay, Red)
• *Pinot Noir* (Barrel Select, Casablanca Valley)

COOPERATIVA AGRICOLA VITIVINICOLA DE CURICÓ
Curicó
★ **V**

This cooperative has been going since 1939, but has recently shown great improvement under the consultancy of flying winemaker Peter Bright, through wines sold under the Viños Los Robles label.

✓ *Chardonnay*
• *Sauvignon-Sémillon*

COOPERATIVA AGRICOLA VITIVINICOLA DE TALCA
Talca

This winery is capable of producing cheap, tasty whites.

COUSIÑO MACUL
Santiago
✫

Chile's one-time best winery has been overtaken by other producers who have not had the luxury of Cousiño Macul's established export business and, hungry to break in, have been receptive to constructive criticism from international markets, and have willingly tailored their wines to suit. Cousiño Macul has not dropped its standards, but seems old-fashioned compared to what we now expect from Chile.

✓ *Cabernet Sauvignon*
(Antigua Reserva)
• *Merlot* (Limited Release)

DOMAINE ORIENTAL
Talca

It was at this 150-year-old property that Rodolfo Donoso planted the first French vines to be cultivated in the Maule Valley. The vineyards remained in the Donoso family, who supplied other wineries, until 1989 when it was purchased by a group of French Polynesian wine enthusiasts, who built a state-of-the-art winery and have only recently begun to sell the wine.

ECHEVERRIA
Molina
✫

This small, family-owned venture has long supplied other wineries with its grapes, but in 1992 began producing wines under its own label, since when it has become one of Chile's fastest-rising stars.

✓ *Cabernet Sauvignon* (Family Reserva) • *Chardonnay* (especially Reserva)
• *Sauvignon Blanc*

ERRAZURIZ
Santiago
★★ **V**

Formerly called Errazuriz-Panquehue, this old winery in the Maule Valley has steadily improved under New Zealander Brian Bicknell (now back home), and it should continue to develop under Ed Flaharty, the gifted Californian who established Cono Sur's reputation. Errazuriz and Robert Mondavi jointly own Caliterra.

✓ *Chardonnay* • *Merlot*
• *Cabernet Sauvignon*

LA FORTUUNA
Lontue
★

The Güell family have owned this winery for more than 50 years, but it has been seriously involved in export markets since only the mid-1990s. Winemaker Claudio Barrio has made some appallingly green Sauvignon Blanc (particularly in 1996), but consistently produces lovely, soft, violety-cherry Malbec.

✓ *Malbec* (Lontue Valley)

LA PALMA
Cachapoal
★✫ **V**

This is the brand name used by Viña la Rosa, a 500-hectare (1,200-acre) vineyard. With a new six-million-dollar winery and Ignacio Recabarren as consultant, success is guaranteed.

✓ *Cabernet Sauvignon*
• *Chardonnay* • *Merlot*

LAS CASAS DEL TOQUI
Rancagua
✫

This is a joint venture between Château Larose-Trintaudon of Bordeaux and the Granella family.

✓ *Cabernet Sauvignon*
(Prestige Reserve)
• *Chardonnay* (Grande Reserve)

LUIS FELIPE
Colchagua
★★ **V**

These mature vineyards produce stunning-value Cabernet Sauvignon and deliciously ripe, tropical fruit-flavoured Chardonnay.

✓ *Cabernet Sauvignon* (especially Reserva) • *Chardonnay*

MONTES
Curicó
★

The brainchild of Aurelio Montes, these wines started out as far too oaky for all but lovers of four-by-two. Their production has now moved from a heavy-handed use of primarily American oak to a more restrained application of French oak. Montes also makes some deliciously fruity unoaked wines.

✓ *Cabernet Sauvignon*
• *Malbec* • *Merlot*

MONTGRAS
Colchagua
★★

An up-and-coming new winery with 250 hectares (600 acres) of vineyards, MontGras is a name to watch.

✓ *Cabernet Sauvignon* (Reserva)
• *Merlot* (Reserva)

PETROA
See Canepa

PORTAL DEL ALTO
Requinoa
★

Owned since 1970 by professor of oenology Alejandero Hernández, this winery produces refined red wines.

✓ *Cabernet Sauvignon*
• *Chardonnay* • *Merlot*

SAN PEDRO
Molina
★ⓥ

The wines of San Pedro, one of the pioneers that earned respect for Chilean wines on export markets, went through a patchy period, but are emerging better than before, thanks to an expensive ultra-modern winery and consultancy from flying winemaker Jacques Lurton. Wines are also sold under the penny-saving Gato Blanco and Gato Negro brands. Santa Helena is an export brand.

✓ *Chardonnay*
(Castillo de Molina Reserva)

SANTA CAROLINA
Santiago
★ⓥ

Fresh, crisp, fruity whites are the best value here. In particular, the cheap Sauvignon-dominated blended white is often better than the Sauvignon Blanc itself. The reds, however, are definitely the best quality here. Santa Carolina owns Viña Casablanca.

✓ *Merlot*
• *Sauvignon Blanc* (Reserve)

SANTA INÉS
Isla de Maipo
This small, quality-minded winery is owned by the De Martino family.

✓ *Carmenère*

SANTA MONICA
Rancagua
Owner-winemaker Emilio de Solminihac (a partner in Domaine Paul Bruno) makes wines with a fat, fruity style at his own winery.

✓ *Sauvignon Blanc*

SANTA RITA
Santiago
★

These wines are fatter and riper than they have been in years, but the "120" range (so-called because Bernardo O'Higgins, the liberator of Chile, and his 120 men hid in these cellars after the battle of Rancagua in 1810) has remained reliable throughout. Santa Rita also owns the Carmen winery, and has a partnership with Lafite-Rothschild in Los Vascos.

✓ *Cabernet Sauvignon* ("120", Casa Real) • *Sauvignon Blanc* (Casa Real) • *Merlot* (Medalla Real, Casablanca, Reserve)

SERGIO TAVERSO
Colchagua
★

Chilean-born Taverso is better known in the US than in his homeland, since he has been a winemaker and winery owner in California for 30 years, but he is quickly establishing a reputation on export markets for these increasingly classy wines, which are also sold under the La Parra label.

✓ *Cabernet Sauvignon*
• *Chardonnay* • *Merlot*

TARAPACA
Santiago
❓

This small winery produced entirely estate-bottled wines until very recently, when it was purchased by the Fosforos Holding Company, who have invested an amazing 30 million dollars in the venture. The first 440 hectares (1,100 acres) of newly planted vineyards came onstream between 1995 and 1997, and while they mature this should be a wine to watch.

TERRA ANDINA
Camino
Produced by Pernod Ricard in partnership with Viña José, Terra Andina is a project with the contradictory aim of producing *terroir* wines blended from different regions of Chile, yet promises to be a successful enterprise.

TERRA NOBLE
Talca
★

With Henri Marionnet, one of Touraine's best winemakers, consulting, Terra Noble has fashioned fine Merlot and Sauvignon Blanc.

✓ *Merlot* • *Sauvignon Blanc*

TORREON DE PAREDES
Rengo
★

This large, efficient, family-owned estate is situated in the Chachapoal Valley (which lies in the Rapel Valley), 100 kilometres (60 miles) south of Santiago. It uses modern stainless-steel vats and exclusively French oak.

✓ *Cabernet Sauvignon* • *Merlot*

MIGUEL TORRES
Curicó
★ⓥ

Although Spain's most innovative winemaker transformed perception of the potential of white wine in this country as long ago as the early 1980s, others failed to follow. His red wines are often misunderstood, particularly in Chile itself, where their slow-evolving style is swamped by the immediacy of more flashy, upfront winemaking methods. The only (relative) disappointment in the entire range has been the Torres Brut Nature, which seemed to show great promise as an experimental 100 per cent Pinot Noir fizz.

✓ *Cabernet Sauvignon* (Bella Terra, Santa Digna) • *Chardonnay* (Cordillera) • *Riesling-Gewürztraminer* (Don Miguel)

UNDURRAGA
Santiago
❓

This was the first Chilean winery to export to the US, but I have seldom found any exciting wines from Undurraga, the attitude of which has been similar to that of Cousiño Macul. Having embarked upon a 1.5-million-dollar renovation and replanting programme, Undurraga may bring about welcome changes.

VALDIVIESO
Santiago
★★ⓥ

Originally called Champagne Alberto Valdivieso, this company still produces large quantities of ordinary Chilean fizz, but has moved into pure varietal, barrel-fermented table wines in a spectacularly successful fashion. Loco is Valivieso's top-of-the-range red, a blend of different grape varieties from various vintages. To distinguish which batch is which (and to enable wine enthusiasts to cellar and follow the wines), they are numbered. I have tasted only Caballo Loco Number One, but it is such a masterly wine that I have no hesitation ranking it as one of South America's finest wines. Cheaper wines are sold under the Casa label.

✓ *Caballo Loco* • *Cabernet Franc*
• *Merlot* • *Pinot Noir*

VILLARD
Casablanca
★

This is a partnership between Thierry Villard (who in 1989 produced what was probably the first truly fine Chilean Chardonnay – Santa Emiliana – which is owned by Concha y Toro) and two growers, one of whom, Pablo Morandé, is Concha y Toro's winemaker.

✓ *Cabernet Sauvignon* • *Merlot*

VIÑA BALDUZZI
San Javier
★ⓥ

Produces fresh, elegant wines with creamy fruit. The Balduzzi family is of *Piemontese* extraction, and

arrived in Chile at the turn of the century, but began exporting wines as recently as 1987.

✓ *Cabernet Sauvignon*
• *Chardonnay*

VIÑA BISQUERTT
Lihueimo
ⓥ

A family-owned venture with large, well-established vineyards in the Colchagua Valley, Viña Bisquertt began bottling its own wines in the early 1990s, and is a rapidly improving producer of soft, easy-drinking, value-for-money wines.

✓ *Cabernet Sauvignon* (Reserve)
• *Sauvignon Blanc*

VIÑA CASABLANCA
Casablanca
★★ⓥ

Owned by Santa Carolina, Viña Casablanca is run by one of Chile's highest-profile winemakers, Ignacio Recabarren, who collaborates in the Penedés region of Spain to produce the Jaume Serra Cava, consults for Viña La Rosa in the Rapel Valley, and is shortly due to release his own premium-quality wine. Viña Casablanca was the first truly gooseberryish Sauvignon Blanc from Chile. In 1996, Recabarren even managed to produce a very good Gewürztraminer with some real spice.

✓ *Cabernet Sauvignon*
• *Chardonnay* • *Gewürztraminer* (Santa Isabella) • *Sauvignon Blanc* (Santa Isabel)

VIÑA FRANCISCO DE AGUIRE
Limari
❓

This ultra-modern venture is the most northerly of Chile's exporting wineries, producing premium varietals just south of the Atacama desert on steep, mineral-rich, drip-irrigated terraces of the Andes foothills. Wines are sold under the Palo Alto, Piedras Atlas, Tierra Arena, and Tierras Atlas labels.

VIÑA GRACIA
Totihue
❓

This is a new winery with 360 hectares (890 acres) of vineyards ranging from the Aconcagua Valley north of Santiago to the Bio Bio Valley in the south. It is too early to make judgement on these wines.

VIÑA LOS VASCOS
Santiago
❓

Originally owned by the Ezyguirre family, Spanish Basques, who purchased this property in 1755 and were part of the Junta who seized power in Chile in 1810, Los Vascos was planted with the native País grape until 1850, when the vineyards were replanted with vines from Bordeaux and Burgundy. It is situated within the Limari Valley, an unproven wine area. In 1988, the Ezyguirre family went into partnership with Lafite-Rothschild:

much was expected, but the results were – relatively – disappointing. In 1996, Santa Rita bought out the Ezyguirre family and, ironically, hopes are now high that this proven Chilean producer can kick-start Lafite into achieving a higher quality.

VIÑA SEGU OLLÉ
Linares

This family-owned winery has 200 hectares (500 acres) in the Maule Valley. The wines are sold under the Caliboro, Doña Consuelo, and La Sierra labels.

VIÑA PORTA
Chachapoal
Ⓥ

These good-value wines are sold under the Casa Porta label.

ARGENTINA

LA AGRICOLA SA
Chuquisaca
★Ⓥ

Australian David Morrison and Californian Ed Flaharty have raised standards here.

✓ *Mission Peak* (Argentinian Red, Argentinian White)
 • *Santa Juliana* (Torrontes)

BIANCHI
Mendoza

This Seagram-owned brand is very popular with the locals.

BODEGAS LOPEZ
Buenos Aires
★

This family firm produces average-quality wines under the Château Montchenot label (known as Don Federico on some export markets).

BODEGAS LA RURAL
Buenos Aires
★

These wines were once heavy and oxidized, but new owners Catena have greatly improved things.

✓ *Chardonnay* • *Malbec* • *Merlot*

BODEGAS LURTON
Buenos Aires
★

The Lurtons of Bordeaux originally came to Chile as flying winemakers for the British supermarket chain Tesco, but liked the potential so much that, together with the omnipresent Nicolas Catena, they purchased their own winery and are now firmly ensconced.

✓ *Tempranillo-Malbec*

BODEGAS NACARI
La Rioja
This small cooperative specializes in Torrontes.

CATENA
Cordoba
★★

Argentina's greatest wine visionary, Nicolas Catena, has produced some

superb wines with the aid of his Californian winemaker Paul Hobbs, who helped to establish the Opus One winery before going to Argentina. Catena is in the premium-priced category, very much upmarket by local standards, while Alta Catena is fine wine by any standard. Superb-value fine wines are also sold under the Alamos Ridge, Bodegas Esmerelda, and Libertad labels. Catena also owns Bodegas La Rural.

✓ *Alta Catena* • *Cabernet Sauvignon* (Agrelo Vineyard)
 • *Chardonnay* (Agrelo Vineyard)
 • *Malbec* (Agrelo Vineyard)

ETCHART
Buenos Aires
★Ⓥ

The very fresh, crisp, and dry Cafayate Torrontes, with its subtle, muscat-like aromas, is a yardstick for this peculiarly Argentinian variety, but Cabernet Sauvignon is by far the best wine here. Etchart is now fully owned by Pernod Ricard.

✓ *Cabernet Sauvignon*
 • *Chardonnay* (Cafayate)
 • *Malbec* • *Torrontes* (Cafayate)

FINCA FLICHMAN
Mendoza
★

After considerable investment in stainless-steel vats and new French oak *barriques*, plus a certain amount of European technical assistance, the quality as well as quantity has increased. Furthermore, emphasis has moved to Latin grape varieties such Barbera, Sangiovese, and Tempranillo, as the choice for blending with local favourites such as Malbec, Cabernet, and Merlot.

✓ *Cabernet Sauvignon* (Caballero de la Cepa)
 • *Sangiovese-Malbec* • *Syrah*

GOYENECHEA
San Rafael

These wines taste old-fashioned, but Goyenechea is always mentioned for its curiously named Aberdeen Angus blend of Cabernet and Syrah.

HUMBERTO CANALE
Rio Negro
★

These are interesting, improving varietal wines from some of the most southerly vineyards in the world.

✓ *Malbec* • *Pinot Noir*

JOSÉ ORFILA
St Martin

Orfila's best wines are sold under its Cautivo label. With beautiful, if unintentional, irony, José Orfila also makes sparkling wines in France, which it exports to Argentina, where they are sold as Champaña!

✓ *Cabernet*

LUIGI BOSCA
Buenos Aires
★

Well above average varietal wines produced by Leoncio Arizu.

✓ *Cabernet Sauvignon*
 • *Chardonnay* • *Malbec* • *Syrah*

NAVARRO CORREAS
Buenos Aires
★

At one time this group of three wineries had a joint venture with Deutz to produce Champaña, but this ceased prior to Roederer taking control of its fellow *grande marque*.

✓ *Malbec* • *Syrah*

NORTON
Buenos Aires
★

Although this firm dates back to 1895, it was not until 1989, when Austrian businessman Gernot Langes-Swarovski purchased the winery from its uninspiring English owners, that these wines started to show their true potential. Sangiovese and Barbera are the most interesting but, regrettably, the most variable as well.

✓ *Cabernet-Merlot* • *Merlot*

PEÑAFLOR
Buenos Aires
★Ⓥ

The quality here has been greatly improved in recent years by a magnum of flying winemakers, in the form of Peter Bright and John Worontschak. The Country Red is a cheap and cheerful blend. Peñaflor also sells wines under the Andean Vineyards, Fond de Cave, Parral, Tio Quinto, and Trapiche labels. *See also* Trapiche.

✓ *Cabernet-Malbec*
 • *Chenin-Chardonnay*
 • *Torrontes* • *Tempranillo*

PIPER
Buenos Aires
When Englishman Trevor Bell was managing Charles Heidsieck and Piper-Heidsieck in France, he blew the whistle on those Champagne houses – including his own – who claimed they were forced by Argentinian law to use the word "Champaña" on their Argentinian sparkling wines. He considered it hypocritical and said that Piper for one would stop the practice.

PROVIAR
Buenos Aires
This long-established arm of Moët & Chandon makes mostly sparkling wines, which are sold shamelessly as Champaña, under the M. Chandon and Baron B. labels. More interesting is the increasing amount of good and improving still wine now being made with an eye on export markets. Other labels include Castel Chandon, Clos du Moulin, Comte de Valmont, Kleinburg, and Renaud Poirier.

✓ *Castel Chandon* (red blend)
 • *Chardonnay* (Renaud Poirier)

SAN TELMO
Maipú
★

This ambitious California-style winery has 230 hectares (570 acres) of vineyards, from which it

consistently produces well-flavoured, fruity wines of very good quality.

✓ *Cabernet Sauvignon*
 • *Chardonnay* • *Chenin Blanc*
 • *Malbec* • *Merlot*

SANTA ANA
Guaymallen
★Ⓥ

Santa Carolina, the Chilean winery, purchased a controlling interest in Santa Ana in 1996. Wines are also sold under the Casa de Campo brand, but much of the emphasis here is placed on supplying own-label wines. Sparkling wines are sold under the Villeneuve label.

✓ *Merlot-Malbec* • *Syrah*

SUTER
San Rafael

This is a Swiss-owned, Seagram-distributed brand of standard quality.

PASCUAL TOSO
San José
★Ⓥ

This long-established winery consistently makes Cabernet of well above average quality.

✓ *Cabernet Sauvignon*

TRAPICHE
Buenos Aires
★Ⓥ

Part of Peñaflor, Trapiche has built a reputation on making a wide variety of fresh-styled wines. Michel Rolland of Château Le Bon Pasteur consults. *See also* Peñaflor.

✓ *Cabernet-Malbec* (Medalla)
 • *Malbec* (Oak Cask Reserve)

VISTALBA
Mendoza
★

This up-and-coming winery makes interesting reds from varieties such as Barbera and Syrah to complement Argentinian faithfuls such as Cabernet and Malbec.

✓ *Cabernet Sauvignon*
 • *Malbec* • *Syrah*

WEINERT
Buenos Aires
★★

Although established as long ago as 1890, this winery emerged as one of Argentina's top two producers only under the present owner, Brazilian-born Bernado Weinert. He renovated the winery in 1975 and shortly after became the first Argentinian producer to reduce yields in order to raise quality. With 850 hectares (2,100 acres) of vineyards it was a huge gamble.

✓ *Cabernet Sauvignon*
 • *Cavas de Weinert*
 (Malbec-Merlot) • *Malbec*

AUTHOR'S CHOICE

I could have filled pages with great Cabernets or Chardonnays from California alone, but have focused on just one or two yardstick examples of the most important or up-and-coming styles in California and the Pacific Northwest. British Columbia and Ontario also have wines worthy of inclusion and, although Chile is the major league player in South America, I felt compelled to include Argentina's best wineries.

PRODUCER	WINE	STYLE	DESCRIPTION	
CALIFORNIA				
Au Bon Climat (*see* p.473)	Sanford & Benedict and Rosemary's Vineyard	RED	These two wines are produced by Jim Clendenen, a world-class Pinot Noir winemaker. Both have a beautiful clarity of fruit and varietal aroma, with Sanford & Benedict showing the greatest finesse, while Rosemary's Vineyard is more upfront, with a riper, fatter style. Both the wines are delectable.	2–5 years
Beringer Vineyards (*see* p.464)	Alluvium	WHITE	This exotic Sauvignon-Sémillon blend illustrates vividly that Californian wines do not have to be pure varietals in order to be successful. The fruit is off-dry and beautifully pure, fresh, and creamy, with a delightful kiss of toasty new oak. Alluvium is a wine best drunk on its own.	2–4 years
Bonny Doon Vineyard (*see* p.471)	Cigare Volant	RED	As one of the original Rhône Rangers, there was no doubt that Bonny Doon had to appear in this selection, but the choice was between Old Telegram (a pun on Vieux Télégraphe) and Cigare Volant. The latter won through due to its sumptuous style and richer, more satisfying fruit. Cigare Volant or 'flying cigar' is made from a Châteauneuf-type blend and was named in honour of the strange-but-true municipal decree issued in 1954, which prevents "flying saucers" and "flying cigars" from landing in Châteauneuf-du-Pape!	3–8 years
De Loach Vineyards (*see* p.460)	O.F.S. Zinfandel	RED	No round-up of Californian wines would be complete without Zinfandel, and De Loach O.F.S. (Our Finest Selection) is my choice for those looking for finesse rather than size (*see also* Ravenswood below). It is a rich, smooth, elegant, and stylish Zinfandel, teeming with deliciously spicy fruit. If you prefer lush Zinfandel with a hint of oak, rather than something bolted together with planks of tannin, this is the wine for you.	3–8 years
Ironstone Vineyards (*see* p.461)	Cabernet Franc	RED	This gorgeously lush, fruity red wine may be silky-smooth, but it has not had its varietal character entirely smoothed out. It is a beautifully expressive wine from Cabernet Franc, a variety that is just beginning to take off in California.	2–4 years
Kistler Vineyards (*see* p.461)	Single-vineyard Chardonnays	WHITE	There is an embarrassingly high number of great Californian Chardonnays, but I chose Kistler to represent this category because it produces so many top-performing, single-vineyard Chardonnays, which include Camp Meeting Ridge, Durell "Sandhill", Dutton Ranch, Kistler, McCrae, and Vine Hill Road. It is hard to choose between these wines because, although some excel more than others, no hierarchical pattern has emerged over the years and even the lowest-performing wines rank among California's top-class Chardonnays. While differences can be quite distinct in a comparative tasting, all these wines possess huge, rich, creamy fruit, with elegant tropical-fruit balancing the acidity and heaps of oaky-malolactic complexity. Some people like to age these wines but, while they do take significant ageing, I always enjoy them most when they still have the vibrancy of youth.	2–7 years
Peter Michael Winery (*see* p.461)	Les Pavots	RED	My choice for the most exciting Bordeaux-style red wine of the moment has to be Sir Peter Michael's Les Pavots. All the products from this winery carry French names, which is indicative of Peter Michael's leaning towards the French, rather than Californian style. Les Pavots means "the poppies", but the wine is built for a much longer life than the ephemeral blossoming poppy suggests. Produced from approximately 70 per cent Cabernet sauvignon, plus Cabernet franc and Merlot, Les Pavots is consistent in offering a classic structure of firm but ripe tannins to support its deep, richly textured fruit. The oak is definitely discernible, but not as obnoxious as that found in most Napa wines, and it provides a smoky-spicy complexity that is useful in the wine's youth, before the slower-developing bottled aromas of the fruit take over.	4–20 years

PRODUCER	WINE	STYLE	DESCRIPTION	
Joseph Phelps Vineyards (*see* p.467)	Vin de Mistral Muscat	WHITE	Although fortified Muscat is prolific throughout the wine world, late-harvest Muscat is a rarity. This refreshing dessert wine, with its vivacious aroma and exotically succulent, exquisitely balanced, peachy fruit is a brilliant example of how late-harvest Muscat should be. It is one of the styles that California excels at, but it has gradually fallen by the wayside. Hopefully with the likes of Phelps promoting this style via its exciting, new Vin de Mistral range, the next generation of drinkers will be enticed by this most luscious of wines.	Upon purchase
Qupé (*see* p.474)	Ben Nacido Syrah	RED	There are plenty of huge Californian Syrahs but, when they are made in a more accessible style, they tend to be jammy, which is fine in an inexpensive wine, but not a premium varietal. Qupé's Ben Nacido Syrah is lovely and rich, but gets my vote for its elegance and finesse. It is a top-notch Syrah, with a wonderfully smooth texture and quite delicate fruit.	3–6 years
Ravenswood (*see* p.462)	Old Hill Zinfandel	RED	For the biggest, top-quality Zinfandel around, look no further than Ravenswood – Old Hill is the most super concentrated.	10–20 years
Ridge Vineyards (*see* p.471)	York Creek Petite Sirah	RED	With the possibility that much of California's Petite Sirah are clones of the classic Syrah, I had to include one in my choice and, if this most massive, dark, tannic, and incredibly age-worthy wine is not a yardstick, I don't know what is.	5–15 years
Roederer Estate (*see* p.457)	Brut	SPARKLING WHITE	Sold under the Quartet label on some export markets, this domaine-bottled sparkling wine is grown in California's Anderson Valley, 240 kilometres (150 miles) north of San Francisco. The first release was a non-vintage blend based on the 1986 vintage and nothing special, but the second blend, based on the 1987 vintage, was stunning. It was as if its winemaker, Michel Salgues, had compressed Louis Roederer's 160 years of Champagne experience into the twelve month period separating the two harvests. I was so impressed by Roederer Estate that I spent the best part of ten weeks the following year trekking around California, Australia, and New Zealand, searching for other world-class sparkling wines. Slow development of bottle aromas after disgorgement is the sign of any classic sparkling wine, wherever it is made, and Roederer Estate requires at least two or three years in bottle, whereas most New World fizz is best drunk on purchase, and starts going fat and blowzy after a couple of years. This wine can taste quite green when first released, but will develop classic, creamy-biscuitiness if given sufficient ageing.	2–6 years
Sanford Winery (*see* p.474)	Barrel Select Sanford & Benedict	RED	I make no excuses for including two Californian Pinot Noir (*see also* Au Bon Climat, p.513), both from Santa Barbara, as this is the most exciting place for the varietal outside Burgundy itself, and Richard Sanford's beautifully balanced, succulently fruity, yet classically structured Barrel Select Sanford & Benedict is consistently one of California's finest Pinot Noirs.	2–7 years
Shafer Vineyards (*see* p.468)	Hillside Select Cabernet Sauvignon	RED	Deciding which Cabernet Sauvignon should represent California was as big a problem as choosing a Californian Chardonnay – if you look at the long list of recommended wines on pp.451–2 you will see what I mean. In the end, I plumped for Shafer because its smooth, rich style with beautifully integrated oak typifies the finest of the California genre. Hillside Select is the epitome of Shafer Cabernet Sauvignon, having dense, purple-fruit and ageing gracefully.	4–20 years
PACIFIC NORTHWEST				
Bethel Heights (*see* p.483) Ⓥ	Pinot Noir	RED	One of the most consistent Oregon Pinot Noirs, Bethel Heights Pinot Noir is smooth and pretty with redcurrant, cherry, and strawberry fruits supported by vanilla-oak.	2–5 years
Domaine Drouhin (*see* p.484)	Pinot Noir	RED	Not the deepest or darkest Oregon Pinot Noir, but certainly the deepest and darkest Oregon Pinot Noir to retain a purity of varietal fruit and, since its inception in 1989, it has been the greatest Oregon Pinot Noir more years than not.	3–10 years
Hedges Cellars (*see* p.486) Ⓥ	Cabernet Merlot	RED	Like all of Tom Hedges' wines, this is lush, succulent, and creamy as soon as it is bottled. There is no doubt that drinking it is pure hedonism!	Upon purchase
Leonetti Cellar (*see* p.486)	Cabernet Sauvignon	RED	Washington is red-wine county and this is the biggest, richest, oakiest Washington red wine produced. Mellow oak-complexity dominates and there is a vast amount of highly extracted flavour.	3–15 years

PRODUCER	WINE	STYLE	DESCRIPTION	🍷
Quilceda Creek (see p.486)	Cabernet Sauvignon	RED	The grandfather of Washington red-wine production, Alex Golitzen is still churning out world-class Cabernet Sauvignon from grapes grown in the suburbs of Seattle, albeit with the help of his son nowadays. Quilceda is a deep, dark, brooding Cabernet that is more reminiscent in tannin structure to the great wines of the Médoc than to those of Washington.	8-20 years
CANADA				
Cave Spring (see p.500)	Chardonnay	WHITE	Cave Springs produces two interesting Chardonnay *cuvées*, one from Chardonnay musqué, which has a delicate floral-muskiness, and Chardonnay Bench Reserve, which is a fine, rich, full, and tasty wine, with heaps of fruit and elegant, toasty oak.	2-4 years
Hainle (see p.499)	Riesling	WHITE	Tilman Hainle might not be the most consistent of Canada's winemakers, but his "go for it" attitude can make him one of the most exciting, and he seldom produces a dull wine. When on form, the Dry Estate Riesling has honeyed-petrolly fruit after bottle-ageing, and the intensely sweet, super-concentrated pineapply Icewine is as unctuous as Riesling can be.	3-5 years, (Dry Estate) 2-20 years (Icewine)
Henry of Pelham (see p.500)	Baco Noir	RED	This is my choice for those who want to know what a top-quality hybrid wine tastes like. It is very rich and fruity with excellent oak complexity and a good food-wine structure.	3-7 years
Inniskillin (see p.500)	Vidal Icewine	WHITE	This is the winery that put the Canadian Icewine bandwagon on the road to international stardom. Vidal Icewine is always an intensely sweet, rich, and racey dessert wine with tingly-tangy acidity balancing the hugely sweet flavour on the finish.	2-20 years
Konzelmann (see p.500)	Gewürtraminer	WHITE	One of the most pungently spicy Gewürtraminers produced outside Alsace, but so little is made and it is so much appreciated that Herbert Konzelmann sells out all too quickly.	1-5 years
Stoney Ridge Cellars (see p.501)	Cabernet Franc	RED	A delicious, smooth, beautifully balanced red wine brimming with soft, succulent fruit. The 1991 vintage was one of the best Cabernet Franc varietal wines produced anywhere in the world.	2-5 years
Sumac Ridge (see p.499)	Gewürtraminer Private Reserve	WHITE	The intensity of true Gewürtraminer spice in this limited bottling has continued to be delightfully surprising since 1992.	3-5 years
CHILE				
Canepa (see p.510) Ⓥ	Cabernet Sauvignon	RED	This is a huge, dark, richly flavoured red wine, well-oaked and packed solid with mouthwatering blackcurranty, liquorice fruit of no little complexity.	3-10 years
Concha y Toro (see p.510)	Casillero del Diablo, Chardonnay	WHITE	Traditionally, Concha y Toro keeps its best wines in the "Devil's Cellar", from which this wine gets its name. Concha Y Toro started the rumour that the cellar was occupied by the devil to scare away pilferers. Casillero del Diablo also happens to be a devil of a good Chardonnay – rich, fresh, and zingy.	2-5 years
Cono Sur (see p.510) Ⓥ	Cabernet Sauvignon	RED	A rich and velvety red, with lots of spicy-plummy fruit and a ripe finish. This wine is nice when released, but improves with a further year or two in bottle.	2-5 years
Errazuriz (see p.510) Ⓥ	Merlot	RED	The first Chilean winery to release a pure Merlot wine, Errazuriz cleverly chose to make this a fresh, juicy-fruity red of no pretensions, just heaps of enjoyment, and positioned it at an inexpensive, super-value price point.	Upon purchase
Viña Casablanca (see p.511) Ⓥ	Sauvignon Blanc	WHITE	Quite how Sauvignon Blanc can be so beautifully juicy and luscious, yet retain the electric-sharp, varietal character and acidity is a mystery, but Viña Casablanca seems to do it every time. In a blind tasting, this wine really stands out.	1-2 years
ARGENTINA				
Catena (see p.512)	Malbec	RED	If Malbec is Argentina's greatest red, then Catena produces the best, although Weinert's Malbec comes close. Both are probably closer to the famous "black wine" of Cahors than anything produced in that French wine area today. A dark wine, although not inky or rustic, its lush, richly flavoured fruit intermingles with violety-floral aromas and creamy oak.	3-8 years
Weinert (see p.512)	Cavas de Weinert	RED	Catena and Weinert are the two most exceptional wine producers in Argentina, and Cavas de Weinert is this winery's top cuvée. It is a deep, dark red wine, full of mellowed cedary-spicy black fruits and creamy-coffee oak.	5-10 years

AUSTRALIA, NEW ZEALAND, and ASIA

WE TEND TO THINK OF AUSTRALIA as the older, more traditional winemaking country, with New Zealand being a much more recent phenomenon. Yet just a 30-year gap separates the viticultural origins of these two countries. Australia's wine industry dates back to 1788, but New Zealand's started not much later, in 1819. It is the considerably larger size and diversity of Australia's wine industry that tends to reinforce the illusion of a much greater divide, although, as most readers will have experienced, the global reputation of both is merely decades old. We know Australia best for the consistency of its Chardonnay, and the creamy-mellow, spicy-cedary style of its Shiraz-cum-Syrah, while New Zealand's fresh, crisp, exhilarating Sauvignon Blanc has put this country firmly on the map. In the meantime, wine styles in Asia continue to evolve.

HENSCHKE'S HILL OF GRACE VINEYARD, EDEN VALLEY
This ancient vineyard dates back to the 1860s. The Church of Gnadenberg can be seen in the background.

✦AUSTRALIA✦

Australian wines have been firm favourites with British consumers since 1985, although it took another decade for these wines to become popular in America. Now sales are soaring in almost every major market.

HOW DO AUSTRALIANS MAINTAIN such consistency and produce such a distinctive, easy-drinking style that you can pick it up even in wines produced by Australians in other countries? The answer is that it is all achieved in the winery, through techniques the Australians have honed to such an extent that every year many of them migrate to become "flying winemakers", a title they invented. These techniques range from such fundamentals as basic cleanliness in every part of the winemaking process, through blending grapes from different regions (the South-Eastern Australian appellation, for example, covers 95 per cent of the country's vineyards). Other techniques include temperature control and acid adjustment to specialist yeasts, and the use of a lot of oak for a relatively short duration. Yeasts in particular seem to impart an Australian character, particularly to white wines such as Chardonnay.

All this is, of course, an over-simplification and one that primarily applies to the bulk of Australia's wines, which are produced at fairly high yields and machine-harvested. It does not apply to the very large number of more expensive, highly individual wines that are usually expressive of a single *terroir*. There are more than 1,200 wineries here, yet only four companies (BRL Hardy, Beringer Blass, Orlando, and Southcorp) account for 80 per cent of the wines produced. Their production is, however, insignificant compared to that of the American Gallo winery, which makes one-and-a-half times the total production of Australia.

THE GROWTH OF AUSTRALIA'S WINE TRADE
The first Australian vineyard was planted at Farm Cove in New South Wales in 1788, with vines originating not from France but from Rio de Janeiro and the Cape of Good Hope. These were collected by the first governor, Captain Arthur Phillip, en route to Sydney. The rich soil of Farm Cove and its humid climate proved

AUSTRALIA
Wine is produced in every state, although most of the vineyards are in the southeastern corner of the country, centred on a semicircular band running from Sydney in New South Wales to Adelaide in South Australia.

● Other wine-producing areas

----- State boundary

▲ Height above sea level (metres)

fine for growing vines, but not for making wine. Phillip persevered, however, and planted another vineyard at Parramatta, just north of Sydney. Soil and climate were more suitable and the success of this new venture encouraged Phillip's official requests for technical assistance. England responded by sending out two French prisoners-of-war, who were offered their freedom in exchange for three years' service in New South Wales, in the belief that all Frenchmen knew something about making wine. This did not prove true: One was so bad at it that he was transported back to England; the other could make only cider, but mistakenly used peaches instead of apples! From these shaky beginnings an industry grew, but with no thanks to the British. At first, Australia's wine trade was monopolized by the needs of the British Empire, later the Commonwealth. It thus gained a

CORIOLE VINEYARDS, McLAREN VALE
McLaren Vale is currently contesting Coonawarra's reputation as the best red-wine region of South Australia, a state that accounts for almost 60 per cent of Australia's total wine output.

HOW TO READ AUSTRALIAN WINE LABELS

Australia's wine labels are among the most straightforward and easy-to-understand in the world, clearly showing the basic details of what the wine is, who made it and where, in addition to further information (often on back labels) supplying details of harvest, vinification, maturation, and tasting notes. Readers should note that many of Australia's most basic terms (such as Burgundy, Champagne, and *Spätlese* etc.) are at present in the process of being phased out, as an appellation guarantee scheme has been negotiated with the European Union is introduced to ensure Australia's exports to the European Union are not hampered. The basic information that is shown on virtually all Australian wine labels includes:

UNWOODED •
The swing away from wood-matured wines has made "Unwooded" a sought-after term for some consumers. Variations on "Wood Matured" will probably mean oak chips, which can be good, but at a price when they should be cheap, whereas the mention of anything indicating the use of real oak barrels will be much more expensive.

GRAPE VARIETY •
Most of Australia's greatest wines are pure varietal wines from classic grape varieties, so the label will reveal names such as Cabernet Sauvignon, Chardonnay, Sémillon, and Shiraz. Some more obscure grape names may be encountered, many of which are synonyms for better-known varieties.

When two or more grapes are indicated on a label, they are listed in order of importance, so that a Sémillon-Chardonnay will have a greater proportion of Sémillon than a Chardonnay-Sémillon, and a Shiraz-Malbec-Cabernet will have more Shiraz than Malbec, and more Malbec than Cabernet.

ADDRESS •
A specific area in the address gives no clues as to the provenance of a wine with a much wider appellation, as there is no requirment that any grapes should come from the same locality as the winery.

BRAND OR COMPANY NAME
The Chapel Hill name on this example is the brand name of Chapel Hill Wines Pty. Ltd., whose name and address are clearly indicated at the bottom of the label.

CAPACITY •
750 ml (which is equal to 75 cl) indicates a standard-sized bottle.

PRODUCT OF AUSTRALIA
All wines exported carry "Product of Australia" or "Produce of Australia".

VINTAGE
At least 85 per cent of the wine will be from the year indicated on the label, which in this case is 1994.

STATE/ZONE, REGION, OR SUBREGION OF ORIGIN
Australian winemakers are open and straightforward when it comes to indicating the origin of their wines. In this case it is South Australia. If individual regions or districts on the label are unknown to you, the name of one of the five mainland states or Tasmania will always be indicated somewhere on the bottle, which should help you to narrow down more specific areas. Indeed, many wines will, like this one, indicate a state of origin only if blended from various areas.

ALCOHOLIC STRENGTH
This is expressed in per cent by volume. This information is more significant in countries that grow wines in baking heat (not all Australian wine areas are extremely hot), since alcoholic strength gives a rough guide to the style – the higher the alcohol the bigger the wine. A high alcohol level invariably indicates a traditionally made wine, while the lower it is, the lighter the wine.

Other information that may be found on Australian wine labels:

BIN NUMBER/CODE, PRIVATE BIN, OR RESERVE BIN
These terms imply a better grade of wine within a company's range, a selected *cuvée*, or reserve quality, but there are no legal requirements.

SHOW OR SHOW RESERVE
Used only on (domestic) award-winning wines. Australian wine competitions are a first-class indication of sources of superior wines. This is not simply because of the highly professional organization of these events and the relatively modest proportion of winners, but because the term can be applied only to wines that come from exactly the same vat, or even barrel, as the prize-winning wine. In theory, this prevents a producer from collecting medals for a *tête de cuvée*, and then blending it into more, inferior wines under the same label, but there seems to be a lot of the "same" Show Reserve wine sold by some companies.

AUSTRALIAN GEOGRAPHICAL INDICATIONS (GIs)

Australia's new appellation system, introduced in 2001, defines boundaries and nothing more. Thankfully it does not attempt to dictate what varieties should be grown, how vines should be pruned or trained, or target yields, alcohol levels, or style of wine produced. Geographical Indications (GIs) were introduced to support the Label Integrity Program. Label Integrity is the simplest, sanest, non-draconian form of wine control invented: if the label states Coonawarra Cabernet Sauvignon, then the wine must be made from Cabernet Sauvignon grown in Coonawarra. But, while Cabernet Sauvignon is Cabernet Sauvignon, where does Coonawarra start and finish? Enter the GIs.

The process of defining GIs has not always been simple, which is why I chose Coonawarra as an example. At present the area recognized as Coonawarra GI sits at some 230 square kilometres, but there are many growers with vineyards bordering this boundary who have asked why not me? With the Coonawarra name attracting such a premium in price, this is only to be expected, but as soon as one boundary is extended, so another raft of growers start asking the same question and so, like Topsy, it just grows and grows. At the time of writing there were more than 45 appeals lodged. Some appeals no doubt are more justified than others, but if they are all upheld Coonawarra would balloon to over 1,200 square kilometres.

Current GIs comprise eight states or territories, one super-zone that covers several states, and 27 zones within states; within these are 61 regions, some encompassing one or more of 31 subregions. At least another 50 subregions are in the pipeline – but this is far more manageable number than the 650 names originally submitted.

The present GIs are as follows (states and territories in bold capitals, zones in bold, regions and subregions in light face):

South Eastern Australia (superzone including the whole of New South Wales, Victoria, and Tasmania, and part of Queensland and South Australia)

NEW SOUTH WALES: Big Rivers: Lachlan Valley, Murray Darling, Perricoota, Riverina, Swan Hill; **Central Ranges:** Cowra, Mudgee, Orange; **Hunter Valley:** Hunter (Allandale, Belford, Broke Fordwich, Dalwood, Pokolbin, Rothbury); **Northern Rivers:** Hastings River; **Northern Slopes; South Coast:** Shoalhaven, Sydney; **Southern New South Wales:** Canberra District, Gundagai, Hilltops, Tumbarumba; **Western Plains**

QUEENSLAND: Granite Belt, South Burnett

SOUTH AUSTRALIA: Adelaide; Barossa: Barossa Valley, Eden Valley (High Eden, Springton); **Far North; Fleurieu:** Currency Creek, Kangaroo Island, Langhorne Creek, McLaren Vale (Clarendon); **Limestone Coast:** Bordertown, Coonawarra, Mount Benson, Padthaway, Wrattonbully; **Lower Murray;** Riverland; **Mount Lofty Ranges:** Adelaide Hills (Gumeracha, Lenswood, Piccadilly Valley), Clare Valley (Auburn, Clare, Hill River, Polish Hill River, Sevenhill, Watervale); **The Peninsulas**

VICTORIA: Central Victoria: Bendigo, Central Victorian Mountain Country, Goulburn Valley (Nagambie Lakes), Heathcote; **Gippsland; North East Victoria:** Alpine Valleys (Beechworth, Kiewa River Valley), Glenrowan, King Valley (Myrrhee, Whitlands), Rutherglen (Wahgunyah); **North West Victoria:** Murray Darling, Swan Hill; **Port Phillip:** Geelong, Macedon Ranges, Mornington Peninsula, Sunbury, Yarra Valley; **Western Victoria:** Grampians (Great Western), Henty, Pyrenees

WESTERN AUSTRALIA: Central Western Australia; Eastern Plains, Inland & North of Western Australia; Greater Perth: Perth Hills, Swan District (Swan Valley); **South West Australia:** Blackwood Valley, Geographe, Great Southern (Albany, Denmark, Frankland River, Mount Barker, Porongurup), Manjimup, Margaret River, Pemberton, Warren Valley; **West Australian South East Coastal**

TASMANIA

NORTHERN TERRITORY

AUSTRALIAN CAPITAL TERRITORY

RECENT AUSTRALIAN VINTAGES

2000 Overall a difficult year in terms of both volume and quality, with South Australia faring worst. Delightful exceptions include Hunter Valley, southern Victoria, Tasmania, and Margaret River.

1999 Another record harvest, but rather uneven in quality, with red wines generally standing up to the dry, hot summer (which was part of a prolonged drought) better than the white wines. Superb reds produced in Margaret River, the Grampians and northern Tasmania.

1998 A great red-wine year for South Australia (at least on a par with 1986, 1990, and 1996), despite another huge increase in production. Victoria, Tasmania, and the Hunter also excelled. Only the Margaret River missed out.

1997 A miserable yield was not compensated for by any special sort of quality except for truly excellent South Australian Rieslings. South and central Victoria were also exceptions, producing nicely concentrated wines. Definitely not a good vintage for the Hunter Valley. This year marked the beginning of a four-year-long drought.

1996 A bumper crop of excellent quality provided the best of both worlds, with all key regions of South Australia excelling. Central Victoria was almost as favourable and other regions did well enough not to take the shine off South Australia's unmitigated success. The vintage was a great relief after 1995 had promised so much, yet failed emphatically.

reputation for cheap fortified wines – not because it could make only such wines, but because Britain wanted them. Unfortunately, Australians also acquired the taste. Although Australia made (and still makes) some of the world's finest dessert wines (botrytized as well as fortified), most wines were heavy, very sweet, and sluggish at a time when the rest of the world was drinking lighter and finer wines. Small quantities of truly fine table wine were produced but, until the 1960s, most of those exported were remarkably similar in style, whatever their grape variety or area of origin.

THE RENAISSANCE OF AUSTRALIAN WINES
Over the last 40 years, the technology of Australian winemaking has soared, taking with it the quality of its wines. Better quality does not necessarily follow in the footsteps of improved technology – not only must there be an understanding of the equipment but also a realization of the potential of grapes and soil conditions, with a certain vision and passion in order to produce finer, more expressive wines. Technology can often "wash out" essential characteristics, but the Australians did not allow this to happen. Once committed to taking part in the international "fine-wine contest", they made such fast progress that Australian wine climbed to the top of the quality ladder before foreign producers realized there was any competition.

Until the early 1980s, as much as 99 per cent of all Australian wine was consumed domestically. When output dramatically increased, producers had to concentrate on exports, which increased tenfold by the late 1980s, and today they represent more than 40 per cent of the country's total production. Even this impressive statistic understates Australia's success because plantings have increased, production has swollen and exports in terms of volume have doubled in the last four years alone.

NEW SOUTH WALES

*From the weighty Hunter Valley Shiraz, through
to honeyed, bottle-aged Sémillon (once sold as Hunter
Riesling), and the easy-drinking Murrumbidgee wines,
to the fast-rising wines from areas such as Orange
and Hilltops – Australian wines are even better in
quality and more varied in style than ever.*

IN THIS DAY AND AGE of clean, vital, and pure-tasting wines,
it is hard to imagine that the Hunter Valley established its once
unassailable reputation on a huge, beefy, red Shiraz that gave
off a strong, gamey, sweat-and-leather odour and possessed
an earthy, almost muddy taste that was "chewed" rather than
swallowed. But the valley grew no other black grape until 1963.
This peculiar aroma, which gave rise to the infamous "sweaty
saddles" description, is supposed to derive from the Hunter
Valley's volcanic basalt soil, although in some areas, this Shiraz
and basalt combination has yielded nothing but pure peppery-
varietal Shiraz with not the slightest hint of "sweaty saddles",
and in the first edition of this book in 1988, I attributed this
phenomenon to hot climate, bad viticultural practices, and sloppy
winemaking. It has since been identified as a mercaptan fault,
which was the result of too much sulphur being used to combat
the effects of heat in the vineyard and winery.

VINEYARDS IN MUDGEE
*Perhaps atypical of the area, these vineyards occupy flatland
rather than the western slopes of the Great Dividing Range.*

NEW SOUTH WALES, *see also* p.518
*North of Sydney, the Lower and Upper Hunter
Valley and the Mudgee area excel, while the
Murrumbidgee Irrigation Area to the
southwest proves that quantity
can, to a certain extent,
co-exist with quality.*

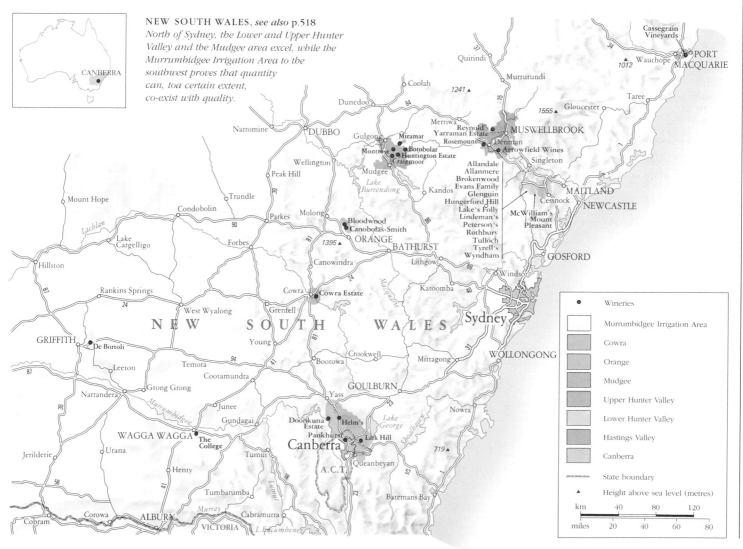

521 •

FACTORS AFFECTING TASTE AND QUALITY

LOCATION
The southern part of Australia's east coast, between Victoria and Queensland.

CLIMATE
Temperatures during the growing season are similar to those of the Languedoc. Cloud cover can temper the heat in the Hunter Valley, but the accompanying rains often promote rot. The growing season is later, and the climate sunnier in Mudgee, Orange and Cowra, while it is relatively hotter and drier in the Murrumbidgee Area.

ASPECT
Vines are grown on generally low-lying, flat or undulating sites, but also on steeper slopes such as the fringes of the Brokenback Range in the Lower Hunter Valley where vines are grown at altitudes of up to 500 m (1,600 ft), and on the western slopes of the Great Dividing Range, where some vineyards can be found at an altitude of 800 m (2,600 ft).

SOIL
Soils are varied with sandy and clay loams of varying fertility found in all areas. Various other types of soil, such as the red-brown volcanic loams, are scattered about the Lower Hunter region and the fertile, but well-drained alluvial sands and silts of the flat valley floors.

VITICULTURE AND VINIFICATION
Irrigation is practised throughout the state, particularly in the mainly bulk-wine-producing inland area of Murrumbidgee. The range of grape varieties is increasing, and the grapes are harvested several days earlier than they used to be, for a crisper style. Temperature-controlled fermentation in stainless-steel vats is common, but new oak is used judiciously.

GRAPE VARIETIES
Cabernet sauvignon, Chardonnay, Clairette, Colombard, Crouchen, Doradillo, Frontignan, Grenache, Marsanne, Mourvedre, Muscat Gordo Blanco, Palomino, Pedro Ximénez, Pinot noir, Riesling, Sauvignon blanc, Sémillon, Shiraz, Muscadelle, Gewürztraminer, Trebbiano, Verdelho

IRRIGATION CANAL AND DE BORTOLI WINERY
A network of irrigation canals like this one, enables Riverina wineries such as De Bortoli to produce vast amounts of modest, easy-drinking wines.

THE APPELLATIONS OF
NEW SOUTH WALES

BIG RIVERS
This zonal GI encompasses the regional GIs of Lachlan Valley, Murray Darling, Perricoota, Riverina and Swan Hill.

CENTRAL RANGES
A zonal GI that encompasses the regional GIs of Cowra, Mudgee and Orange.

CANBERRA
Australian Capital Territory
Technically not part of New South Wales, Canberra is, however, physically surrounded by this state, and since its 18 wineries do not warrant their own chapter, it is included here. It seems strange that the wines of Australia's Capital Territory can be overlooked, but they often are. This area is 40 kilometres (25 miles) north-northwest of the city itself, clustered around a small settlement called Murrumbateman. The area's early downfall was due to its inability to compete with vineyards in warmer areas, but it is a widespread misconception that Canberra is cool in viticultural terms. The summers are warm and dry, and the new generation of winegrowers has accepted that irrigation is indispensable. The only reason for Canberra's reputation for inconsistency is the variable skill and experience of its winemakers, which is apt to show up when there are so few of them. The imminent arrival of BRL Hardy with a substantial new winery will help in this respect. However, a great improvement in the quality of Canberra's smaller producers was evident by 2000, especially in their French-like Shiraz and snappy Rieslings.

COWRA
This is a small but growing viticultural area, which is sometimes referred to as the Central West district. Cowra is situated some 120 miles (180 km) inland and west from Sydney, and nearly the same distance north of Canberra.

FORBES-COWRA
A name sometimes given to vineyards within the Forbes-Cowra-Wellington triangle. Roughly speaking, this area is bounded on the south by the Lachlan River, on the north by the Macquarie River, on the west by Highway 39 and on the east by Highway 81.

HASTINGS VALLEY
Hastings Valley at Port Macquarie is a minor but expanding wine area that supported several vineyards in the 1860s. Production ceased around 1930 and vines were not cultivated here again until John Cassegrain, formerly of Tyrrell's, established a vineyard in 1980.

HUNTER
Subregions: *Allandale, Belford, Broke Fordwich, Dalwood, Pokolbin, Rothbury*
The Hunter sounds as if it should encompass the Hunter Valley, not the other way around, yet while theoretically the Hunter encompasses the Hunter Valley, in practical terms these areas are the same! The Hunter covers the areas popularly known as the Lower Hunter Valley and the Upper Hunter Valley.
See **Lower Hunter Valley and Upper Hunter Valley**

HUNTER VALLEY
This zonal GI encompasses the regional GI of Hunter.

LOWER HUNTER VALLEY
This is the "original" Hunter Valley. Its vineyards were pioneered in the 1820s by such growers as William Kelman of Kirkton and George Wyndham of Dalwood, over 130 years before the Upper Hunter Valley was opened up. The area has long been famous for its rich Sémillons and for its forceful Shiraz, the Syrah of Côte Rôtie and Hermitage. The Lower Hunter Valley is not ideal grape country, being too hot and humid, although the nightly air-drainage from the Brokenback Range cools the vines and prevents the acidity of ripening grapes from dropping too rapidly. After a period of slow growth in the 1980s, the Hunter Valley has enjoyed the same rejuvenation as the Barossa Valley. In 1990 there were 45 wineries, now there are over 100 and a dozen more in the pipeline.

MUDGEE

With a continuous history of grape growing since 1856, this is the oldest district on this side of the Great Dividing Range. Mudgee produces rich and succulent red wines, particularly from Shiraz and Cabernet Sauvignon.

MURRUMBIDGEE IRRIGATION AREA (MIA)

By flooding and pumping the Murrumbidgee River, this district, also known as Griffith-Leeton Riverina, is irrigated in much the same way as the Murray River irrigates South Australia's Riverland. This previously infertile land now cultivates rice and many fruits, including enough grapes to make one-tenth of all the wine in Australia. These wines are not all cheap plonk and include some of Australia's best botrytized wines.

NORTHERN RIVERS

This zonal GI consists of New South Wales' northern coastal strip and encompasses the regional GI of Hastings Valley.

NORTHERN SLOPES

Almost as barren as the Western Plains, this area is sandwiched between it and the Northern Rivers GI.

ORANGE

When entering this town, the first thing you see is a huge sign saying "Welcome to Orange" with a large fruit underneath – an apple! That's right, Orange is famous for apples, and in recent years for grapes. As in the New World everywhere, the best potential vineyard areas have invariably turned out to be those that initially became famous for their orchards. The vines grow 600-900 metres (1,970-2,950 ft) above sea-level on an extinct volcano called Mount Canobolas, which is itself part of the Great Dividing Range. When I first visited the area in the late 1980s, the only local wine was Bloodwood, grown on a very small vineyard owned by Stephen Doyle, a lecturer at Orange Agricultural College. Now there are 15 vineyards commercializing their own wine, with many more growers likely to follow suit when Orange Agricultural College builds a winery on its property, as this is intended to provide contract winemaking services for vineyard owners. Like most famous regions, Orange has expanded beyond its place of origin; its most recent and most important plantings being found at Little Boomey, northeast of Molong.

RIVERINA

See **Murrumbidgee Irrigation Area**

SOUTHERN NEW SOUTH WALES

This zonal GI encompasses the regional GIs of Canberra District, Gundagai, Hilltops and Tumbarumba.

UPPER HUNTER VALLEY

The Upper Hunter Valley was pioneered in the 1960s by Penfolds and put on the map internationally by the sensational performance of Rosemount Estate, easily the district's largest producer. It was Rosemount's sweet-ripe-vanilla Show Reserve Chardonnay that took export markets by storm in the early 1980s. Later, it made its mark with a super-concentrated, more complex Chardonnay from Roxburgh, a prized vineyard acquired some years before. Although this district is just as hot as the Lower Hunter Valley and the growing season very similar, the climate is drier and the vineyards need irrigation. Yet, with irrigation, fertile alluvial soils, and high yields – the two latter factors not auguring well for quality – some very fine wines are made.

WESTERN PLAINS

A virtual wilderness as far as wine today is concerned, this zonal GI covers more than one-third of the entire state, anchored onto the northwestern corner of New South Wales.

THE WINE PRODUCERS OF
NEW SOUTH WALES

ALLANDALE
Lower Hunter Valley
★ ☆ Ⓥ

Amazingly good quality. Also uses grapes from Mudgee and Hilltops.

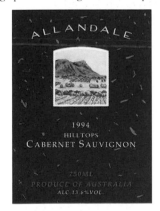

✓ *Chardonnay • Riesling • Sémillon*

ARROWFIELD WINES
Upper Hunter Valley
☆ Ⓥ

This estate dates back to 1824 when Governor Macquarie granted the land to one George Bowman, who named the huge fields on his property after variations of his family name, hence Arrowfield. Now Japanese-owned. Wines are sold under various labels: Arrowfield, Simon Whitlam, Wollombi Brook.

✓ *Chardonnay* (Reserve) *• Sémillon*

BLOODWOOD
Orange
★ ☆ Ⓥ

Owned by Stephen Doyle, a pioneer of Orange, Bloodwood makes wines at the Reynolds Yarraman Estate in the Upper Hunter Valley.

✓ *Cabernet • Merlot*

BOTOBOLAR VINEYARD
Mudgee
☆ Ⓥ

These interesting, good-quality, organically produced wines come from the highest vineyard in the Mudgee district. Botobolar tends to make oddities such as a two-year-old-Shiraz re-fermented on the skins of freshly picked Shiraz!

✓ *Marsanne • Rhine Riesling • St. Gilbert* (Shiraz-Cabernet blend) *• Shiraz*

BRANGAYNE OF ORANGE
Orange
★ ☆ Ⓥ

Don and Pamela Hoskins make supremely stylish wines from their 25-hectare (75-acre) vineyard.

✓ *Chardonnay • Cabernet-Shiraz-Merlot* (The Tristan)

BRINDABELLA HILLS
Canberra
★

Owner Dr Roger Harris produces some of Canberra's most elegant wines.

✓ *Chardonnay • Cabernet Sauvignon • Shiraz*

BROKENWOOD
Lower Hunter Valley
★ ★

This vineyard produces good-quality blends under the Cricket Pitch label, but truly outstanding wines from the low-yielding Graveyard and Rayner vineyards.

✓ *Cabernet Sauvignon* (Graveyard Vineyard) *• Sauvignon Blanc/Sémillon* (Cricket Pitch) *• Sémillon • Shiraz* (Graveyard Vineyard *• Rayner Vineyard)*

CANOBOLAS-SMITH
Orange
★ ★ ☆

Established in 1986 by Murray Smith, these intensely ripe complex wines are a delightful, recent find for me, and further evidence of the great potential of Orange.

✓ *Alchemy* (classic red blend) *• Chardonnay*

CASSEGRAIN VINEYARDS
Port Macquarie
★

The Cassegrain family established this winery back in 1980, yet it still has a frontier feel about it, not the least because of the bracing effect of sea breezes and lashing rain. Some believe the maritime climate is far too marginal for viticulture, but although there are disappointments, some exciting wines are made.

✓ *Chambourcin • Chardonnay • Fromenteau-Chardonnay • Merlot • Sémillon • Shiraz*

CHATEAU PATO
Lower Hunter Valley
★ ☆

This tiny estate produces one of the Hunter Valley's finest Shiraz.

✓ *Shiraz*

COWRA ESTATE
Cowra
★ Ⓥ

Owned by South African businessman John Geber, who is batty about cricket and has thus introduced the new Classic Bat series of wines.

✓ *Cabernet-Merlot* (Classic Bat) *• Chardonnay* (Classic Bat) *• Pinot Noir* (Classic Bat)

DE BORTOLI WINES
MIA
★ ☆ Ⓥ

De Bortoli produces a vast amount of modest wines, which are sold under numerous labels, but it is also capable of producing some excellent wines in large quantities particularly in botrytis styles. De Bortoli produces some stunning wines in the Yarra and King valleys.

✓ *Cabernet-Merlot* (Yarra Valley) *• Chardonnay* (Vat 7, Windy Peak, Yarra Valley) *• Liqueur Muscat* (10 Year Old) *• Sémillon* (Noble One) *• Shiraz* (Yarra Valley)

DOONKUNA ESTATE
Canberra
★

One of the most consistent Canberra wineries, Doonkuna Estate was founded by the late Sir Brian Murray. Now owned and run by Barry and Maureen Moran.

✓ *Cabernet Sauvignon* • *Chardonnay* • *Shiraz*

EVANS FAMILY
Lower Hunter Valley
★ ☆

Len Evans' private vineyard produces top-quality, age-worthy Chardonnay wines.

✓ *Chardonnay*

ANDREW HARRIS
Mudgee
★★

One of Mudgee's fastest rising stars.

✓ *Cabernet-Shiraz* (The Vision)

HELMS
Canberra
★

The irrepressible Ken Helms upset just about everybody when he published a well-documented paper asserting that Phylloxera is not harmful to vines in well-irrigated areas.

✓ *Cabernet-Merlot* • *Riesling*

HUNGERFORD HILL VINEYARDS
Lower Hunter Valley
Ⓥ

Hungerford Hill always used to make blends (of Hunter Valley and Coonawarra, which, at 1,100 kilometres [700 miles] apart, is rather like blending a Rioja with a wine from the Great Hungarian plains), but now it has been sold and is merely a Southcorp brand. It is now sourced from Hilltops, Cowra, Gundagai, and Tumbarumba, all on the western side of the Great Dividing Range, and the results are equally good.

✓ *Shiraz*

HUNTINGTON ESTATE
Mudgee
★ ☆ Ⓥ

Bob Roberts entered the business with a law degree and learned winemaking through a British-based correspondence course. Not the strongest base for success, perhaps, but his clean, fleshy, well-balanced, stylish wines regularly outshine wines made by highly qualified professionals.

✓ *Cabernet Sauvignon* • *Sémillon*

KYEEMA ESTATE
Canberra
★

Consistent award-winning wines.

LAKE'S FOLLY
Lower Hunter Valley
★★

Founded by Sydney surgeon Max Lake who had no winemaking experience, hence the name, yet he introduced the use of new oak to the region and consistently produced vivid, vibrant and stylish wines. Now sold to a Perth resident

for A$8 million, although Lake's son Stephen, who has made the wines for the last 10 years, will remain as consultant for a year or so.

✓ *Cabernet Sauvignon* • *Chardonnay*

LARK HILL
Canberra
★ ☆

This is the highest vineyard in the Canberra district.

✓ *Cabernet-Merlot* • *Pinot Noir* • *Riesling*

LINDEMAN'S WINES
Lower Hunter Valley
★★ Ⓥ

This vast winery is now part of Southcorp and produces wine from almost everywhere, but the Hunter Valley is its historical home. The wines range from good value to great quality. Those from Padthaway in South Australia are the most striking, and some old vintages of Hunter Riesling (Sémillon, *see* Lower Hunter Valley, p.522) are amazing.

✓ *Cabernet-Merlot* (Padthaway) • *Chardonnay* (Classic Release, Coonawarra, Padthaway) • *Pyrus* (classic Bordeaux style) • *Riesling* (Nursery Vineyard Coonawarra, Padthaway Botrytis) • *Sémillon* (Classic Release) • *Shiraz* (Bin 50, Nyrang) • *Shiraz-Cabernet* (Limestone Ridge) • *Verdelhao* (*sic* – Padthaway)

McWILLIAM'S MOUNT PLEASANT
Lower Hunter Valley
★★ Ⓥ

This is the Hunter arm of McWilliam's Wines, whose vast production network also includes wineries at Brand's in Coonawarra, Lillydale in the Yarra Valley, Barwang in the Hilltop's region, and Hanwood/Yenda in the Riverina. Good-value wines, but Mount Pleasant Elizabeth, a bottle-aged Sémillon is one of Australia's finest examples of this unique wine style and one of its greatest bargains too.

✓ *Chardonnay* • *Sémillon* (Elizabeth) • *Sparkling Wines* (Brut)

MARGAN FAMILY
Lower Hunter Valley
★

Although the vineyard has been established in 1989, the winery is brand new and the quality excellent.

✓ *Chardonnay* • *Shiraz*

MIRAMAR WINES
Mudgee
★ ☆ Ⓥ

These are fine-quality wines made in big, rich, true Mudgee style.

✓ *Cabernet Sauvignon* • *Chardonnay* • *Sémillon*

MONTROSE WINES
Mudgee
★

Owned by the Orlando group, Montrose produces quality wines.

✓ *Aleatico* (Reserve Classico) • *Cabernet-Merlot* • *Chardonnay* • *Poets Corner* (classic white blend) • *Sauternes*

PANKHURST
Canberra
★

Since establishing this vineyard in 1986, Allan and Christine Pankhurst have built up the best reputation for Pinot Noir in the Canberra district. Cabernet Sauvignon can be good.

✓ *Pinot Noir*

PETERSONS
Lower Hunter Valley
★

Petersons went through a difficult patch in the early 1990s, but has returned to form.

✓ *Chardonnay* • *Sémillon* • *Shiraz* (Back Block)

REYNOLDS YARRAMAN ESTATE
Upper Hunter Valley
★ ☆ Ⓥ

This former Wybong Estate is now owned by ex-Houghton winemaker Jon Reynolds, who has vineyards in the fast-rising Orange area.

✓ *Cabernet-Merlot* • *Chardonnay*

ROSEMOUNT ESTATE
Denman
★★ Ⓥ

A fastidiously high level of winemaking expertise and an aggressive export marketing policy have made Rosemount a world leader, and the chance-taking curiosity of the indefatigable Philip Shaw and Chris Hancock have kept it ahead. In February 2001 Rosemount merged with Southcorp.

✓ *Cabernet Sauvignon* (especially Coonawarra Show Reserve, Kirri Billi) • *Chardonnay* (especially Orange, Roxburgh, Show Reserve) • *Merlot* (Kirri Billi) • *Sémillon* (Wood Matured) • *Shiraz* (McClaren Vale) • *Syrah* (Balmoral)

ROTHBURY ESTATE
Lower Hunter Valley
★★ Ⓥ

Once owned by Len Evans, this has long been a public company, and under his chairmanship it

continued to produce wines of an extraordinarily high quality, while increasing volume and purchasing other wineries (Bailey's, St. Huberts, and Saltram). Evans left in 1996, when Rothbury was taken over by Mildara-Blass.

✓ *Chardonnay* (Barrel Fermented, Cowra) • *Sémillon* (Reserve) • *Shiraz* (especially Reserve)

SOUTHCORP
Millers Point

Created in 1994 after Penfolds had acquired Lindemans and was then taken over by the owners of Seppelt. In addition to these three famous brands, this huge group also includes: Leo Buring, Coldstream Hills, Devil's Lair, Great Western, Hungerford Hill, Kaiser Stuhl, Killawarra, Matthew Lang, Minchinbury, Queen Adelaide, Rouge Homme, Ryecroft, Seaview, Tollana, Tulloch, Woodley, Wynns, Wynvale, and the low-alcohol brand Loxton, and Laperouse in France. In February 2001 Southcorp merged with Rosemount.

TRENTHAM ESTATE
Murray River
★ ☆ Ⓥ

The red wines in particular offer beautiful quality, great consistency, and terrific value.

✓ *Merlot* • *Shiraz*

TULLOCH
Lower Hunter Valley

Once one of the most traditional wineries in the Hunter Valley, now little more than a brand belonging to Southcorp, although the quality is generally good, with the occasional star-performer.

TYRRELL'S VINEYARDS
Lower Hunter Valley
★★

This long-established winery is still family owned, and although some critics believe that Tyrrell's Chardonnay Vat 47 is not quite as outstanding as it was in the 1970s and 1980s, that is because Australia now makes many great Chardonnay wines, and not in fact because the quality has dropped. The best wines produced here are as uncompromising in their richness and complexity as they have always been.

✓ *Cabernet-Merlot* (Old Winery) • *Chardonnay* (Vat 47) • *Sémillon* (Vat 1) • *Shiraz* (Old Winery, Vat 9)

WYNDHAM ESTATE WINES
Lower Hunter Valley
Ⓥ

Part of the French-owned Orlando group since 1990, Wyndham offers a great source of good-value wines.

✓ *Chardonnay* (Bin 222, Oak Cask)

VICTORIA AND TASMANIA

From Tasmania, Australia's newest wine region, to Victoria, one of its oldest and most traditional, the quality of the wines being produced is ever-improving. Victoria is perhaps most famous for such specialities as its intensely sweet, rich, and sticky liqueur Muscat and Tokay, but between them, these states probably have a greater range of wine styles than anywhere else on the entire continent.

THE WINES OF THESE TWO STATES range from deep-coloured, *cassis*-flavoured Cabernet Sauvignon to some surprisingly classy Pinot Noir, through light and delicate aromatic whites, to rich, oaky, yet finely structured Chardonnay and Sémillon; sparkling wines in both areas are rapidly gaining in reputation.

VICTORIA

John Batman established Melbourne in 1834, and within four years, William Ryrie, a pastoralist, planted the first Yarra Valley vineyard in a place that became known as Yering. The most

PIPERS BROOK VINEYARD, TASMANIA
This world famous winery dominates Pipers Brook, the most successful wine-producing district of Tasmania.

VICTORIA AND TASMANIA, *see also p.518*
The relatively small state of Victoria lies beneath New South Wales and neighbouring South Australia. The island of Tasmania lies due south, on the same latitude as New Zealand's South Island. This area covers a wide variety of climates, terrains, and wines.

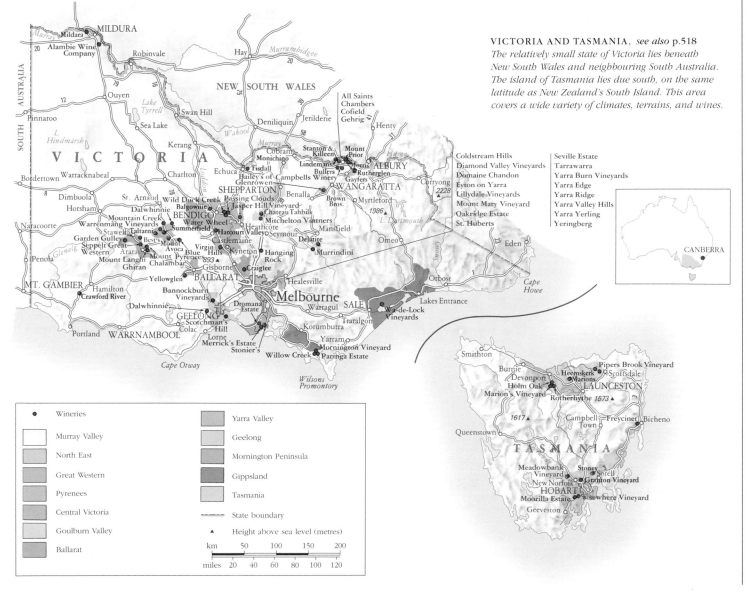

525

CHÂTEAU TAHBILK, GOULBURN VALLEY
This well-known Victorian winery's huge output consists of traditionally made wines. Its Cabernets can be very tannic, requiring at least ten years in bottle.

important sequence of events in the viticultural history of the state began with the appointment of Swiss-born Charles La Trobe as Superintendent of Melbourne in 1839 and culminated in the arrival of 11 fellow Swiss *vignerons* from his home canton of Neufchâtel in 1846, who formed the great foundation of Victoria's future wine industry when they settled in the Geelong district and planted vineyards around their homes.

TASMANIA

Although this is really a new wine region, the first vines planted here were established in 1823 at Prospect Farm by Bartholomew Broughton, an extraordinary convict who had been granted a pardon and eventually came to own a substantial amount of property. By 1827 the quality of his wines had prompted the *Colonial Times* to contrast them with those of Gregory Blaxland, whose Parramatta River vineyard near Sydney had already produced Australia's first exported and first medal-winning wine. The paper reported that a Dr. Shewin, who had tasted Blaxland's famous wine, remarked that by comparison Broughton's was "as far superior

as fine Port to Blackstrap". But such was the cruelty of Britain's penal system in the colonies that it took its toll on Broughton's lifespan. His successful attempt to be pardoned suggests that he probably suffered less than most convicts at the time, but it was sufficient to cut short the luxury of his freedom. He died in 1828, aged 32. Captain Charles Swanston purchased Broughton's property, and by 1865 there were no less than 45 different varieties of vines flourishing at various sites on the island. Yet, by the end of the same decade, virtually all the vineyards had disappeared. Swanston's successor was not interested in viticulture and a combination of personal ruin and Gold Rush fever disposed of the rest. Except for an ephemeral resurgence in the 1880s, Tasmania's wine industry was non-existent until the renaissance of the 1950s, led by a Frenchman called Jean Miguet.

Miguet was not a *vigneron* by profession; he came to Tasmania to work on the construction of a hydro-electric plant, but his new home at La Provence, north of Launceston, reminded him of his native Haute-Savoie and, since it was protected from ocean winds by trees, he believed that grapes might ripen there. In 1956 he cleared his bramble-strewn land and planted vines that grew successfully enough to encourage another European, Claudio Alcorso, to establish a vineyard on the Derwent River in 1958. Alcorso and his Moorilla Estate are still prospering, but after fifteen years, ill-health forced Miguet to abandon his vineyard and return to France, where he sadly died from leukaemia in 1974.

The Tasmanian wine industry is still relatively tiny, but has undergone a rapid and exciting transformation over the last five years and the quality just gets better. It is an island whose destiny is to produce Australia's finest *méthode champenoise*. As far as red wines are concerned, Pinot Noir offers the greatest potential.

GREAT DIVIDING RANGE, VICTORIA
Vines grow on the main upland areas of Victoria, a continuation of Eastern Australia's Great Dividing Range, which is up to 300 kilometres (190 miles) wide.

THE APPELLATIONS OF
VICTORIA AND TASMANIA

ALPINE VALLEYS

Subregions: *Beechworth, Kiewa River Valley*
New GI south of Rutherglen, the wines of which have yet to shake out.

AVOCA

See Pyrenees

BALLARAT

This district is situated within Central Victoria, some 120 kilometres (75 miles) northwest of Melbourne. Ballarat includes vineyards at an altitude of 430 metres (1,400 feet) in Scarsdale, Creswick, and Ballan. The climate is cooler than at Bendigo. Ballarat could become one of Australia's best sparkling wine areas.

BENDIGO

North of Ballarat, situated about 160 kilometres (100 miles) northwest of Melbourne, this part of the Central Victoria region has a dry climate, although only some of its vines are irrigated, with the roots of others having to dig deep into the water-retentive subsoil to survive. This is goldmining country, and viticulture began here at the time of the 1850s Gold Rush. The main growing areas are in Baynton, Big Hill, Bridgewater, Heathcote, Harcourt, Kingower, Maiden Gully, Mandurang, and Mount Ida. Primarily known for its menthol-eucalyptus-tasting red wines, the red-clay, quartz, and ironstone soil is suited to producing fine Shiraz, but Cabernet sauvignon and Chardonnay can also excel and, as Domaine Chandon (known as Green Point on export markets) has shown, the potential for premium-quality sparkling wines also exists.

CENTRAL VICTORIA

Formerly used as an umbrella appellation for Ballarat, Bendigo, and Macedon. *See* separate entries.

COASTAL VICTORIA

See Gippsland

CORIO BAY

See Geelong

DRUMBORG

See Henty

GEELONG

South of Ballarat, along the coast from the Yarra Valley, the vineyards of this district fan out through the hinterland of Corio Bay. Originally worked by Swiss immigrants in the mid-1800s, Geelong underwent a viticultural revival in 1966, somewhat earlier than did other rediscovered areas of Australia, when the Seftons planted the Idyll vineyard. A combination of cool climate and volcanic soil produces wines with fine acidity and varietal character. Bannockburn and Scotchman's Hill are the best producers.

GIPPSLAND

This remote region, which encompasses East Gippsland and South Gippsland and is sometimes simply called Gippsland, was revived in the 1970s when Dacre Stubbs planted the Lulgra vineyard. Apart from occasional fine Cabernet Sauvignon, Pinot Noir, or Chardonnay from one or two tiny wineries, little is happening as yet in this backwater wine region.

GLENROWAN

Part of the North East region, this district is probably best known outside of Australia as Milawa – the use of this alternative name is preferred by Brown Brothers, who put it on their widely exported wines. Glenrowan is, however, more widely used by other winemakers. This is a classic dessert-wine area, but individual vineyards such as Koombahla and Meadow Creek produce scintillating, *cassis*-rich Cabernet Sauvignon and other premium varietals.

GOULBURN VALLEY

Subregion: *Nagambie Lakes*

For years, the excellent Château Tahbilk was the solitary exponent of fine wines in this traditional wine district 120 kilometres (75 miles) north of Melbourne. Now, a number of new wineries are attracting attention. Cabernet Sauvignon is the best wine produced here – a pure varietal or, more traditionally, blended with Shiraz. Chardonnay and Riesling can be terrific and Mitchelton produces excellent wood-matured Marsanne.

GRAMPIANS

This famous old sparkling-wine district of Great Western has been renamed Grampians under the GI scheme, but it is still utilized as a subregional appellation. The entire Grampians region has been revitalized by increasing interest from new ventures. Although best known for sparkling wines, the Grampians name should allow the region's finest varietal, Shiraz, to shine without being lumbered with any preconception that it comes from an essentially fizz region. Cabernet Sauvignon, Chardonnay, and Riesling can also be excellent. Top-performing wineries are Best's, Mount Langhi Ghiran, and Seppelt.

GREAT WESTERN

See Grampians

HENTY

Formerly known as Drumborg, then Far South West and now a GI by the name of Henty, this remote district might have an identity problem, but is still best known for its Seppelts Drumborg winery. This was established when the firm was looking for new supplies of grapes to furnish its growing production of sparkling wines in the 1960s, and the grapes from this area have been very useful components in many an Aussie fizz blend since. The soil is volcanic and the climate so cold that some varieties did not ripen. It is surprising, therefore, that the Cabernet sauvignon and Merlot should be so successful here, but it can be excellent; Riesling and Pinot Noir are also very good. A number of other wineries have now opened up.

KING VALLEY

Subregions: *Myrrhee, Whitlands*
Until 1989 Brown Brothers were the exclusive buyers of grapes in King Valley, but they are now sold far and wide and other wineries have been built here, thus it is now a fully-fledged GI. Chardonnay, Riesling, and Cabernet are the most important varieties, but Nebiolo, Sangiovese and Barolo have shown the greatest potential. Sparkling wine is also produced.

MACEDON

A developing district within the Central Victoria region, Macedon encompasses about 90 hectares (220 acres) of vineyards in and around Mount Macedon, Sunbury, Romsey, Lancefield, and Kyneton. Soil and topography vary greatly and strong winds are the only common climatic factor. Cabernet sauvignon, Chardonnay, and Rhine riesling are the most successful grape varieties so far, and Craiglee Vineyards and Virgin Hills the best wineries.

MILAWA

This name is now used as the bottom-end anchor to King Valley.

MORNINGTON PENINSULA

After an early, but unsuccessful, start in the 1950s, a number of growers have established vineyards in this area overlooking Port Phillip Bay, south of Melbourne. Although only a handful established wineries initially, there are more than 40 facilities in the area now. Provided the vineyards are adequately protected from strong sea winds that whip up over the bay, Mornington Peninsula's cool, often wet, climate shows great potential for first-class winemaking.

MURRAY DARLING

This regional GI overlaps two zonal GIs, North West Victoria and Big Rivers (New South Wales). The region takes its name from one of Australia's great wine rivers. Further upstream is the Rutherglen area, while just downstream is Riverland. The Murray River region brings together several areas of mainly irrigated vineyards dotted along the banks of the middle section of the river. Vineyard plantings soared in the late 1990s, creating a major switch of emphasis from white to red, with some impressive and, frankly, unexpected, results coming through.

PYRENEES

Formerly known as the Avoca district, the vineyards around Mount Avoca, Redbank, and Moonambel are now called Pyrenees, although the former name will no doubt remain in use for a while. Pyrenees, the name of a nearby mountain range, was chosen by local wine growers as an expressive marketing "hook" upon which to "hang" their wines. By whatever name, this area was originally perceived to be red-wine country, making wines of a distinctive and attractive minty character. There was a time in the early 1990s when white wine and even sparkling wine were thought to be the region's best propects, but the original perceptions have since been proven right. Shiraz, Cabernet Sauvignon, and Merlot are the outstanding wines, with Chardonnay and perhaps Pinot Noir on the next rung of quality.

RUTHERGLEN

Subregion: *Wahgunyah*

Rutherglen, whose area is sometimes considered to include Milawa/Glenrowan, has always been the heart of the North East region and the soul of Victoria's wine industry. It is the hub around which the entire state's viticultural activities revolve, and comprises a collection of wineries and vineyards clustered either side of the Murray Valley Highway between Lake Mulwala and Albury, on the left bank of the Murray River. The right bank is also cultivated, but is actually in New South Wales, although most people would consider the two as a pair, and this should be officially recognized if and when any appellation system is undertaken.

Rutherglen has an exciting emergent light-wine industry, whose innovative winegrowers exploit the district's cooler areas. Chardonnay and Sémillon are clean, fresh, and vibrant, Gewürztraminer is performing well, and Durif, Carignan, Shiraz, and Cabernet Sauvignon all show promise to one degree or another. Rutherglen is, however, Australia's greatest dessert-wine country. Its liqueur Muscats and Tokays know no peers.

SUNRAYSIA

Formerly a sub-region of the Murray River, it encompassed the former districts of Mildura, Robinvale, Merbein, Irymple, and Karadoc. *See also* Murray River.

TASMANIA

Tasmania is Australia's ultimate cool-climate location. The first vines were planted at Prospect Farm near Hobart in 1823 by Bartholomew Broughton, but viticulture did not last long on what was then Van Dieman's Land. The wine industry was gradually rekindled in the 1950s. Hopes of international recognition were raised in the late 1980s, when Champagne producer Louis Roederer invested in Heemskerk to produce a premium sparkling wine called Jansz, but Roederer pulled out in 1994 amid patently untrue rumours that the grapes would not ripen. Heemskerk was purchased by Dr. Andrew Pirie of Pipers Brook, Tasmania's largest and best winery. Pirie kept the vineyards, but sold on the Jansz brand to Yalumba, since when his own fizz, the eponymously named Pirie, has established itself as one of the greatest sparkling wines in the world. The reputation of Tasmanian sparkling wine is here to stay, but this island state also produces some intensely flavoured Chardonnay, Riesling, and Pinot Noir. There has even been some fine Cabernet Sauvignon.

YARRA VALLEY

The vines growing on the grey- and red-loam soils of the newly established vineyards in this area benefit not only from the enriching after-

effect of former sheep-farming, but also from one of the coolest climates in Australia. The growing season is long and the yields light. These factors, in the hands of some of the country's most talented winemakers, result in some fine Chardonnay and Cabernet Sauvignon, rare but lettuce-crisp Riesling, and exciting Pinot Noir. Shiraz and Merlot are also very good and, of course, with the presence of Domaine Chandon, Yarrabank, and Devaux Yering Station, this is without doubt sparkling wine country.

THE WINE PRODUCERS OF
VICTORIA AND TASMANIA

ALAMBIE WINE COMPANY
Mildura
⭐
These wines are sold under the Castle Crossing, Milburn Park, and Salisbury Estate labels.
✓ *Chardonnay* (Show Reserve) • *Sparkling Wine* (Milburn Park Brut)

ALL SAINTS
Rutherglen
⭐⭐ V
Taken over in 1992 by Brown Brothers, All Saints became its specialist fortified label.
✓ *Madeira* (Show Reserve) • *Port* (Vintage, Old Tawny) • *Sherry* (Show Reserve Amontillado) • *Sparkling Wine* (Cabernet Sauvignon) • *Tokay* (Show Reserve)

BAILEYS OF GLENROWAN
Glenrowan
⭐⭐
Baileys is now part of the Rothbury group, but continues to produce rich and stunning dessert wines.
✓ *Liqueur Muscat* (Founder, Winemaker's Selection) • *Shiraz* (1920s Block) • *Liqueur Tokay* (Winemaker's Selection)

BALGOWNIE
Bendigo
❓
Balgownie went through a patchy period in the early 1990s, but now seems to be pulling out of it as far as the reds are concerned. The whites are disappointing.
✓ *Cabernet Sauvignon* (Estate) • *Shiraz* (Estate Hermitage)

BANNOCKBURN VINEYARDS
Geelong
⭐⭐ V
Winemaker Gary Farr's experience at Domaine Dujac in Burgundy shows through in the finesse of these wines, which are probably better appreciated in Europe than they are in Australia.
✓ *Cabernet Merlot* • *Chardonnay* • *Pinot Noir* • *Shiraz*

BERINGER-BLASS
South Eastern Australia
One of the "big four" Australian producers, this conglomerate makes wines under the following brands: Benjamin Port, Black Opal, Eaglehawk, Flanagan's Run, Andrew Garrett, Jamiesons Run, Krondorf, Mildara Coonawarra, Pepperjack, Tisdall, Wolf Blass, and Yellowglen.

BEST'S WINES
Great Western
⭐ V
This is a large range that includes a few gems such as the stunning Shiraz and the lovely, zesty-fresh lime-scented Riesling.
✓ *Shiraz* (Bin 0) • *Riesling*

BLACKJACK VINEYARD
Bendigo
⭐ V
Blackjack Vineyard was named after an American sailor who caught gold fever in the 1850s and jumped ship.
✓ *Shiraz*

BLUE PYRENEES
Avoca
⭐
French winemaker Vincent Gere tended to make his sparkling wines on the sweet side until the 1990 vintage, when they became more classic in style. The winemaker is now Kim Hart and the emphasis of production under the Blue Pyrenees label is moving over to still wines.
✓ *Sparkling* (Vintage Reserve)

BROWN BROTHERS
Milawa
⭐⭐ V
The size of this family-owned firm is deceptive until you visit Brown Brothers' so-called micro-vinification winery, which is bigger and better equipped than 70 per cent of the wineries I regularly visit. The big problem with micro-vinification is that there are certain dynamics involved in the fermentation process that determine a minimum size of vat, as well as temperature control and other factors. This is why home-brewers seldom make a polished product and also illustrates why most wines made in research stations are dull and

boring, even if the work the stations do leads to exciting commercial developments. At Brown Brothers, however, the micro-vinification tanks are like a battery of boutique wineries, thus the experimental wines they produce are as polished as any commercially produced wine, which explains why this is one of Australia's most innovative wine producers. The Whitland vineyards are cool, and the wines are lean and crisp. King Valley vineyard is much warmer, which is great for reds, and even the Riesling that is made fat to appeal to Chardonnay drinkers is strangely successful. Blends are often best. Brown Brothers also owns All Saints.

✓ *Barbera* • *Cabernet Sauvignon* (especially Classic Vintage Release) • *Chardonnay* (Family Reserve) • *Dolcetto* • *Liqueur Muscat* • *Liqueur Tokay* (Very Old) • *Muscat* (Blanc, Late Harvest, Orange) • *Nebbiolo* • *Port* (Very Old, Vintage) • *Riesling* (King Valley, Noble, Whitland) • *Shiraz*

BULLER
Rutherglen
★

Forget the table wines, and just buy the beautiful fortified wines.

✓ *Liqueur Muscat* (Museum Release) • *Liqueur Tokay* (Museum Release)

CAMPBELLS WINERY
Rutherglen
★★

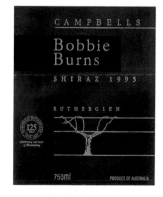

This outstanding fortified wine specialist has expanded into varietal wines with brilliant success.

✓ *Cabernet Merlot* • *Chardonnay* (Bobbie Burns) • *Durif* (The Barkly) • *Liqueur Muscat* (especially Merchant Prince) • *Liqueur Tokay* (especially Isabella) • *Pedro Ximénez* • *Sémillon* (Limited Release) • *Shiraz* (Bobbie Burns)

CHAMBERS
Rutherglen
★★

Bill Chambers is one of the all-time great producers of fortified wine.

✓ *Liqueur Muscat* (especially Old) • *Liqueur Tokay* (especially Old)

CHATEAU TAHBILK
Goulburn Valley
★★✰ ⓥ

This is the oldest winery in Victoria, and makes very traditional wines that always improve in bottle.

✓ *Cabernet Sauvignon* • *Marsanne* • *Shiraz*

COFIELD
Rutherglen
★

Cofield specializes in small quantities of high-quality red fizz.

✓ *Muscat* • *Shiraz* • *Sparkling Wine* (Shiraz)

COLDSTREAM HILLS
Yarra Valley
★★

James Halliday, the doyen of Australia's wine writers, has sold this property to Southcorp but still runs the business. Well known for beautiful Pinot Noir and classic Chardonnay, James Halliday also produces some stunning selected wines under his eponymous label, his secret being that he always goes for length through to elegance and finesse, rather than just weight or punch.

✓ *Cabernet-Merlot* • *Cabernet Sauvignon* (James Halliday) • *Chardonnay* • *Pinot Noir*

CRAIGLEE
Macedon
✰

This famous 19th-century, four-storey, bluestone winery was re-established in 1976 by Pat Carmody.

✓ *Shiraz*

CRAIGOW
Tasmania
✰

Wines of exciting quality are produced here by Hobart surgeon Barry Edwards.

✓ *Pinot Noir*

CRAWFORD RIVER
Western District
★★

This property was established in 1982 by John Thomson, who quickly built a reputation for Riesling, particularly in the botrytis style, but is also very consistent these days with Cabernet.

✓ *Cabernet Sauvignon* • *Riesling*

DALWHINNIE
Pyrenees
★★

Intensely rich and well-structured wines are consistently produced from these vineyards adjacent to Taltarni.

✓ *Cabernet Sauvignon* • *Chardonnay* • *Shiraz*

DELATITE WINERY
Central Victorian High Country
✰ ⓥ

Situated on its own, in the Great Divide, Delatite has produced some

very good-value wines that always show rich, tangy fruit.

✓ *Chardonnay* • *Pinot Noir* • *Riesling*

DIAMOND VALLEY VINEYARDS
Yarra Valley
★✰

David Lance is well known for great Pinot Noir produced here, but his other wines should not be overlooked.

✓ *Chardonnay* • *Pinot Noir* • *Sémillon-Sauvignon*

DOMAINE CHANDON
Yarra Valley
★★✰ ⓥ

Moët & Chandon's Australian winery was set up later than its California venture, but overtook it in quality. Much of the credit should go to Dr. Tony Jordan, who ran the enterprise at that time, but even he will admit that, with sources stretching across an entire continent, he had a wider choice of quality components to choose from. Jordan left to take over at Wirra Wirra. The wines are known in export markets as Green Point.

✓ *Sparkling Wine* (Blanc de Blancs, Vintage Brut)

DROMANA ESTATE
Mornington Peninsula
★ ⓥ

Gary Crittenden produces good and improving wines, particularly under the Schinus Molle label.

✓ *Chardonnay* (Dromana) • *Dolcetto* (Schinus Molle) • *Nebbiolo* (Schinus Molle) • *Riesling* (Schinus Molle) • *Sauvignon Blanc* (Schinus Molle)

ELSEWHERE VINEYARD
Tasmania
✰

Superb Pinot Noir from the Huon Valley has been a Gold Medal winner at the Tasmanian Wine Show.

✓ *Pinot Noir*

EYTON ON YARRA
Yarra Valley
★✰

Matt Aldridge's Yarra Valley wines are as lush, elegant, and stylish as you would expect from this fashionable wine area.

✓ *Cabernet-Merlot* • *Chardonnay* • *Merlot* • *Sparkling* (Pinot Chardonnay)

FREYCINET
Tasmania
★✰

Geoff Bull makes a surprisingly big and beautiful Cabernet Sauvignon for Tasmania's cool climate, but his exquisitely crafted, sumptuous Chardonnay and Pinot Noir surpass it in quality and style.

✓ *Cabernet Sauvignon* • *Chardonnay* • *Pinot Noir*

GARDEN GULLEY
Great Western
★

Former Seppelt winemaker Brian Fletcher runs Garden Gulley, a syndicate-owned boutique winery that excels at fizz.

✓ *Sparkling Wines* (Sparkling Burgundy)

GIACONDA
Wangaretta
★★✰

These are exquisitely crafted, highly sought after wines.

✓ *Chardonnay* • *Pinot Noir*

GEHRIG
Rutherglen
★

Owned by Brian and Bernard Gehrig, this is one of Victoria's very oldest vineyards, and used to be known for its fortified wines, but the most consistent wine now is certainly the elegant Shiraz table wine.

✓ *Shiraz*

HANGING ROCK
Macedon
★

The largest winery in the Macedon area, Hanging Rock specializes in, and is best at, bottle-fermented sparkling wine.

✓ *Sparkling Wines* (Brut)

HOLM OAK
Tasmania
★

Red-wine specialist Nick Butler makes one of Tasmania's best Cabernet Sauvignons.

✓ *Cabernet Sauvignon*

JANSZ
Tasmania
❓

Jansz now belongs to Samuel Smith & Sons, which has entered into a long-term contract with Piper's Brook to buy grapes from the Heemskerk vineyards. Geoff Linton stepped in to make the 1998 vintage, and Tony Davis is now permanent winemaker. Davis has added a non-vintage Jansz *cuvée*.

✓ *Sparkling Wine*

JASPER HILL VINEYARD
Bendigo
★

This vineyard is best known for big, muscular, complex Shiraz and Shiraz-based reds.

✓ *Shiraz* (Georgia's Paddock) • *Shiraz-Cabernet Franc* (Emily's Paddock)

KARA KARA
St. Arnaud
★ ⓥ

Although established since 1977, I must confess that I have only just come across Kara Kara, which seems to be doing good things with Sauvignon Blanc, pure and blended.

✓ *Sauvignon Blanc • Sauvignon-Sémillon* (Fumé Blanc)

LILLYDALE VINEYARDS
Yarra Valley
★ Ⓥ

Owned by McWilliams, Lillydale produces a rich and stylish Chardonnay, which is great value for a Yarra Valley wine. Although I have heard good things about this winery's Gewürztraminer, I am wary of New World opinions of that varietal, but check it out – I will.

✓ *Chardonnay*

MARION'S VINEYARD
Tasmania
★

Mark and Marion Semmens established this winery in the backwoods of Tasmania, with an idyllic view over the Tamar Valley.

✓ *Cabernet Sauvignon*

MEADOWBANK VINEYARD
Tasmania
★

Classic cherry-flavoured Pinot Noir just north of Hobart.

✓ *Chardonnay • Pinot Noir*

MERRICKS ESTATE
Mornington Peninsula
★ ✫

Consistently stunning Shiraz!

✓ *Shiraz • Cabernet Sauvignon*

MILBURN PARK
See Alambie Wine Company

MITCHELTON VINTNERS
Goulburn Valley
★ ✫ Ⓥ

This winery is owned by Petaluma. Innovative Rhône-style blends are adding to Mitchelton's reputation as one of Australia's greatest value-for-money brands. All it needs now is a couple of expensive, top-notch wines of megastar quality and it will become an unstoppable force.

✓ *Marsanne* (Reserve)
• *Marsanne-Viognier-Roussanne* (III)
• *Merlot* (Chinaman's Ridge)
• *Riesling* (Blackwood Park)
• *Shiraz* (Print Label)
• *Shiraz-Mourvèdre-Grenache* (III)

MOORILLA ESTATE
Tasmania
★ ✫

This pioneering Tasmanian winery still produces fabulous Chardonnay and exhilarating Riesling. New winemaker Alain Rousseau has lifted the quality even further.

✓ *Chardonnay*
• *Riesling* (including Botrytis)

MORRIS WINES
Rutherglen
★★ Ⓥ

Mick Morris is one of the real characters of the Australian wine trade and his Liqueur Muscats and Tokays are some of the greatest, some say the very greatest, wines of their type. Morris Wines is now owned by Orlando.

✓ *Liqueur Muscat* (especially Show Blend, Very Old)
• *Liqueur Tokay* (especially Cellar Door, Old Premium, Show Blend)

MOUNTAIN CREEK
Pyrenees

Rich, ripe, and exotic Sauvignon can be produced here.

✓ *Sauvignon Blanc*

MOUNT AVOCA VINEYARD
Avoca
★

The father-and-son team John and Matthew Barry make some vividly fruity wines here, although they can go over the top with Sauvignon Blanc.

✓ *Cabernet Sauvignon*
• *Sauvignon Blanc*
• *Shiraz*

MOUNT LANGHI GHIRAN
Great Western
★ Ⓥ

This vineyard produces hugely rich, extremely ripe, blockbusting reds, particularly Shiraz.

✓ *Merlot • Shiraz*

MOUNT MARY VINEYARD
Yarra Valley
★★

Only small quantities of reds are made at Mount Mary, but these are outstanding with a well-deserved cult-following.

✓ *Pinot Noir*
• *Cabernet* (red Bordeaux-style)

MOUNT PRIOR VINEYARD
Rutherglen

Founded in 1860 and re-established in 1974, Mount Prior is best for white wines.

✓ *Chardonnay • Liqueur Muscat*

MURRINDINI
Murrindini
★ ✫ ✫

Owner-winemaker Hugh Cuthbertson makes wines of an extraordinary consistency and quality, from a tiny vineyard between the Yarra Valley and the Strathbogie Ranges

✓ *Cabernets* (red Bordeaux style)
• *Chardonnay*

OAKRIDGE ESTATE
Yarra Valley
★ ✫

I have in the past enjoyed excellent Chardonnay, but Merlot is the best wine here.

✓ *Chardonnay • Merlot* (Reserve)

PARINGA ESTATE
Mornington Peninsula
★ ✫

Established in 1985, Lindsay McCall's Paringa Estate is one of the fastest-rising stars of Mornington Peninsula.

✓ *Pinot Noir • Shiraz*

PASSING CLOUDS
Bendigo
★ Ⓥ

I gave up smoking when my father caught me at the age of 14, but the name of this winery brought back memories of Passing Cloud cigarettes, which I purchased only because of the attractive packet. It gave me great pleasure, then, to find that this winery makes great Shiraz-Cabernet.

✓ *Shiraz-Cabernet*

PIPERS BROOK VINEYARD
Tasmania
★ ✫ Ⓥ

This winery continues to produce delightful, stylish wines of considerable finesse and quality.

Wines under second label Ninth Island sell at higher prices than some wineries' first labels.

✓ *Pinot Noir • Chardonnay*
• *Riesling • Sauvignon Blanc*

ROTHERHYTHE
Tasmania
❓

A variable producer whose wines, especially Cabernet Sauvignon, can be very good when on form.

ST. HUBERTS
Yarra Valley
★ ✫ Ⓥ

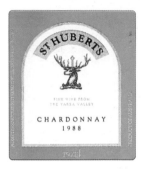

This winery does not hit the high notes it once did, but is more consistent in quality. It is now owned by Beringer-Blass.

✓ *Cabernet Sauvignon*
• *Chardonnay*

SCOTCHMAN'S HILL
Geelong
★ Ⓥ

This winery is owned by David and Vivienne Browne, whose Burgundian-style specialist vineyard and winery overlook the Bellarine Peninsula and benefit from cool maritime breezes.

✓ *Chardonnay • Pinot Noir*

SEPPELT GREAT WESTERN
Great Western
★★ Ⓥ

This winery produces expertly made cheap lime and lavender fizz, great value inexpensive-premium *cuvées*, a fine-quality upmarket Salinger *cuvée*, as well as one of Australia's biggest, brashest, and most brilliant sparkling "Burgundies". At the basic and middle level, sister brand Seaview has a definite edge, but both make underrated still wines and deserve their star ratings. It is part of the giant Southcorp group.

✓ *Cabernet Sauvignon* (Dorrien)
• *Chardonnay* (Partalunga)
• *Pinot Noir* (Sunday Creek)
• *Shiraz* (Chalambar) • *Riesling*
• *Sparkling Wine* (Chardonnay Blanc de Blancs, Pinot Rosé, Premier Cuvée and especially, Salinger, Shiraz, Show Reserve Burgundy)

SEVILLE ESTATE
Yarra Valley
★ ✫

This winery made its name on minuscule releases of its superb botrytis Riesling, but now concentrates on the more marketable premium varietals. Owned by Brokenwood.

✓ *Chardonnay*
• *Pinot Noir*
• *Shiraz*

SORRENBERG
Beechworth
★

This winery is located east of Milawa. Sorrenberg's owner-winemaker Barry Morey began making wine as recently as 1989, but has quickly achieved success.

✓ *Cabernet Sauvignon*
• *Chardonnay*
• *Sauvignon-Sémillon*

STANTON & KILLEEN
Rutherglen
★★ ⓥ

According to *The Penguin Good Australian Wine Guide*, this firm is affectionately known as "Stomp it and Kill it", and this certainly does convey the unashamed style of these brashly flavoured wines.

✓ *Cabernet-Shiraz* (Moodemere)
• *Liqueur Muscat*
• *Liqueur Tokay*
• *Port* (Old Tawny)
• *Shiraz* (Moodemere)

STONIER'S
Mornington Peninsula
★★

This winery has thankfully changed name since the late 1980s, when confusingly it was one of two wineries named Merricks. Stonier's is now majority owned by Petaluma, and still makes excellent wines under Tod Dexter.

✓ *Cabernet Sauvignon*
• *Chardonnay*
• *Pinot Noir*

SUMMERFIELD
Pyrenees
★★ ⓥ

Some of the best red wines in the Pyrenees are made here.

✓ *Cabernet Sauvignon*
• *Shiraz*

TALTARNI VINEYARDS
Pyrenees
★★

Taltarni's wines are always rich in extract, but so lean they demand time in bottle. Sometimes they never come together, but when they do, they can rank among Australia's

best wines. Taltarni is Aboriginal for "red earth", the soil in this vineyard being an iron-rich siliceous clay and duly red.

✓ *Cabernet Sauvignon*
• *Merlot*
• *Sauvignon Blanc* (Fumé Blanc)
• *Shiraz*

TARRAWARRA
Yarra Valley
★★★ ⓥ

The marvellously rich and complex wines of this Burgundian-style specialist are neither cheap nor very expensive, although they are difficult to find. Its second label Tunnel Hill is superb.

✓ *Chardonnay*
• *Pinot Noir*

VIRGIN HILLS VINEYARDS
Macedon
★★

The creation of Hungarian-born Melbourne restaurateur Tom Lazar, this "one-wine-winery" owned by Marcel Gilbert must be unique in Australia. The wine had no indication of varietal or generic character; in fact it was approximately 75 per cent Cabernet Sauvignon, blended with Syrah and a little Merlot and Malbec. Lazar did not even learn his winemaking from a correspondence course, he simply read a book, planted a vineyard, and made his wine. When he retired, Mark Sheppard took over the wine-making, and continued to follow Lazar's methods, making it one of the country's best. Sheppard left to join Vincorp, but returned when Vincorp purchased Virgin Hill in 1998. At that time Vincorp made it clear that "one-wine-winery" would be turned into a brand. However, Vincorp went bust and the future of Virgin Hill was uncertain at the time of writing.

✓ *Virgin Hills*

WA-DE-LOCK VINEYARDS
Gippsland
★★ ⓥ

Since establishing these vineyards in 1989, owner-winemaker Graeme Little has gone from producing poor-quality wines to making some that are very classy.

✓ *Cabernet-Merlot* • *Pinot Noir*

WARRENMANG VINEYARD
Pyrenees
★ ⓥ

The Grand Pyrenees does not indicate the nature of its blend on the label, but contains Merlot, Cabernet franc, and Shiraz.

✓ *Chardonnay* • *Grand Pyrenees* (classic red blend) • *Shiraz*
• *Cabernet Sauvignon*

WATER WHEEL
Bendigo
★ ⓥ

Owner-winemaker Peter Cumming established this vineyard in 1972, and makes well-crafted wines at very reasonable prices.

✓ *Cabernet Sauvignon*
• *Chardonnay*

WILD DUCK CREEK
Bendigo
★ ⓥ

Wild Duck Creek was established in 1980 by David and Diana Anderson, whose rich, yet elegant red wines are fast developing a reputation.

✓ *Cabernets* (Alan's)
• *Shiraz* (Springflat)

WILLOW CREEK
Mornington Peninsula
★

Willow Creek is housed in a historic building with magnificent views.

✓ *Cabernet Sauvignon*
• *Chardonnay* (Tulum)

YARRABANK
★★

This venture is co-owned by Yering Station and Champagne Devaux and produces sparkling wines that are capable of ageing much longer than most Australian fizz.

YARRA BURN VINEYARDS
Yarra Junction
❓

Now owned by BRL Hardy, this range is currently being restructured thus judgement is reserved.

YARRA EDGE
Yarra Valley
★ ⓥ

Although this vineyard was established in 1982, wines bearing the Yarra Edge label commenced with the 1990 vintage. Now leased to Yering Station, where the wines are made.

✓ *Cabernets*

YARRA RIDGE
Yarra Valley
★

Founded in 1982, Beringer-Blass now has a controlling interest, but continues to make elegant red wines in a firm yet accessible style.

✓ *Cabernet Sauvignon* • *Shiraz*

YARRA VALLEY HILLS
Yarra Valley
★★ ⓥ

Established as recently as 1993, owner-winemaker Terry Hill has already turned out some truly fine, relatively inexpensive wines.

✓ *Pinot Noir* • *Riesling*

YARRA YARRA
Yarra Valley
★★

So good they named it twice!

✓ *Cabernet Blend* (Cabernets)
• *Cabernet Sauvignon* (Reserve)

YARRA YERING
Yarra Valley
★★

The first in a number of Yarra-named wineries, Yarra Yering was founded in 1969 by Dr. Bailey Carrodus, whose blended reds are legendary.

✓ *Cabernet Sauvignon*
• *Chardonnay*

✓ *Chardonnay*
• *Dry Red No.1* (Cabernet-based blend)
• *Dry Red No. 2* (Shiraz-based blend)
• *Pinot Noir*

YELLOWGLEN VINEYARDS
Ballarat
★★ ⓥ

This operation was started by Australian Ian Home and *champenois* Dominique Landragin, but is now owned by Beringer-Blass. The wines showed excellent potential ten years ago and have improved enormously, especially since the early 1990s.

✓ *Sparkling Wines* (Crémant, Pinot-Chardonnay, Vintage Brut, Vintage Victoria, "Y" Chardonnay Pinot Noir Premium)

YERINGBERG
Yarra Valley
★★

The oldest winery in the Yarra Valley, Yeringberg was established in 1862 by Guillaume, Baron de Pury, and re-established in 1969 by his grandson, Guillaume de Pury, who has consistently produced fine, sometimes exceptionally fine wines.

✓ *Dry Red* (red Bordeaux style)
• *Pinot Noir*
• *Marsanne*

SOUTH AUSTRALIA

This is Australia's most productive wine region, accounting for almost 50 per cent of the country's total wine output, including the majority of its cheapest wines, although this does not restrict it to the bottom end of the market – South Australia also makes some of the country's finest and most expensive wines.

THE BEGINNINGS OF THIS VAST MARKET-GARDEN of grapes can be traced back to a certain Barton Hack, who planted vines at Launceston in lower North Adelaide in 1837. In the following year a George Stevenson established a vineyard in North Adelaide. However, Hack's vines were removed in 1840, in order to make way for urbanization, starting an incessant trend. Virtually all of Adelaide's metropolitan vineyards have since been uprooted in the name of the city's creeping concrete progress, leaving part of just one, Penfold's historic Magill. The variety of the state's output ranges from Grange, Australia's greatest and most expensive wine, to the cheapest and least heard-of cask-wines.

REMUAGE, BAROSSA VALLEY
Giant gyropalettes are indicative of the scale of the operation at the Southcorp-owned Barossa Valley cooperative.

SOUTH AUSTRALIA
See also p.518
The state perches over the eastern half of the Great Australian Bight, a bay whose climatic influence decreases further inland.

Key

- Wineries
- Clare/Watervale
- Riverland
- Adelaide Plains
- Barossa-Eden and Adelaide Hills
- Southern Vales-Langhorne Creek
- Coonawarra
- Keppoch/Padthaway
- ~~~ State boundary
- ▲ Height above sea level (metres)

km 20 40 60 80 100
miles 20 40 60

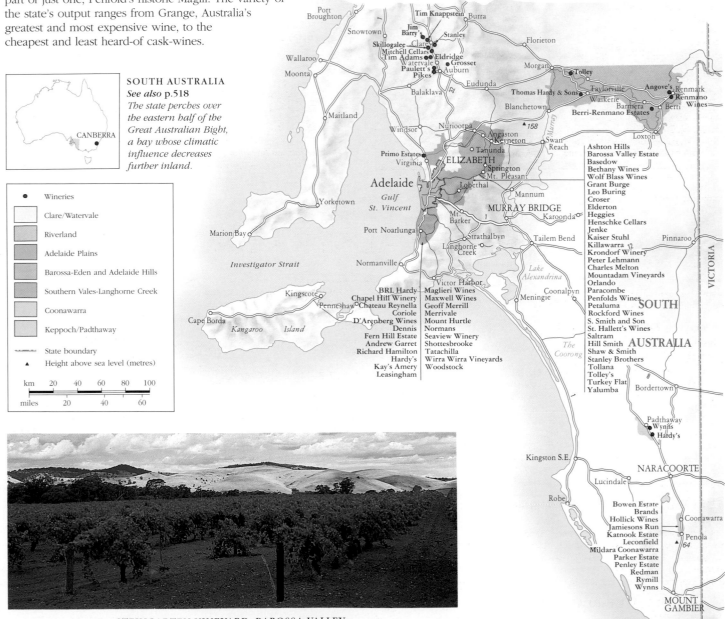

STEINGARTEN VINEYARD, BAROSSA VALLEY
Wide-spaced vines at Orlando's Steingarten vineyard set against the backdrop of the rolling Eastern Barossa Ranges.

FACTORS AFFECTING TASTE AND QUALITY

LOCATION
This is the southern central part of the country, with Australia's five other mainland states to the east, north, and west, and half of the Great Australian Bight forming the coastline to the south.

CLIMATE
The climate varies greatly, from the intensely hot continental conditions of the largely cask-wine producing Riverland area, through the less extreme but still hot and dry Barossa Valley, to the cooler but still dry Coonawarra region. Sea breezes reduce humidity in the plains around Adelaide, which receives low annual rainfall, as does the whole region.

ASPECT
Vines are grown on all types of land, from the flat coastal plain around Adelaide and flat interior Riverland district to the varied locations of the Barossa Valley, where vines are grown from the valley floor at 250 m (820 ft), up to the slopes to a maximum of 600 m (1,970 ft) at Pewsey Vale.

SOIL
Soils are varied, ranging from sandy loam over red earth (terra rossa) on a limestone-marl subsoil in the Adelaide and Riverland areas (the latter having suffered for some time from excess salinity); through variable sand, loam, and clay topsoils, over red-brown loam and clay subsoils in the Barossa Valley, to the thin layer of weathered limestone, stained red by organic and mineral matter, over a thick limestone subsoil in the Coonawarra area.

VITICULTURE AND VINIFICATION
This varies enormously, from the bulk-production methods of the large modern wineries that churn out vast quantities of clean, well-made, inexpensive wine from grapes grown in Riverland's high-yielding irrigated vineyards, to the use of new oak on restricted yields of premium quality varietals by top estate wineries in areas such as Coonawarra, the Barossa Valley, and the up-and-coming Padthaway or Keppoch districts, which produce some of Australia's greatest wines.

GRAPE VARIETIES
Cabernet sauvignon, Chardonnay, Crouchen, Doradillo, Frontignan, Grenache, Malbec, Mataro, Merlot, Muscat d'Alexandrie, Palomino, Pedro Ximénez, Pinot noir, Rhine riesling, Sémillon, Shiraz, Sauvignon blanc, Gewürztraminer, Ugni blanc

THE HARVEST, BAROSSA VALLEY
Many of the best premium varietal producers in South Australia have some sort of interest in the Barossa Valley, the state's most important wine area.

THE APPELLATIONS OF
SOUTH AUSTRALIA

ADELAIDE
A zonal GI that encompasses Adelaide Metropolitan Area and the Adelaide Plains.

ADELAIDE HILLS
Subregions: *Gumeracha, Lenswood, Piccadilly Valley*

This region in the hills overlooks Adelaide, the Adelaide Plains, and McLarenVale. Along with Clare Valley, it is part of the much larger Mount Lofty Ranges GI. With vineyards situated at 450 metres (1,460 feet), there are many different *terroirs* according to the soil and aspect, but in general Chardonnay, Riesling, Pinot Noir, and bottle-fermented sparkling wines are the classics here. Cabernet Franc and Merlot seem to fare better than Cabernet Sauvignon.

ADELAIDE METROPOLITAN AREA
This area has been urbanized to such an extent that very few vines are left; those that remain belong to Penfolds' legendary Magill vineyard, the one-time base for Penfolds' remarkable Grange Hermitage. Wines produced solely from Magill grapes are now sold as The Magill Estate.

ADELAIDE PLAINS
The Adelaide Plains is described by James Halliday as "one of the least appealing, most frequently visited regions in Australia". It is, as he also states, laser flat and searingly hot in summer. Nevertheless, its best winery, Primo Estate, makes exceedingly good wines.

BAROSSA
A zonal GI encompassing the Barossa Valley and Eden Valley regional GIs.

BAROSSA VALLEY
This district is the oldest and most important of South Australia's premium varietal areas. With a hot, dry climate, the vines mostly grow on flatlands at an altitude of between 240 and 300 metres (800–1,000 feet) and produce firmly structured reds in the very best traditional Australian styles. It is strange, therefore, that more white-grape vines, particularly Rhine riesling, are planted than red. The white wines range from full bodied to quite delicate.

CLARE VALLEY
Subregions: *Auburn, Clare, Hill River, Polish Hill River, Sevenhill, Watervale*

Clare Valley is the most northerly vinegrowing district in South Australia and its climate is correspondingly hotter and drier. Many of the vineyards are not irrigated, however, and the result is a low yield of very intensely flavoured, big-bodied, often strapping wines. The Rhine riesling is the valley's most important variety

and botrytis-affected wines are rich, fine, and mellifluous. Other good wines are Cabernet Sauvignon (often blended with Malbec or Shiraz), Sémillon, and Shiraz.

COONAWARRA
This famous district is the most southerly in South Australia. Coonawarra is Aboriginal for "wild honeysuckle"; it also happens to be easy on Anglo-Saxon tongues and this has been useful when it comes to marketing wine from the district in English-speaking countries. The Coonawarra's vines grow on red earth, or *terra rossa*, over a limestone subsoil with a high water table, and this combination, together with the district's unique climate, is responsible for some of Australia's outstanding Cabernet Sauvignon wines. However, in a mistaken bid to make wines better suited to more sophisticated markets, some larger companies have tended to pick too early and make the wines too light.

EDEN VALLEY
Subregions: *High Eden, Springton*

Part of the Mount Lofty Ranges, together with the Adelaide Hills region, the Eden Valley has a rockier, more acid soil than that found in the neighbouring Barossa Valley, with a much wetter climate. Whilst the pre-eminence of

Henschke might suggest that the Eden Valley is world-class Shiraz country, that is very much due to one vineyard, Hill of Grace, and the 130-year-old Shiraz vines planted there. Above all else, Eden Valley is best known for Riesling, and deservedly so.

FAR NORTH

Everything north of an imaginary line running east from Anxious Bay.

FLEURIEU

This zonal GI consists of the peninsula jutting out towards Kangaroo Island, and encompasses the regional GIs of Currency Creek, Kangaroo Island, Langhorne Creek and McClaren Vale.

LANGHORNE CREEK

This once tiny, traditional area, located southeast of Adelaide on the Bremer River, has expanded rapidly since 1995, when Orlando started sourcing grapes from here for huge brands such as Jacob's Creek. This district was named after Alfred Langhorne, a cattle-herder from New South Wales, who arrived in 1841. The meagre rainfall of 35 centimetres (14 inches) means that the vineyards require irrigation. This area is reputed for its beefy reds and for its dessert wines.

LIMESTONE COAST

This zonal GI encompasses the regional GIs of Bordertown, Coonawarra, Mount Benson, Padthaway and Wrattonbully.

LOWER MURRAY

A zonal GI that encompasses the regional GI of Riverland.

MCLAREN VALE

Subregion: *Clarendon*

The rolling green hills of McLaren Vale's vineyards and orchards begin south of Adelaide and extend to south of Morphett Vale. With 56 centimetres (22 inches) of rain and a complex range of soils, including sand, sandy loam, limestone, red clay, and many forms of rich alluvium, there is great potential for quality in a range of styles from various grapes. This is perhaps why it is the most volatile wine district, attracting a lot of new talent, but also seeing wineries close or change hands. McLaren Vale produces big red wines of excellent quality from Shiraz and Cabernet sauvignon (often blended with Merlot), with some increasingly fresh and vital white wines from Chardonnay, Sémillon, and Sauvignon blanc. Fine dessert wines are also produced.

MOUNT LOFTY RANGES

This newly created zonal GI encompasses the regional GIs of Adelaide Hills and Clare Valley.

PADTHAWAY

This district is also known as Keppoch. The development of the area has been carried out almost exclusively by the larger companies (Hardy's built Australia's largest winery for 20 years here in 1998), using a considerable amount of marketing muscle. Provided the smaller businesses are not unreasonably prevented from buying land within the area, this should benefit all types of operation. The success of small ventures should be welcomed by the larger companies because it endorses the intrinsic quality-potential of the district they are promoting.

POLISH HILL RIVER

This appellation is used by some wineries in the Clare Valley region.

RIVERLAND

The wine areas that cluster around the Murray River in Victoria continue into South Australia with Riverland, South Australia's irrigated answer to Riverina in New South Wales and Mildura in Victoria. Although a lot of cheap cask-wine is made in the Riverland district, rarely is a bad one encountered. Cabernet sauvignon, Cabernet sauvignon-Malbec, Chardonnay, and Rhine riesling all fare well, and some relatively inexpensive wines are produced in the area.

SPRINGTON

Part of Eden Valley GI, Springton lies just south of the valley itself and on the edge of the Adelaide Hills. The wine's quality is good, with Shiraz being the best.

WATERVALE

Effectively the smaller, southern half of the Clare Valley GI, the Watervale district is best known for its fine Shiraz and Cabernet Sauvignon, either pure or blended.

THE WINE PRODUCERS OF
SOUTH AUSTRALIA

TIM ADAMS
Clare Valley
★ ☆ ⓥ

Tim Adams's sensational pure-lime Sémillon is probably Australia's very greatest example of a high-quality, ready-to-drink wine, which is made from this grape.

✓ *Sémillon* • *Shiraz* (Aberfeldy)
• *The Fergus* (classic red blend)

ANGOVE'S
Riverland
★ ⓥ

This long-established winery makes many of the UK's best-value own-label wines, but its own *cuvées* are brilliant bargain-wines that cost just a little more.

✓ *Cabernet Sauvignon* (Sarnia Farm) • *Chardonnay* (Classic Reserve) • *Colombard* • *Riesling* • *Shiraz-Cabernet* (Butterfly Ridge)

ASHTON HILLS
Adelaide Hills
★ ☆ ⓥ

Owner-winemaker Stephen George has honed his style into one of

great elegance over the period since this winery was established in the early 1990s. The white wines from this producer are always very crisp, especially its Chablis-like Chardonnay.

✓ *Cabernet Merlot* • *Chardonnay* • *Pinot Noir* • *Riesling* • *Sparkling wines* (Salmon Brut)

BAROSSA VALLEY ESTATE
Barossa Valley
★

Owned by BRL Hardy, Barossa Valley Estate continues to make one of the biggest, oakiest sparkling Shiraz in the country from the low-yielding Barossa vineyards of Elmor Roehr and Elmore Schulz (E & E).

✓ *Shiraz* (Black Pepper)
• *Sparkling wines*
(E & E Sparkling Shiraz)

JIM BARRY'S WINES
Clare Valley
★ ★ ⓥ

Run by Mark and Peter, who are the sons of the eponymous Jim Barry, and their top Shiraz, The Amagh, is one of Australia's greatest wines. It is also one of the country's most expensive wines and, at one-third of the price and almost as good quality as The Amagh, the McRae Wood Shiraz is better value. Virtually every other wine produced by Jim Barry is sold at bargain prices.

✓ *Chardonnay* (especially Personal Selection) • *Port* (Old Walnut Tawny, Sentimental Bloke) • *Riesling* (Watervale) • *Shiraz* (especially The Amagh, McRae Wood)

BASEDOW WINES
Barossa Valley
★ ⓥ

This long-established winery produces brilliant bargains for drinkers of modern-style wines.

✓ *Cabernet Sauvignon*
• *Sémillon*
• *Shiraz Chardonnay*

BERRI-RENMANO ESTATES
Riverland
★ ⓥ

This huge winery now belongs to BRL Hardy, but it still produces bargain-basement wines under the Berri Estates brand, as well as various own-label wines, while its superior wines that are slightly more expensive – but of even greater value – are sold as Renmano.

✓ *Cabernet Sauvignon* (Chardonnay)
• *Port*

BETHANY WINES
Barossa Valley
★ ☆ ⓥ

Bethany produces some big, chewy, and often incredibly jammy red wines.

✓ *Cabernet-Merlot*
• *Grenache* (Pressings)
• *Riesling* (Late Harvest Cut, Steinbruch)

WOLF BLASS WINES
Barossa Valley
☆

This property is now part of Beringer-Blass, but its range is still huge and the wines are marketed as aggressively as ever. Wolf Blass wines are mostly graded according to the colour of their label, which works well enough, although the Yellow Label tends to be more cheap than cheerful these days.

✓ *Cabernet Sauvignon-Shiraz* (Black Label, Grey Label) • *Riesling* (Gold Label) • *Shiraz* (Brown Label)

BOWEN ESTATE
Coonawarra
★☆Ⓥ

Doug Bowen, owner of Bowen Estate, continues to produce some truly exceptional wines.

✓ *Cabernet Sauvignon • Cabernet Sauvignon-Merlot-Cabernet Franc • Chardonnay • Shiraz*

BRANDS
Coonawarra

Since McWilliams purchased Brands, only the Cabernet Sauvignon gives me the degree of pleasure that most of these wines used to, although they are still made by Jim Brand.

✓ *Cabernet Sauvignon* (Laira)

BRL HARDY
McLaren Vale

One of Australia's four largest wine producers, BRL Hardy owns: Berri Estate, Reynell, Hardy's, Houghton, Leasingham, Moondah Brook, Renmano, Stanley, and, in France, Chais Baumière and Philippe de Baudin.

GRANT BURGE
Barossa Valley
★★Ⓥ

Although owner-winemaker Grant Burge launched this venture as recently as 1988, he has quickly built up a reputation for the richness, quality, and consistency of the wines he produces.

✓ *Cabernet-Mataro* (Oakland) • *Chardonnay • Merlot* • *Riesling • Sémillon* (Old Vine) • *Sémillon-Shiraz* (Oakland) • *Shiraz* (Old Vine but especially Meshach) • *Shiraz-Cabernet* (Oakland)

LEO BURING
★Ⓥ

Orlando took over the Leo Buring winery (which now operates as Richmond Grove), but Southcorp bought the Leo Buring name. Although just one of Southcorp's many brands, Leo Buring has kept its identity, and continued to produce great-value wines.

✓ *Cabernet Sauvignon* (DR 150) • *Riesling* (Eden Valley, Watervale)

CHAPEL HILL WINERY
McLaren Vale
★

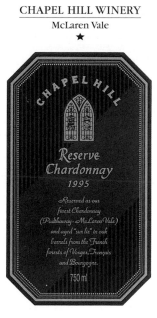

This Chapel Hill has no connection with the Australian-made wines of the same name from Hungary, but instead derives its name from the de-consecrated hilltop chapel which is used as its winery.

✓ *Cabernet Sauvignon* • *Chardonnay • Shiraz*

CORIOLE
McLaren Vale
★★Ⓥ

This is an underrated producer of full-throttle reds, including the New World's best Sangiovese.

✓ *Cabernet Sauvignon* • *Cabernet-Shiraz* (Redstone) • *Chardonnay • Chenin Blanc* • *Mary Kathleen* (red Bordeaux style) • *Sangiovese • Shiraz*

CROSER
See Petaluma

D'ARENBERG WINES
McLaren Vale
★★

Even more voluptuous than before. Stunning Shiraz, unbelievable Grenache.

✓ *Chardonnay • Grenache* • *Shiraz*

DENNIS
McLaren Vale

I have not tasted these wines, but I have heard great things from a very reliable source about the Cabernet Sauvignon and Shiraz.

ELDERTON
Barossa Valley
★★Ⓥ

Established in 1984, Elderton has gained close to superstar status since the early 1990s for its very impressive Cabernet Sauvignon.

✓ *Cabernet Sauvignon* • *Cabernet-Shiraz-Merlot* • *Merlot* • *Shiraz* (especially Command) • *Sparkling wines* (Pinot Pressings)

ELDRIDGE
Clare Valley
★★

Tim Adams acts as consultant to this up-and-coming winery.

✓ *Cabernet Sauvignon* • *Riesling* (Watervale)

ANDREW GARRETT
McLaren Vale
★☆Ⓥ

Ordinary basic wines sell on the reputation of this winery's best *cuvées*, which are themselves inexpensive, and represent the best value in the range. Andrew Garrett is now part of Beringer-Blass.

✓ *Cabernet-Merlot* • *Cabernet Sauvignon* • *Riesling* • *Sémillon* (wood aged) • *Shiraz* (Black, Bold Style)

GROSSET
Clare Valley
★★☆

Owner-winemaker Jeffrey Grosset makes skilfully crafted wines.

✓ *Cabernet-Merlot* (Gaia) • *Chardonnay* (Piccadilly) • *Riesling* (Polish Hill)

RICHARD HAMILTON
McLaren Vale
★★☆Ⓥ

Plastic surgeon Dr. Richard Hamilton makes stunning wines. However, the emphasis in quality has definitely shifted from white to red. He also owns Leconfield.

✓ *Cabernet Sauvignon* (Hut Block) • *Cabernet-Merlot • Chardonnay* • *Grenache-Shiraz* (Burton Vineyard) • *Shiraz* (Old Vines)

HARDY'S
McLaren Vale
★★☆Ⓥ

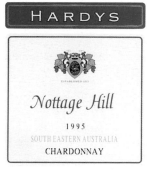

This large company is the basis of the BRL Hardy group (*see* BRL Hardy), which continues to produce a number of wines under various labels bearing the Hardy's name. This diverse selection ranges from penny-pinchers through penny-savers to premium-quality wines. Hardy's Eileen Hardy Chardonnay (a wine named after the late but much-loved matriarch of the family for 40 years) consistently retains its reputation as one of Australia's very greatest wines.

✓ *Cabernet Sauvignon* (Coonawarra, Thomas Hardy) • *Chardonnay* (Eileen Hardy) • *Grenache* (Bankside) • *Port* (Show, Tall Ships Tawny) • *Shiraz* (Eileen Hardy)

HEGGIES
See Yalumba

HENSCHKE
Eden Valley
★★

One of Australia's older wine producers, Henschke makes wines that have become turbo-charged over the last ten years, particularly the reds, yet they manage to retain an amazing amount of finesse for their size and weight.

✓ *Cabernet Sauvignon* (Cyril Henschke) • *Chardonnay* (especially Croft's) • *Merlot-Cabernet* (Abbot's Prayer Lenswood Vineyard) • *Riesling* (especially Green's Hill) • *Sémillon • Shiraz* (Mount Edelstone, Hill of Grace)

HILL-SMITH
See Yalumba

HOLLICK WINES
Coonawarra
★Ⓥ

Owner-viticulturist Ian Hollick set up his venture in 1983 and has produced some fresh, clean, well-focused wines, including a red Bordeaux-style blend that is simply sold by its Coonawarra appellation.

✓ *Cabernet Sauvignon* (Ravenswood) • *Chardonnay* • *Coonawarra* (red Bordeaux-style) • *Riesling* (Botrytis) • *Sparkling Wines* (Cornel Vintage Brut)

JAMIESONS RUN
Coonawarra
★★Ⓥ

One of the most underrated brands in the Beringer-Blass stable.

✓ *Coonawarra* (red Bordeaux style) • *Chardonnay* • *Sauvignon Blanc*

JENKE
Barossa Valley
★☆Ⓥ

This winery produces one of Australia's very best Cabernet Franc wines. The whites need to improve, however.

✓ *Cabernet Franc*

KATNOOK ESTATE
Coonawarra
★★

Katnook is an upmarket producer of intensely flavoured wines that display remarkable finesse. Less expensive wines are sold under the Riddoch label (which should not be confused with Wynn's John Riddoch), and some Riddoch reds are almost the same outstanding quality.

✓ *Cabernet Sauvignon • Merlot* • *Riesling • Sauvignon Blanc* • *Riddoch* (Cabernet Sauvignon, Shiraz)

KAY'S AMERY
McLaren Vale
★✦♥

Kay's Amery is proving a fast-rising star, thanks in no small part to a block of incredibly low-yielding Shiraz vines planted in 1982!

✓ *Grenache* • *Shiraz* (Block 6)

KNAPPSTEIN
Clare Valley
★✦

Part of Petaluma, and although no longer under the helm of Tim Knappstein, who has moved to Lenswood in the Adelaide Hills, the wines produced here are going from strength to strength in the hands of Andrew Hardy.

✓ *Cabernet Sauvignon*
• *Riesling*
• *Shiraz*

KRONDORF
Barossa Valley
★✦♥

This brand belongs to the Beringer-Blass group and consists of a large range of extremely fine, excellent-value wines.

✓ *Cabernet Shiraz* (Show Reserve)
• *Chardonnay* (especially Show Reserve) *Riesling*
• *Sémillon* (Wood Aged)

LEASINGHAM
Clare Valley
★✦♥

Part of the BRL Hardy group, Leasingham makes wines that offer outstanding quality and value.

✓ *Cabernet-Malbec* (Bin 56)
• *Cabernet Sauvignon* (Classic Clare)
• *Shiraz* (Bin 61, Classic Shiraz, Domaine)

LECONFIELD
Coonawarra
★✦♥

Owned by Dr. Richard Hamilton (*see* Richard Hamilton), the wines are now made by his winemaker Philippa Treadwell.

✓ *Cabernet Sauvignon*
• *Shiraz*

PETER LEHMANN
Barossa Valley
★✦♥

Peter Lehmann is a large producer of excellent-value and mostly brilliant-quality wines.

✓ *Cabernet Sauvignon*
• *Cabernet-Malbec* (Cellar Collection) • *Shiraz* (especially Cellar Collection Stonewall)
• *Riesling* (Cellar Collection)
• *Sémillon*

MAGLIERI WINES
McLaren Vale
★✦♥

These are extraordinary bargain wines, which are at last finding their way into mainstream outlets on export markets. (Now owned by Beringer-Blass.)

✓ *Sémillon* (Ingleburn) • *Shiraz*

MAXWELL WINES
McLaren Vale
★✦♥

Founded in 1979, this is a fairly well-established winery, but has suddenly become an Aladdin's Cave of wonderful vinous treasures. Some stunningly rich wines are produced, especially under the top-of-the-range Mount Bold label.

✓ *Cabernet Sauvignon* (Lime Cave) • *Chardonnay* (especially Mount Bold)
• *Sémillon* • *Shiraz* (Ellen Street, Mount Bold, Reserve)

CHARLES MELTON
Barossa Valley
★✦♥

Most famous for his Châteauneuf-du-Pape-type blend, cheekily named Nine Popes, but all the reds produced here are high-flyers.

✓ *Cabernet Sauvignon* • *Nine Popes* (Grenache-Shiraz) • *Rose of Virginia* (Grenache-Cabernet blend) • *Shiraz*

GEOFF MERRILL
★

It is debatable which is the biggest, Geoff Merrill's reputation or his moustache, but there is no mistaking the quality of his wines. Merrill and Château Tahbilk are joint owners of this winery, which is now the primary brand. Second wines are sold under the Cockatoo Ridge label. Mount Hurtle is now an exclusive brand.

✓ *Chardonnay*
• *Sémillon-Chardonnay*

MERRIVALE
McLaren Vale
★

This property was established in 1971, but I have only just come across the wines of owner-winemaker Brian Light, who uses American oak in a delicious way.

✓ *Shiraz* (Tapestry)

MILDARA COONAWARRA
Coonawarra
★✦♥

These wines are now underrated due to the ever-expanding size of Beringer-Blass (*see* map p.528).

✓ *Cabernet-Malbec-Merlot* (Alexanders) • *Cabernet Sauvignon* (especially Alexanders)
• *Riesling* • *Shiraz* (Hermitage)

MITCHELL
Clare Valley
★✦

A small winery, Mitchell produces classic-quality wines, even from the somewhat common Grenache grape.

✓ *Cabernet Sauvignon* • *Grenache* (Growers) • *Shiraz* (Pepper Tree Vineyard) • *Riesling*

MOUNT HURTLE
McLaren Vale
★

Once Geoff Merrill's primary brand, these wines are still made by him in partnership with Château Tahbilk, but are now sold exclusively by the Vintage Cellars chain.

MOUNTADAM VINEYARD
Eden Valley
★✦

Recently purchased by LVMH, these wines are rich, yet lean and of excellent quality. They come from vineyards that once belonged to Adam Wynn, son of the founder of the almost legendary Wynns Coonawarra estate (now belonging to Southcorp). Adam Wynn is still very active in the day-to-day running of Mountadam. The sparkling wine is very well respected in Australia, but has for me been too dominated by malo aromas.

✓ *Cabernet-Merlot* (The Red)
• *Chardonnay* • *Pinot Noir*
• *Riesling*

NORMANS
McLaren Vale
★

This once family-owned winery became a public listed company in 1994, but still produces a wide range of consistently good wines, particularly reds.

✓ *Cabernet Sauvignon* (Chais Clairendon)
• *Port* (King William Tawny)
• *Shiraz* (Chais Clairendon)

ORLANDO
Barossa Valley
★♥

One of Australia's four largest wineries, Orlando is owned by Pernod-Ricard, so the French, probably wary of Australian competition on export markets, now own Craigmoor, Gramps, Hunter Hill, Jacob's Creek, Montrose, Morris, Orlando, Richmond Grove, Wickham Hill, and Wyndham Estate, and through these brands control a quarter of the country's production. Most wines are well made and good

value for money, including those not special enough to recommend below (the gluggy Carrington Rosé fizz and the crisp, fruity Jacob's Creek Sémillon-Chardonnay are typical), but Orlando can also produce the odd gem.

✓ *Cabernet Sauvignon* (Jacaranda Ridge, St. Hugo) • *Chardonnay* (RF) • *Port* (Liqueur) • *Shiraz* (Lawson's, Richmond Grove Limited Release) • *Shiraz-Cabernet* (Jacob's Creek)

PARACOMBE
Adelaide Hills
★♥

Owner-viticulturist-winemaker Paul Drogemuller produces one of Australia's best Cabernet Franc wines.

✓ *Cabernet Franc*

PARKER ESTATE
Coonawarra
★✦

Even though this winery has had several name changes, it has settled down to produce wines of a very high standard.

✓ *Cabernet Sauvignon*

PAULETT'S
Clare Valley
★

Owner-winemaker Neil Paulett produces beautifully focused white wines from his hilltop winery.

✓ *Riesling* (Polish Hill)
• *Sauvignon Blanc* (Polish Hill)

PENFOLDS WINES
Barossa Valley
★★✦♥

Penfolds' superb Grange (formerly Grange Hermitage) is Australia's finest wine, created by the late and legendary Max Schubert, and through this single masterpiece Penfolds itself has become a living legend. Naturally enough, Grange is a very expensive product – the price of a Bordeaux First Growth – but there are other far less expensive Penfolds wines you can enjoy that are minor masterpieces in their own right, and they include many great bargain wines, such as Rawson's Retreat and Koonunga Hill. There is also a reasonably priced, award-winning Organic range. However, some wines, such as Bin 707 and The Magill, have become very pricey (though nowhere near as expensive as Grange), and The Magill is, in terms of its origin, more Grange than Grange has ever been. It is now part of Southcorp. The most recent important addition to the range is RWT, which stands for Red Wine Trial. Positioned between Grange and Magill, RWT is a Shiraz of incredible finesse for its size.

✓ *Cabernet Sauvignon* (Bin 407, Coonawarra, but especially Bin 707) • *Cabernet-Shiraz* (Block 42, Bin 389)
• *Chardonnay* (Padthaway)
• *Port* (Grandfather)
• *Sémillon* (Barrel Fermented)
• *Shiraz* (Coonawarra Bin 28,

but especially Kalimna Bin 28, The Magill Estate, RWT, and, of course, Grange) • *Shiraz-Grenache-Mourvèdre* (Old Vine)

PENLEY ESTATE
Coonawarra
★ ✦

Established in 1988 by Kym Tolley (whose mother was a Penfolds and father a Tolley, hence the cheeky name of Penley), Penley Estates leans towards Penfolds in style as Kym's penchant is clearly for red wines.

✓ *Cabernet Sauvignon*
• *Shiraz-Cabernet*

PETALUMA
Adelaide hills
★★✦ Ⓥ

This is Brian Croser's domaine. It was Croser and his friend Tony Jordan who were the world's first flying winemakers, when this was a domestic function involving flying from one winery to another to act as wine consultants. Croser is a master of beautifully ripe, dry, classic-quality Rhine Riesling that ages slowly and gracefully, and he is one of the best sparkling-wine exponents in the New World (and in Oregon as well, *see* Argyle Winery p.483). He also produces Australia's best Merlot. His greatest strength is the excellence he achieves across the range. Petaluma might not have a Grange that scores 20 out of 20, but every one of its wines would rate at least 19. Excellent second wines are sold under the Bridgewater Mill label. Petaluma now owns outright Mitcheltons and Knappstein, some 75% of Smithbrook, and 70% of Stoniers.

✓ *Cabernet-Merlot* (Coonawarra)
• *Chardonnay* • *Merlot*
• *Riesling* (including occasional Botrytis)
• *Sparkling Wine* (Croser)

PIKES
Clare Valley
★★✦

These excellent-quality red wines are made by winemaker Neil Pike, formerly of Mitchell's.

✓ *Cabernet Sauvignon* • *Shiraz*

PRIMO
Adelaide Plains
✦

This is the only winery in the world named after a cabbage. Owner-winemaker Joe Grilli produces some good wines, but only his botrytized Riesling stands out as truly great.

✓ *Cabernet-Merlot* (Joseph)
• *Riesling* (Botrytis)
• *Sparkling Shiraz* (Joseph)

REDMAN
Coonawarra

Of Bruce Redman's four red wines, his straight Cabernet stands out.

✓ *Cabernet Sauvignon*

REYNELL
McLaren Vale
★★

This long-established firm now belongs to BRL Hardy; it was formerly known as Chateau Reynella. Wines are made and kept separately and are consistently fine.

✓ *Cabernet-Merlot* (Basket Pressed)
• *Chardonnay*
• *Merlot*
• *Port* (Vintage)

ROCKFORD WINES
Barossa Valley
★

The very traditional reds from low-yielding vines might be a bit soupy for some, but the Black Shiraz will be admired by anyone who enjoys Australia's wonderfully eccentric sparkling "Burgundy" style.

✓ *Grenache* (Dry Country)
• *Shiraz* (Basket Press)
• *Sparkling wine* (Black Shiraz)

RYMILL
Coonawarra
★

This property is owned and run by the descendants of John Riddoch, who planted the first Coonawarra vineyard in 1861.

✓ *Cabernet Sauvignon*
• *Chardonnay* • *Shiraz*

ST. HALLET'S WINES
Barossa Valley
★★✦

This long-established winery still makes splendidly rich wines.

✓ *Merlot* • *Shiraz* (Old Block from low-yielding 100-year-old vines)

SALTRAM
Barossa Valley
★

Once known for its red wines, Saltram now concentrates on luscious white wines, although they can sometimes be excessively rich.

✓ *Chardonnay* (Mamre Brook, Pinnacle) • *Port* (Mr. Pickwick's Particular) • *Riesling* (Pinnacle)
• *Sémillon* (Classic)

SEAVIEW WINERY
McLaren Vale
★★✦ Ⓥ

Now part of Southcorp, Seaview has the edge over its sister Seppelt

brand (with the exception of Salinger, Shiraz, and Show Reserve Burgundy), and has a growing reputation for its still wines, particularly under the recently launched, top-performing Seaview Edwards & Chaffey label. Southcorp seems to be trying to replace Seaview with the Edwards & Chaffey label, but Seaview is still big on export markets.

✓ *Cabernet Sauvignon* (Edwards & Chaffey) • *Chardonnay*
• *Riesling* • *Shiraz* (Edwards & Chaffey) • *Sparkling wine* (Pinot Noir Chardonnay)

SHAW & SMITH
Adelaide Hills
★✦ Ⓥ

This up-and-coming venture was set up in 1989 by Martin Shaw, who is well known for his flying winemaker activities, and Michael Hill-Smith, the first Australian to become a Master of Wine.

✓ *Chardonnay* • *Sauvignon Blanc*

SHOTTESBROKE
McLaren Vale
★★✦

A beautifully crafted Merlot, this is made by Nick Holmes, one of Rosemount's winemakers.

✓ *Merlot*

S. SMITH & SON
See Yalumba

STANLEY BROTHERS
Barossa Valley
★

This small operation got underway in the mid-1980s and produces rich, oaky Cabernet Sauvignon.

✓ *Cabernet Sauvignon*

TATACHILLA
McLaren Vale
★ Ⓥ

This long-established winery has recently blossomed under the management of Keith Smith, Wolf Blass's former marketing manager.

✓ *Chardonnay*
• *Grenache-Shiraz* (Keystone)
• *Shiraz-Cabernet* (Partners)

TOLLANA
Barossa Valley
★★✦ Ⓥ

Once entirely estate produced, Tollana is now part of Southcorp, but the wines have retained a certain identity, their quality remains very good, and the value is even greater.

✓ *Cabernet Sauvignon* (Bin TR222)
• *Chardonnay* (Eden Valley)
• *Riesling* (Botrytis) • *Sémillon*
• *Shiraz* (Hermitage Bin TR16)

TURKEY FLAT
Barossa Valley
★★✦

Turkey Flat is a recently established, high-flying winery producing several exceptionally rich, lush, complex red wines.

✓ *Grenache Noir* • *Shiraz*

WIRRA WIRRA
McLaren Vale
★★✦

Owner-viticulturist Greg Trott makes stylish reds of exciting quality.

✓ *Cabernet Sauvignon* (The Angelus)
• *Grenache-Shiraz* (Original)
• *Shiraz* (RSW)

WOODSTOCK
McLaren Vale
★★✦

Woodstock was established in 1974 by Doug Collet, whose son Scott makes wines with great flair.

✓ *Cabernet Sauvignon*
• *Sauvignon Blanc*
• *Sémillon*
• *Shiraz* (The Stocks)

WYNNS
Coonawarra
★★✦ Ⓥ

John Riddoch is supposed to be the top wine here, but, superb as it is, the straight Cabernet Sauvignon, although disappointingly thin during the 1980s, is often the epitome of elegance and always half the price of John Riddoch. Wynns is now part of Southcorp.

✓ *Cabernet-Shiraz-Merlot*
• *Cabernet Sauvignon*
• *Chardonnay*
• *Shiraz*
• *Riesling*

YALUMBA
Barossa Valley
★★✦ Ⓥ

Also known as S. Smith & Sons, this winery produces a vast range of styles and qualities. Yalumba is essentially a sparkling-wine brand, known for fizz, especially Rosé; a serious fizz called Yalumba D also exists and started to show potential in vintages of the late 1980s. The Heggies label is for wine grown from cool-climate grapes on high-altitude vineyards. Yalumba also owns Nautilus in New Zealand.

✓ *Heggies-Chardonnay*
• *Pinot Noir*
• *Riesling*
• *Viognier*
• *Hill-Smith Cabernet-Shiraz*
• *Chardonnay*
• *Riesling*
• *Sauvignon Blanc* (especially Air-Strip Block)
• *Yalumba-Cabernet-Shiraz* (The Signature)
• *Shiraz* (The Octavius)
• *Sparkling Wine* (Yalumba D)

WESTERN AUSTRALIA

Australia's most stylish wines come from the Margaret River region, where the climate and soil combine to produce grapes of unparalleled ripeness, with purity of fruit and balance, and its winemakers are fanatics who care only about quality and finesse.

As THIS STATE WAS FOUNDED a few years before Victoria and South Australia, the vineyards of Western Australia were established correspondingly earlier, in 1829, by either Thomas Waters or Captain John Septimus Roe. If the founder was Roe, he would not have made any wine; his vines were grown to produce table grapes and raisins. Waters, on the other hand, bought eight hectares (20 acres) of land that was to become Olive Farm.

Waters was a botanist who had learned his winemaking skills from the Boers in South Africa. He arrived in Australia with numerous seeds and plants, and by 1842 was making and bartering wine. In 1835, King William IV granted over 3,000 hectares (7,400 acres) of Swan Valley land to one Henry Revett Bland, who sold it to a trio of British army officers soon afterwards. These new owners, Messrs Lowis, Yule, and Houghton, were stationed in India, but Yule was despatched by the senior officer, Colonel Houghton, to run the property. Thus Houghton Wines, the first commercial winery in Western Australia, takes its name from a man who never set foot in the country.

The Swan Valley remained the hub of the state's wine industry and, with an influx of Europeans, notably from Dalmatia, all experienced in viticultural and winemaking techniques, the

VASSE FELIX WINERY
A modern pioneering vineyard in the Margaret River region, Australia's first appellation of origin, Vasse Felix still produces a fine Cabernet Sauvignon.

WESTERN AUSTRALIA
See also p.518
Situated at Australia's southwestern tip, this state's winemaking areas are remote from those to the east. The Margaret River region produces some of Australia's finest wines.

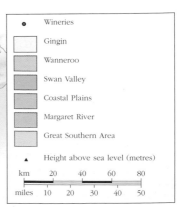

•	Wineries
	Gingin
	Wanneroo
	Swan Valley
	Coastal Plains
	Margaret River
	Great Southern Area
▲	Height above sea level (metres)

expertise of this industry grew. Gradually Mount Barker evolved as a wine area, then Frankland, and last, but certainly not least, the Margaret River. For most foreign wine drinkers, it is the last of these appellations that has given the most excitement and pleasure. There are still people in the more traditional winelands of southeastern Australia who refuse to accept the intrinsic quality of Margaret River, dismissing it as so far away that it might as well be in a different country, but that is just sour grapes.

FACTORS AFFECTING TASTE AND QUALITY

LOCATION
Western Australia's vine-growing areas include the Swan Valley behind Perth, the coastal plain mainly to the south of the city, and the Margaret River Valley and Lower Great Southern areas moving south and east around the coast to Albany.

CLIMATE
This is very variable, from the long, very hot, dry summers and short, wet winters of the Swan Valley, one of the hottest wine-growing areas of the world, through the Mediterranean-type conditions of the Margaret River, with a higher rainfall and summer heat tempered by ocean breezes, to the even cooler Lower Great Southern Area, which also has some light rainfall in summer. Ocean winds can exacerbate salinity problems and high coastal humidity helps with the development of botrytis.

ASPECT
Most vines are planted on the relatively flat coastal plain and river valley basins, but also on some rather more undulating hilly areas, such as those around Denmark and Mount Barker near Albany in the south and east of the region.

SOIL
Soils are fairly homogenous, being mainly deep, free-draining, alluvial, and clay loams over clay subsoils. The Southwest Coastal area has a fine, white-grey topsoil called tuart sand over a base of limestone with gravel in parts of the Margaret River.

VITICULTURE AND VINIFICATION
Drip irrigation is widespread because of the general lack of summer rain and the free-draining nature of the soil, although, ironically, winter water-logging due to clay subsoils is also a problem. Wide planting, mechanized harvesting, and the use of the most modern vinification techniques typify the area, which has generally concentrated on developing the cooler regions away from the Swan Valley in recent years. Well-equipped boutique wineries dominate the Margaret River wine regions.

GRAPE VARIETIES
Cabernet franc, Cabernet sauvignon, Chardonnay, Chenin blanc, Pinot noir, Malbec, Merlot, Riesling, Sauvignon blanc, Sémillon, Shiraz, Verdelho, Zinfandel

SWAN VALLEY VINEYARDS
This flat plain belongs to one of the hottest winegrowing regions in the world, and the first of Western Australia's wine districts to be established.

THE APPELLATIONS OF
WESTERN AUSTRALIA

BLACKWOOD VALLEY
This GI is the least known and one of the newest of Western Australia's wine regions. Sandwiched between Manjimup and Geographe, the first vineyard was Blackwood Crest in 1976 and by 2000 there were over 50 vineyards and five wineries. Cabernet Sauvignon is the most widely planted variety and the most successful, although Shiraz plantings are growing rapidly.

CENTRAL WESTERN AUSTRALIA
This zonal GI covers a vast area of the Darling Ranges, from the Great Southern GI to north of the Swan District, but size is the only impressive aspect of what is currently a viticultural wasteland.

EASTERN PLAINS, INLAND & NORTH OF WESTERN AUSTRALIA
Hardly rolls off the tongue, does it? I'll bet a pound to a penny that we won't see any wines sold under this ludicrous zonal GI, which bureaucratically covers all areas of Western Australia not already covered.

FRANKLAND
A small area on the western edge of the Great Southern Area, known for its Houghton Frankland River Winery. Good Cabernet sauvignon, and promising Rhine Riesling.

GEOGRAPHE
Formed by cutting off the northern and south-eastern extremities of the old Coastal Plains region, this GI is likely to adopt at least three subregions in the future (Capel, Donnybrook, and Ferguson Valley). Chardonnay is perhaps the most successful variety, followed by Cabernet sauvignon and Merlot.

GINGIN
This small area is just north of Perth in the Southwest Coastal Plain district.

GREATER PERTH
This zonal GI encompasses the regional GIs of the Perth Hills and Swan District.

GREAT SOUTHERN
Subregions: *Albany, Denmark, Frankland River, Mount Barker, Porongurup*

This is the coolest of Western Australia's winegrowing areas, although it has similar climatic influences to the Margaret River, but with a lower rainfall. The vineyards are scattered throughout a vast area, and mostly consist of Riesling, Cabernet sauvignon, Shiraz, Malbec, Pinot noir, and Chardonnay.

MANJIMUP
This region is immediately north of Pemberton, on the same latitude as the Margaret River, with which it shares some climatic similarities, although Manjimup is more continental and higher in altitude. Chardonnay is the widest planted variety, but Cabernet Sauvignon and

Merlot fare best. There is more hope than promise for Pinot Noir, even though Picardy, the region's top producer, makes excellent wines from this grape.

MARGARET RIVER

This is Australia's premier region for wine lovers who seek class and finesse, rather than weight and glory. Situated south of Perth, the Margaret River district attracted much attention in 1978 when it established Australia's first Appellation of Origin system. Like similar schemes, it was unsuccessful.

The first vineyard was planted in the Margaret River area at Bunbury as long ago as 1890. However, it was a vineyard planted by Dr. Tom Cullity at Vasse Felix in 1967 that was the first step in the Margaret River's journey to success. Although relatively minor problems do exist in the area, notably oïdium, parrots, wind, and, most serious, dry summers. The oïdium seems to be under control, and the vineyard workers plant sunflowers to distract the parrots from the vines, while rye grass acts as a windbreak. A lot of vines experience water-stress, not a heat-related problem, but dry-summer induced, and one that is exacerbated by the wind factor. The greatness of Margaret River wines cannot be disputed. This is because the quality of fruit is better than elsewhere in Australia. The best varieties are Cabernet sauvignon, Chardonnay, Sémillon-Sauvignon, and Shiraz.

MOUNT BARKER

The wineries here have a reputation for varietals, such as Rhine Riesling and Cabernet Sauvignon, but other grape varieties also fare well. The only factor limiting the potential here is that most of the wines are made by a handful of people.

PEMBERTON

This GI south of Manjimup is one of Western Australia's less consistent wine regions, but it is a young area and there is a lot of hope locally. Supposedly a Pinot Noir area, but yet to prove itself.

PERTH HILLS

This regional GI is adjacent to the Swan Valley and consists of a strip of the lower slopes of the Darling Ranges. The area is much cooler than the Swan Valley, with grapes ripening some two weeks later.

SOUTH WEST AUSTRALIA

This zonal GI encompasses the majority of Western Australia's most exciting wine areas, including the regional GIs of Blackwood Valley, Geographe, Great Southern, Manjimup, Margaret River, Pemberton, and Warren Valley.

SWAN DISTRICT

Subregion: *Swan Valley*

This regional GI contains the Swan Valley itself, but also extends northwards from Perth encompassing former unclassified areas such as Gingin and Moondah Brook.

SWAN VALLEY

Located in the eastern suburbs of Perth, the Swan Valley has the distinction of being one of the hottest winegrowing regions in the world. Partly because of this and partly as a reaction to the phenomenal success of the Margaret River, several producers have deserted the area and the number of vineyards is shrinking. What was once the traditional centre of Western Australia's wine industry is now a waning force, although the best areas are cooled by the so-called Freemantle Doctor (sea breezes!), allowing the old-fashioned, foursquare wines to be replaced by lighter and fresher styles.

WARREN VALLEY

This region challenges Pemberton for Western Australia's Pinot Noir crown, although neither has demonstrated itself a worthy contender.

WEST AUSTRALIAN SOUTH EAST COASTAL

This zonal GI covers a large swathe of coastal area that lies immediately to the east of the Great Southern zone.

THE WINE PRODUCERS OF

WESTERN AUSTRALIA

ALKOOMI WINES
Frankland
★ ❶

Sheep farmers Mervyn and Judy Lange regularly produce fresh, fruity, rich-flavoured wines.

✓ *Cabernet Sauvignon • Cabernet-Shiraz-Merlot-Malbec* (Classic Red) • *Malbec • Riesling • Shiraz*

AMBERLEY ESTATE
Margaret River
☆

Former Brown Brothers' winemaker doing his own thing with some 40 hectares (100 acres) of vineyards.

✓ *Sauvignon-Sémillon*
• *Sémillon-Sauvignon*

BROOKLAND VALLEY
Margaret River

This small winery is now owned by BRL Hardy. It has its own restaurant overlooking the vineyard and lake.

✓ *Chardonnay*
• *Sauvignon Blanc*

CAPE CLAIRAULT
Margaret River

Ian and Ani Lewis have been busily extending everything here, from the vineyards through to the winery and tasting area, and have added a small café called Food in the Forest.

✓ *Cabernet Sauvignon*
• *Sauvignon Blanc • Sémillon*

CAPEL VALE WINES
Southwest Coastal Plain
★★☆

Peter Pratten, a former radiologist, had no experience whatsoever when he began making wine on the banks of the Capel River, but his delicious, vibrantly fruity wines are some of Western Australia's finest. It is worth the expense.

✓ *Cabernet Sauvignon • Merlot*
• *Riesling • Shiraz*

CAPE MENTELLE
Margaret River
★★★☆ ❶

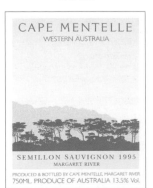

Referred to by locals as the "Mentelle Asylum", this is where David Hohnen started his cultish empire. In the process he established the Cloudy Bay

phenomenon, which has shot to international stardom, but sold out to Veuve Clicquot, although he still owns a share in the business and remains in day-to-day charge. Hohnen is perplexingly capable of straddling both Old and New World styles; he respects tradition, understanding restraint and finesse, but does not allow this to hold back Margaret River's ripe fruit flavours. He is also one of Australia's most innovative winemakers. Wines are also sold under the Ironstone Vineyards label.

✓ *Cabernet-Merlot* (Trinders)
• *Cabernet Sauvignon*
• *Chardonnay*
• *Sémillon-Sauvignon*
• *Shiraz*
• *Zinfandel*

CHATEAU XANADU
Margaret River
★

At least you know they're crazy at Cape Mentelle, but even the locals find Xanadu a bit spooky. If you imagine a philosophical discussion in one corner as to whether the grapes that have just arrived were actually picked, or just appeared out of thin air because nobody saw them delivered, while in the other they're chanting something amid a haze of sweet-smelling blue smoke, you wouldn't even be close. The fine quality of the wine is, thankfully, much easier to discern.

✓ *Cabernet Franc • Cabernet Sauvignon • Chardonnay*
• *Sauvignon Blanc*

CHATSFIELD
Mount Barker
★ ❶

Irish-born Dr. Ken Lynch has a well-established record for easy-drinking wines, especially his ripe, peachy Riesling.

✓ *Cabernet Franc* (Soft Red)
• *Chardonnay • Riesling • Shiraz*

PAUL CONTI
Wanneroo

Paul Conti is a rather low-key winery, capable of surprising finesse.

✓ *Frontignac* (Late Picked)
• *Shiraz*

CULLEN
Margaret River
★★

Vanya Cullen makes an outstanding wine, but don't stay in her guest house unless you've got a four-wheel drive and like snakes.

✓ *Cabernet-Merlot • Chardonnay*
• *Sauvignon Blanc*

DEVIL'S LAIR
Margaret River
★

Planted in 1981, Devil's Lair is a long-established vineyard in Margaret River terms, but I have only recently encountered its wines. I have tasted only two reds but they are both deep, dark, and yet finely structured, showing great potential. Obviously Southcorp think the same, since this group purchased Devil's Lair in 1997.

✓ *Cabernet-Merlot*
• *Cabernet Sauvignon*

EVANS & TATE
Margaret River
★ ☆

This winery used to own vineyards in the Swan Valley as well as the Margaret River, but has sold off its Swan Valley holdings. Stunning wines that combine richness with finesse.

✓ *Cabernet-Merlot* (Barrique 61)
• *Chardonnay*
• *Merlot*
• *Sémillon*
• *Sémillon-Sauvignon*
• *Shiraz*

FERMOY ESTATE
Margaret River

Fermoy Estate consistently produces a very elegant Cabernet-Merlot, and the Pinot Noir is improving in quality.

✓ *Cabernet-Merlot*

FRANKLAND ESTATE
Frankland

Frankland Estate is best for its blended red, which consists of both Cabernets, Merlot, and Malbec. It is dedicated to the late Professor Olmo, California's famous grape breeder, not for creating varieties such as Ruby Cabernet, but because he was instrumental in selecting areas of Frankland best suited to viticulture in the early days of this wine region.

✓ *Olmo's Reward*
(red Bordeaux-style)

GALAFREY
Great Southern
☆ Ⓥ

Anyone who names a winery after Dr. Who's mythical planet of the Time Lords should be locked up in a dark place – preferably with a good supply of Galafrey wines.

✓ *Cabernet Sauvignon*
• *Riesling*
• *Shiraz*

GOUNDREY WINES
Great Southern
★ Ⓥ

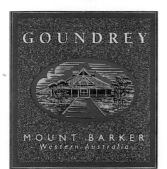

This is now owned by Perth-based US millionaire Jack Bendat, who has invested millions in Goundrey and is intent on driving sales ever upwards.

✓ *Cabernet Sauvignon* (Reserve)
• *Chardonnay*
• *Sauvignon Blanc*

HAPP'S VINEYARD
Margaret River
☆

Erland Happ makes several wines, all of which are eminently drinkable, but you can tell that he puts his heart into the Merlot.

✓ *Merlot*

HOUGHTON WINES
Swan Valley
★ Ⓥ

Because of this winery's huge production and the fact that it is part of the even more gigantic BRL Hardy, the quality of these wines is often underestimated.

✓ *Cabernet Sauvignon* (Gold Reserve)
• *Chardonnay* (Gold Reserve)
• *Riesling*
• *White Burgundy* (Show Reserve)
• *Verdelho* (Show Reserve)

HOWARD PARK
★

Now owned by the Burch family, who also have vineyards in Margaret River.

✓ *Chardonnay* • *Riesling*

JINGALLA PORONGURUP
Porongurup
☆

Jingalla Porongurup produces crisp, vibrantly fruity whites and soft Shiraz sprinkled with fresh-ground black pepper.

✓ *Shiraz* (Oak Matured)
• *Verdelho*

KARRIVALE
Great Southern
★ Ⓥ

Winemaker John Wade makes a deliciously fresh, zesty style of Riesling at this Mount Barker Winery.

✓ *Riesling*

KILLERBY
Southwest Coastal Plain

Established in 1973, Killerby sells most of its wines under its April Classic label.

✓ *Shiraz*

LEEUWIN ESTATE
Margaret River
★★

No expense was spared building this high-tech winery, which has an excellent restaurant and an idyllic setting for concerts. Leeuwin Estate produces lush, stylish, and very classy wines.

✓ *Cabernet Sauvignon*
• *Chardonnay*
• *Pinot Noir*
• *Riesling*
• *Sauvignon Blanc*

LENTON BRAE
Margaret River
❷

Only one wine tasted – Cabernet Sauvignon – and that just once, but it was so complete and complex, it was one of the very greatest Margaret River Cabernets I have tasted, and I have come across quite a lot of exceptional ones from this top wine area.

✓ *Cabernet Sauvignon*

MOONDAH BROOK
Gingin (Vineyards only)
★★ Ⓥ

This good value brand belongs to BRL Hardy and the wines are made at the Houghton winery.

✓ *Cabernet Sauvignon*
• *Chardonnay*
• *Chenin Blanc*
• *Verdelho*

MOSS WOOD
Margaret River
★★

One of the very best Margaret River wineries, Moss Wood was the first in the area to perfect Pinot Noir.

✓ *Cabernet Sauvignon*
• *Chardonnay*
• *Pinot Noir*
• *Sémillon*

OLD KENT RIVER
Great Southern
❷

Although Mark and Deborah Noack established this vineyard in 1985, they have only recently started releasing wines. Fortunately, the big, bold-flavoured Pinot Noir has been worth the wait, and is a wine to watch.

✓ *Pinot Noir*

PATTERSONS
Great Southern
❷

These up-and-coming new wines are made by Arthur Patterson, who planted this vineyard in 1982.

✓ *Chardonnay*

PIERRO
Margaret River
★ ☆

Mike Perkin, who is a genius with white wines, makes the best Chardonnay in Margaret River.

✓ *Chardonnay*
• *Guillotine Red* (Bordeaux-style)
• *Sémillon-Sauvignon*

PLANTAGENET WINES
Great Southern
★ ☆

A winery named after the shire in which it is situated, Plantagenet was the first to cultivate Mount Barker and is the leading winery in the area today. John Wade established this reputation and Gavin Berry has continued to improve on it.

✓ *Cabernet Sauvignon*
• *Chardonnay* • *Pinot Noir*
• *Riesling* • *Shiraz*

SANDALFORD
Margaret River
☆

A historic winery dating back to 1840, at which former Evans & Tate winemaker Bill Crappsley really made improvements, but has recently moved on.

✓ *Verdelho*

SANDSTONE
Margaret River
☆

This tiny vineyard and winery was established in 1988 by owner-winemakers Mike and Jan Davies. The style is rich, oaky, and upfront, yet capable of complexity.

✓ *Cabernet Sauvignon* • *Sémillon*

SMITHBROOK
Manjimup
★ ☆

Now owned by Petaluma, who use the Pinot Noir for sparkling wine. Croser believes Manjimup is best for Merlot and Sauvignon Blanc.

✓ *Merlot*

VASSE FELIX
Margaret River
★ ☆

One of the Margaret River's modern-era pioneering wineries, Vasse Felix's speciality has always been its long-lived Cabernet Sauvignons, and remains so today, although since the change of ownership, they are softer and easier to drink at a younger age than they used to be. The new Classic White blend makes a fine food wine. Good and improving Mount Barker wines are sold under the Forest Hill label.

✓ *Cabernet Sauvignon* (including Forest Hill) • *Classic White*
• *Riesling* (Forest Hill)

WILLESPIE
Margaret River
★

From this expanding winery, Kevin and Marian Squance make lovely smoky-mulberry Cabernet, wonderfully fresh Sémillon, and a fine enough Verdelho to match Sandalford's.

✓ *Cabernet Sauvignon*
• *Sauvignon Blanc*
• *Sémillon* • *Verdelho*

WOODY NOOK
Margaret River
☆

Neil Gallagher of Woody Nook makes a lovely Cabernet Sauvignon, which has an elegant balance of fruit and tannin.

✓ *Cabernet Sauvignon*

QUEENSLAND AND NORTHERN TERRITORY

Queensland and Northern Territory cover nearly half of Australia, but contain just 15 per cent of its population, and the majority live in Brisbane. The rest is a sparsely populated, swelteringly-hot outback, yet a serious vine-growing area is located high up in the Granite Belt, where due to its high altitude the climate is much cooler than many other Australian wine regions, allowing the vines to survive and flourish.

QUEENSLAND

One of the last places on earth that one might expect to find a vineyard, Queensland actually has some 40 wineries (with another 20 licensed to open soon) and a small wine industry dating back to the 1850s. Surprisingly, summers are much cooler than in many other, far more famous Australian regions, which explains why Queensland is enjoying a revival of its wine industry. Heat is not a problem, rain is. Indeed, the relatively wet weather between the *veraison* and harvest-time makes the vines prone to rot.

NORTHERN TERRITORY

A less likely location for a winemaking area than Queensland is hard to imagine, but its western neighbour, Northern Territory, is such a place. Very hot and dry for the most part, the land elsewhere is crocodile-infested swamp – the local tourist board advises visitors to run in a zig-zag when chased by a crocodile! Curiously it is illegal to drink alcohol in a public place within 2 kilometres (1 mile) of a licensed bar (except, of course, in one). Outback machismo might be expected to preclude wine drinking, bearing in mind the cooling properties attributed to some of Australia's beers. Despite all this, the town of Alice Springs is home to Chateau Hornsby and its 3 hectares (7 acres) of vineyards.

FACTORS AFFECTING TASTE AND QUALITY

LOCATION
Queensland is situated in the northeastern corner of Australia, with the Coral Sea to the east, and the Northern Territory, the north central state, to the west.

CLIMATE
Annual rainfall at Roma is only 51 cm (20 in), but the Granite Belt receives 79 cm (31 in). Much of it often falls at vintage time and can be a problem, but frost and hail pose a greater danger. Temperatures are high (similar to the Margaret River in Western Australia) but not unduly so, due to the tempering effect of altitude. Alice Springs has a very hot, dry, continental climate.

ASPECT
The 600 m (2,000 ft) altitude of Alice Springs and Stanthorpe, where the surrounding vineyards lie between 750 and 900 m (2,500–3,000 ft) above sea level, helps to temper the otherwise scorching summer heat in both areas. Around Stanthorpe, vines are generally grown in the hilly area, on sloping sites.

SOIL
The soils of Queensland are phylloxera-free. As the name suggests, they are granitic in the Granite Belt around Stanthorpe. The area around Alice Springs shares the same infertile red soils common to much of central Australia.

VITICULTURE AND VINIFICATION
Irrigation is necessary to produce wines near Alice Springs and, indeed, at Roma. The most modern technology is used in these areas to combat the problems of heat and oxidation. As a result, quite good wines are produced. Queensland has strict quarantine laws regarding the importation of rootstocks (to avoid phylloxera), although this is slowing down the development of different wine styles.

GRAPE VARIETIES
Cabernet sauvignon, Chardonnay, Chenin blanc, Emerald riesling, Malbec, Mataro, Muscat, Riesling, Sémillon, Servante, Shiraz, Sylvaner, Traminer

AN OUTBACK STATION IN ALICE SPRINGS
The hot dry climate means irrigation is necessary for the area's red-sand soil, but there is an abundant supply of water underground.

THE APPELLATIONS OF
QUEENSLAND AND NORTHERN TERRITORY

ALICE SPRINGS

Chateau Hornsby, located at Alice Springs, is the only winery in Northern Territory. The vines, which grow on red sand-ridges include: Cabernet sauvignon, Chardonnay, Riesling, Sémillon, and Syrah. They are all drip-irrigated from wells (water is plentiful in the area if you dig deep enough) and the harvest is in January.

GRANITE BELT

The vines here are grown in an area that surrounds the town of Ballandean, on an elevated granite plateau 240 kilometres (150 miles) west of Brisbane. It is the altitude of this district, between 790 and 940 metres (2,600–3,100 feet), that provides a sufficiently cool climate. Indeed, at Felsberg, located at an altitude of 850 metres (2,763 feet), the grapes sometimes struggle to ripen. The good quality varietal-wine industry of the Granite Belt was once described as Queensland's greatest secret. The most suitable variety is Riesling, but the most successful individual wine is, believe it or not, Ballandean's late-harvest Sylvaner. Other varieties that do well include Cabernet sauvignon, Chardonnay, Sémillon, and Shiraz.

ROMA

This hot, dry area in Queensland is as inappropriate a place as could be found to grow grapes, but there are some 25 hectares (62 acres) of vines. This is meant to be fortified wine country, so I was surprised to be greeted by a sign proclaiming "Welcome to Roma, Champagne Country". Apparently in 1864 a certain Mayor Mitchell was so struck by Roma's resemblance to the Champagne area that he mentioned the fact in despatches, and the description stuck, which means that he had obviously never visited Champagne in his life.

THE WINE PRODUCERS OF
QUEENSLAND AND NORTHERN TERRITORY

BALD MOUNTAIN
Granite Belt
Owned by Denis and Jackie Parsons, whose vineyards near Girraween National Park produce award-winning wines under the careful eye of contract winemaker Simon Gilbert.

BALLANDEAN
Granite Belt
★ ✔
Ballandean is really buzzing, and while its light and elegant Liqueur Muscat has always been excellent value and its late-harvested Sylvaner a very special wine indeed, the varietal wines lacked fruit and freshness until the early 1990s. Since then, however, owner-winemaker Angelo Puglisi has been producing better and better varietal wines. They might not be great wines, but they do not pretend to be and their inexpensive, easy-drinking style is very welcome. Since 1991 every wine produced seems to have at least a touch of botrytis and has consequently been superior to any of the previous vintages.
✔ *Cabernet Sauvignon*
• *Sauvignon Blanc* • *Sémillon*
• *Liqueur Muscat*
• *Sylvaner* (Late Harvest)

BASSETTS ROMAVILLA WINERY
Roma
Chenin Blanc can be fresh with nice tropical fruit, but the Shiraz is too big and alcoholic, as might be expected in such an extremely hot wine area. However, this is supposed to be fortified wine country and although the Very Old Port and Very Old Liqueur Muscat are very rich and intense with big finishes, there are few other fortified wines of interest. I thought this solitary winery was not exploiting its potential for fortified wines, and the use of sulphur was heavy-handed. I also experienced a higher incidence of corked wines here than anywhere else in Australia.

BUNGAWARRA
Granite Belt
Originally founded in the 1920s by Angelo Barbagello, this winery was re-established in 1979 by Alan Dorr and purchased in 1993 by Jeff Harden, a Brisbane pharmacist. The winery is currently being upgraded.

CHATEAU HORNSBY
Northern Territory
There are people in the Australian wine trade who do not believe that a vineyard actually exists at Alice Springs, but I have visited Denis Hornsby twice now and can assure readers that vines grow there. And, contrary to the rumour that started out as a joke within the trade, the vines are not planted in trenches to provide shade. Every year Denis Hornsby makes his Early Red from Shiraz grapes picked at one minute past midnight on 1 January, which makes it the earliest harvested *nouveau* in the world, yet he has picked these Shiraz grapes even earlier. With no winter in mid-1996, the vines became disorientated, his Chardonnay ripened a month early, and his 1997 was actually harvested on 7 December 1996, so he labelled it "Sixes and Sevens".
✔ *Early Red* • *Port* (Horny Tawny)

FELSBERG VINEYARDS-WINERY
Granite Belt
The Chardonnay is not very special as a varietal wine, but has a lean structure that would make it an ideal base wine for a quality fizz.

GOLDEN GROVE ESTATE
Granite Belt
★
Sam and Grace Costanzo have quickly made a name for themselves since establishing this winery in 1992.
✔ *Cabernet* (Reserve)
• *Chardonnay* • *Merlot* • *Shiraz*

IRONBARK RIDGE
Purga
This winery was established in 1984, initially with the help of Peter Scudamore-Smith, Queensland's only Master of Wine, in an isolated area between Brisbane and the Great Divide, where Robert Le Grand had planted vines back in 1991.

KOMINOS WINES
Granite Belt
Tony and Mary Comino's award-winning wines enjoy good sales in Asian markets. The Shiraz produced here is well thought of by enthusiasts of *macération carbonique* wines.
✔ *Cabernet Sauvignon* • *Riesling*

MOUNT MAGNUS
Granite Belt
This is Australia's highest vineyard.
✔ *Shiraz*

MOUNTVIEW
Granite Belt
★ ★ ✔
When I visited this immaculate, tiny, red-cedar barn, I was surprised by the 1991 Shiraz, which was only Mountview's second vintage, yet was arguably one of Australia's most elegant examples of the variety, with its lush, sweet, creamy fruit, and certainly one of its cheapest. Mountview subsequently won "Best Queensland Red" three years in a row. David and Linda Price sold up in 2000, but hopefully the new owners will build on this legacy.
✔ *Shiraz*

OLD CAVES WINERY
Granite Belt
The premium varietals made by Old Caves Winery are really quite good.
✔ *Riesling* • *Shiraz*

ROBINSONS FAMILY
Ballandean
John Robinson got his passion for wine when living in France, close to the Beaujolais region, then studied wine science at Riverina College under Brian Croser.
✔ *Cabernet-Shiraz*

RUMBALARA VINEYARDS
Fletcher
★
Chris Gray is the undisputed king of Granite Belt Sémillon for both unoaked and barrel-fermented styles.
✔ *Cabernet Sauvignon* • *Sémillon*

STONE RIDGE VINEYARD
Granite Belt
Shiraz offers the best potential, but is annoyingly inconsistent.

VIOLET CANE VINEYARD
★
One of Queensland's more recent and most exciting of wineries.
✔ *Merlot* • *Sparkling Shiraz*
• *Viognier*

WINEWOOD
Granite Belt
Ian and Jeanette Davis can be a bit heavy on the coconutty oak character of their wines at times.
✔ *Shiraz* • *Shiraz-Marsanne*

❖ NEW ZEALAND ❖

In the first edition I wrote that New Zealand's Sauvignon Blanc "competes on equal terms with the very best that Sancerre and Pouilly Fumé have to offer" but this is no longer true – New Zealand's Sauvignon Blanc now surpasses anything the French could possibly produce. And, at long last, Pinot Noir is starting to shine.

SOME WOULD ARGUE that Sauvignon blanc is not even New Zealand's greatest grape variety (some consider Chardonnay and more recently Pinot noir to be their most prestigious grape variety, since these wines command substantially higher prices than Sauvignon blanc) but this country is now the world's greatest source of top-quality Sauvignon Blanc and it would be a mistake if its winemakers played down this fact.

FIRST EXPORTS

Cooks and Montana started exporting in the late 1970s, and by 1982 numerous New Zealand producers were trickling Chardonnay, Chenin Blanc, Gewürztraminer, Pinot Gris, Riesling, and Sémillon wines on to export markets. There were several Gewürztraminer-Riesling blends, which were quite a novelty at the time, and even a Furmint. The styles ranged from dry, through off-dry and medium-sweet, to late-picked. There were also some wines with various degrees of oak influence, some being barrel-fermented, others just cask-aged, and there were even some artificial "Icewines" that had been made with the help of a chest freezer! The range of red wines included Cabernet Sauvignon, Pinotage, and Pinot Noir, which were produced with and without new oak.

The first time I tasted such a range was in 1982. The standard was very high, the styles were both attractive and interesting, but nothing came through as being intrinsically New Zealand in style. It might seem strange now, but at the first of what was to become one of the most exciting annual tastings, the New Zealanders showed just one Sauvignon Blanc! We had no idea this variety would become synonymous with New Zealand. Indeed, by the mid-1980s, the rumour was that this country's greatest hope would be Pinot Noir. This, however, is only just being realized.

THE FUTURE NEW ZEALAND

The number of wineries has trebled since the late 1980s, but the industry is still dominated by just three companies: Montana (which also owns Deutz Marlborough), Corbans (which includes Cooks and Robard & Butler), and Villa Maria (encompassing Vidals and Esk Valley). The balance of some

MISSION VINEYARDS, NORTH ISLAND
The Hawkes Bay winery has recently upgraded its wines.

NEW ZEALAND
Although South Island has a younger wine trade, it boasts a slightly more favourable winegrowing climate than North Island, having a lighter rainfall.

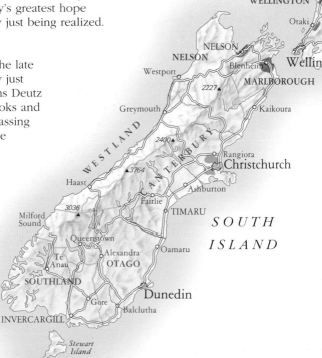

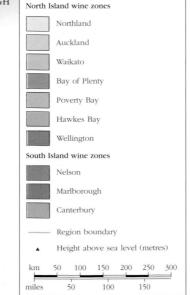

North Island wine zones	
	Northland
	Auckland
	Waikato
	Bay of Plenty
	Poverty Bay
	Hawkes Bay
	Wellington

South Island wine zones	
	Nelson
	Marlborough
	Canterbury

Region boundary

▲ Height above sea level (metres)

km 50 100 150 200 250 300
miles   50   100   150

FACTORS AFFECTING TASTE AND QUALITY

LOCATION
With the exception of Waiheke Island, all New Zealand's grape-growing areas are on the mainland of its two principal islands, North Island and South Island. Otago is the most southerly location.

CLIMATE
North Island generally has a cool maritime climate similar to that of Bordeaux in temperature, but with a much higher rainfall. The crucial autumn periods are rarely dry; heavy rains and high humidity lead to problems of grape damage and rot. South Island is significantly cooler, but sunnier and drier. Marlborough is the warmest area, and often has the country's most hours of sunshine. Rainfall is variable. Using the Californian heat summation system, the most important viticultural areas in both islands are all Region 1 (see p.448).

ASPECT
Most vines are planted on flat or gently sloping land, and are easy to work. Some north-facing slopes have been planted in Auckland and Te Kauwhata; these provide better drainage and longer hours of intensive sunlight. Some steep vineyards are found in South Island's Otago district.

SOIL
Varied soils, mostly clay or loam based, often sandy or gravelly, with volcanic subsoils in parts of Hawke's Bay and around Canterbury.

VITICULTURE AND VINIFICATION
Harvests begin in March and April, six months ahead of wine regions in the Northern Hemisphere. Although the emphasis is very much on higher-quality varietals such as Chardonnay, Sauvignon Blanc, Cabernet Sauvignon, and Pinot Noir, the ubiquitous Müller-Thurgau still dominates the cheap blends, which usually sell in large 1.5-litre (2½-pint) bottles or bag-in-the-box, and are traditionally made in an off-dry style by back-blending with sweet, sterilized, unfermented grape juice. Most winemakers have studied oenology in Australia, and done at least one stage in Europe, and it is this straddling of Old and New World, tradition and technique, that has helped shape New Zealand's exciting wine reputation.

GRAPE VARIETIES
Primary varieties: Cabernet sauvignon, Chardonnay, Merlot, Pinot noir, Riesling, Sauvignon blanc
Secondary varieties: Cabernet franc, Chenin blanc, Gewürztraminer, Malbec, Muscat (various, mostly Dr. Hogg), Pinotage, Pinot gris, Sémillon, Syrah
Others: Auxerrois, Baco blanc, Bacchus, Blauberger, Breidecker, Chambourcin, Grenache, Meunier, Müller-Thurgau, Optima, Palomino, Petit verdot, Reichensteiner, Siebel, Sylvaner

COOPERS CREEK WINERY, NORTH ISLAND
Situated in the Huapi Valley, this winery produces exceptionally stylish wines. Talented North Island winemakers use both traditional and high-tech methods.

360 wineries contribute just ten per cent of the production, but with some 6,000 different wines in total there are plenty to choose from and, with an average of 20 new boutique wineries setting up each year, the choice can only increase.

As word of these vibrantly fruity, pure flavoured wines has circulated, so demand has increased, with exports increasing by almost eight-fold over the last ten years. Sauvignon Blanc and Chardonnay will continue to increase in popularity, as will red wines such as Pinot Noir and Cabernet-Merlot blends. The plantation of Müller-Thurgau has probably bottomed out, but it remains important for cheap blends, particularly of the boxed variety. Contrary to the situation in Australia, Sémillon is not a common varietal, but it has undergone a substantial expansion over the last ten years, which can be explained by its role as an adjunct to Sauvignon. Some producers will harvest it early, when it is more grassy and Sauvignon-like than Sauvignon Blanc itself. A small proportion can greatly improve the varietal character of New Zealand Sauvignon Blanc.

RECENT NEW ZEALAND VINTAGES

2000 New Zealand's largest ever harvest, the 2000 ripening was marked by warm days and cool nights. Even though Marlborough was affected by rain, this diurnal difference provided intense, exceptionally focused varietal flavours, with Chardonnay and Sauvignon Blanc excelling. Rain also affected various North Island regions.

1999 A small increase on New Zealand's 1998 record harvest, with good to very good quality in general, although South Island fared better than North Island, and some reds from Gisborne and Hawkes Bay were disappointing.

1998 A very hot year followed by a record crop produced the best red wines in New Zealand's recent history, with exciting, lush, high quality wines in every style from Cabernet sauvignon to Pinot Noir. Some good, full-bodied Chardonnays, but white wines were variable in Auckland and most Sauvignon Blanc were poor and flabby.

1997 A small harvest of generally disappointing quality, the exceptions being Wairarapa and Nelson, both of which excelled in all styles. Hawkes Bay was variable, although some reds were excellent, as they were throughout South Island. Marlborough also produced some fine, crisp Sauvignon Blanc.

1996 The largest vintage of the decade due not to excessive rain or overcropping, but to newly planted vineyards coming into production. Variable in many areas, but particularly good quality for reds in Auckland and Wairarapa.

NEUDORF VINEYARD, SOUTH ISLAND
The Neudorf Vineyard on South Island produces 2,000 cases annually from its 4.5 hectares (11 acres) of land.

NEW ZEALAND

Note In 1996, New Zealand created a new appellation system, granting geographical regions Certified Origin (CO) status, which have been incorporated in the entries below.

NORTH ISLAND

The more important of the country's two islands, supporting some 70 per cent of the population, North Island is where New Zealand's wine industry began and was confined to until as recently as 1973.

AUCKLAND CO

Sub-regions of Certified Origin
Greater Auckland, Kumeu-Huapai, Henderson, Waiheke Island, Northland-Matakana

In the 1960s, a decade before the first vines were planted in Marlborough, Auckland possessed more than half of New Zealand's vineyards. Today it claims less than four per cent. It does, however, remain the traditional centre of New Zealand's wine industry by virtue of the large number of wineries that are still located here. There are no less than 80 wineries and many of them source their wines from almost every wine region in the country, thus their bottling lines churn out a large percentage of New Zealand's total production. While Auckland's vineyards are insignificant in terms of volume, its various wine districts still produce some of the country's very finest wines. The Kumeu-Huapai district has long been established as a source of premium varietal wines and Waiheke Island, which is much drier and sunnier than mainland Auckland, is one of New Zealand's most exciting red-wine districts. Tiny quantities of Cabernet-Merlot have been produced on Great Barrier Island, which is way out in the Pacific, well beyond Waiheke Island. There are still whispers about the promising future of Clevedon and Whitford, in the eastern outskirts of Auckland, and Northland, where the first New Zealand vines were planted in 1819.

GISBORNE CO

Gisborne is synonymous with Poverty Bay, and has been dubbed "carafe country" due to the enormous yields of Müller-Thurgau, which traditionally formed the basis of New Zealand's bag-in-the-box wines. But even at 25 tonnes per hectare (10 tons per acre), Gisborne Müller-Thurgau has become uneconomical for the cheapest blends, and producers now rely on bulk wine imported at half the price from Australia and Europe. This has caused a shift upwards from the not so cheap Müller-Thurgau towards lower-yielding, but more profitable classic varieties. A large proportion of Gisborne grapes will still be purchased by wineries outside the region for blending, but for more upmarket premium varietals, rather than bag-in-the-box wines. Pure Gisborne wines have already begun to make their mark, some winning medals, which suggests that Gisborne might have more fine-wine potential than has been thought. The traditional Gisborne classic is the Gewürztraminer grown around Matawhero, but although this is justly famous by New Zealand's standards, Chardonnay is far more successful from a truly objective sense, with Villa Maria and Robard & Butler its most consistent exponents. Aotea, Villa Maria, and Coopers have produced some good Sauvignon Blanc. Red wines have been less successful.

HAWKES BAY CO

The driest wine region in the country, this is second only in size to Marlborough and its growth is almost as fast. No one should be fooled, however, into thinking that Hawkes Bay is inferior to Marlborough, as it offers more potential for Cabernet Sauvignon and its derivative blends, is at least as exciting for Chardonnay, and a handful of producers even compete with Marlborough's best Sauvignon Blancs. Stonecroft's promising start with Syrah indicates that Hawkes Bay might have potential for other Rhône varietals. Hawkes Bay is also the country's most sought after source for those wineries that seek the highest-quality components to craft medal-winning multi-regional varietals.

WAIKATO CO

Situated inland, around the northern shore of Lake Waikere, this region is some 65 kilometres (40 miles) southeast of Auckland and encompasses the Te Kauwhata district, where yields are lower, and the climate hotter and more humid, making it suitable for botrytized wines.

WELLINGTON CO

Sub-regions of Certified Origin
Martinborough, Te Horo, Wairarapa

Wellington consists of two distinctly different viticultural districts, Te Horo, a one-winery district to the west of the Taraua Range, and Wairarapa, which encompasses Martinborough on the eastern side. The most important district, however, is Martinborough, just east of Lake Wairapara. It is astonishing to think that I could describe Martinborough as being of minor importance in the first edition of this book, for although the number of vineyards is tiny, the reputation of Pinot Noir has, over the last ten years, given Martinborough a cult following. The area has, however, at least as much potential for various other grape varieties, particularly when better-quality vinestock can be imported. Its free-draining, gravelly soil is very similar to Marlborough's, and ideally suited to viticulture.

OTHER NORTH ISLAND AREAS

Apart from Kanuka Forest's pioneering three hectares (seven acres) at Whakatane, and a few token rows of vines surrounding the Morton Estate Winery at Katikati, viticulture is not a serious consideration in the Bay of Plenty, even though it warrants Certified Origin status. At Galatea CO, some 80 kilometres (50 miles) south of Whakatane, the up-and-coming Covell Estate produces intensely flavoured Pinot Noir, Chardonnay, Cabernet-Merlot, and Riesling from five hectares (12 acres).

SOUTH ISLAND

South Island has a much lower population than North Island and, due to transport difficulties, was not cultivated until 1973, but has quickly demonstrated exciting potential for premium varietals.

CANTERBURY CO

Sub-regions of Certified Origin *Banks Peninsula, Christchurch, Gibbston Valley, Waipara*

Although the summer here can be as warm as in Marlborough, the autumn is cooler and overall temperatures are lower. At just 62 centimetres (24 inches), the annual rainfall here is substantially lower than in Marlborough and less than half that received in Auckland. Most vineyards are located on the plains surrounding Christchurch, New Zealand's third-largest city, or at Waipara, a coastal area to the north. Quality is inconsistent, but this area shows promise.

CENTRAL OTAGO CO

Sub-regions of Certified Origin
Queenstown, Gibbston Valley, Wanaka

In the 1997 edition I reported that "New Zealand's most marginal viticultural area has produced quite a few excellent wines, but they have been few and far between", and just four years later Central Otage Pinot Noir is the hottest development in the New Zealand wine industry! How quickly things have changed! This is now the hottest spot on the Kiwi wine map. Or should that be the coolest? With a climate colder than the Mosel, Central Otago is indeed the country's coolest wine region. It is the hottest, hippest, coolest place to invest in vineyards, with Auckland financiers flocking here as they flocked to Marlborough in the late 1980s. Some of the highest and most southerly Otago vineyards are almost 200 degree days below the theoretical minimum for viticulture. There are, however, sheltered areas of exceptional aspect that provide warmer microclimates, such as Bannockburn, and it is the exciting-quality Pino Noir from these vineyards that has attracted investors. Bendigo is an area to watch. Quartz Reef is showing the way for sparkling wine, but has yet to prove itself as a regional rather than single-producer product. Riesling and other aromatic varieties may also have potential.

MARLBOROUGH CO

Sub-regions of Certified Origin *Awatere Valley*

Although the first vines were planted here as recently as 1973, Marlborough has become New Zealand's most famous wine region, and Marlborough Sauvignon Blanc its greatest asset. New Zealand's wine industry is growing fast, but nowhere faster than in Marlborough, which has fostered a cult-following throughout the rest of the world. Cloudy Bay has become a cult-within-a-cult, although there are many other equally exciting wineries. The collaboration between Deutz and Montana put Marlborough on the sparkling-wine map. However, Sauvignon Blanc remains the superstar, even if Marlborough's gravelly soil and dry, sunny climate make it equally ideal for Chardonnay as Sauvignon Blanc, and Cabernet can also do well.

NELSON CO

Sub-regions of Certified Origin
Moutere Valley, Rabbit Island, Redwood Valley

Although Nelson is overshadowed by the fame of Marlborough, on the other side of Mount Richmond, it is the second-fastest-growing New Zealand wine region and has much to offer. Formerly known for hops and tobacco, its unique topography prevents widescale mechanized cultivation and this, combined with a stony, well-drained soil, makes it one of the country's best areas for small "boutique" wineries. Wetter than Marlborough yet significantly drier than Auckland, Nelson is known for long warm summers, cool autumn nights, and being one of the sunniest places in New Zealand. Pinot noir, Chardonnay, and Sauvignon blanc offer most potential.

THE WINE STYLES OF
NEW ZEALAND

CABERNET AND MERLOT
Pure and Blended

Not so long ago, New Zealand suffered from a reputation for green, aggressive red wines. It was white-wine country and its cool climate was thought to be too cool to ripen such thick-skinned grapes as Cabernet sauvignon; today, however, almost every wine region in New Zealand has become a goldmine for rich, ripe red wines of the most serious and sensual quality. Cabernet sauvignon is the widest-planted variety, but the amount of Merlot cultivated has increased by well over 300 per cent. Even volume-selling brands such as Montana Cabernet Sauvignon are big, full, and spicy, with more quality and character than you can find in Bordeaux for one-and-a-half times the price. The most exciting Cabernet and Merlot wines are produced by strict selection from top vineyards or crafted by smaller boutique wineries.

⌛ 2–5 years (up to 10 for exceptional wines)

✓ *Alpha Domus* (The Navigator) • *Babich* (Irongate Cabernet-Merlot, Patriarch Cabernet Sauvignon) • *Church Road* (Cabernet Sauvignon) • *Clearview* (Reserve Merlot, Cabernet Sauvignon) • *Cloudy Bay* (Cabernet-Merlot) • *Dashwood* (Cabernet Sauvignon) • *Delegat's* (Estate Reserve Merlot, Estate Reserve Cabernet Sauvignon, Proprietor's Reserve Merlot) • *Esk Valley* (Reserve Merlot-Malbec-Cabernet, The Terraces) • *Forrest Estate* (Merlot) • *Goldwater Estate* (Cabernet-Merlot, Cabernet-Merlot-Franc, Esslin Merlot) • *Heron's Flight* (Cabernet Sauvignon) • *Huthlee* (Merlot) • *Hyperion* (Gaia Merlot) • *Kemblefield* (Merlot Cabernet) • *Kumeu River* (Cabernet-Merlot) • *Matua Valley* (Ararimu Cabernet-Merlot, Dartmoor Smith Estate Merlot) • *Mills Reef* (all Elspeth cuvées) • *Morton Estate* (Black Label Cabernet-Merlot) • *Ngtatarawa* (Alwyn Merlot Cabernet) • *C. J. Pask* (all Gimblett Road cuvées) • *Sacred Hill* (Brokenstone Reserve Merlot, Whitecliff Vineyards Merlot) • *Saint Clair Estate* (Merlot) • *St. Jérôme* (Cabernet-Merlot) • *Shingle Peak* (Merlot) • *Stonyridge* (Larose) • *Sileni* (Merlot Cabernets) • *Te Kairanga* (Cabernet Sauvignon) • *Te Mata* (Cabernet-Merlot, Awatea Cabernet-Merlot, Coleraine Cabernet-Merlot) • *Thornbury* (Hawkes Bay Merlot) • *Trinity Hill* • *Unison Vineyard* (Unison Selection) • *Vidal* (Cabernet-Merlot) • *Villa Maria* (Private Bin Cabernet-Merlot, Reserve Cabernet Sauvignon) • *Waimarama Estate* (Cabernet Sauvignon, Undercliffe Cabernet-Merlot)

CHARDONNAY

This ubiquitous grape really does produce something special in New Zealand, which is why its cultivation has increased from 350 hectares (865 acres) in the late 1980s to more than 1,400 hectares (3,458 acres) today, making it the country's most important grape variety. It is generally less predictable, more expressive, and capable of a slower, more classic rate of maturation than its Australian equivalent. This is due not only to cooler climatic conditions, but also hand-picking, whole-bunch pressing, a wider use of natural (local) yeast fermentation, and less obvious oak, although some producers can spoil the natural elegance of these wines by various permutations of malolactic and lees-contact that turn out too heavy-handed.

⌛ 1–4 years

✓ *Ata Rangi* • *Babich* (Irongate) • *Cairnbrae* • *Clearview* • *Cloudy Bay* • *Collards* (Hawkes Bay, Rothesay Vineyard) • *Corbans Marlborough* • *Delegat's* (Proprietors Reserve) • *Hunter's* • *Kumeu River* • *Lawson's Dry Hills* • *Martinborough Vineyards* • *Matua Valley* (Ararimu) • *Montana* (Ormand Estate) • *Morton Estate* (Black Label) • *Neudorf* (Moutere) • *Nobilo* (Dixon Vineyard) • *Oyster Bay* • *C. J. Pask* • *Robard & Butler* (Gisborne) • *Allan Scott* • *Te Mata* (Castle Hill, Elston) • *Trinity Hill* • *Vavasour* (Reserve) • *Vidal* (Reserve) • *Villa Maria* (Reserve Barrique Fermented Gisborne)

PINOT NOIR

Far more fussy than Cabernet sauvignon about where and how it should be grown, Pinot noir has taken some time to find its feet in New Zealand, especially in more marginal regions. The grape was first thought to excel in Martinborough, but although some excellent Pinot Noir have been and still are being made there, it certainly has not turned out to be a second Burgundy. South Island has produced most of the best Pinot Noir wines on a consistent basis. First it was Nelson that showed the most promise, particularly from the likes of Neudorf, whose Moutere Pinot Noir rarely fails to please. Then Canterbury, followed by Marlborough and, most exciting of all, Central Otago. So now New Zealand Pinot Noir has gone full circle, starting off so hesitatingly due to the country's marginal climate, only to end up with success in Central Otago, its most marginal of wine regions. However, before we can be confident that New Zealand Pinot Noir has at last arrived, we must see what happens after all the 1998s have completely disappeared from the shelves. Then we will know whether the Kiwis have cracked it or are merely riding the crest of that wondrous red-wine vintage.

⌛ 1–4 years

✓ *Ata Rangi* • *Chard Farm* • *Felton Road* • *Giesen* (Reserve Barrel Selection) • *Highfield Estate* (Elstree Reserve) • *Isabel Estate* • *Kaituna Valley* • *Martinborough Vineyard* • *McCashin's* • *Mt Difficulty* • *Mud House* • *Neudorf* (Moutere) • *Palliser Estate* • *Pegasus Bay* • *Quartz Reef* • *Rippon* • *Daniel Schuster* (Omihi Hills Selection) • *Te Kairanga* (Reserve) • *Two Paddocks*

SAUVIGNON BLANC

The once-famous grape of the Loire is now firmly the property of New Zealand. Hacking through just a dozen wines from any of the supposedly top Loire Sauvignon appellations is a nightmare, but tasting as many as 50 of their antipodean cousins is one of life's joys. The secret is not simply that New Zealand can ripen this grape, but the fact that they add a drop of early-harvested Sémillon, which is so grassy it is more Sauvignon than Sauvignon itself, thus it turbo-charges the wine's varietal character. This is perfectly legal, as the law in New Zealand allows up to 15 per cent of another grape variety, and the European Union, USA, and most other export countries recognize this. A vivacious crispness and purity of varietal fruit should be the priority of any Sauvignon Blanc winemaker and in New Zealand they have respected this. This country in general, but Marlborough in particular, has the rare capability of being able to ripen Sauvignon blanc to a near-perfect state, enabling a large number of wineries to produce ultra-fresh wines with intense, ripe gooseberry fruit and an electrifying balance of mouthwatering acidity. However, with the emergence of the more complex Chardonnay wines, which attract higher prices than Sauvignon wines, there has been a move towards less fruit-driven, more subtle styles of Sauvignon Blanc. Hopefully such wines will not dominate the market because any

SAUVIGNON BLANC GRAPES, CLOUDY BAY
Cloudy Bay makes one of Marlborough's greatest Sauvignon Blancs and its cult-following has benefited the reputation of the entire New Zealand wine industry.

wholesale attempt to convert New Zealand's flagship wine into something that does not hit between the eyes will kill the Golden Goose. Sauvignon blanc is not exactly a subtle grape. It has no pretensions, hardly any capacity for complexity, and is not improved by either oak or ageing. Sauvignon is an unashamedly upfront and blatantly uncomplicated grape, and letting it do what comes naturally has been the key to its phenomenal popularity, forcing a five-fold increase in the cultivation of this variety during the last decade. Cloudy Bay's cult-following for its high-flying Sauvignon Blanc was probably the catalyst for New Zealand's overall success story, but although many consider that wine to be the country's best Sauvignon Blanc (and I do not hesitate to say that one of the best it certainly is), Jackson Estate is, I think, better and even more consistent in quality. And, of course, many wines achieve a similar quality this year or that.

🍷— 1–2 years (not older, unless you like the asparagus or tinned-peas character that quickly develops with bottle-age in these wines, particularly when from the ripest vintages)

✓ *Aotea* • *Cairnbrae* (The Stones) • *Clifford Bay* • *Cloudy Bay* • *Collard* • *Coopers Creek* (Marlborough) • *Kim Crawford* • *Delegat's* • *Esk Valley* • *Hunter's* • *Isabel Vineyard* • *Jackson Estate* • *Lawson Dry Hills* • *Montana* • *Nautilus* • *Neudorf* • *Oyster Bay* • *Palliser Estate* • *Selaks* • *Stoneleigh* • *Te Mata* (Castle Hill) • *Vavasour* • *Villa Maria* • *Whitehaven* (Single Vineyard Reserve)

SPARKLING WINES

At one time Montana's Lindauer Brut and Rosé exemplified New Zealand's sparkling-wine industry, and it's not bad for a fat, creamy, easy-drinking wine made by the Transfer Method. However, it took collaboration between Montana and Deutz to put this country on the bottle-fermented sparkling-wine map but, although this wine has steadily improved, it was *champenois* Daniel Le Brun who actually demonstrated Marlborough's true potential for serious sparkling wine. Daniel Le Brun's star shone so bright in the early 1990s that he eclipsed even Montana. With the benefit of hindsight, however, we can see that his

reputation was built on just three vintages: 1989, 1990, and 1991. It was the quality of these particular vintages and the speed with which Daniel achieved this quality that grabbed the wine media's attention. Cloudy Bay's Pelorus has now developed a cult following to match that of its Sauvignon Blanc and when Hunter's released its deliciously fresh and easy-drinking Miru Miru, the international wine press was finally seduced by the notion of Kiwi fizz. Quartz Reef now promises to put Central Otago on the sparkling-wine map, although Marlborough still reigns supreme.

🍷— 1–2 years (from purchase)

✓ *Daniel Le Brun* (as from 1997 vintage) • *Le Brun Family Vineyards* • *Hunter's* • *Montana* (all Deutz *cuvées*, Lindauer Special Reserve) • *Pelorus* • *Quartz Reef*

BOTRYTIZED WINES

There is no such thing as a dedicated dessert-wine area in New Zealand, although Te Kauwhata comes close, owing to its high humidity, but botrytis or "noble rot" appears on an unpredictable basis throughout all of New Zealand's wine regions. Riesling is, without doubt, the premier grape for this style in New Zealand, producing wines of the most vivid flavour enhanced by a scintillating acidity to produce a razor-sharp sweetness. Chardonnay is surprisingly the second-most successful variety, and came about by chance, after Hunters produced the first Botrytis Chardonnay in 1987. All peaches and cream, it stunned those lucky enough to taste it, and encouraged other New Zealanders to perfect this unusual wine. Botrytized Sémillon has yet to make its mark, but should do so now that less grassy clones are coming into production.

🍷— 1–15 years

✓ *Corbans* (Botrytis Selected Noble Rhine Riesling) • *Dry River* (Botrytized Chardonnay, Botrytized Riesling) • *Esk Valley* (Botrytis Selection Chenin Blanc) • *Fromm* (Le Strada Riesling) • *Giesen* (Botrytized Riesling) • *Neudorf* (Moutere Late Harvest Riesling) • *Redwood Valley* (Botrytized Riesling) • *Rongopai* (Botrytized Chardonnay, Botrytized Riesling) • *Allan Scott* (Late-Harvest Riesling) • *Seresin (Noble Riesling)* • *Te Whare Ra* (Botrytis Bunch Selection) • *Villa Maria* (Noble Riesling Botrytis Selection) • *Charles Wiffen* (Late Harvest Riesling)

CLASSIC WHITE-WINE BLENDS

New Zealand winemakers who like to experiment with oak, malolactic, and lees-contact on something other than Chardonnay should not interfere with the purity of Sauvignon Blanc, but apply such techniques to classic white-wine blends, which is one of New Zealand's slowest-developing yet ultimately rewarding niches. The most logical partner for Sauvignon is Sémillon, of course, although until recently the only Sémillon vines cultivated in New Zealand were aggressively aromatic and unsuited for blending unless used in a covert way to emphasize the character of a seemingly pure Sauvignon Blanc wine. For classic blends, however, where a more neutral base is required, New Zealand's traditional late-ripening Swiss clone is much too grassy. As more classic Sémillon clones come into production, so the number of successful New Zealand blends will rapidly increase, especially if less overtly aromatic Sauvignon is used (Auckland, Hawkes

Bay, Martinborough, and the north side of Marlborough would seem to be the best bet). In the meantime, Sémillon is blended with Chardonnay to tone down the former's aromatics. The popular Australian Chardonnay-Sémillon blend is not a common combination in New Zealand, where Chardonnay does not need to be crisped up, but Chenin Blanc and Chardonnay have proved to be surprisingly good bed-mates in New Zealand.

🍷— 1–3 years

✓ *Alpha Domus* (Sémillon-Sauvignon) • *Kumeu River* (Sauvignon-Sémillon) • *Pegasus Bay* (Sauvignon Sémillon Oak Aged on Lees) • *Selaks* (Sauvignon Blanc-Sémillon) • *Villa Maria* (Chenin-Chardonnay)

OTHER WHITE-WINE STYLES

No one in New Zealand makes really good Chenin Blanc, but Millton Barrel Fermented is as good as it gets. No New Zealand Gewürztraminer has ever really impressed me; Cloudy Bay, Dry River, Montana Putatahi Estate, and Stonecroft have come closest. New Zealand's Gewürztraminer are more musky-floral and lychee than truly pungent spice, but it would take an imagination the size of Texas to see more than a smidgen of spice in any of the country's Pinot Gris. Dry River makes the best Pinot Gris, and nice, elegant wine it is, but it is not real Pinot Gris. Quartz Reef and Martinborough Vineyards have also produced good wine from this grape. Truly dry Riesling is still a relatively recent phenomenon, but there are an increasing number of fine examples of this style coming on to the market, with Corbans (Private Bin Amberley), Felton Road, Neudorf (Moutere), Rippon, Selaks, Seresin, and Vavasour the best so far. There are many more top-quality off-dry Rieslings, including Collards (Queen Charlotte), Coopers Creek, Kim Crawford, Dry River (Craighill), Lawson's Dry Hills, Martinborough Vineyards, Millton Vineyard (Opou Vineyard), Montana (Marlborough Reserve), Nga Waka, Palliser Estate, Rippon, Allan Scott, Stoneleigh Vineyard, Stratford, Villa Maria (Private Bin, Reserve), and Charles Wiffen. It is often a moot point trying to distinguish between botrytis-affected and medium-sweet Riesling, but Collards, Cooper's Creek (Reserve), Grove Mill, Framingham, Pegasus Bay, and De Redcliffe lead the latter category. With less herbaceously aggressive clones of Sémillon coming into production, we should see a rapidly increasing number of classic renditions of this varietal, which when ripe is greatly enhanced by fermentation in small oak *barriques*. Until then Collards and Villa Maria have established the best track record for this grape. Viognier waits in the wings.

OTHER RED-WINE STYLES

Syrah has come a long way in the last few years. The first commercial release of any New Zealand wine produced from this grape was by Stonecroft from Hawkes Bay. The early vintages were tight and green, but showed potential and this has been realized since the 1996 vintage. Stonecroft is still considered the best by some, although I would place Trinity Hill (Gimblett Road) and Fromm (La Strada) above it, with Babich (Mara Estate), Denton, Dry River, Framingham, Matariki, Okahu, and Peninsula Estate (Gilmour) at least its equal. There is a very good Malbec from Fromm (La Strada), a stunning Montepulciano from Framingham, and Pinotage to see off most Cape renditions from Okahu (Paula's Reserve) and Sanctuary.

ATA RANGI, MARTINBOROUGH
Consistent Pinot Noir is produced here.

THE WINE PRODUCERS OF
NEW ZEALAND

ALPHA DOMUS
Hawkes Bay
★☆

This family-owned enterprise made its first wine in 1995, doubled its capacity in 1999, and had impressed a lot of people in a very short time.

✓ *Chardonnay* (AD) • *Merlot Cabernet• The Navigator* • *Sémillon-Sauvignon*

AOTEA
Gisborne
Ⓥ

A brand, not a winery, owned by Margaret Harvey, a British Master of Wine, Aotea is short for Aotearoa, which is Maori for "land of the long, white cloud". Although not in the same class as those from Marlborough, Aotea Sauvignon Blanc is nonetheless the best wine to come out of Gisborne so far.

✓ *Sauvignon Blanc*

ATA RANGI
Martinborough
★☆Ⓥ

Clive Paton and Phyll Pattie are famous for their beautifully crafted Pinot Noir, but the Chardonnay is also one of Martinborough's best.

✓ *Cabernet-Merlot* (Célèbre) • *Chardonnay • Pinot Noir*

BABICH
Henderson
★

The Irongate Cabernet-Merlot and Irongate Chardonnay have never been better and now there is an exciting Syrah.

✓ *Cabernet-Merlot* (Irongate) • *Cabernet Sauvignon* (The Patriarch) • *Chardonnay* (Irongate) • *Syrah* (Mara Estate)

BENFIELD & DELAMARE
Martinborough
★☆

Located in the heart of Pinot Noir country, this estate makes a Merlot-dominated Bordeaux blend of consistently high quality.

✓ *Red Wine*

BLOOMFIELD VINEYARDS
Masterton
Another specialist in red wine, Bloomfield's Bordeaux varieties may prove to be as successful as Martinborough's Pinot Noir.

BROOKFIELDS VINEYARDS
Napier
☆

A firm, deep-flavoured, oaky Cabernet-Merlot and a ripe, gentle, satisfying Pinot Gris are made here.

✓ *Cabernet-Merlot*

LE BRUN
Marlborough
★

It is now evident that Daniel Le Brun's reputation at Cellier Le Brun was built on wines produced over just three years: 1989, 1990 and 1991. Forget the vintages from 1992 to 1996, when Daniel was enjoying the media spotlight so much that he took his eye of the bulle and allowed his grapes to be harvested far too green. That includes the 1996, which the new owners that year did not consider good enough and was sold as a non-vintage under the Terrace Road label. Inexplicably that Terrace Road *cuvée* won a number of awards, but did not deserve any (I often despair at the medals dished out for fizzed-up dishwater at New World wine competitions). However, the quality and reputation of Cellier Le Brun is destined to return following the 1997 releases, albeit with another wine-maker, Alan MacWilliams, and thus a different style. Look for more tropical, less biscuity-champenois style.

✓ *Sparkling Wines* (from 1997 vintage)

LE BRUN FAMILY ESTATE
Marlborough
★

When Daniel Le Brun's ties with Cellier Le Brun were severed in 1996 he was not allowed to commercialize wine under his own name for three years. In 1999, three years later to the day, Daniel cheekily opened up Le Brun Family Estate around the corner and launched his No. 1 cuvée. He was, after all, the first Le Brun and many of his loyal customers still think that he's the best. However, I couldn't recomm-end the first release (it contained some wine from 1996, when his attention was not focused), but the second release is fine and early tastings of his Daniel 1997 Virginie very promising. It would be nice to see Daniel become a Marlborough superstar for a second time, but we shall have to wait and see.

✓ *Sparkling Wines* (from 1997)

CAIRNBRAE
Marlborough
★☆

This small, boutique winery was established in 1992 and soon made a name for high-quality white wines.

✓ *Chardonnay* • *Riesling Reserve* • *Sauvignon Blanc* (The Stones)

CHARD FARM
Central Otago
Chard Farm is dramatically situated and must be approached along a rough-hewn track that bends around a mountainside, with a steep gorge on one side, and there is barely enough room to drive a car.

✓ *Pinot Noir*

CHURCH ROAD
Taradale
★☆

Montana's high-tech Hawkes Bay boutique winery is housed in the old but lovingly restored Church Winery. With the help of Cordier, the Bordeaux producer, Church Road has produced wines that combine the restrained exuberance of cool-climate New World fruit with the classic Old World structure, promising an exciting future.

✓ *Cabernet Sauvignon* • *Chardonnay*

CLEARVIEW ESTATE
Hawkes Bay
★☆

A very young winery, Clearview Estate has achieved its destiny to be one of New Zealand's star producers in the near future, especially for its stunning Chardonnay and Merlot (Reserve).

✓ *Cabernet Merlot* • *Chardonnay* • *Merlot* • *Sauvignon Blanc*

CLIFFORD BAY
Marlborough
★

With its first wine produced as recently as 1997, Clifford Bay has swiftly seduced everybody, particularly with its Sauvignon Blanc.

✓ *Chardonnay* • *Sauvignon Blanc*

CLOUDY BAY
Marlborough
★★

This winery was established by David Hohnen of Cape Mentelle in Western Australia. His Cloudy Bay Sauvignon Blanc quickly acquired cult status, which is a just reward for Kevin Judd, Hohnen's talented winemaker and partner. The perfect combination of high quality and individual craftsman-ship has turned Cloudy Bay into the southern hemisphere's fastest-rising star. Hohnen and Judd have cleverly evoked a boutique image, which was necessary to attract a cult-following, but a minor PR miracle considering that Cloudy Bay is, in fact, one of Marlborough's largest wineries. This was achieved by developing such a wide distribution that the wines had to be rationed on a strict quota basis, which meant that they quickly sold out, giving the impression of a limited production. Cloudy Bay's Chardonnay has always been at least as good as its Sauvignon, it is world famous for its Pelorus sparkling wine, and continues to surprise with wines like Pinot Noir and even Gewürztraminer.

✓ *Cabernet-Merlot* • *Chardonnay* • *Gewürztraminer* • *Pinot Noir* • *Sauvignon Blanc* • *Sparkling Wines* (Pelorus)

COLLARDS
Henderson
★☆Ⓥ

This winery, founded by English horticulturist J. W. Collard, is still in family ownership. Brothers Bruce and Geoffrey Collard have maintained the winery's reputation for consistency across the range. The wines have a rich vibrancy of fruit, notably the text book Hawkes Bay Chardonnay, which displays a fine youthful complexity.

✓ *Chardonnay* (Hawkes Bay) • *Riesling* • *Sauvignon Blanc*

COOPERS CREEK
Huapai
★☆

One of New Zealand's most prestigious wineries, Coopers Creek was involved in a damaging mis-labelling scandal over some of the wines it produced in 1995 and 1996. There was wrongdoing according to the findings of an audit of the production in question, yet Kim Crawford, the winemaker since 1980, made some splendid, award-winning wines up to and throughout this period, and he continues to do so under his own label today. Crawford's assistant, Simon Nunns, has since taken over and the wines remain excellent. I have absolutely no idea whether I ever tasted one of Coopers Creek's mislabelled wines, but if I did it was bloody good!

✓ *Cabernet Sauvignon* • *Chardonnay* (Swamp Reserve) • *Merlot Cabernet Franc* • *Riesling* • *Sauvignon Blanc* (Marlborough)

CORBANS
Wineries *Auckland, Gisborne, Napier, Blenheim*
★☆Ⓥ

When a Lebanese man called Assid Abraham Corban set sail for New Zealand he was a stonemason and could not have contemplated that wine might be his destiny, but in 1902, after ten years and almost as many jobs, he planted a vineyard in the Henderson area and turned out to be a natural-born winemaker. Corbans was the second-largest wine group in the country until November 2000, when it was purchased by Montana. Quality regional labels include Longridge for Hawkes Bay and Stoneleigh for Marlborough, in addition to which a wide range of wines is sold under various brands, including Chasseur, Cooks, Liebstraum, Montel, Robard & Butler, St. Arnaud, Seven Oaks, and Velluto. Readers should note that many of the wines previously sold as Private Bin are now under the Cottage Block label.

✓ *Cabernet-Merlot* (Cottage Block) • *Chardonnay* (especially Cottage Block) • *Merlot* (Cottage Block) • *Pinot Noir* (Private Bin) • *Riesling* (Botrytized, Private Bin Botrytis Selected Noble, Private Bin Amberley Dry, Stoneleigh) • *Sauvignon Blanc* (Stoneleigh)

COVELL ESTATE
Galatea
⭐

This is the only winery located in the Galatea area of the Bay of Plenty. An up-and-coming biodynamic producer, Bob Covell makes intensely flavoured wines, which sometimes have a noticeable oakiness, but always age well.

✓ *Cabernet-Merlot* • *Chardonnay* • *Pinot Noir* • *Riesling*

KIM CRAWFORD
Hawkes Bay
⭐⭐

One of New Zealand's most experienced, talented, and award-winning winemakers, Kim Crawford has had his own winery since 1996. His best wines are Chardonnay, Riesling and Sauvignon Blanc. The quality of his reds is climbing fast, but all the wines are good here. A very fruity non-vintage sparkling wine called Rory is as bad as it gets, and that ain't so bad.

✓ *Cabernet Franc* (Wicken) • *Chardonnay* (Tietjen) • *Merlot Cabernet Franc* (Tane) • *Riesling* • *Sauvignon Blanc*

DELEGAT'S
Henderson
⭐⭐

Most wines from this medal-winning producer are sourced from Hawkes Bay, although the style is generally more restrained than would be expected from such fruit, with more elegance than richness, but never lacking depth or length. It also sells some fine Marlborough wines under the Oyster Bay label.

✓ *Chardonnay* (Oyster Bay, Proprietors Reserve, Vicarage Road) • *Merlot* (Proprietors Reserve) • *Sauvignon Blanc* (including Oyster Bay)

DENTON
Nelson
⭐

The first harvest here was as recent as 1996, yet Richard and Alexandra Denton have already charmed us with delightful Chardonnay and Riesling. It is, however, their Syrah that has grabbed most of the attention.

✓ *Chardonnay* • *Riesling* • *Syrah*

DRY RIVER
Martinborough
⭐⭐

Neil McCallum makes very elegant Pinot Noir and Chardonnay. Capable of producing one of New Zealand's most delicately perfumed dry Rieslings, his true forte is, however, the crafting of decadently rich botrytized wines. James Halliday once told me, "Some would say he (McCallum) is New Zealand's top wine producer," in a way that suggested he did. Or, at least, he would not want to argue the point.

✓ *Chardonnay* (Botrytized) • *Gewürztraminer* • *Pinot Gris* • *Pinot Noir* • *Riesling* (Botrytized, Craighall Estate Dry) • *Syrah*

ESK VALLEY
Napier
⭐

This was not one of my favourite producers prior to the late 1980s, but the range of Esk Valley wines has become very impressive under the ownership of Villa Maria.

✓ *Chenin Blanc* (Botrytis Selection) • *Sauvignon Blanc* • *The Terraces* (red Bordeaux style)

FELTON ROAD
Central Otago
⭐⭐

With the first harvest in 1997, it is far too early to make definitive statements about Felton Road, but the quality so far from this Bannockburn producer is very exciting indeed.

✓ *Pinot Noir* • *Riesling*

FORREST ESTATE
Marlborough
⭐

An interesting range of fine wines is produced here, especially the soft, classic Sauvignon Blanc.

✓ *Gewürztraminer* • *Merlot* • *Sauvignon Blanc*

FOXES ISLAND WINES
Marlborough
⭐

John Belsham, Hunter's former winemaker, set up a designer-wine service called Rapaura Vintners, where he makes literally any style of wine to order, be it for a grape grower with no winery, a wholesaler, retailer, or restaurant. He is an exceptionally gifted winemaker, and this enterprise has been amazingly successful, making Rapaura a name in small print for the *cognoscenti* to look out for. Belsham is also building up his own outstanding range, starting with minute quantities of sought-after Chardonnay from his own vineyard on Foxes Island.

✓ *Chardonnay* • *Pinot Noir*

FRAMINGHAM
Marlborough
⭐⭐

Marlborough's fastest-rising star has produced one of New Zealand's finest dry Rieslings and tends to specialize in this grape. It also offers a large and fascinating range of other varietal wines.

✓ *Gewürztraminer* • *Merlot* • *Montepulciano* • *Pinot Gris* • *Riesling* (Dry, Classic, Late Harvest) • *Syrah*

FROMM
Marlborough
⭐⭐

Owned by Georg and Ruth Fromm, a Swiss couple who, with the help of winemaker Hätsch Kalberer, have carved out a cosy red-wine niche for themselves.

✓ *Malbec* (La Strada) • *Pinot Noir* (La Strada) • *Syrah* (La Strada)

GIBBSTON VALLEY
Central Otago

A restaurant-winery in an idyllic setting, with steadily improving wines, especially Pinot Noir.

GIESEN WINE ESTATE
Christchurch
⭐⭐Ⓥ

Canterbury's largest winery includes 35 hectares (86 acres) of vineyards, which produce a wide range of wines, with luscious Pinot Noir the most exciting wine of the moment, although it is Giesen's botrytized wines that consistently excel.

✓ *Chardonnay* (Isabel Estate Reserve) • *Pinot Noir* • *Riesling* (Botrytized)

GILLAN
Marlborough

Terry "Telboy" Gillan produces gorgeously crisp and tasty white wines. Also serves a great British breakfast in the winery.

✓ *Chardonnay* • *Sauvignon Blanc*

GOLDWATER ESTATE
Waiheke Island
⭐⭐

There is no doubt that proprietors Kim and Jeanette Goldwater produce one of New Zealand's greatest red wines. Goldwater Cabernet-Merlot is a wine of classic quality, which has the richness, finesse, longevity, and potential complexity to compete with the best wines, whether of California, Australia, or Bordeaux.

✓ *Cabernet-Merlot* (sometimes Cabernet-Merlot-Franc) • *Chardonnay*

GROVE MILL
Marlborough
⭐Ⓥ

Grove Mill's scintillating Sauvignon Blanc is the wine to buy.

✓ *Sauvignon Blanc* • *Riesling*

HERON'S FLIGHT
Matakana
⭐

The sensational Cabernet Sauvignon produced by this winery since the 1991 vintage has confirmed the potential of Matakana.

✓ *Cabernet Sauvignon*

HIGHFIELD ESTATE
Marlborough
⭐

Fine, stylish white wines are made at this Anglo-Japanese-New Zealand owned estate, which overlooks the Omaka Valley. Champagne Drappier helped in the development of Highfield's rich, creamy-vanilla sparkling wine, which is sold under the Elstree label.

✓ *Chardonnay* • *Pinot Noir* (Elstree) • *Sauvignon Blanc* • *Sparkling Wines* (Elstree)

HUNTER'S
Marlborough
⭐⭐

Jane Hunter is a gifted viticulturist whose vineyard is one of Marlborough's uncontested *grands crus*. Her winery sets medal-winning standards that have earned her the respect of her neighbours and international renown. When Jane launched her international fizz Miru Miru with the 1995 it was not only better than her more expensive, longer-aged Hunter's sparkling wine, it was so moreish I just could not get hold of enough of the stuff. This was obviously a watershed year for sparkling wine quality at Hunter's because the eponymous brand was the best yet. Until that vintage I was not at all impressed by the wine, which was supposed to be a mature, complex sparkling wine, yet was merely foursquare and often quite dull. However, if the progress in the 1995 pleased me, the 1996 totally bowled me over: this was everything that Jane had always told me she was trying to make. Mind you, it did not pick up a single medal! What do New World competitions expect from a classic sparkling wine?

√ *Chardonnay* • *Pinot Noir* • *Riesling* • *Sauvignon Blanc* • *Sparkling Wine* (Hunter's, Miru Miru)

HUTHLEE
Hawkes Bay
★

Excellent reds including a Merlot that vies with the very best that New Zealand has to offer.

√ *Cabernet Franc* • *Cabernet Sauvignon Merlot* • *Cabernet Sauvignon Merlot Cabernet Franc* • *Merlot*

HYPERION
Northland
☆

John Crone makes wine in a cowshed north of Auckland!

√ *Merlot* (Gaia)

ISABEL ESTATE
Marlborough
☆

Boutique winery and vineyard on gravelly Hawksberry Terrace soil.

√ *Pinot Noir* • *Sauvignon Blanc*

JACKSON ESTATE
Marlborough
★☆ⓥ

As far as I am concerned, John and Warwick Stichbury produce

Marlborough's consistently greatest Sauvignon Blanc, and have done so since their first vintage in 1991. It has a most intense, vibrantly fruity flavour of extraordinary finesse. Chardonnay promises almost equal potential, albeit in a restrained and somewhat complex style. Pinot Noir is delightful, with elegant strawberry and vanilla fruit. Ironically, these wines were an afterthought for what was supposed to be a specialist sparkling-wine venture.

√ *Chardonnay* • *Pinot Noir* • *Riesling* (Botrytized) • *Sauvignon Blanc*

KAITUNA VALLEY
Canterbury
★

Owner-winemakers Grant and Helen specialize in Pinot Noir and Chardonnay.

√ *Pinot Noir*

KEMBLEFIELD
Hawkes Bay
★☆

John Kemble produces excellent Chardonnay and Merlot-Cabernet. His Gewürztraminer is supposed to be very Alsace-like.

√ *Chardonnay* • *Merlot Cabernet*

KUMEU RIVER
Auckland
★☆

Master of Wine Michael Braijkovitch regularly produces one of New Zealand's greatest Chardonnays. Excellent value easy-drinking wines are sold under the Brajkovich label.

√ *Chardonnay* • *Merlot-Cabernet* • *Sauvignon-Sémillon*

LAWSON'S DRY HILLS
Marlborough
★☆

This winery is capable of producing intensely flavoured white wines.

√ *Chardonnay* • *Riesling* • *Sauvignon Blanc*

LINCOLN VINEYARDS
Henderson
☆

Although most critics opt for the Chardonnay or oak-aged Chenin Blanc, I prefer the richer reds with their minty, fruitcake flavours.

√ *Cabernet-Merlot* (Home Vineyards, Vintage Selection)

McCASHIN'S
Nelson
☆

McCashin's is a well-known brewery in Nelson, but it has only just got into winemaking, with its first vintage as recent as 1998. Bearing in mind the exceptional red wines that that very special vintage produced all over New Zealand, I should be cautious in bestowing any ranking; however, the Pinot Noir was simply too stunning to miss out.

√ *Pinot Noir*

MARTINBOROUGH VINEYARDS
Martinborough
★☆

This winery's reputation was established by Larry McKenna, but he recently left to set up his own winery and the new winemaker, Claire Mulholland (ex-Gibbston Valley), has yet to prove herself. However, as Larry's wines will not be available until I write the next update, Martinborough Vineyards' ranking remains pro tem.

√ *Chardonnay* • *Pinot Noir* • *Riesling*

MATARIKI
Hawkes Bay
★

This fast-rising boutique winery has made some of New Zealand's best Syrah since its first vintage, as recent as 1997, and intends producing Sangiovese in the near future.

√ *Anthology* • *Chardonnay* • *Syrah*

MATAWHERO WINES
Gisborne

Owner Denis Irwin crops his vineyards at a low level, hand harvests, and uses natural yeasts to express the individual *terroir* of his product. Occasionally this produces something stunning, but the results are not infrequently disappointing – a pity for someone of such passion and commitment. Gewürztraminer is his most consistent wine and many believe it to be New Zealand's finest example of this grape.

MATUA VALLEY
Waimauku
★★

This high-tech winery produces a range of fine, expressive wines that are full of exuberant fruit and a pure pleasure to drink. The recently launched Ararimu label is reserved for Matua Valley's top-quality wines made in only the very best vintages. Excellent Marlborough wines are sold under the Shingle Peak label.

√ *Cabernet-Merlot* (Ararimu) • *Chardonnay* (Ararimu) • *Cabernet Sauvignon* (Dartmoor Smith Estate) • *Chardonnay* (Judd Estate) • *Chenin-Chardonnay* (Judd Estate) • *Merlot* (Dartmoor Smith Estate, Shingle Peak) • *Sauvignon Blanc*

MILLS REEF
Hawkes Bay
★

The huge publicity surrounding one over-hyped, over-oaked sparkling wine distracts deserved attention from the deliciously rich, vibrantly fruity Sauvignon Blanc and some stunning Bordeaux blends.

√ *Riesling* • *Sauvignon Blanc* (plus all Elspeth *cuvées*)

THE MILLTON VINEYARD
Gisborne
☆

This biodynamic producer is justly famous for its award winning, lightly-botrytized, medium-sweet Opou Riesling. It also produces a stylish barrel-fermented Chardonnay, and is appreciated locally for Chenin Blanc.

√ *Chardonnay* (Barrel Fermented) • *Riesling* (Opov Vineyard)

MISSION VINEYARDS
Taradale

Although the Society of Mary occasionally makes a real gem, as the Jewelstone Chardonnay 1992, lacklustre products still dominate the range of Hawkes Bay wines from this long-established winery.

√ *Chardonnay* (Jewelstone)

MONTANA
Wineries *Auckland, Gisborne, Marlborough*
★★☆ⓥ

The largest wine producer in the country just got bigger when, in November 2000, Montana purchased Corbans, New Zealand's second-largest wine group. Montana now owns in excess of 2,400 hectares (6,000 acres) and sells through various brands some 55 per cent of all New Zealand's wines. The quality and consistency of the wines produced, even at the bottom of the range, is breathtaking, and sets an example for what every large winery should aspire to.

√ *Cabernet Sauvignon* (Fairhall, Marlborough) • *Chardonnay* (Marlborough, Gisborne, Ormand Estate, Renwick Estate) • *Gewürztraminer* (Pututahi) • *Pinot Noir* (Reserve) • *Riesling* (Reserve) • *Sauvignon Blanc* (Stoneleigh) • *Sparkling Wines* (all Deutz *cuvées*, Lindauer Special Reserve)

MORTON ESTATE
Bay of Plenty
★☆

Although essentially a white-wine specialist, Morton Estate produces one of New Zealand's most stunning Cabernet-Merlot blends and periodically markets an excellent, pure varietal Merlot, although Chardonnay really rules supreme here, whether the young, pineapple-tasting, basic White Label Cuvée, or the richer, riper, more succulent Black Label.

√ *Cabernet-Merlot* (Black Label) • *Chardonnay* (especially Black Label) • *Sauvignon Blanc* (Black Label Fumé Blanc) • *Sparkling Wine* (Méthode Champenoise)

MT DIFFICULTY
Central Otago
★

Another possible Bannockburn star in the making.

✓ *Pinot Noir*

NAUTILUS
Marlborough
☆

This brand belongs to the Australian Yalumba group. Although there is a vineyard, and cellar-door sales, there is no Nautilus winery, the wines being produced by a local winemaker. The rich, ripe, Sauvignon Blanc hits between the eyes, and the Chardonnay is a fulsome wine.

✓ *Sauvignon Blanc • Sparkling Wines* (Nautilus Estate)

NEUDORF VINEYARDS
Nelson
★☆

Tim and Judy Finn make the best pair of Burgundian-style wines in the country. Somebody might make a better Chardonnay or a finer Pinot Noir, this year or that, but no one consistently produces both varietals to such a high standard.

✓ *Chardonnay* (Moutere) *• Pinot Noir* (Moutere*) • Riesling* (Dry Moutere, Late Harvest Moutere) *• Sauvignon Blanc*

NGATARAWA WINES
Hastings
★

This is a quality-conscious Hawkes Bay winery making its mark with distinctive red wines, but with the exception of Alwyn Riesling and Glazebrook Chardonnay, its whites are so understated that their subtlety is lost on me.

✓ *Cabernet Merlot* (Glazebrook) *• Chardonnay* (Glazebrook*) • Riesling* (Alwyn*)*

NGA WAKA VINEYARD
Martinborough
★

This vineyard was established in 1988 by Francophile Roseworthy college graduate Roger Parkinson. Its wines are intense with crisp fruit.

✓ *Riesling • Sauvignon Blanc*

NOBILO
Auckland
★

Now owned by BRL Hardy, which is planning to invest heavily in a new winery and planting vineyards. Best wines at the moment are the Dixon Vineyard Chardonnay and the Marlborough Sauvignon Blanc; this should be a range to watch.

✓ *Chardonnay* (Dixon Vineyard) *• Sauvignon Blanc* (Marlborough)

OKAHU ESTATE
Northland
☆

The most northerly vineyard in New Zealand, the Okahu Estate overlooks Ninety Mile Beach.

✓ *Pinotage* (Paula's Reserve) *• Syrah*

PALLISER ESTATE
Martinborough
★ⓥ

Palliser makes consistently successful Sauvignon Blanc and elegant Pinot Noir, but its Chardonnay is rather hit-and-miss (with the hits, for some reason, often confined to odd-numbered years).

✓ *Pinot Noir • Riesling • Sauvignon Blanc*

C. J. PASK
Hastings
★★

Ex-cropduster Chris Pask was a grower for seven years before setting up his own winery in 1989. His 35 hectares (86 acres) of deep-gravel vineyards are in the prime Gimblett Road area of Hawkes Bay. They form the foundation of the superb quality this winery has already produced, although it is relatively unknown on export markets. Pask's ace up his sleeve is, however, Kate Radburnd, the exceptionally talented, former Vidal winemaker, who has expertly crafted the potential of Pask's vineyard into rich, complex wines that are destined for greater international fame.

✓ *Cabernet-Merlot • Chardonnay*

PEGASUS BAY
Waipara
★☆

A successful new winery owned by wine writer and neurologist Professor Ivan Donaldson.

✓ *Cabernet-Merlot • Chardonnay • Pinot Noir • Riesling • Sauvignon Sémillon Oak Aged on Lees*

PENINSULA ESTATE
Waiheke Island

Brave or stupid, there is no doubting the viticultural risk taken by Doug Hamilton in planting this Cabernet-blend vineyard, which sticks out into the Pacific, exposed to salt-bearing sea-breezes on three sides.

✓ *Peninsula Estate Red* (red Bordeaux style) *• Syrah* (Gilmour)

QUARTZ REEF
Central Otago

Owned by Rudi Bauer and Clotilde Chauvet (who also makes Champagne in Rilly-la-Montagne), who own vineyards at Bendigo and produce excellent Pinot Noir and sparkling wine. Quartz Reef's non-vintage fizz contains a majority of Marlborough fruit and has an unashamedly fruit-driven style with a soft, breezy mousse, but develops a more complex style after a year or so cellaring. A pre-commercial tasting of the first vintage (1998) showed great promise, not only for Quartz Reef, but also for Central Otago, since this is the first successful sparkling wine to be made exclusively from local-grown grapes.

✓ *Pinot Noir* (Reserve) *• Sparkling Wine*

DE REDCLIFFE ESTATES
Mangatawhiri Valley
★

This Waikato winery makes disappointing reds, but good-quality and flavoursome whites, especially Riesling. De Redcliffe Estates offers one of the best winery visits in the country, with a fine Hotel du Vin, restaurant, tennis court, and guest swimming pool.

✓ *Chardonnay* (Mangatawhiri) *• Riesling*

RIPPON
Wanaka

In 1974, against all expert advice, Lois and Rolfe Mills chose one of the most beautiful areas in the world to grow vines, and have certainly succeeded, although it took until 1989 to make their first commercial wine. Chardonnay and possibly Riesling or Gewürztraminer appeared to have most potential, but Pinot Noir was the first wine to establish any consistently fine reputation. A sparkling wine is due to be released.

✓ *Pinot Noir • Riesling*

RONGOPAI
Te Kauwhata
☆

A brilliant source for botrytized wines, Rongopai has just bought the old research station at Te Kauwhata.

✓ *Chardonnay* (Botrytized) *• Riesling* (Botrytized)

SACRED HILL
Hawkes Bay
★

A substantial range of good-quality varietals, the whites of which used to dominate, but now motoring on reds as well.

✓ *Chardonnay* (Rifleman's Reserve) *• Merlot* (Brokenstone Reserve, Whitecliff Vineyards)

• Riesling (XS Noble) *• Sémillon* (Botrytis)

ST. CLAIR
Marlborough
★

Several interesting wines suggest that this could be one of New Zealand's best wineries in the future, particularly when its large holding in the potentially exciting Awatere Valley comes on stream.

✓ *Merlot • Sauvignon Blanc*

ST. HELENA WINE ESTATE
Christchurch

At one time St. Helena was New Zealand's leading Pinot Noir exponent, but although it occasionally still manages to produce excellent wines from this variety, the consistency is not there.

ST. JÉRÔME
Henderson
★

This is a top-quality Bordeaux blend made in a big, blockbuster style from a small boutique winery.

✓ *Cabernet-Merlot*

DANIEL SCHUSTER
Christchurch
★☆

This Waipara winery is owned by Danny Schuster, who makes one of New Zealand's best Pinot Noirs, a very good Chardonnay, and an interesting Pinot Blanc.

✓ *Chardonnay* (Omihi Hills) *• Pinot Noir* (Omihi Hills)

ALLAN SCOTT
Marlborough
★

Allan Scott established Marlborough's very first vineyard, Stoneleigh, in 1973 when he was Corban's Chief Viticulturist. Allan produces good Sauvignon Blanc and launched his own fizz in 1999, but truly excels at Chardonnay and Riesling.

✓ *Chardonnay • Riesling*

SEIFRIED ESTATE
Nelson
★☆ⓥ

Consumers outside of New Zealand will know these wines as Redwood Valley. Seifried is best for white wines, especially the superb botrytized Riesling, and one of this country's better dry Rieslings.

✓ *Chardonnay* (Old Coach Road) *• Riesling* (Botrytis Dry Riesling)

SELAKS
Auckland
★☆ⓥ

Selaks consistently produces fine-quality, stylish wines across the range, especially whites, although its sparkling wine has been curiously uninspiring.

✓ *Chardonnay* (Birchwood, Founder's Reserve) *• Riesling* (Dry) *• Sauvignon Blanc • Sauvignon-Sémillon*

SERESIN
Marlborough
★☆

This is an organic estate: the vines are all hand-tended and some wines are fermented with wild yeasts. The winemaker is Brian Bicknell, known for his flying winemaker exploits, but nothing he has made under contract compares with the wines from Seresin, some of which rank amongst the very best from Marlborough.

✓ *Merlot • Pinot Gris • Pinot Noir • Riesling* (Dry, Noble) *• Sauvignon Blanc*

SILENI
Hawkes Bay
★☆

Hi-tech megastar in the making, Sileni crushed its first crop as recently as 1998 yet has already spellbound wine critics with its Merlot Cabernets.

✓ *Chardonnay • Merlot Cabernets • Sémillon*

STONECROFT
Hastings
☆

This winery has produced a deep, concentrated Syrah, closer in style to the Rhône than an Australian Shiraz, although the early vintages are let down by the youthfulness of the vines and a need for more bottle-age prior to release. Stonecroft is, however, ground-breaking.

✓ *Cabernet • Syrah*

STONYRIDGE
Waiheke Island
★★

Stephen White's pastel-pink winery produces a deep-black red wine called Larose on the verdant isle of Waiheke. He trained in Tuscany, California, and Bordeaux, but was most influenced by the latter region, as demonstrated by his Bordeaux-blend called Larose, which always sells out *en primeur*.

✓ *Larose*

STRATFORD WINES OF MARLBOROUGH
Marlborough
★☆

The first wines produced here were from the 1997 vintage and were sold under the Wakefield Vineyard label, but Strat Canning's Stratford

Wines are well worth digging out whatever he calls them, especially his wonderfully racy Riesling.

✓ *Chardonnay • Pinot Noir • Riesling*

TE KAIRANGA
Martinborough
★★

Since the 1993 vintage, Te Kairanga has produced impressive Pinot Noir with creamy fruit and fine varietal perfume. Now making award-winning Cabernet Sauvignon.

✓ *Cabernet Sauvignon • Chardonnay • Pinot Noir*

TE MATA
Hawkes Bay
★★

The oldest winery in New Zealand, Te Mata Estate was purchased in 1978 by John Buck, who with the help of winemaker Peter Cowley has fashioned two of the country's greatest red wines, Awatea and Coleraine. The blending components of Coleraine have finesse and are nicely structured, while those of Awatea are more generous and accessible. Te Mata's basic Cabernet-Merlot is more easy-drinking in style, although some years can develop a surprising concentration in the bottle. The whites are often overlooked, but should not be, as they are always rich, with racy fruit and mouthwatering acidity.

✓ *Cabernet-Merlot* (especially Awatea, Coleraine) *• Chardonnay* (Castle Hill, Elston) *• Sauvignon Blanc* (Castle Hill)

TE WHARE RA
Marlborough
This vineyard has a well-deserved reputation for luscious dessert style wines.

✓ *Botrytis Bunch Selection*

TRINITY HILL
Hastings
★★

Part-owner and managing director John Hancock, who helped establish Morton Estate's reputation, is now doing well here, along with his winemaker Warren Gibson. Watch out for the Pinot Noir. The first vintage, 2000, was made with help from Hancock's old mucker Larry McKenna (ex-Martinborough Vineyard). More unusual varieties are waiting in the wings. Gimblett Road is the top label, but the quality of the less expensive Shepherds Croft wines is better than the best found at many other wineries. So far I have not found any wine from Trinity Hill I wouldn't like to drink.

✓ *Cabernet Sauvignon* (Gimblett Road) *• Cabernet Sauvignon Merlot* (Gimblett Road, Shepherds Croft) *• Merlot Cabernet Franc Syrah* (Shepherds Croft) *• Riesling* (Wairarapa) *• Syrah* (Gimblett Road)

TWO PADDOCKS
Gibbston Valley
★★

Owned by actor Sam Neill, Two Paddocks has produced some stunning Pinot Noir under the auspices of Dean Shaw, who took over from Rudi Bauer as contract winemaker. During an unannounced visit to one of the so-called paddocks in Bannockburn it was easy to discern Mr Neill's vineyard, it being completely covered in netting while flocks of birds were greedily gobbling up his neighbour's grapes. The other paddock is in Bannockburn and I hear that land has been purchased in Alexandra (very much the growth place in Central Otago, especially for those who think Bannockburn too warm). So will there be an addition to the range or will the wine simply become Three Paddocks?

✓ *Pinot Noir*

UNISON VINEYARD
Hawkes Bay
★☆

This high density vineyard (5,000 vines per hectare) produces just two wines, both a blend of Merlot, Cabernet Sauvignon and Syrah, one simply called Unison, the other Unison Selection. Both are brilliant.

✓ *Unison • Unison Selection*

VAVASOUR
Marlborough
★★

In terms of exports, this is probably New Zealand's most underrated producer. Vavasour opened up the Awatere Valley, about a half-hour's drive south of Blenheim. It is believed to be one of the country's most successful sub-regions. The whites and reds both share intense fruit flavour and excellent structure. Excellent wines are also sold under the Dashwood label.

✓ *Chardonnay • Pinot Noir • Riesling* (Dry) *• Sauvignon Blanc*

VIDAL
Hastings
★★ⓥ

Vidal was founded by a Spaniard, but is now owned by George Fistonich, the son of a Dalmatian immigrant and proprietor of Villa Maria. This winery consistently produces some of the most exciting red wines in the Hawkes Bay area, but the whites often lack finesse, although they are usually very gluggy and easy to drink; Vidal does produce one of New Zealand's better Gewürztraminers.

✓ *Cabernet-Merlot* (Reserve) *• Cabernet Sauvignon* (Reserve) *• Chardonnay* (Reserve)

VILLA MARIA
Auckland
★★★ⓥ

Probably the best all-round producer in New Zealand, Villa Maria has a vast range of wines, yet they are all

beautifully crafted to enhance fruit and finesse. Where oak is used, the touch is light and impeccably integrated. If the quality is super, the consistency is supernatural. Proprietor George Fistonich also owns Esk Valley and Vidals, making this the third-largest group of wineries in New Zealand.

✓ *Cabernet-Merlot* (Private Bin) *• Cabernet Sauvignon* (Reserve) *• Chardonnay* (Reserve Barrique Fermented) *• Chenin-Chardonnay • Riesling* (Noble Botrytis Selection, Private Bin) *• Sauvignon Blanc*

WAIPARA SPRINGS
Waipara
★

This winery has settled down to produce a solid range of consistently fine-quality wines. Riesling is best, but both red and white excel.

✓ *Cabernet Sauvignon • Chardonnay • Pinot Noir • Riesling • Sauvignon Blanc*

WAITAKERE ROAD VINEYARD
Kumeu
This little-known winery has good red-wine potential.

✓ *Harrier Rise*

WHITEHAVEN
Marlborough
★☆

Sensational Riesling and Sauvignon Blanc, particularly Single Vineyard Reserve.

✓ *Chardonnay • Riesling • Sauvignon Blanc*

CHARLES WIFFEN
Canterbury
★☆

Although grape growers since 1980, the Wiffen family did not launch its own wine until 1997, since when the Rieslings have been nothing less than stunning, especially the Late Harvest. Also very good Chardonnay and Sauvignon Blanc.

✓ *Chardonnay • Riesling* (Late Harvest) *• Sauvignon Blanc*

WITHER HILLS
Henderson
If the name and address of this rapidly rising Antipodean star confuse, it is because the vineyards are in South Island's Marlborough while the winery is at Henderson, Auckland, on North Island.

✓ *Chardonnay • Sauvignon Blanc*

AUTHOR'S CHOICE

My selection of Australian wines is not a definitive list of the greatest, although it does include some of the very best. What they have in common is that they are my personal favourites. I had to do two selections for New Zealand; my first was so strict I felt quite mean, yet it resulted in no less than 54 fabulous wines. To reduce it to the following 20 I had to rudely expel wines that would thrash the best available in many more important wine regions of the world.

PRODUCER	WINE	STYLE	DESCRIPTION	⌧
AUSTRALIA				
Grant Burge (*see* p.535) Ⓥ	Meshach Barossa Valley, Shiraz	RED	I can forgive the Australian tendency to over oak their wines when they are as classy as this – an intense, compact, concentrated wine with luscious, long, warm, spicy fruit.	3–7 years
Cape Mentelle (*see* p.540) Ⓥ	Shiraz	RED	It was hard to decide which of my Cape Mentelle favourites to choose, but I opted for Shiraz because it is Australia's most elegant rendering of this classic Rhône variety. Shiraz is a wine of great complexity and finesse, with perfectly integrated oak and precision tannin balance.	3–10 years
Coldstream Hills (*see* p.529)	James Halliday Coonawarra, Cabernet Sauvignon	RED	Not actually made at Coldstream Hills, this wine is selected by its former owner (and still its winemaker) James Halliday, who sells this wine under his name, rather than the estate's. As you would expect of anything bearing the great man's name, this is a wine of tremendous elegance. Halliday looks more for finesse and length than style or power, and the gentle, dry-oak finish makes this wine particularly superb with food.	4–8 years
Coldstream Hills (*see* p.529)	Pinot Noir	RED	These wines usually show an attractive richness of piquant, cherry, and red-fruit flavours with a sweet kiss of oak on the finish and just enough grippy tannins to accompany food.	2–4 years
Cullens (*see* p.540)	Chardonnay	WHITE	A very stylish Chardonnay, with exceptionally rich, exuberantly fruity flavour, underpinned with tingling-ripe acidity.	2–4 years
Lindeman's Wines (*see* p.524) Ⓥ	Limestone Ridge, Shiraz-Cabernet	RED	This fabulously rich, blackcurranty wine has superb acidity and tannin structure, enabling it to age gracefully for an extraordinary length of time, starting with huge toasty-oaky complexity, then taking on vanilla-coffee and black-fruit finesse before gradually gaining great bottle-aged aromas.	5–25 years
Lindeman's Wines (*see* p.524) Ⓥ	Padthaway, Chardonnay	WHITE	For an out-and-out Aussie Chardonnay, this is quite simply one of the most classy and immensely enjoyable New World Chardonnays on the market. Even the upfront oak reeks class.	2–5 years
Morris Wines (*see* p.5) Ⓥ	Old Premium, Liqueur Tokay	FORTIFIED	I cannot put a glass of any Mick Morris wine under my nose without seeing in my mind's eye the wizened face of this diminutive man chuckling away, but his legendary fortified wines are very serious indeed, and this liquorous Tokay with its honeyed complexity and refreshing acidity is just the right choice to toast him with.	Upon opening
Penfolds Wines (*see* p.537) Ⓥ	Bin 407, Cabernet Sauvignon	RED	Seriously priced, but not expensive, this is Penfolds greatest-value red wine. It has amazing finesse for its massive flavour – I cannot imagine a wine of this size having a better balance.	4–20 years
Penfolds Wines (*see* p.537) Ⓥ	Magill Estate, Shiraz	RED	This is expensively priced, but only one quarter the price of Penfolds Grange. Although Grange is considered to be Australia's greatest wine bar none if, in 20 years' time, a new generation of wine writers held a comparative blind tasting of the eighties' vintages of both wines, I would not be surprised if this firmer, cleaner wine came out on top.	8–30 years
Petaluma (*see* p.537) Ⓥ	Riesling	WHITE	Australia's most remarkable dry Riesling wine, this is made ina classic age-worthy style. With simple floral aromas in its youth, Petaluma Riesling achieves an exquisitely rich, petrolly aroma after four or five years in bottle, when the fruit gains intensity and is kept fresh and lively by heaps of ripe acidity.	5–12 years
Rosemount Estate (*see* p.5) Ⓥ	Orange Vineyard, Chardonnay	WHITE	This massively dimensioned Chardonnay has such rich, saturated flavours that it can be difficult to drink at times during its evolution, when the most that you can do is to sip it in awe. However, with ageing, the wine gains a sublime, nutty complexity akin to a great old Côte de Nuits white Burgundy.	1–15 years

PRODUCER	WINE	STYLE	DESCRIPTION	𝛽~
Rosemount Estate (see p.5) ⓥ	Balmoral, Syrah	RED	It was a toss-up between Balmoral, Syrah and the McClaren Vale Shiraz, but I chose this. In fact, I could fill the page with Rosemount wines. I adore them. Rosemount Syrah and Shiraz have a black-fruit, silky-smooth texture that separates them from the mainstream of Australian Shiraz, and this wine is pure heaven.	2–5 years
NEW ZEALAND				
Ata Rangi (see p.549) ⓥ	Pinot Noir	RED	No matter how ripe and full the vintage, Ata Rangi is always elegant with beautifully clear, creamy-cherry, Pinot noir fruit and a barely perceptible soft, sweet kiss of oak.	2–5 years
Daniel le Brun (see p.549)	Blanc de Blancs	SPARKLING	Since the 1989 vintage, this *cuvée*, has become equal to good-quality Champagne. It is sumptuously rich with creamy-toasty fruit, yet is complex, classically balanced, and shows great finesse.	2–7 years (estimated maximum)
Church Road (see p.549)	Cabernet Sauvignon	RED	This is a top-of-the-range red wine with smoky-rich fruit, great potential complexity, and outstanding finesse.	3–8 years
Cloudy Bay (see p.549)	Chardonnay	WHITE	Everyone knows how special Cloudy Bay's Sauvignon Blanc is, but the oak-fermented Chardonnay has always been the better, more serious wine. It is amazingly full, yet beautifully balanced.	2–6 years
Cloudy Bay (see p.549)	Pinot Noir	RED	The deliciously vibrant cherry fruit in this wine perfectly expresses its Marlborough *terroir* and is beautifully underpinned by well-integrated, creamy oak.	3–6 years
Goldwater (see p.550)	Cabernet-Merlot	RED	Since 1990, the Goldwaters have achieved a quality that would stand out at a tasting of *Cru Classé* Bordeaux even in a great vintage. Despite its classic structure of firm but ripe tannins and slowly evolving complexity, this is no Bordeaux lookalike.	2–10 years
Hunter's (see p.550)	Oak-aged Sauvignon Blanc	WHITE	I adore the luscious, zesty, tropical fruits in this wine that are supported, but never dominated, by the deliciously rich oak, which gains a coconutty-creaminess after a little time in bottle.	2–3 years
Jackson Estate (see p.551) ⓥ	Sauvignon Blanc	WHITE	Cloudy Bay and one or two others may come close, but no one makes a more vivacious and vibrant Sauvignon Blanc year in and year out than Jackson Estate.	1–2 years
Kumeu River (see p.551)	Merlot-Cabernet	RED	Wayward wine genius Michael Brajkovich uses Cabernet to back up Merlot to produce a soft, sensuous combination of complex berry and barrel flavours.	3–6 years
Martinborough (see p.551)	Chardonnay	WHITE	Oodles of luscious, buttery fruit teeming with malolactic complexity and barrel-fermented finesse, this will be a controversial choice for those who favour Larry McKenna's famous Pinot Noir, but it is more consistently the better wine.	2–5 years
Matua Valley (see p.551)	Ararimu, Chardonnay	WHITE	Some might think Matua Valley's Sauvignon Blanc deserves pride of place, but it was a toss-up between the well-established Dartmoor Smith Estate Cabernet Sauvignon, with its wonderful tobacco aromas, and the up-and-coming Ararimu Chardonnay.	2–5 years
Neudorf (see p.552)	Moutere, Pinot Noir and Moutere, Chardonnay	RED/WHITE	No matter the vintage, both these wines always have a sumptuous richness of fruit and exquisite varietal purity.	2–5 years
Stonyridge (see p.553)	Larose	RED	A classic blend of Cabernet Sauvignon, Merlot, Cabernet Franc, Malbec, and Petit Verdot, this is a dark, dense, tannic wine of great finesse and cedary-minty complexity.	4–10 years
Te Mata (see p.553)	Awatea and Coleraine Cabernet-Merlot	RED	This supple, generous, and very seductive Cabernet-Merlot is theoretically second in terms of quality to Te Wata's Coleraine, which has first call on all the best fruit, yet the Awatea does not lack elegance and is at least as pleasurable.	3–8 years
Te Mata (see p.553)	Elston, Chardonnay	WHITE	Considered first and foremost a red-wine producer, Te Mata's whites are all too often underestimated, yet this big, firm wine is so rich in toasty fruit with lots of smoky-toasty complexity that it unquestionably belongs with New Zealand's very best.	2–5 years
Villa Maria (see p.553) ⓥ	Reserve	RED/WHITE	Villa Maria's Reserve wines are all fabulous, from the ripe, stylish Chardonnay, through the extravagantly rich and complex Cabernet Sauvignon and more sappy-plummy Cabernet-Merlot to the fabulously concentrated Noble Riesling Botrytis Selection.	2–10 years

◆ ASIA ◆

In Eastern countries tastes are swinging towards drier styles, and the wines produced there now reflect this change. This is the only parallel that can be drawn between such diverse winemaking countries as China, Japan, and India.

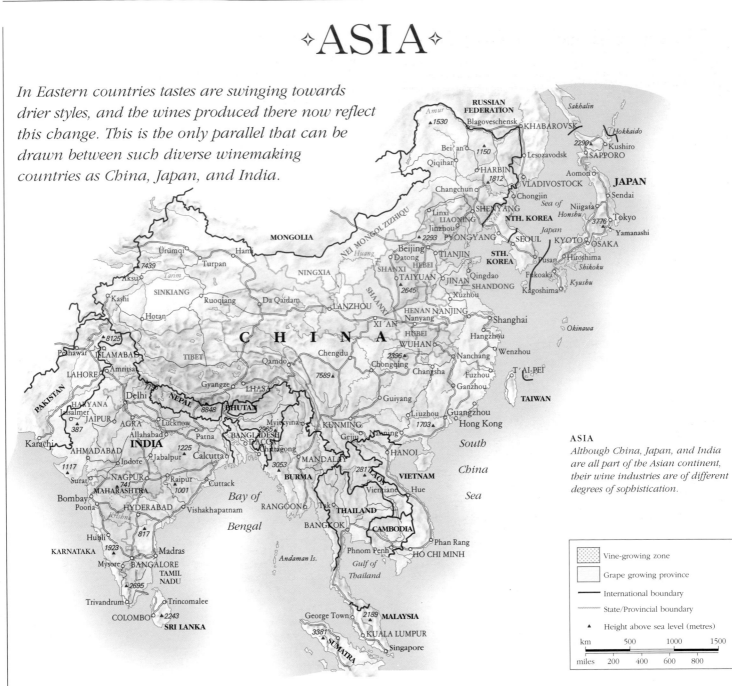

ASIA
Although China, Japan, and India are all part of the Asian continent, their wine industries are of different degrees of sophistication.

▒	Vine-growing zone
□	Grape growing province
——	International boundary
——	State/Provincial boundary
▲	Height above sea level (metres)

THE MAJOR WINEMAKING COUNTRIES in Asia are: China, Japan, and India. Vietnam joined the international fraternity in 1997, when Allied Domecq took a majority shareholding in a newly constructed winery outside Phan Rang. Cardinal table grapes are being used here to make wines for sale on the domestic market. Also, in Korea at least one Champagne house has dabbled with fizz.

CHINA

Main wine districts *Hebei, Shandong (the best areas of which are Lao Shan and Da Za Shan), and Xinjiang.*
Other areas *These include the North East, where "Mountain" wine is made from the hardy* Vitis amurensis, *and Henan, where the land is even more difficult to cultivate.*

It is assumed that Chinese grape-winemaking (as opposed to rice-winemaking) began in 128 BC, when General Chang planted *vinifera* seeds at the Imperial Palace in Chang An (now called Xian), which is 1,000 kilometres (600 miles) south of Beijing, although there is no evidence of wine having been made. The first documented proof of wines, rather than vines, comes from AD 674, when a spectacular grape variety was sent to Emperor

Tai-Tsung by a Turkish people known as the Yagbu. Called Mare's Nipple, this variety had purple grapes and grew in bunches up to 60 centimetres (two feet) long and the wine made from it was described as fiery. During his travels between 1271 and 1294, the explorer Marco Polo noted numerous vineyards in and around Tai-Yuan, the capital of the Shansi province. In 1373 the first Ming emperor officially decreed that wine should be produced in China. Few further developments occurred until 1892, when Zhang Bishi, a Chinese businessman, brought cuttings of ten *vinifera* grape varieties from Europe, and built the Zhang Yu winery at Yantai in the Shandong province. In 1910, a French priest opened a winery in Beijing called Shangyi (now the Beijing Friendship Winery), and in 1914 a German company called Melchers established a winery at Tsingtao (now Quindao) on the Shandong Peninsula.

In more recent times, the French Cognac company Rémy Martin was brought in to give expert technical assistance to the first Franco–Chinese joint venture. This resulted in the first European-style wine being produced in China. It goes by the name of Dynasty and was developed in conjunction with the Tianjin Winery in 1980. In 1987, the Pernod-Ricard group created

FACTORS AFFECTING TASTE AND QUALITY

LOCATION
Asia encompasses the principal winemaking areas of India (Maharashtra State), China (north), and Japan. For reference, Beijing is the same latitude as Madrid.

CLIMATE
India hot throughout the year with no real winter and little rain in the growing season, although the altitude of Maharashtra makes it relatively cool.

China these vineyards have a climate that is classified as "humid micro-thermal cool", a type similar to those of Michigan, Ontario, Austria, and Hungary, where continental conditions are heavily influenced by great water masses, creating hot, damp summers and very cold, dry winters.

Japan suffers extremes of climate, freezing in harsh winter winds, with monsoon rains in the spring and autumn, and typhoons in the summer. Its mean temperatures drop as one moves northwards towards Hokkaido.

ASPECT
India Maharashtra's vineyards are generally located on the gentle east-facing slopes of the Sahyadri Mountains at an altitude of approximately 750 m (2,460 ft).

China recent plantings have been on well-drained, south-facing slopes to overcome the earlier problem of high water-tables on the flatter sites.

Japan in the most important wine area of Honshu Island, the best vineyards are planted on the south-facing slopes of the valley around Kofu.

SOIL
India the Maharashtra vineyards of India are planted on lime-rich soils.

China soils are generally alluvial.

Japan has predominantly acidic soils that are unsuitable for viticulture, except around Kofu, where soil is gravelly and of volcanic origin.

VITICULTURE AND VINIFICATION
India in Maharashtra, vines are grown using the Lenz Moser high system (see p.124) and the *méthode champenoise* has been introduced by experts from Champagne.

Japan recent developments have concentrated on the growing of top European varietals, but the biggest problem is rain, which is often overcome by covering clusters of grapes with a waxed paper disc that acts as an umbrella, avoiding the rot that would otherwise be rampant. This is, however, a very expensive labour-intensive operation.

China this country does not have a cohesive wine industry, but no doubt one will develop as more foreign technology and expertise is brought in. At the moment, however, except for international ventures and some of the bigger domestic wineries, production consists of very low quality wines, which are cut with water and mixed with alcohol to provide the high volumes and low prices demanded by China's internal market. Even the more quality-orientated wineries have problems due to the high-yielding varieties cultivated (some yield up to 150 hl/ha) and susceptibility to rot during the wet summers. However, with Hong Kong returned to Chinese sovereignty, the country could develop as an exciting new wine centre in the 21st century.

GRAPE VARIETIES
India Anab-e-shahi, Arka shyam, Arka Kanchan, Arkavti, Bangalore blue, Cabernet sauvignon, Chardonnay, Karachi gulabi, Pinot noir, Ruby red, Thompson seedless, Ugni blanc

China Beichun, Cabernet sauvignon, Cabernet franc, Carignan, Chardonnay, Chasan, Chenin blanc, Mare's nipple, Cock's heart, Dragon's Eye (*syn.* Longyan), Gamay, Gewürztraminer, Marsanne, Muscat à petits grains, Muscat d'Hambourg, Merlot, Pinot noir, Rkatsiteli, Saperavi, Sauvignon blanc, Sémillon, Sylvaner, Syrah, Welschriesling

Japan Campbell's early, Cabernet sauvignon, Chardonnay, Delaware, Koshu, Merlot, Müller-Thurgau, Muscat Bailey, Riesling, Sémillon

Vietnam Cardinal

---

continuously being reappraised so that, at the moment of writing, official statistics claim 124,400 hectares (307,000 acres) of vineyards, yet more reliable trade sources estimate the true figure to be closer to 174,000 hectares (430,000 acres), with wine grapes accounting for one-third of this area. The two most important grape varieties, for both winemaking and table grapes, are Muscat d'Hambourg and Dragon's Eye.

The best Chinese wine is the soft, fruity Dragon Seal Cabernet Sauvignon. I could easily drink a bottle without getting bored, and the soft, buttery Chardonnay is not bad either. Other wines include Tsingtao (from the Huadong Winery), Great Wall (from Hebei), Marco Polo (an Italian venture at Yantai), and Summer Palace (Seagram), but unless quality is dramatically improved, they would be best advised to concentrate on the Chinese market. Even though the Chinese drink 50 times as much beer as wine, consumption of the latter in China is growing at a healthy 15 per cent per year, and with the handing over of Hong Kong, the future growth of the Chinese wine industry looks rosy.

INDIA

Wine has been made in parts of India on a sporadic basis for more than 2,000 years, but very little wine is produced there today. The country has 12,500 hectares (31,000 acres) of vineyards, but wine production is so small that there are no official statistics. Until the early 1970s, the wine produced was thick, sweet, and not very pleasant. Most is still as unappealing, but in 1972, an Indo–French company called Vinedale was set up and began marketing red wines under the "Shah-Eh-Shah" label. It was a further ten years before another Indo–French venture really shook up the wine world. In 1982, self-made Bombay millionaire Sham Chougule, whose Indage Group controls a chain of hotels and is heavily involved in engineering and shipping, asked Piper-Heidsieck to provide technical assistance in a project aimed at producing fine, sparkling *méthode champenoise* Indian wines. Piper-Heidsieck despatched to India a young oenologist called Raphael Brisbois, who was then attached to the firm's subsidiary company, Champagne Technologie. Brisbois chose a site at Narayangaon, west of Bombay and north of Puna, in the state of Maharashtra, and constructed a £4 million high-tech winery set into the side of the Sahyadri Mountains.

Sold under the Omar Khayyam label, this wine was so good that ten years ago I used it to help launch the first edition of this book. Before doing that I had to visit the winery to see that, the vines were indeed Chardonnay, and to check that wines were present at every stage of the *méthode champenoise*. This was at a time when hardly anyone in the New World was making a decent fizz. I had visited producers in Australia and California many times who complained that they could not get any autolytic character in their wines, despite keeping them on yeast for between three and five years, and here was an Indian wine that underwent autolysis in less than a year. Was it a hoax?

No, it was not a hoax. After landing during a monsoon storm, and enduring one of the most hazardous taxi drives of my life, I was met by Abhay Kewadkar (in the absence of Brisbois), the resident Indian-born winemaker who had spent six months at Piper-Heidsieck in Reims before taking up his position. He showed me the vineyards, which are located on east-facing slopes of the Sahyadri Mountains, where the lime-rich clay soil and altitude of some 750 metres (2,460 feet) are particularly well suited to growing wine grapes. I identified Chardonnay growing there, although it represented only 30 per cent of the blend at the time, the balance being Ugni blanc to increase acidity. Since then, however, the amount of Chardonnay has been increased and a small amount of Pinot noir is also used. Tasting from tank through each phase of production in order to a complete vertical tasting of every vintage produced – an exercise I repeated on a subsequent visit – every stage of the *méthode champenoise*

---

the Dragon Seal brand in association with the Beijing Friendship Winery. This has been more of a success and has achieved much higher standards than Dynasty.

The internal market for European-style wines began as recently as 1992, and has been driven by the big four – Dynasty and Dragon Seal (see opposite), the entirely Chinese-owned Great Wall in Hebei, and Huadong in Quindao, which is now state-owned, although Allied Domecq purchased a 40 per cent stake in 1990. There are some 34 wineries of significant size in China, but also many more smaller facilities – there are at least 100 small wineries in the Shandong province alone. Most vineyards are either state owned or cooperatives of several families in the same village. The area of vines planted in China is constantly under-estimated and passed the test, and I could happily use Omar Khayyam at my launch without worrying about the possibility of it having been concocted from imported wines.

I met Brisbois later, when he was working at Iron Horse in California, and he confessed that his first *cuvée* of Omar Khayyam was 100 per cent composed of Thompson seedless grapes, and many people thought it was almost entirely Chardonnay.

This is an awe-inspiring revelation as to Brisbois's expertise and the sparkling-wine potential of Narayangaon, but although the wine is just as good today as it was in the early days, it has not moved on while the rest of the world's sparkling wines have. The wines now seem rather dull and foursquare compared to the elegance and finesse of modern fizz, which is a pity.

JAPAN

Wine districts of Honshu *Aichi, Akita, Aomori, Hyogo, Iwate, Nagano* (the best area being the Kofu Valley), *Niigata, Okayama, Osaka, Shimane, Yamagata, Yamanashi*
Wine districts of Hokkaido *Kushiro, Sapporo*
Wine districts of Kyushu *Fukuoka, Oita*

Japanese wine production was first documented by the Portuguese in the 16th century, but as winemaking in Japan was already in existence, it obviously dates back to much earlier times. In the 17th century, under the all-powerful Tokugawa shogunate, which even controlled the emperor, Japanese wine virtually became extinct. At this time all things perceived as Christian or western were condemned. Only after Yoshinobu, the last Shogun, handed back military and civil powers to the emperor in 1867 were conditions right to rebuild Japan's wine industry and, in 1875, the first commercial winery was established west of Tokyo in the Yamanashi district, which still accounts for 40 per cent of Japanese vineyards today.

Due to this history, wine drinking in modern Japan was not felt to be natural in Japanese society, and has been slow to take off, but the westernization of its society led to a doubling of wine consumption throughout the 1980s, and it has doubled again since. This has led the industry to improve quality and come clean on the provenance of its products. Once notorious for bottling imported bulk wine as "Produce of Japan" (when I enquired how they could defend such a practice, I was asked how a British motor car was made – point taken), the industry now has a voluntary code that ensures the labelling of all imported wines as *yunyu san,* Japanese-fermented wines as *kokunai san,* and any blends of the two must be clearly indicated.

Although this self-regulated system is adhered to by all the producers of any note, *kokunai san* can still be fermented from imported grapes, grape juice, or concentrate. It is, however, self-evident from the price of a wine whether it is, in fact, a genuine Japanese product, since costs are so high, but an official guarantee-of-origin scheme must evolve one day and, in some areas, this is already underway on a local scale.

The largest wine companies in Japan are Suntory (the winery looks like a James Bond set and the best wine is an extraordinarily good botrytis wine at such a ridiculous price that it works out more expensive than Château d'Yquem), Mercian (owned by Sanacru), Polaire (the wine brand of Sapporo, the giant Japanese brewery), and Mann's (subsidiary of the Kikkoman soy-sauce manufacturers). Some of these wines can be very good indeed, but the best authentic Japanese wines are made at Château Lumière, which is owned by Toshihiko Tsukamoto. The winery was established in 1885 and extended to 28 hectares (70 acres) until 27 hectares (66 acres) were confiscated under General McArthur. Toshihiko Tsukamoto has built his vineyard up to 6 hectares (16 acres), planting Cabernet sauvignon, Cabernet franc, and Merlot cuttings from Château Margaux, Riesling from Schloss Johannisberg, and Syrah from Chapoutier in Hermitage. When I visited, the vineyard was littered with bunches that had

been green pruned to reduce yields and it shows in his red Bordeaux-style blend, which is very fine by any standard. The botrytized Sémillon-Sauvignon (Kohkijuku) is also good, though not up to Suntory's offering, while the basic white is to be avoided.

OTHER ASIAN WINES

The largest concentration of Kazakhstan's vineyards are between Chimkent and Alma Alta, in the foothills of the Tien Shan mountains, very close to the Chinese border, where 17,000 hectares (42,000 acres) produce just over 270,000 hectolitres (three million cases) of wine. There are more than 20 wineries operating in the central Asian state of Tajikistan, mostly in Leninabad, Ghissar, and Vakhsh, where 39,000 hectares (96,000 acres) of vineyards produce almost 315,000 hectolitres (3.5 million cases). In another Central Asian Republic, Uzbekistan, there are a number of wineries in Bukhara, Samarkand, and Tashkent, where 125,000 hectares (308,000 acres) of vineyards produce just over 990,000 hectolitres (11 million cases). Between China and Kazakhstan, the vineyards of Kyrgyzstan amount to just 7,000 hectares (17,000 acres) and produce just over 135,000 hectolitres (1.5 million cases). There are 16,000 hectares (40,000 acres) of vine in Korea and 4,000 hectares (10,000 acres) in Pakistan, but both countries utilize their vineyards primarily for table grapes and dried fruit.

A VINEYARD IN THE YAMANASHI-KEN DISTRICT, JAPAN
In the Yamanashi wine district west of Tokyo on the island of Honshu, where the vines are trained high on slightly sloping, south-facing slopes.

SERVING WINE

TRADITIONALLY, WHITE WINES have been served chilled and red wines at room temperature, or *chambré*. At higher temperatures, the odorous compounds found in all wines are more volatile, so the practice of serving full-bodied red wines *chambré* has the effect of releasing more aromatics into the bouquet. One major effect of chilling wine is that more carbonic gas is retained at lower temperatures. This enhances the crispness and freshness and tends to liven the impression of fruit on the palate. It is thus vital to serve a sparkling wine sufficiently chilled, as this keeps it bubbling longer. However the now-widespread use of refrigerators and central heating means that white wines are all too frequently served too cold, and red wines too warm.

Controversy surrounds the subject of the temperature at which wines are served. Over-chilling wine kills its flavour and aroma as well as making the cork difficult to remove because the wax on a cork adheres to the bottle. Over-warm wine, on the other hand, is bland to taste. The rough guide below is more than you need to know. I prefer not to complicate life with specific temperatures and simply think in terms of "putting a chill on" white or rosé wines and "taking the chill off" red wines.

WINE TYPE	SERVING TEMPERATURE	
Sparkling (red, white, and rosé)	4.5–7°C	(40–45°F)
White	7–10°C	(45–50°F)
Rosé and light-bodied red	10–12.5°C	(50–55°F)
Medium-bodied red	12.5–15.5°C	(55–60°F)
Full-bodied red	15.5–18°C	(60–65°F)

RAPID CHILLING AND INSTANT CHAMBRÉ

It is fine to chill wine in a refrigerator for a couple of hours, but not for much longer because the cork may stick. Long-term refrigeration should never be attempted, as the process extracts moisture from a cork, which shrinks, oxidizing the wine.

Unlike the cumulative effect of wide temperature variations, 10 or 15 minutes in the deep-freeze has never done a wine any harm. The belief that a deep-freeze will "burn" a wine is unfounded; the cold creeps evenly into the bottle. A great innovation since the first edition has been the rapid-chill sheaths that can be kept in the freezer and slid over the bottle when needed. Unlike cooling, warming a wine by direct heat is not an even process; whether standing a bottle by a fire or putting it under a hot tap, some of the wine gets too hot, leaving the rest too cold. The best way of "taking the chill off" is 60 to 90 seconds in a microwave on medium power.

DECANTING

With increasing age, many wines, especially red, throw a natural deposit of tannins and colouring pigments that collect in the base of the bottle. Both red and white wines, particularly white, can also shed a crystalline deposit due to a precipitation of tartrates. Although these deposits are harmless, their appearance is distracting and decanting will be necessary to remove them.

Preparing the bottle and pouring the wine

Several hours prior to decanting, move the bottle to an upright position. This allows the sediment lying along the side of the bottle to fall to the bottom. Cut away the top quarter-inch or so of capsule. This could well reveal a penicillin growth or, if the wine is an old vintage, a fine black deposit, neither of which will have had contact with the wine, but to avoid any unintentional contamination when removing the cork it is wise to wipe the lip of the bottle neck and the top of the cork with a clean, damp cloth.

Insert a cork-screw and gently withdraw the cork. Place a clean finger inside the top of the bottle and carefully remove any pieces of cork or any tartrate crystals adhering to the inside of the neck, then wipe the lip of the bottle neck with a clean, dry cloth.

Lift the bottle slowly in one hand and the decanter in the other and bring them together over a light source, such as a candle or torch, which will reveal any sediment as the wine is poured. Aim to pour the wine in a slow, steady flow so that the bottle does not jerk and wine does not "gulp for air". Such mishaps will disturb the sediment, spreading it through a greater volume of liquid.

Filtering dregs

Personally, I flout tradition by pouring cloudy dregs through a fine-grade coffee filter paper. I always attempt to decant the maximum volume, thereby filtering the minimum, but I have never been able to tell the difference between the pure-decanted wine and that augmented by a small volume of filtered wine. In fact, none of my friends and colleagues who have doubted my assertion have been able to score higher than 50 per cent in blind tastings.

ALLOWING WINE TO BREATHE

As soon as you open a bottle of wine, it will be "breathing" – exposed to the air. Wine "feeds" on the small amount of air trapped inside the bottle between the wine and the cork, and on the oxygen naturally absorbed by the wine itself. It is during this slow oxidation that, over a period of time, various elements and compounds are formed or changed in a complex chemical process known as maturation. Thus, allowing a wine to breathe is, in effect, creating a rapid, but less sophisticated, maturation.

This artificial ageing may or may not be beneficial to specific still wines for numerous reasons, only some of which are known. About the only generalization that generally holds true is that breathing is likely to improve young, full-bodied, tannic red wines.

OPENING A BOTTLE OF CHAMPAGNE

• Remove the foil from the bulbous top end of the neck. Quite often there is a little foil tail sticking out, which you merely pull. Failing this, you may have to look for the circular imprint of the end of the wire cage, which will have been twisted, folded upwards, and pressed into the neck. When you find this, simply pull it outwards, as this will rip the foil, enabling you to remove a section from just below the level of the wire cage.

• Holding the bottle slightly upright, keep one hand firmly on the cork to make sure it will not surprise you by shooting out, untwist the tail with the other hand, and loosen the bottom of the wire cage so that there is a good space all round. A good tip is not to remove the wire cage, not only because that is when most bottles fire their corks unexpectedly, but also because it acts as a good grip, which you need when a Champagne cork is stuck tight.

• Transfer your grip on the cork to the other hand, which should completely enclose the cork and cage and, holding the base of the bottle with your other hand, twist both ends in opposite directions. As soon as you feel pressure forcing the cork out try to hold it in, but continue the twisting operation until, almost reluctantly, you release the cork from the bottle. The mark of a professional is that the cork comes out with a sigh, not a bang.

Keep a firm grip on the cork and cage while twisting

Twist bottle and cork in opposite directions, backwards and forwards

WINE AND FOOD

There is only one golden rule when you are selecting a wine to accompany a dish. The more delicately flavoured the dish, the more delicate the wine should be, whereas fuller-flavoured foods can take fuller-flavoured wines. It's as simple as that.

THIS RULE IS VERY FLEXIBLE because it is capable of adapting to personal circumstances. We all have different ways of perceiving tastes and smells, therefore if one person has a blind spot for, or is especially sensitive to, a particular characteristic such as acidity, sweetness, or bitterness, then their perception of the delicacy or fullness of a certain dish or wine will be somewhat different from other people's. The best approach is to start with conventional food-and-wine combinations, but use them as a launch pad for your own experimentation.

When using the food-and-wine combinations below to plan a menu, always aim to ascend in quality and flavour, serving white before red, dry before sweet, light-bodied before full-bodied, and young before old. The reason for this is twofold. Obviously, a step back in quality will be noticed. Equally, if you go straight to a reasonably fine wine, without first trying a lesser wine, you are likely to miss many of the better wine's subtle qualities.

Try also to make the sequence of wines proceed in some sort of logical order or according to a theme. The most obvious one is to remain faithful to the wines of one area, region, country, or grape variety. You could plan a dinner around the Pinot Noirs of the New World, or the Cabernet Sauvignons of Italy for example. The theme could be one wine type or style, perhaps just Champagne or Sauternes, a popular ploy in those regions. It could be even more specific, such as different vintages of one specific grower's vineyard or a comparison of the "same" wine from different growers.

APERITIFS

Whether you are serving a one-course supper, or a full dinner menu, you might like to start with an aperitif. This should not be an after-thought. Inevitably, the most delicate dishes in a meal arrive first and nobody will be able to appreciate them if palates have been saturated with strong spirits or highly flavoured concoctions. Choose the most suitable aperitif according to your taste; do not offer a choice.

SHERRY

Fino Sherry is a traditional aperitif, but its use has been abused. If the first course is sufficiently well-flavoured, then Sherry can be an admirable choice, and may sometimes be used as an ingredient. Mostly, however, even the lightest *Fino* will have too much alcohol and flavour.

PROPRIETARY APERITIFS AND SPIRITS

Proprietary brands of aromatized aperitif such as Vermouths, inevitably also fall into the trap of being too alcoholic and too strong-tasting. All spirits, especially if they are not mixed, are too aggressive to allow the palate to appreciate the types of food usually served as a first course.

WINES

It is customary in a few countries, notably France, to serve a sweet wine such as Sauternes as an aperitif. For most occasions, this choice would be inappropriate, but sometimes it can be effective.

STARTERS

When matching wines to starters, it is important to consider the next course and its accompanying wine.

White wines that are light-bodied, dry or off-dry, still or sparkling, make perfect all-purpose aperitifs, although a rosé may be suitable if the first wine served with the meal is also a rosé or a light red wine. Excellent choices for a white-wine aperitif may include Mâcon Blanc or Mâcon Villages, good Muscadet, lighter Alsace wines such as Pinot Blanc or Sylvaner, new-wave Rioja, aromatic dry whites from Northeastern Italy, many English wines, young Mosel (up to *Spätlese*) or Rhine (up to *Kabinett*), and light-bodied Chardonnay, Sauvignon, Chenin, or Colombard from California, Australia, New Zealand, or South Africa. The list is endless. If the choice is to be a rosé, try to choose one from the same area, and preferably made from same grape, as the first wine of the meal. The aperitif par excellence in every conceivable situation is Champagne, with Crémant de Bourgogne or Crémant d'Alsace making excellent alternatives.

✓ **Budget choice** *Cava Brut*

STARTERS

At one time, it was customary to get well into the first course before it was permitted to serve the wine. Nowadays, each stage of a meal is seen to play a vital part in the taste experience, leading on to the next taste, or following on from the previous one.

ARTICHOKE

If artichoke is served with butter, a light but slightly assertive, dry Sauvignon Blanc from the Loire is best. The same wine might also accompany artichokes with Hollandaise sauce, although a dry rosé with a highish balance of acidity such as a Coteaux d'Ancenis Rosé from the Loire, Arbois Rosé from the Jura, or Schilcher from Austria is also suitable.

✓ **Budget choice** *Sauvignon de Haut-Poitou*

ASPARAGUS

Fine Champagne or a young Muscat d'Alsace are perfect accompaniments. Medium-weight white Burgundy and Californian or Pacific Northwest Chardonnay also work well.

✓ **Budget choice** *Raimat Chardonnay Blanc de Blanc Brut*

AVOCADO

Although many wines of excellent acidity, such as Champagne or Chablis, are extremely successful partners of this food, Alsace Gewurztraminer, which is naturally low in acidity, is the best choice.

✓ **Budget choice** *Muscadet*

CAVIAR

Champagne is the classic partner.

✓ **Budget choice** *Mineral water*

GARLIC BUTTER

Choose the general style of wine recommended for the main ingredient, but opt for one with more body and a more assertive flavour or higher acidity.

PÂTÉS

Whether fish, fowl, or meat, pâté should be partnered according to its main ingredient or flavour. Look in the appropriate entry and choose a recommended wine. Foie gras is fabulous with a fine vintage Champagne or mature Sauternes and, although diverse in character, Alsace Gewurztraminer and Pinot Gris are both perfect partners.

SALADS

Plain green salads normally need little more than a light, dry white such as a Muscadet, unless there is a predominance of bitter leaves, in which case something more assertive but just as light, such as a lesser Loire Sauvignon, should be chosen. A firm Champagne is the best accompaniment to salads that include warm ingredients.

✓ **Budget choice** *Cava Brut*

SNAILS

Modest village Burgundy from the Côte d'Or, either red or white.

✓ Budget choice *Côtes de Roussillon*

SOUPS

Champagne or any fine sparkling wine is ideal with most purée, velouté, or cream soups, especially with the more delicately flavoured recipes favoured by nouvelle cuisine. It is virtually essential with a chilled soup, whether a jellied consommé or a cold purée soup such as Vichyssoise. Most sparkling wines can match the flavour of a shellfish bisque, but a good pink Champagne makes a particularly picturesque partner. Rich-flavoured soups can take full wines, most often red. A good game soup, for example, can respond well to the heftier reds of the Rhône, Bordeaux, Burgundy, and Rioja. The frothy character of Lambrusco cuts through the texture of a genuine minestrone. The sweet cherry flavour of Lambrusco also matches the soup's rich tomato tang.

✓ Budget choice *Blanquette de Limoux*

TERRINES

Fish, shellfish, and meat terrines should be partnered with a wine according to their main ingredient or flavour (*see* appropriate entry). Most vegetable terrines go well with young, dry or off-dry, light-bodied, still, sparkling, or aromatic white wines from the Loire, Alsace, Germany, Austria, Northeastern Italy, New Zealand, and England.

✓ Budget choice *Crémant d'Alsace*

VINAIGRETTE

Starters with vinaigrette are difficult to partner. Conventional wisdom suggests a *Fino* or *Manzanilla* Sherry, or Montilla, although many believe it best not to serve any wine. I have found that an Alsace Gewurztraminer is one of the very few wines that can really take on vinaigrette and come out on top.

✓ Budget choice *Supermarket Gewurztraminer*

EGG, RICE, AND PASTA DISHES

Champagne is the perfect foil to the bland flavour of any egg dish, the texture of which is cut by the wine's effervescence. Dishes such as omelettes, quiches, soufflés, eggs cooked en cocotte, coddled, fried, scrambled, or poached can also be accompanied by any good sparkling wine. Savoury mousses and mousselines, whether hot or cold, fish or fowl, should be partnered by a wine with slightly less body and at least as much acidity or effervescence (if this is applicable) than those suitable to accompany their main ingredient.

Good sparkling wine is equally useful for many rice and pasta dishes, particularly the more delicately flavoured ones, but light red wines – not too fruity and with nice grippy tannins – can make a surprisingly good accompaniment. Richer ingredients should be matched by the wine.

✓ Budget choice *Saumur Brut and Saumur Rouge*

FISH

Most fish and shellfish go well with dry white wines, but red, rosé, sparkling, and sweet styles are all possible accompaniments in certain circumstances.

FISH WITH SAUCES AND PAN-FRIED FISH

Whatever the fish, pan-fried, cream sauce, or butter sauce dishes require wines with more acidity or effervescence than normal. If the sauce is very rich, then consider wines with more intense flavours.

✓ Budget choice *Crémant de Loire*

FISH STEWS

Although red wine and fish usually react violently in the mouth, dishes cooked in red wine, such as highly-flavoured Mediterranean fish stews, present no such problems.

MACKEREL

An assertive but modest Loire Sauvignon is needed for mackerel, although a richer Sauvignon from various New World countries is preferable with smoked mackerel.

✓ Budget choice *Sauvignon de Touraine*

RIVER FISH

Generally, most river fish go well with a fairly assertive rosé, since both the fish and the wine have a complementary earthiness, but an assertive white such as Sancerre is just as effective. Sancerre, white Graves, and Champagne are especially successful with pike. Champagne or Montrachet is classic with salmon or salmon-trout, whether baked, grilled, pan-fried, poached, or smoked, but any good-quality dry sparkling wine or white Burgundy will be excellent, as will top Chardonnay wines from California, the Pacific Northwest, New Zealand, Australia, and South Africa. Riesling, whether Alsace or German, is almost obligatory with trout, particularly when it is cooked au bleu (rapidly, in stock with plenty of vinegar).

✓ Budget choice *Pink Cava Brut*

SARDINES

Vinho Verde is the ideal wine with sardines, especially if freshly caught and cooked on a beach in Portugal.

✓ Budget choice *Vinho Verde*

SHELLFISH

Choose a top estate Muscadet, a Bourgogne Aligoté from a sunny vintage, a Loire Sauvignon, an English wine, or a Mosel with most modest forms of shellfish (prawns, shrimps, mussels etc.); a fine but assertive Sancerre or Pouilly Fumé with crayfish; a *Grand Cru* Chablis or a good Champagne with crab, lobster, oysters, and scallops. Choose a wine with more acidity or effervescence if the dish you are eating includes a cream sauce.

✓ Budget choice *Crémant de Bourgogne*

SMOKED FISH

A good tip is oaked for smoked. For smoked fish drink an oak-matured version of the wine you would drink with an unsmoked dish of the same fish. It does not work every time, as some wines are not oak-matured, but oakiness in wine does blend well with the smokiness in food, so pick any oaked wine you think suitable.

✓ Budget choice *cheap Ryman-produced oaked Chardonnay from anywhere*

WHITE FISH

White fish have the very lightest flavours and it would be a pity to overwhelm their delicate nuances with a dominant wine. Grilled sole, plaice, and mullet are enhanced by a youthful *blanc de blancs* Champagne, top-quality estate Muscadet, Savennières, Pinot Blanc from Alsace, Pinot Grigio from Northeastern Italy, and fine estate Vinho Verde with authentically tart dryness and just the barest prickle. Haddock, hake, halibut, turbot, cod, and sea bream are good with all the wines mentioned above, but can take slightly richer dry whites.

✓ Budget choice *Crémant d'Alsace*

MEAT DISHES

Few people have not heard the old maxim "red wine with dark meat, white wine with light", but it is quite acceptable to reverse the rule and drink white wine with dark meat and red wine with light meat, providing that the golden rule mentioned in the introduction is observed.

BEEF

Claret is the classic accompaniment to roast beef. Choose a younger, perhaps lighter and livelier, style if the meat is served cold. A good Cabernet Sauvignon from Australia, California, Chile, Italy, New Zealand, or South Africa would do just as well and would be preferable in the case of steaks that are charred on the outside and pink in the middle. For pure beef burgers, an unpretentious, youthful red Côtes-du-Rhône with an honest, chunky, peppery flavour is ideal. But, frankly, almost any drinkable red wine of medium, medium-full, or full body from anywhere will accompany all beef dishes with some degree of competence, as will most full-bodied and rich-flavoured white wines.

✓ Budget choice *Bulgarian Cabernet Sauvignon*

CASSEROLES, DARK

Dark meat casseroles require full-bodied red wines from Bordeaux, Burgundy, the Rhône, or Rioja. Chateau Musar from Lebanon and Chateau Carras from Greece are both ideal, as are many Italian wines, from the Nebbiolo wines of Piedmont, through the fuller Sangiovese wines of Chianti, Carmignano, and Montalcino, to the Montepulciano wines of Abruzzi and the Aglianico del Vulture, not to mention all the super *barrique* wines that are popping up in Tuscany and Northeastern Italy. The richer the casserole, the more robust can be the flavour of the wine, and the more tannin needed.

✓ Budget choice *Inexpensive Zinfandel*

SHELLFISH
A variety of white wines including good Muscadet, Loire Sauvignon, and Mosel can accompany the Spanish dish paella.

POULTRY

Poultry has such a delicate flavour that how it is cooked will be the most important consideration when choosing a wine, particularly if it is served with a sauce, as even the most bland ancillary flavours can dominate.

CASSEROLES, LIGHT

Light meat casseroles are best with young Beaujolais, Loire reds (particularly Bourgueil or Chinon), various medium-bodied reds from Southwest France and Coteaux du Languedoc, Pinot Noir from Alsace, and soft-styled Chianti. For the white-wine drinker, new-wave Rioja, Mâcon Blanc, Tokay d'Alsace and inexpensive French Colombard or Chenin Blanc from California or South Africa are all worth trying.

✓ **Budget choice** *Californian dry white jug wine*

CHILLI CON CARNE

If it is a good chilli, forget wine and stick to ice-cool lager or water.

CHINESE DISHES

Good-quality German Riesling *Kabinett* wines are very useful for partnering many Chinese dishes, particularly those in black bean, ginger, or oyster sauces or with any gingery or sweet pepper flavouring. Spare ribs require a *Spätlese*, sweet-and-sour an *Auslese*, chillies and other hotter flavours an Alsace Gewurztraminer, preferably *Vendange Tardive*. For duck or goose try a good-quality Vouvray *demi-sec*, still or sparkling. If delicate or bland ingredients such as water chestnuts, bamboo shoots, or cashew nuts dominate, choose a fresh or soft white such as a light Australian Chardonnay. With spring rolls, choose a good dry fizz. Iced water makes a good substitute for any of the above.

DUCK

Roast duck is very versatile, but the best accompaniments include certain *Crus* Beaujolais such as

Morgan or Moulin-à-Vent, fine red and white Burgundy, especially from the Côte de Nuits, and mature Médoc. With cold duck, a lighter *Cru* Beaujolais such as Fleurie should be considered. Duck in orange sauce goes extremely well with softer styles of red and white Burgundy, southern Rhône wines, especially Châteauneuf-du-Pape, red Rioja, and Zinfandel.

✓ **Budget choice** *Quinta da Bacalhôa*

GAME

For lightly hung winged game, choose the same wines as for poultry. If it is mid-hung, try a fullish *Cru* Beaujolais. Well-hung birds require a full-bodied red Bordeaux or Burgundy. Pomerol is the classic choice with well-hung pheasant. Treat lightly hung ground game in the same way as lamb and mid-hung meat in the same way as beef. Well-hung ground game can take the biggest Hermitage, Côte Rôtie, Cornas, Châteauneuf-du-Pape, red Rioja, or an old vintage of Château Musar. White-wine drinkers should opt for old vintages of Rhône or Rioja or a Alsace Pinot Gris *Vendange Tardive* (vinified dry).

✓ **Budget choice** *Australian Shiraz*

GOOSE

I find it hard to choose between Chinon, Bourgueil, Anjou Rouge, and (sometimes) Chianti on the red side, and Vouvray (still or sparkling), Riesling (preferably, but not necessarily, Alsace) and Champagne on the white. The one trait they all share is plenty of acidity, which is needed for this fatty bird. If the goose is served in a fruity sauce,

stick to white wines; a little sweetness in the wine will do no harm.

✓ **Budget choice** *South African Chenin Blanc*

GOULASH

When on form, "Bull's Blood" is the obvious choice, otherwise any East European full-bodied, robustly flavoured red wine will suffice.

✓ **Budget choice** *Bulgarian Kadarka*

HAM AND BACON

Ham can react adversely in the mouth with some red wines, particularly if it is unsmoked, but young Beaujolais, Loire Gamay, and Chianti are safe bets. Sparkling white wine is perhaps best of all, although I have known that to react strangely at times.

✓ **Budget choice** *Cava Brut*

INDIAN DISHES

Surprisingly enough, a light and slightly tannic red wine can go well with a number of Indian dishes, such as chicken tikka, korma, pasanda, tandoori, and even rogan josh. You need something fresh and crisp such as a Côtes de Gascogne or one of the lighter New Zealand Sauvignon Blancs to wash down a vegetable tikka or a Madras curry, and something fruitier such as German Riesling *Kabinett* for a vindaloo.

✓ **Budget choice** *Iced water*

LAMB

Claret is as classic with lamb as it is with beef, although Burgundy works at least as well, particularly when the meat is a little pink. It is well known in the wine trade that lamb brings out every nuance of flavour in the finest of wines, which is why it is served more often than any other meat when a merchant is organizing a special meal. Rack of lamb with rosemary seems to be favourite. As with beef, almost any red wine can accompany lamb well, although this meat is perhaps best with slightly lighter wines.

✓ **Budget choice** *Bourgogne Rouge* (Buxy)

MEAT PIES

For hot pies and puddings, treat as for dark-or light-meat casseroles. Cold pork, veal-and-ham, or ham-and- turkey pies require a light- or medium-bodied red that has a firm acidity, such as Chinon or Bourgueil, while cold game pies call for something at least as rich, but softer, such as a New Zealand Cabernet Sauvignon.

✓ **Budget choice** *Saumur Brut*

MOUSSAKA

For romantic association, choose one of the better, medium- to- full-bodied reds from Greece, such as Naousa, Goumenissa or Côtes de Meliton. White-wine drinkers require something of substance, that is not too full or oxidative. A few Greek wines fit the bill (Lac

des Roches from Boutari comes to mind), but something Spanish might be better, such as one of the "inbetweenie" white Riojas.

✓ **Budget choice** *Bulgarian Merlot*

OFFAL

Kidneys go with full, well-flavoured, but round wines, such as a mature red or white Châteauneuf-du-Pape or a Rioja. But much depends on what kidneys they are and how they are cooked: a ragout of lamb's kidneys, for example, requires something with the finesse of a mature *Cru Classé* Médoc.

The finest livers go well with a good but not too heavy Syrah, such as a mature Côte Rôtie or Hermitage from a top producer in a medium-good vintage. Chicken livers are quite strong and require something with a penetrating flavour such as a good Gigondas, Fitou, or Zinfandel. Pig and ox livers are the coarsest in texture and flavour and require a full, robust, but not too fussy red – maybe a modest *vin de pays* from the Pyrénées-Orientales. Either red or dry- to- medium- dry white wine may be served with sweetbreads. Lamb's sweetbreads are the best, and take well to fine St.-Émilion or St.-Julien, if in a sauce, or a good white Burgundy if pan-fried.

✓ **Budget choice** *Crémant de Bourgogne*

PORK, POULTRY, AND VEAL

These meats are flexible and can take a diverse range of wines from modest *méthode champenoise*, through almost every type of medium or full-bodied dry or off-dry white wine, to light reds from Beaujolais, Champagne, Alsace, and Germany, literally any medium-bodied red wine, whatever its origin, and a large number of full-bodied ones too. For chops, cutlets, or escalopes, grilled, pan-fried, or in a cream sauce, it is advisable to choose something with a higher acidity balance or some sparkle. Beaujolais is perhaps the best all-round choice; it works well with roast pork, particularly served cold.

✓ **Budget choice** *Gamay de Touraine*

POT-ROAST

Consult the appropriate entry for meat, and choose a wine listed there. Because of the extra flavour from added vegetables, it is possible, though by no means necessary, to serve a slightly less fine wine than with the straight roast.

✓ **Budget choice** *Côtes de Duras*

STROGANOFF

An authentic Stroganoff requires a full red with a good depth of flavour, but with some finer characteristics, not too robust, and preferably well-rounded with age. Try a modest Médoc, a good Cahors, or a Bergerac.

✓ **Budget choice** *Bulgarian Cabernet Sauvignon-Merlot* (Oriahovica)

THAI DISHES

Much spicier than Chinese, with a more intricate mix of flavours, these dishes are far more difficult to match wine to. For the very hottest chilli-charged dishes, forget wine and stick to beer or, better still, iced water, but with mildly hot Thai dishes, you can get away with a New Zealand Sauvignon Blanc or a Champagne, which will also go with dishes that include coconut milk. When lemon grass, lime, and other zesty ingredients dominate, try an unoaked Australian Sémillon.

✓ **Budget choice** *Iced water*

DESSERTS

While a dessert wine can easily be drunk on its own, there is no reason why it has to be, although there are those who believe that the finest points of a great dessert wine are lost or overshadowed by a sweet. But this only happens if the golden rule of partnering food and wine is not followed.

CAKES, GÂTEAUX, PUDDINGS, AND PASTRIES

Many cakes, sponges, and gâteaux do not require wine, but I have found that Tokaji enhances those with coffee or vanilla flavours, various Iberian Moscatels are very good when almonds or walnuts are present, and sweet sparkling Vouvray or Coteaux du Layon go well with fruit-filled, fresh cream gâteaux and fruit-flavoured cheese-cakes. Iberian Moscatels are superb with Christmas or plum pudding and, on a similar theme, Asti is ideal with mince pies. Chocolate is more difficult, and although some people consider it possible to drink wines ranging from Sauternes to *brut* Champagne with chocolate fudge cake or profiteroles, I am not one of them.

✓ **Budget choice:** *Iced water*

CRÈME BRÛLÉE AND CRÈME CARAMEL

Something sweet and luxurious is required to accompany crème brulée. German or Austrian wines would be too tangy, a top Sauternes or one of the richer Barsacs would be excellent, but perhaps best of all would be an Alsace Pinot Gris Sélection de Grains Nobles or a great Malmsey Madeira.

✓ **Budget choice** *Australian Liqueur Muscat*

FRUIT

A fresh peach, plump and juicy, makes the ideal partner for a Rheingau Riesling *Auslese* or *Beerenauslese*, or a late-harvest, botrytized Riesling from California or Australia. Asti, Californian Muscat Canelli, and Clairette de Die may also partner peaches, especially if it is served with strawberries and raspberries. These wines go well to one degree or another with virtually every other fruit, including fresh fruit salad. Lighter Sauternes and Barsacs, Coteaux du Layon, and sweet sparkling Vouvrays are also good with fruit salad and are the best choice for apple, pear, or peach pies, tarts, and flans.

An Austrian Grüner Veltliner or Gewürztraminer *Auslese* with strawberries and fresh coarse-ground black pepper (no cream) is a revelation. A fine claret or Burgundy with fresh raspberries that have been macerated in the same wine is liked by some, as is a top-quality Mosel *Auslese* with strawberries and fresh raspberry purée (no cream). Apple Strudel, Dutch Apple Pie, and other spicy fruit desserts need to be eaten with a Tokay, Iberian Moscatel, or an Austrian Gewürztraminer *Beerenauslese*. Pies made with dark, rich fruits require full Sauternes, Bonnezeaux, or Quarts de Chaume.

✓ **Budget choice** *Moscato Spumante*

ICE CREAM

When ice cream is part of a dessert, the other ingredients should be considered when choosing a wine. Ice cream on its own rarely calls for any accompaniment, but there is one perfect combination – Muscat de Beaum de Venise with Brown Bread Ice Cream.

✓ **Budget choice** *Moscatel de Valencia*

MERINGUE

For meringue served as part of a vacherin or pavlova, choose a still or sparkling Moscato, Californian Muscat Canelli or late-harvested botrytized Riesling, a top Mosel *Beerenauslese*, a sweet Vouvray, or a good Sauternes. For meringue desserts with nutty, coconutty, or biscuity ingredients, then a Tokay Essencia, Alsace Pinot Gris Sélection de Grains Nobles, Torcolato from Veneto, or Malmsey Madeira would be equally successful. Lightly poached meringue that is served as floating islands or snow eggs needs something of somewhat less intensity, such as a Alsace Pinot Gris *Vendange Tardive* perhaps. An *Eiswein* is the perfect partner for lemon meringue pie – a dessert that demands luxury, acidity, and a vibrant sweetness.

✓ **Budget choice** *Iberian Moscatel*

CHEESES AND CHEESE DISHES

There is a school of thought that decries the traditional concept of cheese and wine as ideal partners. I am not one of its pupils – most cheeses are flattered by many wines; only the most delicate or the most powerful of either cheeses or wines require careful consideration before trying to partner them.

BLUE-VEINED CHEESES

A good-quality blue cheese is best partnered by a sweet wine, which produces a piquant combination of flavours not dissimilar to that found in sweet-and-sour dishes. Many different dessert wines will suffice and the choice will often depend on personal taste, but I find that hard blues such as Stilton and Blue Cheshire are best with Port, while soft blues are greatly enhanced by sweet white wines. Lighter Barsacs, Coteaux du Layon, German *Beerenauslese*, or a mature Sélection de Grains Nobles from Alsace for Bleu de Bresse cheeses, and Sauternes, Austrian Gewürztraminer *Trockenbeerenauslese* or Tokay are needed for more powerful-flavoured Roquefort and Gorgonzola.

✓ **Budget choice** *Moscatel de Valencia*

SOFT AND SEMI-SOFT MILD CHEESES

A light Beaujolais Nouveau or an elegant Pinot Noir from Alsace (as opposed to the deep-coloured, oak-aged reds that are now being made in increasing numbers) will partner most soft and semi-soft cheeses of the mild type, although something even more delicate, such as one of the many fragrant dry white wines of Northeastern Italy or a soft-styled Champagne Rosé should be considered for double- and triple-cream cheeses.

✓ **Budget choice** *Blanquette de Limoux*

SOFT AND SEMI-SOFT STRONG CHEESES

Munster demands a strong Gewürztraminer; and the most decadent way to wash down a perfectly ripe Brie de Meaux or Brie de Melun is with a 20-year-old vintage Champagne. Washed-skin cheeses (that have been bathed in water, brine, or alcohol while ripening), need an assertive red Burgundy or a robust claret.

✓ **Budget choice** *Young Côtes du Rhône*

HARD CHEESES

Dry and off-dry English wines are ideal with Caerphilly, while the sweeter styles of English wine are perfect with Wensleydale served with a slice of homemade apple pie. Mature Cheddar and other well-flavoured, hard English cheeses demand something full and red such as a fine claret or, if it has a bite, Châteauneuf-du-Pape or Château Musar. Sangiovese-based wines bring out the sweet flavour of fresh (but mature) Parmesan. Alsace Pinot Gris and Gewurztraminer are ideal with Gruyère, although something with a little more acidity, such as a Californian Sauvignon Blanc, is better with Emmental.

✓ **Budget choice** *New World Macération carbonique*

GOAT CHEESES

These cheeses require an assertive, dry white wine such as Sancerre or Gewurztraminer, although a firm but light *Cru* Beaujolais would also suit.

✓ **Budget choice** *Sauvignon de Haut-Poitou*

CHEESE FONDUE

It is possible to drink a wide range of red, dry white, and sparkling wines with fondue, but it is fitting to serve a wine from the same area of origin as the dish; Fendant from the Valais with a Swiss fondue, for example, and Apremont or Crépy with fondue Savoyarde.

✓ **Budget choice** *Edelzwicker*

CHEESE SOUFFLÉ

A cheese soufflé requires a good sparkling wine, preferably Champagne. If it is a very rich soufflé, such as soufflé Roquefort, then the wine must have the power to match it – a *blanc de noirs* such as Bollinger's "Vieilles Vignes" would be superb.

✓ **Budget choice** *Blanquette de Limoux*

FRUIT PASTRIES
Sweet wines, particularly Sauternes, are well suited to fruit pies, tarts, and pastries.

TASTE CHART

A TASTE CHART IS A USEFUL mind-jogging aid for identifying elusive aromas and flavours that you may have encountered in a wine, but cannot put a name to – something perhaps that leaps out of the glass and is instantly recognizable yet, at the same time, is frustratingly unidentifiable.

Even the most experienced wine tasters are prone to this baffling experience but, if we analyze the problem carefully, logic tells us that anything ringing bells of recognition in the brain must be well known to it, and the odds are it is an everyday aroma or flavour, rather than something obscure, rare, or esoteric. From this we can conclude that it is not, in fact, the aroma itself that is elusive, merely its name. This is not surprising, since we all have the sensory profile of more than a thousand everyday aromas locked away in our brain – the difficulty lies in assessing the information. I realized this long ago, which is why my personal tasting books always have a list of mind-jogging aromas and flavours. When I am on my travels and find that I cannot immediately identify a flower, fruit, spice, or whatever, I simply run my finger down the list until the brain connects with the aroma that is literally in front of my nose or the flavour that is on the tip of my tongue. This new edition of the Encyclopedia seems the ideal opportunity to pass on the benefits of this system to readers.

HOW TO USE THE CHART

Whenever you encounter a wine with an elusive characteristic, the quickest way of identifying it is through the checklist below. If you instinctively know the category (flower, fruit, spice etc.), go straight to the appropriate section, otherwise start at the beginning. Take the glass in one hand, swirl the wine, and take a sniff. If it is a flavour you are seeking, take a sip, while methodically running a finger down through the list, until one jogs your memory. **Note** Some faults that are detectable on the nose or palate are included here as well as in the Troubleshooter's Guide (*see* p.567), because you will need to identify them first.

THE ORIGIN OF EVERYDAY AROMAS IN WINE

Although no wines actually contain fruits (other than grapes, of course), flowers, vegetables, herbs, spices *et al*, it is perfectly reasonable to use their aromas and flavours when describing wines. To the uninitiated it might sound rather fanciful to say that a wine is buttery, but diacetyl, which is used as an artificial flavouring to make margarine smell and taste buttery, is created naturally in wine as a by-product of the malolactic process. Wines, in fact, contain varying amounts of many chemical compounds that can be linked directly to a vast number of characteristic aromas or flavours.

Some of the compounds involved can evoke different aromas depending on the levels found and the presence of other compounds that can also exert an influence; and various unrelated compounds can induce the same aroma. The amount involved can be minuscule; a strong presence of the aromatic compounds responsible for peas and bell peppers or capsicums of the green variety can be detected, for example, at levels of one part in 100 billion!

Do not get carried away in the search for these aromas and flavours. It is far more important to concentrate on just one or two descriptors than to record a fruit cocktail or pot pourri of aromas and flavours. When you read elaborate descriptions (not too many in this book, I hope), just ask yourself what such concoctions would actually smell like and whether it would be possible to discern any of the component parts.

Note Whether we perceive any of a wine's characteristics as aromas or flavours, technically they are all aromas (*see* The taste or "palate" of a wine, p.17). However, textural and tactile impressions made in the mouth, and true tastes sensed by the tongue (sweetness, acidity or sourness, bitterness, and saltiness), also influence our perception. Where specific chemical compounds are known to be responsible for an aroma or flavour, they are mentioned in the appropriate entry, and are italicized so that those who are interested can identify the possible cause, while those who are not can skim across without interruption to the text. These compounds are not necessarily the cause however, as other chemical compounds could also be responsible.

FLOWERS

Floral aromas are primarily found in young white wines, and may be the major aromatic thrust of an agreeably modest wine or merely a component of finesse in a more complex product. Violet is the most significant floral anomaly in red wine.

ACACIA

This is the flowery autolytic aroma on a recently disgorged sparkling wine. It can be found in other white wines (*paratolylmethyl ketone*).

ELDERFLOWER

Found in wines made from aromatic grape varieties, elderflower is good only when the aroma is clean and fresh, and the fruit ripe, but can verge on cat's pee when the grapes are unacceptably underripe.

GERANIUM

Commonly a sweet wine fault (*2-ethoxyhexa-3, 5-diene*), but also the sign of an Asti that is too old (*geraniol* degradation), it is always distinctive (also *glycyrrhizin* or *hexanedienol*).

LAVENDER

Lavender is often found with lime on Australian wines, particularly Riesling, Muscat, or sparkling wines, and occasionally in German Riesling and even Vinho Verde.

ROSE

Rose petals can be found in many wines, particularly delicate Muscats and understated Gewürztraminers (*damascanone, diacetyl, geraniol, irone, nerol, or phenylethylic acid*).

VIOLET

Violets can often be found as part of the finesse on the finish of Cabernet-based red wines, notably Bordeaux, especially from Graves. It is possibly more tactile-based than a volatile aroma.

FRUITS

In general, fruitiness suggests riper grapes and more bottle-age than floral aromas and flavours, which often evolve into fruity characteristics. Fruitiness is enhanced by sweetness and acidity.

APPLE

Apple is a white-wine aroma that ranges from green apple (*malic acid*) in underripe wines to soft, red-apple flavours in riper wines, where 50-odd known compounds might or might not be responsible.

APRICOT

A pithy apricot character is less ripe and more bottle-aged than peachiness, which is a finer, juicier, more succulent fruitiness. Apricot is often found in Loire or German whites (*4-decanolide*).

BANANA

Banana is found in cool-fermented whites and reds made by carbonic maceration (*amyl acetate* or *isoamyl acetate*, also known as "banana oil" and "pear oil", which, in excess, can lead to a nail-varnish aroma).

BLACKCURRANT

Characteristic of classic Cabernet, blackcurrant is also found in grapes such as Syrah, particularly when bottle-aged (*ethyl acetate, ethyl formate*, various acids and esters).

CHERRY

Tart, red cherries are classic in cool-climate Pinot Noir, while black cherries can be part of the complexity of a great Cabernet or Syrah (*cyanhydrin benzaldehyde*).

DRIED FRUIT

The aroma of sultanas or currants is most commonly found in Italian Recioto or Amarone wines, whereas the aroma of raisins is characteristic of fortified Muscat.

FIG

A fig-like aroma is sometimes a characteristic of potential complexity in a youthful Chardonnay and may be found in combination with nuances of apple or melon.

GOOSEBERRY

The classic aroma of a truly ripe, yet exceedingly fresh, crisp, and vibrant Sauvignon Blanc, gooseberry is most widely found in white wines from New Zealand, particularly Marlborough.

GRAPE

Few wines are actually grapey, but grapiness is found in cheap German wines, young Gewürztraminer, and Muscat or Muscat-like wines (*ethyl caprylate, ethyl heptanoate,* and *ethyl perargonate*).

GRAPEFRUIT

Grapefruit is found in the Jurançon Sec and Alsace Gewurztraminer, German or English Scheurebe and Huxelrebe, and Swiss Arvine wines (a combination of terpenes, such as *linalool* or *citronellal*).

LEMON

Not as distinctive in wine as freshly cut lemon would suggest, many young white wines have simple, ordinary, almost mild lemony fruit or acidity (*limonene* or *citronellal*).

LIME

A truly distinctive aroma and flavour found in good-quality Australian Sémillon and Riesling, in the latter often turning to lavender in bottle (*limonene, citronellal,* or *linalool*).

LYCHEE

Fresh lychee is depicted as the classic varietal character of Gewürztraminer, but is not widely encountered, whereas tinned lychee is commonly found in precocious white wines from off-vintages.

MELON

A characteristic of young, cool-fermented, New World Chardonnay, melon may be found in combination with nuances of apple or fig (*limonene, citronellal,* or *linalool*).

ORANGE

A good blind-tasting tip is that orange can be found in Muscat, but never Gewürztraminer. It is also found in some fortified wines and Ruby Cabernet (*limonene, citronellal,* or *linalool*).

PEACH

Found in ripe Riesling and Muscat, very ripe Sauvignon Blanc, true Viognier, Sézannais Champagne, New World Chardonnay, and botrytized wines (*piperonal* or *undecalactone*).

PEAR

Pear is found in cool-fermented whites and reds made by carbonic maceration (*amyl acetate* or *isoamyl acetate,* also known as "banana oil" or "pear oil", which, in excess, can lead to a nail-varnish aroma).

PINEAPPLE

Pineapple is found in very ripe Chardonnay, Chenin blanc, and Sémillon, especially in the New World, and almost any botrytized wine. It implies good acidity for the ripeness (*ethyl caprylate*).

RASPBERRY

This is sometimes found in Grenache, Loire Cabernet, Pinot noir, and Syrah (evolving into blackcurrant in bottle) (*ethyl acetate, ethyl formate,* various acids and esters).

STRAWBERRY

Succulent, ripe strawberry fruit is found in classic Pinot noir from a warm climate or top vintage. It is also found in Loire Cabernet (*ethyl acetate, ethyl formate,* various acids and esters).

TOMATO

We tend to think of tomato as a vegetable, but it is really a fruit and, although not a common feature in wines, it is found in bottle-aged Sylvaner and, with blood-orange, in Ruby Cabernet.

VEGETATIVE, HERBACEOUS

In small doses vegetative and herbaceous aromas can add to a wine's complexity but few are pleasant on their own; most are, in fact, faults.

ASPARAGUS

Asparagus is common in Sauvignon Blanc made from overripe grapes or kept too long in bottle. Some people adore this style, but most do not. It can develop into canned peas aroma (*isobutyl* or *segbutyl*).

BEETROOT

This fruity-vegetal earthiness may be found in some red wines, mostly Pinot Noir grown in unsuitable areas, and aged too long in bottle, or Cabernet Franc (*geosmin*).

BELL PEPPER OR CAPSICUM

This can be found in a slightly grassy-herbaceous Sauvignon, a Loire Cabernet Franc, or a Cabernet Sauvignon from high-vigour vines. It used to be a big problem in New Zealand (*isobutyl* or *segbutyl*).

CABBAGE OR CAULIFLOWER

The presence of cabbage or cauliflower usually denotes a Chardonnay wine or a wine from the Pinot family. Some people think mature unfiltered Burgundy should have this aroma or even one that is farmyardy or evocative of manure (*methylmercaptan*).

CUT GRASS

Can be aggressive, but if fresh, light, and pleasant, it is a positive attribute of deliberately early-picked Sauvignon blanc or Sémillon grapes (*methoxy-pyrazine* or *hexanedienol*).

HAY

Like dull, flat or oxidized grassiness, the hay characteristic can be found in sparkling wines that have undergone a slight oxidation prior to their second fermentation (*linalool oxides*).

MANURE

This aroma is a very extreme form of the "farmyardy" aroma, which some people (not this author) believe to be characteristic of great Pinot Noir (*see* Anthony Hanson quoted, p.133). Certain New World winemakers try to emulate this aroma in their wines, but it is probably a fixed-sulphur fault, and quite possibly a *mercaptan*.

MUSHROOM

A beautifully clean mushroom aroma is an indication of Pinot meunier in a fine old Champagne, but if the aroma is musty, it will be a contamination fault such as infected staves or a corked wine.

ONION OR GARLIC

A serious wine fault created when ethyl alcohol reacts with hydrogen sulphide, another wine fault, to form a foul-smelling compound called *ethylmercaptan*.

PEAS, CANNED

Common in Sauvignon Blanc made from overripe grapes or kept too long in bottle. Some people adore this style, but most do not. Can develop from an asparagus aroma (*isobutyl* or *segbutyl*).

POTATO PEELINGS

More earthy and less fruity than beetroot, potato peelings is found in a wide range of red wines, and could be an indication of infected staves or corkiness (*geosmin*).

SPICY, HERBAL, RESINOUS

These aromas will either be part of the varietal character of a grape or a component of the wine's complexity, but in both cases they are enhanced by dryness and masked by sweetness.

CINNAMON

Part of the aged complexity of many fine red wines, especially Rhône, cinnamon is also found in oak-aged whites, particularly those made from botrytized grapes (*cinnamic aldehyde*).

CLOVE

Clove is found in wines that have been matured or aged in new oak *barriques,* which gain this aroma during the process of being toasted (*see* p.40). In addition, clove is found in Gewürztraminer from certain *terroirs,* such as Soultzmatt and Bergbieten in Alsace (*eugenol* or *eugenic acid*).

CURRANT LEAF

Although associated with Sauvignon Blanc, this herbaceous character can be found in any wine made from underripe grapes or grapes from high-vigour vines. Can be green and mean on the finish.

EUCALYPTUS

This aroma is noticeable in many Australian Cabernet Sauvignon and Shiraz and could originate from leaves falling off eucalyptus trees into grape-pickers' baskets.

GINGERBREAD

Found in mature Gewürztraminer of the highest quality, when the true spiciness of this variety is mellowed by bottle-age.

LIQUORICE

This can be part of the complexity of red, white, and fortified wines of great concentration, particularly those that are made from late-harvested or sun-dried grapes (*geraniol* or *glycyrrhizin*).

MINT

Although it is occasionally found in Bordeaux, mint is actually far more redolent in full-bodied New World reds, particularly Californian Cabernet (especially Napa) and Coonawarra Shiraz.

PEPPERCORN

Many young reds have a basic peppery character, but Syrah evokes the distinctive fragrance of crushed black peppercorns, while for top-quality Grüner Veltliner it is ground white pepper.

SPICY

Many wines have a hint of spiciness, which is more exotic than peppery, but, after a few years bottle-age, the spiciness of Gewürztraminer should almost burn the palate.

TAR

Like liquorice with a touch of smoke, a tarry aroma in some full-bodied reds, typically Barolo and Northern Rhône, could indicate a wine that has not been racked, fined, or filtered.

OTHER AROMAS AND FLAVOURS

These include oaky, smoky, creamy, nutty, biscuity, baked, roasted, and woody characteristics, all produced by the wine's ageing. Other aromas and flavours defy classification.

BISCUITY

Found in fine-quality, well-matured Champagnes, biscuitiness is the post-disgorgement bottle-aroma that typifies Pinot Noir, although many pure Chardonnay Champagnes develop a creamy-biscuitiness (*acetal, acetoin, diacetyl, benzoic aldehyde,* and *undecalactone*).

BREADY

The second stage of autolysis, as the flowery acacia-like aromas take on more substance and a certain creaminess (*diacetyl, undecalactone,* or *paratolylmethyl ketone*).

BUBBLEGUM

Found in cool-fermented whites and reds made by carbonic maceration (*amyl acetate* or *isoamyl acetate*, also known as "banana oil" or "pear oil", which, in excess, can lead to a nail-varnish aroma).

BURNT MATCH

A burnt match aroma is the clean, if somewhat choking, whiff produced by free sulphur. This is not a fault as such in a young or recently bottled wine, and it can be dispersed by swirling the wine around in the glass (*sulphur dioxide*).

BURNT RUBBER

This is a serious wine fault created by the reaction between ethyl alcohol and hydrogen sulphide, another wine fault, which produces a foul-smelling compound called *ethylmercaptan*.

BUTTER

This charcteristic is usually found in Chardonnay, and is caused by *diacetyl*, an artificial flavouring that is used by the food industry, but it is also produced naturally during the malolactic process (also *undecalactone*). It is inappropriate for classic sparkling wine, so the *champenois* utilize special low-*diacetal*-forming bacteria.

BUTTERSCOTCH

Butterscotch is produced when very ripe, exotically fruity white wines are aged in well-toasted new oak *barriques*, and is most commonly found in New World wines (*cyclotene, diacetyl, maltol,* or *undecalactone*).

CARAMEL

This may be either a mid-palate flavour in young wines aged in new *barriques* or, as in Tawny Port, an aftertaste achieved through considerable ageing in used barrels (*cyclotene* or *maltol*).

CANDLE WAX

Candle wax is a more accurate descriptor for Sémillon wines than the more commonly employed lanolin, since lanolin possesses no smell, even though it has a connotation of one (*aprylate, caproate,* or *ethyl capryate*).

CARDBOARD

This characteristic can literally be produced by storing glasses in a cardboard box. It may also be caused by heavy-handed filtration or by leaving a wine to mature for too long in old wood.

CHEESE

Occasionally a wine can have a clean cheese aroma (Emmenthal or blue-veined being most common), but a strong cheesy smell will be the result of a bacterial fault (*ethyl butryrate* or *S-ethythioacetate*)

CHOCOLATE OR CHOCOLATE-BOX

This is the aroma or flavour typical of youngish Cabernet Sauvignon or Pinot Noir wines, when they are rich and soft with a high alcohol content and low acidity level. It may also be detected as part of the complexity of a mature wine.

COFFEE

A sign of a great old Champagne, maybe 20- or 50-year-old or more, coffee is now increasingly found on the finish of inexpensive red wines made with medium- or high-toast American oak chips.

COCONUT

This characteristic is another found in great old Champagne. Pungent coconutty aromas are also produced by various wood lactones that are most commonly found in American oak (could also be *capric acid*).

EARTHY

Wines can have an earthiness on the palate that some people incorrectly attribute to the *terroir*, but this undesirable taste is unclean and not expressive of origin (*geosmin*).

EGG, HARD-BOILED

Sulphur is added to wine in order to prevent oxidation, which it does by fixing itself to any oxygen that is present in the wine but, if it fixes with hydrogen, it creates *hydrogen sulphide*, which smells of hard-boiled or rotten eggs.

FOXY

Foxy is the term used to describe the very distinctive, cloyingly sweet, and perfumed character of certain indigenous American grape varieties (*methyl anthranilate* or *ethyl anthranilate*).

FLINTY OR WET PEBBLES

This is a subjective connotation for the finest Sauvignon Blanc that only those who have been without water and had to suck a smooth pebble to keep the saliva going are likely to comprehend.

HONEY

Almost every fine white wine becomes honeyed with age, but particularly great Burgundy, classic German Riesling, and botrytized wines (*phenylethylic acid*).

JAM

Any red wine can be jammy, but Grenache has a particular tendency towards raspberry jam, while Pinot Noir has a distinct tendency to evoke strawberry jam. A jammy flavour is not typical of a really fine wine, but can be characteristic of a wine that is upfront and lip-smacking.

LEATHER

A suggestion of leather can be a complex element of many high-quality wines, but the "sweaty-saddle" aroma of old-fashioned Hunter Valley Shiraz is a *methylmercaptan* fault.

MACAROONS

The almondy-coconutty taste of macaroons is a typical characteristic of a great old Champagne, being similar to a coconutty taste, but sweeter and more complex (*undecalactone* or *capric acid*).

NAIL POLISH

Nail polish is the pungent, peardrop aroma produced by intensive carbonic maceration. It is found on the worst Beaujolais Nouveau (*amyl acetate* or *isoamyl acetate*, otherwise known as "banana oil" or 'pear oil").

NUTS

This ranges from the generic nuttiness of mature Burgundy, and the walnuts or hazelnuts in Champagne *blanc de blancs*, to the almondy fruit of young Italian red (*acetoin, diacetyl,* or *undecalactone*).

PETROL OR KEROSENE

Anyone who has syphoned-off petrol will know that the classic petrolly aroma of mature Riesling has nothing in common with the real thing. Yet for those who know and enjoy the zesty-honeyed richness of a great Riesling, petrolly is one of the most evocative words in the wine tasting vocabulary (various *terpenes*).

SAUERKRAUT

The lactic smell of a wine that has undergone excessive malolactic, sauerkraut is actually even more unacceptable in wine than the sour milk or sour cream aroma (*diacetyl* or *lactic acid*).

SHERRY

This is the tell-tale sign of excessive *acetaldehyde*, which could turn a wine into vinegar unless it is Sherry or another type of fortified wine, which will be protected by its high alcohol content.

SMOKE

Smoke is a complexity that might be varietal, as in the case of Syrah, but can be induced by stirring less during barrel fermentation, suggesting that the wine has not been racked, fined, or filtered.

SOUR MILK OR SOUR CREAM

The lactic smell of a wine that has undergone excessive malolactic, the sour-milk character may develop into a more pronounced sauerkraut aroma (*diacetyl* or *lactic acid*).

TOAST

Toastiness is commonly associated with Chardonnay and mature Champagne, particularly *blanc de blanc*, but it can be found in many wines. Toastiness can either be a slow-developing bottle-aroma or an instant gift of new oak (*furanic aldehydes*). Current theory among research chemists is that the toastiness in Chardonnay wines is technically a fixed-sulphur fault, although it is a fault that many wine lovers have come to enjoy.

VANILLA

Oak often adds a vanilla taste to wine due to a substance called vanillin, which also gives vanilla pods their vanilla aroma (also *lactones* or *capric acid*).

TROUBLESHOOTER'S GUIDE

SYMPTOM	CAUSE	REMEDY
Bits of floating cork	You are the cause, and this is not a corked wine! Tiny bits of cork have become dislodged when opening the bottle.	Fish them out and drink the wine. If it happens frequently, buy a Screwpull corkscrew.
Sediment	All wines shed a deposit in time; most are drunk before they do.	Decant the bottle.
Coating on the inside of the bottle	Full-bodied reds from hot countries or exceptionally hot vintages in cool-climate countries are prone to shedding a deposit that adheres to the inside of the bottle.	You can check to see whether the wine pours clear. However, there is bound to be some loose sediment and, even when there is not, it is always safest to decant.
Cloudy haze	If it is not sediment, it will not drop out and is either a metal or protein haze.	Seek a refund. Home winemakers can try bentonite but, although this removes a protein haze, it could make a metal haze worse!
A film or slick on the surface	This is an oil slick caused by glasses or a decanter. Either they have not been properly rinsed or a minuscule amount of grease has come from the glass-cloth used to polish them.	Use detergent to clean glasses and rinse them thoroughly in hot water. Never use a glass-cloth for anything other than polishing glasses and never dry them with general-purpose tea-towels.
Still wine with tiny bubbles clinging to the glass	An unwanted second fermentation or malolactic can make some still wines as fizzy as Champagne.	If the wine is really fizzy then take it back but, if the fault is just a spritz or prickle, use a Vacu-vin to suck the gas out.
Asparagus or canned-peas aromas	Sauvignon Blanc from overripe grapes or kept too long in bottle.	No technical fault – buy a more recent vintage next time.
Cabbage, cauliflower, farmyardy, or manure aromas	Technically a fault (methylmercaptan), but half the wine trade would argue it is part of the complexity of some wines, particularly Burgundy.	Some retailers will refund you, but those who have personally selected this "traditional" style may not.
Currant leaf aromas or flavours	Caused by underripe grapes or high-vigour vines, this may be deliberate if wine is from a hot country and green on the finish.	Not a fault as such, although it is not exactly good winemaking so, if you cannot force yourself to drink the wine, throw it away.
Bubblegum, peardrops, or nail varnish aromas	Produced by cool-fermentation in white wines and carbonic maceration in reds, and found in the worst Beaujolais Nouveau.	This is not a fault, so drink the wine or give it away.
Burnt match aromas (or a tickle in the nose or throat)	The clean whiff of free sulphur, which protects the wine, as opposed to fixed-sulphur faults, which are pungent pongs.	Swirl the glass or pour the wine vigorously into a jug and back into the bottle, to disperse the aroma through aeration.
Burnt rubber or skunk	A serious wine fault created when ethyl alcohol reacts with hydrogen sulphide, a fixed-sulphur fault, to form a foul-smelling compound called ethylmercaptan.	Take the wine back for a full refund.
Cardboard aromas	This can be due to storing glasses in a cardboard box, heavy-handed filtration, or leaving a wine too long in old wood.	If the wine is still cardboardy in a clean, untainted glass, you could seek a refund, but may have to put it down to experience.
Cheese aromas	Occasionally a wine has a clean cheese aroma (Emmenthal or blue-veined being most common), but a real cheesy smell will be a bacterial fault (ethyl butryrate or S-ethythioacetate).	Take the wine back for a full refund.
Earthy aromas	Unclean, but not exactly a known fault.	As the wine was probably purchased by someone who reckoned it had a *goût de terroir*, you are unlikely to get a refund.
Hard-boiled or rotten-egg aromas	Sulphur is added to wine to prevent oxidation by fixing itself to any oxygen, but if it fixes with hydrogen it creates hydrogen sulphide, which is the stuff of stink-bombs.	Theoretically, if you put a brass or copper object into the wine, the smell should drop out as a very fine brown sediment, but frankly it is quicker and easier to ask for a refund.
Geranium aromas	In a sweet wine, this is a sorbic acid and bacterial infection fault. In Asti or any other Muscat wine, the geraniol that gives the wine its classic flowery-peach character has degraded with age.	Take the wine back for a full refund.
Maderized (in any wine other than Madeira)	Maderization is undesirable in any ordinary, light table wine. Such a wine will have been affected by light or heat, or both.	Take the wine back for a full refund, unless you have kept it under bad conditions yourself (*see* Cellar Conditions p.11).
Mushroom aromas	A clean mushroom aroma indicates Pinot meunier in a fine old Champagne but, if musty, it will be a contamination fault.	If a contamination fault, take the wine back for a full refund.
Musty aromas, as in an old church	The wine is corked (or at least it is suffering from a corky taint).	Smell the wine an hour later: a corked wine will get worse and you should seek a refund. Harmless bottle mustiness disappears.
Mousy aromas	Caused by Brettanomyces yeast and malolactic bacteria, this is feared in the New World but some Old World wineries use Brettanomyces yeast deliberately to add to a wine's complexity.	Give it to someone you do not like.
Onion or garlic aromas	A serious wine fault created when ethyl alcohol reacts with hydrogen sulphide, a fixed-sulphur fault, to form a foul-smelling compound called ethylmercaptan.	Take the wine back for a full refund.
Sauerkraut aromas	The smell of a wine that has undergone excessive malolactic, this is more unacceptable than sour milk or sour cream aromas.	Take the wine back for a full refund.
Sherry aromas (in any wine other than Sherry)	Excessive acetaldehyde: the wine is oxidized. An ordinary wine with excessive acetaldehyde turns into vinegar, but Sherry and other fortified wines are protected by a high alcohol content.	Take the wine back for a full refund.
Vinegar aromas	The distinctive aroma of acetic acid: the wine has oxidized.	Use it for salad dressing.

GUIDE TO GOOD VINTAGES

This chart provides a useful fingertip reference to the comparative performance of over 850 vintages, covering 28 different categories of wine. As with any vintage chart, the ratings should merely be seen as "betting odds". They express the likelihood of what might reasonably be expected from a wine of a given year and should not be used as a guide to buying specific wines. No blanket rating can highlight the many exceptions that exist in every vintage, although the higher the rating, the fewer the exceptions; quality and consistency do to some extent go hand in hand.

KEY TO VINTAGE RATINGS

90 – 100*	Excellent to superb
80 – 89	Good to very good
70 – 79	Average to good
60 – 69	Disappointing
40 – 59	Very bad
0 – 39	Disastrous

100* No vintage can be accurately described as perfect, but those achieving a maximum score are truly great vintages.

Remember that some wines are not particularly enjoyable, nor even superior, in so-called "great years". Such wines, which are normally light-bodied, aromatic whites that are best drunk while young, fresh, and grapey (e.g. Muscat d'Alsace, German QbA, or *Kabinett* etc.), favour vintages with ratings of between 70 and 85, or lower.

VINTAGE	2000	1999	1998	1997	1996	1995	1994	1993	1992	1991	1990	1989	1988	1987	1986	1985	1984	1983	1982	1981	1980	1979
BORDEAUX – MÉDOC and GRAVES	90	85	85	83	95	90	85	82	78	78	90	95	88	78	90	92	75	88	98	82	78	85
BORDEAUX – ST.-ÉMILION and POMEROL	90	88	90	80	90	90	85	85	78	75	92	95	88	75	85	92	65	85	98	82	75	85
BORDEAUX – SAUTERNES and BARSAC	87	87	89	95	90	95	79	60	65	60	92	95	95	60	90	85	60	100	70	70	80	80
BURGUNDY – CÔTE D'OR – red	85	90	89	88	97	90	70	80	85	82	95	92	98	70	78	100	70	88	80	75	60	75
BURGUNDY – CÔTE D'OR – white	87	90	90	92	97	92	80	80	95	70	98	95	92	80	92	90	80	88	86	85	72	80
BURGUNDY – BEAUJOLAIS – red	87	88	83	85	90	85	90	85	92	85	90	90	85	78	85	90	70	90	72	74	55	60
CHAMPAGNE	80	80	85	85	95	90	70	85	85	80	100	89	90	–	80	95	–	90	92	90	70	90
ALSACE	85	85	85	90	90	90	90	85	80	75	90	95	90	78	75	90	65	100	80	89	60	85
LOIRE – sweet white	60	60	60	91	90	95	90	55	55	50	90	90	90	60	85	87	65	90	85	70	65	55
LOIRE – red	85	80	75	90	92	90	60	60	40	40	90	90	85	40	85	90	75	85	85	80	70	60
RHÔNE – NORTHERN RHÔNE	95	91	89	85	85	92	75	65	75	85	96	95	95	88	86	95	70	98	92	75	78	81
RHÔNE – SOUTHERN RHÔNE	95	88	96	70	85	90	80	80	75	70	90	95	92	70	88	90	70	92	88	87	83	78
GERMANY – MOSEL-SAAR-RUWER	80	87	75	90	85	92	92	94	92	88	100	98	95	75	93	95	50	100	70	75	50	85
GERMANY – RHINE	80	87	85	95	84	90	85	90	90	90	95	95	90	78	93	95	50	98	73	75	50	88
ITALY – BAROLO	85	89	94	92	91	90	88	85	75	80	93	95	95	88	82	95	55	90	95	80	60	85
ITALY – CHIANTI	87	86	85	93	80	88	90	85	75	80	90	65	90	83	80	93	60	85	90	80	70	85
SPAIN – RIOJA	85	84	80	85	75	87	95	87	85	85	78	85	80	80	80	80	75	88	100	85	80	60
PORTUGAL – VINTAGE PORT	92	–	–	90	–	88	95	–	85	95	–	–	–	–	95	–	95	80	–	85	–	
US – CALIFORNIA – red	90	95	88	87	88	92	94	88	91	93	80	80	85	90	88	98	92	90	88	85	88	80
US – CALIFORNIA – white	90	89	88	88	88	92	88	89	92	85	80	82	88	85	90	84	95	86	86	88	90	80
US – PACIFIC NORTHWEST – red	96	95	90	85	90	88	88	87	89	85	85	85	85	86	96	50	95	84	88	88	80	
US – PACIFIC NORTHWEST – white	90	90	88	85	90	85	75	69	85	85	88	80	85	80	85	90	70	95	83	80	87	80
AUSTRALIA – HUNTER VALLEY – red	88	80	90	65	95	85	70	90	65	95	80	85	80	88	95	90	80	90	80	80	90	98
AUSTRALIA – HUNTER VALLEY – white	88	80	90	65	95	85	85	90	75	90	75	90	90	90	95	90	80	90	80	85	98	90
AUSTRALIA – BAROSSA VALLEY – red	80	80	94	90	95	70	80	80	80	90	95	85	85	80	90	95	95	70	80	85	80	92
AUSTRALIA – BAROSSA VALLEY – white	85	80	90	90	95	80	80	70	80	90	90	70	80	90	90	95	95	85	90	70	80	92
AUSTRALIA – MARGARET RIVER – red	89	90	87	90	90	95	95	85	90	98	88	85	88	88	88	90	80	80	90	85	80	80
AUSTRALIA – MARGARET RIVER – white	88	85	85	85	95	93	93	85	88	86	85	88	85	88	88	90	80	80	90	85	90	80

LOW-RATED VINTAGES

These should be treated with extreme caution, but not ignored. Although wine investors buy only great vintages of blue-chip wines, the clever wine-drinker makes a beeline for unfashionable vintages at a tasting and searches for the exceptions. This is because no matter how successful the wine, if it comes from a modest year it will be relatively inexpensive.

CLOSE SCORING WINES

Obviously, the smaller the gap between two scores, the less difference one might expect in the quality of the wines, but many readers may think that to discriminate by as little as one point is to split hairs. Certainly a one-point difference reveals no great divide but, on balance, it indicates which vintage has the edge.

UNRATED VINTAGES

It is impossible to rate generally undeclared vintages of Port and Champagne because the few wines released often prove to be truly exceptional anomalies. Take the Champagne vintage of 1951: this was one of the worst vintages in Champagne's history. According to almost everyone who remembers the harvest, no pure vintaged Champagnes were produced, yet my researches have uncovered three. If I were to rank 1951 on the two I actually tasted (Clos des Goisses and Salon), the 1951 would be one of the finest vintages of the century, which is clearly a nonsense. Port vintages pose a similar problem: should 1992 be judged on the basis of the superb Taylors, by the handful of other good, but distinctly lesser, 1992s, or by the majority of shippers, who did not produce good enough wine to declare a vintage.

1978	1977	1976	1975	1974	1973	1972	1971	1970	1969	1968	1967	PRE-1967 GREAT VINTAGES	
90	45	80	90	60	80	40	83	90	62	25	65	1961, 1953, 1949, 1945, 1929, 1928, 1900	BORDEAUX – MÉDOC and GRAVES
80	45	80	90	60	78	40	83	87	60	25	70	1961, 1953, 1949, 1945, 1929, 1928, 1900	BORDEAUX – ST.-ÉMILION and POMEROL
65	50	85	90	50	65	55	85	85	60	30	88	1962, 1959, 1955, 1949, 1947, 1945, 1937	BORDEAUX – SAUTERNES and BARSAC
85	40	88	20	70	65	85	90	80	98	10	75	1961, 1959, 1949, 1945, 1929, 1919, 1915	BURGUNDY – CÔTE D'OR – red
88	50	80	80	75	72	80	85	80	90	20	82	1962, 1928, 1921	BURGUNDY – CÔTE D'OR – white
90	55	90	50	55	82	70	85	75	88	45	70	1961, 1959, 1957, 1949, 1945, 1929	BURGUNDY – BEAUJOLAIS – red
80	–	90	90	60	88	–	95	85	85	–	–	1964, 1959, 1947, 1945, 1928, 1921, 1914	CHAMPAGNE
40	33	10	92	50	85	40	90	84	90	40	70	1961, 1959, 1953, 1949 1945, 1937, 1921	ALSACE
75	30	92	90	20	85	10	90	84	90	10	65	1961, 1959, 1949, 1945, 1921	LOIRE – sweet white
80	45	90	92	85	80	10	85	85	90	10	70	1961	LOIRE – red
100	50	85	72	78	85	90	86	93	87	30	88	1961	RHÔNE – NORTHERN RHÔNE
98	72	85	68	80	86	90	85	90	87	45	95	1961	RHÔNE – SOUTHERN RHÔNE
55	50	100	98	45	90	40	98	85	90	40	85	1959, 1953, 1949, 1945, 1921	GERMANY – MOSEL-SAAR-RUWER
55	50	98	100	40	88	40	100	85	92	40	88	1959, 1953, 1949, 1945, 1921	GERMANY – RHINE
100	40	80	70	83	50	20	90	85	80	82	88	1958, 1947, 1931, 1922	ITALY – BAROLO
88	75	40	85	75	70	65	98	86	85	85	60	1947, 1931, 1928, 1911	ITALY – CHIANTI
80	25	85	85	84	75	30	45	95	75	95	45	1964, 1962, 1942, 1934, 1924, 1920, 1916	SPAIN – RIOJA
80	99	–	75	–	–	78	–	98	–	–	75	1963, 1945, 1935, 1931, 1927, 1908	PORTUGAL – VINTAGE PORT
88	80	88	86	95	88	80	70	90	79	90	80	1951, 1946	US – CALIFORNIA – red
88	85	80	88	90	88	65	85	92	78	80	90		US – CALIFORNIA – white
88	80	88	90	88	–	–	–	–	–	–	–		US – PACIFIC NORTHWEST – red
88	80	88	88	88	–	–	–	–	–	–	–		US – PACIFIC NORTHWEST – white
80	80	70	100	45	80	45	25	70	80	45	80	1965	AUSTRALIA – HUNTER VALLEY – red
70	70	80	70	80	88	80	20	80	80	80	92		AUSTRALIA – HUNTER VALLEY – white
70	80	90	80	20	20	–	–	–	–	–	–		AUSTRALIA – BAROSSA VALLEY – red
90	70	90	70	20	25	–	–	–	–	–	–		AUSTRALIA – BAROSSA VALLEY – white
70	90	45	30	45	–	–	–	–	–	–	–		AUSTRALIA – MARGRET RIVER – red
45	70	65	30	45	–	–	–	–	–	–	–		AUSTRALIA – MARGRET RIVER – white

GLOSSARY OF TASTING AND TECHNICAL TERMS

Terms that are explained more comprehensively within the main body of the book are accompanied by a cross-reference to the appropriate page. Terms that appear within a Glossary entry and that have their own separate entry appear set in **bold** type.

Key to abbreviations: Fr. = French; Ger. = German; Gr. = Greek; It. = Italian; Port. = Portuguese; Sp. = Spanish; S. Afr. = South African.

ABC An acronym for "Anything But Cabernet" or "Anything But Chardonnay", ABC was a more than acceptable term when originally conceived by Randall Grahm of Bonny Doon. Grahm was selling Cabernet at the time, but saw it as a rut that every California winery was in. He wanted to explore the quality potential of other grapes, particularly Rhône varieties, but was severely restricted by the public demand for Cabernet and Chardonnay. While Cabernet walked off the shelf, Grahm had to work hard at selling the virtues of anything more exotic. Compelled to sell Cabernet to fund other activities, he came up with the ABC term. Everyone loved it when Grahm invented it. It has since been hijacked by inverted snobs and myopic critics, however, who have been zealots in their crusade to rid the world of two great wine grapes.

ABV Abbreviation of alcohol by volume.

AC (Port., Gr.) Short for Adega Cooperativa in Portugal and Agricultural Cooperative in Greece, or other titles denoting a local or regional cooperative in these countries.

ACCESSIBLE Literally that the wine is easy to approach, with no great barriers of **tannin**, **acidity**, or undeveloped **extract** to prevent enjoyment of drinking. This term is often used for young, fine-quality wine that will undoubtedly improve with age but whose tannins are **supple** and thus approachable.

ACETALDEHYDE The principal **aldehyde** in all wines, but found in much greater quantities in Sherry. In light, unfortified table wines, a small amount of acetaldehyde enhances the **bouquet**, but an excess is undesirable because it is unstable, halfway to complete **oxidation**, and evokes a Sherry-like smell.

ACETIC ACID The most important volatile acid found in wine, apart from **carbonic acid**. Small amounts contribute positively to the attractive flavour of a wine, but large quantities produce a taste of vinegar.

ACETIFICATION The production of **acetic acid** in a wine.

ACETOBACTER The vinegar *bacillus* that can cause **acetification**.

ACIDITY Essential for the life and vitality of all wines. Too much will make wine too **sharp** (not sour, that's a fault), but not enough will make it taste **flat** and dull, and the flavour will not last in the mouth. *See* **Total acidity** and **pH**.

ACTIVE ACIDITY Acids contain positively charged hydrogen ions, the concentration of which determines the **total acidity** of a wine. The **pH** is the measure of the electrical charge of a given solution (positive acidity hydrogen ions buffered by negative alkalinity hydrogen ions). Thus the pH of a wine is a measure of its active acidity.

ADEGA (Port.) Cellar or winery. Often used as part of a firm's title.

AEROBIC In the presence of air.

AFTERTASTE A term for the flavour and **aroma** left in the mouth after wine has been swallowed. When the aftertaste is attractive, it could be the reason why you prefer one wine to a similar wine with no aftertaste as such.

AGES GRACEFULLY Describes wine that retains **finesse** as it matures and that sometimes may even increase in finesse.

AGGRESSIVE The opposite of **soft** and **smooth**.

ALBARIZA (Sp.) A white-surfaced soil formed by diatomaceous deposits, which is found in the Sherry-producing area of Spain. *See* Southern Spain, p.366.

ALCOHOL In wine terms, this is **ethyl alcohol**; a colourless flammable liquid. Alcohol is essential to the flavour and **body** of alcoholic products, thus a de-alcoholized wine is intrinsically difficult to perfect.

ALCOHOLIC This is usually employed in a pejorative rather than a literal sense and implies that a wine has too much **alcohol** and is thus out of **balance**.

ALDEHYDE The midway stage between an **alcohol** and an acid, formed during the **oxidation** of an alcohol. **Acetaldehyde** is the most important of the common wine aldehydes, and forms as wine alcohol oxidizes to become **acetic acid** (vinegar). Small amounts of acetaldehyde add to the **complexity** of a wine, but too much will make a table wine smell like Sherry.

AMPELOGRAPHER An expert who studies, records, and identifies grapevines.

ANAEROBIC In the absence of air.

ANBAUGEBIET (Ger.) A wine region in Germany such as Rheinpfalz or Mosel-Saar-Ruwer that is divided into districts or *Bereiche*. All **QbA** and **QmP** wines must show their *Anbaugebiet* of origin on the label.

ANTHOCYANINS The second-most important group of phenolic compounds found in wine, anthocyanins are colour pigments located in the grape's skins.

ANTI-OXIDANT Any chemical that prevents grapes, **must**, or wine from **oxidizing**, such as **ascorbic acid** or **sulphur dioxide**.

AOC (Fr.) *Appellation d'Origine Contrôlée* is the top-rung in the French wine-quality system, although in practice it includes everything from the greatest French wines to the worst, thus it is always better to pay for an expensive *vin de pays* than buy a cheap AOC wine.

APERITIF Originally used exclusively to describe a beverage prescribed purely for laxative purposes, aperitif now describes any drink that is taken before a meal in order to stimulate the appetite.

APPELLATION Literally a name, this usually refers to an official geographically-based designation for a wine.

AQUIFER A water-retaining geological formation into which rainfall from the surrounding area drains.

AROMA This should really be confined to the fresh and fruity smells reminiscent of grapes, rather than the more winey or bottle-mature complexities of **bouquet**; but it is not always possible to use this word in its purest form, hence aroma and bouquet may be thought of as being synonymous.

AROMATIC GRAPE VARIETIES The most aromatic classic grape varieties are Gewürztraminer, Muscat, Riesling, and Sauvignon blanc. There are a number of exceptions to the rule, but aromatic grapes are generally most successful when vinified at low temperatures, under **anaerobic** conditions, and drunk while they are still young and **fresh**.

AROMATIZED WINE Usually fortified, these wines are flavoured by as few as one, or as many as fifty, aromatic substances and range from bitter-sweet vermouth to *retsina*. The various herbs, fruits, flowers, and other less appetizing ingredients used include: strawberries, orange peel, elderflowers, wormwood, quinine, and pine-resin.

ASCORBIC ACID Otherwise known as Vitamin C, ascorbic acid is an **anti-oxidant**, which is often used in conjunction with sulphur. It has a more freshening effect than sulphur, which tends to dampen the aromatics in wine. It also enables there to be a reduction in the amount of sulphur used in the vinification process. Not to be confused with **sorbic acid**.

ASEPTIC A particular characteristic of a substance such as **sorbic acid** or **sulphur dioxide** that can kill bacteria.

ASSEMBLAGE (Fr.) A blend of base wines that creates the final *cuvée*.

ATMOSPHERES A measure of atmospheric pressure: 1 atmosphere = 15 pounds per square inch. The average internal pressure of a bottle of Champagne is six atmospheres.

ATTACK A wine with good attack suggests one that is **complete** and readily presents its full armament of taste characteristics to the **palate**. The wine is likely to be youthful rather than mature and its attack augurs well for its future.

AUSLESE (Ger.) Category of German **QmP** wine, that is very sweet, made from late-picked grapes, and which may also contain some botrytized grapes.

AUSTERE This term is used to describe wine that lacks fruit and is dominated by harsh **acidity** and/or **tannin**.

AUTOLYSIS The enzymatic breakdown of **yeast** cells that increases the possibility of bacterial spoilage; the autolytic effect of ageing a wine on its **lees** is therefore undesirable in most wines, exceptions being those bottled *sur lie* (mostly Muscadet) and sparkling wines.

BACK-BLEND To blend fresh, unfermented grape juice into a fully-fermented wine, with the aim of adding a certain fresh, grapey sweetness commonly associated with German wines. Synonymous with the German practice of adding *Süssreserve*.

BACKWARD Describes a wine that is slow to develop (the opposite of precocious).

BAKED Applies to wines of high alcoholic content that give a sensory perception of grapes harvested in great heat, either from a hot country, or from a classic wine area in a sweltering hot year. This characteristic can be controlled to some extent by the following methods: early harvesting, night harvesting, rapid transport to the winery, and modern cool-fermentation techniques.

BALANCE Refers to the harmonious relationship between acids, **alcohol**, fruit, **tannin**, and other natural elements. If you have two similar wines but you definitely prefer one of them, its balance is likely to be one of the two determining factors (**length** being the other).

BAN DE VENDANGE (Fr.) Official regional start of grape-picking for the latest vintage.

BARREL-FERMENTED Some white wines are still traditionally fermented in oak barrels – new for top-quality Bordeaux, Burgundy, and premium **varietal** wines, old for middle-quality wines and top-quality Champagnes. New barrels impart oaky characteristics. The older the barrels, the less oaky and more **oxidative** the influence. Barrel-fermented wines have more complex **aromas** than wines that have simply been matured in wood. *See* Stainless Steel or Oak?, p.33.

BARRIQUE (Fr.) This literally means "barrel", but is used generically in English-speaking countries for any small **oak** cask and often denotes the use of new oak.

BAUMÉ (Fr.) A scale of measurement used to indicate the amount of sugar in grape **must**.

BEERENAUSLESE (Ger.) A category of German QmP wine that comes above *Auslese*, but beneath *Trockenbeerenauslese* and is made from botrytized grapes. It has more **finesse** and **elegance** than any other intensely sweet wine, with the possible exception of *Eiswein*.

BENCH or **BENCHLAND** The flat land between two slopes, this term describes a form of natural, rather than artificial, terrace.

BENTONITE This is a fine clay containing a volcanic ash derivative called montromillonite, which is a hydrated silicate of magnesium that activates a precipitation in wine when used as a fining agent. *See* **Fining**.

BEREICH (Ger.) A wine district in Germany that contains smaller *Grosslagen* and is itself part of a larger *Anbaugebiet*.

BIG VINTAGE or **YEAR**. These terms are usually applied to great years, because the exceptional weather conditions produce bigger (i.e., fuller, richer) wines than normal. They may also be used literally to describe a year with a big crop.

BIG WINE This term describes a full-bodied wine with an exceptionally rich flavour.

BIO-DYNAMIC Wines produced bio-dynamically are grown without the aid of chemical or synthetic sprays or fertilizers and vinified with natural **yeast** and the minimum use of **filtration**, **sulphur dioxide**, and **chaptalization**.

BISCUITY A desirable aspect of **bouquet** found in some Champagnes, particularly well-matured, Pinot-Noir-dominated blends (Chardonnay-dominated Champagnes tend to go toasty)

BITE A very definite qualification of **grip**. Usually a desirable characteristic, but an unpleasant bite is possible.

BITTERNESS This quality may be either an unpleasant aspect of a poorly made wine or an expected characteristic of an as yet undeveloped concentration of flavours that should, with maturity, become rich and delicious.

BLACKSTRAP A derogatory term that originated when Port was an unsophisticated product, coloured by elderberries and very **coarse**.

BLANC DE BLANCS (Fr.) This literally means "white of whites", and describes a white wine made from white grapes. It is a term often, but not exclusively, used for sparkling wines.

BLANC DE NOIRS (Fr.) This literally means "white of blacks", and describes a white wine made from black grapes. It is a term that is often, but not exclusively, used for sparkling wines. In the New World, such wines usually have a tinge of pink, often no different from a fully-fledged rosé, but a classic *blanc de noirs* should be as white as possible without artificial means.

BLIND, BLIND TASTING A winetasting at which the identity of wines is unknown to the taster until after he or she has made notes and given scores. All competitive tastings are blind.

BLOWZY An overblown and exaggerated fruity **aroma**, such as fruit jam, which may be attractive in a cheap wine, but would indicate a lack of **finesse** in a more expensive product.

BLUSH WINE A rosé wine that is probably cheap.

BOB An acronym for "Buyer's Own Brand", under which many retailers and restaurants sell wine of increasingly good value, particularly in the supermarket sector, in which the selection process has been increasingly honed to a fine art since the early 1980s.

BODEGA (Sp.) The Spanish equivalent of Adega (i.e., cellar or winery).

BODY The **extract** of fruit and alcoholic strength together give an impression of weight in the mouth.

BOTA (Sp.) A Sherry butt (cask) with a capacity of between 600 and 650 litres.

BOTRYTIS A generic term for rot, but is often used as an abbreviation of *Botrytis cinerea*.

BOTRYTIS CINEREA The technically correct name for **noble rot**, the only rot that is welcomed by winemakers, particularly in sweet-wine areas, as it is responsible for the world's greatest sweet wines. *See* Sauternes, p.92.

BOTRYTIZED GRAPES Literally "rotten grapes", but commonly used for grapes that have been affected by *Botrytis cinerea*.

BOTTLE-AGE The length of time a wine spends in bottle before it is consumed. A wine that has good bottle-age is one that has sufficient time to mature properly. Bottle-ageing has a mellowing effect.

BOUQUET This should really be applied to the combination of smells directly attributable to a wine's maturity in bottle – thus "aroma" for grape and "bouquet" for bottle. But it is not always possible to use these words in their purest form, hence aroma and bouquet may be considered synonymous.

BOURGEOIS (Fr.) *Cru Bourgeois* is a Bordeaux château classification beneath *Cru Classé*.

BREATHING A term used to describe the interaction between a wine and the air after a bottle has been opened and before it is drunk.

BREED The **finesse** of a wine that is due to the intrinsic quality of grape and *terroir* combined with the irrefutable skill and experience of a great winemaker.

BRUT (Fr.) Normally reserved for sparkling wines, *brut* literally means raw or bone dry. Even the driest wines, however, contain a little residual sugar.

BURNT Synonymous with **baked**, and marginally uncomplimentary.

BUTT *See* BOTA.

BUTTERY This is normally a rich, **fat**, and positively delicious character found in white wines, particularly those that have undergone **malolactic** fermentation.

BUYER'S OWN BRAND BOB for short, this is a brand that belongs to the buyer (in the eyes of the producer – the buyer is the seller as far as the consumer is concerned), which could be a wine merchant, supermarket, or restaurant.

CA (Sp.) Short for Cooperativa Agricola and other titles denoting a local or regional cooperative.

CANTINA (It.) A winery.

CANTINA SOCIALE (It.) A grower's cooperative.

CAP The cap or manta of skins that rises to the top of the vat during *cuvaison*.

CARBON DIOXIDE *See* **Carbonic gas**.

CARBONIC ACID The correct term for carbon dioxide (CO_2) when it dissolves in the water content of wine (to become H_2CO_3). Although sometimes referred to as a volatile acid, it is held in equilibrium with the gas in its dissolved state and cannot be isolated in its pure form.

CARBONIC GAS Synonymous with CO_2 (carbon dioxide), this gas is naturally produced during the **fermentation** process (when the sugar is converted into almost equal parts of **alcohol** and carbonic gas), but is normally allowed to escape during fermentation, although a tiny amount will always be present in its dissolved form (carbonic acid) in any wine, even a still one, otherwise it would taste dull, **flat**, and lifeless. If the gas is prevented from escaping, the wine becomes sparkling.

CARBONIC SEMI-MACERATION An adaption of the traditional *macération carbonique* method of fermentation, in which whole bunches of grapes are placed in a vat that is then sealed while its air is displaced with CO_2.

CASEIN A milk protein sometimes used for fining. *See* Fining.

CASK-FERMENTED Synonymous with barrel-fermented.

CASSIS (Fr.) Literally "blackcurrant". If "*cassis*" is used by winetasters in preference to "blackcurrant", it probably implies a richer, more concentrated, and viscous character.

CEDARWOOD A purely subjective word applied to a particular **bouquet** associated with the bottle-maturity of a wine previously stored or fermented in wood, usually **oak**.

CENTRIFUGAL FILTRATION Not filtration in the pure sense, but a process in which unwanted matter is separated from wine or grape juice by so-called "centrifugal force". *See* **Filtration**.

CÉPAGE (Fr.) Literally "grape variety", this is sometimes used on the label immediately prior to the variety, while in the plural format (*cepages*) it is used to refer to the **varietal** recipe of a particular *cuvée*.

CERAMIC FILTRATION An ultra-fine depth-filtration that utilizes **perlite**.

CHAI or **CHAIS** (Fr.) A building or buildings in which wine is stored.

CHAPTALIZATION The addition of sugar to fresh grape juice in order to raise a wine's alcoholic potential. Theoretically it takes 1.7 kilograms of sugar per hectolitre of wine to raise its alcoholic strength by one per cent, but red wines actually require two kilograms to allow for evaporation during the *remontage*. The term is named after Antoine Chaptal, a brilliant chemist and technocrat who served under Napoleon as minister of the interior from 1800 to 1805 and instructed winegrowers on the advantages of adding sugar at pressing time.

CHARM This is a subjective term: if a wine charms, it appeals without attracting in an obvious fashion.

CHARMAT METHOD Invented in 1907 by Eugène Charmat, this is a bulk-production method of making inexpensive sparkling wine through a natural **second fermentation** inside a sealed vat. Also known as the Tank Method or *Cuve Close*.

CHÂTEAU (Fr.) Literally "castle" or "stately home". Whereas many château-bottled wines do actually come from magnificent buildings that could truly be described as châteaux, many may be modest one-storey villas; some are no more than purpose-built *cuveries*; while a few are merely tin sheds! The legal connotation is the same as for any domaine-bottled wine.

CHEESY This is a characteristic element in the **bouquet** of a very old Champagne, although other wines that have an extended contact with their **lees**, possibly those that have not been racked or filtered, may also possess it. It is probably caused by the production during **fermentation** of a very small amount of butyric acid that may later develop into an ester called ethyl butyrate.

CHEWY An extreme qualification of **meaty**.

CHIP-BUDDING A method of propagating vines in which a vine bud with a tiny wedge-shape of phloem (live bark) and xylem (inner wood) is inserted into a rootstock with an existing root system.

CHLOROSIS A vine disorder caused by mineral imbalance (too much active lime, not enough iron or magnesium) that is often called "green sickness".

CHOCOLATY, CHOCOLATE-BOX This is a subjective term often used to describe the odour and flavour of Cabernet Sauvignon or Pinot Noir wines. Sometimes "chocolate-box" is used to describe the bouquet of fairly mature Bordeaux. The fruity character of a wine may also be described as chocolaty in wines with a **pH** above 3.6.

CHRISTMAS CAKE A more intense version of the term **fruitcake**.

CIGAR-BOX A subjective term often applied to a certain complex **bouquet** in wines that have been matured in **oak**, usually red Bordeaux, and have received good bottle-age.

CITROUS This describes **aromas** and flavours of far greater **complexity** in a wine than mere **lemony** can suggest.

CLAIRET (Fr.) A wine that falls somewhere between a dark rosé and a light red wine.

CLARET An English term for a red Bordeaux wine. Etymologically, it has the same roots as the French term *clairet*.

CLASSIC, CLASSY These are both subjective words to convey an obvious impression of quality. These terms are applied to wines that not only portray the correct characteristics for their type and origin, but also possess the **finesse** and **style** indicative of top-quality wines.

CLASSICO (It.) This term may be used only for wines produced in the historic, or classic, area of an **appellation**, usually a small, hilly area at the centre of a DOC.

CLEAN A straightforward term applied to any wine devoid of any unwanted or unnatural undertones of **aroma** and flavour.

CLIMAT (Fr.) A single plot of land with its own name, located within a specific vineyard.

CLONE A variety of vine that has developed differently to other vines of the same variety due to a process of selection, either natural, as in the case of a vine adapting to local conditions, or artificial. *See* Clones and Cloning, p.42.

CLOS (Fr.) Synonymous with *climat*, except that this plot of land is, or was, enclosed by walls.

CLOSED Refers to the **nose** or **palate** of a wine that fails to open or show much character. It also implies that the wine has some qualities, even if they are "hidden", that should open up as the wine develops in bottle.

CLOVES Often part of the complex **bouquet** found on a wine **fermented** or matured in **oak**, the **aroma** of cloves is actually caused by eugenic acid, which is created during the toasting of oak barrels.

CLOYING Describes the sickly and sticky character of a poor sweet wine, where the **finish** is heavy and often unclean.

CO$_2$ *See* **Carbonic gas**.

COARSE Applies to a "rough and ready" wine, not necessarily unpleasant but certainly not fine.

COATES LAW OF MATURITY Master of Wine Clive Coates claims that a wine remains at its **peak** for as long as it took to arrive at this point in its maturity. This law is infinitely variable according to both the wine and individual consumers. If you find a specific wine drinking to your liking in, say, its fifth month, year, or decade, it will remain within the bounds of this taste profile until its tenth month, year, or decade. If you think about it, "Coates Law of Maturity" has a logic and whereas I do not let it influence my optimal drinking recommendations in this book, I have yet to find an anomaly serious enough to debunk the theory.

COCONUTTY-OAK Coconutty aromas are produced by various wood lactones that are most commonly found in American **oak**.

COMMERCIAL A commercial wine is blended to a widely acceptable formula. At its worst it may be bland and inoffensive, at its best it will be fruity, quaffable, and uncomplicated.

COMPACT FRUIT This term suggests a good weight of fruit with a correct **balance** of **tannin** (if red) and **acidity** that is presented on the **nose** and palate in a distinct manner that is opposite to **open-knit**.

COMPLETE Refers to a wine that has everything (fruit, **tannin**, **acidity**, **depth**, **length**, etc.) and thus feels satisfying in the mouth.

COMPLEXITY An overworked word that refers to many different nuances of smell or taste. Great wines in their youth may have a certain complexity, but it is only with maturity in bottle that a wine will eventually achieve full potential in terms of complexity.

CONCOCTION Usually a derogatory term, but can be used in a positive sense for a medley of flavours in an inexpensive wine.

COOKED Similar to **baked**, but may also imply the addition of grape concentrate to the wine during **fermentation**.

COOL-FERMENTED An obviously cool-fermented wine is very **fresh**, with simple aromas of apples, pears, and bananas.

CORKED The term corked applies to a penicillin infection inside the cork, which gives an unpleasant musty character, spoiling an otherwise good wine. It should be highly improbable to have two consecutive corked bottles of the same wine, but every day scientists are discovering "corky" smelling compounds that have nothing to do with a cork, so it is possible for entire batches of wine to smell or taste corked. No wine merchant should, however, put such wines on the shelf.

CORRECT Describes a wine with all the correct characteristics for its type and origin. Not necessarily an exciting wine.

CÔTE, CÔTES (Fr.) Slope(s) or hillside(s) of one contiguous slope or hill.

COTEAUX (Fr.) Slopes and hillsides in a hilly area, not contiguous.

COULURE (Fr.) A physiological disorder of the vine that occurs as a result of alternating periods of warm and cold, dry and wet conditions after bud-break. If this culminates in a flowering during which the weather is too sunny, the sap rushes past the embryo bunches to the shoot-tips, causing vigorous growth of foliage, but denying the clusters an adequate supply of essential nutrients. The barely formed berries dry up and drop to the ground.

COUPAGE (Fr.) To blend by cutting one wine with another.

CREAMY A subjective term used to convey the impression of a creamy flavour that may be indicative of the variety of grape or method of vinification. I tend to use this word in connection with the fruitiness or oakiness of a wine.

CREAMY-OAK A more subtle, lower-key version of the vanilla-oak character that is most probably derived from wood lactones during maturation in small **oak** barrels.

CRÉMANT (Fr.) Although traditionally ascribed to a Champagne with a low-pressure and a soft, creamy *mousse*, this term has now been phased out in Champagne as part of the bargain struck with other producers of French sparkling wines who have agreed to drop the term *Méthode Champenoise*. In return they have been exclusively permitted to use this old Champagne term to create their own appellations, such as Crémant de Bourgogne, Crémant d'Alsace etc.

CRISP A clean wine, with good **acidity** showing on the **finish**, yielding a refreshing, clean taste.

CROSS A vine that has been propagated by crossing two or more varieties within the same

species (*Vitis vinifera* for example), while a hybrid is a cross between two or more varieties from more than one species.

CROSS-FLOW FILTRATION A relatively new, high-speed form of micro-filtration in which the wine flows across (not through), a **membrane filter**, thus avoiding build-up.

CRYPTOGAMIC Refers to a fungus-based disease such as grey rot.

CRU or **CRÛ** (Fr.) Literally means growth, as in *Cru Bourgeois* or *Cru Classé*.

CRU BOURGEOIS (Fr.) A non-classified growth of the Médoc.

CRU CLASSÉ (Fr.) An officially classified French vineyard.

CS (It.) Short for *Cantina Sociale* and other titles denoting a local or regional cooperative.

CULTIVAR A term used mainly in South Africa for a cultivated variety of wine grape.

CUT 1. In blending, a wine of a specific character may be used to cut a wine dominated by an opposite quality. This can range from a bland wine that is cut by a small quantity of very acidic wine, to a white wine that is cut with a little red wine to make a rosé, as in pink Champagne. The most severe form of cutting is also called stretching and involves diluting wine with water, an illegal practice. 2. A cut in pressing terms is a point at which the quality of juice changes, the term deriving from the days of old vertical presses when the lid of the press would be lifted and workers would cut up the compacted mass with sharp spades, piling in the middle so that more juice may be extracted. 3. In matching food and wine, a wine with high acidity may be used to cut the **organoleptic** effect of grease from a grilled or fried dish, or an oily fish, just as the effervescence of a fine sparkling wine cuts the creamy texture of certain soups and sauces.

CUVAISON (Fr.) The fermentation period in red-wine production during which the juice is kept in contact with its skins. *See* **Fermentation**.

CUVE (Fr.) A vat; *cuve* should not be confused with *cuvée*.

CUVE CLOSE (Fr.) A method of producing sparkling wine that involves a **second fermentation** in a vat. *Cuve Close* is synonymous with Charmat Method or Tank Method.

CUVÉE (Fr.) This originally meant the wine of one *cuve* or vat, but now refers to a specific blend or product which, in current commercial terms, will be from several vats.

CUVERIE, CUVIER (Fr.) The room or building housing the fermenting vats.

CV (Fr.) Short for Coopérative de Vignerons and various other titles that denote a local or regional cooperative.

DEFINITION A wine with good definition is one that is not just clean with a correct **balance**, but that also has a positive expression of its grape variety or origin.

DÉGORGEMENT (Fr.) *See* **Disgorgement**

DEGREE-DAYS *See* **Heat summation**

DELICATE Describes the quieter characteristics of quality that give a wine **charm**.

DEMI-MUID (Fr.) A large oval barrel with a capacity of 300 litres (600 litres in Champagne).

DEMI-SEC (Fr.) This literally means "semi-dry" but such wines actually taste quite sweet.

DÉPARTEMENT (Fr.) A geopolitical division of France, similar to a county in the UK and a state in the US.

DEPTH This refers primarily to a wine's depth of flavour and secondarily to its depth of interest.

DIATOMACEOUS EARTH Also known as kieselguhr, this is a fine, powdered, silaceous earth evolved from decomposed deep-sea algae called diatoms. *See also* **Perlite, Ceramic filtration**, and **Polishing**.

DIRTY This applies to any wine with an unpleasant off-taste or off-smell, and is probably the result of poor vinification or bad bottling.

DISGORGEMENT This is part of the process of making a bottle-fermented sparkling wine such as Champagne. After **fermentation** the **yeast** forms a deposit, which must be removed. To allow this, the bottles are inverted in a freezing brine for just long enough for the sediment to form a semi-frozen slush that adheres to the neck of the bottle. This enables the bottle to be re-inverted without disturbing the wine. The temporary cap used to seal the bottle is removed and the internal pressure is sufficient to eject or disgorge the slush of sediment without losing very much wine at all. The wine is then topped up and a traditional Champagne cork used to seal the bottle.

DISTINCTIVE Describes a wine with a positive character. All fine wines are distinctive to some degree, but not all distinctive wines are fine.

DIURNAL DIFFERENCE In viticulture, a diurnal or daily difference referred to will invariably be one of temperature, comparing the highest daytime temperature with the lowest nightime temperature – the greater the difference, the better the grapes' acidity retention. This happens in relatively cool wine areas such as Champagne, as well as essentially hot ones such as Idaho.

DO (Sp.) This stands for Spain's *Denominacíon de Origen*, which is theoretically the equivalent of the French AOC.

DOC (It., Port., and Sp.) Confusingly, this stands for Italy's *Denominazione di Origine Controllata* and Portugal's *Denominaçao de Origem Controlada*, which are theoretically the equivalent of the French AOC. It also stands for Spain's *Denominacíon de Origen Calificada*, which is the equivalent of the Italian DOCG.

DOCG (It.) Italy's *Denominazione di Origine Controllata e Garantita* is theoretically one step above the French AOC. Ideally it should be similar to, say, a *Premier* or *Grand Cru* in Burgundy or a *Cru Classé* in Bordeaux, but in reality, it is almost as big a sop as Italy's *Denominazione di Origine Controllata* itself.

DOBLE PASTA (Sp.) Red wines macerated with double the normal proportion of grape skins to juice during fermentation. *See* How to read Spanish wine labels, p.348.

DOPPELSTÜCK (Ger.) A very large oval cask with a capacity of 2,400 litres.

DOSAGE (Fr.) Sugar added to a sparkling wine after *dégorgement*, the amounts of which are controlled by the terminology used on the label – *brut, demi-sec* etc.

DOUX (Fr.) Sweet, as applied to wines.

DRIP IRRIGATION Various forms exist, but at its most sophisticated, this is a computer-controlled watering system programmed with the vine's general water requirement and constantly amended by a continuous flow of data from soil sensors. The water is supplied literally drip-by-drip through a complex system of pipes with metered valves.

DRYING UP Describes a wine that has dried up has lost some of its freshness and fruit through ageing in the bottle. It may still be enjoyable, but remaining bottles should not be kept long.

DUSTY Akin to "peppery" in a red wine; a blurring of **varietal** definition in a white wine.

EARTH FILTRATION This term is synonymous with depth filtration.

EARTHY Describes a drying impression in the mouth. Some wines can be enjoyably earthy, but the finest-quality wines should be as clean as a whistle. When a wine is very earthy, it is usually due to a preponderance of geosmin, which can

occur naturally in grapes, but in excess can give a wine a **corked** taste.

EASY This term is synonymous to a certain extent with **accessible**, but probably implies a cheaper, value-for-money wine, whereas "accessible" often applies to finer wines.

EAU-DE-VIE (Fr.) Literally, "water of life"; specifically a grape-derived spirit.

EDELFÄULE (Ger.) The German term for noble rot. *See Botrytis cinerea*.

EDELKEUR (S. Afr.) The South African term for noble rot. *See Botrytis cinerea*.

EDGE Almost, but not quite, synonymous with **grip**; wine can have an edge of **bitterness** or **tannin**. Edge usually implies that a wine has the capacity to develop, while grip may be applied to a wine in various stages of development, including fully mature wine.

EDGY Synonymous with "nervous".

EGG WHITE A traditional fining agent that fines out negatively charged matter. *See* **Fining**.

EINZELLAGE (Ger.) A single-vineyard wine area; the smallest geographical unit allowed under German wine law.

EISWEIN (Ger.) Originally a German concept but now used in the New World as well, this rare wine resulted from the tradition of leaving grapes on the vine in the hope of attracting *Botrytis cinerea*. The grapes are frozen by frost or snow, then harvested, and pressed while frozen. This is done because only the ice freezes and, as this rises to the top of the vat, it can be scraped off to leave a concentrated juice that produces a wine with a unique balance of sweetness, acidity, and extract.

ELEGANT A subjective term applied to wines that may also be described as stylish or possessing finesse.

ELEVEUR, ÉLEVAGE (Fr.) Literally "bringing up" or "raising" the wine. Both terms refer to the traditional function of a *négociant*, as it originated in France, namely to buy ready-made wines after the harvest and take care of them until they are ready to be bottled and sold. The task involves racking the wines and blending them into a marketable product as each house sees fit.

EMBRYO BUNCHES In spring, the vine develops little clusters of miniature green berries that will form a bloom a few weeks later. If a berry successfully flowers, it is capable of developing into a grape and the embryo bunch is thus an indication of the potential size of the crop.

ENCÉPAGEMENT (Fr.) The proportion of grape varieties in a blend.

ENOLOGIST, ENOLOGY (Am.) The American spelling of oenology, oenologist. *See* **Oenology**.

EN PRIMEUR (Fr.) Classic wines such as Bordeaux are offered for sale *en primeur*, which is to say within a year of the harvest, before the final blending and bottling has taken place. For experienced buyers given the opportunity to taste, this is a calculated risk and the price should reflect this element of chance.

ESTERS Sweet-smelling compounds, formed during **fermentation** and throughout maturation, that contribute to a wine's **aroma** and **bouquet**.

ESTUFAGEM (Port.) The process whereby Madeira is heated in ovens called *estufas*, then cooled. *See* Madeira, p.383.

ETHANOIC ACID Synonymous with **acetic acid**.

ETHANOL Synonymous with **ethyl alcohol**.

ETHYL ALCOHOL The main alcohol in wine is so important in quantitative terms that to speak of a wine's alcohol is to refer purely to its ethyl alcohol content.

EU LOT NUMBER Proposed by an EC directive in 1989 and implemented by all member states of the Community by 1992, this Lot Number must be indicated on every bottle of wine produced in or

sold to the EU. Should a wine have to be removed from general distribution for any reason, this code can save unnecessary waste by pinpointing the shipment involved.

EVERYDAY WINES These are inexpensive, easy-drinking wines.

EX-CELLARS Wines offered *en primeur* are usually purchased ex-cellars; the cost of shipping the wine to the importer's cellars is extra, on top of which any duty and taxes will be added.

EXPANSIVE Describes a wine that is **big**, but open and **accessible**.

EXPRESSIVE A wine that is expressive is true to its grape variety and area of origin.

EXTRACT Sugar-free soluble solids that give **body** to a wine. The term covers everything from proteins and vitamins to **tannins**, calcium, and **iron**.

FALL BRIGHT A liquid that becomes limpid after cloudy matter falls as sediment to the bottom of the vessel is said to fall bright.

FALLS OVER A wine that goes past its peak, starts to decline at a relatively young age, and at a faster than normal rate, is said to fall over.

FARMYARDY A term used by many people to describe a wine, quite often Chardonnay or Pinot, that has matured beyond its initial freshness of fruit, past the desired stage of roundness and the pleasing phase when it acquires certain vegetal undertones. The wine is still healthy and drinkable, and for some it is at the very peak of perfection.

FAT A wine full in body and extract.

FATTY ACIDS A term sometimes used for volatile acids.

FEMININE A subjective term used to describe a wine with a preponderance of delicately attractive qualities, rather than weight or strength. Descibes a wine of striking beauty, grace, and **finesse** with a silky texture and exquisite style.

FERMENTATION The biochemical process by which enzymes secreted by **yeast** cells convert sugar molecules into almost equal parts of **alcohol** and **carbonic gas**. *See* Fermentation, p.32.

FEUILLETTE (Fr.) A small Burgundian barrel with a capacity of 114 litres (132 litres in Chablis).

FILTER, FILTRATION There are three basic methods of filtration: depth filtration (also known as earth filtration); pad filtration (also known as sheet filtration), and membrane filtration (also known as micro-porous filtration). There is also centrifugal filtration, which is not filtration in the pure sense but achieves the same objective of removing unwanted particles suspended in wine or grape juice.

FINESSE That elusive, indescribable quality that separates a fine wine from those of lesser quality.

FINE WINES Quality wines, representing only a small percentage of all wines produced.

FINING The clarification of fresh grape juice or wine is often speeded up by the use of various fining agents that operate by an electrolytic reaction to fine out oppositely charged matter. *See* Fining p.34.

FINISH The quality and enjoyment of a wine's aftertaste.

FIRM Refers to a certain amount of grip. A firm wine is a wine of good constitution, held up with a certain amount of tannin and acidity.

FIRST PRESSING The first pressing yields the sweetest, cleanest, clearest juice.

FIXED ACIDITY This is the total acidity less the volatile acidity.

FIXED SULPHUR The principal reason why SO_2 (sulphur dioxide) is added to grape juice and wine is to prevent oxidation, but only free sulphur can do this. Upon contact with wine, some SO_2

immediately combines with oxygen and other elements, such as sugars and acids, and is known as fixed or bound sulphur. What remains is free sulphur, capable of combining with molecules of oxygen at some future date.

FLABBY The opposite of crisp, referring to a wine lacking in acidity and consequently dull, weak, and short.

FLASH PASTEURIZATION A sterilization technique that should not be confused with full pasteurization. It involves subjecting the wine to a temperature of about 80°C (176°F) for between 30 and 60 seconds. *See* Heat, p.22.

FLAT 1. A sparkling wine that has lost all of its *mousse*. **2.** A term that is interchangeable with flabby, especially when referring to a lack of acidity on the finish.

FLESHY This term refers to a wine with plenty of fruit and extract and implies a certain underlying firmness.

FLOR (Sp.) A scum-like yeast film that naturally occurs and floats on the surface of some Sherries as they mature in part-filled wooden butts. It is the flor that gives Fino Sherry its inimitable character.

FLURBEREINIGUNG (Ger.) A modern viticultural method of growing vines in rows running vertically up and down slopes rather than across, in terraces.

FLYING WINEMAKER The concept of the flying winemaker was born in Australia, where due to the size of this continent and the staggered picking dates, highly sought-after consultants Brian Croser (now Petaluma) and Tony Jordan (now Green Point) would hop by plane from harvest to harvest. Riding on the success of Australian wines in the UK market, other Australian wine wizards began to stretch their wings, flying in and out of everywhere from Southern Italy to Moldova, usually at the behest of British supermarkets. Like the spread of Chardonnay and Cabernet, the flying winemakers were at first welcomed by wine writers, then turned upon for standardizing wine wherever they went. The truth is that before the arrival of international grapes and international winemakers, the peasant cooperatives in these countries had no idea that they could even produce wines to compete on the international market. Now that they have established a certain standard with known grape varieties and modern technology, they are beginning to turn to their roots, to see what indigenous varieties might have the potential to produce more expressive wines. Few winemakers do more flying than Moët & Chandon's Richard Geoffroy, but the term is usually attributed to the mercenaries of the trade, who work for a supermarket, a supplier to a supermarket, or more than one company. Well-known flying winemakers include Peter Bright, Nick Butler, Steve Donnelly, Michael Goundrey, Lynette Hudson, Jacques and François Lurton, Geoff Merril, Kym Milne, Martin Shaw, Brenden Smith, Adrian Wing, and John Worontschak. Famous Bordeaux professors Peynaud and Ribereau-Gayon have both avoided the flying-winemaker tag, despite the fact that they have each consulted for more companies in more countries over more years than the entire flock of flying winemakers listed above, perhaps because today's mercenaries have a more hands-on approach to their job than was traditional for consultants in the past.

FORTIFIED Fortification with pure alcohol (usually very strong grape spirit of between 77 and 98 per cent) can take place either before fermentation (as in Ratafia de Champagne and Pineau des Charentes), during fermentation (as in Port and Muscat de Beaumes de Venise), or after fermentation (as in Sherry).

FOUDRE (Fr.) A large wooden cask or vat.

FOXY The very distinctive, highly perfumed character of certain indigenous American grape

varieties that can be sickly sweet and cloying to unconditioned palates.

FREE-RUN JUICE *See* Vin de goutte.

FREE SULPHUR The active element of sulphur dioxide in wine, produced by free sulphur combining with intruding molecules of oxygen.

FRENCH PARADOX In 1991, Morley Safer, host of the CBS show *60 Minutes*, screened a programme about the so-called "French Paradox". This described how the high-cholesterol-consuming, high-alcohol-drinking, low-exercising French have a very low mortality rate from heart disease compared to health-conscious Americans, who have low-cholesterol diets, exercise frequently, and drink relatively little alcohol. Part of the explanation was attributed to the Mediterranean diet, in which milk plays an insignificant role, and wine, particularly red wine, a very important one. Although it is a complete food for the young, milk is unnatural for adults, who cannot digest it properly. The more milk an adult drinks (and Americans are particularly high consumers of milk), the greater the risk of cardiovascular disease, while three glasses of wine a day has a proven protective effect against cardiovascular disease. *See* Health benefits of wine.

FRESH Describes wines that are clean and still vital with youth.

FRIZZANTE (It.) Semi-sparkling.

FRIZZANTINO (It.) Very lightly sparkling, between still and semi-sparkling (i.e. *perlant*).

FRUIT Wine is made from grapes and must therefore be 100 per cent fruit, yet it will not have a fruity flavour unless the grapes used have the correct combination of ripeness and acidity.

FRUITCAKE This is a subjective term for a wine that tastes, smells, or has the complexity of the mixed dried-fruit richness and spices found in fruit cake.

FÜDER (Ger.) A large oval cask with a capacity of 1,000 litres, more prevalent in the Mosel areas than those of the Rhine.

FULL This term usually refers to body, e.g., "full-bodied". But a wine can be light in body yet full in flavour.

FULLY FERMENTED A wine that is allowed to complete its natural course of fermentation and so yield a totally dry wine.

FÛT (Fr.) A wooden cask, usually made of oak, in which wines are aged, or fermented and aged.

GARRIGUE (Fr.) A type of moorland found in Languedoc-Roussillon.

GELATINE A positively charged fining agent used for removing negatively charged suspended matter in wines, especially an excess of tannin. *See* Fining.

GENERIC Describes a wine, usually blended, of a general appellation.

GENEROUS A generous wine gives its fruit freely on the palate, while an ungenerous wine is likely to have little or no fruit and, probably, an excess of tannin. All wines should have some degree of generosity.

GENUS The botanical family *Ampelidaceae* has ten *genera*, one of which, *Vitis*, through the sub-genus *Euvites*, contains the species *Vitis vinifera*, to which all the famous wine-making grape varieties belong.

GLUGGY Easy to guzzle.

GOOD GRIP A healthy structure of **tannin** supporting the fruit in a wine.

GOUT DE TERROIR (Fr.) Literally "taste of earth", a term that denotes a particular flavour imparted by certain soils, not necessarily the taste of the soil itself, in a wine.

GRANDE MARQUE (Fr.) Literally a great or famous brand, in the world of wine the term *Grande Marque* is specific to Champagne and applies to members of the Syndicat de Grandes Marques, which include of course all the famous names.

GRAFT The joint between the rootstock and the scion of the producer vine.

GRAND CRU (Fr.) Literally "great growth"; in regions such as Burgundy, where its use is strictly controlled, it has real meaning (i.e., the wine should be great – relative to the quality of the year), but in other winemaking areas where there are no controls, it will mean little.

GRAND VIN (Fr.) Normally used in Bordeaux, this applies to the main wine sold under the château's famous name, and will have been produced from only the finest barrels. Wines excluded during this process go into second, third, and sometimes fourth wines that are sold under different labels.

GRAPEY This term may be applied to an aroma or flavour that is reminiscent of grapes rather than wine, and is particular characteristic of German wines and wines made from various Muscat or Muscat-like grapes.

GRASSY Often used to describe certain Gewürztraminer, Scheurebe, and Sauvignon wines portraying a grassy type of fruitiness.

GREEN Young and tart, as in Vinho Verde. It can be either a derogatory term, or simply an description of youthful wine that might well improve.

GREEN PRUNING Pruning is a bit of a misnomer, as this is really a method of reducing yields by thinning out the potential crop when the grapes are green (unripe) by cutting off a certain percentage of the bunches, so that what remains achieves a quicker, greater, and more even ripening. Also called **Summer Pruning**.

GRIP This term applies to a firm wine with a positive **finish**. A wine showing grip on the finish indicates a certain bite of **acidity** in white wines and of **tannin** in red wines.

GRIPPY Good grippy **tannins** imply ripe tannins that have a nice grippy tactile effect without seeming in the least **firm**, **harsh**, or **austere**.

GROSSLAGE (Ger.) A wine area in Germany that is part of a larger district or *Bereich*.

GROWTH *See* Cru.

GUTSY A wine full in **body**, fruit, **extract** and, usually, **alcohol**. The term is normally applied to wines of ordinary quality.

GUZZLY This term is synonymous with **gluggy**.

HALBFÜDER (Ger.) An oval cask with a capacity of 500 litres, more prevalent in the Mosel areas than those of the Rhine.

HALBSTÜCK (Ger.) An oval cask with a capacity of 600 litres.

HARD Indicates a certain severity, often due to excess **tannin** and **acidity**.

HARSH A more derogatory term than **coarse**.

HEALTH BENEFITS OF WINE Wine consumed in moderation flushes out the cholesterol and fatty substances that can build up inside the artery walls. It does this through the powerful anti-oxidant properties of various chemical compounds found naturally in wine (through contact with grapeskins), the most important of which are polyphenols such as procyanidins and rytoalexins such as reservatol. Most chloresterol in the body is carried around the body on LDLs (low density lipoproteins), which clog up the arteries. By contrast, HDLs (high density lipoproteins) do not clog-up the arteries, but take the cholesterol straight to the liver, where it is processed out of the system. The anti-oxidants convert LDL into HDL, literally flushing away the cholesterol and other fatty substances. Together with alcohol itself, these anti-oxidants also act as an anti-coagulant on the blood, diminishing its clotting ability, which reduces the chances of a stroke to 50 per cent that of non-drinkers.

HEAT SUMMATION A system of measuring the growth potential of vines in a specific area in terms of the environmental temperature, expressed in degree-days. A vine's vegetative cycle is activated only above a temperature of 10°C (50°F). The time during which these temperatures persist equates to the vine's growing season. To calculate the number of degree-days, the proportion of the daily mean temperature significant to the vine's growth – the daily mean minus the inactive 10°C (50°F) – is multiplied by the number of days of the growing season. For example, a growing season of 200 days with a daily mean temperature of 15°C (59°F) gives a heat summation of 1,000 degree-days Celsius (1,800 degree-days Fahrenheit) based on the following calculation: (15 - 10) x 200 = 1,000.

HERBACEOUS A green-leaf or white-currant characteristic that is usually associated with too much **vigour** in the vine's canopy, which can cause under-ripeness, but can also be the result of aggressive extraction techniques employed for red wines fermented in stainless steel.

HERBAL, HERBAL-OAK These terms apply to wines matured in cask, but unlike vanilla-oak, creamy-oak, smoky-oak, and spicy-oak, their origin is unknown. A herbal character devoid of oak is usually derived from the **varietal** character of a grape and is common to many varieties.

HIGH-DENSITY VINES Vines planted close together compete with each other to yield higher-quality fruit, but less of it per vine, than vines planted further apart. Initial planting costs are higher and more labour is required for pruning and other activities, but if the vineyard is in balance, the greater number of vines should produce the same overall volume per hectare, even though the output per vine is reduced. Quantity can therefore be maintained while significantly raising quality, although there is a threshold density which vineyards must reach before real benefits appear. For example, more than half the vineyards in the New World are planted at less than 2,000 vines per hectare (800 per acre) and 1,200–1,500 per hectare is very common, whereas in Champagne, 6,666 vines per hectare is the minimum allowed by law, 7–8,000 the average, and 11,000 possible. In pre-Phylloxera times, it was something like 25,000 vines per hectare. Indeed, before California's vineyards were mechanized, the average density was twice what it is now because every other row was ripped up to allow entry for tractors. When Joseph Drouhin planted his vineyard in Oregon, he planted 7,450 vines per hectare and brought over French tractors that straddled the rows of vines, rather than went between them. All of a sudden, high-density vineyards entered the American vocabulary, although to Drouhin they were not high density, merely a matter of course.

HIGH-TONE A term used in this book to describe aromas of bouquet that aspire to elegance, but that can become too exaggerated and be slightly reminiscent of vermouth.

HOGSHEAD A barrel with a capacity of between 300 and 315 litres, commonly found in Australia and New Zealand.

HOLLOW A wine that appears to lack any real flavour in the mouth compared to the promise shown on the nose. Usually due to a lack of body, fruit, or acidity.

HONEST Applied to any wine, but usually to one that is of a fairly basic quality, honest implies it is true in character and typical of its type and origin. It also implies that the wine does not give any indication of being souped-up or mucked about in any unlawful way. The use of the word honest is, however, a way of damning with faint praise for it does not suggest a wine of any special or truly memorable quality.

HONEYED Many wines develop a honeyed character through bottle-age, particularly sweet wines and more especially those with some **botrytis** character, but some dry wines can also become honeyed, a mature Riesling being the classic example.

HOT Synonym for **baked**.

HOUSE CLARET An unpretentious, and not too expensive, everyday-drinking red Bordeaux.

HYBRID A cross between two or more grape varieties from more than one species.

HYDROGEN SULPHIDE When hydrogen combines with **sulphur dioxide**, the result is a smell of bad eggs. If this occurs prior to bottling and is dealt with immediately, it can be rectified. If allowed to progress, the hydrogen sulphide can develop into **mercaptans** and ruin the wine.

ICEWINE See **Eiswein**.

INKY Can refer either to a wine's opacity of colour, or to an inkiness of character indicating a deep flavour with plenty of supple **tannin**.

IPR (Port.) Short for Indicaçao de Provência Regulamentada, a Portuguese quality designation that falls between DOC and VR.

IRON This is found as a trace element in fresh grapes grown in soils in which relatively substantial ferrous deposits are located. Wines from such sites may naturally contain a tiny amount of iron barely perceptible on the palate. If there is too much, the flavour becomes medicinal. Above seven milligrams per litre for white, ten milligrams per litre for red, there is a danger of the wine going cloudy. But wines of such iron levels should have been blue-fined prior to bottling. See **Fining**.

ISINGLASS A gelatinous fining agent obtained from the swim-bladder of freshwater fish and used to clear hazy, low-tannin wines. See **Fining**.

JAMMY Commonly used to describe a fat and eminently drinkable red wine rich in fruit, if perhaps a bit contrived and lacking elegance.

JUG WINE California's mass-produced *vin de table*, synonymous with carafe wine.

KABINETT The first rung of predication in Germany's **QmP** range, one below *Spätlese*, and often drier than a QbA.

LACTIC ACID The acid that develops in sour milk, and which is also created in wine during the **malolactic** fermentation.

LAGAR (Port.) A rectangular concrete receptacle in which people tread grapes.

LAID-BACK A term that has come into use since the arrival of Californian wines on the international scene in the early 1980s. It usually implies that a wine is very relaxed, easy to drink, and confident of its own quality.

LANDWEIN German equivalent of *vin de pays*.

L.D. A sparkling-wine term that stands for "late disgorged" and paradoxically means the same as "recently disgorged". The use of L.D. implies that the wine in question is of a mature vintage that has been kept on its yeast deposit for an extended period. See **R.D.**

LEACHING A term that is sometimes used when referring to the deliberate removal of **tannin** from new oak by steaming, or when discussing certain aspects of soil, such as **pH**, that can be affected when carbonates are leached, or removed, by rainwater.

LEES Sediment that accumulates in the bottom of a vat during the **fermentation** of a wine.

LEMONY Many dry and medium-sweet wines have a tangy, fruity **acidity** that is suggestive of lemons.

LENGTH A wine that has length is one whose flavour lingers in the mouth a long time after swallowing. If two wines taste the same, yet you definitely prefer one, but do not understand why, it is probably because the one you prefer has a greater length.

LIE (Fr.) The French for **lees**: *sur lie* refers to a wine kept in contact with its lees.

LIEU-DIT (Fr.) A named site (plural: *lieux-dits*). This term is commonly used for wines of specific growths that do not have *Grand Cru* status.

LIGHT VINTAGE A light vintage or year produces relatively light wines. Not a great vintage, but not necessarily a bad one either.

LIME This is the classic character of Sémillon and Riesling grape varietes when grown in many areas of Australia, which explains why Sémillon from the Hunter Valley used to be sold as Hunter Riesling.

LINALOOL A compound found in some grapes, particularly the Muscat and Riesling varieties. It contributes to the peachy-flowery fragrance that is characteristic of Muscat wines.

LINGERING Normally applied to the finish of a wine – an aftertaste that literally lingers.

LIQUEUR DE TIRAGE (Fr.) The bottling *liqueur*: wine, yeast, and sugar added to still Champagne to induce the **mousse**.

LIQUOREUX (Fr.) Literally "liqueur-like", this term is often applied to dessert wines of an unctuous quality. (Sometimes also "liquorous".)

LIQUORICE This characteristic is often detected in Monbazillac, but it may be found in any rich sweet wine. It refers to concentration of flavours from heat-shrivelled, rather than botrytized, grapes.

LIVELINESS A term that usually implies a certain youthful freshness of fruit due to good **acidity** and a touch of **carbonic gas**.

LONGEVITY Potentially long-lived wines may owe their longevity to a significant content of one or more of the following: **tannin**, **acidity**, **alcohol**, and **sugar**.

LUSCIOUS, LUSCIOUSNESS Almost synonymous with voluptuous, although more often used for an unctuous, sweet white wine than a succulently rich red.

MACERATION A term that is usually applied to the period during the vinification process when the fermenting juice is in contact with its skins. This traditionally involves red-winemaking, but it on the increase for white wines utilizing pre-fermentation maceration techniques.

MACÉRATION CARBONIQUE (Fr.) A generic term covering several methods of vinifying wine under the pressure of **carbonic gas**. Such wines, Beaujolais Nouveau being the archetypal example, are characterized by amylic **aromas** (peardrops, bubble-gum, nail-varnish). If this vinification method is used for just a small part of a blend, however, it can lift the fruit and soften a wine without leaving such tell-tale aromas. See Macération Carbonique p.36.

MADERIZED All Madeiras are maderized by the *estufagem*, in which the wines are slowly heated in specially constructed ovens, then cooling them. This is undesirable in all wines except for certain Mediterranean wines that are deliberately made in a *rancio* style. Any ordinary, light, table wine that is maderized will often be erroneously diagnosed as oxidized, but there is a significant difference in the symptoms: maderized wines have a duller **nose**, rarely hint of any Sherry-like character of **acetaldehyde**, and are flatter on the **palate**. All colours and styles of wine are capable of maderizing and the likely cause is storage in bright sunlight or too much warmth.

MALIC A tasting term that describes the green apple **aroma** and flavour found in some young wines, due to the presence of malic acid, the dominant acid found in apples.

MALIC ACID A very strong-tasting acid that diminishes during the fruit's ripening process, but still persists in ripe grapes and, although reduced by **fermentation**, in wine too. The quantity of malic acid present in a wine may be considered too much, particularly in a red wine, and the smoothing effect of replacing it with just two-thirds the quantity of the much weaker lactic acid is often desirable. See Malolactic Fermentation. p.33.

MALOLACTIC The so-called malolactic fermentation is sometimes referred to as a secondary fermentation, but it is actually a biochemical process that converts the hard malic acid of unripe grapes into soft **lactic acid** and **carbonic gas**. *See* Malolactic Fermentation, p.33.

MANURE A very extreme form of **farmyardy**.

MANNOPROTEIN Nitrogenous matter secreted from yeast during **autolysis**.

MANTA *See* **Cap**.

MARC 1. The residue of skins, pips, and stalks after pressing. 2. The name given to a four-tonne load of grapes in Champagne. 3. A rough brandy made from the residue of skins, pips, and stalks after pressing.

MARQUE A brand or make.

MATURE, MATURITY Refers to a wine's development in bottle, as opposed to **ripe**, which describes the maturity of the grape itself.

MEAN An extreme qualification of **ungenerous**.

MEATY This term suggests a wine so rich in **body** and **extract** that the drinker feels almost able to chew it. Wines with a high **tannin** content are often meaty.

MELLOW Describes a wine that is **round** and nearing its peak of **maturity**.

MEMBRANE FILTER A thin screen of biologically inert material, perforated with micro-sized pores that occupy 80 per cent of the membrane. Anything larger than these holes is denied passage when the wine is pumped through during **filtration**.

MERCAPTANS Methyl and ethyl alcohols can react with hydrogen sulphide to form mercaptans, which are foul-smelling compounds, often impossible to remove, that can ruin a wine. Mercaptans can smell of garlic, onion, burnt rubber, or stale cabbage.

MÉTHODE CHAMPENOISE (Fr.) The process in which an effervescence is produced through a secondary **fermentation** in the same bottle the wine is sold in (i.e., not the Transfer Method). This procedure is used for Champagne and other good-quality sparkling wines. In Europe the term is forbidden on the label of any wine other than Champagne, which never uses it anyway.

MÉTHODE GAILLAÇOISE (Fr.) A variant of *Méthode Rurale* involving *dégorgement*.

MÉTHODE RURALE (Fr.) The precursor of *Méthode Champenoise*, this method involves no secondary **fermentation**. The wine is bottled before the first alcoholic fermentation has finished, and **carbonic gas** is produced during the continuation of fermentation in the bottle. There is also no *dégorgement*.

METODO CHAMPENOIS (It.) *See Méthode Champenoise*.

MICROCLIMATE Due to a combination of shelter, exposure, proximity to mountains, water mass, and other topographical features unique to a given area, a vineyard can enjoy (or be prone to) a specific microclimate.

MICRO-POROUS FILTER Synonymous with **membrane filter**.

MICRO-VINIFICATION This technique involves **fermentation** in small, specialized vats, which are seldom bigger than a washing machine. The process is often used to make experimental wines. There are certain dynamics involved in fermentation that determine a minimum optimum size of vat, which is why home-brewers seldom make a polished product and why most wines made in research stations are dull.

MID-PALATE 1. The centre-top of your tongue. 2. A subjective term to describe the middle of the taste sensation when taking a mouthful of wine. It could be hollow, if the wine is thin and lacking, or full, if it is rich and satisfying.

MILLERANDAGE (Fr.) A physiological disorder of the vine that occurs after cold or wet weather at the time of the flowering. This makes fertilization very difficult, and consequently many berries fail to develop. They remain small and seedless even when the rest of the bunch is full-sized and ripe.

MINERAL Some wines have a minerally aftertaste that can be unpleasant. Vinho Verde has an attractive, almost tinny, aftertaste when made from certain grape varieties.

MISTELLE (Fr.) Fresh grape juice that has been muted with **alcohol** before any **fermentation** can take place.

MOELLEUX (Fr.) Literally soft or smooth, this term usually implies a rich, medium-sweet style in most French areas, except the Loire, where it is used to indicate a truly rich, sweet **botrytis** wine, thereby distinguishing it from **demi-sec**.

MONOPOLE (Fr.) Denotes the single ownership of one vineyard.

MOUSSE (Fr.) The effervescence of a sparkling wine, which is best judged in the mouth; a wine may appear to be flat in one glass and vigorous in another due to the different surfaces. The bubbles of a good *mousse* should be small and persistent; the strength of effervescence depends on the style of wine.

MOUSSEUX (Fr.) Literally "sparkling".

MOUTH-FILL Literally meaning a wine that easily fills the mouth with a satisfying flavour. There is no holding back, but it does not quite imply anything upfront or too obvious.

MUID (Fr.) A large oval barrel with a capacity of 600 litres.

MUST Unfermented or partly fermenting grape juice.

MUST WEIGHT The amount of sugar in ripe grapes or grape must.

MUTAGE (Fr.) The addition of pure **alcohol** to a wine or to fresh grape juice either before **fermentation** can take place, as in the case of a *vin de liqueur*, or during fermentation, as in the case of *vin doux naturel*. *See* Mutage, p.38.

NÉGOCIANT (Fr.) Trader or merchant. The name is derived from the traditional practice of negotiating with growers (to buy wine) and wholesalers or customers (to sell it).

NÉGOCIANT-ÉLEVEUR (Fr.) A wine firm that buys in ready-made wines for *élevage*. The wines are then blended and bottled under the *négociant's* label.

NERVY, NERVOUS A subjective term usually applied to a dry white wine that is **firm** and vigorous, but not quite settled down.

NEUTRAL GRAPE VARIETIES Such grapes include virtually all the minor, nondescript varieties that produce bland tasting, low-quality wines, but also encompass better known varieties such as the Melon de Bourgogne, Aligoté, Pinot blanc, Pinot meunier, and even classics such as Chardonnay and Sémillon. The opposite of aromatic grapes, these varieties are ideal for oak-maturation, bottling *sur lie* and turning into fine sparkling wines because their characteristics are enhanced rather than hidden by these processes.

NOBLE ROT A condition caused by the fungus *Botrytis cinerea* under certain conditions.

NOSE The smell or odour of a wine, encompassing both **aroma** and **bouquet**.

OAK Many wines are **fermented** or aged in wooden casks and the most commonly used wood is oak. There are two main categories of oak, French and American, and they are both used the world over. Although the French always use French oak, the greatest California wines are also usually made in French oak barrels. American oak is traditional in Spain, particularly Rioja, and Australia, although both these countries have a growing usage of French oak. Oak often gives a **vanilla** taste to wine because it contains a substance called **vanillin**, which also gives vanilla pods their vanilla aroma. French oak, however, is perceived to be finer and more refined, while American oak is generally considered to have a more upfront, obvious character. This difference in character is due not to intrinsic qualities in the two types of oak (although American oak grows more quickly than French and has a bigger grain, which does have some influence), but to the traditional weathering of French oak in the open for several years, which leaches out the most volatile **aromatics**. American oak is kiln-dried, therefore not leached, and sawn (unlike French oak, which is split), which ruptures the grain, exposing the wine to the oak's most volatile elements in a relatively short time. If French oak were to be kiln-dried and sawn, and American weathered and split, I suspect our perception of the two forms of oak might well be reversed. American oak is often highly charred in the construction of a barrel (wine makers can order it lightly toasted, medium toasted, or highly charred), and this too has an effect, adding caramel, toffee, and smoky-toasty aromas to a wine. The toastiness in oak is different to any toastiness derived from the grape itself. Strangely, oak can produce a cedary taste, although this is probably confined to wines made from spicy black-grape varieties that are fermented and/or matured in relatively old wood. If you get a very strong impression of coconut, it's a good bet that the oak used was American. Oak barrels are very expensive to buy and labour intensive to work with, so if you find a very cheap wine with obvious oak character, it will inevitably be due to the use of oak chips or shavings, which are chucked into a huge, gleaming stainless-steel vat of wine. Cheating this may be, but it is legal, and if people like the taste of oak-aged wine, but cannot afford to pay much for a bottle, what is wrong with it? *See* Stainless Steel or Oak, p.33.

OECHSLE LEVEL (Ger.) A system of measuring the sugar content in grapes for wine categories in Germany and Austria.

OENOLOGIST, OENOLOGY Oenology is the scientific study of wine, which is a branch of chemistry, but with practical consequences, hands-on production experience and an understanding of viticulture.

OFF VINTAGE An off vintage or year is one in which many poor wines are produced due to adverse climatic conditions, such as very little sunshine during the summer, which can result in unripe grapes, and rain or humid heat at the harvest, which can result in rot. Generally this means a vintage to be avoided, but approach any opportunity to taste the wines with an open mind because there are always good wines made in every vintage, however poor, and they have to be sold at bargain prices due to the vintage's widespread bad reputation.

OIDIUM A fungal disease of the vine that turns leaves powdery grey and dehydrates grapes.

OILY Subjective term meaning **fat** and viscous, often also **flat** and **flabby**.

OLOROSO (Sp.) A Sherry style, naturally dry but usually sweetened for export markets.

OPEN-KNIT An open and enjoyable **nose** or **palate**, usually a modest wine, not capable of much development.

OPULENT Suggestive of a rather luxurious **varietal** aroma, very rich, but not quite **blowzy**.

ORGANIC WINES A generic term for wines produced using the minimum amount of sulphur dioxide, from grapes grown without the use of chemical fertilizers, pesticides, or herbicides.

ORGANOLEPTIC Affecting a bodily organ or sense, usually taste or smell.

OSMOTIC PRESSURE When two solutions are separated by a semi-permeable membrane, water will leave the weaker solution for the other in an endeavour to equalize the differing solution strengths. In winemaking this is most usually encountered when yeast cells are expected to work in grape juice with an exceptionally high sugar content. Since water accounts for 65 per cent of a yeast cell, osmotic pressure causes the water to escape through its semi-permeable exterior. The cell caves in (a phenomenon called plasmolysis), and the yeast dries up and eventually dies.

OVERTONE A dominating element of **nose** and **palate** and often one that is not directly attributable to the grape or wine.

OXIDATIVE A wine that openly shows the character of maturation on the **nose** or **palate**. This can range from various buttery, biscuity, spicy characteristics to a hint of nuttiness.

OXIDATION, OXIDIZED These terms are ambiguous; as soon as grapes are pressed or crushed, oxidation sets in and the juice or wine will be oxidized to a certain and increasing extent. Oxidation is also an unavoidable part of **fermentation** and an essential to the maturation process. In order not to mislead, however, it is best to speak of a mature or, at the extreme, an oxidative wine because when the word oxidized is used, even among experts, it will invariably be in an extremely derogatory manner, to highlight the Sherry-like odour of a wine that is in a prematurely advanced stage of oxidation.

PAD FILTRATION A filtration system utilizing a series of cellulose, asbestos, or paper sheets through which wine is passed.

PALATE The flavour or taste of a wine.

PASSERILLAGE (Fr.) Grapes without **noble rot** that are left on the vine are cut off from the plant's metabolic system as its sap withdraws into its roots. The warmth of the day, followed by the cold of the night, causes the grapes to dehydrate and concentrate in a process known as *passerillage*. The sweet wine produced from these grapes is prized in certain areas. A *passerillage* wine from a hot autumn will be totally different to one from a cold autumn.

PASSITO (It.) The equivalent of *passerillage*. *Passito* grapes are semi-dried, either outside on the vine, or on mats; or inside a warm building. This concentrates the pulp and produces strong, often sweet wines.

PASTEURIZATION A generic term for various methods of stabilization and sterilization. *See* Heat, p.22.

PEAK The so-called peak in the maturity of a wine. Those liking fresher, crisper wines will perceive an earlier peak (in the same wine) than drinkers who prefer mature wines. As a rule of thumb that applies to all extremes of taste, a wine will remain at its peak for as long as it took to reach it.

PEARDROP *See* Macération carbonique.

PEPPERY A term applied to young wines whose components are raw and not yet in harmony, sometimes quite fierce and prickly on the **nose**, it also describes the characteristic odour and flavour of southern French wines, particularly Grenache-based ones. Syrah can smell of freshly crushed black pepper, while white pepper is the character of great Grüner Veltliner. Young Ports and light red Riojas can also be very peppery.

PERFUME An agreeable scented quality of a wine's bouquet.

PERLANT (Fr.) Very slightly sparkling, less so than *crémant* and *pétillant*.

PERLITE A fine, powdery, light, and lustrous substance of volcanic origin with similar properties to **diatomaceous earth**. When perlite is used for filtration, it is sometimes referred to as **ceramic filtration**.

PÉTILLANCE, PÉTILLANT (Fr.) This term describes a wine with sufficient **carbonic gas** to create a light sparkle.

PETIT CHÂTEAU (Fr.) Literally "small château", this term is applied to any wine château that is neither a *Cru Classé* nor a *Cru Bourgeois*.

PETROL, PETROLLY With some bottle-age, the finest Rieslings have a vivid and zesty bouquet that some call petrolly. This petrolly character has an affinity with various zesty and citrussy odours, but many **lemony, citrussy, zesty** smells are totally different from one another and the Riesling's petrolly character is both singular and unmistakable. As great Riesling matures, so it also develops a honeyed character, bringing a classic, honeyed-petrol richness to the wine.

pH A commonly used chemical abbreviation of "potential hydrogen-ion concentration", a measure of the **active acidity** or alkalinity of a liquid. It does not give any indication of the **total acidity** in a wine, but neither does the human **palate**. When we perceive the acidity in wine through taste, it is more closely associated with the pH than the total acidity.

PHENOLS, PHENOLIC Compounds found in the skin, pips, and stalks of grapes, the most common being **tannin** and **anthocyanins**.

PHYLLOXERA A vine louse that spread from America to virtually every viticultural region in the world during the late 19th century, destroying many vines. New vines had (and still have) to be grafted on to phylloxera-resistant American rootstocks.

PIPE (Port.) The most famous Portuguese barrel, a Douro pipe has a capacity of 550 litres.

PIQUANT (Fr.) Usually applied to a pleasing white wine with a positive underlying fruit and **acidity**.

PLUMMY An elegant, juicy flavour and texture that resembles the fleshiness of plums.

PLUM-PUDDING A subjective term for rich and spicy red wine; a more intense term than **Christmas cake**.

POLISHED Describes a wine that has been skilfully crafted, leaving no rough edges. It is **smooth** and refined to drink.

POLISHING The very last, ultra-fine **filtration** of a wine, usually with kieselguhr or **perlite**, is so called because it leaves the wine bright; many high-quality wines are not polished because the process can wash out natural flavours.

POURRITURE NOBLE (Fr.) **Noble rot**, which is caused by the fungus *Botrytis cinerea* under certain conditions.

PRE-FERMENTATION MACERATION The practice of maceration of juice in grape skins prior to fermentation, to enhance the **varietal** character of the wine. This maceration is usually cold and normally employed for aromatic white varieties, but can be warm and even quite hot for red wines.

PREMIER CRU (Fr.) Literally "First Growth", this term is of relevance only in those areas where it is controlled, e.g. Burgundy, Champagne.

PRESS WINE *See* Vin de presse.

PRICKLE, PRICKLY This term describes a wine with residual **carbonic gas**, but with less than the light sparkle of a *pétillant* wine. It can be desirable in some fresh white and rosé wines, but it is usually taken as a sign of an undesirable **secondary fermentation** in red wines, although it is deliberately created in certain South African examples.

PRODUCER VINE Vines are usually grafted on to phylloxera-resistant rootstock, but the grapes produced are characteristic of the above-ground producer vine or scion, which is normally a variety of *Vitis vinifera*.

PVPP (POLYVINYLPOLYPYRROLIDONE) A **fining** agent used to remove compounds sensitive to browning from white wines.

PROTEIN HAZE Protein is present in all wines. Too much protein can react with **tannin** to cause a haze, in which case bentonite is usually used as a fining agent to remove it. *See* Fining.

PUNCHEON This type of barrel, which is commonly found in Australia and New Zealand, has a capacity of 450 litres.

QbA (Ger.) Germany's *Qualitätswein bestimmter Anbaugebiete* is the theoretical equivalent of the French AOC.

QmP (Ger.) A common abbreviation of *Qualitätswein mit Prädikat*. Literally a "quality wine with predication", this term is used for any German wine above **QbA**, from *Kabinett* upwards. The predication carried by a QmP wine depends upon the level of ripeness of the grapes used in the wine.

QUAFFING WINE Describes an unpretentious wine that is easy and enjoyable to drink.

QUINTA (Port.) A wine estate.

R2 A yeast strain (*Saccharomyces cerevisiae race bayanus*) discovered by Danish-born winemaker Peter Vinding-Diers.

RACKING The draining of a wine off its **lees** into a fresh cask or vat. *See* Racking, p.34.

RACY Often applied to wines of the Riesling grape. It accurately suggests the liveliness, vitality, and **acidity** of this grape.

RANCIO Description of a *vin doux naturel* stored in oak casks for at least two years, often with the barrels exposed to direct sunlight. This imparts a distinctive flavour that is popular in the Roussillon area of France.

RATAFIA A *liqueur* made by combining **marc** with grape juice, Ratafia de Champagne being the best-known.

R.D. A sparkling-wine term that stands for "recently disgorged", the initials R.D. are the trademark of Champagne Bollinger. *See* L.D.

RECIOTO (It.) A strong, sweet wine made in Italy from *passito* grapes.

REDOX The ageing process of wine was originally conceived as purely **oxidative**, but it was then discovered that when one substance in wine is oxidized (gains oxygen), another is reduced (loses oxygen). This is known as a reductive-oxidative, or redox reaction. **Organoleptically**, however, wines reveal either oxidative or **reductive** characters. In the presence of air, a wine is prone to oxidative character, but shut off from a supply of oxygen, reductive characteristics begin to dominate, thus the bouquet of bottle-age is a reductive one and the aroma of a fresh, young wine is more oxidative than reductive.

REDUCTIVE The less exposure it has to air, the more reductive a wine will be. Different as they are in basic character, Champagne, Muscadet *sur lie*, and Beaujolais Nouveau are all examples of reductive, as opposed to **oxidative**, wines, from the vividly autolytic Champagne, through Muscadet *sur lie* with its barest hint of autolytic character, to the amylic aroma of Beaujolais Nouveau. A good contrast is Madeira, which is reductive, while Sherry is oxidative. The term is, however, abused, as many tasters use it to describe a fault, when the wine is heavily reduced.

REFRACTOMETER An optical device used to measure the sugar content of grapes when out in the field.

REMONTAGE (Fr.) The pumping of wine over the **cap** or manta of skins during the *cuvaison* of red wine.

REMUAGE (Fr.) An intrinsic part of the *méthode champenoise*; deposits thrown off during **secondary fermentation** are eased down to the neck of the bottle and are then removed at *dégorgement*.

RESERVE WINES Still wines from previous vintages that are blended with the wines of one principal year to produce a balanced non-vintage Champagne.

RETICENT This term suggests that the wine is holding back on its **nose** or **palate**, perhaps through youth, and may well develop with a little more maturity.

RICH, RICHNESS A balanced wealth of fruit and depth on the palate and finish.

RIPASSO (It.) Re-fermentation of wine on the **lees** of a *recioto* wine.

RIPE Grapes ripen, and wines mature, although the fruit and even **acidity** in wine can be referred to as ripe. Tasters should, however, be careful not to mistake a certain residual sweetness for ripeness.

RIPE ACIDITY The main acidic component in ripe grapes (**tartaric acid**) tastes refreshing and fruity, even in large proportions, whereas the main acidity in unripe grapes (**malic acid**) tastes hard and unpleasant.

ROASTED This term describes the character of grapes subjected to the shrivelling or roasting of **noble rot**.

ROBUST A milder form of "aggressive", which may often be applied to a mature product; the wine is robust by nature, rather than aggressive through youth.

ROOTSTOCK The lower rooting part of a grafted vine, usually phylloxera-resistant. *See* Rootstock, p.21.

ROUND A wine that has rounded off all its edges of **tannin**, **acidity**, **extract**, etc. through maturity in bottle.

SACCHAROMETER A laboratory device used for measuring the sugar content of grape juice, based on specific gravity.

SAIGNÉE (Fr.) The process of drawing off surplus liquid from the fermenting vat in order to produce a rosé wine from the free-run juice. In cooler wine regions, the remaining mass of grape pulp may be used to make a darker red wine than would normally be possible because of the greater ratio of solids to liquid, providing more colouring pigment.

SASSY Should be a less cringing version of the cheeky, audacious character found in a wine with bold, brash but not necessarily **big** flavour.

SCION *See* Producer vine.

SEC (Fr.) Dry, as applied to wines, means wines without any sweetness. This does not mean there is no fruit: wines with plenty of very ripe fruit can seem so rich they may appear to have some sweetness.

SECOND FERMENTATION, SECONDARY FERMENTATION Strictly speaking, this is the fermentation that occurs in bottle during the *Méthode Champenoise*. The term is sometimes also used, mistakenly, to refer to the **malolactic** fermentation.

SEKT (Ger.) Sparkling wine.

SELECTION DE GRAINS NOBLES (Fr.) In Alsace, a rare, intensely sweet, botrytized wine.

SHARP This term applies to **acidity**, whereas **bitterness** applies to **tannin** and, sometimes, other natural solids. An immature wine might be sharp, but, if used by professional tasters, the term is usually a derogatory one. Good acidity is usually described as **ripe acidity**, which can make the fruit refreshingly tangy.

SHEET FILTRATION Synonymous with **pad filtration**.

SHERRY-LIKE This term refers to the odour of a wine in an advanced state of oxidation, which is undesirable in low-strength or unfortified wines. It is caused by excessive **acetaldehyde**.

SHORT Refers to a wine that may have a good **nose** and initial flavour, but falls short on the **finish**, its taste quickly disappearing after the wine has been swallowed.

SKIN-CONTACT The **maceration** of grape skins in **must** or fermenting wine can extract varying

amounts of colouring pigments, **tannin**, and various aromatic compounds.

SMOKINESS, SMOKY, SMOKY-COMPLEXITY, SMOKY-OAK Some grapes have a smoky character (particularly Syrah and Sauvignon blanc). This character can also come from well-toasted oak casks, but may also indicate an unfiltered wine. Some talented winemakers do not rack their wines and sometimes do not filter them in a passionate bid to retain maximum character and create an individual and expressive wine.

SMOOTH The opposite of **aggressive** and more extreme than **round**.

SO₂ A commonly used chemical formula for sulphur dioxide, an **anti-oxidant** with aseptic qualities used in the production of wine. It should not be noticeable in the finished product, but sometimes a whiff may be detected on recently bottled wine. A good swirl in the glass or a vigorous decanting should remove this trace and after a few months in bottle it ought to disappear altogether. The acrid odour of sulphur in a wine should, if detected, be akin to the smell of a recently extinguished match. If it has a rotten egg aroma, the sulphur has been reduced to **hydrogen sulphide** and the wine may well have formed **mercaptans** that you will not be able to remove. *See* The Use of Sulphur, p.32.

SOFT Interchangeable with **smooth**, although it usually refers to the fruit on the palate, whereas smooth is more often applied to the **finish**. Soft is very desirable, but "extremely soft" may be derogatory, inferring a weak and flabby wine.

SOLERA (Sp.) A system of continually refreshing an established blend with a small amount of new wine (equivalent in proportion to the amount extracted from the *solera*) to effect a wine of consistent quality and character. Some existing *soleras* were laid down in the 19th century and whereas it would be true to say that every bottle of that *solera* sold now contains a little of that first vintage, it would not even be a teaspoon. You would have to measure in molecules, but there would be infinitesimal amounts of each and every vintage from the date of its inception to the year before bottling.

SOLID This term is interchangeable with **firm**.

SOLUMOLOGICAL The science of the soil and, in the context of wine, the relationship between specific soil types and vine varieties.

SORBIC ACID A yeast-inhibiting compound found in the berries of mountain ash, sorbic acid is sometimes added to sweet wines to prevent re-fermentation, but can give a powerful geranium odour if the wine subsequently undergoes **malolactic** fermentation.

SOUPED UP or **SOUPY** Implies a wine has been blended with something richer or more robust. A wine may well be legitimately souped-up, or it could mean that the wine has been played around with. The wine might not be correct, but it could still be very enjoyable.

SOUS MARQUE (Fr.) Another type of *marque* under which wines, usually second-rate in quality, are offloaded.

SOUTHERN-STYLE Describes the obvious characteristics of a wine from the sunny south of France. For reds, it may be complimentary at an **honest** basic level, indicating a full-bodied, full-flavoured wine with a **peppery** character. For whites, it will probably be derogatory, implying a flabby wine with too much **alcohol** and too little **acidity** and freshness.

SOUTIRAGE (Fr.) Racking.

SPARGING A process in which **carbonic gas** is introduced into a wine prior to its bottling, often simply achieved through a valve in the pipe between the vat and the bottling line. *See* Carbonation, p.38.

SPÄTLESE (Ger.) A QmP wine that is one step above *Kabinett*, but one below *Auslese*. It is fairly sweet and made from late-picked grapes.

SPICY 1. A varietal characteristic of some grapes, such as Gewürztraminer. 2. An aspect of a complex **bouquet** or **palate**, probably derived from bottle-age after time in wood.

SPICY-OAK A subjective term describing complex **aromas** derived from **fermentation** or maturation in oak that can give the impression of various spices, usually "creamy" ones such as cinnamon or nutmeg, and that are enhanced by bottle-age.

SPRITZ, SPRITZIG (Ger.) A term synonymous with *pétillant*.

SPUMANTE (It.) Fully sparkling.

STAGE A period of practical experience. It has long been traditional for vineyard owners to send their sons on a stage to a great château in Bordeaux. Now the *bordelais* send their sons on similar stages to California and Australia.

STALKY 1. A **varietal** characteristic of Cabernet grapes. 2. Literally applies to wines made from grapes which were pressed with the stalks. 3. Could be indicative of a **corked** wine.

STRETCHED This term describes a wine that has been diluted by or cut with water (or significantly inferior wine), which is usually illegal in an official appellation. It can also refer to wine that has been produced from vines that have been stretched to yield a high volume of attenuated fruit.

STRUCTURE The structure of a wine is literally composed of its solids (**tannin**, **acidity**, sugar, and **extract** or density of fruit flavour) in balance with the **alcohol**, and how positively they form and feel in the mouth.

STUCK FERMENTATION A stuck, literally halted, **fermentation** is always difficult to rekindle and, even when successful, the wine can taste strangely bitter. The most common causes are: 1. temperatures of 35°C (95°F) or above; 2. nutrient deficiency, which can cause yeast cells to die; 3. high sugar content, which results in high **osmotic pressure**, which can cause yeast cells to die.

STÜCK (Ger.) A large oval cask with a capacity of 1,200 litres.

STYLISH Describes wines possessing all the subjective qualities of **charm**, **elegance**, and **finesse**. A wine might have the "style" of a certain region or type, but a wine is either stylish or it is not. It defies definition.

SUBTLE Although this description should mean a significant yet understated characteristic, it is often employed by wine snobs and frauds who taste a wine with a famous label and know that it should be special, but cannot detect anything exceptional and need an ambiguous word to get out of the hole they have dug for themselves.

SULPHUR DIOXIDE *See* SO₂.

SUMMER PRUNING *See* **Green pruning**

SUPER-TUSCAN This term was coined in the 1980s for the Cabernet-boosted *vini da tavola* blends in Italy that were infinitely better and far more expensive than Tuscany's traditional Sangiovese-based wines. *See* Birth of the Super-Tuscans, p.327.

SUPER-SECOND A term that evolved when Second-Growth châteaux, such as Palmer and Cos d'Estournel, started making wines that came close to First-Growth quality at a time when certain First Growths were not always performing well. The first such super-second was Palmer 1961, but the term did not evolve until some time during the early 1980s.

SUPPLE Describes a wine that is easy to drink, not necessarily soft, but suggests more ease than simply **round** does. With age, the **tannin** in wine becomes supple.

SUPPLE TANNIN Tannins are generally perceived to be harsh and mouth-puckering, but the tannins in a ripe grape are supple, whereas those in an unripe grape are not.

SUR LIE (Fr.) Describes wines, usually Muscadet, that have been kept on their **lees** and have not been racked or filtered prior to bottling. Although this increases the possibility of bacterial infection, the risk is worth taking for those wines made from neutral grape varieties. In the wines of Muscadet, for example, this practice enhances the fruit of the normally bland Melon de Bourgogne grape and adds a yeasty dimension of depth that can give the flavour of a modest white Burgundy. It also avoids aeration and retains more of the **carbonic gas** created during **fermentation**, imparting a certain liveliness and freshness.

SÜSSRESERVE (Ger.) This is unfermented, fresh grape juice commonly used to sweeten German wines up to and including *Spätlese* level, and is also added to cheaper *Auslesen*. It is far superior to the traditional French method of sweetening wines, which utilizes grape concentrate instead of grape juice. *Süssreserve* provides a fresh and grapey character that is desirable in inexpensive medium-sweet wines.

TABLE WINE A term that often implies a wine is modest, even poor-quality because it is the literal translation of *vin de table*, the lowest level of French wine. However, it is not necessarily a derogatory term as it may also be used to distinguish between a light and a fortified wine.

TAFELWEIN (Ger.) Table wine or *vin de table*.

TALENTO (It.) Since March 1996, producers of Italian *Méthode Champenoise* wines may utilize the new term "Talento", which has been registered as a trademark by the Instituto Talento Metado Classico, which was established in 1975 and formerly called the Instituto Spumante Classico Italiano. Talento is almost synonymous with the Spanish term Cava, although to be fully compatible it would have to assume the mantle of a DOC and to achieve that would require mapping all the areas of production. However, it will take all the Talento they can muster to turn most Italian Spumante *brut* into an international class of sparkling wine.

TANK METHOD *See* **Cuve Close**.

TANNIC, TANNIN Tannins are various phenolic substances found naturally in wine that come from the skin, pips, and stalks of grapes. They can also be picked up from casks, particularly new ones. Grape tannins can be divided into "ripe" and "unripe", the former being most desirable. In a proper balance, however, both types are essential to the structure of red wines, in order to knit the many flavours together. Unripe tannins are not water-soluble and will remain harsh no matter how old the wine is, whereas ripe tannins are water-soluble, have a suppleness or, at most, a grippy feel, from an early age and will drop out as the wine matures. Ripe grape tannin softens with age, is vital to the structure of a serious red wine, and is useful when matching food and wine.

TART Refers to a noticeable **acidity** between **sharp** and **piquant**.

TARTARIC ACID The ripe acid of grapes that increases slightly when the grapes increase in sugar during the *véraison*.

TARTRATES, TARTRATE CRYSTALS Tartaric acid deposits look very much like sugar crystals at the bottom of a bottle and may be precipitated when a wine experiences low temperatures. Tartrates are also deposited simply through the process of time, although seldom in a still or sparkling wine that has spent several months in contact with its **lees**, as this produces a mannoprotein called MP32, which prevents the precipitation of tartrates. A fine deposit of glittering crystals can also be deposited on the base of a cork if it has been soaked in a sterilizing solution of metabisulphite prior to bottling. Both are harmless. *See* Cold Stabilization, p.32.

TASTEVIN (Fr.) A shallow, dimpled, silver cup used for tasting, primarily in Burgundy.

TbA (Ger.) A commonly abbreviation of *Trockenbeerenauslese*, this category is for wines produced from individually picked, botrytized grapes that have been left on the vine to shrivel. The wine is golden-amber to amber in colour, intensely sweet, viscous, very complex and as different from *Beerenauslese* as that wine is from *Kabinett*.

TCA Short for trichloroanisole, the prime, but by no means only, culprit responsible for corked wines, TCA is found in oak staves as well as cork. *See* Corked.

TEINTURIER A grape variety with coloured (red), as opposed to clear, juice.

TERPENE Various terpenes and terpene alcohols are responsible for some of the most aromatic characteristics in wine, ranging from the floral aromas of Muscat to the petrol or kerosene character of a wonderfully mature Riesling. In sparkling wine, a terpene character may indicate Riesling in the blend, but is more likely to be due to part or all the base wine being kept unduly long in tank prior to the **second fermentation**.

TERROIR (Fr.) This literally means "soil", but in a viticultural sense *terroir* actually refers in a more general way to a vineyard's complete growing environment, which also includes altitude, aspect, climate, and any other significant factors that may affect the quality of a vine, and thereby the quality of the grapes it produces.

TÉTE DE CUVÉE (Fr.) The first flow of juice during the pressing, and the cream of the *cuvée*. It is the easiest juice to extract and the highest in quality, with the best balance of acids, sugars, and minerals.

THIN A wine lacking in **body**, fruit, and other properties.

TIGHT A **firm** wine of good **extract** and possibly significant **tannin** that seems to be under tension, like a wound spring waiting to be released. Its potential is far more obvious than that of reticent or closed wines.

TOAST 1. A slow-developing bottle-induced **aroma** commonly associated with the Chardonnay, but can develop in wines made from other grapes, including red wines. Toasty bottle aromas are initially noticeable on the **aftertaste**, often with no indication on the **nose**. **2.** A fast-developing oak-induced aroma. **3.** Barrels are toasted during their construction to one of three grades: light or low, medium, and heavy or high.

TOBACCO A subjective **bouquet**/tasting term that is often applied to oak-matured wines, usually Bordeaux.

TOTAL ACIDITY The total amount of **acidity** in a wine is usually measured in grams per litre and, because each acid is of a different strength, expressed either as sulphuric or **tartaric acid**.

TRANSVASAGE (Fr.) A method whereby non-*Méthode Champenoise* sparkling wines undergo a **second fermentation** in bottle, and are then decanted, filtered, and re-bottled under pressure to maintain the *mousse*.

TRIE (Fr.) This term usually refers to the harvesting of selected overripe or botrytized grapes by numerous sweeps or **tries**, through the vineyard.

TROCKENBEERENAUSLESE *See* **TbA**.

TYPICAL An over-used and less than honest form of **honest**.

TYPICITY A wine that shows good typicity is one that accurately reflects its grape and soil.

UC (Fr.) Short for Union Coopérative or other titles denoting a local or regional cooperative.

UC DAVIS Short for the University of California's oenology department at Davis.

ULLAGE (Fr.) **1.** The space between the top of the wine and the head of the bottle or cask. An old bottle of wine with an ullage beneath the shoulder of the bottle is unlikely to be any good. **2.** The practice of topping up wine in a barrel to keep it full and thereby prevent excessive **oxidation**.

UNDERTONE A subtle and supporting characteristic that does not dominate like an **overtone**. In a fine wine, a strong and simple overtone of youth can evolve into a delicate undertone with maturity, adding to a vast array of other nuances that give the wine **complexity**.

UNGENEROUS A wine that lacks generosity has little or no fruit and also far too much **tannin** (if red) or **acidity** for a correct and harmonious **balance**.

UNRIPE ACID Malic acid, as opposed to **tartaric** or **ripe acid**.

UPFRONT This term suggests a wine with an attractive, simple, immediately recognizable quality that says it all. Such a wine may initially be interesting, but it will not develop further and the last glass would say nothing more about its characteristics than the first.

UVAGGIO (It.) Wine blended from various grape varieties.

VALUE-FOR-MONEY The difference between penny-saving and penny-pinching, true value-for-money can exist in a wine that costs £50 (or fifty dollars, deutschemarks *et al*) as much as it can in one that costs £5, and the decision whether to buy will depend on how deep your pocket is. It is, however, facile to ask if the first wine is ten times better than the second. You can get value-for-money when buying a house for £500,000, but will it be ten times better than a £50,000 property?

VANILLA, VANILLA-OAK Often used to describe the **nose** and sometimes **palate** of an oak-aged wine, especially Rioja. It is the most basic and obvious of oak-induced characteristics. *See* Oak.

VANILLIN An aldehyde with a vanilla aroma that is found naturally in **oak** to one degree or another.

VARIETAL, VARIETAL AROMA, VARIETAL CHARACTER The unique and distinctive character of a single grape variety as expressed in the wine it produces.

VC (Sp.) Short for *vino comarcal*, which literally means a "local wine" and can be compared to the *vin de pays* of France.

VDL A common abbreviation of *vin de liqueur*, a fortified wine that is normally muted with alcohol before **fermentation** can begin.

VDLT (Sp.) Short for *vino de la tierra*, which literally means a "country wine", but is closer to the VdQS of France than its *vin de pays*.

VDN A common abbreviation for *vin doux naturel*. This is, in fact, a fortified wine, such as Muscat de Beaumes de Venise, that has been muted during the **fermentation** process, after it has achieved a level of between five and eight per cent alcohol.

VDQS A common abbreviation for *vin délimité de qualité supérieure*, which is a quality-control system below AOC, but above *vin de table* and *vin de pays*.

VDT (It.) Short for *vino da tavola*, supposedly the lowest rung in Italy's appellation system, it does however, in practice, encompass some of the country's greatest wines. *See* p.307.

VEGETAL Applied to wines of a certain maturity, often Chardonnay or Pinot, that are well rounded in style and have taken on a bouquet pleasingly reminiscent of vegetation, rather than fruit.

VENDANGE TARDIVE (Fr.) Late harvest.

VÉRAISON (Fr.) The ripening period during which the grapes do not actually change very much in size, but do gain in colour, if black, and increase in sugar and **tartaric acid**, while at the same time decreasing in unripe **malic acid**.

VERMOUTH An aromatized wine. The name originates from *Wermut*, the German for wormwood, its principal ingredient. Earliest examples made in Germany in the 16th century were for local consumption only, the first commercial vermouth being Punt-é-Mes, created by Antonio Carpano of Turin in 1786. Traditionally, Italian vermouth is red and sweet, while French is white and dry, but both countries make both styles. Vermouth is made by blending very bland base wines (two or three years old, from Apulia and Sicily in Italy and Languedoc-Roussillon in France) with an extract of aromatic ingredients, then sweetening with sugar and fortified with pure alcohol. Chambéry, a pale and delicately aromatic wine made in the Savoie, France, is the only vermouth with an official **appellation**.

VIERTELSTÜCK (Ger.) A small oval cask with a capacity of 300 litres.

VIGNERON (Fr.) Vineyard worker.

VIGNOBLE (Fr.) Vineyard.

VIGOUR Although this term could easily apply to wine, it is invariably used when discussing the growth of a vine, particularly its canopy. In order to ripen grapes properly, a vine needs about 50 sq. cm. of leaf surface to every gram of fruit, but if a vine is too vigorous (known as high vigour), the grapes will have an over-**herbaceous** character even when they are theoretically **ripe**.

VIN DE CAFÉ (Fr.) This category of French wine is sold by the carafe in cafés, bistros etc.

VIN DE GARDE (Fr.) Wine capable of significant improvement if allowed to age.

VIN DE GLACE (Fr.) French equivalent of *Eiswein*.

VIN DE GOUTTE (Fr.) Free-run juice. In the case of white wine, this is the juice that runs free from the press before the actual pressing operation begins. With red wine, it is fermented wine drained off from the manta or **cap**.

VIN DÉLIMITÉ DE QUALITÉ SUPÉRIEUR *See* VdQS.

VIN DE L'ANNÉE (Fr.) This term is synonymous with *vin primeur*.

VIN DE LIQUEUR *See* VdL.

VIN DE PAILLE (Fr.) Literally "straw wine". Complex sweet wine produced by leaving late-picked grapes to dry and shrivel in the sun on straw mats. *See* The Jura and Savoie, p.222.

VIN DE PAYS (Fr.) A rustic style of country wine that is one step above *vin de table*, but one beneath VdQS. *See* Vin de Pays, p.246.

VIN DE PRESSE (Fr.) Very dark, tannic, red wine pressed out of the manta or **cap**, after the *vin de goutte* has been drained off.

VIN DE QUALITÉ PRODUIT DANS UNE RÉGION DÉLIMITÉE *See* VQPRD.

VIN DE TABLE (Fr.) Literally "table wine", although not necessarily a direct translation of this term. It is used to describe the lowest level of wine in France and is not allowed to give either the grape variety or the area of origin on the label. In practice, it is likely to consist of various varieties from numerous areas that have been blended in bulk in order to produce a wine of consistent character, or lack of it, as the case may be.

VIN DOUX NATUREL *See* VdN.

VIN D'UNE NUIT (Fr.) A rosé or very pale red wine that is allowed contact with the manta or cap for one night only.

VIN GRIS (Fr.) A delicate, pale version of rosé.

VINIFICATION Far more than simply describing **fermentation**, vinification involves the entire process of making wine, from the moment the grapes are picked to the point at which the wine is finally bottled.

VINIMATIC This is an enclosed, rotating **fermentation** tank with blades fixed to the inner surface, that works on the same principle as a cement-mixer. Used initially to extract the maximum colour from the grape skins with the minimum **oxidation**, it is now being utilized for *pre-fermentation macération*.

VIN JAUNE (Fr.) This is the famous "yellow wine" of the Jura that derives its name from its honey-gold colour that results from a deliberate **oxidation** beneath a **Sherry**-like **flor**. The result is similar to an aged Fino Sherry, although it is not fortified.

VIN MOUSSEUX (Fr.) This literally means "sparkling wine" without any particular connotation of quality one way or the other, but because all fine sparkling wines in France utilize other terms, for all practical purposes it implies a cheap, low-quality product.

VIN NOUVEAU (Fr.) This term is synonymous with *vin primeur*.

VIN ORDINAIRE (Fr.) Literally "an ordinary wine", this term is most often applied to a French *vin de table*, although it can be used in a rather derogatory way to describe any wine from any country.

VIN PRIMEUR Young wine made to be drunk within the year in which it is produced. Beaujolais Primeur is the official designation of the most famous *vin primeur*, but export markets see it labelled as Beaujolais Nouveau most of the time.

VINO DA TAVOLA (It.) *Vin de table*, table wine.

VINO DE MESA (Sp.) Table wine, *vin de table*.

VINO NOVELLO (It.) Synonymous with *vin nouveau* (as in Beaujolais Nouveau).

VINOUS Of, or relating to, or characteristic of wine. When used to describe a wine, this term implies basic qualities only.

VINTAGE 1. A wine of one year. **2.** Synonymous with harvest. A vintage wine is the wine of one year's harvest only (or at least 85 per cent according to EU regulations) and the year may be anything from poor to exceptional. It is, for this reason, a misnomer to use the term vintage for the purpose of indicating a wine of special quality.

VITIS VINIFERA A species covering all varieties of vines that provide classic winemaking grapes.

VIVID The fruit in some wines can be so **fresh**, ripe, clean-cut, and **expressive** that it quickly gives a vivid impression of complete character in the mouth.

VOLATILE ACIDS These acids, sometimes called fatty acids, are capable of evaporating at low temperatures. Too much volatile acidity is always a sign of instability, but small amounts do actually play a significant role in the taste and aroma of a wine. Formic, butyric, and proprionic are all volatile acids that may be found in wine, but **acetic acid** and **carbonic acid** are the most important.

VQPRD A common abbreviation for *vin de qualité produit dans une région délimitée*.

VR (Port.) Short for *vinho regional*, the lowest rung in Portugal's appellation system, a VR can be compared to the regional *vin de pays* category in France.

WARM, WARMTH These terms are suggestive of a good-flavoured red wine with a high alcoholic content or, if this term is used with an accompanying description of cedary or **creamy**, can mean well-matured in **oak**.

WATERSHED A term used for an area where water drains into a river system, lake, or some other body of water.

WATERY An extreme qualification of **thin**.

WEISSHERBST (Ger.) A single-variety rosé wine produced from black grapes only.

WINE LAKE A common term for the EU surplus of low-quality table wine.

WINKLER SCALE Synonymous with **heat summation** system.

WOOD LACTONES These are various **esters** that are picked up from new oak and that may be the source of certain **creamy-oak** and coconutty characteristics.

WOOD-MATURED This term normally refers to a wine that has been aged in new oak.

YEAST A kind of fungus that is absolutely vital in all winemaking. Yeast cells excrete a number of enzymes, some 22 of which are necessary to complete the chain reaction that is known as **fermentation**. *See* Yeast the Fermenter, p.32.

YEAST ENZYMES Each enzyme acts as a catalyst for one particular activity and is specific for that task only and no other in the **fermentation** process.

YEASTY This is not a complimentary term for most wines, but a yeasty **bouquet** can sometimes be desirable in a good-quality sparkling wine, especially if it is young.

YIELD There are two forms of yield: **1.** the quantity of grapes produced from a given area of land; **2.** how much juice is pressed from it. Wine people in Europe measure yield in hl/ha (hectolitres per hectare – a hectolitre equals 1,000 litres), referring to how much juice has been extracted from the grapes harvested from an area of land. This is fine when the amount of juice that can be pressed from grapes is controlled by European-type **appellation** systems, but in the New World, where this seldom happens, they tend to talk in tons per acre. It can be difficult trying to make exact conversions in the field, particularly after a heavy tasting session, when even the size of a ton or gallon can become quite elusive. This is why, as a rough guide, I multiply the tons or divide the hectolitres by 20 to convert one to the other. This is based on the average extraction rates for both California and Australia, which makes it a good rule-of-thumb. Be aware that white wines can benefit from higher yields than reds (although sweet wines should have the lowest of all yields) and that sparkling wines can get away with relatively high yields. For example, Sauternes averages 25 hl/ha, Bordeaux 50 hl/ha, and Champagne 80 hl/ha.

ZESTY A lively characteristic found in some wines that is suggestive of a **zippy** tactile impression combined, maybe, with a distinctive hint of citrussy aroma.

ZING, ZINGY, ZIP, ZIPPY Terms that are all indicative of something that is noteable for being refreshing, lively, and vital in character, resulting from a high balance of ripe fruit acidity in the wine.

INDEX

Wine producing areas and producer profiles are shown in **bold**, illustration captions in *italic*.

583

ACKNOWLEDGMENTS

AUTHOR'S ACKNOWLEDGMENTS (1997 EDITION)

My first thanks must go to my agent, Michael Sissons. This Encyclopedia was not my first book by any means, but it was the very first contract Michael came up with after I signed with his agency, and I am greatly ashamed that I have only just noticed the omission of his name in my acknowledgments in the last edition.

The maps are still a major feature of the book, and I could not have updated them so easily had it not been for the meticulous groundwork put in by my great friend Michael Schmidt for the first edition, and by Peter Markley of Lovell Johns, who worked on both editions and is one of the best cartographers in the world. Particular thanks go to John Noble, the Indexer, who has done a marvellously comprehensive job.

I would also like to thank everyone I have contact with in the international wine trade, especially those who helped coordinate my trips around the world, or sent me wines from all four corners of the earth, but particularly Gerard and JoAnn Bentryn, Vicky Bishop, Eric Blondeau, Dick Boushey, Véronique Bramaud, Daniel Brennan, Myriam Broggi, Steve Burns, Larry Challacombe, Christine Coletta, Charles Cunningham, François Duhamel, Marjorie Dundas Ruhf, Ricardo Ewertz, David Forbes, Monty Friendship, Christina Fuggit, Peter Gamble, Marie Hardie, Michael Hasslacher, Professor George Hess, Bill Huisman, Mel Knox, Roxanne Langer, Kit Lindlar, Harry MacWatters, Jean-Laurent Maillard, Cathérine Manac'h, Nico Manessis, Archie McClaren, David McCulloch, Lucy Meager, Fiona Morrison MW, Hazel Murphy, Christine Pascal, Michael Parry, Thomas Perry, Jennifer Sanguiliano, Michael Schmidt, Peter Scudamore-Smith MW, Simon Siegl, Con Simos, Tony Skuriat, Don Ziraldo, and Larry Walker.

AUTHOR'S ACKNOWLEDGMENTS (2001 EDITION)

For the 2001 revision, I would particularly like to thank Clive Coates MW, Michael Fridjhon, James Halliday, David Peppercorn MW, John Radford, and Michael Schmidt.

PHOTOGRAPHIC CREDITS

t = top, b = bottom, l = left, r = right, c = centre
Bildagentur Mauritius E. Gebhardt 265 r; Koch 285; Rossenbach 280. **Cephas:** Kevin Argue 499; Nigel Blythe 52, 292, 293, 302, 558; Andy Christodolo 260, 264, 503, 505, 520 b, 540, 548; Bruce Flemming 440; Kevin Judd 2, 547; Alain Proust 428; Mick Rock 1, 2, 5, 6, 22, 28 t, 29, 29, 29, 33, 33, 34, 38, 58 c, 61, 62, 63, 76, 86 bl, 121 t, 121 b, 135 t, 135 b, 136, 138, 139, 144 b, 151, 155, 157, 159, 165 l, 167 tr, 169, 170, 181 b, 186, 207, 211, 246, 255, 258, 269, 290, 291 t, 291 b, 298 t, 300, 304, 306, 308, 318, 319, 320, 336, 338, 343, 346, 350 t, 359, 364, 366, 367, 371, 377, 388, 390, 391, 406 t, 406 b, 407, 408, 409, 411, 412, 420, 422, 475 t, 481, 487, 516, 522; Ted Stefanski 6, 449. **Click Chicago:** Peter Fronk 442 t, 480, 488; John Lawlor 444; Chuck O'Rear 447. **Horizon:** Milton Wordley 533. **Imagebank:** S. Barbosa 504. **Impact:** Pamla Toler 545 t, 545 b. **Landscape Only:** Charlie Waite 194, 327 t, 327 b. **Picture Index:** Guy Gravett 192. **Scope:** Jean-Luc Barde 131, 152, 158, 227; Jacques Guillard 24, 180, 196 t, 198 t Michel Guillard 4, 30 tr, 30 bl, 31 bl, 36 b, 37 l, 58 t, 58 b, 73, 77 t, 77 b, 81, 82 l, 82 r, 86 tr, 86 cr, 90 t, 91 tr, 92 t, 114 tr, 114 bl, 241; Jacques Sierpinski 233; Jean-Daniel Sudres 31 tr. **Susan Griggs Agency:** Adam Woolfitt 400 t. **Visionbank:** Michael Freeman 456; Colin Maher 66, 93. **Zefa:** Armstrong 463; F. Damm 37 r; Eigen 298 b; Fotostudio 401, 405; Harlicek 400 b; Justitz 395; W.H. Mueller 23 l; K. Oster 273; W. Rötzel 270; Haro Schumacher 424; Til 271. Jason Bell back jacket flap; Anthony Blake 113, 114 bl, 196 b, 199 t, 282. Anthony Blake / G. Buntro 350 b. Harry Baker 30 tl. Bernard Breuer 28 t1, 281 b. Michail Busselle 85. Martin Cameron 566. Champagne Bureau 30 br, 31 tl, 164 t, 167 tl. Champagne Deutz 166 tr. Champagne Pommery 165 r. Chateau Haut-Brion 90 b. CIVC Epernay 164 t, 166 t. Stephanie Colasanti 383. Bruce Coleman / Herbet Kranwetter 378. Bruce Coleman / Sandro Prato 425 l. Andy Crawford 16, 16, 17, 17, 39, 40 b, 41, 559. Pedro Domecq 502. Patrick Eagar 23 r, 124 t, 193, 193, 538. Neil Fletcher p 563, 564. Food and Wine from France 31 br, 198 b. French Government Tourist Office 222. Steve Gorton 265 l. Sonia Halliday 419. Sonia Halliday / F.H.C. Birch 21. Margaret Harvey 544. Hudson Picture Library 417. Denis Hughes-Gilbey 31 cr, 199 b. Dave King 564, 565. Krug 166 tl. Laurent Perrier 166 b, 166 b. Ian O'Leary 7, 18-19. David Murray p.561, p.562. David Murray / Jules Felmes p.35, p.560. Piper's Brook Vineyard 525. Janet Price 6, 36 t, 86 br, 103 t, 103 b, 124 b, 130, 132, 133, 144 t, 182, 210 t, 210 b, 507, 519, 520 t, 521, 526 t, 532 t, 532 b. Louis Roederer 167 br. Kim Sayer 7. Sotheby's 9, 10, 11, 12, 13. Tom Stevenson 28 b, 40 t, 91 bl, 91 br, 92 b, 181 t. Tony Stone 539. Tony Stone / Fritz Prenzl 542. J.C. Tordai 415. Trip 416. Jon Wyand 284, 311, 442 b, 458, 469, 475 b. Yapp Brothers 212.

ILLUSTRATION CREDITS

Glossary of grape varieties by Sandra Fernandez, all other illustrations by Kuo Kang Chen.